AIRLINE FLEETS
2004

Edited by Tony Pither
in collaboration with Colin Frost, Peter Gerhardt, Alain Gosset,
Rolf Larsson, Ken Marshall, Kiyoshi Sato, Terry Smith, Martin Stepanek,
Tony Wheeler and John Wilkinson

Published by Air-Britain (Historians) Ltd

Sales Department: 41 Penshurst Road, Leigh,
Tonbridge, Kent TN11 8HL

Membership Enquiries: 1 Rose Cottages, 179 Penn Road
Hazlemere,Bucks HP15 7NE

Further information is available on our website: http://www.air-britain.co.uk

PHOTO CAPTIONS:

Front cover: Boeing 737-76N PR-GOO of Gol lifting off from Belo Horizonte/Pampulha 10.4.03 (Richard Hewitt)

Rear cover: Top: Frontier Airlines Airbus A319-111 N916FR on finals at Tampa, Florida on 12.4.03 (Rod Simpson)

Middle: Fokker 50 OO-VLM of VLM in sponsor's colour scheme at Manchester 15.5.03 (Denis Norman)

Bottom: China Airlines (Taiwan) Boeing 747-409F B-18702 arriving at Manchester 13.6.03 (Denis Norman)

ISBN   0 85130 350 1   ISSN   0262-1657

Printed by Cromwell Press Ltd, Trowbridge BA14 0XB

Air-Britain supports the fight against terrorism and the efforts of the Police and other Authorities in protecting airports and airfields from criminal activity.

If you see anything suspicious do not hesitate to call the
Anti-Terrorist Hotline 0800 789321
or alert a Police Officer

INTRODUCTION

Additional Information and Changes for the 2004 Edition

This year's edition of Airline Fleets follows the pattern established in recent years.

It seems that the world's airlines may have turned the corner in terms of recovery. While some of the US majors are still struggling (Delta and American have reported large losses for 2003), other US airlines are starting to return to profit. Interestingly it is anticipated that those who will benefit most in the next year will be those operating international services rather than the short-haul and low-cost operators. US Airways emerged from Chapter 11 protection as planned while United have set a deadline of 30 June 2004 to leave their protection. US Airways have reached agreements with their pilots' union over the scope clause and are planning to introduce a large number of regional jets for their Express operation; most of the new orders are for wholly-owned subsidiaries rather than the 'bought-in' services.

In Europe we have the first link-up of national carriers with Air France and KLM coming together (officially not a take-over) to form a new holding company although both will continue to operate independently and it is possible Alitalia will join them. Similar tie-ups are possible with British Airways and Iberia considering a similar arrangement, at the moment BA are providing support to struggling Swiss International.

The Australian and New Zealand regulators blocked Qantas's attempt to purchase a bigger stake in Air New Zealand on the grounds that it would not be in the best interest of the travelling public. As a result Qantas have increased their own operations in New Zealand and now Virgin Blue have formed their own NZ subsidiary, Pacific Blue, to begin trans-Tasman services as well as NZ domestic services. Qantas have also announced plans to form their own low cost carrier, Jetstar, to operate internal services in competition with Virgin Blue. How this will affect Qantaslink is unsure as Jetstar will start with the Boeing 717s currently operated by Impulse for the feeder. In Asia the efffects of the SARS outbreak and Iraq war seem to have passed and traffic is picking up.

Aviation in Africa is still relatively dangerous with 28% of all fatal accidents occuring on the continent while it accounts for only 3% of departures. Indeed during 2003 the three worst accidents were in Africa and 2004 started badly with the loss of the Flash 737. This accident highlighted a potential problem within Europe as the aircraft had been banned from operating to Switzerland but cleared by the French; as a result the UK named the airlines who are banned from operating into British airports but more openness is required.

The Russian authorities are still requesting their airlines to merge and create larger, more efficient carriers but it seems to fall on deaf ears. The high import duties on Western aircraft are still preventing many airlines from updating their fleets but as the Tupolev Tu-134 and Tu-154 are banned from Europe on environmental grounds this may have to change. Aeroflot are heading to a mainly Western fleet with the remaining Tupolevs to be withdrawn in the next few years when the only Russian aircraft operated will be Ilyushin Il-96s (plus RRJs if the project proceeds).

For the first time Airbus delivered more aircraft in 2003 than Boeing (305 versus 281) and also booked more orders (254 versus 239); however Boeing have the bigger backlog (2,564 versus 1,454). During the year the Airbus A340-500 entered service with Emirates on services to Australia and the A318 also commenced airline operations with initially Frontier and, later, Air France. Progress is continuing with the A380 and further orders were received during the year from Korean Air and Malaysia Airlines. As predicted last year the end has been announced for the Boeing 757, the last example will roll off the production line later this year. The Boeing 767 order for 100 tanker/transport aircraft has been held up by a Congressional committee following possible unethical dealings at Boeing during the bidding process - as a result the CEO was fired from Boeing and Phil Condit, the chairman resigned. The UK tanker competition has been awarded to the EADS team and the A330, rather than the 767. One bright point for Boeing is the Board's decision to allow the new 7E7 to be offered to airliners prior to a formal launch later this year. This aircraft will have a high percentage of composites to reduce weight as well as efficient engines and will have up to 30% workshare in Japan although final assembly will be in Seattle.

Other manufacturers are continuing with existing models although Canadair are now providing the CRJ-900 as a 74-seat aircraft (CRJ-705) to beat the seat clauses of the US majors. They are also looking, again, at the 100-seat market but may have left it too late as the Embraer 170 is due to enter service soon and its big brother, the 190 will arrive next year. BAE Systems delivered the last RJ and this is the final four-engined jet airliner produced in Britain. Finally a sad day on 24 October 2003 when BA002 landed at Heathrow to mark the final Concorde service; within a couple of weeks the fleet had been dispersed to museums around the world.

Details included

Details are included for almost 3000 operators in nearly 200 countries - also included in the main text are those airlines whose fleets have been deleted this year, along with the reason. As a general guideline, the complete fleets of all operators with an IATA two- or three-letter code are now included, together with non-IATA coded operators of regular services where fleets are known. Many of the world's helicopter fleets down to Bell 206 size are included, with the large majority of all twin-engined aircraft and many single-engined aircraft down to Cessna 180/Piper Cherokee Six also operated on passenger or express freight services. Civil registered jet and turboprop airliners in non-airline use, i.e. those owned and operated by the manufacturers or used as executive or special purpose, are again included in this year's edition. This section does not include details of the stored ex-airline aircraft as mentioned above. The component parts of Northwest Airlink, United Express and US Airways Express have again been grouped together under the airline heading and cross-referenced to the individual feeder carriers although this is becoming more difficult as some operators provide feeder services to a range of airlines. As a result some of the feeders are listed separately for at least part of their fleets although they are cross-referenced to the majors as appropriate.

Where known, first service dates of recent operator start-ups are included. There continue to be some re-appearances where previously removed airlines have either relaunched services or their active status has been confirmed. We also continue with the appearance of 'virtual' airlines where an operator may hold an operator's licence and have a two or three letter code but no aircraft!, these are leased in as required. Also listed this year are a number of airlines who have IATA or ICAO codes allocated but where fleet details are unknown at the time of publication.

Five indices are provided: a national index in alphabetical order of country name; an airline index in alphabetical order, and indices of ICAO and IATA designators for airlines and for those airline bases referred to in the text.

Credits

I am indebted to the following for contributions, corrections, assistance and the use of information, Dave Buck, Ian Burnett, Colin Frost, Rolf Larsson, Terry Smith, Chris Swan, and all contributors to the Commercial Scene section of Air-Britain News edited by Tony Wheeler; Aviation Letter, and the various Air-Britain publications as well as relevant web-sites. I am grateful to Kiyoshi Sato and his contacts within FedEx who have spent time and effort checking names of their aircraft and to Ken Marshall for information on the Canadian fire-fighting fleets. Thanks are also extended to Peter Hillman, Stuart Jessop, Tony Morris and Guus Ottenhof for allowing data from their book 'Half a Century Soviet Transports' to be used in this, and subsequent, editions of Fleets. Final thanks are also due to my wife, Carolyn, without whose forbearance and understanding in the run-up to publication date a volunteer production such as this, which requires in excess of 1000 hours to produce, would be impossible.

Update Information

For readers who are not already members of Air-Britain, this edition can be kept up to date by reading Commercial Scene and other sections of our regular publications. Details of the many benefits of membership are included at the end of this book.

Where possible, information received up to 24th January 2004 has been incorporated in the main text. Naturally, in a work of this complexity and scope, some errors and omissions will occur, and any reader who can add to, amend or correct the information included in this publication is invited to write to the address below.

Users are advised that the information in this publication cannot be reproduced, stored in a retrieval system or transmitted in the form in which it appears, by any means electronic, photocopying, recording or otherwise, without the express prior permission of the Copyright owner. Individual items of information may be used in other publications with due acknowledgement to Air-Britain (Historians).

Tony Pither, 65 Dacombe Drive, Upton, Poole, Dorset BH16 5JJ
E-mail: tonypither@aol.com

EXPLANATORY NOTES

1 Noise Regulations

With effect from 01Jan85 FAR Part 36 Stage 2 regulations came into force with respect to four-engined aircraft. These prevented any further civil operations of Boeing 707/720 and DC-8 (except -70 series) aircraft to or from US airports unless they were fitted with hushkits so that they conformed to the new noise standards. Similar regulations applied in the UK from 01Jan88. Stage 3 requirements are now implemented with all non-compliant aircraft required to be hush-kitted or re-engined; this applies to 707s, 727s, 737s (srs-100/200s), DC-8/9s, 1-11s, Tu-134/154s and Il-62/76s. Many of these aircraft are being withdrawn from service as the economic situation makes it uneconomic to undertake the costly conversions (indeed some of the planned hush-kitting schemes have been abandoned). In the main text of the book reference is made, where known, to the type of hush-kit fitted to Boeing 707, 727, early 737s and Douglas DC-8s and 9s and whether it is Stage 2 or Stage 3 compliant. (For example FedEx 3 means a 727 fitted with a Stage 3 compliant FedEx hush-kit).

2 Chapter 11

In the US section of this book reference is sometimes made to 'Chapter 11'. This refers to a section of the US bankruptcy code designed to give a company protection from its creditors while it attempts a financial reorganisation. Plans for such a reorganisation have to be submitted to and approved by the bankruptcy court. A Chapter 11 filing may or may not be accompanied by a cessation of operations. If operations do continue, then it is usually at a very much reduced level. If they are suspended, then it is possible that they may be restarted in some form at a future date. If the reorganisation plan fails, then an application for liquidation under Chapter 7 will be made.

Since a Chapter 11 filing does not automatically result in a permanent cessation of operations (although many do), airlines are only deleted from this book if at the time of writing it appears that resumption of operations in the near future is unlikely.

3 Boeing 747 Suffixes

An M suffix after Boeing 747-200s indicates that the aircraft is a Combi (Mixed) version fitted with a Side Cargo Door. While not used officially in national registers, the M suffix convention is used in Boeing official literature and is therefore adopted in this publication. Suffixes SCD and EUD indicate converted Side Cargo Door and Extended Upper Deck versions. SF indicates that the aircraft is a 'Special Freighter' conversion.

4 Boeing 737 Test Registrations

The majority of Boeing 737s complete their first flights from Renton (PAE) to Boeing Field (BFI) with the registration N1786B. As a result only those using a different registration are listed in Fleets.

5 German Spellings

German place names appear in anglicised form for operator bases but in the native German spelling for aircraft names (e.g. in the Lufthansa fleet).

6 Description of entries

Countries are listed in alphabetical order of nationality prefix, with the airlines in each country also in alphabetical order. Fleets are listed in alphabetical order of aircraft manufacturer where five or more of the same type occur, otherwise they are listed in registration order. Aircraft type descriptions generally quote the manufacturer currently considered responsible for producing the aircraft. The immediate previous identity appears after the constructor's number and helps determine the source of newly acquired aircraft.

Each Country is identified in bold and italics and enclosed in a shadowed box; followed by airlines in alphabetical order, again enclosed in a box. The details listed for each airline are it's name (and any trading or alternative name where appropriate); the two letter IATA designator and three-letter ICAO codes (where allocated and known); whether they are a member of IATA, and their main operating base(s), again with the recognised three letter code (where allocated). Also listed are the call-sign (as allocated by ICAO) and their IATA membership number (where known).

Each individual entry, from the left, lists current registration (or that known to be reserved and likely to be taken up with that operator in brackets), followed by type. The next column lists the construction number, preceded, for Boeing and McDonnell-Douglas types, by the line number separated by a slash (/). There then appears the immediate past identity (where known) followed by any fleet number or name. The final entry indicates any lease arrangements or other comments; any three-letter designation refers to another airline. Aircraft on order are listed where either delivery is due in the year following the date of publication or where details of the aircraft are known. Otherwise details of aircraft on order for delivery in subsequent years are listed at the bottom of the aircraft type or airline entry; also listed there are any alliances, franchises or ownership details of interest.

Leased (lsd) aircraft will be found in the owner's fleet as well as that of the leasing airline. Where it is known that an aircraft is due to change operator during the currency of this book, it is shown in both fleets with a suitable note. Aircraft that have been withdrawn from service (wfs) are listed unless they are known to have been broken up or are beyond repair. Likewise, aircraft that have been involved in accidents but not confirmed as written off are still included.

7   Abbreviations

Abbreviations used in the text have the following meanings:

AOC	Air Operators Certificate
Avn	Aviation
c/s	colour scheme
dam	damaged
dbr	damaged beyond repair
fr	from
ACMI	Aircraft, Maintenance, Crew and Insurance
lsd	leased
Intl	International
Mgt	Management
o/o	on order (followed by date of delivery when known)
op	operate(d)
ops	operates/operations
resd	reserved
std	stored
Svs	Services
sublsd	subleased
wfs	withdrawn from service (i.e. unlikely to return to operational status with that operator)
w/o	written off

Other abbreviations relate to specific lessors as follows:

AIFS	Airbus Industrie Financial Services
ATR	Aerospatiale/Alenia (manufacturers)
AWAS	Ansett Worldwide Air Services (includes AWMS and operating arm)
BAES	BAE Systems Asset Management Jet/Turboprop
BBAM	Babcock & Brown Aircraft Management
CLPK	Credit Lyonnais PK
FUNB	First Union National Bank
GATX	GATX Inc or GATX Flightlease
GECAS	General Electric Capital Aircraft Services (including GECC, GPA and Aero USA)
GPA ATR	Joint venture between GPA and manufacturer (Similar for Fokker 100)
IAL Inc	International Air Lease Group
ILFC	International Lease Finance Corp
MDFC	McDonnell-Douglas Finance Corp
SALE	Singapore Aircraft Leasing
WFBN	Wells Fargo Bank Northwest
WTCo	Wilmington Trust Co

Other lessors include AAR Corp, AerFi, Bavaria, Boullioun, CIT Leasing, debis, Finova, Interlease, Intrepid, Itochu, Mitsui, MSA Corp, ORIX, Pegasus Aviation, Pembroke, Polaris, Sunrock, Tombo, Triton and Volvo Aviation. Other organisations listed on the right are banks holding trust to the aircraft, such as BancOne, BancBoston, WTCo, FUNB, Wachovia Bank etc

AP - PAKISTAN (Islamic Republic of Pakistan)

AERO ASIA INTERNATIONAL

Aero Asia (E4/RSO) (IATA 532)   *Karachi (KHI)*

RA-42345	Yakovlev Yak-42D	4520422708304	ex LY-AAR		Lsd fr AKT
RA-42354	Yakovlev Yak-42D	4520424711397	ex LY-AAU		Lsd fr AKT
RA-42415	Yakovlev Yak-42D	4520422219089	ex CCCP-42416		Lsd fr AKT
RA-42417	Yakovlev Yak-42D	4520423219110	ex CCCP-42417		Lsd fr AKT
RA-42433	Yakovlev Yak-42D	4520421301017	ex CCCP-42433		Lsd fr AKT
EX-006	Boeing 737-2T5	642/21960	ex N71PW		Lsd fr PHG
EX-450	Boeing 737-281	262/20450	ex PK-JHA		Lsd fr PHG
EX-451	Boeing 737-281	266/20451	ex PK-JHD		Lsd fr PHG
EX-632	Boeing 737-2T5	847/22632	ex N75PW		Lsd fr PHG
AP-BFC	Rombac/BAC One-Eleven 561RC	401	ex YR-BRA	stored OTP	
AP-BFD	Rombac/BAC One-Eleven 561RC	404	ex YR-BRD	stored KHI	
AP-BFE	Rombac/BAC One-Eleven 561RC	406	ex YR-BRF	stored KHI	
AP-BFF	Rombac/BAC One-Eleven 561RC	407	ex YR-BRG	stored KHI	
UR-BYL	Douglas DC-9-51	787/47657	ex N2248F		Lsd fr KHO
UR-CCK	Douglas DC-9-51 (ABS 3)	827/47736	ex OH-LYR		Lsd fr KHO

AIR BLUE

Karachi (KHI)

AP-	Airbus Industrie A320-200		ex	on order	Lsd fr
AP-	Airbus Industrie A320-200		ex	on order	Lsd fr
AP-	Airbus Industrie A320-200		ex	on order	Lsd fr

Due to commence operations as low-cost carrier

AIR PEARL

Karachi (KHI)

AP-	Boeing 737-291 (Nordam 3)	521/21509	ex N978UA	

PAKISTAN INTERNATIONAL AIRLINES

Pakistan (PK/PIA) (IATA 214)   *Karachi (KHI)*

AP-BAX	Airbus Industrie A300B4-203	096	ex F-WZEP		
AP-BAY	Airbus Industrie A300B4-203	098	ex F-WZER		
AP-BAZ	Airbus Industrie A300B4-203	099	ex F-WZET	City of Rawalpindi	
AP-BBA	Airbus Industrie A300B4-203	114	ex F-WZEN		
AP-BBM	Airbus Industrie A300B4-203	064	ex D-AHLA		
AP-BBV	Airbus Industrie A300B4-203	144	ex G-BIMC		
AP-BEL	Airbus Industrie A300B4-203	269	ex EI-CBW		Lsd fr GECAS
AP-BEY	Airbus Industrie A300B4-203	146	ex F-BVGQ		
AP-BDZ	Airbus Industrie A310-308	585	ex F-WWCH	City of Ziarat	
AP-BEB	Airbus Industrie A310-308	587	ex F-WWCT	City of Murree	
AP-BEC	Airbus Industrie A310-308	590	ex F-WWCX	City of Swat	
AP-BEG	Airbus Industrie A310-308	653	ex F-WWCZ		
AP-BEQ	Airbus Industrie A310-308	656	ex F-WWCB		
AP-BEU	Airbus Industrie A310-308	691	ex F-WWCD	City of Skarda	
AP-BGN	Airbus Industrie A310-324ER	684	ex 9V-STD		Lsd fr SIA
AP-BGO	Airbus Industrie A310-324ER	678	ex F-WQTC		Lsd fr AIrbus
AP-BGP	Airbus Industrie A310-324ER	682	ex F-WQTF		Lsd fr Airbus
AP-	Airbus Industrie A310-324ER	676	ex 6Y-JAB	on order	Lsd fr Airbus
AP-	Airbus Industrie A310-324ER	686	ex 6Y-JAE	on order	Lsd fr Airbus
AP-	Airbus Industrie A310-324ER		ex F-OG	on order 04	Lsd fr Airbus
AP-	Airbus Industrie A310-324ER		ex F-OG	on order 04	Lsd fr Airbus
AP-BCA	Boeing 737-340	1114/23294			
AP-BCB	Boeing 737-340	1116/23295			
AP-BCC	Boeing 737-340	1121/23296			
AP-BCD	Boeing 737-340	1122/23297			
AP-BCF	Boeing 737-340	1235/23299			
AP-BFT	Boeing 737-340	1123/23298	ex AP-BCE		
AP-BAK	Boeing 747-240M	383/21825			
AP-BAT	Boeing 747-240M	429/22077			
AP-BFU	Boeing 747-367	634/23392	ex B-HIJ		
AP-BFV	Boeing 747-367	659/23534	ex B-HIK		
AP-BFW	Boeing 747-367	615/23221	ex B-HII		
AP-BFX	Boeing 747-367	671/23709	ex B-HOL		
AP-BFY	Boeing 747-367	690/23920	ex B-HOM		
AP-BGG	Boeing 747-367	709/24215	ex B-HON		

AP-ALW	Fokker F.27 Friendship 400	10187	ex PH-FDB		
AP-ATU	Fokker F.27 Friendship 200	10278	ex PH-FGV		
AP-AUR	Fokker F.27 Friendship 200	10307	ex PH-FKB		
AP-AXB	Fokker F.27 Friendship 200	10288	ex I-ATIG		
AP-BAL	Fokker F.27 Friendship 200	10243	ex F-BUFE		
AP-BAO	Fokker F.27 Friendship 200	10230	ex F-BVTE		
AP-BCT	Fokker F.27 Friendship 200	10289	ex G-BDDH		
AP-BCZ	Fokker F.27 Friendship 200	10305	ex VH-FNP		
AP-BDB	Fokker F.27 Friendship 200	10292	ex VH-FNM		
AP-BDQ	Fokker F.27 Friendship 200	10253	ex PT-LDJ		
AP-BDR	Fokker F.27 Friendship 200	10134	ex PT-LGH		
AP-BDS	Fokker F.27 Friendship 200	10133	ex PT-LCX		

All believed withdrawn from service and stored at Karachi

AP-AXG	Boeing 707-340C (Comtran 2)	849/20488	ex G-AZRO	Freighter, wfs KHI	
AP-BCG	de Havilland DHC-6 Twin Otter 300	726	ex C-GCVZ		
AP-BGJ	Boeing 777-240ER	467/33775			
AP-BGK	Boeing 777-240ER	469/33776			
AP-BGL	Boeing 777-240ER	33777		on order 04	

Two Boeing 777-240LRs are on order for delivery from 2007 plus three Boeing 777-340ERs for delivery from 2005.

PIONEER CARGO AIRLINES

(PER) — *Karachi (KHI)*

UR-26676	Antonov An-26B	8602	ex CCCP-26676		Lsd fr URP

ROYAL AIRLINES

Royal Pakistan (RPK) — *Karachi (KHI)*

EX-160	Antonov An-12BP	401901	ex D2-FCV	Irena	Lsd fr BGK
UR-BWY	Antonov An-26	8205	ex		Lsd fr URP
UR-26581	Antonov An-26B	13503	ex RA-26581		Lsd fr URP

SHAHEEN AIR INTERNATIONAL

Shaheen Air (NL/SAI) — *Karachi (KHI)*

EW-85509	Tupolev Tu-154B-2	81A-509	ex UN-85509		Lsd fr BRU
EW-85538	Tupolev Tu-154B-2	82A-538	ex 4K-85538		Lsd fr BRU
UR-42358	Yakovlev Yak-42	4520422811413	ex CCCP-42358		Lsd fr UKW
UR-42369	Yakovlev Yak-42	4520422914190	ex CCCP-42369		Lsd fr UKW
RA-42376	Yakovlev Yak-42D	4520424914477	ex UR-42376		Lsd fr UDN
UR-42403	Yakovlev Yak-42D	4520422116588	ex CCCP-42403	no titles	Lsd fr UKW
UR-42409	Yakovlev Yak-42D	4520421216709	ex ER-42409		Lsd fr UDN
UR-42449	Yakovlev Yak-42D	4520421401018	ex EP-CPC		Lsd fr UDN

Also operates cargo flights using Antonov An-12s and Ilyushin Il-76s leased from other operators as required

STAR AIR AVIATION

(URJ) — *Karachi (KHI)*

Current status is uncertain as sole aircraft has been written off

A2 - BOTSWANA (Republic of Botswana)

AIR BOTSWANA

Botswana (BP/BOT) (IATA 636) — *Gaborone (GBE)*

A2-ABD	British Aerospace 146 Srs.100	E1101	ex (G-CBAE)		
A2-ABN	Aerospatiale/Alenia ATR 42-500	507	ex F-WQNG	Chobe	
A2-ABO	Aerospatiale/Alenia ATR 42-500	511	ex F-WQNC	Okavango	
A2-ABP	Aerospatiale/Alenia ATR 42-500	512	ex F-WQNI	Makgadikgadi	
A2-NAC	Beech 1900D	UE-325	ex ZS-OYM		Lsd fr NAC Charter

ATR's leased from ATR Asset Management

DEBSWANA

Gaborone (GBE)

A2-OLM	Beech 1900D	UE-423	ex N3241X	

DELTA AIR

Maun (MUB)

A2-AGR	Cessna U206F Stationair	U20601837	ex ZS-OCC	

A2-AHN	Cessna U206G Stationair 6	U20606432	ex ZS-LKX
A2-AID	Cessna U206G Stationair 6	U20605755	ex N9353Z
A2-AIW	Cessna 210N Centurion	21064163	ex ZS-MYC
A2-AJA	Britten-Norman BN-2A Islander	271	ex ZS-LKE
A2-AJB	Piper PA-31-350 Chieftain	31-8152047	ex N6261N

KALAHARI AIR SERVICES AND CHARTER

Gaborone (GBE)

A2-ACP	Beech 58 Baron	TH-171	ex 9J-ADA
A2-ACR	Piper PA-31-350 Navajo Chieftain	31-7405246	ex ZS-ISZ
A2-AEZ	Beech 200 Super King Air	BB-421	ex N4488L
A2-AFK	Cessna 210N Centurion	21064203	ex N5427Y
A2-AHM	Cessna 210L Centurion	21061481	ex ZS-LOT
A2-AHS	Beech 58 Baron	TH-859	ex N18405
A2-AHZ	Beech 200 Super King Air	BB-95	ex ZS-JPD
A2-DBH	Beech C90 King Air	LJ-988	ex ZS-LUU
A2-KAS	Beech 200 Super King Air	BB-614	ex ZS-LKA

(Kalahari Air Service and Charter is the trading name of Air Charter Botswana)

MACK AIR

Maun (MUB)

A2-AIC	Cessna U206G Stationair 6	U20606419	ex N9353Z
A2-AJI	Cessna U206G Stationair 6	U20606842	ex ZS-NSS
A2-AKB	Cessna U206F Stationair	U20601889	ex A2-ZHJ
A2-ZFF	Cessna U206D Super Skywagon	U206-1263	ex ZS-FPD
A2-MAC	Cessna 210N Centurion	21063337	ex V5-MRW
A2-MEG	Cessna 208B Caravan I	208B0944	

MOREMI AIR SERVICES

Maun (MUB)

A2-AFE	Cessna U206F Stationair	U20602452	
A2-DOG	Cessna U206G Stationair 6 II	U20604819	ex A2-DOW
A2-NAP	Cessna 208B Caravan I	208B0727	ex ZS-NAP
A2-TEN	Cessna 210L Centurion	21061141	ex A2-AIY
A2-ZED	Britten-Norman BN-2A-21 Islander	736	ex ZS-XGF

NAC EXECUTIVE CHARTER

Gaborone (GBE)

A2-AJO	Beech 58 Baron	TH-614	ex ZS-OGB	
A2-BHM	Beech B200 Super King Air	BB-903	ex ZS-LBE	
A2-EAH	Beech 95-B55 Baron	TC-1794	ex ZS-GMC	
A2-MXI	Beech 200T Super King Air	BT-5	ex N205EC	
A2-NAC	Beech 1900D	UE-325	ex ZS-OYM	Air Botswana colours

NORTHERN AIR

Maun (MUB)

A2-ADK	Cessna U206G Stationair	U20606056	ex ZS-KUO
A2-AER	Cessna U206G Stationair	U20606324	ex ZS-KXE
A2-NAB	Cessna U206G Stationair	U20605439	ex ZS-KDA

SEFOFANE AIR CHARTER

Maun (MUB)

A2-AIV	Cessna U206G Stationair 6	U20606110	ex ZS-LUA	
A2-BEE	Cessna U206G Stationair 6	U20605665	ex ZS-KUL	
A2-BUG	Cessna U206G Stationair 6	U20604700	ex N27MF	
A2-FOX	Cessna U206G Stationair 6	U20604927	ex N735JM	
A2-OWL	Cessna U206G Stationair 6	U20606978	ex ZS-NXR	
A2-XIG	Cessna U206G Stationair 6	U20605528	ex ZS-NSU	
Z-OOT	Cessna U206G Stationair 6	U20604475	ex V5-AHC	
ZS-ANT	Cessna U206G Stationair 6	U20606237	ex A2-ANT	
V5-BAT	Cessna T210N Turbo Centurion	21064543	ex ZS-MUG	
V5-BUF	Cessna T210N Turbo Centurion	21063539	ex ZS-OXI	
V5-FOX	Cessna T210N Turbo Centurion	21064168	ex ZS-MKM	stored ERS
V5-KUD	Cessna 210N Centurion	21063834	ex ZS-KUD	
V5-MTB	Cessna T210N Turbo Centurion	21062923		
V5-ORX	Cessna 210L Centurion	21060795	ex A2-AIM	
V5-OWL	Cessna 210 Centurion	21063068	ex ZS-NCW	

A2-BUF	Cessna 208B Caravan I	208B0815	ex ZS-BUF	Kwatale
A2-BVR	Cessna 310R	310R2134	ex ZS-KUY	
A2-GNU	Cessna 208B Caravan I	208B0848	ex N1287Y	
V5-ELE	Cessna 208B Caravan I	208B0818	ex N1289Y	
ZS-SUN	Cessna 208B Caravan I	208B0307	ex V5-SUN	

(Also has bases at Lilongwe (Malawi) [LLW], Windhoek (Namibia) [ERS] and Harare (Zimbabwe) [HRE])

XUGANA AIR

Maun (MUB)

A2-AIX	Cessna U206F Stationair	U20601944	ex ZS-MAD	
A2-AJC	Cessna 210L Centurion	21060321	ex ZS-MUS	
A2-AJM	Britten-Norman BN-2B-21 Islander	862	ex ZS-KLK	Safari Air titles
A2-AJQ	Gippsland GA8 Airvan	GA8-02-023	ex VH-DTA	
A2-CEX	Cessna 207 Skywagon	20700154	ex ZS-IDG	
A2-TAU	Britten-Norman BN-2B-20 Islander	2173	ex N999BR	
A2-ZIB	Cessna U206G Stationair 6	U20606845	ex ZS-OBE	

A3 - TONGA (Kingdom of Tonga)

ROYAL TONGAN AIRLINES

Tonga Royal (WR/HRH) (IATA 971)   *Nuku'alofa (Tongatapu-Fua'amotu International) (TBU)*

A3-BFK	Short SD.3-60	SH3693	ex C6-BFK	
A3-FQL	de Havilland DHC-6 Twin Otter 300	685	ex ZK-FQL	Lsd fr GECAS
V8-RBB	Boeing 757-2M6	100/23453		Lsd fr RBA

Royal Tongan Airlines is the trading name of Friendly Islands Airways

A4O - OMAN (Sultanate of Oman)

GULF AIR

Gulf Air (GF/GFA) (IATA 072)   *Bahrain (BAH)*

A4O-EA	Airbus Industrie A320-212	0313	ex TC-ABG		
A4O-EB	Airbus Industrie A320-212	0325	ex F-WWDI	802; Bahla	
A4O-ED	Airbus Industrie A320-212	0375	ex F-WWDT	804; Sitra	
A4O-EE	Airbus Industrie A320-212	0419	ex F-WWDP	805; Al-Rumaitha	
A4O-EF	Airbus Industrie A320-212	0421	ex F-WWIO	806; Al Jasra	Lsd fr Oasis Intl
A4O-EG	Airbus Industrie A320-212	0438	ex F-WWDT	807	Lsd fr Oasis Intl
A4O-EH	Airbus Industrie A320-212	0445	ex F-WWBZ	808	Lsd fr Oasis Intl
A4O-EI	Airbus Industrie A320-212	0459	ex F-WWDK	809	
A4O-EJ	Airbus Industrie A320-212	0466	ex F-WWBB	810	
A4O-EL	Airbus Industrie A320-212	0497	ex F-WWDF	812	
A4O-EN	Airbus Industrie A320-212	0537	ex F-WWBX	814	
A4O-EO	Airbus Industrie A320-212	0409	ex N409MX	815	Lsd fr ILFC
A4O-KA	Airbus Industrie A330-243	276	ex F-WWKD	501	
A4O-KB	Airbus Industrie A330-243	281	ex F-WWKI	502	
A4O-KC	Airbus Industrie A330-243	286	ex F-WWKL	503	
A4O-KD	Airbus Industrie A330-243	287	ex PT-MSE	504	
A4O-KE	Airbus Industrie A330-243	334	ex PT-MSD	505	
A4O-KF	Airbus Industrie A330-243	340	ex F-WWYY	506; Aldafra	
A4O-LB	Airbus Industrie A340-312	039	ex F-WWJZ	402; Al Fateh	
A4O-LC	Airbus Industrie A340-312	040	ex F-WWJA	403; Doha	
A4O-LD	Airbus Industrie A340-312	097	ex F-WWJT	404; Abu Dhabi	
A4O-LE	Airbus Industrie A340-312	103	ex F-WWJG	405	
A4O-LF	Airbus Industrie A340-312	133	ex F-WWJP	406	
A4O-LG	Airbus Industrie A340-313X	212	ex D-ABGM		Lsd fr Boeing
A4O-LH	Airbus Industrie A340-313X	215	ex D-ASIJ		Lsd fr Boeing
A4O-LI	Airbus Industrie A340-313X	554	ex 9V-SJQ		Lsd fr Boeing
A4O-	Airbus Industrie A340-313X	282	ex D-ASIL		Lsd fr Boeing
A4O-GI	Boeing 767-3P6ER	264/24485		604; Al Khor	Lsd fr Oasis Intl
A4O-GJ	Boeing 767-3P6ER	267/24495		605; Al Muharraq	Lsd fr Oasis Intl
A4O-GK	Boeing 767-3P6ER	270/24496		606; Al Burami	Lsd fr Oasis Intl
A4O-GS+	Boeing 767-3P6ER	436/26236		613; Al Ain	
A4O-GT	Boeing 767-3P6ER	440/26238		614; Al Wakrah	
A4O-GU	Boeing 767-3P6ER	501/26233		615	Lsd fr GECAS
A4O-GV	Boeing 767-3P6ER	502/26235		616; Dukhan	
A4O-GY+	Boeing 767-3P6ER	538/26234		619	
A4O-GZ	Boeing 767-3P6ER	544/26237		620; Hilli	

+Operates as all-economy subsidiary, Gulf Traveller
Multinational airline of Abu Dhabi, Bahrain and Oman

OMANAIR

Khanjar (WY/OAS) (IATA 910)   Muscat-Seeb Intl (MCT)

A4O-BN	Boeing 737-8Q8	1018/30652	ex N1795B		Lsd fr ILFC
A4O-BO	Boeing 737-71M	1154/33103	ex N6066Z		
A4O-BR	Boeing 737-81M	1337/33104			
A4O-BS	Boeing 737-7Q8	1048/30649			Lsd fr ILFC
A4O-BT	Boeing 737-7Q8	1142/28250	ex (A4O-BS)		Lsd fr ILFC
A4O-	Boeing 737-71M			on order May04	
OK-TVC	Boeing 737-86Q	963/30278	ex N289CD		Lsd fr TVS
A4O-AL	Aerospatiale/Alenia ATR 42-500	497	ex OY-CIJ		Lsd fr CIM
A4O-AM	Aerospatiale/Alenia ATR 42-500	501	ex OY-CIK		Lsd fr CIM
A4O-AS	Aerospatiale/Alenia ATR 42-500	574	ex F-WWEO		
A4O-AT	Aerospatiale/Alenia ATR 42-500	576	ex F-WWEP		

(Omanair is the trading name of Oman Aviation Services)

A5 - BHUTAN (Kingdom of Bhutan)

DRUK AIR

Royal Bhutan (KB/DRK)   Paro (PBH)

A5-RGD	British Aerospace 146 Srs.100	E1095	ex G-6-095	
A5-RGE	British Aerospace 146 Srs.100	E1199	ex G-RJET	
A5-	Airbus Industrie A319-110		ex D-AV	on order 04
A5-	Airbus Industrie A319-110		ex D-AV	on order 04

A6 - UNITED ARAB EMIRATES (Al Imarat al-Arabiya al-Muttahida)

ABU DHABI AVIATION

Abu Dhabi-Bateen (AZI)

A6-BAB	Bell 212	31227	
A6-BAC	Bell 212	31231	
A6-BBA	Bell 212	30773	ex N9997K
A6-BBC	Bell 212	30777	
A6-BBE	Bell 212	30783	ex N9937K
A6-BBK	Bell 212	30802	
A6-BBL	Bell 212	30822	
A6-BBO	Bell 212	30903	
A6-BBP	Bell 212	30917	
A6-BBQ	Bell 212	30942	
A6-BBR	Bell 212	30976	
A6-BBS	Bell 212	30977	
A6-BBU	Bell 212	31183	
A6-BBV	Bell 212	31189	
A6-BBW	Bell 212	32123	
A6-BBY	Bell 212	32125	
A6-BBZ	Bell 212	32141	

Some based in Spain for fire-fighting duties in summer

A6-BAE	Bell 412HP	36072	
A6-BAF	Bell 412HP	36082	
A6-BAG	Bell 412HP	36061	ex N6173M
A6-BAH	Bell 412HP	36119	ex C-GBUP
A6-BAI	Bell 412HP	36122	
A6-BAK	Bell 412HP	36123	
A6-BAL	Bell 412HP	36150	
A6-BAO	Bell 412HP	36152	
A6-BAP	Bell 412HP	36189	
A6-BAQ	Bell 412HP	36190	
A6-BAS	Bell 412EP	36215	
A6-BAT	Bell 412EP	36216	
A6-HBM	Bell 412EP	36280	ex C-GJCO

A6-ADA	de Havilland DHC-8Q-202	471	ex C-GLOT
A6-ADC	de Havilland DHC-8Q-202	473	ex C-GFRP
A6-BCE	Bell 206B JetRanger II	2185	
A6-BCF	Bell 206B JetRanger III	2423	
A6-BCK	Bell 206B JetRanger III	2426	
A6-	de Havilland DHC-6 Twin Otter 320	758	ex VH-KZP
A6-	de Havilland DHC-6 Twin Otter 320	759	ex VH-KZQ

AEROGULF SERVICES

Aerogulf   *Dubai (DXB)*

A6-ALA	Bell 212	30664	ex N71AL	
A6-ALC	Bell 212	30790	ex N2781A	
A6-ALD	Bell 212	30809	ex N143AL	
A6-ALU	Bell 212	30729	ex C-GBKC	
A6-ALV	Bell 212	30703	ex A6-HMR	
A6-ALW	Bell 212	35065	ex N62200	
A6-ALP	Bell 206B JetRanger III	2495	ex (A6-BCJ)	

AIR ARABIA

(G9)   *Sharjah (SHJ)*

A6-ABX	Airbus Industrie A320-211	0371	ex C-FTDD	Lsd fr Triton
A6-ABY	Airbus Industrie A320-211	0112	ex 9H-ABP	Lsd fr ILFC
A6-	Airbus Industrie A320-		ex	on order Feb04	Lsd fr ILFC
A6-	Airbus Industrie A320-		ex	on order Mar04	Lsd fr ILFC
A6-	Airbus Industrie A320-		ex	on order Oct04	Lsd fr ILFC

One more is on order for delivery in January 2005

DOLPHIN AIR

(FDN)   *Sharjah (SHJ)*
Previously listed as Flying Dolphin Airlines and Santa Cruz Imperial under Liberia

A6-ZYA	Boeing 737-2S2C	597/21926	ex N720A		Lsd to TSG
A6-ZYB	Boeing 737-2S2C	603/21928	ex N715A	stored SHJ	
A6-ZYC	Boeing 737-2X2	807/22679	ex N719A	stored SHJ	
A6-ZYD	Boeing 707-3J6C	872/20718	ex B-513L	all-white	

EMIRATES

Emirates (EK/UAE) (IATA 176)   *Dubai (DXB)*

A6-EAA*	Airbus Industrie A330-243	348	ex F-WWYK		
A6-EAB*	Airbus Industrie A330-243	365	ex F-WWKB		
A6-EAC*	Airbus Industrie A330-243	372	ex F-WWYQ		
A6-EAD+	Airbus Industrie A330-243	382	ex F-WWYR		
A6-EAE+	Airbus Industrie A330-243	384	ex F-WWYS		
A6-EAF+	Airbus Industrie A330-243	392	ex F-WWYX		
A6-EAG+	Airbus Industrie A330-243	396	ex F-WWKJ		
A6-EAH+	Airbus Industrie A330-243	409	ex F-WWKT		
A6-EAI+	Airbus Industrie A330-243	437	ex F-WWYI		Lsd fr Credit Agricole
A6-EAJ+	Airbus Industrie A330-243	451	ex F-WWKE		
A6-EAK+	Airbus Industrie A330-243	452	ex F-WWKF		
A6-EAL*	Airbus Industrie A330-243	462	ex F-WWKK		Lsd fr ILFC
A6-EAM+	Airbus Industrie A330-243	491	ex F-WWYO		
A6-EAN+	Airbus Industrie A330-243	494	ex F-WWKJ		
A6-EAO*	Airbus Industrie A330-243	509	ex F-WWYX		
A6-EAP+	Airbus Industrie A330-243	525	ex F-WWKV		
A6-EAQ+	Airbus Industrie A330-243	518	ex F-WWKT		
A6-EAR	Airbus Industrie A330-243	536	ex F-WWYF		
A6-EAS+	Airbus Industrie A330-243	455	ex F-WWKH		
A6-EAT+	Airbus Industrie A330-243		ex F-WW	on order	
A6-EKQ*	Airbus Industrie A330-243	248	ex F-WWYX		
A6-EKR*	Airbus Industrie A330-243	251	ex F-WWKO		
A6-EKS+	Airbus Industrie A330-243	283	ex F-WWKH		
A6-EKT+	Airbus Industrie A330-243	293	ex F-WWKR		
A6-EKU+	Airbus Industrie A330-243	295	ex F-WWYF		
A6-EKV+	Airbus Industrie A330-243	314	ex F-WWYR		
A6-EKW+	Airbus Industrie A330-243	316	ex F-WWYS		
A6-EKX+	Airbus Industrie A330-243	326	ex F-WWYV		
A6-EKY*	Airbus Industrie A330-243	328	ex F-WWYX		
A6-EKZ*	Airbus Industrie A330-243	345	ex F-WWYI		
A6-ERM	Airbus Industrie A340-313X	236	ex D-AIFL		
A6-ERN	Airbus Industrie A340-313X	166	ex D-ASIC		Lsd fr Boeing Capital
A6-	Airbus Industrie A340-313X	117	ex D-ASIA	on order	Lsd fr Boeing Capital
A6-	Airbus Industrie A340-313X	139	ex D-ASIM	on order	Lsd fr Boeing Capital
A6-	Airbus Industrie A340-313X	149	ex D-A	on order	Lsd fr Boeing Capital
A6-	Airbus Industrie A340-313X	163	ex D-ASIB	on order	Lsd fr Boeing Capital
A6-	Airbus Industrie A340-313X	185	ex D-AGBM	on order	Lsd fr Boeing Capital
A6-	Airbus Industrie A340-313X	190	ex D-AJGP	on order	Lsd fr Boeing Capital

A6-ERA	Airbus Industrie A340-541	457	ex F-WWTI		
A6-ERB	Airbus Industrie A340-541	471	ex F-WWTK		
A6-ERC	Airbus Industrie A340-541	485	ex F-WWTL		
A6-ERD	Airbus Industrie A340-541	520	ex F-WWTS		
A6-ERF	Airbus Industrie A340-541	572	ex F-WWTV	on order Jul04	
A6-ER	Airbus Industrie A340-541	445	ex F-WWTH	on order	
A6-ER	Airbus Industrie A340-541	464	ex F-WWTJ	on order	
A6-ER	Airbus Industrie A340-541	608	ex F-WW	on order 04	
A6-ER	Airbus Industrie A340-541	611	ex F-WW	on order 04	

26 Airbus Industrie A340-642s are on order for delivery from 2005 plus two to be leased from ILFC in March 2005 and February 2006

43 Airbus Industrie A380-800s are on order for delivery beginning in 2006- and two A380-800Fs in 2008, the first 21 being registered A7-EDA to -EDZ with A7-EDK/L being the freighters

A6-EMD*	Boeing 777-21H	30/27247		
A6-EME*	Boeing 777-21H	33/27248		
A6-EMF*	Boeing 777-21H	42/27249		
A6-EMG+	Boeing 777-21HER	63/27252	ex N5020K	
A6-EMH+	Boeing 777-21HER	54/27251		
A6-EMI+	Boeing 777-21HER	47/27250	ex N5028Y	
A6-EMJ+	Boeing 777-21HER	91/27253		
A6-EMK+	Boeing 777-21HER	171/29324		
A6-EML+	Boeing 777-21HER	176/29325		
A6-EMM+	Boeing 777-31H	256/29062		Lsd fr SALE
A6-EMN+	Boeing 777-31H	262/29063		Lsd fr SALE
A6-EMO+	Boeing 777-31H	300/28680		Lsd fr ILFC
A6-EMP+	Boeing 777-31H	326/29395	ex N50281	Lsd fr ILFC
A6-EMQ+	Boeing 777-31H	396/32697		Lsd fr ILFC
A6-EMR+	Boeing 777-31H	402/29396		Lsd fr ILFC
A6-EMS+	Boeing 777-31H	408/29067	ex N50281	Lsd fr SALE
A6-EMT+	Boeing 777-31H	414/32699	ex N5014K	Lsd fr ILFC
A6-EMU+	Boeing 777-31H	418/29064		Lsd fr SALE
A6-EMV+	Boeing 777-31H	432/28687		Lsd fr ILFC
A6-EMW+	Boeing 777-31H	434/32700		Lsd fr ILFC
A6-EMX+	Boeing 777-31H	444/32702		Lsd fr ILFC

*have 2-class configured cabins; + have 3-class cabins
Twenty six Boeing 777-331HERs are on order for delivery between March 2005 and September 2007, 12 leased from ILFC and 14 on lease from GECAS

A6-EKL	Airbus Industrie A310-308	667	ex F-WWCZ	For TSC

EMIRAT LINK AVIATION suspended operations in late 2002

ETIHAD AIRWAYS

(EY/ETD) — *Abu Dhabi (AUH)*

A6-EYA	Airbus Industrie A330-222	361	ex PT-MVE		Lsd fr TAM
A6-EYB	Airbus Industrie A330-222	259	ex PT-MVD		Lsd fr TAM
A6-EYC	Airbus Industrie A340-313X	117	ex 7T-VKL		
A6-	Airbus Industrie A330-2			on order 04	
A6-	Airbus Industrie A330-2			on order 04	
A6-	Airbus Industrie A330-2			on order 04	
A6-	Airbus Industrie A330-2			on order 04	

First service 12 November 2003

FALCON EXPRESS CARGO AIRLINES

(FC) (IATA 553) — *Dubai (DXB)*

A6-FCA	Beech 1900C-1	UC-57	ex OY-GED
A6-FCB	Beech 1900C-1	UC-66	ex OY-GEI
A6-FCC	Beech 1900C-1	UC-68	ex OY-GEJ
A6-FCD	Beech 1900C-1	UC-71	ex OY-GEK
A6-FCE	Beech 1900C-1	UC-79	ex N79GL

Operates for Federal Express - all freighters

MENAJET

(IM/MNJ)

A7-	Airbus Industrie A320-214	2158	ex F-WWDF	on order 04	Lsd fr ILFC
A7-	Airbus Industrie A320-214	2166	ex F-WWDR	on order 04	Lsd fr ILFC

NOVA GULF current status is uncertain; sole aircraft sold

A7 - QATAR (State of Qatar)

GULF HELICOPTERS

(GF)   *Doha Heliport*

A7-HAH	Bell 212	30861		
A7-HAJ	Bell 212	30902		Lsd to GESCO as VT-HGA
A7-HAL	Bell 212	30918		Lsd to GESCO as VT-HGD
A7-HAM	Bell 212	30911		Lsd to H.S.O. as EP-HUE
A7-HAN	Bell 212	31124		Lsd to GESCO as VT-HGB
A7-HAS	Bell 212	31130	ex C-GLZG	Lsd to GESCO as VT-HGE
A7-HAT	Bell 212	31149	ex VT-HGC	Lsd to GESCO as VT-HGC
A7-HAQ	Bell 412SP	36017	ex N66104	
A7-HAR	Bell 412SP	36016	ex N6611A	Lsd to H.S.O. as EP-HUF
A7-HAU	Bell 412SP	33116	ex VH-EEH	Lsd to H.S.O. as EP-HUD
A7-HAV	Bell 412SP	33205	ex D-HHNN	
A7-HAW	Bell 412HP	36046	ex N9142N	
A7-HAY	Bell 412EP	36126	ex N2045S	
A7-HAZ	Bell 412HP	36041	ex N92801	
A7-HBA	Bell 412SP	33117	ex B-55525	Lsd to H.S.O. as EP-HUC
A7-HBB	Bell 412EP	36259	ex N9026K	
A7-HBC	Bell 412EP	36276	ex N9154J	
A7-HBD	Bell 412EP	36088	ex N4324X	
A7-HBE	Bell 412EP	36206	ex N4438D	
A7-HAO	Agusta-Bell 206B JetRanger II	8044	ex A4O-DC	
A7-HBF	Bell 230	23015	ex N236X	

QATAR AIR CARGO

Qatar Cargo (QAC)   *Doha (DOH)*

Operates cargo charters with Antonov An-12 and Ilyushin Il-18 leased as required

QATAR AIRWAYS

Qatari (QR/QTR) (IATA 157)   *Doha (DOH*

A7-ABN	Airbus Industrie A300B4-622R	664	ex VH-PWD	Al-Shaqab	Lsd fr AWAS
A7-ABO	Airbus Industrie A300B4-622R	668	ex VH-OPW	Al-Wajbah	Lsd fr AWAS
A7-ABV	Airbus Industrie A300B4-622R	690	ex VH-CLL	Al-Merqab	Lsd fr AWAS
A7-ABW	Airbus Industrie A300B4-622R	688	ex VH-CLM	Al-Ruwais	Lsd fr AWAS
A7-ABX	Airbus Industrie A300B4-622R	554	ex HL7537	Al-Dawha	Lsd fr Avequis
A7-ABY	Airbus Industrie A300B4-622R	560	ex HL7294	Fwairit	Lsd fr Avequis
A7-AFA	Airbus Industrie A300B4-622R	630	ex VH-JBN		Lsd fr AWAS
A7-AFB	Airbus Industrie A300B4-622RF	614	ex HL7298	Cargo titles	
A7-AFC	Airbus Industrie A300B4-622R	611	ex N611AN		Lsd fr AWMS I
A7-AFD	Airbus Industrie A300B4-622R	613	ex N613AN		Lsd fr AWMS I
A7-AAG	Airbus Industrie A320-232	0927	ex F-WWBA	Laffan; op for Government	
A7-ABR	Airbus Industrie A320-232	0928	ex F-WWIK	Al-Khour	Lsd fr SALE
A7-ABS	Airbus Industrie A320-232	0932	ex F-WWIG	Al-Udaid	Lsd fr SALE
A7-ABT	Airbus Industrie A320-232	0943	ex F-WWIV	Al-Ghariya	Lsd fr SALE
A7-ABU	Airbus Industrie A320-232	0977	ex F-WWDB	Al-Wakrah	Lsd fr SALE
A7-ADA	Airbus Industrie A320-232	1566	ex F-WWBG	Al-Zubareh	Lsd fr Doha Lsg
A7-ADB	Airbus Industrie A320-232	1648	ex F-WWDU	Dukhan	Lsd fr Doha Lsg
A7-ADC	Airbus Industrie A320-232	1773	ex F-WWDG	Mesaieed	Lsd fr Doha Lsg
A7-ADD	Airbus Industrie A320-232	1895	ex F-WWBT	Halul	Lsd fr Doha Lsg
A7-ADE	Airbus Industrie A320-232	1957	ex F-WWIG	Al-Gharrafah	Lsd fr Doha Lsg
A7-ADF	Airbus Industrie A320-232	2097	ex F-WWIP		Lsd fr Doha Lsg
A7-ADG	Airbus Industrie A320-232	2121	ex F-WWIT		Lsd fr A Prime
A7-ADH	Airbus Industrie A320-232	2138	ex F-WWBI		
A7-ADI	Airbus Industrie A320-232	2161	ex F-WWBK		
A7-ADJ	Airbus Industrie A320-232		ex F-WW	on order 04	
A7-ADS	Airbus Industrie A321-231	1928	ex F-WWBU		Lsd fr debis
A7-ADT	Airbus Industrie A321-231	2107	ex D-AVXD		
A7-ACA	Airbus Industrie A330-203	473	ex F-WWKR	Al Wajbah	Lsd fr Doha Lsg
A7-ACB	Airbus Industrie A330-203	489	ex F-WWYN	Al-Majdah	Lsd fr Doha Lsg
A7-ACC	Airbus Industrie A330-203	511	ex F-WWKR	Al-Shahhaniya	
A7-ACD	Airbus Industrie A330-203	521	ex F-WWKU	Al-Wosail	Lsd fr Doha Lsg
A7-ACE	Airbus Industrie A330-203	571	ex F-WWKF		
A7-ACF	Airbus Industrie A330-203		ex F-WW	on order 04	
A7-ACG	Airbus Industrie A330-203		ex F-WW	on order 04	
A7-ACH	Airbus Industrie A330-203	441	ex F-WWYK		Lsd fr Al Khawr Lsg
A7-AEA	Airbus Industrie A330-303	616	ex F-WW	on order 04	
A7-AEB	Airbus Industrie A330-303	623	ex F-WW	on order 04	
A7-AEC	Airbus Industrie A330-303		ex F-WW	on order 04	
A7-AFL	Airbus Industrie A330-203	612	ex F-WW	on order Jul04	

A7-AFM	Airbus Industrie A330-203	616	ex F-WW	on order Aug04	
A7-	Airbus Industrie A330-203	605	ex F-WW	on order 04	
A7-	Airbus Industrie A330-203		ex	on order 04	Lsd fr GECAS
A7-	Airbus Industrie A330-203		ex	on order 04	Lsd fr GECAS
A7-HJJ	Airbus Industrie A330-203	487	ex F-WWYM	Al-Rayan	Op for Govt
EI-DDU	Airbus Industrie A330-203	463	ex I-VLEG		Lsd fr GECAS
EI-DDV	Airbus Industrie A330-203	504	ex I-VLEH		Lsd fr GECAS

Six more Airbus Industrie A330-203s (including one leased from GECAS in June 2005) and seven more Airbus industrie A330-303s are on order

A7-AAF	Airbus Industrie A310-324	473	ex F-ODSV	Al-Saad; op for Govt	
A7-HHJ	Airbus Industrie A319-133X	1335	ex A7-ABZ	Op for Government	[CJ]
A7-HHK	Airbus Industrie A340-211	026	ex F-WWJQ	Op for Government	
A7-HHH	Airbus Industrie A340-541	495	ex F-WWTQ	Op for Government	
A7-CJA	Airbus Industrie A319-133LR	1656	ex D-AVYT	on order Jun03	Lsd fr Doha Lsg
A7-CJB	Airbus Industrie A319-133LR	2236	ex D-AV	on order Jun04	

Two Airbus Industrie A340-642s [A7-AGA/B] and two Airbus Industrie A380-800s on order for delivery from June 2006 & 2009 respectively

A8 - LIBERIA (Republic of Liberia)

INTERNATIONAL AIR SERVICES

Monrovia (ROB)

| A8-AAA | Lockheed L-1011- Tristar | 1101 | ex 3C-QRQ | | Lsd fr DWA |

WEASUA AIR TRANSPORT

Watco (WTC)   *Freetown/Monrovia (FNA/ROB)*

| UN-46438 | Antonov An-24B | 87304308 | ex CCCP-46438 | | Lsd fr Aqualine |

A9C - BAHRAIN (State of Bahrain)

DHL INTERNATIONAL AVIATION

Dilmun (ES/DHX) (IATA 155)   *Bahrain (BAH)*

| A9C-DHA | Swearingen SA.227AC Metro III | AC-788B | ex A9C-DHL1 | Freighter |

Division of DHL International; associated with SNAS Aviation (HZ)

B- CHINA (People's Republic of China)

AIR CHINA

Air China (CA/CCA) (IATA 999)   *Beijing-Capital (PEK)*

B-2223	Airbus Industrie A319-112	1679	ex D-AVWI		Lsd fr CIT Leasing
B-2225	Airbus Industrie A319-112	1654	ex D-AVYS		Lsd fr CIT Leasing
B-2339	Airbus Industrie A319-112	1753	ex D-AVYJ		Lsd fr CIT Leasing
B-6022	Airbus Industrie A319-132	2000	ex D-AVYZ		
B-6023	Airbus Industrie A319-132	2007	ex D-AVWM		
B-6024	Airbus Industrie A319-132	2015	ex D-AVWT		
B-	Airbus Industrie A319-132	2172	ex D-AVWW		
B-	Airbus Industrie A319-132	2202	ex D-AV	on order 04	
B-	Airbus Industrie A319-132	2205	ex D-AV	on order 04	
B-	Airbus Industrie A319-132	2237	ex D-AV	on order 04	
B-	Airbus Industrie A319-132	2269	ex D-AV	on order 04	

Four more Airbus Industrie A319-132s are on order for delivery up to 2006

B-2210	Airbus Industrie A320-214	1296	ex F-WWBG		
B-2354	Airbus Industrie A320-214	0707	ex F-WWIN		Lsd fr GECAS
B-2355	Airbus Industrie A320-214	0724	ex F-WWBN		Lsd fr GECAS
B-2376	Airbus Industrie A320-214	0876	ex F-WWIF		Lsd fr GECAS
B-2377	Airbus Industrie A320-214	0921	ex F-WWDY		Lsd fr GECAS

B-2385	Airbus Industrie A340-313X	192	ex B-HMX		
B-2386	Airbus Industrie A340-313X	199	ex B-HMY		
B-2387	Airbus Industrie A340-313X	201	ex B-HMZ		
B-2388	Airbus Industrie A340-313X	242	ex F-WWJD		
B-2389	Airbus Industrie A340-313X	243	ex F-WWJE		
B-2390	Airbus Industrie A340-313X	264	ex F-WWJY		

B-2519	Boeing 737-3Z0	1168/23448	ex N5573P		
B-2520	Boeing 737-3Z0	1184/23449	ex N1789B		
B-2521	Boeing 737-3Z0	1196/23450	ex N1790B		
B-2522	Boeing 737-3Z0	1240/23451	ex N5573K		
B-2530	Boeing 737-3Z0	2252/27046			

Reg	Type	c/n	ex	status	lease
B-2531	Boeing 737-3J6	1224/23302	ex N1792B		
B-2532	Boeing 737-3J6	1237/23303	ex N5573B		
B-2533	Boeing 737-3Z0	2436/27138			
B-2535	Boeing 737-3J6	2002/25078			
B-2536	Boeing 737-3J6	2016/25079			
B-2537	Boeing 737-3Z0	2027/25089			
B-2580	Boeing 737-3J6	2254/25080			
B-2581	Boeing 737-3J6	2263/25081			
B-2584	Boeing 737-3J6	2385/25891			
B-2585	Boeing 737-3J6	2384/27045			
B-2586	Boeing 737-3Z0	2357/27047			
B-2587	Boeing 737-3J6	2396/25892		based TSN	
B-2588	Boeing 737-3J6	2489/25893		based TSN	
B-2590	Boeing 737-3Z0	2370/27126			
B-2597	Boeing 737-3Z0	2495/27176			
B-2598	Boeing 737-3J6	2493/27128		based TSN	
B-2599	Boeing 737-3Z0	2558/25896			
B-2905	Boeing 737-33A	2360/25506	ex N403AW		
B-2906	Boeing 737-33A	2373/25507	ex N404AW		
B-2907	Boeing 737-33A	2414/25508	ex N405AW		
B-2947	Boeing 737-33A	2599/25511			
B-2948	Boeing 737-3J6	2631/27361			
B-2949	Boeing 737-3J6	2650/27372		based TSN	
B-2950	Boeing 737-3Z0	2647/27374			
B-2951	Boeing 737-3Z0	2658/27373			
B-2953	Boeing 737-3J6	2710/27523			
B-2954	Boeing 737-3J6	2768/27518			
B-2957	Boeing 737-3Z0	2738/27521			
B-5035	Boeing 737-36N	2976/28672	ex F-GRFA		Lsd fr GECAS
B-5036	Boeing 737-36N	2995/28673	ex F-GRFB		Lsd fr GECAS
B-	Boeing 737-36E	2706/26315	ex F-GNFC	on order	Lsd fr ILFC
B-	Boeing 737-36E	2719/26317	ex F-GNFD	on order	Lsd fr ILFC
B-2155	Boeing 737-66N	887/28649			Lsd fr GECAS
B-2156	Boeing 737-66N	932/28650			Lsd fr GECAS
B-2160	Boeing 737-66N	938/28652	ex N1787B		Lsd fr GECAS
B-2161	Boeing 737-86N	965/28655			Lsd fr GECAS
B-2509	Boeing 737-8Z0	466/30072	ex N1787B		
B-2510	Boeing 737-8Z0	381/30071			
B-2511	Boeing 737-8Z0	487/30073			
B-2641	Boeing 737-89L	337/29876			
B-2642	Boeing 737-89L	359/29877			
B-2643	Boeing 737-89L	379/29878			
B-2645	Boeing 737-89L	427/29879			
B-2648	Boeing 737-89L	511/29880			
B-2649	Boeing 737-89L	572/30159	ex N1784B		
B-2650	Boeing 737-89L	594/30160			
B-2657	Boeing 737-89L	1224/30517			
B-2670	Boeing 737-89L	1055/30514			
B-2671	Boeing 737-89L	1165/30515			
B-2672	Boeing 737-89L	1168/30516			
B-2673	Boeing 737-86N	1133/29888			Lsd fr GECAS
B-2690	Boeing 737-86N	1153/29889			Lsd fr GECAS
B-5023	Boeing 737-66N	1276/29890			Lsd fr GECAS
B-5027	Boeing 737-66N	1294/29891			Lsd fr GECAS
B-5037	Boeing 737-66N	1305/29892			Lsd fr GECAS
B-5043	Boeing 737-79L	1331/33408			
B-5044	Boeing 737-79L	1351/33409			
B-5045	Boeing 737-79L	1354/33410			
B-	Boeing 737-79L			on order 04	
B-	Boeing 737-79L			on order 04	
B-	Boeing 737-79L			on order 04	
B-	Boeing 737-8Z0			on order 04	

Two more Boeing 737-800s are on order for delivery in 2005 plus five Boeing 737-700s in 2005/6

Reg	Type	c/n	ex	status	lease
B-2409	Boeing 747-412F	1052/26560	ex 9V-SFC		Lsd fr SQC
B-2443	Boeing 747-4J6	957/25881			
B-2445	Boeing 747-4J6	1021/25882			
B-2446	Boeing 747-2J6B(SF)	591/23071	ex N1781B		
B-2447	Boeing 747-4J6	1054/25883			
B-2448	Boeing 747-2J6B(SF)	628/23461	ex N60668		
B-2450	Boeing 747-2J6B(SF)	670/23746	ex N6018N		
B-2456	Boeing 747-4J6M	743/24346			
B-2458	Boeing 747-4J6M	775/24347			
B-2460	Boeing 747-4J6M	792/24348			
B-2462	Boeing 747-2J6F	814/24960			
B-2467	Boeing 747-4J6M	1119/28754			
B-2468	Boeing 747-4J6M	1128/28755			
B-2469	Boeing 747-4J6M	1175/28756			
B-2470	Boeing 747-4J6M	1181/29070			
B-2471	Boeing 747-4J6M	1229/29071			
B-2472	Boeing 747-4J6	1243/30158			

B-2820	Boeing 757-2Z0	476/25885		
B-2821	Boeing 757-2Z0	480/25886		
B-2826	Boeing 757-2Y0	495/26155		Lsd fr GECAS
B-2832	Boeing 757-2Z0	554/25887		
B-2836	Boeing 757-2Z0	595/27258		
B-2837	Boeing 757-2Z0	609/27259		
B-2839	Boeing 757-2Z0	615/27269		
B-2840	Boeing 757-2Z0	622/27270		
B-2841	Boeing 757-2Z0	624/27367		
B-2844	Boeing 757-2Z0	669/27511		
B-2845	Boeing 757-2Z0	674/27512		
B-2855	Boeing 757-2Z0	822/29792		
B-2856	Boeing 757-2Z0	833/29793		Lsd to RNA
B-2493	Boeing 767-3Q8ER	692/28132	ex N634TW	Lsd fr ILFC
B-2496	Boeing 767-3Q8ER	762/30301	ex B-2494	Lsd fr ILFC
B-2499	Boeing 767-332ER	797/30597	ex B-4025	Op for Govt
B-2551	Boeing 767-2J6ER	126/23307	ex N6065Y	
B-2553	Boeing 767-2J6ER	155/23744	ex N60659	
B-2554	Boeing 767-2J6ER	156/23745	ex N6009F	
B-2555	Boeing 767-2J6ER	204/24007	ex N60668	
B-2556	Boeing 767-2J6ER	253/24157	ex N6018N	
B-2557	Boeing 767-3J6	429/25875		
B-2558	Boeing 767-3J6	478/25876		
B-2559	Boeing 767-3J6	530/25877		
B-2560	Boeing 767-3J6	569/25878		
B-2059	Boeing 777-2J6	168/29153		
B-2060	Boeing 777-2J6	173/29154		
B-2061	Boeing 777-2J6	179/29155		
B-2063	Boeing 777-2J6	214/29156		
B-2064	Boeing 777-2J6	240/29157		
B-2065	Boeing 777-2J6	280/29744		
B-2066	Boeing 777-2J6	290/29745		
B-2067	Boeing 777-2J6	338/29746		
B-2068	Boeing 777-2J6	344/29747		
B-2069	Boeing 777-2J6	349/29748		
B-	Tupolev Tu-204-120C		on order	Lsd fr Sirocco Aerospace
B-	Tupolev Tu-204-120C		on order	Lsd fr Sirocco Aerospace
B-	Tupolev Tu-204-120C		on order	Lsd fr Sirocco Aerospace

Merged with China Southwest Airlines and CNAC-Zhejiang Airlines on 11 October 2002 and fleets combined in 2003.
All are wholly owned subsidiaries of China National Aviation

AIR GUIZHOU merged into China Southern Airlines in 2003

CHANG AN AIRLINES

Changan (2Z/CGN)   *Xi'an (SIA)*

B-3444	Xian Y-7-100	09701		
B-3445	Xian Y-7-100C	09705		
B-3475	Xian Y-7-100C	06703		
B-3707	Xian Y-7-100C	12701		
B-3708	Xian Y-7-100C	11705		
B-3720	Xian Y-7-200A	200-0001		
B-3721	Xian Y-7-200A	200-0003		
B-3569	de Havilland DHC-8Q-402	4039	ex C-	

Subsidiary of Hainan Airlines; some Dornier 328s are operated by the parent on its behalf

CHINA CARGO AIRLINES

Cargo King (CK/CKK) (IATA 112)   *Shanghai (SHA)*

70% owned by China Eastern Airlines; operates Boeing 747F aircraft on ACMI lease from Atlas Air

CHINA EASTERN AIRLINES

China Eastern (MU/CES) (IATA 781)   *Shanghai (SHA)*

B-2301	Airbus Industrie A310-222	311	ex F-WZEJ	Lsd fr Pratt & Whitney
B-2302	Airbus Industrie A310-222	320	ex F-WZER	Lsd fr Pratt & Whitney
B-2303	Airbus Industrie A310-222	419	ex LZ-JXB	Lsd fr Pratt & Whitney
B-2306	Airbus Industrie A300B4-605R	521	ex F-WWAF	
B-2307	Airbus Industrie A300B4-605R	525	ex F-WWAJ	
B-2308	Airbus Industrie A300B4-605R	532	ex F-WWAH	
B-2317	Airbus Industrie A300B4-605R	741	ex F-WWAY	
B-2318	Airbus Industrie A300B4-605R	707	ex F-WWAU	
B-2319	Airbus Industrie A300B4-605R	732	ex F-WWAT	
B-2320	Airbus Industrie A300B4-605R	709	ex N190PL	Lsd fr GECAS
B-2321	Airbus Industrie A300B4-605R	713	ex N191PL	Lsd fr GECAS

B-2322	Airbus Industrie A300B4-605R	715	ex N192PL	Lsd fr GECAS
B-2324	Airbus Industrie A300B4-622R	725	ex F-WWAR	
B-2325	Airbus Industrie A300B4-605R	746	ex F-WWAA	
B-2326	Airbus Industrie A300B4-605R	754	ex F-WWAY	
B-2330	Airbus Industrie A300B4-605R	763	ex F-WWAH	
B-2215	Airbus Industrie A319-112	1541	ex D-AVWI	Lsd fr GECAS
B-2216	Airbus Industrie A319-112	1551	ex D-AVWN	Lsd fr GECAS
B-2217	Airbus Industrie A319-112	1601	ex D-AVWX	Lsd fr GECAS
B-2222	Airbus Industrie A319-112	1603	ex D-AVWY	Lsd fr GECAS
B-2226	Airbus Industrie A319-112	1786	ex D-AVYP	Lsd fr GECAS
B-2227	Airbus Industrie A319-112	1778	ex D-AVYE	Lsd fr GECAS
B-2331	Airbus Industrie A319-112	1285	ex D-AVYT	Lsd fr GECAS
B-2332	Airbus Industrie A319-112	1303	ex D-AVWN	Lsd fr GECAS
B-2333	Airbus Industrie A319-112	1377	ex D-AVWE	Lsd fr GECAS
B-2334	Airbus Industrie A319-112	1386	ex D-AVWC	Lsd fr GECAS
B-2201	Airbus Industrie A320-214	0914	ex F-WWDV	Lsd fr CIT Leasing
B-2202	Airbus Industrie A320-214	0925	ex F-WWID	Lsd fr GECAS
B-2203	Airbus Industrie A320-214	1005	ex F-WWDL	Lsd fr GECAS
B-2205	Airbus Industrie A320-214	0984	ex F-WWDI	Lsd fr ILFC
B-2206	Airbus Industrie A320-214	0986	ex F-WWDJ	Lsd fr CIT Group
B-2207	Airbus Industrie A320-214	1028	ex F-WWDG	
B-2208	Airbus Industrie A320-214	1070	ex F-WWBH	
B-2209	Airbus Industrie A320-214	1030	ex F-WWDU	
B-2211	Airbus Industrie A320-214	1041	ex F-WWID	Lsd fr debis
B-2212	Airbus Industrie A320-214	1316	ex F-WWDG	
B-2213	Airbus Industrie A320-214	1345	ex F-WWDX	
B-2219	Airbus Industrie A320-214	1532	ex F-WWIP	
B-2220	Airbus Industrie A320-214	1542	ex F-WWIV	
B-2221	Airbus Industrie A320-214	1639	ex F-WWDZ	
B-2228	Airbus Industrie A320-214	1906	ex F-WWDK	
B-2229	Airbus Industrie A320-214	1911	ex F-WWDT	
B-2230	Airbus Industrie A320-214	1964	ex F-WWDR	
B-2335	Airbus Industrie A320-214	1312	ex F-WWBZ	
B-2336	Airbus Industrie A320-214	1330	ex F-WWDV	
B-2337	Airbus Industrie A320-214	1357	ex F-WWBF	
B-2338	Airbus Industrie A320-214	1361	ex F-WWBU	
B-2356	Airbus Industrie A320-214	0665	ex F-WWBB	
B-2357	Airbus Industrie A320-214	0754	ex F-WWIY	
B-2358	Airbus Industrie A320-214	0838	ex F-WWBB	
B-2359	Airbus Industrie A320-214	0854	ex F-WWBK	
B-2360	Airbus Industrie A320-214	0772	ex F-WWDK	Lsd fr CIT Leasing
B-2361	Airbus Industrie A320-214	0799	ex F-WWDI	Lsd fr CIT Leasing
B-2362	Airbus Industrie A320-214	0828	ex F-WWIM	Lsd fr GECAS
B-2363	Airbus Industrie A320-214	0883	ex F-WWDC	Lsd fr CIT Leasing
B-2372	Airbus Industrie A320-214	0897	ex F-WWDK	
B-2375	Airbus Industrie A320-214	0909	ex F-WWDS	
B-2378	Airbus Industrie A320-214	0939	ex F-WWIQ	
B-2379	Airbus Industrie A320-214	0967	ex F-WWBN	Lsd fr ILFC
B-2398	Airbus Industrie A320-214	1108	ex F-WWDH	Lsd fr GECAS
B-2399	Airbus Industrie A320-214	1093	ex F-WWIZ	Lsd fr GECAS
B-2400	Airbus Industrie A320-214	1072	ex F-WWBI	Lsd fr GECAS
B-6001	Airbus Industrie A320-214	1981	ex F-WWDL	
B-6002	Airbus Industrie A320-214	2022	ex F-WWIF	
B-6003	Airbus Industrie A320-214	2034	ex F-WWIZ	
B-6005	Airbus Industrie A320-214	2036	ex F-WWIZ	
B-6006	Airbus Industrie A320-214	2068	ex F-WWIL	
B-6007	Airbus Industrie A320-214	2056	ex F-WWIR	
B-6008	Airbus Industrie A320-214	2049	ex F-WWII	
B-	Airbus Industrie A320-214	2171	ex F-WWDG	on order 04
B-	Airbus Industrie A320-214	2182	ex F-WWIO	on order 04
B-	Airbus Industrie A320-214	2199	ex F-WW	on order 04
B-	Airbus Industrie A320-214	2212	ex F-WW	on order 04
B-	Airbus Industrie A320-214		ex OO-S	on order
B-	Airbus Industrie A320-214	2219	ex F-WW	on order 04	Lsd fr ILFC
B-	Airbus Industrie A320-214	2221	ex F-WW	on order 04	Lsd fr ILFC
B-	Airbus Industrie A320-214	2235	ex F-WW	on order 04	Lsd fr ILFC
B-	Airbus Industrie A320-214	2239	ex F-WW	on order 04	Lsd fr ILFC
B-	Airbus Industrie A320-214	2244	ex F-WW	on order 04	Lsd fr ILFC

Four more Airbus Industrie A320-214s are on order for delivery in 2005

B-2380	Airbus Industrie A340-313X	129	ex F-WWJQ	
B-2381	Airbus Industrie A340-313X	131	ex F-WWJO	
B-2382	Airbus Industrie A340-313X	141	ex F-WWJC	
B-2383	Airbus Industrie A340-313X	161	ex F-WWJQ	
B-2384	Airbus Industrie A340-313X	182	ex F-WWJM	
B-6050	Airbus Industrie A340-642	468	ex F-WWCP	
B-6051	Airbus Industrie A340-642	488	ex F-WWCT	
B-6052	Airbus Industrie A340-642	514	ex F-WWCU	
B-	Airbus Industrie A340-642	577	ex F-WW	on order
B-	Airbus Industrie A340-642	586	ex F-WW	on order

B-2517	Boeing 737-3W0	1166/23396	ex N5573K	
B-2518	Boeing 737-3W0	1193/23397	ex N1791B	
B-2538	Boeing 737-3W0	2040/25090		
B-2571	Boeing 737-39P	3053/29410		
B-2572	Boeing 737-39P	3071/29411		
B-2573	Boeing 737-39P	3080/29412		
B-2589	Boeing 737-3W0	2377/27127		
B-2594	Boeing 737-341	2275/26853	ex (PP-VPB)	
B-2918	Boeing 737-3Q8	2192/24986	ex N551LF	Lsd fr ILFC
B-2919	Boeing 737-3Q8	2268/24987	ex N561LF	Lsd fr ILFC
B-2928	Boeing 737-3Q8	2550/26294	ex N261LF	Lsd fr ILFC
B-2955	Boeing 737-33A	2687/27453		Lsd fr AWAS
B-2956	Boeing 737-33A	2690/27907		Lsd fr AWAS
B-2958	Boeing 737-3W0	2727/27522		
B-2966	Boeing 737-33A	2765/27462		Lsd fr AWAS
B-2969	Boeing 737-36R	3108/30102	ex N1787B	
B-2976	Boeing 737-3S3	3059/29244	ex N244SR	Lsd fr Sunrock
B-2977	Boeing 737-36N	2888/28560		Lsd fr GECAS
B-2978	Boeing 737-36N	2896/28561		Lsd fr GECAS
B-2979	Boeing 737-36N	2908/28562		Lsd fr GECAS
B-2981	Boeing 737-3W0	2919/28972		
B-2983	Boeing 737-3W0	2941/28973		
B-2985	Boeing 737-3W0	2945/29068		
B-2986	Boeing 737-3W0	2951/29069		
B-2988	Boeing 737-36R	2970/29087		
B-2502	Boeing 737-7W0	292/30075		
B-2503	Boeing 737-7W0	311/30074		
B-2639	Boeing 737-7W0	140/29912	ex N1787B	
B-2640	Boeing 737-7W0	148/29913	ex N1800B	
B-2660	Boeing 737-86R	786/30494		Lsd fr CIT Leasing
B-2665	Boeing 737-86R	876/30495	ex N1784B	Lsd fr CIT Leasing
B-2680	Boeing 737-76Q	1143/30282	ex N706BA	Lsd fr Boullioun
B-2681	Boeing 737-79P	1198/33037		
B-2682	Boeing 737-79P	1219/33038		
B-2683	Boeing 737-79P	1247/28253		Lsd fr ILFC
B-2684	Boeing 737-79P	1227/33039		
B-2685	Boeing 737-79P	1244/33040		
B-2686	Boeing 737-8Q8	1200/28251		Lsd fr ILFC
B-5030	Boeing 737-79P	1267/30651		Lsd fr ILFC
B-5031	Boeing 737-79P	1284/28255		Lsd fr ILFC
B-5032	Boeing 737-79P	1288/30035		Lsd fr ILFC
B-5033	Boeing 737-79P	1319/30657		Lsd fr ILFC
B-5034	Boeing 737-79P	1336/30036		Lsd fr ILFC
B-2701	British Aerospace 146 Srs.100	E1019	ex G-XIAN	
B-2702	British Aerospace 146 Srs.100	E1026	ex G-5-026	
B-2703	British Aerospace 146 Srs.100	E1032	ex G-5-032	
B-2711	British Aerospace 146 Srs.300	E3207	ex G-BUHV	
B-2712	British Aerospace 146 Srs.300	E3212	ex G-6-212	
B-2715	British Aerospace 146 Srs.300	E3214	ex G-6-214	
B-2717	British Aerospace 146 Srs.300	E3216	ex G-6-216	
B-2718	British Aerospace 146 Srs.300	E3222	ex G-6-222	
B-2719	British Aerospace 146 Srs.300	E3218	ex G-6-218	
B-2720	British Aerospace 146 Srs.300	E3219	ex G-6-219	
B-3013	Canadair CL-600-2B19	7571	ex C-FVAZ	
B-3019	Canadair CL-600-2B19	7581	ex C-	
B-3021	Canadair CL-600-2B19	7596	ex C-FMNW	
B-3070	Canadair CL-600-2B19	7647	ex C-FMLB	special c/s
B-3071	Canadair CL-600-2B19	7684	ex C-FMMT	special c/s
B-3072	Canadair CL-600-2B19	7697	ex C-FMML	
B-3078	Canadair CL-600-2B19	7704		
B-	Canadair CL-600-2B19			on order
B-2170	McDonnell-Douglas MD-11F	475/48461		
B-2171	McDonnell-Douglas MD-11	461/48495		
B-2172	McDonnell-Douglas MD-11F	496/48496		
B-2173	McDonnell-Douglas MD-11F	512/48497		
B-2174	McDonnell-Douglas MD-11F	522/48498		
B-2175	McDonnell-Douglas MD-11F	541/48520	ex N9134D	
B-2256	McDonnell-Douglas MD-90-30	2198/53582		
B-2257	McDonnell-Douglas MD-90-30	2200/53583		
B-2258	McDonnell-Douglas MD-90-30	2203/53584		
B-2262	McDonnell-Douglas MD-90-30	2224/53585		
B-2263	McDonnell-Douglas MD-90-30	2233/53586		
B-2265	McDonnell-Douglas MD-90-30	2240/53587		
B-2268	McDonnell-Douglas MD-90-30	2248/53588		
B-2269	McDonnell-Douglas MD-90-30	2259/53589		
B-2270	McDonnell-Douglas MD-90-30	2261/53590		

B-3442	Xian Y-7-100C	08701	
B-3443	Xian Y-7-100C	08702	
B-3471	Xian Y-7-100C	05706	
B-3472	Xian Y-7-100C	05707	
B-3490	Xian Y-7-100C	07709	
B-3491	Xian Y-7-100C	07710	
B-2127	McDonnell-Douglas MD-82	1537/49511	SAIC c/n 12
B-2129	McDonnell-Douglas MD-82	1568/49513	SAIC c/n 14
B-2131	McDonnell-Douglas MD-82	1609/49515	SAIC c/n 16
B-2568	Boeing 767-3W0ER	620/28148	
B-2569	Boeing 767-3W0ER	627/28149	
B-5001	Boeing 767-3W0ER	644/28264	
B-	Tupolev Tu-204-120C		on order Lsd fr Sirocco Aerospace
B-	Tupolev Tu-204-120C		on order Lsd fr Sirocco Aerospace

Owns 70% of China Cargo Airlines and 40% of Wuhan Airlines. Merged with China Northwest Airlines and China Yunnan Airlines on 11 October 2002 and fleets combined in 2003.

CHINA FLYING DRAGON AVIATION CO

Feilong (CFA)   *Harbin - Ping Fang*

B-7420	Aerospatiale AS.350B-2 Ecureuil	2522	
B-7421	Aerospatiale AS.350B-2 Ecureuil	2523	
B-7422	Aerospatiale AS.350B-2 Ecureuil	2534	
B-7423	Aerospatiale AS.350B-2 Ecureuil	2538	
B-7424	Aerospatiale AS.350B-2 Ecureuil	2547	
B-7425	Aerospatiale AS.350B-2 Ecureuil	2554	
B-7427	Aerospatiale AS.350B-2 Ecureuil	2566	

All operated for Ministry of Forestry

B-3201	Harbin Y-11B	003	
B-3862	Harbin Y-11	0407	
B-3863	Harbin Y-11	0408	
B-3864	Harbin Y-11	0409	
B-3874	Harbin Y-11	0102	
B-3875	Harbin Y-11	0105	
B-3876	Harbin Y-11	0106	
B-3877	Harbin Y-11	0107	
B-3878	Harbin Y-11	0110	
B-3879	Harbin Y-11	0201	
B-3880	Harbin Y-11	0202	
B-3881	Harbin Y-11	0203	
B-3882	Harbin Y-11	0204	
B-3883	Harbin Y-11	0205	
B-3884	Harbin Y-11	0210	

All possibly withdrawn from service

B-3801	Harbin Y-12 II	0006	Freighter
B-3803	Harbin Y-12 II	0003	Surveyor
B-3804	Harbin Y-12 II	0011	Surveyor
B-3805	Harbin Y-12 II	0005	Surveyor
B-3806	Harbin Y-12 II	0008	Freighter
B-3807	Harbin Y-12 II	0016	Op for Maritime Service
B-3808	Harbin Y-12 II	0017	Op for Maritime Service
B-3819	Harbin Y-12 II	0004	
B-3822	Harbin Y-12 II	0001	

B-3501	de Havilland DHC-6 Twin Otter 300	563	ex B-512	
B-3502	de Havilland DHC-6 Twin Otter 300	565	ex B-514	
B-3503	de Havilland DHC-6 Twin Otter 300	602	ex B-516	
B-3504	de Havilland DHC-6 Twin Otter 300	564	ex B-510	
B-7109	Harbin Z-9A Haitun (SA.365N)	045		Op for Ministry of Forestry
B-7110	Harbin Z-9A Haitun (SA.365N)	047		Op for Ministry of Forestry

(China Feilong Airlines trading as a division of Harbin Aircraft Manufacturing Plant)

CHINA NORTHERN AIRLINES merged into China Southern Airlines in 2003

CHINA NORTHWEST AIRLINES merged into China Eastern Airlines in 2003

CHINA POSTAL AIRLINES

China Postair (CYZ)   *Tianjin (TSN)*

B-3101	Yunshuji Y-8F-100	10(08)01		
B-3102	Yunshuji Y-8F-100	10(08)02		
B-3103	Yunshuji Y-8F-100	10(08)03		
B-3109	Yunshuji Y-8F-100	13(08)03		
B-3110	Yunshuji Y-8F-100			
B-	Boeing 737-341F	1645/24276	ex N276HE	Lsd fr CSN
B-	Boeing 737-341F	1660/24278	ex N278HE	Lsd fr CSN

49% owned by China Southern Airlines

CHINA SOUTHERN AIRLINES

China Southern (CZ/CSN) (IATA 784)   *Guangzhou (CAN)*

B-3022	Aerospatiale/Alenia ATR 72-212A	521	ex F-WWED	
B-3023	Aerospatiale/Alenia ATR 72-212A	531	ex F-WWLK	
B-3025	Aerospatiale/Alenia ATR 72-212A	547	ex F-WWLO	
B-3026	Aerospatiale/Alenia ATR 72-212A	552	ex F-WWLP	
B-3027	Aerospatiale/Alenia ATR 72-212A	555	ex F-WWLL	
B-2315	Airbus Industrie A300B4-622R	733	ex F-WWAU	
B-2316	Airbus Industrie A300B4-622R	734	ex F-WWAE	
B-2323	Airbus Industrie A300B4-622R	739	ex F-WWAB	
B-2327	Airbus Industrie A300B4-622R	750	ex HL7583	
B-2328	Airbus Industrie A300B4-622R	756	ex HL7580	
B-2329	Airbus Industrie A300B4-622R	762	ex HL7581	
B-6018	Airbus Industrie A319-132	1971	ex D-AVYC	Lsd fr ILFC
B-6019	Airbus Industrie A319-132	1986	ex D-AVYJ	Lsd fr ILFC
B-6020	Airbus Industrie A319-132	2004	ex D-AVWB	Lsd fr ILFC
B-6021	Airbus Industrie A319-132	2008	ex D-AVWN	Lsd fr ILFC
B-	Airbus Industrie A319-132	2200	ex	
B-	Airbus Industrie A319-132	2203	ex	
B-2343	Airbus Industrie A320-232	0696	ex F-WWII	Lsd to CSC
B-2345	Airbus Industrie A320-232	0698	ex F-WWBT	
B-2346	Airbus Industrie A320-232	0704	ex F-WWDY	
B-2347	Airbus Industrie A320-232	0705	ex F-WWIL	
B-2350	Airbus Industrie A320-232	0712	ex F-WWDI	
B-2351	Airbus Industrie A320-232	0718	ex F-WWBI	
B-2352	Airbus Industrie A320-232	0720	ex F-WWBU	
B-2353	Airbus Industrie A320-232	0722	ex F-WWBM	
B-2365	Airbus Industrie A320-232	0849	ex F-WWBI	
B-2366	Airbus Industrie A320-232	0859	ex F-WWBO	
B-2367	Airbus Industrie A320-232	0881	ex F-WWDB	
B-2368	Airbus Industrie A320-232	0895	ex F-WWDJ	
B-2369	Airbus Industrie A320-232	0900	ex F-WWDM	
B-2391	Airbus Industrie A320-232	0950	ex F-WWIZ	
B-2392	Airbus Industrie A320-232	0966	ex F-WWBK	
B-2393	Airbus Industrie A320-232	1035	ex F-WWDX	
B-2395	Airbus Industrie A320-232	1039	ex F-WWDZ	
B-2396	Airbus Industrie A320-232	1057	ex F-WWIO	
B-2401	Airbus Industrie A320-232	0710	ex F-OHCY	Lsd fr CIT Leasing
B-2448	Airbus Industrie A320-232	0709	ex F-OHCX	
B-2280	Airbus Industrie A321-231	1596	ex D-AVZL	
B-2281	Airbus Industrie A321-231	1614	ex D-AVZA	
B-2282	Airbus Industrie A321-231	1776	ex D-AVZC	
B-2283	Airbus Industrie A321-231	1788	ex D-AVZE	
B-2284	Airbus Industrie A321-231	1974	ex D-AVYN	
B-2285	Airbus Industrie A321-231	1995	ex D-AVZZ	
B-	Airbus Industrie A321-231	2067	ex D-AVZP	
B-2287	Airbus Industrie A321-231	2080	ex D-AVZW	on order 04

Two more Airbus Industrie A321-231s are on order for delivery in 2005

B-2526	Boeing 737-3Y0	2089/25172		Lsd fr GECAS
B-2527	Boeing 737-3Y0	2097/25173		Lsd fr GECAS
B-2528	Boeing 737-3Y0	2168/25174		Lsd fr GECAS
B-2539	Boeing 737-3Y0	2306/26068		Lsd fr BBAM
B-2541	Boeing 737-5Y0	1960/24696		Lsd fr Citicorp
B-2542	Boeing 737-5Y0	2003/24897		Lsd fr GECAS
B-2543	Boeing 737-5Y0	2079/24898		Lsd fr BBAM
B-2544	Boeing 737-5Y0	2093/24899		Lsd fr GECAS
B-2545	Boeing 737-5Y0	2095/24900		Lsd fr GECAS
B-2546	Boeing 737-5Y0	2150/25175		Lsd fr GECAS
B-2547	Boeing 737-5Y0	2155/25176		Lsd fr GECAS
B-2548	Boeing 737-5Y0	2211/25182		Lsd fr GECAS
B-2549	Boeing 737-5Y0	2218/25183		Lsd fr GECAS
B-2550	Boeing 737-5Y0	2238/25188		Lsd fr GECAS
B-2574	Boeing 737-37K	3100/29407		
B-2575	Boeing 737-37K	3104/29408	ex N1800B	
B-2582	Boeing 737-31B	2499/25895		
B-2583	Boeing 737-31B	2554/25897		
B-2596	Boeing 737-31B	2437/27151		
B-2909	Boeing 737-3Y0	2456/26082		Lsd fr GECAS
B-2910	Boeing 737-3Y0	2459/26083		Lsd fr GECAS
B-2911	Boeing 737-3Y0	2460/26084		Lsd fr GECAS
B-2912	Boeing 737-5Y0	2538/26100	ex N35108	Lsd fr GECAS
B-2915	Boeing 737-5Y0	2544/26101		Lsd fr GECAS
B-2920	Boeing 737-3Q8	2523/27271		
B-2921	Boeing 737-3Q8	2528/27286		
B-2922	Boeing 737-31B	2555/27272		

B-2923	Boeing 737-31B	2565/27275			
B-2924	Boeing 737-31B	2575/27287			
B-2926	Boeing 737-31B	2593/27289			
B-2927	Boeing 737-31B	2595/27290			
B-2929	Boeing 737-31B	2619/27343			
B-2935	Boeing 737-37K	2547/27283			
B-2936	Boeing 737-37K	2609/27335			
B-2946	Boeing 737-37K	2655/27375			
B-2941	Boeing 737-31B	2622/27344			
B-2952	Boeing 737-31B	2678/27519			
B-2959	Boeing 737-31B	2775/27520			
B-	Boeing 737-341F	1645/24276	ex N276HE		Lsd to CYZ
B-	Boeing 737-341QC	1658/24277	ex N277HE		
B-	Boeing 737-341F	1660/24278	ex N278HE		Lsd to CYZ
B-	Boeing 737-341QC	1673/24279	ex N279HE		
N999CZ	Boeing 737-3Y9	2405/25604	ex N1784B		Lsd fr C Itoh
B-2162	Boeing 737-7K9	909/30041			Lsd fr Bavaria
B-2163	Boeing 737-7K9	931/30042			Lsd fr Bavaria
B-2930	Boeing 737-31L	2556/27273			
B-2931	Boeing 737-31L	2567/27276			
B-2693	Boeing 737-81B	1187/32921	ex N6065Y		
B-2694	Boeing 737-81B	1199/32922			
B-2695	Boeing 737-81B	1213/32923			
B-2696	Boeing 737-81B	1230/32924			
B-2697	Boeing 737-81B	1250/32925			
B-2698	Boeing 737-76N	994/32583	ex N583SF		Lsd fr GECAS
B-2699	Boeing 737-76N	1028/32596			Lsd fr GECAS
B-5020	Boeing 737-81B	1268/32926			
B-5021	Boeing 737-81B	1290/32927			
B-5022	Boeing 737-81B	1323/32928			
B-5040	Boeing 737-81B	1348/32929			
B-5041	Boeing 737-81B	1355/32930			
B-5042	Boeing 737-81B	1362/32931			
B-5067	Boeing 737-81B	1395/32932			
B-5068	Boeing 737-71B	1430/32933			
B-5069	Boeing 737-71B	32934		on order	
B-5070	Boeing 737-71B	32935		on order	
B-	Boeing 737-81B			on order	
B-	Boeing 737-81B			on order	
B-	Boeing 737-81B			on order	

Five more Boeing 737-81Bs are on order for delivery in 2005

B-2801	Boeing 757-21B	144/24014	ex N1792B		
B-2802	Boeing 757-21B	148/24015	ex N5573B		
B-2803	Boeing 757-21B	150/24016	ex N5573K		
B-2804	Boeing 757-21B	200/24330			Lsd fr Tombo
B-2805	Boeing 757-21B	203/24331			Lsd fr Tombo
B-2806	Boeing 757-21B	232/24401	ex N6067B		
B-2807	Boeing 757-21B	233/24402	ex N6069D		
B-2811	Boeing 757-21B	262/24714			
B-2812	Boeing 757-28S	961/32341			
B-2813	Boeing 757-28S	966/32342			
B-2815	Boeing 757-21B	288/24774			
B-2816	Boeing 757-21B	359/25083			
B-2817	Boeing 757-21B	389/25258			
B-2818	Boeing 757-21B	392/25259			
B-2822	Boeing 757-21B	461/25884			
B-2823	Boeing 757-21B	575/25888			
B-2824	Boeing 757-21B	583/25889			
B-2825	Boeing 757-21B	585/25890			
B-2827	Boeing 757-2Y0	503/26156			Lsd fr GECAS
B-2830	Boeing 757-28S	1015/32343	ex N60668		
B-2831	Boeing 757-2Y0	482/26153			Lsd fr GECAS
B-2835	Boeing 757-236	445/25598	ex N5573P		
B-2838	Boeing 757-2Z0	613/27260			
B-2851	Boeing 757-28S	797/29215			
B-2852	Boeing 757-2Q8	782/28833	ex N711LF		Lsd fr ILFC
B-2853	Boeing 757-28S	811/29216			
B-2859	Boeing 757-28S	868/29217			
B-2051	Boeing 777-21B	20/27357			
B-2052	Boeing 777-21B	24/27358	ex N5017V		
B-2053	Boeing 777-21B	46/27359			
B-2054	Boeing 777-21B	48/27360			
B-2055	Boeing 777-21B	55/27524			
B-2056	Boeing 777-21B	66/27525			
B-2057	Boeing 777-21B	106/27604	ex N5022E	Pearl of The South	
B-2058	Boeing 777-21B	110/27605	ex N5028Y		
N688CZ	Boeing 777-21B	121/27606	ex B-2062		Lsd fr ILFC
	Boeing 777-21B			on order Mar04	Lsd fr ILFC

B-2104	McDonnell-Douglas MD-82	1240/49425	ex N1005T		
B-2105	McDonnell-Douglas MD-82	1241/49428	ex N1005U		
B-2108	McDonnell-Douglas MD-82	1300/49502		SAIC c/n 3	
B-2121	McDonnell-Douglas MD-82	1381/49505		SAIC c/n 6	
B-2122	McDonnell-Douglas MD-82	1400/49506		SAIC c/n 7	
B-2126	McDonnell-Douglas MD-82	1514/49510		SAIC c/n 11	
B-2128	McDonnell-Douglas MD-82	1548/49512		SAIC c/n 13	
B-2130	McDonnell-Douglas MD-82	1589/49514		SAIC c/n 15	
B-2132	McDonnell-Douglas MD-82	1622/49516		SAIC c/n 17	
B-2134	McDonnell-Douglas MD-82	1647/49518		SAIC c/n 19	
B-2136	McDonnell-Douglas MD-82	1671/49520		SAIC c/n 21	
B-2139	McDonnell-Douglas MD-82	1724/49523		SAIC c/n 24	
B-2140	McDonnell-Douglas MD-82	1746/49524		SAIC c/n 25	
B-2142	McDonnell-Douglas MD-82	1798/49850		SAIC c/n 27	
B-2143	McDonnell-Douglas MD-82	1807/49851		SAIC c/n 28	
B-2145	McDonnell-Douglas MD-82	1981/49853		SAIC c/n 35	
B-2146	McDonnell-Douglas MD-82	2010/53162	ex N831US		
B-2147	McDonnell-Douglas MD-82	2025/53163	ex N832AU		
B-2148	McDonnell-Douglas MD-82	2063/53169	ex N838AU		
B-2149	McDonnell-Douglas MD-82	2065/53170	ex N839AU		
B-2150	McDonnell-Douglas MD-82	2067/53171	ex N840AU		
B-2151	McDonnell-Douglas MD-82	1959/49852	ex B-2144	SAIC c/n 34	
B-2152	McDonnell-Douglas MD-82	2041/53164	ex N833AU		Lsd fr GECAS
B-2100	McDonnell-Douglas MD-90-30	4001/60001			
B-2103	McDonnell-Douglas MD-90-30	4002/60002			
B-2250	McDonnell-Douglas MD-90-30	2143/53523			
B-2251	McDonnell-Douglas MD-90-30	2146/53524			Lsd fr Boeing FC
B-2252	McDonnell-Douglas MD-90-30	2150/53525			
B-2253	McDonnell-Douglas MD-90-30	2170/53526			
B-2254	McDonnell-Douglas MD-90-30	2175/53527			
B-2255	McDonnell-Douglas MD-90-30	2177/53528			
B-2259	McDonnell-Douglas MD-90-30	2220/53529			
B-2260	McDonnell-Douglas MD-90-30	2222/53530			
B-2261	McDonnell-Douglas MD-90-30	2228/53531			
B-2266	McDonnell-Douglas MD-90-30	2253/53532			
B-2267	McDonnell-Douglas MD-90-30	2258/53533			
B-3446	Xian Y-7-100C	09703			
B-3466	Xian Y-7-100	04707			
B-3467	Xian Y-7-100	05701			
B-3468	Xian Y-7-100	05703			
B-3477	Xian Y-7-100C	06705			
B-3478	Xian Y-7-100	06707			
B-3484	Xian Y-7-100C	07703			
B-3486	Xian Y-7-100C	07705			
B-3488	Xian Y-7-100	07707			
B-3495	Xian Y-7-100C	08706			
B-2016	Ilyushin Il-86	51483210097	ex RA-86145?	stored URC	
B-2018	Ilyushin Il-86	51483210099		stored URC	
B-2019	Ilyushin Il-86	51483210100		stored URC	
B-	Embraer EMB.145			Harbin built	
B-2473	Boeing 747-41BF	1306/32803	ex N1788B		
B-2461	Boeing 747-41BF	1312/32804			
N412MC	Boeing 747-47UF	1244/30559			Lsd fr/op by GTI

Owns 49% of China Postal Airlines, 60% of Guizhou Airlines while Zhongyuan Airlines is wholly owned subsidiary of parent Group. Five Airbus Industrie A330-200s are on order for delivery from 2005. Merged with China Northern Airlines and China Xinjiang Airlines on 11 October 2003 and fleets combined in 2003.

CHINA SOUTHWEST AIRLINES merged into Air China in 2003

CHINA UNITED AIRLINES

Lianhang (CUA)   *Beijing-Nanyuan/Beijing Xi Jiao (NAY/-)*

B-4008	Boeing 737-3T0	1507/23839	ex N19357	Op for Govt
B-4009	Boeing 737-3T0	1516/23840	ex N27358	Op for Govt
B-4018	Boeing 737-33A	2310/25502		Lsd fr AWAS
B-4019	Boeing 737-33A	2313/25503		Lsd fr AWAS
B-4020	Boeing 737-34N	2746/28081		Op for North China Admin
B-4021	Boeing 737-34N	2747/28082		Op for North China Admin
B-4025	Boeing 737-76D	1334/33470	ex B-5048	
B-4052	Boeing 737-3Q8	1957/24701	ex PK-GWI	Lsd fr ILFC
B-4053	Boeing 737-3Q8	1994/24702	ex PK-GWJ	Lsd fr ILFC
B-4005	Canadair CL-600-2B19	7138	ex C-FZAT	Op for Govt
B-4006	Canadair CL-600-2B19	7149	ex C-FZIS	Op for Govt
B-4007	Canadair CL-600-2B19	7180	ex C-GATM	Op for Govt
B-4010	Canadair CL-600-2B19	7189	ex C-GATY	Op for Govt
B-4011	Canadair CL-600-2B19	7193	ex C-GBFR	Op for Govt

B-4030	Ilyushin Il-76MD	1013407233	
B-4031	Ilyushin Il-76MD	1013408254	
B-4032	Ilyushin Il-76MD	1013409289	
B-4033	Ilyushin Il-76MD	1033416512	
B-4034	Ilyushin Il-76MD	1033416524	
B-4035	Ilyushin Il-76MD	1033416529	
B-4036	Ilyushin Il-76MD	1033417550	
B-4037	Ilyushin Il-76MD	1033417557	
B-4038	Ilyushin Il-76MD	1033417567	
B-4039	Ilyushin Il-76MD	1043418576	
B-4040	Ilyushin Il-76MD	1053419656	ex 19656
B-4041	Ilyushin Il-76MD	1053420663	
B-4042	Ilyushin Il-76MD	1063418587	
B-4043	Ilyushin Il-76MD	1063420671	

Also reported are B-4044 to B-4049 but not confirmed
Commercial division of Chinese Air Force, operates flights for the Chinese military and Government, flying some charters

CHINA XINHUA AIRLINES

Xinhua (XW/CXH) (IATA 779)   *Tianjin (TSN)*

B-2908	Boeing 737-341	2303/26854	ex (F-OGRT)	
B-2934	Boeing 737-39K	2559/27274		
B-2942	Boeing 737-332	2506/25997	ex N304DE	
B-2943	Boeing 737-332	2510/25998	ex N305DE	
B-2945	Boeing 737-39K	2639/27362		
B-2982	Boeing 737-36Q	2859/28657		Lsd fr Boullioun
B-2987	Boeing 737-46Q	2922/28663		Lsd fr Boullioun
B-2989	Boeing 737-46Q	2939/28758		Lsd fr Boullioun
B-2993	Boeing 737-46Q	2981/28759		Lsd fr SALE
B-5081	Boeing 737-86N	515/30231	ex N302LS	Lsd fr GECAS

51% owned by Hainan Airlines

CHINA XINJIANG AIRLINES merged into China Southern Airlines in 2003

CHINA YUNNAN AIRLINES merged into China Eastern Airlines in 2003

CITIC OFFSHORE HELICOPTERS

China Helicopter (CHC)   *Shenzhen Heliport*

B-7951	Aerospatiale AS.332L Super Puma	2165	ex F-WYMQ	
B-7956	Aerospatiale AS.332L1 Super Puma	2356	ex HL9201	
B-7957	Aerospatiale AS.332L1 Super Puma	9000		constructed from parts
B-7958	Aerospatiale AS.332L1 Super Puma	9001	ex F-WQDT	constructed from parts
B-7959	Aerospatiale AS.332L1 Super Puma	2087	ex F-WYMR	
B-7101	Aerospatiale SA.365N Dauphin 2	6012	ex B-730	
B-7102	Aerospatiale SA.365N Dauphin 2	6013	ex B-731	
B-7103	Aerospatiale SA.365N Dauphin 2	6041	ex B-738	
B-7106	Aerospatiale SA.365N Dauphin 2	6047	ex B-741	
B-7107	Aerospatiale SA.365N Dauphin 2	6027	ex B-734	
B-7007	Eurocopter EC.135T2	0246		
B-	Eurocopter EC.135T2			on order
B-	Eurocopter EC.135T2			on order

Also leases other Aerospatiale AS.332Ls from Bristow Helicopters (BHL)

CNAC-ZHEJIANG AIRLINES merged into Air China during 2003

EASTERN GENERAL AVIATION current fleet outside *Airline Fleets 2004* reference criteria

GUANGDONG GENERAL AVIATION current fleet outside *Airline Fleets 2004* reference criteria

HAINAN AIRLINES

Hainan (HU/CHH) (IATA 880)   *Haikou (HAK)*

B-2501	Boeing 737-44P	3067/29914		
B-2576	Boeing 737-44P	3106/29915		
B-2578	Boeing 737-33A	2333/25603	ex N401AW	
B-2579	Boeing 737-33A	2342/25505	ex N402AW	
B-2937	Boeing 737-3Q8	2557/26295		Lsd fr ILFC
B-2938	Boeing 737-3Q8	2581/26296		Lsd fr ILFC
B-2960	Boeing 737-4Q8	1866/24332	ex N191LF	Lsd fr ILFC
B-2963	Boeing 737-3Q8	2769/26325		Lsd fr ILFC
B-2965	Boeing 737-4Q8	2782/26334		Lsd fr ILFC
B-2967	Boeing 737-4Q8	2793/26335		Lsd fr ILFC
B-2970	Boeing 737-4Q8	2811/26337		Lsd fr ILFC
B-2990	Boeing 737-48E	2543/25766	ex HL7231	Lsd fr Sunrock

B-5055	Boeing 737-330(QC)	1677/24283	ex N283A	Lsd fr Automatic Lsg
B-5056	Boeing 737-330(QC)	1508/23836	ex N836Y	Lsd fr Automatic Lsg
B-5057	Boeing 737-330(QC)	1514/23837	ex N837Y	Lsd fr Automatic Lsg
B-5058	Boeing 737-330(QC)	1465/23835	ex N835A	Lsd fr Automatic Lsg

Model 737-330QCs are subleased to Yangtze River Express (a wholly owned subsidiary)

B-2157	Boeing 737-84P	1015/32600		
B-2158	Boeing 737-84P	1033/32601		
B-2159	Boeing 737-84P	972/32599	ex N1787B	
B-2636	Boeing 737-86N	67/28574	ex N574GE	Lsd fr GECAS
B-2637	Boeing 737-86N	103/28576	ex N576GE	Lsd fr GECAS
B-2638	Boeing 737-8Q8	212/28220	ex N361LF	Lsd fr ILFC
B-2646	Boeing 737-8Q8	273/28056	ex N371LF	Lsd fr ILFC
B-2647	Boeing 737-84P	345/29947	ex N1787B	
B-2651	Boeing 737-84P	607/30474	ex N1787B	
B-2652	Boeing 737-84P	731/30475		
B-2675	Boeing 737-86Q	1147/32885		Lsd fr Boullioun
B-2676	Boeing 737-84P	1170/32602		
B-2677	Boeing 737-84P	1191/32604		
B-5060	Boeing 737-76N	154/28582	ex N582HE	Lsd fr GECAS
B-5061	Boeing 737-76N	163/28583	ex N583HE	Lsd fr GECAS
B-5062	Boeing 737-76N	173/28585	ex N585HE	Lsd fr GECAS
B-5080	Boeing 737-86N	477/28614	ex TC-SUB	Lsd fr GECAS
B-5083	Boeing 737-883	548/28319	ex LN-RCO	
B-5089	Boeing 737-883	551/28320	ex OY-KKU	
B-5090	Boeing 737-883	577/28321	ex LN-RCR	
B-	Boeing 737-883	587/30193	ex LN-RCS	on order 04

Eight more Boeing 737-800s are on order for delivery in 2005/06

B-3946	Dornier 328-300	3208	ex D-BDXI	
B-3948	Dornier 328-300	3204	ex D-BDXT	
B-3949	Dornier 328-300	3198	ex N328AB	
B-3960	Dornier 328-300	3123	ex D-BDXJ	
B-3961	Dornier 328-300	3128	ex D-BDXK	
B-3962	Dornier 328-300	3143	ex D-BDXX	
B-3963	Dornier 328-300	3138	ex D-BDXT	
B-3965	Dornier 328-300	3140	ex D-BDXW	
B-3966	Dornier 328-300	3135	ex D-BDXQ	
B-3967	Dornier 328-300	3144	ex D-BDXB	
B-3968	Dornier 328-300	3148	ex D-BDXE	
B-3969	Dornier 328-300	3153	ex D-BDXN	
B-3970	Dornier 328-300	3154	ex D-BDXP	
B-3971	Dornier 328-300	3172	ex D-BDXJ	
B-3972	Dornier 328-300	3175	ex D-BDXK	
B-3973	Dornier 328-300	3158	ex D-BDXQ	
B-3975	Dornier 328-300	3159	ex D-BDXU	
B-3976	Dornier 328-300	3177	ex D-BDXY	
B-3977	Dornier 328-300	3182		
B-3978	Dornier 328-300	3187		
B-3979	Dornier 328-300	3191	ex D-BDXJ	
B-3982	Dornier 328-300	3195	ex D-BDXJ	
B-	Dornier 328-300		ex D-BDXV	o/o
B-	Dornier 328-300	3203	ex D-BXXX	o/o
B-	Dornier 328-300	3211	ex D-BEUU	o/o
B-	Dornier 328-300		ex D-BDXJ	o/o
B-	Dornier 328-300	3215	ex D-BHUU	o/o
B-	Dornier 328-300	3217	ex D-BJUU	o/o
B-	Dornier 328-300	3218	ex N328QR	o/o

Some operate for subsidiary Chang An

B-2490	Boeing 767-34PER	889/33047		
B-2491	Boeing 767-34PER	891/33048		
B-2492	Boeing 767-34PER	893/33049		

To purchase 51% of China Xinhua Airlines; Yangtze River Express is a wholly owned subsidiary
To code share with Malev on flights using Boeing 767-300s to Budapest from August 2004

JIANGNAN UNIVERSAL AVIATION

Changzhou (CZX)

B-3865	Harbin Y-11	0410
B-3866	Harbin Y-11	0104
B-3867	Harbin Y-11	0206
B-3868	Harbin Y-11	0109
B-	Harbin Y-12-II	0032
B-	Harbin Y-12-II	0096

Subsidiary of Changzhou Aircraft Factory

NANJING AIRLINES merged into China Eastern Airlines during 2003

SHANDONG AIRLINES

Shandong (SC/CDG) (IATA 324)   Jinan (TNA)

B-2534	Boeing 737-3Y0	2349/26070		Lsd fr GECAS
B-2961	Boeing 737-35N	2774/28156		
B-2962	Boeing 737-35N	2778/28157		
B-2968	Boeing 737-35N	2818/28158		
B-2995	Boeing 737-35N	3054/29315		
B-2996	Boeing 737-35N	3065/29316		
B-5065	Boeing 737-36Q	2940/28664	ex N286CH	Lsd fr Boullioun
B-5066	Boeing 737-36N	2976/28671	ex N287CH	Lsd fr Boullioun

Three Boeing 737-700s and four Boeing 737-800s are on order for delivery in 2005/6

B-3005	Canadair CL-600-2B19	7435	ex C-FMKW	
B-3006	Canadair CL-600-2B19	7443	ex C-FMLV	
B-3007	Canadair CL-600-2B19	7498	ex C-FMLF	
B-3008	Canadair CL-600-2B19	7512	ex C-FMND	
B-3009	Canadair CL-600-2B19	7522	ex C-FMMY	
B-3010	Canadair CL-600-2B19	7557	ex C-FMLB	Lsd fr GECAS
B-3016	Canadair CL-600-2B19	7614	ex C-FMKV	Lsd fr GECAS
B-3076	Canadair CL-600-2B19	7690	ex C-GZJY	Lsd fr GECAS
B-3078	Canadair CL-600-2B19	7704	ex C-GZKA	
B-3080-	Canadair CL-600-2B19	10120	ex C-F	

B-3630	Cessna 208B Caravan I	208B0883	ex N12285	
B-3631	Cessna 208 Caravan I	20800333	ex N1228V	Floatplane
B-3632	Cessna 208 Caravan I	20800332	ex N1284F	Floatplane
B-3636	Cessna 208 Caravan I	20800338	ex N1321L	
B-3637	Cessna 208B Caravan I	208B0919	ex N1294D	
B-3640	Cessna 208B Caravan I	208B0952	ex N1132X	
B-3641	Cessna 208B Caravan I	208B0953	ex N1133B	
B-3651	SAAB SF.340B	289	ex SE-G89	ZS-PDP reserved
B-3652	SAAB SF.340B	292	ex SE-G92	ZS-PDR reserved
B-3653	SAAB SF.340B	296	ex SE-G96	ZS-PDO reserved
B-3654	SAAB SF.340B	302	ex SE-CO2	ZS-PDS reserved
B-3079	Canadair CL-600-2C10	10118	ex C-F	on order
B-3080	Canadair CL-600-2C10	10129	ex C-F	on order
B-	Canadair CL-600-2C10			on order

A total of ten Canadair CL-600-2C10s are on order

SHANGHAI AIRLINES

Shanghai Air (FM/CSH) (IATA 774)   Shanghai (SHA)

B-2153	Boeing 737-8Q8	942/28242			Lsd fr ILFC
B-2167	Boeing 737-8Q8	1047/30631			Lsd fr ILFC
B-2168	Boeing 737-8Q8	1086/30632			Lsd fr ILFC
B-2577	Boeing 737-76D	600/30168			
B-2631	Boeing 737-7Q8	35/28212	ex N301LF		Lsd fr ILFC
B-2632	Boeing 737-7Q8	122/28216	ex N1795B		Lsd fr ILFC
B-2663	Boeing 737-7AD	72/28437	ex N701EW		Lsd fr PALS I
B-2686	Boeing 737-8Q8	28251		on order 04	Lsd fr ILFC
B-2689	Boeing 737-76D	1343/33472			
B-2913	Boeing 737-76D	550/30167			
B-2997	Boeing 737-7Q8	272/28223			Lsd fr ILFC
B-2688	Boeing 737-86D	1192/33471			
B-	Boeing 737-8Q8	30666		on order 04	Lsd fr ILFC
B-5076	Boeing 737-86N	1434/32739			Lsd fr GECAS
B-5077	Boeing 737-86N	32742		on order 04	Lsd fr GECAS

B-2808	Boeing 757-26D	231/24471	ex N1792B		Lsd fr ILFC
B-2809	Boeing 757-26D	235/24472	ex N5573B		Lsd fr ILFC
B-2810	Boeing 757-26D	301/24473			
B-2833	Boeing 757-26D	560/27152			
B-2834	Boeing 757-26D	576/27183			
B-2842	Boeing 757-26D	626/27342			
B-2843	Boeing 757-26D	684/27681			
B-2850	Boeing 757-231	891/30338	ex N725TW		Lsd fr WFBN
B-	Boeing 757-26D			on order 04	
B-	Boeing 757-26D			on order 04	
B-	Boeing 757-26D			on order 04	
B-	Boeing 757-26D			on order 04	
B-	Boeing 757-26D			on order 04	
B-	Boeing 757-26D			on order 04	

B-2498	Boeing 767-36D	849/27684		
B-2563	Boeing 767-36D	546/27309		
B-2567	Boeing 767-36D	686/27685		
B-2570	Boeing 767-36D	770/27941		
B-5018	Boeing 767-3Q8ER	695/28207	ex N635TW	Lsd fr ILFC

B-3011	Canadair CL-600-2B19	7556	ex C-FFMKZ		
B-3018	Canadair CL-600-2B19	7453	ex C-FMNQ		
B-3020	Canadair CL-600-2B19	7459	ex C-FMMQ		
B-	Canadair CL-600-2B19	7226	ex G-DUOF	on order Jun04	Lsd fr GECAS
B-	Canadair CL-600-2B19	7247	ex G-DUOG	on order Dec04	Lsd fr GECAS

SHANXI AVIATION

Shanxi (CXI) *Taiyuan-Wusu (TYN)*

B-3701	Xian Y-7-100C	12705	stored
B-3702	Xian Y-7-100C	12707	stored
B-3703	Xian Y-7-100C	12708	stored

All flights operated in conjuction with Hainan Airlines using HU call-sign

SHENZHEN AIRLINES

Shenzen Air (ZH/CSZ) (IATA 479) *Shenzhen (SZX)*

B-2932	Boeing 737-3K9	2302/25787	ex N41069	Lsd fr Bavaria
B-2933	Boeing 737-3K9	2331/25788	ex N4113D	Lsd fr Bavaria
B-2939	Boeing 737-31L	2625/27345		
B-2940	Boeing 737-31L	2636/27346		
B-2971	Boeing 737-3Q8	2290/25373	ex N221LF	Lsd fr ILFC
B-2972	Boeing 737-33A	2831/27463		Lsd fr AWAS
B-2633	Boeing 737-79K	110/29190		
B-2635	Boeing 737-79K	127/29191		
B-2666	Boeing 737-78S	631/30169		
B-2667	Boeing 737-78S	654/30170		
B-2668	Boeing 737-78S	681/30171		
B-2669	Boeing 737-77L	1023/32722		
B-2678	Boeing 737-76N	895/32244	ex N315ML	Lsd fr Avn Financial Svs
B-2679	Boeing 737-76N	710/29893	ex N313ML	Lsd fr Avn Financial Svs
B-2691	Boeing 737-8Q8	841/28241	ex N802SY	Lsd fr ILFC
B-2692	Boeing 737-8Q8	808/30628	ex N803SY	Lsd fr ILFC
B-5025	Boeing 737-7BX	823/30741	ex N366ML	Lsd fr GECAS
B-5026	Boeing 737-7BX	864/30742	ex N367ML	Lsd fr GECAS
B-5049	Boeing 737-86N	772/28639	ex N639SH	Lsd fr GECAS
B-5050	Boeing 737-86N	828/28643	ex N643SH	Lsd fr GECAS
B-5073	Boeing 737-8Q8	1402/30680		Lsd fr ILFC
B-5075	Boeing 737-8Q8	1410/30692		Lsd fr ILFC
B-5078	Boeing 737-8Q8	1414/30690	ex N1779B	Lsd fr ILFC
B-5079	Boeing 737-8Q8	1422/30693		Lsd fr ILFC

Five Boeing 737-900s are on order for delivery in 2005/6

SHUANGYANG AVIATION

Shuangyuang (CSY) *Anshun (AOG)*

B-3811	Harbin Y-12 II	0012	Combi
B-3812	Harbin Y-12 II	0024	Sprayer
B-3813	Harbin Y-12 II	0025	Sprayer
B-3814	Harbin Y-12-II	0026	Sprayer
B-3895	Harbin Y-11	0401	
B-3896	Harbin Y-11	0402	
B-3897	Harbin Y-11	0403	
B-3898	Harbin Y-11	0404	

SICHUAN AIRLINES

Sichuan (3U/CSC) *Chengdu (CTU)*

B-2286	Airbus Industrie A321-131	0550	ex N550BR	Lsd fr ILFC
B-2340	Airbus Industrie A320-232	0540	ex F-WWDK	Lsd fr ILFC
B-2341	Airbus Industrie A320-232	0551	ex F-WWBI	Lsd fr ILFC
B-2342	Airbus Industrie A320-232	0556	ex F-WWIL	Lsd fr ILFC
B-2343	Airbus Industrie A320-232	0696	ex F-WWII	Lsd fr CSN
B-2370	Airbus Industrie A321-231	0878	ex D-AVZF	
B-2371	Airbus Industrie A321-231	0915	ex D-AVZM	
B-2373	Airbus Industrie A320-232	0919	ex F-WWIC	
B-2397	Airbus Industrie A320-232	1013	ex F-WWDP	
B-6025	Airbus Industrie A320-232	0573	ex B-MAD	Lsd fr ILFC
B-6026	Airbus Industrie A320-232	0582	ex B-MAE	Lsd fr ILFC
B-6027	Airbus Industrie A320-233	1007	ex N460TA	Lsd fr Pegasus
B-	Airbus Industrie A319-1		ex D-AV	on order
B-	Airbus Industrie A319-1		ex D-AV	on order

Two more Airbus Industrie A319-100s are on order for delivery in 2005

| B-3040 | Embraer EMB.145LR | 145317 | ex PT-SMI |
| B-3041 | Embraer EMB.145LR | 145349 | ex PT-SNP |

B-3042	Embraer EMB.145LR	145352	ex PT-SNR
B-3043	Embraer EMB.145LR	145377	ex PT-SQB
B-3045	Embraer EMB.145LR	145470	ex PT-SVP

B-3425	Xian MA 60	0101	
B-3426	Xian MA 60		
B-	Xian MA 60		on order
B-	Xian MA 60		on order
B-	Xian MA 60		on order

All leased from Shenzhen Financial Leasing

| B-3498 | Xian Y-7-100C | 06706 |

WUHAN AIRLINES merged into China Eastern Airlines during 2003

XIAMEN AIRLINES

Xiamen Air (MF/CXA) (IATA 731)   Xiamen (XMN)

B-2516	Boeing 737-2T4	1167/23447	ex N5573B	dbr 12Mar03?	
B-2529	Boeing 737-505	2578/26297	ex LN-BUA		Lsd fr BRA
B-2591	Boeing 737-505	2353/25792	ex LN-BRW		Lsd fr BRA
B-2592	Boeing 737-505	2516/27153	ex LN-BRZ		Lsd fr BRA
B-2593	Boeing 737-505	2449/27155	ex LN-BRY		Lsd fr BRA
B-2655	Boeing 737-3Q8	2480/26288	ex B-2904		Lsd fr ILFC
B-2656	Boeing 737-3Q8	2519/26292	ex B-2903		Lsd fr ILFC
B-2661	Boeing 737-3Q8	2418/26284	ex B-2901		Lsd fr ILFC
B-2662	Boeing 737-3Q8	2466/24988	ex B-2902		Lsd fr ILFC
B-2973	Boeing 737-505	2805/26336			Lsd fr ILFC
B-2975	Boeing 737-505	2822/26338			Lsd fr ILFC

B-2658	Boeing 737-75C	637/30512		
B-2659	Boeing 737-75C	676/30513		
B-2991	Boeing 737-75C	90/29085		
B-2992	Boeing 737-75C	108/29086		
B-2998	Boeing 737-75C	73/29042		
B-2999	Boeing 737-75C	86/29084	ex N1796B	
B-5028	Boeing 737-75C	1275/30034		Lsd fr ILFC
B-5029	Boeing 737-75C	1229/30634		Lsd fr ILFC
B-5038	Boeing 737-7Q8	1304/30656	ex N1787B	Lsd fr ILFC
B-5039	Boeing 737-75C	1315/28258		Lsd fr ILFC

Five more Boeing 737-75Cs are on order for delivery in 2005/6

B-2819	Boeing 757-25C	475/25898	
B-2828	Boeing 757-25C	565/25899	
B-2829	Boeing 757-25C	574/25900	
B-2848	Boeing 757-25C	685/27513	
B-2849	Boeing 757-25C	698/27517	
B-2868	Boeing 757-25C	993/32941	
B-2869	Boeing 757-25C	1009/32942	
B-	Boeing 757-25C		on order 3Q04
B-	Boeing 757-25C		on order 3Q04

Partially owned by China Southern; in turn owns Fujian Airlines

XINJIANG GENERAL AVIATION

Shihezi

B-3869	Harbin Y-11	0501
B-3870	Harbin Y-11	0502
B-3885	Harbin Y-11	0301
B-3886	Harbin Y-11	0302
B-3887	Harbin Y-11	0303
B-3888	Harbin Y-11	0304
B-3889	Harbin Y-11	0305
B-3890	Harbin Y-11	0306
B-3891	Harbin Y-11	0307
B-3892	Harbin Y-11	0308
B-3893	Harbin Y-11	0309
B-3894	Harbin Y-11	0310

All combination Freighter/Sprayers

B-3810	Harbin Y-12 II	0009	Geological survey
B-3815	Harbin Y-12 II	0023	Geological survey
B-3817	Harbin Y-12 II	0029	Photographic survey
B-3818	Harbin Y-12 II	0030	Photographic survey

Subsidiary of China Xinjiang Airlines

YANGTZE RIVER EXPRESS

Yangtze River (Y8/YZR) (IATA 871)   *Shanghai-Hongqiao*

B-5055	Boeing 737-330(QC)	1677/24283	ex N283A	Lsd fr CHH
B-5056	Boeing 737-330(QC)	1508/23836	ex D-ABWE	Lsd fr CHH
B-5057	Boeing 737-330(QC)	1514/23837	ex N837Y	Lsd fr CHH
B-5058	Boeing 737-330(QC)	1465/23835	ex N835A	Lsd fr CHH

A wholly owned subsidiary of Hainan Airlines

ZHONGFEI AIRLINES

Zhongfei (CFZ)   *Xi'an-Yanliang*

B-3820	Harbin Y-12 II	0031

Division of Chinese Test Flight Establishment, also operates Cessna 550 Citation II calibrators

ZHONGYUAN AIRLINES merged into China Southern Airlines during 2003

B-H, B-K CHINA - HONG KONG

AIR HONG KONG

Air Hong Kong (LD/AHK) (IATA 288)   *Hong Kong (HKG)*

B-HMD	Boeing 747-2L5SF	435/22105	ex VR-HMD		Lsd fr CPA
B-	Airbus Industrie A300F4-605R	855	ex F-WW	on order 04	
B-	Airbus Industrie A300F4-605R	856	ex F-WW	on order 04	
B-	Airbus Industrie A300F4-605R	857	ex F-WW	on order 04	
N371PC	Airbus Industrie A300B4-203F	157	ex D-ASAG		Lsd fr XNA
TF-ELG	Airbus Industrie A300C4-605R	758	ex D-ANDY	DHL titles	Lsd fr ICB

70% owned by Cathay Pacific Airways and 30% by DHL. Three more Airbus Industrie A300F4-605Fs are on order for
regional services; delivery is due in 2005. May lease other aircraft as interim measure

CATHAY PACIFIC AIRWAYS

Cathay (CX/CPA) (IATA 160)   *Hong Kong (HKG)*

B-HLA	Airbus Industrie A330-342	071	ex VR-HLA	
B-HLB	Airbus Industrie A330-342	083	ex VR-HLB	
B-HLC	Airbus Industrie A330-342	099	ex VR-HLC	
B-HLD	Airbus Industrie A330-342	102	ex VR-HLD	
B-HLE	Airbus Industrie A330-342	109	ex VR-HLE	
B-HLF	Airbus Industrie A330-342	113	ex VR-HLF	
B-HLG	Airbus Industrie A330-342	118	ex VR-HLG	
B-HLH	Airbus Industrie A330-342	121	ex VR-HLH	
B-HLI	Airbus Industrie A330-342	155	ex VR-HLI	
B-HLJ	Airbus Industrie A330-342	012	ex VR-HLJ	
B-HLK	Airbus Industrie A330-342	017	ex VR-HLK	
B-HLL	Airbus Industrie A330-342	244	ex F-WWKG	
B-HLM	Airbus Industrie A330-343X	386	ex F-WWYT	
B-HLN	Airbus Industrie A330-343X	389	ex F-WWYV	
B-HLO	Airbus Industrie A330-343X	393	ex F-WWYY	
B-HLP	Airbus Industrie A330-343X	418	ex F-WWKV	
B-HLQ	Airbus Industrie A330-343X	420	ex F-WWYB	
B-HLR	Airbus Industrie A330-343X	421	ex F-WWYC	
B-HLS	Airbus Industrie A330-343X	423	ex F-WWYD	
B-HLT	Airbus Industrie A330-343X	439	ex F-WWYJ	
B-HLU	Airbus Industrie A330-343X	539	ex F-WWYG	
B-HLV	Airbus Industrie A330-343X	548	ex F-WWYI	
B-HLW	Airbus Industrie A330-343X	565	ex F-WWYR	
B-HXA	Airbus Industrie A340-313X	136	ex VR-HXA	
B-HXB	Airbus Industrie A340-313X	137	ex VR-HXB	
B-HXC	Airbus Industrie A340-313X	142	ex VR-HXC	
B-HXD	Airbus Industrie A340-313X	147	ex VR-HXD	
B-HXE	Airbus Industrie A340-313X	157	ex VR-HXE	
B-HXF	Airbus Industrie A340-313X	160	ex VR-HXF	
B-HXG	Airbus Industrie A340-313X	208	ex F-WWJC	
B-HXH	Airbus Industrie A340-313X	218	ex F-WWJT	
B-HXI	Airbus Industrie A340-313X	220	ex F-WWJO	
B-HXJ	Airbus Industrie A340-313X	227	ex F-WWJL	
B-HXK	Airbus Industrie A340-313X	228	ex F-WWJI	
B-HXL	Airbus Industrie A340-313X	381	ex F-WWJB	Lsd fr ILFC
B-HXM	Airbus Industrie A340-313X	123	ex 9V-SJA	Lsd fr Boeing
B-HXN	Airbus Industrie A340-313X	126	ex 9V-SJB	Lsd fr Boeing
B-HXO	Airbus Industrie A340-313X	128	ex 9V-SJC	Lsd fr Boeing
B-HQA	Airbus Industrie A340-642	436	ex F-WWCJ	Lsd fr ILFC
B-HQB	Airbus Industrie A340-642	453	ex F-WWCN	Lsd fr ILFC
B-HQC	Airbus Industrie A340-642	475	ex F-WWCQ	Lsd fr ILFC
B-	Airbus Industrie A340-642		ex F-WW	on order	Lsd fr ILFC

B-HIA	Boeing 747-267B	446/21966	ex VR-HIA	Lsd to ABD as TF-ATD
B-HIB	Boeing 747-267B	466/22149	ex VR-HIB	Lsd to ABD as TF-ATC
B-HIC	Boeing 747-267B	493/22429	ex VR-HIC	Lsd to ABD as TF-ABP
B-HID	Boeing 747-267B	531/22530	ex VR-HID	Lsd to ABD as TF-ABA
B-HIH	Boeing 747-267B(SF)	596/23120	ex VR-HIH	stored Avalon
B-HMD	Boeing 747-2L5B(SF)	435/22105	ex VR-HMD	Lsd to AHK
B-HME	Boeing 747-2L5B(SF)	443/22106	ex VR-HME	
B-HMF	Boeing 747-2L5B(SF)	469/22107	ex VR-HMF	
B-HOO	Boeing 747-467	705/23814	ex VR-HOO	
B-HOP	Boeing 747-467	728/23815	ex VR-HOP	
B-HOR	Boeing 747-467	771/24631	ex VR-HOR	
B-HOS	Boeing 747-467	788/24850	ex VR-HOS	
B-HOT	Boeing 747-467	813/24851	ex VR-HOT	
B-HOU	Boeing 747-467	834/24925	ex VR-HOU	
B-HOV	Boeing 747-467	849/25082	ex VR-HOV	Lsd fr Whirlpool
B-HOW	Boeing 747-467	873/25211	ex VR-HOW	
B-HOX+	Boeing 747-467	877/24955	ex VR-HOX	Lsd fr AWAS
B-HOY	Boeing 747-467	887/25351	ex VR-HOY	Asia's World City c/s
B-HOZ	Boeing 747-467	925/25871	ex VR-HOZ	
B-HUA	Boeing 747-467	930/25872	ex VR-HUA	
B-HUB	Boeing 747-467	937/25873	ex VR-HUB	
B-HUD	Boeing 747-467	949/25874	ex VR-HUD	
B-HUE	Boeing 747-467	970/27117	ex VR-HUE	
B-HUF	Boeing 747-467	993/25869	ex VR-HUF	
B-HUG	Boeing 747-467	1007/25870	ex VR-HUG	
B-HUH	Boeing 747-467F	1020/27175	ex VR-HUH	
B-HUI	Boeing 747-467	1033/27230	ex VR-HUI	
B-HUJ	Boeing 747-467	1061/27595	ex VR-HUJ	Lsd fr ILFC
B-HUK	Boeing 747-467F	1065/27503	ex VR-HUK	
B-HUL	Boeing 747-467F	1255/30804		
B-HUO	Boeing 747-467F	1271/32571	ex B-HUM	
B-HUP	Boeing 747-467F	1282/30805	ex (B-HUN)	
B-HVX	Boeing 747-267F	776/24568	ex VR-HVX	
B-HVY	Boeing 747-236F	480/22306	ex VR-HVY	
B-HVZ	Boeing 747-267F	687/23864	ex VR-HVZ	

+ Special colours, named Spirit of Hong Kong
One more Boeing 747-467F is on order; five 747-467s are to be converted to 747-467SFs for delivery from December 2005 to 2007. Is looking to purchase up to 15 secondhand RR powered Boeing 747-400s

B-HNA	Boeing 777-267	14/27265	ex VR-HNA
B-HNB	Boeing 777-267	18/27266	ex VR-HNB
B-HNC	Boeing 777-267	28/27263	ex VR-HNC
B-HND	Boeing 777-267	31/27264	ex VR-HND
B-HNE	Boeing 777-367	94/27507	ex N5014K
B-HNF	Boeing 777-367	102/27506	ex N5016R
B-HNG	Boeing 777-367	118/27505	ex N5017V
B-HNH	Boeing 777-367	136/27504	
B-HNI	Boeing 777-367	204/27508	
B-HNJ	Boeing 777-367	224/27509	
B-HNK	Boeing 777-367	248/27510	
B-HNL	Boeing 777-267	1/27116	ex N7771
B-HNM	Boeing 777-367	456/33702	
B-HNN	Boeing 777-367	462/33703	
B-HNO	Boeing 777-367	470/33704	

Owns 20% of Dragonair and 70 % of Air Hong Kong

CR AIRWAYS

Bauhina (N8/CRK)   Hong Kong (HKG)

B-KBJ	Canadair CL-600-2B19	7565	ex B-3012	Lsd fr GECAS

DRAGONAIR

Dragonair (KA/HDA) (IATA 043)   Hong Kong (HKG)

B-HSD	Airbus Industrie A320-232	0756	ex F-WWBC	Lsd fr ILFC
B-HSE	Airbus Industrie A320-232	0784	ex F-WWDL	Lsd fr ILFC
B-HSF	Airbus Industrie A320-232	0816	ex F-WWIT	Lsd fr ILFC
B-HSG	Airbus Industrie A320-232	0812	ex B-22315	Lsd fr ILFC
B-HSH	Airbus Industrie A320-232	0877	ex F-WWIH	Lsd fr ILFC
B-HSI	Airbus Industrie A320-232	0930	ex F-WWIE	Lsd fr ILFC
B-HSJ	Airbus Industrie A320-232	1253	ex F-WWIU	Lsd fr ILFC
B-HSK	Airbus Industrie A320-232	1721	ex F-WWDF	Lsd fr Boullioun
B-	Airbus Industrie A320-232	2238	ex F-WW	on order 04
B-	Airbus Industrie A320-232		ex F-WW	on order 04

One more Airbus Industrie A320-232 is on order for delivery in 2005

B-HTD	Airbus Industrie A321-231	0993	ex D-AVZF	Lsd fr ILFC
B-HTE	Airbus Industrie A321-231	1024	ex D-AVZD	Lsd fr ILFC
B-HTF	Airbus Industrie A321-231	0633	ex G-OZBC	Lsd fr ILFC
B-HTG	Airbus Industrie A321-231	1695	ex D-AVZA	Lsd fr ILFC

B-HTH	Airbus Industrie A321-231	1984	ex D-AVZX		
B-HTI	Airbus Industrie A321-231	2021	ex D-AVXJ		
B-HYA	Airbus Industrie A330-342	098	ex VR-HYA		Lsd fr ILFC
B-HYB	Airbus Industrie A330-342	106	ex VR-HYB		
B-HYD	Airbus Industrie A330-342	132	ex VR-HYD		
B-HYE	Airbus Industrie A330-342	177	ex VR-HYE		Lsd fr ILFC
B-HYF	Airbus Industrie A330-342	234	ex F-WWKF		Lsd fr ILFC
B-HYG	Airbus Industrie A330-343X	405	ex F-WWKQ		Lsd fr ILFC
B-HYH	Airbus Industrie A330-343X	407	ex F-WWKR		Lsd fr ILFC
B-HYI	Airbus Industrie A330-343X	479	ex F-WWKU		
B-HYJ	Airbus Industrie A330-343X	512	ex F-WWYR		
B-HYK	Airbus Industrie A330-343X	581	ex F-WWKK		Lsd fr ILFC
B-KAA	Boeing 747-312M	666/23769	ex 9V-SKP	Freighter	
B-KAB	Boeing 747-312M	637/23409	ex 9V-SKM	Freighter	
B-KAC	Boeing 747-3H6M	650/23600	ex N73741	Freighter	
B-	Boeing 747-209F	752/24308	ex B-18771		

Other cargo flights operated by Atlas Air on ACMI lease
35.9% owned by China National Aviation Corp and 20% by Cathay Pacific
Dragonair is the trading name of Hong Kong Dragon Airlines

HELI HONG KONG

HeliHongKong (HHK)   Hong Kong Central Heliport

B-HJR	Sikorsky S-76C+	760497	
B-KCC	Sikorsky S-76C+	760521	ex N9017M
B-KCD	Aerospatiale AS.350B3 Ecureuil	3466	ex N94GH
B-KCE	Aerospatiale AS.350B3 Ecureuil	3511	ex N30224

Associated with EAA Helicopters

B-M CHINA - MACAU

AIR MACAU

Air Macau (NX/AMU) (IATA 675)   Macau (MFM)

B-MAK	Airbus Industrie A319-132	1758	ex D-AVYF	Rio Yangtze	Lsd fr ILFC
B-MAL	Airbus Industrie A319-132	1790	ex D-AVYR	Rio Amarelo	Lsd fr ILFC
B-MAM	Airbus Industrie A319-112	1893	ex D-AVYJ	Lago Sul Lua	Lsd fr ILFC
B-MAN	Airbus Industrie A319-132	1912	ex D-AVWZ	Rio Huang Pu	Lsd fr ILFC
B-MAO	Airbus Industrie A319-132	1962	ex D-AVWU	Rio Yaluzangbu	Lsd fr ILFC
B-MAF	Airbus Industrie A321-131	0620	ex CS-MAF	Macau East Asia Games	Lsd fr ILFC
B-MAG	Airbus Industrie A321-131	0631	ex CS-MAG	Ilha de Coloane	Lsd fr ILFC
B-MAH	Airbus Industrie A320-232	0805	ex CS-MAH	Ilha de Madeira	Lsd fr ILFC
B-MAJ	Airbus Industrie A321-131	0908	ex CS-MAJ	Macau East Asia Games	
B-MAP	Airbus Industrie A321-131	1850	ex D-AVZX		Lsd fr ILFC
B-MAQ	Airbus Industrie A321-131	1926	ex D-AVZS	Lago Tai	Lsd fr ILFC
9M-TGA	Boeing 727-2F2F (Duganair 3)	1808/22993	ex TC-JCB	Air Macau Cargo	Lsd fr TSE
9M-TGB	Boeing 727-2F2F (Duganair 3)	1810/22998	ex TC-JCD	Air Macau Cargo	Lsd fr TSE

25% owned by Air Portugal and 5% by EVA Airlines but control rests with CNAC

EAA HELICOPTERS

(3E/EMU)   Macau Heliport

B-MHF	Sikorsky S-76C+	760474	ex CS-MHF
B-MHG	Sikorsky S-76C+	760475	ex CS-MHG
B-MHH	Sikorsky S-76C+	760476	ex CS-MHH

East Asia Airlines trading as EAA Helicopters; associated with Heli Hong Kong

B - CHINA - TAIWAN (Republic of China)

ASIA PACIFIC AIRLINES

Taipei-Sung Shen (TSA)

| B-66121 | Bell 412HP | 36023 | ex N887H |
| B-66168 | Bell 412SP | 33185 | |

CHINA AIRLINES

China Airlines (CI/CAL) (IATA 297)   Taipei-Chiang Kai Shek/Sung Shen (TPE/TSA)

B-18501	Airbus Industrie A300B4-622R	767	ex F-WWAL
B-18502	Airbus Industrie A300B4-622R	775	ex F-WWAT
B-18503	Airbus Industrie A300B4-622R	788	ex F-WWAE

B-18551	Airbus Industrie A300B4-622R	666	ex B-1806	
B-18571	Airbus Industrie A300B4-622R	529	ex B-1800	Lsd fr Fuyo Lsg
B-18572	Airbus Industrie A300B4-622R	533	ex B-1802	Lsd fr Fuyo Lsg
B-18573	Airbus Industrie A300B4-622R	536	ex B-1804	Lsd fr Fuyo Lsg
B-18575	Airbus Industrie A300B4-622R	559	ex B-18505	Lsd fr Airbus
B-18576	Airbus Industrie A300B4-622R	743	ex N88881	Lsd fr WFBN
B-18578	Airbus Industrie A300B4-622R	625	ex N88887	Lsd fr MSA V
B-18757	Airbus Industrie A300B4-622R	677	ex N8888B	Lsd fr ILFC
B-18759	Airbus Industrie A300B4-622R	555	ex N8888P	Lsd fr ILFC
B-18801	Airbus Industrie A340-313X	402	ex F-WWJC	
B-18802	Airbus Industrie A340-313X	406	ex F-WWJK	
B-18803	Airbus Industrie A340-313X	411	ex F-WWJL	
B-18804	Airbus Industrie A340-313X	163	ex D-ASIB	
B-18805	Airbus Industrie A340-313X	415	ex F-WWJO	
B-18806	Airbus Industrie A340-313X	433	ex F-WWJS	
B-18807	Airbus Industrie A340-313X	541	ex F-WWJK	
B-18851	Airbus Industrie A340-313X	528	ex D-ASIH	
B-16805	Boeing 737-8Q8	768/30636		Lsd fr MDA
B-18601	Boeing 737-809	113/28402	ex N1787B	
B-18605	Boeing 737-809	130/28404	ex N1784B	
B-18606	Boeing 737-809	132/28405		
B-18607	Boeing 737-809	139/29104		
B-18608	Boeing 737-809	141/28406		
B-18609	Boeing 737-809	161/28407		
B-18610	Boeing 737-809	295/29105		
B-18611	Boeing 737-809	302/29106	ex N1787B	
B-18612	Boeing 737-809	695/30173	ex N1785B	
B-18615	Boeing 737-809	1175/30174		
B-18616	Boeing 737-809	1182/30175		
B-	Boeing 737-809			on order Apr04
B-	Boeing 737-809			on order Apr04
B-18201	Boeing 747-409	1114/28709		
B-18202	Boeing 747-409	1132/28710		
B-18203	Boeing 747-409	1136/28711		
B-18205	Boeing 747-409	1137/28712		
B-18206	Boeing 747-409	1145/29030		
B-18207	Boeing 747-409	1176/29219		
B-18208	Boeing 747-409	1186/29031		
B-18209	Boeing 747-409	1219/29906		
B-18251	Boeing 747-409	1063/27965	ex B-16801	
B-18271*	Boeing 747-409	766/24309	ex B-161	
B-18272*	Boeing 747-409	778/24310	ex B-162	
B-18273*	Boeing 747-409	869/24311	ex B-163	
B-18275*	Boeing 747-409	954/24312	ex B-164	
B-18701	Boeing 747-409F	1249/30759		
B-18702	Boeing 747-409F	1252/30760		
B-18703	Boeing 747-409F	1254/30761		
B-18705	Boeing 747-409F	1263/30762		
B-18706	Boeing 747-409F	1267/30763		
B-18707	Boeing 747-409F	1269/30764		
B-18708	Boeing 747-409F	1288/30765		
B-18709	Boeing 747-409F	1294/30766		
B-18710	Boeing 747-409F	1300/30767		
B-18711	Boeing 747-409F	1314/30768		
B-18712	Boeing 747-409F	1332/33729		
B-18715	Boeing 747-409F	1334/33731		
B-18716	Boeing 747-409F	1339/33732		
B-18717	Boeing 747-409F	30769		on order
B-18718	Boeing 747-409F	30770		on order
B-	Boeing 747-409			on order 04
B-	Boeing 747-409			on order 04

*May be converted to 747-409SF (special freighters) in 2005
Two more Boeing 747-409s are on order for delivery in 2005 and 2006 plus four more Boeing 747-409Fs in 2005 (3) and 2007 (1).

B-18172	McDonnell-Douglas MD-11	519/48469	ex B-151	stored MHV; for sale
B-	Airbus Industrie A330-300	607	ex F-WW	on order 04
B-	Airbus Industrie A330-300		ex F-WW	on order 04

Twelve more Airbus Industrie A330-300s are on order for delivery in 2005 (4), 2006 (3) and 2007 (3) to replace the Airbus Industrie A300-600Rs
Owns 19% of FEAT while Mandarin Airlines is wholly owned
Leases 747-400Fs from Atlas Air on ACMI lease

EVA AIRWAYS

EvaAir (BR/EVA) (IATA 695)   *Taipei-Chiang Kai Shek (TPE)*

B-16301	Airbus Industrie A330-203	530	ex F-WWYA	Lsd fr GECAS
B-16302	Airbus Industrie A330-203	535	ex F-WWYE	Lsd fr GECAS

B-16303	Airbus Industrie A330-203	573	ex F-WW		Lsd fr GECAS
B-16304	Airbus Industrie A330-203	587	ex F-WWKL		Lsd fr GECAS
B-16305	Airbus Industrie A330-203	555	ex F-WWYL		Lsd fr GECAS
B-	Airbus Industrie A330-203		ex F-WW	on order	Lsd fr GECAS

Four more Airbus Industrie A330-203s are on order for delivery in 2005, two leased from GECAS

B-16401	Boeing 747-45E	942/27062			Lsd fr Chailease
B-16402	Boeing 747-45E	947/27063			Lsd fr Chailease
B-16403	Boeing 747-45EM	976/27141	ex N403EV		Lsd fr WFBN
B-16405	Boeing 747-45EM	982/27142	ex N405EV		Lsd fr WFBN
B-16406	Boeing 747-45EM	1051/27898	ex N406EV		
B-16407	Boeing 747-45EM	1053/27899	ex N407EV		
B-16408	Boeing 747-45EM	1076/28092	ex N408EV		Lsd fr WFBN
B-16409	Boeing 747-45EM	1077/28093	ex N409EV		Lsd fr WFBN
B-16410	Boeing 747-45E	1140/29061			
B-16411	Boeing 747-45E	1151/29111			Lsd fr Chailease
B-16412	Boeing 747-45E	1159/29112			
B-16461	Boeing 747-45EM	994/27154			Lsd fr HHL Lease
B-16462	Boeing 747-45EM	998/27173			
B-16463	Boeing 747-45EM	1004/27174			
B-16465	Boeing 747-45EM	1016/26062			Lsd fr Chailease
B-16481	Boeing 747-45EF	1251/30607			
B-16482	Boeing 747-45EF	1279/30608			
B-16483	Boeing 747-45EF	1309/30609			

B-16603	Boeing 767-35EER	434/26063			Lsd fr HHL Lease
B-16605	Boeing 767-35EER	438/26064			Lsd fr HHL Lease
B-16621	Boeing 767-25E	524/27192	ex (B-16606)		Lsd fr GECAS
B-16622	Boeing 767-25E	527/27193	ex (B-16607)		Lsd fr GECAS
B-16623	Boeing 767-25E	532/27194	ex (B-16608)		Lsd fr GECAS
B-16625	Boeing 767-25E	535/27195	ex (B-16609)		Lsd fr GECAS
N601EV	Boeing 767-3T7ER	366/25076	ex B-16601		Lsd fr SALE
N602EV	Boeing 767-3T7ER	370/25117	ex B-16602		Lsd fr SALE

B-16101	McDonnell-Douglas MD-11F	570/48542			
B-16102	McDonnell-Douglas MD-11F	572/48543			
B-16103	McDonnell-Douglas MD-11F	576/48415	ex N103EV	on order Aug04	Lsd fr GECAS
B-16106	McDonnell-Douglas MD-11F	587/48545			
B-16107	McDonnell-Douglas MD-11F	589/48546			
B-16108	McDonnell-Douglas MD-11F	619/48778			
B-16109	McDonnell-Douglas MD-11F	620/48779			
B-16110	McDonnell-Douglas MD-11F	630/48786			
B-16111	McDonnell-Douglas MD-11F	631/48787			
B-16112	McDonnell-Douglas MD-11F	633/48789	ex N90178		
B-16113	McDonnell-Douglas MD-11F	634/48790	ex N9030Q		
N105EV	McDonnell-Douglas MD-11F	580/48544			Lsd fr WFBN

B-27017	Boeing 757-27A	904/29610			Lsd fr FEA
B-27021	Boeing 757-27A	910/29611	ex N1787B		Lsd fr FEA

Three Boeing 777-25ELRs and twelve Boeing 777-35EERs are on order for delivery from late 2007 and January 2005 respectively

Owns 20% of Great China Airlines, 5% of Air Macau and also controls UNI Air

---

FAR EASTERN AIR TRANSPORT

FAT (EF/FEA) (IATA 265)   *Taipei-Sung Shan (TSA)*

B-27001	Boeing 757-2Q8	369/25044	ex N341LF		Lsd fr ILFC
B-27007	Boeing 757-29J	591/27204	ex (SU-RAD)		
B-27011	Boeing 757-27A	832/29607		Toyota Camry c/s	
B-27013	Boeing 757-27A	835/29608		Warner Bros c/s	
B-27015	Boeing 757-27A	876/29609			
B-27017	Boeing 757-27A	904/29610			Lsd to EVA
B-27021	Boeing 757-27A	910/29611	ex N1787B		Lsd to EVA

B-17917	McDonnell-Douglas MD-90-30ER	2217/53572			Lsd fr UIA
B-17918	McDonnell-Douglas MD-90-30ER	2193/53571			Lsd fr UIA
B-17923	McDonnell-Douglas MD-90-30ER	2153/53534	ex B-16901		Lsd fr UIA

B-28007	McDonnell-Douglas MD-83	1829/49807	ex N6200N		Lsd fr Sino Pac
B-28011	McDonnell-Douglas MD-82	1954/53118	ex N6202S	TransAsia Tele c/s	Lsd fr Sino Pac
B-28017	McDonnell-Douglas MD-82	2052/53166	ex N835AU		Lsd fr Mach I
B-28021	McDonnell-Douglas MD-82	2056/53167	ex N836AU		Lsd fr Mach I
B-28023	McDonnell-Douglas MD-83	1934/49952	ex G-TONW		Lsd fr GECAS
B-28025	McDonnell-Douglas MD-83	2214/53602			
B-28027	McDonnell-Douglas MD-83	2218/53603	ex N6200N		
B-28031	McDonnell-Douglas MD-83	1913/49950	ex P4-MDE		Lsd fr GECAS
B-28033	McDonnell-Douglas MD-82	2189/53577	ex B-88988		Lsd fr Centrel Lsg

19% owned by China Airlines

GREAT WING AIRLINES

Taipei-Sung Shan (TSA)

B-69832	Britten-Norman BN-2A-26 Islander	2039	ex B-12232

MANDARIN AIRLINES

Mandarin Air (AE/MDA) (IATA 803)

Taipei-Sung Shan (TSA)

B-12270	Fokker 50	20316	ex PT-MLF		Lsd fr Lazard
B-12271	Fokker 50	20284	ex PH-MXG		
B-12272	Fokker 50	20286	ex PH-MXH		
B-12273	Fokker 50	20303	ex PH-JCF		
B-12275	Fokker 50	20306	ex PH-JPB		
B-12276	Fokker 50	20312	ex PH-JCR		
B-12279	Fokker 50	20317	ex PT-MLG		Lsd fr Lazard
B-11152	Dornier 228-212	8234	ex D-CBDO		Lsd fr UIA
B-11156	Dornier 228-212	8235	ex D-CBDP		Lsd fr UIA
B-12253	Dornier 228-212	8215	ex D-CJOH	stored	
B-12259	Dornier 228-212	8224	ex D-CLFC	stored	
B-12291	Fokker 100	11500	ex PH-JCO		
B-12292	Fokker 100	11496	ex PH-JCP		
B-16802	Boeing 737-8Q8	739/28236			Lsd fr ILFC
B-16803	Boeing 737-8Q8	743/30664	ex N1787B		Lsd fr ILFC
B-16805	Boeing 737-8Q8	768/30636			Lsd fr ILFC; sublsd to CAL

Wholly owned by China Airlines; leases Boeing 737-8Q8s to President Airlines when required

TRANSASIA AIRWAYS

Transasia (GE/TNA) (IATA 170)

Taipei-Sung Shan (TSA)

B-22712	Aerospatiale/Alenia ATR 72-202	364	ex F-WWEA	for sale	
B-22715	Aerospatiale/Alenia ATR 72-201	381	ex F-WWEG	for sale	
B-27716	Aerospatiale/Alenia ATR 72-201	389	ex F-WWEH		
B-22801	Aerospatiale/Alenia ATR 72-212A	517	ex F-WWLK		
B-22802	Aerospatiale/Alenia ATR 72-212A	525	ex F-WWLB		
B-22803	Aerospatiale/Alenia ATR 72-212A	527	ex F-WWLC		
B-22805	Aerospatiale/Alenia ATR 72-212A	558	ex F-WQIU		
B-22806	Aerospatiale/Alenia ATR 72-212A	560	ex F-WQIY		Lsd fr Sean-Ho Lsg
B-22807	Aerospatiale/Alenia ATR 72-212A	567	ex F-WQIZ		
B-22810	Aerospatiale/Alenia ATR 72-212A	642	ex F-WQMF		
B-22306	Airbus Industrie A320-231	0441	ex F-WQBC		Lsd fr Kawasaki
B-22310	Airbus Industrie A320-232	0791	ex F-WWDR		Lsd fr HHL Leasing
B-22311	Airbus Industrie A320-232	0822	ex F-WWBY		Lsd fr HHL Leasing
B-22601	Airbus Industrie A321-131	0538	ex F-WGYZ	Special colours	
B-22602	Airbus Industrie A321-131	0555	ex F-WFYZ		
B-22605	Airbus Industrie A321-131	0606	ex F-WGYY		
B-22606	Airbus Industrie A321-131	0731	ex F-WQGL		
B-22607	Airbus Industrie A321-131	0746	ex F-WQGM		

UNI AIR

Glory (B7/UIA)

Taipei-Sung Shan (TSA)

B-15217	de Havilland DHC-8-311A	379	ex C-GEOA	Lsd fr Chailease
B-15219	de Havilland DHC-8-311A	381	ex C-FDHD	Lsd fr Sunshine Finance
B-15221	de Havilland DHC-8-311A	325	ex C-FNJD	Lsd fr AeroCentury
B-15223	de Havilland DHC-8-311B	404	ex C-GDKL	Lsd fr AeroCentury
B-15225	de Havilland DHC-8-311B	405	ex C-GFHZ	Lsd fr Hwa-Hsia Lsg
B-15227	de Havilland DHC-8-311B	406	ex C-FDHD	Lsd fr Hwa-Hsia Lsg
B-15229	de Havilland DHC-8-311B	407	ex C-GFEN	Lsd fr Hwa-Hsia Lsg
B-15231	de Havilland DHC-8-311B	414	ex C-GFBW	Lsd fr Chailease
B-15233	de Havilland DHC-8-311B	402	ex C-GDFT	Lsd fr Chailease
B-15235	de Havilland DHC-8Q-311B	443	ex C-FWBB	Lsd fr Hwa Hsia Lsg
B-15237	de Havilland DHC-8Q-311B	467	ex C-GELN	Lsd fr Hwa-Hsia Lsg
B-15239	de Havilland DHC-8Q-311B	571	ex C-GEWI	
B-17201	de Havilland DHC-8Q-202	522	ex C-FDHV	
B-17911	McDonnell-Douglas MD-90-30	2158/53535		Lsd fr Hwa-Hsia Lsg
B-17913	McDonnell-Douglas MD-90-30	2162/53537		Lsd fr Chailease
B-17915	McDonnell-Douglas MD-90-30	2168/53538		Lsd fr Chailease
B-17916	McDonnell-Douglas MD-90-30	2172/53539		Lsd fr Chailease
B-17917	McDonnell-Douglas MD-90-30ER	2217/53572		Lsd to FEA
B-17918	McDonnell-Douglas MD-90-30ER	2193/53571		Lsd fr Chailease; sublsd to FEA
B-17919	McDonnell-Douglas MD-90-30	2173/53569	ex N6206F	
B-17920	McDonnell-Douglas MD-90-30	2186/53574		
B-17921	McDonnell-Douglas MD-90-30	2166/53554	ex SU-BNN	
B-17922	McDonnell-Douglas MD-90-30	2243/53601	ex SU-BMT	

B-17923	McDonnell-Douglas MD-90-30ER	2153/53534	ex B-16901	Lsd fr FCB Lsg; sublsd to FEA
B-17925	McDonnell-Douglas MD-90-30ER	2171/53568	ex B-16902	Lsd fr FCB Lsg
B-17926	McDonnell-Douglas MD-90-30ER	2169/53567	ex B-15301	Lsd fr Chailease
B-11156	Dornier 228-212	8235	ex D-COAX	Lsd to MDA

C- CANADA

AC JETZ

Specialist sports charter division of Air Canada. For details see parent's fleet

ADLAIR AVIATION

Cambridge Bay, NWT/Yellowknife, NWT (YCB/YZF)

C-FGYN	de Havilland DHC-2 Beaver	134		Floats/Skis	
C-GBFP	Lear Jet 25B	25B-167	ex N664CL	Ernie Lyall	EMS
C-GBYN	Beech B200 Super King Air	BB-1232	ex N209CM		
C-GFYN	de Havilland DHC-6 Twin Otter 200	209	ex N915SA		
C-GSYN	Beech 100 King Air	B-61	ex N418LA		

ADLER AVIATION

Shockwave (SWH)   *Kitchener-Waterloo, Ont (YKF)*

C-GMOZ	Piper PA-31-350 Chieftain	31-8052067	ex N3556B
C-GTGR	Cessna 421C Golden Eagle II	421C0061	ex N15LW

ADVENTURE AIR

Pine Falls, Man

C-FVQD	de Havilland DHC-3 Turbo Otter	466		
C-FXPC	de Havilland DHC-2 Turbo Beaver	1196	ex HK-1014	Floats
C-GSUV	de Havilland DHC-3 Otter	376	ex N445FD	Floats

AERO ARCTIC suspended operations

AERO GOLFE suspended operations

AERO PENINSULE now trades as Air Optima

AEROPRO

Aeropro (APO)   *Montreal-Trudeau, Que (YUL)*

C-GAWN	Cessna 310R II	310R0957	ex N37211
C-GAWT	Cessna 310R II	310R1600	ex N36846
C-GMCR	Cessna 310R II	310R1424	ex N5149C
C-GSVI	Cessna 310R II	310R0833	ex N58JB
C-GYOT	Cessna 310R II	310R0912	ex (N3750G)
CF-DPQ	Cessna 337G Super Skymaster	33701519	ex N72091
C-GIGB	Cessna 337G Super Skymaster	33701599	ex N72478
C-GILW	Cessna 337G Super Skymaster II	33701781	ex 6Y-JNF
C-GJOD	Cessna 337G Super Skymaster II	33701694	ex N53551
C-GTEL	Cessna 337G Super Skymaster II	33701659	ex C-FKTN
C-GYOB	Cessna 337G Super Skymaster II	33701780	
C-FTIW	Piper PA-31-350 Navajo Chieftain	31-7752123	ex N39CA
C-GBYL	Piper PA-31-350 Navajo Chieftain	31-7752144	ex N456JB
C-GHMG	Piper PA-31-350 Navajo Chieftain	31-7652153	ex N62895
C-GQAM	Piper PA-31 Turbo Navajo C	31-7912093	ex N3536Z
C-GQZE	Piper PA-31 Turbo Navajo C	31-7912065	ex N3520E
C-GRFJ	Piper PA-31 Turbo Navajo C	31-7812031	ex N27485
C-GRYE	Piper PA-31-350 Navajo Chieftain	31-7852155	
C-FCGN	Beech 65-A90 King Air	LJ-313	
C-FGIN	Beech A100 King Air	B-164	ex N164RA
C-GDLG	Cessna 425 Conquest I	425-0063	ex N425TY
C-GJBQ	Beech A100 King Air	B-191	ex N214CK
C-GLPG	Beech A100 King Air	B-159	ex N110KF
C-GRSL	Beech 65-C90 King Air	LJ-609	ex Z-WSG

AIR 500

Boomerang (ERM)   Toronto-Pearson Intl, Ont (YYZ)

C-FFSS	Mitsubishi MU-2B-60 Marquise	783SA	ex N81604
C-GFFH	Mitsubishi MU-2B-60 Marquise	1522SA	ex N902M
C-GGDC	Mitsubishi MU-2B-60 Marquise	796SA	ex N700MA

All leased from IMP Group

AIR ALLIANCE

Georgian (ZX/GGN)   Toronto-Pearson Intl, Ont (YYZ)

C-GAAR	Beech 1900D	UE-207	ex N10625	964	Lsd to LAL
C-GAAS	Beech 1900D	UE-209	ex N10659	965	
C-GAAT	Beech 1900D	UE-217	ex N1564J	963	
C-GAAU	Beech 1900D	UE-232	ex N10705	904	
C-GGGA	Beech 1900D	UE-291	ex N20704	951	
C-GHGA	Beech 1900D	UE-293	ex N21063	953	
C-GMGA	Beech 1900D	UE-315	ex N22890	956	
C-GORA	Beech 1900D	UE-326	ex N23164	957	
C-GORC	Beech 1900D	UE-320	ex N22976	959	
C-GORF	Beech 1900D	UE-330	ex N23222	958	
C-GVGA	Beech 1900D	UE-292	ex N20707	952	
C-GWGA	Beech 1900D	UE-309	ex N22874	955	
C-GXGX	Beech 1900D	UE-16	ex N83700		Lsd fr Raytheon
C-GZGA	Beech 1900D	UE-306	ex N22700	954	
C-GKGA	Beech 1900C-1	UC-117	ex N117ZR	963	
C-GTGA	Beech 1900C-1	UC-62	ex N62YV	Freighter	

Operates feeder service for Air Canada Jazz using code ZX. Some aircraft also operate as Simo Air
Air Alliance is the trading name of Air Georgian

AIR BELLEVUE

Bellevue SPB/Roberval, Que (-/YRJ)

C-GABM	Cessna 208 Caravan I	20800308	ex N12712	Floatplane

AIR CAB

Vancouver-Coal Harbour, BC (CXH)

C-FBMO	Cessna A185E Skywagon	18501627	ex N1934U	
C-FOES	de Havilland DHC-2 Turbo Beaver	1673/TB43		Lsd fr CBE Construction
C-FQGZ	Cessna A185E Skywagon	18501691	ex N1967U	
C-FRJG	de Havilland DHC-2 Beaver	1550		
C-GJGC	de Havilland DHC-2 Beaver	88	ex CF-GQM	
C-GJZE	de Havilland DHC-2 Beaver	1276	ex N87780	

All Floatplanes

AIR CANADA

Air Canada (AC/ACA((IATA 014)   Montreal-Mirabel/Montreal-Trudeau, Que (YMX/YUL)

C-FWTF	Airbus Industrie A319-112	1963	ex D-AVYA	298	Lsd fr GECAS
C-FYIY	Airbus Industrie A319-114	0634	ex D-AVYP	252	
C-FYJB	Airbus Industrie A319-114	0639	ex D-AVYU	253	
C-FYJD	Airbus Industrie A319-114	0649	ex D-AVYW	254; Kid's Horizons c/s
C-FYJE	Airbus Industrie A319-114	0656	ex D-AVYZ	255	
C-FYJG	Airbus Industrie A319-114	0670	ex D-AVYE	256	
C-FYJH	Airbus Industrie A319-114	0672	ex D-AVYF	257	
C-FYJI	Airbus Industrie A319-114	0682	ex D-AVYH	258	
C-FYJP	Airbus Industrie A319-114	0688	ex D-AVYJ	259	
C-FYKC	Airbus Industrie A319-114	0691	ex D-AVYP	260	
C-FYKR	Airbus Industrie A319-114	0693	ex D-AVYQ	261	
C-FYKW	Airbus Industrie A319-114	0695	ex D-AVYS	262	
C-FYNS	Airbus Industrie A319-114	0572	ex D-AVYK	251	
C-FZUG	Airbus Industrie A319-114	0697	ex D-AVYT	263	
C-FZUH	Airbus Industrie A319-114	0711	ex D-AVYV	264; TCA c/s
C-FZUJ	Airbus Industrie A319-114	0719	ex D-AVYW	265	
C-FZUL	Airbus Industrie A319-114	0721	ex D-AVYY	266	
C-GAPY	Airbus Industrie A319-114	0728	ex D-AVYE	267	
C-GAQL	Airbus Industrie A319-114	0732	ex D-AVYX	268	
C-GAQX	Airbus Industrie A319-114	0736	ex D-AVYG	269	
C-GAQZ	Airbus Industrie A319-114	0740	ex D-AVYH	270	
C-GARG	Airbus Industrie A319-114	0742	ex D-AVYM	271	
C-GARJ	Airbus Industrie A319-114	0752	ex D-AVYP	272	
C-GARO	Airbus Industrie A319-114	0757	ex D-AVYQ	273	
C-GBHM	Airbus Industrie A319-114	0769	ex D-AVYB	274	

C-GBHN	Airbus Industrie A319-114	0773	ex D-AVYK	275	
C-GBHO	Airbus Industrie A319-114	0779	ex D-AVYT	276	
C-GBHR	Airbus Industrie A319-114	0785	ex D-AVYU	277	
C-GBHY	Airbus Industrie A319-114	0800	ex D-AVYE	278	
C-GBHZ	Airbus Industrie A319-114	0813	ex D-AVYG	279	
C-GBIA	Airbus Industrie A319-114	0817	ex D-AVYM	280	
C-GBIJ	Airbus Industrie A319-114	0829	ex D-AVYH	281	
C-GBIK	Airbus Industrie A319-114	0831	ex D-AVYI	282	
C-GBIM	Airbus Industrie A319-114	0840	ex D-AVYQ	283	
C-GBIN	Airbus Industrie A319-114	0845	ex D-AVYA	284	
C-GBIP	Airbus Industrie A319-114	0546	ex D-AVYV	285	
C-GITP	Airbus Industrie A319-112	1562	ex D-AVYR	286	Lsd fr ILFC
C-GITR	Airbus Industrie A319-112	1577	ex D-AVWR	287	Lsd fr ILFC
C-GITT	Airbus Industrie A319-112	1630	ex D-AVYD	288	Lsd fr ILFC
C-GJTA	Airbus Industrie A319-112	1673	ex D-AVWE	290	Lsd fr ILFC
C-GJTC	Airbus Industrie A319-112	1668	ex D-AVWA	289	
C-GJVS	Airbus Industrie A319-112	1718	ex D-AVWO	291	Lsd fr GECAS
C-GJVY	Airbus Industrie A319-112	1742	ex F-WWIJ	292	Lsd fr ILFC
C-GJWE	Airbus Industrie A319-112	1756	ex D-AVYC	293	Lsd fr GECAS
C-GJWF	Airbus Industrie A319-112	1765	ex D-AVYO	294	Lsd fr ILFC
C-GKNW	Airbus Industrie A319-112	1805	ex D-AVWF	295	Lsd fr ILFC
C-GKOB^	Airbus Industrie A319-112	1853	ex D-AVWY	296	Lsd fr GECAS
C-GKOC	Airbus Industrie A319-112	1886	ex D-AVWB	297	Lsd fr GECAS
C-	Airbus Industrie A319-112	2103	ex D-AV	298 on order	Lsd fr GECAS
C-FDCA	Airbus Industrie A320-211	0232	ex F-WWIY	405 Tango	Lsd fr GECAS
C-FDQQ	Airbus Industrie A320-211	0059	ex F-WWDI	201	Lsd fr GECAS
C-FDQV	Airbus Industrie A320-211	0068	ex F-WWDO	202	
C-FDRH	Airbus Industrie A320-211	0073	ex F-WWDC	203	
C-FDRK	Airbus Industrie A320-211	0084	ex F-WWDP	204	
C-FDRP	Airbus Industrie A320-211	0122	ex F-WWIP	205	Lsd fr GECAS
C-FDSN	Airbus Industrie A320-211	0126	ex F-WWIU	206	
C-FDST	Airbus Industrie A320-211	0127	ex F-WWIV	207	Lsd fr GECAS
C-FDSU	Airbus Industrie A320-211	0141	ex F-WWDH	208	Lsd fr GECAS
C-FFWI	Airbus Industrie A320-211	0149	ex F-WWDP	209	Lsd fr GECAS
C-FFWJ	Airbus Industrie A320-211	0150	ex F-WWDQ	210	
C-FFWM	Airbus Industrie A320-211	0154	ex F-WWDY	211	Lsd fr GECAS
C-FFWN+	Airbus Industrie A320-211	0159	ex F-WWIG	212; 65th colours	Lsd fr GECAS
C-FGYL	Airbus Industrie A320-211	0254	ex F-WWBF	218	
C-FGYS	Airbus Industrie A320-211	0255	ex F-WWBG	219	
C-FKAJ	Airbus Industrie A320-211	0333	ex F-WWBJ	227	
C-FKCK	Airbus Industrie A320-211	0265	ex F-WWDR	220	
C-FKCO	Airbus Industrie A320-211	0277	ex F-WWDX	221	
C-FKCR	Airbus Industrie A320-211	0290	ex F-WWBY	222	
C-FKOJ	Airbus Industrie A320-211	0330	ex F-WWIB	226	
C-FKPO	Airbus Industrie A320-211	0311	ex F-WWIL	224	
C-FKPS	Airbus Industrie A320-211	0310	ex F-WWIK	223	
C-FKPT	Airbus Industrie A320-211	0324	ex F-WWDC	225	
C-FLSF	Airbus Industrie A320-211	0279	ex G-MONY	406 Tango	Lsd fr ILFC
C-FLSS	Airbus Industrie A320-211	0284	ex F-WWBU	408	Lsd fr GECAS
C-FLSU	Airbus Industrie A320-211	0309	ex F-WWIJ	411 Tango	Lsd fr GECAS
C-FMEQ	Airbus Industrie A320-211	0302	ex F-WWIY	409 Tango	
C-FMES	Airbus Industrie A320-211	0305	ex F-WWDE	410 Tango	
C-FMJK	Airbus Industrie A320-211	0342	ex F-WWDB	229	
C-FMST	Airbus Industrie A320-211	0350	ex F-WWDF	230	
C-FMSV	Airbus Industrie A320-211	0359	ex F-WWIT	231	
C-FMSX	Airbus Industrie A320-211	0378	ex F-WWIY	232	
C-FMSY	Airbus Industrie A320-211	0384	ex F-WWBG	233	
C-FNNA	Airbus Industrie A320-211	0426	ex F-WWBU	234	
C-FNVU	Airbus Industrie A320-211	0403	ex F-WWBO	415 Tango	Lsd fr GECAS
C-FNVV	Airbus Industrie A320-211	0404	ex F-WWDF	416 Tango	Lsd fr GECAS
C-FPDN	Airbus Industrie A320-211	0341	ex F-WWBR	228	
C-FPWD	Airbus Industrie A320-211	0231	ex F-WWDV	404 Tango	Lsd fr GECAS
C-FPWE	Airbus Industrie A320-211	0175	ex F-WWIN	402 Tango	Lsd fr GECAS
C-FTJO	Airbus Industrie A320-211	0183	ex F-WWIX	213	Lsd fr GECAS
C-FTJP	Airbus Industrie A320-211	0233	ex F-WWIQ	214	Lsd fr GECAS
C-FTJQ	Airbus Industrie A320-211	0242	ex F-WWDJ	215	
C-FTJR	Airbus Industrie A320-211	0248	ex F-WWDT	216	Lsd fr GECAS
C-FTJS	Airbus Industrie A320-211	0253	ex F-WWBE	217	
C-FXCD	Airbus Industrie A320-211	2018	ex F-WWBV	239	Lsd fr GECAS
C-FZQS	Airbus Industrie A320-214	2145	ex F-WWDI	240	Lsd fr GECAS
C-FZUB	Airbus Industrie A320-214	1940	ex F-WWIP	238	Lsd fr GECAS
C-GJVT	Airbus Industrie A320-211	1719	ex F-WWBC	235	Lsd fr ILFC
C-GKOD	Airbus Industrie A320-211	1864	ex F-WWIE	236	Lsd fr ILFC
C-GKOE	Airbus Industrie A320-211	1874	ex F-WWBN	237	Lsd fr ILFC
C-GPWG	Airbus Industrie A320-211	0174	ex F-WWIM	401 Tango	Lsd fr GECAS
C-GQCA	Airbus Industrie A320-211	0210	ex F-WWIC	403 AC Jetz	Lsd fr GECAS
C-	Airbus Industrie A320-214	2145	ex F-WWDI	on order	Lsd fr GECAS

+Named 'Symphony of voices', maple leaf on each side of tail composed of 40000 employee signatures.
Sold 16 Airbus Industrie A320-211s and one Airbus Industrie A319-111 to GECAS for lease back. Will also trade six old A320s to GECAS in exchange for new A319/A320s

C-FZUY	Airbus Industrie A321-211	2025	ex D-AVXK	462	
C-FZVF	Airbus Industrie A321-211	1794	ex D-AVZF	461	
C-GITU	Airbus Industrie A321-211	1602	ex D-AMTA	451	Lsd fr Mobilien Verwaltungs
C-GITY	Airbus Industrie A321-211	1611	ex D-AVZO	452	
C-GIUB	Airbus Industrie A321-211	1623	ex D-AMTB	453	Lsd fr Mobilien Verwaltungs
C-GIUE	Airbus Industrie A321-211	1632	ex D-AMTC	454	Lsd fr Mobilien Verwaltungs
C-GIUF	Airbus Industrie A321-211	1638	ex D-AMTD	455	Lsd fr Mobilien Verwaltungs
C-GJVX	Airbus Industrie A321-211	1726	ex D-AVXC	456	Lsd fr debis
C-GJWD	Airbus Industrie A321-211	1748	ex D-AVXE	457	Lsd fr debis
C-GJWI	Airbus Industrie A321-211	1772	ex D-AVZA	458	
C-GJWN	Airbus Industrie A321-211	1783	ex D-AVZD	459	
C-GJWO	Airbus Industrie A321-211	1811	ex D-AVZI	460	Lsd fr Oasis Lsg
C-GKOH	Airbus Industrie A321-211	0674	ex D-AMTG	465	Lsd fr Mobilien Verwaltungs
C-GKOI	Airbus Industrie A321-211	0675	ex D-AMTF	466	Lsd fr Mobilien Verwaltungs
C-GKOJ	Airbus Industrie A321-211	0684	ex D-AMTE	467	Lsd fr Mobilien Verwaltungs
C-GFAF	Airbus Industrie A330-343X	277	ex F-WWKO	931	
C-GFAH	Airbus Industrie A330-343X	279	ex F-WWYB	932	
C-GFAJ	Airbus Industrie A330-343X	284	ex F-WWYA	933	
C-GFUR	Airbus Industrie A330-343X	344	ex F-WWYC	934	
C-GHKR	Airbus Industrie A330-343X	400	ex F-WWKM	935	
C-GHKW	Airbus Industrie A330-343X	408	ex F-WWKS	936	
C-GHKX	Airbus Industrie A330-343X	412	ex F-WWKU	937	
C-GHLM	Airbus Industrie A330-343X	419	ex F-WWYA	938	
C-FTNQ	Airbus Industrie A340-313	088	ex F-WWJV		Lsd fr ILFC to Mar04
C-FYKX	Airbus Industrie A340-313X	150	ex F-WWJT	901	
C-FYKZ	Airbus Industrie A340-313X	154	ex F-WWJI	902	
C-FYLC	Airbus Industrie A340-313X	167	ex F-WWJZ	903	
C-FYLD	Airbus Industrie A340-313X	170	ex F-WWJF	904; Star Alliance c/s	
C-FYLG	Airbus Industrie A340-313X	175	ex F-WWJE	905	
C-FYLU	Airbus Industrie A340-313X	179	ex F-WWJY	906	
C-GDVW	Airbus Industrie A340-313X	273	ex F-WWJT	909	
C-GDVZ	Airbus Industrie A340-313X	278	ex F-WWJV	910	
C-GKOO	Airbus Industrie A340-642	592	ex F-WW	961 on order Jul04	
C-GKOU	Airbus Industrie A340-642	596	ex F-WW	962 on order Aug04	
C-GKOV	Airbus Industrie A340-642		ex F-WW	963 on order Sep04	
C-FACP	Boeing 737-2L9	623/22072	ex C2-RN9	Zip	
C-FCPM	Boeing 737-2T7	850/22761	ex G-DWHH	stored	
C-FCPN	Boeing 737-2T7	856/22762	ex G-DGDP	Zip orange	
C-FHCP	Boeing 737-2T5	641/22024	ex EI-BPV	Zip fuschia	
C-GCPM	Boeing 737-217	560/21716	ex N1262E	Zip blue	
C-GCPN	Boeing 737-217	581/21717		Zip green	
C-GCPO	Boeing 737-217	584/21718		Zip orange	
C-GCPP	Boeing 737-217	666/22255		Zip fuschia	
C-GCPQ	Boeing 737-217	672/22256		Zip green	
C-GCPT	Boeing 737-217	770/22258		Zip	Lsd fr Arkia Lsg
C-GEPW	Boeing 737-275	425/21115	ex N129AW	stored MHV	
C-GFCP	Boeing 737-217	874/22659		Zip fucshia	
C-GIPW	Boeing 737-275	556/21712		Tango ; stored YEG	
C-GJCP	Boeing 737-217	911/22728	ex N178EE	Zip blue	
C-GKCP	Boeing 737-217	915/22729		Zip	Lsd fr Arkia Lsg
C-GMCP	Boeing 737-217	945/22864		Zip fuschia	Lsd fr Arkia Lsg
C-GQCP	Boeing 737-217	960/22865		Zip orange	Lsd fr Triton
C-GUPW	Boeing 737-275	898/22873		stored MHV	Lsd fr GECAS
C-GVPW	Boeing 737-275	904/22874		stored MHV	
C-GWPW	Boeing 737-275	1109/23283		Zip green	

All fitted with AvAero Stage 3 hushkits
All retired from main-line service in 2002 with 4 transfered to AC Jetz offering sports charter flights
Tango by Air Canada is low-cost operations in East Canada while Zip Air is low cost operation based in Calgary

C-GAGL+	Boeing 747-433M	840/24998	ex N6018N	341	
C-GAGM	Boeing 747-433M	862/25074		342	
C-GAGN+	Boeing 747-433M	868/25075	ex N6009F	343	

+Leased from GECAS until March 2004

C-FBEF	Boeing 767-233ER	250/24323	ex N6009F	617	
C-FBEG	Boeing 767-233ER	252/24324	ex N6009F	618	
C-FBEM	Boeing 767-233ER	254/24325	ex N6038E	619	
C-FCAB	Boeing 767-375ER	213/24082	ex N6055X	681	
C-FCAE	Boeing 767-375ER	215/24083	ex N6046P	682	
C-FCAF	Boeing 767-375ER	219/24084	ex N6038E	683	
C-FCAG	Boeing 767-375ER	220/24085	ex N6009F	684	
C-FMWP	Boeing 767-333ER	508/25583		631	
C-FMWQ	Boeing 767-333ER	596/25584		632	
C-FMWU	Boeing 767-333ER	597/25585		633	
C-FMWV	Boeing 767-333ER	599/25586		634	
C-FMWY	Boeing 767-333ER	604/25587		635	
C-FMXC	Boeing 767-333ER	606/25588		636	
C-FOCA	Boeing 767-375ER	311/24575		640	
C-FPCA	Boeing 767-375ER	258/24306		637	

C-FTCA	Boeing 767-375ER	259/24307		638	
C-FUCL	Boeing 767-209ER	60/22682	ex N682SH	622	Lsd fr Boullioun
C-FVNM	Boeing 767-209ER	18/22681	ex ZK-NBF	621; std MHV	Lsd fr Aerospace Fin
C-FXCA	Boeing 767-375ER	302/24574		639	
C-GAUB	Boeing 767-233	16/22517		601; Star Alliance colours	
C-GAUE	Boeing 767-233	22/22518		602	
C-GAUH	Boeing 767-233	40/22519		603	
C-GAUN	Boeing 767-233	47/22520		604	
C-GAUP	Boeing 767-233	66/22521	ex N1791B	605; stored YUL	
C-GAUS	Boeing 767-233	75/22522	ex N60659	606; stored MHV	
C-GAUU	Boeing 767-233	87/22523	ex N1784B	607; stored MHV	
C-GAUW	Boeing 767-233	88/22524	ex N6038E	608; stored MHV	
C-GAVC	Boeing 767-233ER	102/22527	ex N1783B	611; stored MHV	
C-GBZR	Boeing 767-38EER	411/25404	ex HL7267	645	Lsd fr ILFC
C-GDSP	Boeing 767-233ER	229/24142	ex N6009F	613; stored YUL	
C-GDSS	Boeing 767-233ER	233/24143	ex N6005C	614	
C-GDSU	Boeing 767-233ER	234/24144	ex N6018N	615	
C-GDSY	Boeing 767-233ER	236/24145	ex N6005C	616	
C-GDUZ	Boeing 767-38EER	399/25347	ex HL7266	646	Lsd fr ILFC
C-GEOQ	Boeing 767-375ER	765/30112		647	Lsd fr GECAS
C-GEOU	Boeing 767-375ER	771/30108		648	Lsd fr GECAS
C-GGMX	Boeing 767-3Y0ER	351/24947	ex N947AC	652	Lsd fr BBAM
C-GGFJ	Boeing 767-3Y0ER	357/24952	ex SE-DKZ	653	Lsd fr BBAM
C-GHLA	Boeing 767-35HER	445/26387	ex VH-BZL	656	Lsd fr Itochu
C-GHLK	Boeing 767-35HER	456/26388	ex VH-BZM	657	Lsd fr Itochu
C-GHLQ	Boeing 767-36NER	832/30846	ex N6009F	658	Lsd fr GECAS
C-GHLT	Boeing 767-36NER	835/30850	ex N6018N	659	Lsd fr GECAS
C-GHLU	Boeing 767-36NER	836/30851	ex N6046P	660	Lsd fr GECAS
C-GHLV	Boeing 767-36NER	843/30852	ex N6055X	661	Lsd fr GECAS
C-GHPA	Boeing 767-3Y0ER	386/25000	ex N250AP	686	Lsd fr WFBN
C-GHPD	Boeing 767-3Y0ER	354/24999	ex N25034	687; stored YUL	Lsd fr GECAS
C-GLCA	Boeing 767-375ER	361/25120		641	
C-GPWA	Boeing 767-275	36/22683		671; stored MHV	
C-GPWB	Boeing 767-275	52/22684	ex N1791B	672	
C-GSCA	Boeing 767-375ER	372/25121	ex B-2564	642	Lsd fr Tombo
C-FRIA	Canadair CL-600-2B19	7045	ex C-FMLQ	101	
C-FRIB	Canadair CL-600-2B19	7047	ex C-FMLT	102	
C-FRID	Canadair CL-600-2B19	7049	ex C-FMLV	103	
C-FRIL	Canadair CL-600-2B19	7051	ex C-FMML	104	
C-FSJF	Canadair CL-600-2B19	7054	ex C-FMMT	105	
C-FSJJ	Canadair CL-600-2B19	7058	ex C-FMNB	106	
C-FSJU	Canadair CL-600-2B19	7060	ex C-FMNH	107	
C-FSKE	Canadair CL-600-2B19	7065	ex C-FMOI	108	
C-FSKM	Canadair CL-600-2B19	7071	ex C-FMKZ	110	
C-FVKM	Canadair CL-600-2B19	7074	ex C-FMLI	111	
C-FVKN	Canadair CL-600-2B19	7078	ex C-FMLU	112	
C-FVKR	Canadair CL-600-2B19	7083	ex C-FMNQ	114	
C-FVMD	Canadair CL-600-2B19	7082		113	
C-FWJB	Canadair CL-600-2B19	7087		115	
C-FWJF	Canadair CL-600-2B19	7095		116	
C-FWJI	Canadair CL-600-2B19	7096		117	
C-FWJS	Canadair CL-600-2B19	7097		118	
C-FWJT	Canadair CL-600-2B19	7098		119	
C-FWRR	Canadair CL-600-2B19	7107		120	
C-FWRS	Canadair CL-600-2B19	7112		121	
C-FWRT	Canadair CL-600-2B19	7118		122	
C-FWSC	Canadair CL-600-2B19	7120		123	
C-FXMY	Canadair CL-600-2B19	7124		124	
C-FZAQ	Canadair CL-600-2B19	7155	ex C-FMMB	151	Lsd fr Oasis Lsg
C-FZSI	Canadair CL-600-2B19	7160	ex LV-WZU	152	Lsd fr Oasis Lsg
C-	Canadair CL-600-2B19			on order Sep04	
C-	Canadair CL-600-2B19			on order 04	
C-	Canadair CL-600-2B19			on order 04	
C-	Canadair CL-600-2B19			on order 04	
C-	Canadair CL-600-2B19			on order 04	

A further ten are on order for future delivery

C-	Canadair CL-600-2D24			on order	
C-	Canadair CL-600-2D24			on order	
C-	Canadair CL-600-2D24			on order	
C-	Canadair CL-600-2D24			on order	
C-	Canadair CL-600-2D24			on order	

A further 25 are on order for future delivery; all to be operated as 74-seat CRJ-705s

CF-TCC	Lockheed L-10A	1116		Trans Canada Airlines colours	

Air Canada Connector feeder services, using AC flight numbers, are op in conjunction with Air Canada Jazz (a wholly owned subsidiary). Founder member of Star Alliance with Lufthansa, United, SAS, Thai Intl and VARIG. Tango by Air Canada is low cost division using Airbus Industrie A320s while Zip Air is low cost operation based in Calgary and four aircraft are operated as AC Jetz for sports charters. Filed for bankruptcy protection in Canada & USA in March 2003; operations continue. Forty-five Embraer 190s are on order for delivery from 4Q05

AIR CANADA JAZZ

TransCan (QK/ARN)   Halifax, NB/Calgary, Alta/London, Ont/Vancouver, BC (YHZ/YYC/YXU/YVR)

Reg	Type	Ser	ex	Notes	Lease
C-FBAB	British Aerospace 146 Srs.200	E2090	ex G-5-090	202	
C-FBAE	British Aerospace 146 Srs.200	E2092	ex G-5-092	207	
C-FBAF	British Aerospace 146 Srs.200	E2096	ex G-5-096	208	
C-FBAO	British Aerospace 146 Srs.200	E2111	ex G-11-111	209; green	
C-FBAV	British Aerospace 146 Srs.200	E2121	ex G-11-121	210	
C-GRNT	British Aerospace 146 Srs.200	E2140	ex G-11-140	206	
C-GRNU	British Aerospace 146 Srs.200	E2139	ex G-5-139	205; green	
C-GRNV	British Aerospace 146 Srs.200	E2133	ex G-5-133	204; red	
C-GRNX	British Aerospace 146 Srs.200	E2130	ex G-5-130	203; yellow	
C-GRNZ	British Aerospace 146 Srs.200	E2106	ex G-5-106	201; red	
C-GKEJ	Canadair CL600-2B19	7269	ex N577ML	180; red	Lsd fr GECAS
C-GKEK	Canadair CL600-2B19	7270	ex N578ML	181; green	Lsd fr GECAS
C-GKEM	Canadair CL600-2B19	7277	ex N579ML	182; yellow	Lsd fr GECAS
C-GKEP	Canadair CL600-2B19	7303	ex N581ML	183; orange	Lsd fr AFS Investments
C-GKER	Canadair CL600-2B19	7368	ex N588ML	184; red	Lsd fr AFS Investments
C-GKEU	Canadair CL600-2B19	7376	ex N589ML	185; green	Lsd fr AFS Investments
C-GKEW	Canadair CL600-2B19	7385	ex N590ML	186 yellow	
C-GKEZ	Canadair CL600-2B19	7327	ex N583ML	187 orange	Lsd fr GECAS
C-GKFR	Canadair CL600-2B19	7330	ex N584ML	188; red	Lsd fr GECAS
C-GKGC	Canadair CL600-2B19	7334	ex N585ML	189; green	Lsd fr GECAS
C-FABA	de Havilland DHC-8-102	092		805; orange	
C-FABG	de Havilland DHC-8-102	147		899	
C-FABN	de Havilland DHC-8-102	044		803	
C-FABT	de Havilland DHC-8-102	049		848; green	Lsd fr Wing-Co Lsg
C-FABW	de Havilland DHC-8-102	097		806	
C-FACD	de Havilland DHC-8-102	150		808	
C-FACF	de Havilland DHC-8-311A	259		308; yellow	
C-FACT	de Havilland DHC-8-311A	262		309; green	
C-FACV	de Havilland DHC-8-311A	278		311	
C-FADF	de Havilland DHC-8-311A	272	ex C-FACU	310	
C-FADJ	de Havilland DHC-8-102A	322		811	
C-FADK	de Havilland DHC-8-102A	324		812	
C-FCON	de Havilland DHC-8-102	179		817	
C-FCTA	de Havilland DHC-8-102	039		823	
C-FDND	de Havilland DHC-8-102	129		850	
C-FGQI	de Havilland DHC-8-102	185		849	
C-FGQK	de Havilland DHC-8-102	193		819	
C-FGRC	de Havilland DHC-8-102	195		821	
C-FGRM	de Havilland DHC-8-102	199		820	
C-FGRP	de Havilland DHC-8-102	207		822	
C-FGRY	de Havilland DHC-8-102	212		844; red	
C-FJFM	de Havilland DHC-8-311A	240		324	
C-FJMG	de Havilland DHC-8-102A	255	ex C-FJMG	824	
C-FJVV	de Havilland DHC-8-311A	271		306	
C-FJXZ	de Havilland DHC-8-311A	264	ex C-FTAQ	326	Lsd fr Avline Lsg
C-FMDW	de Havilland DHC-8-311A	269		305	
C-FPON	de Havilland DHC-8-102	171		836	
C-FTAK	de Havilland DHC-8-311A	246		323	
C-FTON	de Havilland DHC-8-102	178		838	
C-FVON	de Havilland DHC-8-102	181		837	
C-FXON	de Havilland DHC-8-102	183		845	
C-GABF	de Havilland DHC-8-102	025		816	
C-GABH	de Havilland DHC-8-102	211		810	
C-GABI	de Havilland DHC-8-102	205		809	
C-GABO	de Havilland DHC-8-311A	248		312; orange	
C-GABP	de Havilland DHC-8-311A	257		307	
C-GANF	de Havilland DHC-8-102	042		802	
C-GANI	de Havilland DHC-8-102	064		830	
C-GANK	de Havilland DHC-8-102	087		831	
C-GANQ	de Havilland DHC-8-102	096		833; yellow	
C-GANS	de Havilland DHC-8-102	057		828	
C-GCTC	de Havilland DHC-8-102	065	ex V2-LEE	846; orange	
C-GETA	de Havilland DHC-8-301	186		321	
C-GEWQ	de Havilland DHC-8-311A	202		325	
C-GHTA	de Havilland DHC-8-301	198		316	
C-GION	de Havilland DHC-8-102	127		832	
C-GJIG	de Havilland DHC-8-102	068		826	
C-GJMI	de Havilland DHC-8-102	077		825	
C-GJMK	de Havilland DHC-8-102	081		804	
C-GJMO	de Havilland DHC-8-102	079		834	
C-GJSV	de Havilland DHC-8-102	085		814	Lsd fr Wing-Or
C-GJSX	de Havilland DHC-8-102	088		835; red	
C-GKON	de Havilland DHC-8-102	130		815	
C-GKTA	de Havilland DHC-8-301	124		317	
C-GLON	de Havilland DHC-8-102	133		847	
C-GLTA	de Havilland DHC-8-301	154		318	

C-GMON	de Havilland DHC-8-301	131		301	
C-GMTA+	de Havilland DHC-8-301	174		319	
C-GNON	de Havilland DHC-8-301	137		302	
C-GOND	de Havilland DHC-8-102	090		840	
C-GONH	de Havilland DHC-8-102	093		813	Lsd fr Wing-Co
C-GONJ	de Havilland DHC-8-102	095	ex V2-LDZ	839	
C-GONN	de Havilland DHC-8-102	101		898	
C-GONO	de Havilland DHC-8-102	102		807	
C-GONR	de Havilland DHC-8-102	109		841	
C-GONW	de Havilland DHC-8-102	112		843	
C-GONX	de Havilland DHC-8-102	118		829	
C-GONY	de Havilland DHC-8-102	115		827	
C-GSTA+	de Havilland DHC-8-301	182		320	
C-GTAE	de Havilland DHC-8-102	073		852	
C-GTAF	de Havilland DHC-8-103	083		854	
C-GTAG	de Havilland DHC-8-301	200		315	
C-GTAI	de Havilland DHC-8-102	078		853	
C-GTAQ	de Havilland DHC-8-301	180	ex C-FGVK	313	
C-GTAT	de Havilland DHC-8-301	188	ex C-FGVT	314; red	
C-GTBP	de Havilland DHC-8-102	066		855	
C-GUON	de Havilland DHC-8-301	143		303	
C-GVON	de Havilland DHC-8-301	149		304	
C-GVTA	de Havilland DHC-8-301	190		322	
C-GWRR	de Havilland DHC-8-102	070		851	

+Leased from Cypress Leasing ^Leased from CIT Financial
A wholly owned subsidiary of Air Canada. Operates Connector feeder services using flight numbers in the range 1200-1999 and 8800-8899. Code-share services also provided by Air Alliance and Central Mountain Air.

AIR CARIBOU

Goose Bay, Nfld (YYR)

C-FXGA	de Havilland DHC-3 Otter	35	ex N511BW	Regd to Nordplus

Current status is uncertain

AIR CREEBEC

Cree (YN/CRQ) (IATA 219) *Val d'Or, Que (YVO)*

C-FCSK	de Havilland DHC-8-102	122	
C-FPCM	Embraer EMB.110P1 Bandeirante	110340	ex LN-TDI
C-FPCU	Embraer EMB.110P1 Bandeirante	110445	ex LN-TDA
C-FTOW	Beech 1900D	UE-130	
C-FTQR	Beech 1900D	UE-129	
C-FYRH	Embraer EMB.110P1 Bandeirante	110259	ex N91PB
C-GIZX	Beech A100 King Air	B-172	ex N753DB
C-GJOP	de Havilland DHC-8-102	121	ex N381BC
C-GQWO	Hawker Siddeley HS.748 Srs.2A/221	1597	ex T-03
C-GZEW	de Havilland DHC-8-103	393	ex N801SA Lsd fr Bombardier Capital

AIR-DALE FLYING SERVICE

Sault Ste Marie, Ont/Wawa Hawk Junction, Ont (YAM/YXZ)

C-FGYT	de Havilland DHC-2 Beaver	182	
CF-ODE	de Havilland DHC-2 Beaver	131	
C-GELP	de Havilland DHC-2 Beaver	780	ex N5318G
C-GQXI	de Havilland DHC-2 Beaver	427	ex N1059

All floatplanes and operate summer services only.
Freight services are operated as Great Northern Freight (q.v.).

AIR INUIT

Air Inuit (3H/AIE) *Kuujjuaq, Que (YVP)*

C-FJFR	de Havilland DHC-6 Twin Otter 300	784	ex HK-2762
C-FTJJ	de Havilland DHC-6 Twin Otter 300	325	ex 8Q-MAJ
C-GKCJ	de Havilland DHC-6 Twin Otter 300	698	ex A6-AMM
C-GMDC	de Havilland DHC-6 Twin Otter 300	763	
C-GNDO	de Havilland DHC-6 Twin Otter 300	430	
C-GTYX	de Havilland DHC-6 Twin Otter 300	631	

All freighters

C-FAIP	Beech A100 King Air	B-193	ex F-GXAB
C-FCJD	de Havilland DHC-8-102	158	
C-FDAO	de Havilland DHC-8-102	123	
C-FDOX	Hawker Siddeley.HS.748 Srs.2A /310LFD	1749	ex TJ-CCD
C-FGET	Hawker Siddeley.HS.748 Srs.2A/244	1724	ex D-AFSG
C-GCUK	Hawker Siddeley.HS.748 Srs.2A /343LFD	1762	ex V2-LAZ
C-GEGJ	Hawker Siddeley.HS.748 Srs.2A/244	1711	ex TF-GMB

C-GHQP	de Havilland DHC-8Q-402	4003	ex C-FPJH	Op for Hydro-Quebec (APZ)
C-GHQQ	de Havilland DHC-8Q-402	4004	ex C-GIHK	Op for Hydro-Quebec (APZ)
C-GHQZ	de Havilland DHC-8-314	370	ex OE-LLY	Op for Hydro-Quebec (APZ)
C-GJNL	de Havilland DHC-8-311	422	ex G-BXPZ	Op for Hydro-Quebec (APZ)

Shares common ownership with Bradley Air Services and scheduled services are operated as First Air

AIR IVANHOE

Foleyet, Ont

C-GERE	de Havilland DHC-2 Beaver	352	ex N62784
C-GPUS	de Havilland DHC-2 Beaver	624	ex 53-2824

AIR KIPAWA

Kipawa, Ont

C-FDNK	de Havilland DHC-3 Otter	385	ex N80945
C-FWXJ	Cessna A185E Skywagon	185-1331	ex (N3379L)
C-GMOI	de Havilland DHC-2 Beaver	1236	ex N6083

All floatplanes

AIR LABRADOR

Lab Air (WJ/LAL)   *Goose Bay, Nfld (YYR)*

C-FGON	de Havilland DHC-6 Twin Otter 300	369		Floats or wheels/skis
C-FPEX	Cessna 208B Caravan I	208B0118	ex (N986FE)	Lsd to Provincial Express
C-FQOS	de Havilland DHC-3T Turbo Otter	398	ex CAF 9418	Floats or wheels/skis
C-FSVP	de Havilland DHC-3T Turbo Otter	28		Floats or wheels/skis
C-GAAR	Beech 1900D	UE-207	ex N10625	Lsd fr GGN
C-GAAV	Beech 1900D	UE-235	ex N10708	
C-GDQY	de Havilland DHC-6 Twin Otter 100	77	ex YA-GAS	Floats or wheels/skis
C-GLAI	de Havilland DHC-6 Twin Otter 300	296	ex N5377G	Floats or wheels/skis
C-GLAL	Beech 1900C-1	UC-168	ex N168GL	
C-GLHO	Beech 1900D	UE-266	ex N10950	Capt Harold Oake
C-GNQY	de Havilland DHC-6 Twin Otter 300	450		Floats or wheels/skis
C-GTMB	Beech 1900D	UE-345	ex N23388	
C-	Beech 1900C-1	UC-149	ex N149YV	

Air Labrador is the trading name of Labrador Airways

AIR LAURENTIAN ceased operations

AIR MELANCON

St Anne-du-Lac, Que

C-FBPB	de Havilland DHC-2 Beaver	1434	ex VH-IDF
C-FQQD	de Havilland DHC-2 Beaver	1580	ex FAP 64-374
C-FZVP	de Havilland DHC-2 Beaver	1033	ex N564
C-GQXH	de Havilland DHC-2 Beaver	536	ex N1579

All operate on floats or wheels/skis

AIR MIKISEW

(V8)   *Fort McMurray, Alta (YMM)*

C-FAAL	Cessna 208 Caravan I	20800320	ex	
C-FAMB	Beec B200 Super King Air	BB-1281	ex N865TC	
C-FKAM	British Aerospace Jetstream 31	724	ex N852JS	Lsd fr Jetcor
C-FKEY	Cessna 208 Caravan I	20800307		
C-FUAM	British Aerospace Jetstream 31	746	ex N404UE	
C-FVGT	Piper PA-31-350 Navajo Chieftain	31-7405133	ex N74981	
C-FXAJ	Beech A100 King Air	B-122	ex N8181Z	Air Ambulance
C-GFJN	Cessna 207A Stationair 7	20700592	ex (N73446)	
C-GURM	Piper PA-31-350 Navajo Chieftain	31-7752184	ex N273RH	
C-GVAM	Cessna U206G Stationair 6	U20606177	ex N918WJ	
C-GVQU	Cessna A185F Skywagon	18503648	ex N8206Q	Floats or wheels/skis
C-GZAM	Beech 99A	U-116	ex N17AL	

AIR MONT-LAURIER

Ste-Veronique, Que

C-FTUR	de Havilland DHC-2 Beaver	1529	
C-GGSC	de Havilland DHC-3 Otter	366	ex N5072F
C-GMGP	Cessna A185F Skywagon	18502077	ex N9054F
C-GUML	de Havilland DHC-2 Beaver	307	ex N1402Z
C-GVLK	Cessna U206G Stationair	U20604329	ex N756SW

All floatplanes

AIR MONTMAGNY

Montmagny, Que

C-GBFU	Britten-Norman BN-2A-27 Islander	535	ex N70JA
C-GCTM	Cessna U206G Stationair	U20603794	ex N8920G
C-GGJG	Britten-Norman BN-2B-26 Islander	2219	ex F-ODUP

Air Montmagny is the trading name of Montmagny Air Services

AIR MUSKOKA

Air Muskoka (AMS)   *Muskoka, Ont (YQA)*

C-FNTJ	Rockwell 700	70023	ex N702SA

AIR NOOTKA

Gold River, BC

C-FIBR	Cessna 180K	18052788	ex N61666	Floatplane
C-FOXD	de Havilland DHC-2 Beaver	807	ex N90723	Floatplane
C-FQEI	de Havilland DHC-3 Otter	397	ex LN-TSC	Floatplane
C-GIUR	Cessna A185F Skywagon	18503290		Floatplane

AIR NORTERRA now listed under trading name, Canadian North

AIR NORTH

Air North (4N/ANT) (IATA 287)   *Whitehorse, YT (YXY)*

C-FAGI	Hawker Siddeley 748 Srs.2A/276	1699	ex G-11-6	
C-FJLB	Boeing 737-201 (Nordam 3)	680/22273	ex N233US	Lsd fr Structures Unlimited
C-FRQI	Beech 99	U-124	ex TF-ELB	
C-FYDU	Hawker Siddeley 748 Srs.2A/273	1694	ex ZK-MCP	stored YXY
C-FYDY	Hawker Siddeley 748 Srs.2A/233	1661	ex ZK-MCJ	
C-GNAU	Boeing 737-201 (Nordam 3)	602/21817	ex N228US	Lsd fr Structures Unlimited

Air North is the trading name of Air North Charter & Training

AIR NUNAVAT

Air Baffin(BFF)   *Iqaluit, Nun (YFB)*

C-FCGW	Beech 200 Super King Air	BB-207	ex N111WH	Conv to CatPass 200
C-FZNQ	Beech 200 Super King Air	BB-264	ex N465CJ	Conv to CatPass 200
C-GYRS	Piper PA-31 Turbo Navajo B	31-7300937	ex N90AB	
C-GZYO	Beech 200 Super King Air	BB-383	ex N384DB	

AIR OPTIMA

Pokemouche, NB

Previously listed as Aero Peninsule

C-FAPL	Piper PA-31Turbo Navajo B	31-7401249	ex N13TL
C-FIML	Cessna 310Q	310Q0758	
C-GABL	Cessna 310R II	310R0927	ex N3840G

Air Optima is the trading name of Aero Peninsule

AIR SAGUENAY

Lac St-Sebastien, Que

C-FIUS	de Havilland DHC-2 Beaver	901	
C-FJAC	de Havilland DHC-2 Beaver	937	
C-FJKI	de Havilland DHC-2 Beaver	992	
C-FKRJ	de Havilland DHC-2 Beaver	1210	
C-GAEF	de Havilland DHC-2 Beaver	372	ex 51-16830
C-GAXL	de Havilland DHC-2 Beaver	1032	ex 56-537
C-GPUO	de Havilland DHC-2 Beaver	810	ex 54-1677
C-GUJI	de Havilland DHC-2 Beaver	1141	ex N68013
C-GUJU	de Havilland DHC-2 Beaver	1639	ex N4600Y
C-FDAK	de Havilland DHC-3 Otter	157	
C-FMPX	de Havilland DHC-3 Otter	280	
C-FODT	de Havilland DHC-3 Otter	218	
C-GLFL	de Havilland DHC-3T Turbo Otter	329	ex 58-1712
C-GLMT	de Havilland DHC-3 Otter	216	ex IM-1716
C-GQDU	de Havilland DHC-3T Turbo Otter	43	ex N94472
C-GUTQ	de Havilland DHC-3 Otter	402	ex HK-3049X
C-FYAO	Cessna A185E Skywagon	18501472	ex (N2722J)

All operate on floats or wheels/skis. Associated with Ashuanipi Aviation and Labrador Air Safaris

AIR SAINT-MAURICE ceased operations

AIR SATELLITE

Satellite (ASJ)   *Baie Comeau, Que (YBC)*

C-FDOS	Beech A100 King Air	B-106		
C-FFJL	Cessna 310R II	310R1616	ex N2631A	
C-GBOE	Cessna 335	335-0020	ex N27066	
C-GGTF	Cessna 310R II	310R0550	ex N87409	
C-GIAS	Cessna 402B	402B0545	ex N678CM	
C-GOXZ	Britten-Norman BN-2A Mk.III Trislander	361	ex G-BBWP	stored
C-GURS	Cessna 402	402-0214	ex N26309	
C-GZAS	Cessna 402B	402B0626	ex N2083K	

AIR SOUTHWEST

Airsouthwest (ASW)   *Chilliwack, BC (YCW)*

C-FQMO	Cessna U206F Stationair	U20603456	ex N8606Q
C-GYTJ	Cessna U206G Stationair	U20603703	ex (N7599N)

AIR-SPRAY

Air Spray (ASB)   *Edmonton-Municipal/Red Deer, Alta (YEG/YQF)*

CF-AGO	Douglas A-26C Invader	28735	ex N330WC	36; Dragon Lady
CF-CBK	Douglas B-26C Invader	28940	ex N9996Z	11
CF-CUI	Douglas B-26C Invader	28803	ex N9401Z	12
C-FKBM	Douglas A-26B Invader	27415	ex N8017E	20
C-FOVC	Douglas RB-26C Invader	28776	ex N3426G	56
C-FPGF	Douglas A-26B Invader	29154	ex 44-35875	1
C-FPGP	Douglas B-26C Invader	29177	ex N332BG	2
C-FTFB	Douglas RB-26C Invader	28723	ex N7656C	4
CF-ZTC	Douglas B-26C Invader	29136	ex N9300R	13; Lucky Jack
C-GHLX	Douglas A-26C Invader	29227	ex N161H	32
C-GHZM	Douglas A-26B Invader	27400	ex N4805E	5; Fire Eater
C-GPTW	Douglas A-26B Invader	18800	ex N9402Z	26
C-GTOX	Douglas A-26B Invader	27802	ex N9174Z	14
C-GWLT	Douglas A-26B Invader	28057	ex N67943	98
C-GXGY	Douglas A-26C Invader	28987	ex N5530V	10
C-FVFH	Lockheed L-188A Electra	1006	ex PK-RLF	89
C-FVFI	Lockheed L-188C Electra	1082	ex PK-RLD	stored YQF
C-FZCS	Lockheed L-188AF Electra	1060	ex HR-SHN	87
C-GFQA	Lockheed L-188A Electra	1040	ex C-GBKT	
C-GHZI	Lockheed L-188C Electra	2007	ex N1968R	stored YQF
C-GYVI	Lockheed L-188CF Electra	1112	ex N360Q	
C-GZCF	Lockheed L-188CF Electra	1091	ex G-CEXS	
C-GZVM	Lockheed L-188A Electra	1036	ex N351Q	
C-GZYH	Lockheed L-188A Electra	1124	ex HR-AMM	stored YQF
C-FEHK	Ted Smith Aerostar 600A	60-0400-140	ex N17LH	307
C-FGWE	Cessna 310Q II	310Q0920	ex (N69686)	302
C-FJCF	Ted Smith Aerostar 600A	60-0153-067	ex N37HA	308
C-FTUE	Ted Smith Aerostar 601	61-0145-076	ex N601RD	311
C-FTUU	Canadair CL-215-1A10	1011	ex CF-PQH	208
C-FTUW	Canadair CL-215-1A10	1030		209
C-FZRQ	Rockwell Commander 690	11025	ex N100LS	51
C-GFPP	Rockwell Commander 690	11032	ex N349AC	52
C-GJFO	Rockwell Commander 690	11035	ex N15VZ	53
C-GKDZ	Rockwell Commander 690	11016	ex N428SJ	
C-GNSA	Cessna 500 Citation I	500-0160	ex N59TS	50
C-GOFR	Canadair CL-215-1A10	1104		268
C-GXJP	Cessna 310P	310P0073	ex N101QC	305
C-GXXN	Cessna T310P	310P0002	ex N5702M	306
C-GZON	Rockwell Commander 690	11020		

AIR TINDI

(8T)   *Yellowknife, NWT (YZF)*

C-FATM*	de Havilland DHC-6 Twin Otter 300	265	ex PJ-ATL	
C-FATO*	de Havilland DHC-6 Twin Otter 310	674	ex A6-MRM	
C-FGOG*	de Havilland DHC-6 Twin Otter 300	348		
C-GMAS*	de Havilland DHC-6 Twin Otter 300	438	ex N546N	
C-GNPS*	de Havilland DHC-6 Twin Otter 300	558		
C-FATA	Beech 200 Super King Air	BB-283	ex N283JP	
C-FATS	Beech 99	U-75	ex C-FEJL	
C-FATW	Beech 65-C90 King Air	LJ-685	ex N110SE	EMS

C-FCGU	Beech 200B Super King Air	BB-301	ex N611SW	CatPass 200 conv
C-FKAY	Cessna 208B Caravan I	208B0470	ex N1294N	
C-FXUY*	de Havilland DHC-3 Turbo Otter	142	ex N214L	
C-GATV	Cessna 208B Caravan I	208B0308		
C-GATY*	Cessna 208 Caravan I	20800305	ex N52627	
C-GDPB	Beech 200C Super King Air	BL-44	ex N18379	EMS
C-GPHO*	Cessna A185F Skywagon	18503099	ex (N80151)	
C-GTUC	Beech 200 Super King Air	BB-268	ex N565RA	
C-GWXI*	Cessna A185F Skywagon	18502818	ex (N1298F)	
C-GZIX*	Cessna A185F Skywagon	18504182	ex N46CR	

*Operates on floats or wheels/skis

AIR TRANSAT

Transat (TS/TSC) (IATA 649)   Montreal-Mirabel (YMX)

C-FDAT	Airbus Industrie A310-308	658	ex A6-EKK		
C-GFAT	Airbus Industrie A310-308	545	ex A6-EKG		
C-GLAT	Airbus Industrie A310-308	588	ex A6-EKI		
C-GPAT	Airbus Industrie A310-308	597	ex A6-EKJ		
C-GSAT	Airbus Industrie A310-308	600	ex 5Y-KQM		
C-GVAT	Airbus Industrie A310-304	485	ex D-AIDC		Lsd fr GOAL
C-	Airbus Industrie A310-304	595	ex D-AIDM	on order	Lsd fr GOAL
C-FTNG	Lockheed L-1011-150 Tristar	1048		507; stored YMX	
C-FTNL	Lockheed L-1011-100 Tristar	1073	ex 4R-TNL	512; stored	
C-FTSW	Lockheed L-1011-500 Tristar	1246	ex V2-LEJ	246	
C-GATH	Lockheed L-1011-500 Tristar	1235	ex 4R-ULA	235	
C-GATM	Lockheed L-1011-500 Tristar	1236	ex 4R-ULB	236	
C-GTSR	Lockheed L-1011-500 Tristar	1239	ex CS-TEA	239	
C-GTSZ	Lockheed L-1011-100 Tristar	1103	ex N703TT	548; stored YMX Lsd fr Fivestar Avn	

All to be retired by 30 April 2004

C-GGTS	Airbus Industrie A330-243	250	ex F-WWKK		Lsd fr ILFC
C-GITS	Airbus Industrie A330-243	271	ex F-WWKY		Lsd fr ILFC
C-GKTS	Airbus Industrie A330-342	111	ex B-HYC		Lsd fr ILFC
C-GPTS	Airbus Industrie A330-243	480	ex F-WWKV		Lsd fr ILFC; sublsd to SEU
C-GTSV	Boeing 757-28A	530/25622	ex S7-AAX	622	Lsd fr ILFC; sublsd to HLN
F-GRSG	Airbus Industrie A320-214	0737	ex F-WWBS		Lsd fr SEU for winter
F-GRSH	Airbus Industrie A320-214	0749	ex F-WWIK		Lsd fr SEU for winter

Transat Group owns Star Europe

AIR WEMINDJI current status uncertain, both aircraft disposed of

---

AIR WEST

Air West (AWT)   Winnipeg, Man (YWG)

C-FTNZ	Cessna 402C II	402C0021	ex N2643W

AIRBORNE ENERGY SOLUTIONS

Whitecourt, Alta (YZU)

C-FAEF	Aerospatiale AS.350B AStar	2152	ex N700YH
C-FPKM	Aerospatiale AS.350B AStar	2426	ex JA6045
C-FWKM	Aerospatiale AS.350BA AStar	2427	ex JA6044
C-GHKM	Aerospatiale AS.350B3 AStar	3155	ex ZK-HYE
C-GREV	Aerospatiale AS.350BA AStar	1039	ex N98TV
C-GTKM	Aerospatiale AS.350BA AStar	2515	ex JA6095
C-FARJ	Bell 206B JetRanger	741	ex N700BH
C-FBKH	Bell 206B JetRanger	575	ex N100FW
C-FHTT	Bell 206B JetRanger	1042	
C-FMAD	Bell 206B JetRanger	408	ex N725BB
C-GABE	Bell 206B JetRanger II	2070	
C-GAHP	Bell 206B JetRanger	805	ex N2959W
C-GJEL	Bell 206B JetRanger	116	ex N855NR
C-GOLT	Bell 206B JetRanger III	3553	
C-GQRQ	Bell 206B JetRanger	582	ex N98SF
C-GTEZ	Bell 206B JetRanger	746	ex N2926W
C-GTQU	Bell 206B JetRanger	766	ex N8199J
C-GXAG	Bell 206B JetRanger	150	ex N6283N
C-GXBY	Bell 206B JetRanger	477	ex N72HP
C-FARA	Cessna U206C Super Skywagon	U206-1009	ex N29011
C-FARQ	Cessna 208B Caravan I	208B0765	ex N5174W
C-FVGV	Cessna U206G Stationair 6	U20604500	ex N1029M
C-GEAH	Bell 205A-1	30096	ex LX-HAH
C-GJKN	Bell 205A-1	30091	ex CS-HEA
C-GQLG	Bell 205A-1	30008	ex A7-HAF

AIRCO AIRCRAFT CHARTERS

Edmonton-Municipal, Alta (YEG)

C-FSFI	Cessna 441 Conquest II	441-0316	ex N800SR
C-FWPG	Beech 100 King Air	B-67	ex N26KW
C-FWYN	Beech 100 King Air	B-47	ex C-GNAX
C-FWYO	Beech 100 King Air	B-28	ex N27JJ
C-GBMI	Piper PA-31-350 Chieftain	31-8352007	ex N23NP
C-GZNB	Piper PA-31-350 Navajo Chieftain	31-7752079	ex N6654B

AIREXPRESS ONTARIO

Oshawa, Ont (YOO)

C-GBBS	Beech 200 Super King Air	BB-757	ex N948MB
C-GRWN	Piper PA-31-350 Chieftain	31-8152044	ex N4076J

AIRSPEED AVIATION

Speedline (SPD)   *Abbotsford, BC (YXX)*

C-GYFG	Cessna 402B II	402B1015	ex N87166
C-GZOI	Cessna 414 II	414-0844	ex N3814C

AIRWAVE TRANSPORT ceased operations

AKLAK AIR

Aklak (6L/AKK)   *Inuvik, NWT (YEV)*

C-GGKG	Douglas DC-3 (C-117D)	43354	ex N2071X	Lsd fr KBA

Also operates scheduled services with Beech 99 and de Havilland DHC-6 aircraft leased from Kenn Borek Air (KBA)

ALBERTA CENTRAL AIRWAYS

Lac la Biche, Alta (YLB)

C-FNED	Beech 65-C90 King Air	LJ-680	ex N928RD	
C-FRDI	Piper PA-31 Turbo Navajo B	31-7401295		
C-FWPN	Beech 100 King Air	B-51	ex N16SW	
C-GACA	Beech 200 Super King Air	BB-1309	ex N4277C	Beech 1300 conv
C-GACN	Beech 200 Super King Air	BB-1384	ex N575T	Beech 1300 conv
C-GEUA	Piper PA-31 Turbo Navajo	31-187	N64JK	
C-GGBZ	Cessna U206G Stationair 6	U20605637	ex (N5318X)	
C-GUWO	Piper PA-31 Turbo Navajo	31-203	ex N9154Y	
C-GWFF	Piper PA-31 TurboNavajo C	31-7512063	ex N61390	
C-GYUW	Cessna U206G Stationair	U20603738	ex (N995GN)	

ALBERTA CITYLINK

Alberta Citylink (ABK)   *Calgary-Intl/Medicine Hat, Alta (YYC/YXH)*

C-FZVY	British Aerospace Jetstream 32	833	ex N833JX		
C-GEAZ	British Aerospace Jetstream 32	843	ex C-GQRO	034	Lsd fr BAES; sublsd to Peace Air

Associated with Bar XH Air; Alberta Citylink is the trading name of Palliser Air

ALBERTA GOVERNMENT AIR TRANSPORTATION SERVICES

Alberta (GOA)   *Edmonton—Municipal, Alta (YXD)*

C-GFSA	Beech B300 Super King Air	FL-174			
C-GFSG	Beech 200 Super King Air	BB-671			
C-GFSH	Beech B200 Super King Air	BB-912			
C-GFSJ	de Havilland DHC-8-103	017			
C-GFSK	Canadair CL-215-1A10	1085	ex C-GKDN	201	Op by CRC
C-GFSL	Canadair CL-215-1A10	1086	ex C-GKDP	202	Op by CRC
C-GFSM	Canadair CL-215-1A10	1098		203	Op by CRC
C-GFSN	Canadair CL-215-1A10	1099		204	Op by CRC

ALKAN AIR

Alkan Air (AKN)   *Whitehorse, YT (YXY)*

C-FAKN	Beech 200 Super King Air	BB-216	ex LN-VIU
C-GHQF	Piper PA-31-350 Chieftain	31-8052050	ex N633WA
C-GMOC	Beech 200 Super King Air	BB-513	ex N513SA
C-GSDT	Piper PA-31-350 Chieftain	31-8152102	ex N120FL
C-GYTB	Cessna U206G Stationair	U20603685	ex (N7579N)

ALL POINTS AIRWAYS

C-FEGE	de Havilland DHC-2 Beaver	1539

ALLCANADA EXPRESS

Canex (CNX)   *Toronto-Pearson Intl, Ont (YYZ)*

C-FACA	Boeing 727-243F (Raisbeck 3)	1568/22052	ex N179PC	
C-FACN	Boeing 727-221F (FedEx 3)	1796/22540	ex N368PA	
C-FACR	Boeing 727217F (Raisbeck 3)	1117/21055	ex C-GRYC	Lsd fr Finova
C-FACX	Boeing 727-27F (Raisbeck 3)	448/19500	ex N727EV	
C-GACC	Boeing 727-277F (Raisbeck 3)	1030/20550	ex C-GRYZ	

ALLEN AIRWAYS

Sioux Lookout, Ont (YXL)

C-GEXS	Cessna A185F Skywagon	18502955	ex (N4437R)
C-GQDO	Cessna A185F Skywagon	18503745	ex (N8585Q)
C-GVHS	de Havilland DHC-2 Beaver	733	ex 53-7922
C-GYEB	Cessna A185F Skywagon	18503017	ex N5186R

All operate on floats or wheels/skis

ALPEN HELICOPTERS

Langley, BC

C-GAHL	Bell 206B JetRanger III	2600	ex N8264U
C-GLMX	Bell 206L-1 LongRanger II	45439	ex N99ZT
C-GRBO	Cessna A185F Skywagon	18503414	ex N903TH
C-GVII	Bell 206L-1 LongRanger II	45158	ex N5004B

ALPINE HELICOPTERS

Kelowna, BC (YLW)

C-FALQ	Bell 206B JetRanger III	1649	ex N181HJ	
C-FALU	Bell 206B JetRanger III	1072		
C-FTED	Bell 206B JetRanger III	3556		
C-GALR	Bell 206B JetRanger III	1892	ex N100YB	
C-GALX	Bell 206B JetRanger III	1046	ex N58096	
C-GALZ	Bell 206B JetRanger III	1563	ex N59640	
C-GJSL	Bell 206B JetRanger III	3557		
C-FAHB	Bell 212	30794	ex A6-BBH	
C-FAHC	Bell 212	31246	ex N212HT	Lsd to Kachina Avn as N214KA
C-FAHG	Bell 212	30940	ex N8530F	
C-FAHI	Bell 212	30776	ex A6-BBB	Lsd to Kachina Avn as N212KA
C-FAHK	Bell 212	30852	ex XA-SSE	
C-FAHL	Bell 212	30588	ex XA-SSJ	
C-FAHP	Bell 212	30933	ex D-HELL	
C-FAHR	Bell 212	30789	ex A6-BBI	
C-FAHZ	Bell 212	30562	ex XA-SSI	
(C-FAHZ)	Bell 212	30651	ex A6-BBN	Lsd to Kachina Avn as N215KA
C-FALK	Bell 212	30982	ex N212EL	
C-FALV	Bell 212	30816	ex N74AL	
C-FNOB	Bell 212	31172	ex N57416	Lsd to Kachina Avn as N213KA
C-GAHO	Bell 212	30937		
C-GAHV	Bell 212	30699	ex N90221	
C-GALI	Bell 212	30525	ex JA9510	
C-GIRZ	Bell 212	30622	ex RP-C1677	
C-GRNR	Bell 212	30999		
C-FAHL	Bell 407	53016	ex N141MA	Lsd to Kachina Avn as N409KA
C-FALA	Bell 407	53115		
C-FALF	Bell 407	53271	ex CC-CWS	
C-FALM	Bell 407	53018	ex N409KA	
C-FNOB	Bell 407	53070		
C-GALG	Bell 407	53059	ex N409PH	
C-GYAA	Bell 407	53152		
C-FALC	Bell 206L-1 LongRanger	45500	ex N104HC	
C-GALH	Bell 206L-3 LongRanger III	51297	ex N753HL	
C-GALJ	Bell 206L-3 LongRanger III	51010	ex N22654	
C-GALL	Bell 206L-3 LongRanger III	51015	ex N22660	
C-GRLK	Bell 206L-3 LongRanger III	51028	ex N42814	

ALTA FLIGHTS

(ALZ)   Edmonton-Intl/Calgary-Intl/Fort McMurray, Alta (YEG/YYC/YMM)

C-FAFE	Beech B100 King Air	BE-72	ex ZS-MZS	
C-FAFS	Beech B100 King Air	BE-31	ex N80DB	
C-FAFZ	Beech B100 King Air	BE-121	ex VT-AVB	
C-GBVX	Beech B100 King Air	BE-99	ex N524BA	
C-GWWQ	Beech 100 King Air	B-76	ex N300DA	
C-FAFM	Swearingen SA.227AC Metro III	AC-674B	ex N359AE	Freighter
C-FAFR	Swearingen SA.227AC Metro III	AC-684	ex N585MA	
C-FAFZ	Swearingen SA.227AC Metro III	AC-676	ex N361AE	Lsd as HK-
C-GAAF	Swearingen SA.227DC Metro 23	DC-891B	ex B-3956	Lsd to Quikair
C-GAFQ	Swearingen SA.227DC Metro 23	DC-890B	ex N30135	
C-GIAF	Swearingen SA.227DC Metro 23	DC-888B	ex ZK-JSJ	
C-GKAF	Swearingen SA.227DC Metro 23	DC-864B	ex B-3950	Lsd to Quikair
C-GSAF	Swearingen SA.227DC Metro 23	DC-866B	ex B-3951	Lsd to Quikair
C-FAFB	Cessna 402C II	402C0266	ex N150PB	
C-FAFC	Cessna 208B Caravan I	208B0663	ex N1229A	
C-FAFF	Cessna 402C II	402C0074	ex N2611Z	
C-FAFJ	Cessna 208B Caravan I	208B0641	ex N52655	
C-FAFT	Beech 200 Super King Air	BB-57	ex N121DA	conv to CatPass 200
C-FAFV	Cessna 208B Caravan I	208B0528	ex N9510W	
C-FCCP	British Aerospace Jetstream 3101	698	ex	Lsd fr Flight-Ops Intl
C-FPSH	Dornier 228-202	8071	ex N253MC	
C-FTEC	Cessna 414A Chancellor II	414A0298	ex N6260C	
C-FWWF	Cessna 402C II	402C0280	ex N189B	
C-FYEV	Dornier 228-202	8133	ex N261MC	
C-GCCZ	British Aerospace Jetstream 3101	712	ex N335PX	stored YXD
C-GCIL	Cessna 441 Conquest	441-0314	ex XB-CSB	
C-GFMX	Cessna 421B Golden Eagle	421B0939	ex N421HA	
C-GSDG	Cessna 208B Caravan I	208B0376	ex N1118P	Lsd to Conair
C-GVZE	Cessna 414A Chancellor III	414A0219	ex N414WB	

ARCTIC SUNWEST

Yellowknife, NWT (YZF)

C-FASC	de Havilland DHC-8-102	038	ex C-GJUZ	
C-	de Havilland DHC-8-102	013	ex N802MX	
C-FASN	Beech B100 King Air	BE-17	ex N178NC	
C-FOEV	de Havilland DHC-2 Turbo Beaver III	1680/TB48		Amphibian
C-FOPE	de Havilland DHC-2 Turbo Beaver III	1691/TB59		Amphibian
C-FQCN	Beech 99	U-126	ex N4302J	
C-FSWN	Piper PA-31-350 Navajo Chieftain	31-7952182	ex C-GREP	
C-FTFX	de Havilland DHC-6 Twin Otter 300	340		
C-FTXQ	de Havilland DHC-6 Twin Otter 300	308	ex N776A	Lsd fr FAB
C-GARW	de Havilland DHC-6 Twin Otter 300	367	ex N200DA	
C-GASW	Beech 99	U-39	ex N99LP	Lsd fr Robinson's Trucking
C-GOZG	Piper PA-32-300 Cherokee Six	32-7540034		
C-GRTA	Eurocopter EC120B Colibri	1076		
C-GSDJ	Cessna A185F Skywagon	18504212	ex N31079	Floats or wheels/skis

ARCTIC WINGS

Artic Wings (AWR)   Inuvik, NWT (YEV)

C-GAQN	Cessna U206F Stationair	U20602687	
C-FAWB	Piper PA-31-350 Chieftain	31-8052029	ex N161SA
C-FAWL	Cessna 207 Stationair	20700103	ex N91179
C-FPIO	Piper PA-31-350 T1020	31-8353007	ex N4112U

ASHUANIPI AVIATION

Wabush, Nfld (YWK)

C-FOCU	de Havilland DHC-2 Beaver	73	
C-FUWJ	de Havilland DHC-2 Beaver	453	ex N7691
C-GLCO	de Havilland DHC-3 Otter	420	ex N17681

All floatplanes; associated with Air Saguenay and Labrador Air Safari

ATIKOKAN AERO SERVICES

Atikokan-Municipal, Ont (YIB)

CF-IPL	de Havilland DHC-2 Beaver	192	
C-GDZH	de Havilland DHC-2 Beaver	356	ex 51-16555

Both operate on floats or wheels/skis

AVIABEC

C-FMPT	de Havilland DHC-2 Beaver	1260
C-GSJO	Cessna U206G Stationair 6	U20606827

All floatplanes

AVIATION BOREAL

C-GDDX	Piper PA-31 Turbo Navajo B	31-770	ex N7245L

AVIATION COMMERCIAL AVIATION

Access (CMS)

C-FGSX	Piper PA-31T2 Cheyenne II XL	31T-8166048	ex N600XL
C-GBFO	Piper PA-31T2 Cheyenne II XL	31T-8166069	ex N511SC
C-GIKA	Piper PA-31-350 Chieftain	31-7952161	ex LN-TEL
C-GPAK	Piper PA-31-350 Chieftain	31-8052070	ex N3558S

AVIATION MAURICIE

C-FASO	Cessna U206F Stationair	U20602081	ex N70558	
C-FIDG	de Havilland DHC-2 Beaver	718	ex N99872	
C-FVDG	Cessna U206B Super Skywagon	U206-0666		R/STOL conversion
C-GOER	de Havilland DHC-2 Beaver	514	ex N99830	

All operate on floats or wheel/skis

AVIATION QUEBEC LABRADOR ceased operations in March 2003

AVIATION STARLINK

Avionair (ANU)

Formerly listed as Avionair, renamed 23 June 2003

C-FDFM	Cessna 421A	421A0053	ex N240PC
C-FDTC	Beech 350 Super King Air	FL-234	ex N3234K
C-GBXX	Swearingen SA.226TC Metro II	TC-293	ex N161SW
C-GQJG	Beech 200 Super King Air	BB-249	

AVIONAIR renamed Aviation Starlink on 23 June 2003

AVNORTH AVIATION

C-FGCU	de Havilland DHC-2 Beaver	503

BAILEY HELICOPTERS

C-FBYD	Bell 206B JetRanger III	2519	ex N5008L
C-FCQD	Bell 206B JetRanger III	534	ex N8146J
C-FPRB	Bell 206B JetRanger III	3232	ex N20EA
C-GAXB	Bell 206B JetRanger III	3527	
C-GBHB	Bell 206B JetRanger III	2415	
C-GTEK	Bell 206B JetRanger III	1684	ex N222ML
C-FBHC	Aerospatiale AS.350B-2 AStar	2850	ex C-FWCH
C-FBHD	Aerospatiale AS.350BA AStar	2166	ex PT-HSE
C-FBHV	Bell 206LR+ LongRanger	45113	ex N403EH
C-GAVL	Aerospatiale AS.350BA AStar	2258	ex N350AH

BAMAJI AIR

C-FHEP	de Havilland DHC-2 Beaver	69	ex C-FIOB	Floats or wheels/skis
C-GFDS	de Havilland DHC-2 Beaver	1269	ex 31343	Floats or wheels/skis
C-GIPR	Cessna 208 Caravan I	20800343		
C-GZBS	de Havilland DHC-2 Beaver	975		Floats or wheels/skis

BAR XH AIR
Palliser (BXH)
Medicine Hat, Alta (YXH)

C-FBID	British Aerospace Jetstream 31	802	ex G-31-802	301	
C-FBIJ	British Aerospace Jetstream 31	817	ex G-31-817	038; stored YXH	Lsd fr BAES
C-FBIP	British Aerospace Jetstream 31	820	ex G-31-820	305	
C-FCPF	British Aerospace Jetstream 31	827	ex G-31-827	039; stored YXH	Lsd fr BAES
C-FZYB	British Aerospace Jetstream 32EP	837	ex C-FYWY	033; stored YXH	Lsd fr BAES
C-GZOS	British Aerospace Jetstream 31	796	ex N424UE		

C-FBHO	Piper PA-31-350 Navajo Chieftain	31-7405466	ex		
C-FCGB	Beech 200 Super King Air	BB-24	ex N183MC	035 conv to Cat Pass 200	
C-GFHG	Beech 95-B55 Baron	TC-1289	ex N155UT		
C-GMDF	Piper PA-31T Cheyenne II	31T-7620019	ex N82000		
C-GXHD	Beech 1300	BB-1338	ex N915YW	conv Super King Air	
C-GXHG	Beech 1300	BB-1383	ex N913YW	conv Super King Air	
C-GXHK	Piper PA-31-350 Navajo Chieftain	31-7752108	ex N115SC		
C-GXHP	Beech A100 King Air	B-132	ex XB-SLG		
C-GXHS	Beech 1300	BB-1302	ex PP-WYY	conv Super King Air	

Sister company of Alberta Citylink

BAXTER AVIATION
Nanaimo SPB, BC (YCD)

C-FAWA	de Havilland DHC-2 Beaver	1430	ex VH-IDR
C-FEBE	de Havilland DHC-2 Beaver	792	ex N9983B
C-FJBP	de Havilland DHC-2 Beaver	942	
C-FWAC	de Havilland DHC-2 Beaver	1356	ex N68089
C-GEZS	de Havilland DHC-2 Beaver	1277	ex 57-6170
C-GFDI	de Havilland DHC-2 Beaver	606	ex 53-2810
C-GOLC	de Havilland DHC-2 Beaver	1392	ex N62354
C-GTBQ	de Havilland DHC-2 Beaver	1316	ex N9036

C-GBTJ	Cessna A185F Skywagon	18503950	ex (N5279E)
C-GMFG	Cessna A185F Skywagon	18503773	ex N8786Q

All floatplanes

BEARSKIN AIRLINES
Bearskin (JV/BLS)
Sioux Lookout (YXL)

C-GDFX	Beech 99A	U-123	ex N18RA	
C-GFQC	Beech B99	U-120	ex N47156	
C-GHVI	Beech B99	U-153	ex N17RX	dbr 29Jan03?
C-GPEM	Beech 99	U-98	ex N991GP	
C-GQAH	Beech B99	U-58	ex N7801R	Spirit of Muskrat Dam

C-FAJV	Pilatus PC-12/45	234	ex HB-FRE	
C-FCJV	Pilatus PC-12/45	240	ex N240PD	
C-FIJV	Pilatus PC-12/45	222	ex C-FKEN	
C-FKAE	Pilatus PC-12/45	195	ex HB-FQD	

C-FAMC	Swearingen SA.227AC Metro III	AC-719B	ex N436MA	
C-FFZN	Swearingen SA.227AC Metro III	AC-785B	ex N30019	Spirit of Service
C-FXUS	Swearingen SA.227CC Metro 23	CC-841B	ex N456LA	
C-FYAG	Swearingen SA.227AC Metro III	AC-670B	ex N670VG	
C-FYWG	Swearingen SA.227AC Metro III	AC-782B	ex N3000S	Spirit of Winnipeg
C-GYHD	Swearingen SA.227AC Metro III	AC-739B	ex N227JH	Spirit of Dryden
C-GYQT	Swearingen SA.227AC Metro III	AC-644B	ex N644VG	
C-GYTL	Swearingen SA.227CC Metro 23	CC-829B	ex N30154	Spirit of Big Trout Lake

C-GEHY	Piper PA-23-250 Aztec C	27-3843	ex N6548Y	
C-GKAJ	Beech A100 King Air	B-232	ex N400WH	Spirit of Marathon
C-GUPP	Beech A100 King Air	B-157	ex N123CS	Spirit of Sioux Lookout
C-GYQK	Beech A100 King Air	B-153	ex N120AS	Spirit of Kenora

BEAVER AIR SERVICES
The Pas, Man (YQD)

C-GADW	Piper PA-31-350 Navajo Chieftain	31-7752078	ex N27191	
C-GEBA	Piper PA-31T Cheyenne II	31T-7620029	ex N177JE	
C-GOGT	Beech B200 Super King Air	BB-535		
C-GTTZ	Cessna A185F Skywagon	18503694	ex N8423Q	Floats or wheels/skis
C-GYQD	Piper PA-31-350 Chieftain	31-8152039	ex N4075T	

BIG RIVER AIR

C-FVVY	de Havilland DHC-3 Turbo Otter	410	ex RCAF9427
C-GAIX*	Cessna A185F Skywagon	18503890	ex (N4855E)
C-GFZT*	Cessna U206F Stationair II	U20603406	ex (N8550Q)
C-GIJL	Cessna 210L Centurion	21061226	ex (N2283S)
C-GJEM	Cessna 208 Caravan	20800152	ex N9728F
C-GTOI*	de Havilland DHC-2 Beaver	712	ex N6084
C-GVYE*	Cessna A185F Skywagon	18503778	ex (N8852Q)

*Operate on floats or wheels/skis

BIG SALMON AIR

C-FZNL	Cessna A185E Skywagon	18501826	ex (N1602M)
C-GJSR	Cessna U206C Super Skywagon	U206-1106	ex N29136

Both operate on floats or wheels/skis

BLACK SHEEP AVIATION

C-GMCW	de Havilland DHC-3 Otter	108	ex N5339G	Floats or wheel/ski

BLACK TUSK HELICOPTER

C-FSAI	Aerospatiale AS.350BA AStar	2176	ex N121KR
C-FWQU	Bell 214B-1 BigLifter	28209	ex N3999N
C-FZVT	Bell 214B-1 BigLifter	28016	ex LN-OSG
C-GSEE	Bell 206B JetRanger	415	ex N95SB

BLUE WATER AVIATION SERVICES

C-FCUW	Cessna 337 Super Skymaster	337-0009	ex N2109X	
C-FEYQ	de Havilland DHC-2 Beaver	465		
C-FIFP	de Havilland DHC-3 Otter	73		Floats or wheels/skis
C-GBTU	de Havilland DHC-3 Otter	209	ex IM-1711	Floats or wheels/skis
C-GFVZ	Cessna A185F Skywagon	18503058	ex (N21451)	Floats or wheels/skis
C-GKYG	de Havilland DHC-3 Otter	261	ex N2750	Floats or wheels/skis

BOLTON LAKE AIR SERVICES

CF-BSB	Noorduyn Norseman V	N29-15	
C-GEIF	Cessna U206F Stationair	U20602938	ex (N1824Q)
C-GRTG	Piper PA-31-350 Navajo Chieftain	31-7652004	ex N180RM
C-GTZK	Piper PA-31 Turbo Navajo	31-381	ex N9SG
C-GYWE	Piper PA-32-260 Cherokee Six	32-141	ex N3305W
C-GYXM	Cessna A185E Skywagon	185-1171	

BUFFALO AIRWAYS

Buffalo (J4/BFL)

C-FNJE	Consolidated PBY-5A Catalina	CV-437		
C-FOFI	Consolidated PBY-5A Catalina	CV-343	ex RCAF 11047	703
C-FPQM	Consolidated PBY-5A Catalina	CV-425	ex CF-GMS	704
C-FUAW	Consolidated PBY-5A Catalina	CV-201	ex (CF-NTK)	708
C-GFFC	Consolidated PBY-5A Catalina	013		
C-FCUE	Douglas DC-3	12983	ex NC41407	Mel Bryan
C-FDTB	Douglas DC-3	12597	ex CF-TEC	stroed YQF
C-FDTH	Douglas DC-3	12591	ex CF-TEB	stored YQF
C-FFAY	Douglas DC-3	4785	ex N47218	stored YQF
C-FLFR	Douglas DC-3	13155	ex KG563	
C-GJKM	Douglas DC-3	13580	ex CAF 12946	6
C-GPNR	Douglas DC-3	13333	ex CAF 12932	2; Murray Crosby
C-GWIR	Douglas DC-3	9371	ex N18262	8
C-GWZS	Douglas DC-3	12327	ex CAF 12913	4
CF-BAA	Douglas C-54D-DC	10653	ex N4994H	stored YZF
C-FIQM	Douglas C-54G	36088	ex N4218S	57; Arctic Trader
C-GBNV	Douglas C-54G	35988	ex N3303F	56 Tanker

C-GBPA	Douglas C-54D	10673	ex N87591	
C-GBSK	Douglas C-54G	36049		
C-GCTF	Douglas C-54E	27281	ex N51819	58
C-GPSH	Douglas C-54A	7458	ex N7171H	1; Arctic Distributor
C-GQIC	Douglas C-54E	27343		
C-GXKN	Douglas DC-4	36090	ex	

C-FAVO	Curtiss C-46D Commando	33242	ex N9891Z	Arctic Thunder
C-FCGE	Beech 65-A90 King Air	LJ-118		
C-FCGH	Beech 65-A90 King Air	LJ-203		
CF-SAN	Noorduyn Norseman V	N29-29		
C-FULX	Beech 95-C55 Baron	TE-147		
C-FUPT	Cessna A185E Skywagon	185-1075	ex (N4568F)	141
C-GBPD	Canadair CL-215-1A10	1084		291 Op for NWT Govt
C-GBYU	Canadair CL-215-1A10	1083	ex C-GKEA	290 Op for NWT Govt
C-GCSX	Canadair CL-215-1A10	1088		295 Op for NWT Govt
C-GDHN	Canadair CL-215-1A10	1089		296 Op for NWT Govt
C-GIWJ	Beech 95 Travel Air	TD-32	ex N2707Y	
C-GTPO	Curtiss C-46F Commando	22556	ex N519AC	
C-GTXW	Curtiss C-46A Commando	30386	ex 5Y-TXW	stored YZF
C-GWCB	Beech B95 Travel Air	TD-369	ex N9914R	
C-GYFM	Beech 95 Travel Air	TD-202	ex N654Q	

BUFFALO NARROWS AIRWAYS listed under trading name, Courtesy Air

BUSHLAND AIRWAYS

Moosonee, Ont (YMO)

C-FBGB	Cessna U206E Super Skywagon	U20601514	ex (N9114M)	Floatplane
C-FYJR	Cessna A185E Skywagon	185-1520	ex (N2770J)	Floatplane
C-GSNU	Cessna 207A Stationair 7	20700491	ex N6DF	
C-GYWE	Piper PA-32-260 Cherokee Six	32-141	ex N3305W	

CALM AIR INTERNATIONAL

Calm Air (MO/CAV) (IATA 622)

Thompson, Man (YTH)

C-FAMO	Hawker Siddeley HS.748 Srs.2A/258LFD	1669		
C-FMAK	Hawker Siddeley HS.748 Srs.2A/257	1668	ex G-11	
C-GDOP	Hawker Siddeley HS.748 Srs.2A/283	1745	ex F-ODQQ	
C-GEPB	Hawker Siddeley HS.748 Srs.2A/254	1686	ex 9G-ABX	304, freighter
C-GHSC	Hawker Siddeley HS.748 Srs.2B/FAA	1790	ex G-BJTL	
C-GSBF	Hawker Siddeley HS.748 Srs.2A/210	1662	ex G-11-3	

C-FTJV	SAAB SF.340B	366	ex SE-C66	
C-FTJW	SAAB SF.340B	377	ex SE-C77	
C-GALP	Piper PA-31-350 Navajo Chieftain	31-7405441	ex N54317	
C-GKRM	Cessna 208B Caravan I	208B0660	ex N73MM	
C-GTJX	SAAB SF.340B	165	ex N586MA	Lsd fr SAAB
C-GTJY	SAAB SF.340B	166	ex N587MA	Lsd fr SAAB

45% owned by Air Canada and operates for Air Canada Jazz using code ZX

CAMERON AIR SERVICE

Toronto-City Centre, Ont (YTZ)

C-FKCA	Cessna 208 Caravan I	20800211	ex N211PA	
C-FXWH	Cessna U206C Super Skywagon	U206-1170		
C-GCGA	Cessna 208 Caravan I	20800242	ex (A6-CGA)	
C-GGSG	Cessna TU206G Stationair 6	U20605852		

CAMPBELL HELICOPTERS

Abbotsford, BC (YXX)

C-FFJY	Bell 205A-1	30002	ex VH-NGM	
C-FJTG	Bell 205A-1	30104	ex N8138J	
C-FMQN	Bell 205A-1	30082		
C-FOAR	Bell 205A-1	30105	ex HI-728SP	
C-GOLE	Bell 205A-1	30182	ex HI-731SP	
C-GPET	Bell 205A-1	30209	ex N205KA	
C-GPRR	Bell 205A-1	30181		

C-FBWR	Bell 204B	2015		
C-FMPZ	Bell 212	30528	ex HC-BOI	
C-GFDV	Bell 212	30842	ex N291B	
C-GFQN	Bell 212	30571	ex N554CR	

CANADA WESTERN AIRLINES

Previously listed as Canadian Western Airlines

C-GXPZ	Cessna 401A	401A0104	ex N6192Q
C-GYXA	Swearingen SA.227TC Metro III	AC-572	ex N718C

CANADIAN AIR-CRANE

C-FCRN	Sikorsky S-64E	64061	ex N172AC
C-GESG	Sikorsky S-64E	64065	ex N157AC
C-GJZK	Sikorsky S-64E	64003	ex N176AC

Subsidiary of Erickson Air Crane and all leased from the parent

CANADIAN HELICOPTERS - CHC

C-FCCA	Aerospatiale AS.350BA AStar	2900	
C-FCHN	Aerospatiale AS.350BA AStar	2921	
C-FETA	Aerospatiale AS.350D AStar	1085	ex N137BH
C-FFBU	Aerospatiale AS.350B AStar	1215	ex N3605B
C-FHVH	Aerospatiale AS.350BA AStar	1256	ex N36075
C-FPBA	Aerospatiale AS.350B2 AStar	2492	ex JA6091
C-FPER	Aerospatiale AS.350B AStar	2552	ex F-WYMK
C-FPLJ	Aerospatiale AS.350D AStar	1060	ex C-FQNS
C-FQNS	Aerospatiale AS.350D AStar	1423	ex N5783Y
C-FSHV	Aerospatiale AS.350B AStar	1287	ex N5143R
C-FSLB	Aerospatiale AS.350B AStar	2142	ex JA9786
C-FVVH	Aerospatiale AS.350BA AStar	2612	
C-FYCO	Aerospatiale AS.350BA AStar	2899	
C-GAHH	Aerospatiale AS.350B AStar	1036	ex XA-...
C-GAHI	Aerospatiale AS.350D AStar	1086	
C-GALD	Aerospatiale AS.350BA AStar	1146	
C-GALE	Aerospatiale AS.350D AStar	1350	
C-GATX	Aerospatiale AS.350BA AStar	1221	
C-GAYX	Aerospatiale AS.350B AStar	1179	
C-GBPS	Aerospatiale AS.350B AStar	1277	ex N3610R
C-GCEC	Aerospatiale AS.350B AStar	1431	ex N666JK
C-GCHH	Aerospatiale AS.350B-2 AStar	2461	ex ZK-HND
C-GCKP	Aerospatiale AS.350D AStar	1138	ex N140BH
C-GCWD	Aerospatiale AS.350BA AStar	2047	ex N844BP
C-GCWW	Aerospatiale AS.350D AStar	1435	ex N340DF
C-GDKD	Aerospatiale AS.350BA AStar	1432	ex N5785H
C-GDSX	Aerospatiale AS.350BA AStar	1134	ex N35972
C-GDUF	Aerospatiale AS.350B AStar	1309	
C-GELC	Aerospatiale AS.350D AStar	1162	ex VH-HRD
C-GEPH	Aerospatiale AS.350B AStar	1193	ex ZK-HET
C-GEVH	Aerospatiale AS.350B AStar	2620	ex F-WYMN
C-GFHS	Aerospatiale AS.350B AStar	1401	
C-GGIE	Aerospatiale AS.350B-2 AStar	3280	
C-GHVD	Aerospatiale AS.350D AStar	1236	ex N3606Y
C-GLNE	Aerospatiale AS.350BA AStar	1128	ex N3599N
C-GLNK	Aerospatiale AS.350D AStar	1261	ex N3608C
C-GLNM	Aerospatiale AS.350D AStar	1262	ex N3608D
C-GLNO	Aerospatiale AS.350D AStar	1264	ex N3608N
C-GMIZ	Aerospatiale AS.350D AStar	1170	
C-GNMN	Aerospatiale AS.350BA AStar	1315	ex XA-SNA
C-GOVH	Aerospatiale AS.350BA AStar	1286	ex N224GA
C-GRBT	Aerospatiale AS.350D AStar	1246	ex N877JM
C-GRGJ	Aerospatiale AS.350B AStar	1171	ex N3600G
C-GRGU	Aerospatiale AS.350D AStar	1213	ex N7172H
C-GSLF	Aerospatiale AS.350D AStar	1310	
C-GTPF	Aerospatiale AS.350BA AStar	2932	
C-GTVH	Aerospatiale AS.350BA AStar	2611	ex N600CH
C-GVHB	Aerospatiale AS.350D AStar	1297	ex N352EH
C-GVYK	Aerospatiale AS.350D AStar	1094	
C-FAHT	Bell 206B JetRanger II	631	
C-FAHU	Bell 206B JetRanger III	624	
C-FAHW	Bell 206B JetRanger II	785	
C-FAJR	Bell 206B JetRanger II	123	
C-FBQH	Bell 206B JetRanger II	745	
C-FCJC	Bell 206B JetRanger II	832	
C-FCQE	Bell 206B JetRanger II	535	ex N8147J
C-FFVC	Bell 206B JetRanger II	934	
C-FHTP	Bell 206B JetRanger II	1024	
C-FHTR	Bell 206B JetRanger II	1036	

C-FHTS	Bell 206B JetRanger II	1037		
C-FKNX	Bell 206B JetRanger III	2440	ex N5003X	
C-FOAN	Bell 206B JetRanger II	791		
C-FPOD	Bell 206B JetRanger II	696		
C-FWTX	Bell 206B JetRanger II	343		
C-GAHC	Bell 206B JetRanger II	468	ex N2959W	
C-GAHR	Bell 206B JetRanger II	873	ex N1488B	
C-GBHE	Bell 206B JetRanger II	1335		
C-GBHI	Bell 206B JetRanger II	1758	ex N49584	
C-GBXK	Bell 206B JetRanger III	3225		
C-GCIR	Bell 206B JetRanger III	3029		
C-GDBA	Bell 206B JetRanger III	2232	ex N16821	
C-GETF	Bell 206B JetRanger III	3036		
C-GFQH	Bell 206B JetRanger II	1090	ex N100JG	
C-GGNC	Bell 206B JetRanger II	2123		
C-GHUQ	Bell 206B JetRanger II	1721	ex N3199G	
C-GIFY	Bell 206B JetRanger II	2008		
C-GIXS	Bell 206B JetRanger III	2304	ex N272RM	
C-GLRA	Bell 206B JetRanger II	1753	ex N300SE	
C-GMKT	Bell 206B JetRanger II	774	ex N101PN	
C-GNLD	Bell 206B JetRanger III	2357	ex N57PH	
C-GNLE	Bell 206B JetRanger III	2358	ex N56PH	
C-GNLG	Bell 206B JetRanger III	2360		
C-GNPH	Bell 206B JetRanger III	2352	ex N58148	
C-GOKE	Bell 206B JetRanger II	1830	ex N49655	
C-GOKJ	Bell 206B JetRanger II	499	ex N2298W	
C-GRGN	Bell 206B JetRanger II	1824	ex N333WW	
C-GSHP	Bell 206B JetRanger II	1259	ex N259CH	
C-GSRX	Bell 206B JetRanger II	1823	ex N999PA	
C-GUMO	Bell 206B JetRanger II	1943	ex N49721	
C-GVTK	Bell 206B JetRanger II	104	ex N6200N	
C-GXHC	Bell 206B JetRanger II	395	ex N28956	
C-GYQH	Bell 206B JetRanger II	1394	ex N111BH	
C-GZQH	Bell 206B JetRanger II	1055	ex N58148	
C-FNYQ	Bell 206L LongRanger	45047	ex N20LT	
C-GBVZ	Bell 206L-1 LongRanger II	45324	ex N6374S	
C-GGZQ	Bell 206L LongRanger	45006	ex N49637	
C-GLMV	Bell 206L-1 LongRanger II	45430	ex N454CH	
C-GLQY	Bell 206L LongRanger	45146		
C-GMHS	Bell 206L LongRanger	45120		
C-GMHT	Bell 206L LongRanger	45127	ex N16847	
C-GNLK	Bell 206L LongRanger	46601	ex N16939	
C-GNMC	Bell 206L LongRanger	45067		
C-GNZR	Bell 206L LongRanger	45118	ex N16809	
C-GPCX	Bell 206L-1 LongRanger II	45554		
C-GQEZ	Bell 206L LongRanger	45038	ex N9942K	
C-GSVH	Bell 206L LongRanger	45072	ex N206U	
C-GTLB	Bell 206L LongRanger	45031	ex N9927K	
C-GTOM	Bell 206L LongRanger	45010		
C-GVHX	Bell 206L LongRanger	45138	ex N90AC	
C-FAOC*	Bell 212	35103		
C-FBHF	Bell 212	30509	ex N7072J	
C-FCAP*	Bell 212	30923	ex ZS-RNH	
C-FKGT*	Bell 212	30901		Lsd to Icaro as HC-CBW
C-FNJJ	Bell 212	30944	ex N2093S	
C-FOKV	Bell 212	30819	ex N16787	
C-FPKW*	Bell 212	30893	ex C-FARC	Lsd as ZS-RNP
C-FRUT*	Bell 212	30891	ex ZK-HID	Lsd to Icaro
C-FRWF*	Bell 212	30894		Lsd to Helicopter Svs as EP-HCH
C-FRWI*	Bell 212	30672	ex N72AL	
C-FRWL*	Bell 212	30829	ex N93AL	Lsd as ZS-RNR
C-FRWM*	Bell 212	30814	ex VH-LAM	Lsd to Icaro as HC-CDD
C-FTAG	Bell 212	30739		
C-GAHD	Bell 212	30570	ex N7034J	
C-GBPH*	Bell 212	30630	ex HC-BZN	
C-GFQP	Bell 212	30578	ex N58120	
C-GHVH	Bell 212	30877	ex N8555V	
C-GMOH	Bell 212	31133		
C-GOKG	Bell 212	30843	ex N16828	
C-GOKL	Bell 212	30597	ex N2990W	
C-GOKY	Bell 212	30698	ex (5H-...)	
C-FIBN	Sikorsky S-61N	61-811	ex PT-HPV	
C-FOKP*	Sikorsky S-61N	61-297	ex HS-HTP	
C-GARC*	Sikorsky S-61N	61-722	ex N225BF	Lsd to Thai Avn as HS-HTC
C-GHJU	Sikorsky S-61N Helipro Short	61-711	ex YV-1032C	
C-GOLH*	Sikorsky S-61N	61-815	ex HS-HTH	Lsd to Thai Avn as HS-HTA
C-GROV*	Sikorsky S-61N	61-222	ex YV-1033C	
C-GSAB*	Sikorsky S-61N	61-823	ex ZS-RFU	
C-GSBL*	Sikorsky S-61N	61-754	ex G-BEDI	based Azerbaijan

C-FABH	Sikorsky S-76A II	760271	ex C-GHJV	
C-FCHC	Sikorsky S-76C	760546	ex N20449	
C-FIHD	Sikorsky S-76A	760187	ex HS-HTG	Lsd Thai Avn as HS-HTD
C-FSBH	Sikorsky S-76A	760168	ex N5427S	
C-GEJL	Sikorsky S-76C	760537	ex N5008M	
C-GFFJ	Sikorsky S-76A	760138	ex VH-HUD	
C-GIHO	Sikorsky S-76A++	760015	ex C-GHJG	Lsd to Thai Avn as HS-HTO
C-GIHR	Sikorsky S-76A+	760032	ex D-HOSC	Lsd to Thai Avn as HS-HTR
C-GIHS	Sikorsky S-76A+	760150	ex D-HOSD	Lsd to Thai Avn as HS-HTS
C-GIHY	Sikorsky S-76A++	760011	ex RP-C276	
C-GIMA	Sikorsky S-76A	760018	ex G-BZAC	EMS
C-GIMB	Sikorsky S-76A	760111	ex G-BIAW	
C-GIME*	Sikorsky S-76A++	760004		
C-GIMJ*	Sikorsky S-76A++	760009	ex N333AA	
C-GIMK	Sikorsky S-76A	760016	ex ZS-REI	Lsd as ZS-REI
C-GIML*	Sikorsky S-76A++	760017	ex HS-HTL	EMS
C-GIMM	Sikorsky S-76A	760044	ex HS-HTM	
C-GIMN	Sikorsky S-76A	760110	ex G-BIAV	
C-GIMQ	Sikorsky S-76A	760102	ex HS-HTQ	Lsd to Thai Avn as HS-HTQ
C-GIMR	Sikorsky S-76A	760079	ex G-BHYB	EMS
C-GIMT	Sikorsky S-76A	760130	ex N1548S	EMS
C-GIMU	Sikorsky S-76A	760131	ex VH-OHA	Lsd as ZS-RNT
C-GIMV	Sikorsky S-76A	760005	ex VH-WXE	
C-GIMW	Sikorsky S-76A	760226	ex N76FB	EMS
C-GIMX	Sikorsky S-76A++	760213	ex G-BVNX	Lsd Thai Avn as HS-HTX
C-GIMY	Sikorsky S-76A	760055	ex N376LL	
C-GIMZ	Sikorsky S-76A	760169	ex N399PK	
C-GKWS*	Sikorsky S-76A++	760297	ex VR-HZB	Lsd to H.S.O as EP-HCS
C-GKWT	Sikorsky S-76A	760295	ex B-HZD	
C-GMNB	Sikorsky S-76C	760490		
RP-C176	Sikorsky S-76A++	760112	ex VH-LAQ	
C-FJSM	Bell 222	47065		
C-GTLC	Aerospatiale AS.355F1 TwinStar	5097	ex N911BR	
C-GVHC	Aerospatiale AS.355F1 TwinStar	5195	ex N5801T	
C-GVHK	Aerospatiale AS.355F1 TwinStar	5098	ex N60031	

*Registered to CHC International which is based at Vancouver, BC
Canadian Helicopters is a trading name of CHC Helicopter Corp
CHC Helicopter Group includes CHC Ireland (EI), CHC-Scotia Helicopters (G), Thai Aviation Services (HS), CHC
Australia (VH), Aerotechnica (YV) and CHC Helicopters (Africa) (ZS)

CANADIAN NORTH

Norterra (5T/ANX) (IATA 518) — Yellowknife, NWT (YZF)

C-GDPA	Boeing 737-2T2C (AvAero 3)	655/22056		584; Spirit of Yellowknife
C-GFPW	Boeing 737-275C (AvAero 3)	481/21294		552
C-GNDU	Boeing 737-242C (AvAero 3)	880/22877		562
C-GOPW	Boeing 737-275C (AvAero 3)	688/22160	ex N8288V	582; Spirit of Nunavut
C-GSPW	Boeing 737-275C (AvAero 3)	813/22618		583
C-FTAR	Fokker F.28 Fellowship 1000	11047	ex VH-ATD	
C-FTAY	Fokker F.28 Fellowship 1000	11084	ex VH-ATG	

Canadian North is the trading name of Air NorTerra

CANADIAN WESTERN AIRLINES now listed as Canada Western Airlines

CANJET

Canjet (C6/CJA) — Halifax-Intl, NS (YHZ)

C-FECJ	Boeing 737-2Q9 (Nordam 3)	612/21975	ex N230AU	230	Lsd fr IMP Group
C-FGCJ	Boeing 737-201 (Nordam 3)	728/22352	ex N236US	236	Lsd fr IMP Group
C-FHCJ	Boeing 737-201 (Nordam 3)	547/21666	ex N224US		Lsd fr Jetran
C-FJCJ	Boeing 737-201 (Nordam 3)	548/21667	ex N225US		Lsd fr IMP Group
C-FMCJ	Boeing 737-296 (Nordam 3)	733/22398	ex N238US	238	Lsd fr IMP Group
C-FVCJ	Boeing 737-201 (Nordam 3)	731/22353	ex N237US	237	Lsd fr IMP Group

CARAVAN AVIATION

Chibougamau, Que

C-GFLN	Cessna 208 Caravan I	20800261	

CARGAARD AVIATION renamed Fugro Aviation Canada

CARGAIR

Ste Michel-des-SaintsMontreal-St Hubert, Que (-/YHU)

C-FDMP	Piper PA-23-250 Aztec C	27-3560	ex N6306Y

C-FGQA	de Havilland DHC-2 Beaver	72		Floatplane
C-FLEO	de Havilland DHC-2 Beaver	1270		Floats or wheels/skis
C-FQQC	de Havilland DHC-2 Beaver	56		Floatplane
C-FSUB	de Havilland DHC-3 Otter	8	ex RCAF 3662	Floatplane
C-FTSJ	Piper PA-23-250 Aztec D	27-4387	ex N9652N	
C-FZAA	Piper PA-23-250 Aztec E	27-4710	ex N14148	
C-GBLT	Piper PA-31 Turbo Navajo	31-102	ex N123TR	
C-GITW	Piper PA-31-350 Navajo Chieftain	31-7652114	ex N59891	
C-GMRG	Piper PA-31 Turbo Navajo C	31-7812051	ex N27563	

CARGOJET CANADA

Winnport (W8/CJT) (IATA 489)   *Winnipeg-Intl, Man/Toronto-Pearson Intl, Que (YWG/YYZ)*

C-FCJF	Boeing 727-223F (FedEx 3)	1653/22011	ex C-GACG	
C-FCJI	Boeing 727-225F (FedEx 3)	1674/22435	ex N804MA	
C-FCJP	Boeing 727-223F (FedEx 3)	1655/22012	ex C-FUAC	Lsd fr Avn Capital Grp
C-FCJU	Boeing 727-260F (FedEx 3)	1789/22759	ex C-FACM	
C-GCJB	Boeing 727-225F (FedEx 3)	1535/21855	ex N886MA	Lsd fr Flagship Intl
C-GCJD	Boeing 727-231F (FedEx 3)	1568/21988	ex N808MA	Lsd fr Flagship Intl
C-GCJQ	Boeing 727-225F (FedEx 3)	1682/22437	ex N806MA	Lsd fr Flagship Intl
C-GCJZ	Boeing 727-225F (FedEx 3)	1532/21854	ex N889MA	
C-GUJC	Boeing 727-260F (FedEx 3)	1534/21979	ex C-FACJ	

Also operates services with other cargo aircraft as required

CARIBOO CHILCOTIN HELICOPTERS

Lillooet, BC

C-FGYQ	Bell 206B JetRanger III	1357	
C-FHTQ	Bell 206B JetRanger III	1030	
C-FKOD	Bell 206B JetRanger II	1228	
C-FSMI	Bell 205A-1	30263	ex (N205HT)
C-FXFT	Kamov K-1200 K-Max	A94-0007	ex N135KA

CARSON AIR

Kelowna, BC (YLW)

C-FBWQ	Swearingen SA.226TC Metro II	TC-379	ex N1011U	
C-FCAV	Piper PA-42 Cheyenne III	42-8001006	ex N131RC	
C-FCAW	Swearingen SA.26AT Merlin IIB	T26-172E	ex N135SR	
C-GCAU	Swearingen SA.226TC Metro II	TC-331E	ex N255AM	Freighter
C-GCAW	Swearingen SA.226TC Metro II	TC-358	ex N1009R	
C-GIDC	Piper PA-42 Cheyenne III	42-8001002	ex N61QR	
C-GKKC	Swearingen SA.226TC Metro II	TC-370	ex N125AV	

CENTENNIAL AIRLINES

Centennial (CNS)   *Edmonton-Municipal, Alta (YXD)*

C-FTNY	Piper PA-31-350 Navajo Chieftain	31-7952245	ex N2169X
C-FVVS	Piper PA-31-350 Navajo Chieftain	31-7952199	ex N35347
C-GBFG	Piper PA-34-220T Seneca II	34-8070006	
C-GFMX	Cessna 421B Golden Eagle	421B0939	ex N421HA
C-GGKJ	Beech B100 King Air	BE-49	ex N400RK
C-GKCB	Piper PA-34-220T Seneca III	34-8133091	ex N83864
C-GLIL	Cessna 182R Skylane II	18267949	ex N9446H
C-GNJX	Piper PA-34-200 Seneca	34-7450212	ex N44574

CENTRAL MOUNTAIN AIR

Glacier (9M/GLR) (IATA 634)   *Smithers, BC (YYD)*

C-FCMB	Beech 1900D	UE-278		916	
C-FCME	Beech 1900D	UE-277		915	
C-FCMN	Beech 1900D	UE-276		914	
C-FCMO	Beech 1900D	UE-281		917	
C-FCMP	Beech 1900D	UE-271	ex N11037	912	
C-FCMR	Beech 1900D	UE-283	ex N21872	918	
C-FCMU	Beech 1900D	UE-285		919	
C-FCMV	Beech 1900D	UE-272	ex N11079	913	
C-GFSV	Beech 1900D	UE-346	ex C-GORI		Lsd to NTA
C-GCMA	Beech 1900D	UE-289		921	
C-GCML	Beech 1900D	UE-243	ex N10879	911	
C-GCMY	Beech 1900D	UE-287		920	
C-GGBY	Beech 1900D	UE-351	ex N23517	923	
C-GGCA	Beech 1900D	UE-359	ex N31559	924	
C-GCMJ	Beech 1900C-1	UC-49	ex N80198	930, stored PWA	Lsd to NTA
C-GCMT	Beech 1900C-1	UC-120	ex N15683	928	Lsd to NTA

C-GCMZ   Beech 1900C-1   UC-61   ex N1568L   929   Lsd to NTA
Operates codeshare services for Air Canada Jazz using AC flight numbers; owns NT AIR (Northern Thunderbird Air)

CHIMO AIR SERVICE
Red Lake SPB, Ont

CF-HZA	Beech D-18S	A-111	
CF-JIN	Noorduyn Norseman V	N29-65	ex CF-LFR
CF-KAO	Noorduyn Norseman IV	636	ex 44-70371
C-FODQ	de Havilland DHC-3 Otter	111	

All operate on floats

CLEARWATER AIRWAYS
Burditt Lake SPB, Ont

C-FCIP	Cessna U206G Stationair 6	U20605815	ex N5538X
C-FGUE	Beech C-18S	8107	ex N480DB
C-GESW	Beech C-18S	7911	ex N4858V

All operate on floats

CLOUD AIR SERVICE
Port Carling, Ont

C-FGLF	Cessna TU206G Stationair 6	U20606317	ex N924JD
C-FLDC	Cessna 208 Caravan I	20800294	ex N15NH
C-GGMG	Cessna TU206G Stationair 6	U20605768	

COAST WESTERN AIRLINES
Sechelt, BC (YHS)

CF-FAQ	de Havilland DHC-2 Beaver	94	ex N2647	Floatplane

COCHRANE AIR SERVICES
Cochrane-Lillabelle Lake, Ont (YCN)

C-FGBF	de Havilland DHC-2 Beaver	168	Floatplane
C-FGYP	de Havilland DHC-2 Beaver	145	Floatplane
C-FITS	de Havilland DHC-3 Otter	90	Floatplane

COMMANDO AIR TRANSPORT ceased operations

CONAIR AVIATION

Conair Canada (CRC)   *Abbotsford, BC (YXX)*

C-FXVF	AT-802 Air Tractor	802-0033		678	
C-FXVL	AT-802 Air Tractor	802-0034		679	
C-GEDO	AT-802 Air Tractor	802-0073		677	
C-GEDR	AT-802 Air Tractor	802-0075		680	
C-GEDZ	AT-802 Air Tractor	802-0076		681	
C-GYZB	AT-802 Air Tractor	802A-0154			
C-FEFK	Conair Firecat	G-360/014	ex F-ZBEH	574	
C-FEFX	Conair Firecat	G-527/031	ex N425DF	575	
C-FJOH	Conair Firecat	G-254/034	ex N424DF	576	
C-FOPU	Conair Firecat	DHC-38/007	ex RCN1539	564	
C-FOPV	Conair Firecat	DHC-34/006	ex RCN1535	566	
C-FOPY	Conair Firecat	DHC-24/019	ex CF-IOF	569	
C-GABC	Conair Firecat	DHC-90/011	ex RCAF12191	567	
C-GHDY	Conair Firecat	G-374/029	ex Bu136465	573	
C-GHPJ	Conair Firecat	G-509/022	ex Bu136600	571	
C-GWUO	Conair Firecat	DHC-39/003	ex N99261	563	
C-GWUP	Conair Firecat	DHC-19/012	ex RCN12120	568	
C-GYQI	Conair Firecat	G-424/030	ex Bu136575	570	
C-FEKF	Convair 580	80	ex C-GEVB	445 Tanker 45	Lsd fr KFA
C-FFKF	Convair 580	179	ex C-GEVC	444 Tanker 44	Lsd fr KFA
C-FHKF	Convair 580	374	ex C-GEUZ	455 Tanker 55	Lsd fr KFA
C-FKFA	Convair 580	100	ex C-FLVY	452 Tanker 52	Lsd fr KFA
C-FKFL	Convair 580	465	ex C-FZQS		Lsd fr KFA
C-FKFM	Convair 580	70	ex N73133	454 Tanker 54	Lsd fr KFA
C-FKFY	Convair 580	129	ex N5814	448 Tanker 48	Lsd fr KFA
C-GKFO	Convair 580	78	ex N5815	453 Tanker 53	Lsd fr KFA
C-FFIF	Piper PA-60 Aerostar 600A	60-0702-7961218	ex N6073K	122	
C-GBBP	Ted Smith Aerostar 600	60-0142-062	ex N17HA	120	
C-GLVG	Piper PA-60 Aerostar 600A	60-0695-7961217	ex N6072U	111	

C-GMGZ	Piper PA-60 Aerostar 600A	60-0708-7961220	ex N6075C	112
C-GOSX	Piper PA-60 Aerostar 600A	60-0863-8161246	ex N3647B	110
C-GRIK	Piper PA-60 Aerostar 600A	60-0563-7961183	ex N8040J	108
C-GRSQ	Piper PA-60 Aerostar 600A	60-0896-8161254	ex N6893S	116
C-GSXX	Ted Smith Aerostar 600A	60-0430-146	ex N9795Q	109
C-GUHK	Piper PA-60 Aerostar 600A	60-0761-8061230	ex N8EA	119
C-GUSZ	Piper PA-60 Aerostar 600A	60-0894-8161253	ex N6893Q	118
C-GUTV	Piper PA-60 Aerostar 600A	60-0722-8061224	ex N8NF	121
C-FCZZ	Rockwell Commander 690A	11106	ex N57106	135
C-GAAL	Rockwell Commander 690A	11104	ex N690AZ	131
C-GDCL	Rockwell Commander 690A	11192		134
C-GHWF	Rockwell Commander 690A	11134	ex N45VT	132
C-GWEW	Rockwell Commander 690	11057	ex N376TC	133
C-FAFG	Cessna 208B Caravan I	208B0724	ex N997Q	
C-GFSK*	Canadair CL-215-1A10	1085	ex C-GKDN	201
C-GFSL*	Canadair CL-215-1A10	1086	ex C-GKDP	202
C-GFSM*	Canadair CL-215-1A10	1098		203
C-GFSN*	Canadair CL-215-1A10	1099		204
C-GHCB	Douglas DC-6B	44893		
C-GHLY	Douglas DC-6B	953/45501	ex OO-VGE	46 Tanker
C-GIBS	Douglas DC-6A/C	1015/45531	ex HB-IBS	51 Tanker
C-GKUG	Douglas DC-6A/B	859/45177	ex N863TA	50 Tanker
C-GSDG	Cessna 208B Caravan I	208B0376	ex N1118P	

*Operated for Alberta Government Air Transportation Services (GOA)

CONFORTAIR

Confort (COF)   *Sept-Iles, Que (YZV)*

C-GAVY	Piper PA-31-350 Navajo Chieftain	31-7752165	ex N27409
C-GBDM	Piper PA-23-250 Aztec	27-7405381	ex N54071

COOPER AIR

Victoria, BC (YWH)

C-GHZP	Cessna A185F Skywagon	18502878	ex N3403R	Floatplane
C-GSAI	Cessna U206G Stationair 6	U20604745	ex N9013N	Floatplane

---

CORILAIR CHARTERS

Whitetown-SPB, BC

C-FWCA	de Havilland DHC-2 Beaver	1285		
C-GACK	de Havilland DHC-2 Beaver	711	ex 53-7903	Lsd fr I&J Logging
C-GTNE	Cessna A185E Skywagon	18501889		

CORPORATE EXPRESS

Penta (CPB)   *Calgary-Intl, Alta (YYC)*

C-FMIP	British Aerospace Jetstream 31	778	ex N778JX	Lsd fr BAES
C-FSAS	British Aerospace Jetstream 31	779	ex N419UE	Lsd fr BAES
C-GKGM	British Aerospace Jetstream 31	727	ex C-FAGM	Lsd fr BAES
C-GXPS	SAAB SF.340A	075	ex N75UW	

Corporate Express is the trading name of Corpac Canada

COUGAR HELICOPTERS

Cougar (CHI)   *Halifax-Waterfront Heliport, NS (YWF)*

C-FDCX	Bell 206B JetRanger II	652	ex N7935J	
C-GFCH	Aerospatiale AS.355F1 TwinStar	5136	ex C-FNML	
C-GKCH	Sikorsky S-76A	760228	ex N117BG	
C-GQCH	Aerospatiale AS.332L Puma	2139	ex LN-OLF	Lsd fr HKS
C-GTCH	Aerospatiale AS.332L Puma	2048	ex LN-OMD	Lsd fr HKS
C-GVCH	Aerospatiale AS.332L Puma	2074	ex LN-OLA	
C-GXCH	Bell 206B JetRanger III	2000	ex N49735	Lsd fr HKS
C-GYCH	Sikorsky S-61N	61762	ex PH-NZI	

COULSON AIRCRANE

Port Alberni, BC (YPB)

C-FBQI	Bell 206B JetRanger II	747		
C-FCLM	Sikorsky S-61N	61492	ex N226BF	Lsd to Pacific H/c as N265F
C-FDYK	Bell 206B JetRanger II	972		
C-FMAG	Sikorsky S-61N	61821	ex N611RM	Lsd to Pacific H/c as N264F
C-FMAY	Sikorsky S-61N	61363	ex N306V	
C-GGHU	Bell 206B JetRanger II	2196		

C-GHHU	Bell 206B JetRanger II	2000	ex N49735
C-GJDR	Sikorsky S-61L Helipro Short	61428	ex N614RM
C-GXOH	Bell 206B JetRanger II	865	ex N14844

COURTESY AIR
Buffalo Narrow, Sask (YVT)

C-FJMF	Beech 99	U-180	ex OY-PAG
C-GDVD	Beech 58 Baron	TH-668	ex N4557S
C-GKLO	Piper PA-31-350 Chieftain	31-8152118	ex N4505N
C-GKNL	Piper PA-31-350 Navajo Chieftain	31-7852083	ex N27607
C-GNRM	Piper PA-31-350 Navajo Chieftain	31-7752145	ex N27315

CROSS LAKE AIR SERVICE now only operate one light Cessna

CROWN CHARTER SERVICES
Brantford, Ont

| C-GBTS | SOCATA TBM-700 | 19 | ex N635DS |
| C-GHRM | Piper PA-31T Cheyenne II | 31T-7620053 | ex N16HA |

Crown Charter Services is a division of Crown Mail and Delivery Services; sister company of Gateway Airlines

CUSTOM HELICOPTERS
Winnipeg-St Andrews, Man

C-FDUV	Bell 206B JetRanger II	70	ex N7883S
C-FJMH	Bell 206B JetRanger II	1331	ex N70711
C-FKBV	Bell 206B JetRanger II	364	ex N465CC
C-FSVG	Bell 206B JetRanger III	2865	ex N1074G
C-GBWN	Bell 206B JetRanger II	2204	
C-GGZS	Bell 206B JetRanger II	1885	
C-GKBU	Bell 206B JetRanger II	386	ex N1448W
C-GQQO	Bell 206B JetRanger II	1096	ex N83182
C-GQQT	Bell 206B JetRanger II	1657	ex N90218
C-GSHJ	Bell 206B JetRanger II	114	ex N125GW
C-GAVH	Bell 206L-1 LongRanger III	45740	ex N385FP
C-GCHI	Bell 206L-1 LongRanger II	45516	ex N141VG
C-GCHZ	Bell 206L-1 LongRanger III	45314	ex N210AH
C-GHUG	Bell 206LR+ LongRanger	45142	ex N286CP
C-GIPG	Bell 206L-1 LongRanger II	45592	ex N3895K
C-GKCW	Bell 206L LongRanger	45122	ex N6139U
C-FCHD	Bell 205A-1	30014	ex N5598M
C-FCHE	Bell 205A-1	30167	ex XA-SSR
C-FCHJ	Aerospatiale AS.350B2 AStar	2603	ex XC-JAK
C-GFHA	Bell 205A-1	30086	ex VH-NHA
C-GRWK	Bell 205A-1	30005	ex N3764U

CYPRESS HELICOPTERS
Bow Island, Alta

C-GIMO	Sikorsky S-58E	58-067	ex N55AR
C-GQCJ	Sikorsky S-58J	58-1097	ex N8292
C-GRNW	Sikorsky S-58E	58-673	ex N41843

DEH CHO AIR ceased operations

DELTA HELICOPTERS
High Level, Alta (YOJ)

C-FCQJ	Bell 206B JetRanger	540	ex N8152J
C-FDYO	Bell 206B JetRanger	994	
C-GDBN	Bell 206B JetRanger III	2467	ex C-GDEN
C-GDJW	Bell 206B JetRanger III	2909	ex N353E
C-GGOZ	Bell 206B JetRanger	443	ex N2162L
C-GPEZ	Bell 206B JetRanger	1130	ex N9JJ
C-GSHN	Bell 206B JetRanger	616	ex N101TF
C-GTIS	Bell 206B JetRanger	827	ex N3YE
C-GWML	Bell 206B JetRanger	269	ex N30AL
C-FAHO	Bell 204B	2060	
C-FKDS	Aerospatiale AS.350BA AStar	2802	ex N6101U
C-FWCL	Aerospatiale AS.350BA AStar	2869	ex C-FWAW
C-GDUK	Bell 204B	2034	ex N636
C-GEOM	Bell 206L-1 LongRanger II	45625	

C-GERI	Bell 206L-1 LongRanger II	45668	
C-GJLV	Bell 204B	2064	ex Thai 918
C-GPGO	Bell 206L-1 LongRanger II	45475	ex N57416
C-GUPH	Aerospatiale AS.350B AStar	1368	ex N99PS
C-GVEX	Bell 204B	2031	ex OY-HBV

DENE CREE AIR

Thompson, Man

C-GYRD	Swearingen SA.226TC Metro II	TC-278	ex N5493M	Jt ops with Perimeter Airways

DERAPS AVIATION

Natashquan, Que (YNA)

C-FLGA	de Havilland DHC-3 Otter	279	
C-GUBN	Cessna U206F Stationair	U20602860	ex (N1185Q)

EAST-WEST TRANSPORTATION

Salmon Arm, BC (YSN)

C-FXNI	Bell 214B-1	28022	ex N214GL
C-GCQT	Bell 206B JetRanger	492	ex N15FD

ENTERPRISE AIR

Oshawa, Ont (YOO)

C-FCLO	Beech E-18S	BA-143	ex N31M	
C-FCRR	Consolidated 28-5ACF Catalina	21996	ex RCAF 9767	Princess des Etoiles
C-FOOW	Douglas DC-3C	13342	ex 8P-OOW	Pacifica Airways
C-FRYZ	Cessna 310J	310J0036	ex G-BPNS	
C-GEAI	Douglas DC-3/TP	33053/16305	ex N200AN	
C-GJMT	Piper PA-31 Turbo Navajo B	31-7400992	ex N614C	

EXPRESSAIR

Gattineau, Ont

C-FKAZ	Cessna 208 Caravan I	20800236	
C-GAWP	Pilatus PC-12/45	187	ex N187PC
C-GCHL	Bell 206B JetRanger III	2082	

FAST AIR

Winnipeg-Intl, Man (YWG)

C-FCAR	Piper PA-31-350 Navajo Chietain	31-7405483	ex N483LA
C-FDGP	Beech 200 Super King Air	BB-1022	ex N220RJ
C-FNWC	Cessna 441 Conquest	441-0216	ex N441DM
C-GFSB	Beech 200 Super King Air	BB-84	
C-GHDP	Beech 200 Super King Air	BB-891	ex N888HG
C-GMDL	Piper PA-31-325 Navajo C/R	31-7512033	ex N775WM
C-GMOB	Piper PA-31-350 Navajo Chieftain	31-7852072	ex N27596
C-GNDI	Piper PA-31T Cheyenne II	31T-7620036	ex N73TB

FIREWEED HELICOPTERS

Whitehorse, YT (YXY)

C-FFWH	Bell 206B JetRanger III	2464	ex N1974T
C-GBJZ	Bell 206B Jet Ranger II	1900	ex N12DY
C-GFWI	Bell 204B	2070	ex C-GEAI

FIRST AIR

(7F/FAB) (IATA 245)   *Carp, Ont/Iqaluit, Nun/Yellowknife, NWT (YRP/YFB/YZF)*

C-FIFA	Boeing 727-225F (FedEx 3)	823/20381	ex N8838E	Lsd to ABR
C-FUFA	Boeing 727-233F (FedEx 3)	1128/20941	ex N727LS	
C-GVFA	Boeing 727-44C (FedEx 3)	854/20475	ex N26879	
C-GXFA	Boeing 727-233F (Raisbeck 3)	1105/20938	ex C-GAAG	
C-GYFA	Boeing 727-2H3F (Raisbeck 3)	1209/21234	ex N724SK	
C-FASG	de Havilland DHC-6 Twin Otter 300	373		floats or wheels/skis
C-FASS	de Havilland DHC-6 Twin Otter 300	362	ex N304EH	floats or wheels/skis
C-FNAN	de Havilland DHC-6 Twin Otter 300	242		floats or wheels/skis

C-FTXQ	de Havilland DHC-6 Twin Otter 300	308	ex N776A	Lsd to Artic Sunwest
C-FUGT	de Havilland DHC-6 Twin Otter 300	382	ex N677A	floats or wheels/skis
				Lsd fr Unaalik Avn

C-GBFA	Hawker Siddeley HS.748 Srs.2B/FAA	1781	ex N117CA	402; stored YRP
C-GDUL	Hawker Siddeley HS.748 Srs.2A/215	1578	ex YV-05C	403
C-GFNW	Hawker Siddeley HS.748 Srs.2A /335LFD	1758	ex 9Y-TFX	405
C-GGNZ	Hawker Siddeley HS.748 Srs.2A/272	1690	ex ZS-SBU	
C-GJVN	Hawker Siddeley HS.748 Srs.2A/209	1640	ex RP-C1018	406
C-GTLD	Hawker Siddeley HS.748 Srs.2A/216	1722	ex PK-IHR	407
C-GYMX	Hawker Siddeley HS.748 Srs.2A/233	1665	ex DQ-FBK	408; stored YRP

C-FIQR	Aerospatiale/Alenia ATR 42-300	133	ex F-WWEE	
C-FIQU	Aerospatiale/Alenia ATR 42-300	138	ex F-WWEK	
C-FNVT	Boeing 737-248C (AvAero 3)	411/21011	ex F-GKTK	
C-FODA	de Havilland DHC-2 Beaver	112		
C-FTCP	Aerospatiale/Alenia ATR 42-300	143	ex F-WWEO	
C-GCFR	de Havilland DHC-7-150	102		Ice recon
C-GHCP	Aerospatiale/Alenia ATR 42-300	123	ex F-WWET	
C-GHPW	Lockheed L-100-30 Hercules	4799		Capt Harry Sorenson
C-GNDC	Boeing 737-242C (AvAero 3)	580/21728		
C-GNWN	Boeing 737-210C	414/21067	ex N4952W	

First Air is the trading name of Bradley Air Services who operate charters using BAR/Bradley callsigns

FLYING TANKERS

Port Alberni-Sproat Lake, BC (YPB)

C-FLYK	Martin JRM-3 Mars	76820	ex Bu76820	Philippine Mars	Tanker
C-FLYL	Martin JRM-3 Mars	76823	ex Bu76823	Hawaii Mars	Tanker
C-FYOA	Cessna 210L Centurion	21060756			

FORDE LAKE AIR SERVICES

Hearst, Ont (YHF)

| C-GGNM | Cessna A185F Skywagon | 18502807 | | Floatplane |
| C-GRAP | de Havilland DHC-2 Beaver | 829 | ex 54-1690 | Floatplane |

FOREST PATROL

Saint John, NB

C-FBED	Ayres S-2R	1767R
C-FBEJ	Ayres S-2R	1768R
C-FZTE	Ayres S-2R	1578R
C-GMQA	Ayres S-2R-T34	T34013
C-GMQB	Ayres S-2R-T34	T34014
C-GMQC	Ayres S-2R-T34	T34015

C-FESS	Bell 407	53129
C-FXZU	Bell 206L-4 LongRanger IV	52164
C-GVDI	Cessna TU206G Stationair 6	U20606490

FOREST PROTECTION

Fredericton, NB (YFC))

C-FFPL	AT-802 Air Tractor	802-0110		620; Sprayer/Tanker
C-FZPV	AT-202 Air Tractor	802-0141	ex N8507T	622; Sprayer
C-GJJK	AT-802 Air Tractor	802-0120		621; Sprayer/Tanker
C-GJJX	AT-802 Air Tractor	802-0121		624; Tanker
C-GZRH	AT-202 Air Tractor	802-0143		623; Sprayer
C-GZUE	AT-202 Air Tractor	802-0147		625; Sprayer

C-FIMR	Grumman TBM-3 Avenger	53610	ex RCN303	23; stored YFC
C-GFPL	Grumman TBM-3E Avenger	86020	ex N7157C	22; stored YFC
C-GFPM	Grumman TBM-3E Avenger	53857	ex N7017C	21; stored YFC
C-GFPS	Grumman TBM-3E Avenger	85460	ex N7032C	3; stored YFC
C-GFPT	Grumman TBM-3E Avenger	53787	ex N3969A	10; stored YFC
C-GLEJ	Grumman TBM-3E Avenger	69323	ex N7961C	24; stored YFC
C-GLEL	Grumman TBM-3 Avenger	53200	ex N9010C	13; stored YFC

C-GJDF	Cessna 337G Super Skymaster	33701516	ex N72488	
C-FIMY	Cessna A188B AgTruck	18801247T	ex N8144G	Sprayer
C-GLFA	Cessna A188B AgTruck	18802222T		Sprayer
C-GMEK	Cessna U206F Stationair II	U20603083	ex N3755C	
C-GMVQ	PZL-Mielec M-18 Dromader	1Z003-03		Sprayer
C-GXJI	Cessna 210J Centurion	21069155	ex N3355S	
C-GXMA	Cessna 337G Super Skymaster	33701644	ex N53468	
C-GXYZ	Cessna 182N Skylane	18260536		

Operated by Government of New Brunswick

FORT FRANCES SPORTSMEN AIRWAYS

Fort Frances, Ont (YAG)

C-GBQC	de Havilland DHC-3 Otter	401	ex RCAF 9420
C-GMDG	de Havilland DHC-3 Otter	302	ex N90575
C-GXWA	Cessna A185F Skywagon	18502491	ex N1772R

All operate on floats or wheels/skis

FUGRO AVIATION CANADA

Ottawa-Rockcliffe, Ont (YRO)

Previously listed as Cargaard Aviation

C-FXCI	Piper PA-31 Turbo Navajo B	31-7300927	ex N255GC	Surveyor
C-FYAU	Cessna 404 Titan II	404-0431	ex N408EX	Surveyor
C-FYTT	Piper PA-31 Turbo Navajo C	31-7512058	ex N700KA	Surveyor
C-FZLK	Cessna 208B Caravan I	208B0569	ex N1210N	Surveyor
C-GAKM	Piper PA-31 Turbo Navajo	31-577	ex N800CM	Surveyor
C-GDPP	CASA 212 Srs 200	CC50-3-265	ex N430CA	Surveyor
C-GEGH	Cessna 421B Golden Eagle	421B0208	ex HC-BZG	Surveyor
C-GNCA	Cessna 208B Caravan I	208B0764	ex N208KC	Surveyor
PR-FAS	Cessna 208B Caravan I	208B0462	ex C-GRCK	Surveyor
P	CASA 212 Srs 200	196	ex C-FDKM	Surveyor

GATEWAY AIRLINES

Brantford, Ont

| C-GDIK | Douglas RD4-8 (C-117D) | 11948/43369 | ex N8538F | |
| C-GGKE | Douglas RD4-8 (C-117D) | 26403/43366 | ex N2577G | stored Brantford |

Gateway Airlines is a division of Crown Mail & Delivery Services; sister company of Crown Charter Services

GEFFAIR CANADA

Montreal-Trudeau, Que (YUL)

C-GDST	Piper PA-31 Turbo Navajo C	31-7612060	ex N59789
C-GIPV	Piper PA-31 Turbo Navao B	31-7300963	ex N7569L
C-GMHZ	Piper PA-31 Turbo Navajo	31-434	ex N712NT

GEORGIAN BAY AIRWAYS

Parry Sound, Ont (YPD)

| C-GBZH | de Havilland DHC-2 Beaver | 1518 | ex HZ-ZAB |

GEORGIAN EXPRESS

Toronto-Buttonville, Ont (YKZ)

C-FFGA	Cessna 208B Caravan I	208B0662	ex N5264E
C-FHGA	Cessna 208B Caravan I	208B0047	ex C-FESH
C-GEGA	Cessna 208B Caravan I	208B0379	ex N1119A
C-GLGA	Cessna 208B Caravan I	208B0350	ex N64AP

Subsidiary of Air Georgian; some operated as freighters for Dynamex

GILLAM AIR SERVICES

Gillam, Man (YGX)

| C-GFZX | Cessna A185F Skywagon | 18503108 | ex (N80245) |
| C-GSAD | Britten-Norman BN-2A-26 Islander | 7 | ex N32JC |

GO AIR EXPRESS

Pembroke, Man (YTA)

| C-GKHB | Beech 1900C | UB-52 | ex N817BE | | Lsd fr KNX |

Subsidiary of KnightHawk Air Express; leased from parent

GOLDAK EXPLORATION TECHNOLOGY

Saskatoon, Sask (YXE)

| C-GJBA | Piper PA-31 Turbo Navajo | 31-159 | ex N9119Y | Surveyer |
| C-GJBB | Piper PA-31 Turbo Navajo | 31-519 | ex N310DS | Surveyer |

GOGAL AIR SERVICE

Snow Lake, Man

CF-ECG	Noorduyn Norseman V	N29-43		Floats or wheels/skis
CF-GLI	Noorduyn Norseman VI	365	ex N88719	Floats or wheels/skis
C-GBAO	Piper PA-31-350 Navajo Chieftain	31-7405234	ex N54309	
C-GCWO	Cessna A185F Skywagon	18503207	ex N93275	Floats or wheels/skis

GREAT SLAVE HELICOPTERS

Yellowknife, NWT (YZF)

C-FGSC	Aerospatiale AS.350BA AStar	3067	
C-FHAF	Aerospatiale AS.350BA Astar	1543	ex N516WW
C-GAVO	Aerospatiale AS.350B3 AStar	3139	ex F-WWOG
C-GGSP	Aerospatiale AS.350B1 AStar	2126	ex N213LA
C-GGSW	Aerospatiale AS.350B2 AStar	2675	
C-GHMZ	Aerospatiale AS.350BA AStar	2325	
C-GIUX	Aerospatiale AS.350BA AStar	1240	ex C-GHRD
C-GRTL	Aerospatiale AS.350BA AStar	1377	ex N577DL
C-GRTM	Aerospatiale AS.350BA AStar	1402	ex C-GAHE
C-FAFL	Bell 206B JetRanger	1256	
C-FGSD	Bell 206B JetRanger	427	ex N83TA
C-FHBH	Bell 206B JetRanger III	3258	ex N904R
C-FHZP	Bell 206B JetRanger	1238	
C-FPQU	Bell 206B JetRanger II	1000	ex N83131
C-FTWM	Bell 206B JetRanger	712	
C-GBAV	Bell 206B JetRanger III	3925	ex N3201R
C-GHPO	Bell 206B JetRanger II	2151	
C-GOMK	Bell 206B JetRanger	1889	
C-GPGF	Bell 206B JetRanger	1836	
C-GTYU	Bell 206B JetRanger II	2144	ex N16627
C-FBFH	Bell 206L-1 LongRanger II	45178	ex N5005G
C-FGSG	Bell 206LR+ LongRanger	45115	ex N405EH
C-FGSL	Bell 206L-1 LongRanger II	45759	ex N3174L
C-GFEG	Bell 206L LongRanger	45150	ex N71JH
C-GHBY	Bell 206LR+ LongRanger	45109	ex N402EH
C-GRFZ	Bell 206L-1 LongRanger II	45610	
C-GSHL	Bell 206L LongRanger	45092	ex N16751
C-GGSM	Bell 212	30741	ex N49676
C-GGSO	Bell 212	30696	ex N90220
C-GKTL	Bell 212	32124	ex A6-BBX
C-GRTN	Eurocopter EC.120B Colibri	1058	
C-GVEL	Bell 204B	2197	ex OY-HCA
C-GVVI	Bell 204B	2196	ex N1304X

GREEN AIRWAYS

Red Lake, Ont (YRL)

C-FLEA	de Havilland DHC-3 Otter	286		PZL engined
C-FOBE	Noorduyn UC-64A Norseman	480	ex 43-35406	
C-FODJ	de Havilland DHC-3 Otter	14		
C-FVIA	de Havilland DHC-2 Beaver	714	ex N9047U	
C-GEZU	de Havilland DHC-2 Beaver	647	ex 53-8159	
C-GEZW	de Havilland DHC-2 Beaver	1217	ex 57-6138	
C-GYUY	Cessna A185F Skywagon	18503731	ex (N8550Q)	

All operate on floats or wheels/skis

GRONDAIR

St Frederic, Que

C-FNNM	Cessna TR182RG Skylane	R18200946	ex N738NR
C-FQTA	Cessna R182RG Skylane	R18200324	ex N4107C
C-FQTC	Cessna R182RG Skylane	R18201717	ex N4608T
C-FRGN	Cessna R182RG Skyland	R18200394	ex N9083C
C-FRYF	Cessna R182RG Skylane	R18201001	ex N65ET
C-FRYP	Cessna R182RG Skylane	R18200479	ex N9879C
C-FRZE	Cessna R182RG Skylane	R18200197	ex N2657C
C-GCJA	Cessna R182RG Skylane	R18201219	
C-GHVC	Cessna R182RG Skylane	R18201886	ex N5532T
C-GOAL	Cessna TR182RG Skylane	R18201127	
C-GRUA	Cessna R182RG Skylane	R18200077	ex N7325X
C-GSCF	Cessna R182RG Skylane	R18201257	ex N757QM
C-GVCV	Cessna R182RG Skylane	R18200030	ex N7343T
C-GWRJ	Cessna TR182RG Skylane	R18211740	ex N736MG

C-FHWI	Beech 65-A90 King Air	LJ-309	ex N329H
C-FNCN	Beech 65-B90 King Air	LJ-468	ex N1FC
C-GAST	Cessna 310R	310R0730	ex N5009J
C-GBRC	Cessna 310R	310R1284	ex N6116X
C-GJGW	Cessna 310R	310R0960	ex N37200
C-GSRW	Piper PA-31 Turbo Navajo	31-262	ex N707FR
C-GUMQ	Piper PA-31 Turbo Navajo	31-84	ex N777GS

HARBOUR AIR SEAPLANES

(H3) (IATA 458)   Vancouver-CoalHarbour, BC (CXH)

C-FAOP	de Havilland DHC-2 Beaver	1249		
C-FAXI	de Havilland DHC-2 Beaver	1514	ex N6535D	
C-FFHQ	de Havilland DHC-2 Beaver	42		
C-FIFQ	de Havilland DHC-2 Beaver	825		
C-FJFQ	de Havilland DHC-2 Beaver	963		
C-FJOS	de Havilland DHC-2 Beaver	1030		
C-FKDC	de Havilland DHC-2 Beaver	1080		
C-FMXS	de Havilland DHC-2 Beaver	1010	ex N43882	
C-FOCN	de Havilland DHC-2 Beaver	44		
C-FOCY	de Havilland DHC-2 Beaver	79		
C-FOCZ	de Havilland DHC-2 Beaver	100	ex N254BD	
C-FOSP	de Havilland DHC-2 Beaver	1501	ex N2961	
C-FTCW	de Havilland DHC-2 Beaver	646	ex VH-SMH	
C-GCYM	de Havilland DHC-2 Beaver	354	ex N63PS	Floatplane
C-GYOK	de Havilland DHC-2 Beaver	677	ex N5152G	
C-FHAA	de Havilland DHC-3 Turbo Otter	357	ex C-GIWT	
C-FIUZ	de Havilland DHC-3 Turbo Otter	135	ex F-OAKK	
C-FODH	de Havilland DHC-3 Turbo Otter	3		
C-FRNO	de Havilland DHC-3 Turbo Otter	21	ex N128F	
C-GHAR	de Havilland DHC-3 Turbo Otter	42	ex N234KA	
C-GHAS	de Havilland DHC-3 Turbo Otter	284	ex (N)	
C-GLCP	de Havilland DHC-3 Otter	422	ex N17682	
C-GOPP	de Havilland DHC-3 Turbo Otter	355	ex N53KA	
C-GUTW	de Havilland DHC-3 Turbo Otter	405	ex CAF 9423	
C-GVNL	de Havilland DHC-3 Turbo Otter	105	ex N5341G	
C-GQDS	Cessna A185FSkywagon	18503754	ex (N8631Q)	
C-GYZK	Cessna 180K	18052864	ex (N64034)	
C-GZSH	Cessna A185F Skywagon	18503482	ex (N1463Q)	

All floatplanes
Leases de Havilland DHC-6 Twin Otters from Kenn Borek in summers

HARBOUR CITY HELICOPTERS ceased operations

HAWK AIR

(BH)   Wawa-Hawk Junction, Ont (YXZ)

C-FBBG	de Havilland DHC-2 Beaver	358-173	ex N2848D	Floatplane
C-FQMN	de Havilland DHC-3 Otter	184	ex N2959W	Floatplane
C-GPPL	de Havilland DHC-3 Otter	7	ex BM-1004	Floatplane

HAWKAIR AVIATION SERVICES

Terrace, BC (YXT)

C-FCJE	de Havilland DHC-8-102	165		Lsd fr IMP Group
C-FDNG	de Havilland DHC-8-102	166		Lsd fr IMP Group
C-GJVB	de Havilland DHC-8-102	046	ex 142802	Lsd fr Field Avn
C-GYQS	Bristol 170 Freighter 31	13060	ex ZK-EPD	for sale

HAYES HELI-LOG SERVICES

Duncan, BC (DUQ)

C-FBHG	Bell 206B JetRanger II	713		
C-FHHD	Sikorsky S-61N	61490	ex ZS-HDK	
C-FHHM	Sikorsky S-61N	61408	ex C-FZLU	
C-FHHR	Sikorsky S-61L	61033	ex C-FZLS	
C-GHHF	Bell 206B JetRanger III	3311	ex C-FNHL	
C-GHHT	Bell 206B JetRanger III	2869	ex C-GFKD	
C-GPCT	Bell 206B JetRanger III	3085		

HEARST AIR SERVICE

Hearst, Ont (YHF)

C-FBTU	de Havilland DHC-2 Beaver	1564	Floats or wheels/skis
C-FDPM	de Havilland DHC-2 Beaver	1247	Floats or wheels/skis

HELICOPTER TRANSPORT SERVICES

C-FCTV	Bell 206B JetRanger	690	ex C-FQCL
C-GIOB	Bell 206B JetRanger III	603	ex N678KG
C-GJHX	Bell 206B JetRanger	754	ex N2941W
C-GJWL	Bell 206B JetRanger III	3660	ex N3171N
C-GQMR	Bell 206B JetRanger II	2207	
C-FDDS	Bell 206L-1 LongRanger II	45773	ex C-FSUE
C-FLRU	Bell 206L-1 LongRanger II	45402	ex G-CINE
C-FLTX	Bell 206LR+ LongRanger	45043	ex N96AT
C-FWGN	Bell 206L-4 LongRanger IV	52010	ex N2292Z
C-GOVB	Bell 206L-1 LongRanger II	45162	
C-FPAZ	Bell 205A-1	30016	ex N1347N
C-GAHZ	Bell 212	30758	ex N5306T
C-GFFY	Bell 205A-1	30123	ex N1084C
C-GSIT	Bell 205A-1	30120	ex N42113

HELIFOR INDUSTRIES

C-FHFB	Boeing Vertol 234UT Chinook	MJ005	ex N238CH	Lsd fr WCO
C-FHFV	Boeing Vertol 107-II	4	ex N6674D	Lsd fr WCO
C-FHFW	Boeing Vertol 107-II	107	ex N189CH	Lsd fr WCO
C-GHFF	Boeing Vertol 107-II	406	ex N195CH	Lsd fr WCO
C-GHFT	Boeing Vertol 107-II	402	ex N193CH	Lsd fr WCO
C-GHFY	Boeing Vertol 107-II	2002	ex N190CH	

HELIJET INTERNATIONAL AIRWAYS

Helijet (JB/JBA)

C-GHJL	Sikorsky S-76A II	760214	ex N101PB	EMS
C-GHJP	Sikorsky S-76A II	760065	ex (C-GHJT)	
C-GHJT	Sikorsky S-76A	760052	ex VH-XHZ	
C-GHJW	Sikorsky S-76A II	760074	ex N586C	
C-FHJJ	Aerospatiale AS.355F1 TwinStar	5053	ex N442PT	
C-GHJG	Aerospatiale AS.350B AStar	1123	ex C-GDWH	
C-GTDF	Aerospatiale AS.355F1 TwinStar	5161	ex N5795M	
C-GZPM	Bell 206B JetRanger II	880	ex N2NU	

HELI-LIFT INTERNATIONAL

C-GMOR	Bell 205A-1	30159	ex LX-HOR
C-GQCW	Aerospatiale AS.350D AStar	1255	ex N3607T
C-GSHK	Bell 204B	2067	ex Thai 920

HELIQWEST AVIATION

C-FHQK	Bell 205A-1	30142	ex C-GXLF
C-FHQT	Bell 204B	2024	ex C-GEAV
C-GEAK	Bell 205A-1	30183	ex N393EH
C-GEAT	Bell 205A-1	30088	ex G-BKGH

HICKS & LAWRENCE

C-FMUM	Rockwell Shrike Commander 500S	3103	ex N37GW	
C-GAYR	Rockwell Shrike Commander 500S	3118	ex N9170N	
C-GETH	Rockwell Shrike Commander 500S	1800-15	ex N732	
C-GETJ	Rockwell Shrike Commander 500S	3275	ex N81450	
C-GETK	Aero Commander 500B	1093-56	ex N102PJ	
C-GIZV	Aero Commander 500B	1440-155	ex N678GH	
C-GJLO	Aero Commander 500S	1796-11	ex	
C-GJMA	Aero Commander 500B	1319-128	ex N330U	
C-FHNL	Rockwell Commander 690B	11477	ex N690SB	
C-FIET	Ayres S-2R	1523R		
C-FNJB	Consolidated PBY-5A Canso	CV-249	ex RCAF 9815	Tanker
C-FIXO	Cessna 337H Super Skymaster II	33701820	ex N1328L	
C-GEOR	Cessna 337G Super Skymaster II	33701730	ex (N53595)	

C-GFSC	Cessna 337G Super Skymaster II	33701793	ex N53699
C-GIOG	Cessna 337G Super Skymaster II	33701746	ex (N53638)
C-GWDU	Cessna 337G Super Skymaster II	3370665	

HIGHLAND HELICOPTERS

Vancouver-Intl, BC (YVR)

C-FHHC	Aerospatiale AS.350B2 AStar	2569	ex N2PW
C-FHHY	Aerospatiale AS.350B2 AStar	1650	ex C-GSKI
C-FJHH	Aerospatiale AS.350B-2 AStar	3279	
C-FKHH	Aerospatiale AS.350B2 AStar	2736	
C-FYYA	Aerospatiale AS.350B2 AStar	2295	ex ZK-HOU
C-GBHH	Aerospatiale AS.350B2 AStar	3180	
C-GHHH	Aerospatiale AS.350B2 AStar	3270	
C-GHHW	Aerospatiale AS.350B2 AStar	3039	
C-GHHZ	Aerospatiale AS.350B2 AStar	3054	
C-GNHH	Aerospatiale AS.350B2 AStar	2737	ex N9446H
C-GSHH	Aerospatiale AS.350B2 AStar	3192	
C-FCDL	Bell 206B JetRanger III	3852	ex N93AJ
C-FCOY	Bell 206B JetRanger III	3280	ex N7023J
C-FHHB	Bell 206B JetRanger	519	
C-FHHI	Bell 206B JetRanger III	2310	ex N101CD
C-GHHD	Bell 206B JetRanger II	1566	ex N90003
C-GHHG	Bell 206B JetRanger II	1396	ex N918TR
C-GHHM	Bell 206B JetRanger II	2712	
C-GHHO	Bell 206B JetRanger II	1690	
C-GHHR	Bell 206B JetRanger II	1963	
C-GHHX	Bell 206B JetRanger II	2714	
C-GHXJ	Bell 206B JetRanger II	1832	
C-GIZO	Bell 206B JetRanger III	2715	
C-GJJA	Bell 206B JetRanger II	2032	ex N9958K
C-GKDG	Bell 206B JetRanger III	2969	
C-GKGI	Bell 206B JetRanger II	1790	ex N49629
C-GKJL	Bell 206B JetRanger III	3005	
C-GMDQ	Bell 206B JetRanger III	3045	
C-GMDX	Bell 206B JetRanger III	3032	
C-GMXE	Bell 206B JetRanger II	1109	ex N58144
C-GMZH	Bell 206B JetRanger III	3203	
C-GNLT	Bell 206B JetRanger III	2973	
C-GNSQ	Bell 206B JetRanger III	3274	
C-GOPF	Bell 206B JetRanger III	3227	
C-GOPK	Bell 206B JetRanger III	3247	
C-FTHH	Bell 206L-3 LongRanger III	51369	
C-GLHH	Bell 206L-3 LongRanger III	51517	

HMY AIRWAYS
Harmony (HQ/HMY)

Vancouver-Intl, BC (YVR)

C-GMYC	Boeing 757-258	152/23917	ex N789BA	Lsd fr Boeing A/c Holding
C-GMYD	Boeing 757-258	185/24254	ex N73724	802	Lsd fr Boeing A/c Holding
C-GMYH	Boeing 757-236	358/25063	ex N253CT	Lsd fr OT Leasing

HORNE AIR

Hornepayne, Ont (YHN)

C-FFHP	de Havilland DHC-2 Beaver	57		Floatplane
C-FIDM	de Havilland DHC-2 Beaver	1323	ex N99871	Floatplane
C-GEWG	de Havilland DHC-2 Beaver	842	ex N87572	Floatplane

HURON AIR AND OUTFITTERS

Armstrong, Ont (YYW)

C-FDPW	de Havilland DHC-2 Beaver	1339	ex 58-2011	Floats or wheels/skis
C-FGSR	Noorduyn Norseman V	N29-47		Floatplane
C-GOFF	de Havilland DHC-3 Otter	65	ex RCAF 3698	Floatplane

HYDRO-QUEBEC (SERVICE TRANSPORT AÉRIEN)
Ampere (APZ)

Montreal-Trudeau, Que (YUL)

C-GHQZ	de Havilland DHC-8-314	370	ex OE-LLY	Op by AIE
C-GJNL	de Havilland DHC-8-311	422	ex G-BXPZ	Op by AIE
C-GHOQ	de Havilland DHC-8Q-402	4003	ex C-FPJH	Op by AIE
C-GHQP	de Havilland DHC-8Q-402	4004	ex C-GIHK	Op by AIE

Used to fly engineers and equipment to remote sites

ICARUS FLYING SERVICE

Ile de la Madelaine, Que (YGR)

C-GFBF	Britten-Norman BN-2B-27 Islander	2125	ex VP-FBF

IGNACE AIRWAYS

Ignace/Thunder Bay, Ont (ZUC/YQT)

C-FAPR	de Havilland DHC-3 Otter	31	ex LN-LMM
CF-TTL	Cessna U206C Super Skywagon	U206-1062	ex N29088
C-GZBR	de Havilland DHC-2 Beaver	1272	ex N434GR
All floatplanes			

INLAND AIR CHARTERS

Prince Rupert, BC (YPR)

C-FGQC	de Havilland DHC-2 Beaver	75	
C-FIAX	de Havilland DHC-2 Beaver	140	ex VH-AAD
C-FJPX	de Havilland DHC-2 Beaver	1076	
C-FRHW	de Havilland DHC-3 Otter	445	ex 5N-ABN
C-GYJX	Cessna A185F Skywagon	18503187	ex (N93161)
All floatplanes			

INTERNATIONAL EXPRESS AIR CHARTER

Norvan (VL/NRV)   *Vancouver-Intl, BC (YVR)*
Previously listed as North Vancouver Air

C-FLGW	Piper PA-31 Turbo Navajo	31-557	ex N6622L
C-GDJR	Piper PA-31 Turbo Navajo	31-289	ex N9223Y
C-GNVB	Beech A100 King Air	B-143	ex N151U

ISLAND WEST AIR

Courtenay, BC (YCA)

C-FDTV	de Havilland DHC-2 Beaver	34	ex C-FDTC
C-FSCM	de Havilland DHC-2 Beaver	1583	
C-GMKG	de Havilland DHC-2 Beaver	1248	ex N8772Z
C-GYMW	Britten-Norman BN-2A-26 Islander	88	ex D-IFDS

JACKSON AIR SERVICES

Jackson (JCK)   *Flin Flon, Man (YFO)*

C-FFVZ	de Havilland DHC-3 Otter	145	ex N80944	Floats or wheels/skis
C-FWEJ	de Havilland DHC-3 Otter	208	ex IM1710	Floats or wheels/skis
C-GADE	de Havilland DHC-2 Beaver	730	ex 53-7919	Floats or wheels/skis
C-GDYR	de Havilland DHC-2 Beaver	18503018		Floats or wheels/skis
C-GGGT	Cessna TU206G Stationair 6	U206-04170	ex N756LF	
C-GISX	Cessna A185F Skywagon	18503836	ex N4669E	Floats or wheels/skis
C-GJMZ	Partenavia P.68B	369-27-OB		
C-GWHW	Piper PA-31-350 Chieftain	31-8052060	ex N233CH	

JAZZ AIR now correctly listed as Air Canada Jazz

JETPORT

Hamilton, Ont (YHM)

C-FAMF	Swearingen SA.226T Merlin IIIA	T-274	ex I-SWAA
C-FHRB	Cessna 208 Caravan I	20800291	
C-GRJZ	Beech Super King Air 350	FL-285	ex N3185J

JETSGO

(SG/JGO)   *Toronto-Pearson Intl, Ont (YYZ)*

C-FKLI	McDonnell-Douglas MD-83	1793/49941	ex N881RA	Lsd fr Aero USA
C-FKLO	McDonnell-Douglas MD-83	2091/53464	ex F-GRMG	
C-FKLT	McDonnell-Douglas MD-83	2089/53463	ex F-GGMF	
C-FKLY	McDonnell-Douglas MD-83	2093/53465	ex F-GRMH	
C-FKLZ	McDonnell-Douglas MD-83	2101/53466	ex F-GRMC	
C-FRYA	McDonnell-Douglas MD-83	2134/53488	ex F-GRMI	
C-GKLC	McDonnell-Douglas MD-83	2114/53468	ex N228BA	Lsd fr Boeing A/c Holding
C-GKLE	McDonnell-Douglas MD-83	1887/49943	ex F-GPZA	
C-GKLJ	McDonnell-Douglas MD-83	2102/53467	ex N73729	Lsd fr Boeing A/c Holding

C-GKLK	McDonnell-Douglas MD-83	1991/53124	ex N834RA	Lsd fr JP Morgan Trust
C-GKLN	McDonnell-Douglas MD-83	2130/53486	ex N705BA	Lsd fr Boeing A/c Holding
C-GKLQ	McDonnell-Douglas MD-83	2132/53487	ex N227BA	Lsd fr Boeing A/c Holding
C-GKLR	McDonnell-Douglas MD-83	2116/53469	ex N224BA	Lsd fr Boeing A/c Holding

JOHNNY MAY'S AIR CHARTER

Kuujjuaq, Que (YVP)

C-FCEE	de Havilland DHC-3 Otter	282	ex 57-6134	
C-FLAP	de Havilland DHC-3 Otter	289		
C-GMAY	de Havilland DHC-2 Beaver	1123	ex 56-0393	Pengo Pallee

All operate on floats or wheels/skis

JUAN AIR

Juan Air   *Victoria, BC (YYJ)*

| C-GRJA | Piper PA-31-350 Navajo Chieftain | 31-7952154 | ex N35282 |
| C-GXPC | Piper PA-34-220T Seneca | 34-7970234 | ex N29076 |

KABEELO AIRWAYS

Confederation Lake, Ont (YMY)

| C-GDYT | de Havilland DHC-2 Beaver | 1109 | ex 56-4403 | Floatplane |
| C-GLSA | de Havilland DHC-2 Beaver | 1389 | ex N94471 | Floatplane |

KAYAIR

Ear Falls, Ont (YMY)

| CF-TBH | Beech 3T | 6226 | ex RCAF HB210 | Floats |

KD AIR

Kay Dee (XC/KDC)   *Port Alberni, BC (YPB)*

| C-GPCA | Piper PA-31 Turbo Navajo | 31-42 | ex N333DG |
| C-GXEY | Piper PA-31-350 Navajo Chieftain | 31-7305044 | ex N74910 |

KEEWATIN AIR

(FK)   *Churchill, Man/Rankin Inlet, Nun (YYQ /YRT)*

C-FCGT	Beech 200 Super King Air	BB-159/8	ex N47FH	EMS; Cat Pass 200 conv
C-FICU	Learjet 35A	35A-249	ex N300DA	EMS Critical Care
C-FZPW	Beech B200 Super King Air	BB-940	ex N519SA	EMS
C-GAJS	Learjet 35A	35A-380	ex N903WJ	EMS Critical Care

Some services are operated as Kivalliq Air with Pilatus PC-12s

KELOWNA FLIGHTCRAFT AIR CHARTER

Flighcraft (KW/KFA)   *Kelowna (YLW)*

C-FKFP	Boeing 727-22C (FedEx 3)	438/19205	ex N109FE	703	Lsd to TSU as N231FL
C-FPKF	Boeing 727-223 (Raisbeck 3)	1473/21524	ex N885AA		
C-GACU*	Boeing 727-225F (Duganair 3)	775/20152	ex N8833E	710	Op for Purolator Courier
C-GGKF	Boeing 727-223 (Raisbeck 3)	1467/21523	ex C-FMKF		
C-GIKF	Boeing 727-227F (FedEx 3)	982/20772	ex N99763	721	Op for Purolator Courier
C-GJKF	Boeing 727-227F (FedEx 3)	1106/21042	ex N10756	722	Op for Purolator Courier
C-GKFA	Boeing 727-22C (FedEx 3)	547/19806	ex N110FE	704	Op for Purolator Courier
C-GKFC	Boeing 727-22C (Duganair 3)	211/18897	ex OB-R-1115	701	Op for Purolator Courier
C-GKFH	Boeing 727-225F (Duganair 3)	779/20153	ex N8834E	711	Op for Purolator Courier
C-GKFN	Boeing 727-25C (Duganair 3)	368/19359	ex N123FE	706	Op for Purolator Courier
C-GKFZ	Boeing 727-22C (FedEx 3)	436/19204	ex N108FE	707	Op for Purolator Courier
C-GKKF	Boeing 727-227F (FedEx 3)	1113/21043	ex N16758	723	Op for Purolator Courier
C-GLKF	Boeing 727-227F (FedEx 3)	1167/21118	ex N14760	724	Op for Purolator Courier
C-GMKF	Boeing 727-227F (FedEx 3)	1175/21119	ex N16761	725	Op for Purolator Courier
C-GNKF	Boeing 727-227F (FedEx 3)	1031/20839	ex N88770	726	Op for Purolator Courier
C-GQKF	Boeing 727-243 (FedEx 3)	1226/21265	ex N17402	720	Op for Purolator Courier
C-GTKF	Boeing 727-225F (FedEx 3)	1435/21580	ex N8883Z	728	Op for Purolator Courier

*Leased from International Air Leases

C-FCIB	Convair 580	327A	ex N8444H		Lsd to CVA as ZK-CIB
C-FEKF	Convair 580	80	ex C-GEVB	Tanker 45	Lsd to CRC
C-FFKF	Convair 580	179	ex C-GEVC	Tanker 44	Lsd to CRC
C-FHKF	Convair 580	374	ex C-GEUZ	Tanker 55	Lsd to CRC
C-FIWN	Convair 580	126	ex N5816		Lsd to Platinum A/L
C-FKFA	Convair 580	100	ex C-FLVY	507	Lsd to CRC

C-FKFB	Convair 580	57	ex N568JA		
C-FKFL	Convair 580	465	ex C-FZQS		Lsd to CRC
C-FKFM	Convair 580	70	ex N73133	Tanker 54	Lsd to CRC
C-FKFS	Convair 5800	276/004	ex N14094		
C-FKFZ	Convair 580	151	ex N11151	510	
C-GKFF	Convair 580	160	ex N9067R	511	Op for Purolator Courier
C-GKFG	Convair 580	22	ex N32KA	516 wfs YLW	
C-GKFO	Convair 580	78	ex N5815	Tanker 53	Lsd to CRC
C-GKFP	Convair 580	446	ex N589PL	514 Woolaston Lake Resort c/s	
C-GKFQ	Convair 580	86	ex N73136	505	Lsd Gulf & Caribbean
C-GKFU	Convair 580	82	ex N90857	516	Op for Purolator Courier
	Convair 580	34	ex N538JA		
	Convair 580	69	ex N569JA		
C-GIHM	Cessna 402B	402B0203	ex N7875Q		Op for Purolator Courier
C-GJRH	Cessna 340	340-0058	ex N340BD		
C-GKFX	Beech A60 Duke	P-235	ex N60GF		
G-XLAE	Boeing 737-8Q8	800/30637	ex D-ABAA		Lsd fr XLA

KENN BOREK AIR

Borek Air (4K/KBA)   Calgary-Intl, Alta/Edmonton-Intl, Alta/ Iqalut, Nun/Resolute Bay, Nun (YYC/YEG/YFB/YRB)

C-FAKB	de Havilland DHC-6 Twin Otter 300	273	ex 8Q-MAD	
C-FBBA*	de Havilland DHC-6 Twin Otter 300	276	ex 8Q-MAK	Lsd as 8Q-MAK
C-FBBV	de Havilland DHC-6 Twin Otter 300	311	ex C-FMPC	
C-FBBW	de Havilland DHC-6 Twin Otter 300	588	ex C-GMPX	
C-FBKB*	de Havilland DHC-6 Twin Otter 300	611	ex 5N-AJR	Lsd as 8Q-MAQ
C-FCSL*	de Havilland DHC-6 Twin Otter 100	64	ex 8Q-CSL	
C-FDHB	de Havilland DHC-6 Twin Otter 300	338		
C-FKBI*	de Havilland DHC-6 Twin Otter 300	259	ex HP-1197APP	Lsd as 8Q-MAO
C-FMYV*	de Havilland DHC-6 Twin Otter 300	374	ex 8Q-MAH	Lsd as 8Q-MAH
C-FOEQ*	de Havilland DHC-6 Twin Otter 100	44	ex 8Q-OEQ	Lsd as 8Q-OEQ
C-FPOQ*	de Havilland DHC-6 Twin Otter 300	464	ex 8Q-MAE	Lsd as 8Q-MAE
C-FQBU*	de Havilland DHC-6 Twin Otter 100	99	ex 8Q-QBU	Lsd as 8Q-QBU
C-FQHC*	de Havilland DHC-6 Twin Otter 100	21	ex N1370T	Lsd as 8Q-QHC
C-FSJB	de Havilland DHC-6 Twin Otter 300	377	ex N4901D	
C-GBBU*	de Havilland DHC-6 Twin Otter 300	321	ex 8Q-MAL	Lsd as 8Q-MAL
C-GCGW*	de Havilland DHC-6 Twin Otter 300	434	ex N927MA	Lsd Sun Express as 8Q-SUM
C-GCKB	de Havilland DHC-6 Twin Otter 300	312	ex C-FMPF	
C-GDHC	de Havilland DHC-6 Twin Otter 300	494		
C-GKBC	de Havilland DHC-6 Twin Otter 300	650	ex N55921	
C-GKBG	de Havilland DHC-6 Twin Otter 300	733		
C-GKBH	de Havilland DHC-6 Twin Otter 300	732	ex G-BIEM	
C-GKBM*	de Havilland DHC-6 Twin Otter 300	279	ex 8Q-MAI	
C-GKBO	de Havilland DHC-6 Twin Otter 300	725	ex HP-1273APP	
C-GKBR*	de Havilland DHC-6 Twin Otter 300	617	ex HP-1167APP	
C-GKBV*	de Havilland DHC-6 Twin Otter 300	287	ex 8Q-MAB	Lsd as 8Q-MAB
C-GKBX*	de Havilland DHC-6 Twin Otter 300	571	ex VP-LVT	Lsd as 8Q-MAP
C-GKCS*	de Havilland DHC-6 Twin Otter 300	693	ex 8Q-MAA	Lsd as 8Q-MAA
C-GNTA*	de Havilland DHC-6 Twin Otter 300	146	ex 8Q-NTA	Lsd as 8Q-NTA
C-GOKB*	de Havilland DHC-6 Twin Otter 300	339	ex 8Q-MAM	Lsd as 8Q-MAM
C-GPAO	de Havilland DHC-6 Twin Otter 300	447	ex N5356A	
C-GTKB*	de Havilland DHC-6 Twin Otter 100	60	ex 8Q-MAC	Lsd as 8Q-MAC
C-GXXB	de Havilland DHC-6 Twin Otter 300	426	ex 8Q-MAN	
C-GZVH	de Havilland DHC-6 Twin Otter 300	671	ex HZ-FO2	

*Leased to Maldivian Air Taxi

C-FAFD	Beech 100 King Air	B-42	ex LN-VIP
C-GAVI	Beech A100 King Air	B-201	ex G-BBVM
C-GHOC	Beech A100 King Air	B-194	ex N57237
C-GKBQ	Beech 100 King Air	B-62	ex LN-NLB
C-GKBZ	Beech 100 King Air	B-85	ex LN-PAJ
C-GWWA	Beech 100 King Air	B-27	ex G-BOFN

C-FBCN	Beech 200 Super King Air	BB-7		
C-FCXQ	Cessna A185F Skywagon	18502235	ex N4350Q	
C-FKBK	Beech 99	U-18	ex HP-1233APP	
C-FKBU	Beech 200 Super King Air	BB-285	ex C-GQXF	
C-FLKB	Embraer EMB.110P1 Bandeirante	110397	ex N903LE	
C-FQHF	Douglas DC-3C	13392		
C-GFKB	Embraer EMB.110P1 Bandeirante	110400	ex 9N-AFF	
C-GGKG	Douglas DC-3 (C-117D)	43354	ex N2071X	Lsd to Aklak Air
C-GKBA	Beech B99	U-164	ex SE-GRB	
C-GKBB	Beech 65-C90 King Air	LJ-607	ex N48DA	
C-GKBN	Beech 200 Super King Air	BB-29	ex LN-ASG	
C-GKBP	Beech 200 Super King Air	BB-505	ex HP-1083P	
C-GKKB	Beech B99	U-149	ex HP-1230APP	
C-GSFM	Beech 65-B90 King Air	LJ-422	ex N513SC	Lsd to UNHCR

Leases de Havilland DHC-6 Twin Otters to Harbour Air in summers

KENORA AIR SERVICE

Kenora-SPB, Ont (YQK)

C-FWDB	Cessna A185E Skywagon	185-1250	ex (N4783Q)	
C-FWMM	Cessna A185F Skywagon	18502238	ex N4361Q	
C-GDQJ	Cessna A185F Skywagon	18503370		
C-GYJY	Cessna A185F Skywagon	18502468	ex N1748R	
C-GYXY	Cessna A185F Skywagon	18503370		
CF-CBA	de Havilland DHC-3 Otter	230	ex C-FCBA	
CF-JEI	de Havilland DHC-2 Beaver	1020		
C-FNOT	de Havilland DHC-2 Beaver	1067	ex N4193A	
CF-TBX	Beech D-18S	A-479	ex N481B	
C-GCQK	de Havilland DHC-3 Otter	141	ex N80939	
C-GIGZ	de Havilland DHC-3 Otter	183	ex OB-1253	PZL engined

All floatplanes

KEYSTONE AIR SERVICE

Keystone (BZ/KEE)   *Swan River, Man (YSE)*

C-FPCD	Beech B99	U-151	ex C-FBRO
C-FXLO	Piper PA-31-350 Chieftain	31-8052022	ex N3547N
C-GBDN	Piper PA-31-350 Navajo Chieftain	31-7652035	ex N59763
C-GCJH	Piper PA-31-350 Navajo Chieftain	31-7952109	ex N42FL
C-GFOL	Beech 200 Super King Air	BB-27	ex N120DP
C-GGQU	Piper PA-31 Turbo Navajo	31-155	ex N9116Y
C-GRUH	Piper PA-34-200 Seneca	34-7350118	ex N16254

KEYWINDS AIR

Little Rapids, Man

C-GMGD	de Havilland DHC-2 Beaver	519	ex N87091

KISSISSING AIR

Kississing Lake/Pine Falls, Man

C-FENB	Noorduyn UC-64A Norseman	324	ex 43-5384
C-GDLO	Cessna TU206B Super Skywagon	U206-0690	ex N4990F

KIVALLIQ AIR

Winnipeg-Intl, Man/Rankin Islet, Nun (YWG/YRT)

C-FYZS	Pilatus PC-12/45	227	ex N227PB
C-GKNR	Pilatus PC-12/45	308	ex HB-FQV
C-GVKC	Pilatus PC-12/45	207	ex ZS-OEV

Division of Keewatin Air

KLAHANIE AIR

Mission, BC

C-FJFL	de Havilland DHC-2 Beaver	898	Floats or wheels/skis

KLUANE AIRWAYS

Whitehorse, YT (YXY)

C-FHAS	de Havilland DHC-3 Otter	382
C-FMPS	de Havilland DHC-2 Beaver	1114

Both operate on floats or wheels/skis

KNEE LAKE AIR SERVICE

Knee Lake, Man (YKE)

C-FKLR	Cessna 208 Caravan I	20800223	ex N899A
C-GMGV	de Havilland DHC-2 Beaver	432	ex N62278

KNIGHTHAWK AIR EXPRESS

Knight Flite (KNX)   *Hamilton, Ont (YHM)*

C-FONX	AMD Falcon 20D	225	ex N102AD	Freighter	
C-GKHA	AMD Falcon 20C	19	ex N41PC	Freighter	
C-GKHB	Beech 1900C	UB-52	ex N817BE		Lsd to Go Air

| C-GRSD | AMD Falcon 20C | 157 | ex C-GRSD-X | Freighter |
| C-GTAK | AMD Falcon 20D | 197 | ex N399SW | Freighter |

All freighters operate services for Airborne Express; Go Air Express is a wholly owned subsidiary
Filed for bankruptcy protection in early January 2004

LABRADOR AIR SAFARI

Baie Comeau, Que (YBC)

C-FAZW	de Havilland DHC-3 Otter	451	ex JW-9101
C-FBEU	de Havilland DHC-3 Otter	119	ex 55-3273
C-FJZN	de Havilland DHC-3 Otter	205	
C-GLJI	de Havilland DHC-3 Otter	150	ex 55-3297
C-GVNX	de Havilland DHC-3 Otter	353	ex N5335G
C-FJGV	de Havilland DHC-2 Beaver	977	
C-FPQC	de Havilland DHC-2 Beaver	873	ex CF-IKQ
C-FYYT	de Havilland DHC-2 Beaver	1569	ex VH-IDZ
C-GUJQ	Cessna A185F Skywagon	18503048	ex (N20913)
C-GWAE	de Havilland DHC-2 Beaver	1094	ex N93434

All operate on floats or wheels/skis
Associated with Air Saguenay and Ashuanipi Aviation

LABRADOR AIRWAYS

Goose Bay, Nfld (YYR)

| C-GAAN | de Havilland DHC-8-102 | 051 |

LAC LA CROIX QUETICO AIR SERVICE

Lac la Croix, Ont/Crane Lake, MN

C-FHAN	de Havilland DHC-2 Beaver	316	ex N11255
C-FNFI	de Havilland DHC-3 Otter	379	
C-FVSF	Cessna A185E Skywagon	185-1223	
C-GDZD	de Havilland DHC-2 Beaver	496	ex 52-6116
C-GUEC	Cessna A185F Skywagon	18503986	ex N5513E

All floatplanes

LAC SEUL AIRWAYS

Ear Falls, Ont (YMY)

CF-HXY	de Havilland DHC-3 Otter	67	
C-FPEN	de Havilland DHC-3 Otter	439	
C-GLLO	Cessna U206F Stationair	U20602913	ex N1602Q

All floatplanes

LAKE CENTRAL AIRWAYS

Toronto-City Center, Ont (YTZ)

| C-GAGE | Cessna 441 Conquest II | 441-0086 | ex N20BF |

LAKELAND AIRWAYS

Temagami, Ont

| C-FJKT | de Havilland DHC-2 Beaver | 1023 | |
| C-GUFH | Cessna A185F Skywagon | 18502857 | ex (N1488F) |

LAUZON AVIATION

Elliot Lake, Ont (YEL)

| C-FRUY | de Havilland DHC-2 Beaver | 687 | ex N74157 | Floatplane |

LAVAL AVIATION

Laval, Que

| C-FAZX | de Havilland DHC-3 Otter | 458 | ex |

LEUENBERGER AIR SERVICE

Nakina, Ont (YQN)

| C-FSOX | de Havilland DHC-3 Otter | 437 | ex UNO 308 |
| C-GEWP | de Havilland DHC-2 Turbo Beaver | 1543/TB2 | ex ET-AKI |

C-GLCS	de Havilland DHC-3 Otter	428	ex N17685
C-GLCW	de Havilland DHC-3 Otter	172	ex 55-3310
All floatplanes			

LIARD AIR

Muncho Lake, BC

C-FAWC	de Havilland DHC-6 Twin Otter 100	108	ex N204E	
C-GUDK	de Havilland DHC-2 Beaver	708	ex 53-7900	Floats
C-GUGE	Cessna A185F Skywagon	18502904		Floats or wheels/skis

LITTLE RED AIR SERVICE

Little Red (LRA)   *Fort Vermilion, Alta*

C-FLRA	Piper PA-31-350 Navajo Chieftain	31-7952091	ex N152MS
C-FLRD	Beech A100 King Air	B-243	ex PT-OFZ
C-FPQQ	Beech B200 Super King Air	BB-1304	ex N3173K
C-FQOV	Beech 100 King Air	B-38	ex N931M
C-GGUH	Cessna 208B Caravan I	208B0827	ex N51478
C-GICJ	Cessna U206F Stationair	U20603044	ex N4318Q
C-GMIC	de Havilland DHC-2 Beaver	791	ex (N5218G)
C-GWVT	Cessna U206F Stationair	U20602918	ex (N1721Q)
C-GXAJ	Cessna U206F Stationair	U20602810	ex N35935

LOCKHART AIR SERVICES

Sioux Lookout, Ont (YXL)

C-FFCC	Cessna 310R	310R1206	ex G-BOBN
C-FKQM	Cessna 404 Titan II	404-0108	ex N37102
G-GFIT	Cessna 310R	310R1865	
C-GIJF	Cessna 310R	310R1875	ex N3208M
C-GOGP	Cessna 402C	402C0516	ex N401SA

MANITOBA GOVERNMENT AIR SERVICES

Winnipeg-Intl/Thompson, Man (YWG/YTH)

C-FTUV	Canadair CL-215-1A10	1020		256
C-FTXI	Canadair CL-215-1A10	1016		255
C-GBOW	Canadair CL-215-1A10	1087	ex C-GKDY	253
C-GMAF	Canadair CL-215-1A10	1044	ex C-GUMW	250
C-GMAK	Canadair CL-215-1A10	1107		254
C-GUMW	Canadair CL-215-1A10	1065		251
C-GYJB	Canadair CL-215-1A10	1068		252
C-FMAU	de Havilland DHC-3 Otter	74		Floats or wheels/skis
C-FMAX	de Havilland DHC-3 Otter	267		Floats or wheels/skis
C-FODY	de Havilland DHC-3 Otter	429		Floats or wheels/skis
C-GDAT	Cessna 310R	310R1883	ex N315U	
C-GMLN	Cessna 310R	310R1884	ex N316U	
C-GRNE	Piper PA-31-350 Navajo Chieftain	31-7952224	ex N91834	
C-GYNE	Cessna 310R	310R1367	ex N4086C	

MATT'S AIR SERVICE current status uncertain, most aircraft transferred to Bamaji Air

MAX AVIATION

Max Aviation (MAX)   *Montreal-St Hubert, Que (YHU)*

C-FOGP	Beech B100 King Air	BE-134	ex N363EA
C-FSIK	Beech B100 King Air	BE-39	ex N129CP
C-GPRU	Beech B100 King Air	BE-26	ex N36WH

MCMURRAY AVIATION

Fort McMurray, Alta (YMM)

C-GHJB	Cessna U206E Stationair	U20601677	ex N9477G
C-GHLI	Cessna 208B Caravan I	208B0565	ex N5858J
C-GZZD	Cessna U206F Stationair	U20601957	ex N50946

MISSIONAIR

Winnipeg-Intl, Man/Sachigo Lake, Ont (YWG/ZPB)

C-FSHA	Piper PA-31-350 Navajo Chieftain	31-7752062	ex PH-NTB
C-GJET	Piper PA-31-350 Navajo Chieftain	31-7752134	ex N27304
C-GPYJ	Piper PA-31-350 Navajo Chieftain	31-7405430	ex N54298
C-GSHO	Piper PA-31-350 Navajo Chieftain	31-7852079	ex N93EE

MONTAIR AVIATION
(UJ)   *Boundary Bay, BC (YDT)*

C-GMAE	Pilatus PC-12/45	276	ex C-FKPI
C-GYPD	Piper PA-34-220T Seneca	34-7870025	ex N47991

MORGAN AIR SERVICES
Calgary-Intl, Alta (YYC)

C-FRQS	Piper PA-30-160 Twin Comanche	30-934	ex N7854Y
C-GSQD	Cessna 401	401-0300	ex (176TC)

MORNINGSTAR AIR EXPRESS
Morningstar (MAL)   *Edmonton-Intl, Alta (YEG)*

C-FEXB	Cessna 208B Caravan I	208B0539	ex N758FX		Op for FDX
C-FEXE	Cessna 208B Caravan I	208B0244	ex N750FE		Op for FDX
C-FEXF	Cessna 208B Caravan I	208B0508	ex N749FX		Op for FDX
C-FEXS	Cessna 208B Caravan I	208B0542	ex N759FX		Op for FDX
C-FEXX	Cessna 208B Caravan I	208B0209	ex (N877FE)		Op for FDX
C-FEXY	Cessna 208B Caravan I	208B0226	ex N896FE		Op for FDX
C-FBWG	Boeing 727-25C (FedEx 3)	478/19719	ex N127FE		Lsd fr/op for FDX
C-FBWY	Boeing 727-22F (FedEx 3)	349/19085	ex N192FE	Shane Christopher	Lsd fr/op for FDX
C-GBWA	Boeing 727-22C (FedEx 3)	630/19890	ex N112FE		Lsd fr/op for FDX
C-GBWS	Boeing 727-22F (FedEx 3)	247/18867	ex N180FE	Jessica	Lsd fr/op for FDX

NAHANNI AIR SERVICES ceased operations

NAKINA OUTPOST CAMPS & AIR SERVICE
Nakina, Ont (YQN)

C-FDGV	de Havilland DHC-6 Twin Otter 200	154	ex TF-JMD	
CF-MIQ	de Havilland DHC-3 Turbo Otter	336		Floats or wheels/skis
C-FTIN	Cessna A185F Skywagon	18503362	ex N732SH	Floats or wheels/skis
C-FZRJ	Cessna 208B Caravan I	208B0597	ex N52609	
C-GEOW	Pilatus PC-12/45	244	ex HB-FRO	
C-GMVB	Cessna 208B Caravan I	208B0317		

NALAIR
Nalair (NLT)   *Corner Brook, Nfld (YNF)*

C-GBBG	Beech B200 Super King Air	BB-1507	ex N233JS

Nalair is the trading name of Newfoundland Labrador Air Transport

NATIONAL HELICOPTERS
Toronto, Ont

C-FFUJ	Bell 206B JetRanger III	2982	ex N525W
C-FLYC	Bell 206L-1 LongRanger II	45478	ex XA-...
C-FNHB	Bell 212	30519	ex N250MH
C-FNHG	Bell 206L-1 LongRanger II	45784	ex N220HC
C-FTCH	Bell 206B JetRanger	860	ex N809JA
C-GIGS	Bell 206B JetRanger	1434	ex N59474
C-GNHX	Bell 212	30983	ex N19FH
C-GSZZ	Bell 206B JetRanger III	2319	ex XA-TCU

NAV AIR CHARTER
Navair (FCV)   *Victoria, BC (YVJ)*

C-FIFE	Mitsubishi MU-2L Cargoliner	683	ex OY-CEF
C-FROM	Mitsubishi MU-2J	601	ex N308MA
C-FROW	Mitsubishi MU-2J Cargoliner	628	ex N4202M
C-FTOO	Mitsubishi MU-2J Cargoliner	549	ex N65198
C-FTWO	Mitsubishi MU-2L Cargoliner	672	ex N709US
C-FBDT	Piper PA-31 Turbo Navajo	31-77	ex N9054Y
C-FCAI	Piper PA-31 Turbo Navajo	31-475	ex N22DC
C-FWAG	Piper PA-31-350 Navajo Chieftain	31-7652165	ex N62913
C-GJNV	Piper PA-31 Turbo Navajo	31-389	ex N9294Y
C-GSIO	Piper PA-31 Turbo Navajo	31-186	ex N823PC
C-GVCP	Piper PA-31-350 Navajo Chieftain	31-7652080	ex N965SC
C-GXHM	Piper PA-31 Turbo Navajo	31-752	ex N7230L

C-GILS	Britten-Norman BN-2A-21 Islander	416	ex N92JA
C-GMET	Swearingen SA.226TC Metro II	TC-380	ex I-FSAG
C-GXJD	Piper PA-32-300 Cherokee Six	32-7340094	ex N16571

NESTOR FALLS FLY-IN OUTPOSTS

Nestor-Falls-SPB, Ont

C-FODK	de Havilland DHC-3 Otter	13	
C-FSOR	de Havilland DHC-3 Otter	239	ex IM 1725
C-FWWV	Beech 3N	CA-18	ex RCAF 1443
C-GDWB	Cessna U206G Stationair	U20604460	ex N756YJ
All floatplanes			

NEWFOUNDLAND & LABRADOR AIR SERVICES

St John's, Nfld (YYT)

C-FAYN	Canadair CL-215-1A10	1105		282
C-FAYU	Canadair CL-215-1A10	1106		283
C-FTXA	Canadair CL-215-1A10	1006		284
C-FYWP	Canadair CL-215-1A10	1002		285
C-GDKW	Canadair CL-215-1A10	1095		280
C-GDKY	Canadair CL-215-1A10	1096		281
C-FIZU	Consolidated PBY-5A Catalina	2019	ex N10014	704 Tanker
C-FNJC	Consolidated PBY-5A Canso	CV-430	ex 44-33929	701 Tanker
C-GLFY	Cessna 337G Super Skymaster	33701700		
C-GNLA	Beech B300 Super King Air	FL-26	ex N59TF	

NOLINOR AVIATION

Nolinor (NRL)   *Montreal-Trudeau, Que (YUL)*

C-FAWV	Convair 580	154	ex C-FMGB	Freighter
C-FTAP	Convair 580	334	ex N580N	
C-GQHB	Convair 580	376	ex ZS-KRX	
C-GRLQ	Convair 580	347	ex N580TA	

NORCANAIR AIRLINES

Fond du Lac, Sask (ZPD)

C-FGYK	de Havilland DHC-2 Beaver	123		Floats/skis
C-GERW	Swearingen SA.227AC Metro III	AC-479	ex N479NE	
C-FIPW	Swearingen SA.227AC Metro III	AC-524	ex N4442F	
Norcanair is a division of North Dene Airways				

NORTH AMERICAN AIRLINES ceased operations

NORTH AMERICAN CHARTERS

Hammer (HMR)   *Thunder Bay, Ont (YQT)*

C-FKSL	Pilatus PC-12/45	324	ex N324PC
C-GFIL	Pilatus PC-12/45	268	ex N268PC
C-GJKS	Beech 100 King Air	B-14	ex N402G

NORTH ATLANTIC AVIATION ceased operations

NORTH CARIBOO AIR

North Caribou (5N/NCB)   *Fort St John, BC (YXJ)*

C-FDAM	Beech 100 King Air	B-8	ex N59T	
C-FIDN	Beech 100 King Air	B-3	ex N128RC	
C-FMXY	Beech 100 King Air	B-40	ex N923K	
C-GPCB	Beech A100 King Air	B-45	ex N704S	
C-GTLS	Beech 100 King Air	B-35	ex N178WM	
C-FCGC	Beech 200 Super King Air	BB-236	ex N46KA	conv to CatPass 200
C-FCGM	Beech 200 Super King Air	BB-217	ex N200CD	conv to CatPass 200
C-FILO	Cessna U206F Stationair	U20602076		Floats or wheels/skis
C-FMKD	Beech 65-B90 King Air	LJ-376	ex N300RV	
C-FSXF	de Havilland DHC-6 Twin Otter 300	521	ex YV-528C	
C-FVAX	Cessna 425 Conquest	425-0178	ex (N90GM)	
C-GCFM	Beech 65-C90 King Air	LJ-886	ex N15SL	
C-GELD	Piper PA-31 Turbo Navajo	31-555	ex N6621L	
C-GHTO	de Havilland DHC-6 Twin Otter 300	238	ex ST-AHT	
C-GHXR	Cessna U206F Stationair	U20603064	ex (N5417Q)	Floats or wheels/skis

C-GIGK	de Havilland DHC-6 Twin Oter 300	492	
C-GLAC	Beech 58 Baron	TH-339	ex N6YC
C-GMJO	Cessna U206G Stationair 6	U20605536	ex (N4778X)	Floats or wheels/skis
C-GNPG	Beech 1900C	UB-71	ex N3069K
C-GZTU	Beech 1900C-1	UC-103	ex N15031
C-	Beech B300 Super King Air	FL-354	ex N354H

NORTH CENTRAL HELICOPTERS

La Ronge, Sask (YVC)

C-FARV	Bell 206L LongRanger	45117	ex N111WR
C-FCYW	Bell 204B	2004	ex N8588F
C-FDZE	Bell 204B	2055	ex N7932S
C-FKEP	Bell 206L LongRanger	45024	ex N111AL
C-FMAO	Bell 206B JetRanger	407	
C-FVVQ	Aerospatiale AS.350BA AStar	1210	
C-FVVR	Aerospatiale AS.350B AStar	1353	ex N9101N
C-GFYA	Bell 205A-1	30060	ex N4317F
C-GMHE	Bell 205A-1	30212	ex PT-HHZ

NORTH STAR AIR

Pickle Lake, Ont (YPL)

C-FLNB	Cessna 208B Caravan I	208B0799	ex N799B
C-GCQA	de Havilland DHC-3 Otter	77	ex N129JH	Floats or wheels/skis
C-GJAS	Cessna 208 Caravan I	20800322	ex N51869	Floats or wheels/skis
C-GMFS	Cessna A185F Skywagon	18503351	ex N7140H	Floats or wheels/skis

NORTH VANCOUVER AIRLINES renamed International Express Air Charter

NORTH WRIGHT AIRWAYS

Northwright (HW/NWL)   *Norman Wells/Good Hope/Deline, NWT (YVQ/-/YWJ)*

C-FBAX	Cessna 207 Skywagon	20700355	ex N1755U	
C-FKHD	Beech 99	U-11	ex F-BRUN	
C-FMOL	de Havilland DHC-6 Twin Otter 300	303	ex C-FUGP	
CF-WHP	Cessna 337C Super Skymaster	337-0895	ex (N2595S)	
CF-ZIZ	Fairchild PC-6/B1-H2 Turbo Porter	2009	ex N353F	Floatplane
C-GAAP	Pilatus PC-6/B1-H2 Turbo Porter	569		Floatplane
C-GBEB	de Havilland DHC-6 Twin Otter 300	272	ex 8Q-SUN	Floats or wheels/skis
C-GDBI	Cessna 207 Skywagon	20700039	ex N91052	
C-GDLC	Cessna 208B Caravan I	208B0767	ex N5151D	
C-GHDT	Helio 295 Super Courier	1401	ex N6327V	
C-GMOK	Cessna 207A Stationair 8	2070673	ex N6373D	
C-GRDD	de Havilland DHC-6 Twin Otter 100	54	ex N8081N	Floats or wheels/skis
C-GZGO	Britten-Norman BN-2A-26 Islander	2017	ex N59360	
C-GZIZ	Cessna 208B Caravan I	208B0546	ex N5262W	
C-GZVX	Cessna U206G Stationair 6	U20604110	ex (N756HT)	

Some aircraft operate as Sahtu Connector on scheduled services in the Sahtu region

NORTHERN AIR CHARTER

Peace River, Alta (YPE)

C-GIRG	Cessna A185F Skywagon	18504181	ex (N61424)	
C-GNAC	Piper PA-31 Turbo Navajo C	31-7812106	ex N27707	
C-GNAJ	Beech A100 King Air	B-107	ex LN-AAH	
C-GNAM	Beech 1300	BB-1339	ex N252AF	conv Super King Air
C-GNAP	Piper PA-23-250 Aztec F	27-8054002	ex C-GTGS	
C-GNAR	Beech A100 King Air	B-190	ex LN-AAG	EMS
C-GNAX	Beech B200 Super King Air	BB-1419	ex N146SB	

NORTHERN DENE AIRWAYS

(U7)   *Prince Albert/Stony Rapids SPB, Sask*

Previously listed under trading name Norcanair Airlines

C-FIFJ	de Havilland DHC-2 Beaver	831		Floatplane
C-FWAK	Piper PA-31 Turbo Navajo	31-255	ex N407CA	
C-FZOW	Piper PA-31 Turbo Navajo	31-743	ex N7223L	
C-GGIQ	Piper PA-31-350 Navajo Chieftain	31-7552082	ex N59989	
C-GICM	Beech 95-C55 Baron	TE-64	ex N171M	
C-GKEN	de Havilland DHC-2 Beaver	1072	ex N751	Floatplane
C-GPNO	Beech 95-B55 Baron	TC-734	ex N174E	
C-GQHV	Piper PA-31-350 Navajo Chieftain	31-7405230	ex N54298	
C-GQXX	Piper PA-31-350 Navajo Chieftain	31-7852009		
C-GWUM	Piper PA-31-350 Navajo Chieftain	31-7405404	ex N66878	
C-GXZA	Cessna A185F Skywagon	18503019	ex N5211R	Floatplane

Norcanair Airlines is a division of Northern Dene Airways

NORTHERN HAWK AVIATION

Richmond, BC

C-GMAG	Beech A100 King Air	B-229	ex N100HC

NORTHERN LIGHTS AIR

Smithers, Man (YYD)

C-GNLL	Cessna 206B Super Skywagon	U206-0192	Floatplane

NORTHWARD AIR

Dawson Creek, BC (YDQ)

C-FOMF	Cessna A185A Skywagon	185-0423	ex (N1623Z)
CF-SLV	Cessna U206 Super Skywagon	U206-0412	ex N8012Z

NORTHWAY AVIATION

Northway (NAL)   *Arnes, Man (YNR)*

C-FBHP	Cessna 207A Stationair 8	20700647	ex N73857	
C-FBKK	Piper PA-31 Turbo Navajo	31-734	ex N101WA	
C-FHDL	Cessna 180	18030430	ex N1730G	
C-FQQG	de Havilland DHC-2 Beaver	1675	ex FAP 383	Floats or wheels/skis
CF-UKN	de Havilland DHC-3 Otter	456		Floats or wheels/skis
CF-ZZP	Cessna A185E Skywagon	18501843	ex (N1633M)	Floats or wheels/skis
C-GJJM	Cessna 208 Caravan I	20800029	ex N9370F	Viking Express
C-GNYD	Cessna 207 Skywagon	20700254	ex N1654U	
C-GYYK	Piper PA-31-350 Navajo Chieftain	31-7752029	ex N63680	

NORTHWESTERN AIR

Polaris (J3/PLR) (IATA 325)   *Fort Smith, NWT (YSM)*

C-FCGI	Beech 65-A90 King Air	LJ-220	
C-FCPE	British Aerospace Jetstream 31	825	ex G-31-825
C-FNAF	British Aerospace Jetstream 31	789	ex N411UE
C-FNAM	British Aerospace Jetstream 31	767	ex N767JX
C-FNAY	British Aerospace Jetstream 31	768	ex N159PC
C-GNAH	Beech 99	U-107	ex N207BH
C-GNAL	Beech 99	U-57	ex TF-ELD
C-GRHV	Cessna 401	401-0228	ex N8083F

NORTHWEST FLYING

Nestor Falls-SPB, Ont

CF-NKL	Beech C-45H	AF-378	ex N9864Z
C-GEBL	de Havilland DHC-2 Beaver	1068	ex N33466
C-GYYS	de Havilland DHC-3 Otter	276	ex N1UW
All Floatplanes			

NT AIR

Thunderbird (NTA)   *Prince George/Smithers, BC (YXS/YYD)*

C-GCMJ	Beech 1900C-1	UC-49	ex N80198	stored PWA	Lsd fr GLR
C-GCMT	Beech 1900C-1	UC-120	ex N15683		Lsd fr GLR
C-GCMZ	Beech 1900C-1	UC-61	ex N1568L		Lsd fr GLR
C-GEFA	Beech 1900C-1	UC-94	ex N80346		Lsd fr Raytheon
C-GFSV	Beech 1900D	UE-346	ex C-GORI		Lsd fr GLR
C-FMWM	Beech A100 King Air	B-59	ex		
CF-GWM	Cessna U206F Stationair	U20601802	ex CF-BZO		
C-GDOX	Cessna 208B Caravan I	208B0541	ex N621BB		
C-GYIS	Cessna A185F Skywagon	18502895	ex N8679Z		

NT Air is the trading name of Northern Thunderbird Air

NUELTIN LAKE AIR SERVICE

Nueltin Lake, Man

C-FDCL	Cessna U206G Stationair	U20603542	ex N8790Q
C-FSAP	Noorduyn Norseman VI	231	ex 43-5240
C-FYLZ	de Havilland DHC-3 Otter	257	ex VH-SBR
All floatplanes			

ONTARIO MINISTRY OF NATURAL RESOURCES AVIATION SERVICES

Trillium (TRI)   *Sault Ste Marie, Ont (YAM)*

C-GOGD	Canadair CL-215-6B11	2028	ex C-GAOI	270
C-GOGE	Canadair CL-215-6B11	2031	ex C-GAUR	271
C-GOGF	Canadair CL-215-6B11	2032	ex C-GBGE	272
C-GOGG	Canadair CL-215-6B11	2033	ex C-GBFY	273
C-GOGH	Canadair CL-215-6B11	2034	ex C-GCNO	274
C-GOGW	Canadair CL-215-6B11	2037	ex C-GBPM	275
C-GOGX	Canadair CL-215-6B11	2038	ex C-GBPU	276
C-GOGY	Canadair CL-215-6B11	2040		277
C-GOGZ	Canadair CL-215-6B11	2043		278

C-FOEH	de Havilland DHC-2 Turbo Beaver	1644/TB24
C-FOEK	de Havilland DHC-2 Turbo Beaver	1650/TB26
C-FOER	de Havilland DHC-2 Turbo Beaver	1671/TB41
C-FOEU	de Havilland DHC-2 Turbo Beaver	1678/TB46
C-FOEW	de Havilland DHC-2 Turbo Beaver	1682/TB50
C-FOPA	de Havilland DHC-2 Turbo Beaver	1688/TB56

C-FOPG	de Havilland DHC-6 Twin Otter 300	232
C-FOPI	de Havilland DHC-6 Twin Otter 300	243
C-FOPJ	de Havilland DHC-6 Twin Otter 300	344
C-GOGA	de Havilland DHC-6 Twin Otter 300	739
C-GOGB	de Havilland DHC-6 Twin Otter 300	761

All Turbo Beavers and Twin Otters operate on floats or wheels/skis

C-FCHZ	Bell 206L-1 LongRanger II	45567	ex N313HL
C-GCJX	Piper PA-31-350 Navajo Chieftain	31-7552064	ex N4WE
C-GOFH	Bell 206L-1 LongRanger II	45359	ex N100U
C-GOFI	Bell 206L-1 LongRanger II	45342	ex N167CP
C-GOGJ	Aerospatiale AS.350B2 AStar	2749	
C-GOGL	Aerospatiale AS.350B2 AStar	2738	
C-GOGQ	Aerospatiale AS.350B2 AStar	3196	
C-GOGS	Beech B300 Super King Air	FL-296	
C-GOIC	Beech B300 Super King Air	FL-272	

OSNABURGH AIRWAYS

Pickle Lake, Ont (YPL)

C-FCZO	de Havilland DHC-3 Otter	71	
C-FFQX	Noorduyn Norseman VI	625	ex N51131
C-GIRN	Cessna A185F Skywagon	18504187	ex (N61435)
C-GMAU	de Havilland DHC-2 Beaver	1134	ex N775E
C-GYBJ	Cessna A185F Skywagon	18503623	ex (N7596Q)

All operate on floats or wheels/skis

OSPREY WINGS

La Ronge, Sask (YVC)

C-FASZ	de Havilland DHC-3 Otter	463	ex IM672
CF-DIZ	de Havilland DHC-3 Otter	460	ex JW-9107
C-FLLL	de Havilland DHC-3 Otter	292	
C-FTCT	de Havilland DHC-2 Beaver	962	
C-FXRI	de Havilland DHC-3 Otter	258	ex VH-SBT
C-FZCO	de Havilland DHC-2 Beaver	1027	ex N8034J
C-GAIJ	de Havilland DHC-2 Beaver	1373	ex N5334G
C-GCIM	Cessna A185F Skywagon	18503953	ex (N5308E)
C-GQOQ	de Havilland DHC-6 Twin Otter 200	155	ex EC-BPE

All operate on floats or wheels/skis

PACIFIC COASTAL AIRLINES

Pasco (8P/PCO)   *Port Hardy, BC (YZT)*

C-GPCE	Short SD.3-60	SH3611	ex G-WACK	704
C-GPCF	Short SD.3-60	SH3620	ex (N366AC)	706
C-GPCG	Short SD.3-60	SH3619	ex N364MQ	701
C-GPCJ	Short SD.3-60	SH3633	ex G-BMAR	705
C-GPCN	Short SD.3-60	SH3621	ex N365MQ	702
C-GPCW	Short SD.3-60	SH3622	ex 8Q-OCA	703

C-FDSG	de Havilland DHC-2 Beaver	892	ex 54-1737	Floatplane
C-FHUZ	Grumman G-21A Goose	B-83	ex BuA37830	
C-FIOL	Grumman G-21A Goose	B-107	ex RCN 397	
C-FJNQ	Cessna A185F Skywagon	18502233	ex N4318Q	Floatplane
C-FMAZ	de Havilland DHC-2 Beaver	1413		Floatplane
C-FPCK	Grumman G-21A Goose	1187	ex N8229	

C-FPCO	Embraer EMB.110P1 Bandeirante	110405	ex LN-TED	503
C-FPCV	Beech 1900C	UB-9	ex N189GA	
C-FUAZ	Grumman G-21A Goose	1077	ex N95400	
C-GASF	de Havilland DHC-2 Beaver	1202	ex 57-2561	Floatplane
C-GPCP	Beech 200 Super King Air	BB-140		302; conv to CatPass 200
C-GPCQ	Embraer EMB.110P1 Bandeirante	110342	ex N486FS	502
C-GPCY	Beech 1900C	UB-45	ex C-FYZD	

PACIFIC EAGLE AVIATION

Port McNeil, BC (YMP)

C-FEYN	de Havilland DHC-2 Beaver	508	ex N6167K
C-FICK	de Havilland DHC-2 Beaver	796	
C-FMXR	de Havilland DHC-2 Beaver	374	ex N7160C
All floatplanes			

PACIFIC WESTERN HELICOPTERS

Prince George, BC (YXS)

C-GIYD	Bell 206B JetRanger III	3790	ex N7ZV
C-GPGM	Bell 206B JetRanger III	3178	ex N38902
C-GPWD	Bell 206B JetRanger III	1124	ex N41AJ
C-GPWH	Bell 206B JetRanger III	3131	ex N81AJ
C-GPWJ	Bell 206B JetRanger III	2240	ex C-GNMM
C-GPWR	Bell 206B JetRanger III	2989	ex N577AH
C-GRWG	Bell 206B JetRanger III	3318	
C-GTES	Bell 206B JetRanger III	2292	ex N16877
C-GBKV	Aerospatiale AS.350B-2 AStar	3027	
C-GHHI	Bell 206L-3 LongRanger III	51037	ex N30EA
C-GPWC	Cessna TU206F Turbo Stationair	U20602644	ex N59290
C-GPWK	Aerospatiale AS.350B AStar	1559	ex N29TV
C-GPWQ	Aerospatiale AS.350B AStar	1099	ex N3596B
C-GPWT	Bell 205A-1	30231	ex N57954

PACIFIC WINGS AIRLINES

Sechelt, BC (YLT)

CF-FHC	de Havilland DHC-2 Beaver	12	ex C-FFHC	Floats or wheels/skis
C-FMPD	de Havilland DHC-2 Beaver	1510		Floatplane
C-FOCQ	de Havilland DHC-2 Beaver	52		Floatplane
C-GMKP	de Havilland DHC-2 Beaver	1374	ex N87775	Floatplane

PARRY SOUND AIR SERVICE

Parry Sound/McKellar SPB, Ont (YPD/-)

C-FOIV	Cessna A185A Skywagon	185-0417
C-GNUH	Cessna A185F Skywagon	18502731

PEACE AIR

Peace River, Alta (YPE)

C-FKPI	Pilatus PC-12/45	250	ex N250PB		
C-FKUL	Pilatus PC-12/45	204	ex		
C-FKVL	Pilatus PC-12/45	307	ex N307PB		
C-GAEN	Piper PA-31-350 Chieftain	31-8052196	ex N3528X		
C-GEAZ	British Aerospace Jetstream 32	843	ex C-GQRO	034	Lsd fr BXH
C-GNSO	Piper PA-31-350 Navajo Chieftain	31-7852128	ex N174E		
C-GPAC	Piper PA-34-220T Seneca	34-8133190	ex N32JP		
C-GRAC	Cessna 210L Centurion	21060605	ex N2560L		

PEM-AIR ceased operations

PERIMETER AIRLINES

Perimeter (PAG)

Winnipeg-Intl (YWG)

C-FIHB	Swearingen SA.226TC Metro II	TC-361	ex N166SW
C-FIHE	Swearingen SA.226TC Metro II	TC-373	ex N1010Z
C-FIIA	Swearingen SA.226TC Metro II	TC-329	ex N236AM
C-FJNW	Swearingen SA.226TC Metro IIA	TC-352	ex N167MA
C-FKEX	Swearingen SA.226TC Metro II	TC-332	ex N237AM
C-FSLZ	Swearingen SA.226TC Metro II	TC-222EE	ex N104GS
C-FTNV	Swearingen SA.226TC Metro II	TC-239E	ex N227AM
C-GIQF*	Swearingen SA.226TC Metro II	TC-279	ex F-GFGE
C-GIQG*	Swearingen SA.226TC Metro II	TC-285	ex F-GFGD

C-GIQK*	Swearingen SA.226TC Metro II	TC-288	ex F-GFGF	
C-GPCL	Swearingen SA.226AT Merlin IV	AT-017	ex N511M	Freighter
C-GQAJ	Swearingen SA.226TC Metro II	TC-295	ex C-FUIF	
C-GQAP	Swearingen SA.226TC Metro II	TC-263	ex N103UR	
C-GYRD	Swearingen SA.226TC Metro II	TC-278	ex N5493M	Jt ops with Dene Cree Air

*Leased from Agence d'Affretement Aerien International

C-FCMJ	Rockwell Commander 681	681-6054	
C-FCNU	Beech D95A Travel Air	TD-668	ex N7957M
C-FDMX	Beech D95A Travel Air	TD-587	ex N5663K
C-FEQK	Beech 95-B55 Baron	TC-1374	
C-FKMZ	Beech E95 Travel Air	TD-708	ex N6223V
C-GASL	Cessna 421C Golden Eagle III	421C0437	ex N901EA
C-GEFX	Beech 95-B55 Baron	TC-1332	ex N4263A
C-GEUJ	Beech B60 Duke	P-498	ex N36RR
C-GQQC	Beech D95A Travel Air	TD-676	ex N7874L

These are operated as Perimeter Aviation

PIM AIR ceased operations

POINTS NORTH AIR

Saskatoon, Sask (YXE)

C-FASD	Cessna 402B	402B1354	ex N6395X
C-FODW	de Havilland DHC-3 Turbo Otter	403	
C-FPNG	Cessna 208B Caravan I	208B0667	ex N5263S
C-GCGQ	Cessna 402C	402C0249	ex (N2749B)
C-GHGN	de Havilland DHC-2 Beaver	80	ex N115LA
C-GIWQ	de Havilland DHC-3 Otter	59	ex N2634Y

PRIMAC COURIERS current status is uncertain; both aircraft sold in USA 13 May 2003

PRINCE EDWARD AIR

Comet (CME)

Charlottetown, PEI (YYG)

C-FFFH	Piper PA-31-350 Navajo Chieftain	31-7552130	ex N54CG
C-GATD	Piper PA-31-350 Navajo Chieftain	31-7405143	ex N74986
C-GGQM	Piper PA-31-350 Navajo Chieftain	31-7952033	ex TF-EGU
C-GIIZ	Piper PA-31-350 Navajo Chieftain	31-7552099	ex N29TW
C-GILJ	Piper PA-31-350 Navajo Chieftain	31-7552010	ex N374SA
C-GRFA	Piper PA-31-350 Navajo Chieftain	31-7405228	ex N54292
C-GYYJ	Piper PA-31-350 Navajo Chieftain	31-7652086	ex N59833

C-FJCC	Beech B99	U-150	ex N999CA	
C-FKAX	Beech 1900C	UB-67	ex N3067X	
C-FKCG	Beech 99	U-23	ex N218BH	
C-FYSJ	Beech 99	U-73	ex N209BH	
C-GDSL	Beech 99	U-92	ex N112PA	
C-GPEA	Beech 200 Super King Air	BB-170	ex N869MA	CatPass 250 conversion

---

PROPAIR

Propair (PRO)

Rouyn-Noranda, Que (YUY)

C-FDOU	Beech A100 King Air	B-112	
C-FPAJ	Beech A100 King Air	B-151	ex N324B
C-FWRM	Beech A100 King Air	B-125	ex N89JM
C-GJLJ	Beech A100 King Air	B-235	ex N23517
C-GJLP	Beech A100 King Air	B-148	ex N67V

C-FAWE	Grumman G.159 Gulfstream 1	188	ex HB-LDT	
C-FKLC	de Havilland DHC-3 Otter	255		
C-FOGY	Beech 200 Super King Air	BB-168	ex N10VW	
C-GDEF	Swearingen SA.226AT Merlin IVA	AT-069	ex N311RV	
C-GLPM	de Havilland DHC-3 Turbo Otter	147	ex C-FJFJ	Floats or wheels/skis
C-GQAB	Cessna A185F Skywagon	18502766	ex (N1203F)	Floats or wheels/skis
C-GUGQ	de Havilland DHC-2 Beaver	400	ex 51-16485	Floatplane

PROVINCIAL AIRLINES

Provincial (PB)

St Johns, Nfld (YYT)

C-FAOU	Britten-Norman BN-2A-21 Islander	4	ex N43MJ	
C-FGFZ	Beech 200 Super King Air	BB-403	ex N147K	
C-FIFO	Beech 200 Super King Air	BB-527	ex N662L	Maritime Patrol
C-FIZD	de Havilland DHC-6 Twin Otter 300	461	ex PK-NUX	Lsd fr 402677 Alberta Ltd
C-FMPV	de Havilland DHC-2 Beaver	1304		Floatplane
C-FPAG	SAAB SF.340A	028	ex N336BE	Lsd fr MCC Financial
C-FPAI	SAAB SF.340A	047	ex N337BE	Lsd fr MCC Financial

C-FWLG	de Havilland DHC-6 Twin Otter 300	731	ex N915MA	
C-GJDE	de Havilland DHC-6 Twin Otter 300	471	ex C-GMPK	
C-GMEW	Swearingen SA.227AC Metro III	AC-668B	ex N668JS	
C-GMWR	Beech 200 Super King Air	BB-68	ex N844N	Maritime Patrol
C-GPCD	Beech 200 Super King Air	BB-76	ex N500DR	Maritime Patrol
C-GTMW	Swearingen SA.226AT Merlin IV	AT-002	ex N39RD	
C-GWLW	Piper PA-31-350 Navajo Chieftain	31-7405221	ex N54277	

PROVINCIAL HELICOPTERS

Lac du Bonnet, Man

C-FOKY	Bell 204B	2043	ex N3357
C-FPHB	Bell 206B JetRanger	1213	ex N62SH
C-FYUN	Aerospatiale AS.350B AStar	1384	ex N666MP
C-FZYH	Bell 206B JetRanger II	1967	ex G-CPRS

QUEBECAIR EXPRESS

Quebec City, Que

C-GQXD	SAAB SF.340A	077	ex N922MA	Lsd fr Banc of America
C-GQXF	SAAB SF.340A	057	ex N401BH	Lsd fr Banc of America

First service 18 April 2003

QUIKAIR

Edmonton-Municipal, Alta (YXD)

C-GAAF	Swearingen SA.227DC Metro 23	DC-891B	ex B-3956	Lsd fr ALZ
C-GCCN	British Aerospace Jetstream 3101	704	ex N333PX	
C-GKAF	Swearingen SA.227DC Metro 23	DC-864B	ex B-3950	Lsd fr ALZ
C-GSAF	Swearingen SA.227DC Metro 23	DC-866B	ex B-3951	Lsd fr ALZ

Quikair is a subsidiary of Telford Aviation Services Group

QUIKWAY AIR SERVICES

Brooks, Alta

C-GPTE	Piper PA-31-325 Navajo C/R	31-7712059	ex N111RC
C-GXHL	Piper PA-31 Turbo Navajo B	31-788	ex N5345G

RCMP - GRC AIR SERVICES

Ottawa, Ont

C-FMPK	Bell 206L-4 LongRanger IV	52036		
C-GMPA	Bell 206L-4 LongRanger IV	52017		
C-GMPM	Bell 206L LongRanger	45098		
C-GMPT	Bell 206L LongRanger	45149		
C-GMPV	Bell 206L-1 LongRanger II	45414		
C-FMPA	Pilatus PC-12/45	164	ex HB-FRZ	
C-FMPB	Pilatus PC-12/45	283	ex N283PC	
C-FMPE	Pilatus PC-12/45	314	ex HB-FQZ	
C-FMPN	Pilatus PC-12/45	296	ex HB-FQK	
C-FMPO	Pilatus PC-12/45	229	ex HB-FRA	
C-FMPW	Pilatus PC-12/45	315	ex HB-FRA	
C-GFLA	Pilatus PC-12/45	293	ex N293PC	
C-GMPE	Pilatus PC-12/45	184	ex HB-FSS	
C-GMPI	Pilatus PC-12/45	239	ex HB-FRJ	
C-GMPP	Pilatus PC-12/45	321	ex HB-FRD	
C-GMPW	Pilatus PC-12/45	274	ex N274PC	
C-GMPY	Pilatus PC-12/45	311	ex N311PB	
C-GMPZ	Pilatus PC-12/45	272	ex N272PC	
C-FDGM	Cessna U206G Stationair 6	U20606864	ex N9450R	Soloy conversion
C-FMOM	Cessna 210R Centurion	21064924		
C-FMPG	Aerospatiale AS.350B3 AStar	3082		
C-FMPL	de Havilland DHC-6 Twin Otter 300	320		
C-FRPH	Cessna 208B Caravan I	208B0377	ex N1118B	
C-FSUJ	Cessna 208B Caravan I	208B0373	ex N973CC	
C-GHVP	Cessna 210R Centurion	21064920		
C-GMPJ	de Havilland DHC-6 Twin Otter 300	534		
C-GMPN	Aerospatiale AS.350B3 AStar	3072		
C-GMPR	Cessna 208 Caravan I	20800253	ex N208CF	
C-GNMK	Cessna 210R Centurion	21064938		
C-GTCT	Cessna 210R Centurion	21064949		

Division of RCMP [Royal Canadian Mounted Police]/GRC [Gendarmarie Royale du Canada]

RED LAKE AIRWAYS

Red Lake, Ont (YRL)

C-FODO	de Havilland DHC-2 Beaver	822	
C-FTBD	Beech D-18S	CA-89	ex RCAF 2291
C-GAQJ	de Havilland DHC-2 Beaver	1130	ex 56-4411
C-GEHX	Beech 3NM	CA-112	ex CAF 5181
C-GGNL	Cessna A185F Skywagon	02804	ex (N1280F)

All floatplanes

REGENCY AIR CHARTER

Boundary Bay, BC (YDT)

C-FDEB	Britten-Norman BN-2A Islander	58	ex N592JA	
C-FZUT	Britten-Norman BN-2A Islander	183	ex G-AYGT	
C-GKAW	Britten-Norman BN-2A-8 Islander	128		Ops as Regency Express
C-GRXX	Piper PA-31-350 Navajo Chieftain	31-7405244	ex N79423	
C-GRXZ	Cessna 208B Caravan I	208B0469	ex N12852	
C-GWFZ	Piper PA-31-350 Navajo Chieftain	31-7405162	ex N74003	

Regency Air Charter is the trading name of International Express Aircharter

REMOTE HELICOPTERS

Slave Lake, NWT (YZH)

C-GRHJ	Aerospatiale AS.350BA AStar	2149	
C-GRHK	Aerospatiale AS.350B Ecureuil	2305	ex F-GGPE
C-GRHL	Aerospatiale AS.350B AStar	1960	ex N5806D
C-GRHN	Aerospatiale AS.350BA AStar	1963	ex N13TV
C-GTAM	Aerospatiale AS.350BA AStar	1232	ex G-MAGI
C-FBJV	Bell 206B JetRanger	1087	
C-GBHG	Bell 206B JetRanger	802	ex N2954W
C-GRHA	Bell 212	30791	ex N82283I
C-GRHM	Bell 206B JetRanger	600	ex N23SP
C-GRHS	Bell 212	30785	ex N8228R
C-GRHW	Bell 204B	2056	ex N204FB
C-GSKX	Bell 206B JetRanger III	2691	

RESOURCE HELICOPTERS

Vancouver-Intl, BC (YVR)

C-FRSR	Bell 204B	2020	
C-FZQB	Bell 212	30629	
C-GSHB	Bell 204B	2038	
C-GZMQ	Bell 212	30820	ex 8Q-MAX

RIVER AIR

Kenora/Menaki, Ont (YQK/-)

C-FAYM	Cessna U206E Skywagon	U20601541	ex (N9141M)
C-GHOJ	Cessna 180K	18053042	ex N2715K
C-GNNO	Cessna A185F Skywagon	18502685	ex (N1016F)
C-GPDS	de Havilland DHC-2 Beaver	1349	ex N62352
C-GYKO	de Havilland DHC-3 Otter	287	ex N22UT

All floatplanes

ROSS AIR SERVICE

Sandy Bay, Sask

C-FAXC	de Havilland DHC-2 Beaver	1048	ex ZK-CMV	Floats or wheels/skis
C-FWXV	Cessna A185E Skywagon	185-1355		Floats or wheels/skis

RUSH AIR current status is uncertain as all aircraft disposed of

RUSTY MYERS FLYING SERVICE

Fort Frances,Ont (YAG)

C-FERM	Beech 3N	CA-62	ex CAF 1487
C-FKSJ	Cessna 208 Caravan I	20800035	ex N9382F
C-FOBT	de Havilland DHC-2 Beaver	3	
C-FOBY	de Havilland DHC-2 Beaver	13	
C-FRPL	Beech 3NM	CA-225	ex CAF 2346
C-FRVL	Beech 3T	7835	ex CAF 1396

CF-ZRI	Beech D-18S	A-940	ex N164U
C-GAGK	Cessna 208 Caravan I	20800342	ex N51744
All floatplanes			

SABOURIN LAKE AIRWAYS

Sabourin Lake, Man

C-FSJX	de Havilland DHC-2 Beaver	1592	
C-GYER	Cessna U206F Stationair	U20603503	ex N8750Q

SANDY LAKE SEAPLANE SERVICE

Sandy Lake, Ont (ZSI)

C-FZQV	Cessna A185E Skywagon	18501853	ex (N1659M)
C-GBBZ	Cessna U206G Stationair	U20605712	ex (N5396X)
C-GTCC	Cessna U206F Stationair	U20602167	ex N7303Q
All operate on floats or wheels/skis			

SAPAWE AIR

Eva Lake, Que

C-FEYR	de Havilland DHC-2 Beaver	497	
C-FOCC	de Havilland DHC-2 Beaver	23	
C-GKBW	de Havilland DHC-2 Beaver	310	ex N1441Z
All Floatplanes			

SASAIR ceased operations

SASKATCHEWAN GOVERNMENT NORTHERN AIR OPERATIONS

Saskatchewan (SGS)   *La Ronge/Saskatoon, Sask (YVC/YXE)*

C-FAFN	Canadair CL-215-1A10	1093	ex C-GKDY	216
C-FAFO	Canadair CL-215-1A10	1094	ex C-GKBO	217
C-FAFP	Canadair CL-215-1A10	1100	ex C-GKEA	218
C-FAFQ	Canadair CL-215-1A10	1101	ex C-GKEE	219
C-FYWO	Canadair CL-215-1A10	1003		214
C-FYXG	Canadair CL-215-1A10	1009		215
C-GEHP	Grumman CS2F-2 Tracker	DHC-97	ex CAF12198	1 Tanker
C-GEHR	Grumman CS2F-2 Tracker	DHC-51	ex CAF12185	3 Tanker
C-GEQC	Grumman CS2F-2 Tracker	DHC-53	ex CAF12187	4 Tanker
C-GEQD	Grumman CS2F-2 Tracker	DHC-98	ex CAF12199	5 Tanker
C-GEQE	Grumman CS2F-2 Tracker	DHC-92	ex CAF12193	6 Tanker
C-GWHK	Grumman CS2F-1 Firecat	DHC-37/016	ex RCN1538	2 Tanker
C-FNAO	Piper PA-60 Aerostar 600A	60-0737-8061227	ex N6079U	
C-FSPM	Beech 95-B55 Baron	TC-1008		
C-GNBA	Beech 95-B55 Baron	TC-1787		
C-GPVD	Beech 95-B55 Baron	TC-1966		
C-GSAA	Piper PA-42-720 Cheyenne IIIA	42-5501057	ex OE-FAA	EMS
C-GSAE	Beech B200 Super King Air	BB-1748	ex N50848	EMS
C-GSAV	Beech B200 Super King Air	BB-1740	ex N4470T	EMS
C-GVDQ	Piper PA-31-350 Chieftain	31-8152119	ex N40869	
C-GZJR	Piper PA-60 Aerostar 600A	60-0764-8061231	ex N6082Y	
EMS flights are conducted by Saskatchewan Government Air Ambulance Service (SLG) using callsign Lifeguard				

SEAIR SEAPLANES

Vancouver-Coal Harbour, BC (CXH)

C-FDHC	de Havilland DHC-2 Turbo Beaver	1677/TB45	ex N164WC
C-FLAC	Cessna 208 Caravan I	20800357	ex N5267J
C-FPCG	de Havilland DHC-2 Beaver	1000	ex N188JM
C-FPMA	de Havilland DHC-2 Turbo Beaver	1625/TB15	ex N1454T
C-GBVR	de Havilland DHC-2 Beaver	1477	ex VH-HAQ
C-GSAS	Cessna 208 Caravan I	20800341	ex N5154J
C-GTMC	de Havilland DHC-2 Beaver	1171	ex N100HF
C-GYIX	Cessna A185F Skywagon	18503162	ex (N93021)
All floatplanes			

SELKIRK AIR

Selkirk, Man

C-FYNW	Cessna U206D Super Skywagon	U206-1370	ex (N72330)
C-GCDX	de Havilland DHC-3 Otter	314	ex 58-1700
C-GCKZ	Cessna A185F Skywagon	18502665	ex (N4949C)

C-GFIQ	de Havilland DHC-2 Beaver	632	ex N90525	
C-GGSL	de Havilland DHC-3 Otter	166	ex N5248G	
C-GPHI	de Havilland DHC-2 Beaver	838	ex N67687	
C-GPVC	de Havilland DHC-2 Beaver	290	ex N9257Z	

Trading name of Enterlake Air Services; all operate on floats or wheels/skis

SERVICE AÉRIEN GOUVERNEMENTAL

Quebec (QUE)   Quebec, Que (YQB)

C-FASE	Canadair CL-215-6B11	1114	ex Greek AF 1114	238
C-FAWQ	Canadair CL-215-6B11	1115	ex Greek AF 1115	239
C-FTXG	Canadair CL-215-6B11	1014		228
C-FTXJ	Canadair CL-215-6B11	1017		230
C-FTXK	Canadair CL-215-6B11	1018		231
C-GQBA	Canadair CL-215-6B11	2005	ex C-GKDN	240
C-GQBC	Canadair CL-215-6B11	2012	ex C-GKET	241
C-GQBD	Canadair CL-215-6B11	2016	ex C-GBPU	242
C-GQBE	Canadair CL-215-6B11	2017	ex C-GKEA	243
C-GQBF	Canadair CL-215-6B11	2019	ex C-FVKV	244
C-GQBG	Canadair CL-215-6B11	2022	ex C-FVLW	245
C-GQBI	Canadair CL-215-6B11	2023	ex C-FVLI	246
C-GQBK	Canadair CL-215-6B11	2026	ex C-FVLY	247
C-FURG	Canadair CL-600-2A12 (Challenger 601)	3063	ex C-GLYH	EMS
C-GBPQ	Bell 206B JetRanger III	2897		
C-GFQB	Canadair CL-215-1A10	1092	ex C-GKDP	237
C-GQBT	de Havilland DHC-8Q-202	470	ex P2-ANL	EMS/VIP
C-GSQA	Bell 206L-4T Twin Ranger	52060		Police
C-GSQL	Bell 412EP	36262		

Operated by Quebec Government on fire-fighting missions

SIMPSON AIR

Commuter Canada (NCS)   Fort Simpson, NWT (YFS)

C-FTFO	Cessna A185E Skywagon	185-1055	ex N4553F
C-GGHU	Cessna U206G Stationair 6	U20605723	ex (N5407X)
C-GPMS	Cessna U206G Stationair 6	U20604207	ex (N756MU)

SIOUX AIR

Sioux Lookout, Ont (YXL)

C-GGRU	Cessna U206G Stationair 6	U20605838	ex N5373X	Floats or wheels/skis

SIOUX NARROWS AIRWAYS ceased operations

SKYLINE HELICOPTERS

Kelowna, BC (YLW)

C-GSLH	Bell 212	30565	ex N94W
C-GSLT	Bell 212	30851	ex JA9527
C-GSLY	Aerospatiale AS.350B AStar	2771	ex N60951
C-GSLZ	Bell 212	30975	ex JA9546

SKYLINK AVIATION

Skylink (SKK)   Toronto-Pearson Intl, Ont (YYZ)

C-FAHX	Bell 212	30535	ex HC-BXV	
C-GARB	Bell 206B JetRanger	1086	ex 4X-BJS	
C-GZRC	Bell 212	30746	ex N50932	Based in Israel as 4X-BJN
N6505	Antonov An-32B	3202	ex ER-AWK	Op for USAF/6SOS

Aircraft often based overseas operating for Relief Agencies; also leases in other aircraft as required

SKYLINK EXPRESS

Toronto-Pearson Intl, Ont (YYZ)

C-GSKA	Beech 1900C	UB-32	ex N317BH	
C-GSKC	Beech 1900C	UB-27	ex N6929M	
C-GSKG	Beech 1900C-1	UC-22	ex N19016	
C-GSKM	Beech 1900C	UB-21	ex N61MK	Lsd fr Raytheon
C-GSKN	Beech 1900C-1	UC-54	ex N31729	Lsd fr Raytheon
C-GSKU	Beech 1900C	UB-35	ex N735GL	
C-GSKW	Beech 1900C	UB-33	ex N318BH	
C-GSKR	Cessna 208B Caravan I	208B0436	ex N677SC	
C-GSKS	Cessna 208B Caravan I	208B0762	ex N52623	

C-GSKV	Cessna 208B Caravan I	208B0847		
N1117G	Cessna 208B Caravan I	208B0370		Lsd fr Textron
All freighters				

SKYSERVICE AIRLINES

Skytour (6J/SSV) (IATA 884)   Montreal-Trudeau, Que (YUL)

C-FRAA	Airbus Industrie A320-232	1411	ex F-WWLR	Alconquin	Lsd fr SALE
C-FTDA	Airbus Industrie A320-212	0795	ex F-WWDX		Lsd fr ILFC
C-FTDF	Airbus Industrie A320-231	0437	ex D-AAMS		
C-FTDQ	Airbus Industrie A320-214	1686	ex N320MW	Conquest c/s	Lsd fr Boullioun
C-FZAZ	Airbus Industrie A320-214	2003	ex G-KKAZ		Lsd fr MYT
C-GJUK	Airbus Industrie A319-112	1598	ex C-GKZA	Conquest c/s	Lsd fr CIT Leasing
C-GJUQ	Airbus Industrie A320-212	0671	ex C-GVXF		Lsd fr ILFC
C-GTDC	Airbus Industrie A320-232	0496	ex F-WWBV		Lsd fr ILFC
C-GTDH	Airbus Industrie A320-214	1605	ex G-OOAT		Lsd fr FCA
C-GTDK	Airbus Industrie A320-231	0338	ex D-AFTI		Lsd fr ORIX
C-GTDL	Airbus Industrie A320-231	0476	ex D-AUKT		
C-GTDM	Airbus Industrie A320-231	0429	ex G-BYTH		Lsd fr MYT
C-GTDP	Airbus Industrie A320-231	1780	ex OY-VKL		Lsd fr VKG
C-GTDS	Airbus Industrie A319-112	1901	ex D-AVYP	Conquest c/s	Lsd fr ILFC
C-GTDT	Airbus Industrie A319-112	1884	ex D-AVYU	Conquest c/s	Lsd fr ILFC
C-GTDX	Airbus Industrie A319-112	1846	ex D-AVWW	Conquest c/s	Lsd fr CIT Lsg
C-FFAN	Boeing 757-21KER	746/28674	ex G-WJAN		Lsd fr MYT
C-FPEP	Boeing 757-2Y0	400/25268	ex G-CPEP		Lsd fr FCA
C-FTDV	Boeing 757-28AER	162/24017	ex G-OOOC		Lsd fr FCA
C-GBOD	Boeing 757-28A	180/24235	ex G-OOOD		Lsd fr FCA
C-GOOG	Boeing 757-23AER	219/24292	ex G-OOOG	on order	Lsd fr FCA
C-GTBB	Boeing 757-28A	950/32446	ex G-OOBB		Lsd fr FCA
C-GUBA	Boeing 757-28A	950/32446	ex G-OOBA		Lsd fr FCA
C-GEOC	British Aerospace Jetstream 31	793	ex N331CA		Op as Skyservice Avn
C-GJPX	British Aerospace Jetstream 31	756	ex N2275S		Op as Skyservice Avn

SKYWARD AVIATION

Skyward (K9/SGK) (IATA 470)   Thompson, Man (YTH)

C-FCGL	Beech 200 Super King Air	BB-190	ex N190MD	CatPass 200 conv	
C-FGMO	Cessna 421C Golden Eagle II	421C0124	ex N421GT		
C-FLTS	Beech A100 King Air	B-149	ex N883CA		
C-FSKA	Beech 100 King Air	B-239	ex N154TC		
C-FSKC	Cessna 441 Conquest	441-0139	ex N441LL		
C-FSKF	Cessna 208B Caravan I	208B0673	ex N5268M		
C-FSKG	Cessna 441 Conquest	441-0120	ex N544AL		
C-FSKJ	Embraer EMB.110P1 Bandeirante	110272	ex N272GA		
C-FSKL	Embraer EMB.110P1 Bandeirante	110353	ex N623KC	ZS-PDA resd	
C-FSKO	Beech 1900D	UE-9	ex N9YV		
C-FSKR	Embraer EMB.110P1 Bandeirante	110331	ex N331GA		
C-FSKS	Cessna 208B Caravan I	208B0722	ex N5268M		
C-FSKT	Beech 1900D	UE-11	ex N11ZV		
C-FSKX	Cessna 208B Caravan I	208B0664	ex C-GSOW		
C-GGRB	Cessna 207A Stationair 8	20700611	ex N73643		
C-GINR	Cessna 402C II	402C0242	ex N2721B		
C-GLHP	Cessna 414	414-0099	ex N8199Q		
C-GSJP	Cessna 310R II	310R0816	ex (N3388G)		
C-GSKD	Embraer EMB.110P1 Bandeirante	110329	ex N850AC	ZS-PDC resd	
C-GSKH	Cessna 441 Conquest	441-0264	ex N264WS		
C-GSKQ	Beech 1900D	UE-361	ex N1865A		
C-GSKY	Beech 1900D	UE-58	ex F-GING		
C-GSRL	Cessna 402B	402B0027	ex N5427M		
C-GTLF	Beech 100 King Air	B-72	ex N5476R		
C-GYWQ	Cessna U206G Stationair 6	U20604439	ex (N756XM)		

SLATE FALLS AIRWAYS

(SYJ)   Sioux Lookout, Ont (YXL)

CF-DIN	de Havilland DHC-2 Beaver	68	
C-FNWX	de Havilland DHC-3 Otter	412	
C-GGRW	Cessna U206G Stationair 6	U20605689	ex N5373X
C-GHEG	Cessna T210M Turbo Centurion	21062795	ex N6607B
C-GPCR	Cessna U206G Stationair 6	U20605082	ex N206JW
C-GSFA	Cessna 208 Caravan I	208000212	ex 8Q-MAT
All operate on floats or wheels/skis			

SLAVE AIR

Slave Lake, Alta (YZH)

C-FOOS	Cessna U206E Stationair	U20601698	ex (N9498G)
C-FSAO	Beech 200 Super King Air	BB-1610	ex N713TA
C-FSAT	Beech 200 Super King Air	BB-1526	ex N417MC
C-GAYZ	Cessna A185F Skywagon	18504040	ex (N6416E)
C-GDZK	de Havilland DHC-2 Turbo Beaver	1586/TB-8	ex C-FOEC
C-GLGD	Cessna U206G Stationair 6	U20606261	ex (N6388Z)
C-GMLP	Cessna A185F Skywagon	18504275	ex (N61920)
C-GSAZ	Piper PA-31 Turbo Navajo	31-8112063	ex N4094Y
C-GXNL	Cessna 210L Centurion	21060909	ex N5327V
C-GYDD	Cessna A185F Skywagon	18503124	ex (N80516)

SONTAIR

Sontair (STI)   *Chatham, Ont (XCM)*

C-FSKQ	Beech 200 Super King Air	BB-99	ex 5Y-SEL	
C-GSKT	Cessna 208B Caravan I	208B0759	ex N5262W	Lsd fr Cessna

SOUTH NAHANNI AIRWAYS

Fort Simpson, NWT (YFS)

C-FAKM	de Havilland DHC-6 Twin Otter 100	78	ex N242GW	Floatplane

SOUTHERN SKIES AVIATION

Penticton, BC (YYF)

C-GCJO	Piper PA-44-180T Seminole	44-8107062	ex D-GIKA
C-GRKK	Cessna 205	205-0203	ex N82033

SOUTH MORESBY AIR CHARTERS

Queen Charlotte City, BC

C-GGLR	Cessna A185F Skywagon II	18504089	
C-GHAO	Cessna A185F Skywagon	18502370	ex N53088
C-GPVB	de Havilland DHC-2 Beaver	871	ex N9253Z

All operate on floats or wheels/skis

STAGE AIR Northern part ceased operations and Southern part renamed Southern Skies Aviation

SUDBURY AVIATION

Whitewater Lake, Ont

C-FHVT	de Havilland DHC-2 Beaver I	1098	ex VP-PAT
C-FIUU	de Havilland DHC-2 Beaver I	945	
C-GQVG	Cessna A185F Skywagon	18503818	ex N4619E

All operate on floats or wheels/skis

SUMMIT AIR CHARTERS

Yellowknife, NWT/Atlin, BC/Whitehorse, YT (YZF/YSQ/YXY)

C-GJGS	Short SC.7 Skyvan 3-200	SH1909	ex N56NS
C-GJPY	Dornier 228-202	8088	ex 6Y-JQM
C-GKOA	Short SC.7 Skyvan	SH1905	ex N52NS

SUNWEST HOME AVIATION

Chinook (CNK)   *Calgary-Intl, Alta (YYC)*

C-FDON	Cessna 208B Caravan I	208B0770	ex N1299P	Lsd fr Aries Avn Svs
C-FGEW	Swearingen SA.226TC Metro II	TC-347	ex N330BA	
C-FPCP	Beech B300 Super King Air	FL-317		
C-FSWT	Swearingen SA.226TC Metro II	TC-382	ex N1011N	196 Spirit of Medicine Hat
C-GHOP	Beech 200 Super King Air	BB-120	ex N6773S	
C-GJFY	Beech 200 Super King Air	BB-812	ex C-GYUI	
C-GPAE	Piper PA-31 TurboNavajo	31-8012086		
C-GPPC	Beech B300 Super King Air	FL-127		
C-GSFI	Cessna 425 Conquest	425-0177	ex C-GRJM	
C-GSHV	Swearingen SA.227DC Metro 23	DC-900B	ex D-CJKO	
C-GSHY	Swearingen SA.227DC Metro 23	DC-897B	ex N3051Q	
C-GSHZ	Swearingen SA.227DC Metro 23	DC-887B	ex N3007C	
C-GSWF	Beech 100 King Air	BE-129	ex LV-VCU	

C-GSWG	Beech B100 King Air	BE-131	ex N6354H
C-GSWK	Swearingen SA.226TC Metro II	TC-368	ex F-GEBU	The Spirit of Medicine Hat
C-GSWS	Beech 3NM	CA-261	ex 2382
C-GSWY	Piper PA-31 Turbo Navajo	31-595	ex C-GPOP
C-GVAG	Piper PA-31-350 Navajo Chieftain	31-7752166	ex N27411

Also operates executive jets

SUPERIOR HELICOPTERS

Longlac, Ont

C-GENZ	Bell 205A-1	30165	
C-GHHY	Bell 206L-3 LongRanger III	51349	
C-GKCA	Bell 206L-3 LongRanger III	51341	
C-GRGY	Bell 204B	2022	ex CF-OKZ
C-GSHD	Bell 205A-1	30058	ex C-FNMQ

SWANBERG AIR

Grande Prairie, Alta (YQU)

C-GCTH	Piper PA-31-350 Navajo Chieftain	31-7752063	ex N37620	
C-GDFW	British Aerospace Jetstream 31	720	ex G-HDGS	Lsd fr Aviation Starlink
C-GPSB	Piper PA-42 Cheyenne III	42-8001030	ex N855GA	
C-GPSN	British Aerospace Jetstream 31	783	ex C-GHGI	
C-GPSV	British Aerospace Jetstream 31	816	ex C-FBII	
C-GPSW	British Aerospace Jetstream 31	735	ex N854JS	

TAL AIR CHARTERS

Jetel (JEL)　　　　　　　　　　　　　　　　　　　　　　　*Toronto-Pearson Intl, Ont (YYZ)*

C-FAMC	Swearingen SA.227AC Metro III	AC-719B	ex N436MA

Tal-Air Charters is a division of Sky Freight Express

TANGO BY AIR CANADA

Montreal-Trudeau, Que (YUL)

Low cost division of Air Canada; for fleet details, see parent

TASMAN HELICOPTERS

Vancouver-Intl, BC (YVR)

C-FNTR	Bell 205A-1	30297	
C-FTHD	Bell 407	53134	
C-FTVL	Bell 212	30551	ex XC-UHE
C-FVTS	Bell 212	30546	ex N2164Z
C-GEEC	Bell 212	30931	ex EC-GOR

THETIS AIR believed to have ceased operations

30,000 ISLAND AIR current status is uncertain as both aircraft disposed of

THUNDER AIRLINES

Air Thunder (THU)　　　　　　　　　　　　　　　　　　　*Thunder Bay, Ont (YQT)*

C-FFFG	Mitsubishi MU-2L	662	ex N5191B
C-FJEL	Mitsubishi MU-2N	706SA	ex N866MA
C-FRWK	Mitsubishi MU-2L	1521SA	ex N437MA
C-GAMC	Mitsubishi MU-2L	785SA	ex N273MA
C-GZNS	Mitsubishi MU-2L	1550SA	ex N64WB
C-FASB	Beech A100 King Air	B-163	ex SE-ING
C-FWVR	Cessna 208B Caravan I	208B0483	exN51426
C-GASI	Beech A100 King Air	B-126	ex N23BW
C-GFKS	Beech A100 King Air	B-247	ex N153TC
C-GNEX	Beech A100 King Air	B-211	ex N9194F

THUNDERBIRD AVIATION

Stony Rapids, Sask (YSF)

CF-PEM	de Havilland DHC-3 Otter	438	
C-GANM	Cessna U206G Stationair	U20603886	ex N7347C

Both floatplanes

TOFINO AIR LINES

C-FGCY	de Havilland DHC-2 Beaver	216	
C-FHRT	de Havilland DHC-2 Beaver	1203	ex N64390
C-FJIM	de Havilland DHC-2 Beaver	462	ex ZK-CPZ
C-GFLT	de Havilland DHC-2 Beaver	279	ex N5149G
C-GHBX	Cessna 180J	18052449	ex (N52029)
C-GHZR	Cessna 180J	18052567	ex (N7542K)
C-GIDX	Cessna 180J	18052709	ex (N7716K)
C-GYFO	Cessna 180J	18052759	ex (N7825K)

All floatplanes

TRANS CAPITAL AIR

C-FWYU	de Havilland DHC-7-103	012	ex N678MA	Op for UN	
C-GGXS	de Havilland DHC-7-102	064	ex 4X-AHB	Op for UN	Lsd fr Aero Lsg & Sales
C-GLPP	de Havilland DHC-7-102	067	ex N939HA		Lsd fr Stolcraft

TRANS FAIR

C-GTFC	Convair VT-29B	279	ex N152PA

TRANS NORTH HELICOPTERS

Trans North (TNT)

C-FCHU	Bell 206B JetRanger III	2213	ex N70TT
C-FDRZ	Bell 206B JetRanger II	764	
C-GFKD	Bell 206B JetRanger III	2869	ex N1072N
C-GMIG	Bell 206B JetRanger II	2186	
C-GMYQ	Bell 206B JetRanger III	2628	
C-GPGH	Bell 206B JetRanger III	4022	
C-GPWI	Bell 206B JetRanger III	2234	ex N347BB
C-GTNY	Bell 206B JetRanger II	990	ex CF-KNY
C-FHHA	Bell 206L-1 LongRanger II	45662	ex C-GBPO
C-GEAG	Bell 205A-1	30262	ex XC-CIC
C-GTNT	Aerospatiale AS.350B2 AStar	3327	

TRANSWEST AIR

Air Sask(9T/ASK) (IATA 909)

C-GALM	Cessna A185F Skywagon	18503711	ex N783A		
C-GCJM	Cessna A185F Skywagon	18503955	ex (N5330E)		
C-GCVJ	Cessna A185F Skywagon	18503964			
C-GMAO	Cessna A185F Skywagon	18502714	ex N1058F		
C-GZVF	Cessna A185F Skywagon	18503202	ex N93256		

All operate on floats or wheels/skis

C-FAAF	Piper PA-31-350 Navajo Chieftain	31-7752096	ex N747SC		
C-FQWP	Piper PA-31-325 Navajo C/R	31-7400990	ex N7082Y		
C-FZPJ	Piper PA-31-350 Navajo Chieftain	31-7752185	ex N27359		
C-GAYY	Piper PA-31 Turbo Navajo	31-8012006			
C-GCTG	Piper PA-31-350 Navajo Chieftain	31-7552087	ex N72ET		
C-GNOV	Piper PA-31 Turbo Navajo C	31-7812087			
C-GUNP	Piper PA-31-350 Chieftain	31-8052048	ex N3554D		

C-FCCE	de Havilland DHC-6 Twin Otter 100	8	ex VH-TGS	Floats or wheels/skis
C-FGHY	de Havilland DHC-2 Beaver	1344	ex 58-2015	Floats or wheels/skis
C-FHPE	de Havilland DHC-3 Turbo Otter	273	ex Burma AF 4651	Floats or wheels/skis
C-FKIO	Mitsubishi MU-2N	725SA	ex N888RH	
C-FOED	de Havilland DHC-2 Turbo Beaver	1591/TB9		Floats or wheels/skis
C-FPGE	de Havilland DHC-6 Twin Otter 200	197	ex N790M	Floats or wheels/skis
C-FQGD	de Havilland DHC-2 Beaver	76		Floates or wheels/skis
C-FSCA	de Havilland DHC-6 Twin Otter 100	17		Floats or wheels/skis
C-FSEW	British Aerospace Jetstream 31	764	ex N223JL	
C-FSGD	de Havilland DHC-3 Turbo Otter	316	ex N521BK	Floats or wheels/skis
C-FVKC	Beech 1900D	UE-160	ex N3216S	
C-FVOG	de Havilland DHC-6 Twin Otter 100	35		Floats or wheels/skis
C-FYID	Bell 206L-1 Long Ranger II	45206	ex N78CF	
C-GAEB	de Havilland DHC-2 Beaver	703	ex 53-7895	Floats or wheels/skis
C-GAON	Cessna 310R II	310R1627	ex N2632Y	
C-GAPK	Beech 100 King Air	B-198		
C-GBGP	Beech 95-E55 Baron	TE-924	ex N1897W	

C-GCNC	Bell 206B JetRanger II	1142	ex N58152	
C-GCTA	Cessna 441 Conquest II	441-0140	ex (N26264)	
C-GELT	Bell 206B JetRanger III	2994	ex N5744V	
C-GJHW	Beech A100 King Air	B-175	ex N92DL	
C-GKCY	SAAB 340A	133	ex SE-ISM	Lsd fr SAAB
C-GMAQ	de Havilland DHC-2 Beaver	234	ex 51-16784	Floats or wheels/skis
C-GPDC	British Aerospace Jetstream 31	766	ex N222JF	
C-GYHY	Bell 206B JetRanger III	2317	ex N16825	
C-GZYJ	Cessna 310R II	310R1311	ex (N6174C)	

TRANSWEST HELICOPTERS

Chilliwack, BC (YCW)

C-GTWH	Bell 214B-1	28017	ex N214MV	
C-GTWI	Bell 214B-1	28011	ex LN-OSW	
C-GTWL	Bell 214B-1	28055	ex N214NS	Lsd as B-
C-GTWV	Bell 214B	28048	ex HB-XVZ	
C-GTWZ	Bell 214B	28032	ex JA9446	
C-GMIN	Cessna A185F Skywagon	18504065		

TRILLIUM AIR parent company, Pem Air, ceased operations

TSAYTA AVIATION

Fort St James,BC (YXJ)

C-GORH	Cessna A185F Skywagon	18504332	
C-GWKX	Cessna A185E Skywagon	18502032	ex N70167
Operate on floats or wheels/skis			

TUNDRA HELICOPTERS

Langley, BC

C-GHOG	Sikorsky S-58ET	58-1662	ex N58BH
C-GHOS	Sikorsky S-58ET	58-1537	ex N58HA
C-GTHK	Bell 212	30641	ex N708H

ULTRA HELICOPTERS

Grimshaw, Alta

C-FALE	Bell 206B JetRanger III	1074	ex N83160
C-FEEN	Bell 206B JetRanger	236	
C-GBPB	Bell 206B JetRanger	321	
C-GHHK	Bell 206B JetRanger	1588	
C-GMXU	Bell 206B JetRanger	1520	ex N15DW
C-GQKU	Bell 206B JetRanger II	2173	
C-GAHM	Bell 205A-1	30215	ex N59607
C-GAHN	Bell 204B	2044	ex N120BX
C-GAPJ	Bell 204B	2012	ex Thai 912
C-GEWR	Bell 206L-1 LongRanger II	45594	ex N3892R
C-GUHZ	Bell 206L-3 LongRanger III	51014	ex N752HL

VALAIR

Montreal-Trudeau (YUL)

C-FCIZ	de Havilland DHC-8-102	138	
First service 30 November 2003			

VANCOUVER ISLAND AIR

Campbell River, BC (YBL)

C-FCSN	Beech D18S	CA-16	ex RCAF1441
C-FGNR	Beech 3NM	CA-191	ex (CF-SIK)
C-FIZB	Cessna 180J	18052409	ex N46262
C-FUVQ	de Havilland DHC-2 Beaver	696	
C-GAIV	Beech TC-45G	AF-80	ex N711KP
C-GSUE	de Havilland DHC-2 Beaver	1199	ex N37AT
C-GVIB	Beech D-18S	A-480	ex N483B
All floatplanes			

VANCOUVER ISLAND HELICOPTERS

Victoria, BC (YYJ)

C-FTDE	Aerospatiale AS.350B2 AStar	2796	
C-FXHS	Aerospatiale AS.350B1 AStar	2248	
C-GEYN	Aerospatiale AS.350B2 AStar	2732	ex VP-BBB
C-GGNU	Aerospatiale AS.350B2 AStar	9002	ex ZK-HWD
C-GNME	Aerospatiale AS.350B2 AStar	2826	ex N351WW
C-GNMJ	Aerospatiale AS.350BA AStar	2829	
C-GNMP	Aerospatiale AS.350B AStar	1040	ex C-GSKI
C-GOLV	Aerospatiale AS.350BA AStar	1108	
C-GPHM	Aerospatiale AS.350B2 AStar	2488	
C-GPHQ	Aerospatiale AS.350B1 AStar	2017	ex N855NM
C-GPHR	Aerospatiale AS.350B1 AStar	2268	
C-GPTL	Aerospatiale AS.350B2 AStar	2103	ex OY-HEH
C-GPWO	Aerospatiale AS.350BA AStar	2236	ex N2BQ
C-GVIA	Aerospatiale AS.350B1 AStar	2297	ex N442BV
C-GVIV	Aerospatiale AS.350B2 AStar	3419	
C-FANC	Bell 206B JetRanger II	1283	
C-FBER	Bell 206B JetRanger III	2648	ex N5018L
C-FBHQ	Bell 206B JetRanger II	970	
C-FIQF	Bell 206B JetRanger II	1110	ex N58144
C-FMCH	Bell 206B JetRanger II	2132	ex N306CK
C-FMPI	Bell 206B JetRanger II	978	
C-FPZI	Bell 206B JetRanger II	1280	
C-GBNS	Bell 206B JetRanger II	1805	ex N49634
C-GCXT	Bell 206B JetRanger II	1551	ex N4432V
C-GGQL	Bell 206B JetRanger II	2117	ex N16723
C-GHCQ	Bell 206B JetRanger II	1302	
C-GHGG	Bell 206B JetRanger	1342	
C-GHHE	Bell 206B JetRanger II	1979	ex N9906K
C-GISE	Bell 206B JetRanger II	839	ex N300FH
C-GJSG	Bell 206B JetRanger II	326	ex N1545V
C-GJTV	Bell 206B JetRanger II	352	ex N1428W
C-GJVU	Bell 206B JetRanger	1731	ex N90304
C-GMGN	Bell 206B JetRanger III	2867	
C-GNMI	Bell 206B JetRanger III	2602	ex N5014F
C-GNMT	Bell 206B JetRanger III	2295	ex N722CH
C-GNMU	Bell 206B JetRanger III	2283	ex N88AM
C-GORO	Bell 206B JetRanger II	2086	ex N15558
C-GRFD	Bell 206B JetRanger III	2332	ex N16887
C-GTPH	Bell 206B JetRanger II	1531	ex N59629
C-GTWP	Bell 206B JetRanger II	946	ex N29979
C-GUYM	Bell 206B JetRanger II	1687	ex N90191
C-GVIH	Bell 206B JetRanger II	1689	
C-GWUF	Bell 206B JetRanger II	1182	ex N52AA
C-FCTD	Bell 206L-1 LongRanger II	45159	ex N2943A
C-FJTO	Bell 206L LongRanger	45085	ex SE-HOP
C-FVIX	Bell 206L LongRanger	45139	ex SE-HTL
C-GENT	Bell 206L LongRanger	45041	ex ZK-HYV
C-GMJS	Bell 206L LongRanger	46608	ex N120RM
C-FNMD	Bell 212	30730	ex PT-HRK
C-FVIK	Bell 212	30990	ex YV-O-CVG-8
C-FWDV	Bell 212	30973	ex N2768N
C-GERH	Bell 212	30768	ex N42434
C-GGAT	Bell 212	30846	ex N16796
C-GTKE	Bell 212	30704	
C-FIGR*	Kamov Ka-32-IIBC	8707	ex B-77299
C-FKHL*	Kamov Ka-32-IIBC	8801	ex RA-31594
C-FPZR*	Sikorsky S-61L	61-362	ex N305V
C-FTIG*	Sikorsky S-61N	61491	ex N613RM
C-GAYB	Bell 205A-1	30295	
C-GFSI	Bell 222U	47504	
C-GLJJ*	Cessna U206G Stationair	U20606205	ex N6257Z	Amphibian
C-GURI*	Kamov Ka-32-IIBC	8810	ex B-77199
C-GUXH	Bell 222UT	47544	ex N61509
C-GVIE	Bell 205B	30188	ex JA9854
C-GVIM	Bell 222UT	47571	ex JA9912
C-GVIY	Bell 222UT	47562	ex JA9665

* Operated by VIH Logging

VENTURE AIR

Thompson, Man

C-GVPB	de Havilland DHC-2 Beaver	1551

VENTURE HELICOPTERS

Calgary-Intl, Alta (YYC)

C-FPTG	Aerospatiale AS.350B2 AStar	2635	ex SE-JCB
C-FVHX	Aerospatiale AS.350B2 AStar	3323	
C-GEMJ	Aerospatiale AS.350D AStar	1411	ex N139EH
C-GILZ	Aerospatiale AS.350B2 AStar	3386	
C-GPHN	Aerospatiale AS.350BA AStar	1251	
C-GPTC	Aerospatiale AS.350B1 AStar	2092	ex OY-HDY
C-GVEI	Aerospatiale AS.350B2 AStar	2671	ex N6095T
C-GXTO	Aerospatiale AS.350B2 AStar	9061	
C-GZGN	Aerospatiale AS.350B2 AStar	9062	
C-FETK	Bell 205A-1	30299	ex OE-BXH
C-FFHB	Bell 205A-1	30294	
C-GVHP	Bell 205A-1	30119	ex N90729
C-GVHQ	Bell 205A-1	30110	

VIKING AIR

Sidney, BC

CF-FHF	de Havilland DHC-2 Beaver	19
C-FJOQ	de Havilland DHC-2 Beaver	1070
C-FJUH	de Havilland DHC-3 Otter	214
C-GJZX	de Havilland DHC-2 Turbo Beaver	1672TB42

VIKING HELICOPTERS

Ottawa, Ont (YOW)

A subsidiary of Canadian Helicopters [CHC Inc] (q.v.)

VILLERS AIR SERVICES

Fort Nelson, BC (YYE)

C-FGAQ	Britten-Norman BN-2A-27 Islander	212	ex G-51-212
C-FJBD	Beech 58 Baron	TH-260	ex N518SW
C-FTUP	Piper PA-31-350 Navajo Chieftain	31-7652101	ex N76DE
C-GEBH	Cessna U206E Stationair	U20601697	ex N8232Q
C-GPPP	Britten-Norman BN-2A-27 Islander	423	ex (N93JA)
C-GZTP	Britten-Norman BN-2B-26 Islander	876	ex

VISION AIR

Vision (VSN) *Vancouver, BC (YVR)*

C-FGES	Cessna 401	0213	ex N7898F
C-GTST	Cessna TU206G Stationair 6	U20605619	

VOYAGE AIR

Fort McMurray, Alta (ZFM)

C-GBNA	de Havilland DHC-3 Otter	125	ex N5368G
C-GDOB	de Havilland DHC-2 Beaver	774	ex C-GEZR
C-GOLB	Cessna A185F Skywagon	18503188	ex N93173
C-GQQJ	de Havilland DHC-2 Beaver	719	ex N202PS
C-GUJW	de Havilland DHC-2 Beaver	1657	ex 305
C-GZSI	de Havilland DHC-2 Beaver	1003	ex N5327

All operate on floats or wheels/skis

VOYAGEUR AIRWAYS

Voyageur (4V/VAL) (IATA 908) *Sudbury/North Bay, Ont (YSB/YYB)*

C-FAMU	Beech A100 King Air	B-166	ex N221SS
C-FAPP	Beech A100 King Air	B-169	ex N305TZ
C-FBGS	Beech A100 King Air	B-204	ex N108JL
C-FCSD	Beech 100 King Air	B-75	ex N24MK
C-GDPI	Beech A100 King Air	B-156	ex N21RX
C-GISH	Beech A100 King Air	B-152	ex N67LC
C-GJBV	Beech A100 King Air	B-100	ex N100S
C-GJJF	Beech A100 King Air	B-123	ex N741EB

All are convertible to air ambulance role

C-FWZV	de Havilland DHC-7-103	81	ex P2-ANP
C-FZKM	de Havilland DHC-7-102	61	ex N903HA
C-GCEV	de Havilland DHC-7-103	63	ex P2-ANN

C-GFFL	de Havilland DHC-7-102	74	ex HB-IVY	Lsd to DAP
C-GFOF	de Havilland DHC-7-102	37	ex N67RM	
C-GGUL	de Havilland DHC-7-102	70	ex N905HA	
C-GGUN	de Havilland DHC-7-110	66	ex N66SU	
C-GJPI	de Havilland DHC-7-102	36	ex N702GW	Op for Fugro Airborne Surveys
C-GLOL	de Havilland DHC-7-102	39	ex HB-IVW	
C-	de Havilland DHC-7-102	24	ex N234SL	
C-FZVW	Beech 200 Super King Air	BB-787	ex N26G	
C-FZVX	Beech 200 Super King Air	BB-231	ex N200FH	
C-GIND	Beech 200C Super King Air B	BL-42	ex N819CD	
C-GJJT	Beech 200 Super King Air	BB-828	ex N62GA	

WAASHESKKUN AIRWAYS

Baie du Poste (Mistassini Lake), Ont

| C-FDIO | de Havilland DHC-3 Otter | 452 | ex TAF 9102 | Floats or wheels/skis |
| C-FEYY | de Havilland DHC-3 Otter | 19 | | Floats or wheels/skis |

WABAKIMI AIR

Armstrong, Ont (YYW)

CF-BJY	de Havilland DHC-2 Beaver	173	ex N4792C
C-FBPC	de Havilland DHC-2 Beaver	144	ex VH-AAS
C-FLLX	de Havilland DHC-2 Beaver	1293	
All operate on floats or wheels/skis			

WABUSK AIR

Moosonee, Ont (YMO)

C-GKMW	Piper PA-31 Turbo Navajo	31-725	ex N231CD
C-GLEW	Piper PA-31 Turbo Navajo	31-685	ex N6775L
C-GMNX	Piper PA-31 Turbo Navajo	31-528	ex N6601L
C-GRVW	Piper PA-31 Turbo Navajo	31-618	ex N123SA

WALSTEN AIR SERVICE

Walsten (WAS)   *Kenora, Ont (YQK)*

C-FCZP	de Havilland DHC-3 Otter	69	
C-FKJI	Beech 200 Super King Air	BB-105	ex N71TZ
C-FMAQ	de Havilland DHC-2 Beaver	14	
C-FWTE	de Havilland DHC-6 Twin Otter 100	96	
C-GFZQ	Cessna U206E Skywagon	U20601543	ex N9143M
C-GHMW	Cessna 402C II	402C0469	ex N68379
C-GJLI	Beech 200 Super King Air	BB-347	ex N424CR
C-GQNJ	Beech 200 Super King Air	BB-275	
C-GTWW	Beech 65-C90 King Air	LJ-657	ex N9030R

WASAYA AIRWAYS

Wasaya (WG/WSG)   *Thunder Bay, Ont (YQT)*

C-FFFS	Hawker Siddeley HS.748 Srs.2A/209LFD	1663	ex G-BHCJ	806; Freighter
C-FTTW	Hawker Siddeley HS.748 Srs.2A/264	1681	ex G-AYIR	805; Freighter
C-GDTD	Hawker Siddeley HS.748 Srs.2B/398	1779	ex 5U-BAR	803; Freighter
C-GLTC	Hawker Siddeley HS.748 Srs.2A/244	1656	ex N57910	801; Tanker
C-GMAA	Hawker Siddeley HS.748 Srs.2A/214LFD	1576	ex TR-LQY	807; Freighter
C-FKRB	Pilatus PC-12/45	233	ex HB-FRD	
C-FPCI	Pilatus PC-12/45	399	ex N399PB	
C-FSRK	Pilatus PC-12/45	202	ex ZS-SRK	
C-FVPC	Pilatus PC-12/45	358	ex	
C-FWAV	Pilatus PC-12/45	280	ex N280PC	
C-GBJV	Pilatus PC-12/45	237	ex HB-FRH	
C-GBXW	Pilatus PC-12/45	170	ex N170PD	
C-GKPL	Pilatus PC-12/45	245	ex ZS-DET	
C-FKAD	Cessna 208B Caravan I	208B0327		
C-FKDL	Cessna 208B Caravan I	208B0240		
C-FWAW	Cessna 208B Caravan I	208B0895	ex N5265B	
C-FWAX	Beech 1900D	UE-297	ex N21679	
C-GSWA	Beech 1900D	UE-34	ex N83801	dam 27Jan03
C-GZVJ	Beech 1900D	UE-223	ex N1123J	

WATSON'S SKYWAYS

Wawa, Ont (YXZ)

C-FAZQ	Cessna U206 Super Skywagon	U206-0337	
C-GIKP	Cessna 208 Caravan I	20800141	ex N524DB
C-GOFB	de Havilland DHC-3 Turbo Otter	39	ex RCAF 3681

WAWEIG AIR

Armstrong, Ont (YYW)

C-FQND	de Havilland DHC-3 Otter	233	ex N5235G
C-FYCX	de Havilland DHC-3 Otter	44	ex N10704
C-GNZO	de Havilland DHC-2 Beaver	399	ex 51-16844

WEST COAST AIR

(8O) (IATA 222)   *Vancouver-Coal Harbor, BC (CXH)*

C-FGQE	de Havilland DHC-6 Twin Otter 100	40	ex 5H-MNK	
C-FGQH	de Havilland DHC-6 Twin Otter 100	106	ex 8Q-MAF	
C-FGQZ	de Havilland DHC-2 Beaver	118		
C-FMHR	de Havilland DHC-6 Twin Otter 100	51	ex N51FW	
C-GJAW	de Havilland DHC-6 Twin Otter 200	176	ex N2261L	607
C-GQKN	de Havilland DHC-6 Twin Otter 100	94	ex PZ-TAV	606
All floatplanes				

WEST COAST HELICOPTERS

Port McNeill, BC (YMP)

C-FNTA	Aerospatiale AS.350B AStar	1356	ex N511FP
C-FQCD	Aerospatiale AS.350B AStar	1854	ex JA9412
C-FSWH	Aerospatiale AS.350B AStar	1990	ex N9007S
C-FWCH	Aerospatiale AS.350B AStar	1696	ex C-FSUL
C-FWCO	Aerospatiale AS.350BA AStar	2868	ex C-FVTM
C-FWCR	Aerospatiale AS.350B2 AStar	2204	ex F-GMBZ
C-GAVU	Aerospatiale AS.350BA AStar	2533	ex PT-YAE
C-GMEP	Bell 206B JetRanger III	3055	
C-GSEB	Bell 206B JetRanger II	1602	ex XA-...

WEST WIND AVIATION

Westwind (WEW)   *Regina, Sask (YQR)*

C-FCPD	British Aerospace Jetstream 31	822	ex G-31-822
C-FCSE	Hawker Siddeley HS.748 Srs.2A/269	1679	ex G-AYFL
C-FDAD	Cessna 401A	401A0058	ex N6601L
C-FQVE	Hawker Siddeley HS.748 Srs.2B/378	1792	ex G-SSFS
C-FWWQ	Beech 200 Super King Air	BB-667	ex N667NA
C-FZJE	Cessna 401B	401B0032	ex (N7931Q)
C-GADI	Beech 200 Super King Air	BB-853	ex N44SR
C-GAXR	Cessna 401B	401B0050	ex N1250C
C-GHGK	British Aerospace Jetstream 31	786	ex N786SC
C-GGPX	Cessna 402C II	402C0260	ex YV-1037P
C-GRSY	Cessna 401	401-0248	ex N8400F
C-GWWB	Cessna 414	414-0514	ex N414DM
C-GWWC	Aerospatiale/Alenia ATR42-300	209	ex N209AT
C-GWWN	Beech 200 Super King Air	BB-14	ex N418CS

WESTAIR AVIATION

Camloops, BC

C-GPIM	Piper PA-31T Cheyenne II	31T-8020065	C-GNAM
C-GVKA	Piper PA-31T Cheyenne II	31T-7920008	ex N9715N

WESTEX AIRLINES

Westex (WES)   *Vancouver-Intl, BC (YVR)*

C-FTIX	Swearingen SA.226AT Merlin IVA	AT-066	ex N5455N	Op for Purolator Canada
C-FVQE	Fairchild F-27F	89	ex N4425B	Op for DHL
C-FWXB	Beech 200 Super King Air	BB-1058	ex N220DK	
C-FWXR	Beech 300 Super King Air	FL-13	ex N301JW	
C-GFWX	Swearingen SA.227AC Metro III	AC-650B	ex N26863	
C-GTLA	Beech 200 Super King Air	BB-1224	ex N94LC	EMS
C-GWXC	Fokker F.27 Friendship 400	10268	ex HB-AAZ	Op for Purolator Canada
C-GWXD	Fokker F.27 Friendship 300M	10156	ex C-6 (Klu)	Op for Purolator Canada

```
C-GWXH    Beech 200 Super King Air            BB-1126    ex C-GTLT    EMS
C-GWXK    Learjet 31                          31A-068    ex N500EW
C-GWXL    Piper PA-31-350 Navajo Chieftain   31-7952036  ex C-GLYG
C-GWXM    Beech 200C Super King Air           BL-130     ex N362TD    Freighter
C-GWXX    Swearingen SA.227AC Metro III       AC-738     ex N2734X    Op for Purolator Canada
C-GWXZ    Swearingen SA.227AC Metro III       AC-701     ex N27119
```
Westex is the trading name of Western Express Air Lines

WESTJET

Westjet (WS/WJA)   *Calgary-Intl, Alta (YYC)*

C-FAWJ	Boeing 737-281 (AvAero 3)	588/21770	ex JA8456	752
C-FCWJ	Boeing 737-2E3 (AvAero 3)	811/22703	ex 9M-VMB	748
C-FIWJ	Boeing 737-2M8 (AvAero 3)	659/21955	ex N141AW	749
C-FKWJ	Boeing 737-2H4 (AvAero 3)	609/21811	ex N59SW	753
C-FLWJ	Boeing 737-2Q8 (AvAero 3)	1059/23148	ex CC-CYV	750	Lsd fr Pegasus
C-FTWJ	Boeing 737-281 (AvAero 3)	585/21767	ex JA8453	751
C-GEWJ	Boeing 737-2T4 (AvAero 3)	633/22055	ex N467AT	745
C-GGWJ	Boeing 737-2B4 (AvAero 3)	491/21500	ex N311VA	738	Lsd fr Polaris
C-GMWJ	Boeing 737-281 (AvAero 3)	594/21771	ex JA8457	739
C-GQWJ	Boeing 737-281 (AvAero 3)	587/21769	ex JA8455	740
C-GSWJ	Boeing 737-2H4 (AvAero 3)	544/21593	ex N55SW	755
C-GUWJ	Boeing 737-204 (Nordam 3)	341/20807	ex N107TR	743	Lsd fr Triton
C-GVWJ	Boeing 737-281 (AvAero 3)	586/21768	ex JA8454	746
C-GWJE	Boeing 737-275 (AvAero 3)	300/20588	ex N861SY	735
C-GWJG	Boeing 737-275 (AvAero 3)	315/20670	ex N862SY	736
C-GWJK	Boeing 737-269 (Nordam 3)	448/21206	ex N500AL	756
C-GWJU	Boeing 737-2H4 (AvAero 3)	423/21117	ex N26SW	733
C-GWWJ	Boeing 737-204 (Nordam 3)	542/21694	ex N109TR	741	Lsd fr Triton
C-GXWJ	Boeing 737-281 (AvAero 3)	583/21766	ex JA8452	742
C-FGWJ	Boeing 737-76N	32764		on order 04	Lsd fr GECAS
C-FIWS	Boeing 737-76N	851/32404		001	Lsd fr GECAS
C-FJWS	Boeing 737-76N	872/28651		002	Lsd fr GECAS
C-FKWS	Boeing 737-76N	905/30134	ex N1787B	003	Lsd fr GECAS
C-FUWS	Boeing 737-7CT	32765		on order 04	
C-FWAD	Boeing 737-7CT	1222/32753		201	
C-FWAF	Boeing 737-7CT	1239/32747		202	
C-FWAI	Boeing 737-7CT	1246/33656		203	
C-FWAO	Boeing 737-7CT	1254/33657		205	
C-FWAQ	Boeing 737-7CT	1266/32748		206	
C-FWBG	Boeing 737-7CT	1281/32749		207	
C-FWBL	Boeing 737-7CT	1286/32750		208	
C-FWBW	Boeing 737-7CT	1303/33697		209	
C-FWBX	Boeing 737-7CT	1333/32751		210	
C-FWCC	Boeing 737-7CT	1339/32752		211	
C-FWCN	Boeing 737-7CT	1346/33698		212	
C-FWSJ	Boeing 737-76N	1431/32758		218	Lsd fr GECAS
C-FWSO	Boeing 737-76N	1445/32759			Lsd fr GECAS
C-FWSV	Boeing 737-76N	32760		on order 04	Lsd fr GECAS
C-FWSX	Boeing 737-7CT	32761		on order 04	
C-FWSY	Boeing 737-76N	32762		on order 04	Lsd fr GECAS
C-FZWS	Boeing 737-76N	1044/32731		006	Lsd fr GECAS
C-GCWJ	Boeing 737-76N	33970		on order 04	Lsd fr GECAS
C-GJWF	Boeing 737-7CT	32766		on order 04	
C-GLWS	Boeing 737-76N	1009/32581	ex N1787B	005	Lsd fr GECAS
C-GRWS	Boeing 737-76N	1155/32881		007	Lsd fr GECAS
C-GTWS	Boeing 737-76N	1179/32883		008	Lsd fr GECAS
C-GUWS	Boeing 737-76N	1206/33378		009	Lsd fr GECAS
C-GWAZ	Boeing 737-76N	32763		on order 04	Lsd fr GECAS
C-GWBF	Boeing 737-76N	1370/32757		213	Lsd fr GECAS
C-GWBJ	Boeing 737-76N	1385/32754	ex N1787B	214	Lsd fr GECAS
C-GWBT	Boeing 737-76N	1396/32755		215	Lsd fr GECAS
C-GWCM	Boeing 737-7CT	1413/32756	ex N1795B	216	Lsd fr GECAS
C-GWJO	Boeing 737-76N	33969		on order 04	Lsd fr GECAS
C-GWSE	Boeing 737-76N	1216/33379		010	Lsd fr GECAS
C-GWSH	Boeing 737-76N	1258/29886		011	Lsd fr GECAS

A further six Boeing 737-76Ns are on order for delivery in 2005 (5) and 2006 (1). All Boeing 737-700s to be retrofitted with blended winglets.

WESTPOINT AIRLINES

Calgary-Intl, Alta (YYC)

```
C-GWPS    de Havilland DHC-8-102    120    ex N928HA
C-GZKH    de Havilland DHC-8-102    117    ex N927HA    on order
C-GZTC    de Havilland DHC-8-102    099    ex N923HA       .
```
First service 15 August 2003

WHISTLER AIR SERVICES

C-FMAW	de Havilland DHC-2 Beaver	1201	
C-FSKZ	de Havilland DHC-2 Beaver	1594	
C-GEJC	Cessna A185F Skywagon	18502823	ex (N1313F)
C-GEND	de Havilland DHC-3 Otter	371	ex C-GHYJ

All floatplanes

WHITE RIVER AIR
(WRA)

CF-FHR	de Havilland DHC-2 Beaver	46
C-FWRA	de Havilland DHC-3 Otter	213

WHITESHELL AIR SERVICE

C-FASH	Cessna A185E Skywagon	185-1489		Floats or wheels/skis
CF-JFA	de Havilland DHC-2 Beaver	1581	ex N5563	Floats or wheels/skis
C-FQZH	Piper PA-31-350 Navajo Chieftain	31-7952070	ex N105TT	
C-GEHD	Cessna A185F Skywagon	18502787	ex (N1225F)	Floats or wheels/skis
C-GGON	de Havilland DHC-3 Otter	225	ex TI-SPG	Floats or wheels/skis
C-GGOR	de Havilland DHC-3 Otter	97	ex TI-SPE	Floats or wheels/skis
C-GUEH	Piper PA-31 Turbo Navajo C	31-7712057	ex N27255	

WILDCAT HELICOPTERS

C-FCAN	Bell 212	30919	ex XA-IOW
C-GSGT	Bell 212	30771	ex C-FSAT
C-GWHO	Bell 206L LongRanger	45013	ex N3GH

WILDCOUNTRY AIRWAYS

C-FPCC	Cessna 208B Caravan I	208B0840	ex N52623
C-GWCA	Cessna 208B Caravan I	208B0892	ex N5181U

WILDERNESS AIR

C-FGMK	de Havilland DHC-2 Beaver	1329	ex 58-2003
C-FJOF	de Havilland DHC-2 Beaver	1053	
C-FODV	de Havilland DHC-3 Otter	411	
C-FZYE	de Havilland DHC-2 Beaver	192	ex N11252
C-GFZF	Cessna A185E Skywagon	18502002	ex N70118
C-GLAB	de Havilland DHC-3 Otter	348	ex 59-2210

All operate on floats or wheels/skis

WILDERNESS HELICOPTERS

C-FALS	Bell 206L LongRanger	45061	ex N56DE
C-FFBV	Bell 206B JetRanger	1016	ex N90819
C-FQCK	Bell 206B JetRanger	692	
C-GMCJ	Bell 206L-3 LongRanger III	51459	
C-GWHA	Bell 206L-1 LongRanger II	45694	ex N82KA

WILLISTON LAKE AIR SERVICES

C-FBAD	Piper PA-31-350 Navajo Chieftain	31-7752101	ex N6196C
C-GRQG	Piper PA-31-350 Navajo Chieftain	31-7952073	
C-GRWP	Piper PA-31-350 Navajo Chieftain	31-7952095	

WOLVERINE AIR

C-FTQB	Cessna A185F Skywagon	18501655	ex (N1948U)
C-GHKB	Cessna 207 Skywagon	20700228	ex N1628U

C-GQOA	Cessna U206G Stationair 6	U20604993	ex (N46UUU)
C-GTUG	Cessna U206G Stationair 6	U20606214	ex (N6282Z)

YELLOWHEAD HELICOPTERS

Valemount, BC

C-FNMW	Bell 206B JetRanger	665	
C-FPQX	Bell 206B Jet Ranger	1330	
C-FYHB	Bell 206B JetRanger	1655	ex C-GCHH
C-FYHJ	Bell 206B JetRanger III	2900	ex N344P
C-GLCD	Bell 206B JetRanger	1284	
C-GVIF	Bell 206B JetRanger	782	
C-GXYH	Bell 206B JetRanger III	2267	ex N130VG
C-GYHL	Bell 206B JetRanger III	1702	
C-GYHR	Bell 206B JetRanger III	2571	ex N5015A
C-GYHT	Bell 206B JetRanger III	4104	ex HL9107
C-FYHN	Bell 206L LongRanger	45050	ex N600FB
C-FYYH	Bell 206L-1 LongRanger	45643	ex N2630
C-GYHP	Bell 206L-1 LongRanger	45400	ex N2621
C-GYHQ	Bell 206L-1 LongRanger	45419	ex N2629
C-GYHX	Bell 206L-3 LongRanger III	51545	ex N206AC
C-GYHZ	Bell 206L LongRanger	45126	ex N16840
C-FNMO	Bell 205A-1	30128	ex N58057
C-GJWC	Cessna T210L Turbo Centurion	21060438	ex N93858
C-GVEG	Bell 204C	2199	ex OY-HCB
C-GYHU	Bell 204C	2053	ex N120LA

ZIP AIR

Zipper (3J/ZIP)   *Calgary-Intl, Alta (YYC)*

C-FACP	Boeing 737-2L9	623/22072	ex C2-RN9	
C-FCPN	Boeing 737-2T7	856/22762	ex G-DGDP	orange
C-FHCP	Boeing 737-2T5	641/22024	ex EI-BPV	fuschia
C-GCPM	Boeing 737-217	560/21716	ex N1262E	blue
C-GCPN	Boeing 737-217	581/21717		green
C-GCPO	Boeing 737-217	584/21718		orange
C-GCPP	Boeing 737-217	666/22255		fuschia
C-GCPQ	Boeing 737-217	672/22256		green
C-GCPT	Boeing 737-217	770/22258		Lsd fr ACA
C-GFCP	Boeing 737-217	874/22659		fucshia
C-GJCP	Boeing 737-217	911/22728	ex N178EE	blue
C-GKCP	Boeing 737-217	915/22729		Lsd fr ACA
C-GMCP	Boeing 737-217	945/22864		fuschia Lsd fr ACA
C-GQCP	Boeing 737-217	960/22865		orange
C-GWPW	Boeing 737-275	1109/23283		green

Low cost operation based in Western Canada, wholly owned by Air Canada. Titles appear as 4321.Zip.com

ZOOM AIRLINES

(OOM)   *Ottawa, Ont (YOW)*

C-GZMM	Boeing 767-328ER	497/27136	ex N221LF	Lsd fr Castle 2003-1A
C-GZUM*	Boeing 767-328ER	493/27135	ex F-GHGI	101 Lsd fr Florita Finance
C-GZXB	Boeing 767-300ER			on order 2Q04

*Named "City of Ottawa"

CC - CHILE (Republic of Chile)

AEROCARDAL

Cardal (CDA)   *Santiago-Tobalaba*

CC-CWA	MBB Bo105LS-A3	2006	ex N96LS
CC-CWB	Bell 206L-3 LongRanger III	51023	ex N38886
CC-CWC	Dornier 228-202K	8162	ex D-CLEE
CC-CWD	Piper PA-31T1 Cheyenne I	31T-8104071	ex CC-CRU
CC-CWE	Cessna 421C Golden Eagle	421C0614	ex CC-PJB
CC-CWI	MBB Bo105CB	S-193	ex C-11
CC-CWW	Cessna S550 Citation S/II	S550-0002	ex N211VP
CC-CWX	Dornier 228-101	7027	ex CC-CSA
CC-CWZ	Cessna 551 Citation II/SP	551-0141	ex N388MA

All operate as passenger or EMS

AEROMET LINEA AEREA

Aeromet (MTE)   Santiago-Los Cerrilos (ULC)

CC-CZA   British Aerospace Jetstream 31   644   ex N644JX   Lsd fr BAES

<u>AEROVIAS DAP</u> now listed under trading name Dap Airways

ALPINE AIR EXPRESS CHILE

Santiago-Los Cerrilos (ULC)

CC-CAS   Beech 1900C   UB-5   ex N198GA
CC-   Beech 99   U-143 ex N399AA
Wholly owned subsidiary of Alpine Air Express and aircraft leased from parent

ASPAR - AEROSERVICIO PARRAGUE

Aspar (PRG)   Santiago-Los Cerrilos (ULC)
Previously lsited as Empresa Aero-Servicios Parrague

CC-CDT   Canadian Vickers PBY-5A Catalina   CV-332 ex F-YCHB   32
CC-CNP   Consolidated PBY-6A Catalina   2029   ex EC-FXN   35
Operates mainly in the firebombing role, aircraft spend time in Europe operated by ATA-Aerocondor

COPTERS - SERVICIOS AEREOS COPTERS

Copters (KOP)   Rancagua

CC-CLB   Bell UH-1H   5892   ex N28BC
CC-CLD   Bell 206B JetRanger II   2534   ex C-GBZL
CC-CLE   Bell UH-1H   8535   ex N46666
CC-CLF   Bell AH-1S   24060 ex N82277
CC-CLI   Bell 204B   2010   ex C-GEAW
CC-CLJ   Aerospatiale AS.365N2 Dauphin 1   6471   ex N64EH
CC-CLK   Bell UH-1H   4902   ex N38CF
CC-CLL   Aerospatiale AS 350B2 Ecureuil   3061
CC-CLQ   Bell 206B JetRanger II   796   ex C-FOAS
CC-CLU   Bell 204B   2037   ex C-FAHA
CC-CLZ   Aerospatiale AS.350B3 Ecureuil   3182
CC-CNA   Bell 407   53268 ex N4431J

DAP AIRWAYS

Punta Arenas (PUQ)
Previously listed as Aerovias Dap

C-GFFL   de Havilland DHC-7-102   74   ex HB-IVY   Lsd fr VAL
CC-CHV   de Havilland DHC-6 Twin Otter 300   709   ex G-BHUY
CC-CLT   CASA C.212-100   A10-1-103 ex E-210
CC-CLV   Cessna 402C   402C0073   ex CC-CDU
CC-CLY   Beech 100 King Air   B-79   ex CC-PIE
CC-COV   Cessna 402C   402C0282   ex CC-CDS
Dap Airways is the trading name of Aerovias Dap

<u>EMPRESA AERO-SERVICIOS PARRAGUE</u> now listed under trading name Aspar

HELICOPTEROS AGROFORESTAL

Agroforestal (HAA)   Santiago-Tobalaba

CC-CAO   Bell UH-1H   4662   ex N106SW
CC-CCE   Bell UH-1H   13408 ex N7043W
CC-CCX   Bell UH-1B   269   ex N6190S
CC-CEH   Bell UH-1H   11445 ex N92530
CC-CWM   Bell UH-1H   5278   ex N165AS
CC-CWO   Bell UH-1B   675   ex N6185W

CC-CCN   Bell 206B JetRanger   527   ex YV-573C
CC-CPH   Bell 206B JetRanger II   2195   ex N177SH

LAN CHILE

LAN (LA/LAN) (IATA 045)   Santiago-Benitez Intl (SCL)

CC-COC   Airbus Industrie A320-233   1304   ex F-WWBV
CC-COD   Airbus Industrie A320-233   1332   ex F-WWDL
CC-COE   Airbus Industrie A320-233   1351   ex F-WWIC
CC-COF   Airbus Industrie A320-233   1355   ex F-WWBE
CC-COH   Airbus Industrie A320-233   1512   ex F-WWBE   Lsd to LXP
CC-COI   Airbus Industrie A320-233   1526   ex F-WWIM

CC-COK	Airbus Industrie A320-233	1548	ex F-WWDB		Lsd to LXP
CC-COM	Airbus Industrie A320-233	1626	ex F-WWDL		Lsd to LXP
CC-COP	Airbus Industrie A320-233	1858	ex F-WWDY		
CC-COQ	Airbus Industrie A320-233	1877	ex F-WWBO		
CC-COT	Airbus Industrie A320-233	1903	ex F-WWDL		
CC-COU	Airbus Industrie A319-132	2089	ex D-AVWL		Lsd to LXP
CC-COX	Airbus Industrie A319-132	2096	ex D-AVYN		Lsd to LXP
CC-	Airbus Industrie A320-233		ex F-WW	on order 03	
CC-	Airbus Industrie A320-233		ex F-WW	on order 03	
CC-	Airbus Industrie A320-233		ex F-WW	on order 03	
CC-	Airbus Industrie A320-233		ex F-WW	on order 03	
CC-	Airbus Industrie A320-233		ex F-WW	on order 04	
CC-	Airbus Industrie A320-233		ex F-WW	on order 04	
CC-	Airbus Industrie A320-233		ex F-WW	on order 04	
CC-	Airbus Industrie A320-233		ex F-WW	on order 04	
CC-	Airbus Industrie A320-233		ex F-WW	on order 04	
VP-BCJ	Airbus Industrie A320-233	1491	ex CC-COG		Lsd to LPE
VP-BCK	Airbus Industrie A320-233	1568	ex CC-COL		Lsd to LPE
VP-BCS	Airbus Industrie A320-233	1854	ex (CC-COO)		Lsd to LPE

Airbus Industrie A320-233's on order may be deferred; a total of 14 Airbus Industrie A319s are on order

CC-CQA	Airbus Industrie A340-313X	359	ex F-WWJY	
CC-CQC	Airbus Industrie A340-313X	363	ex F-WWJZ	
CC-CQE	Airbus Industrie A340-313X	429	ex F-WWJQ	
CC-CQF	Airbus Industrie A340-313X	442	ex F-WWJY	
CC-	Airbus Industrie A340-313X		on order	
CC-	Airbus Industrie A340-313X		on order	

CC-CRP	Boeing 737-230	777/22134	ex D-ABHF	Lsd fr Milena Intl
CC-CRQ	Boeing 737-230	781/22135	ex D-ABHH	Lsd fr Larissa Industries
CC-CRR	Boeing 737-230	657/22114	ex D-ABFA	Lsd fr Roxana
CC-CRS	Boeing 737-230	791/22139	ex D-ABHN	Lsd fr Valenti Intl
CC-CSH	Boeing 737-204	316/20632	ex G-BADP	Lsd fr TNH Leasing
CC-CSI	Boeing 737-204	318/20633	ex G-BADR	Lsd fr TNH Leasing; sublsd to LXP
CC-CSP	Boeing 737-204	342/20808	ex 9Q-COW	Lsd fr Clipper Lsg; sublsd to LXP
CC-CVC	Boeing 737-229	529/21596	ex OO-SBQ	Lsd fr Glendale; sublsd to LXP
CC-CVD	Boeing 737-229	617/21840	ex OO-SBT	
CC-CVG	Boeing 737-291	909/22743	ex VP-BBL	Lsd fr Hawk Avn Mgt; sublsd to LXP
CC-CVI	Boeing 737-2Q3	706/22367	ex VP-BBO	Lsd fr European Capital Avn
CC-CVJ	Boeing 737-2Q3	896/22736	ex VP-BBP	Lsd fr European Capital Avn
CC-CYC	Boeing 737-219	428/21131	ex G-BGNW	all-white, std SCL Lsd fr ILFC
CC-CYK	Boeing 737-205	506/21445	ex N7031F	Lsd fr A/c Lsd Finance; sublsd LXP
CC-CZK	Boeing 737-236	686/21804	ex G-BGDP	Lsd fr GECAS; sublsd to LXP
CC-CZO	Boeing 737-236	693/22030	ex G-BGJI	Lsd fr Polaris; sublsd to LXP

*Leased to LANPeru

CC-CBJ	Boeing 767-316ER	652/27613		Lsd fr ILFC
CC-CDP	Boeing 767-316ER	602/27597		Lsd fr ILFC
CC-CEB	Boeing 767-316ER	621/26327		Lsd fr ILFC
CC-CEK	Boeing 767-316ER	641/26329		Lsd fr ILFC
CC-CRG	Boeing 767-375ER	430/25865	ex B-2561	Lsd fr CIT Leasing
CC-CRH	Boeing 767-375ER	426/25864	ex B-2562	Lsd fr GECAS
CC-CRT	Boeing 767-316ER	681/27615		Lsd fr ILFC
CC-CZT	Boeing 767-316ER	699/29228		Lsd fr ILFC
CC-CZU	Boeing 767-316ER	729/29229		Lsd fr ILFC
CC-CZW	Boeing 767-316ER	698/29227		Lsd fr ILFC
CC-CEN	Boeing 767-3Q8ER	570/26265	ex TF-ARB	Lsd fr ILFC
CC-	Boeing 767-3Q8ER	694/28206	ex TF-ARA	Lsd fr ILFC

Owns 73.3% of ABSA, 25% of MAS Cargo and 25% of Florida West International. Cargo services are operated by LANChile Cargo (wholly owned) while LANExpress is low cost domestic operation.. LANEcuador is wholly owned Member of oneworld Alliance

LANCHILE CARGO

LAN Cargo (UC/LCO) (IATA 527)   **Santiago-Benitez Intl (SCL)**

CC-CZX	Boeing 767-316ERF	778/29881	Lsd to TUS as PR-ABB
CC-CZY	Boeing 767-316ERF	806/30780	
CC-CZZ	Boeing 767-316ERF	712/25756	Lsd fr Condor Lsg
N312LA	Boeing 767-316ERF	846/32572	Lsd fr Bluebird Lsg
N314LA	Boeing 767-316ERF	848/32573	Lsd fr Bluebird Lsg; op by MAA
N316LA	Boeing 767-316ERF	860/30842	Lsd fr GECAS; op by FWL

Wholly owned by LANChile, part of LANChile Cargo Group with MAS Air; Florida West International and ABSA

LANEXPRESS

LANExpres (LXP)   **Santiago-Benitez Intl (SCL)**

CC-CSI	Boeing 737-204	318/20633	ex G-BADR
CC-CSP	Boeing 737-204	342/20808	ex 9Q-COW
CC-CVC	Boeing 737-229	529/21596	ex OO-SBQ

CC-CVG	Boeing 737-291	965/23024	ex VP-BBL
CC-CYK	Boeing 737-205	506/21445	ex N7031F
CC-CZK	Boeing 737-236	686/21804	ex G-BGDP
CC-CZO	Boeing 737-236	693/22030	ex G-BGJI

CC-COH	Airbus Industrie A320-233	1512	ex F-WWBE
CC-COK	Airbus Industrie A320-233	1548	ex F-WWDB
CC-COM	Airbus Industrie A320-233	1626	ex F-WWDL
CC-COU	Airbus Industrie A319-132	2089	ex D-AVWL
CC-COX	Airbus Industrie A319-132	2096	ex D-AVYN

Wholly owned subsidiary of LANChile and operates aircraft leased from the parent

LASSA - LINEAS DE AEROSERVICIOS

(LSE)   *Santiago-Tobalaba*

CC-CIZ	Bell UH-1B	1124	ex EC-EOH
CC-CNF	Bell UH-1H	5949	ex N1214B
CC-CNG	Bell UH-1H	5054	ex N7232D
CC-CNH	Bell UH-1YH	10484	ex EC-GOH
CC-CNJ	Bell UH-1H	5146	ex N8154G
CC-CNK	Garrick-Bell UH-1B	755	ex LV-WGS
CC-CNL	Garrick-Bell UH-1B	318	ex LV-WNR
CC-CNM	Bell UH-1H	4609	ex N1216Y

CC-CFY	Piper PA-31 Turbo Navajo	31-600	ex E-203
CC-CJG	Aerospatiale SA.315B Lama	2556	ex N3835Q
CC-CNE	Aerospatiale SA.315B Lama	2516	ex H-12
CC-CNN	Bell 206B JetRanger III	3597	ex N22675
CC-CNW	Dornier 228-202K	8063	ex G-BMMR

SKY AIRLINE

(H2/SKU)   *Santiago-Los Cerillos (ULC)*

CC-CAP	Boeing 737-236	654/22027	ex CC-CZM	Lsd fr AerGo Capital
CC-CTB	Boeing 737-2Q3	1241/23481	ex N381AC	Lsd fr WFBN
CC-CTD	Boeing 737-2Q3	1033/23117	ex N380AC	
CC-CTH	Boeing 737-230 (Nordam 3)	808/22636	ex N271LR	
CC-CTK	Boeing 737-230 (Nordam 3)	744/22402	ex N261LR	
CC-CTM	Boeing 737-2H4 (Nordam 3)	303/20583	ex (CC-CTO)	Lsd fr debis
CC-CTO	Boeing 737-2H6 (Nordam 3)	307/20586	ex (CC-CTD)	Lsd fr debis
CC-CTU	Boeing 737-2H6 (Nordam 3)	302/20582	ex (CC-CTM)	Lsd fr debis

| N8892Z | Boeing 727-225F (Raisbeck 3) | 1554/21861 | ex (CC-CTW) | Lsd fr JTI Engines Lsg |

Sky Airline is the trading name of Sky Service

VARMONT EXPRESS

           Santiago-Los Cerillos (ULC)

CC-CEW	Rockwell Commander 680FL	1441-76	ex N4704E
CC-CGO	Rockwell Commander 680FL	1794-149	ex N113NA
CC-CHF	Rockwell Commander 680FL	1430-72	ex N6344U
CC-COA	Rockwell Commander 680FL	1640-121	ex N680AC

All freighters

CN - MOROCCO (Kingdom of Morocco)

AIR ATLAS EXPRESS current status is uncertain, sole aircraft returned to lessor 16 January 2004

MONDAIR

Mondair (MMA)   *Agadir (AGA)*

| CN-RDA | Boeing 737-329 | 1711/24356 | ex OO-SYB | Lsd fr EAST Trust |
| CN-RDB | Boeing 737-329 | 1430/23771 | ex OO-SDV | Lsd fr SLR SA |

MOROCCO AIRWAYS despite issuance of ICAO code, airline did not start operations

REGIONAL AIR LINES

Maroc Regional (FN/RGL)   *Casablanca-Anfa (CAS)*

| CN-RLA | Beech 1900D | UE-259 | ex N10863 | |
| CN-RLD | Beech 1900D | UE-267 | ex N10999 | Lsd fr Raytheon |

ROYAL AIR MAROC
Royalair Maroc (AT/RAM) (IATA 147)
Casablanca-Mohamed V (CMN)

CN-RMF	Boeing 737-4B6	1880/24807		Lsd fr CLS Garnet Lsg
CN-RMG	Boeing 737-4B6	1888/24808		Lsd fr CLS Garnet Lsg
CN-RMI	Boeing 737-2B6 (Nordam 3)	449/21214		El Ayoun; std CAS
CN-RMJ	Boeing 737-2B6 (Nordam 3)	452/21215		Oujda; std CAS
CN-RML	Boeing 737-2B6 (Nordam 3)	851/22767		Lsd to SNG as 6V-AHK
CN-RMM	Boeing 737-2B6C (Nordam 3)	951/23049		
CN-RMN	Boeing 737-2B6C (Nordam 3)	975/23050		
CN-RMV	Boeing 737-5B6	2157/25317		Lsd fr RAM2 Lsg
CN-RMW	Boeing 737-5B6	2166/25364		Lsd fr RAM2 Lsg
CN-RMX	Boeing 737-4B6	2219/26526		
CN-RMY	Boeing 737-5B6	2209/26525		
CN-RNA	Boeing 737-4B6	2453/26531		Lsd fr RAM3 Lsg
CN-RNB	Boeing 737-5B6	2472/26527		Lsd fr RAM3 Lsg
CN-RNC	Boeing 737-4B6	2584/26529		Lsd fr RAM4 Lsg
CN-RND	Boeing 737-4B6	2588/26530		Lsd fr RAM4 Lsg
CN-RNF	Boeing 737-4B6	2733/27678	ex (CN-RNE)	Lsd fr RAM7 Lsg
CN-RNG	Boeing 737-5B6	2734/27679	ex (CN-RNF)	Lsd fr RAM5 Lsg
CN-RNH	Boeing 737-5B6	2855/27680		Lsd fr RAM6 Lsg
CN-RNJ	Boeing 737-8B6	55/28980		Lsd fr RAM7 Lsg
CN-RNK	Boeing 737-8B6	60/28981		Lsd fr RAM7 Lsg
CN-RNL	Boeing 737-7B6	236/28982		Lsd fr RAM8 Lsg
CN-RNM	Boeing 737-7B6	294/28984		Lsd fr RAM8 Lsg
CN-RNP	Boeing 737-8B6	492/28983		Lsd fr RAM10 Lsg
CN-RNQ	Boeing 737-7B6	501/28985		Lsd fr RAM10 Lsg
CN-RNR	Boeing 737-7B6	519/28986	ex N1787B	Lsd fr RAM10 Lsg
CN-RNU	Boeing 737-8B6	1095/28987		
CN-RNV	Boeing 737-7B6	1261/28988		
CN-RNW	Boeing 737-8B6	1347/33057	ex N1787B	
CN-RNZ	Boeing 737-8B6	1432/33058		
CN-ROA	Boeing 737-8B6	1457/33059		

A further seven 737-8B6s are on order for delivery up to December 2008

CN-CDF	Beech 200 Super King Air	BB-577		Trainer	
CN-CDN	Beech 200 Super King Air	BB-713	ex N36741	Trainer	
CN-CDU	Aerospatiale/Alenia ATR 42-300	134	ex F-WWEF	stored CAS	Lsd fr Intl Leasing
CN-CDV	Aerospatiale/Alenia ATR 42-300	137	ex F-WWEI	stored CAS	Lsd fr Intl Leasing
CN-RGA	Boeing 747-428	956/25629	ex F-OGTG		Lsd fr RAM9 Lsg
CN-RME	Boeing 747-2B6M	338/21615		stored	
CN-RMT	Boeing 757-2B6	103/23686	ex N32831	Lsd fr Chemco Equipment Finance	
CN-RMZ	Boeing 757-2B6	106/23687		Lsd fr Chemco Equipment Finance	
CN-RNS	Boeing 767-36NER	863/30115		Lsd fr GECAS	
CN-RNT	Boeing 767-36NER	867/30843		Lsd fr GECAS	
CN-RNX	Airbus Industrie A321-211	2064	ex D-AVZO		
CN-RNY	Airbus Industrie A321-211	2076	ex D-AVZS		
CN-	Airbus Industrie A321-211			on order 04	

A further Airbus Industrie A321 is on order for delivery in 2005
Air Senegal International operates as a franchise operation

CP - BOLIVIA (Republic of Bolivia)

AEROESTE
Santa Cruz-El Trompillo (SRZ)

CP-2266	Rockwell Commander 690B	11395	ex N816PC
CP-2328	LET L-410UVP-E	912536	ex S9-TAY
CP-2349	LET L-410UVP-E20	912530	ex S9-TBM
CP-2382	LET L-410UVP-E	861727	ex S9-TBH
CP-2393	LET L-410UVP-E	872020	

AEROSUR
Aerosur (5L/RSU) (IATA 275)
Santa Cruz-Viru Viru (VVI)

CP-2377	Boeing 727-23	592/20044	ex N1969	status?	Lsd fr JIS A/C Co
CP-2422	Boeing 727-264 (FedEx 3)	1696/22411	ex XA-MEJ		Lsd fr MXA
CP-2423	Boeing 727-264 (FedEx 3)	1607/22156	ex XA-MED		
CP-2427	Boeing 727-2B7 (FedEx 3)	1743/22164	ex XA-TMA		Lsd fr Pegasus
CP-2429	Boeing 727-259 (FedEx 3)	1690/22475	ex N289SC		Lsd fr Aircraft Lease Finance
XA-HON	Boeing 727-264 (FedEx 3)	1416/21617			
XA-HOX	Boeing 727-264 (FedEx 3)	1457/21638			
CP-2244	LET L-410UVP	912534	ex OK-WDD	stored	
CP-2245	LET L-410UVP	912535	ex OK-WDE	stored	
CP-2246	LET L-410UVP	892313	ex SP-FGK	stored	

CP-2438   Boeing 737-201 (Nordam 3)   589/21815 ex C-FNAX   Lsd fr Jetran Intl
Also leases an Airbus Industrie A319 from TACA International
Aerosur is the trading name of Cia Boliviana de Transporte Aereo Privado

FRIGORIFICO REYES

La Paz (LPB)

CP-1207	Douglas DC-4 (C-54G)	10790	ex N62441
CP-1651	Douglas DC-6B	516/44433	ex OB-R-527

FRIGORFICO SANTA RITA current status is uncertain, believed to have ceased operations

LAB AIRLINES - LLOYD AÉREO BOLIVIANO

LloydAereo (LB/LLB) (IATA 051)   *Cochabamba (CBB)*

CP-861"	Boeing 727-1A0	748/20279		Sucre	
CP-1223"	Boeing 727-78 (Stage 3)	104/18795	ex N306BN	Trinidad	
CP-1276"	Boeing 727-2K3	1124/21082	ex N48054	Cochabamba	
CP-1366"	Boeing 727-2K3 (Duganair 3)	1373/21494		La Paz	winglets
CP-1367"	Boeing 727-2K3	1403/21495		Santa Cruz	
CP-2324	Boeing 727-2M7	1591/21823	ex N918PG	Virgen dr Urkupina	
CP-2429	Boeing 727-259 (FedEx 3)	1690/22475	ex N289SC		Lsd fr A/c Lease Finance
CP-	Boeing 727-2M7F	1339/21502	ex N725RW		Lsd fr Pacific AirCorp
"names prefixed 'City of'					
CP-2013	Fokker F.27Friendship 200	10138	ex 286 Bolivia	Reina Beatrix	
CP-2232	Airbus Industrie A310-304	562	ex F-GKTE		Lsd fr ILFC
CP-2313	Boeing 737-3A1	2836/28389		Paititi	Lsd fr VSP
CP-2391	Boeing 737-382	1699/24366	ex N934PG		Lsd fr Pegasus
CP-2425	Boeing 767-3P6ER	158/23764	ex N964PG		Lsd fr Pegasus
CP-2426	Boeing 767-3P6ER	244/24349	ex N957PG		Lsd fr Pegasus

LABSA correctly listed under Venezuela

LINEAS AÉREAS CANEDO

Cochabamba (CBB)

CP-744	Rockwell Commander 680	341-34	ex OB-M-573	JS Gaviota
CP-973	Curtiss C-46C Commando	32941	ex N32227	
CP-1960	Douglas DC-3C	18993	ex PT-KVN	
CP-2421	Douglas DC-3S	12979/43365	ex N545CT	

SAPSA - SERVICIOS AÉREOS PETROLEROS

Santa Cruz-El Trompillo (SRZ)

CP-1019	de Havilland DHC-6 Twin Otter 300	368		stored OPF	ZS-OUH reserved
CP-1106	Twin Commander 690A	11193	ex N9149N		
CP-2176	Dornier 228-202	8163	ex D-CIKI	dbr 07Jul93, rebuilt?	

SAVE - SERVICIO AERO VARGAS ESPANA

Santa Cruz-El Trompillo (SRZ)

CP-2405	British Aerospace Jetstream 31	676	ex N309PX
CP-2441	British Aerospace Jetstream 32EP	832	ex NLV-WCZ

TAB AIRLINES

Bol (BOL)   *La Paz (LPB)*

CP-1376	Lockheed C-130H Hercules	4759	ex TAM-91
CP-2184	Lockheed C-130A Hercules	3228	ex TAM-69

Also operates cargo services with Douglas DC-8-62F aircraft leased from Arrow Air as required; a division of Fuerza Aérea Boliviano

TAM - TRANSPORTES AÉREO MILITAR

La Paz (LPB)

FAB-90	Fokker F.27M Troopship 400M	10578	ex TAM-90	stored LPB
FAB-91	Fokker F.27M Troopship 400M	10580	ex TAM-91	
FAB-92	Fokker F.27M Troopship 400M	10584	ex TAM-92	
FAB-93	Fokker F.27M Troopship 400M	10599	ex TAM-93	
FAB-94	Fokker F.27M Troopship 400M	10600	ex CP-2282	
FAB-71	Convair 580	370	ex TAM-71	stored LPB

| FAB-72 | Convair 580 | 132 | ex TAM-72 |
| FAB-73 | Convair 580 | 170 | ex TAM-73 |

Transport branch of Fuerza Aerea Boliviana, which operates scheduled flights to remote parts of the country

CS - PORTUGAL (Republic of Portugal)

ACEF CARGO

Acef (CFM)   Evora

| CS-TML | Convair 440 | 484 | ex N357SA | | Lsd to AAG |
| CS-TMM | Convair 580 | 375 | ex C-FHEN | stored Evora | |

Possibly ceased operations, current status is uncertain

AEROCONDOR

AeroCondor (2B/EAD) (IATA 088)   Cascais-Tires

CS-TLJ	Short SD.3-60	SH2716	ex OY-MUG		
CS-TMH	Short SD.3-60	SH3694	ex G-BMNJ	Porto Santo	Lsd fr Lynrise Air Lease
CS-TMN	Short SD.3-60	SH3638	ex G-ISLE	Freighter	
CS-TMY	Short SD.3-60	SH3632	ex G-BLCP		Lsd to HWY
G-EXPS	Short SD.3-60	SH3661	ex TC-AOA		
OY-MUD	Short SD.3-60	SH3692	ex N693PC		Lsd fr VIS
CS-AYT	Dornier 228-200	8084	ex VP-FBK		
CS-DCF	Piper PA-31-350 Chieftain	31-8052174	ex PH-ECO		Lsd fr TLP
CS-DCP	Beech 65-A90-1 King Air	LM-22	ex N7034K	Fly sprayer	Lsd fr Dynamic
CS-TGG	Dornier 228-202K	8160	ex D-CORA		Lsd fr Erskine

Operates feeder services for Air Portugal using TP flight numbers. Also operate Catalinas of ASPAR for firefighting duties during European summer. Aerocondor is the trading name of ATA Aerocondor Transportes Aereos

AIR LUXOR

Air Luxor (LK/LXR) (IATA 040)   Lisbon (LIS)

CS-TMW	Airbus Industrie A320-214	1667	ex F-WWII	For TAP Mar04	Lsd fr GATX
CS-TNB	Airbus Industrie A320-211	0191	ex F-WWDH	Vinga Göteborg	Lsd fr Bavaria
CS-TNE	Airbus Industrie A320-212	0395	ex F-WWBJ	For TAP Mar04	Lsd fr GATX
CS-TQA	Airbus Industrie A320-214	1439	ex EI-CWU		Lsd fr SALE Ireland
CS-TQB	Airbus Industrie A320-214	1450	ex EI-CWV		Lsd fr Cladaborg Lease
CS-TQD	Airbus Industrie A320-214	0870	ex HB-IJT		Lsd fr St Leman Ltd
CS-TQE	Airbus Industrie A320-212	0221	ex OY-CNB		
CS-	Airbus Industrie A320-211	0022	ex N220AN		
CS-	Airbus Industrie A320-211	0023	ex N230AN		
CS-TMT	Airbus Industrie A330-322	096	ex F-WQSA		Lsd fr ILFC
CS-TQF	Airbus Industrie A330-322	087	ex C-FRAP		Lsd fr ILFC
SE-RBF	Airbus Industrie A330-223	353	ex F-WWYN		Lsd fr NVR

Planned to set-up Air Luxor Lite as low cost carrier operating eight Airbus Industrie A320s from 26 October 2003 but fleet not expanded

AIR PORTUGAL

Air Portugal (TP/TAP) (IATA 047)   Lisbon (LIS)

CS-TEH	Airbus Industrie A310-304	483	ex F-WWCS	Bartolomeu Dias	Lsd fr NBB
CS-TEI	Airbus Industrie A310-304	495	ex F-WWCO	Fernao de Magalhaes	
					Lsd fr FG Echo Lsg
CS-TEJ	Airbus Industrie A310-304	494	ex F-WWCM	Pedro Nunes	Lsd fr DAP Lease
CS-TEW	Airbus Industrie A310-304	541	ex F-WWCR	Vasco da Gama	Lsd fr DTP Lease
CS-TEX	Airbus Industrie A310-304	565	ex F-WWCC	Joa Xo XXI	Lsd fr ILFC
CS-TEZ	Airbus Industrie A310-304	472	ex VP-BAF		Lsd fr GECAS
CS-TJE	Airbus Industrie A321-211	1307	ex D-AVZM	Pero Vaz de Caminha	
CS-TJF	Airbus Industrie A321-211	1399	ex D-AVZI	Luis Vaz de Camoes	
CS-TJG	Airbus Industrie A321-211	1713	ex D-AVZS	Amalia Rodrigues	
CS-TMW	Airbus Industrie A320-214	1667	ex F-WWII	on order Mar04	Lsd fr GATX
CS-TNA	Airbus Industrie A320-211	0185	ex F-WWDB	Grao Vasco	Lsd fr Bavaria
CS-TNE	Airbus Industrie A320-212	0395	ex F-WWBJ	on order Mar04	Lsd fr GATX
CS-TNG	Airbus Industrie A320-214	0945	ex F-WWIX	Mouzinho de Silveira	Lsd fr ILFC
CS-TNH	Airbus Industrie A320-214	0960	ex F-WWBH	Almada Negreiros	Lsd fr ILFC
CS-TNI	Airbus Industrie A320-214	0982	ex F-WWDF	Aquilino Ribeiro	
CS-TNJ	Airbus Industrie A320-214	1181	ex F-WWDS	Florbela Espanca	
CS-TNK	Airbus Industrie A320-214	1206	ex F-WWIL	Teofilo Braga	
CS-TNL	Airbus Industrie A320-214	1231	ex F-WWIJ	Vitorino Nermesio	
CS-TNM	Airbus Industrie A320-214	1799	ex F-WWIF	Natalia Correira	Lsd fr GATX
CS-TNN	Airbus Industrie A320-214	1816	ex F-WWID	Gil Vicente	Lsd fr GATX
CS-TTA	Airbus Industrie A319-111	0750	ex D-AVYO	Vierra da Silva	
CS-TTB	Airbus Industrie A319-111	0755	ex D-AVYJ	Gago Coutinho	

CS-TTC^	Airbus Industrie A319-111	0763	ex D-AVYS	Fernando Pessoa
CS-TTD^	Airbus Industrie A319-111	0790	ex D-AVYC	Amadeo de Souza Cardoso
CS-TTE	Airbus Industrie A319-111	0821	ex D-AVYN	Francisco d'Ollanda
CS-TTF	Airbus Industrie A319-111	0837	ex D-AVYL	Calouste Gulbenkion
CS-TTG	Airbus Industrie A319-111	0906	ex D-AVYN	Humberto Delgado
CS-TTH	Airbus Industrie A319-111	0917	ex D-AVYJ	Antonio Sergio
CS-TTI	Airbus Industrie A319-111	0933	ex D-AVYP	Eça de Queirós
CS-TTJ^	Airbus Industrie A319-111	0979	ex D-AVYM	Viana da Mota; special c/s
CS-TTK	Airbus Industrie A319-111	1034	ex D-AVYL	Miguel Torga
CS-TTL	Airbus Industrie A319-111	1100	ex D-AVYX	Almeida Garrett
CS-TTM	Airbus Industrie A319-111	1106	ex D-AVWR	Alexandre Herculano
CS-TTN	Airbus Industrie A319-111	1120	ex D-AVYI	Camilo Castelo Branco
CS-TTO	Airbus Industrie A319-111	1127	ex D-AVYH	Antero de Quental
CS-TTP	Airbus Industrie A319-111	1165	ex D-AVWV	Josefa d'Obidos

^Leased from ILFC

CS-TOA	Airbus Industrie A340-312	041	ex F-WWJB	Fernao Mendes Pinto
CS-TOB	Airbus Industrie A340-312	044	ex F-WWJN	D. Joao de Castro
CS-TOC	Airbus Industrie A340-312	079	ex F-WWJS	Wenceslau de Moraes
CS-TOD	Airbus Industrie A340-312	091	ex F-WWJA	D. Francisco de Almeida

Feeder services are operated by AeroCondor using TP flight numbers in Madeira
Owns 25% of Air Macau while Yes is a wholly owned subsidiary
Air Portugal is the trading name of Transportes Aereos Portugueses

EUROATLANTIC AIRWAYS
EuroAtlantic (MM/MMZ)   Lisbon (LIS)

CS-TEB	Lockheed L-1011-500 Tristar	1240	ex V2-LEO	Naughton Simao
CS-TLI	Boeing 737-33A	1462/23830	ex PR-BRA		Lsd fr BRB; sublsd to BBG
CS-TMZ	Boeing 737-33A	1444/23827	ex PT-TEX	winglets	Lsd fr AWAS; sublsd to MPD
PP-VTE	Boeing 767-3Y0ER	505/26208	ex N639TW		Jt ops with VRG
PR-BRE	Boeing 737-3K9	1794/24213	ex CS-TIG		Lsd fr BRB

The Boeing 767 is operated on charter services using Varig's AOC

HELIBRAVO AVIACAO
HeliBravo (HIB)   Cascais-Tires

| CS-HED | Aerospatiale AS.350B2 Ecureuil | 2669 | ex D-HJOE |
| CS-HFA | PZL Swidnik W-3AM Sokol | 370705 | ex SP-SYI |

HELISUL
Helis (HSU)   Cascais-Tires

CS-HEN	Aerospatiale AS.350BA Ecureuil	1845	ex LN-OPC		
CS-HEZ	Bell 212	30557	ex EC-GHP		Lsd fr HSE
CS-HFB	Bell 206B JetRanger III	3640	ex D-HSBA		
EC-GPA	Bell 412SP	36071	ex N7238Y	EMS	Lsd fr HSE

Bell 212 operated for Fire Fighting National Corps

HTA HELICOPTERS
Heliapra (AHT)   Morgado de Apre

CS-HEE	Aerospatiale AS.355F1 Ecureuil 2	5006	
CS-HEK	Bell 206B Jet Ranger III	2914	ex N6280J
CS-HEP	Bell 206B Jet Ranger III	2800	ex N27785
CS-HEY	Aerospatiale AS.350B2 Ecureuil	9027	ex D-HXST

LUZAIR
                                                         Lisbon (LIS)

| CS-TMP | Lockheed L-1011-500 Tristar | 1248 | ex SE-DVI |
| CS-TMR | Lockheed L-1011-500 Tristar | 1241 | ex SE-DVF |

OMNI - AVIACAO E TECNOLOGIA
Omni (OC/OAV)   Cascais-Tires

CS-ASG	Twin Commander 690B	11452	ex N115SB	EMS
CS-DDF	Beech B200 Super King Air	BB-1129	ex N66404	CatPass 250 conv
CS-HCC	Bell 205A-1	30013	ex F-GINO	
CS-HCO	Agusta-Bell 206B Jet Ranger III	8678	ex I-BDPL	
CS-HDH	Bell 205A-1	30121	ex N25AL	
CS-HDS	Bell 222	47028	ex G-META	EMS
CS-HDT	Bell 222	47050	ex G-METC	EMS
CS-HDU	Bell 222	47055	ex G-METB	EMS
CS-HDX	Bell 222	47071	ex N307CK	EMS

CS-HET	Bell 205A-1	30038	ex C-GFHC		
CS-TMU	Beech 1900D	UE-335	ex N23269	Castor	Op as PGA Express
CS-TMV	Beech 1900D	UE-341	ex N23309	Esquilio	Op as PGA Express
PP-MEA	Sikorsky S-76A	76007	ex N2634		based Brazil
PP-MED	Sikorsky S-76A	760119	ex N16GH		based Brazil
PP-MEF	Bell 212	30591	ex CS-HDY		based Brazil

Some helicopters operate for Fire Fighting National Corp

PGA EXPRESS

Lisbon (LIS)

CS-TMU	Beech 1900D	UE-335	ex N23269	Castor	Op by OAV
CS-TMV	Beech 1900D	UE-341	ex N23309	Esquilio	Op by OAV

Providing feeder services to Portugalia

PORTUGALIA AIRLINES

Portugalia (NI/PGA) (IATA 685)   Lisbon (LIS)

CS-TPG	Embraer EMB.145EP	145014	ex PT-SYK	Melro	
CS-TPH	Embraer EMB.145EP	145017	ex PT-SYN	Pardal	
CS-TPI	Embraer EMB.145EP	145031	ex PT-SYZ	Cuco	
CS-TPJ	Embraer EMB.145EP	145036	ex PT-SZC	Chapim	Lsd to GNT
CS-TPK	Embraer EMB.145EP	145041	ex PT-SZG	Gaio	
CS-TPL	Embraer EMB.145EP	145051	ex PT-SZQ	Pisco	
CS-TPM	Embraer EMB.145EP	145095	ex PT-SBR	Rola	
CS-TPN	Embraer EMB.145EP	145099	ex PT-SBV	Brigao	
CS-TPA	Fokker 100	11257	ex PH-LMF	Albatroz	Lsd fr GECAS
CS-TPB	Fokker 100	11262	ex PH-EZE	Pelicano	Lsd fr GECAS
CS-TPC	Fokker 100	11287	ex PH-LML	Flamingo	Lsd fr GECAS
CS-TPD	Fokker 100	11317	ex EP-IDK	Condor	Lsd fr GECAS
CS-TPE	Fokker 100	11342	ex PH-LNJ	Gaviao	Lsd fr GECAS
CS-TPF	Fokker 100	11258	ex PH-EZD	Grifo	Lsd fr GECAS

PGA Express provides feeder services

SATA AIR ACORES

SATA (SP/SAT) (IATA 737)   Ponta Delgada (PDL)

CS-TGL	British Aerospace ATP	2019	ex G-BRTG	Santa Maria	
CS-TGN	British Aerospace ATP	2031	ex G-11-031	Flores	
CS-TGO	Dornier 228	8119	ex D-CMUC		Lsd fr Dornier
CS-TGX	British Aerospace ATP	2025	ex G-BRLY	Faial	Lsd fr BAES
CS-TGY	British Aerospace ATP	2049	ex G-BTZJ		Lsd fr BAES

Owns SATA Internacional; SATA Air Acores is the trading name of Servico Acoreano de Transportes Aereos

SATA INTERNACIONAL

Air Azores (S4/RZO) (ICAO 331)   Ponto Delgada (PDL)

CS-TGP	Boeing 737-3Q8	1641/24131	ex OO-LTX	Corvo	Lsd fr GECAS
CS-TGU	Airbus Industrie A310-304	571	ex F-GJKQ	Terceira	Lsd fr Credit Lyonnais
CS-TGV	Airbus Industrie A310-304	651	ex F-WQKR	Sao Miguel	Lsd fr Credit Lyonnais
CS-TGW	Boeing 737-4Y0	1678/23981	ex TC-AFZ	Pico	Lsd fr GECAS
CS-TGZ	Boeing 737-430	2832/28491	ex N120AF	Sao Jorge	Lsd fr GECAS
CS-TKI	Airbus Industrie A310-304	448	ex C-GRYA		Lsd fr Type 72 Avn
CS-	Airbus Industrie A320-200		ex	on order Apr04	

Wholly owned subsidiary of SATA Air Acores; is a trading name of Servicio Acoreano de Transportes Aereos
Boeing 737s to be returned to GECAS by the end of summer 2005 and replaced by further A320s

YES

Young Sky (YSS) (IATA 097)   Lisbon (LIS)

CS-TMX	Lockheed L-1011-500 Tristar	1206	ex N765DA		

Wholly owned subsidiary of Air Portugal; Yes is the trading name of Linhas Aereas Charter

CU - CUBA (Republic of Cuba)

AERO CARIBBEAN

AeroCaribbean (7L/CRN)   Havana (HAV)

CU-T1203	Yakovlev Yak-40	9641450	ex YV-598C		
CU-T1211	Yakovlev Yak-40	9731554			
CU-T1213	Yakovlev Yak-40	9731954			
CU-T1220	Yakovlev Yak-40	9841059		stored SCU	
CU-T1221	Yakovlev Yak-40	9841159	ex YV-594C		

CU-T1534	Yakovlev Yak-40	9731754	ex CU-T1212	
CU-T1537	Yakovlev Yak-40	9021360	ex CU-T1450	
CU-T1538	Yakovlev Yak-40	9021260	ex CU-T1449	
CU-T1269	Ilyushin Il-18V	185007801	ex CCCP-75562	special c/s
CU-T1296	Aerospatiale/Alenia ATR 42-300	009	ex F-WQGV	
CU-T1297	Aerospatiale/Alenia ATR 42-300	014	ex F-WQIE	
CU-T1501	Antonov An-26	87307207	ex CU-T111	
CU-T1505	Ilyushin Il-18 (F)			
CU-T1506	Antonov An-26	87306710	ex CU-T110	
CU-T1512	Aerospatiale/Alenia ATR 42-300	136	ex CU-T1298	
CU-C1515	Ilyushin Il-18D (F)	188010805	ex CU-T110	
CU-T1532	Ilyushin Il-18D	188010904	ex CU-T131	Cargo
CU-T1536	Antonov An-24RV			

AEROGAVIOTA

Gaviota (GTV)   *Havana (HAV)*

CU-T1240	Aerospatiale/Alenia ATR 42-500	617	ex F-WWLB	VIP	Op in CUB c/s
CU-T1454	Aerospatiale/Alenia ATR 42-500	616	ex F-WWLA		
CU-T1455	Aerospatiale/Alenia ATR 42-500	618	ex F-WWLC		
CU-T1456	Aerospatiale/Alenia ATR 42-500	619	ex F-WWLD		
CU-T1401	Antonov An-26B	12604	ex 14-01		
CU-T1402	Antonov An-26B	12605	ex 14-02		
CU-T1403	Antonov An-26B	12905	ex 14-03		
CU-T1404	Antonov An-26B	12906	ex 14-04		
CU-T1405	Antonov An-26B	13501	ex 14-05		
CU-T1406	Antonov An-26B	13502	ex 14-06		
CU-T1408	Antonov An-26	6903	ex 14-28		
CU-T1417	Antonov An-26				
CU-T1420	Antonov An-26	87306607	ex 14-20		
CU-T1421	Antonov An-26	6610	ex 14-21	status uncertain	
CU-T1425	Antonov An-26	6904	ex 14-25		
CU-T1426	Antonov An-26	5603	ex 14-26		
CU-T1428	Antonov An-26B	11303	ex 14-28		
CU-T1429	Antonov An-26	87307006	ex 14-29		
CU-T1432	Antonov An-26	7306	ex 14-32	status uncertain	
CU-T1433	Antonov An-26	7309	ex 14-33	status uncertain	
CU-T1434	Antonov An-26	7701	ex 14-34		
CU-T1435	Antonov An-26	97307702	ex 14-35		
CU-T1232	Yakovlev Yak-40	9011060			
CU-F1444	Antonov An-30		ex FAR-1444		
CU-T1445	Antonov An-30				

AEROTAXI

Seraer (CNI)   *Havana (HAV)*

CU-T127	Douglas DC-3	11645	ex CU-T113	
CU-T1058	Douglas DC-3	12445	ex CU-T123	Varadero
CU-T1059	Douglas DC-3	15916/32664	ex CU-T124	
CU-T1108	Embraer EMB.110P1 Bandeirante	110091	ex PT-GKB	
CU-T1109	Embraer EMB.110P1 Bandeirante	110116	ex PT-GKN	
CU-T1194	LET L-410UVP	871915	ex OK-SDF	

Aerotaxi is the trading name of Empresa Nacional de Servicios Aéreos

CUBANA DE AVIACIÓN

Cubana (CU/CUB) (IATA 136)   *Havana (HAV)*

CU-T1236	Antonov An-24RV	27308102	ex RA-46484	
CU-T1237	Antonov An-24RV	37308909	ex RA-46641	
CU-T1260	Antonov An-24RV	57310307	ex CCCP-47307	
CU-T1263	Antonov An-24RV	47309610	ex RA-46678	
CU-T1267	Antonov An-24RV	47309907	ex CCCP-46696	
CU-T1295	Antonov An-24RV	27307508	ex RA-47691	
CU-T1243	Yakovlev Yak-42D	4520423303016	ex RA-42425	
CU-T1272	Yakovlev Yak-42D	4520424811442	ex RA-42364	Lsd fr WLG
CU-T1273	Yakovlev Yak-42D	4520424914340	ex RA-42364	Lsd fr KAZ
CU-T1274	Yakovlev Yak-42D	4520422606204	ex RA-42335	Lsd fr KAZ
CU-T1278	Yakovlev Yak-42D	4520423016269		
CU-T1279	Yakovlev Yak-42D	4520424914057		
CU-T1222	Tupolev Tu-154B-2	80A-447		
CU-T1237	Antonov An-26	7704	ex CCCP-47340	
CU-T1280	Ilyushin Il-62M	3749648		15 de Febrero
CU-T1282	Ilyushin Il-62M	2052456		

CU-T1283	Ilyushin Il-62M	4053823		
CU-T1284	Ilyushin Il-62M	4053732		
CU-T1443	Yakovlev Yak-40	9710752		
CU-T1539	Ilyushin Il-18D	2964017102	ex YL-LAO	
CU-	Ilyushin Il-96-300			on order 04
EI-TAA	Airbus Industrie A320-233	0912	ex N458TA	Lsd fr TAI
EI-TAB	Airbus Industrie A320-233	1624	ex N485TA	Lsd fr TAI

Also leases other Airbus Industrie A320-233 and Boeing 767-300 aircraft as required, these operate with Cubana stickers. One more Ilyushin Il-96-300 is on order for delivery in 2005

CX - URUGUAY (Republic of Uruguay)

AEROLINEAS URUGUAYAS
Ausa (AUY) *Montevideo (MVD)*

Leases Boeing 767-316F aircraft from LANChile-Cargo as required

AEROMAS
Aeromas Express (MSM) *Montevideo (MVD)*

CX-BDI	Piper PA-23-250 Aztec B	27-2265		
CX-BRM	Beech A80 Queen Air	LD-200	ex N326JB	Excalibur Queenaire conv; std MVD
CX-MAS	Embraer EMB.110P1 Bandeirante	110393	ex N91DA	
CX-MAX	Cessna 208A Caravan I	20800042	ex ZP-TYT	

Aeromas is the trading name of MaxAir

PLUNA LINEAS AÉREAS URUGUAYAS
Pluna (PU/PUA) (IATA 286) *Montevideo (MVD)*

CX-BON	Boeing 737-2A3	830/22737	ex PH-TSI	Gen Jose Artigas
CX-BOO	Boeing 737-2A3	834/22738	ex PH-TSA	Brig Gen Juan A Lavalleja
CX-BOP	Boeing 737-2A3	844/22739	ex PH-TSB	Gen Fructuoso Rivera
CX-PUA	Boeing 737-3Q8	1924/24700	ex TF-FDA	Lsd fr PLM Transportation
CX-PUB	Boeing 767-33AER	643/28495	ex N284AN	Lsd fr AMWS
CX-PUD	Boeing 757-23A	215/24291	ex N541NA	Lsd fr AMWS

Domestic services are operated by TAMU (q.v.); part owned by VARIG

TAMU - TRANSPORTE AÉREO MILITAR URUGUAYO
Montevideo (MVD)

CX-BHW	Fokker F-27 Friendship 100	10202	ex PH-FDR	also wears T-561
CX-BJC	Embraer EMB.110C Bandeirante	110082	ex PT-GJL	also wears T-583
CX-BJJ	Embraer EMB.110C Bandeirante	110076	ex PT-GJI	also wears T-580
CX-BKF	Embraer EMB.110B1 Bandeirante	110187		also wears T-585
CX-BOG	CASA C.212-200	CC28-2-187		also wears T-531
CX-BPI	CASA C.212-200	A28-1-189		also wears T-532
CX-BPJ	CASA C.212-200	A28-2-198		also wears T-533
CX-BQW	Lockheed C-130B Hercules	3668	ex 61-0971	also wears T-591
CX-BQX	Lockheed C-130B Hercules	3596	ex 60-0295	also wears T-592
CX-BTZ	Embraer EMB.120ER Brasilia	120089	ex N12705	also wears T-550

A division of Fuerza Aérea Uruguaya, operates domestic services for PLUNA

TRANSCONTINENTAL SUR
Trans-Cont (TCT) *Montevideo (MVD)*

| CX-BSB | Boeing 707-321C (Comtran 2) | 372/18766 | ex P4-CCG | Lsd fr Race Avn |

UAIR
Montevideo (MVD)

| PT-MQD | Fokker 100 | 11383 | ex B-2231 | Lsd fr TAM |

VIP AIR
Acla (QD/QCL) *Montevideo (MVD)*

| CX-VIP | Embraer EMB.110P1 Bandeirante | 110258 | ex OH-EBC | |

VIP Air is the trading name of Air Class Lineas Aereas

C2 - NAURU (Republic of Nauru)

AIR NAURU

Air Nauru (ON/RON) (IATA 123)			Nauru (INU)

VH-RON	Boeing 737-4L7	2483/26960 ex C2-RN10	Op for Norfolk Jet Express

C3 - ANDORRA (Principality of Andorra)

HELILAND

La Massana Heliport

F-GODJ	Aerospatiale AS350B3 Ecureuil	3458	Lsd fr/ op by SAF Helicopteres

HELITRANS

La Massana Heliport

Leases helicopters from other operators as and when required

C5 - GAMBIA

AFRINAT INTERNATIONAL despite code being allocated believed not to have commenced operations

AIR GAMBIA

Banjul (BJL)

C5-GNM	Ilyushin Il-62M	3036142 ex TL-ACL	Op for Govt

CONTINENTAL WINGS ceased operations

GAMBIA INTERNATIONAL AIRWAYS

Gambia International (GC/GNR) (IATA 034)			Banjul (BJL)

EC-HMK	Boeing 737-86N	585/28624	Lsd fr FUA

Also operates with Aerospatiale/Alenia ATR 42-300 leased from TACV-Cabo Verde Airlines as required

GAMBIA NEW MILLENNIUM AIR ceased operations

MAHFOOZ AVIATION

Mahfooz (M2/MZS)			Banjul/Jeddah (BJL/JED)

C5-ABM	Boeing 727-256	1501/21781	ex N904RF	stored IGM
C5-DMB	Boeing 727-228	847/20411	ex J2-KBH	stored ADD
C5-SBM	Boeing 727-256	1369/21609	ex N908RF	
C5-SMM	Boeing 727-251	665/19973	ex HK-3871X	all-white Lsd to SUD
C5-AMM	Boeing 707-323B (Comtran 2)	817/20176	ex N712PC	
C5-MBM	Boeing 707-347C (Comtran 2)	743/19966	ex OD-AGU	all-white

C6 - BAHAMAS (Commonwealth of the Bahamas)

OPERATOR NOT KNOWN:

C6-NFS	Cessna 208B Caravan I	208B0994		
C6-PDX	Embraer EMB.110P1 Bandeirante	110		
C6-	Swearingen SA.227AC Metro III	AC-746B	ex N46NE	
C6-	Swearingen SA-227AC Metro III	AC-595	ex N385PH	Lsd fr Leaseco 2
C6-	Cessna 208B Caravan I	208B0841	ex N1295G	

ABACO AIR

Marsh Harbour (MHH)

C6-BFQ	Britten-Norman BN-2A-8 Islander	347	ex N69HA
C6-BFR	Aero Commander 500	825	ex N846VK
C6-BHH	Britten-Norman BN-2B-26 Islander	2021	ex N599MS
C6-BHY	Aero Commander 500	834	ex (C6-BFP)

AIR STREAM current status uncertain

BAHAMASAIR

Bahamas (UP/BHS)   *Nassau (NAS)*

C6-BFG	de Havilland DHC-8-311A	288	ex C-GESR	
C6-BFH	de Havilland DHC-8-311A	291	ex C-GFOD	
C6-BFI	de Havilland DHC-8-311A	295	ex C-GFHZ	
C6-BFN	de Havilland DHC-8-301	159	ex N801XV	Lsd fr Aviaco Lsg
C6-BFO	de Havilland DHC-8-301	164	ex N802XV	Lsd fr Aviaco Lsg
C6-	de Havilland DHC-8Q-311	323	ex N538DS	
C6-	de Havilland DHC-8Q-314	309	ex N994DC	
C6-BGK	Boeing 737-275	667/22086	ex C-GLPW	
C6-BGL	Boeing 737-275 (AvAero 3)	673/22087	ex C-GMPW	

Some local flights are operated by Sky Unlimited

CARIBBEAN AVIATION current status uncertain, both aircraft believed operated by Major's Air Service

CAT ISLAND AIR

Nassau (NAS)

C6-CAB	Embraer EMB.110P1 Bandeirante	110198	ex G-ONEW	
C6-CAH	Embraer EMB.110P1 Bandeirante	110249	ex C6-BHA	Lsd fr BAC Lsg
C6-CAP	Embraer EMB.110P1 Bandeirante	110304	ex J8-VAZ	Lsd fr Asahi Enterprises
C6-CAT	Piper PA-23-250 Aztec E	27-7554083	ex N54779	
N360CL	Embraer EMB.110P1 Bandeirante	110287	ex N63CZ	stored OPF
				Lsd fr Las Vegas VIP Service

FLAMINGO AIR

Nassau (NAS)

C6-ASA	Britten-Norman BN-2A-26 Islander	599	ex N178SC
C6-BGI	Piper PA-23-250 Aztec D	27-4246	
C6-BGZ	Piper PA-23-250 Aztec D		

LAKER AIRWAYS

Laker Bahamas (7Z/LBH) (IATA 569)   *Nassau (NAS)*

N706AA	Boeing 727-223 (FedEx 3)	1755/22463	Lsd fr Avn Capital
N707AA	Boeing 727-223 (FedEx 3)	1758/22464	Lsd fr Avn Capital

Laker Airways is the trading name of LB Limited. Officially registered in Fort Lauderdale, FL

MAJOR'S AIR SERVICES

Freeport (FPO)

C6-RAM	Cessna 404 Titan II	404-0223	ex C6-BGE	
C6-RRM	Beech C99	U-231	ex N141RM	Lsd fr Raytheon
C6-TOM	Cessna 404 Titan II	404-0410	ex N3TU	

QUALITY AIR current status is uncertain as sole aircraft transferred to Seair Airways

SANDPIPER AIR

Nassau (NAS)

N61PB	Cessna 402C II	402C0298	
N555AE	Cessna 402B	402B0822	ex N3945C
N5715C	Cessna 402C II	402C0024	
N98756	Cessna 402B	402B1068	

SEAIR AIRWAYS

Nassau (NAS)

C6-BUS	Britten-Norman BN-2A-26 Islander	2040	exx N23US

SKY UNLIMITED

Nassau (NAS)

N2YV	Beech 1900D	UE-2		Lsd fr Raytheon
N38SU	Beech 1900C-1	UC-38	ex N32018	Lsd fr Raytheon
N555AD	Piper PA-23-250 Aztec E	27-7305006		Lsd fr Sky Unlimited Inc

Operates some local services for Bahamasair

SOUTHERN AIR CHARTER
(PL)   *Nassau (NAS)*

| N79YV | Beech 1900C | UB-41 | ex OB-1694 | Lsd fr Plane 1 Lsg |
| N378SA | Beech 1900C | UB-31 | ex N196GA | Lsd fr JODA Inc |

TAINO AIR ceased operations

WESTERN AIR
Freeport (FPO)

C6-REX	Swearingen SA.227AC Metro III	AC-649	ex N26861	
C6-SAD	Swearingen SA.227AC Metro III	AC-746B	ex N46NE	
C6-SAQ	Swearingen SA.227AC Metro III	AC-661B	ex N661FA	
C6-SAR	Swearingen SA.227AC Metro III	AC-598	ex N3116Z	
C6-WAL	Piper PA-31 Navajo			
N565M	Beech 1900C	UB-43	ex N34GT	Lsd fr Raytheon Aircraft Credit

C9 - MOZAMBIQUE (Republic of Mozambique)

ASAS DE MOZAMBIQUE ceased operations

LAM - LINHAS AEREAS DE MOCAMBIQUE
Mozambique (TM/LAM) (IATA 068)   *Maputo (MPM)*

C9-BAC	Boeing 737-2B1C	289/20536	ex CR-BAC	Lugenda	
C9-BAG	Boeing 737-2N0	1313/23677	ex Z-WPA	Mbuya Nehanda	Lsd fr AZW
C9-BAH	Boeing 737-236	712/21808	ex N808GE		Lsd fr Polaris
C9-BAI	Boeing 737-2K9	1178/23405	ex N405BC		Lsd fr Boeing Capital
C9-BAJ	Boeing 737-205	1223/23464	ex N464BA		Lsd fr Celtic Capital
C9-BAF	Boeing 767-2B1ER	511/26471	ex ZS-SRA	Zambeze	
3D-ALM	Fokker 100	11335	ex PH-EZR	Lambeluzi; stored MPM	
3D-BIN	Embraer EMB.120RT Brasilia	120129	ex OY-PAU		Lsd fr NACT

MOCAMBIQUE EXPRESS
Maputo (MPM)

C9-ASU	CASA 212-200	CC34-1-195	ex HB-LNG		
C9-ASV	Beech 200C Super King Air	BL-21	ex N3831T		
C9-ASX	Beech 200C Super King Air	BL-32	ex N821CA	all-white	stored HLA
C9-AUK	British Aerospace Jetstream 41	41044	ex ZS-NUO		Lsd fr/op by LNK

STA - SOCIEDADE DE TRANSPORTS AÉREOS
Maputo (MPM)

ZS-BRO	Cessna 310Q	310Q0257	ex N7757Q	
ZS-IKL	Piper PA-23-250 Aztec E	27-4666	ex N14055	
ZS-JJB	Piper PA-31-350 Navajo Chieftain	31-7405245	ex N54736	
ZS-MVY	Cessna 208 Caravan I	20800177	ex N9757F	
ZS-RAN	Cessna 402B	402B0439	ex ZS-XAV	Lsd fr VSA Avn

TRANSAIRWAYS
(TWM)   *Maputo/Beira (MPM/BEW)*

C9-SAB	Piper PA-31-350 Navajo Chieftain	31-7552061	ex 9Q-CSG	
N148YV	Beech 1900C-1	UC-148		Lsd fr Raytheon
3D-NVA	LET L-410UVP-E3	882035	ex 2035	
3D-NVE	LET L-410UVP	841219	ex 3D-RAB	

TTA - SOCIEDADE DE TRANSPORTE E TRABALHO SEREO
Kanimanbo (TTA)   *Maputo (MPM)*

C9-ALS	Britten-Norman BN-2A-6 Islander	174	ex G-AYDL
C9-AME	Britten-Norman BN-2A-6 Islander	118	ex G-AYIV
C9-AOV	Britten-Norman BN-2A-3 Islander	624	ex G-AYJF
C9-APD	Britten-Norman BN-2A-9 Islander	683	ex G-AZXO
C9-APO	Britten-Norman BN-2A-2 Islander	687	ex G-AZXT
C9-TAH	Britten-Norman BN-2T Turbine Islander	2120	ex G-BJEE
C9-TAJ	Britten-Norman BN-2T Turbine Islander	2124	ex G-BJEJ
C9-TAK	Britten-Norman BN-2T Turbine Islander	2121	ex G-BJEI
C9-AMH	Piper PA-32-300 Cherokee Six C	32-40682	wx ZS-IGO

D - GERMANY (Federal Republic of Germany)

ADVANCED AVIATION

Bad Saulgau/Africa

D-FLIP	Cessna 208B Caravan I	208B0331	ex N3331
D-FROG	Cessna 208B Caravan I	208B0012	ex SE-LER

Aircraft are based overseas assisting aid organisations; not a certified aviation organisation

AEROLINE

Sylt-Air (7E/AWU)

Westerland (GWT)

D-GFPG	Partenavia P.68B	170		Lsd fr Skroch
D-IOLB	Cessna 404 Titan II	404-0691	ex SE-IVG	

AERO LLOYD

Aero Lloyd (YP/AEF)

Frankfurt (FRA)

D-ALAB	Airbus Industrie A320-232	0575	ex F-WWDO	Lsd fr Bavaria; sublsd to RYN	
D-ALAC	Airbus Industrie A320-232	0580	ex F-WWDV	stored FRA	
D-ALAE	Airbus Industrie A320-232	0659	ex F-WWIV	Lsd fr MMV GmbH; sublsd to RYN	
D-ALAJ	Airbus Industrie A320-232	0990	ex F-WWBC	stored FRA	Lsd fr SALE
D-ALAR	Airbus Industrie A320-232	1459	ex F-WWIR		Lsd to RYN
D-ALAT	Airbus Industrie A320-232	1996	ex F-WWIM	Lsd fr SALE; sublsd to RYN	
D-ABLC	Airbus Industrie A321-211	1012	ex F-WQRS		
D-ALAK*	Airbus Industrie A321-231	1004	ex D-AVZI	Trigema c/s; stored FRA	
D-ALAL	Airbus Industrie A321-231	1195	ex D-AVZK		Lsd to RYN
D-ALAM*	Airbus Industrie A321-231	1199	ex D-AVZM	FC Bayern Munich c/s	
D-ALAN*	Airbus Industrie A321-231	1218	ex D-AVZA	stored FRA	
D-ALAO*	Airbus Industrie A321-231	1408	ex D-AVZE	stored FRA	
D-ALAQ*	Airbus Industrie A321-231	1438	ex D-AVZL		Lsd to RYN

* Leased from ILFC

Suspended operations 16 October 2003 but recommenced limited operations on 23 October 2003. Several aircraft are leased to Ryan International (RYN) for the winter and may reform as Aero Flight in April 2004.

AIR BERLIN

Air Berlin (AB/BER) (IATA 745)

Berlin-Tegel (TXL)

D-ABAH	Boeing 737-46J	2694/27826			Lsd fr Euconus
D-ABAI	Boeing 737-46J	2794/28038			Lsd fr AB Erste
D-ABAK	Boeing 737-46J	2801/28271			Lsd fr Hunold
D-ABAL	Boeing 737-46J	2802/28334			Lsd fr Hunold
D-ABAM	Boeing 737-46J	2879/28867			Lsd fr AB Dritte
D-AABJ	Boeing 737-87Q	30385		on order	Lsd fr Boullioun
D-ABAA	Boeing 737-76Q	740/30271	ex N271CH		Lsd fr Boullioun
D-ABAB	Boeing 737-76Q	947/30277	ex N277CH		Lsd fr Boullioun
D-ABAC	Boeing 737-86J	619/30501			
D-ABAD	Boeing 737-86J	759/30876			
D-ABAE	Boeing 737-86J	782/30877			
D-ABAF	Boeing 737-86J	844/30878	ex N1787B		
D-ABAG	Boeing 737-86J	871/30879			
D-ABAN	Boeing 737-86J	36/28068	ex N35153		Lsd fr AB Erste
D-ABAO	Boeing 737-86J	42/28069	ex N5573B		Lsd fr Hunold
D-ABAP	Boeing 737-86J	106/28070			Lsd fr SALE
D-ABAQ	Boeing 737-86J	133/28071			Lsd fr Boullioun
D-ABAR	Boeing 737-86J	147/28072			Lsd fr Boullioun
D-ABAS	Boeing 737-86J	200/28073	ex N1795B		Lsd fr SALE
D-ABAT	Boeing 737-86J	202/29120			Lsd fr Hunold
D-ABAU	Boeing 737-86J	239/29121			Lsd fr Hunold
D-ABAV	Boeing 737-86J	450/30498			
D-ABAW	Boeing 737-86J	485/30062			
D-ABAX	Boeing 737-86J	517/30063			
D-ABAY	Boeing 737-86J	567/30499	ex N1795B		
D-ABAZ	Boeing 737-86J	593/30500	ex N1787B		
D-ABBA	Boeing 737-86J	879/30570		Dancing Queen	Lsd fr GATX Corp
D-ABBB	Boeing 737-86J	961/32624	ex N1798B		
D-ABBC	Boeing 737-86J	995/32625			
D-ABBD	Boeing 737-86J	1043/30880			
D-ABBE	Boeing 737-86J	1067/30881			
D-ABBF	Boeing 737-86J	1210/32917			
D-ABBG	Boeing 737-86J	1255/32918			
D-ABBH	Boeing 737-86J	1279/32919			
D-ABBI	Boeing 737-86J	1293/32920			
D-ABBJ	Boeing 737-86Q	1280/30286	ex N1787B		Lsd fr Boullioun

D-ABBK	Boeing 737-8BK	1317/33013		Lsd fr CIT Leasing
D-AHFO	Boeing 737-8K5	499/27987		Lsd fr HLF
D-AHFS	Boeing 737-86N	556/28623		Lsd fr HLF
D-AHIA	Boeing 737-73S	229/29082	ex D-ASKH	Lsd fr/op by HHI
D-AHIC	Boeing 737-7BK	812/30617	ex N1787B	Lsd fr/op by HHI
D-AHIE	Boeing 737-73S	215/29081	ex TC-SUF	Lsd fr/op by HHI
PH-HZA	Boeing 737-8K2	51/28373		Lsd fr TRA
PH-HZL	Boeing 737-8K2	814/30391		Lsd fr TRA
PH-HZM	Boeing 737-8K2	833/30392		Lsd fr TRA
All 737NG's retrofitted with winglets		Owns 24% of NIKI		

AIR OMEGA

(OE) *Altenburg (AOC)*

D-CAOA	Embraer EMB.120ER Brasilia	120013	ex N122AM	Nobitz	Freighter; sublsd to AAG
D-CAOB	Embraer EMB.120ER Brasilia	120012	ex N120AM	Stadt Schmölln	
					Freighter; sublsd to EXS

Both leased from Boeing Capital Corp, Air Omega's AOC withdrawn 25 July 2003 and aircraft stored at Coventry and Cologne respectively; later returned to service

AIR SERVICE BERLIN

Berlin-Tempelhof (THF)

D-CXXX	Douglas DC-3	16124/32872	ex G-AMPZ	Jack Bennett

ANTARES AIRTRANSPORT

Antares (ANM) *Rothenburg*

D-CLED	LET L-410UVP-E20	912533	ex OY-TCL
D-CLET	LET L-410UVP-E20	912603	ex S9-TBY
D-COXB	LET L-410UVP	820924	ex DDR-SXB
D-COXC	LET L-410UVP	820925	ex S9-TBT

ARCUS AIR

Arcus Air (AZE) *Mannheim (MHG)*

D-CAAM	Dornier 228-212	8205	ex D-CBDH
D-CUTT	Dornier 228-212	8200	ex D-CBDC

AUGSBURG AIRWAYS

Augsburg Air (IQ/AUB) (IATA 614) *Augsburg (AGB)*

D-BACH	de Havilland DHC-8Q-314A	365	ex VH-TQA	
D-BDTM	de Havilland DHC-8Q-314	545	ex C-FSCG	
D-BEBA	de Havilland DHC-8Q-314	543	ex C-	
D-BHAL	de Havilland DHC-8-202	463	ex C-GFOD	Lsd to ANG
D-BHAS	de Havilland DHC-8Q-314	503	ex C-GDLD	Lsd fr BAWAG Lsg; sublsd to AWS
D-BHAT	de Havilland DHC-8Q-311	505	ex C-GDFT	Lsd fr BAWAG Lsg
D-BHOQ	de Havilland DHC-8Q-311	544	ex C-GHRI	
D-BLEJ	de Havilland DHC-8Q-314	521	ex C-FDHU	Lsd fr CA Lsg; sublsd to ISK
D-BMUC	de Havilland DHC-8-314A	350	ex C-GUAY	Lsd fr Elveden Investments
D-BPAD	de Havilland DHC-8Q-314	523	ex C-FDHW	Lsd fr BAWAG Lsg
D-BTHF	de Havilland DHC-8Q-202	536	ex (VT-VAA)	Lsd to ANG
D-ADHA	de Havilland DHC-8-402Q	4028	ex C-GFBW	
D-ADHB	de Havilland DHC-8-402Q	4029	ex C-GFCA	
D-ADHC	de Havilland DHC-8-402Q	4045	ex C-GDIW	
D-ADHD	de Havilland DHC-8-402Q	4056	ex C-GFYI	
D-ADHE	de Havilland DHC-8-402Q	4066	ex C-GEOA	

Operates feeder service as Lufthansa Regional

AUGUSTA AIR

Augusta (AUF) *Augsburg (AGB)*

D-CAAA	Beech B300 Super King Air	FL-116	ex N350EA	Lsd to Windrose Air
D-CBBB	Beech B300 Super King Air	FL-120	ex N1512H	

AVANTI AIR

Euroexpress (EEX) *Frankfurt (FRA)*

D-BCRP	Aerospatiale/Alenia ATR 42-300QC	158	ex F-WWEE	
D-CARA	Beech 1900C	UB-59	ex N72391	Lsd fr BKM Luftfahrt
D-CBIG	Beech 1900D	UE-288	ex N11320	Lsd fr BKM Luftfahrt, sublsd to HHN
D-CBSF	Beech 1900D	UE-8	ex N55778	Lsd fr BKM Luftfahrt

BERLINJET

Berlin-Schönefeld (SXF)

TF-MDB   McDonnell-Douglas MD-83   1354/49449   ex D-ALLE   Lsd fr MDI
Recommenced services 10 February 2003 with aircraft operated under MD Airlines AOC, but cancelled again after ten
days

BINAIR

(BID)   *Munich (MUC)*

D-CBIN	Swearingen SA.226AT Merlin IV	AT-440B	ex I-FSAD	
D-CCCC	Swearingen SA.227AT Merlin IVC	AT-511	ex N600N	Lsd fr NAG
D-ICRK	Swearingen SA.226TC Metro II	TC-333	ex 4X-CSD	Lsd fr LHG Leasing
PH-RAZ	Swearingen SA.226TC Metro II	TC-252	ex OY-AZW	

BLUE WINGS

(BWG)   *Düsseldorf (DUS)*

| D-ANJA | Airbus Industrie A321-231 | 0519 | ex HB-IOB | Lsd fr ILFC |
| D-ANNE | Airbus Industrie A320-232 | 0530 | ex D-ALTA | Lsd fr ILFC |

CIRRUS AIRLINES

Cirrus Air (C9/RUS) (IATA 251)   *Saarbrücken-Ensheim (SCN)*

D-BHAM	de Havilland DHC-8-314	313	ex OE-LEC	Lsd fr Elveden Investments
D-BIER	de Havilland DHC-8-103	310	ex OE-LEA	Lsd fr AUB
D-BKIM	de Havilland DHC-8-311	356	ex C-GFOD	Lsd fr Eheim; sublsd to FlyBaboo
D-BOBL	de Havilland DHC-8-102A	225	ex C-GFQL	Lsd fr Lipicar
D-BOBO	de Havilland DHC-8-102	153	ex C-GFOD	Lsd fr LGS Leasing
D-BOBU	de Havilland DHC-8-311A	252	ex C-GFCF	Lsd fr ITM Vermögen
D-BOBY	de Havilland DHC-8-102	177	ex C-GFQL	Lsd fr Lipicar

D-ACIR	Embraer EMB.145MP	145230	ex PT-SHT	Saarbrucken
D-CCIR	Dornier 328-130	3100	ex D-CDXA	
D-CIRA	Dornier 328-120	3077	ex HB-AEJ	
D-CIRB	Dornier 328-110	3017	ex HB-AEF	
D-CIRC	Dornier 328-100	3041	ex HB-AEI	Lsd fr Aircraft Asset Mgt
D-CIRD	Dornier 328-110	3011	ex HB-AEG	
D-COSA	Dornier 328-110	3085	ex D-CDXR	Lsd fr Bahag AG
D-	Embraer 170			on order Dec04

One Dornier 328-100 leased to Air Dolomiti

CITY-AIR GERMANY

Cityways (6E/CIP) (IATA 493)   *Paderborn (PAD)*
Previously listed as TAG City Air

D-BKKK	Aerospatiale/Alenia ATR 42-500	532	ex F-WWLP	
D-CEBR	Swearingen SA.227DC Metro 23	DC-899B	ex N3060H	Graf Bernhard	Lsd fr EBR
D-COLC	Swearingen SA.227AC Metro III	AC-689	ex N706C		Lsd fr OLT
D-CSAL	Swearingen SA.227AC Metro III	AC-601	ex I-FSAH	
D-CASB	SAAB SF.340B	223	ex SE-KSI	Lsd fr Handelsbanken Finans
D-CASC	SAAB SF.340B	229	ex SE-KSK	Lsd fr Handelsbanken Finans
D-CASD	SAAB SF.340B	221	ex F-GPKM	

CONDOR BERLIN now listed under trading name Thomas Cook Airlines

CONDOR FLUG now listed under trading name Thomas Cook Airlines

CONTACT AIR

Contactair (3T/KIS)   *Stuttgart (STR)*

D-AFFX	Fokker 50	20142	ex EC-GAF	
D-AFFY	Fokker 50	20141	ex EC-GAE	
D-AFFZ	Fokker 50	20133	ex EC-GAD	
D-AFKK	Fokker 50	20205	ex PH-EXN	
D-AFKL	Fokker 50	20213	ex PH-EXC	
D-AFKM	Fokker 50	20214	ex PH-EXD	
D-AFKN	Fokker 50	20223	ex PH-EXX	
D-AFKO	Fokker 50	20234	ex PH-JXO	
D-AFKP	Fokker 50	20235	ex PH-EXE	

D-BMMM	Aerospatiale/Alenia ATR 42-500	546	ex F-WWLE	Lsd fr LFL Lsg
D-BNNN	Aerospatiale/Alenia ATR 42-500	551	ex F-WWLL	Lsd fr EWG
D-BOOO	Aerospatiale/Alenia ATR 42-500	559	ex F-WWLM	Lsd fr EWG

| D-BRRR | Aerospatiale/Alenia ATR 42-500 | 601 | ex F-WWEC | Lsd fr EWG |
| D-BSSS | Aerospatiale/Alenia ATR 42-500 | 602 | ex F-WWLA | Lsd fr EWG |

24.8% owned by Lufthansa Cityline from whom all aircraft, which operate in Lufthansa Regional colours, are leased.

DBA

Speedway (DI/BAG) (IATA 944)   Munich (MUC)
Previously listed as Deutsche BA

D-ADBM*	Boeing 737-31S	2942/29057		Schrifttanz	
D-ADBN*	Boeing 737-31S	2946/29058		Wolkenschreiber	
D-ADBO*	Boeing 737-31S	2967/29059		Himmelsbrief	
D-ADBP*	Boeing 737-31S	2979/29060		Federtraum	
D-ADBQ*	Boeing 737-31S	2982/29099		Paradiesvogel	
D-ADBR*	Boeing 737-31S	2984/29100		Sternschnuppe	
D-ADBS*	Boeing 737-31S	3005/29116		Windspiel	
D-ADBT*	Boeing 737-31S	3070/29264	ex N1795B	Phantasia	
D-ADBU*	Boeing 737-31S	3073/29265	ex N1787B	Kosmopolit	
D-ADBV"	Boeing 737-31S	3092/29266		Sterntaler	
D-ADBW"	Boeing 737-31S	3093/29267	ex N60436	Wolkenreiter	
D-ADIA+	Boeing 737-33Q	3117/30333		Edelweiss	
D-ADIB+	Boeing 737-36Q	3120/30334		Enzian	
D-ADIC+	Boeing 737-36Q	3129/30335		Alpenrose	
D-ADID	Boeing 737-329	1441/23773	ex OO-SDX	To be retd to lessor	Lsd fr CIT Lsg
D-ADIE	Boeing 737-329	1443/23774	ex OO-SDY	To be retd to lessor	Lsd fr CIT Lsg
D-ADIF	Boeing 737-3L9	2059/25125	ex G-BZZB	on order Feb04	Lsd fr Pembroke
D-ADIG	Boeing 737-3L9	2250/26441	ex G-BZZA		Lsd fr Shananda Ltd
D-ADI^	Boeing 737-35B	1626/24238	ex D-AGEE		Lsd fr GMI
D-ADI^	Boeing 737-35B	1624/24237	ex D-AGEG		Lsd fr GMI
D-ADI^	Boeing 737-3M8	1991/25015	ex D-AGEK		Lsd fr GMI
D-AGEJ	Boeing 737-3L9	1604/24221	ex OO-SEJ		Lsd fr Pembroke

^To possibly be reregistered D-ADII/J/K (tie-ups not confirmed)
+Leased from Boullioun   * Leased from Deutsche Structured Finance
" Leased from FSC Ltd

D-AGP	Fokker 100	11	ex PH-CX	Lsd fr GMI
D-AGP	Fokker 100	11	ex PH-CX	Lsd fr GMI
D-AGP	Fokker 100	11	ex PH-CX	Lsd fr GMI
D-AGP	Fokker 100	11	ex PH-CX	Lsd fr GMI

To be leased for the summer of 2004

__DEUTSCHE BA__   rebranded as dba following sale by British Airways

---

EUROPEAN AIR EXPRESS

Noris (EA/EAL) (IATA 024)   Mönchengladbach (MGL)

D-BCRQ	Aerospatiale/Alenia ATR 42-300	233	ex F-WWEO
D-BCRR	Aerospatiale/Alenia ATR 42-300	255	ex F-WWEC
D-BCRS	Aerospatiale/Alenia ATR 42-300	287	ex F-WWLL
D-BCRT	Aerospatiale/Alenia ATR 42-300QC	289	ex F-WWLN
D-BJJJ	Aerospatiale/Alenia ATR 42-300	278	ex F-WWEC

EUROWINGS

Eurowings (EW/EWG) (IATA 104)   Dortmund/Nuremberg (DTM/NUE)

D-AEWG	Aerospatiale/Alenia ATR 72-212	347	ex F-WWEC	
D-AEWH	Aerospatiale/Alenia ATR 72-212	359	ex F-WWEV	
D-AEWI	Aerospatiale/Alenia ATR 72-212	404	ex F-WWLO	
D-AEWK	Aerospatiale/Alenia ATR 72-212	446	ex F-WWEA	Lsd fr BKL Lsg
D-ANFA	Aerospatiale/Alenia ATR 72-202	224	ex F-WWEQ	
D-ANFB	Aerospatiale/Alenia ATR 72-202	229	ex F-WWEX	
D-ANFC	Aerospatiale/Alenia ATR 72-202	237	ex F-WWEG	Lsd fr Lease Trend
D-ANFD	Aerospatiale/Alenia ATR 72-202	256	ex F-WWEE	
D-ANFE	Aerospatiale/Alenia ATR 72-202	294	ex F-WWLS	
D-ANFF	Aerospatiale/Alenia ATR 72-202	292	ex F-WWLT	Lsd fr LFL Lsg
D-ANFG	Aerospatiale/Alenia ATR 72-212A	658	ex F-WWEL	Lsd fr ATR Asset Mgt
D-ANFH	Aerospatiale/Alenia ATR 72-212A	660	ex F-WWEM	Lsd fr ATR Asset Mgt
D-ANFI	Aerospatiale/Alenia ATR 72-212A	662	ex F-WWEN	Lsd fr ATR Asset Mgt
D-ANFJ	Aerospatiale/Alenia ATR 72-212A	664	ex F-WWEO	Lsd fr ATR Asset Mgt
D-ANFK	Aerospatiale/Alenia ATR 72-212A	666	ex F-WWEP	Lsd fr ATR Asset Mgt
D-ANFL	Aerospatiale/Alenia ATR 72-212A	668	ex F-WWEQ	Lsd fr ATR Asset Mgt
D-BCRO	Aerospatiale/Alenia ATR 42-300QC	122	ex F-WWES	Lippstadt
D-BLLL	Aerospatiale/Alenia AIR 42-500	549	ex F-WWLB	Lsd fr RBS Avn
D-BNNN	Aerospatiale/Alenia ATR 42-500	551	ex F-WWLL	Lsd to CLH
D-BOOO	Aerospatiale/Alenia ATR 42-500	559	ex F-WWLM	Lsd to CLH
D-BPPP	Aerospatiale/Alenia ATR 42-500	581	ex F-WWLE	Lsd fr LFL Lsg
D-BQQQ	Aerospatiale/Alenia ATR 42-500	584	ex F-WWEP	Lsd fr Lease Trend
D-BRRR	Aerospatiale/Alenia ATR 42-500	601	ex F-WWEC	Lsd to CLH
D-BSSS	Aerospatiale/Alenia ATR 42-500	602	ex F-WWLA	Lsd to CLH

D-BTTT	Aerospatiale/Alenia ATR 42-500	603	ex F-WWLD		Lsd fr Commerzleasing

All ATR 42-500s are for sale

D-ACFA	British Aerospace 146 Srs.200	E2200	ex G-BTVT		Lsd fr Trident
D-AEWA	British Aerospace 146 Srs.300	E3163	ex G-BTJG		Lsd fr Celaeno
D-AEWB	British Aerospace 146 Srs.300	E3183	ex G-BUHB		Lsd fr Knight Lsg
D-AEWD	British Aerospace 146 Srs.200	E2069	ex OO-DJC		Lsd fr RBS Avn
D-AEWE	British Aerospace 146 Srs.200	E2077	ex OO-DJD		Lsd fr RBS Avn
D-AHOI	British Aerospace 146 Srs.300	E3187	ex G-BSYT	all-white	Lsd fr Maia Lsg
D-AJET	British Aerospace 146 Srs.200	E2201	ex G-6-201		Lsd fr Lease Trend
D-AQUA	British Aerospace 146 Srs.300	E3118	ex G-OAJF		Lsd fr Trident

D-ACRA	Canadair CL-600-2B19	7567	ex C-FMNX		Lsd fr GOAL
D-ACRB	Canadair CL-600-2B19	7570	ex C-FMOW		Lsd fr GOAL
D-ACRC	Canadair CL-600-2B19	7573	ex C-FMNQ		Lsd fr GOAL
D-ACRD	Canadair CL-600-2B19	7583	ex C-FMNB		Lsd fr GOAL
D-ACRE	Canadair CL-600-2B19	7607	ex C-FMML		Lsd fr GOAL
D-ACRF	Canadair CL-600-2B19	7619	ex C-FMLI	special c/s	Lsd fr GOAL
D-ACRG	Canadair CL-600-2B19	7630	ex C-FMOW		Lsd fr GOAL
D-ACRH	Canadair CL-600-2B19	7738	ex C-FMLF		Lsd fr GOAL
D-ACRI	Canadair CL-600-2B19	7862	ex C-GZPA		Lsd fr GOAL
D-ACRJ	Canadair CL-600-2B19	7864	ex C-GZOZ		Lsd fr GOAL

Germanwings is wholly owned subsidiary. 49% owned by Lufthansa and operates as Lufthansa Regional

EXPRESS AIRWAYS

(EPA)   *Hahn (HHN)*

D-CFXD	Short SD.3-60	SH3749	ex N262GA
D-CRAS	Short SD.3-60	SH3744	ex N825BE

FARNAIR GERMANY reformed as Express Airways

FLUGDIENST FEHLHABER

Witchcraft (FFG)   *Cologne (CGN)*

D-IAAD	Reims Cessna F406 Caravan II	F406-0047	ex N6589A	Freighter
D-INUS	Reims Cessna F406 Caravan II	F406-0043		Freighter
D-ISHY	Reims Cessna F406 Caravan II	F406-0027	ex PH-FWH	Freighter

FRISIA LUFTVERKEHR

Norden-Norddeich (NOE)

D-IFKU	Britten-Norman BN-2B-20 Islander	2290	ex G-BVXY	Norderney
D-IFLN	Britten-Norman BN-2B-20 Islander	2241	ex G-BSPU	Norden
D-IFTI	Britten-Norman BN-2B-20 Islander	2299	ex G-BWYY	Norddeich

GERMANIA FLUG

Germania (ST/GMI)   *Cologne (CGN)*

D-AGPA	Fokker 100	11276	ex PH-CXA		Lsd fr Pembroke
D-AGPB	Fokker 100	11278	ex PH-CXB		Lsd fr Pembroke
D-AGPC	Fokker 100	11280	ex PH-CXC		Lsd fr Pembroke
D-AGPD	Fokker 100	11281	ex PH-CXD		Lsd fr Pembroke
D-AGPE	Fokker 100	11300	ex PH-CXE		Lsd fr Pembroke
D-AGPF	Fokker 100	11303	ex PH-CXF		Lsd fr Pembroke
D-AGPG	Fokker 100	11306	ex PH-CXG		Lsd fr Pembroke
D-AGPH	Fokker 100	11308	ex PH-CXH		Lsd fr Pembroke
D-AGPI	Fokker 100	11310	ex PH-CXI		Lsd fr Pembroke
D-AGPJ	Fokker 100	11312	ex PH-CXJ		Lsd fr Pembroke
D-AGPK	Fokker 100	11313	ex PH-CXK		Lsd fr Pembroke
D-AGPL	Fokker 100	11314	ex PH-CXL		Lsd fr Pembroke
D-AGPM	Fokker 100	11331	ex PH-CXM		Lsd fr Pembroke
D-AGPN	Fokker 100	11333	ex PH-CXN		Lsd fr Pembroke
D-AGPO	Fokker 100	11334	ex PH-CXO		Lsd fr Pembroke
D-AGPP	Fokker 100	11337	ex PH-CXP		Lsd fr Pembroke
D-AGPQ	Fokker 100	11338	ex PH-CXQ		Lsd fr Pembroke
D-AGPR	Fokker 100	11391	ex PH-CXR	on order	Lsd fr Pembroke
D-AGPS	Fokker 100	11399	ex PH-CXS	on order	Lsd fr Pembroke

Four to be leased to dba for the summer

D-AGEE	Boeing 737-35B	1626/24238	ex UR-GAG	Lsd fr Pembroke; sublsd to BAG
D-AGEG	Boeing 737-35B	1624/24237	ex UR-GAF	Lsd fr Pembroke; sublsd to BAG
D-AGEK	Boeing 737-3M8	1991/25015	ex SX-BLB	Lsd to BAG
D-AGEL*	Boeing 737-75B	5/28110	ex N1791B	Lsd to HLX
D-AGEN*	Boeing 737-75B	16/28100	ex N1789B	Lsd to HLX
D-AGEP*	Boeing 737-75B	18/28102	ex N5573B	Lsd to HLX
D-AGEQ*	Boeing 737-75B	23/28103	ex N1787B	Lsd to HLX

D-AGER	Boeing 737-75B	27/28107	ex N1002R	Lsd to HLX
D-AGES	Boeing 737-75B	28/28108		Lsd to HLX
D-AGET*	Boeing 737-75B	31/28109		Lsd to HLX
D-AGEU*	Boeing 737-75B	39/28104		Lsd to HLX
D-AGEY	Boeing 737-73S	98/29076	ex N102UN	
D-AGEZ*	Boeing 737-73S	104/29077	ex N103UN	

*Leased from SAT Flug

GERMANWINGS

Shark (4U/GWI)   Cologne (CGN)

D-AIPC	Airbus Industrie A320-211	0071	ex F-WWIO	Lsd fr DLH
D-AIPD	Airbus Industrie A320-211	0072	ex F-WWIP	Lsd fr DLH
D-AIPH	Airbus Industrie A320-211	0086	ex F-WWDJ	Spirit of Cologne	Lsd fr DLH
D-AIPX	Airbus Industrie A320-211	0147	ex F-WWDN		Lsd fr DLH
D-AIQR	Airbus Industrie A320-211	0382	ex F-WWIZ		Lsd fr DLH
D-AKNF^	Airbus Industrie A319-112	0646	ex D-AVYB	Albrecht Dürer	
D-AKNG^	Airbus Industrie A319-112	0654	ex D-AVYX	Johann Wolfgang von Goethe	
D-AKNH+	Airbus Industrie A319-112	0794	ex D-AVYD	Heinrich Heine	
D-AKNI*	Airbus Industrie A319-112	1016	ex D-AVYK	Johannes Gutenberg	
D-AKNJ^	Airbus Industrie A319-112	1172	ex D-AVWF	Kurt Tucholsky	
D-AKNK	Airbus Industrie A319-112	2207	ex D-AV	on order Mar04	

^Leased from Lease Air GmbH   * Leased from Laria Vermietung
+Leased from Mobilien Lsg   Wholly owned by Eurowings

HAHN AIR LINES

Rooster (HR/HHN) (IATA 169)   Hahn (HHN)

D-CBIG	Beech 1900D	UE-288	ex N11320		Lsd fr EEX
D-CNAY	Swearingen SA.227AT Metro III	AT-493	ex PH-RAX		Lsd fr NAG
D-CSWF	Swearingen SA.227DC Metro 23	DC-896B	ex N3042E		
D-CAHR	SAAB SF.340A	074	ex SE-E74	on order	
D-	SAAB SF.340A			on order	
EC-GPS	Swearingen SA.227AC Metro III	AC-722	ex N439MA	Freighter	Lsd fr ECN

HAMBURG INTERNATIONAL AIRLINES

Hamburg Jet (4R/HHI)   Hamburg (HAM)

D-AHIA	Boeing 737-73S	229/29082	ex D-ASKH	Lsd fr Pembroke; op for BER
D-AHIB	Boeing 737-73S	392/29083	ex D-AWOH	Rostock Olympic Lsd fr Pembroke
D-AHIC	Boeing 737-7BK	812/30617	ex N1787B	Lsd fr CIT Leasing; op for BER
D-AHID	Boeing 737-73S	211/29080	ex EI-CRQ	Lsd fr Pembroke
D-AHIE	Boeing 737-73S	215/29081	ex TC-SUF	Lsd fr Pembroke; op for BER
D-AHIF	Boeing 737-73S	194/29079	ex TC-SUE	Lsd fr Pembroke

Appointed as the national carrier of Kosovo and one (D-AHIF) is based at Pristina with Kosovo Airlines titles

HAPAG-LLOYD

Hapag Lloyd (HF/HLF) (IATA 617)   Hannover (HAJ)

D-AHLA*	Airbus Industrie A310-304	520	ex F-WWCI		
D-AHLC*	Airbus Industrie A310-308	620	ex F-WWCC		Lsd to QSC
D-AHLV*	Airbus Industrie A310-204	430	ex F-WWBL		
D-AHLW*	Airbus Industrie A310-204	427	ex F-WWBK		
D-AHLX*	Airbus Industrie A310-204	487	ex F-WWBO		
D-AHLZ*	Airbus Industrie A310-204	468	ex F-WWBM		
D-AIDD	Airbus Industrie A310-304	488	ex F-WWCE	on order	Lsd fr DLH
D-AHLD*	Boeing 737-5K5	1966/24926	ex HA-LER		Lsd to HLX
D-AHLF*	Boeing 737-5K5	1968/24927		Tbilisi	Sublsd to TGZ
D-AHLG*	Boeing 737-5K5	1848/24776	ex HA-LEP		Lsd to HLX
D-AHLI*	Boeing 737-5K5	2022/25037		Kakheti	Sublsd to TGZ
D-AHLJ	Boeing 737-4K5	1687/24125	ex SP-KEI		Lsd to FUA
D-AHLK*	Boeing 737-4K5	1697/24126	ex SP-KEI	Zakopane	Sublsd to MNG
D-AHLL*	Boeing 737-4K5	1707/24127	ex SP-KEK		For Sunrise
D-AHLN*	Boeing 737-5K5	2044/25062	ex 6V-AHM		Sub-lsd to HLX
D-AHLU*	Boeing 737-4K5	2677/27831			Sublsd to ADF
D-AHFA*	Boeing 737-8K5	7/27981	ex N737BX		
D-AHFB*	Boeing 737-8K5	8/27982	ex N35030		
D-AHFC*	Boeing 737-8K5	9/27977	ex N5573P		
D-AHFD*	Boeing 737-8K5	40/27978	ex N35161		
D-AHFE*	Boeing 737-8K5	44/27979	ex N3502P		
D-AHFF*	Boeing 737-8K5	45/27980	ex N3509J		
D-AHFG*	Boeing 737-8K5	59/27989			
D-AHFH*	Boeing 737-8K5	218/27983			
D-AHFI*	Boeing 737-8K5	220/27984	ex N1787B		
D-AHFJ*	Boeing 737-8K5	246/27990			

D-AHFK*	Boeing 737-8K5	248/27991	
D-AHFL*	Boeing 737-8K5	470/27985	
D-AHFM*	Boeing 737-8K5	474/27986	
D-AHFN	Boeing 737-8K5	484/28228	Lsd fr ILFC
D-AHFO*	Boeing 737-8K5	499/27987	Sublsd to BER
D-AHFP*	Boeing 737-8K5	508/27988	
D-AHFQ*	Boeing 737-8K5	523/27992	
D-AHFR*	Boeing 737-8K5	528/30593 ex N1787B	
D-AHFS	Boeing 737-86N	556/28623	Lsd fr GECAS; sublsd to BER
D-AHFT	Boeing 737-8K5	636/30413 ex N1015B	
D-AHFU	Boeing 737-8K5	703/30414 ex N1787B	
D-AHFV	Boeing 737-8K5	719/30415	
D-AHFW	Boeing 737-8K5	760/30882	
D-AHFX	Boeing 737-8K5	778/30416	
D-AHFY	Boeing 737-8K5	781/30417 ex N1787B	
D-AHFZ	Boeing 737-8K5	783/30883	
D-AHLH	Boeing 737-8K5	804/30783	Lsd fr Tombo
D-AHLP	Boeing 737-8K5	1046/32905 ex N6065Y	
D-AHLQ	Boeing 737-8K5	1087/32906	
D-AHLR	Boeing 737-8K5	1117/32907	
D-ATUI	Boeing 737-86Q	1308/30287	Lsd fr Boullioun

*Leased from Defag   All 737-8K5s retrofitted with winglets
Aircraft being repainted in 'World of TUI' colours [owner, also owns Britannia Airways, Corsair, White Eagle and NEOS]
Hapag-Lloyd Express is wholly owned low-cost subsidiary

HAPAG-LLOYD EXPRESS

(3H/HLX)   Cologne (CGN)

D-AGEL	Boeing 737-75B	5/28110 ex N1791B	Lsd fr GMI
D-AGEN	Boeing 737-75B	16/28100 ex N1789B	Lsd fr GMI
D-AGEP	Boeing 737-75B	18/28102 ex N5573B	Lsd fr GMI
D-AGEQ	Boeing 737-75B	23/28103 ex N1787B	Lsd fr GMI
D-AGER	Boeing 737-75B	27/28107 ex N1002R	Lsd fr GMI
D-AGES	Boeing 737-75B	28/28108	Lsd fr GMI
D-AGET	Boeing 737-75B	31/28109	Lsd fr GMI
D-AGEU	Boeing 737-75B	39/28104	Lsd fr GMI
D-AHLD	Boeing 737-5K5	1966/24926 ex HA-LER	Lsd fr GMI
D-AHLG	Boeing 737-5K5	1848/24776 ex HA-LEP	Lsd fr GMI
D-AHLN	Boeing 737-5K5	2044/25062 ex 6V-AHM	Lsd fr HLF

HELGOLAND AIRLINES

(LE)   Wilhelmshaven (WVN)

D-IAEB	Britten-Norman BN-2A-8 Islander	218 ex OH-BNB	
D-IORF	Britten-Norman BN-2A -26Islander	2020 ex N100DA	stored Bremerhaven

LGW – LUFTFAHRTGESELLSCHAFT WALTER

Walter (HE/LGW)   Dortmund (DTM)

D-IKBA	Dornier 228-200	8066 ex D-CBDR	Lsd fr Dornier
D-ILKA	Dornier 228-100	7005 ex LN-HTB	
D-ILWB	Dornier 228-200	8035 ex D-CDIZ	
D-ILWD	Dornier 228-200	8069 ex D-CHOF	
D-ILWS	Dornier 228-200	8002 ex D-CBDU	
D-IMIK	Dornier 228-200	8058 ex D-CMIC	Lsd fr Franke

LOWFARE JET did not start operations

LTU INTERNATIONAL AIRWAYS

LTU (LT/LTU) (IATA 266)   Düsseldorf (DUS)

D-ALSA	Airbus Industrie A321-211	1629 ex D-AVZC	Lsd fr GATX
D-ALSB	Airbus Industrie A321-211	1994 ex D-AVZR	
D-ALSC	Airbus Industrie A321-211	2005 ex D-AVXI	
D-ALTB*	Airbus Industrie A320-214	1385 ex F-WWIT	Lsd fr CIT Ireland Lse
D-ALTC"	Airbus Industrie A320-214	1441 ex F-WWBQ	Lsd fr Mystic River A/c Finance
D-ALTD+	Airbus Industrie A320-214	1493 ex F-WWDY	Lsd fr GECAS
D-ALTE	Airbus Industrie A320-214	1504 ex F-WWIH	Lsd fr GATX
D-ALTF	Airbus Industrie A320-214	1553 ex F-WWBH	Lsd fr GATX
D-ALTG	Airbus Industrie A320-214	1762 ex F-WWBR	Lsd fr CIT Lsg
D-ALTH	Airbus Industrie A320-214	1797 ex F-WWDV	
D-ALTI	Airbus Industrie A320-214	1806 ex F-WWIJ	Lsd fr CIT Lsg
D-ALTJ	Airbus Industrie A320-214	1838 ex F-WWBM	
D-ALTK	Airbus Industrie A320-214	1931 ex F-WWIH	
D-ALTL	Airbus Industrie A320-214	2009 ex F-WWBO	

*Borrussia Mönchengladbach titles   +Hertha BSC Berlin titles
"Bayer 04 Leverkusen titles

D-AERF	Airbus Industrie A330-322	082	ex F-WWKD		Lsd fr JL Arcadia
D-AERK	Airbus Industrie A330-322	120	ex F-WWKN		Lsd fr JL Emi Lsg
D-AERQ	Airbus Industrie A330-322	127	ex F-WWKO		Lsd fr JL Elm Lsg
D-ALPA	Airbus Industrie A330-223	403	ex F-WWKO		Lsd fr CIT Leasing
D-ALPB	Airbus Industrie A330-223	432	ex F-WWYG		Lsd fr ILFC
D-ALPC	Airbus Industrie A330-223	444	ex F-WWKD		Lsd fr ILFC
D-ALPD	Airbus Industrie A330-223	454	ex F-WWKG		Lsd fr ILFC
D-ALPE	Airbus Industrie A330-223	469	ex F-WWKO		Lsd fr ILFC
D-ALPF	Airbus Industrie A330-223	476	ex F-WWKT		Lsd fr ILFC
D-ALPG	Airbus Industrie A330-223	493	ex F-WWKI		Lsd fr ILFC

LUFTHANSA

Lufthansa (LH/DLH) (IATA 220)   *Frankfurt (FRA)*

D-AIAH	Airbus Industrie A300B4-603	380	ex F-WWAA	Lindau/Bodensee	stored MUC
D-AIAI	Airbus Industrie A300B4-603	391	ex F-WWAL	Erbach/Odenwald	
D-AIAK	Airbus Industrie A300B4-603	401	ex F-WWAO	Kronberg im Taunus	stored HAM
D-AIAL	Airbus Industrie A300B4-603	405	ex F-WWAP	Stade	stored HAM
D-AIAM	Airbus Industrie A300B4-603	408	ex F-WWAQ	Rosenheim	stored FRA
D-AIAN	Airbus Industrie A300B4-603	411	ex F-WWAR	Nördlingen	
D-AIAP	Airbus Industrie A300B4-603	414	ex F-WWAS	Donauwörth	
D-AIAR	Airbus Industrie A300B4-603	546	ex F-WWAP	Bingen am Rhein	
D-AIAS	Airbus Industrie A300B4-603	553	ex F-WWAX	Mönchengladbach	stored MUC
D-AIAT	Airbus Industrie A300B4-603	618	ex F-WWAM	Bottrop	
D-AIAU	Airbus Industrie A300B4-603	623	ex F-WWAT	Bocholt	
D-AIAW	Airbus Industrie A300B4-605R	764	ex F-WWAJ	Witten	Lsd fr ILFC, std MUC
D-AIAX	Airbus Industrie A300B4-605R	773	ex F-WWAO	Fürth	Lsd fr Lufthansa Lsg
D-AIAY	Airbus Industrie A300B4-605R	608	ex A6-EKF		
D-AIAZ	Airbus Industrie A300B4-605R	701	ex A6-EKM		

D-AIDD	Airbus Industrie A310-304	488	ex F-WWCE	Emden; for HLF	
D-AIDF	Airbus Industrie A310-304	524	ex F-WWCA	Aschaffenburg	stored TXL
D-AIDH	Airbus Industrie A310-304	527	ex F-WWCD	Wetzlar	stored STR
D-AIDL	Airbus Industrie A310-304	547	ex F-WWCU	Oberstdorf	
D-AIDN	Airbus Industrie A310-304	599	ex F-WWCZ	Gütersloh	

D-AILA	Airbus Industrie A319-114	0609	ex D-AVYF	Frankfurt an der Oder	
D-AILB	Airbus Industrie A319-114	0610	ex D-AVYG	Lutherstadt / Wittenberg	
D-AILC	Airbus Industrie A319-114	0616	ex D-AVYI	Rüsselsheim	
D-AILD	Airbus Industrie A319-114	0623	ex D-AVYL	Dinkelsbühl	
D-AILE	Airbus Industrie A319-114	0627	ex D-AVYO	Kelsterbach	
D-AILF	Airbus Industrie A319-114	0636	ex D-AVYS	Trier	
D-AILH	Airbus Industrie A319-114	0641	ex D-AVYV	Norderstedt; canx 10.03	stored SXF
D-AILI	Airbus Industrie A319-114	0651	ex D-AVYY	Ingolstadt; canx 10.03	
D-AILK	Airbus Industrie A319-114	0679	ex D-AVYG	Landshut	stored SXF
D-AILL	Airbus Industrie A319-114	0689	ex D-AVYL	Marburg	
D-AILM	Airbus Industrie A319-114	0694	ex D-AVYR	Friedrichshafen	stored SXF
D-AILN	Airbus Industrie A319-114	0700	ex D-AVYU	Idar-Oberstein	
D-AILP	Airbus Industrie A319-114	0717	ex D-AVYA	Tübingen	
D-AILR	Airbus Industrie A319-114	0723	ex D-AVYD	Tegernsee	
D-AILS	Airbus Industrie A319-114	0729	ex D-AVYF	Heide	
D-AILT	Airbus Industrie A319-114	0738	ex D-AVYN	Straubing	
D-AILU	Airbus Industrie A319-114	0744	ex D-AVYI	Verden	
D-AILW	Airbus Industrie A319-114	0853	ex D-AVYO	Donaueschingen	
D-AILX	Airbus Industrie A319-114	0860	ex D-AVYS	Fellbach	
D-AILY	Airbus Industrie A319-114	0875	ex D-AVYC	Schweinfurt	
D-APAC	Airbus Industrie A319-132LR	1727	ex D-AVWQ	48-seat	Lsd fr/op by PTI
D-APAD	Airbus Industrie A319-132LR	1880	ex D-AVYM	48-seat	Lsd fr/op by PTI

First service, Munich-Newark, by Airbus Industrie A319-132LR on 19 May 2003

D-AIPA	Airbus Industrie A320-211	0069	ex F-WWII	Buxtehude	
D-AIPB	Airbus Industrie A320-211	0070	ex F-WWIJ	Heidelberg	
D-AIPC	Airbus Industrie A320-211	0071	ex F-WWIO	Braunschweig	Lsd to GWI
D-AIPD	Airbus Industrie A320-211	0072	ex F-WWIP	Freiburg	Lsd to GWI
D-AIPE	Airbus Industrie A320-211	0078	ex F-WWIU	Kassel	
D-AIPF	Airbus Industrie A320-211	0083	ex F-WWDE	Deggendorf	
D-AIPH	Airbus Industrie A320-211	0086	ex F-WWDJ	Münster	Lsd to GWI
D-AIPK	Airbus Industrie A320-211	0093	ex F-WWDQ	Wiesbaden	stored STR
D-AIPL	Airbus Industrie A320-211	0094	ex 7T-VKO	Ludwigshafen am Rhein	stored SXF
D-AIPM	Airbus Industrie A320-211	0104	ex F-WWIG	Troisdorf	
D-AIPP	Airbus Industrie A320-211	0110	ex F-WWID	Starnberg	
D-AIPR	Airbus Industrie A320-211	0111	ex F-WWIE	Kaufbeuren	
D-AIPS	Airbus Industrie A320-211	0116	ex F-WWIK	Augsburg	
D-AIPT	Airbus Industrie A320-211	0117	ex F-WWIL	Cottbus	
D-AIPU	Airbus Industrie A320-211	0135	ex F-WWDB	Dresden	
D-AIPW	Airbus Industrie A320-211	0137	ex F-WWDD	Schwerin	
D-AIPX	Airbus Industrie A320-211	0147	ex F-WWDN	Mannheim	Lsd to GWI
D-AIPY	Airbus Industrie A320-211	0161	ex F-WWIA	Magdeburg	
D-AIPZ	Airbus Industrie A320-211	0162	ex F-WWDS	Erfurt	
D-AIQA	Airbus Industrie A320-211	0172	ex F-WWIK	Mainz	

D-AIQB	Airbus Industrie A320-211	0200	ex F-WWDJ	Bielefeld	
D-AIQC	Airbus Industrie A320-211	0201	ex F-WWDL	Zwickau	
D-AIQD	Airbus Industrie A320-211	0202	ex F-WWDM	Jena	
D-AIQE	Airbus Industrie A320-211	0209	ex F-WWDY	Gera	
D-AIQF	Airbus Industrie A320-211	0216	ex F-WWDR	Halle an der Saale	
D-AIQH	Airbus Industrie A320-211	0217	ex F-WWDS	Dessau	
D-AIQK	Airbus Industrie A320-211	0218	ex F-WWDX	Rostock	
D-AIQL	Airbus Industrie A320-211	0267	ex F-WWDY	Stralsund	
D-AIQM	Airbus Industrie A320-211	0268	ex F-WWIB	Nordenham	
D-AIQN	Airbus Industrie A320-211	0269	ex F-WWIC	Laupheim	
D-AIQP	Airbus Industrie A320-211	0346	ex F-WWDX	Suhl	
D-AIQR	Airbus Industrie A320-211	0382	ex F-WWIZ	Lahr/Schwarzwald	Lsd to GWI
D-AIQS	Airbus Industrie A320-211	0401	ex F-WWBD	Eisenach	
D-AIQT	Airbus Industrie A320-211	1337	ex F-WWDO	Gotha	
D-AIQU	Airbus Industrie A320-211	1365	ex F-WWIG	Backnang	
D-AIQW	Airbus Industrie A320-211	1367	ex F-WWIH	Kleve	
D-AIRA	Airbus Industrie A321-131	0458	ex F-WWIQ	Finkenwerder	
D-AIRB	Airbus Industrie A321-131	0468	ex F-WWIS	Baden-Baden	
D-AIRC	Airbus Industrie A321-131	0473	ex D-AVZC	Erlangen	
D-AIRD	Airbus Industrie A321-131	0474	ex D-AVZD	Coburg	
D-AIRE	Airbus Industrie A321-131	0484	ex D-AVZF	Osnabrück	
D-AIRF	Airbus Industrie A321-131	0493	ex D-AVZH	Kempten	
D-AIRH	Airbus Industrie A321-131	0412	ex D-AVZA	Garmisch-Partenkirchen	
D-AIRK	Airbus Industrie A321-131	0502	ex D-AVZL	Freudenstadt/Schwarzwald	
D-AIRL	Airbus Industrie A321-131	0505	ex D-AVZM	Kulmbach	
D-AIRM	Airbus Industrie A321-131	0518	ex D-AVZT	Darmstadt	
D-AIRN	Airbus Industrie A321-131	0560	ex D-AVZK	Kaiserslautern	
D-AIRO	Airbus Industrie A321-131	0563	ex D-AVZN	Konstanz	
D-AIRP	Airbus Industrie A321-131	0564	ex D-AVZL	Lüneburg	
D-AIRR	Airbus Industrie A321-131	0567	ex D-AVZM	Wismar	
D-AIRS	Airbus Industrie A321-131	0595	ex D-AVZX	Husum	Lsd fr Lufthansa Lsg
D-AIRT	Airbus Industrie A321-131	0652	ex D-AVZI	Regensburg	
D-AIRU	Airbus Industrie A321-131	0692	ex D-AVZT	Würzburg	
D-AIRW	Airbus Industrie A321-131	0699	ex D-AVZY	Heilbronn	Lsd fr Lufthansa Lsg
D-AIRX	Airbus Industrie A321-131	0887	ex D-AVZI	Weimar	
D-AIRY	Airbus Industrie A321-131	0901	ex D-AVZK	Flensburg	
D-AISB	Airbus Industrie A321-231	1080	ex D-AVZP	Hameln	
D-AISC	Airbus Industrie A321-231	1161	ex D-AVZG	Speyer	
D-AISD	Airbus Industrie A321-231	1188	ex F-WWDD	Chemnitz	
D-AISE	Airbus Industrie A321-231	1214	ex D-AVZS	Neudstadt an der Weinstrasse	
D-AISF	Airbus Industrie A321-231	1260	ex D-AVZI	Lippstadt	
D-AISG	Airbus Industrie A321-231	1273	ex D-AVZU	Dormagen	
D-AIMA	Airbus Industrie A330-223	305	ex HB-IQL		Lsd fr Kayo Ltd
D-AIMB	Airbus Industrie A330-223	308	ex HB-IQM		Lsd fr Kayo Ltd
D-AIMC	Airbus Industrie A330-223	312	ex HB-IQN		Lsd fr Kayo Ltd
D-AIMD	Airbus Industrie A330-223	322	ex F-WIHM		Lsd fr Airbus
D-AIME	Airbus Industrie A330-223	324	ex F-GHYI		Lsd fr Commuter Lease
D-AIKA	Airbus Industrie A330-343X	570	ex F-WWYV	on order 04	
D-AIKB	Airbus Industrie A330-343X	576	ex F-WWKN	on order 04	
D-AIKC	Airbus Industrie A330-343X	579	ex F-WWKG	on order 04	
D-AIKD	Airbus Industrie A330-343X	634	ex F-WW	on order 04	
D-AIKE	Airbus Industrie A330-343X	645	ex F-WW	on order 04	

Airbus Industrie A330-223s leased until five more new Airbus Industrie A330-341s (D-AIKF to AIKJ) are delivered in 2005 (two are c/nos 657 and 668)

D-AIBF	Airbus Industrie A340-211	006	ex F-WWBE	Lübeck	stored HAM
D-AIFA	Airbus Industrie A340-313X	352	ex F-WWJU	Dorsten	
D-AIFB	Airbus Industrie A340-313X	355	ex F-WWJX	Gummersbach	
D-AIFC	Airbus Industrie A340-313X	379	ex F-WWJJ	Gander/Halifax	
D-AIFD	Airbus Industrie A340-313X	390	ex F-WWJE	Giessen	
D-AIFE	Airbus Industrie A340-313X	434	ex F-WWJT	Passau	
D-AIFF	Airbus Industrie A340-313X	447	ex F-WWJB	Delmenhorst	
D-AIGA	Airbus Industrie A340-311	020	ex F-WWJK	Oldenburg	
D-AIGB	Airbus Industrie A340-311	024	ex F-WWJO	Recklinghausen	
D-AIGC	Airbus Industrie A340-311	027	ex F-WWJR	Wilhelmshaven	Star Alliance c/s
D-AIGD	Airbus Industrie A340-311	028	ex F-WWJS	Remscheid	
D-AIGF	Airbus Industrie A340-311	035	ex F-WWJV	Göttingen	
D-AIGH	Airbus Industrie A340-311	052	ex F-WWJQ	Koblenz	
D-AIGI	Airbus Industrie A340-311	053	ex F-WWJJ	Worms	
D-AIGK	Airbus Industrie A340-311	056	ex F-WWJK	Bayreuth	
D-AIGL	Airbus Industrie A340-313X	135	ex F-WWJS	Herne	
D-AIGM	Airbus Industrie A340-313X	158	ex F-WWJN	Görlitz	
D-AIGN	Airbus Industrie A340-313X	213	ex F-WWJM	Solingen	
D-AIGO	Airbus Industrie A340-313X	233	ex F-WWJJ	Offenbach	
D-AIGP	Airbus Industrie A340-313X	252	ex F-WWJM	Paderborn	
D-AIGR	Airbus Industrie A340-313X	274	ex F-WWJI	Leipzig	stored STR
D-AIGS	Airbus Industrie A340-313X	297	ex F-WWJK	Bergisch-Gladbach	
D-AIGT	Airbus Industrie A340-313X	304	ex F-WWJY	Viersen	
D-AIGU	Airbus Industrie A340-313X	321	ex F-WWJM	Castrop-Rauxel	
D-AIGV	Airbus Industrie A340-313X	325	ex F-WWJN	Dinslaken	
D-AIGW	Airbus Industrie A340-313X	327	ex F-WWJO	Gladbeck	

D-AIGX	Airbus Industrie A340-313X	354	ex F-WWJV	Düren	
D-AIGY	Airbus Industrie A340-313X	335	ex F-WWJS	Lünen	
D-AIGZ	Airbus Industrie A340-313X	347	ex F-WWJT	Villingen-Schwenningen	
D-AIHA	Airbus Industrie A340-642	482	ex F-WWCS	Nurnberg	
D-AIHB	Airbus Industrie A340-642	517	ex F-WWCR	Bremerhaven	
D-AIHC	Airbus Industrie A340-642	523	ex F-WWCV	Essen	Star Alliance c/s
D-AIHD	Airbus Industrie A340-642	537	ex F-WWCZ	Stuttgart	
D-AIHE	Airbus Industrie A340-642	540	ex F-WWCF		
D-AIHF	Airbus Industrie A340-642	543	ex F-WWCE		
D-AIHH	Airbus Industrie A340-642	566	ex F-WWCJ		
D-AIHI	Airbus Industrie A340-642	569	ex F-WWCB		
D-AIHK	Airbus Industrie A340-642	580	ex F-WWCN	on order 04	
D-AIHL	Airbus Industrie A340-642	583	ex F-WWCQ	on order 04	
D-AIMF	Airbus Industrie A340-311	047	ex F-WQRH		Lsd fr GIE Lara
D-AIMG	Airbus Industrie A340-311	051	ex F-WQRI		Lsd fr GIE Lara
D-ABEA	Boeing 737-330	1818/24565		Saarbrücken	
D-ABEB	Boeing 737-330	2077/25148		Xanten	
D-ABEC	Boeing 737-330	2081/25149		Karlsruhe	
D-ABED	Boeing 737-330	2082/25215		Hagen	
D-ABEE	Boeing 737-330	2084/25216		Ulm	
D-ABEF	Boeing 737-330	2094/25217		Weiden	
D-ABEH	Boeing 737-330	2102/25242		Bad Kissingen	
D-ABEI	Boeing 737-330	2158/25359	ex (D-ABJK)	Bamberg	
D-ABEK	Boeing 737-330	2164/25414	ex (D-ABJL)	Wuppertal	
D-ABEL	Boeing 737-330	2175/25415	ex (D-ABJM)	Pforzheim	
D-ABEM	Boeing 737-330	2182/25416	ex (D-ABJN)	Eberswalde-Finow	
D-ABEN	Boeing 737-330	2196/26428	ex (D-ABJP)	Neubrandenburg	
D-ABEO	Boeing 737-330	2207/26429	ex (D-ABJR)	Plauen	stored BUD
D-ABEP	Boeing 737-330	2216/26430	ex (D-ABJS)	Naumburg/Saale	
D-ABER	Boeing 737-330	2242/26431	ex TC-SUK	Merseburg	
D-ABES	Boeing 737-330	2247/26432	ex (D-ABJU)	Köthen/Anhalt	stored BUD
D-ABET	Boeing 737-330	2682/27903		Gelsenkirchen	
D-ABEU	Boeing 737-330	2691/27904		GoslarIn	stored SXF
D-ABEW	Boeing 737-330	2705/27905		Detmold	
D-ABIA	Boeing 737-530	1933/24815	ex N3521N	Greifswald	Lsd fr CIT Leasing
D-ABIB	Boeing 737-530	1958/24816		Esslingen	Lsd fr CIT Leasing
D-ABIC	Boeing 737-530	1967/24817		Krefeld	Lsd fr CIT Leasing
D-ABID	Boeing 737-530	1974/24818		Aachen	
D-ABIE	Boeing 737-530	1979/24819		Hildesheim	
D-ABIF	Boeing 737-530	1985/24820		Landau	stored SXF
D-ABIH	Boeing 737-530	1993/24821		Bruchsal	stored PRG
D-ABII	Boeing 737-530	1997/24822		Lörrach	
D-ABIK	Boeing 737-530	2000/24823		Rastatt	
D-ABIL	Boeing 737-530	2006/24824		Memmingen	stored NUE
D-ABIM	Boeing 737-530	2011/24937		Salzgitter	
D-ABIN	Boeing 737-530	2023/24938		Langenhagen	
D-ABIO	Boeing 737-530	2031/24939		Wesel	
D-ABIP	Boeing 737-530	2034/24940		Oberhausen	
D-ABIR	Boeing 737-530	2042/24941		Anklam	
D-ABIS	Boeing 737-530	2048/24942		Rendsburg	
D-ABIT	Boeing 737-530	2049/24943		Neumünster	
D-ABIU	Boeing 737-530	2051/24944		Limburg	
D-ABIW	Boeing 737-530	2063/24945		Bad Nauheim	
D-ABIX	Boeing 737-530	2070/24946		Iserlohn	
D-ABIY	Boeing 737-530	2086/25243		Lingen	
D-ABIZ	Boeing 737-530	2098/25244		Kirchheim/Teck	
D-ABJA	Boeing 737-530	2116/25270		Bad Segeberg	
D-ABJB	Boeing 737-530	2117/25271		Rheine	
D-ABJC	Boeing 737-530	2118/25272		Erding	
D-ABJD	Boeing 737-530	2122/25309		Freising	
D-ABJE	Boeing 737-530	2126/25310		Ingelheim am Rhein	
(D-ABJF)^	Boeing 737-530	2128/25311		Aalen	Lsd as LZ-BOI
D-ABJH	Boeing 737-530	2141/25357		Heppenheim/Bergstrasse	
D-ABJI	Boeing 737-530	2151/25358		Siegburg	
D-ABWH	Boeing 737-330(QC)	1685/24284		Rothenburg	Lsd fr GOAL
D-ABXD	Boeing 737-330(QC)	1278/23525	ex TF-ABL	Siegen	
D-ABXE	Boeing 737-330	1282/23526		Hamm	
D-ABXF	Boeing 737-330	1285/23527	ex PK-IAB	Minden; stored SXF	
(D-ABXI)^	Boeing 737-330	1293/23529		Berchtesgaden;	Lsd as LZ-BOG
(D-ABXK)^	Boeing 737-330	1297/23530		Ludwigsburg	Lsd as LZ-BOH
D-ABXL	Boeing 737-330	1307/23531		Neuss	
D-ABXM	Boeing 737-330	1433/23871		Herford	
D-ABXN	Boeing 737-330	1447/23872		Böblingen	
D-ABXO	Boeing 737-330	1489/23873		Schwäbisch Gmünd	
D-ABXP	Boeing 737-330	1495/23874		Fulda	
D-ABXR	Boeing 737-330	1500/23875		Celle	Lsd fr GOAL
D-ABXS	Boeing 737-330	1656/24280		Sindelfingen	
D-ABXT	Boeing 737-330	1664/24281		Reutlingen	
D-ABXU	Boeing 737-330	1671/24282		Seeheim-Jugenheim	
D-ABXW	Boeing 737-330	1785/24561		Hanau	stored SXF
D-ABXX	Boeing 737-330	1787/24562		Bad Homburg v d Höhe	

D-ABXY	Boeing 737-330	1801/24563	Hof	stored SXF
D-ABXZ	Boeing 737-330	1807/24564	Bad Mergentheim	

^Leased to Bulgaria Air

D-ABTA	Boeing 747-430M	747/24285	Sachsen	
D-ABTB	Boeing 747-430M	749/24286	Brandenburg	
D-ABTC	Boeing 747-430M	754/24287	Mecklenburg-Vorpommern	
D-ABTD	Boeing 747-430M	785/24715	Hamburg	
D-ABTE^	Boeing 747-430M	846/24966	ex N6046P	Sachsen-Anhalt Lsd fr Aero Crane
D-ABTF	Boeing 747-430M	848/24967		Thüringen Lsd fr Ward FSC
D-ABTH*	Boeing 747-430M	856/25047		Duisburg Lsd fr Overseas Lsg FSC
D-ABTK	Boeing 747-430	1293/29871	ex (D-ABVI)	Kiel
D-ABTL	Boeing 747-430	1299/29872	ex (D-ABVG)	
D-ABTM	Boeing 747-430	33430		on order
D-ABTN	Boeing 747-430	33431		on order
D-ABTO	Boeing 747-430	33432		on order
D-ABTP	Boeing 747-430	33433		on order
D-ABVA	Boeing 747-430	723/23816	ex N6055X	Berlin
D-ABVB	Boeing 747-430	700/23817	ex N5573S	Bonn
D-ABVC	Boeing 747-430	757/24288		Baden-Württemberg
D-ABVD	Boeing 747-430	786/24740	ex N60668	Bochum
D-ABVE	Boeing 747-430	787/24741		Potsdam
D-ABVF	Boeing 747-430	796/24761	ex N6018N	Frankfurt am Main
D-ABVH	Boeing 747-430	845/25045	ex N6018N	Düsseldorf Lsd fr Luke FSC
D-ABVK	Boeing 747-430	847/25046	ex N6009F	Hannover Lsd fr Tower FSC
D-ABVL	Boeing 747-430	898/26425	ex N60659	München Lsd fr Overseas Lsg FSC
D-ABVM	Boeing 747-430	1143/29101	ex (V8-AC2)	Hessen
D-ABVN	Boeing 747-430	915/26427		Dortmund Lsd fr DB Export-Lsg
D-ABVO	Boeing 747-430	1080/28086		Mülheim an der Ruhr
D-ABVP	Boeing 747-430	1103/28284		Bremen
D-ABVR	Boeing 747-430	1106/28285		Köln
D-ABVS	Boeing 747-430	1109/28286		Saarland
D-ABVT	Boeing 747-430	1110/28287		Rheinland-Pfalz
D-ABVU	Boeing 747-430	1191/29492		Bayern
D-ABVW	Boeing 747-430	1205/29493		Wolfsburg
D-ABVX	Boeing 747-430	1237/29868		Schleswig-Holstein
D-ABVY	Boeing 747-430	1261/29869		Nordrhein-Westfalen
D-ABVZ	Boeing 747-430	1264/29870		Niedersachsen
D-ABZD	Boeing 747-230B	639/23407	ex N6005C	Kiel stored MZJ
D-ABZE	Boeing 747-230M	663/23509	ex N6038E	Lsd to PLM
D-ABZH	Boeing 747-230B	665/23622	ex N6046P	stored MZJ

^First commercial aircraft with broadband internet on board; uses Connexion by Boeing
The stored 747-230s may be broken up for spares   *Star Alliance colours

HB-IIQ	Boeing 737-7CN	451/30752	ex N1026G	D-ABPA resd Lsd fr/op by PTI [BBJ]
D-ABUV	Boeing 767-3Z9ER	731/29867	ex OE-LAY	Lsd fr/op by CFG
D-ABUW	Boeing 767-3Z9ER	759/30331	ex OE-LAZ	Lsd fr/op by CFG
D-CDLH*	Junkers Ju52/3m g8e	130714	ex N52JU	Tempelhof

*Painted as D-AQUI

Lufthansa is the trading name of Lufthansa German Airlines
Fifteen Airbus Industrie A380-841s are on order for delivery from 3Q 2007
Owns 20% of Lauda Air, 30% of British Midland, 13% of Luxair and 98.8% of Air Dolomiti while Eurowings, Lufthansa
Cargo Airline and Lufthansa CityLine are wholly owned subsidiaries. Lufthansa Regional (feeder) services are operated
by Augsburg Airways, Eurowings, Lufthansa CityLine and Contact Air
Founder member of Star Alliance with Air Canada, United, Thai Intl, SAS and VARIG

LUFTHANSA CARGO

Lufthansa Cargo (LH/GEC) (IATA020)   Frankfurt (FRA)

D-ABYO	Boeing 747-230F	347/21592		America	Lsd fr Lufthansa Lsg
D-ABYU	Boeing 747-230F	538/22668	ex N1785B	Asia	Lsd fr Lufthansa Lsg
D-ABYZ	Boeing 747-230B (SF)	614/23286	ex I-DEMX		Lsd fr Lufthansa Lsg
D-ABZA	Boeing 747-230B (SF)	617/23287	ex N6038E		Lsd fr Lufthansa Lsg
D-ABZB	Boeing 747-230F	625/23348	ex N747MC	New York	For ABD
D-ABZC	Boeing 747-230B (SF)	633/23393	ex N6046P		
D-ABZF	Boeing 747-230B (SF)	660/23621	ex N6046P	std MZJ	For ABD
D-ABZI	Boeing 747-230F	706/24138	ex N6005C	Shanghai	For ABD

Three freighters are to be sold to Air Atlanta Icelandic and leased back until 'new' MD-11Fs are delivered; remainder to
be disposed of

D-ALCA	McDonnell-Douglas MD-11F	625/48781	ex N9020Q	Wilhelm Althen
D-ALCB	McDonnell-Douglas MD-11F	626/48782	ex N9166N	
D-ALCC	McDonnell-Douglas MD-11F	627/48783		Karl-Ulrich Garnadt
D-ALCD	McDonnell-Douglas MD-11F	628/48784		
D-ALCE	McDonnell-Douglas MD-11F	629/48785		
D-ALCF	McDonnell-Douglas MD-11F	637/48798		
D-ALCG	McDonnell-Douglas MD-11F	639/48799		
D-ALCH	McDonnell-Douglas MD-11F	640/48801		
D-ALCI	McDonnell-Douglas MD-11F	641/48800		

D-ALCJ	McDonnell-Douglas MD-11F	642/48802		
D-ALCK	McDonnell-Douglas MD-11F	643/48803	ex N9166N	
D-ALCL	McDonnell-Douglas MD-11F	644/48804		
D-ALCM	McDonnell-Douglas MD-11F	645/48805	ex N6069R	
D-ALCN	McDonnell-Douglas MD-11F	646/48806		
D-	McDonnell-Douglas MD-11F		ex PP-	on order 04
D-	McDonnell-Douglas MD-11F		ex PP-	on order 04

Three more McDonnell-Douglas MD-11Fs are on order in January (2) and February (1) 2005
A wholly owned subsidiary of Lufthansa; operate with WOW titles

LUFTHANSA CITYLINE

Hansaline (CL/CLH) (IATA 683)   *Frankfurt/Cologne (FRA/CGN)*

D-AVRA	Avro RJ85	E2256	ex G-6-256		Lsd fr Lufthansa Lsg
D-AVRB	Avro RJ85	E2253	ex G-BVWD		Lsd fr Lufthansa Lsg
D-AVRC	Avro RJ85	E2251	ex G-6-251		Lsd fr Lufthansa Lsg
D-AVRD	Avro RJ85	E2257	ex G-6-257		Lsd fr Lufthansa Lsg
D-AVRE	Avro RJ85	E2261	ex G-6-261		Lsd fr Lufthansa Lsg
D-AVRF	Avro RJ85	E2269	ex G-JAYV		Lsd fr Lufthansa Lsg
D-AVRG	Avro RJ85	E2266	ex G-6-266		Lsd fr Lufthansa Lsg
D-AVRH	Avro RJ85	E2268	ex G-OCLH		Lsd fr Lufthansa Lsg
D-AVRI	Avro RJ85	E2270	ex G-CLHX		Lsd fr Lufthansa Lsg
D-AVRJ	Avro RJ85	E2277	ex G-BWKY		
D-AVRK	Avro RJ85	E2278	ex G-6-278		
D-AVRL	Avro RJ85	E2285	ex G-6-285		
D-AVRM	Avro RJ85	E2288	ex G-6-288		
D-AVRN	Avro RJ85	E2293	ex G-6-293		
D-AVRO	Avro RJ85	E2246	ex G-6-246		Lsd fr Lufthansa Lsg
D-AVRP	Avro RJ85	E2303	ex G-6-303		
D-AVRQ	Avro RJ85	E2304	ex G-6-304		
D-AVRR	Avro RJ85	E2317	ex G-6-317		

All to be transferred to Eurowings

D-ACHA	Canadair CL-600-2B19	7378	ex C-FMLF	Murrhardt	
D-ACHB	Canadair CL-600-2B19	7391	ex C-GGKF	Meersburg	
D-ACHC	Canadair CL-600-2B19	7394	ex C-GGKD	Füssen	
D-ACHD	Canadair CL-600-2B19	7403	ex C-FMNB	Lutherstadt Eisleben	
D-ACHE	Canadair CL-600-2B19	7407	ex C-FMLB	Meissen	
D-ACHF	Canadair CL-600-2B19	7431	ex C-FMLI	Montabaur	
D-ACHG	Canadair CL-600-2B19	7439	ex C-FMMX	Weil am Rhein	
D-ACHH	Canadair CL-600-2B19	7449	ex C-FMOS	Kronach	
D-ACHI	Canadair CL-600-2B19	7464	ex C-FMKV	Deidesheim	
D-ACHK	Canadair CL-600-2B19	7499	ex C-FMLI	Schkeuditz	
D-ACJA	Canadair CL-600-2B19	7122	ex C-FMKT		Lsd fr Lufthansa Lsg
D-ACJB	Canadair CL-600-2B19	7128	ex C-FMMQ		Lsd fr Lufthansa Lsg
D-ACJC	Canadair CL-600-2B19	7130	ex C-FMMW		Lsd fr Lufthansa Lsg
D-ACJD	Canadair CL-600-2B19	7135	ex C-FMNH		Lsd fr Lufthansa Lsg
D-ACJE	Canadair CL-600-2B19	7165	ex C-FMNH		
D-ACJF	Canadair CL-600-2B19	7200	ex C-F...		
D-ACJG	Canadair CL-600-2B19	7220	ex C-FMMW		
D-ACJH	Canadair CL-600-2B19	7266	ex C-F...	DLH 50th anniversary c/s	
D-ACJI	Canadair CL-600-2B19	7282	ex C-FMMY		
D-ACJJ	Canadair CL-600-2B19	7298	ex C-F...		
D-ACLA	Canadair CL-600-2B19	7004	ex C-GRJJ		Lsd fr JL Silvia Lse
D-ACLB	Canadair CL-600-2B19	7005	ex C-GRJN		Lsd fr JL Petra Lse
D-ACLC	Canadair CL-600-2B19	7006	ex C-GRJO		Lsd fr JL Rita Lse
D-ACLD	Canadair CL-600-2B19	7009	ex C-FMKW		Lsd fr JL Lisa Lse
D-ACLE	Canadair CL-600-2B19	7010	ex C-GRJW		Lsd fr Vera Lse
D-ACLF	Canadair CL-600-2B19	7015	ex C-FMLQ	Helmstedt	Lsd fr Lufthansa Lsg
D-ACLG	Canadair CL-600-2B19	7016	ex C-FMLS		Lsd fr JL Rosa Lse
D-ACLH	Canadair CL-600-2B19	7007	ex C-FMKV		Lsd fr JL Eva Lse
D-ACLI	Canadair CL-600-2B19	7019	ex C-FMLV		Lsd fr Lufthansa Lsg
D-ACLJ	Canadair CL-600-2B19	7021	ex C-FMML		Lsd fr Munda Verwaltung
D-ACLK	Canadair CL-600-2B19	7023	ex C-FMMQ		Lsd fr Lufthansa Lsg
D-ACLL	Canadair CL-600-2B19	7024	ex C-FMMT		Lsd fr JL Sarah Lse
D-ACLM	Canadair CL-600-2B19	7025	ex C-FMMW		Lsd fr JL Lena Lse
D-ACLP	Canadair CL-600-2B19	7064	ex C-FMNX		Lsd fr JL Anna Lse
D-ACLQ	Canadair CL-600-2B19	7073	ex C-FMLF		Lsd fr JL Carina Lse
D-ACLR	Canadair CL-600-2B19	7086	ex C-FMLU		Lsd fr JL Laura Lse
D-ACLS	Canadair CL-600-2B19	7090	ex C-F...		Lsd fr JL Tanja Lse
D-ACLT	Canadair CL-600-2B19	7093	ex C-F...		Lsd fr JL Ulla Lse
D-ACLU	Canadair CL-600-2B19	7104	ex C-FXPI		Lsd fr Lufthansa Lsg
D-ACLV	Canadair CL-600-2B19	7113	ex C-FMMQ		Lsd fr Lufthansa Lsg
D-ACLW	Canadair CL-600-2B19	7114	ex C-FMMT		Lsd fr Lufthansa Lsg
D-ACLY	Canadair CL-600-2B19	7119	ex C-FMND		Lsd fr Lufthansa Lsg
D-ACLZ	Canadair CL-600-2B19	7121	ex C-FMNQ		Lsd fr Lufthansa Lsg

Other Canadair CL-600-2B19s are operated by Eurowings

D-ACPA	Canadair CL-600-2C10	10012	ex C-GHZV	Westerland/Sylt	
D-ACPB	Canadair CL-600-2C10	10013	ex C-GHZY	Rüdesheim am Rhein	

D-ACPC	Canadair CL-600-2C10	10014	ex C-GISW	Espelkamp
D-ACPD	Canadair CL-600-2C10	10015	ex C-GISZ	Vilshofen
D-ACPE	Canadair CL-600-2C10	10027	ex C-GIAZ	Beizig
D-ACPF	Canadair CL-600-2C10	10030	ex C-GIBI	Uhingen
D-ACPG	Canadair CL-600-2C10	10034	ex C-GIBO	Leinfelden-Echterdingen
D-ACPH	Canadair CL-600-2C10	10043	ex C-GHZY	Eschwage
D-ACPI	Canadair CL-600-2C10	10046	ex C-GIAE	Viernheim
D-ACPJ	Canadair CL-600-2C10	10040	ex C-GKCO	Neumarkt in der Oberpfalz
D-ACPK	Canadair CL-600-2C10	10063	ex C-GIBN	
D-ACPL	Canadair CL-600-2C10	10076	ex C-GIAE	
D-ACPM	Canadair CL-600-2C10	10080	ex C-FZRA	
D-ACPN	Canadair CL-600-2C10	10083	ex C-GIAU	
D-ACPO	Canadair CL-600-2C10	10085	ex C-FZYS	
D-ACPP	Canadair CL-600-2C10	10086	ex C-GIGJ	
D-ACPQ	Canadair CL-600-2C10	10091	ex C-GZJA	
D-ACPR	Canadair CL-600-2C10	10098	ex C-GI	
D-ACPS	Canadair CL-600-2C10	10100	ex C-GI	Star Alliance c/s
D-ACPT	Canadair CL-600-2C10	10103	ex C-GJLZ	Star Alliance c/s

Fokker 50s operated by Contact Air on behalf of Lufthansa Cityline (q.v.)
Wholly owned by Lufthansa and operates in Lufthansa Regional colours

LUFTTAXI FLUG

Garfield (DV/LTF)   Dortmund (DTM)

| D-CNRX | British Aerospace Jetstream 31 | 616 | ex G-BKUY |
| D-IGKN | Beech C90A King Air | LJ-1077 | ex N4B |

Also operates executive jets

LUFTVERKEHR FRIESLAND HARLE

Harle

D-ILFA	Britten-Norman BN-2B-26 Islander	2243	ex G-BSWO
D-ILFB	Britten-Norman BN-2B-26 Islander	2271	ex G-BUBO
D-ILFH	Britten-Norman BN-2B-26 Islander	2212	ex G-BPXS

NIGHTEXPRESS

Executive (EXT)   Frankfurt (FRA)

| D-CCAS | Short SD.3-60 | SH3737 | ex G-OLBA |
| D-IEXB | Beech 99 | U-70 | ex G-NUIT |

NORTHERN AIR CHARTER

Stardust (NAG)   Flensburg (FLF)

D-CCCC	Swearingen SA.227AT Merlin IVC	AT-511	ex N600N	City of Flensburg; EMS	Lsd to BID
D-CNAC	Swearingen SA.227DC Metro 23	DC-895B	ex N30384	Erfurt	Lsd to OLT
D-CNAF	Swearingen SA.227AC Metro III	AC-505B	ex TF-BBG		

OLT – OSTFRIESISCHE LUFTTRANSPORT

Oltra (OL/OLT)   Emden/Bremen (EME/BRE)

D-AOLA	SAAB 2000	008	ex SE-008		Lsd fr Swedish A/c Holdingst
D-AOLB	SAAB 2000	005	ex SE-005		Lsd fr Huskvarna Aircraft
D-AOLT	SAAB 2000	037	ex HB-IZU	Emden	Lsd fr SAAB, op for Airbus
D-CMUC	Dornier 328-110	3096			Lsd fr Millennium Lsg
D-CNAC	Swearingen SA.227DC Metro 23	DC-895B	ex N30384	Erfurt	Lsd fr NAG
D-COLB	Swearingen SA.227AC Metro III	AC-754B	ex N54NE		
D-COLD	Swearingen SA.227AC Metro III	AC-421B	ex SE-LIM		
D-COLE	SAAB SF.340A	144	ex LV-WTF	Bremen	
D-COLT	Swearingen SA.227AC Metro III	AC-690	ex N715C		
D-FOLE	Cessna 208B Caravan I	208B0523	ex N5197A		
D-IBOS	Cessna 404 Titan II	404-0809	ex SE-IRB		
D-IFBN	Britten-Norman BN-2B-26 Islander	2185	ex G-BLNF	Juist	
D-IFOX	Britten-Norman BN-2B-26 Islander	2186	ex G-BLNG	Büsum	
D-IOLA	Britten-Norman BN-2B-26 Islander	2187	ex G-BLNH	Kap Arkona	

PRIVATE WINGS

Private Wings (PWF)   Berlin-Schönefeld (SXF)

D-COCA	Beech 1900D	UE-224	ex N224YV	
D-COKE	LearJet 35A	35A-447	ex N300FN	EMS
D-COLA	Beech B300 Super King Air	FL-75	ex HB-GJB	EMS
D-CPWF	Dornier 328-110	3112	ex D-CFWF	

PTL LUFTFAHRTUNTERNEHMEN

King Star (PQ/KST) — Landshut

D-IBAD	Beech B200 Super King Air	BB-1229

REGIO-AIR

German Link (RAG) — Trollenhagen

D-IBIJ	Cessna 402B	402B0327	ex YU-BIJ	Lsd fr Goller
D-IESS	Swearingen SA.226TC Metro II	TC-338	ex N90141	

THOMAS COOK AIRLINES (GERMANY)

Condor (DE/CIB/CFG) — Frankfurt/Berlin-Schönefeld (FRA/SXF)

Reg	Type	c/n	ex	Notes	
D-AICA	Airbus Industrie A320-212	0774	ex F-WWDN	Lsd fr Lufthansa Lsg	
D-AICB	Airbus Industrie A320-212	0793	ex F-WWDU	Lsd fr Lufthansa Lsg	
D-AICC	Airbus Industrie A320-212	0809	ex F-WWIE	Lsd fr Lufthansa Lsg	
D-AICD	Airbus Industrie A320-212	0884	ex F-WWDE	Lsd fr Lufthansa Lsg	
D-AICE	Airbus Industrie A320-212	0894	ex F-WWDI	Lsd fr Lufthansa Lsg	
D-AICF	Airbus Industrie A320-212	0905	ex F-WWDP	Lsd fr Lufthansa Lsg; sublsd to TCW	
D-AICG	Airbus Industrie A320-212	0957	ex F-WWBE		
D-AICH	Airbus Industrie A320-212	0971	ex F-WWBY		
D-AICI	Airbus Industrie A320-212	1381	ex F-WWIP		
D-AICJ	Airbus Industrie A320-212	1402	ex F-WWDB		
D-AICK	Airbus Industrie A320-212	1416	ex F-WWDZ		
D-AICL	Airbus Industrie A320-212	1437	ex F-WWBG		
OO-TCB	Airbus Industrie A320-231	0357	ex G-BVYB	Explore	Lsd fr TCW
OO-TCH	Airbus Industrie A320-214	1929	ex F-WWID	Experience	Lsd fr TCW
(D-ABNB)	Boeing 757-230	274/24738			Lsd to DBR
(D-ABNC)	Boeing 757-230	275/24747		Lsd fr Lufthansa Lsg; sublsd to DBR	
(D-ABND)	Boeing 757-230	285/24748			Lsd to DBR
D-ABNE*	Boeing 757-230	295/24749	ex N35153		Lsd fr Lufthansa AG
D-ABNF	Boeing 757-230	382/25140			Lsd fr Havel Aircraft
D-ABNH*	Boeing 757-230	419/25436			
D-ABNI*	Boeing 757-230	422/25437		std QLA	Lsd fr Spruce Operation
D-ABNK*	Boeing 757-230	428/25438		Lsd fr Mosel & Lahn; sublsd to RYN	
D-ABNL*	Boeing 757-230	437/25439			
D-ABNM*	Boeing 757-230	443/25440		stored FRA	Lsd fr DIA Ltd
D-ABNN*	Boeing 757-230	446/25441			Lsd to RYN
D-ABNO*	Boeing 757-230	464/25901			
D-ABNP*	Boeing 757-230	521/26433		stored MZJ	
D-ABNR*	Boeing 757-230	532/26434		stored FRA	
D-ABNS*	Boeing 757-230	537/26435		stored FRA	
D-ABNT*	Boeing 757-230	587/26436	ex N3502P	stored MZJ	Lsd fr Lufthansa Lsg

*Sold to Center Capital in Russia with five believed for VIM Airlines

Reg	Type	c/n	ex	Notes
D-ABOA	Boeing 757-330	804/29016	ex N757X	
D-ABOB	Boeing 757-330	810/29017	ex N6067B	
D-ABOC	Boeing 757-330	818/29015	ex N6069B	
D-ABOE	Boeing 757-330	839/29012	ex N1012N	
D-ABOF	Boeing 757-330	846/29013		
D-ABOG	Boeing 757-330	849/29014		
D-ABOH	Boeing 757-330	855/30030	ex N1787B	
D-ABOI	Boeing 757-330	909/29018	ex N1002R	
D-ABOJ	Boeing 757-330	915/29019		Lsd fr NBB Lease
D-ABOK	Boeing 757-330	918/29020	ex N1795B	
D-ABOL	Boeing 757-330	923/29021		Lsd fr NBB Lease
D-ABOM	Boeing 757-330	926/29022		Lsd fr NBB Lease
D-ABON	Boeing 757-330	929/29023	ex N1003M	
D-ABUA	Boeing 767-330ER	455/26991		Lsd fr NBB Lease
D-ABUB	Boeing 767-330ER	466/26987		Lsd fr CG-Kumiai
D-ABUC	Boeing 767-330ER	470/26992		Lsd fr NBB Lease
D-ABUD	Boeing 767-330ER	471/26983		Lsd fr NBB Lease
D-ABUE	Boeing 767-330ER	518/26984	ex N1788B	Lsd fr Lufthansa Lsg
D-ABUF	Boeing 767-330ER	537/26985		
D-ABUH	Boeing 767-330ER	553/26986	ex N6046P	
D-ABUI	Boeing 767-330ER	562/26988		
D-ABUV	Boeing 767-3Z9ER	731/29867	ex OE-LAY	Lsd fr LDA; op for DLH
D-ABUW	Boeing 767-3Z9ER	759/30331	ex OE-LAZ	Lsd fr LDA; op for DLH
D-ABUZ	Boeing 767-330ER	382/25209	ex (N634TW)	

Owns 40% of SunExpress. Sister company of Thomas Cook Airlines in UK and Belgium; some interchange between fleets take place. Wear 'powered by Condor' titles

WDL AVIATION

WDL (WE/WDL) Cologne (CGN)

D-ADEP	Fokker F.27 Friendship 600	10318	ex OY-CCK		
D-ADOP	Fokker F.27 Friendship 600	10316	ex OY-BVF	Bassan	
D-AELE	Fokker F.27 Friendship 600	10477	ex OY-SLE		
D-AELG	Fokker F.27 Friendship 600	10338	ex VR-BLZ		
D-AELH	Fokker F.27 Friendship 400	10340	ex VR-BLX	Jude	
D-AELJ	Fokker F.27 Friendship 600	10342	ex F-BYAB	Flying Dutchman	
D-AELK	Fokker F.27 Friendship 600	10361	ex F-GCJV	Petra	
D-AELM	Fokker F.27 Friendship 600	10450	ex OY-CCL	Dietmar Rabe von Papenheim	
D-AISY	Fokker F.27 Friendship 600	10391	ex OY-CCR		
D-BAKB	Fokker F.27 Friendship 600	10261	ex F-GHRC	Hully Gully	
D-BAKC	Fokker F.27 Friendship 600	10195	ex F-GFJS	TNT c/s	
D-BAKD	Fokker F.27 Friendship 600	10179	ex SP-FNF		
All freighters					
D-AMAJ	British Aerospace 146 Srs.200	E2028	ex G-BZBA	Edelweiss c/s	
D-AMGL	British Aerospace 146 Srs.200	E2055	ex G-CBFL		Lsd fr BAES
D-AWBA	British Aerospace 146 Srs.300A	E3134	ex ZK-NZF		
D-AWDL	British Aerospace 146 Srs.100	E1011	ex G-UKJF		
D-AWUE	British Aerospace 146 Srs.200	E2050	ex PK-PJP		

DQ - FIJI (Republic of Fiji)

AIR FIJI

Fijiair (PC/FAJ) (IATA) Suva (SUV)

DQ-AFO	Embraer EMB.110P1 Bandeirante	110419	ex EI-BVX		
DQ-LCM	Embraer EMB.110P1 Bandeirante	110410	ex VH-XFN		
DQ-TLC	Embraer EMB.110P1 Bandeirante	110417	ex VH-TLD		
DQ-WBI	Embraer EMB.110P1 Bandeirante	110292	ex VH-WBI	stored BWU	
DQ-YES	Embraer EMB.110P1 Bandeirante	110307	ex VH-FNR		
DQ-AFM	de Havilland DHC-6 Twin Otter 310	448	ex N234SA	VistaLiner	
DQ-FBS	Beech 95-C55 Baron	TE-445	ex VH-ARY		
DQ-FET	Britten-Norman BN-2A-21 Islander	661	ex ZK-NNE		
DQ-FHC	Harbin Y-12 II	0056		Danny Jorgensen	
DQ-FHD	Beech 95-C55 Baron	TE-329	ex F-GCVT		
DQ-FHF	Harbin Y-12 II	0047	ex B-531L	Waisale Serevi	
DQ-FIC	Britten-Norman BN-2A-20 Islander	511	ex ZK-KHB		
DQ-MUM	Embraer EMB.120RT Brasilia	120079	ex VH-XFH		
DQ-TRI	Britten-Norman BN-2A Mk.III-2 Trislander	1041	ex G-BEFO		
Air Fiji is the trading name of Fiji Air Services					

AIR KATAFANGA

Suva (SUV)

DQ-FIK	Piper PA-31-350 Navajo Chieftain	31-7752090	ex N7088C

AIR PACIFIC

Pacific (FJ/FJI) (IATA 260) Nadi (NAN)

DQ-FJC	Boeing 767-3X2ER	552/26260		Island of Taveuni	Lsd fr ILFC
DQ-FJF	Boeing 737-7X2	96/28878		Island of Koro	Lsd fr APL Finance
DQ-FJG	Boeing 737-8X2	275/29968		Island of Kadavu	Lsd fr APL Finance
DQ-FJH	Boeing 737-8X2	339/29969		Island of Gau	Lsd fr APL Finance
DQ-FJK	Boeing 747-412	755/24064	ex 9V-SMD	Island of Vanua Levu	Lsd fr SIA
DQ-FJL	Boeing 747-412	722/24062	ex 9V-SMB	Island of Viti Levu	Lsd fr SIA
46% owned by Qantas					
Two Airbus Industrie A330-300s are on order for delivery in 2005 and 2007					

AIR WAKAYA

Suva (SUV)

DQ-FHG	Britten-Norman BN-2B-26 Islander	2230	ex G-BSAC

PACIFIC ISLAND AIR

Nadi (NAN)

DQ-GEE	de Havilland DHC-2 Beaver	1358	ex C-GSKY	Floatplane	
DQ-GLL	de Havilland DHC-3 Turbo Otter	288	ex N68086	Floatplane	
DQ-GWW	de Havilland DHC-2 Beaver	124	ex A3-GQW	Floatplane	
DQ-YIR	Britten-Norman BN-2A-8 Islander	845	ex VH-FCO		Lsd fr Yasawa Island Resort

SUN AIR

Sunflower (PI/SUF) (IATA)   *Nadi (NAN)*

DQ-FCX*	Britten-Norman BN-2A-27 Islander	833	ex G-BEMJ	Adi Yasawa
DQ-FDV*	Britten-Norman BN-2A-26 Islander	41	ex 9M-MDA	Bui Ni Gone
DQ-FDW*	Britten-Norman BN-2A-26 Islander	602	ex 9M-MDC	Adi Makutu
DQ-FEW	Beech 65 Queen Air	LC-168	ex YJ-RV17	Excalibur Queenaire conv
DQ-FEY*	de Havilland DHC-6 Twin Otter 100	87	ex N64NB	Spirit of the North
DQ-FEZ*	de Havilland DHC-6 Twin Otter 100	9	ex F-OCFJ	Spirit of the West
DQ-FIE*	de Havilland DHC-6 Twin Otter 300	660	ex N933CL	Spirit of Nadi
DQ-FIN	Britten-Norman BN-2A-26 Islander	159	ex VH-ISA	

*Leased from Colombine Holdings
Sun Air is the trading name of Regional Pacific Airlines

TURTLE AIRWAYS

Turtle (TLT)   *Nadi-Newtown Beach*

DQ-FEX	Cessna U206G Stationair 6	U20605706	ex ZK-FHE
DQ-TAN	Cessna U206G Stationair 6	U20605574	ex VH-HBX
DQ-TAL	de Havilland DHC-2 Beaver	1255	ex C-GLED
DQ-TAM	de Havilland DHC-2 Beaver	1433	ex VH-IME

All floatplanes

D2 - ANGOLA (Republic of Angola)

AIR GEMINI

Twins (GLL)   *Luanda (LAD)*

D2-ERL	Douglas DC-9-32	715/47601	ex N925LG
S9-BAH	Boeing 727-173C	449/19507	ex PT-ITM
S9-BAQ	Boeing 727-22C	293/19093	ex N831RC	Op for UN Humanitarian Airlift
S9-BAR	Boeing 727-22C	318/19098	ex N832RC
S9-BAU	Boeing 727-25C (FedEx 3)	367/19358	ex S9-IAU
S9-BOE	Boeing 727-22C (FedEx 3)	388/19192	ex N706DH

AIR NACOIA ceased operations

AIR TRANSWORLD ceased operations

AIRJET

                                                                      Luanda (LAD)

D2-FEE	Yakovlev Yak-40	

ALADA EMPRESA DE TRANSPORTES AEREOS

Air Alada (RAD)   *Luanda (LAD)*

D2-FAM	Ilyushin Il-18V	184007401	ex UR-75475	
D2-FAP	Antonov An-32B	2903		stored HLA
D2-FAR	Antonov An-12BP	402810		stored PNR
D2-FAX	Antonov An-32B	1510	ex RA-48115	Kimoka
D2-FDY	Ilyushin Il-18E	185008503	ex UR-75850	
D2-FED	Antonov An-32			operator not confirmed
D2-FFR	Ilyushin Il-18D	0393607150	ex UR-75896	
D2-FRB	Antonov An-32			
D2-FRG	Antonov An-12V	00347202		stored PNR

ANGOLA AIR CHARTER

Angola Charter (AGO)   *Luanda (LAD)*

D2-FCI	Boeing 727-23F	26/18429	ex HP-1229PFC		
D2-FCK	Boeing 727-44F	148/18892	ex N94GS	dam NZA 10May01	Lsd fr IASG
D2-FCL	Boeing 727-151C (FedEx 3)	514/19867	ex N432EX		
D2-FFA	Boeing 727-22C (FedEx 3)	324/19199	ex N429EX		
D2-FFB	Boeing 727-51C (FedEx 3)	294/19206	ex N413EX		
D2-FCM	Ilyushin Il-76TD	0063470107	ex UR-76694	Op for Angolan Air Force	
D2-FCN	Ilyushin Il-76TD	0053462872	ex UR-76651	Op for Angolan Air Force	
D2-FDX	Ilyushin Il-76T	063407170	ex RA-86747	Op for Angolan Air Force	
D2-TBI	Boeing 737-214	68/19681	ex N7380F		Lsd fr Avn Consultants

A subsidiary of TAAG Angola Airlines

DIEXIME EXPRESS

Luanda (LAD)

D2-FFI	Embraer EMB.120RT Brasilia	120035	ex N331JS

NATIONAL COMMUTER AIRLINES believed to have ceased operations

SAL – SOCIEDADE DE AVIACAO LIGEIRA

Luanda (LAD)

D2-ECN	Cessna F406 Caravan II	F406-0002	ex PH-MNS		Lsd fr Iber Avn
D2-ECO	Cessna F406 Caravan II	F406-0011	ex D-IDAA		Lsd fr Iber Avn
D2-ECP	Cessna F406 Caravan II	F406-0016	ex PH-LAS		Lsd fr Iber Avn
D2-ECQ	Cessna F406 Caravan II	F406-0019	ex G-CVAN		Lsd fr Iber Avn
D2-ECX	Beech B200 Super King Air	BB-1362	ex N1565F		Lsd fr B.N.A.
D2-ECY	Beech B200C Super King Air	BL-135	ex S9-NAP		Lsd fr GIAS
D2-EDA	Cessna 208B Caravan I	208B0568	ex N1215K		
D2-EDB	Cessna 208B Caravan I	208B0665	ex N1256G		
D2-EOD	Short SC.7 Skyvan 3	SH1938	ex CR-LOD	ENEANA titles	

Also leases Beech 1900C/Ds from SAL Express as and when required

SAVANAIR ceased operations

SONAIR

Luanda (LAD)

D2 EQD	Aerospatiale SA.365N2 Dauphin	6521	ex F-GJIA		
D2-EQE	Aerospatiale SA.365N2 Dauphin	6531	ex F-GJIK		
D2-EVE	Aerospatiale SA.365N2 Dauphin	6418	ex F-GHRZ		
D2-EVF	Aerospatiale SA.365N2 Dauphin	6410	ex F-GHRX	stored Toussus	
F-GFYU	Aerospatiale SA.365N Dauphin 2	6082	ex F-ODTC		Lsd fr HLU
D2-EVJ	Beech 1900D	UE-111	ex N3119U		
D2-EVK	Beech 1900D	UE-121	ex N3221A		
D2-EVL	Beech 1900D	UE-312	ex N312RC		
D2-	Beech 1900D	UE-412	ex N44828		
D2-	Beech 1900D	UE-108	ex N118SK		Lsd fr General Avn Svs
D2-EVA	de Havilland DHC-6 Twin Otter 310	728	ex V2-LDD		
D2-EVB	de Havilland DHC-6 Twin Otter 310	810	ex V2-LDH		
D2-EVC	de Havilland DHC-6 Twin Otter 310	809	ex V2-LDG		
D2-EVH	de Havilland DHC-6 Twin Otter 300	511	ex HB-LOM		
D2-FVM	de Havilland DHC-6 Twin Otter 310	794	ex HB-LRF		
D2-FVN	de Havilland DHC-6 Twin Otter 310	817	ex N817L		
D2-FVO	de Havilland DHC-6 Twin Otter 310	821	ex N821L		
D2-FVP	de Havilland DHC-6 Twin Otter 310	743	ex 5Y-TMF		
D2-FVQ	de Havilland DHC-6 Twin Otter 310	704	ex 5N-ASP		
D2-EXF	Sikorsky S-76A	760160	ex ZS-RJS		
D2-EXG	Sikorsky S-76A	760042	ex ZS-RKE		
D2-EXH	Sikorsky S-76A	760268	ex ZS-RBE		
D2-EXK	Sikorsky S-76C	760525	ex N9017U		
D2-EXL	Sikorsky S-76C	760526	ex N9007U		
D2-	Sikorsky S-76A	760036	ex ZS-RNG		
D2-EDA	Cessna 208B Caravan I	0568	ex N1215K		
D2-EDB	Cessna 208B Caravan I	0665	ex N1256G		
D2-ESN	Fokker F.27 Friendship 500	10610	ex PH-FTY	Kwanda	
D2-ESQ	Beech B200 Super King Air	BB-1407		Luanda	
D2-ESR	Fokker 50	20240	ex PH-RPK	Lombo Este; stored	
D2-ESU	Boeing 727-23F	372/19431	ex N516FE		
D2-ESW	Fokker 50	20241	ex PH-RRM		
D2-ESZ	Aerospatiale AS.332L2 Super Puma II	2503			
D2-EVD	Boeing 727-29C	435/19403	ex CB-02		
D2-EVG	Boeing 727-29C	415/19402	ex N70PA		
D2-FSA	Boeing 727-29C	634/19987	ex HZ-HE4	Freighter	

Sonair is a subsidiary of Sonangol State Corporation

TAAG ANGOLA AIRLINES / LINHAS AEREAS DE ANGOLA

DTA (DT/DTA) (IATA 118)

Luanda (LAD)

D2-TBC	Boeing 737-2M2C	447/21173	ex D2-TAB		
D2-TBD	Boeing 737-2M2	567/21723	ex D2-TAH	Joao Paulo II	Lsd to GCB
D2-TBO	Boeing 737-2M2	891/22776	ex N1782B		
D2-TBP	Boeing 737-2M2	1084/23220		Nelson Mandela	
D2-TBX	Boeing 737-2M2	1117/23351			

| D2-TEA | Boeing 747-312M | 653/23410 | ex 9V-SKN | Cidade de Kuito |
| D2-TEB | Boeing 747-357M | 686/23751 | ex N375TC | |

Owns Angola Air Charter

URALINTERAVIA STAR ceased operations

D4 - CAPE VERDE ISLANDS (Republic of Cape Verde)

CABO VERDE EXPRESS

Sal (SID)

| D4-CBL | LET L-410UVP-E10 | 902511 | ex 9Q-CUM |
| D4-JCA | LET L-410UVP-E | 912604 | ex OY-PEY |

TACV – TRANSPORTES AEREOS DE CABO VERDE / CAPE VERDE AIRLINES

Cabo Verde (VR/TCV)   *Praia (RAI)*

D4-CAY	de Havilland DHC-6 Twin Otter 300	663	ex CR-CAY		
D4-CBE	Aerospatiale/Alenia ATR 42-320	382	ex F-WWEA	Joaquim Ribeiro	
D4-CBF	Aerospatiale/Alenia ATR 42-320	386	ex F-WWEK	Rebil	
D4-CBG	Boeing 757-2Q8	696/27599		B Leza	Lsd fr ILFC
D4-CBH	Aerospatiale/Alenia ATR 42-320	415	ex F-WWLA	Alex	
D4-CBN	Boeing 737-3Q8	2786/26333	ex N263LF		Lsd fr ILFC

D6 - COMOROS (Federal Islamic Republic of the Comoros)

COMORES AIR SERVICE

Moroni (YVA)

| D6-CAM | LET L-410UVP | 851336 | ex D6-GDH |
| D6-CAN | LET L-410UVP | 841331 | ex 9L-LCZ |

COMORES AIRLINES ceased operations

COMORES AVIATION

Moroni (YVA)

| D6-CAK | LET L-410UVP | | |
| D6-CAL | LET L-410UVP | 800526 | ex HA-LAB |

COMPLEX AIRWAYS ceased operations

GLOBAL AIR OPERATIONS

Global Airgroup (GAG)   *Moroni (YVA)*

| D6-OZX | Boeing 747SP-27 | 473/22302 | ex VH-OZX |

OCEAN AIRLINES

(4O)   *Moroni (YVA)*

Current fleet details unknown at time of publication

EC - SPAIN (Kingdom of Spain)

AEBAL – AEROLINEAS BALEARES

Air Balear (DF/ABH)   *Palma de Mallorca (PMI)*

EC-HNY	Boeing 717-2CM	5023/55059	ex N6203U	Formentor	Lsd
EC-HNZ	Boeing 717-2CM	5026/55060	ex N9010L	Espalmador	Lsd
EC-HOA	Boeing 717-2CM	5029/55061		Macarella	
EC-HUZ	Boeing 717-23S	5054/55066		Valdemossa	Lsd fr Pembroke
EC-	Boeing 717-200			on order	
EC-	Boeing 717-200			on order	

Wholly owned subsidiary and operates services on behalf of Spanair as AeBal Spanair Link using JK flight number

AERO NOVA

Aeronova (OVA)   *Valencia (VLC)*

EC-GVE	Swearingen SA.227AC Metro III	AC-669	ex N2702Z
EC-HCH	Swearingen SA.227AC Metro III	AC-658B	ex N2692P
EC-HZH	Swearingen SA.227AC Metro III	AC-720	ex N2724S

AIR CATALUNYA

Gerona-Costa Brava (GRO)

EC-INU	SAAB SF.340A	117	ex OH-SAE		Op by Gestavi
EC-IRD	SAAB SF.340A	081	ex OH-SAC	Ciudad de Leon	Op by Gestavi
EC-IRR	SAAB SF.340A	143	ex OH-SAF		Op by Gestavi

Also operates flights with Metro III leased from Gestair as required

AIR EUROPA LINEAS AEREAS

Europa (UX/AEA) (IATA 996)　　　　　　　　　　　　　　　　*Palmade Mallorca (PMI)*

EC-FXP"	Boeing 737-4Q8	1996/24706	ex EC-644	Villanueva del Conde	
EC-FXQ	Boeing 737-4Q8	2057/24707	ex EC-645	Salamanca	Lsd fr MSA V
EC-GMY*	Boeing 737-36Q	2865/28658		Camino de Santiago	
EC-GUO	Boeing 737-4Q8	2416/26285	ex N402KW		Lsd fr Boeing Capital
EC-HNB	Boeing 737-4Q8	2239/26280	ex G-OBMO		Lsd fr Tombo
EC-HXT	Boeing 737-4K5	1839/24769	ex D-ABAB		Lsd fr KG Aircraft
EC-IRA	Boeing 737-4Y0	1963/24692	ex N692HE		

"Leased from Triton　　　　　　　　　　　　*Leased from Geonet Avn Svs

EC-HBL	Boeing 737-85H	250/28381		Travelspan	Lsd fr RBS Avn
EC-HBM	Boeing 737-85H	256/28382			Lsd fr Itochu
EC-HBN	Boeing 737-85H	266/28383		Llucmajor	Lsd fr RBS Avn
EC-HGO	Boeing 737-85P	420/28384			Lsd fr RBS Avn
EC-HGP	Boeing 737-85P	421/28385			Lsd fr RBS Avn
EC-HGQ	Boeing 737-85P	426/28386			Lsd fr SA Victoria
EC-HJP	Boeing 737-85P	480/28535	ex N1800B		Lsd fr Itochu
EC-HJQ	Boeing 737-85P	522/28387			Lsd fr Itochu
EC-HKQ	Boeing 737-85P	533/28388			Lsd fr Itochu
EC-HKR	Boeing 737-85P	540/28536	ex N1787B	winglets	Lsd fr Itochu
EC-HZS	Boeing 737-86Q	920/30276	ex N747BX	winglets	Lsd fr Boullioun
EC-ICD	Boeing 737-81Q	1007/30785	ex N308TA	winglets	Lsd fr Tombo
EC-IDA	Boeing 737-86Q	1051/32773	ex N73792	winglets	Lsd fr Boullioun
EC-IDT	Boeing 737-86Q	1076/30281	ex N73793	winglets	Lsd fr Boullioun
EC-III	Boeing 737-86Q	1233/30284		winglets	Lsd fr Boullioun
EC-IND	Boeing 737-683	290/28305	ex OY-KKE		Lsd fr SAS
EC-ING	Boeing 737-683	329/28306	ex OY-KKY		Lsd fr SAS
EC-INT	Boeing 737-683	270/28304	ex SE-DNX	Pepecar titles	Lsd fr SAS
EC-ISE	Boeing 737-76Q	1406/30290			Lsd fr Boullioun
EC-ISN	Boeing 737-76Q	1435/30291			Lsd fr Boullioun
EC-	Boeing 737-85P			on order 04	Lsd fr Itochu
EC-	Boeing 737-85P			on order 04	Lsd fr Itochu
EC-	Boeing 737-85P			on order 04	Lsd fr Itochu
EC-	Boeing 737-85P			on order 04	Lsd fr Itochu

Two more Boeing 737-800s (lessor unknown) are on order for delivery in May and July 2005 [c/nos 33975/33976].
Further Boeing 737-800s are on order to replace the Boeing 737 Classics

EC-HKS	Boeing 767-3Q8ER	793/27686			Lsd fr ILFC
EC-HPU	Boeing 767-3Q8ER	828/30048			Lsd fr ILFC
EC-HSV	Boeing 767-3Q8ER	840/29387			Lsd fr ILFC
EC-IQA	Boeing 767-33AER	545/27310	ex N310AN		Lsd fr AWAS

Member of Wings Alliance

AIR MADRID

Madrid-Barajas (MAD)

EC-	Airbus Industrie A330-202	205	ex I-VLEC	on order	Lsd fr Precision Avn
EC-	Airbus Industrie A330-202	211	ex I-VLED	on order	Lsd fr Precision Avn

AIR NOSTRUM / LINEAS AEREAS DEL MEDITERRANEO

Nostrum Air (YW/ANS) (IATA 694)　　　　　　　　　　　　　　　*Valencia (VLC)*

EC-HBY	Aerospatiale/Alenia ATR 72-212A	578	ex F-WWEA	Abeto
EC-HCG	Aerospatiale/Alenia ATR 72-212A	580	ex F-WWEC	Castano
EC-HEI	Aerospatiale/Alenia ATR 72-212A	570	ex F-WWEG	Eucalipto
EC-HEJ	Aerospatiale/Alenia ATR 72-212A	565	ex F-WWEE	Carrasca
EC-HJI	Aerospatiale/Alenia ATR 72-212A	562	ex F-WWLZ	

All leased from ATR Asset Management

EC-GYI	Canadair CL-600-2B19	7249	ex C-GDDM	Pinazo
EC-GZA	Canadair CL-600-2B19	7252	ex C-GDDO	Beniliure
EC-HEK	Canadair CL-600-2B19	7320	ex C-GFCN	Cecilio Pla
EC-HHI	Canadair CL-600-2B19	7343	ex C-GFKQ	Genaro Lahuerta Lopez
EC-HHV	Canadair CL-600-2B19	7350	ex C-GFKR	Sorolla
EC-HPR	Canadair CL-600-2B19	7430	ex C-GHDM	
EC-HSH	Canadair CL-600-2B19	7466	ex C-GHWD	J Michavilla
EC-HTZ	Canadair CL-600-2B19	7493	ex C-GIHJ	Ricardo Verde

EC-HXM	Canadair CL-600-2B19	7514	ex C-GIQL	Encina	
EC-HYG	Canadair CL-600-2B19	7529	ex C-GIXG	E Sales Frances	
EC-HZR	Canadair CL-600-2B19	7547	ex C-GJFR	Jose Ribera	
EC-IAA	Canadair CL-600-2B19	7563	ex C-GJIZ	A Munoz Degrain	
EC-IBM	Canadair CL-600-2B19	7591	ex C-GJQZ	J Navarro Llorens	
EC-IDC	Canadair CL-600-2B19	7622	ex C-GJYV	Francisco Ribalta	
EC-IGO	Canadair CL-600-2B19	7661	ex C-FVAZ		
EC-IJE	Canadair CL-600-2B19	7700	ex C-GZJZ		
EC-IJF	Canadair CL-600-2B19	7705	ex C-GZKC		
EC-IJS	Canadair CL-600-2B19	7706	ex C-GZKD	Manuel Benedito	
EC-IKZ	Canadair CL-600-2B19	7732	ex C-GZUR	Tomas Yepes	
EC-ILF	Canadair CL-600-2B19	7746	ex C-FZQR	Vincente Lopez	
EC-INF	Canadair CL-600-2B19	7785	ex C-GYVM		
EC-IRI	Canadair CL-600-2B19	7851	ex C-GZNF	Benjamin Palencia	
EC-ITU	Canadair CL-600-2B19	7866	ex C-GZSQ		
EC-IBS	de Havilland DHC-8Q-315	560	ex PH-DME		
EC-IBT	de Havilland DHC-8Q-315	561	ex PH-DMI	Cezero	
EC-ICA	de Havilland DHC-8Q-315	562	ex PH-DML	Sabina	
EC-ICX	de Havilland DHC-8Q-315	563	ex PH-DMM	Higurea	
EC-IDK	de Havilland DHC-8Q-315	564	ex PH-DMP	Roble	
EC-IFK	de Havilland DHC-8Q-315	574	ex PH-DMX		
EC-IGE	de Havilland DHC-8Q-315	576	ex PH-DMY	Alamo	
EC-IGS	de Havilland DHC-8Q-315	586	ex PH-DEI		
EC-IIA	de Havilland DHC-8Q-315	587	ex C-GDIU		
EC-IIB	de Havilland DHC-8Q-315	588	ex C-GDIW		
EC-IJD	de Havilland DHC-8Q-315	589	ex C-GDKL	Nispero	
EC-IJP	de Havilland DHC-8Q-315	582	ex PH-DMZ		
EC-IKA	de Havilland DHC-8Q-315	590	ex C-GDLD		
EC-IOV	de Havilland DHC-8Q-315	581	ex PH-DEJ	Cedro	
PH-DEJ	de Havilland DHC-8Q-315	581	ex C-FDHU		Lsd fr/op by DNM
PH-DMQ	de Havilland DHC-8Q-315	567	ex C-GDOE	Almendro	Lsd fr/op by DNM
PH-DMR	de Havilland DHC-8Q-315	569	ex C-GETI		Lsd fr/op by DNM
PH-DMU	de Havilland DHC-8Q-315	568	ex C-GERL		Lsd fr/op by DNM
PH-DMV	de Havilland DHC-8Q-315	570	ex C-GEVP		Lsd fr/op by DNM
PH-DMW	de Havilland DHC-8Q-315	573	ex C-GFCF	Francisco Domingo	Lsd fr/op by DNM
PH-FZG	Fokker 50	20202	ex EC-HZA		Lsd fr DNM
PH-FZH	Fokker 50	20210		Olivo	Lsd fr DNM
PH-JXK	Fokker 50	20233			Lsd fr DNM
PH-JXN	Fokker 50	20239			Lsd fr DNM
PH-LMT	Fokker 50	20192	ex EC-HYJ-		Lsd fr DNM
PH-RRF	Fokker 50	20220	ex EC-HNS		Lsd fr DNM

Operates under franchise agreement with Iberia as Iberia Regional

AIR PLUS COMET

Red Comet (A7/MPD)   *Palma de Mallorca (PMI)*

EC-GMU	Airbus Industrie A310-324	451	ex N571SW		Lsd fr Airbus
EC-GOT	Airbus Industrie A310-324	455	ex N572SW	Andalucia	Lsd fr Airbus
EC-IPN	Boeing 747-212B	436/21938	ex LV-YPC		Lsd fr Pacific
EC-IPS	Boeing 737-33A (winglets)	1444/23827	ex CS-TMZ		Lsd fr MMZ
EC-IPT	Airbus Industrie A310-325ET	642	ex N642KS		Lsd fr ILFC

Affiliated with Spanair. Parent group purchased 92.1% of Aerolineas Argentinas and 90% of Cielos del Sur-Austral

AIR PULLMANTUR

                                           Madrid-Barajas (MAD)

| EC-IUA | Boeing 747-230M | 663/23509 | ex D-ABZE | | Lsd fr DLH |
| EC-IOO | Boeing 747-341 | 701/24106 | ex TF-ATH | | Lsd fr AWAS |

First service May03

ALAIRE

(ALR)   *Madrid-Cuatro Vientos*

| EC-IHD | Cessna 208B Caravan I | 208B0934 | ex D-FOKM | Lucas | |

ARTAC AVIATION

Artac (AVS)   *Madrid-Barajas (MAD)*

| EC-GEN | Swearingen SA.227AC Metro III | AC-688 | ex EC-126 | Juan Salvador | |
| EC-GJM | Swearingen SA.227TC Metro III | BC-772B | ex EC-307 | | |

ATLANTIC AIRWAYS ceased operations

AUDELI AIR EXPRESS

Audeli (ADI)   *Madrid-Barajas (MAD)*

EC-EHC   AMD Falcon 20DC   46 ex N46VG   Freighter
VIP flights are operated as Audeli Executive Jet using Falcon and Hawker executive jets

AVIONES Y HELICOPTEROS ILLES BALEARES

Aviocoba (AIM)   *Palma-Son Sant Juan/Mahon (/MAH)*

EC-ECK   Cessna 402   402-0284   ex D-IFAK
EC-EPS   Rockwell Commander 690   11034   ex N400JJ
EC-HHD   Agusta A109A II   7357   ex VP-CCK
EC-HIO   Agusta A109A II   7319   ex I-CARR
All EMS

AVISER taken over by TAF Helicopters in 2002 and operations subsequently merged

BINTER CANARIAS

(NT/IBB)   *Las Palmas-Gran Canaria/Tenerife-Sur Reine Sofia (LPA/TFS)*

EC-ESS   Aerospatiale/Alenia ATR 72-202   154   ex EC-383
EC-EUJ   Aerospatiale/Alenia ATR 72-202   157   ex EC-384
EC-EYK   Aerospatiale/Alenia ATR 72-202   183   ex EC-515
EC-FIV   Aerospatiale/Alenia ATR 72-201   260   ex EC-873
EC-FJX   Aerospatiale/Alenia ATR 72-201   267   ex EC-874
EC-FKQ   Aerospatiale/Alenia ATR 72-201   276   ex EC-935
EC-GQF   Aerospatiale/Alenia ATR 72-202   489   ex F-WWLJ
EC-GRP   Aerospatiale/Alenia ATR 72-202   488   ex F-WWLI
EC-GRU   Aerospatiale/Alenia ATR 72-202   493   ex F-WWLN
EC-HBU   Aerospatiale/Alenia ATR 72-212   459   ex N12903
EC-HEZ   Aerospatiale/Alenia ATR 72-212A   582   ex F-WWEL   Montana del Fuego
EC-IMH   Aerospatiale/Alenia ATR 72-212   367   ex F-GJRQ
EC-IPJ   Aerospatiale/Alenia ATR 72-202   307   ex F-GKOC   Lsd fr ATR Asset Mgt
EC-   Aerospatiale/Alenia ATR 72-212A   ex F-W   on order 4Q04
EC-   Aerospatiale/Alenia ATR 72-212A   ex F-W   on order 4Q04
EC-   Aerospatiale/Alenia ATR 72-212A   ex F-W   on order 4Q04
EC-   Aerospatiale/Alenia ATR 72-212A   ex F-W   on order 1Q05
EC-   Aerospatiale/Alenia ATR 72-212A   ex F-W   on order 1Q05

BKS AIR

Cosmos (CKM)   *Bilbao (BIO)*

EC-GOY   Beech 65-C90 King Air   LJ-527   ex N55SG
EC-HJO   Swearingen SA.227AC Metro III   AC-615B   ex N972GA   Lsd to MDF
EC-HMA   Beech 65-C90 King Air   LJ-577   ex N57KA
EC-HXY   Swearingen SA.227AC Metro III   AC-461B   ex N25LD
BKS Air is the trading name of Rivaflecha

CEGISA

                                                                        Salamanca-Matacan (SLM)

EC-GBP   Canadair CL-215-6B-11   1031   ex EC-957   Tanker
EC-GBQ   Canadair CL-215-6B-11   1033   ex EC-958   Tanker
EC-GBR   Canadair CL-215-6B-11   1051   ex UD.13-11   Tanker
EC-GBS   Canadair CL-215-6B-11   1052   ex UD.13-12   Tanker
EC-GBT   Canadair CL-215-6B-11   1054   ex UD.13-14   Tanker

EC-HET   Canadair CL-215-1A10   1034   ex I-SISB   Tanker
EC-HEU   Canadair CL-215-1A10   1038   ex I-SISC   Tanker
Member of Grupo Gestair

CYGNUS AIR

Regional Lineas (RGN)   *Madrid-Barajas (MAD)*

EC-EMD   Douglas DC-8-62F (BAC 3)   407/46023   ex EC-217
EC-EMX   Douglas DC-8-62F (BAC 3)   322/45921   ex EC-230
EC-IGZ   Douglas DC-8-73CF   534/46133   ex N961R   Lsd fr US Bank NA
Member of Grupo Gestair

EURO CONTINENTAL AIR

Euro Continental (ECN)   *Barcelona (BCN)*

EC-GPS   Swearingen SA.227AC Metro III   AC-722   ex N439MA   Freighter   Lsd to HHN

FAASA AVIACION

FAASA (FAM)   Palma del Rio-Cordoba (ODB)

EC-EOI	Bell UH-1B	408	ex N5023U
EC-EOX	Bell UH-1B	1214	ex N90632
EC-GAS	Bell 205A-1	30081	ex EC-844
EC-GDM	Bell UH-1H	5398	ex N205UD
EC-GDO	Bell UH-1H	8800	ex N205UE
EC-GKY	Bell UH-1H	13274	ex HE.10B-37
EC-GKZ	Bell UH-1H	13275	ex HE.10B-38
EC-GOE	Bell UH-1H	5272	ex N19UH
EC-GOG	Bell UH-1H	9960	ex N17UH

EC-DVR	Agusta A.109A	7231		EMS
EC-FGL	Bell 206L-3 Long Ranger III	51379	ex N65108	EMS
EC-HBJ	Agusta A.109C	7646	ex D-HBRK	EMS
EC-HFV	Bell 212	30818	ex N25UH	
EC-HNJ	Air Tractor AT-802	802-0096	ex N9075U	
EC-HNK	Air Tractor AT-802	802-0097	ex N9094Z	
EC-HXL	Bell 222UT	47570	ex TC-HLS	
EC-IFB	Bell 222			

FAASA Aviacion is the trading name of Fumigaciion Aerea Andaluza SA

FLIGHTLINE

Flight-Avia (FTL)   Barcelona (BCN)

EC-GBB	Beech 200 Super King Air	BB-182	ex EC-727		
EC-GFK	Swearingen SA.226AT Merlin IVA	AT-062	ex EC-125		Lsd to IBT
EC-HBF	Swearingen SA.226AT Merlin IVA	AT-074	ex EC-GDR	MRW Courier titles	Lsd to IBT

FUTURA INTERNATIONAL

Futura (FH/FUA)   Palma de Mallorca (PMI)

EC-GNZ	Boeing 737-4Y0	2199/25178	ex D-ABAD	Lsd fr GECAS
EC-GRX	Boeing 737-46B	1663/24123	ex G-OBMN	Lsd fr CIT Leasing
EC-GUG	Boeing 737-4S3	2061/25116	ex EI-CNE	Lsd fr KM Associates
EC-HBZ	Boeing 737-4Y0	2201/25180	ex N251RY	Lsd fr GECAS; sublsd to RYN
EC-HVY	Boeing 737-4Y0	1885/24690	ex	Lsd fr GECAS; sublsd to RYN
EC-IFN	Boeing 737-46B	1679/24124	ex EI-CRC	Lsd fr CIT Group; sublsd to ICE
EC-IHI	Boeing 737-4S3	2083/25134	ex G-BUHL	Lsd fr ACG Acquisitions
EC-INQ	Boeing 737-4Q8	2237/25169	ex G-BSNW	
EC-IOU	Boeing 737-4Y0	1883/24689	ex PK-MBK	Lsd fr GECAS
EC-IPF	Boeing 737-4K5	1687/24125	ex D-AHLJ	Lsd fr HLF

EC-HHG	Boeing 737-86N	410/28608		Lsd fr GECAS
EC-HHH	Boeing 737-86N	449/28610		Lsd fr Halvana
EC-HJJ	Boeing 737-86N	504/28617	ex N1787B	Lsd fr GECAS; sublsd to RYN
EC-HLN	Boeing 737-86N	534/28619	ex N255RY	Lsd fr WFBN; sublsd to RYN
EC-HMJ	Boeing 737-86N	570/28621		Lsd fr Halvana
EC-HMK	Boeing 737-86N	585/28624		Lsd fr GECAS; ops for GNR
EC-IEN	Boeing 737-86N	258/28592	ex CN-RNN	Lsd fr GECAS; sublsd to RYN
EC-INP	Boeing 737-804	1127/32903	ex SE-DZN	Lsd fr BLX
EC-ISL	Boeing 737-86N	1444/32740		Lsd fr GECAS

20% owned by Aer Lingus; some aircraft are leased to RYN for winter (via EIN). All 737NGs retrofitted with winglets
Futura International is the trading name of Compania Hispano Irlandesa de Aviacion

GESTAVI

Gestavi (GEV)   Palma de Mallorca (PMI)

EC-EZD	Swearingen SA.226TC Metro II	TC-319	ex EC-487	Freighter; stored BCN
EC-EZE	Swearingen SA.226TC Metro II	TC-314	ex EC-488	Freighter; stored BCN
EC-GUS	Swearingen SA.227AC Metro III	AC-648	ex N2685L	Lsd fr FINOVA
EC-HUN	Cessna 207A Skywagon	20700367	ex CS-AUL	
EC-INU	SAAB SF.340A	083	ex OH-SAD	Op for Air Catalunya

GIR JET

                                                                                Madrid

EC-IPV	Fokker 100	11451	ex PH-ZDJ	
EC-	Fokker 100		ex	on order

GIRJet is the trading name of Gestion Aerea Ejecutiva (GAE Aviacion)

HELICSA HELICOPTEROS

Helicsa (HHH) *Albacete-Helicsa Heliport/Madrid*

EC-DXM	Aerospatiale SA.365C2 Dauphin	5007	ex PH-SSL	
EC-DYU	Aerospatiale SA.365C1 Dauphin	5053	ex PH-SSC	
EC-FOX	Aerospatiale SA.365C2 Dauphin	5024	ex EC-136	EMS
EC-GCZ	Aerospatiale SA.365C2 Dauphin	5037	ex EC-887	EMS
EC-GJE	Aerospatiale SA.365N1 Dauphin	6308	ex LX-HUM	EMS
EC-GXY	Aerospatiale SA.365N1 Dauphin	6242	ex N12AE	EMS
EC-HCL	Aerospatiale AS.365N2 Dauphin	6416	ex SE-JAE	SAR
EC-HIM	Aerospatiale AS.365N2 Dauphin	6478	ex SE-JCE	SAR
EC-HRL	Aerospatiale AS.365C2 Dauphin	5055	ex PH-SSY	
EC-IEL	Aerospatiale SA.365C3 Dauphin	5017	ex F-GHXF	
EC-IGY	Aerospatiale SA.365C2 Dauphin	5049	ex 5N-ALJ	
EC-ILN	Aerospatiale SA.365N1 Dauphin	6234	ex LV-WLU	
EC-EEQ	Bell 212	30612	ex D-HOBB	EMS
EC-FBM	Bell 212	30574	ex EC-552	SAR
EC-GIC	Bell 212	30775	ex LN-OQD	SAR
EC-GID	Bell 212	31150	ex OY-HCS	SAR
EC-GLS	Bell 212	31155	ex OY-HCU	SAR
EC-GVP	Bell 212	30572	ex LN-OQG	SAR
EC-GXA	Bell 212	30812	ex LN-OQJ	SAR
EC-HFX	Bell 212	30639	ex G-BCMC	
EC-FJJ	Sikorsky S-61N	61299	ex EC-862	Op for SASEMAR
EC-FMZ	Sikorsky S-61N	61361	ex LN-ORH	Op for SASEMAR
EC-FTB	Sikorsky S-61N	61741	ex LN-OSY	Op for SASEMAR
EC-FVO	Sikorsky S-61N	61756	ex EC-575	Op for SASEMAR
EC-FZJ	Sikorsky S-61N	61758	ex EC-717	Op for SASEMAR
EC-DVK	MBB Bo.105CB	S-630	ex D-HDSZ	Argos I
EC-DVL	MBB Bo.105CB	S-631	ex D-HDTA	Argos II
EC-ESX	MBB BK.117B-1	7176	ex D-HBHS	
EC-FFV	MBB Bo.105CBS	S-852	ex D-HFHJ	
EC-GHY	Aerospatiale AS.355F1 Ecureuil 2	5089	ex EC-293	EMS
EC-GSK	Bell 412	33092	ex SE-HVL	
EC-HXZ	Bell 412	33106	ex PK-HMT	
EC-IKY	Eurocopter EC.135T2	0255	ex D-HECO	

Associated with Helikopter Service and Schreiner

HELISURESTE / HELICOPTEROS DEL SURESTE

Helisureste (UV/HSE) *Alicante-San Vincente Heliport*

EC-DNM	Agusta A.109A	7222	ex N4210X	EMS
EC-DZT	Agusta A.109A	7159	ex HB-XIU	EMS
EC-ETF	Agusta A.109C	7605	ex 3A-MOR	EMS
EC-FQJ	Agusta A.109C	7664	ex N1YU	Fishery Patrol
EC-FUY	Agusta A.109C	7670	ex EC-453	Fishery Patrol
EC-GCQ	Agusta A.109C	7665	ex EC-895	Fishery Patrol
EC-GRA	Agusta A.109C	7676	ex EC-GJD	
EC-HAO	Agusta A.109C Max	7642	ex D-HAAC	EMS
EC-HBQ	Agusta A.109A II Max	7399	ex I-SOCC	EMS
EC-HHQ	Agusta A.109E Power	11058		EMS
EC-IJR	Agusta A.109E Power	11137		EMS
EC-IKN	Agusta A.109A II Max	7391	ex I-AGSL	EMS
EC-ILA	Augusta A.109A II Max			
EC-FBL	Bell 212	30558	ex EC-553	
EC-GHP	Bell 212	30557	ex EC-256	Lsd to HSU as CS-HEZ
EC-HOX	Bell 212	32254	ex 4X-BCF	
EC-HOY	Bell 212	32225	ex 4X-BCN	
EC-HPJ	Bell 212	32217	ex 4X-BCI	
EC-HTJ	Bell 212	30648	ex PK-HMC	
EC-HXV	Bell 212	30547	ex FAP 74-614	
EC-HZG	Bell 212	32224		
EC-IEM	Bell 212	30684	ex CS-HEJ	
EC-IFA	Bell 212	30989	ex N1074C	
EC-GOP	Bell 412HP	36031	ex N4603T	Lsd to HSU
EC-GPA	Bell 412	36071	ex N7238Y	Lsd to HSU
EC-FEL	Agusta-Bell 412SP	25576	ex EC-607	
EC-GBE	Agusta-Bell 412	25503	ex EC-757	
EC-HFD	Bell 412EP	36183	ex N52247	
EC-HXX	Bell 412	33062	ex N4014U	
EC-HXZ	Bell 412	33106	ex PK-HMT	
EC-HYM	Bell 412	33045	ex C-FTDM	
EC-HZD	Bell 412	33056	ex N4031F	

EC-DEK	Agusta-Bell 206B JetRanger III	8568			
EC-FOL	Bell 206L-3 LongRanger III	51417	ex N6605R		
EC-FRY	Bell 206L-3 LongRanger III	51330	ex N43904		
EC-GAA	Bell 205A-1	30134	ex EC-756		
EC-GCU	Bell 206LT TwinRanger	52105	ex EC-843	EMS	
EC-GNR	Bell 206LT TwinRanger	52051	ex N41060	EMS	
EC-HCT	Bell 206LT TwinRanger	52062	ex G-BXMP	EMS	
EC-INX	CASA C.212-400MP	472			

HOLA AIRLINES

Hola (HOA)   Palma de Mallorca (PMI)

EC-IEZ	Boeing 737-33A	1304/23628	ex N167AW	Trives	Lsd fr AWAS
EC-IFV	Boeing 737-33A	1284/23626	ex N165AW		Lsd fr AWAS
EC-IOR	Boeing 737-382	1857/24449	ex LY-BAG		Lsd fr ILFC
EC-ISY	Boeing 757-236	572/26241	ex N26ND		Lsd fr WFBN

IBERIA LINEAS AEREAS DE ESPANA

Iberia (IB/IBE) (IATA 075)   Madrid-Barajas (MAD)

EC-HGR^	Airbus Industrie A319-111	1154	ex D-AVYY	Ribeira Sacra	Lsd fr ILFC
EC-HGS^	Airbus Industrie A319-111	1180	ex D-AVWR	Bardenas Reales	Lsd fr ILFC
EC-HGT^	Airbus Industrie A319-111	1247	ex D-AVYV	Ignitas de Enciso	Lsd fr ILFC
EC-HKO^	Airbus Industrie A319-111	1362	ex D-AVWJ	Gorbea	Lsd fr ILFC
EC-	Airbus Industrie A319-111	2264	ex D-AV	on order	Lsd fr ILFC
EC-	Airbus Industrie A319-111	2270	ex D-AV	on order	Lsd fr ILFC

^Based Miami, FL   Three more are on order

EC-FCB	Airbus Industrie A320-211	0158	ex EC-579	Montana de Covadonga	
EC-FDA	Airbus Industrie A320-211	0176	ex EC-581	Lagunas de Ruidera	
EC-FDB	Airbus Industrie A320-211	0173	ex EC-580	Lago de Sanabria	
EC-FGH	Airbus Industrie A320-211	0223	ex EC-585	Caldera de Taburiente	
EC-FGR	Airbus Industrie A320-211	0224	ex EC-586	Dehesa de Moncayo	
EC-FGV	Airbus Industrie A320-211	0207	ex EC-584	Monfrague	
EC-FLP	Airbus Industrie A320-211	0266	ex EC-881	Torcal de Antequera	
EC-FLQ	Airbus Industrie A320-211	0274	ex EC-882	Dunas de Liencres	
EC-FNR	Airbus Industrie A320-211	0323	ex EC-885	Monte el Valle	
EC-FQY	Airbus Industrie A320-211	0356	ex EC-886	Joan Miro	
EC-GRE	Airbus Industrie A320-211	0134	ex EC-FAS	Sierra de Cazorla	Lsd fr Julyco
EC-GRF	Airbus Industrie A320-211	0136	ex EC-FBQ	Montseny	Lsd fr Julyco
EC-GRG	Airbus Industrie A320-211	0143	ex EC-FBS	Timanfaya	Lsd fr Julyco
EC-GRH	Airbus Industrie A320-211	0146	ex EC-FBR	Sierra de Segura	Lsd fr Julyco
EC-GRI	Airbus Industrie A320-211	0177	ex EC-FEO	Delta del Ebro	Lsd fr Julyco
EC-GRJ+	Airbus Industrie A320-211	0246	ex EC-FKH	Canon del Rio Lobos	
EC-HAB	Airbus Industrie A320-214	0994	ex F-WWBM	Cabaneros	Lsd fr ILFC
EC-HAD	Airbus Industrie A320-214	0992	ex F-WWBS	Garajonay	Lsd fr SALE
EC-HAF	Airbus Industrie A320-214	1047	ex F-WWIE	Santiago de Compostela	
EC-HAG	Airbus Industrie A320-214	1059	ex F-WWIP	Senorio de Bertiz	
EC-HDK	Airbus Industrie A320-214	1067	ex F-WWBF	Mar de Ontigola	
EC-HDL	Airbus Industrie A320-214	1063	ex F-WWBL	Corredor del Duero	Lsd fr SALE
EC-HDN^	Airbus Industrie A320-214	1087	ex F-WWIY	Parque National de Somiedo	
EC-HDO	Airbus Industrie A320-214	1099	ex F-WWDR	Formentera	
EC-HDP	Airbus Industrie A320-214	1101	ex F-WWBZ	Parque de Cabarceno	
EC-HDT	Airbus Industrie A320-214	1119	ex F-WWBO	Museo Guggenheim Bilbao	
EC-HGY	Airbus Industrie A320-214	1200	ex F-WWII	Albarracin	Lsd fr ILFC
EC-HGZ	Airbus Industrie A320-214	1208	ex F-WWIM	Boi Taull	Lsd fr ILFC
EC-HHA	Airbus Industrie A320-214	1221	ex F-WWBF	Serrania de Ronda	Lsd fr ILFC
EC-HQG	Airbus Industrie A320-214	1379	ex F-WWIO	Las Hurdes	Lsd fr ILFC
EC-HQI	Airbus Industrie A320-214	1396	ex F-WWIX	La Albufera	Lsd fr ILFC
EC-HQJ	Airbus Industrie A320-214	1430	ex F-WWBR	Bosque de Muniellos	Lsd fr ILFC
EC-HQK	Airbus Industrie A320-214	1454	ex F-WWBZ	Caraella	Lsd fr ILFC
EC-HQL	Airbus Industrie A320-214	1461	ex F-WWDD	Liebana	Lsd fr ILFC
EC-HQM	Airbus Industrie A320-214	1484	ex F-WWDM	Rio Jucar	Lsd fr ILFC
EC-HSE	Airbus Industrie A320-214	1229	ex EC-HHB	Hoces de Gabriel	Lsd fr ILFC
EC-HSF	Airbus Industrie A320-214	1255	ex EC-HHC	Mar Menor	
EC-HTA	Airbus Industrie A320-214	1516	ex F-WWIK	Cadaques	
EC-HTB	Airbus Industrie A320-214	1530	ex F-WWIO	Playa de las Americas	
EC-HTC	Airbus Industrie A320-214	1540	ex F-WWIU	Alpujarra	
EC-HTD	Airbus Industrie A320-214	1550	ex F-WWDC	Calblanque	Lsd fr ILFC
EC-HUJ	Airbus Industrie A320-214	1292	ex EC-HKL	Getaria	
EC-HUK	Airbus Industrie A320-214	1318	ex EC-HKM	Laguna Negra	Lsd fr ILFC
EC-HUL	Airbus Industrie A320-214	1347	ex EC-HKN	Monasterio de Rueda	Lsd fr ILFC
EC-HYC	Airbus Industrie A320-214	1262	ex EC-HKI	Ciudad de Ceuta	
EC-HYD	Airbus Industrie A320-214	1288	ex EC-HKX	Maspalomas	
EC-ICQ	Airbus Industrie A320-211	0199	ex EC-FGU	Sierra Espuna	
EC-ICR	Airbus Industrie A320-211	0240	ex EC-FIA	Isla de la Cartuja	
EC-ICS	Airbus Industrie A320-211	0241	ex EC-FIC	Sierra de Grazalema	
EC-ICT	Airbus Industrie A320-211	0264	ex EC-FKD	Monte Alhoya	
EC-ICU	Airbus Industrie A320-211	0303	ex EC-FML	Hayedo de Tejara Negra	

EC-ICV	Airbus Industrie A320-211	0312	ex EC-FMN	Cadi Moixeroi	
EC-IEF	Airbus Industrie A320-214	1655	ex F-WWDY	Castillo de Loarre	
EC-IEG	Airbus Industrie A320-214	1674	ex F-WWIL	Costa Brava	
EC-IEI	Airbus Industrie A320-214	1694	ex F-WWBT	Monasterio de Valllllidigna	
EC-ILQ	Airbus Industrie A320-214	1736	ex F-WWDJ	La Pedrera	
EC-ILR	Airbus Industrie A320-214	1793	ex F-WWIM	San Juan de la Pena; std TLS	
EC-ILS	Airbus Industrie A320-214	1809	ex F-WWBC	Sierra de Cameros; std TLS	
EC-I	Airbus Industrie A320-214	2104	ex F-WWBE	Trujillo; on order 04	
EC-I	Airbus Industrie A320-214	2143	ex F-WWBV	Valle de Ricote; on order 04	
EC-I	Airbus Industrie A320-214	2242	ex F-WW	on order 04	
EC-I	Airbus Industrie A320-214		ex F-WW	on order 04	
EC-I	Airbus Industrie A320-214		ex F-WW	on order 04	
EC-I	Airbus Industrie A320-214		ex F-WW	on order 04	
EC-I	Airbus Industrie A320-214		ex F-WW	on order 04	

A further two Airbus Industrie A320-214s are on order for delivery in 2005
^Leased from ILFC   +Leased from CIT Leasing

EC-HUH	Airbus Industrie A321-211	1021	ex EC-HAC	Benidorm	
EC-HUI	Airbus Industrie A321-211	1027	ex EC-HAE	Comunidad Autonoma de la Rioja	
EC-IGK	Airbus Industrie A321-211	1572	ex EC-HTF	Costa Calida	
EC-IIG	Airbus Industrie A321-211	1554	ex EC-HTE	Ciudad de Siguenza	
EC-IJN	Airbus Industrie A321-211	1836	ex D-AVZN	Merida	
EC-ILO	Airbus Industrie A321-211	1681	ex D-AVZW	Cueva de Nerja	
EC-ILP	Airbus Industrie A321-211	1716	ex D-AVZT	Pensicola	
EC-ITN	Airbus Industrie A321-211	2115	ex D-AVXG		
EC-I	Airbus Industrie A321-211	2220	ex D-AV	on order 04	
EC-I	Airbus Industrie A321-211		ex D-AV	on order 04	
EC-I	Airbus Industrie A321-211		ex D-AV	on order 04	
EC-I	Airbus Industrie A321-211		ex D-AV	on order 04	
EC-I	Airbus Industrie A321-211		ex D-AV	on order 04	

Two more Airbus Industrie A321-211s are on order for delivery in 2005

EC-GGS	Airbus Industrie A340-313	125	ex EC-154	Concha Espina	
EC-GHX	Airbus Industrie A340-313	134	ex EC-155	Rosalia de Castro	
EC-GJT	Airbus Industrie A340-313	145	ex EC-156	Rosa Chacel	
EC-GLE	Airbus Industrie A340-313	146	ex EC-157	Concepcion Arenal	
EC-GPB	Airbus Industrie A340-313X	193	ex F-WWJR	Teresa de Avila	
EC-GQK	Airbus Industrie A340-313X	197	ex F-WWJL	Emelia Pardo Bazan	
EC-GUP	Airbus Industrie A340-313X	217	ex F-WWJG	Augustina de Aragon	
EC-GUQ	Airbus Industrie A340-313X	221	ex F-WWJA	Beatriz Galindo	
EC-HDQ	Airbus Industrie A340-313X	302	ex F-WWJU	Sor Juana Ines de la Cruz	
EC-HGU	Airbus Industrie A340-313X	318	ex F-WWJL	Maria de Molina	
EC-HGV	Airbus Industrie A340-313X	329	ex F-WWJP	Maria Guerrero	
EC-HGX	Airbus Industrie A340-313X	332	ex F-WWJR	Maria Pita	
EC-HQF	Airbus Industrie A340-313X	378	ex F-WWJI	Maria de Zayas y Sotomayor	
EC-HQH	Airbus Industrie A340-313X	387	ex F-WWJD	Mariana de Silva	
EC-HQN	Airbus Industrie A340-313X	414	ex F-WWJN	Luisa Carvajal y Mendoza	
EC-ICF	Airbus Industrie A340-313X	459	ex F-WWJU	Maria Zambrano	
EC-IDF	Airbus Industrie A340-313X	474	ex F-WWJG	Mariana Pineda	
EC-IIH	Airbus Industrie A340-313X	483	ex F-WWJI	Maria Barbara de Braganza	
EC-INO	Airbus Industrie A340-642	431	ex F-WWCI	Gaudi	Lsd fr Airbus
EC-IOB	Airbus Industrie A340-642	440	ex F-WWCL	Pablo Picasso	Lsd fr Airbus
EC-IQR	Airbus Industrie A340-642	460	ex F-WWCO	Salvador Dali	Lsd fr Airbus
EC-	Airbus Industrie A340-642	606	ex F-WW	on order 04	
EC-	Airbus Industrie A340-642	617	ex F-WW	on order 04	
EC-	Airbus Industrie A340-642	619	ex F-WW	on order 04	

Two more Airbus Industrie A340-642s are on order, leased from ILFC, for delivery in February and March 2005

EC-DIA	Boeing 747-256B	450/22238		Tirso de Molina	
EC-DIB	Boeing 747-256B	451/22239		Cervantes	
EC-DNP	Boeing 747-256B	554/22764	ex N8296V	Juan Ramon Jimenez	
EC-HVD	Boeing 747-256M	509/22454	ex TF-ATL	Francisco de Quevedo	
TF-ATI	Boeing 747-341	702/24107	ex N824DS	Gonzalo de Berceo	Lsd fr ABD
TF-ATJ	Boeing 747-341	703/24108	ex N420DS	Jose Zorrilla	Lsd fr ABD
EC-FTR	Boeing 757-256	553/26239	ex EC-420	Sierra de Guadarrama	
EC-FXV	Boeing 757-256	572/26241	ex EC-618	Argentina; stored GYR	
EC-GZY	Boeing 757-256	860/26247	ex N1795B	Santo Domingo	
EC-GZZ	Boeing 757-256	863/26248		Peru	
EC-HAA	Boeing 757-256	881/26249		Ecuador	
EC-HDM	Boeing 757-256	889/26250		Brasil	
EC-HDR	Boeing 757-256	897/26251		Puente Aereo	
EC-HDS	Boeing 757-256	900/26252		Paraguay	
EC-HDU	Boeing 757-256	902/26253		Uruguay	
EC-HDV	Boeing 757-256	905/26254	ex N1786B	Nicaragua	
EC-HIP	Boeing 757-256	920/29306		Panama	
EC-HIQ	Boeing 757-256	924/29307		Honduras	
EC-HIR	Boeing 757-256	935/29308	ex N1795B	El Salvador	
EC-HIS	Boeing 757-256	936/29309		Bolivia	
EC-HIT	Boeing 757-256	938/29310		Guatemala	
EC-HIU	Boeing 757-256	940/29311		Colombia	
EC-HIV	Boeing 757-256	943/29312		Ville de Bilbao	
EC-HIX	Boeing 757-256	948/30052		Cuba	

EC-EXF	McDonnell-Douglas MD-87	1703/49832	ex EC-295	Ciudad de Pamplona	
EC-EXG	McDonnell-Douglas MD-87	1706/49833	ex EC-296	Ciudad de Almeria	
EC-EXM	McDonnell-Douglas MD-87	1717/49835	ex EC-298	Ciudad de Zaragoza	
EC-EXN	McDonnell-Douglas MD-87	1721/49836	ex EC-299	Ciudad de Badajoz	
EC-EXR	McDonnell-Douglas MD-87	1714/49834	ex EC-297	Ciudad de Oviedo	
EC-EXT	McDonnell-Douglas MD-87	1730/49837	ex EC-300	Ciudad de Albacete	
EC-EYB	McDonnell-Douglas MD-87	1733/49838	ex EC-301	Cangas de Onis	
EC-EYX	McDonnell-Douglas MD-87	1739/49839	ex EC-302	Ciudad de Caceres	
EC-EYY	McDonnell-Douglas MD-87	1745/49840	ex EC-303	Ciudad de Barcelona	
EC-EYZ	McDonnell-Douglas MD-87	1751/49841	ex EC-304	Ciudad de Las Palmas	
EC-EZA	McDonnell-Douglas MD-87	1763/49842	ex EC-305	Ciudad de Segovia	
EC-EZS	McDonnell-Douglas MD-87	1771/49843	ex EC-306	Ciudad de Mahon	
EC-FEY	McDonnell-Douglas MD-87	1865/53208	ex EC-634	Ciudad de Jaen	
EC-FEZ	McDonnell-Douglas MD-87	1862/53207	ex EC-633	Ciudad de Malaga	
EC-FFA	McDonnell-Douglas MD-87	1867/53209	ex EC-635	Ciudad de Avila	
EC-FFH	McDonnell-Douglas MD-87	1874/53211	ex EC-637	Ciudad de Logrono	
EC-FFI	McDonnell-Douglas MD-87	1871/53210	ex EC-636	Ciudad de Cuenca	
EC-FGM	McDonnell-Douglas MD-88	1890/53193	ex EC-751	Torre de Hercules	
EC-FHD	McDonnell-Douglas MD-88	1877/53212	ex EC-638	Ciudad de Leon	
EC-FHG	McDonnell-Douglas MD-88	1911/53194	ex EC-752	La Almudaina	
EC-FHK	McDonnell-Douglas MD-87	1879/53213	ex EC-639	Ciudad de Tarragona	
EC-FIG	McDonnell-Douglas MD-88	1929/53195	ex EC-753	Penon de Ifach	
EC-FIH	McDonnell-Douglas MD-88	1930/53196	ex EC-754	Albaicin	
EC-FJE	McDonnell-Douglas MD-88	1940/53197	ex EC-755	Gibraltaro	
EC-FLK	McDonnell-Douglas MD-88	1975/53304	ex EC-946	Palacio de la Magdalena	
EC-FLN	McDonnell-Douglas MD-88	1974/53303	ex EC-945	Puerta de Tierra	Canarias c/s
EC-FND	McDonnell-Douglas MD-88	2001/53305	ex EC-964	Playa de la Concha	
EC-FOF	McDonnell-Douglas MD-88	2015/53307	ex EC-966	Puerta de Alcala	
EC-FOG	McDonnell-Douglas MD-88	2014/53306	ex EC-965	Cesar Manrique Lanzarote	
EC-FOZ	McDonnell-Douglas MD-88	2022/53308	ex EC-987	Montjuic	
EC-FPD	McDonnell-Douglas MD-88	2023/53309	ex EC-988	Lago de Coradonga	
EC-FPJ	McDonnell-Douglas MD-88	2024/53310	ex EC-989	Ria de Vigo	
EC-GRK	McDonnell-Douglas MD-87	1654/49827	ex EC-EUE	Ciudad de Sevilla	Lsd fr Julyco
EC-GRL	McDonnell-Douglas MD-87	1667/49828	ex EC-EUD	Ciudad de Toledo	Lsd fr Julyco
EC-GRM	McDonnell-Douglas MD-87	1678/49829	ex EC-EUC	Ciudad de Burgos	Lsd fr Julyco
EC-GRN	McDonnell-Douglas MD-87	1684/49830	ex EC-EUL	Ciudad de Cadiz	Lsd fr Julyco
EC-GRO	McDonnell-Douglas MD-87	1688/49831	ex EC-EVB	Arrecife de Lanzarote	Lsd fr Julyco
TC-ONM	McDonnell-Douglas MD-88	2167/53546			Lsd fr OHY

10% owned by British Airways and American Airlines, member of oneworld alliance.

IBERLINE

Madrid-Barajas (MAD)

SE-KUT	SAAB SF.340A	087	ex LN-NNF

Wholly owned subsidiary of Swedline Express; 1st service June 2003. Sole service Logrono - Madrid suspended 26.1.04

IBERTRANS AEREA

Ibertrans (IBT)   *Madrid-Barajas (MAD)*

EC-GQA	Embraer EMB-120ER Brasilia	120027	ex EC-GMT	Margarita Tur; freighter	
EC-HHN	Embraer EMB-120ER Brasilia	120103	ex N127AM		
EC-HFZ	Embraer EMB.120RT Brasilia	120261	ex LX-LGK		Lsd fr RGI
EC-HSO	Embraer EMB.120ER Brasilia	120214	ex F-GHEY		
EC-HUP	Embraer EMB.120ER Brasilia	120209	ex F-GHEX		
EC-GFK	Swearingen SA.226AC Merlin IVA	AT-062	ex EC-125		Lsd fr FTL
EC-HBF	Swearingen SA.226AT Merlin IVA	AT-074	ex EC-GDR	MRW Courier titles	Lsd fr FTL

IBERWORLD

(TY/IWD)   *Palma de Mallorca (PMI)*

EC-GZD	Airbus Industrie A320-214	0879	ex F-WWDD	Costa Adeje	Lsd fr GECAS
EC-HZU	Airbus Industrie A320-214	1578	ex F-WWBO		Lsd fr GECAS
EC-IAG	Airbus Industrie A320-214	1597	ex F-WWBY		Lsd fr GECAS
EC-ICK	Airbus Industrie A320-214	1657	ex F-WWID		Lsd fr GECAS
EC-IEQ	Airbus Industrie A320-214	1767	ex F-WWBV		Lsd fr GECAS
EC-IMU	Airbus Industrie A320-214	1130	ex SE-RCD		Lsd fr GECAS
EC-INZ	Airbus Industrie A320-214	2011	ex F-WWBR		Lsd fr Boullioun
EC-IDB	Airbus Industrie A330-243	461	ex F-WWKL	Sabine Thienemann	Lsd fr CIT Lsg
EC-IJH	Airbus Industrie A330-322	072	ex D-AERG	Gloria Fluxa	Lsd fr ILFC

INTERMEDIACION AEREA

Intermed (IEA)   *Barcelona (BCN)*

EC-GMG	Swearingen SA.226TC Metro II	TC-371	ex OY-BJT	Freighter	
EC-HVR	Aerospatiale/Alenia ATR 42-300	025	ex F-GLIB		Lsd fr Aviation Enterprises

EC-IDG	Aerospatiale/Alenia ATR 42-300	130	ex F-WQNE	Costa Brava Girona
				Lsd fr ATR Asset Mgt

ISLAS AIRWAYS

Pintadera (IF/ISW)   *Tenerife Norte Los Rodeos (TNR)*

EC-IKK	Aerospatiale/Alenia ATR 72-201	198	ex F-WQND
EC-IKQ	Aerospatiale/Alenia ATR 72-202	477	ex F-WQNM

LAGUN AIR

(N7)   *León*

EC-IRD	SAAB SF.340A	081	ex OH-SAC		
EC-IRR	SAAB SF.340A	144	ex OH-SAF		
EC-	SAAB SF.340A	055	ex SE-KPE		
EC-	SAAB SF.340A	051	ex N325PX	on order	Lsd fr State Street
EC-	SAAB SF.340A	034	ex N338BE	on order	Lsd fr State Street
EC-	SAAB SF.340A	044	ex N339BE	on order	Lsd fr State Street

LANZAROTE AEROCARGO

(LZT)   *Lanzarote-Arrecife (ACE)*

EC-IKM	Cessna 208B Caravan I	208B0948	ex D-FMCG

LTE INTERNATIONAL AIRWAYS renamed Volar Airlines

NAYSA AEROTAXIS

Naysa (NAY)   *Las Palmas-Gran Canaria (LPA)*

EC-GTM	Beech 1900C	UB-30	ex N7210R	Lsd fr Raytheon
EC-GUD	Beech 1900C-1	UC-156	ex N156YV	Lsd fr Raytheon
EC-GZG	Beech 1900C-1	UC-161	ex N55635	Lsd fr Raytheon
EC-HCM	Beech 1900C-1	UC-124	ex N122GP	Lsd fr Raytheon
EC-IAH	Beech 1900C-1	UC-166	ex N166GL	
EC-IJO	Beech 1900D	UE-300	ex F-GRPM	Lsd fr Kansas Beech Lsg

Naysa Aerotaxis is the trading name of Navegacion y Servicios Aereos Canarios

PANAIR LINEAS AEREAS

Skyjet (PNR)   *Madrid-Barajas (MAD)*

EC-FZE	British Aerospace 146 Srs.200QT	E2105	ex EC-719
EC-GQO	British Aerospace 146 Srs.200QT	E2086	ex D-ADEI
EC-HDH	British Aerospace 146 Srs.200QT	E2056	ex G-TNTA
EC-HJH	British Aerospace 146 Srs.200QT	E2112	ex G-BOMK
EC-HQT	Airbus Industrie A300B4-203F	124	ex G-TNTS
EC-HVZ	Airbus Industrie A300B4-203F	227	ex N223KW

Operate on behalf of TNT Airways in full colours

SAESA / SERVICIOS AEREOS ESPANOLES

Saesa (SSS)   *Madrid-Cuatro Vientos*

EC-ERK	Bell UH-1E	6069	ex N151LC	
EC-EVK	Consolidated PBY-5A Catalina	2008	ex EC-359	Tanker, op for ICONA
EC-FMC	Consolidated PBY-5A Catalina	2134	ex EC-940	Tanker, op for ICONA
EC-HDD	Bell UH-1H	13551	ex HE.10B-51	
EC-HNG	Bell UH-1H			

SPANAIR

Spanair (JK/JKK) (IATA 680)   *Palma de Mallorca (PMI)*

EC-HPM	Airbus Industrie A321-231	1276	ex D-AVZO	Camilo Jose Cela	
EC-HQZ	Airbus Industrie A321-231	1333	ex D-AVZB		
EC-HRG	Airbus Industrie A321-231	1366	ex D-AVZC	Placido Domingo	Lsd fr ILFC
EC-HRP	Airbus Industrie A320-232	1349	ex F-WWBD	Juan de Avalos	
EC-HXA	Airbus Industrie A320-232	1497	ex F-WWID		
EC-IAZ	Airbus Industrie A320-232	1631	ex F-WWDP		
EC-ICL	Airbus Industrie A320-232	1682	ex F-WWBD		Lsd fr ILFC
EC-IEJ	Airbus Industrie A320-232	1749	ex F-WWBO		Lsd fr ILFC
EC-IIZ	Airbus Industrie A320-232	1862	ex F-WWDZ		Lsd fr ILFC
EC-IJU	Airbus Industrie A321-231	1843	ex D-AVZR		
EC-ILH	Airbus Industrie A320-232	1914	ex F-WWDU	Star Alliance c/s	
EC-IMB	Airbus Industrie A320-232	1933	ex F-WWII		
EC-INB	Airbus Industrie A321-231	1946	ex D-AVXD		Lsd fr ILFC

EC-INM	Airbus Industrie A320-232	1979	ex F-WWBE	Star Alliance c/s	
EC-IOH	Airbus Industrie A320-232	1998	ex F-WWIV		
EC-IPI	Airbus Industrie A320-232	2027	ex F-WWDP	Star Alliance c/s	
EC-	Airbus Industrie A320-232	2168	ex F-WWDA	on order 04	
EC-	Airbus Industrie A320-232	2210	ex F-WW	on order 04	
EC-FTS	McDonnell-Douglas MD-83	1495/49621	ex EC-479	Sunbird	Lsd fr Uninter Lsg
EC-FXA	McDonnell-Douglas MD-83	1785/49938	ex EC-592	Sunstar	Lsd fr GECAS
EC-FXI	McDonnell-Douglas MD-83	1591/49630	ex EC-638	Sunseeker a/w	Lsd fr FINOVA
EC-FXY	McDonnell-Douglas MD-83	1580/49627	ex EC-646	Sunbeam	Lsd fr GECAS
EC-FZC	McDonnell-Douglas MD-83	1643/49790	ex EC-742	Sunflower	Lsd fr GECAS
EC-GAT	McDonnell-Douglas MD-83	1542/49709	ex EC-835	Sunmyth	Lsd fr GECAS
EC-GBA	McDonnell-Douglas MD-83	1538/49626	ex EC-805	Sungod	Lsd fr GECAS
EC-GCV	McDonnell-Douglas MD-82	2042/53165	ex EC-894	Sunburst	Lsd fr GECAS
EC-GGV	McDonnell-Douglas MD-83	1644/49791	ex EC-166	Sunbow	Lsd fr GECAS
EC-GHE	McDonnell-Douglas MD-83	1332/49398	ex EC-245	Sunset	Lsd fr GECAS
EC-GHH	McDonnell-Douglas MD-83	1455/49578	ex EC-291	Sundance	Lsd fr GECAS
EC-GNY	McDonnell-Douglas MD-83	1305/49396	ex N396GE	Sunflash	Lsd fr GECAS
EC-GOM	McDonnell-Douglas MD-83	1465/49579	ex EC-EIG	Sunlight	Lsd fr Finans Scandic
EC-GOU	McDonnell-Douglas MD-83	1847/53198	ex SE-DLS	Sunlover	Lsd fr GECAS
EC-GQG	McDonnell-Douglas MD-83	1454/49577	ex EC-FSY	Sunrise	Lsd fr Finans Scandic
EC-GQZ	McDonnell-Douglas MD-83	1458/49571	ex HB-INY	Sunbear	Lsd fr Flightlease
EC-GTO	McDonnell-Douglas MD-82	1440/49570	ex HB-INX	Sunjet	Lsd fr Air Fleet Credit
EC-GVI	McDonnell-Douglas MD-83	1778/49936	ex EI-CPA	Sunup	Lsd fr GECAS
EC-GVO	McDonnell-Douglas MD-83	1421/49642	ex N462GE	Sunspot	Lsd fr GECAS
EC-GXU	McDonnell-Douglas MD-83	1498/49622	ex EC-FTT	Sunray	Lsd fr Finans Scandic
EC-HBP	McDonnell-Douglas MD-83	1583/49629	ex HB-IKP	Sunglow	Lsd fr Credit Agricole
EC-HFP	McDonnell-Douglas MD-82	2072/53148	ex HL7548	Sunbreeze	Lsd fr GECAS
EC-HFS+	McDonnell-Douglas MD-83	1633/49517	ex EI-CTE	Sunbeach	Lsd fr GECAS
EC-HFT+	McDonnell-Douglas MD-82	1690/49521	ex EI-CTF	Sunspirit	Lsd fr GECAS
EC-HGA	McDonnell-Douglas MD-83	1731/53052	ex N942AS	Sunisland	Lsd fr ILFC
EC-HGJ+	McDonnell-Douglas MD-82	1658/49519	ex EI-CTQ	Sunworld	Lsd fr GECAS
EC-HHF+	McDonnell-Douglas MD-82	1482/49509	ex EI-CTP	Sunward	Lsd fr GECAS
EC-HHP+	McDonnell-Douglas MD-82	1292/49501	ex EI-CTV	Sunshiny	Lsd fr GECAS
EC-HJB+	McDonnell-Douglas MD-82	1425/49507	ex EI-CUF	Suntrek	Lsd fr GECAS
EC-HKP	McDonnell-Douglas MD-83	1502/49624	ex EI-CGI	Suntrail	Lsd fr GECAS
EC-HMI	McDonnell-Douglas MD-87	1404/49403	ex OH-LMA	Sunblessed	Lsd fr Craycroft
EC-HNC	McDonnell-Douglas MD-82	1484/49620	ex D-ALLV	Sunplace	Lsd fr GECAS
EC-HOV	McDonnell-Douglas MD-82	1271/49416	ex HL7543	Sunspeed	Lsd fr GECAS
SE-DIX	McDonnell-Douglas MD-82	1800/49998			Lsd fr SAS

+Assembled by SAIC; also have c/ns SAIC 18/22/20/10/2/8 respectively
94.9% owned by SAS and affiliated with Air Plus Comet
Regional services operated by Aerolineas de Baleares (Aebal), a wholly owned subsidiary, as Aebal SpanairLink
Member of Star Alliance

STELLAIR / COMPANIA DE ACTIVIDADES Y SERVICIOS DE AVIACION

Stellair (LCT)   **Madrid-Cuatro Vientos**

EC-EVJ	Grumman G-159 Gulfstream I	039		Freighter	
EC-EXB	Grumman G-159 Gulfstream I	153	ex EC-433	Freighter	
EC-EZO	Grumman G-159 Gulfstream I	041	ex EC-494	Freighter	
EC-FIO	Grumman G-159 Gulfstream I	040	ex EC-493	Freighter	

SWIFTAIR

Swift (SWT) (IATA 227)   **Madrid-Barajas (MAD)**

EC-HAH	Boeing 727-223F (FedEx 3)	1199/21084	ex OO-DHV	Virgen del Carmen	Lsd fr BCS
EC-HHU	Boeing 727-277F (FedEx 3)	1768/22644	ex (OO-DLJ)		Lsd fr BCS
EC-HJV	Boeing 727-264F (FedEx 3)	1049/20895	ex N623DH		Lsd fr BCS
EC-HLP	Boeing 727-264F (FedEx 3)	1051/20896	ex N622DH		Lsd fr BCS
EC-IFC	Boeing 727-277F (FedEx 3)	1762/22643	ex OO-DHK	no titles	Lsd fr BCS
EC-IMY	Boeing 727-225 (FedEx 3)	1241/21293	ex N8875Z	pax aircraft	Lsd fr Finova
EC-GBF	Convair 580	458	ex EC-830		Lsd fr BCS
EC-GDY	Convair 580	25	ex EC-943		Lsd fr BCS
EC-GHN	Convair 580	186	ex EC-255		Lsd fr BCS
EC-GKH	Convair 580	135	ex OO-DHD		Lsd fr BCS
EC-GSJ	Convair 580	130	ex OO-HUB		Lsd fr BCS
EC-HJU	Convair 580	147	ex OO-DHF		Lsd fr BCS
EC-HLD	Convair 580	52	ex OO-DHE		Lsd fr BCS
EC-HMR	Convair 580	68	ex OO-DHC		Lsd fr BCS
EC-HMS	Convair 580	459	ex OO-DHL		Lsd fr BCS
EC-HAK	Embraer EMB-120RT Brasilia	120008	ex N212AS		Lsd fr Leasing Catalunya
EC-HCF	Embraer EMB.120RT Brasilia	120007	ex N211AS		Lsd fr Leasing Catalunya
EC-HFK	Embraer EMB.120RT Brasilia	120063	ex N7215U		
EC-HMY	Embraer EMB.120RT Brasilia	120009	ex N214AS		
EC-HTS	Embraer EMB.120RT Brasilia	120168	ex N168CA		Lsd fr Avn Consultants
EC-IMX	Embraer EMB.120RT Brasilia	120158	ex N312FV		

EC-FZB	Swearingen SA.226TC Metro II	TC-221	ex EC-666		Lsd fr BCS
EC-GXE	Swearingen SA.227AC Metro III	AC-694	ex N457AM		
EC-IEV	Cessna 208B Caravan I	208B0936	ex N40753		
EC-IEX	Cessna 208B Caravan I	208B0937	ex N4057D		
EC-IKU	Cessna 208B Caravan 1	208B0769	ex N106VE		Lsd fr ASA Lease
EC-INV	Aerospatiale/Alenia ATR 72-201	274	ex N274AT		
EC-ISX	Aerospatiale/Alenia ATR 42-320	242	ex N242AT		

All freighters; operates freight services for DHL usually in full colours

TADAIR

Tadair (TDC)   Barcelona (BCN)

EC-CDS	Piper PA-31 Turbo Navajo B	31-7300951	ex N7561L	Freighter
EC-CEY	Piper PA-34-200 Seneca	34-7350311	ex N56279	
EC-CGE	Piper PA-34-200 Seneca	34-7350324	ex N56378	Freighter
EC-FPC	Swearingen SA.226TC Metro II	TC-408	ex EC-243	Freighter; stored BCN
EC-HOK	Piper PA-34-200 Seneca	34-7350320	ex F-BUTT	Freighter

TAF HELICOPTERS

Helitaf (HET)   Barcelona (BCN)

EC-DRG	Aerospatiale AS.350B Ecureuil	1597		
EC-ERD	Aerospatiale AS.350B Ecureuil	1530	ex G-JORR	EMS
EC-EVM	Aerospatiale AS.350B2 Ecureuil	2312		
EC-EZP	Aerospatiale AS.350B Ecureuil	2413	ex EC-562	
EC-FOA	Aerospatiale AS.350BA Ecureuil	2626	ex EC-990	
EC-IHX	Aerospatiale AS.350B3 Ecureuil	3587	ex F-WQRN	06 EMS
EC-DSU	MBB Bo105CBS-5	S-623	ex D-HDSS	02 EMS
EC-EVT	MBB BK117A-4	7074	ex D-HBNV	03 EMS
EC-FQO	Bell 205A-1	30011	ex N43162	
EC-FYV	MBB Bo105CBS-5	S-896	ex EC-705	01 EMS
EC-GUH	Aerospatiale AS.355F2 Ecureuil 2	5474	ex N6040U	
EC-GUZ	Aerospatiale AS.355F2 Ecureuil 2	5454	ex N26ET	
EC-HNT	MBB Bo105CBS	S-414	ex D-HDMA	EMS
EC-IFU	Eurocopter EC.135P2	0223		EMS
EC-IKT	MBB Bo105CBS	S-672	ex EC-HPB	EMS
EC-	Bell 412	33050	ex C-GKJT	

EMS flights for Catalunyan Government use the call-sign Bomberos

TOP-FLY

Topfly (TLY)   Barcelona (BCN)

EC-EYV	Piper PA-34-220T Seneca III	34-8233109	ex OE-FYB
EC-GAN	Swearingen SA.226TC Metro II	TC-203	ex EC-701
EC-GDB	Agusta-Bell 206B JetRanger	8095	ex F-GJAU
EC-GXJ	Swearingen SA.226TC Metro II	TC-374	ex OY-AUO
EC-HZM	Piper PA-34-200 Seneca	34-7250169	ex F-GFJE
EC-IRSI	Swearingen SA.227BC Metro III	BC-786B	ex N61AJ

TRAVEL SERVICE ESPANA

Las Palmas-Gran Canaria (LPA)

| EC-ILX | Boeing 737-86N | 514/28618 | ex OK-TVQ | Unimex Group titles | Lsd fr TVS |

Travel Service Espana is a wholly owned subsidiary of Travel Service Airlines

VOLAR AIRLINES

Fun Jet (XO/LTE)   Palma de Mallorca (PMI)
Previously listed as LTE International Airways

EC-ICN	Airbus Industrie A320-214	1717	ex F-WWDC		Lsd fr GECAS
EC-IEP	Airbus Industrie A320-214	1775	ex F-WWDL		Lsd fr GECAS
EC-ILG	Airbus Industrie A321-211	1233	ex G-VKIS		
EC-IMA	Airbus Industrie A321-211	1219	ex G-VATH	all-white	
EC-ISI	Airbus Industrie A320-214	2123	ex F-WWIE		Lsd fr GECAS
EC-HQV	Boeing 757-2G5	36/23118	ex D-AMUA		
EC-HQX	Boeing 757-2G5	116/23651	ex D-AMUC		
EC-HRB	Boeing 757-2G5	51/23119	ex D-AMUB		

Wholly owned subsidiary of Volare Group

ZOREX

Zorex (ORZ)   Madrid-Barajas (MAD)

| EC-GPE | Swearingen SA.226TC Metro II | TC-273 | ex OY-JER |

| EC-HJC | Swearingen SA.226TC Metro II | TC-318 | ex OY-JEO |
| XA-SCS | Swearingen SA.227BC Metro III | BC-786B | ex N3002K |

EI - IRELAND (Eire)

AER ARANN

Aer Arann (RE/REA) (IATA 809)   *Connemara (NNR)*
Renamed Aer Arann 28 May 2003 when Express was dropped from airline name

EI-BYO	Aerospatiale/Alenia ATR 42-310	161	ex OY-CIS	Lsd fr Magellan
EI-CBK	Aerospatiale/Alenia ATR 42-310	199	ex F-WWEM	Lsd fr Magellan
EI-CPT	Aerospatiale/Alenia ATR 42-300	191	ex (SE-KCX)	Lsd fr Magellan
EI-CVR	Aerospatiale/Alenia ATR 42-300	022	ex F-GGLK	Lsd fr Magellan
EI-CVS	Aerospatiale/Alenia ATR 42-300	033	ex F-GIRC	Lsd fr Magellan
EI-REA	Aerospatiale/Alenia ATR 72-201	441	ex F-WQNC	Lsd fr ATR Asset Mgt
EI-REB	Aerospatiale/Alenia ATR 72-201	470	ex F-WQNH	Lsd fr ATR Asset Mgt
EI-RED	Aerospatiale/Alenia ATR 72-201	373	ex F-GJRX	
EI-REE	Aerospatiale/Alenia ATR 72-202	342	ex G-BVTJ	Lsd fr ATR Asset Mgt
EI-AYN	Britten-Norman BN-2A-8 Islander	704	ex G-BBFJ	
EI-BCE	Britten-Norman BN-2A-26 Islander	519	ex G-BDUV	
EI-CUW	Britten-Norman BN-2B-26 Islander	2293	ex G-BWYW	

Aer Arran is the trading name of Galway Aviation Services. Islanders operate as Aer Arann Islands and are based at Galway

AER LINGUS

Shamrock (EI/EIN) (IATA 053)   *Dublin (DUB)*

EI-CPC	Airbus Industrie A321-211	0815	ex D-AVZT	St Fergus/Faergus	Lsd fr ILFC
EI-CPD	Airbus Industrie A321-211	0841	ex D-AVZA	St Davnet/Damhnat	Lsd fr ILFC
EI-CPE	Airbus Industrie A321-211	0926	ex D-AVZQ	St Enda/Eanna	
EI-CPF	Airbus Industrie A321-211	0991	ex D-AVZE	St Ida/Ide	Lsd fr ILFC
EI-CPG	Airbus Industrie A321-211	1023	ex D-AVZR	St Aidan/Aodhan	
EI-CPH	Airbus Industrie A321-211	1094	ex F-WWDD	St Dervilla/Dearbhile	
EI-CVA	Airbus Industrie A320-214	1242	ex F-WWIT	St Schira/Scire	
EI-CVB	Airbus Industrie A320-214	1394	ex F-WWIV	St Mobhi	
EI-CVC	Airbus Industrie A320-214	1443	ex F-WWBS	St Kealin/Caolfhionn	
EI-CVD	Airbus Industrie A320-214	1467	ex F-WWDG	St Kevin/Caoimhin	
EI-CZV	Airbus Industrie A320-214	0553	ex HB-IJD	St Cormac/Cormac	Lsd to Jun04
EI-CZW	Airbus Industrie A320-214	0559	ex HB-IJE	St Fiacra/Fiachra	Lsd to Aug04
EI-DEA	Airbus Industrie A320-214	2191	ex F-WWBX	on order May04	Lsd fr ILFC
EI-DEB	Airbus Industrie A320-214	2206	ex F-WW	on order May04	Lsd fr ILFC
EI-DEC	Airbus Industrie A320-214	2217	ex F-WW	on order Jun04	Lsd fr ILFC
EI-DEE	Airbus Industrie A320-214	2250	ex F-WW	on order Aug04	
EI-DEF	Airbus Industrie A320-214	2256	ex F-WW	on order Sep04	
EI-DEG	Airbus Industrie A320-214	2284	ex F-WW	on order Oct04	

A further ten Airbus Industrie A320-214s are on order for future delivery (registered EI-DEH to EI-DES)

EI-CRK*	Airbus Industrie A330-301	070	ex F-WWKV	St Patrick/Padraig	
EI-DAA	Airbus Industrie A330-202	397	ex F-WWKK	St Keeva/Caoimhe	
EI-DUB*	Airbus Industrie A330-301	055	ex F-WWKP	St Brigid/Brighid	
EI-EWR*	Airbus Industrie A330-202	330	ex F-WWKV	Laurence O'Toole/Lorcan O'Tuathail	
EI-JFK*	Airbus Industrie A330-301	086	ex F-WWKH	St Colmcille	
EI-LAX	Airbus Industrie A330-202	269	ex F-WWKV	St Mella	
EI-ORD	Airbus Industrie A330-301	059	ex F-GMDD	St Maeve/Maedh	

*Leased from ILFC

EI-BXD^	Boeing 737-448	1867/24866		St Colman	
EI-BXI	Boeing 737-448	2036/25052		St Finnian	
EI-BXK^	Boeing 737-448	2269/25736		St Caimin	
EI-CDA	Boeing 737-548	1939/24878	ex YR-BGZ	St Columba/Colum	
EI-CDB^	Boeing 737-548	1970/24919	ex EI-BXF	St Albert/Ailbhe	
EI-CDC^	Boeing 737-548	1975/24968	ex EI-BXG	St Munchin/Maincin	
EI-CDD*	Boeing 737-548	1989/24989	ex EI-BXH	St Macartan/Macarthaln	
EI-CDE	Boeing 737-548	2050/25115	ex PT-SLM	St Jarlath/Iarflaith	
EI-CDF	Boeing 737-548	2232/25737		St Cronan	
EI-CDG	Boeing 737-548	2261/25738		St Moling	
EI-CDH	Boeing 737-548	2271/25739		St Ronan	

*Leased from ILFC   ^aerlingus.com titles
To sell seven Boeing 737s to ILFC and lease back through 2004, other four to be sold
Four Airbus Industrie A319-112s are on order for future delivery
Owns 20% of Futura
Member of oneworld alliance

AER TURAS TEORANTA entered receivership 02 July 2003

AIR CONTRACTORS (IRELAND)

Contract (AG/ABR) (IATA912)   *Dublin (DUB)*

EI-HCI	Boeing 727-223F (FedEx 3)	705/20183	ex N6830	no titles	Lsd fr TTC Hunt
EI-JIV	Lockheed L-382G Hercules	4673	ex ZS-JIV		Lsd fr SFR
EI-OZA	Airbus Industrie A300B4-103F	148	ex F-GOZA		Op for FPO
EI-OZB	Airbus Industrie A300B4-103F	184	ex F-GOZB		
EI-OZC	Airbus Industrie A300B4-103F	189	ex F-GOZC		Op for FPO
EI-SLE	Aerospatiale/Alenia ATR 42-310F	024	ex F-WQNE		
EI-SLF	Aerospatiale/Alenia ATR 72-202	210	ex OY-RUA		Lsd fr ATR Asset Mgt

Other Hercules are leased from Safair as required

AVIAJET

Dublin (DUB)

SE-RBE	McDonnell-Douglas MD-82	1089/49152	ex OH-LMP	Lsd fr/op by NDC
SE-RDL	McDonnell-Douglas MD-83	1740/53014	ex TF-MDC	Lsd fr/op by NDC

Aviajet is an Irish-based tour operator

CHC IRELAND

Dublin (DUB)

EI-CNL	Sikorsky S-61N	61746	ex ZS-RBU	IMES Rescue	Lsd fr OLOG
EI-CZN	Sikorsky S-61N	61740	ex G-CBWC		Lsd fr SHZ
EI-MES	Sikorsky S-61N	61776	ex G-BXAE	IMES Rescue	Lsd fr OLOG
EI-RCG	Sikorsky S-61N	61807	ex G-87-1	IMES Rescue	Lsd fr SHZ
EI-SAR	Sikorsky S-61N	61143	ex G-AYOM	IMES Rescue	Lsd fr OLOG
EI-MIP	Aerospatiale SA.365N2 Dauphin	6119	ex G-BLEY		

Wholly owned subsidiary of CHC Helicopter Corp. IMES Rescue is Irish Marine Emergency Service

CITYJET

City-Ireland (WX/BCY) (IATA 689)   *Dublin (DUB)*

EI-CMS	British Aerospace 146 Srs.200	E2044	ex N184US	
EI-CMY	British Aerospace 146 Srs.200	E2039	ex N177US	
EI-CNB	British Aerospace 146 Srs.200	E2046	ex N187US	
EI-CNQ	British Aerospace 146 Srs.200	E2031	ex G-OWLD	
EI-CSK	British Aerospace 146 Srs.200	E2062	ex N810AS	Lsd fr BAES
EI-CSL	British Aerospace 146 Srs.200	E2074	ex N812AS	Lsd fr BAES
EI-CWA	British Aerospace 146 Srs.200	E2058	ex G-ECAL	Lsd fr BAES
EI-CWB	British Aerospace 146 Srs.200	E2051	ex SE-DRE	Lsd fr BAES
EI-CWC	British Aerospace 146 Srs.200	E2053	ex SE-DRC	Lsd fr BAES
EI-CWD	British Aerospace 146 Srs.200	E2108	ex SE-DRK	Lsd fr BAES
EI-CZO	British Aerospace 146 Srs.200	E2024	ex G-FLTB	Lsd fr BAES
EI-DDE	British Aerospace 146 Srs.200	E2060	ex G-CCJC	
EI-DDF	British Aerospace 146 Srs.200	E2047	ex G-OZRH	on order May04
EI-PAT	British Aerospace 146 Srs.200	E2030	ex G-ZAPL	Lsd fr AWC
G-DEBE	British Aerospace 146 Srs.200	E2022	ex N163US	Lsd fr FLT until May04

Wholly owned by Air France and operated in their colours

EUJET

Euro Airways (EUY)   *Shannon (SNN)*

EI-DBE	Fokker 100	11329	ex G-BYDN	Lsd fr debis
EI-DBR	Fokker 100	11323	ex G-BYDO	Lsd fr debis

EUJet is the trading name of EU-JetOps

FRESHAER AIRLINES Planned to commence operations October 2003 with Boeing 757-200s but later abandoned

IRISH CARGO AIRLINES entered receivership 02 July 2003, one aircraft unserviceable and the other stored

IRISH HELICOPTERS

Dublin/Cork (DUB/ORK)

EI-BKT	Agusta-Bell 206B Jet Ranger III	8562	ex D-HAFD
EI-BLD	MBB Bo105DB	S-381	ex D-HDLQ
EI-CUG	Bell 206B JetRanger III	4177	ex N248BC
EI-HER	Bell 206B JetRanger		
EI-LIT	MBB Bo105CBS	S-434	ex A6-DBH

A wholly owned subsidiary of Bristow Helicopters

JETMAGIC

Jetmagic (GX/JMG)   *Cork (ORK)*

EI-GXA	*Embraer EMB.145LU*	*145588*	*ex HB-JAX*	*Lsd fr SWR*
EI-GXB	*Embraer EMB.145LU*	*145601*	*ex HB-JAY*	*Lsd fr SWR*
EI-LCY	*Embraer EMB-135ER*	*145376*	*ex PP-SQA* *on order*	*Lsd fr Embraer*
EI-ORK	*Embraer EMB-135ER*	*145431*	*ex PP-SUC*	*Lsd fr LCY Flight*

First service 26 April 2003 using Swiss-registered aircraft due to delays in obtaining its own AOC; ceased operations on 28 January 2004

RYANAIR

Ryanair (FR/RYR) (IATA)   *Dublin (DUB)*

EI-CJC	Boeing 737-204 (Nordam 3)	867/22640	ex G-BJCV	Hertz c/s	
EI-CJD	Boeing 737-204 (Nordam 3)	946/22966	ex G-BKHE	Eircell c/s	
EI-CJE	Boeing 737-204 (Nordam 3)	863/22639	ex G-BJCU	Jaguar c/s	
EI-CJF	Boeing 737-204 (Nordam 3)	953/22967	ex G-BTZF		
EI-CJG	Boeing 737-204 (Nordam 3)	629/22058	ex G-BGYK		
EI-CJI	Boeing 737-2E7 (Nordam 3)	917/22875	ex G-BMDF	stored SEN	
EI-CKP	Boeing 737-2K2 (Nordam 3)	668/22296	ex PH-TVS	stored DUB	
EI-CKQ	Boeing 737-2K2 (Nordam 3)	888/22906	ex PH-TVU	stored PIK	
EI-CKR	Boeing 737-2K2 (Nordam 3)	647/22025	ex PH-TVR	stored PIK	
EI-CKS	Boeing 737-2T5 (Nordam 3)	636/22023	ex PH-TVX	stored PIK	
EI-CNT	Boeing 737-230 (Nordam 3)	694/22115	ex D-ABFC	Vodafone c/s	
EI-CNV	Boeing 737-230 (Nordam 3)	752/22128	ex D-ABFX		
EI-CNW	Boeing 737-230 (Nordam 3)	772/22133	ex D-ABHC		
EI-CNX	Boeing 737-230 (Nordam 3)	745/22127	ex D-ABFW		
EI-CNY	Boeing 737-230 (Nordam 3)	649/22113	ex D-ABFB	Kilkenny Beer c/s	
EI-CNZ	Boeing 737-230 (Nordam 3)	735/22126	ex D-ABFU		
EI-COA	Boeing 737-230 (Nordam 3)	848/22637	ex CS-TES		Lsd fr debis
EI-COB	Boeing 737-230 (Nordam 3)	727/22124	ex D-ABFR		
EI-CON	Boeing 737-2T5 (Nordam 3)	730/22396	ex PK-RIW		
EI-COX	Boeing 737-230 (Nordam 3)	726/22123	ex D-ABFP		
G-BZZE	Boeing 737-3Q8	2680/26310	ex N14381		Lsd fr ILFC
G-BZZF	Boeing 737-3Q8	2681/26311	ex N19382		Lsd fr Cirrus
G-BZZG	Boeing 737-3Q8	2693/26312	ex N14383		Lsd fr ILFC
G-BZZH	Boeing 737-3Q8	2704/26313	ex N14384		Lsd fr ILFC
G-BZZI	Boeing 737-3Q8	2707/26314	ex N73385		Lsd fr ILFC
G-BZZJ	Boeing 737-3Q8	2764/26321	ex N17386		Lsd fr Cirrus

Operated by 'Buzz Stansted' / 'Buzzaway' using FR callsigns and Ryanair titles

EI-CSA	Boeing 737-8AS	210/29916	ex N5573L		
EI-CSB	Boeing 737-8AS	298/29917			
EI-CSC	Boeing 737-8AS	307/29918			
EI-CSD	Boeing 737-8AS	341/29919			
EI-CSE	Boeing 737-8AS	362/29920			
EI-CSF	Boeing 737-8AS	560/29921			
EI-CSG	Boeing 737-8AS	571/29922			
EI-CSH	Boeing 737-8AS	576/29923	ex N1787B		
EI-CSI	Boeing 737-8AS	578/29924			
EI-CSJ	Boeing 737-8AS	588/29925			
EI-CSM	Boeing 737-8AS	722/29926			
EI-CSN	Boeing 737-8AS	727/29927			
EI-CSO	Boeing 737-8AS	735/29928	ex N1784B		
EI-CSP	Boeing 737-8AS	753/29929			
EI-CSQ	Boeing 737-8AS	757/29930			
EI-CSR	Boeing 737-8AS	1020/29931			
EI-CSS	Boeing 737-8AS	1030/29932			
EI-CST	Boeing 737-8AS	1038/29933			
EI-CSV	Boeing 737-8AS	1050/29934		City of Nyköping	
EI-CSW	Boeing 737-8AS	1061/29935			Lsd fr RL Leasing IV
EI-CSX	Boeing 737-8AS	1140/32778			
EI-CSY	Boeing 737-8AS	1167/32779			
EI-CSZ	Boeing 737-8AS	1178/32780			
EI-CTA	Boeing 737-8AS	1236/29936			
EI-CTB	Boeing 737-8AS	1238/29937			
EI-DAC	Boeing 737-8AS	1240/29938			
EI-DAD	Boeing 737-8AS	1249/33544			
EI-DAE	Boeing 737-8AS	1252/33545			
EI-DAF	Boeing 737-8AS	1262/29939			
EI-DAG	Boeing 737-8AS	1265/29940			
EI-DAH	Boeing 737-8AS	1269/33546			
EI-DAI	Boeing 737-8AS	1271/33547			
EI-DAJ	Boeing 737-8AS	1274/33548			
EI-DAK	Boeing 737-8AS	1310/33717			
EI-DAL	Boeing 737-8AS	1311/33718			
EI-DAM	Boeing 737-8AS	1312/33719			
EI-DAN	Boeing 737-8AS	1361/33549			

EI-DAO	Boeing 737-8AS	1366/33550	ex N1800B	Pride of Scotland titles
EI-DAP	Boeing 737-8AS	1368/33551	ex N6066U	
EI-DAR	Boeing 737-8AS	1371/33552	ex EI-DAQ	
EI-DAS	Boeing 737-8AS	1372/33553	ex EI-DAR	
EI-DAT	Boeing 737-8AS	1418/33554		
EI-DAV	Boeing 737-8AS	1426/33555		
EI-DAW	Boeing 737-8AS	1428/33556		
EI-DAX	Boeing 737-8AS	1438/33557		
EI-DAY	Boeing 737-8AS	1441/33558		
EI-DAZ	Boeing 737-8AS	1443/33559		
EI-DCB	Boeing 737-8AS	1447/33560		
EI-DCC	Boeing 737-8AS	1463/33561		on order 04
EI-DCD	Boeing 737-8AS	1466/33562		on order 04
EI-DCE	Boeing 737-8AS	33563		on order 04
EI-DCF	Boeing 737-8AS	33804		on order 04
EI-DCG	Boeing 737-8AS	33806		on order 04
EI-	Boeing 737-8AS			on order 04
EI-	Boeing 737-8AS			on order 04
EI-	Boeing 737-8AS			on order 04
EI-	Boeing 737-8AS			on order 04
EI-	Boeing 737-8AS			on order 04
EI-	Boeing 737-8AS			on order 04
EI-	Boeing 737-8AS			on order 04
EI-	Boeing 737-8AS			on order 04
EI-	Boeing 737-8AS			on order 04
EI-	Boeing 737-8AS			on order 04
G-XLAF	Boeing 737-86N	1083/29883		Lsd fr XLA
G-XLAG	Boeing 737-86N	1121/33003		Lsd fr XLA

A total of 155 Boeing 737-8AS's are on order for delivery up to 2009. 10 to be sold to RBS Aviation and leased back

SKYNET AIRLINES

Bluejet(SI/SIH) (IATA 597)   *Dublin (DUB)*

| EI-CXK | Boeing 737-4S3 | 2255/25596 | ex G-OGBA | Lsd fr Sunrock |
| EI-CZK | Boeing 737-4Y0 | 1781/24519 | ex N519AP | |

EK - ARMENIA (Republic of Armenia)

AIR ARMENIA

(QN/ARR)   *Yerevan-Zvartnots (EVN)*

| EK-12001 | Antonov An-12TB | 401801 | ex RA-11345 | |

AIRCOMPANY VETERAN current status uncertain, code no longer current

ARMAVIA

Armavia (U8/RNV) (IATA669)   *Yerevan-Zvartnots (EVN)*

EK-32007	Airbus Industrie A320-211	0726	ex P4-VNF		Lsd fr SIB
EK-32008	Airbus Industrie A320-211	0229	ex N229AN		Lsd fr WTCo
EK-32009	Airbus Industrie A320-211	0547	ex F-WQSB	on order	
EK-32010	Airbus Industrie A320-211	0622	ex F-WQSG		
EK-42001	Aerospatiale/Alenia ATR 42-300	178	ex F-OHRP		Lsd fr WTCo
EK-65575	Tupolev Tu-134A	62350	ex RA-65575		Lsd fr CMK

Partially owned by Sibir Airlines

ARMENIAN AIRLINES ceased operations 15 April 2003 and filed for bankruptcy

ARMENIAN INTERNATIONAL AIRWAYS

(MV/RML) (IATA904)   *Yerevan-Erebuni*

| EK-32001 | Airbus Industrie A320-212 | 397 | ex N320AW | Lsd fr AWAS |

ATLANTIS EUROPEAN AIRWAYS

(LUR)   *Yerevan-Erebuni*

Fleet details unknown at time of printing

AVIASERVICE current status uncertain, code now reallocated

AVIA-URARTU

Urartu Air (URT)   *Yerevan-Erebuni*

EK-13399	Antonov An-26	2606	ex RA-13399	Lsd to TLR
EK-46630	Antonov An-24RV	37308809	ex UR-46630	
EK-98116	Antonov An-24T	7910403		Lsd to TLR

DVIN-AVIA ceased operations

JUPITER AVIA ceased operations

O.I.L. AIRWAYS

Yerevan-Erebuni

| EK-87662 | Yakovlev Yak-40 | 9240625 | ex RA-87662 | Op for Grand Holdings |

PHOENIX AVIA current status uncertain, sole aircraft disposed of

SOUTH AIRLINES

Sharjah (SHJ)

EK-12222	Antonov An-12
EK-12555	Antonov An-12
EK-12777	Antonov An-12

YEREVAN AVIA

Yerevan-Avia (ERV)   *Yerevan-Zvartnots (EVN)*

| EK-86724 | Ilyushin Il-76M | 073410284 | ex EP-TPZ |
| EK-86817 | Ilyushin Il-76M | 063407191 | ex EP-TPO |

EL - LIBERIA (Republic of Liberia)

Register has been suspended due to illegal registrations and new national registration marks A8 allocated.

DUCOR WORLD AIRWAYS now correctly listed under Equatorial Guinea (3C-)

EAST WEST current status uncertain, presumed to have been grounded

FLYING DOLPHIN AIRLINES now listed as Dolphin Aviation (A6-)

SANTA CRUZ IMPERIAL AIRLINES now listed under Dolphin Aviation (A6-)

TRANSWAY AIR INTERNATIONAL current status uncertain, believed to have ceased operations

WEST AFRICA AIR SERVICE current status unknown, believed to have been grounded

EP - IRAN (Islamic Republic of Iran)

ARAM AIRLINE Status uncertain as sole aircraft sold in Laos and later crashed

ARIA AIR

Aria (IRX)   *Lar/Bandar Abbas (-/BND)*

| EP-EAC | Tupolev Tu-154M | 89A-814 | ex B-2619 | is not confirmed |
| EP-EAD | Tupolev Tu-154M | 92A-930 | ex RA-85747 | |

ATLAS AIR ceased operations

CASPIAN AIRLINES

Caspian (CPN)   *Rasht (RAS)*

EP-CPE	Yakovlev Yak-42D			
EP-CPG	Tupolev Tu-154M	87A-748	ex YA-TAR	Lsd fr UDN
EP-CPN	Tupolev Tu-154M	91A-898	ex EP-JAZ	
EP-CPO	Tupolev Tu-154M	91A-899	ex EP-ARG	
EP-CPR	Yakovlev Yak-42D	4520421219029	ex UR-42410	

Leases Tu-154Ms to Mahan Air as required

CHABAHAR AIRLINE ceased operations and planned to restart but no recorded sightings

HELICOPTER SERVICES

Teheran

EP-HBJ	Bell 212	30504		
EP-HCH	Bell 212	30894	ex C-FRWF	Lsd fr CHC Helicopters
EP-HTN	Bell 212	30885	ex N5009K	
EP-HUA	Bell 212	31176	ex HB-XPO	
EP-HUE	Bell 212	30911	ex A7-HAM	Lsd fr Gulf H/c
EP-HCS	Sikorsky S-76A	760297	ex C-GKWS	
EP-HDS	Aerospatiale AS.365N2 Dauphin 2	6540	ex F-GIZU	
EP-HEB	Aerospatiale AS.350B Ecureuil	3050	ex F-WQDA	
EP-HGC	Aerospatiale AS.330G Puma	1287		
EP-HTQ	Bell 205A-1	30189	ex N90039	
EP-HUC	Bell 412SP	33117	ex A7-HBA	Lsd fr Gulf H/c
EP-HUD	Bell 412SP	33116	ex A7-HAU	Lsd fr Gulf H/c
EP-HUF	Bell 412SP	36016	ex A7-HAR	Lsd fr Gulf H/c

IRAN AIR – THE AIRLINE OF THE ISLAMIC REPUBLIC OF IRAN

Iranair (IR/IRA) (IATA 096)　　　　　　　*Teheran-Mehrabad (THR)*

EP-IBA	Airbus Industrie A300B4-605R	723	ex F-WWAL	
EP-IBB	Airbus Industrie A300B4-605R	727	ex F-WWAZ	
EP-IBS	Airbus Industrie A300B2-203	080	ex F-WZEO	
EP-IBT	Airbus Industrie A300B2-203	185	ex F-WZMB	
EP-IBV	Airbus Industrie A300B2-203	187	ex F-WZMD	
EP-IBZ	Airbus Industrie A300B2-203	226	ex F-WZME	
EP-IBK	Airbus Industrie A310-304	671	ex SU-MWB	
EP-IBL	Airbus Industrie A310-304	436	ex A6-EKB	
EP-IBM	Airbus Industrie A310-203	338	ex TC-JCL	
EP-IBN	Airbus Industrie A310-203	375	ex TC-JCM	
EP-IBO	Airbus Industrie A310-203	379	ex TC-JCN	
EP-IBP	Airbus Industrie A310-203	370	ex TC-JCR	
EP-IBQ	Airbus Industrie A310-203	389	ex TC-JCS	
EP-IBX	Airbus Industrie A310-203	390	ex TC-JCU	
EP-IRB	Boeing 727-86	323/19172		Abadan; stored THR
EP-IRC	Boeing 727-86	505/19816		Ramsar
EP-IRP	Boeing 727-286	1048/20945		
EP-IRR	Boeing 727-286	1052/20946		
EP-IRS	Boeing 727-286	1070/20947		
EP-IRT	Boeing 727-286	1114/21078		
EP-IDA	Fokker 100	11292	ex PH-LMG	
EP-IDB	Fokker 100	11299	ex PH-LMO	PH-CXS reserved
EP-IDD	Fokker 100	11294	ex PH-LMM	
EP-IDF	Fokker 100	11298	ex PH-LMN	
EP-IDG	Fokker 100	11302	ex PH-LMW	
EP-IAA	Boeing 747SP-86	275/20998		Kurdistan
EP-IAB	Boeing 747SP-86	278/20999		Khorasan
EP-IAC	Boeing 747SP-86	307/21093		Fars
EP-IAD	Boeing 747SP-86	371/21758	ex N1800B	Khorasan
EP-IAG	Boeing 747-286M	291/21217		Azarabadegan
EP-IAH	Boeing 747-286M	300/21218		Khuzestan
EP-IAM	Boeing 747-186B	381/21759	ex N5573P	
EP-ICC	Boeing 747-2J9F	343/21514	ex 5-8116	
EP-IRF	Boeing 737-286C	283/20498		Bisotun
EP-IRH	Boeing 737-286C	286/20500		Rey
EP-IRI	Boeing 737-286C	321/20740		Chelsotun
TS-INA	Airbus Industrie A320-214	1121	ex F-WWBT	Dora　Lsd fr LBT
TS-INC	Airbus Industrie A320-214	1744	ex F-WWBS	Youssef　Lsd fr LBT

IRANAIR TOURS

(B9/IRB)　　　　　　　*Teheran-Mehrabad/Mashad (THR/MHD)*

EP-MAT	Tupolev Tu-154M	92A-928	ex RA-85745	Lsd fr OMS
EP-MBK	Tupolev Tu-154M	89A-802	ex LZ-LTD	
EP-MBL	Tupolev Tu-154M	89A-799	ex 11+01	Lsd fr VARZ 400
EP-MBM	Tupolev Tu-154M	92A-931	ex RA-85749	Lsd fr NKZ
EP-MBN	Tupolev Tu-154M	92A-940	ex RA-85758	Lsd fr NKZ
EP-MBP	Tupolev Tu-154M	89A-800	ex LZ-BTY	Lsd fr VARZ 400
EP-MBU	Tupolev Tu-154M	90A-855	ex RA-85085	
EP-MBV	Tupolev Tu-154M	91A-877	ex RA-85702	
EP-MBZ	Tupolev Tu-154M	91A-902	ex RA-85720	

Joint venture between Iran Air and Tajik Air

IRAN ASEMAN AIRLINES
(EP/IRC) (IATA 815)   Teheran-Mehrabad (THR)

EP-ATA	Aerospatiale/Alenia ATR 72-212	334	ex F-WWLQ	
EP-ATH	Aerospatiale/Alenia ATR 72-212	339	ex F-WWLU	
EP-ATS	Aerospatiale/Alenia ATR 72-212	391	ex F-WWED	
EP-ATZ	Aerospatiale/Alenia ATR 72-212	398	ex F-WWEK	
F-GKOA	Aerospatiale/Alenia ATR 72-202	201		Lsd fr ATR Asset Mgt
F-OIRA	Aerospatiale/Alenia ATR 72-212A	697	ex F-WWET	Lsd fr Zahra Ltd
F-OIRB	Aerospatiale/Alenia ATR 72-212A	573	ex F-WWEK	Lsd fr Zahra Ltd
EP-ASE	Fokker F.28 Fellowship 4000	11144	ex F-GDUZ	
EP-PAT	Fokker F.28 Fellowship 4000	11164	ex PH-ZCA	
EP-PAU	Fokker F.28 Fellowship 4000	11166	ex PH-ZCB	
EP-PAX	Fokker F.28 Fellowship 1000C	11102	ex F-GEXX	
EP-PAZ	Fokker F.28 Fellowship 1000	11104	ex F-GIAK	VIP, op for Govt
EP-PBJ	Fokker F.28 Fellowship 4000	11135	ex F-GDFD	
EP-ASG	Fokker 100	11438	ex HL7210	
EP-ASH	Fokker 100	11439	ex HL7211	
EP-ASI	Fokker 100	11378	ex HL7206	
EP-ASJ	Fokker 100	11388	ex HL7208	
EP-ASK	Fokker 100	11519	ex HL7215	
EP-ASL	Fokker 100	11432	ex HL7209	
EP-ASA	Boeing 727-228	1594/22081	ex LX-IRA	
EP-ASB	Boeing 727-228	1603/22082	ex LX-IRB	
EP-ASC	Boeing 727-228	1638/22084	ex LX-IRC	
EP-ASD	Boeing 727-228	1665/22085	ex LX-IRD	

KISH AIR
Kishair (Y9/IRK)   Teheran-Mehrabad (THR)

EP-LBR	Tupolev Tu-154M	90A-938	ex OK-VCG	Lsd fr VARZ 400
EP-LBS	Tupolev Tu-154M	91A-901	ex UN-85719	Lsd fr VARZ 400
EP-LBV	Fokker 50	20158	ex VP-CSE	
EP-LCA	Fokker 50	20273	ex EC-GKU	
EP-LCB	Fokker 50	20274	ex EC-GKV	
EP-LCC	Fokker 50	20275	ex EC-GKX	Lsd fr PLM Tpt
EP-LCD	Tupolev Tu-154M	89A-825	ex RA-85667	Lsd fr MNL

To merge with Mahan Air

MAHAN AIR
Mahan Air (W5/IRM) (IATA 537)   Kerman (KER)

EP-MHH	Airbus Industrie A310-304ER	586	ex TC-JDD	
EP-MHI	Airbus Industrie A310-304ER	537	ex TC-JDC	
EP-	Airbus Industrie A310-304	476	ex TC-JCV	on order
EP-	Airbus Industrie A310-304	478	ex TC-JCY	on order
EP-	Airbus Industrie A310-304	480	ex TC-JCZ	on order
EP-	Airbus Industrie A310-304	496	ex TC-JDA	on order
EP-	Airbus Industrie A310-304	497	ex TC-JDB	on order
EP-MHE	Airbus Industrie A300B4-103	035	ex S7-AAY	
EP-MHF	Airbus Industrie A300B4-103	055	ex S7-AAZ	
EP-MHG	Airbus Industrie A300B4-203	204	ex AP-BFL	
EP-MHS	Tupolev Tu-154M	89A-821	ex RA-85830	Lsd fr OMS
EP-MHU	Yakovlev Yak-40			
EP-MHZ	Tupolev Tu-154M	91A-890	ex RA-85714	Lsd fr OMS
RA-85754	Tupolev Tu-154M	92A-936	ex EP-MHX	Lsd fr ENK

Also lease Tupolev Tu-154Ms from Caspian Airlines as required; to merge with Kish Air. Has option on all Turkish Airlines Airbus Industrie A310s

NAFT AIR LINES
NAFT (IRG)   Ahwaz (AWZ)

EP-GAS	Fokker 50	20224	ex PH-JXA	
EP-IOP	de Havilland DHC-6 Twin Otter 300	577		
EP-IOS	Fokker F.27 Friendship 300	10151	ex PH-IOS	
EP-OIL	Fokker 50	20222	ex PH-LNZ	

(Operates for the National Iranian Oil Company)

PAYAM INTERNATIONAL AIR
Payamair (8P/IRP)   Karaj-Payam

EP-TPH	Embraer EMB.110P1A Bandeirante	110453	ex EP-TPM	Tehran
EP-TPI	Embraer EMB.110P1 Bandeirante	110438	ex EP-TPA	Kerrian

EP-TPJ	Embraer EMB.110P1 Bandeirante	110442	ex EP-TPT	Kashan
EP-TPK	Embraer EMB.110P1 Bandeirante	110386	ex EP-TPG	Esfahan
EP-TPL	Embraer EMB.110P1 Bandeirante	110423	ex EP-TPL	Semnan

QESHM AIR
Faraz Air (IRQ)   *Teheran-Mehrabad (THR)*

EP-TQG	Yakovlev Yak-40	9240625	ex RA-87662
EP-TQI	Ilyushin Il-76TD	1013409321	ex EP-MAH
EP-TQJ	Ilyushin Il-76TD	1013409297	ex EP-JAY

SAFIRAN AIRLINES
Safiran (SFN)   *Teheran-Mehrabad (THR)*

Operates cargo flights with Ilyushin Il-76s leased from other operators as and when required

SAHA AIRLINE
Saha (IRZ)   *Teheran-Mehrabad (THR)*

EP-IRK	Boeing 707-321C	541/19267	ex N445PA	
EP-IRL	Boeing 707-386C	832/20287		
EP-IRM	Boeing 707-386C	839/20288		
EP-IRN	Boeing 707-386C	866/20741	ex N1785B	
EP-SHE	Boeing 707-3J9C	915/21127	ex 5-8311	
EP-SHG	Boeing 707-3J9C	876/20830	ex 5-8301	also '301'
EP-SHK	Boeing 707-3J9C	917/21128	ex 5-8312	
EP-SHP	Boeing 707-3J9C	908/21123	ex 5-8307	
EP-SHU	Boeing 707-3J9C	914/21126	ex 5-8310	
EP-SHV	Boeing 707-3J9C	912/21125	ex	ID not confirmed
EP-SHA	Boeing 747-2J9F	340/21507	ex 5-8115	
EP-SHB	Boeing 747-2J9F	315/21486	ex 5-8113	
EP-SHD	Boeing 747-131F	85/20081	ex 5-8105	
EP-SHH	Boeing 747-2J9F	319/21487	ex 5-8114	
EP-SHL	Fokker F.27Friendship 600	10474	ex 5-8801	
EP-SHM	Fokker F.27Friendship 600	10475	ex 5-8802	
EP-SHN	Fokker F.27 Friendship 400M	10491	ex 5-8811	

Operates IIAF aircraft mainly on freight charters

TAFTAN AIR

| EP-TFN | Fokker 50 | 20302 | ex PH-JCE |
| EP-TFT | Fokker 50 | 20298 | ex PH-MXR |

TEHERAN AIRWAYS current status uncertain, code no longer current

ER - MOLDOVA (Republic of Moldova)

AERIANTUR-M AIRLINES
Aerem (MBV)   *Kishinev-Chisinau (KIV)*

| ER-26068 | Antonov An-26B | 11308 | ex CCCP-26068 |

AEROCOM
(MCC)   *Kishinev-Chisinau (KIV)*

ER-AFB	Antonov An-24RV	87310810B	ex UK.98823	
ER-AWC	Antonov An-24RV	27307504	ex RA-46846	
ER-AWD	Antonov An-24RV	1117306907	ex RA-47805	Getra titles
ER-AWR	Antonov An-24RV	37308605	ex LZ-MNE	
ER-AZG	Antonov An-24RV	57310105	ex YR-ARA	
ER-AZH	Antonov An-24RV	57310405	ex YR-ARB	
ER-AFE	Antonov An-26	17310905	ex RA-26050	
ER-AFH	Antonov An-26	67303901	ex UR-26505	no titles
ER-AFQ	Antonov An-26B	27312503	ex UR-26124	for sale
ER-AWN	Antonov An-26B	87307408	ex RA-46574	
ER-AWV	Antonov An-26			
ER-ACI	Antonov An-12BP	6343707	ex UR-PWH	July Morning
ER-AXE	Antonov An-12BK	7345201		Lsd to Pacific Air Express
ER-AZF	Antonov An-26	07309510	ex UR-KRB	
ER-IBE	Ilyushin Il-76TD	0043454615	ex CU-T1419	no titles
ER-IBV	Ilyushin Il-76T	0033423699	ex RA-76521	

AIR BRIDGE GROUP

ER-AXA	Antonov An-12	01347907	ex RA-11112

AIRLINE TRANSPORT
Aerotitan (RIN))   *Kishinev-Chisinau (KIV)*

ER-AFU	Antonov An-26B	12603	ex RA-26125
ER-IBB	Ilyushin Il-76TD	0063471147	ex UR-76703

AIR MOLDOVA
Air Moldova (9U/MLD)   *Kishinev-Chisinau (KIV)*

ER-46417	Antonov An-24B	87304102	ex RA-46417	stored KIV
ER-46508	Antonov An-24RV	37308404	ex CCCP-46508	
ER-46599	Antonov An-24B	97305109	ex CCCP-46599	
ER-46685	Antonov An-24RV	47309710	ex CCCP-46685	
ER-47698	Antonov An-24RV	27307606	ex CCCP-47698	
ER-65036	Tupolev Tu-134A-3	48700	ex CCCP-65036	
ER-65050	Tupolev Tu-134A-3	49756	ex CCCP-65050	
ER-65051	Tupolev Tu-134A-3	49758	ex CCCP-65051	
ER-65094	Tupolev Tu-134A-3	60255	ex CCCP-65094	Op for Govt
ER-65707	Tupolev Tu-134A-3	63435	ex CCCP-65707	
ER-65791	Tupolev Tu-134A-3	63110	ex CCCP-65791	
ER-	Airbus Industrie A320-211		ex F-W	on order 04
ER-EMA	Embraer EMB.120RT Brasilia	120223	ex N246CA	Lsd fr A/c Consultants
ER-JGD	Yakovlev Yak-40	9421334	ex RA-88307	
ER-YCA	Yakovlev Yak-42D	4520424306017	ex RA-42435	
ER-YCB	Yakovlev Yak-42D	4520424304017	ex RA-42422	
ER-26046	Antonov An-26B	10807	ex CCCP-26046	
ER-26068	Antonov An-26B	11308	ex CCCP-26068	

AIR SERVICE INTERNATIONAL
Sharjah (SHJ)

ER-TAI	Tupolev Tu-154M	82A-546	ex UR-85546	stored SHJ
ER-AZP	Antonov An-24RV	17307002	ex RA-47810	

AIRWEST current status uncertain, believed to have ceased operations

ALIT AIRLINES current status uncertain, believed to have ceased operations

CENTRAL AIRWAYS

ER-AFL	Antonov An-26B	11705	ex RA-26082	all-white

JETLINE INTERNATIONAL
Moldjet (MJL)   *Kishinev-Chisinau (KIV)*

ER-IBF	Ilyushin Il-76T	073410390	ex HA-TCI

MOLDAVIAN AIRLINES
Moldavian (2M/MDV)   *Kishinev-Chisinau (KIV))*

ER-SBA	SAAB 2000	038	ex HB-IZV	
ER-SFA	SAAB 2000	056	ex HB-IYA	
ER-SGB	SAAB SF.340B	182	ex HB-AKF	Lsd fr CRX
ER-SGC	SAAB SF.340B	160	ex HB-AKA	Lsd fr CRX

MTA – MOLDTRANSAVIA current status uncertain, believed to have ceased operations

PECOTEX

ER-ICB	Ilyushin Il-18D	187010603	ex RA-74269

RENAN AIR
Renan (/RAN)   *Kishinev-Chisinau (KIV)*

ER-AES	Antonov An-32	2509	ex RA-48123	Lsd to SDK as HK-4136X
ER-AEU	Antonov An-32B	2109	ex 4K-66756	

ER-AFI	Antonov An-32B	3205	ex ER-ADI	Lsd to African Business
ER-AFM	Antonov An-32B	3305	ex ER-ACM	
ER-AWL	Antonov An-32	3110	ex S9-GRJ	
ER-AWM	Antonov An-32	3009	ex	
ER-AWY	Antonov An-32	2103		
ER-AEJ	Antonov An-72	36572094889	ex ER-ACA	
ER-AEN	Antonov An-74	36547095898	ex ER-CAN	also reported with UMK
ER-AFY	Antonov An-24RV	47309809	ex YR-AMY	
ER-AJD	PZL-WZL/Antonov An-28	1AJ010-19	ex SP-DFA	
ER-AZA	Antonov An-26	77305509	ex	
ER-ICG	Ilyushin Il-18V	184007301	ex YR-IMG	
ER-ICJ	Ilyushin Il-18E	186009102	ex YR-IMJ	Lsd to Sevastopol Avia
ER-ICM	Ilyushin Il-18D	182004804	ex EX-7504	all-white
ER-LIA	LET L-410UVP	810623	ex UR-67022	

TANDEM-AERO

Tandem *(TQ/TDM) (IATA 038)* Kishinev-Chisinau (KIV)

Operates cargo charter flights with aircraft leased from other operators as required

TEPAVIA TRANS AIRLINE

Tepavia *(TET)* Kishinev-Chisinau (KIV)

ER-AJA	WSK-PZL/Antonov An-28	1AJ003-07	ex RA-28743	based WIL
ER-AJC	WSK-PZL/Antonov An-28	1AJ003-12	ex RA-28748	
ER-AJE	WSK-PZL/Antonov An-28	1AJ006-12	ex RA-28701	
ER-AJF	WSK-PZL/Antonov An-28	1AJ005-25	ex RA-28792	
ER-AJH	WSK-PZL/Antonov An-28	1AJ004-07	ex RA-28758	
ER-AJI	WSK-PZL/Antonov An-28	1AJ004-01	ex RA-28752	based WIL
ER-AJK	WSK-PZL/Antonov An-28	1AJ005-12	ex RA-28779	

TIRAMAVIA

Tiramavia *(TVI)* Kishinev-Chisinau (KIV)

ER-ACA	Antonov An-12BP	00347102		
ER-ADN	Antonov An-12BP	3341606	ex RA-11328	DHL titles
ER-AWS	Antonov An-72	36572093876	ex RA-93876	
ER-AXF	Antonov An-32	1704	ex RA-48976	
ER-AXG	Antonov An-12			

VALAN INTERNATIONAL CARGO

Valan *(VLN)* Kishinev-Chisinau (KIV)

ER-AEC	Antonov An-32B	3003	ex (ZS-OIT)	based JNB-Rand	
ER-AEW	Antonov An-32A	2601	ex RA-48090		Air Andemar titles
ER-AFG	Antonov An-32B	3004	ex D2-FVK	based JNB-Rand	Aero Gem titles
ER-AWA	Antonov An-32A	2510	ex RA-48089		
ZS-OWX	Antonov An-32B	2806	ex ER-AWB	based JNB-Rand	
ER-AEZ	Antonov An-24RV	47309705	ex D2-FVL	LA Nationale titles	

Valan International Cargo Charter (ZS) uses code VLA

VICHI AIRLINES

Vivhi *(VIH)* Kishinev-Chisinau (KIV)

ER-AFV	Antonov An-26	47313807		
ER-AFW	Antonov An-72	36572070696	ex ER-72932	
ER-AFZ	Antonov An-72			
ER-TCF	Tupolev Tu-134A-3	62390	ex EL-AAZ	
ER-75929	Ilyushin Il-18D	187010505	ex CCCP-74251	

ES - ESTONIA (Republic of Estonia)

AERO AIRLINES

Reval *(EE/EAY) (IATA 350)* Tallinn-Ylemiste (TLL)

| OH-KRE | Aerospatiale/Alenia ATR 72-201 | 174 | ex F-WWEE | Lsd fr FIN |
| OH-KRK | Aerospatiale/Alenia ATR 72-201 | 251 | ex B-22706 | Lsd fr FIN |

Wholly owned subsidiary of Finnair

AIREST

Elka (S8/AIT) *Tallinn-Ylemiste (TLL)*

ES-LLB	LET L-410UVP-E20C	912608	ex OK-WDG	
ES-LLC	LET L-410UVP-E20C	912609	ex OK-WDH	Lsd to

Air Est is the trading name of Estonian Aviation Company

AIR LIVONIA

Livonia (LIV) *Pärnu*

ES-DAA*	WSK-PZL/Antonov An-28	1AJ009-15	ex YL-KAB
ES-DAB	WSK-PZL/Antonov An-28	1AJ005-13	ex RA-28780

*Also reported as c/n 1AJ007-16 ex CCCP-28731

AVIES AIR COMPANY

Avies (AIA) *Tallinn-Ylemiste (TLL)*

ES-PAH	Piper PA-31-350 Navajo Chieftain	31-7405156	ex SE-GDI	
ES-PLB	LET L-410UVP	851413	ex LY-AVY	
ES-PJG	British Aerospace Jetstream 31	701	ex ES-LJD	Lsd fr Optiva Lsg
ES-PLI	LET L-410UVP	851438	ex LY-AIL	

ENIMEX

Enimex (ENI) *Tallinn-Ylemiste (TLL)*

ES-NOB	Antonov An-72-100	36572080695	ex CCCP-72931	
ES-NOC	Antonov An-72-100	36572010952	ex CCCP-71052?	Lsd fr Antonov
ES-NOG	Antonov An-72-100	36572080786	ex RA-72942	Lsd to United Nations as UNO-21
ES-NOH	Antonov An-72	36572095909	ex EL-ALX	Lsd to Air Co Shar
ES-NOK	Antonov An-72-100	36572080780	ex RA-72939	
ES-NOD	WSK-PZL/Antonov An-28	1AJ002-06	ex RA-28808	
ES-NOW	WSK-PZL/Antonov An-28PD	1AJ002-07	ex FLARF02726	

ESTONIAN AIR

Estonian (OV/ELL) (IATA 960) *Tallinn-Ylemiste (TLL)*

ES-ABC	Boeing 737-5Q8	2772/26324		Koit	Lsd fr ILFC
ES-ABD	Boeing 737-5Q8	2735/26323		Hämarik	Lsd fr ILFC
ES-ABF	Boeing 737-5L9	1816/24778	ex OY-MAA		Lsd fr ORIX
ES-ABG	Boeing 737-505	2245/25790	ex LN-BRU	Virmaline	Lsd fr ILFC
ES-ABH	Boeing 737-53S	3086/29074	ex F-GJNT		Lsd fr MC Europe

49% owned by SAS

ET - ETHIOPIA (Federal Democratic Republic of Ethiopia)

ETHIOPIAN AIRLINES

Ethiopian (ET/ETH) (IATA 071) *Addis Ababa (ADD)*

ET-AJS	Boeing 757-260PF	300/24845	ex N3519L	
ET-AJX	Boeing 757-260	348/25014		
ET-AKC	Boeing 757-260	408/25353		
ET-AKE	Boeing 757-260ER	444/26057		
ET-AKF	Boeing 757-260ER	496/26058		
ET-AIE	Boeing 767-260ER	90/23106	ex N1792B	stored VCV
ET-AIF	Boeing 767-260ER	93/23107	ex N6065Y	
ET-AKW	Boeing 767-33AER	403/25346	ex V8-RBE	Lsd fr BBAM
ET-ALC	Boeing 767-33AER	734/28043		Lsd fr AWAS
ET-ALH	Boeing 767-3BGER	802/30565	ex HB-IHW	Lsd fr Pembroke
ET-ALJ	Boeing 767-360ER	918/33767	ex N5020K	
ET-ALL	Boeing 767-3BGER	798/30564	ex OO-IHV	Lsd fr Roxy Ltd
ET-ALO	Boeing 767-360ER	33768		on order 04
ET-AKR	Fokker 50	20313	ex PH-LOP	
ET-AKS	Fokker 50	20328	ex PH-EXB	
ET-AKT	Fokker 50	20331	ex PH-EXC	
ET-AKU	Fokker 50	20333	ex PH-EXD	
ET-AKV	Fokker 50	20335	ex PH-EXE	
ET-AIN	de Havilland DHC-6 Twin Otter 310	816	ex C-GDFT	
ET-AIT	de Havilland DHC-6 Twin Otter 310	820	ex C-GDNG	
ET-AIX	de Havilland DHC-6 Twin Otter 300	835	ex C-GDFT	

ET-AJB	Boeing 737-260	1583/23915			
ET-AJC	Aerospatiale/Alenia ATR 42-320	071	ex F-WWEZ		stored ADD
ET-AJD	Aerospatiale/Alenia ATR 42-320	076	ex F-WWEB		stored ADD
ET-AJK	Lockheed L-382G Hercules	5022	ex N4272M		
ET-AKG	Lockheed L-382G Hercules	5306			
ET-ALE	Boeing 737-2T4	1165/23446	ex B-2515		Lsd fr debis
ET-ALK	Boeing 737-760	1408/33764			
ET-ALQ	Boeing 737-76N	33420		on order 04; winglets	Lsd fr GECAS
ET-ALU	Boeing 737-76N	32741		on order 04; winglets	Lsd fr GECAS

MIDROC AIR

Addis Ababa/Jeddah (ADD/JED)

ET-AKZ	de Havilland DHC-8Q-202	469	ex C-GLOT

EW - BELARUS (Republic of Belarus)

BAS / BELARUSSKY AVIATSIONNY SERVIS ceased operations

BELAVIA BELARUSSIAN AIRLINES

Belarus Avia (B2/BRU) (IATA 628)   *Minsk 1 (MSQ)*

EW-65085	Tupolev Tu-134A	60123	ex CCCP-65085	
EW-65106	Tupolev Tu-134A	60315	ex CCCP-65106	
EW-65133	Tupolev Tu-134A-3	60645	ex CCCP-65133	
EW-65145	Tupolev Tu-134A	60985	ex 65145	
EW-65149	Tupolev Tu-134A-3	61033	ex CCCP-65149	
EW-65754	Tupolev Tu-134A	62154	ex CCCP-65754	
EW-65772	Tupolev Tu-134A-3	62472	ex CCCP-65772	
EW-85509	Tupolev Tu-154B-2	81A-509	ex UN-85509	Lsd to SAI
EW-85538	Tupolev Tu-154B-2	82A-538	ex 4K-85538	Lsd to SAI
EW-85545	Tupolev Tu-154B-2	82A-545	ex CCCP-85545	
EW-85580	Tupolev Tu-154B-2	83A-580	ex CCCP-85580	
EW-85581	Tupolev Tu-154B-2	83A-581	ex CCCP-85581	
EW-85703	Tupolev Tu-154M	91A-878	ex CCCP-85703	
EW-85706	Tupolev Tu-154M	91A-881	ex CCCP-85706	
EW-85741	Tupolev Tu-154M	91A-896	ex ES-LTC	
EW-85748	Tupolev Tu-154M	92A-924	ex CCCP-85748	
EW-85815	Tupolev Tu-154M	95A-1010	Op for Govt	

Leases Tupolev Tu-154Ms to ALT (UN) as and when required

EW-46483	Antonov An-24RV	27308101	ex CCCP-46483	
EW-46615	Antonov An-24RV	37308702	ex CCCP-46615	
EW-47291	Antonov An-24RV	07306601	ex CCCP-47291	
EW-87330	Yakovlev Yak-40	9510139	ex CCCP-87330	
EW-88161	Yakovlev Yak-40	9611546	ex CCCP-88161	
EW-88187	Yakovlev Yak-40	9620748	ex CCCP-88187	
EW-88202	Yakovlev Yak-40	9630449	ex ER-88202	
EW-250PA	Boeing 737-524	2748/26319	ex N427LF	Lsd fr ILFC

GOMELAVIA

Gomel (GOM)   *Gomel (GME)*

EW-46631	Antonov An-24RV	37308810	ex CCCP-46631	
EW-46829	Antonov An-24RV	17306706	ex CCCP-46829	
EW-46835	Antonov An-24RV	17306802	ex CCCP-46835	
EW-47697	Antonov An-24RV	27307604	ex CCCP-47697	
EW-47808	Antonov An-24RV	17306910	ex CCCP-47808	Lsd to Inter Tropic
EW-85591	Tupolev Tu-154B-2	81A-581	ex CCCP-85591	

MOGILEV AERO ceased operations

TRANS AVIA EXPORT CARGO AIRLINES

Transexport (AL/TXC)   *Minsk-Machulishchy*

EW-76710	Ilyushin Il-76TD	0063473182	ex CCCP-76710	Lsd to KRI as RA-76710
EW-76711	Ilyushin Il-76TD	0063473187	ex CCCP-76711	Joint ops with AYZ
EW-76712	Ilyushin Il-76TD	0063473190	ex CCCP-76712	Lsd to ILV
EW-76734	Ilyushin Il-76TD	0073476312	ex RA-76734	Joint ops with AYZ
EW-76735	Ilyushin Il-76TD	0073476314	ex CCCP-76735	
EW-76737	Ilyushin Il-76TD	0073477323	ex CCCP-76737	Lsd to AUV
EW-78769	Ilyushin Il-76MD	0083487607	ex CCCP-78769	
EW-78779	Ilyushin Il-76TD	0083489662	ex CCCP-78779	Lsd to AYZ

EW-78787	Ilyushin Il-76MD	0083490698	ex CCCP-78787	
EW-78792	Ilyushin Il-76TD	0093490718	ex EP-CFA	
EW-78799	Ilyushin Il-76TD	0093491754	ex CCCP-78799	Lsd to Aerosatars
EW-78801	Ilyushin Il-76TD	0093492763	ex CCCP-78801	
EW-78808	Ilyushin Il-76TD	0093493794	ex CCCP-78808	Lsd to ESL
EW-78819	Ilyushin Il-76TD	0093495883	ex CCCP-78819	Lsd to DOB
EW-78826	Ilyushin Il-76TD	1003499991	ex CCCP-78826	Lsd to DOB
EW-78827	Ilyushin Il-76TD	1003499997	ex CCCP-78827	Lsd to AUV
EW-78828	Ilyushin Il-76TD	1003401004	ex CCCP-78828	Lsd to KRI as RA-78828
EW-78836	Ilyushin Il-76TD	0093499986	ex CCCP-78836	
EW-78839	Ilyushin Il-76TD	1003402047	ex CCCP-78839	
EW-78843	Ilyushin Il-76TD	1003403082	ex CCCP-78843	Lsd to ESL
EW-78848	Ilyushin Il-76TD	1003405159	ex CCCP-78848	Lsd to ILV
EW-78849	Ilyushin Il-76TD	1013405192	ex CCCP-78849	

EX - KYRGHYZSTAN (Republic of Kyrgyzstan)

AERO SERVICE current status uncertain, believed to have ceased operations

AEROVISTA AIRLINES
(AAP)   Sharjah (SHJ)

EX-87226	Yakovlev Yak-40K	9841459	ex RA-87226		
EX-87228	Yakovlev Yak-40D	9841659	ex RA-87228	Sara	Lsd to TLR
EX-87412	Yakovlev Yak-40	9420434	ex CCCP-87412		Lsd to TLR
EX-87426	Yakovlev Yak-40	9420235			Lsd to TLR
EX-87664	Yakovlev Yak-40	9240825	ex CCCP-87664		Lsd to TLR
EX-88270	Yakovlev Yak-40	9720853	ex RA-88270		Lsd to TLR
EX-001	Antonov An-12BP	5343606	ex UK 06105	no titles	
EX-004	Antonov An-24	89901506	ex ER-AEM		
EX-011	Ilyushin Il-18D	182004804	ex ER-ICM		
EX-24807	Antonov An-24RV	77310807	ex S9-CDA		Lsd to RNL as 4R-SEL
EX-24808	Antonov An-24RV	77310808	ex YR-BMN		

ALTYN AIR
Altyn Avia (QH/LYN)   Bishkek-Manas (FRU)

EX-014	Antonov An-24RV				
EX-020	Tupolev Tu-134A-3	61042	ex RA-65750		
EX-24805	Antonov An-24RV	77310805	ex S9-CBA	all-white	
EX-85718	Tupolev Tu-154M	91A-900	ex CCCP-85718		
EX-87631	Yakovlev Yak-40	9141219	ex CCCP-87631		
EX-87632	Yakovlev Yak-40	9141319	ex CCCP-87632		

Also leases Antonov An-24s from Aerovista as and when required

ASTRAL
                                                                           Bishkek-Manas (FRU)

EK-46741	Antonov An-12BK	8345408	ex EX-46741		Jt ops with PHG

BOTIR-AVIA
Botir-Avia (B8/BTR)   Bishkek-Manas (FRU)

EX-86916	Ilyushin Il-76TD	0023438120	ex UR-86916	no titles
EX-86917	Ilyushin Il-76TD	0023438122	ex CCCP-86917	Madina
EX-86919	Ilyushin Il-76TD	0023438129	ex UR-76319	
EX-87640	Yakovlev Yak-40	9140120	ex RA-87640	

BRITISH GULF INTERNATIONAL AIRLINES
Gulf Inter (BGK)   Bishkek-Manas/Sharjah (FRU/SHJ)

EX-160	Antonov An-12BP	401901	ex D2-FCV	Irena	Lsd to RPK
EX-161	Antonov An-12BP	5343305	ex S9-BOT		
EX-163	Antonov An-12B	01347704	ex S9-BOS		
EX-164	Antonov An-12	5343703	ex UN-11002	Alex	
S9-CAQ	Antonov An-12BP	3341408	ex D2-FRT	all-white, no titles	

CLICK AIRWAYS
                                                                           Click (CGK)

EX-78130	Ilyushin Il-76MD	0043454611	ex 4K-78130		
RA-12976	Antonov An-12V	9346510	ex CCCP-12976	no titles	Op for United Nations

INTER TRANS AVIA CARGO – ITA

Seitek (ITD)   *Bishkek-Manas/Sharjah (FRU/SHJ)*

| (ER-AXD) | Antonov An-12BP | 9346602 | ex EX-12960 | |
| EX-11760 | Antonov An-12 | 4342404 | | (c/n not confirmed) |

ITEK AIR

Itek Air (GI/IKA)   *Bishkek-Manas (FRU))*

| EX-65119 | Tupolev Tu-134A-3 | 60475 | ex CCCP-65119 | Lsd fr KGA |
| EX-85369 | Tupolev Tu-154B-2 | 79A-369 | ex CCCP-85369 | Lsd fr KGA |

KAS AIR COMPANY ceased operations

KYRGHYZ AIR

Air Shoumkar (KT/KAF)   *Bishkek-Manas (FRU)*

| 3D-ABV | McDonnell-Douglas MD-82 | 1070/49119 | ex N820US | stored IST | Lsd fr Jetran |
| 3D- | McDonnell-Douglas MD-82 | | ex N | on order | Lsd fr Jetran |

Operating cerificate was suspended by Government on 16 July 2003

KYRGHYZSTAN AIRLINES

Kyrgyz (R8/KGA) (IATA 758)   *Bishkek-Manas (FRU)*

EX-85257	Tupolev Tu-154B-2	77A-257	ex CCCP-85257	
EX-85259	Tupolev Tu-154B-1	77A-259	ex CCCP-85259	
EX-85294	Tupolev Tu-154B-1	78A-294	ex 85294	
EX-85369	Tupolev Tu-154B-2	79A-369	ex CCCP-85369	Lsd to IKA
EX-85444	Tupolev Tu-154B-2	80A-444	ex CCCP-85444	
EX-85497	Tupolev Tu-154B-2	81A-497	ex CCCP-85497	
EX-85519	Tupolev Tu-154B-2	81A-519	ex CCCP-85519	
EX-85590	Tupolev Tu-154B-2	83A-590	ex RA-85590	
EX-85762	Tupolev Tu-154M	93A-945	ex RA-85762	
(EX-28728)	WSK-PZL/Antonov An-28	1AJ007-13	ex 28728	wfs & stored
EX-28729	WSK-PZL/Antonov An-28	1AJ007-14	ex CCCP-28729	wfs & stored
EX-28738	WSK-PZL/Antonov An-28	1AJ008-01	ex CCCP-28738	wfs & stored
EX-28917	WSK-PZL/Antonov An-28	1AJ008-03	ex CCCP-28917	wfs & stored
EX-28934	WSK-PZL/Antonov An-28	1AJ008-21	ex UN-28934	
EX-28946	WSK-PZL/Antonov An-28	IAJ009-12	ex CCCP-28946	
EX-87250	Yakovlev Yak-40	9310726	ex CCCP-87250	Lsd fr TLR
EX-87259	Yakovlev Yak-40	9311626	ex CCCP-87259	
EX-87275	Yakovlev Yak-40	9311127	ex UN-87275	
EX-87293	Yakovlev Yak-40	9320828	ex CCCP-87293	
EX-87331	Yakovlev Yak-40	9510239	ex CCCP-87331	
EX-87379	Yakovlev Yak-40	9411030	ex CCCP-87379	
EX-87442	Yakovlev Yak-40	9431935	ex CCCP-87442	
EX-87445	Yakovlev Yak-40	9430236	ex CCCP-87445	
EX-87470	Yakovlev Yak-40	9441537	ex CCCP-87470	dam 21Oct01; fate?
EX-87529	Yakovlev Yak-40	9521141	ex CCCP-87529	dam 14Aug98; fate?
EX-87538	Yakovlev Yak-40	9530342	ex CCCP-87538	
EX-87555	Yakovlev Yak-40	9210621	ex CCCP-87555	
EX-87571	Yakovlev Yak-40	9221521	ex CCCP-87571	
EX-87589	Yakovlev Yak-40	9220123	ex CCCP-87589	
EX-87820	Yakovlev Yak-40	9231224	ex RA-87820	
EX-87836	Yakovlev Yak-40	9240226	ex CCCP-87836	
EX-26036	Antonov An-26B	10606	ex CCCP-26036	
EX-65119	Tupolev Tu-134A-3	60475	ex CCCP-65119	Lsd to IKA
EX-65779	Tupolev Tu-134A-3	62602	ex CCCP-65779	
EX-65789	Tupolev Tu-134A-3	62850	ex CCCP-65789	
EX-76815	Ilyushin Il-76TD	1013409310	ex CCCP-76815	
UR-CAP	Ilyushin Il-76TD	0063466989	ex UR-76394	Jt ops with UKL

KYRGYZ INTERNATIONAL AIRLINES

Kyrmal (N5/KYL)   *Bishkek-Manas (FRU)*

Fleet details unknown after original aircraft returned; planned to restart operations in 2003

KYZYL ORGA

| EX-007 | Yakovlev Yak-40 | 9640152 | ex RA-88248 | |

PHOENIX AVIATION

Phoenix Group (P3/PHG)   Sharjah (SHJ)

EX-006	Boeing 737-2T5	642/21960	ex N71PW		Lsd to RSO
EX-009	Boeing 737-219	676/22088	ex HP-1288CMP		Lsd fr Intl Aircraft Investors
EX-012*	Boeing 737-219	535/21645	ex HP-1297CMP		Lsd fr Intl Aircraft Investors
EX-015	Boeing 737-275	627/21819	ex C-GKPW	all-white	
EX-450	Boeing 737-281	262/20450	ex PK-JHA		Lsd to RSO
EX-451	Boeing 737-281	266/20451	ex PK-JHD		Lsd to RSO
EX-632	Boeing 737-2T5	847/22632	ex N75PW		Lsd to RSO

*Operated for UN World Food Programme

EX-005	Ilyushin Il-18D	188011105	ex EX-105		Jt ops with JUB
EX-201	Ilyushin Il-18D	188011201	ex EX-74268		Jt ops with JUB
EX-405	Ilyushin Il-18D	184007405	ex T9-ABB	no titles	Jt ops with BIO
EX-601	Ilyushin Il-18E	185008601	ex EL-ALD		Lsd to DJB
EX-75427	Ilyushin Il-18V	183005905	ex LZ-BFU	no titles	Lsd fr BFB
EX-75442	Ilysuhin Il-18D	187009702	ex RA-75442	no titles	
EX-75449	Ilyushin Il-18D	187010004	ex RA-75449	no titles	
EX-75466	Ilyushin Il-18D	187010403	ex RA-75466	Freighter	
EX-75905	Ilyushin Il-18D	186008905		Freighter	

EK-46419	Antonov An-24V	87303704	ex RA-46419	
EK-46741	Antonov An-12BK	8345408	ex EX-46741	Jt ops withAstral
EX-11010	Antonov An-12TB			
ST-CAC	Ilyushin Il-76TD	0023437076	ex T9-CAC	Jt ops with BIO

Leases aircraft to other operators, including Jubba Air Cargo

QUADROTUR AERO

Pegaso (QVR)   Bishkek-Minas/Almaty (FRU/ALA)

EX-62100	Ilyushin Il-62	51902	UN-86503

SERENDIP EXPRESS correctly listed under Sri Lanka

EY - TAJIKISTAN (Republic of Tajikstan)

SAN AIR

EX-65778	Tupolev Tu-134A-3	62590	ex CCCP-65778

TAJIKISTAN AIRLINES / TAJIK AIR

Tajikistan (7J/TZK) (ICAO 502)   Dushanbe/Khudzhand (DYU/LBD)

EY-46365	Antonov An-24B	07305906	ex CCCP-46365	
EY-46399	Antonov An-24B	07306303	ex CCCP-46399	
EY-46602	Antonov An-24RV	37308509	ex CCCP-46602	Lsd to COG
EY-47693	Antonov An-24RV	27307510	ex CCCP-47693	Lsd to DAO
EY-47802	Antonov An-24RV	17306901	ex UN-47802	

EY-65003	Tupolev Tu-134A-3	44040	ex CCCP-65003	Lsd to AYZ
EY-65022	Tupolev Tu-134A-3	48395	ex ES-AAE	
EY-65763	Tupolev Tu-134A-3	62299	ex CCCP-65763	
EY-65788	Tupolev Tu-134A-3	62835	ex CCCP-65788	
EY-65835	Tupolev Tu-134A-3	17112	ex CCCP-65835	
EY-65876	Tupolev Tu-134A-3	31220	ex CCCP-65876	

EY-85385	Tupolev Tu-154B-2	79A-385	ex CCCP-85385	
EY-85466	Tupolev Tu-154B-2	81A-466	ex CCCP-85466	
EY-85469	Tupolev Tu-154B-2	81A-469	ex CCCP-85469	
EY-85475	Tupolev Tu-154B-2	81A-475	ex CCCP-85475	
EY-85487	Tupolev Tu-154B-2	81A-487	ex CCCP-85487	
EY-85511	Tupolev Tu-154B-2	81A-511	ex CCCP-85511	
EY-85651	Tupolev Tu-154M	88A-793	ex RA-85651	
EY-85691	Tupolev Tu-154M	90A-864	ex EP-EAG	
EY-85692	Tupolev Tu-154M	90A-865	ex EP-TUE	Op for Govt
EY-85717	Tupolev Tu-154M	91A-897	ex EP-EAA	stored VKO

EY-87214	Yakovlev Yak-40K	9640851	ex HA-LJB	
EY-87217	Yakovlev Yak-40	9510340	ex EP-EAL	stored DYU
EY-87356	Yakovlev Yak-40	9431035	ex CCCP-87356	
EY-87434	Yakovlev Yak-40	9431035	ex EP-TQF	stored DYU
EY-87446	Yakovlev Yak-40	9430336	ex CCCP-87446	
EY-87522	Yakovlev Yak-40	9510441	ex CCCP-87522	
EY-87922	Yakovlev Yak-40K	9731355	ex EP-EAM	stored DYU

EY-87963	Yakovlev Yak-40K	9831058	ex EP-EAK	
EY-87967	Yakovlev Yak-40K	9831158	ex EP-CPI	
EY-88196	Yakovlev Yak-40	9631648	ex CCCP-88196	Lsd fr IRQ as EP-TQR

EY-26205	Antonov An-26B	14107	ex CCCP-26205
EY-26658	Antonov An-26	7904	ex CCCP-26658

Part owner of Iran Air Tours

TAJIKSTAN INTERNATIONAL AIRLINES current status uncertain, possibly absorbed into Tajikistan Airlines

EZ - TURKMENISTAN (Republic of Turkmenistan)

TURKMENISTAN AIRLINES

Turkmenistan (T5/TUA) (IATA 542)   Askhabad (ASB)

EZ-A101	Boeing 717-22K	5072/55153	ex N6202S		
EZ-A102	Boeing 717-22K	5078/55154			
EZ-A103	Boeing 717-22K	5086/55155			
EZ-	Boeing 717-22K			on order 04	
EZ-	Boeing 717-22K			on order 04	
EZ-A001	Boeing 737-341	2305/26855	ex EK-A001		
EZ-A002	Boeing 737-332	2439/25994	ex N301DE		
EZ-A003	Boeing 737-332	2455/25995	ex N302DE		
EZ-A010	Boeing 757-23A	412/25345	ex N58AW	Lsd fr AWAS	Op for govt
EZ-A011	Boeing 757-22K	725/28336			
EZ-A012	Boeing 757-22K	726/28337			
EZ-A014	Boeing 757-22K	952/30863			
EZ-F423	Ilyushin Il-76TD	1033418608			
EZ-F426	Ilyushin Il-76TD	1033418609			
EZ-F427	Ilyushin Il-76TD	1033418620			
EZ-F428	Ilyushin Il-76TD	1043418624			
EZ-26055	Antonov An-26	17311001			
EZ-26527	Antonov An-26	7209	ex CCCP-26527		
EZ-46490	Antonov An-24RV	27308108	ex UR-46490		
EZ-47301	Antonov An-24RV	57310205	ex CCCP-47301		
EZ-47314	Antonov An-24	57310501	ex CCCP-47314		
EZ-47322	Antonov An-24RV	67310508	ex UR-47322		
EZ-85549	Tupolev Tu-154B-2	82A-549	ex CCCP-85549		
EZ-87548	Yakovlev Yak-40	9531342	ex CCCP-87548		
EZ-87668	Yakovlev Yak-40	9021460	ex CCCP-87668		
EZ-88178	Yakovlev Yak-40K	9621847	ex CCCP-88178		
EZ-88230	Yakovlev Yak-40	9641950	ex CCCP-88230		
EZ-	Boeing 767-300			on order; op for Govt	

E3 - ERITREA (State of Eritrea)

ERITREAN AIRLINES

Eritrean (B8/ERT) (IATA 637)   Asmara (ASM)

E3-AAO	Boeing 767-366ER	275/24541	ex N73730	Lsd fr Boeing Aircraft Holding Co

F - FRANCE (French Republic)

AERIS Filed for bankruptcy protection 29 September 2003 but operations continued until 07 November 2003 when it ceased flying

AEROLINAIR

Perigueux

F-GTKJ	Beech 1900D	UE-348	ex N23406
F-GTVC	Beech 1900D	UE-349	ex N23430

Sister company of Airlinair

AIGLE AZUR TRANSPORTS AERIENS

Aigle Azur (ZI/AAF)   Paris-Orly (ORY)

F-GIXH	Boeing 737-3S3(QC)	1393/23788	ex N271LF	Lsd fr MSA 1
F-GLXI	Boeing 737-4Y0	2301/26066	ex TC-JDZ	Lsd fr Aerco Ireland
F-GLXJ	Boeing 737-4Y0	2176/25177	ex G-OBMM	Lsd fr Leblon Sales
F-GUAA	Airbus Industrie A321-211	0808	ex G-JSJX	Lsd fr GATX

AIR ATLANTIQUE

Charente (KI/APB)   *La Rochelle/Cherbourg (LRH/CER)*

F-GEQJ	Aerospatiale/Alenia ATR 42-300	008	ex PH-ATR	Lsd fr TAT Lsg
F-GHPK	Aerospatiale/Alenia ATR 42-300	218	ex F-WWEC	Lsd fr Abbey National Services
F-GKND	Aerospatiale/Alenia ATR 42-300	231		Lsd fr Prop Bail
F-GPIA	Aerospatiale/Alenia ATR 42-310	018	ex TR-LEW	Lsd fr ATR Asset Mgt

AIR BRETAGNE CENTRAL ceased operations

AIR FRANCE

Airfrans (AF/AFR) (IATA 057)   *Paris Charles de Gaulle/Orly (CDG/ORY)*

F-GUGA	Airbus Industre A318-111	2035	ex D-AUAD		
F-GUGB	Airbus Industre A318-111	2059	ex D-AUAF		
F-GUGC	Airbus Industre A318-111	2071	ex D-AUAG		
F-GUGD	Airbus Industre A318-111	2081	ex D-AUAH		
F-GUGE	Airbus Industre A318-111	2100	ex D-AUAI		
F-GUGF	Airbus Industre A318-111	2109	ex D-AUAJ		
F-GUGG	Airbus Industre A318-111	2213	ex D-AUA	on order 04	
F-GUGH	Airbus Industre A318-111	2228	ex D-AUA	on order 04	
F-GUGI	Airbus Industre A318-111			on order 04	
F-GUGJ	Airbus Industre A318-111			on order 04	
F-GUGK	Airbus Industre A318-111			on order 04	
F-GUGL	Airbus Industre A318-111			on order 04	
F-GUGM	Airbus Industre A318-111			on order 04	
F-GUGN	Airbus Industre A318-111			on order 04	
F-GUGIO	Airbus Industre A318-111			on order 04	
F-GPMA	Airbus Industrie A319-113	0598	ex D-AVYD		Lsd fr Takeoff 8 Ltd
F-GPMB	Airbus Industrie A319-113	0600	ex D-AVYC		Lsd fr Takeoff 9 Ltd
F-GPMC	Airbus Industrie A319-113	0608	ex D-AVYE		Lsd fr Takeoff 10 Ltd
F-GPMD	Airbus Industrie A319-113	0618	ex D-AVYJ		Lsd fr Takeoff 11 Ltd
F-GPME	Airbus Industrie A319-113	0625	ex D-AVYQ		Lsd fr Takeoff 12 Ltd
F-GPMF	Airbus Industrie A319-113	0637	ex D-AVYT		Lsd fr Takeoff 13 Ltd
F-GPMG	Airbus Industrie A319-113	0644	ex D-AVYA		Lsd fr ACG Acquisition
F-GPMH	Airbus Industrie A319-113	0647	ex D-AVYD		Lsd fr Castle 2003-1A
F-GPMI	Airbus Industrie A319-113	0660	ex D-AVYC		Lsd fr ILFC
F-GRHA	Airbus Industrie A319-111	0938	ex D-AVYS		Lsd fr ILFC
F-GRHB	Airbus Industrie A319-111	0985	ex D-AVYO		
F-GRHC	Airbus Industrie A319-111	0998	ex D-AVYW		Lsd fr ILFC
F-GRHD	Airbus Industrie A319-111	1000	ex D-AVYP		Lsd fr ILFC
F-GRHE	Airbus Industrie A319-111	1020	ex D-AVYX		
F-GRHF	Airbus Industrie A319-111	1025	ex D-AVYE		
F-GRHG	Airbus Industrie A319-111	1036	ex D-AVYS		
F-GRHH	Airbus Industrie A319-111	1151	ex D-AVWK		
F-GRHI	Airbus Industrie A319-111	1169	ex D-AVYX		Lsd fr ILFC
F-GRHJ	Airbus Industrie A319-111	1176	ex D-AVWN		Lsd fr ILFC
F-GRHK	Airbus Industrie A319-111	1190	ex D-AVYQ		Lsd fr ILFC
F-GRHL	Airbus Industrie A319-111	1201	ex D-AVWT		Lsd fr Sierra Lsg
F-GRHM	Airbus Industrie A319-111	1216	ex D-AVYF		Lsd fr ILFC
F-GRHN	Airbus Industrie A319-111	1267	ex D-AVWB		
F-GRHO	Airbus Industrie A319-111	1271	ex D-AVWC		
F-GRHP	Airbus Industrie A319-111	1344	ex D-AVYQ		Lsd fr ORIX Lunabase
F-GRHQ	Airbus Industrie A319-111	1404	ex D-AVYB		Lsd fr ORIX Indus
F-GRHR	Airbus Industrie A319-111	1415	ex D-AVYF		Lsd fr ORIX
F-GRHS	Airbus Industrie A319-111	1444	ex D-AVWA		Lsd fr Takeoff 14 Ltd
F-GRHT	Airbus Industrie A319-111	1449	ex D-AVWD		Lsd fr Takeoff 15 Ltd
F-GRHU	Airbus Industrie A319-111	1471	ex D-AVYR		Lsd fr ILFC
F-GRHV	Airbus Industrie A319-111	1505	ex D-AVYF		Lsd fr Eleonore Bail
F-GRHX	Airbus Industrie A319-111	1524	ex D-AVWC		Lsd fr Eleonore Bail
F-GRHY	Airbus Industrie A319-111	1616	ex D-AVWG		
F-GRHZ	Airbus Industrie A319-111	1622	ex D-AVYO		Lsd fr ILFC
F-GRXA	Airbus Industrie A319-111	1640	ex D-AVYJ		Lsd fr Avn Financial Svs
F-GRXB	Airbus Industrie A319-111	1645	ex D-AVYC		Lsd fr ILFC
F-GRXC	Airbus Industrie A319-111	1677	ex D-AVWF		Lsd fr ILFC
F-GRXD	Airbus Industrie A319-111	1699	ex D-AVYG		Lsd fr ILFC
F-GRXE	Airbus Industrie A319-111	1733	ex D-AVWT		Lsd fr ILFC
F-GRXF	Airbus Industrie A319-111	1938	ex D-AVWG	o/o 04; stored XFW	Lsd fr ILFC
F-GRXG	Airbus Industrie A319-111	2213	ex D-AV	on order	Lsd fr ILFC
F-	Airbus Industrie A319-115		ex D-AV	on order May04	Lsd fr ILFC
F-	Airbus Industrie A319-115		ex D-AV	on order May04	Lsd fr ILFC
F-	Airbus Industrie A319-111	2228	ex D-AV	on order Oct 04	Lsd fr ILFC
F-GYAS	Airbus Industrie A319-133LR	1999	ex D-AVYQ	[CJ]	Op by Aero Service
F-GFKA	Airbus Industrie A320-111	0005	ex F-WWDI	Ville de Paris	Lsd fr Durus
F-GFKB	Airbus Industrie A320-111	0007	ex F-WWDJ		Lsd fr Orado
F-GFKD	Airbus Industrie A320-111	0014	ex F-WWDO	Ville de Londres	
F-GFKE	Airbus Industrie A320-111	0019		Ville de Bonn	

F-GFKF	Airbus Industrie A320-111	0020		Ville de Madrid
F-GFKG	Airbus Industrie A320-111	0021		Ville d'Amsterdam
F-GFKH	Airbus Industrie A320-211	0061		Ville de Bruxelles
F-GFKI	Airbus Industrie A320-211	0062		Ville de Lisbonne
F-GFKJ	Airbus Industrie A320-211	0063		Ville de Copenhague
F-GFKK	Airbus Industrie A320-211	0100		Ville d'Athènes
F-GFKL	Airbus Industrie A320-211	0101		Ville de Dublin Lsd fr Clemence Bail
F-GFKM	Airbus Industrie A320-211	0102		Ville de Luxembourg Lsd fr Marie Bail
F-GFKN	Airbus Industrie A320-211	0128		Ville de Strasbourg
F-GFKO	Airbus Industrie A320-211	0129		Ville de Milan
F-GFKP	Airbus Industrie A320-211	0133		Ville de Nice
F-GFKQ	Airbus Industrie A320-111	0002	ex F-WWDA	Ville de Berlin
F-GFKR	Airbus Industrie A320-211	0186		Ville de Barceloune
F-GFKS	Airbus Industrie A320-211	0187		
F-GFKT	Airbus Industrie A320-211	0188		Ville de Lyon
F-GFKU	Airbus Industrie A320-211	0226		Ville de Manchester Lsd fr DB Export
F-GFKV	Airbus Industrie A320-211	0227		Ville de Bordeaux Lsd fr DB Export
F-GFKX	Airbus Industrie A320-211	0228		Ville de Francfort
F-GFKY	Airbus Industrie A320-211	0285		Ville de Toulouse Lsd fr Frantz CRP
F-GFKZ	Airbus Industrie A320-211	0286		Ville de Turin Lsd fr Frantz CRP
F-GGEA	Airbus Industrie A320-111	0010	ex F-WWDL	
F-GGEB	Airbus Industrie A320-111	0012	ex F-WWDM	
F-GGEC	Airbus Industrie A320-111	0013	ex F-WWDN	
F-GGEE	Airbus Industrie A320-111	0016	ex F-WWDQ	
F-GGEF	Airbus Industrie A320-111	0004	ex F-WWDC	
F-GGEG	Airbus Industrie A320-111	0003	ex F-WWDB	
F-GHQA	Airbus Industrie A320-211	0033	ex F-GGEF	
F-GHQB	Airbus Industrie A320-211	0036	ex F-GGEG	
F-GHQC	Airbus Industrie A320-211	0044	ex F-GGEH	
F-GHQD	Airbus Industrie A320-211	0108		
F-GHQE	Airbus Industrie A320-211	0115		
F-GHQF	Airbus Industrie A320-211	0130		Lsd fr ITAB
F-GHQG	Airbus Industrie A320-211	0155		
F-GHQH	Airbus Industrie A320-211	0156		
F-GHQI	Airbus Industrie A320-211	0184		Lsd fr ITAB
F-GHQJ	Airbus Industrie A320-211	0214		
F-GHQK	Airbus Industrie A320-211	0236		
F-GHQL	Airbus Industrie A320-211	0239		
F-GHQM	Airbus Industrie A320-211	0237		
F-GHQO	Airbus Industrie A320-211	0278		
F-GHQP	Airbus Industrie A320-211	0337		
F-GHQQ	Airbus Industrie A320-211	0352		
F-GHQR	Airbus Industrie A320-211	0377		
F-GJVA	Airbus Industrie A320-211	0144	ex F-WWDK	Lsd fr GATX/CL Air
F-GJVB	Airbus Industrie A320-211	0145	ex F-WWDL	Lsd fr GATX/CL Air
F-GJVC	Airbus Industrie A320-211	0204		Lsd fr debis
F-GJVD	Airbus Industrie A320-211	0211		Lsd fr debis
F-GJVE	Airbus Industrie A320-211	0215		Lsd fr ILFC
F-GJVF	Airbus Industrie A320-211	0244		Lsd fr ILFC
F-GJVG	Airbus Industrie A320-211	0270		Lsd fr ILFC
F-GJVW	Airbus Industrie A320-211	0491		Lsd fr MDFC
F-GKXA	Airbus Industrie A320-211	0287		Ville de Nantes
F-GKXB	Airbus Industrie A320-212	0235	ex F-OHFX	Lsd fr GATX
F-GKXC	Airbus Industrie A320-214	1502	ex F-WWIG	based Antilles
F-GKXD	Airbus Industrie A320-214	1873	ex F-WWDV	Lsd fr NBB Cherbourg
F-GKXE	Airbus Industrie A320-214	1879	ex F-WWDX	on order; stored TLS
F-GKXF	Airbus Industrie A320-214	1885		Lsd fr RAFT Co
F-GKXG	Airbus Industrie A320-214	1894	ex F-WWDV	on order; stored TLS
F-GKXH	Airbus Industrie A320-214	1924		Lsd fr ILFC
F-GKXI	Airbus Industrie A320-214	1949		Lsd fr ILFC
F-GKXJ	Airbus Industrie A320-214	1900		Lsd fr CL Capricorn
F-	Airbus Industrie A320-214	2140	ex F-WWBR	on order
F-GLGG	Airbus Industrie A320-211	0203	ex ZS-NZP	Lsd fr Aero USA
F-GLGH	Airbus Industrie A320-211	0220	ex ZS-NZR	Lsd fr Aero USA
F-GLGM	Airbus Industrie A320-212	0131	ex N481GX	Lsd fr GATX
F-GMZA	Airbus Industrie A321-111	0498	ex D-AVZK	Lsd fr FT Global Lsg
F-GMZB	Airbus Industrie A321-111	0509	ex D-AVZN	
F-GMZC	Airbus Industrie A321-211	0521	ex D-AVZW	
F-GMZD	Airbus Industrie A321-111	0529	ex D-AVZA	
F-GMZE	Airbus Industrie A321-111	0544	ex D-AVZF	
F-GTAD	Airbus Industrie A321-211	0777	ex D-AVZI	Lsd fr Takeoff 5 Ltd
F-GTAE	Airbus Industrie A321-211	0796	ex D-AVZN	
F-GTAG	Airbus Industrie A321-211	0956	ex D-AVZO	Lsd fr GECC
F-GTAH	Airbus Industrie A321-211	1133	ex D-AVZD	
F-GTAI	Airbus Industrie A321-211	1299	ex D-AVZP	Lsd fr ILFC
F-GTAJ	Airbus Industrie A321-211	1476	ex D-AVZF	Lsd fr ILFC
F-GTAK	Airbus Industrie A321-211	1658	ex D-AVZP	Lsd fr ILFC
F-GTAL	Airbus Industrie A321-211	1691	ex D-AVZY	Lsd fr ILFC
F-GTAM	Airbus Industrie A321-211	1859	ex D-AVZY	std XFW
F-GTAN	Airbus Industrie A321-211		ex D-AV	on order	Lsd fr debis
F-GTAO	Airbus Industrie A321-211		ex D-AV	on order

156

F-GZCA	Airbus Industrie A330-203	422			Lsd fr Estelle Bail
F-GZCB	Airbus Industrie A330-203	443			Lsd fr ILFC
F-GZCC	Airbus Industrie A330-203	448			Lsd fr ILFC
F-GZCD	Airbus Industrie A330-203	458	ex (F-WWJH)		Lsd fr ILFC
F-GZCE	Airbus Industrie A330-203	465	ex F-WWKM		Lsd fr ILFC
F-GZCF	Airbus Industrie A330-203	481			Lsd fr ILFC
F-GZCG	Airbus Industrie A330-203	498	ex F-WWKI	std CHR	Lsd fr ILFC
F-GZCH	Airbus Industrie A330-203	500			Lsd fr RBS Avn
F-GZCI	Airbus Industrie A330-203	502	ex F-WWKJ	std CHR	Lsd fr ILFC
F-GZCJ	Airbus Industrie A330-203	503			Lsd fr ILFC
F-GZCK	Airbus Industrie A330-203	516			Lsd fr ILFC
F-GZCL	Airbus Industrie A330-203	519			Lsd fr ILFC
F-GZCM	Airbus Industrie A330-203	567			
F-GZCN	Airbus Industrie A330-203	584			
F-GLZA	Airbus Industrie A340-211	005	ex F-WWCA		Lsd fr Marseilles A/c to Apr04
F-GLZB	Airbus Industrie A340-211	007			Lsd fr ILFC to May04
F-GLZC	Airbus Industrie A340-211	029			Lsd fr ILFC to Apr05
F-GLZG	Airbus Industrie A340-211	049			Lsd fr Castle 2003-1A to May05
F-GLZH	Airbus Industrie A340-211	078			Lsd fr BBV Lsg
F-GLZI	Airbus Industrie A340-211	084			Lsd fr BBV Lsg
F-GLZJ	Airbus Industrie A340-313X	186			Lsd fr DB Export
F-GLZK	Airbus Industrie A340-313X	207			
F-GLZL	Airbus Industrie A340-313X	210			
F-GLZM	Airbus Industrie A340-313X	237			Lsd fr Sylvie Bail
F-GLZN	Airbus Industrie A340-313X	245			
F-GLZO	Airbus Industrie A340-313X	246			
F-GLZP	Airbus Industrie A340-313X	260			
F-GLZQ	Airbus Industrie A340-313X	289			Lsd fr Apollo Finance
F-GLZR	Airbus Industrie A340-313X	307			Lsd fr Apollo Finance
F-GLZS	Airbus Industrie A340-313X	310			
F-GLZT	Airbus Industrie A340-313X	319			
F-GLZU	Airbus Industrie A340-313X	377			
F-GNIF	Airbus Industrie A340-313X	168			Lsd fr ILFC
F-GNIG	Airbus Industrie A340-313X	174			Lsd fr ILFC
F-GNIH	Airbus Industrie A340-313X	373			Lsd fr ILFC
F-GNII	Airbus Industrie A340-313X	399			Lsd fr ILFC
F-GFUA	Boeing 737-33A	1436/23635	ex G-OUTA	SE-RCO resd	Lsd fr AWMS I
F-GFUD	Boeing 737-33A	1597/24027			Lsd fr AWAS
F-GFUJ	Boeing 737-33A	2065/25118	ex (F-GBYR)		Lsd fr ILFC
F-GHVM	Boeing 737-33A	1595/24026	ex G-MONT	SE-RCR resd	Lsd fr AWAS
F-GHVO	Boeing 737-33A	1556/24025	ex G-MONU	SE-RCP resd	Lsd fr AWMS I
F-GHXM	Boeing 737-53A	1921/24788			Lsd fr Laure Bail
F-GJNA	Boeing 737-528	2099/25206			Lsd fr GECC
F-GJNB	Boeing 737-528	2108/25227			Lsd fr GECC
F-GJNC	Boeing 737-528	2170/25228			Lsd fr Sandhill Finances
F-GJND	Boeing 737-528	2180/25229			Lsd fr Piedmont Finance
F-GJNE	Boeing 737-528	2191/25230			Lsd fr GECC
F-GJNF	Boeing 737-528	2208/25231			Lsd fr Castle Harbor Lsg
F-GJNG	Boeing 737-528	2231/25232			Lsd fr Golf 737 Bail
F-GJNH	Boeing 737-528	2251/25233			Lsd fr Golf 737 Bail
F-GJNI	Boeing 737-528	2411/25234			Lsd fr Castle Harbor Lsg
F-GJNJ	Boeing 737-528	2428/25235			Lsd fr Castle Harbor Lsg
F-GJNK	Boeing 737-528	2443/25236			
F-GJNL	Boeing 737-5H6	2484/26448	ex 9M-MFC		Lsd fr GECAS
F-GJNM	Boeing 737-528	2464/25237	ex (F-GJNL)		
F-GJNN	Boeing 737-528	2572/27304			Lsd fr FC Uncle Lsg
F-GJNO	Boeing 737-528	2574/27305			Lsd fr FC Uncle Lsg
F-GJNP	Boeing 737-5H6	2654/27356	ex 9M-MFI		Lsd fr GECAS
F-GJNU	Boeing 737-53S	3101/29075			Lsd fr Pembroke
F-GJNV	Boeing 737-548	2427/26287	ex EI-CDS		Lsd fr Triton
F-GJNX	Boeing 737-5H6	2511/26454	ex 9M-MFE		Lsd fr A320 A/c Lsg
F-GJNY	Boeing 737-5H6	2527/26456	ex 9M-MFF		Lsd fr A320 A/c Lsg
F-GJNZ	Boeing 737-5H6	2503/26450	ex 9M-MFD		Lsd fr A320 A/c Lsg
F-GJUA	Boeing 737-548	2463/25165	ex LN-TUX		Lsd fr ILFC
F-BPVR	Boeing 747-228F	295/21255	ex N1783B	Air France Cargo	
F-BPVU	Boeing 747-228B	333/21537	ex N1252E		
F-BPVY	Boeing 747-228B	370/21745			
F-BPVZ	Boeing 747-228F	398/21787		Air France Cargo	
F-BTDG	Boeing 747-2B3M (EUD)	518/22514			
F-BTDH	Boeing 747-2B3M (EUD)	521/22515			
F-GBOX	Boeing 747-2B3F	388/21835		Air France Cargo	Lsd fr Arkia Lsg
F-GCBA	Boeing 747-228B	428/21982			
F-GCBB	Boeing 747-228M	463/22272	ex N1289E		Lsd fr WTCo
F-GCBD	Boeing 747-228B (SF)	503/22428	ex N1305E	Air France Cargo	
F-GCBF	Boeing 747-228M	558/22794	ex N4506H		
F-GCBG	Boeing 747-228F	569/22939	ex N4544F	Air France Cargo	Lsd fr First Trust
F-GCBH	Boeing 747-228B (SF)	656/23611	ex N6046P	Air France Cargo	
F-GCBI	Boeing 747-228M	661/23676	ex N6009F		
F-GCBJ	Boeing 747-228M	698/24067	ex N6018N		

F-GCBK	Boeing 747-228F	714/24158	ex N6055X	Air France Cargo	
F-GCBL	Boeing 747-228F	772/24735		Air France Cargo Asie	
F-GCBM	Boeing 747-228F	822/24879		Air France Cargo	
F-GETA	Boeing 747-3B3M	632/23413	ex N6009F		
F-GETB	Boeing 747-3B3M	641/23480	ex N6018N	Big Boss	
F-GEXA	Boeing 747-4B3	741/24154			
F-GEXB	Boeing 747-4B3M	864/24155			
F-GISA	Boeing 747-428M	872/25238		Air France Asie	
F-GISB	Boeing 747-428M	884/25302			
F-GISC	Boeing 747-428M	899/25599			
F-GISD	Boeing 747-428M	934/25628			
F-GISE	Boeing 747-428M	960/25630			
F-GITA	Boeing 747-428	836/24969			
F-GITB	Boeing 747-428	843/24990	ex N6009F		
F-GITC	Boeing 747-428	889/25344			
F-GITD	Boeing 747-428	901/25600			
F-GITE	Boeing 747-428	906/25601			
F-GITF	Boeing 747-428	909/25602		Lsd fr CIT Leasing	
F-GITH	Boeing 747-428	1325/32868		Lsd fr ILFC	
F-GITI	Boeing 747-428	1327/32869		Lsd fr ILFC	
F-GITJ	Boeing 747-428ER	1343/32871		Lsd fr ILFC	
F-GIUA	Boeing 747-428ERF	1315/32866	ex N5017Q	Lsd fr JLI-I Inc	
F-GIUB	Boeing 747-428ERF	1317/33096		Lsd fr ILFC	
F-GIUC	Boeing 747-428ERF	1318/32867		Lsd fr ILFC	
F-GIUD	Boeing 747-428ERF	32870		on order 04	Lsd fr ILFC

One more Boeing 747-428ERF is on order for delivery in September 2005, also leased from ILFC

F-GSPA	Boeing 777-228ER	129/29002			
F-GSPB	Boeing 777-228ER	133/29003			
F-GSPC	Boeing 777-228ER	138/29004		Lsd fr Fatewood Ltd	
F-GSPD	Boeing 777-228ER	187/29005			
F-GSPE	Boeing 777-228ER	189/29006			
F-GSPF	Boeing 777-228ER	201/29007			
F-GSPG	Boeing 777-228ER	195/27609		Lsd fr ILFC	
F-GSPH	Boeing 777-228ER	210/28675		Lsd fr ILFC	
F-GSPI	Boeing 777-228ER	258/29008			
F-GSPJ	Boeing 777-228ER	263/29009			
F-GSPK	Boeing 777-228ER	267/29010		Lsd fr Eurolease	
F-GSPL	Boeing 777-228ER	284/30457	ex N50281	Lsd fr Takeoff 2 LLC	
F-GSPM	Boeing 777-228ER	307/30456		Lsd fr Takeoff 1 LLC	
F-GSPN	Boeing 777-228ER	314/29011		Lsd fr ILFC	
F-GSPO	Boeing 777-228ER	320/30614		Lsd fr Takeoff 3 LLC	
F-GSPP	Boeing 777-228ER	327/30615		Lsd fr Takeoff 4 LLC	
F-GSPQ	Boeing 777-228ER	331/28682		Lsd fr ILFC	
F-GSPR	Boeing 777-228ER	367/28683		Lsd fr ILFC	
F-GSPS	Boeing 777-228ER	370/32306			
F-GSPT	Boeing 777-228ER	382/32308		Lsd fr ILFC	
F-GSPU	Boeing 777-228ER	383/32309		Lsd fr RBS Avn	
F-GSPV	Boeing 777-228ER	385/28684		Lsd fr ILFC	
F-GSPX	Boeing 777-228ER	392/32698		Lsd fr ILFC	
F-GSPY	Boeing 777-228ER	395/32305			
F-GSPZ	Boeing 777-228ER	401/32310			
F-GSQA	Boeing 777-328ER	466/32723	ex N5017Q	on order Apr04	Lsd fr ILFC
F-GSQB	Boeing 777-328ER	32724		on order 04	Lsd fr ILFC
F-GSQC	Boeing 777-328ER	32727		on order 04	Lsd fr ILFC
F-GSQD	Boeing 777-328ER			on order 04	
F-GSQE	Boeing 777-328ER			on order 04	
F-GSQF	Boeing 777-328ER			on order 04	
F-GSQG	Boeing 777-328ER			on order 04	
F-GSQH	Boeing 777-328ER			on order 04	

Four more Boeing 777-328ERs are on order for delivery in 2005
Ten Airbus Industrie A380-800s are on order for delivery from 2007
Air France has agreement with Brit'Air, flybe. , CCM Airlines, Cityjet and Regional , for the operation of services on their behalf; aircraft wear full Air France colours and use AF flight numbers
Owns 34% of Air Austral, 45% of Air Caraibes, 11.2% of Air Gabon, 12.8% of Air Mauritius, 33.7% of Air Tchad, 28% of MEA, 11.95% of CCM Airlines and smaller shares in Air Caledonie, Air Comores, Air Madagascar, Air Tahiti, Austrian Airlines, Cameroon Airlines, Royal Air Maroc and Tunis Air while Brit'Air, Cityjet and Regional Airlines are wholly owned. Founder member of SkyTeam alliance with Delta, Aeromexico and Korean Air
Signed Letter of Intent 20 September 2003 with KLM Royal Dutch Airlines to form a new holding company Air France-KLM in 2Q04 with two separate operating units; Air France will hold 37% of the new company and KLM will hold 19%.

AIR FRANCE REGIONAL

Various

F-GGLR	Aerospatiale/Alenia ATR 42-300	043		Brit'Air	Lsd to PTN as PT-MFY
F-GHJE	Aerospatiale/Alenia ATR 42-300	070	ex F-WWEW	Brit'Air	Lsd to PTN as PT-MFU
F-GHPI	Aerospatiale/Alenia ATR 42 300	214	ex F-WWEB	Brit'Air	Lsd to RAL
F-GKPC	Aerospatiale/Alenia ATR 72-201	171	ex F-WWEA	CCM Airlines	
F-GKPD	Aerospatiale/Alenia ATR 72-201	177	ex F-WWEH	CCM Airlines	

EI-CMS	British Aerospace 146 Srs.200	E2044	ex N184US	Cityjet
EI-CMY	British Aerospace 146 Srs.200	E2039	ex N177US	Cityjet
EI-CNB	British Aerospace 146 Srs.200	E2046	ex N187US	Cityjet
EI-CNQ	British Aerospace 146 Srs.200	E2031	ex G-OWLD	Cityjet
EI-CSK	British Aerospace 146 Srs.200	E2062	ex N810AS	Cityjet	Lsd fr BAES
EI-CSL	British Aerospace 146 Srs.200	E2074	ex N812AS	Cityjet	Lsd fr BAES
EI-CWA	British Aerospace 146 Srs.200	E2058	ex G-ECAL	Cityjet	Lsd fr BAES
EI-CWB	British Aerospace 146 Srs.200	E2051	ex SE-DRE	Cityjet	
EI-CWC	British Aerospace 146 Srs.200	E2053	ex SE-DRC	Cityjet	
EI-CWD	British Aerospace 146 Srs.200	E2108	ex SE-DRK	Cityjet	
EI-PAT	British Aerospace 146 Srs.200	E2030	ex G-ZAPL	Cityjet	Lsd fr AWC
G-JEAK	British Aerospace 146 Srs.200	E2103	ex G-OLCB	flybe.	
G-JEAM	British Aerospace 146 Srs.300	E3128	ex G-BTJT	flybe.	
G-JEBA	British Aerospace 146 Srs.300	E3181	ex HS-TBL	flybe.	
G-JEBB	British Aerospace 146 Srs.300	E3185	ex HS-TBK	flybe.	
F-GPTF	Canadair CL-600-2B19	7197	ex C-FMLB	Brit'Air	Lsd fr Lerins
F-GRJA	Canadair CL-600-2B19	7070	ex C-FMKW	Brit'Air	Lsd fr MADB Owner Ltd
F-GRJB	Canadair CL-600-2B19	7076	ex C-FMLS	Brit'Air	Lsd fr MADB Owner Ltd
F-GRJC	Canadair CL-600-2B19	7085		Brit'Air	Lsd fr MADB Owner Ltd
F-GRJD	Canadair CL-600-2B19	7088	ex C-FMLU	Brit'Air	Lsd fr MADB Owner Ltd
F-GRJE	Canadair CL-600-2B19	7106	ex C-FMNQ	Brit'Air	Lsd fr MADB Owner Ltd
F-GRJF	Canadair CL-600-2B19	7108	ex C-FMLU	Brit'Air	Lsd fr MADB Owner Ltd
F-GRJG	Canadair CL-600-2B19	7143	ex C-FMMQ	Brit'Air	Lsd fr St Gonven
F-GRJH	Canadair CL-600-2B19	7162		Brit'Air	Lsd fr St.Gonven
F-GRJI	Canadair CL-600-2B19	7147	ex C-FZAL	Brit'Ai	Lsd fr St.Gonven
F-GRJJ	Canadair CL-600-2B19	7190	ex C-GBFF	Brit'Air	Lsd fr Guengat
F-GRJK	Canadair CL-600-2B19	7219	ex C-FMMQ	Brit'Air	Lsd fr Guengat
F-GRJL	Canadair CL-600-2B19	7221		Brit'Air	Lsd fr Guengat
F-GRJM	Canadair CL-600-2B19	7222		Brit'Air	Lsd fr Guengat
F-GRJN	Canadair CL-600-2B19	7262	ex C-FMLT	Brit'Air	
F-GRJO	Canadair CL-600-2B19	7296		Brit'Air	Lsd fr Rosko Lse
F-GRJP	Canadair CL-600-2B19	7301		Brit'Air	Lsd fr Rosko Lse
F-GRJQ	Canadair CL-600-2B19	7321	ex C-FMLS	Brit'Air	Lsd fr Rosko Lse
F-GRJR	Canadair CL-600-2B19	7375	ex C-FMKW	Brit'Air	
F-GRJT	Canadair CL-600-2B19	7389	ex C-FMOS	Brit'Air	Lsd fr Marie Bail
F-GRZA	Canadair CL-600-2C10	10006	ex C-GHCE	Brit'Air	Lsd fr Hermine Bail
F-GRZB	Canadair CL-600-2C10	10007	ex C-GHCF	Brit'Air	
F-GRZC	Canadair CL-600-2C10	10008	ex C-GHCO	Brit'Air	
F-GRZD	Canadair CL-600-2C10	10016	ex C-GJEZ	Brit'Air	Lsd fr Triskel Bail
F-GRZE	Canadair CL-600-2C10	10032	ex C-GJEZ	Brit'Air	
F-GRZF	Canadair CL-600-2C10	10036	ex C-GIBQ	Brit'Air	Lsd fr Mirabel Bail
F-GRZG	Canadair CL-600-2C10	10037	ex C-GIBT	Brit'Air	Lsd fr Skravig Bail
F-GRZH	Canadair CL-600-2C10	10089	ex C-GIBI	Brit'Air	Lsd fr Fulmar Bail
F-GRZI	Canadair CL-600-2C10	10093	ex C-GI	Brit'Air	Lsd fr Fulmar Bail
F-GRZJ	Canadair CL-600-2C10	10096	ex C-GI	Brit'Air	Lsd fr Emerillon Avn
F-GRZK	Canadair CL-600-2C10			on order Brit'Air	
F-GRZL	Canadair CL-600-2C10			on order Brit'Air	

Four Canadair CL-600-2D24s (RJ-900) are also on order

F-GFEO	Embraer EMB.120ER Brasilia	120062	ex PT-SKF	Regional	Lsd fr ATR Asset Mgt
F-GHIA	Embraer EMB.120ER Brasilia	120154	ex PT-SPT	Regional	
F-GHIB	Embraer EMB.120ER Brasilia	120162	ex PT-SQA	Regional	Lsd fr Atrium Capital
F-GIVK	Embraer EMB.120ER Brasilia	120112	ex C-FKOE	Regional; all-white	Lsd fr Acti Bail
F-GJAK	Embraer EMB.120ER Brasilia	120215	ex PT-SSJ	Regional	Lsd fr Atrium Capital
F-GLRG	Embraer EMB.120ER Brasilia	120149	ex PH-MGX	Regional	Lsd fr SNVB Financements
F-GTSG	Embraer EMB.120ER Brasilia	120087	ex PH-BRS	Regional	Lsd fr Regiair
F-GTSH	Embraer EMB.120ER Brasilia	120104	ex OO-DTH	Regional	Lsd fr Regiair
F-GTSI	Embraer EMB.120ER Brasilia	120123	ex OO-DTJ	Regional	Lsd fr Regiair
F-GTSJ	Embraer EMB.120ER Brasilia	120116	ex OO-DTL	Regional	Lsd fr Regiair
F-GTSK	Embraer EMB.120ER Brasilia	120213	ex OO-MTD	Regional	Lsd fr Regiair
F-GTSN	Embraer EMB.120ER Brasilia	120099	ex LX-RGI	Regional	Lsd fr ATR Asset Mgt
F-GTSO	Embraer EMB.120ER Brasilia	120097	ex LX-NVL	Regional	Lsd fr ATR Asset Mgt
F-GTSP	Embraer EMB.120ER Brasilia	120235	ex LX-RCT	Regional	Lsd fr ATR Asset Mgt
F-GOHA	Embraer EMB.135ER	145189		Regional	Lsd fr AFS Investments
F-GOHB	Embraer EMB.135ER	145198		Regional	Lsd fr AFS Investments
F-GOHC	Embraer EMB.135ER	145243		Regional	
F-GOHD	Embraer EMB.135ER	145252	ex PT-SJJ	Regional	Lsd fr Eurojet
F-GOHE	Embraer EMB.135ER	145335	ex PT-SNB	Regional	
F-GOHF	Embraer EMB.135ER	145347	ex PT-SNN	Regional	Lsd fr Eurojet
F-GRGP	Embraer EMB.135ER	145188		Regional	
F-GRGQ	Embraer EMB.135ER	145233		Regional	
F-GRGR	Embraer EMB.135ER	145236		Regional	
F-GRGA	Embraer EMB.145EU	145008	ex PT-SYE	Regional	Lsd fr Samba Avn
F-GRGB	Embraer EMB.145EU	145010	ex PT-SYG	Regional	Lsd fr Samba Avn
F-GRGC	Embraer EMB.145EU	145012	ex PT-SYI	Regional	Lsd fr Samba Avn
F-GRGD	Embraer EMB.145EU	145043	ex PT-SZI	Regional	Lsd fr Naoned
F-GRGE	Embraer EMB.145EU	145047	ex PT-SZM	Regional	Lsd fr Naoned
F-GRGF	Embraer EMB.145EU	145050	ex PT-SZP	Regional	Lsd fr Goeland

F-GRGG	Embraer EMB.145EU	145118	ex PT-SCT	Regional	Lsd fr Askell
F-GRGH	Embraer EMB.145EU	145120	ex PT-SCW	Regional	Lsd fr Parilease
F-GRGI	Embraer EMB.145EU	145152	ex PT-SED	Regional	Lsd fr Keltia
F-GRGJ	Embraer EMB.145EU	145297	ex PT-SKO	Regional	Lsd fr Surcourf
F-GRGK	Embraer EMB.145EU	145324	ex PT-SMQ	Regional	Lsd fr Keltia
F-GRGL	Embraer EMB.145EU	145375	ex PT-SOZ	Regional	Lsd fr Surcourf
F-GRGM	Embraer EMB.145EU	145418	ex PT-STP	Regional	Lsd fr AFS Investments
F-	Embraer EMB.145EU		ex PT-S	Regional, on order	
F-	Embraer EMB.145EU		ex PT-S	Regional, on order	
F-	Embraer EMB.145EU		ex PT-S	Regional, on order	
F-	Embraer EMB.145EU		ex PT-S	Regional, on order	
F-	Embraer EMB.145EU		ex PT-S	Regional, on order	
F-	Embraer EMB.145EU		ex PT-S	Regional, on order	
F-	Embraer EMB.145EU		ex PT-S	Regional, on order	
F-	Embraer EMB.145EU		ex PT-S	Regional, on order	
F-GUAM	Embraer EMB.145MP	145266	ex PT-SIY	Regional	Lsd fr Eurojet
F-GUBA	Embraer EMB.145MP	145398	ex PT-SQV	Regional	Lsd fr RBS Avn
F-GUBB	Embraer EMB.145MP	145419	ex PT-STQ	Regional	Lsd fr RBS Avn
F-GUBC	Embraer EMB.145MP	145556	ex PT-SZR	Regional	
F-GUBD	Embraer EMB.145MP	145333	ex PT-SMZ	Regional	
F-GUBE	Embraer EMB.145MP	145668	ex PT-SFC	Regional	Lsd fr Investima 7
F-GUBF	Embraer EMB.145MP	145669	ex PT-SFD	Regional	
F-GUEA	Embraer EMB.145MP	145342	ex PT-SNI	Regional	Lsd fr Eurojet
F-GUFD	Embraer EMB.145MP	145197	ex PT-S	Regional	Lsd fr Catalina Bail
F-GUJA	Embraer EMB.145MP	145407	ex PT-S	Regional	Lsd fr AFS Investments
F-GUMA	Embraer EMB.145MP	145405	ex PT-S	Regional	Lsd fr AFS Investments
F-GUPT	Embraer EMB.145MP	145294	ex PT-SKL	Regional	Lsd fr Eurojet
F-GVGS	Embraer EMB.145MP	145385	ex PT-SQJ	Regional	
F-GVHD	Embraer EMB.145MP	145178	ex	Regional	Lsd fr Catalina Bail
F-GIOG	Fokker 100	11364	ex	Regional	Lsd fr Jet Trading & Lsg
F-GKHD	Fokker 100	11381	ex HB-IVI	Brit'Air	Lsd fr Air Group Finance
F-GLIR	Fokker 100	11509	ex PH-EZF	Regional	Lsd fr DB Export Lsg
F-GNLI	Fokker 100	11315	ex	Regional	Lsd fr Jet Trading & Lsg
F-GNLJ	Fokker 100	11344	ex D-ADFD	CCM Airlines	
F-GNLK	Fokker 100	11307	ex D-ADFA	Regional	Lsd fr Jet Trading & Lsg
F-GPNK	Fokker 100	11324	ex SE-DUC	Regional	Lsd fr debis
F-GPNL	Fokker 100	11325	ex SE-DUD	Regional	Lsd fr debis
F-GPXA	Fokker 100	11487	ex PH-EZN	Brit'Air	Lsd fr Lufthansa Lsg
F-GPXB	Fokker 100	11492	ex PH-EZK	Brit'Air	Lsd fr Lufthansa Lsg
F-GPXC	Fokker 100	11493	ex PH-EZY	Brit'Air	Lsd fr Lufthansa Lsg
F-GPXD	Fokker 100	11494	ex PH-EZO	Brit'Air	Lsd fr Lufthansa Lsg
F-GPXE	Fokker 100	11495	ex PH-EZP	Brit'Air	Lsd fr Lufthansa Lsg
F-GPXF	Fokker 100	11330	ex F-WQJX	Brit'Air	Lsd fr Lufthansa Lsg
F-GPXG	Fokker 100	11387	ex SX-BGL	Brit'Air	Lsd fr Biblos Ltd
F-GPXH	Fokker 100	11476	ex SX-BGM	Brit'Air	Lsd fr Biblos Ltd
F-GMVB	SAAB 2000	019	ex SE-019	Regional	Lsd fr Nordbanken
F-GMVC	SAAB 2000	021	ex SE-021	Regional	Lsd fr Nordbanken
F-GMVD	SAAB 2000	034	ex SE-034	Regional	Lsd fr Nordbanken
F-GMVE	SAAB 2000	040	ex SE-040	Regional	Lsd fr Nordbanken
F-GMVG	SAAB 2000	049	ex SE-049	Regional	Lsd fr SAAB
F-GMVU	SAAB 2000	045	ex LX-RAC	Regional	Lsd fr SAAB
F-GNEH	SAAB 2000	016	ex EI-CPW	Regional	Lsd fr SAAB

The services are operated in full Air France colours with titles Air France by ..(the apprpropriate airline, Brit'Air, Flybe and Cityjet)

AIR JET suspended operations in early March 2003 and later entered receivership

---

AIR LITTORAL

Air Littoral (FU/LIT) (IATA 659)   Montpellier (MPL)

F-GPYD	Aerospatiale/Alenia ATR 42-500	490	ex F-WWLJ	stored	Lsd fr Brice Bail
F-GPYL	Aerospatiale/Alenia ATR 42-500	542	ex F-WWLH		Lsd fr Callen; lsd to MSR
F-GPYM	Aerospatiale/Alenia ATR 42-500	520	ex F-WWLR		Lsd fr Callen
F-GPYN	Aerospatiale/Alenia ATR 42-500	539	ex F-WWLO		Lsd fr Callen
F-GPYO	Aerospatiale/Alenia ATR 42-500	544	ex F-WWLH		Lsd fr Callen; sublsd to MSR
F-GLIJ+	Canadair CL-600-2B19	7081			
F-GLIK+	Canadair CL-600-2B19	7084	ex C-FMMT		
F-GLIY+	Canadair CL-600-2B19	7053	ex C-FMMQ	white	
F-GLIZ+	Canadair CL-600-2B19	7057	ex C-FMMY		
F-GNMN	Canadair CL-600-2B19	7003	ex C-GVRJ		Lsd fr RJ Finance
F-GPTB	Canadair CL-600-2B19	7177			Lsd fr WFBN
F-GPTC	Canadair CL-600-2B19	7182			Lsd fr WFBN
F-GPTD	Canadair CL-600-2B19	7184			Lsd fr Bombardier
F-GPTE	Canadair CL-600-2B19	7183			Lsd fr Bombardier
F-GPTG	Canadair CL-600-2B19	7223			Lsd fr Bombardier
F-GPTJ^	Canadair CL-600-2B19	7323	ex C-FMLV		
F-GPTK+	Canadair CL-600-2B19	7332	ex C-FMND		

F-GPTM	Canadair CL-600-2B19	7020	ex EC-GTG	all-white	Lsd fr RJ Finance
F-GPYP*	Canadair CL-600-2B19	7126	ex C-FMML	all-white	Lsd fr RJ Finance
F-GPYQ	Canadair CL-600-2B19	7144	ex C-FMMT		Lsd fr Regional A/c Finance
F-GPYR	Canadair CL-600-2B19	7164	ex C-FMND		Lsd fr Regional A/c Finance

+Leased from Deutsche Operations Leasing   *Subleased to Brit'Air
^Leased from Deutsche Structured Finance

| F-GLIS | Fokker 70 | 11540 | ex PH-RRS | Lsd fr DB Export Lsg |
| F-GLIT | Fokker 70 | 11541 | ex PH-RRT | Lsd fr DB Export Lsg |

Filed for bankruptcy protection in August 2003 but operations continued

AIR LITTORAL EXPRESS ceased operations

AIR MEDITERRANÉE

Mediterranée (ZN/BIE)   *Tarbes (LDE)*

F-GCJL	Boeing 737-222 (Nordam 3)	71/19067	ex N9029U	
F-GCSL	Boeing 737-222 (Nordam 3)	69/19066	ex N9028U	
F-GGVQ	Boeing 737-2K2C (AvAero 3)	408/20944	ex VT-EKD	Lsd fr/op for FPO
F-GIXA	Boeing 737-2K2C (AvAero 3)	354/20836	ex PH-TVC	Lsd fr/op for FPO
F-GOAF	Boeing 737-242C (Nordam 3)	84/19847	ex N847TA	Lsd fr Ardennes Alpha
F-GYAM	Boeing 737-505	1917/24652	ex LN-BRF	Lsd tr CIT Leasing
F-GYAN	Airbus Industrie A321-111	0535	ex F-WQQU	Lsd fr Encore Lsg
F-GYAO	Airbus Industrie A321-111	0642	ex F-WQQV	Lsd fr ILFC
F-GYAP	Airbus Industrie A321-111	0517	ex HB-IOA	Lsd fr ILFC
F-GYAQ	Airbus Industrie A321-111	0827	ex HB-IOI	Lsd fr ILFC

AIR PROVENCE taken over by West Air Sweden and renamed West Air.FR

AIR SERVICE VOSGES

Air Service Vosges (VGE)   *Epinal (EPL)*

| F-GDAK | Beech 65-F90 King Air | LA-141 |

AIRBUS TRANSPORT INTERNATIONAL

Super Transport (BGA)   *Toulouse-Blagnac (TLS)*

F-GSTA	Airbus Industrie A300B4-608ST Beluga	655/001	ex F-WAST	Super Transporter 1
F-GSTB	Airbus Industrie A300B4-608ST Beluga	751/002	ex F-WSTB	Super Transporter 2
F-GSTC	Airbus Industrie A300B4-608ST Beluga	765/003	ex F-WSTC	Super Transporter 3 Lsd fr BBV Lsg
F-GSTD	Airbus Industrie A300B4-608ST Beluga	776/004	ex F-WSTD	Super Transporter 4 Lsd fr BBV Lsg
F-GSTF	Airbus Industrie A300B4-608ST Beluga	796/005	ex F-WSTF	Super Transporter 5 Lsd fr SLB Lsg

AIRLEC AIR ESPACE

AirLec (ARL)   *Bordeaux (BOD)*

F-GGRV	Piper PA-31T Cheyenne II	31T-7720036	ex N41RC	Lsd fr Natiolocation
F-GGVG	Swearingen SA.226T Merlin IIIB	T-293	ex D-IBBB	Lsd fr PEA
F-GLPT	Swearingen SA.226T Merlin IIIB	T-298	ex VH-AWU	

AIRLIB ceased operations 06 February 2003

AIRLINAIR

Airlinair (A5/RLA) (IATA 163)   *Paris-Orly (ORY)*

F-GHPI	Aerospatiale/Alenia ATR 42-310	214	ex F-WWEB		Lsd fr BZH, op for AFR
F-GKNB	Aerospatiale/Alenia ATR 42-300	226			Lsd fr Prop Bail
F-GKNC	Aerospatiale/Alenia ATR 42-300	230			Lsd fr Prop Bail
F-GKOB	Aerospatiale/Alenia ATR 72-202	232			Lsd fr A/c Intl Renting
F-GKYN	Aerospatiale/Alenia ATR 42-300	095	ex F-ODUL		Lsd fr ATR Asset Mgt
F-GPOA	Aerospatiale/Alenia ATR 72-202F	204	ex F-ORAC	all-white	Op for FPO
F-GPOB	Aerospatiale/Alenia ATR 72-202F	207	ex F-ORAN	all-white	Op for FPO
F-GPOC	Aerospatiale/Alenia ATR 72-202F	311	ex B-22707	all-white	Op for FPO
F-GPOD	Aerospatiale/Alenia ATR 72-202F	361	ex B-22711		Op for FPO
F-GVZA	Aerospatiale/Alenia ATR 42-300	503	ex F-WQLJ		Lsd fr ATR Asset Mgt; op for TDH
F-GVZF	Aerospatiale/Alenia ATR 72-212	461	ex F-OGXF		Lsd fr Air Vendee, op for AFR
F-GVZX	Aerospatiale/Alenia ATR 42-300	011	ex F-WWZX		Lsd fr ATR Asset Mgt
F-GVZY	Aerospatiale/Alenia ATR 42-300	080	ex F-WWZY		Lsd fr ATR Asset Mgt
F-GVZZ	Aerospatiale/Alenia ATR 42-300	055	ex F-WWZZ		Lsd fr ATR Asset Mgt

Operates services for Air France; sometimes in full colours. Aerolinair is a sister company

ALSAIR

Alsair (AL/LSR)   Colmar (CMR)

F-GEOU	Beech 65-C90 King Air	LJ-941	ex N3804C
F-GJMJ	Beech 200 Super King Air	BB-1032	ex I-CUVI
F-HALS	Beech 1900D	UE-379	ex N31525

ATLANTIQUE AIR ASSISTANCE

Triple A (TLB)   Nantes (NTE)

F-GIZB	Beech C90 King Air	LJ-955	ex N786SB	
F-GNBR	Beech 1900D	UE-327	ex N23154	Lsd fr Raytheon
F-GPYY	Beech 1900C-1	UC-115	ex N115YV	

AXIS AIRWAYS

Axis (AXY)   Marseille (MRS)

F-GFUI	Boeing 737-3M8	1675/24023	ex PH-TSR		Lsd fr GECAS
F-GIXG	Boeing 737-382(QC)	1657/24364	ex F-OGSX		Lsd fr Aircraft Holding
F-GLNI	British Aerospace 146 Srs.200QC	E2188	ex G-BTDO		Lsd fr TNT Jet Svs
F-GOMA	British Aerospace 146 Srs.200QC	E2211	ex G-6-211		Lsd fr TNT Jet Svs
F-	Boeing 737-36C	2068/25159	ex N319FL	on order 04	

BLUE LINE

Paris-Charles de Gaulle (CDG)

F-GNLG	Fokker 100	11363	ex D-ADFE	Lsd fr Jet Trading & Lsg
F-GNLH	Fokker 100	11311	ex D-ADFB	Lsd fr Jet Trading & Lsg

BRIT'AIR

Brit Air (DB/BZH)   Morlaix (MXN)

Wholly owned by Air France and aircraft operate feeder services in their colours using AF call-signs; for fleet see Air France Regional

CCM AIRLINES

Corsica (XK/CCM) (IATA 146)   Ajaccio (AJA)

F-GKPC*	Aerospatiale/Alenia ATR 72-201	171	ex F-WWEA		
F-GKPD*	Aerospatiale/Alenia ATR 72-201	177	ex F-WWEH		Lsd fr Corse Bail
F-GKPE	Aerospatiale/Alenia ATR 72-201	192	ex F-WWEE		Lsd fr Piana Bail
F-GKPF	Aerospatiale/Alenia ATR 72-201	222			
F-GKPH	Aerospatiale/Alenia ATR 72-202	352	ex F-WWEJ		Lsd fr Corse Bail
F-GMGK*	Aerospatiale/Alenia ATR 72-202	365	ex F-WQIX		Lsd fr ATR Asset Mgt
F-GKHE	Fokker 100	11388	ex HB-IVK		Lsd fr Air Group Finance
F-GMPG	Fokker 100	11362	ex PH-EZT		Lsd fr Campo del'Oro Bail
F-GNLJ*	Fokker 100	11344	ex D-ADFD		Lsd fr Jet Fonce Bail
F-GYFM	Airbus Industrie A319-112	1068	ex F-WQRR		Lsd fr Magritte Lsg
F-GYFN	Airbus Industrie A319-112	1086	ex F-OHJX		
F-GYJM	Airbus Industrie A319-112	1145	ex F-WQRT		Lsd fr Magritte Lsg
F-	Airbus Industrie A319-112		ex	on order 04	
F-	Airbus Industrie A320-		ex	on order 04	
F-	Airbus Industrie A320-		ex	on order 04	

*Operate feeder services for Air France in their colours and using AF call-signs.
CCM Airlines is the tradining name of Compagnie Corse Mediterranee

CHAMPAGNE AIRLINES

Champagne (CPH)   Reims (RHE)

F-BXON	Beech 65-E90 King Air	LW-161	
F-GJPN	Swearingen SA.227AC Metro III	AC-757B	ex N57NE
F-GPSN	Swearingen SA.227AC Metro III	AC-758B	ex N58NE
F-GTRB	Swearingen SA.227AC Metro III	AC-519	ex EC-GJV

CORSAIR

Corsair (SS/CRL) (IATA 923)   Ajaccio (AJA)

F-GJSV	Airbus Industrie A330-322	171	ex C-FRAV		Lsd fr CIT Leasing
F-HBIL	Airbus Industrie A330-243	320			Lsd fr Parangue Bail
F-HCAT	Airbus Industrie A330-243	285	ex F-WWKB		Lsd fr CIT Leasing
F-	Airbus Industrie A330-322			on order	
F-	Airbus Industrie A330-322			on order	

F-GSEA	Boeing 747-312	603/23032	ex N121KG	Lsd fr WTCo
F-GSEX	Boeing 747-312	584/23028	ex N117KC	Lsd fr WTCo
F-GSKY	Boeing 747-312	621/23244	ex TF-ATG	Lsd fr VIC-23244
F-GSUN	Boeing 747-312	593/23030	ex N119KE	Lsd fr WTCo
F-HJAC	Boeing 747-312	612/23243	ex (F-OJAC)	

F-GFUG	Boeing 737-4B3	1916/24750	
F-GFUH	Boeing 737-4B3	2107/24751	

Member of TUI Group which includes Hapag Lloyd, Britannia Airways, Neos and White Eagle
Six Boeing 747-422s are on possible order for delivery from June 2004

CROSSAIR EUROPE

Cigogne (QE/ECC)   *Basle-Mulhouse (MLH)*

F-GPKD				
F-GPKG	SAAB SF.340B	185	ex HB-AKG	Lsd fr SWR
F-GPKM	SAAB SF.340B	221	ex HB-AKM	Lsd fr SWR

35% owned by Swiss International Air Lines; Crossair Europe is the trading name of Europe Continental Airways

EAGLE AVIATION

French Eagle (EGN)   *St Nazairre/Paris-Orly (-/ORY)*

F-GEMO	Airbus Industrie A310-304	504	F-WWCF		Lsd fr ILFC; sublsd to FBN
F-GVVV	Airbus Industrie A300B4-103	069	ex 5V-TTT	stored BOD	Lsd fr Hamloc
F-GYYY	Airbus Industrie A310-204	486	ex 5B-DAX		Lsd fr ILFC

EURALAIR HORIZONS

Euralair (RN/EUH)   *Paris-Le Bourget (LBG)*

F-GRNA	Boeing 737-85F	174/28823	ex N1784B	Op for FRAM	Lsd fr GATX
F-GRNB	Boeing 737-85F	180/28824	ex N500GX	Op for Go Vacs	Lsd fr GATX
F-GRNC	Boeing 737-85F	151/28821		Op for FRAM	Lsd fr GATX
F-GRND	Boeing 737-85F	467/28827	ex N1787B	Op for Go Vacs	Lsd fr GATX
F-GRNE	Boeing 737-85F	793/30568		Op for FRAM	Lsd fr GATX

F-GRNS	Airbus Industrie A310-304	432	ex C-GRYI	stored CHR	Lsd fr EFG Aircraft

Sister company, Euralair, operates charter and VIP services with bizjets using designator ERL
Filed for bankruptcy protection 03 November 2003 but operations continue

EUROFLY   To lease a Fokker 100 from EUJet for mid-2004 start-up

EUROJET AIRLINES

(EUF)   *Basel-Mulhouse (MLH)*

F-GNAO	Boeing 737-4Q8	2210/25168	ex F-WNAO	Avione titles	Lsd fr IAI III LLC

EUROPE AIRPOST

French Post (FPO)   *Paris-Charles de Gaulle (CDG)*

F-GFUE	Boeing 737-3B3(QC)	1693/24387			
F-GFUF	Boeing 737-3B3(QC)	1725/24388			
F-GGVQ	Boeing 737-2K2C (AvAero 3)	408/20944	ex VT-EKD		Lsd to/op by BIE
F-GIXA	Boeing 737-2K2C (AvAero 3)	354/20836	ex PH-TVC		Lsd to/op by BIE
F-GIXB	Boeing 737-33A(QC)	1953/24789	ex F-OGSD		
F-GIXC	Boeing 737-38B(QC)	2047/25124	ex F-OGSS	Saint-Louis	
F-GIXD	Boeing 737-33A(QC)	2198/25744	ex N3213T		Lsd fr CIT Leasing
F-GIXE	Boeing 737-3B3(QC)	2235/26850	ex N854WT		Lsd fr CIT Leasing
F-GIXF	Boeing 737-3B3(QC)	2267/26851	ex N4361V		Lsd fr CIT Leasing
F-GIXI	Boeing 737-348(QC)	1458/23809	ex F-OGSY		Lsd fr NBB Lse
F-GIXJ	Boeing 737-3Y0(QC)	1357/23685	ex G-MONH	Cap-Juby	Lsd fr ACG Acquisitions
F-GIXL	Boeing 737-348(QC)	1474/23810	ex F-OHCS		Lsd fr NBB Lse
F-GIXO	Boeing 737-3Q8(QC)	1555/24132	ex N241LF		Lsd fr ILFC
F-GIXR	Boeing 737-3H6F	2415/27125	ex 9M-MZA		Lsd fr Aviacargo Lsg
F-GIXS	Boeing 737-3H6F	2615/27347	ex 9M-MZB		Lsd fr Aviacargo Lsg

EI-OZA	Airbus Industrie A300B4-103F	148	ex F-GOZA		Op by ABR
EI-OZC	Airbus Industrie A300B4-103F	189	ex F-GOZC		Op by ABR
F-GPOA	Aerospatiale/Alenia ATR 72-202F	204	ex F-ORAC	all white	Op by RLA
F-GPOB	Aerospatiale/Alenia ATR 72-202F	207	ex F-ORAN	all-white	Op by RLA
F-GPOC	Aerospatiale/Alenia ATR 72-202F	311	ex B-22707	all-white	Op by RLA
F-GPOD	Aerospatiale/Alenia ATR 72-202F	361	ex B-22711		Op by RLA

Wholly owned by Poste France.

FINIST'AIR

Finistair (FTR)   *Brest (BES)*

| F-GHGZ | Cessna 208A Caravan I | 20800188 | ex (N9769F) |
| F-GJFI | Cessna 208B Caravan I | 208B0230 | ex N208GC |

FLYECO French Eco (FLO) Beauvais. Intended to commence operations in 2003 with Boeing 737-300 or MD-83 aircraft but did not start operations

HELI-UNION

Heli Union (HLU)   *Paris-Heliport/Toussus-le-Noble (JDP/TNF)*

F-GEPN	Aerospatiale SA.365C3 Dauphin 2	5073	ex D-HELY	
F-GERJ	Aerospatiale SA.365N Dauphin 2	6066	ex F-ODRA	
F-GFCH	Aerospatiale SA.365C2 Dauphin 2	5072	ex F-OCCD	
F-GFEC	Aerospatiale SA.365C2 Dauphin 2	5071	ex F-ODBV	
F-GFPA	Aerospatiale SA.365C2 Dauphin 2	5063	ex LV-AIE	
F-GFPB	Aerospatiale SA.365C2 Dauphin 2	5064	ex F-ODNJ	
F-GFYU	Aerospatiale SA.365N Dauphin 2	6082	ex F-ODTC	Lsd to Sonair
F-GIZU	Aerospatiale AS.365N2 Dauphin 2	6540		Lsd to Helicopter Svs as EP-HDS
F-GJDV	Aerospatiale SA.365N Dauphin 2	6065	ex I-SINV	Lsd to Sonair
F-GJPZ	Aerospatiale SA.365N Dauphin 2	6115	ex LN-OLN	
F-GKCU	Aerospatiale SA.365N Dauphin 2	6011	ex PH-SEC	
F-GLMZ	Aerospatiale SA.365N2 Dauphin 2	6467	ex 3A-MSY	
F-GLNU	Aerospatiale SA.365N Dauphin 3	6327	ex ZS-HVI	
F-GMAY	Aerospatiale SA.365N Dauphin 2	6137		
F-GMHI	Aerospatiale SA.365N Dauphin 2	6037	ex PH-SED	
F-GSYA	Aerospatiale SA.365N Dauphin 2	6220	ex JA9913	
F-GINQ	Aerospatiale SA.330J Puma	1583	ex LX-HUL	
F-GONB	Aerospatiale SA.330J Puma	1571	ex F-WQPM	
F-GRRU	Sikorsky S-76A	760186	ex LX-HUE	
F-GRSU	Sikorsky S-76A	760170	ex LX-HUA	based Luanda

HEX'AIR

Hex Airline (UD/HER) (IATA 848)   *Le Puy (LPY)*

F-GOPE	Beech 1900D	UE-103	ex N82930	La Fayette	Lsd fr PEA
F-GYPE	Embraer EMB.135LR	145492	ex PT-SXL	Savoie titles	Lsd fr PEA
F-HAPE	Beech 1900D	UE-367	ex N30515		Lsd fr PEA

OCCITANIA

Occitania (OJF)   *Paris-Le Bourget (LBG)*

F-GVBR*	Embraer EMB.120ER Brasilia	120014	ex LX-PTU		Lsd fr Regourd Avn
F-GLPJ*	Beech 1900C-1	UC-40	ex OY-BVG	VIP	Lsd fr Regourd Avn
F-HAAA*	Beech 65-E90 King Air	LW-175	ex F-BXSN		Lsd fr Citicapital
F-HBCA	Beech 1900D	UE-188	ex SE-KXV	Lsd fr Bail Materiel; sublsd to 5E	

*Leased to Octavia Airlines, a sister company

OCEAN AIRWAYS

(OG/OCW)   *Nantes (NTE)*

| F- | Airbus Industrie A340-300 | | ex F-WW | on order 04 |

Due to commence operations in early 2004

OCTAVIA AIRLINES

Octaflight (OCN)   *Paris-le Bourget (LBG)*

F-GVBR	Embraer EMB.120ER Brasilia	120014	ex LX-PTU	
F-GLPJ	Beech 1900C-1	UC-40	ex OY-BVG	VIP
F-HAAA	Beech 65-E90 King Air	LW-175	ex F-BXSN	

A sister company of Occitania who operate the aircraft

PAN EUROPÉENNE AIR SERVICE

(PEA)   *Chambery (CMF)*

F-GOPE	Beech 1900D	UE-103	ex N82930	La Fayette	
F-GUPE	Beech 1900D	UE-248	ex N10882		Lsd to HER
F-GVPE	Beech 300 Super King Air	FA-94	ex I-AZME		
F-GYPE	Embraer EMB.135LR	145492	ex PT-SXL		Lsd fr Papa Echo
F-GZPE	Piaggio 180	1064			
F-HAPE	Beech 1900D	UE-367	ex N30515		Lsd to HER

PREST'AFFAIR   current status is uncertain; both aircraft returned to lessors

REGIONAL

Regional Europe (YS/RAE) (IATA)   Nantes (NTE)

F-GIYH	Embraer EMB.120ER Brasilia	120239	ex OM-FLY	Lsd to ESK
F-GIYI	Embraer EMB.120ER Brasilia	120244	ex OM-SAY	Lsd to ESK

Wholly owned by Air France and aircraft operate feeder services in their colours as Air France by Regional using AF call-signs; for fleet see Air France Regional . Regional is the trading name of Regional Compagnie Aerienne Europeenne

R-LINES   ceased operations

SECURITÉ CIVILE

Marseille (MRS)

F-ZBEG	Canadair CL-215-6B11	2015	ex C-FXBH	P-39
F-ZBEO	Canadair CL-215-6B11	2011	ex C-FWPD	P-36
F-ZBEU	Canadair CL-215-6B11	2024	ex C-FZDE	P-42
F-ZBEZ	Canadair CL-215-6B11	2018	ex C-FXBX	P-41
F-ZBFN	Canadair CL-215-6B11	2006	ex C-FVUK	P-33
F-ZBFP	Canadair CL-215-6B11	2002	ex C-FBET	P-31
F-ZBFS	Canadair CL-215-6B11	2001	ex C-GSCT	P-32
F-ZBFV	Canadair CL-215-6B11	2013	ex C-FWPE	P-37
F-ZBFW	Canadair CL-215-6B11	2014	ex C-FWZH	P-38
F-ZBFX	Canadair CL-215-6B11	2007	ex C-FVUJ	P-34
F-ZBFY	Canadair CL-215-6B11	2010	ex C-FVDY	P-35
F-ZBAA	Conair Turbo Firecat	456/027	ex F-WEOL	T-22
F-ZBAP	Conair Turbo Firecat	567/026	ex F-ZBDA	T-12
F-ZBAU	Conair Firecat	DHC-32/009	ex F-WZLQ	T-2
F-ZBAZ	Conair Turbo Firecat	DHC-57/008	ex F-WEOL	T-01
F-ZBBL	Conair Turbo Firecat	626/024	ex F-WEOK	T-19
F-ZBCZ	Conair Turbo Firecat	DHC-94/036	ex F-ZBCA	T-23
F-ZBEH	Conair Turbo Firecat	410/035	ex F-WEOJ	T-20
F-ZBET	Conair Turbo Firecat	703/028	ex F-WEOJ	T-15
F-ZBEW	Conair Turbo Firecat	621/025	ex F-WEOL	T-11
F-ZBEY	Conair Turbo Firecat	400/017	ex F-WEOK	T-7
F-ZBFE	Conair Turbo Firecat	656/032	ex F-WEOK	T-17
F-ZBMA	Conair Turbo Firecat	461/021	ex C-GFZG	T-24
F-Z	Conair Turbo Firecat	DHC-58/	ex C-FLRA	on order
F-ZBFF	Fokker F.27 Friendship 600	10432/3	ex C-FGDS	P-71; Conair Firebomber conv
F-ZBFG*	Fokker F.27 Friendship 600	10440/2	ex C-FBDY	P-72; Conair Firebomber conv
F-ZBFJ	Beech B200 Super King Air	BB-1102	ex D-IWAN	B-98
F-ZBFK	Beech B200 Super King Air	BB-876	ex F-GHSC	B-96
F-ZBMB	Beech B200 Super King Air	BB-1379	ex F-GJFD	B-97

*stored Dinard

STAR AIRLINES

Starway (2R/SEU) (IATA 473)   *Paris-Orly (ORY)*

F-GRSD	Airbus Industrie A320-214	0653	ex F-GJDY	Lsd fr GATX
F-GRSE	Airbus Industrie A320-214	0657	ex F-WWIR	Lsd fr GATX
F-GRSG	Airbus Industrie A320-214	0737	ex F-WWBS	Lsd fr GECAS; sublsd to TSC
F-GRSH	Airbus Industrie A320-214	0749	ex F-WWIK	Lsd fr GECAS; sublsd to TSC
F-GRSI	Airbus Industrie A320-214	0973	ex F-WWBR	Lsd fr ILFC
F-GRSN	Airbus Industrie A320-214	1692	ex F-WWIN	Lsd fr NOE Lsg
C-GPTS	Airbus Industrie A330-243	480	ex F-WWKV	Lsd fr TSC for winter
F-GRSQ	Airbus Industrie A330-243	501	ex F-WWKG	Lsd fr ILFC
F-	Airbus Industrie A330-243		ex F-WW	on order Nov04 Lsd fr ILFC

Owned by Transat Group;

SUD AIRLINES

F-BTDG	Douglas DC-10-30	288/46997	ex TU-TAN

TAXI AIR FRET

Paris-Le Bourget (LBG)

F-BTME	Beech 99	U-79	ex N551GP	Op for BRE
F-GFPE	Beech 99	U-21	ex OO-WAY	Lsd fr private
F-GHVF	Swearingen SA.227AT Merlin IVC	AT-429	ex N10NB	

TWIN JET

(T7/TJT) (IATA 294)   *Marseille (MRS)*

F-GLNH	Beech 1900D	UE-73	ex YR-BLB		Lsd fr RAE
F-GLPL	Beech 1900C-1	UC-92	ex N15382	all-white	Lsd fr RAE
F-GRYL	Beech 1900CD	UE-301	ex		Lsd fr RAE

WESTAIR current status uncertain, possibly a tour operator

WEST-AIR FRANCE

West Azur (FWA)   *Marseille (MRS)*
Previously lisred as Provence Airways

SE-LIA	Hawker Siddeley HS.748 Srs.2A/264	1717	ex F-GFYM	Mademoiselle
SE-LGU	British Aerospace ATP	2022	ex N853AW	
SE-LPU	British Aerospace ATP	2060	ex G-OBWO	

Wholly owned subsidiary of West Air Sweden; may be liquidated

F-O PACIFIC TERRITORIES (French Polynesia and New Caledonia)

AIR ARCHIPELS

Archipels (RHL)   *Papeete (PPT)*

F-OHJK	Beech 200 Super King Air	BB-1544	ex N1094S
F-OHJL	Beech 200 Super King Air	BB-1592	ex N6148X

Owned by Air Tahiti

AIR CALÉDONIE

AirCal (TY/TPC)   *Noumea (NOU)*

F-ODYB	Dornier 228-212	8191	ex D-CORK
F-ODYD	Aerospatiale/Alenia ATR 42-320	221	
F-ODYE	Aerospatiale/Alenia ATR 42-320	335	ex F-WWLW
F-OIAM	Aerospatiale/Alenia ATR 42-320	403	ex F-WWLD

Partially owned by Air France

AIRCALIN - AIR CALÉDONIE INTERNATIONAL

AirCalin (SB/ACI) (IATA 063)   *Noumea (NOU)*

F-OCQZ	de Havilland DHC-6 Twin Otter 300	412			
F-ODGX	Boeing 737-33A	1729/24094		For Palau Air	Lsd fr Volito
F-OHSD	Airbus Industrie A330-202	507	ex F-WWYS		
F-OJSB	Airbus Industrie A320-232	2152			
F-OJSE	Airbus Industrie A330-202	510	ex F-WWYT		
F-	Airbus Industrie A330-202		ex F-WW	on order Mar04	

AIR MOOREA

Air Moorea (QE/TAH)   *Papeete (PPT)*

F-ODBN	de Havilland DHC-6 Twin Otter 300	470		Lsd fr VTA
F-ODUQ	Britten-Norman BN-2B-26 Islander	2220	ex G-BRGC	
F-ODUR	Britten-Norman BN-2B-26 Islander	2217	ex G-BRFZ	
F-OHAA	Dornier 228-212	8198	ex D-CDWK	
F-OHJF	de Havilland DHC-6 Twin Otter 300	500	ex N929MA	
F-OHJG	de Havilland DHC-6 Twin Otter 300	603	ex Fr AF 603	Lsd fr SNC Twin 1

A subsidiary of Air Tahiti

AIR TAHITI

Air Tahiti (VT/VTA) (IATA 135)   *Papeete (PPT)*

F-OHJB	Aerospatiale/Alenia ATR 42-500	513	ex F-WWLL	Lsd fr Airinvest
F-OHJC	Aerospatiale/Alenia ATR 42-500	528	ex F-WWLF	Lsd fr Airinvest
F-OHJD	Aerospatiale/Alenia ATR 42-500	556	ex F-WWLM	Lsd fr Tahiti 2009
F-OHJJ	Aerospatiale/Alenia ATR 42-500	614	ex F-WWLU	Lsd fr Antin Participation
F-OHJN	Aerospatiale/Alenia ATR 72-212A	535	ex F-WWEC	Lsd fr Vavin Tahiti Bail
F-OHJO	Aerospatiale/Alenia ATR 72-212A	553	ex F-WWLC	Lsd fr Air Bail
F-OHJS	Aerospatiale/Alenia ATR 72-212A	696	ex F-WWES	Lsd fr Antin Participation
F-OHJT	Aerospatiale/Alenia ATR 72-212A	590	ex F-WWET	Lsd fr Credit a l'Ind
F-OHJU	Aerospatiale/Alenia ATR 72-212A	563	ex F-WWEA	Lsd fr Doumer Tahiti Bail
F-OIQB	Aerospatiale/Alenia ATR 72-212A	621	ex F-WWLB	
F-OI	Aerospatiale/Alenia ATR 72-212A		ex F-WW	on order Jun04

F-ODBN	de Havilland DHC-6 Twin Otter 300	470		Lsd to TAH
F-OHAF	Dornier 228-212	8199	ex D-CBDZ	Lsd fr Tahiti Investments

Owns Air Archipels and Air Moorea

AIR TAHITI NUI

Tahiti Airlines (TN/THT) (IATA 244)   *Papeete (PPT)*

F-OITQ	Aerospatiale/Alenia ATR 42-500	622	ex		Lsd fr Government
F-OJGF	Airbus Industrie A340-313X	385	ex F-WWJC	Mangareva	
F-OJTN	Airbus Industrie A340-313X	395	ex C-GZIA	Bora Bora	Lsd fr ILFC
F-OSEA	Airbus Industrie A340-313X	438	ex F-WWJV	Rangiroa	Lsd fr Rangiroa Bail
F-OSUN	Airbus Industrie A340-313X	446	ex F-WWJA	Moorea	Lsd fr Moorea Bail

AVIAZUR

Iazur (VZR)   *Noumea (NOU)*

F-OIAY	de Havilland DHC-6 Twin Otter 300	507	ex P2-KSR	Lsd fr Regional Avn

WANAIR

Wanair (3W/VNR)   *Papeete (PPT)*

F-OHJM	Dornier 328-300	3129	ex D-BDXL
F-OHRX	Beech 1900D	UE-282	ex N11296

F-O ATLANTIC / INDIAN OCEAN TERRITORIES (St Pierre & Miquelon and Reunion)

AIR AUSTRAL

Reunion (UU/REU) (IATA 760)   *St Denis-Gilot (RUN)*

F-ODZJ	Boeing 737-53A	1943/24877	ex F-GHXN		
F-ODZY	Boeing 737-33A	2679/27452			
F-ODZZ	Boeing 737-39M (QC)	2906/28898	ex N35153		
F-OHSF	Aerospatiale/Alenia ATR 72-212A	650	ex F-WWEC		
F-OPAR	Boeing 777-2Q8ER	229/29908	ex EI-CRS	Marcel Goulette	Lsd fr ILFC
F-ORUN	Boeing 777-2Q8ER	246/28676	ex EI-CRT		Lsd fr ILFC

34% owned by Air France

AIR BOURBON

(ZN/BUB)   *St Denis-Gilot (RUN)*

F-OITN	Airbus Industrie A340-211	031	ex F-GLZD	Lsd fr Airbus

AIR ST PIERRE

Saint-Pierre (PJ/SPM) (IATA 638)   *St Pierre et Miquelon (FSP)*

F-OBYN	Piper PA-31-350 Chieftain	31-8152005	ex N4046M	
F-OHGL	Aerospatiale/Alenia ATR 42-320	323	ex F-WWET	Lsd fr St Pierre Investments
F-OSPJ	Reims Cessna F406 Caravan II	F406-0091		Lsd fr St Pierre Investments

F-O FRENCH CARIBBEAN
(Guadeloupe & Saint-Barthelemy, Martinique and French Guyana)

AIR ANTILLES EXPRESS

(3S)   *Pointe-a-Pitre (PTP)*

F-GHPZ	Aerospatiale/Alenia ATR 42-300	005	ex OY-CIA	Lsd fr Danish Air Tpt
F-OIJJ	Aerospatiale/Alenia ATR 42-310QC	059	ex TF-ELK	Lsd fr AL Avn Lsg

AIR CARAIBES

French West (TX/FWI) (IATA 427)   Pointe a Pitre/Fort de France/St Barthelemy/St Martin (PTP/FDF/SBH/-)

F-OGXY	Cessna 208B Caravan I	208B0574	ex (F-OHXJ)	Lsd fr ING Lease
F-OGXZ	Cessna 208B Caravan I	208B0586	ex (F-OHXK)	Lsd fr ING Lease
F-OHQM	Cessna 208B Caravan I	208B0726		Lsd fr ING Lease
F-OHQN	Cessna 208B Caravan I	208B0715	ex N1285H	Lsd fr ING Lease
F-OHQU	Cessna 208B Caravan I	208B0725	ex N12326	Lsd fr Kara Snc
F-ODZH	Dornier 228-202K	8077	ex N2255Y	
F-OGOL	Dornier 228-202K	8139	ex D-CACC	
F-OGVA	Dornier 228-212	8236	ex D-CBDB	
F-OGVE	Dornier 228-212	8237	ex D-CBDD	Lsd fr Guadaero
F-OHQK	Dornier 228-212	8238	ex D-CBDH	Lsd fr ING Lease France

F-OGUO	Aerospatiale/Alenia ATR 72-212	475	ex F-WWEH		Lsd fr ING Lease
F-OHQV	Aerospatiale/Alenia ATR 42-500	571	ex F-WWEM		
F-OIJE	Embraer EMB.145MP	145360	ex PT-SNZ		
F-OIJF	Embraer EMB.145MP	145362	ex PT-SON		
F-OIJG	Aerospatiale/Alenia ATR 72-212A	654	ex F-WWEI		Lsd fr ATR Asset Mgt
F-OIJH	Aerospatiale/Alenia ATR 72-212A	682	ex F-WWEE		Lsd fr Le Gosier SNC
F-OPTP	Airbus Industrie A330-223	240	ex HB-IQB		Lsd fr ILFC
F-	Airbus Industrie A330-223		ex	on order 04	Lsd fr ILFC

45% owned by Air France; Air Caraibes is the trading name of Societe Nouvelle Air Guadeloupe

AIR GUYANE EXPRESS

Air Guyane (3S/GUY)   *Cayenne (CAY)*

F-OIJB	Aerospatiale/Alenia ATR 42-500	579	ex F-WWLF	
F-OIJI	de Havilland DHC-6 Twin Otter 310	277	ex HB-LSU	Lsd fr Topscore
F-OIJL	de Havilland DHC-6 Twin Otter 310	281	ex HB-LSV	Lsd fr Topscore

AIR TROPICAL

French Hopper (DZ/NOE)   *St Francois (SFC)*

F-OPCL	Partenavia P.68B	142	ex TU-TLQ

Air Tropical is the trading name of Transcaraibes Air International

ST BARTH COMMUTER

Black Fin (PV/SBU)   *St Barthélemy (SBH)*

F-OGXB	Britten-Norman BN-2A-2 Islander	303	ex D-IHVH
F-OHQX	Britten-Norman BN-2A-26 Islander	3009	ex F-OHQW
F-OHQY	Britten-Norman BN-2B-20 Islander	2251	ex V2-LFE
F-OIJS	Britten-Norman BN-2B-20 Islander	2294	ex VH-CSS

G - UNITED KINGDOM (United Kingdom of Great Britain and Northern Ireland)

AIR 2000 renamed First Choice Airways on 21 October 2003 but operated as Air 2000 until 14 January 2004

AIR ATLANTA EUROPE

Snowbird (EUK)   *London-Gatwick/Manchester (LGW/MAN)*

(G-DAAE)	Boeing 767-3Y0ER	464/26204	ex TF-ATU	Lsd to XLA
G-SATR	Boeing 767-204ER	256/24457	ex TF-ATR	Lsd to XLA

Wholly owned subsidiary of Air Atlanta Iceland; aircraft leased from the parent

AIR ATLANTIQUE

Atlantic (AAG)   *Coventry (CVT)*

G-AGTM	de Havilland DH.89A Dragon Rapide	6746	ex JY-ACL	Historic flight	
G-AIDL	de Havilland DH.89A Dragon Rapide	6968	ex TX310	Historic flight	
G-AMRA	Douglas DC-3	26735	ex XE280		
G-ANAF	Douglas DC-3	16688/33436	ex N170GP	Lsd to Thales	
G-APRS	Scottish Aviation Twin Pioneer 3	561	ex G-BCWF	Primrose; ETPS colours	
G-APSA	Douglas DC-6A	995/45997	ex 4W-ABQ		
G-BXES	Percival P.66 Pembroke C.1	P66/101	ex N4234C	Historic flight	
G-CONV	Convair 440	484	ex CS-TML	stored CVT	Lsd fr GRR
G-DHDV	de Havilland DH.104 Dove	04205	ex VP981	Historic flight; as VP981	
G-SIXC	Douglas DC-6A/B	1032/45550	ex N93459		
G-VROE	Avro 652 Anson T.21	3634	ex G-BFIR	Historic flight; as WD413	

Associated with Atlantic Airlines, Atlantic Express and Atlantic Reconnaissance

AIR CORDIAL

Cordial (ORC)   *Manchester (MAN)*

Operates Airbus A300's on behalf of Air Scandic

AIR SCANDIC

Airscan (SCY)   *Manchester (MAN)*

G-SWJW	Airbus Industrie A300B4-203	302	ex OH-LAB
G-TTMC	Airbus Industrie A300B4-203	299	ex OH-LAA

Airbus A300's operated by Air Cordial (ORC) on behalf of Air Scandic.

AIR SCOTLAND

Edinburgh/Glasgow (EDI/GLA)

| PH-AHS | Boeing 757-28A | 530/25622 | ex C-GTSV | Lsd fr HLN |
| SX-BLV | Boeing 757-2G5 | 671/26278 | ex G-JMCG | Lsd fr Greek A/l |

Commenced services 29 March 2003

AIR SOUTHWEST

(WOW)   Plymouth (PLH)

| G-WOWA | de Havilland DHC-8-311 | 296 | ex C-GZOF | Lsd fr Avmax |
| G-WOWB | de Havilland DHC-8-311 | 334 | ex C-GZOU | Lsd fr Avmax |

Commenced operations on 26 October 2003

AIR WALES

Red Dragon (6G/AWW)   Cardiff-Wales (CWL)

G-KNNY	Aerospatiale/Alenia ATR 42-300	291	ex G-ORFH	Lsd fr Aeronautics Lsg
G-SSEA	Aerospatiale/Alenia ATR 42-310	196	ex OY-CIT	
G-TAWE	Aerospatiale/Alenia ATR 42-300	371	ex G-BVJP	Lsd fr Aeronautics Lsg
G-WLSH	Aerospatiale/Alenia ATR 42-300	329	ex PT-MFX	

AIR X renamed RockHopper 29 August 2003

AIRFREIGHT EXPRESS Grounded by CAA and entered administration; current status is uncertain

ASTRAEUS

Flystar (5W/AEU)   London-Gatwick (LGW)

G-STRA	Boeing 737-3S3	1517/24059	ex G-OBWY	Lsd fr KG Aircraft Lsg
G-STRB*	Boeing 737-3Y0	1625/24255	ex G-OBWX	Lsd fr Starlight Investments
G-STRC	Boeing 737-7BX	658/30736	ex N361ML	Lsd fr Wachovia Bank
G-STRD	Boeing 737-7BX	687/30737	ex N362ML	Lsd fr Wachovia Bank
G-STRE	Boeing 737-36N	3031/28572	ex G-XBHX	

*Leased to Iceland Express 26 February 2003

ATLANTIC AIR LINES

LofCargo (ALH)   Coventry (CVT)

G-FIJR	Lockheed L-188PF Electra	1138	ex EI-HCF	
G-FIJV	Lockheed L-188CF Electra	1129	ex EI-HCE	
G-FIZU	Lockheed L-188CF Electra	2014	ex EI-CHY	
G-LOFB	Lockheed L-188CF Electra	1131	ex N667F	
G-LOFC	Lockheed L-188CF Electra	1100	ex N665F	
G-LOFD	Lockheed L-188AC Electra	1143	ex LN-FOG	
G-LOFE	Lockheed L-188CF Electra	1144	ex EI-CET	
G-LOFF	Lockheed L-188CF Electra	1128	ex LN-FON	
G-LOFG	Lockheed L-188CF Electra	1116	ex LN-FOL	stored CVT
(G-LOFH)	Lockheed L-188PF Electra	1140	ex N4HG	Lsd fr European Aero Leases
(G-LOFI)	Lockheed L-188PF Electra	2010	ex N2RK	Lsd fr Electra Aero Inc
G-IONA	Aerospatiale/Alenia ATR 42-300	017	ex N971NA	Freighter Lsd fr European Airleases
YL-RAB	Antonov An-26	07310508	ex RA-26032	Lsd fr RAF Avia
YL-RAC	Antonov An-26	07309903	ex CCCP-79169	Lsd fr RAF Avia
UR-74057	Antonov An-74-200	36547098960		Lsd fr CBI

Also trades as Air Atlantique, Atlantic Express and Atlantic Reconnaissance, while Highland Airways is an associated company

ATLANTIC EXPRESS

Atlantic (RYM)   Coventry (CVT)

D-CAOA	Embraer EMB.121ER Brasilia	121013	ex N122AM	stored CVT Lsd fr Air Omega
G-BUKA	Swearingen SA.227AC Metro III	AC-706B	ex ZK-NSQ	Atlantic Express titles
G-FIND	Reims Cessna F406 Caravan II	F406-0045	ex OY-PEU	
G-LEAF	Reims Cessna F406 Caravan II	F406-0018	ex EI-CKY	
G-NOSE	Cessna 402B	402B0823	ex N98AR	Pollution control

Also trades as Air Atlantique, Atlantic Airlines and Atlantic Reconnaissance while Highland Airways is an associated company

ATLANTIC RECONNAISSANCE

Atlantic (AAG)   Coventry (CVT)

| G-BCEN | Britten-Norman BN-2A-26 Islander | 403 | ex 4X-AYG | Op for MCA |
| G-EXEX | Cessna 404 Titan | 404-0037 | ex SE-GZF | Op for Dept of Transport |

G-EYES	Cessna 402C	402C0008	ex SE-IRU	Op for Environment Agency
G-MIND	Cessna 404 Titan	404-0004	ex G-SKKC	
G-SURV	Britten-Norman BN-2T-4S Islander	4005		Op for NERC
G-TASK	Cessna 404 Titan	404-0829	ex PH-MPC	Op for DETR
G-TURF	Reims Cessna F406 Caravan II	F406-0020	ex PH-FWF	

Also trades as Air Atlantique, Atlantic Airlines and Atlantic Express while Highland Airways is an associated company

AURIGNY AIR SERVICES

Ayline (GR/AUR)   *Guernsey (GCI)*

G-BDTN	Britten-Norman BN-2A Mk.III Trislander	1026	ex S7-AAN	stored GCI
G-BDTO	Britten-Norman BN-2A Mk.III Trislander	1027	ex G-RBSI	Merrill Lynch c/s
G-BEVT	Britten-Norman BN-2A Mk.III Trislander	1057		Aberdeen Asset Mgt c/s
G-FTSE	Britten-Norman BN-2A Mk.III Trislander	1053	ex G-BEPI	Morgan Stanley Quilter c/s
G-JOEY	Britten-Norman BN-2A Mk.III Trislander	1016	ex G-BDGG	Joey
G-PCAM	Britten-Norman BN-2A Mk.III Trislander	1052	ex G-BEPH	ABN AMRO Bank c/s
G-RBCI	Britten-Norman BN-2A Mk.III Trislander	1035	ex G-BDWV	Royal Bank of Canada c/s
G-RLON	Britten-Norman BN-2A Mk.III Trislander	1008	ex G-ITEX	Royal London Asset Management c/s
G-XTOR	Britten-Norman BN-2A Mk.III Trislander	359/1065	ex G-BAXD	

G-BPFN	Short SD.3-60	SH3747	ex N747HH	
G-BWDA	Aerospatiale/Alenia ATR 72-202	444	ex F-WQNG	
G-BWDB	Aerospatiale/Alenia ATR 72-202	449	ex F-WQNI	
G-GNTC	SAAB SF.340A	020	ex HB-AHE	Lsd fr SAAB
G-RUNG	SAAB SF.340A	086	ex F-GGBV	Lsd fr DTR

AV8AIR

(MNF)   *Manchester (MAN)*

| G-OAVB | Boeing 757-23A | 209/24289 | ex N289AN | Lsd fr AMWS I |

| TF-FIA | Boeing 767-3Y0ER | 405/24953 | ex N632TW | Lsd fr ICE |
| TF-FIB | Boeing 767-383ER | 25365 | ex N365SR | Lsd fr ICE |

First service 27 November 2003. AV8air.com is the trading name of Man-Air.com

BAC EXPRESS AIRLINES

Rapex (RPX)   *London-Gatwick (LGW)*

G-BKMX	Short SD.3-60	SH3608	ex G-14-3608	City of Bristol	Lsd fr BAC Lsg
G-BNMU	Short SD.3-60	SH3724	ex N161DD	stored EXT	
G-BOEG	Short SD.3-60	SH3733	ex D-CFXE		Lsd fr Lynrise A/c Financing
G-BOEI	Short SD.3-60	SH3735	ex D-CFLX		Lsd fr AeroCentury
G-BPKW	Short SD.3-60	SH3753	ex D-CFXG		
G-BPKZ	Short SD.3-60	SH3756	ex D-CFXB		
G-CEAL	Short SD.3-60	SH3761	ex N161CN	City of Belfast	Lsd fr BAC Lsg
G-CLAS	Short SD.3-60	SH3635	ex EI-BEK	City of Cardiff	Lsd fr BAC Lsg
G-OBLK	Short SD.3-60	SH3712	ex G-BNDI	City of Liverpool	
G-OCEA	Short SD.3-60	SH3762	ex N162CN		Lsd fr BAC Lsg
G-OLAH	Short SD.3-60	SH3604	ex G-BPCO		Lsd to REA
G-VBAC	Short SD.3-60	SH3736	ex VH-MJU	City of Norwich	Lsd fr BAC Lsg
G-XPSS	Short SD.3-60	SH3713	ex EI-CPR	City of Derby	

G-BMXD	Fokker F.27 Friendship 500	10417	ex TF-FLR	Scottish Trader	
G-BVOB	Fokker F.27 Friendship 500	10366	ex PH-FMN	Euro Trader	
G-JEAE	Fokker F.27 Friendship 500F	10633	ex VH-EWV		Lsd fr BAC Lsg
G-	Aerospatiale/Alenia ATR 42-300F		ex	on order 04	

BAC Leasing also operate aircraft under own designator BAC.

BMIBABY

Baby(WW/BMI)   *East Midlands (EMA)*

G-BVKA	Boeing 737-59D	1834/24694	ex SE-DNA		Lsd fr BMA
G-BVKB	Boeing 737-59D	2592/27268	ex SE-DNM		Lsd fr BMA
G-BVKC	Boeing 737-59D	1872/24695	ex SE-DNB		Lsd fr BMA
G-BVKD	Boeing 737-59D	2279/26421	ex SE-DNK	Wales logojet	Lsd fr BMA
G-BVZE	Boeing 737-59D	2412/26422	ex SE-DNL	little costa baby	Lsd fr BMA
G-BVZG	Boeing 737-5Q8	2114/25160	ex SE-DNF	Wales logojet	Lsd fr BMA
G-BVZH	Boeing 737-5Q8	2129/25166	ex SE-DNG	baby blue skies	Lsd fr BMA
G-BVZI	Boeing 737-5Q8	2173/25167	ex SE-DNH		Lsd fr BMA
G-BYZJ	Boeing 737-3Q8	2139/24962	ex G-COLE		Lsd fr BMA
G-ECAS	Boeing 737-36N	2835/28554		golden jubilee baby	Lsd fr BMA
G-OBMP	Boeing 737-3Q8	2193/24963		baby ET	Lsd fr BMA
G-ODSK	Boeing 737-37Q	2904/28537		baby dragon fly	Lsd fr BMA
G-OGBD	Boeing 737-3L9	2688/27853	ex OY-MAR		Lsd fr BMA
G-OJTW	Boeing 737-36N	2876/28558		rock-a-bye-baby	Lsd fr BMA

Wholly owned by bmi-british midland international; operates as no-frills airline.

BMI - BRITISH MIDLAND INTERNATIONAL

Midland (BD/BMA) (IATA 236)   East Midlands (EMA)

G-MIDA	Airbus Industrie A321-231	0806	ex D-AVZQ	Lsd fr ILFC
G-MIDC	Airbus Industrie A321-231	0835	ex D-AVZZ	
G-MIDE	Airbus Industrie A321-231	0864	ex D-AVZB	Lsd fr debis
G-MIDF	Airbus Industrie A321-231	0810	ex D-AVZS	Lsd fr ILFC
G-MIDH	Airbus Industrie A321-231	0968	ex D-AVZX	Lsd fr ILFC
G-MIDI	Airbus Industrie A321-231	0974	ex D-AVZA	Lsd fr ILFC
G-MIDJ	Airbus Industrie A321-231	1045	ex D-AVZO	Lsd fr debis
G-MIDK	Airbus Industrie A321-231	1153	ex D-AVZF	Star Alliance c/s
G-MIDL	Airbus Industrie A321-231	1174	ex D-AVZH	Star Alliance c/s	Lsd fr debis
G-MIDM	Airbus Industrie A321-231	1207	ex D-AVZR	
G-MIDO	Airbus Industrie A320-232	1987	ex F-WWIR	Lsd fr ILFC
G-MIDP	Airbus Industrie A320-232	1732	ex F-WWBK	Lsd fr ILFC
G-MIDR	Airbus Industrie A320-232	1697	ex F-WWIQ	Lsd fr ILFC
G-MIDS	Airbus Industrie A320-232	1424	ex F-WWBO	Lsd fr ILFC
G-MIDT	Airbus Industrie A320-232	1418	ex F-WWBI	Lsd fr ILFC
G-MIDU	Airbus Industrie A320-232	1407	ex F-WWDC	Lsd fr ILFC
G-MIDV	Airbus Industrie A320-232	1383	ex F-WWIQ	Lsd fr ILFC
G-MIDW	Airbus Industrie A320-232	1183	ex F-WWDT	Star Alliance c/s	Lsd fr debis
G-MIDX	Airbus Industrie A320-232	1177	ex F-WWDP	Star Alliance c/s	Lsd fr ILFC
G-MIDY	Airbus Industrie A320-232	1014	ex F-WWDQ	
G-MIDZ	Airbus Industrie A320-232	0934	ex F-WWII	Lsd fr debis
G-	Airbus Industrie A321-231		ex D-AV	on order 03	Lsd fr ILFC
G-	Airbus Industrie A320-232		ex F-WW	on order Mar03	Lsd fr ILFC
G-	Airbus Industrie A320-232		ex F-WW	on order 03	
G-	Airbus Industrie A320-232		ex F-WW	on order 03	
G-	Airbus Industrie A320-232		ex F-WW	on order 03	
G-DBCA	Airbus Industrie A319-132	2098	ex D-AVYV	Lsd fr ILFC
G-DBCB	Airbus Industrie A319-132	2188	ex D-AVYA	Lsd fr ILFC
G-DBCC	Airbus Industrie A319-132	2194	ex D-AVYT	on order Apr04	Lsd fr ILFC
G-	Airbus Industrie A319-132		ex D-AV	on order May04	Lsd fr ILFC
G-BVKA	Boeing 737-59D	1834/24694	ex SE-DNA	Lsd fr BBAM; sublsd to BMI
G-BVKB	Boeing 737-59D	2592/27268	ex SE-DNM	Lsd to BMI
G-BVKC	Boeing 737-59D	1872/24695	ex SE-DNB	Lsd fr BBAM; sublsd to BMI
G-BVKD	Boeing 737-59D	2279/26421	ex SE-DNK	Lsd to BMI
G-BVZE	Boeing 737-59D	2412/26422	ex SE-DNL	Lsd to BMI
G-BVZG	Boeing 737-5Q8	2114/25160	ex SE-DNC	Lsd fr BBAM; sublsd to BMI
G-BVZH	Boeing 737-5Q8	2129/25166	ex SE-DNG	Lsd fr BBAM; sublsd to BMI
G-BVZI	Boeing 737-5Q8	2173/25167	ex SE-DNH	Lsd fr BBAM; sublsd to BMI
G-BYZJ	Boeing 737-3Q8	2139/24962	ex G-COLE	Lsd fr GECAS; sublsd to BMI
G-ECAS	Boeing 737-36N	2835/28554		Lsd fr GECAS; sublsd to BMI
G-OBMP	Boeing 737-3Q8	2193/24963		Lsd fr Tombo; sublsd to BMI
G-ODSK	Boeing 737-37Q	2904/28537		Lsd fr GECAS; sublsd to BMI
G-OJTW	Boeing 737-36N	2876/28558		Lsd fr GECAS; sublsd to BMI
G-BVJA	Fokker 100	11489	ex PH-EZE	Lsd fr A/c Finance & Trading
G-BVJB	Fokker 100	11488	ex PH-EZD	Lsd fr A/c Finance & Trading
G-BVJC	Fokker 100	11497	ex PH-EZJ	Lsd fr A/c Finance & Trading
G-BVJD	Fokker 100	11503	ex PH-EZO	Lsd fr A/c Finance & Trading
G-BXWE	Fokker 100	11327	ex PH-CFE	for sale
G-BXWF	Fokker 100	11328	ex PH-CFF	for sale
G-WWBB	Airbus Industrie A330-243	404	ex F-WWKP	Lsd fr ILFC
G-WWBD	Airbus Industrie A330-243	401	ex F-WWKN	Lsd fr ILFC
G-WWBM	Airbus Industrie A330-243	398	ex F-WWKL	Lsd fr ILFC

A subsidiary of The Airlines of Britain Group, in which SAS and Lufthansa have a 20% and 30% holding respectively.
bmi Regional is a wholly owned subsidiary while bmibaby is low-cost subsidiary. Member of Star Alliance.

BMI REGIONAL

Granite (WW/GNT)   Aberdeen/East Midlands (ABZ/EMA)

G-RJXA	Embraer EMB.145EP	145136		
G-RJXB	Embraer EMB.145EP	145142		
G-RJXC	Embraer EMB.145EP	145153	ex PT-SEE	
G-RJXD	Embraer EMB.145EP	145207		
G-RJXE	Embraer EMB.145EP	145245		
G-RJXF	Embraer EMB.145EP	145280	ex PT-SJW	
G-RJXG	Embraer EMB.145EP	145390	ex PT-SQO	
G-RJXH	Embraer EMB.145EP	145442	ex PT-SUN	Star Alliance c/s
G-RJXI	Embraer EMB.145EP	145454	ex PT-SUZ	Star Alliance c/s
G-RJXJ	Embraer EMB.135EP	145473	ex PT-SVS	
G-RJXK	Embraer EMB.135EP	145494	ex PT-SXN	Star Alliance c/s
G-RJXL	Embraer EMB.135EP			on order
G-RJXM	Embraer EMB.145EP			on order
G-	Embraer EMB.145EP			on order
G-	Embraer EMB.135EP			on order

CS-TPJ   Embraer EMB.145EP   145036 ex PT-SZC   Chapim   Lsd fr PGA until Mar04
Subsidiary of bmi-british midland international, operates feeder flights for them in full colours and other Star Alliance partners

BOND AIR SERVICES

Bond (BND)   *Gloucestershire (GLO)*

Reg	Type	Serial		Notes
G-BZRS	Eurocopter EC-135T1	0166		back-up
G-KRNW	Eurocopter EC-135T1	0175		EMS; Cornwall Air Ambulance
G-SASA*	Eurocopter EC-135T1	0147		EMS
G-SASB*	Eurocopter EC-135T1	0151		EMS
G-SPAU	Eurocopter EC-135T1	0142	ex D-HECF	Op for Strathclyde Police
G-WMAS	Eurocopter EC-135T1	0174		EMS; County Air Ambulance
G-	Eurocopter EC-135T1			on order
G-	Eurocopter EC-135T1			on order

A further six Eurocopter EC-135T1s are on order for future delivery
*Operated for Scottish Ambulance Service

Reg	Type	Serial		Notes
G-BAMF*	MBB Bo105DB	S-36	ex D-HDAM	based Sullom Voe
G-BATC	MBB Bo105DB	S-45	ex D-HDAW	back-up
G-BTHV	MBB Bo105DBS-4	S-855	ex D-HMBV	EMS; County Air Ambulance
G-BUXS	MBB Bo105DBS-4	S-41/913	ex G-PASA	EMS; based ABZ
G-CDBS	MBB Bo105DBS-4	S-738	ex D-HDRZ	EMS; County Air Ambulance
G-NAAA	MBB Bo105DBS-4	S-34/912	ex G-BUTN	EMS; Lancashire Air Ambulance
G-NAAB	MBB Bo105DBS-4	S-416	ex D-HDMO	EMS; Dorset & Somerset Air Amb'ce
G-THLS	MBB Bo105DBS-4	S-80/859	ex G-BCXO	Trinity House
G-TVAM	MBB Bo105DBS-4	S-392	ex G-SPOL	EMS; Thames Valley Air Ambulance
G-WAAN	MBB Bo105DB	S-20	ex G-AZOR	EMS
G-WAAS	MBB Bo105DBS-4	S-138/911	ex G-ESAM	EMS
G-WMAA	MBB Bo105DBS-4	S-135/914	ex G-PASB	EMS; Devon Air Ambulance

*Pollution control   "Humberside Police
Bond Offshore Helicopters is a sister organisation

BOND OFFSHORE HELICOPTERS

Gloucestershire/Aberdeen-Dyce (GLO/ABZ)

Reg	Type		Notes
G-	Eurocopter SA.332L2 Super Puma II		on order 04
G-	Eurocopter SA.332L2 Super Puma II		on order 04
G-	Eurocopter SA.332L2 Super Puma II		on order 04
G-	Eurocopter SA.332L2 Super Puma II		on order 04
G-	Eurocopter SA.332L2 Super Puma II		on order 04
G-	Eurocopter SA.332L2 Super Puma II		on order 04

Sister company of Bond Air Services; to commence operations on 01 August 2004

BRISTOW HELICOPTERS

Bristow (BHL/BHN/BMH)   *Redhill/Aberdeen-Dyce (KRH/ABZ)*

Reg	Type	Serial		Notes	
G-BLPM	Aerospatiale AS.332L Super Puma	2122	ex LN-ONB		
G-BLRY	Aerospatiale AS.332L Super Puma	2111	ex LN-ONA		
G-BLXR	Aerospatiale AS.332L Super Puma	2154		Cromarty	
G-BMCW	Aerospatiale AS.332L Super Puma	2161	ex F-WYMG	Monifieth	
G-BMCX	Aerospatiale AS.332L Super Puma	2164		Lossiemouth	
G-BRXU	Aerospatiale AS.332L Super Puma	2092	ex VH-BHV	Crail	
G-BWMG	Aerospatiale AS.332L Super Puma	2046	ex OY-HMG	Catterline	
G-BWWI	Aerospatiale AS.332L Super Puma	2040	ex OY-HMF	Johnshaven	
G-BWZX	Aerospatiale AS.332L Super Puma	2120	ex F-WQDE	Muchalls	
G-JSAR	Aerospatiale AS.332L-2 Super Puma	2576	ex F-WQRE	based Den Helda	
G-PUMH	Aerospatiale AS.332L Super Puma	2101		Gardenstown; stored ABZ	
G-PUMI	Aerospatiale AS.332L Super Puma	2170		stored ABZ	
G-TIGB	Aerospatiale AS.332L Super Puma	2023	ex G-BJXC	City of Aberdeen	
G-TIGC	Aerospatiale AS.332L Super Puma	2024	ex (G-BJYH)	Royal Burgh of Montrose	
G-TIGE	Aerospatiale AS.332L Super Puma	2028	ex (G-BJYJ)	City of Dundee	
G-TIGF	Aerospatiale AS.332L Super Puma	2030	ex F-WKQJ	Peterhead	
G-TIGG	Aerospatiale AS.332L Super Puma	2032	ex F-WXFT	Macduff	
G-TIGI	Aerospatiale AS.332L Super Puma	2036	ex F-WTNP	Fraserburgh	based China
G-TIGJ	Aerospatiale AS.332L Super Puma	2042	ex VH-BHT	Rosehearty	
G-TIGL	Aerospatiale AS.332L Super Puma	2050		Portsoy	
G-TIGM	Aerospatiale AS.332L Super Puma	2045		Banff	based China
G-TIGO	Aerospatiale AS.332L Super Puma	2061	ex PP-MIM		
G-TIGP	Aerospatiale AS.332L Super Puma	2064		Carnoustie	based China
G-TIGR	Aerospatiale AS.332L Super Puma	2071	ex F-WTNW	Stonehaven	
G-TIGS	Aerospatiale AS.332L Super Puma	2086		Findochty	
G-TIGT	Aerospatiale AS.332L Super Puma	2078		Portknockie	
G-TIGV	Aerospatiale AS.332L Super Puma	2099	ex LN-ONC	Burghead	
VH-BHH	Aerospatiale AS.332L Super Puma	2059	ex G-TIGW	Nairn	
VH-BHK	Aerospatiale AS.332L Super Puma	2096	ex G-TIGU		
VH-BHX	Aerospatiale AS.332L Super Puma	2079	ex G-BRWE		
VH-BHY	Aerospatiale AS.332L Super Puma	2129	ex B-HZY		

5N-AJC	Bell 206L LongRanger	45095	ex (5N-ALB)	
5N-AMQ	Bell 206L-1 LongRanger II	45746	ex N3173U	
5N-AQB	Bell 206L-1 LongRanger II	45506	ex N5749X	
5N-AQP	Bell 206L-1 LongRanger II	45604	ex N3907E	
5N-BAS	Bell 206L-1 LongRanger II	45367	ex N1076K	
5N-BFE	Bell 206L-4 LongRanger IV	52272	ex N20796	Lsd fr ALG
5N-BFF	Bell 206L-4 LongRanger IV	52273	ex N2080C	Lsd fr ALG
5N-BFG	Bell 206L-4 LongRanger IV	52274	ex N2080W	Lsd fr ALG
5N-BFH	Bell 206L-4 LongRanger IV	52275	ex N2081K	Lsd fr ALG
5N-BFV	Bell 206L-4 LongRanger IV	52160	ex 5N-ESC	
5N-PAA	Bell 206L-1 LongRanger II	45659	ex N39118	
G-BALZ	Bell 212	30542	ex EC-IPD	
G-BFER	Bell 212	30835	ex N18099	
G-BGLJ	Bell 212	30548	ex ZJ969	
G-BIXV	Bell 212	30870	ex N16931	Based Kazakhstan
ZH814	Bell 212HP	30512	ex G-BGMH	Based Brunei
ZH815	Bell 212HP	30668	ex G-BGCZ	Based Brunei
ZH816	Bell 212HP	30549	ex G-BGMG	Based Brunei
ZJ964	Bell 212	31170	ex G-BJGU	Based Belize
ZJ965	Bell 212	31171	ex G-BJGV	Based Belize
ZJ966	Bell 212	32134	ex G-BJJO	Based Belize
VT-DAM	Bell 212HP	31191	ex G-BXIK	Based Yanam, India
XA-TRK	Bell 212	31225	ex G-BWLE	Lsd to OLOG
XA-TQG	Bell 212	30687	ex 9Y-TFA	Lsd to OLOG
5N-ALQ	Bell 212	30670	ex G-BGMF	
5N-ALU	Bell 212	31197	ex G-BJIT	
5N-AOF	Bell 212	31200	ex G-BJIU	
5N-AQV	Bell 212	30782	ex VR-BIJ	
5N-AXX	Bell 212HP	30787	ex G-BSOA	
5N-AYX	Bell 212	30599	ex N212NK	
5N-BEN	Bell 212HP	30681	ex G-BOEP	
5N-BHE	Bell 212HP	30666	ex G-BMVF	
5N-BHO	Bell 212HP	30866	ex G-BLDY	
9Y-TEY	Bell 212	30640	ex VR-BFE	
9Y-TIF	Bell 212	30615	ex G-BTYA	
9Y-TIG	Bell 212	30544	ex G-BHDL	
5N-BDH	Eurocopter EC.155B	6591		
5N-BDI	Eurocopter EC.155B	6602		
5N-BDJ	Eurocopter EC.155B	6607		
5N-BDK	Eurocopter EC.155B	6608	ex F-WQDA	
5N-BDL	Eurocopter EC.155B	6610	ex F-WQDD	
5N-BDM	Eurocopter EC.155B	6611	ex F-WQDH	

All operated for Shell Petroleum

G-BBHL^	Sikorsky S-61N II	61712	ex N4032S	Glamis	
G-BBVA+^	Sikorsky S-61N II	61718		Vega	
G-BCLC^	Sikorsky S-61N II	61737		Craigievar	Based LSI
G-BCLD	Sikorsky S-61L	61739		Slains; stored ABZ	
G-BDIJ+^	Sikorsky S-61N II	61751	ex 9M-AYF	Crathes	
G-BDOC^	Sikorsky S-61N II	61765		Tolquhoun	Based LSI
G-BFRI	Sikorsky S-61N II	61809		Braeriach; based ABZ	
G-BGWJ	Sikorsky S-61N II	61819		Monadh Mor; stored ABZ	
G-BGWK	Sikorsky S-61N II	61820	ex N1346C	Dun Robin; stored ABZ	
G-BHOG	Sikorsky S-61N II	61825	ex PT-YEK	stored ABZ	
G-BHOH	Sikorsky S-61N II	61827		Ben Avon; stored ABZ	
G-BIMU^	Sikorsky S-61N II	61752	ex N8511Z	Stac Pollaidh	Based SYY
G-BPWB*	Sikorsky S-61N II	61822	ex EI-BHO	Druminnor	based Portland
PT-MNL	Sikorsky S-61N II	61745	ex G-BFMY	Diamond	Lsd to OLOG

+Based Lee on Solent   ^Operated for Marine & Coastguard Agency

G-BHBF	Sikorsky S-76A+	760022	ex N4247S	Spirit of Paris; based Kazakhstan	
G-BIBG	Sikorsky S-76A+	760083	ex 5N-BCE	stored KRH	
G-BIEJ	Sikorsky S-76A+	760097		Glen Lossie	
G-BISZ	Sikorsky S-76A+	760156			
G-BJFL	Sikorsky S-76A+	760056	ex N106BH	Glen Moray	based in Kazakhstan
G-BJGX	Sikorsky S-76A+	760026	ex N103BH	Glen Elgin	
G-BVKR	Sikorsky S-76A	760115	ex RJAF 734		
G-BXZS	Sikorsky S-76A+	760287	ex N190AL		
VH-BHI	Sikorsky S-76A	760118	ex G-BVKS		
VH-BHL	Sikorsky S-76A+	760046	ex G-BHLY	Glenrothes	
VH-BHM	Sikorsky S-76A	760107	ex G-BVKO		
VH-BHQ	Sikorsky S-76A	760090	ex G-BVKN		
VH-BZW	Sikorsky S-76A+	760157	ex G-BITR		
5N-BBO	Sikorsky S-76A+	760014	ex (5N-OOY)		
5N-BCF	Sikorsky S-76A+	760084			
5N-BCT	Sikorsky S-76A	760109	ex G-BZJT		
5N-SKY	Sikorsky S-76A+	760084	ex G-BJVZ		
5N-BGD	Sikorsky S-76C+	760540	ex N864AL		
5N-BGE	Sikorsky S-76C+	760545	ex N20509		
5N-BGF	Sikorsky S-76C+	760560	ex N867AL		

G-AVII	Agusta-Bell 206B Jet Ranger II	8011		Brighton Belle	based KRH
G-BKFN	Bell 214ST	28109	ex LZ-CAW	stored ABZ	
N	Bell 214ST	28110	ex G-BKFP	stored New Iberia, LA	
VH-BHO	Bell 206L-3 Long Ranger	51354	ex JA9893		
5N-AMW	Cessna 425 Conquest	425-0067	ex N6844V		
5N-AQO	Bell 206B JetRanger III	3765	ex N31800		
5N-BAG	Bell 206B JetRanger III	2728	ex N2760T		
5N-BCV	Bell 206B JetRanger	2782	ex ZS-HIC		
5N-BCZ	Bell 412EP	33179	ex B-55521		Lsd ft OLOG
5N-BDD	Bell 412EP	33046	ex N395AL		Lsd fr OLOG
5N-BDY	Bell 412EP	36267	ex N506AL		Lsd fr OLOG
5N-BDZ	Bell 412EP	36278	ex 9Y-ALI		Lsd fr OLOG
5N-BEM	Bell 407	53246	ex N567AL		Lsd fr OLOG
5N-BEO	Bell 407	53190	ex N467AL		Lsd fr OLOG
5N-BEP	Bell 407	53107	ex N427AL		Lsd fr OLOG
5N-BES	Bell 206B JetRanger III	3216	ex N139H		
5N-BFI	Bell 407	53550	ex N2531G		
5N-CES	Cessna 208 Caravan	20800249	ex N1288Y		
5N-SPE	Dornier 328-300	3151	ex D-BDXT	Op for Shell Petroleum	
5N-SPM	Dornier 328-300	3141	ex D-BDXR	Op for Shell Petroleum	
5N-SPN	Dornier 328-300	3120	ex D-BABA	Op for Shell Petroleum	

Two Bell-Boeing 609's are on order
Irish Helicopters is a wholly owned subsidiary. Itself is a wholly owned subsidiary of Offshore Logistics (OLOG). Operates as Bristow Helicopter Group (BHL); Bristow Helicopters [Nigeria] (BHN), Bristow Caribbean and Bristow Masayu Helicopters (BMH)

BRITANNIA AIRWAYS

Britannia *(BY/BAL)*   London-Luton *(LTN)*

G-BYAD	Boeing 757-204ER	450/26963			
G-BYAE	Boeing 757-204ER	452/26964			
G-BYAF	Boeing 757-204ER	514/26266			Lsd fr ILFC
G-BYAH	Boeing 757-204	520/26966		Lsd fr Thompson Intl Finance	
G-BYAI	Boeing 757-204	522/26967		Lsd fr Thompson Intl Finance	
G-BYAJ	Boeing 757-28AER	528/25623			Lsd fr ILFC
G-BYAK	Boeing 757-204	538/26267			Lsd fr ILFC
G-BYAL	Boeing 757-204	549/25626			Lsd fr ILFC
G-BYAN	Boeing 757-204	596/27219			Lsd fr ILFC
G-BYAO	Boeing 757-204	598/27235			Lsd fr ITID Leasing
G-BYAP	Boeing 757-204	600/27236		John Lennon	
G-BYAR	Boeing 757-204	602/27237	ex PH-AHT		Lsd fr Itochu
G-BYAS	Boeing 757-204	604/27238			
G-BYAT	Boeing 757-204	606/27208			Lsd fr ILFC
G-BYAU	Boeing 757-204	618/27220			Lsd fr ILFC
G-BYAW	Boeing 757-204	663/27234		Philip Stanley	
G-BYAX	Boeing 757-204	850/28834			Lsd fr ILFC
G-BYAY	Boeing 757-204	861/28836			Lsd fr ILFC
G-CDUO	Boeing 757-236	279/24792	ex SE-DUO		Lsd fr BBAM
G-CDUP	Boeing 757-236	292/24793	ex SE-DUP		Lsd fr ACG Acquistion
G-BRIF	Boeing 767-204ER	296/24736	ex (PH-AHM)	Lord Horatio Nelson	
G-BRIG	Boeing 767-204ER	299/24757	ex (PH-AHN)	Eglantyne Jebb	
G-BYAA	Boeing 767-204ER	362/25058	ex PH-AHM	Sir Matt Busby CBE	
G-BYAB	Boeing 767-204ER	373/25139		Brian Johnston CBE MC	
G-OBYB	Boeing 767-304ER	613/28040		Bobby Moore OBE	
G-OBYC	Boeing 767-304ER	614/28041	ex D-AGYC	Roy Castle OBE Lsd fr ITID Leasing	
G-OBYD	Boeing 767-304ER	649/28042	ex SE-DZG	Lsd fr ALE-Four Ltd; sublsd to BLX	
G-OBYE	Boeing 767-304ER	691/28979	ex D-AGYE	Bill Travers	
G-OBYF	Boeing 767-304ER	705/28208	ex D-AGYF		Lsd fr ILFC
G-OBYG	Boeing 767-304ER	733/29137			Lsd fr ILFC
G-OBYH	Boeing 767-304ER	737/28883	ex SE-DZO		Lsd fr ILFC
G-OBYI	Boeing 767-304ER	783/29138			
G-OBYJ	Boeing 767-304ER	784/29384			Lsd fr ILFC

Controls Britannia AB (SE); all aircraft being repainted in 'World of TUI' colours [owner, also owns Hapag-Lloyd, White Eagle and NEOS] but with Thomson.co.uk titles. Thomsonfly.com is wholly owned

BRITISH AIRWAYS

Speedbird & Shuttle *(BA/BAW/SHT) (IATA 125)*   London-Heathrow/Gatwick & Manchester *(LHR/LGW/MAN)*

G-EUOA	Airbus Industrie A319-131	1513	ex D-AVYE	
G-EUOB	Airbus Industrie A319-131	1529	ex D-AVWH	
G-EUOC	Airbus Industrie A319-131	1537	ex D-AVYP	
G-EUOD	Airbus Industrie A319-131	1558	ex D-AVYJ	
G-EUOE	Airbus Industrie A319-131	1574	ex D-AVWF	
G-EUOF	Airbus Industrie A319-131	1590	ex D-AVYW	
G-EUOG	Airbus Industrie A319-131	1594	ex D-AVVWU	
G-EUOH	Airbus Industrie A319-131	1604	ex D-AVYM	
G-EUOI	Airbus Industrie A319-131	1606	ex D-AVYN	
G-EUOJ	Airbus Industrie A319-131		ex D-AV	on order Apr04

G-EUOK	Airbus Industrie A319-131		ex D-AV	on order 04
G-EUOL	Airbus Industrie A319-131		ex D-AV	on order 04
G-EUPA	Airbus Industrie A319-131	1082	ex D-AVYK	
G-EUPB	Airbus Industrie A319-131	1115	ex D-AVYT	
G-EUPC	Airbus Industrie A319-131	1118	ex D-AVYU	
G-EUPD	Airbus Industrie A319-131	1142	ex D-AVWG	
G-EUPE	Airbus Industrie A319-131	1193	ex D-AVYT	
G-EUPF	Airbus Industrie A319-131	1197	ex D-AVWS	
G-EUPG	Airbus Industrie A319-131	1222	ex D-AVYG	
G-EUPH	Airbus Industrie A319-131	1225	ex D-AVYK	
G-EUPJ	Airbus Industrie A319-131	1232	ex D-AVYJ	
G-EUPK	Airbus Industrie A319-131	1236	ex D-AVYO	
G-EUPL	Airbus Industrie A319-131	1239	ex D-AVYP	
G-EUPM	Airbus Industrie A319-131	1258	ex D-AVYR	
G-EUPN	Airbus Industrie A319-131	1261	ex D-AVWA	
G-EUPO	Airbus Industrie A319-131	1279	ex D-AVYU	
G-EUPP	Airbus Industrie A319-131	1295	ex D-AVWU	
G-EUPR	Airbus Industrie A319-131	1329	ex D-AVYH	
G-EUPS	Airbus Industrie A319-131	1338	ex D-AVYM	
G-EUPT	Airbus Industrie A319-131	1380	ex D-AVWH	
G-EUPU	Airbus Industrie A319-131	1384	ex D-AVWP	
G-EUPV	Airbus Industrie A319-131	1423	ex D-AVYE	
G-EUPW	Airbus Industrie A319-131	1440	ex D-AVYP	
G-EUPX	Airbus Industrie A319-131	1445	ex D-AVWB	
G-EUPY	Airbus Industrie A319-131	1466	ex D-AVYK	
G-EUPZ	Airbus Industrie A319-131	1510	ex D-AVYY	
G-BUSB	Airbus Industrie A320-111	0006	ex (G-BRSA)	
G-BUSC	Airbus Industrie A320-111	0008	ex (G-BRSB)	
G-BUSD	Airbus Industrie A320-111	0011	ex F-WWDF	
G-BUSE	Airbus Industrie A320-111	0017	ex F-WWDG	
G-BUSF	Airbus Industrie A320-111	0018	ex F-WWDH	
G-BUSG	Airbus Industrie A320-211	0039	ex F-WWDM	
G-BUSH	Airbus Industrie A320-211	0042	ex F-WWDT	
G-BUSI	Airbus Industrie A320-211	0103	ex F-WWDB	
G-BUSJ	Airbus Industrie A320-211	0109	ex F-WWIC	
G-BUSK	Airbus Industrie A320-211	0120	ex F-WWIN	
G-EUUA	Airbus Industrie A320-232	1661	ex F-WWIH	
G-EUUB	Airbus Industrie A320-232	1689	ex F-WWBE	
G-EUUC	Airbus Industrie A320-232	1696	ex F-WWIO	
G-EUUD	Airbus Industrie A320-232	1760	ex F-WWBN	
G-EUUE	Airbus Industrie A320-232	1782	ex F-WWDO	
G-EUUF	Airbus Industrie A320-232	1814	ex F-WWIY	Lsd fr Itochu
G-EUUG	Airbus Industrie A320-232	1829	ex F-WWIU	Lsd fr Itochu
G-EUUH	Airbus Industrie A320-232	1665	ex F-WWIG	
G-EUUI	Airbus Industrie A320-232	1871	ex F-WWBI	Lsd fr Itochu
G-EUUJ	Airbus Industrie A320-232	1883	ex F-WWBQ	
G-EUUK	Airbus Industrie A320-232	1899	ex F-WWDO	Lsd fr Itochu
G-EUUL	Airbus Industrie A320-232	1708	ex F-WWIV	
G-EUUM	Airbus Industrie A320-232	1907	ex F-WWDN	Lsd fr Itochu
G-EUUN	Airbus Industrie A320-232	1910	ex F-WWDP	
G-EUUO	Airbus Industrie A320-232	1958	ex F-WWIT	
G-EUUP	Airbus Industrie A320-232	2038	ex F-WWDB	
G-EUUR	Airbus Industrie A320-232	2040	ex F-WWID	
G-EUWA	Airbus Industrie A321-131		ex D-AV	on order Nov04
G-EUWB	Airbus Industrie A321-131		ex D-AV	on order 04
G-EUWC	Airbus Industrie A321-131		ex D-AV	on order 04
G-EUWD	Airbus Industrie A321-131		ex D-AV	on order 04

Six more Airbus Industrie A321-131s are on order for delivery in 2005 (3) and 2006 (3); to be registered
G-EUWE to G-EUWJ

G-BVNO	Boeing 737-4S3	1736/24167	ex G-BPKE	Lsd fr Lanie A/c
G-DOCA	Boeing 737-436	2131/25267		
G-DOCB	Boeing 737-436	2144/25304		
G-DOCD	Boeing 737-436	2156/25349		
G-DOCE	Boeing 737-436	2167/25350		
G-DOCF	Boeing 737-436	2178/25407		
G-DOCG	Boeing 737-436	2183/25408		
G-DOCH	Boeing 737-436	2185/25428		
G-DOCI	Boeing 737-436	2188/25839		
G-DOCL	Boeing 737-436	2228/25842		
G-DOCM	Boeing 737-436	2244/25843		
G-DOCN	Boeing 737-436	2379/25848		
G-DOCO	Boeing 737-436	2381/25849		
G-DOCP	Boeing 737-436	2386/25850		
G-DOCR	Boeing 737-436	2387/25851		
G-DOCS	Boeing 737-436	2390/25852		
G-DOCT	Boeing 737-436	2409/25853		
G-DOCU	Boeing 737-436	2417/25854		
G-DOCV	Boeing 737-436	2420/25855		
G-DOCW	Boeing 737-436	2422/25856		

G-DOCX	Boeing 737-436	2451/25857		
G-DOCY	Boeing 737-436	2514/25844	ex OO-LTQ	
G-DOCZ	Boeing 737-436	2522/25858	ex EC-FXJ	
G-GBTA	Boeing 737-436	2532/25859	ex G-BVHA	
G-GBTB	Boeing 737-436	2545/25860	ex OO-LTS	
G-GFFA	Boeing 737-59D	1969/25038	ex G-BVZF	Lsd fr BBAM
G-GFFB	Boeing 737-505	2229/25789	ex LN-BRT	Lsd fr debis
G-GFFC	Boeing 737-505	1923/24272	ex LN-BRG	Lsd fr BBAM
G-GFFD	Boeing 737-59D	2186/26419	ex LY-BFV	Lsd fr Charlston Partners
G-GFFE	Boeing 737-528	2720/27424	ex LX-LGR	Lsd fr Itochu
G-GFFF	Boeing 737-53A	1868/24754	ex G-OBMZ	Lsd fr BBAM
G-GFFG	Boeing 737-505	1792/24650	ex LN-BRC	Lsd fr BBAM
G-GFFH	Boeing 737-5H6	2637/27354	ex VT-JAW	Lsd fr GECAS
G-GFFI	Boeing 737-528	2730/27425	ex LX-LGS	Lsd fr Itochu
G-GFFJ	Boeing 737-5H6	2646/27355	ex VT-JAZ	Lsd fr GECAS
G-LGTE	Boeing 737-3Y0	2015/24908	ex TC-SUP	Lsd fr GECAS
G-LGTF	Boeing 737-382	1873/24450	ex N115GB	Lsd fr ORIX
G-LGTG	Boeing 737-3Q8	1765/24470	ex N696BJ	Lsd fr WFBN
G-LGTH	Boeing 737-3Y0	1542/23924	ex OO-LTV	Lsd fr BBAM
G-LGTI	Boeing 737-3Y0	1544/23925	ex OO-LTY	Lsd fr BBAM
G-BNLA	Boeing 747-436	727/23908	ex N60665	
G-BNLB	Boeing 747-436	730/23909		
G-BNLC	Boeing 747-436	734/23910		
G-BNLD	Boeing 747-436	744/23911	ex N6018N	
G-BNLE	Boeing 747-436	753/24047		
G-BNLF	Boeing 747-436	773/24048		
G-BNLG	Boeing 747-436	774/24049		
G-BNLH	Boeing 747-436	779/24050	ex VH-NLH	
G-BNLI	Boeing 747-436	784/24051		
G-BNLJ	Boeing 747-436	789/24052	ex N60668	
G-BNLK	Boeing 747-436	790/24053	ex N6009F	
G-BNLL	Boeing 747-436	794/24054		
G-BNLM	Boeing 747-436	795/24055	ex N6009F	
G-BNLN	Boeing 747-436	802/24056		
G-BNLO	Boeing 747-436	817/24057		
G-BNLP	Boeing 747-436	828/24058		
G-BNLR	Boeing 747-436	829/24447	ex N6005C	
G-BNLS	Boeing 747-436	841/24629		
G-BNLT	Boeing 747-436	842/24630		
G-BNLU	Boeing 747-436	895/25406		
G-BNLV	Boeing 747-436	900/25427		
G-BNLW	Boeing 747-436	903/25432		
G-BNLX	Boeing 747-436	908/25435		
G-BNLY	Boeing 747-436	959/27090	ex N60659	
G-BNLZ	Boeing 747-436	964/27091		
G-BYGA	Boeing 747-436	1190/28855		
G-BYGB	Boeing 747-436	1194/28856		
G-BYGC	Boeing 747-436	1195/25823		
G-BYGD	Boeing 747-436	1196/28857		
G-BYGE	Boeing 747-436	1198/28858		
G-BYGF	Boeing 747-436	1200/25824		
G-BYGG	Boeing 747-436	1212/28859		
G-CIVA	Boeing 747-436	967/27092		
G-CIVB	Boeing 747-436	1018/25811		
G-CIVC	Boeing 747-436	1022/25812		
G-CIVD	Boeing 747-436	1048/27349		stored CWL
G-CIVE	Boeing 747-436	1050/27350		
G-CIVF	Boeing 747-436	1058/25434	ex (G-BNLY)	
G-CIVG	Boeing 747-436	1059/25813	ex N6009F	
G-CIVH	Boeing 747-436	1078/25809		
G-CIVI	Boeing 747-436	1079/25814		
G-CIVJ	Boeing 747-436	1102/25817		
G-CIVK	Boeing 747-436	1104/25818		
G-CIVL	Boeing 747-436	1108/27478		
G-CIVM	Boeing 747-436	1116/28700		
G-CIVN	Boeing 747-436	1129/28848		
G-CIVO	Boeing 747-436	1135/28849	ex N6046P	
G-CIVP	Boeing 747-436	1144/28850		
G-CIVR	Boeing 747-436	1146/25820		
G-CIVS	Boeing 747-436	1148/28851		
G-CIVT	Boeing 747-436	1149/25821		
G-CIVU	Boeing 747-436	1154/25810		
G-CIVV	Boeing 747-436	1156/25819	ex N6009F	
G-CIVW	Boeing 747-436	1157/25822		
G-CIVX	Boeing 747-436	1172/28852		
G-CIVY	Boeing 747-436	1178/28853		
G-CIVZ	Boeing 747-436	1183/28854		

See also Global Supply System

G-BPEC	Boeing 757-236ER	323/24882	
G-BPED	Boeing 757-236	363/25059	

G-BPEE	Boeing 757-236ER	364/25060	Lsd fr BBAM
G-BPEI	Boeing 757-236	601/25806	
G-BPEJ	Boeing 757-236	610/25807	
G-BPEK	Boeing 757-236	665/25808	
G-CPEL	Boeing 757-236	224/24398 ex N602DF	
G-CPEM	Boeing 757-236	747/28665	
G-CPEN	Boeing 757-236	751/28666	
G-CPEO	Boeing 757-236	752/28667	
G-CPER	Boeing 757-236	784/29113	
G-CPES	Boeing 757-236	793/29114	
G-CPET	Boeing 757-236	798/29115	
G-BNWA	Boeing 767-336ER	265/24333 ex N6009F	
G-BNWB	Boeing 767-336ER	281/24334 ex N6046P	
G-BNWC	Boeing 767-336ER	284/24335	
G-BNWD	Boeing 767-336ER	286/24336 ex N6018N	
G-BNWH	Boeing 767-336ER	335/24340 ex N6005C	
G-BNWI	Boeing 767-336ER	342/24341	
G-BNWM	Boeing 767-336ER	376/25204	
G-BNWN	Boeing 767-336ER	398/25444	
G-BNWO	Boeing 767-336ER	418/25442	
G-BNWR	Boeing 767-336ER	421/25732	
G-BNWS	Boeing 767-336ER	473/25826 ex N6018N	
G-BNWT	Boeing 767-336ER	476/25828	
G-BNWU	Boeing 767-336ER	483/25829	
G-BNWV	Boeing 767-336ER	490/27140	
G-BNWW	Boeing 767-336ER	526/25831	
G-BNWX	Boeing 767-336ER	529/25832	
G-BNWY	Boeing 767-336ER	608/25834 ex N5005C	
G-BNWZ	Boeing 767-336ER	648/25733	
G-BZHA	Boeing 767-336ER	702/29230	
G-BZHB	Boeing 767-336ER	704/29231	
G-BZHC	Boeing 767-336ER	708/29232	
G-RAES	Boeing 777-236ER	76/27491 ex (G-ZZZP)	
G-VIIA	Boeing 777-236ER	41/27483 ex N5022E	
G-VIIB	Boeing 777-236ER	49/27484 ex (G-ZZZG)	
G-VIIC	Boeing 777-236ER	53/27485 ex (G-ZZZH)	
G-VIID	Boeing 777-236ER	56/27486 ex (G-ZZZI)	
G-VIIE	Boeing 777-236ER	58/27487 ex (G-ZZZJ)	
G-VIIF	Boeing 777-236ER	61/27488 ex (G-ZZZK)	
G-VIIG	Boeing 777-236ER	65/27489 ex (G-ZZZL)	
G-VIIH	Boeing 777-236ER	70/27490 ex (G-ZZZM)	
G-VIIJ	Boeing 777-236ER	111/27492 ex (G-ZZZN)	
G-VIIK	Boeing 777-236ER	117/28840	
G-VIIL	Boeing 777-236ER	127/27493	
G-VIIM	Boeing 777-236ER	130/28841	
G-VIIN	Boeing 777-236ER	157/29319	
G-VIIO	Boeing 777-236ER	182/29320	
G-VIIP	Boeing 777-236ER	193/29321	
G-VIIR	Boeing 777-236ER	203/29322	
G-VIIS	Boeing 777-236ER	206/29323	
G-VIIT	Boeing 777-236ER	217/29962	
G-VIIU	Boeing 777-236ER	221/29963	
G-VIIV	Boeing 777-236ER	228/29964	
G-VIIW	Boeing 777-236ER	233/29965	
G-VIIX	Boeing 777-236ER	236/29966	
G-VIIY	Boeing 777-236ER	251/29967	
G-YMMA	Boeing 777-236ER	242/30302 ex N5017Q	
G-YMMB	Boeing 777-236ER	265/30303	
G-YMMC	Boeing 777-236ER	268/30304	
G-YMMD	Boeing 777-236ER	269/30305	
G-YMME	Boeing 777-236ER	275/30306	
G-YMMF	Boeing 777-236ER	281/30307	
G-YMMG	Boeing 777-236ER	301/30308	City of Chicago
G-YMMH	Boeing 777-236ER	303/30309	
G-YMMI	Boeing 777-236ER	308/30310	
G-YMMJ	Boeing 777-236ER	311/30311	
G-YMMK	Boeing 777-236ER	312/30312	
G-YMML	Boeing 777-236ER	334/30313	
G-YMMM	Boeing 777-236ER	342/30314	
G-YMMN	Boeing 777-236ER	346/30316	
G-YMMO	Boeing 777-236ER	361/30317	
G-YMMP	Boeing 777-236ER	369/30315	
G-ZZZA	Boeing 777-236	6/27105 ex N77779	
G-ZZZB	Boeing 777-236	10/27106 ex N77771	
G-ZZZC	Boeing 777-236	12/27107 ex N5014K	

Franchise services are operated by British Airways CitiExpress, plus Loganair in full British Airways colours and by British Mediterranean Airways, Comair, Sun Air, GB Airways and Zambian Air Services
Owns 22.5% of Qantas, 12.8% of Air Mauritius and 18.3% of Comair; British Asia Airways and British Airways CitiExpress are wholly owned. British Airways Santa flights are operated with designator XMS while SHT is used for shutltle flights
Founder member of oneworld alliance with American Airlines

BRITISH AIRWAYS CITIEXPRESS
(TH/BRT) *Various*

G-BXAR	Avro RJ100	E3298	ex G-6-298
G-BXAS	Avro RJ100	E3301	ex G-6-301
G-BZAT	Avro RJ100	E3320	ex G-6-320
G-BZAU	Avro RJ100	E3328	ex G-6-328
G-BZAV	Avro RJ100	E3331	ex G-6-331
G-BZAW	Avro RJ100	E3354	ex G-6-354
G-BZAX	Avro RJ100	E3356	ex G-6-356
G-BZAY	Avro RJ100	E3368	
G-BZAZ	Avro RJ100	E3369	ex G-6-369
G-CFAA*	Avro RJ100	E3373	
G-CFAB*	Avro RJ100	E3377	
G-CFAC	Avro RJ100	E3379	
G-CFAD	Avro RJ100	E3380	
G-CFAE*	Avro RJ100	E3381	
G-CFAF*	Avro RJ100	E3382	
G-CFAH*	Avro RJ100	E3384	

*operate into and out of London City

G-GNTZ	British Aerospace 146 Srs.200	E2036	ex G-CLHB	
G-MABR	British Aerospace 146 Srs.100	E1015	ex G-DEBN	
G-MANS	British Aerospace 146 Srs.200	E2088	ex G-CLHC	Lsd fr BAES
G-MIMA	British Aerospace 146 Srs.200	E2079	ex G-CNMF	
G-OINV	British Aerospace 146 Srs.300	E3171	ex VH-EWI	

G-MANE	British Aerospace ATP	2045	ex G-LOGB	
G-MANF	British Aerospace ATP	2040	ex G-LOGA	
G-MANG	British Aerospace ATP	2018	ex G-LOGD	To leave fleet Sep04
G-MANH	British Aerospace ATP	2017	ex G-LOGC	To leave fleet Aug04
G-MANJ	British Aerospace ATP	2004	ex G-LOGE	for Loganair
G-MANL	British Aerospace ATP	2003	ex G-ERIN	for Loganair
G-MANM	British Aerospace ATP	2005	ex G-OATP	for Loganair
G-MANP	British Aerospace ATP	2023	ex OK-VFO	for Loganair
G-MAUD	British Aerospace ATP	2002	ex G-BMYM	for Loganair

All to be withdrawn from service by March 2004 and stored pending disposal

G-BRYI	de Havilland DHC-8-311A	256	ex C-GEOA
G-BRYJ	de Havilland DHC-8-311A	319	ex C-GEOA
G-BRYU	de Havilland DHC-8Q-311A	458	ex C-GFEN
G-BRYV	de Havilland DHC-8Q-311A	462	ex C-GFHZ
G-BRYW	de Havilland DHC-8Q-311A	474	ex C-GDIU
G-BRYX	de Havilland DHC-8Q-311A	508	ex C-GDOE
G-BRYY	de Havilland DHC-8Q-311A	519	ex C-FDHD
G-BRYZ	de Havilland DHC-8Q-311A	464	ex C-FCSG
G-NVSA	de Havilland DHC-8Q-311A	451	ex C-GDNG
G-NVSB	de Havilland DHC-8Q-311A	517	ex C-GHRI

All for disposal; to be withdrawn from use by March 2004

G-EMBC	Embraer EMB.145EU	145024	ex PT-SYU
G-EMBD	Embraer EMB.145EU	145039	
G-EMBE	Embraer EMB.145EU	145042	
G-EMBF	Embraer EMB.145EU	145088	
G-EMBG	Embraer EMB.145EU	145094	ex PT-SBQ
G-EMBH	Embraer EMB.145EU	145107	
G-EMBI	Embraer EMB.145EU	145126	ex PT-SDG
G-EMBJ	Embraer EMB.145EU	145134	
G-EMBK	Embraer EMB.145EU	145167	
G-EMBL	Embraer EMB.145EU	145177	ex PT-SEY
G-EMBM	Embraer EMB.145EU	145196	ex PT-SGL
G-EMBN	Embraer EMB.145EP	145201	ex PT-SGQ
G-EMBO	Embraer EMB.145EU	145219	ex PT-SHF
G-EMBP	Embraer EMB.145EU	145300	ex PT-SKR
G-EMBS	Embraer EMB.145EU	145357	ex PT-SNW
G-EMBT	Embraer EMB.145EU	145404	ex PT-STB
G-EMBU	Embraer EMB.145EU	145458	ex PT-SVD
G-EMBV	Embraer EMB.145EU	145482	ex PT-SXB
G-EMBW	Embraer EMB.145EU	145546	ex PT-SZJ
G-EMBX	Embraer EMB.145EU	145573	ex PT-SBJ
G-EMBY	Embraer EMB.145EU	145617	ex PT-SDF
G-ERJA	Embraer EMB.145EP	145229	ex PT-SHS
G-ERJB	Embraer EMB.145EP	145237	ex PT-SIC
G-ERJC	Embraer EMB.145EP	145253	ex PT-SIN
G-ERJD	Embraer EMB.145EP	145290	ex PT-SKH
G-ERJE	Embraer EMB.145EP	145315	ex PT-SMG
G-ERJF	Embraer EMB.145EP	145325	ex PT-SMR
G-ERJG	Embraer EMB.145EP	145394	ex PT-SQR

G-LGNA	SAAB SF.340B	199	ex N592MA	Lsd fr SAAB A/c Lsg
G-LGNB	SAAB SF.340B	216	ex N595MA	Lsd fr SAAB A/c Lsg

G-LGNC	SAAB SF.340B	318	ex SE-KXC		Lsd fr SAAB A/c Lsg
G-LGND	SAAB SF.340B	169	ex G-GNTH		Lsd fr SAAB
G-LGNE	SAAB SF.340B	172	ex G-GNTI		Lsd fr SAAB
G-LGNF	SAAB SF.340B	192	ex N192JE		Lsd fr SAAB
G-LGNG	SAAB SF.340B	327	ex SE-C27		Lsd fr SAAB
G-	SAAB SF.340A	082	ex G-GNTB		Lsd fr Swedish Aircraft

Operated by Loganair in full British Airways colours

BRITISH ASIA AIRWAYS

Speedbird (BA/BAW)   *London-Heathrow (LHR)*

A subsidiary of British Airways, aircraft leased from parent

BRITISH INTERNATIONAL

Brintel (BS/BIH)   *Cardiff, Penzance & Plymouth (CWL/PZE/PLH)*

G-ATBJ	Sikorsky S-61N	61269			Lsd to CHC Scotia
G-ATFM	Sikorsky S-61N	61270	ex CF-OKY	based PSY	
G-AYOY	Sikorsky S-61N	61476			
G-BCEA	Sikorsky S-61N	61721		based PSY	
G-BCEB	Sikorsky S-61NM	61454	ex N4023S	The Isles of Scilly	based PZE
G-BFFJ	Sikorsky S-61N	61777	ex N6231	Tresco	based PZE

G-BTKL	MBB Bo.105DBS-4	S-422	ex D-HDMU		
G-SEWP	Aerospatiale AS.355F2 Twin Squirrel	5480	ex G-OFIN		
ZJ164	Aerospatiale AS.365N2 Dauphin 2	6406	ex G-BTLC		Op for RN-Flag Officer
ZJ165	Aerospatiale AS.355N2 Dauphin 2	6372	ex G-NTOO		Op for RN Flag Officer

British International is the trading name of Veritair

BRITISH MEDITERRANEAN AIRWAYS

Bee Med (KJ/LAJ)   *London-Heathrow (LHR)*

G-MEDA	Airbus Industrie A320-231	0480	ex N480RX		Lsd fr ORIX
G-MEDE	Airbus Industrie A320-232	1194	ex F-WWDY		Lsd fr SALE
G-MEDF	Airbus Industrie A321-131	1690	ex D-AVZX		Lsd fr debis
G-MEDG	Airbus Industrie A321-131	1711	ex D-AVZK		Lsd fr debis
G-MEDH	Airbus Industrie A320-232	1922	ex F-WWBX		Lsd fr SALE
G-MEDI	Airbus Industrie A321-231	2190	ex D-AVZD	on order	

Operates services for British Airways in BA colours under a franchise agreement

BUZZ STANSTED Purchased by Ryanair, operations ceased for April 03 but resumed 01May03 on routes as a sub-service for Ryanair

CHANNEL EXPRESS

Channex (LS/EXS)   *Bournemouth (BOH)*

G-CELA	Boeing 737-377	1323/23663	ex VH-CZK	stored BOH	
G-CELB	Boeing 737-377	1326/23664	ex VH-CZL	stored BOH	
G-CELC	Boeing 737-33A	1471/23831	ex N190FH		Op for Jet2
G-CELD	Boeing 737-33A	1473/23832	ex N191FH	stored BOH	
G-CELE	Boeing 737-33A	1601/24029	ex VH-CZX	stored BOH	
G-CELP	Boeing 737-330(QC)	1246/23522	ex TF-ELP		
G-CELR	Boeing 737-330(QC)	1271/23523	ex TF-ELR		
G-CELS	Boeing 737-377	1294/23660	ex VH-CZH		Op for Jet2
G-CELU	Boeing 737-377	1280/23657	ex VH-CZE		Op for Jet2
G-CELV	Boeing 737-377	1314/23661	ex VH-CZI		Op for Jet2
G-CELW	Boeing 737-377(QC)	1292/23659	ex N659DG		
G-CELX	Boeing 737-377	1273/23654	ex VH-CZB		Op for Jet2
G-CELY	Boeing 737-377 (QC)	1316/23662	ex N622DG		
G-CELZ	Boeing 737-377	1281/23658	ex VH-CZF		
TF-ELC	Boeing 737-3M8	2024/25041	ex OO-LTL		Jt ops with ISL
TF-ELM	Boeing 737-3M8(QC)	1630/24021	ex F-GIXP		Lsd fr ISL

*Operated for Flyglobespan.com

G-BNIZ	Fokker F.27 Friendship 600F	10405	ex OY-SRA		
G-CEXA	Fokker F.27 Friendship 500RF	10503	ex N703A		
G-CEXB	Fokker F.27 Friendship 500RF	10550	ex N743A		
G-CEXD	Fokker F.27 Friendship 600	10351	ex PH-KFE		
G-CEXE	Fokker F.27 Friendship 500	10654	ex SU-GAF		
G-CEXF	Fokker F.27 Friendship 500	10660	ex SU-GAE		
G-CEXG	Fokker F.27 Friendship 500	10459	ex G-JEAP		

D-CAOB	Embraer EMB.120ER Brasilia	120012	ex N120AM	Lsd fr Air Omega
G-CEXH	Airbus Industrie A300B4-203F	117	ex D-ASAZ	
G-CEXI	Airbus Industrie A300B4-203F	121	ex D-ASAA	
G-CEXJ	Airbus Industrie A300B4-203F	147	ex N300FV	Lsd fr GATX
G-CEXK	Airbus Industrie A300B4-103F	105	ex PH-ABF	Lsd fr Finova

Owned by Dart Group and operates Boeing 737-377s for sister company Jet 2

CHC SCOTIA HELICOPTERS

Helibus (BS/SHZ)   *Aberdeen-Dyce (ABZ)*

G-BKZE	Aerospatiale AS.332L Super Puma	2102	ex F-WKQE	based ABZ	Lsd fr Heliworld Lsg
G-BKZG	Aerospatiale AS.332L Super Puma	2106	ex HB-ZBT		
G-BKZH	Aerospatiale AS.332L Super Puma	2107			Lsd as VH-LHK
G-BOZK	Aerospatiale AS.332L Super Puma	2179	ex LN-OMQ		Lsd as OY-HHC
G-BUZD	Aerospatiale AS.332L Super Puma	2069	ex C-GSLJ	based ABZ	
G-BWHN*	Aerospatiale AS.332L Super Puma	2017	ex C-GSLC		Lsd as OY-HDT
G-CHCA*	Aerospatiale AS.332L Super Puma	2007	ex C-GSEM		Lsd as OY-HEO
G-CHCB*	Aerospatiale AS.332L Super Puma	2015	ex C-GYGX		Lsd as OY-HHA
G-CHCF	Eurocopter AS.332L2 Super Puma	2567			
G-CHCG	Eurocopter AS.332L2 Super Puma	2592			
G-PUMA	Aerospatiale AS.332L Super Puma	2038	ex F-WMHB	based ABZ	
G-PUMB	Aerospatiale AS.332L Super Puma	2075		based ABZ	
G-PUMD	Aerospatiale AS.332L Super Puma	2077	ex F-WXFD	based ABZ	
G-PUME	Aerospatiale AS.332L Super Puma	2091		based ABZ	
G-PUMG	Aerospatiale AS.332L Super Puma	2018	ex F-ODOS	based ABZ	
G-PUMK	Aerospatiale AS.332L Super Puma	2067	ex LN-OMF		Lsd fr HKS
G-PUML	Aerospatiale AS.332L Super Puma	2073	ex LN-ODA		Lsd fr HKS
G-PUMM	Aerospatiale AS.332L2 Super Puma	2477			
G-PUMN	Aerospatiale AS.332L2 Super Puma	2474	ex LN-OHF		Lsd fr HKS
G-PUMO	Aerospatiale AS.332L2 Super Puma	2467			
G-PUMS	Aerospatiale AS.332L2 Super Puma	2504			
G-TIGZ	Aerospatiale AS.332L Super Puma	2115	ex C-GQKK	based ABZ	

*Leased to Danish International Helicopters

G-BKXD	Aerospatiale SA.365N Dauphin 2	6088	ex F-WMHD	based BPL	
G-BLEZ	Aerospatiale SA.365N Dauphin 2	6131			
G-BLUM	Aerospatiale SA.365N Dauphin 2	6101		based HUY	
G-BLUN	Aerospatiale SA.365N Dauphin 2	6114	ex PH-SSS	based LPL	
G-BTEU	Aerospatiale SA.365N2 Dauphin 2	6392		based HUY	
G-BTNC	Aerospatiale SA.365N2 Dauphin 2	6409		based HUY	
G-BTUX	Aerospatiale SA.365N2 Dauphin 2	6424		based HUY	
G-NTWO	Aerospatiale SA.365N2 Dauphin 2	6358			Lsd as LN-ODB

G-BHGK	Sikorsky S-76A+	760049	ex N1545Y		Lsd as ZS-RPR
G-BMAL	Sikorsky S-76A+	760120	ex F-WZSA	based HUY	
G-BVCX	Sikorsky S-76A+	760183	ex N951L		Lsd as OY-HIW
G-CHCD	Sikorsky S-76A+	760101	ex (ZS-RNH)		
G-CHCE	Sikorsky S-76A+	760036	ex (ZS-RNG)		
G-DRNT	Sikorsky S-76A+	760201	ex N93WW		
G-SSSC	Sikorsky S-76C	760408		based ABZ	
G-SSSD	Sikorsky S-76C	760415		based ABZ	
G-SSSE	Sikorsky S-76C	760417		based ABZ	
ZS-	Sikorsky S-76A+	760036	ex G-CHCE		Lsd to Court H/c

G-ATBJ	Sikorsky S-61N	61269			Lsd fr British Intl
G-BEJL	Sikorsky S-61N	61224	ex EI-BPK	stored ABZ	
G-BZSN	Sikorsky S-61N	61807	ex LN-OQB	Lsd fr HKS; sublsd to CHC Ireland	
G-CBKZ	Sikorsky S-61N II	61816	ex LN-OQU	Lsd to CHC Ireland	
G-CBWC	Sikorsky S-61N	61740	ex OY-HDO	Lsd fr HKS; sublsd to CHC Ireland	
ZS-RLK	Sikorsky S-61N	61772	ex G-BEWM	Lsd to Court H/c	
ZS-RLL	Sikorsky S-61N	61778	ex G-BFFK	Lsd to Court H/c	

G-BPPM*	Beech 200 Super King Air	BB-1044	ex N7061T	based ABZ	

*Operated by GAMA Aviation
Controls CHC Helicopters Australia (VH-); member of CHC International (Canada)

CITYFLYER EXPRESS absorbed into British Airways CitiExpress

COUGAR AIRLINES ceased operations 17 May 2003

COYNE AIRWAYS

Coyne Air (7C/COY)   *Ostend (OST)*

Operates cargo services with aircraft leased from other operators as required

DHL AIR

World Express (ER/DHK)   *East Midlands (EMA)*

G-BIKC	Boeing 757-236SF	11/22174		Lsd fr BCS
G-BIKF	Boeing 757-236SF	16/22177		Lsd fr BCS
G-BIKG	Boeing 757-236SF	23/22178		Lsd fr BCS
G-BIKI	Boeing 757-236SF	25/22180	ex OO-DLO	Lsd fr BCS
G-BIKJ	Boeing 757-236SF	29/22181		Lsd fr BCS
G-BIKK	Boeing 757-236SF	30/22182		Lsd fr BCS
G-BIKM	Boeing 757-236SF	33/22184	ex N8293V	Lsd fr BCS

G-BIKN	Boeing 757-236SF	50/22186		Lsd fr BCS
G-BIKO	Boeing 757-236SF	52/22187		Lsd fr BCS
G-BIKP	Boeing 757-236SF	54/22188		Lsd fr BCS
G-BIKS	Boeing 757-236SF	63/22190		Lsd fr BCS
G-BIKU	Boeing 757-236SF	78/23399		Lsd fr BCS
G-BIKV	Boeing 757-236SF	81/23400		Lsd fr BCS
G-BIKZ	Boeing 757-236SF	98/23532		Lsd fr BCS
G-BMRA	Boeing 757-236SF	123/23710		Lsd fr BCS
G-BMRB	Boeing 757-236SF	145/23975		Lsd fr BCS
G-BMRC	Boeing 757-236SF	160/24072		Lsd fr BCS
G-BMRD	Boeing 757-236SF	166/24073		Lsd fr BCS
G-BMRE	Boeing 757-236SF	168/24074		Lsd fr BCS
G-BMRF	Boeing 757-236SF	175/24101		Lsd fr BCS
G-BMRH	Boeing 757-236SF	210/24266		Lsd fr BCS
G-BMRJ	Boeing 757-236SF	214/24268		Lsd fr BCS

Wholly owned subsidiary of DHL Holdings

DIRECTFLIGHT

(DCT) *Norwich (NWI)*

G-LUXE	British Aerospace 146 Srs.301	E3001	ex G-5-300	Atmospheric Research
G-MAFA	Reims Cessna F406 Caravan II	F406-0036	ex G-DFLT	Op for DEFRA
G-MAFB	Reims Cessna F406 Caravan II	F406-0080		Op for DEFRA
G-SFPA*	Reims Cessna F406 Caravan II	F406-0064		
G-SFPB*	Reims Cessna F406 Caravan II	F406-0065		

*Operated for Scottish Fisheries Protection

DUO AIRWAYS

Bluestar (VB/DAW) (IATA 702) *Birmingham (BHX)*
Formerly listed as Maersk Air , subject to management buyout on 12 May 2003

G-DUOF	Canadair CL-600-2B19	7226	ex G-MSKK	For CSH Jun04	Lsd fr GECAS
G-DUOG	Canadair CL-600-2B19	7247	ex G-MSKL	For CSH Dec04	Lsd fr GECAS
G-DUOH	Canadair CL-600-2B19	7248	ex G-MSKM		
G-DUOA	Canadair CL-600-2C10	10028	ex G-MRSK		
G-DUOB	Canadair CL-600-2C10	10029	ex G-MRSJ		
G-DUOC	Canadair CL-600-2C10	10039	ex G-MRSI		
G-DUOD	Canadair CL-600-2C10	10048	ex G-MRSH		
G-DUOE	Canadair CL-600-2C10	10052	ex G-MRSG		

Operated as British Airways Express until 31 October 2003. Relaunched services next day in its own right.

EASTERN AIRWAYS

Eastflight (T3/EZE) *Humberside (HUY)*

G-BLKP	British Aerospace Jetstream 31	634	ex (G-BLEX)	Lsd fr Global Avn, op for BAES
G-BUVC	British Aerospace Jetstream 32	970	ex F-GMVP	Lsd fr BAES
G-BUVD	British Aerospace Jetstream 32	977	ex F-GMVK	Lsd fr BAES
G-BYMA	British Aerospace Jetstream 32	840	ex OH-JAE	Lsd fr BAES
G-BYRA	British Aerospace Jetstream 32	845	ex OH-JAG	Lsd fr BAES
G-BYRM	British Aerospace Jetstream 32	847	ex OH-JAF	Lsd fr BAES
G-BZYP	British Aerospace Jetstream 32	978	ex F-GMVL	Lsd fr BAES
G-CBCS	British Aerospace Jetstream 32	842	ex SE-LHA	Lsd fr BAES
G-CBDA	British Aerospace Jetstream 32	986	ex JA8590	
G-IJYS	British Aerospace Jetstream 31	715	ex G-BTZT	Flying Scotsman	Op by AKI
G-OAKJ	British Aerospace Jetstream 32	795	ex G-BOTJ		Lsd fr BAES
G-MAJA	British Aerospace Jetstream 41	41032	ex G-4-032	
G-MAJB	British Aerospace Jetstream 41	41018	ex G-BVKT	
G-MAJC	British Aerospace Jetstream 41	41005	ex G-LOGJ	
G-MAJD	British Aerospace Jetstream 41	41006	ex G-WAWR	
G-MAJE	British Aerospace Jetstream 41	41007	ex G-LOGK	
G-MAJF	British Aerospace Jetstream 41	41008	ex G-WAWL	
G-MAJG	British Aerospace Jetstream 41	41009	ex G-LOGL	
G-MAJH	British Aerospace Jetstream 41	41010	ex G-WAYR	
G-MAJI	British Aerospace Jetstream 41	41011	ex G-WAND	
G-MAJJ	British Aerospace Jetstream 41	41024	ex G-WAFT	
G-MAJK	British Aerospace Jetstream 41	41070	ex G-4-070	
G-MAJL	British Aerospace Jetstream 41	41087	ex G-4-087	
G-MAJM	British Aerospace Jetstream 41	41096	ex G-4-096	

To be operated from ex British Airways bases to complement BAW

| SE-DZC | Embraer EMB.145EP | 145169 | ex PT-S | Lsd fr SKX |
| SE-LOX | SAAB 2000 | 009 | ex SE-009 | Lsd fr GAO |

Eastern Airways is a trading name of Air Kilroe

EASYJET AIRLINES

Easy (U2/EZY)   London-Luton (LTN)

G-EZEA	Airbus Industrie A319-111	2119	ex D-AVWZ	
G-EZEB	Airbus Industrie A319-111	2120	ex D-AVYK	
G-EZEC	Airbus Industrie A319-111	2129	ex D-AVWR	
G-EZED	Airbus Industrie A319-111	2170	ex D-AVWT	on order
G-EZEE	Airbus Industrie A319-111	2176	ex D-AVYS	on order
	Airbus Industrie A319-111	2181	ex D-AVWF	on order
	Airbus Industrie A319-111	2184	ex D-AVWO	on order
	Airbus Industrie A319-111	2214	ex D-AV	on order
	Airbus Industrie A319-111	2224	ex D-AV	on order
	Airbus Industrie A319-111	2230	ex D-AV	on order
	Airbus Industrie A319-111	2245	ex D-AV	on order
	Airbus Industrie A319-111	2249	ex D-AV	on order
	Airbus Industrie A319-111	2265	ex D-AV	on order
	Airbus Industrie A319-111	2271	ex D-AV	on order

A total of 120 Airbus Industrie A319-11s are on order for delivery up to 2007

G-EZYB	Boeing 737-3M8	1614/24020	ex N797BB	Lsd fr BBAM
G-EZYC	Boeing 737-3Y0	1691/24462	ex G-BWJA	
G-EZYD	Boeing 737-3M8	1662/24022	ex N798BB	Lsd fr BBAM
G-EZYF	Boeing 737-375	1395/23708	ex D-AGEX	Lsd fr BBAM
G-EZYG	Boeing 737-33V	3062/29331		
G-EZYH	Boeing 737-33V	3072/29332		
G-EZYI	Boeing 737-33V	3084/29333	ex N1787B	
G-EZYJ	Boeing 737-33V	3089/29334		
G-EZYK	Boeing 737-33V	3094/29335		
G-EZYL	Boeing 737-33V	3102/29336	ex N1787B	
G-EZYM	Boeing 737-33V	3113/29337	ex HB-IIK	Lsd fr Alnitak FSC
G-EZYN	Boeing 737-33V	3114/29338	ex HB-III	
G-EZYN	Boeing 737-33V	3114/29338	ex HB-III	
G-EZYO	Boeing 737-33V	3119/29339	ex HB-IIT	
G-EZYP	Boeing 737-33V	3121/29340		
G-EZYR	Boeing 737-33V	3125/29341	ex N1787B	
G-EZYS	Boeing 737-33V	3127/29342	ex HB-IIJ	
G-EZYT	Boeing 737-3Q8	2664/26307	ex HB-IIE	Lsd fr EZS
G-IGOA	Boeing 737-3Y0	1853/24678	ex EI-BZK	Lsd fr ORIX
G-IGOB	Boeing 737-36Q	2883/28660	ex EC-GNU	Lsd fr Boullioun
G-IGOG	Boeing 737-3Y0	1580/23927	ex F-GLLE	Lsd fr BBAM
G-IGOH	Boeing 737-3Y0	1562/23926	ex F-GLLD	Lsd fr BBAM
G-IGOI	Boeing 737-33A	1669/24092	ex G-OBMD	wfs 28Sep03	Lsd fr BBAM
G-IGOJ	Boeing 737-36N	3082/28872	ex N1795B	Lsd fr GECAS
G-IGOK	Boeing 737-36N	3107/28594		Lsd fr GECAS
G-IGOL	Boeing 737-36N	3112/28596	ex N1015X	Lsd fr GECAS
G-IGOM	Boeing 737-36N	3115/28599	ex N1796B	Lsd fr GECAS
G-IGOO	Boeing 737-36N	2862/28557	ex G-SMDB	Lsd fr GECAS
G-IGOP	Boeing 737-36N	3118/28602	ex N1787B	Lsd fr GECAS
G-IGOR	Boeing 737-36N	3124/28606		Lsd fr GECAS
G-IGOS	Boeing 737-3L9	2587/27336	ex D-ADBH	Lsd fr GECAS
G-IGOT	Boeing 737-3L9	1815/24571	ex N2393W	Lsd fr WFBN
G-IGOU	Boeing 737-3L9	2594/27337	ex D-ADBI	Lsd fr GECAS
G-IGOV	Boeing 737-3M8	2005/25017	ex N250GE	Lsd fr GECAS
G-IGOW	Boeing 737-3Y0	1540/23923	ex N923AP	Lsd fr
G-IGOX	Boeing 737-3L9	1600/24219	ex N219TY	Lsd fr CIT Leasing
G-IGOY	Boeing 737-36N	3010/28570	ex CS-TGQ	Lsd fr GECAS
G-IGOZ	Boeing 737-3Q8	1886/24699	ex G-OBWZ	Lsd fr ILFC
G-ODUS	Boeing 737-36Q	2880/28659	ex D-ADBX	Lsd fr Boullioun
G-OFRA	Boeing 737-36Q	3023/29327		Lsd fr Boullioun
G-OGVA	Boeing 737-3M8	1689/24024	ex HB-IIB	Lsd fr GECAS
G-OHAJ	Boeing 737-36Q	3035/29141		Lsd fr Boullioun
G-OMUC	Boeing 737-36Q	3047/29405		Lsd fr Boullioun
G-EZJA	Boeing 737-73V	672/30235	ex N1787B	Lsd fr GECAS
G-EZJB	Boeing 737-73V	715/30236	ex N1787B	Lsd fr GECAS
G-EZJC	Boeing 737-73V	730/30237		
G-EZJD	Boeing 737-73V	890/30242		
G-EZJE	Boeing 737-73V	913/30238	ex N1787B	
G-EZJF	Boeing 737-73V	919/30243	ex N1785B	
G-EZJG	Boeing 737-73V	944/30239		
G-EZJH	Boeing 737-73V	974/30240		
G-EZJI	Boeing 737-73V	1034/30241		
G-EZJJ	Boeing 737-73V	1058/30245		
G-EZJK	Boeing 737-73V	1064/30246		
G-EZJL	Boeing 737-73V	1066/30247		
G-EZJM	Boeing 737-73V	1118/30248		Lsd fr IEM Airfinance
G-EZJN	Boeing 737-73V	1128/30249		Lsd fr IEM Airfinance
G-EZJO	Boeing 737-73V	1148/30244		Lsd fr IEM Airfinance
G-EZJP	Boeing 737-73V	1151/32412		
G-EZJR	Boeing 737-73V	1202/32413		

G-EZJS	Boeing 737-73V	1214/32414			
G-EZJT	Boeing 737-73V	1260/32415			
G-EZJU	Boeing 737-73V	1270/32416	ex N6046P		
G-EZJV	Boeing 737-73V	1285/32417			
G-EZJW	Boeing 737-73V	1300/32418			
G-EZJX	Boeing 737-73V	1321/32419			
G-EZJY	Boeing 737-73V	1341/32420			Lsd fr SALE
G-EZJZ	Boeing 737-73V	1357/32421			Lsd fr SALE
G-EZKA	Boeing 737-73V	1363/32422	ex (G-ESYA)		Lsd fr SALE
G-EZKB	Boeing 737-73V	1433/32423	ex (G-ESYB)		Lsd fr SALE
G-EZKC	Boeing 737-73V	32424	ex (G-ESYC)	on order 04	Lsd fr SALE
G-EZKD	Boeing 737-73V	32425	ex (G-ESYD)	on order 04	Lsd fr SALE
G-EZKE	Boeing 737-73V	32426	ex (G-ESYE)	on order 04	Lsd fr SALE
G-EZKF	Boeing 737-73V	32427	ex (G-ESYF)	on order 04	Lsd fr SALE
G-EZKG	Boeing 737-73V	32428	ex (G-ESYG)	on order 04	Lsd fr SALE
G-OSLH	Boeing 737-76Q	1156/30283			Lsd fr Boullioun

Owns 40% of easyJet Switzerland

EMERALD AIRWAYS

Gemstone (JEM)   Liverpool (LPL)

G-JEMA	British Aerospace ATP	2028	ex N854AW	
G-JEMB	British Aerospace ATP	2029	ex N855AW	
G-JEMC	British Aerospace ATP	2032	ex N856AW	
G-JEMD	British Aerospace ATP	2026	ex S2-ACX	on order
G-JEME	British Aerospace ATP	2027	ex S2-ACY	on order

Plans to acquire five British Aerospace ATP freighters in 2004

G-ATMJ	Hawker Siddeley HS.748 Srs.2A/225	1593	ex VP-LAJ	dam 11Apr02	
G-AYIM	Hawker Siddeley HS.748 Srs.2A/270	1687	ex G-11-687		
G-BEJD*	Hawker Siddeley HS.748 Srs.1/105	1543	ex LV-HHE	Sisyphus	
G-BGMN	Hawker Siddeley HS.748 Srs.2A/347	1766	ex PK-OCH		
G-BGMO	Hawker Siddeley HS.748 Srs.2A/347	1767	ex ZK-MCB		
G-BIUV	Hawker Siddeley HS.748 Srs.2A/275LFD				
		1701	ex 5W-FAN	City of Liverpool	
G-BVOU	Hawker Siddeley HS.748 Srs.2A/270	1721	ex CS-TAH	Lynx c/s	
G-BVOV	Hawker Siddeley HS.748 Srs.2A/372	1777	ex CS-TAO		
G-OPFW	Hawker Siddeley HS.748 Srs.2A/266	1714	ex G-BMFT	Parcel force c/s	
G-ORAL*	Hawker Siddeley HS.748 Srs.2A/334	1756	ex G-BPDA	John J Goodall	
G-ORCP	Hawker Siddeley HS.748 Srs.2A/	1647	ex ZS-OCF	Freighter	Lsd fr Clewer Avn
G-OSOE	Hawker Siddeley HS.748 Srs.2A/242	1697	ex G-AYYG	Securicor Omega Express c/s	
G-OTBA	Hawker Siddeley HS.748 Srs.2A/242	1712	ex A3-MCA		Lsd fr Clewer Avn
G-SOEI	Hawker Siddeley HS.748 Srs.2A/242	1689	ex ZK-DES		

G-BMLC	Short SD.3-60	SH3688	ex SE-LDA	
G-OBHD	Short SD.3-60	SH3714	ex G-BNDK	
G-ROND	Short SD.3-60	SH3604	ex EI-CWG	Lsd fr RPX
G-SSWB	Short SD.3-60	SH3690	ex C6-BFT	
G-SSWC	Short SD.3-60	SH3686	ex SE-LGE	
G-SSWE	Short SD.3-60	SH3705	ex SE-IXE	Laura
G-SSWM	Short SD.3-60	SH3648	ex SE-KCI	
G-SSWO	Short SD.3-60	SH3609	ex SE-KLO	
G-SSWR	Short SD.3-60	SH3670	ex SE-KGV	
G-SSWX	Short SD.3-60	SH3715	ex N711PM	
G-SSWA	Short SD.3-30	SH3042	ex D-CTAG	
G-SSWP	Short SD.3-30	SH3030	ex CS-DBY	

*Reed Aviation colours

EUROMANX

Euromanx (3W/EMX)   Ronaldsway (IOM)

PH-RAH	Beech 1900D	UE-31	ex (OY-GEP)	Lsd fr/op by TRQ
PH-RAK	Aerospatiale/Alenia ATR 42-300	032	ex ZS-OUY	Lsd fr ROS
PH-RAR	Beech 1900D	UE-372	ex ZS-ONS	Lsd fr/op by TRQ
PH-RAT	Beech 1900D	UE-350	ex ZS-OOV	Lsd fr/op by TRQ

Subsidiary of Woodgate Executive Air Services

EUROPEAN AIRCHARTER

European (E7/EAF)   Bournemouth (BOH)

G-CEAC*	Boeing 737-229 (Nordam 3)	360/20911	ex OO-SDE	
G-CEAD	Boeing 737-229 (Nordam 3)	421/21137	ex OO-SDM	
G-CEAE	Boeing 737-229 (Nordam 3)	365/20912	ex OO-SDF	
G-CEAF*	Boeing 737-229 (Nordam 3)	358/20910	ex G-BYRI	
G-CEAG	Boeing 737-229 (Nordam 3)	420/21136	ex OO-SDL	
G-CEAH	Boeing 737-229 (Nordam 3)	418/21135	ex OO-SDG	
G-CEAI	Boeing 737-229 (Nordam 3)	431/21176	ex OO-SDN	all-white

| G-CEAJ | Boeing 737-229 (Nordam 3) | 433/21177 | ex OO-SDO | VIP | |
| G-GPFI | Boeing 737-229 (Nordam 3) | 351/20907 | ex F-GVAC | | Lsd fr European Skybus |

*Operated by Palmair Flightline under European Aircharter EAF code

G-BDXE	Boeing 747-236B	321/21350			
G-BDXF	Boeing 747-236B	323/21351			
G-BDXG	Boeing 747-236B	328/21536			
G-BDXH	Boeing 747-236B	365/21635			
G-BDXJ	Boeing 747-236B	440/21831	ex N1792B		
G-BDXO	Boeing 747-236B	677/23799			
G-CCMA	Boeing 747-267B	566/22872	ex G-VCAT		
G-CCMB	Boeing 747-267B	582/23048	ex G-VRUM	on order	

All 747s registered to European Skybus; operate services for other airlines or tour operators

EXCEL AIRWAYS

Expo (JN/XLA)   *London-Gatwick (LGW)*

G-XLAA	Boeing 737-8Q8	77/28226	ex G-OKDN		Lsd fr ILFC
G-XLAB	Boeing 737-8Q8	160/28218	ex G-OJSW	Tinks	Lsd fr ILFC
G-XLAC	Boeing 737-81Q	479/29051	ex G-LFJB		Lsd fr Tombo; sublsd to BSK
G-XLAD	Boeing 737-81Q	557/29052	ex G-ODMW		Lsd fr Tombo; sublsd to BSK
G-XLAE	Boeing 737-8Q8	800/30637	ex D-ABAA		Lsd fr ILFC; sublsd to KFA
G-XLAF	Boeing 737-86N	1083/29883			Lsd fr GECAS; sublsd to RYR
G-XLAG	Boeing 737-86N	1121/33003			Lsd fr GECAS; sublsd to RYR
G-XLAH	Boeing 737-8Q8	29351		on order Apr04	Lsd fr ILFC
G-OXLA	Boeing 737-81Q	856/30619	ex N733MA	Elaine	Lsd fr BSK for summers

| (G-DAAE) | Boeing 767-3Y0ER | 464/26204 | ex TF-ATU | | Lsd fr EUK |
| G-SATR | Boeing 767-204ER | 256/24457 | ex TF-ATR | | Lsd fr EUK |

Fleet varies between summer and winter

FIRST CHOICE AIRWAYS

Jet Set (DP/FCA)   *Manchester (MAN)*

Formerly known as Air 2000 but renamed 21 October 2003 although operated as Air 2000 until 14 January 2004

G-OOAE	Airbus Industrie A321-211	0852	ex G-UNIF		Lsd fr Unijet Leisure
G-OOAF	Airbus Industrie A321-211	0677	ex G-UNID		Lsd fr NBB Lease
G-OOAH	Airbus Industrie A321-211	0781	ex G-UNIE		Lsd fr Castle Harbour Lsg
G-OOAI	Airbus Industrie A321-211	1006	ex D-AVZJ		Lsd fr GECAS
G-OOAJ	Airbus Industrie A321-211	1017	ex D-AVZM		Lsd fr GECAS
G-OOAP	Airbus Industrie A320-214	1306	ex F-WWBY		Lsd CIT Leasing
G-OOAR	Airbus Industrie A320-214	1320	ex F-WWDT		Lsd CIT Leasing
G-OOAS	Airbus Industrie A320-214	1571	ex C-GTDG		Lsd fr ILFC
G-OOAT	Airbus Industrie A320-214	1605	ex C-GTDH		Lsd fr ILFC; sublsd to SSV
G-OOAU	Airbus Industrie A320-214	1637	ex F-WWDM		Lsd fr ILFC
G-OOAV	Airbus Industrie A321-211	1720	ex D-AVXA		Lsd fr ILFC
G-OOAW	Airbus Industrie A320-214	1777	ex F-WWDM		Lsd fr ILFC
G-OOAX	Airbus Industrie A320-214	2180	ex F-WWDY	on order	

C-FTDV	Boeing 757-28AER	162/24017	ex G-OOOC		Lsd fr Crawley Co; sublsd to SSV
G-CPEP*	Boeing 757-2Y0	400/25268	ex C-GTSU		
G-CPEU	Boeing 757-236	864/29941			Lsd fr CIT Leasing
G-CPEV	Boeing 757-236	871/29943	ex N1795B	Stored MAN	Lsd fr CIT Leasing
G-OOBA*	Boeing 757-28A	950/32446	ex N446GE		Lsd fr Castle Harbour Lsg
G-OOBB*	Boeing 757-28A	951/32447	ex N447GE		Lsd fr Castle Harbour Lsg
G-OOBC	Boeing 757-28A	1026/33098			Lsd fr CIT Leasing
G-OOBD	Boeing 757-28A	1029/33099			Lsd fr CIT Leasing
G-OOBE	Boeing 757-28A	1029/33100			Lsd fr CIT Leasing
G-OOBF	Boeing 757-28A	33101		on order	Lsd fr CIT Leasing
G-OOBG	Boeing 757-236	871/29442	ex N545NA		Lsd fr Pembroke
G-OOBH	Boeing 757-236	872/29944	ex N544NA		Lsd fr Pembroke
G-OOOB	Boeing 757-28A	130/23822	ex C-FRYH		Lsd fr Dean Avn Co
G-OOOD*	Boeing 757-28A	180/24235	ex C-GRYU		Lsd fr West Sussex Co
G-OOOG*	Boeing 757-23AER	219/24292	ex C-FOOG		Lsd fr AWAS
G-OOOK	Boeing 757-236	362/25054	ex SE-DUK		
G-OOOX	Boeing 757-2Y0ER	526/26158			Lsd fr ALPS Ltd
G-OOOY	Boeing 757-28AER	802/28203			Lsd fr ILFC
G-OOOZ	Boeing 757-236	466/25593	ex N593RA		Lsd fr BBAM

| G-OOAL | Boeing 767-38AER | 741/29617 | | Sunrise | Lsd fr AFT Trust-Sub |
| G-OOAN | Boeing 767-39HER | 484/26256 | ex G-UKLH | Caribbean Star | Lsd fr MSA 1 |

*Subleased to Skyservice

FLIGHTLINE

Flightline (B5/FLT)   Southend/Aberdeen (SEN/ABZ)

G-BPNT	British Aerospace 146 Srs.300	E3126			Lsd fr BAES
G-DEBE	British Aerospace 146 Srs.200	E2022	ex N163US		Lsd fr BAES
G-DEFM	British Aerospace 146 Srs.200	E2016	ex G-DEBM	stored SEN	Lsd fr IMP Group
G-FLTA	British Aerospace 146 Srs.200	E2048	ex N189US	IAC titles	
(G-FLTC)	British Aerospace 146 Srs.200	E2023	ex G-CLHD	IAC titles	Lsd fr Finova
G-JEBH	British Aerospace 146 Srs.300	E3205	ex G-BTVO		Lsd to BEE
G-OZRH	British Aerospace 146 Srs.200	E2047	ex N188US	for CityJet May04	
G-TBIC	British Aerospace 146 Srs.200	E2025	ex N167US		Lsd fr TBI Lse

FLYBE

Jersey (BE/BEE) (IATA 267)   Jersey/Exeter (JER/EXT)

G-BTUY	British Aerospace 146 Srs.300	E3202	ex G-NJIC		
G-BVCE	British Aerospace 146 Srs.300	E3209	ex G-NJIE		
G-JEAJ*	British Aerospace 146 Srs.200	E2099	ex G-OLCA	Pride of Guernsey	
G-JEAK*	British Aerospace 146 Srs.200	E2103	ex G-OLCB	Pride of Birmingham	
G-JEAM	British Aerospace 146 Srs.300	E3128	ex G-BTJT	Pride of Jersey	Op for AFR
G-JEAS	British Aerospace 146 Srs.200	E2020	ex G-OLHB		
G-JEAT	British Aerospace 146 Srs.100	E1071	ex N171TR	stored EXT for spares	
G-JEAU	British Aerospace 146 Srs.100	E1035	ex N135TR	stored EXT	
G-JEAV*	British Aerospace 146 Srs.200	E2064	ex (N764BA)		
G-JEAW*	British Aerospace 146 Srs.200	E2059	ex (N759BA)		
G-JEAX*	British Aerospace 146 Srs.200	E2136	ex N136JV		
G-JEAY*	British Aerospace 146 Srs.200	E2138	ex SE-DRL		
G-JEBA+	British Aerospace 146 Srs.300	E3181	ex HS-TBL		Op for AFR
G-JEBB+	British Aerospace 146 Srs.300	E3185	ex HS-TBK		Op for AFR
G-JEBC+	British Aerospace 146 Srs.300	E3189	ex HS-TBO		
G-JEBD+	British Aerospace 146 Srs.300	E3191	ex HS-TBJ		
G-JEBE+	British Aerospace 146 Srs.300	E3206	ex HS-TBM		
G-JEBH	British Aerospace 146 Srs.300	E3205	ex G-BTVO		Lsd fr FLT
*Leased from BAES			+Leased from Walker Aviation Finance		

G-JEDC	de Havilland DHC-8Q-311A	532	ex C-GEOA		
G-JEDD	de Havilland DHC-8Q-311A	533	ex C-GERC		
G-JEDE	de Havilland DHC-8Q-311A	534	ex C-GERL		
G-JEDF	de Havilland DHC-8Q-311B	548	ex C-GDIW		
G-JEDI	de Havilland DHC-8-402Q	4052	ex C-GFOD		
G-JEDJ	de Havilland DHC-8-402Q	4058	ex C-FDHZ		
G-JEDK	de Havilland DHC-8-402Q	4065	ex C-GEMU		
G-JEDL	de Havilland DHC-8-402Q	4067	ex C-GEOZ		
G-JEDM	de Havilland DHC-8-402Q	4077	ex C-FGNP		
G-JEDN	de Havilland DHC-8-402Q	4078	ex C-FNGB		
G-JEDO	de Havilland DHC-8-402Q	4079	ex C-GDFT		
G-JEDX	de Havilland DHC-8Q-201B	541	ex C-FDHV		
G-JEDY	de Havilland DHC-8Q-201B	542	ex C-FNGB		
G-JEDZ	de Havilland DHC-8Q-201B	547	ex C-GDIU		
G-	de Havilland DHC-8-402Q		ex C-	on order	
G-	de Havilland DHC-8-402Q		ex C-	on order 04	
G-	de Havilland DHC-8-402Q		ex C-	on order 04	
G-	de Havilland DHC-8-402Q		ex C-	on order 04	
G-	de Havilland DHC-8-402Q		ex C-	on order 04	
G-	de Havilland DHC-8-402Q		ex C-	on order 04	
G-	de Havilland DHC-8-402Q		ex C-	on order 04	
G-	de Havilland DHC-8-402Q		ex C-	on order 04	
G-	de Havilland DHC-8-402Q		ex C-	on order 04	

Five more de Havilland DHC-8-402Qs are on order for delivery in 2005 (2) and 2006 (3)
flybe. is the trading name of Jersey European Airways

FLY EUROPA current status uncertain, code is no longer current

FLYGLOBESPAN

                                                                      Prestwick (PIK)

G-CELP	Boeing 737-330(QC)	1246/23522	ex TF-ELP		
G-CELR	Boeing 737-330(QC)	1271/23523	ex TF-ELR		
G-	Boeing 737-329	1441/23773	ex D-ADID	on order 04	Lsd fr CIT Lsg
G-	Boeing 737-329	1443/23774	ex D-ADIE	on order 04	Lsd fr CIT Lsg
TF-ELC	Boeing 737-3M8	2024/25041	ex OO-LTL		

The two ex dba aircraft are to be G-SPAN and G-OTDA but tie-up not known
Aircraft are operated by Channel Express (jointly with Islandsflug) using the former's EXS code

FLYJET

(FJE)   *Gatwick/Manchester (LGW/MAN)*

| G-FJEA | Boeing 757-23AER | 259/24636 | ex G-LCRC | Lsd fr AWAS |
| G-FJEB | Boeing 757-23A | 212/24290 | ex N290AN | |

GB AIRWAYS

GeeBee Airways (GT/GBL) (IATA 171)   *London-Gatwick/Gibraltar (LGW/GIB)*

G-TTIA	Airbus Industrie A321-231	1428	ex D-AVZA	
G-TTIB	Airbus Industrie A321-231	1433	ex D-AVZC	
G-TTIC	Airbus Industrie A321-231	1869	ex D-AVZZ	
G-TTOA	Airbus Industrie A320-231	1215	ex F-WWDB	Lsd fr SALE
G-TTOB	Airbus Industrie A320-232	1687	ex F-WWIM	Lsd fr RBS Avn
G-TTOC	Airbus Industrie A320-232	1715	ex F-WWDB	Lsd fr RBS Avn
G-TTOD	Airbus Industrie A320-232	1723	ex F-WWBH	Lsd fr RBS Avn
G-TTOE	Airbus Industrie A320-232	1754	ex F-WWDH	Lsd fr RBS Avn
G-TTOF	Airbus Industrie A320-232	1918	ex F-WWIS	
G-TTOG	Airbus Industrie A320-232	1969	ex F-WWDZ	
G-TTOH	Airbus Industrie A320-232	1993	ex F-WWDO	
G-TTOI	Airbus Industrie A320-232	2137	ex F-WWBN	
G-TTOJ	Airbus Industrie A320-232	2157	ex F-WW	

Operates services for British Airways in BAW colours under a franchise agreement

GLOBAL SUPPLY SYSTEM

JetLift (GSS)   *London-Stansted (STN)*

G-GSSA	Boeing 747-47UF	1213/29256	ex N495MC	Lsd fr/op by GTI
G-GSSB	Boeing 747-47UF	1165/29252	ex N491MC	Lsd fr/op by GTI
G-GSSC	Boeing 747-47UF	1184/29255	ex N494MC	Lsd fr/op by GTI

Operated by Atlas Air, (who own 49%), on behalf of British Airways

GO FLY taken over by easyJet and fleets merged 31 March 2003

HEBRIDEAN AIR SERVICES

       Cumbernauld

| G-BCWO | Britten-Norman BN-2B-21 Islander | 431 | ex SE-LAX |
| G-BLNL | Britten-Norman BN-2T Turbine Islander | 2191 | ex PH-PRN |

HIGHLAND AIRWAYS

HiWay (HWY)   *Inverness (INV)*

CS-TMY	Short SD.3-60	SH3632	ex G-BLCP		Lsd fr EAD
G-BTXG	British Aerospace Jetstream 31	719	ex SE-FVP		
G-JURA	British Aerospace Jetstream 31	772	ex SE-LDH	City of Inverness	
G-TWIG	Reims Cessna F406 Caravan II	F406-0014	ex PH-FWD	Wee Dram	
G-UIST	British Aerospace Jetstream 31	750	ex N190PC		Lsd fr BAE Systems

Associated with Atlantic Airways

ISLANDAIR

(IAJ)   *Jersey (JSY)*

Current status is uncertain

ISLAND FLYER

(IAV)   *Jersey (JSY)*

Current status is uncertain, fleet details unknwon

ISLES OF SCILLY SKYBUS

Scillonia (IOS)   *Lands End-St Just (LEQ)*

G-BIHO	de Havilland DHC-6 Twin Otter 310	738	ex A6-ADB	
G-BUBN	Britten-Norman BN-2B-20 Islander	2270		
G-CBML	de Havilland DHC-6 Twin Otter 300	695	ex C-FZSP	Lsd fr Beau Del Lsg
G-SBUS	Britten-Norman BN-2A-26 Islander	3013	ex G-BMMH	
G-SSKY	Britten-Norman BN-2B-26Islander	2247	ex G-BSWT	

JET 2

(LS)   *Leeds-Bradford (LBA)*

G-CELC	Boeing 737-33A	1471/23831	ex N190FH		Op by EXS
G-CELS	Boeing 737-377	1294/23660	ex VH-CZH	Jet Leeds-Bradford	Op by EXS
G-CELU	Boeing 737-377	1280/23657	ex VH-CZE		Op by EXS
G-CELV	Boeing 737-377	1314/23661	ex VH-CZI		Op by EXS
G-CELX	Boeing 737-377	1273/23654	ex VH-CZB		Op by EXS

First service 12 February 2003
Wholly owned by Dart Group, owners of Channel Express,

JMC AIRLINES renamed Thomas Cook Airlines 01 March 2003

KEEN AIRWAYS

Keenair (5Q/JFK)   *Liverpool (LPL)*
Previously listed as Keen Air Charter

G-BGYT	Embraer EMB.110P1 Bandeirante	110234	ex N104VA
G-FLTY	Embraer EMB.110P1 Bandeirante	110215	ex G-ZUSS

KLM CITYHOPPER UK fleet integrated into Dutch parent

LOGANAIR

Logan (LOG)   *Glasgow (GLA)*

G-MANJ	British Aerospace ATP	2004	ex G-LOGE	on order
G-MANL	British Aerospace ATP	2003	ex G-ERIN	on order
G-MANM	British Aerospace ATP	2005	ex G-OATP	on order
G-MANP	British Aerospace ATP	2023	ex OK-VFO	on order
G-MAUD	British Aerospace ATP	2002	ex G-BMYM	on order
G-BJOP	Britten-Norman BN-2B-26 Islander	2132		Capt EE Freeson
G-BLDV	Britten-Norman BN-2B-26 Islander	2179	ex D-INEY	
G-BLNJ	Britten-Norman BN-2B-26 Islander	2189		EL Gander Dower, Esq
G-BOMG	Britten-Norman BN-2B-26 Islander	2205		
G-BPCA	Britten-Norman BN-2B-26 Islander	2198	ex G-BLNX	Capt David Barclay MBE
G-BVVK	de Havilland DHC-6 Twin Otter 300	666	ex LN-BEZ	
G-BZFP	de Havilland DHC-6 Twin Otter 300	696	ex C-GGNF	

Operates British Airways services under a franchise agreement in full colours although Islander services due to come out with effect from February 2004. Will operate all internal Scottish routes with effect from 01 March 2004

LOVE AIR did not recommence operations as planned

LYDD AIR

Lyddair (LYD)   *Lydd (LYX)*

G-BDOT	Britten-Norman BN-2A Mk111-2 Trislander		
		1025	ex ZS-SFF
G-BEDP	Britten-Norman BN-2A Mk111-2 Trislander		
		1039	ex ZS-SFG
G-OJAV	Britten-Norman BN-2A Mk111-2 Trislander		
		1024	ex G-BDOS

MAERSK AIR renamed Duo Airways 12 May 2003 after management buy-out

MCALPINE AVIATION SERVICES renamed Premiair Aviation Services

MONARCH AIRLINES

Monarch (ZB/MON)   *London-Luton (LTN)*

G-MARA	Airbus Industrie A321-231	0983	ex D-AVZB		
G-MONX	Airbus Industrie A320-212	0392	ex F-WWDR		Lsd fr GECAS
G-MPCD	Airbus Industrie A320-212	0379	ex C-GZCD		Lsd fr GECAS
G-OJEG	Airbus Industrie A321-231	1015	ex D-AVZN		
G-OZBB	Airbus Industrie A320-212	0389	ex C-GZUM		Lsd fr ILFC
G-OZBE	Airbus Industrie A321-231	1707	ex D-AVZH		
G-OZBF	Airbus Industrie A321-231	1763	ex D-AVZB		
G-OZBG	Airbus Industrie A321-231	1941	ex D-AVXC		
G-OZBH	Airbus Industrie A321-231	2105	ex D-AVXB		
G-OZBI	Airbus Industrie A321-231	2234	ex D-AV	on order Apr04	
G-DAJB	Boeing 757-2T7ER	125/23770			
G-MONB	Boeing 757-2T7ER	15/22780			
G-MONC	Boeing 757-2T7ER	18/22781	ex PH-AHO		
G-MOND	Boeing 757-2T7	19/22960	ex D-ABNZ		

G-MONE	Boeing 757-2T7ER	56/23293		
G-MONJ	Boeing 757-2T7ER	170/24104		
G-MONK	Boeing 757-2T7ER	172/24105		

G-EOMA	Airbus Industrie A330-242	265	ex F-WWKU	
G-MAJS	Airbus Industrie A300B4-605R	604	ex F-WWAX	
G-MONR	Airbus Industrie A300B4-605R	540	ex VH-YMJ	
G-MONS	Airbus Industrie A300B4-605R	556	ex VH-YMK	
G-OJMR	Airbus Industrie A300B4-605R	605	ex F-WWAY	
G-SMAN	Airbus Industrie A330-242	261	ex F-WWKR	

MYTRAVEL AIRWAYS

Kestrel (VZ/MYT)   Manchester (MAN)

G-BYTH	Airbus Industrie A320-231	0429	ex C-GTDM		Lsd to SSV
G-CRPH	Airbus Industrie A320-231	0424	ex C-GJUU		Lsd fr Hare Ltd
G-CTLA	Airbus Industrie A321-211	1887	ex D-AVZC		Lsd fr Boullioun
G-DHJH	Airbus Industrie A321-211	1238	ex D-AVZL		Lsd fr GECAS
G-DHJZ	Airbus Industrie A320-214	1965	ex F-WWDY		Lsd fr GECAS
G-DHRG	Airbus Industrie A320-214	1942	ex F-WWIY		Lsd fr GECAS
G-DJAR	Airbus Industrie A320-231	0164	ex OY-CNE		Lsd fr Frid Lsg
G-EFPA	Airbus Industrie A321-211	1960	ex D-AVZG		Lsd fr debis
G-HBAP*	Airbus Industrie A320-212	0294	ex G-HAGT		Lsd fr GPAA Funding
G-JANM*	Airbus Industrie A320-212	0301	ex G-KMAM		Lsd fr Airplanes A320 Ltd
G-JOEE	Airbus Industrie A321-211	2060	ex D-AVZH		Lsd fr Boullioun
G-JOEM	Airbus Industrie A320-231	0449	ex G-OUZO		Lsd fr ORIX
G-KKAZ	Airbus Industrie A320-214	2003	ex F-WWBN		Lsd fr GECAS; sublsd to SSV
G-NIKO	Airbus Industrie A321-211	1250	ex D-AVZF		Lsd fr GECAS
G-OMYA	Airbus Industrie A321-211	2117	ex D-AVZB		Lsd fr Boullioun
G-OMYB	Airbus Industrie A321-211	2227	ex D-AV	on order	
G-SMTJ	Airbus Industrie A321-211	1972	ex D-AVXG		Lsd fr Boullioun
G-SSAS+	Airbus Industrie A320-231	0230	ex C-GDTO		Lsd fr ORIX
G-SUEW	Airbus Industrie A320-214	1961	ex F-WWIX		Lsd fr GECAS
G-TICL	Airbus Industrie A320-231	0169	ex OY-CNG	all-white	Lsd fr Odin Lsg
G-VCED	Airbus Industrie A320-231	0193	ex OY-CNI		Lsd fr Thor Lsg
G-VOLH	Airbus Industrie A321-211	0823	ex D-AVZX	all-white	Lsd fr GATX
G-YJBM^	Airbus Industrie A320-231	0362	ex G-IEAF		Lsd fr ALPS 94/1
G-YLBM	Airbus Industrie A320-214	1954	ex F-WWIL		Lsd fr GECAS
OY-VKA	Airbus Industrie A321-211	1881	ex D-AVZO		Lsd fr debis, sublsd to VKG
OY-VKB	Airbus Industrie A321-211	1921	ex D-AVZQ		Lsd fr debis; sublsd to VKG
OY-VKC	Airbus Industrie A321-211	1932	ex D-AVXB		Lsd fr debis; sublsd to VKG
OY-VKL	Airbus Industrie A320-231	1780	ex F-WWDN		Lsd fr ILFC; sublsd to VKG
OY-VKM	Airbus Industrie A320-231	1889	ex F-WWBV		Lsd fr GECAS; sublsd to VKG
OY-VKN	Airbus industrie A320-231	2114	ex F-WWDZ		Lsd fr Boullioun; sublsd to VKG
G-	Airbus Industrie A320-214	2180	ex F-WWDY	on order	
G-	Airbus Industrie A320-214	2162	ex F-WWBM	on order	Lsd fr Boullioun

*Subleased as OY-CNP/CNM respectively
+Operated as MyTravel Lite
^Leased to Ryan Intl/Skyservice USA

G-MDBD	Airbus Industrie A330-243	266	ex F-WWKG		
G-MLJL	Airbus Industrie A330-243	254	ex F-WWKT	Ben Crossland	
G-OMYT	Airbus Industrie A330-243	301	ex G-MOJO		
OY-VKF	Airbus Industrie A330-243	309	ex G-CSJS		Lsd fr VKG
OY-VKG	Airbus Industrie A330-343X	349	ex F-WWYG		Lsd fr SL Ibis; sublsd to VKG
OY-VKH	Airbus Industrie A330-343X	356	ex F-WWYJ		Lsd fr SL Ibis; sublsd to VKG
OY-VKI	Airbus Industrie A330-343X	357	ex F-WWKA		Lsd fr Kovenhavn; sublsd to VKG

G-JALC	Boeing 757-225	5/22194	ex N504EA	stored QLA	Lsd fr Anfield Ltd
G-MCEA	Boeing 757-225	20/22200	ex N510EA		Lsd fr Goodison Ltd
G-PIDS	Boeing 757-225	6/22195	ex N505EA		Lsd fr Elland Ltd
G-RJGR	Boeing 757-225	8/22197	ex N701MG		Lsd fr Ewood Ltd
G-WJAN	Boeing 757-21KER	746/28674			Lsd fr Alcudia Lsg; sublsd to SSV

G-BYDA	Douglas DC-10-30	260/46990	ex OY-CNO		Lsd fr Finova
G-DAJC	Boeing 767-31KER	533/27206			Lsd fr Bluebird Lsg
G-DIMB	Boeing 767-31KER	637/28865			
G-SJMC	Boeing 767-31KER	528/27205	ex N6038E		Lsd fr Crown Green Ltd

Owns share of Ryan International. See also MyTravel Airways (OY). MyTravel Lite operates low-cost scheduled services

MYTRAVEL LITE

(VZ/MYL)   Birmingham (BHX)

G-SSAS	Airbus Industrie A320-231	0230	ex C-GDTO		

Low cost division using aircraft leased from parent

NOW AIRLINES

London-Luton (LTN)

| G- | Boeing 737-3Y0 | 1811/24546 | ex G-IGOC | Lsd fr ORIX |
| G- | Boeing 737-3Y0 | 1813/24547 | ex G-IGOE | Lsd fr ORIX |

Due to commence operations during 2004

PALMAIR

Bournemouth (BOH)

| G-CEAC | Boeing 737-229 (Nordam 3) | 360/20911 | ex OO-SDE |
| G-CEAF | Boeing 737-229 (Nordam 3) | 358/20910 | ex G-BYRI |

Leased from European Aircharter and operates under EAF flight numbers;other EAF aircraft leased as and when required

PLANET AIR failed to commence operations

POLICE AVIATION SERVICES

Special (PLC)   Gloucester (GLO)

G-GMPA	Aerospatiale AS.355F2 Twin Squirrel	5409	ex G-BPOI	EMS
G-NAAS	Aerospatiale AS.355F1 Twin Squirrel	5203	ex G-BPRG	Op for North East Air Ambulance
G-PASH	Aerospatiale AS.355F1 Twin Squirrel	5040	ex F-GHLI	Op for Dyfed-Powys Police
G-SYPA	Aerospatiale AS.355F2 Twin Squirrel	5193	ex LV-WHC	Op for South Yorkshire Police
G-WMPA	Aerospatiale AS.355F2 Twin Squirrel	5401		EMS

G-BXZK	MD Helicopters MD.902 Explorer	900-00057	ex N9238T	Op for Dorset Police
G-KAAT	MD Helicopters MD.902 Explorer	900-00056	ex G-PASS	Op for Kent Air Ambulance
G-LNAA	MD Helicopters MD.902 Explorer	900-00074	ex G-76-074	Op for Lincs & Notts Air Ambulance
G-SUSX	MD Helicopters MD.902 Explorer	900-00065	ex N3065W	Op for Sussex Police
G-WMID	MD Helicopters MD.902 Explorer	900-00062	ex N3063T	Op for West Midlands Police
G-WPAS	MD Helicopters MD.902 Explorer	900-00053		Op for Wiltshire Police
G-YPOL	MD Helicopters MD.902 Explorer	900-00078	ex N7038S	Op for West Yorkshire Police

G-CHEZ	Britten-Norman BN-2B-20 Islander	2234	ex 9M-TAM	Op for Cheshire Police
G-NESU	Britten-Norman BN-2B-20 Islander	2260	ex G-BTVN	Op for North East Police
G-PASG	MBB Bo.105DBS-4	S-819	ex G-MHSL	EMS Op for Yorkshire Air Ambulance
G-PASV	Britten-Norman BN-2B-21 Islander	2157	ex G-BKJH	
G-PASX	MBB Bo.105DBS-4	S-814		EMS
G-WCAO	Eurocopter EC.135T1	0204	ex D-HECU	Op for Western Counties Police
G-WYPA	MBB Bo.105DBS-4	S-815		EMS

PREMIER AVIATION SERVICES

Denham

Previously listed as McAlpines Aviation Services

G-CCAU	Eurocopter EC.135T1	0040		Central Counties Police
G-ESEX	Eurocopter EC.135 T2	0267	ex	
G-FTWO	Aerospatiale AS.355F2 Twin Squirrel	5347	ex G-OJOR	Police back-up
G-GMPS	MD Helicopters MD 902 Explorer	900-00081	ex N7033K	Greater Manchester Police
G-SSSX	Eurocopter EC.135T2	0270	ex G-SSSX	Sussex Police
G-SURY	Eurocopter EC.135T2	0283		Surrey Police

Also operate charter services with other helicopters, including the Royal Squadron

QUEST AIRLINES

Coventry (CVT)

| G-BYMA | British Aerospace Jetstream 32 | 840 | ex (G-OESU) |
| G-OEST | British Aerospace Jetstream 32EP | 836 | ex OH-JAD |

Quest Airlines is the trading name of Aceline Air

REED AVIATION

Reed Aviation (RAV)   London-Luton (LTN)

| G-BEJD | Hawker Siddeley HS.748 Srs.1/105 | 1543 | ex LV-HHE | Sisyphus | Op by JEM |
| G-ORAL | Hawker Siddeley HS.748 Srs.2A/334 | 1756 | ex G-BPDA | The Paper Plane | Op by JEM |

ROCKHOPPER

Blue Island (XAX)   Alderney/Bournemouth (ACI/BOH)

Previously listed as Air X, renamed 29 August 2003

G-BIIP	Britten-Norman BN-2B-27 Islander	2103	ex 6Y-JQJ	Op for LeCocq Air Link
G-LCOC	Britten-Norman BN-2A Mk.III Trislander	366	ex G-BCCU	Op for LeCocq Air Link
G-XAXA	Britten-Norman BN-2A-26 Islander	530	ex G-LOTO	Op for LeCocq Air Link

SCOTAIRWAYS

Suckling (CB/SAY) (IATA 969)   Cambridge (CBG)

G-BWIR	Dornier 328-100	3023	ex D-CDXF	
G-BWWT	Dornier 328-110	3022	ex D-CDXO	
G-BYHG	Dornier 328-110	3098	ex D-CDAE	
G-BYMK	Dornier 328-110	3062	ex LN-ASK	
G-BYML	Dornier 328-110	3069	ex D-CDUL	
G-BYTY	Dornier 328-120	3104	ex D-CDXJ	
G-BZIF	Dornier 328-110	3053	ex F-GNBS	Lsd fr Dornier

ScotAirways is the trading name of Suckling Airways. Operates feeder services to Amsterdam for KLM

SKYDRIFT AIRCHARTER

Skydrift (SDL)   Norwich (NWI)

G-TABS	Embraer EMB.110P1 Bandeirante	110212	ex G-PBAC

THOMAS COOK AIRLINES

Globe (MT/TCX)   Manchester (MAN)

G-BVYA+	Airbus Industrie A320-231	0354	ex F-WQAY	Lsd fr debis
G-BVYB+	Airbus Industrie A320-231	0357	ex F-WQAZ	Lsd fr NSJ Grp
G-BVYC+	Airbus Industrie A320-231	0411	ex F-WQBA	Lsd fr NSJ Grp
G-BXKA^	Airbus Industrie A320-214	0714	ex N714AW	Lsd fr GECAS
G-BXKB	Airbus Industrie A320-214	0716	ex N716AW	Lsd fr GECAS
G-BXKC^	Airbus Industrie A320-214	0730	ex F-WWBQ	Lsd fr GECAS
G-BXKD	Airbus Industrie A320-214	0735	ex F-WWBV	Lsd fr GECAS
G-CVYE+	Airbus Industrie A320-231	0394	ex B-HYP	Lsd fr ILFC
G-CVYG	Airbus Industrie A320-231	0443	ex OO-TCG	Lsd fr ILFC
G-TCKE	Airbus Industrie A320-231	1968	ex F-WWBD	

*Subleased to Ryan International for winter season   +Subleased to Thomas Cook Belgium Airlines
^Subleased to USA 3000 for winter season

G-FCLA	Boeing 757-28A	738/27621	ex N1789B	Lsd fr ILFC
G-FCLB	Boeing 757-28A	749/28164	ex N751NA	Lsd fr ILFC
G-FCLC	Boeing 757-28A	756/28166		Lsd fr ILFC
G-FCLD	Boeing 757-25F	752/28718		Lsd fr GATX
G-FCLE	Boeing 757-28A	805/28171		Lsd fr ILFC
G-FCLF	Boeing 757-28A	858/28835	ex N1787B	Lsd fr ILFC
G-FCLG	Boeing 757-28A	208/24367	ex N701LF	Lsd fr ILFC
G-FCLH	Boeing 757-28A	676/26274	ex N751LF	Lsd fr ILFC
G-FCLI	Boeing 757-28A	672/26275	ex N161LF	Lsd fr ILFC
G-FCLJ	Boeing 757-2Y0	555/26160	ex N160GE	Lsd fr GECAS
G-FCLK	Boeing 757-2Y0	557/26161	ex EI-CJY	Lsd fr GECAS
G-JMAA	Boeing 757-3CQ	960/32241	ex N5002K	
G-JMAB	Boeing 757-3CQ	963/32242	ex N1795B	Lsd fr BBAM
G-JMCD	Boeing 757-25F	928/30757		Lsd fr GATX; sublsd to RYN
G-JMCE	Boeing 757-25F	932/30758		Lsd fr GATX; sublsd to RYN
G-JMCF	Boeing 757-28A	226/24369	ex C-FOOE	Lsd fr ILFC

G-OJMB	Airbus Industrie A330-243	427	ex F-WWYH	Lsd fr CIT Leasing
G-OJMC	Airbus Industrie A330-243	456	ex F-WWKI	Lsd fr CIT Leasing

THOMSONFLY

Coventry (CVT)

G-	Boeing 737-5L9	1919/24859	ex N859CT	Op by BAL
G-	Boeing 737-5L9	1961/24928	ex N928CT	Op by BAL

Due to commence low-cost operations on 31 March 2004 with aircraft operated by Britannia Airways

TITAN AIRWAYS

Zap (AWC)   London-Stansted (STN)

G-ZAPK	British Aerospace 146 Srs.200QC	E2148	ex G-BTIA	
G-ZAPL	British Aerospace 146 Srs.200	E2030	ex G-WLCY	Lsd to BCY as EI-PAT
G-ZAPN	British Aerospace 146 Srs.200QT	E2119	ex ZK-NZC	
G-ZAPO	British Aerospace 146 Srs.200QC	E2176	ex F-GMMP	Lsd fr Trident Lsg
G-ZAPR	British Aerospace 146 Srs.200QT	E2114	ex VH-JJZ	

G-BUPS	Aerospatiale/Alenia ATR 42-300	109	ex DQ-FEP	Lsd fr GECAS
G-ZAPJ	Aerospatiale/Alenia ATR 42-310	113	ex EI-CIQ	Lsd fr GECAS
G-ZAPM	Boeing 737-33A	2608/27285	ex DQ-FJD	Lsd fr AWAS
G-ZAPT	Beech 200C Super King Air	BL-141	ex N200KA	
G-ZAPU	Boeing 757-2Y0	472/26151	ex EI-MON	Lsd fr GECAS
G-ZAPV	Boeing 737-3Y0	1811/24546	ex G-IGOC	Lsd fr Orix

VIRGIN ATLANTIC AIRWAYS
Virgin (VS/VIR) (IATA 932)   *London-Gatwick/Heathrow (LGW/LHR)*

G-VAEL	Airbus Industrie A340-311	015	ex F-WWJG	Maiden Toulouse	
G-VAIR	Airbus Industrie A340-313X	164	ex F-WWJA	Maiden Tokyo	Lsd fr ILFC
G-VBUS	Airbus Industrie A340-311	013	ex F-WWJE	Lady in Red; for French AF 10/03	
G-VELD	Airbus Industrie A340-313X	214	ex F-WWJY	African Queen	Lsd fr ILFC
G-VFAR	Airbus Industrie A340-313X	225	ex F-WWJZ	Diana	
G-VFLY	Airbus Industrie A340-311	058	ex F-WWJE	Dragon Lady; for French AF 10/03	
G-VHOL	Airbus Industrie A340-311	002	ex F-WWAS	Jetstreamer	Lsd fr debis
G-VSEA	Airbus Industrie A340-311	003	ex F-WWDA	Plane Sailing	Lsd fr debis
G-VSUN	Airbus Industrie A340-311	114	ex F-WWJI	Rainbow Lady	Lsd fr ILFC
G-VATL	Airbus Industrie A340-642	376	ex F-WWCC	Miss Kitty	
G-VEIL	Airbus Industrie A340-642	575	ex F-WWCK	Dancing Girl on order	
G-VFOX	Airbus Industrie A340-642	449	ex F-WWCM	Silver Lady	
G-VGOA	Airbus Industrie A340-642	371	ex F-WWCB	Indian Princess	
G-VMEG	Airbus Industrie A340-642	391	ex F-WWCK	Mystic Maiden	
G-VOGE	Airbus Industrie A340-642	416	ex F-WWCF	Cover Girl	
G-VSHY	Airbus Industrie A340-642	383	ex F-WWCD	Madam Butterfly	
G-VSSH	Airbus Industrie A340-642	615	ex F-WW	Sweet Dreamer on order	
G-	Airbus Industrie A340-642		ex F-WWCI	on order	
G-	Airbus Industrie A340-642	622		on order	

Six Airbus Industrie A380-841s are on order for delivery in 2006 (2), 2007 (2) and 2008 (2)

G-VAST	Boeing 747-41R	1117/28757		Ladybird	Lsd fr ILFC
G-VBEE	Boeing 747-219B	527/22723	ex ZK-NZW	Honeypie	Lsd to ABD
G-VBIG	Boeing 747-4Q8	1081/26255		Tinker Belle	Lsd fr ILFC
G-VFAB	Boeing 747-4Q8	1028/24958		Lady Penelope	Lsd fr ILFC
G-VGAL	Boeing 747-443	1272/32337	ex (EI-CVH)	Jersey Girl	Lsd fr GECAS
G-VHOT	Boeing 747-4Q8	1043/26326		Tubular Belle	Lsd fr ILFC
G-VIBE^	Boeing 747-219B	568/22791	ex ZK-NZZ	Spirit of New York	stored MZJ
G-VLIP	Boeing 747-443	1274/32338	ex (EI-CVI)	Hot Lips	Lsd fr GECAS
G-VPUF^	Boeing 747-219B	563/22725	ex ZK-NZY	High as a Kite	
G-VROC	Boeing 747-41R	1336/32746		Mustang Sally	Lsd fr GECAS
G-VROM	Boeing 747-443	1275/32339	ex (EI-CVJ)	Barbarella	Lsd fr GECAS
G-VROS	Boeing 747-443	1268/30885	ex (EI-CVG)	English Rose	Lsd fr GECAS
G-VROY	Boeing 747-443	1277/32340	ex (EI-CVK)	Pretty Woman	Lsd fr GECAS
G-VTOP	Boeing 747-4Q8	1100/28194		Virginia Plain	Lsd fr ILFC
G-VWOW	Boeing 747-41R	1287/32745		Cosmic Girl	Lsd fr GECAS
G-VXLG	Boeing 747-41R	1177/29406		Ruby Tuesday	
G-VZZZ^	Boeing 747-219B	523/22722	ex ZK-NZV	Morning Glory	
TF-ATW	Boeing 747-219B	528/22724	ex G-VSSS	stored MSE	Lsd to/op by ABD

^Stored Mojave, CA
49% owned by Singapore Airlines

WOODGATE EXECUTIVE AIR SERVICES
Woodair (3W/WOD)   *Belfast-Aldergrove (BFS)*

G-JAJK   Piper PA-31-350 Navajo Chieftain 31-8152014 ex G-OLDB   Lsd fr Keen leasing
See also EuroManx

HA - HUNGARY (Hungarian Republic)

ABC AIR HUNGARY
ABC Hungary (AHU)   *Budapest (BUD)*

HA-LAY   LET L-410UVP   841326 ex LZ-MNG

AIR HUNGARIA AIR TRANSPORT ceased operations

ATLANT HUNGARY
Atlant-Hungary (ATU)   *Budapest (BUD)*

HA-TCG	Ilyushin Il-76TD	0023436048	ex RA-76382
HA-TCH	Ilyushin Il-76MD	0083483513	ex UR-76438
HA-TCK	Ilyushin Il-76TD	1023409280	ex 4Z-AK11

AVIAEXPRESS sole aircraft now operates as Cityline Hungary

BUDAPEST AIRCRAFT SERVICES
Base (BPS)   *Budapest (BUD)*

HA-LAF	LET L-410UVP-E8A	902518		Flight Inspection Services
HA-LAV	LET L-410UVP	892215	ex SP-KTA	
HA-LAZ	LET L-410UVP-E	902504	ex RA-67651	Lsd to WEA as SP-KTB
HA-YFD	LET L-410UVP-E17	892324	EMS	

CITYLINE HUNGARY

(CNB)
Budapest (BUD)

HA-TCN	Antonov An-26	97307705	ex UR-26244	all-white	Lsd fr KRO

Operates freight flights on behalf of Malev as and when required

FARNAIR HUNGARY

Blue Strip (FAH)
Budapest (BUD)

HA-LAC	LET L-410UVP-E3	871828	ex 21 red		
HA-LAD	LET L-410UVP-E8A	902516		Swiss HQ Support titles	
HA-LAE	LET L-410UVP-E8A	902517			Lsd to BST
HA-LAQ	LET L-410UVP-E4	841332	ex HAF-332	based UK for skydiving	
HA-LAR	LET L-410UVP-E4	871923	ex HAF-923		Lsd to LPS
HA-YFC	LET L-410FG	851528		Para	Based Cark, UK
HA-ACN	Cessna 402B II	402B1037	ex OO-SVD		
HA-FAB	Fokker F.27 Friendship 500	10370	ex HB-ISY		Lsd fr FAT
HA-FAC	Fokker F.27 Friendship 500F	10341	ex PH-FLM		Lsd fr FAT

Part of Farnair Europe Group

HUNAIR HUNGARIAN AIRLINES

Silver Eagle (HUV)
Budapest (BUD)

HA-TCB	Ilyushin Il-76TD	1013408257	ex UR-78736

HUNGARIAN UKRAINIAN HEAVYLIFT

Big Bird (HUK)
Budapest (BUD)

HA-TCI	Ilyushin Il-76T	083410300	ex RA-76430	no titles	Lsd fr Jet Line Intl
HA-TCJ	Ilyushin Il-76TD	0083484527	ex UR-76437		Lsd fr Ecopatrol

LINAIR - HUNGARIAN REGIONAL AIRLINES ceased operations

MALEV – HUNGARIAN AIRLINES

Malev (MA/MAH) (IATA 182)
Budapest (BUD)

HA-LED	Boeing 737-3Y0	2021/24909			Lsd fr GECAS
HA-LEF	Boeing 737-3Y0	2054/24914			Lsd fr BBAM
HA-LEG	Boeing 737-3Y0	2066/24916		Szent Istvan/Sanctus	Lsd fr GECAS
HA-LEJ	Boeing 737-3Q8	2635/26303			Lsd fr ILFC
HA-LEN	Boeing 737-4Y0	2352/26069	ex UR-GAA		Lsd fr GECAS
HA-LEV	Boeing 737-4Y0	1988/24904	ex TC-JDE	Charter Services	Lsd fr Aero Ireland
HA-LEX	Boeing 737-3Y0	1973/24902	ex CS-TGR		Lsd fr GECAS
HA-LEY	Boeing 737-4Y0	1824/24682	ex 5B-DBG		Lsd fr State Street
HA-LEZ	Boeing 737-4Q8	2482/26290	ex TC-APB	Charter Services	Lsd fr Triton
HA-LOA	Boeing 737-7Q8	1283/28254			Lsd fr ILFC
HA-LOB	Boeing 737-7Q8	1264/29346	ex N5573L		Lsd fr ILFC
HA-LOC	Boeing 737-7Q8	1287/32797			Lsd fr ILFC
HA-LOD	Boeing 737-6Q8	1378/28259			Lsd fr ILFC
HA-LOE	Boeing 737-6Q8	1400/28260			Lsd fr ILFC
HA-LOF	Boeing 737-6Q8	1415/29348			Lsd fr ILFC
HA-LOG	Boeing 737-6Q8	1437/28261			Lsd fr ILFC
HA-LOH	Boeing 737-8Q8	30667		on order 04	Lsd fr ILFC
HA-LOI	Boeing 737-7Q8	29350		on order 04	Lsd fr ILFC
HA-LOJ	Boeing 737-6Q8	29349		on order 04	Lsd fr ILFC
HA-LOK	Boeing 737-7Q8	29352		on order 04	Lsd fr ILFC
HA-LOL	Boeing 737-8Q8	30669		on order 04	Lsd fr ILFC
HA-LOM	Boeing 737-6Q8	29353		on order 04	Lsd fr ILFC
HA-LON	Boeing 737-8Q8	30672		on order 04	Lsd fr ILFC
HA-LOP	Boeing 737-7Q8	29354		on order 04	Lsd fr ILFC
HA-LOR	Boeing 737-7Q8	29355		on order 04	Lsd fr ILFC
HA-LOS	Boeing 737-7Q8	30682		on order 04	Lsd fr ILFC
HA-LOU	Boeing 737-8Q8	30684		on order 04	Lsd fr ILFC
HA-LMA	Fokker 70	11564	ex PH-EZR		Lsd fr ILFC
HA-LMB	Fokker 70	11565	ex PH-EZX		Lsd fr ILFC
HA-LMC	Fokker 70	11569	ex PH-EZA		Lsd fr ILFC
HA-LMD*	Fokker 70	11563	ex PH-WXD		
HA-LME*	Fokker 70	11575	ex PH-WXB		
HA-LMF*	Fokker 70	11571	ex PH-RVE		

*Leased from Aircraft Financing and Trading

HA-LHA	Boeing 767-27GER	475/27048	ex N6009F
HA-LHB	Boeing 767-27GER	482/27049	ex N60668
HA-LHD	Boeing 767-3P6ER	260/24484	

Also operates freight flights with Antonov An-26 aircraft leased from Aviaexpress as and when required. Malev Express is wholly owned subsidiary
To code share with Hainan Airlines on flights using Boeing 767-300s to Beijing from August 2004

MALEV EXPRESS

(MA/MEH)   *Budapest (BUD)*

HA-LNA	Canadair CL-600-2B19	7676	ex C-FMKZ
HA-LNB	Canadair CL-600-2B19	7686	ex C-FMNW
HA-LNC	Canadair CL-600-2B19	7784	ex C-FMLU
HA-LND	Canadair CL-600-2B19		

SKYEUROPE AIRLINES

(5P)   *Budapest (BUD)*

HA-LKO	Boeing 737-5Y0	2220/25185	ex N185FR	Lsd fr GECAS

Commenced operations 15 November 2003; wholly owned subsidiary of Slovak parent

TRAVEL SERVICE HUNGARY

Travel Service (TVL)   *Budapest (BUD)*

HA-LKA	Boeing 737-4Y0	2033/24911	ex OK-TVS	Lsd fr TVS

HB - SWITZERLAND & LIECHTENSTEIN (Swiss Confederation)

AIR AVANCE

Altenrhein

HB-	British Aerospace Jetstream 31		ex	on order

AIR GLACIERS

Air Glaciers (7T/AGV)   *Sion (SIR)*

HB-CGW	Cessna U206G Stationair 6	U20604822	ex D-ELML
HB-FCT	Pilatus PC-6/B2-H2 Turbo Porter	637	
HB-FDU	Pilatus PC-6/B1-H2 Turbo Porter	663	
HB-FFW	Pilatus PC-6/B2-H2 Turbo Porter	735	
HB-GIL	Beech 200 Super King Air	BB-194	ex N502EB
HB-GJI	Beech 200 Super King Air	BB-451	ex D-IBOW
HB-GJM	Beech 200 Super King Air	BB-255	ex N32KD
HB-XSO	Aerospatiale AS.350B2 Ecureuil	1950	ex D-HACC
HB-ZCZ	Aerospatiale AS.350B3 Ecureuil	3434	
HB-ZEP	Eurocopter EC.120B Colibri	1336	

AIR ZERMATT

Air Zermatt (AZF)   *Zermatt Heliport*

HB-XSU	Aerospatiale AS.350B2 Ecureuil	2115	
HB-ZCC	Aerospatiale AS.350B2 Ecureuil	2107	ex I-REGL
HB-ZCX	Aerospatiale AS.350B2 Ecureuil	3105	ex I-AOLA
HB-ZEF	Eurocopter EC-135T2	0259	ex D-HECA

ASTRA AIRLINES Current status is uncertain as aircraft returned to lessors

BELAIR

Belair (4T/BHP)   *Zurich (ZRH)*

HB-IHR	Boeing 757-2Q8ER	919/29379		Solemar	Lsd fr ILFC
HB-IHS	Boeing 757-2Q8ER	922/30394		Horizonte	Lsd fr ILFC
HB-ISE	Boeing 767-3Q8ER	655/27600	ex EI-CNS		Lsd fr ILFC

CLASSIC AIR

Classic Air (CLC)   *Zurich (ZRH)*

HB-ISB	Douglas DC-3	4666	ex C-FTAS
HB-ISC	Douglas DC-3	9995	ex N88YA

EASYJET SWITZERLAND

Topswiss (DS/EZS)
Geneva (GVA)

HB-JZA	Airbus Industrie A319-111	2037	ex (G-CCKA)		Lsd fr EZY
HB-JZB	Airbus Industrie A319-111	2043	ex (G-CCKB)	on order 03	Lsd fr EZY
HB-JZC	Airbus Industrie A319-111	2050	ex (G-CCKC)	on order 03	Lsd fr EZY
HB-JZD	Airbus Industrie A319-111	2053	ex (G-CCKD)	on order 03	Lsd fr EZY
HB-JZE	Airbus Industrie A319-111	2062	ex (G-CCKE)	on order 03	Lsd fr EZY
HB-IIE	Boeing 737-3Q8	2664/26307	ex N721LF	Island of Kos	Lsd to EZY

40% owned by easyJet

EDELWEISS AIR

Edelweiss (8R/EDW)
Zurich (ZRH)

HB-IHX	Airbus Industrie A320-214	0942	ex F-WWIU	Calvaro	Lsd fr Alp Air
HB-IHY	Airbus Industrie A320-214	0947	ex F-WWIY	Upali	Lsd fr Alp Air
HB-IHZ	Airbus Industrie A320-214	1026	ex F-WWDD	Viktoria	Lsd fr Alp Air
HB-IQZ	Airbus Industrie A330-243	369	ex F-WWKG	Barart	Lsd fr CIT Leasing

EUROBLUE

Zurich (ZRH)

Plans to operate Airbus Industrie A319s on business class services to the Middle East

FARNAIR SWITZERLAND

Farner (FAT)
Basle (BSL)

HB-AFC	Aerospatiale/Alenia ATR 42-320(F)	087	ex F-WQLF	
HB-AFD	Aerospatiale/Alenia ATR 42-320	121	ex (LZ-ATA)	
HB-AFF	Aerospatiale/Alenia ATR-42-320	264	ex F-GOBK	
HB-AFG	Aerospatiale/Alenia ATR 72-201(F)	108	ex F-WQNA	Lsd fr OFSB Ltd
HB-AFH	Aerospatiale/Alenia ATR 72-202	313	ex F-GJKP	Lsd fr Dreieck Lsg
HB-ISY	Fokker F.27 Friendship 500	10370	ex F-BPUB	Lsd to FAH as HA-FAB
HB-ITQ	Fokker F.27 Friendship 400	10295	ex HA-ACK	Lsd to MNL as I-MLQT
HB-ITY	Fokker F.27 Friendship 500	10448	ex (D-AAAC)	Lsd fr OFSB Ltd
HB-IVQ	Fokker F.27 Friendship 500	10425	ex PH-FOZ	Lsd fr OFSB Ltd
PH-JLN	Fokker F.27 Friendship 500	10449	ex F-BSUO	Lsd to EPA as D-AAAF

Operates services for Federal Express and TNT
Farnair Europe Group includes Farnair Hungary (HA); Farnair Switzerland (HB), Miniliner (I) and Tulip Air (PH)

FLYBABOO

Geneva (GVA)

D-BKIM	de Havilland DHC-8-311	356	ex C-GFOD	Lsd fr RUS

First service 17 November 2003

HELISWISS

Heliswiss (HSI)
Bern (BRN)

HB-XKE	Kamov Ka-32A	8709	ex RA-31587

HELOG

Helog (HLG)
Küssnacht

HB-ZBA	Bell 407	53324	ex C-GEQC

HELVETIC AIRWAYS

Zurich (ZRH)

HB-JVA	Fokker 100	11460	ex N1451N	
HB-	Fokker 100	11446	ex N1443A	on order
HB-	Fokker 100	11448	ex N1445B	on order
HB-	Fokker 100	11465	ex N1453D	on order
HB-	Fokker 100	11466	ex N1454D	on order
HB-	Fokker 100	11478	ex N1458H	on order
HB-	Fokker 100	11483	ex N1463A	on order
HB-	Fokker 100	11490	ex N1464A	on order
HB-	Fokker 100	11491	ex N1465K	on order
HB-	Fokker 100	11498	ex N1466A	on order
HB-	Fokker 100	11499	ex N1467A	on order
HB-	Fokker 100	11501	ex N1468A	on order
HB-	Fokker 100	11502	ex N1469D	on order

| HB- | Fokker 100 | 11515 | ex N1473K | on order |
| HB- | Fokker 100 | 11520 | ex N1474D | on order |

Operated under Odette Airways AOC; first service 28 November 2003

INTERSKY

(ISK)   *Bern (BRN)*

| D-BLEJ | de Havilland DHC-8Q-314 | 521 | ex C-FDHU | Lsd fr AUB |

ODETTE AIRWAYS

Arabella (OAW)   *Zurich (ZRH)*

| HB-INV | McDonnell-Douglas MD-83 | 1349/49359 |

Plans to acquire Fokker 100s but they will be operated as Helvetic Airways

PRIVATAIR

PrivatAir (PTI)   *Geneva (GVA)*

D-APAA*	Airbus Industrie A319-132LR	1947	ex D-AVWI		Lsd fr CIT Lsg
D-APAB*	Airbus Industrie A319-132LR	1955	ex D-AVWD		Lsd fr CIT Lsg
D-APAC	Airbus Industrie A319-132LR	1727	ex D-AVWQ		Lsd fr CIT Lsg; sublsd to DLH
D-APAD	Airbus Industrie A319-132LR	1880	ex D-AVYM		Lsd fr CIT Lsg; sublsd to DLH

*Operated as corporate shuttle between Airbus plants, principally in Toulouse, Hamburg, Filton and Hawarden

HB-IEE	Boeing 757-23A	249/24527	ex HB-IHU		
HB-IIO	Boeing 737-7AK	241/29865			[BBJ]
HB-IIP	Boeing 737-7AK	408/29866	ex N1779B		[BBJ]
HB-IIQ*	Boeing 737-7CN	451/30752	ex N1026G	D-ABPA reserved	[BBJ]

*Operates transatlantic flights for Lufthansa

SWISS INTERNATIONAL AIR LINES

Swiss (LX/SWR) (IATA 724)   *Basle, Lugano, Geneva, Zurich (BSL/LUG/GVA/ZRH)*

HB-IPR	Airbus Industrie A319-112	1018	ex D-AVYQ	Clariden	Lsd fr Sierra Lsg
HB-IPS*	Airbus Industrie A319-112	0734	ex D-AVYZ	Piz Morteratsch	
HB-IPT+	Airbus Industrie A319-112	0727	ex D-AVYC	Les Ordons	
HB-IPU+	Airbus Industrie A319-112	0713	ex D-AVYB	Schrattenflue	
HB-IPV	Airbus Industrie A319-112	0578	ex D-AVYA	Mont Racine, all-white	Lsd fr WFBN
HB-IPX	Airbus Industrie A319-112	0612	ex D-AVYH	Rotsandnollen	Lsd fr Dritte Lsg Svs
HB-IPY+	Airbus Industrie A319-112	0621	ex D-AVYK	Schafnase	

*Leased from ILFC   +Leased from Merlan Mobilien Verwaltungs

HB-IJI+	Airbus Industrie A320-214	0577	ex F-WWDT	Creux de Van	
HB-IJJ	Airbus Industrie A320-214	0585	ex F-WWIV	Ruchstock	Lsd fr ILFC
HB-IJK+	Airbus Industrie A320-214	0596	ex F-WWBH	Wissigstock	
HB-IJL+	Airbus Industrie A320-214	0603	ex F-WWBK	Pizol	
HB-IJM+	Airbus Industrie A320-214	0635	ex F-WWDD	Randen	
HB-IJN+	Airbus Industrie A320-214	0643	ex F-WWDI	Hasenmatt	
HB-IJO+	Airbus Industrie A320-214	0673	ex F-WWBF	Grisset	
HB-IJP+	Airbus Industrie A320-214	0681	ex F-WWBH	Nollen	
HB-IJQ+	Airbus Industrie A320-214	0701	ex F-WWDL	Basodino	
HB-IJR+	Airbus Industrie A320-214	0703	ex F-WWDS	Dammastock	
HB-IJS	Airbus Industrie A320-214	0782	ex F-WWDS	Les Diablerets	Lsd fr ILFC
HB-IJU^	Airbus Industrie A320-214	1951	ex D-AVVD	Bietschhorn	
HB-IJV^	Airbus Industrie A320-214	2024	ex F-WWDK	Wildspitz	
HB-IJW^	Airbus Industrie A320-214	2134	ex F-WWBO	Bachtel	
HB-IJZ^	Airbus Industrie A320-214	2177	ex F-WW	Grenzchopf on ored 04	

+Leased from Merlan Mobilien Verwaltungs   ^Leased from ILFC and subleased to Swiss Sun

HB-IOC+	Airbus Industrie A321-111	0520	ex D-AVZV	St Chrischona	
HB-IOH+	Airbus Industrie A321-111	0664	ex D-AVZL	Kaiseregg; stdZRH	
HB-IOJ	Airbus Industrie A321-111	0891	ex D-AVXJ	Piz Palü	Lsd fr ILFC
HB-IOK	Airbus Industrie A321-111	0987	ex D-AVZC	Les Sommytres	Lsd fr ILFC
HB-IOL	Airbus Industrie A321-111	1144	ex D-AVZE	Bratterstock	Lsd fr Sierra Lsg

+Leased from Merlan Mobilien Verwaltungs

HB-IQA	Airbus Industrie A330-223	229	ex	Novartis	
HB-IQC+	Airbus Industrie A330-223	249	ex F-WWKI	Breithorn	
HB-IQD	Airbus Industrie A330-223	253	ex F-WWKM	Jungfrau	Lsd fr Sierra Lsg
HB-IQG	Airbus Industrie A330-223	275	ex F-WWKF	Pollux	Lsd fr Sierra Lsg
HB-IQH	Airbus Industrie A330-223	288	ex F-WWKX	Obergabelhorn	
HB-IQI^	Airbus Industrie A330-223	291	ex F-WWKS	Piz Bernina	
HB-IQJ^	Airbus Industrie A330-223	294	ex F-WWYJ	Lauteraarhorn	
HB-IQK^	Airbus Industrie A330-223	299	ex F-WWYD	Allainhorn	
HB-IQO	Airbus Industrie A330-223	343	ex F-WWYA	Weissmies	Lsd fr Rubicon Finance
HB-IQP	Airbus Industrie A330-223	366	ex F-WWYZ	Lagginhorn	Lsd fr ILFC

+Leased from Merlan Mobilien Verwaltungs   ^Leased from Broad River Aircraft Finance

HB-JMA	Airbus Industrie A340-313X	538	ex F-WWJJ	Matterhorn	Lsd fr Matterhorn Fin
HB-JMB	Airbus Industrie A340-313X	545	ex F-WWJL	Dufourspitze	
HB-JMC	Airbus Industrie A340-313X	546	ex F-WWJM	Zumsteinspitze	Lsd fr Dufourspitze
HB-JMD	Airbus Industrie A340-313X	556	ex F-WWJN	Signalkuppe	
HB-JME	Airbus Industrie A340-313X	559	ex F-WWJP	Dom	
HB-JMF	Airbus Industrie A340-313X	561	ex F-WWJQ	Liskamm	
HB-JMG	Airbus Industrie A340-313X	562	ex F-WWJR	Weisshorn	
HB-JMH	Airbud Industrie A340-313X	585	ex F-WWJV	Parrotspitze	
HB-JMI	Airbus Industrie A340-313X	598	ex F-WWJX	Dent Blanche on order	
HB-JMJ	Airbus Industrie A340-313X		ex F-WW	Nadelhorn on order	
HB-JMK	Airbus Industrie A340-313X		ex F-WW	Lenzspitze on order	
HB-JML	Airbus Industrie A340-313X		ex F-WW	Finsteraarhorn on order	

HB-IXF	Avro RJ85	E2226	ex G-CROS	Karpf	
HB-IXG	Avro RJ85	E2231	ex G-6-231	Piz Julier	
HB-IXH	Avro RJ85	E2233	ex G-6-233	Montchaibeux	
HB-IXK	Avro RJ85	E2235	ex G-XAIR	Lindenberg	
HB-IXN	Avro RJ100	E3286	ex G-6-286	Silberen	
HB-IXO	Avro RJ100	E3284	ex G-6-284	Ottenberg	Lsd fr Kulan Mobilien
HB-IXP	Avro RJ100	E3283	ex G-6-283	Corno Gries	Lsd fr Kulan Mobilien
HB-IXQ	Avro RJ100	E3282	ex G-6-282	Stucklistock	Lsd fr Kulan Mobilien
HB-IXR	Avro RJ100	E3281	ex G-6-281	Tour d'Ai	Lsd fr Kulan Mobilien
HB-IXS	Avro RJ100	E3280	ex G-6-280	Mont Velan Lsd fr Euter Verwaltfungs	
HB-IXT	Avro RJ100	E3259	ex G-BVYS	Pfannensteil	
					Lsd fr Harpalus Verwaltflung
HB-IXU	Avro RJ100	E3276	ex G-6-276	Chestenberg	Lsd fr Melik Mobilien
HB-IXV	Avro RJ100	E3274	ex G-6-274	Saxer First	Lsd fr Lauren Mobilien
HB-IXW	Avro RJ100	E3272	ex G-6-272	Salmhorn	Lsd fr Lakuna Mobilien
HB-IXX	Avro RJ100	E3262	ex G-6-262	Schafarnisch	Lsd fr Metra Mobilien
HB-IYW	Avro RJ100	E3359	ex G-6-359	Brisen	Lsd fr Kevin Ltd
HB-IYX	Avro RJ100	E3357	ex G-6-357	Titlis	Lsd fr Kevin Ltd
HB-IYY	Avro RJ100	E3339	ex G-6-339	Spitzmellon	
HB-IYZ	Avro RJ100	E3338	ex G-6-338	Hohe Winde	

HB-JAC*	Embraer EMB.145LU	145255	ex PT-SIP	stored	
HB-JAG*	Embraer EMB.145LU	145321	ex PT-SMM	Furkahorn	
HB-JAH*	Embraer EMB.145LU	145341	ex PT-SNH	Chatilon	
HB-JAI*	Embraer EMB.145LU	145351	ex PT-SNQ		Lsd to Finn Comm
HB-JAJ*	Embraer EMB.145LU	145382	ex PT-SQG	Albishorn	
HB-JAK*	Embraer EMB.145LU	145387	ex PT-SQL	Staffelegg	
HB-JAL	Embraer EMB.145LU	145400	ex PT-SQX	Nedlenspitz	Lsd fr SL Planet
HB-JAM	Embraer EMB.145LU	145420	ex PT-STR	Silberhorn	Lsd fr SL Planet
HB-JAN	Embraer EMB.145LU	145434	ex PT-SUF	Schopfenspitz	Lsd fr SL Canopus
HB-JAO	Embraer EMB.145LU	145456	ex PT-SVB	Zwolfihorn	Lsd fr SL Canopus
HB-JAS	Embraer EMB.145LU	145559	ex PT-SZU	Ochsenhorn	
HB-JAT	Embraer EMB.145LU	145564	ex PT-SZZ	Arnihaaggen	
HB-JAU	Embraer EMB.145LU	145570	ex PT-SBG	Rotrufner	
HB-JAV	Embraer EMB.145LU	145574	ex PT-SBK	Geisflue	
HB-JAW	Embraer EMB.145LU	145580	ex PT-SBR	Marenspitz	
HB-JAX	Embraer EMB.145LU	145588	ex PT-SBZ	Pizzo del Sole	Lsd to JMG
HB-JAY	Embraer EMB.145LU	145601	ex PT-SCK	600th titles;Germsstock	Lsd to JMG

*Leased from State Street Trust and Bank

HB-JCA	Embraer 170		ex PT-S	on order 04	
HB-JCB	Embraer 170		ex PT-S	on order 04	
HB-JCC	Embraer 170		ex PT-S	on order 04	
HB-JCD	Embraer 170		ex PT-S	on order 04	
HB-JCE	Embraer 170		ex PT-S	on order 04	

Ten more on order for delivery in 2005/2006, the next registered HB-JCF to HB-JCO. Whole order may be postponed

HB-IWA	McDonnell-Douglas MD-11	458/48443	ex N517MD	Zinairothorn	Lsd fr CIT Leasing
HB-IWC	McDonnell-Douglas MD-11	460/48445		Finsteraarhorn	Lsd fr Samedan Lsg
HB-IWE	McDonnell-Douglas MD-11	464/48447		Nadelhorn	
					Lsd fr Outer Banks Finance
HB-IWI	McDonnell-Douglas MD-11	477/48454		Dent Blanche	Lsd fr CIT Leasing
HB-IWK	McDonnell-Douglas MD-11	487/48455		Parrotspitze	Lsd fr Bandung
HB-IWL	McDonnell-Douglas MD-11	494/48456		Weisshorn	Lsd fr Bandung
HB-IWN*	McDonnell-Douglas MD-11	571/48539		Dom	Lsd fr Bandung
HB-IWO	McDonnell-Douglas MD-11	611/48540		Signalkuppe	Lsd fr Bandung
HB-IWQ	McDonnell-Douglas MD-11	621/48541		Dufourspitze	Lsd fr Bandung

*Swiss Asia titles

HB-INW	McDonnell-Douglas MD-83	1405/49569	ex (RA-....)	stored ZRH	Lsd fr Germania Flug
HB-INZ	McDonnell-Douglas MD-83	1468/49572	ex (RA-....)	stored ZRH	Lsd fr Germania Flug
HB-ISX	McDonnell-Douglas MD-83	1579/49844		stored	Lsd fr SAT Flug
HB-ISZ	McDonnell-Douglas MD-83	1720/49930		stored	Lsd fr SAT Flug
HB-IUG	McDonnell-Douglas MD-83	1817/53149		stored ZRH	Lsd fr SAT Flug
HB-IUH	McDonnell-Douglas MD-83	1831/53150		stored ZRH	Lsd fr SAT Flug
HB-IUP	McDonnell-Douglas MD-83	1675/49856	ex D-ALLM	Grande Lui; stored	Lsd fr GECAS

All retired by September 2003 and replaced by Airbus Industrie A320-214s for charter operations

HB-AKA	SAAB SF.340B	160	ex SE-F60		Lsd to MDV as ER-SGC
HB-AKB	SAAB SF.340B	161	ex SE-F61		Lsd to SLI as XA-AEM
HB-AKC	SAAB SF.340B	164	ex SE-F64		Lsd to SLI as XA-AAO
HB-AKD	SAAB SF.340B	173	ex F-GKPD		
HB-AKE	SAAB SF.340B	176	ex SE-F76		Lsd to SLI as XA-AKE
HB-AKF	SAAB SF.340B	182	ex SE-F82		Lsd to MDV as ER-SGB
HB-AKG	SAAB SF.340B	185	ex SE-F85		Lsd to QE as F-GPKG
HB-AKH	SAAB SF.340B	200	ex SE-E02		Lsd to KRP as YR-VGN
HB-AKI	SAAB SF.340B	208	ex SE-G08		Lsd to KRP as YR-VGM
HB-AKL	SAAB SF.340B	215	ex SE-G15		Lsd to KRP as YR-VGO
HB-AKN	SAAB SF.340B	225	ex SE-G25		Lsd to KRP as YR-VGR
HB-AKO	SAAB SF.340B	228	ex SE-G28		Lsd to KRP as YR-VGP
HB-AKP	SAAB SF.340B	168	ex ER-SGA		Lsd to KRP
HB-IYB	SAAB 2000	057	ex SE-057	Ruchen	
HB-IYC	SAAB 2000	058	ex SE-058	Pizzo Badlie	
HB-IYD	SAAB 2000	059	ex SE-059	Stierenberg	Lsd to KRP
HB-IYE	SAAB 2000	060	ex SE-060	Tomlishorn	
HB-IYF	SAAB 2000	061	ex SE-061	Astelhorn	
HB-IZA	SAAB 2000	004	ex SE-004	L'Argentine	
HB-IZH	SAAB 2000	011	ex SE-011	stored ZUR	Lsd fr SL Scorpio Ltd
HB-IZI	SAAB 2000	012	ex SE-012	Piz Buin	Lsd fr SL Capricorn Aircraft
HB-IZJ	SAAB 2000	015	ex SE-015	Burgenstock	Lsd fr SL Aquarius Acft
HB-IZL	SAAB 2000	022	ex SE-022	Bonistock	Lsd fr SL Garnet
HB-IZM	SAAB 2000	024	ex SE-024	Alvier	
HB-IZN	SAAB 2000	026	ex SE-026	Passwang	
HB-IZO	SAAB 2000	029	ex SE-029	Fronalpstock	Lsd to KRP
HB-IZR	SAAB 2000	033	ex SE-033	stored	
HB-IZW	SAAB 2000	039	ex SE-039	Le Chamossaire	
HB-IZX	SAAB 2000	041	ex SE-041	Monte Leone	
HB-IZZ	SAAB 2000	048	ex SE-048	Doldenhorn	

15 Embraer 190s are on order for delivery from August 2006 (four in 2006, 6 in 2007 and remaining 5 in 2008,
registrations HB-JGA to JGO reserved) but the whole order may be postponed
Swiss Sun is a wholly owned charter subsidiary. To join oneworld alliance

SWISS SUN

Zurich (ZRH)

HB-IJU	Airbus Industrie A320-214	1951	ex F-WWIQ	Bietschhorn	Lsd fr SWR
HB-IJV	Airbus Industrie A320-214	2024	ex F-WWDK	Wildspitz	Lsd fr SWR
HB-IJW	Airbus Industrie A320-214	2134	ex F-WWBO	Bachtel	
HB-IJX	Airbus Industrie A320-214		ex F-WW	Heltersberg on order 04	
HB-IJY	Airbus Industrie A320-214		ex F-WW	Lisengrat; on order 04	
HB-IJZ	Airbus Industrie A320-214		ex F-WW	Grenzchopf on ored 04	

Wholly owned charter subsidiary of Swiss International

ZIMEX AVIATION

Zimex (C4/IMX)

Zurich (ZRH)

HB-LOK	de Havilland DHC-6 Twin Otter 300	658	ex D-IASL		
HB-LQV	de Havilland DHC-6 Twin Otter 300	643	ex 5Y-LQV		
HB-LRF	de Havilland DHC-6 Twin Otter 300	794	ex N794CC		Lsd to Sonangol as D2-FVP
HB-LRN	de Havilland DHC-6 Twin Otter 310	636	ex PK-YPE		Lsd to/op for Sirte Oil
HB-LRO	de Havilland DHC-6 Twin Otter 300	523	ex F-GKTO		
HB-LRR	de Havilland DHC-6 Twin Otter 300	505	ex 5Y-KZT		
HB-LRS	de Havilland DHC-6 Twin Otter 300	502	ex 5Y-UAU		
HB-LTD	de Havilland DHC-6 Twin Otter 300	717	ex C-GIED		Lsd fr Avisto
HB-LTG	de Havilland DHC-6 Twin Otter 300	628	ex D-IFLY		based Weston-on-the-Green
HB-GJD	Beech 200C Super King Air	BL-7	ex F-GJBJ		

HC - ECUADOR (Republic of Ecuador)

AEROGAL – AEROLINEAS GALAPAGOS

Aerogal (2K/GLG)

Shell-Mera/Quito (-/UIO)

HC-BSL	Fairchild F-27F	56	ex N28FA	stored UIO	
HC-BSV	Fairchild F-27F	71	ex N870HA	stored UIO	
HC-CDJ	Boeing 727-227	1216/21246	ex N14GA	Piquero	
HC-CED	Boeing 737-2B7 (Nordam 3)	976/22887	ex N275AU		Lsd fr British Avn Grp

AEROMASTER AIRWAYS

Quito (UIO)

HC-BNI	Bell 206L LongRanger II	45305	ex N2771D		Lsd fr Jaguar Avn
HC-CBH	Bell 206L-1 LongRanger III	45354	ex N213HC		Lsd fr Rainier Heli-Lift

HC-CBP	Bell 407	53473	ex N9160M
HC-CBT	Bell 427	56028	ex N40560
HC-CDO	Aerospatiale SA.330J Puma	1478	ex N505R

AUSTRO AEREO

Austro Aereo (UST)   *Cuenca (CUE)*

| HC-CBE | Embraer EMB.120RT Brasilia | 120178 | ex N341JS | orange | |
| HC-CBX | Embraer EMB.120RT Brasilia | 120172 | ex N340JS | green | Lsd fr BCC Equipment Lsg |

ECUATORIANA DE AVIACION

Ecuatoriana (EU/EEA) (IATA 341)   *Quito (UIO)*

50.1% owned by VASP but for sale; sole aircraft returned and operates services in code-share agreement with LANChile but see LANEcuador

ECUAVIA

(ECU)   *Quito (UIO)*

| HC-BJP | Piper PA-44-180 Seminole | 44-8195023 | |
| HC-BXQ | Bell 407 | 53133 | ex N53095 |

ICARO EXPRESS

(X8)   *Quito (UIO)*

HC-BYO	Beech 1900D	UE-317	ex N22908	
HC-CAO	Beech 1900D	UE-371	ex N31712	Lsd fr Raytheon
HC-CBW	Bell 212	30901	ex C-FKGT	Lsd fr CHC Helicopters
HC-CDA	Fokker F.28 Fellowship 4000	11230	ex N481US	Lsd fr WFBN
HC-CDD	Bell 212	30814	ex C-FRMM	Lsd fr CHC Helicopters
HC-CDG	Fokker F.28 Fellowship 4000	11240	ex N488US	Lsd fr WFBN
HC-CDT	Fokker F.28 Fellowship 4000	11222	ex N475AU	Lsd fr Capital A/c
HC-CDW	Fokker F.28 Fellowship 4000	11224	ex N476US	Lsd fr Capital A/c
HC-CEC	Aerospatiale AS.350BA Ecureuil	3009	ex N483AE	
HC-CEF	Bell 212	30630	ex C-GBPH	
HC-C	Bell 212	30891	ex C-FRUT	

LAN ECUADOR

Aerolane (XL/LNE) (IATA 462)   *Quito (UIO)*

Wholly owned by LANChile; operates services with Airbus Industrie A320 & Boeing 767-300ER leased from the parent as and when required. LANEcuador is the trading name of Lineas Aeras Nacionales del Ecuador

SAEREO / SERVICIOS AEREOS EJECUTIVOS

Saereo (SRO)   *Quito (UIO)*

HC-BUD	Rockwell Commander 690C	11669	ex N844MA
HC-BVN	Beech 1900C	UB-53	ex N814BE
HC-BYH	Cessna T207A Turbo Stationair 8	20700749	ex N9905M
HC-BZO	Bell 407	53302	ex N8226A
HC-CAC	Pilatus PC6-B2/H4 Turbo Porter	928	ex HB-FLT
HC-CBC	Beech 1900D	UE-17	ex N17YV
HC-CDM	Embraer EMB.120ER Brasilia	120088	ex N193SW

TACA ECUADOR

(YZ)   *Quito (UIO)*

Wholly owned subsidiary of TACA International Airlines; due to start operations with aircraft leased from the parent

TAME / TRANSPORTES AEREOS MILITARES ECUATORIANAS

Tame (EQ/TAE)   *Quito (UIO)*

HC-BHM	Boeing 727-2T3	1644/22078	ex N1293E	Cotopaxi
HC-BLE	Boeing 727-134	487/19691	ex RP-C1240	Manabi
HC-BLV	Boeing 727-17	806/20328	ex G-BKCG	Azuay
HC-BRI	Boeing 727-230	887/20560	ex D-ABHI	Guayas
HC-BSC	Boeing 727-230	1011/20788	ex D-ABRI	Galapogas
HC-BZR	Boeing 727-230	1404/21618	ex TC-AFT	Esmeraldas
HC-BZS	Boeing 727-230 (FedEx 3)	1419/21620	ex TC-AFO	Imbabura
HC-BZU	Fokker F.28 Fellowship 4000	11112	ex SE-DGE	Moronoa Santiago	
HC-CDY	Airbus Industrie A320-233	2014	ex F-WWBT		Lsd fr GATX

HC-CDZ	Airbus Industrie A320-233	2044	ex F-WWIC		Lsd fr GATX
HC-CEH	Fokker F.28 Fellowship 4000	11228	ex N479AU		

Note: TAME aircraft also carry a Fuerza Aerea Ecuador serial corresponding with the c/n

TRANS AM

Aero Transam (7T/RTM)
Guayaquil (GYE)

HC-BSS	AMD Falcon 20C	150	ex TG-RBW	Op for DHL
HC-CDX	Aerospatiale/Alenia ATR 42-300F	081	ex YV-914C	Op for DHL

VUELOS INTERNOS PRIVADOS

(VUR)
Quito (UIO)

HC-BXO	Dornier 328-120	3076	ex D-CDXE

HH - HAITI (Republic of Haiti)

AIR ADEAH

Air Adeah (HJA)
Port au Prince (PAP)

Operates cargo flights with DC-8Fs leased from Arrow Air as required

HAITI AMBASSADOR AIRLINES   current status is uncertain

HAITI CARIBBEAN AIRLINES

(9C)
Port au Prince (PAP)

N751PA	Boeing 757-2G5	146/23928	ex D-AMUV	on order	Lsd fr PCE

HAITI REGIONAL   current status is uncertain, believed to have ceased operations

TROPICAL AIRWAYS D'HAITI

(M7/TBG)
Port-au-Prince (PAP)

HH-PRT	LET-L-410-UVP	851412	ex TI-AYH
HH-TAH	LET L-41OUVP	831105	ex HI-670CT
HH-TRA	LET L-410UVP	841308	ex RA-67483

HI - DOMINICAN REPUBLIC (Republica Dominicana)

AERO CONTINENTE DOMINICANA

(9D/CND) (IATA 609)
Santo Domingo-Las Americas (SDQ)

Wholly owned by Aero Continente

AEROCHAGO AIRLINES

Aerochago (AHG) (IATA 926)
Santo Domingo-Las Americas (SDQ)

Operates cargo flights with leased Douglas DC-8Fs as required

AERO DOMCA

Santo Domingo-Las Americas (SDQ)

HI-761CT	LET 410UVP	871938	ex 9L-LCF

AEROMAR AIRLINES   ceased operations 26 December 2003

AIR SANTO DOMINGO

Aero Domingo (EX/SDO)
Santo Domingo-Herrara (HEX)

HI-681CT	LET L-410UVP-E3	882025	ex HI-681CA	stored Deland	
HI-688CT	LET L-410UVP-E	861616	ex HI-688CA		
HI-695CT	LET L-410UVP-E	861615	ex HI-695CA		
HI-717CT	Beech 1900D	UE-352	ex N23519		
N521NA	Boeing 757-236	453/25592	ex N592KA		Lsd fr TRZ
N522NA	Boeing 757-236	374/25133			Lsd fr TRZ
N906PG	Boeing 727-281 (FedEx 3)	969/20728	ex OB-1573		Lsd fr TRZ

| N23317 | Beech 1900D | UE-340 | | Lsd fr Raytheon |
| N729PC | Snort SD.3-60 | SH3729 ex 6Y-JMY | on order | |

Operates feeder services for Air Europa within Caribbean. Officially registered as Aerolineas Santo Domingo

AT AIR TAXI

Santo Domingo-Herrara (HEX)

| HI-640CA | Britten-Norman BN-2A-21 Islander | 849 | ex A2-AEA |

CARIBAIR

Caribair (CBC)   *Santo Domingo-Herrara (HEX)*

HI-666CT	LET L-410UVP	851517	ex RA-67550	
HI-697CT	LET L-410UVP-E9A	882040	ex S9-TAV	
HI-698CT	LET L-410UVP-E9A	882040	ex S9-TAU	
HI-713CA	LET L-410UVP	851340	ex HI-676CA	
HI-569CT	Piper PA-31 Turbo Navajo	31-700	ex HI-569CA	
HI-585CA	Piper PA-31 Turbo Navajo B	31-850	ex N333GT	
HI-653CA	Britten-Norman BN-2A-26 Islander	8	ex N28BN	
HI-746CA	British Aerospace Jetstream 31	692	ex N692JX	no titles
HI-	British Aerospace Jetstream 31	660	ex N411MX	

LAN DOMINICANA

(4M/LNC)   *Santo Domingo-Las Americas (SDQ)*

Wholly owned subsidiary of LANChile; operates services with Boeing 767-300ER aircraft leased from parent

QUEEN AIR

(OQ)   *Santo Domingo*

Queen Air is the trading name of Aeronaves Queen SA, current status is uncertain

SAPAIR / SERVICIOS AEREOS PROFESIONALES

Proservicios (5S/PSV)   *Santo Domingo Herrar (HEX)*

HI-690CT	LET L-410UVP	831106	ex S9-TAR	
HI-691CT	LET L-410UVP	831107	ex S9-TAW	
HI-693CT	LET L-410UVP	851439	ex S9-TBC	
HI-722CT	LET L-410UVP-E	861729	ex Russ AF 1729	
HI-723CT	LET L-410UVP-E	861730	ex LY-AZI	
HI-724CT	LET L-410UVP-E	882032	ex LY-AZN	
HI-644CT	de Havilland DHC-6 Twin Otter 100	46	ex CS-TFG	
HI-658CT	Short SD.3-60	SH3674	ex B-3607	
HI-678CT	Grumman G-159 Gulfstream 1	323	ex HI-678CA	
HI-704CT	Britten-Norman BN-2A-27 Islander	504	ex VH-LRX	
HI-719CT	Beech 1900C-1	UC-84	ex N84GL	
HI-720CT	Embraer EMB.120RT Brasilia	120038	ex N332JS	Lsd fr DLT USA Inc
HI-760CT	Cessna 208B Caravan I	208B0802	ex N1326D	
N10876	Beech 1900D	UE-241		Lsd fr Raytheon
N23045	Beech 1900D	UE-322		Lsd fr Raytheon

TAINO TOURS

Taino (TIN)   *Santo Domingo-Las Americas (SDQ)*

Operates cargo services with aircraft leased from other operators as and when required

HK - COLOMBIA (Republic of Columbia)

ACES COLOMBIA – AEROLINEAS CENTRALES DE COLOMBIA ceased operations 20 Aug 03 and
liquidated by Allianza Summa which was later dissolved

ADA - AEROLINEAS DE ANTIOQUA

HK-2548	de Havilland DHC-6 Twin Otter 300	718	ex C-GDIW
HK-2603	de Havilland DHC-6 Twin Otter 300	749	
HK-2669	de Havilland DHC-6 Twin Otter 300	760	
HK-3972	Dornier 28D-2	4156	
HK-4000	Dornier 28D-2	4177	ex YS-404P
HK-4073	Dornier 28D-2	4114	ex N952

ADES COLOMBIA

Villavicencio (VVC)

HK-1149	Douglas C-47B	15148/26593	ex N69
HK-2279	Cessna U206G Stationair 6	U20604885	
HK-2663	Douglas DC-3	12352	ex C-FXUS
HK-2430	Cessna TU206G Stationair 6	U20605166	
HK-3462	Douglas DC-3	11759	ex N130W

AEROLINEAS ANDINAS now listed under trading name Aliansa

AEROREPUBLICA COLOMBIA

Aerorepublica (P5/RPB)　　　　　　　　　　　　　　　　　　*Bogota-Eldorado (BOG)*

EI-CMM	McDonnell-Douglas MD-83	1784/49937	ex VP-BGH	Lsd fr Irish Aerospace
HK-4237X	McDonnell-Douglas MD-81	48008	ex N480AC	Lsd fr Finova
HK-4238X	McDonnell-Douglas MD-81	48009	ex N489AC	Lsd fr Finova
HK-4255X	McDonnell-Douglas MD-81	950/48004	ex N834F	Lsd fr Finova
HK-4259X	McDonnell-Douglas MD-81	957/48005	ex N825F	Lsd fr Finova
HK-4265X	McDonnell-Douglas MD-81	938/48002	ex N832F	Lsd fr Finova
HK-4230X	Douglas DC-9-31 (ABS 3)	603/47526	ex N934ML	

AEROSUCRE

Aerosucre (6N/KRE)　　　　　　　　　　　　　　　　　　　*Barranquilla (BAQ)*

HK-727	Boeing 727-59F	243/19127		
HK-3667X	Boeing 727-23F	366/19430	ex N934FT	
HK-3985X	Boeing 727-224F	814/20465	ex N32723	
HK-4216X	Boeing 737-230C (Nordam 3)	223/20253	ex HP-1408PVI	
HK-4253	Boeing 737-2H6C	436/21109	ex HP-1311CMP	Lsd fr CIT Leasing
HK-4262X	Boeing 727-2F9F (FedEx 3)	1291/21427	ex N299AJ	Lsd fr American Avn Grp
HK-	Boeing 737-2S5C	663/22148	ex N802AL	

All freighters

AEROTACA EXPRESS / AEROTRANSPORTES CASANARE
current status uncertain, aircraft returned to owner

AEROVANGUARDIA

Villavicencio (VVC)

HK-1503	Douglas DC-3	17064/34331	ex N54336	El Viejto
HK-3199	Douglas DC-3	26044	ex FAC1123	

AIR COLOMBIA

Bogota-Eldorado (BOG)

HK-3292	Douglas DC-3	19661	ex C-GABG
HK-3293	Douglas DC-3	9186	ex N46877
HK-4046X	Douglas C-118A	347/43708	ex HK-3531X

AIRES – AEROVIAS DE INTEGRACION REGIONAL

Aires (4C/ARE)　　　　　　　　　　　　　　　　　　　*Bogota-Eldorado (BOG)*

HK-3942X*	de Havilland DHC-8-103	136	ex N4101T	Dario Echanda
HK-3946X*	de Havilland DHC-8-103	076	ex N4101Z	
HK-3951X*	de Havilland DHC-8-301	184	ex N184CL	Gustavo Artunduaga
HK-3952X*	de Havilland DHC-8-301	169	ex N169CL	
HK-4030X*	de Havilland DHC-8-301	100	ex N100CQ	
HK-4107X	de Havilland DHC-8Q-311	224	ex D-BELT	Lsd fr GECAS
HK-4258X*	de Havilland DHC-8-102	018	ex N909HA	

*Leased from Volvo Aero Services

ALIANSA

Villavicencio (VVC)

HK-122	Douglas DC-3	4414	ex C-122
HK-2820	Douglas DC-3	20171	ex N151D
HK-3215	Douglas DC-3	14466/26111	ex N124SF

ALLIANZA SUMMA Formed by the merger of ACES Colombia, Avianca and SAM Columbia and aircraft painted with Allianza Summa logo but individual flights continue. ACES Colombia ceased operations 20 Aug 03 and liquidated and Allianza Summa later dissolved

APSA – AEROEXPRESO BOGOTA

Aeroexpreso (ABO)   Bogota-Guayamaral

HK-3736X	Bell 212	31144	ex N3895P		Lsd fr OLOG
HK-3990X	Beech B200 Super King Air	BB-1376	ex N914YW	Catpass 200 conv	Lsd fr Raytheon
HK-4076X	Bell 212	30826	ex N62AL		Lsd fr OLOG
HK-4222X	Bell 212	30815	ex N24HL		Lsd fr OLOG

ARALL – AEROLINEAS LLANERAS

Villavicencio (VVC)

HK-1018	de Havilland DHC-2 Beaver	93	ex HK-240
HK-1231	Cessna TU206D Skywagon	U206-1391	ex (N72389)
HK-2257	Cessna U206G Stationair 6	U20604600	ex (N9950M)
HK-2373	de Havilland DHC-2 Beaver	61	ex HK-84
HK-2708	Cessna U206G Stationair 6	U20606167	
HK-2868	Cessna TU206G Stationair 6	U20606626	ex (N9724Z)

ATC COLOMBIA ceased operations

AVIANCA – AEROVIAS NACIONALES DE COLOMBIA

Avianca (AV/AVA) (IATA 134)   Bogota-Eldorado (BOG)

EI-CEY	Boeing 757-2Y0ER	478/26152			Lsd fr GECAS
EI-CEZ	Boeing 757-2Y0ER	486/26154			Lsd fr GECAS
N506NA	Boeing 757-236	272/24771	ex TC-AJA		Lsd fr CIT Lsg
N517NA	Boeing 757-28A	204/24260	ex N757GA		Lsd fr MSA 1
N767AN	Boeing 757-28A	127/23767	ex G-OOOA		Lsd fr MSA 1
N951PG	Boeing 757-236	34/22185	ex EC-GCA		Lsd fr Pegasus
N958PG	Boeing 757-236	163/24118	ex C-GRYO		Lsd fr TRZ
N421AV	Boeing 767-2B1ER	407/25421	ex PT-TAK		Lsd fr GECAS
N535AW	Boeing 767-33AER	491/25535	ex VH-NOE		Lsd fr MSA 1
N984AN	Boeing 767-383ER	262/24357	ex LN-RCB	Astrid	Lsd fr Pegasus
N985AN	Boeing 767-259ER	292/24618		Cristobal Colon	Lsd fr Pacific
N986AN	Boeing 767-259ER	321/24835		Amerigo Vespucio	Lsd fr Pacific
N988AN	Boeing 767-284ER	303/24742	ex VH-RMA	Simon Bolivar	Lsd fr AWMS 1
PH-AVG	Fokker 50	20278	ex (PH-LXS)		
PH-AVH	Fokker 50	20281			
PH-AVJ	Fokker 50	20285			Sublsd to SAM
PH-AVN	Fokker 50	20296			
PH-AVO	Fokker 50	20297			
PH-LXW	Fokker 50	20266			Sublsd to SAM
PH-MXJ	Fokker 50	20288			Sublsd to SAM
PH-MXS	Fokker 50	20299			
PH-MXZ	Fokker 50	20301			

All leased from debis

EI-CBR*	McDonnell-Douglas MD-83	1787/49939		Ciudad de Bucaramanga	
EI-CBS*	McDonnell-Douglas MD-83	1799/49942		Ciudad de Cucuta	Sublsd to SAM
EI-CBY*	McDonnell-Douglas MD-83	1888/49944		Ciudad de Barranquilla	
EI-CBZ*	McDonnell-Douglas MD-83	1889/49945	ex N6206F	Ciudad de Santiago de Cali	
EI-CCC*	McDonnell-Douglas MD-83	1898/49946		Ciudad de Pereira	
EI-CCE*	McDonnell-Douglas MD-83	1900/49947		Ciudad de Medellin	
EI-CDY*	McDonnell-Douglas MD-83	1905/49948		Ciudad de Santa Maria	Sublsd to SAM
EI-CEP*	McDonnell-Douglas MD-83	1984/53122		San Andres Isla	
EI-CEQ*	McDonnell-Douglas MD-83	1987/53123		Ciudad de Leticia	
EI-CER*	McDonnell-Douglas MD-83	1993/53125		Ciudad de Monteria	
EI-CFZ*	McDonnell-Douglas MD-83	1964/53120	ex N6206F	Ciudad de San Juan de Pasto	
N190AN	McDonnell-Douglas MD-83	2148/53190	ex HK-4137X	Ciudad de Cartagena	Lsd fr AWMS
N583AN	McDonnell-Douglas MD-83	2071/53183	ex HK-4184X	Ciudad de Valledupar	Lsd fr AWMS
N593AN+	McDonnell-Douglas MD-83	2066/53093	ex HK-4167X	Ciudad de Riohacha	Lsd fr AWMS
N632CT	McDonnell-Douglas MD-83	1603/49632	ex 9Y-THV	Retro c/s	Lsd fr CIT Leasing

*Leased from GECAS
Helicol and SAM are both wholly owned subsidiaries
Member of Allianza Summa although continued to operate its own aircraft. Filed US Chapter 11 on 21 March 2003 but continues to operate; Allianza Summa later dissolved

HELIANDES

Medellin-Herrara (EOH)

HK-4187X	LET L-410UVP-E	902432	ex HA-LAT
HK-4191	Bell 206B JetRanger lii	3410	ex N206KT
HK-4223	Bell 206B JetRanger	303	ex HP-1321HC
HK-4224X	LET L-410UVP	902420	ex S9-BOZ

202

HELICOL

Helicol (HEL)   *Bogota-Eldorado (BOG)*

HK-3111G	de Havilland DHC-7-102	87	ex C-GFBW	Op for Intercor/Carbocol
HK-3183X	Bell 212	32137	ex N21505	
HK-3303X	Bell 212	30654	ex N59608	
HK-3336X	Bell 212	31207	ex N2180J	
HK-3340W	de Havilland DHC-7-102	108	ex C-GFBW	Op for Intercor/Carbocol
HK-3357G	Bell 206L-2 LongRanger III	51231		
HK-3578G	Bell 412	33203		
HK-3633X	Bell 206L-1 LongRanger II	45510	ex N57497	
HK-4031X	Bell 212	31203	ex HK-3184X	
HK-4140X	Bell 206L-1 LongRanger II	45721	ex N20898	
HK-4141X	Bell 206L-3 LongRanger III	51303	ex N141BH	
HK-4213G	Bell 407	53405	ex (N2382Z)	

A subsidiary of AVIANCA

HELITAXI COLOMBIA

Bogota-Guaymaral

HK-3730X	Mil Mi-8TV-1	95728	
HK-3731X	Mil Mi-8TV-1	95586	
HK-3732X	Mil Mi-8TV-1	95729	
HK-3758X	Mil Mi-8TV-1	95908	ex HC-BSG
HK-3779X	Mil Mi-8TV-1	95645	
HK-3780X	Mil Mi-8TV-1	95909	
HK-3782X	Mil Mi-8TV-1	95910	ex HC-BSH
HK-3862	Mil Mi-8TV-1	95923	
HK-3863	Mil Mi-8TV-1	95894	
HK-3864	Mil Mi-8TV-1	95893	
HK-3865	Mil Mi-8TV-1	95892	
HK-3882X	Mil Mi-8TV-1	96018	
HK-3888X	Mil Mi-8TV-1	95838	
HK-3908X	Mil Mi-8TV-1	95823	
HK-3910X	Mil Mi-8TV-1	96008	
HK-3911X	Mil Mi-8TV-1	96124	
HK-3250	Bell 212	31219	ex HC-BSI
HK-3262	Bell 222UT	47556	
HK-3723	Bell 212	32122	ex N1080V
HK-3742	Bell 212	30847	
HK-4208X	Beech 1900C-1	UC-152	ex N152GL

HELITEC / HELICOPTEROS TERRITORIALES DE COLOMBIA

Cali (CLO)

HK-3341	Bell 212	31287	ex N3204H
HK-4025X	Bell 212	31143	ex HC-BSQ
HK-3851	Kamov Ka-32T	9001	
HK-4231X	Kamov Ka-32S	9101	ex N40475

HELIVALLE / HELICOPTEROS DEL VALLE

Palmira

HK-2383E	Bell 206B JetRanger III	2841	
HK-3693	Piper PA-42 Cheyenne III	42-8001075	ex N4998M
HK-3978X	Bell 206L-3 LongRanger III	51446	
HK-4015X	Bell 206L-4 LongRanger IV	52092	ex N4268G
HK-4026X	Bell 212	35055	ex N4354J
HK-4129X	Bell 212	30926	ex N412AX

INTER / INTERCONTINENTAL DE AVIACION

Contavia (RS/ICT)   *Bogota-Eldorado (BOG)*

HK-2865X	Douglas DC-9-15	55/45722	ex FAC-1142	Lsd fr Largo Lsg
HK-3752X	Douglas DC-9-15	101/45781	ex N1067T	Lsd fr Largo Lsg
HK-3827X	Douglas DC-9-15	35/47048	ex G-BMAA	Lsd fr Largo Lsg
HK-3859X	Douglas DC-9-14	28/45843	ex N8962	Lsd fr Largo Lsg
HK-3958X	Douglas DC-9-15	54/45738	ex G-BMAB	Lsd fr Largo Lsg
HK-4270X	Douglas DC-9-15 (ABS 3)	46/45841	ex N900ME	
HK-4271X	Douglas DC-9-14 (ABS 3)	23/45842	ex N800ME	
HK-	Douglas DC-9-32 (ABS 3)	230/47133	ex N401ME	
HK-4061X	de Havilland DHC-8-301	192	ex C6-BFL	Lsd fr Aviaco Traders

LAP COLOMBIA / LINEAS AÉREAS PETROLERAS

LAP (APT)   *Bogota-Eldorado (BOG)*

HK-2503   Piper PA-31 Turbo Navajo   31-8012056

LATINA DE AVIACIÓN

Villavicencio (VVC)

HK-2006	Douglas DC-3	43086	ex N43A	
HK-4173X	Beech 1900C-1	UC-14	ex N38015	Lsd fr Raytheon

LINEAS AÉREAS SURAMERICANAS COLOMBIA

Suramericano (LAU)   *Bogota-Eldorado (BOG)*

HK-1271	Boeing 727-24C (Raisbeck 3)	428/19524	ex N1781B	Pegasus; lascargo.com titles
HK-1273	Boeing 727-24C (Raisbeck 3)	442/19526	ex N8320	Voyager
HK-3745	Boeing 727-1C3F (Raisbeck 3)	819/20420	ex PP-CJG	Pegasus; stored BOG
HK-3814X	Boeing 727-25F (Raisbeck 3)	79/18270	ex N5111Y	Skipper
HK-4154	Boeing 727-51F (Raisbeck 3)	162/18804	ex N5607	Orion
HK-4261X	Boeing 727-251F (FedEx 3)	1170/21156	ex N296AJ	Lsd fr American Avn Grp
HK-4245X	Douglas DC-9-15RC (ABS 3)	115/47012	ex N562PC	Lsd fr Flying Air Cargo

All freighters

OLOG / AIRLOG

El Yopal (EYP)

Subsidiary of Offshore Logistics; helicopters are also leased from/or operated for other operators as required

ORION AIR CARGO

Villavicencio (VVC)

HK-1700   Douglas DC-6B   491/44419   ex

SADELCA / SOCIEDAD AÉREA DEL CAQUETA

Sadelca (SDK)   *Neiva (NVA)*

HK-1514	Douglas DC-3	11741	ex N100RW	
HK-2494	Douglas DC-3	16357/33105	ex Bu99826	
HK-2665X	Douglas DC-3	19433	ex CF-XPK	El Condor
HK-3286	Douglas DC-3	6144	ex HP-86	Liliana
HK-4189	Douglas DC-3	4319	ex HK-3994	Miguel Angel
HK-4136X	Antonov An-32B	2509	ex ER-AES	Lsd fr RAN

SADI / SOCIEDAD AÉREA DE IBAGUÉ

Ibagué (IBE)

HK-3154	Cessna TU206G Stationair 6	U20606836		
HK-3829	Bell 222	47076	ex N50RX	
HK-4013	LET L-410UVP-E	861601	ex TG-TJS	
HK-4055	LET L-410UVP-E10A	902521	ex S9-TAX	

SAEP / SERVICIOS AÉREOS ESPECIALIZADOS EN TRANSPORTES PETROLEROS

SAEP (KSP)   *Bogota-Eldorado (BOG)*

HK-4117X   Antonov An-32B   2909   ex RA-48071

SAM / SOCIEDAD AERONAUTICA DE MEDELLIN CONSOLIDADA

SAM (MM/SAM)   *Medellin-Olaya Herrara (MDE)*

PH-AVJ	Fokker 50	20285	Lsd fr AVA
PH-LXW	Fokker 50	20266	Lsd fr AVA
PH-MXJ	Fokker 50	20288	Lsd fr AVA
PH-MXT	Fokker 50	20300	Lsd fr AVA
PH-MXZ	Fokker 50	20301	Lsd fr AVA
EI-CBS	McDonnell-Douglas MD-83	1799/49942	Lsd fr AVA
EI-CDY	McDonnell-Douglas MD-83	1905/49948	Lsd fr AVA

A wholly owned subsidiary of AVIANCA; also operates other MD-83s leased from parent as and when required.
Member of Allianza Summa although this was later dissolved

204

SATENA / SERVICIO DE AERONAVEGACION Y TERRITORIOS NACIONALES

Satena (9N/NSE)   *Bogota-Eldorado (BOG)*

FAC-1160	Dornier 328-120	3079	ex D-CDXB	Maipures
FAC-1161	Dornier 328-120	3080	ex D-CDXH	La Macarena
FAC-1162	Dornier 328-120	3082	ex D-CDXP	Bahia Solano
FAC-1163	Dornier 328-120	3081	ex D-CDXM	
FAC-1164	Dornier 328-120	3092	ex D-CDXO	El Antioqueño
FAC-1165	Dornier 328-120	3103	ex D-CDXW	
FAC-1141	Fokker F.28 Fellowship 3000C	11162	ex PH-EZL	El Llanero
FAC-1156	CASA C.212-300	370		Vaupes
FAC-1157	CASA C.212-300	372		Amazonas
FAC-1170	Embraer EMB-145ER	145003	ex PT-ZJD	Milenium
FAC-1171	Embraer EMB.145LR	145774	ex PT-SME	
FAC-1172	Embraer EMB.145LR	145776	ex PT-SMG	

The airline wing of the Fuerza Aerea Colomiana (Colombian AF) operating social services throughout Colombia

SEARCA COLOMBIA / SERVICIO AÉREO DE CAPURGANA

Searca (SRC)   *Medellin-Olaya Herrara (MDE)*

HK-4038X	LET L-410UVP-E	851323	ex OK-022
HK-4048	LET L-410UVP-E	912626	ex TG-TJT
HK-4094X	LET L-410UVP-E	861707	ex N5857T
HK-4105X	LET L-410UVP-E	861613	ex N5957N
HK-4196X	LET L-410UVP-E	861617	ex CCCP-67577
HK-4235	LET L-410UVP-E	902423	ex S9-BAD
HK-3953X	Dornier 28D-2	4196	
HK-4108X	Beech 200 Super King Air	BB-60	ex N530JA
HK-4282X	Beech 1900C-1	UC-60	ex N901SC

SELVA / SERVICIOS AEREOS DEL VAUPES

Selva (SDV)   *Villavicencio (VVC)*

HK-4052X	Antonov An-32B	1805	ex YN-CBU	Margarita Maria
HK-4240X	Antonov An-32B	3204	ex OB-1625	Juan Pabla
HK-4295X	Antonov An-26		ex LZ-HNA	

TAMPA AIRLINES / TRANSPORTES AÉREOS MERCANTILES PANAMERICANOS

Tampa (QT/TPA) (IATA 729)   *Medellin-Olaya Herrara (MDE)*

HK-3785X	Douglas DC-8-71F	462/46066	ex N8099U		Lsd fr GECAS
HK-3786X	Douglas DC-8-71F	289/45849	ex N8074U		Lsd fr GECAS
HK-4176X	Douglas DC-8-71F	337/45945	ex N945GE		Lsd fr GECAS
HK-4277X	Douglas DC-8-71F	372/45976	ex N976AL		Lsd fr WFBN
HK-4294X	Douglas DC-8-71F	449/46040	ex N872SJ		Lsd fr AerCo USA
HK-	Boeing 767-241SF		ex	on order 04	Lsd fr GECAS
HK-	Boeing 767-241SF		ex	on order 04	Lsd fr GECAS

Two more Boeing 767-241SF freighters are on order, leased from GECAS

TAS / TRANSPORTE AEREO DE SANTANDER

Bucaramanga (BGA)

HK-4102	Dornier 28D-2 Skyservant	4187	ex D-IDES
HK-4104	Dornier 28D-2 Skyservant	4193	ex D-IDRV
HK-4139	Dornier 28D-2 Skyservant	4153	ex D-IDRF

TAXI AÉREO CUSIANA

Bogota-Eldorado (BOG)

HK-2522	Cessna 402C II	402C0322	
HK-3916	Cessna 208B Caravan I	208B0372	ex N1117P
HK-4225X	LET L-410UVP	871929	ex S9-CBB
HK-4260	LET L-410UVP-E3	871933	ex OK-SDQ

TRANS ORIENTE / TRANSPORTE AÉREO REGULAR SECUNDARIO ORIENTAL

Villavicencio (VVC)

HK-3981	Dornier 28D-2 Skyservant	4162	ex D-IDND
HK-3982	Dornier 28D-2 Skyservant	4169	ex D-IDNC
HK-3991X	Dornier 28D-2 Skyservant	4148	ex D-IDNF

HK-3992X	Dornier 28D-2 Skyservant	4161	ex D-IDNE
HK-4053X	Dornier 28D-1 Skyservant	4105	ex D-IDNH

TRANSPORTE AÉREO DEL PACIFICO

HK-	Boeing 727-151C	529/19868	ex N433EX

VIARCO / VIAS AÉREAS COLOMBIANAS

Villavicencio (VVC)

HK-1212	Douglas DC-3	4987	ex N76B
HK-1315	Douglas DC-3	4307	ex PP-ANG
HK-1842	Cessna U206F Stationair	U20603487	
HK-3349	Douglas DC-3	11825	ex FAE 92066/HC-AVC

WEST CARIBBEAN AIRWAYS

(YH/WCW)   *San Andres (ADZ)*

HK-4125X	LET L-410UVP-E	912606	ex OK-WDZ		Lsd fr Full Mark Co
HK-4146X	LET L-410UVP-E	902426	ex HP-1325	Old Providence	
HK-4147X	LET L-410UVP-E	892341	ex HP-1326		Lsd fr Millenium Corp
HK-4151X	LET L-410UVP-E	861610	ex N16100		
HK-4159X	LET L-410UVP-E	861717	ex Russ AF 1717	Saint Catalina	Lsd fr Full Mark Co
HK-4161X	LET L-410UVP-E	861612	ex N9968L		Lsd fr Full Mark Co
HK-4187X	LET L-410UVP-E	902432	ex HA-LAT		
HK-4224X	LET-L-410UVP-E	902420	ex S9-BOX		
HK-3678X	Aerospatiale/Alenia ATR 42-320	261	ex F-WWEI		Lsd fr GECAS
HK-3943X	Aerospatiale/Alenia ATR 42-320	142	ex EI-BXS		Lsd fr GECAS
HK-4302	McDonnell-Douglas MD-81	973/48027	ex N37882		Lsd fr Finova
HK-4305X	McDonnell-Douglas MD-82	1144/49237	ex N825US		Lsd fr Finova
VP-BBC	Aerospatiale/Alenia ATR 42-300	077	ex F-WQJM		Lsd fr Panoramix Lsg
VP-BNH	Aerospatiale/Alenia ATR 42-320	296	ex VR-BNH		Lsd fr GECAS

West Caribbean Costa Rica uses code WCR

HL - SOUTH KOREA (Republic of Korea)

AIR KOREA   ceased operations

ASIANA AIRLINES

Asiana (OZ/AAR) (IATA 988)   *Seoul-Incheon/Kimpo (ICN/SEL)*

HL7549	Airbus Industrie A321-231	1293	ex D-AVZK		Lsd fr ILFC
HL7588	Airbus Industrie A321-231	0771	ex D-AVZE		
HL7589	Airbus Industrie A321-231	0855	ex F-WWDS		Lsd fr Airbus
HL7590	Airbus Industrie A321-231	1060	ex D-AVZC		Lsd fr ILFC
HL7594	Airbus Industrie A321-231	1356	ex D-AVZA		Lsd fr CIT Leasing
HL7703	Airbus Industrie A321-231	1511	ex D-AVZA		
HL7711	Airbus Industrie A321-231	1636	ex D-AVZG		Lsd fr debis
HL7712	Airbus Industrie A321-231	1670	ex D-AVZU		LSd fr CIT Leasing
HL7713	Airbus Industrie A321-231	1734	ex D-AVXD		Lsd fr ILFC
HL7722	Airbus Industrie A321-231	2041	ex D-AVZA		
HL7723	Airbus Industrie A321-231	2045	ex D-AVZC		
HL7729	Airbus Industrie A321-231	2110	ex D-AVXF	on order 04	
HL7730	Airbus Industrie A321-231	2226		on order 04	Lsd fr ILFC
HL7731	Airbus Industrie A321-231	2247		on order 04	Lsd fr ILFC

Two more Airbus Industrie A321-231s plus two Airbus Industrie A320s are on order for delivery in 2005/2006

HL7227	Boeing 737-48E	2314/25764	
HL7228	Boeing 737-48E	2335/25765	
HL7232	Boeing 737-58E	2614/25767	Lsd fr CIT Leasing
HL7233	Boeing 737-58E	2724/25768	Lsd fr debis
HL7250	Boeing 737-58E	2737/25769	
HL7253	Boeing 737-4Y0	1655/23977	Lsd fr GECAS
HL7257	Boeing 737-4Y0	1749/24469	Lsd fr GECAS
HL7258	Boeing 737-4Y0	1751/24493	Lsd fr GECAS
HL7259	Boeing 737-4Y0	1757/24494	Lsd fr GECAS
HL7260	Boeing 737-4Y0	1803/24520	Lsd fr GECAS
HL7508	Boeing 737-48E	2791/25772	Lsd fr OZ Alpha Lsg
HL7509	Boeing 737-48E	2806/28198	Lsd fr ILFC
HL7510	Boeing 737-48E	2816/25771	Lsd fr ILFC
HL7511	Boeing 737-48E	2848/27630	Lsd fr Avn Capital
HL7512	Boeing 737-48E	2857/27632	Lsd fr ILFC
HL7513	Boeing 737-48E	2860/25776	Lsd fr OZ Gamma Lsg
HL7517	Boeing 737-48E	2909/25774	Lsd fr ILFC

HL7518	Boeing 737-48E	2954/28053		Lsd fr ILFC
HL7527	Boeing 737-4Q8	2602/26299	ex TC-JEK	Lsd fr ILFC
HL7591	Boeing 737-4Q8	2513/26291	ex TC-JEF	Lsd fr ILFC
HL7592	Boeing 737-4Q8	2562/26320	ex TC-JEH	Lsd fr ILFC
HL7593	Boeing 737-43Q	2837/28492	ex B-10001 (RoCAF)	Lsd fr Boullioun
HL7413	Boeing 747-48EM	880/25405		
HL7414	Boeing 747-48EM	892/25452		
HL7415	Boeing 747-48EM	946/25777		
HL7417	Boeing 747-48EM	1006/25779		
HL7418	Boeing 747-48E	1035/25780	ex N6018N	
HL7419	Boeing 747-48EF	1044/25781		Lsd fr Seagalt A/c
HL7420	Boeing 747-48EF	1064/25783		Lsd fr Eagle A/c
HL7421	Boeing 747-48EM	1086/25784		
HL7422	Boeing 747-48EF	1096/28367		Lsd fr SALE
HL7423	Boeing 747-48EM	1115/25782		Lsd fr OZ Delta Lsg
HL7426	Boeing 747-48EF	1210/27603	ex N6003C	Lsd fr ILFC
HL7428	Boeing 747-48E	1160/28552	ex N6018N	Lsd fr GECAS
HL7436	Boeing 747-48EF	1305/29170	ex N1785B	Lsd fr SALE

Two more Boeing 747-48EFs are on order for delivery in 2005/6

HL7200	Boeing 767-328ER	531/27212	ex OO-STF	Lsd fr Sunrock
HL7247	Boeing 767-38E	523/25757		
HL7248	Boeing 767-38E	582/25758		
HL7263	Boeing 767-38EER	328/24797		
HL7268	Boeing 767-38EER	417/25132	ex EI-CPV	Lsd fr Greenfly
HL7506	Boeing 767-38EFER	639/25760		Lsd fr OZ Gamma Lsg
HL7507	Boeing 767-38EFER	616/25761	ex N6005C	Lsd fr OZ Alpha Lsg
HL7514	Boeing 767-38E	656/25763		Lsd fr OZ Everest Lsg
HL7515	Boeing 767-38E	658/25762	ex N6055X	Lsd fr OZ Delta Lsg
HL7516*	Boeing 767-38E	668/25759		Lsd fr OZ Everest Lsg
HL7528	Boeing 767-38E	693/29129	ex N6005C	
HL7595	Boeing 767-36NER	829/30840		Lsd fr GECAS

*Painted in Star Alliance colours

HL7596	Boeing 777-28EER	322/28681		Lsd fr ILFC
HL7597	Boeing 777-28EER	359/28686		Lsd fr ILFC
HL7500	Boeing 777-28EER	400/28685		Lsd fr ILFC
HL7700	Boeing 777-28EER	403/30859	ex N5014K	
HL	Boeing 777-28EER		on order	
HL	Boeing 777-28EER		on order	Lsd fr ILFC

Four more Boeing 777-28EERs and six Airbus Industrie A330-323Xs are on order for future delivery.
Member of Star Alliance with effect from 01 March 2003

KOREAN AIR

Koreanair (KE/KAL) (IATA 180)

Seoul-Incheon/Kimpo (ICN/SEL)

HL7239	Airbus Industrie A300B4-622R	627	ex F-WWAD	
HL7240	Airbus Industrie A300B4-622R	631	ex F-WWAB	
HL7241	Airbus Industrie A300B4-622R	662	ex F-WWAT	
HL7242	Airbus Industrie A300B4-622R	685	ex F-WWAG	
HL7243	Airbus Industrie A300B4-622R	692	ex F-WWAR	
HL7244	Airbus Industrie A300B4-622R	722	ex F-WWAH	
HL7245	Airbus Industrie A300B4-622R	731	ex F-WWAK	
HL7278	Airbus Industrie A300B4-203F	277	ex F-WZME	Lsd to MNB
HL7279	Airbus Industrie A300B4-203F	292	ex F-WZMS	Lsd to MNB
HL7291*	Airbus Industrie A300B4-622	417	ex F-WWAT	Lsd fr Intrepid Avn
HL7295	Airbus Industrie A300B4-622R	582	ex F-WWAM	
HL7297	Airbus Industrie A300B4-622R	609	ex F-WWAE	
HL7299	Airbus Industrie A300B4-622R	717	ex F-WWAY	

*sold for future delivery to FedEx for freighter conversion

HL7524	Airbus Industrie A330-322	206	ex HL7552	
HL7525	Airbus Industrie A330-322	219	ex F-WWKO	
HL7538	Airbus Industrie A330-223	222	ex F-WWKP	Lsd fr debis
HL7539	Airbus Industrie A330-223	226	ex F-WWKR	Lsd fr debis
HL7540	Airbus Industrie A330-322	241	ex F-WWKF	
HL7550	Airbus Industrie A330-322	162	ex F-WWKK	
HL7551	Airbus Industrie A330-322	172	ex F-WWKI	
HL7552	Airbus Industrie A330-223	258	ex F-WWKQ	Lsd fr debis
HL7553	Airbus Industrie A330-322X	267	ex F-WWKZ	
HL7554	Airbus Industrie A330-322X	256	ex F-WWKN	
HL7584	Airbus Industrie A330-322X	338	ex F-WWKP	
HL7585	Airbus Industrie A330-322X	350	ex F-WWYF	
HL7586	Airbus Industrie A330-322X	351	ex F-WWYH	
HL7587	Airbus Industrie A330-322X	368	ex F-WWKF	
HL7701	Airbus Industrie A330-323X	425	ex F-WWYE	
HL7702	Airbus Industrie A330-323X	428	ex F-WWYF	
HL7709	Airbus Industrie A330-323X	484	ex F-WWKD	
HL7710	Airbus Industrie A330-323X	490	ex F-WWKF	

Reg	Type	Line/MSN	ex	Notes
HL7720	Airbus Industrie A330-323X	550	ex F-WWKP	
HL7555	Boeing 737-86N	460/30230		Lsd fr GECAS
HL7557	Boeing 737-86N	562/28622		Lsd fr GECAS
HL7558	Boeing 737-86N	590/28625		Lsd fr GECAS
HL7559	Boeing 737-86N	611/28626		Lsd fr GECAS
HL7560	Boeing 737-8B5	622/29981		
HL7561	Boeing 737-8B5	663/29982		
HL7562	Boeing 737-8B5	678/29983		
HL7563	Boeing 737-86N	756/28636		Lsd fr GECAS
HL7564	Boeing 737-86N	765/28638		Lsd fr GECAS
HL7565	Boeing 737-8B5	848/29984		
HL7566	Boeing 737-8B5	852/29985		
HL7567	Boeing 737-86N	878/28647		Lsd fr GECAS
HL7568	Boeing 737-8B5	891/29986		
HL7569	Boeing 737-9B5	999/29987		
HL7599	Boeing 737-9B5	1026/29988	ex N1795B	
HL7704	Boeing 737-9B5	1082/29989		
HL7705	Boeing 737-9B5	1162/29990		
HL7706	Boeing 737-9B5	1188/29991		
HL7707	Boeing 737-9B5	1190/29992		
HL7708	Boeing 737-9B5	1208/29993		
HL7716	Boeing 737-9B5	1320/29994		
HL7717	Boeing 737-9B5	1332/29995		
HL7718	Boeing 737-9B5	1338/29996		
HL7719	Boeing 737-9B5	1416/29997		
HL7724	Boeing 737-9B5	29998		on order 04
HL7725	Boeing 737-9B5	29999		on order 04
HL7727	Boeing 737-9B5	30000		on order 04
HL	Boeing 737-9B5			on order 04
HL	Boeing 737-9B5			on order 04
HL7400	Boeing 747-4B5F	1295/26414		
HL7402	Boeing 747-4B5	1155/26407	ex N6038E	
HL7403	Boeing 747-4B5	1163/26408	ex N60659	
HL7404	Boeing 747-4B5	1170/26409	ex N6009F	Lsd to AIC as VT-AIC
HL7405	Boeing 747-2B5F	718/24195	ex HL7475	Lsd fr KI Freight Ltd
HL7407	Boeing 747-4B5	729/24198	ex HL7477	Lsd fr KI Freight Ltd
HL7408	Boeing 747-2B5F	720/24196	ex HL7476	
HL7409	Boeing 747-4B5	739/24199	ex HL7478	Lsd fr Aircraft Owner B; sublsd to IAC
HL7412	Boeing 747-4B5	748/24200	ex HL7479	Lsd to AIC as VT-AID
HL7434	Boeing 747-4B5F	1316/32809		
HL7437	Boeing 747-4B5ERF	1323/32808		
HL7438	Boeing 747-4B5ERF	1329/33515	ex N6005X	
HL7439	Boeing 747-4B5ERF	1338/33516		
HL7443	Boeing 747-2B5B	363/21772		
HL7448	Boeing 747-4B5F	1246/26416		Lsd fr GECAS
HL7449	Boeing 747-4B5F	1248/26411		Lsd fr GECAS
HL7452	Boeing 747-2B5F	454/22481	ex N5573F	For Orbit Express 04
HL7459	Boeing 747-2B5F	520/22486		For Orbit Express 04
HL7460	Boeing 747-4B5	1107/26404		Lsd fr KE Apollo Lsg
HL7461	Boeing 747-4B5	1118/26405		
HL7462	Boeing 747-4B5F	1123/26406		
HL7465	Boeing 747-4B5	1284/26412		
HL7466	Boeing 747-4B5F	1286/26413		
HL7467	Boeing 747-4B5F	1291/27073		
HL7469	Boeing 747-3B5	611/22489	ex N6009F	
HL7470	Boeing 747-3B5SF	713/24194	ex N6038E	Cargo titles
HL7472	Boeing 747-4B5	1095/26403		
HL7473	Boeing 747-4B5	1098/28335		
HL7480	Boeing 747-4B5M	793/24619	ex N6009F	
HL7481	Boeing 747-4B5	830/24621		
HL7482	Boeing 747-4B5	853/25205		
HL7483	Boeing 747-4B5	874/25275		
HL7484	Boeing 747-4B5	893/26392		Lsd fr OLC Air Lsg
HL7485	Boeing 747-4B5	922/26395		
HL7486	Boeing 747-4B5	951/26396		
HL7487	Boeing 747-4B5	958/26393		
HL7488	Boeing 747-4B5	986/26394		
HL7489	Boeing 747-4B5	1013/27072		
HL7490	Boeing 747-4B5	1019/27177		
HL7491	Boeing 747-4B5	1037/27341		
HL7492	Boeing 747-4B5	1055/26397		
HL7493	Boeing 747-4B5	1057/26398		
HL7494	Boeing 747-4B5	1067/27662		
HL7495	Boeing 747-4B5	1073/28096		
HL7497	Boeing 747-4B5F	1087/26401		
HL7498	Boeing 747-4B5	1092/26402		
HL7499	Boeing 747-4B5ERF	1340/33517		
HL	Boeing 747-4B5ERF			on order May04
HL	Boeing 747-4B5ERF			on order 04

HL7526	Boeing 777-2B5ER	148/27947	ex N50217
HL7530	Boeing 777-2B5ER	59/27945	Lsd fr KE Apollo Lsg
HL7531	Boeing 777-2B5ER	62/27946	Lsd fr KE Apollo Lsg
HL7532	Boeing 777-3B5	162/28371	
HL7533	Boeing 777-3B5	178/27948	
HL7534	Boeing 777-3B5	120/27950	ex N5020K
HL7573	Boeing 777-3B5	288/27952	
HL7574	Boeing 777-2B5ER	305/28444	
HL7575	Boeing 777-2B5ER	309/28445	
HL7598	Boeing 777-2B5ER	356/27949	
HL7714	Boeing 777-2B5ER	411/27951	
HL7715	Boeing 777-2B5ER	416/28372	
HL7721	Boeing 777-2B5ER	452/33727	
HL7732	Boeing 777-2B5ER	29174	on order

Eight more Boeing 777-2B5ERs are on order for delivery from 2005

HL5253	CASA C.212-100	CB16-1-125		
HL7213	Fokker 100	11504	ex PH-EZP	
HL7214	Fokker 100	11513	ex PH-EZI	
HL7216	Fokker 100	11522	ex PH-EZG	Lsd fr ORIX
HL7217	Fokker 100	11523	ex PH-EZM	Lsd fr ORIX
HL7371	McDonnell-Douglas MD-11F	456/48407		
HL7372	McDonnell-Douglas MD-11F	457/48408	dam SYD 09Jan02	Lsd fr Pegasus
HL7374	McDonnell-Douglas MD-11F	495/48410		Lsd fr Pegasus
HL7375	McDonnell-Douglas MD-11F	521/48523		Lsd fr GECAS
HL7541	McDonnell-Douglas MD-82	1201/49373	ex HL7272	Lsd fr GECAS

McDonnell-Douglas MD-82s are being replaced by 737-8B5/9B5. Five Airbus Industrie A380s are on order for delivery between 4Q 2007 and 2009.
Founder member of Sky Team Alliance with Air France, Delta and Aeromexico

SEOUL AIR INTERNATIONAL ceased operations

HP - PANAMA (Republic of Panama)

AEROPER

Panama City-Paitilla (PAC)

HP-1445	Canadair CL-66B Cosmopolitan	CL66B-7	ex N4FY	Lsd fr PMA Aeronautical Support

AEROPERLAS / AEROLINEAS PACIFICO ATLANTICO

Aeroperlas (WL/APP)   *Panama City-Paitilla (PAC)*

HP-1355APP	Cessna 208B Caravan	208B0681		
HP-1358APP	Cessna 208B Caravan I	208B0710		
HP-1359APP	Cessna 208B Caravan I	208B0711		
HP-1397APP	Cessna 208B Caravan I	208B0613	ex TI-LRT	Lsd fr FSBN
HP-1399APP	Cessna 208B Caravan I	208B0640	ex TI-LRA	Lsd fr FSBN
HP-1402APP	Cessna 208B Caravan I	208B0789	ex N1318L	Lsd fr Cessna Finance
HP-1251APP	Short SD.3-60	SH3610	ex N715NC	
HP-1280APP	Short SD.3-60	SH3665	ex N190SB	
HP-1315APP	Short SD.3-60	SH3614	ex N363MQ	
HP-1317APP	Short SD.3-60	SH3602	ex N360MQ	Lsd to La Costena
HP-1318APP	Short SD.3-60	SH3612	ex N362MQ	Lsd to La Costena
HP-1319APP	Short SD.3-60	SH3607	ex N361MQ	
HP-1326APP	Short SD.3-60	SH3631	ex N360MM	
HP-747APP	de Havilland DHC-6 Twin Otter 300	403		Isla del Rey
HP-1281APP	de Havilland DHC-6 Twin Otter 300	407	ex C-FVFK	
HP-1283APP	de Havilland DHC-6 Twin Otter 300	269	ex C-GKBO (1)	
HP-1336APP	Beech A100 King Air	B-173	ex C-GAST	
HP-1445APP	Canadair CL-66B Cosmopolitan	CL66B-7	ex	
HP-1468APP	Canadair CL-66B Cosmopolitan	CL66B-4	ex 9XR-NB	
HP-1473APP	Canadair CL-66B Cosmopolitan	CL66B-9	ex C-GNCB	

Member of Grupo TACA

AIR SERVICES CARGO

HP-1479	Sud Aviation SE.210 Caravelle 10B-1R	255	ex HK-3948X

AVIATUR / AVIACIÓN DE TURISMO

Panama City-Paitilla (PAC)

HP-1156AR	Britten-Norman BN-2B-27 Islander	879	ex HP-1156P	Lsd fr Aircraft Lsg
HP-1284AR	Britten-Norman BN-2A-26 Islander	170	ex N140FS	Lsd fr Aircraft Lsg
HP-1312AR	Britten-Norman BN-2A-6 Islander	641	ex D-IORS	Lsd fr Aircraft Lsg

HP-1332AR	Cessna U206G Stationair 6	U20604857	ex C-GNTB		Lsd fr Aircraft Lsg
HP-1345AR	Cessna 208B Caravan I	208B0380	ex YN-CEJ		Lsd fr Aircraft Lsg
HP-1360AR	Cessna 208B Caravan I	208B0719			Lsd fr Caravan Investment
HP-1460AR	El Gavilan EL-1 Gavilan 358	11			Lsd fr Aircraft Lsg Intl

COPA AIRLINES

Copa (CM/CMP) (IATA 230)   *Panama City-Tocumen Intl (PTY)*

HP-1163CMP	Boeing 737-204	541/21693	ex G-BFVA		Lsd fr Orbit Avn
HP-1195CMP	Boeing 737-204	338/20806	ex G-BAZG		Lsd fr Orbit Avn
HP-1234CMP	Boeing 737-2S3	849/22660	ex VR-HYK		Lsd fr Interlease
HP-1255CMP	Boeing 737-2P6	500/21359	ex HR-SHQ		Lsd fr GECAS
HP-1322CMP	Boeing 737-2P5	794/22667	ex AP-BEV		Lsd fr Interjet Lsg
HP-1324CMP	Boeing 737-2P5	1010/23113	ex HS-TBE		Lsd fr Interjet Lsg
HP-1369CMP	Boeing 737-71Q	235/29047	ex N8251R	669	Lsd fr Tombo
HP-1370CMP	Boeing 737-71Q	288/29048	ex N82521	670	Lsd fr Tombo
HP-1371CMP	Boeing 737-7V3	388/30049	ex N1787B	671	Lsd fr GECAS
HP-1372CMP	Boeing 737-7V3	399/28607		672	Lsd fr GECAS
HP-1373CMP	Boeing 737-7V3	459/30458		673	
HP-1374CMP	Boeing 737-7V3	494/30459	ex N1787B	674	
HP-1375CMP	Boeing 737-7V3	558/30460	ex N1787B	675	
HP-1376CMP	Boeing 737-7V3	574/30497		676	
HP-1377CMP	Boeing 737-7V3	1161/30462		677	
HP-1378CMP	Boeing 737-7V3	1173/30461		678	
HP-1379CMP	Boeing 737-7V3	1221/30463			
HP-1380CMP	Boeing 737-7V3	1241/30464			
HP-1520CMP	Boeing 737-7V3	1376/33707			
HP-1521CMP	Boeing 737-7V3	1379/33708			
HP-1522CMP	Boeing 737-8V3	1387/33709			
HP-1523CMP	Boeing 737-8V3	1397/33710			
HP-	Boeing 737-7V3			on order 04	
HP	Boeing 737-7Q8	30676		on order Dec04	Lsd fr ILFC

All retrofitted with winglets
49% owned by Continental

DHL AERO EXPRESSO

(D5/DAE)   *Panama City-Tocumen Intl (PTY)*

HP-1310DAE	Boeing 727-264F (FedEx 3)	1047/20894	ex N9184X	El Gato	Lsd fr Volvo Aero Services
HP-1510DAE	Boeing 727-264F (FedEx 3)	950/20709	ex N624DH		Lsd fr BCS
HP-1610DAE	Boeing 727-264F (FedEx 3)	986/20780	ex N625DH		Lsd fr BCS
HP-1710DAE	Boeing 727-2Q4F (FedEx 3)	1683/22424	ex OO-DHZ		Lsd fr SWT

MAPIEX AERO

Panama City-Paitilla (PAC)

HP-1458MAM	British Aerospace Jetstream 31	679	ex N311PX	Lsd fr Bas Norton
HP-1477MAM	British Aerospace Jetstream 31	760	ex N844JS	Lsd fr Bas Norton

PANAVIA PANAMA

Panavia (6Z/PNV)   *Panama City-Tocumen Intl (PTY)*

HP-1261PVI	Boeing 727-25F	205/18965	ex N8141N	Lsd fr Aero Inversiones

HR - HONDURAS (Republic of Honduras)

AERO HONDURAS believed not to have started operations

AEROLINEAS SOSA

Sosa (P4/VSU)   *La Ceiba (LCE)*

HR-AQR	LET L-410UVP	851516	ex S9-TBD
HR-ARE	LET L-410UVP	841312	ex S9-TBL
HR-ARJ	Nord 262A-14	15	ex N417SA
HR-ARP	Nord 262A-27	33	ex N274A
HR-ARU	Nord 262A-21	21	ex TG-ANP
HR-ASI	LET L-410UVP-E	871925	ex OK-SDJ
HR-ASR	Fairchild F-27F	84	ex 3C-QQA
HR-ASZ	LET L-410UVP	851530	ex HR-AQO

ATLANTIC AIRLINES

(ZF/HHA)   *Tegucigalpa (TGU)*

HR-ASD	LET L-410UVP	882034	ex YS-15C
HR-ASE	LET L-410UVP	861611	ex YS-10C
HR-ASF	LET L-410UVP	831136	ex YS-04C
HR-ASG	LET L-410UVP-E	861710	ex YV-13C
HR-ASH	LET L-410UVP	861716	ex YS-14C
HR-ASI	LET L-410UVP-E	871925	ex N888LT
HR-ASJ	LET L-410UVP	861724	ex YS-12C
HR-ASM	LET L-410UVP-E	861711	ex YS-05C
HR-ASN	LET L-410UVP-E	861701	ex YS-06C
HR-ASS	LET L-410UVP	831137	ex TG-AGW
HR-ASW	LET L-410UVP-E	871916	ex CU-T1193
HR-ASX	LET L-410UVP-E	871915	ex CU-T1194
HR-ASK	Fairchild-Hiller FH-227B	524	ex N155JB
HR-ATI	Fairchild F.27F Friendship	95	ex N19FF

HONDURAS AIRLINES believed not to have started operations

ISLENA AIRLINES

(WC/ISV)   *La Ceiba (LCE)*

HR-ARY	Aerospatiale/Alenia ATR 42-300	030	ex N423MQ	Lsd fr CIT Leasing
HR-IAP	Short SD.3-60	SH3616	ex N345MV	
HR-IAW	Short SD.3-60	SH3669	ex N361PA	
HR-IAX	Aerospatiale/Alenia ATR 42-300	004	ex F-WEGD	Lsd fr ATR Asset Mgt
HR-IAY	Aerospatiale/Alenia ATR 42-300	120	ex F-WQHM	Lsd fr ATR Asset Mgt

Islena Airlines is the trading name of Islena de Inversiones
20% owned by Grupo TACA

LINEAS AEREAS NACIONALES DE HONDURAS ceased operations

ROLLINS AIR ceased operations

SETCO / SERVICIOS EJECUTIVOS TURISTICOS COMMANDER

Tegucigalpa (TGU)

HR-AFB	Shrike Commander 500S	3268	ex HR-315
HR-AFC	Shrike Commander 500S	3271	ex HR-317
HR-AKF	Aero Commander 560E	560E-592	ex N6215B
HR-AKM	Shrike Commander 500S	3098	ex TG-CNA

SOL AIR

(4S)   *La Ceiba (LCE)*

N371FA	Boeing 737-33A	1337/23631	ex N172AW	Gabriela	Lsd fr FAO
N54348	Boeing 727-231 (Super 27)	1563/21967		Alicia	Lsd fr FAO

HS - THAILAND (Kingdom of Thailand)

AIR ANDAMAN

(2Y/ADW)   *Phuket (HKT)*

HS-KLA	British Aerospace Jetstream 31	638	ex SE-LHP	
HS-KLB	British Aerospace Jetstream 31	629	ex ZK-OSW	stored BKK
HS-KLD	Fokker 50	20188	ex PH-ZDD	
HS-KLE	Fokker 50	20193	ex PH-ZDE	

Fokker 50s leased from Aircraft Financing and Trading

AIR PEOPLE INTERNATIONAL

Air People (3D)   *Bangkok (BKK)*

3C-QRN	Antonov An-12BP	7344705	ex ER-AXB	Lsd fr Aquiline

ANGEL AIRLINES

Angel Air (8G/NGE)   *Bangkok (BKK)*

Operated services using aircraft leased from other operators as and when required but current status uncertain

BANGKOK AIRWAYS
Bangkok Air (PG/BKP)　　　　　　　　　　　　　　　　　　　　　　Bangkok (BKK)

HS-PGA*	Aerospatiale/Alenia ATR 72-212A	710	ex F-WWEJ	Kut	
HS-PGB	Aerospatiale/Alenia ATR 72-212A	708	ex F-WWEH	Phuket	
HS-PGC*	Aerospatiale/Alenia ATR 72-202	452	ex F-WWEW		Lsd fr Dorabella
HS-PGD*	Aerospatiale/Alenia ATR 72-202	455	ex F-WWLM		Lsd fr Dorabella
HS-PGE*	Aerospatiale/Alenia ATR 72-202	450	ex F-WWEH		Lsd fr Dorabella
HS-PGF*	Aerospatiale/Alenia ATR 72-212A	700	ex F-WWEW	Hua Hin	
HS-PGG*	Aerospatiale/Alenia ATR 72-212A	692	ex F-WWEO	Chang	
HS-PGK*	Aerospatiale/Alenia ATR 72-212A	680	ex F-WWEV	Apsara	
HS-PGL	Aerospatiale/Alenia ATR 72-212A	670	ex F-WWER	Pha Ngan	
HS-PGM*	Aerospatiale/Alenia ATR 72-212A	704	ex F-WWEC	Tao	

*Carry joint Bangkok Airways and Siam Reap Air titles

HS-PGO	Boeing 717-23S	5059/55067		Angkor	Lsd fr Pembroke
HS-PGP	Boeing 717-23S	5037/55064	ex N9014S	Samui	Lsd fr Pembroke
HS-PGQ	Boeing 717-231	5045/55081	ex N2414E	Sukhothai Lsd fr BCC Equipment Lsg	
HS-PGR	Boeing 717-231	5030/55074	ex N407TW	Luang Prabang	Lsd fr Hawk Lsg
HS-	Airbus Industrie A320-		ex	on order Sep04	Lsd fr debis
HS-	Airbus Industrie A320-		ex	on order Nov04	Lsd fr debis

Siem Reap Air (SRH) is a wholly owned subsidiary, aircraft used may vary

HOLIDAY AIR
　　　　　　　　　　　　　　　　　　　　　　　　　　　　　　　　　Phuket (HKT)

Holiday Air is a subsidiary of Phuket Airlines and uses Boeing 747s from the parent as required

ONE- TWO- GO
　　　　　　　　　　　　　　　　　　　　　　　　　　　　　　　　　Bangkok (BKK)

HS-OTA	Boeing 757-28AER	213/24368	ex N521AT
HS-UTK	Boeing 747-306M	600/23137	ex PH-BUV
XU-123	Boeing 757-23A	250/24528	ex G-CCMY

First service 5 December 2003. Wholly owned low-cost subsidiary of Orient Thai Airlines

ORIENT THAI AIRLINES
Orient Express (OX/OEA)　　　　　　　　　　　　　　　　　　　　　Bangkok (BKK)

HS-UTB	Boeing 747-246B	192/20529	ex N910BW	Lsd fr Cuda Ray Investments
HS-UTC	Boeing 747-238B	341/21658	ex N165UA	Lsd fr Grandmax Group
HS-UTD	Boeing 747-146A	259/21029	ex JA8128	
HS-UTH	Boeing 747-146	199/20532	ex JA8116	Lsd fr Boeing Aircraft Holding
HS-UTI	Boeing 747-246B	255/21031	ex JA8127	
HS-UTJ	Boeing 747-246B	361/21678	ex JA8219	
HS-UTK*	Boeing 747-306M	600/23137	ex PH-BUV	
HS-UTP	Boeing 747-246B	196/20530	ex JA8114	Lsd fr Boeing Aircraft Holding
HS-OTA*	Boeing 757-28AER	213/24368	ex N521AT	Lsd fr ACG Acquisitions
HS-UTA	Lockheed L-1011 Tristar 1	1225	ex XU-222	
HS-UTE	Lockheed L-1011 Tristar 1	1199	ex N730DA	
HS-UTF	Lockheed L-1011 Tristar 1	1213	ex N1732D	
HS-UTG	Lockheed L-1011 Tristar 1	1226	ex N735D	
XU-123*	Boeing 757-23A	250/24528	ex G-CCMY	Lsd fr Tombo

*Operates for One-Two-Go; a wholly owned low-cost subsidiary

PB AIR
Peebee Air (9Q/PBA)　　　　　　　　　　　　　　　　　　　　　　Bangkok (BKK)

HS-PBE	Embraer EMB.145LU	145597	ex PT-SCH	Lsd fr Embraer
HS-PBF	Embraer EMB.145LU	145607	ex PT-SCQ	Lsd fr Embraer

PHUKET AIRLINES
Phuket Air (9R/VAP)　　　　　　　　　　　　　　　　　　　　　　　Phuket (HKT)

HS-AKO	Boeing 737-281	282/20507	ex PK-JHG	Similan
HS-AKU*	Boeing 737-2B7 (Nordam 3)	998/23115	ex N282AU	Kavida-Urawan
HS-KUO	NAMC YS-11A-523	2146	ex JA8772	
HS-KVA	NAMC YS-11A-513	2133	ex JA8761	
HS-KVO	NAMC YS-11A-213	2116	ex JA8744	stored Don Muang
HS-KVU*	NAMC YS-11A	2097	ex JA8729	stored BKK
HS-VAA	Boeing 747-206B (EUD)	397/21848	ex PH-BUO	
HS-VAK	Boeing 747-2U3B	468/22249	ex PK-GSD	
HS-VA	Boeing 747-2U3B			
HS-VAU	Boeing 747-2U3B			
HS-VAV	Boeing 747-206M (EUD)	369/21659	ex PH-BUM	

HS-VKK*   Boeing 737-2B7 (Nordam 3)   1039/23131 ex N284AU   Komrit-Urawan
The other two ex Garuda aircraft are 452/22246, 459/22247 ex PK-GSA, GSB
*Leased from Suwanaphumi Airlines; Holiday Air is a wholly owned subsidiary

SKY EYES

Sky Eyes (SEQ)   *Bangkok (BKK)*

HS-SEA   Piper PA-31-350 Navajo Chieftain 31-7852102
XU-375   Antonov An-24B   Lsd fr PSD

SUWANAPHUMI AIRLINES

Phuket (HKT)

HS-AKU   Boeing 737-2B7 (Nordam 3)   998/23115   ex N282AU   Lsd to VAP
HS-KVU   NAMC YS-11A   2097   ex JA8729   Lsd to VAP
HS-VKK   Boeing 737-2B7 (Nordam 3)   1039/23131   ex N284AU   Lsd to VAP
Possibly only a leasing company

THAI AIR ASIA

Bangkok (BKK)

9M-AAN   Boeing 737-301   1208/23234 ex N338US
Subisidary of Air Asia and due to commence operations in February 2004

THAI AIR CARGO

Thai Cargo (T2/TCG)   *Bangkok (BKK)*

Leases DC-10-30F from Gemini Air Cargo as and when required.

THAI AIRWAYS INTERNATIONAL

Thai (TG/THA) (IATA 217)   *Bangkok (BKK)*

HS-TAA	Airbus Industrie A300B4-601	368	ex F-WWAG	Suwannaphum	wfs UTP
HS-TAB	Airbus Industrie A300B4-601	371	ex F-WWAH	Sri Anocha	
HS-TAC	Airbus Industrie A300B4-601	377	ex F-WWAI	Sri Ayutthaya	
HS-TAD	Airbus Industrie A300B4-601	384	ex F-WWAK	U Thong	
HS-TAE	Airbus Industrie A300B4-601	395	ex F-WWAM	Sukhothai	
HS-TAF	Airbus Industrie A300B4-601	398	ex F-WWAN	Ratchasima	
HS-TAG	Airbus Industrie A300B4-605R	464	ex F-WWAL	Srinapha	
HS-TAH	Airbus Industrie A300B4-605R	518	ex F-WWAE	Napachinda	
HS-TAK	Airbus Industrie A300B4-622R	566	ex F-WWAB	Phaya Thai	
HS-TAL	Airbus Industrie A300B4-622R	569	ex F-WWAD	Sri Trang	
HS-TAM	Airbus Industrie A300B4-622R	577	ex F-WWAG	Chiang Mai	
HS-TAN	Airbus Industrie A300B4-622R	628	ex F-WWAE	Chiang Rai	
HS-TAO	Airbus Industrie A300B4-622R	629	ex F-WWAF	Chanthaburi	
HS-TAP	Airbus Industrie A300B4-622R	635	ex F-WWAP	Pathum Thani	stored BKK
HS-TAR	Airbus Industrie A300B4-622R	681	ex F-WWAB	Yasothon	
HS-TAS	Airbus Industrie A300B4-622R	705	ex F-WWAT	Yala	
HS-TAT	Airbus Industrie A300B4-622R	782	ex F-WWAY	Srimuang	
HS-TAW	Airbus Industrie A300B4-622R	784	ex F-WWAL	Suranaree	
HS-TAX	Airbus Industrie A300B4-622R	785	ex F-WWAO	Thepsatri	
HS-TAY	Airbus Industrie A300B4-622R	786	ex F-WWAQ	Srisoonthorn	
HS-TAZ	Airbus Industrie A300B4-622R	787	ex F-WWAB	Srisubhan	
HS-TEA	Airbus Industrie A330-321	050	ex F-WWKI	Manorom	
HS-TEB	Airbus Industrie A330-321	060	ex F-WWKQ	Sri Sakhon	
HS-TEC	Airbus Industrie A330-321	062	ex F-WWKR	Bang Rachan	
HS-TED	Airbus Industrie A330-321	064	ex F-WWKS	Donchedi	
HS-TEE	Airbus Industrie A330-321	065	ex F-WWKT	Kusuman	
HS-TEF	Airbus Industrie A330-321	066	ex F-WWKJ	Song Dao	
HS-TEG	Airbus Industrie A330-321	112	ex F-WWKM	Lam Plai Mat	
HS-TEH	Airbus Industrie A330-321	122	ex F-WWKG	Sai Buri	
HS-TEJ	Airbus Industrie A330-322	209	ex F-WWKN	Sudawadi	Lsd fr debis
HS-TEK+	Airbus Industrie A330-322	224	ex F-WWKD	Srichulalak	
HS-TEL	Airbus Industrie A330-322	231	ex F-WWKU	Thepamart	Star Alliance c/s
HS-TEM	Airbus Industrie A330-323X	346	ex F-WWYE	Jiraprabha	
HS-TDA	Boeing 737-4D7	1899/24830		Songkhla	
HS-TDB	Boeing 737-4D7	1922/24831		Phuket	
HS-TDD	Boeing 737-4D7	2318/26611		Chumphon	
HS-TDE	Boeing 737-4D7	2330/26612		Surin	
HS-TDF	Boeing 737-4D7	2338/26613		Si Sa Ket	
HS-TDG	Boeing 737-4D7	2481/26614		Kalasin	
HS-TDH	Boeing 737-4D7	2962/28703		Lopburi	
HS-TDJ	Boeing 737-4D7	2968/28704		Nakhon Chaisi	
HS-TDK	Boeing 737-4D7	2977/28701		Sri Surat	
HS-TDL	Boeing 737-4D7	2978/28702		Srikarn	

HS-TGA	Boeing 747-4D7	1273/32369		Srisuriyothai
HS-TGB	Boeing 747-4D7	1278/32370		Si Satchanalai
HS-TGD	Boeing 747-3D7	681/23721	ex N6046P	Suchada
HS-TGE	Boeing 747-3D7	688/23722	ex N60668	Chutamat
HS-TGF	Boeing 747-4D7	1335/33770		Sri Ubon
HS-TGG	Boeing 747-4D7	1337/33771		Pathoomawadi
HS-TGH	Boeing 747-4D7	769/24458		Chaiprakarn
HS-TGJ+	Boeing 747-4D7	777/24459		Hariphunchai
HS-TGK	Boeing 747-4D7	833/24993		Alongkorn
HS-TGL	Boeing 747-4D7	890/25366		Theparat
HS-TGM	Boeing 747-4D7	945/27093		Chao Phraya
HS-TGN	Boeing 747-4D7	950/26615		Simongkhon
HS-TGO+	Boeing 747-4D7	1001/26609		Bowonrangsi
HS-TGP	Boeing 747-4D7	1047/26610		Thepprasit
HS-TGR	Boeing 747-4D7	1071/27723		Siriwatthna
HS-TGT	Boeing 747-4D7	1097/26616		Watthanothai
HS-TGW^	Boeing 747-4D7	1111/27724		Visuthakasatriya
HS-TGX	Boeing 747-4D7	1134/27725		Sirisobhakya
HS-TGY	Boeing 747-4D7	1164/28705	ex N60697	Dararasmi
HS-TGZ	Boeing 747-4D7	1214/28706		Phimara

+ 'Royal Barge' colours   ^Star Alliance colours
Seven ex United Boeing 747-422s are on order but sale may be blocked by United creditors

HS-TJA	Boeing 777-2D7	25/27726		Lamphun
HS-TJB	Boeing 777-2D7	32/27727		U Thaithani
HS-TJC	Boeing 777-2D7	44/27728		Nakhon Nayok
HS-TJD	Boeing 777-2D7	51/27729		Mukdahan
HS-TJE^	Boeing 777-2D7	89/27730		Chaiyaphum
HS-TJF^	Boeing 777-2D7	95/27731		Phanom Sarakham
HS-TJG	Boeing 777-2D7	100/27732		Pattani
HS-TJH	Boeing 777-2D7	113/27733		Suphan Buri
HS-TKA	Boeing 777-3D7	156/29150	ex N5028Y	Sriwanna
HS-TKB	Boeing 777-3D7	170/29151		Chainarai
HS-TKC	Boeing 777-3D7	250/29211		Kwanmuang
HS-TKD	Boeing 777-3D7	260/29212		Thepalai
HS-TKE	Boeing 777-3D7	304/29213		Sukhirin
HS-TKF	Boeing 777-3D7	310/29214		Chutamai

^Leased from Palomino Leasing

HS-TMD	McDonnell-Douglas MD-11	466/48416		Phra Nakhon
HS-TME	McDonnell-Douglas MD-11	467/48417		Pathum Wan
HS-TMF	McDonnell-Douglas MD-11	501/48418		Phichit
HS-TMG	McDonnell-Douglas MD-11	505/48451		Nakhon Sawan; stored
HS-TRA	Aerospatiale/Alenia ATR 72-201	164	ex F-WWEO	Lampang
HS-TRB	Aerospatiale/Alenia ATR 72-201	167	ex F-WWEU	Chai Nat
HS-	Airbus Industrie A340-541	624	ex F-WW	on order 04

Two more Airbus Industrie A340-541s and five Airbus Industrie A340-642s are on order for delivery from 2005
Founder member of Star Alliance with Air Canada, Lufthansa, United, SAS and VARIG

THAI AVIATION SERVICES

Songkhla (SGZ)

HS-HTD	Sikorsky S-76A++	760187	ex C-FIHD	Lsd fr CHC Helicopters
HS-HTI	Sikorsky S-76A++	760148	ex VH-JXL	Lsd fr CHC Lloyd
HS-HTO	Sikorsky S-76A++	760015	ex C-GIHO	Lsd fr CHC Helicopters
HS-HTQ	Sikorsky S-76A	760102	ex C-GIMQ	Lsd fr CHC Helicopters
HS-HTR	Sikorsky S-76A+	760032	ex C-GIHR	Lsd fr CHC Helicopters
HS-HTS	Sikorsky S-76A+	760150	ex C-GIHS	Lsd fr CHC Helicopters
HS-HTU	Sikorsky S-76A++	760010	ex VH-HUB	Lsd fr CHC Lloyd
HS-HTX	Sikorsky S-76A++	760213	ex C-GIMX	Lsd fr CHC Helicopters
HS-HTA	Sikorsky S-61N	61815	ex C-GOLH	
HS-HTC	Sikorsky S-61N	61722	ex C-GARC	Lsd fr CHC Helicopters

Subsidiary of CHC International

THAI FLYING SERVICE

Thai Flying (TFT)

Bangkok (BKK)

HS-ITD	Beech Super King Air 350	FL-151	ex N10817	Lsd fr Italian/Thai Co
HS-TFE	Piper PA-23-250 Aztec F	27-7954045	ex HS-SKF	
HS-TFG	Rockwell Commander 690B	11482	ex N745T	

Also operates as Thai Flying Helicopter Service with designator TFH

THAI PACIFIC AIRLINES

(3P/TPV)

Bangkok (BKK)

Current fleet details unknown. Intended to lease two Boeing 747-200s for BKK-SYD service originally planned to begin 1 December 2003

THAIJET

(THJ) *Bangkok (BKK)*

HS-OGA	Boeing 757-225	115/22688	ex TC-OGA	Lsd fr OGE
HS-OGB	Boeing 757-225	161/23983	ex TC-OGC	Lsd fr OGE

HZ - SAUDI ARABIA (Kingdom of Saudi Arabia)

SAUDI ARABIAN AIRLINES

Saudia (SV/SVA) (IATA 065) *Jeddah (JED)*

HZ-AJA	Airbus Industrie A300B4-620	284	ex F-WZLS
HZ-AJB	Airbus Industrie A300B4-620	294	ex F-WZYA
HZ-AJC	Airbus Industrie A300B4-620	301	ex F-WZYB
HZ-AJD	Airbus Industrie A300B4-620	307	ex F-WZYC
HZ-AJE	Airbus Industrie A300B4-620	312	ex F-WZYD
HZ-AJF	Airbus Industrie A300B4-620	317	ex F-WZYE
HZ-AJG	Airbus Industrie A300B4-620	321	ex F-WZYF
HZ-AJH	Airbus Industrie A300B4-620	336	ex F-WZYI
HZ-AJI	Airbus Industrie A300B4-620	341	ex F-WZYJ
HZ-AJJ	Airbus Industrie A300B4-620	348	ex F-WZYL
HZ-AJK	Airbus Industrie A300B4-620	351	ex F-WZYB
HZ-AIA	Boeing 747-168B	512/22498	ex N8281V
HZ-AIB	Boeing 747-168B	517/22499	
HZ-AIC	Boeing 747-168B	522/22500	
HZ-AID	Boeing 747-168B	525/22501	
HZ-AIE	Boeing 747-168B	530/22502	ex N8284V
HZ-AIF	Boeing 747SP-68	529/22503	
HZ-AIG	Boeing 747-168B	551/22747	
HZ-AII	Boeing 747-168B	557/22749	
HZ-AIK	Boeing 747-368	616/23262	ex N6005C
HZ-AIL	Boeing 747-368	619/23263	ex N6009F
HZ-AIM	Boeing 747-368	620/23264	ex N6046P
HZ-AIN	Boeing 747-368	622/23265	ex N6046P
HZ-AIP	Boeing 747-368	630/23267	ex N6055X
HZ-AIQ	Boeing 747-368	631/23268	ex N6005C
HZ-AIR	Boeing 747-368	643/23269	ex N6038E
HZ-AIS	Boeing 747-368	645/23270	ex N6046P
HZ-AIT	Boeing 747-368	652/23271	ex N6038N
HZ-AIU	Boeing 747-268F	724/24359	ex N6018N
HZ-AIV	Boeing 747-468	1122/28339	ex N6005C
HZ-AIW	Boeing 747-468	1138/28340	
HZ-AIX	Boeing 747-468	1182/28341	
HZ-AIY	Boeing 747-468	1216/28342	ex N6009F
HZ-AIZ	Boeing 747-468	1265/28343	
HZ-AKA	Boeing 777-268ER	98/28344	ex N50217
HZ-AKB	Boeing 777-268ER	99/28345	ex N5023Q
HZ-AKC	Boeing 777-268ER	101/28346	
HZ-AKD	Boeing 777-268ER	103/28347	
HZ-AKE	Boeing 777-268ER	109/28348	
HZ-AKF	Boeing 777-268ER	114/28349	
HZ-AKG	Boeing 777-268ER	119/28350	
HZ-AKH	Boeing 777-268ER	124/28351	
HZ-AKI	Boeing 777-268ER	143/28352	
HZ-AKJ	Boeing 777-268ER	147/28353	
HZ-AKK	Boeing 777-268ER	154/28354	
HZ-AKL	Boeing 777-268ER	166/28355	
HZ-AKM	Boeing 777-268ER	175/28356	
HZ-AKN	Boeing 777-268ER	181/28357	
HZ-AKO	Boeing 777-268ER	186/28358	
HZ-AKP	Boeing 777-268ER	194/28359	
HZ-AKQ	Boeing 777-268ER	219/28360	ex N5016R
HZ-AKR	Boeing 777-268ER	236/28361	ex N5017V
HZ-AKS	Boeing 777-268ER	255/28362	
HZ-AKT	Boeing 777-268ER	298/28363	
HZ-AKU	Boeing 777-268ER	306/29364	
HZ-AKV	Boeing 777-268ER	323/28365	
HZ-AKW	Boeing 777-268ER	351/28366	
HZ-APA	McDonnell-Douglas MD-90-30	2191/53491	
HZ-APB	McDonnell-Douglas MD-90-30	2205/53492	ex N9012S
HZ-APC	McDonnell-Douglas MD-90-30	2209/53493	ex N9014S
HZ-APD	McDonnell-Douglas MD-90-30	2213/53494	ex N9010L
HZ-APE	McDonnell-Douglas MD-90-30	2215/53495	ex N6203D
HZ-APF	McDonnell-Douglas MD-90-30	2216/53496	ex N9012S
HZ-APG	McDonnell-Douglas MD-90-30	2219/53497	
HZ-APH	McDonnell-Douglas MD-90-30	2221/53498	ex N6202D

HZ-API	McDonnell-Douglas MD-90-30	2223/53499	
HZ-APJ	McDonnell-Douglas MD-90-30	2225/53500	
HZ-APK	McDonnell-Douglas MD-90-30	2226/53501	
HZ-APL	McDonnell-Douglas MD-90-30	2227/53502	
HZ-APM	McDonnell-Douglas MD-90-30	2229/53503	
HZ-APN	McDonnell-Douglas MD-90-30	2230/53504	
HZ-APO	McDonnell-Douglas MD-90-30	2231/53505	ex N9012S
HZ-APP	McDonnell-Douglas MD-90-30	2232/53506	
HZ-APQ	McDonnell-Douglas MD-90-30	2235/53507	
HZ-APR	McDonnell-Douglas MD-90-30	2237/53508	
HZ-APS	McDonnell-Douglas MD-90-30	2250/53509	ex N6203D
HZ-APT	McDonnell-Douglas MD-90-30	2251/53510	ex N6203U
HZ-APU	McDonnell-Douglas MD-90-30	2255/53511	
HZ-APV	McDonnell-Douglas MD-90-30	2256/53512	
HZ-APW	McDonnell-Douglas MD-90-30	2257/53513	ex N9010L
HZ-APX	McDonnell-Douglas MD-90-30	2260/53514	ex N6200N
HZ-APY	McDonnell-Douglas MD-90-30	2262/53515	ex N9014S
HZ-APZ	McDonnell-Douglas MD-90-30	2263/53516	ex N9075H
HZ-AP3	McDonnell-Douglas MD-90-30	2289/53518	ex N6203D
HZ-AP4	McDonnell-Douglas MD-90-30	2290/53519	ex N9075H
HZ-AP7	McDonnell-Douglas MD-90-30	2288/53517	ex HZ-AP2
HZ-ANA	McDonnell-Douglas MD-11F	609/48773	ex N90187
HZ-ANB	McDonnell-Douglas MD-11F	616/48775	ex N91566
HZ-ANC	McDonnell-Douglas MD-11F	617/48776	ex N91078
HZ-AND	McDonnell-Douglas MD-11F	618/48777	ex N9166N

Also operates a fleet of executive and EMS aircraft for the Saudi Royal Family and the Government
Owns 49% of Yemenia

SNAS AVIATION

Red Sea (RSE)   *Riyadh/Bahrain (RUH/BAH)*

HZ-SN7	Swearingen SA.227AC Metro III	AC-565B	ex N3113G	Freighter	SNAS c/s
HZ-SN8	Swearingen SA.227AT Merlin IVC	AT-434	ex N3110F	Freighter	SNAS c/s
HZ-SN10	Swearingen SA.227AC Metro III	AC-769B	ex HZ-SN1	Freighter	DHL c/s
HZ-SN11	Convair 580	385	ex C-FKFA	Freighter	DHL c/s
HZ-SN14	Convair 580	361	ex OO-DHJ	Freighter	DHL c/s

Operates for DHL

H4 - SOLOMON ISLANDS

PACIFIC AIR EXPRESS

Solpac (PAQ)   *Honiara (HIR)*

Operates cargo flights with Antonov An-12 aircraft leased from Aerocom or Douglas DC-4 leased from Pacific Air Freighters as required

SOLOMONS

Solomon (IE/SOL) (IATA 193)   *Honiara (HIR)*

H4-AAH	Britten-Norman BN-2A-8 Islander	75	ex VH-TZH
H4-AAI	Britten-Norman BN-2A-9 Islander	355	ex N355BN
H4-FNT	de Havilland DHC-6 Twin Otter 310	280	ex VH-FNT
H4-SIB	de Havilland DHC-6 Twin Otter 310	256	ex N661MA
H4-SID	de Havilland DHC-6 Twin Otter 310	442	ex VH-XFE

WESTERN PACIFIC AIRLINK

Honiara (HIR)

H4-WPG	Britten-Norman BN-2B-21 Islander	2177	ex VH-BNX

I - ITALY (Italian Republic)

AIR BLU Was due to start operations in September 2003 with Canadair CL-600-2B19 and a Aerospatiale/Alenia ATR 42-500 leased from Air Littoral but latter entered receivership; current status uncertain

AIR COLUMBIA changed name to TAI-Transporte Aerei Italiana

AIR DOLOMITI

Dolomiti (EN/DLA) (IATA 101)   *Trieste (TRS)*

I-ADLF	Aerospatiale/Alenia ATR 42-500	462	ex F-OHFF	
I-ADLG	Aerospatiale/Alenia ATR 42-500	476	ex F-OHFG	
I-ADLH	Aerospatiale/Alenia ATR 42-500	445	ex F-OHFM	Lsd fr Locafit

I-ADLI	Aerospatiale/Alenia ATR 42-500	515	ex F-OHFN		Lsd fr Locafit
I-ADLJ	Aerospatiale/Alenia ATR 72-212A	686	ex F-WQMO		
I-ADLK	Aerospatiale/Alenia ATR 72-212A	706	ex F-W	on order 04	
I-ADLL	Aerospatiale/Alenia ATR 42-500	518	ex F-OHFP		Lsd fr San Paolo Lsg
I-ADLM	Aerospatiale/Alenia ATR 72-212A	543	ex F-WWLB		Lsd fr Locafit
I-ADLN	Aerospatiale/Alenia ATR 72-212A	557	ex F-WWLV		Lsd fr Intesa Lsg
I-ADLO	Aerospatiale/Alenia ATR 72-212A	585	ex F-WQJH		Lsd fr Italease
I-ADLP	Aerospatiale/Alenia ATR 42-500	604	ex F-WQKY		Lsd fr Finagem
I-ADLQ	Aerospatiale/Alenia ATR 42-500	606	ex F-WQMA		
I-ADLS	Aerospatiale/Alenia ATR 72-212A	634	ex F-WQMB		Lsd fr Locat
I-ADLT	Aerospatiale/Alenia ATR 72-212A	638	ex F-WQME		Lsd fr Italease
I-ADLU	Aerospatiale/Alenia ATR 42-500	609	ex F-WQMH		Lsd fr Locafit
I-ADLV	Aerospatiale/Alenia ATR 42-500	610	ex F-OHJI		Lsd fr Sanpaolo Leasint
I-ADLW	Aerospatiale/Alenia ATR 72-212A	707	ex F-W	on order 04	
I-ADLZ	Aerospatiale/Alenia ATR 42-500	611	ex F-WQM.		Lsd fr Roma Lsg
I-ADJA	Canadair CL-600-2B19	7478	ex C-GIDJ		
I-ADJB	Canadair CL-600-2B19	7486	ex C-GIGH		
I-ADJC	Canadair CL-600-2B19	7494	ex C-GIHG		
I-ADJD	Canadair CL-600-2B19	7625	ex C-GJYW		
I-ADJE	Canadair CL-600-2B19	7629	ex C-GJYX		

98.8% owned by Lufthansa; leases a Dornier 328-100 from Cirrus Aviation

AIR EMILIA

Parma

| PH-ACZ | Beech B200 Super King Air | BB-1215 | ex D-IEEE | Lsd fr ROS |
| PH-RAE | Beech 1900D | UE-21 | ex ZS-OLX | Lsd fr ROS |

First service 14 April 2003 but ceased operations 30 November 2003

AIR EUROPE ITALY

Air Europe (PE/AEL)   *Milan-Malpensa (MXP)*

| I-VIMQ | Boeing 767-3Q8ER | 619/27993 | ex I-PIMQ | Lsd fr Pegasus |

AIR INDUSTRIA

(7Y/IDU)   *Naples (NAP)*

I-ATRF	Aerospatiale/Alenia ATR 42-300	034	ex F-WWEP	dam 06Mar03
I-ATRG	Aerospatiale/Alenia ATR 42-300	042	ex F-WWEW	stored NAP
I-ATRJ	Aerospatiale/Alenia ATR 42-300	057	ex F-WWEL	stored NAP
I-ATRL	Aerospatiale/Alenia ATR 42-300	068	ex F-WWES	

AIR ITALICA

Orio Al Serio (BGY)

| F-OHFQ | Aerospatiale/Alenia ATR 72-202 | 509 | ex F-WQNH | Lsd fr Alisea |

Commenced operations July 03 under Alisea Airlines AOC but ceased operations after 3 months

AIR ONE

Heron (AP/ADH) (IATA 867)   *Pescara (PSR)*

D-AGMR	Boeing 737-430	2367/27007	ex TC-SUS	Lsd fr GOAL
EI-CLW	Boeing 737-3Y0	2248/25187	ex XA-SAB	Lsd fr GECAS
EI-CLZ	Boeing 737-3Y0	2205/25179	ex XA-RJR	Lsd fr GECAS
EI-COH	Boeing 737-430	2316/27001	ex D-ABKB	Lsd fr GATX
EI-COI	Boeing 737-430	2323/27002	ex D-ABKC	Lsd fr GOAL
EI-COJ	Boeing 737-430	2359/27005	ex D-ABKK	Lsd fr GOAL
EI-COK	Boeing 737-430	2328/27003	ex F-GRNZ	Lsd fr Flightlease
EI-CRZ	Boeing 737-36E	2770/26322	ex EC-GGE	Lsd fr ILFC
EI-CSU	Boeing 737-36E	2792/27626	ex EC-GGZ	Lsd fr ILFC
EI-CWE	Boeing 737-42C	2060/24232	ex PH-BPE	Lsd fr Rockshaw
EI-CWF	Boeing 737-42C	2270/24814	ex PH-BPG	Lsd fr Rockshaw
EI-CWW	Boeing 737-4Y0	2064/24912	ex EC-GBN	Lsd fr Airplane Holdings
EI-CWX	Boeing 737-4Y0	2009/24906	ex EC-GAZ	Lsd fr Airplane Holdings
EI-CXI	Boeing 737-46Q	2910/28661	ex EC-GPI	Lsd fr Bellevue A/c Lsg
EI-CXJ	Boeing 737-4Q8	2447/25164	ex N164LF	Lsd fr ILFC
EI-CXL	Boeing 737-46N	2886/28723	ex G-SFBH	Lsd fr Monroe Aircraft
EI-CXM	Boeing 737-4Q8	2620/26302	ex VH-VOZ	Lsd fr ILFC
EI-CZG	Boeing 737-4Q8	2461/25740	ex VH-VGB	Lsd fr ILFC
F-GKTA	Boeing 737-3M8	1884/24413	ex (OO-LTH)	Lsd fr Alter Bail Avn
F-GKTB	Boeing 737-3M8	1895/24414	ex (OO-LTI)	Lsd fr Alter Bail Avn
I-JETA	Boeing 737-229 (Nordam 3)	593/21839	ex OO-SBS	
I-JETC	Boeing 737-230 (Nordam 3)	1075/23153	ex D-ABMA	
I-JETD	Boeing 737-230 (Nordam 3)	1089/23158	ex D-ABMF	Lsd fr Sardaleasing

EI-CXP	Boeing 737-883	634/30467	ex LN-RPO	Lsd fr SAS
EI-CXT	Boeing 737-883	668/30468	ex OY-KKT	Lsd fr Challey Ltd
EI-CXU	Boeing 737-883	625/28323	ex LN-RPD	Lsd fr Challey Ltd
EI-CXW	Boeing 737-883	666/30194	ex LN-RPP	Lsd fr Challey Ltd

AIR SICILIA ceased operations

AIR VALLÉE / SERVICES AÉRIENS DU VAL D'AOSTE

Air Vallee (DO/RVL) (IATA 965) *Aosta (AOT)*

I-AIRJ	Dornier 328-300	3186		
I-AIRX	Dornier 328-300	3142	ex D-BDXS	Lsd fr Locat

ALIDAUNIA

Lid (D4/LID) *Foggia (FOG)*

I-AGSE	Agusta A.109A II	7354	
I-AGSH	Agusta A.109A II	7384	
I-LIDC	MBB BK117C-1	7529	ex D-HMB.
I-LIDD	Agusta A.109E Power	11107	
I-MSTR	Agusta A.109A	7227	ex N4256P
I-RMDV	Sikorsky S-76A	760235	ex N760P

ALIEUROPE

Alieurope (TOO) *Uggiate*

I-EMEB	Aerospatiale AS.332C Super Puma	2001	ex C-GOOH

ALISEA

Alisea (FZ/BBG) *Palermo (PMO)*

CS-TLI	Boeing 737-33A	1462/23830	ex PR-BRA	Lsd fr MMZ
F-OHFQ	Aerospatiale/Alenia ATR 72-202	509	ex F-WQNH	Lsd fr ATRiam Capital;
OE-LNH	Boeing 737-4Z9	2043/25147	ex (I-BPAC)	Lsd fr LDI

ALITALIA

Alitalia (AZ/AZA) (IATA 055) *Rome-Fiumicino (FCO)*

I-BIMA	Airbus Industrie A319-112	1722	ex D-AVWP	Isola d'Elba
I-BIMB	Airbus Industrie A319-112	2033	ex D-AVYP	
I-BIMC	Airbus Industrie A319-112	2057	ex D-AVYC	
I-BIMD	Airbus Industrie A319-112	2074	ex D-AVYM	Isola di Capri
I-BIME	Airbus Industrie A319-112	1740	ex D-AVWW	Isola di Panarea
I-BIMF	Airbus Industrie A319-112	2083	ex D-AVYZ	Isola Tremiti
I-BIMG	Airbus Industrie A319-112	2086	ex D-AVWD	Isola di Pantelleria
I-BIMH	Airbus Industrie A319-112	2101	ex D-AVYY	on order
I-BIMI	Airbus Industrie A319-112	1745	ex D-AVWZ	Isola di Ponza
I-BIMJ	Airbus Industrie A319-112	1779	ex D-AVYG	Isola di Caprera
I-BIMO	Airbus Industrie A319-112	1770	ex D-AVWC	Isola d'Ischia
I-BIML	Airbus Industrie A319-112	2127	ex D-AVWN	
I-BIKA	Airbus Industrie A320-214	0951	ex F-WWBT	Johann Sebastian Bach
I-BIKB	Airbus Industrie A320-214	1226	ex F-WWIG	Wolfgang Amadeus Mozart
I-BIKC	Airbus Industrie A320-214	1448	ex F-WWBV	Maschio Angioino Napoli
I-BIKD	Airbus Industrie A320-214	1457	ex F-WWDE	Torre di Pisa
I-BIKE	Airbus Industrie A320-214	0999	ex F-WWBZ	Franz Liszt
I-BIKF	Airbus Industrie A320-214	1473	ex F-WWDP	Grecale
I-BIKG	Airbus Industrie A320-214	1480	ex F-WWDT	Scirocco
I-BIKI	Airbus Industrie A320-214	1138	ex F-WWDJ	Girolamo Frescobaldi
I-BIKL	Airbus Industrie A320-214	1489	ex F-WWDN	Libeccio
I-BIKO	Airbus Industrie A320-214	1168	ex F-WWDL	George Bizet
I-BIKU	Airbus Industrie A320-214	1217	ex F-WWBD	Fryderyk Chopin Lsd fr ILFC
I-BIXA	Airbus Industrie A321-112	0477	ex D-AVZE	Piazza del Duomo-Milano
I-BIXB	Airbus Industrie A321-112	0524	ex D-AVZY	Piazza Castello-Torino
I-BIXC	Airbus Industrie A321-112	0526	ex D-AVZZ	Piazza del Campo-Siena
I-BIXD	Airbus Industrie A321-112	0532	ex D-AVZB	Piazza Pretorio-Palermo
I-BIXE	Airbus Industrie A321-112	0488	ex D-AVZG	Piazza di Spagna-Roma
I-BIXF	Airbus Industrie A321-112	0515	ex D-AVZQ	Piazza Maggiore-Bologna
I-BIXG	Airbus Industrie A321-112	0516	ex D-AVZR	Piazza del Miracoli-Pisa
I-BIXH	Airbus Industrie A321-112	0940	ex D-AVZS	Piazza del Municipio-Noto
I-BIXI	Airbus Industrie A321-112	0494	ex D-AVZI	Piazza San Marco-Venezia
I-BIXJ	Airbus Industrie A321-112	0959	ex D-AVZP	Piazza Ducale-Vigeevano
I-BIXK	Airbus Industrie A321-112	1220	ex D-AVZC	Piazza Ducale Vigevano
I-BIXL	Airbus Industrie A321-112	0513	ex D-AVZO	Piazza del Duomo-Lecce
I-BIXM	Airbus Industrie A321-112	0514	ex D-AVZP	Piazza S Francesco -Assisi

I-BIXN	Airbus Industrie A321-112	0576	ex D-AVZR	Piazza del Duomo-Catania
I-BIXO	Airbus Industrie A321-112	0495	ex D-AVZJ	Piazza Plebiscito-Napoli
I-BIXP	Airbus Industrie A321-112	0583	ex D-AVZT	Carlo Morelli
I-BIXQ	Airbus Industrie A321-112	0586	ex D-AVZU	Domenico Calapietro
I-BIXR	Airbus Industrie A321-112	0593	ex D-AVZW	Piazza del Campidoglio-Roma
I-BIXS	Airbus Industrie A321-112	0599	ex D-AVZZ	Piazza San Martino-Lucca
I-BIXT	Airbus Industrie A321-112	0765	ex D-AVZW	Piazza del Signori-Vizenza
I-BIXU	Airbus Industrie A321-112	0434	ex D-AVZB	Piazza della Signoria-Gubbio
I-BIXV	Airbus Industrie A321-112	0819	ex D-AVZU	Piazza del Rinaccimento-Urbino
I-BIXZ	Airbus Industrie A321-112	0848	ex D-AVZO	Piazza del Duomo Orvieto

I-DEMC	Boeing 747-243M	492/22506		Atlante freighter
I-DEMR	Boeing 747-243F	545/22545		Titano

Also leases Atlas Air 747F-on ACMI lease. Both for sale to Volga-Dnepr Airlines

EI-CRD	Boeing 767-31BER	534/26259	ex B-2565		Lsd fr ILFC
EI-CRF	Boeing 767-31BER	542/25170	ex B-2566		Lsd fr ILFC
EI-CRL	Boeing 767-343ER	743/30008		Leonardo da Vinci	GECAS
EI-CRM	Boeing 767-343ER	746/30009	ex (I-DEIB)	Amerigo Vespucci	GECAS
EI-CRO	Boeing 767-3Q8ER	747/29383		Francesco de Pinedo	ILFC
EI-CTW	Boeing 767-341ER	774/30342	ex (PP-)	Roberto Pau	Lsd fr GECAS
EI-DBP	Boeing 767-35HER	459/26389	ex C-GGBJ	Duca degli Abruzzi	Lsd fr CIT Lsg
EI-DDW	Boeing 767-3S1ER	559/26608	ex N979PG		Lsd fr Pegasus
I-DEIB*	Boeing 767-33AER	560/27376	ex G-OITA	Pier Paolo Racchetti	
I-DEIC*	Boeing 767-33AER	561/27377	ex G-OITB	Alberto Nassetti	
I-DEID*	Boeing 767-33AER	584/27468	ex G-OITC	Marco Polo	
I-DEIF^	Boeing 767-33AER	578/27908	ex G-OITF	Cristoforo Colombo	Lsd SALE
I-DEIG	Boeing 767-33AER	603/27918	ex G-OITG	Francesco Agello	Lsd fr SALE
I-DEIL	Boeing 767-33AER	611/28147	ex G-OITL	Arturo Ferraria	

*Leased from Ansett Worldwide Group (AWAS)   ^Stored GSO

EI-DBK	Boeing 777-243ER	455/32783		Ostuni	Lsd fr GECAS
EI-DBL	Boeing 777-243ER	459/32781		Sestriere	Lsd fr GECAS
EI-DBM	Boeing 777-243ER	463/32782		Argentario	Lsd fr GECAS
EI-DDH	Boeing 777-243ER	32784		on order	Lsd fr GECAS
I-DISA	Boeing 777-243ER	413/32855		Taormina	
I-DISB	Boeing 777-243ER	426/32859		Porto Rotundo	
I-DISD	Boeing 777-243ER	439/32860		Cortina d'Amprezzo	
I-DISE	Boeing 777-243ER	421/32856		Portofino	
I-DISO	Boeing 777-243ER	424/32857	ex N5014K	Positano	
I-DISU	Boeing 777-243ER	425/32858		Madonna de Campiglio	

I-DUPA	McDonnell-Douglas MD-11C	468/48426	ex N9020Z	Gioacchino Rossini
I-DUPB	McDonnell-Douglas MD-11C	534/48431		Pietro Mascagni
I-DUPC	McDonnell-Douglas MD-11	565/48581		Vincente Bellini
I-DUPD	McDonnell-Douglas MD-11	567/48630		Gaetano Donizetti
I-DUPE	McDonnell-Douglas MD-11C	471/48427	ex N9020Z	Giuseppe Verdi
I-DUPI	McDonnell-Douglas MD-11C	474/48428		Giacomo PuccinI
I-DUPO	McDonnell-Douglas MD-11C	500/48429		Nicolo Paccanini
I-DUPU	McDonnell-Douglas MD-11C	508/48430		Antonio Vivaldi

I-DACM	McDonnell-Douglas MD-82	1755/49971	La Spezia
I-DACN	McDonnell-Douglas MD-82	1757/49972	Rieti
I-DACP	McDonnell-Douglas MD-82	1762/49973	Padova
I-DACQ	McDonnell-Douglas MD-82	1774/49974	Taranto
I-DACR	McDonnell-Douglas MD-82	1775/49975	Carrara
I-DACS	McDonnell-Douglas MD-82	1806/53053	Maratea
I-DACT	McDonnell-Douglas MD-82	1856/53054	Valtellina
I-DACU	McDonnell-Douglas MD-82	1857/53055	Brindisi
I-DACV	McDonnell-Douglas MD-82	1880/53056	Riccione
I-DACW	McDonnell-Douglas MD-82	1894/53057	Vieste
I-DACX	McDonnell-Douglas MD-82	1944/53060	Piacenza
I-DACY	McDonnell-Douglas MD-82	1942/53059	Novara
I-DACZ	McDonnell-Douglas MD-82	1927/53058	Castelfidardo
I-DAND	McDonnell-Douglas MD-82	1957/53061	Bolzano
I-DANF	McDonnell-Douglas MD-82	1960/53062	Sassari
I-DANG	McDonnell-Douglas MD-82	1972/53176	Benevento
I-DANH	McDonnell-Douglas MD-82	1973/53177	Massina
I-DANL	McDonnell-Douglas MD-82	1994/53178	Cosenza
I-DANM	McDonnell-Douglas MD-82	1997/53179	Vicenza
I-DANP	McDonnell-Douglas MD-82	2002/53180	Fabriano
I-DANQ	McDonnell-Douglas MD-82	2005/53181	Lecce
I-DANR	McDonnell-Douglas MD-82	2007/53203	Matera
I-DANU	McDonnell-Douglas MD-82	2009/53204	Trapani
I-DANV	McDonnell-Douglas MD-82	2028/53205	Forte del Marmi
I-DANW	McDonnell-Douglas MD-82	2034/53206	Siena
I-DATA	McDonnell-Douglas MD-82	2048/53216	Gubbio
I-DATB	McDonnell-Douglas MD-82	2079/53221	Bergamo
I-DATC	McDonnell-Douglas MD-82	2080/53222	Foggia
I-DATD	McDonnell-Douglas MD-82	2081/53223	Savona
I-DATE	McDonnell-Douglas MD-82	2053/53217	Grosseto
I-DATF	McDonnell-Douglas MD-82	2084/53224	Vittoria Veneto

I-DATG	McDonnell-Douglas MD-82	2086/53225		Arezzo
I-DATH	McDonnell-Douglas MD-82	2087/53226		Pescara
I-DATI	McDonnell-Douglas MD-82	2060/53218		Siracausa
I-DATJ	McDonnell-Douglas MD-82	2103/53227		Lunigiana
I-DATK	McDonnell-Douglas MD-82	2104/53228		Ravenna
I-DATL	McDonnell-Douglas MD-82	2105/53229		Alghero
I-DATM	McDonnell-Douglas MD-82	2106/53230		Cividale del Friuli
I-DATN	McDonnell-Douglas MD-82	2107/53231		Sondrio
I-DATP	McDonnell-Douglas MD-82	2108/53232		Latina
I-DATQ	McDonnell-Douglas MD-82	2110/53233		Modena
I-DATR	McDonnell-Douglas MD-82	2111/53234		Livorno
I-DATS	McDonnell-Douglas MD-82	2113/53235	ex N9021J	Foligno
I-DATU	McDonnell-Douglas MD-82	2073/53220		Verona
I-DAVA	McDonnell-Douglas MD-82	1253/49215		Cunero
I-DAVB	McDonnell-Douglas MD-82	1262/49216		Ferrara
I-DAVC	McDonnell-Douglas MD-82	1268/49217		Lucca
I-DAVD	McDonnell-Douglas MD-82	1274/49218	ex N6203D	Mantova
I-DAVF	McDonnell-Douglas MD-82	1310/49219		Oristano
I-DAVG	McDonnell-Douglas MD-82	1319/49220		Pesara
I-DAVH	McDonnell-Douglas MD-82	1330/49221		Salerno
I-DAVI	McDonnell-Douglas MD-82	1334/49430		Assisi
I-DAVJ	McDonnell-Douglas MD-82	1377/49431		Parma
I-DAVK	McDonnell-Douglas MD-82	1378/49432		Pompei
I-DAVL	McDonnell-Douglas MD-82	1428/49433		Reggio Calabria
I-DAVM	McDonnell-Douglas MD-82	1446/49434		Caserta
I-DAVP	McDonnell-Douglas MD-82	1544/49549		Gorizia
I-DAVR	McDonnell-Douglas MD-82	1584/49550		Piza
I-DAVS	McDonnell-Douglas MD-82	1586/49551		Catania
I-DAVT	McDonnell-Douglas MD-82	1597/49552		Cormo
I-DAVU	McDonnell-Douglas MD-82	1600/49794		Udine
I-DAVV	McDonnell-Douglas MD-82	1639/49795		Pavia
I-DAVW	McDonnell-Douglas MD-82	1713/49796		Camerino
I-DAVX	McDonnell-Douglas MD-82	1719/49969		Asti
I-DAVZ	McDonnell-Douglas MD-82	1737/49970		Brescia
I-DAWA	McDonnell-Douglas MD-82	1126/49192	ex N19B	Roma
I-DAWB	McDonnell-Douglas MD-82	1138/49197		Cagliari
I-DAWC	McDonnell-Douglas MD-82	1142/49198		Campobasso
I-DAWD	McDonnell-Douglas MD-82	1143/49199		Catanzaro
I-DAWE	McDonnell-Douglas MD-82	1127/49193	ex N13627	Milano
I-DAWF	McDonnell-Douglas MD-82	1147/49200		Firenze
I-DAWG	McDonnell-Douglas MD-82	1148/49201		L'Aquila
I-DAWH	McDonnell-Douglas MD-82	1170/49202		Palermo
I-DAWI	McDonnell-Douglas MD-82	1130/49194		Ancona
I-DAWJ	McDonnell-Douglas MD-82	1174/49203		Genova
I-DAWL	McDonnell-Douglas MD-82	1179/49204		Perugia
I-DAWM	McDonnell-Douglas MD-82	1184/49205		Potenza
I-DAWO	McDonnell-Douglas MD-82	1136/49195		Bari
I-DAWP	McDonnell-Douglas MD-82	1188/49206		Torino
I-DAWQ	McDonnell-Douglas MD-82	1189/49207		Trieste
I-DAWR	McDonnell-Douglas MD-82	1190/49208		Venezia
I-DAWS	McDonnell-Douglas MD-82	1191/49209		Aosta
I-DAWT	McDonnell-Douglas MD-82	1192/49210		Napoli
I-DAWU	McDonnell-Douglas MD-82	1137/49196		Bologna
I-DAWV	McDonnell-Douglas MD-82	1202/49211		Trento
I-DAWW	McDonnell-Douglas MD-82	1233/49212		Riace
I-DAWY	McDonnell-Douglas MD-82	1243/49213		Agrigento
I-DAWZ	McDonnell-Douglas MD-82	1245/49214		Avellino

Five McDonnell-Douglas MD-82s to be transferred to Eurofly
All McDonnell-Douglas MD-11s to be phased out of service and replaced by 767-300s and 777s
Owns 45% of Eurofly while Alitalia Express is a wholly owned subsidiary. Member of SkyTeam alliance but may join
new Air France-KLM group in 2005

ALITALIA EXPRESS

Cee-Cee Express (XM/SMX)   **Rome-Fiumicino (FCO)**

EI-CLB	Aerospatiale/Alenia ATR 72-212	423	ex F-WWEB	Lago di Bracciano	Lsd fr NBB Milan
EI-CLC	Aerospatiale/Alenia ATR 72-212	428	ex F-WWEF	Fiume Simeto	Lsd fr NBB Naples
EI-CLD	Aerospatiale/Alenia ATR 72-212	432	ex F-WWEL	Fiume Piave	Lsd fr NBB Rome
EI-CMJ	Aerospatiale/Alenia ATR 72-212	467	ex F-WWLU	Fiume Volturno	Lsd fr NBB Fregene
I-ATLR	Aerospatiale/Alenia ATR 72-212A	701	ex F-WWEA	Fiume Tevere	
I-ATMC	Aerospatiale/Alenia ATR 72-212A	588	ex F-WWED	Fiume Arno	
I-ATPA	Aerospatiale/Alenia ATR 72-212A	626	ex F-WWLC	Lago Trasimeno	Lsd fr Lsg Roma
I-ATPM	Aerospatiale/Alenia ATR 72-212A	705	ex F-WWED	Fiume Po	
I-ATSL	Aerospatiale/Alenia ATR 72-212A	592	ex F-WWEM	Lago di Garda	Lsd fr Lsg Roma
I-ATSM	Aerospatiale/Alenia ATR 72-212A	702	ex F-WWEX	Lago di Nemi	
I-NOWA	Aerospatiale/Alenia ATR 42-300	051	ex F-WWEF	Fiume Po	
I-NOWT	Aerospatiale/Alenia ATR 42-300	054	ex F-WWEI	Fiume Tevere	
I-EXMA	Embraer EMB.145LR	145250	ex PT-SIN	Giosué Carducci	
I-EXMB	Embraer EMB.145LR	145330	ex PT-SMW	Salvatore Quasidomo	

I-EXMC	Embraer EMB.145LR	145436	ex PT-SUH	Emilio Gino Segre	
I-EXMD	Embraer EMB.145LR	145445	ex PT-SUQ	Eugenio Montale	
I-EXME	Embraer EMB.145LR	145282	ex PT-SJY	Guglialmo Marconi	
I-EXMF	Embraer EMB.145LR	145641	ex PT-SED	Giulio Natta	
I-EXMG	Embraer EMB.145LR	145652	ex PT-SEM	Daniel Bovet	
I-EXMH	Embraer EMB.145LR	145665	ex PT-SEZ	Camillo Golgi	
I-EXMI	Embraer EMB.145LR	145286	ex PT-SKD	Grazia Deledda	
I-EXML	Embraer EMB.145LR	145709	ex PT-S	Ernesto Teodoro Monetta	
I-EXMM	Embraer EMB.145LR	145738	ex PT-SHS	Anna Magnani	
I-EXMN	Embraer EMB.145LR	145750	ex PT-SJJ	Vittorio de Sica	
I-EXMO	Embraer EMB.145LR	145299	ex PT-SKQ	Luigi Pirandello	
I-EXMU	Embraer EMB.145LR	145316	ex PT-SMH	Enrico Fermi	
I-EMCX	Embraer 170-100ST	170-0008	ex PT-	Via Aurelia	on order
I-EMMX	Embraer 170-100ST	170-0011	ex PT-	Via Emilia	on order
I-EMRX	Embraer 170-100ST	170-0010	ex PT-	Via Cassia	on order
I-EMSX	Embraer 170-100ST	170-0009	ex PT-	Via Appia	on order
I-	Embraer 170-100ST		ex PT-	Via Salaria	on order
I-	Embraer 170-100ST		ex PT-	Via Flaminia	on order

Wholly owned by Alitalia; operates feeder services in full colours and using AZ flight numbers

ALPI EAGLES

Alpi Eagles (E8/ELG) (IATA 789)   *Venice (VCE)*

I-ALPK	Fokker 100	11244	ex F-WQHE	Sant Antonio	Lsd fr San Paolo Lsg
I-ALPL*	Fokker 100	11250	ex F-WQHG	San Marco	Lsd fr San Paolo Lsg
I-ALPQ	Fokker 100	11256	ex F-WQFP	San Lorenzo	Lsd fr San Paolo Lsg
I-ALPS	Fokker 100	11254	ex F-WQHK	San Zeno	Lsd fr San Paolo Lsg
I-ALPW	Fokker 100	11255	ex PH-FYB	Sant Agusta Jolly Motors c/s	
I-ALPX	Fokker 100	11251	ex F-WQFL	San Efisio	Lsd fr Ithifly
I-ALPZ	Fokker 100	11252	ex F-WQBP	San Pietro	Lsd fr Ithifly
I-ELGF	Fokker 100	11253	ex PH-FYA	Jolly Motors c/s	

*'Casino' de Venezia' titles
Some services are operated by Dornier 328-300s operated by Gandalf Airlines

AZZURRA AIR

Azzurra Air (ZS/AZI) (IATA 864)   *Bergamo (BGY)*

EI-CNI*	Avro RJ-85	E2299	ex G-6-299	Lombardia	
EI-CNJ*	Avro RJ-85	E2300	ex G-6-300	Piemonte	
EI-CNK*	Avro RJ-85	E2306	ex G-6-306	Lazio	
EI-COQ*	Avro RJ-70	E1254	ex 9H-ACM	Sardegna	
EI-CPJ*	Avro RJ-70	E1258	ex 9H-ACN	Puglia	
EI-CPK*	Avro RJ-70	E1260	ex 9H-ACO	Calabria	
EI-CPL*	Avro RJ-70	E1267	ex 9H-ACP	Veneto	

*Leased from Peregrine Aviation Leasing; all stored EXT following loss of Alitalia feeder contract

EI-DBC	Airbus Industrie A320-214	1787	ex SE-RCB	Manchester	Lsd fr GATX
EI-DBD	Airbus Industrie A320-214	1975	ex F-WWBI	Paris	Lsd fr GATX

From 15 January 2004 the two Irish registered examples were operated by Air Malta on behalf of AzzurraAir leaving the airline with no equipment; both ferried to MLA 16 January 2004 so current status is uncertain
Owned by Seven Group

BLUE

Milan-Linate (MIL)

PH-RAH	Beech 1900D	UE-31	ex (OY-GEP)		Lsd fr ROS

BLUE LINE did not commence operations

BLUE PANORAMA AIRLINES

Blue Panorama (BV/BPA) (IATA 004)   *Rome-Fiumicino (FCO)*

D-AHLU	Boeing 737-4K5	2677/27831			Lsd fr HLF; sublsd to AAW
EI-CUA	Boeing 737-4K5	1854/24901	ex D-AHLR		Lsd fr Gustav Lsg
EI-CUD	Boeing 737-4Q8	2564/26298	ex TC-JEI		Lsd fr ILFC
EI-CUN	Boeing 737-4K5	2281/27074	ex D-AHLS	Juventus colours	Lsd fr Gustav Lsg
UR-GAL	Boeing 737-341	1637/24275	ex PP-VOD		Lsd fr AUI
EI-CXO	Boeing 767-3G5ER	612/28111	ex (I-BPAB)		Lsd fr ILFC
EI-CZH	Boeing 767-3G5ER	720/29435	ex (I-BPAD)		Lsd fr ILFC
F-GLOV	Boeing 767-304ER	610/28039	ex G-OBYA		Lsd fr Itochu

BRIXIA AIRWAYS believed to have ceased operations

221

CITYFLY

City Fly (CII) | Rome-Urbe (ROM)

I-DEPE	Britten-Norman BN-2B-26 Islander	2253	ex G-BTLY
I-LACO	Britten-Norman BN-2A-6 Islander	17	ex G-AWBY
I-NEGL	Cessna 421A	421A0138	ex OO-EDB

CLUBAIR SIXGO

(6P/ISG) | Brescia (VBS)

EI-DBY	British Aerospace 146 Srs.200	E2012	ex G-DEFK	Michael	Lsd fr IMP Group
EI-DBZL	British Aerospace 146 Srs.200	E2014	ex G-DEFL	Scarlet	Lsd fr IMP Group
G-CCJP	British Aerospace 146 Srs.200	E2066	ex D-ALOA		
I-SIXA	Fokker F.27 Friendship 500F	10637	ex G-JEAF		Lsd fr Locafit

DOLPHIN AIR EXPRESS

Parma (PMF)

| I-DZPO | CASA C.212DD | 387 | ex F-ZVMR |

Current status uncertain

EASY ISLANDS

Cagliari (CAG)

LN-FAJ	British Aerospace Jetstream 31	621	ex G-BTXL	Bokn	Lsd fr CST
LN-FAM	British Aerospace Jetstream 31	740	ex (N2247R)	Feoy	Lsd fr CST
LN-FAV	British Aerospace Jetstream 31	606	ex OY-CLB	Bomlo	Lsd fr CST

Also operated services with Fokker 50 leased from Gee Bee Air

ELIDOLOMITI

Elidolomiti (EDO) | Belluno-Heliport

I-AGKK	Agusta A109K2	10021		EMS; Falco	
I-FLAG	Aerospatiale AS.350B2 Ecureuil	2621	ex F-GPFE		Lsd fr Locafit
I-REMR	Agusta A109E Power	11133		EMS	
I-REMV	Agusta A109E Power	11119		EMS	

ELIFLY

Elifly (EBS) | Esine-Heliport

| F-OIOL | Bell 414HP | 33160 | ex N4380K | Lsd fr TFC Textron |
| I-SARB | Bell 412SP | 33078 | | |

ELIFRIULA

Elifriula (EFG) | Trieste (TRS)

I-HAVE	Aerospatiale AS.350B3 Ecureuil	3205	
I-HOLD	Aerospatiale AS.350B3 Ecureuil	3566	
I-HOOK	Aerospatiale AS.350B3 Ecureuil	3090	
I-HORT	Aerospatiale AS.350B Ecureuil	3699	
I-HPLC	Aerospatiale AS.350B Ecureuil	3702	
I-HIFI	Eurocopter EC-135T1	0085	EMS
I-HSAR	Agusta A.109E	11125	
I-ORAO	Aerospatiale AS.355N Twin Squirrel	5583	

ELILARIO ITALIA

Lario (ELH) | Colico/Bergamo-Orio al Serio

I-AGSF	Agusta-Bell 412	25542		
I-AGUI	Agusta-Bell 412	25507	ex Fv11337	
I-CGCL	Agusta-Bell 412SP	25600		
I-MAGM	Agusta-Bell 412SP	25602	ex Fv11338	Lsd fr Elicaffaro
I-NUBJ	Agusta-Bell 412EP	25913		Lsd fr Palladio
I-	Agusta-Bell 412EP		on order	
I-ESUE	Agusta A.109E Power	11124		
I-FASH	Agusta A.109E Power	11153		
I-FLAK	Agusta A.109E Power	11076		
I-GEMI	Agusta A.109E	11095		
I-ISBE	Agusta A.109E Power	11222		
I-MUNA	Agusta A.109E	11052		

I-PCLE	Agusta A.109A	7164			

I-PCLE					
D-HBHG	MBB BK117B-2	7164			Lsd fr Eurocopter
D-HECD	MBB BK117C-1	7500		EMS	Lsd fr Eurocopter
D-HIMT	MBB BK117B-2	7203			Lsd fr Eurocopter
D-HSML	MBB BK117C-1	7514	ex N40027	EMS	Lsd fr Eurocopter
D-HSTP	MBB BK117C-1	7541			Lsd fr Eurocopter
I-AICO	MBB BK117C-1	7542	ex D-HZBV		Lsd fr Sanpaolu Lsg
I-AVJF	MBB BK117C-1	7525	ex D-HMBI		Lsd fr Palladio
I-BKBS	MBB BK117C-1	7504	ex D-HOTZ	EMS	Lsd fr San Paolo Lsg
I-DENI	MBB BK117C-1	7539			
I-HVEN	MBB BK117C-1	7526	ex D-HVEN	EMS	Lsd fr Italease
I-MESO	MBB BK117C-1	7532	ex D-HMB.		
I-HMED	Aerospatiale EC.135T1	0082	ex D-HBYI	EMS	Lsd fr Intesa Lsg
N158AC	Sikorsky S-64F Skycrane	64081	ex HL9260	Firefighter	Lsd fr Erickson
N159AC	Sikorsky S-64F Skycrane	64084	ex 69-18476	Firefighter	Lsd fr Erickson
N217AC	Sikorsky S-64F Skycrane	64066	ex N542SB	Firefighter	Lsd fr Erickson
N229AC	Sikorsky S-64F Skycrane	64018	ex N4099Y	Firefighter	Lsd fr Erickson

EUROFLY

Siriofly (GJ/EEZ)   **Milan-Malpensa (MXP)**

I-EEZC	Airbus Industrie A320-214	1852	ex F-WWIT		Lsd fr GATX Capital
I-EEZD	Airbus Industrie A320-214	1920	ex F-WWDJ		Lsd fr GATX Capital
I-EEZE	Airbus Industrie A320-214	1937	ex F-WWIO		Lsd fr GATX Capital
I-EEZF	Airbus Industrie A320-214	1983	ex F-WWDM		Lsd fr GECAS
I-EEZG	Airbus Industrie A320-214	2001	ex F-WWBB		Lsd fr GECAS
I-DATO	McDonnell-Douglas MD-82	2062/53219			
I-EEZA	Airbus Industrie A330-223	358	ex EI-CXF		Lsd fr ILFC
I-EEZB	Airbus Industrie A330-223	364	ex EI-CXG		Lsd fr ILFC

Operate for Alitalia in full colours   45% owned by Alitalia but share for sale
To receive five McDonnell-Douglas MD-82s from Alitalia

FREEAIR ITALY ceased operations

GANDALF AIRLINES

Gandalf (G7/GNF)   **Bergamo (BGY)**

D-BGAB	Dornier 328-300	3134	ex D-BDXP	Lsd fr Unicredito
D-BGAE	Dornier 328-300	3146	ex D-BDXC	
D-BGAG	Dornier 328-300	3133	ex D-BDXO	Lsd fr Unicredito
D-BGAL	Dornier 328-300	3131	ex D-BDXN	Lsd fr Unicredito
D-BGAQ	Dornier 328-300	3130	ex D-BDXM	Lsd fr Unicredito
D-BGAR	Dornier 328-300	3152	ex D-BDXO	Lsd fr Unicredito
D-BGAS	Dornier 328-300	3139	ex D-BDXC	Lsd fr Unicredito

Operates Dornier 328-300s on behalf of Alpi Eagles

D-CGAP	Dornier 328-110	3107	ex D-CDXD	Lsd fr Dornier

To move operating base to Brescia and relaunch as a low-cost airline using Boeing 737-500s; however cut most of its routes in 4Q03

HELI-ITALIA

Helitalia (HIT)   **Florence (FLR)**

I-HBFI	Agusta A.109E Power	11048			Lsd fr GECAS
I-HBHA	Agusta A.109K2	10023	ex I-ECAM	EMS	
I-HBHB	Agusta A.109K2	10025		EMS	
I-HBHC	MBB BK117B-1	7251	ex D-HITZ	EMS	Lsd fr Eligestione
I-HBMC	MBB BK117C-1	7528	ex D-HBMC	EMS	Lsd fr Elisoccorso
I-HBMS	MBB BK117C-1	7531	ex D-HMBB		Lsd fr Leasing Roma
I-MAFP	Agusta A.109E Power	11121			

Helitalia also operate Agusta A109s for Government of Greece

ICARO

Icarfly (ICA)   **Forli (FRL)**

I-VICY	Swearingen SA.227DC Metro 23	DC-849B	ex N451LA	Lsd fr Leasing Roma

ITALY FIRST

Riviera (IF/IFS)   **Rimini (RMI)**

I-RIML	Aerospatiale/Alenia ATR 42-300	206	ex G-BYHB	Leonardo
I-RIMS	Aerospatiale/Alenia ATR 42-300	190	ex G-BYHA	Lorenzo

LAUDA AIR ITALY

Lauda Italy (L4/LDI) (IATA 372)   Milan-Malpensa (MXP)

OE-LAT	Boeing 767-31AER	393/25273	ex PH-MCK	Enzo Ferrari	Lsd fr LDA
OE-LAW	Boeing 767-3Z9ER	448/26417		Imagination	Lsd fr LDA
I-	Airbus Industrie A330-243	597	ex F-WWKQ	on order	Lsd fr ILFC

Scheduled services operated as Livingston

LIVINGSTON

Lauda Italy (NG/LVG) (IATA 372)   Milan-Malpensa (MXP)

I-LIVA	Airbus Industrie A321-231	1950	ex D-AVXE		Lsd fr SALE
I-LIVB	Airbus Industrie A321-231	1970	ex D-AVZK	Jacaranda	Lsd fr SALE
I-LIVM	Airbus Industrie A330-243	551	ex F-WWKE		Lsd fr ILFC
I-	Airbus Industrie A330-243	627	ex F-WW	on order 04	Lsd fr ILFC
I-LLAG	Boeing 767-330ER	377/25137	ex N691LF		Lsd fr ILFC

New name for scheduled services of Lauda Air Italy; commenced operations 10 May 2003

MERIDIANA

Merair (IG/ISS) (IATA 191)   Olbia (OLB)

EI-CIW	McDonnell-Douglas MD-83	1628/49785	ex HL7271	Lsd fr GECAS
EI-CKM	McDonnell-Douglas MD-83	1655/49792	ex TC-INC	Lsd fr GECAS
EI-CRE	McDonnell-Douglas MD-83	1601/49854	ex D-ALLL	Lsd fr AAR Ireland
EI-CRH	McDonnell-Douglas MD-83	1773/49935	ex HB-IKM	Lsd fr GECAS
EI-CRJ	McDonnell-Douglas MD-83	1738/53013	ex D-ALLP	Lsd fr CA Aviation
EI-CRW	McDonnell-Douglas MD-83	1915/49951	ex HB-IKN	Lsd fr GECAS
I-SMEB	McDonnell-Douglas MD-82	1908/53064	ex B-28001	
I-SMEC	McDonnell-Douglas MD-83	1836/49808	ex N183NA	Lsd fr ILFC
I-SMED	McDonnell-Douglas MD-83	2068/53182	ex N875RA	Lsd fr AWAS
I-SMEL	McDonnell-Douglas MD-82	1151/49247	ex HB-IKK	
I-SMEM	McDonnell-Douglas MD-82	1152/49248	ex HB-IKL	
I-SMEP	McDonnell-Douglas MD-82	1618/49740		
I-SMER	McDonnell-Douglas MD-82	1766/49901	ex N6202S	
I-SMES	McDonnell-Douglas MD-82	1948/49902		
I-SMET	McDonnell-Douglas MD-82	1362/49531		
I-SMEV	McDonnell-Douglas MD-82	1493/49669		
I-SMEZ	McDonnell-Douglas MD-82	1949/49903	ex PH-SEZ	

Plans to replace the McDonnell_Douglas MD-82s with 17 Airbus Industrie A320s but timescale uncertain

I-FLRE	British Aerospace 146 Srs.200	E2210	ex G-BVMP	Lsd fr JL Starship
I-FLRI	British Aerospace 146 Srs.200	E2220	ex G-BVMT	Lsd fr JL Airrose
I-FLRO	British Aerospace 146 Srs.200	E2227	ex G-BVMS	Lsd fr JL Mayflower
I-FLRU	British Aerospace 146 Srs.200	E2204	ex I-FLRA	

MINERVA AIRLINES

Air Minerva (N4/MTC)   Trieste (TRS)

D-CPRP	Dornier 328-110	3066	ex D-CDXL	
D-CPRS	Dornier 328-110	3046	ex D-CDXM	
D-CPRT	Dornier 328-110	3042	ex D-CDXI	Riviera di Rimini colours
D-CPRU	Dornier 328-110	3091	ex D-CDXN	
D-CPRV	Dornier 328-110	3093	ex D-CDXD	
D-CPRW	Dornier 328-110	3097	ex D-CDXV	
D-CPRX	Dornier 328-110	3101	ex D-CDXR	
D-CPRY	Dornier 328-110	3106	ex D-CDXC	

All leased from Millennium Leasing
Operates as Alitalia Express in full colours and using AZ flight numbers. Ceased operations 26 October 2003 but
planned to restart 09 November 2003. Majority of aircraft stored at Innsbruck so status is uncertain

MINILINER

Miniliner (MNL)   Bergamo (BGY)

I-MLQT	Fokker F.27 Friendship 400	10295	ex HB-ITQ	Lsd fr FAT; op for UPS
I-MLRT	Fokker F.27 Friendship 500	10377	ex F-BPUE	
I-MLTT	Fokker F.27 Friendship 500	10378	ex F-BPUF	
I-MLUT	Fokker F.27 Friendship 500	10369	ex F-BPUA	
I-MLVT	Fokker F.27 Friendship 500	10373	ex F-BPUC	all white
I-MLXT	Fokker F.27 Friendship 500	10374	ex F-BPUD	

Status of above fleet uncertain as all Farnair F.27 Friendships to be retired in 2003
Part of Farnair Europe

MISTRAL AIR

Airmerci (MSA)   Rome-Ciampino (CIA)

| I-MSAA | British Aerospace 146 Srs.200QT | E2109 | ex I-TPGS | Op for TNT |
| I-TNTC | British Aerospace 146 Srs.200QT | E2078 | ex G-5-078 | Op for TNT |

NEOS

(NO/NOS)   Milan-Malpensa (MXP)

I-NEOS	Boeing 737-86N	1078/32733	Citta di Milano	Lsd fr GECAS
I-NEOT	Boeing 737-86N	1144/33004	Citta di Torino	Lsd fr GECAS
I-NEOU	Boeing 737-86N	1263/29887	Citta di Verona	Lsd fr GECAS
I-NEOX	Boeing 737-86N	33677	on order Apr04	Lsd fr GECAS

Owned by Pressuag, operated in World of TUI colours, sister company of Britannia, Corsair and Hapag-Lloyd. Due to leave TUI Group in 2004

PANAIR ceased airliner services and reverted to bizjet operations

SOREM – SOCIETA RICHERCHE ESPERIENZE METEOROLOGICHE

Rome-Ciampano/Urbe (CIA/ROM)

I-DPCD	Canadair CL-215-6B11	2003	ex C-FTUA
I-DPCE	Canadair CL-215-6B11	2004	ex C-FTUS
I-DPCO	Canadair CL-215-6B11	2009	ex C-FVRA
I-DPCP	Canadair CL-215-6B11	2020	ex C-FYCY
I-DPCQ	Canadair CL-215-6B11	2021	ex C-FYDA
I-DPCT	Canadair CL-215-6B1	2029	ex C-FZYS
I-DPCU	Canadair CL-215-6B11	2030	ex C-GALV
I-DPCV	Canadair CL-215-6B11	2035	ex C-GCXG
I-DPCW	Canadair CL-215-6B11	2036	ex C-GDHW
I-DPCX	Canadair CL-215-6B11	2045	ex C-GFPX
I-DPCY	Canadair CL-215-6B11	2047	ex C-GFUS
I-DPCZ	Canadair CL-215-6B11	2048	ex C-GGCW
I-	Canadair CL-215-1A10	1004	ex C-FYWQ
I-	Canadair CL-215-1A10	1012	ex C-FTXE

All Tankers, leased from and operated for Protezione Civile

TAI-TRANSPORTI AEREI ITALIANI

Spada (9X/ACO)   Pescara (PSR)
Previously listed as Air Columbia

| I-BSTI | Swearingen SA.227AC Metro III | AC-470 | ex N5818T | |
| I-BSTS | Swearingen SA.227AC Metro III | AC-603 | ex N3117S | Lsd fr Locafit |

Due to commence services 14 July 2003

VOLARE AIRLINES

Revola (VA/VLE) (IATA 263)   Verona (VRN)

EI-CTD	Airbus Industrie A320-211	0085	ex F-GJVZ		Lsd fr GECAS
EI-CUQ*	Airbus Industrie A320-214	1259	ex F-WWIZ		Lsd fr Flightlease
F-GJVU*	Airbus Industrie A320-211	0436	ex G-BXAT		Lsd fr GATX
F-GJVX	Airbus Industrie A320-211	0420	ex (PH-GCX)		Lsd fr GATX
F-OHFR*	Airbus Industrie A320-212	0189	ex G-UKLL		Lsd fr GATX
F-OHFT	Airbus Industrie A320-212	0343	ex G-UKLK		Lsd fr GATX
F-OHFU	Airbus Industrie A320-212	0190	ex PH-DVR		Lsd fr GATX
I-PEKE	Airbus Industrie A320-214	1308	ex F-WWBS		Lsd fr Flightlease
I-PEKF	Airbus Industrie A320-214	1322	ex F-WWDS		Lsd fr Flightlease
I-PEKG	Airbus Industrie A320-214	1132	ex I-PEKA		Lsd fr Flightlease
I-PEKH	Airbus Industrie A320-214	1162	ex I-PEKZ		Lsd fr Flightlease
I-PEKI	Airbus Industrie A320-214	1179	ex I-PEKC		Lsd fr Flightlease
I-PEKL	Airbus Industrie A320-214	1244	ex I-PEKD		Lsd fr Flightlease
I-PEKN	Airbus Industrie A321-211	1607	ex D-AVZN		Lsd fr SALE
I-PEKQ*	Airbus Industrie A320-214	1757	ex F-WWIR		Lsd fr ILFC
I-PEKR*	Airbus Industrie A320-212	0446	ex N446AN		Lsd fr ILFC
I-PEKS*	Airbus Industrie A320-232	1856	ex F-WQSK		Lsd fr SALE
I-PEKT*	Airbus Industrie A320-232	1909	ex F-WQSL		Lsd fr SALE
I-VELA*	Airbus Industrie A320-214	1125	ex I-VLEO	impounded	Lsd fr Flightlease
	Airbus Industrie A320-214	2123	ex F-WWIE	on order	

*Operates with Volareweb.com titles
Volareweb.com is low cost subsidiary which commenced operations in April 2003 using Airbus A320s leased from the parent.

VOLAREWEB.COM

Verona (VRN)

EI-CUQ	Airbus Industrie A320-214	1259	ex F-WWIZ
F-GJVU	Airbus Industrie A320-211	0436	ex G-BXAT
F-OHFR	Airbus Industrie A320-212	0189	ex G-UKLL
I-PEKQ	Airbus Industrie A320-214	1757	ex F-WWIR
I-PEKR	Airbus Industrie A320-212	0446	ex N446AN
I-PEKS	Airbus Industrie A320-232	1856	ex F-WQSK
I-PEKT	Airbus Industrie A320-232	1909	ex F-WQSL
I-VLEA	Airbus Industrie A320-214	1125	ex I-VLEO

Low cost subsidiary of Volare Airlines; all aircraft leased from parent. First service April 2003

WINDJET

(IV/JET)

Catania

I-LINB	Airbus Industrie A320-231	0363	ex G-SUEE	Lsd fr Oasis
I-LINF	Airbus Industrie A320-231	0393	ex N393NY	Lsd fr ILFC
I-LING	Airbus Industrie A320-231	0414	ex 5B-DBJ	Lsd fr ILFC
I-LINH	Airbus Industrie A320-231	0163	ex G-RDVE	Lsd fr Beowolf Lsg
I-LINP	Airbus Industrie A320		ex	on order

First service 26 July 03

JA - JAPAN

AIR DO / HOKKAIDO INTERNATIONAL AIRLINES

Air Do (HD/ADO)

Sapporo-New Chitose (CTS)

JA01HD	Boeing 767-33AER	689/28159	ex OO-CTQ	Lsd fr Hotaru Holding
JA98AD	Boeing 767-33AER	687/27476	ex N767AN	Lsd fr Nikuokusu
JA8251	Boeing 767-281	143/23431	ex N6009F	Sublsd fr ANA

Filed for creditor protection 25 June 2002; operations continue and entered code-share with All Nippon

AIR DOLPHIN

Okinawa-Naha (OKA)

JA3428	Cessna P206C Super Skylane	P206-0517	ex N1610C
JA5306	Britten-Norman BN-2B-26 Islander	2236	ex G-BSPO
JA5320	Britten-Norman BN-2B-20 Islander	2269	ex G-BUBM

AIR JAPAN

Air Japan (NQ/AJX)

Osaka-Itami/Kansi (ITM/KIX)

JA603A	Boeing 767-381	877/32972	ex N6046P	Lsd fr ANA
JA604A	Boeing 767-381	881/32973		Lsd fr ANA
JA605A	Boeing 767-381	882/32974		Lsd fr ANA
JA606A	Boeing 767-381	883/32975		Lsd fr ANA
JA607A	Boeing 767-381	884/32976		Lsd fr ANA
JA608A	Boeing 767-381	886/32977		Lsd fr ANA
JA609A	Boeing 767-381	888/32978		Lsd fr ANA
JA610A	Boeing 767-381	895/32979		Lsd fr ANA
JA611A	Boeing 767-381	914/32980		Lsd fr ANA
JA8323	Boeing 767-381ER	463/25654		Lsd fr ANA
JA8356	Boeing 767-381ER	379/25136		Lsd fr ANA
JA8362	Boeing 767-381ER	285/24632		Lsd fr ANA
JA8664	Boeing 767-381ER	556/27339		Lsd fr ANA
JA8970	Boeing 767-381ER	645/25619		Lsd fr ANA
JA8971	Boeing 767-381ER	651/27492		Lsd fr ANA

Wholly owned by All Nippon Airways and operates services from Osaka to Seoul; aircraft carry titles of all members of ANA Group (Air Japan, Air Nippon and ANA) and can be operated by any airline

AIR NIPPON

ANK Air (EL/ANK)

Tokyo-Haneda (HND)

JA300K	Boeing 737-54K	2872/27434		Lsd fr ANA
JA301K	Boeing 737-54K	2875/27435		Lsd fr ANA
JA302K	Boeing 737-54K	3002/28990	ex N1787B	Lsd fr ANA
JA303K	Boeing 737-54K	3017/28991		Lsd fr Sky Dolphin
JA304K	Boeing 737-54K	3030/28992		Lsd fr MNE Lease
JA305K	Boeing 737-54K	3075/28993	ex N1781B	Lsd fr Star Dolphin
JA306K	Boeing 737-54K	3109/29794		Lsd fr ANA
JA307K	Boeing 737-54K	3116/29795	ex N60436	Lsd fr ANA
JA351K	Boeing 737-5Y0	2240/25189	ex N189NK	Lsd fr Ageha Holding
JA352K	Boeing 737-5Y0	2534/26097	ex N97NK	Lsd fr Ageha Holding
JA353K	Boeing 737-5Y0	2552/26104	ex N104NK	Lsd fr Ageha Holding

JA354K	Boeing 737-5Y0	2553/26105	ex N105NK	Lsd fr Ageha Holding
JA355K	Boeing 737-5L9	2823/28129	ex N8129L	Lsd fr IS Air Investment
JA356K	Boeing 737-5L9	2784/28083	ex N8083N	Lsd fr GL Natural Lsg
JA357K	Boeing 737-5L9	2828/28131	ex N88131	Lsd fr GL Omega Lsg
JA358K	Boeing 737-5L9	2825/28130	ex N8130J	Lsd fr GL Pearl Lsg
JA359K	Boeing 737-5L9	2817/28128	ex N8128R	Lsd fr GL Juneau Lsg
JA391K^	Boeing 737-4Y0	1805/24545	ex N545NK	Lsd fr Ageha Holding
JA392K^	Boeing 737-46M	2847/28550	ex N8550F	Lsd fr GL Quality Lsg
JA8195	Boeing 737-54K	2815/27433		Lsd fr Air Dolphin
JA8196	Boeing 737-54K	2824/27966		Lsd fr ANA
JA8404	Boeing 737-54K	2708/27381	ex N35108	Lsd fr ANA
JA8419	Boeing 737-54K	2723/27430		Lsd fr Mitsui Lse Jigyo
JA8500	Boeing 737-54K	2751/27431		Lsd fr Mitsui Sumitomo Gin Lse
JA8504	Boeing 737-54K	2783/27432		Lsd fr ANA
JA8595	Boeing 737-54K	2850/28461		Lsd fr ANA
JA8596	Boeing 737-54K	2853/28462		Lsd fr JL Hawk Lse

^Flying Dolphins colour scheme. Being repainted in full ANA colours and small titles

JA8797	de Havilland DHC-6 Twin Otter 300	285	ex 9V-BCL
JA8799	de Havilland DHC-6 Twin Otter 300	420	ex C-GOWO

Member of ANA Group; Air Nippon Network is a wholly owned subsidiary

AIR NIPPON NETWORK

(EH/AKX)   *Sapporo-Okadama (OKD)*

JA801K	de Havilland DHC-8Q-314	565	ex C-GDFT	Tsubaki c/s	
JA802K	de Havilland DHC-8Q-314	577	ex C-FDHD	Himawari c/s	Lsd fr YT Aero
JA803K	de Havilland DHC-8Q-314	583	ex C-FDHW	Suzuran c/s	Lsd fr NL Scorpio Lsg
JA804K	de Havilland DHC-8Q-314	591	ex C-GFUM	Cosmos c/s	Lsd fr NL Orion
JA805K	de Havilland DHC-8Q-314	592	ex C-GFYI	Hamanasu c/s	Lsd fr NL Phoenix
JA841A	de Havilland DHC-8Q-402	4080	ex C-GDLK		Lsd fr NL Centaurus
JA842A	de Havilland DHC-8Q-402	4082	ex C-GFOD		Lsd fr Maple Lease
JA843A	de Havilland DHC-8Q-402	4084	ex C-GFQL	not confirmed	
JA	de Havilland DHC-8Q-402		ex C-	on order 04	

Wholly owned subsidiary of Air Nippon; operates in ANA colours and A-net titles

AIR SHENPIX

                                                    Sapporo-Okadama (OKD)

JA22PT	Swearingen SA.226TC Metro	TC-211EEEE	ex N200PT
JA8866	Dornier 228-200	8124	ex D-IAHD

ALL NIPPON AIRWAYS

All Nippon (NH/ANA) (IATA 205)   *Tokyo-Haneda (HND)*

JA201A	Airbus Industrie A320-211	1973	ex F-WWBQ	Lsd fr FG Rose Lsg
JA202A	Airbus Industrie A320-211	2054	ex F-WWIS	Lsd fr FG Sky Lsg
JA203A	Airbus Industrie A320-211	2061	ex F-WWDC	Lsd fr Tombo Capital
JA8300	Airbus Industrie A320-211	0549	ex F-WWIT	Lsd fr Kogin Lse
JA8304	Airbus Industrie A320-211	0531	ex F-WWDY	Lsd fr Fuyo Sogo Lse
JA8313	Airbus Industrie A320-211	0534	ex F-WWBC	Lsd fr Global Lse
JA8381	Airbus Industrie A320-211	0138	ex F-WWDE	EXPO 2005 titles
JA8382	Airbus Industrie A320-211	0139	ex F-WWDF	
JA8383	Airbus Industrie A320-211	0148	ex F-WWDO	
JA8384	Airbus Industrie A320-211	0151	ex F-WWDR	
JA8385	Airbus Industrie A320-211	0167	ex F-WWIE	
JA8386	Airbus Industrie A320-211	0170	ex F-WWII	
JA8387	Airbus Industrie A320-211	0196	ex F-WWDE	Lsd to ANK
JA8388	Airbus Industrie A320-211	0212	ex F-WWIG	
JA8389	Airbus Industrie A320-211	0219	ex F-WWDZ	Lsd to ANK
JA8390	Airbus Industrie A320-211	0245	ex F-WWDE	Lsd to ANK
JA8391	Airbus Industrie A320-211	0300	ex F-WWDD	Lsd to ANK
JA8392	Airbus Industrie A320-211	0328	ex F-WWDR	
JA8393	Airbus Industrie A320-211	0365	ex F-WWBZ	Lsd to ANK
JA8394	Airbus Industrie A320-211	0383	ex F-WWBF	
JA8395	Airbus Industrie A320-211	0413	ex F-WWIM	
JA8396	Airbus Industrie A320-211	0482	ex F-WWIO	
JA8400	Airbus Industrie A320-211	0554	ex F-WWIG	Lsd fr Mach Lsg Intl
JA8609	Airbus Industrie A320-211	0501	ex F-WWIN	Lsd fr Global Lse
JA8654	Airbus Industrie A320-211	0507	ex F-WWBT	Lsd fr Mitsui Sumitomo Gin Lse
JA8946	Airbus Industrie A320-211	0669	ex F-WWBD	Lsd fr FI Honey Lsg
JA8947	Airbus Industrie A320-211	0685	ex F-WWDR	Lsd fr Marmaid Lse
JA8997	Airbus Industrie A320-211	0658	ex F-WWIU	Lsd fr FI Lemon Lsg
JA101A	Airbus Industrie A321-131	0802	ex D-AVZO	Lsd fr Tombo Capital
JA102A	Airbus Industrie A321-131	0811	ex D-AVZR	Lsd fr Spider Lsg
JA103A	Airbus Industrie A321-131	0963	ex D-AVZW	Lsd fr Tateha A/c Holding
JA104A	Airbus Industrie A321-131	1008	ex D-AVZK	Lsd fr Tateha A/c Holding

JA105A	Airbus Industrie A321-131	1042	ex D-AVZA	Lsd fr Tateha A/c Holding
JA106A	Airbus Industrie A321-131	1204	ex D-AVZQ	Lsd fr Tateha A/c Holding
JA107A	Airbus Industrie A321-131	1227	ex D-AVZT	Lsd fr Tateha A/c Holding

To be removed from service by the end of March 2004 and replaced by Boeing 767-300ERs

JA300K	Boeing 737-54K	2872/27434		Lsd to ANK
JA301K	Boeing 737-54K	2875/27435		Lsd to ANK
JA302K	Boeing 737-54K	3002/28990	ex N1787B	Lsd to ANK
JA306K	Boeing 737-54K	3109/29794		Lsd to ANK
JA307K	Boeing 737-54K	3116/29795	ex N60436	Lsd to ANK
JA8196	Boeing 737-54K	2824/27966		Lsd to ANK
JA8404	Boeing 737-54K	2708/27381	ex N35108	Lsd to ANK
JA8504	Boeing 737-54K	2783/27432		Lsd to ANK
JA8595	Boeing 737-54K	2850/28461		Lsd to ANK

45 Boeing 737-781s are on order for delivery from 2005

JA401A	Boeing 747-481D	1133/28282		
JA402A	Boeing 747-481D	1142/28283		
JA403A	Boeing 747-481	1199/29262		Lsd fr Falcan Lsg
JA404A	Boeing 747-481	1204/29263		
JA405A	Boeing 747-481	1250/30322		
JA8094	Boeing 747-481	805/24801		
JA8095	Boeing 747-481	812/24833		
JA8096	Boeing 747-481	832/24920		
JA8097	Boeing 747-481	863/25135		
JA8098	Boeing 747-481	870/25207		
JA8099	Boeing 747-481D	891/25292		
JA8147	Boeing 747SR-81	477/22293	ex N5973L	
JA8148	Boeing 747SR-81	481/22294		
JA8152	Boeing 747SR-81	511/22594		
JA8153	Boeing 747SR-81	516/22595		
JA8157	Boeing 747SR-81	544/22710		
JA8159	Boeing 747SR-81	572/22712		
JA8174	Boeing 747-281B	648/23501	ex N6055X	
JA8175	Boeing 747-281B	649/23502	ex N60659	
JA8192	Boeing 747-2D3B(SF)	514/22579	ex G-CITB	Lsd to NCA
JA8955	Boeing 747-481D	914/25639		
JA8956	Boeing 747-481D	920/25640		
JA8957	Boeing 747-481D	927/25642		
JA8958	Boeing 747-481	928/25641	ex N6009F	Lsd fr Afuko
JA8959	Boeing 747-481D	952/25646		
JA8960	Boeing 747-481D	972/25643		Lsd fr Global Lse
JA8961	Boeing 747-481D	975/25644		Lsd fr Mitsui Lse Jigyo
JA8962*	Boeing 747-481	979/25645		Lsd fr UFJ Business Finance
JA8963	Boeing 747-481D	991/25647	ex N6055X	Lsd fr Mitsui Lse Jigyo
JA8964*	Boeing 747-481D	996/27163	ex N5573S	Lsd fr Mitsui Sumitomo Gin Lse
JA8965	Boeing 747-481D	1060/27436		Lsd fr Mitsui Sumitomo Gin Lse
JA8966	Boeing 747-481D	1066/27442		Lsd fr Fuyo Sogo Lse

*Painted in Pocket Monsters colour scheme

JA601A	Boeing 767-381	669/27943		Lsd fr FI Strewberry Lse
JA601F	Boeing 767-381ERF	885/33404		Jt ops with NCA; lsd fr Baxter Avn
JA602A	Boeing 767-381	684/27944		Lsd fr F1 Strawberry Lsg
JA603A*	Boeing 767-381	877/32972	ex N6046P	
JA604A*	Boeing 767-381	881/32973		Lsd fr SMBCL Chameleon
JA605A*	Boeing 767-381	882/32974		Lsd fr Lavender
JA606A*	Boeing 767-381	883/32975		Lsd fr FK Soraru
JA607A*	Boeing 767-381	884/32976		
JA608A*	Boeing 767-381	886/32977		
JA609A*	Boeing 767-381	888/32978		Lsd fr SMBC Kefeusu
JA610A*	Boeing 767-381	895/32979		Lsd fr Tulip Blossom Lsg
JA611A*	Boeing 767-381	914/32980		Lsd fr Orix Star Cluster
JA612A	Boeing 767-381	920/33506		
JA613A	Boeing 767-381	33507		on order 04
JA614A	Boeing 767-381			on order 04
JA8240	Boeing 767-281	110/23142	ex N6038E	Lsd fr Marubeni Aerospace
JA8251	Boeing 767-281	143/23431	ex N6009F	Lsd fr KC Six; sublsd to ADO
JA8255	Boeing 767-281	171/23434	ex N6046P	Lsd to SKY
JA8256	Boeing 767-381	176/23756	ex N6005C	
JA8257	Boeing 767-381	177/23757	ex N6038E	
JA8258	Boeing 767-381	179/23758	ex N6055X	
JA8259	Boeing 767-381	185/23759	ex N6038E	
JA8271	Boeing 767-381	199/24002	ex N60668	
JA8272	Boeing 767-381	212/24003	ex N6038E	
JA8273	Boeing 767-381	218/24004	ex N6055X	
JA8274	Boeing 767-381	222/24005	ex N6046P	
JA8275	Boeing 767-381	223/24006	ex N6018N	
JA8285	Boeing 767-381	245/24350	ex N1789B	
JA8286	Boeing 767-381ER	269/24400		
JA8287	Boeing 767-381	271/24351		
JA8288	Boeing 767-381	276/24415		
JA8289	Boeing 767-381	280/24416		

JA8290	Boeing 767-381	290/24417	Star Alliance c/s
JA8291	Boeing 767-381	295/24755	
JA8322	Boeing 767-381	458/25618	Lsd fr Global Lse
JA8323*	Boeing 767-381ER	463/25654	Lsd fr Fuyo Sogo Lse
JA8324	Boeing 767-381	465/25655	Lsd fr Mitsui Sumitomo Gin Lse
JA8342	Boeing 767-381	573/27445	Lsd fr Kogin Lse
JA8356*	Boeing 767-381ER	379/25136	
JA8357	Boeing 767-381	401/25293	ANA Woody Jet c/s
JA8358	Boeing 767-381ER	432/25616	Yokosa Japan
JA8359	Boeing 767-381	439/25617	
JA8360	Boeing 767-381	352/25055	
JA8362*	Boeing 767-381ER	285/24632	
JA8363	Boeing 767-381	300/24756	
JA8368	Boeing 767-381	336/24880	
JA8567	Boeing 767-381	510/25656	Lsd fr Mach Lsg Intl
JA8568	Boeing 767-381	515/25657	Lsd fr Diamond Lse
JA8569	Boeing 767-381	516/27050	Lsd fr Fuyo Sogo Lse
JA8578	Boeing 767-381	519/25658	Lsd fr Global Lse
JA8579	Boeing 767-381	520/25659	Lsd fr Kogin Lse
JA8664*	Boeing 767-381ER	556/27339	Lsd fr ORIX Aircraft
JA8669	Boeing 767-381	567/27444	Lsd fr Mitsui Sumitomo Gin Lease
JA8670	Boeing 767-381	539/25660	
JA8674	Boeing 767-381	543/25661	Lsd fr Fuyo Sogo Lse
JA8677	Boeing 767-381	551/25662	Lsd fr Kogin Lse
JA8970*	Boeing 767-381ER	645/25619	Lsd fr Fl Orchard Lse
JA8971*	Boeing 767-381ER	651/27942	

Four more Boeing 767-300ERs are on order for delivery in 2005 (3) and 2006 (1)
*Leased to Air Japan and operated with joint titles along with Air Nippon

JA701A	Boeing 777-281	77/27938		Lsd fr Alpine Rose
JA702A	Boeing 777-281	75/27033		
JA703A	Boeing 777-281	81/27034	ex N50217	Lsd fr SBL Aqua Marine
JA704A	Boeing 777-281	131/27035		Lsd fr Phoenix Lsg
JA705A	Boeing 777-281	137/29029		Lsd fr Dia Zepha
JA706A	Boeing 777-281	141/27036		Lsd fr FO Paradise Lsg
JA707A	Boeing 777-281ER	247/27037		
JA708A	Boeing 777-281ER	278/28277		Lsd fr Arcadia Lsg
JA709A	Boeing 777-281ER	286/28278		
JA710A	Boeing 777-281ER	302/28279		
JA731A	Boeing 777-381ER	28281		on order Nov04
JA	Boeing 777-381ER			on order Dec04
JA751A	Boeing 777-381	142/28272	ex N5017Q	Lsd fr CL Orion
JA752A	Boeing 777-381	160/28274		Lsd fr FO Serenade Lsg
JA753A	Boeing 777-381	132/28273		Lsd fr ORIX Sky Blue
JA754A	Boeing 777-381	172/27939		Lsd fr ORIX Sky Lark
JA755A	Boeing 777-381	104/28275	ex N5017Q	
JA756A	Boeing 777-381	440/27039		
JA757A	Boeing 777-381	442/27040		
JA758A	Boeing 777-381			on order 04
JA759A	Boeing 777-381			on order 04
JA8197	Boeing 777-281	16/27027	ex N5016R	Lsd fr Global Lse
JA8198	Boeing 777-281	21/27028		Lsd fr Mitsui Sumitomo Gin Lse
JA8199	Boeing 777-281	29/27029		Lsd fr Global Lse
JA8967	Boeing 777-281	37/27030		
JA8968	Boeing 777-281	38/27031		Lsd fr Mach Lsg Intl
JA8969	Boeing 777-281	50/27032		Lsd fr Fl Kiwi Lsg

Four more Boeing 777-381ERs are on order for delivery 2005 (2), 2006 and 2007 plus five Boeing 777-281s for 2005-06
Member of Star Alliance; Air Japan and Air Nippon are members of ANA Group and are wholly owned subsidiaries
Services operated by Fair Inc as ANA Connection

AMAKUSA AIRLINES

Kumamoto (KMJ)

| JA81AM | de Havilland DHC-8Q-103 | 537 | ex C-FCSG |

FAIR LINK

Fair (FW/FRI)   *Sendai (SDJ)*

JA01RJ	Canadair CL-600-2B19	7052	ex OE-LRD	
JA02RJ	Canadair CL-600-2B19	7033	ex OE-LRB	
JA03RJ	Canadair CL-600-2B19	7624	ex C-GJZF	Lsd fr CL Regulus
JA04RJ	Canadair CL-600-2B19	7798	ex C-FMLF	

Fair Link is the trading name of The Fair Inc; operates feeder operations for ANA Connection

HARLEQUIN AIR

Harlequin (JH/HLQ)   *Fukuoka (FUK)*

Wholly owned by Japan Airlines System and operates flights with McDonnell-Douglas MD-81 leased from the parent

HOKKAIDO AIR SYSTEM

North Air (NTH)   *Sapporo-Chitose (CTS)*

JA01HC	SAAB SF.340B	432	ex SE-B32	
JA02HC	SAAB SF.340B	440	ex SE-B40	
JA03HC	SAAB SF.340B	458	ex SE-B58	Lsd fr MLD Commuter Lse

Partially owned by Japan Airlines System

IKI INTERNATIONAL AIRLINES

(IKK)   *Iki (IKI)*

| JA8835 | Dornier 228-200 | 8007 | ex D-IDID |

J-AIR

Nagasaki (NGS)

JA201J	Canadair CL-600-2B19	7452	ex C-FMND	Lsd fr CL Raibura
JA202J	Canadair CL-600-2B19	7484	ex C-FMLU	Lsd fr Majoka Avn
JA203J	Canadair CL-600-2B19	7626	ex C-FMNW	Lsd fr Pisces Flight Svs
JA204J	Canadair CL-600-2B19	7643	ex C-	Lsd fr Phoenix Avn
JA205J	Canadair CL-600-2B19	7767	ex C-FMLB	Lsd fr DIA Canary
JA206J	Canadair CL-600-2B19	7834	ex C-FMMT	Lsd fr NL Crux
JA207J	Canadair CL-600-2B19		ex C-	on order Mar04

Wholly owned by Japan Airlines System and operates commuter flights on behalf of JAL using JL flight numbers

JAL EXPRESS

Janex (JC/JEX)   *Tokyo-Haneda (HND)*

JA8991	Boeing 737-446	2718/27916		
JA8992	Boeing 737-446	2729/27917	ex N1792B	
JA8993	Boeing 737-446	2812/28087		Lsd fr Zonet Avn Financial Service
JA8994	Boeing 737-446	2907/28097		Lsd fr Zonet Avn Financial Service
JA8995	Boeing 737-446	2911/28831		Lsd fr Zonet Avn Financial Service
JA8996	Boeing 737-446	2953/28832		Lsd fr Zonet Avn Financial Service
JA8998	Boeing 737-446	3044/28994		
JA8999	Boeing 737-446	3111/29864		Lsd fr SBL Zeus

Wholly owned by Japan Airlines Systems

JAL WAYS

Jalways (JO/JAZ) (IATA 708)   *Tokyo-Narita (NRT)*

JA8150	Boeing 747-246B	496/22479	ex N1783B	Reso'cha c/s	Lsd to JAL
JA8186	Boeing 747-346	694/24018	ex N6018N		Lsd fr JAL
JA8187	Boeing 747-346	695/24019	ex N6038E	Reso'cha c/s	
JA8541	Douglas DC-10-40	308/47824	ex N10020		Lsd to JAL
JA8544	Douglas DC-10-40	340/47852		Reso'cha c/s	

Wholly owned by Japan Airlines System

JAPAN AIR COMMUTER

Commuter (3X/JAC)   *Amami (ASJ)*

JA841C	de Havilland DHC-8-402Q	4072	ex C-GEWI		Lsd fr NL Bago Lse
JA842C	de Havilland DHC-8-402Q	4073	ex C-GFCA		Lsd fr NL Cassiopea
JA843C	de Havilland DHC-8-402Q	4076	ex C-GFHZ		
JA844C	de Havilland DHC-8-402Q	4082	ex C-GFOD	on order	
JA845C	de Havilland DHC-8-402Q		ex C-	on order	
JA846C	de Havilland DHC-8-402Q		ex C-	on order	
JA8717	NAMC YS-11A-217	2092			Lsd fr JAS
JA8759	NAMC YS-11A-227	2152	ex JQ2152		Lsd fr JAS
JA8763	NAMC YS-11A-227	2135	ex JQ2135		Lsd fr JAS
JA8766	NAMC YS-11A-227	2142	ex JQ2142		Lsd fr JAS
JA8768	NAMC YS-11A-222	2147	ex PK-IYS		Lsd fr JAS
JA8771	NAMC YS-11A-227	2149			Lsd fr JAS
JA8777	NAMC YS-11A-227	2163			Lsd fr JAS
JA8781	NAMC YS-11A-217	2166			Lsd fr JAS
JA8788	NAMC YS-11A-217	2176			Lsd fr JAS
JA001C	SAAB SF.340B	419	ex SE-B19		
JA002C	SAAB SF.340B	459	ex SE-B59		Lsd fr MLD Commuter Lse
JA8594	SAAB SF.340B	399	ex SE-C99		
JA8642	SAAB SF.340B	365	ex SE-C65		Lsd fr Tajima Kuko Terminal
JA8649	SAAB SF.340B	368	ex SE-C68		Lsd fr Central Lease
JA8703	SAAB SF.340B	355	ex SE-C55		Lsd fr JL Wood Side Park Lse
JA8704	SAAB SF.340B	361	ex SE-C61		Lsd fr Mitsui Lse Jigyo

JA8886	SAAB SF.340B	281	ex SE-G81	Lsd fr Mitsui Lse Jigyo
JA8887	SAAB SF.340B	308	ex SE-C08	Lsd fr NTT Lease
JA8888	SAAB SF.340B	331	ex SE-C31	
JA8900	SAAB SF.340B	378	ex SE-C78	Lsd fr Kogin Lease

Owned by Japan Airlines System

JAPAN AIR LINES

Japanair (JL/JAL) (IATA 131)　　　　　　　　　　　　　　　　　　*Tokyo-Haneda/Narita (HND/NRT)*

JA8993	Boeing 737-446	2812/28087		Lsd fr Zonet Avn Finacial Service
JA8994	Boeing 737-446	2907/28097		Lsd fr Zonet Avn Finacial Service
JA8995	Boeing 737-446	2911/28831		Lsd fr Zonet Avn Finacial Service
JA8996	Boeing 737-446	2953/28832		Lsd fr Zonet Avn Finacial Service
JA8998	Boeing 737-446	3044/28994		
JA8999	Boeing 737-446	3111/29864		Lsd fr SBL Zeus

Operated by either Japan Air Lines or JAL Express

JA811J	Boeing 747-246F	571/22989	ex N211JL	JAL Cargo	Lsd fr JAL Capital
JA812J	Boeing 747-346	588/23067	ex N212JL		Lsd fr JAL Capital
JA813J	Boeing 747-346	589/23068	ex N213JL		Lsd fr JAL Capital
JA8071	Boeing 747-446	758/24423			
JA8072	Boeing 747-446	760/24424			
JA8073	Boeing 747-446	767/24425			
JA8074	Boeing 747-446	768/24426			
JA8075	Boeing 747-446	780/24427			
JA8076	Boeing 747-446	797/24777	ex N6046P		Lsd fr JAL Capital
JA8077	Boeing 747-446	798/24784			Lsd fr JAL Capital
JA8078	Boeing 747-446	821/24870	ex N60697		
JA8079	Boeing 747-446	824/24885	ex N6005C		Lsd fr JAL Capital
JA8080	Boeing 747-446	825/24886			Lsd fr JAL Capital
JA8081	Boeing 747-446	851/25064			
JA8082	Boeing 747-446	871/25212			
JA8083	Boeing 747-446D	844/25213	ex N60668		
JA8084	Boeing 747-446D	879/25214			
JA8085	Boeing 747-446	876/25260			
JA8086	Boeing 747-446	885/25308			
JA8087	Boeing 747-446	897/26346			Lsd fr NI Aircraft Lsg
JA8088	Boeing 747-446	902/26341			Lsd fr UFJ Business Finance
JA8089	Boeing 747-446	905/26342		Yokosa titles	Lsd fr NI Aircraft Lsg
JA8090	Boeing 747-446D	907/26347			Lsd fr NI Aircraft Lsg
JA8130	Boeing 747-246B	376/21679			Lsd fr Zonet Avn Finacial Service
JA8131	Boeing 747-246B	380/21680			Lsd fr Zonet Avn Finacial Service
JA8132	Boeing 747-246F	382/21681	ex N1782B	JAL Cargo	Lsd fr Stabilizer Lsg
JA8141	Boeing 747-246B	411/22065			Lsd fr Zonet Avn Finacial Service
JA8150	Boeing 747-246B	496/22479	ex N1783B	Reso'cha c/s	Lsd fr JAZ
JA8160	Boeing 747-221F	392/21744	ex N905PA	JAL Cargo	
JA8161	Boeing 747-246B(SF)	579/22990	ex N6046B	JAL Cargo	
JA8162	Boeing 747-246B	581/22991	ex N5573K		
JA8163	Boeing 747-346	599/23149	ex N5573B		
JA8164	Boeing 747-146B	601/23150	ex N1781B		
JA8165	Boeing 747-221F	384/21743	ex N904PA	JAL Cargo	
JA8166	Boeing 747-346	607/23151	ex N1786B		
JA8169	Boeing 747-246B(SF)	635/23389	ex N6018N	JAL Cargo	
JA8170	Boeing 747-346SR	636/23390	ex N6009F		
JA8171	Boeing 747-246F	654/23391	ex N6038E	JAL Cargo	Lsd fr New Matic Lsg
JA8173	Boeing 747-346	640/23482	ex N6009F		
JA8176	Boeing 747-346SR	655/23637	ex N60668		
JA8177	Boeing 747-346	658/23638	ex N6009F		
JA8178	Boeing 747-346	664/23639	ex N6009F		
JA8179	Boeing 747-346	668/23640	ex N6009F		
JA8180	Boeing 747-246F	684/23641		JAL Cargo	
JA8183	Boeing 747-346	692/23967	ex N6005C	Reso'cha c/s	
JA8184	Boeing 747-346	693/23968	ex N6055X	Reso'cha c/s	
JA8185	Boeing 747-346	691/23969	ex N6005C		Lsd to JAZ
JA8186	Boeing 747-346	694/24018	ex N6018N	Reso'cha c/s	Lsd to JAZ
JA8193	Boeing 747-212B(SF)	457/21940	ex 9V-SQO	JAL Cargo	Lsd fr JAL Capital
JA8901	Boeing 747-446	918/26343			
JA8902	Boeing 747-446	929/26344	ex N6018N		
JA8903	Boeing 747-446D	935/26345			Lsd fr UFJ Business Finance
JA8904	Boeing 747-446D	941/26348			
JA8905	Boeing 747-446D	948/26349			
JA8906	Boeing 747-446	961/26350			Lsd fr Charlotte A/c
JA8907	Boeing 747-446D	963/26351			Lsd fr JAL Capital
JA8908	Boeing 747-446D	978/26352			Lsd fr JAL Capital
JA8909	Boeing 747-446	980/26353			
JA8910	Boeing 747-446	1024/26355			
JA8911	Boeing 747-446	1026/26356			
JA8912	Boeing 747-446	1031/27099			Lsd fr Illinois Aircraft Lsg
JA8913	Boeing 747-446	1153/26359			
JA8914	Boeing 747-446	1166/26360			
JA8915	Boeing 747-446	1188/26361			'JAL's 100th 747' titles

JA8916	Boeing 747-446	1202/26362			Lsd fr Uranus Lsg
JA8917	Boeing 747-446	1208/29899	ex N6009F		Lsd fr Twin Crane Lsg
JA8918	Boeing 747-446	1234/27650			Lsd fr Twin Crane Lsg
JA8919	Boeing 747-446	1236/27100			Lsd fr Twin Crane Lsg
JA8920	Boeing 747-446	1253/27648			
JA8921	Boeing 747-446	1262/27645	ex N747BA		
JA8922	Boeing 747-446	1280/27646	ex N747BJ		
JA	Boeing 747-446F			on order	
JA	Boeing 747-446F			on order	
JA8937	Boeing 747-246F	494/22477	ex N740SJ	JAL Cargo	Lsd fr JAL Capital
JA601J	Boeing 767-346ER	875/32886	ex N60697		Lsd fr Emerald Lsg
JA602J	Boeing 767-346ER	879/32887			Lsd fr DIA Peach
JA603J	Boeing 767-346ER	880/32888			Lsd fr DIA Lavender
JA604J	Boeing 767-346ER	905/33493			Lsd fr TRM Aircraft Lsg
JA605J	Boeing 767-346ER	911/33494			Lsd fr TRM Aircraft Lsg
JA606J	Boeing 767-346ER	915/33495			Lsd fr TRM Aircraft Lsg
JA607J	Boeing 767-346ER	917/33496			Lsd fr TRM Aircraft Lsg
JA608J	Boeing 767-346ER	919/33497			
JA609J	Boeing 767-346ER	33845			
JA8231	Boeing 767-246	117/23212	ex N6046P		
JA8232	Boeing 767-246	118/23213	ex N6038E		
JA8233	Boeing 767-246	122/23214	ex N6038E		
JA8234	Boeing 767-346	148/23216	ex N6005C		Lsd fr Zonet Avn Financial Service
JA8235	Boeing 767-346	150/23217	ex N60659		
JA8236	Boeing 767-346	132/23215	ex N767S		
JA8253*	Boeing 767-346	174/23645	ex N6038E		Lsd fr Zonet Avn Financial Service
JA8264	Boeing 767-346	186/23965	ex N6018N		
JA8265	Boeing 767-346	192/23961	ex N6005C		Lsd fr Zonet Avn Financial Service
JA8267	Boeing 767-346	193/23962	ex N6038E		Lsd fr Zonet Avn Financial Service
JA8268	Boeing 767-346	224/23963	ex N6055X		Lsd fr Zonet Avn Financial Service
JA8269	Boeing 767-346	225/23964	ex N6046P		Lsd fr Zonet Avn Financial Service
JA8299	Boeing 767-346	277/24498	ex N6055X		
JA8364	Boeing 767-346	327/24782			Lsd fr JAL Capital
JA8365	Boeing 767-346	329/24783			Lsd fr JAL Capital
JA8397	Boeing 767-346	547/27311			
JA8398	Boeing 767-346	548/27312			Lsd fr Mitsui Sumitomo Gin Lease
JA8399	Boeing 767-346	554/27313			Lsd fr JAL Capital
JA8975	Boeing 767-346	581/27658			
JA8980	Boeing 767-346	673/28837			
JA8986	Boeing 767-346	680/28838			
JA8988	Boeing 767-346	772/29863			Lsd fr Twin Crane Lsg

*EXPO 2005 Aichi Japan logo; Eight more Boeing 767-346ERs are on order for delivery up to 2006

JA701J	Boeing 777-246ER	410/32889	ex (JA8989)		Lsd fr DIA Marguerite
JA702J	Boeing 777-246ER	417/32890	ex (JA8990)		Lsd fr TLCDG
JA703J	Boeing 777-246ER	427/32891	ex N5023Q		Lsd fr DIA Sea Gulf
JA704J	Boeing 777-246ER	435/32892	ex N50281		Lsd fr FK Rapid Lsg
JA705J	Boeing 777-246ER	446/32893			Lsd fr DIA Gurausu
JA706J	Boeing 777-246ER	464/33394			Lsd fr TLC Laurel
JA707J	Boeing 777-246ER	32894		on order Apr04	
JA708J	Boeing 777-246ER	32895		on order Jun04	
JA709J	Boeing 777-246ER	32896		on order Sep04	
JA731J	Boeing 777-346ER	423/32430	ex N5017V	on order Jun04	
JA732J	Boeing 777-346ER	429/32431	ex N5016R	on order Jun04	
JA733J	Boeing 777-346ER	32432		on order Jun05	
JA751J	Boeing 777-346	458/27654			Lsd fr Saffron
JA752J	Boeing 777-346	460/27655			Lsd fr Dia Olive
JA771J	Boeing 777-246ER	437/27656	ex (JA711J)		Lsd fr SMLC Pixies
JA8941	Boeing 777-346	152/28393		Regulus	Lsd fr DIA Eminence
JA8942	Boeing 777-346	158/28394	ex N50284	Spica	Lsd fr FO Harvest Lsg
JA8943	Boeing 777-346	196/28395		Acturus	Lsd fr DIA Crane
JA8944	Boeing 777-346	212/28396		Antares	Lsd fr Pluto Lsg
JA8945	Boeing 777-346	238/28397			Lsd fr Saturn Lsg
JA8981	Boeing 777-246	23/27364	ex (JA8195)	Sirius	
JA8982	Boeing 777-246	26/27365	ex (JA8196)	Vega	
JA8983	Boeing 777-246	39/27366		Altair	
JA8984	Boeing 777-246	68/27651		Betelgeuse	Lsd fr Skywalk Lsg
JA8985	Boeing 777-246	72/27652		Procyon	

Two more Boeing 777-246ERs are on order for delivery in 2005 [JA710J-JA711J] plus eight more 777-346ER's for delivery from 2005 to 2008 [including JA734J to JA740J]

JA8531	Douglas DC-10-40	216/46923	ex N8703Q		Lsd fr JAA
JA8532	Douglas DC-10-40	220/46660	ex N8705Q		Lsd fr JAA
JA8534	Douglas DC-10-40	206/46913	ex N54652		Lsd fr JAA
JA8535	Douglas DC-10-40	230/46662	ex N19B		
JA8537	Douglas DC-10-40	265/46967			Lsd fr JAA
JA8538	Douglas DC-10-40	274/46974			
JA8541	Douglas DC-10-40	308/47824	ex N10020		Lsd fr JAZ
JA8542	Douglas DC-10-40	310/47825			
JA8543	Douglas DC-10-40	313/47826			
JA8545	Douglas DC-10-40	343/47853			

All sold to 40-Ten Inc (Omega Air) for future delivery and conversion to freighters

JA8582^	McDonnell-Douglas MD-11	559/48573	Tancho/Red Crowned Crane
JA8586+	McDonnell-Douglas MD-11	583/48577	Kounotori/White Stork
JA8587+*	McDonnell-Douglas MD-11	588/48578	Pryer's Woodpecker

+2-class configuration, ^3-class configuration   * Leased from Mitsui Sumitomo Gin lease
All sold to Boeing for freighter conversion for UPS; delivery due through 2004 although conversion programme delayed

Owns 90.5% of Japan Asia Airways, 51% of Japan TransOcean Air, 8.5% of Hawaiian Airlines and 5% of Air New Zealand while JAL Express and JAL Ways are wholly owned
Merged with Japan Air System on 2 October 2002 as Japan Airlines System as holding company; to create new subsidiaries Japan Airlines International, Japan Airlines Domestic and Japan Airlines Cargo in 2004

JAPAN AIR SYSTEM

Air System (JD/JAS) (IATA 234)   *Tokyo-Haneda (HND)*

JA011D	Airbus Industrie A300B4-622R	783	ex F-WWAA	
JA012D	Airbus Industrie A300B4-622R	797	ex F-WWAQ	Lsd fr NL Saturn Lse
JA014D	Airbus Industrie A300B4-622R	836	ex F-WWAF	Lsd fr Signet Lease
JA015D	Airbus Industrie A300B4-622R	837	ex F-WWAK	Lsd fr Darwitch Lease
JA016D	Airbus Industrie A300B4-622R	838	ex F-WWAL	Lsd fr SMBCL Cygnus
JA8237	Airbus Industrie A300C4-2C	256	ex F-WZMA	
JA8263	Airbus Industrie A300B4-2C	151	ex VH-TAB	
JA8369	Airbus Industrie A300B4-203	239	ex SU-GAA	
JA8375	Airbus Industrie A300B4-622R	602	ex F-WWAT	Lsd fr Mitsui Lse Jigyo
JA8376	Airbus Industrie A300B4-622R	617	ex F-WWAK	
JA8377	Airbus Industrie A300B4-622R	621	ex F-WWAA	
JA8464	Airbus Industrie A300B2K-3C	082	ex F-WZEQ	Lsd fr Air Hawk
JA8466	Airbus Industrie A300B2K-3C	090	ex F-WZEG	Lsd fr Air Hawk
JA8471	Airbus Industrie A300B2K-3C	160	ex F-WZMI	
JA8473	Airbus Industrie A300B2K-3C	176	ex F-WZMU	
JA8476	Airbus Industrie A300B2K-3C	209	ex F-WZMH	
JA8477	Airbus Industrie A300B2K-3C	244	ex F-WZMS	
JA8478	Airbus Industrie A300B2K-3C	253	ex F-WZMX	
JA8527	Airbus Industrie A300B4-622R	724	ex F-WWAQ	
JA8529	Airbus Industrie A300B4-622R	729	ex F-WWAM	Lsd fr JL Wood Side Park Lse
JA8558	Airbus Industrie A300B4-622R	637	ex F-WWAX	
JA8559	Airbus Industrie A300B4-622R	641	ex F-WWAM	
JA8560	Airbus Industrie A300B4-2C	178	ex F-BVGS	Lsd fr Dia Air System
JA8561	Airbus Industrie A300B4-622R	670	ex F-WWAD	
JA8562	Airbus Industrie A300B4-622R	679	ex F-WWAL	
JA8563	Airbus Industrie A300B4-622R	683	ex F-WWAJ	
JA8564	Airbus Industrie A300B4-622R	703	ex F-WWAO	Lsd fr JL Wood Sidepark Lse
JA8565	Airbus Industrie A300B4-622R	711	ex F-WWAE	Lsd fr Mitsui Sumitomo Gin Lse
JA8566	Airbus Industrie A300B4-622R	730	ex F-WWAV	
JA8573	Airbus Industrie A300B4-622R	737	ex F-WWAF	
JA8574	Airbus Industrie A300B4-622R	740	ex F-WWAG	
JA8657	Airbus Industrie A300B4-622R	753	ex F-WWAD	Lsd fr Kogin Lse
JA8659	Airbus Industrie A300B4-622R	770	ex F-WWAQ	Lsd fr Kogin Lse

JA007D	Boeing 777-289	134/27639		
JA008D	Boeing 777-289	146/27640		
JA009D	Boeing 777-289	159/27641	ex N5017V	Lsd fr Sony Finance Intl
JA010D	Boeing 777-289	213/27642		Lsd fr Sony Finance Intl
JA8977	Boeing 777-289	45/27636		Lsd fr Mitsui Sumitomo Gin Lse
JA8978	Boeing 777-289	79/27637		
JA8979	Boeing 777-289	107/27638		

JA8260	McDonnell-Douglas MD-81	1359/49461		
JA8261	McDonnell-Douglas MD-81	1477/49462		Lsd fr Orange Air One
JA8262	McDonnell-Douglas MD-81	1488/49463		Lsd fr Intec Lse
JA8278	McDonnell-Douglas MD-87	1476/49464		
JA8279	McDonnell-Douglas MD-87	1604/49465		
JA8280	McDonnell-Douglas MD-87	1727/49466		
JA8281	McDonnell-Douglas MD-87	1742/49467		
JA8294	McDonnell-Douglas MD-81	1598/49820		Lsd fr Air Sun
JA8295	McDonnell-Douglas MD-81	1615/49821		Lsd fr Air Eagle
JA8296	McDonnell-Douglas MD-81	1734/49907		
JA8297	McDonnell-Douglas MD-81	1749/49908		dbr 01 January 2004?
JA8370	McDonnell-Douglas MD-87	1881/53039	ex N5168X	Lsd fr Mitsui Lse Jigyo
JA8371	McDonnell-Douglas MD-87	1897/53040		Lsd fr Mitsui Lse Jigyo
JA8372	McDonnell-Douglas MD-87	1945/53041		
JA8373	McDonnell-Douglas MD-87	1969/53042	ex N90126	
JA8374	McDonnell-Douglas MD-81	1982/53043		
JA8496	McDonnell-Douglas MD-81	1194/49280		Lsd fr Shin Capital Egg
JA8497	McDonnell-Douglas MD-81	1200/49281		Lsd fr Air Sun
JA8498	McDonnell-Douglas MD-81	1282/49282	ex N6202S	
JA8499	McDonnell-Douglas MD-81	1299/49283		
JA8552	McDonnell-Douglas MD-81	2040/53297		
JA8553	McDonnell-Douglas MD-81	2045/53298		
JA8554	McDonnell-Douglas MD-81	2075/53299		Lsd fr JL Wood Side Park Lse
JA8555	McDonnell-Douglas MD-81	2076/53300		Lsd fr JL Wood Side Park Lse

JA8556	McDonnell-Douglas MD-81	2082/53301		Lsd fr Mitsui Lse Jigyo
JA8557	McDonnell-Douglas MD-81	2085/53302		Lsd fr Mitsui Sumitomo Gin Lse
JA001D	McDonnell-Douglas MD-90-30	2210/53555		
JA002D	McDonnell-Douglas MD-90-30	2207/53556		
JA003D	McDonnell-Douglas MD-90-30	2211/53557		Lsd fr Sony Finance Intl
JA004D	McDonnell-Douglas MD-90-30	2212/53558		Lsd fr Kogin Lse
JA005D	McDonnell-Douglas MD-90-30	2236/53559		
JA006D	McDonnell-Douglas MD-90-30	2245/53560		
JA8004	McDonnell-Douglas MD-90-30	2184/53359		
JA8020	McDonnell-Douglas MD-90-30	2190/53360		
JA8029	McDonnell-Douglas MD-90-30	2202/53361		Lsd fr Central Lse
JA8062	McDonnell-Douglas MD-90-30	2098/53352		
JA8063	McDonnell-Douglas MD-90-30	2120/53353		
JA8064	McDonnell-Douglas MD-90-30	2125/53354		
JA8065	McDonnell-Douglas MD-90-30	2131/53355		
JA8066	McDonnell-Douglas MD-90-30	2157/53356		
JA8069	McDonnell-Douglas MD-90-30	2164/53357		
JA8070	McDonnell-Douglas MD-90-30	2179/53358		
JA8717	NAMC YS-11A-217	2092		Lsd to JAC
JA8759	NAMC YS-11A-227	2152	ex JQ2152	Lsd to JAC
JA8763	NAMC YS-11A-227	2135	ex JQ2135	Lsd to JAC
JA8766	NAMC YS-11A-227	2142	ex JQ2142	Lsd to JAC
JA8768	NAMC YS-11A-222	2147	ex PK-IYS	Lsd to JAC
JA8771	NAMC YS-11A-227	2149		Lsd to JAC
JA8777	NAMC YS-11A-227	2163		Lsd to JAC
JA8781	NAMC YS-11A-217	2166		Lsd to JAC
JA8788	NAMC YS-11A-217	2176		Lsd to JAC

Owns Japan Air Commuter and 10% of Air Philippines
Merged with Japan Air Lines on 2 October 2002 as Japan Airlines System as new holding company; will create new subsidiaries Japan Airlines International, Japan Airlines Domestic and Japan Airlines Cargo. Aircraft are being repainted in new JAL colours

JAPAN ASIA AIRWAYS

Asia (EG/JAA) **Tokyo-Narita (NRT)**

JA8154	Boeing 747-246B	547/22745		Lsd fr Niaruko Avn
JA8155	Boeing 747-246B	548/22746		
JA8189	Boeing 747-346	716/24156	ex N6046P	
JA8266	Boeing 767-346	191/23966	ex N6018N	Yokoso Japan
JA8531	Douglas DC-10-40	216/46923	ex N8703Q	Lsd to JAL
JA8532	Douglas DC-10-40	220/46660	ex N8705Q	Lsd to JAL
JA8534	Douglas DC-10-40	206/46913	ex N54652	Lsd to JAL
JA8537	Douglas DC-10-40	255/46967		Lsd to JAL
JA8976	Boeing 767-346	667/27659		
JA8987	Boeing 767-346	668/28553		

90.5% owned by Japan Airlines System

JAPAN REGIONAL AIRLINES

Yamaguchi (GAJ)

| JA8229 | Cessna 208 Caravan I | 20800137 | ex N1570C |
| JA8890 | Cessna 208 Caravan I | 20800195 | ex N9776F |

JAPAN TRANSOCEAN AIR

JAI Ocean (NU/JTA) **Okinawa-Naha (OKA)**

JA8523	Boeing 737-4Q3	2618/26603		
JA8524	Boeing 737-4Q3	2684/26604		Lsd fr JAL Capital
JA8525	Boeing 737-4Q3	2752/26605		Lsd fr Zonet Avn Financial Service
JA8526	Boeing 737-4Q3	2898/26606		Lsd fr JAL Capital
JA8597	Boeing 737-4Q3	3043/27660		Lsd fr SA Southern Lsg
JA8930	Boeing 737-4K5	2394/27102	ex D-AHLM	Papas Island c/s Lsd fr TLC Begonia
JA8931	Boeing 737-429	2106/25247	ex N931NU	Lsd fr Hibuscus Lsg
JA8932	Boeing 737-429	2120/25248	ex N932NU	Lsd fr Churashima Lsg
JA8933	Boeing 737-429	2104/25226	ex N933NU	
JA8934	Boeing 737-4K5	2670/27830	ex N934NU	
JA8938	Boeing 737-4Q3	3085/29485		Lsd fr JAL Capital
JA8939	Boeing 737-4Q3	3088/29486	ex N1800B	Lsd fr SA Southern Wind Lse
JA8940	Boeing 737-4Q3	3122/29487		Lsd fr SKL Reberaito Lsg
JA8953	Boeing 737-4K5	1783/24129	ex D-AHLP	Lsd fr JAL Capital
JA8954	Boeing 737-4K5	1827/24130	ex D-AHLQ	Papas Island c/s Lsd fr Central Lse

51% owned by Japan Airlines System

LEQUOIS AIRLINES Although painted up in full colours, their aircraft was not delivered and operations did not commence

234

NAKANIHON AIRLINE SERVICE
(NV)   *Nagoya (NGO)*

JA01NV	Fokker 50	20257 ex PH-KXY	Lsd fr Meitetsu Property
JA8200	Fokker 50	20307 ex PH-JCN	Lsd fr Meitetsu Property
JA8875	Fokker 50	20196 ex PH-LMS	Lsd fr Meitetsu Property
JA8889	Fokker 50	20259 ex PH-EXX	Lsd fr Meitetsu Property

20% owned by All Nippon Airways and operates some feeder services for them

NIPPON CARGO AIRLINES
Nippon Cargo (KZ/NCA) (IATA 933)   *Tokyo-Narita (NRT)*

JA8158	Boeing 747SR-81(SF)	559/22711	
JA8167	Boeing 747-281F	604/23138 ex N6066Z	
JA8168	Boeing 747-281F	608/23139 ex N6046P	
JA8172	Boeing 747-281F	623/23350 ex N6018N	
JA8181	Boeing 747-281B(SF)	667/23698 ex N6055C	
JA8182	Boeing 747-281B(SF)	683/23813 ex N60659	
JA8188	Boeing 747-281F	689/23919 ex N6009F	
JA8190	Boeing 747-281B(SF)	750/24399	
JA8191	Boeing 747-281F	818/24576	
JA8192	Boeing 747-2D3B(SF)	514/22579 ex G-CITB	Lsd fr ANA
JA8194	Boeing 747-281F	886/25171	

Three Boeing 747-481Fs are on order for delivery in 2005 (2) and 2006 (1)

JA601F	Boeing 767-381ERF	33404	Jt ops with ANA; lsd fr Baxter Avn

13.2% owned by All Nippon Airways

ORANGE CARGO
(ORJ)   *Nagasaki (NGS)*

JA190A	Beech 1900C-1	UC-151 ex N151YV	Lsd fr Central Lease
JA190B	Beech 1900C-1	UC-106 ex N106YV	Lsd fr Central Lease
JA190C	Beech 1900C-1	UC-75 ex N75YV	Lsd fr Central Lease
JA190D	Beech 1900C-1	UC-134 ex N134YV	Lsd fr Central Lease

All freighters

ORIENTAL AIR BRIDGE
Oriental Bridge (NGK)   *Nagasaki (NGS)*

JA801B	de Havilland DHC-8Q-201	566 ex C-GDNG
JA802B	de Havilland DHC-8Q-201	579 ex C-FDHO
JA5316	Britten-Norman BN-2B-20 Islander	2240 ex G-BSPT
JA5318	Britten-Norman BN-2B-20 Islander	2267 ex G-BUBJ
JA5323	Britten-Norman BN-2B-20 Islander	2291 ex G-BVYD

RYUKYU AIR COMMUTER
Okinawa-Naha (OKA)

JA5281	Britten-Norman BN-2B-26 Islander	2154 ex N667J
JA5282	Britten-Norman BN-2B-26 Islander	2129 ex N655J
JA5324	Britten-Norman BN-2B-20 Islander	2297 ex G-BWNG
JA5325	Britten-Norman BN-2B-20 Islander	2298 ex G-BWYX
JA8935	de Havilland DHC-8Q-103B	593 ex C-GSAH
JA8972	de Havilland DHC-8Q-103	472 ex C-GDKL
JA8973	de Havilland DHC-8Q-103	501 ex C-GDLD
JA8974	de Havilland DHC-8Q-103B	540 ex C-FDHP

SHIN CHUO KOKU / NEW CENTRAL AVIATION
Tokyo-Chofu

JA31CA	Dornier 228-212	8242 ex D-CBDO	
JA32CA	Dornier 228-212	8243 ex D-CBDP	
JA5195	Britten-Norman BN-2A-20 Islander	302 ex G-AZUR	Lsd fr Intl A/c Lsg & Finance
JA5290	Britten-Norman BN-2B-20 Islander	2172 ex G-BKOI	
JA5305	Britten-Norman BN-2B-20 Islander	2239 ex G-BSPS	
JA5319	Britten-Norman BN-2B-20 Islander	2268 ex G-BUBK	Lsd fr ORIX Alpha

SKYMARK AIRLINES
Skymark (BC/SKY)   *Osaka-Itami (ITM)*

JA767A	Boeing 767-3Q8ER	714/27616	Yamato Shaken c/s Lsd fr Sky Aircraft
JA767B	Boeing 767-3Q8ER	722/27617	Lsd fr Sky Aircraft
JA767C	Boeing 767-3Q8ER	870/29390 ex N1018N	Lsd fr Sky Aeroplane
JA767D	Boeing 767-36NER	902/30847 ex N847SF	Lsd fr SC Air One
JA8255	Boeing 767-281	171/23434 ex N6046P	Lsd fr ANA

SKYNET ASIA AIRLINES
(6J/SNJ)   *Miyazaki (KMI)*

JA737A	Boeing 737-46Q	3033/29000	ex N56CD	Lsd fr Vinus Aircraft
JA737B	Boeing 737-46Q	3040/29001	ex N89CD	Lsd fr Vinus Aircraft
JA737C	Boeing 737-4H6	2426/27086	ex N270AZ	Lsd fr Coral Reef Avn
JA737D	Boeing 737-4H6	2435/27168	ex N271AZ	Lsd fr Coral Reef Avn

JU - MONGOLIA (State of Mongolia)

AERO MONGOLIA
(MNG)   *Ulan Bator (ULN)*

JU-8251	Fokker 50	20251	ex PH-WXH
JU-8258	Fokker 50	20258	ex PH-KXU

Commenced operations March 2003

CENTRAL MONGOLIAN AIRWAYS
(CEM)

JU-5444	Mil Mi-8T	20409	ex JU-1024
JU-5445	Mil Mi-8T	98103227	ex JU-1025
JU-5446	Mil Mi-8T	20411	ex JU-1026

HANGARD AIRLINES
Hangard (HGD)   *Ulan Bator (ULN)*

JU-7048	Antonov An-24B	07306307	ex MT-7048
JU-7050	Antonov An-24B		

MIAT – MONGOLIAN AIRLINES
Mongol Air (OM/MGL) (IATA 289)   *Ulan Bator (ULN)*

JU-1005	Antonov An-24RV	47309310	ex MT-1005		
JU-1006	Antonov An-24RV	47309807	ex MT-1006		
JU-1007	Antonov An-24RV	57310102	ex MT-10102		
JU-1009	Antonov An-24RV	57310104	ex MT-1009		
JU-1010	Antonov An-24RV	57310209	ex MT-1010		
JU-1011	Antonov An-24RV	57310301	ex MT-1011		
EI-CXV	Boeing 737-8CX	1166/32364			Lsd fr GATX JetPartners
JU-1014	Antonov An-26	14101	ex MT-1014		
JU-1024	Mil Mi-8T	20409	ex MT-1024		
JU-1025	Mil Mi-8T	20410	ex MT-1025		
JU-1026	Mil Mi-8T	20411	ex MT-1026		
JU-2030	LET L-410UVP	861801	ex OK-RDE		
F-OHPT	Airbus Industrie A310-304	526	ex (JU-1069)	Chinggis Khan	Lsd fr Airbus

JY - JORDAN (Hashemite Kingdom of Jordan)

AIR RUM
(RUM)   *Amman (AMM)*

5Y-RUM	Lockheed L-1011 Tristar 1	1200	ex XU-200	Op by SEK

Current status uncertain as aircraft reregistered in Sierra Leone

JORDANIAN AVIATION
Jordan Aviation (JAV)   *Amman (AMM)*

JY-JAB	Boeing 737-33A	1312/23630	ex N169AW	Lsd to Aqaba
JY-JAR	Airbus Industrie A320-211	0234	ex CS-TNC	
JY-JAV	Airbus Industrie A310-222	357	ex 3B-STK	Op for SUD

Also lease Boeing 737s from Air Malta or Travel Service as and when required

ROYAL JORDANIAN
Jordanian (RJ/RJA) (IATA 512)   *Amman (AMM)*

F-ODVF	Airbus Industrie A310-304F	445		Princess Raiyah
F-ODVG	Airbus Industrie A310-304F	490		Prince Faisal	Lsd fr Waha Lse
F-ODVH	Airbus Industrie A310-304	491		Prince Hamzeh	Lsd fr Waha Lse
F-ODVI	Airbus Industrie A310-304	531		Princess Haya
JY-AGK	Airbus Industrie A310-304	573	ex A6-EKN		Lsd fr GATX

JY-AGL	Airbus Industrie A310-304	661	ex CP-2307		Lsd fr ILFC
JY-AGP	Airbus Industrie A310-304	416	ex 5Y-BEL		
JY-AGU	Airbus Industrie A310-203	295	ex 7T-VJE		Lsd to LAA as 5A-AGU
JY-AGV	Airbus Industrie A310-203	306	ex 7T-VJF		Lsd to LAA
F-OGYC	Airbus Industrie A320-212	0569	ex F-WWDG		
F-OHGB	Airbus Industrie A320-212	0289	ex A4O-MC	40th anniversary c/s	Lsd fr GATX
F-OHGC	Airbus Industrie A320-211	0407	ex CS-TNF		Lsd fr IBIS
JY-AYA	Airbus Industrie A320-212	0087	ex F-OGYA	Cairo	
JY-AYB	Airbus Industrie A320-212	0088	ex F-OGYB	Baghdad	
F-OHLP	Airbus Industrie A340-212	014	ex F-WQRG		Lsd fr GIE Lizad
F-OHLQ	Airbus Industrie A340-212	022	ex F-WQRF		Lsd fr GIE Lizad
JY-AIA	Airbus Industrie A340-211	038	ex F-GLZE		Lsd fr Airbus
JY-AIB	Airbus Industrie A340-211	043	ex F-GLZF		Lsd fr Airbus

ROYAL WINGS

Royal Wings (AWS) *Amman (AMM)*

JY-RWB	de Havilland DHC-8-311B	401	ex N7985B	Lsd fr Bombardier
JY-RWC	de Havilland DHC-8Q-315	549	ex SU-YAN	Lsd fr Bombardier
JY-RWD	de Havilland DHC-8Q-314	503	ex D-BHAS	Lsd fr AUB

A subsidiary of Royal Jordanian

SKYGATE INTERNATIONAL

Amman/Sharjah (AMM/SHJ)

| JY-SGI | Lockheed L1011 Trisat-1 | 1234 | ex N1738D | Al Saafa |

J2 - DJIBOUTI (Republic of Djibouti)

DAALLO AIRLINES

Dalo Airlines (D3/DAO) *Djibouti/Dubai (JIB/DAB)*

| EY-47693 | Antonov An-24RV | 27307510 | ex CCCP-47693 | Lsd fr TZK |
| EX-47252 | Antonov An-24RV | 27307704 | ex RA-47252 | Lsd fr STB |

DJIBOUTI AIRLINES

Djibouti Air (D8/DJB) *Djibouti (JIB)*

| EX-008 | Antonov An-24RV | 37308307 | ex RA-46502 |

Also leases Antonov An-24 and other Ilyushin Il-18 aircraft as required

J5 - GUINEA BISSAU (Republic of Guinea Bissau)

AIR LUXOR GB

(L8/LXG) *Bissau (OXB)*

Presumed to lease aircraft from Air Luxor

GUINEA BISSAU AIRLINES

Bissau Airlines (G6/BSR) *Bissau (OXB)*

Plans to recommence services in 2003/4

J8 - ST VINCENT & GRENADINES (State of St. Vincent & Grenadines)

MUSTIQUE AIRWAYS

Mustique (Q4/MAW) *Mustique (MQS)*

J8-VAH	Britten-Norman BN-2B-26 Islander	2018	ex VP-VAH	
J8-VAM	Britten-Norman BN-2B-26 Islander	2165	ex N670J	Lsd fr Locaiman
J8-VBD	Aero Commander 500U	1670-18	ex N75CG	
J8-VBE	Shrike Commander 500S	3253	ex N808AC	

SVG AIR

Grenadines (SVD) *Kingston, St Vincent (SVD)*

J8-VAQ	Cessna 402B II STOL	402B1038	ex N400XY
J8-VAX	Shrike Commander 500S	1869-45	ex N9033N
J8-VAY	Aero Commander 500U	1637-2	ex N6531V

J8-VBG	Aero Commander 500U	1660-13	ex C-FWPR	
J8-VBI	Britten-Norman BN-2B-26 Islander	2025	ex J3-GAF	
J8-VBJ	Britten-Norman BN-2A Islander	163	ex J3-GAG	
J8-VBL	Cessna 402C II	402C0640	ex N404MN	
J8-VBK	Britten-Norman BN-2A-26 Islander	570	ex J3-GAH	
J8-VBN	Britten-Norman BN-2A-26 Islander	384	ex J6-SLY	
J8-VBO	de Havilland DHC-6 Twin Otter 310	772	ex N235SA	Lsd fr N285SA LLC

SVG Air is the trading name of St Vincent Grenadines Air

LN - NORWAY (Kingdom of Norway)

AIR NORWAY

Oslo-Gardermoen (GEN)

OY-NPB	Swearingen SA.227AC Metro III	AC-420	ex N67TC	Lsd fr NFA

AIRLIFT

Foerde (FDE)

LN-OBX	Aerospatiale AS.332C Puma	2001	ex I-EMEB
LN-OCO	Aerospatiale AS.365N Dauphin 2	6420	ex OY-HLL
LN-OLK	Bell 212	30722	ex C-GOKT
LN-OMX	Aerospatiale AS.332L1 Super Puma	2351	ex G-BTNZ

ARCTIC AIR suspended operations and filed for bankruptcy

BENAIR NORWAY

Sccop (HAX)   *Oslo-Gardermoen (GEN)*

LN-PBD	Cessna 208 Caravan I	20800105	ex OY-TCA	Lsd fr Alebco
LN-PBE	Cessna 208B Caravan I	208B0587	ex (OY-PBE)	Lsd fr Alebco
LN-PBF	Cessna 208B Caravan I	208B0584	ex OY-PBF	Lsd fr Alebco
LN-PBJ	Cessna 208B Caravan I	208B0859	ex N5188W	Lsd fr Alebco
LN-PBK	Cessna 208B Caravan I	208B0914	ex N5196U	Lsd fr Alebco
LN-PBL	Cessna 208B Caravan I	208B0988	ex N52655	Lsd fr Alebco

LN-PBG	Reims Cessna F406 Caravan II	F406-0015	ex OY-PBG	Lsd fr Alebco

BenAir Noway is the trading name of Hangar 5 Airservices

BERGEN AIR TRANSPORT

Bergen Air (BGT)   *Bergen (BGO)*

LN-BAT	Cessna 421B Golden Eagle	421B0915	ex N421L
LN-BAU	Cessna 421C Golden Eagle	421C0099	ex OE-FCA

BRAATHENS AIRWAYS

Braathens (BU/BRA) (IATA 154)   *Oslo (OSL)*

LN-BRD	Boeing 737-505	1842/24651		Harald Gille	Lsd fr debis
LN-BRE	Boeing 737-405	1860/24643		Hakon V Magnusson	Lsd fr BBAM
LN-BRH+	Boeing 737-505	1925/24828	ex D-ACBB	Haaken den gode	
LN-BRI	Boeing 737-405	1938/24644	ex 9M-MLL	Harald Harfagre	
					Lsd fr Greenwich Kahala
LN-BRJ	Boeing 737-505	2018/24273	ex D-ACBC	Olav Tryggvason	
					Lsd fr Magens Bay Co; sublsd to BTI
LN-BRK	Boeing 737-505	2035/24274		Magnus Barfot	Lsd fr ORIX
LN-BRM	Boeing 737-505	2072/24645		Olav den Helige	Lsd fr Trongheim
LN-BRN	Boeing 737-505	2138/24646		Hakon Herdebrei	Lsd fr NBB Nord
LN-BRO	Boeing 737-505	2143/24647		Magnus Haraldsson	Lsd Engaly
LN-BRP	Boeing 737-405	2137/25303	ex 9M-MLK	Harald Hardrade; std Lsd fr Pegasus	
LN-BRQ	Boeing 737-405	2148/25348		Harald Grafell	Lsd fr NBB Troms
LN-BRR	Boeing 737-505	2213/24648		Halvdan Svarte	Lsd fr Engaly
LN-BRS	Boeing 737-505	2225/24649		Olav Kyrre	Lsd fr Engaly
LN-BRV	Boeing 737-505	2351/25791		Hakon Sverresson	
					Lsd fr Avn Financial Svs
LN-BRX	Boeing 737-505	2434/25797		Sigurd Munn	Lsd fr NBB Oslo Lsg
LN-BUC*	Boeing 737-505	2649/26304		Magnus Erlingsson	
LN-BUD*	Boeing 737-505	2803/25794		Inge Krokrygg	Lsd fr Intec Lsg
LN-BUE*	Boeing 737-505	2800/27627		Erling Skjalgsson	
LN-BUF*	Boeing 737-405	2867/25795		Magnus den Gode	I
LN-BUG*	Boeing 737-505	2866/27631		Øystein Haraldsson	
LN-TUA"	Boeing 737-705	33/28211		Ingeborg Eriksdatter	
LN-TUD*	Boeing 737-705	142/28217		Magrete Skulesdatter	
LN-TUF*	Boeing 737-705	245/28222		Tyra Haraldsdatter	

LN-TUH>	Boeing 737-705	471/29093		Margrete Ingesdatter
LN-TUI<	Boeing 737-705	507/29094	ex N1787B	Kristin Knudsdatter Lsd fr Larrett Ltd
LN-TUJ	Boeing 737-705	773/28095		Eirik Blodoks
LN-TUK	Boeing 737-705	794/28096		Inge Berdsson
LN-TUL	Boeing 737-705	1072/29097		
LN-TUM^	Boeing 737-705	1116/29098		Oystein Magnusson

*Leased from ILFC/Castle 2003-1A LLC   +Leased from CIT Leasing
<Leased from NBB Oslo Lease Partnership Three   "Leased from ACG Acquisitions
^Leased from BBAM Aircraft Holdings   >Leased from NBB Narvik Co Ltd
Wholly owned by SAS ; in turn Malmo Aviation is wholly owned but for sale

CHC HELIKOPTER SERVICE

Helibus (L5/HKS)   Stavanger/Bergen (SVG/BGO)

LN-OAW	Aerospatiale AS.332L Super Puma	2053	ex VH-LHD			
LN-OBF	Aerospatiale AS.332L Super Puma 2	2381	ex F-WTNH			Lsd fr Helicopter Lease
LN-ODA	Aerospatiale AS.332L Super Puma	2073	ex G-PUML			Lsd to SHZ as G-PUML
LN-OHA	Aerospatiale AS.332L Super Puma 2	2396	ex F-WYMS			Lsd fr GECAS
LN-OHB	Aerospatiale AS.332L Super Puma 2	2398	ex F-WYMD			Lsd fr GECAS
LN-OHC	Aerospatiale AS.332L Super Puma 2	2393				Lsd fr Helicopter Lease
LN-OHD	Aerospatiale AS.322L Super Puma 2	2395				Lsd fr FinansSkandic
LN-OHF	Aerospatiale AS.332L2 Super Puma	2474				Lsd to SHZ as G-PUMN
LN-OHG	Aerospatiale AS.332L2 Super Puma	2493				
LN-OHH	Aerospatiale AS.332L2 Super Puma	2366	ex VN-8609			Lsd fr SFC Vietnam
LN-OHI	Aerospatiale AS.332L2 Super Puma	2582	ex F-WW			Lsd fr SEB Finans
LN-OHJ	Aerospatiale AS.332L2 Super Puma	2594				
LN-OLB	Aerospatiale AS.332L Super Puma	2082	ex OY-HMJ			
LN-OLD	Aerospatiale AS.332L Super Puma	2103	ex OY-HMI			
LN-OMF	Aerospatiale AS.332L Super Puma	2067	ex G-PUMK			Lsd to SHZ as G-PUMK
LN-OMH	Aerospatiale AS.332L Super Puma	2113	ex HZ-RH4			
LN-OMT	Aerospatiale AS.332L1 Super Puma	2468				Lsd fr Westbroker Finans
LN-OPH	Aerospatiale AS.332L1 Super Puma	2347				Lsd fr GECAS
LN-OQB	Sikorsky S-61N II	61807				Lsd to SHZ as G-BZSN
LN-OQH	Sikorsky S-61N II	61757				Lsd Aeroleo Taxi Aero as PT-YCF
LN-OQM	Sikorsky S-61N II	61764	ex (D-HOSA)			
LN-OQQ	Sikorsky S-61N II	61814	ex OY-HGG			
LN-ORC	Sikorsky S-61N II	61817				
LN-ORR	Sikorsky S-61N II	61810	ex (D-HOSB)			Lsd as PT-YAF
LN-OSJ	Sikorsky S-61N II	61715	ex N53094	Paul		
LN-OST	Sikorsky S-61N II	61738		Morten		
LN-OSU	Sikorsky S-61N II	61740		Per		Lsd to SHZ as G-CBWC
LN-ODB	Aerospatiale AS.365N2 Dauphin	6358	ex G-NTWO			Lsd fr SHZ
LN-OMJ	Aerospatiale AS.365N2 Dauphin	6301	ex F-WQEZ	SAR		
LN-OMM	Bell 214ST	28199		SAR		
LN-OMN	Aerospatiale SA.365N2 Dauphin	6423	ex F-GHXG	SAR		

Associated with CHC Scotia Helicopters (G-) and CHC Australia (VH-); part of CHC Helicopter Group

COAST AIR

Coast Center (BX/CST)   Haugesund (HAU)

LN-FAI	Aerospatiale/Alenia ATR 42-300	331	ex G-BVEF		Lsd fr Tarnwood Trading
LN-FAJ	British Aerospace Jetstream 31	621	ex G-BTXL	Bokn	Lsd fr Vestfly
LN-FAM	British Aerospace Jetstream 31	740	ex (N2247R)	Feoy	Lsd fr Kystfly A/S
LN-FAO	Aerospatiale/Alenia ATR 42-320	148	ex F-WQKX	Karmoy	Lsd fr Vestfly
LN-FAP	Aerospatiale/Alenia ATR 42-320	110	ex F-WQKQ		Lsd fr Vestfly
LN-FAV	British Aerospace Jetstream 31	606	ex OY-CLB	Bomlo	Lsd fr Vestfly
LN-FAZ	British Aerospace Jetstream 31	749	ex C-GJPU		Lsd fr Kystfly A/S

Jetstreams leased to Easy Island

HELITRANS

Scanbird (HTA)   Trondheim (TRD)

LN-OPO	Bell 214B	28053	ex N18091		Lsd fr Helitrans Heavy Lift
LN-ORM	Bell 214B-1	28054	ex SE-HLE		

KATO AIRLINE

Kato-Air (6SKAT)   Harstad (EVE)

LN-KAT	Cessna 208B Caravan I	208B0970	ex N12295		
LN-KJK	Cessna 208B Caravan I	208B0554	ex N1267A		Lsd fr GE Capital Equipment

LUFTTRANSPORT

Luft Transport (L5/LTR)   Bardufoss (BDU)

LN-MOA	Beech 200 Super King Air	BB-582	ex N47PA	Lsd fr Elcon Finans
LN-MOB	Beech 200 Super King Air	BB-584	ex (N490WP)	Lsd fr Elcon Finans
LN-MOC	Beech B200 Super King Air	BB-1449	ex N200KA	Lsd fr Elcon Finans
LN-MOD	Beech B200 Super King Air	BB-1459	ex N8163R	Lsd fr Elcon Finans
LN-MOE	Beech B200 Super King Air	BB-1460	ex N8164G	Lsd fr Elcon Finans
LN-MOF	Beech B200 Super King Air	BB-1461	ex N8261E	Lsd fr Elcon Finans
LN-MOG	Beech B200 Super King Air	BB-1465	ex N8214T	Lsd fr Elcon Finans
LN-MOH	Beech B200 Super King Air	BB-1466	ex N8216Z	Lsd fr Elcon Finans
LN-MOI	Beech B200 Super King Air	BB-1470	ex N8225Z	Lsd fr Elcon Finans
LN-MOJ	Beech B200 Super King Air	BB-1334	ex TC-SKO	
LN-MON	Beech B200 Super King Air	BB-1537	ex ZS-ARL	Lsd fr SEB Finans
LN-LYR	Dornier 228-202K	8166	ex D-CICA	Lsd fr Elcon Finans
LN-MOL	Dornier 228-202K	8156	ex TF-ELA	
LN-OLE	Aerospatiale SA.365N2 Dauphin	6405	ex VT-CKR	
LN-OLJ	Aerospatiale SA.365N2 Dauphin	6404	ex D-HNIK	
LN-OLT	Aerospatiale SA.365N Dauphin 2	6140	ex G-BLUP	Lsd fr Elcon Finans
LN-OPD	Aerospatiale SA.365N Dauphin 2	6067		Lsd fr Elcon Finans

Operates as a wholly owned subsidiary of Norwegian Air Shuttle. All except Dorniers operate in EMS role

NORSK HELIKOPTER

Norske (NOR)   Stavanger (SVG)

LN-OBA	Aerospatiale AS.332L1 Super Puma	2384		Lsd fr Brilog
LN-OLC	Aerospatiale AS.332L Super Puma	2083	ex JA6782	Lsd fr Brilog
LN-OMI	Aerospatiale AS.332L Super Puma	2123	ex G-BLZJ	Lsd fr AirLog Intl
LN-OND	Aerospatiale AS.322L Super Puma	2157	ex G-BLXS	Lsd fr BHL
LN-ONE	Aerospatiale AS.332L1 Super Puma	9002		Lsd fr Knut Axel Ugland
LN-ONH	Aerospatiale AS.332L2 Super Puma	2488		Lsd fr Heliair
LN-ONI	Aerospatiale AS.332L2 Super Puma	2500		Lsd fr Heliair
LN-ONZ	Sikorsky S-76C+	760456		Lsd fr Heliair

Associated with Bristow Helicopters, wholly owned by OLOG (Offshore Logistics)

NORSK LUFTAMBULANCE

Helidoc (DOC)   Oslo/Dröbak (OSL/-)

LN-OOA	Eurocopter EC.135P1	0125	ex D-HECF	EMS	Lsd fr Elcor Finance
LN-OOB	Eurocopter EC.135P2	0165			
LN-	Eurocopter EC.135P2			on order 04	
LN-	Eurocopter EC.135P2			on order 04	
LN-	Eurocopter EC.135P2			on order 04	
LN-OSB	MBB Bo105CBS-4	S-606	ex N2913Z	EMS	Lsd fr GE Capital Finance
LN-OSE	MBB Bo105CBS-4	S-634	ex N2784V	EMS	Lsd fr GE Capital Finance
LN-OSI	MBB Bo105CBS-4	S-609	ex N29144	EMS	Lsd fr GE Capital Finance
LN-OSZ	MBB Bo105CBS-4	S-666	ex N4573A	EMS	Lsd fr GE Capital Finance
LN-OTD	MBB Bo105CBS-4	S-433	ex D-HDMG	EMS	Lsd fr GE Capital Finance
LN-OPJ	Aerospatiale SA.365N1 Dauphin 2	6228	ex 9M-TAF		Lsd fr Airlift
LN-OPL	Aerospatiale SA.365N1 Dauphin 2	6346	ex F-WQDP		Lsd fr Airlift
LN-OPM	Aerospatiale SA.365N1 Dauphin 2	6264	ex CS-HCG		Lsd fr Airlift

NORWEGIAN AIR SHUTTLE

Nor Shuttle (DY/NAX)   Oslo (OSL)

LN-KKF	Boeing 737-3K2	1683/24326	ex N730BC	Fridtjof Nansen	
					Lsd fr BCC Mafolie Hill Co
LN-KKG	Boeing 737-3K2	1712/24327	ex PH-HVN	Gidsken Jakobsen	Lsd fr Jetscape
LN-KKH	Boeing 737-3K2	1856/24328	ex PH-HVT	Otto Sverdrup	Lsd fr Castle 2003-1A
LN-KKI	Boeing 737-3K2	1858/24329	ex PH-HVV	Helge Ingstad	Lsd fr Avn Capital
LN-KKJ	Boeing 737-36N	2936/28564	ex N564SR	Sonja Henie	Lsd fr AFT Trust-Sub
LN-KKL	Boeing 737-36N	2955/28671	ex N671SR	Roald Amundsen	Lsd fr LIFT VG Brazil
LN-KKM	Boeing 737-3Y0	1829/24676	ex HA-LES	Thor Heyerdahl	Lsd fr GECAS
LN-KKN	Boeing 737-3Y0	2030/24910	ex HA-LET	Sigrid Undset	Lsd fr Little River A/c

Names prefixed 'Real Norwegian '

LN-BBA	Fokker 50	20130	ex (LN-AKE)	Lsd fr Elcon Finans
LN-BBB	Fokker 50	20131	ex (LN-AKF)	Lsd fr Elcon Finans
LN-BBC	Fokker 50	20134	ex (LN-AKG)	Lsd fr Elcon Finans
LN-KKA	Fokker 50	20117	ex PH-DLT	Lsd fr GECAS
LN-KKD	Fokker 50	20230	ex PT-SLR	Lsd fr Brazilian A/C Fin
LN-KKE	Fokker 50	20226	ex PT-SLQ	Lsd fr Brazilian A/C Fin

Lufttransport is a wholly owned subsidiary; Norwegian.no is the trading name of Norwegian Air Shuttle

SCANDINAVIAN AIRLINE SYSTEM

Scandinavian (SK/SAS) (IATA 117)

See fleet details under Sweden (SE-)

TEDDY AIR ceased operations

TRANS WING

Transwing Cargo (TWG)				Oslo (OSL)
LN-TWL	Beech B200 Super King Air	BB-1144	ex N120AJ	

WIDERØE'S FLYVESELSKAP

Widerøe (WF/WIF) (IATA 701)   Bodo (BOO)

LN-WFA	de Havilland DHC-8-311A	342	ex C-FTUY		Lsd fr GECAS
LN-WFB	de Havilland DHC-8-311A	293	ex PH-SDS		Lsd fr GECAS
LN-WFC	de Havilland DHC-8-311A	236	ex D-BEYT		Lsd fr ABB New Finance
LN-WFE	de Havilland DHC-8Q-311	491	ex C-GFCA	Sandefjord	Lsd fr Bank Austria
LN-WFH	de Havilland DHC-8-311A	238	ex C-FZOH	all-white	Lsd fr ABB New Finance
LN-WFO	de Havilland DHC-8Q-311	493	ex C-GERC		Lsd fr Nordea Finans Sverige
LN-WFP	de Havilland DHC-8Q-311	495	ex C-GFUM		Lsd fr Nordea Finans Sverige
LN-WFR	de Havilland DHC-8Q-311	385	ex N383DC		Lsd fr Bombardier
LN-WFS	de Havilland DHC-8Q-311	535	ex C-GEWI		Lsd fr CRAF
LN-WIA	de Havilland DHC-8-103B	359	ex C-GHRI	Nordland	
LN-WIB	de Havilland DHC-8-103B	360	ex C-GFBW	Finnmark	
LN-WIC	de Havilland DHC-8-103B	367	ex C-GDNG	Sogn og Fjordane	
LN-WID	de Havilland DHC-8-103B	369	ex C-FDHD	More og Romsdal	
LN-WIE	de Havilland DHC-8-103B	371	ex C-GFYI	Hordoland	
LN-WIF	de Havilland DHC-8-103B	372	ex C-GFOD	Nord-Trondelag	
LN-WIG	de Havilland DHC-8-103B	382	ex C-GLOT	Troms	
LN-WIH	de Havilland DHC-8-103B	383	ex C-GFYI	Oslo	
LN-WII	de Havilland DHC-8-103B	384	ex C-GFOD	Nordkapp	
LN-WIJ	de Havilland DHC-8-103B	386	ex C-GFQL	Hammerfest	
LN-WIK	de Havilland DHC-8-103B	394	ex C-GDNG	Bodo	
LN-WIL	de Havilland DHC-8-103B	398	ex C-GFCF	Floro	
LN-WIM	de Havilland DHC-8-103B	403	ex C-GDIU	Vesterälen	
LN-WIN	de Havilland DHC-8-103B	409	ex C-GDNG	Alstadhaug/Lofoten	
LN-WIO	de Havilland DHC-8-103B	417	ex C-GFQL	Rost/Askerhus	
LN-WIP	de Havilland DHC-8-103A	239	ex C-FXNE	Alstahaug	Lsd fr AeroCentury
LN-WIR	de Havilland DHC-8-103A	273	ex C-FZNU	Nordkyn	
LN-WDA	de Havilland DHC-8Q-402	4069	ex C-GERL		
LN-WDB	de Havilland DHC-8Q-402	4070	ex C-GETI		
LN-WDC	de Havilland DHC-8Q-402	4071	ex C-GEVP		
LN-WDS	de Havilland DHC-8Q-402	4016	ex C-GELN		

96.4% owned by SAS

LV - ARGENTINA (Republic of Argentina)

AEROLINEAS ARGENTINAS

Argentina (AR/ARG) (IATA 044)   Buenos Aires-Ezeizal (EZE)

LV-JMX	Boeing 737-287	243/20404		Ciudad de Bariloche	std EZE
LV-JMY	Boeing 737-287	248/20405		Ciudad de Posadas	std EZE
LV-JND	Boeing 737-287C	263/20407		Ciudad de Comodoro Rivadavia	
LV-JTD*	Boeing 737-287F	285/20523	ex LV-PRQ	Ciudad de Tucuman; VIP	
LV-JTO	Boeing 737-287	291/20537		Ciudad de Jujuy	
LV-LEB	Boeing 737-287	331/20768		Ciudad de Esquel	
LV-LIV	Boeing 737-287	381/20965		Ciudad de Ushuaia	std EZE
LV-WSY+	Boeing 737-281	293/20562	ex JA8416		
LV-WTX+	Boeing 737-281	292/20561	ex LV-PMI		
LV-ZEC	Boeing 737-236	648/21796	ex N921PG		Lsd fr Pegasus
LV-ZIE	Boeing 737-236	658/21798	ex N922PG		Lsd fr Pegasus
LV-ZRE	Boeing 737-236	1077/23168	ex N927PG		Lsd fr Pegasus
LV-ZRO	Boeing 737-236	1060/23164	ex N925PG		Lsd fr Pegasus
LV-ZSD	Boeing 737-236	1088/23171	ex N930PG		Lsd fr Pegasus
LV-ZSW	Boeing 737-236	1086/23170	ex N937PG		Lsd fr Pegasus
LV-ZTD	Boeing 737-236	1102/23225	ex N939PG		Lsd fr Pegasus
LV-ZTE	Boeing 737-228	1135/23349	ex LV-PIJ		Lsd fr Triton
LV-ZTG	Boeing 737-236	1081/23169	ex N938PG		Lsd fr Pegasus
LV-ZTI+	Boeing 737-228	937/23002	ex LV-PIM		Lsd fr Triton
LV-ZTJ+	Boeing 737-236	1091/23172	ex N948PG		Lsd fr Pegasus
LV-ZTT+	Boeing 737-236	699/21806	ex N947PG		Lsd fr Pegasus
LV-ZTX+	Boeing 737-228	1267/23504	ex LV-PIP		Lsd fr Triton
LV-ZTY	Boeing 737-236	1047/23159	ex N949PG		Lsd fr Pegasus

LV-ZXB	Boeing 737-228	958/23009	ex LV-PIS		Lsd fr Triton
LV-ZXC	Boeing 737-236	1053/23160	ex N950PG		Lsd fr Pegasus
LV-ZXH+	Boeing 737-228	1256/23503	ex LV-PIU		Lsd fr Triton
LV-ZXP	Boeing 737-228	939/23003	ex LV-PIV		Lsd fr Triton
LV-ZXU	Boeing 737-236	1105/23226	ex N952PG		Lsd fr Pegasus
LV-ZXV+	Boeing 737-228	1426/23793	ex LV-PIX		Lsd fr Triton
LV-ZYG	Boeing 737-236	645/21795	ex N954PG		Lsd fr Pegasus
LV-ZYI+	Boeing 737-228	959/23010	ex LV-PJC		Lsd fr Triton
LV-ZYN	Boeing 737-236	643/21794	ex N900PG		Lsd fr Pegasus
LV-ZYY	Boeing 737-236	660/21799	ex N941PG	stored AEP	Lsd fr Pegasus
LV-ZZD	Boeing 737-228	971/23011	ex N247TR		Lsd fr Triton
LV-ZZD+	Boeing 727-228	971/23011	ex LV-P		Lsd fr Triton
LV-ZZI+	Boeing 737-236	1097/23166	ex N956PG		Lsd fr Pegasus

*Operated as Aerolineas Executive Jet; two more planned
+Operates with Aerolineas titles on left side and Austral on right side

LV-MLO	Boeing 747-287B	349/21725	ex N1789B	stored EZE	
LV-MLP	Boeing 747-287B	403/21726			
LV-MLR	Boeing 747-287B	404/21727			
LV-OEP	Boeing 747-287B	487/22297			
LV-OOZ	Boeing 747-287B	532/22592			
LV-OPA	Boeing 747-287B	552/22593			
LV-	Boeing 747-475	912/25422	ex N971PG		Lsd fr Pegasus

LV-VBX*	McDonnell-Douglas MD-88	2016/53047		Parque Nacional Lanin	
LV-VBZ*	McDonnell-Douglas MD-88	2031/53049		Parque Baritu	
LV-VCB	McDonnell-Douglas MD-88	2043/53351		Parque Iguazu	
LV-VGB	McDonnell-Douglas MD-88	2046/53446		Parque Nahuel Huapi	
LV-VGC*	McDonnell-Douglas MD-88	2064/53447		Parque Caliliegua	
LV-WFN*	McDonnell-Douglas MD-81	952/48025	ex N10027	Isla de los Estados	
LV-WGN*	McDonnell-Douglas MD-83	1764/49934	ex N907MD		Lsd fr Boeing
LV-WPY*	McDonnell-Douglas MD-81	948/48024	ex N10022	Estrecho San Carlos	

*Joint colours - Aerolineas Argentinas and Austral

LV-AIV	Airbus Industrie A310-325ET	640	ex EC-IHV		Lsd fr ILFC
LV-ZPJ	Airbus Industrie A340-211	074	ex F-OHPG		
LV-ZPO	Airbus Industrie A340-211	063	ex F-OHPF		
LV-ZPX	Airbus Industrie A340-211	080	ex F-OHPH		
LV-ZRA	Airbus Industrie A340-211	085	ex F-OHPI		

6 Airbus Industrie A340-642s on order
92.1% owned by owners of Air Plus Comet. Member of oneworld alliance. Feeder services operated by Aero VIP as Aerolineas Argentinas Express and Southern Winds as Aerolineas Argentinas Connection.
Plans to launch subsidiaries in Bolivia, Chile, Paraguay and Uruguay. Austral to be merged with parent in 2003 but name retained for low-cost operation; some aircraft are in joint colours.

AERO VIP

Airvip (2D/AOG)   Cordoba (COR)

LV-ZOW	British Aerospace Jetstream 32EP	869	ex N869AE	Lsd fr BAES
LV-ZPW	British Aerospace Jetstream 32EP	861	ex N861AE	Lsd fr BAES
LV-ZPZ	British Aerospace Jetstream 32EP	931	ex N931AE	Lsd fr BAES
LV-ZRL	British Aerospace Jetstream 32EP	928	ex N928AE	Lsd fr BAES
LV-ZSB	British Aerospace Jetstream 32EP	942	ex N942AE	Lsd fr BAES
LV-ZST	British Aerospace Jetstream 32EP	941	ex N941AE	Lsd fr BAES
LV-	British Aerospace Jetstream 32EP	830	ex N22NC	

Operates as Aerolineas Argentinas Express but aircraft in own colours

AIRMAN

Buenos Aires-San Fernando

| LV-YIC | Swearingen SA.227AC Metro III | AC-448 | ex LV-PNF |
| LV-ZEB | Swearingen SA.226TC Metro II | TC-393 | ex N867MA |

AIR TANGO

Buenos Aires-Aeroparque (AEP)

| LV-WEO | Swearingen SA.226TC Metro II | TC-346 | ex N52EA |

AMERICAN FALCON

American Falcon (WK/AFB)   Buenos Aires-Aeroparque (AEP)

LV-LZN	Fokker F.28 Fellowship 1000	11048	ex		
LV-WGX	Boeing 737-2P6	498/21358	ex N930CA	Macloula	Lsd fr Capital A/c
LV-WZC	Fokker F.28 Fellowship 1000	11017	ex N802PH	Nazira	Lsd fr Capital A/L Lsg
LV-ZXS	Boeing 737-201	141/20211	ex		
LV-ZYJ	Boeing 737-291	923/22744	ex CC-CDE	Virgen de Halisa	Op for LPR

AMERICAN JET

Buenos Aires-Aeroparque (AEP)

LV-WTD	Dornier 228-200	8094	ex D-CBDR	Lsd fr Dornier
LV-WTV	Dornier 228-200	8093	ex N228AM	Lsd fr Dornier
N3027B	Swearingen SA.227DC Metro 23	DC-856B	ex OE-LIA	Lsd fr PC Air Charter

BAIRES FLY

Buenos Aires-Aeroparque (AEP)

LV-VDJ	Swearingen SA.227AC Metro III	AC-729	ex N27823	
LV-WHG	Swearingen SA.226TC Metro II	TC-344	ex N44CS	
LV-WJT	Swearingen SA.227AC Metro III	AC-776B	ex N776NE	
LV-WRA	Swearingen SA.227AC Metro III	AC-429	ex C-FJLF	
LV-WTE	Swearingen SA.227AC Metro III	AC-584	ex LV-PMF	
LV-ZMG	Swearingen SA.227AC Metro III	AC-425	ex N721MA	Lsd fr JODA

All freighters

CATA LINEAS AEREAS

CATA

Buenos Aires-Aeroparque (AEP)

LV-AZV	Fairchild F-27J	65	ex LV-PAD	
LV-RBO	Fairchild F-27J	78	ex LV-PAG	
LV-RLB	Fairchild F-27J	42	ex N102FJ	

Current status uncertain as ICAO code has been cancelled

CIELOS DEL SUR – AUSTRAL

Austral (AU/AUT) (IATA 143)

Buenos Aires-Aeroparque (AEP)

LV-WGM	McDonnell-Douglas MD-83	1627/49784	ex N509MD	Lsd fr Boeing

90% owned by owners of Air Plus Comet. Aircraft being repainted with joint colours; see Aerolineas Argentinas

DINAR LINEAS AEREAS ceased operations 01 October 2002 and assets subsequently sold to American Falcon

HAWK AIR

Air Hawk (HKR)

Buenos Aires-Aeroparque (AEP)

LV-WHX	Piper PA-31Turbo Navajo	31-353	ex N716DR	
LV-WIR	Swearingen SA.226T Merlin III	T-232	ex N56TA	Freighter
LV-WNC	Swearingen SA.226AT Merlin IVA	AT-036	ex N642TS	Freighter
LV-WXW	Swearingen SA.226TC Metro II	TC-419	ex N7205L	Freighter

LADE / LINEAS AEREAS DEL ESTADO

Lade (5U/LDE) (IATA 022)

Comodoro Rivadavia (CRD)

T-82	de Havilland DHC-6 Twin Otter 200	167	
T-84	de Havilland DHC-6 Twin Otter 200	214	ex LV-JMN
T-85	de Havilland DHC-6 Twin Otter 200	173	
T-86	de Havilland DHC-6 Twin Otter 200	225	
T-89	de Havilland DHC-6 Twin Otter 200	185	ex LV-JPX
T-90	de Havilland DHC-6 Twin Otter 200	178	ex LV-JMR
LV-ISD	Boeing 707-387B	556/19241	ex TC-95
LV-LGO	Boeing 707-372C	721/20076	ex TC-93
LV-WXL	Boeing 707-365C (Comtran 2)	654/19590	ex JY-AJM
T-41	Fokker F.27 Friendship 600	10345	ex T-80
T-43	Fokker F.27 Friendship 600	10451	ex PH-EXA
T-44	Fokker F.27 Friendship 600	10454	ex PH-EXB
T-45	Fokker F.27 Friendship 600	10368	ex PH-FMP
TC-52	Fokker F.28 Fellowship 1000C	11074	ex LV-RCS
TC-53	Fokker F.28 Fellowship 1000C	11020	ex PH-EXX
TC-54	Fokker F.28 Fellowship 1000C	11018	ex LV-VCS
TC-55	Fokker F.28 Fellowship 1000C	11024	ex PH-EXZ
TC-91	Boeing 707-387B	897/21070	ex T-91

LADE is the "airline" wing of the Argentine AF and operates social services in Patagonia

LAFSA – LINEA AÉREAS FEDERALES

Being formed by Argentinian government to replace LAPA; several aircraft operated by Southern Winds wear these titles

LAPA - LINEA PRIVADA ARGENTINA

Lapa (MJ/LPR) (IATA 069)   *Buenos Aires-Aeroparque (AEP)*

LV-VGF	Boeing 737-2M6	422/21138	ex ZK-NAL	Altair	Lsd fr Aerospace Fin
LV-YXB	Boeing 737-204	487/21335	ex LV-PMO		Lsd fr Triton
LV-YZA	Boeing 737-204	489/21336	ex LV-PNS		Lsd fr Triton
LV-ZYJ	Boeing 737-291	923/22744	ex CC-CDE	Virgen de Halisa	Op by AFB

Filed for bankruptcy protection 20 April 2001, operations continue but to be replaced by LAFSA - Lineas Aereas Federales

SAPSA - SERVICIOS AÉREOS PATAGONICAS

Viedma (VDM)

LV-ZXA	Swearingen SA.227DC Metro 23	DC-901B	ex N3070F

SOUTHERN WINDS AIRLINES

Southern Winds (A4/SWD) (IATA 242)   *Cordoba (COR)*

LV-AGC	Boeing 737-241	394/21005	ex PP-VMJ		Lsd fr PLM Intl
LV-YBS*	Boeing 737-266	453/21193	ex LV-PNI	Litoral	Lsd fr Patagonia Air
LV-YGB*	Boeing 737-2S3	746/22633	ex N633GP	Malvinas	Lsd fr La Rioja Air
LV-YXB	Boeing 737-204	487/21335	ex LV-PNO	LAFSA	
LV-YZA	Boeing 737-204	489/21336	ex LV-PNS	LAFSA	
LV-ZYX	Boeing 737-2M6	399/20913	ex CC-CYW		Lsd fr ACG Aquisition
LV-ZZA*	Boeing 737-205	460/21219	ex CC-CYD		Lsd fr A/c Lse Fin
LV-ZZC*	Boeing 737-2E1	424/21112	ex CC-CYT		Lsd fr ACG Acquisitions
LV-	Boeing 737-2C3	410/21017	ex PP-CJT		Lsd fr PLM Intl

*Wear additional Federales titles, see LAFSA

LV-WXT	Canadair CL-600-2B19	7041	ex F-GPYZ	Salta	Lsd fr Bombardier

Operates as Aerolineas Argentinas Connection

STAF CARGA / SERVICICOS DE TRANSPORTES AÉREOS FUEGINOS

(FS) (IATA 278)   *Buenos Aires-Ezeiza (EZE)*

Operates charter flights with aircraft leased from other operators as required. Owns Cielos de Peru

TAPSA AVIACIÓN

LV-LSI	de Havilland DHC-6 Twin Otter 300	456	ex

TRANSPORTES BRAGADO

Buenos Aires-Aeroparque (AEP)

LV-MGD	Piper PA-31T Cheyenne II	31T-7720059	ex LV-PXD
LV-ZNU	Cessna 208B Caravan I	208B0718	ex LV-POC

LX - LUXEMBOURG (Grand Duchy of Luxembourg)

CARGOLUX AIRLINES INTERNATIONAL

Cargolux (CV/CLX) (IATA172)   *Luxembourg (LUX)*

LX-FCV	Boeing 747-4R7F	1002/25866	ex N1785B	Luxembourg	Lsd fr Elena Lsg
LX-GCV	Boeing 747-4R7F	1008/25867		Esch/Alzette	Lsd fr Geraldine Lsg
LX-ICV	Boeing 747-428F	968/25632	ex N6005C	Ettlebrück	
LX-KCV	Boeing 747-4R7F	1125/25868		Dudelange	
LX-LCV	Boeing 747-4R7F	1139/29053		Grevenmacher	
LX-MCV	Boeing 747-4R7F	1189/29729		Echternach	
LX-NCV	Boeing 747-4R7F	1203/29730		Vianden	
LX-OCV	Boeing 747-4R7F	1222/29731		Differdange	
LX-PCV	Boeing 747-4R7F	1231/29732		Diekirch	
LX-RCV	Boeing 747-4R7F	1235/30400		Schengen	Lsd fr Bellami Ltd
LX-SCV	Boeing 747-4R7F	1281/29733		Niederanven	Lsd fr Allwright
LX-TCV	Boeing 747-4R7F	1311/30401	ex N6046P	Sandweiler	Lsd fr Valerie Lsg
LX-UCV	Boeing 747-4R7F	33827		on order 2Q04	

24.5% owned by Luxair   All names prefixed 'City of'

LUXAIR

Luxair (LG/LGL) (IATA 149)   *Luxembourg (LUX)*

LX-LGF+	Boeing 737-4C9	2215/25429		Chateaus de Vianden	
LX-LGG+	Boeing 737-4C9	2249/26437		Chateau de Bourscheid	
LX-LGN	Boeing 737-59D	2028/25065	ex G-OBMX		Lsd fr NBB Luxembourg Lse
LX-LGO	Boeing 737-5C9	2413/26438		Chateau de Clervaux	

LX-LGP	Boeing 737-5C9	2444/26439		Chateau de Bourglinster	
LX-LGQ	Boeing 737-7C9	1442/33802			
LX-	Boeing 737-7C9			on order 04	
LX-	Boeing 737-7C9			on order	

+Leased from Volito Aviation for 3 years from late 2003

LX-LGI	Embraer EMB.145LU	145369	ex PT-SOU		
LX-LGJ	Embraer EMB.145LU	145395	ex PT-S		
LX-LGU	Embraer EMB.145LR	145084	ex PT-S	Prince Sebastian	
LX-LGV	Embraer EMB.145LU	145129	ex PT-SDG		
LX-LGW	Embraer EMB.145LU	145135	ex PT-SDM		
LX-LGX	Embraer EMB.145LU	145147	ex PT-SDX		
LX-LGY	Embraer EMB.145LU	145242	ex PT-SIH		
LX-LGZ	Embraer EMB.145LU	145258	ex PT-SIR		

LX-LGC	Fokker 50	20168	ex PH-EXH	Prince Guillaume	Lsd fr Slux (One)
LX-LGD	Fokker 50	20171	ex PH-EXJ	Prince Felix	Lsd fr Slux (One)
LX-LGE	Fokker 50	20180	ex PH-EXF	Prince Louis	Lsd fr Slux (Two)

13% owned by Lufthansa; in turn owns 24.5% of Cargolux International

LUXAVIATION
Red Lion (LXA)   *Luxembourg (LUX)*

| LX-GDE | Embraer EMB.120ER Brasilia | 120184 | ex LX-EAC | | Lsd fr CIT Lsg |

WEST AIR LUXEMBOURG
Luxembourg (LUX)

| LX-WAL | British Aerospace ATP | 2059 | ex SE-LHZ | | Lsd fr SWN |

LY - LITHUANIA (Republic of Lithuania)

AIR LITHUANIA
Kainas (TT/KLA)   *Kaunus-Karmelava (KUN)*

LY-AAY	Yakovlev Yak-40	9720753	ex CCCP-88269	
LY-AAZ	Yakovlev Yak-40	9641851	ex SP-FYT	
LY-ARI	Aerospatiale/Alenia ATR 42-300	012A	ex F-WQBT	Lsd fr ATR Asset Mgt
LY-ARY	Aerospatiale/Alenia ATR 42-300	118	ex TF-ELJ	

Wholly owned by Lithuanian Airlines but for sale

APATAS
Apatas (LYT)   *Kaunus-Karmelava (KUN)*

LY-AVA	LET L-410UVP-E3	882036	ex Soviet AF 2036
LY-AVP	LET L-410UVP	851514	ex RA-67547
LY-AVT	LET L-410UVP-E3	882033	ex Soviet AF 2033 stored BRS
LY-AVV	LET L-410UVP-E	892335	ex RA-67609
LY-AVZ	LET L-410UVP-E	892336	ex RA-67610

AURELA
Aurela (LSK)   *Vilnius (VNO)*

| LY-SKB | Yakovlev Yak-42D | 4520424811431 | ex LY-AAX |

AVIAVILSA
Aviailsa (LVR)   *Vilnius (VNO)*

LY-APC	Antonov An-26B	17311107	ex RA-26060	DHL titles	Lsd fr PSW
LY-APK	Antonov An-26B	27312201	ex RA-26114		
LY-APN	Antonov An-26B	27312010	ex UR-BXF		
LY-FTL	Antonov An-26	77305002	ex SP-FTL	DHL c/s	
LY-LVR	Antonob An-26B	12008	ex RA-26107		Lsd fr PSW

Operate for DHL

LITHUANIAN AIRLINES / LITOVSKIE AVALINII
Lithuania Air (TE/LIL) (IATA 874)   *Vilnius (VNO)*

LY-AGQ	Boeing 737-524	2771/26339	ex N33635		Lsd fr ILFC
LY-AGZ	Boeing 737-524	2777/26340	ex N19636		Lsd fr ILFC
LY-BSD	Boeing 737-2T4	886/22701	ex N4569N	Steponas Darius	
LY-BSG	Boeing 737-2T2	892/22793	ex N4571M	Stasys Girénas	
LY-SBC	SAAB 2000	025	ex F-GTSE	Suvalkietis	Lsd fr SAAB
LY-SBD	SAAB 2000	023	ex F-GTSD	Dzukas	Lsd fr SAAB
LY-SBG	SAAB 2000	032	ex HB-IZQ	Aukstaities	Lsd fr SAAB

Owns Air Lithuania but for sale

LZ - BULGARIA (Republic of Bulgaria)

AIR MAX

Aeromax (RMX) *Plovdiv (PDV)*

LZ-RMF	LET L-410UVP	831104	ex UR-67416		
LZ-RMI	LET L-410UVP	831113	ex UR-67422	no titles	

AIR NOVE

Air Nove (NHA) *Sofia (SOF)*

LZ-NHA	Antonov An-26	67304702	ex UR-26605	Yves Duval

AIR SOFIA

Air Sofia (CT/SFB) *Sofia (SOF)*

LZ-SFA	Antonov An-12BP	02348007	ex LZ-SGA		
LZ-SFF	Antonov An-12BP				
LZ-SFK	Antonov An-12BP	2341901	ex CCCP-11511	all-white, no titles	Lsd to ALK
LZ-SFL	Antonov An-12BP	4342101	ex Z3-AFA	DHL titles	
LZ-SFN	Antonov An-12BP	2340806	ex RA-11307		
LZ-SFS	Antonov An-12BP	6344308	ex SP-LZB	all-white	
LZ-SFT	Antonov An-12BP	9346904	ex LZ-SAA		
LZ-SFW	Antonov An-12BP				
LZ-SFH	Antonov An-26	3904	ex RA-26570	all white	Lsd to Mandala

AVIOSTART

Aviostart (VSR) *Sofia (SOF)*

LZ-ANC	Antonov An-24B	67302808		
LZ-ASZ	Antonov An-24B	27307903	ex UR-49290	Lsd fr UKL

BALKAN AIR TOURS renamed Bulgaria Air

BF AIRLINES curent status uncertain

BH AIR

(BGH) *Sofia (SOF)*

LZ-HMF	Tupolev Tu-154M	88A-777	ex CU-T1275	
LZ-HMI	Tupolev Tu-154M	85A-706	ex LZ-BTI	Lsd fr HMS
LZ-HMN	Tupolev Tu-154M	90A-832	ex LZ-BTN	Lsd fr HMS
LZ-HMQ	Tupolev Tu-154M	87A-743	ex LZ-BTQ	Lsd fr HMS
LZ-HMW	Tupoelv Tu-154M	85A-707	ex LZ-BTW	Lsd fr HMS
LZ-BHA	Airbus Industrie A320-211	0029	ex N290SE	Lsd fr WFBN
Operate in Balkan Holiday colours				

BRIGHT AVIATION SERVICES

Bright Services (BRW) *Sofia (SOF)*

LZ-BRA	Antonov An-12BP	8346006	ex LZ-ITB	
LZ-BRC	Antonov An-12BP	8345510	ex ER-ACW	aircharter.co.uk titlles
LZ-BRP	Antonov An-12BP			

BULGARIAN AIR CHARTER

Bulgarian Charter (BUC) *Sofia (SOF)*

LZ-LCA	Tupolev Tu-154M	89A-829		Lsd fr VARZ 400
LZ-LCI	Tupolev Tu-154M	88A-788	ex RA-85650	Lsd fr VARZ 400
LZ-LCS	Tupolev Tu-154M	86A-727	ex 4K-727	Lsd fr URN
LZ-LCT	Tupolev Tu-154M	85A-717	ex EP-LBN	Lsd fr VARZ 400
LZ-LCV	Tupolev Tu-154M	86A-733	ex 4K-733	Lsd fr URN
LZ-LCX	Tupolev Tu-154M	86A-744	ex LZ-LTX	Lsd fr VARZ 400
LZ-	Tupolev Tu-154M	85A-717	ex EP-LBN	Lsd fr VARZ 400

BULGARIA AIR

(FB/LZB) (IATA 623) *Sofia (SOF)*

LZ-BOG	Boeing 737-330	1293/23529	ex D-ABXI	Lsd fr DLH
LZ-BOH	Boeing 737-330	1297/23530	ex D-ABXK	Lsd fr DLH

LZ-BOI	Boeing 737-530	2128/25311	ex D-ABJF	Lsd fr DLH
LZ-BOJ	Boeing 737-3L9	1402/23718	ex N377PA	Lsd fr CIT Leasing

Fly with Bulgari@Air.BG titles

FLYING DANDY AIRLINES

(ZD/DDD)   *Sofia (SOF)*

LZ-CBC	Antonov An-24B	07305810	ex 040

HELI-AIR

Heli Bulgaria (HLR)   *Sofia (SOF)*

LZ-CBA	Antonov An-26	8007	ex UR-26659	
LZ-CBB	Antonov An-24RV	37309008	ex 030	
LZ-CBE	Antonov An-12BP	6343708	ex LZ-BAC	
LZ-CBG	Antonov An-12A	2340804	ex RA-11370	Bansko
LZ-CBH	Antonov An-12BP	9346807	ex LZ-BAH	Melnik
LZ-CCA	Cessna 421C Golden Eagle	421C0272	ex N6390G	
LZ-CCF	LET L-410UVP-E	861722	ex 1722	

HEMUS AIR

Hemus Air (DU/HMS) (IATA 748)   *Sofia (SOF)*

LZ-TUH	Tupolev Tu-134A	60142	ex OK-HFM		Op for ADA
LZ-TUJ	Tupolev Tu-134A	49913	ex OK-HFL		Lsd to LBC
LZ-TUL	Tupolev Tu-134A-3	4352303			
LZ-TUN	Tupolev Tu-134A-3	4352307			
LZ-TUT	Tupolev Tu-134B-3	63987			
LZ-HMI	Tupolev Tu-154M	85A-706	ex LZ-BTI		Lsd to BGH
LZ-HMN	Tupolev Tu-154M	90A-832	ex LZ-BTN		Lsd to BGH
LZ-HMQ	Tupolev Tu-154M	87A-743	ex LZ-BTQ		Lsd to BGH
LZ-HMS	Tupolev Tu-154M	87A-751	ex CU-T1265		Lsd to LBC
LZ-HMW	Tupolev Tu-154M	85A-707	ex LZ-BTW		Lsd to BGH
LZ-HMY	Tupolev Tu-154M	91A-875	ex UR-85700		
LZ-DOB	Yakovlev Yak-40	9340432			Lsd to LBC
LZ-DOC	Yakovlev Yak-40	9340532			
LZ-DOE	Yakovlev Yak-40	9521441			
LZ-DOF	Yakovlev Yak-40	9521541			
LZ-DOM	Yakovlev Yak-40	9620447			Lsd to ADE
LZ-DOR	Yakovlev Yak-40	9231623			
LZ-DOS	Yakovlev Yak-40	9231423		Nova Composit c/s	Lsd to BLV
LZ-LSB	LET L-410UVP-E2	861802		DHL colours	
ZA-MAL	British Aerospace 146 Srs.200	E2054	ex G-BZWP		Op for ADA
ZA-MEV	British Aerospace 146 Srs.300	E3197	ex VH-EWS		Op for ADA

49% owned by Bulgarian government but stake for sale

INTER TRANS AIR

Inter Transair (ITT)   *Sofia (SOF)*

LZ-ITA	Antonov An-12BP	3341004	
LZ-ITS	Antonov An-12BP	3341505	ex 4R-SKL

RILA AIRLINES Current status is uncertain as sole aircraft now with Vega Airlines

OCEAN AIR

LZ-VPD	Antonov An-24RV	47309703

SKORPION AIR

Air Scorpic (SPN)   *Sofia (SOF)*

LZ-CBA	Antonov An-26	8007	ex UR-26659	
LZ-MNG	LET L-410UVP	841326	ex UR-67100	Lsd to AHU as HA-LAY
LZ-MNK	Antonov An-12BK	8345802	ex 53 red	
LZ-MNL	Antonov An-26	1309	ex UR-26233	
LZ-MNN	Antonov An-12P	0901409	ex UR-11322	
LZ-MNO	LET L-410UVP	800507		
LZ-MNP	Antonov An-12BK	9346309	ex CCCP-12113	
LZ-MNQ	Antonov An-12BP	3341402	ex 70 black	
LZ-MNR	Antonov An-26	87307504	ex LZ-NHC	
LZ-MNS	Antonov An-26	47302203	ex 203	

LZ-MNT	Antonov An-26	47302209	ex 209	
LZ-RMK	LET L-410UVP	851406	ex UR-67502	
LZ-VEB	Antonov An-12V	01347701	ex RA-12999	DHL c/s

SOLIS AVIATION

Solis (SOF)　　　　　　　　　　　　　　　　　　　　　　　　　*Sofia (SOF)*

Operates cargo flights with Antonov An-12 aircraft leased from other companies as and when required

TRANSAIR believed to have ceased operations

VEGA AIRLINES

Vega Airlines (VEA)　　　　　　　　　　　　　　　　　　　　*Sofia (SOF)*

LZ-VEA	Antonov An-12BP	01340106	ex RA-11976	Chan Asparuch	
LZ-VEB	Antonov An-12TB	01347701	ex RA-12999	Tsar Boris II	Lsd to SPN
LZ-VEC	Antonov An-12	06344610	ex UR-93920	Tsar Simoon Boliki	
LZ-VED	Antonov An-12B	02348207	ex D2-FDB	Thor Ivan-Asen	
LZ-VEE	Antonov An-12BP	402410	ex LZ-RAA	Patriach Eftimil	

VIA – AIR VIA BULGARIAN AIRWAYS

(VL/VIM)　　　　　　　　　　　　　　　　　　　　　　　　　*Varna (VAR)*

LZ-MIG	Tupolev Tu-154M	90A-840
LZ-MIK	Tupolev Tu-154M	90A-844
LZ-MIL	Tupolev Tu-154M	90A-845
LZ-MIR	Tupolev Tu-154M	90A-852
LZ-MIS	Tupolev Tu-154M	90A-863

VIAGGIO AIR

(VM/VOA)

| LZ-ATR | Aerospatiale/Alenia ATR 42-300 | 151 | ex F-WQNC | Lsd fr ATR Asset Management |

VIVANT AIRLINES

| LZ-VVI | Antonov An-24B |

N - UNITED STATES OF AMERICA

ABBE AIR CARGO

Palmer, AK (PAQ)

| N59314 | Douglas DC-3 | 12363 | ex C-GABE | stored PAQ |

ABX AIR see Airborne Express

ACADEMY AIRLINES

Academy (ACD)　　　　　　　　　　　　　　*Hampton-Clayton Co/Tara Field, GA*

| N143D | Douglas DC-3 | 2054 | ex N2817D | Miss Ali Gater | Lsd fr private |

Subsidiary of Airline Aviation Academy

ADIRONDACK FLYING SERVICE

Lake Placid, NY (LKP)

N372WP	Cessna 310R	310R0904
N402AF	Cessna 402B	402B1337
N8091Q	Cessna 402B	402B0369
N33247	Cessna U206F Stationair	U20602692

Adirondack Flying Service is the trading name of Lake Placid Airways

AERO CHARTER

Char Tran (CTA)　　　　　　　　　*Albuquerque-International Sunport, NM (ABQ)*

N588DM	Cessna 310Q	310Q0624	
N589DM	Cessna 310Q II	310Q1048	
N590DM	Cessna 310Q	310Q0059	
N591DM	Cessna 310Q	310Q0006	ex N7506Q

N592DM	Cessna T310R II	310R0681	ex N828P		
N25BH	Cessna 402B II	402B1228			
N38CJ	Cessna 402C II	402C0023			
N594DM	Cessna 402C II	402C0068	ex N2610Z		
N596DM	Cessna 402C II	402C0255	ex N7011X		
N598DM	Cessna 402C II	402C0114	ex N81970		
N635MA	Cessna 402C II	402C0634	ex 5H-TGA		
N775RC	Cessna 402C II	402C0311			
N22LT	Ted Smith Aerostar 601	61-0321-098	ex N22LL		

AERO DYNAMICS

Aero Dynamic (DYN)   *Dallas-Love Field, TX (DAL)*

N457TC	Beech B200 Super King Air	BB-1458	ex N883SW	Lsd fr Big Bird A/c Lsg
N762KA	Beech 200 Super King Air	BB-762	ex RP-C4650	Lsd fr Farris Air
N35890	Piper PA-31-350 Chieftain	31-8052139		

AERO FLITE

Kingman, AZ (IGM)

N82FA	Douglas C-54G	35960	ex N14BA	161 Tanker
N262NR	Canadair CL-215-1A10	1081	ex C-GDRS	
N3054V	Douglas DC-4	10547	ex N76AU	
N96358	Douglas C-54E	27284	ex Bu90398	160 Tanker

AERO FREIGHT

El Paso, TX (ELP)

N472AF	Douglas DC-3	13485	ex N272AF	CAF colours

Sister company of Aero-Juarez

AERO INDUSTRIES

Wabash (WAB)   *Richmond, VA (RIC)*

N1439T	Piper PA-32-300 Cherokee Six	32-7200039	
N3073W	Piper PA-32-300 Cherokee Six	32-7940081	Lsd fr L&J Air
N3521S	Piper PA-31-350 Navajo Chieftain	31-7952107	
N9211K	Piper PA-34-200T Seneca II	34-7670191	
N27508	Piper PA-31-350 Navajo Chieftain	31-7852031	

AERO UNION

Chico-Municipal, CA (CIC)

N701AU	Lockheed P2V-7 Neptune	726-7190	ex N920AU	01 Tanker	
N702AU	Lockheed SP-2H Neptune		ex Bu147968		
N703AU	Lockheed SP-2H Neptune	726-7217	ex N702AU	03 Tanker	Lsd as CC-CHU
N713AU	Lockheed SP-2H Neptune		ex Bu145903		
N716AU	Lockheed P2V-7 Neptune	726-7065	ex N90YY	16 Tanker	
N718AU	Lockheed SP-2H Neptune	726-7214	ex N964L	18 Tanker	
N9804P	Lockheed P2V-7 Neptune		ex Bu140980		
N900AU	Lockheed P-3A Orion	185-5104	ex N406TP	00 Tanker	
N920AU	Lockheed P-3A Orion	185-5039	ex Bu150513	20 Tanker	
N921AU	Lockheed P-3A Orion	185-5098	ex Bu151385	21 Tanker	
N922AU	Lockheed P-3A Orion	185-5100	ex N181AU	22 Tanker	
N923AU	Lockheed P-3A Orion	185-5085	ex N185AU	23 Tanker	
N925AU	Lockheed P-3A Orion	185-5074	ex N183AU	25 Tanker	
N926AU	Lockheed P-3A Orion	185-5171	ex Bu152731	26 Tanker	
N927AU	Lockheed P-3A Orion	185-5082	ex N182AU	27 Tanker	
N183PL	Lockheed PV-1	5492			
N690TB	Rockwell Commander 690A	11109			
N2742G	Douglas C-54G	36089	ex N54577	15 Tanker	
N4096W	Piper PA-32-300 Cherokee Six	32-40159			
N4112W	Piper PA-32-300 Cherokee Six	32-40175			
N4958M	Douglas C-54G	36009	ex N427NA		
N5938Y	Piper PA-23-250 Aztec C	27-3103			
N8234Y	Piper PA-30-160B Twin Comanche	30-1360			
N62297	Douglas C-54E	27328	ex Bu90402	14 Tanker	

AEX AIR

Desert (DST)   Phoenix-Sky Harbor, AZ/La Verne, CA (PHX/PDC)

N57AS	Piper PA-31 Turbo Navajo	31-113
N57D	Piper PA-31 Turbo Navajo	31-260
N370RC	Piper PA-31 Turbo Navajo	31-268
N626JD	Piper PA-32R-300 Lance II	32R-7680084
N1656H	Piper PA-34-200T Seneca II	34-7770131
N2817T	Piper PA-34-200 Seneca	34-7250170
N55549	Piper PA-34-200 Seneca	34-7350228
N75053	Piper PA-34-200T Seneca II	34-7670233
All freighters	AEX Air is the trading name of Air Desert Pacific	

AIRBORNE EXPRESS

Abex (GB/ABX)   Wilmington-Airborne Airpark, OH (ILN)

N702AX	Boeing 767-231ER	29/22566	ex N603TW	
N707AX	Boeing 767-231ER	63/22570	ex N607TW	
N708AX	Boeing 767-231ER	64/22571	ex N608TW	
N709AX	Boeing 767-231ER	65/22572	ex N609TW	
N713AX	Boeing 767-205ER	101/23058	ex N651TW	
N767AX	Boeing 767-281	51/22785	ex JA8479	
N768AX	Boeing 767-281	54/22786	ex JA8480	
N769AX	Boeing 767-281	58/22787	ex JA8481	
N773AX	Boeing 767-281	61/22788	ex JA8482	
N774AX	Boeing 767-281	67/22789	ex JA8483	
N775AX	Boeing 767-281	69/22790	ex JA8484	
N783AX	Boeing 767-281	80/23016	ex JA8485	
N784AX	Boeing 767-281	82/23017	ex JA8486	Lsd fr WFBN
N785AX	Boeing 767-281	84/23018	ex JA8487	Lsd fr WFBN
N786AX	Boeing 767-281	85/23019	ex JA8488	Lsd fr WFBN
N787AX	Boeing 767-281	96/23020	ex JA8489	
N788AX	Boeing 767-281	103/23021	ex JA8490	
N789AX	Boeing 767-281	104/23022	ex JA8491	Lsd fr GECAS
N790AX	Boeing 767-281	106/23140	ex JA8238	Lsd fr GECAS
N791AX	Boeing 767-281	108/23141	ex JA8239	
N792AX	Boeing 767-281	110/23142	ex JA8240	on order
N793AX	Boeing 767-281	114/23143	ex JA8241	
N794AX	Boeing 767-281	115/23144	ex JA8242	
N795AX	Boeing 767-281	116/23145	ex JA8243	
N796AX	Boeing 767-281	121/23146	ex JA8244	
N797AX	Boeing 767-281	123/23147	ex JA8245	
N798AX	Boeing 767-281	143/23431	ex JA8251	on order
N799AX	Boeing 767-281	145/23432	ex JA8252	

Those on order from All Nippon originally for delivery up to 03 but programme slowed and possibly the last two above will not be delivered. Those in use are converted to freighter configuration but without cargo door. Some of latter deliveries may be converted to full freighters

N811AX	Douglas DC-8-63F	521/46113	ex N818EV	
N812AX	Douglas DC-8-63F	524/46126	ex N819EV	
N813AX	Douglas DC-8-63F	509/46136	ex N795AL	
N814AX	Douglas DC-8-63F	439/46041	ex N792AL	
N815AX	Douglas DC-8-63PF	503/46097	ex N793AL	
N816AX	Douglas DC-8-63PF	496/46093	ex N790AL	Lsd fr Aerolease Fin
N817AX	Douglas DC-8-63F	334/45928	ex N780AL	stored ILN
N818AX	Douglas DC-8-63F	484/46075	ex N512FP	
N819AX	Douglas DC-8-63F	327/45927	ex N783AL	
N820AX	Douglas DC-8-63F	529/46155	ex C-GQBA	
N821AX	Douglas DC-8-63F	518/46116	ex C-GQBF	stored ILN
N823AX	Douglas DC-8-63F	506/46122	ex 5Y-ZEB	stored ILN
N824AX	Douglas DC-8-63F	533/46141	ex HB-IBF	stored ILN
N825AX	Douglas DC-8-63F	530/46115	ex ZP-CCH	
N826AX	Douglas DC-8-63CF	480/46061	ex N952R	
N828AX	Douglas DC-8-63F	377/45999	ex N788AL	Lsd fr Aerolease Fin
N842AX	Douglas DC-8-61F (BAC 2)	405/46015	ex N766RD	
N843AX	Douglas DC-8-61F (BAC 2)	418/46017	ex N64RD	
N847AX	Douglas DC-8-61F (BAC 2)	435/46031	ex N28UA	
N848AX	Douglas DC-8-61F (QNC 2)	436/46032	ex N51UA	
N849AX	Douglas DC-8-61F (QNC 2)	305/45891	ex N21UA	
N850AX	Douglas DC-8-61F (BAC 2)	297/45894	ex N915CL	stored ILN
N853AX	Douglas DC-8-61F (QNC 2)	419/46037	ex ZP-CCR	

All DC-8-62s and -63s are fitted with BAC Stage 3 hushkits

N900AX	Douglas DC-9-32	514/47380	ex N1284L	
N901AX	Douglas DC-9-32	519/47381	ex N1285L	
N902AX	Douglas DC-9-32	572/47426	ex N1286L	
N903AX	Douglas DC-9-32	573/47427	ex N1287L	
N904AX	Douglas DC-9-32CF	172/47040	ex N931F	
N905AX	Douglas DC-9-32CF	208/47147	ex N933F	

N906AX	Douglas DC-9-31	270/47072	ex VH-TJM
N907AX	Douglas DC-9-31	401/47203	ex VH-TJN
N908AX	Douglas DC-9-31F	98/47008	ex VH-TJK
N909AX	Douglas DC-9-32CF	246/47148	ex N934F
N923AX	Douglas DC-9-31	260/47165	ex N8942E
N924AX	Douglas DC-9-31	507/47403	ex N8987E
N925AX	Douglas DC-9-15	14/45728	ex I-TIGA
N927AX	Douglas DC-9-15	20/45717	ex I-TIGE
N928AX	Douglas DC-9-33RC	447/47392	ex YU-AJB
N929AX	Douglas DC-9-31	351/45874	ex N965ML
N930AX	Douglas DC-9-33RC	445/47363	ex N502MD
N931AX	Douglas DC-9-33F	543/47384	ex HB-IFW
N932AX	Douglas DC-9-33RC	584/47465	ex N7465B
N933AX	Douglas DC-9-33RC	343/47291	ex N94454
N934AX	Douglas DC-9-33RC	564/47462	ex N32UA
N935AX	Douglas DC-9-33F	521/47413	ex N939F
N936AX	Douglas DC-9-31	371/47269	ex N970ML
N937AX	Douglas DC-9-31	376/47074	ex N973ML
N938AX	Douglas DC-9-31	152/47009	ex VH-TJL
N939AX	Douglas DC-9-32	459/47201	ex EC-ECU
N941AX	Douglas DC-9-31	602/47419	ex VH-TJQ
N943AX	Douglas DC-9-31	617/47528	ex VH-TJR
N944AX	Douglas DC-9-31	623/47550	ex VH-TJS
N945AX	Douglas DC-9-31	634/47551	ex VH-TJT
N946AX	Douglas DC-9-31	86/47003	ex N535MD
N947AX	Douglas DC-9-31	81/47004	ex N537MD
N948AX	Douglas DC-9-31	269/47065	ex N534MD
N949AX	Douglas DC-9-31	515/47325	ex N540MD
N952AX	Douglas DC-9-41	751/47615	ex JA8432
N953AX	Douglas DC-9-41	732/47608	ex JA8427
N954AX	Douglas DC-9-41	736/47612	ex JA8428
N955AX	Douglas DC-9-41	768/47619	ex JA8436
N956AX	Douglas DC-9-41	777/47620	ex JA8437
N957AX	Douglas DC-9-41	871/47759	ex JA8439
N958AX	Douglas DC-9-41	874/47760	ex JA8440
N959AX	Douglas DC-9-41	875/47761	ex JA8441
N960AX	Douglas DC-9-41	876/47762	ex JA8442
N962AX	Douglas DC-9-41	887/47768	ex JA8449
N963AX	Douglas DC-9-41	894/47780	ex JA8450
N964AX	Douglas DC-9-41	895/47781	ex JA8451
N965AX	Douglas DC-9-41	566/47498	ex SE-DAL
N966AX	Douglas DC-9-41	645/47510	ex OY-KGK
N967AX	Douglas DC-9-41	643/47509	ex SE-DAO
N968AX	Douglas DC-9-41	568/47499	ex SE-DAM
N969AX	Douglas DC-9-41	575/47464	ex SE-DAN
N970AX	Douglas DC-9-41	601/47494	ex OY-KGI
N971AX	Douglas DC-9-41	604/47497	ex LN-RLB
N972AX	Douglas DC-9-41	743/47631	ex SE-DAX
N973AX	Douglas DC-9-41	677/47511	ex LN-RLU
N974AX	Douglas DC-9-41	728/47623	ex LN-RLS
N975AX	Douglas DC-9-41	678/47512	ex SE-DAP
N976AX	Douglas DC-9-41	714/47596	ex SE-DAR
N977AX	Douglas DC-9-41	679/47513	ex LN-RLX
N978AX	Douglas DC-9-41	740/47628	ex OY-KGN
N979AX	Douglas DC-9-41	559/47492	ex SE-DAK
N980AX	Douglas DC-9-32	314/47176	ex N3335L
N981AX	Douglas DC-9-32	347/47273	ex N3337L
N982AX	Douglas DC-9-32	385/47317	ex N1261L
N983AX	Douglas DC-9-32	386/47257	ex N1262L
N984AX	Douglas DC-9-32	387/47258	ex N1263L
N985AX	Douglas DC-9-32	606/47522	ex EC-BYD
N986AX	Douglas DC-9-32	654/47543	ex EC-BYG
N987AX	Douglas DC-9-32	484/47364	ex EC-BPF
N988AX	Douglas DC-9-32	179/47084	ex EC-BIL
N989AX	Douglas DC-9-32	279/47314	ex EC-BIU
N990AX	Douglas DC-9-41	562/47493	ex SE-DLC

All fitted with ABS Partnership Stage 3 hushkits
Airborne Express is the trading name of ABX Air Inc   15% controlled by TNT

AIR BORINQUEN

Abex (GB/ABX)   *San Jian/Isla Grande, PR (SIG)*

N1253K	Cessna 208B Caravan I	208B0648
N1253Y	Cessna 208B Caravan I	208B0649

Also trades as Inter Island Express

AIR CARGO CARRIERS

Night Cargo (2Q/SNC) (IATA 883)   Milwaukee-General Mitchell Intl, WI (MKE)

N55AN	Short SD.3-30	SH3025	ex N373HA	stored MKE
N58DD	Short SD.3-30	SH3008	ex TG-TJA	
N166RC	Short SD.3-30	SH3021	ex N5132T	stored MKE
N167RC	Short SD.3-30	SH3038	ex N690RA	
N260AG	Short SD.3-30	SH3107	ex 84-0461	stored MKE
N261AG	Short SD.3-30	SH3117	ex 84-0470	
N330AC	Short SD.3-30	SH3007	ex C-GSKW	
N334AC	Short SD.3-30	SH3029	ex VH-LSI	
N335MV	Short SD.3-30	SH3017	ex PJ-DDA	
N336MV	Short SD.3-30	SH3018	ex PJ-DDB	
N390GA	Short SD.3-30	SH3077	ex 4X-CSP	
N936MA	Short SD.3-30	SH3036	ex G-BGNI	
N938MA	Short SD.3-30	SH3046	ex G-BHJJ	
N939MA	Short SD.3-30	SH3047	ex G-BHSH	
N2629P	Short SD.3-30	SH3079	ex G-BJLL	
N124CA	Short SD.3-60	SH3652	ex G-BLJS	
N151CA	Short SD.3-60	SH3653	ex G-BLJT	
N360RW	Short SD.3-60	SH3613	ex C-FCRB	
N360SA	Short SD.3-60	SH3601	ex G-WIDE	
N367AC	Short SD.3-60	SH3626	ex VH-MVW	
N368AC	Short SD.3-60	SH3651	ex VH-BWO	
N601CA	Short SD.3-60	SH3623	ex G-BKWM	
N691A	Short SD.3-60	SH3618	ex G-BKUG	
N4498Y	Short SD.3-60	SH3625	ex G-BKZN	
N	Short SD.3-60	SH3728	ex VH-SUR	
N	Short SD.3-60	SH3720	ex VH-SUM	
N	Short SD.3-60	SH3752	ex VH-SUL	
N	Short SD.3-60	SH3764	ex VH-SUF	

All freighters

N20EF	Swearingen SA.26AT Merlin IIB	T26-157	ex N20ER

Associated with North Star Air Cargo

AIR CARGO EXPRESS renamed Everts Air Cargo

AIR CARGO EXPRESS

Turbo Dog (TDG)   Fort Wayne-Intl, IN (FWA)

N992TD	Lear Jet 23	23-035	ex (N10QX)
N993TD	Lear Jet 24	24-166	ex N124HF
N994TD	Lear Jet 24	24-179	ex XA-RQP
N995TD	Lear Jet 24	24-149	ex N64HB
N996TD	Lear Jet 24D	24D-320	ex S5-BAB

All freighters

AIR CARGO MASTERS

N702M	Swearingen SA.227AC Metro III	AC-702	ex N2712B	Lsd fr Interair Lease
N704C	Swearingen SA.227AC Metro III	AC-704		Lsd fr Interair Lease

Status uncertain as both stored at Billings, MT in Big Sky colours

AIR CARRIERS

Fast Check (FCI)   Bessemer, AL (EKY)

N756JX	Cessna U206G Stationair 6 II	U20604138	
N8630Z	Cessna P206C Super Skylane	P206-0430	
N9599G	Cessna U206F Stationair	U20601799	
N24013	Cessna 206H Stationair	20608087	
N72700	Cessna T206H Turbo Stationair	T20608248	
N7PJ	Cessna 210L Centurion II	21060754	
N10HL	Cessna 210L Centurion II	21060646	
N27JR	Cessna 210L Centurion II	21059706	
N521SC	Cessna 210M Centurion II	21062343	
N732QA	Cessna 210M Centurion II	21061679	
N761PS	Cessna 210M Centurion II	21062415	
N823AR	Cessna 210M Centurion II	21062661	
N9163M	Cessna 210M Centurion II	21062067	
N9455M	Cessna 210K Centurion II	21059355	
N93885	Cessna 210L Centurion II	21060444	
N29PK	Cessna 310L	310L0001	ex N2201F

N333BS	Cessna 310R II	310R0865		
N4140Q	Cessna 310N	310N0040		
N5817M	Cessna 310P	310P0117		
N7754Q	Cessna 310Q	310Q0254		
N7940Q	Cessna 310Q	310Q0623		
N2BZ	Shrike Commander 500S	3227		
N91WW	Ted Smith Aerostar 600A	60-0262-105	ex N90416	
N92ST	Mitsubishi MU-2J	610	ex N342MA	Cavanaugh SCD conversion
N499BA	Cessna 208B Caravan I	208B0689		
N699RF	Ted Smith Aerostar 600A	60-0169-074	ex N74GD	
N900DT	Shrike Commander 500S	3056		
N1399G	Cessna 402B	402B0573		
N1532T	Cessna 402B	402B0307		
N8536	Shrike Commander 500S	3267		
N8554C	Piper PA-32R-300 Lance	32R-7680122		
N9096N	Shrike Commander 500S	3076		

AIR CARRIERS EXPRESS sole aircraft written off, status uncertain

AIR CERBERUS current status uncertain

AIR CHARTER

San Juan-Fernando Luis Ribas Dominicci, PR (SIG)

N901GD	Britten-Norman BN-2A-26 Islander	855	ex XA-JEK	The Spirit of Culebra
N902GD	Britten-Norman BN-2A-27 Islander	905	ex VP-AAE	
N903GD	Britten-Norman BN-2A-6 Islander	625	ex HI-636CT	
N904GD	Britten-Norman BN-2B-26 Islander	2128	ex N902VL	
N905GD	Britten-Norman BN-2A-9 Islander	339	ex C-FTAM	

Air Charter also operates as Air Flamenco

AIR CHARTER

Wausau-Central Wisconsin, WI (CWA)

N266M	Swearingen SA.227TT Merlin IIIC	TT-426	ex N900AK	

AIR COLORADO

Westavia (WTV)   *Grand Junction-Walker Field, CO (GJT)*

N106RE	Piper PA-31-350 Navajo Chieftain	31-7752056		
N159SW	Piper PA-31-350 Navajo Chieftain	31-7405229		
N494SC	Piper PA-31-350 Navajo Chieftain	31-7752099		
N495SC	Piper PA-31-350 Chieftain	31-8052062	ex N3555Y	
N4051X	Swearingen SA.26TC Merlin IIB	T26-124		

Air Colorado is the trading name of Western Aviators

AIR CRANE

Winder-Barrow County/Loganville, GA (WDR/-)

N47B	Sikorsky S-58BT	58-530	ex EC-CYJ	
N72B	Sikorsky S-58T	58-1626	ex	
N85HJ	Sikorsky S-58E	58-1716	ex N58WH	
N1038G	Bell 204	7316	ex 66-1240	

AIR DIRECT

Rhinelander-Oneida County, WI (RHI)

N100YR	Cessna 421B Golden Eagle	421B0437		
N102CT	Cessna 310R II	310R0136	ex C-GNKT	
N5456S	Cessna 337B Super Skymaster	337-0556		
N87395	Cessna 310R	310R0543		

Air Direct is the trading name of Rhinelander Flying Services

AIR FLORIDA EXPRESS

(FD)   *Miami-International, FL (MIA)*

N371R	Cessna 402C	402C0028	ex VH-ANO	
N404PJ	Cessna 402C	402C0513	ex N7884J	
N1123S	Cessna 208B Caravan I	208B0396		Lsd fr Plane 1 Lsg

AIR GLOBAL INTERNATIONAL current status is uncertain

AIR GRAND CANYON

N6308H	Cessna T207A Turbo Stationair 7	20700476
N6491H	Cessna T207A Turbo Stationair 7	20700543
N7311U	Cessna T207A Turbo Skywagon	20700395
N91085	Cessna T207 Turbo Skywagon	20700066

AIR LAUGHLIN

Operates charters with Boeing 737-200s leased from (and operated by) Casino Express (a sister company)

AIR LOGISTICS (ALSO AIR LOGISTICS OF ALASKA)

Airlog (ALG)   *New Iberia-Arcadia, LA/Anchorage-Intl, AK/Fairbanks-Intl, AK (ARA/ANC/FAI)*

N9AT	Bell 206B JetRanger III	3854		
N15Q	Bell 206B JetRanger III	2235	ex N15CT	
N35WH	Bell 206B JetRanger III	2736	ex D-HHUN	stored ARA
N42AL	Bell 206B JetRanger	918		
N53AL	Bell 206B JetRanger	1092		
N56AL	Bell 206B JetRanger	1402		
N65AL	Bell 206B JetRanger	1443		
N70Q	Bell 206B JetRanger III	3160	ex N5859V	
N113AL	Bell 206B JetRanger III	2380		
N116AL	Bell 206B JetRanger III	2389	ex PT-HTZ	
N117AL	Bell 206B JetRanger II	2391	ex PT-HUA	
N158H	Bell 206B JetRanger III	2974	ex N10857	
N167H	Bell 206B JetRanger III	2968	ex N227EH	stored ARA
N168H	Bell 206B JetRanger III	3453	ex N711NM	stored ARA
N198H	Bell 206B JetRanger III	3647	ex N3897Q	
N209AL	Bell 206B JetRanger III	1044	ex N31AL	
N1078Y	Bell 206B JetRanger III	2924		
N2155Z	Bell 206B JetRanger III	3476		
N2201W	Bell 206B JetRanger III	3477		stored ARA
N2295F	Bell 206B JetRanger III	3579		
N3896W	Bell 206B JetRanger III	3197		
N3912Q	Bell 206B JetRanger III	3271		
N4847	Bell 206B JetRanger III	4004	ex C-FBBQ	
N5008G	Bell 206B JetRanger III	2506		based Alaska
N5008K	Bell 206B JetRanger III	2524		stored ARA
N5011F	Bell 206B JetRanger III	2564		stored ARA
N5743B	Bell 206B JetRanger III	3056		
N27574	Bell 206B JetRanger III	2562		
N58111	Bell 206B JetRanger	1082		
N59485	Bell 206B JetRanger	1266		
N59541	Bell 206B JetRanger	1412		
N90228	Bell 206B JetRanger	1720		
5N-AQO	Bell 206B JetRanger III	3765	ex N31800	based Escravos
5N-BAG	Bell 206B JetRanger III	2728	ex N2760T	based Escravos
5N-BCV	Bell 206B JetRanger III	2782	ex ZS-HIC	based Escravos
5N-BES	Bell 206B JetRanger III	3216	ex N139H	based Escravos
N8WH	Bell 206L-1 LongRanger	45318	ex N2775D	stored ARA
N40LP	Bell 206L-1 LongRanger	45233	ex N289JH	stored ARA
N41GH	Bell 206L-1 LongRanger II	45502	ex N5748N	
N60WJ	Bell 206L-1 LongRanger	45276	ex N4470K	
N69AL	Bell 206L-4 LongRanger IV	52139	ex PT-YBH	
N76AL	Bell 206L-4 LongRanger IV	52165	ex N15EW	
N130AL	Bell 206L-3 LongRanger III	51132		based Alaska
N133AL	Bell 206L-3 LongRanger III	51133		based Alaska
N170AL	Bell 206L-4 LongRanger IV	52063		
N171AL	Bell 206L-4 LongRanger IV	52064		
N173AL	Bell 206L-4 LongRanger IV	52066		
N174AL	Bell 206L-4 LongRanger IV	52067		
N175AL	Bell 206L-4 LongRanger IV	52117		
N176AL	Bell 206L-4 LongRanger IV	52146	ex C-FOFE	
N177AL	Bell 206L-4 LongRanger IV	52157	ex C-GLZU	
N178AL	Bell 206L-4 LongRanger IV	52191	ex N86549	
N179AL	Bell 206L-4 LongRanger IV	52102	ex PT-HTH	
N180AL	Bell 206L-4 LongRanger IV	52104	ex C-FTJZ	
N182AL	Bell 206L-3 LongRanger III	52057	ex D-HSDA	
N187AL	Bell 206L-3 LongRanger III	51135	ex N134AL	
N194H	Bell 206L-1 LongRanger	45660	ex N39121	
N206DB	Bell 206L-4 LongRanger IV	52127		
N206SL	Bell 206L-2 LongRanger II	45245	ex N5086L	
N211EL	Bell 206L-1 LongRanger II	45251	ex N27511	stored ARA
N265AL	Bell 206L-4 LongRanger IV	52280		

N266AL	Bell 206L-4 LongRanger IV	52281	ex C-GFNY	
N272M	Bell 206L-1 LongRanger III	45365		stored ARA
N330P	Bell 206L-3 LongRanger III	51295		
N343AL	Bell 206L-3 LongRanger III	51372		
N346AL	Bell 206L-3 LongRanger III	51378		based Alaska
N349AL	Bell 206L-3 LongRanger III	51388		
N351AL	Bell 206L-3 LongRanger III	51431		
N355AL	Bell 206L-3 LongRanger III	51444		
N358AL	Bell 206L-3 LongRanger III	51460		based Alaska
N359AL	Bell 206L-3 LongRanger III	51461		
N360AL	Bell 206L-3 LongRanger III	51462		based Alaska
N361AL	Bell 206L-3 LongRanger III	51212	ex N552BM	
N362AL	Bell 206L-3 LongRanger III	51471		
N363AL	Bell 206L-3 LongRanger III	51472		based Alaska
N364AL	Bell 206L-3 LongRanger III	51434	ex XA-RVD	
N365AL	Bell 206L-3 LongRanger III	51376		
N367AL	Bell 206L-3 LongRanger III	51443	ex XA-RVX	
N414LV	Bell 206L-4 LongRanger IV	52006		
N577E	Bell 206L-1 LongRanger	45577	ex ZS-HJR	stored ARA
N1067D	Bell 206L-1 LongRanger II	45435		
N1075W	Bell 206L-1 LongRanger II	45377	ex PT-HAD	
N1075Y	Bell 206L-1 LongRanger II	45378		
N1078N	Bell 206L-1 LongRanger II	45389		
N1081G	Bell 206L-1 LongRanger II	45405		stored ARA
N1081K	Bell 206L-1 LongRanger II	45407	ex PT-HVR	stored ARA
N1084Y	Bell 206L-1 LongRanger II	45433		
N2025G	Bell 206L-1 LongRanger II	45690		stored ARA
N2081K	Bell 206L-4 LongRanger IV	52275		Lsd to BHN as 5N-BFH
N2611	Bell 206L-1 LongRanger	45417		stored ARA
N2618	Bell 206L-1 LongRanger	45503		
N2619	Bell 206L-3 LongRanger III	51375		
N2654	Bell 206L-1 LongRanger	45482		stored ARA
N2755F	Bell 206L-1 LongRanger II	45237		
N2756A	Bell 206L-1 LongRanger II	45256		
N2759N	Bell 206L-1 LongRanger II	45271		
N2762D	Bell 206L-1 LongRanger II	45280		
N3179S	Bell 206L-1 LongRanger II	45781		
N3184P	Bell 206L-1 LongRanger II	45774		
N3185P	Bell 206L-1 LongRanger II	45775		
N3186P	Bell 206L-1 LongRanger II	45776		
N3188P	Bell 206L-1 LongRanger II	45778		
N3190P	Bell 206L-1 LongRanger II	45779		
N3192P	Bell 206L-1 LongRanger II	45780	ex XA-SIP	
N3199P	Bell 206L-1 LongRanger II	45790		
N3899C	Bell 206L-1 LongRanger	45596		stored ARA
N5734M	Bell 206L-1 LongRanger II	45449		
N5756N	Bell 206L-1 LongRanger II	45546		
N5759M	Bell 206L-1 LongRanger II	45555		stored ARA
N20796	Bell 206L-4 LongRanger IV	52272		Lsd BHN as 5N-BFE
N27483	Bell 206L-1 LongRanger II	45230		
N27545	Bell 206L-1 LongRanger II	45234		
N27554	Bell 206L-1 LongRanger II	45246		stored ARA
N57510	Bell 206L-1 LongRanger II	45530		
5N-AJC	Bell 206L LongRanger	45095	ex 5N-ALB	based Escravos
5N-AMQ	Bell 206L-1 LongRanger	45746	ex N3173U	based Escravos
5N-AQB	Bell 206L-1 LongRanger	45506	ex N5749X	based Escravos
5N-AQP	Bell 206L-1 LongRanger	45604	ex N3907E	based Escravos
5N-BAS	Bell 206L-1 LongRanger	45367	ex N1076K	based Escravos
5N-BFE	Bell 206L-4 LongRanger IV	52272	ex N20796	based Escravos
5N-BFF	Bell 206L-4 LongRanger IV	52273	ex N2080C	based Escravos
5N-BFG	Bell 206L-4 LongRanger IV	52274	ex N2080W	based Escravos
5N-BFH	Bell 206L-4 LongRanger IV	52275	ex N2081K	based Escravos
5N-BFV	Bell 206L-4 LongRanger IV	52160	ex 5N-ESC	based Escravos
5N-PAA	Bell 206L-1 LongRanger	45659	ex N39118	based Escravos

Other Bell 206Ls are operated on lease

N24HL	Bell 212	30569			Lsd to ABO as HK-4222X
N29AL	Bell 212	30569			
N62AL	Bell 212	30826	ex N5139U	stored	Lsd to ABO as HK-4076X
N212AL	Bell 212	30932	ex XA-TLY		Lsd to ABO as HK-4221X
N361EH	Bell 212	30554	ex XA-TRY		
N399EH	Bell 212	30810	ex XA-AAM		
N874AL	Bell 212	31225			
N522EH	Bell 212	31199	ex XA-TRZ		
N3895P	Bell 212	31144			Lsd to ABO as HK-3736X
N3895U	Bell 212	31153			Lsd to ABO as HK-3737X

N403AL	Bell 407	53478		
N404AL	Bell 407	53479	ex N40410	
N407AL	Bell 407	53044		
N416AL	Bell 407	53046	ex N1116H	
N417AL	Bell 407	53054		

Registration	Type	C/n	ex/notes	
N436AL	Bell 407	53069	ex N58236	
N437AL	Bell 407	53141		
N457AL	Bell 407	53151		
N477AL	Bell 407	53203		
N487AL	Bell 407	53204		
N497AL	Bell 407	53172		
N507AL	Bell 407	53103	ex N407ST	
N527AL	Bell 407	53211		
N537AL	Bell 407	53230		
N547AL	Bell 407	53240		
N557AL	Bell 407	53243		
N577AL	Bell 407	53247		
N587AL	Bell 407	53248		
N607AL	Bell 407	53264		
N617AL	Bell 407	53265		
N627AL	Bell 407	53284		
N647AL	Bell 407	53357		
N677AL	Bell 407	53015	ex EC-GJC	
N687AL	Bell 407	53366		
N697AL	Bell 407	53374		
N847AL	Bell 407	53150	ex N407XS	
N917AL	Bell 407	53381		
N937AL	Bell 407	53383		
N2531G	Bell 407	53550		
5N-BEM	Bell 407	53246	ex N567AL	based Escravos
5N-BEO	Bell 407	53190	ex N467AL	based Escravos
5N-BEP	Bell 407	53107	ex N427AL	based Escravos
5N-BFI	Bell 407	53550	ex N2531G	based Escravos
N1TY	Eurocopter EC.120B	1244	ex N988AL	
N510AL	Eurocopter EC.120B	1251	ex N442AE	
N511AL	Eurocopter EC.120B	1252	ex N443AE	
N512AL	Eurocopter EC.120B	1148	ex N446AE	
N513AL	Eurocopter EC.120B	1261		
N514AL	Eurocopter EC.120B	1266		
N515AL	Eurocopter EC.120B	1165	ex N512AL	
N516AL	Eurocopter EC.120B	1157		
N523AL	Eurocopter EC.120B	1262		
N524AL	Eurocopter EC.120B	1263		
N526AL	Eurocopter EC.120B	1281		
N41N	MBB Bo105CBS	S-344	ex N777VE	
N107AL	MBB Bo105CBS	S-772		
N492HL	MBB Bo105CBS-4	S-803	ex N124PW	
N494HL	MBB Bo105CBS-4	S-813	ex N234JL	
N495HL	MBB Bo105CBS-4	S-817	ex N126PP	
N496HL	MBB Bo105CBS-4	S-822	ex N246HA	
N501AL	MBB Bo105C	S-58	ex N205BB	
N502AL	MBB Bo105C	S-103	ex N1818S	
N505AL	MBB Bo105C	S-113	ex XA-TME	
N2785R	MBB Bo105CBS	S-642		
N4572V	MBB Bo105CBS	S-665	ex D-HDUG	
N5412J	MBB Bo105CBS-4	S-784		
N5416F	MBB Bo105CBS-4	S-794	ex D-HDZD	
N164AG	Sikorsky S-76A	760290	ex N154AE	
N518AL	Sikorsky S-76A+	760134	ex G-BGVM	
N519AL	Sikorsky S-76A	760058	ex N38PP	
N521AL	Sikorsky S-76A	760132	ex ZS-RGX	
N522AL	Sikorsky S-76A	760236	ex N202SR	
N701AL	Sikorsky S-76A	760238		
N702AL	Sikorsky S-76A	760243		
N705AL	Sikorsky S-76A	760267		
N707AL	Sikorsky S-76A	760189	ex N989QS	
N709AL	Sikorsky S-76A	760278		
N712AL	Sikorsky S-76A	760280		Lsd to Aeroleo as PR-LCL
N717AL	Sikorsky S-76A	760221	ex G-BWIM	
N741SW	Sikorsky S-76A	760070	ex N721SW	
N768AL	Sikorsky S-76A	760031	ex VH-EMM	
N769AL	Sikorsky S-76A	760048		
N860AL	Sikorsky S-76C+	760527	ex N9024W	
N861AL	Sikorsky S-76C+	760529	ex N2032W	
N862AL	Sikorsky S-76C+	760531	ex N2021W	
N863AL	Sikorsky S-76C+	760536	ex N5009K	
N868AL	Sikorsky S-76C+			on order
N869AL	Sikorsky S-76C+			on order
N870AL	Sikorsky S-76C+			on order
N871AL	Sikorsky S-76C+			on order
N872AL	Sikorsky S-76C+			on order
N873AL	Sikorsky S-76C+			on order
N917QS	Sikorsky S-76A	760217	ex N127BG	
N1547K	Sikorsky S-76A	760085		Lsd to Aeroleo as PR-NLF

N1547N	Sikorsky S-76A	760088			
N7912L	Sikorsky S-76A	760054			
N20509	Sikorsky S-76C	760545			
N31211	Sikorsky S-76A	760225			
5N-BGC	Sikorsky S-76C+	760481	ex LN-ONY		Lsd fr Norsk Helikopter
5N-BGD	Sikorsky S-76C+	760540	ex N864AL	based Lagos	
5N-BGE	Sikorsky S-76C+	760545	ex N20509	based Lagos	
5N-BGF	Sikorsky S-76C+	760560	ex N867AL	based Lagos	
N161AL	Sikorsky S-61N II	61-761	ex G-BXSN		Lsd in Brazil
N252AL	Cessna U206G Stationair	U20603612	ex N7322N	based Alaska	
N390AL	Bell 214ST	28198	ex N3217H		
N391AL	Bell 214ST	28103	ex N2091E		
N392AL	Bell 214ST	28114	ex G-BKJD		
N393AL	Bell 214ST	28117	ex N214EV		
N395AL	Bell 412EP	33046			Lsd to BHL as 5N-BDD
N416EH	Bell 412	33011			
N506AL	Bell 412	36267			Lsd to BHL as 5N-BDY
N509AL	Bell 412EP	36278	ex 9Y-ALI		Lsd to BHL as 5N-BDZ
N690L	Beech B200 Super King Air	BB-1573	ex N702TA		
N7022F	Bell 412	36318			
5N-AMW	Cessna 425 Conquest I	425-0067	ex N6844V		
5N-BEL	Cessna S550 Citation IISP	S5500079	ex N79LB	based Escravos	
5N-CES	Cessna 208 Caravan I	20800249	ex N1288Y		

Both companies are subsidiaries of Offshore Logistics (OLOG)

AIR MARBRISA no details known, believed not to have commenced operations

---

AIR METHODS

Denver-Centennial, CO (DIA)

N21UM	Aerospatiale AS.350B AStar	1674	ex N5801B		
N22UM	Aerospatiale AS.350BA AStar	1065	ex N29888	EMS	
N92LG	Aerospatiale AS.350B2 AStar	2575		EMS	
N93LG	Aerospatiale AS.350B2 AStar	2654	ex N60662	EMS	
N94LG	Aerospatiale AS.350B2 AStar	2728	ex N60928	EMS	
N96LG	Aerospatiale AS.350B2 AStar	2817	ex N6098S	EMS	Lsd fr debis
N97LG	Aerospatiale AS.350B2 AStar	2917	ex N4030W	EMS	
N101LN	Aerospatiale AS.350B2 AStar	3038	ex N4060Z	EMS	Lsd fr GECAS
N102LN	Aerospatiale AS.350B2 AStar	3065	ex N4064Z	EMS	Lsd fr GECAS
N103LN	Aerospatiale AS.350B2 AStar	3128	ex N4069B	EMS	Lsd fr GECAS
N104LN	Aerospatiale AS.350B2 AStar	3134	ex N5206S	EMS	Lsd fr GECAS
N105LN	Aerospatiale AS.350B2 AStar	3249	ex N52281	EMS	Lsd fr PNC Leasing
N106LN	Aerospatiale AS.350B3 AStar	3251	ex N52285	EMS	Lsd fr PNC Leasing
N110LN	Aerospatiale AS.350B2 AStar	2828	ex N213LP	EMS	Lsd fr CIT Leasing
N151AD	Aerospatiale AS.350D AStar	1173	ex N151AC		
N152AC	Aerospatiale AS.350BA AStar	1101	ex N139BH		
N350RM	Aerospatiale AS.350D AStar	1024			
N392LG	Aerospatiale AS.350B3 AStar	3252	ex N5229Y	EMS	Lsd fr PNC Leasing
N397LG	Aerospatiale AS.350B3 AStar	3268	ex N404AE	EMS	Lsd fr WFBN
N415AE	Aerospatiale AS.350B3 AStar	3336			
N779LF	Aerospatiale AS.350D Astar II	1621	ex N85230		
N781LF	Aerospatiale AS.350B AStar	1178			
N792LF	Aerospatiale AS.350B AStar	1035	ex N9004M		
N852HW	Aerospatiale AS.350B2 AStar	2630	ex N352HW		Lsd fr CIT Lsg
N911LR	Aerospatiale AS.350B2 AStar	2404	ex N93GT	EMS	
N3593X	Aerospatiale AS.350B AStar	1081			
N5771C	Aerospatiale AS.350B AStar	1369			Lsd fr GECAS
N5797T	Aerospatiale AS.350D AStar	1472	ex N3944S		
N6099P	Aerospatiale AS.350B2 AStar	2818			Lsd fr debis
N57731	Aerospatiale AS.350D AStar II	1434			
N58045	Aerospatiale AS.350D AStar	1602			
N28MS	Beech 65-E90 King Air	LW-100	ex N31FN		
N92DV	Beech 65-E90 King Air	LW-292	ex N7MA		
N228RA	Beech 65-E90 King Air	LW-197	ex N222JD		
N987GM	Beech 65-E90 King Air	LW-65	ex N3065W		
N989GM	Beech 65-E90 King Air	LW-108	ex N388SC		
N206AL	Bell 206L-1 LongRanger II	45446	ex N5735M		
N206UH	Bell 206L-3 LongRanger III	51167			
N220LL	Bell 206L-3 LongRanger III	51039	ex N3175R		
N771AM	Bell 206L-3 LongRanger III	51065			
N772AM	Bell 206L-3 LongRanger III	51036	ex N3174S		
N206CM	Bell 222U	47558	ex N7643S		
N208CM	Bell 222U	47518	ex N773AM		
N222AM	Bell 222U	47547	ex N221HX		
N222LL	Bell 222	47060	ex N222LG		
N224LL	Bell 222U	47552	ex N776AM		

N226LL	Bell 222UT	47537	ex N781SA		
N404EM	Bell 222U	47514	ex N7XM		Lsd fr debis
N611SJ	Bell 222U	47564	ex N222MT		
N885AL	Bell 222U	47542	ex N772AM		
N911ED	Bell 222U	47551	ex N3204L		
N911NM	Bell 222U	47569	ex N4181X		
N407AM	Bell 407	53309			
N407GA	Bell 407	53104	ex C-FSPD		
N407LN	Bell 407	53181	ex N5984L		
N407LR	Bell 407	53279			
N407SJ	Bell 407	53422			
N407UH	Bell 407	53345			
N407VV	Bell 407	53476			
N408AM	Bell 407	53445			
N408GA	Bell 407	53392			
N772AL	Bell 407	53040			
N773AL	Bell 407	53160	ex N176PA		
N811AL	Bell 407	53144	ex N70829		
N911LN	Bell 407	53446			
N911WB	Bell 407	53176	ex N72402		
N911WN	Bell 407	53360	ex N6298N		
N412FH	Bell 412HP	36027			
N412LG	Bell 412SP	33209			
N554AL	Bell 412	33017	ex N20703		
N555BA	Bell 412HP	36015			
N556UH	Bell 412SP	33178	ex N2024Z		
N586AC	Bell 412SP	36008	ex N402MA		
N778AM	Bell 412	33033	ex N565AC		
N135N	Eurocopter EC135P1	0086	ex N52268		Lsd fr Memorial Mission H/c
N135SJ	Eurocopter EC135P1	0054	ex N4056V		Lsd fr GECC
N426AE	Eurocopter EC135P1	0159			
N427AE	Eurocopter EC135P1	0162			
N5233N	Eurocopter EC135P1	0133			
N10UM	MBB BK117B-1	7231	ex N65541		Lsd fr Merrill Lynch
N61LF	MBB BK117B-1	7230	ex N17SJ		Lsd fr Merrill Lynch
N62LF	MBB BK117B-1	7163	ex N5188B		Lsd fr State Street
N117BK	MBB BK117B-2	7229			
N117CW	MBB BK117A-4	7125	ex N9021D		
N117MA	MBB BK117A-3	7107	ex N529MB		Lsd fr DRL Enterprises
N117MV	MBB BK117A-3	7089	ex N492MB		
N117NY	MBB BK117A-3	7110	ex N9017Z		
N117SU	MBB BK117C-1	7527	ex N5217M		Lsd fr WFBN
N118NY	MBB BK117A-4	7115	ex N202HN		
N118LF	MBB BK117A-4	7137	ex N9025N	EMS	Lsd fr Fifth Third Lsg
N127HH	MBB BK117A-3	7060	ex N160BK		
N128HH	MBB BK117A-1	7036	ex N118HH		Lsd fr Merrill Lynch
N137HH	MBB BK117A-4	7107	ex N117MB		
N155SC	MBB BK117A-3	7065	ex N155BK		Lsd fr Merrill Lynch
N158BK	MBB BK117A-3	7058			
N163BK	MBB BK117A-3	7063	ex D-HBNK		Lsd fr Merrill Lynch
N202HN	MBB BK117A-3	7115	ex N90184		
N417BK	MBB BK117B-1	7143			Lsd fr WFBN
N420MB	MBB BK117A-3	7077			
N424MB	MBB BK117A-3	7082			
N527RM	MBB BK117A-4	7111	ex N527SF		
N528SF	MBB BK117A-3	7104	ex N528MB		Lsd fr DRL Enterprises
N586BH	MBB BK117A-4	7129	ex N9022E		
N625MB	MBB BK117A-4	7108			Lsd fr DRL Enterprises
N770SL	MBB BK117B-1	7135	ex N117VH		
N911BY	MBB BK117A-4	7127	ex N11UM		
N911SX	MBB BK117B-2	7232	ex N411MA		
N911VU	MBB BK117B-1	7141	ex N90263		Lsd fr WFBN
N951AM	MBB BK117A-4	7017	ex N317RM		
N990SL	MBB BK117B-2	7057	ex N911KD		
N5194C	MBB BK117B-1	7169			Lsd fr State Street
N7059N	MBB BK117B-1	7154			Lsd fr State Street
N7060G	MBB BK117B-1	7173			
N71703	MBB BK117B-1	7227			Lsd fr Merrill Lynch
N90260	MBB BK117B-1	7140			Lsd fr Fifth Third Lsg
N105LC	MBB Bo105CBS-4	S-789	ex N5414F		Op for LEC Medical Center
N105NC	MBB Bo105CBS-4	S-790	ex N301LG		Lsd fr MDFC
N485EC	MBB Bo105CBS-4	S-754	ex N722MB		
N825LF	MBB Bo105CBS-4	S-796	ex N5417E		Lsd fr State Street
N911BH	MBB Bo105CBS	S-685			Lsd fr debis
N299AM	Pilatus PC-12/45	236	ex HB-FRG		
N399AM	Pilatus PC-12/45	249	ex HB-FRT		

N852AL	Pilatus PC-12/45	213	ex N213WA		
N853AL	Pilatus PC-12/45	168	ex N168WA		
N854AL	Pilatus PC-12/45	397	ex N397WA		

N26PK	Cessna 441 Conquest II	441-0143	ex N2627K		Lsd fr Haut-Monts Avn
N30LG	Aerospatiale AS.355F1 TwinStar	5065			Lsd fr GECAS
N53LH	Aerospatiale AS.355F1 TwinStar	5093	ex N57898		Lsd fr Hauts-Monts Avn
N130LN	Eurocopter EC.130B4	3506			
N185GA	Cessna 441 Conquest II	441-0066	ex D-INKA		Lsd fr Hauts-Monts Avn
N220TB	Beech B200 Super King Air	BB-1057	ex F-GILY		
N430UH	Bell 430	49056	ex N430UM		
N441RC	Cessna 441 Conquest II	441-0076			Lsd fr Hauts-Monts Avn
N451AE	Eurocopter EC130B4	3453			
N452AE	Eurocopter EC130B4	3470			
N791DC	Beech B200 Super King Air	BB-1402	ex N91CD		
N793DC	Beech B200 Super King Air	BB-1404	ex N93CD		
N901CF	McDonnell Helicopters MD.900	900-00012	ex N9212Z	EMS	Lsd fr Regional Emergency
N902AM	McDonnell Helicopters MD.902	900-00092			
N8970N	Cessna 441 Conquest II	441-0092			Lsd fr Hauts-Monts Avn

Integrated Rocky Mountain Helicopters during 2003

AIR MIDWEST

Air Midwest (ZV/AMW) (IATA 471)   *Wichita-Mid Continent, KS (ICT)*

N3YV	Beech 1900D	UE-3		Mesa Airlines	Lsd fr ASH
N5YV	Beech 1900D	UE-5		US Airways Express	Lsd fr ASH
N6YV	Beech 1900D	UE-6		US Airways Express	Lsd fr ASH
N13ZV	Beech 1900D	UE-13		US Airways Express	Lsd fr ASH
N15YV	Beech 1900D	UE-15		US Airways Express	Lsd fr ASH
N23YV	Beech 1900D	UE-23		US Airways Express	Lsd fr ASH
N26YV	Beech 1900D	UE-26		Mesa Airlines	Lsd fr ASH
N95YV	Beech 1900D	UE-95		all-white	Lsd fr ASH
N99YV	Beech 1900D	UE-99		Mesa Airlines	Lsd fr ASH
N104YV	Beech 1900D	UE-104		Mesa Airlines	Lsd fr ASH
N105YV	Beech 1900D	UE-105		Mesa Airlines	Lsd fr ASH
N110YV	Beech 1900D	UE-110		US Airways Express	Lsd fr ASH
N112ZV	Beech 1900D	UE-112		Mesa Airlines	Lsd fr ASH
N114YV	Beech 1900D	UE-114		Mesa Airlines	Lsd fr ASH
N120YV	Beech 1900D	UE-120		US Airways Express	Lsd fr ASH
N123YV	Beech 1900D	UE-123		Mesa Airlines	Lsd fr ASH
N125YV	Beech 1900D	UE-125		US Airways Express	Lsd fr ASH
N131YV	Beech 1900D	UE-131			
N133YV	Beech 1900D	UE-133		US Airways Express	Lsd fr ASH
N135YV	Beech 1900D	UE-135			
N138YV	Beech 1900D	UE-138		US Airways Express	Lsd fr ASH
N139ZV	Beech 1900D	UE-139		US Airways Express	Lsd fr ASH
N140ZV	Beech 1900D	UE-140	ex (N137ZV)	US Airways Express	Lsd fr ASH
N143YV	Beech 1900D	UE-143		US Airways Express	Lsd fr ASH
N144ZV	Beech 1900D	UE-144		US Airways Express	Lsd fr ASH
N146ZV	Beech 1900D	UE-146		Mesa Airlines	Lsd fr ASH
N155ZV	Beech 1900D	UE-155		US Airways Express	Lsd fr ASH
N159YV	Beech 1900D	UE-159		all-white	Lsd fr ASH
N161YV	Beech 1900D	UE-161		US Airways Express	Lsd fr ASH
N162ZV	Beech 1900D	UE-162		US Airways Express	Lsd fr ASH
N163YV	Beech 1900D	UE-163		US Airways Express	Lsd fr ASH
N165YV	Beech 1900D	UE-165		US Airways Express	Lsd fr ASH
N166YV	Beech 1900D	UE-166		US Airways Express	Lsd fr ASH
N167YV	Beech 1900D	UE-167		US Airways Express	Lsd fr ASH
N171ZV	Beech 1900D	UE-171		US Airways Express	Lsd fr ASH
N173YV	Beech 1900D	UE-173		US Airways Express	Lsd fr ASH
N174YV	Beech 1900D	UE-174	ex N17541	US Airways Express	Lsd fr ASH
N176YV	Beech 1900D	UE-176		US Airways Express	Lsd fr ASH
N178YV	Beech 1900D	UE-178		US Airways Express	Lsd fr ASH
N190YV	Beech 1900D	UE-190		US Airways Express	Lsd fr ASH
N218YV	Beech 1900D	UE-218		US Airways Express	Lsd fr ASH
N231YV	Beech 1900D	UE-231		US Airways Express	Lsd fr ASH
N237YV	Beech 1900D	UE-237		US Airways Express	Lsd fr ASH
N242YV	Beech 1900D	UE-242		US Airways Express	Lsd fr ASH
N244YV	Beech 1900D	UE-244		US Airways Express	Lsd fr ASH
N3199Q	Beech 1900D	UE-213		US Airways Express	Lsd fr ASH
N10675	Beech 1900D	UE-229		US Airways Express	Lsd fr ASH

Wholly owned by Mesa Air, operates aircraft for America West Express and US Airways Express, the latter in full colours

---

AIRNET SYSTEMS

Star Check (USC) (IATA 116)   *Columbus-Port Columbus Intl, OH/Dallas-Love Field, TX (CMH/DAL)*

N4AW	Beech 58 Baron	TH-450
N21ES	Beech 58 Baron	TH-1123
N26CC	Beech 58 Baron	TH-136

N27MT	Beech 58 Baron	TH-1120	
N33DK	Beech 58 Baron	TH-372	
N33WC	Beech 58 Baron	TH-170	
N58TA	Beech 58 Baron	TH-596	
N58WA	Beech 58 Baron	TH-201	
N65FS	Beech 58 Baron	TH-1084	
N78DM	Beech 58 Baron	TH-281	ex N78MM
N78RE	Beech 58 Baron	TH-371	
N95BB	Beech 58 Baron	TH-333	
N140S	Beech 58 Baron	TH-1155	
N158MT	Beech 58P Baron	TH-1186	
N297AT	Beech 58 Baron	TH-1349	
N367S	Beech 58 Baron	TH-1393	
N400RP	Beech 58 Baron	TH-319	
N456WW	Beech 58 Baron	TH-444	
N525GW	Beech 58 Baron	TH-557	
N696BD	Beech 58 Baron	TH-352	
N858LG	Beech 58 Baron	TH-518	
N882MT	Beech 58 Baron	TH-1343	
N1653W	Beech 58 Baron	TH-252	
N1814W	Beech 58 Baron	TH-287	
N1847F	Beech 58 Baron	TH-1291	
N1859K	Beech 58 Baron	TH-1299	
N2027V	Beech 58 Baron	TH-965	
N2064V	Beech 58 Baron	TH-1004	
N2892W	Beech 58 Baron	TH-389	
N3695V	Beech 58 Baron	TH-1183	
N3703Q	Beech 58 Baron	TH-1189	
N4098S	Beech 58 Baron	TH-600	
N6573K	Beech 58 Baron	TH-1369	
N6650D	Beech 58 Baron	TH-1375	
N6758C	Beech 58 Baron	TH-1080	
N7383R	Beech 58 Baron	TH-502	
N9044V	Beech 58 Baron	TH-216	
N9189Q	Beech 58 Baron	TH-148	
N9367Q	Beech 58 Baron	TH-192	
N17708	Beech 58 Baron	TH-813	
N36673	Beech 58 Baron	TH-1143	
N36901	Beech 58 Baron	TH-1173	
N62500	Beech 58 Baron	TH-1347	
N102AN	Cessna 208B Caravan I	208B0906	
N103AN	Cessna 208B Caravan I	208B0928	
N104AN	Cessna 208B Caravan I	208B0918	
N105AN	Cessna 208B Caravan I	208B0956	
N106AN	Cessna 208B Caravan I	208B0917	ex N5207V
N107AN	Cessna 208B Caravan I	208B0993	
N108AN	Cessna 208B Caravan I	208B0975	
N28NT	Cessna 310R	310R0243	
N35H	Cessna 310R	310R0953	
N310CS	Cessna 310R	310R0239	
N1346G	Cessna 310R	310R0029	
N3597G	Cessna 310R	310R0875	
N3700G	Cessna 310R	310R0899	
N5113J	Cessna 310R	310R0233	
N5119JC	Cessna 310R	310R1420	
N5215C	Cessna 310R	310R1515	
N5238J	Cessna 310R	310R0810	
N5338C	Cessna 310R	310R1544	
N5461J	Cessna 310R	310R0259	
N6121C	Cessna 310R	310R1288	
N6122C	Cessna 310R	310R1290	
N6160X	Cessna 310R	310R1305	
N8251G	Cessna 310R	310R0931	
N37223	Cessna 310R	310R0963	
N37575	Cessna 310R	310R1207	
N15WH	Lear Jet 35A	35A-085	
N25AN	Lear Jet 35A	35A-259	ex HK-3983X
N27BL	Lear Jet 35A	35A-163	ex YV-173CP
N27TT	Lear Jet 35A	35A-122	ex OE-GMP
N31WR	Lear Jet 35A	35A-313	ex TR-LZI
N39DK	Lear Jet 35A	35A-480	ex N35CK
N40AN	Lear Jet 35A	35A-271	ex LV-OAS
N51LC	Lear Jet 35A	35A-302	ex N631CW
N55F	Lear Jet 35A	35A-147	ex N717W
N56JA	Lear Jet 35A	35A-342	ex YV-15CP
N64CP	Lear Jet 35A	35A-264	ex VR-CDI
N72JF	Lear Jet 35A	35A-088	ex OE-GBR
N81FR	Lear Jet 35A	35A-081	ex N118DA
N88BG	Lear Jet 35A	35A-090	ex I-FIMI

N98LC	Lear Jet 35A	35A-077	ex ZS-NRZ
N100WN	Lear Jet 25D	25D-288	ex N40BC
N118DA	Lear Jet 35A	35A-081	ex JY-AFF
N122JW	Lear Jet 35A	35A-217	ex N111RF
N130F	Lear Jet 35	35-044	ex N44VW
N228SW	Lear Jet 25D	25D-228	
N279DM	Lear Jet 35A	35A-214	
N400JE	Lear Jet 35A	35A-120	
N684HA	Lear Jet 35A	35A-113	ex N684LA
N700SJ	Lear Jet 35A	35A-082	ex N700GB
N701AS	Lear Jet 35A	35A-047	ex N13MJ
N800AW	Lear Jet 35A	35A-149	ex N600AW
N813AS	Lear Jet 35A	35A-167	ex N725P
N924BW	Lear Jet 25B	25B-158	ex N71RB
N959SA	Lear Jet 35A	35A-076	
N1140A	Lear Jet 35	35-045	ex N304AT
N4358N	Lear Jet 35	35-065	ex N425DN
N8040A	Lear Jet 35	35-048	ex F-GHMP
N2KC	Piper PA-31-350 Navajo Chieftain	31-7952217	ex N3540X
N4UE	Piper PA-31-350 Chieftain	31-8152061	
N42HD	Piper PA-31-350 Chieftain	31-8152031	
N106TG	Piper PA-31-350 Chieftain	31-8052002	
N225TM	Piper PA-31-350 Chieftain	31-8152133	ex XA-MAU
N525AA	Piper PA-31-350 Chieftain	31-8052111	
N711LH	Piper PA-31-350 Chieftain	31-8152174	
N3547C	Piper PA-31-350 Chieftain	31-8052018	
N3587P	Piper PA-31-350 Chieftain	31-8052120	
N3590D	Piper PA-31-350 Chieftain	31-8052144	
N4079Y	Piper PA-31-350 Chieftain	31-8152079	
N22427	Piper PA-31-350 Chieftain	31-8152065	
N35453	Piper PA-31-350 Chieftain	31-8052006	
N35551	Piper PA-31-350 Chieftain	31-8052063	
N35584	Piper PA-31-350 Chieftain	31-8052076	
N35871	Piper PA-31-350 Chieftain	31-8052123	
N40919	Piper PA-31-350 Chieftain	31-8152162	
N40978	Piper PA-31-350 Chieftain	31-8152199	
N222KD	Ted Smith Aerostar 600A	60-0557-181	ex N8074J
N3643D	Piper PA-60 Aerostar 600A	0835-8161238	
N3645M	Piper PA-60 Aerostar 600A	0847-8161243	
N3645T	Piper PA-60 Aerostar 600A	0852-8161244	
N6069T	Piper PA-60 Aerostar 600A	0887-8161251	
N6076L	Piper PA-60 Aerostar 600A	0713-7961221	
N6892R	Piper PA-60 Aerostar 600A	0887-8161521	ex (N32TY)
N6896B	Piper PA-60 Aerostar 600A	0919-8161260	
N7512S	Ted Smith Aerostar 600A	60-0144-064	
N8073J	Ted Smith Aerostar 600A	60-0556-180	
N8229J	Piper PA-60 Aerostar 600A	0631-7961200	ex C-GFEI
N90349	Ted Smith Aerostar 600A	60-0202-090	

All are freighters.

AIR NOW

Sky Courier (BEN)   *Burlington-Intl, VT (BTV)*

N49BA	Embraer EMB.110P1 Bandeirante	110301	ex N401AS	
N51BA	Embraer EMB.110P1 Bandeirante	110404	ex N903FB	Lsd fr WFBN
N59BA	Embraer EMB.110P1 Bandeirante	110396	ex N900FB	Lsd fr WFBN
N62CZ	Embraer EMB.110P1 Bandeirante	110388	ex PT-SFF	Lsd fr Keycorp Lsg
N64CZ	Embraer EMB.110P1 Bandeirante	110399	ex PT-SFQ	Lsd fr Keycorp Lsg
N83BA	Embraer EMB.110P1 Bandeirante	110351	ex N405AS	Lsd fr WFBN
N97BA	Embraer EMB.110P1 Bandeirante	110322	ex N403AS	
N101TN	Embraer EMB.110P1 Bandeirante	110271	ex PT-SBI	
N621KC	Embraer EMB.110P1 Bandeirante	110335	ex PT-SDL	
N710NH	Embraer EMB.110P1 Bandeirante	110250	ex PT-SAQ	
N790RA	Embraer EMB.110P1 Bandeirante	110278	ex G-SWAG	
N830AC	Embraer EMB.110P1 Bandeirante	110205	ex N524MW	
N7801Q	Embraer EMB.110P1 Bandeirante	110228	ex C-FZAU	
N7DD	Mitsubishi MU-2B	297	ex N106GB	
N28AN	Cessna 208B Caravan	208B0751		
N29AN	Cessna 208B Caravan	208B0753		Lsd fr WFBN
N9339B	Cessna 208B Caravan I	208B0057		

AirNow is the trading name of Business Air

AIR ONE EXPRESS

N372PH	Swearingen SA.227AC Metro III	AC-532	ex N3110B	Lsd fr Air Support
N26959	Swearingen SA.227AC Metro III	AC-662		Lsd fr GAS Wilson

AIR RESPONSE

Mesa-Falcon Field, AZ (MSC)

N99AS	Douglas C-54D	22203	ex Bu56549	Sprayer
N438NA	Douglas C-54G	36031	ex Bu45578	Sprayer
N67017	Douglas C-54B	10438	ex Bu39122	Sprayer
N67019	Douglas C-54B	10520	ex Bu50865	Sprayer
N99AS	Douglas C-54D	22203	ex Bu56549	Sprayer
N438NA	Douglas C-54G	36031	ex Bu45578	Sprayer
N67017	Douglas C-54B	10438	ex Bu39122	Sprayer
N67019	Douglas C-54B	10520	ex Bu50865	Sprayer
N99AS	Douglas C-54D	22203	ex Bu56549	Sprayer
N438NA	Douglas C-54G	36031	ex Bu45578	Sprayer
N67017	Douglas C-54B	10438	ex Bu39122	Sprayer
N67019	Douglas C-54B	10520	ex Bu50865	Sprayer

AIR RESPONSE NORTH renamed Global Air Response

AIR ST THOMAS

Paradise (ZP/STT)   *St Thomas-Cyril E King, VI (STT)*

N329SD	Piper PA-23-250 Aztec C	27-3512	ex N6268Y	Lsd fr Virgin Air
N5623Y	Piper PA-23-250 Aztec C	27-2733		Lsd fr Virgin Air
N6389Y	Piper PA-23-250 Aztec C	27-3675		
N8125F	Cessna 402	402-0231		

AIR SUNSHINE

Air Sunshine (YI/RSI)   *Fort Lauderdale-Hollywood Intl, FL (FLL)*

N122TA	Cessna 402C	402C0122	ex N2712P
N220RS	Cessna 402C	402C0220	ex N2716L
N251RS	Cessna 402C	402C0251	ex N166PB
N347AB	Cessna 402C	402C0347	ex N26548
N351AB	Cessna 402C	402C0351	ex N26629
N402RS	Cessna 402C	402C0402	ex N2663N
N603AB	Cessna 402C	402C0603	ex N84PB
N123HY	Embraer EMB.110P1 Bandeirante	110321	ex N619KC

Associated with Tropical Transport Services

AIR TAHOMA

Tahoma (5C/HMA)   *Columbus-Rickenbacker, OH (LCK)*

N581P	Convair 580	29	ex C-FBHW	Lsd fr R&R Holdings
N582P	Convair 580	475	ex N969N	Lsd fr N582P Inc
N583P	Convair 580	454	ex C-GKFR	Lsd fr Kasi Intl
N584E	Convair 580	24	ex C-FAUF	Lsd fr US Contract Financing
N585P	Convair 580	163	ex N718RA	
N327UW	Convair T-29	53-16	ex	

All freighters

AIR TRANSPORT

Coyote (CYO)   *El Paso-Intl, TX (ELP)*

N22WE	Cessna 402B	402B0004	ex C-GULD		Lsd fr CIT Lsg
N26AT	Lear Jet 25B	25B-130	ex N25PL	EMS	Lsd fr FJM Nevada
N35WE	Lear Jet 35A	35A-156	ex N190DA		Lsd fr CIT Lsg
N273LR	Lear Jet 25	25-058	ex N273LP	EMS	Lsd fr FJM Nevada
N761JP	Cessna T210M Turbo Centurion	21062296			Lsd fr VGT LLC
N976BS	Lear Jet 25	25-016	ex N8FF		Lsd fr FJM Nevada
N3855C	Cessna 421C Golden Eagle	421C0121			
N77404	Cessna 404 Titan	404-0005	ex N3933C		

Conducts EMS flights as Air Med El Paso

AIR TRANSPORT INTERNATIONAL now listed as ATI-Air Transport International

AIR VEGAS AIRLINES

Air Vegas (6V/VGA)   *Las Vegas-North, NV (VGT)*

N174AV	Beech C99	U-174	ex N99CJ	
N189AV	Beech C99	U-189	ex N516DM	
N191AV	Beech C99	U-191	ex VR-CIB	
N206AV	Beech C99	U-206	ex N216EE	
N227AV	Beech C99	U-227	ex N2225H	
N234AV	Beech C99	U-234	ex N234BH	
N235AV	Beech C99	U-235	ex N235BH	special Centennial c/s
N330AV	Beech C99	U-230	ex N3063W	
N388AV	Beech C99	U-188	ex N799GL	

All leased from Pacific Aircraft Finance LLC

AIR WISCONSIN

Air Wisconsin (ZW/AWI) (IATA 303)   Appleton-Outagamie Co, WI (ATW)

N156TR	British Aerospace 146 Srs.200	E2156	ex N884DV	United Express	Lsd fr BAES
N179US	British Aerospace 146 Srs.200	E2041	ex N358PS	United Express	Lsd fr WTCo
N181US	British Aerospace 146 Srs.200	E2042	ex N359PS	United Express	Lsd fr WTCo
N183US	British Aerospace 146 Srs.200	E2043	ex N360PS	United Express	Lsd fr WTCo
N290UE	British Aerospace 146 Srs.200	E2080	ex N814AS	United Express	Lsd fr BAES
N291UE	British Aerospace 146 Srs.200	E2084	ex N815AS	United Express	Lsd fr BAES
N292UE	British Aerospace 146 Srs.200	E2087	ex N816AS	United Express	Lsd fr BAES
N463AP	British Aerospace 146 Srs.100	E1063	ex N70NA	United Express	Lsd fr WFBN
N606AW	British Aerospace 146 Srs.200	E2033	ex G-5-033	United Express	Lsd fr WFBN
N607AW	British Aerospace 146 Srs.200	E2052	ex G-5-001	United Express; Kitty	
N608AW	British Aerospace 146 Srs.200	E2049	ex G-5-002	United Express	
N609AW	British Aerospace 146 Srs.200	E2070	ex G-BNKK	United Express	
N610AW	British Aerospace 146 Srs.200	E2082	ex G-5-082	United Express	
N611AW	British Aerospace 146 Srs.300	E3120	ex N146UK	United Express	
N612AW	British Aerospace 146 Srs.300	E3122	ex G-5-122	United Express	
N614AW	British Aerospace 146 Srs.300	E3132	ex G-5-132	United Express	
N615AW	British Aerospace 146 Srs.300	E3141	ex G-5-141	United Express	
N616AW	British Aerospace 146 Srs.300	E3145	ex G-5-145	United Express	
N401AW	Canadair CL-600-2B19	7280	ex C-FMMW	401 United Express	
N402AW	Canadair CL-600-2B19	7281	ex C-FMMX	402 United Express	
N403AW	Canadair CL-600-2B19	7288	ex C-FMLF	403 United Express	
N404AW	Canadair CL-600-2B19	7294	ex C-FMMT	404 United Express	
N405AW	Canadair CL-600-2B19	7362	ex C-FMND	405 United Express	
N406AW	Canadair CL-600-2B19	7402	ex C-FMMY	406 United Express	
N407AW	Canadair CL-600-2B19	7424	ex C-FMLU	407 United Express	
N408AW+	Canadair CL-600-2B19	7568	ex C-FMNY	408 United Express	
N409AW	Canadair CL-600-2B19	7447	ex C-FMNX	409 United Express	
N410AW	Canadair CL-600-2B19	7490	ex C-FMMW	410 United Express	
N411ZW+	Canadair CL-600-2B19	7569	ex C-F	411 United Express	
N412AW+	Canadair CL-600-2B19	7582	ex C-FMMY	412 United Express	
N413AW+	Canadair CL-600-2B19	7585	ex C-FMKW	413 United Express	
N414ZW+	Canadair CL-600-2B19	7586	ex C-FMKZ	414 United Express	
N415AW+	Canadair CL-600-2B19	7593	ex C-FMLV	415 United Express	
N416ANQ+	Canadair CL-600-2B19	7603	ex C-FMNQ	416 United Express	
N417AW+	Canadair CL-600-2B19	7610	ex C-FMMW	417 United Express	
N418AW+	Canadair CL-600-2B19	7618	ex C-FMLF	418 United Express	
N419AW+	Canadair CL-600-2B19	7633	ex C-FMNQ	419 United Express	
N420AW+	Canadair CL-600-2B19	7640	ex C-FMMW	420 United Express	
N421ZW*	Canadair CL-600-2B19	7346	ex N587ML	421 United Express	
N422AW*	Canadair CL-600-2B19	7341	ex N586ML	422 United Express	
N423AW+	Canadair CL-600-2B19	7636	ex C-FMMB	423 United Express	
N424AW+	Canadair CL-600-2B19	7656	ex C-FMNW	424 United Express	
N425AW+	Canadair CL-600-2B19	7663	ex C-FMNQ	425 United Express	
N426AW+	Canadair CL-600-2B19	7669	ex C-FMMQ	426 United Express	
N427ZW+	Canadair CL-600-2B19	7685	ex C-FMNH	427 United Express	
N428AW+	Canadair CL-600-2B19	7695	ex C-FMOI	428 United Express	
N429AW+	Canadair CL-600-2B19	7711	ex CFMLS	429 United Express	
N430AW+	Canadair CL-600-2B19	7719	ex C-FMOS	430 United Express	
N431AW+	Canadair CL-600-2B19	7256	ex N575ML	AirTran Jet Connect	
N432AW+	Canadair CL-600-2B19	7257	ex N576ML	AirTran Jet Connect	
N433AW	Canadair CL-600-2B19	7289	ex N580ML	AirTran Jet Connect	
N434AW	Canadair CL-600-2B19	7322	ex N582ML	AirTran Jet Connect	
N435AW+	Canadair CL-600-2B19	7724	ex C-FMLU	435 United Express	
N436AW	Canadair CL-600-2B19	7734	ex C-FMKV	436 United Express	
N437AW	Canadair CL-600-2B19	7744	ex C-FMMT	437 United Express	
N438AW	Canadair CL-600-2B19	7748	ex C-GFAX	AirTran JetConnect	
N439AW	Canadair CL-600-2B19	7753	ex C-FZZO	AirTran JetConnect	
N440AW	Canadair CL-600-2B19	7766	ex C-FMKZ	440 United Express	
N441ZW	Canadair CL-600-2B19	7777	ex C-FMNX	441 United Express	
N442AW	Canadair CL-600-2B19	7778	ex C-FMNY	442 United Express	
N443AW	Canadair CL-600-2B19	7781	ex C-FVAZ	443 United Express	
N444ZW	Canadair CL-600-2B19	7788	ex C-FMMN	444 United Express	
N445AW	Canadair CL-600-2B19	7804	ex C-FMMT	AirTran JetConnect	
N446AW	Canadair CL-600-2B19	7806	ex C-FMNV	446 United Express	
N447AW	Canadair CL-6002-B19	7812	ex C-FMND	447 United Express	
N448AW	Canadair CL-6002-B19	7814	ex C-FMLU	448 United Express	
N449AW	Canadair CL-6002-B19	7818	ex C-FMMN	AirTran JetConnect	
N450AW	Canadair CL-600-2B19	7823	ex C-	450 United Express	
N451AW	Canadair CL-600-2B19	7832	ex C-FMLT	451 United Express	
N452AW	Canadair CL-600-2B19	7835	ex C-FMNH	452 United Express	
N453AW	Canadair CL-600-2B19	7838	ex C-FMNY	AirTran JetConnect	
N454AW	Canadair CL-600-2B19	7842	ex C-FMND	454 United Express	
N455AW	Canadair CL-600-2B19	7848	ex C-FMMN		
N456ZW	Canadair CL-600-2B19	7849	ex C-FMMQ	456 United Express	
N457AW	Canadair CL-600-2B19	7854	ex C-FMKV	AirTran JetConnect	
N458AW	Canadair CL-600-2B19	7861	ex C-FMLS	458 United Express	

N459AW	Canadair CL-600-2B19	7863	ex C-FMLV	459 United Express		
N460AW	Canadair CL-600-2B19	7867	ex C-GZTD	460 United Express		
N461SW	Canadair CL-600-2B19	7870	ex C-FMOW	461 United Express		
N462AW	Canadair CL-600-2B19	7875	ex C-FMOI	462 United Express		
N463AW	Canadair CL-600-2B19	7878	ex C-FMMN	463 United Express		
N464AW	Canadair CL-600-2B19	7890	ex C-FMLQ	464 United Express		
N465AW	Canadair CL-600-2B19	7893	ex C-	465 United Express		
N466AW	Canadair CL-600-2B19	7899	ex C-			
N467AW	Canadair CL-600-2B19	7900	ex C-			
N	Canadair CL-600-2B19		ex C-	on order		
N	Canadair CL-600-2B19		ex C-	on order		
N	Canadair CL-600-2B19		ex C-	on order		

+Leased from Wachovia Trust

N328LS*	Dornier 328-120	3025	ex D-CDHK	321 United Express	Lsd fr WFBN
N328MX	Dornier 238-120	3071	ex D-CDXX	301 United Express	Lsd fr WFBN
N329MX	Dornier 328-120	3049	ex D-CAOS	302 United Express	Lsd fr WFBN
N330MX	Dornier 328-120	3067	ex D-CDXN	303 United Express	Lsd fr WFBN
N331MX	Dornier 328-120	3074	ex D-CDXA	304 United Express	Lsd fr WFBN
N334PH*	Dornier 328-120	3012	ex D-CASI	309 United Express	Lsd fr WFBN
N335LS*	Dornier 328-120	3025	ex D-CDAU	United Express	Lsd fr WFBN
N335PH*	Dornier 328-120	3013	ex D-CALT	314 United Express	Lsd fr WFBN
N336PH*	Dornier 328-120	3014	ex D-CANO	310 United Express	Lsd fr WFBN
N337PH*	Dornier 328-120	3020	ex D-CDHE	312 United Express	Lsd fr WFBN
N338PH*	Dornier 328-120	3029	ex D-CDHO	313 United Express	Lsd fr WFBN
N339PH*	Dornier 328-120	3015	ex D-CALT	311 United Express	Lsd fr WFBN
N340LS*	Dornier 328-120	3040	ex D-CDXF	317 United Express	Lsd fr WFBN
N340PH*	Dornier 328-120	3064	ex D-CDXG	United Express	Lsd fr WFBN
N341PH*	Dornier 328-120	3065	ex D-CDXJ	315 United Express	Lsd fr WFBN
N350AD*	Dornier 328-120	3050	ex G-BYHF	318 United Express	Lsd fr WFBN

Operates as a United Express carrier (q.v.) using flight numbers in the range 5000-5299 and 5400-5499 and as AirTran Connect from Orlando, FL   *Stored Oklahoma City

AIRPAC AIRLINES

Airpac (APC)   **Seattle-Boeing Field, WA (BFI)**

N36PB	Piper PA-31-350 Navajo Chieftain	31-7405128		
N40ST	Piper PA-31-350 Navajo Chieftain	31-7405183		Lsd fr Pioneer Lsg
N627HA	Piper PA-31-350 Navajo Chieftain	31-7952241		
N777KT	Piper PA-31-350 Navajo Chieftain	31-7552053	ex N1TW	
N3582X	Piper PA-31-350 Chieftain	31-8052105		
N27594	Piper PA-31-350 Navajo Chieftain	31-7852070		

N41SA	Cessna 404 Titan	404-0023	ex N5271J
N2880A	Beech 99	U-109	
N5278J	Cessna 404 Titan	404-0635	
N4377X	Piper PA-34-200T Seneca II	34-7670035	
N4490F	Piper PA-34-200T Seneca II	34-7670339	
N8107D	Piper PA-34-200T Seneca II	34-8070010	
N36319	Piper PA-34-200T Seneca II	34-7870318	

All freighters

AIRPRO FLIGHT SERVICES ceased operations

AIRSERV INTERNATIONAL

Warrenton, VA

N17SE	Beech 65-E90 King Air	LW-169	ex N600KC	Lsd fr First Capital Group
N115DT	Beech A100 King Air	B-212	ex N115D	
N740GL	Beech 200 Super King Air	BB-650	ex N33TJ	
N756GQ	Cessna TU206G Stationair 6	U20604083		
N899AS	de Havilland DHC-6 Twin Otter 300	347	ex LN-FKB	Op for United Nations
N9008U	Beech A200 Super King Air	BD-05	ex 73-1219	
N9324F	Cessna 208 Caravan I	20800013		
N9732F	Cessna 208 Caravan I	20800156		

Usually based overseas operating relief flights

AIRTRAN AIRWAYS

Citrus (FL/TRS)   **Orlando-Intl, FL/Atlanta-Hartsfield Intl, GA (MCO/ATL)**

N	Boeing 717-22A	5074/55127	ex N482HA		Lsd fr WFBN
N604AT	Boeing 717-22A	5079/55128	ex N483HA		Lsd fr WFBN
N717JL	Boeing 717-2BD	5115/55042	ex N983AT	740	Lsd fr WFBN
N906AT	Boeing 717-231	5060/55087	ex N420TW	795	Lsd fr BCC Equipment Lsg
N910AT	Boeing 717-231	5056/55086	ex N2419C		Lsd fr BCC Equipment Lsg
N915AT	Boeing 717-231	5055/55085	ex N418TW		Lsd fr BCC Equipment Lsg
N919AT	Boeing 717-231	5052/55084	ex N2417F		Lsd fr BCC Equipment Lsg
N920AT	Boeing 717-231	5049/55083	ex N416TW		

Reg	Type	c/n	ex	Fleet	Lease
N921AT	Boeing 717-231	5046/55082	ex N415TW		
N924AT	Boeing 717-231	5043/55080	ex N413TW		Lsd fr BCC Equipment Lsg
N925AT	Boeing 717-231	5042/55079	ex N412TW		Lsd fr BCC Equipment Lsg
N926AT	Boeing 717-231	5039/55078	ex N411TW		Lsd fr Hawk Lsg
N927AT	Boeing 717-231	5038/55077	ex N2410W		Lsd fr WFBN
N928AT	Boeing 717-231	5035/55076	ex N409TW		Lsd fr Hawk Lsg
N929AT	Boeing 717-231	5032/55075	ex N408TW		Lsd fr Hawk Lsg
N930AT	Boeing 717-231	5025/55072	ex N405TW		Lsd fr Hawk Lsg
N932AT	Boeing 717-231	5028/55073	ex N406TW		Lsd fr WFBN
N933AT	Boeing 717-231	5024/55071	ex N2404A		Lsd fr Hawk Lsg
N934AT	Boeing 717-231	5022/55070	ex N403TW		Lsd fr Hawk Lsg
N935AT	Boeing 717-231	5019/55069	ex N402TW		Lsd fr Hawk Lsg
N936AT	Boeing 717-231	5017/55058	ex N401TW		Lsd fr Hawk Lsg
N937AT	Boeing 717-231	5075/55091	ex N424TW		Lsd fr BCC Equipment Lsg
N940AT	Boeing 717-2BD	5005/55004	ex N717XE	702	Lsd fr WFBN
N942AT	Boeing 717-2BD	5006/55005		703	Lsd fr WFBN
N943AT	Boeing 717-2BD	5007/55006		704	Lsd fr WFBN
N944AT	Boeing 717-2BD	5008/55007		705	Lsd fr WFBN
N945AT	Boeing 717-2BD	5009/55008		706	Lsd fr WFBN
N946AT	Boeing 717-2BD	5010/55009		707	Lsd fr WFBN
N947AT	Boeing 717-2BD	5011/55010		708	Lsd fr WFBN
N948AT	Boeing 717-2BD	5012/55011		709	Lsd fr WFBN
N949AT	Boeing 717-2BD	5004/55003	ex N717XD	701	Lsd fr WFBN
N950AT	Boeing 717-2BD	5018/55012		710	Lsd fr WFBN
N951AT	Boeing 717-2BD	5021/55013		711	Lsd fr WFBN
N952AT	Boeing 717-2BD	5027/55014		712	
N953AT	Boeing 717-2BD	5033/55015		713	Lsd fr WFBN
N954AT	Boeing 717-2BD	5036/55016		714	Lsd fr WFBN
N955AT	Boeing 717-2BD	5040/55017		715	Lsd fr WFBN
N956AT	Boeing 717-2BD	5044/55018		716	Lsd fr WFBN
N957AT	Boeing 717-2BD	5047/55019		717	Lsd fr WFBN
N958AT	Boeing 717-2BD	5051/55020		718	Lsd fr WFBN
N959AT	Boeing 717-2BD	5057/55021		719	Lsd fr WFBN
N960AT	Boeing 717-2BD	5058/55022		720	Lsd fr WFBN
N961AT	Boeing 717-2BD	5062/55023		721	Lsd fr WFBN
N963AT	Boeing 717-2BD	5066/55024			Lsd fr WFBN
N964AT	Boeing 717-2BD	5071/55025			Lsd fr WFBN
N965AT	Boeing 717-2BD	5076/55026			Lsd fr WFBN
N966AT	Boeing 717-2BD	5081/55027			Lsd fr WFBN
N967AT	Boeing 717-2BD	5082/55028			Lsd fr WFBN
N968AT	Boeing 717-2BD	5091/55029			Lsd fr WFBN
N969AT	Boeing 717-2BD	5094/55030			Lsd fr WFBN
N970AT	Boeing 717-2BD	5096/55031			Lsd fr WFBN
N971AT	Boeing 717-2BD	5097/55032			Lsd fr WFBN
N972AT	Boeing 717-2BD	5099/55033			Lsd fr WFBN
N974AT	Boeing 717-2BD	5101/55034			Lsd fr WFBN
N975AT	Boeing 717-2BD	5102/55035			Lsd fr WFBN
N977AT	Boeing 717-2BD	5106/55036			Lsd fr WFBN
N978AT	Boeing 717-2BD	5108/55037			Lsd fr WFBN
N979AT	Boeing 717-2BD	5109/55038			
N980AT	Boeing 717-2BD	5111/55039			Lsd fr WFBN
N981AT	Boeing 717-2BD	5113/55040			Lsd fr WFBN
N982AT	Boeing 717-2BD	5114/55041			Lsd fr WFBN
N985AT	Boeing 717-231	5068/55090	ex N423TW		Lsd fr BCC Equipment Lsg
N986AT	Boeing 717-231	5067/55089	ex N422TW		Lsd fr BCC Equipment Lsg
N987AT	Boeing 717-231	5063/55088	ex N2421A		Lsd fr BCC Equipment Lsg
N988AT	Boeing 717-23S	5065/55068	ex (EI-CWJ)		Lsd fr WFBN
N989AT	Boeing 717-23S	5085/55152	ex (EI-CWK)		Lsd fr WFBN
N990AT	Boeing 717-23S	5088/55134	ex (EI-CWM)		Lsd fr WFBN
N991AT	Boeing 717-23S	5090/55135	ex N6202S		Lsd fr WFBN
N992AT	Boeing 717-2BD	5100/55136	ex N6202D		LSd fr WFBN
N993AT	Boeing 717-2BD	5103/55137			Lsd fr WFBN
N994AT	Boeing 717-2BD	5104/55138			Lsd fr WFBN
N995AT	Boeing 717-2BD	5105/55139			Lsd fr WFBN
N996AT	Boeing 717-2BD	5107/55140			Lsd fr WFBN
N997AT	Boeing 717-23S	5110/55141			Lsd fr WFBN
N998AT	Boeing 717-2BD	5112/55142			Lsd fr WFBN

Six more Boeing 717s are on order

Reg	Type	c/n	Status	Lease
N126AT	Boeing 737-76N	32679	on order 04	Lsd fr GECAS
N149AT	Boeing 737-76N	32681	on order 04	Lsd fr GECAS
N166AT	Boeing 737-7BD	33817	on order 04	
N	Boeing 737-7BD		on order 04	
N	Boeing 737-7BD		on order 04	
N	Boeing 737-7BD		on order 04	

A further 44 are on order for delivery at a rate of one a month; 22 in total will be leased from GECAS

Reg	Type	c/n	ex	Lease
N381LF	Airbus Industrie A320-232	0640	ex F-OHMO	Lsd fr/op by RYN
N391LF	Airbus industrie A320-232	0676	ex F-OHMR	Lsd fr/op by RYN
N821AT	Douglas DC-9-32 (ABS 3)	413/47284	ex N921VV	
N836AT	Douglas DC-9-32 (ABS 3)	636/47397	ex N936VV	
N846AT	Douglas DC-9-32 (ABS 3)	333/47226	ex N946VV	

N849AT	Douglas DC-9-32 (ABS 3)	648/47484	ex N949VV	Lsd fr WFBN
N941LF	Airbus Industrie A320-233	0461	ex F-WWDP	Lsd fr/op by RYN
N951LF	Airbus Industrie A320-233	0460	ex F-WWDN	Lsd fr/op by RYN

Last Douglas DC-9 flight on 16 December 2003. AirTran JetConnect provides feeder services in Florida

AIRTRAN JETCONNECT

Orlando-Intl, FL (MCO)

N431AW	Canadair CL-600-2B19	7257	ex N576ML
N432AW	Canadair CL-600-2B19	7256	ex N575ML
N433AW	Canadair CL-600-2B19	7289	ex N580ML
N434AW	Canadair CL-600-2B19	7322	ex N581ML
N438AW	Canadair CL-600-2B19	7748	ex C-GFAX
N439AW	Canadair CL-600-2B19	7753	ex C-FZZO
N445AW	Canadair CL-600-2B19	7804	ex C-FMMT
N446AW	Canadair CL-600-2B19	7806	ex C-FMNW
N449AW	Canadair CL-6002-B19	7818	ex C-FMMN
N453AW	Canadair CL-600-2B19	7838	ex C-FMNY
N457AW	Canadair CL-600-2B19	7854	ex C-FMKV

Operated by Air Wisconsin to provide feeder services in Florida

ALASKA AIRLINES

Alaska (AS/ASA) (IATA 027)   *Seattle-Tacoma Intl, WA (SEA)*

N703AS	Boeing 737-490	3039/28893	ex (N747AS)		Lsd fr WFBN
N705AS	Boeing 737-490	3043/29318	ex (N748AS)		Lsd fr WFBN
N706AS	Boeing 737-490	3050/28894	ex (N749AS)		Lsd fr WFBN
N708AS	Boeing 737-490	3058/28895	ex N1786B		
N709AS	Boeing 737-490	3099/28896	ex N1787B		
N713AS	Boeing 737-490	3110/30161	ex N1787B		
N730AS	Boeing 737-290C (Nordam 3)	760/22577			
N740AS	Boeing 737-290C (Nordam 3)	767/22578			
N741AS	Boeing 737-2Q8C (Nordam 3)	610/21959	ex N206FE		
N742AS	Boeing 737-290C (Nordam 3)	1032/23136			
N743AS	Boeing 737-210C (Nordam 3)	590/21821	ex N492WC		
N744AS	Boeing 737-210C (Nordam 3)	605/21822	ex N493WC		
N745AS	Boeing 737-298C (Nordam 3)	346/20794	ex N87WA		
N746AS	Boeing 737-2X6C (Nordam 3)	1042/23123	ex N672MA		
N747AS	Boeing 737-2X6C (Nordam 3)	1046/23124	ex 9M-PMU		
N754AS	Boeing 737-4Q8	2266/25095		Spirit of Alaska	Lsd fr WFBN
N755AS	Boeing 737-4Q8	2278/25096			Lsd fr WFBN
N756AS	Boeing 737-4Q8	2299/25097			
N760AS	Boeing 737-4Q8	2320/25098			Lsd fr WFBN
N762AS	Boeing 737-4Q8	2334/25099			Lsd fr ILFC
N763AS	Boeing 737-4Q8	2346/25100			
N764AS	Boeing 737-4Q8	2348/25101			Lsd fr Interlease
N765AS	Boeing 737-4Q8	2350/25102			Lsd fr Interlease
N767AS	Boeing 737-490	2354/27081			
N768AS	Boeing 737-490	2350/27082			
N769AS	Boeing 737-4Q8	2452/25103			Lsd fr WFBN
N771AS	Boeing 737-4Q8	2476/25104			Lsd fr ILFC
N772AS	Boeing 737-4Q8	2505/25105			Lsd fr MSA V
N773AS	Boeing 737-4Q8	2518/25106			Lsd fr ACG Acquisition
N774AS	Boeing 737-4Q8	2526/25107			Lsd Castle 2003-1B
N775AS	Boeing 737-4Q8	2551/25108			Lsd fr Castle 2003-2A
N776AS	Boeing 737-4Q8	2561/25109			Lsd fr BCC Equipment Lsg
N778AS	Boeing 737-4Q8	2586/25110			Lsd fr ILFC
N779AS	Boeing 737-4Q8	2605/25111			Lsd fr ILFC
N780AS	Boeing 737-4Q8	2638/25112			Lsd fr ILFC
N782AS	Boeing 737-4Q8	2656/25113		stored PAE	Lsd fr WFBN
N783AS	Boeing 737-4Q8	2666/25114			Lsd fr WFBN
N784AS	Boeing 737-4Q8	2826/28199		Spirit of Disneyland c/s	Lsd fr ILFC
N785AS	Boeing 737-4Q8	2858/27628			Lsd fr ILFC
N786AS	Boeing 737-4S3	1870/24795	ex TF-FIE		Lsd fr WFBN
N788AS	Boeing 737-490	2891/28885			Lsd fr WFBN
N791AS	Boeing 737-490	2902/28886			Lsd fr WFBN
N792AS	Boeing 737-490	2903/28887			Lsd fr WFBN
N793AS	Boeing 737-490	2990/28888			Lsd fr WFBN
N794AS	Boeing 737-490	3000/28889			Lsd fr WFBN
N795AS	Boeing 737-490	3006/28890			Lsd fr WFBN
N796AS	Boeing 737-490	3027/28891			Lsd fr WFBN
N797AS	Boeing 737-490	3036/28892			Lsd fr WFBN
N799AS	Boeing 737-490	3038/29270			Lsd fr WFBN
N607AS	Boeing 737-790	313/29751			
N609AS	Boeing 737-790	350/29752			
N611AS	Boeing 737-790	385/29753			
N612AS	Boeing 737-790	406/30162	ex N1787B		
N613AS	Boeing 737-790	430/30163			

N614AS	Boeing 737-790	439/30343			
N615AS	Boeing 737-790	472/30344	ex N1787B		
N617AS	Boeing 737-790	532/30542			
N618AS	Boeing 737-790	536/30543	ex N1787B		
N619AS	Boeing 737-790	597/30164			
N622AS	Boeing 737-790	661/30165			
N623AS	Boeing 737-790	700/30166			
N624AS	Boeing 737-790	724/30778			
N625AS	Boeing 737-790	754/30792			
N626AS	Boeing 737-790	763/30793			
N627AS	Boeing 737-790	796/30794			
N629AS	Boeing 737-790	1273/30626			Lsd fr CIT Lsg
N644AS	Boeing 737-790	1277/30795			
N645AS	Boeing 737-7BK	1291/33011			Lsd fr CIT Lsg
N647AS	Boeing 737-7BK	1306/33012			Lsd fr CIT Lsg
N648AS	Boeing 737-790	1382/30662			Lsd fr ILFC
N649AS	Boeing 737-790	1386/30663			Lsd fr ILFC
N302AS	Boeing 737-990	596/30017	ex N737X		
N303AS	Boeing 737-990	683/30016	ex N672AS		
N305AS	Boeing 737-990	774/30013	ex (N673AS)		
N306AS	Boeing 737-990	802/30014	ex (N674AS)		
N307AS	Boeing 737-990	838/30015	ex (N675AS)		
N309AS	Boeing 737-990	902/30857			
N315AS	Boeing 737-990	1218/30019			
N317AS	Boeing 737-990	1296/30856			
N318AS	Boeing 737-990	1326/30018			
N319AS	Boeing 737-990	1344/33679			
N320AS	Boeing 737-990	1380/33680			
N323AS	Boeing 737-990	1454/30021			
N324AS	Boeing 737-990			on order	
N	Boeing 737-990			on order	
N931AS	McDonnell-Douglas MD-83	1178/49232			
N933AS	McDonnell-Douglas MD-83	1204/49234		stored MHV	
N934AS	McDonnell-Douglas MD-83	1234/49235			
N935AS	McDonnell-Douglas MD-83	1235/49236			
N937AS	McDonnell-Douglas MD-83	1276/49364			Lsd fr WFBN
N943AS	McDonnell-Douglas MD-83	1779/53018			
N944AS	McDonnell-Douglas MD-83	1783/53019			
N947AS	McDonnell-Douglas MD-83	1789/53020			
N948AS	McDonnell-Douglas MD-83	1801/53021			
N949AS	McDonnell-Douglas MD-83	1809/53022			Lsd fr WFBN
N950AS	McDonnell-Douglas MD-83	1821/53023			
N951AS	McDonnell-Douglas MD-82	1064/49111	ex N781JA	stored MHV	Lsd fr Finova
N953AS	McDonnell-Douglas MD-82	1287/49386	ex N784JA	stored MHV	
N954AS	McDonnell-Douglas MD-82	1288/49387	ex N785JA	stored MHV	
N958AS	McDonnell-Douglas MD-83	1825/53024			
N960AS	McDonnell-Douglas MD-83	1976/53074			Lsd fr WFBN
N961AS	McDonnell-Douglas MD-83	1977/53075			Lsd fr WFBN
N962AS	McDonnell-Douglas MD-83	1988/53076			Lsd fr WFBN
N964AS	McDonnell-Douglas MD-83	1996/53078			Lsd fr WFBN
N965AS	McDonnell-Douglas MD-83	2004/53079			Lsd fr WFBN
N967AS	McDonnell-Douglas MD-82	1083/49103	ex N782JA		Lsd fr WFBN
N968AS	McDonnell-Douglas MD-83	1850/53016			
N969AS	McDonnell-Douglas MD-83	1851/53063			
N972AS	McDonnell-Douglas MD-83	2074/53448			Lsd fr WFBN
N973AS	McDonnell-Douglas MD-83	2077/53449			
N974AS	McDonnell-Douglas MD-83	2078/53450			
N975AS	McDonnell-Douglas MD-83	2083/53451			
N976AS	McDonnell-Douglas MD-83	2109/53452			Lsd fr WFBN
N977AS	McDonnell-Douglas MD-83	2112/53453			Lsd fr WFBN
N979AS	McDonnell-Douglas MD-83	2139/53471			
N981AS	McDonnell-Douglas MD-83	2178/53472			
N982AS	McDonnell-Douglas MD-83	2183/53473			

Alaska Airlines operates feeder services in conjunction with ERA Aviation, Horizon Air and Peninsula Airways under the
name Alaska Airlines Commuter and using AS flight numbers
Horizon Air is a subsidiary of Alaska Air Group
15% owned by ILFC

ALASKA CENTRAL EXPRESS

Ace Air (KO/AER)   Fairbanks-Intl, AK (FAI)

N111AX	Beech 1900C-1	UC-81	ex N5632C	
N112AX	Beech 1900C-1	UC-45	ex N45GL	dam 24Nov03
N113AX	Beech 1900C-1	UC-41	ex N41UE	
N114AX	Beech 1900C-1	UC-36	ex N1566C	
N5632C	Beech 1900C-1	UC-81	ex N15189	
N9874M	Cessna 207A Stationair 8	20700745		

| N9957M | Cessna 207A Stationair 8 | 20700764 |
| N75941 | Cessna 207A Stationair 8 | 20700656 |

All freighters

ALASKA COASTAL AIRLINES taken over by Wings of Alaska and fleets merged

ALASKA WEST AIR

Kenai Island Lake, AK (ENA)

N87AW	de Havilland DHC-3 Otter	52	ex C-FMPO
N211AW	de Havilland DHC-2 Beaver	1360	ex CF-XGG
N222RL	de Havilland DHC-2 Turbo Beaver	1570/TB5	ex C-FOEB
N1432Z	de Havilland DHC-2 Beaver	797	ex 54-1668

ALLEGHENY AIRLINES

Allegheny (US/ALO) (IATA 395) *Harrisburg-Intl, PA (MDT)*

N804EX	de Havilland DHC-8-102A	227	ex C-GFYI		
N805EX	de Havilland DHC-8-102A	228	ex C-GLOT		
N806EX	de Havilland DHC-8-102A	263	ex C-GEVP	ESC	
N807EX	de Havilland DHC-8-102A	292	ex C-GFQL		
N808EX	de Havilland DHC-8-102A	299	ex C-GDKL	ESE	
N809EX	de Havilland DHC-8-102A	302	ex PT-MFI	ESF	
N810EX	de Havilland DHC-8-102A	308	ex C-GDKL		Lsd to TCF
N811AW	de Havilland DHC-8-102A	201	ex C-GDNG		Lsd fr WFBN
N812EX	de Havilland DHC-8-102A	312	ex C-GDNG	ESH	
N814EX	de Havilland DHC-8-102A	318	ex C-GDNG	ESI	
N815EX	de Havilland DHC-8-102A	321	ex C-GDFT		Lsd to TCF
N816EX	de Havilland DHC-8-102A	329	ex C-GEVP		Lsd to TCF
N817EX	de Havilland DHC-8-102A	191	ex N810AW	ESL	
N818EX	de Havilland DHC-8-102A	235	ex N812AW		
N819EX	de Havilland DHC-8-102	016	ex N803MX		Lsd fr WFBN
N820EX	de Havilland DHC-8-102	019	ex N804MX	ESO	Lsd fr WFBN
N821EX	de Havilland DHC-8-102	173	ex N808AW	ESP	Lsd fr JP Morgan
N822EX	de Havilland DHC-8-102	187	ex N809AW		Lsd fr Boeing Capital
N824EX	de Havilland DHC-8-102	387		ESS	Lsd fr WFBN
N825EX	de Havilland DHC-8-102A	388	ex G-GHRI		Lsd fr WFBN
N826EX	de Havilland DHC-8-102A	389	ex C-GDNG		Lsd fr WFBN
N827EX	de Havilland DHC-8-102A	390	ex C-GEOA		Lsd fr WFBN
N828EX	de Havilland DHC-8-102A	392	ex C-GEVP		Lsd fr WFBN
N829EX	de Havilland DHC-8-102	146	ex N805AW	ESY	Lsd fr JP Morgan
N830EX	de Havilland DHC-8-102	155	ex N806AW		Lsd fr JP Morgan
N831EX	de Havilland DHC-8-102	160	ex N807AW	ERB	Lsd fr JP Morgan
N832EX	de Havilland DHC-8-102A	280	ex N415AW		
N833EX	de Havilland DHC-8-102A	282	ex N416AW	ERD	Lsd fr WFBN
N834EX	de Havilland DHC-8-102A	285	ex N417AW	ERE	Lsd fr WFBN
N835EX	de Havilland DHC-8-102A	289	ex N418AW		Lsd fr WFBN
N836EX	de Havilland DHC-8-102A	297	ex N419AW		Lsd fr WFBN
N837EX	de Havilland DHC-8-102A	217	ex N976HA		
N838EX	de Havilland DHC-8-102A	220	ex N977HA	ERK	
N839EX	de Havilland DHC-8-102A	226	ex N978HA	ERL	
N840EX	de Havilland DHC-8-102A	327	ex N824MA		Lsd fr Bombardier
N841EX	de Havilland DHC-8-102A	249	ex N817MA		Lsd fr Bombardier
N842EX	de Havilland DHC-8-102	341	ex N832MA		Lsd fr Bombardier
N843EX	de Havilland DHC-8-102	335	ex N829MA		Lsd fr Bombardier
N844EX	de Havilland DHC-8-102	339	ex N831MA		Lsd fr Bombardier
N845EX	de Havilland DHC-8-102	344	ex N846MA		Lsd fr Bombardier
N846EX	de Havilland DHC-8-102A	326	ex N960HA	EBC	Lsd fr Bombardier
N847EX	de Havilland DHC-8-102A	333	ex N961HA		Lsd fr Bombardier
N848EX	de Havilland DHC-8-102A	331	ex N962HA		Lsd fr Bombardier
N849EX	de Havilland DHC-8-102A	337	ex N963HA		Lsd fr Bombardier
N851EX	de Havilland DHC-8-102	343	ex N964HA	EBG	Lsd fr Bombardier

A wholly owned subsidiary of US Airways Group and operates commuter services as US Airways Express (q.v.) using US flight numbers in the range 3500-3999. Allegheny Airlines is the trading name of Pennyslvania Commuter Airlines. Parent plans to merge it into Piedmont Airlines by April 2004

ALLEGIANT AIR

Allegiant (G4/AAY) *Fresno Air Terminal, CA (FAT)*

N860GA	McDonnell-Douglas MD-83	1631/49786	ex 9Y-THW	Lsd fr BBAM
N861GA	McDonnell-Douglas MD-83	1436/49557	ex SE-DPI	Lsd fr WFBN
N862GA	McDonnell-Douglas MD-83	1415/49556	ex LN-RMF	Lsd fr WFBN
N863GA	McDonnell-Douglas MD-82	1653/49911	ex OY-KHL	Lsd fr WFBN
N890GA	McDonnell-Douglas MD-82	1207/49371	ex N33817	Lsd fr Cedar River A/c Finance
N891GA	McDonnell-Douglas MD-82	1283/49423	ex LN-RLG	Lsd fr WFBN
N945MA	McDonnell-Douglas MD-87	1552/49725	ex VP-BOP	Lsd fr DFO Partnerships
N948MA	McDonnell-Douglas MD-87	1646/49778	ex VP-BOO	Lsd fr WFBN
N	McDonnell-Douglas MD-82	1800/49998	ex SE-DIX	Lsd fr WFBN

N   McDonnell-Douglas MD-82   1659/49912 ex LN-RMJ   on order
Filed Chapter 11 on 13th December 2000; operations continue

ALLWEST FREIGHT

Sterling-South Gasline, AK

N50DA	Short SC.7 Skyvan	SH1852	ex G-AWWM	Freighter
N549WB	Short SC.7 Skyvan	SH1911	ex XA-SRD	Freighter
N754BD	Short SC.7 Skyvan	SH1907	ex G-BKMD	Freighter

ALOHA AIRLINES

Aloha (AQ/AAH) (IATA 327)   *Honolulu-Intl, HI (HNL)*

N805AL	Boeing 737-2M6C	637/21809	ex V8-UEB	Hoapili	
N807AL	Boeing 737-2T4	1151/23443	ex B-2511	Ke'opuolani	Lsd fr debis
N808AL	Boeing 737-2T4	1155/23445	ex B-2514	Kaleleonalani	Lsd fr debis
N810AL	Boeing 737-2Y5	1523/24031	ex 9H-ABG	Lu'ukia	Lsd fr WFBN
N816AL	Boeing 737-2X6C	1036/23122	ex TF-ABE	David Kalakaua	Lsd fr Jetlease
N817AL	Boeing 737-2X6C	1113/23292	ex N674MA	Kalanikupule	Lsd fr Jetlease
N818AL	Boeing 737-230	703/22117	ex D-ABFF	Kaumuali'i	
N819AL	Boeing 737-25A	1486/23791	ex N685MA	Kekaulike	Lsd fr Boeing
N820AL	Boeing 737-230	790/22138	ex D-ABHM	Pai'ea	
N821AL	Boeing 737-230 (Nordam 3)	1079/23155	ex D-ABMC	La'a Maikahiki	Lsd fr WFBN
N823AL	Boeing 737-230 (Nordam 3)	1078/23154	ex D-ABMB	Liholiho	Lsd fr WFBN
N824AL	Boeing 737-282	978/23045	ex CS-TEO	Kalani'opu'u	Lsd fr WFBN
N826AL	Boeing 737-282C	1002/23051	ex CS-TEQ	Kahuhihewa	Lsd fr WFBN
N827AL	Boeing 737-209	1579/23913	ex PK-RIO	Malaio Kekuanaoa	Lsd fr WFBN

*Leased from ACG Acquisition

N738AL	Boeing 737-73A	390/28499		Kuapaka'a	Lsd fr AWAS
N739AL	Boeing 737-73A	414/28500	ex N1787B	Mo'ikeha	Lsd fr AWAS
N740AL	Boeing 737-76N	799/28640			Lsd fr GECAS
N741AL	Boeing 737-76N	809/28641	ex N1781B		Lsd fr GECAS
N742AL	Boeing 737-76N	855/30830			Lsd fr Castle Harbor Lsg
N743AL	Boeing 737-76N	986/28654	ex N316ML		Lsd fr Aircraft 28654
N744AL	Boeing 737-76N	1013/32582	ex (N1795B)		Lsd fr Aircraft 32582
N745AL	Boeing 737-76N	347/29904	ex LV-ZRC		Lsd fr AFS Investments
N746AL	Boeing 737-76N	372/29905	ex LV-ZRP	Kaha'l	Lsd fr AFS Investments
N748AL	Boeing 737-76N	429/30050	ex LV-ZSN		Lsd fr AFS Investments
N749AL	Boeing 737-76N	1392/32738			Lsd fr AFS Investments
N750AL	Boeing 737-76N	32743		on order Jun04	Lsd fr ILFC
N751AL	Boeing 737-7Q8	30674		on order 04	

Feeder services operated by Island airHonolulu. Boeing 737NGs being retrofitted with blended winglets

ALPINE AIR EXPRESS

Alpine Air (5A/AIP)   *Provo-Municipal, UT (PVU)*

N14MV	Beech 99	U-59	ex C-FGJT		Lsd fr CLB Corp
N24BH	Beech 99	U-67	ex C-GVNQ		Lsd fr CLB Corp
N95WA	Beech 99	U-6	ex N19RA		Lsd fr CLB Corp
N99CA	Beech 99A	U-127	ex N22AT		Lsd fr CLB Corp
N99GH	Beech 99A	U-112	ex N86569		Lsd fr CLB Corp
N99TH	Beech B99	U-155		no titles	Lsd fr CLB Corp
N199GL	Beech 99	U-15	ex C-GJEZ		Lsd fr CLB Corp
N216CS	Beech C99	U-216	ex C-GGPP		Lsd fr CLB Corp
N236AL	Beech C99	U-236	ex RP-C2317		Lsd fr Mallette Family
N237SL	Beech C99	U-237	ex RP-C2370		Lsd fr CLB Corp
N238AL	Beech C99	U-238			Lsd fr Mallette Family
N239AL	Beech C99	U-239	ex RP-C2390		Lsd fr CLB Corp
N326CA	Beech B99	U-135	ex N10RA		Lsd fr CLB Corp
N399AA*	Beech 99A	U-143	ex CC-PNO		Lsd fr CLB Corp
N899CA	Beech B99	U-104	ex N1922T		Lsd fr CLB Corp
N950AA	Beech B99	U-159	ex C-FCBU		Lsd fr CLB Corp
N955AA	Beech 99A	U-128	ex J6-AAE		Lsd fr CLB Corp
N4381Y	Beech 99	U-71	ex N216BH		

All freighters

N153GA	Beech 1900C	UB-34	ex N734GL		Lsd fr Mallette Family
N154GA	Beech 1900C	UB-25	ex N315BH		Lsd fr Mallette Family
N172GA	Beech 1900C	UB-11	ex N11ZR		Lsd fr Mallette Family
N190GA	Beech 1900C	UB-1	ex N1YW		Lsd fr Mallette Family
N192GA	Beech 1900C	UB-17	ex N17ZR		Lsd fr Mallette Family
N194GA	Beech 1900C	UB-8	ex CC-CAF		Lsd fr Mallette Family
N195GA	Beech 1900C	UB-65	ex CC-CAK		Lsd fr Mallette Family
N197GA	Beech 1900C	UB-16	ex N16ZR		Lsd fr Mallette Family
N198GA*	Beech 1900C	UB-5	ex N5ZR		Lsd fr Mallette Family

All freighters. Associated with Sundance Air

N700TS   Piper PA-31-350 Chieftain   31-8152157   Lsd fr CLB Corp
Alpine Air Express Chile is a wholly owned subsidiary and those marked * are leased to same. Operates some
services on behalf of USPS (US Postal Service)

AMERICAN AIRLINES

American (AA/AAL) (IATA 001)   *Dallas-Fort Worth, TX (DFW)*

Reg	Type	MSN	ex	Fleet	Notes
N3075A	Airbus Industrie A300B4-605R	606	ex F-WWAA	075	
N7055A	Airbus Industrie A300B4-605R	462	ex F-WWAC	055	Lsd fr AFS Investments
N7062A	Airbus Industrie A300B4-605R	474	ex F-WWAK	062	
N7076A	Airbus Industrie A300B4-605R	610	ex F-WWAF	076	
N7082A	Airbus Industrie A300B4-605R	643	ex F-WWAN	082	
N7083A	Airbus Industrie A300B4-605R	645	ex F-WWAO	083	
N8067A	Airbus Industrie A300B4-605R	510	ex F-WWAU	067	
N11060	Airbus Industrie A300B4-605R	470	ex F-WWAA	060	
N14056	Airbus Industrie A300B4-605R	463	ex F-WWAO	056	
N14061	Airbus Industrie A300B4-605R	471	ex F-WWAH	061	
N14065	Airbus Industrie A300B4-605R	508	ex F-WWAR	065 stored ROW	
N14068	Airbus Industrie A300B4-605R	511	ex F-WWAV	068	
N14077	Airbus Industrie A300B4-605R	612	ex F-WWAH	077	
N18066	Airbus Industrie A300B4-605R	509	ex F-WWAS	066	
N19059	Airbus Industrie A300B4-605R	469	ex F-WWAF	059	
N25071	Airbus Industrie A300B4-605R	514	ex F-WWAY	071	Lsd fr AFS Investments
N33069	Airbus Industrie A300B4-605R	512	ex F-WWAC	069	
N34078	Airbus Industrie A300B4-605R	615	ex F-WWAO	078	
N40064	Airbus Industrie A300B4-605R	507	ex F-WWAQ	064	
N41063	Airbus Industrie A300B4-605R	506	ex F-WWAP	063	
N50051	Airbus Industrie A300B4-605R	459	ex F-WWAX	051	
N59081	Airbus Industrie A300B4-605R	639	ex F-WWAV	081	
N70054	Airbus Industrie A300B4-605R	461	ex F-WWAZ	054	
N70072	Airbus Industrie A300B4-605R	515	ex F-WWAZ	072	
N70073	Airbus Industrie A300B4-605R	516	ex F-WWAA	073	Lsd fr AFS Investments
N70074	Airbus Industrie A300B4-605R	517	ex F-WWAD	074	
N70079	Airbus Industrie A300B4-605R	619	ex F-WWAU	079	
N77080	Airbus Industrie A300B4-605R	626	ex F-WWAR	080	
N80052	Airbus Industrie A300B4-605R	460	ex F-WWAY	052	
N80057	Airbus Industrie A300B4-605R	465	ex F-WWAM	057	Lsd fr AFS Investments
N80058	Airbus Industrie A300B4-605R	466	ex F-WWAE	058	
N80084	Airbus Industrie A300B4-605R	675	ex F-WWAE	084	
N90070	Airbus Industrie A300B4-605R	513	ex F-WWAX	070 stored ROW	
N91050	Airbus Industrie A300B4-605R	423	ex F-WWAV	050	
N901AN	Boeing 737-823	184/29503		3AA	
N902AN	Boeing 737-823	190/29504		3AB	
N903AN	Boeing 737-823	196/29505		3AC	
N904AN	Boeing 737-823	207/29506		3AD	
N905AN	Boeing 737-823	231/29507		3AE	
N906AN	Boeing 737-823	240/29508		3AF	
N907AN	Boeing 737-823	254/29509		3AG	
N908AN	Boeing 737-823	263/29510		3AH	
N909AN	Boeing 737-823	267/29511	ex (N909AM)	3AJ	
N910AN	Boeing 737-823	271/29512		3AK	
N912AN	Boeing 737-823	289/29513		3AL	
N913AN	Boeing 737-823	293/29514		3AM	
N914AN	Boeing 737-823	316/29515		3AN	
N915AN	Boeing 737-823	322/29516		3AP	
N916AN	Boeing 737-823	332/29517		3AR	
N917AN	Boeing 737-823	344/29518		3AS	
N918AN	Boeing 737-823	353/29519		3AT	
N919AN	Boeing 737-823	363/29520		3AU	
N920AN	Boeing 737-823	378/29521		3AV	
N921AN	Boeing 737-823	383/29522		3AW	
N922AN	Boeing 737-823	398/29523		3AX	
N923AN	Boeing 737-823	405/29524		3AY	
N924AN	Boeing 737-823	434/29525		3BA	
N925AN	Boeing 737-823	440/29526		3BB	
N926AN	Boeing 737-823	453/29527		3BC	
N927AN	Boeing 737-823	462/30077		3BD	
N928AN	Boeing 737-823	473/29528		3BE	
N929AN	Boeing 737-823	488/30078		3BF	
N930AN	Boeing 737-823	503/29529		3BG	
N931AN	Boeing 737-823	509/30079		3BH	
N932AN	Boeing 737-823	527/29530		3BJ	
N933AN	Boeing 737-823	531/30080		3BK	
N934AN	Boeing 737-823	553/29531		3BL	
N935AN	Boeing 737-823	559/30081		3BM	
N936AN	Boeing 737-823	575/29532		3BN	
N937AN	Boeing 737-823	579/30082		3BP	
N938AN	Boeing 737-823	608/29533		3BR	
N939AN	Boeing 737-823	612/30083		3BS	

N940AN	Boeing 737-823	616/30598		3BT
N941AN	Boeing 737-823	624/29534		3BU
N942AN	Boeing 737-823	629/30084		3BV
N943AN	Boeing 737-823	635/30599		3BW
N944AN	Boeing 737-823	645/29535		3BX
N945AN	Boeing 737-823	649/30085		3BY
N946AN	Boeing 737-823	655/30600		3CA
N947AN	Boeing 737-823	671/29536	ex (N2292Z)	3CB
N948AN	Boeing 737-823	679/30086	ex (N2294B)	3CC
N949AN	Boeing 737-823	699/29537		3CD
N950AN	Boeing 737-823	704/30087		3CE
N951AA	Boeing 737-823	720/29538		3CF Astrojet c/s
N952AA	Boeing 737-823	726/30088		3CG
N953AN	Boeing 737-823	741/29539		3CH
N954AN	Boeing 737-823	745/30089		3CJ
N955AN	Boeing 737-823	762/29540		3CK
N956AN	Boeing 737-823	764/30090		3CL
N957AN	Boeing 737-823	788/29541		3CM
N958AN	Boeing 737-823	797/30091		3CN
N959AN	Boeing 737-823	801/30828		3CP
N960AN	Boeing 737-823	818/29542		3CR
N961AN	Boeing 737-823	822/30092		3CS
N962AN	Boeing 737-823	825/30858		3CT
N963AN	Boeing 737-823	834/29543		3CU
N964AN	Boeing 737-823	837/30093		3CV
N965AN	Boeing 737-823	860/29544		3CW
N966AN	Boeing 737-823	863/30094		3CX
N967AN	Boeing 737-823	883/29545		3CY
N968AN	Boeing 737-823	886/30095		3DA
N969AN	Boeing 737-823	910/29546		3DB	Lsd fr Avn Financial Svs
N970AN	Boeing 737-823	915/30096		3DC	Lsd fr Avn Financial Svs
N971AN	Boeing 737-823	937/29547		3DD	Lsd fr Avn Financial Svs
N972AN	Boeing 737-823	941/30097		3DE	Lsd fr Avn Financial Svs
N973AN	Boeing 737-823	971/29548		3DF	Lsd fr Avn Financial Svs
N974AN	Boeing 737-823	977/30098		3DG	Lsd fr WFBN
N975AN	Boeing 737-823	992/29549		3DH	Lsd fr WFBN
N976AN	Boeing 737-823	1001/30099		3DJ	Lsd fr WFBN
N977AN	Boeing 737-823	1019/29550		3DK	Lsd fr WFBN
N978AN	Boeing 737-823	1022/30100		3DL	Lsd fr Silvermine River Finance

A further forty-two Boeing 737-823s are on order for future delivery in 2005 (21) and 2006 (21), fleet numbers 3DM to 3FH

N172AJ	Boeing 757-223	1012/32400		5FT
N173AN	Boeing 757-223	1005/32399		5FS
N174AA	Boeing 757-223	998/31308		5FR
N175AN	Boeing 757-223	992/32394		5FK
N176AA	Boeing 757-223	994/32395		5FL
N177AN	Boeing 757-223	996/32396		5FM
N178AA	Boeing 757-223	1002/32397	ex (N20140)	5FN
N179AA	Boeing 757-223	1000/32398	ex (N20171)	5FP
N181AN	Boeing 757-223	852/29591	ex N5573L	5EN
N182AN	Boeing 757-223	853/29592		5EP
N183AN	Boeing 757-223ER	862/29593		5ER
N184AN	Boeing 757-223ER	866/29594	ex N1787B	5ES
N185AN	Boeing 757-223	962/32379		5ET
N186AN	Boeing 757-223	964/32380		5EU
N187AN	Boeing 757-223	965/32381		5EV
N188AN	Boeing 757-223	969/32382		5EW
N189AN	Boeing 757-223	970/32383		5EX
N190AA	Boeing 757-223	973/32384		5EY
N191AN	Boeing 757-223	977/32385		5FA
N192AN	Boeing 757-223	979/32386		5FB
N193AN	Boeing 757-223	981/32387		5FC
N194AA	Boeing 757-223	983/32388		5FD
N195AN	Boeing 757-223	984/32389		5FE
N196AA	Boeing 757-223	986/32390		5FF
N197AN	Boeing 757-223	988/32391		5FG
N198AA	Boeing 757-223	989/32392		5FH
N199AN	Boeing 757-223	991/32393		5FJ
N601AN	Boeing 757-223	661/27052		5DU
N602AN	Boeing 757-223	664/27053		5DV
N603AA	Boeing 757-223	670/27054		5DW
N604AA	Boeing 757-223	677/27055		5DX
N605AA	Boeing 757-223	680/27056		5DY
N606AA	Boeing 757-223	707/27057		5EA
N607AM	Boeing 757-223	712/27058		5EB
N608AA	Boeing 757-223ER	720/27446		5EC
N609AA	Boeing 757-223ER	722/27447		5ED
N610AA	Boeing 757-223	234/24486		610
N611AM	Boeing 757-223	236/24487		611
N612AA	Boeing 757-223	240/24488		612
N613AA	Boeing 757-223	242/24489		613
N614AA	Boeing 757-223	243/24490		614	Lsd fr WTCo

N615AM	Boeing 757-223	245/24491	615	Lsd fr WTCo
N616AA	Boeing 757-223	248/24524	616	Lsd fr WTCo
N617AM	Boeing 757-223	253/24525	617	
N618AA	Boeing 757-223	260/24526	618	Lsd fr Wachovia Bank
N619AA	Boeing 757-223	269/24577	619	Lsd fr Wachovia Bank
N620AA	Boeing 757-223	276/24578	620	Lsd fr Wachovia Bank
N621AM	Boeing 757-223	283/24579	621	
N622AA	Boeing 757-223	289/24580	622	
N623AA	Boeing 757-223	296/24581	623	
N624AA	Boeing 757-223	297/24582	624	
N625AA	Boeing 757-223	303/24583	625	
N626AA	Boeing 757-223	304/24584	626	
N627AA	Boeing 757-223	308/24585	627	
N628AA	Boeing 757-223	309/24586	628	
N629AA	Boeing 757-223	315/24587	629	Lsd fr Wachovia Bank
N630AA	Boeing 757-223	316/24588	630	Lsd fr Wachovia Bank
N631AA	Boeing 757-223	317/24589	631	
N632AA	Boeing 757-223	321/24590	632	
N633AA	Boeing 757-223	324/24591	633	
N634AA	Boeing 757-223	327/24592	634	
N635AA	Boeing 757-223	328/24593	635	
N636AM	Boeing 757-223	336/24594	636	
N637AM	Boeing 757-223	337/24595	637	
N638AA	Boeing 757-223	344/24596	638	
N639AA	Boeing 757-223	345/24597	639	
N640A	Boeing 757-223	350/24598	640	
N641AA	Boeing 757-223	351/24599	641	Lsd fr WTCo
N642AA	Boeing 757-223	357/24600	642	
N643AA	Boeing 757-223	360/24601	643	
N645AA	Boeing 757-223	370/24603	5BR	
N646AA	Boeing 757-223	375/24604	5BS	
N647AM	Boeing 757-223	378/24605	5BT	
N648AA	Boeing 757-223	379/24606	5BU	
N649AA	Boeing 757-223	383/24607	5BV	
N650AA	Boeing 757-223	384/24608	5BW	Lsd fr Wachovia Bank
N652AA	Boeing 757-223	391/24610	5BY	Lsd fr Wachovia Bank
N653A	Boeing 757-223	397/24611	5CA	
N654A	Boeing 757-223	398/24612	5CB	
N655AA	Boeing 757-223	402/24613	5CC	
N656AA	Boeing 757-223	404/24614	5CD	
N657AM	Boeing 757-223	409/24615	5CE	
N658AA	Boeing 757-223	410/24616	5CF	
N659AA	Boeing 757-223	417/24617	5CG Pride of American	
N660AM	Boeing 757-223	418/25294	5CH	
N661AA	Boeing 757-223	423/25295	5CJ	
N662AA	Boeing 757-223	425/25296	5CK	
N663AM	Boeing 757-223	432/25297	5CL	
N664AA	Boeing 757-223	433/25298	5CM	
N665AA	Boeing 757-223	436/25299	5CN	
N666A	Boeing 757-223	451/25300	5CP	
N668AA	Boeing 757-223	460/25333	5CS	
N669AA	Boeing 757-223	463/25334	5CT	
N670AA	Boeing 757-223	468/25335	5CU	
N671AA	Boeing 757-223	473/25336	5CV	
N672AA	Boeing 757-223	474/25337	5CW	
N673AN	Boeing 757-223	812/29423	5EE	
N674AN	Boeing 757-223	816/29424	5EF	
N675AN	Boeing 757-223	817/29425	5EG	
N676AN	Boeing 757-223	827/29426 ex N1798B	5EH	
N677AN	Boeing 757-223	828/29427	5EJ	
N678AN	Boeing 757-223	837/29428 ex N1787B	5EK	
N679AN	Boeing 757-223	842/29589 ex N1800B	5EL Astrojet c/s	
N680AN	Boeing 757-223	847/29590	5EM	
N681AA	Boeing 757-223	483/25338	5CX	
N682AA	Boeing 757-223	484/25339	5CY	
N683A	Boeing 757-223	491/25340	5DA	
N684AA	Boeing 757-223	504/25341	5DB	
N685AA	Boeing 757-223	507/25342	5DC	
N686AA	Boeing 757-223	509/25343	5DD	
N687AA	Boeing 757-223ER	536/25695	5DE	
N688AA	Boeing 757-223ER	548/25730	5DF	
N689AA	Boeing 757-223ER	562/25731	5DG	
N690AA	Boeing 757-223ER	566/25696	5DH	
N691AA	Boeing 757-223ER	568/25697	5DJ	
N692AA	Boeing 757-223	578/26972	5DK	
N693AA	Boeing 757-223	580/26973	5DL	
N694AN	Boeing 757-223	582/26974	5DM	
N695AN	Boeing 757-223	621/26975	5DN	
N696AN	Boeing 757-223	627/26976	5DP	
N697AN	Boeing 757-223	633/26977	5DR	
N698AN	Boeing 757-223	635/26980	5DS	
N699AN	Boeing 757-223	660/27051	5DT	

N701TW	Boeing 757-2Q8	721/28160	5TA	Lsd fr MSA V
N702TW	Boeing 757-2Q8	732/28162	5TB	Lsd fr ILFC
N703TW	Boeing 757-2Q8ER	736/27620	5TC	Lsd fr ILFC
N704X	Boeing 757-2Q8	741/28163	5TD	Lsd fr ILFC
N705TW	Boeing 757-231	742/28479	5TE; stored	Lsd fr Pegasus
N706TW	Boeing 757-2Q8	743/28165	5TF	Lsd fr ILFC
N707TW	Boeing 757-2Q8ER	744/27625	5TG	Lsd fr ILFC
N709TW^	Boeing 757-2Q8	754/28168	5TJ	Lsd fr ILFC
N710TW	Boeing 757-2Q8	757/28169	5TK	Lsd fr ILFC
N711ZX	Boeing 757-231	758/28481	5TL	Lsd fr WFBN
N712TW	Boeing 757-2Q8ER	760/27624	5TM	Lsd fr Castle 2003-1A LLC
N713TW	Boeing 757-2Q8	764/28173	5TN	Lsd fr Castle 2003-2A LLC
N714P	Boeing 757-231	770/28482	5TP; stored	Lsd fr Pegasus
N715TW	Boeing 757-231	777/28483	5TR; stored	Lsd fr Pegasus
N716TW	Boeing 757-231	825/28484 ex N1799B	5TS	Lsd fr WFBN
N717TW	Boeing 757-231	854/28485	5TT; stored	Lsd fr Pegasus
N718TW	Boeing 757-231	869/28486	5TU; stored	Lsd fr WFBN
N719TW*	Boeing 757-231	878/28487	5TV; stored	
N720TW*	Boeing 757-231	883/30319	5TW; stored	
N721TW	Boeing 757-231	874/29954	5TX	Lsd fr ILFC
N722TW	Boeing 757-231	893/29385 ex N1795B	5TY; stored	Lsd fr ILFC
N723TW	Boeing 757-231	907/29378	5WA	Lsd fr ILFC
N724TW	Boeing 757-231	884/28488 ex N1787B	5WB; stored	Lsd fr Pegasus
N726TW	Boeing 757-231	896/30339	5WD; stored	Lsd fr WFBN
N727TW	Boeing 757-231	901/30340	5WE; stored	Lsd fr Pegasus
N7667A	Boeing 757-223	459/25301	5CR	

*Leased from Aerospace Finance   ^St Louis Rams colours
The ex-TWA aircraft are being reconfigured to American standards, including cockpits

N301AA	Boeing 767-223	8/22307	301; stored ROW	
N302AA	Boeing 767-223	19/22308	302; stored ROW	
N303AA	Boeing 767-223	23/22309	303; stored ROW	
N304AA	Boeing 767-223	25/22310	304; stored ROW	
N305AA	Boeing 767-223	34/22311	305; stored ROW	
N306AA	Boeing 767-223	44/22312	306; stored ROW	
N307AA	Boeing 767-223	72/22313	307; stored ROW	
N308AA	Boeing 767-223	73/22314	308; stored ROW	
N312AA	Boeing 767-223	94/22315	312; stored ROW	
N313AA	Boeing 767-223ER	95/22316	313; stored ROW	
N315AA	Boeing 767-223ER	109/22317	315; stored ROW	
N316AA	Boeing 767-223ER	111/22318	316; stored ROW	
N317AA	Boeing 767-223ER	112/22319	317; stored ROW	
N319AA	Boeing 767-223ER	128/22320	319; stored ROW	
N320AA	Boeing 767-223ER	130/22321	320	
N321AA	Boeing 767-223ER	139/22322	321	
N322AA	Boeing 767-223ER	140/22323	322	
N323AA	Boeing 767-223ER	146/22324	323	
N324AA	Boeing 767-223ER	147/22325	324	
N325AA	Boeing 767-223ER	157/22326	325	
N327AA	Boeing 767-223ER	159/22327	327	Lsd fr Wachovia Bank
N328AA	Boeing 767-223ER	160/22328	328	
N329AA	Boeing 767-223ER	164/22329	329	Lsd fr State Street
N330AA	Boeing 767-223ER	166/22330	330	
N332AA	Boeing 767-223ER	168/22331	332	
N335AA	Boeing 767-223ER	194/22333	335	
N336AA	Boeing 767-223ER	195/22334	336	
N338AA	Boeing 767-223ER	196/22335	338	
N339AA	Boeing 767-223ER	198/22336	339	
N342AN	Boeing 767-323	896/33081	342	
N343AN	Boeing 767-323	899/33082	343	
N344AN	Boeing 767-323	900/33083	344	
N345AN	Boeing 767-323	906/33084	345	
N346AN	Boeing 767-323ER	907/33085	346	
N347AN	Boeing 767-323ER	908/33086	347	
N348AN	Boeing 767-323ER	910/33087	348	
N349AN	Boeing 767-323ER	913/33088	349	
N350AN	Boeing 767-323ER	916/33089	350	
N351AA	Boeing 767-323ER	202/24032	351	
N352AA	Boeing 767-323ER	205/24033	352	
N353AA	Boeing 767-323ER	206/24034	353	
N354AA	Boeing 767-323ER	211/24035	354	
N355AA	Boeing 767-323ER	221/24036	355	
N357AA	Boeing 767-323ER	227/24038	357	
N358AA*	Boeing 767-323ER	228/24039	358	
N359AA	Boeing 767-323ER	230/24040	359	
N360AA	Boeing 767-323ER	232/24041	360	
N361AA	Boeing 767-323ER	235/24042	361	
N362AA*	Boeing 767-323ER	237/24043	362	
N363AA	Boeing 767-323ER	238/24044	363	
N366AA	Boeing 767-323ER	388/25193	366	Lsd fr Wachovia Bank
N368AA	Boeing 767-323ER	404/25195	368	Lsd fr WTCo
N369AA	Boeing 767-323ER	422/25196	369	Lsd fr JP Morgan Trust

N370AA	Boeing 767-323ER	425/25197	370	
N371AA	Boeing 767-323ER	431/25198	371	Lsd fr Wachovia Bank
N372AA	Boeing 767-323ER	433/25199	372	
N373AA	Boeing 767-323ER	435/25200	373	
N374AA	Boeing 767-323ER	437/25201	374	
N376AN	Boeing 767-323ER	447/25445	376	
N377AN	Boeing 767-323ER	453/25446	377	
N378AN	Boeing 767-323ER	469/25447	378	
N379AA	Boeing 767-323ER	481/25448	379	
N380AN	Boeing 767-323ER	489/25449	380	
N381AN	Boeing 767-323ER	495/25450	381	
N382AN	Boeing 767-323ER	498/25451	382	
N383AN	Boeing 767-323ER	500/26995	383	
N384AA	Boeing 767-323ER	512/26996	384	
N385AM	Boeing 767-323ER	536/27059	385	
N386AA	Boeing 767-323ER	540/27060	386	
N387AM	Boeing 767-323ER	541/27184	387	
N388AA	Boeing 767-323ER	563/27448	388	
N389AA	Boeing 767-323ER	564/27449	389	
N390AA	Boeing 767-323ER	565/27450	390	
N391AA	Boeing 767-323ER	566/27451	391	
N392AN*	Boeing 767-323ER	700/29429	392	
N393AN*	Boeing 767-323ER	701/29430	393	
N394AN*	Boeing 767-323ER	703/29431	394	
N395AN*	Boeing 767-323ER	709/29432	395	
N396AN	Boeing 767-323ER	739/29603	396	
N397AN	Boeing 767-323ER	744/29604	397	
N398AN	Boeing 767-323ER	748/29605	398	
N399AN	Boeing 767-323ER	752/29606	399	
N7375A	Boeing 767-323ER	441/25202	375	
N39356	Boeing 767-323ER	226/24037	356	
N39364*	Boeing 767-323ER	240/24045	364	
N39365*	Boeing 767-323ER	241/24046	365	
N39367	Boeing 767-323ER	394/25194	367	Lsd fr Wachovia Bank

*Configured for Hawaiian services

N750AN	Boeing 777-223ER	332/30259	ex (N798AN)	7BJ
N751AN	Boeing 777-223ER	333/30798		7BK
N752AN	Boeing 777-223ER	339/30260	ex (N799AN)	7BL
N753AN	Boeing 777-223ER	341/30261	ex (N750AN)	7BM
N754AN	Boeing 777-223ER	345/30262		7BN
N755AN	Boeing 777-223ER	354/30263		7BP
N756AM	Boeing 777-223ER	358/30264		7BR
N757AN	Boeing 777-223ER	363/32636		7BS
N758AN	Boeing 777-223ER	371/32637		7BT
N759AN	Boeing 777-223ER	376/32638		7BU
N760AN	Boeing 777-223ER	379/31477		7BV
N761AJ	Boeing 777-223ER	393/31478		7BW
N762AN	Boeing 777-223ER	399/31479		7BX
N765AN	Boeing 777-223ER	433/32879		7CB
N766AN	Boeing 777-223ER	445/32880		7CC
N770AN	Boeing 777-223ER	185/29578		7AA
N771AN	Boeing 777-223ER	190/29579		7AB
N772AN	Boeing 777-223ER	198/29580		7AC
N773AN	Boeing 777-223ER	199/29583		7AD
N774AN	Boeing 777-223ER	208/29581		7AE
N775AN	Boeing 777-223ER	209/29584		7AF
N776AN	Boeing 777-223ER	215/29582		7AG
N777AN	Boeing 777-223ER	218/29585		7AH
N778AN	Boeing 777-223ER	223/29587		7AJ
N779AN	Boeing 777-223ER	225/29955		7AK
N780AN	Boeing 777-223ER	241/29956		7AL
N781AN	Boeing 777-223ER	266/29586		7AM
N782AN	Boeing 777-223ER	270/30003		7AN
N783AN	Boeing 777-223ER	271/30004		7AP
N784AN	Boeing 777-223ER	272/29588		7AR
N785AN	Boeing 777-223ER	274/30005		7AS
N786AN	Boeing 777-223ER	276/30250		7AT
N787AL	Boeing 777-223ER	277/30010		7AU
N788AN	Boeing 777-223ER	283/30011		7AV
N789AN	Boeing 777-223ER	285/30252		7AW
N790AN	Boeing 777-223ER	287/30251		7AX
N791AN	Boeing 777-223ER	289/30254		7AY
N792AN	Boeing 777-223ER	292/30253		7BA
N793AN	Boeing 777-223ER	299/30255		7BB
N794AN	Boeing 777-223ER	313/30256		7BC
N795AN	Boeing 777-223ER	315/30257		7BD
N796AN	Boeing 777-223ER	316/30796		7BE
N797AN	Boeing 777-223ER	321/30012	ex (N796AN)	7BF; American Spirit
N798AN	Boeing 777-223ER	324/30797		7BG
N799AN	Boeing 777-223ER	328/30258	ex (N797AN)	7BH

Nine more Boeing 777-223ERs are on order but delivery deferred until 2006 at the earliest

N1400H+	Fokker 100	11340	ex PH-LNI	2AA; stored MHV
N1401G+	Fokker 100	11352	ex PH-EZZ	2AB; stored MHV
N1402K	Fokker 100	11353	ex PH-EZA	2AC
N1403M	Fokker 100	11354	ex PH-EZC	2AD
N1404D	Fokker 100	11355	ex PH-EZI	2AE
N1405J	Fokker 100	11356	ex PH-EZJ	2AF
N1406A+	Fokker 100	11359	ex PH-EZG	2AG
N1407D+	Fokker 100	11360	ex PH-EZO	2AH
N1408B+	Fokker 100	11361	ex PH-EZS	2AJ
N1409B	Fokker 100	11367	ex PH-EZI	2AK
N1410E	Fokker 100	11368	ex PH-EZJ	2AL
N1411G	Fokker 100	11369	ex PH-EZB	2AM
N1412A	Fokker 100	11370	ex PH-EZD	2AN	Lsd fr Aircraft N1412A Trust
N1413A	Fokker 100	11376	ex PH-EZO	2AP	Lsd fr Aircraft N1413A Trust
N1414D	Fokker 100	11377	ex PH-EZS	2AR	Lsd fr Aircraft N1414D Trust
N1415K+	Fokker 100	11385	ex PH-EZY	2AS
N1416A+	Fokker 100	11395	ex PH-EZC	2AT
N1417D+	Fokker 100	11396	ex PH-EZE	2AU
N1418A	Fokker 100	11397	ex PH-EZI	2AV
N1420D+	Fokker 100	11403	ex PH-EZO	2AX
N1421K	Fokker 100	11404	ex PH-EZB	2AY
N1422J	Fokker 100	11405	ex PH-EZG	2BA	Lsd fr Aircraft N1422J Trust
N1423A	Fokker 100	11406	ex PH-EZP	2BB
N1424M	Fokker 100	11407	ex PH-EZS	2BC	Lsd fr Aircraft N1424M Trust
N1425A	Fokker 100	11408	ex PH-EZE	2BD
N1426A+	Fokker 100	11411	ex PH-EZB	2BE	Lsd fr Aircraft N1426A Trust
N1427A	Fokker 100	11412	ex PH-EZC	2BF	Lsd fr Aircraft N1427A Trust
N1428D	Fokker 100	11413	ex PH-EZI	2BG	Lsd fr Aircraft M1428D Trust
N1429G+	Fokker 100	11414	ex PH-EZJ	2BH	Lsd fr Aircraft N1429G Trust
N1430D+	Fokker 100	11415	ex PH-EZL	2BJ	Lsd fr Aircraft N1430D Trust
N1431B	Fokker 100	11416	ex PH-EZY	2BK	Lsd fr Aircraft N1431B Trust
N1432A+	Fokker 100	11417	ex PH-EZZ	2BL	Lsd fr Aircraft N1432A Trust
N1433B+	Fokker 100	11418	ex PH-EZO	2BM	Lsd fr Aircraft N1433B Trust
N1434A+	Fokker 100	11419	ex PH-EZM	2BN	Lsd fr Aircraft N1434A Trust
N1435D+	Fokker 100	11425	ex PH-EZD	2BP	Lsd fr Aircraft N1435D Trust
N1436A+	Fokker 100	11426	ex PH-EZE	2BR	Lsd fr Aircraft N1436A Trust
N1437B+	Fokker 100	11427	ex PH-EZG	2BS	Lsd fr Aircraft N1437B Trust
N1438H+	Fokker 100	11428	ex PH-EZP	2BT
N1439A+	Fokker 100	11434	ex PH-EZA	2BU
N1440A+	Fokker 100	11435	ex PH-EZB	2BV	Lsd fr Aircraft N1440A Trust
N1441A+	Fokker 100	11436	ex PH-EZC	2BW	Lsd fr Aircraft N1441A Trust
N1442E+	Fokker 100	11437	ex PH-EZI	2BX
N1443A+	Fokker 100	11446	ex PH-EZN	2BY
N1444N+	Fokker 100	11447	ex PH-EZO	2CA
N1445B+	Fokker 100	11448	ex PH-EZP	2CB
N1446A	Fokker 100	11449	ex PH-EZS	2CC	Lsd fr Aircraft N1446A Trust
N1447L	Fokker 100	11456	ex PH-EZA	2CD	Lsd fr Aircraft N1447L Trust
N1448A+	Fokker 100	11457	ex PH-EZB	2CE	Lsd fr Aircraft N1448A Trust
N1449D	Fokker 100	11458	ex PH-EZC	2CF	Lsd fr Aircraft N1449D Trust
N1452B+	Fokker 100	11464	ex PH-EZI	2CJ	Lsd fr Aircraft N1452B Trust
N1453D	Fokker 100	11465	ex PH-EZJ	2CK	Lsd fr Aircraft N1453D Trust
N1455K	Fokker 100	11467	ex PH-EZL	2CM	Lsd fr Aircraft N1455K Trust
N1456D	Fokker 100	11468	ex PH-EZM	2CN	Lsd fr Aircraft N1456D Trust
N1457B	Fokker 100	11469	ex PH-EZN	2CP	Lsd fr Aircraft N1457B Trust
N1459A	Fokker 100	11479	ex PH-EZB	2CS	Lsd fr Aircraft N1459A Trust
N1460A+	Fokker 100	11480	ex PH-JCA	2CT
N1461C+	Fokker 100	11481	ex PH-JCB	2CU	Lsd fr Aircraft N1461C Trust
N1462C+	Fokker 100	11482	ex PH-JCC	2CV	Lsd fr Aircraft N1462C Trust
N1463A+	Fokker 100	11483	ex PH-JCD	2CW	Lsd fr Aircraft N1463A Trust
N1464A+	Fokker 100	11490	ex PH-EZU	2CX	Lsd fr WFBN
N1467A	Fokker 100	11499	ex PH-EZL	2DB
N1469D	Fokker 100	11502	ex PH-EZN	2DD
N1470K	Fokker 100	11506	ex PH-EZF	2DE	Lsd fr Aircraft N1470K Trust
N1471G+	Fokker 100	11507	ex PH-EZG	2DF
N1472B	Fokker 100	11514	ex PH-EZZ	2DG	Lsd fr Aircraft N1472B Trust
N1473K	Fokker 100	11515	ex PH-EZY	2DH
N1474D+	Fokker 100	11520	ex PH-EZV	2DJ	Lsd fr WFBN

+ stored at Mojave, CA; all to be retired between 3Q 2003 and 3Q 2005

N110HM"	McDonnell-Douglas MD-83	1636/49787	ex HL7274	4WT
N203AA	McDonnell-Douglas MD-82	1097/49145		203
N205AA	McDonnell-Douglas MD-82	1103/49155		205
N207AA	McDonnell-Douglas MD-82	1106/49158		207
N208AA	McDonnell-Douglas MD-82	1107/49159		208
N210AA	McDonnell-Douglas MD-82	1109/49161		210
N214AA	McDonnell-Douglas MD-82	1110/49162		214	Lsd fr CIT Leasing
N216AA	McDonnell-Douglas MD-82	1099/49167		216
N218AA	McDonnell-Douglas MD-82	1100/49168		218
N219AA	McDonnell-Douglas MD-82	1112/49171		219	Lsd fr CIT Leasing
N221AA	McDonnell-Douglas MD-82	1113/49172		221	Lsd fr CIT Leasing
N223AA	McDonnell-Douglas MD-82	1114/49173		223	Lsd fr CIT Leasing
N224AA	McDonnell-Douglas MD-82	1115/49174		224	Lsd fr CIT Leasing

N225AA	McDonnell-Douglas MD-82	1116/49175	225	Lsd fr CIT Leasing
N226AA	McDonnell-Douglas MD-82	1120/49176	226	
N227AA	McDonnell-Douglas MD-82	1121/49177	227	
N228AA	McDonnell-Douglas MD-82	1122/49178	228	
N232AA	McDonnell-Douglas MD-82	1123/49179	232	
N233AA	McDonnell-Douglas MD-82	1124/49180	233	
N234AA	McDonnell-Douglas MD-82	1125/49181	234	Lsd fr CIT Leasing
N236AA	McDonnell-Douglas MD-82	1154/49251	236	Lsd fr State Street
N237AA	McDonnell-Douglas MD-82	1155/49253	237	Lsd fr State Street
N241AA	McDonnell-Douglas MD-82	1156/49254	241	Lsd fr State Street
N242AA	McDonnell-Douglas MD-82	1157/49255	242	Lsd fr State Street
N244AA	McDonnell-Douglas MD-82	1158/49256	244	Lsd fr State Street
N245AA	McDonnell-Douglas MD-82	1160/49257	245	Lsd fr State Street
N246AA	McDonnell-Douglas MD-82	1161/49258	246	Lsd fr State Street
N248AA	McDonnell-Douglas MD-82	1162/49259	248	Lsd fr State Street
N249AA	McDonnell-Douglas MD-82	1164/49269	249	
N251AA	McDonnell-Douglas MD-82	1165/49270	251	
N253AA	McDonnell-Douglas MD-82	1175/49286	253	
N255AA	McDonnell-Douglas MD-82	1176/49287	255	
N258AA	McDonnell-Douglas MD-82	1187/49288	258	
N259AA	McDonnell-Douglas MD-82	1193/49289	269	
N262AA	McDonnell-Douglas MD-82	1195/49290	262	
N266AA	McDonnell-Douglas MD-82	1210/49291	266	
N269AA	McDonnell-Douglas MD-82	1211/49292	269	
N271AA	McDonnell-Douglas MD-82	1212/49293	271	
N274AA	McDonnell-Douglas MD-82	1166/49271	274	
N275AA	McDonnell-Douglas MD-82	1167/49272	275	
N276AA	McDonnell-Douglas MD-82	1168/49273	276	
N278AA	McDonnell-Douglas MD-82	1213/49294	278	
N279AA	McDonnell-Douglas MD-82	1214/49295	279	
N283AA	McDonnell-Douglas MD-82	1215/49296	283	
N285AA	McDonnell-Douglas MD-82	1216/49297	285	
N286AA	McDonnell-Douglas MD-82	1217/49298	286	
N287AA	McDonnell-Douglas MD-82	1218/49299	287	
N288AA	McDonnell-Douglas MD-82	1219/49300	288	
N289AA	McDonnell-Douglas MD-82	1220/49301	289	
N290AA	McDonnell-Douglas MD-82	1221/49302	290	
N291AA	McDonnell-Douglas MD-82	1222/49303	291	
N292AA	McDonnell-Douglas MD-82	1223/49304	292	
N293AA	McDonnell-Douglas MD-82	1226/49305	293	
N294AA	McDonnell-Douglas MD-82	1227/49306	294	Lsd fr State Street
N295AA	McDonnell-Douglas MD-82	1228/49307	295	Lsd fr State Street
N296AA	McDonnell-Douglas MD-82	1229/49308	296	Lsd fr State Street
N297AA	McDonnell-Douglas MD-82	1246/49309	297	
N298AA	McDonnell-Douglas MD-82	1247/49310	298	
N400AA	McDonnell-Douglas MD-82	1248/49311	400	
N402A	McDonnell-Douglas MD-82	1255/49313	402	
N403A	McDonnell-Douglas MD-82	1256/49314	403	
N405A	McDonnell-Douglas MD-82	1258/49316	405	
N406A	McDonnell-Douglas MD-82	1259/49317	406	
N407AA	McDonnell-Douglas MD-82	1265/49318	407	
N408AA	McDonnell-Douglas MD-82	1266/49319	408	
N409AA	McDonnell-Douglas MD-82	1267/49320	409	
N410AA	McDonnell-Douglas MD-82	1273/49321	410	
N411AA	McDonnell-Douglas MD-82	1280/49322	411	
N412AA	McDonnell-Douglas MD-82	1281/49323	412	
N413AA	McDonnell-Douglas MD-82	1289/49324	413	
N415AA	McDonnell-Douglas MD-82	1295/49326	415	
N416AA	McDonnell-Douglas MD-82	1296/49327	416	
N417AA	McDonnell-Douglas MD-82	1301/49328	417	
N418AA	McDonnell-Douglas MD-82	1302/49329	418	
N419AA	McDonnell-Douglas MD-82	1306/49331	419	
N420AA	McDonnell-Douglas MD-82	1307/49332	420	
N422AA	McDonnell-Douglas MD-82	1312/49334	422	
N423AA	McDonnell-Douglas MD-82	1320/49335	423	
N424AA	McDonnell-Douglas MD-82	1321/49336	424	
N426AA	McDonnell-Douglas MD-82	1327/49338	426	
N427AA	McDonnell-Douglas MD-82	1328/49339	427	
N428AA	McDonnell-Douglas MD-82	1329/49340	428	
N429AA	McDonnell-Douglas MD-82	1336/49341	429	
N430AA	McDonnell-Douglas MD-82	1337/49342	430	
N431AA	McDonnell-Douglas MD-82	1339/49343	431	
N432AA	McDonnell-Douglas MD-82	1376/49350	432	
N433AA	McDonnell-Douglas MD-83	1388/49451	433	
N434AA	McDonnell-Douglas MD-83	1389/49452	434	
N435AA	McDonnell-Douglas MD-83	1390/49453	435	
N436AA	McDonnell-Douglas MD-83	1391/49454	436	
N437AA	McDonnell-Douglas MD-83	1392/49455	437	
N438AA	McDonnell-Douglas MD-83	1393/49456	438	
N439AA	McDonnell-Douglas MD-83	1398/49457	439	
N440AA	McDonnell-Douglas MD-82	1407/49459	440	
N441AA	McDonnell-Douglas MD-82	1408/49460	441	

N442AA	McDonnell-Douglas MD-82	1409/49468	442	
N443AA	McDonnell-Douglas MD-82	1410/49469	443	
N445AA	McDonnell-Douglas MD-82	1418/49471	445	
N446AA	McDonnell-Douglas MD-82	1426/49472	446	
N447AA	McDonnell-Douglas MD-82	1427/49473	447	
N448AA	McDonnell-Douglas MD-82	1431/49474	448	
N449AA	McDonnell-Douglas MD-82	1432/49475	449	
N450AA	McDonnell-Douglas MD-82	1439/49476	450	
N451AA	McDonnell-Douglas MD-82	1441/49477	451	
N452AA	McDonnell-Douglas MD-82	1450/49553	452	Lsd fr WFBN
N453AA	McDonnell-Douglas MD-82	1451/49558	453	Lsd fr WFBN
N454AA	McDonnell-Douglas MD-82	1460/49559	454	
N455AA	McDonnell-Douglas MD-82	1462/49560	455	
N456AA	McDonnell-Douglas MD-82	1474/49561	456	
N457AA	McDonnell-Douglas MD-82	1475/49562	457	
N458AA	McDonnell-Douglas MD-82	1485/49563	458	
N459AA	McDonnell-Douglas MD-82	1486/49564	459	
N460AA	McDonnell-Douglas MD-82	1496/49565	460	
N461AA	McDonnell-Douglas MD-82	1497/49566	461	
N462AA	McDonnell-Douglas MD-82	1505/49592	462	
N463AA	McDonnell-Douglas MD-82	1506/49593	463	
N464AA	McDonnell-Douglas MD-82	1507/49594	464	
N465A	McDonnell-Douglas MD-82	1509/49595	465	
N466AA	McDonnell-Douglas MD-82	1510/49596	466	
N467AA	McDonnell-Douglas MD-82	1511/49597	467	
N468AA	McDonnell-Douglas MD-82	1513/49598	468	
N469AA	McDonnell-Douglas MD-82	1515/49599	469	
N470AA	McDonnell-Douglas MD-82	1516/49600	470	
N471AA	McDonnell-Douglas MD-82	1518/49601	471	
N472AA	McDonnell-Douglas MD-82	1520/49647	472	
N473AA	McDonnell-Douglas MD-82	1521/49648	473	
N474	McDonnell-Douglas MD-82	1526/49649	474	
N475AA	McDonnell-Douglas MD-82	1527/49650	475	
N476AA	McDonnell-Douglas MD-82	1528/49651	476	
N477AA	McDonnell-Douglas MD-82	1529/49652	477	
N478AA	McDonnell-Douglas MD-82	1534/49653	478	
N479AA	McDonnell-Douglas MD-82	1535/49654	479	
N480AA	McDonnell-Douglas MD-82	1536/49655	480	
N481AA	McDonnell-Douglas MD-82	1545/49656	481	
N482AA	McDonnell-Douglas MD-82	1546/49675	482	
N483A	McDonnell-Douglas MD-82	1550/49676	483	
N484AA	McDonnell-Douglas MD-82	1551/49677	484	
N485AA	McDonnell-Douglas MD-82	1555/49678	485	
N486AA	McDonnell-Douglas MD-82	1557/49679	486	
N487AA	McDonnell-Douglas MD-82	1558/49680	487	
N488AA	McDonnell-Douglas MD-82	1560/49681	488	
N489AA	McDonnell-Douglas MD-82	1562/49682	489	
N490AA	McDonnell-Douglas MD-82	1563/49683	490	
N491AA	McDonnell-Douglas MD-82	1564/49684	491	
N492AA	McDonnell-Douglas MD-82	1565/49730	492	
N493AA	McDonnell-Douglas MD-82	1566/49731	493	
N494AA	McDonnell-Douglas MD-82	1567/49732	494	
N495AA	McDonnell-Douglas MD-82	1607/49733	495	
N496AA	McDonnell-Douglas MD-82	1619/49734	496	
N497AA	McDonnell-Douglas MD-82	1635/49735	497	
N498AA	McDonnell-Douglas MD-82	1640/49736	498	
N499AA	McDonnell-Douglas MD-82	1641/49737	499	
N501AA	McDonnell-Douglas MD-82	1648/49738	501	
N505AA	McDonnell-Douglas MD-82	1652/49799	505	
N510AM	McDonnell-Douglas MD-82	1669/49804	510	
N513AA	McDonnell-Douglas MD-82	1686/49890	513	Lsd fr Arkia Lsg
N516AM	McDonnell-Douglas MD-82	1696/49893	516	
N552AA	McDonnell-Douglas MD-82	1826/53034	552	
N553AA	McDonnell-Douglas MD-82	1828/53083	553	
N554AA	McDonnell-Douglas MD-82	1830/53084	554	
N555AN	McDonnell-Douglas MD-82	1839/53085	555	
N556AA	McDonnell-Douglas MD-82	1840/53086	556	
N557AN	McDonnell-Douglas MD-82	1841/53087	557	
N558AA	McDonnell-Douglas MD-82	1852/53088	558	
N559AA	McDonnell-Douglas MD-82	1853/53089	559	
N560AA	McDonnell-Douglas MD-82	1858/53090	560	
N561AA	McDonnell-Douglas MD-82	1863/53091	561	
N562AA	McDonnell-Douglas MD-83	1370/49344	562	Lsd fr State Street
N563AA	McDonnell-Douglas MD-83	1371/49345	563	Lsd fr State Street
N564AA	McDonnell-Douglas MD-83	1372/49346	564	
N565AA	McDonnell-Douglas MD-83	1373/49347	565	
N566AA	McDonnell-Douglas MD-83	1374/49348	566	
N567AM	McDonnell-Douglas MD-83	2021/53293	567	
N568AA	McDonnell-Douglas MD-83	1375/49349	568	
N569AA	McDonnell-Douglas MD-83	1385/49351	569	
N570AA	McDonnell-Douglas MD-83	1386/49352	570	
N571AA	McDonnell-Douglas MD-83	1387/49353	571	

Registration	Type	Line/MSN	Notes	Fleet	Extra
N572AA	McDonnell-Douglas MD-83	1406/49458		572	
N573AA	McDonnell-Douglas MD-82	1864/53092		573	
N574AA	McDonnell-Douglas MD-82	1866/53151		574	
N575AM	McDonnell-Douglas MD-82	1875/53152		575	
N576AA	McDonnell-Douglas MD-82	1876/53153		576	
N577AA	McDonnell-Douglas MD-82	1878/53154		577	
N578AA	McDonnell-Douglas MD-82	1883/53155		578	
N579AA	McDonnell-Douglas MD-82	1884/53156		579	
N580AA	McDonnell-Douglas MD-82	1885/53157		580	
N581AA	McDonnell-Douglas MD-82	1891/53158		581	
N582AA	McDonnell-Douglas MD-82	1892/53159		582	
N583AA	McDonnell-Douglas MD-82	1893/53160		583	
N584AA	McDonnell-Douglas MD-82	1902/53247		584	
N585AA	McDonnell-Douglas MD-82	1903/53248		585	
N586AA	McDonnell-Douglas MD-82	1904/53249		586	
N587AA	McDonnell-Douglas MD-82	1907/53250		587	
N588AA	McDonnell-Douglas MD-83	1909/53251		588	
N589AA	McDonnell-Douglas MD-83	1910/53252		589	
N590AA	McDonnell-Douglas MD-83	1919/53253		590	
N591AA	McDonnell-Douglas MD-83	1920/53254		591	
N592AA	McDonnell-Douglas MD-83	1932/53255		592	
N593AA	McDonnell-Douglas MD-83	1933/53256		593	
N594AA	McDonnell-Douglas MD-83	1966/53284		594	
N595AA	McDonnell-Douglas MD-83	1989/53285		595	
N596AA	McDonnell-Douglas MD-83	2000/53286		596	
N597AA	McDonnell-Douglas MD-83	2006/53287		597	
N598AA	McDonnell-Douglas MD-83	2011/53288		598	
N599AA	McDonnell-Douglas MD-83	2012/53289		599	
N901TW	McDonnell-Douglas MD-82	1098/49166		4TA; stored	
N902TW	McDonnell-Douglas MD-82	1101/49153		4TB; stored ROW	Lsd fr CIT Leasing
N903TW	McDonnell-Douglas MD-82	1102/49154		4TC; stored	
N904TW	McDonnell-Douglas MD-82	1104/49156		4TD; stored ROW	
N905TW	McDonnell-Douglas MD-82	1105/49157		4TE	Lsd fr CIT Leasing
N906TW	McDonnell-Douglas MD-82	1108/49160		4TF	Lsd fr CIT Leasing
N907TW	McDonnell-Douglas MD-82	1117/49165		4TG	Lsd fr PLM Intl
N908TW	McDonnell-Douglas MD-82	1118/49169		4TH; stored ROW	
N909TW	McDonnell-Douglas MD-82	1119/49170		4TJ; stored ROW	
N911TW	McDonnell-Douglas MD-82	1128/49182		4TK	Lsd fr PLM Intl
N912TW	McDonnell-Douglas MD-82	1129/49183		4TL	Lsd fr PLM Intl
N913TW	McDonnell-Douglas MD-82	1131/49184		4TM; stored ROW	
N914TW	McDonnell-Douglas MD-82	1132/49185		4TN; stored ROW	
N915TW	McDonnell-Douglas MD-82	1133/49186		4TP; stored ROW	
N916TW	McDonnell-Douglas MD-82	1134/49187		4TR; stored ROW	
N917TW	McDonnell-Douglas MD-82	1196/49366		4TS; stored DFW	
N918TW	McDonnell-Douglas MD-82	1197/49367		4TT; stored ROW	
N919TW	McDonnell-Douglas MD-82	1198/49368		4TU	Lsd fr East Trust
N920TW	McDonnell-Douglas MD-82	1199/49369		4TV; stored ROW	
N921TW	McDonnell-Douglas MD-82	1051/49101	ex N531MD	4UL std	Lsd fr BCC Equipment Lsg
N922TW	McDonnell-Douglas MD-82	1000/48013	ex HB-INO	4UM std	Lsd fr BCC Equipment Lsg
N923TW	McDonnell-Douglas MD-82	1205/49379	ex D-ALLS	4UN std	Lsd fr ACG Acquisitions
N924TW	McDonnell-Douglas MD-82	1025/49100	ex HB-INA	4UP stored ROW	Lsd fr Pacific
N925TW	McDonnell-Douglas MD-82	1251/49357	ex HB-INT	4UR	
N926TW	McDonnell-Douglas MD-82	1250/49356	ex HB-INS	4US; stored ROW	
N927TW	McDonnell-Douglas MD-82	1294/49358	ex HB-INU	4UT; stored STL	
N928TW	McDonnell-Douglas MD-82	997/48012	ex HB-INN	4UU; stored ROW	
N929TW	McDonnell-Douglas MD-82	1013/48014	ex HB-INP	4UV; std	Lsd fr BCC Equipment Lsg
N940AS	McDonnell-Douglas MD-83	1577/49825	ex N940AS	4UJ	Lsd fr ILFC
N941AS	McDonnell-Douglas MD-83	1616/49925		4UK	Lsd fr ILFC
N948TW*	McDonnell-Douglas MD-83	1414/49575	ex EI-BWD	4WS	Lsd fr Aero USA
N950U	McDonnell-Douglas MD-82	1141/49230		4TW	Lsd fr Mitsubishi
N951TW	McDonnell-Douglas MD-83	2135/53470	ex N978AS	4XA	
N951U"	McDonnell-Douglas MD-82	1145/49245		4TX	
N952U"	McDonnell-Douglas MD-82	1238/49266		4TY	
N953U	McDonnell-Douglas MD-82	1239/49267		4UA	Lsd fr Mitsubishi
N954U	McDonnell-Douglas MD-82	1399/49426	ex N786JA	4UB	Lsd fr Bank of NY
N955U	McDonnell-Douglas MD-82	1401/49427	ex N787JA	4UC	Lsd fr Bank of NY
N956U	McDonnell-Douglas MD-82	1478/49701		4UD	Lsd fr GECAS
N957U	McDonnell-Douglas MD-82	1479/49702		4UE	Lsd fr GECAS
N958U	McDonnell-Douglas MD-82	1489/49703		4UF	Lsd fr GECAS
N959U	McDonnell-Douglas MD-82	1490/49704		4UG	Lsd fr GECAS
N960TW	McDonnell-Douglas MD-82	1177/49231	ex N930AS	4UH stored ROW	Lsd fr ACG Grp
N961TW'	McDonnell-Douglas MD-83	2264/53611		4XT	
N962TW'	McDonnell-Douglas MD-83	2265/53612		4XU	
N963TW'	McDonnell-Douglas MD-83	2266/53613		4XV	
N964TW'	McDonnell-Douglas MD-83	2267/53614		4XW	
N965TW'	McDonnell-Douglas MD-83	2268/53615		4XX	
N966TW'	McDonnell-Douglas MD-83	2269/53616		4XY	
N967TW'	McDonnell-Douglas MD-83	2270/53617		4YA	
N968TW'	McDonnell-Douglas MD-83	2271/53618		4YB	
N969TW'	McDonnell-Douglas MD-83	2272/53619		4YC	
N970TW'	McDonnell-Douglas MD-83	2273/53620		4YD; stored TUL	
N971TW'	McDonnell-Douglas MD-83	2274/53621		4YE; stored TUL	

N972TW'	McDonnell-Douglas MD-83	2275/53622		4YF	
N973TW	McDonnell-Douglas MD-83	2276/53623		4YG	Lsd fr East Trust
N974TW	McDonnell-Douglas MD-83	2277/53624		4YH	Lsd fr East Trust
N975TW'	McDonnell-Douglas MD-83	2278/53625		4YJ	
N976TW'	McDonnell-Douglas MD-83	2279/53626		4YK	
N978TW'	McDonnell-Douglas MD-83	2281/53628		4YM	
N979TW'	McDonnell-Douglas MD-83	2282/53629		4YN	
N980TW'	McDonnell-Douglas MD-83	2283/53630		4YP	
N982TW'	McDonnell-Douglas MD-83	2285/53632		4YR	
N983TW'	McDonnell-Douglas MD-83	2286/53633		4YS	
N984TW'+	McDonnell-Douglas MD-83	2287/53634		4YT	
N3507A	McDonnell-Douglas MD-82	1661/49801		507	
N3515	McDonnell-Douglas MD-82	1695/49892		515	
N7506	McDonnell-Douglas MD-82	1660/49800		506	
N7508	McDonnell-Douglas MD-82	1662/49802		508	
N7509	McDonnell-Douglas MD-82	1663/49803		509	
N7512A	McDonnell-Douglas MD-82	1673/49806		512	
N7514A	McDonnell-Douglas MD-82	1694/49891		514	Lsd fr Arkia Lsg
N7517A	McDonnell-Douglas MD-82	1697/49894		517	Lsd fr Wachovia Bank
N7518A	McDonnell-Douglas MD-82	1698/49895		518	
N7519A	McDonnell-Douglas MD-82	1707/49896		519	
N7520A	McDonnell-Douglas MD-82	1708/49897		520	
N7521A	McDonnell-Douglas MD-82	1709/49898		521	
N7522A	McDonnell-Douglas MD-82	1722/49899		522	Lsd fr Wachovia Bank
N7525A	McDonnell-Douglas MD-82	1735/49917		525	
N7526A	McDonnell-Douglas MD-82	1743/49918		526	
N7527A	McDonnell-Douglas MD-82	1744/49919		527	
N7528A	McDonnell-Douglas MD-82	1750/49920		528	
N7530	McDonnell-Douglas MD-82	1753/49922		530	
N7531A	McDonnell-Douglas MD-82	1758/49923		531	
N7532A	McDonnell-Douglas MD-82	1759/49924		532	
N7533A	McDonnell-Douglas MD-82	1760/49987		533	
N7534A	McDonnell-Douglas MD-82	1768/49988		534	
N7535A	McDonnell-Douglas MD-82	1769/49989		535	
N7536A	McDonnell-Douglas MD-82	1770/49990		536	
N7537A	McDonnell-Douglas MD-82	1780/49991		537	
N7538A	McDonnell-Douglas MD-82	1781/49992		538	Lsd fr Wachovia Bank
N7539A	McDonnell-Douglas MD-82	1782/49993		539	
N7540A	McDonnell-Douglas MD-82	1790/49994		540	Lsd fr Arkia Lsg
N7541A	McDonnell-Douglas MD-82	1791/49995		541	Lsd fr Arkia Lsg
N7542A	McDonnell-Douglas MD-82	1792/49996		542	Lsd fr Arkia Lsg
N7543A	McDonnell-Douglas MD-82	1802/53025		543	
N7544A	McDonnell-Douglas MD-82	1804/53026		544	
N7546A	McDonnell-Douglas MD-82	1813/53028		546	
N7547A	McDonnell-Douglas MD-82	1814/53029		547	
N7548A	McDonnell-Douglas MD-82	1816/53030		548	
N7549A	McDonnell-Douglas MD-82	1819/53031		549	
N7550	McDonnell-Douglas MD-82	1820/53032		550	
N9302B	McDonnell-Douglas MD-83	1383/49528		4WB; stored	Lsd fr AWMS I
N9304C	McDonnell-Douglas MD-83	1397/49530		4WD stored ROW	Lsd fr AWMS I
N9305N	McDonnell-Douglas MD-83	1286/49395	ex YV-36C	4WE	
N9306T	McDonnell-Douglas MD-83	1367/49567	ex YV-38C	4WF	
N9307R	McDonnell-Douglas MD-83	1437/49663	ex SE-DPH	4WG; stored	Lsd fr Lancelot Lsg
(N9308R)	McDonnell-Douglas MD-83	1459/49657	ex N939AS	4WH	Lsd fr MSA V
N9401W	McDonnell-Douglas MD-83	1872/53137	ex N9001L	4WJ	Lsd fr BCC Equipment Lsg
N9402W	McDonnell-Douglas MD-83	1886/53138	ex N9001D	4WK	Lsd fr BCC Equipment Lsg
N9403W	McDonnell-Douglas MD-83	1899/53139	ex N9035C	4WL	Lsd fr BCC Equipment Lsg
N9404V	McDonnell-Douglas MD-83	1923/53140	ex N9075H	4WM	Lsd fr BCC Equipment Lsg
N9405T	McDonnell-Douglas MD-83	1935/53141		4WN	Lsd fr BCC Equipment Lsg
N9406W	McDonnell-Douglas MD-83	2026/53126	ex N6203U	4WP	Lsd fr BCC Equipment Lsg
N9407R	McDonnell-Douglas MD-83	1356/49400	ex EI-CKB	4WR	
N9409F	McDonnell-Douglas MD-83	1971/53121	ex N532MD	4WS	Lsd fr BCC Equipment Lsg
N9412W	McDonnell-Douglas MD-83	2118/53187		4WU	Lsd fr AWAS
N9413T	McDonnell-Douglas MD-83	2119/53188		4WV	Lsd fr AWAS
N9414W	McDonnell-Douglas MD-83	2121/53189		4WX	Lsd fr AWAS
N9420D	McDonnell-Douglas MD-83	1554/49824	ex 9Y-THU	4WY	Lsd fr ILFC
N9615W^	McDonnell-Douglas MD-83	2192/53562		4XB	
N9616G^	McDonnell-Douglas MD-83	219/653563		4XC	
N9617R^	McDonnell-Douglas MD-83	2199/53564		4XD	
N9618A"	McDonnell-Douglas MD-83	2201/53565		4XE	
N9619V"	McDonnell-Douglas MD-83	2206/53566		4XF	
N9620D"	McDonnell-Douglas MD-83	2208/53591		4XG	
N9621A"	McDonnell-Douglas MD-83	2234/53592		4XH	
N9622A"	McDonnell-Douglas MD-83	2239/53593		4XJ	
N9624T"	McDonnell-Douglas MD-83	2241/53594		4XK	
N9625W"	McDonnell-Douglas MD-83	2244/53595		4XL	
N9626F"	McDonnell-Douglas MD-83	2247/53596		4XM	
N9627R"	McDonnell-Douglas MD-83	2249/53597		4XN	
N9628W"	McDonnell-Douglas MD-83	2252/53598		4XP	
N9629H"	McDonnell-Douglas MD-83	2254/53599		4XR	
N9630A"	McDonnell-Douglas MD-83	2174/53561	ex N90126	4XS	
N9677W'	McDonnell-Douglas MD-83	2280/53627		4YL	

N9681B"	McDonnell-Douglas MD-83	2284/53631	ex (N981TW)	4XT
N14551	McDonnell-Douglas MD-82	1822/53033		551
N16545	McDonnell-Douglas MD-82	1805/53027		545
N33414	McDonnell-Douglas MD-82	1290/49325		414
N33502	McDonnell-Douglas MD-82	1649/49739		502
N44503	McDonnell-Douglas MD-82	1650/49797		503
N59523	McDonnell-Douglas MD-82	1723/49915		523
N70401	McDonnell-Douglas MD-82	1249/49312		401
N70404	McDonnell-Douglas MD-82	1257/49315		404
N70425	McDonnell-Douglas MD-82	1325/49337		425
N70504	McDonnell-Douglas MD-82	1651/49798		504
N70524	McDonnell-Douglas MD-82	1729/49916		524
N70529	McDonnell-Douglas MD-82	1752/49921		529
N73444	McDonnell-Douglas MD-82	1417/49470		444
N76200	McDonnell-Douglas MD-83	2013/53290		200
N76201	McDonnell-Douglas MD-83	2019/53291		201
N76202	McDonnell-Douglas MD-83	2020/53292		202
N77421	McDonnell-Douglas MD-82	1311/49333		421
N90511	McDonnell-Douglas MD-82	1672/49805		511

+Named Spirit of Long Beach last MD-80 built   *Named Wings of Pride
^Leased from MDFC Equipment Leasing Corp   "Leased from Boeing Capital Corp
Up to twenty-eight to be parked in early 2003. Seating configuations on Boeing 767/777s to be standardised
Owns 5% of Iberia. Founder member of oneworld alliance with British Airways.
Feeder services operated by American Eagle (wholly owned subsidiary) with other services operated by Trans State,
Executive Airlines and Chautauqua as American Connection

AMERICAN CONNECTION

Red Bird (AX/RBD)   *Indianapolis, IN/St Louis-Lambert Intl, MO (IND/STL)*

N856TE	British Aerospace Jetstream 32EP	856	ex N422AM	Corporate Airlines
N860AE	British Aerospace Jetstream 32EP	860	ex G-31-860	Corporate Airlines
N871JX	British Aerospace Jetstream 32EP	871	exN871AE	Corporate Airlines
N872AE	British Aerospace Jetstream 32EP	872	ex G-31-872	Corporate Airlines
N875JX	British Aerospace Jetstream 32EP	875	ex N875AE	Corporate Airlines
N880TE	British Aerospace Jetstream 32EP	880	ex N430AM	Corporate Airlines
N883CH	British Aerospace Jetstream 32EP	883	ex N432AM	Corporate Airlines
(N917CX)	British Aerospace Jetstream 32EP	917	ex N917AE	Corporate Airlines
(N921CX)	British Aerospace Jetstream 32EP	921	ex N921AE	Corporate Airlines
N922CX	British Aerospace Jetstream 32EP	922	ex N922AE	Corporate Airlines
(N924CX)	British Aerospace Jetstream 32EP	924	ex N924AE	Corporate Airlines
N926AE	British Aerospace Jetstream 32EP	926	ex G-31-926	Corporate Airlines
N933CX	British Aerospace Jetstream 32EP	933	ex N933AE	Corporate Airlines
(N936CX)	British Aerospace Jetstream 32EP	936	ex N936AE	Corporate Airlines
(N937CX)	British Aerospace Jetstream 32EP	937	ex N937AE	Corporate Airlines
(N938CX)	British Aerospace Jetstream 32EP	938	ex N938AE	Corporate Airlines
(N944CX)	British Aerospace Jetstream 32EP	944	ex N944AE	Corporate Airlines
N551HK	British Aerospace Jetstream 41	41040	ex G-4-040	Trans State
N552HK	British Aerospace Jetstream 41	41057	ex G-4-057	Trans State
M553HK	British Aerospace Jetstream 41	41066	ex G-4-066	Trans State
N555HK	British Aerospace Jetstream 41	41072	ex G-4-072	Trans State
N556HK	British Aerospace Jetstream 41	41073	ex G-4-073	Trans State
N557HK	British Aerospace Jetstream 41	41074	ex G-4-074	Trans State
N558HK	British Aerospace Jetstream 41	41071	ex G-4-071	Trans State
N559HK	British Aerospace Jetstream 41	41075	ex G-4-075	Trans State
N560HK	British Aerospace Jetstream 41	41076	ex G-4-076	Trans State
N561HK	British Aerospace Jetstream 41	41077	ex G-4-077	Trans State
N564HK	British Aerospace Jetstream 41	41081	ex G-4-081	Trans State
N565HK	British Aerospace Jetstream 41	41082	ex G-4-082	Trans State
N566HK	British Aerospace Jetstream 41	41084	ex G-4-084	Trans State
N567HK	British Aerospace Jetstream 41	41085	ex G-4-085	Trans State
N568HK	British Aerospace Jetstream 41	41086	ex G-4-086	Trans State
N569HK	British Aerospace Jetstream 41	41088	ex G-4-088	Trans State
N570HK	British Aerospace Jetstream 41	41089	ex G-4-089	Trans State
N571HK	British Aerospace Jetstream 41	41090	ex G-4-090	Trans State
N573HK	British Aerospace Jetstream 41	41092	ex G-4-092	Trans State
N574HK	British Aerospace Jetstream 41	41093	ex G-4-093	Trans State
N295SK	Embraer EMB.135KL	145513	ex PT-SYF	Chautauqua
N297SK	Embraer EMB.135KL	145522	ex PT-SYN	Chautauqua
N299SK	Embraer EMB.135KL	145532	ex PT-STW	Chautauqua
N371SK	Embraer EMB.135KL	145535	ex PT-STZ	Chautauqua
N372SK	Embraer EMB.135KL	145538	ex PT-SZC	Chautauqua
N373SK	Embraer EMB.135KL	145543	ex PT-SZG	Chautauqua
N374SK	Embraer EMB.135KL	145544	ex PT-SZH	Chautauqua
N375SK	Embraer EMB.135KL	145569	ex PT-S	Chautauqua
N376SK	Embraer EMB.135KL	145578	ex PT-SBO	Chautauqua
N377SK	Embraer EMB.135KL	145579	ex PT-SBP	Chautauqua
N378SK	Embraer EMB.135KL	145593	ex PT-S	Chautauqua
N379SK	Embraer EMB.135KL	145606	ex PT-SCP	Chautauqua

N380SK	Embraer EMB.135KL	145613	ex PT-SCX	Chautauqua
N381SK	Embraer EMB.135KL	145619	ex PT-SDH	Chautauqua
N382SK	Embraer EMB.135KL	145624	ex PT-SDM	Chautauqua

A further twenty-three Embraer EMB.135KLs are on order for Chautauqua plus ten for Trans State

N270SK	Embraer EMB.145LR	145304	ex PT-SKV	Chautauqua
N272SK	Embraer EMB.145LR	145306	ex PT-SKX	Chautauqua
N277SK	Embraer EMB.145LR	145355	ex PT-SNU	Chautauqua
N279SK	Embraer EMB.145LR	145379	ex PT-SQD	Chautauqua
N296SK	Embraer EMB.145LR	145497	ex PT-SXQ	Chautauqua
N801HK	Embraer EMB.145ER	145053	ex PT-SZS	Trans State
N802HK	Embraer EMB.145ER	145066	ex PT-SAJ	Trans State
N803HK	Embraer EMB.145ER	145077	ex PT-S	Trans State
N804HK	Embraer EMB.145ER	145082	ex PT-S	Trans State
N805HK	Embraer EMB.145ER	145096	ex PT-s	Trans State
N806HK	Embraer EMB.145ER	145112	ex PT-SCO	Trans State
N807HK	Embraer EMB.145ER	145119	ex PT-SCV	Trans State
N808HK	Embraer EMB.145ER	145157	ex PT-	Trans State
N809HK	Embraer EMB.145ER	145187	ex PT-S	Trans State
N810HK	Embraer EMB.145LR	145231	ex PT-SHV	Trans State
N811HK	Embraer EMB.145ER	145256	ex PT-SIQ	Trans State
N812HK	Embraer EMB.145ER	145373	ex PT-S	Trans State
N813HK	Embraer EMB.145MR	145044	ex N600BK	Trans State
N814HK	Embraer EMB.145MR	145046	ex N601GH	Trans State
N815HK	Embraer EMB.145LR	145048	ex N602AE	Trans State
N816HK	Embraer EMB.145LR	145055	ex N603AE	Trans State
N817HK	Embraer EMB.145LR	145058	ex N604DG	Trans State
N818HK	Embraer EMB.145LR	145059	ex N605RR	Trans State
N819HK	Embraer EMB.145LR	145062	ex N606AE	Trans State
N820HK	Embraer EMB.145LR	145064	ex N607AE	Trans State
N821HK	Embraer EMB.145LR	145068	ex N608AE	Trans State
N822HK	Embraer EMB.145LR	145069	ex N609AE	Trans State
N824HK	Embraer EMB.145LR	145498	ex HB-JAQ	Trans State
N825HK	Embraer EMB.145LR	145510	ex HB-JAR	Trans State
N826HK	Embraer EMB.145EP	145016	ex VP-CZB	Trans State
N827HK	Embraer EMB.145EP	145021	ex VP-CZA	Trans State
N829HK	Embraer EMB.145LU	145281	ex HB-JAE	Trans State
N830HK	Embraer EMB.145LU	145313	ex HB-JAF	Trans State
N831HK	Embraer EMB.145LU	145232	ex HB-JAA	Trans State
N833HK	Embraer EMB.145LU	145240	ex HB-JAB	Trans State
N834HK	Embraer EMB.145LU	145269	ex HB-JAD	Trans State

Other services are operated by Corporate Airlines

AMERICAN EAGLE

Eagle Flight (MQ/EGF)   Dallas-Fort Worth, TX (DFW)

N4AE	Aerospatiale/Alenia ATR 72-212	244	ex N244AT		
N135MQ	Aerospatiale/Alenia ATR 42-310	135	ex N429MQ		Lsd fr AMR Leasing
N141AE	Aerospatiale/Alenia ATR 42-300	141	ex N431MQ		Lsd fr AMR Leasing
N246AE	Aerospatiale/Alenia ATR 42-320	243	ex N243AT		Lsd fr AMR Leasing
N248AT	Aerospatiale/Alenia ATR 72-212	248	ex F-WWEN		Lsd fr debis
N252AM	Aerospatiale/Alenia ATR 72-212	253	ex N253AT		Lsd fr GPA ATR
N255AE	Aerospatiale/Alenia ATR 42-300	254	ex N254AT	stored YUL	Lsd fr GPA ATR
N260AE	Aerospatiale/Alenia ATR 72-201	263	ex N263AT		Lsd fr GPA ATR
N262AT	Aerospatiale/Alenia ATR 42-300	262	ex F-WWEL		Lsd fr AMR Leasing
N265AE	Aerospatiale/Alenia ATR 42-320	266	ex N266AT		Lsd fr AMR Leasing
N270AT	Aerospatiale/Alenia ATR 72-212	270	ex F-WWEL		
N271AT	Aerospatiale/Alenia ATR 42-320	273	ex N273AT		Lsd fr AMR Leasing
N274AT	Aerospatiale/Alenia ATR 72-212	274	ex F-WWLC	stored Calgary	Lsd fr AerFi Corp
N282AT	Aerospatiale/Alenia ATR 42-320	282	ex F-WWLI	stored MCO	Lsd fr AMR Leasing
N288AM	Aerospatiale/Alenia ATR 72-212	288	ex F-WWLP		
N308AE	Aerospatiale/Alenia ATR 72-212	309	ex N309AM		
N310DK	Aerospatiale/Alenia ATR 42-300	310	ex F-WWEC		Lsd fr AMR Leasing
N314AM	Aerospatiale/Alenia ATR 42-300	314	ex F-WWEK		Lsd fr AMR Leasing
N319AM	Aerospatiale/Alenia ATR 42-300	319	ex F-WWER		Lsd fr AMR Leasing
N322AC	Aerospatiale/Alenia ATR 72-212	320	ex N320AT	stored MQT	
N325AT	Aerospatiale/Alenia ATR 42-320	325	ex F-WWLK		Lsd fr AMR Leasing
N327AT	Aerospatiale/Alenia ATR 42-320	327	ex F-WWLM		Lsd fr AMR Leasing
N342AT	Aerospatiale/Alenia ATR 72-212	345	ex N345AT		
N348AE	Aerospatiale/Alenia ATR 72-212	349	ex N349AT		
N355AT	Aerospatiale/Alenia ATR 72-212	355	ex F-WWEQ		
N369AT	Aerospatiale/Alenia ATR 72-212	369	ex F-WWEC		
N377AT	Aerospatiale/Alenia ATR 72-212	377	ex F-WWLA		
N399AT	Aerospatiale/Alenia ATR 72-212	399	ex F-WWLK		
N407AT	Aerospatiale/Alenia ATR 72-212	407	ex F-WWEL		
N408AT	Aerospatiale/Alenia ATR 72-212	408	ex F-WWEM		
N410AT	Aerospatiale/Alenia ATR 72-212	410	ex F-WWLS		
N414WF	Aerospatiale/Alenia ATR 72-212	414	ex F-WWLD		
N417AT	Aerospatiale/Alenia ATR 72-212	417	ex F-WWLT		
N420AT	Aerospatiale/Alenia ATR 72-212	420	ex F-WWLY		

N425MJ	Aerospatiale/Alenia ATR 72-212	425	ex F-WWEC
N426AT	Aerospatiale/Alenia ATR 72-212	426	ex F-WWED
N429AT	Aerospatiale/Alenia ATR 72-212	429	ex F-WWEH
N431AT	Aerospatiale/Alenia ATR 72-212	431	ex F-WWEI
N434AT	Aerospatiale/Alenia ATR 72-212	434	ex F-WWEM
N438AT	Aerospatiale/Alenia ATR 72-212	438	ex F-WWEO
N440AM	Aerospatiale/Alenia ATR 72-212	440	ex F-WWEP
N447AM	Aerospatiale/Alenia ATR 72-212	447	ex F-WWEC
N448AM	Aerospatiale/Alenia ATR 72-212	448	ex F-WWED
N451AT	Aerospatiale/Alenia ATR 72-212	451	ex F-WWES
N494AE	Aerospatiale/Alenia ATR 72-212A	494	ex F-WWLS
N498AT	Aerospatiale/Alenia ATR 72-212A	498	ex F-WWLW
N499AT	Aerospatiale/Alenia ATR 72-212A	499	ex F-WWLY	Special '500th' colours
N529AM	Aerospatiale/Alenia ATR 72-212A	529	ex F-WWLR	stored MCO
N533AT	Aerospatiale/Alenia ATR 72-212A	533	ex F-WWLO
N536AT	Aerospatiale/Alenia ATR 72-212A	536	ex F-WWLZ
N538AT	Aerospatiale/Alenia ATR 72-212A	538	ex F-WWEA
N540AM	Aerospatiale/Alenia ATR 72-212A	540	ex F-WWLJ
N541AT	Aerospatiale/Alenia ATR 72-212A	541	ex F-WWLA
N545AT	Aerospatiale/Alenia ATR 72-212A	545	ex F-WWLE
N548AT	Aerospatiale/Alenia ATR 72-212A	548	ex F-WWLI
N550LL	Aerospatiale/Alenia ATR 72-212A	550	ex F-WWLK

All Aerospatiale/Alenia ATR 42-320s are for sale to FedEx

N500AE	Canadair CL-600-2C10	10025	ex C-GJEX
N501BG	Canadair CL-600-2C10	10017	ex C-GIAH
N502AE	Canadair CL-600-2C10	10018	ex C-GJUI
N503AE	Canadair CL-600-2C10	10021	ex C-GIAP
N504AE	Canadair CL-600-2C10	10044	ex C-GHZZ
N505AE	Canadair CL-600-2C10	10053	ex C-GIAU
N506AE	Canadair CL-600-2C10	10056	ex C-GIAX
N507AE	Canadair CL-600-2C10	10059	ex C-GIBH
N508AE	Canadair CL-600-2C10	10072	ex C-GHZV
N509AE	Canadair CL-600-2C10	10078	ex C-GZUC
N510AE	Canadair CL-600-2C10	10105	ex C-
N511AE	Canadair CL-600-2C10	10107	ex C-
N512AE	Canadair CL-600-2C10	10110	ex C-
N513AE	Canadair CL-600-2C10	10114	ex C-
N514AE	Canadair CL-600-2C10	10119	ex C-
N515AE	Canadair CL-600-2C10	10121	ex C-
N516AE	Canadair CL-600-2C10	10123	ex C-
N517AE	Canadair CL-600-2C10	10124	ex C-
N518AE	Canadair CL-600-2C10	10126	ex C-
N519AE	Canadair CL-600-2C10	10131	ex C-
N520DC	Canadair CL-600-2C10		on order Mar04
N521AE	Canadair CL-600-2C10		on order Apr04
N522AE	Canadair CL-600-2C10		on order May04
N523AE	Canadair CL-600-2C10		on order Jun04
N524AE	Canadair CL-600-2C10		on order Jul04

N700LE	Embraer EMB.135LR	145156	ex PT-SFC
N701MH	Embraer EMB.135LR	145162	ex PT-SFD
N702AE	Embraer EMB.135LR	145164	ex PT-SFE
N703MR	Embraer EMB.135LR	145173	ex PT-SFG
N704PG	Embraer EMB.135LR	145174	ex PT-SFH
N705AE	Embraer EMB.135LR	145184	ex PT-SFJ
N706RG	Embraer EMB.135LR	145194	ex PT-SFO
N707EB	Embraer EMB.135LR	145195	ex PT-SFP
N708AE	Embraer EMB.135LR	145205	ex PT-SFR
N709GB	Embraer EMB.135LR	145211	ex PT-SFV
N710TB	Embraer EMB.135LR	145224	ex PT-SFZ
N711PH	Embraer EMB.135LR	145235	ex PT-SJC
N712AE	Embraer EMB.135LR	145247	ex PT-SJG
N713AE	Embraer EMB.135LR	145249	ex PT-SJH
N715AE	Embraer EMB.135LR	145262	ex PT-SIV
N716AE	Embraer EMB.135LR	145264	ex PT-SIW
N717AE	Embraer EMB.135LR	145272	ex PT-SJO
N718AE	Embraer EMB.135LR	145275	ex PT-SJR
N719AE	Embraer EMB.135LR	145276	ex PT-SJS
N720AE	Embraer EMB.135LR	145279	ex PT-SJV
N721HS	Embraer EMB.135LR	145283	ex PT-S JZ
N722AE	Embraer EMB.135LR	145287	ex PT-SKE
N723AE	Embraer EMB.135LR	145288	ex PT-SKF
N724AE	Embraer EMB.135LR	145301	ex PT-SKS
N725AE	Embraer EMB.135LR	145312	ex PT-SMD
N726AE	Embraer EMB.135LR	145314	ex PT-SMF
N727AE	Embraer EMB.135LR	145326	ex PT-SMS
N728AE	Embraer EMB.135LR	145328	ex PT-SMU
N729AE	Embraer EMB.135LR	145343	ex PT-SNJ
N730KW	Embraer EMB.135LR	145346	ex PT-SNM
N731BE	Embraer EMB.135LR	145356	ex PT-SNV
N732DH	Embraer EMB.135LR	145358	ex PT-SNX

N733KR	Embraer EMB.135LR	145368	ex PT-SOT	
N734EK	Embraer EMB.135LR	145371	ex PT-SOW	
N735TS	Embraer EMB.135LR	145386	ex PT-SQK	
N736DT	Embraer EMB.135LR	145388	ex PT-SQM	
N737MW	Embraer EMB.135LR	145396	ex PT-SQT	
N738NR	Embraer EMB.135LR	145401	ex PT-SQY	
N739AE	Embraer EMB.135LR	145402	ex PT-SQZ	
N800AE	Embraer EMB.135KL	145425	ex PT-XGF	special c/s
N801AE	Embraer EMB.135KL	145469	ex PT-SVO	
N802AE	Embraer EMB.135KL	145471	ex PT-SVQ	
N803AE	Embraer EMB.135KL	145483	ex PT-SXC	100th RJ Spirit of Eagle titles
N804AE	Embraer EMB.135KL	145487	ex PT-SXG	
N805AE	Embraer EMB.135KL	145489	ex PT-SXI	
N806AE	Embraer EMB.135KL	145503	ex PT-SXW	
N807AE	Embraer EMB.135KL	145506	ex PT-SXZ	Make A Wish colours
N808AE	Embraer EMB.135KL	145519	ex PT-SYK	
N809AE	Embraer EMB.135KL	145521	ex PT-SYM	
N810AE	Embraer EMB.135KL	145525	ex PT-SYQ	
N811AE	Embraer EMB.135KL	145529	ex PT-STT	
N812AE	Embraer EMB.135KL	145531	ex PT-STV	
N813AE	Embraer EMB.135KL	145539	ex PT-SZD	
N814AE	Embraer EMB.135KL	145541	ex PT-SZF	
N815AE	Embraer EMB.135KL	145545	ex PT-SZI	
N816AE	Embraer EMB.135KL	145552	ex PT-SZO	
N817AE	Embraer EMB.135KL	145554	ex PT-SZQ	
N818AE	Embraer EMB.135KL	145561	ex PT-SZW	
N819AE	Embraer EMB.135KL	145566	ex PT-SBC	
N820AE	Embraer EMB.135KL	145576	ex PT-SBM	
N821AE	Embraer EMB.135KL	145577	ex PT-SBN	
N822AE	Embraer EMB.135KL	145581	ex PT-SBS	
N823AE	Embraer EMB.135KL	145582	ex PT-SBT	
N824AE	Embraer EMB.135KL	145584	ex PT-SBV	
N825AE	Embraer EMB.135KL	145589	ex PT-SBZ	
N826AE	Embraer EMB.135KL	145592	ex PT-SCA	
N827AE	Embraer EMB.135KL	145602	ex PT-SCL	
N828AE	Embraer EMB.135KL	145604	ex PT-SCN	
N829AE	Embraer EMB.135KL	145609	ex PT-SCS	
N830AE	Embraer EMB.135KL	145615	ex PT-SDD	
N831AE	Embraer EMB.135KL	145616	ex PT-SDE	
N832AE	Embraer EMB.135KL	145627	ex PT-SDP	
N833AE	Embraer EMB.135KL	145629	ex PT-SDR	
N834AE	Embraer EMB.135KL	145631	ex PT-SDT	
N835AE	Embraer EMB.135KL	145634	ex PT-SDW	
N836AE	Embraer EMB.135KL	145635	ex PT-SDX	
N837AE	Embraer EMB.135KL	145647	ex PT-SEH	
N838AE	Embraer EMB.135KL	145651	ex PT-SEL	
N839AE	Embraer EMB.135KL	145653	ex PT-SEN	
N840AE	Embraer EMB.135KL	145656	ex PT-SEQ	
N841AE	Embraer EMB.135KL	145667	ex PT-SFB	
N842AE	Embraer EMB.135KL	145673	ex PT-SFG	
N843AE	Embraer EMB.135KL	145680	ex PT-SFM	
N844AE	Embraer EMB.135KL	145682	ex PT-SFO	
N845AE	Embraer EMB.135KL	145685	ex PT-SFR	
N846AE	Embraer EMB.135KL	145692	ex PT-SFY	
N847AE	Embraer EMB.135KL	145707	ex PT-SGK	
N848AE	Embraer EMB.135KL	145710	ex PT-SGO	
N849AE	Embraer EMB.135KL	145716	ex PT-SGT	
N850AE	Embraer EMB.135KL	145722	ex PT-SGY	
N851AE	Embraer EMB.135KL	145734	ex PT-SHK	
N852AE	Embraer EMB.135KL	145736	ex PT-SHM	
N853AE	Embraer EMB.135KL	145742	ex PT-SJB	
N854AE	Embraer EMB.135KL	145743	ex PT-SJC	
N855AE	Embraer EMB.135KL	145747	ex PT-SJG	
N856AE	Embraer EMB.135KL	145748	ex PT-SJH	
N857AE	Embraer EMB.135KL	145752	ex PT-S	
N858AE	Embraer EMB.135KL	145754	ex PT-S	
N600BK	Embraer EMB.145LR	145044	ex PT-SZJ	Lsd to LOF as N813HK
N601GH	Embraer EMB.145LR	145046	ex PT-SZL	Lsd to LOF as N814HK
N602AE	Embraer EMB.145LR	145048	ex PT-SZN	Lsd to LOF as N815HK
N603AE	Embraer EMB.145LR	145055	ex PT-SZU	Lsd to LOF as N816HK
N604DG	Embraer EMB.145LR	145058	ex PT-SZX	Lsd to LOF as N817HK
N605RR	Embraer EMB.145LR	145059	ex PT-SZY	Lsd to LOF as N818HK
N606AE	Embraer EMB.145LR	145062	ex PT-SAF	Lsd to LOF as N819HK
N607AE	Embraer EMB.145LR	145064	ex PT-SAH	Lsd to LOF as N820HK
N608AE	Embraer EMB.145LR	145068	ex PT-SAM	Lsd to LOF as N821HK
N609AE	Embraer EMB.145LR	145069	ex PT-SAN	Lsd to LOF as N822HK
N610AE	Embraer EMB.145LR	145073	ex PT-SAR	
N611AE	Embraer EMB.145LR	145074	ex PT-SAS	
N612AE	Embraer EMB.145LR	145079	ex PT-S	
N613AE	Embraer EMB.145LR	145081	ex PT-S	
N614AE	Embraer EMB.145LR	145086	ex PT-S	

N615AE	Embraer EMB.145LR	145087	ex PT-S		
N616AE	Embraer EMB.145LR	145092	ex PT-S		
N617AE	Embraer EMB.145LR	145093	ex PT-SBP		
N618AE	Embraer EMB.145LR	145097	ex PT-SBT		
N619AE	Embraer EMB.145LR	145101	ex PT-S		
N620AE	Embraer EMB.145LR	145102	ex PT-S		
N621AE	Embraer EMB.145LR	145105	ex PT-S		
N622AE	Embraer EMB.145LR	145108	ex PT-S		
N623AE	Embraer EMB.145LR	145109	ex PT-S		
N624AE	Embraer EMB.145LR	145111	ex PT-S		
N625AE	Embraer EMB.145LR	145115	ex PT-SCR		
N626AE	Embraer EMB.145LR	145117	ex PT-SCT		
N627AE	Embraer EMB.145LR	145121	ex PT-SCX		
N628AE	Embraer EMB.145LR	145124	ex PT-SDA		
N629AE	Embraer EMB.145LR	145130	ex PT-SDH		
N630AE	Embraer EMB.145LR	145132	ex PT-SDJ		
N631AE	Embraer EMB.145LR	145139	ex PT-SDQ		
N632AE	Embraer EMB.145LR	145143	ex PT-SDT		
N633AE	Embraer EMB.145LR	145148	ex PT-SDY		
N634AE	Embraer EMB.145LR	145150	ex PT-SEB		
N635AE	Embraer EMB.145LR	145158	ex PT-S		
N636AE	Embraer EMB.145LR	145160	ex PT-S		
N637AE	Embraer EMB.145LR	145170	ex PT-S		
N638AE	Embraer EMB.145LR	145172	ex PT-S		
N639AE	Embraer EMB.145LR	145182	ex PT-SGE		
N640AE	Embraer EMB.145LR	145183	ex PT-SGF		
N641AE	Embraer EMB.145LR	145191	ex PT-SGJ		
N642AE	Embraer EMB.145LR	145193	ex PT-SGK		
N643AE	Embraer EMB.145LR	145200	ex PT-S	200th titles	
N644AE	Embraer EMB.145LR	145204	ex PT-SGW		
N645AE	Embraer EMB.145LR	145212	ex PT-SGZ		
N646AE	Embraer EMB.145LR	145213	ex PT-SHA		
N647AE	Embraer EMB.145LR	145222	ex PT-SHH		
N648AE	Embraer EMB.145LR	145225	ex PT-SHJ		
N649PP	Embraer EMB.145LR	145234	ex PT-SIB		
N650AE	Embraer EMB.145LR	145417	ex PT-STO		
N651AE	Embraer EMB.145LR	145422	ex PT-STT		
N652RS	Embraer EMB.145LR	145432	ex PT-SUD		
N653AE	Embraer EMB.145LR	145433	ex PT-SUE		
N654AE	Embraer EMB.145LR	145437	ex PT-SUI		
N655AE	Embraer EMB.145LR	145452	ex PT-SUX		
N656AE	Embraer EMB.145LR	145740	ex PT-SHV		
N657AE	Embraer EMB.145LR	145744	ex PT-SJD		
N658AE	Embraer EMB.145LR	145760	ex PT-SJO		
N659AE	Embraer EMB.145LR	145762	ex PT-SJT		
N660CL	Embraer EMB.145LR	145764	ex PT-SJV		
N661JA	Embraer EMB.145LR	145766	ex PT-SJX		
N662EH	Embraer EMB.145LR	145777	ex PT-		
N663AR	Embraer EMB.145LR	145778	ex PT-		
N664MS	Embraer EMB.145LR	145779	ex PT-		
N	Embraer EMB.145LR		ex PT-S	on order 04	
N	Embraer EMB.145LR		ex PT-S	on order 04	
N	Embraer EMB.145LR		ex PT-S	on order 04	
N	Embraer EMB.145LR		ex PT-S	on order 04	
N	Embraer EMB.145LR		ex PT-S	on order 04	
N	Embraer EMB.145LR		ex PT-S	on order 04	
N	Embraer EMB.145LR		ex PT-S	on order 04	
N	Embraer EMB.145LR		ex PT-S	on order 04	
N	Embraer EMB.145LR		ex PT-S	on order 04	
N	Embraer EMB.145LR		ex PT-S	on order 04	
N	Embraer EMB.145LR		ex PT-S	on order 04	
N	Embraer EMB.145LR		ex PT-S	on order 04	
N	Embraer EMB.145LR		ex PT-S	on order 04	
N	Embraer EMB.145LR		ex PT-S	on order 04	
N	Embraer EMB.145LR		ex PT-S	on order 04	
N	Embraer EMB.145LR		ex PT-S	on order 04	
N	Embraer EMB.145LR		ex PT-S	on order 04	
N	Embraer EMB.145LR		ex PT-S	on order 04	
N	Embraer EMB.145LR		ex PT-S	on order 04	
N	Embraer EMB.145LR		ex PT-S	on order 04	
N	Embraer EMB.145LR		ex PT-S	on order 04	
N	Embraer EMB.145LR		ex PT-S	on order 04	

Fifty-six more Embraer EMB.145s are on order, converted from an order for EMB.135KLs including 24 in 2005

N174AE	SAAB SF.340B	174	ex SE-F74	stored ABI	Lsd fr AMR Leasing
N177AE	SAAB SF.340B	177	ex SE-F77	stored ABI	Lsd fr AMR Leasing
N180AE	SAAB SF.340B	180	ex SE-F80	stored ABI	Lsd fr AMR Leasing
N211NE	SAAB SF.340B	211	ex SE-G11	stored IGM	Lsd fr AMR Leasing
N218AE	SAAB SF.340B	218	ex SE-G18	stored IGM	Lsd fr AMR Leasing

N219AE	SAAB SF.340B	219	ex SE-G19	stored IGM	Lsd fr AMR Leasing
N222NE	SAAB SF.340B	222	ex SE-G22		Lsd fr AMR Leasing
N227AE	SAAB SF.340B	227	ex SE-G27		Lsd fr AMR Leasing
N231LN	SAAB SF.340B	231	ex SE-G31	stored LAW	Lsd fr AMR Leasing
N232AE	SAAB SF.340B	232	ex SE-G32	stored IGM	Lsd fr AMR Leasing
N234AE	SAAB SF.340B	234	ex SE-G34	stored ABI	Lsd fr AMR Leasing
N235AE	SAAB SF.340B	235	ex SE-G35	stored IGM	
N236AE	SAAB SF.340B	236	ex SE-G36	stored IGM	
N238AE	SAAB SF.340B	238	ex SE-G38	stored IGM	
N240DS	SAAB SF.340B	240	ex SE-G40	stored IGM	
N241AE	SAAB SF.340B	241	ex SE-G41		
N243AE	SAAB SF.340B	243	ex SE-G43	stored ABI	
N244AE	SAAB SF.340B	244	ex SE-G44	stored ABI	
N245AE	SAAB SF.340B	245	ex SE-G45	stored ABI	
N247AE	SAAB SF.340B	247	ex SE-G47	stored ABI	
N250AE	SAAB SF.340B	250	ex SE-G50	stored IGM	
N253AE	SAAB SF.340B	253	ex SE-G53	stored IGM	
N254AE	SAAB SF.340B	254	ex SE-G54		
N256AE	SAAB SF.340B	256	ex SE-G56		
N259AE	SAAB SF.340B	259	ex SE-G59	stored IGM	
N261AE	SAAB SF.340B	261	ex SE-G61		
N263AE	SAAB SF.340B	263	ex SE-G63	stored ABI	
N264AE	SAAB SF.340B	264	ex SE-G64	stored LAW	
N266AE	SAAB SF.340B	266	ex SE-G66	stored ABI	
N268AE	SAAB SF.340B	268	ex SE-G68	stored ABI	
N272AE	SAAB SF.340B	272	ex SE-G72		
N273AE	SAAB SF.340B	273	ex SE-G73		
N278AE	SAAB SF.340B	278	ex SE-G78		
N280AE	SAAB SF.340B	280	ex SE-G80		
N283AE	SAAB SF.340B	283	ex SE-G83	stored IGM	
N284AE	SAAB SF.340B	284	ex SE-G84		
N286AE	SAAB SF.340B	286	ex SE-G86	stored IGM	
N297AE	SAAB SF.340B	297	ex SE-G97	stored ABI	
N298AE	SAAB SF.340B	298	ex SE-G98	stored IGM	
N301AE	SAAB SF.340B	301	ex SE-C01	stored IGM	
N304AE	SAAB SF.340B	304	ex SE-C04	stored IGM	
N305AE	SAAB SF.340B	305	ex SE-C05		
N306AE	SAAB SF.340B	306	ex SE-C06	stored ABI	
N307AE	SAAB SF.340B	307	ex SE-C07		
N309AE	SAAB SF.340B	309	ex SE-C09	stored ABI	
N312AE	SAAB SF.340B	312	ex SE-C12	stored ABI	
N313AE	SAAB SF.340B	313	ex SE-C13		
N317AE	SAAB SF.340B	317	ex SE-C17	stored ABI	
N320AE	SAAB SF.340B	320	ex SE-C20		
N323AE	SAAB SF.340B	323	ex SE-C23	stored IGM	
N324AE	SAAB SF.340B	324	ex SE-C24	stored ABI	
N326AE	SAAB SF.340B	326	ex SE-C26	stored ABI	
N329AE	SAAB SF.340B	329	ex SE-C29	stored ABI	
N330AE	SAAB SF.340B	330	ex SE-C30	stored ABI	
N332AE	SAAB SF.340B	332	ex SE-C32		
N338SB	SAAB SF.340B	338	ex SE-C38		Lsd fr AMR Leasing
N339SB	SAAB SF.340B	339	ex SE-C39		Lsd fr AMR Leasing
N340RC	SAAB SF.340B	340	ex SE-C40	stored ABI	Lsd fr AMR Leasing
N341SB	SAAB SF.340B	341	ex SE-C41		Lsd fr AMR Leasing
N344SB	SAAB SF.340B	344	ex SE-C44		Lsd fr AMR Leasing
N345SB	SAAB SF.340B	345	ex SE-C45		Lsd fr AMR Leasing
N346SB	SAAB SF.340B	346	ex SE-C46	stored IGM	Lsd fr AMR Leasing
N347SB	SAAB SF.340B	347	ex SE-C47	stored ABI	Lsd fr AMR Leasing
N350CF	SAAB SF.340B	350	ex SE-C50		Lsd fr AMR Leasing
N356SB	SAAB SF.340B	356	ex SE-C56		Lsd fr AMR Leasing
N359SB	SAAB SF.340B	359	ex SE-C59		Lsd fr AMR Leasing
N371AE	SAAB SF.340B	371	ex SE-C71		Lsd fr SAAB
N373AE	SAAB SF.340B	373	ex SE-C73		Lsd fr SAAB
N374AE	SAAB SF.340B	374	ex SE-C74	stored ABI	Lsd fr SAAB
N375AE	SAAB SF.340B	375	ex SE-C75	stored ABI	Lsd fr SAAB
N376AE	SAAB SF.340B	376	ex SE-C76	stored ABI	Lsd fr SAAB
N380AE	SAAB SF.340B	380	ex SE-C80	stored LAW	Lsd fr SAAB
N381AE	SAAB SF.340B	381	ex SE-C81		Lsd fr SAAB
N382AE	SAAB SF.340B	382	ex SE-C82	stored ABI	Lsd fr SAAB
N383AE	SAAB SF.340B	383	ex SE-C83	stored LAW	Lsd fr SAAB
N384AE	SAAB SF.340B	384	ex SE-C84	stored LAW	Lsd fr SAAB
N386AE	SAAB SF.340B	386	ex SE-C86	stored ABI	Lsd fr SAAB
N387AE	SAAB SF.340B	387	ex SE-C87	stored ABI	Lsd fr SAAB
N388AE	SAAB SF.340B	388	ex SE-C88	stored LAW	Lsd fr SAAB
N389AE	SAAB SF.340B	389	ex SE-C89		Lsd fr SAAB
N390AE	SAAB SF.340B	390	ex SE-C90	stored LAW	Lsd fr SAAB
N391AE	SAAB SF.340B	391	ex SE-C91	stored ABI	Lsd fr SAAB
N392AE	SAAB SF.340B	392	ex SE-C92	stored ABI	Lsd fr SAAB
N393AE	SAAB SF.340B	393	ex SE-C93	stored ABI	Lsd fr SAAB
N394AE	SAAB SF.340B	394	ex SE-C94	stored ABI	Lsd fr SAAB
N396AE	SAAB SF.340B	396	ex SE-C96	stored ABI	Lsd fr SAAB
N397AE	SAAB SF.340B	397	ex SE-C97	stored ABI	Lsd fr SAAB

N398AM	SAAB SF.340B	398	ex SE-C98	stored ABI	Lsd fr SAAB
N400BR	SAAB SF.340B	400	ex SE-400	stored ABI	Lsd fr SAAB
N901AE	SAAB SF.340B	401	ex SE-B01		Lsd fr SAAB
N902AE	SAAB SF.340B	269	ex N269AE	Spirit of Nashville	
N903AE	SAAB SF.340B	282	ex N282AE	stored ABI	
N904AE	SAAB SF.340B	314	ex N314AE	stored ABI	
N905AE	SAAB SF.340B	319	ex N319AE	stored ABI	

Ten SAAB SF.340Bs are to be sub-leased to Colgan Air from 2Q04
American Eagle operates feeder services for American Airlines from hubs at Nashville, TN, Dallas-Fort Worth, TX and San Luis Obispo, CA. Also operates some feeder services for Delta Air Lines

AMERICAN TRANS AIR – ATA renamed as ATA Airlines on 19 March 2003

AMERICA WEST AIRLINES

Cactus (HP/AWE) (IATA 401)   *Phoenix-Sky Harbor Intl, AZ (PHX)*

N801AW	Airbus Industrie A319-132	0889	ex D-AVYM		
N802AW	Airbus Industrie A319-132	0924	ex D-AVYR		
N803AW	Airbus Industrie A319-132	0931	ex D-AVYK		
N804AW	Airbus Industrie A319-132	1043	ex D-AVYY		Lsd fr State Street
N805AW	Airbus Industrie A319-132	1049	ex D-AVYU		Lsd fr State Street
N806AW	Airbus Industrie A319-132	1056	ex D-AVYO		Lsd fr State Street
N807AW	Airbus Industrie A319-132	1064	ex D-AVWB		Lsd fr State Street
N808AW	Airbus Industrie A319-132	1088	ex D-AVWM		Lsd fr State Street
N809AW	Airbus Industrie A319-132	1111	ex D-AVWT		Lsd fr State Street
N810AW	Airbus Industrie A319-132	1116	ex D-AVWV		Lsd fr State Street
N812AW	Airbus Industrie A319-132	1178	ex D-AVWP		Lsd fr State Street
N813AW	Airbus Industrie A319-132	1223	ex D-AVYH		Lsd fr ILFC
N814AW	Airbus Industrie A319-132	1281	ex D-AVYC		
N815AW	Airbus Industrie A319-132	1323	ex D-AVWW		Lsd fr ILFC
N816AW	Airbus Industrie A319-132	1350	ex D-AVYV		Lsd fr State Street
N817AW	Airbus Industrie A319-132	1373	ex D-AVWA		Lsd fr State Street
N818AW	Airbus Industrie A319-132	1375	ex D-AVWB		Lsd fr State Street
N819AW	Airbus Industrie A319-132	1395	ex D-AVYX		Lsd fr State Street
N820AW	Airbus Industrie A319-132	1397	ex D-AVWQ		Lsd fr State Street
N821AW	Airbus Industrie A319-132	1406	ex D-AVYC		Lsd fr State Street
N822AW	Airbus Industrie A319-132	1410	ex D-AVYD		Lsd fr State Street
N823AW	Airbus Industrie A319-132	1463	ex D-AVYJ		Lsd fr ILFC
N824AW	Airbus Industrie A319-132	1490	ex D-AVYA		Lsd fr State Street
N825AW	Airbus Industrie A319-132	1527	ex D-AVWG		Lsd fr State Street
N826AW	Airbus Industrie A319-132	1534	ex D-AVYO		Lsd fr State Street
N827AW	Airbus Industrie A319-132	1547	ex D-AVWL		Lsd fr State Street
N828AW	Airbus Industrie A319-132	1552	ex D-AVWO		Lsd fr State Street
N829AW	Airbus Industrie A319-132	1563	ex D-AVYS		Lsd fr State Street
N830AW	Airbus Industrie A319-132	1565	ex D-AVYT		Lsd fr State Street
N831AW	Airbus Industrie A319-132	1576	ex D-AVWQ		Lsd fr State Street
N832AW	Airbus Industrie A319-132	1643	ex D-AVYA		Lsd fr State Street
N833AW	Airbus Industrie A319-132	1844	ex D-AVWV		Lsd fr State Street
N834AW	Airbus Industrie A319-132		ex D-AV	on order 04	
N601AW	Airbus Industrie A320-232	1935	ex D-ALAU		Lsd fr Boullioun
N604AW	Airbus Industrie A320-232	1196	ex F-WWDZ		Lsd fr SALE
N605AW	Airbus Industrie A320-232	0543	ex OO-COH		Lsd fr ILFC
N619AW	Airbus Industrie A320-232	0527	ex HC-BUJ		Lsd fr Castle 2003-1A LLC
N620AW	Airbus Industrie A320-231	0052	ex N901BN		Lsd fr GECAS
N621AW	Airbus Industrie A320-231	0053	ex N902BN		Lsd fr GECAS
N622AW	Airbus Industrie A320-231	0054	ex N903BN		Lsd fr GECAS
N624AW	Airbus Industrie A320-231	0055	ex N904BN		Lsd fr GECAS
N625AW	Airbus Industrie A320-231	0064	ex N905BN		Lsd fr GECAS
N626AW	Airbus Industrie A320-231	0065	ex N906BN		Lsd fr GECAS
N627AW	Airbus Industrie A320-231	0066	ex N907GP		Lsd fr GECAS
N628AW	Airbus Industrie A320-231	0067	ex N908GP		Lsd fr GECAS
N629AW	Airbus Industrie A320-231	0076	ex N910GP		Lsd fr GECAS
N631AW	Airbus Industrie A320-231	0077	ex N911GP		Lsd fr GECAS
N632AW	Airbus Industrie A320-231	0081	ex N912GP		Lsd fr GECAS
N633AW	Airbus Industrie A320-231	0082	ex N913GP		Lsd fr GECAS
N634AW	Airbus Industrie A320-231	0091	ex N914GP		Lsd fr GECAS
N636AW	Airbus Industrie A320-231	0098	ex N916GP		Lsd fr GECAS
N637AW	Airbus Industrie A320-231	0099	ex N917GP		Lsd fr GECAS
N638AW	Airbus Industrie A320-232	0455	ex F-WWBK		Lsd fr GECAS
N639AW	Airbus Industrie A320-232	0471	ex F-WWIR		Lsd fr GECAS
N640AW	Airbus Industrie A320-232	0448	ex N931LF		Lsd fr ACG Acquisitions
N642AW	Airbus Industrie A320-232	0584	ex F-WWDZ		Lsd fr CIT Leasing
N644AW*	Airbus Industrie A320-231	0317	ex N300ML		Lsd fr ORIX
N645AW	Airbus Industrie A320-231	0238	ex N238RX		Lsd fr ORIX
N646AW	Airbus Industrie A320-231	0271	ex N271RX	stored GYR	Lsd fr ORIX
N647AW	Airbus Industrie A320-232	0762	ex F-WWDE		Lsd fr SALE
N648AW	Airbus Industrie A320-232	0770	ex F-WWDJ		Lsd fr SALE
N649AW	Airbus Industrie A320-232	0803	ex F-WWDZ		Lsd fr SALE
N650AW	Airbus Industrie A320-232	0856	ex F-WWBM		Lsd fr SALE

N651AW	Airbus Industrie A320-232	0866	ex F-WWBS		Lsd fr SALE
N652AW	Airbus Industrie A320-232	0953	ex F-WWDR		Lsd fr SALE
N653AW	Airbus Industrie A320-232	1003	ex F-WWDK		
N654AW	Airbus Industrie A320-232	1050	ex F-WWIL		Lsd fr State Street
N655AW	Airbus Industrie A320-232	1075	ex F-WWIG		Lsd fr State Street
N656AW	Airbus Industrie A320-232	1079	ex F-WWIQ		Lsd fr State Street
N657AW	Airbus Industrie A320-232	1083	ex F-WWIU		Lsd fr State Street
N658AW	Airbus Industrie A320-232	1110	ex F-WWDI		Lsd fr ILFC
N659AW	Airbus Industrie A320-232	1166	ex F-WWDG		Lsd fr State Street
N660AW	Airbus Industrie A320-232	1234	ex F-WWIO		
N661AW	Airbus Industrie A320-232	1284	ex F-WWBK		Lsd fr State Street
N662AW	Airbus Industrie A320-232	1274	ex F-WWDR		Lsd fr State Street
N663AW	Airbus Industrie A320-232	1419	ex F-WWBJ		Lsd fr State Street
N664AW	Airbus Industrie A320-232	1621	ex F-WWDK		Lsd fr State Street
N665AW	Airbus Industrie A320-232	1644	ex F-WWDN		Lsd fr State Street
N667AW	Airbus Industrie A320-232	1710	ex F-WWIX		
N668AW	Airbus Industrie A320-232	1764	ex F-WWBZ		Lsd fr State Street
N669AW	Airbus Industrie A320-232	1792	ex F-WWDX		Lsd fr State Street
N670AW	Airbus Industrie A320-232	2029	ex F-WWDX		
N671AW	Airbus Industrie A320-232	2077	ex F-WWIY		Lsd fr US Bank NA
N672AW	Airbus Industrie A320-232		ex F-WW	on order 04	
N	Airbus Industrie A320-232		ex F-WW	on order 04	Lsd fr Boullioun
N	Airbus Industrie A320-232	0565	ex D-ALAA	on order Mar04	Lsd fr ILFC
N	Airbus Industrie A320-232	0661	ex D-ALAD	on order Mar04	Lsd fr ILFC
N	Airbus Industrie A320-232	2193	ex F-WW	on order Apr04	Lsd fr ILFC

Two more Airbus Industrie A320-232s are on order for delivery in 2007 (deferred from 2004)

N138AW	Boeing 737-2E3 (Nordam 3)	887/22792	ex CC-CIY	stored GYR	
N149AW	Boeing 737-2U9 (Nordam 3)	749/22575	ex ZK-NEF	stored GYR	
N154AW	Boeing 737-3G7	1417/23776			Lsd fr WFBN
N155AW	Boeing 737-3G7	1419/23777			Lsd fr WFBN
N156AW	Boeing 737-3G7	1455/23778			Lsd fr WFBN
N157AW	Boeing 737-3G7	1457/23779			Lsd fr WFBN
N158AW	Boeing 737-3G7	1459/23780			Lsd fr WFBN
N160AW	Boeing 737-3G7	1496/23782			
N164AW	Boeing 737-33A	1283/23625	ex (N3281Y)		Lsd fr AWMS 1
N166AW	Boeing 737-33A	1302/23627	ex (N3281Y)		Lsd fr AWMS 1
N168AW	Boeing 737-33A	1311/23629	ex (N3282N)		Lsd fr AWMS 1
N173AW	Boeing 737-33A	1344/23632	ex (N3282V)		Lsd fr AWMS 1
N174AW	Boeing 737-33A	1421/23633	ex (N3282W)		Lsd fr AWMS 1
N175AW	Boeing 737-33A	1423/23634	ex (N3282X)		Lsd fr AWMS 1
N178AW	Boeing 737-277 (Nordam 3)	768/22645	ex VH-CZM		Lsd fr IBM Corp
N180AW	Boeing 737-277 (Nordam 3)	785/22647	ex VH-CZO		Lsd fr Pacificorp
N182AW	Boeing 737-277 (Nordam 3)	801/22649	ex VH-CZQ		Lsd fr Pacificorp
N184AW	Boeing 737-277 (Nordam 3)	819/22651	ex VH-CZS	stored PHX	
N186AW	Boeing 737-277 (Nordam 3)	832/22653	ex VH-CZU		Lsd fr EDS Leasing
N187AW	Boeing 737-277 (Nordam 3)	862/22654	ex VH-CZV		Lsd fr EDS Leasing
N188AW	Boeing 737-277 (Nordam 3)	872/22655	ex VH-CZW		Lsd fr IBM Corp
N189AW	Boeing 737-277 (Nordam 3)	876/22656	ex VH-CZX		Lsd fr CIT Leasing
N302AW	Boeing 737-3G7	1578/24009			
N303AW	Boeing 737-3G7	1606/24010			Lsd fr Bank of NY
N305AW	Boeing 737-3G7	1612/24012			Lsd fr PS Group
N306AW	Boeing 737-3G7	1809/24633			
N307AW	Boeing 737-3G7	1823/24634			
N308AW	Boeing 737-3G7	1825/24710			
N309AW	Boeing 737-3G7	1843/24711			
N311AW	Boeing 737-3G7	1869/24712			
N312AW	Boeing 737-3S3	1519/24060	ex N200KG		Lsd fr KG Aircraft Lsg
N313AW	Boeing 737-3S3	1336/23712	ex EC-EBZ		Lsd fr Boullioun
N314AW	Boeing 737-3S3	1345/23733	ex G-BMTG		Lsd fr Boullioun
N315AW	Boeing 737-3S3	1359/23734	ex G-BMTH		Lsd fr Boullioun
N316AW	Boeing 737-3S3	1341/23713	ex G-BMTF		Lsd fr Boullioun
N322AW	Boeing 737-3G7	2112/25400			Lsd fr GECAS
N323AW	Boeing 737-3Y0	1353/23684	ex EC-FQB		Lsd fr GECAS
N324AW	Boeing 737-301	1157/23261	ex N583US		Lsd fr GECAS
N325AW	Boeing 737-301	1146/23260	ex N582US		Lsd fr GECAS
N326AW	Boeing 737-301	1126/23258	ex N579US		Lsd fr GECAS
N327AW	Boeing 737-3Q8	1252/23507	ex N398US		Lsd fr GECAS
N328AW	Boeing 737-3B7	1320/23377	ex N502AU		Lsd fr East Trust-Sub
N331AW	Boeing 737-3Y0	1363/23747	ex EI-CKV		Lsd fr GECAS
N332AW	Boeing 737-3B7	1427/23384	ex N953WP		Lsd fr LIFTArizona
N334AW	Boeing 737-3Y0	1381/23748	ex N962WP		Lsd fr ACG Acquisitions
N335AW	Boeing 737-3U3	3003/28740	ex N1790B		Lsd fr GECAS
N336AW	Boeing 737-375	1388/23707	ex EC-FKI		Lsd fr AFT Trust

*To be returned to lessor in 2003

N901AW^	Boeing 757-2S7	76/23321	ex N601RC	Arizona c/s; City of Phoenix	
N902AW^''	Boeing 757-2S7	79/23322	ex N602RC		
N903AW*	Boeing 757-2S7	80/23323	ex N603RC		
N904AW*	Boeing 757-2S7	96/23566	ex N604RC	Arizona Diamondbacks c/s	
N905AW*	Boeing 757-2S7	97/23567	ex N605RC	Ohio c/s; City of Columbus	
N906AW*	Boeing 757-2S7	99/23568	ex N606RC		

N907AW	Boeing 757-225	155/22691	ex XA-TCD	Lsd fr CIT
N908AW	Boeing 757-2G7	244/24233	Arizona Cardinals c/s	
N909AW	Boeing 757-2G7	252/24522		Lsd fr WFBN
N910AW	Boeing 757-2G7	256/24523		Lsd fr PLC Lsg
N913AW+	Boeing 757-225	35/22207	ex N517EA	Lsd fr Linc Capital
N914AW+	Boeing 757-225	38/22208	ex N518EA	
N915AW+	Boeing 757-225	40/22209	ex N747BJ	Nevada c/s; City of Las Vegas

^Leased from Wachovia Bank and Reno
*Leased from Boeing   +Leased from WTCo
"Stored Goodyear (GYR)

Fifteen Airbus Industrie A318s are on order for delivery from 2006 along with one A319 and one A320 deferred from 2003-4 to 2004-7. Commuter services are op by America West and Freedom Airlines divisions of Mesa Airlines as America West Express and by Chautauqua Airlines (from Columbus, OH) using Embraer ERJ-145s and Canadair RJ-200/700/900s. 17.7% owned by Continental and 7.6% by Mesa Airlines

AMERICA WEST EXPRESS

(HP)   *Farmington-Four Corners, NM/Phoenix-Sky Harbor Intl, AZ (FMN/PHX)*

N7264V	Canadair CL-600-2B19	7264		
N7291Z	Canadair CL-600-2B19	7291		
N7305V	Canadair CL-600-2B19	7305		
N17231	Canadair CL-600-2B19	7231		
N17275	Canadair CL-600-2B19	7275	ex C-FMQI	
N17337	Canadair CL-600-2B19	7337		
N17358	Canadair CL-600-2B19	7358	ex C-FMNY	
N27172	Canadair CL-600-2B19	7172		
N27173	Canadair CL-600-2B19	7173		
N27314	Canadair CL-600-2B19	7314	ex C-FMKV	
N27318	Canadair CL-600-2B19	7318	ex C-FMLF	
N37178	Canadair CL-600-2B19	7178	ex C-GAVO	
N37208	Canadair CL-600-2B19	7208	ex C-FMNY	
N37218	Canadair CL-600-2B19	7218		
N37228	Canadair CL-600-2B19	7228	ex C-FMLF	
N47239	Canadair CL-600-2B19	7239		
N77195	Canadair CL-600-2B19	7195	ex C-FMKV	all-white
N77260	Canadair CL-600-2B19	7260	ex C-FMLQ	
N77278	Canadair CL-600-2B19	7278	ex C-FMMN	
N77286	Canadair CL-600-2B19	7286	ex C-FMKZ	
N77302	Canadair CL-600-2B19	7302		
N77331	Canadair CL-600-2B19	7331	ex C-FVAZ	all-white
N87353	Canadair CL-600-2B19	7353	ex C-FMLV	
N97325	Canadair CL-600-2B19	7325		
N	Canadair CL-600-2B19			on order

Operated by Mesa Airlines; some are operated in Mesa colours

N502MJ	Canadair CL-600-2C10	10050	ex C-GIAO	
N503MJ	Canadair CL-600-2C10	10058	ex C-GIBG	
N504MJ	Canadair CL-600-2C10	10066	ex C-GIBR	
N505MJ	Canadair CL-600-2C10	10070	ex C-GICN	
N506MJ	Canadair CL-600-2C10	10073	ex C-GHZY	
N507MJ	Canadair CL-600-2C10	10077	ex C-GIAH	
N508MJ	Canadair CL-600-2C10	10087	ex C-FZZE	
N509MJ	Canadair CL-600-2C10	10094	ex C-	

Operated by Freedom Airlines

N902FJ	Canadair CL-600-2D24	15002	ex C-GDNH	
N903FJ	Canadair CL-600-2D24	15003	ex C-GZQA	
N904FJ	Canadair CL-600-2D24	15004	ex C-GZQB	
N905J	Canadair CL-600-2D24	15005	ex C-GZQC	
N906FJ	Canadair CL-600-2D24	15006	ex C-GZQE	
N907FJ	Canadair CL-600-2D24	15007	ex C-GZQF	
N908FJ	Canadair CL-600-2D24	15008	ex C-GZQG	
N909FJ	Canadair CL-600-2D24	15009	ex C-GZQI	Lsd fr WFBN
N910FJ	Canadair CL-600-2D24	15010	ex C-GZQJ	
N911FJ	Canadair CL-600-2D24	15011	ex C-GZQK	
N912FJ	Canadair CL-600-2D24	15012	ex C-	
N913FJ	Canadair CL-600-2D24	15013	ex C-	
N914FJ	Canadair CL-600-2D24	15014	ex C-	
N	Canadair CL-600-2D24		ex C-	on order 04
N	Canadair CL-600-2D24		ex C-	on order 04
N	Canadair CL-600-2D24		ex C-	on order 04
N	Canadair CL-600-2D24		ex C-	on order 04
N	Canadair CL-600-2D24		ex C-	on order 04
N	Canadair CL-600-2D24		ex C-	on order 04

Operated by Freedom Airlines; five more are on order for delivery in 2005

N436YV	de Havilland DHC-8-202	436	ex C-GDNG	
N437YV	de Havilland DHC-8-202	437	ex C-FDHD	
N444YV	de Havilland DHC-8Q-202	444	ex C-GFRP	
N445YV	de Havilland DHC-8Q-202	445	ex C-GFEN	

N446YV	de Havilland DHC-8Q-202	446	ex C-GEOA
N449YV	de Havilland DHC-8Q-202	449	ex C-GFHZ
N454YV	de Havilland DHC-8Q-202	454	ex C-
N455YV	de Havilland DHC-8Q-202	455	ex C-
N456YV	de Havilland DHC-8Q-202	456	ex C-GFOD

All operated by Mesa Airlines

| N123YV | Beech 1900D | UE-123 |
| N135YV | Beech 1900D | UE-135 |

Operated by Chautauqua
Other Beech 1900Ds from Mesa Airlines fleet may operate services for America West Express
America West Express is the operating name for the network of feeder services op by America West Airlines and
Freedom Airlines divisions of Mesa Airlines plus Chautauqua Airlines

---

AMERIFLIGHT

Ameriflight (AMF)   Burbank Glendale-Passadena, CA (BUR)

N20FW*	Beech 99A	U-111		
N21FW	Beech 99A	U-117		
N34AK	Beech 99A	U-105	ex N4099A	
N51RP	Beech C99	U-212		
N52RP	Beech C99	U-210	ex N66305	
N53RP	Beech C99	U-195	ex N64997	
N54RP	Beech C99	U-218		
N55RP	Beech C99	U-198	ex N64002	
N68TA	Beech C99	U-177	ex N177EE	Lsd fr Key Corporate Credit
N96AV	Beech C99	U-201		Lsd fr Fleet Capital
N102GP	Beech C99	U-208	ex N6628K	
N104BE	Beech C99	U-221	ex N7203L	Lsd fr Fleet Capital
N106SX	Beech C99	U-166		
N107SX	Beech C99	U-176		Lsd fr Fleet Capital
N108SX	Beech C99	U-184	ex N6787P	
N130GP	Beech C99	U-222	ex N818FL	Lsd fr Fleet Capital
N134PM	Beech 99	U-34	ex N852SA	
N164HA	Beech B99	U-60	ex N72TC	
N193SU	Beech C99	U-193	ex C-GFAT	Lsd fr Key Corporate Credit
N199AF	Beech B99	U-161	ex N12AK	
N204AF	Beech C-99	U-204	ex N575W	
N221BH	Beech C99	U-168	ex N18AK	
N223BH	Beech C99	U-173	ex N6460D	
N225BH	Beech C99	U-181	ex N62936	
N226BH	Beech C99	U-182	ex N6263D	
N228BH	Beech C99	U-229		Lsd fr Key Corporate Credit
N261SW	Beech C99	U-202		
N802BA	Beech 99	U-29	ex N800BE	
N805BA	Beech 99A	U-147	ex N803BE	
N949K	Beech 99A	U-36		
N990AF	Beech C99	U-211	ex N113GP	Lsd fr Fleet Capital
N991AF	Beech C99	U-214	ex N112GP	Lsd fr Fleet Capital
N992AF	Beech C99	U-203	ex N541JC	Lsd fr Fleet Capital
N997SB	Beech C99	U-192	ex N6534A	
N1049C	Beech 99	U-9		Lsd fr Fleet Capital
N1924T	Beech 99A	U-115	ex N24AT	
N4199C	Beech C99	U-50	ex N7940	
N4299A	Beech B99	U-146		
N6199D*	Beech C99	U-169		
N6724D	Beech C99	U-215		
N7200Z	Beech C99	U-219		
N7209W	Beech C99	U-224		Lsd fr Fleet Capital
N7862R	Beech 99A	U-85		
N8226Z	Beech C99	U-190	ex 6Y-JVB	Lsd fr Key Corporate Credit
N8227P	Beech C99	U-194	ex 6Y-JVA	Lsd fr Key Corporate Credit
N62989*	Beech C99	U-183		
N63978*	Beech C99	U-171		
N81820	Beech C99	U-232	ex J6-AAG	Lsd fr Key Corporate Credit

*Leased from Tucker Commercial Lease Funding

N330AF	Beech 1900C	UB-38	ex N805BE	
N331AF	Beech 1900C	UB-44	ex N807BE	
N3052K	Beech 1900C	UB-70		
N3071A	Beech 1900C	UB-46	ex N10RA	Lsd fr BancOne
N3229A	Beech 1900C	UB-51		
N7203C	Beech 1900C	UB-28		Lsd fr BancOne
N31701	Beech 1900C	UB-2	ex N121CZ	Lsd fr BancOne
N31702	Beech 1900C	UB-3	ex N122CZ	
N31703	Beech 1900C	UB-10	ex N123CZ	
N31704	Beech 1900C	UB-12	ex N124CZ	
N31705	Beech 1900C	UB-60		

| N8FB | Cessna 402B | 402B1372 |

N49PB	Cessna 402B	402B1361		
N108GP	Cessna 402B	402B1235		
N141MC	Cessna 402B	402B0547		
N3826C	Cessna 402B	402B0814		
N3997C	Cessna 402B	402B0864		
N4188G	Cessna 402B	402B1234		
N5550K	Cessna 402B	402B1226		
N6384X	Cessna 402B	402B1347		
N7162J	Cessna 402B	402B1229		
N7162K	Cessna 402B	402B1208		
N29854	Cessna 402B	402B0878		
N98635	Cessna 402B	402B1024		
N98702	Cessna 402B	402B1054		
N98764	Cessna 402B	402B1069		
N179CA	Embraer EMB.120ER Brasilia	120179		Lsd fr BancOne
N189CA	Embraer RMB.120ER Brasilia	120189		Lsd fr BancOne
N201YW	Embraer EMB.120RT Brasilia	120201	ex N142EB	Lsd fr Keycorp Lsg
N246AS	Embraer EMB.120ER Brasilia	120100	ex PP-SMS	
N247CA	Embraer EMB.120ER Brasilia	120225	ex PT-SSU	Lsd fr Key Corporate Capital
N257AS	Embraer EMB.120ER Brasilia	120126	ex PT-SNS	Lsd fr Key Corporate Capital
N258AS	Embraer EMB.120ER Brasilia	120131	ex PT-SNX	Lsd fr Key Corporate Capital
N94AF	Lear Jet 35A	35A-094	ex N94GP	
N128CA	Lear Jet 35A	35A-248	ex C-GBFA	
N237AF	Lear Jet 35A	35A-262	ex N237GA	
N535AF	Lear Jet 35A	35A-191	ex N35SE	
N754GL	Lear Jet 35A	35A-197		
N199DS	Piper PA-31 Turbo Navajo B	31-7400980		
N500CF	Piper PA-31 Turbo Navajo	31-425	ex N6467L	
N6480L	Piper PA-31 Turbo Navajo	31-443		
N6733L	Piper PA-31 Turbo Navajo	31-636		
N6759L	Piper PA-31 Turbo Navajo	31-661		
N7434L	Piper PA-31 Turbo Navajo B	31-822		
N7441L	Piper PA-31 Turbo Navajo B	31-844		
N9132Y	Piper PA-31 Turbo Navajo	31-178		
N27275	Piper PA-31 Turbo Navajo C	31-7712066		
N3BT	Piper PA-31-350 Navajo Chieftain	31-7752172	ex N27422	
N29UM	Piper PA-31-350 Navajo Chieftain	31-7652127	ex N29JM	
N555RG	Piper PA-31-350 Navajo Chieftain	31-7305103	ex N555RC	
N600TS	Piper PA-31-350 Navajo Chieftain	31-7305047		
N777MP	Piper PA-31-350 Navajo Chieftain	31-7552072	ex N59983	
N961CA	Piper PA-31-350 Navajo Chieftain	31-7652014	ex N961PS	
N3525G	Piper PA-31-350 Navajo Chieftain	31-7952123		Lsd fr Quebec Enterprises
N3527D	Piper PA-31-350 Navajo Chieftain	31-7952137		
N3540N	Piper PA-31-350 Navajo Chieftain	31-7952214		
N3548B	Piper PA-31-350 Chieftain	31-8052025		
N3553F	Piper PA-31-350 Chieftain	31-8052044		
N3555D	Piper PA-31-350 Chieftain	31-8052059		Lsd fr Quebec Enterprises
N4044P	Piper PA-31-350 Chieftain	31-8152004		
N4078B	Piper PA-31-350 Chieftain	31-8152055		
N4087J	Piper PA-31-350 Chieftain	31-8152128		
N4098A	Piper PA-31-350 Chieftain	31-8152200		
N4502Y	Piper PA-31-350 Chieftain	31-8052189		
N27426	Piper PA-31-350 Navajo Chieftain	31-7752175		
N27579	Piper PA-31-350 Navajo Chieftain	31-7852063		
N27677	Piper PA-31-350 Navajo Chieftain	31-7852101		
N27996	Piper PA-31-350 Navajo Chieftain	31-7952083		
N35336	Piper PA-31-350 Navajo Chieftain	31-7952189		
N35805	Piper PA-31-350 Chieftain	31-8052090		
N42076	Piper PA-31-350 Navajo Chieftain	31-7405209	ex N54362	
N42079	Piper PA-31-350 Navajo Chieftain	31-7405488	ex G-BCOD	
N45004	Piper PA-31-350 Chieftain	31-8052163		
N45014	Piper PA-31-350 Chieftain	31-8052171		
N59820	Piper PA-31-350 Navajo Chieftain	31-7652073		
N59973	Piper PA-31-350 Navajo Chieftain	31-7552079		
N62858	Piper PA-31-350 Navajo Chieftain	31-7652115		
N62959	Piper PA-31-350 Navajo Chieftain	31-7752008		
N66859	Piper PA-31-350 Navajo Chieftain	31-7405168		
N123KC	Piper PA-32R-300 Lance	32R-7680431		
N188SP	Piper PA-32R-300 Lance	32R-7780309		
N1333H	Piper PA-32R-300 Lance	32R-7780154		
N1512X	Piper PA-32R-300 Lance	32R-7680002		
N2165M	Piper PA-32R-300 Lance	32R-7880053		
N3609Q	Piper PA-32R-300 Lance	32R-7780319		
N4085F	Piper PA-32R-300 Lance	32R-7680427		
N4342F	Piper PA-32R-300 Lance	32R-7680140		
N4588F	Piper PA-32R-300 Lance	32R-7680462		
N5363F	Piper PA-32R-300 Lance	32R-7680510		

N6812J	Piper PA-32R-300 Lance	32R-7680352		
N6851J	Piper PA-32R-300 Lance	32R-7680370		
N7612F	Piper PA-32R-300 Lance	32R-7780063		
N7838C	Piper PA-32R-300 Lance	32R-7680064		
N8456F	Piper PA-32R-300 Lance	32R-7780100		
N8701E	Piper PA-32R-300 Lance	32R-7680160		
N8929C	Piper PA-32R-300 Lance	32R-7680144		
N9226K	Piper PA-32R-300 Lance	32R-7680199		
N75195	Piper PA-32R-300 Lance	32R-7680277		
N75397	Piper PA-32R-300 Lance	32R-7680301		
N155AF	Swearingen SA.227AC Metro III	AC-455	ex N356AE	Lsd fr BancBoston
N191AF	Swearingen SA.227AC Metro III	AC-481	ex N209CA	
N240DH	Swearingen SA.227AT Expediter	AT-602B	ex N3117P	
N241DH	Swearingen SA.227AT Expediter	AT-607B	ex N3118A	
N242DH	Swearingen SA.227AT Expediter	AT-608B	ex N3118G	
N243DH	Swearingen SA.227AT Expediter	AT-609B	ex N3118H	
N244DH	Swearingen SA.227AT Expediter	AT-618B		Lsd fr Fifth Third Lsg
N245DH	Swearingen SA.227AT Expediter	AT-624B		Lsd fr Fifth Third Lsg
N246DH	Swearingen SA.227AT Expediter	AT-625B		Lsd fr Fifth Third Lsg
N247DH	Swearingen SA.227AT Expediter	AT-626B		Lsd fr Fifth Third Lsg
N248DH	Swearingen SA.227AT Expediter	AT-630B		Lsd fr Fifth Third Lsg
N249DH	Swearingen SA.227AT Expediter	AT-631B		Lsd fr Fifth Third Lsg
N360AE	Swearingen SA.227AC Metro III	AC-675		Lsd fr BancBoston
N362AE	Swearingen SA.227AC Metro III	AC-677		Lsd fr BancBoston
N377PH	Swearingen SA.227AC Metro III	AC-574	ex (D-CABG)	
N421MA	Swearingen SA.227AC Metro III	AC-634	ex N3119Q	Lsd fr BancBoston
N422MA	Swearingen SA.227AC Metro III	AC-635	ex N3119T	Lsd fr BancBoston
N423MA	Swearingen SA.227AC Metro III	AC-636	ex N26823	Lsd fr BancBoston
N424MA	Swearingen SA.227AC Metro III	AC-639		
N426MA	Swearingen SA.227AC Metro III	AC-645		
N428MA	Swearingen SA.227AC Metro III	AC-646		
N443AF	Swearingen SA.227AC Metro III	AC-443	ex N443NE	
N473AF	Swearingen SA.227AC Metro III	AC-473	ex N473NE	
N475AF	Swearingen SA.227AC Metro III	AC-475	ex N475NE	
N476AF	Swearingen SA.227AC Metro III	AC-476	ex N476NE	
N488AF	Swearingen SA.227AC Metro III	AC-488	ex N488NE	
N544UP	Swearingen SA.227AT Expediter	AT-544	ex N68TA	Lsd fr BancBoston
N548UP	Swearingen SA.227AT Expediter	AT-548	ex N548SA	Lsd fr BancBoston
N556UP	Swearingen SA.227AT Expediter	AT-556	ex N3113B	
N560UP	Swearingen SA.227AT Expediter	AT-560	ex N3113A	
N561UP	Swearingen SA.227AT Expediter	AT-561	ex N3113F	
N566UP	Swearingen SA.227AT Expediter	AT-566	ex N3113N	
N569UP	Swearingen SA.227AT Expediter	AT-569	ex N31134	
N573G	Swearingen SA.227AT Merlin IVC	AT-446B	ex N3008L	
N578AF	Swearingen SA.227AC Metro III	AC-578	ex C-FJLE	
N671AV	Swearingen SA.227AC Metro III	AC-671	ex N671AV	Lsd fr BancBoston
N672AV	Swearingen SA.227AC Metro III	AC-672		Lsd fr BancBoston
N673AV	Swearingen SA.227AC Metro III	AC-673	ex N673AV	Lsd fr BancBoston
N807M	Swearingen SA.227AT Merlin IVC	AT-454B	ex N3013T	
N200AF	Beech 200 Super King Air	BB-102	ex N997MA	Lsd fr Quebec Enterprises
All freighters				

AMERIJET INTERNATIONAL

Amerijet (M6/AJT) — Fort Lauderdale-Hollywood Intl, FL (FLL)

N199AJ	Boeing 727-2F9F (Duganair 3)	1285/21426	ex N83428	Lsd fr SFG Equipment
N395AJ	Boeing 727-233F (Duganair 3)	1148/21100	ex N727SN	Lsd fr JODA LLC
N495AJ	Boeing 727-233F (FedEx 3)	1103/20937	ex C-GAAD	Lsd fr JODA LLC
N598AJ	Boeing 727-212F (Duganair 3)	1506/21947	ex N86430	Lsd fr WFBN
N794AJ	Boeing 727-227F (Duganair 3)	1197/21243	ex N567PE	Lsd fr SFG Equipment
N994AJ	Boeing 727-233F (Duganair 3)	1130/20942	ex N727JH	Lsd fr JODA LLC
All fitted with winglets				

AMERISTAR JET CHARTER

Ameristar (AJI) — Dallas-Addison, TX (ADS)

N147TW	Lear Jet 25	25-023	ex N767SC	Lsd fr Sierra America Corp
N157TW	Lear Jet 24	24-157	ex N659AT	Lsd fr Sierra America Corp
N222TW	Lear Jet 24	24-161	ex N24KF	Lsd fr Sierra America Corp
N233TW	Lear Jet 24B	24B-221	ex N59JG	Lsd fr Sierra America Corp
N237TW	Lear Jet 24D	24D-237	ex N825DM	Lsd fr Sierra America Corp
N265TW	Lear Jet 25D	25D-265	ex N69GF	Lsd fr Chaparral Lsg
N266TW	Lear Jet 24D	24D-266	ex N266BS	Lsd fr Sierra America Corp
N277TW	Lear Jet 24D	24D-277	ex N57BC	Lsd fr Sierra America Corp
N299TW	Lear Jet 24D	24D-299	ex XB-GJS	Lsd fr Chaparral Lsg
N324TW	Lear Jet 24D	24D-324	ex XA-SCY	Lsd fr Chaparral Lsg
N330TW	Lear Jet 24E	24E-330	ex N511AT	Lsd fr Sierra America Corp

N333TW	Lear Jet 24	24-168	ex N155BT	Lsd fr Sierra America Corp
N444TW	Lear Jet 24F	24F-348	ex N8BG	Lsd fr Sierra America Corp
N525TW	Lear Jet 25	25-011	ex N108GA	Lsd fr Sierra America Corp
N666TW	Lear Jet 25C	25C-116	ex N819GY	Lsd fr Sierra America Corp
N888TW	Lear Jet 24D	24D-292	ex N800PC	Lsd fr Sierra America Corp
N148TW	AMD Falcon 20C	148	ex N148WC	Lsd fr Sierra America Corp
N158TW	AMD Falcon 20C	158	ex N450MA	Lsd fr Sierra America Corp
N165TW	AMD Falcon 20C	65	ex C-GSKN	Lsd fr Sierra America Corp
N204TW	AMD Falcon 20DC	204	ex EC-EGM	Lsd fr Sierra America Corp
N221TW	AMD Falcon 20DC	221	ex EC-EIV	Lsd fr Sierra America Corp
N223TW	AMD Falcon 20C	123	ex N45MR	Lsd fr Sierra America Corp
N232TW	AMD Falcon 20C	32	ex F-GIVT	Lsd fr Sierra America Corp
N240TW	AMD Falcon 20C	40	ex C-GSKQ	Lsd fr Sierra America Corp
N285TW	AMD Falcon 20EF	285	ex N285AP	Lsd fr Sierra America Corp
N295TW	AMD Falcon 20C	5	ex F-GJPR	Lsd fr Sierra America Corp
N314TW	AMD Falcon 20E	314	ex F-GDLU	Lsd fr Sierra America Corp
N699TW	AMD Falcon 20DC	50	ex EC-EDO	Lsd fr Sierra America Corp
N977TW	AMD Falcon 20C	13	ex F-BTCY	Lsd fr Sierra America Corp
N176TW	Beech 65-E90 King Air	LW-76	ex ZS-LJF	Lsd fr Sierra America Corp
N206TW	Bell 206B JetRanger II	2403		Lsd fr Sierra America Corp
N737TW	Boeing 737-230C (Nordam 3)	274/20257	ex TF-ABX	Lsd fr Sierra America Corp
N742TW	Boeing 737-242 (Nordam 3)	438/21186	ex N159PL	Lsd fr Conway Avn
N767TW	Boeing 737-230C (Nordam 3)	276/20258	ex TF-ABF	Lsd fr Sierra America Corp
N783TW	Douglas DC-9-15F	97/47010	ex N916R	
N784TW	Douglas DC-9-15F	141/47014	ex N923R	
N785TW	Douglas DC-9-15F	156/47015	ex N5373G	
N3867N	Rockwell Commander 681	6010	ex XB-PAO	

All freighters Boeing 737s registered to sister company Ameristar Air Cargo and Douglas DC-9s to Ameristar Airways

ANDERSON AVIATION

Andax (4Q/ADX) *Anderson-Municipal, IN (AID)*

N208AD	Cessna 208B Caravan I	208B0063	ex C-FESO
N208SD	Cessna 208B Caravan I	208B0491	

ANDREW AIRWAYS

Kodiac, AK

N13VF	de Havilland DHC-2 Beaver	1613	ex ZK-CRE
N1544	de Havilland DHC-2 Beaver	1230	ex N67686
N1545	de Havilland DHC-2 Beaver	1493	ex N123UA
N5303X	Cessna U206G Stationair 6	U20605622	

All operate on floats or wheel/skis

ARCTIC CIRCLE AIR SERVICE

Air Arctic (5F/CIR) *Aniak/Bethel/Dillingham-Municipal/Fairbanks-Intl, AK (ANI/BET/DLG/FAI)*

N916AC	Cessna 207 Skywagon	20700061	ex ZK-JFJ	
N917AC	Cessna 207A Stationair 7	20700517	ex ZK-ETC	
N6480H	Cessna 207A Stationair 7	20700540		
N7305U	Cessna 207A Skywagon	20700392		
N9936M	Cessna 207A Stationair 8	20700752		
N9965M	Cessna 207A Stationair 8	20700767		
N73467	Cessna 207A Stationair 8	20700594		
N73533	Cessna 207A Stationair 8	20700602		
N251RC	Cessna 402C	402C0490	ex 5H-MAF	
N402ET	Cessna 402C	402C0054	ex C-GTKJ	
N419RC	Cessna 402C	402C0419	ex VH-NGG	
N4630N	Cessna 402C	402C0001		
N6790B	Cessna 402C	402C0442		
N101WA	Short SC.7 Skyvan 3	SH1859	ex (PH-DAF)	Freighter
N168LM	Short SD.3-30	SH3104	ex N174Z	
N456TA	Cessna U206G Stationair 6	U20605034		
N1906	Short SC.7 Skyvan 3A	SH1906	ex HS-DCC	Freighter
N2088Z	Short SC.7 Skyvan 3	SH1963	ex 9M-PIF	Freighter
N5187B	Cessna 208B Caravan I	208B0270	ex F-OGRO	
N7721C	Piper PA-32-300R Lance	32R-7680060		

All registered to Arctic Air Group

ARCTIC TRANSPORTATION SERVICES

Arctic Transport (7S/RYA) *Unalakleet-Municipal, AK (UNK)*

N19TA	Cessna 207A Stationair 7	20700468	ex N6289H
N26TA	Cessna 207A Stationair 8	20700725	

N7605U	Cessna 207A Stationair 7	20700443		
N9475M	Cessna 207A Stationair 8	20700695		
N9699H	Cessna 207A Stationair 8	20700718		
N9736M	Cessna 207A Stationair 8	20700722		
N9829M	Cessna 207A Stationair 8	20700741		
N9956M	Cessna 207A Stationair 8	20700763		
N73217	Cessna 207A Stationair 8	20700572		
N73503	Cessna 207A Stationair 8	20700599		
N73789	Cessna 207A Stationair 8	20700629		
N424CA	CASA 212-200	CC20-7-242		Lsd fr E2R LLC
N437CA	CASA 212-200	CC21-2-166	ex TI-SAC	
N2719A	Cessna 402C	402C0233		

ARDCO AVIATION

Tucson-Ryan Field, AZ

N406WA	Douglas C-54G	35944	ex N460WA	119 Tanker
N460WA	Douglas C-54E	27359	ex 44-9133	151 Tanker
N9015Q	Douglas C-54D	22178	ex 43-17228	152 Tanker
N49451	Douglas C-54D	10722	ex 42-72617	

Ardco Aviation is the trading name of Aerial Retardant Delivery Co

ARIS HELICOPTERS

San Jose-Intl, CA (SJC)

N58AH	Sikorsky S-58ET	58-328	ex N39790
N549W	Bell 206B JetRanger II	2604	ex N484Z
N1168U	Sikorsky S-58ET	58-1070	
N3597T	Aerospatiale AS.350D AStar	1126	
N3609N	Aerospatiale AS.350B AStar	1248	

ARIZONA EXPRESS AIRWAYS

Tempe (K7/TMP)   *Phoenix-Sky Harbor Intl, AZ (PHX)*

N168AZ	Beech 1900D	UE-68	ex N68ZV

ARROW AIR

Big A (JW/APW)   *Miami Intl, FL (MIA)*

Previously listed as Fine Air

N29UA	Douglas DC-8-61F (QTV 3)	544/46159	ex (TC-GUL)		Lsd fr Agro Air
N30UA	Douglas DC-8-61F (QTV 3)	290/45888	ex EC-DYY	stored OPF	Lsd fr Agro Air
N345JW	Douglas DC-8-63F (BAC 3)	421/46042	ex N7043U		Lsd fr Agro Air
N441J	Douglas DC-8-63CF (BAC 3)	416/45988	ex N941JW	Andrew	Lsd fr Agro Air
N661AV	Douglas DC-8-63CF (BAC 3)	396/45969	ex N6161A		Lsd fr Agro Air
N784AL	Douglas DC-8-63F (BAC 3)	531/46135	ex TU-TCF		Lsd fr WTCo
N791AL	Douglas DC-8-62F (BAC 3)	539/46150	ex RTAF 60109	Pride of Miami	Lsd fr Agro Air
N802BN	Douglas DC-8-62F (BAC 3)	307/45909	ex XA-AMT		Lsd fr Agro Air
N810BN	Douglas DC-8-62F (BAC 3)	298/45905	ex EC-ELM		Lsd fr Agro Air
N906R	Douglas DC-8-63F (BAC 3)	454/46087	ex N774FT		Lsd fr WTCo
N8968U	Douglas DC-8-62F (BAC 3)	465/46069	ex EC-GEE	Pearl Harbor	Lsd fr Agro Air
N8969U	Douglas DC-8-62F (BAC 3)	467/46070	ex PP-AIY	Sir Willy	Lsd fr Interair
N8974U	Douglas DC-8-62F (BAC 3)	487/46110	ex HI-576CT		Lsd fr Aeroengine Support
N260FA	Lockheed L-1011-200F Tristar	1158	ex N851MA	stored ROW	Lsd fr ILFC
N307GB	Lockheed L-1011-200F Tristar	1131	ex A4O-TW	San Juan	Lsd fr Agro Air
N308GB	Lockheed L-1011-200F Tristar	1133	ex A4O-TX		Lsd fr Agro Air

ASCEND AVIATION

San Bernardino, CA

N410BN	Boeing 727-223 (Raisbeck 3)	1335/21387	ex N875AA	stored ICT	Op by RYN
N415BN	Boeing 727-227 (Raisbeck 3)	929/20613	ex N720AA		Op by RYN
N416BN	Boeing 727-227 (Raisbeck 3)	955/20729	ex N721AA		
N417BN	Boeing 727-227 (Raisbeck 3)	956/20730	ex N722AA		
N419BN	Boeing 727-227 (Raisbeck 3)	963/20732	ex N725AA		
N422BN	Boeing 727-227 (Raisbeck 3)	973/20735	ex N728AA	stored ICT	Op by RYN
N423BN	Boeing 727-227 (Raisbeck 3)	977/20738	ex N731AA	stored ICT	Op by RYN
N723AA	Boeing 727-227 (Raisbeck 3)	957/20731	ex N418BN	stored SAT	
N727AA	Boeing 727-227 (Raisbeck 3)	965/20734	ex N421BN		
N868AA	Boeing 727-223 (Raisbeck 3)	1279/21373			
N869AA	Boeing 727-223 (Raisbeck 3)	1280/21374			
N873AA	Boeing 727-223 (Raisbeck 3)	1331/21385			
N878AA	Boeing 727-223 (Raisbeck 3)	1361/21390			Op by RYN

Some painted in Braniff old style colours; Ascend Aviation is the trading name of KCP Leasing & Sales

ASIA PACIFIC AIRLINES

Magellan (ML/MGE) (IATA 046)   Guam (GUM)

N281US	Boeing 727-251 (FedEx 3)	1180/21160		Lsd fr JRW Aviation
N319NE	Boeing 727-212F (Duganair 3)	1289/21349	ex N591DB	
N705AA	Boeing 727-223F (Raisbeck 3)	1751/22462		on order
N86425	Boeing 727-212F(Duganair 3)	1329/21459	ex N296AS	

Asia Pacific Airlines is the trading name of Aero Micronesia

ASPEN HELICOPTERS

Aspen (AHF)   Oxnard, CA

N383SH	Bell 206L-3 LongRanger III	51073	
N999AH	Bell 206L-3 LongRanger III	51046	ex C-GALM
N1085T	Bell 206L-1 LongRanger III	45376	
N5736N	Bell 206L-1 LongRanger II	45418	
N8057B	Bell 206L LongRanger	45045	
N228AH	Bell 222UT	47530	ex N422RM
N300LF	Partenavia P.68C	295	
N3832K	Partenavia P.68C	272	
N4107Q	Piper PA-31-350 T1020	31-8253008	
N5006Y	Bell 206B JetRanger III	2485	
N5012F	Bell 206B JetRanger III	2559	
N6602L	Partenavia P.68 Observer	326-19-OB	
N8131	Piper PA-31-350 Chieftain	31-8152032	
N39049	Bell 206B JetRanger III	3101	
N49643	Bell 206B JetRanger	1813	

ASTAR AIR CARGO

Dhl (ER/DHL)   Cincinnati-Northern Kentucky Intl, OH (CVG)
Previously listed as DHL Airways; renamed 14 Jul 03

N362DH	Airbus Industrie A300B4-103F	084	ex HS-THP		Lsd fr WFBN
N363DH	Airbus Industrie A300B4-103F	085	ex HS-THR		
N364DH	Airbus Industrie A300B4-203F	141	ex HS-THT		Lsd fr WTCo
N365DH	Airbus Industrie A300B4-203F	149	ex HS-THW		Lsd fr WTCo
N366DH	Airbus Industrie A300B4-203F	249	ex F-WIHZ		Lsd fr WTCo
N367DH	Airbus Industrie A300B4-203F	265	ex F-WIHY		Lsd fr WTCo
N368DH	Airbus Industrie A300B4-203F	207	ex N506TA		Lsd fr TDX
N622DH	Boeing 727-264F (FedEx 3)	1051/20896	ex XA-DUK		Op by SWT
N623DH	Boeing 727-264F (FedEx 3)	1049/20895	ex XA-DUJ		Op by SWT
N624DH	Boeing 727-264F (FedEx 3)	950/20709	ex XA-CUB		Op by DAE
N625DH	Boeing 727-264F (FedEx 3)	986/20780	ex XA-CUN		Op by DAE
N626DH	Boeing 727-277F (FedEx 3)	1768/22644	ex N72381		Op by SWT
N627DH	Boeing 727-277F (FedEx 3)	1753/22641	ex (N436DH)		Op by SWT
N720DH	Boeing 727-228F (FedEx 3)	562/19544	ex N606AR		
N721DH	Boeing 727-228F (FedEx 3)	564/19545	ex N605AR		
N726DH	Boeing 727-228F (FedEx 3)	845/20409	ex N604AR		
N727DH	Boeing 727-228F (FedEx 3)	778/20204	ex F-BPJM	stored IGM	
N740DH	Boeing 727-2Q9F (FedEx 3)	1508/21930	ex N200AV		
N741DH	Boeing 727-2Q9F (FedEx 3)	1531/21931	ex N202AV		
N742DH	Boeing 727-225F (FedEx 3)	1238/21290	ex N8872Z		
N743DH	Boeing 727-225F (FedEx 3)	1685/22438	ex N928PG		Lsd fr Pegasus
N745DH	Boeing 727-224F (FedEx 3)	1149/20665	ex N69736		Lsd fr Aerospace Finance
N746DH	Boeing 727-224F (Raisbeck 3)	1697/22252	ex N79743		Lsd fr Pacific AirCorp
N747DH	Boeing 727-224F (FedEx 3)	1702/22253	ex N79744		Lsd fr Pacific AirCorp
N748DH	Boeing 727-225F (FedEx 3)	1692/22440	ex XA-TCX		Lsd fr Pacific AirCorp
N749DH	Boeing 727-223F (FedEx 3)	1659/22013	ex N897AA		Lsd fr Pacific AirCorp
N750DH	Boeing 727-2M7 (FedEx 3)	1680/21951	ex A7-ABC		Lsd fr Pacific AirCorp
N751DH	Boeing 727-264 (FedEx 3)	1802/22982	ex A7-ABD		Lsd fr ART 22982
N752DH	Boeing 727-223F (FedEx 3)	1763/22466	ex N709AA		Lsd fr Aviation Capital Corp
N753DH	Boeing 727-223F (FedEx 3)	1766/22468	ex N712AA		Lsd fr Aviation Capital Corp
N754DH	Boeing 727-223F (FedEx 3)	1646/22008	ex N892AA		Lsd fr Aviation Capital Corp
N755DH	Boeing 727-225F (FedEx 3)	1539/21857	ex N887MA		Lsd fr Aviation Capital Corp
N780DH	Boeing 727-223F (FedEx 3)	1636/22006	ex N890AA		Lsd fr Aviation Capital Corp
N781DH	Boeing 727-227F (FedEx 3)	1571/21996	ex N768AT		Lsd fr WFBN
N782DH	Boeing 727-227F (FedEx 3)	1577/21998	ex N769AT		Lsd fr WFBN
N783DH	Boeing 727-227F (FedEx 3)	1581/21999	ex N766AT		Lsd fr WFBN
N784DH	Boeing 727-227F (FedEx 3)	1585/22001	ex N767AT		Lsd fr WFBN
N	Boeing 727-264F (FedEx 3)	1816/23014	ex N765AT		Lsd fr WFBN
N801DH	Douglas DC-8-73AF	431/46033	ex C-FTIK	New York Transit	
N802DH	Douglas DC-8-73AF	451/46076	ex C-FTIO		Lsd fr WFBN
N803DH	Douglas DC-8-73AF	508/46123	ex C-FTIQ		Lsd fr WFBN
N804DH	Douglas DC-8-73AF	511/46124	ex C-FTIR		
N805DH	Douglas DC-8-73AF	515/46125	ex C-FTIS	Los Angeles Express	Lsd fr WFBN

N806DH	Douglas DC-8-73CF	394/46002	ex N815UP	
N807DH	Douglas DC-8-73CF	375/45990	ex N816UP	
N873SJ	Douglas DC-8-73F	519/46091	ex F-GESM	Lsd fr GECAS

Operates on behalf of DHL Worldwide Couriers

ATA AIRLINES

AmTran (TZ/AMT)   *Indianapolis-Intl, IN (IND)*
Previously listed as American Trans Air; renamed 19 March 2003

N126AT	Boeing 737-76N	32679		on order	Lsd fr GECAS
N149AT	Boeing 737-76N	32681		on order	Lsd fr GECAS
N166AT	Boeing 737-76N	33817		on order	Lsd fr GECAS
N301TZ	Boeing 737-83N	847/28239	ex N1784B		Lsd fr Castle 2003-2A LLC
N302TZ	Boeing 737-83N	875/32576	ex N1787B		Lsd fr GECAS
N303TZ	Boeing 737-83N	888/28648	ex N1787B		Lsd fr GECAS
N304TZ	Boeing 737-83N	898/30675			Lsd fr ILFC
N305TZ	Boeing 737-83N	929/30706	ex N1787B		Lsd fr ILFC
N306TZ	Boeing 737-83N	933/32348	ex N1787B		Lsd fr GECAS
N307TZ	Boeing 737-83N	948/28653	ex N1787B		Lsd fr GECAS
N308TZ	Boeing 737-83N	958/28244	ex N1787B		Lsd fr ILFC
N309TZ	Boeing 737-83N	973/32577			Lsd fr GECAS
N310TZ	Boeing 737-83N	984/28243			Lsd fr Castle 2003-2A LLC
N311TZ	Boeing 737-83N	998/32578			Lsd fr GECAS
N312TZ	Boeing 737-83N	1002/32579	ex N1787B		Lsd fr GECAS
N313TZ	Boeing 737-83N	1024/32580			Lsd fr GECAS
N314TZ	Boeing 737-83N	1035/30640			Lsd fr ILFC
N315TZ	Boeing 737-83N	1054/28245			Lsd fr ILFC
N316TZ	Boeing 737-83N	1059/32609			Lsd fr GECAS
N317TZ	Boeing 737-83N	1081/28246			Lsd fr ILFC
N318TZ	Boeing 737-83N	1091/28247			Lsd fr ILFC
N319TZ	Boeing 737-83N	1106/30643			Lsd fr ILFC
N320TZ	Boeing 737-83N	1110/32610			Lsd fr GECAS
N321TZ	Boeing 737-83N	1123/28249			Lsd fr ILFC
N322TZ	Boeing 737-83N	1135/32611			Lsd fr GECAS
N323TZ	Boeing 737-83N	1149/30033			Lsd fr ILFC
N324TZ	Boeing 737-83N	1163/32882			Lsd fr GECAS
N325TZ	Boeing 737-83N	1181/32884			Lsd fr GECAS
N326TZ	Boeing 737-83N	1184/32612			Lsd fr GECAS
N327TZ	Boeing 737-83N	1197/32613			Lsd fr GECAS
N328TZ	Boeing 737-83N	1201/32614			Lsd fr GECAS
N329TZ	Boeing 737-83N	1207/32615			Lsd fr GECAS
N330TZ	Boeing 737-83N	1212/32616			Lsd fr GECAS
N331TZ	Boeing 737-83N	1330/30660			Lsd fr ILFC
N332TZ	Boeing 737-83N	1404/30679			
N333TZ	Boeing 737-83N	30673		on order 04	
N334TZ	Boeing 737-83N	32620		on order 04	
N335TZ	Boeing 737-83N	32621		on order 04	
N336TZ	Boeing 737-83N			on order 04	Lsd fr ILFC
N337TZ	Boeing 737-83N	32622		on order 04	
N338TZ	Boeing 737-83N	32623		on order 04	
N339TZ	Boeing 737-83N			on order 04	
N	Boeing 737-83N	30673		on order May04	Lsd fr ILFC
N512TZ	Boeing 757-2K2	608/26635	ex PH-TKC		Lsd fr AFS Investments
N513AT	Boeing 757-28A	974/32449	ex N449GE		Lsd fr WFBN
N514AT	Boeing 757-23N	690/27971			Lsd fr GATX
N515AT	Boeing 757-23N	692/27598			Lsd fr WFBN
N516AT	Boeing 757-23N	694/27972			Lsd fr WFBN
N517AT	Boeing 757-23N	735/27973			Lsd fr WFBN
N518AT	Boeing 757-23N	737/27974			Lsd fr WFBN
N519AT	Boeing 757-23N	779/27975			Lsd fr WFBN
N520AT	Boeing 757-23N	814/27976			Lsd fr WFBN
N521AT	Boeing 757-28AER	213/24368	ex G-MCKE	stored MHV	Lsd fr ACG Acquisitions
N522AT	Boeing 757-23N	843/29330			Lsd fr debis
N523AT	Boeing 757-23N	888/30232			Lsd fr WFBN
N524AT	Boeing 757-23N	895/30233			Lsd fr WFBN
N525AT	Boeing 757-23N	930/30548	ex N1795B		Lsd fr WFBN
N526AT	Boeing 757-23N	931/30735			Lsd fr WFBN
N527AT	Boeing 757-23N	945/30886			Lsd fr WFBN
N528AT	Boeing 757-23N	946/30887			Lsd fr WFBN
N550TZ	Boeing 757-33N	972/32584			Lsd fr WFBN
N551TZ	Boeing 757-33N	976/32585			Lsd fr WFBN
N552TZ	Boeing 757-33N	978/32586			Lsd fr WFBN
N553TZ	Boeing 757-33N	980/32587			Lsd fr WFBN
N554TZ	Boeing 757-33N	985/32588			Lsd fr WFBN
N555TZ	Boeing 757-33N	1003/32589			Lsd fr WFBN
N556TZ	Boeing 757-33N	1017/32590			Lsd fr WFBN
N557TZ	Boeing 757-33N	1007/32591			Lsd fr WFBN
N558TZ	Boeing 757-33N	1008/32592			Lsd fr WFBN
N559TZ	Boeing 757-33N	1018/32593			Lsd fr WFBN

N560TZ	Boeing 757-33N	1031/33525		Lsd fr WFBN
N561TZ	Boeing 757-33N	1032/33526	ex N1795B	Lsd fr WFBN
N160AT	Lockheed L-1011-500 Tristar	1217	ex JY-AGA	stored ROW
N161AT	Lockheed L-1011-500 Tristar	1219	ex JY-AGB	
N162AT	Lockheed L-1011-500 Tristar	1220	ex JY-AGC	
N163AT	Lockheed L-1011-500 Tristar	1229	ex JY-AGD	
N164AT	Lockheed L-1011-500 Tristar	1238	ex JY-AGE	
N186AT	Lockheed L-1011-50 Tristar	1074	ex N706DA	stored ROW
N188AT	Lockheed L-1011-50 Tristar	1078	ex N708DA	
N189AT	Lockheed L-1011-50 Tristar	1081	ex N709DA	stored ROW
N191AT	Lockheed L-1011-50 Tristar	1084	ex N710DA	stored ROW
N194AT	Lockheed L-1011-100 Tristar	1230	ex N8034T	Lsd fr State Street
N195AT	Lockheed L-1011-150 Tristar	1041	ex N701TT	stored ROW
N196AT	Lockheed L-1011-50 Tristar	1076	ex N31022	stored ROW
N197AT	Lockheed L-1011-50 Tristar	1082	ex N763BE	Big Ed; stored ROW
N198AT	Lockheed L-1011-500 Tristar	1111	ex N31030	stored ROW

All Tristars retired from scheduled services and now used for charters

ATI - AIR TRANSPORT INTERNATIONAL

Air Transport (8C/ATN)
Previously listed as Air Transport International

Little Rock-Adams Field, AR (LIT)

N21CX	Douglas DC-8-62F (BAC 3)	365/45955	ex N163CA	
N31CX	Douglas DC-8-62F (BAC 3)	318/45911	ex N1806	
N41CX	Douglas DC-8-62CF (BAC 3)	523/46129	ex N798AL	Lsd fr Aerospace Finance; op for BAX
N71CX	Douglas DC-8-62F (BAC 3)	361/45961	ex N818CK	
N602AL	Douglas DC-8-73F	380/45991	ex D-ADUI	Lsd fr WTCo
N603AL	Douglas DC-8-73F	401/46003	ex D-ADUA	Lsd fr WTCo
N605AL	Douglas DC-8-73F	490/46106	ex D-ADUC	Lsd fr WFBN
N606AL	Douglas DC-8-73F	432/46044	ex D-ADUI	op for BAX
N728PL	Douglas DC-8-62F (BAC 3)	353/45918	ex F-BOLF	Jerry 'Pete' Zerkel
N786AL	Douglas DC-8-63CF (BAC 3)	500/46121	ex EI-CAK	Lsd fr Skytrade Intl
N799AL	Douglas DC-8-62F (BAC 3)	335/45922	ex RTAF 60112	Lsd fr WTCo, op for BAX
N820BX+	Douglas DC-8-71F	460/46065	ex N8098U	Lsd fr GECAS, op for BAX
N821BX	Douglas DC-8-71F	262/45811	ex N8071U	Lsd fr GECAS
N822BX	Douglas DC-8-71F	284/45813	ex N8073U	Lsd fr GECAS, op for BAX
N823BX	Douglas DC-8-71F	459/46064	ex N8097U	Lsd fr GECAS, op for BAX
N824BX	Douglas DC-8-71F	339/45946	ex N8078U	std ROW Lsd fr GECAS, op for BAX
N825BX	Douglas DC-8-71F	381/45978	ex N8088U	Lsd fr GECAS, op for BAX
N826BX	Douglas DC-8-71F	399/45998	ex N8094U	std ROW Lsd fr GECAS, op for BAX
N827BX	Douglas DC-8-71F	356/45971	ex SE-DLM	std ROW Lsd fr GECAS, op for BAX
N828BX	Douglas DC-8-71F	382/45993	ex N8089U	Lsd fr GECAS
N829BX	Douglas DC-8-71F	387/45994	ex N501SR	Lsd fr GECAS, op for BAX
N830BX	Douglas DC-8-71F	358/45973	ex N783UP	Lsd fr GECAS, op for BAX
N867BX	Douglas DC-8-63CF (BAC 3)	479/46049	ex TF-FLC	Lsd fr and op for BAX
N870BX	Douglas DC-8-63F (BAC 3)	445/46036	ex C-FTIN	stored MZJ Lsd fr and op for BAX

+Named 'Larry LJ Johnston'
Wholly owned subsidiary of BAX Global

ATLANTIC AIR CARGO

Miami-Intl, FL (MIA)

N437GB	Douglas DC-3	19999	ex HR-LAD	Freighter	Lsd fr J&E Avn
N705GB	Douglas DC-3	13854	ex CF-HBX	Freighter	Lsd fr J&E Avn

ATLANTIC COAST AIRLINES

Blue Ridge (DH/BLR) (IATA 480)

Washington-Reagan National, DC (DCA)

N301UE	British Aerospace Jetstream 41	41012	ex G-4-012	Blue Ridge Highlander
N302UE	British Aerospace Jetstream 41	41013	ex G-4-013	
N303UE*	British Aerospace Jetstream 41	41015	ex G-4-015	
N305UE*	British Aerospace Jetstream 41	41019	ex G-4-019	
N306UE	British Aerospace Jetstream 41	41020	ex G-4-020	
N307UE	British Aerospace Jetstream 41	41021	ex G-4-021	
N308UE	British Aerospace Jetstream 41	41023	ex G-4-023	
N309UE	British Aerospace Jetstream 41	41022	ex G-4-022	
N311UE	British Aerospace Jetstream 41	41029	ex G-4-029	
N312UE	British Aerospace Jetstream 41	41025	ex G-4-025	
N313UE	British Aerospace Jetstream 41	41026	ex G-4-026	
N314UE	British Aerospace Jetstream 41	41027	ex G-4-027	
N315UE	British Aerospace Jetstream 41	41033	ex G-4-033	
N316UE^	British Aerospace Jetstream 41	41055	ex G-4-055	
N317UE	British Aerospace Jetstream 41	41031	ex G-4-031	
N318UE^	British Aerospace Jetstream 41	41041	ex G-4-041	
N319UE^	British Aerospace Jetstream 41	41042	ex G-4-042	
N320UE^	British Aerospace Jetstream 41	41043	ex G-4-043	
N321UE	British Aerospace Jetstream 41	41045	ex G-4-045	

N322UE^	British Aerospace Jetstream 41	41058	ex G-4-058
N324UE*	British Aerospace Jetstream 41	41017	ex N304UE
N325UE^	British Aerospace Jetstream 41	41063	ex G-4-063
N326UE^	British Aerospace Jetstream 41	41064	ex G-4-064
N327UE	British Aerospace Jetstream 41	41080	ex G-4-080
N328UE	British Aerospace Jetstream 41	41083	ex G-4-083
N329UE	British Aerospace Jetstream 41	41097	ex G-4-097
N330UE+	British Aerospace Jetstream 41	41098	ex G-4-098
N331UE+	British Aerospace Jetstream 41	41099	ex G-4-099
N332UE+	British Aerospace Jetstream 41	41100	ex G-4-100
N333UE	British Aerospace Jetstream 41	41101	ex G-4-101

*Leased from Banc of America   ^ Leased from WFBN
+Leased from Wachovia Bank
All were operated for United Express; to be retired by 30 April 2004

N620BR	Canadair CL-600-2B19	7179	ex C-	620
N621BR	Canadair CL-600-2B19	7186	ex C-FMML	621
N622BR	Canadair CL-600-2B19	7187	ex C-	622
N623BR	Canadair CL-600-2B19	7192	ex C-	623
N624BR	Canadair CL-600-2B19	7211	ex C-	624
N625BR	Canadair CL-600-2B19	7214	ex C-FMLU	625
N626BR*	Canadair CL-600-2B19	7225	ex C-FMKW	626
N627BR*	Canadair CL-600-2B19	7233	ex C-	627
N628BR*	Canadair CL-600-2B19	7240	ex C-	628
N629BR*	Canadair CL-600-2B19	7251	ex C-	629
N630BR	Canadair CL-600-2B19	7255	ex C-	630
N631BR	Canadair CL-600-2B19	7261	ex C-FMLS	631
N632BR*	Canadair CL-600-2B19	7268	ex C-FMNY	632
N633BR	Canadair CL-600-2B19	7274	ex C-FMLU	633
N634BR	Canadair CL-600-2B19	7287	ex C-FMLB	634
N635BR*	Canadair CL-600-2B19	7295	ex C-	635
N636BR*	Canadair CL-600-2B19	7307	ex C-	636
N637BR	Canadair CL-600-2B19	7308	ex C-	637
N638BR*	Canadair CL-600-2B19	7311	ex C-	638
N639BR*	Canadair CL-600-2B19	7313	ex C-FMNB	639
N640BR	Canadair CL-600-2B19	7340	ex C-FMMW	640
N641BR*	Canadair CL-600-2B19	7349	ex C-FMLI	641
N642BR*	Canadair CL-600-2B19	7356	ex C-FMNW	642
N643BR*	Canadair CL-600-2B19	7363	ex C-FMNO	643
N644BR*	Canadair CL-600-2B19	7379	ex C-FMLI	644
N645BR*	Canadair CL-600-2B19	7383	ex C-FMLV	645
N646BR*	Canadair CL-600-2B19	7392	ex C-FMND	646
N647BR*	Canadair CL-600-2B19	7399	ex C-FMMQ	647
N648BR*	Canadair CL-600-2B19	7406	ex C-FMKZ	648
N649BR*	Canadair CL-600-2B19	7414	ex C-FMMT	649
N650BR*	Canadair CL-600-2B19	7418	ex C-FMNY	650
N651BR*	Canadair CL-600-2B19	7426	ex C-FMMB	651
N652BR*	Canadair CL-600-2B19	7429	ex C-FMMQ	652
N653BR*	Canadair CL-600-2B19	7438	ex C-FMLF	653
N654BR*	Canadair CL-600-2B19	7454	ex C-FMLU	654
N655BR*	Canadair CL-600-2B19	7457	ex C-FMML	655
N656BR*	Canadair CL-600-2B19	7485	ex C-FMOI	656
N657BR*	Canadair CL-600-2B19	7491	ex C-FMMX	657
N658BR*	Canadair CL-600-2B19	7500	ex C-FMLQ	658
N659BR*	Canadair CL-600-2B19	7509	ex C-FMOS	659
N660BR*	Canadair CL-600-2B19	7519	ex C-FMMQ	660
N661BR*	Canadair CL-600-2B19	7520	ex C-FMMW	661
N662BR*	Canadair CL-600-2B19	7526	ex C-FMKZ	662
N663BR*	Canadair CL-600-2B19	7527	ex C-FMLB	663
N664BR*	Canadair CL-600-2B19	7528	ex C-FMLF	664
N665BR*	Canadair CL-600-2B19	7534	ex C-FMMT	665
N667BR*	Canadair CL-600-2B19	7535	ex C-FMNH	667
N668BR*	Canadair CL-600-2B19	7544	ex C-FMLU	668
N669BR*	Canadair CL-600-2B19	7545	ex C-FMOI	669
N670BR*	Canadair CL-600-2B19	7561	ex C-FMLS	670
N671BR*	Canadair CL-600-2B19	7572	ex C-FMND	671
N672BR*	Canadair CL-600-2B19	7594	ex C-FMMT	672
N673BR*	Canadair CL-600-2B19	7599	ex C-FMOS	673
N674BR*	Canadair CL-600-2B19	7601	ex C-FVAZ	674
N675BR*	Canadair CL-600-2B19	7635	ex C-FMOI	675
N676BR*	Canadair CL-600-2B19	7644	ex C-FMKV	676
N677BR*	Canadair CL-600-2B19	7652	ex C-FMLT	677
N678BR*	Canadair CL-600-2B19	7653	ex C-FMLV	678
N679BR*	Canadair CL-600-2B19	7662	ex C-FMND	679
N680BR*	Canadair CL-600-2B19	7679	ex C-FMLI	680
N681BR*	Canadair CL-600-2B19	7680	ex C-FMLQ	681
N682BR*	Canadair CL-600-2B19	7691	ex C-FVAZ	682
N683BR*	Canadair CL-600-2B19	7692	ex C-FMND	683
N684BR*	Canadair CL-600-2B19	7708	ex C-FMLF	684
N685BR*	Canadair CL-600-2B19	7712	ex C-FMLT	685
N686BR*	Canadair CL-600-2B19	7715	ex C-FMNH	686
N687BR*	Canadair CL-600-2B19	7720	ex C-FMOW	687

N688BR*	Canadair CL-600-2B19	7723	ex C-FMNQ	688	
N689BR*	Canadair CL-600-2B19	7737	ex C-FMLB	689	
N690BR*	Canadair CL-600-2B19	7739	ex C-FMLI	690	
N691BR*	Canadair CL-600-2B19	7740	ex C-FMLQ	691	
N692BR*	Canadair CL-600-2B19	7759	ex C-FMMQ	692	
N693BR	Canadair CL-600-2B19	7761	ex C-GYXS	693	
N694BR	Canadair CL-600-2B19	7768	ex C-FMLI	694	
N695BR	Canadair CL-600-2B19	7772	ex C-GYYA	695	
N696BR	Canadair CL-600-2B19	7779	ex C-FJKK	696	
N697BR	Canadair CL-600-2B19	7787	ex C-FSDZ	697	
N698BR	Canadair CL-600-2B19	7799	ex C-FMLI	698	
N699BR	Canadair CL-600-2B19	7801	ex C-FMLS	699	
N701BR*	Canadair CL-600-2B19	7448	ex N850FJ	701	
N702BR*	Canadair CL-600-2B19	7462	ex N851FJ	702	
N703BR*	Canadair CL-600-2B19	7467	ex N852FJ	703	
N705BR*	Canadair CL-600-2B19	7470	ex N853FJ	705	
N706BR*	Canadair CL-600-2B19	7553	ex C-GJJP	706	
N708BR*	Canadair CL-600-2B19	7575	ex C-GJOT	708	
N709BR	Canadair CL-600-2B19	7850	ex C-FMMW	709	
N710BR	Canadair CL-600-2B19	7852	ex C-FMMY	710	
N712BR	Canadair CL-600-2B19		ex C-	712	on order
N713BR	Canadair CL-600-2B19		ex C-	713	on order
N715BR	Canadair CL-600-2B19		ex C-	715	on order
N716BR	Canadair CL-600-2B19		ex C-	716	on order
N717BR	Canadair CL-600-2B19		ex C-	717	on order
N718BR	Canadair CL-600-2B19		ex C-	718	on order
N719BR	Canadair CL-600-2B19		ex C-	719	on order
N720BR	Canadair CL-600-2B19		ex C-	720	on order
N721BR	Canadair CL-600-2B19		ex C-	721	on order 04
N722BR	Canadair CL-600-2B19		ex C-	722	on order 04
N723BR	Canadair CL-600-2B19		ex C-	723	on order 04
N724BR	Canadair CL-600-2B19		ex C-	724	on order 04
N725BR	Canadair CL-600-2B19		ex C-	725	on order 04
N726BR	Canadair CL-600-2B19		ex C-	726	on order 04
N	Canadair CL-600-2B19		ex C-		on order 04
N	Canadair CL-600-2B19		ex C-		on order 04

Twenty-five more Canadair CL-600-2B19s are on order for delivery in 2005; to be transferred to Independence Air
*Leased from Wachovia Bank   +Leased fr State Street Bank & Trust

N401FJ	Dornier 328-310	3145	ex D-BDX.	401 Delta Connection
N402FJ	Dornier 328-310	3147	ex D-BDX.	402 Delta Connection
N403FJ	Dornier 328-310	3149	ex D-BDX.	403 Delta Connection
N404FJ	Dornier 328-310	3150	ex D-BDX.	404 Delta Connection
N405FJ	Dornier 328-310	3155	ex D-BDXJ	405 Delta Connection
N406FJ	Dornier 328-310	3156	ex D-BDXK	406 Delta Connection
N407FJ	Dornier 328-310	3157	ex D-BDXL	407 Delta Connection
N408FJ	Dornier 328-310	3160	ex D-BDX.	408 Delta Connection
N409FJ	Dornier 328-310	3161	ex D-BDX.	409 Delta Connection
N410FJ	Dornier 328-310	3165	ex D-BDXV	410 Delta Connection
N411FJ	Dornier 328-310	3166	ex D-BDXW	411 Delta Connection
N412FJ	Dornier 328-310	3167	ex D-BDXA	412 Delta Connection
N413FJ	Dornier 328-310	3168	ex D-BDXB	413 Delta Connection
N414FJ	Dornier 328-300	3169	ex D-BDXC	414 Delta Connection
N415FJ	Dornier 328-310	3170	ex D-BDXZ	415 Delta Connection
N416FJ	Dornier 328-310	3171	ex D-BDXE	416 Delta Connection
N417FJ	Dornier 328-310	3174	ex D-BDXH	417 Delta Connection
N418FJ	Dornier 328-310	3176	ex D-BDXI	418 Delta Connection
N419FJ	Dornier 328-310	3173	ex D-BDX	419 Delta Connection
N420FJ	Dornier 328-310	3178		420 Delta Connection
N421FJ	Dornier 328-310	3189		421 Delta Connection
N422FJ	Dornier 328-310	3180		422 Delta Connection
N423FJ	Dornier 328-310	3181		423 Delta Connection
N424FJ	Dornier 328-310	3185		424 Delta Connection
N425FJ	Dornier 328-310	3189		425 Delta Connection
N426FJ	Dornier 328-310	3190		426 Delta Connection
N427FJ	Dornier 328-310	3192		427 Delta Connection
N428FJ	Dornier 328-310	3193		428 Delta Connection
N429FJ	Dornier 328-310	3194	ex D-BDXQ	429 Delta Connection
N430FJ	Dornier 328-310	3209		430 Delta Connection
N451FJ	Dornier 328-310	3205	ex D-BDXX	VIP shuttle
N452FJ	Dornier 328-310	3214	ex D-BDXC	VIP shuttle
N500FJ	Dornier 328-310	3197	ex D-BDXA	VIP shuttle
N502FJ	Dornier 328-310	3206	ex D-BDXY	stored OBF
N503FJ	Dornier 328-310	3207	ex D-BDXE	VIP shuttle; stored OBF

All leased from Wachovia Bank
Operates as Delta Connection with Dornier 328s. Ceased United Express flights at the end of 2003 and will begin low-cost operations in its own right as Independence Air using Airbus Industrie A320 family as well as Canadair Regional Jets (has signed MoU to purchase 10 new A319s and 5 new A320s direct from Airbus and lease a further 10)

ATLANTIC SOUTHEAST AIRLINES

Candler (EV/CAA) (IATA 862)   *Atlanta-Hartsfield Intl, GA/Orlando-Intl, FL (ATL/MCO*

N530AS+	Aerospatiale/Alenia ATR 72-212	453	ex F-WQLC	
N531AS+	Aerospatiale/Alenia ATR 72-212	454	ex F-WQLH	
N532AS+	Aerospatiale/Alenia ATR 72-212	458	ex F-WQLK	
N533AS+	Aerospatiale/Alenia ATR 72-212	460	ex F-WQLL	
N534AS+	Aerospatiale/Alenia ATR 72-212	463	ex F-WQLM	
N535AS+	Aerospatiale/Alenia ATR 72-212	464	ex F-WQKS	
N536AS+	Aerospatiale/Alenia ATR 72-212	465	ex F-WQLB	
N630AS+	Aerospatiale/Alenia ATR 72-212	336	ex F-WWLS	
N631AS+	Aerospatiale/Alenia ATR 72-212	362	ex F-WWEZ	
N632AS+	Aerospatiale/Alenia ATR 72-212	338	ex F-WWLT	
N633AS+	Aerospatiale/Alenia ATR 72-212	344	ex F-WWLC	
N634AS+	Aerospatiale/Alenia ATR 72-212	370	ex F-WWEF	
N635AS+	Aerospatiale/Alenia ATR 72-212	372	ex F-WWEP	
N636AS+	Aerospatiale/Alenia ATR 72-212	375	ex F-WWLW	
N637AS+	Aerospatiale/Alenia ATR 72-212	383	ex F-WWEB	
N640AS	Aerospatiale/Alenia ATR 72-212	405	ex F-WWLP	
N641AS	Aerospatiale/Alenia ATR 72-212	387	ex F-WWLG	
N642AS	Aerospatiale/Alenia ATR 72-212	395	ex F-WWLJ	
N643AS	Aerospatiale/Alenia ATR 72-212	413	ex F-WWLC	

+Leased from WFBN

N820AS~	Canadair CL-600-2B19	7188		820
N821AS~	Canadair CL-600-2B19	7194	ex C-FMKV	821
N823AS~	Canadair CL-600-2B19	7196		823
N824AS~	Canadair CL-600-2B19	7203		824
N825AS~	Canadair CL-600-2B19	7207		825
N826AS	Canadair CL-600-2B19	7210	ex C-FMOW	826
N827AS	Canadair CL-600-2B19	7212	ex C-FMND	827
N828AS	Canadair CL-600-2B19	7213	ex C-FMNQ	828
N829AS	Canadair CL-600-2B19	7232		829
N830AS	Canadair CL-600-2B19	7236		830
N832AS	Canadair CL-600-2B19	7243		832
N833AS	Canadair CL-600-2B19	7246	ex C-FMMB	833
N834AS	Canadair CL-600-2B19	7254		834
N835AS	Canadair CL-600-2B19	7258	ex C-FMLF	835
N836AS	Canadair CL-600-2B19	7263	ex C-FMLU	836
N837AS	Canadair CL-600-2B19	7271	ex C-FVAZ	837
N838AS	Canadair CL-600-2B19	7276	ex C-FMMB	838
N839AS	Canadair CL-600-2B19	7284	ex C-FMKV	839
N840AS	Canadair CL-600-2B19	7290	ex C-FMLQ	840
N841AS	Canadair CL-600-2B19	7300	ex C-FMOW	841
N842AS	Canadair CL-600-2B19	7304		842
N843AS^	Canadair CL-600-2B19	7310	ex C-FMMW	843
N844AS^	Canadair CL-600-2B19	7317	ex C-FMLB	844
N845AS^	Canadair CL-600-2B19	7324		845
N846AS^	Canadair CL-600-2B19	7328	ex C-FMNY	846
N847AS^	Canadair CL-600-2B19	7335		847
N848AS^	Canadair CL-600-2B19	7339		848
N849AS'^	Canadair CL-600-2B19	7347	ex C-FMLB	849
N850AS^	Canadair CL-600-2B19	7355	ex C-FMNH	850
N851AS^	Canadair CL-600-2B19	7360	ex C-FMOW	851
N852AS^	Canadair CL-600-2B19	7369	ex C-FMMQ	852
N853AS^	Canadair CL-600-2B19	7374	ex C-FMKV	853
N854AS^	Canadair CL-600-2B19	7382	ex C-FMLT	854
N855AS^	Canadair CL-600-2B19	7395	ex C-GGKY	855
N856AS^	Canadair CL-600-2B19	7404	ex C-FMKV	856
N857AS^	Canadair CL-600-2B19	7411	ex C-FMLS	857
N858AS^	Canadair CL-600-2B19	7417	ex C-FMNX	858
N859AS^	Canadair CL-600-2B19	7421	ex C-FVAZ	859
N860AS^	Canadair CL-600-2B19	7433	ex C-FMNB	860
N861AS^	Canadair CL-600-2B19	7445	ex C-FMNH	861
N862AS	Canadair CL-600-2B19	7476	ex C-FMNW	862
N863AS	Canadair CL-600-2B19	7487	ex C-FMML	863
N864AS	Canadair CL-600-2B19	7502	ex C-FMLT	864
N865AS	Canadair CL-600-2B19	7507	ex C-FMNX	865
N866AS	Canadair CL-600-2B19	7517	ex C-FMML	866
N867AS^	Canadair CL-600-2B19	7463	ex C-FMNB	867
N868AS>	Canadair CL-600-2B19	7474	ex C-FMMT	868
N869AS<	Canadair CL-600-2B19	7479	ex C-FMOS	869
N870AS^	Canadair CL-600-2B19	7530	ex C-FMLQ	870
N871AS^	Canadair CL-600-2B19	7537	ex C-FMNX	871
N872AS	Canadair CL-600-2B19	7542	ex C-FMND	872
N873AS	Canadair CL-600-2B19	7549	ex C-GJLI	873
N874AS	Canadair CL-600-2B19	7551	ex C-GJLK	874
N875AS	Canadair CL-600-2B19	7559	ex C-FJLQ	875
N876AS	Canadair CL-600-2B19	7576	ex C-	876
N877AS	Canadair CL-600-2B19	7579	ex C-FMMQ	877

N878AS	Canadair CL-600-2B19	7590	ex C-FMLQ	878
N879AS	Canadair CL-600-2B19	7600	ex C-FMOW	879
N880AS	Canadair CL-600-2B19	7606	ex C-FMMB	880
N881AS	Canadair CL-600-2B19	7496	ex C-GIXF	881
N882AS	Canadair CL-600-2B19	7503	ex C-GJAO	882
N883AS	Canadair CL-600-2B19	7504	ex C-GIZD	883
N884AS	Canadair CL-600-2B19	7513	ex C-GIZF	884
N885AS	Canadair CL-600-2B19	7521	ex C-GJDX	885
N886AS	Canadair CL-600-2B19	7531	ex C-GJJC	886
N889AS	Canadair CL-600-2B19	7538	ex C-GJJG	889
N901EV	Canadair CL-600-2B19	7616	ex C-FMKZ	901
N902EV	Canadair CL-600-2B19	7620	ex C-FMLQ	902
N903EV	Canadair CL-600-2B19	7621	ex C-FMLI	903
N904EV	Canadair CL-600-2B19	7628	ex C-FMNY	904
N905EV	Canadair CL-600-2B19	7632	ex C-FMND	905
N906EV	Canadair CL-600-2B19	7642	ex C-FMMY	906
N907EV	Canadair CL-600-2B19	7648	ex C-FMLF	907
N908EV	Canadair CL-600-2B19	7654	ex C-FMMT	908
N909EV	Canadair CL-600-2B19	7658	ex C-FMNY	909
N910EV	Canadair CL-600-2B19	7727	ex C-FMML	910
N912EV	Canadair CL-600-2B19	7728	ex C-FMMN	912
N913EV	Canadair CL-600-2B19	7731	ex C-FMMX	913
N914EV	Canadair CL-600-2B19	7752	ex C-FMND	914
N915EV	Canadair CL-600-2B19	7754	ex C-FMLU	915
N916EV	Canadair CL-600-2B19	7757	ex C-FMML	916
N917EV	Canadair CL-600-2B19	7769	ex C-FMLI	917
N919EV	Canadair CL-600-2B19	7780	ex C-FMOW	919
N920EV	Canadair CL-600-2B19	7810	ex C-FMOW	920
N921EV	Canadair CL-600-2B19	7819	ex C-FMMQ	921
N922EV	Canadair CL-600-2B19	7822	ex C-FMMY	922
N923EV	Canadair CL-600-2B19	7826	ex C-FMKZ	923
N924EV	Canadair CL-600-2B19	7830	ex C-FMLQ	924
N925EV	Canadair CL-600-2B19	7831	ex C-FMLS	925
N926EV	Canadair CL-600-2B19	7843	ex C-FMNQ	926
N927EV	Canadair CL-600-2B19	7844	ex C-FMLU	927

^Leased from State Street   ~Leased from Wachovia Bank NA
*Cincinnati - the Jet Hub c/s   'Special 20th Anniversary c/s, named City of Atlanta
>Texas Bluebonnet colours

N701EV	Canadair CL-600-2C10	10020	ex C-GIAB	
N702EV	Canadair CL-600-2C10	10035	ex C-GIBQ	
N703EV	Canadair CL-600-2C10	10038	ex C-GICB	
N705EV	Canadair CL-600-2C10	10051	ex C-GIAP	
N706EV	Canadair CL-600-2C10	10054	ex C-GIAZ	
N707EV	Canadair CL-600-2C10	10057	ex C-GIAZ	
N708EV	Canadair CL-600-2C10	10060	ex C-GIBI	
N709EV	Canadair CL-600-2C10	10068	ex C-GICB	
N710EV	Canadair CL-600-2C10	10071	ex C-GICP	
N712EV	Canadair CL-600-2C10	10074	ex C-GHZZ	
N713EV	Canadair CL-600-2C10	10081	ex C-GIAP	
N716EV	Canadair CL-600-2C10	10084	ex C-GIAV	
N717EV	Canadair CL-600-2C10	10088	ex C-GIBH	
N718EV	Canadair CL-600-2C10	10095	ex C-	
N719EV	Canadair CL-600-2C10	10099	ex C-GICL	
N720EV	Canadair CL-600-2C10	10115	ex C-GIAW	
N722EV	Canadair CL-600-2C10	10127	ex C-	
N723EV	Canadair CL-600-2C10	10132	ex C-	
N724EV	Canadair CL-600-2C10			on order
N727EV	Canadair CL-600-2C10			on order
N730EV	Canadair CL-600-2C10			on order
N738EV	Canadair CL-600-2C10			on order
N740EV	Canadair CL-600-2C10			on order
N741EV	Canadair CL-600-2C10			on order
N744EV	Canadair CL-600-2C10			on order
N748EV	Canadair CL-600-2C10			on order
N750EV	Canadair CL-600-2C10			on order
N751EV	Canadair CL-600-2C10			on order
N752EV	Canadair CL-600-2C10			on order
N753EV	Canadair CL-600-2C10			on order
N754EV	Canadair CL-600-2C10			on order

N238AS	Embraer EMB.120RT Brasilia	120053	ex PT-SJW
N261AS	Embraer EMB.120RT Brasilia	120141	ex PT-SPH
N262AS	Embraer EMB.120RT Brasilia	120146	ex PT-SPM
N263AS	Embraer EMB.120RT Brasilia	120157	ex PT-SPW
N264AS	Embraer EMB.120ER Brasilia	120165	ex PT-SQD
N265AS	Embraer EMB.120RT Brasilia	120170	ex PT-SQI
N266AS	Embraer EMB.120RT Brasilia	120188	ex PT-SRB
N268AS	Embraer EMB.120RT Brasilia	120202	ex PT-SRS
N269AS	Embraer EMB.120RT Brasilia	120210	ex PT-SSE
N274AS	Embraer EMB.120RT Brasilia	120229	ex PT-STB
N280AS	Embraer EMB.120ER Brasilia	120231	ex PT-STD

N281AS	Embraer EMB.120ER Brasilia	120224	ex PT-SST	
N282AS	Embraer EMB.120ER Brasilia	120226	ex PT-SSV	
N283AS	Embraer EMB.120ER Brasilia	120236	ex PT-STI	
N285AS	Embraer EMB.120RT Brasilia	120265	ex PT-SUL	
N286AS	Embraer EMB.120ER Brasilia	120268	ex PT-SUO	
N503AS	Embraer EMB.120RT Brasilia	120275	ex PT-SUV	
N638AS	Embraer EMB.120RT Brasilia	120282	ex PT-SVC	
N639AS	Embraer EMB.120RT Brasilia	120283	ex PT-SVD	

Last Embraer EMB.120 Brasilia service 31 Jul 03 and all stored
Wholly owned subsidiary of Delta Air Lines and operates as Delta Connection

ATLAS AIR

Giant (5Y/GTI) (IATA 369)   New York-JFK Intl, NY (JFK)

N354MC	Boeing 747-341SF	627/23394	ex PP-VNH		Lsd fr Nissho Iwai; sublsd to PAC
N355MC	Boeing 747-341SF	629/23395	ex PP-VNI		Lsd fr Nissho Iwai; sublsd to PAC
N408MC	Boeing 747-47UF	1192/29261	ex (N495MC)		Lsd fr WFBN
N409MC	Boeing 747-47UF	1242/30558			Lsd fr WFBN; sublsd to PAC
N412MC	Boeing 747-47UF	1244/30559			Lsd fr WFBN, op for CSN
N415MC	Boeing 747-47UF	1304/32837			Lsd fr US Bank
N416MC	Boeing 747-47UF	1307/32838			Lsd fr Tuolumme River A/c
N418MC	Boeing 747-47UF	1319/32840			Lsd fr AFS Investments
N491MC	Boeing 747-47UF	1165/29252			Lsd fr WFBN; sublsd to GSS
N492MC	Boeing 747-47UF	1169/29253		no titles	Lsd fr WFBN
N493MC	Boeing 747-47UF	1179/29254			Lsd fr WFBN
N494MC	Boeing 747-47UF	1184/29255	ex OO-TJA		Lsd to GSS as G-GSSC
N495MC	Boeing 747-47UF	1213/29256			Lsd to GSS as G-GSSA
N496MC	Boeing 747-47UF	1217/29257			Lsd fr WFBN; sublsd to PAC
N497MC	Boeing 747-47UF	1220/29258			Lsd fr WFBN
N498MC	Boeing 747-47UF	1227/29259			Lsd fr WFBN
N499MC	Boeing 747-47UF	1240/29260			Lsd fr WFBN
N505MC	Boeing 747-2D3M	296/21251	ex F-GFUK		Lsd fr Atlas Freighter Lsg; sublsd PAC
N506MC	Boeing 747-2D3M	297/21252	ex LX-ZCV		Lsd fr WFBN
N507MC	Boeing 747-230M	320/21380	ex D-ABYL	stored ROW	Lsd fr WFBN
N508MC	Boeing 747-230M	356/21644	ex D-ABYS		Lsd fr State Street
N509MC	Boeing 747-230M	299/21221	ex D-ABYK		
N512MC	Boeing 747-230M	294/21220	ex D-ABYJ		Lsd fr Atlas Freighter Lsg
N516MC	Boeing 747-243M	497/22507	ex I-DEMD		
N517MC	Boeing 747-243B (SF)	613/23300	ex I-DEMT		
N518MC	Boeing 747-243M	647/23476	ex I-DEMW	all-white	Lsd fr Wachovia Bank
N522MC	Boeing 747-2D7B (SF)	417/21783	ex HS-TGB		
N523MC	Boeing 747-2D7B (SF)	402/21782	ex N323MC	std ROW	Lsd fr Atlas Freighter Lsg
N524MC	Boeing 747-2D7B (SF)	424/21784	ex HS-TGC		Lsd fr Atlas Freighter Lsg
N526MC	Boeing 747-2D7B (SF)	479/22337	ex HS-TGF		Lsd fr Atlas Freighter Lsg
N527MC	Boeing 747-2D7B (SF)	504/22471	ex HS-TGG	all-white	Lsd fr Atlas Freighter Lsg
N528MC	Boeing 747-2D7B (SF)	597/22472	ex HS-TGS		
N534MC	Boeing 747-2F6B (SF)	421/21832	ex N741PR		
N535MC	Boeing 747-2F6B (SF)	423/21833	ex N742PR		
N536MC	Boeing 747-228F	334/21576	ex F-GPVV		
N537MC	Boeing 747-271C	524/22403	ex LX-BCV		Op for CLX
N538MC	Boeing 747-271C	416/21964	ex LX-ACV		Lsd to ICL as 4X-ICL
N539MC	Boeing 747-271C	438/21965	ex LX-ECV		Lsd to ICL as 4X-ICM
N540MC	Boeing 747-243M	499/22508	ex I-DEMF		
N808MC	Boeing 747-212B SCD	253/21048	ex N726PA		Lsd fr Atlas Freighter Lsg
N809MC	Boeing 747-228F	245/20887	ex LX-DCV		Lsd fr Atlas Freighter Lsg
N24837	Boeing 747-329M	810/24837	ex OO-SGD		Lsd fr EAST Trust; sublsd to PAC

One Boeing 747-47UF is on order for delivery in September 2006

Operates ACMI freight services for other airlines including Alitalia, British Airways, Dragonair, EVA Airlines, Emirates, China Airlines, Federal Express, Korean Air and Thai International; aircraft sometimes carry these airlines' colours, but leases vary
Subsisiary of Atlas Air Worldwide Holdings as is Polar Air Cargo

BAKER AVIATION

Baker Aviation (8Q/BAJ)   Kotzebue-Wien Memorial, AK (OTZ)

N5293X	Cessna U206G Stationair 6	U20605612	
N6908M	Cessna 207A Stationair 8	20700672	Lsd fr Alaska A/c Lsg
N9942M	Cessna 207A Stationair 8	20700756	Lsd fr Alaska A/c Lsg

BALTIMORE AIR TRANSPORT now listed under trading name as CorpJet

BANCSERVE AIR

Bessemer, AL (EKY)

Sister company of Air Carriers and leases aircraft as and when required

BANKAIR

Bankair (B4/BKA)   Columbia-Owens Field, SC (CUB)

N21CJ	Mitsubishi MU-2L	789SA	ex N278MA	
N21JA	Mitsubishi MU-2J	614	ex N998CA	Lsd fr MU-2 LLC
N27TJ	Mitsubishi MU-2B	1511SA	ex N418MA	
N44KU	Mitsubishi MU-2J	647	ex N44KS	
N102BX	Mitsubishi MU-2L	748SA	ex N102BG	
N174MA	Mitsubishi MU-2B	753SA	ex N100BY	
N334EB	Mitsubishi MU-2J	568	ex N99SL	
N535WM	Mitsubishi MU-2J	655		
N610CA	Mitsubishi MU-2B	788SA	ex N277MA	
N637WG	Mitsubishi MU-2J	637	ex N951MS	
N823MA	Mitsubishi MU-2L	663	ex YV-409P	Lsd fr Turbine A/c Marketing
N920S	Mitsubishi MU-2G	534	ex (N78V)	Lsd fr Turbine A/c Marketing
N942ST	Mitsubishi MU-2B	745SA	ex N942MA	
N33PT	Lear Jet 25D	25D-240	ex N83EA	Lsd fr Lear 25 LLC
N58EM	Lear Jet 35	35-046	ex VH-LJL	Lsd fr 58EM LLC
N58HC	Lear Jet 25D	25D-341	ex XA-SAE	
N67PA	Lear Jet 35A	35A-208	ex (N39DJ)	Lsd fr 67PA LLC
N82TS	Lear Jet 25B	25B-154	ex N210NC	Lsd fr Lear 25 LLC
N86BE	Lear Jet 35A	35A-194	ex N86BL	Lsd fr Dickerson Associates
N88BY	Lear Jet 25B	25B-168	ex N88BT	Lsd fr Lear 25 LLC
N135AG	Lear Jet 35A	35A-132	ex N37TJ	Lsd fr 135AG LLC
N155AM	Lear Jet 35A	35A-131	ex N26GD	Lsd fr 155AM LLC
N326DD	Lear Jet 35A	35A-173	ex YU-BPY	Lsd fr 326DD LLC
N333RY	Lear Jet 24B	24B-202	ex N814JR	Lsd fr Lear 25 LLC
N369BA	Lear Jet 35A	35A-312	ex LV-OFV	Lsd fr 369BA LLC
N399BA	Lear Jet 35A	35A-371	ex LV-ALF	Lsd fr MU-2 LLC
N465NW	Lear Jet 35A	35A-465		Lsd fr 465MW LLC
N500ED	Lear Jet 35A	35A-241	ex N500EX	Lsd fr 500ED LLC
N688GS	Lear Jet 25B	25B-123	ex N906SU	Lsd fr Lear 25 LLC
N900BJ	Lear Jet 35A	35A-123	ex N900JE	Lsd fr 900BJ LLC

All leasing companies believed associated with Dickerson Associates

N345AC	Piper PA-34-200T Seneca II	34-7870087	Lsd fr Management Co LLC
N8313C	Piper PA-34-200T Seneca II	34-7570226	
N8564E	Piper PA-32-300 Cherokee Six	32-7640072	
N41336	Piper PA-34-200 Seneca	34-7450109	Lsd fr Dickerson Associates

All freighters

BARON AVIATION SERVICES

Show-Me (BVN)   Rolla-Vichy-National, MO (VIH)

N702FX	Cessna 208B Caravan I	208B0422	
N718FX	Cessna 208B Caravan I	208B0448	
N719FX	Cessna 208B Caravan I	208B0450	
N723FX	Cessna 208B Caravan I	208B0456	
N738FX	Cessna 208B Caravan I	208B0482	
N741FX	Cessna 208B Caravan I	208B0486	
N745FX	Cessna 208B Caravan I	208B0495	
N749FE	Cessna 208B Caravan I	208B0242	
N751FX	Cessna 208B Caravan I	208B0514	
N753FX	Cessna 208B Caravan I	208B0520	
N756FE	Cessna 208B Caravan I	208B0251	
N765FE	Cessna 208B Caravan I	208B0259	
N770FE	Cessna 208B Caravan I	208B0265	
N773FE	Cessna 208B Caravan I	208B0269	
N774FE	Cessna 208B Caravan I	208B0271	
N786FE	Cessna 208B Caravan I	208B0284	
N793FE	Cessna 208B Caravan I	208B0291	
N841FE	Cessna 208B Caravan I	208B0144	
N845FE	Cessna 208B Caravan I	208B0152	
N861FE	Cessna 208B Caravan I	208B0183	
N866FE	Cessna 208B Caravan I	208B0189	
N889FE	Cessna 208B Caravan I	208B0218	
N894FE	Cessna 208B Caravan I	208B0224	
N900FE	Cessna 208B Caravan I	208B0054	ex SE-KLX
N902FE	Cessna 208B Caravan I	208B0002	
N912FE	Cessna 208B Caravan I	208B0012	
N922FE	Cessna 208B Caravan I	208B0022	
N928FE	Cessna 208B Caravan I	208B0028	
N929FE	Cessna 208B Caravan I	208B0029	
N934FE	Cessna 208B Caravan I	208B0034	
N939FE	Cessna 208B Caravan I	208B0180	
N950FE	Cessna 208B Caravan I	208B0056	ex (N956FE)
N957FE	Cessna 208B Caravan I	208B0070	ex (N970FE)
N961FE	Cessna 208B Caravan I	208B0077	

N970FE   Cessna 208B Caravan I   208B0093
N978FE   Cessna 208B Caravan I   208B0105
N994FE   Cessna 208B Caravan I   208B0132
Operates Cessna 208/208B Caravans on behalf of Federal Express

BASLER AIRLINES

Basler (BFC)   *Oshkosh-Wittman Regional, WI (OSH)*

N300BF   Douglas DC-3/Basler BT-67   15299/26744 ex N300TX   Turbo-Express
A division of Basler Turbo Conversions; several more aircraft are registered to parent but not operated by BFC

BAX GLOBAL

(8W)   *Toledo-Express, OH (TOL)*

N41CX*   Douglas DC-8-62CF (BAC 3)   523/46129 ex N798AL
N606AL*   Douglas DC-8-73F   432/46044
N799AL*   Douglas DC-8-62F (BAC 3)   335/45922 ex RTAF 60112
N820BX*   Douglas DC-8-71F   460/46065 ex N8098U   Larry LJ Johnston
N823BX*   Douglas DC-8-71F   459/46064 ex N8097U
N824BX*   Douglas DC-8-71F   339/45946 ex N8078U   stored ROW
N825BX*   Douglas DC-8-71F   381/45978 ex N8088U
N826BX*   Douglas DC-8-71F   399/45998 ex N8094U   stored ROW
N827BX*   Douglas DC-8-71F   356/45971 ex SE-DLM
N829BX*   Douglas DC-8-71F   387/45994 ex N501SR
N830BX*   Douglas DC-8-71F   358/45973 ex N783UP
N867BX*   Douglas DC-8-63CF (BAC 3)   479/46049 ex TF-FLC
N868BX*   Douglas DC-8-63F (BAC 3)   434/46034 ex C-FTIL   stored MZJ   Lsd fr ALG Transport
N869BX*   Douglas DC-8-63F (BAC 3)   438/46035 ex C-FTIM   stored MZJ
N870BX*   Douglas DC-8-63F (BAC 3)   445/46036 ex C-FTIN   stored MZJ
*Leased from and operated by ATI-Air Transport International, a wholly owned subsidiary

N858AA   Boeing 727-223F (FedEx 3)   1200/21085   Op by KHA
N6806   Boeing 727-223F (FedEx 3)   548/19481 ex N719CK   Op by KHA
N6816   Boeing 727-223F (FedEx 3)   611/19491   Op by KHA
N6831   Boeing 727-223F (FedEx 3)   707/20184   Op by KHA
Also leases McDonnell-Douglas DC-10-30F from Gemini Air Cargo as and when required

BELLAIR

(7G)   *Sitka, AK (SIT)*

N31PR   Piper PA-31-350 Navajo Chieftain 31-7952049
N76RL   Piper PA-32-300 Cherokee Six   32-7540024
N107TA   Piper PA-32-300 Cherokee Six   32-7540099
N401CK   Volpar Turboliner   AF-60 ex N401TH
N732XR   Cessna U206G Stationair 6   U20604735   Floats/wheels
N1924H   Piper PA-32R-300 Lance   32R-7780206
N59722   Piper PA-31-350 Navajo Chieftain 31-7652002

BEMIDJI AIRLINES

Bemidji (CH/BMJ)   *Bemidji, MN (BJI)*

N55SA   Beech 65-A80 Queen Air   LD-243 ex N794A   Queenaire 8800 conversion
N95LL   Beech 65-A80 Queen Air   LD-235   Queenaire 8800 conversion
N103BA   Beech 65-B80 Queen Air   LD-435 ex N103EE   Queenaire 8800 conversion
N106BA   Beech 65-B80 Queen Air   LD-409 ex N1338T   Queenaire 8800 conversion
N107BA   Beech 65-B80 Queen Air   LD-358 ex N7838L   Queenaire 8800 conversion
N110BA   Beech 65-B80 Queen Air   LD-279 ex N102KK   Queenaire 8800 conversion
N111AR*   Beech 65-B80 Queen Air   LF-68   ex 62-3870
N112AR*   Beech 65-B80 Queen Air   LF-16   ex 60-3586
N131BA   Beech 65-B80 Queen Air   LD-297 ex N1555M   Queenaire 8800 conversion
N132BA*   Beech 65-B80 Queen Air   LD-331 ex C-GRID   Queenaire 8800 conversion
N134BA   Beech 65-A80 Queen Air   LD-202 ex N848S   Queenaire 8800 conversion
N135BA   Beech 65-80 Queen Air   LD-68   ex N29RG   Queenaire 8800 conversion
N777GA   Beech 65-B80 Queen Air   LF-72   ex N777ZA
N778GA   Beech 65-B80 Queen Air   LF-62   ex 62-3864
N5078E*   Beech 65-80 Queen Air   LF-76
N5078N   Beech 65-80 Queen Air   LF-16   ex 60-0347
N5078U   Beech 65-80 Queen Air   LF-32   ex 62-3834
N5079E   Beech 65-80 Queen Air   LF-52   ex 62-3854
N5080L   Beech 65-80 Queen Air   LF-59   ex 62-3861

N70NP*   Beech 99   U-14   ex N914Y
N108BA   Beech 99   U-40   ex C-GQFD
N125DP*   Beech 99   U-12   ex C-GPCE
N130BA   Beech 99A   U-80   ex N51PA   Freighter, no titles
N133BA*   Beech 99   U-142 ex C-GAVV
N137BA   Beech 99   U-137 ex C-GAWW

| N139BA | Beech 99 | U-76 | ex N983MA |
| N7207E | Beech C99 | U-223 | |

N60BA	Beech 65-E90 King Air	LW-79	ex N12AK
N70DD	Beech 58 Baron	TH-370	ex N25660
N204RD	Piper PA-23-250 Aztec C	27-3994	
N4016A	Beech 58 Baron	TH-9	
N6451Y	Piper PA-23-250 Aztec D	27-4230	
N6513Y	Piper PA-23-250 Aztec C	27-3804	
N6881Y	Piper PA-23-250 Aztec D	27-4230	

*Leased from Air Direct Aircraft

BERING AIR

Bering Air (8E/BRG)   Nome, AK (OME)

N205BA	Cessna 208B Caravan I	208B0890	
N806BA	Cessna 208B Caravan I	208B0943	
N1123R	Cessna 208B Caravan I	208B0395	Lsd fr Norton Basin Services
N1128L	Cessna 208B Caravan I	208B0536	
N1263Y	Cessna 208B Caravan I	208B0731	

N141ME	Piper PA-31-350 Chieftain	31-8152117	
N4112D	Piper PA-31-350T-1020	31-8353004	
N4112E	Piper PA-31-350T-1020	31-8353005	
N4118G	Piper PA-31-350T-1020	31-8453001	
N41189	Piper PA-31-350T-1020	31-8553002	
N45052	Piper PA-31-350 Chieftain	31-8152063	

N79CF	Beech 200 Super King Air	BB-441		CatPass 250 conv
N326KW	Beech 200 Super King Air	BB-1360	ex HK-3703X	CatPass 250 conv
N349TA	CASA 212-200	CC60-9-349	ex N316CA	Freighter
N9964M	Cessna 207A Stationair 8	20700766	
N9988M	Cessna 207A Stationair 8	20700776	

BERRY AVIATION

Berry (BYA)   San Marcos-Municipal, TX (HYI)

N227LJ	Swearingen SA.227AC Metro III	AC-522	ex N3109B	Lsd fr Metro-Jet LLC
N373PH	Swearingen SA.227AC Metro III	AC-538	ex N732C	
N589BA	Swearingen SA.227AC Metro III	AC-589	ex (XA-)	
N590BA	Swearingen SA.227AC Metro III	AC-590	ex (XA-)	
N680AX	Swearingen SA.227AC Metro III	AC-680	ex N365AE	
N691AX	Swearingen SA.227AC Metro III	AC-691		
N697AX	Swearingen SA.227AC Metro III	AC-697		
N729C	Swearingen SA.227AC Metro III	AC-571	ex N374PH	
N789C	Swearingen SA.227AC Metro III	AC-540	ex N389PH	
N27442	Swearingen SA.227AC Metro III	AC-750		

N123LH	Swearingen SA.227TT Merlin IIIC	TT-433	ex C-GFCE	Lsd fr North Park Avn
N189GA	Beech 1900C	UB-9	ex N9ZR	
N226BA	Swearingen SA.226TC Metro II	TC-321	ex N105UR	
N323BA	Swearingen SA.226TC Metro II	TC-280	ex N303TL	Freighter
N911HF	Swearingen SA.226TC Metro II	TC-215	ex N62SA	

BIGHORN AIRWAYS

Bighorn Air (BHR) (IATA 405)   Sheridan-County, WY/Casper-Natrona Co, WY (SHR/CPR)

N107BH	CASA C.212-200	CC20-4-165	ex N212TH
N114BH	Cessna 340A	340A1230	ex N6228X
N115BH	Cessna 340A	340A1531	ex N2688Q
N117BH	CASA C.212-200	CC23-1-171	ex N349CA
N118BH	Cessna 340A	340A0003	ex N5168J
N257MC	Dornier 228-202	8102	ex YV-648C
N263MC	Dornier 228-202	8141	ex N116DN
N266MC	Dornier 228-202	8150	ex D-CBDL
N276MC	Dornier 228-202	8109	ex YV-649C
N543CC	Bell 206B JetRanger III	3593	ex N2295W
N700WJ	Cessna 425 Conquest	425-0036	ex F-GCQN
N4091D	Piper PA-31-350 Chieftain	31-8152154	
N6266C	Cessna T210N Turbo Centurion	21063849	
N27956	Piper PA-31-350 Navajo Chieftain	31-7852064	

BIG ISLAND AIR

Big Isle (BIG)   Kailua-Keahole Kona Intl, HI (KOA)

| N281A | Cessna 208 Caravan 1 | 20800271 | ex LV-WYX |

BIG SKY AIRLINES

Big Sky (GQ/BSY) (IATA 387)   Billings-Logan Intl, MT (BIL)

N60NE	Swearingen SA.227AC Metro III	AC-760B	ex N307NE		Lsd fr Patti A Goody
N158MC	Swearingen SA.227AC Metro III	AC-726B			Lsd fr Patti A Goody
N159MC	Swearingen SA.227AC Metro III	AC-728B			Lsd fr Patti A Goody
N160MC	Swearingen SA.227AC Metro III	AC-733B		stored BIL	Lsd fr Patti A Goody
N184SW	Swearingen SA.227AC Metro III	AC-647	ex CX-TAA		Lsd fr EDB Air
N425MA	Swearingen SA.227AC Metro III	AC-640			
N430MA	Swearingen SA.227AC Metro III	AC-710	ex N2710T		Lsd fr Campbell County
N453LA	Swearingen SA.227DC Metro 23	DC-852B	ex EC-GLI		Lsd fr CIT Leasing
N459AM	Swearingen SA.227AC Metro III	AC-700			Lsd fr Finova
N850LS	Swearingen SA.227DC Metro 23	DC-850B	ex N3025B		Lsd fr Gas Wilson
N853LS	Swearingen SA.227DC Metro 23	DC-853B	ex N3025Y		Lsd fr Gas Wilson
N854LS	Swearingen SA.227DC Metro 23	DC-854B	ex N3026R		Lsd fr Gas Wilson
N2728G	Swearingen SA.227AC Metro III	AC-731		Freighter	Lsd to PKW
N27465	Swearingen SA.227AC Metro III	AC-755B			Lsd fr Patti A Goody

Wholly owned by Mesaba Holdings, owner of Mesaba Airlines but operates independently

BIMINI ISLAND AIR

(BMY)   Fort Lauderdale-Executive, FL (FXE)

N46ZP	Cessna 402B	402B1004		
N98EB	Swearingen SA.227AC Metro III	AC-497	ex N110AV	Lsd fr SHO Enterprises
N807MA	Cessna 208B Caravan I	208B0323	ex F-OGUX	Lsd fr Maxfly Avn
N991PH	Cessna 402B	402B1329		Lsd fr JBH Enterprises

BLM AVIATION MANAGEMENT

Boise Air Terminal, ID (BOI)

N91LM	Rockwell OV-10A Bronco	321-137	ex 68-3811	Birddog	
N93LM	Rockwell OV-10A Bronco	305A-23	ex 67-14615	Birddog	
N97LM	Rockwell OV-10A Bronco	305-17	ex 155426	Birddog	
N168LM	Short SD.3-30	SH3104	ex N174Z	Smokejumper	
N188LM	Short SD.3-30	SH3112	ex N172Z	Smokejumper	Lsd fr Avn Services

Division of Bureau of Land Management, controlled by US Department of the Interior

BORINQUEN AIR

San Juan-Munoz Marin Intl, PR (SJU)

N28PR	Douglas DC-3	6323	ex N18916	Freighter
N1019B	Beech E-18S	BA-254		Freighter
N86553	Douglas DC-3	4715	ex 41-18590	Freighter

All leased from Del Caribbean Corp; also trades as Air Puerto Rico

BOSTON-MAINE AIRWAYS

Clipper Express (E9/CXS/NLE)   Portsmouth-Pease Intl, NH (PSM)

N507PA	British Aerospace Jetstream 31	673	ex N307PX	Lsd fr Guilford Transportation
N508PA	British Aerospace Jetstream 31	674	ex N308PX	Lsd fr Guilford Transportation
N509PA	British Aerospace Jetstream 31	675	ex N161PC	Lsd fr Guilford Transportation
N510PA	British Aerospace Jetstream 31	677	ex N162PC	Lsd fr Guilford Transportation
N512PA	British Aerospace Jetstream 31	678	ex N163PC	Lsd fr Guilford Transportation
N514PA	British Aerospace Jetstream 31	682	ex N164PC	Lsd fr Guilford Transportation
N515PA	British Aerospace Jetstream 31	652	ex N300PX	Lsd fr Guilford Transportation
N517PA	British Aerospace Jetstream 31	654	ex N301PX	Lsd fr Guilford Transportation
N518PA	British Aerospace Jetstream 31	658	ex N658MA	Lsd fr Guilford Transportation
N521PA	British Aerospace Jetstream 31	702	ex N332PX	Lsd fr Guilford Transportation
N522PA	British Aerospace Jetstream 31	663	ex N304PX	Lsd fr Guilford Transportation
N525PA	British Aerospace Jetstream 31	666	ex N305PX	Lsd fr Guilford Transportation
N528PA	British Aerospace Jetstream 31	670	ex N306PX	Lsd fr Guilford Transportation
N529PA	British Aerospace Jetstream 31	771	ex N846JS	Lsd fr Guilford Transportation
N530PA	British Aerospace Jetstream 31	732	ex N836JS	Lsd fr Guilford Transportation
N531PA	British Aerospace Jetstream 31	748	ex N839JS	Lsd fr Guilford Transportation
N532PA	British Aerospace Jetstream 31	750	ex N840JS	Lsd fr Guilford Transportation
N534PA	British Aerospace Jetstream 31	731	ex N835JS	Lsd fr Guilford Transportation
N535PA	British Aerospace Jetstream 31	687	ex N316PX	Lsd fr Guilford Transportation
N536PA	British Aerospace Jetstream 31	681	ex N461CE	Lsd fr Guilford Transportation
N537PA	British Aerospace Jetstream 31	684	ex N462CE	Lsd fr Guilford Transportation
N538PA	British Aerospace Jetstream 31	751	ex N841JS	Lsd fr Guilford Transportation
N539PA	British Aerospace Jetstream 31	741	ex N838JS	Lsd fr Guilford Transportation

Operates feeder services for Pan American as Pan Am Clipper Connection in full colours and using PA flight numbers

BOWMAN AVIATION

Bowman (BMN)   Fort Wayne-Smith Field, IN (FWA)

N25SC	Cessna 414A Chancellor II	414A0114		Lsd fr Abby A/c Lsg
N3284M	Cessna 310R	310R1892		Lsd fr Lan A/c Lsg
N5033J	Cessna 310R	310R0153		Lsd fr Carma Leasing
N5119J	Cessna 310R	310R0996		Lsd fr Rock Island Contractors
N6787V	Cessna 402C	402C0421		
N37167	Cessna 404A Titan II	404-0129		
N87403	Cessna 310R	310R0547		Lsd fr M&K Investments

BROOKS FUEL

Fairbanks-Intl, AK (FAI)

N898AT	Aviation Traders ATL.98A Carvair	20/42994	ex C-GAAH	on overhaul
N44911	Douglas C-54S	10461	ex Bu50857	Fuel Tanker

BUSINESS AIR CHARTER ceased operations

BUSINESS AVIATION COURIER

Dakota (DKT)   Sioux Falls-Joe Foss Field, SD (FSD)

N76MD	Cessna 402B	402B1055		
N402BP	Cessna 402B	402B0353		
N402SS	Cessna 402B	402B0562		
N624CA	Cessna 402B	402B0876		
N780MB	Cessna 402B	402B0249		
N1048	Cessna 402B	402B0628		
N3729C	Cessna 402B	402B0589		
N3796C	Cessna 402B	402B0803		
N3813	Cessna 402B	402B0807		
N366AE	Swearingen SA.227AC Metro III	AC-681B		Lsd fr Daedalus
N371PH	Swearingen SA.227AC Metro III	AC-576	ex N3119W	Lsd fr GAS Wilson
N387PH	Swearingen SA.227AC Metro III	AC-531	ex N31094	Lsd fr GAS Wilson
N620PA	Swearingen SA.227AC Metro III	AC-533	ex N3110H	Lsd fr Career Avn
N685BA	Swearingen SA.227AC Metro III	AC-685	ex N685AV	Lsd fr Daedalus
N3108B	Swearingen SA.227AC Metro III	AC-509	ex XA-TAK	Lsd fr GAS Wilson
N3116N	Swearingen SA.227AC Metro III	AC-596		
N80BS	Cessna 404	404-0048		
N500FS	Cessna 310R	310R0630		
N1324G	Cessna 208B Caravan I	208B0777		Lsd fr Atlantic Aero
N1533T	Cessna 310R	310R0111		
N1761G	Cessna 310R	310R0630		
N3482G	Cessna 310R	310R0850		

All other aircraft leased from Daedalus Inc, the parent company. All are freighters

BUTLER AIRCRAFT

Redmond, OR (RDM)

N401US	Douglas DC-7	767/45145	ex N6331C	62 Tanker
N531BA	Lockheed C-130A Hercules	3139	ex 56-0531	67 Tanker
N6353C	Douglas DC-7	964/45486		66 Tanker
N60018	Cessna TU206F Turbo Stationair	U20602002		

C&M AIRWAYS

Red Wing (RWG)   El Paso-Intl, TX (ELP)

N640CM	Convair 640	104	ex C-GCWY
N640R	Convair 640	332	ex PH-MAL
N3410	Convair 640	27	
N3417	Convair 640	48	
N3420	Convair 640	64	
N5515K	Convair 640	133	ex PH-CGM
N73137	Convair 640	88	
N563PC	Douglas DC-9-15RC (ABS 3)	194/47055	ex N1305T

All aircraft leased from Century Airlines (a leasing company, not an operator)

CAPE AIR

Cair (9K/KAP) (IATA 306)   Hyannis-Barnstaple Municipal, MA/Naples-Municipal, FL (HYA/APF)

N69SC	Cessna 402C	402C0041		
N83PB	Cessna 402C	402C0350	ex N26627	Lsd fr Hyannis Air Lsg

N106CA	Cessna 402C	402C1020	ex TJ-AHO	
N120PC	Cessna 402C	402C0079		Lsd fr Hyannis Air Lsg
N121PB	Cessna 402C	402C0507	ex N6874X	Lsd fr Hyannis Air Lsg
N161TA	Cessna 402C	402C0070		
N223PB	Cessna 402C	402C0105	ex N2615T	
N401TJ	Cessna 402C	402C0109		
N402VN	Cessna 402C	402C0488	ex (N6840D)	
N406GA	Cessna 402C	402C0329	ex N2642D	
N514NC	Cessna 402C	402C0514		
N524CA	Cessna 402C	402C0522	ex C-GSKG	
N548GA	Cessna 402C	402C0653		
N618CA	Cessna 402C	402C0620	ex VH-RGK	
N660CA	Cessna 402C	402C0406		
N760EA	Cessna 402C	402C0056	ex PZ-TAE	
N762EA	Cessna 402C	402C0061	ex N5872C	
N763EA	Cessna 402C	402C0497	ex N763AN	
N764EA	Cessna 402C	402C0237	ex N2719T	
N769EA	Cessna 402C	402C0303	ex N3283M	
N770CA	Cessna 402C	402C0432	ex C-GIBL	
N771EA	Cessna 402C	402C0046	ex N5809C	
N780EA	Cessna 402C	402C0257	ex N821AN	
N781EA	Cessna 402C	402C0310	ex N822AN	
N812AN	Cessna 402C	402C0229	ex N2718P	
N818AN	Cessna 402C	402C0501	ex N6842Q	
N991AA	Cessna 402C	402C0317	ex N36916	Lsd fr Ocean Air
N1361G	Cessna 402C	402C0270		
N1376G	Cessna 402C	402C0271		Lsd fr Hyannis Air Lsg
N2611X	Cessna 402C	402C0072		
N2615G	Cessna 402C	402C0101		
N2714B	Cessna 402C	402C0210		
N2714M	Cessna 402C	402C0211		
N4652N	Cessna 402C	402C0011		
N6813J	Cessna 402C	402C0641		
N6837Y	Cessna 402C	402C0467		Lsd fr Hyannis Air Lsg
N6875D	Cessna 402C	402C0511		
N6879R	Cessna 402C	402C0611		
N7037E	Cessna 402C	402C0471	ex C-GGXH	
N26514	Cessna 402C	402C0344		
N26632	Cessna 402C	402C0404		
N36911	Cessna 402C	402C0314		
N67786	Cessna 402C	402C0631		
N67886	Cessna 402C	402C0435		
N68391	Cessna 402C	402C0483		
N68752	Cessna 402C	402C0518		
N88833	Cessna 402C	402C0265		

Cape Air is a trading name of Hyannis Air Services; also trades as Nantucket Airlines and Key West Express

CAPE SMYTHE AIR SERVICE

Cape Smythe Air (6C/CMY)   Barrow-Wiley Post (Will Rogers Memorial), AK (BRW)

N207DH	Cessna 207 Skywagon	20700345	ex N1745U	
N6295H	Cessna 207A Stationair 7	20700471		
N7396U	Cessna 207A Stationair 7	20700438		
N9620M	Cessna 207A Stationair 7	20700711		
N9641M	Cessna 207A Stationair 7	20700714		
N9950M	Cessna 207A Stationair 7	20700760		
N73100	Cessna 207A Stationair 7	20700559		

N22VF	Piper PA-31T2 Cheyenne IIXL	31T-8166018	ex N5UB	
N137CS	Piper PA-31-350 Chieftain	31-8152137	ex C-GVPP	Lsd fr US Bancorp
N207CS	Beech C99	U-207	ex C-GGLE	
N217CS	Piper PA-31T3-T1040	31T-8275014	ex C-FYPL	
N223CS	Piper PA-31T3-T1040	31T-8275008	ex N315CS	Lsd fr US Bancorp
N995SB	Beech C99	U-179	ex (N998SB)	
N3535F	Piper PA-31-350 Navajo Chieftain	31-7952200		
N4585U	Piper PA-31-350 Chieftain	31-8052198	ex C-GPIJ	
N20752	Cessna A185F Skywagon	18503041		

CAPITAL CARGO INTERNATIONAL AIRLINES

Cappy (PT/CCI)   Orlando-Intl, FL (MCO)

N227JL	Boeing 727-214F (FedEx 3)	1020/20875	ex N375PA	Angie; stored
N286SC	Boeing 727-2A1F (FedEx 3)	1694/21601	ex N328AS	Lsd fr Avn Capital Group
N287SC	Boeing 727-2A1F (FedEx 3)	1673/21345	ex N327AS	Lsd fr ACG Acquisition
N308AS	Boeing 727-227F (FedEx 3)	1627/22002	ex N479BN	
N357KP	Boeing 727-230F (FedEx 3)	924/20675	ex G-BPNY	Princess Kendall
N708AA	Boeing 727-223F (FedEx 3)	1761/22465		Lsd fr Avn Capital Group
N713AA	Boeing 727-223F (FedEx 3)	1769/22469		Lsd fr ACG Acquisition
N715AA	Boeing 727-223F (FedEx 3)	1771/22470		Lsd fr ACG Acquisition

N808EA	Boeing 727-225F(FedEx 3)	1689/22439	ex TC-DEL		Lsd fr IAL
N898AA	Boeing 727-223F (FedEx 3)	1663/22014		Roberta	Lsd fr ACG Acquisition
N899AA	Boeing 727-223F (FedEx 3)	1666/22015		Barbara	Lsd fr ACG Acquisition
N89427	Boeing 727-227F (FedEx 3)	1273/21365	ex N323AS		

CAPITAL CITY AIR CARRIER

Cap City (CCQ)   *Pierre-Regional, SD (PIR)*

N13PB	Piper PA-34-200T Seneca II	34-7870003	
N6597F	Piper PA-34-200T Seneca II	34-7770032	
N8017C	Piper PA-34-220T Seneca III	34-8133200	
N8180G	Piper PA-34-200T Seneca II	34-8070174	
N9638K	Piper PA-34-200T Seneca II	34-7670212	
N36369	Piper PA-34-200T Seneca II	34-7870323	
N300VF	Piper PA-31-350 Navajo Chieftain	31-7852050	
N305SK	Piper PA-31-350 Navajo Chieftain	31-7652039	
N400RA	Piper PA-31-350 Navajo Chieftain	31-7405167	ex N22AE
N777ZM	Piper PA-31-350 Chieftain	31-8052193	
N984PA	Piper PA-31-350 Navajo Chieftain	31-7305104	
N27537	Piper PA-31-350 Navajo Chieftain	31-7852053	
N126BP	Cessna 414A Chancellor	414A0214	
N402RM	Cessna 402B	402B0607	
N8745E	Piper PA-32-300 Cherokee Six	32-7640073	
N75156	Piper PA-32R-300 Lance	32R-7680272	

All aircraft leased from Aircraft International

CARIB-AIR CARGO ceased operations

CARIBBEAN AIR SERVICES current status is uncertain

CARIBBEAN SUN AIRLINES

(ZQ/SFG) IATA 521   *San Juan-Munos Marin Intl, PR (SJU)*

C-FABN	de Havilland DHC-8-102	044			
C-GTBP	de Havilland DHC-8-102	066			
N803WP	de Havilland DHC-8-102	141	ex C-FDNE		
	de Havilland DHC-8-106	351	ex V2-LFN	on order	Lsd fr Bombardier Capital
	de Havilland DHC-8-103	277	ex N880CC		
	de Havilland DHC-8-102A	294	ex N881CC		Lsd fr TIC Trust

Sister company of Caribbean Star Airways

CARSON HELICOPTERS

Perkasie-Heliport, PA/Jackonsville Heliport, OR

N116AZ	Sikorsky S-61N	61242	ex VH-BHO	
N612RM	Sikorsky S-61N	61744	ex C-FSYH	
N3173U	Sikorsky S-61A	61186		
N4263A	Sikorsky S-61R	61551	ex 65-5700	
N4263F	Sikorsky S-61R	61533		
N4503E	Sikorsky S-61N	61220	ex G-ASNL	
N7011M	Sikorsky S-61N	61216	ex G-AWFX	
N8167B	Sikorsky S-61A	61137		
N8174J	Sikorsky S-61R	61584		stored
N9260A	Sikorsky S-61D	61442	ex Bu156496	
N9271A	Sikorsky S-61D	61449	ex Bu156486	
N13491	Sikorsky S-61A	61129		
N42626	Sikorsky S-61R	61522		
N81661	Sikorsky S-61A	61272		
N81692	Sikorsky S-61A	61074		
N81697	Sikorsky S-61A	61147		
N81701	Sikorsky S-61R	61529		stored
N81702	Sikorsky S-61R	61608		stored
N81743	Sikorsky S-61R	61575		
N82702	Sikorsky S-61D	61432	ex N92592	
N92590	Sikorsky S-61D	61351	ex Bu152691	
N239Z	de Havilland DHC-6 Twin Otter 300	239	ex N15239	
N920R	de Havilland DHC-6 Twin Otter 100	45	ex HC-BYK	

CASCADE AIR

Ephrata-Municipal, WA (EPH)

N272R	Douglas DC-3	13678	ex N88824	Lsd fr Kestrel Inc
N60154	Douglas DC-3	16007		
N91314	Douglas DC-3	4538	ex NC17884	Lsd fr Comanche Air

CASINO AIRLINES

Casair (CSO)

Santa Maria-Public, CA (SMX)

N650JX	British Aerospace Jetstream 31	650	ex N405AE	
N653JX	British Aerospace Jetstream 31	653	ex N407AE	
Joint operations with Pacific Skyway				

CASINO EXPRESS

Casino Express (XP/CXP)

Elko-JC Harris Field, NV (EKO)

N222TM	Boeing 737-2K9 (AVA 3)	1176/23404	ex PR-ACT		Lsd fr Boeing Capital
N233TM*	Boeing 737-282 (AVA 3)	972/23043	ex CS-TEM		
N344TM	Boeing 737-282 (AVA 3)	973/23044	ex CS-TEN	Red Lion-1	Lsd fr McClaskey Avn
N789TM	Boeing 737-282 (AVA 3)	981/23046	ex CS-TEP		
*Subleased to Air Laughlin					

CASTLE AVIATION

Castle (CSJ)

Akron-Canton Regional, OH (CAK)

N24MG	Cessna 208B Caravan I	208B0850		Freighter	
N27MG	Cessna 208B Caravan I	208B0650		Freighter	
N28MG	Cessna 208B Caravan I	208B0732		Freighter	
N29MG	Cessna 208B Caravan I	208B0812	ex N52229	Freighter	
N35WT	Piper PA-31 Turbo Navajo B	31-817	ex D-IFLG	Freighter	
N52MG	Ted Smith Aerostar 600A	60-0530-172	ex N8047J		
N25677	Swearingen SA.226T Merlin IIIA	T-254	ex N58018		Lsd fr Kolar Avn
Operates some freight services for Purolator Couriers					

CATALINA FLYING BOATS

Catalina Air (CBT)

Long Beach-Daugherty Field, CA (LGB)

N18R	Beech E-18S	BA-312		Lsd fr Phoenix Air Tpt
N62TP	Beech E-18S	BA-45		Lsd fr Phoenix Air Tpt
N103AF	Beech G-18S	BA-526	ex N277S	Lsd fr Phoenix Air Tpt
N335WB	Piper PA-31-350 Navajo Chieftain	31-7952135	ex N35268	
N403JB	Douglas DC-3	16943/34202	ex N17778	
N2298C	Douglas DC-3	16453/33201	ex (N352SA)	
N9375Y	Beech G-18S	BA-584		Lsd fr Phoenix Air Tpt
All freighters				

CDF AVIATION – CALIFORNIA DEPT OF FORESTRY AND FIRE PROTECTION

Sacramento-Mather, CA (MHR)

N481DF	Bell UH-1H	13318	ex 72-21019	104
N489DF	Bell UH-1H	12224	ex 69-15936	
N490DF	Bell UH-1H	12375	ex 70-15765	205
N491DF	Bell UH-1H	12146	ex 69-15858	301
N492DF	Bell UH-1H	11433	ex 69-15145	
N493DF	Bell UH-1H	12001	ex 69-15713	
N494DF	Bell UH-1H	11303	ex 69-15015	404
N495DF	Bell UH-1H	12218	ex 69-15930	106
N496DF	Bell UH-1H	11964	ex 69-15676	102
N497DF	Bell UH-1H	11553	ex 69-15265	202
N498DF	Bell UH-1H	12153	ex 69-15865	406
N499DF	Bell UH-1H	12846	ex 72-20022	101
N404DF	Grumman S-2A Tracker	455	ex Bu136546	80
N406DF	Grumman S-2A Tracker	293	ex Bu133322	73
N411DF	Grumman S-2A Tracker	476	ex Bu136567	74
N412DF	Grumman S-2A Tracker	222	ex Bu133251	78
N417DF	Grumman S-2A Tracker	061	ex Bu133090	76
N420DF	Grumman S-2A Tracker	388	ex Bu136479	75
N436DF	Grumman S-2A Tracker	445	ex Bu136536	100
N443DF	Grumman S-2A Tracker	195	ex Bu133224	72
N446DF	Grumman S-2A Tracker	175	ex Bu133204	94
N447DF	Grumman S-2A Tracker	417	ex Bu136508	81
N453DF	Grumman S-2A Tracker	572	ex Bu136663	86
N422DF	Marsh S-2T Turbo Tracker	0341/017	ex Bu 152817	82
N424DF	Marsh S-2T Turbo Tracker	0341/024	ex Bu152820	83
N425DF	Marsh S-2T Turbo Tracker		ex Bu152825	89
N426DF	Marsh S-2T Turbo Tracker	0341/028	ex Bu152824	88
N427DF	Marsh S-2T Turbo Tracker	0382/011	ex Bu153570	70
N428DF	Marsh S-2T Turbo Tracker	0865/018	ex Bu149862	91
N431DF	Marsh S-2T Turbo Tracker		ex Bu149265	

N432DF	Marsh S-2T Turbo Tracker			ex Bu149268	71
N433DF	Marsh S-2T Turbo Tracker	0865/011			
N434DF	Marsh S-2T Turbo Tracker	0382/034			90
N435DF	Marsh S-2T Turbo Tracker	0382/029			72
N437DF	Marsh S-2T Turbo Tracker	0865/004			73
N438DF	Marsh S-2T Turbo Tracker	0229/003			
N439DF	Marsh S-2T Turbo Tracker	0865/010			74
N440DF	Marsh S-2T Turbo Tracker			ex Bu149873	
N441DF	Marsh S-2T Turbo Tracker			ex Bu152808	71
N445DF	Marsh S-2T Turbo Tracker			ex Bu152345	
N449DF	Marsh S-2T Turbo Tracker			ex Bu152838	
N400DF	Rockwell OV-10A Bronco	305A-65		ex Bu155454	440
N401DF	Rockwell OV-10A Bronco	305A-68		ex Bu155457	310
N402DF	Rockwell OV-10A Bronco	305A-70		ex Bu155459	210
N403DF	Rockwell OV-10A Bronco	305A-78		ex Bu155467	240
N407DF	Rockwell OV-10A Bronco	305A-86		ex Bu155475	430
N408DF	Rockwell OV-10A Bronco	305A-91		ex Bu155480	230
N409DF	Rockwell OV-10A Bronco	305A-11		ex Bu155401	330
N410DF	Rockwell OV-10A Bronco	305A-82		ex Bu155471	110
N413DF	Rockwell OV-10A Bronco	305A-13		ex Bu155402	120
N414DF	Rockwell OV-10A Bronco	305A-16		ex Bu155415	140
N415DF	Rockwell OV-10A Bronco	305A-38		ex Bu155427	460
N418DF	Rockwell OV-10A Bronco	305A-39		ex Bu155428	340
N419DF	Rockwell OV-10A Bronco	305A-56		ex Bu155445	410
N421DF	Rockwell OV-10A Bronco	305A-107			
N429DF	Rockwell OV-10A Bronco			ex Bu155400	
N430DF	Rockwell OV-10A Bronco	305A-60		ex Bu155449	

CENTRAL AIR SOUTHWEST

Central Commuter (CTL) — Kansas City-Downtown, KS/Cushing-Municipal, OK (MKC/CUH)

N23BQ	Aero Commander 500B	1065-46	
N30MB	Aero Commander 500B	1453-160	ex N6376U
N107DF	Aero Commander 500B	1191-97	ex N88PC
N127KH	Aero Commander 500B	1027-38	ex N801TC
N159BM	Aero Commander 500B	1523-185	ex N1159Z
N272CA	Aero Commander 500B	1409-146	
N304JT	Aero Commander 500B	1494-175	ex N222AV
N315TG	Aero Commander 500B	1460-163	ex N9260N
N324RR	Aero Commander 500B	1386-139	ex N471A
N411ET	Aero Commander 500B	1621-214	ex N445CA
N411JF	Aero Commander 500B	1014-35	ex N6178X
N411JT	Shrike Commander 500S	3097	ex N9134N
N411PT	Aero Commander 500B	1207-99	ex N291CA
N415BH	Aero Commander 500B	918-5	ex N6129X
N444CA	Aero Commander 500B	1458-162	ex N6326U
N477CC	Aero Commander 500B	1480-172	ex N477CA
N516DT	Aero Commander 500B	1574-200	ex N134X
N524HW	Aero Commander 500B	1533-191	ex N324MA
N553RA	Aero Commander 500B	1315-124	ex N153K
N607MM	Aero Commander 500U	1712-25	
N615MT	Aero Commander 500B	911-2	ex N193CA
N630KC	Aero Commander 500B	997-28	
N662MW	Aero Commander 500B	1235-106	ex N106CA
N667CA	Aero Commander 500B	1468-166	ex C-FRJU
N712AT	Aero Commander 500B	1118-68	ex N6213X
N716TC	Aero Commander 500B	1225-102	ex N192CA
N724LH	Aero Commander 500B	1613-211	ex N13M
N777CM	Aero Commander 500B	1412-147	ex N120BL
N780SP	Aero Commander 500B	1362-133	ex N510SP
N888CA	Aero Commander 500B	1318-127	ex N621RM
N917GT	Aero Commander 500B	1137-77	ex N177CA
N922BS	Aero Commander 500B	1598-207	ex N1193Z
N1153C	Aero Commander 500B	1474-169	
All freighters			
N690AT	Rockwell Commander 690A	11202	ex N600PB

CENTURION AIR CARGO

Centurion Cargo (WE/CWC) — Miami-Intl, FL (MIA)

N140WE	Douglas DC-10-40F	212/46920	ex N157DM	Lsd fr Air-Lease Intl
N142WE	Douglas DC-10-40F	262/46966	ex JA8536	no titles	Lsd fr Air Lease Intl

CHALKS OCEAN AIRWAYS

Chalks (OP/CHK)   Miami-Watson Island, FL (MPB)

N130FB	Grumman G-73 Turbo Mallard	J-30	ex N135PA
N142PA	Grumman G-73 Turbo Mallard	J-42	ex N51151
N1208	Grumman G-73 Turbo Mallard	J-44	ex N2977
N2969	Grumman G-73 Turbo Mallard	J-27	ex (N200SZ)
N2974	Grumman G-73 Turbo Mallard	J-36	

All leased from Seaplane Leasing

CHAMPION AIR

Champion Air (MG/CCP)   MinneapolisSt Paul Intl, MN/Los Angeles-Intl, CA (MSP/LAX)

N292AS	Boeing 727-212	1327/21458	ex HK-4047		Lsd fr CIT Leasing
N293AS	Boeing 727-212	1287/21348	ex N26729		Lsd fr CIT Leasing
N294AS	Boeing 727-290	1621/22146	ex PP-OPR		Lsd fr CIT Leasing
N295AS*	Boeing 727-290	1623/22147			Lsd fr CIT Leasing
N681CA	Boeing 727-2S7	1592/22020	ex N712RC		Lsd fr Pegasus
N682CA	Boeing 727-2S7	1584/22019	ex N715RC		Lsd fr Pegasus
N683CA	Boeing 727-2S7	1721/22490	ex N719RC		Lsd fr NWA
N684CA	Boeing 727-2S7	1726/22491	ex N720RC		Lsd fr NWA
N685CA	Boeing 727-2S7	1729/22492	ex N721RC		Lsd fr NWA
N686CA	Boeing 727-2S7	1617/22021	ex N716RC	stored OKC	Lsd fr NWA
N688CA	Boeing 727-2S7	1654/22344	ex N718RC		Lsd fr NWA
N696CA	Boeing 727-2J4	1733/22574	ex C-GRYQ		Lsd fr Finova
N697CA	Boeing 727-270	1817/23052	ex OY-SBI		Lsd fr Finova
N8877Z	Boeing 727-225	1308/21450		stored OKC	Lsd fr GECAS

*Named 1st Lt. Joseph Page Jr.;   All fitted with FedEx Stage 3 hushkits
Champion Air is the trading name of Grand Holdings

CHAMPLAIN AIR

                                                         Plattsburg-Clinton County, NY (PLB)

N59NA	Douglas DC-3	9043	ex G-AKNB	
N122CA	Douglas DC-3	4827	ex N32PB	stored PLB
N700CA	Douglas DC-3	12438	ex N107AD	Mary Lou
N922CA	Douglas DC-3	2204	ex N34PB	

CHANNEL ISLANDS AVIATION

Channel (CHN)   Camarillo, CA (CMA)

N55JA	Britten-Norman BN-2A-8 Islander	295	ex G-51-295	
N599MT	Britten-Norman BN-2A-8 Islander	427	ex XA-CAZ	
N2722D	Cessna 441 Conquest II	441-0168		
N2727L	Cessna 414A Chancellor III	414A0602		Lsd fr JBL Charter
N6844D	Cessna 425 Conquest	425-0062		
N60078	Beech 76 Duchess	ME-139		

CHARLIE HAMMONDS FLYING SERVICE now listed under trading name, Hammonds Flying Service

CHARTER SERVICES believed to be a leasing company

CHAUTAUQUA AIRLINES

Chautauqua (RP/CHQ)   Indianapolis-Intl, IN (IND)

N831RP	Embraer EMB.135LR	145663	ex PT-SEX	Delta Connection	
N832RP	Embraer EMB.135LR	145676	ex PT-SFJ	Delta Connection	
N833RP	Embraer EMB.135LR	145687	ex PT-SFT	Delta Connection	Lsd fr Solitair
N834RP	Embraer EMB.135LR	145696	ex PT-SGB	Delta Connection	
N835RP	Embraer EMB.135LR	145702	ex PT-SGG	Delta Connection	
N836RP	Embraer EMB.135LR	145713	ex PT-SGQ	Delta Connection	
N837RP	Embraer EMB.135LR	145715	ex PT-SGS	Delta Connection	
N838RP	Embraer EMB.135LR	145720	ex PT-SGW	Delta Connection	
N839RP	Embraer EMB.135LR	145724	ex PT-SHA	Delta Connection	
N840RP	Embraer EMB.135LR	145725	ex PT-SHB	Delta Connection	
N841RP	Embraer EMB.135LR	145737	ex PT-SHQ	Delta Connection	
N842RP	Embraer EMB.135LR	145661	ex PT-SEV	Delta Connection	
N843RP	Embraer EMB.135LR	145599	ex PT-SAO	Delta Connection	
N844RP	Embraer EMB.135LR	145725	ex PT-SDI	Delta Connection	
N845RP	Embraer EMB.135LR	145551	ex PT-SZN	Delta Connection	
N295SK	Embraer EMB.135KL	145513	ex PT-SYF	American Connection	Lsd fr Solitair
N297SK	Embraer EMB.135KL	145522	ex PT-SYN	American Connection	Lsd fr Solitair
N299SK	Embraer EMB.135KL	145532	ex PT-STW	American Connection	Lsd fr Solitair
N371SK	Embraer EMB.135KL	145535	ex PT-STZ	American Connection	Lsd fr Solitair

N372SK	Embraer EMB.135KL	145538	ex PT-SZC	American Connection	Lsd fr Solitair
N373SK	Embraer EMB.135KL	145543	ex PT-SZG	American Connection	Lsd fr Solitair
N374SK	Embraer EMB.135KL	145544	ex PT-SZH	American Connection	Lsd fr Solitair
N375SK	Embraer EMB.135KL	145569	ex PT-SBF	American Connection	Lsd fr Solitair
N376SK	Embraer EMB.135KL	145578	ex PT-SBO	American Connection	
N377SK	Embraer EMB.135KL	145579	ex PT-SBP	American Connection	
N378SK	Embraer EMB.135KL	145593	ex PT-SCB	American Connection	
N379SK	Embraer EMB.135KL	145606	ex PT-SCP	American Connection	Lsd fr Solitair
N380SK	Embraer EMB.135KL	145613	ex PT-SCX	American Connection	
N381SK	Embraer EMB.135KL	145619	ex PT-SDH	American Connection	
N382SK	Embraer EMB.135KL	145624	ex PT-SDM	American Connection	
N258JQ	Embraer EMB.145LR	145768	ex PT-SJZ	USA Express	Lsd fr WFBN
N259JQ	Embraer EMB.145LR	145763	ex PT-SJU	JBH; USA Express	Lsd fr WFBN
N260SK	Embraer EMB.145LR	145128	ex PT-SDF	US Airways Express	Lsd fr ICX Corp
N261SK	Embraer EMB.145LR	145144	ex PT-SDU	US Airways Express	Lsd fr Solitair
N262SK	Embraer EMB.145LR	145168	ex PT-S	US Airways Express	Lsd fr Solitair
N263SK	Embraer EMB.145LR	145199	ex PT-SGP	US Airways Express	Lsd fr FINOVA
N264SK	Embraer EMB.145LR	145221	ex PT-SHG	US Airways Express	Lsd fr FINOVA
N265SK	Embraer EMB.145LR	145226	ex PT-SHL	US Airways Express	Lsd fr Solitair
N266SK	Embraer EMB.145LR	145241	ex PT-SIG	US Airways Express	Lsd fr Solitair
N267SK	Embraer EMB.145LR	145268	ex PT-SJK	US Airways Express	Lsd fr Solitair
N268SK	Embraer EMB.145LR	145270	ex PT-SJM	US Airways Express	Lsd fr Solitair
N269SK	Embraer EMB.145LR	145293	ex PT-SKK	Delta Connection	Lsd fr Solitair
N270SK	Embraer EMB.145LR	145304	ex PT-SKV	Delta Connection	Lsd fr Solitair
N271SK	Embraer EMB.145LR	145305	ex PT-SKW	Delta Connection	Lsd fr Solitair
N272SK	Embraer EMB.145LR	145306	ex PT-SKX	Delta Connection	Lsd fr Solitair
N273SK	Embraer EMB.145LR	145331	ex PT-SMX	Delta Connection	Lsd fr Solitair
N274SK	Embraer EMB.145LR	145344	ex PT-SNK	Delta Connection	Lsd fr Solitair
N275SK	Embraer EMB.145LR	145345	ex PT-SNL	US Airways Express	Lsd fr Solitair
N276SK	Embraer EMB.145LR	145348	ex PT-SNO	Delta Connection	Lsd fr Solitair
N277SK	Embraer EMB.145LR	145355	ex PT-SNU	US Airways Express	Lsd fr Solitair
N278SK	Embraer EMB.145LR	145370	ex PT-SOV	US Airways Express	Lsd fr Solitair
N279SK	Embraer EMB.145LR	145379	ex PT-SQD	US Airways Express	Lsd fr Solitair
N280SK	Embraer EMB.145LR	145381	ex PT-SQF	US Airways Express	Lsd fr Solitair
N281SK	Embraer EMB.145LR	145391	ex PT-SQP	US Airways Express	Lsd fr Solitair
N282SK	Embraer EMB.145LR	145409	ex PT-STG	US Airways Express	
N283SK	Embraer EMB.145LR	145424	ex PT-STV	US Airways Express	Lsd fr Solitair
N284SK	Embraer EMB.145LR	145427	ex PT-STY	US Airways Express	
N285SK	Embraer EMB.145LR	145435	ex PT-SUG	US Airways Express	Lsd fr Solitair
N286SK	Embraer EMB.145LR	145443	ex PT-SUO	US Airways Express	Lsd fr Solitair
N287SK	Embraer EMB.145LR	145460	ex PT-SVF	US Airways Express	Lsd fr Solitair
N288SK	Embraer EMB.145LR	145461	ex PT-SVG	US Airways Express	Lsd fr Solitair
N289SK	Embraer EMB.145LR	145463	ex PT-SVI	US Airways Express	Lsd fr Solitair
N290SK	Embraer EMB.145LR	145474	ex PT-SVT	Delta Connection	Lsd fr Solitair
N291SK	Embraer EMB.145LR	145486	ex PT-SXF	US Airways Express	Lsd fr Solitair
N292SK	Embraer EMB.145LR	145488	ex PT-SXH	Delta Connection	Lsd fr Solitair
N293SK	Embraer EMB.145LR	145500	ex PT-SXT	US Airways Express	Lsd fr Solitair
N294SK	Embraer EMB.145LR	145497	ex PT-SXQ	Delta Connection	Lsd fr Solitair
N296SK	Embraer EMB.145LR	145514	ex PT-SYG	Delta Connection	Lsd fr Solitair
N298SK	Embraer EMB.145LR	145508	ex PT-SYA	US Airways Express	Lsd fr Solitair
N370SK	Embraer EMB.145LR	145515	ex PT-SYH	Chautauqua	Lsd fr Solitair
N561RP	Embraer EMB.145LR	145447	ex PT-S	Delta Connection	Lsd fr Mitsui
N562RP	Embraer EMB.145LR	145451	ex PT-SUW	Delta Connection	Lsd fr Mitsui
N563RP	Embraer EMB.145LR	145509	ex PT-SYB	Delta Connection	
N564RP	Embraer EMB.145LR	145524	ex PT-SYP	Delta Connection	
N565RP	Embraer EMB.145LR	145679	ex PT-SFL	Delta Connection	
N566RP	Embraer EMB.145LR	145691	ex PT-S	Delta Connection	
N567RP	Embraer EMB.145LR	145698	ex PT-S	Delta Connection	
N971RP	Embraer EMB.145LR	145426	ex SX-BLO	US Airways Express	
N972RP	Embraer EMB.145LR	145440	ex SX-BLP	US Airways Express	
N973RP	Embraer EMB.145LR	145444	ex SX-BLR	US Airways Express	
N974RP	Embraer EMB.145MP	145203	ex OE-LSR	US Airways Express	Lsd fr WFBN
N975RP	Embraer EMB.145MP	145337	ex OE-LSP		Lsd fr WFBN
N976RP	Embraer EMB.145MP	145322	ex OE-LSM		Lsd fr WFBN
N	Embraer EMB.145LR		ex PT-	on order 04	
N	Embraer EMB.145LR		ex PT-	on order 04	
N	Embraer EMB.145LR		ex PT-	on order 04	
N	Embraer EMB.145LR		ex PT-	on order 04	
N	Embraer EMB.145LR		ex PT-	on order 04	
N	Embraer EMB.145LR		ex PT-	on order 04	
N	Embraer EMB.145LR		ex PT-	on order 04	
N	Embraer EMB.145LR		ex PT-	on order 04	
N	Embraer EMB.145LR		ex PT-	on order 04	
N	Embraer EMB.145LR		ex PT-	on order 04	
N	Embraer EMB.145LR		ex PT-	on order 04	
N95CQ	SAAB SF.340A	095	ex N95MQ	Lsd fr SAAB; sublsd to TCF	
N104CQ	SAAB SF.340A	104	ex N344BE	Lsd fr Fairbrook Lsg; sublsd to TCF	
N108CQ	SAAB SF.340A	108	ex N345BE	Lsd fr Fairbrook Lsg; sublsd to TCF	
N140CQ	SAAB SF.340A	140	ex N140N	Lsd fr Fairbrook Lsg; sublsd to TCF	
N150CN	SAAB SF.340A	150	ex N346BE	Lsd fr Fairbrook Lsg; sublsd to TCF	

| N152CQ | SAAB SF.340A | 152 | ex N749BA | Lsd fr Fairbrook Lsg; sublsd to TCF |
| N340SF | SAAB SF.340A | 014 | ex SE-E14 | Lsd fr Fairbrook Lsg; sublsd to TCF |

Chautauqua operates as US Airways Express using flight numbers in the range 4750-4999. Also operates as American Connection from Knoxville, TN and Lincoln, NE, Delta Connection from Orlando, FL and Columbus, OH

CHERRY-AIR

Cherry (CCY)   Dallas-Addison, TX (ADS)

N207CA	AMD Falcon 20C	153	ex N70MD	
N216CA	AMD Falcon 20C	11	ex N983AJ	
N218CA	AMD Falcon 20DC	218	ex EC-EEU	
N219CA	AMD Falcon 20D	193	ex 9Q-CTT	
N220CA	AMD Falcon 20DC	220	ex EC-EDL	
N234CA	AMD Falcon 20C	17	ex N55TH	
N235CA	AMD Falcon 20C	139	ex N900WB	
N140CA*	Lear Jet 25	25B-140	ex N403AC	
N151WW	Lear Jet 24	24-170	ex N200DH	Lsd fr Addison Avn Svs
N213CA*	Lear Jet 25D	25D-241	ex N713LJ	
N233CA*	Lear Jet 25B	25B-133	ex XA-RZY	
N236CA*	Lear Jet 25B	25B-161	ex N61EW	
N238CA*	Lear Jet 25	25-040	ex N23FN	
N239CA*	Lear Jet 25B	25B-149	ex N149J	
N273CA*	Lear Jet 25	25-039	ex N308AJ	
N343CA	Lear Jet 25B	25B-202	ex YU-BRA	
N344CA	Lear Jet 25B	25B-203	ex YU-BRB	
N8005Y*	Lear Jet 25B	25B-121	ex XA-SIO	

*Leased from Source Investments; all freighters

CHICAGO EXPRESS AIRLINES

(C8) (IATA 488)   Chicago-Midway, IL (MDW)

N300CE	SAAB SF.340B	184	ex N184AE	Lsd fr WFBN
N301CE	SAAB SF.340B	191	ex N191AE	Lsd fr WFBN
N302CE	SAAB SF.340B	193	ex N193AE	Lsd fr Firstar Bank
N303CE	SAAB SF.340B	194	ex N194AE	Lsd fr US Bancorp
N304CE	SAAB SF.340B	198	ex N198AE	Lsd fr US Bancorp
N305CE	SAAB SF.340B	202	ex N202KD	Lsd fr Firstar Bank
N306CE	SAAB SF.340B	203	ex N203NE	Lsd fr US Bancorp
N307CE	SAAB SF.340B	204	ex N204NE	Lsd fr Firstar Bank
N308CE	SAAB SF.340B	210	ex N210AE	Lsd fr US Bancorp
N309CE	SAAB SF.340B	201	ex N201AE	
N311CE	SAAB SF.340B	214	ex N214DA	
N312CE	SAAB SF.340B	334	ex N334AE	
N314CE	SAAB SF.340B	335	ex N335AE	
N315CE	SAAB SF.340B	343	ex N343SB	Lsd fr AMR Leasing
N316CE	SAAB SF.340B	348	ex N906AE	
N317CE	SAAB SF.340B	352	ex N352SB	
N318CE	SAAB SF.340B	358	ex N358RZ	

Three more SAAB 340s are on order from American Eagle
Owned by ATA Airlines and operates as ATA Connection using TZ flight numbers

CIMARRON AIRE

Cimmaron Aire (CMN)   McAlester-Regional, OK (MLC)

| N737SW | Beech E-18S | BA-402 | | Freighter |

COASTAL AIR TRANSPORT

Trans Coastal (TCL)   Fairhope-Municipal, AL

| N154JR | Convair 340 | 47 | ex N454GA | no titles |

COASTAL AIR TRANSPORT

Coastal (DQ/CXT) (IATA 457)   St Croix-Alexander Hamilton, VI (STX)

| N676MF | Cessna 402B | 402B0106 | ex N7856Q | Cruzan Queen |

COLGAN AIR

(9L) (IATA 426)   Manassas-Regional, VA (MNZ)

N60MJ	Beech 1900D	UE-60	ex N85445		Lsd fr Raytheon
N119CJ	Beech 1900C-1	UC-19	ex N1552C	LVC	Lsd fr Raytheon
N124CJ	Beech 1900D	UE-24	ex N575D		Lsd fr Raytheon
N129CJ	Beech 1900C-1	UC-129	ex N15615	LVE	

N152MJ	Beech 1900D	UE-52	ex N84703		Lsd fr Raytheon
N155CJ	Beech 1900D	UE-55	ex N85230	LVX	Lsd fr Raytheon
N171CJ	Beech 1900D	UE-71	ex N85704		Lsd fr Raytheon
N172MJ	Beech 1900D	UE-72	ex N85804		Lsd fr Raytheon
N191CJ	Beech 1900D	UE-19	ex N83005		Lsd fr Raytheon
N207CJ	Beech 1900C-1	UC-107	ex N15539		
N210CJ	Beech 1900C-1	UC-110	ex N132GP	LVD	Lsd fr Raytheon
N221CJ	Beech 1900D	UE-221			
N243CJ	Beech 1900D	UE-43	ex N84307		Lsd fr Raytheon
N550CJ	Beech 1900C-1	UC-50	ex N1568C	LVA; std MZJ	Lsd fr Raytheon
N32017	Beech 1900C-1	UC-37		LVS	Lsd fr Raytheon
N9CJ	SAAB SF.340B	224			Lsd fr
N233CJ	SAAB SF.340B	233	ex N233CH		Lsd fr Fairbrook Lsg
N237MJ	SAAB SF.340B	237	ex N351BE		Lsd fr SAAB
N239CJ	SAAB SF.340B	239	ex N352BE		Lsd fr SAAB
N242CJ	SAAB SF.340B	242	ex N353BE		Lsd fr SAAB
N252CJ	SAAB SF.340B	252	ex N252CH		Lsd fr SAAB
N275CJ	SAAB SF.340B	275	ex N356BE	stored BNA	Lsd fr SAAB
N277MJ	SAAB SF.340B	277	ex N357BE		Lsd fr SAAB
N294CJ	SAAB SF.340B	294	ex N364BE		Lsd fr Fairbrook Lsg
N299CJ	SAAB SF.340B	299	ex N365BE		
N	SAAB SF.340			on order 2Q04	Lsd fr EGF
N	SAAB SF.340			on order 2Q04	Lsd fr EGF
N	SAAB SF.340			on order 2Q04	Lsd fr EGF
N	SAAB SF.340			on order 2Q04	Lsd fr EGF
N	SAAB SF.340			on order 2Q04	Lsd fr EGF
N	SAAB SF.340			on order 2Q04	Lsd fr EGF
N	SAAB SF.340			on order 2Q04	Lsd fr EGF
N	SAAB SF.340			on order 2Q04	Lsd fr EGF
N	SAAB SF.340			on order 2Q04	Lsd fr EGF
N	SAAB SF.340			on order 2Q04	Lsd fr EGF

All operated on behalf of US Airways as US Airways Express

COLUMBIA HELICOPTERS

Columbia Heli (WCO)   *Aurora-State, OR/Lake Charles-Regional, LA (-/LCH)*

N184CH	Kawasaki KV107-II	4001	ex Thai 4001	
N185CH	Kawasaki KV107-II	4003	ex Thai 4003	
N186CH	Kawasaki KV107-II	4005	ex P2-CHA	
N187CH	Kawasaki KV107-II	4012	ex HC-BZP	
N189CH	Boeing Vertol 107-II	107	ex P2-CHB	Lsd to Helifor as C-FHFW
N190CH	Boeing Vertol 107-II	2002	ex ex C-GHFY	Lsd to Helifor as C-GHFY
N191CH	Boeing-Vertol 107-II	2003	ex P2-CHD	
N192CH	Kawasaki KV107-II	4011	ex JA9505	
N193CH	Boeing-Vertol 107-II	402	ex 04452	Lsd to Helifor as C-GHFT
N194CH	Boeing-Vertol 107-II	404	ex 04454	
N195CH	Boeing-Vertol 107 II	406	ex 04456	Lsd to Helifor as C-GHFF
N6672D	Boeing Vertol 107-II	2		
N6674D	Boeing-Vertol 107-II	4		Lsd to Helifor as C-FHFV
N6675D	Boeing-Vertol 107-II	5	ex C-GHFI	
N6682D	Boeing-Vertol 107-II	101	ex JA9500	
N235CH	Boeing-Vertol 234UT Chinook	MJ-002	ex G-BISO	
N237CH	Boeing-Vertol 234UT Chinook	MJ-003	ex G-BISR	Lsd to MBA as P2-CHI
N238CH	Boeing-Vertol 234UT Chinook	MJ-005	ex P2-CHY	Lsd to Helifor as C-FHFB
N239CH	Boeing-Vertol 234UT Chinook	MJ-006	ex C-FHFJ	
N241CH	Boeing-Vertol 234UT Chinook	MJ-016	ex HC-CAW	
N242CH	Boeing-Vertol 234UT Chinook	MJ-023	ex HC-BYF	
N245CH	Boeing-Vertol 234UT Chinook	MJ-022	ex LN-OMA	
N246CH	Boeing-Vertol 234UT Chinook	MJ-017	ex LN-OMK	
N247AC	Sikorsky S-64	64052	ex N2270B	stored
N543CH	Sikorsky S-64	64016	ex N4409U	
N544CH	Sikorsky S-64	64022	ex N22696	
(N545CH)	Sikorsky S-64	64027	ex N4410K	stored
(N546CH)	Sikorsky S-64	64042	ex N7073C	stored
N548CH	Sikorsky S-64		ex N4410N	
N111NS	Beech 200C Super King Air	BL-36		
N3697F	Beech 200C Super King Air	BL-14		

COMAIR

Comair (OH/COM)   *Cincinnati-Northern Kentucky Intl, OH (CVG)*

N403CA~	Canadair CL-600-2B19	7428	ex N896AS	7428
N408CA~	Canadair CL-600-2B19	7440	ex C-FMLQ	7440
N409CA~	Canadair CL-600-2B19	7441	ex C-FMLS	7441
N416CA~	Canadair CL-600-2B19	7450	ex N493SW	7450

N420CA~	Canadair CL-600-2B19	7451	ex C-FVAZ	7451
N427CA~	Canadair CL-600-2B19	7460	ex N897AS	7460
N430CA~	Canadair CL-600-2B19	7461	ex N898AS	7461
N431CA~	Canadair CL-600-2B19	7472	ex C-FMLT	7472
N435CA	Canadair CL-600-2B19	7473	ex N496SW	7473
N436CA	Canadair CL-600-2B19	7482	ex N497SW	7482
N442CA	Canadair CL-600-2B19	7483	ex C-FMNQ	7483	Lsd to SKW
N443CA	Canadair CL-600-2B19	7539	ex C-GJJH	7539
N446CA	Canadair CL-600-2B19	7546	ex C-FMMB	7546
N447CA	Canadair CL-600-2B19	7552	ex C-GJLL	7552
N451CA	Canadair CL-600-2B19	7562	ex C-FMLT	7562; 25 th Anniversary colours
N455CA	Canadair CL-600-2B19	7592	ex C-FMLT	7592
N457CA	Canadair CL-600-2B19	7612	ex C-FMMY	7612
N458CA	Canadair CL-600-2B19	7613	ex C-FMNB	7613
N466CA	Canadair CL-600-2B19	7627	ex C-FMNX	7627
N467CA	Canadair CL-600-2B19	7637	ex C-FMML	7637
N468CA	Canadair CL-600-2B19	7649	ex C-FMLI	7649
N470CA	Canadair CL-600-2B19	7650	ex C-FMLQ	7650
N471CA	Canadair CL-600-2B19	7655	ex C-FMNH	7655
N472CA	Canadair CL-600-2B19	7667	ex C-FMML	7667
N473CA	Canadair CL-600-2B19	7668	ex C-FMMN	7668
N477CA	Canadair CL-600-2B19	7670	ex C-FMMW	7670
N478CA	Canadair CL-600-2B19	7671	ex C-FMMX	7671
N479CA	Canadair CL-600-2B19	7675	ex C-FMKW	7675
N483CA	Canadair CL-600-2B19	7689	ex C-FMLV	7689
N484CA	Canadair CL-600-2B19	7702	ex C-FMMY	7702
N486CA	Canadair CL-600-2B19	7707	ex C-FMLB	7707
N487CA	Canadair CL-600-2B19	7729	ex C-FMMQ	7729
N488CA	Canadair CL-600-2B19	7730	ex C-FMMW	7730
N489CA	Canadair CL-600-2B19	7755	ex C-FMOI	7755
N491CA	Canadair CL-600-2B19	7756	ex C-FMMB	7756
N492CA	Canadair CL-600-2B19	7763	ex C-FMNB	7763
N494CA	Canadair CL-600-2B19	7765	ex C-FMKW	7765
N495CA	Canadair CL-600-2B19	7774	ex C-FMMT	7774
N496CA	Canadair CL-600-2B19	7791	ex C-FMMX	7791
N498CA	Canadair CL-600-2B19	7792	ex C-FMMY	7792
N506CA	Canadair CL-600-2B19	7793	ex C-FMNB	7793
N507CA	Canadair CL-600-2B19	7796	ex C-GZFC	7796
N510CA	Canadair CL-600-2B19	7802	ex C-GZFH	7802
N514CA	Canadair CL-600-2B19	7809	ex C-FMOS	7809
N518CA	Canadair CL-600-2B19	7816	ex C-FMMB	7816
N523CA	Canadair CL-600-2B19	7821	ex C-FMMX	7821
N526CA	Canadair CL-600-2B19	7824	ex C-FMKV	7824
N528CA	Canadair CL-600-2B19	7841	ex C-FVAZ	7841
N533CA	Canadair CL-600-2B19		ex C-		on order 03
N536CA	Canadair CL-600-2B19		ex C-		on order 03
N537CA	Canadair CL-600-2B19		ex C-		on order 03
N538CA	Canadair CL-600-2B19		ex C-		on order 03
N539CA	Canadair CL-600-2B19		ex C-		on order 04
N548CA	Canadair CL-600-2B19		ex C-		on order 04
N549CA	Canadair CL-600-2B19		ex C-		on order 04
N574CA	Canadair CL-600-2B19		ex C-		on order 04
N576CA	Canadair CL-600-2B19		ex C-		on order 04
N708CA~	Canadair CL-600-2B19	7235		7235
N709CA~	Canadair CL-600-2B19	7238		7238
N710CA~	Canadair CL-600-2B19	7241		7241
N712CA~	Canadair CL-600-2B19	7244		7244
N713CA~	Canadair CL-600-2B19	7245		7245
N716CA~	Canadair CL-600-2B19	7250	ex C-FMMW	7250
N719CA~	Canadair CL-600-2B19	7253		7253
N721CA~	Canadair CL-600-2B19	7259	ex C-FMLI	7259
N729CA~	Canadair CL-600-2B19	7265		7265
N735CA~	Canadair CL-600-2B19	7267		7267 Cincinnati The Jet Hub colours
N739CA~	Canadair CL-600-2B19	7273	ex C-FMNQ	7273
N759CA~	Canadair CL-600-2B19	7279	ex C-FMMQ	7279	Sublsd to SKW
N767CA~	Canadair CL-600-2B19	7285	ex C-FMKW	7285	Sublsd to SKW
N769CA~	Canadair CL-600-2B19	7292	ex C-FMLT	7292	Sublsd to SKW
N776CA~	Canadair CL-600-2B19	7293		7293	Sublsd to SKW
N778CA	Canadair CL-600-2B19	7297		7297	Lsd to SKW
N779CA~	Canadair CL-600-2B19	7306	ex C-FMMB	7306
N781CA~	Canadair CL-600-2B19	7312	ex C-FMMY	7312
N783CA~	Canadair CL-600-2B19	7315	ex C-FMKW	7315
N784CA~	Canadair CL-600-2B19	7319	ex C-FMLI	7319
N785CA~	Canadair CL-600-2B19	7326	ex C-	7326
N786CA~	Canadair CL-600-2B19	7333	ex C-	7333
N796CA~	Canadair CL-600-2B19	7338	ex C-	7338
N797CA~	Canadair CL-600-2B19	7344	ex C-	7344
N798CA	Canadair CL-600-2B19	7348	ex C-FMLF	7348
N804CA	Canadair CL-600-2B19	7352	ex C-FMLT	7352
N805CA	Canadair CL-600-2B19	7354	ex C-FMMT	7354
N806CA	Canadair CL-600-2B19	7359	ex C-FMOS	7359
N807CA	Canadair CL-600-2B19	7364	ex C-FMLU	7364

N809CA~	Canadair CL-600-2B19	7366	ex C-FMMB	7366
N810CA~	Canadair CL-600-2B19	7370	ex C-FMMW	7370
N811CA~	Canadair CL-600-2B19	7380	ex C-FMLQ	7380
N812CA~	Canadair CL-600-2B19	7381	ex C-FMLS	7381
N814CA~	Canadair CL-600-2B19	7387	ex C-GFVM	7387
N815CA~	Canadair CL-600-2B19	7397	ex C-FMML	7397
N818CA~	Canadair CL-600-2B19	7408	ex C-FMLF	7408
N819CA~	Canadair CL-600-2B19	7415	ex C-FMNH	7415
N821CA~	Canadair CL-600-2B19	7420	ex C-FMOW	7420
N868CA	Canadair CL-600-2B19	7427	ex C-FMML	7427
N912CA#	Canadair CL-600-2B19	7011	ex C-FMKZ	7011	Lsd fr WFBN
N914CA#	Canadair CL-600-2B19	7012	ex C-FMLB	7012	Lsd fr WFBN
N915CA#	Canadair CL-600-2B19	7013	ex C-FMLQ	7013	Lsd fr WFBN
N916CA#	Canadair CL-600-2B19	7014	ex C-FMLI	7014	Lsd fr WFBN
N917CA#	Canadair CL-600-2B19	7017	ex C-FMLT	7017	Lsd fr WFBN
N918CA#	Canadair CL-600-2B19	7018	ex C-FMLU	7018	Lsd fr WFBN
N920CA#	Canadair CL-600-2B19	7022	ex C-FMMN	7022	Lsd fr WFBN
N924CA#	Canadair CL-600-2B19	7026	ex C-FMMX	7026	Lsd fr WFBN
N926CA#	Canadair CL-600-2B19	7027	ex C-FMMY	7027	Lsd fr WFBN
N927CA#	Canadair CL-600-2B19	7031	ex C-FMNQ	7031	Lsd fr WFBN
N929CA#	Canadair CL-600-2B19	7035	ex C-FMOI	7035	Lsd fr WFBN
N931CA#	Canadair CL-600-2B19	7037	ex C-FMOS	7037	Lsd fr WFBN
N932CA#	Canadair CL-600-2B19	7038	ex C-FMOW	7038	Lsd fr WFBN
N933CA#	Canadair CL-600-2B19	7040	ex C-FMKW	7040	Lsd fr WFBN
N934CA#	Canadair CL-600-2B19	7042	ex C-FMLB	7042	Lsd fr WFBN
N936CA	Canadair CL-600-2B19	7043	ex C-FMLF	7043
N937CA	Canadair CL-600-2B19	7044	ex C-FMLI	7044
N938CA	Canadair CL-600-2B19	7046	ex C-FMLS	7046
N940CA	Canadair CL-600-2B19	7048	ex C-FMLU	7048
N941CA	Canadair CL-600-2B19	7050	ex C-FMMB	7050
N943CA#	Canadair CL-600-2B19	7062	ex C-FMNW	7062	Lsd to SKW
N945CA#	Canadair CL-600-2B19	7069	ex C-FMKV	7069	Lsd to SKW
N946CA#	Canadair CL-600-2B19	7072	ex C-FMLB	7072	Lsd to SKW
N947CA#	Canadair CL-600-2B19	7077	ex C-FMLT	7077	Lsd to SKW
N948CA#	Canadair CL-600-2B19	7079	ex C-FMLV	7079	Lsd to SKW
N949CA#	Canadair CL-600-2B19	7080	ex C-FMMB	7080
N951CA#	Canadair CL-600-2B19	7091		7091
N952CA#	Canadair CL-600-2B19	7092		7092
N954CA#	Canadair CL-600-2B19	7100	ex C-FXFB	7100; 100 th RJ special colours
N956CA#	Canadair CL-600-2B19	7105	ex C-FMNH	7105
N957CA~	Canadair CL-600-2B19	7109	ex C-FMLV	7109
N958CA~	Canadair CL-600-2B19	7111	ex C-FMML	7111
N959CA~	Canadair CL-600-2B19	7116	ex C-FMMX	7116
N960CA~	Canadair CL-600-2B19	7117	ex C-FMMY	7117
N962CA~	Canadair CL-600-2B19	7123	ex C-FMLU	7123
N963CA~	Canadair CL-600-2B19	7127	ex C-FMMN	7127
N964CA~	Canadair CL-600-2B19	7129	ex C-FMMT	7129
N965CA	Canadair CL-600-2B19	7131	ex C-FMMX	7131
N966CA~	Canadair CL-600-2B19	7132	ex C-FMMY	7132
N967CA~	Canadair CL-600-2B19	7134	ex C-FMND	7134
N969CA	Canadair CL-600-2B19	7141	ex C-FMML	7141
N971CA	Canadair CL-600-2B19	7145	ex C-FMMW	7145
N973CA	Canadair CL-600-2B19	7146	ex C-FMMX	7146
N975CA	Canadair CL-600-2B19	7150	ex C-FMNH	7150
N976CA	Canadair CL-600-2B19	7151	ex C-FMNQ	7151
N977CA#	Canadair CL-600-2B19	7157	ex C-	7157	Lsd fr WFBN
N978CA#	Canadair CL-600-2B19	7158	ex C-FMNQ	7158	Lsd fr WFBN
N979CA'	Canadair CL-600-2B19	7159	ex C-FMMT	7159
N981CA#	Canadair CL-600-2B19	7163	ex C-FMOS	7163	Lsd fr WFBN
N982CA#	Canadair CL-600-2B19	7168	ex C-FMLU	7168	Lsd fr WFBN
N983CA~	Canadair CL-600-2B19	7169	ex C-	7169
N984CA~	Canadair CL-600-2B19	7171	ex C-	7171
N986CA	Canadair CL-600-2B19	7174	ex C-FMMT	7174
N987CA~	Canadair CL-600-2B19	7199	ex C-	7199
N988CA~	Canadair CL-600-2B19	7204	ex C-	7204
N989CA~	Canadair CL-600-2B19	7215	ex C-FMOI	7215
N991CA~	Canadair CL-600-2B19	7216	ex C-	7216
N995CA~	Canadair CL-600-2B19	7229	ex C-	7229
N999CA~	Canadair CL-600-2B19	7230	ex C-	7230

"Leased from Bank of America   #Leased from WFBN
~Leased from Wachovia Bank NA   'Special 20th Anniversary c/s, named City of Atlanta

N317CA	Canadair CL-600-2C10	10055	ex C-GZXI	10055
N331CA	Canadair CL-600-2C10	10061	ex C-GIBJ	10061
N340CA	Canadair CL-600-2C10	10062	ex C-GIBL	10062
N354CA	Canadair CL-600-2C10	10064	ex C-GIBO	10064
N355CA	Canadair CL-600-2C10	10067	ex C-GIBT	10067
N367CA	Canadair CL-600-2C10	10069	ex C-GICL	10069
N368CA	Canadair CL-600-2C10	10075	ex C-GIAD	10075
N369CA	Canadair CL-600-2C10	10079	ex C-GZUD	10079
N371CA	Canadair CL-600-2C10	10082	ex C-GIAR	10082
N374CA	Canadair CL-600-2C10	10090	ex C-	10090

N378CA	Canadair CL-600-2C10	10097	ex C-GIAJ	10097	
N379CA	Canadair CL-600-2C10	10102	ex C-	10102	
N390CA	Canadair CL-600-2C10	10106	ex C-	10106	
N391CA	Canadair CL-600-2C10	10108	ex C-	10108	
N398CA	Canadair CL-600-2C10	10112	ex C-	10112	
N625CA	Canadair CL-600-2C10	10113	ex C-	10113	
N641CA	Canadair CL-600-2C10	10122	ex C-	10122	
N642CA	Canadair CL-600-2C10	10125	ex C-	10125; 1000 th CRJ	
N653CA	Canadair CL-600-2C10	10129	ex C-GZUC	10129	
N	Canadair CL-600-2C10			10...	on order
N	Canadair CL-600-2C10			10...	on order
N	Canadair CL-600-2C10			10...	on order
N	Canadair CL-600-2C10			10...	on order
N	Canadair CL-600-2C10			10...	on order
N	Canadair CL-600-2C10			10...	on order
N	Canadair CL-600-2C10			10...	on order

Wholly owned subsidiary of Delta Air Lines and operates as Delta Connection in full colours and using DL flight numbers.

COMMERCIAL FLYER

Honolulu-Intl, HI (HNL)

N300EE	Piper PA-31-350 Chieftain	31-8052112
N500EE	Piper PA-31-350 Chieftain	31-8052131
N4576Q	Cessna 402A	402A0076

COMMUTAIR

Commutair (C5/UCA)   *Plattsburgh-Clinton County, NY (PLB)*

N830CA	Beech 1900D	UE-393	ex N43939		
N831CA	Beech 1900D	UE-395	ex N44695	stored SLN	Lsd fr Raytheon
N832CA	Beech 1900D	UE-406	ex N44703	stored PLB	
N833CA	Beech 1900D	UE-377	ex N31477		Lsd fr Raytheon
N834CA	Beech 1900D	UE-378	ex N44578		Lsd fr Raytheon
N835CA	Beech 1900D	UE-400	ex N44640		
N836CA	Beech 1900D	UE-407	ex N44739		
N837CA	Beech 1900D	UE-397	ex N42957		
N838CA	Beech 1900D	UE-396	ex N43596		
N839CA	Beech 1900D	UE-385	ex N32290		Lsd fr Raytheon
N840CA	Beech 1900D	UE-401	ex N44871		
N841CA	Beech 1900D	UE-391	ex N44810	stored PLB	Lsd fr Raytheon
N842CA	Beech 1900D	UE-402	ex N43442	stored PLB	
N843CA	Beech 1900D	UE-382	ex N32022		Lsd fr Raytheon
N844CA	Beech 1900D	UE-410	ex N44812		
N845CA	Beech 1900D	UE-388	ex N32571		Lsd fr Raytheon
N846CA	Beech 1900D	UE-363	ex N31136		Lsd fr Raytheon
N847CA	Beech 1900D	UE-386	ex N40486		Lsd fr Raytheon
N848CA	Beech 1900D	UE-387	ex N44687		Lsd fr Raytheon
N850CA	Beech 1900D	UE-215	ex N215CJ		
N852CA	Beech 1900D	UE-389	ex N40484		Lsd fr Raytheon
N853CA	Beech 1900D	UE-390	ex N40729	stored SLN	Lsd fr Raytheon
N854CA	Beech 1900D	UE-399	ex N44679		
N855CA	Beech 1900D	UE-392	ex N44102		
N856CA	Beech 1900D	UE-405	ex N44666		
N857CA	Beech 1900D	UE-403	ex N44644		
N858CA	Beech 1900D	UE-408	ex N44762		

Operates as Continental Connection in full colours and using CO flight numbers. Fleet to be trimmed to 14 aircraft with remainder being returned to Raytheon
Commutair is a trading name of Champlain Enterprises

CONTINENTAL AIRLINES

Continental (CO/COA) (IATA 005)   *Houston-George Bush Intercontinental, TX (IAH)*

N16301	Boeing 737-3T0	1119/23352	301	Lsd fr US Bank Trust
N59302	Boeing 737-3T0	1129/23353	302	Lsd fr US Bank Trust
N77303	Boeing 737-3T0	1130/23354	303	Lsd fr US Bank Trust
N61304	Boeing 737-3T0	1131/23355	304	Lsd fr US Bank Trust
N63305	Boeing 737-3T0	1133/23356	305	Lsd fr Linc Capital
N17306	Boeing 737-3T0	1141/23357	306; stored HOU	
N14307	Boeing 737-3T0	1142/23358	307; stored HOU	
N14308	Boeing 737-3T0	1144/23359	308; stored GYR	
N17309	Boeing 737-3T0	1147/23360	309	
N16310	Boeing 737-3T0	1150/23361	310	
N69311	Boeing 737-3T0	1152/23362	311	
N60312	Boeing 737-3T0	1153/23363	312	
N12313	Boeing 737-3T0	1158/23364	313	
N71314	Boeing 737-3T0	1159/23365	314; stored HOU	
N34315	Boeing 737-3T0	1174/23366	315	

Registration	Type	Serial	ex	No.	Notes
N17316	Boeing 737-3T0	1180/23367		316	
N17317	Boeing 737-3T0	1181/23368		317; stored HOU	
N12318	Boeing 737-3T0	1188/23369		318	Lsd fr CIT Leasing
N12319	Boeing 737-3T0	1190/23370		319	Lsd fr CIT Leasing
N14320	Boeing 737-3T0	1191/23371		320	Lsd fr State Street
N17321	Boeing 737-3T0	1192/23372		321	Lsd fr State Street
N12322	Boeing 737-3T0	1202/23373		322	
N10323	Boeing 737-3T0	1204/23374		323	
N14324	Boeing 737-3T0	1207/23375		324	
N14325	Boeing 737-3T0	1228/23455		325	
N17326	Boeing 737-3T0	1230/23456		326	
N12327	Boeing 737-3T0	1238/23457		327	
N17328	Boeing 737-3T0	1244/23458		328	Lsd fr GECAS
N17329	Boeing 737-3T0	1247/23459		329	
N70330	Boeing 737-3T0	1253/23460		330	
N47332	Boeing 737-3T0	1263/23570		332	
N69333	Boeing 737-3T0	1276/23571		333	
N14334	Boeing 737-3T0	1296/23572		334	
N14335	Boeing 737-3T0	1298/23573		335	
N14336	Boeing 737-3T0	1328/23574		336	Lsd fr WFBN
N14337	Boeing 737-3T0	1333/23575		337	Lsd fr WFBN
N59338	Boeing 737-3T0	1338/23576		338	Lsd fr WFBN
N16339	Boeing 737-3T0	1340/23577		339	Lsd fr GECAS
N14341	Boeing 737-3T0	1368/23579		341	Lsd fr WFBN
N14342	Boeing 737-3T0	1373/23580		342	Lsd fr WFBN
N39343	Boeing 737-3T0	1376/23581		343	Lsd fr WFBN
N17344	Boeing 737-3T0	1383/23582		344	Lsd fr WFBN
N17345	Boeing 737-3T0	1385/23583		345	Lsd fr WFBN
N14346	Boeing 737-3T0	1396/23584		346	
N14347	Boeing 737-3T0	1404/23585		347	
N69348	Boeing 737-3T0	1411/23586		348	
N12349	Boeing 737-3T0	1413/23587		349	
N18350	Boeing 737-3T0	1448/23588		350	Lsd fr WFBN
N69351	Boeing 737-3T0	1466/23589		351	Lsd fr WFBN
N70352	Boeing 737-3T0	1468/23590		352	Lsd fr WFBN
N70353	Boeing 737-3T0	1472/23591		353	Lsd fr WFBN
N76354	Boeing 737-3T0	1476/23592		354	Lsd fr Wachovia Bank
N76355	Boeing 737-3T0	1478/23593		355	Lsd fr WFBN
N17356	Boeing 737-3T0	1522/23942	ex N320AW	356	Lsd fr ICX Corp
N19357	Boeing 737-3T0	1518/23841	ex N301AL	357	Lsd fr GECAS
N14358	Boeing 737-3T0	1558/23943	ex N302AL	358	Lsd fr GECAS
N73380	Boeing 737-3Q8	2674/26309		380 stored MHV	Lsd fr MSA V
N14601	Boeing 737-524	2566/27314		601	Lsd fr WFBN
N69602	Boeing 737-524	2571/27315		602	Lsd fr WFBN
N69603	Boeing 737-524	2573/27316		603	Lsd fr WFBN
N14604	Boeing 737-524	2576/27317		604	Lsd fr WFBN
N14605	Boeing 737-524	2582/27318		605	Lsd fr WFBN
N58606	Boeing 737-524	2590/27319		606	Lsd fr WFBN
N16607	Boeing 737-524	2596/27320		607	Lsd fr WFBN
N33608	Boeing 737-524	2597/27321		608	Lsd fr WFBN
N14609	Boeing 737-524	2607/27322		609	Lsd fr WFBN
N27610	Boeing 737-524	2616/27323		610	Lsd fr WFBN
N18611	Boeing 737-524	2621/27324		611	Lsd fr WFBN
N11612	Boeing 737-524	2630/27325		612	Lsd fr WFBN
N14613	Boeing 737-524	2633/27326		613	Lsd fr WFBN
N17614	Boeing 737-524	2634/27327		614	Lsd fr Castle Harbor Lsg
N37615	Boeing 737-524	2640/27328		615	Lsd fr WFBN
N52616	Boeing 737-524	2641/27329		616	Lsd fr WFBN
N16617	Boeing 737-524	2648/27330		617	Lsd fr Castle Harbor Lsg
N16618	Boeing 737-524	2652/27331		618	Lsd fr WFBN
N17619	Boeing 737-524	2659/27332		619	Lsd fr WFBN
N17620	Boeing 737-524	2660/27333	ex N1790B	620	Lsd fr GECAS
N19621	Boeing 737-524	2661/27334		621	Lsd fr WFBN
N18622	Boeing 737-524	2669/27526		622	Lsd fr WFBN
N19623	Boeing 737-524	2672/27527		623	Lsd fr GECAS
N13624	Boeing 737-524	2675/27528		624	Lsd fr GECAS
N46625	Boeing 737-524	2683/27529		625	Lsd fr GECAS
N32626	Boeing 737-524	2686/27530		626	Lsd fr GECAS
N17627	Boeing 737-524	2700/27531		627	Lsd fr GECAS
N14628	Boeing 737-524	2712/27532		628	Lsd fr WFBN
N14629	Boeing 737-524	2725/27533		629	Lsd fr WFBN
N59630	Boeing 737-524	2726/27534		630	Lsd fr WFBN
N62631	Boeing 737-524	2728/27535		631	Lsd fr GECAS
N16632	Boeing 737-524	2736/27900		632	Lsd fr GECAS
N24633	Boeing 737-524	2743/27901		633	Lsd fr GECAS
N33637	Boeing 737-524	2776/27540		637	
N19638	Boeing 737-524	2912/28899		638	Lsd fr WFBN
N14639	Boeing 737-524	2913/28900		639	Lsd fr WFBN
N17640	Boeing 737-524	2924/28901		640	Lsd fr WFBN
N11641	Boeing 737-524	2926/28902		641	Lsd fr WFBN
N16642	Boeing 737-524	2927/28903		642	Lsd fr WFBN

N17644	Boeing 737-524	2934/28905	644	Lsd fr WFBN
N14645	Boeing 737-524	2935/28906	645	Lsd fr WFBN
N16646	Boeing 737-524	2956/28907	646	Lsd fr WFBN
N16647	Boeing 737-524	2958/28908	647	Lsd fr WFBN
N16648	Boeing 737-524	2960/28909	648	Lsd fr WFBN
N16649	Boeing 737-524	2972/28910	649	Lsd fr WFBN
N16650	Boeing 737-524	2973/28911	650	Lsd fr WFBN
N11651	Boeing 737-524	2980/28912 ex (N16651)	651	Lsd fr WFBN
N14652	Boeing 737-524	2985/28913	652	Lsd fr WFBN
N14653	Boeing 737-524	2986/28914	653	Lsd fr WFBN
N14654	Boeing 737-524	2993/28915	654	
N14655	Boeing 737-524	2994/28916	655	
N11656	Boeing 737-524	3019/28917	656	
N23657	Boeing 737-524	3026/28918 ex N1787B	657	
N18658	Boeing 737-524	3045/28919	658	
N15659	Boeing 737-524	3048/28920	659	
N14660	Boeing 737-524	3052/28921	660	
N23661	Boeing 737-524	3055/28922	661	
N14662	Boeing 737-524	3060/28923	662	
N17663	Boeing 737-524	3063/28924	663	
N14664	Boeing 737-524	3066/28925	664	
N13665	Boeing 737-524	3069/28926	665	
N14667	Boeing 737-524	3074/28927	667	
N14668	Boeing 737-524	3077/28928	668	
N16701	Boeing 737-724	29/28762	701	Lsd fr WFBN
N24702	Boeing 737-724	32/28763	702	Lsd fr WFBN
N16703	Boeing 737-724	37/28764	703	Lsd fr WFBN
N14704	Boeing 737-724	43/28765	704	
N25705	Boeing 737-724	46/28766	705	Lsd fr WFBN
N24706	Boeing 737-724	47/28767	706	Lsd fr WFBN
N23707	Boeing 737-724	48/28768 ex N1787B	707	Lsd fr WFBN
N23708	Boeing 737-724	52/28769	708	Lsd fr WFBN
N16709	Boeing 737-724	93/28779	709	Lsd fr WFBN
N15710	Boeing 737-724	94/28780	710	Lsd fr WFBN
N54711	Boeing 737-724	97/28782	711	Lsd fr WFBN
N15712	Boeing 737-724	105/28783	712	Lsd fr WFBN
N16713	Boeing 737-724	107/28784	713	Lsd fr WFBN
N33714	Boeing 737-724	119/28785	714	Lsd fr WFBN
N24715	Boeing 737-724	125/28786 ex N1795B	715	Lsd fr WFBN
N13716	Boeing 737-724	156/28787	716	Lsd fr WFBN
N29717	Boeing 737-724	182/28936	717	
N13718	Boeing 737-724	185/28937	718	
N17719	Boeing 737-724	195/28938	719	
N13720	Boeing 737-724	214/28939	720	
N23721	Boeing 737-724	219/28940	721	
N27722	Boeing 737-724	247/28789	722	
N21723	Boeing 737-724	253/28790 ex N1787B	723	
N27724	Boeing 737-724	283/28791 ex N1787B	724	Lsd fr WFBN
N39726	Boeing 737-724	315/28796 ex N1787B	726	Lsd fr WFBN
N38727	Boeing 737-724	317/28797	727	Lsd fr WFBN
N39728	Boeing 737-724	321/28944	728	
N24729	Boeing 737-724	325/28945 ex N1784B	729	
N17730	Boeing 737-724	338/28798	730	Lsd fr WFBN
N14731	Boeing 737-724	346/28799	731	Lsd fr WFBN
N16732	Boeing 737-724	352/28948 ex N60436	732	
N27733	Boeing 737-724	364/28800	733; Sir Samuel J LeFrak	
				Lsd fr WFBN
N27734	Boeing 737-724	371/28949	734	
N14735	Boeing 737-724	376/28950	735	
N24736	Boeing 737-724	380/28803	736	
N13750	Boeing 737-724	286/28941	750	
N15751	Boeing 737-724		751 on order	
N17752	Boeing 737-724		752 on order	
N17753	Boeing 737-724		753 on order	
N12754	Boeing 737-724		754 on order	
N13755	Boeing 737-724		755 on order	
N16756	Boeing 737-724		756 on order	
N18757	Boeing 737-724		757 on order	
N15758	Boeing 737-724		758 on order	

Twelve more Boeing 737-724s are on order but delivery deferred to 2008 and beyond

N25201*	Boeing 737-824	443/28958	201	
N24202	Boeing 737-824	581/30429	202	Lsd fr WFBN
N33203	Boeing 737-824	591/30613	203	Lsd fr WFBN
N35204	Boeing 737-824	606/30576 ex N1795B	204	Lsd fr WFBN
N27205	Boeing 737-824	615/30577	205	Lsd fr WFBN
N11206	Boeing 737-824	618/30578	206	Lsd fr WFBN
N36207	Boeing 737-824	627/30579	207	Lsd fr WFBN
N26208	Boeing 737-824	644/30580	208	Lsd fr WFBN
N33209	Boeing 737-824	647/30581	209	
N26210	Boeing 737-824	56/28770	210	

N24211	Boeing 737-824	58/28771		211	
N24212	Boeing 737-824	63/28772		212	
N27213	Boeing 737-824	65/28773		213	
N14214	Boeing 737-824	74/28774		214	Lsd fr WFBN
N26215	Boeing 737-824	76/28775		215	
N12216	Boeing 737-824	79/28776		216	Lsd fr WFBN
N16217	Boeing 737-824	81/28777		217	Lsd fr WFBN
N12218	Boeing 737-824	84/28778		218	Lsd fr WFBN
N14219	Boeing 737-824	88/28781		219	Lsd fr WFBN
N18220	Boeing 737-824	134/28929	ex N60436	220	Lsd fr WFBN
N12221	Boeing 737-824	153/28930	ex N1796B	221	Lsd fr WFBN
N34222	Boeing 737-824	159/28931		222	Lsd fr WFBN
N18223	Boeing 737-824	162/28932		223	Lsd fr WFBN
N24224	Boeing 737-824	165/28933		224	Lsd fr WFBN
N12225	Boeing 737-824	168/28934		225	Lsd fr WFBN
N26226	Boeing 737-824	171/28935		226	
N13227*	Boeing 737-824	262/28788	ex N1787B	227	
N14228*	Boeing 737-824	281/28792	ex N1787B	228	Lsd fr WFBN
N17229	Boeing 737-824	287/28793		229	Lsd fr WFBN
N14230	Boeing 737-824	296/28794	ex N1787B	230	Lsd fr WFBN
N14231	Boeing 737-824	300/28795	ex N1787B	231	Lsd fr WFBN
N26232*	Boeing 737-824	304/28942		232	
N17233	Boeing 737-824	328/28943	ex N1787B	233	Lsd fr GECAS
N16234	Boeing 737-824	334/28946	ex N1787B	234	Lsd fr WFBN
N14235*	Boeing 737-824	342/28947		235	
N35236*	Boeing 737-824	367/28801		236	
N14237	Boeing 737-824	374/28802		237	Lsd fr WFBN
N12238	Boeing 737-824	386/28804		238	Lsd fr WFBN
N27239	Boeing 737-824	391/28951	ex N1787B	239	Lsd fr WFBN
N14240*	Boeing 737-824	394/28952		240	Lsd fr WFBN
N54241	Boeing 737-824	395/28953	ex N1787B	241	Lsd fr WFBN
N14242	Boeing 737-824	402/28805		242	Lsd fr WFBN
N18243	Boeing 737-824	403/28806		243	
N17244	Boeing 737-824	409/28954	ex N1787B	244	Lsd fr WFBN
N17245	Boeing 737-824	411/28955		245	Lsd fr WFBN
N27246*	Boeing 737-824	413/28956		246	
N36247	Boeing 737-824	431/28807		247	Lsd fr WFBN
N13248*	Boeing 737-824	435/28808		248	Lsd fr WFBN
N14249	Boeing 737-824	438/28809		249	
N14250	Boeing 737-824	441/28957		250	
N73251	Boeing 737-824	650/30582		251	Lsd fr WFBN
N37252	Boeing 737-824	656/30583		252	
N37253	Boeing 737-824	660/30584		253	
N76254	Boeing 737-824	667/30779		254	
N37255	Boeing 737-824	686/30610	ex N1787B	255	Lsd fr WFBN
N73256	Boeing 737-824	692/30611	ex N1787B	256	Lsd fr WFBN
N38257	Boeing 737-824	706/30612		257	Lsd fr WFBN
N77258	Boeing 737-824	708/30802		258	
N73259	Boeing 737-824	854/30803		259	Lsd fr WFBN
N35260	Boeing 737-824	862/30855		260	Lsd fr WFBN
N77261	Boeing 737-824	897/31582		261	Lsd fr WFBN
N33262	Boeing 737-824	901/32402		262	Lsd fr WFBN
N37263	Boeing 737-824	906/31583		263	Lsd fr WFBN
N33264	Boeing 737-824	916/31584		264	
N76265	Boeing 737-824	928/31585		265	
N33266	Boeing 737-824	930/32403		266	
N37267	Boeing 737-824	939/31586		267	Lsd fr WFBN
N38268	Boeing 737-824	957/31587		268	Lsd fr WFBN
N76269	Boeing 737-824	966/31588		269	Lsd fr WFBN
N73270	Boeing 737-824	970/31632	ex N1787B	270	Lsd fr WFBN
N35271	Boeing 737-824	982/31589		271	Lsd fr WFBN
N36272	Boeing 737-824	987/31590	ex N1795B	272	
N37273	Boeing 737-824	1012/31591		273	
N37274	Boeing 737-824	1062/31592		274	Lsd fr WFBN
N73275	Boeing 737-824	1077/31593		275	Lsd fr WFBN
N73276	Boeing 737-824	1079/31594		276	Lsd fr WFBN
N37277	Boeing 737-824	1099/31595		277	
N73278	Boeing 737-824	1390/31596		278	
N79279	Boeing 737-824	1411/31597	ex N1787B	279	
N36280	Boeing 737-824	1423/31598		280	
N37281	Boeing 737-824	1425/31599		281	
N34282	Boeing 737-824	1440/31634		282	
N73283	Boeing 737-824	1456/31606		283	
N33284	Boeing 737-824	31635		284 on order	
N78285	Boeing 737-824			285 on order	
N33286	Boeing 737-824			286 on order	
N37287	Boeing 737-824			287 on order	
N76288	Boeing 737-824			288 on order	
N33289	Boeing 737-824			289 on order	
N37290	Boeing 737-824			290 on order	
N73291	Boeing 737-824			291 on order	
N33292	Boeing 737-824			292 on order	

N	Boeing 737-824			293 on order	

Thirty more Boeing 737-824s are on order but delivery defered to 2008 and beyond
*Based Guam and operated for Continental Micronesia

N30401	Boeing 737-924	820/30118		401	Lsd fr WFBN
N79402	Boeing 737-924	857/30119		402	
N38403	Boeing 737-924	884/30120		403	
N32404	Boeing 737-924	893/30121		404	Lsd fr WFBN
N72405	Boeing 737-924	911/30122		405	
N73406	Boeing 737-924	943/30123		406	
N35407	Boeing 737-924	951/30124		407	
N37408	Boeing 737-924	962/30125	ex N1787B	408	Lsd fr WFBN
N37409	Boeing 737-924	1004/30126	ex N1787B	409	Lsd fr WFBN
N75410	Boeing 737-924	1021/30127		410	
N71411	Boeing 737-924	1052/30128		411	
N31412	Boeing 737-924	1112/30129		412	
N37413	Boeing 737-924			413 on order	
N30414	Boeing 737-924			414 on order	
N73415	Boeing 737-924			415 on order	
N58101	Boeing 757-224	614/27291		101	Lsd fr WFBN
N14102	Boeing 757-224	619/27292		102	Lsd fr WFBN
N33103	Boeing 757-224	623/27293		103	Lsd fr WFBN
N17104	Boeing 757-224	629/27294		104	Lsd fr GECAS
N17105	Boeing 757-224	632/27295		105	Lsd fr GECAS
N14106	Boeing 757-224	637/27296		106; Sam E Ashmore	Lsd fr GECAS
N14107	Boeing 757-224	641/27297		107	Lsd fr GECAS
N21108	Boeing 757-224	645/27298		108	Lsd fr GECAS
N12109	Boeing 757-224	648/27299		109	Lsd fr GECAS
N13110	Boeing 757-224	650/27300		110	Lsd fr GECAS
N57111	Boeing 757-224	652/27301		111	Lsd fr WFBN
N18112	Boeing 757-224	653/27302		112	Lsd fr GECAS
N13113	Boeing 757-224	668/27555		113	Lsd fr GECAS
N12114	Boeing 757-224	682/27556		114	Lsd fr WFBN
N14115	Boeing 757-224	686/27557		115	Lsd fr WFBN
N12116	Boeing 757-224	702/27558		116	Lsd fr WFBN
N19117	Boeing 757-224	706/27559		117	Lsd fr WFBN
N14118	Boeing 757-224	748/27560	(ex (N19118)	118	Lsd fr WFBN
N18119	Boeing 757-224	753/27561		119	Lsd fr WFBN
N14120	Boeing 757-224	761/27562		120	Lsd fr WFBN
N14121	Boeing 757-224	766/27563		121	Lsd fr WFBN
N17122	Boeing 757-224	768/27564		122	Lsd fr WFBN
N26123	Boeing 757-224	781/28966		123	Lsd fr WFBN
N29124	Boeing 757-224	786/27565		124	Lsd fr WFBN
N12125	Boeing 757-224	788/28967	ex N1787B	125	Lsd fr WFBN
N17126	Boeing 757-224ER	790/27566		126	
N48127	Boeing 757-224ER	791/28968		127	
N17128	Boeing 757-224ER	795/27567		128	
N29129	Boeing 757-224ER	796/28969		129	
N19130	Boeing 757-224ER	799/28970		130	
N34131	Boeing 757-224	806/28971		131	
N33132	Boeing 757-224	809/29281		132	
N17133	Boeing 757-224	840/29282		133	Lsd fr WFBN
N67134	Boeing 757-224	848/29283	ex N1800B	134	
N41135	Boeing 757-224	851/29284		135	
N19136	Boeing 757-224	856/29285		136	
N34137	Boeing 757-224	899/30229		137	
N13138	Boeing 757-224	903/30351	ex N1795B	138	
N17139	Boeing 757-224	911/30352		139	
N41140	Boeing 757-224	913/30353		140	
N19141	Boeing 757-224	933/30354		141	
N75851	Boeing 757-324	990/32810		851	
N57852	Boeing 757-324	995/32811		852	
N75853	Boeing 757-324	997/32812		853	
N75854	Boeing 757-324	999/32813		854	
N75855	Boeing 757-324	1038/32814		855	
N74856	Boeing 757-324	1039/32815		856	
N57857	Boeing 757-324	1040/32816		857	
N75858	Boeing 757-324			858 on order 04	
N56859	Boeing 757-324			859 on order 04	
N76151	Boeing 767-224ER	811/30430	ex (N37165)	151	
N73152	Boeing 767-224ER	815/30431	ex (N37166)	152	
N76153	Boeing 767-224ER	819/30432	ex (N37167)	153	
N69154	Boeing 767-224ER	823/30433	ex (N37168)	154	
N68155	Boeing 767-224ER	825/30434	ex (N37169)	155	
N76156	Boeing 767-224ER	827/30435	ex (N37170)	156	
N67157	Boeing 767-224ER	833/30436		157	Lsd fr WFBN
N67158	Boeing 767-224ER	839/30437		158	
N68159	Boeing 767-224ER	845/30438		159	
N68160	Boeing 767-224ER	851/30439		160	

321

Reg	Type	Ln/Cn	ex	Fleet	Notes
N66051	Boeing 767-424ER	799/29446	ex (N76401)	051	
N67052	Boeing 767-424ER	805/29447	ex (N87402)	052	
N59053	Boeing 767-424ER	809/29448	ex (N47403)	053	
N76054	Boeing 767-424ER	816/29449	ex (N87404)	054	Lsd fr WFBN
N76055	Boeing 767-424ER	826/29450		055	Lsd fr WFBN
N66056	Boeing 767-424ER	842/29451		056	
N66057	Boeing 767-424ER	859/29452		057	
N67058	Boeing 767-424ER	862/29453		058	
N69059	Boeing 767-424ER	864/29454		059	
N78060	Boeing 767-424ER	866/29455		060	
N68061	Boeing 767-424ER	868/29456		061	
N76062	Boeing 767-424ER	869/29457		062	
N69063	Boeing 767-424ER	872/29458		063	
N76064	Boeing 767-424ER	873/29459		064	
N76065	Boeing 767-424ER	876/29460		065	
N77066	Boeing 767-424ER	878/29461		066	
N78001	Boeing 777-224ER	161/27577		001	Lsd fr WFBN
N78002	Boeing 777-224ER	165/27578		002	Lsd fr WFBN
N78003	Boeing 777-224ER	167/27579		003	Lsd fr WFBN
N78004	Boeing 777-224ER	169/27580		004	Lsd fr WFBN
N78005	Boeing 777-224ER	177/27581		005	Lsd fr WFBN
N77006	Boeing 777-224ER	183/29476		006	
N74007	Boeing 777-224ER	197/29477		007	Lsd fr WFBN
N78008	Boeing 777-224ER	200/29478		008	Lsd fr WFBN
N78009	Boeing 777-224ER	211/29479		009	
N76010	Boeing 777-224ER	220/29480		010	Lsd fr WFBN
N79011	Boeing 777-224ER	227/29859		011	
N77012	Boeing 777-224ER	234/29860		012	Lsd fr WFBN
N78013	Boeing 777-224ER	243/29861		013	
N77014	Boeing 777-224ER	253/29862		014	Lsd fr WFBN
N27015	Boeing 777-224ER	273/28678		015	Lsd fr ILFC
N57016	Boeing 777-224ER	279/28679		016	Lsd fr ILFC
N78017	Boeing 777-224ER	391/31679		017	
N37018	Boeing 777-224ER	397/31680		018	
N477AC	McDonnell-Douglas MD-82	1015/48062		885; stored MHV	Lsd fr ILFC
N478AC	McDonnell-Douglas MD-82	1020/48063		886; stored MHV	Lsd fr ILFC
N819NY	McDonnell-Douglas MD-82	1297/49479		819	
N936AS	McDonnell-Douglas MD-83	1275/49363		842; stored MHV	
N937MC	McDonnell-Douglas MD-82	1324/49450		877; stored MHV	Lsd fr Sequoia
N938AS	McDonnell-Douglas MD-83	1277/49365		843; stored MHV	
N938MC	McDonnell-Douglas MD-83	1340/49525		878; stored MHV	Lsd fr AWAS
N10801	McDonnell-Douglas MD-82	1082/49127	ex N801NY	801;std MHV	Lsd fr Kuta Two
N16806	McDonnell-Douglas MD-82	1150/49260	ex N806NY	806 Lsd fr Lone Star Air Partners	
N12811	McDonnell-Douglas MD-82	1185/49265	ex N811NY	811	
N17812	McDonnell-Douglas MD-82	1186/49250	ex N812NY	812; stored MHV	Lsd fr Kuta Two
N14818	McDonnell-Douglas MD-82	1293/49478	ex N818NY	818; stored MHV	Lsd fr Linc Capital
N15820	McDonnell-Douglas MD-82	1298/49480	ex N820NY	820; stored GYR	
N72821	McDonnell-Douglas MD-82	1308/49481		821	Lsd fr WFBN
N72822	McDonnell-Douglas MD-82	1309/49482		822	Lsd fr Pacific
N76823	McDonnell-Douglas MD-82	1314/49483	ex N6200N	823 sored GYR	Lsd fr WFBN
N72824	McDonnell-Douglas MD-82	1315/49484		824; stored MHV	
N72825	McDonnell-Douglas MD-82	1316/49485		825	
N69826	McDonnell-Douglas MD-82	1317/49486		826; stored TUS	Lsd fr Pacific
N77827	McDonnell-Douglas MD-82	1335/49487		827	
N71828	McDonnell-Douglas MD-82	1350/49488		828	Lsd fr Potomac
N72829	McDonnell-Douglas MD-82	1351/49489		829; stored MHV	Lsd fr WFBN
N72830	McDonnell-Douglas MD-82	1352/49490		830	Lsd fr WFBN
N14831	McDonnell-Douglas MD-82	1360/49491		831	Lsd fr Potomac
N35832	McDonnell-Douglas MD-82	1361/49492		832	Lsd fr Wachovia Bank
N18833	McDonnell-Douglas MD-82	1364/49493		833	
N10834	McDonnell-Douglas MD-82	1368/49494		834; stored MHV	
N18835	McDonnell-Douglas MD-82	1318/49439	ex N6200N	835	Lsd fr Kuta Two
N35836	McDonnell-Douglas MD-82	1322/49441	ex N6202D	836; stored GYR	
N57837	McDonnell-Douglas MD-82	1411/49582		837; stored MHV	
N34838	McDonnell-Douglas MD-82	1419/49634		838; stored GYR	Lsd fr WFBN
N14840	McDonnell-Douglas MD-82	1369/49580		840	Lsd fr Wachovia Bank
N15841	McDonnell-Douglas MD-82	1384/49581		841	
N83870	McDonnell-Douglas MD-82	1012/48056	ex N930MC	870; stored MHV	
N14871	McDonnell-Douglas MD-82	1079/48022	ex N80UA	871	
N92874	McDonnell-Douglas MD-82	1073/49122	ex N934MC	874	
N14879	McDonnell-Douglas MD-83	1342/49526	ex N939MC	879; stored IAH	Lsd fr WFBN
N14880	McDonnell-Douglas MD-81	967/48044	ex N809HA	880; stored MHV	
					Lsd fr Wachovia Bank
N13881	McDonnell-Douglas MD-81	970/48045	ex N819HA	881; stored MHV	
N16883	McDonnell-Douglas MD-81	1018/48073	ex N849HA	883	

All McDonnell-Douglas MD-80s will be retired by 2005
Owned 14% by Northwest Airlines but stake for sale. In turn owns 17.7% of America West, 28% of Gulfstream International Airlines and 49% of COPA Airlines, while ExpressJet Airlines, (trading as Continental Express), is wholly owned. Feeder services also operated by Commutair and Gulfstream International as Continental Connection
See also Continental Micronesia

CONTINENTAL CONNECTION

(CO/COA)

N16540	Beech 1900D	UE-172		
N17534	Beech 1900D	UE-141		stored MZJ
N17541	Beech 1900D	UE-203		
N38537	Beech 1900D	UE-158		
N47542	Beech 1900D	UE-198		
N48544	Beech 1900D	UE-183		
N49543	Beech 1900D	UE-181		
N53545	Beech 1900D	UE-185		
N69547	Beech 1900D	UE-189		
N69548	Beech 1900D	UE-193		
N69549	Beech 1900D	UE-194		
N81533	Beech 1900D	UE-137	N137ZV	
N81535	Beech 1900D	UE-147		Grand Bahama Island colours
N81536	Beech 1900D	UE-152		
N81538	Beech 1900D	UE-199		
N81546	Beech 1900D	UE-187		
N81553	Beech 1900D	UE-222		
N81556	Beech 1900D	UE-239		
N82539	Beech 1900D	UE-168		
N87550	Beech 1900D	UE-205		
N87551	Beech 1900D	UE-206		
N87552	Beech 1900D	UE-216		
N87554	Beech 1900D	UE-227		
N87555	Beech 1900D	UE-234		
N87557	Beech 1900D	UE-246		

All leased from Raytheon Aircraft Credit Corp; operated by Gulfstream International using CO callsigns

N582SW	Embraer EMB.120ER Brasilia	120350		Skywest
N583SW	Embraer EMB.120ER Brasilia	120351		Skywest
N15732	Embraer EMB.120ER Brasilia	120195	ex PT-	Skywest

CONTINENTAL EXPRESS

Jet Link (CO/BTA) (IATA 565)
Cleveland-Hopkins Intl, OH/Houston-George Bush Intercontinental, TX/Denver-Centennial, CO (CLE/IAH/DEN)

N16501	Embraer EMB.135ER	145145	ex PT-SDV	501	Lsd fr WFBN
N16502	Embraer EMB.135ER	145166	ex PT-SFF	502	Lsd fr WFBN
N19503	Embraer EMB.135ER	145176	ex PT-SFI	503	Lsd fr WFBN
N22504	Embraer EMB.135ER	145186	ex PT-SFK	504	Lsd fr WFBN
N14505	Embraer EMB.135ER	145192	ex PT-SFN	505	Lsd fr WFBN
N27506	Embraer EMB.135ER	145206	ex PT-SFT	506	Lsd fr WFBN
N17507	Embraer EMB.135ER	145215	ex PT-SFW	507	Lsd fr WFBN
N14508	Embraer EMB.135ER	145220	ex PT-SFY	508	Lsd fr WFBN
N15509	Embraer EMB.135ER	145238	ex PT-SID	509	Lsd fr WFBN
N16510	Embraer EMB.135ER	145251	ex PT-SJI	510	Lsd fr WFBN
N16511	Embraer EMB.135ER	145267	ex PT-SIZ	511	Lsd fr WFBN
N27512	Embraer EMB.135ER	145274	ex PT-SJQ	512	Lsd fr WFBN
N17513	Embraer EMB.135LR	145292	ex PT-SKJ	513	Lsd fr WFBN
N14514	Embraer EMB.135LR	145303	ex PT-SKU	514	Lsd fr WFBN
N29515	Embraer EMB.135LR	145309	ex PT-SMA	515	Lsd fr WFBN
N14516	Embraer EMB.135LR	145323	ex PT-SMP	516	Lsd fr WFBN
N24517	Embraer EMB.135LR	145332	ex PT-SMY	517	Lsd fr WFBN
N28518	Embraer EMB.135LR	145334	ex PT-SNA	518	Lsd fr WFBN
N12519	Embraer EMB.135LR	145366	ex PT-SOQ	519	Lsd fr WFBN
N16520	Embraer EMB.135LR	145372	ex PT-SOX	520	Lsd fr WFBN
N17521	Embraer EMB.135LR	145378	ex PT-SQC	521	Lsd fr WFBN
N14522	Embraer EMB.135LR	145383	ex PT-SQH	522	Lsd fr WFBN
N27523	Embraer EMB.135LR	145389	ex PT-SQN	523	Lsd fr WFBN
N17524	Embraer EMB.135LR	145399	ex PT-SQW	524	Lsd fr WFBN
N16525	Embraer EMB.135LR	145403	ex PT-STA	525	Lsd fr WFBN
N11526	Embraer EMB.135LR	145410	ex PT-STH	526	Lsd fr WFBN
N15527	Embraer EMB.135LR	145413	ex PT-STJ	527	Lsd fr WFBN
N12528	Embraer EMB.135LR	145504	ex PT-SXX	528	Lsd fr WFBN
N28529	Embraer EMB.135LR	145512	ex PT-SYE	529	Lsd fr WFBN
N12530	Embraer EMB.135LR	145533	ex PT-STX	530	
N11535	Embraer EMB.145LR	145518	ex PT-SYJ	535	Lsd fr WFBN
N11536	Embraer EMB.145LR	145520	ex PT-SYL	536	Lsd fr WFBN
N21537	Embraer EMB.145LR	145523	ex PT-SYO	537	Lsd fr WFBN
N12538	Embraer EMB.145LR	145527	ex PT-STS	538	Lsd fr WFBN
N11539	Embraer EMB.145LR	145536	ex PT-SZA	539	Lsd fr WFBN
N12540	Embraer EMB.145LR	145537	ex PT-SZB	540	Lsd fr WFBN
N16541	Embraer EMB.145LR	145542	ex PT-SZF	541	Lsd fr WFBN
N14542	Embraer EMB.145LR	145547	ex PT-SZK	542	Lsd fr WFBN
N14543	Embraer EMB.145LR	145553	ex PT-SZP	543	Lsd fr WFBN
N11544	Embraer EMB.145LR	145557	ex PT-SZS	544	Lsd fr WFBN

N26545	Embraer EMB.145LR	144558	ex PT-SZT	545	Lsd fr WFBN
N16546	Embraer EMB.145LR	145562	ex PT-S	546	Lsd fr WFBN
N11547	Embraer EMB.145LR	145563	ex PT-S	547	Lsd fr WFBN
N11548	Embraer EMB.145LR	145565	ex PT-SBB	548	Lsd fr WFBN
N26549	Embraer EMB.145LR	145571	ex PT-SBH	549	Lsd fr WFBN
N13550	Embraer EMB.145LR	145575	ex PT-SBL	550	Lsd fr WFBN
N11551	Embraer EMB.145LR	145411	ex PT-STI	551	Lsd fr WFBN
N12552	Embraer EMB.145LR	145583	ex PT-SBU	552	Lsd fr WFBN
N13553	Embraer EMB.145LR	145585	ex PT-SBW	553	Lsd fr WFBN
N19554	Embraer EMB.145LR	145587	ex PT-SBX	554	Lsd fr WFBN
N15555	Embraer EMB.145LR	145594	ex PT-SCD	555	Lsd fr WFBN
N18556	Embraer EMB.145LR	145595	ex PT-SCE	556	Lsd fr WFBN
N18557	Embraer EMB.145LR	145596	ex PT-SCF	557	Lsd fr WFBN
N14558	Embraer EMB.145LR	145598	ex PT-SCG	558	Lsd fr WFBN
N16559	Embraer EMB.145LR	145603	ex PT-SCM	559	Lsd fr WFBN
N17560	Embraer EMB.145LR	145605	ex PT-SCO	560	Lsd fr WFBN
N16561	Embraer EMB.145LR	145610	ex PT-S	561	Lsd fr WFBN
N14562	Embraer EMB.145LR	145611	ex PT-S	562	Lsd fr WFBN
N12563	Embraer EMB.145LR	145612	ex PT-S	563	Lsd fr WFBN
N12564	Embraer EMB.145LR	145618	ex PT-SDG	564	Lsd fr WFBN
N11565	Embraer EMB.145LR	145621	ex PT-SDJ	565	Lsd fr WFBN
N13566	Embraer EMB.145LR	145622	ex PT-SDK	566	Lsd fr WFBN
N12567	Embraer EMB.145LR	145623	ex PT-SDL	567	Lsd fr WFBN
N14568	Embraer EMB.145LR	145628	ex PT-SDQ	568	Lsd fr WFBN
N12569	Embraer EMB.145LR	145630	ex PT-SDS	569	Lsd fr WFBN
N14570	Embraer EMB.145LR	145632	ex PT-SDU	570	Lsd fr WFBN
N16571	Embraer EMB.145LR	145633	ex PT-SDV	571	Lsd fr WFBN
N15572	Embraer EMB.145LR	145636	ex PT-SDY	572	Lsd fr WFBN
N14573	Embraer EMB.145LR	145638	ex PT-SDZ	573	Lsd fr WFBN
N15574	Embraer EMB.145LR	145639	ex PT-S	574	Lsd fr WFBN
N10575	Embraer EMB.145LR	145640	ex PT-SEC	575	Lsd fr WFBN
N12900	Embraer EMB.145LR	145511	ex PT-SYD	900	
N48901	Embraer EMB.145LR	145501	ex PT-SXU	901	Lsd fr WFBN
N14902	Embraer EMB.145LR	145496	ex PT-SXO	902	Lsd fr WFBN
N13903	Embraer EMB.145LR	145479	ex PT-SVY	903	Lsd fr WFBN
N14904	Embraer EMB.145LR	145477	ex PT-SVW	904	Lsd fr WFBN
N14905	Embraer EMB.145LR	145476	ex PT-	905	Lsd fr WFBN
N29906	Embraer EMB.145LR	145472	ex PT-SVR	906	Lsd fr WFBN
N10907	Embraer EMB.145LR	145468	ex PT-SVN	907	Lsd fr WFBN
N13908	Embraer EMB.145LR	145465	ex PT-SVK	908	Lsd fr WFBN
N22909	Embraer EMB.145LR	145459	ex PT-SVE	909	Lsd fr WFBN
N15910	Embraer EMB.145LR	145455	ex PT-SVA	910	Lsd fr WFBN
N16911	Embraer EMB.145LR	145446	ex PT-SUR	911	Lsd fr WFBN
N14912	Embraer EMB.145LR	145439	ex PT-SUK	912	Lsd fr WFBN
N13913	Embraer EMB.145LR	145438	ex PT-SUJ	913	Lsd fr WFBN
N13914	Embraer EMB.145LR	145430	ex PT-SUB	914	Lsd fr WFBN
N36915	Embraer EMB.145LR	145421	ex PT-STS	915	Lsd fr WFBN
N14916	Embraer EMB.145LR	145415	ex PT-STL	916	Lsd fr WFBN
N29917	Embraer EMB.145LR	145414	ex PT-STK	917	Lsd fr WFBN
N16918	Embraer EMB.145LR	145397	ex PT-SQU	918	Lsd fr WFBN
N16919	Embraer EMB.145LR	145393	ex PT-S	919	Lsd fr WFBN
N14920	Embraer EMB.145LR	145380	ex PT-SQE	920	Lsd fr WFBN
N12921	Embraer EMB.145LR	145354	ex PT-SNT	921	Lsd fr WFBN
N12922	Embraer EMB.145LR	145338	ex PT-SNE	922	Lsd fr WFBN
N14923	Embraer EMB.145LR	145318	ex PT-SMJ	923	Lsd fr WFBN
N12924	Embraer EMB.145LR	145311	ex PT-SMC	924	Lsd fr WFBN
N14925	Embraer EMB.145ER	145004	ex PT-SYA	925	Lsd fr WFBN
N15926	Embraer EMB.145ER	145005	ex PT-SYB	926	Lsd fr WFBN
N16927	Embraer EMB.145ER	145006	ex PT-SYC	927	Lsd fr WFBN
N17928	Embraer EMB.145ER	145007	ex PT-SYD	928	Lsd fr WFBN
N13929	Embraer EMB.145ER	145009	ex PT-SYF	929	Lsd fr WFBN
N14930	Embraer EMB.145ER	145011	ex PT-SYH	930	Lsd fr WFBN
N15932	Embraer EMB.145ER	145015	ex PT-SYL	932	Lsd fr WFBN
N14933	Embraer EMB.145ER	145018	ex PT-SYO	933	Lsd fr WFBN
N12934	Embraer EMB.145ER	145019	ex PT-SYP	934	Lsd fr WFBN
N13935	Embraer EMB.145ER	145022	ex PT-SYS	935	Lsd fr WFBN
N13936	Embraer EMB.145ER	145025	ex PT-SYV	936	Lsd fr WFBN
N14937	Embraer EMB.145ER	145026	ex PT-SYW	937	Lsd fr WFBN
N14938	Embraer EMB.145ER	145029	ex PT-SYZ	938	Lsd fr WFBN
N14939	Embraer EMB.145ER	145030	ex PT-SYY	939	Lsd fr WFBN
N14940	Embraer EMB.145ER	145033	ex PT-SZA	940	Lsd fr WFBN
N15941	Embraer EMB.145ER	145035	ex PT-SZB	941	Lsd fr WFBN
N14942	Embraer EMB.145ER	145037	ex PT-SZD	942	Lsd fr WFBN
N14943	Embraer EMB.145ER	145040	ex PT-SZE	943	Lsd fr WFBN
N16944	Embraer EMB.145ER	145045	ex PT-SZK	944	Lsd fr WFBN
N14945	Embraer EMB.145ER	145049	ex PT-SZO	945	Lsd fr WFBN
N12946	Embraer EMB.145ER	145052	ex PT-SZR	946	Lsd fr WFBN
N14947	Embraer EMB.145ER	145054	ex PT-SZT	947	Lsd fr WFBN
N15948	Embraer EMB.145FR	145056	ex PT-SZV	948	Lsd fr WFBN
N13949	Embraer EMB.145LR	145057	ex PT-SZW	949	Lsd fr WFBN
N14950	Embraer EMB.145LR	145061	ex PT-SAE	950	Lsd fr WFBN
N16951	Embraer EMB.145LR	145063	ex PT-SAG	951	Lsd fr WFBN

N14952	Embraer EMB.145LR	145067	ex PP-SAK	952	Lsd fr WFBN
N14953	Embraer EMB.145LR	145071	ex PT-SAP	953	Lsd fr WFBN
N16954	Embraer EMB.145LR	145072	ex PT-SAQ	954	Lsd fr WFBN
N13955	Embraer EMB.145LR	145075	ex PT-SAT	955	Lsd fr WFBN
N13956	Embraer EMB.145LR	145078	ex PT-SA	956	Lsd fr WFBN
N12957	Embraer EMB.145LR	145080	ex PT-S	957	Lsd fr WFBN
N13958	Embraer EMB.145LR	145085	ex PT-S	958	Lsd fr WFBN
N14959	Embraer EMB.145LR	145091	ex PT-S	959	Lsd fr WFBN
N14960	Embraer EMB.145LR	145100	ex PT-S	960; 100th c/s	Lsd fr WFBN
N16961	Embraer EMB.145LR	145103	ex PT-S	961	Lsd fr WFBN
N27962	Embraer EMB.145LR	145110	ex PT-S	962	Lsd fr WFBN
N16963	Embraer EMB.145LR	145116	ex PT-SCS	963	Lsd fr WFBN
N13964	Embraer EMB.145LR	145123	ex PT-SCZ	964	Lsd fr WFBN
N13965	Embraer EMB.145LR	145125	ex PT-SDC	965	Lsd fr WFBN
N19966	Embraer EMB.145LR	145131	ex PT-SDI	966	Lsd fr WFBN
N12967	Embraer EMB.145LR	145133	ex PT-SDK	967	Lsd fr WFBN
N13968	Embraer EMB.145LR	145138	ex PT-SDP	968	Lsd fr WFBN
N13969	Embraer EMB.145LR	145141	ex PT-SDR	969	Lsd fr WFBN
N13970	Embraer EMB.145LR	145146	ex PT-SDW	970	Lsd fr WFBN
N22971	Embraer EMB.145LR	145149	ex PT-SDZ	971	Lsd fr WFBN
N14972	Embraer EMB.145LR	145151	ex PT-SEC	972	Lsd fr WFBN
N15973	Embraer EMB.145LR	145159	ex PT-S	973	Lsd fr WFBN
N14974	Embraer EMB.145LR	145161	ex PT-S	974	Lsd fr WFBN
N13975	Embraer EMB.145LR	145163	ex PT-S	975	
N16976	Embraer EMB.145LR	145171	ex PT-S	976	
N14977	Embraer EMB.145LR	145175	ex PT-S	977	
N13978	Embraer EMB.145LR	145180	ex PT-S	978	
N13979	Embraer EMB.145LR	145181	ex PT-S	979	
N15980	Embraer EMB.145LR	145202	ex PT-S	980	
N16981	Embraer EMB.145LR	145208	ex PT-S	981	
N18982	Embraer EMB.145LR	145223	ex PT-S	982	
N15983	Embraer EMB.145LR	145239	ex PT-SIE	983	
N17984	Embraer EMB.145LR	145246	ex PT-SIK	984	
N15985	Embraer EMB.145LR	145248	ex PT-SIL	985	Lsd fr WFBN
N15986	Embraer EMB.145LR	145254	ex PT-SIO	986	
N16987	Embraer EMB.145ER	145261	ex PT-SIU	987	
N13988	Embraer EMB.145LR	145265	ex PT-SIX	988	
N13989	Embraer EMB.145LR	145271	ex PT-SJN	989	
N13990	Embraer EMB.145LR	145277	ex PT-SJT	990	
N14991	Embraer EMB.145LR	145278	ex PT-SJU	991	
N13992	Embraer EMB.145LR	145284	ex PT-S	992	
N13993	Embraer EMB.145LR	145289	ex PT-SKG	993	
N13994	Embraer EMB.145LR	145291	ex PT-SKI	994	Lsd fr WFBN
N13995	Embraer EMB.145LR	145295	ex PT-SKM	995	Lsd fr WFBN
N12996	Embraer EMB.145LR	145296	ex PT-SKN	996	Lsd fr WFBN
N13997	Embraer EMB.145LR	145298	ex PT-SKP	997	Lsd fr WFBN
N14998	Embraer EMB.145LR	145302	ex PT-SKT	998	Lsd fr WFBN
N16999	Embraer EMB.145LR	145307	ex PT-SKY	999	Lsd fr WFBN
N18101	Embraer EMB.145XR	145590	ex PT-XHF	101	Lsd fr WFBN
N18102	Embraer EMB.145XR	145643	ex PT-SEE	102	Lsd fr WFBN
N24103	Embraer EMB.145XR	145645	ex PT-SEF	103	Lsd fr WFBN
N41104	Embraer EMB.145XR	145646	ex PT-SEG	104	Lsd fr WFBN
N14105	Embraer EMB.145XR	145649	ex PT-SEJ	105	Lsd fr WFBN
N11106	Embraer EMB.145XR	145650	ex PT-SEK	106	Lsd fr WFBN
N11107	Embraer EMB.145XR	145654	ex PT-SEO	107	Lsd fr WFBN
N17108	Embraer EMB.145XR	145655	ex PT-SEP	108	Lsd fr WFBN
N11109	Embraer EMB.145XR	145657	ex PT-SER	109	Lsd fr WFBN
N34110	Embraer EMB.145XR	145658	ex PT-SES	110	Lsd fr WFBN
N34111	Embraer EMB.145XR	145659	ex PT-SET	111	Lsd fr WFBN
N16112	Embraer EMB.145XR	145660	ex PT-SEU	112	Lsd fr WFBN
N11113	Embraer EMB.145XR	145662	ex PT-SEW	113	Lsd fr WFBN
N18114	Embraer EMB.145XR	145664	ex PT-SEY	114	Lsd fr WFBN
N17115	Embraer EMB.145XR	145666	ex PT-SFA	115	Lsd fr WFBN
N14116	Embraer EMB.145XR	145672	ex PT-SFF	116	Lsd fr WFBN
N14117	Embraer EMB.145XR	145674	ex PT-SFH	117	Lsd fr WFBN
N13118	Embraer EMB.145XR	145675	ex PT-SFI	118	Lsd fr WFBN
N11119	Embraer EMB.145XR	145677	ex PT-SFK	119	Lsd fr WFBN
N18120	Embraer EMB.145XR	145681	ex PT-SFN	120	Lsd fr WFBN
N11121	Embraer EMB.145XR	145683	ex PT-SFP	121	Lsd fr WFBN
N12122	Embraer EMB.145XR	145684	ex PT-SFQ	122	
N13123	Embraer EMB.145XR	145688	ex PT-SFU	123	
N13124	Embraer EMB.145XR	145689	ex PT-SFV	124	
N14125	Embraer EMB.145XR	145690	ex PT-SFW	125	
N12126	Embraer EMB.145XR	145693	ex PT-SFZ	126	
N11127	Embraer EMB.145XR	145697	ex PT-SGC	127	Lsd fr WFBN
N24128	Embraer EMB.145XR	145700	ex PT-SGE	128	Lsd fr WFBN
N21129	Embraer EMB.145XR	145703	ex PT-SGH	129	
N21130	Embraer EMB.145XR	145704	ex PT-SGI	130	
N31131	Embraer EMB.145XR	145705	ex PT-SGJ	131	
N13132	Embraer EMB.145XR	145708	ex PT-SGL	132	
N13133	Embraer EMB.145XR	145712	ex PT-SGP	133	

N25134	Embraer EMB.145XR	145714	ex PT-SGR	134	
N12135	Embraer EMB.145XR	145718	ex PT-SSU	135	
N12136	Embraer EMB.145XR	145719	ex PT-SGV	136	
N11137	Embraer EMB.145XR	145721	ex PT-SGX	137	
N17138	Embraer EMB.145XR	145727	ex PT-SHD	138	
N23139	Embraer EMB.145XR	145731	ex PT-SHH	139	
N11140	Embraer EMB.145XR	145732	ex PT-SHI	140	
N26141	Embraer EMB.145XR	145733	ex PT-SHJ	141	
N12142	Embraer EMB.145XR	145735	ex PT-SHL	142	
N14143	Embraer EMB.145XR	145739	ex PT-SHT	143	
N21144	Embraer EMB.145XR	145741	ex PT-SJA	144	
N12145	Embraer EMB.145XR	145745	ex PT-SJE	145	
N17146	Embraer EMB.145XR	145746	ex PT-SJF	146	
N16147	Embraer EMB.145XR	145749	ex PT-SJI	147	Lsd fr WFBN
N14148	Embraer EMB.145XR	145751	ex PT-S	148	Lsd fr WFBN
N16149	Embraer EMB.145XR	145753	ex PT-SJM	149	Lsd fr WFBN
N11150	Embraer EMB.145XR	145756	ex PT-SJP	150	Lsd fr WFBN
N16151	Embraer EMB.145XR	145758	ex PT-SJQ	151	Lsd fr WFBN
N27152	Embraer EMB.145XR	145759	ex PT-S	152	
N14153	Embraer EMB.145XR	145761	ex PT-SJS	153	
N21154	Embraer EMB.145XR	145772	ex PT-SMC	154	
N11155	Embraer EMB.145XR	145782	ex PT-S	155	
N10156	Embraer EMB.145XR		ex PT-S	156 on order	
N12157	Embraer EMB.145XR		ex PT-S	157 on order	
N14158	Embraer EMB.145XR		ex PT-S	158 on order 04	
N17159	Embraer EMB.145XR		ex PT-S	159 on order 04	
N12160	Embraer EMB.145XR		ex PT-S	160 on order 04	
N13161	Embraer EMB.145XR		ex PT-S	161 on order 04	
N14162	Embraer EMB.145XR		ex PT-S	162 on order 04	
N12163	Embraer EMB.145XR		ex PT-S	163 on order 04	
N11164	Embraer EMB.145XR		ex PT-S	164 on order 04	
N11165	Embraer EMB.145XR		ex PT-S	165 on order 04	
N12166	Embraer EMB.145XR		ex PT-S	166 on order 04	
N12167	Embraer EMB.145XR		ex PT-S	167 on order 04	
N14168	Embraer EMB.145XR		ex PT-S	168 on order 04	
N17169	Embraer EMB.145XR		ex PT-S	169 on order 04	
N16170	Embraer EMB.145XR		ex PT-S	170 on order 04	
N14171	Embraer EMB.145XR		ex PT-S	171 on order 04	
N12172	Embraer EMB.145XR		ex PT-S	172 on order 04	
N14173	Embraer EMB.145XR		ex PT-S	173 on order 04	
N14174	Embraer EMB.145XR		ex PT-S	174 on order 04	
N12175	Embraer EMB.145XR		ex PT-S	175 on order 04	

29 more Embraer EMB.145XRs are on order for delivery in 2005 (21) plus final eight in 2006)
Continental Express is the trading name of ExpressJet Airlines

CONTINENTAL MICRONESIA

Air Mike (CS/CMI) (IATA 596)   Guam, GU (GUM)

N25201	Boeing 737-824	443/28958		201	
N13227	Boeing 737-824	262/28788	ex N1787B	227	
N14228	Boeing 737-824	281/28792	ex N1787B	228	
N26232	Boeing 737-824	304/28942		232	
N14235	Boeing 737-824	342/28947		235	
N35236	Boeing 737-824	367/28801		236	
N14240	Boeing 737-824	394/28952		240	
N27246	Boeing 737-824	413/28956		246	
N13248	Boeing 737-824	435/28808		248	

A subsidiary of Continental Airlines and operates Boeing 737-824's and Boeing 767-424ERs leased from the parent as required

CONTRACT AIR CARGO

Trans Auto (TSU)   Pontiac-Oakland, MI (PTK)

N131FL	Convair 580	151	ex N5804	Freighter
N141FL	Convair 580	111	ex N302K	Freighter
N151FL	Convair 580	51	ex N5810	Freighter
N161FL	Convair 580	430	ex N303K	Freighter
N171FL	Convair 580	318	ex N300K	Freighter
N181FL	Convair 580	387	ex N301K	Freighter
N191FL	Convair 580	326	ex N923DR	Freighter
N371FL	Convair 5800	309	ex C-FMKF	Freighter
N381FL	Convair 5800	276	ex C-FKFS	Freighter
N391FL	Convair 5800	278	ex C-GKFD	Freighter
N631MB	Convair 580	176	ex C-GFHF	Freighter
N631MW	Convair 580	137	ex C-GQBP	Freighter
N723ES	Convair 580	217	ex N7146X	Freighter
N991FL	Convair 580	508	ex C-GTTG	Freighter
N3UW	Convair 580	343	ex N90	for conv to 5800

N211FL	Boeing 727-172C (Dugan 3)	575/19807	ex C-GKFT	Lsd fr Intl Trading Co of Yukon
N221FL	Boeing 727-22C (FedEx 3)	543/19805	ex C-GKFW	Lsd fr Intl Trading Co of Yukon
N231FL	Boeing 727-22C (FedEx 3)	438/19205	ex C-GKFP	Lsd fr Intl Trading Co of Yukon

Contract Air Cargo is an operating name of IFL Group

CORPJET

Beewee (BWE) — Baltimore-Martin State, MD (MTN)

Previously listed as Baltimore Air Transport

N208HF	Cessna 208 Caravan I	20800116	ex C-GMPR	Freighter	Lsd fr CE Lsg
N715BT	Cessna 208B Caravan I	208B0835		Freighter	Lsd fr Hummingbird Lsg
N716BT	Cessna 208B Caravan I	208B0843		Freighter	Lsd fr Cardinal Lsg LLC
N717BT	Cessna 208B Caravan I	208B0863		Freighter	Lsd fr Tarene Lsg
N718BT	Cessna 208B Caravan I	208B0881		Freighter	Lsd fr C&R Lsg
N719BT	Cessna 208B Caravan I	208B0898		Freighter	Lsd fr KC Lsg
N1301K	Cessna 208B Caravan I	208B0488		Freighter	Lsd fr Sea Hawk Lsg
N917BT	Beech 200 Super King Air	BB-225	ex N8534W		Lsd fr CE Lsg
N2698C	Swearingen SA.227AC Metro III	AC-665			Lsd fr Sparrow Lsg

CorpJet is the trading name of Baltimore Air Transport

CORPORATE AIR

Air Spur (CPT) — Billings-Logan Intl, MT (BIL)

N710FX	Cessna 208B Caravan I	208B0431			
N716FX	Cessna 208B Caravan I	208B0442			
N724FX	Cessna 208B Caravan I	208B0458			
N730FX	Cessna 208B Caravan I	208B0477			
N751FE	Cessna 208B Caravan I	208B0245			
N794FE	Cessna 208B Caravan I	208B0292			
N796FE	Cessna 208B Caravan I	208B0212	ex C-FEXY		
N797FE	Cessna 208B Caravan I	208B0042	ex C-FEXH		
N798FE	Cessna 208B Caravan I	208B0174	ex C-FEDY		
N799FE	Cessna 208A Caravan I	20800065	ex C-FEXF		
N800FE	Cessna 208 Caravan I	20800007	ex (N9300F)		
N812FE	Cessna 208A Caravan I	20800040	ex (N9401F)		
N827FE	Cessna 208A Caravan I	20800072	ex (N9491F)		
N846FE	Cessna 208B Caravan I	208B0154			
N851FE	Cessna 208B Caravan I	208B0166			
N863FE	Cessna 208B Caravan I	208B0186			
N864FE	Cessna 208B Caravan I	208B0187			
N867FE	Cessna 208B Caravan I	208B0191			
N877FE	Cessna 208B Caravan I	208B0232			
N885FE	Cessna 208B Caravan I	208B0185			
N890FE	Cessna 208B Caravan I	208B0219			
N903FE	Cessna 208B Caravan I	208B0003			
N904FE	Cessna 208B Caravan I	208B0004			
N910FE	Cessna 208B Caravan I	208B0010			
N916FE	Cessna 208B Caravan I	208B0016			
N924FE	Cessna 208B Caravan I	208B0024			
N926FE	Cessna 208B Caravan I	208B0026			
N933FE	Cessna 208B Caravan I	208B0033			
N936FE	Cessna 208B Caravan I	208B0036			
N948FE	Cessna 208B Caravan I	208B0052			
N952FE	Cessna 208B Caravan I	208B0060	ex (N960FE)		
N964FE	Cessna 208B Caravan I	208B0083			
N971FE	Cessna 208B Caravan I	208B0094			
N972FE	Cessna 208B Caravan I	208B0096			
N977FE	Cessna 208B Caravan I	208B0104			
N980FE	Cessna 208B Caravan I	208B0108			
N990FE	Cessna 208B Caravan I	208B0125			
N991FE	Cessna 208B Caravan I	208B0127			
N997FE	Cessna 208B Caravan I	208B0197			

All leased from and operated on behalf of FedEx

N125AM	Embraer EMB.120RT Brasilia	120017	ex PT-SIM	Freighter	
N210AS	Embraer EMB.120RT Brasilia	120006	ex PT-SIA	Freighter	
N217AS	Embraer EMB.120RT Brasilia	120011	ex PT-SIF	Freighter, for spares?	
N218AS	Embraer EMB.120RT Brasilia	120015	ex PT-SIK	Freighter	Lsd to VSC
N223AS	Embraer EMB.120RT Brasilia	120021	ex PT-SIQ	Freighter	
N199CA	Beech 99A	U-96	ex N503TF	Freighter	Lsd fr Molo Lsg
N223CA	Beech C99	U-200	ex SE-IZX	Freighter	Lsd fr Molo Lsg
N279CA	Beech 200 Super King Air	BB-279	ex 4X-ARD		Lsd fr Air Services
N319BH	Beech 1900C	UB-36	ex N19RA		Lsd fr Skywalker Intl
N330US	Short SD.3-30	SH3013	ex N330SB	Freighter	Lsd fr Molo Lsg
N331SB	Short SD.3-30	SH3015	ex N331CA	Freighter	
N411FS	Aero Commander 500B	1162-85		Freighter	
N533SW	de Havilland DHC-6 Twin Otter 300	533	ex 4X-AHZ		Lsd fr LOPS LLC

N617FB	Short SD.3-60	SH3617	ex G-BKUF	Freighter	
N701A	Short SD.3-60	SH3627	ex G-BKZP	Freighter	
N702PV*	de Havilland DHC-6 Twin Otter 300	702			Lsd fr LOPS LLC
N715GL	Beech 1900C	UB-15	ex N309BH	Freighter	Lsd fr Molo Lsg
N789US	Short SD.3-30	SH3002	ex N330US	Freighter	Lsd fr Molo Lsg
N972SW*	de Havilland DHC-6 Twin Otter 300	356	ex JA8790		Lsd fr LOPS LLC
N4298S	Beech 200 Super King Air	BB-198			
N7212P	Beech C99	U-220		Freighter	
N7254R	Beech 1900C	UB-22		Freighter	
N38535	de Havilland DHC-6 Twin Otter 300	414	ex G-BDHC		Lsd fr LOPS LLC

*Subleased to Corporate Air, Philippines

CORPORATE AIRLINES

Corp-X (3C)   Nashville-Intl, TN (BNA)

N856TE	British Aerospace Jetstream 32EP	856	ex N422AM	Lsd fr BAES
N860AE	British Aerospace Jetstream 32EP	860	ex G-31-860	Lsd fr BAES
N871JX	British Aerospace Jetstream 32EP	871	exN871AE	Lsd fr BAES
N872AE	British Aerospace Jetstream 32EP	872	ex G-31-872	Lsd fr BAES
N875JX	British Aerospace Jetstream 32EP	875	ex N875AE	Lsd fr BAES
N880TE	British Aerospace Jetstream 32EP	880	ex N430AM	Lsd fr BAES
N883CH	British Aerospace Jetstream 32EP	883	ex N432AM	Lsd fr BAES
(N917CX)	British Aerospace Jetstream 32EP	917	ex N917AE	Lsd fr BAES
(N921CX)	British Aerospace Jetstream 32EP	921	ex N921AE	Lsd fr BAES
N922CX	British Aerospace Jetstream 32EP	922	ex N922AE	Lsd fr BAES
(N924CX)	British Aerospace Jetstream 32EP	924	ex N924AE	Lsd fr BAES
N926AE	British Aerospace Jetstream 32EP	926	ex G-31-926	Lsd fr BAES
N933CX	British Aerospace Jetstream 32EP	933	ex N933AE	Lsd fr BAES
(N936CX)	British Aerospace Jetstream 32EP	936	ex N936AE	Lsd fr BAES
(N937CX)	British Aerospace Jetstream 32EP	937	ex N937AE	Lsd fr BAES
(N938CX)	British Aerospace Jetstream 32EP	938	ex N938AE	Lsd fr BAES
(N944CX)	British Aerospace Jetstream 32EP	944	ex N944AE	Lsd fr BAES

Operated as American Connection using AA flight numbers

CORPORATE EXPRESS

Eifel (IFL)   Pontiac-Oakland, MI (PTK)

| N801FL | Cessna 208B Caravan I | 0809 | ex N5264E |
| N811FL | Cessna 208B Caravan I | 0813 | ex N5151D |

Corporate Express is an operating division of IFL Group; sister company of Contract Air Cargo

CSA AIR

Iron Air (IRO)   Iron Mountain-Kingsford-Ford, MI (IMT)

N703FX	Cessna 208B Caravan I	208B0423	
N706FX	Cessna 208B Caravan I	208B0426	
N712FX	Cessna 208B Caravan I	208B0435	
N717FX	Cessna 208B Caravan I	208B0445	
N727FX	Cessna 208B Caravan I	208B0468	
N752FE	Cessna 208B Caravan I	208B0247	
N761FE	Cessna 208B Caravan I	208B0254	
N767FE	Cessna 208B Caravan I	208B0262	
N784FE	Cessna 208B Caravan I	208B0282	
N795FE	Cessna 208B Caravan I	208B0293	
N828FE	Cessna 208B Caravan I	208B0122	ex F-GHHD
N830FE	Cessna 208A Caravan I	20800075	ex (N9502F)
N843FE	Cessna 208B Caravan I	208B0147	
N858FE	Cessna 208B Caravan I	208B0178	
N871FE	Cessna 208B Caravan I	208B0198	
N883FE	Cessna 208B Caravan I	208B0210	
N884FE	Cessna 208B Caravan I	208B0233	
N893FE	Cessna 208B Caravan I	208B0223	
N906FE	Cessna 208B Caravan I	208B0006	
N907FE	Cessna 208B Caravan I	208B0007	
N914FE	Cessna 208B Caravan I	208B0014	
N923FE	Cessna 208B Caravan I	208B0023	
N925FE	Cessna 208B Caravan I	208B0025	
N927FE	Cessna 208B Caravan I	208B0027	
N946FE	Cessna 208B Caravan I	208B0048	ex (N948FE)
N954FE	Cessna 208B Caravan I	208B0064	ex (N964FE)
N986FE	Cessna 208B Caravan I	208B0194	
N993FE	Cessna 208B Caravan I	208B0130	

All leased from and operated on behalf of FedEx

CUSTOM AIR SERVICE

N89FA	Aviation Traders ATL-98 Carvair	27249/9	ex G-ASHZ	Fat Annie	Lsd fr Gator Global F/S

CUSTOM AIR TRANSPORT

Catt (5R/CTT)

Fort Lauderdale-Hollywood Intl, FL (FLL)

N128NA	Boeing 727-2J7F (FedEx 3)	1033/20879			Lsd fr ART 20879
N220NE	Boeing 727-31F (Raisbeck 3)	160/18905	ex N840TW		Lsd fr Charter America
N511PE	Boeing 727-232F (FedEx 3)	917/20634	ex N452DA		Lsd fr ART 20634
N742RW	Boeing 727-2M7F (FedEx 3)	1693/21952			Lsd fr Pacific Air
N902PG	Boeing 727-281F (Raisbeck 3)	958/20725	ex OY-TNT		Lsd fr Pegasus
N1279E	Boeing 727-2Q8F (FedEx 3)	1540/21971			Lsd fr ART 21971
N8887Z	Boeing 727-281F (FedEx 3)	1537/21856			Lsd fr Pegasus
N24343	Boeing 727-231F (Super 27)	1458/21630			Lsd fr Pacific AirCorp
N54354	Boeing 727-231F (super 27)	1580/21986			Lsd fr ART 21986

Some operated for Charter America as and when required

DELTA AIR LINES

Delta (DL/DAL) (IATA 006)

Atlanta-Hartsfield Intl, GA (ATL)

N235WA	Boeing 737-2J8	890/22859	ex N4562N	359; stored GYR	Lsd fr WFBN
N236WA	Boeing 737-247	1061/23184		360; stored GYR	
N237WA	Boeing 737-247	1065/23185		361; stored GYR	
N238WA	Boeing 737-247	1066/23186		362	
N239WA	Boeing 737-247	1070/23187		363; stored GYR	
N242WA	Boeing 737-247	1257/23516		364; stored MHV	Lsd fr WFBN
N243WA	Boeing 737-247	1261/23517		365; stored MHV	Lsd fr WFBN
N244WA	Boeing 737-247	1265/23518		366; stored MHV	Lsd fr WFBN
N245WA	Boeing 737-247	1299/23519		372	
N301DL	Boeing 737-232	991/23073		301	
N302DL	Boeing 737-232	993/23074		302; stored GYR	
N303DL	Boeing 737-232	994/23075		303	
N304DL	Boeing 737-232	995/23076		304	
N305DL	Boeing 737-232	996/23077		305	
N306DL	Boeing 737-232	1000/23078		306	
N307DL	Boeing 737-232	1003/23079		307	
N308DL	Boeing 737-232	1004/23080		308	
N309DL	Boeing 737-232	1005/23081		309; stored GYR	
N310DA	Boeing 737-232	1006/23082		310	
N311DL	Boeing 737-232	1008/23083		311	
N312DL	Boeing 737-232	1009/23084		312	
N313DL	Boeing 737-232	1011/23085		313	
N314DA	Boeing 737-232	1012/23086		314	
N315DL	Boeing 737-232	1013/23087		315	
N316DL	Boeing 737-232	1018/23088		316; stored GYR	
N317DL	Boeing 737-232	1019/23089		317	
N318DL	Boeing 737-232	1020/23090		318	
N319DL	Boeing 737-232	1021/23091		319; stored GYR	
N320DL	Boeing 737-232	1023/23092		320	
N321DL	Boeing 737-232	1024/23093		321	
N322DL	Boeing 737-232	1026/23094		322 stored GYR	
N323DL	Boeing 737-232	1027/23095		323	
N324DL	Boeing 737-232	1028/23096		324	
N325DL	Boeing 737-232	1029/23097		325	
N326DL	Boeing 737-232	1031/23098		326; stored GYR	
N327DL	Boeing 737-232	1035/23099		327	
N328DL	Boeing 737-232	1038/23100		328; stored GYR	
N329DL	Boeing 737-232	1041/23101		329	Lsd fr GECAS
N330DL	Boeing 737-232	1045/23102		330; stored GYR	
N331DL	Boeing 737-232	1051/23103		331	
N332DL	Boeing 737-232	1062/23104		332	
N334DL	Boeing 737-232	1068/23105		334; stored GYR	
N373DL	Boeing 737-247	1329/23520	ex N246WA	373	
N374DL	Boeing 737-247	1342/23521	ex N247WA	374; stored GYR	
N375DL	Boeing 737-247	1347/23602	ex N248WA	375	
N376DL	Boeing 737-247	1361/23603	ex (N249WA)	376	
N377DL	Boeing 737-247	1369/23604	ex (N254WA)	377	
N378DL	Boeing 737-247	1371/23605	ex (N255WA)	378	
N379DL	Boeing 737-247	1379/23606	ex (N256WA)	379	
N380DL	Boeing 737-247	1387/23607	ex (N257WA)	380	
N381DL	Boeing 737-247	1399/23608	ex (N258WA)	381; stored GYR	
N382DL	Boeing 737-247	1403/23609	ex (N259WA)	382	

All fitted with Nordam Stage 3 hushkits

N221DL	Boeing 737-35B	1467/23970	ex D-AGEA	221	Lsd fr CIT Lsg
N222DZ	Boeing 737-35B	1482/23971	ex D-AGEB	222	Lsd fr CIT Lsg

N223DZ	Boeing 737-35B	1537/23972	ex D-AGEC	223	Lsd fr Pembroke
N224DA	Boeing 737-35B	1628/24269	ex D-AGED	224	Lsd fr Pembroke
N225DL	Boeing 737-35B	2053/25069	ex D-AGEF	225	Lsd fr Pembroke
N231DN	Boeing 737-35B	1365/23717	ex D-AGEH	231	Lsd fr Pembroke
N232DZ	Boeing 737-35B	1602/24220	ex D-AGEI	232	Lsd fr Pembroke
N241DL	Boeing 737-330	1439/23833	ex D-ABWA	241	Lsd fr Pembroke
N242DL	Boeing 737-330	1454/23834	ex D-ABWB	242	Lsd fr Pembroke
N302WA	Boeing 737-347	1106/23182		202; Wally Bird	Lsd fr BCI A/c Lsg
N303WA	Boeing 737-347	1108/23183		203; Salt Lake City	
N304WA	Boeing 737-347	1170/23345		204	
N305WA	Boeing 737-347	1172/23346		205	
N306WA	Boeing 737-347	1173/23347		206	
N307WA	Boeing 737-347	1218/23440		207	Lsd fr BCI A/c Lsg
N308WA	Boeing 737-347	1220/23441		208	Lsd fr BCI A/c Lsg
N309WA	Boeing 737-347	1239/23442		209	Lsd fr BCI A/c Lsg
N311WA	Boeing 737-347	1287/23597		211	
N312WA	Boeing 737-347	1289/23598		212	
N313WA	Boeing 737-347	1324/23599		213	Lsd fr State Street
N947WP	Boeing 737-3B7	1308/23376	ex N501AU	253	Lsd fr LIFT Georgia
N948WP	Boeing 737-301	1132/23259	ex N581US	252	Lsd fr GECAS
N951WP	Boeing 737-3B7	1007/22951	ex N372US	251	Lsd fr GECAS
N952WP	Boeing 737-3B7	1339/23378	ex N503AU	254	Lsd fr GECAS
N2310	Boeing 737-347	1269/23596		210	
N3301	Boeing 737-347	1087/23181		201; Larry Lee	Lsd fr BCI A/c Lsg
N371DA	Boeing 737-832	115/29619	ex N1787B	3701 stored GYR	
N372DA	Boeing 737-832	118/29620	ex N1782B	3702	
N373DA	Boeing 737-832	123/29621	ex N1800B	3703 stored GYR	
N374DA	Boeing 737-832	128/29622	ex N1787B	3704 stored GYR	
N375DA	Boeing 737-832	145/29623		3705 stored GYR	
N376DA	Boeing 737-832	176/29624		3706 stored GYR	
N377DA	Boeing 737-832	264/29625		3707 stored GYR	
N378DA	Boeing 737-832	340/30265		3708 stored GYR	
N379DA	Boeing 737-832	351/30349		3709	
N380DA	Boeing 737-832	361/30266		3710	
N381DN	Boeing 737-832	365/30350	ex (N381DA)	3711	
N382DA	Boeing 737-832	389/30345		3712	
N383DN	Boeing 737-832	393/30346	ex (N383DA)	3713	
N384DA	Boeing 737-832	412/30347		3714	
N385DA	Boeing 737-832	418/30348		3715	
N386DA	Boeing 737-832	446/30373	ex N1780B	3716	
N387DA	Boeing 737-832	457/30374	ex N1795B	3717	
N388DA	Boeing 737-832	469/30375		3718	
N389DA	Boeing 737-832	513/30376	ex N1787B	3719	
N390DA	Boeing 737-832	518/30536	ex N6063S	3720	
N391DA	Boeing 737-832	535/30560	ex N1787B	3721	
N392DA	Boeing 737-832	564/30561		3722	
N393DA	Boeing 737-832	584/30377	ex N1782B	3723	
N394DA	Boeing 737-832	589/30562		3724	
N395DN	Boeing 737-832	604/30773		3725	Delta Shuttle
N396DA	Boeing 737-832	632/30378	ex N1795B	3726	Delta Shuttle
N397DA	Boeing 737-832	638/30537		3727	Delta Shuttle
N398DA	Boeing 737-832	641/30774		3728	Delta Shuttle
N399DA	Boeing 737-832	657/30379		3729	Delta Shuttle
N3730B	Boeing 737-832	662/30538		3730	Delta Shuttle
N3731T	Boeing 737-832	665/30775		3731	Delta Shuttle
N3732J	Boeing 737-832	674/30380		3732	Delta Shuttle
N3733Z	Boeing 737-832	685/30539		3733	Delta Shuttle
N3734B	Boeing 737-832	689/30776		3734	Delta Shuttle
N3735D	Boeing 737-832	694/30381	ex (N3735J)	3735	Delta Shuttle
N3736C	Boeing 737-832	709/30540		3736	Delta Shuttle
N3737C	Boeing 737-832	712/30799		3737	Delta Shuttle
N3738B	Boeing 737-832	723/30382		3738	Delta Shuttle
N3739P	Boeing 737-832	729/30541		3739	Delta Shuttle
N3740C	Boeing 737-832	732/30800		3740	Delta Shuttle
N3741S	Boeing 737-832	750/30487		3741	
N3742C	Boeing 737-832	755/30835		3742	
N3743H	Boeing 737-832	770/30836		3743	
N3744F	Boeing 737-832	805/30837		3744	
N3745B	Boeing 737-832	831/32373		3745	
N3746H	Boeing 737-832	842/30488		3746	
N3747D	Boeing 737-832	846/32374		3747	
N3748Y	Boeing 737-832	865/30489		3748	
N3749D	Boeing 737-832	867/30490		3749	
N3750D	Boeing 737-832	870/32375	ex N1787B	3750	
N3751B	Boeing 737-832	892/30491		3751	
N3752	Boeing 737-832	894/30492		3752	
N3753	Boeing 737-832	899/32626		3753	
N3754A	Boeing 737-832	907/29626		3754	
N3755D	Boeing 737-832	914/29627		3755	
N3756	Boeing 737-832	917/30493	ex N1799B	3756	
N3757D	Boeing 737-832	921/30813		3757	

N3758Y	Boeing 737-832	923/30814	3758	
N3759	Boeing 737-832	949/30815	3759	
N3760C	Boeing 737-832	952/30816	3760	
N3761R	Boeing 737-832	964/29628	3761	
N3762Y	Boeing 737-832	968/30817	3762	
N3763D	Boeing 737-832	1003/29629	3763	
N3764D	Boeing 737-832	1006/30818	3764	
N3765	Boeing 737-832	1008/30819	3765	
N3766	Boeing 737-832	1029/30820	3766	
N3767	Boeing 737-832	1031/30821	3767	
N3768	Boeing 737-832	1053/29630	3768	
N3769L	Boeing 737-832	1057/30822	3769	
N3771K	Boeing 737-832	1103/29632	3771	
N37700	Boeing 737-832	1074/29631	3770	

A further 50 Boeing 737-832s are on order for delivery in 2006 (19), 2007 (23) and 2008 (8)

N601DL	Boeing 757-232	37/22808	601	
N602DL	Boeing 757-232	39/22809	602	
N603DL	Boeing 757-232	41/22810	603	
N604DL	Boeing 757-232	43/22811	604	
N605DL	Boeing 757-232	46/22812	605	
N606DL	Boeing 757-232	49/22813	606	
N607DL	Boeing 757-232	61/22814	607	
N608DA	Boeing 757-232	64/22815	608	
N609DL	Boeing 757-232	65/22816	609	
N610DL	Boeing 757-232	66/22817	610	
N611DL	Boeing 757-232	71/22818	611	
N612DL	Boeing 757-232	73/22819	612	
N613DL	Boeing 757-232	84/22820	613	
N614DL	Boeing 757-232	85/22821	614	
N615DL	Boeing 757-232	87/22822	615	
N616DL	Boeing 757-232	91/22823	616	
N617DL	Boeing 757-232	92/22907	617	
N618DL	Boeing 757-232	95/22908	618	
N619DL	Boeing 757-232	101/22909	619	
N620DL	Boeing 757-232	111/22910	620	
N621DL	Boeing 757-232	112/22911	621	
N622DL	Boeing 757-232	113/22912	622	
N623DL	Boeing 757-232	118/22913	623	
N624DL	Boeing 757-232	120/22914	624	
N625DL	Boeing 757-232	126/22915	625	
N626DL	Boeing 757-232	128/22916	626	
N627DL	Boeing 757-232	129/22917	627	
N628DL	Boeing 757-232	133/22918	628	
N629DL	Boeing 757-232	134/22919	629	
N630DL	Boeing 757-232	135/22920	630	
N631DL	Boeing 757-232	138/23612	631	
N632DL	Boeing 757-232	154/23613	632	
N633DL	Boeing 757-232	157/23614	633	
N634DL	Boeing 757-232	158/23615	634	
N635DL	Boeing 757-232	159/23762 ex 'N635DA'	635	
N636DL	Boeing 757-232	164/23763	636	
N637DL	Boeing 757-232	171/23760	637	
N638DL	Boeing 757-232	177/23761	638	
N639DL	Boeing 757-232	198/23993	638	
N640DL	Boeing 757-232	201/23994	640	
N641DL	Boeing 757-232	202/23995	641	Lsd fr Arkia Lsg
N642DL	Boeing 757-232	205/23996	642	
N643DL	Boeing 757-232	206/23997	643	
N644DL	Boeing 757-232	207/23998	644	
N645DL	Boeing 757-232	216/24216	645; Song	Lsd fr Arkia Lsg
N646DL	Boeing 757-232	217/24217	646	
N647DL	Boeing 757-232	222/24218	647	
N648DL	Boeing 757-232	223/24372	648	
N649DL	Boeing 757-232	229/24389	649; Song	
N650DL	Boeing 757-232	230/24390	650	
N651DL	Boeing 757-232	238/24391	651; Song	
N652DL	Boeing 757-232	239/24392	652	
N653DL	Boeing 757-232	261/24393	653	Lsd fr Arkia Lsg
N654DL	Boeing 757-232	264/24394	654	
N655DL	Boeing 757-232	265/24395	655	
N656DL	Boeing 757-232	266/24396	656	
N657DL	Boeing 757-232	286/24419	657	
N658DL	Boeing 757-232	287/24420	658	Lsd fr WFBN
N659DL	Boeing 757-232	293/24421	659	
N660DL	Boeing 757-232	294/24422	660	
N661DN	Boeing 757-232	335/24972	661	
N662DN	Boeing 757-232	342/24991	662	
N663DN	Boeing 757-232	343/24992	663	
N664DN	Boeing 757-232	347/25012	664	
N665DN	Boeing 757-232	349/25013	665	
N666DN	Boeing 757-232	354/25034	666	

N667DN	Boeing 757-232	355/25035	667
N668DN	Boeing 757-232	376/25141	668
N669DN	Boeing 757-232	377/25142	669
N670DN	Boeing 757-232	415/25331	670
N671DN	Boeing 757-232	416/25332	671
N672DL	Boeing 757-232	429/25977	672
N673DL	Boeing 757-232	430/25978	673
N674DL	Boeing 757-232	439/25979	674
N675DL	Boeing 757-232	448/25980	675
N676DL	Boeing 757-232	455/25981	676
N677DL	Boeing 757-232	456/25982	677
N678DL	Boeing 757-232	465/25983	678
N679DA	Boeing 757-232	500/26955	679
N680DA	Boeing 757-232	502/26956	680
N681DA	Boeing 757-232	516/26957	681
N682DA	Boeing 757-232	518/26958	682
N683DA	Boeing 757-232	533/27103	683
N684DA	Boeing 757-232	535/27104	684; Song
N685DA	Boeing 757-232	667/27588	685; Song
N686DA	Boeing 757-232	689/27589	686
N687DL	Boeing 757-232	800/27586	687
N688DL	Boeing 757-232	803/27587	688
N689DL	Boeing 757-232	807/27172	689
N690DL	Boeing 757-232	808/27585	690
N692DL	Boeing 757-232	820/29724 ex N1799B	692
N693DL	Boeing 757-232	826/29725 ex N1799B	693; Song
N694DL	Boeing 757-232	831/29726	694
N695DL	Boeing 757-232	838/29727 ex N1795B	695; Song
N696DL	Boeing 757-232	845/29728 ex N1795B	696
N697DL	Boeing 757-232	880/30318 ex N1795B	697; Song
N698DL	Boeing 757-232	885/29911	698; Song
N699DL	Boeing 757-232	887/29970 ex N1795B	699
N750AT	Boeing 757-212ER	45/23126 ex 9V-SGL	6902
N751AT	Boeing 757-212ER	44/23125 ex 9V-SGK	6901
N752AT	Boeing 757-212ER	48/23128 ex 9V-SGN	6904
N757AT	Boeing 757-212ER	47/23127 ex 9V-SGM	6903
N900PC	Boeing 757-26D	740/28446	691
N6700	Boeing 757-232	890/30337	6700
N6701	Boeing 757-232	892/30187	6701
N6702	Boeing 757-232	898/30188	6702; Song
N6703D	Boeing 757-232	908/30234 ex N1795B	6703
N6704Z	Boeing 757-232	914/30396 ex N1795B	6704; Song
N6705Y	Boeing 757-232	917/30397	6705; Song
N6706Q	Boeing 757-232	921/30422	6706; Song
N6707A	Boeing 757-232	927/30395	6707
N6708D	Boeing 757-232	934/30480	6708
N6709	Boeing 757-232	937/30481	6709; Song
N6710E	Boeing 757-232	939/30482	6710
N6711M	Boeing 757-232	941/30483	6711
N6712B	Boeing 757-232	942/30484	6712; Song
N6713Y	Boeing 757-232	944/30777	6713
N6714Q	Boeing 757-232	949/30485	6714
N6715C	Boeing 757-232	953/30486	6715; Song
N6716C	Boeing 757-232	955/30838	6716; Song
N67171	Boeing 757-232	959/30839	6717; Song

36 to be converted to 199 seater aircraft for use by new low-fare Song

N101DA	Boeing 767-232	6/22213	101
N102DA	Boeing 767-232	12/22214	102 Spirit of Delta
N103DA	Boeing 767-232	17/22215	103; stored GYR
N104DA	Boeing 767-232	26/22216	104
N105DA	Boeing 767-232	27/22217	105
N106DA	Boeing 767-232	31/22218	106; stored GYR
N107DL	Boeing 767-232	37/22219	107
N108DL	Boeing 767-232	38/22220	108
N109DL	Boeing 767-232	53/22221	109
N110DL	Boeing 767-232	56/22222	110
N111DN	Boeing 767-232	74/22223	111
N112DL	Boeing 767-232	76/22224	112; stored GYR
N113DA	Boeing 767-232	77/22225	113
N114DL	Boeing 767-232	78/22226	114; stored GYR
N115DA	Boeing 767-232	83/22227	115; stored GYR
N116DL	Boeing 767-332	136/23275	116
N117DL	Boeing 767-332	151/23276	117
N118DL	Boeing 767-332	152/23277	118
N119DL	Boeing 767-332	153/23278	119
N120DL	Boeing 767-332	154/23279	120
N121DE	Boeing 767-332	162/23435	121
N122DL	Boeing 767-332	163/23436	122
N123DN	Boeing 767-332	188/23437	123
N124DE	Boeing 767-332	189/23438	124
N125DL	Boeing 767-332	200/24075	125

N126DL	Boeing 767-332	201/24076		126	
N127DL	Boeing 767-332	203/24077		127	
N128DL	Boeing 767-332	207/24078		128	
N129DL	Boeing 767-332	209/24079		129	
N130DL	Boeing 767-332	216/24080		130	
N131DN	Boeing 767-332	320/24852		131	
N132DN	Boeing 767-332	345/24981		132	
N133DN	Boeing 767-332	348/24982		133	
N134DL	Boeing 767-332	353/25123		134	
N135DL	Boeing 767-332	356/25145		135	
N136DL	Boeing 767-332	374/25146		136	
N137DL	Boeing 767-332	392/25306		137	
N138DL	Boeing 767-332	410/25409		138	
N139DL	Boeing 767-332	427/25984		139	
N140LL	Boeing 767-332	499/25988		1401	
N143DA	Boeing 767-332	721/25991		1403	
N144DA	Boeing 767-332	751/27584		1404	
N152DL	Boeing 767-3P6ER	339/24984	ex A4O-GM	1502	
N153DL	Boeing 767-3P6ER	340/24985	ex A4O-GN	1503	
N154DL	Boeing 767-3P6ER	389/25241	ex A4O-GO	1504	
N155DL	Boeing 767-3P6ER	390/25269	ex A4O-GP	1505	
N156DL	Boeing 767-3P6ER	406/25354	ex A4O-GR	1506	
N169DZ	Boeing 767-332ER	706/29689		1601	
N171DN	Boeing 767-332ER	304/24759		171	
N171DZ	Boeing 767-332ER	717/29690		1701	
N172DN	Boeing 767-332ER	312/24775		172	
N172DZ	Boeing 767-332ER	719/29691		1702	
N173DN	Boeing 767-332ER	313/24800		173	
N173DZ	Boeing 767-332ER	723/29692		1703	
N174DN	Boeing 767-332ER	317/24802		174; stored GYR	
N174DZ	Boeing 767-332ER	725/29693		1704	
N175DN	Boeing 767-332ER	318/24803		175	
N175DZ	Boeing 767-332ER	740/29696		1705	
N176DN	Boeing 767-332ER	341/25061		176	
N176DZ	Boeing 767-332ER	745/29697		1706	
N177DN	Boeing 767-332ER	346/25122		177	
N177DZ	Boeing 767-332ER	750/29698		1707	
N178DN	Boeing 767-332ER	349/25143		178	
N178DZ	Boeing 767-332ER	795/30596		1708	
N179DN	Boeing 767-332ER	350/25144		179	
N180DN	Boeing 767-332ER	428/25985		180	
N181DN	Boeing 767-332ER	446/25986		181	
N182DN	Boeing 767-332ER	461/25987		182	
N183DN	Boeing 767-332ER	492/27110		183	
N184DN	Boeing 767-332ER	496/27111		184	
N185DN	Boeing 767-332ER	576/27961		185	
N186DN	Boeing 767-332ER	585/27962		186	
N187DN	Boeing 767-332ER	617/27582		187	
N188DN	Boeing 767-332ER	631/27583		188	
N189DN	Boeing 767-332ER	646/25990		189	
N190DN	Boeing 767-332ER	653/28447		190	
N191DN	Boeing 767-332ER	654/28448		191	
N192DN	Boeing 767-332ER	664/28449		192	
N193DN	Boeing 767-332ER	671/28450		193	
N194DN	Boeing 767-332ER	675/28451		194	
N195DN	Boeing 767-332ER	676/28452		195	
N196DN	Boeing 767-332ER	679/28453		196	
N197DN	Boeing 767-332ER	683/28454		197	
N198DN	Boeing 767-332ER	685/28455		198	
N199DN	Boeing 767-332ER	690/28456		199	
N394DL	Boeing 767-324ER	572/27394	ex HL7505	1521	Lsd fr GECAS
N1200K	Boeing 767-332ER	696/28457		200	
N1201P	Boeing 767-332ER	697/28458		201	
N1402A	Boeing 767-332	506/25989		1402	
N1501P	Boeing 767-3P6ER	334/24983	ex A4O-GL	1501	
N1602	Boeing 767-332ER	735/29694		1602	
N1603	Boeing 767-332ER	739/29695		1603	
N1604R	Boeing 767-332ER	749/30180		1604	
N1605	Boeing 767-332ER	753/30198		1605	
N1607B	Boeing 767-332ER	787/30388		1607	
N1608	Boeing 767-332ER	788/30573		1608	
N1609	Boeing 767-332ER	789/30574		1609	
N1610D	Boeing 767-332ER	790/30594		1610	
N1611B	Boeing 767-332ER	794/30595		1611	
N1612T	Boeing 767-332ER	838/30575		1612	
N1613B	Boeing 767-332ER	847/32776		1613	
N16065	Boeing 767-332ER	755/30199		1606	
N825MH	Boeing 767-432ER	758/29703	ex N6067U	1801	
N826MH	Boeing 767-432ER	769/29713		1802	
N827MH	Boeing 767-432ER	773/29705	ex N76400	1803	
N828MH	Boeing 767-432ER	791/29699		1804	

N829MH	Boeing 767-432ER	801/29700		1805
N830MH	Boeing 767-432ER	803/29701		1806
N831MH	Boeing 767-432ER	804/29702		1807
N832MH	Boeing 767-432ER	807/29704		1808
N833MH	Boeing 767-432ER	810/29706		1809
N834MH	Boeing 767-432ER	813/29707		1810
N835MH	Boeing 767-432ER	814/29708		1811
N836MH	Boeing 767-432ER	818/29709		1812
N837MH	Boeing 767-432ER	820/29710		1813
N838MH	Boeing 767-432ER	821/29711		1814
N839MH	Boeing 767-432ER	824/29712		1815
N840MH	Boeing 767-432ER	830/29718		1816
N841MH	Boeing 767-432ER	855/29714		1817
N842MH	Boeing 767-432ER	856/29715		1818
N843MH	Boeing 767-432ER	865/29716		1819
N844MH	Boeing 767-432ER	871/29717		1820
N845MH	Boeing 767-432ER	874/29719		1821
N860DA	Boeing 777-232ER	202/29951		7001
N861DA	Boeing 777-232ER	207/29952		7002
N862DA	Boeing 777-232ER	235/29734	ex N5022E	7003
N863DA	Boeing 777-232ER	245/29735	ex N5014K	7004
N864DA	Boeing 777-232ER	249/29736	ex N50217	7005 Soaring Spirit c/s
N865DA	Boeing 777-232ER	257/29737		7006
N866DA	Boeing 777-232ER	261/29738		7007
N867DA	Boeing 777-232ER	387/29743		7008

Five more Boeing 777-232ERs are on order for delivery in 2005 (2) and 2006 (3)

N801DE	McDonnell-Douglas MD-11	480/48472		801	
N802DE	McDonnell-Douglas MD-11	481/48473		802; dbf 11Dec03?	
N803DE	McDonnell-Douglas MD-11	485/48474	ex N30075	803;	Lsd to WOA
N804DE	McDonnell-Douglas MD-11	489/48475		804	Lsd to WOA
N805DE	McDonnell-Douglas MD-11	510/48476		805; stored GYR	
N806DE	McDonnell-Douglas MD-11	511/48477		806	
N807DE	McDonnell-Douglas MD-11	514/48478		807; stored GYR	
N808DE	McDonnell-Douglas MD-11	536/48479		808; stored GYR	
N809DE	McDonnell-Douglas MD-11	538/48480		809; stored GYR	
N810DE	McDonnell-Douglas MD-11	542/48565		810; stored GYR	
N811DE	McDonnell-Douglas MD-11	543/48566		811	
N812DE	McDonnell-Douglas MD-11	560/48600	ex N90178	812 stored GYR	
N813DE	McDonnell-Douglas MD-11	562/48601	ex N6202S	813	
N814DE	McDonnell-Douglas MD-11	605/48623		814; stored GYR	
N815DE	McDonnell-Douglas MD-11	622/48624		815; stored GYR	

All retired by 02 January 2004, but planned to return to service at a later date

N900DE	McDonnell-Douglas MD-88	1970/53372	9000
N901DE	McDonnell-Douglas MD-88	1980/53378	9001
N901DL	McDonnell-Douglas MD-88	1338/49532	901
N902DE	McDonnell-Douglas MD-88	1983/53379	9002
N902DL	McDonnell-Douglas MD-88	1341/49533	902
N903DE	McDonnell-Douglas MD-88	1986/53380	9003
N903DL	McDonnell-Douglas MD-88	1344/49534	903
N904DE	McDonnell-Douglas MD-88	1990/53409	9004
N904DL	McDonnell-Douglas MD-88	1347/49535	904
N905DE	McDonnell-Douglas MD-88	1992/53410	9005
N905DL	McDonnell-Douglas MD-88	1348/49536	905
N906DE	McDonnell-Douglas MD-88	2027/53415	9006
N906DL	McDonnell-Douglas MD-88	1355/49537	906
N907DE	McDonnell-Douglas MD-88	2029/53416	9007
N907DL	McDonnell-Douglas MD-88	1365/49538	907
N908DE	McDonnell-Douglas MD-88	2032/53417	9008
N908DL	McDonnell-Douglas MD-88	1366/49539	908
N909DE	McDonnell-Douglas MD-88	2033/53418	9009
N909DL	McDonnell-Douglas MD-88	1395/49540	909
N910DE	McDonnell-Douglas MD-88	2036/53419	9010
N910DL	McDonnell-Douglas MD-88	1416/49541	910
N911DE	McDonnell-Douglas MD-88	2037/49967	9011
N911DL	McDonnell-Douglas MD-88	1433/49542	911
N912DE	McDonnell-Douglas MD-88	2038/49997	9012
N912DL	McDonnell-Douglas MD-88	1434/49543	912
N913DE	McDonnell-Douglas MD-88	2039/49956	9013
N913DL	McDonnell-Douglas MD-88	1443/49544	913
N914DE	McDonnell-Douglas MD-88	2049/49957	9014
N914DL	McDonnell-Douglas MD-88	1444/49545	914
N915DE	McDonnell-Douglas MD-88	2050/53420	9015
N915DL	McDonnell-Douglas MD-88	1447/49546	915
N916DE	McDonnell-Douglas MD-88	2051/53421	9016
N916DL	McDonnell-Douglas MD-88	1448/49591	916
N917DE	McDonnell-Douglas MD-88	2054/49958	9017
N917DL	McDonnell-Douglas MD-88	1469/49573	917
N918DE	McDonnell-Douglas MD-88	2055/49959	9018
N918DL	McDonnell-Douglas MD-88	1470/49583	918

N919DE	McDonnell-Douglas MD-88	2058/53422	9019
N919DL	McDonnell-Douglas MD-88	1471/49584	919
N920DE	McDonnell-Douglas MD-88	2059/53423	9020
N920DL	McDonnell-Douglas MD-88	1473/49644	920
N921DL	McDonnell-Douglas MD-88	1480/49645	921
N922DL	McDonnell-Douglas MD-88	1481/49646	922
N923DL	McDonnell-Douglas MD-88	1491/49705	923
N924DL	McDonnell-Douglas MD-88	1492/49711	924
N925DL	McDonnell-Douglas MD-88	1500/49712	925
N926DL	McDonnell-Douglas MD-88	1523/49713	926
N927DA	McDonnell-Douglas MD-88	1524/49714	927
N928DL	McDonnell-Douglas MD-88	1530/49715	928
N929DL	McDonnell-Douglas MD-88	1531/49716	929
N930DL	McDonnell-Douglas MD-88	1532/49717	930
N931DL	McDonnell-Douglas MD-88	1533/49718	931
N932DL	McDonnell-Douglas MD-88	1570/49719	932
N933DL	McDonnell-Douglas MD-88	1571/49720	933
N934DL	McDonnell-Douglas MD-88	1574/49721	934
N935DL	McDonnell-Douglas MD-88	1575/49722	935
N936DL	McDonnell-Douglas MD-88	1576/49723	936
N937DL	McDonnell-Douglas MD-88	1588/49810	937
N938DL	McDonnell-Douglas MD-88	1590/49811	938
N939DL	McDonnell-Douglas MD-88	1593/49812	939
N940DL	McDonnell-Douglas MD-88	1599/49813	940
N941DL	McDonnell-Douglas MD-88	1602/49814	941
N942DL	McDonnell-Douglas MD-88	1605/49815	942
N943DL	McDonnell-Douglas MD-88	1608/49816	943
N944DL	McDonnell-Douglas MD-88	1612/49817	944
N945DL	McDonnell-Douglas MD-88	1613/49818	945
N946DL	McDonnell-Douglas MD-88	1629/49819	946
N947DL	McDonnell-Douglas MD-88	1664/49878	947
N948DL	McDonnell-Douglas MD-88	1666/49879	948
N949DL	McDonnell-Douglas MD-88	1676/49880	949
N950DL	McDonnell-Douglas MD-88	1677/49881	950
N951DL	McDonnell-Douglas MD-88	1679/49882	951
N952DL	McDonnell-Douglas MD-88	1683/49883	952
N953DL	McDonnell-Douglas MD-88	1685/49884	953
N954DL	McDonnell-Douglas MD-88	1689/49885	954
N955DL	McDonnell-Douglas MD-88	1691/49886	955
N956DL	McDonnell-Douglas MD-88	1699/49887	956
N957DL	McDonnell-Douglas MD-88	1700/49976	957
N958DL	McDonnell-Douglas MD-88	1701/49977	958
N959DL	McDonnell-Douglas MD-88	1710/49978	959
N960DL	McDonnell-Douglas MD-88	1711/49979	960
N961DL	McDonnell-Douglas MD-88	1712/49980	961
N962DL	McDonnell-Douglas MD-88	1725/49981	962
N963DL	McDonnell-Douglas MD-88	1726/49982	963
N964DL	McDonnell-Douglas MD-88	1747/49983	964
N965DL	McDonnell-Douglas MD-88	1748/49984	965
N966DL	McDonnell-Douglas MD-88	1795/53115	966
N967DL	McDonnell-Douglas MD-88	1796/53116	967
N968DL	McDonnell-Douglas MD-88	1808/53161	968
N969DL	McDonnell-Douglas MD-88	1810/53172	969
N970DL	McDonnell-Douglas MD-88	1811/53173	970
N971DL	McDonnell-Douglas MD-88	1823/53214	971
N972DL	McDonnell-Douglas MD-88	1824/53215	972
N973DL	McDonnell-Douglas MD-88	1832/53241	973
N974DL	McDonnell-Douglas MD-88	1833/53242	974
N975DL	McDonnell-Douglas MD-88	1834/53243	975
N976DL	McDonnell-Douglas MD-88	1845/53257	976
N977DL	McDonnell-Douglas MD-88	1848/53258	977
N978DL	McDonnell-Douglas MD-88	1849/53259	978
N979DL	McDonnell-Douglas MD-88	1859/53266	979
N980DL	McDonnell-Douglas MD-88	1860/53267	980
N981DL	McDonnell-Douglas MD-88	1861/53268	981
N982DL	McDonnell-Douglas MD-88	1870/53273	982
N983DL	McDonnell-Douglas MD-88	1873/53274	983
N984DL	McDonnell-Douglas MD-88	1912/53311	984
N985DL	McDonnell-Douglas MD-88	1914/53312	985
N986DL	McDonnell-Douglas MD-88	1924/53313	986
N987DL	McDonnell-Douglas MD-88	1926/53338	987
N988DL	McDonnell-Douglas MD-88	1928/53339	988 stored SAT
N989DL	McDonnell-Douglas MD-88	1936/53341	989
N990DL	McDonnell-Douglas MD-88	1939/53342	990
N991DL	McDonnell-Douglas MD-88	1941/53343	991
N992DL	McDonnell-Douglas MD-88	1943/53344	992
N993DL	McDonnell-Douglas MD-88	1950/53345	993
N994DL	McDonnell-Douglas MD-88	1952/53346	994
N995DL	McDonnell-Douglas MD-88	1955/53362	995
N996DL	McDonnell-Douglas MD-88	1958/53363	996
N997DL	McDonnell-Douglas MD-88	1961/53364	997
N998DL	McDonnell-Douglas MD-88	1963/53370	998

N999DN	McDonnell-Douglas MD-88	1965/53371		999

N901DA	McDonnell-Douglas MD-90-30	2100/53381	ex N902DC	9201
N902DA	McDonnell-Douglas MD-90-30	2094/53382		9202
N903DA	McDonnell-Douglas MD-90-30	2095/53383		9203
N904DA	McDonnell-Douglas MD-90-30	2096/53384		9204
N905DA	McDonnell-Douglas MD-90-30	2097/53385		9205
N906DA	McDonnell-Douglas MD-90-30	2098/53386		9206
N907DA	McDonnell-Douglas MD-90-30	2115/53387		9207
N908DA	McDonnell-Douglas MD-90-30	2117/53388		9208
N909DA	McDonnell-Douglas MD-90-30	2122/53389		9209
N910DN	McDonnell-Douglas MD-90-30	2123/53390		9210
N911DA	McDonnell-Douglas MD-90-30	2126/53391		9211
N912DN	McDonnell-Douglas MD-90-30	2136/53392		9212
N913DN	McDonnell-Douglas MD-90-30	2154/53393		9213
N914DN	McDonnell-Douglas MD-90-30	2156/53394		9214
N915DN	McDonnell-Douglas MD-90-30	2159/53395		9215
N916DN	McDonnell-Douglas MD-90-30	2161/53396		9216

Services are also operated in conjunction with Atlantic Southeast and Comair (wholly owned subsidiaries), Atlantic Coast, Trans States and Skywest as the "Delta Connection". Also operates corporate jet-charter subsidiary Delta AirElite Business Jets [EBU]
Founder member of Sky Team alliance with Air France, Korean Air and Aeromexico

---

DELTA CONNECTION

Cincinnati-Northern Kentucky Intl, OH/Atlanta-Hartsfield Intl, GA/Orlando-Intl, FL (CVG/ATL/MCO)

N530AS+	Aerospatiale/Alenia ATR 72-212	453	ex F-WQLC	Atlantic Southeast
N531AS+	Aerospatiale/Alenia ATR 72-212	454	ex F-WQLH	Atlantic Southeast
N532AS+	Aerospatiale/Alenia ATR 72-212	458	ex F-WQLK	Atlantic Southeast
N533AS+	Aerospatiale/Alenia ATR 72-212	460	ex F-WQLL	Atlantic Southeast
N534AS+	Aerospatiale/Alenia ATR 72-212	463	ex F-WQLM	Atlantic Southeast
N535AS+	Aerospatiale/Alenia ATR 72-212	464	ex F-WQKS	Atlantic Southeast
N536AS+	Aerospatiale/Alenia ATR 72-212	465	ex F-WQLB	Atlantic Southeast
N630AS+	Aerospatiale/Alenia ATR 72-212	336	ex F-WWLS	Atlantic Southeast
N631AS+	Aerospatiale/Alenia ATR 72-212	362	ex F-WWEZ	Atlantic Southeast
N632AS+	Aerospatiale/Alenia ATR 72-212	338	ex F-WWLT	Atlantic Southeast
N633AS+	Aerospatiale/Alenia ATR 72-212	344	ex F-WWLC	Atlantic Southeast
N634AS+	Aerospatiale/Alenia ATR 72-212	370	ex F-WWEF	Atlantic Southeast
N635AS+	Aerospatiale/Alenia ATR 72-212	372	ex F-WWEP	Atlantic Southeast
N636AS+	Aerospatiale/Alenia ATR 72-212	375	ex F-WWLW	Atlantic Southeast
N637AS+	Aerospatiale/Alenia ATR 72-212	383	ex F-WWEB	Atlantic Southeast
N640AS	Aerospatiale/Alenia ATR 72-212	405	ex F-WWLP	Atlantic Southeast
N641AS	Aerospatiale/Alenia ATR 72-212	387	ex F-WWLG	Atlantic Southeast
N642AS	Aerospatiale/Alenia ATR 72-212	395	ex F-WWLJ	Atlantic Southeast
N643AS	Aerospatiale/Alenia ATR 72-212	413	ex F-WWLC	Atlantic Southeast

+Leased from WFBN

N403CA~	Canadair CL-600-2B19	7428	ex N896AS	7428 Comair
N403SW	Canadair CL-600-2B19	7028	ex C-FMNB	7028 Skywest
N405SW	Canadair CL-600-2B19	7029	ex C-FMND	7029 Skywest
N406SW	Canadair CL-600-2B19	7030	ex C-FMNH	7030 Skywest
N407SW	Canadair CL-600-2B19	7034	ex C-FMNY	7034 Skywest
N408CA~	Canadair CL-600-2B19	7440	ex C-FMLQ	7440 Comair
N408SW	Canadair CL-600-2B19	7055	ex C-FMMW	7055 Skywest
N409CA~	Canadair CL-600-2B19	7441	ex C-FMLS	7441 Comair
N409SW	Canadair CL-600-2B19	7056	ex C-FMMX	7056 Skywest
N410SW	Canadair CL-600-2B19	7066	ex C-FMOL	7066 Skywest
N411SW	Canadair CL-600-2B19	7067	ex C-FMOS	7067 Skywest
N412SW	Canadair CL-600-2B19	7101		7101 Skywest
N413SW	Canadair CL-600-2B19	7102		7102 Skywest
N416SW	Canadair CL-600-2B19	7089	ex N60SR	7089 Skywest
N417SW	Canadair CL-600-2B19	7400	ex C-FMMW	7400 Skywest
N418SW	Canadair CL-600-2B19	7446	ex C-FMNW	7446 Skywest
N420CA~	Canadair CL-600-2B19	7451	ex C-FVAZ	7451 Comair
N423SW	Canadair CL-600-2B19	7456	ex C-FMMB	7456 Skywest
N426SW	Canadair CL-600-2B19	7468	ex C-FMLF	7468 Skywest
N427CA~	Canadair CL-600-2B19	7460	ex N897AS	7460 Comair
N427SW	Canadair CL-600-2B19	7497	ex C-FMLB	7497 Skywest
N429SW	Canadair CL-600-2B19	7518	ex C-FMMN	7518 Skywest
N430CA~	Canadair CL-600-2B19	7461	ex N898AS	7461 Comair
N430SW	Canadair CL-600-2B19	7523	ex C-FMNB	7523 Skywest
N431CA~	Canadair CL-600-2B19	7472	ex C-FMLT	7472 Comair
N431SW	Canadair CL-600-2B19	7536	ex C-FMNW	7536 Skywest
N432SW	Canadair CL-600-2B19	7548	ex C-GJFG	7548 Skywest
N433SW	Canadair CL-600-2B19	7550	ex C-GJFH	7550 Skywest
N435CA	Canadair CL-600-2B19	7473	ex N496SW	7473 Comair
N435SW	Canadair CL-600-2B19	7555	ex C-GJHK	7555 Skywest
N436CA	Canadair CL-600-2B19	7482	ex N497SW	7482 Comair
N437SW	Canadair CL-600-2B19	7564	ex C-GJIA	7564 Skywest
N438SW	Canadair CL-600-2B19	7574	ex C-FMLU	7574 Skywest

Reg	Type	MSN	Ex	Notes	Extra
N439SW	Canadair CL-600-2B19	7578	ex C-FMMN	7578 Skywest	
N440SW	Canadair CL-600-2B19	7589	ex C-FMLI	7589 Skywest	
N441SW	Canadair CL-600-2B19	7602	ex C-FMND	7602 Skywest	
N442CA<	Canadair CL-600-2B19	7483	ex N498SW	7483 Comair	
N442SW	Canadair CL-600-2B19	7609	ex C-FMMQ	7609 Skywest	
N443CA	Canadair CL-600-2B19	7539	ex C-GJJH	7539 Comair	
N443SW	Canadair CL-600-2B19	7638	ex C-FMMN	7638 30th anniversary colours	
N445SW	Canadair CL-600-2B19	7651	ex C-FMLS	7651 Skywest	
N446CA	Canadair CL-600-2B19	7546	ex C-FMMB	7546 Comair	
N446SW	Canadair CL-600-2B19	7666	ex C-FMMB	7666 Skywest	
N447CA	Canadair CL-600-2B19	7552	ex C-GJLL	7552 Comair	
N447SW	Canadair CL-600-2B19	7677	ex C-FMLB	7677 Skywest	
N448SW	Canadair CL-600-2B19	7678	ex C-FMLF	7678 Skywest	
N449SW	Canadair CL-600-2B19	7699	ex C-FMMQ	7699 Skywest	
N451CA	Canadair CL-600-2B19	7562	ex C-FMLT	7562 Comair	
N452SW	Canadair CL-600-2B19	7716	ex C-FMNW	7716 Skywest	
N453SW	Canadair CL-600-2B19	7743	ex C-FMLV	7743 Skywest	
N454SW	Canadair CL-600-2B19	7749	ex C-FMOS	7749 SKywest	
N455CA	Canadair CL-600-2B19	7592	ex C-FMLT	7592 Comair	
N455SW	Canadair CL-600-2B19	7760	ex C-FMMW	7760 Skywest	
N457CA	Canadair CL-600-2B19	7612	ex C-FMMY	7612 Comair	
N457SW	Canadair CL-600-2B19	7773	ex C-FMLV	7773 Skywest	
N458CA	Canadair CL-600-2B19	7613	ex C-FMNB	7613 Comair	
N459SW	Canadair CL-600-2B19	7782	ex C-FMND	7782 Skywest	
N460SW	Canadair CL-600-2B19	7803	ex C-FMLV	7803 Skywest	
N461SW	Canadair CL-600-2B19	7811	ex C-FVAZ	7811 Skywest	
N463SW	Canadair CL-600-2B19	7820	ex C-FMMW	7820 Skywest	
N464SW	Canadair CL-600-2B19	7827	ex C-FMLB	7827 Skywest	
N465SW	Canadair CL-600-2B19	7845	ex C-FMOI	7845 Skywest	
N466CA	Canadair CL-600-2B19	7627	ex C-FMNX	7627 Comair	
N466SW	Canadair CL-600-2B19	7856	ex C-FMKZ	7856 Skywest	
N467CA	Canadair CL-600-2B19	7637	ex C-FMML	7637 Comair	
N468CA	Canadair CL-600-2B19	7649	ex C-FMLI	7649 Comair	
N470CA	Canadair CL-600-2B19	7650	ex C-FMLQ	7650 Comair	
N471CA	Canadair CL-600-2B19	7655	ex C-FMNH	7655 Comair	
N472CA	Canadair CL-600-2B19	7667	ex C-FMML	7667 Comair	
N473CA	Canadair CL-600-2B19	7668	ex C-FMMN	7668 Comair	
N477CA	Canadair CL-600-2B19	7670	ex C-FMMW	7670 Comair	
N478CA	Canadair CL-600-2B19	7671	ex C-FMMX	7671 Comair	
N479CA	Canadair CL-600-2B19	7675	ex C-FMKW	7675 Comair	
N483CA	Canadair CL-600-2B19	7689	ex C-FMLV	7689 Comair	
N484CA	Canadair CL-600-2B19	7702	ex C-FMMY	7702 Comair	
N486CA	Canadair CL-600-2B19	7707	ex C-FMLB	7707 Comair	
N487CA	Canadair CL-600-2B19	7729	ex C-FMMQ	7729 Comair	
N488CA	Canadair CL-600-2B19	7730	ex C-FMMW	7730 Comair	
N489CA	Canadair CL-600-2B19	7755	ex C-FMOI	7755 Comair	
N491CA	Canadair CL-600-2B19	7756	ex C-FMMB	7756 Comair	
N492CA	Canadair CL-600-2B19	7763	ex C-FMNB	7763 Comair	
N494CA	Canadait CL-600-2B19	7765	ex C-FMKW	7765 Comair	
N495CA	Canadair CL-600-2B19	7774	ex C-FMMT	7774 Comair	
N496CA	Canadair CL-600-2B19	7791	ex C-FMMX	7791 Comair	
N498CA	Canadair CL-600-2B19	7792	ex C-FMMY	7792 Comair	
N506CA	Canadair CL-600-2B19	7793	ex C-FMNB	7793 Comair	
N507CA	Canadair CL-600-2B19	7796	ex C-GZFC	7796 Comair	
N510CA	Canadair CL-600-2B19	7802	ex C-GZFH	7802 Comair	
N514CA	Canadair CL-600-2B19	7809	ex C-FMOS	7809 Comair	
N518CA	Canadair CL-600-2B19	7816	ex C-FMMB	7816 Comair	
N523CA	Canadair CL-600-2B19	7821	ex C-FMMX	7821 Comair	
N526CA	Canadair CL-600-2B19	7824	ex C-FMKV	7824 Comair	
N528CA	Canadair CL-600-2B19	7841	ex C-FVAZ	7841 Comair	
N533CA	Canadair CL-600-2B19		ex C-	7 Comair	on order
N536CA	Canadair CL-600-2B19		ex C-	7 Comair	on order
N537CA	Canadair CL-600-2B19		ex C-	7 Comair	on order
N538CA	Canadair CL-600-2B19		ex C-	7 Comair	on order
N539CA	Canadair CL-600-2B19		ex C-	7 Comair	on order
N548CA	Canadair CL-600-2B19		ex C-	7 Comair	on order
N549CA	Canadair CL-600-2B19		ex C-	7 Comair	on order
N574CA	Canadair CL-600-2B19		ex C-	7 Comair	on order
N576CA	Canadair CL-600-2B19		ex C-	7 Comair	on order
N587SW	Canadair CL-600-2B19	7062	ex N943CA	7062 Skywest	Lsd fr COM
N588SW	Canadair CL-600-2B19	7069	ex N945CA	7069 Skywest	Lsd fr COM
N589SW	Canadair CL-600-2B19	7072	ex C-FMLB	7072 Skywest	Lsd fr COM
N590SW	Canadair CL-600-2B19	7077	ex N947CA	7077 Skywest	Lsd fr COM
N591SW	Canadair CL-600-2B19	7079	ex N948CA	7079 Skywest	Lsd fr COM
N592SW	Canadair CL-600-2B19	7279	ex N759CA	7279 Skywest	Lsd fr COM
N594SW	Canadair CL-600-2B19	7285	ex N767CA	7285 Skywest	Lsd fr COM
N595SW	Canadair CL-600-2B19	7292	ex N769CA	7292 Skywest	Lsd fr COM
N597SW	Canadair CL-600-2B19	7293	ex N776CA	7293 Skywest	Lsd fr COM
N708CA~	Canadair CL-600-2B19	7235		7235 Comair	
N709CA~	Canadair CL-600-2B19	7238		7238 Comair	
N710CA~	Canadair CL-600-2B19	7241		7241 Comair	
N712CA~	Canadair CL-600-2B19	7244		7244 Comair	

N713CA~	Canadair CL-600-2B19	7245		7245 Comair	
N716CA~	Canadair CL-600-2B19	7250	ex C-FMMW	7250 Comair	
N719CA~	Canadair CL-600-2B19	7253		7253 Comair	
N721CA~	Canadair CL-600-2B19	7259	ex C-FMLI	7259 Comair	
N720SW	Canadair CL-600-2B19	7297	ex N778CA	7297 Skywest	Lsd fr COM
N729CA~	Canadair CL-600-2B19	7265		7265 Comair	
N735CA~	Canadair CL-600-2B19	7267		7267 Comair	
N739CA~	Canadair CL-600-2B19	7273	ex C-FMNQ	7273 Comair	
N759CA~	Canadair CL-600-2B19	7279	ex C-FMMQ	7279 Comair	Sublsd to SKW
N767CA~	Canadair CL-600-2B19	7285	ex C-FMKW	7285 Comair	Sublsd to SKW
N769CA~	Canadair CL-600-2B19	7292	ex C-FMLT	7292 Comair	Sublsd to SKW
N776CA~	Canadair CL-600-2B19	7293		7293 Comair	Sublsd to SKW
N778CA	Canadair CL-600-2B19	7297		7297 Comair	Lsd to SKW
N779CA~	Canadair CL-600-2B19	7306	ex C-FMMB	7306 Comair	
N781CA~	Canadair CL-600-2B19	7312	ex C-FMMY	7312 Comair	
N783CA~	Canadair CL-600-2B19	7315	ex C-FMKW	7315 Comair	
N784CA~	Canadair CL-600-2B19	7319	ex C-FMLI	7319 Comair	
N785CA~	Canadair CL-600-2B19	7326		7326 Comair	
N786CA~	Canadair CL-600-2B19	7333		7333 Comair	
N796CA~	Canadair CL-600-2B19	7338		7338 Comair	
N797CA~	Canadair CL-600-2B19	7344		7344 Comair	
N798CA	Canadair CL-600-2B19	7348	ex C-FMLF	7348 Comair	
N804CA	Canadair CL-600-2B19	7352	ex C-FMLT	7352 Comair	
N805CA	Canadair CL-600-2B19	7354	ex C-FMMT	7354 Comair	
N806CA	Canadair CL-600-2B19	7359	ex C-FMOS	7359 Comair	
N807CA	Canadair CL-600-2B19	7364	ex C-FMLU	7364 Comair	
N809CA~	Canadair CL-600-2B19	7366	ex C-FMMB	7366 Comair	
N810CA~	Canadair CL-600-2B19	7370	ex C-FMMW	7370 Comair	
N811CA~	Canadair CL-600-2B19	7380	ex C-FMLQ	7380 Comair	
N812CA~	Canadair CL-600-2B19	7381	ex C-FMLS	7381 Comair	
N814CA~	Canadair CL-600-2B19	7387	ex C-GFVM	7387 Comair	
N815CA~	Canadair CL-600-2B19	7397	ex C-FMML	7397 Comair	
N816CA	Canadair CL-600-2B19	7398	ex N499SW	7398 Comair	
N818CA~	Canadair CL-600-2B19	7408	ex C-FMLF	7408 Comair	
N819CA~	Canadair CL-600-2B19	7415	ex C-FMNH	7415 Comair	
N820AS~	Canadair CL-600-2B19	7188		820 Atlantic Southeast	
N821AS~	Canadair CL-600-2B19	7194	ex C-FMKV	821 Atlantic Southeast	
N821CA~	Canadair CL-600-2B19	7420	ex C-F	7420 Comair	
N823AS~	Canadair CL-600-2B19	7196		823 Atlantic Southeast	
N824AS~	Canadair CL-600-2B19	7203		824 Atlantic Southeast	
N825AS~	Canadair CL-600-2B19	7207		825 Atlantic Southeast	
N826AS	Canadair CL-600-2B19	7210	ex C-FMOW	826 Atlantic Southeast	
N827AS	Canadair CL-600-2B19	7212	ex C-FMND	827 Atlantic Southeast	
N828AS	Canadair CL-600-2B19	7213	ex C-FMNQ	828 Atlantic Southeast	
N829AS	Canadair CL-600-2B19	7232		829 Atlantic Southeast	
N830AS	Canadair CL-600-2B19	7236		830 Atlantic Southeast	
N832AS	Canadair CL-600-2B19	7243		832 Atlantic Southeast	
N833AS	Canadair CL-600-2B19	7246	ex C-FMMB	833 Atlantic Southeast	
N834AS	Canadair CL-600-2B19	7254		834 Atlantic Southeast	
N835AS	Canadair CL-600-2B19	7258	ex C-FMLF	835 Atlantic Southeast	
N836AS	Canadair CL-600-2B19	7263	ex C-FMLU	836 Atlantic Southeast	
N837AS	Canadair CL-600-2B19	7271	ex C-FVAZ	837 Atlantic Southeast	
N838AS	Canadair CL-600-2B19	7276	ex C-FMMB	838 Atlantic Southeast	
N839AS	Canadair CL-600-2B19	7284	ex C-FMKV	839 Atlantic Southeast	
N840AS	Canadair CL-600-2B19	7290	ex C-FMLQ	840 Atlantic Southeast	
N841AS	Canadair CL-600-2B19	7300	ex C-FMOW	841 Atlantic Southeast	
N842AS	Canadair CL-600-2B19	7304		842 Atlantic Southeast	
N843AS^	Canadair CL-600-2B19	7310	ex C-FMMW	843 Atlantic Southeast	
N844AS^	Canadair CL-600-2B19	7317	ex C-FMLB	844 Atlantic Southeast	
N845AS^	Canadair CL-600-2B19	7324		845 Atlantic Southeast	
N846AS^	Canadair CL-600-2B19	7328	ex C-FMNY	846 Atlantic Southeast	
N847AS^	Canadair CL-600-2B19	7335		847 Atlantic Southeast	
N848AS^	Canadair CL-600-2B19	7339		848 Atlantic Southeast	
N849AS'^	Canadair CL-600-2B19	7347	ex C-FMLB	849 Atlantic Southeast	
N850AS^	Canadair CL-600-2B19	7355	ex C-FMNH	850 Atlantic Southeast	
N851AS^	Canadair CL-600-2B19	7360	ex C-FMOW	851 Atlantic Southeast	
N852AS^	Canadair CL-600-2B19	7369	ex C-FMMQ	852 Atlantic Southeast	
N853AS^	Canadair CL-600-2B19	7374	ex C-FMKV	853 Atlantic Southeast	
N854AS^	Canadair CL-600-2B19	7382	ex C-FMLT	854 Atlantic Southeast	
N855AS^	Canadair CL-600-2B19	7395	ex C-GGKY	855 Atlantic Southeast	
N856AS^	Canadair CL-600-2B19	7404	ex C-FMKV	856 Atlantic Southeast	
N857AS^	Canadair CL-600-2B19	7411	ex C-FMLS	857 Atlantic Southeast	
N858AS^	Canadair CL-600-2B19	7417	ex C-FMNX	858 Atlantic Southeast	
N859AS^	Canadair CL-600-2B19	7421	ex C-FVAZ	859 Atlantic Southeast	
N860AS^	Canadair CL-600-2B19	7433	ex C-FMNB	860 Atlantic Southeast	
N861AS^	Canadair CL-600-2B19	7445	ex C-FMNH	861 Atlantic Southeast	
N862AS	Canadair CL-600-2B19	7476	ex C-FMNW	862 Atlantic Southeast	
N863AS	Canadair CL-600-2B19	7487	ex C-FMML	863 Atlantic Southeast	
N864AS	Canadair CL-600-2B19	7502	ex C-FMLT	864 Atlantic Southeast	
N865AS	Canadair CL-600-2B19	7507	ex C-FMNX	865 Atlantic Southeast	
N866AS	Canadair CL-600-2B19	7517	ex C-FMML	866 Atlantic Southeast	
N867AS^	Canadair CL-600-2B19	7463	ex C-FMNB	867 Atlantic Southeast	

N868CA	Canadair CL-600-2B19	7427	ex C-FMML	7427 Comair	
N868AS>	Canadair CL-600-2B19	7474	ex C-FMMT	868 Atlantic Southeast	
N869AS<	Canadair CL-600-2B19	7479	ex C-FMOS	869 Atlantic Southeast	
N870AS^	Canadair CL-600-2B19	7530	ex C-FMLQ	870 Atlantic Southeast	
N871AS^	Canadair CL-600-2B19	7537	ex C-FMNX	871 Atlantic Southeast	
N872AS	Canadair CL-600-2B19	7542	ex C-FMND	872 Atlantic Southeast	
N873AS	Canadair CL-600-2B19	7549	ex C-GJLI	873 Atlantic Southeast	
N874AS	Canadair CL-600-2B19	7551	ex C-GJLK	874 Atlantic Southeast	
N875AS	Canadair CL-600-2B19	7559	ex C-FJLQ	875 Atlantic Southeast	
N876AS	Canadair CL-600-2B19	7576	ex C-	876 Atlantic Southeast	
N877AS	Canadair CL-600-2B19	7579	ex C-FMMQ	877 Atlantic Southeast	
N878AS	Canadair CL-600-2B19	7590	ex C-FMLQ	878 Atlantic Southeast	
N879AS	Canadair CL-600-2B19	7600	ex C-FMOW	879 Atlantic Southeast	
N880AS	Canadair CL-600-2B19	7606	ex C-FMMB	880 Atlantic Southeast	
N881AS	Canadair CL-600-2B19	7496	ex C-GIXF	881 Atlantic Southeast	
N882AS	Canadair CL-600-2B19	7503	ex C-GJAO	882 Atlantic Southeast	
N883AS	Canadair CL-600-2B19	7504	ex C-GIZD	883 Atlantic Southeast	
N884AS	Canadair CL-600-2B19	7513	ex C-GIZF	884 Atlantic Southeast	
N885AS	Canadair CL-600-2B19	7521	ex C-GJDX	885 Atlantic Southeast	
N886AS	Canadair CL-600-2B19	7531	ex C-GJJC	886 Atlantic Southeast	
N889AS	Canadair CL-600-2B19	7538	ex C-GJJG	889 Atlantic Southeast	
N901EV	Canadair CL-600-2B19	7616	ex C-FMKZ	901 Atlantic Southeast	
N902EV	Canadair CL-600-2B19	7620	ex C-FMLQ	902 Atlantic Southeast	
N903EV	Canadair CL-600-2B19	7621	ex C-FMLI	903 Atlantic Southeast	
N904EV	Canadair CL-600-2B19	7628	ex C-FMNY	904 Atlantic Southeast	
N905EV	Canadair CL-600-2B19	7632	ex C-FMND	905 Atlantic Southeast	
N906EV	Canadair CL-600-2B19	7642	ex C-FMMY	906 Atlantic Southeast	
N907EV	Canadair CL-600-2B19	7648	ex C-FMLF	907 Atlantic Southeast	
N908EV	Canadair CL-600-2B19	7654	ex C-FMMT	908 Atlantic Southeast	
N909EV	Canadair CL-600-2B19	7658	ex C-FMNY	909 Atlantic Southeast	
N910EV	Canadair CL-600-2B19	7727	ex C-FMML	910 Atlantic Southeast	
N912CA	Canadair CL-600-2B19	7011	ex C-FMKZ	7011 Comair	Lsd fr WFBN
N912EV	Canadair CL-600-2B19	7728	ex C-FMMN	912 Atlantic Southeast	
N913EV	Canadair CL-600-2B19	7731	ex C-FMMX	913 Atlantic Southeast	
N914CA	Canadair CL-600-2B19	7012	ex C-FMLB	7012 Comair	Lsd fr WFBN
N914EV	Canadair CL-600-2B19	7752	ex C-FMND	914 Atlantic Southeast	on order
N915CA	Canadair CL-600-2B19	7013	ex C-FMLQ	7013 Comair	Lsd fr WFBN
N915EV	Canadair CL-600-2B19	7754	ex C-FMLU	915 Atlantic Southeast	on order
N916CA	Canadair CL-600-2B19	7014	ex C-FMLI	7014 Comair	Lsd fr WFBN
N916EV	Canadair CL-600-2B19	7757	ex C-FMML	916 Atlantic Southeast	
N917CA	Canadair CL-600-2B19	7017	ex C-FMLT	7017 Comair	Lsd fr WFBN
N917EV	Canadair CL-600-2B19	7769	ex C-FMLI	917 Atlantic Southeast	
N918CA	Canadair CL-600-2B19	7018	ex C-FMLU	7018 Comair	Lsd fr WFBN
N919EV	Canadair CL-600-2B19	7780	ex C-FMOW	919 Atlantic Southeast	
N920CA	Canadair CL-600-2B19	7022	ex C-FMMN	7022 Comair	Lsd fr WFBN
N920EV	Canadair CL-600-2B19	7810	ex C-FMOW	920 Atlantic Southeast	
N921EV	Canadair CL-600-2B19	7819	ex C-FMMQ	921 Atlantic Southeast	
N922EV	Canadair CL-600-2B19	7822	ex C-FMMY	922 Atlantic Southeast	
N923EV	Canadair CL-600-2B19	7826	ex C-FMKZ	923 Atlantic Southeast	
N924CA	Canadair CL-600-2B19	7026	ex C-FMMX	7026 Comair	Lsd fr WFBN
N924EV	Canadair CL-600-2B19	7830	ex C-FMLQ	924 Atlantic Southeast	
N925EV	Canadair CL-600-2B19	7831	ex C-FMLS	925 Atlantic Southeast	
N926CA	Canadair CL-600-2B19	7027	ex C-FMMY	7027 Comair	Lsd fr WFBN
N926EV	Canadair CL-600-2B19	7843	ex C-FMNQ	926 Atlantic Southeast	
N927CA	Canadair CL-600-2B19	7031	ex C-FMNQ	7031 Comair	Lsd fr WFBN
N927EV	Canadair CL-600-2B19	7844	ex C-FMLU	927 Atlantic Southeast	
N929CA	Canadair CL-600-2B19	7035	ex C-FMOI	7035 Comair	Lsd fr WFBN
N931CA	Canadair CL-600-2B19	7037	ex C-FMOS	7037 Comair	Lsd fr WFBN
N932CA	Canadair CL-600-2B19	7038	ex C-FMOW	7038 Comair	Lsd fr WFBN
N933CA	Canadair CL-600-2B19	7040	ex C-FMKW	7040 Comair	Lsd fr WFBN
N934CA	Canadair CL-600-2B19	7042	ex C-FMLB	7042 Comair	Lsd fr WFBN
N936CA	Canadair CL-600-2B19	7043	ex C-FMLF	7043 Comair	
N937CA	Canadair CL-600-2B19	7044	ex C-FMLI	7044 Comair	
N938CA	Canadair CL-600-2B19	7046	ex C-FMLS	7046 Comair	
N940CA	Canadair CL-600-2B19	7048	ex C-FMLU	7048 Comair	
N941CA	Canadair CL-600-2B19	7050	ex C-FMMB	7050 Comair	
N943CA#	Canadair CL-600-2B19	7062	ex C-FMNW	7062 Comair	Lsd to SKW
N945CA#	Canadair CL-600-2B19	7069	ex C-FMKV	7069 Comair	Lsd to SKW
N946CA#	Canadair CL-600-2B19	7072	ex C-FMLB	7072 Comair	Lsd to SKW
N947CA#	Canadair CL-600-2B19	7077	ex C-FMLT	7077 Comair	Lsd to SKW
N948CA#	Canadair CL-600-2B19	7079	ex C-FMLV	7079 Comair	Lsd to SKW
N949CA#	Canadair CL-600-2B19	7080	ex C-FMMB	7080 Comair	
N951CA#	Canadair CL-600-2B19	7091		7091 Comair	
N952CA#"	Canadair CL-600-2B19	7092		7092 Comair	
N954CA#	Canadair CL-600-2B19	7100	ex C-FXFB	7100 Comair	
N956CA#	Canadair CL-600-2B19	7105	ex C-FMNH	7105 Comair	
N957CA~	Canadair CL-600-2B19	7109	ex C-FMLV	7109 Comair	
N958CA~	Canadair CL-600-2B19	7111	ex C-FMML	7111 Comair	
N959CA~	Canadair CL-600-2B19	7116	ex C-FMMX	7116 Comair	
N960CA~	Canadair CL-600-2B19	7117	ex C-FMMY	7117 Comair	
N962CA~	Canadair CL-600-2B19	7123	ex C-FMLU	7123 Comair	
N963CA~	Canadair CL-600-2B19	7127	ex C-FMMN	7127 Comair	

N964CA~	Canadair CL-600-2B19	7129	ex C-FMMT	7129 Comair	
N965CA	Canadair CL-600-2B19	7131	ex C-FMMX	7131 Comair	
N966CA~	Canadair CL-600-2B19	7132	ex C-FMMY	7132 Comair	
N967CA~	Canadair CL-600-2B19	7134	ex C-FMND	7134 Comair	
N969CA	Canadair CL-600-2B19	7141	ex C-FMML	7141 Comair	
N971CA	Canadair CL-600-2B19	7145	ex C-FMMW	7145 Comair	
N973CA	Canadair CL-600-2B19	7146	ex C-FMMX	7146 Comair	
N975CA	Canadair CL-600-2B19	7150	ex C-FMNH	7150 Comair	
N976CA	Canadair CL-600-2B19	7151	ex C-FMNQ	7151 Comair	
N977CA	Canadair CL-600-2B19	7157		7157 Comair	Lsd fr WFBN
N978CA	Canadair CL-600-2B19	7158	ex C-FMNQ	7158 Comair	Lsd fr WFBN
N979CA	Canadair CL-600-2B19	7159	ex C-FMMT	7159 Comair	
N981CA	Canadair CL-600-2B19	7163	ex C-FMOS	7163 Comair	Lsd fr WFBN
N982CA	Canadair CL-600-2B19	7168	ex C-FMLU	7168 Comair	Lsd fr WFBN
N983CA~	Canadair CL-600-2B19	7169		7169 Comair	
N984CA~	Canadair CL-600-2B19	7171		7171 Comair	
N986CA	Canadair CL-600-2B19	7174	ex C-FMMT	7174 Comair	
N987CA~	Canadair CL-600-2B19	7199		7199 Comair	
N988CA~	Canadair CL-600-2B19	7204		7204 Comair	
N989CA~	Canadair CL-600-2B19	7215	ex C-FMOI	7215 Comair	
N991CA~	Canadair CL-600-2B19	7216		7216 Comair	
N995CA~	Canadair CL-600-2B19	7229		7229 Comair	
N999CA~	Canadair CL-600-2B19	7230		7230 Comair	

^Leased from State Street
#Leased from WFBN
*Cincinnati - the Jet Hub c/s
>Texas Bluebonnet colours

"Leased from Bank of America
~Leased from Wachovia Bank NA
'Special 20th Anniversary c/s, named City of Atlanta

N317CA	Canadair CL-600-2C10	10055	ex C-GZXI	10055 Comair	
N331CA	Canadair CL-600-2C10	10061	ex C-GIBJ	10061 Comair	
N340CA	Canadair CL-600-2C10	10062	ex C-GIBL	10062 Comair	
N354CA	Canadair CL-600-2C10	10064	ex C-GIBO	10064 Comair	
N355CA	Canadair CL-600-2C10	10067	ex C-GIBT	10067 Comair	
N367CA	Canadair CL-600-2C10	10069	ex C-GICL	10069 Comair	
N368CA	Canadair CL-600-2C10	10075	ex C-GIAD	10075 Comair	
N369CA	Canadair CL-600-2C10	10079	ex C-GZUD	10079 Comair	
N371CA	Canadair CL-600-2C10	10082	ex C-GIAR	10082 Comair	
N374CA	Canadair CL-600-2C10	10090	ex C-	10090 Comair	
N378CA	Canadair CL-600-2C10	10097	ex C-GIAJ	10097 Comair	
N379CA	Canadair CL-600-2C10	10102	ex C-	10102 Comair	
N390CA	Canadair CL-600-2C10	10106	ex C-	10106 Comair	
N391CA	Canadair CL-600-2C10	10108	ex C-	10108 Comair	
N398CA	Canadair CL-600-2C10	10112	ex C-	10112 Comair	
N625CA	Canadair CL-600-2C10	10113	ex C-	10113 Comair	
N641CA	Canadair CL-600-2C10	10122	ex C-	10122 Comair	
N642CA	Canadair CL-600-2C10	10125	ex C-	10125 Comair	
N653CA	Canadair CL-600-2C10	10129	ex C-GZUC	10129 Comair	
N	Canadair CL-600-2C10			10... Comair	on order
N	Canadair CL-600-2C10			10... Comair	on order
N	Canadair CL-600-2C10			10... Comair	on order
N	Canadair CL-600-2C10			10... Comair	on order
N	Canadair CL-600-2C10			10... Comair	on order
N	Canadair CL-600-2C10			10... Comair	on order
N	Canadair CL-600-2C10			10... Comair	on order
N701EV	Canadair CL-600-2C10	10020	ex C-GIAB	Atlantic Southeast	
N702EV	Canadair CL-600-2C10	10035	ex C-GIBQ	Atlantic Southeast	
N703EV	Canadair CL-600-2C10	10038	ex C-GICB	Atlantic Southeast	
N705EV	Canadair CL-600-2C10	10051	ex C-GIAP	Atlantic Southeast	
N706EV	Canadair CL-600-2C10	10054	ex C-GIAZ	Atlantic Southeast	
N707EV	Canadair CL-600-2C10	10057	ex C-GIAZ	Atlantic Southeast	
N708EV	Canadair CL-600-2C10	10060	ex C-GIBI	Atlantic Southeast	
N709EV	Canadair CL-600-2C10	10068	ex C-GICB	Atlantic Southeast	
N710EV	Canadair CL-600-2C10	10071	ex C-GICP	Atlantic Southeast	
N712EV	Canadair CL-600-2C10	10074	ex C-GHZZ	Atlantic Southeast	
N713EV	Canadair CL-600-2C10	10081	ex C-GIAP	Atlantic Southeast	
N716EV	Canadair CL-600-2C10	10084	ex C-GIAV	Atlantic Southeast	
N717EV	Canadair CL-600-2C10	10088	ex C-GIBH	Atlantic Southeast	
N718EV	Canadair CL-600-2C10	10095	ex C-G	Atlantic Southeast	
N719EV	Canadair CL-600-2C10	10099	ex C-GICL	Atlantic Southeast	
N720EV	Canadair CL-600-2C10	10115	ex C-GIAW	Atlantic Southeast	
N722EV	Canadair CL-600-2C10			Atlantic Southeast	on order
N723EV	Canadair CL-600-2C10			Atlantic Southeast	on order
N724EV	Canadair CL-600-2C10			Atlantic Southeast	on order
N727EV	Canadair CL-600-2C10			Atlantic Southeast	on order
N730EV	Canadair CL-600-2C10			Atlantic Southeast	on order
N738EV	Canadair CL-600-2C10			Atlantic Southeast	on order
N740EV	Canadair CL-600-2C10			Atlantic Southeast	on order
N741EV	Canadair CL-600-2C10			Atlantic Southeast	on order
N744EV	Canadair CL-600-2C10			Atlantic Southeast	on order
N748EV	Canadair CL-600-2C10			Atlantic Southeast	on order
N750EV	Canadair CL-600-2C10			Atlantic Southeast	on order
N751EV	Canadair CL-600-2C10			Atlantic Southeast	on order

N752EV	Canadair CL-600-2C10			Atlantic Southeast	on order
N753EV	Canadair CL-600-2C10			Atlantic Southeast	on order
N754EV	Canadair CL-600-2C10			Atlantic Southeast	on order
N401FJ	Dornier 328-310	3145	ex D-BDX.	401 Atlantic Coast	
N402FJ	Dornier 328-310	3147	ex D-BDX.	402 Atlantic Coast	
N403FJ	Dornier 328-310	3149	ex D-BDX.	403 Atlantic Coast	
N404FJ	Dornier 328-310	3150	ex D-BDX.	404 Atlantic Coast	
N405FJ	Dornier 328-310	3155	ex D-BDXJ	405 Atlantic Coast	
N406FJ	Dornier 328-310	3156	ex D-BDXK	406 Atlantic Coast	
N407FJ	Dornier 328-310	3157	ex D-BDXL	407 Atlantic Coast	
N408FJ	Dornier 328-310	3160	ex D-BDX.	408 Atlantic Coast	
N409FJ	Dornier 328-310	3161	ex D-BDX.	409 Atlantic Coast	
N410FJ	Dornier 328-310	3165	ex D-BDXV	410 Atlantic Coast	
N411FJ	Dornier 328-310	3166	ex D-BDXW	411 Atlantic Coast	
N412FJ	Dornier 328-310	3167	ex D-BDXA	412 Atlantic Coast	
N413FJ	Dornier 328-310	3168	ex D-BDXB	413 Atlantic Coast	
N414FJ	Dornier 328-300	3169	ex D-BDXC	414 Atlantic Coast	
N415FJ	Dornier 328-310	3170	ex D-BDXZ	415 Atlantic Coast	
N416FJ	Dornier 328-310	3171	ex D-BDXE	416 Atlantic Coast	
N417FJ	Dornier 328-310	3174	ex D-BDXH	417Atlantic Coast	
N418FJ	Dornier 328-310	3176	ex D-BDXI	418Atlantic Coast	
N419FJ	Dornier 328-310	3173	ex D-BDX	419 Atlantic Coast	
N420FJ	Dornier 328-310	3178		420 Atlantic Coast	
N421FJ	Dornier 328-310	3179		421 Atlantic Coast	
N422FJ	Dornier 328-310	3180		422 Atlantic Coast	
N423FJ	Dornier 328-310	3181		423 Atlantic Coast	
N424FJ	Dornier 328-310	3185		424 Atlantic Coast	
N425FJ	Dornier 328-310	3189		425 Atlantic Coast	
N426FJ	Dornier 328-310	3190		426 Atlantic Coast	
N427FJ	Dornier 328-310	3192		427 Atlantic Coast	
N428FJ	Dornier 328-310	3193		428 Atlantic Coast	
N429FJ	Dornier 328-310	3194	ex D-BDXQ	429 Atlantic Coast	
N430FJ	Dornier 328-310	3209		430 Atlantic Coast	

All leased from Wachovia Bank

N229AS	Embraer EMB.120RT Brasilia	120042	ex PT-SJK	Atlantic Southeast	Lsd fr Bombardier
N235AS	Embraer EMB.120RT Brasilia	120047	ex PT-SJQ	Atlantic Southeast	Lsd fr AGES
N237AS	Embraer EMB.120RT Brasilia	120051	ex PT-SJU	Atlantic Southeast	
N238AS	Embraer EMB.120RT Brasilia	120053	ex PT-SJW	Atlantic Southeast	
N239AS	Embraer EMB.120RT Brasilia	120057	ex PT-SKA	Atlantic Southeast	
N240AS	Embraer EMB.120RT Brasilia	120060	ex PT-SKD	Atlantic Southeast	
N245AS"	Embraer EMB.120RT Brasilia	120075	ex PT-SKS	Atlantic Southeast	
N260AS"	Embraer EMB.120RT Brasilia	120132	ex PT-SNY	Atlantic Southeast	
N261AS	Embraer EMB.120RT Brasilia	120141	ex PT-SPH	Atlantic Southeast	
N262AS	Embraer EMB.120RT Brasilia	120146	ex PT-SPM	Atlantic Southeast	
N263AS	Embraer EMB.120RT Brasilia	120157	ex PT-SPW	Atlantic Southeast	
N264AS	Embraer EMB.120ER Brasilia	120165	ex PT-SQD	Atlantic Southeast	
N265AS	Embraer EMB.120RT Brasilia	120170	ex PT-SQI	Atlantic Southeast	
N266AS	Embraer EMB.120RT Brasilia	120188	ex PT-SRB	Atlantic Southeast	
N268AS	Embraer EMB.120RT Brasilia	120202	ex PT-SRS	Atlantic Southeast	
N268CA	Embraer EMB.120RT Brasilia	120262	ex PT-SUI	Comair	Lsd fr WFBN
N269AS	Embraer EMB.120RT Brasilia	120210	ex PT-SSE	Atlantic Southeast	
N274AS	Embraer EMB.120RT Brasilia	120229	ex PT-STB	Atlantic Southeast	
N280AS	Embraer EMB.120ER Brasilia	120231	ex PT-STD	Atlantic Southeast	
N281AS	Embraer EMB.120ER Brasilia	120224	ex PT-SST	Atlantic Southeast	
N282AS	Embraer EMB.120ER Brasilia	120226	ex PT-SSV	Atlantic Southeast	
N283AS	Embraer EMB.120ER Brasilia	120236	ex PT-STI	Atlantic Southeast	
N285AS	Embraer EMB.120RT Brasilia	120265	ex PT-SUL	Atlantic Southeast	
N286AS	Embraer EMB.120ER Brasilia	120268	ex PT-SUO	Atlantic Southeast	
N503AS	Embraer EMB.120RT Brasilia	120275	ex PT-SUV	Atlantic Southeast	
N638AS	Embraer EMB.120RT Brasilia	120282	ex PT-SVC	Atlantic Southeast	
N639AS	Embraer EMB.120RT Brasilia	120283	ex PT-SVD	Atlantic Southeast	

"Leased from Bombardier Services Corp; all Atlantic Southeast examples retired by 3Q03

N831RP	Embraer EMB.135LR	145663	ex PT-SEX	Chautauqua	
N832RP	Embraer EMB.135LR	145676	ex PT-SFJ	Chautauqua	
N833RP	Embraer EMB.135LR	145687	ex PT-SFT	Chautauqua	Lsd fr Solitair
N834RP	Embraer EMB.135LR	145696	ex PT-SGB	Chautauqua	
N835RP	Embraer EMB.135LR	145702	ex PT-SGG	Chautauqua	
N836RP	Embraer EMB.135LR	145713	ex PT-SGQ	Chautauqua	
N837RP	Embraer EMB.135LR	145715	ex PT-SGS	Chautauqua	
N838RP	Embraer EMB.135LR	145720	ex PT-SGW	Chautauqua	
N839RP	Embraer EMB.135LR	145724	ex PT-SHA	Chautauqua	
N840RP	Embraer EMB.135LR	145725	ex PT-SHB	Chautauqua	
N841RP	Embraer EMB.135LR	145737	ex PT-SHQ	Chautauqua	
N842RP	Embraer EMB.135LR	145661	ex PT-SEV	Chautauqua	
N843RP	Embraer EMB.135LR	145599	ex PT-SAO	Chautauqua	
N844RP	Embraer EMB.135LR	145725	ex PT-SDI	Chautauqua	
N845RP	Embraer EMB.135LR	145551	ex PT-SZN	Chautauqua	
N270SK	Embraer EMB.145LR	145304	ex PT-SKV	Chautauqua	

N271SK	Embraer EMB.145LR	145305	ex PT-SKW	Chautauqua
N272SK	Embraer EMB.145LR	145306	ex PT-SKX	Chautauqua
N273SK	Embraer EMB.145LR	145331	ex PT-SMX	Chautauqua
N274SK	Embraer EMB.145LR	145344	ex PT-SNK	Chautauqua
N276SK	Embraer EMB.145LR	145348	ex PT-SNO	Chautauqua
N278SK	Embraer EMB.145LR	145370	ex PT-SOV	Chautauqua
N290SK	Embraer EMB.145LR	145474	ex PT-SVT	Chautauqua
N292SK	Embraer EMB.145LR	145488	ex PT-SXH	Chautauqua
N296SK	Embraer EMB.145LR	145514	ex PT-S	Chautauqua
N561RP	Embraer EMB.145LR	145447	ex PT-SUS	Chautauqua
N562RP	Embraer EMB.145LR	145451	ex PT-SUW	Chautauqua
N563RP	Embraer EMB.145LR	145509	ex PT-SYB	Chautauqua
N564RP	Embraer EMB.145LR	145524	ex PT-SYP	Chautauqua
N565RP	Embraer EMB.145LR	145679	ex PT-SFL	Chautauqua
N566RP	Embraer EMB.145LR	145691	ex PT-SFX	Chautauqua
N567RP	Embraer EMB.145LR	145698	ex PT-SGD	Chautauqua
N973RP	Embraer EMB.145MP	145444	ex	

Services operated by Comair using flight numbers in the range DL3000-3699 and Atlantic Southeast Airlines using flight numbers in the range DL7000-7999. Other services operated by American Eagle (at Los Angeles, CA), Chautauqua Airlines (at Orlando, FL), Trans State (at St Louis, MO) and Skywest

DESERT AIR ceased operations

DHL AIRWAYS renamed AStar Air Cargo 14 July 2003 following management buy-out

DISCOVER AIR ceased operations 27 February 2003

DODITA AIR CARGO

San Juan-Munoz Marin Intl, PR (SJU)

N912AL	Convair 440	353	ex PZ-TGA	
N4826C	Convair 440	391		
N31325	Convair 240	52-8	ex 52-1183	stored SJU

All freighters

DODSON INTERNATIONAL AIR ceased operations

DWYAIR AIR CHARTER ceased operations

DYNAMIC AIR

Bridgewater-Air Park, VA

N16NM	Beech 65-E90 King Air	LW-62	ex N96DA	
N28C	Beech A100 King Air	B-216	ex JDF-T3	
N41J*	Beech 65-A90-1 King Air	LM-89	ex N7113Z	
N61U*	Beech 65-A90-1 King Air	LM-92	ex N7123C	
N70U*	Beech 65-A90-1 King Air	LM-51	ex N7063W	
N75V	Beech 65-A90-1 King Air	LM-103	ex N7143Y	
N76Q*	Beech 65-A90-1 King Air	LM-15	ex N7026H	
N77SS	Beech 65-A90 King Air	LJ-230	ex N93BA	Lsd fr K&K Aircraft
N87V	Beech 65-A90-1 King Air	LM-130	ex N71764	
N89F	Beech 65-A90-1 King Air	LM-124	ex N72014	
N91S	Beech 65-A90-4 King Air	LU-15	ex N71998	
N92S*	Beech 65-A90-4 King Air	LU-05	ex N7199B	
N117CP*	Beech 65-A90-1 King Air	LM-68		
N412MA	Beech 65-A90 King Air	LJ-214	ex N985AA	Lsd fr K&K Aircraft
N500NA	Beech 65-B90 King Air	LJ-401	ex N8NM	Lsd fr K&K Aircraft
N553MA	Beech 65-E90 King Air	LW-147		
N611ND*	Beech 65-A90-1 King Air	LM-11	ex 66-18010	
N7000B*	Beech 65-A90-1 King Air	LM-1	ex 66-18000	
N7007G*	Beech 65-A90-1 King Air	LM-2	ex 66-18001	
N7007Q*	Beech 65-A90-1 King Air	LM-5	ex 66-18004	
N7010L*	Beech 65-A90-1 King Air	LM-7	ex 66-18006	
N7014L*	Beech 65-A90-1 King Air	LM-10	ex 66-18009	
N7018F*	Beech 65-A90-1 King Air	LM-13	ex 66-18012	
N7031F*	Beech 65-A90-1 King Air	LM-19	ex 66-18018	
N7031L*	Beech 65-A90-1 King Air	LM-21	ex 66-18020	
N7035B*	Beech 65-A90-1 King Air	LM-24	ex 66-18023	
N7036L*	Beech 65-A90-1 King Air	LM-26	ex 66-18025	
N7038Y	Beech 65-A90-1 King Air	LM-28	ex 66-18027	
N7039T	Beech 65-A90-1 King Air	LM-30	ex 66-18029	
N7040J	Beech 65-A90-1 King Air	LM-31	ex 66-18030	Lsd fr Dynamic Avlease
N7040V*	Beech 65-A90-1 King Air	LM-32	ex 66-18031	
N7041M*	Beech 65-A90-1 King Air	LM-33	ex 66-18032	
N7043D*	Beech 65-A90-1 King Air	LM-35	ex 66-18034	
N7043G*	Beech 65-A90-1 King Air	LM-37	ex 66-18036	Lsd fr Dynamic Avlease
N7043N*	Beech 65-A90-1 King Air	LM-38	ex 66-18037	
N7043Y*	Beech 65-A90-1 King Air	LM-39	ex 66-18038	

N7047D*	Beech 65-A90-1 King Air	LM-41	ex 66-18040	
N7051K*	Beech 65-A90-1 King Air	LM-44	ex 66-18043	
N7052X*	Beech 65-A90-1 King Air	LM-45	ex 66-18044	
N7052Y*	Beech 65-A90-1 King Air	LM-47	ex 66-18046	
N7059H*	Beech 65-A90-1 King Air	LM-48	ex 66-18047	Lsd fr Dynamic Avlease
N7062W*	Beech 65-A90-1 King Air	LM-49	ex 67-18048	
N7063D*	Beech 65-A90-1 King Air	LM-50	ex 67-18049	
N7064Q*	Beech 65-A90-1 King Air	LM-52	ex 67-18051	
N7066X*	Beech 65-A90-1 King Air	LM-54	ex 67-18053	
N7067S*	Beech 65-A90-1 King Air	LM-55	ex 67-18054	
N7069F*	Beech 65-A90-1 King Air	LM-56	ex 67-18055	
N7070Z*	Beech 65-A90-1 King Air	LM-57	ex 67-18056	
N7071H*	Beech 65-A90-1 King Air	LM-58	ex 67-18057	
N7071N*	Beech 65-A90-1 King Air	LM-59	ex 67-18058	Lsd fr Dynamic Avlease
N7076X*	Beech 65-A90-1 King Air	LM-60	ex 67-18059	
N7078J*	Beech 65-A90-1 King Air	LM-67	ex 67-18066	
N7078L*	Beech 65-A90-1 King Air	LM-69	ex 67-18068	
N7079S*	Beech 65-A90-1 King Air	LM-70	ex 67-18069	Lsd fr Dynamic Avlease
N7087U*	Beech 65-A90-1 King Air	LM-74	ex 67-18073	
N7089Q*	Beech 65-A90-1 King Air	LM-77	ex 67-18076	Lsd fr Dynamic Avlease
N7092K*	Beech 65-A90-1 King Air	LM-83	ex 67-18083	Lsd fr Dynamic Avlease
N7112M*	Beech 65-A90-1 King Air	LM-87	ex 67-18090	
N7112T*	Beech 65-A90-1 King Air	LM-88	ex 67-18091	
N7120P*	Beech 65-A90-1 King Air	LM-90	ex 67-18094	
N7126U*	Beech 65-A90-1 King Air	LM-93	ex 67-18097	
N7128H	Beech 65-A90-1 King Air	LM-94	ex 67-18098	
N7132Z*	Beech 65-A90-1 King Air	LM-95	ex 67-18099	
N7136M*	Beech 65-A90-1 King Air	LM-98	ex 67-18102	Lsd fr Dynamic Avlease
N7137G*	Beech 65-A90-1 King Air	LM-99	ex 67-18103	
N7139Z	Beech 65-A90-1 King Air	LM-101	ex 67-18105	
N7146X	Beech 65-A90-1 King Air	LM-104	ex 67-18108	
N7148A	Beech 65-A90-1 King Air	LM-105	ex 67-18109	Lsd fr Dynamic Avlease
N7154W	Beech 65-A90-1 King Air	LM-106	ex 67-18110	Lsd fr Dynamic Avlease
N7155P*	Beech 65-A90-1 King Air	LM-107	ex 67-18111	Lsd fr Dynamic Avlease
N7155S*	Beech 65-A90-1 King Air	LM-112	ex 67-18116	
N7156J*	Beech 65-A90-1 King Air	LM-113	ex 67-18117	
N7157K	Beech 65-A90-1 King Air	LM-115	ex 67-18119	
N7165J*	Beech 65-A90-1 King Air	LM-119	ex 67-18123	
N7165Y*	Beech 65-A90-1 King Air	LM-120	ex 67-18124	Lsd fr Dynamic Avlease
N7169U*	Beech 65-A90-1 King Air	LM-122	ex 67-18126	
N7169Z*	Beech 65-A90-1 King Air	LM-123	ex 67-18127	
N7170A	Beech 65-A90-1 King Air	LM-125	ex 70-15891	
N7173K*	Beech 65-A90-1 King Air	LM-127	ex 70-15893	
N7173Y	Beech 65-A90-1 King Air	LM-128	ex 70-15894	
N7174J	Beech 65-A90-1 King Air	LM-129	ex 70-15895	
N7181E	Beech 65-A90-1 King Air	LM-132	ex 70-15898	
N7181H	Beech 65-A90-1 King Air	LM-134	ex 70-15900	
N7181J	Beech 65-A90-1 King Air	LM-135	ex 70-15901	
N7182H	Beech 65-A90-1 King Air	LM-137	ex 70-15903	
N7191W	Beech 65-A90-1 King Air	LM-138	ex 70-15904	
N7193M*	Beech 65-A90-1 King Air	LM-139	ex 70-15905	
N7198B*	Beech 65-A90-1 King Air	LM-141	ex 70-15907	
N7198S*	Beech 65-A90-4 King Air	LU-1	ex 70-15875	Lsd fr Dynamic Avlease
N7198Y*	Beech 65-A90-4 King Air	LU-2	ex 70-15876	
N7199B	Beech 65-A90-4 King Air	LU-5	ex 70-15879	
N7199D	Beech 65-A90-4 King Air	LU-6	ex 70-15880	
N7199H	Beech 65-A90-4 King Air	LU-7	ex 70-15881	
N7199J	Beech 65-A90-4 King Air	LU-8	ex 70-15882	
N7199L*	Beech 65-A90-4 King Air	LU-9	ex 70-15883	Lsd fr Dynamic Avlease
N7199N	Beech 65-A90-4 King Air	LU-10	ex 70-15884	
N7199S*	Beech 65-A90-4 King Air	LU-11	ex 70-15885	Lsd fr Dynamic Avlease
N7201S*	Beech 65-A90-1 King Air	LM-61	ex 67-18060	Lsd fr Dynamic Avlease
N7201Z*	Beech 65-A90-1 King Air	LM-100	ex 67-18104	
N7202D	Beech 65-A90-1 King Air	LM-133	ex 70-15899	
N7644R	Beech 65-B90 King Air	LJ-335		Lsd fr K&K Aircraft
N70088*	Beech 65-A90-1 King Air	LM-6	ex 66-18005	
N70135	Beech 65-A90-1 King Air	LM-9	ex 66-18008	
N70224*	Beech 65-A90-1 King Air	LM-14	ex 66-18013	Lsd fr Dynamic Avlease
N70292*	Beech 65-A90-1 King Air	LM-18	ex 66-18017	
N70356*	Beech 65-A90-1 King Air	LM-25	ex 66-18024	
N70503	Beech 65-A90-1 King Air	LM-43	ex 67-18042	
N70648*	Beech 65-A90-1 King Air	LM-53	ex 67-18052	
N70876*	Beech 65-A90-1 King Air	LM-75	ex 67-18074	
N70879*	Beech 65-A90-1 King Air	LM-76	ex 67-18075	
N70890*	Beech 65-A90-1 King Air	LM-78	ex 67-18077	
N70926*	Beech 65-A90-1 King Air	LM-84	ex 67-18083	
N71347*	Beech 65-A90-1 King Air	LM-96	ex 67-18100	
N71351	Beech 65-A90-1 King Air	LM-97	ex 67-18101	
N71581*	Beech 65-A90-1 King Air	LM-116	ex 67-18120	
N71597*	Beech 65-A90-1 King Air	LM-118	ex 67-18122	
N71797*	Beech 65-A90-1 King Air	LM-131	ex 70-15897	
N71982	Beech 65-A90-4 King Air	LU-3	ex 70-15877	

N71984	Beech 65-A90-4 King Air	LU-4	ex 70-15878	
N71992	Beech 65-A90-4 King Air	LU-12	ex 70-15886	
N71996	Beech 65-A90-4 King Air	LU-13	ex 70-15887	

Those with LM- c/ns were US Army U-21As while those with LU- c/ns were RU-21Hs. Actual purpose uncertain

N45A	Beech A200 Super King Air	BC-48	ex 77-22937	
N48A	Beech A200 Super King Air	BC-12	ex N254AG	
N49K	Beech A200 Super King Air	BD-26	ex N49A	
N321F	Beech A200 Super King Air	BC-70	ex 78-23134	
N321P	Beech 200 Super King Air	BP-6	ex 78-23149	
N380SA	Beech A200 Super King Air	BC-7	ex N253AG	
N390SA	Beech A200 Super King Air	BD-2	ex N200EA	
N399SA	Beech 200 Super King Air	BB-5	ex N200KE	
N612SA	Beech A200 Super King Air	BC-29	ex N255AG	

N38L*	Hamilton Westwind III (TC-45J)	51132		Lsd fr K&K Aircraft
N202GW*	Hamilton Westwind III	BA-321	ex N63E	Lsd fr K&K Aircraft
N909GP*	Hamilton Westwind III (E-18S)	BA-236		Lsd fr K&K Aircraft
N961GP*	Hamilton Westwind III (G-18S)	BA-559		Lsd fr K&K Aircraft
N1400E	Beech E-18S	BA-227		Lsd fr K&K Aircraft
N5653D*	Hamilton Westwind III (E-18S)	BA-385		Lsd fr K&K Aircraft

N47E	Douglas DC-3	13816	ex N7043N	Lsd fr K&K Aircraft
N56KS	Douglas DC-3	25769	ex N2566B	Lsd fr K&K Aircraft
N321L	Douglas DC-3	43345	ex N307SF	Lsd fr Nord Aviation
N17334	Douglas DC-3	1920	ex N177H	Lsd fr K&K Aircraft

*Freighters or stored pending freighter conversion.

EAGLE AIR TRANSPORT operates Skydive flights only

EDB AIR

Denver-Centennial, CO (DEN)

N161RB	Piper PA-31-350 Navajo Chieftain	31-7952097		
N3549X	Piper PA-31-350 Chieftain	31-8052034		
N411BJ	Piper PA-31-350 Navajo Chieftain	31-7952043		Lsd to LYM
N9247L	Piper PA-31-350 Chieftain	31-8152160		
N27989	Piper PA-31-350 Navajo Chieftain	31-7952077		

N184SW	Swearingen SA.227AC Metro III	AC-647	ex CX-TAA	Lsd to BSY
N542FA	Swearingen SA.227AC Metro III	AC-542	ex ZK-NSX	Lsd to OKAir
N765FA	Swearingen SA.227AC Metro III	AC-765B	ex ZK-NSI	Lsd to OKAir
N779BC	Swearingen SA.227AC Metro III	BC-779B	ex XA-RXW	
N787KL	Swearingen SA.227BC Metro III	BC-787B	ex XA-SAQ	Lsd to LYM
N882DC	Swearingen SA.227DC Metro 23	DC-882	ex C-GAFQ	Lsd to LYM
N2691W	Swearingen SA.227AC Metro III	AC-655B		Lsd to LYM

N60U	Swearingen SA.226TC Metro II	TC-232	ex N5389M		Lsd to LYM
N62Z	Swearingen SA.226TC Metro II	TC-237	x N5437M		Lsd to LYM
N103BM	Piper PA-44-180T Seminole	44-8107007			
N509SS	Swearingen SA.226TC Metro II	TC-206	ex N261S		Lsd to LYM
N770S	Swearingen SA.226TC Metro II	TC-248		Freighter	Lsd to LYM
N8303P	Piper PA-44-180T Seminole	44-8107031			
N37127	Cessna 404 Titan	404-0114			

Current status is uncertain, possibly only a Leasing Company

EDWARDS JET CENTER OF MONTANA

Edwards (EDJ)   *Billings-Logan Intl, MT (BIL)*
Previously listed as Lynch Flying Services

N53MD	Beech 100 King Air	B-86	ex N500Y	
N102LF	Beech 100 King Air	B-65	ex N102RS	
N277JD	Cessna 310R	310R0581	ex N77JD	
N401NA	Cessna 402B	402B0035	ex SE-FXI	
N552R	Beech 65-C90 King Air	LJ-749	ex N93BA	
N911SR	Beech 200 Super King Air	BB-898	ex N98GA	
N2703U	Cessna 340A	340A0914		
N5774C	Cessna 402C	402C0039		
N6316X	Cessna 340A	340A0487		
N6839Y	Cessna 402C	402C0481		
N9781S	Cessna 414A Chancellor III	414A0515	ex D-IFLO	

Edwards Jet Center of Montana is the trading name of Lynch Flying Service

---

ELLISON AIR

Anchorage-Lake Hood SPB, AK

N7375N	Cessna U206G Stationair	U20603641		Wheels or skis
N59352	Cessna U206F Stationair	U20603221		Wheels or skis

Operates seasonal flights

EMPIRE AIRLINES

Empire Air (EM/CFS)   *Coeur d'Alene, ID/Missoula, MT (COE/MSO)*

N700FX	Cessna 208B Caravan I	208B0419	
N705FX	Cessna 208B Caravan I	208B0425	
N709FX	Cessna 208B Caravan I	208B0430	
N711FX	Cessna 208B Caravan I	208B0433	
N720FX	Cessna 208B Caravan I	208B0452	
N728FX	Cessna 208B Caravan I	208B0471	
N746FX	Cessna 208B Caravan I	208B0498	
N752FX	Cessna 208B Caravan I	208B0517	
N753FE	Cessna 208B Caravan I	208B0248	
N756FX	Cessna 208B Caravan I	208B0532	
N775FE	Cessna 208B Caravan I	208B0272	
N778FE	Cessna 208B Caravan I	208B0275	
N779FE	Cessna 208B Caravan I	208B0276	
N788FE	Cessna 208B Caravan I	208B0286	
N833FE	Cessna 208A Caravan I	20800084	ex EI-FDX
N850FE	Cessna 208B Caravan I	208B0164	
N856FE	Cessna 208B Caravan I	208B0176	
N859FE	Cessna 208B Caravan I	208B0181	
N873FE	Cessna 208B Caravan I	208B0202	
N875FE	Cessna 208B Caravan I	208B0206	
N876FE	Cessna 208B Caravan I	208B0207	
N880FE	Cessna 208B Caravan I	208B0215	
N882FE	Cessna 208B Caravan I	208B0208	
N895FE	Cessna 208B Caravan I	208B0015	ex C-FEXG
N897FE	Cessna 208B Caravan I	208B0227	
N899FE	Cessna 208B Caravan I	208B0235	
N918FE	Cessna 208B Caravan I	208B0018	
N940FE	Cessna 208B Caravan I	208B0040	
N953FE	Cessna 208B Caravan I	208B0062	ex (N962FE)
N956FE	Cessna 208B Caravan I	208B0068	ex (N968FE)
N960FE	Cessna 208B Caravan I	208B0075	
N965FE	Cessna 208B Caravan I	208B0084	
N976FE	Cessna 208B Caravan I	208B0103	
N983FE	Cessna 208B Caravan I	208B0113	
N992FE	Cessna 208B Caravan I	208B0128	
N701FE	Fokker F.27 Friendship 600	10419	ex OO-FEF
N702FE	Fokker F.27 Friendship 600	10350	ex OO-FEG
N703FE	Fokker F.27 Friendship 600	10420	ex D-AFEH
N707FE	Fokker F.27 Friendship 500	10371	ex G-FEBZ
N708FE	Fokker F.27 Friendship 500	10372	ex G-BOMV
N711FE	Fokker F.27 Friendship 500	10383	ex F-BPNI
N720FE	Fokker F.27 Friendship 500	10464	ex 9M-MCE
N729FE	Fokker F.27 Friendship 600	10385	ex EI-FEA
N730FE	Fokker F.27 Friendship 600	10386	ex I-FEAB
N740FE	Fokker F.27 Friendship 600	10329	ex HB-ISJ
N741FE	Fokker F.27 Friendship 600	10387	ex G-FEAD
N742FE	Fokker F.27 Friendship 600	10349	ex G-FEAE

Cessna 208 Caravans, and Fokker F.27 Friendship 500s leased from and operated on behalf of FedEx

EPPS AIR SERVICE

Epps Air (EPS)   *Atlanta-De Kalb-Peachtree, GA (PDK)*

N10HT	Mitsubishi MU-2B-60	778SA	ex N264MA
N42AF	Mitsubishi MU-2B-60	1539SA	ex ZS-MRJ
N46AK	Mitsubishi MU-2B-60	754SA	ex N942ST
N755AF	Mitsubishi MU-2B-60	755SA	ex SE-KGO
N772DA	Mitsubishi MU-2B-60	772SA	ex I-MPLT
N888RH	Mitsubishi MU-2B-60	737SA	ex N315MA
N888SE	Mitsubishi MU-2B-60	1549SA	ex N475MA
N941MA	Mitsubishi MU-2B-60	744SA	
N984RE	Mitsubishi MU-2B-60	787SA	ex N267PC
N1164F	Mitsubishi MU-2B-60	1562SA	ex D-ICDG
N8083A	Mitsubishi MU-2B-60	739SA	ex N707EZ

All Cavanaugh SCD conversions

N23WJ	Beech B200 Super King Air	BB-1297	ex N21VF
N27GA	Beech 200 Super King Air	BB-477	ex F-GILB
N72PK	Beech 65-C90 King Air	LJ-1449	
N74WM	Beech 58 Baron	TH-653	
N601CF	Beech 200 Super King Air	BB-25	ex N1555N
N795CA	Beech 200 Super King Air	BB-559	ex N559BM

ERA HELICOPTERS / JET ALASKA

Erah (7H/ERH)   *Anchorage-Intl South, AK/Lake Charles-Regional, FL (ANC/LCH)*

Reg	Type	MSN	ex	Notes	More
N161EH	Aerospatiale AS.350B2 AStar	2144			
N162EH	Aerospatiale AS.350B2 AStar	2147			
N165EH	Aerospatiale AS.350B-1 AStar	2185			
N166EH	Aerospatiale AS.350B2 AStar	2194			
N178EH	Aerospatiale AS.350B2 AStar	2264			
N181EH	Aerospatiale AS.350B2 AStar	2680			
N182EH	Aerospatiale AS.350B2 AStar	2681			
N183EH	Aerospatiale AS.350B2 AStar	2752			
N185EH	Aerospatiale AS.350B2 AStar	2823			
N186EH	Aerospatiale AS.350B2 AStar	2844			
N187EH	Aerospatiale AS.350B2 AStar	2839			
N188EH	Aerospatiale AS.350B2 AStar	2954			
N189EH	Aerospatiale AS.350B2 AStar	2956			
N190EH	Aerospatiale AS.350B2 AStar	2974			
N191EH	Aerospatiale AS.350B2 AStar	2505			
N192EH	Aerospatiale AS.350B2 AStar	2582			
N193EH	Aerospatiale AS.350B2 AStar	2599			
N194EH	Aerospatiale AS.350B2 AStar	2608			
N195EH	Aerospatiale AS.350B2 AStar	2615			
N196EH	Aerospatiale AS.350B2 AStar	2976			
N197EH	Aerospatiale AS.350B2 AStar	2983			
N212EH	Aerospatiale AS.350B2 AStar	3151			
N213EH	Aerospatiale AS.350B2 AStar	3158			
N214EH	Aerospatiale AS.350B2 AStar	3163			
N215EH	Aerospatiale AS.350B2 AStar	3172			
N216EH	Aerospatiale AS.350B2 AStar	3184			
N217EH	Aerospatiale AS.350B2 AStar	3197			
N357EH	Bell 212	31209			
N358EH	Bell 212	31211			
N359EH	Bell 212	31212	ex C-GRVN		
N360EH	Bell 212	31213			
N361EH	Bell 212	30554	ex N213AH		Lsd to Airlog as XA-TRY
N362EH	Bell 212	30853	ex XA-TRX		
N370EH	Bell 212	30624			
N399EH	Bell 212	30810			Lsd to Airlog as XA-AAM
N500EH	Bell 212	30945			
N507EH	Bell 212	30950			
N508EH	Bell 212	30908			
N509EH	Bell 212	30925			
N510EH	Bell 212	31113			
N511EH	Bell 212	31118			
N522EH	Bell 212	31199			Lsd to Airlog as XA-TRZ
N523EH	Bell 212	31214	ex C-GRWX		
N164EH	Bell 412	33004	ex N58RC		
N167EH	Bell 412	33089	ex VH-NSO		
N168EH	Bell 412	33058	ex VH-NSI		
N169EH	Bell 412	33064	ex C-GBHH		
N174EH	Bell 412	33085	ex JA9583		
N177EH	Bell 412	33037	ex N177LG		
N412EH	Bell 412	33001			
N415EH	Bell 412	33009			Lsd as PR-NNL
N417EH	Bell 412	33031	ex N3911E		
N418EH	Bell 412	33032	ex N3911J		Based Trinidad
N419EH	Bell 412	33043			
N421EH	Bell 412	33067	ex N57413		
N422EH	Bell 412	33068			
N57RD	Convair 580	509	ex N12FV	VIP	Lsd to RDC Marine
N565EA	Convair 580	399	ex N57RD		
N566EA	Convair 580	381	ex N73167	Jet Alaska	
N201EH	de Havilland DHC-6 Twin Otter 200	217	ex N4901W		
N203EH	de Havilland DHC-6 Twin Otter 100	97	ex N2715R		
N206EH	de Havilland DHC-6 Twin Otter 200	194	ex N995SA		
N302EH	de Havilland DHC-6 Twin Otter 300	576	ex N57AN		
N320EA	de Havilland DHC-6 Twin Otter 300	625	ex C-GCVI		
N321EA	de Havilland DHC-6 Twin Otter 300	299	ex C-GNTH		
N885EA	de Havilland DHC-6 Twin Otter 300	454	ex N454MG		
N886EA	de Havilland DHC-6 Twin Otter 300	756	ex N126AS		
N887EA	de Havilland DHC-6 Twin Otter 300	467	ex N404X		
N124EH	MBB Bo.105CBS	S-559	ex 9Y-TJE		
N125EH	MBB Bo.105CBS	S-562	ex N9376Y		
N127EH	MBB Bo.105CBS	S-571	ex D-HDPT		
N128EH	MBB Bo.105CBS	S-572	ex D-HDPU		

N129EH	MBB Bo.105CBS	S-580	ex N29077	
N130EH	MBB Bo.105CBS	S-588	ex N2910H	
N131EH	MBB Bo.105CBS	S-595	ex N3129U	
N133EH	MBB Bo.105CBS	S-598	ex N29128	
N134EH	MBB Bo.105CBS	S-635	ex N2785A	
N135EH	MBB Bo.105CBS	S-675	ex N4573D	
N148EH	MBB Bo.105CBS	S-703	ex PH-NZX	Op for Air Med Services
N149EH	MBB Bo.105CBS	S-705	ex N968MB	
N151EH	MBB Bo.105CBS	S-706	ex N955MB	
N152EH	MBB Bo.105CBS	S-701	ex N954MB	
N153EH	MBB Bo.105CBS	S-702	ex PH-NZY	
N154EH	MBB Bo-105CBS	S-704	ex N141LG	
N290EH	MBB Bo.105CBS-4	S-850	ex N6554Y	
N291EH	MBB Bo.105CBS-4	S-842	ex N65962	
N292EH	MBB Bo.105CBS-4	S-843	ex N7170C	
N293EH	MBB Bo.105CBS-4	S-844	ex N6612K	
N294EH	MBB Bo.105CBS-4	S-846	ex N6559A	
N296EH	MBB Bo.105CBS-4	S-849	ex N65385	
N298EH	MBB Bo.105CBS-4	S-845	ex N4186F	
N423EH	MBB Bo.105CBS	S-543	ex N42018	
N424EH	MBB Bo.105CBS	S-548	ex N42001	
N426EH	MBB Bo.105CBS	S-552	ex N93173	
N427EH	MBB Bo.105CBS	S-554	ex N93205	
N573EH	Sikorsky S-76B	760373	ex N76TH	
N574EH	Sikorsky S-76B	760369	ex N369AG	
N575EH	Sikorsky S-76A++	760366	ex N621LH	
N576EH	Sikorsky S-76A+	760212	ex N15458	
N577EH	Sikorsky S-76A+	760222	ex N15459	
N578EH	Sikorsky S-76A+	760099	ex N223BF	
N579EH	Sikorsky S-76A+	760274	ex ZS-RLG	
N170EH	Aerospatiale AS.332L Super Puma	2016	ex C-GSLB	
N171EH	Aerospatiale AS.332L Super Puma	2058	ex C-GSLA	
N404EH	Bell 206L Long Ranger	45114		
N514RD	Beech 200C Super King Air	BL-5	ex N143LG	
N561EH	Sikorsky S-61N	61471	ex ZS-RAX	
N562EH	Sikorsky S-61N	61257	ex PH-NZA	
N563EH	Sikorsky S-61N	61808	ex PH-NZR	
N564EH	Sikorsky S-61N	61365	ex C-GBSF	
N881EA	de Havilland DHC-8-102A	233	ex C-GFOD	
N882EA	de Havilland DHC-8-102	098	ex D-BERT	
N883EA	de Havilland DHC-8-102	260	ex C-GGEW	
N1944H	Douglas DC-3	17111/34378	ex N54542	Spirit of Alaska
N1944M	Douglas DC-3	19394	ex N394CA	Spirit of the North

Services are operated in conjunction with Alaska Airlines using AS flight numbers in the range 4800-4899
DC-3s are operated as ERA Classic Airlines

ERICKSON AIR CRANE

Central Point, OR

N154AC	Sikorsky S-64E Skycrane	64037	ex 68-18435	
N157AC	Sikorsky S-64E Skycrane	64065		Lsd as C-GESG
N158AC	Sikorsky S-64F Skycrane	64081	ex HL9260	
N159AC	Sikorsky S-64F Skycrane	64084	ex 68-18476	
N163AC	Sikorsky S-64E Skycrane	64093	ex 70-18485	
N164AC	Sikorsky S-64E Skycrane	64034	ex C-FCRN	The Incredible Hulk
N171AC	Sikorsky S-64F Skycrane	64090	ex 69-18482	
N172AC	Sikorsky S-64E Skycrane	64061	ex	Lsd as C-FCRN
N173AC	Sikorsky S-64E Skycrane	64015	ex 68-18413	
N174AC	Sikorsky S-64E Skycrane	64080	ex N7094X	
N178AC	Sikorsky S-64E Skycrane	64097	ex 69-18489	Isabelle
N179AC	Sikorsky S-64E Skycrane	64091	ex C-GFAH	
N189AC	Erickson/Sikorsky S-64E Skycrane	641001		
N194AC	Sikorsky S-64E Skycrane	64017	ex C-GFLH	
N197AC	Sikorsky S-64E Skycrane	64067	ex N7028U	
N198AC	Sikorsky S-64E Skycrane	64098	ex N70280	
N213AC	Sikorsky S-64E Skycrane	64088	ex 69-18480	
N217AC	Sikorsky S-64E Skycrane	64066	ex N542SB	
N218AC	Sikorsky S-64E Skycrane	64033	ex N545SB	
N227AC	Sikorsky S-64E Skycrane	64078	ex 69-18471	
N229AC	Sikorsky S-64E Skycrane		ex 67-18716	731
N236AC	Sikorsky S-64E Skycrane	64089	ex 69-18481	
N237AC	Sikorsky S-64E Skycrane	64095	ex 69-18487	
N4099D	Sikorsky S-64E Skycrane		ex 68-14448	
N4099L	Sikorsky S-64E Skycrane		ex 68-18436	
N4099M	Sikorsky S-64E Skycrane		ex 67-18426	
N6962R	Sikorsky S-64E Skycrane	64058	ex HC-CAT	

The two Canadian examples are leased to subsidiary Canadian Air Crane; several are stored awaiting conversion

N126AC	Garlick-Bell 205A-1 (UH-1H)	5645	ex 66-01162	
N149AC	Garlick-Bell 205A-1 (UH-1H)	5229	ex 66-00746	Lsd to Layang-Layang
N543CH	Sikorsky CH-54A		ex 67-18414	
N544CH	Sikorsky CH-54A		ex 67-18420	
N564AC	Cessna 441 Conquest	441-0147	ex N999BE	
N4410K	Sikorsky CH-54A		ex 67-18425	
N7073C	Sikorsky CH-54A		ex 67-18440	

EVERGREEN HELICOPTERS

McMinnville, OR/Anchorage-Merrill, AK/ Galveston, TX (RNC/MRI/-)

N350EV	Aerospatiale AS.350B2 Ecureuil	2961	ex C-FZWB			
N352EV	Aerospatiale AS.350B2 Ecureuil	2555	ex JA6112			
N353EV	Aerospatiale AS.350B2 Ecureuil	2444	ex C-GJVG			
N354EV	Aerospatiale AS.350B3 Ecureuil	3664				
N355EV	Aerospatiale AS.350B3 Ecureuil	3550				
N356EV	Aerospatiale AS.350B3 Ecureuil	3649				
N917JT	Aerospatiale AS.350B2 Ecureuil	2759	ex N6096P			
N85TC	Bell 206L-3 LongRanger III	51143				
N255EV	Bell 206L-3 LongRanger III	51488				
N5000G	Bell 206L-1 Long Ranger III	45163				
N5007F	Bell 206L-1 Long Ranger III	45186				
N5748H	Bell 206L-1 Long Ranger II	45490				
N212EV	Bell 212	30881	ex P2-HCA			
N398EH	Bell 212	30766				
N827MS	Bell 212	31205	ex N711EV			
N5017H	Bell 212	30930				
N5410N	Bell 212	31206	ex VH-CUZ			
N16973	Bell 212	30882	ex VH-CRO			
N16974	Bell 212	30886				
N59633	Bell 212	30676				
N22MS	Lear Jet 35A	35A-209	ex N711DS			
N60EV	Sikorsky S-61 (H-3)	61642	ex 69-5799			
N61EV	Sikorsky S-61 (CH-3E)	61566	ex 65-12791			
N62EV	Sikorsky S-61 (HH-3F)	61670	ex USCG 1493			
N63EV	Sikorsky S-61 (HH-3F)	61674	ex USCG 1497			
N108FH	Bell 206B JetRanger III	2770	ex N301GP			
N131EV	Lockheed C-130E Hercules	3688	ex 61-2365	stored MZJ		
N202EV	Lockheed P2V-5 Neptune	726-5387	ex Bu131502	141 Tanker		
N204BB	MBB Bo105C	S-57	ex D-HDBH			
N348CA	CASA C.212-200	CC20-7-175				
N352CA	CASA C.212-200	CC40-1-190		Lsd to US Air Force		
N422CA	CASA C.212-200	CC40-5-238				
N423CA	CASA C.212-200	S1-1-240		Lsd to US Air Force		
N500KM	MBB Bo105C	S-76				
N2777Q	Bell 206B JetRanger III	2805				
N3889Y	Bell 206B JetRanger III	3099				
N4750R	Bell 205A-1	30009	N6979R	Sikorsky S-64E	64079	
N9688G	Cessna U206F Stationair	U20601888				
N10729	Bell 206B JetRanger III	2876				

EVERGREEN INTERNATIONAL AIRLINES

Evergreen (EZ/EIA)   *McMinnville, OR/Marana-Pinal Airpark, AZ (RNC/MZJ)*

N470EV	Boeing 747-273C	237/20653	ex N749WA	
N471EV	Boeing 747-273C	209/20651	ex N747WR	
N477EV	Boeing 747SR-46 (SCD)	231/20784	ex N688UP	
N478EV	Boeing 747SR-46 (SCD)	254/21033	ex PT-TDE	
N479EV	Boeing 747-132 (SCD)	94/19898	ex N725PA	
N480EV	Boeing 747-121 (SCD)	106/20348	ex N690UP	
N481EV	Boeing 747-132 (SCD)	72/19896	ex N902PA	
N482EV	Boeing 747-212B (SCD)	219/20713	ex N729PA	
N485EV	Boeing 747-212B (SCD)	218/20712	ex N728PA	
N486EV	Boeing 747-212B (SCD)	240/20888	ex N745SJ	
N915F	Douglas DC-9-15RC (ABS 3)	207/47061	ex EC-EYS	
N916F	Douglas DC-9-15RC (ABS 3)	165/47044	ex OH-LYH	
N933F	Douglas DC-9-33RC (ABS 3)	280/47191	ex N33UA	
N941F	Douglas DC-9-33F (ABS 3)	311/47193	ex VH-IPC	Lsd fr Venture Acquistions
N942F	Douglas DC-9-33F (ABS 3)	467/47408	ex VH-IPF	
N944F	Douglas DC-9-33RC (ABS 3)	324/47194	ex PH-DNP	
N945F	Douglas DC-9-33RC (ABS 3)	337/47279	ex PH-DNR	

Evergreen own Pinal Airpark, Marana [MZJ] and aircraft regularly enter short-term storage. Several Boeing 727s are also still registered but all are believed withdrawn from service

EVERTS AIR ALASKA

Everts (3K/VTS)   *Fairbanks-Intl, AK (FAI)*

N108NS	Piper PA-32R-300 Lance	32R-7680288			
N148RF	Piper PA-32R-300 Lance	32R-7680076			
N575JD	Cessna 208B Caravan I	208B0595	ex N5268V		Lsd fr C&R Leasing
N1063H	Piper PA-32R-300 Lance	32R-7780129			
N6969J	Piper PA-32R-300 Lance	32R-7680398			
N41185	Piper PA-31-350 T1020	31-8553001			
N444CE	Douglas DC-6B	962/45478	ex C-GHLZ	Spirit of America	
N451CE	Douglas C-118B	358/43712	ex N840CS		
N3050P	Douglas C-118B	406/44073	ex C-		

EVERTS AIR CARGO

Cargo Express (3K/VTS) (IATA 029)   *Fairbanks-Intl, AK (FAI)*
Previously listed as Air Cargo Express

N28CA	Douglas DC-6B	934/45321	ex EP-AEW		
N151	Douglas DC-6B	992/45496	ex C-GICD		
N251CE	Douglas C-118A	532/44612	ex Bu153693		
N351CE	Douglas C-118A	505/44599	ex 53-3228		
N400UA	Douglas DC-6A	467/44258			
N555SQ	Douglas DC-6B	830/45137	ex N37585		
N888DG	Douglas C-118A	642/44675	ex 53-3304		
N951CE	Douglas C-118A	328/43696	ex	USN colours	
N3047V	Douglas DC-6A	451/44658	ex C-GBYS		
N3050P	Douglas DC-6A	406/44073	ex C-GBYB		
N6586C	Douglas DC-6BF	849/45222			
N1837M	Curtiss C-46F Commando	22388	ex CF-FNC	Hot Stuff	Everts Air Fuel titles
N7848B	Curtiss C-46R Commando	273	ex HP-238	Dumbo	
N54514	Curtiss C-46D Commando	33285	ex 51-1122	Maid in Japan	

Division of Tatonduk Outfitters, all freighters; see also Tatonduk Air Services

EXECUTIVE AIRLINES sale not completed due to overall scope clause agreements at American Airlines; remains as part of American Eagle

EXECUTIVE AIRLINES

Long Island (YL/ORA)   *Farmington-Republic Field, NY (FRG)*

N16EN	British Aerospace Jetstream 31	743	ex N403UE	Lsd fr Millennium Jetstream
N16EX	British Aerospace Jetstream 31	826	ex N850JS	Lsd fr Millennium Jetstream
N404GJ	British Aerospace Jetstream 31	754	ex N754JX	Lsd fr Millennium Jetstream

Also trades as East Coast Aviation Services

EXPRESS.NET AIRLINES

Expressnet (XNA)   *Detroit-Willow Run, MI (YIP)*

N224KW	Airbus Industrie A300B4-203F	073	ex D-ASAF	all-white	Lsd fr BBAM
N370PC	Airbus Industrie A300B4-203F	134	ex D-ASAE		Lsd fr PACE
N371PC	Airbus Industrie A300B4-203F	157	ex D-ASAG		Lsd fr PACE; sublsd to AHK
N372PC	Airbus Industrie A300B4-203F	196	ex D-ASAH		Lsd fr PACE
N373PC	Airbus Industrie A300B4-203F	218	ex VH-TAD		Lsd fr PACE
N472AS	Airbus Industrie A300B4-203F	125	ex RP-C3003		Lsd fr DMCMAG
N473AS	Airbus Industrie A300B4-203F	203	ex RP-C3004		Lsd fr DMCMAG
N474AS	Airbus Industrie A300B4-203F	219	ex RP-C3005		Lsd fr DMCMAG
N13974	Airbus Industrie A300B4-203F	126	ex N968C		Lsd fr GATX
N704A	Boeing 727-173C	427/19504	ex N690WA		Lsd fr Clark Avn Holdings
N792A	Boeing 727-22C	406/19195	ex N727CK	all white	Lsd fr Clark Avn Holdings
N793A	Boeing 727-227	997/20774	ex N926TS		Lsd fr Clark Avn Holdings
N73751	Boeing 727-227F	1217/21247	ex N446BN		Lsd fr Finova Capital
N76752	Boeing 727-227F	1218/21248	ex N447BN		Lsd fr Finova Capital
N76753	Boeing 727-227F	1219/21249	ex N448BN		Lsd fr Finova Capital
N79754	Boeing 727-227F	1258/21363			Lsd fr Finova Capital

All fitted with Raisbeck Stage 3 hushkits

EXPRESS ONE INTERNATIONAL

Longhorn (EO/LHN)   *Dallas-Love Field, TX (DAL)*

Entered Chapter 11 early in 2002; ceased operations in 2002 but planned to restart in 2003

EXPRESSJET AIRLINES

Jet Link (CO/BTA) (IATA 565)
Cleveland-Hopkins Intl, OH/Houston-George Bush Intercontinental, TX/Denver-Centennial, CO (CLE/IAH/DIA)

Operates (and listed) under trading name Continental Express; subsidiary of Continental Airlines

FALCON AIR EXPRESS

Panther (F2/FAO)   Miami-Intl, FL (MIA)

N203AV	Boeing 727-259 (FedEx 3)	1688/22474		Lillian; std TUS	Lsd fr ART 22474
N266US	Boeing 727-251 (FedEx 3)	745/19985		Lillian; std TUS	Lsd fr ART19985
N296SC	Boeing 727-224 (FedEx 3)	1756/22449	ex N79746	Carolina	Lsd fr ART 22449
					sublsd toSol Air
N521DB	Boeing 727-243 (FedEx 3)	1227/21266	ex N573PE		Lsd to DHL Avn Americas
N908PG	Boeing 727-276 (FedEx 3)	1101/20951	ex TF-AIA	Cecilia	Lsd fr ART 20951
N54348	Boeing 727-231 (FedEx 3)	1563/21967		Alicia	Lsd fr ART 21967;
					sublsd to Sol Air
N64346*	Boeing 727-231 (FedEx 3)	1464/21633			Lsd fr ART 21633
N79749*	Boeing 727-224 (FedEx 3)	1767/22451		Christine	Lsd fr ART 22451
N79750*	Boeing 727-224 (FedEx 3)	1772/22452		Patricia	Lsd fr ART 22452

*Subleased to Aeropostal

N371FA	Boeing 737-33A	1337/23631	ex N172AW	Lsd fr AWMS I; sublsd to Sol Air
N550FA	Boeing 737-3K2	1196/23411	ex TC-ESA	Lsd fr Pegasus

FARWEST AIRLINES

(FRW)   Chandler-Memorial, AZ (CHD)

N701AC	de Havilland DHC-7-102	18	ex N895S	Lsd fr FWA Investors
N703MG	de Havilland DHC-7-102	103	ex N773BE	Lsd fr FWA Investors

FEDERICO HELICOPTERS

(FDE)   Fresno-Air Terminal, CA/Mariposa-Yosemite, CA (FAT/-)

N111VF	Cessna T210N Centurion II	21064005	ex N7067N
N205JG	Bell UH-1H (204)	9884	ex 67-17686
N747A	Sikorsky S-58T	58910	
N752A	Sikorsky S-58T	58981	ex C-GRXA
N1386L	Bell UH-1B (204)	652	ex 62-4592
N2610G	Cessna 402C II	402C0064	

FEDEX EXPRESS

FedEx (FX/FDX) (IATA023)   Memphis-Intl, TN (MEM)

N47AE	Aerospatiale/Alenia ATR 42-300	047	ex N425MQ	
N135MQ	Aerospatiale/Alenia ATR 42-310	135	ex N429MQ	on order
N141AE	Aerospatiale/Alenia ATR 42-300	141	ex N431MQ	on order
N246AE	Aerospatiale/Alenia ATR 42-320	243	ex N243AT	on order
N251AE	Aerospatiale/Alenia ATR 42-320	250	ex N250AA	
N255AE	Aerospatiale/Alenia ATR 42-300	254	ex N254AT	on order
N262AT	Aerospatiale/Alenia ATR 42-300	262	ex F-WWEL	on order
N265AE	Aerospatiale/Alenia ATR 42-320	266	ex N266AT	on order
N269AT	Aerospatiale/Alenia ATR 42-320	269	ex F-WWEA	
N271AT	Aerospatiale/Alenia ATR 42-320	273	ex N273AT	on order
N277AT	Aerospatiale/Alenia ATR 42-300	277	ex F-WWLA	
N282AT	Aerospatiale/Alenia ATR 42-320	282	ex F-WWLI	on order
N293AT	Aerospatiale/Alenia ATR 42-300	293	ex F-WWLR	
N310DK	Aerospatiale/Alenia ATR 42-300	310	ex F-WWEC	on order
N314AM	Aerospatiale/Alenia ATR 42-300	314	ex F-WWEK	on order
N319AM	Aerospatiale/Alenia ATR 42-300	319	ex F-WWER	on order
N325AT	Aerospatiale/Alenia ATR 42-320	325	ex F-WWLK	on order
N327AT	Aerospatiale/Alenia ATR 42-320	327	ex F-WWLM	on order
N351AT	Aerospatiale/Alenia ATR 42-320	354	ex N354AT	on order
N424MQ	Aerospatiale/Alenia ATR 42-300	045	ex F-WWEY	
N721TE	Aerospatiale/Alenia ATR 72-202	217	ex F-WWEM	
N722TE	Aerospatiale/Alenia ATR 72-202	220	ex F-ODQP	
N900FX	Aerospatiale/Alenia ATR 42-320	170	ex N14825	
N901FX	Aerospatiale/Alenia ATR 42-320	172	ex N26826	
N902FX	Aerospatiale/Alenia ATR 42-320	175	ex N15827	
N903FX	Aerospatiale/Alenia ATR 42-320	179	ex N14828	
N904FX	Aerospatiale/Alenia ATR 42-320	259	ex N99838	
N905FX	Aerospatiale/Alenia ATR 42-320	271	ex N93840	
N906FX	Aerospatiale/Alenia ATR 42-320	280	ex N97841	
N907FX	Aerospatiale/Alenia ATR 42-320	286	ex N86842	
N908FX	Aerospatiale/Alenia ATR 42-300	023	ex N972NA	
N909FX	Aerospatiale/Alenia ATR 42-300	275	ex N275BC	

N650FE	Airbus Industrie A300F4-605R	726	ex F-WWAP	Molly Mickler	
N651FE	Airbus Industrie A300F4-605R	728	ex F-WWAJ	Diane Kathleen	Lsd fr WFBN
N652FE	Airbus Industrie A300F4-605R	735	ex F-WWAN	Rachael Patricia	
N653FE	Airbus Industrie A300F4-605R	736	ex F-WWAD	Samantha Massey	
N654FE	Airbus Industrie A300F4-605R	738	ex F-WWAX	Richard	
N655FE	Airbus Industrie A300F4-605R	742	ex F-WWAJ	Dion	
N656FE	Airbus Industrie A300F4-605R	745	ex F-WWAP	Devin	Lsd fr WFBN
N657FE	Airbus Industrie A300F4-605R	748	ex F-WWAM	Lizzie	Lsd fr WFBN
N658FE	Airbus Industrie A300F4-605R	752	ex F-WWAE	Tristian	Lsd fr WFBN
N659FE	Airbus Industrie A300F4-605R	757	ex F-WWAF	Calvin	Lsd fr WFBN
N660FE	Airbus Industrie A300F4-605R	759	ex F-WWAG	Zack	

N661FE	Airbus Industrie A300F4-605R	760	ex F-WWAL	Whitney	
N662FE	Airbus Industrie A300F4-605R	761	ex F-WWAK	Tessa	Lsd fr WFBN
N663FE	Airbus Industrie A300F4-605R	766	ex F-WWAO	Domenick	
N664FE	Airbus Industrie A300F4-605R	768	ex F-WWAA	Amanda	Lsd fr WFBN
N665FE	Airbus Industrie A300F4-605R	769	ex F-WWAM	Ethan	Lsd fr WFBN
N667FE	Airbus Industrie A300F4-605R	771	ex F-WWAF	Sean	Lsd fr WFBN
N668FE	Airbus Industrie A300F4-605R	772	ex F-WWAP	Tianna	Lsd fr WFBN
N669FE	Airbus Industrie A300F4-605R	774	ex F-WWAE	Kaitlyn	Lsd fr WFBN
N670FE	Airbus Industrie A300F4-605R	777	ex F-WWAQ	Amrit	
N671FE	Airbus Industrie A300F4-605R	778	ex F-WWAV	Drew	
N672FE	Airbus Industrie A300F4-605R	779	ex F-WWAZ		
N673FE	Airbus Industrie A300F4-605R	780	ex F-WWAU	Mark	
N674FE	Airbus Industrie A300F4-605R	781	ex F-WWAN	Thea	
N675FE	Airbus Industrie A300F4-605R	789	ex F-WWAZ	Byron	
N676FE	Airbus Industrie A300F4-605R	790	ex F-WWAV	Jade	
N677FE	Airbus Industrie A300F4-605R	791	ex F-WWAD	Clifford	
N678FE	Airbus Industrie A300F4-605R	792	ex F-WWAF	Allison	
N679FE	Airbus Industrie A300F4-605R	793	ex F-WWAG	Ty	
N680FE	Airbus Industrie A300F4-605R	794	ex F-WWAH	Tierney	
N681FE	Airbus Industrie A300F4-605R	799	ex F-WWAJ	Kaci	
N682FE	Airbus Industrie A300F4-605R	800	ex F-WWAK		
N683FE	Airbus Industrie A300F4-605R	801	ex F-WWAL	Xenophon	
N684FE	Airbus Industrie A300F4-605R	802	ex F-WWAM	Daniel	Lsd fr State Street
N685FE	Airbus Industrie A300F4-605R	803	ex F-WWAB	Landon Ostlie	
N686FE	Airbus Industrie A300F4-605R	804	ex F-WWAO	Alex	Lsd fr State Street
N716FD	Airbus Industrie A300B4-622F	358	ex HL7287	Halle	
N717FD	Airbus Industrie A300B4-622F	361	ex HL7280		
N718FD	Airbus Industrie A300B4-622F	365	ex HL7281		
N719FD	Airbus Industrie A300B4-622	388	ex HL7290		
N720FD	Airbus Industrie A300B4-622F	417	ex HL7291		
N721FD	Airbus Industrie A300B4-622RF	477	ex D-ASAE	Kathryn	
N722FD	Airbus Industrie A300B4-622RF	479	ex HL7535		
N723FD	Airbus Industrie A300B4-622RF	543	ex HL7536		
N401FE	Airbus Industrie A310-203F	191	ex D-AICA	Mickey	Lsd fr WFBN
N402FE	Airbus Industrie A310-203F	201	ex D-AICB	Carlye	
N403FE	Airbus Industrie A310-203F	230	ex D-AICC	Maddison	Lsd fr WFBN
N404FE	Airbus Industrie A310-203F	233	ex D-AICD	Sarah	Lsd fr WFBN
N405FE	Airbus Industrie A310-203F	237	ex D-AICF	Mariah	
N407FE	Airbus Industrie A310-203F	254	ex D-AICH	Stacey Denise	
N408FE	Airbus Industrie A310-203F	257	ex D-AICK	Patrice	Lsd fr WFBN
N409FE	Airbus Industrie A310-203F	273	ex D-AICL	Jake	
N410FE	Airbus Industrie A310-203F	356	ex D-AICM	Jerel	
N411FE	Airbus Industrie A310-203F	359	ex D-AICN	Barbara	
N412FE	Airbus Industrie A310-203F	360	ex D-AICP	Corina	
N413FE	Airbus Industrie A310-203F	397	ex D-AICR	Skip Mayer	
N414FE	Airbus Industrie A310-203F	400	ex D-AICS	Tanner	
N415FE	Airbus Industrie A310-203F	349	ex PH-MCB	Jacquelyn	
N416FE	Airbus Industrie A310-222F	288	ex N801PA	Patrick	
N417FE	Airbus Industrie A310-222F	333	ex N802PA	Kyle	
N418FE	Airbus Industrie A310-222F	343	ex N803PA	Rachel	
N419FE	Airbus Industrie A310-222F	345	ex N804PA	Krystle	
N420FE	Airbus Industrie A310-222F	339	ex N805PA	Molly	
N421FE	Airbus Industrie A310-222F	342	ex N806PA	Caitlin	
N422FE	Airbus Industrie A310-222F	346	ex N807PA	Joseph	
N423FE	Airbus Industrie A310-203F	281	ex PH-MCA	Trey	
N424FE	Airbus Industrie A310-203F	241	ex PH-AGA	Kendall	
N425FE	Airbus Industrie A310-203F	264	ex PH-AGD	Jerome	
N426FE	Airbus Industrie A310-203F	245	ex PH-AGB	Shana	
N427FE	Airbus Industrie A310-203F	362	ex PH-AGH	Zackary	
N428FE	Airbus Industrie A310-203F	248	ex PH-AGC	Kristina	
N429FE	Airbus Industrie A310-203F	364	ex PH-AGI	Conner	
N430FE	Airbus Industrie A310-203F	394	ex PH-AGK	Kelleen	
N431FE	Airbus Industrie A310-203	316	ex F-WWAD		
N432FE	Airbus Industrie A310-203F	326	ex F-GEMB	stored MHV; all white	
N433FE	Airbus Industrie A310-203F	335	ex F-GEMC	under conversion	
N434FE	Airbus Industrie A310-203	355	ex F-GEMD	stored MHV; all white	
N435FE	Airbus Industrie A310-203	369	ex F-GEME	stored MHV; all white	
N436FE	Airbus Industrie A310-203F	454	ex F-GEMG		
N442FE	Airbus Industrie A310-203F	353	ex PH-AGG	Breanna	
N443FE	Airbus Industrie A310-203F	283	ex PH-AGE	Katelin	
N445FE	Airbus Industrie A310-203F	297	ex PH-AGF	Nicholas	
N446FE	Airbus Industrie A310-222F	224	ex HB-IPA	Kyler	Lsd fr ILFC
N447FE	Airbus Industrie A310-222F	251	ex HB-IPB	Shaunna	Lsd fr ILFC
N448FE	Airbus Industrie A310-222F	260	ex HB-IPD	Augustine	
N449FE	Airbus Industrie A310-222F	217	ex F-GOCJ	Treydn	
N450FE	Airbus Industrie A310-222F	162	ex F-GPDJ	Selna	
N451FE	Airbus Industrie A310-222F	303	ex OO-SCA	Reis	
N452FE	Airbus Industrie A310-222F	313	ex OO-SCB	Ashley	
N453FE	Airbus Industrie A310-222F	267	ex D-ASAL	Rush	
N454FE	Airbus Industrie A310-222F	278	ex F-OGYX		
N455FE	Airbus Industrie A310-222F	331	ex F-WWAH	Sara	

N456FE	Airbus Industrie A310-222F	318	ex F-OHPQ		
N801FD	Airbus Industrie A310-324F	539	ex D-ASAD	Amos	
N802FD	Airbus Industrie A310-324F	542	ex D-ASAD		
N102FE	Boeing 727-22C	392/19193	ex N7418U	Laura Lane	
N103FE	Boeing 727-22C	414/19199	ex N7424U	Jennifer	
N107FE	Boeing 727-22C	424/19202	ex N7427U	Kira	
N112FE	Boeing 727-22C	630/19890	ex N7433U	Alicia	Lsd to MAL as C-GBWA
N113FE	Boeing 727-22C	647/19894	ex N7437U	Jarrod	
N114FE	Boeing 727-24C	460/19527	ex CC-CAN	Rollin III	
N119FE	Boeing 727-25C	352/19301	ex N8154G	Stefani Lynn	
N120FE	Boeing 727-25C	356/19356	ex N8156G	April Dawn; stored MEM	
N124FE	Boeing 727-25C	371/19360	ex N8160G	Marcella	
N127FE	Boeing 727-25C	478/19719	ex N8163G	Sidney Lewis	
					Lsd to MAL as C-FBWG
N133FE	Boeing 727-25C	510/19851	ex N8168G	Kimberly Ann	
N135FE	Boeing 727-25C	522/19853	ex N8170G	Annie	
N136FE	Boeing 727-25C	632/19855	ex N8172G	Christopher	
N144FE	Boeing 727-21C	316/19137	ex N723EV	Spencer	
N149FE	Boeing 727-22F	359/19087	ex N7074U	Holly	
N150FE	Boeing 727-22F	370/19141	ex N7077U	Amber	
N151FE	Boeing 727-22F	472/19147	ex N7083U	Rob	
N166FE	Boeing 727-22F	227/18863	ex N7056U	Katy	
N168FE	Boeing 727-22F	232/18865	ex N7058U	William	
N169FE	Boeing 727-22F	241/18866	ex N7059U	Skyler	
N180FE	Boeing 727-22F	247/18867	ex N7060U	Alayna	Lsd to MAL as C-GBWS
N185FE	Boeing 727-22F	259/18871	ex N7064U	Casey	
N186FE	Boeing 727-22F	261/18872	ex N7065U	Clayton	
N187FE	Boeing 727-22F	268/19079	ex N7066U	Aaron	
N188FE	Boeing 727-22F	275/19081	ex N7068U	Austin	
N189FE	Boeing 727-22F	279/19082	ex N7069U	Micah	
N190FE	Boeing 727-22F	281/19083	ex N7070U	Curtis	
N191FE	Boeing 727-22F	337/19084	ex N7071U	Thomas	
N192FE	Boeing 727-22F	349/19085	ex N7072U	Kellye	Lsd to MAL as C-FBWY
N193FE	Boeing 727-22F	440/19142	ex N7078U	Anna	
N194FE	Boeing 727-22F	446/19143	ex N7079U	Lindsay	
N198FE	Boeing 727-22F	512/19154	ex N7090U	Faye	
N199FE	Boeing 727-173C	459/19509	ex TZ-ADR	Ms Mali	
N201FE	Boeing 727-2S2FRE	1818/22924		Bridgette Patrice	
N203FE	Boeing 727-2S2F	1819/22925		Jonathan Richard	
N204FE	Boeing 727-2S2F	1820/22926		Rebecca Rose	
N205FE	Boeing 727-2S2FRE	1821/22927		Robert Christopher	
N206FE	Boeing 727-2S2FRE	1822/22928		Joshua Gene	
N207FE	Boeing 727-2S2FRE	1823/22929		Vivien	
N208FE	Boeing 727-2S2FRE	1824/22930		Audrey	
N209FE	Boeing 727-2S2FRE	1825/22931		Kasey Sue-Ellen	
N210FE	Boeing 727-2S2FRE	1826/22932		Missy	
N211FE	Boeing 727-2S2F	1827/22933		Adam Bradley	
N212FE	Boeing 727-2S2FRE	1828/22934		Jeremy David	
N213FE	Boeing 727-2S2F	1829/22935		Christine	
N215FE	Boeing 727-2S2FRE	1830/22936		Billy	
N216FE	Boeing 727-2S2FRE	1831/22937		Wade	
N217FE	Boeing 727-2S2FRE	1832/22938		Sonja	
N218FE	Boeing 727-233F	1150/21101	ex C-GAAM	Christin Leigh	
N219FE	Boeing 727-233F	1152/21102	ex C-GAAN	Jakob	
N220FE	Boeing 727-233F	1074/20934	ex C-GAAC	Emily	
N221FE	Boeing 727-233F	1069/20932	ex C-GAAA	Megan Nicole	
N222FE	Boeing 727-233F	1071/20933	ex C-GAAB	Michael	
N223FE	Boeing 727-233F	1076/20935	ex C-GAAD	Dustin	
N233FE	Boeing 727-247F	1249/21327	ex N2822W	Monika	
N234FE	Boeing 727-247F	1251/21328	ex N2823W		
N235FE	Boeing 727-247F	1254/21329	ex N2824W	Stephanie	
N236FE	Boeing 727-247F	1260/21330	ex N2825W		
N237FE	Boeing 727-247F	1266/21331	ex N2826W		
N240FE	Boeing 727-277F	1083/20978	ex VH-RMY	Baron	
N241FE	Boeing 727-277F	1098/20979	ex VH-RMZ	Jill	
N242FE	Boeing 727-277F	1237/21178	ex VH-RMK	Brittney	
N243FE	Boeing 727-277F	1352/21480	ex VH-RML	Braden	
N244FE	Boeing 727-277F	1436/21647	ex VH-RMM	Crystal	
N245FE	Boeing 727-277F	1566/22016	ex VH-RMO	Kelsey	
N246FE	Boeing 727-277F	1660/22068	ex VH-RMP	Daisy	
N254FE	Boeing 727-233F	1078/20936	ex C-GAAE	Courtney	
N257FE	Boeing 727-233F	1112/20939	ex C-GAAH	Kurt	
N258FE	Boeing 727-233F	1120/20940	ex C-GAAI	Ivie	
N262FE	Boeing 727-233F	1468/21624	ex C-GAAO	Betsy	
N263FE	Boeing 727-233F	1470/21625	ex C-GAAP	Marc	
N264FE	Boeing 727-233F	1472/21626	ex C-GAAQ	Chastity	
N265FE	Boeing 727-233F	1523/21671	ex C-GAAR	Paul	
N266FE	Boeing 727-233F	1538/21672	ex C-GAAS	Steven	
N267FE	Boeing 727-233F	1541/21673	ex C-GAAT		
N268FE	Boeing 727-233F	1543/21674	ex C-GAAU	Ginger	
N269FE	Boeing 727-233F	1555/21675	ex C-GAAV		

N270FE	Boeing 727-233F	1578/22035	ex C-GAAW	Benjamin
N271FE	Boeing 727-233F	1596/22036	ex C-GAAX	Andrew
N272FE	Boeing 727-233F	1600/22037	ex C-GAAY	Payton
N273FE	Boeing 727-233F	1612/22038	ex C-GAAZ	Samantha
N274FE	Boeing 727-233F	1614/22039	ex C-GYNA	Jessica
N275FE	Boeing 727-233F	1626/22040	ex C-GYNB	Skylar
N276FE	Boeing 727-233F	1628/22041	ex C-GYNC	Devon
N277FE	Boeing 727-233F	1630/22042	ex C-GYND	Tineka
N278FE	Boeing 727-233F	1699/22345	ex C-GYNE	Jeffrey
N279FE	Boeing 727-233F	1704/22346	ex C-GYNF	Ryan
N280FE	Boeing 727-223F	1708/22347	ex C-GYNG	Chad
N281FE	Boeing 727-233F	1714/22348	ex C-GYNH	Ivie
N282FE	Boeing 727-233F	1722/22349	ex C-GYNI	Dominique
N283FE	Boeing 727-233F	1745/22350	ex C-GYNJ	Randall
N284FE	Boeing 727-233F	1791/22621	ex C-GYNK	Victoria
N285FE	Boeing 727-233F	1792/22622	ex C-GYNL	Jordann
N286FE	Boeing 727-233F	1803/22623	ex C-GYNM	Charlsi
N287FE	Boeing 727-2D4F	1527/21849	ex N361PA	Lsd fr Lone Star Air Partners
N288FE	Boeing 727-2D4F	1536/21850	ex N362PA	Lsd fr WFBN
N461FE	Boeing 727-225F	1734/22548	ex N811EA	
N462FE	Boeing 727-225F	1739/22550	ex N813EA	
N463FE	Boeing 727-225F	1744/22551	ex N814EA	
N464FE	Boeing 727-225F	1234/21288	ex N8870Z	Blake
N465FE	Boeing 727-225F	1235/21289	ex N8871Z	
N466FE	Boeing 727-225F	1240/21292	ex N8874Z	
N467FE	Boeing 727-225F	1306/21449	ex N8876Z	Joy
N468FE	Boeing 727-225F	1312/21452	ex N8879Z	
N469FE	Boeing 727-225F	1437/21581	ex N8884Z	
N477FE	Boeing 727-227F	1281/21394	ex N453BN	Walter
N478FE	Boeing 727-227F	1283/21395	ex N454BN	Nikki
N479FE	Boeing 727-227F	1337/21461	ex N455BN	Norah
N480FE	Boeing 727-227F	1342/21462	ex N456BN	Warren
N481FE	Boeing 727-227F	1353/21463	ex N457BN	Tiffany
N482FE	Boeing 727-227F	1355/21464	ex N458BN	Natalie
N483FE	Boeing 727-227F	1363/21465	ex N459BN	David
N484FE	Boeing 727-227F	1372/21466	ex N460BN	Hallie
N485FE	Boeing 727-227F	1388/21488	ex N461BN	Kirsten
N486FE	Boeing 727-227F	1390/21489	ex N462BN	Hunter
N487FE	Boeing 727-227F	1396/21490	ex N463BN	Britney
N488FE	Boeing 727-227F	1402/21491	ex N464BN	Olivia
N489FE	Boeing 727-227F	1440/21492	ex N465BN	Timothy
N490FE	Boeing 727-227F	1442/21493	ex N466BN	Chase
N491FE	Boeing 727-227F	1444/21529	ex N467BN	Tobias
N492FE	Boeing 727-227F	1446/21530	ex N468BN	Two Bears
N493FE	Boeing 727-227F	1450/21531	ex N469BN	Maxx
N494FE	Boeing 727-227F	1453/21532	ex N470BN	Ian
N495FE	Boeing 727-227F	1484/21669	ex N471BN	Leslie
N496FE	Boeing 727-227F	1486/21670	ex N472BN	Zachary
N498FE	Boeing 727-232F	1068/20867	ex CS-TCI	Aidan
N499FE	Boeing 727-232F	1095/21018	ex CS-TCJ	Sierra

All 727s are fitted with FedEx Stage 3 hushkits except those marked FRE which are Super 27 variants (re-engined with P&W JT8D-217C outboard and -17A engine centre).

N700FX	Cessna 208B Caravan I	208B0419	Op by CFS
N701FX	Cessna 208B Caravan I	208B0420	Op by WIG
N702FX	Cessna 208B Caravan I	208B0422	Op by BVN
N703FX	Cessna 208B Caravan I	208B0423	Op by IRO
N705FX	Cessna 208B Caravan I	208B0425	Op by CFS
N706FX	Cessna 208B Caravan I	208B0426	Op by IRO
N707FX	Cessna 208B Caravan I	208B0427	Op by PCM
N708FX	Cessna 208B Caravan I	208B0429	Op by MTN
N709FX	Cessna 208B Caravan I	208B0430	Op by CFS
N710FX	Cessna 208B Caravan I	208B0431	Op by CPT
N711FX	Cessna 208B Caravan I	208B0433	Op by CFS
N712FX	Cessna 208B Caravan I	208B0435	Op by IRO
N713FX	Cessna 208B Caravan I	208B0438	Op by PCM
N715FX	Cessna 208B Caravan I	208B0440	Op by MTN
N716FX	Cessna 208B Caravan I	208B0442	Op by CPT
N717FX	Cessna 208B Caravan I	208B0445	Op by IRO
N718FX	Cessna 208B Caravan I	208B0448	Op by BVN
N719FX	Cessna 208B Caravan I	208B0450	Op by BVN
N720FX	Cessna 208B Caravan I	208B0452	Op by CFS
N721FX	Cessna 208B Caravan I	208B0453	Op by MTN
N722FX	Cessna 208B Caravan I	208B0454	Op by PCM
N723FX	Cessna 208B Caravan I	208B0456	Op by BVN
N724FX	Cessna 208B Caravan I	208B0458	Op by CPT
N725FX	Cessna 208B Caravan I	208B0460	Op by WIG
N726FX	Cessna 208B Caravan I	208B0465	Op by PCM
N727FX	Cessna 208B Caravan I	208B0468	Op by IRO
N728FX	Cessna 208B Caravan I	208B0471	Op by CFS
N729FX	Cessna 208B Caravan I	208B0474	Op by MTN
N730FX	Cessna 208B Caravan I	208B0477	Op by CPT

N731FX	Cessna 208B Caravan I	208B0480		Op by WIG
N738FX	Cessna 208B Caravan I	208B0482		Op by BVN
N740FX	Cessna 208B Caravan I	208B0484		Op by MTN
N741FX	Cessna 208B Caravan I	208B0486		Op by BVN
N742FX	Cessna 208B Caravan I	208B0489		Op by MTN
N744FX	Cessna 208B Caravan I	208B0492		Op by PCM
N745FX	Cessna 208B Caravan I	208B0495		Op by BVN
N746FX	Cessna 208B Caravan I	208B0498		Op by CFS
N747FE	Cessna 208B Caravan I	208B0238		Op by MTN
N747FX	Cessna 208B Caravan I	208B0501		Op by MTN
N748FE	Cessna 208B Caravan I	208B0241		Op by WIG
N748FX	Cessna 208B Caravan I	208B0503		Op by PCM
N749FE	Cessna 208B Caravan I	208B0242		Op by BVN
N749FX	Cessna 208B Caravan I	208B0508		Op by MAL as C-FEXF
N750FX	Cessna 208B Caravan I	208B0511		Op by PCM
N751FE	Cessna 208B Caravan I	208B0245		Op by CPT
N751FX	Cessna 208B Caravan I	208B0514		Op by BVN
N752FE	Cessna 208B Caravan I	208B0247		Op by IRO
N752FX	Cessna 208B Caravan I	208B0517		Op by CFS
N753FE	Cessna 208B Caravan I	208B0248		Op by CFS
N753FX	Cessna 208B Caravan I	208B0520		Op by BVN
N754FX	Cessna 208B Caravan I	208B0526		Op by PCM
N755FE	Cessna 208B Caravan I	208B0250		Op by MTN
N755FX	Cessna 208B Caravan I	208B0529		Op by WIG
N756FE	Cessna 208B Caravan I	208B0251		Op by BVN
N756FX	Cessna 208B Caravan I	208B0532		Op by CFS
N757FX	Cessna 208B Caravan I	208B0535		Op by WIG
N758FX	Cessna 208B Caravan I	208B0539		Op by MAL as C-FEXB
N759FX	Cessna 208B Caravan I	208B0542		Op by MAL as C-FEXS
N760FE	Cessna 208B Caravan I	208B0252		Op by Corp Air, Philippines
N761FE	Cessna 208B Caravan I	208B0254		Op by IRO
N762FE	Cessna 208B Caravan I	208B0255		Op by PCM
N763FE	Cessna 208B Caravan I	208B0256		Op by PCM
N764FE	Cessna 208B Caravan I	208B0258		Op by MTN
N765FE	Cessna 208B Caravan I	208B0259		Op by BVN
N766FE	Cessna 208B Caravan I	208B0260		Op by Corp Air, Philippines
N767FE	Cessna 208B Caravan I	208B0262		Op by IRO
N768FE	Cessna 208B Caravan I	208B0263		Op by PCM
N769FE	Cessna 208B Caravan I	208B0264		Op by MTN
N770FE	Cessna 208B Caravan I	208B0265		Op by BVN
N771FE	Cessna 208B Caravan I	208B0267		Op by PCM
N772FE	Cessna 208B Caravan I	208B0268		Op by PCM
N773FE	Cessna 208B Caravan I	208B0269		Op by BVN
N774FE	Cessna 208B Caravan I	208B0271		Op by BVN
N775FE	Cessna 208B Caravan I	208B0272		Op by CFS
N776FE	Cessna 208B Caravan I	208B0273		Op by MTN
N778FE	Cessna 208B Caravan I	208B0275		Op by CFS
N779FE	Cessna 208B Caravan I	208B0276		Op by CFS
N780FE	Cessna 208B Caravan I	208B0277		Op by WIG
N781FE	Cessna 208B Caravan I	208B0278		Op by PCM
N782FE	Cessna 208B Caravan I	208B0280		Op by PCM
N783FE	Cessna 208B Caravan I	208B0281		Op by WIG
N784FE	Cessna 208B Caravan I	208B0282		Op by IRO
N785FE	Cessna 208B Caravan I	208B0283		Op by PCM
N786FE	Cessna 208B Caravan I	208B0284		Op by BVN
N787FE	Cessna 208B Caravan I	208B0285		Op by MTN
N788FE	Cessna 208B Caravan I	208B0286		Op by CFS
N789FE	Cessna 208B Caravan I	208B0287		Op by WIG
N790FE	Cessna 208B Caravan I	208B0288		Op by PCM
N792FE	Cessna 208B Caravan I	208B0290		Op by MTN
N793FE	Cessna 208B Caravan I	208B0291		Op by BVN
N794FE	Cessna 208B Caravan I	208B0292		Op by CPT
N795FE	Cessna 208B Caravan I	208B0293		Op by IRO
N796FE	Cessna 208B Caravan I	208B0212	ex C-FEXY	Op by CPT
N797FE	Cessna 208B Caravan I	208B0042	ex C-FEXH	Op by CPT
N798FE	Cessna 208B Caravan I	208B0174	ex C-FEDY	Op by CPT
N799FE	Cessna 208A Caravan I	20800065	ex C-FEXF	Op by CPT
N800FE	Cessna 208 Caravan I	20800007	ex (N9300F)	Op by CPT
N801FE	Cessna 208A Caravan I	20800009	ex (N9305F)	Op by MTN
N804FE	Cessna 208B Caravan I	208B0039	ex F-GETN	Op by WIG
N807FE	Cessna 208B Caravan I	208B0041	ex F-GETO	Op by WIG
N812FE	Cessna 208A Caravan I	20800040	ex (N9401F)	Op by CPT
N819FE	Cessna 208A Caravan I	20800056	ex (N9451F)	Op by MTN
N820FE	Cessna 208B Caravan I	208B0111	ex F-GHHC	Op by MTN
N827FE	Cessna 208A Caravan I	20800072	ex (N9491F)	Op by CPT
N828FE	Cessna 208B Caravan I	208B0122	ex F-GHHD	Op by IRO
N830FE	Cessna 208A Caravan I	20800075	ex (N9502F)	Op by IRO
N831FE	Cessna 208B Caravan I	208B0225	ex F-GHHE	Op by MTN
N832FE	Cessna 208 Caravan I	20800081	ex (N9518F)	Op by BVN
N833FE	Cessna 208A Caravan I	20800084	ex EI-FDX	Op by CFS
N835FE	Cessna 208A Caravan I	20800016	ex EI-FEX	Op by WIG
N841FE	Cessna 208B Caravan I	208B0144		Op by BVN

N842FE	Cessna 208B Caravan I	208B0146	Op by MTN
N843FE	Cessna 208B Caravan I	208B0147	Op by IRO
N844FE	Cessna 208B Caravan I	208B0149	Op by PCM
N845FE	Cessna 208B Caravan I	208B0152	Op by BVN
N846FE	Cessna 208B Caravan I	208B0154	Op by CPT
N847FE	Cessna 208B Caravan I	208B0156	Op by MTN
N848FE	Cessna 208B Caravan I	208B0158	Op by MTN
N849FE	Cessna 208B Caravan I	208B0162	Op by MTN
N850FE	Cessna 208B Caravan I	208B0164	Op by CFS
N851FE	Cessna 208B Caravan I	208B0166	Op by CPT
N852FE	Cessna 208B Caravan I	208B0168	Op by MTN
N853FE	Cessna 208B Caravan I	208B0170	Op by MTN
N855FE	Cessna 208B Caravan I	208B0203	Op by MTN
N856FE	Cessna 208B Caravan I	208B0176	Op by CFS
N857FE	Cessna 208B Caravan I	208B0177	Op by PCM
N858FE	Cessna 208B Caravan I	208B0178	Op by IRO
N859FE	Cessna 208B Caravan I	208B0181	Op by CFS
N860FE	Cessna 208B Caravan I	208B0182	Op by Corp Air, Philippines
N861FE	Cessna 208B Caravan I	208B0183	Op by BVN
N862FE	Cessna 208B Caravan I	208B0184	Op by MTN
N863FE	Cessna 208B Caravan I	208B0186	Op by CPT
N864FE	Cessna 208B Caravan I	208B0187	Op by CPT
N865FE	Cessna 208B Caravan I	208B0188	Op by WIG
N866FE	Cessna 208B Caravan I	208B0189	Op by BVN
N867FE	Cessna 208B Caravan I	208B0191	Op by CPT
N869FE	Cessna 208B Caravan I	208B0195	Op by MTN
N870FE	Cessna 208B Caravan I	208B0196	Op by WIG
N871FE	Cessna 208B Caravan I	208B0198	Op by IRO
N872FE	Cessna 208B Caravan I	208B0200	Op by PCM
N873FE	Cessna 208B Caravan I	208B0202	Op by CFS
N874FE	Cessna 208B Caravan I	208B0205	Op by MTN
N875FE	Cessna 208B Caravan I	208B0206	Op by CFS
N876FE	Cessna 208B Caravan I	208B0207	Op by CFS
N877FE	Cessna 208B Caravan I	208B0232	Op by CPT
N878FE	Cessna 208B Caravan I	208B0211	Op by MTN
N879FE	Cessna 208B Caravan I	208B0213	Op by PCM
N880FE	Cessna 208B Caravan I	208B0215	Op by CFS
N881FE	Cessna 208B Caravan I	208B0204	Op by MTN
N882FE	Cessna 208B Caravan I	208B0208	Op by CFS
N883FE	Cessna 208B Caravan I	208B0210	Op by IRO
N884FE	Cessna 208B Caravan I	208B0233	Op by IRO
N885FE	Cessna 208B Caravan I	208B0185	Op by CPT
N886FE	Cessna 208B Caravan I	208B0190	Op by PCM
N887FE	Cessna 208B Caravan I	208B0216	Op by MTN
N888FE	Cessna 208B Caravan I	208B0217	Op by WIG
N889FE	Cessna 208B Caravan I	208B0218	Op by BVN
N890FE	Cessna 208B Caravan I	208B0219	Op by CPT
N891FE	Cessna 208B Caravan I	208B0221	Op by PCM
N892FE	Cessna 208B Caravan I	208B0222	Op by PCM
N893FE	Cessna 208B Caravan I	208B0223	Op by IRO
N894FE	Cessna 208B Caravan I	208B0224	Op by BVN
N895FE	Cessna 208B Caravan I	208B0015 ex C-FEXG	Op by CFS
N896FE	Cessna 208B Caravan I	208B0226	Op by MAL as C-FEXY
N897FE	Cessna 208B Caravan I	208B0227	Op by CFS
N898FE	Cessna 208B Caravan I	208B0228	Op by WIG
N899FE	Cessna 208B Caravan I	208B0235	Op by CFS
N900FE	Cessna 208B Caravan I	208B0054 ex SE-KLX	Op by BVN
N901FE	Cessna 208B Caravan I	208B0001 ex N9767F	Op by WIG
N902FE	Cessna 208B Caravan I	208B0002	Op by BVN
N903FE	Cessna 208B Caravan I	208B0003	Op by CPT
N904FE	Cessna 208B Caravan I	208B0004	Op by CPT
N905FE	Cessna 208B Caravan I	208B0005	Op by MTN
N906FE	Cessna 208B Caravan I	208B0006	Op by IRO
N907FE	Cessna 208B Caravan I	208B0007	Op by IRO
N908FE	Cessna 208B Caravan I	208B0008	Op by PCM
N909FE	Cessna 208B Caravan I	208B0009	Op by WIG
N910FE	Cessna 208B Caravan I	208B0010	Op by CPT
N911FE	Cessna 208B Caravan I	208B0011	Op by WIG
N912FE	Cessna 208B Caravan I	208B0012	Op by BVN
N914FE	Cessna 208B Caravan I	208B0014	Op by IRO
N916FE	Cessna 208B Caravan I	208B0016	Op by CPT
N917FE	Cessna 208B Caravan I	208B0017	Op by MTN
N918FE	Cessna 208B Caravan I	208B0018	Op by CFS
N919FE	Cessna 208B Caravan I	208B0019	Op by WIG
N920FE	Cessna 208B Caravan I	208B0020	Op by PCM
N921FE	Cessna 208B Caravan I	208B0021	Op by MTN
N922FE	Cessna 208B Caravan I	208B0022	Op by BVN
N923FE	Cessna 208B Caravan I	208B0023	Op by IRO
N924FE	Cessna 208B Caravan I	208B0024	Op by CPT
N925FE	Cessna 208B Caravan I	208B0025	Op by IRO
N926FE	Cessna 208B Caravan I	208B0026	Op by CPT
N927FE	Cessna 208B Caravan I	208B0027	Op by IRO

N928FE	Cessna 208B Caravan I	208B0028		Op by BVN
N929FE	Cessna 208B Caravan I	208B0029		Op by BVN
N930FE	Cessna 208B Caravan I	208B0030		Op by PCM
N931FE	Cessna 208B Caravan I	208B0031		Op by WIG
N933FE	Cessna 208B Caravan I	208B0033		Op by CPT
N934FE	Cessna 208B Caravan I	208B0034		Op by BVN
N935FE	Cessna 208B Caravan I	208B0035		Op by WIG
N936FE	Cessna 208B Caravan I	208B0036		Op by CPT
N937FE	Cessna 208B Caravan I	208B0037		Op by WIG
N938FE	Cessna 208B Caravan I	208B0038		Op by MTN
N939FE	Cessna 208B Caravan I	208B0180		Op by BVN
N940FE	Cessna 208B Caravan I	208B0040		Op by CFS
N943FE	Cessna 208B Caravan I	208B0043		Op by MTN
N946FE	Cessna 208B Caravan I	208B0048	ex (N948FE)	Op by IRO
N947FE	Cessna 208B Caravan I	208B0050	ex (N950FE)	Op by WIG
N950FE	Cessna 208B Caravan I	208B0056	ex (N956FE)	Op by BVN
N952FE	Cessna 208B Caravan I	208B0060	ex (N960FE)	Op by CPT
N953FE	Cessna 208B Caravan I	208B0062	ex (N962FE)	Op by CFS
N954FE	Cessna 208B Caravan I	208B0064	ex (N964FE)	Op by IRO
N955FE	Cessna 208B Caravan I	208B0066	ex (N966FE)	Op by MTN
N956FE	Cessna 208B Caravan I	208B0068	ex (N968FE)	Op by CFS
N957FE	Cessna 208B Caravan I	208B0070	ex (N970FE)	Op by BVN
N958FE	Cessna 208B Caravan I	208B0071		Op by WIG
N959FE	Cessna 208B Caravan I	208B0073		Op by WIG
N960FE	Cessna 208B Caravan I	208B0075		Op by CFS
N961FE	Cessna 208B Caravan I	208B0077		Op by BVN
N962FE	Cessna 208B Caravan I	208B0078		Op by MTN
N963FE	Cessna 208B Caravan I	208B0080		Op by WIG
N964FE	Cessna 208B Caravan I	208B0083		Op by CPT
N965FE	Cessna 208B Caravan I	208B0084		Op by CFS
N966FE	Cessna 208B Caravan I	208B0086		Op by WIG
N967FE	Cessna 208B Caravan I	208B0088		Op by MTN
N968FE	Cessna 208B Caravan I	208B0090		Op by PCM
N969FE	Cessna 208B Caravan I	208B0092		Op by PCM
N970FE	Cessna 208B Caravan I	208B0093		Op by BVN
N971FE	Cessna 208B Caravan I	208B0094		Op by CPT
N972FE	Cessna 208B Caravan I	208B0096		Op by CPT
N973FE	Cessna 208B Caravan I	208B0098		Op by MTN
N975FE	Cessna 208B Caravan I	208B0101		Op by MTN
N976FE	Cessna 208B Caravan I	208B0103		Op by CFS
N977FE	Cessna 208B Caravan I	208B0104		Op by CPT
N978FE	Cessna 208B Caravan I	208B0105		Op by BVN
N979FE	Cessna 208B Caravan I	208B0106		Op by MTN
N980FE	Cessna 208B Caravan I	208B0108		Op by CPT
N981FE	Cessna 208B Caravan I	208B0110		Op by WIG
N983FE	Cessna 208B Caravan I	208B0113		Op by CFS
N984FE	Cessna 208B Caravan I	208B0115		Op by PCM
N985FE	Cessna 208B Caravan I	208B0117		Op by PCM
N986FE	Cessna 208B Caravan I	208B0194		Op by IRO
N987FE	Cessna 208B Caravan I	208B0201		Op by PCM
N989FE	Cessna 208B Caravan I	208B0124		Op by WIG
N990FE	Cessna 208B Caravan I	208B0125		Op by CPT
N991FE	Cessna 208B Caravan I	208B0127		Op by CPT
N992FE	Cessna 208B Caravan I	208B0128		Op by CFS
N993FE	Cessna 208B Caravan I	208B0130		Op by IRO
N994FE	Cessna 208B Caravan I	208B0132		Op by BVN
N995FE	Cessna 208B Caravan I	208B0133		Op by PCM
N996FE	Cessna 208B Caravan I	208B0135		Op by WIG
N997FE	Cessna 208B Caravan I	208B0197		Op by CPT
N998FE	Cessna 208B Caravan I	208B0139		Op by WIG
N999FE	Cessna 208B Caravan I	208B0231		Op by MTN
N701FE	Fokker F.27 Friendship 600	10419	ex OO-FEF	Op by CFS
N702FE	Fokker F.27 Friendship 600	10350	ex OO-FEG	Op by CFS
N703FE	Fokker F.27 Friendship 600	10420	ex D-AFEH	Op by CFS
N705FE	Fokker F.27 Friendship 500	10367	ex G-FEDX	Op by MTN
N706FE	Fokker F.27 Friendship 500	10384	ex G-OFEC	Op by MTN
N707FE	Fokker F.27 Friendship 500	10371	ex G-FEBZ	Op by CFS
N708FE	Fokker F.27 Friendship 500	10372	ex G-BOMV	Op by CFS
N709FE	Fokker F.27 Friendship 500	10375	ex F-BPNE	Op by MTN
N710FE	Fokker F.27 Friendship 500	10380	ex F-BPNG	Op by MTN
N711FE	Fokker F.27 Friendship 500	10383	ex F-BPNI	Op by CFS
N712FE	Fokker F.27 Friendship 500F	10613	ex 9M-MCK	dam 08Mar03	Op by MTN
N713FE	Fokker F.27 Friendship 500F	10615	ex 9M-MCL		Op by MTN
N714FE	Fokker F.27 Friendship 500	10461	ex 9M-MCD		Op by MTN
N715FE	Fokker F.27 Friendship 500	10468	ex 9M-MCG		Op by MTN
N716FE	Fokker F.27 Friendship 500	10471	ex 9M-MCI		Op by MTN
N717FE	Fokker F.27 Friendship 500	10455	ex 9M-MCA		Op by MTN
N718FE	Fokker F.27 Friendship 500	10470	ex 9M-MCH		Op by MTN
N719FE	Fokker F.27 Friendship 500	10467	ex 9M-MCF		Op by MTN
N720FE	Fokker F.27 Friendship 500	10464	ex 9M-MCE		Op by CFS
N721FE	Fokker F.27 Friendship 500	10460	ex 9M-MCC		Op by MTN

Reg	Type	MSN	ex	Name	Notes
N722FE	Fokker F.27 Friendship 500	10472	ex 9M-MCJ		Op by MTN
N723FE	Fokker F.27 Friendship 500	10682	ex OO-FEI		Op by MTN
N724FE	Fokker F.27 Friendship 500	10677	ex OO-FEK		Op by MTN
N725FE	Fokker F.27 Friendship 500	10658	ex N514AW		Op by MTN
N726FE	Fokker F.27 Friendship 500	10683	ex (OO-FEN)		Op by MTN
N727FE	Fokker F.27 Friendship 500	10661	ex (OO-FEM)		Op by MTN
N728FE	Fokker F.27 Friendship 500	10657	ex OO-FEL		Op by MTN
N729FE	Fokker F.27 Friendship 600	10385	ex EI-FEA		Op by CFS
N730FE	Fokker F.27 Friendship 600	10386	ex I-FEAB		Op by CFS
N740FE	Fokker F.27 Friendship 600	10329	ex HB-ISJ		Op by CFS
N741FE	Fokker F.27 Friendship 600	10387	ex G-FEAD		Op by CFS
N742FE	Fokker F.27 Friendship 600	10349	ex G-FEAE		Op by CFS
N301FE	McDonnell-Douglas MD-10-30CF	96/46800	ex N101TV	Tara Lynn	
N302FE	Douglas DC-10-30CF	103/46801	ex N102TV	Brian Jr	
N303FE	McDonnell-Douglas MD-10-30CF	110/46802	ex N103TV	Amanda Marie	
N304FE	Douglas DC-10-30CF	257/46992	ex EC-DSF	Alison	
N306FE	Douglas DC-10-30F	409/48287		John Peter Jr	
N307FE	Douglas DC-10-30F	412/48291		Erin Lee	
N308FE	Douglas DC-10-30F	416/48297		Ann	
N309FE	Douglas DC-10-30F	419/48298		Stacey	
N310FE	Douglas DC-10-30F	422/48299		John Shelby	
N311FE	McDonnell-Douglas MD-10-30CF	219/46871	ex LN-RKB	Abe	Lsd fr WFBN
N312FE	McDonnell-Douglas MD-10-30CF	433/48300		Angela	
N313FE	Douglas DC-10-30F	440/48311		Brandon Parksl	
N314FE	Douglas DC-10-30F	442/48312		Caitlin Ann	
N315FE	Douglas DC-10-30F	443/48313		Kevin	
N316FE	McDonnell-Douglas MD-10-30F	444/48314		Brandon	
N317FE	Douglas DC-10-30CF	277/46835	ex N106WA	Madison	Lsd fr Wachovia Bank
N318FE	Douglas DC-10-30CF	282/46837	ex N108WA	Mason	Lsd fr McDD A/C Finance
N319FE	Douglas DC-10-30CF	317/47820	ex N112WA		Lsd fr Mitsui
N320FE	Douglas DC-10-30F	326/47835	ex OO-SLD	Maura	Lsd fr Potomac
N321FE	Douglas DC-10-30F	330/47836	ex OO-SLE	Athena	Lsd fr Potomac
N322FE	Douglas DC-10-30CF	215/47908	ex OO-SLC	Gerald	Lsd fr CIT Leasing
N323FE	Douglas DC-10-30F	302/47811	ex N1852U	basic UA colours, no titles	
N326FE	Douglas DC-10-30F	312/47813	ex N1854U		
N357FE	McDonnell-Douglas MD-10-10F	203/46939	ex N1849U		
N358FE	McDonnell-Douglas MD-10-10F	297/46633	ex N1839U		
N359FE	McDonnell-Douglas MD-10-10F	307/46635	ex N1842U		
N360FE	McDonnell-Douglas MD-10-10F	309/46636	ex N1843U		
N361FE	McDonnell-Douglas MD-10-10F	344/48260	ex N1844U		
N362FE	McDonnell-Douglas MD-10-10F	347/48261	ex N1845U	Cole	
N363FE	McDonnell-Douglas MD-10-10F	353/48263	ex N1847U	Carter	
N365FE	Douglas DC-10-10F	6/46601	ex N1802U	Joey	
N366FE	Douglas DC-10-10F	8/46602	ex N1803U	Gretchen	
N367FE	Douglas DC-10-10F	15/46605	ex N1806U	Lathan	
N368FE	Douglas DC-10-10F	17/46606	ex N1807U	Cindy	
N369FE	Douglas DC-10-10	25/46607	ex N1808U	stored GYR	
N370FE	McDonnell-Douglas MD-10-10F	26/46608	ex N1809U		
N371FE	Douglas DC-10-10F	27/46609	ex N1810U	Vincent	
N372FE	McDonnell-Douglas MD-10-10F	32/46610	ex N1811U		
N373FE	Douglas DC-10-10F	35/46611	ex N1812U		
N374FE	Douglas DC-10-10	39/46612	ex N1813U		
N375FE	Douglas DC-10-10	42/46613	ex N1814U		
N377FE	McDonnell-Douglas MD-10-10F	59/47965	ex N1833U	Shelby	
N381FE	Douglas DC-10-10	76/46615	ex N1816U	stored GYR	
N383FE	McDonnell-Douglas MD-10-10F	86/46616	ex N1817U	Cody	
N384FE	McDonnell-Douglas MD-10-10F	89/46617	ex N1818U	Kelly	
N385FE	Douglas DC-10-10F	119/46619	ex N1820U	Lindsey	
N386FE	McDonnell-Douglas MD-10-10F	138/46620	ex N1821U	First MD-10 conversion	
N387FE	Douglas DC-10-10F	140/46621	ex N1822U	Joel	
N388FE	McDonnell-Douglas MD-10-10F	144/46622	ex N1823U	Izzul	
N389FE	Douglas DC-10-10F	154/46623	ex N1824U		
N390FE	McDonnell-Douglas MD-10-10F	155/46624	ex N1825U	Rasik	
N391FE	McDonnell-Douglas MD-10-10F	169/46625	ex N1826U	Chandra	
N392FE	McDonnell-Douglas MD-10-10F	198/46626	ex N1827U	Axton	
N393FE	McDonnell-Douglas MD-10-10F	205/46627	ex N1828U		
N394FE	McDonnell-Douglas MD-10-10F	207/46628	ex N1829U		
N395FE	Douglas DC-10-10F	208/46630	ex N1830U		
N396FE	McDonnell-Douglas MD-10-10F	209/46631	ex N1831U		
N397FE	Douglas DC-10-10F	210/46632	ex N1832U	Stefani	
N398FE	McDonnell-Douglas MD-10-10F	298/46634	ex N1841U		
N399FE	McDonnell-Douglas MD-10-10F	351/48262	ex N1846U		
N550FE	McDonnell-Douglas MD-10-10F	55/45521	ex N121AA	Adam	
(N553FE)	Douglas DC-10-10	61/46707	ex N152AA	stored MHV	
N554FE	Douglas DC-10-10	62/46708	ex N153AA	stored MHV	
N556FE	Douglas DC-10-10	70/46710	ex N160AA	stored MHV	
(N557FE)	Douglas DC-10-10	72/46525	ex N125AA	stored MHV	
N559FE	MdDonnell-Douglas MD-10-10F	112/46930	ex N167AA		
N560FE	McDonnell-Douglas MD-10-10F	153/46938	ex N168AA		
(N562FE)	Douglas DC-10-10	247/46947	ex N126AA	stored MHV	
(N563FE)	Douglas DC-10-10	249/46948	ex N127AA	stored MHV	

(N564FE)	Douglas DC-10-10	250/46984	ex N128AA	stored MHV	
(N565FE)	Douglas DC-10-10	270/46996	ex N129AA	stored MHV	
N566FE	McDonnell-Douglas MD-10-10F	271/46989	ex N130AA	Ben	
(N567FE)	Douglas DC-10-10	273/46994	ex N131AA	stored MHV	
(N568FE)	Douglas DC-10-10	294/47827	ex N132AA	stored MHV	
N569FE	McDonnell-Douglas MD-10-10F	319/47828	ex N133AA		
N570FE	McDonnell-Douglas MD-10-10F	321/47829	ex N134AA		
(N571FE)	Douglas DC-10-10	323/47830	ex N135AA	stored MHV	
N10060	Douglas DC-10-10F	269/46970	ex N581LF	Haylee	Lsd fr CIT Leasing
N40061	Douglas DC-10-10F	272/46973	ex N591LF	Garrett	Lsd fr CIT Leasing
N68049	McDonnell-Douglas MD-10-10CF	139/47803		Dusty	
N68050	Douglas DC-10-10CF	142/47804		Merideth Allison	
N68051	Douglas DC-10-10CF	145/47805		Todd	
N68052	Douglas DC-10-10CF	148/47806		Janette Louise	
N68053	Douglas DC-10-10CF	173/47807		Chayne	
N68054	Douglas DC-10-10CF	177/47808		Dani Elena	
N68056	Douglas DC-10-10CF	194/47810		Valerie Ann	
N68057	McDonnell-Douglas MD-10-10CF	379/48264	ex N1848U	under MD-10 conversion	
N68058	Douglas DC-10-10F	33/46705	ex TC-JAU		
N68059	Douglas DC-10-10F	78/46907	ex TC-JAY		Lsd fr JP Morgan Trust

60 ex-passenger DC10s being converted to MD-10 freighters with two man cockpits and same type rating as MD-11

N578FE	McDonnell-Douglas MD-11F	449/48458	ex N489GX	Stephen	
N579FE	McDonnell-Douglas MD-11	546/48470	ex B-18151	Nash	
N580FE	McDonnell-Douglas MD-11F	558/48471	ex B-18152	Asthon	
N582FE	McDonnell-Douglas MD-11F	451/48420	ex N1751A	Jamie	
N583FE	McDonnell-Douglas MD-11F	452/48421	ex N1752K	Nancy	
N584FE	McDonnell-Douglas MD-11F	483/48436	ex N1768D	Jeffrey Wellington	
N585FE	McDonnell-Douglas MD-11F	482/48481	ex N1759	Katherine	
N586FE	McDonnell-Douglas MD-11F	469/48487	ex N1753	Dylan	Lsd fr WFBN
N587FE	McDonnell-Douglas MD-11F	492/48489	ex N1754	Jeanna	
N588FE	McDonnell-Douglas MD-11F	499/48490	ex N1755	Kondic	Lsd fr WFBN
N589FE	McDonnell-Douglas MD-11F	503/48491	ex N1756	Shaun	
N590FE	McDonnell-Douglas MD-11F	462/48505	ex N1757A	Stan	
N591FE	McDonnell-Douglas MD-11F	504/48527	ex N1758B	Giovanni	Lsd fr Wachovia Bank
N592FE	McDonnell-Douglas MD-11F	526/48550	ex N1760A	Joshua	
N593FE	McDonnell-Douglas MD-11F	527/48551	ex N1761R	Harrison	
N594FE	McDonnell-Douglas MD-11F	530/48552	ex N1762B	Derek	
N595FE	McDonnell-Douglas MD-11F	531/48553	ex N1763	Avery	
N596FE	McDonnell-Douglas MD-11F	535/48554	ex N1764B	Pegton	Lsd fr WFBN
N597FE	McDonnell-Douglas MD-11F	537/48596	ex N1765B	Corbin	
N598FE	McDonnell-Douglas MD-11F	540/48597	ex N1766A	Kate	
N599FE	McDonnell-Douglas MD-11F	550/48598	ex N1767A	Merisac	
N601FE	McDonnell-Douglas MD-11F	447/48401	ex N111MD	Jim Riedmeyer	
N602FE	McDonnell-Douglas MD-11F	448/48402	ex N211MD	Malcolm Baldrige 1990	
N603FE	McDonnell-Douglas MD-11F	470/48459		Elizabeth	
N604FE	McDonnell-Douglas MD-11F	497/48460		Hollis	
N605FE	McDonnell-Douglas MD-11F	515/48514		April Star	
N606FE	McDonnell-Douglas MD-11F	549/48602		Charles & Teresa	
N607FE	McDonnell-Douglas MD-11F	517/48547		Louis III	
N608FE	McDonnell-Douglas MD-11F	521/48548		Karen	
N609FE	McDonnell-Douglas MD-11F	545/48549		Scott	
N610FE	McDonnell-Douglas MD-11F	551/48603		Marisa	
N612FE	McDonnell-Douglas MD-11F	555/48605		Algies	
N613FE	McDonnell-Douglas MD-11F	598/48749		Krista	
N614FE	McDonnell-Douglas MD-11F	507/48528		Christy Allison	
N615FE	McDonnell-Douglas MD-11F	602/48767		Max	
N616FE	McDonnell-Douglas MD-11F	594/48747		Shanita	Lsd fr MDFC
N617FE	McDonnell-Douglas MD-11F	595/48748		Travis	Lsd fr MDFC
N618FE	McDonnell-Douglas MD-11F	604/48754		Justin	
N619FE	McDonnell-Douglas MD-11F	607/48770		Tara Lynn	
N620FE	McDonnell-Douglas MD-11F	635/48791		Grady	
N621FE	McDonnell-Douglas MD-11F	636/48792		Connor	
N623FE	McDonnell-Douglas MD-11F	638/48794		Meghan	

Ten Airbus Industrie A380-800Fs are on order for delivery in 2008 (3), 2009 (3), 2010 (3) and 2011 (1).

FINA AIR

Puerto Rico

N112PX	SAAB SF.340A	025	ex N344CA	Lsd fr AeroCentury
N935MA	SAAB SF.340A	073	ex	Lsd fr State Street

FINE AIR SERVICES reorganised and reverted to previous trading name Arrow Air

FIRST FLIGHT OUT

Charlotte-Douglas Intl, NC (CLT)

N58NA	Douglas DC-3	12970	ex G-BLXV	Waawka, as 293096
N115SA	Douglas DC-3	13310	ex C-GRTM	

N12907	Douglas DC-3	15742/27187	ex C-FPIK	As 349926
N79017	Douglas DC-3	19227	ex NC79017	

FLIGHT ALASKA

(4Y/TUD)   *Dillingham-Memorial, AK (DLG)*

N36CF	Cessna 207 Skywagon	20700269		Lsd fr M&M Leasing
N755AB	Cessna 207A Stationair 8	20700622		Lsd fr M&M Leasing
N1704U	Cessna 207 Skywagon	20700304		Lsd fr Flight Capital
N1750U	Cessna 207 Skywagon	20700350		Lsd fr M&M Leasing
N6470H	Cessna 207A Stationair 7	20700534		Lsd fr Flight Capital
N7336U	Cessna 207A Skywagon	20700405		Lsd fr Flight Capital
N7384U	Cessna 207A Stationair 7	20700431		Lsd fr Flight Capital
N7438U	Cessna T207A Stationair 7	20700464		Lsd fr M&M Leasing
N73036	Cessna 207A Stationair 7	20700555		Lsd fr Johnson Services
N73128	Cessna 207A Stationair 7	20700562		Lsd fr M&M Leasing
N205FN	CASA 212 Aviocar Srs 300	379	ex N897FL	Lsd fr Flight Capital
N3516A	Piper PA-31-350 Navajo Chieftain	31-7952106		Lsd fr Aviation Co

FLIGHT EXPRESS

Flight Express (EXR)   *Orlando-Executive, FL (ORL)*

N6BW	Beech 58 Baron	TH-292	
N31CE	Beech 58 Baron	TH-220	
N31T	Beech 58 Baron	TH-121	
N38CL	Beech 58 Baron	TH-829	
N46US	Beech 58 Baron	TH-294	
N80AC	Beech 58 Baron	TH-56	
N93DF	Beech 58 Baron	TH-61	
N103GA	Beech 58 Baron	TH-213	
N112BS	Beech 58 Baron	TH-628	
N112KB	Beech 58 Baron	TH-1007	
N159TH	Beech 58 Baron	TH-159	
N225TA	Beech 58 Baron	TH-64	
N258TJ	Beech 58 Baron	TH-988	
N329H	Beech 58 Baron	TH-219	
N703MC	Beech 95-E55 Baron	TE-974	
N752P	Beech 58 Baron	TH-422	
N796Q	Beech 58 Baron	TH-43	
N950JP	Beech 58 Baron	TH-432	ex (N982DC)
N1888W	Beech 58 Baron	TH-340	
N4099S	Beech 95-E55 Baron	TE-1037	
N4174S	Beech 58 Baron	TH-621	
N4492F	Beech 95-E55 Baron	TE-1097	
N4626A	Beech 58 Baron	TH-39	
N4675S	Beech 58 Baron	TH-689	
N8195R	Beech 58 Baron	TH-529	
N9098Q	Beech 58 Baron	TH-109	
N18447	Beech 58 Baron	TH-883	
N8WE	Cessna 210L Centurion	21060766	
N70TC	Cessna 210MCenturion	21061707	
N102CR	Cessna T210N Turbo Centurion	21064745	
N115WL	Cessna 210L Centurion	21060949	
N210CT	Cessna 210L Centurion	21060356	
N221AT	Cessna 210N Centurion	21064567	
N274CS	Cessna 210L Centurion	21060148	
N300EW	Cessna 210L Centurion	21061219	
N318JP	Cessna 210L Centurion	21060770	
N640AJ	Cessna 210L Centurion	21060758	
N732CQ	Cessna 210L Centurion	21061413	
N732HN	Cessna T210L Turbo Centurion	21061527	
N732LW	Cessna 210M Centurion	21061606	
N732ST	Cessna 210M Centurion	21061744	
N732YA	Cessna 210M Centurion	21061870	
N761AT	Cessna 210M Centurion	21062108	
N761AY	Cessna 210M Centurion	21062113	
N761BQ	Cessna 210M Centurion	21062129	
N761DW	Cessna T210M Turbo Centurion	21062183	
N777BK	Cessna 210L Centurion	21060560	
N778VK	Cessna 210M Centurion	21062895	
N965B	Cessna 210M Centurion	21061580	
N1666X	Cessna 210L Centurion	21060701	
N2013S	Cessna 210L Centurion	21060981	
N2110S	Cessna 210L Centurion	21061074	
N2137S	Cessna 210L Centurion	21061098	
N2145U	Cessna T210N Turbo Centurion	21064776	
N2255S	Cessna 210L Centurion	21061199	

N2263S	Cessna 210L Centurion	21061207		
N2280S	Cessna 210L Centurion	21061223		
N2437S	Cessna 210L Centurion	21061281		
N2495S	Cessna 210L Centurion	21061304		
N2667S	Cessna 210L Centurion	21061347		
N4637Y	Cessna 210N Centurion	21063965		
N4672Y	Cessna 210N Centurion	21063977		
N4673C	Cessna 210N Centurion	21063586		
N4702C	Cessna T210N Turbo Centurion	21063591		
N4781C	Cessna 210N Centurion	21063624		
N5171V	Cessna 210L Centurion	21060846		
N5229A	Cessna 210N Centurion	21063320		
N5307A	Cessna 210N Centurion	21063360		
N5489V	Cessna 210L Centurion	21060961		
N6108Y	Cessna T210N Turbo Centurion	21064254		
N6149B	Cessna T210M Turbo Centurion	21062694		
N6195N	Cessna 210N Centurion	21062966		
N6490N	Cessna 210N Centurion	21063064		
N6598Y	Cessna T210N Turbo Centurion	21064451		
N6611C	Cessna T210N Turbo Centurion	21063930		
N6622N	Cessna 210N Centurion	21063125		
N7398M	Cessna 210M Centurion	21062018		
N7660E	Cessna 210M Centurion	21062692		
N7874J	Cessna 210L Centurion	21060597		
N8134L	Cessna 210L Centurion	21060621		
N8427M	Cessna 210M Centurion	21062043		
N9073M	Cessna 210M Centurion	21062058		
N9489M	Cessna 210M Centurion	21062081		
N29209	Cessna 210L Centurion	21059832		
N29278	Cessna 210L Centurion	21059852		
N30326	Cessna 210L Centurion	21059914		
N59130	Cessna 210L Centurion	21060110		
N59141	Cessna 210L Centurion	21060118		
N59240	Cessna 210L Centurion	21060174		
N59299	Cessna 210L Centurion	21060199		
N93111	Cessna 210L Centurion	21060266		
N93887	Cessna 210L Centurion	21060445		
N60FX	Beech A65 Queen Air	LC-312	ex N277JJ	Excalibur Queenaire conv
All freighters				

FLIGHT INTERNATIONAL AVIATION

Invader Jack (IVJ)   *Newport News-Williamsburg Intl, VA (PHF)*

N10FN	Lear Jet 36	36-015	ex N14CF	Lsd fr Flight Capital
N12FN	Lear Jet 36	36-016	ex N616DJ	Lsd fr Flight Capital
N14FN	Lear Jet 25C	25C-126	ex N114CC	Lsd fr Flight Capital
N26FN	Lear Jet 36	36-011	ex N26MJ	Lsd fr Flight Capital
N39FN	Lear Jet 35	35-006	ex N39DM	Lsd fr Flight Capital
N48FN	Lear Jet 24D	24D-238	ex N49DM	Lsd fr Flight Capital
N48GP	Lear Jet 35A	35A-069	ex N35NW	Lsd fr Aviation Co
N50FN	Lear Jet 35A	35A-070	ex N543PA	Lsd fr Flight Capital
N54FN	Lear Jet 25C	25C-083	ex N200MH	Lsd fr Aviation Co
N55FN	Lear Jet 35A	35A-202	ex D-CGPD	Lsd fr Flight Capital
N58FN	Lear Jet 24B	24B-184	ex N58DM	Lsd fr Flight Capital
N83FN	Lear Jet 36	36-007	ex N83DM	Lsd fr Flight Capital
N84FN	Lear Jet 36	36-002	ex N84DM	Lsd fr Flight Capital
N96FN	Lear Jet 35A	35A-186	ex N96DM	Lsd fr Flight Capital
N97FN	Lear Jet 25	25-003	ex N97DM	Lsd fr Flight Capital
N99FN	Lear Jet 35A	35A-071		Lsd fr Flight Capital
N118FN	Lear Jet 35A	35A-118	ex N88JA	Lsd fr Flight Capital
N508GP	Lear Jet 35A	35A-424	ex N2844	Lsd fr Flight Capital
N611TW	Lear Jet 35A	35A-611	ex N622WG	Lsd fr Flight Capital
N710GS	Lear Jet 35	35-032	ex N711MA	Lsd fr Flight Capital
N4415S	Lear Jet 35	35-021	ex N442JT	Lsd fr Flight Capital
N175SW	Swearingen SA.227AC Metro III	AC-621		Lsd fr GAS/Wilson
N766C	Swearingen SA.227AC Metro III	AC-559	ex N170SW	Lsd fr Flight Capital
N781C	Swearingen SA.227AC Metro III	AC-535	ex N3110J	Lsd fr Flight Capital
N782C	Swearingen SA.227AC Metro III	AC-525	ex N31078	Lsd fr Flight Capital
N784C	Swearingen SA.227AC Metro III	AC-482	ex N482SA	Lsd fr Flight Capital
N26974	Swearingen SA.227AC Metro III	AC-664		Lsd fr Joda Lsg
N707ML	Piper PA-31T Cheyenne	31T-7520017	ex N502RH	Lsd fr Flight Capital
N59924	Piper PA-31 Turbo Navajo	31-7512042		Lsd fr Flight Capital

FLIGHT LINE

American Check (ACT)   Denver-Centennial, CO/Salt Lake City, UT (DIA/SLC)

N6KF	Mitsubishi MU-2L	659	ex N5JE
N34AL	Mitsubishi MU-2B	792SA	ex N66LA
N35RR	Mitsubishi MU-2B	1525SA	ex N442MA
N60FL	Mitsubishi MU-2B	1512SA	ex HB-LQB
N132BK	Mitsubishi MU-2B	1529SA	ex N818R
N157CA	Mitsubishi MU-2B	1558SA	ex N5PQ
N361JA	Mitsubishi MU-2L	681	ex C-GJWM
N454MA	Mitsubishi MU-2B	1535SA	
N538EA	Mitsubishi MU-2B	1538SA	ex N538MC

N68ST	Piper PA-31 Turbo Navajo	31-729
N103BU	Piper PA-31-350 Navajo Chieftain	31-7405202
N350FL	Piper PA-31-350 Navajo Chieftain	31-7752182
N405PA	Piper PA-31 Turbo Navajo	31-424
N800SA	Piper PA-31-350 Chieftain	31-8152012
N35614	Piper PA-31-350 Navajo Chieftain	31-7952090
N62869	Piper PA-31-350 Navajo Chieftain	31-7652145

All freighters

FLORIDA AIR CARGO

Miami-Opa Locka, FL (OPF)

N15MA	Douglas DC-3	19286		
N81B	Douglas DC-3	7382	ex 42-5688	stored OPF
N123DZ	Douglas DC-3	12004	ex N337AF	no titles
N130D	Douglas DC-3	19800		Animal Crackers
N255D	Beech E-18S	BA-16		
N967	Beech E-18S (tri-gear)	BA-395	ex N94FB	Lsd fr TMF Aircraft

All aircraft leased from South Florida Aircraft Leasing

FLORIDA AIR TRANSPORT

Fort Lauderdale-Executive, FL (FXE)

N70BF	Douglas C-118B	373/43720	ex XA-SCZ	
N381AA	Douglas DC-7BF	666/44921	ex N101LM	Lsd fr Turks Air
N836D	Douglas DC-7B	928/45345		Eastern colours Op by Legendary A/L

FLORIDA COASTAL AIRLINES

Fort Pierce-St Lucis, FL (FPR)

N77FC	Cessna 402C	402C0044	ex N440RC
N78FC	Cessna 402C	402C0496	ex C-FFCH
N6787V	Cessna 402C	402C0421	

FLORIDA WEST INTERNATIONAL AIRLINES

Flo West (RF/FWL)   Miami-Intl, FL (MIA)

N316LA	Boeing 767-316ERF	860/30842	Lsd fr LCO

25% owned by LANChile

FLORIDA WINGS

Fort Lauderdale Executive (FXE)

N54EW	Britten-Norman BN-2T Islander	2145	ex G-BOBC

Current status is uncertain

40 MILE AIR

Mile-Air (Q5/MLA)   Tok-Junction, AK (TKJ)

N87TS	Piper PA-31 Turbo Navajo B	31-7300969	Lsd fr RWR Air
N207DG	Cessna T207 Turbo Skywagon	20700070	Lsd fr RWR Air
N734WG	Cessna U206G Stationair 6	U20604832	Lsd fr RWR Air
N1541F	Cessna 185D Skywagon	185-0896	Lsd fr RWR Air
N5200X	Cessna U206G Stationair 6	U20605591	Lsd fr Charlie Inc
N8515Q	Cessna U206F Stationair	U20603372	Lsd fr Charlie Inc
N9935M	Cessna 207A Stationair 8	20700751	

Associated with Travelair
Operates services for DHL and UPS

361

FOUR STAR AVIATION

Four Star (HK/FSC) — St Thomas-Cyril E King, VI (STT)

Reg	Type	Serial	ex	Notes	
N131FS	Douglas DC-3	16172/32920	ex N67PA	Freighter	
N132FS	Douglas DC-3	14333/25778	ex N333EF	Freighter	
N133FS	Douglas DC-3	15757/27202	ex N53NA	Freighter	
N135FS	Douglas DC-3	20063	ex N63107	Freighter	
N136FS	Douglas DC-3	10267	ex N58296	Freighter	
N138FS	Douglas DC-3	9967	ex N303SF	Freighter	
N153JR	Convair 440	117	ex N53GA	Freighter	Jt ops with Fresh Air
N155JR	Convair 440	433	ex N455GA	Freighter	Jt ops with Fresh Air
N323CF	Convair 440	323	ex SE-CCU	Freighter	Jt ops with Fresh Air

FREEDOM AIR

Freedom (FP/FRE) — Guam, GU (GUM)

Reg	Type	Serial	ex
N4168R	Piper PA-32-300 Cherokee Six C	32-40484	
N4171R	Piper PA-32-300 Cherokee Six C	32-40504	
N8628N	Piper PA-32-300 Cherokee Six	32-7140021	
N8938N	Piper PA-32-300 Cherokee Six C	32-40736	
N8969N	Piper PA-32-300 Cherokee Six	32-40769	
N44FA	Cessna 207A Stationair 8	20700659	ex N75975
N72FA	Piper PA-31 Turbo Navajo C	31-7812023	ex JA5278
N76NF	Short SD.3-30	SH3044	ex N344SB
N121PC	Short SD.3-60	SH3721	ex F-OHQG
N131FA	Piper PA-23-250 Aztec D	27-4097	ex N234SP

All leased from Aviation Services

FREEDOM AIRLINES

Freedom (F8/FRL) — Phoenix-Sky Harbor Intl, AZ (PHX)

Reg	Type	Serial	ex	Notes
N501MJ	Canadair CL-600-2C10	10047	ex C-FZVM	all-white
N502MJ	Canadair CL-600-2C10	10050	ex C-GIAO	
N503MJ	Canadair CL-600-2C10	10058	ex C-GIBG	Lsd fr WFBN
N504MJ	Canadair CL-600-2C10	10066	ex C-GIBR	Lsd fr WFBN
N505MJ	Canadair CL-600-2C10	10070	ex C-GICN	Lsd fr WFBN
N506MJ	Canadair CL-600-2C10	10073	ex C-GHZY	Lsd fr WFBN
N507MJ	Canadair CL-600-2C10	10077	ex C-GIAH	Lsd fr WFBN
N509MJ	Canadair CL-600-2C10	10094	ex C-	
N902FJ	Canadair CL-600-2D24	15002	ex C-GDNH	Lsd fr WFBN
N903FJ	Canadair CL-600-2D24	15003	ex C-GZQA	
N904FJ	Canadair CL-600-2D24	15004	ex C-GZQB	
N905J	Canadair CL-600-2D24	15005	ex C-GZQC	
N906FJ	Canadair CL-600-2D24	15006	ex C-GZQE	
N907FJ	Canadair CL-600-2D24	15007	ex C-GZQF	
N908FJ	Canadair CL-600-2D24	15008	ex C-GZQG	
N909FJ	Canadair CL-600-2D24	15009	ex C-GZQI	
N910FJ	Canadair CL-600-2D24	15010	ex C-GZQJ	
N911FJ	Canadair CL-600-2D24	15011	ex C-GZQK	
N912FJ	Canadair CL-600-2D24	15012	ex C-	
N913FJ	Canadair CL-600-2D24	15013	ex C-	
N914FJ	Canadair CL-600-2D24	15014	ex C-	
N	Canadair CL-600-2D24		ex C-	on order 04
N	Canadair CL-600-2D24		ex C-	on order 04
N	Canadair CL-600-2D24		ex C-	on order 04
N	Canadair CL-600-2D24		ex C-	on order 04
N	Canadair CL-600-2D24		ex C-	on order 04
N	Canadair CL-600-2D24		ex C-	on order 04

Five more are on order for delivery in 2005; some are believed operated by Mesa Airlines
Wholly owned subsidiary of Mesa Airlines operates Canadair CL-600-2C10s and Canadair CL-600-2D24s for America West Express

FREIGHT RUNNERS EXPRESS

Freight Runners (FRG) — Milwaukee-General Mitchell Intl, WI (MKE)

Reg	Type	Serial	ex
N199CZ	Beech 99	U-30	ex N3RP
N299CZ	Beech 99	U-74	ex C-FCVJ
N399CZ	Beech B99	U-52	ex ZK-LLA
N499CZ	Beech 99A	U-81	ex N36AK
N599CZ	Beech B99	U-89	ex 5Y-BJW
(N699CZ)	Beech B99	U-133	ex N27AL
N75GB	Cessna 402B	402B0912	
N727CA	Cessna 402A	402A0102	ex N7802Q

N933T	Beech H-18S	BA-665
N1517U	Cessna 207 Skywagon	20700117
N1518U	Cessna 207 Skywagon	20700118
N4504B	Cessna 402B	402B1370

FRONTIER AIRLINES

Frontier Flight (F9/FFT) — Denver-Centiennal, CO (DEN)

N801FR	Airbus Industrie A318-111	1939	ex D-AUAA		Lsd fr ILFC
N802FR	Airbus Industrie A318-111	1991	ex D-AUAB		
N803FR	Airbus Industrie A318-111	2017	ex D-AUAC		
N804FR	Airbus Industrie A318-111	2051	ex D-AUAE		
N805FR	Airbus Industrie A318-111	1660	ex F-WWIB	on order May04	Lsd fr ILFC

One more Airbus Industrie A318-111 is on order for delivery in March 2005, leased from ILFC; also wear 'A whole different animal' titles

N901FR	Airbus Industrie A319-111	1488	ex D-AVYW		Lsd fr GECAS
N902FR	Airbus Industrie A319-111	1515	ex D-AVYM		Lsd fr GECAS
N903FR	Airbus Industrie A319-111	1560	ex D-AVYK		Lsd fr GECAS
N904FR	Airbus Industrie A319-111	1579	ex D-AVWS		Lsd fr GECAS
N905FR	Airbus Industrie A319-111	1583	ex D-AVYC		Lsd fr GECAS
N906FR	Airbus Industrie A319-111	1684	ex D-AVWK		Lsd fr Avn Financial Svs
N907FR	Airbus Industrie A319-111	1743	ex D-AVWY		Lsd fr GECAS
N908FR	Airbus Industrie A319-111	1759	ex D-AVYL		Lsd fr AFS Investments
N909FR	Airbus Industrie A319-111	1761	ex D-AVYM		Lsd fr GECAS
N910FR	Airbus Industrie A319-111	1781	ex D-AVYK		Lsd fr GECAS
N912FR	Airbus Industrie A319-111	1803	ex D-AVWE		Lsd fr AFS Investments
N913FR	Airbus Industrie A319-111	1863	ex D-AVWU		Lsd fr GECAS
N914FR	Airbus Industrie A319-111	1841	ex D-AVWE		Lsd fr GECAS
N915FR	Airbus Industrie A319-111	1851	ex D-AVWX		Lsd fr GECAS
N916FR	Airbus Industrie A319-111	1876	ex D-AVYL		
N917FR	Airbus Industrie A319-111	1890	ex D-AVYD		Lsd fr GECAS
N918FR	Airbus Industrie A319-111	1943	ex D-AVWH		Lsd fr WFBN
N919FR	Airbus Industrie A319-111	1980	ex D-AVYD		Lsd fr AFS Investments
N920FR	Airbus Industrie A319-111	1997	ex D-AVYO		Lsd fr AFS Investments
N921FR	Airbus Industrie A319-111	2010	ex D-AVWO		Lsd fr SALE
N922FR	Airbus Industrie A319-111	2012	ex D-AVWR		Lsd fr AFS Investments
N923FR	Airbus Industrie A319-111	2019	ex D-AVWV		Lsd fr AFS Investments
N924FR	Airbus Industrie A319-111	2030	ex D-AVYG		Lsd fr AFS Investments
N925FR	Airbus Industrie A319-111	2103	ex D-AVWH	on order 04	Lsd fr GECAS
N926FR	Airbus Industrie A319-111	2198	ex D-AV	on order 04	Lsd fr ILFC
N	Airbus Industrie A319-111	2209	ex D-AV	on order 04	Lsd fr ILFC
N	Airbus Industrie A319-111	2218	ex D-AV	on order 04	Lsd fr ILFC
N	Airbus Industrie A319-111	2240	ex D-AV	on order 04	
N	Airbus Industrie A319-111	2241	ex D-AV	on order 04	Lsd fr ILFC
N	Airbus Industrie A319-111	2251	ex D-AV	on order 04	
N	Airbus Industrie A319-111	2253	ex D-AV	on order 04	Lsd fr ILFC
N	Airbus Industrie A319-111	2258	ex D-AV	on order 04	Lsd fr ILFC
N	Airbus Industrie A319-111	2260	ex D-AV	on order 04	Lsd fr ILFC

Seven more are on order for future delivery including two from ILFC and one from GECAS in 2005. Also operates 56 seat VIP aircraft for Blue Moon Aviation

N1PC	Boeing 737-2P6 (Nordam 3)	530/21613	ex A6-AAA	272; stored MZJ	Lsd fr Interlease
N237TR	Boeing 737-228 (Nordam 3)	948/23007	ex F-GBYH	274	Lsd fr Triton
N302FL	Boeing 737-317	1216/23177	ex EI-CHH	302	Lsd fr GECAS
N303FL	Boeing 737-3M8	2007/25039	ex OO-LTJ	303	Lsd fr WFBN
N304FL	Boeing 737-3Q8	2878/27633		304	Lsd fr ILFC
N305FA	Boeing 737-36Q	2914/28662		305; stored ROW	Lsd fr Rain III
N306FL	Boeing 737-36N	2921/28563		306	Lsd fr AFT Trust
N307FL	Boeing 737-36Q	2989/28760		307	Lsd fr Rain III
N310FL	Boeing 737-3L9	2234/26440	ex D-ADBB	310	Lsd fr debis
N311FL	Boeing 737-3S1	1911/24856	ex N372TA	311	Lsd fr Amerilease
N312FL	Boeing 737-3L9	1775/24569	ex OY-MMD	312	Lsd fr CIT Lsg
N313FL	Boeing 737-3L9	2277/26442	ex D-ADBC	313	Lsd fr debis
N316FL	Boeing 737-36E	2194/25264	ex EC-FLG	316	Lsd fr Avn Financial Svs
N317FL	Boeing 737-36E	2187/25263	ex EC-FLF	317	Lsd fr GECAS
N319FL	Boeing 737-3Q8	2623/26301	ex N362PR	319	Lsd fr Castle 2003-1B LLC
N578US	Boeing 737-301	1124/23257	ex N305P	301	Lsd fr WFBN

Tails are painted in wildlife schemes with different picture on each side

Feeder services at Denver are operated by Horizon Airlines as Frontier JetExpress; also operates some code-share services with Great Lakes

FRONTIER FLYING SERVICE

Frontier Air (2F/FTA) — Fairbanks-Intl, AK (FAI)

N200AK	Piper PA-31-350 Chieftain	31-8052180	ex N8529T	
N234CE	Piper PA-31-350 Chieftain	31-8052003		Lsd fr Northern Alaska Tours
N3536B	Piper PA-31-350 Navajo Chieftain	31-7952205		
N4112K	Piper PA-31-350 T-1020	31-8353006		

N4301C	Piper PA-31-350 T-1020	31-8353001			
N575A	Beech 1900C-1	UC-83	ex N80334		
N575F	Beech 1900C-1	UC-99	ex N80598		
N575G	Beech 1900C-1	UC-155	ex N155YV		
N575L	Grumman G-44 Widgeon	1463			
N575P	Beech 1900C-1	UC-95	ex N80532		Lsd fr Raytheon
N575Q	Beech 1900C-1	UC-160	ex N160AM		
N575X	Beech 1900C-1	UC-149	ex N149YV		
N575Y	Beech 1900C-1	UC-162	ex N162YV		
N1785U	Cessna 207A Skywagon	20700385			

FRONTIER JETEXPRESS

Denver-Centennial, CO (DEN)

N601QX	Canadair CL-600-2C10	10009	ex C-GHCS	601
N608QX	Canadair CL-600-2C10	10026	ex C-GIAX	608

Operated by Horizon Airlines

FS AIR SERVICE

Sockeye (4A/EYE)   *Anchorage-Intl, AK (ANC)*

N55ZP	Swearingen SA.226T Merlin IIIB	T-299	ex N81QH	dam Soldotna, AK 18Dec02
N95AC	Swearingen SA.226T Merlin IIIB	T-381	ex N80MJ	
N502FS	CASA C.212-200	C058-1-294	ex N31BR	
N505FS	Swearingen SA.227AC Metro III	AC-591	ex N176SW	
N509FS	Piper PA-31-350 Navajo Chieftain	31-7952162	ex N35249	
N74923	Piper PA-31-350 Navajo Chieftain	31-7305066		

GEMINI AIR CARGO

Gemini (GR/GCO) (IATA 358)   *Minneapolis-St Paul Intl, MN (MSP)*

N600GC	Douglas DC-10-30F	245/46965	ex D-ADMO	Christopher	Lsd fr Gemini Lsg
N601GC	Douglas DC-10-30F	117/47921	ex D-ADAO	Molly; stored MHV	Lsd fr Gemini Lsg
N602GC	Douglas DC-10-30F	123/47923	ex D-ADCO	Ariana	Lsd fr Gemini Lsg
N603GC	Douglas DC-10-30F	122/47922	ex D-ADBO	Leslie; std MHV	Lsd fr Gemini Lsg
N604GC	Douglas DC-10-30F	129/47924	ex D-ADDO	Eric	Lsd fr Gemini Lsg
N605GC	Douglas DC-10-30F	166/47925	ex D-ADFO	Ryan; std MHV	Lsd fr Gemini Lsg
N606GC	Douglas DC-10-30F	196/47929	ex PP-AJM	Kirk	Lsd fr Gemini Lsg
N607GC	Douglas DC-10-30F	256/46978	ex N777SJ	stored MHV	Lsd fr Gemini Lsg
N609GC	Douglas DC-10-30F	158/46932	ex G-NIUK	Alyssa	Lsd fr Finova
N612GC	Douglas DC-10-30F	337/47840	ex G-BHDJ	Jessica	Lsd fr Finova
N614GC	Douglas DC-10-30F	137/46931	ex N832LA		Lsd fr WFBN; sublsd to CIU

Douglas DC-10s occassionaly enter short term storage at Mojave

N701GC	McDonnell-Douglas MD-11F	476/48434	ex PP-VOP	Emilie	Lsd fr debis
N702GC	McDonnell-Douglas MD-11F	478/48435	ex PP-VOQ	Mary	Lsd fr debis
N703GC	McDonnell-Douglas MD-11F	453/48411	ex PP-SPD	Penny	Lsd fr Tombo
N705GC	McDonnell-Douglas MD-11F	454/48412	ex PP-SPE	Tracy	Lsd fr Tombo

Operates cargo services for other carriers; usually under ACMI conditions Underwent restructuring in late 2003 and now operates only 10 DC-10Fs as well as the four MD-11Fs.

GEO-AIR believed to have ceased operations

GLOBAL AIR RESPONSE

Response (RPS)   *Denver-Centennial, CO/Albany-County, NY (DIA/ALB)*
Formerly listed as Air Response North & Air Response

N54JA	Lear Jet 36A	36A-044	ex N44LJ	EMS
N75GC	Beech 65-C90 King Air	LJ-727	ex N888BK	EMS
N160GC	Lear Jet 36A	36A-030	ex N36PJ	EMS
N180GC	Lear Jet 36	36-004	ex N50DT	EMS
N190GC	Lear Jet 35	35-014	ex N77LJ	EMS
N621PG	Piper PA-31-350 Navajo Chieftain	31-7652049		

GRAND AIRE EXPRESS

Grand Express (GAE)   *Toledo-Express, OH/Monroe-Regional, LA (TOL/MLU)*

N175GA	AMD Falcon 20	45	ex N202KH	
N258PE	AMD Falcon 20	163	ex N178GA	
N326VW	AMD Falcon 20C-5	27	ex N174GA	
N345FH	AMD Falcon 20CF	146	ex N182GA	
N510BM	AMD Falcon 20DC	215	ex N619GA	Lsd fr Czars Inc
N566YT	AMD Falcon 20C	94	ex N614GL	Lsd fr N614GA LLC
N611GA	AMD Falcon 20C	9	ex LV-WMF	

N612GA	AMD Falcon 20C	8	ex N190BD	Lsd fr National City Lsg
N617GA	AMD Falcon 20DC	88	ex N41CD	
N764LA	AMD Falcon 20DC	211	ex N618GA	Lsd fr Czars Inc
N844SL	AMD Falcon 20C-5	77	ex N613GA	
N168GA	Swearingen SA.226TC Metro	TC-207	ex N501AB	
N396RY	Swearingen SA.226TC Metro II	TC-281	ex N164GA	
N479VK	Swearingen SA.226AT Merlin IV	AT-009	ex N615GA	Lsd fr Metroliner
N629EK	Swearingen SA.226TC Metro II	TC-396	ex N165GA	
N637PJ	Swearingen SA.226TC Metro II	TC-376	ex N169GA	
N742ES	Swearingen SA.226TC Metro II	TC-377	ex N616GA	Lsd fr Metroliner
N851LH	Swearingen SA.226TC Metro II	TC-337	ex N166GA	
N158GA	Piper PA-60 Aerostar	60-0608-7961195	ex N8208J	
N160EA	Swearingen SA.26AT Merlin IIB	T26-165	ex C-GMZG	
N160GA	Ted Smith Aerostar 601	61-0021-50	ex N7436S	
N161GA	Piper PA-61P Aerostar	61P-0629-7963287	ex N321GB	
N601GA	Ted Smith Aerostar 601P	61P-0282-064	ex N76AC	
N610GA	Lear Jet 35A	35A-073	ex N352TX	
All freighters				

GRAND CANYON AIRLINES

Canyon View (CVU)   *Grand Canyon-National Park, AZ/Valle-J Robidoux, AZ (GCN/VLE)*

N72GC	de Havilland DHC-6 Twin Otter 300	264	ex N264Z	VistaLiner conv
N74GC	de Havilland DHC-6 Twin Otter 300	559	ex J6-AAK	VistaLiner conv
N173GC	de Havilland DHC-6 Twin Otter 300	295	ex C-GLAZ	VistaLiner conv
N177GC	de Havilland DHC-6 Twin Otter 300	263	ex N102AC	VistaLiner conv

GRANT AVIATION

(GS)   *Emmonak, AK (EMK)*

N8NZ	Cessna T207A Turbo Stationair 7	20700421	
N48CF	Cessna T207A Turbo Skywagon	20700366	
N207DF	Cessna 207A Stationair 8	20700728	ex ZK-EAL
N562CT	Cessna 207A Stationair 7	20700487	ex HI-562CT
N1684	Cessna 207A Stationair 7	20700526	
N9651M	Cessna 207A Stationair 8	20700715	
N9728M	Cessna 207A Stationair 8	20700721	
N9973M	Cessna 207A Stationair 8	20700771	
N91090	Cessna 207 Skywagon	20700069	
N77HV	Piper PA-31-350 Chieftain	31-8152193	ex C-GLCN
N90PB	Beech 200 Super King Air	BB-125	ex TG-UGA
N417PM	Piper PA-31-350 Chieftain	31-8052051	
N454SF	Cessna 208B Caravan I	208B0797	ex N5180C
N1276P	Cessna 208B Caravan I	208B0852	
N4105D	Piper PA-31-350 Chieftain	31-8252027	
N27739	Piper PA-31-350 Navajo Chieftain	31-7852135	

GREAT LAKES AIRLINES

Lakes Air (ZK/GLA)   *Cheyenne, WY (CYS)*

N94GL	Beech 1900D	UE-94	ex N94UX		
N96UX	Beech 1900D	UE-96			
N97UX	Beech 1900D	UE-97			
N100UX	Beech 1900D	UE-100			
N101UX	Beech 1900D	UE-101		stored MZJ	Lsd fr Raytheon
N118GL	Beech 1900D	UE-118	ex N118UX		
N122UX	Beech 1900D	UE-122	ex N122YV	stored CYS	
N150GL	Beech 1900D	UE-150	ex N150UX		
N153GL	Beech 1900D	UE-153	ex N153ZV		
N154GL	Beech 1900D	UE-154	ex N154ZV		
N169GL	Beech 1900D	UE-169			
N170GL	Beech 1900D	UE-170	ex N170YV		
N179GL	Beech 1900D	UE-179	ex N179YV		
N182YV	Beech 1900D	UE-182			
N184UX	Beech 1900D	UE-184	ex N184YV		
N192GL	Beech 1900D	UE-192	ex N192YV		
N195GL	Beech 1900D	UE-195	ex N195YV		Lsd fr Raytheon
N201GL	Beech 1900D	UE-201	ex N201YQ		
N202UX	Beech 1900D	UE-202	ex (N202GV)		
N204GL	Beech 1900D	UE-204	ex N204YV		
N208GL	Beech 1900D	UE-208	ex N208YV		
N210GL	Beech 1900D	UE-210	ex N210UX		
N211GL	Beech 1900D	UE-211	ex N211UX		
N219GL	Beech 1900D	UE-219	ex N219YV		
N220UX	Beech 1900D	UE-220	ex N220YV		

N226GL	Beech 1900D	UE-226	ex N226YV		Lsd fr Raytheon
N228GL	Beech 1900D	UE-228	ex N228YV		Lsd fr Raytheon
N240GL	Beech 1900D	UE-240	ex N240YV	Devil's Tower titles	
N245GL	Beech 1900D	UE-245	ex N245YV		
N247GL	Beech 1900D	UE-247	ex N247YV		
N249GL	Beech 1900D	UE-249	ex N249YV		Lsd fr Raytheon
N251GL	Beech 1900D	UE-251	ex N251ZV	Grand Tetons titles	
N253GL	Beech 1900D	UE-253	ex N253YV		
N254GL	Beech 1900D	UE-254	ex N10840		
N255GL	Beech 1900D	UE-255	ex N10860		
N257GL	Beech 1900D	UE-257	ex N257YV		
N261GL	Beech 1900D	UE-261	ex N261YV		
N71GL	Embraer EMB.120ER Brasilia	120071	ex N267UE		
N85GL	Embraer EMB.120ER Brasilia	120085	ex N279UE	stored CYS	Lsd fr FINOVA
N96ZK	Embraer EMB.120ER Brasilia	120096	ex N452UE		
N108UX	Embraer EMB.120ER Brasilia	120108	ex N451UE		
N293UX	Embraer EMB.120ER Brasilia	120293	ex PT-SVN		Lsd fr Boeing
N297UX	Embraer EMB.120ER Brasilia	120297	ex PT-SVQ		Lsd fr Boeing
N299UX	Embraer EMB.120RT Brasilia	120299	ex PT-SVT		
N101UE	Beech 1900C-1	UC-101	ex (N162RB)		Lsd fr Raytheon
N167GL	Beech 1900C-1	UC-167		stored BEC	Lsd fr Raytheon

Airline is headquarted in Cheyenne, WY but aircraft operate at major hubs

GREAT PLAINS AIRLINES

Ozark (ZO/OZR) (IATA 507)   Columbia-Regional, MO (COU)

N335PH	Dornier 328-120	3013	ex (N335PC)	
N410Z	Dornier 328-300	3125	ex D-BDXF	Lsd fr WFBN
N430Z	Dornier 328-300	3127	ex D-BDXH	Lsd fr WFBN
N473PS	Dornier 328-110	3010	ex N332PH	Lsd fr WFBN

Operated by Ozark Airlines

GRIFFING FLYING SERVICE

Sandusky-Griffing, OH (SKY)

N425S	Cessna U206E Stationair	U20601692	ex N9492G	
N426S	Piper PA-31-350 Chieftain	31-8152190	ex N426SC	
N427SX	Piper PA-31-350 Chieftain	31-8152173	ex N427S	
N428S	Piper PA-32-301 Saratoga	32-8106021		
N430S	Piper PA-31-350 Chieftain	31-8252048	ex N86AJ	
N442S	Britten-Norman BN-2A-20 Islander	770	ex N6863G	
N443S	Britten-Norman BN-2A-20 Islander	766	ex N25SA	

All leased from Griffing Sandusky Airport Inc

GULF AND CARIBBEAN AIR

(8G)   Fort Lauderdale-Hollywood Intk, FL (FLL)

| C-GKFQ | Convair 580 | 86 | ex N73136 | | Lsd fr KFA |
| N4753B | Convair 440 | 340 | ex 55-4753 | std | Lsd fr Intl Trading Co of Yukon |

GULFSTREAM INTERNATIONAL

Gulf Flight (3M/GFT) (IATA 449)   Miami Intl, FL (MIA)

N16540	Beech 1900D	UE-172		
N17534	Beech 1900D	UE-141		
N17541	Beech 1900D	UE-203		
N38537	Beech 1900D	UE-158		
N47542	Beech 1900D	UE-198		
N48544	Beech 1900D	UE-183		
N49543	Beech 1900D	UE-181		
N53545	Beech 1900D	UE-185		
N69547	Beech 1900D	UE-189		
N69548	Beech 1900D	UE-193	stored MZJ	
N69549	Beech 1900D	UE-194		
N81533	Beech 1900D	UE-137	N137ZV	
N81535	Beech 1900D	UE-147	Grand Bahama Island colours	
N81536	Beech 1900D	UE-152		
N81538	Beech 1900D	UE-199		
N81546	Beech 1900D	UE-187		
N81553	Beech 1900D	UE-222	stored MZJ	
N81556	Beech 1900D	UE-239		
N82539	Beech 1900D	UE-168		
N87550	Beech 1900D	UE-205		
N87551	Beech 1900D	UE-206		

N87552	Beech 1900D	UE-216	
N87554	Beech 1900D	UE-227	
N87555	Beech 1900D	UE-234	
N87557	Beech 1900D	UE-246	

All leased from Raytheon Aircraft Credit Corp
28% owned by Continental Airlinesand operates as Continental Connection

HAGELAND AVIATION SERVICES

Hageland (H6/HAG) — St Mary's, Bethel, AK (KSM)

N17GN*	Cessna 207A Stationair 8	20700693	
N23CF	Cessna 207 Skywagon	20700276	
N104K*	Cessna 207 Skywagon	20700122	
N207SE*	Cessna 207 Skywagon	20700237	
N327CT*	Cessna 207A Stationair 7	20700535	
N747SQ*	Cessna 207A Skywagon	20700387	
N5277J*	Cessna 207A Stationair 8	20700772	
N6207H*	Cessna 207A Stationair 7	20700551	
N6439H*	Cessna 207A Stationair 7	20700525	
N7340U*	Cessna T207A Turbo Skywagon	20700407	
N9399M	Cessna 207A Stationair 8	20700652	ex VH-UAA
N9400M	Cessna 207A Stationair 8	20700687	
N9869M*	Cessna 207A Stationair 8	20700744	
N73067	Cessna 207A Stationair 7	20700558	
N303GV*	Cessna 208B Caravan I	208B0581	
N407GV*	Cessna 208B Caravan I	208B0616	
N410GV*	Cessna 208B Caravan I	208B0632	ex N5264U
N411GV*	Cessna 208B Caravan I	208B0672	
N715HE*	Cessna 208B Caravan I	208B0603	ex N715HL
N717PA	Cessna 208B Caravan I	208B0804	
N1232Y*	Cessna 208B Caravan I	208B0566	ex N5246Z
N402QA*	Cessna 402C	402C0338	
N404GV	Beech 1900C-1	UC-154	ex N154YV
N406GV*	Reims Cessna F406 Caravan II	F406-0049	ex 9M-PMS
N1553C	Beech 1900C-1	UC-24	ex N31226
N6590Y*	Reims Cessna F406 Caravan II	F406-0052	
N6591L*	Reims Cessna F406 Caravan II	F406-0053	
N6591R*	Reims Cessna F406 Caravan II	F406-0054	
N9575G*	Cessna U206F Stationair	U20601775	
N91361	Cessna 180F	180-52045	
N15503*	Beech 1900C-1	UC-72	

*Leased from Gussic Ventures

HAMMONDS FLYING SERVICE

Hammond (HMD) — Houma-Terrebone, LA (HUM)

Previously listed as Charlie Hammonds Flying Service

N2906Q	Cessna A185F Skywagon	18503542	
N9866Q	Cessna A185F Skywagon	18503794	
N61181	Cessna A185F Skywagon	18504120	

HAWAIIAN AIRLINES

Hawaiian (HA/HAL) — Honolulu-Intl, HI (HNL)

N475HA	Boeing 717-22A	5050/55121		I'Iwi	Lsd fr WFBN
N476HA	Boeing 717-22A	5053/55118		'Elepalo	Lsd fr WFBN
N477HA	Boeing 717-22A	5061/55122		'Apapane	Lsd fr WFBN
N478HA	Boeing 717-22A	5064/55123		'Amakihi	Lsd fr WFBN
N479HA	Boeing 717-22A	5069/55124		'Akepa	Lsd fr WFBN
N480HA	Boeing 717-22A	5070/55125		Pueo	Lsd fr WFBN
N481HA	Boeing 717-22A	5073/55126		'Alauahio	Lsd fr WFBN
N484HA	Boeing 717-22A	5080/55129		'Oma'o	Lsd fr WFBN
N485HA	Boeing 717-22A	5089/55130		Palila	Lsd fr WFBN
N486HA	Boeing 717-22A	5092/55131		'Akiki	Lsd fr WFBN
N487HA	Boeing 717-22A	5098/55132		'Lo	Lsd fr WFBN
N580HA	Boeing 767-33AER	850/28140		Kolea	Lsd fr AWMS 1
N581HA	Boeing 767-33AER	853/28141		Manu o Ku	Lsd fr AWMS 1
N582HA	Boeing 767-33AER	857/28139		Ake Ake	Lsd fr AWMS 1
N583HA	Boeing 767-33AER	423/25531	ex D-AMUP	'A	Lsd fr ILFC
N584HA	Boeing 767-3G5ER	255/24258	ex D-AMUS	Kioea	Lsd fr ILFC
N585HA	Boeing 767-3G5ER	251/24257	ex D-AMUR	Noio	Lsd fr ILFC
N586HA	Boeing 767-3G5ER	268/24259	ex D-AMUN	Ou	Lsd fr ILFC
N587HA	Boeing 767-33AER	887/33421		Pakalakala	Lsd fr AWMS
N588HA	Boeing 767-3CBER	890/33466		'Iwa	Lsd fr Boeing Capital
N589HA	Boeing 767-33AER	892/33422		Moli	Lsd fr AWMS

N590HA	Boeing 767-3CBER	894/33467		Koa'e Ula	Lsd fr Boeing Capital
N591HA	Boeing 767-33AER	897/33423		Ake keke	Lsd fr AWMS
N592HA	Boeing 767-3CBER	898/33468		Hunakai	Lsd fr BCC Equipment Lsg
N593HA	Boeing 767-33AER	901/33424		Nene	Lsd fr AWMS

Filed Chapter 11 on 21 March 2003 but operations continue

HAWAII HELICOPTERS ceased operations

HAWKINS & POWERS AVIATION

Greybull, WY/Fairbanks-Fort Wainright, AK (GEY/FBK)

N122HP	Lockheed SP-2H Neptune	726-7226	ex N2216K	122	Lsd fr D&G Inc
N125HP	Lockheed SP-2H Neptune	726-7035	ex N4846N	125	Lsd fr D&G Inc
N128HP	Lockheed P2V-7 Neptune	726-7073	ex N2215G	128	Lsd fr D&G Inc
N129HP	Lockheed P-2V-7 Neptune	726-7200	ex N22154	129	Lsd fr D&G Inc
N138HP	Lockheed SP-2H Neptune	726-7223	ex N22166	138	Lsd fr D&G Inc
N139HP	Lockheed P2V-7 Neptune	726-7168	ex N8064A	139	
N140HP	Lockheed P2V-7 Turbo Neptune	726-7102	ex N8063S	140	
N2218A	Lockheed P2V-7 Neptune	726-7243	ex Bu148355	under conv to Turbo	
N131FF	Lockheed C-130A Hercules	3142	ex N132FF	131 stored GEY	
N132HP	Lockheed C-130A Hercules	3115	ex N4172Q	132 stored GEY	
N133HP	Lockheed C-130A Hercules	3189	ex N8026J	130 stored GEY	
N134HP	Lockheed C-130A Hercules	3218	ex 57-0511	134 stored GEY	
N135HP	Lockheed C-130A Hercules	3166		Georgia Box	
N112HP	Cessna 310I	310I0104	ex N199W		
N123HP	Bell 206L-1 LongRanger II	45394	ex N93ZT		
N401HP	Bell 206B JetRanger III	3314			
N1365N	Boeing KC-97L Stratotanker	16729	ex 52-2698	97	
N2751U	Bell 206B JetRanger III	2689			
N2751X	Bell 206L-1 LongRanger II	45252			
N2871G	Consolidated PBY4-2 Privateer	66302	ex Bu66302	121 Tanker	
N2872G	Consolidated PBY4-2 Privateer	66300	ex Bu66300	124 Tanker	
N6643T	Bell 206L-3 LongRanger III	51453			
N6884C	Consolidated PBY4-2 Privateer	59701	ex N3432G	127 Tanker	
N7962C	Consolidated PBY4-2 Privateer	59882	ex Bu59882	126 Tanker	
N8043Z	Bell UH-1B	198	ex 60-3552		
N90203	Douglas C-54G	35934	ex 45-0481	166	

HEARTLAND AVIATION

Night Chase (NTC)   *Eau Claire-Chippewa Valley Regional, WI (EAU)*

N310JZ	Cessna 310R	310R1623
N1448Z	Cessna 310R	310R1527
N1551G	Cessna 402B	402B1072
N3286M	Cessna 310R	310R1894
N26635	Cessna 414A Chancellor III	414A0531

HEAVY LIFT HELICOPTERS

Apple Valley, CA/Ketchikan, AK (APV/KTN)

N408HL	Sikorsky S-64 Skycrane	64010	ex N6156Y
N811KA	Bell 212	30656	ex N59630
N873HL	Bell 212	30873	ex N910KW
N6156U	Sikorsky S-64 Skycrane	64012	ex 66-18410
N6156Z	Sikorsky S-64 Skycrane	64029	ex 67-18427
N44094	Sikorsky S-64 Skycrane	64023	ex 67-18421

HELI-FLITE

Corona-Municipal, CA (AJO)

N1078Q	Bell 206B JetRanger III	2425	ex N5002X	Lsd fr Sunwest Inc
N9043N	Sikorsky S-58 (SH-34G)	58761	ex Bu143957	
N87717	Sikorsky S-58 (SH-34G)	581269	ex Bu148011	

HELI-JET

Eugene-Private Heliport, OR

N28HJ	Bell 205A-1	30006	ex PK-UHI	Lsd fr WFBN
N58HJ	Bell 205A-1	30314		Lsd fr WFBN
N66HJ	Bell 205A-1	30239	ex N49766	Lsd fr WFBN
N73HJ	Bell 212	30552	ex XC-EDM	Lsd fr WFBN
N97HJ	Bell 205A-1	30173	ex C-GFHG	Lsd fr WFBN

HELICOPTER TRANSPORT SERVICES

Baltimore-Martin State, MD (MTN)

N89FB	Bell 206B JetRanger II	1980		
N206YP	Bell 206B JetRanger II	1981	ex C-GLLA	
N2168S	Bell 206B JetRanger III	3490		Lsd fr US Leaseco
N16917	Bell 206B JetRanger III	2303		Lsd fr Fleetwind Inc
N70523	Bell 206B JetRanger III	3162	ex C-GDKN	
N76LP	Sikorsky S-76A	760133		
N208WB	Bell 206L-1 LongRanger II	45550	ex C-GBHZ	
N219AC	Sikorsky S-61N	61755	ex G-BDKI	
N467KG	Sikorsky S-64 Skycrane	64074		Lsd fr US Leaseco
N484KG	Sikorsky S-64 Skycrane	64092	ex 70-18484	Lsd fr US Leaseco
N664Y	Sikorsky S-61R	61501		
N91158	Sikorsky S-61N Helipro Short	61424	ex G-AZDC	

HELIFLIGHT

Fort Lauderdale-Hollywood Intl, FL (FLL)

N33HF	Bell 206B JetRanger II	2192	ex N16732	Lsd fr Prospect Lsg
N58HF	Sikorsky S-58J		ex 57-1692	Lsd fr Helicrane

HIRTH AIR TANKERS

Buffalo-Johnson County, WY (BYG)

N7080C	Lockheed PV-2 Harpoon	15-1465	ex Bu37499	39
N7272C	Lockheed PV-2 Harpoon	15-1242	ex Bu37276	40
N7458C	Lockheed PV-2 Harpoon	15-1200	ex Bu37234	37
N7670C	Lockheed PV-2 Harpoon	15-1438	ex Bu37472	36

HOMER AIR

(HB)　　　　　　　　　　　　　　　　　　　　　　　　　　　　　　*Homer, AK (HOM)*

N6522T	Britten-Norman BN-2A-8 Islander	136	ex F-OCOZ	
N7138Q	Cessna U206F Stationair	U20603074		Lsd fr C&L Inc
N8337Q	Cessna U206F Stationair	U20703198		Lsd fr C&L Inc
N9815M	Cessna U206G Stationair 6	U20604572		Lsd fr C&L Inc

HOOTERS AIR

Myrtle Beach, SC (CRE)

N250TR	Boeing 737-2K5 (Nordam 3)	779/22597	ex F-GFLV	Lsd fr/op by PCE
N252TR	Boeing 737-228 (Nordam 3)	936/23001	ex F-GBYB	Lsd fr/op by PCE
N751PA	Boeing 757-2G5	146/23928	ex D-AMUV	Lsd fr/op by PCE

Began operations 06 March 2003; aircraft operated by Pace Air a wholly owned subsidiary

HORIZON AIRLINES

Horizon Air (QX/QXE)　　　　　　　　　　　　　　　　　*Seattle-Tacoma Intl, WA (SEA)*

N600QX	Canadair CL-600-2C10	10005	ex C-GCRA	600	Lsd fr WFBN
N601QX	Canadair CL-600-2C10	10009	ex C-GHCS	601; Frontier	Lsd fr WFBN
N602QX	Canadair CL-600-2C10	10010	ex C-GHCV	602	Lsd fr WFBN
N603QX	Canadair CL-600-2C10	10011	ex C-GHCZ	603	Lsd fr WFBN
N604QX	Canadair CL-600-2C10	10019	ex C-GIAJ	604	Lsd fr WFBN
N605QX	Canadair CL-600-2C10	10022	ex C-GIAR	605	Lsd fr WFBN
N606QX	Canadair CL-600-2C10	10023	ex C-GISU	606	Lsd fr WFBN
N607QX	Canadair CL-600-2C10	10024	ex C-GIZG	607	Lsd fr WFBN
N608QX	Canadair CL-600-2C10	10026	ex C-GIAX	608; Frontier	Lsd fr WFBN
N609QX	Canadair CL-600-2C10	10031	ex C-GIBJ	609	Lsd fr WFBN
N610QX	Canadair CL-600-2C10	10033	ex C-GIBN	610	Lsd fr WFBN
N611QX	Canadair CL-600-2C10	10041	ex C-GICP	611	Lsd fr WFBN
N612QX	Canadair CL-600-2C10	10042	ex C-GHZV	612	Lsd fr WFBN
N613QX	Canadair CL-600-2C10	10045	ex C-GIAD	613	Lsd fr WFBN
N614QX	Canadair CL-600-2C10	10049	ex C-GIAJ	614	Lsd fr WFBN
N615QX	Canadair CL-600-2C10	10065	ex C-GIBQ	615	Lsd fr WFBN
N616QX	Canadair CL-600-2C10	10128	ex C-		Lsd fr WFBN
N617QX	Canadair CL-600-2C10	10130	ex C-	617	Lsd fr WFBN
N618QX	Canadair CL-600-2C10			on order 04	
N619QX	Canadair CL-600-2C10			on order 04	

A further six are on order for delivery from 2005

N345PH^	de Havilland DHC-8Q-202	476	ex C-GFYI	City of Wenatchee
N346PH^	de Havilland DHC-8Q-202	477	ex C-GEOA	City of Redmond/Bend
N347PH^	de Havilland DHC-8Q-202	480	ex C-FWBB	City of Moses Lake

N348PH^	de Havilland DHC-8Q-202	484	ex C-FWBB
N349PH^	de Havilland DHC-8Q-202	486	ex C-GEOA
N350PH^	de Havilland DHC-8Q-202	488	ex C-GFQL	City of Pendleton
N351PH^	de Havilland DHC-8Q-202	490	ex C-GFUM	City of Eugene
N352PH^	de Havilland DHC-8Q-202	494	ex C-GHRI
N353PH^	de Havilland DHC-8Q-202	496	ex C-GFRP
N354PH^	de Havilland DHC-8Q-202	498	ex C-FCSG	Cities of North Bend/Coos Bay
N355PH^	de Havilland DHC-8Q-202	500	ex C-GEMU
N356PH^	de Havilland DHC-8Q-202	502	ex C-GEOZ
N357PH^	de Havilland DHC-8Q-202	504	ex C-GFRP	City of Portland
N358PH^	de Havilland DHC-8Q-202	506	ex C-FWBB
N359PH^	de Havilland DHC-8Q-202	514	ex C-GEOA	City of Kelowna
N360PH^	de Havilland DHC-8Q-202	515	ex C-GEWI	City of Medford
N361PH^	de Havilland DHC-8Q-202	516	ex C-GFOD	City of Sun Valley
N362PH^	de Havilland DHC-8Q-202	518	ex C-FDHI
N363PH^	de Havilland DHC-8Q-202	520		City of Boise
N364PH^	de Havilland DHC-8Q-202	524		Cities of Seattle/Tacoma
N365PH^	de Havilland DHC-8Q-202	526		City of Pocatello
N366PH^	de Havilland DHC-8Q-202	510	ex C-GELN	City of Redding
N367PH^	de Havilland DHC-8Q-202	511	ex C-GDLD
N368PH^	de Havilland DHC-8Q-202	512	ex C-GDFT	City of Idaho Falls
N369PH^	de Havilland DHC-8Q-202	513	ex C-FWBB
N374PH^	de Havilland DHC-8Q-202	528	ex C-GDIU
N375PH^	de Havilland DHC-8Q-202	529	ex C-GDKL
N379PH^	de Havilland DHC-8Q-202	530	ex C-GDLK

*Leased from Finova
+Leased from CIT Group
^Leased from WFBN
'Lsd fr PB leasing
"Leased from Mellon Bank
All names prefixed The Great

N400QX	de Havilland DHC-8-401Q	4030	ex C-GFCF	Lsd fr BCC Equipment Lsg
N401QX	de Havilland DHC-8-401Q	4031	ex C-GFCW	Lsd fr BCC Equipment Lsg
N402QX	de Havilland DHC-8-401Q	4032	ex C-GFOD	Lsd fr BCC Equipment Lsg
N403QX	de Havilland DHC-8-401Q	4037	ex C-FDHP	Lsd fr BCC Equipment Lsg
N404QX	de Havilland DHC-8-401Q	4046	ex C-GDKL	Lsd fr BCC Equipment Lsg
N405QX	de Havilland DHC-8-401Q	4047	ex C-GDLD	Lsd fr BCC Equipment Lsg
N406QX	de Havilland DHC-8-401Q	4048	ex C-GDLK	Lsd fr WFBN
N407QX	de Havilland DHC-8-401Q	4049	ex C-GDNK	Lsd fr WFBN
N408QX	de Havilland DHC-8-401Q	4050	ex C-GFCA	Lsd fr WFBN
N409QX	de Havilland DHC-8-401Q	4051	ex C-GFCW	Lsd fr WFBN
N410QX	de Havilland DHC-8-401Q	4053	ex C-GFQL	Lsd fr WFBN
N411QX	de Havilland DHC-8-401Q	4055	ex C-GFUM	Lsd fr WFBN
N412QX	de Havilland DHC-8-401Q	4059		Lsd fr BCC Eqpt Lsg
N413QX	de Havilland DHC-8-401Q	4060	ex C-FNGB	Lsd fr WFBN
N414QX	de Havilland DHC-8-401Q	4061	ex C-GDFT	Lsd fr WFBN
N416QX	de Havilland DHC-8-402Q	4083	ex C-	Lsd fr Bombardier Capital
N546DS	de Havilland DHC-8-402Q	4017	ex	Lsd fr Bombardier Capital
N	de Havilland DHC-8-402Q		ex C-	on order 04

Horizon is a wholly owned subsidiary of the Alaska Air Group and operates services as Alaska Airlines Commuter using flight numbers in the range 2000-2699 and 2800-2849. Horizon also has a code-sharing agreement with Northwest Airlines using flight numbers in the range 2000-2899 plus operating for Frontier Airlines

---

HOUSTON HELICOPTERS

Houston Heli (HHO)   *Pearland-Heliport, TX*

N107CC	Bell 206B JetRanger III	2374	ex N16977
N2949W	Bell 206B JetRanger II	824	
N5007E	Bell 206B JetRanger III	2484	
N6139Q	Bell 206B JetRanger	1276	
N16770	Bell 206B JetRanger II	2147	
N16814	Bell 206B JetRanger III	2229	
N49742	Bell 206B JetRanger II	1972	
N59531	Bell 206B JetRanger II	1352	
N59518	Bell 206B JetRanger	1322	
N59589	Bell 206B JetRanger	1482	
N59604	Bell 206B JetRanger	1276	
N1071A	Bell 206L-1 LongRanger II	45340	
N2135Y	Bell 206L-1 LongRanger II	45640	
N2774V	Bell 206L-1 LongRanger II	45308	
N4246Z	Bell 206L-3 LongRanger III	51475	
N5737V	Bell 206L-1 LongRanger II	45457	
N5755N	Bell 206L-1 LongRanger II	45535	
N42489	Bell 206L-3 LongRanger III	51474	
N57377	Bell 206L-1 LongRanger II	45458	
N57400	Bell 206L-1 LongRanger II	45464	
N407HH	Bell 407	53460	
N5009M	Sikorsky S-76A	760041	
N8145Y	Bell 212	30795	ex C-FSAU
N8223V	Bell 212	30728	ex C-FRUQ

N8224V	Bell 212	30808	ex C-FRUP
N9937K	Bell 212	30778	
N90421	Sikorsky S-76A	760039	ex C-GMQD

IBC AIRWAYS

Chasqui (II/CSQ)   *Miami-Intl, FL (MIA)*

N811BC	Swearingen SA.227AC Metro III	AC-463	ex N630PA	
N821BC	Swearingen SA.227AC Metro III	AC-642	ex N355AE	
N831BC	Swearingen SA.227AC Metro III	AC-654B	ex N26906	
N841BC	Swearingen SA.227TC Metro II	TC-282	ex N248AM	
N861BC	Swearingen SA.227AC Metro III	AC-487B	ex N550TD	
N871BC	Swearingen SA.227AC Metro III	AC-659B	ex N2693C	
N891BC	Swearingen SA.227AC Metro III	AC-709B	ex N2708D	Lsd fr CRI Lsg
N921BC	Swearingen SA.227AC Metro III	AC-682	ex N682AV	
(N941BC)	Swearingen SA.227AC Metro III	AC-678	ex N363AE	stored MIA

| N881BC | Short SD.3-60 | SH3691 | ex C6-BFW |
| N901BC | Cessna 402B | 402B0379 | |

IBC Airways is a division of International Bonded Couriers

ILIAMNA AIR TAXI

Iliamna Air (V8/IAR)   *Iliamna, AK (ILI)*

N38KC	Piper PA-31-350 Chieftain	31-8352033		
N121AK	de Havilland DHC-2 Beaver	121	ex C-FDJO	Floatplane
N715HL	Pilatus PC-12/45	292	ex N292PB	
N76SU	de Havilland DHC-2 Beaver	483	ex 52-6107	Floatplane
N3682Z	Beech 58 Baron	TH-1159		
N1748U	Cessna 207 Skywagon	20700348		
N7379U	Cessna 207A Stationair 7	20700427		
N9720M	Cessna 207A Stationair 8	20700720		
N62230	de Havilland DHC-2 Beaver	707	ex 53-7899	Floatplane
N68088	de Havilland DHC-2 Beaver	1197		Floatplane

INDEPENDENCE AIR

                                                                                   Washington-Dulles, DC (DUL)

N620BR	Canadair CL-600-2B19	7179		620
N621BR	Canadair CL-600-2B19	7186	ex C-FMML	621
N622BR	Canadair CL-600-2B19	7187		622
N623BR	Canadair CL-600-2B19	7192		623
N624BR	Canadair CL-600-2B19	7211		624
N625BR	Canadair CL-600-2B19	7214	ex C-FMLU	625
N626BR*	Canadair CL-600-2B19	7225	ex C-FMKW	626
N627BR*	Canadair CL-600-2B19	7233		627
N628BR*	Canadair CL-600-2B19	7240		628
N629BR*	Canadair CL-600-2B19	7251		629
N630BR	Canadair CL-600-2B19	7255		630
N631BR	Canadair CL-600-2B19	7261	ex C-FMLS	631
N632BR*	Canadair CL-600-2B19	7268	ex C-FMNY	632
N633BR	Canadair CL-600-2B19	7274	ex C-FMLU	633
N634BR	Canadair CL-600-2B19	7287	ex C-FMLB	634
N635BR*	Canadair CL-600-2B19	7295		635
N636BR*	Canadair CL-600-2B19	7307		636
N637BR	Canadair CL-600-2B19	7308		637
N638BR*	Canadair CL-600-2B19	7311		638
N639BR*	Canadair CL-600-2B19	7313	ex C-FMNB	639
N640BR	Canadair CL-600-2B19	7340	ex C-FMMW	640
N641BR*	Canadair CL-600-2B19	7349	ex C-FMLI	641
N642BR*	Canadair CL-600-2B19	7356	ex C-FMNW	642
N643BR*	Canadair CL-600-2B19	7363	ex C-FMNO	643
N644BR*	Canadair CL-600-2B19	7379	ex C-FMLI	644
N645BR*	Canadair CL-600-2B19	7383	ex C-FMLV	645
N646BR*	Canadair CL-600-2B19	7392	ex C-FMND	646
N647BR*	Canadair CL-600-2B19	7399	ex C-FMMQ	647
N648BR*	Canadair CL-600-2B19	7406	ex C-FMKZ	648
N649BR*	Canadair CL-600-2B19	7414	ex C-FMMT	649
N650BR*	Canadair CL-600-2B19	7418	ex C-FMNY	650
N651BR*	Canadair CL-600-2B19	7426	ex C-FMMB	651
N652BR*	Canadair CL-600-2B19	7429	ex C-FMMQ	652
N653BR*	Canadair CL-600-2B19	7438	ex C-FMLF	653
N654BR*	Canadair CL-600-2B19	7454	ex C-FMLU	654
N655BR*	Canadair CL-600-2B19	7457	ex C-FMML	655
N656BR*	Canadair CL-600-2B19	7485	ex C-FMOI	656
N657BR*	Canadair CL-600-2B19	7491	ex C-FMMX	657
N658BR*	Canadair CL-600-2B19	7500	ex C-FMLQ	658
N659BR*	Canadair CL-600-2B19	7509	ex C-FMOS	659

N660BR*	Canadair CL-600-2B19	7519	ex C-FMMQ	660
N661BR*	Canadair CL-600-2B19	7520	ex C-FMMW	661
N662BR*	Canadair CL-600-2B19	7526	ex C-FMKZ	662
N663BR*	Canadair CL-600-2B19	7527	ex C-FMLB	663
N664BR*	Canadair CL-600-2B19	7528	ex C-FMLF	664
N665BR*	Canadair CL-600-2B19	7534	ex C-FMMT	665
N667BR*	Canadair CL-600-2B19	7535	ex C-FMNH	667
N668BR*	Canadair CL-600-2B19	7544	ex C-FMLU	668
N669BR*	Canadair CL-600-2B19	7545	ex C-FMOI	669
N670BR*	Canadair CL-600-2B19	7561	ex C-FMLS	670
N671BR*	Canadair CL-600-2B19	7572	ex C-FMND	671
N672BR*	Canadair CL-600-2B19	7594	ex C-FMMT	672
N673BR*	Canadair CL-600-2B19	7599	ex C-FMOS	673
N674BR*	Canadair CL-600-2B19	7601	ex C-FVAZ	674
N675BR*	Canadair CL-600-2B19	7635	ex C-FMOI	675
N676BR*	Canadair CL-600-2B19	7644	ex C-FMKV	676
N677BR*	Canadair CL-600-2B19	7652	ex C-FMLT	677
N678BR*	Canadair CL-600-2B19	7653	ex C-FMLV	678
N679BR*	Canadair CL-600-2B19	7662	ex C-FMND	679
N680BR*	Canadair CL-600-2B19	7679	ex C-FMLI	680
N681BR*	Canadair CL-600-2B19	7680	ex C-FMLQ	681
N682BR*	Canadair CL-600-2B19	7691	ex C-FVAZ	682
N683BR*	Canadair CL-600-2B19	7692	ex C-FMND	683
N684BR*	Canadair CL-600-2B19	7708	ex C-FMLF	684
N685BR*	Canadair CL-600-2B19	7712	ex C-FMLT	685
N686BR*	Canadair CL-600-2B19	7715	ex C-FMNH	686
N687BR*	Canadair CL-600-2B19	7720	ex C-FMOW	687
N688BR*	Canadair CL-600-2B19	7723	ex C-FMNQ	688
N689BR*	Canadair CL-600-2B19	7737	ex C-FMLB	689
N690BR*	Canadair CL-600-2B19	7739	ex C-FMLI	690
N691BR*	Canadair CL-600-2B19	7740	ex C-FMLQ	691
N692BR*	Canadair CL-600-2B19	7759	ex C-FMMQ	692
N693BR	Canadair CL-600-2B19	7761	ex C-GYXS	693
N694BR	Canadair CL-600-2B19	7768	ex C-FMLI	694
N695BR	Canadair CL-600-2B19	7772	ex C-GYYA	695
N696BR	Canadair CL-600-2B19	7779	ex C-FJKK	696
N697BR	Canadair CL-600-2B19	7787	ex C-FSDZ	697
N698BR	Canadair CL-600-2B19	7799	ex C-FMLI	698
N699BR	Canadair CL-600-2B19	7801	ex C-FMLS	699
N701BR*	Canadair CL-600-2B19	7448	ex N850FJ	701
N702BR*	Canadair CL-600-2B19	7462	ex N851FJ	702
N703BR*	Canadair CL-600-2B19	7467	ex N852FJ	703
N705BR*	Canadair CL-600-2B19	7470	ex N853FJ	705
N706BR*	Canadair CL-600-2B19	7553	ex C-GJJP	706
N708BR*	Canadair CL-600-2B19	7575	ex C-GJOT	708
N709BR	Canadair CL-600-2B19	7850	ex C-FMMW	709
N710BR	Canadair CL-600-2B19	7852	ex C-FMMY	710
N712BR	Canadair CL-600-2B19			712	on order
N713BR	Canadair CL-600-2B19			713	on order
N715BR	Canadair CL-600-2B19			715	on order
N716BR	Canadair CL-600-2B19			716	on order
N717BR	Canadair CL-600-2B19			717	on order
N718BR	Canadair CL-600-2B19			718	on order
N719BR	Canadair CL-600-2B19			719	on order
N720BR	Canadair CL-600-2B19			720	on order
N721BR	Canadair CL-600-2B19			721	on order 04
N722BR	Canadair CL-600-2B19			722	on order 04
N723BR	Canadair CL-600-2B19			723	on order 04
N724BR	Canadair CL-600-2B19			724	on order 04
N725BR	Canadair CL-600-2B19			725	on order 04
N726BR	Canadair CL-600-2B19			726	on order 04
N	Canadair CL-600-2B19				on order 04
N	Canadair CL-600-2B19				on order 04

Twenty-five more Canadair CL-600-2B19s are on order for delivery in 2005
*Leased from Wachovia Bank   +Leased fr State Street Bank & Trust
New low-cost operator formed by Atlantic Coast Airlines in January 2004 following loss of United Express franchise. To lease six new Airbus Industrie A319-13x from ILFC as part of plan to lease 10 in total (plus 10 A319s and 5 A320s from Airbus direct).

INLAND AVIATION SERVICES

(7N)   *Aniak, AK (ANI)*

N910SP	Helio H-395 Super Courier	627
N1673U	Cessna 207 Skywagon	20700273
N1754U	Cessna T207 Turbo Skywagon	20700354
N42472	Cessna 207 Skywagon	20700148
N91099	Cessna 207 Skywagon	20700073

All leased from Inland Holdings

INTER ISLAND EXPRESS

San Juan/Isla Grande, PR (SIG)

N391EC	Pilatus PC-12/45	391	ex HB-FQG	
N1253K	Cessna 208B Caravan I	208B0648		Regd to Air Borinquen
N1253Y	Cessna 208B Caravan I	208B0649		Regd to Air Borinquen

Also trades as Air Borinquen

INTERMOUNTAIN HELICOPTERS

Columbia, CA (COA)

| N9121Z | Bell 212 | 30582 | ex C-GJDC |
| N9122Z | Bell 212 | 30716 | ex C-GFRS |

INTERNATIONAL AIR RESPONSE

Chandler-Memorial, AZ (CHD)

N117TG	Lockheed C-130A Hercules	3018	ex 54-1631	31; Iron Butterfly
N118TG	Lockheed C-130A Hercules	3219	ex 57-0512	32; stored CHD
N796AL	Douglas DC-8-63F (BAC 3)	453/46054	ex OY-SBL	
N797AL	Douglas DC-8-63F (BAC 3)	556/46163	ex SE-DBL	stored VCV
N995CF	Douglas DC-8-62F (BAC 3)	528/46024	ex N815ZA	stored VCV
N4887C	Douglas DC-7C	903/45351		33

ISLAND AIR CHARTERS

Barracuda (ISC)   Fort Lauderdale-Hollywood Intl, FL (FLL)

| N138LW | Britten-Norman BN-2A-27 Islander | 138 | ex YR-BNF | |
| N779KS | Britten-Norman BN-2A-27 Islander | 779 | ex YR-BNE | stored FLL |

ISLAND AIR HONOLULU

Moku (WP/PRI)   Honolulu-Intl, HI (HNL)

N805WP	de Havilland DHC-8-102A	353	ex N853MA	Lsd fr Willis Lease
N806WP	de Havilland DHC-8-102A	357	ex N854MA	Lsd fr Willis Lease
N807WP	de Havilland DHC-8-102	023	ex N811PH	Lsd fr Willis Lease
N808WP	de Havilland DHC-8-103	026	ex N812PH	Lsd fr Willis Lease

Operates feeder services for Aloha Airlines using AQ flight numbers in the range 1000-1699

ISLAND AIRLINES

Island (IS/ISA)   Nantucket-Memorial, MA (ACK)

N175TT	Cessna 402C	402C1006		Lsd fr B&K Lsg
N401BK	Cessna 402C	402C0297	ex N3252M	Lsd fr B&K Lsg
N402BK	Cessna 402C	402C0689	ex N550CQ	Lsd fr B&K Lsg
N403BK	Cessna 402C	402C0330	ex N26436	Lsd fr B&K Lsg
N405BK	Cessna 402C	402C0459	ex N459RC	Lsd fr B&K Lsg
N406BK	Cessna 402C	402C0907	ex N1235A	Lsd fr B&K Lsg
N407BK	Cessna 402C	402C0238	ex N279CB	Lsd fr B&K Lsg
N409BK	Cessna 402C	402C0651	ex N67220	Lsd fr B&K Lsg
N408BK	Beech H-18	BA-653	ex N8451	

ISLAND AIR SERVICE

Kodiak-Municipal, AK (ADQ)

N27MR	Britten-Norman BN-2A-26 Islander	884	ex XC-DUN
N1162W	Beech B80 Queen Air	LD-350	
N2233Z	Britten-Norman BN-2A-26 Islander	23	ex C-FXYK
N756BW	Cessna U206G Stationair 6	U20605559	
N3941W	Piper PA-32-260 Cherokee Six	32-890	
N3983W	Piper PA-32-260 Cherokee Six	32-953	
N5891V	Britten-Norman BN-2A-26 Islander	3011	ex J8-VAN
N8152Z	Piper PA-32-301 Saratoga	32-8006004	

ISLAND AIRWAYS

Charlevoix-Municipal, MI (CVX)

N19WA	Britten-Norman BN-2A-8 Islander	524	ex N307SK
N80KM	Britten-Norman BN-2A Islander	80	ex G-BNXA
N95BN	Britten-Norman BN-2A-8 Islander	95	ex G-AXKB

N137MW	Britten-Norman BN-2A Islander	137	ex G-AXWH	
N866JA	Britten-Norman BN-2A-6 islander	185	ex G-31-185	Lsd fr Gemini Air Service
N371MC	Piper PA-31-350 Navajo Chieftain	31-7405409		Lsd fr Inter Midwest Inc
N707BT	Piper PA-34-200T Seneca II	34-7570110		

Islands Airways is the trading name of McPhillips Flying Service

ISLAND EXPRESS

Sandy Isle (2S/SDY) — Fort Lauderdale-Hollwood Intl, FL (FLL)

N402DD	Cessna 402C	402C0485	ex N94MM
N803RC	Cessna 402C	402C0803	ex ZK-VAB

ISLA NENA AIR SERVICES

Vieques , PR (VQS)

N229BN	Britten-Norman BN-2A-6 Islander	229	ex	
N555DM	Britten-Norman BN-2A-26 Islander	129	ex C-GGYY	
N678TA	Britten-Norman BN-2A-26 Islander	77	ex J6-SLZ	
N787DM	Cessna 208B Caravan I	208B0868	ex N1311A	Lsd fr San Juan Jet
N1202S	Britten-Norman BN-2A-26 islander	193	ex J6-SLV	

JETBLUE AIRWAYS

JetBlue (B6/JBU) — New York-JFK Intl, NY (JFK)

N503JB	Airbus Industrie A320-232	1123	ex F-WWBR	Bluebird	Lsd fr WFBN
N504JB	Airbus Industrie A320-232	1156	ex F-WWBV	Shades of Blue	Lsd fr ILFC
N505JB	Airbus Industrie A320-232	1173	ex F-WWDN	Blue Skies	Lsd fr WFBN
N506JB	Airbus Industrie A320-232	1235	ex F-WWIN	Born to be Blue	Lsd fr Castle LLC
N507JB	Airbus Industrie A320-232	1240	ex F-WWIP	Blue Crew	
N508JB	Airbus Industrie A320-232	1257	ex F-WWIY	Canard Blue	Lsd fr ILFC
N509JB	Airbus Industrie A320-232	1270	ex F-WWDF	True Blue	Lsd fr ILFC
N510JB	Airbus Industrie A320-232	1280	ex F-WWBA	Out of the Blue	Lsd fr ILFC
N516JB	Airbus Industrie A320-232	1302	ex F-WWBQ	Royal Blue	Lsd fr Mitsui
N517JB	Airbus Industrie A320-232	1327	ex F-WWDU	Blue Moon	Lsd fr Mitsui
N519JB	Airbus Industrie A320-232	1398	ex F-WWIY	It had to be Blue	Lsd fr ILFC
N520JB	Airbus Industrie A320-232	1446	ex F-WWBT	Blue Velvet	Lsd fr Castle LLC
N521JB	Airbus Industrie A320-232	1452	ex F-WWBY	Baby Blue	Lsd fr ILFC
N522JB	Airbus Industrie A320-232	1464	ex F-WWDG	Blue Ribbon	Lsd fr ILFC
N523JB	Airbus Industrie A320-232	1506	ex F-WWII	Born to be Blue	Lsd fr Mitsui
N524JB	Airbus Industrie A320-232	1528	ex F-WWIN	Blue Belle	Lsd fr Mitsui
N526JB	Airbus Industrie A320-232	1546	ex F-WWIY	Cool Blue	
N527JB	Airbus Industrie A320-232	1557	ex F-WWDF	Midnight Blue	
N528JB	Airbus Industrie A320-232	1591	ex F-WWBS	Mi Corazon Azul	
N529JB	Airbus Industrie A320-232	1610	ex F-WWDE	Ole Blue Eyes	
N531JB	Airbus Industrie A320-232	1650	ex F-WWDV	Rhapsody in Blue	
N533JB	Airbus Industrie A320-232	1652	ex F-WWDX	Usto Schulz	
N534JB	Airbus Industrie A320-232	1705	ex F-WWIU	Bada Bing Bada Blue	
N535JB	Airbus Industrie A320-232	1739	ex F-WWBQ	Estrella Azul	
N536JB	Airbus Industrie A320-232	1784	ex F-WWDS	Canyon Blue	Lsd fr Mitsui
N537JB	Airbus Industrie A320-232	1785	ex F-WWDP	Red, White and Blue	
N542JB	Airbus Industrie A320-232	1802	ex N513JB	Deja Blue	
N543JB	Airbus Industrie A320-232	1823	ex F-WWIP	Only Blue	
N544JB	Airbus Industrie A320-232	1835	ex F-WWBH	Blue Jean Baby	
N546JB	Airbus Industrie A320-232	1827	ex F-WWBE	Blue Traveller	
N547JB	Airbus Industrie A320-232	1849	ex F-WWDF	Forever Blue	Lsd fr WFBN
N548JB	Airbus Industrie A320-232	1868	ex F-WWIQ	Bluberry	
N550JB	Airbus Industrie A320-232	1891	ex F-WWBR	Blue Bayou	
N552JB	Airbus Industrie A320-232	1861	ex F-WWDM	Blue Jay	Lsd fr WFBN
N553JB	Airbus Industrie A320-232	1896	ex F-WWBY	Got Blue?	
N554JB	Airbus Industrie A320-232	1898	ex F-WWBK	Sacre' Bleu!	Lsd fr WFBN
N556JB	Airbus Industrie A320-232	1904	ex F-WWDO	Betty Blue	
N558JB	Airbus Industrie A320-232	1915	ex F-WWIF	Song Sung Blue	
N559JB	Airbus Industrie A320-232	1917	ex F-WWIR	Here's looking at Blue, Kid	
N561JB	Airbus Industrie A320-232	1927	ex F-WWIC	La vie en Blue	
N562JB	Airbus Industrie A320-232	1948	ex F-WWDF	The name is Blue, Jetblue	Lsd fr WFBN
N563JB	Airbus Industrie A320-232	2006	ex F-WWBY	Blue Chip	
N564JB	Airbus Industrie A320-232	2020	ex F-WWBZ	Absolute Blue	
N565JB	Airbus Industrie A320-232	2031	ex F-WWDT	Bippity Boppity Blue	
N566JB	Airbus Industrie A320-232	2042	ex F-WWDU	Blue Suede Shoes	
N568JB	Airbus Industrie A320-232	2063	ex F-WWDE	Blue Sapphire	
N569JB	Airbus Industrie A320-232	2075	ex F-WWDF	Blues Brothers	Lsd fr WFBN
N570JB	Airbus Industrie A320-232	2099	ex F-WWBD		
N570JB	Airbus Industrie A320-232	2099	ex F-WWBD	Devil with a Blue Dress On	
N571JB	Airbus Industrie A320-232	2125	ex F-WWIX		
N579JB	Airbus Industrie A320-232	2132	ex F-WWDB		Lsd fr WFBN
N580JB	Airbus Industrie A320-232	2136	ex F-WWBB		Lsd fr WFBN

N581JB	Airbus Industrie A320-232	2141	ex F-WWBR		
N582JB	Airbus Industrie A320-232	2147	ex F-WWDS	Mystic Blue	
N583JB	Airbus Industrie A320-232	2150	ex F-WWII		
N584JB	Airbus Industrie A320-232	2149	ex F-WWID		
N585JB	Airbus Industrie A320-232	2159	ex F-WWIC	on order	
N586JB	Airbus Industrie A320-232	2160	ex F-WWIN	on order	
N587JB	Airbus Industrie A320-232	2177	ex F-WWIL	on order	
N	Airbus Industrie A320-232	2201	ex F-WWIT	on order	
N	Airbus Industrie A320-232	2215	ex F-WW	on order	
N	Airbus Industrie A320-232		ex F-WW	on order	
N	Airbus Industrie A320-232		ex F-WW	on order	

A total of 143 Airbus Industrie A320-232s are on order for delivery up to 2011. Have differing tail colour schemes, namely harlequin diamonds, white dots, horizontal stripes, circular patches and plaid, all on a blue background
100 Embraer 190s are on order for delivery from 2005 to 2011

JIM HANKINS AIR SERVICE

Hankins (HKN)   Jackson-Hawkins Field, MS (JAN)

N22BR	Beech H-18	BA-729	ex N402AP	Freighter	
N123MD	Beech H-18	BA-701	ex N251R	Freighter	
N811BF	Beech H-18	BA-659	ex N13AW	Freighter	
N958B	Beech H-18	BA-651		Freighter	
N8476H	Beech H-18	BA-749	ex F-OCUU	Freighter	
N92756	Beech H-18	BA-728	ex JA5133	Freighter	
N99799	Beech H-18	BA-758	ex JA5147	Freighter	
N3BA	Douglas DC-3	12172	ex N94530	Freighter	
N40XL	Beech 58 Baron	TH-400			
N46JH	Short SD.3-30	SH3101	ex 83-0513	Freighter	
N95PC	Beech 65-C90A King Air	LJ-1109			
N899DD	Beech 58 Baron	TH-899			
N958JH	Beech 65-C90A King Air	LJ-1108	ex N438SP		
N3106W	Beech 58 Baron	TH-408			
N6652A	Beech 58 Baron	TH-1045			
N8061A	Douglas DC-3	6085	ex (N351SA)	Freighter	

JOHNSON AVIATION

N215BB	Aerospatiale/Alenia ATR 42-320F		ex N985MA

KACHINA AVIATION

Boise Air Terminal, ID

N212KA	Bell 212	30776	ex C-FAHI
N213KA	Bell 212	31172	ex C-FNOB
N214KA	Bell 212	30827	ex C-FAHC
N215KA	Bell 212	30651	ex C-FAHZ
N409KA	Bell 407	53016	ex C-FAHL

All leased from Alpine Helicopters, Canada

KALITTA AIR

Connie (L1/CKS)   Detroit-Willow Run, MI (YIP)

N702CK	Boeing 747-146 (SCD)	161/20332	ex JA8107	
N704CK	Boeing 747-209F	462/22299	ex B-18752	
N705CK	Boeing 747-246 (SCD)	243/21034	ex JA8123	
N707CK	Boeing 747-269B(SF)	332/21541	ex 9K-ADA	Lsd fr Kitty Hawk Collateral Trust
N708CK	Boeing 747-269BF	359/21542	ex 9K-ADB	Lsd fr Kitty Hawk Collateral Trust
N709CK	Boeing 747-132 (SCD)	159/20247	ex N625PL	
N710CK	Boeing 747-2B4BF	262/21097	ex OD-AGH	
N712CK	Boeing 747-122 (SCD)	60/19754	ex N854FT	Lsd fr Kelsey Investments
N713CK	Boeing 747-2B4B(SF)	264/21099	ex OD-AGH	
N714CK	Boeing 747-209B(SF)	519/22446	ex B-18753	
N715CK	Boeing 747-209B(SF)	556/22447	ex B-18755	
N716CK	Boeing 747-122 (SCD)	52/19753	ex N853FT	Lsd fr Kelsey Investments
N717CK	Boeing 747-123SF	125/20325	ex N673UP	
N	Boeing 747-246B(SF)	116/19823	ex N570SW	
N727CK	Boeing 747-246B	489/22478	ex JA8149	
N	Boeing 747-233M	250/20977	ex C-GAGA	stored MZJ
N720CK	Boeing 727-2B6F (FedEx 3)	1246/21298	ex N721SK	

KALITTA CHARTERS

Kalitta (CB/KFS) *Detroit-Willow Run, MI/Morristown, TN/El Paso, TX (YIP/-/ESP)*

N20TA	Lear Jet 23	23-062	ex N670MF
N28CK	Lear Jet 25	25-045	ex N24FN
N39CK	Lear Jet 25	25-005	ex XA-SDQ
N49CK	Lear Jet 23	23-009	ex N13SN
N50CK	Lear Jet 25B	25B-157	ex N57CK
(N68CK)	Lear Jet 25	25-047	ex N222B
N71CK	Lear Jet 36A	36A-035	ex VH-BIB
N72CK	Lear Jet 35A	35A-165	ex N16BJ
N75CK	Lear Jet 25D	25D-256	ex N6LL
N76CK	Lear Jet 25	25-020	ex N500JS
N80CK	Lear Jet 24D	24D-309	ex N789AA
N83CK	Lear Jet 25B	25B-183	ex N5LL
N96CK	Lear Jet 23	23-016	ex N7GF
N130CK	Lear Jet 25	25-038	ex N813JW
N147CK	Lear Jet 24	24-147	ex N147KH
N248CK	Lear Jet 25D	25D-248	ex N95CK
N555LB	Lear Jet 24	24-177	ex N555LA
N588CG	Lear Jet 24D	24D-304	ex N500CG
N70CK	AMD Falcon 20C	128	ex N228CK
N108R	AMD Falcon 20DC	108	ex N101ZE
N192R	AMD Falcon 20C	192	ex N910W
N212R	AMD Falcon 20DC	212	ex N31FE
N226R	AMD Falcon 20DC	226	ex N21FE
N227CK	AMD Falcon 20DC	227	ex N227R
N229R	AMD Falcon 20DC	229	ex N25EV
N230RA	AMD Falcon 20DC	230	ex N26EV
N301R	AMD Falcon 20C	3	ex N92MH
N560RA	AMD Falcon 20C	56	ex N388AJ
N810RA	AMD Falcon 20C	81	ex N93RS
N950RA	AMD Falcon 20C	95	ex N664B
N980R	AMD Falcon 20C	98	ex N781AJ
N54CK	Mitsubishi MU-2F	135	ex N66CL
N915CK	Douglas DC-9-15RC	219/47086	ex N915R

All freighters

KAMAKA AIR

Honolulu-Intl, HI (HNL)

N231H	Beech E-18S	BA-281	
N954RJ	Beech C-45G	AF-5	ex N8839Z
N9881Z	Beech C-45H	AF-851	ex 52-10921

KAPOWSIN AIR SPORT

Kapowsin, WA

N21SC	Cessna U206F Stationair 6	U20605278		Soloy conv Lsd fr Aircraft Guaranty
N52FW	de Havilland DHC-6 Twin Otter 100	52	ex N952	
N430A	Cessna 208B Caravan I	208B0415	ex LN-TWF	
N9641F	Cessna 208 Caravan I	20800122		
N9652F	Cessna 208 Caravan I	20800113		

KATMAI AIR

Anchorage-Lake Hood, AK

N491K	de Havilland DHC-3 Otter	434	ex N49KA	Floats
N492K	Piper PA-31-350 Chieftain	31-8052176	ex C-GAWL	Lsd fr Katmailand Inc
N495K	Cessna U206F Stationair	U20602730	ex N35566	Floats
N496K	Cessna U206G Stationair	U20603953	ex N756BE	Floats Lsd fr Katmailand Inc
N498K	Cessna T207A Turbo Stationair 8	20700624	ex N73762	Floats
N499K	Cessna T207A Turbo Stationair 8	20700632	ex N73835	Floats
N9644G	Cessna U206F Stationair	U20601844		Floats
N35851	Cessna U206F Stationair	U20602757		Floats Lsd fr Katmailand Inc

KENMORE AIR

(M5) *Kenmore SPB, WA (KEH)*

N900KA	de Havilland DHC-2 Turbo Beaver III	1676	ex LN-BFH
N1018F	de Havilland DHC-2 Beaver	710	ex N62SJ
N1018U	de Havilland DHC-2 Beaver	1381	ex 58-2049
N1455T	de Havilland DHC-2 Turbo Beaver III	1647/TB26	ex CF-OEI

N2513N	de Havilland DHC-2 Beaver	1521	ex C-FTPH	
N2516D	de Havilland DHC-2 Beaver	1519	ex C-FASF	
N6781L	de Havilland DHC-2 Beaver	788	ex N10LU	
N6782L	de Havilland DHC-2 Beaver	820	ex N23LU	
N9271Z	de Havilland DHC-2 Beaver	1380	ex 58-2048	
N9744T	de Havilland DHC-2 Turbo Beaver III	1692/TB60	ex N1944	
N9766Z	de Havilland DHC-2 Beaver	504	ex N13454	
N17598	de Havilland DHC-2 Beaver	1129	ex VP-FAH	
N25149	de Havilland DHC-2 Beaver	1520	ex C-FASY	
N72355	de Havilland DHC-2 Beaver	1164	ex N62355	
N50KA	de Havilland DHC-3 Turbo Otter	221	ex IM-1720	
N58JH	de Havilland DHC-3 Otter	131	ex N8510Q	
N87KA	de Havilland DHC-3 Turbo Otter	11	ex N8262V	
(N707KA)	de Havilland DHC-3 Otter	106	ex N888KA	
N3125S	de Havilland DHC-3 Turbo Otter	407	ex N9424	
N90422	de Havilland DHC-3 Turbo Otter	152	ex 55-3296	Expedia.com titles
All floatplanes				

KETCHUM AIR SERVICE

Anchorage-Lake Hood, AK

N340KA	de Havilland DHC-2 Beaver	1127	ex N1018N	
N342KA	de Havilland DHC-3 Turbo Otter	465	ex N32910	
N345KA	de Havilland DHC-2 Beaver	1306	ex N67678	
N756QG	Cessna U206G Stationair 6	U20604267		
N836KA	de Havilland DHC-2 Beaver	604	ex N727KA	Lsd fr ATS Leasing
N8340Q	Cessna U206F Stationair	U20603201		
N62469	de Havilland DHC-2 Beaver	1237	ex 57-6147	

KEY LIME AIR

Key Lime (LYM)

Denver-Centennial, CO (DEN)

N60U	Swearingen SA.226TC Metro II	TC-232	ex N5389M		Lsd fr EDB Air
N62Z	Swearingen SA.226TC Metro II	TC-237	ex N5437M		Lsd fr EDB Air
N332BA	Swearingen SA.226TC Metro II	TC-222E	ex N639S	Freighter	
N509SS	Swearingen SA.226TC Metro II	TC-206	ex N261S		Lsd fr EDB Air
N770S	Swearingen SA.226TC Metro II	TC-248			Lsd fr EDB Air
N81418	Swearingen SA.226TC Metro II	TC-223	ex EC-GNM		
N411BJ	Piper PA-31-350 Navajo Chieftain	31-7952043			Lsd fr EDB Air
N3549X	Piper PA-31-350 Chieftain	31-8052034	ex C-FAWT		Lsd fr EDB Air
N9247L	Piper PA-31-350 Chieftain	31-8152160			Lsd fr EDB Air
N27989	Piper PA-31-350 Navajo Chieftain	31-7952077			Lsd fr EDB Air
N66906	Piper PA-31-350 Navajo Chieftain	31-7405197			
N74952	Piper PA-31-350 Navajo Chieftain	31-7305100			Lsd fr Western Aero
N27BJ	Lear Jet 24B	24B-227	ex N28AT		
N340AE	Swearingen SA.227AC Metro III	AC-510	ex N3108E		Lsd fr GAS/Wilson
N404MG	Cessna 404	404-0813			Lsd fr Western Aero
N787KL	Swearingen SA.227BC Metro III	BC-787B	ex XA-SAQ		Lsd fr EDB Air
N882DC	Swearingen SA.227DC Metro 23	DC-882	ex C-GAFQ		Lsd fr EDB Air
N2691W	Swearingen SA.227AC Metro III	AC-655B			Lsd fr EDB Air

KING AIRELINES

Las Vegas-Henderson Executive, NV (HSH)

N1570U	Cessna 207 Skywagon	20700170	
N1783U	Cessna T207A Turbo Skywagon	20700383	
N3156X	Cessna T207 Turbo Skywagon	20700376	
N3728B	Cessna T207 Turbo Skywagon	20700298	
N70437	Cessna 207A Stationair 7	20700552	
N73320	Cessna T207A Turbo Stationair 7	20700577	
N57SA	Cessna 402A	402A0101	ex N7801Q
N69PB	Cessna 402B	402B1248	
N82TA	Cessna 402	402-0156	
N99AT	Cessna 402A	402A0022	
N402SW	Cessna 402	402-0036	ex N8236Q
N2966Q	Cessna 402B	402B0321	
N3278Q	Cessna 402	402-0078	
N4010Q	Cessna 402	402-0110	
N5098G	Cessna 402A	402A0056	
N5210J	Cessna 402B	402B0897	
N9901F	Cessna 402B	402B0402	
N69341	Cessna 402B	402B0449	

N8467Q	Cessna U206F Stationair	U20603325
N8564Q	Cessna U206F Stationair	U20603420
N8785Q	Cessna TU206G Stationair	U20603537

All registered to Skyventure LLC

KING FLYING SERVICE

Naknek, AK (NNK)

| N38186 | Piper PA-32-300 Cherokee Six | 32-7740077 |
| N44851 | Piper PA-32-300 Cherokee Six | 32-7740107 |

KITTY HAWK AIR CARGO

Air Kittyhawk (KR/KHA)

Dallas-Fort Forth, TX (DFW)

N90AX	Boeing 727-222F	729/20040	ex N7646U	stored ROW	
N180AX	Boeing 727-222F	732/20041	ex N7647U	stored ROW	
N252US*	Boeing 727-251F	655/19971			
N255US	Boeing 727-251F	667/19974			
N264US	Boeing 727-251F	741/19983		stored TUS	Lsd fr Pegasus
N278US*	Boeing 727-251F	1173/21157			
N279US*	Boeing 727-251F	1177/21158			
N281KH*	Boeing 727-2J0F	1158/21105	ex 6Y-JMM		
N284KH*	Boeing 727-2J0F	1174/21108	ex 6Y-JMP		
N579PE	Boeing 727-243F	1421/21662	ex (N10409)		Lsd fr ART 21662
N854AA*	Boeing 727-223F	1192/20995			
N750US	Boeing 727-214F	1343/21512	ex N555PS		
N751US	Boeing 727-214F	1365/21513	ex N556PS		
N855AA*	Boeing 727-223F	1193/20996		stored ROW	
N856AA	Boeing 727-223F	1195/20997			
N858AA	Boeing 727-223F	1200/21085			
N916PG	Boeing 727-287F	1469/21690	ex CC-CSK	std ROW	Lsd fr ART 21690
N936PG	Boeing 727-222F	1695/22441	ex F-GKDZ		Lsd fr ART 22441
N1269Y	Boeing 727-2A1F	1230/21269	ex OY-SEU		
N6806	Boeing 727-223F	548/19481	ex N719CK		
N6807	Boeing 727-223F	557/19482	ex N729CK	stored DFW	
N6808	Boeing 727-223F	558/19483	ex (N744CK)	stored ROW	
N6809*	Boeing 727-223F	560/19484			
N6810	Boeing 727-223F	571/19485	ex N722CK	stored ROW	
N6812	Boeing 727-223F	579/19487	ex N720CK		
N6816	Boeing 727-223F	611/19491		stored ROW	Lsd to BAX
N6821	Boeing 727-223F	669/19496	ex N706CA		
N6827*	Boeing 727-223F	698/20180		stored ROW	
N6831	Boeing 727-223F	707/20184			Lsd to BAX
N6833*	Boeing 727-223F	721/20186			
N6838	Boeing 727-223F	739/20191	ex N723CK	stored ROW	
N69735	Boeing 727-224F	1079/20664		stored ROW	
N69739*	Boeing 727-224F	1153/20667			
N69740*	Boeing 727-224F	1154/20668			
N77780	Boeing 727-232F	918/20635	ex N13780	stored ROW	
N79748	Boeing 727-224F	1760/22450			Lsd fr Art 22450 LLC

All fitted with FedEx Stage 3 hushkits   *Leased from Kitty Hawk Collateral Liquidating Trust

| N563PC | Douglas DC-9-15RC (ABS 3) | 194/47055 | ex N1305T | | Lsd fr Century A/L |
| N564PC | Douglas DC-9-15RC (ABS 3) | 223/47062 | ex N1307T | stored VCV | Lsd fr Aircraft Lsg |

Associated with Martinaire; subsidiary of Kitty Hawk Inc.

KNIGHTHAWK EXPRESS

Rizz (KHX)

Boston-Logan Intl, MA (BOS)

| N63TT | Piper PA-31-350 Chieftain | 31-8152026 | Lsd fr United Business Jet A/c |

LAB FLYING SERVICE

LAB (JF/LAB)

Juneau-Intl, AK/Haines-Municipal, AK (JNU/HNS)

N23LA	Piper PA-32-300 Cherokee Six	32-7840045	
N54KA	Piper PA-32-300 Cherokee Six	32-7840197	
N666EB	Piper PA-32-300 Six	32-7940115	ex N2116G
N2181Z	Piper PA-32-300 Six	32-7940104	
N2897X	Piper PA-32-300 Six	32-7940187	
N2930Q	Piper PA-32R-300 Lance	32R-7780269	
N3957X	Piper PA-32-300 Cherokee Six	32-7640003	
N4485X	Piper PA-32-300 Cherokee Six	32-7640026	
N5686V	Piper PA-32R-300 Lance	32R-7780361	
N6117J	Piper PA-32-300 Cherokee Six	32-7640095	
N6968J	Piper PA-32R-300 Lance	32R-7680397	
N7718C	Piper PA-32-300 Cherokee Six	32-7640049	

N8127Q	Piper PA-32-300 Six	32-7940269		
N8493C	Piper PA-32R-300 Lance	32R-7680118		
N9795C	Piper PA-32-300 Cherokee Six	32-7840118		
N39636	Piper PA-32-300 Cherokee Six	32-7840172		
N3523Y	Piper PA-31-350 Navajo Chieftain	31-7952115		
N3835Z	Britten-Norman BN-2A-26 Islander	2010	ex G-BEJW	Lsd fr L&A Bennett Fouth Family LP
N7333L	Piper PA-34-200T Seneca II	34-7670099		
N27513	Piper PA-31-350 Navajo Chieftain	31-7852033		
N29884	Britten-Norman BN-2A-26 Islander	847	ex G-BESH	Lsd fr L&A Bennett Fouth Family LP
N54732	Piper PA-31-350 Navajo Chieftain	31-7405254		

Operates services in conjunction with Alaska Airlines using AS flight numbers in the range 4400-4499

LAKE & PENINSULA AIRLINES

Port Alsworth, AK (PTA)

N9602F	Cessna U206G Stationair 6	U20606740	Floats/Wheels or skis
N9909Z	Cessna 208 Caravan 1	20800103	

LAKE CLARK AIR

Port Alsworth, AK (PTA)

N76RA	Piper PA-31-350 Navajo Chieftain	31-7752089	
N200VF	Piper PA-31-350 Navajo Chieftain	31-7405445	
N206AR	Cessna U206G Stationair 6	U20604766	ex N733GH
N733KD	Cessna U206G Stationair 6	U20604772	Floatplane
N8300Q	Cessna U206F Stationair	U20603161	Floatplane
N27231	Piper PA-31-350 Navajo Chieftain	31-7752106	
N70076	Cessna 207A Stationair 7	20700547	
N91028	Cessna 207 Skywagon	20700019	

LAKE MEAD AIR

Boulder City-Municipal, NV (BLD)

N70Y	Cessna U206B Super Skywagon	U206-0828	ex N701
N2082U	Cessna U206F Stationair	U20602327	
N3259R	Cessna U206F Stationair	U20602215	
N3467L	Cessna U206B Super Skywagon	U206-0767	
N4769U	Cessna TU206G Stationair 6	U20605093	ex VH-WDZ
N5337U	Cessna TU206G Stationair 6	U20605218	
N9681G	Cessna U206F Stationair	U20601881	
N72218	Cessna U206D Super Skywagon	U206-1328	
N801AN	Cessna 207A Stationair	20700640	ex N111LS
N1653U	Cessna 207 Super Skywagon	20700253	
N1675U	Cessna T207 Super Skywagon	20700275	
N6328H	Cessna T207A Turbo Stationair 7	20700485	
N6427H	Cessna T207A Turbo Stationair 7	20700522	
N6460H	Cessna T207A Turbo Stationair 7	20700530	
N9100D	Cessna 207 Skywagon	20700001	ex N91000
N73445	Cessna 207A Stationair 7	20700591	
N73612	Cessna T207A Turbo Stationair 8	20700608	
N91038	Cessna 207 Super Skywagon	20700027	
N2138S	Cessna T210L Turbo Centurion	21061099	

All leased from Riffey Co

LAKELAND AIR TRANSPORT

Lakeland, FL

N267AS	Embraer EMB.120RT Brasilia	120198	ex PT-SRO

LARRY'S FLYING SERVICE

(J6) *Fairbanks-Intl, AK (FAI)*

N1824Q	Cessna 207A Stationair 8	20700788
N4375B	Piper PA-32R-301 Saratoga SP	32R-8413023
N9243K	Piper PA-32R-300 Lance	32R-7680201
N9996M	Cessna 207A Stationair 8	20700779
N27501	Piper PA-31-359 Navajo Chieftain	31-7852028
N31657	Piper PA-32-300 Cherokee Six	32-7840139

LEGEND AIRWAYS OF COLORADO

Denver-Centennial, CO (DIA)

N341A	Douglas DC-3	2145	ex N14RD
N25641	Douglas DC-3	9059	ex 42-32833

LINEAS AEREA PUERTORIQUENA

San Juan-Muzon Marin Intl, PR (SJU)

N127LB	Britten-Norman BN-2A Mk.III-2 Trislander	1010	ex DQ-FCG	w/o Sep95, status?
N650LP	Britten-Norman BN-2A Mk.III-2 Trislander	1029	ex VQ-TAD	
N7094T	Britten-Norman BN-2A-21	643	ex C-GPAB	
Current status is uncertain				

LINDSAY AVIATION

Lindsay Air (LSY)   *Buffalo-Intl, NY (BUF)*

N85DS	Cessna 310Q	310Q0080
N310SA	Cessna 310R II	310R1565
N1852E	Cessna 310R II	310R1587
N2640F	Cessna 310R II	310R1676
N3376G	Cessna 310R II	310R0818
N6096C	Cessna 310R II	310R1263
N8669G	Cessna 310R II	310R0948
N37289	Cessna 310R II	310R1203

LONE STAR CONTRACT AIR CARGO

Port Isabel-Cameron County, TX

N3427	Convair 340	90		Freighter	Lsd fr Aviones Inc
N7813B	Convair 340	265	ex 53-7813	Freighter	Lsd fr Aviones Inc

LYNCH FLYING SERVICE now listed under trading name Edwards Jet Center of Montana

LYNDEN AIR CARGO

Lynden (L2/LYC)   *Anchorage-Intl, AK (ANC)*

N401LC	Lockheed L-100-30 Hercules	4606	ex ZS-RSJ
N402LC	Lockheed L-100-30 Hercules	4698	ex ZS-JJA
N403LC	Lockheed L-100-30 Hercules	4590	ex N903SJ
N404LC	Lockheed L-100-30 Hercules	4763	ex N909SJ
N405LC	Lockheed L-100-30 Hercules	5025	ex ZS-OLG

LYNX AIR INTERNATIONAL

Lynx Flight (LXF)   *Fort Lauderdale-Hollwood Intl, FL (FLL)*

N61NE	Swearingen SA.227AC Metro III	AC-761B	Lsd fr LAI Lsg
N63NE	Swearingen SA.227AC Metro III	AC-763B	Lsd fr Textron Financial
N5441F	Swearingen SA.227AC Metro III	AC-528	Lsd fr North Delaware Corp

MAC DAN AVIATION

Mac Dan (MCN)   *Caldwell-Essex County, NJ (CDW)*

N99EF	Cessna 414A Chancellor III	414A0666		Lsd fr Urban Transportation
N186DD	Beech 65-F90 King Air	LA-83	ex N771JB	
N245JS	Beech 200 Super King Air	BB-693	ex N60SQ	
N718MA	Cessna 310Q	310Q1153	ex N1312G	
N1537T	Cessna 421B Golden Eagle	421B0307		
N1921G	Cessna 310R	310R0062		
N2651S	Cessna 402C	402C0342		
N3237W	Cessna 310R	310R0070		
N32211	Beech 65-C90B King Air	LJ-1581		
N69610	Cessna 310R	310R0102		
Associated with Primac Courier (PMC), Teterboro, NJ				

MAJESTIC AIR CARGO ceased operations

M & N AVIATION

(W4)   *San Juan-Munoz Marin Intl, PR (SJU)*

N405MN	Cessna 402C	402C0221	ex N2717B
N408MN	Cessna 208B Caravan I	208B0830	

N409MN	Cessna 208B Caravan I	208B0846	
N1131G	Cessna 208B Caravan I	208B0661	Lsd fr M&N Aviation
N1241X	Cessna 208B Caravan I	208B0657	Lsd fr First Capital Group

MARTINAIRE

Martex (MRA) — *Dallas-Addison, TX (ADS)*

N1031P	Cessna 208B Caravan I	208B0404		Lsd fr Avion Capital
N1116W	Cessna 208B Caravan I	208B0411		Lsd fr Avion Capital
N4591B	Cessna 208B Caravan I	208B0137	ex (N997FE)	
N4602B	Cessna 208B Caravan I	208B0140	ex (N999FE)	
N4625B	Cessna 208B Caravan I	208B0159		
N4655B	Cessna 208B Caravan I	208B0160		
N4662B	Cessna 208B Caravan I	208B0161		
N4687B	Cessna 208B Caravan I	208B0167		
N9331B	Cessna 208B Caravan I	208B0055	ex (N995FE)	
N9469B	Cessna 208B Caravan I	208B0079		
N9471B	Cessna 208B Caravan I	208B0081		
N9505B	Cessna 208B Caravan I	208B0085		
N9546B	Cessna 208B Caravan I	208B0126		
N9623B	Cessna 208B Caravan I	208B0138		
N9714B	Cessna 208B Caravan I	208B0153		
N9738B	Cessna 208B Caravan I	208B0097		
N9760B	Cessna 208B Caravan I	208B0102		
N9761B	Cessna 208B Caravan I	208B0107		
N9762B	Cessna 208B Caravan I	208B0109		
N9766B	Cessna 208B Caravan I	208B0112		
N9956B	Cessna 208B Caravan I	208B0119		

MAY AIR X-PRESS

Beechnut (MXP) — *Dallas-Love Field, TX (DAL)*

| N25646 | Douglas DC-3 | 2234 | ex NC25646 |

MCCALL & WILDERNESS AIR

McCall, ID

N555JA	Britten-Norman BN-2A Islander	20	ex N585JA
N634MA	Britten-Norman BN-2A-20 Islander	464	ex C-GEVX
N848MA	Britten-Norman BN-2B-20 Islander	2210	ex 8P-TAJ

MCNEELY CHARTER SERVICE

Mid-South(MDS) — *West Memphis-Municipal, AR/Malden, MO (AWM/MAW)*

N32EC	Mitsubishi MU-2N	699SA	ex N859MA
N103RC	Mitsubishi MU-2L	673	ex N4565E
N106GA	Beech Baron 58	TH-437	
N120SC	Swearingen SA.226TC Merlin IVA	AT-067	ex C-FJTL
N212SA	Cessna 208B Caravan I	208B0466	
N262AG	Short SD.3-30	SH3120	ex 84-0473
N700RH	Cessna 208B Caravan I	208B0700	
N856JC	Mitsubishi MU-2B	430SA	ex N170MA
N866D	Mitsubishi MU-2L	656	ex N666D
N2699Y	Swearingen SA.227AC Metro III	AC-666	

All leased from River City Aviation

MERCAIR current status is uncertain and believed to have ceased operations

MERLIN AIRWAYS

Avalon (MEI) — *Billings-Logan Intl, MT (BIL)*

N364AE	Swearingen SA.227AC Metro III	AC-679			Lsd fr Finova
N378PH	Swearingen SA.227AC Metro III	AC-575	ex N3114X		Lsd fr Molo Lsg
N445MA	Swearingen SA.227AC Metro III	AC-687B	ex N455AM		Lsd fr Molo Lsg
N446MA	Swearingen SA.227AC Metro III	AC-693B	ex N456AM		Lsd fr Molo Lsg
N768ML	Swearingen SA.227BC Metro III	BC-768B	ex XA-SBN		Lsd fr Molo Lsg
N770ML	Swearingen SA.227BC Metro III	BC-770B	ex XA-RWS		Lsd fr Molo Lsg
N781ML	Swearingen SA.227BC Metro III	BC-781B	ex XA-RYY		Lsd fr Molo Lsg
N783ML	Swearingen SA.227BC Metro III	BC-783B	ex XA-RSB		Lsd fr Molo Lsg
N787C	Swearingen SA.227AC Metro III	AC-550	ex N31110		Lsd fr GAS/Wilson
N1119K	Swearingen SA.227DC Metro 23	DC-830B	ex XA-TFF	stored BIL	Lsd fr Textron Financial
N3114G	Swearingen SA.227AC Metro III	AC-583			Lsd fr GAS Wilson
N27188	Swearingen SA.227AC Metro III	AC-708B			Lsd fr Molo Lsg

All freighters

MESA AIRLINES

Air Shuttle (YV/ASH)   Phoenix-Sky Harbor Intl, AZ/Albuquerque-Intl, NM (PHX/ABQ)

N3YV	Beech 1900D	UE-3			Lsd to AMW
N5YV	Beech 1900D	UE-5			Lsd to AMW
N6YV	Beech 1900D	UE-6			Lsd to AMW
N13ZV	Beech 1900D	UE-13			Lsd to AMW
N15YV	Beech 1900D	UE-15			Lsd to AMW
N23YV	Beech 1900D	UE-23			Lsd to AMW
N26YV	Beech 1900D	UE-26			Lsd to AMW
N95YV	Beech 1900D	UE-95			Lsd to AMW
N98YV	Beech 1900D	UE-98		stored INT	Lsd to AMW
N99YV	Beech 1900D	UE-99			Lsd to AMW
N104YV	Beech 1900D	UE-104			Lsd to AMW
N105YV	Beech 1900D	UE-105			Lsd to AMW
N110YV	Beech 1900D	UE-110			Lsd to AMW
N112ZV	Beech 1900D	UE-112			Lsd to AMW
N114YV	Beech 1900D	UE-114			Lsd to AMW
N123YV	Beech 1900D	UE-123			Lsd to AMW
N124YV	Beech 1900D	UE-124		stored INT	Lsd to AMW
N125YV	Beech 1900D	UE-125			Lsd to AMW
N126YV	Beech 1900D	UE-126		stored SLN	Lsd to AMW
N131YV	Beech 1900D	UE-131			Lsd to AMW
N132YV	Beech 1900D	UE-132		stored MCO	Lsd to AMW
N133YV	Beech 1900D	UE-133			Lsd to AMW
N135YV	Beech 1900D	UE-135			Lsd to AMW
N138YV	Beech 1900D	UE-138			Lsd to AMW
N139ZV	Beech 1900D	UE-139			Lsd to AMW
N140ZV	Beech 1900D	UE-140	ex (N137ZV)		Lsd to AMW
N142YV	Beech 1900D	UE-142		stored MCO	Lsd to AMW
N143YV	Beech 1900D	UE-143			Lsd to AMW
N144ZV	Beech 1900D	UE-144			Lsd to AMW
N146ZV	Beech 1900D	UE-146			Lsd to AMW
N155ZV	Beech 1900D	UE-155			Lsd to AMW
N159YV	Beech 1900D	UE-159			Lsd to AMW
N161YV	Beech 1900D	UE-161			Lsd to AMW
N162ZV	Beech 1900D	UE-162			Lsd to AMW
N163YV	Beech 1900D	UE-163			Lsd to AMW
N165YV	Beech 1900D	UE-165			Lsd to AMW
N166YV	Beech 1900D	UE-166			Lsd to AMW
N167YV	Beech 1900D	UE-167			Lsd to AMW
N171ZV	Beech 1900D	UE-171			Lsd to AMW
N173YV	Beech 1900D	UE-173			Lsd to AMW
N174YV	Beech 1900D	UE-174	ex N17541		Lsd to AMW
N176YV	Beech 1900D	UE-176			Lsd to AMW
N178YV	Beech 1900D	UE-178			Lsd to AMW
N190YV	Beech 1900D	UE-190			Lsd to AMW
N218YV	Beech 1900D	UE-218			Lsd to AMW
N231YV	Beech 1900D	UE-231			Lsd to AMW
N237YV	Beech 1900D	UE-237			Lsd to AMW
N242YV	Beech 1900D	UE-242			Lsd to AMW
N244YV	Beech 1900D	UE-244			Lsd to AMW
N3199Q	Beech 1900D	UE-213			Lsd to AMW
N10675	Beech 1900D	UE-229			Lsd to AMW

N501MJ*	Canadair CL-600-2C10	10047	ex C-FZVM	all-white	
N508MJ	Canadair CL-600-2C10	10087	ex C-		Lsd fr WFBN
N510MJ	Canadair CL-600-2C10	10101	ex C-	United Express	Lsd fr WFBN
N512MJ	Canadair CL-600-2C10	10109	ex C-	United Express	
N513MJ	Canadair CL-600-2C10	10111	ex C-	United Express	
N514MJ	Canadair CL-600-2C10	10116	ex C-	United Express	
N515MJ	Canadair CL-600-2C10	10117	ex C-	United Express	

*Used for either United Express or America West Express

N434YV	de Havilland DHC-8-202	434	ex C-GDNG	YDB, US Airways Express
N436YV	de Havilland DHC-8-202	436	ex C-GDNG	America West Express
N437YV	de Havilland DHC-8-202	437	ex C-FDHD	America West Express
N444YV	de Havilland DHC-8Q-202	444	ex C-GFRP	America West Express
N445YV	de Havilland DHC-8Q-202	445	ex C-GFEN	America West Express
N446YV	de Havilland DHC-8Q-202	446	ex C-GEOA	America West Express
N447YV	de Havilland DHC-8Q-202	447	ex C-GFYI	America West Express
N448YV	de Havilland DHC-8Q-202	448	ex C-GLOT	United Express
N449YV	de Havilland DHC-8Q-202	449	ex C-GFHZ	America West Express
N454YV	de Havilland DHC-8Q-202	454	ex C-	America West Express
N455YV	de Havilland DHC-8Q-202	455	ex C-	America West Express
N456YV	de Havilland DHC-8Q-202	456	ex C-GFOD	America West Express

Three more to be assigned to United Express for operations from Denver

N825MJ*	Embraer EMB.145LR	145179	YRA, US Airways Express
N826MJ*	Embraer EMB.145LR	145214	YRB, US Airways Express

N827MJ*	Embraer EMB.145LR	145217		YRC, US Airways Express
N828MJ*	Embraer EMB.145LR	145218		YRD, US Airways Express
N829MJ*	Embraer EMB.145LR	145228	ex PT-SHQ	YRE, US Airways Express
N830MJ*	Embraer EMB.145LR	145259	ex PT-SIS	YRF, US Airways Express
N831MJ*	Embraer EMB.145LR	145273	ex PT-SJP	YRG, US Airways Express
N832MJ*	Embraer EMB.145LR	145310	ex PT-SMB	YRH, US Airways Express
N833MJ*	Embraer EMB.145LR	145327	ex PT-SMT	YRI, US Airways Express
N834MJ*	Embraer EMB.145LR	145340	ex PT-SNG	YRJ, US Airways Express
N835MJ*	Embraer EMB.145LR	145353	ex PT-SNS	YRK, US Airways Express
N836MJ*	Embraer EMB.145LR	145359	ex PT-SNY	YRL, US Airways Express
N837MJ*	Embraer EMB.145LR	145367	ex PT-SOR	YRM, US Airways Express
N838MJ	Embraer EMB.145LR	145384	ex PT-SQI	YRN, US Airways Express
N839MJ	Embraer EMB.145LR	145416	ex PT-STM	YRO, US Airways Express
N840MJ	Embraer EMB.145LR	145429	ex PT-SUA	YRP, US Airways Express
N841MJ	Embraer EMB.145LR	145448	ex PT-SUT	YRR, US Airways Express
N842MJ*	Embraer EMB.145LR	145457	ex PT-SVC	YRS, US Airways Express
N843MJ*	Embraer EMB.145LR	145478	ex PT-SVX	YRT, US Airways Express
N844MJ*	Embraer EMB.145LR	145481	ex PT-SXA	YRU, US Airways Express
N845MJ*	Embraer EMB.145LR	145502	ex PT-SXV	YRV, US Airways Express
N846MJ*	Embraer EMB.145LR	145507	ex PT-SXZ	YRW, US Airways Express
N847MJ*	Embraer EMB.145LR	145517	ex PT-SYI	YRX, US Airways Express
N848MJ*	Embraer EMB.145LR	145530	ex PT-STU	YRY, US Airways Express
N849MJ*	Embraer EMB.145LR	145534	ex PT-STY	YRZ, US Airways Express
N850MJ*	Embraer EMB.145LR	145568	ex PT-SBE	YSA, US Airways Express
N851MJ*	Embraer EMB.145LR	145572	ex PT-S	YSB, US Airways Express
N852MJ*	Embraer EMB.145LR	145567	ex PT-SBD	YSC, US Airways Express
N853MJ*	Embraer EMB.145ER	145464	ex PT-SVJ	YSD, US Airways Express
N854MJ*	Embraer EMB.145ER	145490	ex PT-SXJ	YSE, US Airways Express
N855MJ*	Embraer EMB.145LR	145614	ex PT-SCZ	YSF, US Airways Express
N856MJ	Embraer EMB.145LR	145626	ex PT-SDO	YSG, US Airways Express
N857MJ	Embraer EMB.145LR	145765	ex PT-SJW	US Airways Express
N858MJ	Embraer EMB.145LR	145767	ex PT-SJY	US Airways Express
N859MJ	Embraer EMB.145LR	145769	ex PT-SMA	US Airways Express
N860MJ	Embraer EMB.145LR	145773	ex PT-SMD	US Airways Express

*Leased from Wells Fargo Bank Northwest

N7264V	Canadair CL-600-2B19	7264			Lsd fr WFBN
N7291Z	Canadair CL-600-2B19	7291			Lsd fr WFBN
N7305V	Canadair CL-600-2B19	7305			Lsd fr WFBN
N17156	Canadair CL-600-2B19	7156	ex C-FZSC	US Airways Express	Lsd fr WFBN
N17217	Canadair CL-600-2B19	7217		United Express	Lsd fr WFBN
N17231	Canadair CL-600-2B19	7231			Lsd fr WFBN
N17275	Canadair CL-600-2B19	7275	ex C-FMQI		Lsd fr WFBN
N17337	Canadair CL-600-2B19	7337			Lsd fr WFBN
N17358	Canadair CL-600-2B19	7358	ex C-FMNY		Lsd fr WFBN
N27172	Canadair CL-600-2B19	7172			Lsd fr WFBN
N27173	Canadair CL-600-2B19	7173			Lsd fr WFBN
N27185	Canadair CL-600-2B19	7185		US Airways Express	Lsd fr WFBN
N27191	Canadair CL-600-2B19	7191		US Airways Express	Lsd fr WFBN
N27314	Canadair CL-600-2B19	7314	ex C-FMKV		Lsd fr WFBN
N27318	Canadair CL-600-2B19	7318	ex C-FMLF		Lsd fr WFBN
N37178	Canadair CL-600-2B19	7178	ex C-GAVO		Lsd fr WFBN
N37208	Canadair CL-600-2B19	7208	ex C-FMNY		Lsd fr WFBN
N37218	Canadair CL-600-2B19	7218			Lsd fr WFBN
N37228	Canadair CL-600-2B19	7228	ex C-FMLF		Lsd fr WFBN
N37342	Canadair CL-600-2B19	7342	ex C-FMMY		Lsd fr WFBN
N47202	Canadair CL-600-2B19	7202		US Airways Express	Lsd fr WFBN
N47239	Canadair CL-600-2B19	7239			Lsd fr WFBN
N75983	Canadair CL-600-2B19	7481	ex C-FZUK		Lsd fr WFBN
N75984	Canadair CL-600-2B19	7489	ex C-GZGX	US Airways Express	Lsd fr WFBN
N75987	Canadair CL-600-2B19	7405	ex C-FZSZ	US Airways Express	Lsd fr WFBN
N75991	Canadair CL-600-2B19	7422	ex C-FZSY	US Airways Express	Lsd fr WFBN
N75992	Canadair CL-600-2B19	7401	ex C-FZTH	US Airways Express	Lsd fr WFBN
N75993	Canadair CL-600-2B19	7372	ex C-FZTT	US Airways Express	Lsd fr WFBN
N75994	Canadair CL-600-2B19	7367	ex C-FZTY	US Airways Express	Lsd fr WFBN
N75998	Canadair CL-600-2B19	7336	ex C-FZTU	US Airways Express	Lsd fr WFBN
N75999	Canadair CL-600-2B19	7471	ex C-FSXX	US Airways Express	Lsd fr WFBN
N	Canadair CL-600-2B19	7357	ex C-FZTZ	on order	
N	Canadair CL-600-2B19	7361	ex C-FZTW	on order	
N77181	Canadair CL-600-2B19	7181		US Airways Express	Lsd fr WFBN
N77195	Canadair CL-600-2B19	7195	ex C-FMKV	all-white	Lsd fr WFBN
N77260	Canadair CL-600-2B19	7260	ex C-FMLQ		Lsd fr WFBN
N77278	Canadair CL-600-2B19	7278	ex C-FMMN		Lsd fr WFBN
N77286	Canadair CL-600-2B19	7286	ex C-FMKZ		Lsd fr WFBN
N77302	Canadair CL-600-2B19	7302			Lsd fr WFBN
N77331	Canadair CL-600-2B19	7331	ex C-FVAZ	all-white	Lsd fr WFBN
N87353	Canadair CL-600-2B19	7353	ex C-FMLV		Lsd fr WFBN
N97325	Canadair CL-600-2B19	7325	ex C-		Lsd fr WFBN

Operated by Mesa Airlines; some are operated in Mesa colours; some also operated for Frontier by Freedom Air (a wholly owned division). A total of 25 are to be opeated for United Express by December 2004 alongside 59 for US Airways Express by early 2004

N501MJ	Canadair CL-600-2C10	10047	ex C-FZVM	all-ahite
N502MJ*	Canadair CL-600-2C10	10050	ex C-GIAO	
N503MJ*	Canadair CL-600-2C10	10058	ex C-GIBG	
N504MJ*	Canadair CL-600-2C10	10066	ex C-GIBR	
N505MJ*	Canadair CL-600-2C10	10070	ex C-GICN	
N506MJ*	Canadair CL-600-2C10	10073	ex C-GHZY	
N507MJ*	Canadair CL-600-2C10	10077	ex C-GIAH	
N508MJ*	Canadair CL-600-2C10	10087	ex C-	
N509MJ	Canadair CL-600-2C10	10094	ex C-	United Express
N510MJ	Canadair CL-600-2C10	10101	ex C-	United Express
N511MJ	Canadair CL-600-2C10	10104	ex C-	United Express
N512MJ	Canadair CL-600-2C10	10109	ex C-	United Express
N513MJ	Canadair CL-600-2C10	10111	ex C-	United Express
N514MJ*	Canadair CL-600-2C10	10116	ex C-	
N515MJ*	Canadair CL-600-2C10	10117	ex C-	

*Operated for America West by Freedom Airlines (a wholly owned division); a total of ten are to be transferred to United Express and 15 to be operated by December 2004 along with 15 CRJ-200s

N902FJ	Canadair CL-600-2D24	15002	ex C-GDNH	Lsd fr WFBN
N903FJ	Canadair CL-600-2D24	15003	ex C-GZQA	
N904FJ	Canadair CL-600-2D24	15004	ex C-GZQB	
N905J	Canadair CL-600-2D24	15005	ex C-GZQC	
N906FJ	Canadair CL-600-2D24	15006	ex C-GZQE	
N907FJ	Canadair CL-600-2D24	15007	ex C-GZQF	
N908FJ	Canadair CL-600-2D24	15008	ex C-GZQG	
N909FJ	Canadair CL-600-2D24	15009	ex C-GZQI	
N910FJ	Canadair CL-600-2D24	15010	ex C-GZQJ	
N911FJ	Canadair CL-600-2D24	15011	ex C-GZQK	
N912FJ	Canadair CL-600-2D24	15012	ex C-	
N913FJ	Canadair CL-600-2D24	15013	ex C-	
N914FJ	Canadair CL-600-2D24	15014	ex C-	
N	Canadair CL-600-2D24		ex C-	on order 04
N	Canadair CL-600-2D24		ex C-	on order 04
N	Canadair CL-600-2D24		ex C-	on order 04
N	Canadair CL-600-2D24		ex C-	on order 04
N	Canadair CL-600-2D24		ex C-	on order 04
N	Canadair CL-600-2D24		ex C-	on order 04

Five more are on order for delivery in 2005; some are believed operated by Freedom Airlines
Divided into divisions aligned to code-share partners as follows: America West A/L, Frontier, United Express and US Airways Express while Air Midwest continue to operate Beech 1900Ds as subsidiary, some in Mesa A/L colours.

MESABA AIRLINES

Mesaba (MES)   Minneapolis-St Paul Int, MN (MSP)

N501XJ	Avro RJ85	E2208	ex G-ISEE	501	Lsd fr BAES
N502XJ	Avro RJ85	E2307	ex G-6-307	502	Lsd fr BAES
N503XJ	Avro RJ85	E2310	ex G-6-310	503	Lsd fr BAES
N504XJ	Avro RJ85	E2311	ex G-6-311	504	Lsd fr BAES
N505XJ	Avro RJ85	E2313	ex G-6-313	505	Lsd fr BAES
N506XJ	Avro RJ85	E2314	ex G-6-314	506	Lsd fr BAES
N507XJ	Avro RJ85	E2316	ex G-6-316	507	Lsd fr BAES
N508XJ	Avro RJ85	E2318	ex G-6-318	508	Lsd fr BAES
N509XJ	Avro RJ85	E2321	ex G-6-321	509	Lsd fr BAES
N510XJ	Avro RJ85	E2323	ex G-6-323	510	Lsd fr BAES
N511XJ	Avro RJ85	E2325	ex G-6-325	511	Lsd fr BAES
N512XJ	Avro RJ85	E2326	ex G-6-326	512	Lsd fr BAES
N513XJ	Avro RJ85	E2329	ex G-6-329	513	Lsd fr BAES
N514XJ	Avro RJ85	E2330	ex G-6-330	514	Lsd fr BAES
N515XJ	Avro RJ85	E2333	ex G-6-333	515	Lsd fr BAES
N516XJ	Avro RJ85	E2334	ex G-6-334	516	Lsd fr BAES
N517XJ	Avro RJ85	E2335	ex G-6-335	517	Lsd fr BAES
N518XJ	Avro RJ85	E2337	ex G-6-337	518	Lsd fr BAES
N519XJ	Avro RJ85	E2344	ex G-6-344	519	Lsd fr BAES
N520XJ	Avro RJ85	E2345	ex G-6-345	520	Lsd fr BAES
N521XJ	Avro RJ85	E2346	ex G-6-346	521	Lsd fr BAES
N522XJ	Avro RJ85	E2347	ex G-6-347	522	Lsd fr BAES
N523XJ	Avro RJ85	E2348	ex G-6-348	523	Lsd fr BAES
N524XJ	Avro RJ85	E2349	ex G-6-349	524	Lsd fr BAES
N525XJ	Avro RJ85	E2350	ex G-6-350	525	Lsd fr WFBN
N526XJ	Avro RJ85	E2351	ex G-6-351	526	
N527XJ	Avro RJ85	E2352	ex G-6-352	527	
N528XJ	Avro RJ85	E2353	ex G-6-353	528 dam 15Oct02	
N529XJ	Avro RJ85	E2363	ex G-6-363	529	
N530XJ	Avro RJ85	E2364	ex G-6-364	530; stored GYR	
N531XJ	Avro RJ85	E2365	ex G-6-365	531; stored GYR	
N532XJ	Avro RJ85	E2366	ex G-6-366	532	
N533XJ	Avro RJ85	E2367	ex G-6-367	533	
N534XJ	Avro RJ85	E2370	ex G-6-370		
N535XJ	Avro RJ85	E2371	ex G-6-371		
N536XJ	Avro RJ85	E2372	ex G-6-372		

Operated as Northwest Jet Airlink

N27XJ	SAAB SF.340A	027	ex N320PX	Lsd fr WFBN
N46XJ	SAAB SF.340A	046	ex N323PX	Lsd fr WFBN
N48XJ	SAAB SF.340A	048	ex N324PX	Lsd fr WFBN
N68XJ	SAAB SF.340A	068	ex N328PX	
N79XJ	SAAB SF.340A	079	ex N340PX	
N89XJ	SAAB SF.340A	089	ex N89MQ	
N98XJ	SAAB SF.340A	098	ex N98MQ	
N99XJ	SAAB SF.340A	099	ex N99RZ	
N106XJ	SAAB SF.340A	106	ex N106PX	
N110XJ	SAAB SF.340A	110	ex N110MQ	dam 21Jul02
N112XJ	SAAB SF.340A	112	ex N112AE	
N114XJ	SAAB SF.340A	114	ex N114SB	
N115XJ	SAAB SF.340A	115	ex N115SB	
N119XJ	SAAB SF.340A	119	ex N119AE	
N142XJ	SAAB SF.340A	142	ex N341PX	Lsd fr Banc of America
N362PX	SAAB SF.340B	258	ex SE-G58	Lsd fr WFBN
N363PX	SAAB SF.340B	260	ex SE-G60	Spirit of the Pine Belt
N365PX	SAAB SF.340B	265	ex SE-G65	
N367PX	SAAB SF.340B	271	ex SE-G71	Spirit of Montgomery
N368PX	SAAB SF.340B	274	ex SE-G74	
N369PX	SAAB SF.340B	295	ex SE-G95	Spirit of Lafayette
N370PX	SAAB SF.340B	300	ex SE-E03	Spirit of Monroe
N402XJ	SAAB SF.340B	402	ex SE-B02	Lsd fr Wachovia Bank
N403XJ	SAAB SF.340B	403	ex SE-B03	Lsd fr Wachovia Bank
N404XJ	SAAB SF.340B	404	ex SE-B04	
N406XJ	SAAB SF.340B	406	ex SE-B06	Lsd fr Wachovia Bank
N407XJ	SAAB SF.340B	407	ex SE-B07	
N408XJ	SAAB SF.340B	408	ex SE-B08	
N410XJ	SAAB SF.340B	410	ex SE-B10	Lsd fr Wachovia Bank
N411XJ	SAAB SF.340B	411	ex SE-B11	Lsd fr Wachovia Bank
N412XJ	SAAB SF.340B	412	ex SE-B12	Lsd fr Wachovia Bank
N413XJ	SAAB SF.340B	413	ex SE-B13	Lsd fr Wachovia Bank
N414XJ	SAAB SF.340B	414	ex SE-B14	Lsd fr Wachovia Bank
N415XJ	SAAB SF.340B	415	ex SE-B15	Lsd fr Wachovia Bank
N416XJ	SAAB SF.340B	416	ex SE-B16	
N417XJ	SAAB SF.340B	417	ex SE-B17	Lsd fr Wachovia Bank
N418XJ	SAAB SF.340B	418	ex SE-B18	Lsd fr Wachovia Bank
N420XJ	SAAB SF.340B	420	ex SE-B20	Lsd fr Wachovia Bank
N421XJ	SAAB SF.340B	421	ex SE-B21	Lsd fr Wachovia Bank
N422XJ	SAAB SF.340B	422	ex SE-B22	
N423XJ	SAAB SF.340B	423	ex SE-B23	
N424XJ	SAAB SF.340B	424	ex SE-B24	
N425XJ	SAAB SF.340B	425	ex SE-B25	
N426XJ	SAAB SF.340B	426	ex SE-B26	
N427XJ	SAAB SF.340B	427	ex SE-B27	
N428XJ	SAAB SF.340B	428	ex SE-B28	
N429XJ	SAAB SF.340B	429	ex SE-B29	
N430XJ	SAAB SF.340B	430	ex SE-B30	
N433XJ	SAAB SF.340B	433	ex SE-B33	
N434XJ	SAAB SF.340B	434	ex SE-B34	
N435XJ	SAAB SF.340B	435	ex SE-B35	
N436XJ	SAAB SF.340B	436	ex SE-B36	
N437XJ	SAAB SF.340B	437	ex SE-B37	
N438XJ	SAAB SF.340B	438	ex SE-B38	
N439XJ	SAAB SF.340B	439	ex SE-B39	
N441XJ	SAAB SF.340B	441	ex SE-B41	25th Anniversary c/s
N442XJ	SAAB SF.340B	442	ex SE-B42	
N443XJ	SAAB SF.340B	443	ex SE-B43	
N444XJ	SAAB SF.340B	444	ex SE-B44	
N445XJ	SAAB SF.340B	445	ex SE-B45	
N446XJ	SAAB SF.340B	446	ex SE-B46	stored
N447XJ	SAAB SF.340B	447	ex SE-B47	
N448XJ	SAAB SF.340B	448	ex SE-B48	
N449XJ	SAAB SF.340B	449	ex SE-B49	
N450XJ	SAAB SF.340B	450	ex SE-B50	
N451XJ	SAAB SF.340B	451	ex SE-B51	500th SAAB regional a/c c/s
N452XJ	SAAB SF.340B	452	ex SE-B52	
N453XJ	SAAB SF.340B	453	ex SE-B53	
N454XJ	SAAB SF.340B	454	ex SE-B54	
N456XJ	SAAB SF.340B	456	ex SE-B56	
N457XJ	SAAB SF.340B	457	ex SE-B57	
N991XJ	SAAB SF.340A	091	ex N91MQ	

Ops services as part of the Northwest Airlink network, using NW flight numbers in the range 3000-3439. Parent company owns Big Sky but operated independently

METHOW AVIATION

Methrow (MER)   Everett-Snohomish County/Paine Field, WA (PAE)

N42D	Beech E-18S	BA-117	Lsd fr Comanche Air
N48K	Beech E-18S	BA-202	Lsd fr Comanche Air

N93CA	Beech G-18S	BA-604	ex N8087	Freighter	
N228A	Beech H-18	BA-629		Freighter	
N251K	Beech E-18S	BA-170			Lsd fr Kestrel Inc
N432U	Hamilton Westwind III	BA-161			Lsd fr Comanche Air
N1827M	Beech D-18S	A-394			Lsd fr Comanche Air
N9001	Beech E-18S	BA-460			Lsd fr Comanche Air
N9210	Beech G-18S	BA-472	ex N92D		Lsd fr Comanche Air
N160RL	Beech 58 Baron	TH-60			Lsd fr Comanche Air

MIAMI AIR INTERNATIONAL

Biscayne (GL/BSK)   Miami-Intl, FL (MIA)

N802MA	Boeing 727-225 (FedEx 3)	1668/22433	ex N802EA	Stacy	
N803MA	Boeing 727-225 (FedEx 3)	1671/22434	ex N803EA	Kim	
G-XLAC	Boeing 737-81Q	479/29051	ex G-LFJB		Lsd fr XLA for winter
G-XLAD	Boeing 737-81Q	557/29052	ex G-ODMW		Lsd fr XLA for winter
N732MA	Boeing 737-81Q	830/30618	ex N1787B		Lsd fr CIT Leasing
N733MA	Boeing 737-81Q	856/30619	ex G-OXLA		Lsd fr CIT Leasing; sublsd to XLA for summers
N734MA	Boeing 737-8Q8	701/30039	ex 5W-SAM	Billie	Lsd fr ILFC
N738MA	Boeing 737-81Q	32799		on order	Lsd fr CIT Leasing
N739MA	Boeing 737-8Q8	30670		on order	Lsd fr ILFC

MIAMI VALLEY AVIATION

Night Owl (OWL)   Middletown-Hook Field Municipal, OH (MWO)

N36AP	Douglas DC-3	13439	ex N11VU	36 no titles
N707BA	Douglas DC-3	16298/33046	ex C-GWUH	70
N907Z	Douglas DC-3	12300	ex N90HA	81
N932H	Douglas DC-3	17101/34368	ex N93HA	93
N8187E	Douglas DC-3	13840	ex N81HA	90
N9923S	Douglas DC-3	14519/25964	ex N99HA	99
All freighters				
N25FM	Lear Jet 25	25-063	ex N24LT	
N27LP	Beech 200 Super King Air	BB-331	ex N111WA	
N108RB	Lear Jet 25A	35A-097	ex N135J	
N131MV	AMD Falcon 20C	31	ex N828AA	freighter
N294NW	Lear Jet 25	25-031		
N8627A	Beech E-18S	BA-283	ex N86HA	freighter
N8711H	Beech E-18S	BA-87	ex N87HA	freighter
N9669N	Beech E-18S	BA-382	ex N96HA	freighter
N62498	Piper PA-23-250 Aztec F	27-7654023		
N62650	Piper PA-23-250 Aztec F	27-7654115		
N63911	Piper PA-23-250 Aztec F	27-7854053		

Associated with Hoganair (HGA) All registered to The Eagle and The Hawks Inc.

MIDATLANTIC AIRWAYS

Pittsburgh-Greater Pittsburgh Intl, PA (PIT)

N801MA	Embraer 170-100LR	170-00012	ex PT-	on order 04
N802MD	Embraer 170-100LR	170-00013	ex PT-	on order 04
N803MD	Embraer 170-100LR	170-00015	ex PT-	on order 04
N804MD	Embraer 170-100LR	170-00016	ex PT-	on order 04
N805MD	Embraer 170-100LR	170-00018	ex PT-	on order 04
N806MD	Embraer 170-100LR	170-00019	ex PT-	on order 04
N807MD	Embraer 170-100LR	170-00020	ex PT-	on order 04
N808MD	Embraer 170-100LR	170-00021	ex PT-	on order 04
N809MD	Embraer 170-100LR	170-00022	ex PT-	on order 04
N810MD	Embraer 170-100LR		ex PT-	on order 04
N811MD	Embraer 170-100LR		ex PT-	on order 04
N812MD	Embraer 170-100LR		ex PT-	on order 04
N813MA	Embraer 170-100LR		ex PT-	on order 04
N814MD	Embraer 170-100LR		ex PT-	on order 04
N815MD	Embraer 170-100LR		ex PT-	on order 04

A further 70 Embraer 170s are on order for delivery up to September 2006 (may be operated by PSA Airlines)
Wholly owned subsidiary of US Airways, due to commence operations as US Airways Express

MID-ATLANTIC FREIGHT

Night Ship (MDC)   Greensboro-Piedmont Triad Intl, NC (GSO)

N250AA	Cessna 208B Caravan I	208B0887	ex C-GIKN
N599BA	Cessna 208B Caravan I	208B0773	
N1041L	Cessna 208B Caravan I	208B0337	

N1058N	Cessna 208B Caravan I	208B0347		
N1114N	Cessna 208B Caravan I	208B0406		
N1203S	Cessna 208B Caravan I	208B0439		
N1324G	Cessna 208B Caravan I	208B0777		Sublsd to DKT
N1958E	Cessna 208B Caravan I	208B0834		
N4667B	Cessna 208B Caravan I	208B0163		
N4698B	Cessna 208B Caravan I	208B0175		
N9452B	Cessna 208B Caravan I	208B0123		
N9525B	Cessna 208B Caravan I	208B0087		
N9594B	Cessna 208B Caravan I	208B0131		
N9653F	Cessna 208 Caravan I	20800114		
N9829B	Cessna 208B Caravan I	208B0116		

Charter flights are sometimes operated as Atlantic Aero; a sister company who own all the aircraft

MIDLINE AIR FREIGHT

Elizabethtown, KY (EKX)

N683LS	Douglas DC-3	43084	ex N121L
N1480K	Beech G-18S	BA-601	ex N1480W

MIDWAY AIRLINES suspended operations 30 October 2003 and liquidated

MIDWEST AIRLINES

Midex (YX/MEP)   *AppletonpOutagamie County, WI/Milwaukee-General Mitchell Intl (ATW/MKE)*

N902ME	Boeing 717-2BL	5116/55166		
N903ME	Boeing 717-2BL	5117/55167		
N904ME	Boeing 717-2BL	5118/55168		Lsd fr US Bank NA
N905ME	Boeing 717-2BL	5119/55169		Lsd fr US Bank NA
N906ME	Boeing 717-2BL	5120/55170		Lsd fr US Bank NA
N907ME	Boeing 717-2BL	5121/55171		Lsd fr US Bank NA
N908ME	Boeing 717-2BL	5122/55172		Lsd fr US Bank NA
N909ME	Boeing 717-2BL	5123/55173		Lsd fr US Bank NA
N910ME	Boeing 717-2BL	5124/55174		Lsd fr US Bank NA
N912ME	Boeing 717-2BL	5125/55175		Lsd fr US Bank NA
N913ME	Boeing 717-2BL	5126/55176		
N914ME	Boeing 717-2BL	55177		
N916ME	Boeing 717-2BL	55178		
N917ME	Boeing 717-2BL	55179	on order Mar04	
N918ME	Boeing 717-2BL	55180	on order 2Q04	
N919ME	Boeing 717-2BL	55181	on order 3Q04	
N920ME	Boeing 717-2BL	55182	on order 4Q04	

A further 8 are on order for delivery at one a quarter until October 2006 (c/ns 55183-85, 26190-94)

N202ME	Douglas DC-9-32	778/47672	ex D-ALLC	Lsd fr Fifth Third Lsg
N203ME	Douglas DC-9-32	779/47673	ex D-ALLA	Lsd fr Banc of America
N207ME	Douglas DC-9-32	915/47794	ex PK-GNX	stored MKE Lsd fr Banc of America
N209ME	Douglas DC-9-32	828/47730	ex PK-GNO	Lsd fr First National
N216ME	Douglas DC-9-32	835/47740	ex PK-GNP	stored MKE Lsd fr Banc of America
N301ME	Douglas DC-9-32	240/47190	ex N942ML	
N302ME	Douglas DC-9-32	198/47102	ex N940ML	
N501ME	Douglas DC-9-32	229/47132	ex N944ML	
N700ME	Douglas DC-9-14	2/45696	ex N3301L	stored MKE

All fitted with ABS Partnership Stage 3 hushkits

N601ME	McDonnell-Douglas MD-88	1624/49762	ex (N159PL)	Lsd fr US Bancorp
N701ME	McDonnell-Douglas MD-88	1620/49760	ex (N157PL)	Lsd fr Fifth Third Lsg
N803ME	McDonnell-Douglas MD-81	953/48029	ex JA8458	Lsd fr WFBN
N804ME	McDonnell-Douglas MD-81	962/48030	ex JA8459	
N805ME	McDonnell-Douglas MD-81	969/48031	ex JA8460	Lsd fr M&I First National Lsg
N806ME	McDonnell-Douglas MD-81	978/48032	ex JA8461	
N807ME	McDonnell-Douglas MD-81	988/48033	ex JA8462	
N808ME	McDonnell-Douglas MD-82	999/48070	ex JA8468	Lsd fr US Bancorp
N809ME	McDonnell-Douglas MD-82	1004/48071	ex JA8469	
N810ME	McDonnell-Douglas MD-81	1011/48072	ex JA8470	
N812ME	McDonnell-Douglas MD-81	966/48006	ex OY-KIG	
N813ME	McDonnell-Douglas MD-81	971/48007	ex OY-KIH	
N814ME	McDonnell-Douglas MD-81	992/48010	ex SE-DMY	

Commuter services are operated by Midwest Connect

MIDWEST AVIATION

Midwest (MWT)   *Marshall-Ryan Field, MN (MML)*

N185MV	Beech 200 Super King Air	BB-1034	ex N185MC	
N711HG	Piper PA-31-350 Chieftain	31-8052110		Lsd fr Southwest Avn Inc
N727SC	Piper PA-31-350 Navajo Chieftain	31-7305110		Lsd fr Southwest Avn Inc
N3558X	Piper PA-31-350 Chieftain	31-8052073		Lsd fr Southwest Avn Inc
N43305	Piper PA-32-301R Saratoga	32R-8413002		Lsd fr Southwest Avn Inc

MIDWEST CONNECT

Skyway-Ex (AL/SYX)   *Milwaukee-General Mitchell Intl, WI (MKE)*

N79SK	Beech 1900D	UE-79	
N81SK	Beech 1900D	UE-81	
N85SK	Beech 1900D	UE-85	Lsd fr WFBN
N87SK	Beech 1900D	UE-87	Lsd fr WFBN
N91SK	Beech 1900D	UE-91	Lsd fr US Bancorp
N92SK	Beech 1900D	UE-92	Lsd fr Boatmens Equipment
N145SK	Beech 1900D	UE-145	Lsd fr Information Leasing
N148SK	Beech 1900D	UE-148	Lsd fr Information Leasing
N801SK	Beech 1900D	UE-80	
N831SK	Beech 1900D	UE-83	
N841SK	Beech 1900D	UE-84	
N881SK	Beech 1900D	UE-88	Lsd fr WFBN
N891SK	Beech 1900D	UE-89	Lsd fr Boatmens Equipment
N901SK	Beech 1900D	UE-90 ex (N90ZV)	Lsd fr US Bancorp
N351SK	Dornier 328-300	3108 ex D-BALU	Lsd fr WFBN
N352SK	Dornier 328-300	3111 ex D-BALI	Lsd fr WFBN
N353SK	Dornier 328-300	3122 ex D-BDXD	Lsd fr WFBN
N354SK	Dornier 328-300	3126 ex D-BDXG	Lsd fr WFBN
N355SK	Dornier 328-300	3124 ex D-BDXI	Lsd fr WFBN
N356SK	Dornier 328-300	3163 ex D-BDX.	
N357SK	Dornier 328-300	3164 ex D-BDX.	
N358SK	Dornier 328-300	3188 ex D-BDX.	
N359SK	Dornier 328-300	3202 ex D-BDX.	
N360SK	Dornier 328-300	3136 ex D-BDXR	

Twenty Embraer EMB.135KLs are on order, (to be registered N530RJ to N549RJ), for delivery from July 2006 (defered from January 2004)
Operates feeder services for Midwest Airlines in full colours and using YX call signs

MIDWEST EXPRESS   renamed Midwest Airlines on 28 February 2003

MIDWEST HELICOPTER AIRWAYS

Hinsdale-Midwest Heliport, IL

N129NH	Sikorsky S-58ET	58555 ex N47781
N2256Z	Sikorsky S-58J	58867 ex 57-1707
N4247V	Sikorsky S-58ET	581547
N4388S	Sikorsky S-58J	581551
N90561	Sikorsky S-58J	581332

MISSIONAIR

Orlando-Kissimee Municipal, FL (ISM)

| N79MA | Douglas DC-3 | 4089 ex N168LG |
| N213MA | Douglas DC-3 | 7320 ex N123BA |

MOUNTAIN AIR CARGO

Mountain (MTN)   *Denver, NC*

N708FX	Cessna 208B Caravan I	208B0429	
N715FX	Cessna 208B Caravan I	208B0440	
N721FX	Cessna 208B Caravan I	208B0453	
N729FX	Cessna 208B Caravan I	208B0474	
N740FX	Cessna 208B Caravan I	208B0484	
N742FX	Cessna 208B Caravan I	208B0489	
N747FE	Cessna 208B Caravan I	208B0238	
N747FX	Cessna 208B Caravan I	208B0501	
N755FE	Cessna 208B Caravan I	208B0250	
N764FE	Cessna 208B Caravan I	208B0258	
N769FE	Cessna 208B Caravan I	208B0264	
N776FE	Cessna 208B Caravan I	208B0273	
N787FE	Cessna 208B Caravan I	208B0285	
N792FE	Cessna 208B Caravan I	208B0290	
N801FE	Cessna 208A Caravan I	20800009 ex (N9305F)	
N819FE	Cessna 208A Caravan I	20800056 ex (N9451F)	
N820FE	Cessna 208B Caravan I	208B0111 ex F-GHHC	
N831FE	Cessna 208B Caravan I	208B0225 ex F-GHHE	
N842FE	Cessna 208B Caravan I	208B0146	
N847FE	Cessna 208B Caravan I	208B0156	
N848FE	Cessna 208B Caravan I	208B0158	
N849FE	Cessna 208B Caravan I	208B0162	
N852FE	Cessna 208B Caravan I	208B0168	
N853FE	Cessna 208B Caravan I	208B0170	

N855FE	Cessna 208B Caravan I	208B0203		
N862FE	Cessna 208B Caravan I	208B0184		
N869FE	Cessna 208B Caravan I	208B0195		
N874FE	Cessna 208B Caravan I	208B0205		
N878FE	Cessna 208B Caravan I	208B0211		
N881FE	Cessna 208B Caravan I	208B0204		
N887FE	Cessna 208B Caravan I	208B0216		
N905FE	Cessna 208B Caravan I	208B0005		
N917FE	Cessna 208B Caravan I	208B0017		
N921FE	Cessna 208B Caravan I	208B0021		
N938FE	Cessna 208B Caravan I	208B0038		
N943FE	Cessna 208B Caravan I	208B0043		
N955FE	Cessna 208B Caravan I	208B0066	ex (N966FE)	
N962FE	Cessna 208B Caravan I	208B0078		
N967FE	Cessna 208B Caravan I	208B0088		
N973FE	Cessna 208B Caravan I	208B0098		
N975FE	Cessna 208B Caravan I	208B0101		
N979FE	Cessna 208B Caravan I	208B0106		
N999FE	Cessna 208B Caravan I	208B0231		
N705FE	Fokker F.27 Friendship 500	10367	ex G-FEDX	
N706FE	Fokker F.27 Friendship 500	10384	ex G-OFEC	
N709FE	Fokker F.27 Friendship 500	10375	ex F-BPNE	
N710FE	Fokker F.27 Friendship 500	10380	ex F-BPNG	
N712FE	Fokker F.27 Friendship 500F	10613	ex 9M-MCK	
N713FE	Fokker F.27 Friendship 500F	10615	ex 9M-MCL	
N714FE	Fokker F.27 Friendship 500	10461	ex 9M-MCD	
N715FE	Fokker F.27 Friendship 500	10468	ex 9M-MCG	
N716FE	Fokker F.27 Friendship 500	10471	ex 9M-MCI	
N717FE	Fokker F.27 Friendship 500	10455	ex 9M-MCA	
N718FE	Fokker F.27 Friendship 500	10470	ex 9M-MCH	
N719FE	Fokker F.27 Friendship 500	10467	ex 9M-MCF	
N721FE	Fokker F.27 Friendship 500	10460	ex 9M-MCC	
N722FE	Fokker F.27 Friendship 500	10472	ex 9M-MCJ	
N723FE	Fokker F.27 Friendship 500	10682	ex OO-FEI	
N724FE	Fokker F.27 Friendship 500	10677	ex OO-FEK	
N725FE	Fokker F.27 Friendship 500	10658	ex N514AW	
N726FE	Fokker F.27 Friendship 500	10683	ex (OO-FEN)	
N727FE	Fokker F.27 Friendship 500	10661	ex (OO-FEM)	
N728FE	Fokker F.27 Friendship 500	10657	ex OO-FEL	
N2679U	Short SD.3-30	SH3071	ex (N330AE)	
N26288	Short SD.3-30	SH3074	ex G-BIYF	

Cessna 208 Caravans and Fokker F.27 Friendship 500s leased from and operated on behalf of FedEx

---

MURRAY AIR

Murray Air (MUA)   Detroit-Willow Run, MI (YIP)

N865F	Douglas DC-8-63F (BAC 3)	464/46088	ex TF-FLC	all-white	Lsd fr EDS Financial
N921R	Douglas DC-8-63F (BAC 3)	548/46145	ex N806WA	all-white	Lsd fr EDS Financial

---

MURRAY AVIATION

Detroit-Willow Run, MI (YIP)

N262MA	CASA C.212-200	CC50-1-262	ex N429CA	Freighter	
N287MA	CASA C.212-200	287	ex N436CA	Freighter	
N290KA	Beech 65-E90 King Air	LW-59	ex N992MA		
N305CW	Mitsubishi MU-2L	667	ex N300CW	Freighter	
N384MA	SAAB SF.340A	102	ex N102XJ		Lsd fr Lambert Lsg
N553MA	Beech 65-E90 King Air	LW-147	ex C-FATX		
N687MA	CASA C.212-200	CC20-6-174	ex N174FB	Freighter	
N695MA	British Aerospace Jetstream 31	695	ex N169PC	Freighter	

*Operated for Chrysler Aviation from Pontiac, IL

NANTUCKET AIRLINES believed to have ceased own operations

NAT AVIATION USA

Miami, FL

N26877	Swearingen SA.227AC Metro III	AC-652	ex (N652AV)	based Colombo	Lsd fr Joda

---

NATIONAL EXPRESS ceased operations

NATIONAL JET AVIATION SERVICES believed to have ceased operations

NATIVE AMERICAN AIR SERVICES

Phoenix-Williams Gateway, AZ

N95NA	Cessna 208B Caravan I	208B0666	ex N1131S	EMS	Lsd fr Cessna Finance
N206MH	Bell 206L-1 LongRanger III	45426	ex N518EH	EMS	Op by Omniflight
N224LF	Bell 206L-1 LongRanger II	45199	ex N5013Y	EMS	Op by Omniflight
N308NA	Pilatus PC-12/45	226	ex N226PC	Air Ambulance	
N314LS	Bell 206L-3 LongRanger III	51006	ex N2210H	EMS	
N317NA	Pilatus PC-12/45	223	ex N223PD	Air Ambulance	
N350GR	Aerospatiale AS.350B AStar	3140		EMS	Op by Omniflight
N562NA	Pilatus PC-12/45	174	ex N174PC	Air Ambulance	
N613NA	Pilatus PC-12/45	197	ex N197PC	Air Ambulance	
N5230J	Aerospatiale AS.350B3 AStar	3256		EMS	

NEPTUNE AVIATION SERVICES

Missoula-Intl, MT (MSO)

N362RR	Lockheed P2V-7 Neptune	726-7260	ex Bu148362	stored
N714AU	Lockheed P2V-7 Neptune	726-7224	ex N339L	stored
N715AU	Lockheed P2V-7 Neptune	726-7228	ex N343RR	stored
N717AU	Lockheed P2V-7 Neptune	726-7209	ex N959LH	stored
N949RR	Lockheed P2V-7 Neptune	726-7199	ex Bu147949	stored
N1386C	Lockheed P2V-5 Neptune	426-5268	ex Bu128422	stored
N1386K	Lockheed P2V-5 Neptune	426-5305	ex Bu131424	07
N4235N	Lockheed SP-2H Neptune	726-7158	ex Bu144681	10
N4235T	Lockheed SP-2H Neptune	726-7285	ex Bu150282	09
N9855F	Lockheed P2V-5 Neptune	426-5326	ex Bu131445	06
N13852	Lockheed P2V-5 Neptune	426-5387	ex Bu131506	stored
N13859	Lockheed P2V-5 Neptune	426-5344	ex Bu131463	stored
N14447	Lockheed P2V-7 Neptune	826-8010	ex RCAF 24110	11
N63819	Lockheed P2V-7 Neptune	726-7215	ex Bu147965	stored
N96264	Lockheed P2V-5 Neptune	426-5192	ex Bu128346	12
N96278	Lockheed P2V-5 Neptune	426-5340	ex Bu131459	05
N308D	Lockheed L-188C Electra	1130	ex N595KR	spares use?

NEW ENGLAND AIRLINES

New England (EJ/NEA)   *Westerly-State, RI (WST)*

N123NE	Britten-Norman BN-2A-26 Islander	46	ex G-BJSA
N304SK	Britten-Norman BN-2A-26 Islander	564	ex N80PA
N345CS	Piper PA-32-300 Cherokee Six	32-7640043	ex N345ES
N598JA	Britten-Norman BN-2A Islander	66	
N4885T	Piper PA-32-300 Cherokee Six	32-7240092	
N8203C	Piper PA-32-300 Cherokee Six	32-7640058	

NIGHT EAGLE AVIATION

Pittsburgh, PA

N903NJ	Swearingen SA.227DC Metro 23	DC-903B	ex N3086H		
N904NJ	Swearingen SA.227DC Metro 23	DC-904B	ex N3094W		Lsd fr RCH Aviation

Current status is uncertain

NORD AVIATION

Santa Teresa-Dona Ana County, NM

N738WB	Beech D50C Twin Bonanza	DH-286		Freighter
N57626	Douglas DC-3	4564	ex NC57626	Freighter

NORTH AMERICAN AIRLINES

North American (NA/NAO)   *New York-JFK Intl, NY (JFK)*

N750NA	Boeing 757-28A	658/26277		Lisa Caroline	Lsd fr ILFC
N752NA	Boeing 757-28A	865/28174	ex N1795B	Alisa Ferrara	Lsd fr ILFC
N753NA	Boeing 757-28A	280/24544	ex N549NA		Lsd fr ILFC
N754NA	Boeing 757-28A	958/29381			Lsd fr ILFC
N755NA	Boeing 757-28A	925/30043	ex N523NA	John Plueger	Lsd fr ILFC
N756NA	Boeing 757-28A	967/32448		Claudette Abrahams	Lsd fr GECAS
N767NA	Boeing 767-324ER	601/27569	ex N569NB		Lsd fr GECAS
N768NA	Boeing 767-36NER	754/29898	ex N898GE	Lisa Caroline	Lsd fr GECAS

NORTHERN AIR CARGO

Yukon (NC/NAC)   *Anchorage-Intl, AK (ANC)*

N434TA	Douglas DC-6BST	515/44434	ex EC-BBK	stored FAI
N779TA	Douglas DC-6A	1035/45529	ex PP-LFC	
N1027N	Douglas C-118A	294/43580	ex 51-3833	stored FAI
N1036F	Douglas C-118A	295/43581	ex 51-3834	stored FAI
N1377K	Douglas C-118A	499/44596	ex 53-3225	
N2907F	Douglas C-118A	574/44636	ex 53-3265	
N4213X	Douglas C-118A	518/44605	ex 53-3234	stored FAI
N6174C	Douglas DC-6A	451/44075	ex C-GBYN	on overhaul
N6204U	Douglas DC-6BF	245/43549	ex C-GBYH	stored ANC
N7780B	Douglas DC-6A	875/45372		Northern Air Fuel titles
N7919C	Douglas DC-6B	247/43554	ex PH-DFM	
N43872	Douglas C-118A	632/44665	ex 53-3294	
N99330	Douglas C-118A	275/43576	ex C-GPEG	
N42NC	Aerospatiale/Alenia ATR 42-300F	067	ex F-OHFH	Lsd fr RNS Leasing
N190AJ	Boeing 727-46F (FedEx 3)	236/18878	ex G-BAJW	stored ANC
N930FT	Boeing 727-23F (FedEx 3)	329/19387	ex N1929	
N992AJ	Boeing 727-23F (FedEx 3)	358/19428	ex N515FE	

NORTH-SOUTH AIRWAYS

Sparkle (SPK)   *Atlanta-De Kalb Peachtree, GA (PDK)*

N283UE	Embraer EMB.110RT Brasilia	120139	ex PT-SPF		Lsd fr IASG
N453UE	Embraer EMB.120FC Brasilia	120148	ex PT-SPN	Freighter	Lsd fr IASG
N8078V	Embraer EMB.120ER Brasilia	120242	ex PT-OQJ		Lsd fr IASG
N12703	Embraer EMB.120FC Brasilia	120084	ex PT-SMB	Freighter	Lsd fr IASG

NORTH STAR AIR CARGO

Sky Box (SBX)   *Milwaukee-General Mitchell Intl, WI (MKE)*

N50NS	Short SC.7 Skyvan	SH1856	ex N50GA	Freighter
N51NS	Short SC.7 Skyvan	SH1843	ex N20DA	Freighter
N53NS	Short SC.7 Skyvan	SH1920	ex C-FPSQ	Freighter
N410AC	Short SC.7 Skyvan	SH1883	ex C-FQSL	Freighter
N731E	Short SC.7 Skyvan	SH1853	ex N80JJ	Freighter

Associated with Air Cargo Carriers

NORTHWEST AIRLINES

Northwest (NW/NWA) (IATA 012)   *Minneapolis/St Paul Intl, MN (MSP)*

N301NB	Airbus Industrie A319-114	1058	ex D-AVYP	3101; City of Duluth	Lsd fr WFBN
N302NB	Airbus Industrie A319-114	1062	ex D-AVWA	3102	Lsd fr WFBN
N303NB	Airbus Industrie A319-114	1071	ex D-AVWF	3103	Lsd fr WFBN
N304NB	Airbus Industrie A319-114	1078	ex D-AVWJ	3104	Lsd fr WFBN
N305NB	Airbus Industrie A319-114	1090	ex D-AVYE	3105	Lsd fr WFBN
N306NB	Airbus Industrie A319-114	1091	ex D-AVYL	3106	Lsd fr WFBN
N307NB	Airbus Industrie A319-114	1126	ex D-AVYW	3107	Lsd fr WFBN
N308NB	Airbus Industrie A319-114	1129	ex D-AVYZ	3108	Lsd fr WFBN
N309NB	Airbus Industrie A319-114	1131	ex D-AVWA	3109	Lsd fr WFBN
N310NB	Airbus Industrie A319-114	1149	ex D-AVWJ	3110	Lsd fr WFBN
N311NB	Airbus Industrie A319-114	1164	ex D-AVWU	3111	Lsd fr WFBN
N312NB	Airbus Industrie A319-114	1167	ex D-AVWW	3112	Lsd fr WFBN
N314NB	Airbus Industrie A319-114	1191	ex D-AVWO	3114	
N315NB	Airbus Industrie A319-114	1230	ex D-AVYM	3115	
N316NB	Airbus Industrie A319-114	1249	ex D-AVYW	3116	
N317NB	Airbus Industrie A319-114	1324	ex D-AVWT	3117	
N318NB	Airbus Industrie A319-114	1325	ex D-AVYF	3118	
N319NB	Airbus Industrie A319-114	1346	ex D-AVYR	3119	
N320NB	Airbus Industrie A319-114	1392	ex D-AVYT	3120	
N321NB	Airbus Industrie A319-114	1414	ex D-AVYL	3121	
N322NB	Airbus Industrie A319-114	1434	ex D-AVYO	3122	
N323NB	Airbus Industrie A319-114	1453	ex D-AVWE	3123	
N324NB	Airbus Industrie A319-114	1456	ex D-AVWF	3124	
N325NB	Airbus Industrie A319-114	1483	ex D-AVYU	3125	
N326NB	Airbus Industrie A319-114	1498	ex D-AVYC	3126	
N327NB	Airbus Industrie A319-114	1501	ex D-AVYD	3127	
N328NB	Airbus Industrie A319-114	1520	ex D-AVYN	3128	
N329NB	Airbus Industrie A319-114	1543	ex D-AVWJ	3129	
N330NB	Airbus Industrie A319-114	1549	ex D-AVWM	3130	
N331NB	Airbus Industrie A319-114	1567	ex D-AVYU	3131	
N332NB	Airbus Industrie A319-114	1570	ex D-AVWD	3132	
N333NB	Airbus Industrie A319-114	1582	ex D-AVYA	3133	
N334NB	Airbus Industrie A319-114	1659	ex D-AVYU	3134	

N335NB	Airbus Industrie A319-114	1662	ex D-AVYW	3135	
N336NB	Airbus Industrie A319-114	1683	ex D-AVWJ	3136	
N337NB	Airbus Industrie A319-114	1685	ex D-AVWL	3137	
N338NB	Airbus Industrie A319-114	1693	ex D-AVYD	3138	
N339NB	Airbus Industrie A319-114	1709	ex D-AVWG	3139	
N340NB	Airbus Industrie A319-114	1714	ex D-AVWN	3140	
N341NB	Airbus Industrie A319-114	1738	ex D-AVWV	3141	
N342NB	Airbus Industrie A319-114	1746	ex D-AVYA	3142	
N343NB	Airbus Industrie A319-114	1752	ex D-AVYH	3143	
N344NB	Airbus Industrie A319-114	1766	ex D-AVYU	3144	
N345NB	Airbus Industrie A319-114	1774	ex D-AVYD	3145	
N346NB	Airbus Industrie A319-114	1796	ex D-AVYX	3146	
N347NB	Airbus Industrie A319-114	1800	ex D-AVYZ	3147	
N348NB	Airbus Industrie A319-114	1810	ex D-AVWH	3148	
N350NB	Airbus Industrie A319-114	1819	ex D-AVWK	3150	
N351NB	Airbus Industrie A319-114	1820	ex D-AVWL	3151	
N352NB	Airbus Industrie A319-114	1824	ex D-AVWM	3152	
N353NB	Airbus Industrie A319-114	1828	ex D-AVWO	3153	
N354NB	Airbus Industrie A319-114	1833	ex D-AVWS	3154	
N355NB	Airbus Industrie A319-114	1839	ex D-AVWA	3155	
N356NB	Airbus Industrie A319-114	1870	ex D-AVYC	3156	
N357NB	Airbus Industrie A319-114	1875	ex D-AVYH	3157	
N358NB	Airbus Industrie A319-114	1897	ex D-AVYK	3158	
N359NB	Airbus Industrie A319-114	1923	ex D-AVWC	3159	
N360NB	Airbus Industrie A319-114	1959	ex D-AVWL	3160	
N361NB	Airbus Industrie A319-114	1976	ex D-AVYB	3161	
N362NB	Airbus Industrie A319-114	1982	ex D-AVYF	3162	
N363NB	Airbus Industrie A319-114	1990	ex D-AVYL	3163	
N364NB	Airbus Industrie A319-114	2002	ex D-AVWA	3164	
N365NB	Airbus Industrie A319-114	2013	ex D-AVWS	3165	
N366NB	Airbus Industrie A319-114	2026	ex D-AVWX	3166	
N367NB	Airbus Industrie A319-114	2028	ex D-AVWY	3167	
N368NB	Airbus Industrie A319-114	2039	ex D-AVYT	3168	
N369NB	Airbus Industrie A319-114	2047	ex D-AVWC	3169	
N370NB	Airbus Industrie A319-114	2087	ex D-AVWI	3170	
N371NB	Airbus Industrie A319-114	2095	ex D-AVYI	3171	
N372NB	Airbus Industrie A319-114		ex D-AV	3172	on order 04
N373NB	Airbus Industrie A319-114		ex D-AV	3173	on order 04
N374NB	Airbus Industrie A319-114		ex D-AV	3174	on order 04
N375NB	Airbus Industrie A319-114		ex D-AV	3175	on order 04
N376NB	Airbus Industrie A319-114		ex D-AV	3176	on order 04
N377NB	Airbus Industrie A319-114		ex D-AV	3177	on order 04

N278NB to N451NB are reserved for potential future deliveries

N301US	Airbus Industrie A320-211	0031	ex F-WWDJ	3201	
N302US	Airbus Industrie A320-211	0032	ex F-WWDK	3202	
N303US	Airbus Industrie A320-211	0034	ex F-WWDL	3203	
N304US	Airbus Industrie A320-211	0040	ex F-WWDD	3204	
N305US	Airbus Industrie A320-211	0041	ex F-WWDS	3205	
N306US	Airbus Industrie A320-211	0060	ex F-WWIE	3206	
N307US	Airbus Industrie A320-211	0106	ex F-WWIA	3207	
N308US	Airbus Industrie A320-211	0107	ex F-WWIB	3208	
N309US	Airbus Industrie A320-211	0118	ex F-WWIM	3209	
N310NW	Airbus Industrie A320-211	0121	ex F-WWIO	3210	
N311US	Airbus Industrie A320-211	0125	ex F-WWIT	3211	
N312US	Airbus Industrie A320-211	0152	ex F-WWDT	3212	
N313US	Airbus Industrie A320-211	0153	ex F-WWDX	3213	
N314US	Airbus Industrie A320-211	0160	ex F-WWDZ	3214	
N315US	Airbus Industrie A320-211	0171	ex F-WWIJ	3215	
N316US	Airbus Industrie A320-211	0192	ex F-WWIY	3216	
N317US	Airbus Industrie A320-211	0197	ex F-WWDF	3217	
N318US	Airbus Industrie A320-211	0206	ex F-WWDK	3218	
N319US	Airbus Industrie A320-211	0208	ex F-WWDT	3219	
N320US	Airbus Industrie A320-211	0213	ex F-WWIB	3220	
N321US	Airbus Industrie A320-211	0262	ex F-WWDI	3221	
N322UQ	Airbus Industrie A320-211	0263	ex F-WWDQ	3222	
N323US	Airbus Industrie A320-211	0272	ex F-WWBP	3223	
N324US	Airbus Industrie A320-211	0273	ex F-WWDS	3224	
N325US	Airbus Industrie A320-211	0281	ex F-WWBS	3225; stored MZJ	
N326US	Airbus Industrie A320-211	0282	ex F-WWIA	3226	
N327NW	Airbus Industrie A320-211	0297	ex F-WWIO	3227	
N328NW	Airbus Industrie A320-211	0298	ex F-WWIP	3228	
N329NW	Airbus Industrie A320-211	0306	ex F-WWDG	3229; stored MZJ	
N330NW	Airbus Industrie A320-211	0307	ex F-WWDJ	3230	
N331NW	Airbus Industrie A320-211	0318	ex F-WWBF	3231	
N332NW	Airbus Industrie A320-211	0319	ex F-WWBG	3232	
N333NW	Airbus Industrie A320-211	0329	ex F-WWDY	3233	
N334NW	Airbus Industrie A320-212	0339	ex F-WWBP	3234; stored MZJ	
N335NW	Airbus Industrie A320-212	0340	ex F-WWBQ	3235; stored MZJ	
N336NW	Airbus Industrie A320-212	0355	ex F-WWIE	3236	
N337NW	Airbus Industrie A320-212	0358	ex F-WWIO	3237	
N338NW	Airbus Industrie A320-212	0360	ex F-WWBY	3238	

N339NW	Airbus Industrie A320-212	0367 ex F-WWDG	3239; based NRT	
N340NW	Airbus Industrie A320-212	0372 ex F-WWIX	3240; based NRT	
N341NW	Airbus Industrie A320-212	0380 ex F-WWIS	3241; based NRT	
N342NW	Airbus Industrie A320-212	0381 ex F-WWIJ	3242	
N343NW	Airbus Industrie A320-212	0387 ex F-WWBV	3243; based NRT	
N344NW	Airbus Industrie A320-212	0388 ex F-WWDC	3244	
N345NW	Airbus Industrie A320-212	0399 ex F-WWIG	3245	
N346NW	Airbus Industrie A320-212	0400 ex F-WWIT	3246	
N347NW	Airbus Industrie A320-212	0408 ex F-WWDN	3247	
N348NW	Airbus Industrie A320-212	0410 ex F-WWDV	3248	
N349NW	Airbus Industrie A320-212	0417 ex F-WWBR	3249	
N350NA	Airbus Industrie A320-212	0418 ex F-WWDG	3250	
N351NW	Airbus Industrie A320-212	0766 ex F-WWDG	3251	
N352NW	Airbus Industrie A320-212	0778 ex F-WWDO	3252	
N353NW	Airbus Industrie A320-212	0786 ex F-WWDP	3253	
N354NW	Airbus Industrie A320-212	0801 ex F-WWDY	3254	
N355NW	Airbus Industrie A320-212	0807 ex F-WWIC	3255	
N356NW	Airbus Industrie A320-212	0818 ex F-WWBD	3256	
N357NW	Airbus Industrie A320-212	0830 ex F-WWIN	3257	
N358NW	Airbus Industrie A320-212	0832 ex F-WWIO	3258	
N359NW	Airbus Industrie A320-212	0846 ex F-WWBH	3259	
N360NW	Airbus Industrie A320-212	0903 ex F-WWDO	3260	
N361NW	Airbus Industrie A320-212	0907 ex F-WWDQ	3261	
N362NW	Airbus Industrie A320-212	0911 ex F-WWDT	3262	
N363NW	Airbus Industrie A320-212	0923 ex F-WWDZ	3263	
N364NW	Airbus Industrie A320-212	0962 ex F-WWBF	3264	Lsd fr WFBN
N365NW	Airbus Industrie A320-212	0964 ex F-WWBJ	3265	Lsd fr WFBN
N366NW	Airbus Industrie A320-212	0981 ex F-WWDE	3266	Lsd fr WFBN
N367NW	Airbus Industrie A320-212	0988 ex F-WWIH	3267	Lsd fr WFBN
N368NW	Airbus Industrie A320-212	0996 ex F-WWBV	3268	Lsd fr WFBN
N369NW	Airbus Industrie A320-212	1011 ex F-WWDO	3269	Lsd fr WFBN
N370NW	Airbus Industrie A320-212	1037 ex F-WWDY	3270	Lsd fr WFBN
N371NW	Airbus Industrie A320-212	1535 ex F-WWIS	3271	
N372NW	Airbus Industrie A320-212	1633 ex F-WWDO	3272	
N373NW	Airbus Industrie A320-212	1641 ex F-WWIR	3273	
N374NW	Airbus Industrie A320-212	1646 ex F-WWDS	3274	
N375NC	Airbus Industrie A320-212	1789 ex F-WWDU	3275	
N376NW	Airbus Industrie A320-212	1812 ex F-WWBB	3276	
N377NW	Airbus Industrie A320-212	2082 ex F-WWIU	3277	
N378NW	Airbus Industrie A319-114	2092 ex F-WWBP	3178	on order
N379NW	Airbus Industrie A320-212	ex F-WW	3279	on order
N380NW	Airbus Industrie A320-212	ex F-WW	3280	on order
N381NW	Airbus Industrie A320-212	ex F-WW	3281	on order
N382NW	Airbus Industrie A320-212	ex F-WW	3282	on order

Two more are on order for delivery in 2005

N801NW	Airbus Industrie A330-323E	524 ex F-WWYZ	
N802NW	Airbus Industrie A330-323E	533 ex F-WWYD	
N803NW	Airbus Industrie A330-323E	542 ex F-WWYH	
N804NW	Airbus Industrie A330-323E	549 ex F-WWYJ	
N805NW	Airbus Industrie A330-323E	552 ex F-WWKQ	
N807NW	Airbus Industrie A330-323E	588 ex F-WWKM	on order 04
N808NW	Airbus Industrie A330-323E	591 ex F-WWKQ	on order Jan04
N809NW	Airbus Industrie A330-323E	ex F-WW	on order 04
N810NW	Airbus Industrie A330-323E	ex F-WW	on order 04

N	Airbus Industrie A330-223	609 ex F-WW	on order 04
N	Airbus Industrie A330-223	614 ex F-WW	on order 04
N	Airbus Industrie A330-223	618 ex F-WW	on order 04
N	Airbus Industrie A330-223	620 ex F-WW	on order 04
N	Airbus Industrie A330-223	621 ex F-WW	on order 04
N	Airbus Industrie A330-223	623 ex F-WW	on order 04
N	Airbus Industrie A330-223	634 ex F-WW	on order 04
N	Airbus Industrie A330-223	641 ex F-WW	on order 04

Five more Airbus Industrie A330-323X's are on order for delivery in 2005 (3) and 2006 (2) plus three more Airbus Industrie A330-223s for delivery in 2006

N201US	Boeing 727-251	1645/22154	2201; stored ROW
N204US	Boeing 727-251	1703/22544	2204; stored Maxton
N275US	Boeing 727-251	1168/21154	2275; stored Maxton
N284US	Boeing 727-251	1284/21323	2284; stored ROW
N285US	Boeing 727-251	1286/21324	2285; stored ROW
N286US	Boeing 727-251	1288/21325	2286; stored ROW
N287US	Boeing 727-251	1290/21375	2287; stored ROW
N289US	Boeing 727-251	1295/21377	2289; stored Maxton
N290US	Boeing 727-251	1297/21378	2290; stored ROW
N291US	Boeing 727-251	1299/21379	2291; stored ROW
N292US	Boeing 727-251	1317/21503	2292; stored Maxton
N293US	Boeing 727-251	1319/21504	2293; stored Maxton
N295US	Boeing 727-251	1392/21506	2295; stored ROW
N296US	Boeing 727-251	1495/21788	2296; stored ROW
N297US	Boeing 727-251	1496/21789	2297; stored ROW

N298US	Boeing 727-251	1599/22152		2298; stored ROW	
N299US	Boeing 727-251	1601/22153		2299; stored Maxton	
N716RC	Boeing 727-2S7	1617/22021		2713	Lsd to CCP
N718RC	Boeing 727-2S7	1654/22344		2714	Lsd to CCP
N719RC	Boeing 727-2S7	1721/22490		2715	Lsd to CCP
N720RC	Boeing 727-2S7	1726/22491		2716	Lsd to CCP
N721RC	Boeing 727-2S7	1729/22492		2717	Lsd to CCP
N722RW	Boeing 727-2M7	1220/21201		2762; stored ROW	
N727RW	Boeing 727-2M7	1455/21656		2767; stored MZJ	
N817EA	Boeing 727-225	1781/22554		2708; stored ROW	Lsd fr GECAS
N820EA	Boeing 727-225	1795/22557		2710; stored ROW	Lsd fr GECAS

All 727s fitted with FedEx Stage 3 hushkits; all retired by 07 January 2003

N613US	Boeing 747-251B	141/20358		6613; stored MZJ	
N615US	Boeing 747-251B	165/20360		6615; stored ROW	
N616US	Boeing 747-251F	258/21120		6716	
N617US	Boeing 747-251F	261/21121		6717	
N618US	Boeing 747-251F	269/21122		6718	
N619US	Boeing 747-251F	308/21321		6719	
N622US	Boeing 747-251B	357/21704		6622; stored MZJ	
N623US	Boeing 747-251B	374/21705		6623	
N624US	Boeing 747-251B	377/21706		6624	
N625US	Boeing 747-251B	378/21707		6625; stored MZJ	
N626US	Boeing 747-251B	379/21708	ex N626NW	6626; stored MZJ	
N627US	Boeing 747-251B	412/21709		6627; stored MZJ	
N628US	Boeing 747-251B	442/22389		6628; stored MZJ	
N629US	Boeing 747-251F	444/22388		6729	
N630US	Boeing 747-2J9F	400/21668	ex N1288E	6730	
N631US	Boeing 747-251B	594/23111		6631	
N632US	Boeing 747-251B	595/23112		6632	
N633US	Boeing 747-227B	437/21991	ex N8284V	6633; stored MHV	
N634US	Boeing 747-227B	465/22234	ex N1607B	6634; stored MZJ	
N635US	Boeing 747-227B	375/21682	ex N602PE	6635	
N636US	Boeing 747-251B	642/23547		6636; stored MZJ	
N637US	Boeing 747-251B	644/23548		6637	
N638US	Boeing 747-251B	651/23549		6638	
N639US	Boeing 747-251F	680/23887		6739	
N640US	Boeing 747-251F	682/23888		6740	
N641NW	Boeing 747-212B	470/21941	ex 9V-SQP	6641	
N642NW^	Boeing 747-212B	471/21942	ex 9V-SQQ	6642	
N643NW^	Boeing 747-249F	458/22245	ex N9401	6743 Pacific Trade special c/s	
N644NW	Boeing 747-212F	710/24177	ex ZS-SBJ	6744	Lsd fr Finova
N645NW	Boeing 747-222B (SF)	673/23736	ex N151UA	6745	
N646NW	Boeing 747-222B (SF)	675/23737	ex N152UA	6746	
N661US	Boeing 747-451	696/23719	ex N401PW	6301	Lsd fr State Street
N662US	Boeing 747-451	708/23720	ex (N302US)	6302	
N663US	Boeing 747-451	715/23818	ex (N303US)	6303	
N664US	Boeing 747-451	721/23819	ex (N304US)	6304 The Spirit of Beijing	
N665US	Boeing 747-451	726/23820	ex (N305US)	6305	
N666US	Boeing 747-451	742/23821	ex (N306US)	6306	
N667US	Boeing 747-451	799/24222	ex (N307US)	6307	
N668US	Boeing 747-451	800/24223	ex (N308US)	6308	
N669US^	Boeing 747-451	803/24224	ex (N309US)	6309	
N670US	Boeing 747-451	804/24225	ex (N311US)	6310 Alliance Spirit	
N671US^	Boeing 747-451	1206/26477		6311 City of Detroit	
N672US^	Boeing 747-451	1223/30267		6312 Spirit of Asia	
N673US^	Boeing 747-451	1226/30268		6313 Spirit of Tokyo	
N674US^	Boeing 747-451	1232/30269		6314 City of Shanghai	
N675NW	Boeing 747-451	1297/33001		6315 Spirit of Northwest People	
N676NW	Boeing 747-451	1303/33002		6316	Lsd fr WFBN

^Leased from WFBN

N501US	Boeing 757-251	53/23190		5501 St Paul	
N502US	Boeing 757-251	55/23191		5502 Minneapolis	
N503US	Boeing 757-251	59/23192		5503 Detroit; stored MZJ	
N504US	Boeing 757-251	60/23193		5504 Los Angeles	
N505US	Boeing 757-251	62/23194		5505 Boston	
N506US	Boeing 757-251	67/23195		5506 New York	
N507US	Boeing 757-251	68/23196		5507 Seattle	
N508US	Boeing 757-251	69/23197		5508 Washington DC	
N509US	Boeing 757-251	70/23198		5509 Anchorage	
N511US	Boeing 757-251	72/23199		5511 Tampa	
N512US	Boeing 757-251	82/23200		5512 Chicago Bay	
N513US	Boeing 757-251	83/23201		5513 Orlando; stored MZJ	
N514US	Boeing 757-251	86/23202		5514 San Francisco; stored MZJ	
N515US	Boeing 757-251	88/23203		5515 Phoenix	
N516US*	Boeing 757-251	104/23204		5516 San Diego; stored MZJ	
N517US*	Boeing 757-251	105/23205		5517 Portland	Lsd fr Linc Capital
N518US	Boeing 757-251	107/23206		5518 Milwaukee; stored MZJ	
N519US	Boeing 757-251	108/23207		5519 Cleveland	
N520US	Boeing 757-251	109/23208		5520 Philadelphia	
N521US	Boeing 757-251	110/23209		5521 Denver	

N522US	Boeing 757-251	119/23616		5522 Spokane; stored MZJ	
N523US	Boeing 757-251	121/23617		5523 Dallas	
N524US	Boeing 757-251	122/23618		5524 Houston; stored MZJ	
N525US	Boeing 757-251	124/23619		5525 Miami	
N526US	Boeing 757-251	131/23620		5526 Memphis	
N527US	Boeing 757-251	136/23842		5527 Fargo	
N528US	Boeing 757-251	137/23843		5528 Toronto	
N529US	Boeing 757-251	140/23844		5529 New Orleans	
N530US	Boeing 757-251	188/23845		5530 Omaha	
N531US	Boeing 757-251	190/23846		5531 Newark	
N532US	Boeing 757-251	192/24263		5532 Fort Myers	
N533US	Boeing 757-251	194/24264		5533 Orange County	
N534US	Boeing 757-251	196/24265		5534 Winnipeg	
N535US	Boeing 757-251	693/26482		5635	Lsd fr WFBN
N536US	Boeing 757-251	695/26483		5636	Lsd fr WFBN
N537US	Boeing 757-251	697/26484		5637	Lsd fr WFBN
N538US	Boeing 757-251	699/26485		5638	Lsd fr WFBN
N539US	Boeing 757-251	700/26486		5639	Lsd fr WFBN
N540US	Boeing 757-251	701/26487		5640	Lsd fr WFBN
N541US	Boeing 757-251	703/26488		5641	Lsd fr WFBN
N542US	Boeing 757-251	705/26489		5642	Lsd fr WFBN
N543US	Boeing 757-251	709/26490		5643	Lsd fr WFBN
N544US	Boeing 757-251	710/26491		5644	
N545US	Boeing 757-251	711/26492		5645	
N546US	Boeing 757-251	713/26493		5646	
N547US	Boeing 757-251	714/26494		5647	
N548US	Boeing 757-251	715/26495		5648	
N549US	Boeing 757-251	716/26496		5649	
N550NW	Boeing 757-251	968/26497		5550	
N551NW	Boeing 757-251	971/26498		5551	
N552NW	Boeing 757-251	975/26499		5552	
N553NW	Boeing 757-251	982/26500		5553	
N554NW	Boeing 757-251	987/26501		5554	
N555NW	Boeing 757-251	1011/33391		5555	
N556NW	Boeing 757-251	1013/33392		5556	
N557NW	Boeing 757-251	1016/33393		5557	

names prefixed 'City of'   *Leased from State Street Bank & Trust

N581NW	Boeing 757-351	1001/32982	ex N753JM	
N582NW	Boeing 757-351	1014/32981		The Bernie Epple
N583NW	Boeing 757-351	1019/32983		
N584NW	Boeing 757-351	1020/32984		
N585NW	Boeing 757-351	1021/32985		
N586NW	Boeing 757-351	1022/32987		
N587NW	Boeing 757-351	1023/32986		
N588NW	Boeing 757-351	1024/32988		
N589NW	Boeing 757-351	1025/32989		
N590NW	Boeing 757-351	1027/32990	ex N1795B	
N591NW	Boeing 757-351	1030/32991		
N592NW	Boeing 757-351	1033/32992		
N593NW	Boeing 757-351	1034/32993	ex N1795B	
N594NW	Boeing 757-351	1035/32994		
N595NW	Boeing 757-351	1036/32995	ex N1795B	
N596NW	Boeing 757-351	1037/32996		

N89S	Douglas DC-9-31	486/47042		9930
N90S	Douglas DC-9-31	498/47244		9931
N401EA	Douglas DC-9-51	788/47682	ex N920VJ	9885
N600TR	Douglas DC-9-51	899/47783	ex YV-40C	9886
N601NW	Douglas DC-9-32	136/47038	ex I-DIBA	9601
N602NW	Douglas DC-9-32	168/47046	ex I-DIBE	9602
N603NW	Douglas DC-9-32	195/47101	ex I-DIBL	9603
N604NW	Douglas DC-9-32	299/47222	ex I-DIBP	9604
N605NW	Douglas DC-9-32	300/47223	ex I-DIBM	9605
N606NW	Douglas DC-9-32	317/47225	ex I-RIFG	9606
N607NW	Douglas DC-9-32	428/47232	ex I-RIFY	9607
N608NW	Douglas DC-9-32	429/47233	ex I-RIFC	9608
N609NW	Douglas DC-9-32	435/47234	ex I-RIFD	9609
N610NW	Douglas DC-9-32	525/47432	ex I-RIFB	9610
N611NA	Douglas DC-9-32	540/47435	ex I-RIFL	9611
N612NW	Douglas DC-9-32	541/47436	ex I-RIFZ	9612
N613NW	Douglas DC-9-32	545/47438	ex I-RIFP	9613
N614NW	Douglas DC-9-32	210/47128	ex I-RIFH	9614
N615NW	Douglas DC-9-32	225/47129	ex I-DIBI	9615
N616NW	Douglas DC-9-32	356/47229	ex I-RIFS	9616
N617NW	Douglas DC-9-32	436/47235	ex I-RIFJ	9617
N618NW	Douglas DC-9-32	526/47433	ex I-RIFU	9618
N619NW	Douglas DC-9-32	614/47518	ex I-RIFE	9619
N620NW	Douglas DC-9-32	641/47533	ex I-RIFV	9620
N621NW	Douglas DC-9-32	676/47544	ex I-RIFM	9621
N622NW	Douglas DC-9-32	680/47575	ex I-RIFW	9622
N623NW	Douglas DC-9-32	706/47591	ex I-RIFT	9623; stored MZJ

N670MC	Douglas DC-9-51	807/47659	ex HB-ISP	9882; stored MZJ	
N671MC	Douglas DC-9-51	810/47660	ex HB-ISR	9883	
N675MC	Douglas DC-9-51	780/47651	ex OE-LDK	9880; stored MZJ	
N676MC	Douglas DC-9-51	798/47652	ex OE-LDL	9881; stored MZJ	
N677MC	Douglas DC-9-51	873/47756	ex OE-LDO	9884	
N750NW	Douglas DC-9-41	218/47114	ex SE-DBX	9750	
N751NW	Douglas DC-9-41	261/47115	ex OY-KGA	9751	
N752NW	Douglas DC-9-41	308/47116	ex LN-RLK	9752	
N753NW	Douglas DC-9-41	319/47117	ex SE-DBW	9753	
N754NW	Douglas DC-9-41	323/47178	ex OY-KGB	9754	
N755NW	Douglas DC-9-41	335/47179	ex LN-RLC	9755	
N756NW	Douglas DC-9-41	354/47180	ex SE-DBU	9756	
N758NW	Douglas DC-9-41	359/47286	ex OY-KGC	9758	Lsd fr Electra
N759NW	Douglas DC-9-41	364/47287	ex LN-RLJ	9759	
N760NC	Douglas DC-9-51	813/47708		9851	
N760NW	Douglas DC-9-41	369/47288	ex SE-DBT	9760	
N761NC	Douglas DC-9-51	814/47709		9852	
N762NC	Douglas DC-9-51	818/47710		9853	
N762NW	Douglas DC-9-41	555/47395	ex OY-KGG	9762	
N763NC	Douglas DC-9-51	832/47716		9854	
N763NW	Douglas DC-9-41	557/47396	ex LN-RLD	9763	
N764NC	Douglas DC-9-51	833/47717		9855	
N765NC	Douglas DC-9-51	834/47718		9856	
N766NC	Douglas DC-9-51	852/47739		9857	
N767NC	Douglas DC-9-51	853/47724		9858	
N768NC	Douglas DC-9-51	854/47729		9859	
N769NC	Douglas DC-9-51	877/47757		9860	
N770NC	Douglas DC-9-51	880/47758		9861	
N771NC	Douglas DC-9-51	881/47769		9862	
N772NC	Douglas DC-9-51	884/47774		9863	
N773NC	Douglas DC-9-51	888/47775		9864	
N774NC	Douglas DC-9-51	889/47776		9865	
N775NC	Douglas DC-9-51	904/47785		9866	Lsd fr GATX
N776NC	Douglas DC-9-51	905/47786		9867	
N777NC	Douglas DC-9-51	912/47787		9868	
N778NC	Douglas DC-9-51	927/48100		9869	Lsd fr GATX
N779NC	Douglas DC-9-51	931/48101		9870	Lsd fr GATX
N780NC	Douglas DC-9-51	932/48102		9871	Lsd fr GATX
N781NC	Douglas DC-9-51	935/48121		9872	
N782NC	Douglas DC-9-51	936/48107		9873	
N783NC	Douglas DC-9-51	937/48108		9874	
N784NC	Douglas DC-9-51	939/48109		9875	
N785NC	Douglas DC-9-51	945/48110		9876	
N786NC	Douglas DC-9-51	984/48148		9877	
N787NC	Douglas DC-9-51	990/48149		9878	
N908H	Douglas DC-9-31	583/47517		9937; stored MZJ	
N914RW	Douglas DC-9-31	492/47362	ex N907H	9962	
N915RW	Douglas DC-9-31	169/47139	ex N8930E	9957	
N916RW	Douglas DC-9-31	239/47144	ex N8935E	9952	
N917RW	Douglas DC-9-31	247/47145	ex N8936E	9958	
N918RW	Douglas DC-9-31	248/47158	ex N8937E	9953	
N919RW	Douglas DC-9-31	255/47162	ex N8939E	9959	
N920RW	Douglas DC-9-31	256/47163	ex N8940E	9960	
N921RW	Douglas DC-9-31	259/47164	ex N8941E	9954	
N922RW	Douglas DC-9-31	271/47182	ex N8946E	9955	
N923RW	Douglas DC-9-31	272/47183	ex N8947E	9956	
N924RW	Douglas DC-9-31	275/47185	ex N8949E	9961	
N925US	Douglas DC-9-32	596/47472	ex YU-AHO	9925; stored MZJ	
N926NW	Douglas DC-9-32	589/47425	ex YU-AHL	9926	
N926RC	Douglas DC-9-32	598/47473	ex YU-AHP	9924	Lsd fr ALG DC-9
N927RC	Douglas DC-9-32	590/47469	ex YU-AHM	9923	
N940N	Douglas DC-9-32	708/47572		9918	
N941N	Douglas DC-9-32	535/47450	ex D-ADIT	9919	
N942N	Douglas DC-9-32	549/47459	ex D-ADIS	9920	
N943N	Douglas DC-9-32	773/47647		9921	
N945N	Douglas DC-9-32	775/47664		9922	
N949N	Douglas DC-9-32	691/47566		9916	
N952N	Douglas DC-9-31	161/47073		9902; stored ROW	
N953N	Douglas DC-9-31	177/47083		9903	
N955N	Douglas DC-9-31	241/47160		9905	
N956N	Douglas DC-9-31	294/47252		9906	
N957N	Douglas DC-9-31	295/47253		9907	
N958N	Douglas DC-9-31	301/47254		9908	
N959N	Douglas DC-9-31	310/47255		9909	
N960N	Douglas DC-9-31	326/47256		9910	
N961N	Douglas DC-9-31	487/47405		9911	
N962N	Douglas DC-9-31	499/47406		9912	
N963N	Douglas DC-9-31	511/47415		9913	
N964N	Douglas DC-9-31	512/47416		9914	
N965N	Douglas DC-9-31	518/47417		9915	
N967N	Douglas DC-9-32	694/47573		9917	
N982US	Douglas DC-9-32	264/45790	ex HB-IFH	9982	

N983US	Douglas DC-9-32	446/47282	ex HB-IFU	9983	Lsd fr WFBN
N984US	Douglas DC-9-32	538/47383	ex HB-IFV	9984	
N985US	Douglas DC-9-32	605/47479	ex HB-IFZ	9985	Lsd fr WFBN
N986US	Douglas DC-9-32	607/47480	ex N988US	9986	Lsd fr ALG DC-9
N987US	Douglas DC-9-32	646/47458	ex OE-LDF	9987	Lsd fr Electra
N994Z	Douglas DC-9-32	193/47097	ex N979NE	9981	
N1308T	Douglas DC-9-31	433/47315		9943	Lsd fr BCC Equipment Lsg
N1309T	Douglas DC-9-31	439/47316		9944	Lsd fr BCC Equipment Lsg
N1332U	Douglas DC-9-31	554/47404		9935	
N1334U	Douglas DC-9-31	597/47280		9933	
N1798U	Douglas DC-9-31	529/47369		9938; stored MZJ	
N1799U	Douglas DC-9-31	551/47370		9936; stored MZJ	
N3322L	Douglas DC-9-32	187/47031	ex YV-68C	9940	
N3324L	Douglas DC-9-32	205/47103	ex YV-70C	9941	
N3991C	Douglas DC-9-32	298/47175	ex PJ-SNE	9942; stored MZJ	Lsd fr ALG DC-9
N8908E	Douglas DC-9-14	50/45749		9150	
N8909E	Douglas DC-9-14	57/45770		9151	
N8911E	Douglas DC-9-14	67/45825		9152	
N8912E	Douglas DC-9-14	68/45829		9153	
N8913E	Douglas DC-9-14	75/45830		9154	
N8914E*	Douglas DC-9-14	76/45831		9155	
N8915E	Douglas DC-9-14	84/45832		9156	
N8920E	Douglas DC-9-31	95/45835		9927	
N8921E	Douglas DC-9-31	96/45836		9928	
N8923E	Douglas DC-9-31	104/45838		9929	
N8925E	Douglas DC-9-31	117/45840		9945	
N8926E	Douglas DC-9-31	124/45863		9946	
N8928E	Douglas DC-9-31	137/45865		9949	
N8929E	Douglas DC-9-31	138/45866		9948	
N8932E	Douglas DC-9-31	227/47141		9996	Lsd fr BCC Equipment Lsg
N8933E	Douglas DC-9-31	232/47142		9997	Lsd fr BCC Equipment Lsg
N8934E	Douglas DC-9-31	238/47143		9998	Lsd fr BCC Equipment Lsg
N8938E	Douglas DC-9-31	249/47161	ex 5N-GIN	9947	
N8944E	Douglas DC-9-31	266/47167		9988	
N8945E	Douglas DC-9-31	267/47181		9989	
N8950E	Douglas DC-9-31	276/47186	ex C-FBKT	9990	
N8957E	Douglas DC-9-31	313/47215		9991	
N8960E	Douglas DC-9-31	331/45869		9992	
N8978E	Douglas DC-9-31	391/47327		9995	
N8979E	Douglas DC-9-31	392/47328		9994	
N8986E	Douglas DC-9-31	482/47402	ex 5N-INZ	9993	
N9330	Douglas DC-9-31	318/47138		9966; stored MZJ	
N9331	Douglas DC-9-31	320/47263	ex (N9106)	9967	
N9332	Douglas DC-9-31	329/47264	ex (N9107)	9968	
N9333	Douglas DC-9-31	292/47246		9969	
N9334	Douglas DC-9-31	342/47247		9970	
N9335	Douglas DC-9-31	415/47337		9971	
N9336	Douglas DC-9-31	416/47338		9972; stored MZJ	
N9337	Douglas DC-9-31	464/47346		9973	
N9338	Douglas DC-9-31	478/47347		9974	
N9339	Douglas DC-9-31	479/47382		9975	
N9340	Douglas DC-9-31	489/47389		9976	
N9341	Douglas DC-9-31	490/47390		9977	
N9342	Douglas DC-9-31	491/47391		9978	
N9343	Douglas DC-9-31	501/47439		9979	
N9344	Douglas DC-9-31	502/47440		9980	
N9346	Douglas DC-9-32	517/47376	ex N394PA	9950	
N9347	Douglas DC-9-32	135/45827	ex HL7201	9951	
N9348	Douglas DC-9-15	127/45787	ex N1793U	9138	

All fitted with ABS Stage 3 hush-kits except one marked *

N211NW*	Douglas DC-10-30	171/46868	ex HB-IHP	1211	Lsd fr Electra
N221NW	Douglas DC-10-30	132/46579	ex HB-IHE	1221	Lsd fr Linc Capital
N223NW	Douglas DC-10-30	183/46580	ex HB-IHF	1223	
N224NW	Douglas DC-10-30	184/46581	ex HB-IHG	1224	
N225NW	Douglas DC-10-30	187/46582	ex HB-IHH	1225	
N226NW	Douglas DC-10-30ER	292/46583	ex HB-IHL	1226	
N227NW	Douglas DC-10-30	241/46969	ex HB-IHI	1227	
N229NW	Douglas DC-10-30	60/46551	ex N4655Y	1229	Lsd fr CIT Leasing
N230NW	Douglas DC-10-30	71/46552	ex N4655Z	1230	Lsd fr CIT Leasing
N232NW	Douglas DC-10-30	236/46961	ex N961GF	1232	Lsd fr Banc of America
N233NW	Douglas DC-10-30	240/46640	ex N962GF	1233	Lsd fr Banc of America
N234NW	Douglas DC-10-30	188/46912	ex HL7316	1234	
N235NW	Douglas DC-10-30	199/46915	ex HL7317	1235	
N236NW	Douglas DC-10-30	160/46934	ex HL7315	1236	
N237NW	Douglas DC-10-30	336/47844	ex PP-VMW	1237	
N238NW	Douglas DC-10-30ER	434/48267	ex HS-TMA	1238	
N239NW	Douglas DC-10-30ER	435/48290	ex HS-TMB	1239	
N240NW	Douglas DC-10-30ER	438/48319	ex HS-TMC	1240	
N241NW	Douglas DC-10-30	355/48282	ex PP-VMY	1241	
N242NW	Douglas DC-10-30	356/47845	ex PP-VMX	1242	
N243NW	Douglas DC-10-30ER	436/48315	ex JA8550	1243	

N244NW   Douglas DC-10-30ER   437/48316 ex JA8551   1244
*Named City of Amsterdam
DC-10-30s to be replaced or relegated to domestic service by Airbus A330-323's
Northwest has a codesharing agreement with Horizon Airlines and tie-up with KLM; owns 14% of Continental Airlines
but stake for sale. Feeder services are operated by Pinaccle Airlines (wholly owned) and Mesaba Airlines as Northwest
Airlink plus Pacific Island

NORTHWEST AIRLINK

Northwest (NW)   **Minneapolis-St Paul Intl/Memphis-Intl/Detroit-Wayne County, (MSP/MEM/DTW)**

Reg	Type	MSN	Ex	Fleet	Notes
N501XJ	Avro RJ85	E2208	ex G-ISEE	501	Lsd fr BAES
N502XJ	Avro RJ85	E2307	ex G-6-307	502	Lsd fr BAES
N503XJ	Avro RJ85	E2310	ex G-6-310	503	Lsd fr BAES
N504XJ	Avro RJ85	E2311	ex G-6-311	504	Lsd fr BAES
N505XJ	Avro RJ85	E2313	ex G-6-313	505	Lsd fr BAES
N506XJ	Avro RJ85	E2314	ex G-6-314	506	Lsd fr BAES
N507XJ	Avro RJ85	E2316	ex G-6-316	507	Lsd fr BAES
N508XJ	Avro RJ85	E2318	ex G-6-318	508	Lsd fr BAES
N509XJ	Avro RJ85	E2321	ex G-6-321	509	Lsd fr BAES
N510XJ	Avro RJ85	E2323	ex G-6-323	510	Lsd fr BAES
N511XJ	Avro RJ85	E2325	ex G-6-325	511	Lsd fr BAES
N512XJ	Avro RJ85	E2326	ex G-6-326	512	Lsd fr BAES
N513XJ	Avro RJ85	E2329	ex G-6-329	513	Lsd fr BAES
N514XJ	Avro RJ85	E2330	ex G-6-330	514	Lsd fr BAES
N515XJ	Avro RJ85	E2333	ex G-6-333	515	Lsd fr BAES
N516XJ	Avro RJ85	E2334	ex G-6-334	516	Lsd fr BAES
N517XJ	Avro RJ85	E2335	ex G-6-335	517	Lsd fr BAES
N518XJ	Avro RJ85	E2337	ex G-6-337	518	Lsd fr BAES
N519XJ	Avro RJ85	E2344	ex G-6-344	519	Lsd fr BAES
N520XJ	Avro RJ85	E2345	ex G-6-345	520	Lsd fr BAES
N521XJ	Avro RJ85	E2346	ex G-6-346	521	Lsd fr BAES
N522XJ	Avro RJ85	E2347	ex G-6-347	522	Lsd fr BAES
N523XJ	Avro RJ85	E2348	ex G-6-348	523	Lsd fr BAES
N524XJ	Avro RJ85	E2349	ex G-6-349	524	Lsd fr BAES
N525XJ	Avro RJ85	E2350	ex G-6-350	525	Lsd fr WFBN
N526XJ	Avro RJ85	E2351	ex G-6-351	526; stored GYR	
N527XJ	Avro RJ85	E2352	ex G-6-352	527; stored GYR	
N528XJ	Avro RJ85	E2353	ex G-6-353	528	
N529XJ	Avro RJ85	E2363	ex G-6-363	529; stored GYR	
N530XJ	Avro RJ85	E2364	ex G-6-364	530; stored GYR	
N531XJ	Avro RJ85	E2365	ex G-6-365	531; stored GYR	
N532XJ	Avro RJ85	E2366	ex G-6-366	532	
N533XJ	Avro RJ85	E2367	ex G-6-367	533	
N534XJ	Avro RJ85	E2370	ex G-6-370	534	
N535XJ	Avro RJ85	E2371	ex G-6-371	535	
N536XJ	Avro RJ85	E2372	ex G-6-372	536	

Operated as Northwest Jet Airlink by Mesaba Airlines

Reg	Type	MSN	Ex	Fleet	Notes
N8390A*	Canadair CL-600-2B19	7390	ex C-FMOW	8390	Spirit of 'Memphis Belle'
N8396A*	Canadair CL-600-2B19	7396	ex C-FMMB	8396	
N8409N*	Canadair CL-600-2B19	7409	ex C-FMLI	8409	
N8412F*	Canadair CL-600-2B19	7412	ex C-FMLT	8412	
N8416B*	Canadair CL-600-2B19	7416	ex C-FMNW	8416	
N8423C*	Canadair CL-600-2B19	7423	ex C-FMNQ	8423	
N8432A*	Canadair CL-600-2B19	7432	ex C-GHRR	8432	
N8444F*	Canadair CL-600-2B19	7444	ex C-FMMT	8444	
N8458A*	Canadair CL-600-2B19	7458	ex C-FMMN	8458	
N8475B*	Canadair CL-600-2B19	7475	ex C-	8475	
N8477R*	Canadair CL-600-2B19	7477	ex C-FMNX	8477	
N8488D*	Canadair CL-600-2B19	7488	ex C-FMMN	8488	
N8492C*	Canadair CL-600-2B19	7492	ex	8492	
N8495B*	Canadair CL-600-2B19	7495	ex C-FMKW	8495	
N8501F	Canadair CL-600-2B19	7501	ex C-FMLS	8501	
N8505Q	Canadair CL-600-2B19	7505	ex C-FMNH	8505	
N8506C	Canadair CL-600-2B19	7506	ex C-FMNW	8506	
N8515F*	Canadair CL-600-2B19	7515	ex C-FMOI	8515	
N8516C*	Canadair CL-600-2B19	7516	ex C-FMMB	8516	
N8524A*	Canadair CL-600-2B19	7524	ex C-FMKV	8524	
N8525B*	Canadair CL-600-2B19	7525	ex C-FMKW	8525	
N8532G*	Canadair CL-600-2B19	7532	ex C-FMLT	8532	
N8533D*	Canadair CL-600-2B19	7533	ex C-FMLV	8533	
N8541D*	Canadair CL-600-2B19	7541	ex C-FVAZ	8541	
N8543F*	Canadair CL-600-2B19	7543	ex C-FMNQ	8543	
N8554A*	Canadair CL-600-2B19	7554	ex C-FMKV	8554	
N8560F*	Canadair CL-600-2B19	7560	ex C-FMLQ	8560	
N8577D*	Canadair CL-600-2B19	7577	ex C-FMML	8577	
N8580A*	Canadair CL-600-2B19	7580	ex C-FMMW	8580	
N8587E*	Canadair CL-600-2B19	7587	ex C-FMLB	8587	
N8588D*	Canadair CL-600-2B19	7588	ex C-GJSZ	8588	First RJ-440
N8598B*	Canadair CL-600-2B19	7598	ex C-FMNY	8598	

N8604C*	Canadair CL-600-2B19	7604	ex C-FMLU	8604	
N8611A*	Canadair CL-600-2B19	7611	ex C-FMMX	8611	
N8623A*	Canadair CL-600-2B19	7623	ex C-FMLV	8623	
N8631E*	Canadair CL-600-2B19	7631	ex C-FVAZ	8631	
N8646A*	Canadair CL-600-2B19	7646	ex C-FMKZ	8646	
N8659B*	Canadair CL-600-2B19	7659	ex C-FMOS	8659	
N8665A*	Canadair CL-600-2B19	7665	ex C-FMOI	8665	
N8672A	Canadair CL-600-2B19	7672	ex C-FMMY	8672	
N8673D*	Canadair CL-600-2B19	7673	ex C-FMNB	8673	
N8674A	Canadair CL-600-2B19	7674	ex C-FMKV	8674	
N8683B	Canadair CL-600-2B19	7683	ex C-FMLV	8683	
N8688C	Canadair CL-600-2B19	7688	ex C-FMNY	6888	
N8694A*	Canadair CL-600-2B19	7694	ex C-FMLU	8694	
N8696C*	Canadair CL-600-2B19	7696	ex C-FMMB	8696	
N8698A*	Canadair CL-600-2B19	7698	ex C-FMMN	8698	
N8709A*	Canadair CL-600-2B19	7709	ex C-FMLI	8709	
N8710A*	Canadair CL-600-2B19	7710	ex C-FMLQ	8710	
N8718E*	Canadair CL-600-2B19	7718	ex C-FMNY	8718	
N8721B*	Canadair CL-600-2B19	7721	ex C-FVAZ	8721	
N8733G	Canadair CL-600-2B19	7733	ex C-FMNB	8733	
N8736A	Canadair CL-600-2B19	7736	ex C-FMKZ	8736	
N8745B	Canadair CL-600-2B19	7745	ex C-FMNH	8745	
N8747B	Canadair CL-600-2B19	7747	ex C-FMNX	8747	
N8751D	Canadair CL-600-2B19	7751	ex C-FVAZ	8751	
N8758D	Canadair CL-600-2B19	7758	ex C-FMMN	8758	
N8771A*	Canadair CL-600-2B19	7771	ex C-FMLS	8771	
N8775A*	Canadair CL-600-2B19	7775	ex C-FMNH	8775	
N8783E*	Canadair CL-600-2B19	7783	ex C-FMNQ	8783	
N8790A*	Canadair CL-600-2B19	7790	ex C-FMMW	8790	
N8794B*	Canadair CL-600-2B19	7794	ex C-FMKV	8794	
N8797A*	Canadair CL-600-2B19	7797	ex C-FMLB	8797	
N8800G*	Canadair CL-600-2B19	7800	ex C-FMLQ	8800	
N8808H*	Canadair CL-600-2B19	7808	ex C-FMNY	8808	
N8828D*	Canadair CL-600-2B19	7828	ex C-FMLF	8828	
N8836A*	Canadair CL-600-2B19	7836	ex C-FMNW	8836	
N8837B*	Canadair CL-600-2B19	7837	ex C-FMNX	8837	
N8839E*	Canadair CL-600-2B19	7839	ex C-FMOS	8839	
N8847A*	Canadair CL-600-2B19	7847	ex C-FMML	8847	
N8855A*	Canadair CL-600-2B19	7855	ex C-FMKW	8855	
N8869B*	Canadair CL-600-2B19	7869	ex C-FMOS	8869	
N8877A*	Canadair CL-600-2B19	7877	ex C-FMML	8877	
N8883E*	Canadair CL-600-2B19	7883	ex C-FMNB	8883	
N8884E*	Canadair CL-600-2B19	7884	ex C-FMKV	8884	
N8886A*	Canadair CL-600-2B19	7886	ex C-FMKZ	8886	
N8888D	Canadair CL-600-2819	7888	ex C-	8888	
N8891A	Canadair CL-600-2B19	7891	ex C-	8891	
N8894A	Canadair CL-600-2B19	7894	ex C-	8894	
N	Canadair CL-600-2B19		ex C-	on order	
N	Canadair CL-600-2B19		ex C-	on order	
N	Canadair CL-600-2B19		ex C-	on order	
N	Canadair CL-600-2B19		ex C-	on order	
N	Canadair CL-600-2B19		ex C-	on order	
N	Canadair CL-600-2B19		ex C-	on order	
N	Canadair CL-600-2B19		ex C-	on order	
N	Canadair CL-600-2B19		ex C-	on order	
N	Canadair CL-600-2B19		ex C-	on order	
N	Canadair CL-600-2B19		ex C-	on order	
N	Canadair CL-600-2B19		ex C-	on order	
N	Canadair CL-600-2B19		ex C-	on order	
N	Canadair CL-600-2B19		ex C-	on order	
N	Canadair CL-600-2B19		ex C-	on order	

All operated by Pinnacle Airlines ; *leased from Wells Fargo Bank Northwest; a further 18 Canadair CL-600-2B19s are on order for future delivery for operation by Pinnacle Airlines. From c/n 7588 aircraft are RJ-440s (44-seaters)

N27XJ*	SAAB SF.340A	027	ex N320PX		Lsd fr WFBN
N46XJ*	SAAB SF.340A	046	ex N323PX		Lsd fr WFBN
N48XJ*	SAAB SF.340A	048	ex N324PX		Lsd fr WFBN
N68XJ*	SAAB SF.340A	068	ex N328PX		
N79XJ*	SAAB SF.340A	079	ex N340PX		
N98XJ*	SAAB SF.340A	098	ex N98MQ		
N99XJ*	SAAB SF.340A	099	ex N99RZ		
N106XJ*	SAAB SF.340A	106	ex N106PX		
N110XJ*	SAAB SF.340A	110	ex N110MQ	dam 21Jul02	
N112XJ*	SAAB SF.340A	112	ex N112AE		
N114XJ*	SAAB SF.340A	114	ex N114SB		
N115XJ*	SAAB SF.340A	115	ex N115SB	stored Loring	
N119XJ*	SAAB SF.340A	119	ex N119AE		
N142XJ*	SAAB SF.340A	142	ex N341PX		Lsd fr Banc of America
N360PX*	SAAB SF.340B	220	ex SE-G20	Spirit of Pensacola	Lsd fr WFBN
N361PX*	SAAB SF.340B	249	ex SE-G49		Lsd fr WFBN
N362PX*	SAAB SF.340B	258	ex SE-G58		Lsd fr WFBN
N363PX*	SAAB SF.340B	260	ex SE-G60	Spirit of the Pine Belt	

N364PX*	SAAB SF.340B	262	ex SE-G62	
N365PX*	SAAB SF.340B	265	ex SE-G65	
N366PX*	SAAB SF.340B	267	ex SE-G67	
N367PX*	SAAB SF.340B	271	ex SE-G71	Spirit of Montgomery
N368PX*	SAAB SF.340B	274	ex SE-G74	
N369PX*	SAAB SF.340B	295	ex SE-G95	Spirit of Lafayette
N370PX*	SAAB SF.340B	300	ex SE-E03	Spirit of Monroe
N402XJ*	SAAB SF.340B	402	ex SE-B02	Lsd fr Wachovia Bank
N403XJ*	SAAB SF.340B	403	ex SE-B03	Lsd fr Wachovia Bank
N404XJ*	SAAB SF.340B	404	ex SE-B04	
N406XJ*	SAAB SF.340B	406	ex SE-B06	Lsd fr Wachovia Bank
N407XJ*	SAAB SF.340B	407	ex SE-B07	
N408XJ*	SAAB SF.340B	408	ex SE-B08	
N410XJ*	SAAB SF.340B	410	ex SE-B10	Lsd fr Wachovia Bank
N411XJ*	SAAB SF.340B	411	ex SE-B11	Lsd fr Wachovia Bank
N412XJ*	SAAB SF.340B	412	ex SE-B12	Lsd fr Wachovia Bank
N413XJ*	SAAB SF.340B	413	ex SE-B13	Lsd fr Wachovia Bank
N414XJ*	SAAB SF.340B	414	ex SE-B14	Lsd fr Wachovia Bank
N415XJ*	SAAB SF.340B	415	ex SE-B15	Lsd fr Wachovia Bank
N416XJ*	SAAB SF.340B	416	ex SE-B16	
N417XJ*	SAAB SF.340B	417	ex SE-B17	Lsd fr Wachovia Bank
N418XJ*	SAAB SF.340B	418	ex SE-B18	Lsd fr Wachovia Bank
N420XJ*	SAAB SF.340B	420	ex SE-B20	Lsd fr Wachovia Bank
N421XJ*	SAAB SF.340B	421	ex SE-B21	Lsd fr Wachovia Bank
N422XJ*	SAAB SF.340B	422	ex SE-B22	
N423XJ*	SAAB SF.340B	423	ex SE-B23	
N424XJ*	SAAB SF.340B	424	ex SE-B24	
N425XJ*	SAAB SF.340B	425	ex SE-B25	
N426XJ*	SAAB SF.340B	426	ex SE-B26	
N427XJ*	SAAB SF.340B	427	ex SE-B27	
N428XJ*	SAAB SF.340B	428	ex SE-B28	
N429XJ*	SAAB SF.340B	429	ex SE-B29	
N430XJ*	SAAB SF.340B	430	ex SE-B30	
N433XJ*	SAAB SF.340B	433	ex SE-B33	
N434XJ*	SAAB SF.340B	434	ex SE-B34	
N435XJ*	SAAB SF.340B	435	ex SE-B35	
N436XJ*	SAAB SF.340B	436	ex SE-B36	
N437XJ*	SAAB SF.340B	437	ex SE-B37	
N438XJ*	SAAB SF.340B	438	ex SE-B38	
N439XJ*	SAAB SF.340B	439	ex SE-B39	
N441XJ*	SAAB SF.340B	441	ex SE-B41	25th Anniversary c/s
N442XJ*	SAAB SF.340B	442	ex SE-B42	
N443XJ*	SAAB SF.340B	443	ex SE-B43	
N444XJ*	SAAB SF.340B	444	ex SE-B44	
N445XJ*	SAAB SF.340B	445	ex SE-B45	
N446XJ*	SAAB SF.340B	446	ex SE-B46	stored
N447XJ*	SAAB SF.340B	447	ex SE-B47	
N448XJ*	SAAB SF.340B	448	ex SE-B48	
N449XJ*	SAAB SF.340B	449	ex SE-B49	
N450XJ*	SAAB SF.340B	450	ex SE-B50	
N451XJ*	SAAB SF.340B	451	ex SE-B51	500th SAAB regional a/c c/s
N452XJ*	SAAB SF.340B	452	ex SE-B52	
N453XJ*	SAAB SF.340B	453	ex SE-B53	
N454XJ*	SAAB SF.340B	454	ex SE-B54	
N456XJ*	SAAB SF.340B	456	ex SE-B56	
N457XJ*	SAAB SF.340B	457	ex SE-B57	
N991XJ*	SAAB SF.340A	091	ex N91MQ	stored BGR

*Operated by Mesaba Airlines
Northwest Airlink is the operating name for a network of feeder services op by Pinnacle Airlines, [9E/FGL] a wholly owned subsidiary, and Mesaba Airlines, [XJ/MES], in conjunction with Northwest Airlines using Northwest's NW designator. Services also provided by Pacific Island Aviation

NORTHWEST SEAPLANES

(2G)				Seattle-Lake Union, WA/Seattle-Renton (LKS/RNT)
N90YC	de Havilland DHC-2 Beaver	1338	ex N67675	
N67681	de Havilland DHC-2 Beaver	1158	ex N215LU	
N67684	de Havilland DHC-2 Beaver	1208	ex N67894	Lsd to Air Rainbow
N67685	de Havilland DHC-2 Beaver	1250	ex N128WA	Lsd fr Air Rainbow
N67687	de Havilland DHC-2 Beaver	1359	ex N301GT	
N67689	de Havilland DHC-2 Beaver	1338	ex N127WA	Lsd to Air Rainbow

All floatplanes

N120JD	Piper PA-31-350 Panther II	31-8152179	
N1030N	Cessna 208B Caravan I	208B0326	

OFFSHORE LOGISTICS (OLOG)

Parent company of helicopter operating companies around the world including Bristow Helicopters (G, PK, VH & 5N), Heliltalia (I), Norsk Helicopter (LN), Air Logistics (N) and Heliservicico (XA).

OKAIR AIRLINES

N508FA	Swearingen SA.227AC Metro III	AC-508	ex ZK-NSW		Lsd fr EDB Air
N542FA	Swearingen SA.227AC Metro III	AC-542	ex ZK-NSX		Lsd fr EDB Air
N765FA	Swearingen SA.227AC Metro III	AC-765B	ex ZK-NSI		Lsd fr EDB Air

OLSON AIR SERVICE

(4B)   *Nome, AK (OME)*

N412CA	Cessna 402C	402C0005
N75773	Cessna T207A Turbo Stationair 8	20700643

OMNI AIR INTERNATIONAL

Omni (X9/OAE)   *Tulsa-Intl, OK (TUL)*

N189AX	Douglas DC-10-30F	354/48277	ex N48277		Lsd fr WFBN
N279AX	Douglas DC-10-30F	316/47816	ex N47816	stored ROW	Lsd fr Prop Three
N450AX	Douglas DC-10-10	162/46942	ex N161AA	stored VCV	
N540AX	Douglas DC-10-30	299/46595	ex D-ADPO		
N630AX	Douglas DC-10-30	301/46596	ex D-ADQO		
N720AX	Douglas DC-10-30	342/48252	ex D-ADSO		
N810AX	Douglas DC-10-30ER	345/48265	ex F-GPVC		
N17085	Douglas DC-10-30	201/47957	ex F-GPVB		
N59083	Douglas DC-10-30	170/47926	ex OO-SLG		
N49082	Douglas DC-10-30	190/47927	ex OO-SLH		
N369AX	Boeing 757-2Q8	723/28161	ex N543NA		Lsd fr ILFC
N459AX	Boeing 757-2Q8	457/25621	ex N551NA		Lsd fr ILFC

OMNIFLIGHT HELICOPTERS

Dallas-Addison, TX (ADS)

N206AZ	Bell 206L-3 LongRanger III	51007	ex N725RE		
N206MH	Bell 206L-1 LongRanger II	45426	ex N518EH	EMS	Op for Native American
N224LF	Bell 206L-1 LongRanger II	45199	ex N5013Y	EMS	Op for Native American
N314LS	Bell 206L-3 LiongRanger III	51006	ex N2210H	EMS	Op for Native American
N519EH	Bell 206L-1 LongRanger III	45429			
N721SP	Bell 206L-1 LongRanger III	45486			
N117AP	MBB BK117A-3	7144	ex N311LS		Lsd fr Textron
N117LF	MBB BK117A-4	7013	ex N3919A		
N117LS	MBB BK117A-3	7113	ex N628MB		
N117M	MBB BK117A-3	7023	ex N39251	EMS	
N117MH	MBB BK117A-3	7112	ex N627MB	EMS	
N117MK	MBB BK117B-2	7196	ex N117BK	EMS	Lsd fr WFBN
N117NG	MBB BK117A-4	7083	ex N312LF		
N117UC	MBB BK117B-1	7206	ex N214AE	EMS	
N117VU	MBB BK117B-1	7211	ex N8194S		
N118LL	MBB BK117A-3	7097	ex N117SJ		
N170MC	MBB BK117B-1	7217	ex N7161S		
N171MU	MBB BK117A-4	7138	ex N313LF		Lsd fr Textron
N217MC	MBB BK117B-1	7195	ex N54113	EMS	Op for Mayo Foundation
N312LS	MBB BK117A-3	7061	ex N117CH		Lsd fr CIT Lsg
N317MC	MBB BK117C-1	7505	ex N117AE	EMS	Op for Mayo Foundation
N460H	MBB BK117B-1	7142	ex N90266	EMS	Lsd fr Textron
N527MB	MBB BK117A-3	7103	ex D-HBPX		
N711FC	MBB BK117A-4	7070	ex N311LF	EMS	Lsd fr IACI Vince
N911MZ	MBB BK117A-3	7098	ex N117UC		
N1140H	MBB BK117A-3	7078	ex N212AE		
N4493X	MBB BK117A-3	7038	ex D-HBMM		Lsd fr CIT Lsg
N75LV	Beech B200 Super King Air	BB-1075	ex C-GTDY	EMS	Lsd fr C-FWC Medical Centre
N219HM	Bell 222UT	47573	ex C-FTIU	EMS	Lsd fr Key Corp Lsg
N222HX	Bell 222UT	47533	ex N3201W		Lsd fr Key Corp Lsg
N230EM	Bell 230	23011			
N350AZ	Aerospatiale AS.350B2 AStar	3127	ex N4037A		
N350GR	Aerospatiale AS.350B AStar	3140		EMS	Op for Native American
N911GF	Aerospatiale AS.350B2 AStar	3140			
N911LW	Bell 222UT	47520		EMS	Lsd fr HCA Health Svs
N911MK	Bell 222UT	47515	ex N4072G		Lsd fr CIT Lsg
N911SV	Eurocopter EC135P1	0070	ex N4066P		Lsd fr WFBN
N911SY	MBB Bo105LS-A3	2033	ex N911SV		Lsd fr debis
N5230J	Aerospatiale AS.350B3 AStar	3256			
N40751	Aerospatiale AS.350B2 AStar	3154			

PACE AIRLINES

Pace (PCE) — Winston-Salem-Smith Reynolds, NC (INT)

Reg	Type	c/n	ex	Notes	Lease
N37NY	Boeing 737-4Y0	1651/23976	ex N773RA	Op for New York Knicks & Rangers	Lsd fr MSG Aircraft Lsg
N219PA	Boeing 737-222 (Nordam 3)	211/19956	ex (N737AP)		
N234TR	Boeing 737-228 (Nordam 3)	941/23004	ex F-GBYE		Lsd fr Triton
N249TR	Boeing 737-2K5 (Nordam 3)	792/22598	ex F-GFLX		Lsd fr Triton
N250TR	Boeing 737-2K5 (Nordam 3)	779/22597	ex F-GFLV	Hooters Air	Lsd fr Triton
N251TR	Boeing 737-228 (Nordam 3)	1397/23792	ex F-GBYP		Lsd fr Triton
N252TR	Boeing 737-228 (Nordam 3)	936/23001	ex F-GBYB	Hooters Air	Lsd fr Triton
N304AW*	Boeing 737-3G7	1608/24011			Lsd fr CIT Leasing
N371PA*	Boeing 737-306	1325/23543	ex PH-BDH		Lsd fr GECAS
N372PA	Boeing 737-306	1349/23546	ex PH-BDL	The Dee Pacemaker	Lsd fr GECAS
N373PA	Boeing 737-3Y0	1389/23749	ex N749AP	The Steffie Pacemaker	Lsd fr Aero USA
N374PA	Boeing 737-36M	2810/28333	ex HB-IIL	all-white	Lsd fr AFT Trust-Sub
N375PA	Boeing 737-3Y0	1511/23812	ex N238CT	The Lisa Pacemaker	Lsd fr CIT Lsg
N920WA	Boeing 737-236 (Nordam 3)	626/21791	ex G-BGDB		Lsd fr Sunwest Intl
N513NA	Boeing 757-2T7	132/23895	ex N513NA	The Grace Evelyn Pacemaker	
N526NA	Boeing 757-236	278/24794	ex		Lsd fr Tombo
N750WL	Boeing 757-2G5	146/23928	ex N751PA	Hooters Air	Lsd fr East Trust-Sub;
N801DM	Boeing 757-256	561/26240	ex N286CD	Op for Dallas Mavericks	Lsd fr MLW Avn

PACE Airlines is owned by Hooters Air.
*Operated for Vacation Express may be switched to provide scheduled domestic charters for Interstate Jet

PACIFIC HELICOPTER SERVICES

Kahului-Heliport, HI

Reg	Type	c/n	ex	Lease
N1076C	Bell TH-1F	6436	ex N64F	
N3280U	Bell UH-1H	9098	ex 66-16904	
N4963F	Bell TH-1L	6404	ex Bu157809	
N6131P	Bell UH-1H	5787	ex 66-16093	
N6226H	Bell UH-1B	3115	ex 66-14420	
N8079E	Bell UH-1H	4762	ex 65-9718	
N80780	Bell UH-1H	4527	ex 64-13820	
N64F	Bell 204B	2027	ex N103CR	
N261F	Sikorsky S-61N	61771	ex G-BEOO	
N264F	Sikorsky S-61N	61821	ex C-FMAG	Lsd fr Coulson Aircrane
N265F	Sikorsky S-61N	61492	ex C-FCLM	Lsd fr Coulson Aircrane
N503AH	Bell 206B JetRanger	686	ex C-FAOL	
N529RS	Bell 206B JetRanger	989	ex JA9102	
N622F	Bell 222U	47543	ex C-GIVU	
N866JH	Ted Smith Aerostar 601	61-0042-83	ex N7471S	
N2011W	Bell 212	30957		
N6651H	Bell 206L-1 LongRanger II	45211		
N8649Z	Cessna TP206C Super Skylane	P206-0449		
N20128	Bell 212	30951		
N38993	Bell 206L-1 LongRanger III	45601		
N73280	Bell 204B	2016		

PACIFIC ISLAND AVIATION

Pacific Isle (9J/PSA) (IATA 321) — Saipan (SPN)

Reg	Type	c/n	ex	Lease
N711HJ	Short SD.3-60	SH3697	ex G-BMUW	Lsd fr WFBN
N711MP	Short SD.3-60	SH3698	ex G-BMUX	Lsd fr WFBN
N711PK	Short SD.3-60	SH3696	ex G-BMUV	Lsd fr WFBN

Operated for Northwest Airlines as Northwest Airlink in full colours using NW flight numbers

PACIFIC SKYWAY

Shreveport, LA/Santa Maria-Public, CA (DTN/SMX)

Reg	Type	c/n	ex
N650JX	British Aerospace Jetstream 31	650	ex N405AE
N653JX	British Aerospace Jetstream 31	653	ex N407AE

Joint operations with Casino Airlines

PACIFIC WINGS

Tsunami (LW/NMI) (IATA 568) — Kahului-Intl, HI (OGG)

Reg	Type	c/n	Lease
N301PW	Cessna 208B Caravan I	208B0983	Lsd fr Aero Wing Equipment
N302PW	Cessna 208B Caravan I	208B0984	Lsd fr Bravo Wing Equipment
N303PW	Cessna 208B Caravan I	208B0985	Lsd fr Coast Wing Equipment

N811PW	Cessna 402C	402C0078	ex N811AN	
N814PW	Cessna 402C	402C0277	ex N814AN	
N815PW	Cessna 402C	402C0098	ex N815AN	
N816PW	Cessna 402C	402C0261	ex N816AN	
N817PW	Cessna 402C	402C0353	ex N817AN	

PAN AM – PAN AMERICAN AIRWAYS

Clipper (PN/PAA)   Portsmouth-Pease Intl, NH (PSM)

N342PA	Boeing 727-222 (FedEx 3)	1503/21893	ex N7298U	Bahamas CI	Lsd fr Guilford
N343PA	Boeing 727-222 (FedEx 3)	1505/21894	ex N7299U		Lsd fr Guilford
N346PA	Boeing 727-222 (FedEx 3)	1528/21904	ex N7450U	CI Lady Thatcher	Lsd fr Guilford
N347PA	Boeing 727-222 (FedEx 3)	1507/21895	ex N7441U	CI Ronald Reagan	Lsd fr Guilford
N348PA	Boeing 727-222 (FedEx 3)	1639/21921	ex N7468U		Lsd fr Guilford
N349PA	Boeing 727-222 (FedEx 3)	1515/21898	ex N7444U		Lsd fr Guilford
N357PA	Boeing 727-222 (FedEx 3)	1511/21896	ex N7442U	CI Dominican	Lsd fr Guilford
N361PA	Boeing 727-225 (Raisbeck 3)	939/20623	ex N8861E	CI A Jay Cristol	Lsd fr Guilford
N362PA	Boeing 727-2J0 (Raisbeck 3)	1160/21106	ex 6Y-JMN		Lsd fr Guilford
N363PA	Boeing 727-221 (Duganair 3)	1764/22535		CI Walt Heimer	Lsd fr Guilford
N364PA	Boeing 727-2J0 (Duganair 3)	1172/21107	ex 6Y-JMO	CI Deschapelles	Lsd fr Guilford
N365PA	Boeing 727-225 (Duganair 3)	948/20628	ex N8866E	CI Portsmouth	Lsd fr Guilford
N367PA	Boeing 727-221 (Raisbeck 3)	1794/22539		CI Egil	Lsd fr Aeron
N369PA	Boeing 727-282 (Raisbeck 3)	1579/21950	ex N609KW	CI Pathfinder	Lsd fr Guilford
N7445U	Boeing 727-222 (FedEx 3)	1517/21899		stored SFM	Lsd fr Guilford
N7446U	Boeing 727-222 (FedEx 3)	1519/21900		stored SFM	Lsd fr Guilford
N7448U	Boeing 727-222 (FedEx 3)	1524/21902		stored SFM	Lsd fr Guilford
N7464U	Boeing 727-222 (FedEx 3)	1625/21918		stored SFM	Lsd fr Guilford

Feeder services provided by Boston-Maine Airways in full colours as Pan Am Services

PAPILLON GRAND CANYON AIRWAYS

(HI) (IATA 563)   Grand Canyon-Heliport, AZ, (JGC)

N121US	Aerospatiale AS.350BA AStar	1447	ex B-HJP		
N170PA	Aerospatiale AS.350B2 AStar	2637	ex ZK-HNG		Lsd fr Zuni LLC
N453NW	Aerospatiale AS.350B2 AStar	2475	ex HB-XYC		Lsd fr Juliet Inc
N911KR	Aerospatiale AS.350B2 AStar	2094	ex N94LH		Lsd fr Zuni LLC
N6093R	Aerospatiale AS.350B2 AStar	2415			Lsd fr Juliet Inc
N7VG	Bell 206L-1 LongRanger III	45463		5	Lsd fr Monarch Enterprises
N177PA	Bell 206L-1 LongRanger III	45194	ex N992PA	17	Lsd fr Foxtrot Inc
N178PA	Bell 206L-1 LongRanger III	45319	ex F-ODUB	18	Lsd fr Monarch Enterprises
N333ER	Bell 206L-1 LongRanger III	45203		12	Lsd fr Monarch Enterprises
N1075S	Bell 206L-1 LongRanger III	45366		10	
N1076T	Bell 206L-1 LongRanger III	45373			
N2072M	Bell 206L-1 LongRanger II	45720			Lsd fr Monarch Enterprises
N3893U	Bell 206L-3 LongRanger III	51020		9	Lsd fr Monarch Enterprises
N3895D	Bell 206L-1 LongRanger II	45590		1	Lsd fr Monarch Enterprises
N4227E	Bell 206L-1 LongRanger III	45702	ex N725RE		Lsd fr Monarch Enterprises
N5743C	Bell 206L-1 LongRanger II	45474			Lsd fr Juliet Inc
N5745Y	Bell 206L-1 LongRanger II	45531		11	Lsd fr Monarch Enterprises
N10761	Bell 206L-1 LongRanger II	45381			Lsd fr Zuni LLC
N20316	Bell 206L-1 LongRanger II	45687			Lsd fr Bravo I Inc
N22425	Bell 206L-1 LongRanger II	45743			Lsd fr Bravo I Inc
N27694	Bell 206L-1 LongRanger II	45282		4	Lsd fr Monarch Enterprises
N38903	Bell 206L-3 LongRanger III	51017			
N50046	Bell 206L-1 LongRanger II	45173			
N57491	Bell 206L-1 LongRanger II	45505		15	Lsd fr Monarch Enterprises
N175PA	Bell 407	53154			Lsd fr Juliet Inc
N179PA	MD Helicopters MD900 Explorer	900-00021	ex N811CM		Lsd fr Gulf Inc
N8533F	Bell 206B JetRanger III	254			Lsd fr Gulf Inc
N17756	Sikorsky S-55QT	V55400T	ex 140958		Lsd fr Monarch Enterprises
N17758	Sikorsky S-55QT	V55396T		19	Op for National Park Service
					Lsd fr Foxtrot Inc
N21507	Bell 206B JetRanger III	3464			Lsd fr Monarch Enterprises
N83037	Bell 206B JetRanger III	1128		7	Lsd fr Monarch Enterprises
N90065	Bell 206B JetRanger III	1572			Lsd fr Monarch Enterprises

PARAGON AIR EXPRESS

Paragon Express (PGX)   Nashville-Intl, TN (BNA)

N702PA	Cessna 208B Caravan I	208B0702	ex (N702SE)	Freighter
N703PA	Cessna 208B Caravan I	208B0776		Freighter

PENAIR

Peninsula(KS/PEN)

N4327P	Piper PA-32-301 Saratoga	32-8406002		
N8004N	Piper PA-32-301 Saratoga	32-8206014		
N8212H	Piper PA-32-301 Saratoga	32-8006046		
N8259V	Piper PA-32-301 Saratoga	32-8006097		
N8305H	Piper PA-32-301 Saratoga	32-8106017		
N8327S	Piper PA-32-301 Saratoga	32-8106039		
N8361Q	Piper PA-32-301 Saratoga	32-8106055		
N8402S	Piper PA-32-301 Saratoga	32-8106075		
N8429N	Piper PA-32-301 Saratoga	32-8106089		
N8470Y	Piper PA-32-301 Saratoga	32-8206012		
N81052	Piper PA-32-301 Saratoga	32-8206023		
N81844	Piper PA-32-301 Saratoga	32-8006012		
N82455	Piper PA-32-301 Saratoga	32-8006079		
N15PR	Piper PA-31-350 Chieftain	31-8352011		
N28KE	Piper PA-31-350 Chieftain	31-8152049	ex N826CB	
N3588Z	Piper PA-31-350 Chieftain	31-8052130		
N27663	Piper PA-31-350 Navajo Chieftain	31-7852094		
N27801	Piper PA-31-350 Navajo Chieftain	31-7852157		
N27987	Piper PA-31 Turbo Navajo C	31-7912054		
N41NE	Swearingen SA.227AC Metro III	AC-741B	ex C-FNAM	
N640PA	Swearingen SA.227AC Metro III	AC-759B	ex N306NE	Lsd fr IMH A/c Lsg
N650PA	Swearingen SA.227AC Metro III	AC-775B		
N892DC	Swearingen SA.227DC Metro 23	DC-892B	ex C-GAFO	
N2719H	Swearingen SA.227AC Metro III	AC-713B		
N655PA	SAAB SF.340B	181	ex N590MA	Lsd fr SAAB
N675PA	SAAB SF.340B	206	ex N593MA	Spirit of Bristol Bay Lsd fr SAAB
N685PA	SAAB SF.340B	212	ex N594MA	Spirit of the Aleutians Lsd fr SAAB
N700RD	Piper PA-31T3-1040	31T-5575001	ex HP-1101P	
N741	Grumman G-21A Goose	B-97		
N750PA	Cessna 208B Caravan I	208B0628		
N7811	Grumman G-21A Goose	B-122		
N9304F	Cessna 208 Caravan I	20800008		Lsd fr GSST LLC
N9481F	Cessna 208 Caravan I	20800070		Lsd fr Avion Corp
N22932	Grumman G-21A Goose	B-139	ex CF-WCP	

Operates services on behalf of Alaska Airlines Commuter using flight numbers in the range 4200-4299
Penair is the trading name of Peninsula Airways

PETROLEUM HELICOPTERS

Petroleum (PHM)

N351LG	Aerospatiale AS.350B3 AStar	3722	ex N580AE	
N499AE	Aerospatiale AS.350B3 AStar	3690		
N732AE	Aerospatiale AS.350B2 AStar	2873	ex N4000L	EMS
N954AE	Aerospatiale AS.350B2 AStar	3248	ex N854PH	
N956AE	Aerospatiale AS.350B2 AStar	3352	ex N856PH	
N970AE	Aerospatiale AS.350B3 AStar	3235		EMS
N971AE	Aerospatiale AS.350B3 AStar	3230		EMS
N972AE	Aerospatiale AS.350B3 AStar	3234		EMS
N973AE	Aerospatiale AS.350B3 AStar	3229		EMS
N974AE	Aerospatiale AS.350B2 AStar	2653	ex N350BZ	
N975AE	Aerospatiale AS.350B2 AStar	2777	ex N6095S	
N4031L	Aerospatiale AS.350B2 AStar	2907		Based Antarctica
N4036H	Aerospatiale AS.350B2 AStar	2919		Based Antarctica
N40466	Aerospatiale AS.350B2 AStar	3004		
N103PH	Bell 206B JetRanger III	3000	ex F-GHRS	
N2268V	Bell 206B JetRanger III	3605		
N2270G	Bell 206B JetRanger III	3610		
N2272J	Bell 206B JetRanger III	3620		
N2275Y	Bell 206B JetRanger III	3626		
N2277A	Bell 206B JetRanger III	3630		
N2753F	Bell 206B JetRanger III	2729		
N22743	Bell 206B JetRanger III	3624		
N22751	Bell 206B JetRanger III	3627		
N30KH	Bell 206L-3 LongRanger III	51527	ex HK-3726X	
N42EA	Bell 206L-3 LongRanger III	51542	ex OM-WIP	
N45RP	Bell 206L-1 LongRanger II	45521	ex HC-BXS	
N49EA	Bell 206L-3 LongRanger III	51507	ex D-HHSG	
N81SP	Bell 206L-3 LongRanger III	51029	ex N82AW	Lsd fr WFBN
N83MT	Bell 206L-1 LongRanger II	45492		
N92MT	Bell 206L-3 LongRanger III	51175		Lsd fr WFBN
N108PH	Bell 206L-3 LongRanger III	51334	ex C-FPUB	Lsd fr WFBN

N129MR	Bell 206L-3 LongRanger III	51129	Lsd fr WFBN
N141BH	Bell 206L-3 LongRanger III	51303	ex HK-4141X
N205FC	Bell 206L-3 LongRanger III	51130	Lsd fr Fifth Third Lsg
N206FS	Bell 206L-3 LongRanger III	51506	Lsd fr CIT Leasing
N206LS	Bell 206L-3 LongRanger III	51070	Lsd fr Fifth Third Lsg
N319E	Bell 206L-3 LongRanger III	51042	ex N3193E	Lsd fr Exxon Corp
N363BH	Bell 206L-3 LongRanger III	51345	ex N997PT
N406EH	Bell 206L-2 LongRanger II	45183	
N436PH	Bell 206L-3 LongRanger III	51436	ex EI-CIO
N515KA	Bell 206L-3 LongRanger III	51048	
N593AE	Bell 206L-2 LongRanger II	45421	ex N513EH
N595AE	Bell 206L-1 LongRanger II	45244	ex N5019F
N979BH	Bell 206L-3 LongRanger III	51403	ex N998PT
N1076Y	Bell 206L-1 LongRanger II	45380	
N1078D	Bell 206L-1 LongRanger II	45397	
N2133X	Bell 206L-1 LongRanger II	45634	Lsd fr Fifth Third Lsg
N2135V	Bell 206L-1 LongRanger II	45657	
N2249Z	Bell 206L-1 LongRanger II	45753	
N2758N	Bell 206L-1 LongRanger II	45267	
N2759U	Bell 206L-1 LongRanger II	45272	
N2761N	Bell 206L-1 LongRanger II	45277	
N2764F	Bell 206L-1 LongRanger II	45279	
N2777D	Bell 206L-1 LongRanger II	45299	
N3107N	Bell 206L-3 LongRanger III	51512	
N3108E	Bell 206L-3 LongRanger III	51498	Lsd fr CIT Leasing
N3116L	Bell 206L-3 LongRanger III	51529	Lsd fr CIT Leasing
N3116P	Bell 206L-3 LongRanger III	51530	Lsd fr CIT Leasing
N3207Q	Bell 206L-3 LongRanger III	51540	Lsd fr Fleet Capital
N3905B	Bell 206L-1 LongRanger II	45598	
N4180F	Bell 206L-3 LongRanger III	51469	
N4282Z	Bell 206L-3 LongRanger III	51499	Lsd fr CIT Leasing
N4835	Bell 206L-3 LongRanger III	51131	
N5000K	Bell 206L-1 LongRanger II	45167	
N5007N	Bell 206L-1 LongRanger II	45184	
N5007Q	Bell 206L-1 LongRanger II	45187	
N5014V	Bell 206L-1 LongRanger II	45217	
N5014Y	Bell 206L-1 LongRanger II	45219	
N5745S	Bell 206L-1 LongRanger II	45491	
N6160Y	Bell 206L-3 LongRanger III	51609	Lsd fr WFBN
N6160Z	Bell 206L-3 LongRanger III	51610	Lsd fr WFBN
N6161A	Bell 206L-3 LongRanger III	51611	Lsd fr WFBN
N6251V	Bell 206L-3 LongRanger III	51404	ex C-FLYD
N6251X	Bell 206L-3 LongRanger III	51552	ex C-FLYF
N6251Y	Bell 206L-3 LongRanger III	51556	ex C-FLYG
N6603X	Bell 206L-3 LongRanger III	51412	
N6610C	Bell 206L-3 LongRanger III	51425	
N6610Y	Bell 206L-3 LongRanger III	51419	Lsd fr WFBN
N6748D	Bell 206L-3 LongRanger III	51106	Lsd fr WFBN
N7074W	Bell 206L-4 LongRanger IV	52033	
N7077F	Bell 206L-4 LongRanger IV	52038	
N8587X	Bell 206L-3 LongRanger III	51464	
N8588X	Bell 206L-3 LongRanger III	51486	
N8589X	Bell 206L-3 LongRanger III	51487	Lsd fr CIT Leasing
N8590X	Bell 206L-3 LongRanger III	51494	Lsd fr CIT Leasing
N8591X	Bell 206L-3 LongRanger III	51495	Lsd fr CIT Leasing
N8592X	Bell 206L-3 LongRanger III	51508	Lsd fr CIT Leasing
N8593X	Bell 206L-3 LongRanger III	51509	Lsd fr CIT Leasing
N8594X	Bell 206L-3 LongRanger III	51531	Lsd fr CIT Leasing
N11027	Bell 206L-1 LongRanger II	45411	ex YV-908C
N20898	Bell 206L-1 LongRanger II	45721	
N21497	Bell 206L-3 LongRanger III	51518	Lsd fr CIT Leasing
N27766	Bell 206L-1 LongRanger II	45312	
N31073	Bell 206L-3 LongRanger III	51520	Lsd fr CIT Leasing
N31077	Bell 206L-3 LongRanger III	51512	
N31801	Bell 206L-3 LongRanger III	51074	
N31821	Bell 206L-3 LongRanger III	51076	
N32041	Bell 206L-3 LongRanger III	51539	Lsd fr Fleet Capital
N41791	Bell 206L-3 LongRanger III	51465	
N53119	Bell 206L-3 LongRanger III	51575	ex XA-SFW
N54641	Bell 206L-3 LongRanger III	51184	ex JA9471
N62127	Bell 206L-4 LongRanger IV	52023	
N81671	Bell 206L-3 LongRanger III	51301	Lsd fr Fifth Third Lsg
N102PH	Bell 212	30899	ex C-FSKS
N3131S	Bell 212	30953	
N3208H	Bell 212	31304	
N5736D	Bell 212	31135	ex N752H
N5736J	Bell 212	31140	
N27805	Bell 212	31106	
N402PH	Bell 407	53159	
N403PH	Bell 407	53267	ex N8595X

N404PH	Bell 407	53188		
N405PH	Bell 407	53207		
N406PH	Bell 407	53198		
N407PH	Bell 407	53003	ex C-FWRD	Lsd fr WFBN
N407XM	Bell 407	53464		
N408PH	Bell 407	53228		
N417PH	Bell 407	53038		
N447PH	Bell 407	53114		
N457PH	Bell 407	53147		
N467PH	Bell 407	53142		
N490PH	Bell 407	53378	ex N6387C	
N491PH	Bell 407	53386		
N492PH	Bell 407	53390		
N493PH	Bell 407	53393		
N494PH	Bell 407	53396		
N495PH	Bell 407	53397		
N496PH	Bell 407	53398		
N498PH	Bell 407	53399		
N499PH	Bell 407	53400		
N501PH	Bell 407	53401		
N510PH	Bell 407	53209		
N612PH	Bell 407	53199		
N719PH	Bell 407	53266		
N720PH	Bell 407	53277		
N721PH	Bell 407	53278		
N722PH	Bell 407	53288		
N723PH	Bell 407	53283		Lsd fr WFBN
N724PH	Bell 407	53327		
N740PH	Bell 407	53435	ex N6077V	
N741PH	Bell 407	53437		
N3193E	Bell 407	53276		Lsd fr Exxon Mobil
N4999	Bell 407	53323		
N107X	Bell 412SP	33113		
N108X	Bell 412SP	33115		
N142PH	Bell 412SP	33150	ex HL9236	
N412PH	Bell 412EP	36140	ex B-55523	
N412SM	Bell 412EP	36213	ex N426DR	EMS
N800Y	Bell 412SP	33134		
N1202T	Bell 412SP	33112	ex D-HHOF	
N2014K	Bell 412	33020	ex YV-922C	
N2148K	Bell 412SP	36001		Lsd fr Fleet Capital
N2149S	Bell 412SP	36002		Lsd fr CIT Leasing
N2258F	Bell 412	33073	ex YV-1030C	
N2261D	Bell 412SP	33076		
N2298Z	Bell 412	33077		
N3893L	Bell 412	33006	ex C-FOQL	Lsd fr RTS Helicopters
N3893N	Bell 412	33010		
N3893P	Bell 412	33012		
N3911L	Bell 412	33023		
N5759N	Bell 412	33002	ex C-FOQK	
N6559Z	Bell 412SP	36019		
N7128R	Bell 412SP	36007		
N21498	Bell 412SP	36003		Lsd fr Fleet Capital
N22347	Bell 412SP	36005	ex XA-RSL	
N22608	Bell 412	33075		
N33008	Bell 412SP	36004		
N135AE	MBB Bo105CBS-4	S-838	ex N7171A	
N205UC	MBB Bo105CB	S-668	ex N9190F	
N800PH	MBB Bo105CBS-4	S-800	ex N133AE	
N851PH	MBB Bo105CBS-4	S-851	ex N137AE	
N911EB	MBB Bo105S	S-812	ex N105WK	Lsd fr Air Med Svs
N911PF	MBB Bo105CBS-4	S-718	ex N5368F	
N911WK	MBB Bo105CBS-4	S-753	ex N818SH	Lsd fr Air Med Svs
N911XS	MBB Bo105CBS	S-757	ex	Lsd fr Air Med Svs
N3071K	MBB Bo105CBS-4	S-859		
N4573B	MBB Bo105S	S-673		
N5031U	MBB Bo105CB	S-678		
N5421E	MBB Bo105CBS-4	S-806		
N6607K	MBB Bo105CBS-4	S-841		
N7136H	MBB Bo105CBS-4	S-833		
N7170D	MBB Bo105CBS-4	S-840		
N8197X	MBB Bo105CBS-4	S-808		
N8199J	MBB Bo105CBS-4	S-826		
N9109Y	MBB Bo105CB	S-669		
N50293	MBB Bo105CB	S-677		
N54191	MBB Bo105CBS-4	S-804		
N81832	MBB Bo105CBS-4	S-828		
N81982	MBB Bo105CBS-4	S-818		
N81992	MBB Bo105CBS-4	S-827		

N89H	Sikorsky S-76C	760406		Lsd fr Exxon Mobil
N127FH	Sikorsky S-76A	760063	ex N402M	
N276X	Sikorsky S-76C	760405		Lsd fr Exxon Mobil
N278X	Sikorsky S-76C	760440		Lsd fr Exxon Mobil
N476X	Sikorsky S-76C	760436		Lsd fr Exxon Mobil
N478X	Sikorsky S-76C	760493		Lsd fr Exxon Mobil
N505PH	Sikorsky S-76C	760505		
N760PH	Sikorsky S-76A	760078	ex VH-BJR	
N761PH	Sikorsky S-76A	760224	ex VH-BJS	
N763P	Sikorsky S-76A	760166	ex C-GHJT	
N764P	Sikorsky S-76A	760276	ex N913UK	
N776P	Sikorsky S-76A	760275	ex N911UK	
N792P	Sikorsky S-76A	760193	ex N792CH	
N911MJ	Sikorsky S-76A	760231	ex N3122D	
N1545K	Sikorsky S-76A	760047		
N1545X	Sikorsky S-76A	760050		
N1546G	Sikorsky S-76A	760076		
N1546K	Sikorsky S-76A	760082		Lsd fr WFBN
N1547D	Sikorsky S-76A	760077		Based Brazil as PP-MCS
N4253S	Sikorsky S-76A	760035		
N5435V	Sikorsky S-76A	760158		
N22342	Sikorsky S-76A	760096	ex C-GHJT	
N14UH	Bell 230	23028	ex XA-IKA	Op for Univ of Mississippi
N32PH	Rockwell Commander 840 (690C)	11691	ex N800BM	
N120PH	Kaman K-1200 K-Max	A94-0027	ex B-55588	
N217AE	MBB BK117B-2	7152	ex N217UC	
N230H	Bell 230	23004	ex N500HG	
N430X	Bell 430	49058		Lsd fr Exxon Mobil
N430XM	Bell 430	49073		Lsd fr Mobil Business Resources
N482PH	Kaman K-1200 K-Max	A94-0028		
N911RC	Bell 230	23037		EMS Op for Palmetto Health Alliance
N911RZ	MBB BK117A-4	7092	ex N520WJ	
N911TL	MBB BK117B-1	7198	ex N911AF	
N912SM	Beech 200 Super King Air	BB-478	ex N789DS	
N3897N	Bell 214ST	28106		Lsd fr WFBN
N5748M	Bell 214ST	28102		
N6992	Bell 222U	47521	ex N911WY	
N8045T	Bell 214ST	28101	ex VH-LHQ	
N8765J	MBB BK117A-3	7054		
N59806	Bell 214ST	28140	ex B-7723	

PHOENIX AIR

Gray Bird (PHA)   Cartersville, GA (VPC)

N164PA	Grumman G-159 Gulfstream I	54	ex N26AJ	
N165PA	Grumman G-159 Gulfstream I	119	ex YV-28CP	
N167PA	Grumman G-159 Gulfstream I	117	ex YV-08CP	
N168PA	Grumman G-159 Gulfstream I	56	ex YV-48CP	
N171PA	Grumman G-159 Gulfstream I	192	ex YV-76CP	
N173PA	Grumman G-159 Gulfstream I	175	ex YV-453CP	
N183PA	Grumman G-159 Gulfstream I	199	ex YV-83CP	
N184PA	Grumman G-159 Gulfstream I	97	ex YV-85CP	
N185PA	Grumman G-159 Gulfstream I	26	ex YV-82CP	
N186PA	Grumman G-159 Gulfstream I	23	ex N193PA	
N190PA	Grumman G-159 Gulfstream I	195	ex N1900W	Freighter
N192PA	Grumman G-159 Gulfstream I	149	ex N684FM	Freighter
N193PA	Grumman G-159 Gulfstream I	125	ex N5NA	
N195PA	Grumman G-159 Gulfstream IC	88	ex C-GPTN	stored VPC as C-GPTN
N196PA	Grumman G-159 Gulfstream I	139	ex C-FRTU	
N197PA	Grumman G-159 Gulfstream I	93	ex N137C	
N198PA	Grumman G-159C Gulfstream I	27	ex N415CA	
N32PA	Lear Jet 36A	36A-025	ex N800BL	
N56PA	Lear Jet 36A	36A-023	ex N6YY	
N62PG	Lear Jet 36A	36A-031	ex N20UG	
N71PG	Lear Jet 36	36-013	ex D-CBRD	
N80PG	Lear Jet 35	35-063	ex N663CA	
N524PA	Lear Jet 35	35-033	ex N31FN	
N527PA	Lear Jet 36A	36A-019	ex N540PA	
N541PA	Lear Jet 35	35-053	ex N53FN	
N544PA	Lear Jet 35A	35A-247	ex N523PA	
N545PA	Lear Jet 36A	36A-028	ex N75TD	
N547PA	Lear Jet 36	36-012	ex N712JE	
N549PA	Lear Jet 35A	35A-119	ex N36FN	
N568PA	Lear Jet 35A	35A-205	ex N59FN	
N456DA	Piper PA-31 Navajo Panther	31-7912103		

PHOENIX AIR TRANSPORT

Phoenix-Sky Harbor Intl, AZ (PHX)

N18R	Beech E-18S	BA-312	
N62TP	Beech E-18S	BA-45	
N103AF	Beech G-18S	BA-526	ex N277S
N9375Y	Beech G-18S	BA-564	

PIEDMONT AIRLINES

Piedmont (US/PDT) (IATA 531)   *Salisbury-Wicomico Regional, MD (SBY)*

N326EN	de Havilland DHC-8-311	234	ex N386DC	HDF	Lsd fr Bombardier Capital
N327EN	de Havilland DHC-8-311A	261	ex N379DC	HDD	Lsd fr Bombardier Capital
N328EN	de Havilland DHC-8-311A	281	ex N380DC	HDC	Lsd fr Bombardier Capital
N329EN	de Havilland DHC-8-311	290	ex SU-UAD	HDG	Lsd fr Bombardier Capital
N330EN	de Havilland DHC-8-311A	274	ex N805SA	HDI	Lsd fr Bombardier Capital
N331EN	de Havilland DHC-8-311	279	ex N806SA	HDJ	Lsd fr Bombardier Capital
N333EN	de Havilland DHC-8-311	221	ex N803SA	HDK	Lsd fr Bombardier Capital
N335EN	de Havilland DHC-8-311	375	ex N804SA	HDN	Lsd fr Bombardier Capital
N336EN	de Havilland DHC-8-311	336	ex N284BC	HDA	Lsd fr Bombardier Capital
N337EN	de Havilland DHC-8-311A	284	ex SU-UAE	HDH	Lsd fr Bombardier Capital
N342EN	de Havilland DHC-8-311A	395	ex N511CL	HDB	Lsd fr Bombardier Capital
N343EN	de Havilland DHC-8-311A	340	ex OE-LLZ	HDE	Lsd fr Bombardier Capital
N906HA	de Havilland DHC-8-102	009	ex C-GHRI	HSA	
N907HA	de Havilland DHC-8-102	011	ex C-GESR	HSB	
N908HA	de Havilland DHC-8-102	015	ex C-GIBQ	HSC	
N911HA	de Havilland DHC-8-102	034	ex C-GEOA	HSF	
N912HA	de Havilland DHC-8-102	040	ex C-GEOA	HSG	
N914HA	de Havilland DHC-8-102	053	ex C-GETI	HSH	
N916HA*	de Havilland DHC-8-102	072	ex C-GEOA	HSJ	
N917HA*	de Havilland DHC-8-102	075	ex C-GEVP	HSK	
N930HA	de Havilland DHC-8-102	126	ex C-GFQL	HSW	
N931HA	de Havilland DHC-8-102	132	ex C-GFOD	HSZ	
N933HA	de Havilland DHC-8-102	134	ex C-GFUM	HBA	
N934HA	de Havilland DHC-8-102	139	ex C-GETI	HBB	
N935HA	de Havilland DHC-8-102	142	ex C-GLOT	HBC	
N936HA	de Havilland DHC-8-102	145	ex C-GFQL	HRA	
N937HA	de Havilland DHC-8-102	148	ex C-GLOT	HRB	
N938HA	de Havilland DHC-8-102	152	ex C-GFUM		
N940HA	de Havilland DHC-8-102	156	ex C-GLOT	HRE	
N941HA	de Havilland DHC-8-102	161	ex C-GETI	HRF	
N942HA	de Havilland DHC-8-102	163	ex C-GFUM	HRG	
N943HA	de Havilland DHC-8-102	167	ex C-GFOD		
N964HA	de Havilland DHC-8-102	343	ex N833MA		Lsd fr Bombardier Capital
N965HA	de Havilland DHC-8Q-202	450	ex C-GFCF	HHL	Lsd fr Wachovia Trust
N966HA	de Havilland DHC-8Q-202	452	ex C-GETI	HHM	Lsd fr Wachovia Trust
N968HA	de Havilland DHC-8Q-202	465	ex C-GFBW	HHN	Lsd fr Wachovia Trust
N969HA	de Havilland DHC-8Q-202	468	ex C-FDHD	HHP	Lsd fr Wachovia Trust
N975HA	de Havilland DHC-8-102	176	ex C-GEWQ	HRI	
N979HA	de Havilland DHC-8-102A	373	ex C-GFQL	HRJ	Lsd fr WFBN
N980HA	de Havilland DHC-8-102A	376	ex C-GFBW		Lsd fr WFBN
N981HA	de Havilland DHC-8-102A	378	ex C-GDNG	HRL	Lsd fr WFBN
N982HA	de Havilland DHC-8-102A	380	ex C-FWBB		Lsd fr WFBN
N983HA	de Havilland DHC-8Q-201	478	ex C-GEMU	HHR	Lsd fr Wachovia Trust
N984HA	de Havilland DHC-8-102A	377	ex N823EX		Lsd fr WFBN
N985HA	de Havilland DHC-8Q-201	479	ex C-GEOZ	HHS	Lsd fr Wachovia Trust
N986HA	de Havilland DHC-8-201	421	ex C-GFYI	HHA	Lsd fr CIT Group
N987HA	de Havilland DHC-8-201	425	ex C-GFHZ	HHB	Lsd fr CIT Group
N988HA	de Havilland DHC-8-201	426	ex C-FDHD	HHC	Lsd fr CIT Group
N989HA	de Havilland DHC-8-201	427	ex C-GFEN		Lsd fr CIT Group
N990HA	de Havilland DHC-8-201	428	ex C-GDKL	HHE	Lsd fr CIT Group
N991HA	de Havilland DHC-8-201	431	ex C-GLOT	HHF	Lsd fr CIT Group
N992HA	de Havilland DHC-8-201	432	ex C-GFQL	HHG	Lsd fr CIT Group
N993HA	de Havilland DHC-8-201	457	ex C-GDIU	HHI	
N994HA	de Havilland DHC-8-201	459	ex C-GFYI	HHJ	
N995HA	de Havilland DHC-8-201	460	ex C-GFBW	HHK	
N996HA	de Havilland DHC-8Q-201	497	ex C-GDIW	HHT	Lsd fr Wachovia Trust
N997HA	de Havilland DHC-8Q-202	507	ex C-GFRP		Lsd fr Wachovia Trust
N998HA	de Havilland DHC-8Q-202	509	ex C-GFYI	HHV	Lsd fr Wachovia Trust

*Leased from Westinghouse Aircraft Leasing
Piedmont is a wholly owned subsidiary of US Airways and uses US Airways Express flight numbers in the range
US3000-3399. To take over Allegheny Airlines (also wholly owned by US Airways) by April 2004.

PINNACLE AIRLINES

Flagship (9E/FLG)   *Memphis-Intl, TN/Minneapolis-St Paul Intl, MN (MEM/MSP)*

N8390A*	Canadair CL-600-2B19	7390	ex C-FMOW	8390 Spirit of 'Memphis Belle'
N8396A*	Canadair CL-600-2B19	7396	ex C-FMMB	8396

408

N8409N*	Canadair CL-600-2B19	7409	ex C-FMLI	8409	
N8412F*	Canadair CL-600-2B19	7412	ex C-FMLT	8412	
N8416B*	Canadair CL-600-2B19	7416	ex C-FMNW	8416	
N8423C*	Canadair CL-600-2B19	7423	ex C-FMNQ	8423	
N8432A*	Canadair CL-600-2B19	7432	ex C-GHRR	8432	
N8444F*	Canadair CL-600-2B19	7444	ex C-FMMT	8444	
N8458A*	Canadair CL-600-2B19	7458	ex C-FMMN	8458	
N8475B*	Canadair CL-600-2B19	7475	ex C-	8475	
N8477R*	Canadair CL-600-2B19	7477	ex C-FMNX	8477	
N8488D*	Canadair CL-600-2B19	7488	ex C-FMMN	8488	
N8492C*	Canadair CL-600-2B19	7492	ex	8492	
N8495B*	Canadair CL-600-2B19	7495	ex C-FMKW	8495	
N8501F	Canadair CL-600-2B19	7501	ex C-FMLS	8501	
N8505Q	Canadair CL-600-2B19	7505	ex C-FMNH	8505	
N8506C	Canadair CL-600-2B19	7506	ex C-FMNW	8506	
N8515F*	Canadair CL-600-2B19	7515	ex C-FMOI	8515	
N8516C*	Canadair CL-600-2B19	7516	ex C-FMMB	8516	
N8524A*	Canadair CL-600-2B19	7524	ex C-FMKV	8524	
N8525B*	Canadair CL-600-2B19	7525	ex C-FMKW	8525	
N8532G*	Canadair CL-600-2B19	7532	ex C-FMLT	8532	
N8533D*	Canadair CL-600-2B19	7533	ex C-FMLV	8533	
N8541D*	Canadair CL-600-2B19	7541	ex C-FVAZ	8541	
N8543F*	Canadair CL-600-2B19	7543	ex C-FMNQ	8543	
N8554A*	Canadair CL-600-2B19	7554	ex C-FMKV	8554	
N8560F*	Canadair CL-600-2B19	7560	ex C-FMLQ	8560	
N8577D*	Canadair CL-600-2B19	7577	ex C-FMML	8577	
N8580A*	Canadair CL-600-2B19	7580	ex C-FMMW	8580	
N8587E*	Canadair CL-600-2B19	7587	ex C-FMLB	8587	
N8588D*	Canadair CL-600-2B19	7588	ex C-GJSZ	8588	First RJ-440
N8598B*	Canadair CL-600-2B19	7598	ex C-FMNY	8598	
N8604C*	Canadair CL-600-2B19	7604	ex C-FMLU	8604	
N8611A*	Canadair CL-600-2B19	7611	ex C-FMMX	8611	
N8623A*	Canadair CL-600-2B19	7623	ex C-FMLV	8623	
N8631E*	Canadair CL-600-2B19	7631	ex C-FVAZ	8631	
N8646A*	Canadair CL-600-2B19	7646	ex C-FMKZ	8646	
N8659B*	Canadair CL-600-2B19	7659	ex C-FMOS	8659	
N8665A*	Canadair CL-600-2B19	7665	ex C-FMOI	8665	
N8672A	Canadair CL-600-2B19	7672	ex C-FMMY	8672	
N8673D*	Canadair CL-600-2B19	7673	ex C-FMNB	8673	
N8674A	Canadair CL-600-2B19	7674	ex C-FMKV	8674	
N8683B	Canadair CL-600-2B19	7683	ex C-FMLV	8683	
N8688C	Canadair CL-600-2B19	7688	ex C-FMNY	6888	
N8694A*	Canadair CL-600-2B19	7694	ex C-FMLU	8694	
N8696C*	Canadair CL-600-2B19	7696	ex C-FMMB	8696	
N8698A*	Canadair CL-600-2B19	7698	ex C-FMMN	8698	
N8709A*	Canadair CL-600-2B19	7709	ex C-FMLI	8709	
N8710A*	Canadair CL-600-2B19	7710	ex C-FMLQ	8710	
N8718E*	Canadair CL-600-2B19	7718	ex C-FMNY	8718	
N8721B*	Canadair CL-600-2B19	7721	ex C-FVAZ	8721	
N8733G	Canadair CL-600-2B19	7733	ex C-FMNB	8733	
N8736A	Canadair CL-600-2B19	7736	ex C-FMKZ	8736	
N8745B	Canadair CL-600-2B19	7745	ex C-FMNH	8745	
N8747B	Canadair CL-600-2B19	7747	ex C-FMNX	8747	
N8751D	Canadair CL-600-2B19	7751	ex C-FVAZ	8751	
N8758D	Canadair CL-600-2B19	7758	ex C-FMMN	8758	
N8771A*	Canadair CL-600-2B19	7771	ex C-FMLS	8771	
N8775A*	Canadair CL-600-2B19	7775	ex C-FMNH	8775	
N8783E*	Canadair CL-600-2B19	7783	ex C-FMNQ	8783	
N8790A*	Canadair CL-600-2B19	7790	ex C-FMMW	8790	
N8794B*	Canadair CL-600-2B19	7794	ex C-FMKV	8794	
N8797A*	Canadair CL-600-2B19	7797	ex C-FMLB	8797	
N8800G*	Canadair CL-600-2B19	7800	ex C-FMLQ	8800	
N8808H*	Canadair CL-600-2B19	7808	ex C-FMNY	8808	
N8828D	Canadair CL-600-2B19	7828	ex C-FMLF	8828	
N8836	Canadair CL-600-2B19	7836	ex C-FMNW	8836	
N8837B	Canadair CL-600-2B19	7837	ex C-FMNX	8837	
N	Canadair CL-600-2B19		ex C-	on order	
N	Canadair CL-600-2B19		ex C-	on order	
N	Canadair CL-600-2B19		ex C-	on order	
N	Canadair CL-600-2B19		ex C-	on order	
N	Canadair CL-600-2B19		ex C-	on order	
N	Canadair CL-600-2B19		ex C-	on order	
N	Canadair CL-600-2B19		ex C-	on order	
N	Canadair CL-600-2B19		ex C-	on order	
N	Canadair CL-600-2B19		ex C-	on order	
N	Canadair CL-600-2B19		ex C-	on order	
N	Canadair CL-600-2B19		ex C-	on order	
N	Canadair CL-600-2B19		ex C-	on order	

*Leased from Wells Fargo Bank Northwest. From c/n 7588 aircraft are RJ-440s (40-seaters)
Wholly owned by Northwest Airlines, operates as Northwest Airlink, using NW flight numbers in the range 5000-5899

PIONEER AIR SERVICE ceased operations

PLANEMASTER AIR CHARTERS

Planemaster (PMS)   *Chicago-Du Page, IL (DPA)*

N208PM	Cessna 208B Caravan I	208B0348	ex VH-NTS	
N274PM	Cessna 208B Caravan I	208B0705	ex N9183L	
N275PM	Cessna 208 Caravan I	20800119	ex N9635F	
N276PM	Cessna 208B Caravan I	208B0074	ex N9457B	Freighter
N278PM	Cessna 208B Caravan I	208B0171	ex N4694B	Freighter
N279PM	Cessna 208B Caravan I	208B0623	ex N104VE	Freighter
N280PM	Cessna 208B Caravan I	208B0564	ex N1256P	
N282PM	Cessna 208B Caravan I	208B0981		Lsd fr Cessna A/c Corp
N286PM	Cessna 208B Caravan I	208B0631		

Flies services for UPS - United Parcel Service   Also operates VIP charters with a range of biz-jets

PLANET AIRWAYS

Planet (PLZ)   *Fort Lauderdale-Hollwood Intl, FL (FLL)*

N893AA	Boeing 727-223 (FedEx 3)	1649/22009	Rene
N894AA	Boeing 727-223 (FedEx 3)	1650/22010	Koster
N1910	Boeing 727-23 (Raisbeck 3)	311/19385	Dominic
N69741	Boeing 727-224 (Raisbeck 3)	1684/22250	Louis
N69742	Boeing 727-224 (Raisbeck 3)	1687/22251	Natasja
N79745	Boeing 727-224 (Raisbeck 3)	1740/22448	Danielle

PLATINUM AIRLINES

Miami-Intl, FL (MIA)

N7455U	Boeing 727-222 (FedEx 3)	1562/21909		Lsd fr Elegaire
N17789	Boeing 727-232F (Raisbeck 3)	951/20643	ex N520PE	stored GYR	Lsd fr Finova

POLAR AIR CARGO

Polar Tiger (PO/PAC) (IATA 403)   *New York-JFK Intl, NY (JFK)*

N354MC	Boeing 747-341SF	627/23394	ex PP-VNH		Lsd fr GTI
N355MC	Boeing 747-341SF	629/23395	ex PP-VNI		Lsd fr GTI
N450PA*	Boeing 747-46NF	1257/30808		The Spirit of Long Beach	
N451PA*	Boeing 747-46NF	1259/30809		Wings of Change	
N452PA*	Boeing 747-46NF	1260/30810		Polar Spirit	
N453PA*	Boeing 747-46NF	1283/30811			
N454PA"	Boeing 747-46NF	1310/30812		Lsd fr Charles River A/c Finance	
N496MC	Boeing 747-47UF	1217/29257			Lsd fr GTI
N505MC	Boeing 747-2D3M	296/21251	ex F-GFUK		Lsd fr GTI
N524UP	Boeing 747-237BSF	318/21446	ex N104TR	all-white	Lsd fr Triton
N858FT	Boeing 747-123 (SCD)	90/20109	ex N9670	std ROW	Lsd fr Arkia Lsg
N859FT	Boeing 747-123 (SCD)	133/20326	ex N9674	std ROW	Lsd fr Arkia Lsg
N920FT"	Boeing 747-249F	460/22237	ex VR-HKO	Thomas G Taaffe	
N921FT	Boeing 747-283M	358/21575	ex N9727N	Raymond B Moe	
N922FT	Boeing 747-2U3B (SCD)	561/22768	ex N105TR	William P Brackett	Lsd fr Triton
N923FT	Boeing 747-2U3B (SCD)	562/22769	ex N106TR		Lsd fr Triton
N924FT	Boeing 747-259B (SCD)	372/21730	ex N527UP		Lsd fr Aero USA
(N925FT)	Boeing 747-245F	396/21841	ex N638FE		Lsd fr Boeing
N926FT	Boeing 747-2R7F	354/21650	ex N639FE		
N24837	Boeing 747-329M	810/24837	ex OO-SGD		Lsd fr GTI

*Leased from GECAS "Leased from Polaris Aircraft (Pacific Rim)
Names change frequently; wholly owned subsidiary of Atlas Air Worldwide Holdings but operates independently

PRIMAC AIR

Primac (PMC)   *Teterboro, NJ (TEB)*

N1285D	Cessna 208B Caravan I	208B0747	Freighter

PRIORITY AIR CHARTER

Kidron-Stolzfus Airfield, OH

N208PA	Cessna 208B Caravan I	208B0312	ex N208PF	Lsd fr Jilco Industries
N208TF	Cessna 208B Caravan I	208B0592		
N218PA	Cessna 208B Caravan I	208B0306	ex N218PF	Lsd fr Jilco Industries
N248PA	Cessna 208B Caravan I	208B0134	ex N208JL	Lsd fr Jilco Industries
N1209X	Cessna 208B Caravan I	208B0443		

PRO MECH AIR

(Z3)

Ketchikan-Harbor SPB, AK (WFB)

N995WA	de Havilland DHC-2 Beaver	1100	ex C-GAEG		
N1108Q	de Havilland DHC-2 Beaver	416	ex 51-16851		
N4787C	de Havilland DHC-2 Beaver	1330	ex C-FGMK		
N64393	de Havilland DHC-2 Beaver	845	ex 54-1701		
N64397	de Havilland DHC-2 Beaver	760	ex 53-7943		
N270PA	de Havilland DHC-3 Turbo Otter	270	ex N51KA		Lsd fr Pantechnicon Avn
N353PM	de Havilland DHC-6 Twin Otter 300	351	ex C-FCST	VistaLiner	Lsd fr 353PM LLC
N409PA	de Havilland DHC-3 Turbo Otter	409	ex C-FLDD		Lsd fr Pantechnicon Avn
N444BA	Cessna A185E Skywagon	185-1433			
N531H	Cessna A185E Skywagon	185-1348			
N959PA	de Havilland DHC-3 Turbo Otter	159	ex N67KA		Lsd fr Pantechnicon Avn
All floatplanes					

PSA AIRLINES

Blue Streak (JIA) (IATA 320)

Dayton-Cox Intl, OH (DAY)

N328JS	Dornier 328-100	3030	ex D-CDHP	PDA	Lsd fr Dornier
N422JS	Dornier 328-100	3018	ex D-CDHC	PDB	Lsd fr Dornier
N423JS	Dornier 328-100	3032	ex D-CDHR	PDC	Lsd fr Dornier
N424JS	Dornier 328-100	3033	ex D-CDHS	PDD	Lsd fr Dornier
N425JS	Dornier 328-100	3037	ex D-CDXC	PDE	Lsd fr Dornier
N426JS	Dornier 328-100	3038	ex D-CDXD	PDF	Lsd fr Dornier
N427JS	Dornier 328-100	3039	ex D-CDXE	PDG	Lsd fr Dornier
N429JS	Dornier 328-100	3043	ex D-CDXJ	PDH	Lsd fr Dornier
N430JS	Dornier 328-100	3044	ex D-CDXK	PDI	Lsd fr Dornier
N431JS	Dornier 328-100	3028	ex D-CDHN	PDJ	Lsd fr Dornier
N432JS	Dornier 328-100	3045	ex D-CDXL	PDK	Lsd fr Dornier
N433JS	Dornier 328-100	3047	ex D-CDXN	PDL	Lsd fr Dornier
N434JS	Dornier 328-100	3051	ex D-CDXS	PDM	Lsd fr Dornier
N436JS	Dornier 328-100	3052	ex D-CDXT	PDN	Lsd fr Dornier
N437JS	Dornier 328-100	3055	ex D-CDXW	PDP	Lsd fr Dornier
N438JS	Dornier 328-100	3056	ex D-CDXX	PDR	Lsd fr Dornier
N439JS	Dornier 328-100	3057	ex D-CDXY	PDS	Lsd fr Dornier
N440JS	Dornier 328-100	3058	ex D-CDXZ	PDT	Lsd fr Dornier
N441JS	Dornier 328-100	3059	ex D-CDXA	PDU	Lsd fr Dornier
N442JS	Dornier 328-100	3060	ex D-CDXC	PDV	Lsd fr Dornier
N457PS	Dornier 328-100	3048	ex D-CDXP	PDW	Lsd fr Dornier
N458PS	Dornier 328-100	3068	ex D-CDXS	PDY; stored OKC	Lsd fr Dornier
N459PS	Dornier 328-100	3070	ex D-CDXW	PDZ	Lsd fr Dornier
N460PS	Dornier 328-100	3061	ex D-CDXD	PEB	Lsd fr Dornier
N461PS	Dornier 328-100	3075	ex D-CDXC	PED; stored OKC	Lsd fr Dornier
N462PS	Dornier 328-110	3084	ex N328ML	PEG	Lsd fr Dornier
N463PS	Dornier 328-110	3087	ex N329ML		Lsd fr Dornier
N470PS	Dornier 328-110	3006	ex N328PH	PEI	Lsd fr Dornier
N471PS	Dornier 328-110	3007	ex N329PH	PEJ	Lsd fr Dornier
N472PS	Dornier 328-110	3008	ex D-CDAN		Lsd fr Dornier
Due to be phased out of service as Canadair CRJ-200s are delivered from December 2003					
N202PS	Canadair CL-600-2B19	7858	ex C-		
N206PS	Canadair CL-600-2B19	7860	ex C-FMLQ		
N207PS	Canadair CL-600-2B19	7873	ex C-		
N209PS	Canadair CL-600-2B19	7874	ex C-FMLU		
N213PS	Canadair CL-600-2B19	7879	ex C-FMMQ		
N215PS	Canadair CL-600-2B19	7880	ex C-FMMW		
N216PS	Canadair CL-600-2B19	7882	ex C-FMMY		
N218PS	Canadair CL-600-2B19	7885	ex C-FMKS		
N220PS	Canadair CL-600-2B19	7887	ex C-FMLB		
N221PS	Canadair CL-600-2B19	7889	ex C-FMLI		
N223JS	Canadair CL-600-2B19		ex C-	on order	
N226JS	Canadair CL-600-2B19		ex C-	on order	
N228PS	Canadair CL-600-2B19		ex C-	on order	
N229PS	Canadair CL-600-2B19		ex C-	on order	
N230PS	Canadair CL-600-2B19		ex C-	on order	
N237PS	Canadair CL-600-2B19		ex C-	on order	
N241PS	Canadair CL-600-2B19		ex C-	on order	
N242JS	Canadair CL-600-2B19		ex C-	on order	
N244PS	Canadair CL-600-2B19		ex C-	on order	
N245PS	Canadair CL-600-2B19		ex C-	on order	
N246PS	Canadair CL-600-2B19		ex C-	on order	
N247JS	Canadair CL-600-2B19		ex C-	on order	
N248PS	Canadair CL-600-2B19		ex C-	on order	
N249PS	Canadair CL-600-2B19		ex C-	on order	
N250PS	Canadair CL-600-2B19		ex C-	on order	
N251PS	Canadair CL-600-2B19		ex C-	on order	
N253PS	Canadair CL-600-2B19		ex C-	on order	

N254PS	Canadair CL-600-2B19	ex C-	on order
N256PS	Canadair CL-600-2B19	ex C-	on order
N257PS	Canadair CL-600-2B19	ex C-	on order
N258PS	Canadair CL-600-2B19	ex C-	on order
N259PS	Canadair CL-600-2B19	ex C-	on order
N260JS	Canadair CL-600-2B19	ex C-	on order
N261PS	Canadair CL-600-2B19	ex C-	on order
N262PS	Canadair CL-600-2B19	ex C-	on order
N263PS	Canadair CL-600-2B19	ex C-	on order
N264PS	Canadair CL-600-2B19	ex C-	on order
N265PS	Canadair CL-600-2B19	ex C-	on order
N266PS	Canadair CL-600-2B19	ex C-	on order
N267JS	Canadair CL-600-2B19	ex C-	on order
N269PS	Canadair CL-600-2B19	ex C-	on order
N270PS	Canadair CL-600-2B19	ex C-	on order
N271PS	Canadair CL-600-2B19	ex C-	on order
N272PS	Canadair CL-600-2B19	ex C-	on order
N273JS	Canadair CL-600-2B19	ex C-	on order
N275PS	Canadair CL-600-2B19	ex C-	on order
N276PS	Canadair CL-600-2B19	ex C-	on order
N277PS	Canadair CL-600-2B19	ex C-	on order
N278PS	Canadair CL-600-2B19	ex C-	on order
N279PS	Canadair CL-600-2B19	ex C-	on order
N280PS	Canadair CL-600-2B19	ex C-	on order
N281PS	Canadair CL-600-2B19	ex C-	on order
N282PS	Canadair CL-600-2B19	ex C-	on order
N283PS	Canadair CL-600-2B19	ex C-	on order
N284PS	Canadair CL-600-2B19	ex C-	on order
N285PS	Canadair CL-600-2B19	ex C-	on order
N286PS	Canadair CL-600-2B19	ex C-	on order
N287PS	Canadair CL-600-2B19	ex C-	on order
N288PS	Canadair CL-600-2B19	ex C-	on order
N289JS	Canadair CL-600-2B19	ex C-	on order
N290PS	Canadair CL-600-2B19	ex C-	on order
N291PS	Canadair CL-600-2B19	ex C-	on order
N292PS	Canadair CL-600-2B19	ex C-	on order
N293PS	Canadair CL-600-2B19	ex C-	on order
N294JS	Canadair CL-600-2B19	ex C-	on order
N295JS	Canadair CL-600-2B19	ex C-	on order
N296JS	Canadair CL-600-2B19	ex C-	on order
N297PS	Canadair CL-600-2B19	ex C-	on order
N298PS	Canadair CL-600-2B19	ex C-	on order
N702PS	Canadair CL-600-2D24	ex C-	on order
N703PS	Canadair CL-600-2D24	ex C-	on order
N705PS	Canadair CL-600-2D24	ex C-	on order
N706PS	Canadair CL-600-2D24	ex C-	on order
N708PS	Canadair CL-600-2D24	ex C-	on order
N709PS	Canadair CL-600-2D24	ex C-	on order
N710PS	Canadair CL-600-2D24	ex C-	on order
N712PS	Canadair CL-600-2D24	ex C-	on order
N716PS	Canadair CL-600-2D24	ex C-	on order
N718PS	Canadair CL-600-2D24	ex C-	on order
N719PS	Canadair CL-600-2D24	ex C-	on order
N720PS	Canadair CL-600-2D24	ex C-	on order
N721PS	Canadair CL-600-2D24	ex C-	on order
N723PS	Canadair CL-600-2D24	ex C-	on order
N724PS	Canadair CL-600-2D24	ex C-	on order
N725PS	Canadair CL-600-2D24	ex C-	on order
N726PS	Canadair CL-600-2D24	ex C-	on order
N728PS	Canadair CL-600-2D24	ex C-	on order
N729PS	Canadair CL-600-2D24	ex C-	on order
N730PS	Canadair CL-600-2D24	ex C-	on order
N731PS	Canadair CL-600-2D24	ex C-	on order
N736PS	Canadair CL-600-2D24	ex C-	on order
N740PS	Canadair CL-600-2D24	ex C-	on order
N741PS	Canadair CL-600-2D24	ex C-	on order
N742PS	Canadair CL-600-2D24	ex C-	on order
N743PS	Canadair CL-600-2D24	ex C-	on order
N744PS	Canadair CL-600-2D24	ex C-	on order
N745PS	Canadair CL-600-2D24	ex C-	on order
N746PS	Canadair CL-600-2D24	ex C-	on order
N748PS	Canadair CL-600-2D24	ex C-	on order
N749PS	Canadair CL-600-2D24	ex C-	on order
N750PS	Canadair CL-600-2D24	ex C-	on order
N751PS	Canadair CL-600-2D24	ex C-	on order
N752PS	Canadair CL-600-2D24	ex C-	on order
N753PS	Canadair CL-600-2D24	ex C-	on order
N754PS	Canadair CL-600-2D24	ex C-	on order
N755PS	Canadair CL-600-2D24	ex C-	on order
N756PS	Canadair CL-600-2D24	ex C-	on order
N762PS	Canadair CL-600-2D24	ex C-	on order

N763PS	Canadair CL-600-2D24	ex C-	on order
N764PS	Canadair CL-600-2D24	ex C-	on order
N765PS	Canadair CL-600-2D24	ex C-	on order
N766PS	Canadair CL-600-2D24	ex C-	on order
N767PS	Canadair CL-600-2D24	ex C-	on order
N768PS	Canadair CL-600-2D24	ex C-	on order
N769PS	Canadair CL-600-2D24	ex C-	on order
N771PS	Canadair CL-600-2D24	ex C-	on order
N772PS	Canadair CL-600-2D24	ex C-	on order
N773PS	Canadair CL-600-2D24	ex C-	on order
N774PS	Canadair CL-600-2D24	ex C-	on order

All to be operated as 74-seat CRJ-705ERs
A wholly owned subsidiary of US Airways operates services as a US Airways Express commuter using US flight numbers in the range 4000-4299

QUEST CARGO INTERNATIONAL ceased operations

RAM AIR FREIGHT

RAM Express (REX)

Raleigh-Durham-Intl, NC (RDU)

N4UT	Beech 58 Baron	TH-	
N11HW	Beech 58 Baron	TH-271	
N44RA	Beech 95-B55 Baron	TC-916	
N707RA	Beech 58 Baron	TH-257	
N958MC	Beech 58 Baron	TH-552	
N7351R	Beech 58 Baron	TH-481	
N884RC	Cessna 402B	402B0884	ex TF-JVC
N6350X	Cessna 402B	402B1317	

All leased from Bellefonte Inc

RAMP 66

Pelican (PPK)

North Myrtle Beach-Grand Strand, NC (CRE)

N31BW	Beech 58 Baron	TH-490	Lsd fr Grand Strand Avn
N6656C	Beech 58 Baron	TH-1060	Lsd fr Grand Strand Avn
N8121R	Beech 58 Baron	TH-690	Lsd fr Grand Strand Avn

RAPID AIR

Grand Rapids-Kent County Intl, MI (GRR)

N1240G	Cessna 310Q	310Q1091	Lsd fr Spartan Avn Sve
N1249G	Cessna 310Q	310Q1100	
N4084L	Cessna 310Q	310Q0493	Lsd fr Spartan Avn Sve
N6362X	Cessna 402B	402B1325	Lsd fr Spartan Avn Sve
N36934	Cessna 414A	414A0486	
N69811	Cessna 310Q	310Q0992	Lsd fr Spartan Avn Sve

RAPID AIR TRANS

Washington-Dulles, DC (DUL)

| N2189M | Lockheed L-382G Hercules | 4582 | ex TR-KKA |
| N8183J | Lockheed L-382G Hercules | 4796 | ex N123GA |

Operates with various US government agencies, both leased to Tepper Aviation

---

RED BARON AVIATION

Red Baron (RBN)

Brooksville-Pilot County, FL

N4345X	Cessna 210B	21058033	
N4667Q	Cessna 210L Centurion	21058567	
N5874F	Cessna 210G Centurion	21058874	
N6585A	Cessna 210N Centurion	21063554	
N8280M	Cessna 210K Centurion	21059280	
N8064J	Ted Smith Aerostar 600A	60-0547-177	

All freighters and leased from Gallops Inc

REDDING AERO ENTERPRISES

Boxer (BXR)

Redding-Municipal, CA (RDD)

N2613B	Cessna 402C	402C0083
N2712F	Cessna 402C	402C0121
N5205J	Cessna 402B	402B0892
N5826C	Cessna 402C	402C0050

N5849C	Cessna 402C	402C0052		
N6814A	Cessna 402C	402C0645		
N36908	Cessna 402C	402C0313		
N12GK	Cessna 340A	340A0309		
N48SA	Cessna 404A Titan II	404-0417	ex C-GSPG	
N6072V	Piper Aerostar 601P	61P-0696-7963332		

RHOADES INTERNATIONAL

Rhoades Express (RDS)
Columbus-Municipal, IN (CLU)

N148JR	Convair 240	232	ex N351JD		Lsd fr K-Air
N151JR	Convair T-29D	52-31	ex N451GA		
N152JR	Convair T-29D	283	ex N452GA		Lsd fr J&R Lsg
N156JR	Convair 440	200	ex N440CF		Lsd fr Starflite Intl
N157JR	Convair 340	284	ex N820TA	stored CLU	Lsd fr J&R Lsg
N587CA	Convair 640	463	ex C-FPWO		Lsd fr J&R Lsg
N866TA	Convair 640	283/409	ex 141000		Lsd fr J&R Lsg
N94226	Convair 600	48		stored CLU	Lsd fr J&R Lsg
N94246	Convair 600	102			Lsd fr J&R Lsg
N94258	Convair 600	119			Lsd fr J&R Lsg
N139JR	Douglas DC-3	20550	ex N16475	Miss Daisy	stored CLU
N141JR	Douglas DC-3	19366	ex C-FCUC		
N142JR	Douglas DC-3	16095/32843	ex CF-CTA		
N376AS	AMI Tutbo DC-3	27047	ex ZS-OBU		Lsd fr Rhoades Partners
All freighters					
N36CC	Lear Jet 25B-XR	25B-079	ex N50DH		
N132JR	Cessna 402B	402B1363	ex (N4606N)	Freighter	
N134JR	Cessna 310R	310R2117	ex N6831X		
N421SM	Cessna 421B Golden Eagle	421B0889			

RIO GRANDE AIR

Grande (E2/GRN)
Albuquerque-Intl Sunport/Taos-Municipal, NM (ABQ/TSM)

N64BP	Cessna 208B Caravan I	208B0604	ex (D-FLAX)
N53642	Cessna 208B Caravan I	208B0878	
Both leased from Edelweiss Holdings; operates as Great Plains Connection			

ROBLEX AVIATION
San Juan-Munoz Marin Intl, PR (SJU)

(N151PR)	Short SD.3-60	SH3725	ex N162DD	
N221LM	Short SD.3-60	SH3722	ex N722PC	
N377AR	Short SD.3-60	SH3755	ex SE-LHY	
N411ER	Short SD.3-60	SH3726	ex G-BNMW	
N875RR	Short SD.3-60	SH3741	ex G-ZAPD	
N948RR	Short SD.3-60	SH3751	ex G-BVMX	
N50E	Douglas DC-3	11657	ex N50EB	El Abuelo
N821RR	Britten-Norman BN-2A-9 Islander	338	ex N146A	

ROCKY MOUNTAIN HELICOPTERS purchased by Air Methods and fleets merged in 2003

ROGERS HELICOPTERS
Clovis-Rogers Heliport, NM

N505WW	Aerospatiale AS.350B2 AStar	2442	ex JA6046
N910VR	Aerospatiale AS.350B2 AStar	3213	ex I-VINO
N911EW	Aerospatiale AS.350B2 AStar	2657	ex I-MUSY
N912KW	Aerospatiale AS.350B2 AStar	2260	ex EC-ESA
N3609J	Aerospatiale AS.350D AStar	1245	
N2292W	Bell 206B JetRanger III	505	
N2762P	Bell 206B JetRanger III	2711	
N2763M	Bell 206B JetRanger III	2646	
N16832	Bell 206B JetRanger III	2243	
N20395	Bell 206B JetRanger III	3301	
N58140	Bell 206B JetRanger III	1108	
N59564	Bell 206B JetRanger III	1389	
N59571	Bell 206B JetRanger III	1433	
N91AL	Bell 212	30821	
N212HL	Bell 212	30621	
N811KA	Bell 212	30656	

N873HL	Bell 212	30873	
N911HW	Bell 212	31101	ex N703H
N911KW	Bell 212	30592	ex N50EW
N911VR	Bell 212	30998	ex N701H

N101MZ	Aerospatiale AS.355F1 TwinStar	5045			
N102UM	Aerospatiale AS.355F1 TwinStar	5075	ex N130US		
N313DH	Bell 206L LongRanger II	45630	ex A6-CAC		
N712M	Bell 206L-3 LongRanger III	51072			
N896SB	Beech A100 King Air	B-160	ex OY-CCS		
N911WL	Bell 222U	47557		EMS	Op as Air Life
N10864	Bell 206L-1 LongRanger III	45434			
N27472	Piper PA-31-350 Navajo Chieftain	31-7852019			
N29176	Cessna T210L Turbo Centurion	21059828			
N45731	Bell UH-1B	330	ex 61-0750		

Also trades as TGR Helicopters

ROSS AVIATION

Energy (NRG)   **Albuquerque-Kirkland AFB, NM**

Operates DHC-6 Twin Otter and Douglas DC-9 aircraft solely for US Dept of Energy

ROYAL AIR FREIGHT

Air Royal (RAX)   **Pontiac-Oakland, MI (PTK)**

N22DM	Cessna T310R	310R0069	ex N7593Q
N22LE	Cessna 310R	310R0033	ex N1398G
N310KS	Cessna 310R	310R1501	
N1591T	Cessna 310R	310R0112	
N2643D	Cessna 310R	310R1686	
N87309	Cessna 310R	310R0510	
N87341	Cessna 310R	310R0520	

N34A	Embraer EMB.110P1 Bandeirante	110350	ex N4361Q
N49RA	Embraer EMB.110P1 Bandeirante	110424	ex C-GPRV
N64DA	Embraer EMB.110P1 Bandeirante	110385	ex PT-SFC
N72RA	Embraer EMB.110P1 Bandeirante	110377	ex C-GHOV
N73RA	Embraer EMB.110P1 Bandeirante	110413	ex C-GPNW

N9RA	Lear Jet 23	23-095	ex N5D
N16KK	Lear Jet 25B	25B-174	ex N412SP
N48L	Lear Jet 24A	24A-107	
N64CE	Lear Jet 24B	24B-205	ex N64CF
N120RA	Lear Jet 24	24-153	ex N153BR
N710TV	Lear Jet 24	24-159	ex N66MR
N876MC	Lear Jet 24B	24B-217	ex C-FZHT
N2094L	Lear Jet 25B	25B-095	ex C-GRCO

N160PB	Cessna 402C	402C0493	ex N6841M
N201UV	Mitsubishi MU-2L	680	ex N201U
N688RA	Mitsubishi MU-2L	688	ex N688MA
N717PS	Mitsubishi MU-2L	686	ex N23RA
N5279J	Cessna 402B	402B1202	ex N6841M
N5373J	Cessna 402B	402B0367	

All freighters

RUSTS FLYING SERVICE

                                                    Anchorage-Lake Hood SPB, AK

N626KT	Cessna U206G Stationair 6	U20604426	ex n756WY
N929KT	de Havilland DHC-3 Otter	461	ex N271PA
N2740X	de Havilland DHC-2 Beaver	579	ex C-GIJO
N2899J	de Havilland DHC-3 Otter	425	ex C-GLCR
N4444Z	de Havilland DHC-2 Beaver	1307	ex N123PG
N4596U	Cessna U206G Stationair 6	U20604990	
N4661Z	Cessna U206G Stationair 6	U20605998	
N4891Z	Cessna U206G Stationair 6	U20606044	
N68083	de Havilland DHC-2 Beaver	1254	ex 57-2580

All floatplanes

RYAN INTERNATIONAL AIRLINES

Ryan International (RD/RYN)   **Wichita-Mid Continent, KS (ICT)**

D-ALAB	Airbus Industrie A320-232	0575	ex F-WWDO	Funjet Vacations	Lsd fr AEF
D-ALAE	Airbus Industrie A320-232	0659	ex F-WWIV	Funjet Vacations	Lsd fr AEF
D-ALAH	Airbus Industrie A321-231	0792	ex D-AVZM		Lsd fr AEF

D-ALAL	Airbus Industrie A321-231	1195	ex D-AVZK	Funjet Vacations	Lsd fr AEF
D-ALAQ	Airbus Industrie A321-231	1438	ex D-AVZL	Trans Global	Lsd fr AEF
D-ALAR	Airbus Industrie A320-232	1459	ex F-WWIR	Funjet Vacations	Lsd fr AEF
D-ALAT	Airbus Industrie A320-232	1996	ex F-WWIM	Funjet Vacations	Lsd fr AEF
N381LF	Airbus Industrie A320-232	0640	ex F-OHMO		Lsd fr ILFC; sublsd to TRS
N391LF	Airbus industrie A320-232	0676	ex F-OHMR		Lsd fr ILFC; sublsd to TRS
N941LF	Airbus Industrie A320-233	0461	ex F-WWDP		Lsd fr ILFC; sublsd to ATS
N951LF	Airbus Industrie A320-233	0460	ex F-WWDN		Lsd fr ACG Acqusitions; sublsd ATS
N54SW	Boeing 737-2H4 (Nordam 3)	543/21535			Lsd fr CL Aircraft
N240AU	Boeing 737-201 (Nordam 3)	741/22355	ex C-GEIM		
N253TR	Boeing 737-228	943/23005	ex F-GBYF		Lsd fr Triton
N251RY	Boeing 737-4Y0	2201/25180	ex EC-HBZ		Lsd fr FUA
N254RY	Boeing 737-4Y0	1885/24690	ex EC-HVY	Trans Global	Lsd fr FUA
N255RY	Boeing 737-86N	534/28619	ex EC-HLN		Lsd fr FUA
N974RY	Boeing 737-86N	504/28617	ex EC-HJJ	Trans Global	Lsd fr FUA
N975RY	Boeing 737-86N	258/28592	ex EC-IEN	Trans Global	Lsd fr Lift Morocco
D-ABNK	Boeing 757-230	428/25438			Lsd fr CFG
D-ABNN	Boeing 757-230	446/25441			Lsd fr CFG
G-JMCD	Boeing 757-25F	928/30757			Lsd fr TCW for winter
G-JMCE	Boeing 757-25F	932/30758		Apple	Lsd fr TCW for winter
N281SC	Boeing 727-282 (FedEx 3)	1494/21949	ex CS-TBW		Lsd fr Mach A/c Lsg
N310FV	Boeing 757-23A	471/25488	ex C-GTSE		Lsd fr Finova
N410BN	Boeing 727-223 (Raisbeck 3)	1335/21387	ex N875AA	stored ICT	Lsd fr KCP Leasing
N415BN	Boeing 727-227 (Raisbeck 3)	929/20613	ex N720AA	stored ICT	Lsd fr KCP Leasing
N422BN	Boeing 727-227 (Raisbeck 3)	973/20735	ex N728AA	stored ICT	Lsd fr KCP Leasing
N423BN	Boeing 727-227 (Raisbeck 3)	977/20738	ex N731AA	stored ICT	Lsd fr KCP Leasing
N571RY	Douglas DC-10-10	283/46645	ex N571SC	Op for Sky Service USA	
N572RY	Douglas DC-10-10	251/46977	ex N572SC	Op for Sky Service USA	

Controlled by MyTravel Airlines; leases aircraft from other operators in the winter.

SABER CARGO AIRLINES current status is uncertain, believed to have ceased operations; all DC-3s registered to First Flight Out Inc

SAINT LOUIS HELICOPTER AIRWAYS

Saint Louis-Spirit of St Louis, MO (SUS)

N26SE	MBB Bo105CBS-2	S-587	ex N2909L		Lsd fr Goldstar EMS
N205LF	MBB Bo105CBS	S-146	ex N770H		Lsd fr Goldstar EMS
N233SL	MBB Bo105CBS	S-387	ex I-EHBB		Lsd fr Goldstar EMS
N692DD	MBB Bo105CS	S-149	ex N21SE		Lsd fr Goldstar EMS
N2784F	MBB Bo105CBS-2	S-621		EMS	Lsd fr St Johns Regional HC
N9107R	MBB Bo105C	S-129			Lsd fr Goldstar EMS
N887	Sikorsky S-58B	58482			
N1078T	Sikorsky S-58HT	581016	ex C-FOHA		
N6488	Sikorsky S-58D	581573			
N6488C	Sikorsky S-58E	58269			
N45726	Sikorsky S-58	58675	ex 56-4037		
N99275	Sikorsky S-58E	58245			
N810F	Bell 206L LongRanger	46603			

SALMON AIR

Salmon-Lemhi County, ID (SMN)

N3528Y	Piper PA-31-350 Navajo Chieftain	31-7952149	
N4237D	Piper PA-31-350 Navajo Chieftain	31-7305055	
N6561B	Britten-Norman BN-2A-20 Islander	520	ex YV-O-GSF-6
N7537N	Cessna TU206G Turbo Stationair	U20603665	
N84859	Piper PA-31-350 Navajo Chieftain	31-7305043	ex N804PC

All leased from Spirit Air

SAMOA AIR

(SE)

Pago Pago, AM Samoa (PPG)

N28SP	de Havilland DHC-6 Twin Otter 300	601		Lsd fr Taylor, Taylor & Assoc
N710AS	Beech A100 King Air	B-127	ex C-GJVK	

SAN JUAN

Hato Rey, PR

N786DM	Cessna 208B Caravan I	208B0922	
N787DM	Cessna 208B Caravan I	208B0868	ex N1311A

SB AIR

S-Bar (SBF)   *Albuquerque-Intl Sunport, NM/Dallas-Love Field, TX (ABQ/DAL)*

N14NM	Beech 65-E90 King Air	LW-35	ex N811JB	
N16NM	Beech 65-E90 King Air	LW-62	ex N96DA	
N17NM	Beech 65-E90 King Air	LW-237	ex N5NM	
N21NM	Beech 65-E90 King Air	LW-336	ex N675J	
N44GK	Beech 65-E90 King Air	LW-298	ex N2029X	N118SB resd
N304LG	Beech 65-E90 King Air	LW-231	ex N4954S	
N676J	Beech 65-E90 King Air	LW-179	ex N211MH	
N11692	Beech 65-C90 King Air	LJ-772	ex F-GFBO	
All EMS				
N65TW	Beech B200 Super King Air	BB-902	ex N5TW	
N114SB	Beech 200 Super King Air	BB-161	ex N131PA	

SCENIC AIRLINES

Scenic (YR/SCE)   *Las Vegas-North, NV/Page, AZ (VGT/PGA)*

N140SA+	de Havilland DHC-6 Twin Otter 300	267	ex N387EX		
N142SA+	de Havilland DHC-6 Twin Otter 300	241	ex N385EX		
N144SA*	de Havilland DHC-6 Twin Otter 300	365	ex N544N		
N146SA+	de Havilland DHC-6 Twin Otter 300	514	ex N27RA		
N147SA	de Havilland DHC-6 Twin Otter 300	537	ex N19RA		Lsd fr Avro Ltd
N148SA+	de Havilland DHC-6 Twin Otter 300	409	ex N548N		
N227SA+	de Havilland DHC-6 Twin Otter 300	517	ex N43SP		
N228SA+	de Havilland DHC-6 Twin Otter 300	253	ex N103AC		
N230SA	de Havilland DHC-6 Twin Otter 300	692	ex N549N		Lsd fr Bristol Ltd
N232SA*	de Havilland DHC-6 Twin Otter 300	421	ex N545N		Lsd fr Fairey Ltd
N237SA	de Havilland DHC-6 Twin Otter 300	683	ex N7020G		Lsd fr Gloster Ltd
N241SA+	de Havilland DHC-6 Twin Otter 300	556	ex N97RA		
N297SA+	de Havilland DHC-6 Twin Otter 300	297	ex N852TB		
N331SA*	de Havilland DHC-6 Twin Otter 300	337	ex N2886Z	stored VGT	
*Leased from Twin Otter International			+Leased from Eagle Canyon Leasing		
All VistaLiner conversions;					
N278MA	Fokker F.27 Friendship 200	10280	ex LX-LGK	stored	Lsd fr Eagle Canyon Lsg
N279MA	Fokker F.27 Friendship 600	10297	ex LX-LGJ	stored	Lsd fr Eagle Canyon Lsg
N280EA	Fokker F.27 Friendship 600	10394	ex OY-SRB	stored	Lsd fr Eagle Canyon Lsg
N283EA	Fokker F.27 Friendship 500F	10522	ex N280MA		Lsd fr Eagle Jet Charter
N284MA	Fokker F.27 Friendship 500F	10560	ex VH-FCF		Lsd fr Eagle Jet Charter
N381CR	Beech 1900C	UB-69	ex N331CR		Lsd fr Yamagata Enterprises
N765EA	Cessna 402B	402B0314	ex N1547T		Lsd fr Upper Limits Sales & Lsg
N766EA	Cessna 402B	402B0401	ex N8049Q		Lsd fr Upper Limits Sales & Lsg
N767EA	Cessna 402B	402B1244	ex N4616G		Lsd fr Canyon Lsg
N773EA	Cessna 402B	402B0544	ex N97158		Lsd fr Canyon Lsg

SEA-AIR believed to have ceased operations

SEABORNE AIRLINES

Seaborne (BB/SBS)   *St Thomas-SPB, VI (SPB)*

N224SA	de Havilland DHC-6 Twin Otter 300	247	ex C-GOES	VistaLiner	Lsd fr Twin Otter Intl
N251SA	de Havilland DHC-6 Twin Otter 300	524	ex N81708	VistaLiner	Lsd fr Seaborne VI Inc
N	de Havilland DHC-6 Twin Otter 300	573	ex C-GMUS		Lsd fr Seaborne VI Inc

SEAPLANES OF KEY WEST

                             Key West-Intl, FL (EYW)

N111KW	Cessna U206F Stationair	U20602460	ex N779A	
N200KW	Cessna U206F Stationair	U20602785	ex N108SM	
N208KW	Cessna 208 Caravan I	20800292		
All floatplanes				

SHORELINE AVIATION

                          New Haven-Tweed, CT (HVN)

N208TW	Cessna 208B Caravan I	208B0671	ex N211SA	Floatplane	Lsd fr Caravan Air
N309SA	Cessna 208 Caravan I	20800309		Floatplane	
N702MJ	Cessna 208 Caravan I	20800054	ex N208RD	Flaotplane	Lsd fr Phaeton LLC
N6844T	Cessna 425 Conquest	425-0066			
N9624F	Cessna TU206G Turbo Stationair 6	U20606907			Lsd fr RK Aviation
N9670F	Cessna 208 Caravan I	20800117		Floatplane	

SHUTTLE AMERICA

Shuttlecraft (S5/TCF) Wilmington-Newcastle, DE/Windsor Locks-Bradley Intl, CT (ILG/BDL)

N19XS	SAAB SF.340A	019	ex N19CQ		Lsd fr Lambert Lsg
N35SZ	SAAB SF.340A	035	ex N35CQ		Lsd fr Lambert Lsg
N40SZ	SAAB SF.340A	040	ex N40CQ		Lsd fr Lambert Lsg
N43SZ	SAAB SF.340A	043	ex N43CQ		Lsd fr Lambert Lsg
N95CQ	SAAB SF.340A	095	ex N95MQ		Lsd fr CHQ
(N101SZ)	SAAB SF.340A	101	ex N101CN		Lsd fr SAAB
N104CQ	SAAB SF.340A	104	ex N344BE		Lsd fr CHQ
N108CQ	SAAB SF.340A	108	ex N345BE		Lsd fr CHQ
N118SD	SAAB SF.340A	118	ex N118CQ		Lsd fr SAAB
N121CQ	SAAB SF.340A	121	ex SE-F21		Lsd fr SAAB
N123XS	SAAB SF.340A	123	ex N123CQ		Lsd fr SAAB
N138SD	SAAB SF.340A	138	ex N138CQ		Lsd fr Bank of America
N140CQ*	SAAB SF.340A	140	ex N140N		Lsd fr CHQ
N146SD	SAAB SF.340A	146	ex N146CQ		Lsd fr Fairbrook Lsg
N148SD	SAAB SF.340A	148	ex N148CQ		Lsd fr Fairbrook Lsg
N149SZ	SAAB SF.340A	149	ex N149CQ		Lsd fr State Street
N150CN	SAAB SF.340A	150	ex N346BE		Lsd fr CHQ
N152CQ	SAAB SF.340A	152	ex N749BA		Lsd fr CHQ
N157SD	SAAB SF.340A	157	ex N157CQ		Lsd fr Bank of America
N158SD	SAAB SF.340A	158	ex N158CQ		Lsd fr Bank of America
N340SZ	SAAB SF.340A	004	ex N340CA		Lsd fr Lambert Lsg
N340SF	SAAB SF.340A	014	ex SE-E14		Lsd fr CHQ
N360SZ	SAAB SF.340A	006	ex N360CA		Lsd fr Lambert Lsg
N810EX	de Havilland DHC-8-102A	308	ex C-GDKL	ESG	Lsd fr ALO
N815EX	de Havilland DHC-8-102A	321	ex C-GDFT		Lsd fr ALO
N816EX	de Havilland DHC-8-102A	329	ex C-GEVP	ESK	Lsd fr ALO

Entered Chapter 11 17 April 2001 but operations continue, operates as US Airways Express

SIERRA PACIFIC AIRLINES

Sierra Pacific (SI/SPA) Tucson-Intl, AZ (TUS)

N703S	Boeing 737-2T4 (AVA 3)	750/22529	ex N703ML
N712S	Boeing 737-2Y5 (AVA 3)	949/23038	ex ZK-NAF

SIERRA WEST AIRLINES

Platinum West (PKW) Stockton-Metropolitan, CA (SCK)

N221TR	Lear Jet 35A	35A-221	ex VH-FSY	Freighter	
N242DR	Lear Jet 35A	35A-242	ex VH-FSZ	Freighter	
N2728G	Swearingen SA.227AC Metro III	AC-731		Freighter	Lsd fr EDB Air
N4019	Swearingen SA.226AT Merlin IV	AT-014	ex C-GSDR	Freighter	
N8897Y	Swearingen SA.226AT Merlin IVC	AT-492	ex C-FJTA	Freighter	

All leased from Career Aviation Academy; Sierra West Airlines is the trading name of Pak West Airlines

SILLER AVIATION

Yuba City-Sutter County, CA

N4196Z	Sikorsky S-61R	61567	ex 65-12792
N4197R	Sikorsky S-61R	61571	ex 65-12796
N4230X	Sikorsky S-61R	61562	ex 66-1787
N5193J	Sikorsky S-61A	61014	ex Bu148036
N15456	Sikorsky S-61N	61826	
N45917	Sikorsky S-61V-1	61271	
N51953	Sikorsky S-61A	61172	ex Bu149903
N429C	Sikorsky CH-54A	64031	ex 67-18429
N2268L	Sikorsky CH-54A	64013	ex 66-18411
N4035S	Sikorsky S-64E Skycrane	64099	ex 70-18491
N4037S	Sikorsky S-64E Skycrane	64101	ex 70-18493
N7095B	Sikorsky CH-54A	64032	ex 67-18430
N9125M	Sikorsky CH-54A	64057	ex 68-18455

SILVERADO AIR TAXI current status is uncertain

SKAGWAY AIR SERVICE

Skagway Air (7J/SGY) Skagway, AK (SGY)

N1132Q	Piper PA-32-300 Cherokee Six	32-7740046
N2884M	Piper PA-32-300 Cherokee Six	32-7840058
N8127K	Piper PA-32-300 Cherokee Six	32-7940268
N30004	Piper PA-32-300 Cherokee Six	32-7840120

N31589	Piper PA-32-300 Cherokee Six	32-7840135	
N40698	Piper PA-32-300 Cherokee Six	32-7440056	
N999SA	Britten-Norman BN-2A-26 Islander	897	ex C-GVKE
N4109D	Piper PA-31-350 T-1020	31-8253012	ex N260SW
N8216T	Piper PA-32-301 Saratoga	32-8206037	
N9540K	Piper PA-34-200T Seneca II	34-7670206	

SKYLINK CHARTER

Hawthorne-Municipal, CA (HHR)

N343AE	Swearingen SA.227AC Metro III	AC-554	ex N3112K	Lsd fr Career Avn

SKYSERVICE USA

Denver-Centennial, CO (DIA)

N571RY	Douglas DC-10-10	283/46645	ex N571SC	Op by RYN
N572RY	Douglas DC-10-10	251/46977	ex N572SC	Op by RYN
Sister company of Skyservice, Canada				

SKY CASTLE AVIATION

New Castle-HenryCounty, IN (MIE)

N38W	Beech H18	BA-580	ex N616T	Freighter
N4231V	Piper PA-31-350 Navajo Chieftain	31-7652162	ex C-GBHM	
N6685S	Beech 58 Baron	TH-718		

SKYWAY ENTERPRISES

Skyway Inc (SKZ)   Orlando-Kissimmee, FL/Detroit-Willow Run, IL (ISM/YIP)

N366MQ	Short SD.3-60	SH3639	ex G-BLEH	
N367MQ	Short SD.3-60	SH3640	ex G-BLGA	
N377MQ	Short SD.3-60	SH3699	ex G-BMUY	
N378MQ	Short SD.3-60	SH3700	ex G-BMXP	stored ISM
N380MQ	Short SD.3-60	SH3702	ex (G-BMXS)	
N381MQ	Short SD.3-60	SH3703	ex (N703AE)	
N382MQ	Short SD.3-60	SH3704	ex (N704AM)	stored ISM
N383MQ	Short SD.3-60	SH3706	ex (G-BNBB)	
N384MQ	Short SD.3-60	SH3711	ex G-BNBG	stored ISM
N385MQ	Short SD.3-60	SH3707	ex G-BNBC	
N386MQ	Short SD.3-60	SH3709	ex G-BNBE	
N387MQ	Short SD.3-60	SH3710	ex G-BNBF	stored ISM
N106SW	Short SD.3-30	SH3072	ex C-GLAT	
N112PS	Douglas DC-9-15F	129/47013	ex N557AS	
N118SW	Short SD.3-30	SH3100	ex 83-0512	
N805SW	Short SD.3-30	SH3055	ex C-FLAC	dam 09Apr03
All freighters				

SKYWEST AIRLINES

(OO/SKW)   Salt Lake City-Intl, UT/Los Angelos-Intl, CA (SLC/LAX)

N403SW	Canadair CL-600-2B19	7028	ex C-FMNB	7028 Delta Connection
N405SW	Canadair CL-600-2B19	7029	ex C-FMND	7029 Delta Connection
N406SW	Canadair CL-600-2B19	7030	ex C-FMNH	7030 Delta Connection
N407SW	Canadair CL-600-2B19	7034	ex C-FMNY	7034 Delta Connection
N408SW	Canadair CL-600-2B19	7055	ex C-FMMW	7055 Delta Connection
N409SW	Canadair CL-600-2B19	7056	ex C-FMMX	7056 Delta Connection
N410SW	Canadair CL-600-2B19	7066	ex C-FMOL	7066 Delta Connection
N411SW	Canadair CL-600-2B19	7067	ex C-FMOS	7067 Delta Connection
N412SW	Canadair CL-600-2B19	7101		7101 Delta Connection
N413SW	Canadair CL-600-2B19	7102		7102 Delta Connection
N416SW	Canadair CL-600-2B19	7089	ex N60SR	7089 Delta Connection
N417SW	Canadair CL-600-2B19	7400	ex C-FMMW	7400 Delta Connection
N418SW	Canadair CL-600-2B19	7446	ex C-FMNW	7446 Delta Connection
N423SW	Canadair CL-600-2B19	7456	ex C-FMMB	7456 Delta Connection
N426SW	Canadair CL-600-2B19	7468	ex C-FMLF	7468 Delta Connection
N427SW	Canadair CL-600-2B19	7497	ex C-FMLB	7497 Delta Connection
N429SW	Canadair CL-600-2B19	7518	ex C-FMMN	7518 Delta Connection
N430SW	Canadair CL-600-2B19	7523	ex C-FMNB	7523 Delta Connection
N431SW	Canadair CL-600-2B19	7536	ex C-FMNW	7536 Delta Connection
N432SW	Canadair CL-600-2B19	7548	ex C-GJFG	7548 Delta Connection
N433SW	Canadair CL-600-2B19	7550	ex C-GJFH	7550 Delta Connection
N435SW	Canadair CL-600-2B19	7555	ex C-GJHK	7555 Delta Connection
N437SW	Canadair CL-600-2B19	7564	ex C-GJIA	7564 Delta Connection

N438SW	Canadair CL-600-2B19	7574	ex C-FMLU	7574 Delta Connection	
N439SW	Canadair CL-600-2B19	7578	ex C-FMMN	7578 Delta Connection	
N440SW	Canadair CL-600-2B19	7589	ex C-FMLI	7589 Delta Connection	
N441SW	Canadair CL-600-2B19	7602	ex C-FMND	7602 Delta Connection	
N442SW	Canadair CL-600-2B19	7609	ex C-FMMQ	7609 Delta Connection	
N443SW	Canadair CL-600-2B19	7638	ex C-FMMN	7638 30th anniversary colours	
N445SW	Canadair CL-600-2B19	7651	ex C-FMLS	7651 Delta Connection	
N446SW	Canadair CL-600-2B19	7666	ex C-FMMB	7666 Delta Connection	
N447SW	Canadair CL-600-2B19	7677	ex C-FMLB	7677 Delta Connection	
N448SW	Canadair CL-600-2B19	7678	ex C-FMLF	7678 Delta Connection	
N449SW	Canadair CL-600-2B19	7699	ex C-FMMQ	7699 Delta Connection	
N452SW	Canadair CL-600-2B19	7716	ex C-FMNW	7716 Delta Connection	
N453SW	Canadair CL-600-2B19	7743	ex C-FMLV	7743 Delta Connection	
N454SW	Canadair CL-600-2B19	7749	ex C-FMOS	7749 Delta Connection	
N455SW	Canadair CL-600-2B19	7760	ex C-FMMW	7760 Delta Connection	
N457SW	Canadair CL-600-2B19	7773	ex C-FMLV	7773 Delta Connection	Lsd fr WFBN
N459SW	Canadair CL-600-2B19	7782	ex C-FMND	7782 Delta Connection	Lsd fr WFBN
N460SW	Canadair CL-600-2B19	7803	ex C-FMLV	7803 Delta Connection	Lsd fr WFBN
N461SW	Canadair CL-600-2B19	7811	ex C-FVAZ	7811 Delta Connection	Lsd fr WFBN
N463SW	Canadair CL-600-2B19	7820	ex C-FMMW	7820 Delta Connection	Lsd fr WFBN
N464SW	Canadair CL-600-2B19	7827	ex C-FMLB	7827 Delta Connection	
N465SW	Canadair CL-600-2B19	7845	ex C-FMOI	7845 Delta Connection	
N466SW	Canadair CL-600-2B19	7856	ex C-FMKZ	7856 Delta Connection	
N499SW	Canadair CL-600-2B19	7398	ex N816CA	7398 Delta Connection	Lsd fr COM
N587SW	Canadair CL-600-2B19	7062	ex N943CA	7062 Delta Connection	Lsd fr COM
N588SW	Canadair CL-600-2B19	7069	ex N945CA	7069 Delta Connection	Lsd fr COM
N589SW	Canadair CL-600-2B19	7072	ex C-FMLB	7072 Delta Connection	Lsd fr COM
N590SW	Canadair CL-600-2B19	7077	ex N947CA	7077 Delta Connection	Lsd fr COM
N591SW	Canadair CL-600-2B19	7079	ex N948CA	7079 Delta Connection	Lsd fr COM
N592SW	Canadair CL-600-2B19	7279	ex N759CA	7279 Delta Connection	Lsd fr COM
N594SW	Canadair CL-600-2B19	7285	ex N767CA	7285 Delta Connection	Lsd fr COM
N595SW	Canadair CL-600-2B19	7292	ex N769CA	7292 Delta Connection	Lsd fr COM
N597SW	Canadair CL-600-2B19	7293	ex N776CA	7293 Delta Connection	Lsd fr COM
N720SW	Canadair CL-600-2B19	7297	ex N778CA	7297 Delta Connection	Lsd fr COM
N903SW	Canadair CL-600-2B19	7425	ec C-FMOI	United Express	
N905SW	Canadair CL-600-2B19	7437	ex C-FMLB	United Express	
N906SW	Canadair CL-600-2B19	7510	ex C-FMOW	United Express	
N907SW	Canadair CL-600-2B19	7511	ex C-FVAZ	United Express	
N908SW	Canadair CL-600-2B19	7540	ex C-FMOW	United Express	
N909SW	Canadair CL-600-2B19	7558	ex C-GJHL	United Express	
N910SW	Canadair CL-600-2B19	7566	ex C-GJHY	United Express	
N912SW	Canadair CL-600-2B19	7595	ex C-FMNH	United Express	
N913SW	Canadair CL-600-2B19	7597	ex C-FMNX	United Express	
N915SW	Canadair CL-600-2B19	7615	ex C-FMKV	United Express	
N916SW	Canadair CL-600-2B19	7634	ex C-FMLU	United Express	
N917SW	Canadair CL-600-2B19	7641	ex C-FMMX	United Express	
N918SW	Canadair CL-600-2B19	7645	ex C-FMKW	United Express	
N919SW	Canadair CL-600-2B19	7657	ex C-FMNX	United Express	
N920SW	Canadair CL-600-2B19	7660	ex C-FMOW	United Express	
N923SW	Canadair CL-600-2B19	7664	ex C-FMLU	United Express	
N924SW	Canadair CL-600-2B19	7681	ex C-FMLS	United Express	Lsd fr WFBN
N925SW	Canadair CL-600-2B19	7682	ex C-FMLT	United Express	Lsd fr WFBN
N926SW	Canadair CL-600-2B19	7687	ex C-FMNX	United Express	Lsd fr WFBN
N927SW	Canadair CL-600-2B19	7693	ex C-FMNQ	United Express	Lsd fr WFBN
N928SW	Canadair CL-600-2B19	7701	ex C-FMMX	United Express	Lsd fr WFBN
N929SW	Canadair CL-600-2B19	7703	ex C-FMNB	United Express	Lsd fr WFBN
N930SW	Canadair CL-600-2B19	7713	ex C-FMLV	United Express	
N932SW	Canadair CL-600-2B19	7714	ex C-FMMT	United Express	Lsd fr WFBN
N934SW	Canadair CL-600-2B19	7722	ex C-FMND	United Express	Lsd fr WFBN
N935SW	Canadair CL-600-2B19	7725	ex C-FMOI	United Express	Lsd fr WFBN
N936SW	Canadair CL-600-2B19	7726	ex C-FMMB	United Express	Lsd fr WFBN
N937SW	Canadair CL-600-2B19	7735	ex C-FMKW	United Express	
N938SW	Canadair CL-600-2B19	7741	ex C-FMLS	United Express	
N939SW	Canadair CL-600-2B19	7742	ex C-FMLS	United Express	
N941SW	Canadair CL-600-2B19	7750	ex C-FMOW	United Express	
N943SW	Canadair CL-600-2B19	7762	ex C-FMMY	United Express	
N944SW	Canadair CL-600-2B19	7764	ex C-FMKV	United Express	Lsd fr WFBN
N945SW	Canadair CL-600-2B19	7770	ex C-FMLQ	United Express	Lsd fr WFBN
N946SW	Canadair CL-600-2B19	7776	ex C-FMNW	United Express	Lsd fr WFBN
N947SW	Canadair CL-600-2B19	7786	ex C-FMMB	United Express	Lsd fr WFBN
N948SW	Canadair CL-600-2B19	7789	ex C-GZTU	United Express	Lsd fr WFBN
N951SW	Canadair CL-600-2B19	7795	ex C-FMKW	United Express	Lsd fr WFBN
N952SW	Canadair CL-600-2B19	7805	ex C-FMNH	United Express	Lsd fr WFBN
N953SW	Canadair CL-600-2B19	7813	ex C-GZGP	United Express	
N954SW	Canadair CL-600-2B19	7815	ex C-FMOI	United Express	Lsd fr WFBN
N955SW	Canadair CL-600-2B19	7817	ex C-	United Express	Lsd fr WFBN
N956SW	Canadair CL-600-2B19	7825	ex C-FMKW	United Express	Lsd fr WFBN
N957SW	Canadair CL-600-2B19	7829	ex C-FMLI	United Express	
N958SW	Canadair CL-600-2B19	7833	ex C-FMLV	United Express	
N959SW	Canadair CL-600-2B19	7840	ex C-FMOW	United Express	
N960SW	Canadair CL-600-2B19	7853	ex C-FMNB	United Express	
N961SW	Canadair CL-600-2B19	7857	ex C-FMLB	United Express	

N962SW	Canadair CL-600-2B19	7859	ex C-FMLI	United Express	
N963SW	Canadair CL-600-2B19	7865	ex C-FMNH	United Express	
N964SW	Canadair CL-600-2B19	7868	ex C-FMNY	United Express	
N965SW	Canadair CL-600-2B19	7871	ex C-FVAZ	United Express	
N967SW	Canadair CL-600-2B19	7872	ex C-FMND	United Express	
N969SW	Canadair CL-600-2B19	7876	ex C-FMMB	United Express	
N970SW	Canadair CL-600-2B19	7881	ex C-GZUJ	United Express	

15 sold to CIT Structured Finance in late 2002 and leased back

N701SK	Canadair CL-600-2C10	10133	ex C-	United Express	
N	Canadair CL-600-2C10		ex C-	on order 04	
N	Canadair CL-600-2C10		ex C-	on order 04	
N	Canadair CL-600-2C10		ex C-	on order 04	
N	Canadair CL-600-2C10		ex C-	on order 04	
N	Canadair CL-600-2C10		ex C-	on order 04	
N	Canadair CL-600-2C10		ex C-	on order 04	
N	Canadair CL-600-2C10		ex C-	on order 04	
N	Canadair CL-600-2C10		ex C-	on order 04	
N	Canadair CL-600-2C10		ex C-	on order 04	
N	Canadair CL-600-2C10		ex C-	on order 04	
N	Canadair CL-600-2C10		ex C-	on order 04	
N	Canadair CL-600-2C10		ex C-	on order 04	
N	Canadair CL-600-2C10		ex C-	on order 04	
N	Canadair CL-600-2C10		ex C-	on order 04	
N	Canadair CL-600-2C10		ex C-	on order 04	
N	Canadair CL-600-2C10		ex C-	on order 04	
N	Canadair CL-600-2C10		ex C-	on order 04	
N	Canadair CL-600-2C10		ex C-	on order 04	
N	Canadair CL-600-2C10		ex C-	on order 04	

N137H	Embraer EMB.120ER Brasilia	120137	ex PT-SPD	stored SGU	Lsd fr WFBN
N156CA	Embraer EMB.120ER Brasilia	120156	ex PT-SPV	stored SGU	Lsd fr WFBN
N161CA	Embraer EMB.120ER Brasilia	120143	ex PT-SPJ	stored SGU	Lsd fr WFBN
N162CA	Embraer EMB.120ER Brasilia	120150	ex PT-SPP	stored SGU	Lsd fr WFBN
N186SW	Embraer EMB.120ER Brasilia	120034	ex PT-SJD		
N187SW	Embraer EMB.120ER Brasilia	120037	ex PT-SJG		
N188SW	Embraer EMB.120ER Brasilia	120039	ex PT-SJI		
N189SW	Embraer EMB.120ER Brasilia	120048	ex PT-SJR		
N190SW	Embraer EMB.120ER Brasilia	120050	ex PT-SJT		
N195SW	Embraer EMB.120ER Brasilia	120127	ex PT-SNT	stored VCV	Lsd fr Boeing
N196CA	Embraer EMB.120ER Brasilia	120196	ex PT-SRL	stored SGU	Lsd fr Boeing
N196SW	Embraer EMB.120ER Brasilia	120151	ex PT-SPQ		
N197SW	Embraer EMB.120ER Brasilia	120186	ex PT-SQY	stored INT	
N199SW	Embraer EMB.120ER Brasilia	120237	ex PT-STJ	stored VCV	Lsd fr WFBN
N203SW	Embraer EMB.120ER Brasilia	120240	ex PT-STM	stored VCV	Lsd fr Boeing Capital
N204SW	Embraer EMB.120ER Brasilia	120243	ex PT-STP		Lsd fr Players Airi
N207SW	Embraer EMB.120ER Brasilia	120266	ex PT-SUM		
N209SW	Embraer EMB.120ER Brasilia	120269	ex PT-SUP		
N212SW	Embraer EMB.120ER Brasilia	120276	ex PT-SUW		
N213SW	Embraer EMB.120ER Brasilia	120277	ex PT-SUX		Lsd fr Aircraft Lse Finance
N214SW	Embraer EMB.120ER Brasilia	120280	ex PT-SVA		
N215SW	Embraer EMB.120ER Brasilia	120281	ex PT-SVB		
N216SW	Embraer EMB.120ER Brasilia	120285	ex PT-SVF		
N217SW	Embraer EMB.120ER Brasilia	120286	ex PT-SVG		
N218SW	Embraer EMB.120ER Brasilia	120287	ex PT-SVH	United Express	
N220SW	Embraer EMB.120ER Brasilia	120288	ex PT-SVI		Lsd fr Banc One
N221SW	Embraer EMB.120ER Brasilia	120290	ex PT-SVK	United Express	Lsd fr WFBN
N223SW	Embraer EMB.120ER Brasilia	120291	ex PT-SVL	United Express	
N224SW	Embraer EMB.120ER Brasilia	120294	ex PT-SVO		Lsd fr Banc One
N226SW+	Embraer EMB.120ER Brasilia	120296	ex PT-SVQ	United Express	
N227SW	Embraer EMB.120ER Brasilia	120304	ex PT-SVW	United Express	
N229SW	Embraer EMB.120ER Brasilia	120305	ex PT-SVX	United Express	
N232SW	Embraer EMB.120ER Brasilia	120306	ex PT-SVY		
N233SW	Embraer EMB.120ER Brasilia	120307	ex PT-SVZ	United Express	
N234SW	Embraer EMB.120ER Brasilia	120308	ex PT-SXA	United Express	Lsd fr WFBN
N235SW	Embraer EMB.120ER Brasilia	120310	ex PT-SXC	United Express	Lsd fr WFBN
N236SW	Embraer EMB.120ER Brasilia	120312	ex PT-SXE		Lsd fr WFBN
N237SW	Embraer EMB.120ER Brasilia	120314	ex PT-SXG	United Express	Lsd fr WFBN
N250YV	Embraer EMB.120ER Brasilia	120250	ex PT-STW	United Express	Lsd fr Norwest
N251UE	Embraer EMB.120RT Brasilia	120108	ex PT-SNA	United Express	
N251YV	Embraer EMB.120ER Brasilia	120251	ex PT-STX	United Express	Lsd fr FUNC
N268UE	Embraer EMB.120ER Brasilia	120207	ex PT-SRZ	United Express	
N270YV	Embraer EMB.120ER Brasilia	120270	ex PT-SUR	United Express	Lsd fr WFBN
N271YV	Embraer EMB.120ER Brasilia	120271	ex PT-SUS	United Express	Lsd fr WFBN
N284YV	Embraer EMB.120ER Brasilia	120284	ex PT-SVE	United Express	Lsd fr WFBN
N288SW+	Embraer EMB.120ER Brasilia	120316	ex PT-SXI	United Express	
N290SW	Embraer EMB.120ER Brasilia	120317	ex PT-SXJ	United Express	Lsd fr WFBN
N291SW	Embraer EMB.120ER Brasilia	120318	ex PT-SXK	United Express	Lsd fr WFBN
N292SW	Embraer EMB.120ER Brasilia	120319	ex PT-SXL	United Express	
N292UX	Embraer EMB.120ER Brasilia	120292	ex PT-SVM	United Express	
N293SW	Embraer EMB.120ER Brasilia	120320	ex PT-SXM	United Express	Lsd fr WFBN
N294SW	Embraer EMB.120ER Brasilia	120321	ex PT-SXN	United Express	Lsd fr WFBN

N295SW	Embraer EMB.120ER Brasilia	120322	ex PT-SXO	United Express	
N295UX+	Embraer EMB.120ER Brasilia	120295	ex PT-SVP		
N296SW	Embraer EMB.120ER Brasilia	120325	ex PT-SXR	United Express	
N297SW	Embraer EMB.120ER Brasilia	120327	ex PT-SXT	United Express	Lsd fr WFBN
N298SW	Embraer EMB.120ER Brasilia	120328	ex PT-SXU		Lsd fr WFBN
N299SW	Embraer EMB.120ER Brasilia	120329	ex PT-SXV	United Express	Lsd fr WFBN
N301YV	Embraer EMB.120ER Brasilia	120301	ex PT-SVV	United Express	
N308SW+	Embraer EMB.120ER Brasilia	120326	ex PT-SXS		
N393SW	Embraer EMB.120ER Brasilia	120330	ex PT-SXW	United Express	
N560SW	Embraer EMB.120ER Brasilia	120334	ex PT-SXX	United Express	Lsd fr WFBN
N561SW	Embraer EMB.120ER Brasilia	120335	ex PT-SXY	United Express	Lsd fr WFBN
N562SW	Embraer EMB.120ER Brasilia	120336	ex PT-SXZ	United Express	Lsd fr WFBN
N563SW	Embraer EMB.120ER Brasilia	120338		United Express	Lsd fr WFBN
N564SW	Embraer EMB.120ER Brasilia	120339		United Express	
N565SW	Embraer EMB.120ER Brasilia	120340			
N566SW	Embraer EMB.120ER Brasilia	120341	ex PT-SAF	United Express	Lsd fr WFBN
N567SW	Embraer EMB.120ER Brasilia	120342		United Express	Lsd fr WFBN
N568SW	Embraer EMB.120ER Brasilia	120343		United Express	
N569SW	Embraer EMB.120ER Brasilia	120344		United Express	
N576SW	Embraer EMB.120ER Brasilia	120345		United Express	
N578SW	Embraer EMB.120ER Brasilia	120346		United Express	Lsd fr US Bancorp
N579SW	Embraer EMB.120ER Brasilia	120347		United Express	Lsd fr WFBN
N580SW	Embraer EMB.120ER Brasilia	120348		United Express	Lsd fr WFBN
N581SW	Embraer EMB.120ER Brasilia	120349			
N582SW	Embraer EMB.120ER Brasilia	120350		Continental Express	Lsd fr WFBN
N583SW	Embraer EMB.120ER Brasilia	120351		Continental Express	Lsd fr WFBN
N584SW	Embraer EMB.120ER Brasilia	120352	ex PT-SEG	United Express	Lsd fr WFBN
N585SW	Embraer EMB.120ER Brasilia	120353		United Express	Lsd fr WFBN
N586SW	Embraer EMB.120ER Brasilia	120354		United Express	Lsd fr WFBN
N1105G	Embraer EMB.120ER Brasilia	120105	ex PT-SMX	stored SGU	
N1110J	Embraer EMB.120ER Brasilia	120110	ex PT-SNC	stored SGU	
N1117H	Embraer EMB.120ER Brasilia	120117	ex PT-SNJ	stored SGU	
N16731	Embraer EMB.120ER Brasilia	120190	ex PT-		Lsd fr US Bank
N15732	Embraer EMB.120ER Brasilia	120195	ex PT-		Lsd fr US Bank
N58733	Embraer EMB.120ER Brasilia	120197	ex PT-	stored FAT	Lsd fr US Bank
N57734	Embraer EMB.120ER Brasilia	120199	ex PT-		Lsd fr US Bank

+Leased from Banc of America Leasing & Capital   +Operates as Continental Connection

All aircraft are operated for Delta Air Lines (as Delta Connection), including some code-shared with Continental Airlines plus United Airlines as United Express from points on the West Coast and Nevada. Note some are in Skywest colours

---

SMITHAIR

Smithair (SMH)   *Hampton-Clayton County, GA*

N140RC	Lear Jet 23	23-048	ex N48MW
N216SA	AMD Falcon 20DC	16	ex N216TW
N283SA	AMD Falcon 20DC	83	ex N20PL
N351N	Lear Jet 23	23-054	ex N351NR
N514SA	AMD Falcon 20DC	30	ex F-GPIM
N900NA	Lear Jet 24A	24A-111	ex N44WD
N7200K	Lear Jet 23	23-099	

Operates for Airborne Express; all leased from RBS Aviation

SMOKEY BAY AIR

(2E)   *Homer, AK (HOM)*

N505SD	Cessna U206C Super Skywagon	U206-0947
N72067	Cessna U206D Super Skywagon	U206-1273

SONG

Boston-Logan Intl, MA/New York-JFK, NY (BOS/JFK)

N645DL	Boeing 757-232	216/24216		645
N649DL	Boeing 757-232	229/24389		649
N651DL	Boeing 757-232	238/24391		651
N684DA	Boeing 757-232	535/27104		684
N685DA	Boeing 757-232	667/27588		685
N693DL	Boeing 757-232	826/29725	ex N1799B	693
N695DL	Boeing 757-232	838/29727	ex N1795B	695
N697DL	Boeing 757-232	880/30318	ex N1795B	697
N698DL	Boeing 757-232	885/29911		698
N6702	Boeing 757-232	898/30188		6702
N6704Z	Boeing 757-232	914/30396	ex N1795B	6704
N6705Y	Boeing 757-232	917/30397		6705
N6706Q	Boeing 757-232	921/30422		6706
N6709	Boeing 757-232	937/30481		6709
N6712B	Boeing 757-232	942/30484		6712
N6715C	Boeing 757-232	953/30486		6715

N6716C	Boeing 757-232	955/30838	6716
N67171	Boeing 757-232	959/30839	6717

Song is a low-cost carrier wholly owned by Delta Air Lines. A total of 36 199 seat Boeing 757s are on order from the parent

SOUTH AERO

Albuquerque-Intl Sunport, NM (ABQ)

N42MG	Cessna 402C	402C0320	
N57PB	Cessna 402C	402C0300	
N305AT	Cessna 402C	402C0030	ex C-GZVM
N402MQ	Cessna 402C	402C0095	
N402SA	Cessna 402C	402C0623	ex C-GHOR
N494BC	Cessna 402C	402C0308	ex N67PB
N525RH	Cessna 402C	402C0525	
N747WS	Cessna 402C	402C0080	ex C-GHYZ
N2649Z	Cessna 402C	402C0333	
N2711X	Cessna 402C	402C0116	
N2713X	Cessna 402C	402C0207	
N3292M	Cessna 402C	402C0304	
N4643N	Cessna 402C	402C0006	
N5820C	Cessna 402C	402C0047	
N6880A	Cessna 402C	402C0616	
N26156	Cessna 402C	402C0112	
N54ZP	Cessna 404 Titan	404-0694	
N165SA	Cessna 404 Titan	404-0622	
N1689X	Cessna 210L Centurion	21060724	
N5388J	Cessna 404 Titan	404-0666	
N6479N	Cessna T210N Turbo Centurion	21063053	
N7213N	Cessna T210N Turbo Centurion	21063207	

SOUTHEAST AIRLINES

Sun King (SNK)

St Petersburg-Clearwater Intl, FL (PIE)

N920LG	Douglas DC-9-32 (ABS 3)	913/47797	ex N12508	Lsd fr Triton
N921LG	Douglas DC-9-32 (ABS 3)	914/47798	ex N27509	Lsd fr Triton
N932MJ	Douglas DC-9-31 (ABS 3)	1052/48156	ex N980VJ	
N933JK	Douglas DC-9-31 (ABS 3)	1058/48159	ex N983VJ	
N934LK	Douglas DC-9-31 (ABS 3)	1054/48157	ex N981VJ	
N935DS	Douglas DC-9-31 (ABS 3)	1056/48158	ex N982VJ	
N12532	Douglas DC-9-32 (ABS 3)	349/45791	ex N532TX	Lsd fr Pacific
N11FQ	McDonnell-Douglas MD-88	1606/49759	ex P4-MDA	Lsd fr Bank of NY
N12FQ	McDonnell-Douglas MD-88	1657/49766	ex P4-MDC	Lsd fr Bank of NY
N374GE	McDonnell-Douglas MD-82	1208/49374	ex HL7542	Lsd fr Castle Harbour Lsg
N418GE	McDonnell-Douglas MD-82	1394/49418	ex HL7545	Lsd fr Castle Harbour Lsg

SOUTHERN AIR

Southern Air (9S/SOO) (IATA 099)

Columbus-Rickenbacker, OH (LCK)

N751SA	Boeing 747-228F	535/22678	ex F-GCBE	all-white	Lsd fr CIT Leasing

Filed Chapter 11 October 2002, operations continue

SOUTHERN SEAPLANE

Southern Skies (SSC)

Belle Chasse-Southern Seaplane SPB, LA (BCS)

N227SS	Cessna U206E Skywagon	U20601516	
N2272X	Cessna U206E Skywagon	U20601556	
N7896S	Cessna U206B Super Skywagon	U206-0814	ex CF-WRI
N21058	de Havilland DHC-2 Beaver	630	ex CF-HOE
N61301	Cessna A185F Skywagon 6	18504144	
N61441	Cessna A185F Skywagon 6	18504191	
N70117	Cessna A185E Skywagon	18501997	
N70822	Cessna U206F Stationair	U20602099	

All floatplanes

SOUTHWEST AIRLINES

Southwest (WN/SWA) (IATA 526)

Dallas-Love Field/Houston-Hobby, TX (DAL/HOU)

N68SW	Boeing 737-2H4 (AVA 3)	725/22357	stored DAL
N73SW	Boeing 737-2H4 (AVA 3)	826/22673	
N74SW	Boeing 737-2H4 (AVA 3)	827/22674	
N81SW	Boeing 737-2H4 (AVA 3)	841/22730	no titles
N82SW	Boeing 737-2H4 (AVA 3)	864/22731	
N83SW	Boeing 737-2H4 (AVA 3)	877/22732	

N85SW	Boeing 737-2H4 (AVA 3)	878/22826			
N86SW	Boeing 737-2H4 (AVA 3)	882/22827			
N90SW	Boeing 737-2H4 (AVA 3)	918/22905			
N91SW	Boeing 737-2H4 (AVA 3)	929/22963			
N92SW	Boeing 737-2H4 (AVA 3)	933/22964			
N93SW	Boeing 737-2H4 (AVA 3)	942/22965			
N94SW	Boeing 737-2H4 (AVA 3)	968/23053			Lsd fr Polaris
N95SW	Boeing 737-2H4 (AVA 3)	969/23054			Lsd fr Polaris
N96SW	Boeing 737-2H4 (AVA 3)	970/23055		The Fred J Jones	
N102SW	Boeing 737-2H4 (AVA 3)	1014/23108			
N103SW	Boeing 737-2H4 (AVA 3)	1016/23109			
N104SW	Boeing 737-2H4 (AVA 3)	1017/23110			
N105SW	Boeing 737-2H4 (AVA 3)	1095/23249			
N129SW	Boeing 737-2K6 (AVA 3)	678/22340	ex N148AW	stored MZJ	Lsd fr WFBN
N702ML	Boeing 737-2T4 (AVA 3)	624/22054	ex G-BJXL		Lsd fr Polaris
N721WN	Boeing 737-2T4 (AVA 3)	817/22697	ex N721ML		Lsd fr Whirlpool
N722WN	Boeing 737-2T4 (AVA 3)	823/22698	ex N722ML		Lsd fr Whirlpool
N300SW	Boeing 737-3H4	1037/22940		The Spirit of Kitty Hawk	
N301SW	Boeing 737-3H4	1048/22941		The Spirit of Kitty Hawk	
N302SW	Boeing 737-3H4	1052/22942		The Spirit of Kitty Hawk	
N303SW	Boeing 737-3H4	1101/22943			
N304SW	Boeing 737-3H4	1138/22944			
N305SW	Boeing 737-3H4	1139/22945			
N306SW	Boeing 737-3H4	1148/22946			
N307SW	Boeing 737-3H4	1156/22947		Rick Evens	
N308SA	Boeing 737-3Y0	1233/23498	ex G-EZYA		
N309SW	Boeing 737-3H4	1160/22948			
N310SW	Boeing 737-3H4	1161/22949			
N311SW	Boeing 737-3H4	1183/23333			
N312SW	Boeing 737-3H4	1185/23334			
N313SW	Boeing 737-3H4	1201/23335			
N314SW	Boeing 737-3H4	1229/23336			
N315SW	Boeing 737-3H4	1231/23337			
N316SW	Boeing 737-3H4	1232/23338			
N317WN	Boeing 737-3Q8	1506/24068	ex G-EZYE		
N318SW	Boeing 737-3H4	1255/23339			Lsd fr BTM Capital
N319SW	Boeing 737-3H4	1348/23340			
N320SW	Boeing 737-3H4	1350/23341			
N321SW	Boeing 737-3H4	1351/23342			
N322SW	Boeing 737-3H4	1377/23343			Lsd fr Colonial Pacific
N323SW	Boeing 737-3H4	1378/23344			
N324SW	Boeing 737-3H4	1384/23414			
N325SW	Boeing 737-3H4	1398/23689			Lsd fr State Street
N326SW	Boeing 737-3H4	1400/23690			
N327SW	Boeing 737-3H4	1407/23691			Lsd fr GECAS
N328SW	Boeing 737-3H4	1521/23692			
N329SW	Boeing 737-3H4	1525/23693			
N330SW	Boeing 737-3H4	1529/23694			
N331SW	Boeing 737-3H4	1536/23695			Lsd fr Colonial Pacific
N332SW	Boeing 737-3H4	1545/23696			Lsd fr WFBN
N333SW	Boeing 737-3H4	1547/23697			Lsd fr WFBN
N334SW	Boeing 737-3H4	1549/23938		Shamu	
N335SW	Boeing 737-3H4	1553/23939			
N336SW	Boeing 737-3H4	1557/23940			
N337SW	Boeing 737-3H4	1567/23959			Lsd fr WFBN
N338SW	Boeing 737-3H4	1571/23960			Lsd fr WFBN
N339SW	Boeing 737-3H4	1591/24090			
N340LV	Boeing 737-3K2	1360/23738	ex PH-HVJ		
N341SW	Boeing 737-3H4	1593/24091			
N342SW	Boeing 737-3H4	1682/24133			
N343SW	Boeing 737-3H4	1686/24151			
N344SW	Boeing 737-3H4	1688/24152			
N345SA	Boeing 737-3K2	1386/23786	ex PH-HVK		
N346SW	Boeing 737-3H4	1690/24153			
N347SW	Boeing 737-3H4	1708/24374			
N348SW	Boeing 737-3H4	1710/24375			
N349SW	Boeing 737-3H4	1734/24408			
N350SW	Boeing 737-3H4	1748/24409			
N351SW	Boeing 737-3H4	1790/24572			
N352SW	Boeing 737-3H4	1942/24888		Lone Star One	
N353SW	Boeing 737-3H4	1947/24889			
N354SW	Boeing 737-3H4	2092/25219			
N355SW	Boeing 737-3H4	2103/25250			
N356SW	Boeing 737-3H4	2105/25251			
N357SW	Boeing 737-3H4	2294/26594			
N358SW	Boeing 737-3H4	2295/26595			
N359SW+	Boeing 737-3H4	2297/26596			
N360SW+	Boeing 737-3H4	2307/26571			
N361SW+	Boeing 737-3H4	2309/26572			
N362SW+	Boeing 737-3H4	2322/26573			
N363SW+	Boeing 737-3H4	2429/26574		Heroes of the Heart	

N364SW	Boeing 737-3H4	2430/26575	
N365SW+	Boeing 737-3H4	2433/26576	The Herbert D Kelleher
N366SW	Boeing 737-3H4	2469/26577	
N367SW	Boeing 737-3H4	2470/26578	
N368SW	Boeing 737-3H4	2473/26579	
N369SW	Boeing 737-3H4	2477/26580	
N370SW	Boeing 737-3H4	2497/26597	
N371SW	Boeing 737-3H4	2500/26598	
N372SW	Boeing 737-3H4	2504/26599	
N373SW	Boeing 737-3H4	2509/26581	
N374SW	Boeing 737-3H4	2515/26582	
N375SW	Boeing 737-3H4	2520/26583	
N376SW	Boeing 737-3H4	2570/26584	
N378SW	Boeing 737-3H4	2579/26585	
N379SW	Boeing 737-3H4	2580/26586	
N380SW	Boeing 737-3H4	2610/26587	
N382SW	Boeing 737-3H4	2611/26588	
N383SW	Boeing 737-3H4	2612/26589	Arizona One
N384SW	Boeing 737-3H4	2613/26590	
N385SW	Boeing 737-3H4	2617/26600	
N386SW	Boeing 737-3H4	2626/26601	
N387SW	Boeing 737-3H4	2627/26602	
N388SW	Boeing 737-3H4	2628/26591	
N389SW	Boeing 737-3H4	2629/26592	
N390SW+	Boeing 737-3H4	2642/26593	
N391SW	Boeing 737-3H4	2643/27378	
N392SW	Boeing 737-3H4	2644/27379	
N394SW	Boeing 737-3H4	2645/27380	
N395SW	Boeing 737-3H4	2667/27689	
N396SW	Boeing 737-3H4	2668/27690	
N397SW	Boeing 737-3H4	2695/27691	
N398SW	Boeing 737-3H4	2696/27692	
N399WN	Boeing 737-3H4	2697/27693	
N600WN	Boeing 737-3H4	2699/27694	
N601WN	Boeing 737-3H4	2702/27695	Jack Vidal
N602SW	Boeing 737-3H4	2713/27953	
N603SW	Boeing 737-3H4	2714/27954	
N604SW	Boeing 737-3H4	2715/27955	
N605SW	Boeing 737-3H4	2716/27956	
N606SW	Boeing 737-3H4	2740/27926	
N607SW	Boeing 737-3H4	2741/27927	June H Morris
N608SW	Boeing 737-3H4	2742/27928	
N609SW	Boeing 737-3H4	2744/27929	California One
N610WN	Boeing 737-3H4	2745/27696	
N611SW	Boeing 737-3H4	2750/27697	
N612SW	Boeing 737-3H4	2753/27930	
N613SW	Boeing 737-3H4	2754/27931	
N614SW	Boeing 737-3H4	2755/28033	
N615SW	Boeing 737-3H4	2757/27698	
N616SW	Boeing 737-3H4	2758/27699	
N617SW	Boeing 737-3H4	2759/27700	
N618WN	Boeing 737-3H4	2761/28034	
N619SW	Boeing 737-3H4	2762/28035	
N620SW	Boeing 737-3H4	2766/28036	
N621SW	Boeing 737-3H4	2767/28037	
N622SW	Boeing 737-3H4	2779/27932	
N623SW	Boeing 737-3H4	2780/27933	Lsd fr Wachovia Bank
N624SW	Boeing 737-3H4	2781/27934	
N625SW	Boeing 737-3H4	2787/27701	Lsd fr Wachovia Bank
N626SW	Boeing 737-3H4	2789/27702	Lsd fr Wachovia Bank
N627SW	Boeing 737-3H4	2790/27935	Lsd fr Wachovia Bank
N628SW	Boeing 737-3H4	2795/27703	Lsd fr Wachovia Bank
N629SW	Boeing 737-3H4	2796/27704	Silver One
N630WN	Boeing 737-3H4	2797/27705	
N631SW	Boeing 737-3H4	2798/27706	
N632SW	Boeing 737-3H4	2799/27707	
N633SW	Boeing 737-3H4	2807/27936	
N634SW	Boeing 737-3H4	2808/27937	
N635SW	Boeing 737-3H4	2813/27708	Lsd fr Wachovia Bank
N636WN	Boeing 737-3H4	2814/27709	
N637SW	Boeing 737-3H4	2819/27710	
N638SW	Boeing 737-3H4	2820/27711	
N639SW	Boeing 737-3H4	2821/27712	
N640SW	Boeing 737-3H4	2840/27713	
N641SW	Boeing 737-3H4	2841/27714	
N642WN	Boeing 737-3H4	2842/27715	
N643SW	Boeing 737-3H4	2843/27716	
N644SW	Boeing 737-3H4	2869/28329	
N645SW	Boeing 737-3H4	2870/28330	
N646SW	Boeing 737-3H4	2871/28331	
N647SW	Boeing 737-3H4	2892/27717	Triple Crown c/s
N648SW	Boeing 737-3H4	2893/27718	

N649SW	Boeing 737-3H4	2894/27719		
N650SW	Boeing 737-3H4	2901/27720		
N651SW	Boeing 737-3H4	2915/27721		
N652SW	Boeing 737-3H4	2916/27722		
N653SW	Boeing 737-3H4	2917/28398		
N654SW	Boeing 737-3H4	2918/28399		
N655WN	Boeing 737-3H4	2931/28400		
N656SW	Boeing 737-3H4	2932/28401		
N657SW	Boeing 737-3L9	1111/23331	ex N960WP	
N658SW	Boeing 737-3L9	1118/23332	ex N961WP	
N659SW	Boeing 737-301	1112/23229	ex N950WP	
N660SW	Boeing 737-301	1115/23230	ex N949WP	Lsd fr WFBN
N661SW	Boeing 737-317	1098/23173	ex N946WP	Lsd fr BBAM
N662SW	Boeing 737-3Q8	1125/23255	ex N327US	Lsd fr MSA V
N663SW	Boeing 737-3Q8	1128/23256	ex N329US	Lsd fr MSA V
N664WN	Boeing 737-3Y0	1206/23495	ex EC-FVT	Lsd fr GECAS
N665WN	Boeing 737-3Y0	1227/23497	ex G-MONF	Lsd fr GECAS
N667SW	Boeing 737-3T5	1092/23063	ex N752MA	Lsd fr National City
N669SW	Boeing 737-3A4	1484/23752	ex N758MA	Lsd fr ACG Corp
N670SW	Boeing 737-3G7	1533/23784	ex N779MA	Lsd fr GECAS
N671SW	Boeing 737-3G7	1535/23785	ex N778MA	Lsd fr GATX
N672SW	Boeing 737-3Q8	1215/23406	ex N755MA	Lsd fr ACG Acquisitions
N673AA	Boeing 737-3A4	1063/23251	ex N307AC	Lsd fr Linc Capital
N674AA	Boeing 737-3A4	1094/23252	ex N776MA	Lsd fr WFBN
N675AA	Boeing 737-3A4	1096/23253	ex (TF-AIC)	Lsd fr Pacific AirCorp
N676SW	Boeing 737-3A4	1100/23288	ex N742MA	
N677AA	Boeing 737-3A4	1182/23289	ex N735MA	
N678AA	Boeing 737-3A4	1205/23290	ex N304AC	Lsd fr GATX
N679AA	Boeing 737-3A4	1211/23291	ex N306AC	
N680AA	Boeing 737-3A4	1318/23505	ex N310AC	Lsd fr AAL
N682SW	Boeing 737-3Y0	1217/23496	ex N67AB	Lsd fr Aeronautics Lsg
N683SW	Boeing 737-3G7	1576/24008	ex N301AW	Lsd fr WFBN
N684WN	Boeing 737-3T0	1520/23941	ex EC-EID	Lsd fr WFBN
N685SW	Boeing 737-3Q8	1209/23401	ex G-BOWR	Lsd fr WFBN
N686SW	Boeing 737-317	1110/23175	ex EI-CHU	Lsd fr debis
N687SW	Boeing 737-3Q8	1187/23388	ex N103GU	Lsd fr WFBN
N688SW	Boeing 737-3Q8	1107/23254	ex N780MA	Lsd fr ILFC
N689SW	Boeing 737-3Q8	1163/23387	ex N734MA	
N690SW	Boeing 737-3G7	1531/23783	ex N785MA	Lsd fr GATX
N691WN	Boeing 737-3G7	1494/23781	ex N784MA	Lsd fr GECAS
N692SW	Boeing 737-3T5	1083/23062	ex N733MA	
N693SW	Boeing 737-317	1104/23174	ex N775MA	Lsd fr WFBN
N694SW	Boeing 737-3T5	1080/23061	ex N744MA	
N695SW	Boeing 737-3Q8	1249/23506	ex N730MA	Lsd fr First Union Comm
N696SW	Boeing 737-3T5	1527/23064	ex N748MA	
N697SW	Boeing 737-3T0	1505/23838	ex N764MA	Lsd fr Cirrus
N698SW	Boeing 737-317	1213/23176	ex EI-CHD	Lsd fr WFBN
N699SW	Boeing 737-3Y0	1372/23826	ex EI-CHE	Lsd fr WFBN
N501SW	Boeing 737-5H4	1718/24178	ex N73700	Shamu Three
N502SW	Boeing 737-5H4	1744/24179		
N503SW	Boeing 737-5H4	1766/24180		
N504SW	Boeing 737-5H4	1804/24181		
N505SW	Boeing 737-5H4	1826/24182		
N506SW	Boeing 737-5H4	1852/24183		
N507SW	Boeing 737-5H4	1864/24184		Shamu Two
N508SW	Boeing 737-5H4	1932/24185		
N509SW	Boeing 737-5H4	1934/24186		
N510SW	Boeing 737-5H4	1940/24187		
N511SW+	Boeing 737-5H4	2029/24188		
N512SW	Boeing 737-5H4	2056/24189		
N513SW	Boeing 737-5H4	2058/24190		
N514SW+	Boeing 737-5H4	2078/25153		
N515SW	Boeing 737-5H4	2080/25154		
N519SW	Boeing 737-5H4	2121/25318		
N520SW	Boeing 737-5H4	2134/25319		
N521SW	Boeing 737-5H4	2136/25320		
N522SW	Boeing 737-5H4	2202/26564		
N523SW	Boeing 737-5H4	2204/26565		
N524SW	Boeing 737-5H4	2224/26566		
N525SW	Boeing 737-5H4	2283/26567		
N526SW	Boeing 737-5H4	2285/26568		
N527SW	Boeing 737-5H4	2287/26569		
N528SW	Boeing 737-5H4	2292/26570		

*Leased from Polaris   +Leased from State Street

N400WN	Boeing 737-7H4	806/27891	
N401WN	Boeing 737-7I I4	810/29813	
N402WN	Boeing 737-7H4	811/29814	
N403WN	Boeing 737-7H4	821/29815	
N404WN	Boeing 737-7H4	880/27892	
N405WN	Boeing 737-7H4	881/27893	

N406WN	Boeing 737-7H4	885/27894		
N407WN	Boeing 737-7H4	903/29817		
N408WN	Boeing 737-7H4	934/27895		
N409WN	Boeing 737-7H4	945/27896	ex N1787B	
N410WN	Boeing 737-7H4	946/27897		
N411WN	Boeing 737-7H4	950/29821		
N412WN	Boeing 737-7H4	956/29818		
N413WN	Boeing 737-7H4	960/29819		
N414WN	Boeing 737-7H4	967/29820		
N415WN	Boeing 737-7H4	980/29836		
N416WN	Boeing 737-7H4	990/33453		
N417WN	Boeing 737-7H4	993/29822		The Rollin W King
N418WN	Boeing 737-7H4	1000/29823		The Winning Spirit
N419WN	Boeing 737-7H4	1017/29824		
N420WN	Boeing 737-7H4	1039/29825		
N421LV	Boeing 737-7H4	1040/33452		
N422WN	Boeing 737-7H4	1093/29826		
N423WN	Boeing 737-7H4	1101/29827		
N424WN	Boeing 737-7H4	1105/29828		
N425LV	Boeing 737-7H4	1109/29829		
N426WN	Boeing 737-7H4	1114/29830		
N427WN	Boeing 737-7H4	1119/29831		
N428WN	Boeing 737-7H4	1243/29844		
N429WN	Boeing 737-7H4	1256/33658		
N430WN	Boeing 737-7H4	1257/33659		
N431WN	Boeing 737-7H4	1259/29845		
N432WN	Boeing 737-7H4	1297/33715		
N433LV	Boeing 737-7H4	1301/33716		
N434WN	Boeing 737-7H4	1313/32454		
N435WN	Boeing 737-7H4	1328/32455		
N436WN	Boeing 737-7H4	1342/32456		
N437WN	Boeing 737-7H4	1349/29832		
N438WN	Boeing 737-7H4	1353/29833		
N439WN	Boeing 737-7H4	1356/29834		The Donald G Ogden
N4440LV	Boeing 737-7H4	1358/29835		
N441WN	Boeing 737-7H4	1360/29837		
N442WN	Boeing 737-7H4	1365/32459	ex (N442LV)	
N443WN	Boeing 737-7H4	1369/29838		
N444WN	Boeing 737-7H4	1374/29839		
N445WN	Boeing 737-7H4	1388/29841		
N446WN	Boeing 737-7H4	1401/29842	ex N1787B	
N447WN	Boeing 737-7H4	1405/33720		
N448WN	Boeing 737-7H4	1409/33721		
N449WN	Boeing 737-7H4	32469	on order 04	
N450WN	Boeing 737-7H4	32470	on order 04	
N451WN	Boeing 737-7H4	1458/32495	on order 04	
N452WN	Boeing 737-7H4	29846	on order 04	
N453WN	Boeing 737-7H4	29847	on order 04	
N454WN	Boeing 737-7H4	29851	on order 04	
N455WN	Boeing 737-7H4	32462	on order 04	
N456WN	Boeing 737-7H4	32463	on order 04	
N457WN	Boeing 737-7H4	33856	on order 04	
N458WN	Boeing 737-7H4	33857	on order 04	
N459WN	Boeing 737-7H4	32497	on order 04	
N460WN	Boeing 737-7H4	32464	on order 04	
N461WN	Boeing 737-7H4	32465	on order 04	
N462WN	Boeing 737-7H4	32466	on order 04	
N463WN	Boeing 737-7H4	32467	on order 04	
N464WN	Boeing 737-7H4	32468	on order 04	
N465WN	Boeing 737-7H4	33829	on order 04	
N466WN	Boeing 737-7H4	30677	on order 04	Lsd fr ILFC
N467WN	Boeing 737-7H4	33830	on order 04	
N468WN	Boeing 737-7H4	33858	on order 04	
N469WN	Boeing 737-7H4	33589	on order 04	
N470WN	Boeing 737-7H4	33860	on order 04	
N471WN	Boeing 737-7H4	32471	on order 04	
N472WN	Boeing 737-7H4	33831	on order 04	
N473WN	Boeing 737-7H4	33832	on order 04	
N474WN	Boeing 737-7H4	33861	on order 04	
N475WN	Boeing 737-7H4	32474	on order 04	
N476WN	Boeing 737-7H4	32475	on order 04	
N477WN	Boeing 737-7H4	33988	on order 04	
N478WN	Boeing 737-7H4	33989	on order 04	
N479WN	Boeing 737-7H4	33990	on order 04	
N480WN	Boeing 737-7H4	33998	on order 04	
N481WN	Boeing 737-7H4	29853	on order 04	
N482WN	Boeing 737-7H4	29852	on order 04	
N483WN	Boeing 737-7H4	32472	on order 04	
N484WN	Boeing 737-7H4	33841	on order 04	
N485WN	Boeing 737-7H4	32473	on order 04	
N486WN	Boeing 737-7H4	33852	on order 04	
N487WN	Boeing 737-7H4	33854	on order 04	

N488WN	Boeing 737-7H4	33853		on order 04
N489WN	Boeing 737-7H4	33855		on order 04
N490WN	Boeing 737-7H4	32476		on order 04
N	Boeing 737-7H4			on order 04
N	Boeing 737-7H4			on order 04
N	Boeing 737-7Q8			on order 04
N700GS	Boeing 737-7H4	4/27835		
N701GS	Boeing 737-7H4	6/27836	ex N35108	
N703SW	Boeing 737-7H4	12/27837		
N704SW	Boeing 737-7H4	15/27838		
N705SW	Boeing 737-7H4	20/27839		
N706SW	Boeing 737-7H4	24/27840		
N707SA	Boeing 737-7H4	1/27841	ex N737X	
N708SW	Boeing 737-7H4	2/27842		
N709SW	Boeing 737-7H4	3/27843		
N710SW	Boeing 737-7H4	34/27844	ex N1787B	
N711HK	Boeing 737-7H4	38/27845		
N712SW	Boeing 737-7H4	53/27846		
N713SW	Boeing 737-7H4	54/27847		
N714CB	Boeing 737-7H4	61/27848		
N715SW	Boeing 737-7H4	62/27849		
N716SW	Boeing 737-7H4	64/27850		
N717SA	Boeing 737-7H4	70/27851		
N718SW	Boeing 737-7H4	71/27852		
N719SW	Boeing 737-7H4	82/27853		
N720WN	Boeing 737-7H4	121/27854	ex N1787B	
N723SW	Boeing 737-7H4	199/27855	ex N1787B	
N724SW	Boeing 737-7H4	201/27856	ex N1787B	
N725SW	Boeing 737-7H4	208/27857		
N726SW	Boeing 737-7H4	213/27858		
N727SW	Boeing 737-7H4	274/27859		Nevada One c/s
N728SW	Boeing 737-7H4	276/27860		
N729SW	Boeing 737-7H4	278/27861		
N730SW	Boeing 737-7H4	284/27862	ex N1795B	
N731SA	Boeing 737-7H4	318/27863		
N732SW	Boeing 737-7H4	319/27864	ex N1787B	
N733SA	Boeing 737-7H4	320/27865	ex N1787B	
N734SA	Boeing 737-7H4	324/27866	ex N1795B	
N735SA	Boeing 737-7H4	354/27867		
N736SA	Boeing 737-7H4	357/27868		
N737JW	Boeing 737-7H4	358/27869		
N738CB	Boeing 737-7H4	360/27870		
N739GB	Boeing 737-7H4	144/29275		
N740SW	Boeing 737-7H4	155/29276		
N741SA	Boeing 737-7H4	157/29277		
N742SW	Boeing 737-7H4	172/29278		
N743SW	Boeing 737-7H4	175/29279	ex N60436	
N744SW	Boeing 737-7H4	232/29490	ex N1781B	
N745SW	Boeing 737-7H4	237/29491	ex "N728SW"	
N746SW	Boeing 737-7H4	299/29798		
N747SA	Boeing 737-7H4	306/29799		
N748SW	Boeing 737-7H4	331/29800		
N749SW	Boeing 737-7H4	343/29801		
N750SA	Boeing 737-7H4	366/29802		
N751SW	Boeing 737-7H4	373/29803		
N752SW	Boeing 737-7H4	387/29804		
N753SW	Boeing 737-7H4	400/29848	ex N1787B	
N754SW	Boeing 737-7H4	416/29849	ex N1787B	
N755SA	Boeing 737-7H4	419/27871	ex N1787B	
N756SA	Boeing 737-7H4	422/27872		
N757LV	Boeing 737-7H4	425/29850		
N758SW	Boeing 737-7H4	437/27873		
N759GS	Boeing 737-7H4	448/30544		
N760SW	Boeing 737-7H4	468/27874		
N761RR	Boeing 737-7H4	495/27875		
N762SW	Boeing 737-7H4	512/27876		
N763SW	Boeing 737-7H4	520/27877		
N764SW	Boeing 737-7H4	521/27878	ex N1787B	
N765SW	Boeing 737-7H4	525/29805		
N766SW	Boeing 737-7H4	537/29806		
N767SW	Boeing 737-7H4	541/29807	ex N1787B	
N768SW	Boeing 737-7H4	580/30587	ex N1002R	
N769SW	Boeing 737-7H4	592/30588		
N770SA	Boeing 737-7H4	595/30589		
N771SA	Boeing 737-7H4	599/27879		
N772SW	Boeing 737-7H4	601/27880		
N773SA	Boeing 737-7H4	603/27881		
N774SW	Boeing 737-7H4	609/27882		
N775SW	Boeing 737-7H4	617/30590		
N776WN	Boeing 737-7H4	620/30591		
N777QC	Boeing 737-7H4	621/30592		
N778SW	Boeing 737-7H4	626/27883		

N779SW	Boeing 737-7H4	628/27884		
N780SW	Boeing 737-7H4	643/27885		
N781WN	Boeing 737-7H4	646/30601		
N782SA	Boeing 737-7H4	670/29808	ex N1787B	
N783SW	Boeing 737-7H4	675/29809	ex N1785B	
N784SW	Boeing 737-7H4	677/29810		
N785SW	Boeing 737-7H4	693/30602		
N786SW	Boeing 737-7H4	698/29811	ex N1787B	
N787SA	Boeing 737-7H4	705/29812		
N788SA	Boeing 737-7H4	707/30603		
N789SW	Boeing 737-7H4	718/29816		
N790SW	Boeing 737-7H4	721/30604		
N791SW	Boeing 737-7H4	736/27886		
N792SW	Boeing 737-7H4	737/27887		
N793SA	Boeing 737-7H4	744/27888		
N794SW	Boeing 737-7H4	748/30605	ex N1781B	
N795SW	Boeing 737-7H4	780/30606		
N796SW	Boeing 737-7H4	784/27889		
N797MX	Boeing 737-7H4	803/27890		
N798SW	Boeing 737-7AD	41/28436	ex N700EW	
N799SW	Boeing 737-7Q8	14/28209	ex 9Y-TJI	Lsd fr Castle 2003-1A LLC

A total of 266 Boeing 737-7H4s are on order including the following: 2005 (25), 2006 (22), 2007 (25) and 2008 (8).
All existing Boeing 737-7H4s to be retrofitted with winglets, new production will have them installed from 3Q04

SOUTHWIND AIRLINES

McAllen-Miller Intl, TX (MFE)

N12BA	Douglas DC-3	10035	ex N55LT	Lsd fr Aviones Inc
N514AC	Douglas DC-3	15113/26558	ex N235GB	Lsd fr Aviones Inc

SPECIAL AVIATION SYSTEMS

Pontiac-Oakland, MI (PTK)

N57DA	Embraer EMB.110P1 Bandeirante	110348	ex PT-SDX
N101RA	Embraer EMB.110P1 Bandeirante	110220	ex PT-GMM
N101WJ	Embraer EMB.110P1 Bandeirante	110203	ex PT-GLT
N102EB	Embraer EMB.110P1 Bandeirante	110354	ex PT-SEC
N127JM	Embraer EMB.110P1 Bandeirante	110218	ex N202RA

All freighters and leased from Ruhe Sales

SPERNAK AIRWAYS

Anchorage-Merrill, AK (MRI)

N29CF	Cessna 207 Skywagon	20700353
N6492H	Cessna 207A Stationair 7	20700544
N7392U	Cessna 207A Stationair 7	20700435
N73047	Cessna 207A Stationair 7	20700556

SPIRIT AIRLINES

Spirit Wings (NK/NKS)

Fort Lauderdale-Hollwood Intl, FL (FLL)

N800NK	McDonnell-Douglas MD-82	1096/49144	ex N500TR		Lsd fr WFBN
N801NK	McDonnell-Douglas MD-82	1005/48048	ex N804RA		Lsd fr Spirit Silver
N802NK	McDonnell-Douglas MD-82	2061/53168	ex B-28015		Lsd fr Spirit Silver
N803NK	McDonnell-Douglas MD-82	1035/48087	ex N805RA		
N804NK	McDonnell-Douglas MD-82	1085/49104	ex N966AS		Lsd fr UT Finance
N805NK	McDonnell-Douglas MD-81	991/48058	ex N981SB		
N806NK	McDonnell-Douglas MD-81	975/48051	ex N980SB		
N807NK	McDonnell-Douglas MD-87	1634/49777	ex N750RA	stored GYR	Lsd fr Finova
N808NK*	McDonnell-Douglas MD-82	1363/49504	ex B-2120		Lsd fr WFBN
N809NK*	McDonnell-Douglas MD-82	1346/49503	ex B-2109		Lsd fr WFBN
N810NK	McDonnell-Douglas MD-82	924/48015	ex OE-LDP		
N811NK	McDonnell-Douglas MD-82	958/48017	ex OE-LDS		Lsd fr Pacific Coast Grp
N812NK	McDonnell-Douglas MD-82	1078/48021	ex OE-LDX		Lsd fr Finova
N814NK	McDonnell-Douglas MD-82	1483/49619	ex D-ALLU	10th Anniversary c/s	Lsd fr WFBN
N815NK*	McDonnell-Douglas MD-82	1260/49415	ex N602CA		Lsd fr Finova
N816NK+	McDonnell-Douglas MD-82	1092/49140	ex B-2101		Lsd fr Avn Financial Svs
N817NK	McDonnell-Douglas MD-82	1093/49141	ex B-2102	st Nimes	Lsd fr Avn Financial Svs
N818NK	McDonnell-Douglas MD-81	995/48018	ex ZS-OBJ		Lsd fr WFBN
N819NK	McDonnell-Douglas MD-81	941/48016	ex ZS-OBI		Lsd fr WFBN
N820NK	McDonnell-Douglas MD-82	1080/49126	ex N957AS	all-white	Lsd fr CIT Leasing
N821NK*	McDonnell-Douglas MD-82	1449/49508	ex N603CA		Lsd fr Finova
N822NK	McDonnell-Douglas MD-83	1272/49392	ex N16893		Lsd fr CS Aviation
N823NK	McDonnell-Douglas MD-82	1045/48020	ex LV-ZSU		Lsd fr WFBN
N824NK	McDonnell-Douglas MD-83	1818/53015	ex D-ALLR		Lsd fr EAST Trust 2
N825NK	McDonnell-Douglas MD-83	1736/53012	ex D-ALLO		Lsd fr WFBN

N826NK	McDonnell-Douglas MD-82	1270/49391	ex N16892	Lsd fr WFBN
N827NK	McDonnell-Douglas MD-83	1658/49793	ex N872RA	Lsd fr Finova
N828NK	McDonnell-Douglas MD-83	1540/49823	ex N823NS	Lsd fr ILFC
N829NK	McDonnell-Douglas MD-83	1754/49931	ex N140NJ	Lsd fr WFBN
N830NK	McDonnell-Douglas MD-82	1756/49932	ex N141NJ	Lsd fr WFBN
N831NK	McDonnell-Douglas MD-83	1464/49617	ex SE-RBS	Lsd fr Finova
N832NK	McDonnell-Douglas MD-83	1611/49618	ex SE-RBT	Lsd fr Finova
N833NK	McDonnell-Douglas MD-83	1354/49449	ex TF-MDB	
N834NK	McDonnell-Douglas MD-83	1585/49847	ex HB-IUM	

*Also SAIC c/nos 5, 4, 1 and 9 respectively   +Named 'Spirit of Freedom'

N131NK	Douglas DC-9-41 (ABS 3)	724/47605	ex LV-ZXY	Lsd fr SSS 131 LLC
N928ML	Douglas DC-9-31 (ABS 3)	516/47326	ex N731L	Lsd fr Homefeld II

Withdrawn by 01 May 2003 and stored at Fort Worth, TX (FTW)

SPRINGDALE AIR SERVICE

Spring Air (SPG)   Springdale-municipal, AR (SPZ)

N208SA	Cessna 208B Caravan I	208B0831	ex N5206T	Lsd fr Arkansas A/c Lse
N684SA	Cessna 208B Caravan I	208B0684		
N685SA	Cessna 208B Caravan I	208B0685		Lsd fr Aire Express
N822SA	Cessna 208B Caravan I	208B0822	ex N5265B	Lsd fr Arkansa A/c Lse
N823SA	Cessna 208B Caravan I	208B0823		Lsd fr Arkansa A/c Lse
N832SA	Cessna 208B Caravan I	208B0832		Lsd fr Arkansa A/c Lse

N269BW	Beech 200 Super King Air	BB-618	ex HB-GID	Lsd fr Big Country Charters
N402BF	Cessna 402B	402B1076	ex N544GA	Lsd fr Canamera Holdings
N812E	Beech G-18S	BA-520		
N5040Q	Cessna 402B	402B0347		Lsd fr Canamera Holdings
N5133J	Cessna 310R	310R0253		
N7886Q	Cessna 402B	402B0214		Lsd fr Canamera Holdings
N26942	Cessna 402B	402B1321		

SUBURBAN AIR FREIGHT

Sub Air (SUB)   OmahaEppley Airfield, NE (OMA)

N31P	Aero Commander 680FL	1646-123	
N114MN	Aero Commander 680FL	1553-107	ex (N2611L)
N290MP	Aero Commander 680FL	1535-104	
N309VS	Aero Commander 680FL	1659-128	
N2828S	Aero Commander 680FL	1329-14	
N4983S	Aero Commander 680FL	1427-70	ex CF-LAC
N5035E	Aero Commander 680FL	1764-147	
N9011N	Aero Commander 680FL	1836-153	

All registered to Airport Management Services

N208QC	Cessna 208B Caravan I	208B0774	ex N5261R
N398A	Cessna 208B Caravan I	208B0390	ex LN-TWE
N864SF	Cessna 208B Caravan I	208B0864	
N895SF	Cessna 208B Caravan I	208B0095	ex N9662B
N1116Y	Cessna 208B Caravan I	208B0368	

N118SF	Beech C99	U-32	ex C-FESU	
N124GP	Beech 1900C	UB-23	ex N23VK	Lsd fr Airport Mgt Svs
N128SF	Beech 99	U-87	ex N59CA	
N147SF	Beech 99	U-47	ex N204BH	
N719GL	Beech 1900C	UB-19	ex N314BH	Lsd fr Airport Mgt Svs
N7994R	Beech C99	U-103		

All freighters

SUNBIRD AIR SERVICES

                                                   Springfield-Beckley Municipal, OH (SGH)

N74GS	Beech 200 Super King Air	BB-1135	ex N399LA
N663AA	Cessna 402C	402C0123	

SUN COUNTRY AIRLINES

Sun Country (SY/SCX) (IATA 337)   Minneapolis/St Paul Intl, MN (MSP)

N801SY	Boeing 737-8Q8	777/30332	ex N1787B	The Phoenix	Lsd fr ILFC
N804SY	Boeing 737-8Q8	908/30689		Laughlin Luck	Lsd fr ILFC
N805SY	Boeing 737-8Q8	985/30032	ex N1781B	The Spirit of Minnesota	Lsd fr ILFC
N806SY	Boeing 737-8Q8	75/28215	ex N800NA		Lsd fr Castle 2003-1A LLC
PH-HZC	Boeing 737-8K2	85/28375			Lsd fr TRA
PH-HZG	Boeing 737-8K2	498/28379			Lsd fr TRA
PH-HZI	Boeing 737-8K2	524/28380			Lsd fr TRA
PH-HZJ	Boeing 737-8K2	549/30389	ex N1796B		Lsd fr TRA
PH-HZV	Boeing 737-8K2	1158/30650			Lsd fr TRA

SUNDANCE AIR

Barnacle Air (BNC)   Denver Centennial, CO (DEN)

N17ZV	Beech 1900C-1	UC-17		Lsd fr Mallette Family
N125BA	Beech 1900C	UB-6	ex N125GP	Lsd fr Mallette Family
N127BA	Beech 1900C	UB-7	ex N126GP	Lsd fr Mallette Family
N410UB	Beech 1900C-1	UC-70	ex LV-WPI	Lsd fr Raytheon
N31764	Beech 1900C-1	UC-53	ex LV-WPH	Lsd fr Raytheon

N491SC	Piper PA-31-350 Navajo Chieftain	31-7405225
N3525B	Piper PA-31-350 Navajo Chieftain	31-7952121
N27309	Piper PA-31-350 Navajo Chieftain	31-7752135
N27413	Piper PA-31-350 Navajo Chieftain	31-7752167

All freighters

SUNRISE AIRLINES   filed Chapter 11 in December 2000; later ceased operations

SUNSHINE AIR TOURS
ceased operations

SUNWORLD INTERNATIONAL AIRLINES

Sunworld (SM/SWI) (IATA 375)   Cincinnati-Northern Kentucky Intl, OH (CVG)

N211DB	Boeing 727-2J4 (Duganair 3)	993/20766	ex C-GRYP	Sports charter
N282US	Boeing 727-251 (Duganair 3)	1181/21161		

SUPERIOR AVIATION

Spend Air (SO/HKA)   Iron Mountain-Kingsford, MI (IMT)

N78SA	Cessna 208B Caravan I	208B0467	ex N5058J
N126HA	Cessna 208B Caravan I	208B0067	ex (N9448B)
N162SA	Cessna 208B Caravan I	208B0548	ex N1219N
N164SA	Cessna 208B Caravan I	208B0530	ex N1248D
N179SA	Cessna 208B Caravan I	208B0594	ex N5268M
N1037N	Cessna 208B Caravan I	208B0334	ex (C-GWFN)
N1119V	Cessna 208B Caravan I	208B0383	
N1120N	Cessna 208B Caravan I	208B0386	
N1120W	Cessna 208B Caravan I	208B0388	
N7580B	Cessna 208B Caravan I	208B0051	ex (N951FE)

N26SA	Cessna 404 Titan	404-0225	ex N20ML)
N27SA	Cessna 404 Titan	404-0038	ex C-GZJQ
N28SA	Cessna 404 Titan	404-0072	ex C-GTNJ
N54SA	Cessna 404 Titan	404-0426	ex N2677N
N167SA	Cessna 404 Titan	404-0639	ex N5292J
N255CS	Cessna 404 Titan	404-0019	ex N47SA
N8754G	Cessna 404 Titan	404-0083	
N37127	Cessna 404 Titan	404-0114	
N37144	Cessna 404 Titan	404-0118	
N41059	Cessna 404 Titan	404-0012	ex Fv87003
N88719	Cessna 404 Titan	404-0235	

N78CP	Swearingen SA.226AT Metro IVA	AT-029	ex N294A
N151SA	Swearingen SA.226TC Metro II	TC-302	ex C-FJTQ
N152SA	Swearingen SA.226TC Metro II	TC-306	ex C-FJTJ
N162SW	Swearingen SA.226TC Metro II	TC-325	
N220AM	Swearingen SA.226TC Metro II	TC-234	ex N160MA
N235BA	Swearingen SA.226TC Metro II	TC-235	ex N61Z
N245AM	Swearingen SA.226TC Metro II	TC-265	ex N5471M
N250AM	Swearingen SA.226TC Metro II	TC-316	ex N505SS
N327BA	Swearingen SA.226TC Metro II	TC-249	ex N5451M
N328BA	Swearingen SA.226TC Metro II	TC-253	ex N5457M
N329BA	Swearingen SA.226TC Metro II	TC-238	ex N5436M

N354AE	Swearingen SA.227AC Metro III	AC-633	ex N3113C
N370AE	Swearingen SA.227AC Metro III	AC-506	ex N87FM
N592BA	Swearingen SA.227AC Metro III	AC-592	ex N384PH
N698FA	Swearingen SA.227AC Metro III	AC-698	ex N2711R
N26932	Swearingen SA.227AC Metro III	AC-660	ex (N660AV)
N31171	Swearingen SA.227AC Metro III	AC-605	

N33NC	Cessna 402B	402B0825	ex N384PH
N300SN	Cessna 402C	402C0060	ex N5871C
N4661N	Cessna 402C	402C0019	
N6851X	Cessna 441 Conquest	441-0212	
N9231F	Cessna 208 Caravan I	20800005	
N98697	Cessna 402B	402B1053	

Owns Air Vantage; all freighters

TAB EXPRESS AIRLINES

Deland, FL

N172TE	Beech 1900C	UB-24	ex N181GA	The Alexandria
(N173TE)	Beech 1900C	UB-55	ex N155GA	
N896FM	Beech 1900C	UB-48		

TANANA AIR SERVICE

Tan Air (4E/TNR)   *Ruby, AK (RBY)*

N97CR	Piper PA-32R-300 Lance	32R-7780078
N200HM	Piper PA-32R-300 Lance	32R-7680025
N4352F	Piper PA-32R-300 Lance	32R-7680441
N4798S	Piper PA-32-260 Cherokee Six B	32-1183
N4803S	Piper PA-32-260 Cherokee Six B	32-1188
N4811T	Piper PA-32-300 Cherokee Six	32-7840137
N7748J	Piper PA-32-260 Cherokee Six B	32-1152
N8506F	Piper PA-32R-300 Lance	32R-7780107
N8698N	Piper PA-32-300 Cherokee Six E	32-7240045
N31606	Piper PA-32-260 Cherokee Six E	32-7240086
N40449	Piper PA-32R-300 Lance	32R-7780519
N75387	Piper PA-32R-300 Lance	32R-7680298
N101LJ	Piper PA-31 Turbo Navajo	31-267
N712MA	Piper PA-31-350 Navajo Chieftain	31-7405217	ex N54269

TAQUAN AIR SERVICE

Taquan (TQN)   *Metlakatla/Ketchikan-Waterfront SPB, AK (MTM/WFB)*

N1018A	de Havilland DHC-2 Beaver	178	ex N52409
N5160G	de Havilland DHC-2 Beaver	236	ex 51-16483
N37756	de Havilland DHC-2 Beaver	1456	ex G-203
N67673	de Havilland DHC-2 Beaver	1284	ex 57-2586
N68010	de Havilland DHC-2 Beaver	1243	ex 57-6150

All floatplanes and leased from S&S Aircraft Leasing

TATONDUK FLYING SERVICES renamed Everts Air Alaska

TBM

Tulare-Mefford Field, CA/Visalia-Municipal, CA (TLR/VIS)

N466TM	Lockheed C-130A Hercules	3173	ex 57-0466	64 Tanker
N473TM	Lockheed C-130A Hercules	3081	ex 56-0473	63 Tanker
N838D	Douglas DC-7B	936/45347		60 Tanker
N8502R	Douglas C-54E	27367	ex Bu90411	65 Tanker
N90739	Douglas DC-6	84/43044		68 Tanker

Also leases Douglas DC-7 and Lockheed Hercules from Butler Aircraft as and when required

TEAM AIR CARGO

Boca Raton, FL (BCT)

| N41527 | Convair CV-440 | 346 | ex C-FPUM |

Current status is uncertain

TED

Denver, CO (DIA)

N495UA	Airbus Industrie A320-232	1842	ex F-WWBP
N	Airbus Industrie A320-232		ex F-WW
N	Airbus Industrie A320-232		ex F-WW
N	Airbus Industrie A320-232		ex F-WW

Low cost operation, wholly owned by United Air Lines. Commenced operations in February 2004

TELFORD AVIATION

Telford (TEL)   *Waterville, ME/Rockland-Knox County, ME (WVL/RKD)*

N8RQ	Cessna 208B Caravan I	208B0363	ex F-OGVJ		
N207TA	Cessna 208B Caravan I	208B0371	ex N1117N		Lsd fr Textron Financial
N208TA	Cessna 208B Caravan I	208B0365	ex N1116R	Freighter	Lsd fr Cessna Finance
N215TA	Cessna 208B Caravan I	208B0447			
N803TH	Cessna 208B Caravan I	208B0321	ex N1027G		Lsd fr Avion Capital
N804TH	Cessna 208B Caravan I	208B0421			Lsd fr Avion Capital

N805TH	Cessna 208B Caravan I	208B0609			Lsd fr Avion Capital
N7392B	Cessna 208B Caravan I	208B0045	ex (N945FE)	Freighter	Lsd fr Avion Capital
N9612B	Cessna 208B Caravan I	208B0136		Freighter	Lsd fr Avion Capital
N216TA	Cessna 208 Caravan I	20800099	ex N9551F		
N249TA	Cessna U206G Stationair 6	U20605865	ex N6400X		
N910TA	Cessna U206G Stationair 6	U20604102	ex N756HK		
N1523U	Cessna U206F Stationair	U20602234			
N8411Q	Cessna U206F Stationair	U20603271			

Operates for UPS

TEMSCO HELICOPTERS

Temsco (TMS)   *Ketchikan-Temsco Heliport, AK*

N94TH	Aerospatiale AS.350B AStar	2548			
N301TH	Aerospatiale AS.350B2 AStar	9022			
N403AE	Aerospatiale AS.350B3 AStar	3281			
N405AE	Aerospatiale AS.350B3 AStar	3286			
N802TH	Aerospatiale AS.350B2 AStar	9023			
N911CV	Aerospatiale AS.350B3 AStar	3142	ex N40729		
N913LP	Aerospatiale AS.350B2 AStar	2383			
N970TH	Aerospatiale AS.350BA AStar	9011			
N4022D	Aerospatiale AS.350B2 AStar	2891			
N6015S	Aerospatiale AS.350BA AStar	1884			
N6052F	Aerospatiale AS.350B2 AStar	2587			
N6080R	Aerospatiale AS.350BA AStar	2685			
N6094E	Aerospatiale AS.350BA AStar	2750			
N6094U	Aerospatiale AS.350BA AStar	2751			
N6180T	Aerospatiale AS.350BA AStar	1149	ex N39GT		
N6302Y	Aerospatiale AS.350B2 AStar	9007			
N26492	Aerospatiale AS.350B AStar	1066	ex G-BGIF		
N57954	Aerospatiale AS.350B AStar	1127	ex N35977		
N57958	Aerospatiale AS.350B AStar	1512			
N60618	Aerospatiale AS.350B2 AStar	2565			
N135NW	Eurocopter EC.135T1	0010	ex N4037A	EMS	
N16920	Bell 212	30865			
N83230	Bell 212	30560			
N99675	Bell UH-1B	661	ex 62-4601		

TEPPER AVIATION

                                                                 Crestview-Bob Sikes, FL (CEW)

N2189M	Lockheed L-382G Hercules	4582	ex TR-KKA		Lsd fr Rapid Air Trans
N8183J	Lockheed L-382G Hercules	4796	ex N123GA		Lsd fr Rapid Air Trans

TIGER CONTRACT CARGO

                                                                 Denton-Municipal, TX (DTO)

N404TC	Convair 340	254	ex N43944	Freighter	Lsd fr N404TC Inc
N973AT	Convair 340	257	ex N92102	Freighter	Lsd fr N973AT Inc

TMC AIRLINES

Willow Run (TMM)   *Detroit-Willow Run (YIP)*

N282F	Lockheed L-188AF Electra	1084	ex N5006K	
N286F	Lockheed L-188AF Electra	1146	ex N5013K	
N290F	Lockheed L-188CF Electra	1133	ex N863U	
N340HA	Lockheed L-188CF Electra	1109	ex N172PS	
N344HA	Lockheed L-188AF Electra	1038	ex N5525	
N346HA	Lockheed L-188AF Electra	1043	ex N61AJ	
N5512	Lockheed L-188AF Electra	1017		
N5522	Lockheed L-188AF Electra	1033		

TMC Airlines is a division of Traffic Management Corp; all allegedly leased from Zantop Airlines

TOLAIR SERVICES

Tol Air (TI/TOL)   *San Juan-Munoz Marin Intl, PR (SJU)*

N87T	Douglas DC-3	6148	ex N346K		
N780T	Douglas DC-3	20865	ex N80617	Freighter	Lsd fr MBD Corp
N781T	Douglas DC-3	4306	ex N92HA	Freighter	
N782T	Douglas DC-3	4382	ex N722A	Freighter	
N783T	Douglas DC-3	4219	ex N783V	Freighter	Lsd fr MBD Corp
N784T	Douglas DC-3	6054	ex N5117X		

N147JR	Convair T-29C	403	ex N154PA		
N728T	Beech E-18S	BA-130	ex N28V	Freighter	Lsd fr MBD Corp
N732T	Beech E-18S	BA-114	ex N52A	Freighter	Lsd fr MBD Corp
N748T	Beech E-18S	BA-329	ex N398B	Freighter	Lsd fr MBD Corp
N779T	Beech H-18	BA-618	ex N220WH	Freighter	Lsd fr MBD Corp
N840T	Cessna 402B	402B1099	ex N87280		

TRADEWINDS AIRLINES

Tradewinds Express (WI/TDX)   *Greensboro-Piedmont Triad Intl, NC (GSO)*

N368DH	Airbus Industrie A300B4-203F	207	ex N506TA	Lsd fr WFBN; sublsd to DHL
N501TR	Airbus Industrie A300B4-203F	053	ex N6254X	Lsd fr WFBN
N502TA	Airbus Industrie A300B4-203F	075	ex N864PA	Lsd fr WFBN
N504TA	Airbus Industrie A300B4-203F	216	ex N861PA	Lsd fr WFBN
N505TA	Airbus Industrie A300B4-203F	271	ex N824SC	Lsd fr WFBN
N510TA	Airbus Industrie A300B4-203F	100	ex C-GICD	Lsd fr C-S Avn
N820SC	Airbus Industrie A300B4-203F	154	ex RP-C8884	Lsd fr C-S Avn
N821SC	Airbus Industrie A300B4-203F	211	ex TC-ALU	Lsd fr C-S Avn
N311EA	Lockheed L-1011-1 Tristar	1012		Sara Kate; Freighter

TRANSAIR

Maui (P6/MUI) (IATA 356)   *Honolulu-Intl, HI (HNL)*

N770Q	Cessna 402A	402A0077		
N808KR	Short SD.3-60	SH3734	ex D-CFAO	
N808TR	Short SD.3-60	SH3718	ex VQ-TSK	
N827BE	Short SD.3-60	SH3746	ex N746SA	Lsd fr Lynrise
N3949C	Cessna 402B	402B0826		
N4544Q	Cessna 402A	402A0044	Touradj	

Transair is the trading name of Trans Executive Airlines of Hawaii

TRANSATLANTIC INTERNATIONAL AIRLINES

Columbus, OH

| N4508H | Boeing 747SP-09 | 534/22547 | ex N1785B | |

TRANSFLORIDA AIRLINES

Trans Florida (TFA)   *Daytona Beach-Intl, FL (DAB)*

N295M	Convair 240	64	ex N3338N	Freighter
N1020C	Convair 240	144	ex HB-IMA	
N1022C	Convair 240	147	ex N2642Z	
N7761	Convair 240	176	ex YE-ABB	stored DAB
N12905	Convair 240	29	ex N12903	stored DAB
N22913	Convair 240 (T-29B)	316	ex 51-7904	Freighter

All leased from Bahamas Air Ferries

TRANSMERIDIAN AIRWAYS

Trans-Meridian (T9/TRZ)   *Chicago-O'Hare, IL/Miami-Intl, FL, (ORD/MIA)*

N288SC	Boeing 727-2J4 (Super 27)	984/20765	ex CS-TKA	Lsd fr ART 20765
N906PG*	Boeing 727-281 (FedEx 3)	969/20728	ex OB-1573	Lsd fr ART 20728
N910PG	Boeing 727-287 (FedEx 3)	1812/22606	ex OB-1647	Lsd fr ART 22606
N919PG	Boeing 727-287 (FedEx 3)	1777/22604	ex XA-TGP	Lsd fr ART 22604
N54344	Boeing 727-231 (Super 27)	1460/21631		Lsd fr ART 21631

*Subleased to Air Santo Domingo

N521NA*	Boeing 757-236	453/25592	ex N592KA	Lsd fr Pegasus
N522NA	Boeing 757-236	374/25133		sublsd to SDO
N708TW	Boeing 757-231	750/2848-	Funjet	
N958PG	Boeing 757-236	163/24118	ex C-GRYO	Lsd fr Pegasus; sublsd to AVA
N962PG	Boeing 757-236	167/24119	ex C-GRYZ	on order
N	McDonnell-Douglas MD-80		ex	on order; op for Funjet
N	McDonnell-Douglas MD-80		ex	on order; op for Funjet
N	McDonnell-Douglas MD-80		ex	on order; op for Funjet
N	McDonnell-Douglas MD-80		ex	on order; op for Funjet
N	McDonnell-Douglas MD-80		ex	on order; op for Funjet

Filed Chapter 11 September 2000; operations continue   *Leased to Travelspan, NY

TRANS NORTH AVIATION

(HX)   *Eagle River, WI (EGV)*

| N4599F | Cessna 340A | 340A0652 | |
| N59773 | Piper PA-31-350 Navajo Chieftain | 31-7652044 | |

TRANSNORTHERN AVIATION

Talkeetna, AK (TKA)

N32TN	Douglas DC-3	43301	ex XA-TMR	Lsd fr Northern 3 LLC
N98RZ	Beech B99	U-49	ex HR-IAL	Lsd fr Warehouse Assoc
N199SD	Beech 99	U-26	ex C-FRQC	Lsd fr Bell Air

TRANS AIR LINK

Sky Truck (GJB)

Miami-Intl, FL (MIA)

N581HG	Convair 580	19	ex C-GTEM	Lsd fr World Avn Svs
N583HG	Convair 580	65	ex C-GJEE	Lsd fr World Avn Svs
N590HG	Lockheed L-188CF Electra	1098	ex LN-FOO	Lsd fr World Avn Svs

TRANS STATES AIRLINES

Waterski (/LOF)

St Louis-Lambert Intl, MO (STL)

N550HK	British Aerospace Jetstream 41	41039	ex G-4-039	American Connection	
N551HK	British Aerospace Jetstream 41	41040	ex G-4-040	American Connection	
N552HK	British Aerospace Jetstream 41	41057	ex G-4-057	American Connection	
N553HK	British Aerospace Jetstream 41	41066	ex G-4-066	American Connection	
N554HK	British Aerospace Jetstream 41	41067	ex G-4-067	American Connection	
N555HK	British Aerospace Jetstream 41	41072	ex G-4-072	American Connection	
N556HK	British Aerospace Jetstream 41	41073	ex G-4-073	American Connection	
N557HK	British Aerospace Jetstream 41	41074	ex G-4-074	American Connection	
N558HK	British Aerospace Jetstream 41	41071	ex G-4-071	American Connection	
N559HK	British Aerospace Jetstream 41	41075	ex G-4-075	American Connection	
N560HK	British Aerospace Jetstream 41	41076	ex G-4-076	American Connection	
N561HK	British Aerospace Jetstream 41	41077	ex G-4-077	American Connection	
N562HK	British Aerospace Jetstream 41	41078	ex G-4-078	US Airways Express	
N563HK	British Aerospace Jetstream 41	41079	ex G-4-079	TUR US Airways Express	
N564HK	British Aerospace Jetstream 41	41081	ex G-4-081	American Connection	
N565HK	British Aerospace Jetstream 41	41082	ex G-4-082	American Connection	
N566HK	British Aerospace Jetstream 41	41084	ex G-4-084	American Connection	
N567HK	British Aerospace Jetstream 41	41085	ex G-4-085	American Connection	
N568HK	British Aerospace Jetstream 41	41086	ex G-4-086	American Connection	
N569HK	British Aerospace Jetstream 41	41088	ex G-4-088	American Connection	
N570HK	British Aerospace Jetstream 41	41089	ex G-4-089	American Connection	
N571HK	British Aerospace Jetstream 41	41090	ex G-4-090	American Connection	
N572HK	British Aerospace Jetstream 41	41091	ex G-4-091	TUW US Airways Express	
N573HK	British Aerospace Jetstream 41	41092	ex G-4-092	American Connection	
N574HK	British Aerospace Jetstream 41	41093	ex G-4-093	American Connection	
N801HK	Embraer EMB.145ER	145053	ex PT-SZS	US Airways Express	Lsd fr WFBN
N802HK	Embraer EMB.145ER	145066	ex PT-SAJ	US Airways Express	
					Lsd fr Bank of Hawaii
N803HK	Embraer EMB.145ER	145077		US Airways Express	
N804HK	Embraer EMB.145ER	145082		US Airways Express	
N805HK	Embraer EMB.145ER	145096	ex PT-SBS	US Airways Express	Lsd fr GATX
N806HK	Embraer EMB.145ER	145112	ex PT-SCO	US Airways Express	Lsd fr WFBN
N807HK	Embraer EMB.145ER	145119	ex PT-SCV	US Airways Express	Lsd fr WFBN
N808HK	Embraer EMB.145ER	145157	ex PT-SEK	US Airways Express	Lsd fr WFBN
N809HK	Embraer EMB.145ER	145187	ex PT-SGH	US Airways Express	Lsd fr WFBN
N810HK	Embraer EMB.145ER	145231	ex PT-SHV	US Airways Express	Lsd fr WFBN
N811HK	Embraer EMB.145ER	145256	ex PT-SIQ	US Airways Express	Lsd fr WFBN
N812HK	Embraer EMB.145ER	145373	ex PT-SOY	US Airways Express	Lsd fr WFBN
N813HK	Embraer EMB.145LR	145044	ex N600BK	American Connection	Lsd fr EGF
N814HK	Embraer EMB.145LR	145046	ex N601GH	American Connection	Lsd fr EGF
N815HK	Embraer EMB.145LR	145048	ex N602AE	American Connection	Lsd fr EGF
N816HK	Embraer EMB.145LR	145055	ex N603AE	American Connection	Lsd fr EGF
N817HK	Embraer EMB.145LR	145058	ex N604DG	American Connection	Lsd fr EGF
N818HK	Embraer EMB.145LR	145059	ex N605RR	American Connection	Lsd fr EGF
N819HK	Embraer EMB.145LR	145062	ex N606AE	American Connection	Lsd fr EGF
N820HK	Embraer EMB.145LR	145064	ex N607AE	American Connection	Lsd fr EGF
N821HK	Embraer EMB.145LR	145068	ex N608AE	American Connection	Lsd fr EGF
N822HK	Embraer EMB.145LR	145069	ex N609AE	American Connection	Lsd fr EGF
N823HK	Embraer EMB.145LR	145475	ex HB-JAP	United Express	Lsd fr GECAS
N824HK	Embraer EMB.145LR	145498	ex HB-JAQ	American Connection	Lsd fr GECAS
N825HK	Embraer EMB.145LR	145510	ex HB-JAR	American Connection	Lsd fr GECAS
N826HK	Embraer EMB.145EU	145016	ex VP-CZB	American Connection	
N827HK	Embraer EMB.145EU	145021	ex VP-CZA	American Connection	
N829HK	Embraer EMB.145LU	145281	ex HB-JAE	American Connection	Lsd fr GECAS
N830HK	Embraer EMB.145LU	145313	ex HB-JAF	American Connection	Lsd fr GECAS
N831HK*	Embraer EMB.145LU	145232	ex HB-JAA	American Connection	Lsd fr GECAS
N832HK	Embraer EMB.145LR	145771	ex PT-SMB	United Express	
N833HK*	Embraer EMB.145LU	145240	ex HB-JAB	American Connection	Lsd fr GECAS
N834HK*	Embraer EMB.145LU	145269	ex HB-JAD	American Connection	Lsd fr GECAS
N835HK	Embraer EMB.145LR	145670	ex PT-SFE	United Express	

N836HK   Embraer EMB-145LR   145695 ex PT-SGA   United Express   Lsd fr WFBN
*Leased from State Street Bank & Trust
Operates commuter services for American Airlines as American Connection and also US Airways Express . To
commence United Express flights from Washington, DC and Chicago-O'Hare, IL

TRAVELAIR believed to have ceased operations

TROPIX EXPRESS believed to have ceased operations

TWIN AIR

Fort Lauderdale-Hollywood Intl, FL (FLL)

N49RB	Piper PA-31-325 Navajo C/R	31-7512031
N146DC	Piper PA-31-350 Navajo Chieftain	31-7305109
N456M	Piper PA-31-350 Chieftain	31-8152081
N537NB	Piper PA-31 Turbo Navajo C	31-90
N27337	Piper PA-31 Turbo Navajo	31-86
N61518	Piper PA-31-350 Navajo Chieftain	31-7552022

UNION FLIGHTS

Union Flights (UNF)

Dayton-Carson City, NV (CSN)

N121HA	Cessna 208B Caravan I	208B0069	ex N6540Q
N127HA	Cessna 208B Caravan I	208B0148	
N208N	Cessna 208B Caravan I	208B0279	ex F-OGRU
N932C	Cessna 208B Caravan I	208B0032	
N1116N	Cessna 208B Caravan I	208B0417	
N9511F	Cessna 208 Caravan I	20800077	
N9634B	Cessna 208B Caravan I	208B0141	
N9655B	Cessna 208B Caravan I	208B0145	
N9680B	Cessna 208B Caravan I	208B0150	
N9750B	Cessna 208B Caravan I	208B0100	
N9762F	Cessna 208 Caravan I	20800181	

All leased from Aero Leasing

N400JM	Piper PA-31-350 Chieftain	31-8152002
N6654Z	Piper PA-31-350 Navajo Chieftain	31-7752143
N7511L	Piper PA-31 Turbo Navajo B	31-837
N27181	Piper PA-31-350 Navajo Chieftain	31-7752068

UNITED AIR LINES

United (UA/UAL) (IATA 016)

Chicago-O'Hare Intl, IL/San Francisco-Intl, CA (ORD/SFO)

N801UA	Airbus Industrie A319-131	0686	ex D-AVYI	4001
N802UA	Airbus Industrie A319-131	0690	ex D-AVYO	4002
N803UA	Airbus Industrie A319-131	0748	ex D-AVYL	4003
N804UA	Airbus Industrie A319-131	0759	ex D-AVYR	4004
N805UA	Airbus Industrie A319-131	0783	ex D-AVYY	4005
N806UA	Airbus Industrie A319-131	0788	ex D-AVYW	4006
N807UA	Airbus Industrie A319-131	0798	ex D-AVYX	4007
N808UA	Airbus Industrie A319-131	0804	ex D-AVYF	4008
N809UA	Airbus Industrie A319-131	0825	ex D-AVYZ	4009
N810UA	Airbus Industrie A319-131	0843	ex D-AVYR	4010
N811UA	Airbus Industrie A319-131	0847	ex D-AVYB	4011
N812UA	Airbus Industrie A319-131	0850	ex D-AVYK	4012
N813UA	Airbus Industrie A319-131	0858	ex D-AVYP	4013
N814UA	Airbus Industrie A319-131	0862	ex D-AVYT	4014
N815UA	Airbus Industrie A319-131	0867	ex D-AVYU	4015
N816UA	Airbus Industrie A319-131	0871	ex D-AVYY	4016
N817UA	Airbus Industrie A319-131	0873	ex D-AVYX	4017
N818UA	Airbus Industrie A319-131	0882	ex D-AVYE	4018
N819UA	Airbus Industrie A319-131	0893	ex D-AVYV	4019
N820UA	Airbus Industrie A319-131	0898	ex D-AVYZ	4020
N821UA	Airbus Industrie A319-131	0944	ex D-AVYC	4021
N822UA	Airbus Industrie A319-131	0948	ex D-AVYE	4022
N823UA	Airbus Industrie A319-131	0952	ex D-AVYF	4023
N824UA	Airbus Industrie A319-131	0965	ex D-AVYH	4024
N825UA	Airbus Industrie A319-131	0980	ex D-AVYN	4025
N826UA	Airbus Industrie A319-131	0989	ex D-AVYU	4026
N827UA	Airbus Industrie A319-131	1022	ex D-AVYD	4027
N828UA	Airbus Industrie A319-131	1031	ex D-AVYF	4028
N829UA	Airbus Industrie A319-131	1211	ex D-AVYC	4029
N830UA	Airbus Industrie A319-131	1243	ex D-AVWI	4030
N831UA	Airbus Industrie A319-131	1291	ex D-AVWF	4031
N832UA	Airbus Industrie A319-131	1321	ex D-AVWQ	4032
N833UA	Airbus Industrie A319-131	1401	ex D-AVYA	4033
N834UA	Airbus Industrie A319-131	1420	ex D-AVYM	4034

N835UA	Airbus Industrie A319-131	1426	ex D-AVYN	4035	
N836UA	Airbus Industrie A319-131	1460	ex D-AVYI	4036	
N837UA	Airbus Industrie A319-131	1474	ex D-AVYS	4037	
N838UA	Airbus Industrie A319-131	1477	ex D-AVYG	4038	
N839UA	Airbus Industrie A319-131	1507	ex D-AVYX	4039	
N840UA	Airbus Industrie A319-131	1522	ex D-AVYZ	4040	
N841UA	Airbus Industrie A319-131	1545	ex D-AVWK	4041	
N842UA	Airbus Industrie A319-131	1569	ex D-AVWA	4042	
N843UA	Airbus Industrie A319-131	1573	ex D-AVWE	4043	
N844UA	Airbus Industrie A319-131	1581	ex D-AVWT	4044	
N845UA	Airbus Industrie A319-131	1585	ex D-AVYD	4045	
N846UA	Airbus Industrie A319-131	1600	ex D-AVWW	4046	
N847UA	Airbus Industrie A319-131	1627	ex D-AVYB	4047	Lsd fr WFBN
N848UA	Airbus Industrie A319-131	1647	ex D-AVYK	4048	
N849UA	Airbus Industrie A319-131	1649	ex D-AVYP	4049	
N850UA	Airbus Industrie A319-131	1653	ex D-AVYR	4050	
N851UA	Airbus Industrie A319-131	1664	ex D-AVYX	4051	
N852UA	Airbus Industrie A319-131	1671	ex D-AVWD	4052	
N853UA	Airbus Industrie A319-131	1688	ex D-AVWM	4053	Lsd fr WFBN
N854UA	Airbus Industrie A319-131	1731	ex D-AVWS	4054	Lsd fr WFBN
N855UA	Airbus Industrie A319-131	1737	ex D-AVWU	4055	Lsd fr WFBN

A further 23 Airbus Industrie A319-131s are on order although all orders deferred to beyond 2005

N401UA	Airbus Industrie A320-232	0435	ex F-WWDD	4701		
N402UA	Airbus Industrie A320-232	0439	ex F-WWIJ	4702		
N403UA	Airbus Industrie A320-232	0442	ex F-WWIY	4703		
N404UA	Airbus Industrie A320-232	0450	ex F-WWII	4704		
N405UA	Airbus Industrie A320-232	0452	ex F-WWBF	4705		
N406UA	Airbus Industrie A320-232	0454	ex F-WWBJ	4706		
N407UA	Airbus Industrie A320-232	0456	ex F-WWDB	4707		
N408UA	Airbus Industrie A320-232	0457	ex F-WWDG	4708		
N409UA	Airbus Industrie A320-232	0462	ex F-WWDQ	4709		
N410UA	Airbus Industrie A320-232	0463	ex F-WWDV	4710		
N411UA	Airbus Industrie A320-232	0464	ex F-WWDX	4711		
N412UA	Airbus Industrie A320-232	0465	ex F-WWIM	4712		
N413UA	Airbus Industrie A320-232	0470	ex F-WWBM	4713		
N414UA	Airbus Industrie A320-232	0472	ex F-WWIU	4614		
N415UA	Airbus Industrie A320-232	0475	ex F-WWBP	4615	Lsd fr US Bank	
N416UA	Airbus Industrie A320-232	0479	ex F-WWDH	4616		
N417UA	Airbus Industrie A320-232	0483	ex F-WWIT	4617		
N418UA	Airbus Industrie A320-232	0485	ex F-WWIZ	4618		
N419UA	Airbus Industrie A320-232	0487		ex F-WWDJ		4619
N420UA	Airbus Industrie A320-232	0489		ex F-WWDM		4620
N421UA	Airbus Industrie A320-232	0500	ex F-WWDZ	4621		
N422UA	Airbus Industrie A320-232	0503	ex F-WWIV	4622		
N423UA	Airbus Industrie A320-232	0504		ex F-WWBO		4623
N424UA	Airbus Industrie A320-232	0506		ex F-WWBQ		4624
N425UA	Airbus Industrie A320-232	0508		ex F-WWBY		4625
N426UA	Airbus Industrie A320-232	0510		ex F-WWBZ		4626
N427UA	Airbus Industrie A320-232	0512		ex F-WWDD		4627
N428UA	Airbus Industrie A320-232	0523	ex F-WWDE	4628		
N429UA	Airbus Industrie A320-232	0539	ex F-WWIX	4629		
N430UA	Airbus Industrie A320-232	0568	ex F-WWDC	4630		
N431UA	Airbus Industrie A320-232	0571	ex F-WWDH	4631		
N432UA	Airbus Industrie A320-232	0587	ex F-WWBB	4632		
N433UA	Airbus Industrie A320-232	0589	ex F-WWBD	4633		
N434UA	Airbus Industrie A320-232	0592	ex F-WWBF	4634		
N435UA	Airbus Industrie A320-232	0613	ex F-WWBQ	4635		
N436UA	Airbus Industrie A320-232	0638	ex F-WWDE	4636		
N437UA	Airbus Industrie A320-232	0655	ex F-WWIK	4637		
N438UA	Airbus Industrie A320-232	0678	ex F-WWBJ	4638		
N439UA	Airbus Industrie A320-232	0683	ex F-WWDQ	4639		
N440UA	Airbus Industrie A320-232	0702	ex F-WWDP	4640		
N441UA	Airbus Industrie A320-232	0751	ex F-WWIU	4641		
N442UA	Airbus Industrie A320-232	0780	ex F-WWDQ	4642		
N443UA	Airbus Industrie A320-232	0820	ex F-WWBT	4643		
N444UA	Airbus Industrie A320-232	0824	ex F-WWBZ	4644		
N445UA	Airbus Industrie A320-232	0826	ex F-WWIL	4645		
N446UA	Airbus Industrie A320-232	0834	ex F-WWIP	4646		
N447UA	Airbus Industrie A320-232	0836	ex F-WWIR	4647		
N448UA	Airbus Industrie A320-232	0842	ex F-WWBF	4648		
N449UA	Airbus Industrie A320-232	0851	ex F-WWBJ	4649		
N451UA	Airbus Industrie A320-232	0865	ex F-WWBR	4651		
N452UA	Airbus Industrie A320-232	0955	ex F-WWBD	4652		
N453UA	Airbus Industrie A320-232	1001	ex F-WWBH	4653		
N454UA	Airbus Industrie A320-232	1104	ex F-WWDC	4654		
N455UA	Airbus Industrie A320-232	1105	ex F-WWDE	4655		
N456UA	Airbus Industrie A320-232	1128	ex F-WWIJ	4656		
N457UA	Airbus Industrie A320-232	1146	ex F-WWBM	4657		
N458UA	Airbus Industrie A320-232	1163	ex F-WWDK	4658		
N459UA	Airbus Industrie A320-232	1192	ex F-WWDX	4659		
N460UA	Airbus Industrie A320-232	1248	ex F-WWIS	4660		

N461UA	Airbus Industrie A320-232	1266	ex F-WWDC	4661
N462UA	Airbus Industrie A320-232	1272	ex F-WWDI	4662
N463UA	Airbus Industrie A320-232	1282	ex F-WWBJ	4663; Jim Briggs
N464UA	Airbus Industrie A320-232	1290	ex F-WWBR	4664
N465UA	Airbus Industrie A320-232	1341	ex F-WWDP	4665
N466UA	Airbus Industrie A320-232	1343	ex F-WWDQ	4666
N467UA	Airbus Industrie A320-232	1359	ex F-WWBH	4667
N468UA	Airbus Industrie A320-232	1363	ex F-WWIE	4668
N469UA	Airbus Industrie A320-232	1409	ex F-WWDF	4669
N470UA	Airbus Industrie A320-232	1427	ex F-WWBN	4670
N471UA	Airbus Industrie A320-232	1432	ex F-WWBA	4671
N472UA	Airbus Industrie A320-232	1435	ex F-WWBC	4672
N473UA	Airbus Industrie A320-232	1469	ex F-WWDL	4673
N474UA	Airbus Industrie A320-232	1475	ex F-WWDQ	4674
N475UA	Airbus Industrie A320-232	1495	ex F-WWIC	4675
N476UA	Airbus Industrie A320-232	1508	ex F-WWBB	4676
N477UA	Airbus Industrie A320-232	1514	ex F-WWBF	4677
N478UA	Airbus Industrie A320-232	1533	ex F-WWIQ	4678
N479UA	Airbus Industrie A320-232	1538	ex F-WWIT	4679
N480UA	Airbus Industrie A320-232	1555	ex F-WWBP	4680
N481UA	Airbus Industrie A320-232	1559	ex F-WWDH	4681	Lsd fr WFBN
N482UA	Airbus Industrie A320-232	1584	ex F-WWBN	4682	Lsd fr WFBN
N483UA	Airbus Industrie A320-232	1586	ex F-WWBR	4683	Lsd fr WFBN
N484UA	Airbus Industrie A320-232	1609	ex F-WWBZ	4684	Lsd fr WFBN
N485UA	Airbus Industrie A320-232	1617	ex F-WWDD	4685	Lsd fr WFBN
N486UA	Airbus Industrie A320-232	1620	ex F-WWDG	4686	
N487UA	Airbus Industrie A320-232	1669	ex F-WWIJ	4687	Lsd fr WFBN
N488UA	Airbus Industrie A320-232	1680	ex F-WWBF	4688	
N489UA	Airbus Industrie A320-232	1702	ex F-WWIT	4689	Lsd fr WFBN
N490UA	Airbus Industrie A320-232	1728	ex F-WWBI	4690	
N491UA	Airbus Industrie A320-232	1741	ex F-WWBU	4691	
N492UA	Airbus Industrie A320-232	1755	ex F-WWDZ	4692	
N493UA	Airbus Industrie A320-232	1821	ex F-WWIO	4693	
N494UA	Airbus Industrie A320-232	1840	ex F-WWDC	4694	
N495UA	Airbus Industrie A320-232	1842	ex F-WWBP	4695; Ted	
N496UA	Airbus Industrie A320-232	1845	ex F-WWDR	4696	
N497UA	Airbus Industrie A320-232	1847	ex F-WWDE	4697	
N498UA	Airbus Industrie A320-232	1865	ex F-WWIK	4968	

20 more Airbus Industrie A320-232s are on order for future delivery,- all deliveries subsequently deferred until beyond 2005
Ted is low cost operation based at Denver, CO; commenced operations February 2004

N202UA	Boeing 737-322	1930/24717	1002
N203UA	Boeing 737-322	1937/24718	1003
N301UA	Boeing 737-322	1300/23642	9901
N302UA	Boeing 737-322	1315/23643	9902
N303UA	Boeing 737-322	1322/23644	9903
N304UA	Boeing 737-322	1330/23665	9904
N305UA	Boeing 737-322	1332/23666	9905
N306UA	Boeing 737-322	1334/23667	9906
N307UA	Boeing 737-322	1346/23668	9907
N308UA	Boeing 737-322	1354/23669	9908
N309UA	Boeing 737-322	1364/23670	9909
N310UA	Boeing 737-322	1370/23671	9910
N311UA	Boeing 737-322	1470/23672	9911
N312UA	Boeing 737-322	1479/23673	9912
N313UA	Boeing 737-322	1481/23674	9913
N314UA	Boeing 737-322	1483/23675	9914
N315UA	Boeing 737-322	1485/23947	9915
N316UA	Boeing 737-322	1491/23948	9916
N317UA	Boeing 737-322	1493/23949	9917
N318UA	Boeing 737-322	1504/23950	9918
N319UA	Boeing 737-322	1532/23951	9919
N320UA	Boeing 737-322	1534/23952	9920
N321UA	Boeing 737-322	1546/23953	9921
N322UA	Boeing 737-322	1548/23954	9922
N323UA	Boeing 737-322	1550/23955	9923
N324UA	Boeing 737-322	1564/23956	9924
N325UA	Boeing 737-322	1566/23957	9925
N326UA	Boeing 737-322	1568/23958	9926
N327UA	Boeing 737-322	1570/24147	9927
N328UA	Boeing 737-322	1572/24148	9928
N329UA	Boeing 737-322	1574/24149	9929
N330UA	Boeing 737-322	1588/24191	9930
N331UA	Boeing 737-322	1590/24192	9931
N332UA	Boeing 737-322	1592/24193	9932
N333UA	Boeing 737-322	1594/24228	9933
N334UA	Boeing 737-322	1605/24229	9934
N335UA	Boeing 737-322	1607/24230	9935
N336UA	Boeing 737-322	1609/24240	9936
N337UA	Boeing 737-322	1611/24241	9937
N338UA	Boeing 737-322	1613/24242	9938

N339UA	Boeing 737-322	1615/24243	9939	
N340UA	Boeing 737-322	1617/24244	9940	
N341UA	Boeing 737-322	1619/24245	9941	
N342UA	Boeing 737-322	1632/24246	9942	
N343UA	Boeing 737-322	1634/24247	9943	
N344UA	Boeing 737-322	1636/24248	9944	
N345UA	Boeing 737-322	1638/24249	9945	
N346UA	Boeing 737-322	1644/24250	9946	
N347UA	Boeing 737-322	1646/24251	9947	
N348UA	Boeing 737-322	1648/24252	9948	
N349UA	Boeing 737-322	1650/24253	9949	
N350UA	Boeing 737-322	1652/24301	9950	
N351UA	Boeing 737-322	1668/24319	9951	
N352UA	Boeing 737-322	1670/24320	9952	
N353UA	Boeing 737-322	1672/24321	9953	
N354UA	Boeing 737-322	1692/24360	9954; stored GYR	
N355UA	Boeing 737-322	1694/24361	9955; stored GYR	
N356UA	Boeing 737-322	1696/24362	9956; stored GYR	
N357UA	Boeing 737-322	1704/24378	9957; stored GYR	
N358UA	Boeing 737-322	1724/24379	1358; stored GYR	
N359UA	Boeing 737-322	1728/24452	9959; stored GYR	
N360UA	Boeing 737-322	1730/24453	9960; stored GYR	
N361UA	Boeing 737-322	1750/24454	9961; stored GYR	
N362UA	Boeing 737-322	1752/24455	9962; stored GYR	
N363UA	Boeing 737-322	1754/24532	9963	
N364UA	Boeing 737-322	1756/24533	9964	
N365UA	Boeing 737-322	1758/24534	9965	
N366UA	Boeing 737-322	1760/24535	1366	
N367UA	Boeing 737-322	1762/24536	1367	
N368UA	Boeing 737-322	1774/24537	9968; stored GYR	
N369UA	Boeing 737-322	1776/24538	1369; stored GYR	
N370UA	Boeing 737-322	1778/24539	1370	
N371UA	Boeing 737-322	1780/24540	1371; stored GYR	
N372UA	Boeing 737-322	1782/24637	1372	
N373UA	Boeing 737-322	1784/24638	1373	
N374UA	Boeing 737-322	1786/24639	1374	
N375UA	Boeing 737-322	1798/24640	1375; stored VCV	
N376UA	Boeing 737-322	1802/24641	1376; stored GYR	
N377UA	Boeing 737-322	1806/24642	1377	
N378UA	Boeing 737-322	1810/24653	1378	
N379UA	Boeing 737-322	1812/24654	1379	
N380UA	Boeing 737-322	1814/24655	1380	Lsd fr Aircraft Trust
N381UA	Boeing 737-322	1822/24656	1381	
N382UA	Boeing 737-322	1830/24657	1382	
N383UA	Boeing 737-322	1832/24658	1383	
N385UA	Boeing 737-322	1838/24660	1385	
N386UA	Boeing 737-322	1840/24661	1386	
N387UA	Boeing 737-322	1862/24662	1387	
N388UA	Boeing 737-322	1875/24663	1388	
N389UA	Boeing 737-322	1877/24664	1389	
N390UA	Boeing 737-322	1889/24665	1390	
N391UA	Boeing 737-322	1891/24666	1391	
N392UA	Boeing 737-322	1893/24667	1392	
N393UA	Boeing 737-322	1905/24668	1393	
N394UA	Boeing 737-322	1907/24669	1394	
N395UA	Boeing 737-322	1909/24670	1395	
N396UA	Boeing 737-322	1913/24671	1396	
N397UA	Boeing 737-322	1915/24672	1397	
N398UA	Boeing 737-322	1920/24673	1398	
N399UA	Boeing 737-322	1928/24674	1399	
N901UA	Boeing 737-522	1948/25001	1601	
N902UA	Boeing 737-522	1950/25002	1602	
N903UA	Boeing 737-522	1952/25003	1603	
N904UA	Boeing 737-522	1965/25004	1604	
N905UA	Boeing 737-522	1976/25005	1605	
N906UA	Boeing 737-522	1981/25006	1606	
N907UA	Boeing 737-522	1983/25007	1607	
N908UA	Boeing 737-522	1987/25008	1608	
N909UA	Boeing 737-522	1999/25009	1609	
N910UA	Boeing 737-522	2073/25254	9710	
N911UA	Boeing 737-522	2075/25255	9711	
N912UA	Boeing 737-522	2096/25290	9712	
N913UA	Boeing 737-522	2101/25291	9713	
N914UA	Boeing 737-522	2110/25381	9714	
N915UA	Boeing 737-522	2119/25382	9715	
N916UA	Boeing 737-522	2146/25383	9716	
N917UA	Boeing 737-522	2149/25384	9717	
N918UA	Boeing 737-522	2152/25385	9718	
N919UA	Boeing 737-522	2154/25386	9719	
N920UA	Boeing 737-522	2179/25387	9720	
N921UA	Boeing 737-522	2181/25388	9721	

N922UA	Boeing 737-522	2189/26642		9722
N923UA	Boeing 737-522	2190/26643		9723
N924UA	Boeing 737-522	2212/26645		9724
N925UA	Boeing 737-522	2214/26646		9725
N926UA	Boeing 737-522	2230/26648		9726
N927UA	Boeing 737-522	2246/26649		9727
N928UA	Boeing 737-522	2257/26651		9728
N929UA	Boeing 737-522	2259/26652		9729
N930UA	Boeing 737-522	2274/26655		9730
N931UA	Boeing 737-522	2289/26656		9731
N932UA	Boeing 737-522	2291/26658		9732
N933UA	Boeing 737-522	2293/26659		9733
N934UA	Boeing 737-522	2312/26662		9734
N935UA	Boeing 737-522	2315/26663		1635
N936UA	Boeing 737-522	2325/26667		1636
N937UA	Boeing 737-522	2329/26668		1637
N938UA	Boeing 737-522	2336/26671		1638
N939UA	Boeing 737-522	2343/26672		1639
N940UA	Boeing 737-522	2345/26675		1640
N941UA	Boeing 737-522	2364/26676		1641
N942UA	Boeing 737-522	2365/26679		1642
N943UA	Boeing 737-522	2366/26680		1643
N944UA	Boeing 737-522	2368/26683		1644
N945UA	Boeing 737-522	2388/26684		1645
N946UA	Boeing 737-522	2402/26687		1646
N947UA	Boeing 737-522	2404/26688		1647
N948UA	Boeing 737-522	2408/26691		1648	Lsd fr WFBN
N949UA	Boeing 737-522	2421/26692		1649
N950UA	Boeing 737-522	2423/26695		1650
N951UA	Boeing 737-522	2440/26696		1651
N952UA	Boeing 737-522	2485/26699		1652
N953UA	Boeing 737-522	2490/26700		1653
N954UA	Boeing 737-522	2494/26739		1654; stored GYR
N955UA	Boeing 737-522	2498/26703		1655
N956UA	Boeing 737-522	2508/26704		1656
N957UA	Boeing 737-522	2512/26707		1657; Capt Don Merucci
N104UA	Boeing 747-422	1141/26902		8104
N105UA	Boeing 747-451	985/26473	ex N60659	8105	Lsd fr WFBN
N106UA	Boeing 747-451	988/26474	ex N60668	8106; stored VCV Lsd to US Bank
N107UA	Boeing 747-422	1168/26900		8107; William A Patterson
N116UA	Boeing 747-422	1193/26908		8116
N117UA	Boeing 747-422	1197/28810		8117
N118UA	Boeing 747-422	1201/28811		8118
N119UA	Boeing 747-422	1207/28812		8119
N120UA	Boeing 747-422	1209/29166		8120
N121UA	Boeing 747-422	1211/29167		8121
N122UA	Boeing 747-422	1218/29168		8122
N127UA	Boeing 747-422	1221/28813		8127
N128UA	Boeing 747-422	1245/30023		8128
N171UA	Boeing 747-422	733/24322		8171	Lsd fr State Street
N172UA	Boeing 747-422	740/24363		8172; stored VCV
N173UA*	Boeing 747-422	759/24380		8173
N174UA*	Boeing 747-422	762/24381		8174
N175UA	Boeing 747-422	806/24382		8175
N176UA	Boeing 747-422	811/24383		8176; stored VCV
N177UA	Boeing 747-422	819/24384		8177
N178UA	Boeing 747-422	820/24385		8178
N179UA	Boeing 747-422	866/25158		8179
N180UA	Boeing 747-422	867/25224		8180
N181UA	Boeing 747-422	881/25278	ex N6005C	8181
N182UA	Boeing 747-422	882/25279		8182
N183UA	Boeing 747-422	911/25379		8183; stored VCV
N184UA	Boeing 747-422	913/25380		8184; stored VCV
N185UA	Boeing 747-422	919/25395		8185; stored VCV
N186UA	Boeing 747-422	931/26875		8186; stored VCV
N187UA	Boeing 747-422	939/26876		8187; stored VCV
N188UA	Boeing 747-422	944/26877		8188; stored VCV
N189UA	Boeing 747-422	966/26878		8189; stored VCV
N190UA	Boeing 747-422	973/26879		8190; stored VCV
N191UA	Boeing 747-422	984/26880		8191; stored VCV
N192UA	Boeing 747-422	989/26881		8192; stored VCV
N193UA	Boeing 747-422	1085/26890		8193
N194UA	Boeing 747-422	1088/26892		8194
N195UA	Boeing 747-422	1113/26899		8195 stored VCV
N196UA	Boeing 747-422	1120/28715		8196
N197UA	Boeing 747-422	1121/26901		8197; stored VCV
N198UA	Boeing 747-422	1124/28716		8198; stored BFM
N199UA	Boeing 747-422	1126/28717		8199

Up to 10 Boeing 747-400s are for future sale

N501UA	Boeing 757-222	241/24622	5401	Lsd fr CIT Leasing
N502UA	Boeing 757-222	246/24623	5402	
N503UA	Boeing 757-222	247/24624	5403	
N504UA	Boeing 757-222	251/24625	5404	
N505UA	Boeing 757-222	254/24626	5405	Lsd fr WFBN
N506UA	Boeing 757-222	263/24627	5406	
N507UA	Boeing 757-222	270/24743	5407	
N508UA	Boeing 757-222	277/24744	5408	
N509UA	Boeing 757-222	284/24763	5409	Lsd fr Tombo
N510UA	Boeing 757-222	290/24780	5410	
N511UA	Boeing 757-222	291/24799	5411	
N512UA	Boeing 757-222	298/24809	5412	
N513UA	Boeing 757-222	299/24810	5413	Lsd fr State Street
N514UA	Boeing 757-222	305/24839	5414	
N515UA	Boeing 757-222	306/24840	5415	
N516UA	Boeing 757-222	307/24860	5416	
N517UA	Boeing 757-222	310/24861	5417	
N518UA	Boeing 757-222	311/24871	5418	
N519UA	Boeing 757-222	312/24872	5419	
N520UA	Boeing 757-222	313/24890	5420	
N521UA	Boeing 757-222	319/24891	5421	Lsd fr Cumberland Lsg
N522UA	Boeing 757-222	320/24931	5422	
N523UA	Boeing 757-222	329/24932	5423	Lsd fr State Street
N524UA	Boeing 757-222	331/24977	5424	
N525UA	Boeing 757-222	338/24978	5425	
N526UA	Boeing 757-222	339/24994	5426	
N527UA	Boeing 757-222	341/24995	5427	
N528UA	Boeing 757-222	346/25018	5428	
N529UA	Boeing 757-222	352/25019	5429	
N530UA	Boeing 757-222	353/25043	5430	
N531UA	Boeing 757-222	361/25042	5431	
N532UA	Boeing 757-222	366/25072	5432	
N533UA	Boeing 757-222	367/25073	5433	
N534UA	Boeing 757-222	372/25129	5434; std GYR	
N535UA	Boeing 757-222	373/25130	5435	
N536UA	Boeing 757-222	380/25156	5436; std GYR	
N537UA	Boeing 757-222	381/25157	5437	
N538UA	Boeing 757-222	385/25222	5438	
N539UA	Boeing 757-222	386/25223	5439; std GYR	
N540UA	Boeing 757-222	393/25252	5440	
N541UA	Boeing 757-222	394/25253	5441; std GYR	
N542UA	Boeing 757-222	396/25276	5442	
N543UA	Boeing 757-222ER	401/25698	5543	
N544UA	Boeing 757-222ER	405/25322	5544	
N545UA	Boeing 757-222ER	406/25323	5545	
N546UA	Boeing 757-222ER	413/25367	5546	
N547UA	Boeing 757-222ER	414/25368	5547	
N548UA	Boeing 757-222ER	420/25396	5548	
N549UA	Boeing 757-222ER	421/25397	5549	
N550UA	Boeing 757-222ER	426/25398	5550	
N551UA	Boeing 757-222ER	427/25399	5551	
N552UA	Boeing 757-222ER	431/26641	5552	
N553UA	Boeing 757-222	434/25277	5453	
N554UA	Boeing 757-222	435/26644	5454	
N555UA	Boeing 757-222	442/26647	5455	Lsd fr State Street
N556UA	Boeing 757-222	447/26650	5456; std GYR	Lsd fr State Street
N557UA	Boeing 757-222	454/26653	5457	Lsd fr State Street
N558UA	Boeing 757-222	462/26654	5458; std GYR	Lsd fr State Street
N559UA	Boeing 757-222	467/26657	5459; std GYR	Lsd fr State Street
N560UA	Boeing 757-222	469/26660	5460	Lsd fr State Street
N561UA	Boeing 757-222	479/26661	5461; std VCV	Lsd fr State Street
N562UA	Boeing 757-222	487/26664	5462; std GYR	
N563UA	Boeing 757-222	488/26665	5463	Lsd fr State Street
N564UA	Boeing 757-222	490/26666	5464	
N565UA	Boeing 757-222	492/26669	5465	
N566UA	Boeing 757-222	494/26670	5466	Lsd fr State Street
N567UA	Boeing 757-222	497/26673	5467	Lsd fr State Street
N568UA	Boeing 757-222	498/26674	5468	Lsd fr State Street
N569UA	Boeing 757-222	499/26677	5469	
N570UA	Boeing 757-222	501/26678	5470	Lsd fr State Street
N571UA	Boeing 757-222	506/26681	5471	
N572UA	Boeing 757-222	508/26682	5472	Lsd fr State Street
N573UA	Boeing 757-222	512/26685	5473	
N574UA	Boeing 757-222	513/26686	5474	
N575UA	Boeing 757-222	515/26689	5475	
N576UA	Boeing 757-222	524/26690	5676	
N577UA	Boeing 757-222	527/26693	5677	
N578UA	Boeing 757-222	531/26694	5678	
N579UA	Boeing 757-222	539/26697	5679	
N580UA	Boeing 757-222	542/26698	5680	
N581UA	Boeing 757-222	543/26701	5681	
N582UA	Boeing 757-222	550/26702	5682	

N583UA	Boeing 757-222	556/26705	5683; std MZJ	Lsd fr WFBN
N584UA	Boeing 757-222	559/26706	5684	
N585UA	Boeing 757-222	563/26709	5685	
N586UA	Boeing 757-222	567/26710	5686	
N587UA	Boeing 757-222	570/26713	5687	
N588UA	Boeing 757-222	571/26717	5688	
N589UA	Boeing 757-222ER	773/28707 ex N3509J	5589	
N590UA	Boeing 757-222ER	785/28708	5590	
N592UA	Boeing 757-222	719/28143	5492	
N593UA	Boeing 757-222	724/28144	5493	
N594UA	Boeing 757-222	727/28145	5494	
N595UA	Boeing 757-222ER	789/28748	5595	
N596UA	Boeing 757-222ER	794/28749	5596	
N597UA	Boeing 757-222ER	841/28750	5597	
N598UA	Boeing 757-222ER	844/28751 ex N1787B	5598	
N601UA	Boeing 767-222	2/21862	6201; stored VCV	
N602UA	Boeing 767-222ER	3/21863	6002; stored VCV	
N603UA	Boeing 767-222	4/21864	6203	
N604UA	Boeing 767-222	5/21865	6204	
N605UA	Boeing 767-222ER	7/21866	6005	
N606UA	Boeing 767-222ER	9/21867	6006; City of Chicago; stored VCV	
N607UA	Boeing 767-222ER	10/21868	6007; City of Denver	
N608UA	Boeing 767-222ER	11/21869	6008; stored VCV	
N609UA	Boeing 767-222ER	13/21870	6009; stored VCV	
N610UA	Boeing 767-222ER	15/21871	6010; stored VCV	
N611UA	Boeing 767-222ER	20/21872	6011; stored LAS	
N613UA	Boeing 767-222	42/21874	6213	
N614UA	Boeing 767-222	43/21875	6214	
N615UA	Boeing 767-222	45/21876	6215; stored VCV	
N617UA	Boeing 767-222	46/21877	6217	
N618UA	Boeing 767-222	48/21878	6218	
N619UA	Boeing 767-222	49/21879	6219	
N620UA	Boeing 767-222	50/21880	6220; stored VCV	
N641UA	Boeing 767-322ER	360/25091	6341	
N642UA	Boeing 767-322ER	367/25092	6342	
N643UA	Boeing 767-322ER	368/25093	6343	
N644UA	Boeing 767-322ER	369/25094	6344	
N645UA	Boeing 767-322ER	391/25280	6345	
N646UA	Boeing 767-322ER	420/25283	6346	
N647UA	Boeing 767-322ER	424/25284	6347	
N648UA	Boeing 767-322ER	443/25285	6348	
N649UA	Boeing 767-322ER	444/25286	6349	
N650UA	Boeing 767-322ER	449/25287	6350	
N651UA	Boeing 767-322ER	452/25389	6351	
N652UA	Boeing 767-322ER	457/25390	6352	
N653UA	Boeing 767-322ER	460/25391	6353; Star Alliance c/s	
N654UA	Boeing 767-322ER	462/25392	6354	
N655UA	Boeing 767-322ER	468/25393	6355	
N656UA	Boeing 767-322ER	472/25394	6356	
N657UA	Boeing 767-322ER	479/27112	6357	Lsd fr GECAS
N658UA	Boeing 767-322ER	480/27113	6358	Lsd fr GECAS
N659UA	Boeing 767-322ER	485/27114	6359	Lsd fr GECAS
N660UA	Boeing 767-322ER	494/27115	6360	Lsd fr GECAS
N661UA	Boeing 767-322ER	507/27158	6361	
N662UA	Boeing 767-322ER	513/27159	6362	
N663UA	Boeing 767-322ER	514/27160	6363	
N664UA	Boeing 767-322ER	707/29236	6764; Bill Baxley Jr retd	
N665UA	Boeing 767-322ER	711/29237	6765	
N666UA	Boeing 767-322ER	715/29238	6766	
N667UA	Boeing 767-322ER	716/29239	6767	
N668UA	Boeing 767-322ER	742/30024	6768	
N669UA	Boeing 767-322ER	757/30025	6769	
N670UA	Boeing 767-322ER	763/29240	6770	
N671UA	Boeing 767-322ER	766/30026	6771	
N672UA	Boeing 767-322ER	777/30027	6772; John Doley retd	
N673UA	Boeing 767-322ER	779/29241	6773	
N674UA	Boeing 767-322ER	782/29242	6774 stored IND	
N675UA	Boeing 767-322ER	800/29243	6775	
N676UA	Boeing 767-322ER	834/30028	6776	
N677UA	Boeing 767-322ER	852/30029	6777	
N204UA	Boeing 777-222ER	191/28713	2704	
N205UA	Boeing 777-222ER	205/28714	2705; stored GYR	
N206UA	Boeing 777-222ER	216/30212	2706; stored GYR	
N207UA	Boeing 777-222ER	232/30213	2707; stored GYR	
N208UA	Boeing 777-222ER	254/30214	2708; stored GYR	
N209UA	Boeing 777-222ER	259/30215	2809	
N210UA	Boeing 777-222ER	264/30216	2510	
N211UA	Boeing 777-222	282/30217	2511; Bill Anderson retd	
N212UA	Boeing 777-222	293/30218	2512	
N213UA	Boeing 777-222	295/30219	2513	

N214UA	Boeing 777-222	296/30220	2514	
N215UA	Boeing 777-222	297/30221	2515	
N216UA	Boeing 777-222ER	291/30549	2816	
N217UA	Boeing 777-222ER	294/30550	2817	
N218UA	Boeing 777-222ER	317/30222	2818	
N219UA	Boeing 777-222ER	318/30551	2819	Lsd fr WFBN
N220UA	Boeing 777-222ER	340/30223	2820	Lsd fr WFBN
N221UA	Boeing 777-222ER	347/30552	2821	Lsd fr WFBN
N222UA	Boeing 777-222ER	352/30553	2822	Lsd fr WFBN
N223UA	Boeing 777-222ER	357/30224	2823	Lsd fr WFBN
N224UA	Boeing 777-222ER	375/30225	2824	
N225UA	Boeing 777-222ER	377/30554	2825; Spirit of United	
N226UA	Boeing 777-222ER	380/30226	2826	
N227UA	Boeing 777-222ER	381/30555	2827	
N228UA	Boeing 777-222ER	384/30556	2828	
N229UA	Boeing 777-222ER	388/30557	2829	
N230UA	Boeing 777-222ER	30227	2830	on order
N766UA	Boeing 777-222	8/26917	ex (N77776)	2366; stored GYR
N767UA	Boeing 777-222	9/26918	2367	Lsd fr US Bank NA
N768UA	Boeing 777-222	11/26919	2368	
N769UA	Boeing 777-222	12/26921	2369	
N770UA	Boeing 777-222	13/26925	2370	
N771UA	Boeing 777-222	3/26932	ex N7773	2371; stored VCV
N772UA	Boeing 777-222	5/26930	ex (N77775)	2372; Bob Boelter, retd
N773UA	Boeing 777-222	4/26929	ex N7774	2373; Richard H Leung
N774UA	Boeing 777-222	2/26936	ex N7772	2374
N775UA	Boeing 777-222	22/26947	2375	
N776UA	Boeing 777-222	27/26937	2376	
N777UA	Boeing 777-222	7/26916	2377; Working Together	
N778UA	Boeing 777-222	34/26940	2378	
N779UA	Boeing 777-222	35/26941	2379	
N780UA	Boeing 777-222	36/26944	2380; Spirit of Adalyn	
N781UA	Boeing 777-222	40/26945	2381	
N782UA	Boeing 777-222ER	57/26948	2782	
N783UA	Boeing 777-222ER	60/26950	2783	
N784UA	Boeing 777-222ER	69/26951	2784	
N785UA	Boeing 777-222ER	73/26954	2785	
N786UA	Boeing 777-222ER	52/26938	2786	
N787UA	Boeing 777-222ER	43/26939	2787	
N788UA	Boeing 777-222ER	82/26942	2788	
N789UA	Boeing 777-222ER	88/26935	2789; stored GYR	
N790UA	Boeing 777-222ER	92/26943	2790	
N791UA	Boeing 777-222ER	93/26933	2791	
N792UA	Boeing 777-222ER	96/26934	2792	
N793UA	Boeing 777-222ER	97/26946	2793	
N794UA	Boeing 777-222ER	105/26953	2794	
N795UA	Boeing 777-222ER	108/26927	2795	
N796UA	Boeing 777-222ER	112/26931	2796	
N797UA	Boeing 777-222ER	116/26924	2797	
N798UA	Boeing 777-222ER	123/26928	2798	
N799UA	Boeing 777-222ER	139/26926	2799	

Founder member of Star Alliance with Air Canada, Thai International, SAS and VARIG. Filed Chapter 11 on 09 December 2002 but operations continue. Code-shares with US Airways on over 250 combined flights. To begin low-cost operations as Ted from Denver, CO in February 2004 using four Airbus Industrie A320s in 156Y configuration

UNITED EXPRESS

United (UA) *various*

N156TR	British Aerospace 146 Srs.200	E2156	ex N884DV	Air Wisconsin	Lsd fr BAES
N179US	British Aerospace 146 Srs.200	E2041	ex N358PS	Air Wisconsin	Lsd fr WTCo
N181US	British Aerospace 146 Srs.200	E2042	ex N359PS	Air Wisconsin	Lsd fr WTCo
N183US	British Aerospace 146 Srs.200	E2043	ex N360PS	Air Wisconsin	Lsd fr WTCo
N291UE	British Aerospace 146 Srs.200	E2084	ex N815AS	Air Wisconsin	Lsd fr BAES
N292UE	British Aerospace 146 Srs.200	E2087	ex N816AS	Air Wisconsin	Lsd fr BAES
N290UE	British Aerospace 146 Srs.200	E2080	ex N814AS	Air Wisconsin	Lsd fr BAES
N463AP	British Aerospace 146 Srs.100	E1063	ex N70NA	Air Wisconsin	Lsd fr WFBN
N606AW	British Aerospace 146 Srs.200	E2033	ex G-5-033	Air Wisconsin	Lsd fr WFBN
N607AW	British Aerospace 146 Srs.200	E2052	ex G-5-001	Air Wisconsin; Kitty	
N608AW	British Aerospace 146 Srs.200	E2049	ex G-5-002	Air Wisconsin	
N609AW	British Aerospace 146 Srs.200	E2070	ex G-BNKK	Air Wisconsin	
N610AW	British Aerospace 146 Srs.200	E2082	ex G-5-082	Air Wisconsin	
N611AW	British Aerospace 146 Srs.300	E3120	ex N146UK	Air Wisconsin	
N612AW	British Aerospace 146 Srs.300	E3122	ex G-5-122	Air Wisconsin	
N614AW	British Aerospace 146 Srs.300	E3132	ex G-5-132	Air Wisconsin	
N615AW	British Aerospace 146 Srs.300	E3141	ex G-5-141	Air Wisconsin	Lsd fr WTCo
N616AW	British Aerospace 146 Srs.300	E3145	ex G-5-145	Air Wisconsin	
N401AW	Canadair CL-600-2B19	7280	ex C-FMMW	401 Air Wisconsin	
N402AW	Canadair CL-600-2B19	7281	ex C-FMMX	402 Air Wisconsin	
N403AW	Canadair CL-600-2B19	7288	ex C-FMLF	403 Air Wisconsin	

N404AW	Canadair CL-600-2B19	7294		404 Air Wisconsin
N405AW	Canadair CL-600-2B19	7362	ex C-FMND	405 Air Wisconsin
N406AW	Canadair CL-600-2B19	7402	ex C-FMMY	406 Air Wisconsin
N407AW	Canadair CL-600-2B19	7424	ex C-FMLU	407 Air Wisconsin
N408AW+	Canadair CL-600-2B19	7568	ex C-FMNY	408 Air Wisconsin
N409AW	Canadair CL-600-2B19	7447	ex C-FMNX	409 Air Wisconsin
N410AW	Canadair CL-600-2B19	7490	ex C-FMMW	410 Air Wisconsin
N411ZW+	Canadair CL-600-2B19	7569	ex C-F	411 Air Wisconsin
N412AW+	Canadair CL-600-2B19	7582	ex C-FMMY	412 Air Wisconsin
N413AW+	Canadair CL-600-2B19	7585	ex C-FMKW	413 Air Wisconsin
N414ZW+	Canadair CL-600-2B19	7586	ex C-FMKZ	414 Air Wisconsin
N415AW+	Canadair CL-600-2B19	7593	ex C-FMLV	415 Air Wisconsin
N416AW+	Canadair CL-600-2B19	7603	ex C-FMNQ	416 Air Wisconsin
N417AW+	Canadair CL-600-2B19	7610	ex C-FMMW	417 Air Wisconsin
N418AW+	Canadair CL-600-2B19	7618	ex C-FMLF	418 Air Wisconsin
N419AW+	Canadair CL-600-2B19	7633	ex C-FMNQ	419 Air Wisconsin
N420AW+	Canadair CL-600-2B19	7640	ex C-FMMW	420 Air Wisconsin
N421ZW*	Canadair CL-600-2B19	7346	ex N587ML	421 Air Wisconsin
N422AW*	Canadair CL-600-2B19	7341	ex N586ML	422 Air Wisconsin
N423AW+	Canadair CL-600-2B19	7636	ex C-FMMB	423 Air Wisconsin
N424AW+	Canadair CL-600-2B19	7656	ex C-FMNW	424 Air Wisconsin
N425AW+	Canadair CL-600-2B19	7663	ex C-FMNQ	425 Air Wisconsin
N426AW+	Canadair CL-600-2B19	7669	ex C-FMMQ	426 Air Wisconsin
N427ZW+	Canadair CL-600-2B19	7685	ex C-FMNH	427 Air Wisconsin
N428AW+	Canadair CL-600-2B19	7695	ex C-FMOI	428 Air Wisconsin
N429AW+	Canadair CL-600-2B19	7711	ex CFMLS	429 Air Wisconsin
N430AW+	Canadair CL-600-2B19	7719	ex C-FMOS	430 Air Wisconsin
N434AW	Canadair CL-600-2B19	7322	ex N582ML	434 Air Wisconsin
N435AW+	Canadair CL-600-2B19	7724	ex C-FMLU	435 Air Wisconsin
N436AW	Canadair CL-600-2B19	7734	ex C-FMKV	436 Air Wisconsin
N437AW	Canadair CL-600-2B19	7744	ex C-FMMT	437 Air Wisconsin
N440AW	Canadair CL-600-2B19	7766	ex C-FMKZ	440 Air Wisconsin
N441ZW	Canadair CL-600-2B19	7777	ex C-FMNX	441 Air Wisconsin
N442AW	Canadair CL-600-2B19	7778	ex C-FMNY	442 Air Wisconsin
N443AW	Canadair CL-600-2B19	7781	ex C-FVAZ	443 Air Wisconsin
N444ZW	Canadair CL-600-2B19	7788	ex C-FMMN	444 Air Wisconsin
N446AW	Canadair CL-600-2B19	7806	ex C-FMNV	446 Air Wisconsin
N447AW	Canadair CL-6002-B19	7812	ex C-FMND	447 Air Wisconsin
N448AW	Canadair CL-6002-B19	7814	ex C-FMLU	448 Air Wisconsin
N450AW	Canadair CL-600-2B19	7823	ex C-	450 Air Wisconsin
N451AW	Canadair CL-600-2B19	7832	ex C-FMLT	451 Air Wisconsin
N452AW	Canadair CL-600-2B19	7835	ex C-FMNH	452 Air Wisconsin
N454AW	Canadair CL-600-2B19	7842	ex C-FMND	454 Air Wisconsin
N456ZW	Canadair CL-600-2B19	7849	ex C-FMMQ	456 Air Wisconsin
N458AW	Canadair CL-600-2B19	7861	ex C-FMLS	458 Air Wisconsin
N459AW	Canadair CL-600-2B19	7863	ex C-FMLV	459 Air Wisconsin
N460AW	Canadair CL-600-2B19	7867	ex C-GZTD	460 Air Wisconsin
N461AW	Canadair CL-600-2B19	7870	ex C-FMOW	461 Air Wisconsin
N462AW	Canadair CL-600-2B19	7875	ex C-FMOI	462 Air Wisconsin
N463AW	Canadair CL-600-2B19	7878	ex C-FMMN	463 Air Wisconsin
N464AW	Canadair CL-600-2B19	7890	ex C-FMLQ	464 Air Wisconsin
N465AW	Canadair CL-600-2B19	7893	ex C-	465 Air Wisconsin
N903SW	Canadair CL-600-2B19	7425	ec C-FMOI	Skywest
N905SW	Canadair CL-600-2B19	7437	ex C-FMLB	Skywest
N906SW	Canadair CL-600-2B19	7510	ex C-FMOW	Skywest
N907SW	Canadair CL-600-2B19	7511	ex C-FVAZ	Skywest
N908SW	Canadair CL-600-2B19	7540	ex C-FMOW	Skywest
N909SW	Canadair CL-600-2B19	7558	ex C-GJHL	Skywest
N910SW	Canadair CL-600-2B19	7566	ex C-GJHY	Skywest
N912SW	Canadair CL-600-2B19	7595	ex C-FMNH	Skywest
N913SW	Canadair CL-600-2B19	7597	ex C-FMNX	Skywest
N915SW	Canadair CL-600-2B19	7615	ex C-FMKV	Skywest
N916SW	Canadair CL-600-2B19	7634	ex C-FMLU	Skywest
N917SW	Canadair CL-600-2B19	7641	ex C-FMMX	Skywest
N918SW	Canadair CL-600-2B19	7645	ex C-FMKW	Skywest
N919SW	Canadair CL-600-2B19	7657	ex C-FMNX	Skywest
N920SW	Canadair CL-600-2B19	7660	ex C-FMOW	Skywest
N923SW	Canadair CL-600-2B19	7664	ex C-FMLU	Skywest
N924SW	Canadair CL-600-2B19	7681	ex C-FMLS	Skywest
N925SW	Canadair CL-600-2B19	7682	ex C-FMLT	Skywest
N926SW	Canadair CL-600-2B19	7687	ex C-FMNX	Skywest
N927SW	Canadair CL-600-2B19	7693	ex C-FMNQ	Skywest
N928SW	Canadair CL-600-2B19	7701	ex C-FMMX	Skywest
N929SW	Canadair CL-600-2B19	7703	ex C-FMNB	Skywest
N930SW	Canadair CL-600-2B19	7713	ex C-FMLV	Skywest
N932SW	Canadair CL-600-2B19	7714	ex C-FMMT	Skywest
N934SW	Canadair CL-600-2B19	7722	ex C-FMND	Skywest
N935SW	Canadair CL-600-2B19	7725	ex C-FMOI	Skywest
N936SW	Canadair CL-600-2B19	7726	ex C-FMMB	Skywest
N937SW	Canadair CL-600-2B19	7735	ex C-FMKW	Skywest
N938SW	Canadair CL-600-2B19	7741	ex C-FMLS	Skywest
N939SW	Canadair CL-600-2B19	7742	ex C-FMLS	Skywest

N941SW	Canadair CL-600-2B19	7750	ex C-FMOW	Skywest		
N943SW	Canadair CL-600-2B19	7762	ex C-FMMY	Skywest		
N944SW	Canadair CL-600-2B19	7764	ex C-FMKV	Skywest		
N945SW	Canadair CL-600-2B19	7770	ex C-FMLQ	Skywest		
N946SW	Canadair CL-600-2B19	7776	ex C-FMNW	Skywest		
N947SW	Canadair CL-600-2B19	7786	ex C-FMMB	Skywest		
N948SW	Canadair CL-600-2B19	7789	ex C-GXTU	Skywest		
N951SW	Canadair CL-600-2B19	7795	ex C-FMKW	Skywest		
N952SW	Canadair CL-600-2B19	7805	ex C-FMNH	Skywest		
N953SW	Canadair CL-600-2B19	7813	ex C-GZGP	Skywest		
N954SW	Canadair CL-600-2B19	7815	ex C-FMOI	Skywest		
N955SW	Canadair CL-600-2B19	7817	ex C-	Skywest		
N956SW	Canadair CL-600-2B19	7825	ex C-FMKW	Skywest		
N957SW	Canadair CL-600-2B19	7829	ex C-FMLI	Skywest		
N958SW	Canadair CL-600-2B19	7833	ex C-FMLV	Skywest		
N959SW	Canadair CL-600-2B19	7840	ex C-FMOW	Skywest		
N960SW	Canadair CL-600-2B19	7853	ex C-FMNB	Skywest		
N961SW	Canadair CL-600-2B19	7857	ex C-FMLB	Skywest		
N962SW	Canadair CL-600-2B19	7859	ex C-FMLI	Skywest		
N963SW	Canadair CL-600-2B19	7865	ex C-FMNH	Skywest		
N964SW	Canadair CL-600-2B19	7867	ex C-GZTD	Skywest		
N965SW	Canadair CL-600-2B19	7871	ex C-FVAZ	Skywest		
N967SW	Canadair CL-600-2B19	7872	ex C-FMND	Skywest		
N969SW	Canadair CL-600-2B19	7876	ex C-	Skywest	on order 04	
N970SW	Canadair CL-600-2B19	7881	ex C-	Skywest	on order 04	
N17217	Canadair CL-600-2B19	7217		Mesa		

*Leased from Wachovia Bank   +Leased fr State Street Bank & Trust
Total of 236 regional jets are on order for delivery by the end of April 2004

N448YV	de Havilland DHC-8Q-202	448	ex C-GLOT	Mesa	
N	de Havilland DHC-8Q-202		ex C	Mesa	
N	de Havilland DHC-8Q-202		ex C-	Mesa	
N	de Havilland DHC-8Q-202		ex C-	Mesa	

Based at Denver

N501MJ	Canadair CL-600-2C10	10047	ex C-FZVM	Mesa; all-white	
N510MJ	Canadair CL-600-2C10	10101	ex C-	Mesa	Lsd fr WFBN
N511MJ	Canadair CL-600-2C10	10104	ex C-	Mesa	
N512MJ	Canadair CL-600-2C10	10109	ex C-	Mesa	
N513MJ	Canadair CL-600-2C10	10111	ex C-	Mesa	
N514MJ	Canadair CL-600-2C10	10116	ex C-	Mesa	
N515MJ	Canadair CL-600-2C10	10117	ex C-	Mesa	
N701SK	Canadair CL-600-2C10	10133	ex C-	United Express	

N328LS	Dornier 328-100	3025	ex D-CDHK	321	Air Wisconsin	Lsd fr WFBN
N328MX	Dornier 238-120	3071	ex D-CDXX	301	Air Wisconsin	Lsd fr WFBN
N329MX	Dornier 328-120	3049	ex D-CAOS	302	Air Wisconsin	Lsd fr WFBN
N330MX	Dornier 328-120	3067	ex D-CDXN	303	Air Wisconsin	
N331MX	Dornier 328-120	3074	ex D-CDXA	304	Air Wisconsin	Lsd fr WFBN
N334PH	Dornier 328-110	3012	ex D-CASI	309	Air Wisconsin	Lsd fr WFBN
N336PH	Dornier 328-110	3014	ex D-CANO	310	Air Wisconsin	Lsd fr WFBN
N337PH	Dornier 328-110	3020	ex D-CDHE	312	Air Wisconsin	Lsd fr WFBN
N338PH	Dornier 328-110	3029	ex D-CDHO	313	Air Wisconsin	Lsd fr WFBN
N339PH	Dornier 328-110	3015	ex D-CALT	311	stored TUL	Lsd fr WFBN
N340LS	Dornier 328-120	3040	ex D-CDXF	317	Air Wisconsin	
N341PH	Dornier 328-110	3065	ex D-CDXJ	315	Air Wisconsin	
N350AD	Dornier 328-120	3050	ex G-BYHF	318	Air Wisconsin	
(N454PS)	Dornier 328-120	3035	ex N335PH	319	Air Wisconsin	Lsd fr WFBN

N823HK	Embraer EMB.145LR	145475	ex HB-JAP	Trans State	
N832HK	Embraer EMB.145LR	145771	ex PT-S	Trans State	
N835HK	Embraer EMB.145LR	145670	ex PT-	Trans Stare	
N836HK	Embraer EMB.145LR	145695	ex PT-	Trans State	

United Express is the operating name for the network of feeder services operated by Air Wisconsin [ZW/AWI], Mesa United Express and Skywest [OO/SKW] in conjunction with United Airlines using UA flight numbers plus Trans State from ORD

UNIVERSAL AIRLINES

(PNA)   *Victoria-Regional, TX (VCT)*

N170UA	Douglas DC-6A	998/45518	ex N870TA	
N500UA	Douglas DC-6A	501/44597	ex N766WC	
N600UA	Douglas DC-6B	651/44894	ex N37570	

UPS AIRLINES

UPS (5X/UPS) (IATA 406)   *Louisville-Intl, KY (SDF)*

N120UP	Airbus Industrie A300F4-622R	805	ex F-WWAR	
N121UP	Airbus Industrie A300F4-622R	806	ex F-WWAP	

N122UP	Airbus Industrie A300F4-622R	807	ex F-WWAX	
N124UP	Airbus Industrie A300F4-622R	808	ex F-WWAT	
N125UP	Airbus Industrie A300F4-622R	809	ex F-WWAU	
N126UP	Airbus Industrie A300F4-622R	810	ex F-WWAB	
N127UP	Airbus Industrie A300F4-622R	811	ex F-WWAD	
N128UP	Airbus Industrie A300F4-622R	812	ex F-WWAE	
N129UP	Airbus Industrie A300F4-622R	813	ex F-WWAF	
N130UP	Airbus Industrie A300F4-622R	814	ex F-WWAG	
N131UP	Airbus Industrie A300F4-622R	815	ex F-WWAH	
N133UP	Airbus Industrie A300F4-622R	816	ex F-WWAJ	
N134UP	Airbus Industrie A300F4-622R	817	ex F-WWAL	
N135UP	Airbus Industrie A300F4-622R	818	ex F-WWAM	
N136UP	Airbus Industrie A300F4-622R	819	ex F-WWAN	
N137UP	Airbus Industrie A300F4-622R	820	ex F-WWAO	
N138UP	Airbus Industrie A300F4-622R	821	ex F-WWAQ	
N139UP	Airbus Industrie A300F4-622R	822	ex F-WWAS	
N140UP	Airbus Industrie A300F4-622R	823	ex F-WWAV	
N141UP	Airbus Industrie A300F4-622R	824	ex F-WWAY	
N142UP	Airbus Industrie A300F4-622R	825	ex F-WWAA	
N143UP	Airbus Industrie A300F4-622R	826	ex F-WWAB	
N144UP	Airbus Industrie A300F4-622R	827	ex F-WWAD	
N145UP	Airbus Industrie A300F4-622R	828	ex F-WWAE	
N146UP	Airbus Industrie A300F4-622R	829	ex F-WWAG	
N147UP	Airbus Industrie A300F4-622R	830	ex F-WWAJ	
N148UP	Airbus Industrie A300F4-622R	831	ex F-WWAM	
N149UP	Airbus Industrie A300F4-622R	832	ex F-WWAN	
N150UP	Airbus Industrie A300F4-622R	833	ex F-WWAO	
N151UP	Airbus Industrie A300F4-622R	834	ex F-WWAP	
N152UP	Airbus Industrie A300F4-622R	835	ex F-WWAQ	
N153UP	Airbus Industrie A300F4-622R	839	ex F-WWAR	
N154UP	Airbus Industrie A300F4-622R	840	ex F-WWAS	
N155UP	Airbus Industrie A300F4-622R	841	ex F-WWAT	
N156UP	Airbus Industrie A300F4-622R	845	ex F-WWAU	on order
N157UP	Airbus Industrie A300F4-622R	846	ex F-WWAV	on order
N158UP	Airbus Industrie A300F4-622R	847	ex F-WWAX	on order 04
N159UP	Airbus Industrie A300F4-622R	848	ex F-WW	on order 04
N160UP	Airbus Industrie A300F4-622R	849	ex F-WW	on order 04
N161UP	Airbus Industrie A300F4-622R		ex F-WW	on order 04
N162UP	Airbus Industrie A300F4-622R		ex F-WW	on order 04
N163UP	Airbus Industrie A300F4-622R		ex F-WW	on order 04
N164UP	Airbus Industrie A300F4-622R		ex F-WW	on order 04
N165UP	Airbus Industrie A300F4-622R		ex F-WW	on order 04
N166UP	Airbus Industrie A300F4-622R		ex F-WW	on order 04
N167UP	Airbus Industrie A300F4-622R		ex F-WW	on order 04
N168UP	Airbus Industrie A300F4-622R		ex F-WW	on order 04
N169UP	Airbus Industrie A300F4-622R		ex F-WW	on order 04
N170UP	Airbus Industrie A300F4-622R		ex F-WW	on order 04

Forty five more Airbus Industrie A300F4-622Rs are on order for future delivery, the last 30 of which can be taken as other Airbus Industrie freighters available at the time

N902UP*	Boeing 727-51C	244/18898	ex N434EX	
N903UP*	Boeing 727-51C	263/18945	ex N415EX	
N904UP*	Boeing 727-51C	274/18946	ex N418EX	
N905UP*	Boeing 727-51C	286/18947	ex N419EX	
N906UP*	Boeing 727-30C	437/19314	ex N423EX	
N907UP*	Boeing 727-27C	379/19118	ex N7279	stored ROW
N908UP*	Boeing 727-27C	312/19114	ex N7275	stored ROW
N909UP*	Boeing 727-27C	328/19115	ex N7276	stored ROW
N910UP*	Boeing 727-27C	376/19117	ex N7278	stored ROW
N911UP*	Boeing 727-27C	393/19119	ex N7280	stored ROW
N912UP*	Boeing 727-62C	338/19244	ex N7284	stored ROW
N913UP*	Boeing 727-62C	342/19245	ex N7286	stored ROW
N914UP*	Boeing 727-62C	423/19246	ex N7287	stored ROW
N915UP*	Boeing 727-27C	475/19533	ex N7296	stored ROW
N916UP*	Boeing 727-172C	615/19808	ex N309BN	stored ROW
N917UP*	Boeing 727-30C	395/19310	ex N701EV	stored ROW
N918UP*	Boeing 727-30C	364/19008	ex N310BN	
N919UP*	Boeing 727-30C	391/19012	ex N311BN	
N920UP*	Boeing 727-180C	604/19873	ex N9516T	
N921UP*	Boeing 727-180C	534/19874	ex OY-UPB	stored ROW
N922UP*	Boeing 727-31C	404/19231	ex N892TW	
N923UP*	Boeing 727-31C	390/19229	ex OY-UPM	stored ROW
N924UP*	Boeing 727-31C	463/19234	ex N895TW	
N925UP*	Boeing 727-31C	402/19230	ex OY-UPC	stored ROW
N926UP*+	Boeing 727-31C	458/19233	ex OY-UPA	
N927UP*+	Boeing 727-31C	425/19232	ex N893TW	
N928UP*	Boeing 727-22C	280/19091	ex N490W	
N929UP*	Boeing 727-22C	291/19092	ex N495WC	stored GYR
N930UP*	Boeing 727-22C	305/19096	ex N497WC	
N931UP*	Boeing 727-25C	645/19858	ex N8175G	stored ROW
N932UP*	Boeing 727-25C	635/19856	ex N8173G	stored ROW
N933UP*	Boeing 727-25C	641/19857	ex N8174G	stored ROW

N934UP*	Boeing 727-21C	301/19135	ex N724PL		
N935UP*	Boeing 727-1A7C	619/20143	ex N2915		
N936UP*	Boeing 727-108C	420/19503	ex N727TG	stored SKF	
N937UP*	Boeing 727-25QC	354/19302	ex TG-ALA		
N938UP*	Boeing 727-173C	447/19506	ex TG-AYA		
N939UP*	Boeing 727-27C	469/19532	ex CC-CGD	stored ROW	
N940UP*	Boeing 727-185C	546/19826	ex TF-FLG		
N941UP*	Boeing 727-22C	407/19196	ex CC-CLB		
N942UP*	Boeing 727-22C	333/19101	ex N430EX		
N943UP*	Boeing 727-22C	336/19102	ex OY-UPJ		
N944UP*+	Boeing 727-22C	341/19103	ex N431EX		
N945UP*	Boeing 727-22C	295/19094	ex OY-UPT		
N946UP*	Boeing 727-25C	490/19721	ex N130FE		
N947UP*	Boeing 727-25C	493/19722	ex N131FE		
N948UP*	Boeing 727-25C	360/19357	ex N121FE		
N949UP*	Boeing 727-25C	468/19717	ex N125FE		
N950UP*	Boeing 727-25C	474/19718	ex N126FE		
N951UP*	Boeing 727-25C	497/19850	ex N132FE		
N954UP*	Boeing 727-185C	527/19827	ex N744EV		

*Fitted with R-R Tay Stage 3 conversion (QF)
+Leased to StarAir as OY-UPM/A/S/D respectively

N520UP	Boeing 747-212SF	475/21943	ex RP-C5746		
N521UP	Boeing 747-212SF	510/21944	ex 9V-SQS	Olympic c/s	
N522UP	Boeing 747-212SF	401/21936	ex VT-ENQ		
N523UP	Boeing 747-283SF	500/22381	ex N155FW		Lsd fr BBAM
N524UP	Boeing 747-237SF	318/21446	ex N104TR		Lsd fr Triton; sublsd to PAC
N525UP	Boeing 747-212SF	449/21939	ex N616FF	all-white	Lsd fr FINOVA
N526UP	Boeing 747-212SF	419/21937	ex N618FF		Lsd fr ILFC
N528UP	Boeing 747-256M	699/24071	ex EC-EEK		Lsd fr Triton
N671UP	Boeing 747-123SF	115/20323	ex N9671	stored ROW	
N672UP	Boeing 747-123SF	119/20324	ex N9672		
N674UP	Boeing 747-123SF	46/20100	ex N9661	stored ROW	
N675UP	Boeing 747-123SF	136/20390	ex N9675		
N676UP	Boeing 747-123SF	57/20101	ex N9676		
N677UP	Boeing 747-123SF	143/20391	ex N629FE		
N680UP	Boeing 747SR-46SF	234/20923	ex JA8121		
N681UP	Boeing 747-121SF	70/19661	ex N628FE		Lsd fr Polaris
N682UP	Boeing 747-121SF	110/20349	ex N626FE		Lsd fr Polaris
N683UP	Boeing 747-121SF	131/20353	ex N627FE	United Way titles	

N401UP	Boeing 757-24APF	139/23723		
N402UP	Boeing 757-24APF	141/23724		
N403UP	Boeing 757-24APF	143/23725		
N404UP	Boeing 757-24APF	147/23726		
N405UP	Boeing 757-24APF	149/23727		
N406UP	Boeing 757-24APF	176/23728		
N407UP	Boeing 757-24APF	181/23729		
N408UP	Boeing 757-24APF	184/23730		
N409UP	Boeing 757-24APF	186/23731		
N410UP	Boeing 757-24APF	189/23732		
N411UP	Boeing 757-24APF	191/23851		
N412UP	Boeing 757-24APF	193/23852		
N413UP	Boeing 757-24APF	195/23853		
N414UP	Boeing 757-24APF	197/23854		
N415UP	Boeing 757-24APF	199/23855		
N416UP	Boeing 757-24APF	318/23903		
N417UP	Boeing 757-24APF	322/23904		
N418UP	Boeing 757-24APF	326/23905		
N419UP	Boeing 757-24APF	330/23906		
N420UP	Boeing 757-24APF	334/23907		
N421UP	Boeing 757-24APF	395/25281		
N422UP	Boeing 757-24APF	399/25324		
N423UP	Boeing 757-24APF	403/25325		
N424UP	Boeing 757-24APF	407/25369		
N425UP	Boeing 757-24APF	411/25370		
N426UP	Boeing 757-24APF	477/25457		
N427UP	Boeing 757-24APF	481/25458		
N428UP	Boeing 757-24APF	485/25459		
N429UP	Boeing 757-24APF	489/25460		
N430UP	Boeing 757-24APF	493/25461		
N431UP	Boeing 757-24APF	569/25462		Lsd to SRR as OY-USA
N432UP	Boeing 757-24APF	573/25463		Lsd to SRR as OY-USB
N433UP	Boeing 757-24APF	577/25464		Lsd to SRR as OY-USC
N434UP	Boeing 757-24APF	579/25465		Lsd to SRR as OY-USD
N435UP	Boeing 757-24APF	581/25466		
N436UP	Boeing 757-24APF	625/25467		
N437UP	Boeing 757-24APF	628/25468		
N438UP	Boeing 757-24APF	631/25469		
N439UP	Boeing 757-24APF	634/25470		
N440UP	Boeing 757-24APF	636/25471		
N441UP	Boeing 757-24APF	638/27386		

N442UP	Boeing 757-24APF	640/27387	
N443UP	Boeing 757-24APF	642/27388	
N444UP	Boeing 757-24APF	644/27389	
N445UP	Boeing 757-24APF	646/27390	
N446UP	Boeing 757-24APF	649/27735	
N447UP	Boeing 757-24APF	651/27736	
N448UP	Boeing 757-24APF	654/27737	
N449UP	Boeing 757-24APF	656/27738	
N450UP	Boeing 757-24APF	659/25472	
N451UP	Boeing 757-24APF	675/27739	
N452UP	Boeing 757-24APF	679/25473	
N453UP	Boeing 757-24APF	683/25474	
N454UP	Boeing 757-24APF	687/25475	
N455UP	Boeing 757-24APF	691/25476	
N456UP	Boeing 757-24APF	728/25477	
N457UP	Boeing 757-24APF	729/25478	
N458UP	Boeing 757-24APF	730/25479	
N459UP	Boeing 757-24APF	733/25480	
N460UP	Boeing 757-24APF	734/25481	
N461UP	Boeing 757-24APF	755/28265	
N462UP	Boeing 757-24APF	759/28266	
N463UP	Boeing 757-24APF	763/28267	
N464UP	Boeing 757-24APF	765/28268	
N465UP	Boeing 757-24APF	767/28269	
N466UP	Boeing 757-24APF	769/25482	
N467UP	Boeing 757-24APF	771/25483	
N468UP	Boeing 757-24APF	774/25484	
N469UP	Boeing 757-24APF	776/25485	
N470UP	Boeing 757-24APF	778/25486	
N471UP	Boeing 757-24APF	813/28842	
N472UP	Boeing 757-24APF	815/28843	
N473UP	Boeing 757-24APF	823/28846	ex N5573L
N474UP	Boeing 757-24APF	879/28844	
N475UP	Boeing 757-24APF	882/28845	
N301UP	Boeing 767-34AFER	580/27239	
N302UP	Boeing 767-34AFER	590/27240	
N303UP	Boeing 767-34AFER	594/27241	
N304UP	Boeing 767-34AFER	598/27242	
N305UP	Boeing 767-34AFER	600/27243	
N306UP	Boeing 767-34AFER	622/27759	
N307UP	Boeing 767-34AFER	624/27760	
N308UP	Boeing 767-34AFER	626/27761	
N309UP	Boeing 767-34AFER	628/27740	
N310UP	Boeing 767-34AFER	630/27762	
N311UP	Boeing 767-34AFER	632/27741	
N312UP	Boeing 767-34AFER	634/27763	
N313UP	Boeing 767-34AFER	636/27764	
N314UP	Boeing 767-34AFER	638/27742	
N315UP	Boeing 767-34AFER	640/27743	
N316UP	Boeing 767-34AFER	660/27744	
N317UP	Boeing 767-34AFER	666/27745	
N318UP	Boeing 767-34AFER	670/27746	
N319UP	Boeing 767-34AFER	672/27758	
N320UP	Boeing 767-34AFER	674/27747	
N322UP	Boeing 767-34AFER	678/27748	
N323UP	Boeing 767-34AFER	682/27749	
N324UP	Boeing 767-34AFER	724/27750	
N325UP	Boeing 767-34AFER	726/27751	
N326UP	Boeing 767-34AFER	728/27752	
N327UP	Boeing 767-34AFER	730/27753	
N328UP	Boeing 767-34AFER	732/27754	
N329UP	Boeing 767-34AFER	756/27755	
N330UP	Boeing 767-34AFER	760/27756	
N331UP	Boeing 767-34AFER	764/27757	
N332UP	Boeing 767-34AFER	854/32843	
N334UP	Boeing 767-34AFER	858/32844	
N700UP	Douglas DC-8-71CF	316/45900	ex N861FT
N701UP	Douglas DC-8-71CF	331/45938	ex N860FT
N702UP	Douglas DC-8-71CF	294/45902	ex N810EV
N703UP	Douglas DC-8-71CF	351/45939	ex N867FT
N705UP	Douglas DC-8-71CF	329/45949	ex N863FT
N706UP	Douglas DC-8-71F	495/46056	ex N1307L
N707UP	Douglas DC-8-71F	288/45907	ex N822E
N708UP	Douglas DC-8-71F	450/46048	ex N1304L
N709UP	Douglas DC-8-71F	292/45914	ex N823E
N713UP	Douglas DC-8-71F	400/46014	ex N1300L	stored ROW
N715UP	Douglas DC-8-71F	295/45915	ex N824E
N718UP	Douglas DC-8-71F	420/46018	ex N1301L
N729UP	Douglas DC-8-71F	425/46029	ex N1302L
N730UP	Douglas DC-8-71F	426/46030	ex N1303L

N744UP	Douglas DC-8-71F	326/45944	ex N825E	
N748UP	Douglas DC-8-71CF	321/45948	ex N862FT	
N750UP	Douglas DC-8-71CF	354/45950	ex N868FT	
N752UP	Douglas DC-8-71CF	338/45952	ex N864FT	
N755UP	Douglas DC-8-71F	492/46055	ex N1306L	
N772UP	Douglas DC-8-71F	477/46072	ex N1305L	
N779UP	Douglas DC-8-71F	363/45979	ex N826E	
N797UP	Douglas DC-8-71CF	313/45897	ex EI-BPF	stored ROW
N798UP	Douglas DC-8-71CF	320/45898	ex N8787R	
N801UP	Douglas DC-8-73CF	489/46101	ex N8630	
N802UP	Douglas DC-8-73AF	502/46100	ex C-FTIP	
N803UP	Douglas DC-8-73CF	485/46073	ex N402FE	
N804UP	Douglas DC-8-73AF	403/46004	ex N784FT	
N805UP	Douglas DC-8-73CF	525/46117	ex N401FE	
N806UP	Douglas DC-8-73AF	413/46006	ex N786FT	
N807UP	Douglas DC-8-73AF	422/46007	ex N787FT	
N808UP	Douglas DC-8-73AF	423/46008	ex N788FT	
N809UP	Douglas DC-8-73CF	493/46109	ex N772FT	
N810UP	Douglas DC-8-73CF	395/46001	ex N404FE	
N811UP	Douglas DC-8-73CF	501/46089	ex N407FE	
N812UP	Douglas DC-8-73CF	520/46112	ex N776FT	
N813UP	Douglas DC-8-73CF	456/46059	ex N703FT	Spirit of Manila
N814UP	Douglas DC-8-73CF	504/46090	ex N405FE	
N818UP	Douglas DC-8-73CF	522/46108	ex N798FT	
N819UP	Douglas DC-8-73F	411/46019	ex TF-VLY	
N836UP	Douglas DC-8-73CF	344/45936	ex N8631	
N840UP	Douglas DC-8-73CF	528/46140	ex N797FT	
N851UP	Douglas DC-8-73CF	440/46051	ex N811EV	
N852UP	Douglas DC-8-73CF	442/46052	ex N31EK	
N866UP	Douglas DC-8-73CF	393/45966	ex N773FT	
N867UP	Douglas DC-8-73CF	385/45967	ex N907CL	
N868UP	Douglas DC-8-73CF	389/45968	ex N871TV	
N874UP	Douglas DC-8-73PF	468/46074	ex HB-IDZ	
N880UP	Douglas DC-8-73F	466/46080	ex TF-VLZ	
N894UP	Douglas DC-8-73CF	482/46094	ex N910CL	
N250UP	McDonnell-Douglas MD-11F	596/48745	ex N798BA	
N251UP	McDonnell-Douglas MD-11F	592/48744	ex N797BA	
N252UP	McDonnell-Douglas MD-11	601/48768	ex PP-SFA	
N253UP	McDonnell-Douglas MD-11F	554/48439	ex PP-VPM	
N254UP	McDonnell-Douglas MD-11F	547/48406	ex PP-VPL	
N270UP	McDonnell-Douglas MD-11F	574/48576	ex JA8585	
N271UP	McDonnell-Douglas MD-11F	556/48572	ex JA8581	
N272UP	McDonnell-Douglas MD-11F	552/48571	ex JA8580	
N273UP	McDonnell-Douglas MD-11F	566/48574	ex JA8583	
N274UP	McDonnell-Douglas MD-11F	568/48575	ex JA8584	
N275UP	McDonnell-Douglas MD-11	610/48774	ex JA8589	stored GYR
N276UP	McDonnell-Douglas MD-11	599/48579	ex JA8588	
N	McDonnell-Douglas MD-11	559/48573	ex JA8582	on order
N	McDonnell-Douglas MD-11	583/48577	ex JA8586	on order
N	McDonnell-Douglas MD-11	588/48578	ex JA8587	on order

Conversion of McDonnell-Douglas MD-11s to freighters has been slowed, originally all due by 2004
UPS Airlines is a division of United Parcel Service

US AIRWAYS

U S Air (US/USA) (IATA 037)   *Pittsburgh-Greater Pittsburgh Intl, PA (PIT)*

N700UW	Airbus Industrie A319-112	0885	ex D-AVYF		Lsd fr WFBN
N701UW	Airbus Industrie A319-112	0890	ex D-AVYG	stored GYR	Lsd fr WFBN
N702UW	Airbus Industrie A319-112	0896	ex D-AVYH	stored GYR	Lsd fr WFBN
N703UW	Airbus Industrie A319-112	0904	ex D-AVYI	stored GYR	Lsd fr WFBN
N704US	Airbus Industrie A319-112	0922	ex D-AVYQ		Lsd fr WFBN
N705UW	Airbus Industrie A319-112	0929	ex D-AVYA		Lsd fr WFBN
N706US	Airbus Industrie A319-112	0946	ex D-AVYD		Lsd fr AFS Investments
N707UW	Airbus Industrie A319-112	0949	ex D-AVYG	stored GYR	Lsd fr AFS Investments
N708UW	Airbus Industrie A319-112	0972	ex D-AVYT		Lsd fr WFBN
N709UW	Airbus Industrie A319-112	0997	ex D-AVYV		Lsd fr WFBN
N710UW	Airbus Industrie A319-112	1019	ex D-AVYR		Lsd fr WFBN
N711UW	Airbus Industrie A319-112	1033	ex D-AVYG		Lsd fr WFBN
N712US	Airbus Industrie A319-112	1038	ex D-AVYW		Lsd fr WFBN
N713UW	Airbus Industrie A319-112	1040	ex D-AVYH		Lsd fr WFBN
N714US	Airbus Industrie A319-112	1046	ex D-AVYZ		Lsd fr WFBN
N715UW	Airbus Industrie A319-112	1051	ex D-AVYV		Lsd fr WFBN
N716UW	Airbus Industrie A319-112	1055	ex D-AVYM		Lsd fr WFBN
N717UW	Airbus Industrie A319-112	1069	ex D-AVWC		Lsd fr WFBN
N718UW	Airbus Industrie A319-112	1077	ex D-AVWI		Lsd fr AFS Investments
N719US	Airbus Industrie A319-112	1084	ex D-AVWK		Lsd fr AFS Investments
N720US	Airbus Industrie A319-112	1089	ex D-AVYC		Lsd fr AFS Investments
N721UW	Airbus Industrie A319-112	1095	ex D-AVYQ		Lsd fr WFBN
N722UW	Airbus Industrie A319-112	1097	ex D-AVYS		Lsd fr WFBN

N723UW	Airbus Industrie A319-112	1109	ex D-AVWP	Lsd fr WFBN
N724UW	Airbus Industrie A319-112	1122	ex D-AVYA	Lsd fr WFBN
N725UW	Airbus Industrie A319-112	1135	ex D-AVWC	Lsd fr WFBN
N726US	Airbus Industrie A319-112	1136	ex D-AVYM	stored GYR
N727UW	Airbus Industrie A319-112	1147	ex D-AVWI	Lsd fr AFS Investments
N728UW	Airbus Industrie A319-112	1155	ex D-AVYS	stored GYR
N728UW	Airbus Industrie A319-112	1155	ex D0AV	stored GYR
N729US	Airbus Industrie A319-112	1170	ex D-AVWQ	stored GYR
N730US	Airbus Industrie A319-112	1182	ex D-AVYD	
N732US	Airbus Industrie A319-112	1203	ex D-AVYA	stored Lake City
N733UW	Airbus Industrie A319-112	1205	ex D-AVYB	
N736US	Airbus Industrie A319-112	1209	ex D-AVYI	
N737US	Airbus Industrie A319-112	1245	ex D-AVYN	Lsd fr WFBN
N738US	Airbus Industrie A319-112	1254	ex D-AVYQ	Lsd fr WFBN
N739US	Airbus Industrie A319-112	1263	ex D-AVYB	
N740UW	Airbus Industrie A319-112	1265	ex D-AVWO	Lsd fr WFBN
N741UW	Airbus Industrie A319-112	1269	ex D-AVWP	Lsd fr WFBN
N742US	Airbus Industrie A319-112	1275	ex D-AVWR	Lsd fr WFBN
N743UW	Airbus Industrie A319-112	1277	ex D-AVWJ	
N744US	Airbus Industrie A319-112	1287	ex D-AVWD	Lsd fr WFBN
N745UW	Airbus Industrie A319-112	1289	ex D-AVWL	Lsd fr WFBN
N746UW	Airbus Industrie A319-112	1297	ex D-AVWV	Lsd fr WFBN
N747UW	Airbus Industrie A319-112	1301	ex D-AVWM	Lsd fr WFBN
N748UW	Airbus Industrie A319-112	1311	ex D-AVYA	Lsd fr WFBN
N749US	Airbus Industrie A319-112	1313	ex D-AVWG	Lsd fr WFBN
N750UW	Airbus Industrie A319-112	1315	ex D-AVWH	Lsd fr WFBN; op for Shuttle
N751UW	Airbus Industrie A319-112	1317	ex D-AVWK	Lsd fr WFBN
N752US	Airbus Industrie A319-112	1319	ex D-AVWS	Lsd fr WFBN
N753US	Airbus Industrie A319-112	1326	ex D-AVYG	Lsd fr WFBN; op for Shuttle
N754UW	Airbus Industrie A319-112	1328	ex D-AVYJ	Lsd fr WFBN
N755US	Airbus Industrie A319-112	1331	ex D-AVYN	Lsd fr WFBN
N756US	Airbus Industrie A319-112	1340	ex D-AVYO	Lsd fr WFBN
N757UW	Airbus Industrie A319-112	1342	ex D-AVYP	Lsd fr WFBN
N758US	Airbus Industrie A319-112	1348	ex D-AVYS	Lsd fr WFBN
N760US	Airbus Industrie A319-112	1354	ex D-AVWI	Lsd fr WFBN
N762US	Airbus Industrie A319-112	1358	ex D-AVWD	
N763US	Airbus Industrie A319-112	1360	ex D-AVWF	
N764US	Airbus Industrie A319-112	1369	ex D-AVWM	stored Lake City, FL
N765US	Airbus Industrie A319-112	1371	ex D-AVWO	
N766US	Airbus Industrie A319-112	1378	ex D-AVWG	
N767UW	Airbus Industrie A319-112	1382	ex D-AVWN	
N768US	Airbus Industrie A319-112	1389	ex D-AVYI	
N769US	Airbus Industrie A319-112	1391	ex D-AVYJ	
N770UW	Airbus Industrie A319-112	1393	ex D-AVYU	

Those used on US Airways Shuttle being replaced by Boeing 737-300s

N101UW	Airbus Industrie A320-214	0936	ex F-WWIT	stored GYR Lsd fr AFS Investments
N102UW	Airbus Industrie A320-214	0844	ex F-WWBG	Lsd fr WFBN
N103US	Airbus Industrie A320-214	0861	ex F-WWBP	stored GYR Lsd fr WFBN
N104UW	Airbus Industrie A320-214	0863	ex F-WWBQ	Lsd fr WFBN; op for Shuttle
N105UW	Airbus Industrie A320-214	0868	ex F-WWBU	Lsd fr WFBN
N106US	Airbus Industrie A320-214	1044	ex F-WWIi	Lsd fr WFBN
N107US	Airbus Industrie A320-214	1052	ex F-WWIM	
N108UW	Airbus Industrie A320-214	1061	ex F-WWBB	
N109UW	Airbus Industrie A320-214	1065	ex F-WWBD	
N110UW	Airbus Industrie A320-214	1112	ex F-WWBJ	
N111US	Airbus Industrie A320-214	1114	ex F-WWBK	Op for Shuttle
N112US	Airbus Industrie A320-214	1134	ex F-WWIV	Op for Shuttle
N113UW	Airbus Industrie A320-214	1141	ex F-WWBC	
N114UW	Airbus Industrie A320-214	1148	ex F-WWBQ	
N115US	Airbus Industrie A320-214	1171	ex F-WWDM	
N116US	Airbus Industrie A320-214	1210	ex F-WWBU	
N117UW	Airbus Industrie A320-214	1224	ex F-WWBH	Lsd fr WFBN
N118US	Airbus Industrie A320-214	1264	ex F-WWDE	Lsd fr WFBN
N119US	Airbus Industrie A320-214	1268	ex F-WWDH	Lsd fr WFBN
N120US	Airbus Industrie A320-214	1286	ex F-WWBN	
N121UW	Airbus Industrie A320-214	1294	ex F-WWBC	Lsd fr WFBN
N122US	Airbus Industrie A320-214	1298	ex F-WWBM	Lsd fr WFBN
N123UW	Airbus Industrie A320-214	1310	ex F-WWBX	Lsd fr WFBN
N124US	Airbus Industrie A320-214	1314	ex F-WWDJ	Lsd fr WFBN
N125US	Airbus Industrie A320-214		ex F-WW	on order
N126US	Airbus Industrie A320-214	1694	ex F-WW	on order

All outstanding Airbus A320 family aircraft [19 A320s and 18 A321s] on order were cancelled and replaced by new order for 6 Airbus Industrie A320-214s and 13 Airbus Industrie A321-211s for delivery between 2007 and 2009

N161UW	Airbus Industrie A321-211	1403	ex D-AVZD	Lsd fr GECAS
N162UW	Airbus Industrie A321-211	1412	ex D-AVZF	
N163US	Airbus Industrie A321-211	1417	ex D-AVZG	
N164UW	Airbus Industrie A321-211	1425	ex D-AVZJ	
N165US	Airbus Industrie A321-211	1431	ex D-AVZB	
N166US	Airbus Industrie A321-211	1436	ex D-AVZK	
N167US	Airbus Industrie A321-211	1442	ex D-AVXA	Lsd fr WFBN

N168US	Airbus Industrie A321-211	1447	ex D-AVXB		Lsd fr WFBN
N169UW	Airbus Industrie A321-211	1455	ex D-AVXD		Lsd fr WFBN
N170US	Airbus Industrie A321-211	1462	ex D-AVZM		
N171US	Airbus Industrie A321-211	1465	ex D-AVZN		Lsd fr WFBN
N172US	Airbus Industrie A321-211	1472	ex D-AVZO		Lsd fr WFBN
N173US	Airbus Industrie A321-211	1481	ex D-AVZI		Lsd fr WFBN
N174US	Airbus Industrie A321-211	1492	ex D-AVZR		Lsd fr WFBN
N175US	Airbus Industrie A321-211	1496	ex D-AVZS		
N176US	Airbus Industrie A321-211	1499	ex D-AVZT		
N177US	Airbus Industrie A321-211	1517	ex D-AVZF		
N178US	Airbus Industrie A321-211	1519	ex D-AVZH		
N179UW	Airbus Industrie A321-211	1521	ex D-AVZJ		
N180US	Airbus Industrie A321-211	1525	ex D-AVZV		
N181UW	Airbus Industrie A321-211	1531	ex D-AVZW		
N182UW	Airbus Industrie A321-211	1536	ex D-AVZB		
N183UW	Airbus Industrie A321-211	1539	ex D-AVZC		
N184US	Airbus Industrie A321-211	1651	ex D-AVZQ		
N185UW	Airbus Industrie A321-211	1666	ex D-AVZI		
N186US	Airbus Industrie A321-211	1701	ex D-AVZD		
N187US	Airbus Industrie A321-211	1704	ex D-AVZE		
N188US	Airbus Industrie A321-211	1724	ex D-AVXB		
N670UW	Airbus Industrie A330-323X	315	ex F-WWKJ		
N671UW	Airbus Industrie A330-323X	323	ex F-WWKN		
N672UW	Airbus Industrie A330-323X	333	ex F-WWKT		
N673UW	Airbus Industrie A330-323X	337	ex F-WWKZ		
N674UW	Airbus Industrie A330-323X	342	ex F-WWYB		
N675US	Airbus Industrie A330-323X	370	ex F-WWKH		
N676UW	Airbus Industrie A330-323X	375	ex F-WWKI		
N677UW	Airbus Industrie A330-323X	380	ex F-WWYL		
N678US	Airbus Industrie A330-323X	388	ex F-WWYU		

Ten Airbus A330-223s are on order for delivery in 2007 (3), 2008 (4) and 2009 (3)

N300AU	Boeing 737-301	1103/23228	ex N301P		Lsd fr JP Morgan Trust
N334US	Boeing 737-301	1164/23231	ex N313P	std MHV	Lsd fr Wachovia Bank
N335US	Boeing 737-301	1169/23232	ex N314P		Lsd fr Wachovia Bank
N340US	Boeing 737-301	1222/23237	ex N320P		Lsd fr Wachovia Bank; op for Shuttle
N346US	Boeing 737-301	1355/23515	ex N326P		Lsd fr AFS Investments
N349US	Boeing 737-301	1382/23552	ex N334P	std MHV	Lsd fr Wachovia Bank
N350US	Boeing 737-301	1406/23553	ex N335P		
N351US	Boeing 737-301	1408/23554	ex N336P	std MHV	Lsd fr Wachovia Bank
N352US	Boeing 737-301	1428/23555	ex N337P	std MHV	Lsd fr Wachovia Bank
N353US	Boeing 737-301	1435/23556	ex N340P		Lsd fr Wachovia Bank
N354US	Boeing 737-301	1437/23557	ex N341P		Lsd fr Wachovia Bank
N355US	Boeing 737-301	1449/23558	ex N342P		Lsd fr Wachovia Bank
N356US	Boeing 737-301	1451/23559	ex N348P		Lsd fr Wachovia Bank
N371US	Boeing 737-3B7	1001/22950	ex N350AU		Lsd fr JP Morgan Trust
N373US	Boeing 737-3B7	1015/22952	ex N352AU		Lsd fr JP Morgan Trust
N374US	Boeing 737-3B7	1022/22953	ex N353AU		Lsd fr JP Morgan Trust
N375US	Boeing 737-3B7	1030/22954	ex N354AU		Lsd fr JP Morgan Trust
N376US	Boeing 737-3B7	1043/22955	ex N355AU		Lsd fr JP Morgan Trust
N383US	Boeing 737-3B7	1057/22956	ex N356AU		Lsd fr JP Morgan Trust
N384US	Boeing 737-3B7	1127/22957	ex N357AU		Lsd fr JP Morgan Trust
N385US	Boeing 737-3B7	1137/22958	ex N358AU		
N387US	Boeing 737-3B7	1140/22959	ex N359AU		Op for Shuttle
N389US	Boeing 737-3B7	1149/23311	ex N361AU		
N390US	Boeing 737-3B7	1162/23312	ex N362AU		stored Lake City, FL
N391US	Boeing 737-3B7	1177/23313	ex N363AU		Lsd fr JP Morgan Trust
N392US	Boeing 737-3B7	1179/23314	ex N364AU		Lsd fr JP Morgan Trust
N393US	Boeing 737-3B7	1210/23315	ex N365AU		Lsd fr JP Morgan Trust
N394US	Boeing 737-3B7	1212/23316	ex N366AU		Lsd fr JP Morgan Trust
N395US	Boeing 737-3B7	1221/23317	ex N367AU		Lsd fr JP Morgan Trust; op Shuttle
N396US	Boeing 737-3B7	1234/23318	ex N368AU		Lsd fr JP Morgan Trust
N397US	Boeing 737-3B7	1250/23319	ex N369AU		Lsd fr JP Morgan Trust; op Shuttle
N504AU	Boeing 737-3B7	1362/23379	ex N373AU		Lsd fr Wachovia Bank
N505AU	Boeing 737-3B7	1366/23380	ex N374AU		Lsd fr Wachovia Bank
N506AU	Boeing 737-3B7	1394/23381	ex N375AU	std MHV	Lsd fr Wachovia Bank
N511AU	Boeing 737-3B7	1442/23594	ex N380AU		Lsd fr Aircraft Statutory Trust
N512AU	Boeing 737-3B7	1450/23595	ex N381AU		Lsd fr Aircraft Statutory Trust
N514AU	Boeing 737-3B7	1461/23700	ex N383AU		Lsd fr Aircraft Statutory Trust
N515AU	Boeing 737-3B7	1464/23701	ex N384AU		Lsd fr Aircraft Statutory Trust
N516AU	Boeing 737-3B7	1475/23702	ex N385AU		
N517AU	Boeing 737-3B7	1480/23703	ex N386AU		Lsd fr Aircraft Statutory Trust
N518AU	Boeing 737-3B7	1488/23704	ex N387AU		Lsd fr Aircraft Statutory Trust
N519AU	Boeing 737-3B7	1497/23705	ex N388AU		
N520AU	Boeing 737-3B7	1499/23706	ex N389AU		
N521AU	Boeing 737-3B7	1501/23856	ex N390AU		
N522AU	Boeing 737-3B7	1503/23857	ex N391AU		
N523AU	Boeing 737-3B7	1509/23858	ex N392AU		Lsd fr CIT Leasing
N524AU	Boeing 737-3B7	1551/23859	ex N393AU		Lsd fr CIT Leasing
N525AU	Boeing 737-3B7	1560/23860	ex N394AU		Lsd fr Aircraft Statutory Trust
N526AU	Boeing 737-3B7	1584/23861	ex N395AU		Lsd fr Aircraft Statutory Trust

N527AU	Boeing 737-3B7	1586/23862	ex N396AU		Lsd fr Aircraft Statutory Trust
N528AU	Boeing 737-3B7	1703/24410			Lsd fr Aircraft Statutory Trust
N529AU	Boeing 737-3B7	1713/24411			Lsd fr Aircraft Statutory Trust
N530AU	Boeing 737-3B7	1735/24412			Lsd fr Aircraft Statutory Trust
N531AU	Boeing 737-3B7	1743/24478			Lsd fr Aircraft Statutory Trust
N532AU	Boeing 737-3B7	1745/24479			Lsd fr Aircraft Statutory Trust
N533AU	Boeing 737-3B7	1767/24515			Lsd fr Aircraft Statutory Trust
N558AU	Boeing 737-301	1291/23512	ex N343US		Lsd fr Wachovia Bank
N560AU	Boeing 737-301	1331/23514	ex N345US		
N563AU	Boeing 737-301	1380/23551	ex N348US	stored MHV	Lsd fr Wachovia Bank
N573US	Boeing 737-301	1463/23560	ex N357US		
N574US	Boeing 737-301	1469/23739	ex N358US		
N575US	Boeing 737-301	1477/23740	ex N359US	stored MHV	Lsd fr Wachovia Bank
N576US	Boeing 737-301	1498/23741	ex N360US		
N577US	Boeing 737-301	1502/23742	ex N361US		
N584US	Boeing 737-301	1510/23743	ex N355P		
N585US	Boeing 737-301	1539/23930	ex N357P		Lsd fr Wachovia Bank
N586US	Boeing 737-301	1552/23931	ex N358P		Lsd fr Wachovia Bank
N587US	Boeing 737-301	1554/23932	ex N359P		Lsd fr Wachovia Bank
N588US	Boeing 737-301	1559/23933	ex (N360P)		Lsd fr Aircraft Statutory Trust
N589US	Boeing 737-301	1563/23934	ex (N361P)		Lsd fr Aircraft Statutory Trust
N590US	Boeing 737-301	1569/23935	ex (N362P)		Lsd fr Aircraft Statutory Trust
N591US	Boeing 737-301	1575/23936	ex (N364P)		Lsd fr Aircraft Statutory Trust
N592US	Boeing 737-301	1587/23937	ex (N365P)		Lsd fr Aircraft Statutory Trust
N404US	Boeing 737-401	1487/23886	ex (N402P)	stored MHV	
N405US	Boeing 737-401	1512/23885	ex (N403P)	stored MHV	
N406US	Boeing 737-401	1528/23876	ex (N404P)	Thomas A Davis, Pacemaker	
					Lsd fr Aircraft Statutory Trust
N409US	Boeing 737-401	1573/23879	ex (N407P)		Lsd fr Aircraft Statutory Trust
N417US	Boeing 737-401	1674/23984		stored MHV	
N418US	Boeing 737-401	1676/23985			
N419US	Boeing 737-401	1684/23986			Lsd fr Aircraft Statutory Trust
N420US	Boeing 737-401	1698/23987			Lsd fr Aircraft Statutory Trust
N421US	Boeing 737-401	1714/23988			Lsd fr Aircraft Statutory Trust
N422US	Boeing 737-401	1716/23989			Lsd fr Aircraft Statutory Trust
N423US	Boeing 737-401	1732/23990			Lsd fr Aircraft Statutory Trust
N424US	Boeing 737-401	1746/23991			Lsd fr Aircraft Statutory Trust
N425US	Boeing 737-401	1764/23992			Lsd fr Aircraft Statutory Trust
N426US	Boeing 737-4B7	1789/24548			Lsd fr WTCo
N427US	Boeing 737-4B7	1791/24549			Lsd fr Aircraft Statutory Trust
N428US	Boeing 737-4B7	1793/24550			Lsd fr CIT Leasing
N429US	Boeing 737-4B7	1795/24551			Lsd fr CIT Leasing
N430US	Boeing 737-4B7	1797/24552			Lsd fr WTCo
N432US	Boeing 737-4B7	1817/24554			Lsd fr Aircraft Statutory Trust
N433US	Boeing 737-4B7	1819/24555			Lsd fr Aircraft Statutory Trust
N434US	Boeing 737-4B7	1821/24556			Lsd fr Aircraft Statutory Trust
N435US	Boeing 737-4B7	1835/24557			Lsd fr Aircraft Statutory Trust
N436US	Boeing 737-4B7	1845/24558			
N437US	Boeing 737-4B7	1847/24559			
N438US	Boeing 737-4B7	1849/24560			Lsd fr AFS Investments XLIV
N439US	Boeing 737-4B7	1874/24781			Lsd fr AFS Investments XLIV
N440US	Boeing 737-4B7	1890/24811			Lsd fr AFS Investments XLIV
N441US	Boeing 737-4B7	1892/24812			
N442US	Boeing 737-4B7	1906/24841			
N443US	Boeing 737-4B7	1908/24842		stored Lake City, FL	
N444US	Boeing 737-4B7	1910/24862			Lsd fr AFS Investments XLIV
N445US	Boeing 737-4B7	1914/24863			
N446US	Boeing 737-4B7	1931/24873		stored Lake City, FL	
N447US	Boeing 737-4B7	1936/24874			
N448US	Boeing 737-4B7	1944/24892			
N449US	Boeing 737-4B7	1946/24893			
N775AU	Boeing 737-4B7	1954/24933			
N776AU	Boeing 737-4B7	1956/24934			
N777AU	Boeing 737-4B7	1980/24979			
N778AU	Boeing 737-4B7	1982/24980			
N779AU	Boeing 737-4B7	1986/24996			
N780AU	Boeing 737-4B7	1990/24997			
N781AU	Boeing 737-4B7	1992/25020			
N782AU	Boeing 737-4B7	1995/25021			
N783AU	Boeing 737-4B7	2010/25022			
N784AU	Boeing 737-4B7	2020/25023			
N785AU	Boeing 737-4B7	2026/25024			
N600AU	Boeing 757-225	3/22192	ex N502EA		Lsd fr GECAS
N601AU	Boeing 757-225	4/22193	ex N503EA		Lsd fr GECAS
N602AU	Boeing 757-225	7/22196	ex N506EA		Lsd fr GECAS
N603AU	Boeing 757-225	12/22198	ex N508EA		Lsd fr GECAS
N604AU	Boeing 757-225	17/22199	ex N509EA		Lsd fr GECAS
N605AU	Boeing 757-225	21/22201	ex N511EA		Lsd fr GECAS
N606AU	Boeing 757-225	22/22202	ex N512EA		Lsd fr GECAS
N607AU	Boeing 757-225	26/22203	ex N513EA		Lsd fr GECAS

N608AU	Boeing 757-225	27/22204	ex N514EA		Lsd fr GECAS
N609AU	Boeing 757-225	28/22205	ex N515EA		Lsd fr GECAS
N610AU	Boeing 757-2B7	525/27122			Lsd fr Aircraft Statutory Trust
N611AU	Boeing 757-2B7	534/27123			Lsd fr Aircraft Statutory Trust
N612AU	Boeing 757-2B7	540/27124			Lsd fr Aircraft Statutory Trust
N613AU	Boeing 757-2B7	544/27144			Lsd fr Aircraft Statutory Trust
N614AU	Boeing 757-2B7	546/27145			Lsd fr Aircraft Statutory Trust
N617AU	Boeing 757-2B7	564/27148			Lsd fr Aircraft Statutory Trust
N618AU	Boeing 757-225	42/22210	ex N520EA	stored MHV	
N619AU	Boeing 757-2B7	584/27198			Lsd fr Aircraft Statutory Trust
N620AU	Boeing 757-2B7	586/27199			Lsd fr Aircraft Statutory Trust
N621AU	Boeing 757-2B7	589/27200			Lsd fr Aircraft Statutory Trust
N622AU	Boeing 757-2B7	605/27201			Lsd fr WTCo
N623AU	Boeing 757-2B7	607/27244			Lsd fr WTCo
N624AU	Boeing 757-2B7	630/27245			Lsd fr WFBN
N625VJ	Boeing 757-2B7	643/27246			Lsd fr WFBN
N626AU	Boeing 757-2B7	647/27303			Lsd fr Q Aviation
N627AU	Boeing 757-2B7	655/27805			Lsd fr Q Aviation
N628AU	Boeing 757-2B7	657/27806			Lsd fr Q Aviation
N629AU	Boeing 757-2B7	662/27807			Lsd fr Q Aviation
N630AU	Boeing 757-2B7	666/27808			Lsd fr Q Aviation
N631AU	Boeing 757-2B7	673/27809			Lsd fr Q Aviation
N632AU	Boeing 757-2B7	678/27810			Lsd fr Q Aviation
N633AU	Boeing 757-2B7	681/27811			Lsd fr WFBN
N645US	Boeing 767-201ER	173/23897	ex N603P		Lsd fr Aircraft Statutory Trust
N646US	Boeing 767-201ER	175/23898	ex N604P		Lsd fr Aircraft Statutory Trust
N648US	Boeing 767-201ER	190/23900	ex N608P		
N649US	Boeing 767-201ER	197/23901	ex N614P		
N650US	Boeing 767-201ER	217/23902	ex N617P		
N651US	Boeing 767-2B7ER	306/24764			
N652US	Boeing 767-2B7ER	308/24765			
N653US	Boeing 767-2B7ER	338/24894			Lsd fr WTCo
N655US	Boeing 767-2B7ER	383/25257			Lsd fr WTCo
N656US	Boeing 767-2B7ER	486/26847			

Code-shares with United Air Lines on over 250 combined flights and approved for Star Alliance membership
Feeder services operated by Allegheny Airlines, Chautauqua Airlines, Colgan Air, Mesa Airlines, MidAtlantic Airways, Piedmont Airlines, , PSA Airlines, Shuttle America and Trans States in full colours as US Airways Express

---

US AIRWAYS EXPRESS

US Air (USX)   *various*

N550HK	British Aerospace Jetstream 41	41039	ex G-4-039	TUA	
N553HK	British Aerospace Jetstream 41	41066	ex G-4-066	TUV	
N554HK	British Aerospace Jetstream 41	41067	ex G-4-067	TUD	
N555HK	British Aerospace Jetstream 41	41072	ex G-4-072	TUF	
N556HK	British Aerospace Jetstream 41	41073	ex G-4-073	TUH	
N558HK	British Aerospace Jetstream 41	41071	ex G-4-071		
N559HK	British Aerospace Jetstream 41	41075	ex G-4-075	TUK	
N562HK	British Aerospace Jetstream 41	41078	ex G-4-078		
N563HK	British Aerospace Jetstream 41	41079	ex G-4-079	TUR	
N564HK	British Aerospace Jetstream 41	41081	ex G-4-081		
N572HK	British Aerospace Jetstream 41	41091	ex G-4-091	TUW	

All leased from WFBN and operated by Trans States

N5YV	Beech 1900D	UE-5		Mesa - US Airways	Lsd fr WFBN
N6YV	Beech 1900D	UE-6		Mesa - US Airways	
N13ZV	Beech 1900D	UE-13		Mesa - US Airways	
N23YV	Beech 1900D	UE-23		Mesa - US Airways	
N62ZV	Beech 1900D	UE-62	stored MZJ	Mesa - US Airways	
N64YV	Beech 1900D	UE-64	stored ABQ	Mesa - US Airways	
N67YV	Beech 1900D	UE-67	stored ABQ	Mesa - US Airways	
N123YV	Beech 1900D	UE-123		Mesa - US Airways	
N126YV	Beech 1900D	UE-126	stored Salina, KS	Mesa - US Airways	
N127ZV	Beech 1900D	UE-127		Mesa - US Airways	
N133YV	Beech 1900D	UE-133		Mesa - US Airways	
N138YV	Beech 1900D	UE-138		Mesa - US Airways	
N140ZV	Beech 1900D	UE-140	ex (N137ZV)	Mesa - US Airways	
N142ZV	Beech 1900D	UE-142		Mesa - US Airways	
N143YV	Beech 1900D	UE-143		Mesa - US Airways	
N144ZV	Beech 1900D	UE-144		Mesa - US Airways	
N146ZV	Beech 1900D	UE-146		Mesa - US Airways	
N155ZV	Beech 1900D	UE-155		Mesa - US Airways	
N159YV	Beech 1900D	UE-159		Mesa - US Airways	
N161YV	Beech 1900D	UE-161		Mesa - US Airways	
N162ZV	Beech 1900D	UE-162		Mesa - US Airways	
N165YV	Beech 1900D	UE-165		Mesa - US Airways	
N167YV	Beech 1900D	UE-167		Mesa - US Airways	
N173YV	Beech 1900D	UE-173		Mesa - US Airways	
N190YV	Beech 1900D	UE-190		Mesa - US Airways	

N218YV	Beech 1900D	UE-218		Mesa - US Airways
N3199Q	Beech 1900D	UE-213		Mesa - US Airways
N10675	Beech 1900D	UE-229		Mesa - US Airways
N202PS	Canadair CL-600-2B19	7858	ex C-	PSA Airlines
N206PS	Canadair CL-600-2B19	7860	ex C-FMLQ	PSA Airlines
N207PS	Canadair CL-600-2B19	7873	ex C-	PSA Airlines
N209PS	Canadair CL-600-2B19	7874	ex C-FMLU	PSA Airlines
N213PS	Canadair CL-600-2B19	7879	ex C-FMMQ	PSA Airlines
N215PS	Canadair CL-600-2B19	7880	ex C-FMMW	PSA Airlines
N216PS	Canadair CL-600-2B19	7882	ex C-FMMY	PSA Airlines
N218PS	Canadair CL-600-2B19	7885	ex C-FMKS	PSA Airlines
N220PS	Canadair CL-600-2B19	7887	ex C-FMLB	PSA Airlines
N221PS	Canadair CL-600-2B19	7889	ex C-FMLI	PSA Airlines
N223JS	Canadair CL-600-2B19		ex C-	on order PSA Airlines
N226JS	Canadair CL-600-2B19		ex C-	on order PSA Airlines
N228PS	Canadair CL-600-2B19		ex C-	on order PSA Airlines
N229PS	Canadair CL-600-2B19		ex C-	on order PSA Airlines
N230PS	Canadair CL-600-2B19		ex C-	on order PSA Airlines
N237PS	Canadair CL-600-2B19		ex C-	on order PSA Airlines
N241PS	Canadair CL-600-2B19		ex C-	on order PSA Airlines
N242JS	Canadair CL-600-2B19		ex C-	on order PSA Airlines
N244PS	Canadair CL-600-2B19		ex C-	on order PSA Airlines
N245PS	Canadair CL-600-2B19		ex C-	on order PSA Airlines
N246PS	Canadair CL-600-2B19		ex C-	on order PSA Airlines
N247JS	Canadair CL-600-2B19		ex C-	on order PSA Airlines
N248PS	Canadair CL-600-2B19		ex C-	on order PSA Airlines
N249PS	Canadair CL-600-2B19		ex C-	on order PSA Airlines
N250PS	Canadair CL-600-2B19		ex C-	on order PSA Airlines
N251PS	Canadair CL-600-2B19		ex C-	on order PSA Airlines
N253PS	Canadair CL-600-2B19		ex C-	on order PSA Airlines
N254PS	Canadair CL-600-2B19		ex C-	on order PSA Airlines
N256PS	Canadair CL-600-2B19		ex C-	on order PSA Airlines
N257PS	Canadair CL-600-2B19		ex C-	on order PSA Airlines
N258PS	Canadair CL-600-2B19		ex C-	on order PSA Airlines
N259PS	Canadair CL-600-2B19		ex C-	on order PSA Airlines
N260JS	Canadair CL-600-2B19		ex C-	on order PSA Airlines
N261PS	Canadair Cl-600-2B19		ex C-	on order PSA Airlines
N262PS	Canadair CL-600-2B19		ex C-	on order PSA Airlines
N263PS	Canadair CL-600-2B19		ex C-	on order PSA Airlines
N264PS	Canadair CL-600-2B19		ex C-	on order PSA Airlines
N265PS	Canadair CL-600-2B19		ex C-	on order PSA Airlines
N266PS	Canadair CL-600-2B19		ex C-	on order PSA Airlines
N267JS	Canadair CL-600-2B19		ex C-	on order PSA Airlines
N269PS	Canadair CL-600-2B19		ex C-	on order PSA Airlines
N270PS	Canadair CL-600-2B19		ex C-	on order PSA Airlines
N271PS	Canadair CL-600-2B19		ex C-	on order PSA Airlines
N272PS	Canadair CL-600-2B19		ex C-	on order PSA Airlines
N273JS	Canadair CL-600-2B19		ex C-	on order PSA Airlines
N275PS	Canadair CL-600-2B19		ex C-	on order PSA Airlines
N276PS	Canadair CL-600-2B19		ex C-	on order PSA Airlines
N277PS	Canadair CL-600-2B19		ex C-	on order PSA Airlines
N278PS	Canadair CL-600-2B19		ex C-	on order PSA Airlines
N279PS	Canadair CL-600-2B19		ex C-	on order PSA Airlines
N280PS	Canadair CL-600-2B19		ex C-	on order PSA Airlines
N281PS	Canadair CL-600-2B19		ex C-	on order PSA Airlines
N282PS	Canadair CL-600-2B19		ex C-	on order PSA Airlines
N283PS	Canadair CL-600-2B19		ex C-	on order PSA Airlines
N284PS	Canadair CL-600-2B19		ex C-	on order PSA Airlines
N285PS	Canadair CL-600-2B19		ex C-	on order PSA Airlines
N286PS	Canadair CL-600-2B19		ex C-	on order PSA Airlines
N287PS	Canadair CL-600-2B19		ex C-	on order PSA Airlines
N288PS	Canadair CL-600-2B19		ex C-	on order PSA Airlines
N289JS	Canadair CL-600-2B19		ex C-	on order PSA Airlines
N290PS	Canadair CL-600-2B19		ex C-	on order PSA Airlines
N291PS	Canadair CL-600-2B19		ex C-	on order PSA Airlines
N292PS	Canadair CL-600-2B19		ex C-	on order PSA Airlines
N293PS	Canadair CL-600-2B19		ex C-	on order PSA Airlines
N294JS	Canadair CL-600-2B19		ex C-	on order PSA Airlines
N295JS	Canadair CL-600-2B19		ex C-	on order PSA Airlines
N296JS	Canadair CL-600-2B19		ex C-	on order PSA Airlines
N297PS	Canadair CL-600-2B19		ex C-	on order PSA Airlines
N298PS	Canadair CL-600-2B19		ex C-	on order PSA Airlines
N17156	Canadair CL-600-2B19	7156	ex C-FZSC	Mesa - US Airways
N17175	Canadair CL-600-2B19	7175	ex LV-WXB	Mesa - US Airways
N27172	Canadair CL-600-2B19	7172		Mesa - US Airways
N27173	Canadair CL-600-2B19	7173	ex C-FMMQ	Mesa - US Airways
N27185	Canadair CL-600-2B19	7185		Mesa - US Airways
N27191	Canadair CL-600-2B19	7191		Mesa - US Airways
N47202	Canadair CL-600-2B19	7202		Mesa - US Airways
N75984	Canadair CL-600-2B19	7489	ex C-GZGX	Mesa - US Airways
N75987	Canadair CL-600-2B19	7405	ex C-FZSZ	Mesa - US Airways

N75991	Canadair CL-600-2B19	7422	ex C-FZSY	Mesa - US Airways	
N75992	Canadair CL-600-2B19	7401	ex C-FZTH	Mesa - US Airways	
N75993	Canadair CL-600-2B19	7372	ex C-FZTT	Mesa - US Airways	
N75994	Canadair CL-600-2B19	7367	ex C-FZTY	Mesa - US Airways	
N75995	Canadair CL-600-2B19	7361	ex C-FZTW	Mesa - US Airways	
N75996	Canadair CL-600-2B19	7357	ex C-FZTZ	Mesa - US Airways	
N75998	Canadair CL-600-2B19	7336	ex C-FZTU	Mesa - US Airways	
N75999	Canadair CL-600-2B19	7471	ex C-FSXX	Mesa - US Airways	
N77181	Canadair CL-600-2B19	7181		Mesa - US Airways	

Those operated by Mesa to be replaced by Embraer EMB.145s and transferred to America West Express/Frontier Jet Express

N702PS	Canadair CL-600-2D24	ex C-	on order PSA Airlines
N703PS	Canadair CL-600-2D24	ex C-	on order PSA Airlines
N705PS	Canadair CL-600-2D24	ex C-	on order PSA Airlines
N706PS	Canadair CL-600-2D24	ex C-	on order PSA Airlines
N708PS	Canadair CL-600-2D24	ex C-	on order PSA Airlines
N709PS	Canadair CL-600-2D24	ex C-	on order PSA Airlines
N710PS	Canadair CL-600-2D24	ex C-	on order PSA Airlines
N712PS	Canadair CL-600-2D24	ex C-	on order PSA Airlines
N716PS	Canadair CL-600-2D24	ex C-	on order PSA Airlines
N718PS	Canadair CL-600-2D24	ex C-	on order PSA Airlines
N719PS	Canadair CL-600-2D24	ex C-	on order PSA Airlines
N720PS	Canadair CL-600-2D24	ex C-	on order PSA Airlines
N721PS	Canadair CL-600-2D24	ex C-	on order PSA Airlines
N723PS	Canadair CL-600-2D24	ex C-	on order PSA Airlines
N724PS	Canadair CL-600-2D24	ex C-	on order PSA Airlines
N725PS	Canadair CL-600-2D24	ex C-	on order PSA Airlines
N726PS	Canadair CL-600-2D24	ex C-	on order PSA Airlines
N728PS	Canadair CL-600-2D24	ex C-	on order PSA Airlines
N729PS	Canadair CL-600-2D24	ex C-	on order PSA Airlines
N730PS	Canadair CL-600-2D24	ex C-	on order PSA Airlines
N731PS	Canadair CL-600-2D24	ex C-	on order PSA Airlines
N736PS	Canadair CL-600-2D24	ex C-	on order PSA Airlines
N740PS	Canadair CL-600-2D24	ex C-	on order PSA Airlines
N741PS	Canadair CL-600-2D24	ex C-	on order PSA Airlines
N742PS	Canadair CL-600-2D24	ex C-	on order PSA Airlines
N743PS	Canadair CL-600-2D24	ex C-	on order PSA Airlines
N744PS	Canadair CL-600-2D24	ex C-	on order PSA Airlines
N745PS	Canadair CL-600-2D24	ex C-	on order PSA Airlines
N746PS	Canadair CL-600-2D24	ex C-	on order PSA Airlines
N748PS	Canadair CL-600-2D24	ex C-	on order PSA Airlines
N749PS	Canadair CL-600-2D24	ex C-	on order PSA Airlines
N750PS	Canadair CL-600-2D24	ex C-	on order PSA Airlines
N751PS	Canadair CL-600-2D24	ex C-	on order PSA Airlines
N752PS	Canadair CL-600-2D24	ex C-	on order PSA Airlines
N753PS	Canadair CL-600-2D24	ex C-	on order PSA Airlines
N754PS	Canadair CL-600-2D24	ex C-	on order PSA Airlines
N755PS	Canadair CL-600-2D24	ex C-	on order PSA Airlines
N756PS	Canadair CL-600-2D24	ex C-	on order PSA Airlines
N762PS	Canadair CL-600-2D24	ex C-	on order PSA Airlines
N763PS	Canadair CL-600-2D24	ex C-	on order PSA Airlines
N764PS	Canadair CL-600-2D24	ex C-	on order PSA Airlines
N765PS	Canadair CL-600-2D24	ex C-	on order PSA Airlines
N766PS	Canadair CL-600-2D24	ex C-	on order PSA Airlines
N767PS	Canadair CL-600-2D24	ex C-	on order PSA Airlines
N768PS	Canadair CL-600-2D24	ex C-	on order PSA Airlines
N769PS	Canadair CL-600-2D24	ex C-	on order PSA Airlines
N771PS	Canadair CL-600-2D24	ex C-	on order PSA Airlines
N772PS	Canadair CL-600-2D24	ex C-	on order PSA Airlines
N773PS	Canadair CL-600-2D24	ex C-	on order PSA Airlines
N774PS	Canadair CL-600-2D24	ex C-	on order PSA Airlines

All are to be operated as CRJ705ERs with 74 seats

N326EN	de Havilland DHC-8-311	234	ex N386DC	Piedmont	
N327EN	de Havilland DHC-8-311A	261	ex N379DC	Piedmont	
N328EN	de Havilland DHC-8-311A	281	ex N380DC	Piedmont	
N329EN	de Havilland DHC-8-311	290	ex SU-UAD	Piedmont	Lsd fr Bombardier Capital
N330EN	de Havilland DHC-8-311A	274	ex N805SA	Piedmont	
N331EN	de Havilland DHC-8-311A	279	ex N806SA	Piedmont	Lsd fr WFBN
N333EN	de Havilland DHC-8-311	221	ex N803SA	Piedmont	
N335EN	de Havilland DHC-8-311	375	ex N804SA	Piedmont	
N336EN	de Havilland DHC-8-311A	336	ex N284BC	Piedmont	
N337EN	de Havilland DHC-8-311A	284	ex SU-UAE	Piedmont	Lsd fr Bombardier Capital
N342EN	de Havilland DHC-8-311A	395	ex N511CL	Piedmont	
N343EN	de Havilland DHC-8-311A	340	ex OE-LLZ	Piedmont	
N434YV	de Havilland DHC-8-202	434	ex C-GDNG	Mesa	Lsd fr WFBN
N447YV	de Havilland DHC-8Q-202	447	ex C-GFYI	Mesa	Lsd fr WFBN
N448YV	de Havilland DHC-8Q-202	448	ex C-GLOT	Mesa	Lsd fr WFBN
N804EX	de Havilland DHC-8-102A	227	ex C-GFYI	Allegheny Airlines	
N805EX	de Havilland DHC-8-102A	228	ex C-GLOT	Allegheny Airlines	
N806EX	de Havilland DHC-8-102A	263	ex C-GEVP	Allegheny Airlines	

N807EX	de Havilland DHC-8-102A	292	ex C-GFQL	Allegheny Airlines	
N808EX	de Havilland DHC-8-102A	299	ex C-GDKL	Allegheny Airlines	
N809EX	de Havilland DHC-8-102A	302	ex PT-MFI	Allegheny Airlines	
N810EX	de Havilland DHC-8-102A	308	ex C-GDKL	Shuttle America	Lsd fr ALO
N811AW	de Havilland DHC-8-102A	201	ex C-GDNG	Allegheny Airlines	Lsd fr WFBN
N812EX	de Havilland DHC-8-102A	312	ex C-GDNG	Allegheny Airlines	
N814EX	de Havilland DHC-8-102A	318	ex C-GDNG	Allegheny Airlines	
N815EX	de Havilland DHC-8-102A	321	ex C-GDFT	Shuttle America	Lsd fr ALO
N816EX	de Havilland DHC-8-102A	329	ex C-GEVP	Shuttle America	Lsd fr ALO
N817EX	de Havilland DHC-8-102A	191	ex N810AW	Allegheny Airlines	Lsd fr WFBN
N818EX	de Havilland DHC-8-102A	235	ex N812AW	Allegheny Airlines	Lsd fr WFBN
N821EX	de Havilland DHC-8-102	173	ex N808AW	Allegheny Airlines	Lsd fr BCCorp
N824EX"	de Havilland DHC-8-102	387	ex C-	Allegheny Airlines	
N825EX"	de Havilland DHC-8-102A	388	ex G-GHRI	Allegheny Airlines	
N826EX"	de Havilland DHC-8-102A	389	ex C-GDNG	Allegheny Airlines	
N827EX"	de Havilland DHC-8-102A	390	ex C-GEOA	Allegheny Airlines	
N828EX"	de Havilland DHC-8-102A	392	ex C-GEVP	Allegheny Airlines	
N829EX	de Havilland DHC-8-102	146	ex N805AW	Allegheny Airlines	Lsd fr BCCorp
N830EX	de Havilland DHC-8-102	155	ex N806AW	Allegheny Airlines	Lsd fr WFBN
N831EX	de Havilland DHC-8-102	160	ex N807AW	Allegheny Airlines	Lsd fr WFBN
N832EX	de Havilland DHC-8-102A	280	ex N415AW	Allegheny Airlines	
N833EX	de Havilland DHC-8-102A	282	ex N416AW	Allegheny Airlines	Lsd fr WFBN
N834EX	de Havilland DHC-8-102A	285	ex N417AW	Allegheny Airlines	Lsd fr WFBN
N835EX	de Havilland DHC-8-102A	289	ex N418AW	Allegheny Airlines	Lsd fr WFBN
N836EX	de Havilland DHC-8-102A	297	ex N419AW	Allegheny Airlines	Lsd fr WFBN
N837EX	de Havilland DHC-8-102A	217	ex N976HA	Piedmont Airlines	
N838EX	de Havilland DHC-8-102A	220	ex N977HA	Piedmont Airlines	
N839EX	de Havilland DHC-8-102A	226	ex N978HA	Piedmont Airlines	
N840EX+	de Havilland DHC-8-102A	327	ex N824MA	Allegheny Airlines	
N841EX+	de Havilland DHC-8-102A	249	ex N817MA	Allegheny Airlines	
N842EX+	de Havilland DHC-8-102	341	ex N832MA	Allegheny Airlines	
N843EX+	de Havilland DHC-8-102	335	ex N829MA	Allegheny Airlines	
N844EX+	de Havilland DHC-8-102A	339	ex N831MA	Allegheny Airlines	
N845EX+	de Havilland DHC-8-102	344	ex N846MA	Allegheny Airlines	
N846EX	de Havilland DHC-8-102A	326	ex N960HA	Piedmont Airlines	
N847EX	de Havilland DHC-8-102A	333	ex N961HA	Piedmont Airlines	
N848EX	de Havilland DHC-8-102A	331	ex N962HA	Piedmont Airlines	
N849EX	de Havilland DHC-8-102A	337	ex N963HA	Piedmont Airlines	
N906HA	de Havilland DHC-8-102	009	ex C-GHRI	Piedmont Airlines	
N907HA	de Havilland DHC-8-102	011	ex C-GESR	Piedmont Airlines	
N908HA	de Havilland DHC-8-102	015	ex C-GIBQ	Piedmont Airlines	
N911HA	de Havilland DHC-8-102	034	ex C-GEOA	Piedmont Airlines	
N912HA	de Havilland DHC-8-102	040	ex C-GEOA	Piedmont Airlines	
N914HA	de Havilland DHC-8-102	053	ex C-GETI	Piedmont Airlines	
N916HA<	de Havilland DHC-8-102	072	ex C-GEOA	Piedmont Airlines	
N917HA<	de Havilland DHC-8-102	075	ex C-GEVP	Piedmont Airlines	
N930HA	de Havilland DHC-8-102	126	ex C-GFQL	Piedmont Airlines	
N931HA	de Havilland DHC-8-102	132	ex C-GFOD	Piedmont Airlines	
N933HA	de Havilland DHC-8-102	134	ex C-GFUM	Piedmont Airlines	
N934HA	de Havilland DHC-8-102	139	ex C-GETI	Piedmont Airlines	
N935HA	de Havilland DHC-8-102	142	ex C-GLOT	Piedmont Airlines	
N936HA	de Havilland DHC-8-102	145	ex C-GFQL	Piedmont Airlines	
N937HA	de Havilland DHC-8-102	148	ex C-GLOT	Piedmont Airlines	
N938HA	de Havilland DHC-8-102	152	ex C-GFUM	Piedmont Airlines	
N940HA	de Havilland DHC-8-102	156	ex C-GLOT	Piedmont Airlines	
N941HA	de Havilland DHC-8-102	161	ex C-GETI	Piedmont Airlines	
N942HA	de Havilland DHC-8-102	163	ex C-GFUM	Piedmont Airlines	
N943HA	de Havilland DHC-8-102	167	ex C-GFOD	Piedmont Airlines	
N964HA+	de Havilland DHC-8-102	343	ex N833MA	Piedmont Airlines	
N965HA>	de Havilland DHC-8Q-202	450	ex C-GFCF	Piedmont Airlines	
N966HA>	de Havilland DHC-8Q-202	452	ex C-GETI	Piedmont Airlines	
N968HA>	de Havilland DHC-8Q-202	465	ex C-GFBW	Piedmont Airlines	
N969HA>	de Havilland DHC-8Q-202	468	ex C-FDHD	Piedmont Airlines	
N975HA	de Havilland DHC-8-102	176	ex C-GEWQ	Piedmont Airlines	
N979HA"	de Havilland DHC-8-102A	373	ex C-GFQL	Piedmont Airlines	
N980HA"	de Havilland DHC-8-102A	376	ex C-GFBW	Piedmont Airlines	
N981HA"	de Havilland DHC-8-102A	378	ex C-GDNG	Piedmont Airlines	
N982HA"	de Havilland DHC-8-102A	380	ex C-FWBB	Piedmont Airlines	
N983HA>	de Havilland DHC-8Q-201	478	ex C-GEMU	Piedmont Airlines	
N984HA"	de Havilland DHC-8-102A	377	ex N823EX	Piedmont Airlines	
N985HA>	de Havilland DHC-8Q-201	479	ex C-GEOZ	Piedmont Airlines	
N986HA^	de Havilland DHC-8-201	421	ex C-GFYI	Piedmont Airlines	
N987HA^	de Havilland DHC-8-201	425	ex C-GFHZ	Piedmont Airlines	
N988HA^	de Havilland DHC-8-201	426	ex C-FDHD	Piedmont Airlines	
N989HA^	de Havilland DHC-8-201	427	ex C-GFEN	Piedmont Airlines	
N990HA^	de Havilland DHC-8-201	428	ex C-GDKL	Piedmont Airlines	
N991HA^	de Havilland DHC-8-201	431	ex C-GLOT	Piedmont Airlines	
N992HA^	de Havilland DHC-8-201	432	ex C-GFQL	Piedmont Airlines	
N996HA>	de Havilland DHC-8Q-201	497	ex C-GDIW	Piedmont Airlines	
N997HA>	de Havilland DHC-8Q-202	507	ex C-GFRP	Piedmont Airlines	
N998HA>	de Havilland DHC-8Q-202	509	ex C-GFYI	Piedmont Airlines	
N+	de Havilland DHC-8-314	290	ex SU-UAD	Piedmont Airlines	

*Leased from GECAS   +Leased from Bombardier
^Leased from CIT Group/Corporate Avn   "Leased fr WFBN
<Leased from Westinghouse Aircraft Leasing   >Leased from Wachovia Trust Co
Thirteen de Havilland DHC-8-100s to be returned; only 82 believed in use

Reg	Type	MSN	ex	Operator	Notes
N328JS	Dornier 328-100	3030	ex D-CDHP	PSA Airlines	Lsd fr WFBN
N422JS	Dornier 328-100	3018	ex D-CDHC	PSA Airlines	Lsd fr WFBN
N423JS	Dornier 328-100	3032	ex D-CDHR	PSA Airlines	Lsd fr WFBN
N424JS	Dornier 328-100	3033	ex D-CDHS	PSA Airlines	Lsd fr WFBN
N425JS	Dornier 328-100	3037	ex D-CDXC	PSA Airlines	Lsd fr WFBN
N426JS	Dornier 328-100	3038	ex D-CDXD	PSA Airlines	Lsd fr WFBN
N427JS	Dornier 328-100	3039	ex D-CDXE	PSA Airlines	Lsd fr WFBN
N429JS	Dornier 328-100	3043	ex D-CDXJ	PSA Airlines	Lsd fr WFBN
N430JS	Dornier 328-100	3044	ex D-CDXK	PSA Airlines	Lsd fr WFBN
N431JS	Dornier 328-100	3028	ex D-CDHN	PSA Airlines	Lsd fr WFBN
N432JS	Dornier 328-100	3045	ex D-CDXL	PSA Airlines	Lsd fr WFBN
N433JS	Dornier 328-100	3047	ex D-CDXN	PSA Airlines	Lsd fr WFBN
N434JS	Dornier 328-100	3051	ex D-CDXS	PSA Airlines	Lsd fr WFBN
N436JS	Dornier 328-100	3052	ex D-CDXT	PSA Airlines	Lsd fr WFBN
N437JS	Dornier 328-100	3055	ex D-CDXW	PSA Airlines	Lsd fr WFBN
N439JS	Dornier 328-100	3057	ex D-CDXY	PSA Airlines	Lsd fr WFBN
N440JS	Dornier 328-100	3058	ex D-CDXZ	PSA Airlines	Lsd fr WFBN
N441JS	Dornier 328-100	3059	ex D-CDXA	PSA Airlines	Lsd fr WFBN
N442JS	Dornier 328-100	3060	ex D-CDXC	PSA Airlines	Lsd fr WFBN
N457PS	Dornier 328-100	3048	ex D-CDXP	PSA Airlines	Lsd fr WFBN
N458PS	Dornier 328-100	3068	ex D-CDXS	PSA Airlines	Lsd fr WFBN
N459PS	Dornier 328-100	3070	ex D-CDXW	PSA Airlines	Lsd fr WFBN
N460PS	Dornier 328-100	3061	ex D-CDXD	PSA Airlines	
N461PS	Dornier 328-100	3075	ex D-CDXC	PSA Airlines	Lsd fr WFBN
N462PS	Dornier 328-110	3084	ex N328ML	PSA Airlines	Lsd fr WFBN
N463PS	Dornier 328-110	3087	ex N329ML	PSA Airlines	Lsd fr Dornier
N470PS	Dornier 328-110	3006	ex N328PH	PSA Airlines	Lsd fr WFBN
N471PS	Dornier 328-110	3007	ex N329PH	PSA Airlines	Lsd fr WFBN
N472PS	Dornier 328-110	3008	ex D-CDAN	PSA Airlines	Lsd fr WFBN
N258JQ	Embraer EMB.145LR	145768	ex PT-SJZ	Chautauqua	
N259JQ	Embraer EMB.145LR	145763	ex PT-SJU	Chautauqua	
N260SK	Embraer EMB.145LR	145128	ex PT-SDF	Chautauqua	
N261SK	Embraer EMB.145LR	145144	ex PT-SDU	Chautauqua	
N262SK	Embraer EMB.145LR	145168	ex PT-S	Chautauqua	
N263SK	Embraer EMB.145LR	145199	ex PT-S	Chautauqua	
N264SK	Embraer EMB.145LR	145221	ex PT-S	Chautauqua	
N265SK	Embraer EMB.145LR	145226	ex PT-S	Chautauqua	
N266SK	Embraer EMB.145LR	145241	ex PT-SIG	Chautauqua	
N267SK	Embraer EMB.145LR	145268	ex PT-SJK	Chautauqua	
N268SK	Embraer EMB.145LR	145270	ex PT-SJM	Chautauqua	
N269SK	Embraer EMB.145LR	145293	ex PT-SKK	Chautauqua	
N280SK	Embraer EMB.145LR	145381	ex PT-SQF	Chautauqua	
N281SK	Embraer EMB.145LR	145391	ex PT-S	Chautauqua	
N282SK	Embraer EMB.145LR	145409	ex PT-STG	Chautauqua	
N283SK	Embraer EMB.145LR	145424	ex PT-STV	Chautauqua	
N284SK	Embraer EMB.145LR	145427	ex PT-STY	Chautauqua	
N285SK	Embraer EMB.145LR	145435	ex PT-SUG	Chautauqua	
N286SK	Embraer EMB.145LR	145443	ex PT-SUO	Chautauqua	
N287SK	Embraer EMB.145LR	145460	ex PT-SVF	Chautauqua	
N288SK	Embraer EMB.145LR	145461	ex PT-SVG	Chautauqua	
N289SK	Embraer EMB.145LR	145463	ex PT-SVI	Chautauqua	
N291SK	Embraer EMB.145LR	145486	ex PT-SXF	Chautauqua	
N293SK	Embraer EMB.145LR	145500	ex PT-SXT	Chautauqua	
N298SK	Embraer EMB.145LR	145508	ex PT-SYA	Chautauqua	
N370SK	Embraer EMB.145LR	145515	ex PT-SYH	Chautauqua	
N971RP	Embraer EMB.145LR	145426	ex SX-BLO	Chautauqua	
N972RP	Embraer EMB.145LR	145440	ex SX-BLP	Chautauqua	
N	Embraer EMB.145LR	145444	ex SX-BLR	Chautauqua	
N	Embraer EMB.145LR			Chautauqua	o/o
N	Embraer EMB.145LR			Chautauqua	o/o
N	Embraer EMB.145LR			Chautauqua	o/o
N	Embraer EMB.145LR			Chautauqua	o/o
N	Embraer EMB.145LR			Chautauqua	o/o
N	Embraer EMB.145LR			Chautauqua	o/o
N	Embraer EMB.145LR			Chautauqua	o/o
N	Embraer EMB.145LR			Chautauqua	o/o
N	Embraer EMB.145LR			Chautauqua	o/o
N825MJ*	Embraer EMB.145LR	145179		Mesa - US Airways	
N826MJ*	Embraer EMB.145LR	145214		Mesa - US Airways	
N827MJ*	Embraer EMB.145LR	145217		Mesa - US Airways	
N828MJ*	Embraer EMB.145LR	145218		Mesa - US Airways	
N829MJ*	Embraer EMB.145LR	145228	ex PT-SHQ	Mesa - US Airways	
N830MJ*	Embraer EMB.145LR	145259	ex PT-SIS	Mesa - US Airways	
N831MJ*	Embraer EMB.145LR	145273	ex PT-SJP	Mesa - US Airways	
N832MJ*	Embraer EMB.145LR	145310	ex PT-SMB	Mesa - US Airways	
N833MJ*	Embraer EMB.145LR	145327	ex PT-SMT	Mesa - US Airways	

N834MJ*	Embraer EMB.145LR	145340	ex PT-SNG	Mesa - US Airways	
N835MJ*	Embraer EMB.145LR	145353	ex PT-SNS	Mesa - US Airways	
N836MJ*	Embraer EMB.145LR	145359	ex PT-SNY	Mesa - US Airways	
N837MJ*	Embraer EMB.145LR	145367	ex PT-SOR	Mesa - US Airways	
N838MJ	Embraer EMB.145LR	145384	ex PT-SQI	Mesa - US Airways	
N839MJ	Embraer EMB.145LR			Mesa - US Airways	on order
N840MJ	Embraer EMB.145LR	145429	ex PT-SUA	Mesa - US Airways	
N841MJ	Embraer EMB.145LR	145448	ex PT-S	Mesa - US Airways	
N842MJ*	Embraer EMB.145LR	145457	ex PT-SVC	Mesa - US Airways	
N843MJ*	Embraer EMB.145LR	145478	ex PT-SVX	Mesa - US Airways	
N844MJ*	Embraer EMB.145LR	145481	ex PT-SXA	Mesa - US Airways	
N845MJ*	Embraer EMB.145LR	145502	ex PT-SXV	Mesa - US Airways	
N846MJ*	Embraer EMB.145LR	145507	ex PT-SXZ	Mesa - US Airways	
N847MJ*	Embraer EMB.145LR	145517	ex PT-SYI	Mesa - US Airways	
N848MJ*	Embraer EMB.145LR	145530	ex PT-STU	Mesa - US Airways	
N849MJ*	Embraer EMB.145LR	145534	ex PT-STY	Mesa - US Airways	
N850MJ*	Embraer EMB.145LR	145568	ex PT-SBE	Mesa - US Airways	
N851MJ*	Embraer EMB.145LR	145572	ex PT-S	Mesa - US Airways	on order
N852MJ*	Embraer EMB.145LR	145567	ex PT-SBD	Mesa - US Airways	
N853MJ*	Embraer EMB.145ER	145464	ex PT-SVJ	Mesa - US Airways	
N854MJ*	Embraer EMB.145ER	145490	ex PT-SXJ	Mesa - US Airways	
N855MJ*	Embraer EMB.145LR	145614	ex PT-SCZ	Mesa - US Airways	
N856MJ*	Embraer EMB.145LR	145626	ex PT-SDO	Mesa - US Airways	
N857MJ*	Embraer EMB.145LR	145765	ex PT-SJW	Mesa - US Airways	
N858MJ*	Embraer EMB.145LR	145767	ex PT-SJY	Mesa - US Airways	
N859MJ*	Embraer EMB.145LR	145769	ex PT-SMA	Mesa - US Airways	
N860MJ*	Embraer EMB.145LR	145773	ex PT-SMD	Mesa - US Airways	

*Leased from Wells Fargo Bank Northwest

N801MA	Embraer 170-100LR	170-00012	ex PT-	MidAtlantic	on order 04
N802MD	Embraer 170-100LR	170-00013	ex PT-	MidAtlantic	on order 04
N803MD	Embraer 170-100LR	170-00015	ex PT-	MidAtlantic	on order 04
N804MD	Embraer 170-100LR	170-00016	ex PT-	MidAtlantic	on order 04
N805MD	Embraer 170-100LR	170-00018	ex PT-	MidAtlantic	on order 04
N806MD	Embraer 170-100LR	170-00019	ex PT-	MidAtlantic	on order 04
N807MD	Embraer 170-100LR	170-00020	ex PT-	MidAtlantic	on order 04
N808MD	Embraer 170-100LR	170-00021	ex PT-	MidAtlantic	on order 04
N809MD	Embraer 170-100LR	170-00022	ex PT-	MidAtlantic	on order 04
N	Embraer 170-100LR		ex PT-	MidAtlantic	on order 04
N	Embraer 170-100LR		ex PT-	MidAtlantic	on order 04
N	Embraer 170-100LR		ex PT-	MidAtlantic	on order 04
N	Embraer 170-100LR		ex PT-	MidAtlantic	on order 04
N	Embraer 170-100LR		ex PT-	MidAtlantic	on order 04
N	Embraer 170-100LR		ex PT-	MidAtlantic	on order 04

A further 70 Embraer 170s are on order for delivery up to September 2006

N19XS	SAAB SF.340A	019	ex N19CQ	Shuttle America	
N35SZ	SAAB SF.340A	035	ex N35CQ	Shuttle America	
N40SZ	SAAB SF.340A	040	ex N40CQ	Shuttle America	
N43SZ	SAAB SF.340A	043	ex N43CQ	Shuttle America	
N95CQ	SAAB SF.340A	095	ex N95MQ	Shuttle America	
(N101SZ)	SAAB SF.340A	101	ex N101CN	Shuttle America	
N104CQ	SAAB SF.340A	104	ex N344BE	Shuttle America	
N108CQ	SAAB SF.340A	108	ex N345BE	Shuttle America	
N118SD	SAAB SF.340A	118	ex N118CQ	Shuttle America	
N123XS	SAAB SF.340A	123	ex N123CQ	Shuttle America	
N138SD	SAAB SF.340A	138	ex N138CQ	Shuttle America	
N140CQ*	SAAB SF.340A	140	ex N140N	Shuttle America	
N146SD	SAAB SF.340A	146	ex N146CQ	Shuttle America	
N148SD	SAAB SF.340A	148	ex N148CQ	Shuttle America	
N149SZ	SAAB SF.340A	149	ex N149CQ	Shuttle America	
N150CN	SAAB SF.340A	150	ex N346BE	Shuttle America	
N152CQ	SAAB SF.340A	152	ex N749BA	Colgan Air	
N157SD	SAAB SF.340A	157	ex N157CQ	Shuttle America	
N158SD	SAAB SF.340A	158	ex N158CQ	Shuttle America	
N233CJ	SAAB SF.340B	233	ex N233CH	Colgan Air	
N237MJ	SAAB SF.340B	237	ex N351BE	Colgan Air	
N239CJ	SAAB SF.340B	239	ex N352BE	Colgan Air	
N242CJ	SAAB SF.340B	242	ex N353BE	Colgan Air	
N252CJ	SAAB SF.340B	252	ex N252CH	Colgan Air	
N277MJ	SAAB SF.340B	277	ex N357BE	Colgan Air	
N294CJ	SAAB SF.340B	294	ex N364BE	Colgan Air	
N299CJ	SAAB SF.340B	299	ex N365BE	ColganAir	
N340SF	SAAB SF.340A	014	ex SE-E14	Shuttle America	
N340SZ	SAAB SF.340A	004	ex N340CA	Shuttle America	
N360SZ	SAAB SF.340A	006	ex N360CA	Shuttle America	
N	SAAB SF.340			on order 2Q04; Colgan Air	
N	SAAB SF.340			on order 2Q04; Colgan Air	
N	SAAB SF.340			on order 2Q04; Colgan Air	
N	SAAB SF.340			on order 2Q04; Colgan Air	
N	SAAB SF.340			on order 2Q04; Colgan Air	
N	SAAB SF.340			on order 2Q04; Colgan Air	

N	SAAB SF.340			on order 2Q04; Colgan Air
N	SAAB SF.340			on order 2Q04; Colgan Air
N	SAAB SF.340			on order 2Q04; Colgan Air
N	SAAB SF.340			on order 2Q04; Colgan Air

*Leased from Banc of America Leasing
USAir Express is the operating name for feeder services operated by Allegheny Airlines, (a subsidiary), Chautauqua, Colgan Air, US Airways division of Mesa Air Group, MidAtlantic Airlines, Piedmont Airlines (a subsidiary), Shuttle America and PSA Airlines (a subsidiary) in conjunction with US Airways using US Airways' US designator. Other services are operated by Trans States Airlines

US AIRWAYS SHUTTLE fleet highlighted in parent US Airways

USA 3000 AIRLINES

Getaway (U5/GWY)   *Philadelphia-Intl, PA (PHL)*

G-BXKA	Airbus Industrie A320-214	0714	ex N714AW		Lsd fr TCW
G-BXKC	Airbus Industrie A320-214	0730	ex F-WWBQ		Lsd fr TCW
N260AV	Airbus Industrie A320-214	1564	ex F-WWBJ		Lsd fr Avn Financial Svs
N261AV	Airbus Industrie A320-214	1615	ex F-WWDR		Lsd fr WFBN
N262AV	Airbus Industrie A320-214	1725	ex F-WWBP	Miss Doreen	Lsd fr WFBN
N263AV	Airbus Industrie A320-214	1860	ex F-WWDQ		Lsd fr AFS Investments
N264AV	Airbus Industrie A320-214	1867	ex F-WWIL	Miss Janine	Lsd fr AFS Investments
N265AV	Airbus Industrie A320-214	0427	ex C-GJUL		Lsd fr ILFC
N266AV	Airbus Industrie A320-214	1152	ex I-PEKO		Lsd fr LIFT Ireland
N267AV	Airbus Industrie A320-214	1198	ex I-PEKP		Lsd fr LIFT Ireland

Seven Airbus Industrie A320-200s in total are to be leased from GECAS and one from GATX.
USA 3000 Airways is the trading name of Brendan Airways

USA JET AIRLINES

Jet USA (U7/JUS)   *Detroit-Willow Run, MI (YIP)*

N811AA	AMD Falcon 20D	187	ex N750R
N812AA	AMD Falcon 20C	57	ex N711KG
N815AA	AMD Falcon 20D	205	ex N4LH
N816AA	AMD Falcon 20E	290	ex I-TIAL
N817AA	AMD Falcon 20DC	233	ex I-TIAG
N818AA	AMD Falcon 20C	36	ex OE-GUS
N819AA	AMD Falcon 20C	26	ex N11827
N820AA	AMD Falcon 20C	118	ex F-GGKE
N821AA	AMD Falcon 20D	203	ex N36P
N822AA	AMD Falcon 20D	195	ex N195MP
N823AA	AMD Falcon 20D	228	ex OE-GRU
N826AA	AMD Falcon 20C	67	ex N821AA
N827AA	AMD Falcon 20E	298	ex OE-GNN
N1501	AMD Falcon 20C	15	
N191US	Douglas DC-9-15 (ABS 3)	17/45718	ex N300ME
N192US	Douglas DC-9-15RC	228/47156	ex N9357
N193US	Douglas DC-9-15RC	242/45828	ex N566PC
N194US	Douglas DC-9-15RC (ABS 3)	173/47016	ex N9349
N195US	Douglas DC-9-15RC (ABS 3)	186/47017	ex N9352
N196US	Douglas DC-9-15RC (ABS 3)	216/47155	ex N9355
N197US	Douglas DC-9-15RC (ABS 3)	201/47154	ex N901CK
N198US	Douglas DC-9-15RC (ABS 3)	184/47045	ex N902CK
N199US	Douglas DC-9-15RC (ABS 3)	185/47153	ex N567PC
N205US	Douglas DC-9-32CF	843/47690	ex N724HB
N207US	Douglas DC-9-32F (ABS 3)	452/47355	ex N932F
N208US	Douglas DC-9-32F (ABS 3)	296/47220	ex N935F
N327US	Douglas DC-9-33F (ABS 3)	536/47414	ex N940F
N829AA	LearJet 25B	25B-100	ex N25TK
N984AA	Beech 65-B90 King Air	LJ-429	ex N811AA

All freighters, shares a common ownership with Active Aero Charter

US FOREST SERVICE

     Boise, ID (BOI)

N110Z	Beech 58P Baron	TJ-213	
N112Z	Beech 58P Baron	TJ-371	
N121Z	Beech 58P Baron	TJ-285	
N123Z	Beech 58P Baron	TJ-211	ex N144Z
N132Z	Beech 58P Baron	TJ-284	
N133Z	Beech 58P Baron	TJ-367	
N135Z	Beech 58P Baron	TJ-247	ex N163Z
N145Z	Beech 58P Baron	TJ-289	
N146Z	Beech 58P Baron	TJ-426	ex N120Z
N150Z	Beech 58P Baron	TJ-425	
N152Z	Beech 58 TC Baron	TK-33	ex N8008A

N153Z	Beech 58P Baron	TJ-322	ex N23RT
N155Z	Beech 58P Baron	TJ-368	
N158Z	Beech 58P Baron	TJ-180	
N159Z	Beech 58P Baron	TJ-178	
N162Z	Beech 58P Baron	TJ-433	ex N63967
N164Z	Beech 58P Baron	TJ-290	
N165Z	Beech 58P Baron	TJ-314	ex N130Z
N166Z	Beech 58P Baron	TJ-442	ex N6559X
N100Z	Cessna 550 Citation Bravo	550-0926	ex N720B
N104Z	Beech 65-B90 King Air	LJ-472	
N106Z	Bell 206B JetRanger	508	ex N950NS
N107Z	Beech B200C Super King Air	BL-124	
N109Z	Bell UH-I	20854	ex 69-16422
N111Z	Cessna TU206F Turbo Stationair	U20602919	
N115Z	Basler Turbo-67 (DC-3TP)	16819/33567	ex 44-77235
N126Z	Cessna TU206F Turbo Stationair	U20602367	ex N2399U
N127Z	Beech A100 King Air	B-179	ex N20EG
N136Z	Cessna TU206G Turbo Stationair 6	U20606923	ex N9659R
N141Z	de Havilland DHC-6 Twin Otter 300	803	
N142Z	Basler Turbo-67 (DC-3TP)	20494	ex N100Z
N143Z	de Havilland DHC-6 Twin Otter 300	437	ex N300LJ
N147Z	Aero Commander 500B	1432-152	
N171Z	Aero Commander 500B	1450-159	
N173Z*	Short SD.3-30	SH3116	ex 84-0469
N175Z*	Short SD.3-30	SH3115	ex 84-0468
N178Z*	Short SD.3-30	SH3119	ex 84-0472
N179Z*	Short SD.3-30	SH3109	ex 84-0462
N181Z	Beech 65-E90 King Air	LW-52	ex N74171
N182Z	Beech 200 Super King Air	BB-402	ex N318W
N191Z	de Havilland DHC-2 Beaver	1006	
N192Z	de Havilland DHC-2 Beaver	1347	
N197Z	de Havilland DHC-2 Beaver	11627	

*Operated for USDA Forest Service   Subsidiary of US Department of Agriculture

VIEQUES AIR LINK

Vieques (VI/VES)   **Vieques, PR (VQS)**

N148ES	Britten-Norman BN-2A-20 Islander	685	ex N143FS	
N663VL	Britten-Norman BN-2B-26 Islander	2110	ex N663J	
N861VL	Britten-Norman BN-2B-26 Islander	2155	ex N861JA	
N903VL	Britten-Norman BN-2A-26 Islander	2019	ex N2159X	
N904VL	Britten-Norman BN-2A-26 Islander	3014	ex HK-3813	no titles
N901VL	Britten-Norman BN-2A Mk.III Trislander	1003	ex N901TA	
N905VL	Britten-Norman BN-2A Mk.III Trislander	1048	ex N905GD	
N906VL	Britten-Norman BN-2A Mk.III Trislander	1060	ex N906GD	

VIKING EXPRESS ceased operations

VILLAGE AIR

Air Camai (R9/CAM)   **Bethel, AK (BET)**

N1668U	Cessna 207 Skywagon	20700268
N1809Q	Cessna 207A Stationair 8	20700787
N6312H	Cessna 207A Stationair 7	20700477
N6314H	Cessna 207A Stationair 7	20700478
N7320U	Cessna 207A Skywagon	20700397
N7389U	Cessna 207A Stationair 7	20700432
N7353Q	Cessna U206F Stationair	U20602180

Possibly changed operating name to Air Camai as code is now in their name

VINTAGE PROPS AND JETS

(VQ)   **New Smyrna Beach-Municipal, FL**

N51HN	Piper PA-31-350 Navajo Chieftain	31-7552068	
N112CH	de Havilland DHC-4A Caribou	63	ex C-GVYZ
N6141V	Beech D95A Travel Air	TD-614	
N7559L	Piper PA-31 Turbo Navajo B	31-7300946	
N59905	Piper PA-31-350 Navajo Chieftain	31-7652135	

VISION AIR

                                   Las Vegas North, NV (VGT)

| N228ST | Dornier 228-212 | 8240 | | Inner Canyon Air titles |
| N402VA | Dornier 228-202K | 8085 | ex G-BWEX | Lsd fr WFBN |

N403VA	Dornier 228-202K	8171	ex 9M-BAS		Lsd fr WFBN
N404VA	Dornier 228-203F	8120	ex N279MC		Lsd fr Vegas Jet Financial
N405VA	Dornier 228-203F	8144	ex N264MC		Lsd fr Vegas Jet Financial
N406VA	Dornier 228-202	8149	ex N265MC	std VGT	Lsd fr Vegas Jet Financial
N407VA	Dornier 228-201	8044	ex HZ-NC11	on order	Lsd fr Dornier One Lsg
N408VA	Dornier 228-201	8045	ex HZ-NC12	on order	Lsd fr Dornier One Lsg

N76CF	Piper PA-31-350 Navajo Chieftain	31-7552052	
N88MG	Piper PA-31-350 Navajo Chieftain	31-7652088	
N444EM	Piper PA-31-350 Navajo Chieftain	31-7752112	
N974CS	Piper PA-31-350 Navajo Chieftain	31-7652120	
N3587Y	Piper PA-31-350 Chieftain	31-8052121	
N27419	Piper PA-31-350 Navajo Chieftain	31-7752170	Spirit of Pearce Canyon
N27877	Piper PA-31-350 Navajo Chieftain	31-7952019	
N27910	Piper PA-31-350 Navajo Chieftain	31-7952044	Spirit of Lake Mead
N61510	Piper PA-31-350 Navajo Chieftain	31-7552019	
N62971	Piper PA-31-350 Navajo Chieftain	31-7752013	

| N401VA | Piper PA-31T3-T1040 | 31T-8275001 | ex N2489Y |
| N911VJ | Piper PA-42-720 Cheyenne III | 42-7800002 | ex N202VJ |

Vision Air (9M) is part owned subsidiary

VIVA AIRLINES did not start operations after backer withdrew support

WARBELOW'S AIR VENTURES

Ventaire (4W/VNA)   *Fairbanks-Intl, AK (FAI)*

N42WP	Piper PA-31-350 Chieftain	31-8252038	
N300ED	Piper PA-31-350 Navajo Chieftain	31-7852008	
N792FC	Piper PA-31-350 Navajo Chieftain	31-7552108	ex N492SC
N3527U	Piper PA-31-350 Navajo Chieftain	31-7952141	
N3582P	Piper PA-31-350 Chieftain	31-8052103	
N4082T	Piper PA-31-350 Chieftain	31-8152089	
N4434D	Piper PA-31-350 Navajo Chieftain	31-7552020	ex PH-ASC
N27755	Piper PA-31-350 Navajo Chieftain	31-7852148	
N59764	Piper PA-31-350 Navajo Chieftain	31-7652037	
N59829	Piper PA-31-350 Navajo Chieftain	31-7652081	

| N756DJ | Cessna U206G Stationair | U20604005 |
| N7380U | Cessna 207A Stationair 7 | 20700428 |

See also 40 Mile Air (Q5/MLA)

WARD AIR

                                                                          Juneau-Intl, AK (JNU)

N62353	de Havilland DHC-2 Beaver	1363	ex 58-2031	Lsd fr Red Leasing
N62355	de Havilland DHC-2 Beaver	1045	ex N67897	
N62357	de Havilland DHC-2 Beaver	1145	ex N64391	
N63354	de Havilland DHC-3 Otter	30	ex C-FWAF	Lsd fr Red Leasing
N93025	Cessna A185F Skywagon	18503163		
N93311	Cessna A185F Skywagon	18503217		

WEST AIR

PAC Valley (PCM)   *Fresno-Air Terminal, CA (FAT)*

N707FX	Cessna 208B Caravan I	208B0427
N713FX	Cessna 208B Caravan I	208B0438
N722FX	Cessna 208B Caravan I	208B0454
N726FX	Cessna 208B Caravan I	208B0465
N744FX	Cessna 208B Caravan I	208B0492
N748FX	Cessna 208B Caravan I	208B0503
N750FX	Cessna 208B Caravan I	208B0511
N754FX	Cessna 208B Caravan I	208B0526
N762FE	Cessna 208B Caravan I	208B0255
N763FE	Cessna 208B Caravan I	208B0256
N768FE	Cessna 208B Caravan I	208B0263
N771FE	Cessna 208B Caravan I	208B0267
N772FE	Cessna 208B Caravan I	208B0268
N781FE	Cessna 208B Caravan I	208B0278
N782FE	Cessna 208B Caravan I	208B0280
N785FE	Cessna 208B Caravan I	208B0283
N790FE	Cessna 208B Caravan I	208B0288
N844FE	Cessna 208B Caravan I	208B0149
N857FE	Cessna 208B Caravan I	208B0177
N872FE	Cessna 208B Caravan I	208B0200
N879FE	Cessna 208B Caravan I	208B0213
N886FE	Cessna 208B Caravan I	208B0190

N891FE	Cessna 208B Caravan I	208B0221
N892FE	Cessna 208B Caravan I	208B0222
N908FE	Cessna 208B Caravan I	208B0008
N920FE	Cessna 208B Caravan I	208B0020
N930FE	Cessna 208B Caravan I	208B0030
N968FE	Cessna 208B Caravan I	208B0090
N969FE	Cessna 208B Caravan I	208B0092
N984FE	Cessna 208B Caravan I	208B0115
N985FE	Cessna 208B Caravan I	208B0117
N987FE	Cessna 208B Caravan I	208B0201
N995FE	Cessna 208B Caravan I	208B0133

All leased from and operated on behalf of FedEx

WESTERN AIR EXPRESS

Western Express (WAE)

Boise, ID (BOI)

N158WA	Swearingen SA.226TC Metro II	TC-411	ex N5974V
N159WA	Swearingen SA.226TC Metro II	TC-334	ex N341PL
N160WA	Swearingen SA.226TC Metro IIA	TC-399	ex N56EA
N161WA	Swearingen SA.226TC Metro	TC-208	ex C-GEMM
N162WA	Swearingen SA.226TC Metro IIA	TC-418	ex C-GRET
N6367X	Cessna 402B	402B1330	
N7947Q	Cessna 402B	402B0397	
N9868	Cessna 402B	402B1044	

WESTERN AIR EXPRESS

Lubbock-Intl, TX (LBB)

N6AQ	Beech 65-A80 Queen Air	LD-214
N20NP	Beech 65-B80 Queen Air	LD-433
N5376M	Beech 65-B80 Queen Air	LD-301
N7817L	Beech 65-B80 Queen Air	LD-340
N8071R	Beech 65-B80 Queen Air	LD-420

All freighters

WEST ISLE AIR

Westisle Air (WIL)

Anacortes, WA (OTS)

N120JD	Piper PA-31-350 Panther	31-8152179		Lsd fr MRR
N1584U	Cessna 207 Skywagon	20700184		
N7405	Cessna T207 Turbo Skywagon	20700147		
N8313Q	Cessna U206F Stationair	U20603174		
N8768Q	Cessna U206F Stationair	U20603521		
N9428G	Cessna U206E Stationair	U20601628		
N29068	Cessna U206C Super Skywagon	U206-1049		

WESTWIND AVIATION

Phoenix-Deer Valley, AZ (DVT)

N208WW	Cessna 208B Caravan I	208B0721		
N402AT	Cessna 402B	402B0612		
N456MA	Cessna U206G Stationair 6	U20604325		
N756LK	Cessna U206G Stationair 6	U20604174		
N785WW	Cessna 208B Caravan I	208B0792	ex N5267T	Lsd fr Ace Avn
N6241B	Cessna T210M Centurion	21062719		
N7255B	Cessna 206H Stationair 6	20608038		
N9317M	Cessna T207A Turbo Stationair 8	20700680		
N9482M	Cessna T207A Turbo Stationair 8	20700698		
N9527M	Cessna T207A Turbo Stationair 8	20700701		
N72436	Cessna TU206D Turbo Skywagon	U206-1403		
N	Aerospatiale/Alenia ATR 42-300	209	ex N209AT	on order

WIGGINS AIRWAYS

Wiggins (WIG)

Norwood-Memorial, MA (OWD)

N191WA	Beech C99	U-136	ex C-GCPF	
N192WA	Beech C99	U-152	ex C-GEOI	
N193WA	Beech 99	U-17	ex N10MV	
N194WA	Beech 99	U-64	ex C-FAWX	
N195WA	Beech 99	U-91	ex N533SK	Freighter
N196WA	Beech 99	U-68	ex N900AR	
N197WA	Beech 99A	U-130	ex C-FOZU	stored YPQ
N199WA	Beech B99	U-154	ex N99CH	

N701FX	Cessna 208B Caravan I	208B0420			
N725FX	Cessna 208B Caravan I	208B0460			
N731FX	Cessna 208B Caravan I	208B0480			
N748FE	Cessna 208B Caravan I	208B0241			
N755FX	Cessna 208B Caravan I	208B0529			
N757FX	Cessna 208B Caravan I	208B0535			
N780FE	Cessna 208B Caravan I	208B0277			
N783FE	Cessna 208B Caravan I	208B0281			
N789FE	Cessna 208B Caravan I	208B0287			
N804FE	Cessna 208B Caravan I	208B0039	ex F-GETN		
N807FE	Cessna 208B Caravan I	208B0041	ex F-GETO		
N835FE	Cessna 208A Caravan I	20800016	ex EI-FEX		
N865FE	Cessna 208B Caravan I	208B0188			
N870FE	Cessna 208B Caravan I	208B0196			
N888FE	Cessna 208B Caravan I	208B0217			
N898FE	Cessna 208B Caravan I	208B0228			
N901FE	Cessna 208B Caravan I	208B0001	ex N9767F		
N909FE	Cessna 208B Caravan I	208B0009			
N919FE	Cessna 208B Caravan I	208B0019			
N931FE	Cessna 208B Caravan I	208B0031			
N935FE	Cessna 208B Caravan I	208B0035			
N937FE	Cessna 208B Caravan I	208B0037			
N947FE	Cessna 208B Caravan I	208B0050	ex (N950FE)		
N958FE	Cessna 208B Caravan I	208B0071			
N959FE	Cessna 208B Caravan I	208B0073			
N963FE	Cessna 208B Caravan I	208B0080			
N966FE	Cessna 208B Caravan I	208B0086			
N981FE	Cessna 208B Caravan I	208B0110			
N989FE	Cessna 208B Caravan I	208B0124			
N996FE	Cessna 208B Caravan I	208B0135			
N998FE	Cessna 208B Caravan I	208B0139			

All leased from and operated on behalf of Fedex

N37WA	Bell 206B Jet Ranger III	3433	ex N70TV		
N505TV	Bell 206B JetRanger	3096	ex N112SC		
N656WA	de Havilland DHC-6 Twin Otter 100	47	ex N56AN	Freighter	
N5749U	Bell 206B JetRanger III	3106			

All, except Caravans, leased from Piper East

WILLOW AIR

Willow-Lake SPB, AK (WOW)

N98JH	de Havilland DHC-2 Beaver	953	ex 5-3 RNAF	

WINGS OF ALASKA

Wings Alaska (K5/WAK)

Juneau-Intl, AK (JNU)

N47AK	de Havilland DHC-2 Beaver	726	ex N43447	
N90AK	de Havilland DHC-2 Beaver	438	ex N5158G	
N91AK	de Havilland DHC-2 Beaver	737	ex C-GAEU	
N450DB	de Havilland DHC-2 Beaver	1309	ex C-GWPF	
N470DB	de Havilland DHC-2 Beaver	917	ex N67669	Lsd fr Wings Airline Sve
N67676	de Havilland DHC-2 Beaver	809	ex N93AK	Lsd fr Venture Travel
N335AK	de Havilland DHC-3 Otter	263	ex C-FOMS	
N336AK	de Havilland DHC-3 Otter	333	ex N567KA	
N337AK	de Havilland DHC-3 Otter	418	ex N2783J	
N338AK	de Havilland DHC-3 Otter	262	ex N62355	
N339AK	de Havilland DHC-3 Otter	454	ex N28TH	
N39AK	Cessna 207A Stationair 8	20700597	ex N73482	
N43AK	Cessna U206G Stationair 6	U20605545	ex N4811X	
N53AK	Cessna U206G Stationair 6	U20604823	ex N734CX	
N62AK	Cessna 207A Stationair 8	20700780	ex N9997M	
N332AK	Cessna 208B Caravan I	208B0779	ex N5264S	Lsd fr Wild Goose Air

Operate on floats or wheels/skis
Wings of Alaska is the trading name of Alaska Juneau Aeronautics

---

WOODS AIR

Palmer, AK (PAQ)

N50CM	Douglas DC-3	13445	ex		
N777YA	Douglas DC-3	25634/14189	ex	Arctic Liner	ski equipped

WORLD AIRWAYS

World (WO/WOA)

N303WL	Douglas DC-10-30F	211/46917	ex N13086	303	Lsd fr ILFC
N304WL	Douglas DC-10-30F	192/47928	ex N17087	304	Lsd fr ILFC
N352WL	Douglas DC-10-30F	338/47838	ex G-GOKT	352	Lsd fr Polaris
N353WL	Douglas DC-10-30	446/48318	ex N117GB	353	Lsd fr Aerospace Finance
N526MD	Douglas DC-10-30F	267/46998	ex OO-LRM	302, std GYR	Lsd fr Boeing Capital
N541SA	Douglas DC-10-30F	281/46541	ex C-GCPD		
N14075	Douglas DC-10-30	221/46922			
N271WA	McDonnell-Douglas MD-11	525/48518		271	Lsd fr ILFC
N272WA	McDonnell-Douglas MD-11	506/48437		272	Lsd fr ILFC, sublsd to EIN
N273WA	McDonnell-Douglas MD-11	539/48519		273	Lsd fr ILFC
N274WA	McDonnell-Douglas MD-11F	563/48633		274	Lsd fr ILFC
N275WA	McDonnell-Douglas MD-11CF	579/48631		275	Lsd fr ILFC
N276WA	McDonnell-Douglas MD-11CF	582/48632		276	Lsd fr ILFC
N277WA	McDonnell-Douglas MD-11ER	590/48743	ex N6203D	277	Lsd fr BCC Equipment Lsg
N278WA	McDonnell-Douglas MD-11ER	597/48746	ex N9020Q	278	Lsd fr BCC Equipment Lsg
N279WA	McDonnell-Douglas MD-11	623/48756	ex	279	Lsd fr CBSA Partners
N803DE	McDonnell-Douglas MD-11	485/48474	ex N30075		Lsd fr DAL
N804DE	McDonnell-Douglas MD-11	489/48475			Lsd fr DAL

World also operate short and long term leases for other airlines
Filed Chapter 11 12 February 1999 but operations continue

WRIGHT AIR SERVICE

(8V)

N32WA	Cessna 208B Caravan I	208B0234	ex C-FKEL
N540ME	Cessna 208B Caravan I	208B0540	
N900WA	Cessna 208B Caravan I	208B0659	ex N52613
N976E	Cessna 208B Caravan I	208B0976	ex N5263D
N1323R	Cessna 208B Caravan I	208b0745	
N4365U	Cessna 208B Caravan I	208B0253	ex N208CC
N4637U	Cessna U206G Stationair 6	U20605017	
N9FW	Piper PA-31-350 Navajo Chieftain	31-7405468	ex N61441
N54WA	Piper PA-31-350 Navajo Chieftain	31-7652067	ex N942LU
N63MB	Piper PA-31-350 Navajo Chieftain	31-7852117	
N4637U	Cessna U206G Stationair 6	U20605017	
N7426L	Piper PA-31 Turbo Navajo B	31-812	
N27532	Cessna A185F Skywagon	18503688	
N73463	Cessna 207A Stationair 8	20700593	
N91027	Cessna 207 Skywagon	20700018	

OB - PERU (Republic of Peru)

AERO ANDINO

OB-1600	Pilatus PC-6/B2-H2 Turbo Porter	789	ex HC-BHL	
OB-	Britten-Norman BN-2A-6 Islander	187	ex C-GKMJ	on rebuild
OB-	Britten-Norman BN-2A-20 Islander	404	ex C-GIRH	on rebuild

AEROCONDOR

Condor-Peru (Q6/CDP)

OB-952	Beech B80 Queen Air	LD-348		Excalibur Queenaire conv
OB-1001	Cessna 207 Skywagon	20700055		
OB-1192	Cessna U206G Stationair 6	U20605538		
OB-1204	Cessna U206G Stationair 6	U20605800		
OB-1297	Beech 65-B90 King Air	LJ-326	ex N7702	Fray Gregorio
OB-1593	Beech 65-B90 King Air	LJ-477	ex N7777	
OB-1594	Beech 65-B90 King Air	LJ-322	ex N45SC	
OB-1616	Cessna U206B Super Skywagon	U206-0878	ex N3878G	
OB-1627	Fokker F.27 Friendship 100	10116	ex YV-929C	for sale
OB-1650	Antonov An-24RV	37308802	ex YR-AMH	stored LIM Lsd fr TAR Aeroregional
OB-1651	Antonov An-24RV	27308303		
OB-1693-P	Fokker F.27 Friendship 200	10181	ex N863MA	Lsd fr Joda
OB-1700	Beech 200 Super King Air	BB-214	ex N26LE	CatPass 250 conv
OB-1740	Cessna 208B Caravan I	208B0735	ex N12652	Lsd fr Cessna
OB-1741	Cessna 208B Caravan I	208B0670	ex N1132D	Lsd fr Cessna
OB-1770	Fokker 50	20280	ex PH-LXU	Lsd fr AeroCentury
OB-	Boeing 737-2S3 (AVA 3)	577/21776	ex N369DL	

AERO CONTINENTE

Aero Continente (N6/ACQ) — Lima-Jorge Chavez Intl (LIM)

OB-1546-P	Boeing 727-22 (Raisbeck 3)	485/19150	ex N283AT	Lsd fr Intl A/l Investors
OB-1570-P^	Boeing 727-22	508/19153	ex N286AT	Lsd fr Intl A/l Investors
OB-1601-P	Boeing 727-51	203/18943	ex N288AT	Lsd fr Intl A/l Investors
OB-1728	Boeing 727-23	44/18433	ex P4-BAA	Lsd fr Air Ventures
OB-1738-P	Boeing 727-23	381/19432	ex P4-BAB	Lsd fr CS Aviation
OB-1759-P	Boeing 727-22 (Raisbeck 3)	507/19152	ex N932PG	Lsd fr Millennium A/c

^Subleased to Aviandina;

CC-CJM	Boeing 737-201	159/20212	ex N212US		Lsd fr Palm Aire Holdings
OB-1544	Boeing 737-2A9	386/20956	ex VT-EWA		Lsd fr Millennium A/c
OB-1620	Boeing 737-247	125/19615	ex N4518W		Lsd fr Intl A/l Investors
OB-1723-P	Boeing 737-204	162/19712	ex P4-ARC		Lsd fr Millennium Aircraft
OB-1729-P	Boeing 737-247	145/20128	ex XA-STB		Lsd fr Intl Pacific Trading
OB-1730-P	Boeing 737-201	61/19422	ex P4-CAD		
OB-1733	Boeing 737-222	50/19059	ex P4-SYX		Lsd fr Intl Pacific Trading
OB-1742-P	Boeing 737-247	126/19616	ex (CC-CJO (1))		Lsd fr Jet Aircraft Lsg
OB-1745	Boeing 737-130	3/19014	ex P4-ASA		Lsd fr Air Sweden
OB-1746-P	Boeing 737-281	235/20277	ex P4-ARA		Lsd fr Intl Pacific Trading
OB-1747	Boeing 737-201	244/20414	ex N219US	stored LIM	
OB-1751	Boeing 737-205	128/19409	ex XA-MAD		Lsd fr Nyckeln Flygleasing
OB-1752-P	Boeing 737-205	320/20711	ex XA-SWL		
OB-1753	Boeing 737-201	172/20214	ex CC-CJN		Lsd fr Palm Aire Holdings
OB-1754	Boeing 737-201	207/20215	ex CC-CJQ	stored LIM	Lsd fr Palm Aire Holdings
OB-1764-P	Boeing 737-201	159/20212	ex CC-CJM		
OB-1783-P	Boeing 737-222 (Nordam 3)	210/19955	ex HI-764CA		Lsd fr Airplane Holdings
	Boeing 737-242 (Nordam 3)	619/22074	ex N127GU	stored GUA	Lsd fr debis
	Boeing 737-2K5 (Nordam 3)	763/22596	ex N231TA	stored GUA	Lsd fr WFBN
	Boeing 737-296 (Nordam 3)	675/22277	ex N232TA		Lsd fr WFBN
	Boeing 737-2K5 (Nordam 3)	833/22601	ex N233TA		Lsd fr WFBN
	Boeing 737-205 (Nordam 3)	595/21765	ex N235TA	stored SAL	Lsd fr WFBN
	Boeing 737-242 (Nordam 3)	630/22075	ex N238TA	stored SAL	Lsd fr WFBN
	Boeing 737-205 (Nordam 3)	572/21729	ex N240TA		Lsd fr WFBN
	Boeing 737-2L9 (Nordam 3)	705/22408	ex N251LF	stored GUA	Lsd fr WFBN
	Boeing 737-2L9 (Nordam 3)	620/22071	ex N281LF		Lsd fr WFBN
	Boeing 737-2T5 (Nordam 3)	729/22395	ex N501NG		Lsd fr WFBN

OB-1735	British Aerospace Jetstream 31	762	ex N407UE		Lsd fr Jet Aircraft
OB-1750-P	Fokker F.28 Fellowship 1000	11097	ex N110AV		Lsd fr Intl A/l Investors
OB-1758-P	Boeing 767-205	81/23057	ex N650TW	Miguel Grau	Lsd fr ILFC
OB-1765-P	Boeing 767-2Q8B	272/24448	ex CC-CJR	Alfonso Ugarte	Lsd fr ILFC
OB-1766-P	Boeing 767-219ER	239/24150	ex CC-CJP	Francisco Bolognesi	Lsd fr ILFC
OB-1779-P	Fokker F.28 Fellowship 1000	11006	ex C-GTUU		Lsd fr Air Ventures
OB-1780-P	Fokker F.28 Fellowship 1000	11087	ex C-FCRK		
OB-1784T	British Aerospace Jetstream 3101	729	ex N401UE	tie-up not confirmed	
OB-1785T	British Aerospace Jetstream 3101	734	ex N402UE		
OB-1788-P	Boeeing 757-2G5	227/24451	ex N451GX		Lsd fr East-Trust Sub

Aero Continente Dominicana is wholly owned

AERO TRANSPORTE

ATSA (AMP) — Lima-Jorge Chavez Intl (LIM)

OB-1629	Piper PA-42 Cheyenne III	42-8001067	ex N183CC
OB-1630	Piper PA-42 Cheyenne III	42-8001022	ex N145CA
OB-1633	Piper PA-42 Cheyenne III	42-7801003	ex N134KM
OB-1667	Beech 1900C	UB-54	ex N815BE
OB-1687	Piper PA-42 Cheyenne III	42-8001016	ex N69PC
OB-1778-P	Antonov An-26B-100	14205	ex OB-1777-T

AERO TURISMO Y PUBLICIDAD   now listed under trading name, Magenta Air

AVIANDINA

Aviandina (SJ) — Lima-Jorge Chavez Intl (LIM)

OB-1570	Boeing 727-22	508/19153	ex N286AT	Lsd fr ACQ
OB-1748-P	Boeing 737-247	107/19547	ex N208AU	Lsd fr Palm Aire Holdings

CIELOS DEL PERU

Cielos (A2/CIU) — Lima-Jorge Chavez Intl (LIM)

N305FE	Douglas DC-10-30F	339/47870	ex (OE-ILD)	
N614GC	Douglas DC-10-30F	137/46931	ex N832LA	Lsd fr GCO
N831LA	Douglas DC-10-30F	147/46936	ex G-BWIN	Lsd fr GECC
N833LA	Douglas DC-10-30F	152/46937	ex N822BP	Lsd fr GECC

OB-1749   Douglas DC-10-30CF   127/46891 ex N105AM   Petete   Lsd fr CIT Leasing
Owned by STAF Carga; operates services for DHL; also leases McDonnell-Douglas MD-11F's from Gemini Air Cargo as and when required

FUERZA AÉREA DEL PERU

(FPR)   *Lima-Jorge Chavez Intl (LIM)*

OB-1379	Antonov An-32	0909		FAP-362; stored LIM
OB-1381	Antonov An-32	1001		FAP-366
OB-1382	Antonov An-32	1002		FAP-367; stored LIM
OB-1383	Antonov An-32	1003		FAP-376; stored LIM
OB-1386	Antonov An-32	1108		FAP-379
OB-1393	Antonov An-32	1305		FAP-387
OB-1640	Antonov An-32B	3002	ex TS-LCA	FAP-322
OB-1641	Antonov An-32B	2809	ex 48052	FAP-323
OB-1642	Antonov An-32B	2907	ex RA-48129	FAP-324
OB-1685	Antonov An-32B	3407		FAP-326
OB-1686	Antonov An-32B	3207	ex RA-48063	FAP-327
OB-1374	Lockheed L-382E Hercules	4706	ex OB-R-1183	FAP-382
OB-1375	Lockheed L-382E Hercules	4715		FAP-384
OB-1376	Lockheed L-382E Hercules	4358	ex N7985S	FAP-394
OB-1378	Lockheed L-382E Hercules	4853	ex N4119M	FAP-398
OB-1395	Lockheed C-130A Hercules	3177	ex 57-0470	FAP-396
OB-	Lockheed L-382E Hercules	4850	ex N4115M	FAP-397

All operated by Grupo Aereo 8 on domestic non-profit services

HELICOPTEROS DEL SUR / HELISUR

Iquitos (IQT)

OB-1584	Mil Mi-17TV	95432	
OB-1585	Mil Mi-8MTV1	223M103	
OB-1586	Mil Mi-8MTV1	223M104	
OB-1691	Mil Mi-17TV	96153	ex RA-27193

HELI-UNION PERU

Lima/Iquitos

Leases helicopters from Frontier Helicopters (C) or parent Heli-Union (F) as and when required

LAN PERU

LanPeru (LP/LPE) (IATA 544)   *Lima-Jorge Chavez Intl (LIM)*

VP-BCJ	Airbus Industrie A320-233	1491	ex CC-COG	Lsd fr LAN
VP-BCK	Airbus Industrie A320-233	1568	ex CC-COL	Lsd fr LAN
VP-BCS	Airbus Industrie A320-233	1854	ex (CC-COO)	Lsd fr LAN

49% owned by LANChile

LC BUSRE

Busre (LCB)   *Lima-Jorge Chavez Intl (LIM)*

N139LC	Swearingen SA.227TC Metro III	AC-732	ex XA-ACT	Lsd fr Joda
N239LC	Swearingen SA.227TC Metro III	AC-735	ex N523WA	Lsd fr Pacific Coast Grp
N386PH	Swearingen SA.227TC Metro III	AC-597	ex N3116T	Lsd fr Joda

MAGENTA AIR

Lima-Jorge Chavez Intl (LIM)

OB-1768	de Havilland DHC-8-102	128	ex C-FDOJ	Lsd fr Air Manitoba

Magenta Air is the trading name of Aero Turismo y Publicidad SA

RELOCATION SERVICE believed to have ceased operations

STAR UP

Star Up (SRU)   *Lima-Jorge Chavez Intl (LIM)*

OB-1717	Antonov An-24RV	27308010	ex ER-AFU	
OB-1734-P	Antonov An-24RV	17307006	ex ER-AFC	
OB-1769	Antonov An-24RV	57310110	ex ER-AWX	Leonid
OB-1772-P	Antonov An-26B	17310704	ex UR-26216	

TACA PERU

Trans Peru (ES/TPU) (IATA 530)   *Lima-Jorge Chavez Intl (LIM)*

N463TA	Airbus Industrie A320-233	1339	ex F-WWDN	Lsd fr TAI
N471TA	Airbus Industrie A319-132	1066	ex D-AVWE	Lsd fr TAI
N472TA	Airbus Industrie A319-132	1113	ex D-AVWU	Lsd fr TAI
N473TA	Airbus Industrie A319-132	1140	ex D-AVYP	Lsd fr TAI
N474TA	Airbus Industrie A319-132	1159	ex D-AVWD	Lsd fr TAI

Member of TACA Grupo; TACA Peru is the trading name of Trans American Airlines

TANS / TRANSPORTES AÉREOS NACIONALES DE LA SELVA

Aereos Selva (TJ/ELV)   *Lima-Jorge Chavez Intl (LIM)*

OB-1713	Boeing 737-244	82/19707	ex XA-SFR	350	
OB-1718	Boeing 737-248	147/19424	ex OB-1314		Lsd fr IAL Inc
OB-1719	Boeing 737-248	227/20221	ex CC-CVB		Lsd fr IAL Inc
OB-1724	Boeing 737-282	967/23042	ex VT-PDC	352	
OB-1781-P	Boeing 737-241	384/21001	ex PP-VMF		
OB-1782-P	Boeing 737-241	385/21002	ex PP-VMG		

Division of Fuerza Aerea del Peru/Peruvian Air Force

TAR AEROREGIONAL – TRANSPORTE AÉREO REGIONAL

Lima-Jorge Chavez Intl (LIM)

OB-1650	Antonov An-24RV	37308802	ex YR-AMH	Sentender	
OB-1651	Antonov An-24RV	27308303	ex OB-1571	Nino Jesus de Praga	
OB-1653	Yakovlev Yak-40	9041860	ex OB-1606	Christo Ascension	Lsd to Aerosur

OD - LEBANON (Republic of Lebanon)

FLYING CARPET

(FCR)   *Beirut (BEY)*

| OD-MAB | Swearingen SA.227AC Metro III | AC-604 | ex C-FNAL | Flying Group titles |

MIDDLE EAST AIRLINES

Cedar Jet (ME/MEA) (IATA 076)   *Beirut (BEY)*

F-OHLO	Airbus Industrie A320-232	0760	ex N681LF	all white	Lsd fr ILFC
F-ORME	Airbus Industrie A321-231	1878	ex D-AVZA		
F-ORMF	Airbus Industrie A321-231	1953	ex D-AVXF		
F-ORMG	Airbus Industrie A321-231	1956	ex D-AVZE		
F-ORMH	Airbus Industrie A321-231	1967	ex D-AVZI		
F-ORMI	Airbus Industrie A321-231	1977	ex D-AVZU		
F-ORMJ	Airbus Industrie A321-231	2055	ex D-AVZE		Lsd fr MEA SPC 6
F-OMEA	Airbus Industrie A330-243	527	ex F-WWKZ		Lsd fr ILFC
F-OMEB	Airbus Industrie A330-243	529	ex F-WWYB		Lsd fr ILFC
F-OMEC	Airbus Industrie A330-243	532	ex F-WWYC		Lsd fr ILFC

TMA CARGO

Tango Lima (TL/TMA) (IATA 270)   *Beirut/Sharjah (BEY/SHJ)*

OD-AGD	Boeing 707-323C (Comtran 2)	437/18939	ex N7560A	
OD-AGO	Boeing 707-321C (Comtran 2)	570/19269	ex N447PA	no titles
OD-AGP	Boeing 707-321C (Comtran 2)	594/19274	ex N452PA	
OD-AGS	Boeing 707-331C (Comtran 2)	626/19214	ex N5773T	
OD-AGX	Boeing 707-327C (Comtran 2)	498/19104	ex N7095	no titles; stored BEY
OD-AGY	Boeing 707-327C (Comtran 2)	499/19105	ex N7096	no titles; stored BEY
3D-JOE	Lockheed L-1011-500 Tristar	1243	ex C-GTSQ	Lsd fr Joasro Avn
3D-	Lockheed L-1011-500 Tristar	1242	ex C-GTSP	

TMA Cargo is the trading name of Trans Mediterranean Airways

OE - AUSTRIA (Republic of Austria)

AERO LLOYD AUSTRIA commenced operations 01 May 2003 but German parent ceased operations 16
October 2003 and Austrian subsidiary purchased by Niki Lauda and reformed as flyniki

AIR ALPS AVIATION

Alpav (A6/LPV)   *Innsbruck (INN)*

OE-LKA	Dornier 328-110	3110	ex D-COXI	Igls-Innsbruck
OE-LKB	Dornier 328-110	3036	ex HB-AEH	Commune di Tortoli'-Arbatax
OE-LKC*	Dornier 328-110	3119	ex D-CDXK	Regio Bodensee
OE-LKD*	Dornier 328-110	3072	ex HS-PBB	Discover the Sky titles
OE-LKE	Dornier 328-110	3063	ex D-CALP	
OE-LKF	Dornier 328-110	3073	ex D-CHOC	Lsd fr Erste Bank
OE-LKG	Dornier 328-110	3089	ex D-CGEP	
OE-	Dornier 328-110	3107	ex D-CGAP	

*Leased from Orest-Immorent Leasing

AMERER AIR

Amer Air (AMK)   *Linz (LNZ)*

OE-ILA	Lockheed L-188AF Electra	1145	ex LN-FOH	
OE-ILB	Lockheed L-188AF Electra	1039	ex N356Q	
OE-ILW	Fokker F.27 Friendship 500	10681	ex N505AW	Sissy; freighter

AUSTRIAN AIRLINES

Austrian (OS/AUA) (IATA 257)   *Vienna-Schwechat (VIE)*

OE-LBA	Airbus Industrie A321-111	0552	ex D-AVZH	Salzkammergut	
OE-LBB	Airbus Industrie A321-111	0570	ex D-AVZQ	Pinzgau	
OE-LBC	Airbus Industrie A321-111	0581	ex D-AVZS	Südtirol	
OE-LBD	Airbus Industrie A321-211	0920	ex D-AVZN	Steirisches Weinland	
OE-LBE	Airbus Industrie A321-211	0935	ex D-AVZR	Wachau	
OE-LBF	Airbus Industrie A321-211	1458	ex D-AVXE	Wien	
OE-LBN	Airbus Industrie A320-214	0768	ex F-WWDH	Ostirrol	
OE-LBO	Airbus Industrie A320-214	0776	ex F-WWDM	Pyhrn-Eisenwürzen	
OE-LBP	Airbus Industrie A320-214	0797	ex F-WWDV	Neusiedlersee	
OE-LBQ	Airbus Industrie A320-214	1137	ex F-WWDF	Wienerwald	
OE-LBR	Airbus Industrie A320-214	1150	ex F-WWBP	Bregenzer Wald; Star Alliance c/s	
OE-LBS	Airbus Industrie A320-214	1189	ex F-WWDV	Waldviertel	
OE-LBT	Airbus Industrie A320-214	1387	ex F-WWIS	Wörthersee	
OE-LBU	Airbus Industrie A320-214	1478	ex F-WWDS	Muhlvierter	
OE-LDA	Airbus Industrie A319-111	2131	ex D-AVWS		
OE-LDB	Airbus Industrie A319-111	2174	ex D-AVYP		
OE-LDC	Airbus Industrie A319-111	2262	ex D-AV	on order Sep04	

Four more Airbus Industrie A319-111s (to be registered OE-LDD to OE-LDG) are on order for delivery in 2005 (3) and 2006

OE-LAG	Airbus Industrie A340-212	075	ex F-WWJR	Europe	
OE-LAH	Airbus Industrie A340-212	081	ex F-WWJO	Asia	
OE-LAK	Airbus Industrie A340-313X	169	ex F-WWJC	Africa	
OE-LAL	Airbus Industrie A340-313X	263	ex F-WWJU	America	
OE-LAM	Airbus Industrie A330-223	223	ex F-WWKQ	Dachstein	
OE-LAN	Airbus Industrie A330-223	195	ex F-WWKJ	Arlberg	
OE-LAO	Airbus Industrie A330-223	181	ex F-WWKA	Grossglockner	Star Alliance c/s
OE-LAP	Airbus Industrie A330-223	317	ex F-WWYQ	Semmering	Lsd fr ILFC

OE-LAD	Airbus Industrie A310-325	624	ex EC-HIF		
OE-LFO	Fokker 70	11559	ex PH-EZV	Wiener Neustadt; dam 05Jan04	
OE-LFP	Fokker 70	11560	ex PH-EZW	Wels	
OE-LFQ	Fokker 70	11568	ex PH-EZC	Dornbirn	
OE-LFR	Fokker 70	11572	ex PH-EZD	Steyr	

OE-LMB	McDonnell-Douglas MD-82	1230/49279	ex (OE-LDQ)	Eisenstadt	Lsd fr Boeing Capital
OE-LMD	McDonnell-Douglas MD-83	1837/49933		Villach	
OE-LME	McDonnell-Douglas MD-83	2057/53377		Krems	
OE-LMK	McDonnell-Douglas MD-87(ER)	1412/49411		St Polten	
OE-LML	McDonnell-Douglas MD-87(ER)	1424/49412		Stadt Salzburg	
OE-LMN	McDonnell-Douglas MD-87	1682/49414		Klagenfurt all-white	
OE-LMO	McDonnell-Douglas MD-87	1692/49888		Bregenz	

Owns 36% of Lauda Air, 50.1% of Rheintalflug and 85.7% of Tyrolean Airways
Member of Star Alliance

AUSTRIAN ARROWS

Vienna-Schwechat (VIE)

Austrian Arrows is the trading name of Tyrolean Airways

BACHFLUG now operate executive charter flights

468

CHARTER AIR

Charter Wien (CHW)
Vienna-Schwecat (VIE)

OE-FRW	Cessna 414	414-0825	ex N98726	EMS
OE-FOW	Swearingen SA.226T Merlin IIIB	T-318	ex D-IBBD	EMS

EAGLE AIRLINES status uncertain, sole aircraft sold in USA

EUROHOPPER
Augsburg (AUB)

PH-JXJ	Fokker 50	20232	ex PT-SLJ	Lsd fr DNM
PH-PRJ	Fokker 50	20212		Lsd fr DNM

First service June 2003

FAIRLINE AIR
Graz (GRZ)

OE-GIF	SAAB SF.340A	100	ex G-GNTD		Lsd fr Teamline Air
OE-	SAAB 2000		ex	on order	Lsd fr Teamline Air

Due to begin operateions with SAAB 2000 from 12 January 2004; Teamline Air is a wholly owned subsidiary

FLYNIKI Renamed NIKI after Air Berlin purchased a 24% stake

FLYING BULLS
Salzburg (SZG)

OE-EDM	Cessna 208 Caravan I	20800257	ex N666CS	Amphibian
N996DM	Douglas DC-6B	1034/45563	ex V5-NCF	Red Bull; on rebuild
N6123C	North American B-25J Mitchell	44-86893A	ex 44-86893A	

Operate some pleasure flights as well as airshow appearances

GROSSMANN AIR SERVICES ceased all operations in May 2003 and filed for bankruptcy

JETALLIANCE now operate corporate charters only

LAUDA AIR

Lauda Air (NG/LDA) (IATA 231)
Vienna-Schwecat (VIE)

OE-LNJ	Boeing 737-8Z9	69/28177		Falco	
OE-LNK	Boeing 737-8Z9	222/28178	ex N1784B	Freddie Mercury	
OE-LNM	Boeing 737-6Z9	546/30138	ex N1795B		
OE-LNN	Boeing 737-7Z9	815/30418			
OE-LNO	Boeing 737-7Z9	874/30419			
OE-LNP	Boeing 737-8Z9	1100/30420		George Harrison	
OE-LNQ	Boeing 737-8Z9	1345/30421		Gregory Peck	

Three Boeing 737-8Z9s are on order for delivery in April 05, April 06 and June 06

OE-LAE	Boeing 767-3Z9ER	812/30383		Louis Armstrong	
OE-LAT	Boeing 767-31AER	393/25273	ex PH-MCK	Enzo Ferrari	Lsd to LDI
OE-LAU	Boeing 767-3Z9ER	165/23765	ex N6009F	Marilyn Monroe	Lsd to LDI
OE-LAW	Boeing 767-3Z9ER	448/26417		Imagination	Lsd to LDI
OE-LAX	Boeing 767-3Z9ER	467/27095		James Dean	
OE-LAY	Boeing 767-3Z9ER	731/29867	ex EC-HVG	Steve McQueen	Lsd to CFG
OE-LAZ	Boeing 767-3Z9ER	759/30331		Frank Sinatra	Lsd to CFG

OE-ILF	Boeing 737-3Z9	1254/23601		John Lennon; Star Alliance c/s	
OE-LNH	Boeing 737-4Z9	2043/25147	ex (I-BPAC)	Elvis Presley	Lsd to BBG
OE-LNI	Boeing 737-4Z9	2432/27094		Janis Joplin	
OE-LPA	Boeing 777-2Z9ER	87/28698	ex N5022E	Pablo Picasso	
OE-LPB	Boeing 777-2Z9ER	163/28699		Ernest Hemmingway	
OE-LPC	Boeing 777-2Z9ER	386/29313			
OE-LRF	Canadair CL-600-2B19	7061	ex C-FMNQ	Oskar Kokoschka	
OE-LRG	Canadair CL-600-2B19	7063	ex C-FMNY	Jean Tinguely	
OE-LRH	Canadair CL-600-2B19	7125	ex C-FMMB	Jochen Rindt	

36% owned by Austrian Airlines and 20% owned by Lufthansa; One Boeing 737 to be based at Bratislava from May 2004

Operates scheduled services for Austrian Airlines using OS/AUA designators in 3000 range. Member of Star Alliance

NIKI
Vienna-Schwecat (VIE)

(OE-LOF)	Airbus Industrie A320-232	0667	ex D-ALAF

469

OE-LOS   Airbus Industrie A321-231   1487 ex D-ALAS   Lsd fr ILFC
OE-   Airbus Industrie A320-2   ex   on order Apr04
OE-   Airbus Industrie A320-2   ex   on order Apr04
Originally wholly owned subsidiary of Aero Lloyd, commenced operations 01 May 2003 using parent's AEF code.
Parent ceased operations 16 October 2003; majority of Austrian subsidiary purchased by Niki Lauda. flyniki was the
trading name of NL Lufthhart. 24% owned by Air Berlin and will start as low-cost operator in April 2004 but renamed
NIKI in January 2004.

STYRIAN SPIRIT

Styrian (Z2/STY)   *Graz (GRZ)*

OE-LSC   Canadair CL-600-2B19   7299 ex N781BC   Lsd fr Bombardier Capital
OE-LSD   Canadair CL-600-2B19   7329 ex N786BC   Lsd fr Bombardier Capital
OE-LSS   Canadair CL-600-2B19   7283 ex N785BC   Lsd fr Bombardier Capital
First service 24 March 2003

TEAMLINE AIR

                                                                                      Augsburg (AGB)

OE-GIF   SAAB SF.340A   100   ex G-GNTD   Lsd to Fairline
OE-   SAAB 2000   ex   on order   Lsd to Fairline
Due to begin operateions with SAAB 2000 from 12 January 2004; Teamline Air is a wholly owned subsidiary of Fairline

TYROLEAN AIRWAYS

Tyrolean (VO/TYR) (IATA 734)   *Innsbruck (INN)*

OE-LCF   Canadair CL-600-2B19   7094   Stadt Düsseldorf
OE-LCG   Canadair CL-600-2B19   7103 ex C-FMNB Stadt Köln
OE-LCH   Canadair CL-600-2B19   7110 ex C-FMMB Stadt Amsterdam
OE-LCI   Canadair CL-600-2B19   7133 ex C-FMNB Stadt Zurich
OE-LCJ   Canadair CL-600-2B19   7142 ex B-3017 Stadt Hanover
OE-LCK   Canadair CL-600-2B19   7148 ex C-FMNB Stadt Brüssel
OE-LCL   Canadair CL-600-2B19   7167 ex B-3015 Stadt Oslo
OE-LCM   Canadair CL-600-2B19   7205   Stadt Bologna
OE-LCN   Canadair CL-600-2B19   7365 ex C-FMOI
OE-LCO   Canadair CL-600-2B19   7371 ex C-FMMX
OE-LCP   Canadair CL-600-2B19   7480 ex C-FMOW
OE-LCQ   Canadair CL-600-2B19   7605 ex C-FMOI
OE-LCR   Canadair CL-600-2B19   ex C-   on order Mar04
OE-LCS   Canadair CL-600-2B19   ex C-   on order Mar04
OE-LRE   Canadair CL-600-2B19   7059
One more Canadair CL-600-2B19 is on order for delivery in March 2005

OE-LGA   de Havilland DHC-8-402Q   4014 ex C-GDNG Land Kärnten
OE-LGB   de Havilland DHC-8-402Q   4015 ex C-GDOE Land Tirol
OE-LGC   de Havilland DHC-8-402Q   4026 ex C-GEVP Land Salzburg   Star Alliance c/s
OE-LGD   de Havilland DHC-8-402Q   4027 ex C-GEWI Land Steiermark
OE-LGE   de Havilland DHC-8-402Q   4042   Land Oberössterreich
OE-LGF   de Havilland DHC-8-402Q   4068 ex C-GERC Land Niederösterreich
OE-LGG   de Havilland DHC-8-402Q   4074 ex C-GFCF Stadt Budapest
OE-LGH   de Havilland DHC-8-402Q   4075 ex C-GFCW
OE-LLE   de Havilland DHC-8-106B   355   ex C-GFEN Ziltertal   Lsd to OAL
OE-LTD   de Havilland DHC-8Q-314   400   ex VH-TQB
OE-LTF   de Havilland DHC-8Q-314   423   ex VH-TQC
OE-LTG   de Havilland DHC-8Q-314   438   ex C-GDFT Land Kärtnen
OE-LTH   de Havilland DHC-8Q-314   442   ex C-GFUM Stadt Kitzbühel
OE-LTI   de Havilland DHC-8Q-314   466   ex C-GFQL
OE-LTJ   de Havilland DHC-8Q-314   481   ex C-GDOE Seefeld
OE-LTK   de Havilland DHC-8Q-314   483   ex C-GDFT Oetztal
OE-LTL   de Havilland DHC-8Q-314   485   ex C-GFYI Land Osterösterreich
OE-LTM   de Havilland DHC-8Q-314   527   ex C-   Achensee
OE-LTN   de Havilland DHC-8Q-314   531   ex C-   St Anton
OE-LTO   de Havilland DHC-8Q-314   553   ex C-FWBB Stadt Kuesstein
OE-LTP   de Havilland DHC-8Q-314   554   ex C-GDLK Stadt Lienz
Two more de Havilland DHC-8-402Qs are on order for delivery in 1H05

OE-LFG   Fokker 70   11549 ex PH-EZW Stadt Innsbruck   Star Alliance c/s
OE-LFH   Fokker 70   11554 ex PH-EZN Stadt Salzburg
OE-LFI   Fokker 70   11529 ex PH-WXF Stadt Klagenfurt
OE-LFJ   Fokker 70   11532 ex PH-WXG Stadt Graz
OE-LFK   Fokker 70   11555 ex PH-EZP Stadt Wien
OE-LFL   Fokker 70   11573 ex PH-WXE Stadt Linz
85.7% owned by Austrian Airlines. Operates scheduled services as 'Austrian Arrows, operated by Tyrolean' using OS/
AUA designators in 5000 range

TYROLEAN JET SERVICE

Tyroljet (TJS)

OE-HMS	Dornier 328-300	3121	ex D-BDXI	
OE-HTJ	Dornier 328-300	3114	ex D-BDXA	

Operates Ambulance flights as Tyrol Air Ambulance using code TYW
Associated with Welcome Air

WELCOME AIR

Welcomeair (2W/WLC)

OE-GBB	Dornier 328-110	3078	ex D-CDXG		Jt ops with Tyrol Air Ambulance
OE-LIR	Dornier 328-110	3115	ex D-CDX.	Phonix	
OE-LJR	Dornier 328-310	3213	ex D-BDX.	Aurora	

Associated with Tyrolean Jet Service

OH - FINLAND (Republic of Finland)

AIR BOTNIA renamed Blue1 on 01 January 2004

AIR FINLAND

Air Finland (OF/FIF)

OH-AFI	Boeing 757-2K2	717/26330	ex PH-TKD	Lsd fr ILFC
OH-AFJ	Boeing 757-28A	612/26269	ex N321LF	Lsd fr ILFC

BLUE1

Botnia (KF/BLW) (IATA 142)
Previously listed as Air Botnia but renamed on 01 January 2004

OH-SAH	Avro RJ-85	E2383	ex G-6-383	Suur-Saimaa	
OH-SAI	Avro RJ-85	E2385	ex G-6-385	PihlaJavesi	
OH-SAJ	Avro RJ-85	E2388	ex G-6-388	Pyhaselka	Lsd fr Steven Ltd
OH-SAK	Avro RJ-85	E2389	ex G-6-389	Nasijarvi	Lsd fr Steven Ltd
OH-SAL	Avro RJ-85	E2392	ex G-6-390	Orivesi	Lsd fr Steven Ltd
OH-SAM	Avro RJ-100	E3386	ex G-NBAA	Pyhäjärvi	Lsd fr BAES
OH-SAN	Avro RJ-100	E3387	ex G-CBMF	Päijänne	Lsd fr BAES
OH-SAO	Avro RJ-85	E2393	ex G-CBMG	Oulujärvi	
OH-SAP	Avro RJ-85	E2394	ex G-CBMH	Pielinen	
OH-SAS	SAAB 2000	044	ex SE-LSC	Inarijärvi	Lsd fr SAAB
OH-SAT	SAAB 2000	042	ex SE-LSA	Vanajavesi	Lsd fr SAAB
OH-SAU	SAAB 2000	043	ex SE-LSB	Kilpsjärvi	Lsd fr SAAB
OH-SAW	SAAB 2000	046	ex SE-LSE	Keitele	Lsd fr SAAB
OH-SAX	SAAB 2000	055	ex SE-LSG	Hiidenvesi	Lsd fr SAAB

Wholly owned by SAS

COPTERLINE

Copterline (AAQ)

OH-HCB	MBB Bo105CBS-4	S-396	ex N10360	
OH-HCC	MBB Bo105CBS-4	S-546	ex AB-6	
OH-HCD	MBB Bo105CBS-4	S-547	ex AB-7	
OH-HKI	MBB Bo105CBS-4	S-731	ex D-HECB	
OH-HMS	MBB Bo105CBS-4	S-703	D-HMBV	
OH-HCH	Eurocopter EC135P1	0008	ex D-HPOZ	
OH-HCI	Sikorsky S-76C	760508	ex N7600P	
OH-HCJ	Sikorsky S-76C	760510		
OH-HIF	Agusta-Bell 206B JetRanger	8372		

DELTACRAFT

Deltacraft (4L/DEC)

OH-BKA	Beech A100 King Air	B-39	ex HB-GEN	
OH-SBA	Short SC.7 Skyvan 3A	SH1906	ex SE-GEY	

FINNCOMMAIRLINES

(FC)

OH-EBE	Embraer EMB.145LU	145351	ex HB-JAI	Lsd fr SWR
OH-FAE	SAAB SF.340A/QC	139	ex SE-F39	Lsd fr FIN

OH-FAF   SAAB SF.340B   167   ex SE-F67   Lsd fr FIN
Operates codeshare flights for Finnair; FinnComm is the trading name of Finnish Commuter Airlines

FINNAIR

Finnair (AY/FIN) (IATA 105)   Helsinki-Vantaa (HEL)

Reg	Type	MSN	ex	note	Lsd
OH-KRA	Aerospatiale/Alenia ATR 72-201	126	ex (OH-LTN)		
OH-KRB	Aerospatiale/Alenia ATR 72-201	140	ex F-WWER		
OH-KRC	Aerospatiale/Alenia ATR 72-201	145	ex F-WWES		
OH-KRD	Aerospatiale/Alenia ATR 72-201	162	ex F-WWEM		
OH-KRE	Aerospatiale/Alenia ATR 72-201	174	ex F-WWEE		
OH-KRF	Aerospatiale/Alenia ATR 72-201	324	ex F-WWEU		
OH-KRH	Aerospatiale/Alenia ATR 72-201	212	ex F-WQIU		
OH-KRK	Aerospatiale/Alenia ATR 72-201	251	ex B-22706		Lsd to EAY
OH-KRL	Aerospatiale/Alenia ATR 72-201	332	ex B-22710		
OH-LVA	Airbus Industrie A319-112	1073	ex F-WWID		
OH-LVB	Airbus Industrie A319-112	1107	ex D-AVWS		
OH-LVC	Airbus Industrie A319-112	1309	ex D-AVWY		
OH-LVD	Airbus Industrie A319-112	1352	ex D-AVYW		
OH-LVE	Airbus Industrie A319-112	1791	ex D-AVYS		Lsd fr ILFC
OH-LVF	Airbus Industrie A319-112	1808	ex D-AVWG		Lsd fr ILFC
OH-LVG	Airbus Industrie A319-112	1916	ex D-AVYG		Lsd fr ILFC
OH-LVH	Airbus Industrie A319-112	1184	ex EI-CZE		Lsd fr Ensor A/c Lsg
OH-LVI	Airbus Industrie A319-112	1364	ex F-WQQZ		
OH-LVK	Airbus Industrie A319-112	2124	ex D-AVWB		Lsd fr ILFC
OH-	Airbus Industrie A319-112	2266	ex D-AV	on order Apr04	Lsd fr ILFC

One more Airbus Industrie A319-112 is on order for delivery in October 2005, leased from ILFC

Reg	Type	MSN	ex	note	Lsd
OH-LXA	Airbus Industrie A320-214	1405	ex F-WWDH		
OH-LXB	Airbus Industrie A320-214	1470	ex F-WWDO		
OH-LXC	Airbus Industrie A320-214	1544	ex F-WWIX		
OH-LXD	Airbus Industrie A320-214	1588	ex F-WWBQ		
OH-LXE	Airbus Industrie A320-214	1678	ex F-WWBB		Lsd fr Rain I LLC
OH-LXF	Airbus Industrie A320-214	1712	ex F-WWIY		Lsd fr SALE
OH-LXG	Airbus Industrie A320-214	1735	ex F-WWBM		Lsd fr Boullioun
OH-LXH	Airbus Industrie A320-214	1913	ex F-WWIZ		Lsd fr ILFC
OH-LXI	Airbus Industrie A320-214	1989	ex F-WWDN		Lsd fr ILFC
OH-LXK	Airbus Industrie A320-214	2065	ex F-WWIQ		Lsd fr ILFC
OH-LXL	Airbus Industrie A320-214	2146	ex F-WWDN		Lsd fr ILFC
OH-LXM	Airbus Industrie A320-214	2154	ex F-WWDP		
OH-LZA	Airbus Industrie A321-211	0941	ex D-AVZT		
OH-LZB	Airbus Industrie A321-211	0961	ex D-AVZU		
OH-LZC	Airbus Industrie A321-211	1185	ex D-AVZI		
OH-LZD	Airbus Industrie A321-211	1241	ex D-AVZG		
OH-LZE	Airbus Industrie A321-211	1978	ex D-AVZV		Lsd fr ILFC
OH-LZF	Airbus Industrie A321-211	2208	ex D-AV	on order Apr04	Lsd fr ILFC
OH-LBO	Boeing 757-2Q8	772/28172	ex N1789B		Lsd fr ILFC
OH-LBR	Boeing 757-2Q8	775/28167			Lsd fr ILFC
OH-LBS	Boeing 757-2Q8	792/27623	ex N5573K		Lsd fr ILFC
OH-LBT	Boeing 757-2Q8	801/28170			Lsd fr ILFC
OH-LBU	Boeing 757-2Q8	857/29377			Lsd fr ILFC
OH-LBV	Boeing 757-2Q8	1006/30046	ex N60659		Lsd fr ILFC
OH-LBX	Boeing 757-2Q8	1010/29382	ex N60668		Lsd fr ILFC
OH-LGA	McDonnell-Douglas MD-11	455/48449			Lsd fr BBAM
OH-LGB	McDonnell-Douglas MD-11	479/48450			Lsd fr BBAM
OH-LGC	McDonnell-Douglas MD-11	529/48512			
OH-LGD	McDonnell-Douglas MD-11	564/48513			
OH-LGE	McDonnell-Douglas MD-11	624/48780	ex P4-SWM		Lsd fr CBSA Partners
OH-	McDonnell-Douglas MD-11		ex	on order 04	Lsd fr Boeing Capital
OH-LMG	McDonnell-Douglas MD-83	1503/49625			Lsd fr PCG Acquisition
OH-LMH	McDonnell-Douglas MD-82	1978/53245			Lsd fr Gustav Lsg
OH-LMS	McDonnell-Douglas MD-83	1169/49252	ex N19B		Lsd fr Aircraft Trade & Investments
OH-LMW	McDonnell-Douglas MD-82	1767/49905			Lsd fr Gustav Lsg
OH-LMX	McDonnell-Douglas MD-82	1786/49906			Lsd fr ACQ Aquisitions
OH-LMY	McDonnell-Douglas MD-82	1901/53244	ex N19B		
OH-LMZ	McDonnell-Douglas MD-82	1918/53246			
OH-LPA	McDonnell-Douglas MD-82	1765/49900	ex EC-FJQ		Lsd fr ATEL Capital Equipment
OH-LPB	McDonnell-Douglas MD-83	2047/49966	ex SE-DLX		Lsd fr AAR International
OH-LPC	McDonnell-Douglas MD-83	2044/49965	ex SE-DLV		
OH-LPD	McDonnell-Douglas MD-83	1547/49710	ex EC-GFJ		Lsd fr Nordea Finans
OH-LPF	McDonnell-Douglas MD-83	1413/49574	ex EC-FVR		
OH-LPG	McDonnell-Douglas MD-83	1561/49708	ex EC-GKS		Lsd fr Nordea Finans
OH-LPH	McDonnell-Douglas MD-83	1499/49623	ex SE-DHN		
OH-FAE	SAAB SF.340A/QC	139	ex SE-F39		Lsd to FinnComm

OH-FAF	SAAB SF.340B	167	ex SE-F67		Lsd to FinnComm
OH-LYT	Douglas DC-9-51 (ABS 3)	830/47738			Lsd to LAV as YV-14C
OH-LYU	Douglas DC-9-51 (ABS 3)	883/47771			Lsd to LAV as YV-15C

Member of oneworld alliance; Aero Airlines is a wholly owned subsidiary while Finncomm operates feeder services

FLYING FINN AIRWAYS

Fly Finn (FFW)   *Helsinki-Vantaa (HEL)*

| OH-LMR | McDonnell-Douglas MD-83 | 1209/49284 | | Lsd fr Aviation 49284 Corp |
| OH-LMS | McDonnell-Douglas MD-83 | 1169/49252 | ex N19B | Lsd fr Aviation 49252 Corp |

Applied for bankruptcy protection 15 January 2004 and suspended international flights

SKAERGARDSFLYG ceased operations

SODER AIR

(SDE)   Tampere

| OH-SRC | SAAB 2000 | 006 | ex SE-006 |

TURKU AIR

Turku (TKU)

OH-PNU	Piper PA-31-350 Navajo Chieftain	31-7752027	ex N62993
OH-PNX	Piper PA-31-350 Chieftain	31-8052040	ex ES-PAG
OH-PNY	Piper PA-31-350 Navajo Chieftain	31-7652079	ex LN-SAB

UTIN LENTO

Utti

| OH-UDZ | Cessna T207A Turbine Skywagon | 20700388 | ex D-EXWG | Soloy conversion |
| OH-USI | Cessna 208 Caravan I | 20800275 | | |

WESTBIRD AVIATION

Westbird (WBA)   *Seinajoki (SJY)*

| OH-STA | Mitsubishi MU-2B | 1515SA | ex LX-TWO |
| OH-WBA | Mitsubishi MU-2N | 718SA | ex N150BA |

OK - CZECH REPUBLIC

ABA-AIR

Bair (ABP)   *Prague-Ruzyne (PRG)*

OK-ABA	Fokker F-27 Friendship 500CRF	10530	ex N737A		Op for UPS
OK-ABB	Fokker F-27 Friendship 500CRF	10531	ex N739A		Op for UPS
OK-BKS	Beech 65-C90 King Air	LJ-1430	ex N3251U	EMS	

BUD AIR

Plzen

| OK-PDC | LET L-410FG | 851524 | ex Czech AF 1524 | Photographic survey |

CSA CZECH AIRLINES

CSA Lines (OK/CSA) (IATA 064)   *Prague-Ruzyne (PRG)*

OK-AFE	Aerospatiale/Alenia ATR 42-420	487	ex F-WWEF	Kolin	To be retd Oct05
OK-AFF	Aerospatiale/Alenia ATR 42-420	491	ex F-WWLC	Kutna Hora	To be retd Nov05
OK-BFG*	Aerospatiale/Alenia ATR 42-320	409	ex F-OKMR	Rakovnik	Lsd fr ATR Asset Mgt
OK-BFH*	Aerospatiale/Alenia ATR 42-320	412	ex F-OKMS	Telc	Lsd fr ATR Asset Mgt
OK-JFJ	Aerospatiale/Alenia ATR42-512	623		on order Mar04	
OK-JFK	Aerospatiale/Alenia ATR42-512	625		on order Apr04	
OK-JFL	Aerospatiale/Alenia ATR42-512			on order Jul04	
OK-VFI	Aerospatiale/Alenia ATR 42-320	173	ex F-WQNE	Sky Rider	Lsd fr ATR Asset Mgt
OK-XFA	Aerospatiale/Alenia ATR 72-202	285	ex F-WWLO	Cesky Krumlov	
OK-XFB	Aerospatiale/Alenia ATR 72-202	297	ex F-WWLW	Znojmo	
OK-XFC	Aerospatiale/Alenia ATR 72-202	299	ex F-WWLX	Nitra	
OK-XFD	Aerospatiale/Alenia ATR 72-202	303	ex F-WWLB	Mlada Boleslav	

Four more Aerospatiale/Alenia ATR 42-512s are on order for delivery in Mar/Apr/Oct/Nov 2005 (OK-KFM-Q)
*To be returned April/June 2004

OK-BGQ	Boeing 737-43Q	2839/28494	ex N462PR	Karlovy Vary	Lsd fr Boullioun
OK-CGH	Boeing 737-55S	2849/28469		Usit nad Labem	
OK-CGI	Boeing 737-49R	2845/28882	ex N461PR	Prostejov	Lsd fr KG A/c Lsg
OK-CGJ	Boeing 737-55S	2861/28470		Hradec Kralove	
OK-CGK	Boeing 737-55S	2885/28471		Pardubice	
OK-CGT	Boeing 737-46M	2844/28549	ex OO-VEC	Pisek	Lsd fr Geonet
OK-DGL	Boeing 737-55S	3004/28472		Tabor; 80th anniversary colours	
OK-DGM	Boeing 737-45S	3014/28473		Trebon	
OK-DGN	Boeing 737-45S	3028/28474		Trebic	
OK-EGO	Boeing 737-55S	3096/28475		Jindrichuv Hradec	
OK-EGP	Boeing 737-45S	3103/28476		Kladno	
OK-FGR	Boeing 737-45S	3131/28477		Ostrava	
OK-FGS*	Boeing 737-45S	3132/28478		Brno	
OK-WGF	Boeing 737-4Y0	1978/24903	ex 9M-MJN	Jihlava	Lsd fr GECAS
OK-WGG	Boeing 737-4Y0	1972/24693	ex 9M-MJM	Liberec	Lsd fr GECAS
OK-XGA	Boeing 737-55S	2300/26539	ex (OO-SYL)	Plzen	
OK-XGB	Boeing 737-55S	2317/26540	ex (OO-SYM)	Olomouc	
OK-XGC	Boeing 737-55S	2319/26541	ex (OO-SYN)	Ceske Budejovice	
OK-XGD	Boeing 737-55S	2337/26542	ex (OO-SYO)	Poprad	
OK-XGE	Boeing 737-55S	2339/26543	ex (OO-SYP)	Kosice	
OK-XGV	Boeing 737-5H6	2327/26445	ex F-GJNQ		Lsd fr GECAS
OK-XGW	Boeing 737-5H6	2358/26446	ex F-GJNR		Lsd fr GECAS
OK-YGU	Boeing 737-4Q8	2486/26289	ex G-BUHK	Melnik	Lsd fr ILFC

*Last 'Classic' 737 built

OK-WAA	Airbus Industrie A310-304	564	ex F-WWCB	Praha	
OK-WAB	Airbus Industrie A310-304	567	ex F-WWCD	Bratislava	
OK-YAC	Airbus Industrie A310-325	672	ex F-OHPX		Lsd fr Airbus

Member of Sky Team alliance

FISCHER AIR

Fischer (8F/FFR) Prague-Ruzyne (PRG)

OK-FAN	Boeing 737-33A	2864/27469			
OK-FIT	Boeing 737-36N	3097/28590	ex N1787B		Lsd fr Boullioun
OK-FUN	Boeing 737-33A	2873/27910			

JOB AIR

Ostrava (OSR)

OK-VDA	LET L-410UVP-E	902403	ex RA-44477	

LR AIRLINES

Lady Racine (LRB) Ostrava (OSR)

OK-LRA	LET L-410UVP-E	882216	ex CCCP-67605	Lady Racine

OLIMEX ceased operations

SILVER AIR

Solid (SLD) Prague-Ruzyne (PRG)

OK-SLD	LET L-410UVP-E9	022634		Ceska Posta titles	
OK-WDT	LET L-410UVP-E	912615	ex CCCP-67684		Lsd fr VZLÚ

SMART WINGS

Prague-Ruzyne (PRG)

OK-	Boeing 737-500		ex	on order

Low-cost carrier, due to start operations 01 May 2004; sister company of Travel Service Airlines

TRAVEL SERVICE AIRLINES

Skytravel (QS/TVS) Prague-Ruzyne (PRG)

OK-TVA	Boeing 737-86N	869/32243			Lsd fr GECAS
OK-TVB	Boeing 737-8CX	1125/32362			Lsd fr GATX
OK-TVC	Boeing 737-86Q	963/30278	ex N289CD		Lsd fr Boullioun; sublsd to OAS
OK-TVD	Boeing 737-86N	285/28595	ex CN-RNO		Lsd fr GECAS
OK-TVQ	Boeing 737-86N	514/28618		Vitava	Lsd fr GECAS; sublsd to VSG
OK-TVR	Boeing 737-4Y0	1647/23870	ex G-OBMG		Lsd fr BBAM
OK-TVS	Boeing 737-4Y0	2033/24911	ex SE-DTB	Bubu	Lsd fr GECAS; sublsd to TVL

OK-	Boeing 767-200		ex	on order 3Q04

Travel Service Hungary (TVL) and Travel Service Espana are wholly owned subsidiaries while Smart Wings is a sister company operating as a low-cost carrier

OM - SLOVAKIA (Slovak Republic)

AIR SLOVAKIA

Slovakia (GM/SVK) *Bratislava-MR Stefanik (BTS)*

OM-DGK	Boeing 757-236	271/24772	ex N88AM	City of the Golden Temple
				Lsd fr IAI V Inc
OM-ERA	Boeing 737-2H4	568/21722	ex N57SW	stored BTS	Lsd fr CL Aircraft
OM-RAN	Boeing 737-230	1082/23156	ex N621AC		Lsd fr Joda LLC

AIR TRANSPORT EUROPE

Trans Europe (EAT) *Tatry-Poprad (TAT)*

| OM-EVA | Mil Mi-8T | 98417157 | ex RA-22896 | Kristina |
| OM-OTO | Aerospatiale AS.355FN Ecureuil 2 | 5113 | ex N5786D | Lucia | EMS |

OLIMEX SLOVAKIAAIR

Slavnica

| OM-ODQ | LET L-410UVP | 841320 | ex OK-ODQ |
| OM-SAB | LET L-410M | 750405 | ex 0405 Slovak AF |

SEAGLE AIR

Seagle (CGL) *Trencin*

| OM-HLB | LET L-410UVP-E3 | 871914 | ex Soviet AF 1914 | Air Becker Avionic titles |
| OM-SDA | LET L-410UVP-E | 872006 | ex Soviet AF 2006 |

SKYEUROPE AIRLINES

Relax (NE/ESK) *Bratislava-MR Stefanik (BTS)*

HA-LKO	Boeing 737-5Y0	2220/25185	ex N185FR	based BUD
OM-DAY	Embraer EMB.120ER Brasilia	120244	ex F-GIYI		Lsd fr RAE
OM-FLY	Embraer EMB.120ER Brasilia	120239	ex F-GIYH		Lsd fr RAE
OM-SHY	Embraer EMB.120ER Brasilia	120253	ex F-GMMU
OM-SKY	Embraer EMB.120ER Brasilia	120175	ex PH-BRP		Lsd fr MPS
OM-SPY	Embraer EMB.120ER Brasilia	120092	ex N92GL		Lsd fr Finova
OM-SEA	Boeing 737-5Y0	2236/25186	ex N186LS		Lsd fr WFBN
OM-	Boeing 737-5Y0	2260/25191	ex N191LS	on order

SkyEurope Airlines (HA) is a wholly owned subisidary

SLOVAK AIRLINES / SLOVENSKIE AEROLINIE

Slov Line (6Q/SLL) *Bratislava-MR Stefanik (BTS)*

| OM-AAD | Boeing 737-33A | 1438/23636 | ex N509DC | Lsd fr AWMS I |

SLOVAK GOVERNMENT FLYING SERVICE

Slovak Government (SSG) *Bratislava-MR Stefanik (BTS)*

OM-BYE	Yakovlev Yak-40	9440338	ex OK-BYE
OM-BYL	Yakovlev Yak-40	9940560	ex OK-BYL
OM-BYO	Tupolev Tu-154M	89A-803	ex OK-BYO
OM-BYR	Tupolev Tu-154M	98A-1012

Operate charter services as well as Government VIP flights

OO - BELGIUM (Kingdom of Belgium)

AIRVENTURE

Venture Liner (RVE) *Antwerp-Deurne (ANR)*

| OO-SXB | Embraer EMB.121A Xingu | 121040 | ex PT-MBH | EMS |
| OO-SXC | Embraer EMB.121A Xingu | 121042 | ex PT-MBJ | EMS |

BIRDY AIRLINES

Bel-Bird (4V/BDY) *Brussels-National (BRU)*

OO-SFM	Airbus Industrie A330-301	030	ex F-GMDA	Lsd fr debis; sublsd to/op for DAT
OO-SFN	Airbus Industrie A330-301	037	ex F-GMDB	Lsd fr debis; sublsd to/op for DAT
OO-SFO	Airbus Industrie A330-301	045	ex F-GMDC	Lsd fr debis; sublsd to/op for DAT

EUROPEAN AIR TRANSPORT

Eurotrans (QY/BCS) (IATA615)   *Brussels-National (BRU)*

OO-DIB	Airbus Industrie A300B4-203F	274	ex EI-DHL	Lsd fr C-S Avn Svcs
OO-DIC	Airbus Industrie A300B4-203F	220	ex EI-SAF	Lsd fr C-S Avn Svcs
OO-DLC	Airbus Industrie A300B4-203F	152	ex N221EA	Lsd fr Safair Lease Finance
OO-DLD	Airbus Industrie A300B4-203F	259	ex N865PA	Lsd fr Safair Lease Finance
OO-DLE	Airbus Industrie A300B4-203F	236	ex N222KW	Lsd fr Safair Lease Finance
OO-DLG	Airbus Industrie A300B4-203F	208	ex N212PA	Lsd fr Safair Lease Finance
OO-DLI	Airbus Industrie A300B4-203F	234	ex F-WHPS	Lsd fr Safair Lease Finance
OO-DLL	Airbus Industrie A300B4-203F	093	ex N225KW	*dam Baghdad Lsd fr PACE
OO-DLR	Airbus Industrie A300B4-203F	095	ex EI-EAE	
OO-DLT	Airbus Industrie A300B4-203F	250	ex EI-EAC	
OO-DLU	Airbus Industrie A300B4-203F	289	ex EI-EAD	Lsd fr Hull 753 Corp
OO-DLV	Airbus Industrie A300B4-203F	150	ex EI-EAA	
OO-DLW	Airbus Industrie A300B4-203F	199	ex EI-EAB	
OO-DLY	Airbus Industrie A300B4-203F	116	ex EI-EAT	

*OO-DLL was hit by SAM-7 missile after take-off from Baghdad, Iraq 22 November 2003; aircraft made emergency landing and badly damaged

EC-HAH	Boeing 727-223F (FedEx 3)	1199/21084	ex OO-DHV	Lsd to SWT
EC-HHU	Boeing 727-277F (FedEx 3)	1768/22644	ex (OO-DLJ)	Lsd to SWT
EC-HJV	Boeing 727-264F (FedEx 3)	1049/20895	ex N623DH	Lsd to SWT
EC-HLP	Boeing 727-264F (FedEx 3)	1051/20896	ex N622DH	Lsd to SWT
EC-IFC	Boeing 727-277F (FedEx 3)	1762/22643	ex OO-DHK	no titles	Lsd to SWT
HP-1510DAE	Boeing 727-264F (FedEx 3)	950/20709	ex N624DH	Lsd to DAE
HP-1610DAE	Boeing 727-264F (FedEx 3)	986/20780	ex N625DH	Lsd to DAE
HP-1710DAE	Boeing 727-2Q4F (FedEx 3)	1683/22424	ex OO-DHZ	Lsd to DAE
OO-DHS	Boeing 727-223F (FedEx 3)	733/20189	ex N6836	
OO-DHU	Boeing 727-223F (FedEx 3)	1187/20992	ex N851AA	
OO-DHW	Boeing 727-223F (FedEx 3)	1189/20993	ex N852AA	
OO-DHX	Boeing 727-223F (FedEx 3)	1190/20994	ex N853AA	
OO-DHY	Boeing 727-230F (FedEx 3)	1091/20905	ex N626DH	
VH-DHE	Boeing 727-2J4F (FedEx 3)	1598/22080	ex N729DH	Lsd to AXF
VH-VLH	Boeing 727-277F (FedEx 3)	1759/22642	ex OO-DLB	Lsd to AUC
VH-VLI	Boeing 727-277F (FedEx 3)	1753/22641	ex EC-HIG	Lsd to AUC
YV-846C	Boeing 727-35F (FedEx 3)	325/19167	ex OO-DHQ	

G-BIKC	Boeing 757-236SF	11/22174		Lsd fr Boeing Capital; sublsd to DHK
G-BIKF	Boeing 757-236SF	16/22177		Lsd fr Boeing Capital; sublsd to DHK
G-BIKG	Boeing 757-236SF	23/22178		Lsd fr Boeing Capital; sublsd to DHK
G-BIKI	Boeing 757-236SF	25/22180	ex OO-DLO	Lsd fr Boeing Capital; sublsd to DHK
G-BIKJ	Boeing 757-236SF	29/22181		Lsd fr Boeing Capital; sublsd to DHK
G-BIKK	Boeing 757-236SF	30/22182		Lsd fr Boeing Capital; sublsd to DHK
G-BIKM	Boeing 757-236SF	33/22184	ex N8293V	Lsd fr Boeing Capital; sublsd to DHK
G-BIKN	Boeing 757-236SF	50/22186		Lsd fr Boeing Capital; sublsd to DHK
G-BIKO	Boeing 757-236SF	52/22187		Lsd fr Boeing Capital; sublsd to DHK
G-BIKP	Boeing 757-236SF	54/22188		Lsd fr Boeing Capital; sublsd to DHK
G-BIKS	Boeing 757-236SF	63/22190		Lsd fr Boeing Capital; sublsd to DHK
G-BIKU	Boeing 757-236SF	78/23399		Lsd fr Boeing Capital; sublsd to DHK
G-BIKV	Boeing 757-236SF	81/23400		Lsd fr Boeing Capital; sublsd to DHK
G-BIKZ	Boeing 757-236SF	98/23532		Lsd fr Boeing Capital; sublsd to DHK
G-BMRA	Boeing 757-236SF	123/23710		Lsd fr Boeing Capital; sublsd to DHK
G-BMRB	Boeing 757-236SF	145/23975		Lsd fr Boeing Capital; sublsd to DHK
G-BMRC	Boeing 757-236SF	160/24072		Lsd fr Boeing Capital; sublsd to DHK
G-BMRD	Boeing 757-236SF	166/24073		Lsd fr Boeing Capital; sublsd to DHK
G-BMRE	Boeing 757-236SF	168/24074		Lsd fr Boeing Capital; sublsd to DHK
G-BMRF	Boeing 757-236SF	175/24101		Lsd fr Boeing Capital; sublsd to DHK
G-BMRH	Boeing 757-236SF	210/24266		Lsd fr Boeing Capital; sublsd to DHK
G-BMRJ	Boeing 757-236SF	214/24268		Lsd fr Boeing Capital; sublsd to DHK
OO-DLJ	Boeing 757-23APF	340/24971	ex N573CA	
OO-DLN	Boeing 757-236SF	9/22172	ex G-BIKA	Lsd fr Boeing Capital
OO-DLP	Boeing 757-236SF	24/22179	ex G-BIKH	Lsd fr Boeing Capital
OO-DLQ	Boeing 757-236SF	13/22175	ex G-BIKD	Lsd fr Boeing Capital
OO-DPB	Boeing 757-236SF	32/22183	ex G-BIKL	Lsd fr Boeing Capital
OO-DPF	Boeing 757-236SF	10/22173	ex G-BIKB	Lsd fr Boeing Capital
OO-DPI	Boeing 757-236SF	179/24102	ex G-BMRG	Lsd fr Boeing Capital
OO-DPJ	Boeing 757-236SF	90/23493	ex G-BIKX	Lsd fr Boeing Capital
OO-DPK	Boeing 757-236SF	89/23492	ex G-BIKW	Lsd fr Boeing Capital
OO-DPL	Boeing 757-236SF	211/24267	ex G-BMRI	Lsd fr Boeing Capital
OO-DPM	Boeing 757-236SF	58/22189	ex G-BIKR	Lsd fr Boeing Capital
OO-DPN	Boeing 757-236SF	93/23533	ex G-BIKY	Lsd fr Boeing Capital
OO-DPO	Boeing 757-236SF	77/23398	ex G-BIKT	Lsd fr Boeing Capital

OO-DHB	Convair 580	458	ex N537SA	Lsd to SWT as EC-GBF
OO-DHC	Convair 580	68	ex N535SA	Lsd to SWT as EC-HMR
OO-DHD	Convair 580	135	ex N536SA	Lsd to SWT as EC-GKH
OO-DHE	Convair 580	52	ex C-GDTE	Lsd to SWT as EC-HLD
OO-DHF	Convair 580	147	ex C-GQHA	Lsd to SWT as EC-HJU
OO-DHG	Convair 580	25	ex N73117	Lsd to SWT as EC-GDY

OO-DHH	Convair 580	186	ex N73156	Lsd to SWT as EC-GHN
OO-DHL	Convair 580	459	ex C-GGWF	Lsd to SWT as EC-HMS
OO-HUB	Convair 580	130	ex C-GGWG	Lsd to SWT as EC-GSJ

A subsidiary of DHL Worldwide Express and aircraft operate in full DHL colours

NOORDZEE HELIKOPTERS VLAANDEREN

Ostend/Antwerp-Deurne/Kortrijk-Wevelgem (OST/ANR/KJK)

OO-ECB	Eurocopter EC120B Colibri	1096	ex F-WQDK	
OO-NHF	MD Helicopters MD900 Explorer	900-00015	ex N9015P	
OO-NHU	Aerospatiale AS.365SR Dauphin	6665		
OO-NHV	Aerospatiale AS.365N2 Dauphin 2	6510	ex F-WWQZ	Flipper 1
OO-NHZ	Aerospatiale AS.365N2 Dauphin 2	6450	ex N4H	

Associated with Sky Service

SKY SERVICE

Sky Service (SKS)   *Kortrijk-Wevelgem (KJK)*

OO-LAC	Beech 200C Super King Air	BL-16	ex F-GLTX
OO-SKL	Beech B200 Super King Air	BB-1348	ex D2-EST
OO-SKM	Beech B200 Super King Air	BB-1407	ex D2-ESQ
OO-VHV	Beech 65-E90 King Air	LW-316	ex N77WZ

SN BRUSSELS AIRLINES

Deltair (SN/DAT) (IATA 082)   *Brussels-National (BRU)*

OO-DJK	Avro RJ-85	E2271	ex G-6-271	
OO-DJL	Avro RJ-85	E2273	ex G-6-273	
OO-DJN	Avro RJ-85	E2275	ex G-6-275	
OO-DJO	Avro RJ-85	E2279	ex G-6-279	
OO-DJP	Avro RJ-85	E2287	ex G-6-287	
OO-DJQ	Avro RJ-85	E2289	ex G-6-289	
OO-DJR	Avro RJ-85	E2290	ex G-6-290	
OO-DJS	Avro RJ-85	E2292	ex G-6-292	
OO-DJT	Avro RJ-85	E2294	ex G-6-294	
OO-DJV	Avro RJ-85	E2295	ex G-6-295	
OO-DJW	Avro RJ-85	E2296	ex G-6-296	
OO-DJX	Avro RJ-85	E2297	ex G-6-297	
OO-DJY	Avro RJ-85	E2302	ex G-6-302	
OO-DJZ	Avro RJ-85	E2305	ex G-6-305	
OO-DWA	Avro RJ-100	E3308	ex G-BXEU	
OO-DWB	Avro RJ-100	E3315	ex G-6-315	
OO-DWC	Avro RJ-100	E3322	ex G-6-322	
OO-DWD	Avro RJ-100	E3324	ex G-6-324	
OO-DWE	Avro RJ-100	E3327	ex G-6-327	
OO-DWF	Avro RJ-100	E3332	ex G-6-332	
OO-DWG	Avro RJ-100	E3336	ex G-6-336	
OO-DWH	Avro RJ-100	E3340	ex G-6-340	
OO-DWI	Avro RJ-100	E3342	ex G-6-342	
OO-DWJ	Avro RJ-100	E3355	ex G-6-355	Lsd fr Jeremy Ltd
OO-DWK	Avro RJ-100	E3360	ex G-6-360	Lsd fr Jeremy Ltd
OO-DWL	Avro RJ-100	E3361	ex G-6-361	Lsd fr Jeremy Ltd
OO-DJE	British Aerospace 146 Srs.200	E2164	ex G-6-164	
OO-DJF	British Aerospace 146 Srs.200	E2167	ex G-6-167	
OO-DJG	British Aerospace 146 Srs.200	E2180	ex G-BSZZ	
OO-DJH	British Aerospace 146 Srs.200	E2172	ex G-BSSG	
OO-DJJ	British Aerospace 146 Srs.200	E2196	ex G-6-196	Lsd to SCM as SE-DRM
OO-MJE	British Aerospace 146 Srs.200	E2192	ex G-6-192	
OO-SFM	Airbus Industrie A330-301	030	ex F-GMDA	Lsd fr/op by BDY
OO-SFN	Airbus Industrie A330-301	037	ex F-GMDB	Lsd fr/op by BDY
OO-SFO	Airbus Industrie A330-301	045	ex F-GMDC	Lsd fr/op by BDY
OO-SSG	Airbus Industrie A319-132	1160	ex EI-CZF	Lsd fr Pembroke
OO-SSK	Airbus Industrie A319-132	1336	ex F-WQRU	Lsd fr Margritte Lsg
OO-SSM	Airbus Industrie A319-132	1388	ex F-WQRV	Lsd fr Margritte Lsg

SOBELAIR liquidated by Belgian courts 19 January 2004 after seeking protection from creditors

SUNRISE

Brussels-National (BRU)

OO-TUA	Boeing 737-4K5	1707/24127	ex D-AHLL	Lsd fr HLF

Wholly owned by TUI, will take over services operated by Sobelair in Jetair titles from March 2004 (however Sobelair liquidated 19 January 2004)

THOMAS COOK AIRLINES BELGIUM

(FQ/TCW) (IATA 583)   *Brussels-National (BRU)*

OO-TCB	Airbus Industrie A320-231	0357	ex G-BVYB	Explore	Lsd to CFG
OO-TCC	Airbus Industrie A320-231	0411	ex G-BVYC	Dream	Lsd fr TCX
OO-TCE	Airbus Industrie A320-231	0394	ex G-CVYE	Inspire	Lsd fr TCX
OO-TCF	Airbus Industrie A320-231	0354	ex G-BVYA	Discover	Lsd fr TCX
OO-TCH	Airbus Industrie A320-214	1929	ex F-WWID	Experience	Lsd to CFG

TNT AIRWAYS

Quality (3V/TAY) (IATA 163)   *Liege (LGG)*

EC-HQT	Airbus Industrie A300B4-203F	124	ex G-TNTS		Op by PNR
EC-HVZ	Airbus Industrie A300B4-203F	227	ex N223KW		Op by PNR
OO-TZA	Airbus Industrie A300B4-203F	155	ex G-TNTI	Ad Scheepdouwer	
OO-TZB	Airbus Industrie A300B4-203F	261	ex N229KW		
OO-TZC	Airbus Industrie A300B4-203F	210	ex N210TN		Lsd fr WFBN
OO-TZD	Airbus Industrie A300B4-203F	247	ex N247TN		Lsd fr WFBN
EC-ELT	British Aerospace 146 Srs.200QT	E2102	ex EC-198		Op by PNR
EC-FVY	British Aerospace 146 Srs.200QT	E2117	ex EC-615		Op by PNR
EC-FZE	British Aerospace 146 Srs.200QT	E2105	ex EC-719		Op by PNR
EC-GQO	British Aerospace 146 Srs.200QT	E2086	ex D-ADEI		Op by PNR
EC-HDH	British Aerospace 146 Srs.200QT	E2056	ex G-TNTA		Op by PNR
EC-HJH	British Aerospace 146 Srs.200QT	E2112	ex G-BOMK		Op by PNR
I-TNTC	British Aerospace 146 Srs.200QT	E2078	ex G-5-078		Op by MSA
I-MSAA	British Aerospace 146 Srs.200QT	E2109	ex I-TPGS		Op by MSA
OO-TAA	British Aerospace 146 Srs.300QT	E3151	ex G-TNTR		
OO-TAD	British Aerospace 146 Srs.300QT	E3166	ex G-TNTM		
OO-TAE	British Aerospace 146 Srs.300QT	E3182	ex G-TNTG		
OO-TAF	British Aerospace 146 Srs.300QT	E3186	ex G-TNTK		
OO-TAH	British Aerospace 146 Srs.300QT	E3168	ex G-TNTL		
OO-TAJ	British Aerospace 146 Srs.300QT	E3153	ex G-TNTE		
OO-TAK	British Aerospace 146 Srs.300QT	E3150	ex G-TJPM		
OO-TAR	British Aerospace 146 Srs.200QT	E2067	ex G-TNTB		
OO-TAS	British Aerospace 146 Srs.300QT	E3154	ex EC-FFY		
OO-TAU	British Aerospace 146 Srs.200QT	E2100	ex EC-GQP		
OO-TAW	British Aerospace 146 Srs.200QT	E2089	ex EC-EPA		
OO-TNA	Boeing 737-3T0F	1258/23569	ex N13331		Lsd fr AFS Investments IX
OO-TNB	Boeing 737-3T0F	1358/23578	ex N39340		Lsd fr Polaris Lsg
OO-	Boeing 737-301F	1327/23513	ex N559AU	on order	Lsd frGECAS
OO-	Boeing 737-301F	1355/23515	ex N346US	on order	Lsd fr GECAS

Three more on order, leased from GECAS, in 2005-7

SU-EAG	Tupolev Tu-204-120C	1450743764028	ex RA-64028		Lsd fr CCE
SU-EAJ	Tupolev Tu-204-120S	1450743164029	ex RA-64029		Lsd fr CCE
SU-EAK	Tupolev Tu-204-120S	1450743164033	ex RA-64033	on order	Lsd fr CCE

Other services are operated on behalf of TNT Express Worldwide by other companies

VIRGIN EXPRESS

Virgin Express (TV/VEX)   *Brussels-National (BRU)*

OO-LTM	Boeing 737-3M8	2037/25070	ex F-GMTM		Lsd fr Locabel
OO-LTU	Boeing 737-33A	2709/27455			Lsd fr AWAS
OO-VBR	Boeing 737-4Y0	1680/24314	ex F-GMBR	all-white	Lsd fr GECAS
OO-VED	Boeing 737-46M	2847/28550	ex C-GBIX		Lsd fr Tombo
OO-VEF	Boeing 737-430	2311/27000	ex D-ABKA		Lsd fr Oasis Intl
OO-VEG	Boeing 737-36N	2987/28568	ex EI-TVQ		Lsd fr GECAS
OO-VEH	Boeing 737-36N	3022/28571	ex EI-TVR		Lsd fr GECAS
OO-VEJ	Boeing 737-405	1738/24271	ex LN-BRB		Lsd fr debis
OO-VEK	Boeing 737-405	1726/24270	ex LN-BRA		Lsd fr CIT Leasing
OO-VEN	Boeing 737-36N	3090/28586	ex EI-TVN		Lsd fr GECAS
OO-VEO	Boeing 737-4Y0	1876/24688	ex SX-BLN		Lsd fr GECAS
OO-VEP	Boeing 737-43Q	2827/28489	ex VH-VGA		Lsd fr AFT Trust
OO-VES	Boeing 737-43Q	2838/28493	ex VH-VGE		Lsd fr Boullioun
OO-VEX	Boeing 737-36N	2948/28670	ex EI-TVS		Lsd fr GECAS

VLM AIRLINES

Rubens (VG/VLM)   *Antwerp-Deurne (ANR)*

OO-VLE	Fokker 50	20132	ex PH-ARG	City of Düsseldorf Lsd fr Frevag
OO-VLJ*	Fokker 50	20105	ex PH-ARE	City of London
OO-VLK+	Fokker 50	20122	ex PH-FZF	City of Hamburg
OO-VLM	Fokker 50	20135	ex PH-VLM	City of Rotterdam; special c/s
OO-VLN	Fokker 50	20145	ex PH-VLN	City of Antwerp Lsd fr Mass Holding

478

OO-VLO	Fokker 50	20127	ex ES-AFL	City of Genève	Lsd fr Finova
OO-VLQ	Fokker 50	20159	ex EC-GBH	City of Brussels	Lsd fr Frevag
OO-VLR*	Fokker 50	20121	ex PH-ARF	Grand Duchy of Luxembourg	
OO-VLS	Fokker 50	20109	ex EC-GBG	Victor Somers	Lsd fr Frevag
OO-VLV	Fokker 50	20160	ex EC-GDD	States of Guernsey	Lsd fr Frevag
OO-VLX	Fokker 50	20177	ex EI-FKC	on order	
OO-VLY	Fokker 50	20181	ex EI-FKD	on order	

+Leased from AeroCentury   *Leased from debis Airfinance

OY - DENMARK (Kingdom of Denmark)

AIR ALPHA GREENLAND

Air Alpha (GD/AHA)   Nuuk-Godthaab (GOH)

OY-HIA	Bell 222UT	47529	ex TC-HCS	
OY-HIB	Bell 222U	47519	ex D-HCED	
OY-HIC	Bell 222U	47522	ex PT-HXC	
OY-HID	Bell 222U	47548	ex D-HCAN	
OY-HIE	Bell 222U	47501	ex D-HUKM	
OY-HIF	Bell 222UT	47512	ex N256SP	
OY-TPC	Cessna 208B Caravan I	208B0805	ex D-FPUL	Ops as Tele Greenland A/S
OY-TPG	Cessna 208B Caravan I	208B0810	ex D-FROG	Ops as Tele Greenland A/S

AIR GREENLAND

Greenlandair (GL/GRL)   Nuuk-Godthaab (GOH)

OY-CBT	de Havilland DHC-7-103	10	ex C-GRQB-X	Papikkaaq
OY-CBU	de Havilland DHC-7-103	20		Nipiki
OY-CTC	de Havilland DHC-7-102	101	ex G-BNDC	Minniki
OY-GRD	de Havilland DHC-7-103	9	ex A6-ALM	Sapangaq
OY-GRE	de Havilland DHC-7-103	106	ex N54026	
OY-GRF	de Havilland DHC-7-102	113	ex OE-LLU	
OY-ATY	de Havilland DHC-6 Twin Otter 300	561	ex C-GRZH	Naaja
OY-GRL+	Boeing 757-236	449/25620	ex TF-GRL	Kunuunnguaq
OY-GRN	Airbus Industrie A330-223	230	ex OO-SFP	Norsaq
				Lsd fr Credit Agricole Indosuez
OY-HAF	Sikorsky S-61N	61267	ex N10045	Nagtoralik
OY-HAG	Sikorsky S-61N	61268	ex N10046	Kussak
OY-HCY	Bell 212	31166		Piseeq 2
OY-HDM	Bell 212	31142	ex N57545	
OY-HDN	Bell 212	31136	ex N5752K	Miteq
OY-HEY	Aerospatiale AS.350B2 Ecureuil	2904	ex N4027Q	
OY-HGA	Aerospatiale AS.350B2 Ecureuil	2600		
OY-HGK	Aerospatiale AS.350B2 Ecureuil	2570	ex C-FNJW	
OY-HGL	Aerospatiale AS.350B2 Ecureuil	2950	ex N4074E	
OY-HMD	Bell 212	31125	ex LN-ORI	
OY-NUK	Beech 200 Super King Air	BB-634	ex N101CP	
OY-POF	de Havilland DHC-6 Twin Otter 300	235	ex N6868	

+Leased from FIH Leasing
50% owned by SAS

ATLANTIC AIRWAYS

Faroeline (RC/FLI)   Vagar (FAE)

OY-CRG	British Aerospace 146 Srs.200A	E2075	ex (N193US)
OY-HMB	Bell 212	30686	ex LN-OSR
OY-HSR	Bell 412EP	36133	ex N62734
OY-RCA	British Aerospace 146 Srs.200	E2045	ex G-CLHE

AVIATION ASSISTANCE

Avia Assist (7W/VIS)   Copenhagen-Roskilde (RKE)

OY-BVB	Beech 200 Super King Air	BB-419	ex N256EN	
OY-CBP	Beech 200 Super King Air	BB-235	ex N9BK	Op for UN
OY-GEB	Beech 200C Super King Air	BL-40	ex VH-NSR	Op for UN
OY-GER*	Beech 1300	BB-1343	ex VT-SAF	Super King Air conv Lsd fr Raytheon
OY-GES*	Beech 1300	BB-1305	ex VT-SAB	Super King Air conv Lsd fr Raytheon
OY-GEU	Beech 1300	BB-1341	ex VT-SAD	Super King Air conv Lsd fr Raytheon
OY-GEW	Beech 1300	BB-1342	ex VT-SAE	Super King Air conv Lsd fr Raytheon
OY-GMA	Beech 1300	BB-1340	ex N256AF	Super King Air conv Lsd fr Raytheon
OY-GRB	Beech 200 Super King Air	BB-845	ex N486DC	Op for UN/WFP
OY-JAR	Beech 200C Super King Air	BL-13	ex PH-ILG	Op for ICRC
OY-JRN	Beech 200 Super King Air	BB-364	ex F-GHYV	Lsd to IKR

*Sub-leased to Aviation Assistance (5Y)

OY-GEG	Beech 1900C-1	UC-132	ex 1180	Op for UN	
OY-GEN	Beech 1900C	UB-4	ex 5Y-DHW		Lsd to IKR
OY-GML	Beech 1900C-1	UC-69	ex F-GPYS	Op for UN	Lsd fr Raytheon
OY-GMM	Beech 1900C-1	UC-172	ex F-GHSE	Op for UN	Lsd fr Raytheon
OY-GMN	Beech 1900C-1	UC-173	ex F-GHSI		Lsd fr Raytheon
OY-ASY	Embraer EMB.110P1 Bandeirante	110308	ex EI-BPI		
OY-BHT	Embraer EMB.110P2 Bandeirante	110161	ex N4942S		
OY-BVB	Beech 200 Super King Air	BB-419	ex N256EN		Lsd to IKR

Some aircraft are based in Africa and often operate for organisations such as UN, WFP and the Red Cross

BENAIR AIR SERVICE

Birdie (BDI)   *Stauning (STA))*

OY-BJP	Swearingen SA.227AC Metro III	AC-499	ex F-GHVG	Lsd fr Alebco
OY-PBH	LET L-410UVP-E20	972736	ex OK-DDC	Lsd fr Alebco
OY-PBI	LET L-410UVP-E20	871936	ex OK-SDM	Lsd fr Alebco

Subsidiary of Hangar 5 Airservices; Benair Air Services is the trading name of Air and Training Center-West

CHC DENMARK

Helibird (HBI)   *Esbjerg (EBJ)*

OY-HDT	Aerospatiale AS.332L Super Puma	2017	ex G-BWHN
OY-HEO	Aerospatiale AS.332L Super Puma	2007	ex G-CHCA
OY-HHA	Aerospatiale AS.332L Super Puma	2015	ex G-CHCB
OY-HHC	Aerospatiale AS.332L Super Puma	2179	ex G-BOZK
OY-HIW	Sikorsky S-76A+	760183	ex G-BVCX

All leased from CHC Scotia

CIMBER AIR

Cimber (QI/CIM) (IATA 647)   *Sonderborg (SGD)*

OY-CIB^	Aerospatiale/Alenia ATR 42-300	007	ex F-WWEC		
OY-CID^	Aerospatiale/Alenia ATR 42-300	079	ex D-BATA		
OY-CIE^	Aerospatiale/Alenia ATR 42-300	082	ex D-BATB		
OY-CIG	Aerospatiale/Alenia ATR 42-300	019	ex YU-ALL	all-white	
OY-CIH	Aerospatiale/Alenia ATR 42-300	238	ex F-WWEC		
OY-CIJ	Aerospatiale/Alenia ATR 42-500	497	ex F-WWLR		Lsd to OAS as A4O-AL
OY-CIK	Aerospatiale/Alenia ATR 42-500	501	ex F-WWEE		Lsd to OAS as A4O-AM
OY-CIL	Aerospatiale/Alenia ATR 42-500	514	ex F-WWLO		
OY-CIM	Aerospatiale/Alenia ATR 72-212A	468	ex F-WWLV		
OY-CIN	Aerospatiale/Alenia ATR 72-212A	568	ex F-WWEH		
OY-CIO	Aerospatiale/Alenia ATR 72-212A	595	ex F-WWEB		
OY-CIP	Aerospatiale/Alenia ATR 72-201	147	ex EI-CBC		Lsd fr GPA-ATR
OY-CIV	Aerospatiale/Alenia ATR 72-201	150	ex EI-CBD		Lsd fr GPA-ATR
OY-CIW	Aerospatiale/Alenia ATR 72-212	422	ex F-WQNR		Lsd fr ATRiam Capital

*Leased from GECAS   ^Leased from Cimber Air Leasing

| D-ACIM | Canadair CL-600-2B19 | 7413 | ex OY-RJA |
| D-ACIN | Canadair CL-600-2B19 | 7419 | ex OY-RJB |

COPENHAGEN AIRTAXI

Aircat (CAT)   *Copenhagen-Roskilde (RKE)*

OY-CAA	Partenavia P.68B	48	
OY-CAC	Partenavia P.68B	179	
OY-CAT	Britten-Norman BN-2B-26 Islander	2224	ex EC-FFZ
OY-CDC	Partenavia P.68C	211	ex D-GEMD

DANISH AIR TRANSPORT

(DX)   *Kolding-Vamdrup*

OY-CIA	Aerospatiale/Alenia ATR 42-300	005	ex F-GHLZ	Lsd fr Shooting Star Investments
				Sublsd to GUY
OY-CIR	Aerospatiale/Alenia ATR 42-310	107	ex F-GHPX	Lsd fr Shooting Star Investments
OY-CIU	Aerospatiale/Alenia ATR 42-310	112	ex C-FIQB	Lsd fr Shooting Star Investments
OY-JRJ	Aerospatiale/Alenia ATR 42-320	036	ex F-WQIS	
OY-JRY	Aerospatiale/Alenia ATR 42-300	063	ex F-WQOC	Lsd fr ATR Asset Mgt
OY-MUK	Aerospatiale/Alenia ATR 42-300	176	ex EI-CBF	Lsd fr GPA-ATR
OY-RUB	Aerospatiale/Alenia ATR 72-202	301	ex F-WQNS	Lsd fr ATR Asset Mgt
(OY-RUC)	Aerospatiale/Alenia ATR 72-201	227	ex F-GHPU	Lsd fr ATR Asset Mgt
OY-RUM	Aerospatiale/Alenia ATR 42-300	010	ex N110VV	Lsd fr Nordic Avn Contractor
G-RUNG	SAAB SF.340A	086	ex F-GGBV	Lsd to AUR

OY-BVS	Beech B90B King Air	LJ-418	ex SE-LEN	
OY-JRF	Beech 1900C	UB-66	ex F-GTOT	Lsd fr Nordic Avn Contractor
OY-JRI	Beech 1900C-1	UC-44	ex SE-KXX	
OY-JRK	Short SC.7 Skyliner	SH1901	ex N8117V	stored
OY-JRN	Beech 200 Super King Air	BB-364	ex F-GHYV	
OY-JRO	Beech 65-C90 King Air	LJ-327	ex N827K	Freighter
OY-JRV	Beech 1900D	UE-338	ex N23381	
OY-SBU	Beech 65-C90 King Air	LJ-768	ex LN-KCG	

IKAROS AIR

Ikaros (IKR)   *CopenhagenRoskilde (RKE)*

| OY-BVB | Beech 200 Super King Air | BB-419 | ex N256EN | Lsd fr VIS |
| OY-GEN | Beech 1900C | UB-4 | ex 5Y-DHW | Lsd fr VIS |

MAERSK AIR

Maerskair (DM/DAN) (IATA 349)   *Copenhagen-Kastrup/Esbjerg (CPH/EBJ)*

OY-APB	Boeing 737-5L9	2788/28084	ex G-MSKE	Lsd fr ORIX Atlas Corp
OY-APH	Boeing 737-5L9	2856/28721		Lsd to RWD
OY-API	Boeing 737-5L9	2868/28722		
OY-APK	Boeing 737-5L9	2947/28995		
OY-APL	Boeing 737-5L9	2998/28996		Lsd to LOT as SP-LKK
OY-APN	Boeing 737-5L9	3008/28997		Lsd fr Sumisho A/c Asset Mgt
OY-APP	Boeing 737-5L9	3068/29234		Lsd fr Sumisho A/c Asset Mgt
OY-APR	Boeing 737-5L9	3076/29235		Lsd fr Sumosho A/c Asset Mgt
OY-MAA	Boeing 737-5L9	1816/24778	ex G-MSKD	Lsd fr ORIX; sublsd to ELL
OY-MAE	Boeing 737-5L9	2038/25066	ex G-MSKC	Lsd fr ORIX
OY-MRC*	Boeing 737-7L9	26/28006	ex N5573K	
OY-MRD*	Boeing 737-7L9	136/28007		
OY-MRE	Boeing 737-7L9	203/28008		
OY-MRF	Boeing 737-7L9	221/28009	ex N1780B	
OY-MRG	Boeing 737-7L9	396/28010		
OY-MRH	Boeing 737-7L9	682/28013		
OY-MRI	Boeing 737-7L9	766/28014		
OY-MRJ	Boeing 737-7L9	785/28015		
OY-MRK	Boeing 737-7L9	1092/28012		Lsd to SNB
OY-MRL	Boeing 737-7L9	1203/28011		

*Leased from Sumisho Aircraft Asset Management

OY-MBI	Canadair CL-600-2B19	7436	ex G-MSKT	
OY-MBJ	Canadair CL-600-2B19	7442	ex G-MSKU	
OY-MBT	Canadair CL-600-2B19	7617	ex C-GKDI	
OY-MBU	Canadair CL-600-2B19	7373	ex G-MSKR	
OY-	Canadair CL-600-2B19	7386	ex G-MSKS	

Owns StarAir

MYTRAVEL AIRWAYS

Viking (DK/VKG)   *Copenhagen-Kastrup (CPH)*

OY-CNM	Airbus Industrie A320-212	0301	ex G-JANM	Lsd fr MYT
OY-CNP	Airbus Industrie A320-212	0294	ex G-HBAP	Lsd fr MYT
OY-VKA	Airbus Industrie A321-211	1881	ex D-AVZO	Lsd fr MYT
OY-VKB	Airbus Industrie A321-211	1921	ex D-AVZQ	Lsd fr MYT
OY-VKC	Airbus Industrie A321-211	1932	ex D-AVXB	Lsd fr MYT
OY-VKL	Airbus Industrie A320-231	1780	ex F-WWDN	Lsd fr MYT; sublsd to SSV
OY-VKM	Airbus Industrie A320-231	1889	ex F-WWBV	Lsd fr MYT
OY-VKN	Airbus Industrie A320-231	2114	ex F-WWDZ	Lsd fr Boullioun
OY-VKO	Airbus Industrie A320-231		ex F-WW	on order Mar04
OY-VKP	Airbus Industrie A320-231		ex F-WW	on order Apr04
OY-VKR	Airbus Industrie A320-231		ex F-WW	on order Jun04
OY-VKF	Airbus Industrie A330-243	309	ex G-CSJS	Lsd to AIH
OY-VKG	Airbus Industrie A330-343X	349	ex F-WWYG	Lsd fr AIH
OY-VKH	Airbus Industrie A330-343X	356	ex F-WWYJ	Lsd fr AIH
OY-VKI	Airbus Industrie A330-343X	357	ex F-WWKA	Lsd fr AIH

See also entry under MyTravel (G)

NEWAIR AIR SERVICE

Newdane (8L/NAW)   *Billund (BLL)*

| OY- | Fokker F.27 Friendship 500 | 10669 | ex G-ECAH | |

NORTH FLYING

North Flying (M3/NFA)
Aalborg (AAL)

OY-DLY	Piper PA-31 Turbo Navajo	31-229	ex G-AWOW		Lsd fr DAX
OY-FRE	Piper PA-31 Turbo Navajo	31-632	ex G-AXYA		
OY-NPA	Swearingen SA.226TC Metro II	TC-258	ex C-GBDF		
OY-NPB	Swearingen SA.227AC Metro III	AC-420	ex N67TC		Lsd to Air Norway
OY-NPD	Swearingen SA.227DC Metro 23	DC-865B	ex 9M-BCH		Lsd fr DAX
OY-NPE	Swearingen SA.227DC Metro 23	DC-867B	ex N23VJ		Lsd fr DAX

SCANDINAVIAN AIRLINE SYSTEM

Scandinavian (SK/SAS) (IATA 117)
Copenhagen-Kastrup (CPH)

For details see under Sweden (SE-)

SCAN-CON AIRWAYS ceased operations and aircraft returned to lessors

STAR AIR

Whitestar (SRR)
Copenhagen-Kastrup (CPH)

OY-UPA	Boeing 727-31C	458/19233	ex N926UP	RR Tay conv	Lsd fr/op for UPS
OY-UPD	Boeing 727-22C	341/19103	ex N944UP	RR Tay conv	Lsd fr/op for UPS
OY-UPS	Boeing 727-31C	425/19232	ex N927UP	RR Tay conv	Lsd fr/op for UPS
OY-USA	Boeing 757-24APF	569/25462	ex N431UP		Lsd fr/op for UPS
OY-USB	Boeing 757-24APF	573/25463	ex N432UP		Lsd fr/op for UPS
OY-USC	Boeing 757-24APF	577/25464	ex N433UP		Lsd fr/op for UPS
OY-USD	Boeing 757-24APF	579/25465	ex N434UP		Lsd fr/op for UPS

Owned by Maersk Air

STERLING EUROPEAN AIRLINES

Sterling (NB/SNB)
Copenhagen-Kastrup (CPH)

OY-MRK	Boeing 737-7L9	1092/28012			Lsd fr DAN
OY-SEA	Boeing 737-8Q8	50/28213	ex N3521N	Blue c/s	
OY-SEB	Boeing 737-8Q8	78/28214		Dark Blue c/s	Lsd fr Castle 2003-1A
OY-SEC	Boeing 737-8Q8	226/28221	ex N1787B	Yellow c/s	Lsd fr ILFC
OY-SED	Boeing 737-8Q8	769/28237		Light Blue c/s	Lsd fr ILFC
OY-SEH	Boeing 737-85H	178/29444	ex N1787B	Green c/s	Lsd fr Itochu
OY-SEI	Boeing 737-85H	186/29445		Red c/s	Lsd fr Itochu
OY-SEJ	Boeing 737-86Q	1399/30289		Red c/s	Lsd fr Boullioun
OY-SEK	Boeing 737-86Q	1451/30292			Lsd fr Boullioun
OY-SEL	Boeing 737-8BK	33018		on order Apr04	Lsd fr CIT Lsg
OY-SEM	Boeing 737-8BK	33019		on order May04	Lsd fr CIT Lsg

SUN-AIR OF SCANDINAVIA

Sunscan (EZ/SUS) (IATA 947)
Billund (BLL)

OY-MUE	British Aerospace Jetstream 31	758	ex G-BTAI		
OY-SVF	British Aerospace Jetstream 31	686	ex G-BSFG	Skien	
OY-SVJ	British Aerospace Jetstream 31	711	ex G-BTYG		
OY-SVR	British Aerospace Jetstream 31	925	ex JA8877		
OY-SVV	British Aerospace Jetstream 31	985	ex JA8591		
OY-SVY	British Aerospace Jetstream 31	981	ex JA8865		
OY-SVZ	British Aerospace Jetstream 31	641	ex G-MACX		
OY-SVI	British Aerospace ATP	2061	ex G-BUYW		Lsd fr Nordania Lsg
OY-SVS	British Aerospace Jetstream 41	41014	ex G-4-014	Spirit of Aarhus	
OY-SVT	British Aerospace ATP	2062	ex G-11-062		
OY-SVU	British Aerospace ATP	2063	ex G-BWYT		
OY-SVW	British Aerospace Jetstream 41	41047	ex G-BVZC	Port of Arhus	

Operates feeder services as franchise for British Airways in full Union Flag colours using BA flight numbers

P - KOREA (Democratic People's Republic of Korea)

AIR KORYO

Air Koryo (JS/KOR) (IATA 120)
Pyongyang (FNJ)

P-527	Antonov An-24B	67302207
P-532	Antonov An-24RV	47309707
P-533	Antonov An-24RV	47309708
P-534	Antonov An-24RV	47309802
P-537	Antonov An-24B	67302408

P-551	Tupolev Tu-154B	75A-129		
P-552	Tupolev Tu-154B	76A-143		
P-553	Tupolev Tu-154B	77A-191		
P-561	Tupolev Tu-154B-2	83A-573		
P-618	Ilyushin Il-62M	2546624		Govt op; no titles
P-881	Ilyushin Il-62M	3647853		
P-882	Ilyushin Il-62M	2850236		Govt op; no titles
P-885	Ilyushin Il-62M	3933913		
P-813	Tupolev Tu-134B-3	66215		
P-814	Tupolev Tu-134B-3	66368		
P-835	Ilyushin Il-18D	188011205	ex 835	
P-836	Ilyushin Il-18V	185008204	ex 836	
P-912	Ilyushin Il-76MD	1003403104		
P-913	Ilyushin Il-76TD	1003404126		
P-914	Ilyushin Il-76TD	1003404146		

PH - NETHERLANDS (Kingdom of the Netherlands)

AIR HOLLAND

Orange (HLN)   *Amsterdam-Schipol (AMS)*

PH-AHE	Boeing 757-27B	165/24135	ex OY-SHE		Lsd fr Finova
PH-AHQ	Boeing 767-383ER	337/24477	ex OY-KDL	on order	Lsd fr SAS
PH-AHS*	Boeing 757-28A	530/25622	ex C-GTSV	Grace	Lsd fr ILFC
PH-AHX	Boeing 767-383ER	315/24847	ex LN-RCD		Lsd fr SAS; jt ops with SLM
PH-AHY	Boeing 767-383ER	325/24848	ex OY-KDN		Lsd fr SAS; jt ops with SLM

*Subleased to and operated for Air Scotland; owned by IMCA Group, may merge with KLMexel
Operates Boeing 767s on behalf of Dutch Caribbean Airlines

BASIQ AIR

     Amsterdam-Schipol (AMS)

Low cost, wholly owned subsidiary of Transavia uses aircraft operated by the parent in full TRA colours

CITY CONNECT

Hunter (6N/TRQ)   *Rotterdam (RTM)*

PH-RAQ	Aerospatiale/Alenia ATR 42-300	139	ex ZS-OSN	Lsd fr/op by ROS

CityConnect was formed from Trans Travel Airlines, commenced operations on 22 April but ceased 06 August 2003

DENIM AIR

Denim (3D/DNM)   *Eindhoven (EIN)*

PH-DMQ+	de Havilland DHC-8Q-315	567	ex C-GDOE		
PH-DMR+	de Havilland DHC-8Q-315	569	ex C-GETI		
PH-DMU+	de Havilland DHC-8Q-315	568	ex C-GERL		
PH-DMV+	de Havilland DHC-8Q-315	570	ex C-GEVP		
PH-DMW+	de Havilland DHC-8Q-315	573	ex C-GFCF	Francisco Domingo	
PH-DMS	Fokker 50	20209	ex EI-FKF		
PH-DMT	Fokker 50	20208	ex EI-FKE		
PH-FZG+	Fokker 50	20202	ex EC-HZA		
PH-FZH+	Fokker 50	20210	ex EC-IAD	Olivo	Lsd fr Volito Avn
PH-JXJ^	Fokker 50	20232	ex PT-SLJ		Lsd fr debis
PH-JXK+	Fokker 50	20233	ex PT-SLK	all-white	
PH-JXN+	Fokker 50	20239			
PH-LMT+	Fokker 50	20192	ex EC-HYJ		
PH-PRH^	Fokker 50	20200			
PH-PRJ^	Fokker 50	20212			Lsd fr A/C Financing & Trading
PH-RRF+	Fokker 50	20220	ex EC-HNS		

+Leased to and operated for Air Nostrum in full Iberia colours as Iberia Regional
^Operated in Eurohopper.com titles

DUTCHBIRD

Dutchbird (5D/DBR)   *Amsterdam-Schipol (AMS)*

PH-BMC	Airbus Industrie A320-214	1081	ex D-ABLA		Lsd fr Bayerische Landesbank
PH-BMD	Airbus Industrie A320-214	1370	ex D-ABLB		Lsd fr Bayerische Landesbank
PH-DBA	Boeing 757-230	275/24747	ex D-ABNC	Gerda Klooster	Lsd fr CFG
PH-DBB	Boeing 757-230	274/24738	ex D-ABNB	Marianne Weber	Lsd fr CFG
PH-DBH	Boeing 757-230	285/24748	ex D-ABND		Lsd fr CFG

Also operates the Airbus Industrie A320-212s for V-Bird until summer 2004

FARNAIR EUROPE

Farnair Europe (FNE)   Rotterdam (RTM)
Previously listed as Farnair Netherlands

PH-FHL	Fokker F.27 Friendship 500F	10634	ex PT-LAK	
PH-FLM	Fokker F.27 Friendship 500F	10341	ex PT-LAL	Lsd to FAH
PH-FYC	Fokker F.27 Friendship 500F	10632	ex PT-LAJ	
PH-JLN	Fokker F.27Friendship 500	10449	ex D-AAAF	

FARNAIR NETHERLANDS now listed as Farnair Europe

KLM CITYHOPPER

City (WA/KLC)   Amsterdam-Schipol (AMS)

PH-KVA*	Fokker 50	20189	ex PH-EXC	City of Bremen	
PH-KVB*	Fokker 50	20190	ex PH-EXD	City of Brussels	
PH-KVC*	Fokker 50	20191	ex PH-EXF	City of Stavanger	
PH-KVD*	Fokker 50	20197		City of Dusseldorf	
PH-KVE^	Fokker 50	20206		City of Amsterdam	
PH-KVF^	Fokker 50	20207		City of Paris	
PH-KVG^	Fokker 50	20211		City of Stuttgart	
PH-KVH^	Fokker 50	20217		City of Hanover	
PH-KVI^	Fokker 50	20218		City of Bordeaux	
PH-KVK^	Fokker 50	20219		City of London	
PH-KXM	Fokker 50	20252	ex PT-SLO	all-white	Lsd fr Volito Avn
PH-LXJ+	Fokker 50	20270	ex G-UKTE	City of Hull	
PH-LXK+	Fokker 50	20271	ex G-UKTF	City of York	
PH-LXP+	Fokker 50	20276	ex G-UKTG	City of Durham	
PH-LXR+	Fokker 50	20277	ex G-UKTH	City of Amsterdam	
PH-LXT+	Fokker 50	20279	ex G-UKTI	City of Stavanger	

*Leased from Libra Leasing   ^Leased from DB Export Leasing
+Leased from Abbey National Leasing

PH-JCH*	Fokker 70	11528	ex OE-LFS		
PH-JCT*	Fokker 70	11537	ex OE-LFT		
PH-KZA	Fokker 70	11567			
PH-KZB	Fokker 70	11562			
PH-KZC	Fokker 70	11566			
PH-KZD	Fokker 70	11582			
PH-KZE	Fokker 70	11576			
PH-KZF	Fokker 70	11577	ex (G-BVTH)		
PH-KZG	Fokker 70	11578	ex (G-BWTI)		
PH-KZH	Fokker 70	11583			
PH-KZI	Fokker 70	11579	ex (I-REJC)		
PH-KZK	Fokker 70	11581	ex (I-REJD)		
PH-KZL	Fokker 70	11536	ex 9V-SLK		Lsd fr debis
PH-KZM	Fokker 70	11561	ex 9V-SLL		Lsd fr debis
PH-KZN	Fokker 70	11553	ex PK-PFE		
PH-KZO*	Fokker 70	11538	ex G-BVTE		
PH-KZP*	Fokker 70	11539	ex G-BVTF		
PH-KZR*	Fokker 70	11551	ex G-BVTG		
PH-WXA	Fokker 70	11570	ex I-REJO		
PH-WXC	Fokker 70	11574	ex I-REJI		

*Leased from Aircraft Financing & Trading

PH-OFA	Fokker 100	11246	ex G-UKFA	Lsd fr ILFC
PH-OFB	Fokker 100	11247	ex G-UKFB	Lsd fr ILFC
PH-OFC	Fokker 100	11263	ex G-UKFC	Lsd fr ILFC
PH-OFD	Fokker 100	11259	ex G-UKFD	Lsd fr ILFC
PH-OFE	Fokker 100	11260	ex G-UKFE	Lsd fr ILFC
PH-OFF	Fokker 100	11274	ex G-UKFF	Lsd fr Pembroke Lsg
PH-OFG	Fokker 100	11275	ex G-UKFG	Lsd fr Pembroke Lsg
PH-OFH	Fokker 100	11277	ex G-UKFH	Lsd fr Pembroke Lsg
PH-OFI	Fokker 100	11279	ex G-UKFI	Lsd fr Pembroke Lsg
PH-OFJ	Fokker 100	11248	ex G-UKFJ	Lsd fr ILFC
PH-OFK	Fokker 100	11249	ex G-UKFK	Lsd fr ILFC
PH-KLD	Fokker 100	11269	ex G-UKFM	
PH-KLE	Fokker 100	11270	ex G-UKFN	
PH-KLG	Fokker 100	11271	ex G-UKFO	
PH-KLI	Fokker 100	11273	ex G-UKFR	

A wholly owned subsidiary of KLM operates scheduled services using KL flight numbers

KLM EXEL

Exel Commuter (XT/AXL)   Maastricht (MST)

PH-XLE	Aerospatiale/Alenia ATR 42-320	090	ex F-WQBR	Lsd fr Lax Bail
PH-XLH	Aerospatiale/Alenia ATR 72-201	195	ex F-WQGO	Lsd fr ATR Asset Mgt
PH-XLI*	Aerospatiale/Alenia ATR 42-320	066	ex F-WQBO	Lsd fr ATR Asset Mgt

PH-XLK	Aerospatiale/Alenia ATR 42-320	093	ex F-WQCZ		Lsd fr ATR Asset Mgt
PH-XLL*	Aerospatiale/Alenia ATR 42-320	374	ex F-OHFD		Lsd fr ATR Asset Mgt
PH-XLM*	Aerospatiale/Alenia ATR 42-320	378	ex F-OHFE		Lsd fr ATR Asset Mgt

Leased to BonairExel

PH-BRL	Embraer EMB.120RT Brasilia	120083	ex N278UE		
PH-BRM	Embraer EMB.120ER Brasilia	120090	ex N280UE	stored SGE	
PH-RXA*	Embraer EMB.145MP	145216		Granda exel titles	
PH-RXB*	Embraer EMB.145MP	145320	ex PT-SML	all-white	
PH-RXC*	Embraer EMB.145LR	145106	ex EC-GZU		
PH-XLB	Embraer EMB.120ER Brasilia	120091	ex F-GFTB	Aquis Grani; stored MST	for sale

*Leased from Regional Jet Leasing. May merge with Air Holland

---

KLM – ROYAL DUTCH AIRLINES

KLM (KL/KLM) (IATA 074)   Amsterdam-Schipol (AMS)

PH-BDA^	Boeing 737-306	1275/23537		William Barentsz	
PH-BDB^	Boeing 737-306	1288/23538		Olivier van Noort	
PH-BDC^	Boeing 737-306	1295/23539		Cornelis de Houtman	
PH-BDD^	Boeing 737-306	1303/23540		Anthonij van Diemen	
PH-BDE^	Boeing 737-306	1309/23541		Abel J Tasman	
PH-BDG^	Boeing 737-306	1317/23542		Michiel A de Ruyter	
PH-BDI^	Boeing 737-306	1335/23544		Maarten H Tromp	
PH-BDK^	Boeing 737-306	1343/23545		Jan H van Linschoten	
PH-BDN	Boeing 737-306	1640/24261		Willem van Ruysbroeck	
PH-BDO	Boeing 737-306	1642/24262		Jacob van Heemskerck	
PH-BDP	Boeing 737-306	1681/24404		Jacob Roggeveen	Lsd fr ORIX
PH-BDR"	Boeing 737-406	1768/24514		Willem C Schouten	
PH-BDS"	Boeing 737-406	1770/24529		Joris van Spilbergen	
PH-BDT+	Boeing 737-406	1772/24530		Gerrit de Veer	
PH-BDU"	Boeing 737-406	1902/24857		Marco Polo	
PH-BDW+	Boeing 737-406	1903/24858		Leifur Eiriksson	
PH-BDY"	Boeing 737-406	1949/24959		Vasco da Gama	
PH-BDZ+	Boeing 737-406	2132/25355		Christophorus Columbus	
PH-BPB^	Boeing 737-4Y0	1723/24344	ex G-UKLB	Jan Tinbergen	
PH-BPC^	Boeing 737-4Y0	1747/24468	ex G-UKLE	Ernest Hemingway	
PH-BTA	Boeing 737-406	2161/25412		Fernao de Magelhaes	
PH-BTB	Boeing 737-406	2184/25423		Henry Hudson	
PH-BTC	Boeing 737-406	2200/25424		David Livingstone	
PH-BTD	Boeing 737-306	2406/27420		James Cook	
PH-BTE	Boeing 737-306	2438/27421		Roald Amundsen	
PH-BTF	Boeing 737-406	2591/27232		Alexander von Humboldt	
PH-BTG	Boeing 737-406	2601/27233		Sir Henry Morton Stanley	
PH-BTH	Boeing 737-306	2930/28719		Heike Kamerling-Onnes	
PH-BTI	Boeing 737-306	2957/28720		Niels Bohr	

^Leased from GECAS   +Leased from Safair Lease Finance
"Leased from BCI Aircraft Leasing

PH-BXA	Boeing 737-8K2	198/29131		Zwann/Swan	
PH-BXB	Boeing 737-8K2	261/29132		Valk/Falcon	
PH-BXC	Boeing 737-8K2	305/29133		Karhoen/Grouse	
PH-BXD	Boeing 737-8K2	355/29134	ex N1784B	Arend/Eagle	
PH-BXE	Boeing 737-8K2	552/29595	ex N1787B	Havik/Hawk	
PH-BXF	Boeing 737-8K2	583/29596	ex N1787B	Zwalluw/Swallow	
PH-BXG	Boeing 737-8K2	605/30357	ex N1787B	Kraanvogel/Crane	
PH-BXH	Boeing 737-8K2	630/29597		Gans/Goose	
PH-BXI	Boeing 737-8K2	633/30358	ex N1787B	Zilvermeeuw/Herring Gull	
PH-BXK	Boeing 737-8K2	639/29598	ex N1015G	Gierzwalluw/Swift	
PH-BXL	Boeing 737-8K2	659/30359		Sperwer/Sparrow Hawk	
PH-BXM	Boeing 737-8K2	714/30355		Kluut/Avocet	
PH-BXN	Boeing 737-8K2	728/30356	ex N1787B	Merel/Blackbird	
PH-BXO	Boeing 737-9K2	866/29599		Plevier/Plover	
PH-BXP	Boeing 737-9K2	924/29600		Merkroet/Crested Coot	
PH-BXR	Boeing 737-9K2	959/29601		Nachtegaal/Nightingale	
PH-BXS	Boeing 737-9K2	982/29602		Buizard/Buzzard	
PH-BXT	Boeing 737-9K2	32944		on order 04	

PH-BFA	Boeing 747-406	725/23999	ex N6018N	City of Atlanta	
PH-BFB	Boeing 747-406	732/24000		City of Bangkok	
PH-BFC*	Boeing 747-406M	735/23982	ex N6038E	City of Calgary	
PH-BFD*	Boeing 747-406M	737/24001		City of Dubai/Doebai	
PH-BFE	Boeing 747-406M	763/24201	ex N6046P	City of Melbourne	Lsd ORIX
PH-BFF*	Boeing 747-406M	770/24202	ex N6046P	City of Freetown	Lsd ORIX
PH-BFG	Boeing 747-406	782/24517		City of Guayaquil	
PH-BFH*	Boeing 747-406M	783/24518	ex N60668	City of Hong Kong	
PH-BFI	Boeing 747-406M	850/25086		City of Jakarta	
PH-BFK	Boeing 747-406	854/25087		City of Karachi	
PH-BFL	Boeing 747-406	888/25356		City of Lima	
PH-BFM*	Boeing 747-406M	896/26373		City of Mexico	Lsd fr CIT Leasing
PH-BFN	Boeing 747-406	969/26372		City of Nairobi	

PH-BFO	Boeing 747-406M	938/25413		City of Orlando	
PH-BFP*	Boeing 747-406M	992/26374		City of Paramaribo	
PH-BFR	Boeing 747-406M	1014/27202		City of Rio de Janeiro	
PH-BFS	Boeing 747-406	1090/28195		City of Seoul	
PH-BFT	Boeing 747-406	1112/28459		City of Tokyo	
PH-BFU	Boeing 747-406	1127/28196		City of Beijing	
PH-BFV	Boeing 747-406	1225/28460		City of Vancouver	
PH-BFW	Boeing 747-406	1258/30454		City of Shanghai	
PH-BFY	Boeing 747-406	1302/30455		City of Johannesburg	
PH-BUK	Boeing 747-206M (EUD)	336/21549		stored	
PH-BUN	Boeing 747-206M (EUD)	389/21660		stored MHV	
PH-BUR	Boeing 747-206B (EUD)	491/22379	ex N1298E	stored MHV	
PH-BUW	Boeing 747-306M	657/23508	ex N6055X	stored MHV	
PH-CKA	Boeing 747-406ERF	1326/33694		Eendracht	
PH-CKB	Boeing 747-406ERF	1328/33695			
PH-CKC	Boeing 747-406ERF	1341/33696		Oranje	

*KLM Asia c/s   ^Freighter configuration with KLM Cargo titles

PH-BZA	Boeing 767-306ER	587/27957		Blauwbrug/Blue Bridge	
PH-BZB	Boeing 767-306ER	589/27958		Pont Neuf	
PH-BZC	Boeing 767-306ER	592/26263		Brooklyn Brug/Bridge	
PH-BZD	Boeing 767-306ER	605/27610		King Hussain Brug/Bridge	
PH-BZE	Boeing 767-306ER	607/28098		Ponte Rialto	
PH-BZF	Boeing 767-306ER	609/27959		Golden Gate Bridge	
PH-BZG	Boeing 767-306ER	625/27960	ex N6009F	Erasmus Burg/Bridge	
PH-BZH	Boeing 767-306ER	633/27611		Tower Bridge	
PH-BZI	Boeing 767-306ER	647/27612		Bosporus Bridge	
PH-BZK	Boeing 767-306ER	661/27614		Zeelandbrug/Zeeland Bridge	
PH-BZM	Boeing 767-306ER	738/28884	ex (PH-BZL)	Garibaldi Bridge	
PH-BZO	Boeing 767-306ER	781/30393		Karmsund Brug/Bridge	

All leased from ILFC

PH-BQA	Boeing 777-206ER	454/33711	ex N5014K	Albert Plesman	
PH-BQB	Boeing 777-206ER	457/33712		Borobudur	
PH-BQC	Boeing 777-206ER	461/29397		Chichen-Itza	Lsd fr ILFC
PH-BQD	Boeing 777-206ER	465/33713		Darjeeling Highway	
PH-BQE	Boeing 777-206ER	468/28691		Epidaurus	Lsd fr ILFC
PH-BQF	Boeing 777-206ER	474/29398		on order Mar04	Lsd fr ILFC
PH-BQG	Boeing 777-206ER	476/32704		on order Apr04	Lsd fr ILFC

Three more Boeing 777-206ERs are on order for delivery in 2005

PH-KCA	McDonnell-Douglas MD-11	557/48555	ex N6202D	Amy Johnson	Lsd fr ILFC
PH-KCB	McDonnell-Douglas MD-11	561/48556		Maria Montessori	
PH-KCC	McDonnell-Douglas MD-11	569/48557		Marie Curie	
PH-KCD	McDonnell-Douglas MD-11	573/48558		Florence Nightingale	
PH-KCE	McDonnell-Douglas MD-11	575/48559	ex N91566	Audrey Hepburn	
PH-KCF	McDonnell-Douglas MD-11	578/48560		Annie Romein	
PH-KCG	McDonnell-Douglas MD-11	585/48561		Maria Callas	
PH-KCH	McDonnell-Douglas MD-11	591/48562		Anna Pavlova	
PH-KCI	McDonnell-Douglas MD-11	593/48563	ex PP-SPM	Mother Theresa	Lsd fr ILFC
PH-KCK	McDonnell-Douglas MD-11	612/48564		Ingrid Bergman	

Six Airbus A330-200s are on order for delivery 2005-06
KLM controls KLM cityhopper and owns 80% of Transavia, and 26% of Kenya Airways while KLM exel, KLM UK and Martinair are wholly owned. Feeder services are operated by KLM cityhopper and KLM exel while freight flights are undertaken by Atlas Air and Martinair. To become member of SkyTeam alliance
Signed Letter of Intent 20 September 2003 to merge with Air France and form a new holding company Air France-KLM in 2Q04 with two separate operating units; Air France will hold 37% of the new company and KLM will hold 19%.

MARTINAIR HOLLAND

Martinair (MP/MPH) | **Amsterdam-Schipol (AMS)**

PH-MCG	Boeing 767-31AER	279/24428		Prins Johan Friso	Lsd fr Mega-Flight
PH-MCH	Boeing 767-31AER	294/24429		Prins Constantijn	Lsd fr Mega Flight
PH-MCI	Boeing 767-31AER	400/25312		Prins Pieter-Christiaan	
					Lsd fr Ruby Aircraft
PH-MCL	Boeing 767-31AER	415/26469		Koningin Beatrix; Fox Kids c/s	
					Lsd fr Zodiac Lease
PH-MCM	Boeing 767-31AER	416/26470		Prins Floris	Lsd fr Apple Aircraft
PH-MCP	McDonnell-Douglas MD-11CF	577/48616	ex N90187		Lsd fr MGF Kumiai
PH-MCR	McDonnell-Douglas MD-11CF	581/48617			Lsd fr Yamasa Planet lease
PH-MCS	McDonnell-Douglas MD-11CF	584/48618			Lsd fr Royal Lease
PH-MCT	McDonnell-Douglas MD-11CF	586/48629			Lsd fr Malc Fin Two
PH-MCU	McDonnell-Douglas MD-11F	606/48757			
PH-MCW	McDonnell-Douglas MD-11CF	632/48788			
PH-AHI	Boeing 757-27B	178/24137	ex G-OAHI		Lsd fr ING Lease
PH-BUH	Boeing 747-206M (EUD/SF)	271/21110			
PH-MCE	Boeing 747-21AC	669/23652	ex N6038E	Prins van Oranje	Lsd fr Mitsui
PH-MCF	Boeing 747-21AM	712/24134	ex N6009F	Prins Claus	Lsd fr Mega-Carrier

PH-MCN	Boeing 747-228F	878/25266	ex (F-GCBN)	Prins Bernhard Junior	Lsd fr Stellar
PH-MPD	Airbus Industrie A320-232	1944	ex F-WWDC		Lsd fr SALE
PH-MPE	Airbus Industrie A320-232	1945	ex F-WWDE		Lsd fr SALE
PH-MPF	Airbus Industrie A320-232	2167	ex F-WWDR		Lsd fr GATX

Wholly owned by KLM.

METROPOLIS REGIONAL AIRLINES ceased operations and aircraft returned to lessors

QUICK AIRWAYS

Quick (QAH)   Groningen-Eelde (GRQ)

PH-BOA	Mitsubishi MU-2B-60	1507SA	ex (N415HH)	EMS
PH-PTC	Piper PA-31-350 Navajo Chieftain	31-7852052	ex G-CLAN	
PH-PTD	Piper PA-31-350 Navajo Chieftain	31-7852066	ex G-BRGV	

ROSSAIR EUROPE

Catcher (ROS)   Lelystad (LEY)

PH-ACY	Beech 1900D	UE-44	ex D-CBSG	Lsd fr Air Cover; sub lsd to MDM
PH-RAE	Beech 1900D	UE-21	ex ZS-OLX	Lsd fr RSS
PH-RAG	Beech 1900D	UE-29	ex OY-GMP	Lsd fr RSS
PH-RAH	Beech 1900D	UE-31	ex (OY-GEP)	Lsd fr RSS
PH-RAR	Beech 1900D	UE-372	ex ZS-ONS	Lsd fr RSS; sublsd to EMX
PH-RAT	Beech 1900D	UE-350	ex ZS-OOV	Lsd fr RSS; sublsd to EMX
PH-ACZ	Beech B200 Super King Air	BB-1215	ex D-IEEE	
PH-RAK	Aerospatiale/Alenia ATR 42-300	032	ex ZS-OUY	Lsd fr RSS; sublsd to EMX
PH-RAQ	Aerospatiale/Alenia ATR 42-300	139	ex ZS-OSN	stored MST Lsd fr RSS

Wholly owned subsidiary of Rossair

SCHREINER AIRWAYS

Schreiner (AW/SCH)   Rotterdam (RTM)

PH-OHN	de Havilland DHC-6 Twin Otter 310	700	ex TJ-OJN	on order
PH-SDH	de Havilland DHC-8-102	222	ex C-GFUM	Op for Mobil Oil
PH-SDK	de Havilland DHC-8-311A	254	ex C-GFYI	Op for Waha Oil

Owns Schreiner Airways Cameroon. See also Aero Contractors (Nigeria) and Indonesia Air Transport

SCHREINER NORTHSEA HELICOPTERS

den Helder

PH-NZS	Sikorsky S-76B	760325	ex G-UKLS	
PH-NZT	Sikorsky S-76B	760326	ex G-UKLT	
PH-NZU	Sikorsky S-76B	760329	ex G-UKLU	
PH-NZV	Sikorsky S-76B	760336	ex G-UKLM	
PH-NZW	Sikorsky S-76B	760381	ex G-OKLE	
PH-NZZ	Sikorsky S-76B	760316	ex N373G	
PH-NZD	Sikorsky S-61N	61489	ex EI-CTK	
PH-NZG	Sikorsky S-61N	61753		
PH-NZK	Sikorsky S-61N	61773	ex LN-OMO	
PH-RVD	MD Helicopters MD.902 Explorer	900-00079	ex N70279	EMS
PH-SHF	MD Helicopters MD.902 Explorer	900-00080		EMS
PH-SSX	Aerospatiale SA.365N Dauphin 2	6030	ex 5N-BAR	

Owned by Schreiner Aviation but to be purchased by CHC Helicopters; all leased from Capital Aviation Services

TRANSAVIA AIRLINES

Transavia (HV/TRA) (IATA 979)   Amsterdam-Schipol (AMS)

PH-HZA	Boeing 737-8K2	51/28373		Lsd to BER
PH-HZB	Boeing 737-8K2	57/28374		
PH-HZC	Boeing 737-8K2	85/28375		City of Rotterdam Lsd to SCX
PH-HZD	Boeing 737-8K2	252/28376		Lsd fr ING Lease
PH-HZE	Boeing 737-8K2	277/28377		City of Rhodos
PH-HZF	Boeing 737-8K2	291/28378	ex N1796B	
PH-HZG	Boeing 737-8K2	498/28379		Lsd fr ING Lease: sublsd to SCX
PH-HZI	Boeing 737-8K2	524/28380		Lsd fr SCX
PH-HZJ	Boeing 737-8K2	549/30389	ex N1796B	Lsd fr Dia Prune; sublsd to SCX
PH-HZK	Boeing 737-8K2	555/30390		Lsd fr Dia Tulip
PH-HZL	Boeing 737-8K2	814/30391		Lsd to BER
PH-HZM	Boeing 737-8K2	833/30392		Lsd to BER
PH-HZN	Boeing 737-8K2	32943		on order
PH-HZO	Boeing 737-8K2	32944		on order
PH-HZP	Boeing 737-8K2	1122/30646		Lsd fr ILFC
PH-HZV	Boeing 737-8K2	1158/30650		Lsd fr ILFC; sublsd to SCX

PH-HZW	Boeing 737-8K2	1132/29345		Lsd fr ILFC; sublsd to PRZ
PH-HZX	Boeing 737-8K2	1126/28248		
PH-HZY	Boeing 737-8K2	1122/30646		Lsd fr ILFC
PH-HZX	Boeing 737-8K2	1126/28248		Lsd fr ILFC
PH-XRA	Boeing 737-7K2	873/30784		Lsd fr Tombo
PH-XRB	Boeing 737-7K2	1298/28256		Lsd fr ILFC
PH-XRC	Boeing 737-7K2	1318/29347		Lsd fr ILFC
PH-XRD	Boeing 737-7K2	1329/30659		Lsd fr ILFC
PH-XRE	Boeing 737-7K2	30668	on order	
PH-XRW	Boeing 737-7K2	1316/33465		Lsd fr ILFC
PH-XRX	Boeing 737-7K2	1299/33464		Lsd fr ILFC
PH-XRY	Boeing 737-7K2	1292/33463		Lsd fr ILFC
PH-XRZ	Boeing 737-7K2	1278/33462		Lsd fr ILFC
PH-	Boeing 737-7K2		on order Apr04	Lsd fr ILFC

A subsidiary of KLM (80%); Basiq Air is a low cost subsidiary but operates in Transavia colours

TRANS TRAVEL AIRLINES ceased operations and reformed as CityConnect

TULIP AIR

Tulipair (TD/TLP)   *Rotterdam (RTM)*

PH-ATM	Beech 200 Super King Air	BB-123	ex N120DA	CatPass 200 conv
PH-DDB	Beech 200 Super King Air	BB-221	ex SE-KYL	
PH-EEF	Piper PA-31-350 Navajo Chieftain	31-7552017	ex SE-GIM	
PH-IDA	Piper PA-31-350 Navajo Chieftain	31-7852160	ex N27806	
PH-KJG	British Aerospace Jetstream 31	690	ex G-LOGT	
PH-MJM	Reims Cessna F406 Caravan II	F406-0037	ex 5Y-BIS	Lsd fr Duvesteijn Avn

V-BIRD

PH-VAC	Airbus Industrie A320-212	0645	ex C-GJUP	Lsd fr ILFC
PH-VAD	Airbus Industrie A320-212	0525	ex C-GTDB	Lsd fr ILFC
PH-VAE	Airbus Industrie A320-212	0579	ex C-GJUM	Lsd fr ILFC

Registered to Dutch Bird as they are operated under their AOC until summer 2004

PJ - NETHERLANDS ANTILLES

BONAIREXEL

(9H/BXL)   *Kralendijk (BON)*

PJ-XLI	Aerospatiale/Alenia ATR 42-320	066	ex PH-XLI	Lsd fr AXL
PJ-XLL	Aerospatiale/Alenia ATR 42-320	374	ex PH-XLL	Lsd fr AXL
PJ-XLM	Aerospatiale/Alenia ATR 42-320	378	ex PH-XLM	Lsd fr AXL

BonairExel is the trading name of Dutch Eagle Express

DIVI DIVI AIR

      St Maartens (SXM)

PJ-BMV	Cessna 402B	402B0865	ex C-GCKB	
PJ-SUN	Britten-Norman BN-2A-8 Islander	377	ex SE-LGN	
PJ-	Britten-Norman BN-2A-26 Islander	82	ex N100NE	

DUTCH CARIBBEAN AIRLINES

Antillean (LM/ALM)   *Curacao-Hato (CUR)*

PJ-SEF	McDonnell-Douglas MD-82	1075/49123	ex (N317RC)	Flamboyant	
PJ-SEG	McDonnell-Douglas MD-82	1077/49124	ex (N319RC)	Kibrahocha	
PJ-SEH	McDonnell-Douglas MD-82	1452/49661	ex EC-EVY	Watapana	Lsd fr GECAS
PJ-SNK	Douglas DC-9-31 (ABS 3)	1039/48144	ex N924VJ		Lsd fr Alameda Corp
PJ-SNL	Douglas DC-9-31 (ABS 3)	1046/48154	ex N927VJ		Lsd fr Jetran Intl
PJ-SNM	Douglas DC-9-31 (ABS 3)	1024/48139	ex N919VJ		Lsd fr Jetran Intl
PJ-SNN	Douglad DC-9-31 (ABS 3)	1021/46138	ex N918VJ		Lsd fr Jetran Intl

Boeing 767s are operated by Air Holland for transatlantic flights

DUTCH CARIBBEAN EXPRESS

Dutch Caribbean (K8/DCE) (IATA 559)   *Curacao-Hato (CUR)*

PJ-DHE	de Havilland DHC-8-311A	242	ex C-FZPS	Lsd fr Avmax
PJ-DHI	de Havilland DHC-8-311A	230	ex C-FZVU	Lsd fr Avmax
PJ-TOC*	de Havilland DHC-6 Twin Otter 300	371	ex C-GGMV	Lsd fr BBS Leasing
PJ-TOD	de Havilland DHC-6 Twin Otter 300	675	ex C-GGKR	Lsd fr BBS Leasing
PJ-	de Havilland DHC-6 Twin Otter 300	359	ex N149SA	

*Ban Boneiru/Bin Korsou titles

DUTCH EAGLE EXPRESS listed under trading name, Bonair Express

WINAIR

Windward (WM/WIA)   *St. Maarten (SXM)*

PJ-AIW	Britten-Norman BN-2A-26 Islander	2038	ex C-GZKG
PJ-WIH	de Havilland DHC-6 Twin Otter 300	766	ex N304CH
PJ-WIL	de Havilland DHC-6 Twin Otter 300	358	ex C-FCSY
PJ-WIM	de Havilland DHC-6 Twin Otter 300	840	ex N840ES

Winair is the trading name of Windward Islands Airways

WINDWARD EXPRESS AIRWAYS

St Maarten (SXM)

PJ-WEA	Britten-Norman BN-2A-27 Islander	659	ex N659CM
PJ-WEB	Britten-Norman BN-2A-26 Islander	2208	ex 8P-TAG

PK - INDONESIA (Republic of Indonesia)

ADAMAIR

PK-KKA	Boeing 737-56N	2944/28565	ex N565LS	Lsd fr GECAS
PK-KKC	Boeing 737-4Y0	2361/26071	ex HA-LEO	Lsd fr GECAS
PK-KKD	Boeing 737-4Y0	1659/23978	ex HL7254	Lsd fr GECAS

Due to commence services 20 December 2003

AIRFAST INDONESIA

Airfast (AFE)   *Singapore-Seletar/Balikpapan/Jayapura (XSP/BPN/DJJ)*

PK-OAQ	Piper PA-23-250 Aztec D	27-4416	ex PK-KSB	
PK-OAT	Agusta-Bell 204B	3169	ex PK-LBC	
PK-OAW	Beech 65-B80 Queen Air	LD-308	ex PK-JBF	
PK-OAZ	Douglas DC-3	19623	ex PK-GDF	
PK-OBA	Bell 204B	2050	ex VH-UTW	
PK-OBG	Bell 206B JetRanger	67	ex VH-UHC	
PK-OBI	Bell 206B JetRanger	48	ex P2-AJJ	
PK-OBN	Sikorsky S-58ET	581492	ex PH-NZE	
PK-OBQ	Hawker Siddeley HS.748 Srs.2A/209	1638	ex RP-C1016	stored HLP
PK-OCA	ITPN Bell 412			
PK-OCC	CASA-Nurtanio C.212	50N/CC4-2-210	ex PK-NZJ	
PK-OCD	Bell 206B JetRanger II	893	ex PK-VBP	
PK-OCE	Bell 212	30981	ex PK-VBZ	
PK-OCI*	Boeing 737-230C	234/20255	ex N800WA	
PK-OCJ	de Havilland DHC-6 Twin Otter 300	522	ex A6-MBM	
PK-OCK	de Havilland DHC-6 Twin Otter 310	616	ex G-BGEN	
PK-OCL	de Havilland DHC-6 Twin Otter 310	689	ex N689WJ	
PK-OCO	Bell 206B JetRanger	580	ex PK-EBL	
PK-OCP*	Boeing 737-27A	1424/23794	ex B-2625	
PK-OCQ*	Boeing 737-2Q8	554/21687	ex B-2615	
PK-OCR	MD Helicopters MD.900	900-00089	ex N70089	
PK-OCS	MD Helicopters MD.900	900-00090	ex N70530	
PK-OSP	British Aerospace 146 Srs 100	E1124	ex G-CBXY	Op for Golkar Party

*Operated for Freeport Indonesia

AIR MARK INDONESIA AVIATION

Jakarta-Halim (HLP)

PK-AIG	Boeing 737-204	696/22364	ex ZK-NAB		Lsd fr IAI Pacific Lsg
PK-AIL	ITPN/CASA 212-200	CC-4-209/49N	ex PK-RRA	Lambarasa	
PK-AIY	Fokker 50	20227	ex OY-EBG		

AIR PARADISE INTERNATIONAL

Radisair (AD/PRZ)   *Banjarmasin (BDJ)*

PH-HZW	Boeing 737-8K2	1132/29345		Lsd fr TRA
PK-K	Airbus Industrie A310-324	500	ex N501RR	Lsd fr Pembroke
PK-KDW	Airbus Industrie A310-324	534	ex N534RR	Lsd fr Pembroke
PK-KDK	Airbus Industrie A300B4-622R	633	ex N633AN	Lsd fr AWAS

First service 16 February 2003

AIR REGIONAL

Wamena

PK-WAR	de Havilland DHC-6 Twin Otter 300	313	ex VH-FNV	dam 28Apr03

AWAIR INTERNATIONAL ceased operations in March 2002 and proposed Boeing 737-400 fleet not delivered

BALI AIR

Biar (BO/BLN)   *Banjarmasin (BDJ)*

PK-IHH	Hawker Siddeley HS.748 Srs.2A/235	1629	ex PP-VDR		
PK-IHJ	Hawker Siddeley HS.748 Srs.2A/235	1630	ex PP-VDS		
PK-IHT	Hawker Siddeley HS.748 Srs.2B/402	1793	ex G-BKLG	stored Surabaya	
PK-IHV	Hawker Siddeley HS.748 Srs.2B/402	1795	ex G-BKLI		
PK-KJM	Boeing 737-2H6	559/21732	ex PK-ALH		Lsd fr Aero Nusantara
PK-KJN	Boeing 737-2K5	814/22599	ex F-GMJD	all-white	Lsd fr BNP Bail
PK-KJO	Boeing 737-2L9 (AvAero 3)	690/22406	ex F-GEXI		Lsd fr Alter Bail

A subsidiary of Bouraq Indonesia Airlines

BATAVIA AIR

(7P/BTV)   *Jakarta-Soekarno Hatto (CGK)*

PK-YTA	Boeing 737-266	451/21192	ex N201YT	Lsd fr Wings of Eagles
PK-YTD	Boeing 737-2T4	901/22802	ex N203YT	
PK-YTE	Boeing 737-405	2137/25303	ex LN-BRP	Lsd fr Pegasus
PK-YTF	Boeing 737-2T5	737/22397	ex N31AU	Lsd fr GECAS
PK-YTI	Boeing 737-2L9	698/22407	ex N30AU	Lsd fr AeroUSA
PK-YTK	Boeing 737-4Y0	1865/24687	ex TC-APT	Lsd fr GECAS
PK-YTP	Boeing 737-4Y0	1731/24345	ex TC-APC	Lsd fr Airplanes Holdings
PK-YTZ	Boeing 737-4Y0	1639/23869	ex N869AP	Lsd fr BBAM
PK-YCM	Fokker F.28 Fellowship 4000	11168	ex PK-KFD	

Batavia Air is the trading name of Metro Batavia

BAYU INDONESIA AIR

Bayu (BYU)   *Medan (MES)*

PK-BYD	Boeing 737-2Q8	522/21518	ex CX-FAT	Lsd fr Residco

BOURAQ INDONESIA AIRLINES

Bouraq (BO/BOU)   *Jakarta-Soekarno Hatta (CGK)*

PK-IJH	Boeing 737-2K2	507/21397	ex PH-TVP	Lsd fr PT Finance
PK-IJI	Boeing 737-230	734/22125	ex D-ABFS	Lsd fr PT Finance
PK-IJJ	Boeing 737-230	762/22130	ex D-ABFZ	Lsd fr PT Finance
PK-IJK	Boeing 737-230	838/22143	ex D-ABHU	Lsd fr PT Finance
PK-IJM	Boeing 737-230	764/22131	ex PK-JHH	Lsd fr PT Finance
PK-IJN	Boeing 737-230	769/22132	ex PK-JHI	
PK-KJK	Boeing 737-266	457/21195	ex SU-AYL	Lsd fr MSR
PK-IMC	McDonnell-Douglas MD-82	1069/49113	ex N16815	Lsd fr EAL Delaware
PK-IMD	McDonnell-Douglas MD-82	1068/49112	ex N14814	Lsd fr EAL Delaware
PK-IME	McDonnell-Douglas MD-82	1019/48066	ex N16813	Lsd fr EAL Delaware

Bali Air is a wholly owned subsidiary

CALTEX PACIFIC

                                                                                                          Denpasar (DPS)

PK-PJK	Fokker F.28 Fellowship 4000	11192	ex PH-EXW	Op by PAS

CELEBES AIRLINES current status is uncertain, believed not to have commenced operations

CITILINK

                                                                                                     Jakarta-Halim (HLP)

PK-GFS	Fokker F.28 Fellowship 3000R	11119	ex PH-EXX	Lsd fr GIA
PK-GFT	Fokker F.28 Fellowship 3000R	11129	ex PH-EXS	Lsd fr GIA
			dam 11Aug03	
PK-GFW	Fokker F.28 Fellowship 3000RC	11134	ex PH-EXZ	Lsd fr GIA
PK-GKQ	Fokekr F.28 Fellowship 4000	11201	ex	Lsd fr GIA
PK-GKZ	Fokker F.28 Fellowship 4000	11216	ex PH-EZD	Lsd fr GIA
PK-GQB	Fokker F.28 Fellowship 4000	11218	ex PH-EZP	Lsd fr GIA
PK-GHS	Boeing 737-3Q8	1846/24698	ex G-IGOF	Lsd fr GIA

Wholly owned low-cost domestic subsidiary of Garuda

491

DERAYA AIR TAXI

Deraya (DRY) Jakarta-Halim (HLP)

PK-DCC	Cessna 402C	402C0250	ex N444DS
PK-DCJ	Cessna 402B	402B0615	ex N3759C
PK-DCK	Cessna 402B	402B0627	ex N3780C
PK-DCY	Cessna 402C	402C0801	ex N1233G
PK-DCZ	Cessna 402B	402B0890	ex N5203J
PK-DCP	CASA-Nurtanio C.212-A4	14N/A4-11-101	ex PK-XCM
PK-DCQ	CASA-Nurtanio C.212-A4	16N/A4-13-112	ex PK-XCO
PK-DSB	Short SD.3-30	SH3056	ex DQ-SUN
PK-DSF	Short SC.7 Skyvan 3	SH1881	ex AF-702
PK-DSR	Short SD.3-30	SH3060	ex DQ-FIJ
PK-DSU	Short SC.7 Skyvan 3	SH1924	ex PK-PSJ
PK-DSV	Short SC.7 Skyvan 3	SH1910	ex PK-PSH
PK-DYR	Piper PA-31T Cheyenne II	31T-7820054	ex VH-MWT

DIRGANTARA AIR SERVICE

Dirgantara (AW/DIR) Jakarta-Halim/Bandarmasin/Pontianak (HLP/BDJ/PNK)

PK-VIA	Britten-Norman BN-2B-20 Islander	2250	ex PK-HNF	
PK-VIB	Britten-Norman BN-2A-21 Islander	545	ex PK-TRC	
PK-VIM	Britten-Norman BN-2A-3 Islander	634	ex 9V-BEB	
PK-VIN	Britten-Norman BN-2A-3 Islander	351	ex G-BBJA	
PK-VIS	Britten-Norman BN-2A-21 Islander	485	ex G-BEGB	
PK-VIU	Britten-Norman BN-2A-21 Islander	781	ex PK-KNH	
PK-VIW	Britten-Norman BN-2A-21 Islander	2026	ex G-BIPD	
PK-VIX	Britten-Norman BN-2A-21 Islander	2027	ex G-BIUF	stored
PK-VIY	Britten-Norman BN-2B-21 Islander	2133	ex G-BJOR	stored
PK-VSA	CASA-Nurtanio C.212	87N/CC4-38-282	ex PK-HJA	
PK-VSB	CASA-Nurtanio C.212	88N/CC4-39-283	ex PK-HJB	
PK-VSC	CASA-Nurtanio C.212	90N/4-410	ex PK-HJC	
PK-VSD	CASA-Nurtanio C.212	91N/4-411	ex PK-HJD	
PK-VSE	CASA-Nurtanio C.212	92N/4-412	ex PK-HJE	
PK-VSF	CASA Nurtanio C.212	93N/4-413	ex PK-HJI	
PK-VSN	CASA-Nurtanio C.212	22N/A4-19-136	ex PK-XCU	
PK-VSP	CASA-Nurtanio C.212	7N/A4-4-78	ex PK-NCE	

EASTINDO

 Jakarta-Halim (HLP)

PK-RGI	Beech B200 Super King Air	BB-1792	ex N23268
PK-RGP	Britten-Norman BN-2B-20 Islander	2249	ex PK-HNG

EastIndo is the trading name of East Indonesian Air Taxi & Charter Service

GARUDA INDONESIA

Indonesia (GA/GIA) (IATA 126) Jakarta-Soerkarno Hatta (CGK)

PK-GPA	Airbus Industrie A330-341	138	ex F-WWKH	
PK-GPC	Airbus Industrie A330-341	140	ex F-WWKU	
PK-GPD	Airbus Industrie A330-341	144	ex F-WWKG	
PK-GPE	Airbus Industrie A330-341	148	ex F-WWKD	
PK-GPF	Airbus Industrie A330-341	153	ex F-WWKY	
PK-GPG	Airbus Industrie A330-341	165	ex F-WWKL	
EI-BZM	Boeing 737-3Y0	1929/24681		Lsd fr GECAS
PK-GGA	Boeing 737-5U3	2920/28726		
PK-GGC	Boeing 737-5U3	2937/28727		
PK-GGD	Boeing 737-5U3	2938/28728		
PK-GGE	Boeing 737-5U3	2950/28729	ex N60436	
PK-GGF	Boeing 737-5U3	2952/28730		
PK-GGG	Boeing 737-3U3	2949/28731		
PK-GGN	Boeing 737-3U3	3029/28735	ex N5573K	
PK-GGO	Boeing 737-3U3	3032/28736	ex N3134C	
PK-GGP	Boeing 737-3U3	3037/28737	ex N1020L	
PK-GGQ	Boeing 737-3U3	3064/28739	ex N1024A	
PK-GGR	Boeing 737-3U3	3079/28741	ex N1026G	
PK-GGS	Boeing 737-33A	2153/25138	ex F-GHVN	Lsd fr GECAS
PK-GGT	Boeing 737-36N	2964/28566	ex N566HE	Lsd fr GECAS
PK-GGU	Boeing 737-36N	2971/28567	ex N567HE	Lsd fr GECAS
PK-GGV	Boeing 737-3Q8	2541/26293	ex N318FL	Lsd fr ILFC
PK-GGW	Boeing 737-36M	2809/28332	ex YR-BGY	Lsd fr Boullioun
PK-GGX	Boeing 737-36N	3041/28573	ex G-XMAN	
PK-GGY	Boeing 737-36N	2846/28555	ex 9M-AAB	Lsd fr GECAS
PK-GHQ	Boeing 737-34S	2983/29108	ex (PK-GHA)	Lsd fr ILFC

PK-GHR	Boeing 737-34S	3001/29109	ex (PK-GHC)		Lsd fr ILFC
PK-GHS	Boeing 737-3Q8	1846/24698	ex G-IGOF		Op by Citilink
PK-GWK	Boeing 737-4U3	2531/25713			
PK-GWL	Boeing 737-4U3	2535/25714	ex N6067B		
PK-GWM	Boeing 737-4U3	2537/25715			
PK-GWN	Boeing 737-4U3	2540/25716			
PK-GWO	Boeing 737-4U3	2546/25717			
PK-GWP	Boeing 737-4U3	2548/25718			
PK-GWQ	Boeing 737-4U3	2549/25719			
PK-GWT	Boeing 737-4K5	2711/26316	ex D-AHLG		Lsd fr ILFC
PK-GWU	Boeing 737-4Q8	2076/24708	ex N708KS		Lsd fr ILFC
PK-GWV	Boeing 737-4Y0	1777/24512	ex N512GE		Lsd fr GECAS
PK-GWW	Boeing 737-470	1901/24683	ex N683GE		Lsd fr GECAS
PK-GWX	Boeing 737-4Y0	1904/24691	ex N691GE		Lsd fr GECAS
PK-GWY	Boeing 737-43Q	2830/28490	ex N490GE		Lsd fr AFT Trust
PK-GWZ	Boeing 737-49R	2833/28881	ex N460PR		Lsd fr GECAS
PK-GZA	Boeing 737-497	2382/25663	ex N663AL		Lsd fr GECAS
PK-GZC	Boeing 737-497	2393/25664	ex N664AL		Lsd fr GECAS
PK-GZF	Boeing 737-4M0	3018/29201	ex VP-BAH		Lsd fr Sailplane Lsg
PK-GZG	Boeing 737-4M0	3025/29202	ex VP-BAI		Lsd fr Sailplane Lsg
PK-GZH	Boeing 737-4M0	3049/29203	ex VP-BAJ		Lsd fr Sailplane Lsg
PK-GZI	Boeing 737-4M0	3051/29204	ex VP-BAL		Lsd fr Sailplane Lsg
PK-GZJ	Boeing 737-4M0	3056/29205	ex VP-BAM		Lsd fr Sailplane Lsg
PK-	Boeing 737-4M0	3058/29206	ex VP-BAN	on order 04	Lsd fr Sailplane Lsg
PK-	Boeing 737-4M0	3078/29207	ex VP-BAO	on order 04	Lsd fr Sailplane Lsg
PK-	Boeing 737-4M0	3081/29208	ex VP-BAP	on order 04	Lsd fr Sailplane Lsg
PK-	Boeing 737-4M0	3087/29209	ex VP-BAQ	on order 04	Lsd fr Sailplane Lsg
PK-	Boeing 737-4M0	3091/29210	ex VP-BAR	on order 04	Lsd fr Sailplane Lsg
PK-	Boeing 737-3Q8	1846/24698	ex G-IGOF		Lsd fr Oasis; sublsd to Citilink
PK-GSA	Boeing 747-2U3B	452/22246			To Orient Thai
PK-GSB	Boeing 747-2U3B	459/22247			To Orient Thai
PK-GSC	Boeing 747-2U3B	461/22248			
PK-GSG	Boeing 747-4U3	1011/25704			
PK-GSH	Boeing 747-4U3	1029/25705	ex N6038E		
PK-GSI	Boeing 747-441	917/24956	ex N791LF		Lsd fr ILFC

Three Boeing 747-2U3Bs are for sale to Phuket Airlines

PK-GIA	Douglas DC-10-30	223/46918			
PK-GIB	Douglas DC-10-30	226/46919			
PK-GIC	Douglas DC-10-30	239/46964			
PK-GID	Douglas DC-10-30	246/46951			
PK-GIF	Douglas DC-10-30	286/46686			

Citilink is a wholly owned low cost domestic subsidiary

GATARI AIR SERVICE

Gatari (GHS)   Jakarta-Halim (HLP)

PK-HMM	Bell 212	30958	ex PK-PGF	
PK-HMP	Bell 412	33102		
PK-HNI	Nurtanio/Bell 412	NB19/34019	ex PK-CND	
PK-HNY	Kawasaki/MBB BK117B-1	1052	ex JA6614	

GT AIR

Jakarta-Halim (HLP)

PK-LTP	Fokker F.27 Friendship 500	10398	ex PH-FNW	Op for Papua Air
PK-LTQ	Fokker F.27 Friendship 500	10528	ex HB-ILQ	Lsd fr Papua A/C
PK-LTY	de Havilland DHC-6 Twin Otter 300	831	ex B-3512	Lsd fr Nordic Avn Lsg
PK-LTZ	de Havilland DHC-6 Twin Otter 100	23	ex PK-KBD	

GT Air is the trading name of Germania Trisila Air

INDONESIA AIR TRANSPORT

Intra (IDA)   Jakarta-Halim (HLP)

PK-TRD	Aerospatiale SA.365C Dauphin 2	5058	ex N3606Q	
PK-TRE	Aerospatiale SA.365C Dauphin 2	5004	ex N3604G	
PK-TRR	Short SC.7 Skyvan Srs.3	SH1926	ex PK-FCD	
PK-TRU	BAC One-Eleven 492GM	262	ex G-BLDH	
PK-TRW	Beech 1900D	UE-177	ex N3237H	
PK-TRX	Beech 1900D	UE-186	ex N3233J	
PK-TSD	Aerospatiale AS.350BA Ecureuil	1818	ex F-GETP	
PK-TSE	Aerospatiale HB.350BA Ecureuil	1581	ex F-GKMD	Helibras built with c/no HB1039
PK-TSF	Bell 212	30974	ex N27664	
PK-TSG	Bell 212	30753	ex N81FC	
PK-TSH	Aerospatiale SA365N-2 Dauphin	6008	ex N801BA	
PK-TSI	Aerospatiale SA365N-2 Dauphin	6026	ex N87SV	
PK-TSJ	Fokker F.27 Friendship 500RFC	10525	ex N702A	

PK-TSK	Fokker F.27 Friendship 600	10441	ex VH-TQS	stored HLM	
PK-TSL	Fokker F.27 Friendship 600	10458	ex VH-TQT		
PK-TSN	Fokker 50	20185	ex PH-ZDA		Lsd fr Pembroke
PT-TSO	Fokker 50	20186	ex PH-ZDB		Lsd fr Pembroke
PK-TST	BAC One-Eleven 423ET	118	ex G-BEJM	VIP	

Affiliate of Schreiner

INDONESIAN AIRLINES

(IO/IAA)   *Jakarta-Soekarno Hatta (CGK)*

PK-IAF	Boeing 727-232 (FedEx 3)	1522/21702	ex N528DA	stored CGK	Lsd fr Aviation Partners
PK-IAT	Boeing 747-312	626/23245	ex N681SW	stored VCV	Lsd fr UT Finance
PK-IAU	Boeing 747-146B	427/22067	ex N553SW	stored RKT	Lsd fr Logistic Air
PK-MBV	Boeing 727-232 (FedEx 3)	1298/21310	ex N508DA		
PK-	Boeing 737-330	1290/23528	ex N35LX		Lsd fr WFBN

Current status uncertain, believed to have ceased operations

INTRA ASIA AIRLINES

Jakarta-Soekarno Hatta (CGK)

PK-YGZ	Boeing 727-31F (FedEx 3)	700/20112	ex OO-DHO	Noble Witness

ISLAND SEAPLANES

Bali-Benoa Harbour

PK-SDL	de Havilland DHC-2 Beaver	413	ex C-GIPL	floatplane

JATAYU AIR

Jatayu (VJ/JTY)   *Jakarta-Soekarno Hatta (CGK)*

PK-JGC	Boeing 727-227 (Raisbeck 3)	974/20736	ex N729AA		Lsd fr Aerospace Finance
PK-JGM	Boeing 727-227 (Raisbeck 3)	1459/21519	ex N880AA		Lsd fr Aerospace Sales & Lsg
PK-JGN	Boeing 727-223 (Raisbeck 3)	1328/21384	ex N872AA		Lsd fr IAL Intl
PK-JGO	Boeing 727-232 (FedEx 3)	1478/21584	ex N524DA		Lsd fr Aviation Partners
PK-JGR	Boeing 737-230	1085/23157	ex OM-ALK		Lsd fr JODA LLC
(PK-JGS)	Boeing 737-222	197/19949	ex N199NA	stored CGK	Lsd fr NAT Avn
PK-JGT	Boeing 727-247 (Duganair 3QWS)	889/20580	ex N580CR		Lsd fr NAT Avn
PK-JGU	Boeing 727-227 (Raisbeck 3)	928/20612	ex N719AA		Lsd fr Aerospace Finance
PK-JGV	Boeing 737-266	466/21227	ex PK-KJL		Lsd fr NAT Avn
PK-JGW	Boeing 737-2N7	458/21226	ex N119SW		Lsd fr BBC Aircraft

KARTIKA AIR

(KAE)   *Jakarta-Soekarno Hatta (CGK)*

PK-KAT	Boeing 737-2B7 (Nordam 3)	1050/23134	ex N287AU	Lsd fr Alameda

Reported as ceased operations but later received the above aircraft

KURA KURA AVIATION

Semarang

PK-WLX	Cessna 402B	402B0549	ex VH-AAP
PK-WLY	Cessna 402B	402B0541	ex VH-PEK

LION AIRLINES

Lion Inter (JT/LNI)   *Jakarta-Soekarno Hatta (CGK)*

PK-LMF	McDonnell-Douglas MD-82	2069/53147	ex EI-CTJ	Lsd fr LIFT Ireland
PK-LMG	McDonnell-Douglas MD-82	1278/49417	ex N417GE	Lsd fr Castle Harbour Lsg
PK-LMH	McDonnell-Douglas MD-82	1403/49419	ex N419GE	Lsd fr WFBN
PK-LMI	McDonnell-Douglas MD-82	1163/49263	ex N809NY	Lsd fr East-Trust
PK-LMJ	McDonnell-Douglas MD-82	1159/49262	ex N16808	Lsd fr East-Trust
PK-LML	McDonnell-Douglas MD-82	1043/48083	ex N10033	Lsd fr CIT Lsg
PK-LMM	McDonnell-Douglas MD-82	1032/48069	ex N480CT	Lsd fr CIT Lsg
PK-LMN	McDonnell-Douglas MD-82	1173/49189	ex N189GE	Lsd fr AFS Investment
PK-LMO	McDonnell-Douglas MD-82	1201/49373	ex N493AP	Lsd fr GECAS
PK-LMP	McDonnell-Douglas MD-82	1076/49102	ex N13891	Lsd fr Polaris
PK-LMQ	McDonnell-Douglas MD-82	1063/49117	ex N35888	Lsd fr Polaris
PK-LMR	McDonnell-Douglas MD-82	1061/49114	ex N16887	Lsd fr Polaris
PK-LMS	McDonnell-Douglas MD-82	1079/48022	ex N14871	Lsd fr Polaris
PK-LMT	McDonnell-Douglas MD-82	1171/49264	ex N14810	Lsd fr Finova
PK-LMU	McDonnell-Douglas MD-82	1242/49429	ex N829US	Lsd fr State Street
PK-	McDonnell-Douglas MD-82	1291/49443	ex N830US	
PK-	McDonnell-Douglas MD-82	1066/49114	ex N14890	Lsd fr Castle Harbour-1

PK-	McDonnell-Douglas MD-82	1065/49118	ex N14889		Lsd fr Castle Harbour-1
PK-	McDonnell-Douglas MD-82	1838/49985	ex F-GHHO	on order	
PK-	McDonnell-Douglas MD-82	1842/49986	ex F-GHHP	on order	

Lion Airlines is the trading name of Lion Mentari Air; feeder services operated by Wings Air

MAF INDONESIA

Maf (MAF)
Irian Jaya

PK-MAA	Cessna TU206G Turbo Stationair 6	U20606093	ex N206MF
PK-MAB	Cessna TU206G Turbo Stationair 6	U20606806	ex N1779R
PK-MAJ	Cessna U206G Stationair 6	U20606868	ex N9461R
PK-MAQ	Cessna TU206G Turbo Stationair 6	U20605164	
PK-MAR	Cessna TU206G Turbo Stationair 6	U20606231	ex N6317Z
PK-MAT	Cessna TU206G Turbo Stationair 6	U20604164	ex N206ST
PK-MAU	Cessna TU206G Turbo Stationair 6	U20606365	ex N7551Z
PK-MCA	Cessna TU206D Turbo Skywagon	U206-1269	ex N72054
PK-MCP	Cessna TU206F Turbo Stationair	U20603000	ex N2818Q
PK-MCZ	Cessna TU206F Turbo Stationair	U20602142	ex PK-OBR
PK-MPO	Cessna TU206G Turbo Stationair 6	U20605255	ex N5347U
PK-MPP	Cessna U206G Stationair	U20603719	ex N9M-AVW
PK-MPR	Cessna U206F Stationair	U20603398	ex N8542Q
PK-MPT	Cessna U206G Stationair 6	U20606987	ex N9933R
PK-MPV	Cessna TU206G Turbo Stationair 6	U20605864	ex N6011W
PK-MPX	Cessna TU206G Turbo Stationair	U20603620	ex N7341N
PK-MPY	Cessna TU206G Turbo Stationair	U20606094	ex N235BD
PK-MPZ	Cessna TU206G Turbo Stationair	U20606130	ex N111CM
PK-MAN	Cessna 208 Caravan I	20800048	ex N88TJ
PK-MAO	Cessna 208 Caravan I	20800162	ex N9738F
PK-MPS	Cessna 208B Caravan I	208B0656	ex N12284

MANDALA AIRLINES

Mandala (RI/MDL)
Jakarta-Soekarno Hatta (CGK)

PK-RIA	Boeing 737-2P6	497/21357	ex LV-WFX	Lsd fr GECAS
PK-RIC	Boeing 737-2S3	646/22278	ex LV-WJS	Lsd fr GECAS
PK-RID	Boeing 737-2T4	906/22803	ex N803SR	Lsd fr Aero USA
PK-RIE	Boeing 737-2T4	908/22804	ex HA-LEM	Lsd fr GECAS
PK-RIF	Boeing 737-2L9	549/21685	ex UR-BFA	Lsd fr GECAS
PK-RIH	Boeing 737-4Y0	1616/23868	ex N868AC	Lsd fr Aero USA
PK-RII	Boeing 737-2E7	922/22876	ex G-BLDE	
PK-RIJ	Boeing 737-210	578/21820	ex G-BKNH	
PK-RIK	Boeing 737-2V5	724/22531	ex N167PL	Lsd fr Polaris
PK-RIL	Boeing 737-230	788/22137	ex D-ABHL	Lsd fr PT Finance
PK-RIM	Boeing 737-230	783/22136	ex D-ABHK	Lsd fr PT Finance
PK-RIQ	Boeing 737-291	957/23023	ex TF-ABI	Lsd fr GECAS
PK-RIR	Boeing 737-2L9	825/22735	ex N164PL	Lsd fr Polaris
PK-RIT	Boeing 737-4Y0	1661/23979	ex F-GLXK	Lsd fr AerCo Ireland
PK-RIY	Boeing 727-232 (FedEx 3)	1479/21585	ex N525DA	Lsd fr Aventura Avn
PK-RIZ	Boeing 727-232 (FedEx 3)	1492/21587	ex N527DA	Lsd fr Aventura Avn

MANUNGGAL AIR

Jakarta-Halim (HLP)

PK-VTQ	Aerospatiale/MBB Transall C-160NG	235	ex PK-PTQ	
PK-VTR	Aerospatiale/MBB Transall C-160NG	233	ex PK-PTO	stored
PK-VTS	Aerospatiale/MBB Transall C-160P	207	ex PK-PTY	

MAPINDO AIR

Jakarta-Halim (HLP)

PK-VRA	Dornier 28D-1 Skyservant	4026	ex PK-LDI
PK-VRB	Dornier 28D-1 Skyservant	4031	ex PK-LDJ

MERPATI NUSANTARA AIRLINES

Merpati (MZ/MNA) (IATA)
Jakarta-Soekarno Hatta (CGK)

PK-MBC	Boeing 737-230	754/22129	ex D-ABFY		Lsd fr PT Finance
PK-MBD	Boeing 737-230	795/22141	ex D-ABHR		Lsd fr PT Finance
PK-MBE	Boeing 737-230	797/22142	ex D-ABHS	Batanta	Lsd fr PT Finance
PK-MBF	Boeing 737-2T4 (Nordam 3)	707/22368	ex N368AP		Lsd fr AeroUSA
PK-MBG	Boeing 737-2T4	708/22369	ex N369AP		Lsd fr AeroUSA
PK-MBH	Boeing 737-2S3	650/22279	ex N279AD		Lsd fr AerGo Capital
PK-MBJ	Boeing 737-2U4	761/22576	ex N576DF		Lsd fr AerGo Capital

PK-MBL	Boeing 737-4Y0	1733/24467	ex N467HE		Lsd fr GECAS
PK-MBM	Boeing 737-4Y0	1779/24513	ex N513HE		Lsd fr GECAS
PK-NCH	CASA-Nurtanio C.212-AB4	30N/AB4-2-173	ex PK-XAD	Weh	
PK-NCL	CASA-Nurtanio C.212-AB4	34N/AB4-6-185	ex PK-XAH	Berbak	
PK-NCN	CASA-Nurtanio C.212-AB4	36N/AB4-8-191	ex PK-XAJ	Seribu	
PK-NCU	CASA-Nurtanio C.212-C4	74N/CC4-24-254	ex PK-XDW	Pantar	dam Mar96
PK-NCV	CASA-Nurtanio C.212-C4	75N/CC4-26-255	ex PK-XDX	Misool	
PK-NCX	CASA-Nurtanio C.212-C4	77N/CC4-28-257	ex PK-XDZ	Batudata	
PK-NCZ	CASA-Nurtanio C.212-C4	79N/CC4-30-274	ex PK-XEC	Tanah Massa	

All reported to be withdrawn from service

PK-MNC	CASA-Nurtanio CN-235	5/N002	ex PK-XND	Wokam	
PK-MND	CASA-Nurtanio CN-235	7/N003	ex PK-XNE	Sermata	
PK-MNE	CASA-Nurtanio CN-235	9/N004	ex PK-XNF	Leti	
PK-MNF	CASA-Nurtanio CN-235-200	10/N005	ex PK-XNG	Wowoni	
PK-MNG	CASA-Nurtanio CN-235	14/N006	ex PK-XNH	Timor	
PK-MNH	CASA-Nurtanio CN-235	18/N008	ex YV-1098C	Kai Besat	
PK-MNI	CASA-Nurtanio CN-235	16/N007	ex PK-XNI	Babar; all-white	
PK-MNJ	CASA-Nurtanio CN-235	19/N009	ex PK-XNK	Damar	
PK-MNK	CASA-Nurtanio CN-235	20/N010	ex PK-XNL	Kobroor	
PK-MNM	CASA-Nurtanio CN-235	26/N012	ex PK-XNN	Moa	
PK-MNP	CASA-Nurtanio CN-235	30/N015	ex PK-XNQ	Kaledupo	

All reported to be withdrawn from service

PK-NUH	de Havilland DHC-6 Twin Otter 300	383		Natuna	
PK-NUO	de Havilland DHC-6 Twin Otter 300	487		Singkep	
PK-NUR	de Havilland DHC-6 Twin Otter 300	484		Muna	
PK-NUS	de Havilland DHC-6 Twin Otter 300	481		Peleng	
PK-NUV	de Havilland DHC-6 Twin Otter 300	472		Tanimbar	
PK-NUZ	de Havilland DHC-6 Twin Otter 300	443	ex PK-NUM	Alor	
PK-MFF	Fokker F.27 Friendship 500	10551	ex ZK-NFA	Tanah Bela	
PK-MFG	Fokker F.27 Friendship 500	10552	ex ZK-NFB	Lingga	
PK-MFJ	Fokker F.27 Friendship 500	10598	ex ZK-NFE	Adonara	
PK-MFK	Fokker F.27 Friendship 500	10607	ex ZK-NFF	Wangi-Wangi	stored SUB
PK-MFN	Fokker F.27 Friendship 500	10618	ex ZK-NFJ	Batanta	
PK-MFQ	Fokker F.27 Friendship 500	10623	ex PK-GRF	Bintan	
PK-MFV	Fokker F.27 Friendship 500	10625	ex PK-GRH	Kabia	
PK-MFW	Fokker F.27 Friendship 500	10626	ex PK-GRI	Maja	
PK-MFY	Fokker F.27 Friendship 500	10629	ex PK-GRK	Halmahera	

All reported to be withdrawn from service

PK-MGE	Fokker F.28 Fellowship 4000	11158	ex PK-GKD	
PK-MGG	Fokker F.28 Fellowship 4000	11170	ex PK-GKF	
PK-MGI	Fokker F.28 Fellowship 4000	11174	ex PK-GKH	
PK-MGJ	Fokker F.28 Fellowship 4000	11175	ex PK-GKL	
PK-MGK	Fokker F.28 Fellowship 4000	11188	ex PK-GKI	
PK-MGL	Fokker F.28 Fellowship 4000	11189	ex PK-GKJ	
PK-MGM	Fokker F.28 Fellowship 4000	11199	ex PK-GKP	
PK-MGP	Fokker F.28 Fellowship 4000	11213	ex PK-GKW	
PK-MGR	Fokker F.28 Fellowship 4000	11215	ex PK-GKY	

*Leased to Citilink; all reported withdrawn from Merpati service

PK-MBV	Boeing 727-232 (FedEx 3)	21587	ex N508DA		Lsd fr Aventura Avn
PK-MBW	Boeing 727-232 (FedEx 3)	1270/21306	ex N504DA		Lsd fr Aventura Avn
PK-MJA	Fokker 100	11453	ex PH-MXO	Bawal	
PK-MJC	Fokker 100	11463	ex PH-EZV	Sabu	
PK-MJD	Fokker 100	11474	ex PH-EZW	Rupat	

NURMAN AIR

(NIN)   *Jakarta-Halim (HLP)*

PK-NAI	Fokker F.28 Fellowship 4000	11133	ex F-GDFC	
PK-NAM	Fokker F.28 Fellowship 4000	11142	ex PK-VFA	

Nurman Air is the trading name of Nurman Avia Indopura

PELITA AIR

Pelita (6D/PAS)   *Jakarta-Halim (HLP)*

PK-PDT	Aerospatiale SA.330G Puma	1264	ex F-WTNB	
PK-PEI	Aerospatiale SA.330G Puma	1299		
PK-PEK	Aerospatiale SA.330G Puma	1283		
PK-PEN	Aerospatiale SA.330G Puma	1275		
PK-PEO	Aerospatiale SA.330G Puma	1261		
PK-PHW	Aerospatiale SA.330G Puma	1082	ex F-OCRQ	
PK-PUG	Aerospatiale AS.332C Super Puma	NSP2/2020	ex PK-XSB	
PK-PUH	Aerospatiale AS.332C Super Puma	NSP3/2021	ex PK-XSC	

PK-PCN	CASA-Nurtanio C.212-A4	56N/CC4-8-216	ex PK-XDE		
PK-PCO	CASA-Nurtanio C.212-A4	55N/CC4-7-215	ex PK-XDD		
PK-PCP	CASA-Nurtanio C.212-A4	48N/AB4-20-208	ex PK-XAV		
PK-PCQ	CASA-Nurtanio C.212-A4	47N/AB4-19-207	ex PK-XAU		
PK-PCR	CASA-Nurtanio C.212-A4	46N/AB4-18-206	ex PK-XAT		
PK-PCS	CASA-Nurtanio C.212-A4	45N/AB4-17-205	ex PK-XAS		
PK-PCT	CASA-Nurtanio C.212-A4	44N/AB4-16-204	ex PK-XAR		
PK-PCU	CASA-Nurtanio C.212-A4	43N/AB4-15-203	ex PK-XAQ		
PK-PSV	de Havilland DHC-7-103	105	ex C-GFOD		
PK-PSW	de Havilland DHC-7-103	100	ex C-GFCF		
PK-PSX	de Havilland DHC-7-103	94	ex C-GFYI		
PK-PSY	de Havilland DHC-7-103	86	ex C-GFUM		
PK-PSZ	de Havilland DHC-7-103	75	ex C-GFCF		
PK-PGJ	Nurtanio/MBB Bo105CB	N56/S-454			
PK-PGQ	Nurtanio/MBB Bo105CB	N60/S-458			
PK-PGR	Nurtanio/MBB Bo105CB	N62/S-460			
PK-PGS	Nurtanio/MBB Bo105CB	N63/S-551			
PK-PGT	Nurtanio/MBB Bo105CB	N64/S-552			
PK-PGU	Nurtanio/MBB Bo105C	N12/S-218	ex PK-XZJ		
PK-PGZ	Nurtanio/MBB Bo105CB	N65/S-553			
PK-PIH	Nurtanio/MBB Bo105CB	N68/S-556			
PK-PIJ	Nurtanio/MBB Bo105CB	N70/S-558	ex PK-XYN		
PK-PIM	Nurtanio/MBB Bo105CB	N72/S-560	ex PK-XYP		
PK-PIO	Nurtanio/MBB Bo105CB	N74/S-562	ex PK-XYR		
PK-PIP	Nurtanio/MBB Bo105CB	N75/S-563	ex PK-XYS		
PK-PIR	Nurtanio/MBB Bo105CB	N77/S-565	ex PK-XYU		
PK-PIT	Nurtanio/MBB Bo105CB	N79/S-567	ex PK-XYW		
PK-PFF	Fokker 100	11475	ex PH-WOL		Lsd fr Fokker Svs
PK-PFG	Fokker 100	11477	ex PH-EUS	Janggah	Lsd fr debis
PK-PFZ	Fokker 100	11486	ex PH-ZFA		
PK-PJN	Fokker 100	11288	ex PH-LMU	Lengguru	Lsd fr debis, op for Caltex
PK-PJO	Fokker 100	11444	ex PH-MXC	Kamodjang	Lsd fr debis
PK-PJX	Fokker 100	11445	ex PH-MXD	Lahendong	Lsd fr debis
PK-PFH^	Fokker 50	20237	ex PH-JXM	Wakatobi	
PK-PFJ^	Fokker 50	20260	ex PH-KXV	Tanjun Santan	
PK-PFK^	Fokker 50	20283	ex PH-MXF		
PK-PJJ	Avro RJ85	E2239	ex G-6-239	Wamema	
PK-PJK	Fokker F.28 Fellowship 4000	11192	ex PH-EXW		Op for Caltex
PK-PJL	Fokker F.28 Fellowship 4000	11111	ex PH-EZA	Kurau	
PK-PJM	Fokker F.28 Fellowship 4000	11178	ex PH-EXW	Matak	
PK-PJY	Fokker F.28 Fellowship 4000	11146	ex PH-EXN	Aceh	
PK-PUA	Sikorsky S-76A	76-0179	ex N5446U		Lsd to Travira
PK-PUD	Sikorsky S-76A	76-0195	ex N3121A		Lsd to Travira
PK-PUE	Sikorsky S-76A	76-0200			Lsd to Travira
PK-PUJ	Bell 412EP	36282	ex N2012Y		
PK-PUK	Bell 412EP	36288	ex N2028L		
PK-PUL	Bell 430	46088	ex N3005J		

Pelita Air is a subsidiary of Pertamina   ^Leased fron Aircraft Financing & Trading

PENAS now operates only one surveyor

POST EKSPRES PRIMA

PK-RJW	Fokker F.28 Friendship 1000	11045	ex	VIP	

REPUBLIC EXPRESS – RPX AIRLINES now listed as RPX Airlines

RIAU AIRLINES

PK-PAS	Fokker 50	20261	ex PT-SRA		Lsd fr Brazilian A/c Finance
PK-RAL	Fokker 50	20282	ex PH-MXE	Bengkalis	

RPX AIRLINES

(RH/RPH)   *Jakarta-Soekarno Hatta (CGK)*
Previously listed as Republic Express

PK-RPH	Boeing 737-2K2C (AvAero 3)	405/20943	ex F-GGVP		
PK-RPX	Boeing 737-230C (AvAero 3)	238/20256	ex F-GFVI	Norman	

RPX Airlines is the trading name of Republic Express Airlines

SABANG MERAUKE RAYA AIR CHARTER

Samer (SMC)   *Medan (MES)*

PK-ZAE	Britten-Norman BN-2A-21 Islander	565	ex G-BEGH
PK-ZAI	CASA-Nurtanio C.212-A4	18N/A4-15-120	ex PK-XCQ
PK-ZAK	Piper PA-31 Turbo Navajo	31-407	ex PK-FJA
PK-ZAN	CASA-Nurtanio C.212-A4	5N/A4-3-60	ex A-2102
PK-ZAO	CASA-Nurtanio C.212-A4	6N/A4-3-64	ex A-2101
PK-ZAP	de Havilland DHC-6 Twin Otter 300	535	ex N477AG

Operates feeder services for Garuda and Merpati in Sumatra

SEULAWAH NAD AIR

(NAD)   *Jakarta-Soekarno Hatta (CGK)*

PK-NAD	Boeing 737-209	1581/24197	ex 9M-PMW	Lsd fr TSE

Joint venture between NAD Province and Transmile

SRIWUAYA AIR

PK-CJH	Boeing 737-2B7 (Nordam 3)	935/22883	ex N271AU	Lsd fr Alameda Corp
N268AU	Boeing 737-2B7	927/22880	ex N312AU	Lsd fr Jetran

STAR AIR

(5H/STQ)   *Jakarta-Soekarno Hatta (CGK)*

PK-ALC	Boeing 737-2H6	1120/23320	ex N9187D		Lsd fr Aero Nusantara
PK-ALK	Boeing 737-236	742/22032	ex RA-73000	Cattleya	Lsd fr Finavion
PK-ALN	Boeing 737-2B7 (Nordam 3)	1044/23132	ex N285AU		
PK-ALV	Boeing 737-2B7 (Nordam 3)	1054/23135	ex N288AU	Vanda	

SUTRA AIRLINES current status uncertain, believed to have ceased operations

TRANSAIR

Jakarta-Halim (HLP)

PK-BAR	Boeing 727-25 (FedEx 3)	229/18970	ex PK-VBA	Lsd fr Bakrie Brothers

TRANSWISATA AIR

Jakarta

PK-TWA	Fokker F.28 Fellowship 4000	11234	ex N484US		
PK-TWC	Fokker 50	20272	ex D-AFFI		
PK-TWI	Fokker 100	11293	ex G-MAMH	Corporate	Op for PT Arutmin

Transwisata Air is the trading name of Transwisata Prima Aviation

TRAVIRA AIR

Denpasar (DPS)

PK-PUA	Sikorsky S-76A	760179	ex N5446U		Lsd fr PAS
PK-PUD	Sikorsky S-76A	760195	ex N3121A		Lsd fr PAS
PK-PUE	Sikorsky S-76A	760200			Lsd fr PAS
PK-TVF	Sikorsky S-76A	760154	ex VH-CPH		
PK-TVG	Sikorsky S-76A	760147	ex C-GSCH		
PK-NZU	ITPN/MBB Bo105CB	N121/S-719	ex PK-IWJ		
PK-TVA	IPTN/MBB Bo105CB	N1/S-124	ex PK-PEE		
PK-TVB	ITPN/MBB Bo105CB	N6/S-177	ex PK-PGV		
PK-TVH	Beech 1900D	UE-364	ex N30469		
PK-TVI	Cessna 208 Caravan I	20800313	ex C-FAMB	floatplane	
PK-TVK	Beech 1900D	UE-375	ex N31424	International SOS titles	
PK-TVL	Beech 1900D	UE-360	ex VH-FOZ		
PK-TVN	Cessna 208 Caravan I	20800358	ex N1229N	floatplane	

TRIGANA AIR SERVICE

(TGN)   *Jakarta-Halim (HLP)*

PK-YPA	Fokker F.27 Friendship 200	10223	ex PK-ZAY		Lsd fr Aviona Lsg
PK-YPN	Fokker F.27 Friendship 400	10299	ex PK-MFT	Morotai	
PK-YPO	Fokker F.27 Friendship 600	10400	ex PK-MFE	stored HLP	
PK-YPU	Fokker F.27 Friendship 200	10222	ex PK-ZAF		
PK-YRA	Fokker F.27 Friendship 500	10506	ex HB-ISQ		
PK-YRG	Fokker F.27 Friendship 500	10297	ex PH-FNV		

PK-YPX	de Havilland DHC-6 Twin Otter 300	684	ex HB-LTF	
PK-YPY	de Havilland DHC-6 Twin Otter 300	535	ex N477AG	
PK-YRE	Aerospatiale/Alenia ATR 42-300	027	ex F-GPZB	Lsd fr Martinique Aero Lease
PK-YRF	de Havilland DHC-6 Twin Otter 300	462	ex D-ISKY	
PK-	de Havilland DHC-6 Twin Otter 310	525	ex C-GATU	

TRI-MG AIRLINES

Trilines (TMG)
Jakarta-Halim (HLP)

PK-YGI	Boeing 727-223F (FedEx 3)	710/20185	ex EI-HCD
PK-YGM	Boeing 737-2A9C	249/20206	ex PK-LIH

WINGS AIR

(WON)
Jakarta-Soekarno Hatta (CGK)

PK-WIA	de Havilland DHC-8-301	194	ex N194TY	Lsd fr CIT Aerospace
PK-WIB	de Havilland DHC-8-301	116	ex N116TY	Lsd f CIT Aerospace
PK-WIC	de Havilland DHC-8-301	108	ex N108TY	Lsd fr CIT Aerospace
PK-WID	de Havilland DHC-8-301			

Wings Air is the trading name of Wings Abadi Air; first service May 03

XPRESS AIR

PK-TXC	Boeing 737-2B7 (Nordam 3)	956/22884	ex N272AU	Lsd fr Alameda Corp

PP-, PR-, PS-, PT- BRAZIL (Federative Republic of Brazil)

ABAETE AEROTAXI
Salvador, BA (SSA)

PT-OGK	Cessna 208A Caravan I	20800078	ex N65575
PT-OGP	Cessna 208A Caravan I	20800050	ex N817FE
PT-OGR	Cessna 208A Caravan I	20800100	ex N838FE
PT-OGS	Cessna 208A Caravan I	20800034	ex N811FE
PT-OGT	Cessna 208A Caravan I	20800038	ex N815FE
PT-OGU	Cessna 208A Caravan I	20800066	ex N826FE
PT-OZA	Cessna 208B Caravan I	208B0157	ex N4615B
PP-ATS	Cessna 402B	402B0372	
PP-ATT	Cessna 402B	402B0631	
PT-IUW	Cessna 402B	402B0380	
PT-JBD	Cessna 402B	402B0404	
PT-JRT	Cessna 402B	402B0552	ex N1634T
PT-JTZ	Cessna 402B	402B0532	
PT-LKZ	Cessna 402B	402B1074	ex N1554G
PT-RGV	Embraer EMB.821 Caraja	820138	ex PT-ZNA
PT-VCH	Embraer EMB.821 Caraja	821012	
PT-VCI	Embraer EMB.821 Caraja	820144	
PT-VKD	Embraer EMB.821 Caraja	820159	
PT-WFL	Embraer EMB.821 Caraja	820150	
PT-ACM	Embraer EMB.121A Xingu	121021	ex PT-MAN
PT-MCA	Embraer EMB.121A Xingu	121058	

Sister company of Abaete Linhas Aereas

ABAETE LINHAS AEREAS

(ABJ)
Salvador, BA (SSA)

PT-GKO	Embraer EMB.110P Bandeirante	110119	
PT-MFO	Embraer EMB.110C Bandeirante	110058	ex FAB2158
PT-MFP	Embraer EMB.110C Bandeirante	110105	ex FAB2181
PT-MFQ	Embraer EMB.110C Bandeirante	110121	ex FAB2188
PT-MFS	Embraer EMB.110C Bandeirante	110054	ex FAB2160

Sister company of Abaete Aerotaxi

ABSA CARGO

Absa Cargo (M3/TUS) (IATA 549)
Sao Paulo-Viracopos, SP (VCP)

PR-ABA	Douglas DC-8-61F (Comtran 2)	374/45980	ex XA-MAA	El Magnifico	Lsd fr ALG Lease
PR-ABB	Boeing 767-316FER	778/29881	ex CC-CZX		Lsd fr LAN
PR-GPT	Douglas DC-8-71F	343/45970	ex N871MY		

73.3% owned by LANChile

AEB TAXI AERO

Porto Alegre, RS (POA)

PT-EVP	Embraer EMB.810C Seneca II	810250	
PT-IUD	Piper PA-31-350 Navajo Chieftain	31-7305037	ex N74915
PT-JEH	Piper PA-31-350 Navajo Chieftain	31-7305057	ex N74928

AEROLEO TAXI AERO

Rio de Janeiro-Santos Dumont, RJ (SDU)

PR-EDA	Sikorsky S-76A	760279	ex N710AL	Lsd fr Airlog Intl
PR-GPC	Sikorsky S-76A	760266	ex N703AL	Lsd fr Airlog Intl
PR-LCL	Sikorsky S-76A	760280	ex N712AL	Lsd fr Airlog Intl
PR-NLF	Sikorsky S-76A	760085	ex N1547K	Lsd fr Airlog Intl
PT-HOR	Sikorsky S-76A	760003	ex N476AL	Lsd fr Airlog Intl
PT-YAU	Sikorsky S-76A	760175	ex N5446E	Lsd fr Airlog Intl
PT-YAY	Sikorsky S-76A	760277	ex N708AL	Lsd fr Airlog Intl
PP-MNL	Sikorsky S-61N	61745	ex G-BFMY	Lsd fr BHL
PR-MDS	Sikorsky S-61N	61761	ex N161AL	Lsd fr Airlog Intl
PR-NNL	Bell 412	33009	ex N415EH	Lsd fr Airlog Intl
PT-HQG	Bell 212	31123	ex N1087B	
PT-HUV	Bell 412SP	33184	ex N32130	Lsd fr Bell Financial
PT-YCF	Sikorsky S-61N	61757	ex LN-OQH	Op for Petrobas

AERO STAR TAXI AEREO

Salvador, BA (SSA)

PT-EDF	Embraer EMB-820C Navajo	820114	
PT-EZN	Embraer EMB-820C Navajo	820106	
PT-FSE	LET L-410UVP	912532	ex OY-TCM
PT-KRO	Britten-Norman BN-2A-21 Islander	742	ex G-BCVL
PT-KTR	Britten-Norman BN-2A-27 Islander	495	ex G-BDNN

AEROTAXI JACAREPAGUA suspended operations

AEROTAXI POTY suspended operations

AIR MINAS

(AMG)   Belo Horizonte-Pampulha, MG (PLU)

PR-MGE	Embraer EMB.120RT Brasilia	120130	ex N130G	on order
PR-PPT	Aerospatiale/Alenia ATR 42-320	091	ex F-WQNS	on order
PR-	Aerospatiale/Alenia ATR 42-320	128	ex F-WQNT	on order

Air Minas is the trading name of Air Minas Linhas Aereas

AMAZONIA LINHAS AEREAS suspended operations

ATA BRASIL

(ABZ)   Recife, PE (REC)

PR-ATA	Cessna 208B Caravan I	208B0880			
PR-LSW	Boeing 737-248C	208/20219	ex CC-CEI	on order	Lsd fr Aalesund
PR-MGA	Boeing 737-204C	245/20282	ex PT-MTC	on order	Lsd fr European Capital

ATA Brasil is the trading name of Atlantico Transporte Aereo

BAHIA TAXI AEREO – BATA

Salvador, BA (SSA)

PT-EHM	Embraer EMB.820C Navajo	820049	
PT-ENY	Embraer EMB.820C Navajo	820077	
PP-SEC	Shrike Commander 500S	3094	

BETA CARGO AIR

Beta Cargo (BET)   Sao Paulo-Guarulhos, SP (GRU)

PP-BRG	Boeing 707-323C (Comtran 2)	670/19586	ex CP-1698	Lsd fr Promodal Logistics
PP-BRI	Boeing 707-351C (Comtran 2)	732/19776	ex N8091J	Lsd fr Promodal Logistics
PP-BRR	Boeing 707-323C (Comtran 2)	727/20088	ex PT-TCN	Lsd fr Omega
PP-BSE	Boeing 707-330C	557/19317	ex PT-TCM	Lsd fr Omega

BETA is the trading name of Brazilian Express Transportes Aereos

BRA – BRASIL RODO AEREO

BRA-Transpaereos (BRB)

Sao Paulo-Guarulhos, SP (GRU)

PR-BRA	Boeing 737-33A	1462/23830	ex CS-TIO	Lsd fr Unicapital; sublsd to MMZ
PR-BRB	Boeing 737-3Q4	1577/24210	ex PT-TEH	Lsd fr Avn Capital Grp
PR-BRC	Boeing 737-46B	2088/25262	ex PH-AAU	Lsd fr Boullioun
PR-BRD	Boeing 737-3M8	1717/24376	ex EC-GGO	Lsd fr Avn Capital Grp
PR-BRE	Boeing 737-3K9	1794/24213	ex CS-TIG	Lsd fr Bavaria Lsg; sublsd to MMZ
PR-BRF	Boeing 737-341	2127/25051	ex PP-VOV	Lsd fr WTCo
PR-BRG	Boeing 737-341	2125/25050	ex PP-VOU	Lsd fr WTCo

BRA - Brasil Rodo Aereo is the trading name of BRA Transportes Aereos

BRASMEX

(BCA)

Belo Horizonte-Tancredo Neves Intl, MG (CNF)

PR-BME	Douglas DC-10-30F	314/47819	ex N1859U	Lsd fr CIT Lsg

Brasmex is the trading name of Brasil-Minas Express

CRUISER TAXI AEREO BRASIL

Curitiba, PR (CWB)

PR-CRX	LET L-410UVP-E20	912617	ex OK-2617
PT-WAK	Embraer EMB.110C Bandeirante	110071	ex FAB 2167
PT-WBR	Embraer EMB.110C Bandeirante	110045	ex FAB 2153
PT-WDM	Embraer EMB.110C Bandeirante	110094	ex FAB2174

FLY LINHAS AEREAS

Aereafly (4H/FLB)

Sao Paulo-Guarulhos, SP (GRU)

PP-BLR	Boeing 727-243	1394/21661	ex N578PE		Lsd fr AeroTurbine
PP-BLS	Boeing 727-224	934/20655	ex N32725	Brigadeiro Bürger	
					Lsd fr CSB Servicios
PP-JUB	Boeing 727-227	1196/21242	ex N15774	stored GRU	Lsd fr Marsh Aviation
PP-LBF	Boeing 727-2B6	945/20705	ex N609AG	stored GRU	

GIRASSOL AEROTAXI

Manaus-Eduardo Gomes, AM (MAO)

PT-DKO	Beech 95-B55 Baron	TC-1335	
PT-EAA	Embraer EMB.810C Minuano	810001	
PT-EBN	Embraer EMB.820C Navajo	820001	
PT-JBT	Piper PA-31-350 Navajo Chieftain	31-7305101	ex N94953
PT-KXV	Shrike Commander 500S	3104	ex PP-FRA
PT-LYH	Piper PA-31-350 Navajo Chieftain	31-7305124	ex PP-EFS

GOL TRANSPORTES AEREOS

Gol Transporte (G9/GLO)

Sao Paulo-Congonhas, SP (CGH)

PR-GOA	Boeing 737-7L9	11/28005	ex OY-MRB		Lsd fr GECAS
PR-GOB	Boeing 737-75B	13/28099	ex D-AGEM		Lsd fr Boeing Capital
PR-GOC	Boeing 737-75B	17/28101	ex D-AGEO		Lsd fr Boeing Capital
PR-GOD	Boeing 737-75B	66/28105	ex D-AGEV		Lsd fr Boeing Capital
PR-GOE	Boeing 737-75B	68/28106	ex D-AGEW		Lsd fr Boeing Capital
PR-GOF	Boeing 737-76Q	843/30273		Aurea	Lsd fr Boullioun
PR-GOG	Boeing 737-76Q	900/30275	ex N795BA		Lsd fr Boullioun
PR-GOH	Boeing 737-76N	954/32440			Lsd fr GECAS
PR-GOI	Boeing 737-76N	983/32574			Lsd fr GECAS
PR-GOJ	Boeing 737-8CX	1041/32359			Lsd fr GATX JetPartners
PR-GOK	Boeing 737-8CX	1084/32360			Lsd fr GATX JetPartners
PR-GOL	Boeing 737-7L9	10/28004	ex OY-MRA		Lsd fr GECAS
PR-GOM	Boeing 737-76N	463/28613	ex N312ML		Lsd fr Yildun A/c Lsg
PR-GON	Boeing 737-76N	436/30051	ex N311ML		Lsd fr Wezen A/c Lsg
PR-GOO	Boeing 737-76N	1068/30135	ex N135SF		Lsd fr Twin Peaks Holdings
PR-GOP	Boeing 737-8BK	1194/30621	ex N461LF	Victoria	Lsd fr CIT Lsg
PR-GOQ	Boeing 737-76N	1215/33417			Lsd fr GECAS
PR-GOR	Boeing 737-76N	1231/33380			Lsd fr GECAS
PR-GOT	Boeing 737-8BK	1248/30625			Lsd fr CIT Leasing
PR-GOU	Boeing 737-7Q8	183/28219	ex N331LF		Lsd fr ILFC
PR-GOV	Boeing 737-76N	135/28580	ex N580HE		Lsd fr GECAS
PR-GOW	Boeing 737-76N	170/28584	ex N584SR		Lsd fr GECAS

GONAIR TAXI AEREO suspended operations

HELISUL TAXI AEREO

Foz do Iguaçu, PR

PR-HTA	Helibras HS.350B Esquito	AS3523		
PT-HLL	Helibras HS.350B Esquito	1426/HB1021		
PT-HLO	Helibras HS.350B Esquito	1498/HB1024		
PT-HMI	Helibras HS.350B Esquito	1639/HB1046		
PT-HML	Helibras HS.350B Esquito	1642/HB1049		
PT-HMP	Helibras HS.350B Esquito	1658/HB1053		
PT-HGB	Bell 206B JetRanger III	4298	ex C-FRIN	
PT-HOY	Bell 206B JetRanger III	4171	ex N4171J	Lsd fr BCN Leasing
PT-HTC	Bell 206B JetRanger III	3449	ex N2113Z	Lsd fr Banestado Lsg
PT-YAP	Bell 206B JetRanger III	3481	ex N215RG	Lsd fr Safra Lsg
PT-YEE	Bell 206L-4 LongRanger IV	52173	ex N6257J	Lsd fr Textron Financial
PT-YEF	Bell 206L-4 LongRanger IV	52171	ex N6257B	Lsd fr Textron Financial
PT-YEL	Bell 206L-4 LongRanger IV	52918	ex N6593X	Lsd fr Textron Financial

Wholly owned by TAM

HELIVIA AERO TAXI

Manaus-Ponta Pelada, AM (PLL)

PT-HVA	MBB Bo105CBS-4	S-795	ex N5416X	Lsd fr Eurocopter
PT-HVB	MBB Bo105CBS-4	S-792	ex N7062W	Lsd fr Eurocopter
PT-HXK	MBB Bo105CBS-4	S-785	ex N54125	Lsd fr Eurocopter
PT-YAW	Aerospatiale SA.330J Puma	1590	ex F-GEQI	

INTERBRASIL STAR did not restart operations as planned

LRC LINHAS AEREAS

(LRN)

Sao Paulo-Marte, SP

PT-MET	Cessna 208B Caravan I	208B0509	ex N5073G	Lsd fr Cessna Finance
PT-MEZ	Cessna 208B Caravan I	208B0519		Lsd fr Cessna Finance

META – MESQUITA TRANSPORTES AEREO

Meta (MSQ)

Boa Vista, RR (BVB)

PT-FLY	Embraer EMB.120ER Brasilia	120044	ex PT-SLI	Lsd fr Embraer
PT-LMZ	Cessna U206F Stationair	U20602184		
PT-LNW	Embraer EMB.110P1 Bandeirante	110346	ex N697RA	
PT-LXN	Embraer EMB.120ER Brasilia	120052	ex D-CEMG	Lsd fr Embraer
PT-OND	Cessna U206G Stationair 6	U20606542	ex N9529Z	

NORDESTE LINHAS AEREAS REGIONAIS

Nordeste (JH/NES)

Salvador, SA (SSA)

PT-MND	Boeing 737-53A	1898/24786	ex HL7561	Lsd fr AWAS
PT-MNE	Boeing 737-53A	1900/24787	ex HL7562	Lsd fr AWAS
PT-MNH	Boeing 737-5Y0	2304/26067	ex DQ-FJB	Lsd fr debis
PT-MNI	Boeing 737-53A	2177/25425	ex N425AN	Lsd fr AWMS I
PT-MNK	Boeing 737-33A	2756/27457	ex N457AN	Lsd fr AWAS
PT-MNL	Boeing 737-33A	2959/27458	ex N458AN	Lsd fr AWAS

Owned by Rio-Sul which in turn is a subsidiary of VARIG who plan to merge the operations.

OCEANAIR LINHAS AEREAS

Oceanair (ONE)

Rio de Janeiro-Santos Dumont, RJ (SDU)

PR-OAN	Embraer EMB.120RT Brasilia	120051	ex N237AS	
PR-OAO	Embraer EMB.120RT Brasilia	120057	ex N239AS	
PR-OAP	Embraer EMB.120RT Brasilia	120060	ex N240AS	
PT-SLC	Embraer EMB.120ER Brasilia	120094	ex PT-SML	Green c/s
PT-SLD	Embraer EMB.120ER Brasilia	120147		Yellow c/s
PT-SLE	Embraer EMB.120ER Brasilia	120161		Blue c/s
PT-SRF	Embraer EMB.120ER Brasilia	120192		on order
PR-OAA	Fokker 50	20254	ex PH-KXN	Lsd fr debis
PR-OAB	Fokker 50	20255	ex PH-KXS	Yellow c/s	Lsd fr debis
PR-OAC	Fokker 50	20262	ex PH-KXX	

PANTANAL LINHAS AEREAS SUL-MATOGROSSENSES

Pantanal (P8/PTN)   *Sao Paulo-Congonhas, SP (CGU)*

PT-MFI	Aerospatiale/Alenia ATR 42-320	302	ex F-OKNG		Lsd fr ATR Asset Mgt
PT-MFJ	Aerospatiale/Alenia ATR 42-320	343	ex F-WQHV		Lsd fr ATR Asset Mgt
PT-MFK	Aerospatiale/Alenia ATR 42-300	225	ex F-GKNA		Lsd fr ATR Asset Mgt
PT-MFM	Aerospatiale/Alenia ATR 42-300	376	ex F-GKNH		Lsd fr ATR Asset Mgt
PT-MFT	Aerospatiale/Alenia ATR 42-320	306	ex G-BXEH		Lsd fr BZH
PT-MFU	Aerospatiale/Alenia ATR 42-310	070	ex F-GHJE		Lsd fr BZH
PT-MFV	Aerospatiale/Alenia ATR 42-300	043	ex F-GGLR		
PT-MFX	Aerospatiale/Alenia ATR 42-320	329	ex G-BXEG		

PENTA – PENA TRANSPORTES AEREOS

Aero Pena (5P/PEP)   *Santarem, PA (STM)*

PT-MPA	Cessna 208B Caravan I	208B0627	ex N5263D	Lsd fr Cessna
PT-MPB	Cessna 208B Caravan I	208B0630	ex N5263A	Lsd fr Cessna
PT-MPD	Cessna 208B Caravan I	208B0644	ex N5267T	Lsd fr Cessna
PT-MPG	Cessna 208B Caravan I	208B0645	ex N5268A	Lsd fr Cessna
PT-OSG	Cessna 208B Caravan I	208B0300	ex N5516B	Lsd fr Cessna
PP-ISE	Embraer EMB.120ER Brasilia	120246	ex N6222Z	
PT-LLC	Embraer EMB.110P1 Bandeirante	110427	ex N302EB	
PT-SOF	Embraer EMB.110P1A Bandeirante	110486		

PUMA LINHAS AEREAS

(PLY)   *Belem, PA (BEL)*

PR-PMA	Cessna 208B Caravan I	208B0907	ex N12171
PR-PMB	Cessna 208B Caravan I	208B0908	ex N1259Z
PR-PMC	Cessna 208B Caravan I	208B0909	ex N12826
PT-STN	Embraer EMB.120ER Brasilia	120241	

RICO LINHAS AEREAS

Rico (C7/RLE)   *Manaus-Eduardo Gomez, AM (MAO)*

PR-RLA	Boeing 737-241	417/21009	ex PP-VMN	on order	Lsd fr PLM Intl
PR-RLB	Boeing 737-241	402/21008	ex PP-VMM		Lsd fr PLM Intl
PT-WDB	Embraer EMB.110C Bandeirante	110051	ex FAB2159		
PT-WGE	Embraer EMB.120RT Brasilia	120004	ex XA-SQN		
PT-WJA	Embraer EMB.110P1 Bandeirante	110265	ex PT-OHF		
PT-WRO	Embraer EMB.120ER Brasilia	120070	ex PT-SLB		Lsd fr Embraer

RIO-SUL SERVICIOS AEREOS REGIONAIS

Riosul (SL/RSL) (IATA)   *Rio de Janaiero-Santos Dumont, RJ (SDU)*

PT-MNJ	Boeing 737-33A	2046/25057	ex PT-TEQ	Turma da Monica colours	
					Lsd fr AWAS
PT-SLW	Boeing 737-53A	1964/24922	ex CN-RMU		Lsd fr AWAS
PT-SSB	Boeing 737-5Q8	2834/27629			Lsd fr ILFC
PT-SSC	Boeing 737-5Q8	2889/27634			Lsd fr ILFC
PT-SSE	Boeing 737-5Q8	2965/28052			Lsd fr ILFC
PT-SSF	Boeing 737-5Q8	2999/28201			Lsd fr ILFC
PT-SSG	Boeing 737-5Q8	3024/28055			Lsd fr ILFC
PT-SSH	Boeing 737-58E	2991/29122	ex N291SR		Lsd fr Sunrock
PT-SSI	Boeing 737-53A	1882/24785	ex 5X-USM		Lsd fr ORIX
PT-SSJ	Boeing 737-33A	1984/24791	ex N791AW		Lsd fr AWAS
PT-SSK	Boeing 737-3Y0	1538/23922	ex OO-VEE		Lsd fr GECAS
PT-SSN	Boeing 737-53A	1945/24881	ex LZ-BOA		Lsd fr AWAS
PT-SSO	Boeing 737-53A	1962/24921	ex LZ-BOB		Lsd fr AWAS
PT-SSP	Boeing 737-33A	1741/24097	ex N497SR		Lsd fr AWMS
PT-SSQ	Boeing 737-33A	2703/27454	ex VH-CZT		Lsd fr AWMS
PT-SPF	Embraer EMB.145ER	145034			
PT-SPH	Embraer EMB.145ER	145060			
PT-SPI	Embraer EMB.145ER	145065			
PT-SPJ	Embraer EMB.145ER	145083			
PT-SPK	Embraer EMB.145ER	145089			
PT-SPL	Embraer EMB.145ER	145090			
PT-SPM	Embraer EMB.145ER	145114			
PT-SPN	Embraer EMB.145ER	145127			
PT-SPO	Embraer EMB.145ER	145137			
PT-SPP	Embraer EMB.145ER	145350			

All leased from River One Ltd and to be returned to Embraer

PR-SAE	Boeing 737-73S	187/29078	ex EI-CRP		Lsd fr Pembroke

PR-SAF	Boeing 737-7Q8	713/30635	ex N461LF	Lsd fr ILFC
PR-SAG	Boeing 737-7Q8	369/28224	ex N411LF	Lsd fr ILFC

A wholly owned subsidiary of VARIG and operates in their colours; controls Nordeste.

SKYMASTER AIRLINES

Skymaster Air (SKC) — *Manaus-Eduardo Gomes, AM/Sao Paulo-Viraacopos, SP (MAO/VCP)*

PT-MTR	Boeing 707-369C (Comtran 2)	758/20084	ex OB-1699	Lsd fr Daedalus Avn
PT-WSZ	Boeing 707-338C (Comtran 2)	404/18808	ex HK-3030	
PT-WUS	Boeing 707-324C (Comtran 2)	576/19352	ex HK-3604X	Lsd fr Comtran
PR-SKC	Douglas DC-8-63F (BAC 3)	547/46143	ex N959R	Lsd fr GM Acceptance
PR-SKI	Douglas DC-8-62F (BAC 3)	554/46154	ex N997CF	Lsd fr Skytrade Intl Enterprises
PR-SKM	Douglas DC-8-63F (BAC 3)	527/46137	ex N957R	Lsd fr GM Acceptance

TAF LINHAS AEREAS

(TSD) — *Fortaleza, CE (FOR)*

PP-KZD	Shrike Commander 500S	3140			
PP-SBF	Embraer EMB.110C Bandeirante	110023			
PR-GMA	Boeing 727-224F	979/20659	ex OY-SEY		
PT-GJD	Embraer EMB.110EJ Bandeirante	110056			
PT-LBU	Embraer EMB.110C Bandeirante	110033	ex PT-FAE		
PT-OGG	Cessna 208A Caravan I	20800041	ex N813FE		Lsd fr Cessna
PT-MTA	Boeing 737-248C	215/20220	ex 9M-PMP	Freighter	Lsd fr TSE
PT-MTB	Boeing 737-230C	230/20254	ex 9M-PMQ	Freighter	Lsd fr TSE
PT-MTC	Boeing 737-204C	245/20282	ex N282AD	Lsd fr Euro Capital; for ATA Brasil	
PT-MTF	Boeing 737-241	400/21007	ex PP-VML		Lsd fr PLM Intl
PT-OGL	Cessna 208A Caravan I	20800102	ex N839FE		Lsd fr Cessna
PT-OGV	Cessna 208A Caravan I	20800019	ex N805FE		Lsd fr Cessna
PT-OQT	Cessna 208B Grand Caravan	208B0314	ex N1018X		Lsd fr Cessna
PT-TAF	Embraer EMB.110 Bandeirante	110103	ex FAB2179		
PT-YPF	Aerospatiale AS.350B2 Ecureuil	3149			

*Operated for Aluminal Quimica de Noroeste

TAM LINHAS AEREAS

TAM (JJ/TAM) (IATA 957) — *Sao Paulo-Congonhas, SP (GGH)*

PR-MAH	Airbus Industrie A319-132	1608	ex D-AIJO	
PR-MAI	Airbus Industrie A319-132	1703	ex D-AIMM	
PR-MAL	Airbus Industrie A319-132	1801	ex D-AVWD	
PR-MAM	Airbus Industrie A319-132	1826	ex D-AVWN	
PR-MAN	Airbus Industrie A319-132	1831	ex D-AVWR	
PR-MAO	Airbus Industrie A319-132	1837	ex D-AVYQ	
PR-MAQ	Airbus Industrie A319-132	1855	ex D-AVYA	
PT-MZA	Airbus Industrie A319-132	0976	ex D-AVYI	Lsd fr Boullioun
PT-MZB	Airbus Industrie A319-132	1010	ex D-AVYA	Lsd fr Boullioun
PT-MZC	Airbus Industrie A319-132	1092	ex D-AVYD	Lsd fr Napoleon Lsg
PT-MZD	Airbus Industrie A319-132	1096	ex D-AVYR	Lsd fr Napoleon Lsg
PT-MZE	Airbus Industrie A319-132	1103	ex D-AVWD	Lsd fr Napoleon Lsg
PT-MZF	Airbus Industrie A319-132	1139	ex D-AVYO	Lsd fr Napoleon Lsg
PR-MAA	Airbus Industrie A320-232	1595	ex F-WWBU	Lsd fr IEM Airfinance
PR-MAB	Airbus Industrie A320-232	1663	ex F-WWIE	
PR-MAC	Airbus Industrie A320-232	1672	ex F-WWIK	
PR-MAD	Airbus Industrie A320-232	1771	ex F-WWDD	
PR-MAE	Airbus Industrie A320-232	1804	ex F-WWII	
PR-MAF	Airbus Industrie A320-231	0249	ex 3B-NBH	Lsd fr Airbus
PR-MAG	Airbus Industrie A320-232	1832	ex F-WWBD	Sao Paulo 450 Anos
PR-MAJ	Airbus Industrie A320-232	1818	ex F-WWIN	
PR-MAK	Airbus Industrie A320-232	1825	ex F-WWIX	
PR-MAP	Airbus Industrie A320-232	1857	ex F-WWBZ	Lsd fr CIT Group
PR-MAR	Airbus Industrie A320-232	1888	ex F-WWBS	Lsd fr SALE
PT-MZG	Airbus Industrie A320-232	1143	ex F-WWBG	Lsd fr Juliana Lsg
PT-MZH	Airbus Industrie A320-232	1158	ex F-WWBY	Flagc/s	Lsd fr Juliana Lsg
PT-MZI	Airbus Industrie A320-232	1246	ex F-WWIR	Lsd fr Amazon Avn
PT-MZJ	Airbus Industrie A320-232	1251	ex F-WWIV	Lsd fr Amazon Avn
PT-MZK	Airbus Industrie A320-232	1368	ex F-WWIJ	Lsd fr Boullioun
PT-MZL	Airbus Industrie A320-232	1376	ex F-WWIN	Lsd fr Boullioun
PT-MZM	Airbus Industrie A320-232	0453	ex N641AW	Lsd fr CIT Group
PT-MZN	Airbus Industrie A320-231	0440	ex ZS-SHG	Lsd fr GATX Flightlease
PT-MZO	Airbus Industrie A320-231	0250	ex ZS-SHC	Lsd fr GATX Flightlease
PT-MZP	Airbus Industrie A320-231	0243	ex ZS-SHA	Lsd fr GATX Flightlease
PT-MZQ	Airbus Industrie A320-231	0335	ex ZS-SHF	Lsd fr GATX Flightlease
PT-MZR	Airbus Industrie A320-231	0334	ex ZS-SHE	Lsd fr GATX Flightlease
PT-MZS	Airbus Industrie A320-231	0251	ex ZS-SHD	Lsd fr GATX Flightlease
PT-MZT	Airbus Industrie A320-232	1486	ex F-WWDV	
PT-MZU	Airbus Industrie A320-232	1518	ex F-WWIJ	

PT-MZV	Airbus Industrie A320-232	0758	ex N758SL		Lsd fr WFBN
PT-MZW	Airbus Industrie A320-232	1580	ex F-WWBK		Lsd fr IEM Airfinance
PT-MZX	Airbus Industrie A320-232	1613	ex F-WWDI		Lsd fr IEM Airfinance
PT-MZY	Airbus Industrie A320-232	1628	ex F-WWDO		
PT-MZZ	Airbus Industrie A320-232	1593	ex F-WWBT		Lsd fr IEM Airfinance
PT-MVA	Airbus Industrie A330-222	232	ex F-WWKV		Lsd fr GECAS; sublsd to SAA
PT-MVB	Airbus Industrie A330-222	238	ex F-WWKY		Lsd fr GECAS; sublsd to SAA
PT-MVC	Airbus Industrie A330-222	247	ex F-WWKH		Lsd fr GECAS
PT-MVD*	Airbus Industrie A330-222	259	ex F-WWKP	The Magic Red Carpet	Lsd fr WFBN
PT-MVE*	Airbus Industrie A330-223	361	ex F-WWYM		Lsd fr Tiago Lsg
PT-MVF	Airbus Industrie A330-223	466	ex F-WWKP		Lsd fr GECAS
PT-MVG	Airbus Industrie A330-223	472	ex F-WWKQ		Lsd fr GECAS
PT-MVH	Airbus Industrie A330-223	477	ex F-WWKS		Lsd fr GECAS
PT-MVK	Airbus Industrie A330-223	486	ex F-WWYL		Lsd fr GECAS
PT-	Airbus Industrie A330-223		ex F-WW	on order	Lsd fr GECAS
PT-	Airbus Industrie A330-223	527	ex F-WW	on order	Lsd fr GECAS

*Subleased to Etihad

PT-MEA	Cessna 208B Caravan I	208B0333	ex N1037L	
PT-MEB	Cessna 208B Caravan I	208B0335	ex N1038G	
PT-MEC	Cessna 208B Caravan I	208B0342	ex N1045C	
PT-MED	Cessna 208B Caravan I	208B0343	ex N1052C	
PT-MEE	Cessna 208B Caravan I	208B0344	ex N1054M	
PT-MEG	Cessna 208B Caravan I	208B0352	ex N1114N	
PT-MEH	Cessna 208B Caravan I	208B0354	ex N1114W	
PT-MEI	Cessna 208B Caravan I	208B0358	ex N1115P	
PT-MEJ	Cessna 208B Caravan I	208B0359	ex N1115V	
PT-MEK	Cessna 208B Caravan I	208B0360	ex N1115W	
PT-MEL	Cessna 208B Caravan I	208B0361	ex N1116G	
PT-MEM	Cessna 208B Caravan I	208B0405		
PT-MEN	Cessna 208B Caravan I	208B0408		
PT-MEO	Cessna 208B Caravan I	208B0412		
PT-MEP	Cessna 208B Caravan I	208B0413		
PT-MER	Cessna 208B Caravan I	208B0506	ex N5071M	
PT-MFS	Cessna 208B Caravan I	208B0507	ex N5261R	
PT-MEU	Cessna 208B Caravan I	208B0510	ex N5076J	
PT-MEV	Cessna 208B Caravan I	208B0512	ex N5076X	
PT-MEX	Cessna 208B Caravan I	208B0515	ex N50820	
PT-MEY	Cessna 208B Caravan I	208B0518		
PT-MHA	Cessna 208B Caravan I	208B0533		
PT-MHB	Cessna 208B Caravan I	208B0534		
PT-MHC	Cessna 208B Caravan I	208B0543		
PT-OGQ	Cessna 208 Caravan I	20800032	ex N809FE	
PT-OGX	Cessna 208 Caravan I	20800076	ex N825FE	

All leased from Cessna Finance Corp

PT-MQB	Fokker 100	11350	ex PH-LNN	Lsd fr GPA Fokker 100
PT-MQC+	Fokker 100	11371	ex PH-JXP	Lsd fr GPA Fokker 100
PT-MQD	Fokker 100	11383	ex B-2231	Lsd fr GPA Fokker 100; sublsd to UAir
PT-MQE	Fokker 100	11389	ex B-2232	Lsd fr GPA Fokker 100
PT-MQF	Fokker 100	11401	ex B-2234	Lsd fr GPA Fokker 100
PT-MQG	Fokker 100	11527	ex F-WQGZ	Lsd fr Jakarta A/c Finance
PT-MQI	Fokker 100	11517	ex F-WQGX	Lsd fr Jakarta A/c Finance
PT-MQJ	Fokker 100	11347	ex PH-LNL	Lsd fr GPA Fokker 100
PT-MQK	Fokker 100	11336	ex PH-LNF	Lsd fr GPA Fokker 100
PT-MQL	Fokker 100	11394	ex B-2233	Lsd fr GPA Fokker 100
PT-MQM	Fokker 100	11301	ex PH-LMV	Lsd fr Baltic Airlease
PT-MQN^	Fokker 100	11409	ex B-2235	Lsd fr GPA Fokker 100
PT-MQO	Fokker 100	11423	ex B-2238	Lsd fr Aircraft Lsg PS
PT-MQP+	Fokker 100	11430	ex B-2236	Lsd fr F100 Lsg
PT-MQQ	Fokker 100	11265	ex PH-SEM	Lsd fr debisBaltic Airlease
PT-MQR	Fokker 100	11421	ex B-2237	Lsd fr F100 Lsg
PT-MQS	Fokker 100	11431	ex B-2240	Lsd fr F100 Lsg
PT-MQT	Fokker 100	11429	ex B-2239	Lsd fr F100 Lsg
PT-MQU	Fokker 100	11264	ex PH-THY	Lsd fr Baltic Lse
PT-MQV^	Fokker 100	11326	ex SE-DUE	Lsd fr AMS Fokker
PT-MRA+	Fokker 100	11284	ex PH-LMI	Lsd fr GPA Fokker 100
PT-MRB +	Fokker 100	11285	ex PH-LMK	Lsd fr GPA Fokker 100
PT-MRC	Fokker 100	11320	ex PH-LND	Lsd fr Baltic Airlease
PT-MRD+	Fokker 100	11322	ex PH-LNE	Lsd fr Baltic Airlease
PT-MRE+	Fokker 100	11348	ex PH-LNM	Lsd fr GPA Fokker 100
PT-MRF+	Fokker 100	11351	ex PH-LNO	Lsd fr GECAS
PT-MRG+	Fokker 100	11304	ex PH-LMX	Lsd fr GPA Fokker 100
PT-MRH	Fokker 100	11305	ex PH-LMY	Lsd fr GPA Fokker 100
PT-MRO	Fokker 100	11470	ex PH-EZR	Lsd fr Brazilian A/c Finance
PT-MRP	Fokker 100	11472	ex PH-EZU	Lsd fr Brazilian A/c Finance
PT-MRR	Fokker 100	11461	ex PH-EZT	Lsd fr Brazilian A/c Finance
PT-MRS	Fokker 100	11462	ex PH-EZX	Lsd fr Brazilian A/c Finance
PT-MRT	Fokker 100	11505	ex PH-JCJ	Lsd fr Brazilian A/c Finance
PT-MRU	Fokker 100	11511	ex PH-JCK	Lsd fr Lazard
PT-MRV	Fokker 100	11516	ex PH-JCL	Lsd fr Lazard

PT-MRW	Fokker 100	11518	ex PH-JCM	Lsd fr Lazard
PT-MRX+	Fokker 100	11341	ex PH-LNH	Lsd fr GPA Fokker 100
PT-MRY	Fokker 100	11343	ex PH-LNK	Lsd fr GPA Fokker 100
PT-WHL ^	Fokker 100	11471	ex PH-MXW	Lsd fr Pembroke

+Stored at TAM maintenance base at Sao Carlos   ^For return to lessor
Member of TAM Group which includes TAM Paraguay and Interexpress T/A Regionais. Announced plans on 18 September 2003 to merge with VARIG but terms still not concluded

TASUL / TAXI AEREO SUL

Alegre-Salgado Filho, RS (PQA)

PT-JGH	Cessna 402B	402B0441	
PT-JJB	Cessna 402B	402B0399	ex N8063Q
PT-KDA	Cessna 310Q	310Q1087	
PT-MAL	Embraer EMB.121A Xingu	121019	

TAVAJ – TRANSPORTES AEREOS REGULARES

Tavaj (4U/TVJ)   *Rio Branco, AC (RBR)*

PT-GJP	Embraer EMB.110EJ Bandeirante	110065		
PT-LRB	Embraer EMB.110P1 Bandeirante	110409	ex N720RA	
PT-LRJ	Embraer EMB.110P1 Bandeirante	110384	ex N699RA	
PT-LTN	Embraer EMB.110P1 Bandeirante	110418	ex N860AC	
PT-OCW	Embraer EMB.110P1 Bandeirante	110273	ex N90PB	
PT-OCX	Embraer EMB.110P1 Bandeirante	110316	ex N94PB	
PT-LAH	Fokker F.27 Friendship 600	10178	ex	
PT-TVA	Fokker F.27 Friendship 600	10334	ex G-BNAL	stored Manaus

TAXI AEREO ITAITUBA

Santarem, PA (STM)

PT-GJR	Embraer EMB.110EJ Bandeirante	110070	
PT-GKE	Embraer EMB.110B1 Bandeirante	110096	ex PP-ZKE

TAXI AEREO KOVACS

Belem, PA (BEL)

PT-BBW	Cessna U206C Super Skywagon	U206-1039
PT-JNG	Cessna 402B	402B0446

TAXI AEREO WEISS

Curitiba, PR (CWB)

PT-EFU	Embraer EMB.820C Navajo	820031
PT-ELY	Embraer EMB.820C Navajo	820063
PT-GKQ	Embraer EMB.110P Bandeirante	110125

TCB / TRANSPORTES CHARTER DO BRASIL

Charter Brasil (TCJ)   *Sao Paulo-Viracopos, SP (VCP)*

PP-TAR	Douglas DC-8F-54 (QNC 2)	187/45668	ex CP-2217	stored VCP	Lsd fr Global
PP-TPC	Douglas DC-8-52 (QNC 2)	233/45752	ex N42920	Daniel; std VCP	Lsd fr Daedalus Intl

Current status is uncertain

TEAM AIRLINES – TEAM TRANSPORTES AEREOS

(TIM)   *Rio de Janeiro-Santos Dumont, RJ (SDU)*

PR-AIA	LET L-410UVP-E	912611	ex CCCP-67680
PR-IMO	LET L-410UVP-E20	922701	ex OK-XDJ

TOTAL LINHAS AEREAS

Total (TTL)   *Belo Horizonte-Pampulha, MG/Manaus-Eduardo Gomes, AM (PLU/MAO)*

PP-ATV	Aerospatiale/Alenia ATR 42-300	298	ex F-WQHA		Lsd fr ATR Asset Mgt
PR-TTA	Aerospatiale/Alenia ATR 42-300	015	ex F-WQNO		Lsd fr ATR Asset Mgt
PR-TTC	Aerospatiale/Alenia ATR 42-300	028	ex F-WQNG		Lsd fr ATR Asset Mgt
PR-TTD	Aerospatiale/Alenia ATR 42-300	038	ex LV-YJA	on order	Lsd fr ATR Asset Mgt
PT-MFE	Aerospatiale/Alenia ATR 42-300	295	ex F-WWLU		Lsd fr ATR Asset Mgt
PT-MTO	Aerospatiale/Alenia ATR 42-320	115	ex XA-TPZ		Lsd fr ATR Asset Mgt
PT-TTL	Aerospatiale/Alenia ATR 42-320	380	ex N988MA		Lsd fr ATR Asset Mgt
PR-TTB	Boeing 727-223 (FedEx 3)	1643/22007	ex N891AA		Lsd fr Avn Capital Grp

PT-JHG	Embraer EMB.110C Bandeirante	110012		stored	
PT-MTQ	Boeing 727-243F	1620/22053	ex N198PC		Lsd fr Pegasus
PT-MTT	Boeing 727-243F	1752/22167	ex N270PC		Lsd fr Pacific

TRANSPORTES REGIONAIS DO INTERIOR PAULISTA / TRIP

(8R)   *Sao Paulo-Viracopos, SP (VCP)*

PP-PTA	Embraer EMB.120RT Brasilia	120061	ex F-GFEN		Lsd fr ATR Asset Mgt
PP-PTB	Embraer EMB.120RT Brasilia	120080	ex F-GFEP		Lsd fr ATR Asset Mgt
PP-PTC	Aerospatiale/Alenia ATR 42-300	035	ex F-ODUD		Lsd fr ATR Asset Mgt
PP-PTD	Aerospatiale/Alenia ATR 42-300	091	ex F-		Lsd fr ATR Asset Mgt

---

VARIG BRASIL

Varig (RG/VRG) (IATA 042)   *Rio de Janeiro-Galeao, RJ/Porto Alegre-Canoas, RS (GIG/POA)*

PP-CJR	Boeing 737-2C3	404/21015		stored GIG	
PP-VME	Boeing 737-241	378/21000	ex (PR-NAD)	stored	Lsd fr PLM Intl
PP-VMH	Boeing 737-241	389/21003			Lsd fr PLM Intl
PP-VMI	Boeing 737-241	390/21004		stored GIG	
PP-VNM	Boeing 737-241	417/21009	ex (PR-NAE)	stored; for RLE	Lsd fr PLM Intl
PP-VNT	Boeing 737-33A	1446/23828			Lsd fr Nordstress
PP-VNX	Boeing 737-33A	1460/23829		stored POA	Lsd fr Nordstress
PP-VNY	Boeing 737-3K9	1918/24864			Lsd fr Bavaria
PP-VNZ	Boeing 737-3K9	1926/24869			Lsd fr Bavaria
PP-VON	Boeing 737-341	1935/24935			Lsd fr Mitsui
PP-VOO	Boeing 737-341	1951/24936			Lsd fr Mitsui
PP-VOR	Boeing 737-33A	1727/24093	ex G-PATE		Lsd fr Ansett
PP-VOT	Boeing 737-341	2091/25049			Lsd fr SR VRG
PP-VOW	Boeing 737-3Q8	2133/24961			Lsd fr WFBN
PP-VOY	Boeing 737-3K9	2090/25210			Lsd fr Bavaria
PP-VOZ	Boeing 737-3K9	2100/25239			Lsd fr Bavaria
PP-VPA	Boeing 737-341	2273/26852			Lsd fr CIT Group
PP-VPB	Boeing 737-341	2321/26856			Lsd fr Bavaria
PP-VPC	Boeing 737-341	2326/26857			Lsd fr Bavaria
PP-VPF	Boeing 737-3S1	1896/24834	ex N371TA		Lsd fr TAI
PP-VPX	Boeing 737-33R	2899/28870	ex N965WP		Lsd fr GATX
PP-VPY	Boeing 737-33R	2900/28871	ex N966WP		Lsd fr NBB Lease
PP-VPZ	Boeing 737-3S3	3061/29245			Lsd fr Sunrock
PP-VQN	Boeing 737-33A	1763/24098	ex N98NG		Lsd fr ING Lease
PP-VQO	Boeing 737-3M8	1719/24377	ex N77NG		Lsd fr ING Lease
PP-VQW	Boeing 737-3S3	1374/23787	ex PP-TEY		Lsd fr ACG Acquisitions
PP-VQZ	Boeing 737-33A	2606/27284	ex YR-BGU		Lsd fr AWAS
PP-VTA	Boeing 737-3K9	1416/23797	ex PT-TEU		Lsd fr Bavaria
PP-VTB	Boeing 737-3K9	1429/23798	ex PT-TEV		Lsd fr Bavaria
PP-VOI	Boeing 767-341ER	289/24752			Lsd fr Nissho Iwai
PP-VOJ	Boeing 767-341ER	291/24753			Lsd fr Nissho Iwai
PP-VOK	Boeing 767-341ER	314/24843		500th c/s	Lsd fr Itoh Lse
PP-VOL	Boeing 767-341ER	324/24844			Lsd fr Itoh Lse
PP-VPW	Boeing 767-375ER	248/24086	ex C-FCAJ		Lsd fr Sunrock
PP-VPW	Boeing 767-375ER	249/24087	ex C-FCAU		Lsd fr CIT Group
PP-VTC	Boeing 767-3Y0ER	408/25411	ex N640TW		Lsd fr debis
PP-VTE	Boeing 767-3Y0ER	505/26208	ex N639TW	Lsd fr LIFT Missouri; jt ops with MMZ	
PP-VAR	Boeing 777-236	17/27108	ex N702BA		Lsd fr Boeing Capital
PP-VRA	Boeing 777-2Q8ER	365/28689		Otto Meyer	Lsd fr ILFC
PP-VRB	Boeing 777-2Q8ER	373/28692			Lsd fr ILFC
PP-VRD	Boeing 777-236	19/27109	ex N703BA		Lsd fr Boeing Capital
PP-VSA	Boeing 737-85F	936/30571			Lsd fr GATX
PP-VSB	Boeing 737-85F	976/30477	ex N1782B		Lsd fr GATX
PP-VPJ	McDonnell-Douglas MD-11	523/48404			Lsd fr Compass Rose Lsg
PP-VPK	McDonnell-Douglas MD-11	524/48405			Lsd fr Compass Rose Lsg
PP-VQF	McDonnell-Douglas MD-11	520/48502	ex N540MD		Lsd fr KUTA
PP-VQG	McDonnell-Douglas MD-11	528/48503	ex N538MD		Lsd fr Dillon
PP-VQH	McDonnell-Douglas MD-11	548/48504	ex N539MD		Lsd fr Akash
PP-VQI	McDonnell-Douglas MD-11ER	608/48753	ex PK-GIK		Lsd fr Boeing
PP-VQJ	McDonnell-Douglas MD-11ER	613/48755	ex PK-GIL		Lsd fr Boeing
PP-VQK	McDonnell-Douglas MD-11ER	615/48758	ex PK-GIM		Lsd fr Boeing
PP-VQL	McDonnell-Douglas MD-11	488/48413	ex PP-SOW		Lsd fr Mitsui
PP-VQM	McDonnell-Douglas MD-11	491/48414	ex PP-SOZ		Lsd fr Mitsui
PP-VQX	McDonnell-Douglas MD-11	603/48769	ex N799BA		Lsd fr RGL-3 Corp
PP-VTF	McDonnell-Douglas MD-11	459/48444	ex HB-IWB		Lsd fr Bandung
PP-VTG	McDonnell-Douglas MD-11	463/48446	ex HB-IWD		Lsd fr Bandung
PP-VTH	McDonnell-Douglas MD-11	498/48457	ex HB-IWM	Star Alliance c/s	Lsd fr Bandung

Founder member of Star Alliance. VARIG Logistica is wholly owned cargo division. To integrate Rio Sul and Nordeste operations into main-line services and return three Embraer EMB.145s and seven EMB.120s to lessors
VARIG Brasil is the trading name of Viaçao Aerea Rio-Grandenses. Announced plans on 18 September 2003 to merge with TAM

VARIG LOGISTICA

(4V/VLO)
Sao Paulo-Guaraulhos, SP/ (GRU)

PP-VLD	Boeing 727-41F	824/20425			
PP-VLE	Boeing 727-172C	480/19666	ex N726AL		
PP-VLG	Boeing 727-41F	810/20423			
PP-VLS	Boeing 727-173C	457/19508	ex N694WA		
PP-VQU	Boeing 727-2J7F	1037/20880	ex PP-SFF		Lsd fr Pegasus
PP-VQV	Boeing 727-243F	1725/22166	ex PP-SFE	Lsd fr Pegasus	
PR-LGB	Boeing 727-2A1F (FedEx 3)	1253/21341	ex N213UP		Lsd fr First Platinum
PR-LGC	Boeing 727-2A1F (FedEx 3)	1256/21342	ex N214UP	Leandra	Lsd fr Second Platinum
PP-VMT	Douglas DC-10-30CF	329/47841			Lsd fr Pegasus
PP-VMU	Douglas DC-10-30CF	332/47842		stored	Lsd fr Pegasus
PP-VQY	Douglas DC-10-30F	179/46949	ex N16949		Lsd fr Prop Five

Wholly owned cargo operations of VARIG but partial stake for sale

VASP

VASP (VP/VSP) (IATA 343)
Sao Paulo-Congonhas, SP (CGH)

CP-2313	Boeing 737-3A1	2836/28389			Lsd to LLB
PP-SFI	Boeing 737-2Q3	591/21478	ex JA8445		
PP-SFJ	Boeing 737-3K9	1633/24212	ex N945WP		Lsd fr Bavaria
PP-SFN	Boeing 737-3L9	2763/27925	ex OY-MAU	Cidade Maravilhosa	
					Lsd fr Vitoria Regis Lsg
PP-SMA	Boeing 737-2A1	161/20092		Rio Grande do Norte	
PP-SMB	Boeing 737-2A1F	169/20093		VASPEX c/s	
PP-SMC	Boeing 737-2A1	182/20094		Para	
PP-SMF	Boeing 737-2A1	301/20589		Ceara	
PP-SMG	Boeing 737-2A1	324/20777		Goias	
PP-SMH	Boeing 737-2A1	325/20778		Alagoas	
PP-SMP	Boeing 737-2A1	327/20779		Parana	
PP-SMQ	Boeing 737-214	180/20155	ex N382PS	Sergipe	
PP-SMR	Boeing 737-214	189/20157	ex N984PS	Maranhao	
PP-SMS	Boeing 737-214	193/20159	ex N986PS	Bahia	
PP-SMT	Boeing 737-214	195/20160	ex N987PS	Rio Grande do Sul	
PP-SMU	Boeing 737-2A1	364/20967		Amazonas	
PP-SMW	Boeing 737-2H4C	258/20346	ex N23SW	VASPEX c/s	
PP-SMZ	Boeing 737-2A1	382/20971		Mato Grosso	
PP-SNA	Boeing 737-2A1	412/21094		Paraiba	
PP-SNB	Boeing 737-2A1F	432/21095		VASPEX c/s	
PP-SOT	Boeing 737-3L9	2074/25150	ex OY-MMY		Lsd fr Vitoria Regis Lsg
PP-SOU	Boeing 737-3L9	2140/25360	ex (OY-MMZ)		Lsd fr Vitoria Regis Lsg
PP-SPF	Boeing 737-2L7C	419/21073	ex C2-RN3		
PP-SPG	Boeing 737-2L7	533/21616	ex C2-RN6		
PP-SPH	Boeing 737-2L9	614/22070	ex C2-RN8		
PP-SPI	Boeing 737-2Q3	519/21476	ex JA8443		
PP-SFC	Boeing 727-264F	1143/21071	ex N171G	VASPEX c/s	
PP-SFG	Boeing 727-2Q4F	1698/22425	ex N63063	VASPEX c/s	
PP-SFQ	Boeing 727-2J4F	1588/22079	ex CP-2294	VASPEX c/s	
PP-SNL	Airbus Industrie A300B2-203	202	ex F-WZMJ		
PP-SNM	Airbus Industrie A300B2-203	205	ex F-WZMP		Lsd fr Rural Leasing
PP-SNN	Airbus Industrie A300B2-203	225	ex F-WZMB		

Owns 80% of TAN and 50.1% of Ecuatoriana
VASP is the trading name of Viaçao Aerea Sao Paulo. VASPEX is the name used for cargo operations

VIA BRASIL current status uncertain as sole aircraft has been wfu

PZ - SURINAME (Republic of Suriname)

GUM AIR
Paramaribo-Zorg en Hoop (ORG)

PZ-TBA	GAF N22B Nomad	N22B-66	
PZ-TBD	Cessna U206G Stationair	U20603786	ex N8286G
PZ-TBE	Cessna U206G Stationair 6	U20606776	ex N9559Z
PZ-TBL	Britten-Norman BN-2B-26 Islander	2153	ex N633BB
PZ-TBM	GAF N24A Nomad	N24A-42	ex ZK-ECN
PZ-TVC	Cessna 404	404-	ex YV-
PZ-TVU	Cessna TU206G Turbo Stationair 6	U20604783	ex PZ-PVU

INTER TROPICAL AVIATION

Tropair (3P/TCU)
Paramaribo-Zorg en Hoop (ORG)

PZ-TGP	Cessna U206G Stationair	U20604041	ex PZ-PGP

PZ-TGT	Britten-Norman BN-2B-21 Islander	2116	ex SAF003
PZ-TGW	PZL-Mielec An-28	1AJ007-21	ex YV-529C
PZ-TLV	Cessna U206G Stationair 6	U20606591	

SURINAM AIRWAYS

Surinam (PY/SLM) (IATA 192)   *Paramaribo-Zanderij International/Zorg en Hoop (PBM/ORG)*

PH-AHX	Boeing 767-383ER	315/24847	ex LN-RCD		Jt ops with HLN
PH-AHY	Boeing 767-383ER	325/24848	ex OY-KDN		Jt ops with HLN
PZ-TCD	de Havilland DHC-6 Twin Otter 300	646			
PZ-TCE	de Havilland DHC-6 Twin Otter 300	656			
PZ-TCK	Douglas DC-9-51	763/47655	ex N54642	stored Lake City, FL	
PZ-TCL	McDonnell-Douglas MD-82	1323/49444	ex N98876		Lsd fr Pegasus

Scheduled services to USA operated with aircraft leased from Miami Air when required

P2 - PAPUA NEW GUINEA (Independent State of Papua New Guinea)

AIRLINES OF PAPUA NEW GUINEA

(CG)   *Port Moresby (POM)*

P2-MBA	de Havilland DHC-6 Twin Otter 300	353	ex C-FWAX		
P2-MCB	de Havilland DHC-6 Twin Otter 300	441	ex C-GNHB	stored CNS	
P2-MCD	de Havilland DHC-6 Twin Otter 300	592	ex C-GOVG		
P2-MCE	de Havilland DHC-6 Twin Otter 300	673	ex C-GHRB		
P2-MCF	de Havilland DHC-6 Twin Otter 300	741	ex C-GRBY		
P2-CHI	Boeing 234UT Chinook	MJ-003	ex N237CH		Lsd fr Columbia H/c
P2-MBX	Beech 1900D	UE-102	ex N82928	Wild Thing	
P2-MBY	Beech 1900D	UE-115	ex N15317		
P2-MCG	de Havilland DHC-8-102	006	ex C-GJCB		
P2-MCH	de Havilland DHC-8-102	012	ex C-GPYD		
P2-MML	Beech Super King Air 200	BB-579	ex VH-AKT		

AIRLINK

(ND)   *Rabaul/Madang (RAB/MAG)*

P2-ALS	Embraer EMB.110P2 Bandeirante	110253	ex VH-UQB	
P2-ALT	Embraer EMB.110P1 Bandeirante	110208	ex VH-UQD	
P2-ALU	Embraer EMB.110P1 Bandeirante	110232	ex VH-UQF	
P2-ALV	Embraer EMB.110P1 Bandeirante	110236	ex VH-UQG	
P2-ALZ	Embraer EMB.110P1 Bandeirante	110233	ex VH-HVS	
P2-ALB	Cessna 402B	402B0006	ex P2-GKL	
P2-ALD	Britten-Norman BN-2A-26 Islander	76	ex P2-DNB	
P2-ALE	Britten-Norman BN-2A-26 Islander	100	ex P2-SAB	
P2-ALG	Cessna 404 Titan	404-0653	ex VH-SON	
P2-ALI	Britten-Norman BN-2A-26 Islander	73	ex P2-ISI	
P2-ALK	Cessna 404 Titan	404-0222	ex VH-TMX	

AIR NIUGINI

Niugini (PX/ANG) (IATA 656)   *Port Moresby (POM)*

P2-AND	Fokker F.28 Fellowship 4000	11118	ex PH-RRJ		
P2-ANE	Fokker F.28 Fellowship 1000	11033	ex C-FTAV		
P2-ANF	Fokker F.28 Fellowship 1000	11038	ex C-FTAY		
P2-ANI	Fokker F.28 Fellowship 4000	11223	ex PH-RRB		
P2-ANJ	Fokker F.28 Fellowship 4000	11219	ex PH-RRA		
P2-ANR	Fokker F.28 Fellowship 4000	11207	ex VH-EWC	W/Cmdr RH (Bobby) Gibbes	
P2-ANS	Fokker F.28 Fellowship 4000	11195	ex VH-EWA		
P2-ANG	Boeing 767-319ER	371/24875	ex ZK-NCE		Lsd fr Pegasus Avn
P2-ANK	de Havilland DHC-8Q-202	461	ex C-GFBW		
P2-ANX	de Havilland DHC-8Q-202	463	ex D-BHAL		Lsd fr AUB
P2-ANY	de Havilland DHC-8Q-202	536	ex D-BTHF		Lsd fr AUB
P2-MCI	de Havilland DHC-8-102	197	ex ZK-NET		
P2-MCJ	de Havilland DHC-8-102	125	ex ZK-NES		
VH-FWH	Fokker 100	11316	ex G-BXNF		Lsd fr/op by DQA

ASIA PACIFIC AIRLINES   Status is uncertain as aircraft are now operated by Fubilan Air Transport

FUBILAN AIR TRANSPORT

     Tabubil (TBG)

P2-NAX	de Havilland DHC-8-102A	229	ex VH-JSI		Lsd fr NJS
P2-NAZ	de Havilland DHC-8-106	316	ex C-GFUM	Spirit of Tabubil	

Both operated for Ok Tedi Mining

HELI NIUGINI

Madang/Mount Hagen(MAG/HGU)

P2-HBG	Bell 206L-3 LongRanger III	51432	ex JA6059
P2-HBH	Bell 206L-3 LongRanger III	51012	ex SE-HOR
P2-HBK	Kawasaki/MBB BK117B-2	1046	ex ZK-HBK
P2-HBL	Kawasaki/MBB BK117B-2	1021	ex ZK-HLU
RA-25503	Mil Mi-8MTV-1	95651	ex CCCP-25503
RA-27101	Mil Mi-8AMT	59489605782	
RA-31031	Kamov Ka-32S/T	6106	ex CCCP-31031
RA-31032	Kamov Ka-32S	6107	ex CCCP-31032
RA-31036	Kamov Ka-32T	6111	ex CCCP-31036
RA-31583	Kamov Ka-32S	8705	ex P2-RAA

HEVI-LIFT

(IU)

Mount Hagen/Cairns (HGU/CNS)

P2-HCC	Bell 206L-1 LongRanger III	45427	ex N5019T
P2-HCD	Bell 206L-1 LongRanger III	45528	ex C-GGHZ
P2-HCE	Bell 206L-3 LongRanger III	51291	
P2-HCO	Bell 206L-3 LongRanger III	51178	ex N3204K
P2-HCU	Bell 206L-3 LongRanger III	51416	ex N254EV
P2-HLT	Bell 206L-3 LongRanger III	51387	ex VH-HQT
P2-HCF	de Havilland DHC-6 Twin Otter 300	528	ex N528SA
P2-HCJ	Bell 212	30799	ex VH-EMJ
P2-HCN	Beech 200C Super King Air	BL-22	ex P2-PJV
P2-HCQ	Bell 212	20860	ex JA9528
P2-HCW	Bell 212	30520	ex PK-EBO
P2-HCX	de Havilland DHC-6 Twin Otter 300	485	ex CP-2035
P2-HLA	Embraer EMB.120ER Brasilia	120030	ex N271UE
P2-HLV	Bell 212	30508	ex VH-BUV
RA-27158	Mil Mi-8AMT	59489611156	

ISLAND AIRWAYS

Madang (MAG)

P2-CBA	Britten-Norman BN-2A-20 Islander	753	ex P2-MFF
P2-CBC	Cessna 402B	402B0909	ex VH-LCF

ISLANDS NATIONAIR

(CN)

Port Moresby (POM)

P2-IHA	Bell 206L-1 LongRanger II	45333	ex VH-BLV	
P2-IHC	Bell 206L-1 LongRanger III	45614	ex VH-HIV	
P2-IHE	Bell 206L-1 LongRanger III	45238	ex N140VG	
P2-IHF	Bell 206L-3 LongRanger III	51322		
P2-IHH	Bell 206L-3 LongRanger III	45255	ex P2-NHD	
P2-IHK	Bell 206L-2 LongRanger II	45450	ex VH-WCS	
P2-IAB	Beech 58 Baron	TH-760	ex VH-NET	
P2-IAJ	Embraer EMB.110P1 Bandeirante	110254	ex VH-FCE	
P2-IAK	Embraer EMB.110P2 Bandeirante	110394	ex ZS-LGM	
P2-IAL	Embraer EMB.110P2 Bandeirante	110412	ex ZS-LGN	ZS-PCZ resd

KIUNGA AVIATION

Lae (LAE)

P2-KAA	Cessna 402C	402C0247	ex N2748X

MAF PAPUA NEW GUINEA

Mount Hagen (HGU)

P2-MAI	Cessna TU206G Stationair 6	U20605734	ex P2-DMH
P2-MAJ	Cessna TU206G Stationair 6	U20606295	ex P2-SIK
P2-MDC	Cessna U206G Stationair	U20602738	ex N1753C
P2-MFG	Cessna TU206G Stationair	U20602675	ex N1759C
P2-MFJ	Cessna TU206G Stationair	U20602447	ex P2-BLA
P2-MFM	Cessna TU206G Stationair 6	U20605380	
P2-MFN	Cessna TU206G Stationair 6	U20605441	ex N6346U
P2-MFP	Cessna TU206G Stationair 6	U20605793	ex N4809M
P2-MFV	Cessna TU206G Stationair 6	U20606252	ex N6359Z

All Robertson STOL conversions

P2-MFB	de Havilland DHC-6 Twin Otter 300	289	ex N910HD	
P2-MFQ	de Havilland DHC-6 Twin Otter 300	174	ex N9762J	
P2-MFR	de Havilland DHC-6 Twin Otter 300	118	ex N63118	
P2-MFU	de Havilland DHC-6 Twin Otter 300	182	ex TJ-AHV	
P2-MFY	de Havilland DHC-6 Twin Otter 300	219	ex VH-BMG	

NORTH COAST AVIATION

(N9)   *Madang (MAG)*

P2-DWA	Britten-Norman BN-2A-26 Islander	113	ex VH-EQE	
P2-IAC	Britten-Norman BN-2A-21 Islander	425	ex P2-KAF	
P2-ISB	Britten-Norman BN-2A-20 Islander	709	ex P2-MKW	stored
P2-ISL	Britten-Norman BN-2A-20 Islander	806	ex G-BDYT	
P2-ISM	Britten-Norman BN-2A-20 Islander	227	ex VH-EDI	
P2-NCE	Britten-Norman BN-2A-20 Islander	768	ex P2-IAD	
P2-SAC	Britten-Norman BN-2A-20 Islander	94	ex P2-DNY	
P2-DQU	Cessna U206B Super Skywagon	U206-0892	ex VH-DQU	
P2-IDK	Cessna U206G Super Skymaster	U206-1415	ex P2-TNK	
P2-NCD	Cessna 402B	402B1027	ex VH-USV	
P2-OHS	Cessna P206B Super Skylane	P206-0392	ex P2-HCM	

PACAIR

Goroka (GKA)

P2-GKW	Beech 95-D55 Baron	TE-618	ex VH-FWJ

PACIFIC HELICOPTERS

Goroka (GKA)

P2-PHA	Aerospatiale AS350BA Ecureuil	1181	ex P2-PHU
P2-PHD	Aerospatiale AS350BA Ecureuil	1067	ex 9N-ACQ
P2-PHG	Aerospatiale AS350BA Ecureuil	1687	
P2-PHH	Aerospatiale AS350BA Ecureuil	1608	ex VH-CHO
P2-PHX	Aerospatiale AS350BA Ecureuil	1817	
P2-PAU	Bell 212	30793	ex A6-BBG
P2-PAV	Bell 212	30913	ex G-GLEN
P2-PAW	Bell 212	30547	ex I-SNAE
P2-PAX	Bell 212	30786	ex A6-BBF
P2-PAY	Aerospatiale SA330J Puma	1502	ex N3263U
P2-PAZ	Aerospatiale SA330J Puma	1459	ex N3263P
P2-PBA	Bell 206L-1 LongRanger III	45642	ex VH-SCV
P2-PBB	Bell 206L-3 LongRanger III	51400	ex N86CE
P2-PBC	Bell 206L-1 LongRanger III	45349	ex N1077N
P2-PBD	Bell 206L-3 LongRanger III	51275	ex VH-CKI
P2-PHZ	Aerospatiale SA330J Puma	1472	ex VH-WOB

REGIONAL PACIFIC AIR

(QT)   *Madang (MAG)*
Previously listed as Sun-Air (Pacific)

P2-KSA	Beech 200 Super King Air	BB-1527	ex N170W
P2-KSG	de Havilland DHC-6 Twin Otter 300	509	ex VH-WPT
P2-KSS	de Havilland DHC-6 Twin Otter 300	578	ex N578SA

SIL AVIATION

Aiyura (AYU)

P2-SIB	Cessna 402C	402C0263	ex N379P	Robertson STOL conversion
P2-SIG	Cessna TU206G Stationair 6	U20606029	ex VH-XAA	Robertson STOL conversion
P2-SIJ	Cessna TU206G Stationair 6	U20605805	ex N5491X	Robertson STOL conversion
P2-SIM	Cessna TU206G Stationair 6	U20606347	ex N6620Z	Robertson STOL conversion
P2-SIR	Cessna 402C	402C0422	ex N67872	Robertson STOL conversion
P2-SIT	Cessna TU206G Stationair 6	U20606158	ex N181PK	Robertson STOL conversion
P2-SIV	Britten-Norman BN-2T Islander	2138	ex 9M-TIR	

SOUTHWEST AIR

(W2)   *Mendi (MDU)*

P2-SHA	Bell 206L-3 LongRanger III	51533	ex VH-IRE	
P2-SHB	Bell 206L-3 LongRanger III	51153		
P2-SWE	de Havilland DHC-6 Twin Otter 300	480	ex P2-RDL	
P2-SWF	Embraer EMB.110P1 Bandeirante	110237	ex N691RA	stored BNE

SUN AIR (PACIFIC) reverted to Region Air name

TRANSNIUGINI AIRWAYS

Port Moresby (POM)

P2-TNC	Cessna A185E Skywagon	185-1233	ex P2-TAC
P2-TND	Britten-Norman BN-2A-21 Islander	813	ex P2-COD

TROPICAIR

Port Moresby (POM)

P2-BEN	Cessna 208B Caravan I	208B0424	ex VH-LSA
P2-SMA	Cessna U206G Stationair 6	U20604227	ex P2-AAC

VAN AIR

Vanimo (VAI)

P2-TSJ	Cessna 208B Caravan I	208B0339	ex N1045Y
P2-VAB	Britten-Norman BN-2A-20 Islander	759	ex P2-MFZ
P2-VAC	Cessna U206F Stationair	U20602408	ex P2-AAC

P4 - ARUBA

AVIA AIR CHARTER SERVICES

Aviair (3R/ARB)   *Oranjestad (AUA)*

P4-AVD	Embraer EMB.110P1 Bandeirante	110336	ex N76CZ	Lsd fr Volvo Aero
P4-AVE	Embraer EMB.110P1 Bandeirante	110283	ex N404AS	Lsd fr Volvo Aero

Current status is uncertain as both the Bandeirantes repossessed by lessor

FIRST INTERNATIONAL AIRWAYS

Ostend/Sharjah (OST/SHJ)

9G-LAD	Boeing 707-323C	439/18940	ex 5N-MXX	Lsd fr/op by JON
9G-NHA	Douglas DC-8-63F (BAC 3)	392/45924	ex EI-CGO	

ROYAL ARUBAN AIRLINES

(V5/RYL)   *Oranjestad (AUA)*

P4-	Douglas DC-9-14	19/45725	ex N600ME	Lsd fr Centec Avn

RA - RUSSIA (Russian Federation)

Please note that several aircraft have, in previous editions, been shown as stored in this section. It has been pointed out that these aircraft may be undergoing maintenance (in Russia line maintenance is performed in the open on the apron, rather than in hangars!) and may not be withdrawn from use. Even aircraft noted minus engines on one visit may be back in service shortly afterwards; as a result comments are made where appropriate to indicate status of certain individual aircraft or a fleet.

ABAKAN-AVIA

Abakan-Avia (ABG)   *Abakan (ABA)*

RA-76504	Ilyushin Il-76T	073411328	ex CCCP-76504	
RA-76505	Ilyushin Il-76T	073411331	ex CCCP-76505	UN/WFP titles

Rumoured to have merged with RusAir but not confirmed

ADYGHEYA AVIA

Adlines (RDD)   *Maikop*

RA-26242	Antonov An-26B	07308608	ex CCCP-26242
RA-46479	Antonov An-24RV	27308007	ex CCCP-46479
RA-47190	Antonov An-24B	99902005	ex CCCP-47190

AEROBRATSK

Aerobra (BRP)   *Bratsk (BTK)*

RA-87414	Yakovlev Yak-40	9420634	ex CCCP-87414
RA-87448	Yakovlev Yak-40	9430536	ex CCCP-87448

RA-87545	Yakovlev Yak-40	9531042	ex CCCP-87545		
RA-87974	Yakovlev Yak-40K	9041960	ex CCCP-87974		
RA-88205	Yakovlev Yak-40	9630749	ex CCCP-88205		
RA-88215	Yakovlev Yak-40K	9630150	ex CCCP-88215		
RA-88228	Yakovlev Yak-40	9641750	ex CCCP-88228		
RA-85429	Tupolev Tu-154B-2	80A-429	ex CCCP-85429		
RA-85660	Tupolev Tu-154M	89A-810	ex LZ-LTK		
RA-85689	Tupolev Tu-154M	90A-860	ex LZ-LTP		Lsd to ESL

AEROFLOT DON AIRLINES

Donavia (D9/DNV)

Rostov-on-Don (ROV)

RA-85149	Tupolev Tu-154M	89A-797	ex B-609L		
RA-85409	Tupolev Tu-154B-2	80A-409	ex CCCP-85409		Lsd to KIL
RA-85425	Tupolev Tu-154B-2	80A-425	ex CCCP-85425		
RA-85435	Tupolev Tu-154B-2	80A-435	ex CCCP-85435		
RA-85436	Tupolev Tu-154B-2	80A-436	ex CCCP-85436		
RA-85452	Tupolev Tu-154B-2	80A-452	ex CCCP-85452		
RA-85527	Tupolev Tu-154B-2	82A-527	ex CCCP-85527		
RA-85626	Tupolev Tu-154M	87A-753	ex CCCP-85626		
RA-85640	Tupolev Tu-154M	88A-772	ex CCCP-85640		
RA-85726	Tupolev Tu-154M	86A-725	ex EP-TQD		
RA-11115	Antonov An-12BP	01348003	ex CCCP-11115		Lsd to FRT
RA-12974	Antonov An-12BP	9346506	ex CCCP-12974		Lsd to FRT
RA-65100	Tupolev Tu-134A-3	60258	ex CCCP-65100		
RA-65771	Tupolev Tu-134A-3	62445	ex CCCP-65771		
RA-65796	Tupolev Tu-134A-3	63150	ex CCCP-65796		
RA-65863	Tupolev Tu-134A-3	28283	ex CCCP-65863		

AEROFLOT RUSSIAN AIRLINES

Aeroflot (SU/AFL) (IATA 555)

Moscow-Sheremetyevo (SVO)

F-OGQQ	Airbus Industrie A310-308	592	ex F-WWCN	Tchaikovski	Lsd fr Alex Bail
F-OGQR	Airbus Industrie A310-308	593	ex F-WWCP	Rachmaninov	Lsd fr Quark Lsg
F-OGQT	Airbus Industrie A310-308	622	ex F-WWCD	Moussorgski	Lsd fr Kat Bail
F-OGQU	Airbus Industrie A310-308	646	ex F-WWCT	Skriabin	Lsd fr Cladel Bail
F-OGYP	Airbus Industrie A310-324	442	ex N812PA	Rymsky Korsakov	Lsd fr Airbus
F-OGYT	Airbus Industrie A310-324	660	ex N836AB	Borodin	Lsd fr Airbus
F-OGYU	Airbus Industrie A310-324	687	ex N842AB	Alyabiev	Lsd fr Airbus
F-OGYV	Airbus Industrie A310-324	689	ex N843AB	Dargomyzhsky	Lsd fr Airbus
VP-BAG	Airbus Industrie A310-304	475	ex N475GE		Lsd fr Polaris
VP-BDK	Airbus Industrie A320-214	2106	ex F-WWDR		Lsd fr GECAS
VP-BDM	Airbus Industrie A319-111	2069	ex D-AVYJ		
VP-BDN	Airbus Industrie A319-111	2072	ex D-AVYL		
VP-BDO	Airbus Industrie A319-111	2091	ex D-AVWU		
VP-BWA	Airbus Industrie A319-111	2052	ex D-AVYA		
VP-BWD	Airbus Industrie A320-214	2116	ex F-WWDY		Lsd fr GECAS
VP-BWE	Airbus Industrie A320-214	2133	ex F-WWDX		Lsd fr GECAS
VP-BWF	Airbus Industrie A320-314	2144	ex F-WWBY		Lsd fr GECAS
VP-BWG	Airbus Industrie A319-111	2093	ex D-AVYE		
VP-BWH	Airbus Industrie A320-314	2151	ex F-WWIR		Lsd fr GECAS
VP-BWI	Airbus Industrie A320-214	2163	ex F-WWBD		Lsd fr GECAS
VP-BWJ	Airbus Industrie A319-111	2179	ex D-AVYU	on order 04	
VP-BWK	Airbus Industrie A319-111	2222	ex D-AV	on order 04	
VP-B	Airbus Industrie A320-214	2233	ex F-WW	on order 04	
VP-B	Airbus Industrie A319-111		ex D-AV	on order 04	

Seven more Airbus A320-214s are on order for delivery in 2005, all leased from GECAS

VP-BAL	Boeing 737-4M0	3051/29204			Lsd fr Sailplane Lsg
VP-BAN	Boeing 737-4M0	3058/29206			Lsd fr Sailplane Lsg
VP-BAO	Boeing 737-4M0	3078/29207			Lsd fr Sailplane Lsg
VP-BAP	Boeing 737-4M0	3081/29208	ex N1003W		Lsd fr Sailplane Lsg
VP-BAQ	Boeing 737-4M0	3087/29209			Lsd fr Sailplane Lsg
VP-BAR	Boeing 737-4M0	3091/29210	ex N1015B		Lsd fr Sailplane Lsg

All for Garuda Indonesia by June 2004

VP-BAV	Boeing 767-36NER	761/30107			Lsd fr GECAS
VP-BAX	Boeing 767-36NER	767/30109			Lsd fr GECAS
VP-BAY	Boeing 767-36NER	775/30110			Lsd fr GECAS
VP-BAZ	Boeing 767-36NER	776/30111			Lsd fr GECAS
VP-BDI	Boeing 767-38AER	29618	ex N618SH		
VP-BAS	Boeing 777-2Q8ER	135/27607	ex N5022E		Lsd fr ILFC
VP-BAU	Boeing 777-2Q8ER	164/27608			Lsd fr ILFC
VP-BDE	Douglas DC-10-40F	306/47823	ex N804AZ		Lsd fr TenForty
VP-BDF	Douglas DC-10-40F	349/47855	ex N805AZ		Lsd fr TenForty

512

Reg	Type	Serial	Ex	Notes	Lease
VP-BDG	Douglas DC-10-40F	224/46661	ex N141WE		Lsd fr TenForty
VP-	Douglas DC-10-40F			on order	Lsd fr TenForty

The freighters are based in Hahn and planned to be replaced by McDonnell-Douglas MD-11s in 2005

Reg	Type	Serial	Ex	Notes
RA-76467	Ilyushin Il-76TD	0023440157	ex CCCP-76467	stored SVO
RA-76468	Ilyushin Il-76TD	0023441195	ex CCCP-76468	stored SVO
RA-76469	Ilyushin Il-76TD	0033444286	ex CCCP-76469	stored SVO
RA-76470	Ilyushin Il-76TD	0033445291	ex CCCP-76470	stored SVO
RA-76478	Ilyushin Il-76TD	0053459788	ex CCCP-76478	stored SVO
RA-76479	Ilyushin Il-76TD	0053460790	ex CCCP-76479	stored SVO
RA-76482	Ilyushin Il-76TD	0053460832	ex CCCP-76482	
RA-76488	Ilyushin Il-76TD	0073479371	ex CCCP-76488	stored SVO
RA-76785	Ilyushin Il-76TD	0093495863	ex CCCP-76785	
RA-76795	Ilyushin Il-76TD	0093498962	ex CCCP-76795	

All removed from scheduled services; six to be scrapped and the remaining four sold

Reg	Type	Serial	Ex	Notes	Lease
RA-86002	Ilyushin Il-86	0103	ex CCCP-86002		
RA-86015	Ilyushin Il-86	51483202013	ex CCCP-86015	stored SVO	
RA-86054	Ilyushin Il-86	51483203021	ex CCCP-86054		
RA-86058	Ilyushin Il-86	51483203025	ex CCCP-86058	stored SVO	
RA-86066	Ilyushin Il-86	51483204033	ex CCCP-86066		Lsd to VSO
RA-86067	Ilyushin Il-86	51483204034	ex CCCP-86067		
RA-86075	Ilyushin Il-86	51483205044	ex CCCP-86075	stored SVO	
RA-86079	Ilyushin Il-86	51483206050	ex CCCP-86079		
RA-86087	Ilyushin Il-86	51483206058	ex CCCP-86087		
RA-86088	Ilyushin Il-86	51483206059	ex CCCP-86088	stored SVO	
RA-86095	Ilyushin Il-86	51483207066	ex CCCP-86095		
RA-86096	Ilyushin Il-86	51483207067	ex CCCP-86096	stored SVO	
RA-86110	Ilyushin Il-86	51483208078	ex CCCP-86110		
RA-86113	Ilyushin Il-86	51483209081	ex CCCP-86113	Wella titles	
RA-86124	Ilyushin Il-86	51483210092	ex CCCP-86124		

Ilyushin Il-86s used for charter flights only; only six are operational for seasonal charters

Reg	Type	Serial	Ex	Lease
RA-96005	Ilyushin Il-96-300	74393201002	ex CCCP-96005	Lsd fr VASO Lsg
RA-96007	Ilyushin Il-96-300	74393201004		
RA-96008	Ilyushin Il-96-300	74393201005		
RA-96010	Ilyushin Il-96-300	74393201007		
RA-96011	Ilyushin Il-96-300	74393201008		
RA-96015	Ilyushin Il-96-300	74393201012		

Six more are on order, leased from Ilyushin Finance

Reg	Type	Serial	Ex	Notes	Lease
RA-65559	Tupolev Tu-134A	49909	ex 101 Polish AF		
RA-65566	Tupolev Tu-134A	63952	ex 11+11 German AF		
RA-65567	Tupolev Tu-134A	63967	ex 11+10 German AF		
RA-65568	Tupolev Tu-134A	66135	ex 11+12 German AF		
RA-65612	Tupolev Tu-134A-3	3352102	ex D-AOBC		Lsd fr KMV
RA-65623	Tupolev Tu-134A	49985	ex SP-LHI		
RA-65694	Tupolev Tu-134A	63235	ex YL-LBD		
RA-65697	Tupolev Tu-134A-3	63307	ex CCCP-65697		
RA-65717	Tupolev Tu-134A-3	63657	ex CCCP-65717	white c/s	
RA-65769	Tupolev Tu-134A-3	62415	ex CCCP-65769		
RA-65770	Tupolev Tu-134A-3	62430	ex CCCP-65770		
RA-65781	Tupolev Tu-134A-3	62645	ex CCCP-65781		
RA-65783	Tupolev Tu-134A-3	62713	ex CCCP-65783		
RA-65784	Tupolev Tu-134A-3	62715	ex CCCP-65784		

Reg	Type	Serial	Ex
RA-85570	Tupolev Tu-154B-2	83A-570	ex CCCP-85570
RA-85637	Tupolev Tu-154M	87A-767	ex CCCP-85637
RA-85638	Tupolev Tu-154M	88A-768	ex CCCP-85638
RA-85639	Tupolev Tu-154M	88A-771	ex CCCP-85639
RA-85641	Tupolev Tu-154M	88A-773	ex CCCP-85641
RA-85642	Tupolev Tu-154M	88A-778	ex CCCP-85642
RA-85643	Tupolev Tu-154M	88A-779	ex CCCP-86643
RA-85644	Tupolev Tu-154M	88A-780	ex MPR-85644
RA-85646	Tupolev Tu-154M	88A-784	ex CCCP-85646
RA-85648	Tupolev Tu-154M	88A-786	ex CCCP-85648
RA-85649	Tupolev Tu-154M	88A-787	ex CCCP-85649
RA-85661	Tupolev Tu-154M	89A-811	ex CCCP-85661
RA-85662	Tupolev Tu-154M	89A-816	ex CCCP-85662
RA-85663	Tupolev Tu-154M	89A-817	ex CCCP-85663
RA-85665	Tupolev Tu-154M	89A-819	ex CCCP-85665
RA-85668	Tupolev Tu-154M	89A-826	ex CCCP-85668
RA-85669	Tupolev Tu-154M	89A-827	ex CCCP-85669
RA-85670	Tupolev Tu-154M	89A-828	ex CCCP-85670
RA-85810	Tupolev Tu-154M	89A-824	ex SP-LCM
RA-85811	Tupolev Tu-154M	89A-831	ex SP-LCN

Reg	Type	Serial
RA-74004	Antonov An-74	36547094890

A total of twenty-five Antonov An-74TK-300s are on order
Took over the passenger services of Rossia State Transport Company in late October 2003
Plans to return the Boeing 777-2Q8ERs, Boeing 737-4M0s and the Airbus Industrie A310s to lessors

AEROFREIGHT AIRLINES
Aerofreight (RS/FRT)   Moscow-Domodedovo (DME)

RA-11115	Antonov An-12BP	01348003	ex CCCP-11115	Lsd fr DNV
RA-11124	Antonov An-12B	02348106	ex CCCP-11124	
RA-12994	Antonov An-12B	00347401	ex CCCP-12994	Lsd fr DNV
RA-62024	Tupolev Tu-204-100S	1450743164024	ATU Cargo	
RA-64032	Tupolev Tu-204-120C	1450743164032		Op in Aviastar colours
RA-85312	Tupolev Tu-154B-1	78A-312	ex CCCP-85312	
RA-85568	Tupolev Tu-154B-2	82A-568	ex CCCP-85568	
RA-	Tupolev Tu-334		on order 04	Lsd fr
RA-	Tupolev Tu-334		on order 04	Lsd fr

Three more Tupolev Tu-334s are on order

AERO-KAMOV
Aerafkam (MSV)   Moscow-Lyubersty

RA-31065	Kamov Ka-32A	8607	ex CCCP-31065	
RA-31072	Kamov Ka-32AT	8903	ex CCCP-31072	Op for Moscow Firebrigade
RA-31073	Kamov Ka-32AT	8904	ex CCCP-31073	Op for Moscow Firebrigade
RA-31098	Kamov Ka-32A	8805	ex CCCP-31098	
RA-31584	Kamov Ka-32S	8706	ex CCCP-31584	
RA-31589	Kamov Ka-32S	8711	ex CCCP-31589	

AEROKUZBASS
Novokuznetsk (NKZ)   Novokuznetsk (NOZ)

RA-85392	Tupolev Tu-154B-2	80A-392	ex CCCP-85392	
RA-85749	Tupolev Tu-154M	92A-931		Lsd to IRB
RA-85758	Tupolev Tu-154M	92A-940	ex EP-TQE	Lsd to IRB

AERO RENT
Moscow-Zhukovsky

RA-65919	Tupolev Tu-134A-3	66380	ex CCCP-65919	
RA-88306	Yakovlev Yak-40D	9640651	ex OK-GEL	Samaratransgaz

AEROSTARS
Morozov (PL/ASE)   Moscow-Domodedovo (DME)

EW-78799	Ilyushin Il-76MD	0093491754	ex CCCP-78799	Lsd fr TXC
RA-76369	Ilyushin Il-76TD	1033414480		
RA-76476	Ilyushin Il-76TD	0043451528	ex CCCP-76476	
RA-76490	Ilyushin Il-76T	093416506	ex YI-AKO	Lsd fr EFR
RA-76750	Ilyushin Il-76TD	0083485561	ex CCCP-76750	
RA-76786	Ilyushin Il-76TD	0093496923	ex CCCP-76786	Lsd fr DMO
RA-76823	Ilyushin Il-76TD	0023441189	ex YI-ALQ	Lsd fr EFR
RA-76842	Ilyushin Il-76TD	1033418616		
RA-13392	Antonov An-12BK	00347210	ex CCCP-13392	all white	Lsd fr KAO

Also reported as Air Stars

AEROTEX aircraft are now operated by Rusline

AEROVOLGA ceased operations

AIR AND SEA TRANSPORT current status uncertain

AIRBRIDGE CARGO

Boeing 747-243M	492/22506	ex I-DEMC	Freighter, on order
Boeing 747-243F	545/22545	ex I-DEMR	on order

Wholly owned subsidiary of Volga-Dnepr; plans to commence operations in April 2004

AIRLINES 400
Remont Air (VAZ)   Moscow-Vnukovo (VKO))

RA-85650	Tupolev Tu-154M	88A-788	ex LZ-LOI	on order	Lsd fr VARZ
RA-85653	Tupolev Tu-154M	88A-795	ex CCCP-85653		Lsd fr VARZ
RA-85671	Tupolev Tu-154M	89A-829	ex LZ-LCA		
RA-85680	Tupolev Tu-154M	90A-843	ex LZ-LCE		Lsd fr MVL
RA-85747	Tupolev Tu-154M	92A-930	ex EP-EAD		
RA-85847	Tupolev Tu-154M	88A-792	ex OK-TCD		Lsd fr BTC

RA-65099	Tupolev Tu-134A-3	63700	ex CCCP-65099	VIP
RA-65939	Tupolev Tu-134A-3	1351409	ex LZ-TUU	
RA-65935	Tupolev Tu-134A-3	66180	ex CCCP-65935	
RA-76472	Ilyushin Il-76TD	0033446350	ex CCCP-76472	Lsd to AYZ
RA-76492	Ilyushin Il-76T	093418548	ex YI-AKT	Lsd to AYZ
RA-76483	Ilyushin Il-76TD	0063468042	ex CCCP-76483	Lsd to TIS
RA-76787	Ilyushin Il-76TD	0093495854	ex EP-CFB	Lsd to AYZ

AIRSTAN ceased operations

AIRSTARS

Moscow-Domodedovo (DME)

RA-86515	Ilyushin Il-62M	2138657	ex CCCP-86515	ECM pod
RA-86568	Ilyushin Il-62M	4256223		

Same company as Aero Stars?

AJT AIR INTERNATIONAL

Turjet (E9/TRJ)   *Moscow-Sheremetyevo (SVO)*

RA-86065	Ilyushin Il-86	51483203032	ex CCCP-86065	
RA-86115	Ilyushin Il-86	51483209083	ex CCCP-86115	
RA-86140	Ilyushin Il-86	51483211102		Lsd fr Vaso Lsg
RA-86141	Ilyushin Il-86	51483211103		Lsd fr Vaso Lsg

Tupolev Tu-154's are leased from other airlines as and when required
AJT Air International is the trading name of Asian Joint Transport

ALANIA AIRLINE

Alania (OST)   *Vladikavkaz (OGZ)*

RA-42339	Yakovlev Yak-42	452042606267	
RA-42341	Yakovlev Yak-42D	4520421706292	ex CCCP-42341
RA-65613	Tupolev Tu-134A	3352106	ex 65613
RA-65622	Tupolev Tu-134A-3	60495	ex CCCP-65622

ALLIANCE AIR

Orbita (NZP)   *Moscow-Zhukovsky*

RA-65554	Tupolev Tu-134A-3	66320	ex CCCP-65554	Lsd fr LLM
RA-74020	Antonov An-74-200	36547195014		
RA-74027	Antonov An-74-200	36547096920	ex UR-74027	Lsd fr LLM
RA-74052	Antonov An-74-200	36547098444		Lsd fr LLM
RA-87502	Yakovlev Yak-40	9510140	ex CCCP-87502	
RA-87530	Yakovlev Yak-40	9521241	ex CCCP-87530	

Alliance Air is the trading name of ATC Alliance Avia Group

ALROSA AVIATION

Alrosa (LRO)   *Mirny (MJZ)*

RA-65693	Tupolev Tu-134B-3	63221	ex YL-LBC	VIP
RA-65715	Tupolev Tu-134B-3	63536	ex 4L-AAC	
RA-65907	Tupolev Tu-134A	63996	ex CCCP-65907	VIP
RA-85757	Tupolev Tu-154M	92A-939	ex EW-85757	Lsd fr VARZ 400

ALROSA MIRNY AIR ENTERPRISE

Mirny (DRU)   *Mirny (MJZ)*

RA-46352	Antonov An-24B	97305801	ex CCCP-46352	
RA-46488	Antonov An-24RV	27308106	ex CCCP-46488	
RA-46501	Antonov An-24RV	37308306	ex CCCP-46501	
RA-46580	Antonov An-24B	97304909	ex CCCP-46580	
RA-46621	Antonov An-24RV	37308708	ex CCCP-46621	
RA-47272	Antonov An-24B	07306402	ex CCCP-47272	
RA-47298	Antonov An-24	.7306701	ex CCCP-47298	
RA-47694	Antonov An-24RV	27307601	ex CCCP-47694	
RA-47807	Antonov An-24B	17306909	ex CCCP-47607	
RA-85654	Tupolev Tu-154M	89A-796	ex CCCP-85654	
RA-85675	Tupolev Tu-154M	90A-835	ex CCCP-85765	
RA-85684	Tupolev Tu-154M	90A-851	ex CCCP-85684	
RA-85728	Tupolev Tu-154M	92A-910	ex CCCP-85728	
RA-85757	Tupolev Tu-154M	92A-939	ex EW-85757	impounded Dubai Lsd fr VARZ 400
RA-26552	Antonov An-26	3107	ex CCCP-26552	

RA-26607	Antonov An-26	470.?	ex CCCP-26607	
RA-26628	Antonov An-26	5309	ex CCCP-26628	
RA-26668	Antonov An-26	8201	ex CCCP-26668	
RA-38004	Antonov An-38-100			
RA-38009	Antonov An-38-100			
RA-65146	Tupolev Tu-134B-3	61000	ex YL-LBA	
RA-65738	Tupolev Tu-134A	2351507	ex CCCP-65738	Lsd fr Novosibisky NII
RA-76357	Ilyushin Il-76TD	1023414467	ex CCCP-76357	
RA-76360	Ilyushin Il-76TD	1033414492		
RA-76373	Ilyushin Il-76TD	1033415507	ex CCCP-76373	Lsd to TIS
RA-76420	Ilyushin Il-76TD	1023413446	ex CCCP-76420	Lsd to TIS

ALTAI AIRLINES

Barnaul (BAX)

RA-87252	Yakovlev Yak-40	9310926	ex CCCP-87252
RA-87297	Yakovlev Yak-40	9321428	ex 87297
RA-87326	Yakovlev Yak-40	9330530	ex CCCP-87326
RA-87460	Yakovlev Yak-40	9431936	ex CCCP-87460
RA-87557	Yakovlev Yak-40	9210821	ex CCCP-87557
RA-87558	Yakovlev Yak-40	9210921	ex CCCP-87558
RA-26692	Antonov An-26		
RA-76833	Ilyushin Il-76TD	1023411363	ex CCCP-76833

AMUR AVIAKOMPANIA

Mar-Kyuel

| RA-26048 | Antonov An-26B | 10901 | ex CCCP-26048 |

AMURAVIATRANS believed to have ceased operations

ANGARA AIRLINES

Sarma (AGU) *Irkutsk (IKT)*

RA-46642	Antonov An-24RV	37308910?	ex CCCP-46642
RA-46659	Antonov An-24RV	47309306	ex CCCP-46659
RA-46660	Antonov An-24RV	47309307	ex CCCP-46660
RA-46697	Antonov An-24RV	47309908	ex CCCP-46697
RA-46712	Antonov An-24RV	57310408	ex EK-24408
RA-47842	Antonov An-24B	37308410	ex CCCP-47842
RA-47848	Antonov An-24B	17307410	ex CCCP-47848

All leased from Irkutsk Aircraft Repair Plant 403

ANTEX-POLUS

Antex-Polus (AKP) *Ermolino*

RA-11098	Antonov An-12B			
RA-11356	Antonov An-12BP	7345206	ex CCCP-11356	
RA-11516	Antonov An-12BP	4341909	ex 84 red	
RA-11768	Antonov An-12BP	5343103	ex Soviet AF	
RA-65908	Tupolev Tu-134A	63870	ex CCCP-65908	Op for Aviazapchast Trade Co

ARKHANGELSK 2ND AVIATION ENTERPRISE

Dvina (OAO) *Arkhangelsk-Vaslearo*

RA-67553	LET L-410UVP-E	851430	ex CCCP-67553	
RA-67562	LET L-410UVP-E	851602	ex CCCP-67562	
RA-67563	LET L-410UVP-E	861603	ex CCCP-67563	Pomor-Tur titles
RA-67564	LET L-410UVP-E	851604	ex CCCP-67564	
RA-67565	LET L-410UVP-E	851605	ex CCCP-67565	
RA-67567	LET L-410UVP-E	861607	ex CCCP-67567	
RA-67569	LET L-410UVP-E	861609	ex CCCP-67569	

ASHAB AIR

| RA-65124 | Tupolev Tu-134A-3 | 60560 | ex CCCP-65124 |

ASTAIR

Astair (SUW) *Moscow-Domodedovo (DME)*

RA-42320	Yakovlev Yak-42	4520421302075	ex CCCP-42320	
RA-42333	Yakovlev Yak-42	4520422606156	ex CCCP-42333	
RA-42411	Yakovlev Yak-42D	4520421219043	ex CCCP-42411	no titles
RA-42429	Yakovlev Yak-42D	4520423407016		no titles

ASTRAKHAN AIRLINES

Air Astrakhan (OB/ASZ)
Astrakhan-Narimanovo (ASF)

RA-65055	Tupolev Tu-134A	49856	ex CCCP-65055	
RA-65080	Tupolev Tu-134A-3	60065	ex CCCP-65080	Lsd to KGL
RA-65102	Tupolev Tu-134A-3	60267	ex CCCP-65102	Lsd to BTC
RA-65825	Tupolev Tu-134A-3	09078	ex CCCP-65825	
RA-65828	Tupolev Tu-134A	12086	ex CCCP-65828	
RA-46687	Antonov An-24RV	47309804	ex CCCP-46687	
RA-46834	Antonov An-24RV	17306801	ex CCCP-46834	
RA-47260	Antonov An-24RV	27307802	ex CCCP-47260	

ASTRAL believed to have ceased operations

ATLANT – SOYUZ AIRLINES

Atlant-Soyuz (3G/AYZ)
Chkalovskaya (CKL)

EW-76711	Ilyushin Il-76TS	0063473187	ex CCCP-76711		Joint ops with TXC
EW-76734	Ilyushin Il-76TD	0073476312	ex RA-76734		Joint ops with TXC
EW-78779	Ilyushin Il-76TD	0083489662	ex CCCP-78779		Lsd fr TXC
RA-76401	Ilyushin Il-76TD	1023412399	ex CCCP-76401		Lsd fr UHS
RA-76409	Ilyushin Il-76TD	1023410355	ex CCCP-76409		Lsd fr KNM
RA-76425	Ilyushin Il-76TD	1003405167	ex CCCP-76425		Lsd fr KNM
RA-76472	Ilyushin Il-76TD	0033446350	ex CCCP-76472		Lsd fr VAZ
RA-76492	Ilyushin Il-76T	093418548	ex YI-AKT		Lsd fr VAZ
RA-76494	Ilyushin Il-76TD	0053465956	ex CCCP-76494		
RA-76666	Ilyushin Il-76TD	0053464934	ex CCCP-76666		
RA-76783	Ilyushin Il-76TD	0093498974	ex CCCP-76783	all-white	Lsd fr UHS
RA-76787	Ilyushin Il-76TD	0093495854	ex EP-CFB		Lsd fr VAZ
RA-76798	Ilyushin Il-76TD	1003403063	ex CCCP-76798		Lsd fr BRZ
RA-78831	Ilyushin Il-76T	0013428831	ex EP-TPF		
RA-86062	Ilyushin Il-86	51483203029	ex EK-86062		Lsd fr UHS
RA-86139	Ilyushin Il-86	51483210098			Joint ops with ESL
RA-96002	Ilyushin Il-96-300	74393201001		Freighter	Lsd fr Ilyushin

Two Ilyushin Il-96-400Ts and five Tupolev Tu-334s are on order

ATRAN – AVIATRANS CARGO AIRLINES

Atran (V8/VAS)
Moscow-Domodedovo (DME)

RA-11868	Antonov An-12B	9346310	ex CCCP-11868	
RA-12990	Antonov An-12B	00347304	ex CCCP-12990	
RA-93912	Antonov An-12B	4341709	ex CCCP-93912	
RA-93913	Antonov An-12B	4342609-	ex CCCP-93913	
RA-93915	Antonov An-12B	4342103	ex CCCP-93915	
RA-98117	Antonov An-12B	402301	ex CCCP-98117	Lsd to SVT
RA-26595	Antonov An-26B	13401	ex CCCP-26595	
RA-27210	Antonov An-26	5410	ex CCCP-27210	
RA-76809	Ilyushin Il-76TD	1013408252	ex CCCP-76809	Lsd to DOB
RA-76820	Ilyushin Il-76TD	1013409295	ex CCCP-76820	Lsd to DOB

ATRUVERA AIR TRANSPORT

Atruvera (AUV)
St Petersburg-Pulkovo (LED)

EW-76737	Ilyushin Il-76TD	0073477323	ex CCCP-76737	Lsd fr TXC
EW-78827	Ilyushin Il-76TD	1003499997	ex CCCP-78827	Lsd fr TXC
RA-76368	Ilyushin Il-76TD	0033447364	ex UR-76561	
RA-76471	Ilyushin Il-76TD	0033446345	ex EP-MKA	
RA-76516	Ilyushin Il-76T	093418556	ex CCCP-76516	
RA-76659	Ilyushin Il-76TD	0053463908	ex CCCP-76659	
RA-76672	Ilyushin Il-76TD	0063466981	ex EP-CFC	
RA-76848	Ilyushin Il-76TD	0033448390	ex CCCP-76848	

ATU CARGO

RA-64021	Tupolev Tu-204-100S	1450743164021	Op in Aviastar colours

AVIACON ZITOTRANS

Zitotrans (ZR/AZS)
Ekaterinburg-Koltsovo (SVX)

RA-76352	Ilyushin Il-76TD	1023411378	ex EP-SFB	
RA-76510	Ilyushin Il-76T	083414432	ex YL-LAJ	Lsd fr TYM
RA-76514	Ilyushin Il-76T	083415453	ex CCCP-76514	Lsd fr TYM

| RA-76527 | Ilyushin Il-76T | 0003427796 | ex CCCP-76527 | | Lsd fr TYM |
| RA-76807 | Ilyushin Il-76TD | 1013405176 | ex CCCP-76807 | | Lsd fr TYM |

AVIAENERGO

Aviaenergo (7U/ERG) *Moscow-Sheremetyevo (SVO)*

RA-65962	Tupolev Tu-134A-3	3351901	ex CCCP-65962	Insat-Aero titles
RA-85797	Tupolev Tu-154M	93A-981		
RA-85809	Tupolev Tu-154M	94A-985		
RA-86130	Ilyushin Il-62M	3255333	ex UN-86130	
RA-86583	Ilyushin Il-62M	1356851	ex CCCP-86583	Executive

AVIAEKPRESSKRUIZ / AVIAEXPRESSCRUISE

Aviacruise (E6/BKS) *Moscow-Vnukovo (VKO)*

RA-85101*	Tupolev Tu-154M	88A-783	ex B-608L	
RA-85109*	Tupolev Tu-154M	88A-790	ex B-606L	
RA-85136*	Tupolev Tu-154M	88A-791	ex B-607L	
RA-85712	Tupolev Tu-154M	91A-888	ex CCCP-85712	
RA-85713	Tupolev Tu-154M	91A-889	ex 4L-85713	

*Leased from Baltiskaya Strakhovaya Kompania

RA-87511	Yakovlev Yak-40	9521340	ex CCCP-87511	
RA-87535	Yakovlev Yak-40	9521941	ex CCCP-87535	VIP
RA-87917	Yakovlev Yak-40	9730755	ex CCCP-87917	

AVIAL AVIATION CO

New Avial (NVI) *Moscow-Domodedovo (DME)*

RA-11324	Antonov An-12BP	2340805	ex Soviet AF 88 red	
RA-11339	Antonov An-12BP	6344310	ex CCCP-11339	Op for Russian Post
RA-11370	Antonov An-12BP			
RA-11408	Antonov An-12BP	3341209	ex CCCP-11408	
RA-11813	Antonov An-12BP	3340908	ex CCCP-11813	

RA-28927	WSK-PZL/Antonov An-28	1AJ008-14	ex CCCP-28927
RA-28937	WSK-PZL/Antonov An-28	1AJ009-03	ex CCCP-28937
RA-28939	WSK-PZL/Antonov An-28	1AJ009-05	ex CCCP-28939

AVIALESOOCHRANA VLADIMIR AIR ENTERPRISE

Vladimir

RA-26040	Antonov An-26B	10703	ex CCCP-26040
RA-26532	Antonov An-26	7410	ex CCCP-26532
RA-47361	Antonov An-24RV	67310705	ex CCCP-47361
RA-47363	Antonov An-24RV	67310707	ex CCCP-47363

AVIAOBSHEMASH AIRCO / AOM AIR COMPANY

Obshemash (OBM) *Omsk-Severny (OMS)*

RA-11830	Antonov An-12BP	4342210	ex CCCP-11830
RA-26090	Antonov An-26	11506	ex CCCP-28090
RA-26191	Antonov An-24	19902309	ex CCCP-26191

AVIAPRAD

Aviaprad (VID) *Ekaterinburg-Koltsovo (SVX)*

| RA-76386 | Ilyushin Il-76TD | 1033418600 | ex UK-76386 |

AVIAST

Ialsi (VVA) *Moscow-Vnukovo (VKO)*

RA-76485	Ilyushin Il-76TD	0063470088	ex 76485	Lsd to ESL
RA-76486	Ilyushin Il-76TD	0073476281	ex CCCP-76486	
RA-76487	Ilyushin Il-76TD	0073479367	ex CCCP-76487	
RA-76754	Ilyushin Il-76T	093421637	ex CCCP-76754	
RA-76797	Ilyushin Il-76TD	1003403052	ex CCCP-76797	
RA-76843	Ilyushin Il-76TD	1013408269	ex RA-76814	
RA-76849	Ilyushin Il-76TD	0023440161	ex UR-86921	

RA-11756	Antonov An-12BP	4342208	ex CCCP-11756	no titles
RA-11962	Antonov An-12BP	5543007	ex CCCP-11962	
RA-69314	Antonov An-12BP	5343004	ex CCCP-69314	

RA-87800   Yakovlev Yak-40   9621547 ex LZ-CBD
Also operates cargo charters with other Antonov An-12 aircraft leased as required
Three Tupolev Tu-214s and one Tu-214F are on order for delivery in 2006/7

AVIASTAR AIRLINES

Aviastar-Volga (FUE)   *Ulyanovsk (ULY)*

RA-26088	Antonov An-26	11209	ex CCCP-26088	Survey/Calibrator
RA-26251	Antonov An-26	07309109		Freighter
RA-26625	Antonov An-26	77305206	ex CCCP-26625	Survey/Calibrator
RA-87227	Yakovlev Yak-40K	9841559	ex CCCP-87227	VIP
RA-87244	Yakovlev Yak-40	9531243	ex CCCP-87244	VIP

AVL – ARKHANGELSKIE LINII / ARCHANGELSK AIRLINES

Archangelsk Air (5N/AUL)   *Arkhangelsk-Talegi (ARH)*

RA-26024	Antonov An-26B	10306	ex CCCP-26024	
RA-26104	Antonov An-26BRL	27312002	ex CCCP-26104	
RA-26135	Antonov An-26B	12806	ex CCCP-26135	
RA-26501	Antonov An-26B	6308	ex CCCP-26501	
RA-26542	Antonov An-26B	2708	ex CCCP-26542	
RA-26551	Antonov An-26B	310.?	ex CCCP-26551	
RA-26556	Antonov An-26B	57303204	ex CCCP-26556	
RA-26601	Antonov An-26B	440.?	ex CCCP-26601	
RA-26615	Antonov An-26B	77305001	ex CCCP-26615	
RA-26682	Antonov An-26B	97308706	ex CCCP-26682	no titles
RA-65052	Tupolev Tu-134A	49825	ex CCCP-65052	Lsd to TMN
RA-65066	Tupolev Tu-134A-3	49898	ex CCCP-65066	
RA-65083	Tupolev Tu-134A-3	60090	ex CCCP-65083	Lsd to TMN
RA-65084	Tupolev Tu-134A-3	60115	ex CCCP-65084	Lsd to TMN
RA-65096	Tupolev Tu-134A-3	60257	ex CCCP-65096	
RA-65103	Tupolev Tu-134A-3	60297	ex CCCP-65103	
RA-65116	Tupolev Tu-134A-3	60420	ex CCCP-65116	
RA-85302	Tupolev Tu-154B-2	78A-302	ex CCCP-85302	
RA-85365	Tupolev Tu-154B-2	79A-365	ex LZ-LTB	
RA-85386	Tupolev Tu-154B-2	79A-386	ex CCCP-85386	
RA-85468	Tupolev Tu-154B-2	81A-468	ex CCCP-85468	
RA-85551	Tupolev Tu-154B-2	82A-551	ex CCCP-85551	Lsd to ESL
RA-46528	Antonov An-24RV	47310007	ex CCCP-46528	
RA-46651	Antonov An-24RV	47309202	ex CCCP-46651	
RA-46667	Antonov An-24RV	47309508	ex CCCP-46667	

BAIKAL AIRLINES ceased operations

BAL – BASHKIRSKIE AVIALINII / BASHKIRIAN AIRLINES

Bashkirian (V9/BTC)   *Ufa (UFA)*

RA-85773	Tupolev Tu-154M	93A-955	ex EP-TUB	
RA-85777	Tupolev Tu-154M	93A-959	ex EP-TUA	
RA-85824	Tupolev Tu-154M	88A-769	ex SP-LCE	
RA-85825	Tupolev Tu-154M	88A-776	ex SP-LCH	
RA-85826	Tupolev Tu-154M	89A-812	ex SP-LCL	
RA-85831	Tupolev Tu-154M	88A-774	ex SP-LCF	
RA-85846	Tupolev Tu-154M	89A-807	ex OK-UCF	
RA-85847	Tupolev Tu-154M	88A-792	ex OK-TCD	Lsd to VAZ
RA-85848	Tupolev Tu-154M	89A-804	ex OK-UCE	
RA-46649	Antonov An-24RV	47309102	ex CCCP-46649	possibly wfs
RA-65028	Tupolev Tu-134A	48490	ex CCCP-65028	
RA-65040	Tupolev Tu-134A	49100	ex LY-ABC	Op for Government
RA-65102	Tupolev Tu-134A-3	60267	ex CCCP-65102	Lsd fr ASZ
RA-74014	Antonov An-74-200	36547098968		
RA-74015	Antonov An-74-200	36547098969		no titles
RA-74046	Antonov An-74	36547097935		

BELGOROD AIR ENTERPRISE

Belgorye (BED)   *Belgorod (EGO)*

RA-87304	Yakovlev Yak-40	9322028	ex CCCP-87304	
RA-87371	Yakovlev Yak-40	9340232	ex CCCP-87371	
RA-87465	Yakovlev Yak-40	9430437	ex CCCP-87465	
RA-87648	Yakovlev Yak-40	9140920	ex CCCP-87648	Executive
RA-87809	Yakovlev Yak-40	9231923	ex CCCP-87809	
RA-87919	Yakovlev Yak-40K	9730955	ex CCCP-87919	

| RA-87959 | Yakovlev Yak-40K | 9822057 | ex CCCP-87959 |
| RA-87993 | Yakovlev Yak-40 | 9541744 | ex CCCP-87993 |

BEREZNIKI AVIATION ENTERPRISE ceased operations

BEREZNIKI MUNICIPAL AIR

Perm (PEE)

| RA-13344 | Antonov An-24RV | 37308310 | ex CCCP-13344 |

BLAGHOVESCHENSK AIRLINES

Blagoveschenk (BQS)

RA-87395	Yakovlev Yak-40	9410733	ex CCCP-87395
RA-87452	Yakovlev Yak-40	9430936	ex CCCP-87452
RA-88153	Yakovlev Yak-40	9610746	ex CCCP-88153

BODAIBO AIR ENTERPRISE

Bodaibo

| RA-26655 | Antonov An-26 | 97307802 | ex CCCP-26655 |

BRAVIA / BRIANSK AVIA ENTERPRISE

Briansk Avia (BRK)   *Bryansk (BZK)*

RA-87373	Yakovlev Yak-40	9410732	ex CCCP-87373	
RA-87440	Yakovlev Yak-40	9431635	ex CCCP-87440	VIP
RA-87510	Yakovlev Yak-40	9521240	ex CCCP-87510	
RA-87513	Yakovlev Yak-40	9521540	ex CCCP-87513	
RA-87904	Yakovlev Yak-40K	9720854	ex CCCP-87904	
RA-87906	Yakovlev Yak-40K	9731054	ex CCCP-87906	
RA-88276	Yakovlev Yak-40	9721453	ex CCCP-88276	VIP
RA-46394	Antonov An-24B	07306208		

BUGULMA AIR ENTERPRISE

Bugavia (BGM)   *Bugulma (UUA)*

RA-87239	Yakovlev Yak-40	9530743	ex CCCP-87239	
RA-87342	Yakovlev Yak-40	9511139	ex CCCP-87342	Tatneft titles; VIP
RA-87447	Yakovlev Yak-40	9430436	ex CCCP-87447	
RA-87462	Yakovlev Yak-40	9430137	ex CCCP-87462	
RA-87505	Yakovlev Yak-40	9510740	ex CCCP-87505	
RA-87517	Yakovlev Yak-40	9521940	ex CCCP-87517	
RA-87588	Yakovlev Yak-40	9222022	ex CCCP-87588	Tatneft titles; VIP
RA-87991	Yakovlev Yak-40	9541544	ex CCCP-87991	
RA-88156	Yakovlev Yak-40	9611046	ex CCCP-88156	
RA-88165	Yakovlev Yak-40	9611946	ex CCCP-88165	
RA-88176	Yakovlev Yak-40	9621447	ex CCCP-88176	
RA-88182	Yakovlev Yak-40	9620248	ex CCCP-88182	Tatneft titles; VIP

Several appear stored at a time

BUGURUSLAN FLYING SCHOOL ceased operations

BURAL

Bural (U4/BUN)   *Ulan Ude (UUD)*

RA-46408	Antonov An-24B	77304003	ex CCCP-46408
RA-46506	Antonov An-24RV	37308402	ex CCCP-46506
RA-46614	Antonov An-24RV	37308701	ex CCCP-46614

BYLINA

(BYL)   *Moscow-Vnukovo (VKO)*

| RA-88263 | Yakovlev Yak-40 | 9711852 | ex CCCP-88263 |
| RA-88274 | Yakovlev Yak-40 | 9721453 | ex CCCP-88274 |

CENTER-SOUTH AIRLINES

Center-South (CTS)   *Belgorod (EGO)*

| RA-87467 | Yakovlev Yak-40 | 9440637 | ex CCCP-87467 |
| RA-87550 | Yakovlev Yak-40 | 9210121 | ex CCCP-87550 |

CENTRAL DISTRICTS AIRLINES Current status is uncertain, sole aircraft disposed of

CENTRE AVIA AIRLINES

Aviacentre (J7/CVC) — *Moscow-Bykovo (BKA)*

RA-42325	Yakovlev Yak-42D	4520424402148	ex CCCP-42325	
RA-42340	Yakovlev Yak-42D	4520424506270	ex CCCP-42340	
RA-42355	Yakovlev Yak-42D	4520424711399	ex LY-AAV	
RA-42360	Yakovlev Yak-42D	4520423811421	ex EP-YAF	
RA-42368	Yakovlev Yak-42D	4520423914166	ex EP-LBT	
RA-42370	Yakovlev Yak-42D	4520422914203	ex CCCP-42370	
RA-42378	Yakovlev Yak-42D	4520421014494	ex TC-FAR	Lsd fr SOV
RA-42385	Yakovlev Yak-42D	4520423016309	ex ER-YCC	
RA-42549	Yakovlev Yak-42D	11040105	ex CCCP-42549	Evgenii Kutscher
RA-46665	Antonov An-24RV	47309506	ex CCCP-46665	

CHEBOKSARY AIR ENTERPRISE

Air Cheboksary (CBK) — *Cheboksary (CSY)*

RA-65007	Tupolev Tu-134A-3	46100	ex CCCP-65007	
RA-65015	Tupolev Tu-134A-3	48325	ex CCCP-65015	
RA-65021	Tupolev Tu-134A-3	48390	ex CCCP-65021	
RA-65024	Tupolev Tu-134A	48420	ex CCCP-65024	Lsd to AKT
RA-65033	Tupolev Tu-134A-3	48540	ex CCCP-65033	Lsd to SIB
RA-46499	Antonov An-24RV	27308302	ex CCCP-46499	
RA-46619	Antonov An-24RV	37306706	ex CCCP-46619	Avia Predpreeyatne titles
RA-47294	Antonov An-24RV	07306604	ex UR-47294	

Will become national airline of Chuvashian Republic

CHERNOMOR AVIA

Cheravia (CMK) — *Sochi-Adler (AER)*

RA-65565	Tupolev Tu-134A	63998	ex EW-65565
RA-65604	Tupolev Tu-134A	62561	ex CCCP-65604
RA-85291	Tupolev Tu-154B-1	78A-291	ex CCCP-85291
RA-85384	Tupolev Tu-154B-2	79A-384	ex ER-85384

CHITAAVIA

Chita (CHF) — *Chita (HTA)*

RA-85133	Tupolev Tu-154B	76A-133	ex YL-LAA	
RA-85280	Tupolev Tu-154B-2	78A-280	ex CCCP-85280	
RA-85506	Tupolev Tu-154B-2	81A-506	ex CCCP-85506	
RA-85766	Tupolev Tu-154M	92A-923	ex EP-MAP	all-white
RA-85802	Tupolev Tu-154M	93A-961	ex EP-MAN	

CHUKOTAVIA

Anadyr (DYR)

RA-26099	Antonov An-26B		ex CCCP-26099
RA-26117	Antonov An-26B		ex CCCP-26117
RA-26128	Antonov An-26B	12702	ex CCCP-26128
RA-26591	Antonov An-26B	14001	ex CCCP-26591
RA-46616	Antonov An-24RV	37308703	ex CCCP-46616
RA-47159	Antonov An-24B	89901701	ex CCCP-47159

CNG TRANSAVIA

Transgaz (CGT) — *Voronezh (VOZ)*

RA-21506	Yakovlev Yak-40KD	9840259	ex CCCP-21506	VIP
RA-87246	Yakovlev Yak-40	9531543	ex CCCP-87246	
RA-87247	Yakovlev Yak-40	9351543	ex CCCP-87247	
RA-87436	Yakovlev Yak-40	9431235	ex CCCP-87436	
RA-88278	Yakovlev Yak-40	9732053	ex CCCP-88278	
RA-98103	Antonov An-12BP	00347003	ex CCCP-98103	Lsd to VCG as 3C-AAL
RA-98119	Antonov An-12BP	7344801	ex CCCP-98119	Lsd to VCG as 3C-AAG

CONTINENTAL AIRWAYS

Contair (PC/PVV) (IATA 922) — *Moscow-Sheremetyevo (SVO)*

RA-85696	Tupolev Tu-154M	91A-869	Lsd fr MVL

RA-85760	Tupolev Tu-154M	92A-942	ex EW-85760	no titles	Lsd fr VARZ 400
RA-86136	Ilyushin Il-86	51483210094		no titles	Lsd fr F-16 Leasing
RA-86138	Ilyushin Il-86	51483210096		no titles	Lsd fr F-16 Leasing

DAGHESTAN AIRLINES

Dagal (DAG) Makhachkala (MCX)

RA-46654	Antonov An-24RV	47309205	ex CCCP-46654	
RA-65569	Tupolev Tu-134B-3	63340	ex 4L-AAB	
RA-65579	Tupolev Tu-134B-3	63295	ex 4L-AAD	
RA-85756	Tupolev Tu-154M	92A-938		
RA-85828	Tupolev Tu-154M	9.A-1009		
RA-85840	Tupolev Tu-154M	98A-1011		Russian National FA titles

DALAVIA

Khabarovsk Air (H8/KHB) (IATA 560) Khabarovsk (KHV)

RA-46474	Antonov An-24RV	27308002	ex CCCP-46474
RA-46522	Antonov An-24RV	47310001	ex CCCP-46522
RA-46529	Antonov An-24RV	57310008	ex CCCP-46529
RA-46565	Antonov An-24B	87304704	ex CCCP-46565
RA-46643	Antonov An-24RV	37309001	ex CCCP-46643
RA-47156	Antonov An-24RB	89901608	ex CCCP-47156
RA-47170	Antonov An-24B	89901802	ex CCCP-47170
RA-47184	Antonov An-24B	99901909	ex CCCP-47184
RA-47188	Antonov An-24B	99902003	ex CCCP-47188
RA-47290	Antonov An-24B	07306510	ex CCCP-47290
RA-47354	Antonov An-24RV	67310603	ex CCCP-47354
RA-47367	Antonov An-24RV	77310806	ex CCCP-47367
RA-47748	Antonov An-24B	79901201	ex CCCP-47748
RA-47758	Antonov An-24B	79901301	ex CCCP-47758
RA-47766	Antonov An-24B	79901401	ex CCCP-47766
RA-47819	Antonov An-24RV	17307108	ex CCCP-47819
RA-47831	Antonov An-24B	17307302	ex CCCP-47831
RA-26000	Antonov An-26	7309604	ex CCCP-26000
RA-26001	Antonov An-26	9705	ex CCCP-26001
RA-26043	Antonov An-26B		ex CCCP-26043
RA-26058	Antonov An-26B	11101	ex CCCP-26058
RA-26500	Antonov An-26	87306307	ex CCCP-26500
RA-26562	Antonov An-26	57303505	ex CCCP-26562
RA-26564	Antonov An-26	3507	ex CCCP-26564
RA-86128	Ilyushin Il-62M	2255719	ex CCCP-86128
RA-86131	Ilyushin Il-62M	4255244	ex CCCP-86131
RA-86471	Ilyushin Il-62M	72504	ex CCCP-86471
RA-86479	Ilyushin Il-62M	4728118	ex CCCP-86479
RA-86481	Ilyushin Il-62M	1829415	ex CCCP-86481
RA-86486	Ilyushin Il-62M	3830123	ex CCCP-86486
RA-86493	Ilyushin Il-62M	4140748	ex CCCP-86493
RA-86503	Ilyushin Il-62M	4934512	ex CCCP-86503
RA-86525	Ilyushin Il-62M	4851612	ex CCCP-86525
RA-86560	Ilyushin Il-62M	2153347	ex CCCP-86560
RA-85178	Tupolev Tu-154B-1	76A-178	ex CCCP-85178
RA-85190	Tupolev Tu-154B-1	76A-190	ex CCCP-85190
RA-85205	Tupolev Tu-154B-1	77A-205	ex CCCP-85205
RA-85206	Tupolev Tu-154B-1	77A-206	ex CCCP-85206
RA-85207	Tupolev Tu-154B-1	77A-207	ex CCCP-85207
RA-85216	Tupolev Tu-154B-1	77A-216	ex CCCP-85216
RA-85220	Tupolev Tu-154B-2	77A-220	ex CCCP-85220
RA-85266	Tupolev Tu-154B-2	78A-266	ex CCCP-85266
RA-85336	Tupolev Tu-154B-2	79A-336	ex CCCP-85336
RA-85341	Tupolev Tu-154B-2	79A-341	ex CCCP-85341
RA-85443	Tupolev Tu-154B-2	80A-443	ex CCCP-85443
RA-85477	Tupolev Tu-154B-2	81A-477	ex CCCP-85477
RA-85607	Tupolev Tu-154M	85A-702	ex EK-85607

RA-64502	Tupolev Tu-214	42625002		Lsd fr Financial Lsg Co
RA-64503	Tupolev Tu-214	42103003		Lsd fr Financial Lsg Co

DAURIA

Chita-Kadala (HTA)

RA-26053	Antonov An-26B	10909	ex CCCP-26053	Lsd to Iraero
RA-26543	Antonov An-26	2709	ex CCCP-26543	
RA-47268	Antonov An-24B	07306306	ex CCCP-47268	
RA-47838	Antonov An-24B	17307210	ex CCCP-47838	Avialinii Zabaikalaya titles

DOBROLET AIRLINES

Dobrolet (G2/DOB) (IATA 847)   *Moscow-Sheremetyevo (SVO)*

EW-78819	Ilyushin Il-76TD	0093495883	ex CCCP-78819	Lsd fr TXC
EW-78826	Ilyushin Il-76TD	1003499991	ex CCCP-78826	Lsd fr TXC
RA-76388	Ilyushin Il-76TD	1013406204	ex RA-78851	
RA-76389	Ilyushin Il-76TD	1013407212	ex RA-78852	
RA-76418	Ilyushin Il-76T	073409237	ex CCCP-86640	
RA-76809	Ilyushin Il-76TD	1013408252	ex CCCP-76809	Lsd fr VAS
RA-76820	Ilyushin Il-76TD	1013409295	ex CCCP-76820	Lsd fr VAS

DOMODEDOVO AIRLINES

Domodedovo (E3/DMO)   *Moscow-Domodedovo (DME)*

RA-86127	Ilyushin Il-62M	1254851	ex CCCP-86127	
RA-86129	Ilyushin Il-62M	2255525		
RA-86475	Ilyushin Il-62M	3727213	ex CCCP-86475	
RA-86484	Ilyushin Il-62M	4727324	ex CCCP-86484	
RA-86494	Ilyushin Il-62M	4140952	ex CCCP-86494	
RA-86499	Ilyushin Il-62M	2932637	ex CCCP-86499	
RA-86509	Ilyushin Il-62M	2036829	ex CCCP-86509	
RA-86516	Ilyushin Il-62M	2139524	ex CCCP-86516	
RA-86519	Ilyushin Il-62M	4140212	ex CCCP-86519	
RA-86521	Ilyushin Il-62M	1241425	ex CCCP-86521	
RA-86526	Ilyushin Il-62M	2951447	ex CCCP-86526	
RA-86530	Ilyushin Il-62M	4242543	ex CCCP-86530	
RA-86535	Ilyushin Il-62M	2444555	ex CCCP-86535	
RA-86541	Ilyushin Il-62M	3951359	ex CCCP-86541	
RA-86542	Ilyushin Il-62M	3952714	ex CCCP-86542	
RA-86552	Ilyushin Il-62M	2052345	ex CCCP-86552	
RA-86673	Ilyushin Il-62M	3154416	ex CCCP-86673	
RA-42359	Yakovlev Yak-42D	4520424811417	ex LY-AAW	
RA-42542	Yakovlev Yak-42	11140804	ex CCCP-42542	
RA-76786	Ilyushin Il-76TD	0093496923	ex CCCP-76786	Lsd to ASE
RA-76799	Ilyushin Il-76TD	1003403037	ex CCCP-76799	Lsd to ESL
RA-76812	Ilyushin Il-76TD	1013407230	ex CCCP-76812	Lsd to ESL
RA-96006	Ilyushin Il-96-300	74393201003	ex CCCP-96006	
RA-96009	Ilyushin Il-96-300	74393201006		
RA-96013	Ilyushin Il-96-300	74393202013		

EAST LINE EXPRESS

Eastline Express (P7/ESL) (IATA 215)   *Moscow-Domodedovo (DME)*

RA-78808	Ilyushin Il-76MD	0093493794	ex CCCP-78808		Lsd fr TXC
EW-78843	Ilyushin Il-76TD	1003403082	ex CCCP-78843		Lsd fr TXC
RA-76381	Ilyushin Il-76TD	1033418596			
RA-76400	Ilyushin Il-76TD	1023413438			Lsd fr VLK
RA-76403	Ilyushin Il-76TD	1023412414		Igor Bykov	Lsd fr VLK
RA-76462	Ilyushin Il-76T	0012432955	ex CCCP-76462		
RA-76474	Ilyushin Il-76TD	0033448407	ex UN-76001		Lsd fr ILV
RA-76485	Ilyushin Il-76TD	0063470088	ex 76485		Lsd fr VVA
RA-76799	Ilyushin Il-76TD	1003403037	ex CCCP-76799		Lsd fr DOB
RA-76806	Ilyushin Il-76TD	1003403121	ex CCCP-76806		Lsd fr Aviastar
RA-76812	Ilyushin Il-76TD	1013407230	ex CCCP-76812		Lsd fr DOB
RA-76817	Ilyushin Il-76TD	1023412387	ex CCCP-76817		
RA-78840	Ilyushin Il-76MD	1003403056			
UK 76448	Ilyushin Il-76TD	1023413443	ex CCCP-76448		Lsd fr UZB
RA-65798	Tupolev Tu-134A-3	63179	ex 4L-65798		
RA-85551	Tupolev Tu-154B-2	82A-551	ex CCCP-85551		Lsd fr AUL
RA-85689	Tupolev Tu-154M	90A-860	ex LZ-LTP		Lsd fr BRP
RA-85788	Tupolev Tu-154M	93A-972	ex EP-ITS		Lsd fr KNI
RA-85789	Tupolev Tu-154M	93A-973		no titles	Lsd fr KNI
RA-85798	Tupolev Tu-154M	93A-982	ex EP-MBO		Lsd fr KAZ
RA-85799	Tupolev Tu-154M	93A-983			Lsd fr KAZ
RA-86567	Ilyushin Il-62M	4256314	ex CCCP-86567		Lsd fr Gosinkor Lsg
RA-86139	Ilyushin Il-86	51483210098	ex B-2017		
RA-86142	Ilyushin Il-86	51483210097	ex B-2016		
RA-86144	Ilyushin Il-86	51483204035	ex UN-86068		Lsd fr KZK

ELBRUS AVIA

Elavia (NLK)   *Nalchik (NAL)*

| RA-42371 | Yakovlev Yak-42D | 4520422914225 | ex CCCP-42371 |
| RA-87500 | Yakovlev Yak-40 | 9511939 | ex CCCP-87500 |

ELF AIR renamed Grizoldubova Air

ENKOR

Enkor (G5/ENK)   *Moscow-Domodedovo (DME)*

RA-85514	Tupolev Tu-154B-2	81A-514	ex CCCP-85514	
RA-85724	Tupolev Tu-154M	92A-906	ex EP-TQM	
RA-85725	Tupolev Tu-154M	92A-907	ex EP-MHB	
RA-85754	Tupolev Tu-154M	92A-936	ex EP-MHX	
RA-85827	Tupolev Tu-154M	87A-745	ex SP-LCC	all-white
RA-85829	Tupolev Tu-154M	89A-755	ex SP-LCD	
RA-42387	Yakovlev Yak-42D	4520424016436	ex CCCP-42387	
RA-42388	Yakovlev Yak-42D	4520424016510	ex CCCP-42388	
RA-42401	Yakovlev Yak-42D	4520421116567	ex CCCP-42401	
RA-42408	Yakovlev Yak-42D	4520424116698	ex EP-YAC	
RA-42412	Yakovlev Yak-42D	4520422219055	ex EP-YAA	
RA-42413	Yakovlev Yak-42D	4520422219066	ex EP-YAB	
RA-42430	Yakovlev Yak-42D	4520423408016		
RA-65118	Tupolev Tu-134A-3	60462	ex CCCP-65118	
RA-65131	Tupolev Tu-134A-3	60637	ex CCCP-65131	
RA-65786	Tupolev Tu-134A-3	62775	ex CCCP-65786	

Some aircraft still in Chelyabinsk Air Enterprise colours and titles

ERMOLINO AIRLINES ceased operations

ETELEAIR COMPANY ceased operations

EURASIA AIR COMPANY reportedly ceased operations on 01 September 2003

EVENKY

RA-87900	Yakovlev Yak-40	9720254	ex CCCP-87900

FLIGHT AIR COMPANY – AVIAKOMPANIA FLAIT

Belouga (FLV)   *Astrakhan (ASF)*

RA-12988	Antonov An-12B	00347206	ex CCCP-12988	
RA-65563	Tupolev Tu-134A-3	60035	ex CCCP-65563	Lsd fr NPO;
				op for AstrakhanGazprom
RA-65682	Tupolev Tu-134A-3	62120	ex CCCP-65682	Op for AstrakhanGazprom

GAZPROMAVIA

Gazprom (4G/GZP)   *Moscow-Ostafyevo/Moscow-Vnukovo (-/VKO)*

RA-74005	Antonov An-74TK-100	36547095892		EMS
RA-74008	Antonov An-74T-100	36547095900	ex UR-74008	
RA-74012	Antonov An-74D	36547098959	ex UR-74055	VIP
RA-74016	Antonov An-74TK-100	365470991034		
RA-74031	Antonov An-74-200	36547098961	ex UN-74031	
RA-74032	Antonov An-74TK-100	36547098962	ex UR-74032	
RA-74035	Antonov An-74TK-100	36547098963		
RA-74036	Antonov An-74-200	36547098965		
RA-74040	Antonov An-74	36547097930		
RA-74044	Antonov An-74TK-100	36547097936	ex UN-74044	
RA-74045	Antonov An-74	36547097938	ex UR-74045	damaged, stored Ostafyevo
RA-74056	Antonov An-74-200	36547098951		
RA-74058	Antonov An-74-200	36547098956		

Several appear out of service at any one time

RA-42436	Yakovlev Yak-42D	4520421605018		
RA-42437	Yakovlev Yak-42D	4520423606018		
RA-42438	Yakovlev Yak-42D	4520423609018		
RA-42439	Yakovlev Yak-42D	4520423904019		
RA-42442	Yakovlev Yak-42D	4520421402019		VIP
RA-42451	Yakovlev Yak-42D	4520422708018		
RA-42452	Yakovlev Yak-42	452042.409016		
RA-21505	Yakovlev Yak-40K	9830159	ex CCCP-21505	
RA-76370	Ilyushin Il-76TD	1033414458	ex CCCP-76370	Joint ops with AYZ
RA-76402	Ilyushin Il-76TD	1023413430		Joint ops with AYZ
RA-76445	Ilyushin Il-76TD	1023410330	ex EK-76445	
RA-65983	Tupolev Tu-134A-3	63350	ex CCCP-65983	
RA-85625	Tupolev Tu-154M	87A-752	ex CCCP-85625	
RA-85751	Tupolev Tu-154M	92A-933		
RA-85774	Tupolev Tu-154M	93A-956		

RA-85778	Tupolev Tu-154M	93A-962		
RA-88186	Yakovlev Yak-40K	9620648	ex CCCP-88186	Op for Tyumentransgaz
RA-88300	Yakovlev Yak-40K	9641451	ex OK-GEO	

Gazpromavia is the fleet of the Russian Gas Exploration and Drilling Co and has subsidiary bases at Kaluga [KLF], Perm [PEE], Samara-Smyshlaevka, Sochi [AER], Ukhta [UCT], Yamburg and Yugorsk

GRIZODUBOVOY AVIATION COMPANY

Elfair (E6/EZD)   Moscow-Zhukovsky
Previously listed as Elf Air

RA-65604	Tupolev Tu-134A	62561	ex CCCP-65604	no titles	Lsd to CMK
RA-75811	Ilyushin Il-18V	182004504	ex CCCP-75811		
RA-75851	Ilyushin Il-18V	182005501	ex CCCP-75851	no titles	Lsd to LDF
RA-75894	Ilyushin Il-18V	182004801	ex CCCP-75894		
RA-76490	Ilyushin Il-76T	093416506	ex YI-AKO		Lsd to ASE
RA-76756	Ilyushin Il-76T	0013428839	ex CCCP-76756	no titles	
RA-76823	Ilyushin Il-76TD	0023441189	ex YI-ALQ		Lsd to ASE

GROMOV AIR

Gromov Airlines (GAI)   Moscow-Zhukovsky

RA-65047	Tupolev Tu-134A	49600	ex CCCP-65047		
RA-65721	Tupolev Tu-134A-3M	66130	ex CCCP-65721	VIP	
RA-65740	Tupolev Tu-134A-3M	2351510	ex CCCP-65740	Research	
RA-65926	Tupolev Tu-134A-1	66101	ex CCCP-65926		
RA-65927	Tupolev Tu-134A	66198	ex CCCP-65927	Youri Sheffer	
RA-65932	Tupolev Tu-134A-3	66405	ex 65932		Lsd fr SDB
RA-11372	Antonov An-12B				
RA-11374	Antonov An-12B				
RA-85317	Tupolev Tu-154M	78A-317	ex CCCP-85317	FACT testbed	
RA-88265	Yakovlev Yak-40	9722052	ex CCCP-88265	VIP	

Gromov Air is a division of the Flight Research Institute MM Gromov

IL-AVIA

Ilavia (ILV)   Moscow-Zhukovsky

EW-76712	Ilyushin Il-76TD	0063473190	ex RA-76712	Lsd fr TXC
EW-78848	Ilyushin Il-76TD	1003405159	ex CCCP-78848	Lsd fr TXC
RA-76474	Ilyushin Il-76TD	0033448407	ex UN-76001	Lsd to ESL
RA-76578	Ilyushin Il-76MD	0043449468	ex	
RA-88294	Yakovlev Yak-40	9331329	ex 031 Polish AF	

Sister company of Ilyushin Design Bureau

IRAERO
                                                                       Irkutsk (IKT)

RA-26053	Antonov An-26B	17310909	ex CCCP-26053	Lsd fr Dauria
RA-26130	Antonov An-26B	27312705	ex CCCP-26130	

IRKUT-AVIA

Irkut (UTK)   Irkutsk (IKT)

RA-11309	Antonov An-12BP	00347510	ex CCCP-11309
RA-11310	Antonov An-12BP	4342601	ex CCCP-11310
RA-12162	Antonov An-12BP	3341509	ex CCCP-12162

Irkut-Avia is the trading name of Irkutsk Aviation Industrial Association

IRON DRAGON FLY ceased operations

IRS-AERO grounded mid-October 2002 by Russian Aviation officicals, did not restart operations

IZHAVIA / IZHEVSK AIRLINES

Izhavia (IZA)   Izhevsk (IJK)

RA-26529	Antonov An-26		ex CCCP-26529
RA-26683	Antonov An-26	8707?	ex CCCP-26683
Ra-42450	Yakovlev Yak-42	4520424601019	
RA-46620	Antonov An-24RV	37308707	ex CCCP-46620
RA-46637	Antonov An-24RV	37308903	ex CCCP-46637
RA-65056	Tupolev Tu-134A-3	49860	ex CCCP-65056
RA-65141	Tupolev Tu-134A-3	60945	ex CCCP-65141

KALININGRAD AVIA
Kaliningrad Air (KD/KNI)

RA-65010	Tupolev Tu-134A	46130	ex CCCP-65010		
RA-65011	Tupolev Tu-134A	46140	ex CCCP-65011		
RA-65019	Tupolev Tu-134A	48375	ex CCCP-65019		
RA-65027	Tupolev Tu-134A	48485	ex CCCP-65027		
RA-65054	Tupolev Tu-134A	49840	ex CCCP-65054		
RA-65087	Tupolev Tu-134A	60155	ex CCCP-65087		
RA-65090	Tupolev Tu-134A-3	60185	ex CCCP-65090		
RA-65824	Tupolev Tu-134A-3	09074	ex HA-LBS		
RA-65870	Tupolev Tu-134A-3	28310	ex CCCP-65870		
RA-85788	Tupolev Tu-154M	93A-972	ex EP-ITS		Lsd to ESL
RA-85789	Tupolev Tu-154M	93A-973		no titles	Lsd to ESL

KAPO / KAZAN AVIATION PRODUCTION ASSOCIATION
Kazavia (KAO)

RA-13392	Antonov An-12BK	00347210	ex CCCP-13392	Lsd to ASE
RA-26597	Antonov An-26B	13310	ex CCCP-26597	
RA-64501	Tupolev Tu-214	44524001		
RA-86126	Ilyushin Il-62M	4154535		
RA-86586	Ilyushin Il-62M	3357947		
RA-86945	Ilyushin Il-62M	3850145	ex OK-BYV	
RA-87341	Yakovlev Yak-40	9511039	ex CCCP-87341	

KARAT AIR COMPANY / AVIAKOMPANIA KARAT
Aviakarat (V2/AKT)

RA-87224	Yakovlev Yak-40	9841259	ex CCCP-87224	Op for Yava Corp
RA-87397	Yakovlev Yak-40	9410933	ex CCCP-87397	
RA-87938	Yakovlev Yak-40K	9710153	ex CCCP-87938	
RA-87496	Yakovlev Yak-40	9541945	ex CCCP-87496	Op for Nizhykamsk Petrol
RA-87966	Yakovlev Yak-40	9820958	ex CCCP-87966	
RA-98109	Yakovlev Yak-40K	9740956	ex CCCP-98109	
RA-42343	Yakovlev Yak-42	4520421708285	ex UR-42343	
RA-42345	Yakovlev Yak-42D	4520422708304	ex LY-AAR	Lsd to RSO
RA-42354	Yakovlev Yak-42D	4520424711397	ex LY-AAU	Lsd to RSO
RA-42415	Yakovlev Yak-42D	4520422219089	ex CCCP-42415	Lsd to RSO
RA-42417	Yakovlev Yak-42D	4520423219110	ex CCCP-42417	Lsd to RSO
RA-42433	Yakovlev Yak-42D	4520421301017	ex CCCP-42433	Lsd to RSO
RA-42440	Yakovlev Yak-42D	45222042..1018		
RA-42443	Yakovlev Yak-42	4520424116664	ex	
RA-42444	Yakovlev Yak-42	4520424116677	ex YL-LBY	
RA-42445	Yakovlev Yak-42	4520424116669	ex YL-LBZ	
RA-46640	Antonov An-24RV	37308908	ex CCCP-46640	
RA-47264	Antonov An-24RV	27307806	ex CCCP-47264	
RA-65024	Tupolev Tu-134A	48420	ex CCCP-65024	Lsd fr CBK
RA-65137	Tupolev Tu-134A-3	60890	ex CCCP-65137	Lsd fr KTA
RA-65830	Tupolev Tu-134A-3	12093	ex CCCP-65830	
RA-65930	Tupolev Tu-134A-3	66500	ex CCCP-65930	
RA-85358	Tupolev Tu-154B-2	79A-358	ex CCCP-85358	

Merged with Tulpar in early November 2003

KATEKAVIA
Katekavia (KTK)

RA-46493	Antonov An-24RV	27308206	ex CCCP-46493
RA-46693	Antonov An-24RV	47309904	ex CCCP-46693
RA-47351	Antonov An-24RV	67310510	ex YL-LCI
RA-47358	Antonov An-24RV	67310607	ex CCCP-47358
RA-48102	Antonov An-24RT	1911804	

KAZAN 2nd AVIATION ENTERPRISE To be renamed Tulpar after merger of Karat and original Tulpar in early November 2003

KHAKASIA AIRLINES ceased operations

KHANTYAVIA

RA-87484	Yakovlev Yak-40	9441238	ex CCCP-87484	Lsd fr VGV
RA-87524	Yakovlev Yak-40	9520641	ex CCCP-87524	
RA-88234	Yakovlev Yak-40	9640351	ex CCCP-88234	

KIROV AVIA ENTERPRISE
Vyatka-Avia (KTA)   Kirov (KVX)

RA-46382	Antonov An-24B	07306105	ex CCCP-46382	
RA-46660	Antonov An-24RV	47309307	ex CCCP-46660	
RA-47154	Antonov An-24B	89901606	ex CCCP-47154	
RA-47295	Antonov An-24RV	07306608	ex CCCP-47295	no titles
RA-26086	Antonov An-26	27312302		
RA-26101	Antonov An-26	17311908	ex CCCP-26101	Op for UN as UN960
RA-26123	Antonov An-26B	12402	ex CCCP-26123	
RA-26134	Antonov An-26B	27312805	ex CCCP-26134	
RA-26664	Antonov An-26	97307905		Op for UN as UN962
RA-26677	Antonov An-26B	97308603	ex CCCP-26677	Op for UN
RA-65060	Tupolev Tu-134A	49872	ex CCCP-65060	
RA-65137	Tupolev Tu-134A-3	60890	ex CCCP-65137	Lsd to AKT

KMPO
Kazan (KZN)

RA-26212	Antonov An-26B	14401	ex CCCP-26212
RA-48110	Yakovlev Yak-40	9230623	ex 48110
RA-69309	Antonov An-32	1605	ex CCCP-69309
Division of Kazan Motors Production Association			

KMV MINERALNYE VODY AIRLINES / KAVMINVODY AVIA
Air Minvody (KV/MVD)   Mineralnye Vody (MRV)

RA-65074	Tupolev Tu-134A-3	49987	ex CCCP-65074
RA-65126	Tupolev Tu-134A-3	60588	ex CCCP-65126?
RA-65139	Tupolev Tu-134A	60915	ex CCCP-65139
RA-65844	Tupolev Tu-134A	18125	ex CCCP-65844
RA-65887	Tupolev Tu-134A	36170	ex CCCP-65887
RA-85226	Tupolev Tu-154B-1	77A-226	ex CCCP-85226
RA-85303	Tupolev Tu-154B-2	78A-303	ex CCCP-85303
RA-85307	Tupolev Tu-154B-2	78A-307	ex CCCP-85307
RA-85330	Tupolev Tu-154B-2	79A-330	ex CCCP-85330
RA-85332	Tupolev Tu-154B-2	79A-332	ex ER-85332
RA-85340	Tupolev Tu-154B-2	79A-340	ex CCCP-85340
RA-85371	Tupolev Tu-154B-2	79A-371	ex CCCP-85371
RA-85373	Tupolev Tu-154B-2	79A-373	ex CCCP-85373
RA-85382	Tupolev Tu-154B-2	79A-382	ex CCCP-85382
RA-85393	Tupolev Tu-154B-2	80A-393	ex CCCP-85393
RA-85457	Tupolev Tu-154B-2	80A-457	ex CCCP-85457
RA-85494	Tupolev Tu-154B-2	81A-494	ex CCCP-85494
RA-85715	Tupolev Tu-154M	91A-891	ex EP-MAX
RA-85722	Tupolev Tu-154M	92A-904	ex EP-MAU
RA-85746	Tupolev Tu-154M	92A-929	ex EP-MAV
RA-64016	Tupolev Tu-204-100	1450742364016	
RA-64022	Tupolev Tu-204-100	1450743164022	

KNAAPO / KOMSOMOLSK NA AMUR AIR ENTERPRISE
Knaapo (KNM)   Komsomolsk na Amure (KXK)

RA-11125	Antonov An-12BP	3341006	ex CCCP-11125	
RA-11230	Antonov An-12BP	5342708	ex LZ-BFA	
RA-11789	Antonov An-12BP	6343905	ex LZ-BFB	
RA-26185	Antonov An-26	8303	ex CCCP-26185	
RA-48101	Antonov An-32	2106	ex CCCP-48101	
RA-48978	Antonov An-12	9346410	ex CCCP-48978	
RA-48979	Antonov An-32	1409	ex CCCP-48979	
RA-65564	Tupolev Tu-134A-3	63165	ex CCCP-65564	
RA-76409	Ilyushin Il-76TD	1023410355	ex CCCP-76409	Lsd to AYZ
RA-76425	Ilyushin Il-76TD	1003405167	ex CCCP-76425	Lsd to AYZ
RA-93927	Tupolev Tu-134A-3	2351508	ex YU-AJD	

KOLAVIA / KOGALYMAVIA
Kogalym (7K/KGL)   Kogalym (KGP)

RA-65045	Tupolev Tu-134A	49500	ex CCCP-65045	VIP
RA-65080	Tupolev Tu-134A-3	60065	ex CCCP-65080	Lsd fr ASZ
RA-65611	Tupolev Tu-134A	3351903	ex CCCP-65611	Lsd fr KMV
RA-65618	Tupolev Tu-134A-3	12095	ex CCCP-65618	

RA-65861	Tupolev Tu-134A-3	1351407	ex EW-65861	VIP
RA-65942	Tupolev Tu-134A-3	17103	ex EW-65942	
RA-65943	Tupolev Tu-134A-3	63580	ex EW-65943	
RA-65944	Tupolev Tu-134A-3	12096	ex EW-65944	
RA-85427	Tupolev Tu-154B-2	80A-427	ex CCCP-85427	
RA-85630	Tupolev Tu-154M	87A-759	ex CCCP-85630	
RA-85761	Tupolev Tu-154M	93A-944		
RA-85784	Tupolev Tu-154M	93A-968		
RA-85786	Tupolev Tu-154M	93A-970		
RA-85787	Tupolev Tu-154M	93A-971		

KOMIINTERAVIA

Kominter (8J/KMV) (IATA 184) Syktyvkar (SCW)

RA-46468	Antonov An-24RV	27307906	ex CCCP-46468		Lsd to SYL
RA-46494	Antonov An-24RV	27308207	ex CCCP-46494		Lsd to SYL
RA-46603	Antonov An-24RV	37308510	ex CCCP-46603		
RA-46692	Antonov An-24RV	47309903	ex CCCP-46692		
RA-47820	Antonov An-24RV	17307201	ex CCCP-47820		Lsd to SYL
RA-65606	Tupolev Tu-134A	46300	ex CCCP-65606		
RA-65607	Tupolev Tu-134A	48560	ex CCCP-65607		
RA-65611	Tupolev Tu-134A	3351903	ex CCCP-65611		Lsd to KGL
RA-65612	Tupolev Tu-134A	3352102	ex D-AOBC		Lsd to AFL
RA-65614	Tupolev Tu-134A	4352207	ex CCCP-65614		Lsd to TMN
RA-65616	Tupolev Tu-134A-3	4352206	ex CCCP-65616	all-white	Lsd to TMN
RA-65620	Tupolev Tu-134A	35180	ex CCCP-65620		
RA-65621	Tupolev Tu-134A-3	48320	ex CCCP-65621		Lsd to TMN
RA-65716	Tupolev Tu-134B-3	63595	ex CCCP-65716		
RA-65755	Tupolev Tu-134A-3	62165	ex CCCP-65755		Lsd to TMN
RA-65777	Tupolev Tu-134A-3	62552	ex CCCP-65777		Lsd to TMN
RA-65780	Tupolev Tu-134A-3	62622	ex CCCP-65780		
RA-65793	Tupolev Tu-134A-3	63128	ex CCCP-65793	no titles	Lsd to TMN
RA-65901	Tupolev Tu-134A-3	63731	ex CCCP-65901		
RA-65902	Tupolev Tu-134A-3	63742	ex CCCP-65902		Lsd to TMN
RA-65977	Tupolev Tu-134A-3	63245	ex CCCP-65977		
RA-87439	Yakovlev Yak-40	9431535	ex CCCP-87439		
RA-88216	Yakovlev Yak-40	9630250	ex CCCP-88216		

KORYAKAVIA

Tilichiki

Previously listed as Koryak Air Enterprise

RA-74039	Antonov An-74	36547097931
RA-74050	Antonov An-74	36547181011

KOSMOS AVIAKOMPANIA

Kosmos (KSM) Moscow-Vnukovo (VKO)

RA-11025	Antonov An-12B	6344103	ex CCCP-11025	
RA-12957	Antonov An-12B	8345508	ex CCCP-12957	no titles
RA-65719	Tupolev Tu-134A	63637	ex CCCP-65719	VIP
RA-65726	Tupolev Tu-134A	63720	ex CCCP-65726	VIP
RA-65956	Tupolev Tu-134A	2351709	ex CCCP-65956	

KOSTROMA AIR ENTERPRISE

Kostroma (KMW)

RA-67143	LET L-410UVP	800409	ex CCCP-67143
RA-67338	LET L-410UVP	820838	ex CCCP-67338
RA-67401	LET L-410UVP	831029	ex CCCP-67401
RA-67402	LET L-410UVP	831030	ex CCCP-67402
RA-67443	LET L-410UVP	841208	ex SP-FTP
RA-67501	LET L-410UVP	851405	ex CCCP-67501

KOTLASAVIA

RA-88308	Yakovlev Yak-40	9230224	ex CCCP-88308

Current status is uncertain

KRAS AIR / KRASNOYARSK AIRLINES

Krasnoyarsky Air (7B/KJC)   *Krasnoyarsk-Yemilianovo (KJA)*

RA-76459	Ilyushin Il-76T	0013430890	ex CCCP-76459	
RA-76463	Ilyushin Il-76T	0013432960	ex 76463	
RA-76464	Ilyushin Il-76TD	0023437090	ex CCCP-76464	
RA-76465	Ilyushin Il-76TD	0023438101	ex CCCP-76465	
RA-76509	Ilyushin Il-76T	083413415	ex CCCP-76509	
RA-76515	Ilyushin Il-76T	093417526	ex CCCP-76515	
RA-76517	Ilyushin Il-76T	093418560	ex CCCP-76517	
RA-76524	Ilyushin Il-76T	0003425746	ex CCCP-76524	Op for UN - WFP
RA-76792	Ilyushin Il-76TD	0093497942	ex CCCP-76792	
RA-86121	Ilyushin Il-86	51483209089	ex CCCP-86121	
RA-86122	Ilyushin Il-86	51483210090	ex CCCP-86122	
RA-86137	Ilyushin Il-86	51483210095		
RA-86143	Ilyushin Il-86	51483210099	ex B-2018	
RA-86145	Ilyushin Il-86	51483211101		
RA-86926	Ilyushin Il-86	51463210100	ex B-2019	
RA-85201	Tupolev Tu-154B-1	77A-201	ex CCCP-85201	
RA-85417	Tupolev Tu-154B-2	80A-417	ex CCCP-85417	
RA-85418	Tupolev Tu-154B-2	80A-418	ex CCCP-85418	
RA-85489	Tupolev Tu-154B-2	81A-489	ex CCCP-85489	
RA-85505	Tupolev Tu-154B-2	81A-505	ex CCCP-85505	
RA-85529	Tupolev Tu-154B-2	82A-529	ex CCCP-85529	
RA-85672	Tupolev Tu-154M	90A-830	ex CCCP-85672	
RA-85678	Tupolev Tu-154M	90A-841	ex EP-MBC	no titles
RA-85679	Tupolev Tu-154M	90A-842	ex EP-LAT	
RA-85682	Tupolev Tu-154M	90A-849	ex CCCP-85682	
RA-85683	Tupolev Tu-154M	90A-850	ex EP-LAQ	
RA-85694	Tupolev Tu-154M	91A-867	ex EP-MAY	
RA-85704	Tupolev Tu-154M	91A-879	ex EP-LAV	stored
RA-85708	Tupolev Tu-154M	91A-883	ex EP-ITJ	
RA-85759	Tupolev Tu-154M	92A-941		Op for Severnikel Co
RA-64014	Tupolev Tu-204-100			Lsd fr Ilyushin Finance
RA-64015	Tupolev Tu-204-100			Lsd fr Ilyushin Finance
RA-64018	Tupolev Tu-204-110	1450743164018		Vassily Surshkov
RA-64019	Tupolev Tu-204-110	1450743164019		Ivan Jarygin
RA-64020	Tupolev Tu-204-100	1450743164024		Alexandr Lebed
RA-65560	Tupolev Tu-134A	3351806	ex CCCP-65560	Lsd fr Ulan-Ude Aviation Plant
RA-65605	Tupolev Tu-134A	09070	ex EW-65605	
RA-65960	Tupolev Tu-134A	3351806	ex CCCP-65960	Lsd fr Novossibisrky-NII
RA-86453	Ilyushin Il-62M	1622323	ex CCCP-86453	
RA-86709	Ilyushin Il-62	62204	ex CCCP-86709	
RA-87916	Yakovlev Yak-40K	9730655	ex CCCP-87916	Lsd to SIB
N769BC	Boeing 767-216ER	144/23624	ex 5R-MFE	Lsd fr Boeing Capital
	Boeing 767-200		ex	on order	Lsd fr Boeing Capital
	Tupolev Tu-334-100			on order	
	Tupolev Tu-334-100			on order	
	Yakovlev Yak-42D			on order	Lsd fr Aviatrading
	Yakovlev Yak-42D			on order	Lsd fr Aviatrading

KRYLO AIR

Krylo (K9/KRI)   *Moscow-Domodedovo (DME)*

RA-76710	Ilyushin Il-76TD	0063473182	ex CCCP-76710	Lsd fr TXC
RA-78828	ilyushin Il-76TD	1003401004	ex EW-78828	Lsd fr TXC

KUBAN AIRLINES / AVIATSIONYYEE LINII KUBANI

Air Kuban (GW/KIL)   *Krasnodar (KRR)*

RA-42331	Yakovlev Yak-42	4520424505128	ex CCCP-42331	
RA-42336	Yakovlev Yak-42	4250422606220	ex CCCP-42336	
RA-42350	Yakovlev Yak-42	4520424711372	ex CCCP-42350	
RA-42363	Yakovlev Yak-42D	4520424811438	ex CCCP-42363	
RA-42367	Yakovlev Yak-42D	4520421914133	ex CCCP-42367	
RA-42375	Yakovlev Yak-42D	4520424914410	ex CCCP-42375	
RA-42386	Yakovlev Yak-42D	4520424016310	ex CCCP-42386	
RA-42421	Yakovlev Yak-42D	4520422303017		
RA-42526	Yakovlev Yak-42	11040803	ex CCCP-42526	
RA-42538	Yakovlev Yak-42	11130404	ex CCCP-42538	
RA-42541	Yakovlev Yak-42	11140704	ex CCCP-42541	
RA-47817	Antonov An-24RV	17307103	ex LZ-VPB	
RA-85318	Tupolev Tu-154B-2	78A-318	ex CCCP-85318	
RA-85409	Tupolev Tu-154B-2	80A-409	ex CCCP-85409	Lsd fr DNV

KVZ – KAZANSKY VERTOLETNY ZAVOD
KAMA (KPH)   *Kazan-Int'l (KZN)*

RA-47715	Antonov An-24B	69900505	ex CCCP-47715

KVZ is a trading name of Kazan Plant of Helicopters

LESAVIA
Seimchany

RA-26002	Antonov An-26	073009706	ex CCCP-26002
RA-26011	Antonov An-26	9808	ex CCCP-26011

LIPETSK AIR ENTERPRISE ceased operations

LUKIAVIATRANS
Velkie Luki/Pskov

RA-30053	Antonov An-30D	1008	ex CCCP-30053
RA-30067	Antonov An-30	1208	ex CCCP-30067
RA-46632	Antonov An-30	0201	ex CCCP-46632

LUKOIL
Lukoil (LUK)   *Moscow-Sheremetyevo (SVO)*

RA-42424	Yakovlev 142	4520421302016	ex UN-42424
Ra-87221	Yakovlev Yak-40	9831958	ex CCCP-87221
RA-87353	Yakovlev Yak-40	9330231	ex CCCP-87353
RA-88297	Yakovlev Yak-40	9530142	ex 01 Red

MAGMA
Moscow-Sheremetyevo (SVO)

RA-46470	Antonov An-24RV	27307908	ex CCCP-46470

MAVIAL / MAGADAN AIRLINES
Mavial (H5/MVL) (IATA 428)   *Magadan-Sokol (GDX)*

RA-85540	Tupolev Tu-154B-2	82A-540	ex CCCP-85540	
RA-85567	Tupolev Tu-154B-2	82A-567	ex CCCP-85567	
RA-85584	Tupolev Tu-154B-2	83A-584	ex CCCP-85584	
RA-85667	Tupolev Tu-154M	89A-825	ex CCCP-85667	Lsd fr VARZ 400; sublsd to IRK
RA-85671	Tupolev Tu-154M	90A-829	ex CCCP-85671	Lsd fr VARZ 400
RA-85677	Tupolev Tu-154M	90A-839	ex CCCP-85677	
RA-85680	Tupolev Tu-154M	90A-843	ex LZ-LCE	Lsd fr VARZ 400; sublsd to VAZ
RA-85696	Tupolev Tu-154M	91A-869		Lsd to PVV
RA-86590	Ilyushin Il-62M	2647737	ex OK-BYZ	

MCHS ROSSII
Sumes (SUM)   *Moscow-Zhukovsky*

RA-76362	Ilyushin Il-76TD	1033416533		
RA-76363	Ilyushin Il-76TD	1033417540		
RA-76429	Ilyushin Il-76TD	1043419639		
RA-76840	Ilyushin Il-76TD	1033417553		
RA-76841	Ilyushin Il-76TD	1033418601		
RA-76845	Ilyushin Il-76TD	1043420696		
RA-42441	Yakovlev Yak-42D	4520421402018	ex EP-LAN	Velery Chkalov
RA-42446	Yakovlev Yak-42D	4520423308017	ex	
RA-74029	Antonov An-74P	36547097940		Alexander Belyakov
RA-74034	Antonov An-74P	36547136012		Georgy Baidukov
RA-86570	Ilyushin Il-62M	1356344		VIP
RA-87482	Yakovlev Yak-40	9441028	ex CCCP-87482	

Operates for Russian Ministry of Civil Aid and Protection; the State Unitary Air Enterprise

MERIDIAN AIR
Moscow-Vnukovo (VKO)

RA-65725	Tupolev Tu-134A-3M	66472	ex CCCP-65725
RA-65917	Tupolev Tu-134A-3M	63991	ex CCCP-65917

MYACHKOVO AIR SERVICES – MAUS

Luber (MKV)
Moscow Myachkovo

RA-30001	Antonov An-30	1402	ex CCCP-30001	
RA-30035	Antonov An-30	0702	ex CCCP-30035	
RA-30039	Antonov An-30	0710	ex CCCP-30039	
RA-30042	Antonov An-30	0901	ex CCCP-30042	
RA-30043	Antonov An-30	0905	ex CCCP-30043	
RA-30047	Antonov An-30	0909	ex CCCP-30047	
RA-30064	Antonov An-30	1203	ex CCCP-30064	
RA-30070	Antonov An-30	1301	ex CCCP-30070	
RA-30073	Antonov An-30	1304	ex CCCP-30073	no titles
RA-30075	Antonov An-30	1306	ex CCCP-30075	

Most aircraft are believed stored

NAPO AVIATRANS

Novsib (NPO)
Novosibirsk-Yeltsovka

RA-12193	Antonov An-12BK	9346805	ex CCCP-12193	
RA-12194	Antonov An-12BK	00347203	ex CCCP-12194	
RA-12195	Antonov An-12BP	00347410	ex CCCP-12195	
RA-65563	Tupolev Tu-134A-3	60035	ex CCCP-65563	Lsd to FLV

NAPO Aviatrans is a division of Novosibirsk Aircraft Production Association

NIKOLAEVSK-NA-AMURE AIR ENTERPRISE

Nikolaevsk-na-Amure

RA-87303	Yakovlev Yak-40	9321928	ex CCCP-87303
RA-87376	Yakovlev Yak-40	9411032	ex CCCP-87376
RA-87647	Yakovlev Yak-40	9140820	ex CCCP-87647
RA-87651	Yakovlev Yak-40	9141220	ex CCCP-87651
RA-88251	Yakovlev Yak-40K	9710552	ex CCCP-88251

NIZHEGORODSKIE AVIALINII / NIZHNY NOVGOROD AIRLINES declared bankrupt and ceased operations

NORILSK AIR ENTERPRISE ceased operations

NOVGOROD AVIA ENTERPRISE

Sadko Avia (NVG)
Novgorod (NVR)

RA-87575	Yakovlev Yak-40	9220722	ex CCCP-87575	Lsd fr KDO Aero

NOVOSIBIRSK AIR ENTERPRISE

Novosibirsk-Severnij

RA-46252	Antonov An-24B	77303304	ex CCCP-46252	
RA-46321	Antonov An-24B	97305407	ex CCCP-46321	
RA-46354	Antonov An-24B	07305804	ex CCCP-46354	
RA-46384	Antonov An-24B	07306107	ex CCCP-46384	
RA-46646	Antonov An-24RV	37309105	ex CCCP-46646	
RA-47185	Antonov An-24B	99901910	ex CCCP-47185	no titles
RA-47275	Antonov An-24B	07306405	ex CCCP-47275	no titles
RA-47306	Antonov An-24RV	57310306	ex CCCP-47306	
RA-47821	Antonov An-24RV	17307202?	ex CCCP-47821	
RA-47839	Antonov An-24B	17307401?	ex CCCP-47839	
RA-30004	Antonov An-30D	1405	ex CCCP-30004	
RA-30007	Antonov An-30D	1408	ex CCCP-30007	
RA-30034	Antonov An-30	0701	ex CCCP-30034	
RA-30037	Antonov An-30	0704	ex CCCP-30037	
RA-30041	Antonov An-30	0805	ex CCCP-30041	
RA-30049	Antonov An-30	1004	ex CCCP-30049	
RA-30051	Antonov An-30	1006	ex CCCP-30051	
RA-30056	Antonov An-30	1102	ex CCCP-30056	
RA-30059	Antonov An-30	1108	ex CCCP-30059	
RA-30063	Antonov An-30D	1202	ex CCCP-30063	
RA-30068	Antonov An-30D	1209?	ex CCCP-30068	
RA-88179	Yakovlev Yak-40	9621947	ex CCCP-88179	

Several aircraft are withdrawn from service

NPP MIR AVIAKOMPANIA

Mir Scientific (NPP)
St Petersburg-Pushkin

RA-65098	Tupolev Tu-134A-3	49860	ex CCCP-65098

```
RA-75411    Ilyushin Il-18V           186009205   ex CCCP-75411
RA-75713    Ilyushin Il-18D           186009403   ex CCCP-75713
RA-75804    Ilyushin Il-18V           182004305   ex CCCP-75804
```
NPP MIR Aviakompania is a division of MIR Scientific Industrial Enterprise

OIL TRANS AIR

Krapivnya

```
RA-28928    WSK-PZL/Antonov An-28     1AJ008-15
```

OMSKAVIA AIRLINE

Omsk (N3/OMS)   *Omsk (OMS)*

RA-85714	Tupolev Tu-154M	91A-890	ex 4L-AAF	Lsd to IRM as EP-MHZ
RA-85730	Tupolev Tu-154M	92A-912	ex CCCP-85730	
RA-85745	Tupolev Tu-154M	92A-928	ex EP-MAT	Lsd to IRB as EP-MAT
RA-85750	Tupolev Tu-154M	92A-932	ex EP-MHV	
RA-85752	Tupolev Tu-154M	92A-934	ex EP-MBF	
RA-85763	Tupolev Tu-154M	92A-946		
RA-85801	Tupolev Tu-154M	93A-960	ex EP-MHT	
RA-85818	Tupolev Tu-154M	85A-719	ex EP-MAJ	
RA-85830	Tupolev Tu-154M	89A-821	ex EP-MBB	Lsd to IRM as EP-MHS
RA-85841	Tupolev Tu-154M	90A-858	ex EP-MBG	
RA-46674	Antonov An-24RV	47309606	ex CCCP-46674	

Four Tupolev Tu-214s are on order for delivery in 2005/6

OREL AIR ENTERPRISE

Orprise (ORM)   *Orel (OEL)*

```
RA-87568    Yakovlev Yak-40           9222021     ex CCCP-87568
RA-87829    Yakovlev Yak-40           9240125     ex CCCP-87829
RA-87838    Yakovlev Yak-40           9240426     ex CCCP-87838
```

ORENBURG AVIA

Orenburg (R2/ORB)   *Orenburg (REN)*

RA-46315	Antonov An-24B	97305401?	ex CCCP-46315	
RA-46339	Antonov An-24B	97305607	ex CCCP-46339	
RA-46388	Antonov An-24B	07306201?	ex CCCP-46388	
RA-46597	Antonov An-24B	97305107	ex CCCP-46597	
RA-47847	Antonov An-24B	17307409	ex CCCP-47847	
RA-65049	Tupolev Tu-134A	49755	ex EW-65049	Lsd to TMN
RA-65101	Tupolev Tu-134A-3	60260	ex CCCP-65101	
RA-65110	Tupolev Tu-134A-3	60343	ex (HA-LBT)	
RA-65117	Tupolev Tu-134A-3	60450	ex (HA-LBU)	
RA-65136	Tupolev Tu-134A-3	60885	ex CCCP-65136	
RA-85595	Tupolev Tu-154B-2	84A-595	ex CCCP-85595	Lsd to TMN
RA-85603	Tupolev Tu-154B-2	84A-603	ex CCCP-85603 no titles	
RA-85604	Tupolev Tu-154B-2	85A-604	ex CCCP-85604	
RA-85768	Tupolev Tu-154M	94A-949		
RA-87272	Yakovlev Yak-40	9330827	ex UN-87272	
RA-87352	Yakovlev Yak-40	9330131	ex UN-87352	
RA-87471	Yakovlev Yak-40	9441637	ex UN-87471	

PERM AIRLINES / PERMSKIE AVIALINII

Perm Air (9D/PGP)   *Perm-Bolshoe Savina (PEE)*

```
RA-65046    Tupolev Tu-134A-3         49550       ex CCCP-65046
RA-65059    Tupolev Tu-134A           49870       ex CCCP-65059
RA-65064    Tupolev Tu-134A-3         49886       ex CCCP-65064
RA-65751    Tupolev Tu-134A-3         61066       ex CCCP-65751

RA-26520    Antonov An-26             87307101    ex CCCP-26520
RA-26636    Antonov An-26             87306306    ex EP-TQB
RA-47152    Antonov An-24B            89901604    ex CCCP-47152
RA-47756    Antonov An-24B            79901209    ex CCCP-47756
RA-85284    Tupolev Tu-154B-1         78A-284     ex CCCP-85284
RA-85287    Tupolev Tu-154B-1         78A-287     ex CCCP-85287
RA-85450    Tupolev Tu-154B-2         80A-450     ex CCCP-85450
RA-87418    Yakovlev Yak-40           9421034     ex CCCP-87418
```

PERMSKIE MOTORY AVIAKOMPANIA ceased own operations

PETROPAVLOVSK-KAMCHATSKY AIR ENTERPRISE

Petrokam (PTK)   *Petropavlovsk-Kamchatsky (PKC)*

RA-87385	Yakovlev Yak-40K	9411632	ex CCCP-87385
RA-87947	Yakovlev Yak-40K	9621145	ex CCCP-87947
RA-87949	Yakovlev Yak-40K	9621345	ex CCCP-87949
RA-87988	Yakovlev Yak-40	9541244	ex CCCP-87988
RA-88241	Yakovlev Yak-40K	9641351	ex CCCP-88241
RA-26122	Antonov An-26B	27312401	ex CCCP-26122
RA-67098	LET L-410UVP	841322	ex CCCP-67098
RA-67482	LET L-410UVP	841307	ex CCCP-67482
RA-67645	LET L-410UVP-E	902438	ex CCCP-67645
RA-67662	LET L-410UVP-E	902520	ex CCCP-67662

POLAR AIRLINES

Batagai

RA-26008	Antonov An-26	9902	ex CCCP-26008
RA-26030	Antonov An-26B	10501	ex CCCP-26030
RA-26061	Antonov An-26B	11108	ex CCCP-26061
RA-26105	Antonov An-26	27312003	ex CCCP-26105
RA-26509	Antonov An-26	6705	ex CCCP-26509
RA-26538	Antonov An-26	2102	ex CCCP-26538
RA-26635	Antonov An-26	6305	ex CCCP-26635
RA-26674	Antonov An-26	8506	ex CCCP-26674
RA-26685	Antonov An-26	1307	ex CCCP-26685
RA-26686	Antonov An-26	87306302	ex CCCP-26686
RA-46333	Antonov An-24B	97305510	ex CCCP-46333
RA-46374	Antonov An-24B	07306005	ex CCCP-46374
RA-47158	Antonov An-24B	89901610	ex CCCP-47158
RA-47161	Antonov An-24B	89901703	ex CCCP-47161
RA-47786	Antonov An-24B	89901601	ex CCCP-47786
RA-74000	Antonov An-74	36547070649	
RA-74003	Antonov An-74	36547070960	
RA-74006	Antonov An-74	36547095896	ex CCCP-74006

POLET AVIAKOMPANIA

Polet (POT)   *Voronezh (VOZ)*

RA-82010	Antonov An-124-100	9773053616017	ex CCCP-82010
RA-82013	Antonov An-124	977305.73203.	ex CCCP-82013
RA-82014	Antonov An-124	9773054732039	ex CCCP-82014
RA-82024	Antonov An-124	19530502033	ex CCCP-82024
RA-82026	Antonov An-124-100	19530502127	ex Soviet AF 10 black
RA-82075	Antonov An-124-100	9773053459147	
RA-82077	Antonov An-124-100	9773054459151	
RA-82080	Antonov An-124-100		on order
RA-87541	Yakovlev Yak-40	9530642	ex CCCP-87541

PRIMAIR

Primavia (PMM)   *Moscow-Domodedovo (DME)*

RA-65097	Tupolev Tu-134A	60540	ex CCCP-65097

PROGRESS AVIAKOMPANIA ceased operations

PSKOVAVIA

Pskovavia (PSW)   *Pskov (PKV)*

RA-26060	Antonov An-26B	11107	ex CCCP-26060	Lsd to LVR
RA-26107	Antonov An-26B	27312008	ex LY-LVR	Lsd to LVR
RA-26120	Antonov An-26B	27312304	ex CCCP-26120	aircharter.co.uk titles
RA-26142	Antonov An-26B	37312904	ex CCCP-26142	

PULKOVO AIRLINES / PULKOVO AVIA ENTERPRISE

Pulkovo (FV/PLK) (IATA 195)   *St Petersburg-Pulkovo (LED)*

RA-86050	Ilyushin Il-86	51483202017	ex CCCP-86050
RA-86061	Ilyushin Il-86	51483203028	ex CCCP-86061
RA-86063	Ilyushin Il-86	51483203030	ex CCCP-86063
RA-86070	Ilyushin Il-86	51483204037	ex CCCP-86070
RA-86073	Ilyushin Il-86	51483204040	ex CCCP-86073
RA-86092	Ilyushin Il-86	51483207063	ex CCCP-86092

RA-86094	Ilyushin Il-86	51483207065	ex CCCP-86094	
RA-86106	Ilyushin Il-86	51483208074	ex CCCP-86106	
RA-65004	Tupolev Tu-134A-3	44060	ex CCCP-65004	
RA-65042	Tupolev Tu-134A-3	49350	ex CCCP-65042	
RA-65068	Tupolev Tu-134A-3	49907	ex ES-AAG	
RA-65088	Tupolev Tu-134A	60172	ex LY-ABF	
RA-65093	Tupolev Tu-134A-3	60215	ex UR-65093	
RA-65109	Tupolev Tu-134A-3	60339	ex UR-65109	
RA-65112	Tupolev Tu-134A-3	60350	ex ES-AAI	
RA-65113	Tupolev Tu-134A	60380	ex ES-AAM	
RA-65128	Tupolev Tu-134A-3	60628	ex LY-ABI	
RA-65144	Tupolev Tu-134A-3	60977	ex ES-AAK	
RA-65759	Tupolev Tu-134A	62239	ex ES-AAO	
RA-85171	Tupolev Tu-154M	92A-893	ex B-2625	
RA-85185	Tupolev Tu-154M	91A-894	ex B-2626	
RA-85187	Tupolev Tu-154M	91A-919	ex B-2629	
RA-85204	Tupolev Tu-154M	91A-896	ex B-2624	
RA-85334	Tupolev Tu-154B-2	79A-334	ex CCCP-85334	
RA-85377	Tupolev Tu-154B-2	79A-377	ex CCCP-85377	
RA-85381	Tupolev Tu-154B-2	79A-381	ex CCCP-85381	
RA-85390	Tupolev Tu-154B-2	79A-390	ex CCCP-85390	
RA-85441	Tupolev Tu-154B-2	80A-441	ex CCCP-85441	
RA-85530	Tupolev Tu-154B-2	82A-530	ex CCCP-85530	
RA-85542	Tupolev Tu-154B-2	82A-542	ex CCCP-85542	
RA-85552	Tupolev Tu-154B-2	82A-552	ex CCCP-85552	
RA-85553	Tupolev Tu-154B-2	82A-553	ex CCCP-85553	
RA-85579	Tupolev Tu-154B-2	83A-579	ex CCCP-85579	
RA-85658	Tupolev Tu-154M	89A-808	ex CCCP-85658	
RA-85695	Tupolev Tu-154M	91A-868	ex CCCP-85695	
RA-85739	Tupolev Tu-154M	92A-922		
RA-85767	Tupolev Tu-154M	93A-948		
RA-85769	Tupolev Tu-154M	93A-951		
RA-85770	Tupolev Tu-154M	93A-952		
RA-85771	Tupolev Tu-154M	93A-953		
RA-85779	Tupolev Tu-154M	93A-963		
RA-85785	Tupolev Tu-154M	93A-969		
RA-85800	Tupolev Tu-154M	94A-984		
RA-85832	Tupolev Tu-154M	92A-908	ex LZ-MNA	
RA-	Tupolev Tu-154M	92A-925	ex B-2628	
RA-85834	Tupolev Tu-154M	98A-1014	ex OM-AAA	on order 1Q04
RA-85835	Tupolev Tu-154M	98A-1015	ex OM-AAB	on order 1Q04
RA-	Tupolev Tu-154M	98A-1018	ex OM-AAC	on order 1Q04

Operates some international services on behalf of Aeroflot Russian Airlines using SU/AFL flight numbers. Works closely with Rossia State Transport Co and may merge

---

ROSNEFT-BALTIKA

Rosbalt (RNB)   **St Petersburg-Pulkovo (LED)**

RA-21500	Yakovlev Yak-40K	9741356	ex CCCP-21500	Op for Baltic Finance Industrial Grp

---

ROSSIA STATE TRANSPORT CO

Rossia (R4/SDM) (IATA 948)   **Moscow-Vnukovo (VKO)**

RA-86466	Ilyushin Il-62M	2749316	ex CCCP-86466	
RA-86467	Ilyushin Il-62M	3749733	ex CCCP-86467	
RA-86468	Ilyushin Il-62M	4749857	ex CCCP-86468	VIP
RA-86536	Ilyushin Il-62M	4445948	ex CCCP-86536	
RA-86537	Ilyushin Il-62M	3546733	ex CCCP-86537	
RA-86540	Ilyushin Il-62M	3546548	ex CCCP-86540	VIP
RA-86559	Ilyushin Il-62M	2153258	ex CCCP-86559	VIP
RA-86561	Ilyushin Il-62M	4154841	ex CCCP-86561	VIP
RA-86710	Ilyushin Il-62M	2647646	ex CCCP-86710	
RA-86712	Ilyushin Il-62M	4648339	ex 86712	VIP
RA-65553	Tupolev Tu-134A-3	66300	ex CCCP-65553	
RA-65555	Tupolev Tu-134A-3	66350	ex CCCP-65555	
RA-65904	Tupolev Tu-134A-3	63953	ex CCCP-65904	
RA-65905	Tupolev Tu-134A-3	63965	ex 65905	
RA-65911	Tupolev Tu-134A-3	63972	ex 65911	
RA-65912	Tupolev Tu-134A-3	63985	ex CCCP-65912	
RA-65921	Tupolev Tu-134A-3	63997	ex CCCP-65921	
RA-65978	Tupolev Tu-134A-3	63357	ex CCCP-65978	
RA-65979	Tupolev Tu-134A-3	63158	ex CCCP-65979	
RA-65994	Tupolev Tu-134A	66207	ex CCCP-65994	
RA-65995	Tupolev Tu-134A-3	66400	ex CCCP-65995	
RA-85565	Tupolev Tu-154B-2	82A-565	ex CCCP-85565	

534

RA-85629	Tupolev Tu-154M	87A-758	ex CCCP-85629	
RA-85631	Tupolev Tu-154M	87A-760	ex CCCP-85631	
RA-85645	Tupolev Tu-154M	88A-782	ex CCCP-85645	
RA-85659	Tupolev Tu-154M	89A-809	ex CCCP-85659	VIP
RA-85666	Tupolev Tu-154M	89A-820	ex 85666	
RA-85686	Tupolev Tu-154M	90A-854	ex 85686	
RA-85843	Tupolev Tu-154M	95A-991		
RA-87203	Yakovlev Yak-40	9741456	ex CCCP-87203	
RA-87807	Yakovlev Yak-40	9231723	ex CCCP-87807	
RA-87968	Yakovlev Yak-40	9831258	ex CCCP-87968	
RA-87969	Yakovlev Yak-40	9831358	ex CCCP-87969	
RA-87970	Yakovlev Yak-40	9831458	ex CCCP-87970	
RA-87971	Yakovlev Yak-40	9831558	ex CCCP-87971	
RA-87972	Yakovlev Yak-40	9921658	ex CCCP-87972	
RA-88200	Yakovlev Yak-40	9630249	ex CCCP-88200	
RA-64504	Tupolev Tu-214	41203004		
RA-64505	Tupolev Tu-214			
RA-64506	Tupolev Tu-214			
RA-75453	Ilyushin Il-18D	187010103	ex CCCP-75453	
RA-75454	Ilyushin Il-18D	187010104	ex CCCP-75454	
RA-75464	Ilyushin Il-18D	187010401	ex CCCP-75464	
RA-96012	Ilyushin Il-96-300	74393201009		Presidential a/c
RA-96016	Ilyushin Il-96-300PU	74393202010	ex (RA-96013)	Presidential a/c

Operates VIP flights on behalf of Russian Government; commercial services taken over by Aeroflot Russian Airlines in October 2003. Works closely with Pulkovo Airlines and may merge

RUSAIR

CGI-Rusair (CGI)   *Moscow-Sheremetyevo (SVO)*

RA-65005	Tupolev Tu-134A-3	44065	ex CCCP-65005		
RA-65035	Tupolev Tu-134A-3	48590	ex CCCP-65035		
RA-65756	Tupolev Tu-134A-3	62179	ex CCCP-65756		
RA-65934	Tupolev Tu-134A-3	66143	ex CCCP-65934		
RA-87248	Yakovlev Yak-40K	9540144	ex CCCP-87248		Lsd fr Priroda
RA-87284	Yakovlev Yak-40	9311927	ex CCCP-87284	VIP	
RA-87311	Yakovlev Yak-40	9320629	ex CCCP-87311		
RA-87429	Yakovlev Yak-40	9420535	ex CCCP-87429		
RA-87533	Yakovlev Yak-40	9511741	ex CCCP-87533	no titles	
RA-87828	Yakovlev Yak-40	9242024	ex CCCP-87828		
RA-88293	Yakovlev Yak-40	9510138	ex CCCP-88293		

All VIP and operated in Aerotex colours
Also quoted as Rusline

RUSSIAN POST AIRLINES / POST ROSSII

            Moscow-Domodedovo (DME)

RA-11128	Antonov An-12BP	02348203	ex CCCP-11128	
RA-11339	Antonov An-12BP	6344310	ex CCCP-11339	Lsd fr NVI

Commenced mail flights on 16 September 2003

RYAZANAVIA TRANS

Ryazan Air (RYZ)   *Ryazan (RZN)*

RA-47359	Antonov An-24RV	67310608	ex UR-47359	
RA-47362	Antonov An-24RV	67310706	ex UR-47362	

SAKHAAVIA renamed Yakutia Airlines

SAKHA AVIATION SCHOOL CENTER ceased commercial operations

SAKHALIN AIRLINES

Air Sakhalan (SVT)   *Yuzhno-Sakhalinsk (UUS)*

RA-11116	Antonov An-12	01348006	ex CCCP-11116	Lsd fr TIS
RA-98117	Antonov An-12B	402301	ex CCCP-98117	Lsd fr VAS
RA-98118	Antonov An-12B	6344304	ex CCCP-98118	

SAMARA AIRLINES

Beryoza (E5/BRZ) (IATA 906)   *Samara (KUF)*

RA-65105	Tupolev Tu-134A-3	60308	ex LY-ABH
RA-65122	Tupolev Tu-134A-3	60518	ex CCCP-65122
RA-65753	Tupolev Tu-134A-3	61099	ex CCCP-65753

RA-65758	Tupolev Tu-134A-3	62230	ex CCCP-65758	
RA-65792	Tupolev Tu-134A-3	63121	ex CCCP-65792	
RA-65797	Tupolev Tu-134A-3	63173	ex CCCP-65797	
RA-65800	Tupolev Tu-134A	3352009	ex CCCP-65800	
RA-65970	Tupolev Tu-134A	3351910	ex CCCP-65970	
RA-85472	Tupolev Tu-154B-2	81A-472	ex CCCP-85472	
RA-85500	Tupolev Tu-154B-2	81A-500	ex CCCP-85500	
RA-85585	Tupolev Tu-154B-2	83A-585	ex CCCP-85585	
RA-85716	Tupolev Tu-154M	91A-892	ex CCCP-85716	
RA-85723	Tupolev Tu-154M	92A-905	ex HA-LGB	
RA-85731	Tupolev Tu-154M	92A-913	ex EP-LBH	
RA-85792	Tupolev Tu-154M	93A-976	ex EP-LAZ	
RA-85817	Tupolev Tu-154M	95A-1007	ex EP-LBM	
RA-85821	Tupolev Tu-154M	89A-805	ex SP-LCI	
RA-85822	Tupolev Tu-154M	89A-806	ex SP-LCK	
RA-85823	Tupolev Tu-154M	88A-775	ex HA-LGA	
RA-42356	Yakovlev Yak-42D	4520422811400	ex CCCP-42356	
RA-42414	Yakovlev Yak-42D	4520423219073	ex CCCP-42414	
RA-42418	Yakovlev Yak-42D	4520423219118	ex CCCP-42418	
RA-42524	Yakovlev Yak-42	11030603	ex CCCP-42524	
RA-76475	Ilyushin Il-76TD	0043451523	ex EP-TPV	stored KUF as EP-TPV
RA-76791	Ilyushin Il-76TD	0093497936	ex EP-TPU	stored KUF as EP-TPU
RA-76798	Ilyushin Il-76TD	1003403063	ex CCCP-76798	Lsd to AYZ
RA-87382	Yakovlev Yak-40	9411332	ex CCCP-87382	
RA-87444	Yakovlev Yak-40	9430136	ex CCCP-87444	
RA-	Antonov An-140			on order
RA-	Antonov An-140-100			on order

SAND INTERNATIONAL current status is uncertain

SARANSK AIR

Saransk (SKX)

RA-46255	Antonov An-24B	77303403	ex CCCP-46255
RA-46480	Antonov An-24RV	27308008?	ex CCCP-46480
RA-46845	Antonov An-24RV	27307503	ex CCCP-46845
RA-47834	Antonov An-24B	17307306?	ex CCCP-47834

SARATOV AVIATION

Sazavia (SVP)   Saratov (RTW)

RA-87317	Yakovlev Yak-40K	9331629	ex CCCP-87317
RA-87621	Yakovlev Yak-40K	9130219	ex CCCP-87621
RA-87849	Yakovlev Yak-40K	9331830	ex CCCP-87849
RA-87952	Yakovlev Yak-40K	9811057	ex CCCP-87952
RA-88301	Yakovlev Yak-40K	9641251	ex EY-1251

Saratov Aviation is the operating arm of Saratov Aviation Plant

---

SARAVIA / SARATOV AIR

Saratov Air (6W/SOV)   Saratov (RTW)

RA-42316	Yakovlev Yak-42	4520422202030	ex CCCP-42316	
RA-42326	Yakovlev Yak-42D	4520424402154	ex CCCP-42326	
RA-42328	Yakovlev Yak-42	4520421505058	ex CCCP-42328	
RA-42329	Yakovlev Yak-42D	4520422505093	ex CCCP-42329	
RA-42361	Yakovlev Yak-42D	4520423811427	ex CCCP-42361	
RA-42365	Yakovlev Yak-42D	4520424811447	ex CCCP-42365	
RA-42378	Yakovlev Yak-42D	4520421014494	ex TC-FAR	Lsd to CVC
RA-42389	Yakovlev Yak-42D	4520424016542	ex CCCP-42389	
RA-42432	Yakovlev Yak-42D	4520424410016	ex TC-ALY	
RA-42550	Yakovlev Yak-42D	1140205	ex CCCP-42550	
RA-42551	Yakovlev Yak-42	11140305	ex CCCP-42551	
RA-47304	Antonov An-24RV	57310304	ex CCCP-47304	

SAT AIRLINES – SAKHALINSKE AVIATRASSY

Satair (HZ/SHU)   Yuzhno-Sakhalinsk (UUS)
Previously listed as SAT-Sakhalin Airlines

RA-46530	Antonov An-24B	57310009	ex CCCP-46530
RA-46618	Antonov An-24RV	37308705	ex CCCP-46618
RA-47198	Antonov An-24RV	27307702	ex CCCP-47198
RA-47317	Antonov An-24RV	67310504	ex CCCP-47317
RA-47366	Antonov An-24RV	77310804	ex CCCP-47366

RA-26131	Antonov An-26B	12707	ex CCCP-26131	
RA-26132	Antonov An-26B	37312708	ex CCCP-26132	
RA-26138	Antonov An-26B	12810	ex CCCP-26138	
RA-67251*	de Havilland DHC-8-102	215	ex C-GZPV	Op for Exxon-Neftegas
RA-67253*	de Havilland DHC-8-102	105	ex C-GZTD	Op for Exxon Neftegas
RA-67255*	de Havilland DHC-8-102	345	ex C-GZKA	
RA-86566	Ilyushin Il-62M	4255152	ex CCCP-86566	

*Leased from Avmax Group

SATURN AVIAKOMPANIA

Rybmotors (RMO)   Rybinsk-Staroselye (RYB)

RA-87225	Yakovlev Yak-40K	9841359	ex CCCP-87225
RA-87936	Yakovlev Yak-40K	9740756	ex CCCP-87936
RA-88289	Antonov An-26B	11804	ex CCCP-88289

Saturn Aviakompania is a division of Rybinsk Aircraft Motors Factory

SEVERSTAL

(D2)   Cherepovets (CEE)

RA-87586	Yakovlev Yak-40	9221822	ex CCCP-87586	
RA-87954	Yakovlev Yak-40	9541844	ex CCCP-87954	
RA-88180	Yakovlev Yak-40	9622047	ex CCCP-88180	
RA-88296	Yakovlev Yak-40	9421634	ex VN-A445	Severstal Metal , VIP

Also leases other Yakovlev Yak-40s from Vologda Air Enterprise as required

SHANS AIR

Shans Air (SNF)   Moscow-Domodedovo (DME)

RA-65570	Tupolev Tu-134A-3	66550	ex RA-64451	Executive	
RA-65692	Tupolev Tu-134B-3	63215	ex YL-LBB	Executive	
RA-65940	Tupolev Tu-134A-3	3351906	ex LZ-TUM	VIP	Lsd fr AFL

SHAR INK

Sharink (UGP)   Moscow-Ostafyevo

ES-NOH	Antonov An-72	36572095909	ex EL-ALX	Lsd fr ENI
RA-42434*	Yakovlev Yak-42	4250424305017		
RA-74001	Antonov An-74TK-100	36547070655	ex CCCP-74001	
RA-74024*	Antonov An-74			
RA-74041	Antonov An-74-200	36547096924		Lsd fr SIB
RA-74060	Antonov An-74-200	36547098966		

Joint operatios for Khrunichev Space Center, has Proton titles

SIBAVIATRANS

Sibavia (5M/SIB)   Krasnoyarsk-Yemelyanovo (KJA)

RA-46520	Antonov An-24RV	37308506	ex CCCP-46520	
RA-46683	Antonov An-24RV	47309706	ex CCCP-46683	
RA-49278	Antonov An-24RV	47309808	ex YR-AMJ	
RA-49279	Antonov An-24RV	17306905	ex YR-AMB	
RA-49287	Antonov An-24RV	27307607	ex YR-AME	
RA-21503	Yakovlev Yak-40K	9832058	ex CCCP-21503	
RA-48113	Antonov An-32	1709	ex CCCP-48113	
RA-65033	Tupolev Tu-134A-3	48540	ex CCCP-65033	Lsd fr CBK
RA-65615	Tupolev Tu-134A-3	4352205		
RA-65571	Tupolev Tu-134A	63995	ex EW-63955	
RA-65845	Tupolev Tu-134A-3	23131	ex CCCP-65845	
RA-65881	Tupolev Tu-134A-3	35220	ex CCCP-65881	
RA-74041	Antonov An-74-200	36547096924		Lsd to UGP
RA-85395	Tupolev Tu-154B-2	80A-395	ex 4K-85395	
RA-87916	Yakovlev Yak-40K	9730655	ex CCCP-87916	Lsd fr KJC
RA-	Antonov An-140		on order	Lsd fr Ilyushin Finance
RA-	Antonov An-140		on order	Lsd fr Ilyushin Finance
RA-	Antonov An-140		on order	Lsd fr Ilyushin Finance

Ten Ilyushin Il-114-100s are on order for future delivery

SIBIR AIRLINES / SIBERIA AIRLINES

Siberia Airlines (S7/SBI) (IATA 421)   Novosibirsk-Tolmachevo (OVB)

RA-86006	Ilyushin Il-86	51483200004	ex CCCP-86006	
RA-86081	Ilyushin Il-86	51483206052	ex CCCP-86081	all white
RA-86084	Ilyushin Il-86	51483206055	ex CCCP-86084	
RA-86085	Ilyushin Il-86	51483208056	ex CCCP-86085	

RA-86089	Ilyushin Il-86	51483207060	ex CCCP-86089	
RA-86091	Ilyushin Il-86	51483207062	ex CCCP-86091	
RA-86102	Ilyushin Il-86	51483207070	ex CCCP-86102	
RA-86104	Ilyushin Il-86	51483208072	ex CCCP-86104	
RA-86105	Ilyushin Il-86	51483208073	ex CCCP-86105	
RA-86107	Ilyushin Il-86	51483208075	ex CCCP-86107	
RA-86108	Ilyushin Il-86	51483208076	ex CCCP-86108	
RA-86109	Ilyushin Il-86	51483208077	ex CCCP-86109	
RA-86112	Ilyushin Il-86	51483208080	ex CCCP-86112	wfs OVB
RA-86120	Ilyushin Il-86	51483209088	ex CCCP-86120	
RA-85237	Tupolev Tu-154B-1	77A-237	ex CCCP-85237	
RA-85402	Tupolev Tu-154B-2	80A-402	ex CCCP-85402	
RA-85437*	Tupolev Tu-154B-2	80A-437	ex CCCP-85437	
RA-85451*	Tupolev Tu-154B-2	80A-451	ex CCCP-85451	
RA-85453	Tupolev Tu-154B-2	80A-453	ex CCCP-85453	
RA-85461	Tupolev Tu-154B-2	80A-461	ex CCCP-85461	
RA-85471	Tupolev Tu-154B-2	81A-471	ex CCCP-85471	
RA-85485	Tupolev Tu-154B-2	81A-485	ex CCCP-85485	
RA-85495*	Tupolev Tu-154B-2	81A-495	ex CCCP-85495	
RA-85556	Tupolev Tu-154B-2	82A-556	ex YL-LAD	
RA-85583	Tupolev Tu-154B-2	83A-583	ex EW-85583	
RA-85610	Tupolev Tu-154M	84A-705	ex CCCP-85610	
RA-85612	Tupolev Tu-154M	86A-721	ex CCCP-85612	
RA-85613	Tupolev Tu-154M	86A-722	ex CCCP-85613	
RA-85615	Tupolev Tu-154M	86A-731	ex CCCP-85615	
RA-85618	Tupolev Tu-154M	86A-737	ex CCCP-85618	
RA-85619	Tupolev Tu-154M	86A-738	ex CCCP-85619	Yulia Fomina
RA-85620	Tupolev Tu-154M	86A-739	ex TC-ACT	
RA-85622	Tupolev Tu-154M	87A-746	ex CCCP-85622	
RA-85623	Tupolev Tu-154M	87A-749	ex CCCP-85623	
RA-85624	Tupolev Tu-154M	87A-750	ex CCCP-85624	
RA-85628	Tupolev Tu-154M	87A-757	ex CCCP-85628	
RA-85632	Tupolev Tu-154M	87A-761	ex CCCP-85632	
RA-85633	Tupolev Tu-154M	87A-762	ex CCCP-85633	
RA-85635	Tupolev Tu-154M	87A-764	ex CCCP-85635	
RA-85647	Tupolev Tu-154M	88A-785	ex CCCP-85647	
RA-85652	Tupolev Tu-154M	88A-794	ex LZ-LTF	
RA-85673	Tupolev Tu-154M	90A-833	ex TC-ACV	
RA-85674	Tupolev Tu-154M	90A-834	ex TC-ACI	
RA-85687	Tupolev Tu-154M	90A-857	ex EP-MAZ	
RA-85688	Tupolev Tu-154M	90A-859	ex OM-VEA	
RA-85690	Tupolev Tu-154M	90A-861	ex CCCP-85690	
RA-85697	Tupolev Tu-154M	91A-870	ex EP-MAQ	
RA-85699	Tupolev Tu-154M	91A-874	ex EP-ITC	
RA-85705	Tupolev Tu-154M	91A-880	ex EP-MBH	
RA-85709	Tupolev Tu-154M	91A-884	ex EP-MAK	
RA-85736	Tupolev Tu-154M	92A-918	ex CCCP-85736	
RA-85743	Tupolev Tu-154M	92A-926	ex CCCP-85743	

* Leased from Aircraft Repair Plant 411

P4-VNF	Airbus Industrie A320-211	0726	ex N726NS	Lsd fr ILFC; sublsd to RNV
RA-26563	Antonov An-26	3506	ex CCCP-26563?	
RA-64011	Tupolev Tu-204-100	1450741364011		
RA-64017	Tupolev Tu-204-100	1450742564017		Lsd fr Aviastar Avn

Part owns Armavia

SIR AERO

Sirair (SRN) *Yakutsk (YKS)*

RA-11130	Antonov An-12BP	02348205	ex CCCP-11130
RA-11892	Antonov An-12BP	402501	ex CCCP-11892
RA-26665	Antonov An-26	8108	ex CCCP-26665

SIRIUS AERO

Sirius Aero (CIG) *Moscow-Vnukovo (VKO)*

RA-65722	Tupolev Tu-134A-3M	66420	ex CCCP-65722	VIP	
RA-65723	Tupolev Tu-134A-3M	66440	ex CCCP-65723	VIP	
RA-65724	Tupolev Tu-134A-3M	66445	ex CCCP-65724	VIP	
RA-65794	Tupolev Tu-134A-3	63135	ex CCCP-65794	VIP	Lsd fr VRN
RA-65880	Tupolev Tu-134A-3	35200	ex CCCP-65880	VIP	Lsd fr VRN
RA-65928	Tupolev Tu-134A-3M	66491	ex CCCP-65928	VIP	

SOKOL now only operate helicopters

SPETSAVIA

Aviaspec (BHV)
Moscow-Bykovo/Khabarovsk

RA-26571	Antonov An-26	3909	ex CCCP-26571	Calibrator/Flying laboratroy
RA-26631	Antonov An-26	77305503	ex CCCP-26631	Calibrator/Flying laboratroy
RA-26673	Antonov An-26	8408	ex CCCP-26673	Calibrator/Flying laboratroy
RA-46395	Antonov An-24B	07306209	ex CCCP-46395	Calibrator/Flying laboratroy
UN 26507	Antonov An-26	87306703		

STAERO

Staero (STB)
Stavropol (STW)

RA-47252	Antonov An-24RV	27307704	ex CCCP-47252	Lsd to DAO as EX-47252

STELA ceased operations

SUKHOI AVIAKOMPANIA ceased own operations

SUKHOI DESIGN BUREAU AIR TRANSPORT COMPANY

Su-Craft (SDB)
Moscow-Zhukovsky

RA-65932	Tupolev Tu-134A-3	66405	ex 65932	Lsd to GAI
RA-87229	Yakovlev Yak-40K	9841759	ex CCCP-87229	
RA-98111	Yakovlev Yak-40	9741656	ex CCCP-98111	

SVB AOLAP AVIAKOMPANIA now listed as Lesavia

SVERDLOVSK 2ND AIR ENTERPRISE

Pyshma (UKU)
Ekaterinburg (SVX)

RA-74048	Antonov An-74	36547098943	
RA-87253	Yakovlev Yak-40	9321026	ex CCCP-87253
RA-87503	Yakovlev Yak-40AT	9520240	ex CCCP-87503
RA-87908	Yakovlev Yak-40	9721354	ex CCCP-87908
RA-88159	Yakovlev Yak-40	9621346	ex CCCP-88159

TAMBOV AVIA
Tambov

RA-	Antonov An-24
RA-	Antonov An-24

TAIMYR AVIA

RA-69355	Antonov An-32

TATARSTAN AIR

(U9/KAZ) (IATA 966)
Kazan (KZN)

RA-85412	Tupolev Tu-154B-2	80A-412	ex CCCP-85412		Lsd to AKT
RA-85488	Tupolev Tu-154B-2	81A-488	ex OK-LCP		
RA-85798	Tupolev Tu-154M	93A-982	ex EP-MBO		Lsd to ESL
RA-85799	Tupolev Tu-154M	93A-983			Lsd to ESL
RA-85804	Tupolev Tu-154B-2	81A-517	ex EP-TQB		
RA-42332	Yakovlev Yak-42	4520421605135	ex CCCP-42332		
RA-42335	Yakovlev Yak-42	4520422606204	ex CCCP-42335		Lsd to CUB
RA-42347	Yakovlev Yak-42	4520423711322	ex CCCP-42347		
RA-42357	Yakovlev Yak-42	4520422811408	ex CCCP-42357		Lsd to CUB
RA-42374	Yakovlev Yak-42D	4520423914340	ex CCCP-42374		
RA-42380	Yakovlev Yak-42D	4520422014549	ex CCCP-42380		
RA-26647	Antonov An-26	7409	ex CCCP-26647		
RA-46526	Antonov An-24RV	47310005	ex CCCP-46526		
RA-46625	Antonov An-24RV	37308804	ex CCCP-46625		
RA-47804	Antonov An-24RV	17306903	ex CCCP-47804		
RA-47818	Antonov An-24RV	17307107	ex CCCP-47818		
RA-65023	Tupolev Tu-134A-3	48415	ex CCCP-65023		
RA-65065	Tupolev Tu-134A-3	49890	ex XU-101		
RA-65691	Tupolev Tu-134A	63195			
RA-65973	Tupolev Tu-134A	3352003	ex LY-ABA		
RA-87209	Yakovlev Yak-40K	9810657	ex CCCP-87209	all-white	
RA-88287	Yakovlev Yak-40K	9940360	ex CCCP-88287	VIP; op for Tatarstan Govt	

TAVIA ceased operations

TESIS

Tesis (UZ/TIS)				*Moscow-Domodedovo (DME)*
RA-76373	Ilyushin Il-76TD	1033415507	ex CCCP-76373	Lsd fr DRU
RA-76380	Ilyushin Il-76TD	0043450493	ex UR-76584	
RA-76420	Ilyushin Il-76TD	1023413446	ex CCCP-76420	Lsd fr DRU
RA-76483	Ilyushin Il-76TD	0063468042	ex CCCP-76483	Lsd fr VAZ
RA-76484	Ilyushin Il-76TD	0063469081	ex CCCP-76484	
RA-76808	Ilyushin Il-76TD	1013405177	ex CCCP-76808	
RA-11116	Antonov An-12	01348006	ex CCCP-11116	Lsd to SVT
RA-85503	Tupolev Tu-154B-2	81A-503	ex CCCP-85503	
RA-85512	Tupolev Tu-154B-2	81A-512	ex CCCP-85512	

TITAN AERO

Rustitan (RTT)			*Moscow-Vnukovo (VKO)*
RA-75834	Ilyushin Il-18V	182005104	ex CCCP-75834
RA-76493	Ilyushin Il-76TD	0043456700	ex CCCP-76493
RA-76822	Ilyushin Il-76MD	0093499982	ex CCCP-76822

TOMSKAVIA

Tomsk Avia (TSK)				*Tomsk (TOF)*
RA-46627	Antonov An-24RV	37308806	ex CCCP-46627	not confirmed
RA-46679	Antonov An-24RV	47309701?	ex CCCP-46679	
RA-47254	Antonov An-24RV	27307706?	ex CCCP-47254	
RA-47255	Antonov An-24RV	27307707?	ex CCCP-47255	
RA-47355	Antonov An-24RV	673106004?	ex CCCP-47355	
RA-47826	Antonov An-24B	173072077?	ex CCCP-47826	
RA-87232	Yakovlev Yak-40	9531742	ex CCCP-87232	
RA-87493	Yakovlev Yak-40	9541645	ex CCCP-87493	
RA-87494	Yakovlev Yak-40	9541745	ex CCCP-87494	
RA-87984	Yakovlev Yak-40	9540744	ex CCCP-87984	
RA-88164	Yakovlev Yak-40	9611846	ex CCCP-88164	
RA-26039	Antonov An-26B		ex CCCP-26039	
RA-26209	Antonov An-26	57314302	ex CCCP-26209	
RA-26566	Antonov An-26		ex CCCP-26566	
RA-26688	Antonov An-26	97309004	ex CCCP-26688	

TRANSAERO AIRLINES

Transoviet (UN/TSO) (IATA 670)					*Moscow-Domodedovo (DME)*
EI-CXN	Boeing 737-329	1432/23772	ex 'N506GX'		Lsd fr GATX
EI-CXR	Boeing 737-329	1709/24355	ex OO-SYA		Lsd fr Embarcadero A/c
EI-DDK	Boeing 737-4S3	1720/24165	ex N758BC		Lsd fr Boeing Capital
N100UN	Boeing 737-7K9	19/28088		Bavaria	Lsd fr Bavaria Lsg
N101UN	Boeing 737-7K9	25/28089		Seattle	Lsd fr Bavaria Lsg
RA-73000	Boeing 737-2C9	516/21444	ex VP-BTB	stored DME	Lsd fr IAS Group
RA-73001	Boeing 737-236	656/22028	ex YL-BAA	stored DME	Lsd fr Finavion
RA-73002	Boeing 737-236	751/22034	ex YL-BAC	stored DME	Lsd fr Finavion
VP-BTA	Boeing 737-2C9	501/21443	ex EI-CLN	stored SVO	Lsd fr IAS Group

The Boeing 737-200s are withdrawn from service

EI-CXZ	Boeing 767-216ER	347/24973	ex N502GX		Lsd fr Embarcadero A/c
EI-CZD	Boeing 767-216ER	142/23623	ex N762TA		Lsd fr ILFC
EI-DBF	Boeing 767-3Q8ER	355/24745	ex F-GHGF		Lsd fr ACG Acquisition
EI-DBG	Boeing 767-3Q8ER	378/24746	ex F-GHGG		Lsd fr Charlie Aircraft Mgt
EI-DBU	Boeing 767-37EER	385/25077	ex F-GHGH		Lsd fr Pegasus Aviation
EI-DBW	Boeing 767-201ER	182/23899	ex N647US		Lsd fr BA Finance
RA-86123	Ilyushin Il-86	51483210091	ex CCCP-86123	Moskva	Lsd to VSO
RA-	Tupolev Tu-204-300			on order 04	Lsd fr Ilyushin Finance
RA-	Tupolev Tu-204-300			on order 04	Lsd fr Ilyushin Finance

Two more Tupolev Tu-204s are on order for delivery in 2004

TRETYAKOVO AIRLINES ceased operations

TULPAR

Previously listed as Kazan 2 nd Aviation Enterprise, renamed after original Tulpar merged with Karat

RA-67006	LET L-410UVP	810607	ex CCCP-67006
RA-67015	LET L-410UVP	810616	ex CCCP-67015
RA-67142	LET L-410UVP	800408	ex CCCP-67142
RA-67171	LET L-410UVP	790207	ex CCCP-67171
RA-67406	LET L-410UVP	831034	ex CCCP-67406
RA-67667	LET L-410UVP-E	902408	ex Soviet AF 2408
RA-67668	LET L-410UVP-E	902413	ex Soviet AF 2413
RA-67669	LET L-410UVP-E	902409	ex Soviet AF 2409
RA-67670	LET L-410UVP-E	902416	ex Soviet AF 2416
RA-67671	LET L-410UVP-E	902410	ex Soviet AF 2410

TULPAR AIRLINE CO merged into Karat in November 2003

TURA AIR

RA-26118	Antonov An-26	27312207
RA-69354	Antonov An-32	1606

TUVA AIRLINES

RA-87425	Yakovlev Yak-40	9420135?	ex CCCP-87425
RA-87443	Yakovlev Yak-40	9432035?	ex CCCP-87443
RA-87476	Yakovlev Yak-40	9440438?	ex CCCP-87476
RA-87477	Yakovlev Yak-40	9440538?	ex CCCP-87477
RA-87495	Yakovlev Yak-40	9541845?	ex CCCP-87495
RA-87519	Yakovlev Yak-40	9520141?	ex CCCP-87519
RA-87915	Yakovlev Yak-40	9730455	ex CCCP-87915
RA-87925	Yakovlev Yak-40	9731655	ex CCCP-87925
RA-88212	Yakovlev Yak-40	9631849	ex CCCP-88212

TYUMEN AIRLINES

Air Tyumen (7M/TYM)

RA-46267	Antonov An-24B	77303510	ex EW-46267	
RA-46297	Antonov An-24B	77303809	ex EW-46297	
RA-47160	Antonov An-24B	89901702	ex CCCP-47160	
RA-47166	Antonov An-24B	89901708	ex CCCP-47166	
RA-47741	Antonov An-24B	79901104	ex CCCP-47741	Lsd to AGE
RA-47745	Antonov An-24B	79901108	ex CCCP-47745	
RA-47780	Antonov An-24B	89901505	ex CCCP-47780	
RA-65009	Tupolev Tu-134A-3	46120	ex CCCP-65009	
RA-65012	Tupolev Tu-134A	46175	ex CCCP-65012	
RA-65017	Tupolev Tu-134A	48360	ex CCCP-65017	
RA-65025	Tupolev Tu-134A	48450	ex CCCP-65025	
RA-65038	Tupolev Tu-134A	48950	ex CCCP-65038	
RA-65063	Tupolev Tu-134A-3	49880	ex UR-65063	
RA-65127	Tupolev Tu-134A-3	60627	ex EY-65127	
RA-65802	Tupolev Tu-134A	3352101	ex CCCP-65802	
RA-65899	Tupolev Tu-134A-3	42225	ex CCCP-65899	
RA-85255	Tupolev Tu-154B-1	77A-255	ex CCCP-85255	
RA-85335	Tupolev Tu-154B-2	79A-335	ex CCCP-85335	
RA-85366	Tupoled Tu-154B-2	79A-366	ex CCCP-85366	
RA-85481	Tupolev Tu-154B-2	81A-481	ex CCCP-85481	
RA-85498	Tupolev Tu-154B-2	81A-498	ex CCCP-85498	
RA-85502	Tupolev Tu-154B-2	81A-502	ex CCCP-85502	
RA-85522	Tupolev Tu-154B-2	82A-522	ex CCCP-85522	
RA-76510	Ilyushin Il-76T	083414432	ex YL-LAJ	Lsd to AZS
RA-76514	Ilyushin Il-76T	083415433	ex CCCP-76514	Lsd to AZS
RA-76527	Ilyushin Il-76T	0003427796	ex CCCP-76527	Lsd to AZS
RA-76807	Ilyushin Il-76TD	1013405176	ex CCCP-76807	Lsd to AZS

TYUMENAVIATRANS renamed Utair Aviation

UDMUTIYA presumed to have ceased oeprations as all aircraft now operated by other airlines

ULYANOVSK HIGHER CIVIL AVIATION SCHOOL

Pilot Air (UHS)   Ulyanovsk (ULY)

RA-85078	Tupolev Tu-154A	74A-078	ex CCCP-85078	
RA-85091	Tupolev Tu-154A	74A-091	ex CCCP-85091	
RA-85315	Tupolev Tu-154B-2	78A-315	ex CCCP-85315	
RA-85388	Tupolev Tu-154B-2	79A-388	ex CCCP-85388	
RA-85470	Tupolev Tu-154B-2	81A-470	ex CCCP-85470	
RA-85609	Tupolev Tu-154M	-704	ex CCCP-85609	
RA-85636	Tupolev Tu-154M	87A-766	ex CCCP-85636	
RA-26025	Antonov An-26B	10308	ex CCCP-26025	
RA-26503	Antonov An-26	6310	ex CCCP-26503	
RA-26513	Antonov An-26	6810	ex CCCP-26513	
RA-26544	Antonov An-26	2710	ex CCCP-26544	
RA-42528	Yakovlev Yak-42D	11041003	ex CCCP-42528	
RA-42539	Yakovlev Yak-42D	11140504	ex CCCP-42539	
RA-42543	Yakovlev Yak-42D	11250904	ex CCCP-42543	
RA-76401	Ilyushin Il-76TD	1023412399	ex CCCP-76401	Lsd to AYZ
RA-76783	Ilyushin Il-76TD	0093498974	ex CCCP-76783	Lsd to AYZ
RA-86062	Ilyushin Il-86	51483203029	ex EW-86062	Lsd to AYZ
RA-86507	Ilyushin Il-62M	2035546	ex CCCP-86507	
RA-87299	Yakovlev Yak-40	9341528	ex CCCP-87299	
RA-87315	Yakovlev Yak-40	9331429	ex CCCP-87315	
RA-87580	Yakovlev Yak-40	9221222	ex CCCP-87580	
RA-87653	Yakovlev Yak-40	9211620	ex CCCP-87653	VIP

URAL AIRLINES

Sverdlovsk Air (U6/SVR)   Ekaterinburg (SVX)

RA-85193	Tupolev Tu-154B-2	77A-193	ex CCCP-85193
RA-85219	Tupolev Tu-154B-2	77A-219	ex CCCP-85219
RA-85319	Tupolev Tu-154B-2	78A-319	ex CCCP-85319
RA-85328	Tupolev Tu-154B-2	79A-328	ex CCCP-85328
RA-85337	Tupolev Tu-154B-2	79A-337	ex UN-85337
RA-85357	Tupolev Tu-154B-2	79A-357	ex CCCP-85357
RA-85374	Tupolev Tu-154B-2	79A-374	ex CCCP-85374
RA-85375	Tupolev Tu-154B-2	79A-375	ex CCCP-85375
RA-85432	Tupolev Tu-154B-2	80A-432	ex CCCP-85432
RA-85439	Tupolev Tu-154B-2	80A-439	ex CCCP-85439
RA-85459	Tupolev Tu-154B-2	80A-459	ex CCCP-85459
RA-85508	Tupolev Tu-154B-2	81A-508	ex CCCP-85508
RA-85807	Tupolev Tu-154M	94A-988	
RA-85814	Tupolev Tu-154M	9.A-994	
RA-85833	Tupolev Tu-154M	01A-1017	
RA-85844	Tupolev Tu-154M	95A-992	
RA-46532	Antonov An-24RV	57310101	ex CCCP-46532
RA-47182	Antonov An-24B	99901907	ex CCCP-47182
RA-47187	Antonov An-24B	99902002	ex CCCP-47187
RA-86078	Ilyushin Il-86	51483205049	ex CCCP-86078
RA-86093	Ilyushin Il-86	51483207064	ex CCCP-86093
RA-86103	Ilyushin Il-86	51483208071	ex CCCP-86103
RA-86114	Ilyushin Il-86	51483209082	ex CCCP-86114

UTAIR AVIATION

U Tair (P2/TMN)   Tyumen (TJM)
Previuosly listed as Tyumenaviatrans

RA-46362	Antonov An-24B	07305903	ex CCCP-46362	
RA-46481	Antonov An-24RV	27308009	ex CCCP-46481	
RA-46609	Antonov An-24RV	37308606	ex CCCP-46609	
RA-46828	Antonov An-24B	17306705	ex CCCP-46828	
RA-47271	Antonov An-24B	07306401	ex CCCP-47271	
RA-47273	Antonov An-24B	07306403	ex CCCP-42473	
RA-47289	Antonov An-24B	07306509	ex CCCP-47289	
RA-47305	Antonov An-24RV	57310305	ex CCCP-47305	
RA-47357	Antonov An-24RV	67310606	ex CCCP-47357	
RA-47827	Antonov An-24B	17307208	ex CCCP-47827	
RA-47829	Antonov An-24B	17307210	ex CCCP-47829	
RA-65049	Tupolev Tu-134A	49755	ex EW-65049	Lsd fr ORB
RA-65052	Tupolev Tu-134A	49825	ex CCCP-65052	Lsd fr AUL
RA-65083	Tupolev Tu-134A-3	60090	ex CCCP-65083	Lsd fr AUL
RA-65084	Tupolev Tu-134A-3	60115	ex CCCP-65084	Lsd fr AUL
RA-65148	Tupolev Tu-134A-3	61025	ex CCCP-65148	
RA-65608	Tupolev Tu-134A	38040	ex CCCP-65608	VIP
RA-65609	Tupolev Tu-134A-3	46155	ex CCCP-65609	

RA-65614	Tupolev Tu-134A	4352207	ex CCCP-65614		Lsd fr KMV
RA-65616	Tupolev Tu-134A-3	4352206	ex CCCP-65616	all-white	Lsd fr KMV
RA-65621	Tupolev Tu-134A-3	48320	ex CCCP-65621		Lsd fr KMV
RA-65755	Tupolev Tu-134A-3	62165	ex CCCP-65755		Lsd fr KMV
RA-65777	Tupolev Tu-134A-3	62552	ex CCCP-65777		Lsd fr KMV
RA-65793	Tupolev Tu-134A-3	63128	ex CCCP-65793	no titles	Lsd fr KMV
RA-65847	Tupolev Tu-134A-3	23135	ex CCCP-65847		
RA-65902	Tupolev Tu-134A-3	63742	ex CCCP-65902		Lsd fr KMV
RA-85504	Tupolev Tu-154B-2	81A-504	ex CCCP-85504		
RA-85557	Tupolev Tu-154B-2	82A-557	ex CCCP-85557		
RA-85595	Tupolev Tu-154B-2	84A-595	ex CCCP-85595		Lsd fr ORB
RA-85602	Tupolev Tu-154B-2	84A-602	ex CCCP-85602		
RA-85727	Tupolev Tu-154M	92A-909	ex ES-LTP		
RA-85733	Tupolev Tu-154M	92A-915	ex EP-MAL	Antonina Grigoreva	
RA-85755	Tupolev Tu-154M	92A-937		Basilii Baxilov	
RA-85796	Tupolev Tu-154M	93A-980			
RA-85805	Tupolev Tu-154M	94A-986			
RA-85806	Tupolev Tu-154M	94A-987			
RA-85808	Tupolev Tu-154M	94A-989			
RA-85813	Tupolev Tu-154M	95A-990			
RA-85820	Tupolev Tu-154M	9.A-995		Roman Maruenko	
RA-21504	Yakovlev Yak-40K	9831758	ex CCCP-21504		
RA-87292	Yakovlev Yak-40	9320728	ex CCCP-87292		
RA-87343	Yakovlev Yak-40	9511239	ex CCCP-87343		
RA-87348	Yakovlev Yak-40	9511739	ex CCCP-87348		
RA-87365	Yakovlev Yak-40	9341531	ex CCCP-87365		
RA-87383	Yakovlev Yak-40	9411432	ex CCCP-87383		
RA-87410	Yakovlev Yak-40	9420234	ex CCCP-87410		
RA-87422	Yakovlev Yak-40	9421834	ex CCCP-87422		
RA-87449	Yakovlev Yak-40	9430636	ex CCCP-87449		
RA-87516	Yakovlev Yak-40	9521840	ex CCCP-87516		
RA-87527	Yakovlev Yak-40	9520941	ex CCCP-87527		
RA-87901	Yakovlev Yak-40	9720354	ex CCCP-87901		
RA-87907	Yakovlev Yak-40	9731254	ex CCCP-87907		
RA-87941	Yakovlev Yak-40	9540545	ex CCCP-87941		
RA-87942	Yakovlev Yak-40K	9540645	ex CCCP-87942		
RA-87997	Yakovlev Yak-40	9540145	ex CCCP-87997		
RA-88209	Yakovlev Yak-40K	9631549	ex CCCP-88209		
RA-88210	Yakovlev Yak-40	9631649	ex CCCP-88210		
RA-88213	Yakovlev Yak-40	9631949	ex CCCP-88213		
RA-88227	Yakovlev Yak-40	9641550	ex CCCP-88227	VIP	
RA-88244	Yakovlev Yak-40	9641751	ex CCCP-88244		
RA-88280	Yakovlev Yak-40	9820658	ex CCCP-88280		
RA-26010	Antonov An-26	9906	ex CCCP-26010		

VASO AIRLINES

Vaso (DN/VSO)   Voronezh (VOZ)

RA-48096	Antonov An-24RV	57310406	ex CCCP-48096		
RA-86066	Ilyushin Il-86	51483204033	ex CCCP-86066		Lsd fr AFL
RA-86123	Ilyushin Il-86	51483210091	ex CCCP-86123		Lsd fr TSO

Vaso Airlines is the trading name of Voronezh Aircraft Manufacturing Society

VILYUI AVIAKOMPANIA merged into Polar Airlines

VIM AIRLINES

MovAir (MOV)   Moscow-Domodedovo (DME)

RA-11529	Antonov An-12B	6344109	ex CCCP-11529		
RA-12992	Antonov An-12B	00347306	ex CCCP-12992		
RA-48984	Antonov An-12BP	402913	ex CCCP-48984		Lsd fr VASO
	Douglas DC-10-15	346/48259	ex N301FV	on order	Lsd fr Finova
	Boeing 757-230		ex D-ABN	on order	Lsd fr Center Capital
	Boeing 757-230		ex D-ABN	on order	Lsd fr Center Capital
	Boeing 757-230		ex D-ABN	on order	Lsd fr Center Capital
	Boeing 757-230		ex D-ABN	on order	Lsd fr Center Capital
	Boeing 757-230		ex D-ABN	on order	Lsd fr Center Capital
RA-86517	Ilyushin Il-62M	3130732	ex CCCP-86517		
RA-86518	Ilyushin Il-62M	3139956	ex CCCP-86517		
RA-86520	Ilyushin Il-62M	1241314	ex CCCP-86520		
RA-86523	Ilyushin Il-62M	2241647	ex CCCP-86523		
RA-86524	Ilyushin Il-62M	3242321	ex CCCP-86524		
RA-86531	Ilyushin Il-62M	4242654	ex CCCP-86531	Ivan	
RA-86563	Ilyushin Il-62M	3036931	ex CCCP-86563		
RA-86565	Ilyushin Il-62M	2546812	ex CCCP-86565	Sarkis	

| RA-86597 | Ilyushin Il-62M | 2932748 | ex OK-JBI | Uliya |
| RA-86935 | Ilyushin Il-62M | 1545951 | ex OK-PBM | Natalya |

VLADIKAVKAZ AIR ENTERPRISE
Irair (OSV)   Vladikavkaz (OGZ)

| RA-87286 | Yakovlev Yak-40 | 9310128 | ex CCCP-87286 |
| RA-87569 | Yakovlev Yak-40 | 9220222 | ex UN 87569 |

VLADIVOSTOK AIR
Vladair (XF/VLK)   Vladivostok (VVO)

RA-87273	Yakovlev Yak-40	9310927	ex CCCP-87273	
RA-87325	Yakovlev Yak-40	9330430	ex CCCP-87325	for sale
RA-87518	Yakovlev Yak-40	9522040	ex CCCP-87518	for sale
RA-87546	Yakovlev Yak-40	9531142	ex CCCP-87546	
RA-87958	Yakovlev Yak-40K	9821957	ex CCCP-87958	for sale
RA-88163	Yakovlev Yak-40	9611746	ex CCCP-88163	for sale
RA-88172	Yakovlev Yak-40	9611047	ex CCCP-88172	for sale
RA-88222	Yakovlev Yak-40K	9630850	ex CCCP-88222	for sale
RA-88223	Yakovlev Yak-40	9640950	ex CCCP-88223	for sale
RA-88232	Yakovlev Yak-40K	9640151	ex CCCP-88232	for sale
RA-88255	Yakovlev Yak-40K	9711052	ex CCCP-88255	for sale
RA-85562	Tupolev Tu-154B-2	82A-562	ex CCCP-85562	Dalnerechensk
RA-85588	Tupolev Tu-154B-2	83A-588	ex CCCP-85588	Artem
RA-85596	Tupolev Tu-154B-2	84A-596	ex CCCP-85596	Spassk-Dalny
RA-85676	Tupolev Tu-154M	90A-836	ex EP-MAM	Sayanogorsk
RA-85681	Tupolev Tu-154M	90A-848	ex LZ-LTE	Abakan
RA-85685	Tupolev Tu-154M	90A-853	ex CCCP-85685	Nakhodka
RA-85710	Tupolev Tu-154M	91A-885	ex UR-85710	Vladivostok
RA-85803	Tupolev Tu-154M	89A-822	ex EK-85803	
RA-85849	Tupolev Tu-154M	89A-815	ex B-2620	Arsenyev
RA-76400	Ilyushin Il-76TD	1023413438		Lsd to ESL
RA-76403	Ilyushin Il-76TD	1023412414	Igor Bykov	Lsd to ESL

VOLGA AVIAEXPRESS
Goumrak (WLG)   Volgograd (VOG)

RA-42364	Yakovlev Yak-42D	4520424811442	ex CCCP-42364	Lsd to CUB as CU-T1272
RA-42382	Yakovlev Yak-42D	4520422016196	ex CCCP-42382	
RA-42384	Yakovlev Yak-42D	4520423016230	ex CCCP-42384	
RA-42406	Yakovlev Yak-42D	4520424116683	ex CCCP-42406	special c/s
RA-46230	Antonov An-24B	77302110	ex CCCP-46230	
RA-46610	Antonov An-24RV	37308607	ex CCCP-46610	
RA-65043	Tupolev Tu-134A-3	49400	ex CCCP-65043	
RA-65086	Tupolev Tu-134A-3	60130	ex CCCP-65086	
RA-65903	Tupolev Tu-134A-3	63750	ex CCCP-65903	

VOLGA-DNEPR AIRLINES
Volga Dnepr (VI/VDA)   Ulyanovsk (ULY)

RA-82042	Antonov An-124-100	9773054055093	ex CCCP-82042	
RA-82043	Antonov An-124-100	9773054155101	ex CCCP-82043	
RA-82044	Antonov An-124-100	9773054155109	ex CCCP-82044	
RA-82045	Antonov An-124-100	9773052255113	ex CCCP-82045	
RA-82046	Antonov An-124-100	9773052255117	ex RA-82067	
RA-82047	Antonov An-124-100	9773053259121	ex CCCP-82068	
RA-82074	Antonov An-124-100	9773051459142		
RA-82078	Antonov An-124-100	9773054559153		
RA-82079	Antonov An-124-100	9773052062157		
RA-82	Antonov An-124-100		on order	
RA-87357	Yakovlev Yak-40	9340631	ex CCCP-87357	Lsd to TLR
RA-87400	Yakovlev Yak-40	9421233	ex CCCP-87400	
RA-87844	Yakovlev Yak-40	9331330	ex CCCP-87844	
RA-87981	Yakovlev Yak-40	9540444	ex ER-YGA	
RA-88240	Yakovlev Yak-40	9641151	ex CCCP-88240	
RA-88243	Yakovlev Yak-40	9641651	ex CCCP-88243	
RA-76366	Ilyushin Il-76TD	1043418628		
RA-76591	Ilyushin Il-76TD	0043452546		
RA-76788	Ilyushin Il-76TD	0033446325	ex CCCP-76788	Lsd fr VARZ

Four Antonov An-140s are on order for delivery in 2003/4 plus three Antonov An-148s in 2005/6. Airbridge Cargo is wholly owned and plans to commence Boeing 747 service in April 2004

VORONEZH AVIA

VOLOGDA STATE AVIATION ENTERPRISE

Vologda Air (VGV)   **Vologda (VGD)**

RA-87277	Yakovlev Yak-40	9321327	ex CCCP-87277	
RA-87433	Yakovlev Yak-40	9420935	ex CCCP-87433	
RA-87484	Yakovlev Yak-40	9441238	ex CCCP-87484	no titles	Lsd to Khantyavia
RA-87582	Yakovlev Yak-40	9221422	ex CCCP-87582	
RA-87606	Yakovlev Yak-40	9120518	ex CCCP-87606	
RA-87611	Yakovlev Yak-40	9131018?	ex CCCP-87611	
RA-87665	Yakovlev Yak-40	9240925	ex CCCP-87665	no titles
RA-87837	Yakovlev Yak-40	9240326	ex CCCP-87837	
RA-87842	Yakovlev Yak-40	9321030	ex CCCP-87842	

VORONEZH AVIA

Voronezhavia (ZT/VRN)   **Voronezh (VOZ)**

RA-65057	Tupolev Tu-134A-3	49865	ex CCCP-65057	no titles
RA-65062	Tupolev Tu-134A	49875	ex CCCP-65062	
RA-65067	Tupolev Tu-134A-3	49905	ex CCCP-65067	VIP; no titles
RA-65762	Tupolev Tu-134A-3	62279	ex CCCP-65762	
RA-65794	Tupolev Tu-134A-3	63135	ex CCCP-65794	VIP	Lsd to CIG
RA-65880	Tupolev Tu-134A-3	35200	ex CCCP-65880	VIP	Lsd to CIG
RA-65918	Tupolev Tu-134A-3CX	63995	ex CCCP-65918	agricultural research
RA-65929	Tupolev Tu-134A	66495	ex CCCP-65929	agricultural research; dam 24Jun03
RA-46639	Antonov An-24RV	37308905	ex CCCP-46639	
RA-46676	Antonov An-24RV	47309608	ex CCCP-46676	
RA-46690	Antonov An-24RV	47309901	ex CCCP-46690	
RA-47321	Antonov An-24RV	67310507	ex TC-TOR	

VOSTOK AVIAKOMPANIA / EASTAIR

Vostok (VTK)   **Khabarovsk-Novy (KHV)**

RA-67308	LET L-410UVP	820808	ex CCCP-67308	
RA-67377	LET L-410UVP	831005	ex CCCP-67377	
RA-67634	LET L-410UVP-E	902427	ex CCCP-67634	
RA-67635	LET L-410UVP-E	902428	ex CCCP-67635	
RA-67636	LET L-410UVP-E	902429	ex CCCP-67636	
RA-67644	LET L-410UVP-E	902437	ex CCCP-67644	
RA-28920	WSK-PZL/Antonov An-28	1AJ008-06	ex CCCP-28920	
RA-28929	WSK-PZL/Antonov An-28	1AJ008-16	ex CCCP-28929	
RA-28931	WSK-PZL/Antonov An-28	1AJ008-18	ex CCCP-28931	
RA-28933	WSK-PZL/Antonov An-28	1AJ008-20	ex CCCP-28933	
RA-28941	WSK-PZL/Antonov An-28	1AJ009-07	ex CCCP-28941	
RA-28942	WSK-PZL/Antonov An-28	1AJ009-08	ex CCCP-28942	
RA-41901	Antonov An-38-100	4163847010001		Lsd to Layang-Layang Aerospace
RA-41902	Antonov An-38-100	4163847010002		
RA-41903	Antonov An-38-100	4163838010003		Lsd to Layang-Layang Aerospace

VYBORG AIRLINES

Vyborg Air (VBG)   **St Petersburg-Pulkovo (LED)**

RA-91014	Ilyushin Il-114	1023823024	ex UK 91014	Lsd fr UzbAviaLizing
RA-91015	Ilyushin Il-114		ex UK-91015	Lsd fr UzbAviaLizing
Two more are on order				

YAK SERVICE

Yak-Service (AKY)   **Moscow-Bykovo (BKA)**

RA-42330	Yakovlev Yak-42	4520422505122	ex UR-42330
RA-42344	Yakovlev Yak-42	4520422708295	ex LY-AAQ
RA-87625	Yakovlev Yak-40	9130619	ex CCCP-87625
RA-88295	Yakovlev Yak-40	9331329	ex 035 Polish AF

YAKUTIA AIRLINES

Air Yakutia (K7/SYL)   **Yakutsk (YKS)**
Previously listed as Sakha Avia and Yakutsk Airlines

RA-46468	Antonov An-24RV	27307906	ex CCCP-46468	Lsd fr KMV
RA-46494	Antonov An-24RV	27308207	ex CCCP-46494	Lsd fr KMV
RA-46519	Antonov An-24RV	37308505	ex CCCP-46519	
RA-46665	Antonov An-24RV	47309506	ex CCCP-46665	
RA-46670	Antonov An-24RV	47309601	ex CCCP-46670	

RA-46690	Antonov An-24RV	47309901	ex CCCP-46690	
RA-47352	Antonov An-24RV	67310601	ex CCCP-47352	
RA-47353	Antonov An-24RV	67310602	ex CCCP-47353	
RA-47820	Antonov An-24RV	17307201	ex CCCP-47820	Lsd fr KMV
RA-47830	Antonov An-24B	17307301	ex CCCP-47830	
RA-47845	Antonov An-24B	17307410	ex CCCP-47845	
RA-85348	Tupolev Tu-154B-2	79A-348	ex CCCP-85348	
RA-85354	Tupolev Tu-154B-2	79A-354	ex CCCP-85354	
RA-85520	Tupolev Tu-154B-2	81A-520	ex CCCP-85520	
RA-85577	Tupolev Tu-154B-2	83A-577	ex CCCP-85577	
RA-85597	Tupolev Tu-154B-2	84A-597	ex CCCP-85597	
RA-85753	Tupolev Tu-154M	92A-935		
RA-85790	Tupolev Tu-154M	93A-974	ex EP-CPL	
RA-85791	Tupolev Tu-154M	93A-975	ex EP-MBR	
RA-85793	Tupolev Tu-154M	93A-977		
RA-85794	Tupolev Tu-154M	92A-978		
RA-85812	Tupolev Tu-154M	9.A-1005		
RA-87205	Yakovlev Yak-40	9810257	ex CCCP-87205	
RA-87656	Yakovlev Yak-40	9211920	ex CCCP-87656	
RA-87903	Yakovlev Yak-40K	9720654	ex CCCP-87903	
RA-88166	Yakovlev Yak-40	9612046	ex CCCP-88166	
RA-88261	Yakovlev Yak-40	9711652	ex CCCP-88261	
RA-11354	Antonov An-12BP	410812	ex CCCP-11354	
RA-11767	Antonov An-12BP	401909	ex CCCP-11767	
RA-11884	Antonov An-12BP	401710	ex CCCP-11884	
RA-26037	Antonov An-26	10608	ex CCCP-26037	
RA-26516	Antonov An-26	7001	ex CCCP-26516	
RA-26660	Antonov An-26	97308008	ex CCCP-26660	

YAKUTSK AIRLINES merged into Yakutia Airlines

YAMAL AIRLINES

Yamal (YL/LLM)   *Selekhard*

RA-65132	Tupolev Tu-134A-3	60639	ex CCCP-65132	RMAA titles
RA-65143	Tupolev Tu-134A	60967	ex CCCP-65143	
RA-65552	Tupolev Tu-134A-3	66270	ex CCCP-65552	
RA-65554	Tupolev Tu-134A-3	66320	ex CCCP-65554	Lsd to NZP
RA-65906	Tupolev Tu-134A	66175	ex CCCP-65906	no titles
RA-65914	Tupolev Tu-134A-3	66109	ex TC-GRD	
RA-65915	Tupolev Tu-134A-3	66120	ex TC-GRE	
RA-65916	Tupolev Tu-134A-3	66152	ex CCCP-65916	
RA-87222	Yakovlev Yak-40K	9832058	ex YL-TRA	
RA-87340	Yakovlev Yak-40	9510939	ex YL-TRA	
RA-87381	Yakovlev Yak-40	9411232	ex CCCP-87381	
RA-87416	Yakovlev Yak-40	9420834	ex CCCP-87416	
RA-88188	Yakovlev Yak-40	9620848	ex CCCP-88188	
RA-88264	Yakovlev Yak-40K	9711952	ex CCCP-88264	
RA-26133	Antonov An-26	37312709	ex CCCP-26133	
RA-46694	Antonov An-24RV	47309905	ex CCCP-46694	
RA-46695	Antonov An-24RV	47309906	ex UN46695	
RA-72918	Antonov An-72			
RA-74027	Antonov An-74-200	36547096920	ex UR-74027	Lsd to NZP
RA-74043	Antonov An-74-200	36547096923	ex UR-74043	
RA-74052	Antonov An-74-200	36547098444		Lsd to NZP
RA-85324	Tupolev Tu-154B-2	79A-324	ex UN-85324	
RA-85819	Tupolev Tu-154M	97A-1008		
RA-85842	Tupolev Tu-154B-2	80A-420	ex 0420 Slovak AF	

YOSHKAR-OLA AIR ENTERPRISE

Yoshkar-Ola

RA-46496	Antonov An-24RV	27308209	ex CCCP-46496	
RA-46509	Antonov An-24RV	37308405?	ex CCCP-46509	
RA-46589	Antonov An-24B	97305009?	ex CCCP-46589	
RA-47285	Antonov An-24B	07306505?	ex CCCP-47285	

ZAPOLYARYE AVIAKOMPANIA

Norlisk-Alykel

RA-11363	Antonov An-12B	00347505	ex CCCP-11363	no titles
RA-11816	Antonov An-12BP	3341003	ex CCCP-11816	
RA-11906	Antonov An-12BP	2340802	ex CCCP-11906	

RA-12981	Antonov An-12B	00347104	ex CCCP-12981	dbr 11Apr03?
RA-26013	Antonov An-26B	10009	ex CCCP-26013	
RA-26056	Antonov An-26B	11005	ex CCCP-26056	
RA-26610	Antonov An-26	4901	ex CCCP-26610	
RA-26620	Antonov An-26	5104	ex CCCP-26620	
RA-46466	Antonov An-24RV	27307904	ex CCCP-46466	
RA-46531	Antonov An-24RV	57310010	ex CCCP-46531	

RDPL - LAOS (Lao People's Democratic Republic)

EURO-ASIA AVIATION current status is uncertain, sole aircraft crashed

EXPRESS AVIA sole aircraft transferred to Euro Asia Aviation; status uncertain

LAO AIRLINES

Vientiane (VTE)

VN-A123	Airbus Industrie A320-211	0024	ex N240SE	Lsd fr SALE; op by HVN

LAO AVIATION

Lao (QV/LAO) *Vientiane (VTE)*

RDPL 34115	Harbin Y-12	0033		
RDPL 34116	Harbin Y-12	0034		
RDPL-34118	Harbin Y-12	0043		
RDPL 34129	Harbin Y-12	0085		
RDPL 34131	Harbin Y-12	0087		
RDPL 34127	Xian Y-7-100C	12706		
RDPL 34128	Xian Y-7-100C	13701		
RDPL 34132	Aerospatiale/Alenia ATR 72-202	396	ex F-OLAO	
RDPL 34137	Aerospatiale/Alenia ATR 72-202	316	ex F-OHOB	

RP - PHILIPPINES (Republic of the Philippines)

AAI ISLAND HOPPER

Manila-Sangley Point (SGL)

RP-C109	Agusta A.109A II	7263	ex I-SEIE	
RP-C143	Cessna 421B Golden Eagle	421B0463	ex N421AS	
RP-C688	Britten-Norman BN-2A-26 Islander	2042		Lsd fr LBC Group; sublsd to Chemtrad
RP-C1502	Beech B200 Super King Air	BB-1500	ex N3199B	

ABOITIZ AIR TRANSPORT

Abair (BO/BOI) *Manila-Nino Aquino Intl (MNL)*

RP-C2253	NAMC YS-11A	2020	ex RP-C1936	Freighter	
RP-C2739	NAMC YS-11A	2090	ex JA8710		
RP-C3202	NAMC YS-11A	2128	ex JA8821	stored MNL	Freighter
RP-C3205	NAMC YS-11	2010	ex JA8644	Isang Araw Ka Lang	Freighter
RP-C3208	NAMC YS-11A	2138	ex JA8769		Lsd to RIT
RP-C3212	NAMC YS-11A	2111	ex JA8736	stored MNL	
RP-C3214	NAMC YS-11A	2158	ex JU-9050		Lsd to RIT
RP-C3590	NAMC YS-11A	2106	ex P4-KFB	Freighter	
RP-C3592	NAMC YS-11A	2078	ex JA8722		

Member of Soriano Group; also operates as Midnight Express

AIR LINK INTERNATIONAL AIRWAYS

Manila-Sangley Point (SGL)

RP-C180	Cessna 414	414-0402	ex RP-180	
RP-C818	Beech 95-55 Baron	TC-88	ex PI-C818	
RP-C1102	Beech 88 Queen Air	LP-44	ex RP-94	
RP-C2252	NAMC YS-11A	2079	ex RP-C1931	
RP-C6699	Beech 95-B55 Baron	TC-893	ex N4E	

AIR PHILIPPINES

Orient Pacific (2P/GAP) *Subic Bay-Intl (SFS)*

RP-C2020	Boeing 737-222	179/19943	ex N9062U	
RP-C2021	Boeing 737-222	6/19039	ex N9001U	

RP-C2022	Boeing 737-222	175/19942	ex N9061U	
RP-C2023	Boeing 737-222	187/19947	ex N9066U	
RP-C2025	Boeing 737-222	103/19077	ex N9039U	
RP-C3011	Boeing 737-2H4	524/21533	ex N52SW	Lsd fr AAR Grp
RP-C3012	Boeing 737-2H4	509/21448	ex N51SW	Lsd fr AAR Grp
RP-C3015	Boeing 737-2H4	526/21534	ex N53SW	Lsd fr AAR Grp
RP-C8001	Boeing 737-2B7 (Nordam 3)	999/23116	ex N283AU	
RP-C8003	Boeing 737-2B7 (Nordam 3)	979/22888	ex N276AU	on order
RP-C8004	Boeing 737-2B7 (Nordam 3)	934/22882	ex N270AU	on order
RP-C	Boeing 737-2B7 (Nordam 3)	974/22886	ex N274US	on order

10% owned by Japan Airlines System

ASIA OVERNIGHT EXPRESS

(OE/AOT)

Current fleet details are unknown, possibly still being set up

ASIAN SPIRIT

Asian Spirit (6K/RIT)   Manila-Sangley Point (SGL)

RP-C2015	NAMC YS-11A-500	2067	ex JA8698	
RP-C3208	NAMC YS-11A-500	2138	ex JA8769	Lsd fr BOI
RP-C3214	NAMC YS-11A-500	2158	ex JU-9050	Lsd fr BOI
RP-C3217	NAMC YS-11A-500	2083	ex JA8794	
RP-C3587	NAMC YS-11A-500	2069	ex P4-KFA	VIP
RP-C3588	NAMC YS-11A-213	2168	ex JA8787	stored MNL
RP-C3589	NAMC YS-11A-213	2078	ex JA8722	
RP-C3592	NAMC YS-11A-213	2108	ex JA8735	
RP-C2786	British Aerospace ATP	2055	ex G-MANB	
RP-	British Aerospace ATP	2054	ex G-MANC	
RP-C2895	de Havilland DHC-7-102	035	ex 7O-ADB	
RP-C2915	de Havilland DHC-7-102	092	ex C-GELY	
RP-C2918	LET L-410UVP	902510	ex 9A-BNZ	
RP-C2978	de Havilland DHC-7-102	079	ex N67DA	
RP-C2988	de Havilland DHC-7-102	078	ex N60RA	stored MNL
RP-C3880	LET L-410UVP-E	892228	ex RA-67601	
RP-C3889	LET L-410UVP-E	851511	ex RA-67544	
RP-C4000	ITPN CASA CN.235	N020	ex PK-XNV	
RP-C5000	ITPN CASA CN.235	N001	ex PK-	

A SORIANO AVIATION

Soriano (SOY)   Manila-Nino Aquino Intl (MNL)

RP-C1008	Dornier 228-212	8193	ex D-CARD	Lsd fr Transvoger Inc
RP-C2282	Dornier 228-202K	8173	ex RP-C2101	all-white

Member of Soriano Group

CEBU PACIFIC AIR

Cebu Air (5J/CEB)   Manila-Nino Aquino Intl (MNL)

RP-C1503	Douglas DC-9-32	906/47789	ex PK-GNS	
RP-C1504	Douglas DC-9-32	910/47792	ex PK-GNV	
RP-C1505	Douglas DC-9-32	911/47793	ex PK-GNW	
RP-C1506	Douglas DC-9-32	916/47795	ex PK-GNY	
RP-C1508	Douglas DC-9-32	176/47070	ex C-FTLR	
RP-C1509	Douglas DC-9-32	188/47071	ex C-FTLS	
RP-C1535	Douglas DC-9-32	352/47266	ex C-FTMA	Paradise c/s
RP-C1536	Douglas DC-9-32	471/47353	ex C-FTMO	Centennial c/s
RP-C1537	Douglas DC-9-32	684/47570	ex S5-ABH	
RP-C1538	Douglas DC-9-32	466/47239	ex S5-ABF	
RP-C1539	Douglas DC-9-32	666/47485	ex C-FTMX	
RP-C1540	Douglas DC-9-32	868/47734	ex N920L	City of Davao; Paradise c/s
RP-C1541	Douglas DC-9-31 (ABS 3)	1036/48143	ex N923VJ	
RP-C1542	Douglas DC-9-31 (ABS 3)	920/48115	ex N935VJ	Lsd fr Finova
RP-C1543	Douglas DC-9-31 (ABS 3)	921/48116	ex N936VJ	Lsd fr Finova
RP-C1544	Douglas DC-9-31 (ABS 3)	922/48117	ex N937VJ	Lsd fr Pacific VI Holdings
RP-C1545	Douglas DC-9-32 (ABS 3)	956/48132	ex N502ME	
RP-C1546	Douglas DC-9-32 (ABS 3)	959/48133	ex N602ME	
RP-C2714	Boeing 757-236	218/24370	ex N903PG	Lsd fr Pegasus
RP-C2715	Boeing 757-236	225/24371	ex N955PG	Lsd fr PALS I Inc
RP-C2716	Boeing 757-236	441/25597	ex EI-CZB	Lsd fr Bellevue A/c Lsg

CHEMTRAD AVIATION

Manila-Nino Aquino Intl (MNL)

RP-C28	Britten-Norman BN-2A-21 Islander	409	ex G-BCLF	
RP-C688	Britten-Norman BN-2A-26 Islander	2042		Lsd fr AAI Island Hopper
RP-C764	Britten-Norman BN-2A-26 Islander	318	ex G-BANL	
RP-C1262	Britten-Norman BN-2A-21 Islander	408	ex G-BCLE	
RP-C2141	Britten-Norman BN-2A-21 Islander	452	ex G-BDDL	
RP-C2201	Britten-Norman BN-2A-26 Islander	718	ex RP-C2207	
RP-C2079	Cessna 207A Stationair 8	20700600	ex N73511	
RP-C3216	Cessna 207 Skywagon	20700333	ex N1793U	

CORPORATE AIR

Subic Bay-Intl (SFS)

N702PV	de Havilland DHC-6 Twin Otter 300	702		Lsd fr CPT
N760FE	Cessna 208B Caravan I	208B0252		Lsd fr/op for FDX
N766FE	Cessna 208B Caravan I	208B0260		Lsd fr/op for FDX
N860FE	Cessna 208B Caravan I	208B0182		Lsd fr/op for FDX
N972SW	de Havilland DHC-6 Twin Otter 300	356	ex JA8790	Lsd fr CPT
RP-C2101	Dornier 228-212	8218	ex 9M-BOR	

Subsidiary of Corporate Air, USA

ISLAND TRANSVOYAGER

Manila

RP-C2289	Dornier 228-212	8177	ex B-11150	Lsd fr Transvoyager Inc

LAOAG INTERNATIONAL AIRWAYS

Laoag Air (L7/LPN)   *Laoag (LAO)*

RP-C3318	LET L-410UVP-E	871934	ex 3C-QRH

PACIFICAIR

(GX) (IATA)   *Manila-Sangley Point (SGL)*

RP-C1320	Britten-Norman BN-2A-21 Islander	569	ex PAF-569
RP-C1321	Britten-Norman BN-2A-21 Islander	547	ex PAF-547
RP-C1323	Britten-Norman BN-2A-21 Islander	502	ex PAF 502
RP-C1324	Britten-Norman BN-2A-21 Islander	539	ex PAF 538
RP-C1325	Britten-Norman BN-2A-21 Islander	593	ex PAF-593
RP-C1801	Britten-Norman BN-2A-21 Islander	739	ex G-BCNI
RP-C2132	Britten-Norman BN-2A-21 Islander	422	ex G-BCSG
RP-C2137	Britten-Norman BN-2A-21 Islander	443	ex G-BCZU
RP-C2138	Britten-Norman BN-2A-21 Islander	445	ex G-BCZW
RP-C2157	Britten-Norman BN-2A-21 Islander	505	
RP-C24	Cessna U206F Stationair	U20603026	ex N3578Q
RP-C108	Cessna 210L Centurion	21060546	ex N94220
RP-C165	Cessna U206F Stationair	U20602016	ex RP-165
RP-C978	Cessna U206E Skywagon	U20601506	ex N9105M
RP-1103	Beech H-18	BA-660	ex N638CZ
RP-C1155	de Havilland DHC-6 Twin Otter 200	134	ex N1373T
RP-C1175	Cessna U206F Stationair	U20601943	ex N50625
RP-C1226	Cessna 207 Skywagon	20700092	ex N519SA
RP-C1358	Beech H-18 Tri-Gear	BA-750	ex RP-C1986
RP-C1611	Cessna 421C Golden Eagle	421C0155	ex N5282J
RP-C2346	Aero Commander 560A	342-78	ex N26403

PHILIPPINE AIRLINES

Philippine (PR/PAL) (IATA 079)   *Manila-Nino Aquino Intl (MNL)*

F-OHZM	Airbus Industrie A330-301	183	ex F-WWKP	Lsd fr Airbus
F-OHZN	Airbus Industrie A330-301	184	ex F-WWKG	Lsd fr Airbus
F-OHZO	Airbus Industrie A330-301	188	ex F-WWKQ	Lsd fr Airbus
F-OHZP	Airbus Industrie A330-301	191	ex F-WWKR	Lsd fr Airbus
F-OHZQ	Airbus Industrie A330-301	189	ex F-WWKS	Lsd fr Airbus
F-OHZR	Airbus Industrie A330-301	198	ex F-WWKT	Lsd fr Airbus
F-OHZS	Airbus Industrie A330-301	200	ex F-WWKH	Lsd fr Airbus
F-OHZT	Airbus Industrie A330-301	203	ex F-WWKI	Lsd fr Airbus
F-OHPJ	Airbus Industrie A340-313X	173	ex F-WWJG	Lsd fr Airbus
F-OHPK	Airbus Industrie A340-313X	176	ex F-WWJB	Lsd fr Airbus
F-OHPL	Airbus Industrie A340-313X	187	ex F-WWJO	Lsd fr Airbus

F-OHPM	Airbus Industrie A340-313X	196	ex F-WWJI	Lsd fr Airbus
RP-C3221	Airbus Industrie A320-214	0706	ex F-WWIM	Lsd fr Airbus
RP-C3223	Airbus Industrie A320-214	0745	ex F-WWIR	Lsd fr Airbus
RP-C3224	Airbus Industrie A320-214	0753	ex F-WWIV	Lsd fr Airbus
EI-BZE	Boeing 737-3Y0	1753/24464		Lsd fr BBAM
EI-BZF	Boeing 737-3Y0	1755/24465		Lsd fr GECAS
EI-BZJ	Boeing 737-3Y0	1837/24677		Lsd fr GECAS
EI-BZL	Boeing 737-3Y0	1927/24680		Lsd fr GECAS
EI-BZN	Boeing 737-3Y0	1941/24770		Lsd fr GECAS
EI-CUL	Boeing 737-36N	2882/28559	ex PH-OZC	Lsd fr GECAS
EI-CVN	Boeing 737-4Y0	1841/24684	ex TC-AFK	Lsd fr Airplanes Finance
EI-CVO	Boeing 737-4S3	2223/25594	ex SP-LLH	Lsd fr AerCo Ireland
EI-CVP	Boeing 737-4Y0	2442/26081	ex TC-AFU	Lsd fr Airplanes Finance
RP-C4007	Boeing 737-332	2488/25996	ex RP-C2000	
RP-C4008	Boeing 737-33A	2025/25033	ex N5033	Lsd fr CIT Leasing
N751PR	Boeing 747-4F6	1005/27261	ex (RP-C5751)	Lsd fr WTCo
N752PR	Boeing 747-4F6	1012/27262	ex (RP-C5752)	Lsd fr WTCo
N753PR	Boeing 747-4F6	1039/27828	ex (N774BE)	Lsd fr WTCo
N754PR	Boeing 747-469M	1068/27663	ex N6009F	Lsd fr WTCo
RP-C8186	Boeing 747-4F6	1038/27827	ex C-FGHZ	Lsd fr GECAS

SEAIR ASIAN AIRWAYS

Seair (DG/SRQ) — Manila-Nino Aquino Intl/Clark Air Base (MNL/CRK)

RP-C728	LET L-410UVP-E	902434	ex RA-67641	Lsd fr Avn Enterprises
RP-C748	LET L-410UVP-E	892342	ex UR-67514	Lsd fr Vivere Isle
RP-C2128	LET L-410UVP-E	882102	ex S9-BOX	
RP-C2328	LET L-410UVP-E3	872004	ex S9-BOY	
RP-C2428	LET L-410UVP-E3	871909	ex 3D-DAM	
RP-C2628	LET L-410UVP-E	871931	ex Russian AF 1931	Lsd fr Avn Enterprises
RP-C2728	LET L-410UVP-E	861708	ex RA-67588 jungle c/s	Lsd fr Avn Enterprises
RP-C2928	LET L-410UVP-E	871821	ex Russian AF 1821	Lsd fr Avn Enterprises
RP-C3328	LET L-410UVP-E	872003	ex Soviet AF 38 red	Lsd fr Avn Enterprises
RP-C1179	Dornier 28D-2	4127	ex D-IDRH	

SOUTH EAST ASIAN AIRLINES entry in error, should have been referenced to Seair Asian Airlines

VICTORIA AIR

Manila-Sangley Point (SGL)

| RP-C535* | Douglas DC-3 | 15571/27016 | ex RP-C95 | |
| RP-C550 | Douglas DC-3 | 14292/25737 | ex 43-48476 | |

*Also quoted as c/n 33294 ex Philippine Air Force 476962

SE - SWEDEN (Kingdom of Sweden)

BRITANNIA AIRWAYS SWEDEN

Bluescan (6B/BLX) (IATA 951) — Stockholm-Arlanda (ARN)

SE-DZH	Boeing 737-804	452/28227		Lsd fr ILFC
SE-DZI	Boeing 737-804	478/28229		Lsd fr ILFC
SE-DZK	Boeing 737-804	538/28231		Lsd fr ILFC
SE-DZL	Boeing 737-804	502/30465	ex NBB-Britannia Lse	Lsd fr NBB-Britannia Lse
SE-DZM	Boeing 737-804	505/30466	ex PH-ABE	Lsd fr Croydon Co
SE-DZN	Boeing 737-804	1127/32903		Lsd fr NBB Berlin Co; sublsd to FUA
SE-DZV	Boeing 737-804	1302/32904		
G-OBYD	Boeing 767-304ER	649/28042	ex SE-DZG	Lsd fr BAL for winter

Controlled by Britannia Airways

CITY AIRLINE

Swedestar (CF/SDR) — Gothenburg-Landvetter (GOT)

SE-RAA	Embraer EMB.135ER	145210		City of Gothenburg Lsd fr Investment AB Janus
SE-RAB	Embraer EMB.135LR	145453	ex PT-SUY	City of Linkoping Lsd fr SEB Finans
SE-RAC	Embraer EMB.145LR	145098	ex N285CD	Lsd fr GATX

EUROPEAN EXECUTIVE EXPRESS

Echo Express (RY/EXC) — Stockholm-Bromma (BMA)

SE-LDI	British Aerospace Jetstream 31	785	ex C-FHOE	Lsd fr Elicon Data
SE-LGB	British Aerospace Jetstream 31	639	ex N639JX	Lsd fr GE Capital
SE-LGC	British Aerospace Jetstream 31	645	ex G-BXLM	Lsd fr GE Capital

550

SE-LGH	British Aerospace Jetstream 31	773	ex (LN-BES)	Lsd fr Enar Lindstrom
SE-LNU	British Aerospace Jetstream 32EP	949	ex VH-XFC	Lsd fr Favora NV
SE-LNV	British Aerospace Jetstream 32EP	951	ex VH-XFD	Lsd fr Skylease Sweden AB

FALCON AVIATION

Falcon (IH/FCN) (IATA 759) — *Malmo-Sturup (MMX)*

SE-DPA	Boeing 737-33A(QC)	2067/25401		Aftonfalken	Lsd fr AWAS
SE-DPB	Boeing 737-33A(QC)	2159/25402	ex N33AW	Pilgrimsfalken	Lsd fr Metsuda Ent
SE-DPC	Boeing 737-33A(QC)	2172/25426	ex N34AW	Tornfalken	Lsd fr Ancon Inc
SE-LST	Aerospatiale/Alenia ATR 42-300F	149	ex F-WQNP	Norrskensfalken	Lsd fr ABR

Domestic mail flights to be transferred to new operator Amapola Flyg by 2006

FLY ME SWEDEN

Gothenburg-Landvetter (GOT)

SE-RCO	Boeing 737-33A	1436/23635	ex F-GFUA	on order	Lsd fr AWMS I
SE-RCP	Boeing 737-33A	1556/24025	ex F-GHVO	on order	Lsd fr AWMS I
SE-RCR	Boeing 737-33A	1595/24026	ex F-GHVM	on order	Lsd fr AWAS
SE-RCS	Boeing 737-3Q8	1598/24299	ex N299NY		Lsd fr

GOLDEN AIR

Golden (DC/GAO) — *Trollhattan (THN)*

SE-ISD	SAAB SF.340A	145	ex ZK-FXQ	
SE-ISE	SAAB SF.340A	156	ex YL-BAP	
SE-ISG	SAAB SF.340B	162	ex SE-F62	Lsd fr Handelsbanken Finans
SE-KTE	SAAB SF.340B	230	ex XA-TQY	
SE-KTK	SAAB SF.340B	276	ex F-GHVT	
SE-LEP	SAAB SF.340A	127	ex B-12200	Lsd fr ABB New Finance
SE-LES	SAAB SF.340A	129	ex B-12299	Lsd fr ABB New Finance
SE-LHO	SAAB SF.340B	364	ex B-12265	Lsd fr ABB New Finance
SE-LMR	SAAB SF.340A	141	ex OK-UFO	Lsd fr ABB New Finance
SE-LSR	SAAB SF.340A	078	ex N407BH	
SE-LOG	SAAB 2000	031	ex HB-IZP	Lsd fr Swedish A/c Holdings
SE-LOM	SAAB 2000	035	ex HB-IZS	Lsd fr Swedish A/c Holdings
SE-LOX	SAAB 2000	009	ex SE-009	Lsd fr Swedish A/c Holdings; Sublsd to EZE

GRAFAIR believed to have ceased operations

HELIKOPTERSERVICE EURO AIR ceased operations

INTERNATIONAL BUSINESS AIR

Interbiz (U5/IBZ) — *Stockholm-Bromma (BMA)*

SE-LEF	Swearingen SA.227AC Metro III	AC-451B	ex VH-NEM	Lsd fr Killarney Management
SE-LIL	Swearingen SA.227AC Metro III	AC-432B	ex F-GLPE	Lsd fr Killarney Management
SE-LKC	Embraer EMB.120ER Brasilia	120046	ex N273UE	Lsd fr CRI Intl

JONAIR

Umea (UME)

| SE-GLE | Piper PA-31 Turbo Navajo C | 31-7512056 | |

LID AIR

(LIQ) — *Stockholm-Bromma (BMA)*

SE-GVI	Piper PA-32R-300 Lance II	32R-7885129		Lsd fr Lidingö Bilcenter
SE-ILY	Piper PA-31-350 Navajo Chieftain	31-7852051	ex G-FTTA	Lsd fr Lidingö Bilcenter
SE-IZT	Piper PA-32R-300 Lance	32R-7780538	ex N701JB	Lsd fr Lidingö Bilcenter
SE-KFR	Piper PA-34-220T Seneca II	34-7870170	ex N9224C	

To operate taxiflight operations under the name of Flygcentrum i Stockholm AB. Three other Navajos on order

MALMÖ AIR TAXI

Logic (LOD) — *Malmö-Sturup (MMX)*

SE-GIN	Piper PA-31 Turbo Navajo C	31-7512039	
SE-IDR	Piper PA-31 Turbo Navajo	31-7712085	ex LN-DAB
SE-IKV	Piper PA-31-350 Navajo Chieftain	31-7405148	ex G-BDFN
SE-KTF	Piper PA-31-350 Navajo Chieftain	31-7852119	ex LN-TSC

MALMÖ AVIATION

Scanwing (TF/SCW)   *Stockholm-Arlanda/Malmö-Sturup (ARN/MMX)*

SE-DRA	British Aerospace 146 Srs 200	E2115	ex G-BRXT	Lsd fr BAES
SE-DRD	British Aerospace 146 Srs 200	E2094	ex G-CSJH	Lsd fr AB Dendera
SE-DRM	British Aerospace 146 Srs.200	E2196	ex OO-DJJ	Lsd fr DAT; sublsd to SKX
SE-DSO	Avro RJ100	E3221	ex N504MM	Lsd fr SCL Juno Co
SE-DSP	Avro RJ100	E3242	ex N505MM	Lsd fr JL Sunflower
SE-DSR	Avro RJ100	E3244	ex N506MM	Lsd fr Air Iris Co
SE-DSS	Avro RJ100	E3245	ex N507MM	Lsd fr SCL Cosmos Co
SE-DST	Avro RJ100	E3247	ex N508MM	Lsd fr SCL Lilac Co
SE-DSU	Avro RJ100	E3248	ex N509MM	Lsd fr JL Brighton Co
SE-DSV	Avro RJ100	E3250	ex N510MM	Lsd fr Air Cosmos Co
SE-DSX	Avro RJ100	E3255	ex N511MM	Lsd fr SCL Crystal
SE-DSY	Avro RJ100	E3263	ex N512MM	Lsd fr Trident Jet

Wholly owned by Braathens but for sale.
Early/late services from Bromma to Gothenburg and Malmo operated under brand name Snålskjutsen

NORDFLYG

Nordex (NEF)   *Eskilstuna (EKT)*

SE-GBO	Piper PA-31 Turbo Navajo	31-7400983		
SE-KYH	Cessna 208B Caravan I	208B0817	ex N5262W	Lsd fr ABB Credit, op for NTDC
SE-KYI	Cessna 208B Caravan I	208B0629	ex N52639	Lsd fr /op for NTDC
SE-LPZ	Cessna 208B Caravan I	208B0561	ex N919C	Lsd fr AB New Finance; Op for November Avn
SE-LSK	Cessna 208B Caravan I	208B1012	ex N5236L	Lsd fr Elcon Finans AS Norge

NORDIC AIRLINK

Nordic (LF/NDC)   *Umeå (UME)*

HB-INR	McDonnell-Douglas MD-82	1181/49277		Lsd fr Germania
SE-DMT	McDonnell-Douglas MD-81	944/48003	ex N312TT	Lsd fr Lugano-Plus Corp
SE-RBE	McDonnell-Douglas MD-82	1089/49152	ex OH-LMP	Lsd fr Lakera Assets
SE-RDL*	McDonnell-Douglas MD-83	1740/53014	ex TF-MDC	Lsd fr debis
SE-RDM	McDonnell-Douglas MD-83	1429/49662	ex N766BC	Lsd fr Boeing Capital
SE-RDR	McDonnell-Douglas MD-82	1088/49151	ex N619DB	Lsd fr Farnell Assets
SE-RDS	McDonnell-Douglas MD-83	1357/49401	ex OH-LPE	Lsd fr WFBN
SE-RDT	McDonnell-Douglas MD-82	1183/49278	ex OE-LMA	Lsd fr Boeing Capital
SE-RDU	McDonnell-Douglas MD-82	1252/49372	ex OE-LMC	Lsd fr Boeing Capital

*Operated on behalf of tour operator Aviajet

SE-LMX	SAAB SF.340A	056	ex 9N-AHK	Lsd fr Viking Leasing

Nordic Regional is a wholly owned subsidiary operating Swedish domestic services

NORDIC REGIONAL

Umeå (UME)

Wholly owned subsidiary of Nordic Airlink, operates Swedish dosmestic services

NORDKALOTTFLYG

Nordflight (8N/NKF)   *Lulea (LLA)*

SE-GBG	Piper PA-31 Turbo Navajo	31-7401234	
SE-KCY	Piper PA-31-350 Navajo Chieftain	31-7752061	ex OY-OLE
SE-KEC	Piper PA-31-350 Navajo Chieftain	31-7952098	ex LN-FAM

NORRLANDSFLYG

Lifeguard Sweden   *Gallivare/Kiruna*

SE-JEZ	Sikorsky S-76A	760215	ex N72WW	EMS	
SE-JUC	Sikorsky S-76A	760219	ex N18KH	EMS	Lsd fr ABB New Finance
SE-JUJ	Sikorsky S-76C	760424	ex N523KH	EMS	
SE-JUS	Sikorsky S-76A	760288	ex PT-YBG	EMS	Lsd fr ABB New Finance
SE-JUY	Sikorsky S-76C	760407	ex N154AE	EMS	Lsd fr SEB Finans
SE-JUZ	Sikorsky S-76A	760282	ex N92RR	EMS	Lsd fr GE Capital Eq Finance
SE-HGZ	Sikorsky S-55T	551252	ex N62540		
SE-HLS	Aerospatiale SA.360C Dauphin	1016	ex F-BZAQ		
SE-JFK	Aerospatiale AS.350B1 Ecureuil	1983	ex F-GPAT		
SE-JUR	Aerospatiale AS.350B3 Ecureuil	3426			Lsd fr ABB New Finance

NOVAIR

Navigator (1I/NVR)   *Stockholm-Arlanda (ARN)*

SE-DVO	Boeing 737-85F	166/28822	ex N1780B		Lsd fr GATX
SE-DVR	Boeing 737-85F	238/28826	ex N1787B		Lsd fr GATX
SE-DVU	Boeing 737-85F	188/28825	ex N501GX		Lsd fr GATX
SE-RBF	Airbus Industrie A330-223	353	ex F-WWYN		Lsd fr CLJ Avenue Ltd
SE-RBG	Airbus Industrie A330-223	362	ex F-WWKD		Lsd fr CLJ Avenue Ltd
SE-	Airbus Industrie A321-231	2211	ex D-AV	on order Apr04	Lsd fr ILFC
SE-	Airbus Industrie A321-231	2216	ex D-AV	on order May04	Lsd fr ILFC

ÖREBRO AVIATION

Bluelight (BUE)   *Örebro-Bofors (ORB)*

SE-FNE	Piper PA-31-350 Navajo Chieftain	31-7405434	ex N54306
SE-GIT	Piper PA-31 Turbo Navajo	31-7512041	

SCANDINAVIAN AIRLINES SYSTEM

Scandinavian (SK/SAS) (IATA 117)   *Copenhagen-Kastrup/Oslo/Stockholm-Arlanda (CPH/OSL/ARN)*

LN-RKI	Airbus Industrie A321-232	1817	ex D-AVZK	Gunnhild Viking	Lsd fr Rurik Ltd
OY-KBB	Airbus Industrie A321-232	1642	ex D-AVZN	Hjörulf Viking	Lsd fr Rurik Ltd
OY-KBE	Airbus Industrie A321-232	1798	ex D-AVZG	Emma Viking	Lsd fr Rurik Ltd
OY-KBF	Airbus Industrie A321-232	1807	ex D-AVZH	Skapti Viking	Lsd fr Rurik Ltd
OY-KBH	Airbus Industrie A321-232	1675	ex D-AVZV	Sulke Viking	Lsd fr Rurik Ltd
OY-KBK	Airbus Industrie A321-232	1587	ex D-AVZK	Arne Viking	Lsd fr Rurik Ltd
OY-KBL	Airbus Industrie A321-232	1619	ex D-AVZB	Gunnbjörn Viking	Lsd fr Rurik Ltd
SE-REG	Airbus Industrie A321-232	1848	ex D-AVZU	Svipdag Viking	Lsd fr Rurik Ltd

Four more are on order, to be registered LN-RKK/RKL, SE-REH/REL, but deferred to 2006/7

LN-RKH	Airbus Industrie A330-343X	497	ex F-WWYP	Emund Viking	Lsd fr USK Grouper
OY-KBN	Airbus Industrie A330-343X	496	ex F-WWKK	Eystein Viking	Lsd fr Rurik Ltd
OY-KBS	Airbus Industrie A330-343X			Erik Viking	on order 04
SE-REE	Airbus Industrie A330-343X	515	ex F-WWYY	Sigrid Viking	Lsd fr Rurik Ltd
SE-REF	Airbus Industrie A330-343X	568	ex F-WWYS	on order	Star Alliance c/s

LN-RKF	Airbus Industrie A340-313X	413	ex SE-REA	Godfred Viking	Lsd fr SG Five Kumiai
LN-RKG	Airbus Industrie A340-313X	424	ex SE-REB	Gudrod Viking	Lsd fr Blueberry Ltd
OY-KBA	Airbus Industrie A340-313X	435	ex F-WWJU	Adalstein Viking	Lsd fr Rurik Ltd
OY-KBC	Airbus Industrie A340-313X	467	ex F-WWJE	Freydis Viking	Lsd fr Rurik Ltd
OY-KBD	Airbus Industrie A340-313X	470	ex F-WWJF	Toste Viking	Lsd fr Rurik Ltd
OY-KBI	Airbus Industrie A340-313X	430	ex F-WWJR	Rurik Viking	Lsd fr Rurik Ltd
OY-KBM	Airbus Industrie A340-313X	450	ex F-WWJD	Astrid Viking	Lsd fr Rurik Ltd

LN-RCN+	Boeing 737-883	529/28318	ex SE-DTK	Hedrun Viking	
LN-RCS+	Boeing 737-883	587/30193	ex SE-DTY	Thorgrim Viking	For CCH 04
LN-RCT*	Boeing 737-683	303/30189	ex OY-KKF	Fridlev Viking	Lsd fr FL Arrow Lsg
LN-RCU*	Boeing 737-683	335/30190	ex SE-DNZ	Sigfrid Viking	Lsd fr LG Olive Lsg
LN-RCW*	Boeing 737-683	333/28308	ex SE-DNY	Yngvar Viking	Lsd fr FG Unity
LN-RCX*"	Boeing 737-683	733/30196	ex SE-DYH	Höttur Viking	Lsd fr SBL Coral
LN-RCY*	Boeing 737-883	767/28324	ex SE-DTT	Eylime Viking	Lsd fr TLC Gentia Co
LN-RCZ+	Boeing 737-883	798/30197	ex SE-DTS	Glitne Viking	Lsd fr SB Starlight
LN-RPA*	Boeing 737-683	100/28290	ex N5002K	Arnljot Viking	Lsd fr Glenhagen
LN-RPB*	Boeing 737-683	137/28294	ex N1787B	Bure Viking	Lsd fr Glenhagen
LN-RPD+^	Boeing 737-683	625/28323	ex SE-DYA	Gyrd Viking	
LN-RPF*	Boeing 737-683	330/28307	ex N1784B	Frede Viking	Lsd fr SBL Chisima
LN-RPG*	Boeing 737-683	255/28310	ex N1787B	Geirmund Viking	Lsd fr Pembroke
LN-RPH*	Boeing 737-683	375/28605		Hamder Viking	Lsd fr Alcyone
LN-RPJ+	Boeing 737-783	486/30192	ex (SE-DTK)	Grimhild Viking	
LN-RPK+	Boeing 737-783	500/28317	ex (SE-DTL)	Heimer Viking	Lsd fr SBL Delta Co
LN-RPL+	Boeing 737-683	673/30469	ex (SE-DYC)	Svanevit Viking	
LN-RPM*	Boeing 737-883	696/30195	ex (SE-DYD)	Frigg Viking	Lsd fr SBL Lambda
LN-RPN*"	Boeing 737-883	717/30470	ex (SE-DYD)	Bergfora Viking	Lsd fr SBL Kappa
LN-RPO+^	Boeing 737-883	634/30467	ex SE-DTN	Thorleif Viking	
LN-RPP+^	Boeing 737-883	666/30194	ex SE-DTO	Gerda Viking	
LN-RPS+	Boeing 737-683	191/28298	ex OY-KKC	Gautrek Viking	Lsd fr NBB Namsos
LN-RPT+	Boeing 737-683	193/28299	ex OY-KKD	Ellida Viking	Lsd fr NBB Molde
LN-RPU*	Boeing 737-683	407/28312	ex OY-KKP	Ragna Viking	Lsd fr SBL Atlantic
LN-RPW*	Boeing 737-683	92/28289	ex OY-KKA	Alvid Viking	Lsd fr Glenhagen
LN-RPX*	Boeing 737-683	112/28291	ex SE-DNN	Nanna Viking	Lsd fr Glenhagen
LN-RPY*	Boeing 737-683	116/28292	ex SE-DNO	Olof Viking	Lsd fr Odda Co
LN-RPZ*	Boeing 737-683	120/28293	ex OY-KKB	Bera Viking	Lsd fr Glenhagen
LN-RRM*	Boeing 737-783	458/28314	ex SE-DTI	Erland Viking	Lsd fr RBS Avn
LN-RRN+	Boeing 737-783	404/30191	ex SE-DTG	Solveig Viking	Lsd fr SMBCL H Lse
LN-RRO*	Boeing 737-683	49/28288	ex SE-DNM	Bernt Viking	
LN-RRP*	Boeing 737-683	382/28311	ex SE-DTU	Vilborg Viking	
LN-RRR*	Boeing 737-683	368/28309	ex SE-DTF	Torbjörn Viking	
LN-RRS+	Boeing 737-883	1014/28325	ex (SE-DYM)	Ymer Viking	

LN-RRT+	Boeing 737-883	1036/28326	ex (SE-DYN)	Lodyn Viking	
LN-RRU+	Boeing 737-883	1070/28327	ex (SE-DYP)	Vingolf Viking	
LN-RRX*	Boeing 737-683	21/28296	ex SE-DNR	Ragnfast Viking Lsd fr Honest Kumiai	
LN-RRY*	Boeing 737-683	30/28297	ex SE-DNS	Signe Viking	Lsd fr FL Titan Lsg
LN-RRZ*	Boeing 737-683	149/28295	ex SE-DNP	Gisla Viking	Lsd fr FL Uranus Lsg
OY-KKE+>	Boeing 737-683	290/28305	ex N1787B	Elisabeth Viking	
OY-KKG+	Boeing 737-683	209/28300	ex (LN-RPC)	Sindre Viking	
OY-KKH+	Boeing 737-683	227/28301	ex N1795B	Embla Viking	
OY-KKI+	Boeing 737-783	464/28315	ex N1796B	Borgny Viking Lsd fr Strakur Europe	
OY-KKR+	Boeing 737-783	476/28316		Gjuke Viking	
OY-KKS+	Boeing 737-683	614/28322	ex LN-RPC	Ramveig Viking	
OY-KKT+^	Boeing 737-883	668/30468	ex LN-RPR	Ore Viking	
OY-KKY*>	Boeing 737-683	329/28306	ex LN-RPE	Edla Viking	
SE-DNT+	Boeing 737-683	243/28302		Snefrid Viking	
SE-DNU+	Boeing 737-683	257/28303		Unn Viking	
SE-DNX+>	Boeing 737-683	270/28304	ex N1787B	Torvald Viking	
SE-DTH*	Boeing 737-683	447/28313	ex (OY-KKI)	Vile Viking	
SE-DTR	Boeing 737-883	32277		Saga Viking	on order
SE-DYC	Boeing 737-883	32276		Cecilia Viking	on order
SE-DYD	Boeing 737-883	30471	ex (SE-DTR)	Dag Viking	on order
SE-DYG+	Boeing 737-883	1169/32278		Gerud Viking	
SE-DYT	Boeing 737-883	1424/28328	ex (SE-DYD)	Jarlabanke Viking; Star Alliance c/s	

*Means Euro version and + means domestic version with regards to seating configuration.
^Leased to Air One　　　　　　　　　　　"Operated by Snowflake
>Leased to Air Europa

LN-RCD	Boeing 767-383ER	315/24847			Lsd fr BBAM; sublsd to HLN
LN-RCF	Boeing 767-383ER	330/24849	ex OY-KDO	stored	AAR Financial Svs
LN-RCH+	Boeing 767-383ER	257/24318	ex SE-DKO	stored	
LN-RCM	Boeing 767-383ER	412/26544	ex SE-DOC	stored	Lsd fr Nordea Finans
OY-KDL	Boeing 767-383ER	337/24477	ex (SE-KDR)	stored	Lsd to HLN
OY-KDN	Boeing 767-383ER	325/24848	ex (LN-RLY)		Lsd fr BBAM; sublsd to HLN

+Leased from SAC-24318 Ltd; last service 30 November 2003

LN-RLE^	McDonnell-Douglas MD-82	1232/49382		Kettil Viking
LN-RLF^	McDonnell-Douglas MD-82	1236/49383	ex VH-LNJ	Finn Viking
LN-RLR^	McDonnell-Douglas MD-82	1345/49437	ex VH-LNL	Vegard Viking
LN-RMA	McDonnell-Douglas MD-82	1379/49554		Hasting Viking
LN-RMD	McDonnell-Douglas MD-82	1402/49555	ex (OY-KHD)	Fenge Viking
LN-RMG	McDonnell-Douglas MD-87	1522/49611		Snorre Viking
LN-RMH^	McDonnell-Douglas MD-87	1827/49612	ex N6203U	Solmund Viking
LN-RMK^	McDonnell-Douglas MD-87	1705/49610		Ragnhild Viking
LN-RML	McDonnell-Douglas MD-82	1835/53002		Aud Viking
LN-RMM	McDonnell-Douglas MD-82	1855/53005		Blenda Viking　　Lsd fr Fornebu A/c
LN-RMN	McDonnell-Douglas MD-82	1922/53295		Ivar Viking; std DNR
LN-RMO	McDonnell-Douglas MD-81	1947/53315		Bergljot Viking
LN-RMP	McDonnell-Douglas MD-87	1962/53337		Reidun Viking
LN-RMR^	McDonnell-Douglas MD-81	1998/53365		Olav Viking
LN-RMS^	McDonnell-Douglas MD-81	2003/53368		Nial Viking
LN-RMT^	McDonnell-Douglas MD-81	1815/53001	ex OY-KHS	Jarl Viking
LN-RMU	McDonnell-Douglas MD-87	1967/53340	ex SE-DMC	Grim Viking
LN-ROM^	McDonnell-Douglas MD-81	1895/53008	ex SE-DIY	Albin Viking
LN-RON^	McDonnell-Douglas MD-81	1979/53347	ex SE-DMD	Holmfrid Viking
LN-ROO^	McDonnell-Douglas MD-81	1999/53366	ex SE-DME	Kristin Viking
LN-ROP^	McDonnell-Douglas MD-82	1237/49384	ex SE-DFS	Bjorn Viking
LN-ROR^	McDonnell-Douglas MD-82	1244/49385	ex SE-DFT	Assur Viking
LN-ROS^	McDonnell-Douglas MD-82	1263/49421	ex SE-DFU	Isulv Viking
LN-ROT^	McDonnell-Douglas MD-82	1264/49422	ex SE-DFR	Ingjald Viking
LN-ROU^	McDonnell-Douglas MD-82	1284/49424	ex SE-DFX	Ring Viking
LN-ROW^	McDonnell-Douglas MD-82	1353/49438	ex SE-DFY	Ottar Viking
LN-ROX^	McDonnell-Douglas MD-82	1442/49603	ex SE-DIA	Ulvrik Viking
LN-ROY^	McDonnell-Douglas MD-82	1543/49615	ex SE-DID	Spjute Viking
LN-ROZ^	McDonnell-Douglas MD-87	1572/49608	ex SE-DIH	Slagfinn Viking
OY-KGT^	McDonnell-Douglas MD-82	1225/49380	ex N845RA	Hake Viking
OY-KGY^	McDonnell-Douglas MD-81	1254/49420		Rollo Viking
OY-KGZ^	McDonnell-Douglas MD-81	1231/49381		Hagbard Viking
OY-KHC^	McDonnell-Douglas MD-82	1303/49436		Faste Viking
OY-KHE^	McDonnell-Douglas MD-82	1456/49604	ex N842RA	Saxo Viking
OY-KHF	McDonnell-Douglas MD-87	1517/49609		Ragnar Viking
OY-KHG^	McDonnell-Douglas MD-82	1519/49613		Alle Viking
OY-KHI^	McDonnell-Douglas MD-87	1556/49614		Torkel Viking
OY-KHK	McDonnell-Douglas MD-82	1638/49910		Roald Viking
OY-KHM	McDonnell-Douglas MD-82	1693/49914		Mette Viking
OY-KHN^	McDonnell-Douglas MD-81	1812/53000		Dan Viking
OY-KHP	McDonnell-Douglas MD-81	1882/53007		Arild Viking
OY-KHR^	McDonnell-Douglas MD-81	1896/53275		Torkild Viking
OY-KHT	McDonnell-Douglas MD-82	1937/53296		Gorm Viking
OY-KHU	McDonnell-Douglas MD-87	1953/53336		Ravn Viking
OY-KHW^	McDonnell-Douglas MD-87	1985/53348		Ingemund Viking
SE-DIB	McDonnell-Douglas MD-87	1501/49605	ex N19B	Varin Viking
SE-DIC	McDonnell-Douglas MD-87	1512/49607		Grane Viking
SE-DIF	McDonnell-Douglas MD-87	1569/49606		Hjorulv Viking

SE-DII	McDonnell-Douglas MD-82	1625/49909		Sigtrygg Viking	
SE-DIK	McDonnell-Douglas MD-82	1553/49728	ex (SE-DIE)	Stenkil Viking	
SE-DIL	McDonnell-Douglas MD-82	1665/49913		Tord Viking	
SE-DIN	McDonnell-Douglas MD-82	1803/49999		Eskil Viking	
SE-DIP	McDonnell-Douglas MD-87	1921/53010	ex N6202D	Margret Viking	
SE-DIR	McDonnell-Douglas MD-81	1846/53004		Nora Viking	
SE-DIS	McDonnell-Douglas MD-81	1869/53006		Sigmund Viking	
SE-DIU	McDonnell-Douglas MD-87	1931/53011		Torsten Viking	
SE-DIZ	McDonnell-Douglas MD-82	1917/53294		Sigyn Viking	
SE-DMB	McDonnell-Douglas MD-81	1946/53314		Bjarne Viking; stored Riga	

^Leased from Commercial Aviation Leasing

LN-ROA	McDonnell-Douglas MD-90-30	2141/53459		Sigurd Viking	Lsd fr SCL Sierra
LN-ROB	McDonnell-Douglas MD-90-30	2149/53462		Isrid Viking	Lsd fr Baltic Aircraft
OY-KIL	McDonnell-Douglas MD-90-30	2140/53458		Kaare Viking	Lsd fr JL Horizon Lse
OY-KIM	McDonnell-Douglas MD-90-30	2142/53460		Jon Viking	Lsd fr SBL Chisima Co
OY-KIN	McDonnell-Douglas MD-90-30	2197/53544		Tormod Viking	
SE-DMF	McDonnell-Douglas MD-90-30	2138/53457		Heidrek Viking	Lsd fr JL Venus Lse
SE-DMG	McDonnell-Douglas MD-90-30	2147/53461		Hervor Viking	Lsd fr JL Bellona Lse
SE-DMH	McDonnell-Douglas MD-90-30	2194/53543		Torolf Viking	

LN-RDA	de Havilland DHC-8-402Q	4013	ex C-GDFT	Frej Viking	Lsd fr SG Three Kumiai
LN-RDB	de Havilland DHC-8-402Q	4018	ex C-FDHU	Kari Viking	Lsd fr SG Four Kumiai
LN-RDC	de Havilland DHC-8-402Q	4019	ex C-FDHW	Hader Viking	Lsd fr TLC Bellflower
LN-RDD	de Havilland DHC-8-402Q	4009	ex C-GFQL	Loge Viking	Lsd fr Aviator
LN-RDE	de Havilland DHC-8-402Q	4020	ex C-FDHX	Dore Viking	Lsd fr TLC Hope
LN-RDF	de Havilland DHC-8-402Q	4021	ex C-FDHZ	Fenja Viking	Lsd fr USK Kumiai
LN-RDG	de Havilland DHC-8-402Q	4022	ex C-FGNP	Greip Viking	Lsd fr USK Sillago
LN-RDH	de Havilland DHC-8-402Q	4023	ex C-FNGB	Gloe Viking	Lsd fr USK Sailfin
LN-RDI	de Havilland DHC-8-402Q	4024	ex C-GERL	Asta Viking	Lsd fr USK Grampus
LN-RDJ	de Havilland DHC-8-402Q	4010	ex N480DC	Toke Viking	Lsd fr SL Pinnacle Ltd
LN-RDK	de Havilland DHC-8-402Q	4025	ex C-GETI	Ingrid Viking	
LN-RDL	de Havilland DHC-8-402Q	4011	ex C-FDHY	Ulv Viking	Lsd fr USK Herring
LN-RDM	de Havilland DHC-8-402Q	4033	ex N481DC	Banke Viking	Lsd fr USK Albacore
LN-RDO	de Havilland DHC-8-402Q	4036	ex C-FDHD	Frid Viking	Lsd fr Aviator
LN-RDP	de Havilland DHC-8-402Q	4012	ex OY-KCA	Huge Viking	Lsd fr SG One Kumiai
LN-RDQ	de Havilland DHC-8-402Q	4008	ex OY-KCB	Herta Viking	Lsd fr SG Two Kumiai
LN-RDR	de Havilland DHC-8-402Q	4034	ex N482DC	Terje Viking	Lsd fr USK Haibut
LN-RDS	de Havilland DHC-8-402Q	4035	ex C-GHRI	Göte Viking	Lsd fr Aviator
LN-RDT	de Havilland DHC-8-402Q	4038	ex N382BC	Kile Viking	Lsd fr USK Trevally
OY-KCD	de Havilland DHC-8-402Q	4054	ex C-GFRP	Bjarrke Viking	
OY-KCE	de Havilland DHC-8-402Q	4057	ex C-GHRI	Alf Viking	
OY-KCF	de Havilland DHC-8-402Q	4062	ex C-GDNG	Åsa Viking	
OY-KCG	de Havilland DHC-8-402Q	4063	ex C-GDSG	Sote Viking	
OY-KCH	de Havilland DHC-8-402Q	4064	ex C-GELZ	Igle Viking	

LN-RNC	Fokker 50	20176	ex PH-EXY	Eivind Viking	
LN-RND	Fokker 50	20178	ex PH-EXZ	Inge Viking	
LN-RNE	Fokker 50	20179	ex PH-EXE	Ebbe Viking	
LN-RNF	Fokker 50	20183	ex PH-EXI	Leif Viking	
LN-RNG	Fokker 50	20184	ex PH-EXJ	Gudrid Viking	
OY-KAE	Fokker 50	20162	ex PH-EXE	Hans Viking	Lsd to BTI as YL-BAS
OY-KAF	Fokker 50	20163	ex PH-EXF	Sigvat Viking	Lsd to BTI as YL-BAT

DHC-8-402s and Fokker 50s are operated by subsidiary SAS Commuter as SAS Commuter Eurolink (based CPH), SAS Commuter Norlink (based in Western Norway) and SAS Commuter Swelink (based ARN).
Owns 94.9% of Spanair; 49% of Estonian Air, 26% of Cimber Air and 96.4% of Wideroe's while Blue1 and Braathens are wholly owned. Snowflake is a wholly owned low-cost subsidiary
Founder member of Star Alliance with Air Canada, Lufthansa, Thai Intl, United and VARIG

SCANDINAVIAN LITE renamed Snowflake before commencing operations

SKYWAYS EXPRESS

Sky Express (JZ/SKX) (IATA 752)　　　　　　　　　　　　**Jönköping /Linköping (JKG/LPI)**

SE-KTC	Fokker 50	20124	ex OY-MMG	
SE-KTD	Fokker 50	20125	ex OY-MMH	
SE-LEA	Fokker 50	20116	ex PH-GHK	Lsd fr Aerocentury
SE-LEB	Fokker 50	20120	ex PH-JHD	Lsd fr SEB Finans AB
SE-LEC	Fokker 50	20112	ex VH-FNG	Lsd fr Ansett Avn
SE-LED	Fokker 50	20111	ex VH-FNF	Lsd fr Ansett Avn
SE-LEH	Fokker 50	20108	ex VH-FNC	Lsd fr Ansett Avn
SE-LEL	Fokker 50	20110	ex VH-FNE	Lsd fr Ansett Avn
SE-LEU	Fokker 50	20115	ex 9M-MGZ	Lsd fr Aerocentury
SE-LEZ	Fokker 50	20128	ex PH-PRA	Lsd fr Aircraft Finance & Trading
SE-LIN	Fokker 50	20138	ex PH-PRB	Lsd fr Aircraft Finance & Trading
SE-LIO	Fokker 50	20146	ex PH-PRC	Lsd fr Aircraft Finance & Trading
SE-LIP	Fokker 50	20147	ex PH-PRD	Lsd fr Aircraft Finance & Trading
SE-LIR	Fokker 50	20151	ex PH-PRE	Lsd fr Aircraft Finance & Trading
SE-LIS	Fokker 50	20152	ex PH-PRF	Lsd fr Aircraft Finance & Trading
SE-LIT	Fokker 50	20194	ex PH-ZDF	Lsd fr Aircraft Finance & Trading

SE-	Fokker 50	20155	ex PH-PRG		Lsd fr Aircraft Finance & Trading
SE-ISL	SAAB SF.340A/QC	130	ex LN-SAA		
SE-ISP	SAAB SF.340A	015	ex SE-E15		Lsd fr ABB New Finance
SE-ISR	SAAB SF.340A	017	ex SE-E17		Lsd fr ABB New Finance
SE-ISV	SAAB SF.340A	045	ex SE-E45		Lsd fr ABB New Finance
SE-ISY	SAAB SF.340A	080	ex SE-E80		Lsd fr ABB New Finance
SE-KCR	SAAB SF.340A/QC	065	ex OH-FAA		
SE-KCS	SAAB SF.340A/QC	066	ex OH-FAB		
SE-KCT	SAAB SF.340A/QC	070	ex OH-FAC		Lsd to SRL
SE-KCU	SAAB SF.340A	135	ex OH-FAD		
SE-KPD	SAAB SF.340A	037	ex PH-KJL		Lsd fr ABB New Finance
SE-KRN	SAAB SF.340A	159	ex D-CHBC		Lsd to NZA
SE-KUT	SAAB SF.340A	087	ex LN-NNF		Lsd fr Commuter Invest; Sublsd to Iberline
SE-DRM	British Aerospace 146 Srs.200	E2196	ex OO-DJJ		Lsd fr SCW
SE-DZA	Embraer EMB.145EP	145070	ex PT-SAO		Lsd fr Corporate A/c Lsg
SE-DZB	Embraer EMB.145EP	145113			Lsd fr Corporate A/c Lsg
SE-DZC	Embraer EMB.145EP	145169			Lsd to EZE
SE-DZD	Embraer EMB.145EP	145185			

Member of Skyways Holding AB

SNOWFLAKE

Stockholm-Arlanda (ARN)

Previously listed as Scandinavian Lite but renamed before operations commenced

LN-RCX	Boeing 737-883	733/30196	ex SE-DYH	Höttur Viking	Lsd fr SBL Coral
LN-RPN	Boeing 737-883	717/30470	ex (SE-DYG)	Bergfora Viking	Lsd fr SBL Kappa

Low cost subsidiary of SAS-Scandinavian Airlines System. First service 30 March 2003

SVENSKA DIREKTFLYG

Skyreg (HS/HSV)   *Hultsfred (HLF)*

SE-LHB	British Aerospace Jetstream 32	844	ex N844JX	Lsd fr BAES
SE-LHC	British Aerospace Jetstream 32	846	ex N846JX	Lsd fr BAES
SE-LHE	British Aerospace Jetstream 32	854	ex N854JX	Lsd fr BAES
SE-LHF	British Aerospace Jetstream 32	855	ex N855JX	Lsd fr BAES
SE-LHG	British Aerospace Jetstream 32EP	857	ex N857JX	Lsd fr BAES
SE-LHH	British Aerospace Jetstream 32EP	848	ex N848JX	Lsd fr BAES
SE-LHI	British Aerospace Jetstream 32EP	841	ex N841JX	Lsd fr BAES
SE-LHK	British Aerospace Jetstream 32EP	864	ex N864AE	Lsd fr BAES

SWEDLINE EXPRESS

Starline (SM/SRL)   *Hultsfred (HLF)*

SE-KCS	SAAB SF.340A/QC	066	ex OH-FAB	Lsd fr SKX
SE-KCT	SAAB SF.340A/QC	070	ex OH-FAC	Lsd fr SKX
SE-KCV	SAAB SF.340B	310	ex SE-C10	Lsd fr Svenska Volkswagen
SE-LGS	SAAB SF.340A	071	ex LN-NVF	Lsd fr Nordea Finans
SE-LSP	SAAB SF.340A	126	ex G-GNTG	Lsd fr Nordea Finans
SE-LCX	Beech 1900D	UE-275	ex N11189	Lsd fr Nordsea Finans Sverige
SE-LTU	SAAB 2000	062	ex HB-IYG	Lsd fr Kalidas
SE-LTV	SAAB 2000	063	ex HB-IYH	Lsd fr SAAB

SWEFLY

Sveaflyg (WV/SVB)   *Nyköping (NYO)*

Previously listed as WestEast Air

SE-IAC	Piper PA-31 Turbo Navajo C	31-7812095		Lsd fr Swefly AB; based KSK
SE-LFO	Fokker 50	20198	ex PH-ZDH	

VIKING AIRLINES

(VIK)

SE-RDE	McDonnell-Douglas MD-83	1687/49857	ex HB-IUO	Lsd fr GECAS
SE-RDF	McDonnell-Douglas MD-83	1559/49769	ex HB-IUN	Lsd fr GECAS

First service May 2003

WALTAIR

Norrköping (NRK)

SE-KOL	Beech 300LW Super King Air	FA-189	ex N7241V
SE-LKY	Beech 200C Super King Air	BL-127	ex D2-ESO

WEST AIR SWEDEN

Air Sweden (PT/SWN)   Lidköping (LDK)

SE-LEG	Hawker Siddeley HS.748 Srs.2A/244	1723	ex D-AFSF	L-G P	
SE-LEK	Hawker Siddeley HS.748 Srs.2A/244	1725	ex D-AFSH	Betty Boop	
SE-LEX	Hawker Siddeley HS.748 Srs.2A/244	1727	ex D-AFSJ		
SE-LIA	Hawker Siddeley HS.748 Srs.2A/264	1717	ex F-GFYM	Mademoiselle	based MRS
SE-LIB	Hawker Siddeley HS.748 Srs.2B/371LFD	1776	ex FAC1108		
SE-LIC	Hawker Siddeley HS.748 Srs.2B/399LFD	1778	ex C-FKTL		
SE-LID	Hawker Siddeley HS.748 Srs.2A/333	1760	ex J5-GAT	African Queen	
SE-LIE	Hawker Siddeley HS.748 Srs.2A/229	1595	ex A10-595		
SE-LIF	Hawker Siddeley HS.748 Srs.2A/229	1596	ex A10-596	Number 10	

All leased from ELCON Finans A/S

SE-LGU	British Aerospace ATP	2022	ex N853AW	West Air Europe titles	based MRS
SE-LGV	British Aerospace ATP	2034	ex N857AW		
SE-LGX	British Aerospace ATP	2036	ex N859AW		
SE-LGY	British Aerospace ATP	2035	ex N858AW		
SE-LGZ	British Aerospace ATP(F)	2021	ex N852AW		
SE-LHX	British Aerospace ATP	2020	ex N851AW		
SE-LHZ	British Aerospace ATP	2059	ex G-OBWN	Lsd fr ABB New Finans; based LUX	
SE-LPR	British Aerospace ATP	2057	ex G-OBWL		
SE-LPS	British Aerospace ATP	2043	ex G-BTPM	Lsd fr Trident Avn Lsg	
SE-LPT	British Aerospace ATP	2058	ex G-OBWM	Lsd fr ABB New Finans	
SE-LPU	British Aerospace ATP	2060	ex G-OBWO	based MRS	
SE-	British Aerospace ATP	2041	ex G-BTPJ	undergoing LFD conversion	

All freighters [except SE-LPS/T/U]; only SE-LGZ has a freight door, others use passenger doors
All aircraft leased from European Turboprop Management except SE-LHZ/LPS/T. West Air France is wholly owned

WESTEAST AIR   renamed Swefly late3Q03

SP - POLAND (Republic of Poland)

AEROGRYF

Aerogryf (GRF)   Szczecina (SZZ)

SP-DDA	PZK Mielec M-28 Skytruck	AJE0001-01	ex SP-FYV	
SP-FFN	WSK-PZL/Antonov An-28	1AJ006-08	ex TC-FEB	
SP-FHP	WSK-PZL/Antonov An-28	1AJ008-04	ex RA-28918	
SP-FHS	WSK-PZL/Antonov An-28	1AJ007-10	ex RA-28725	stored SZZ

AIR POLONIA

(APN)   Warsaw-Okecie (WAW)

SP-KPI	Boeing 737-4Q8	3009/28202	ex TC-APP	Lsd fr ILFC
SP-KPK	Boeing 737-4Q8	2653/26306	ex TC-AFA	Lsd fr ILFC
SP-KPY	LET L-410UVP	902439	ex OK-VDF	Freighter
SP-KPS	LET L-410UVP	831138	ex OK-NDG	Freighter
SP-KPZ	LET L-410UVP	902431	ex OK-VDE	Freighter

EUROLOT

Eurolot (K2/ELO)   Warsaw-Okecie (WAW)

SP-EDA	Aerospatiale/Alenia ATR 42-500	516	ex F-GPYG	Lsd fr Brice Bail
SP-EDB	Aerospatiale/Alenia ATR 42-500	522	ex F-GPYH	Lsd fr Brice Bail
SP-EDC	Aerospatiale/Alenia ATR 42-500	526	ex F-GPYI	Lsd fr Brice Bail
SP-EDD	Aerospatiale/Alenia ATR 42-500	530	ex F-GPYJ	Lsd fr Brice Bail
SP-EDE	Aerospatiale/Alenia ATR 42-500	443	ex F-WWEZ	Lsd fr Brice Bail
SP-LFA	Aerospatiale/Alenia ATR 72-202	246	ex F-WWEM	Lsd fr Polska Bail
SP-LFB	Aerospatiale/Alenia ATR 72-202	265	ex F-WWEJ	Lsd fr Polska Bail
SP-LFC	Aerospatiale/Alenia ATR 72-202	272	ex F-WWEN	Lsd fr Polska Bail
SP-LFD	Aerospatiale/Alenia ATR 72-202	279	ex F-WWLD	Lsd fr Polska Bail
SP-LFE	Aerospatiale/Alenia ATR 72-202	328	ex F-WWLJ	Lsd fr Polska Bail
SP-LFF	Aerospatiale/Alenia ATR 72-202	402	ex F-WWLM	Lsd fr Polska Bail
SP-LFG	Aerospatiale/Alenia ATR 72-202	411	ex F-WWEO	Lsd fr Chopin Lease
SP-LFH	Aerospatiale/Alenia ATR 72-202	478	ex F-WWEK	Lsd fr Polska Bail

Eight Embraer EMB.145s to be transferred from parent when it's Embraer 170s are delivered from January 2004
Wholly owned by LOT-Polish Airlines and operates feeder services using LO flight numbers

EXIN

Exin (EXN)   Katowice-Muchoeiec (KTW)

SP-FDO	Antonov An-26	10503	ex RA-26031	
SP-FDP	Antonov An-26	11903	ex RA-26098	DHL colours
SP-FDR	Antonov An-26	11305	ex RA-26067	DHL colours

| SP-FDS | Antonov An-26B | 12102 | ex RA-26110 |
| SP-FDT | Antonov An-26B | 27312205 | ex RA-26116 |

Also operates Ilyushin Il-76s leased from other operators as required

GETJET

Warsaw-Okecie (WAW)

| SP- | Airbus Industrie A320-211 | 0026 | ex SU-PBD | on order | Lsd |

GLOBUS AIRLINES

| SP-KTR | Aerospatiale/Alenia ATR 42-300 | 092 | ex D-BAAA | | Lsd fr ING BSK Lsg |

LOT – POLISH AIRLINES / LOT – POLSKIE LINIE LOTNICZE

LOT (LO/LOT) (IATA 080)

Warsaw-Okecie (WAW)

SP-LKA	Boeing 737-55D	2389/27416			Lsd fr Marta Lsg
SP-LKB	Boeing 737-55D	2392/27417			Lsd fr Marta Lsg
SP-LKC	Boeing 737-55D	2397/27418			Lsd fr Marta Lsg
SP-LKD	Boeing 737-55D	2401/27419			Lsd fr Marta Lsg
SP-LKE	Boeing 737-55D	2448/27130		Star Alliance c/s	Lsd fr Marta Lsg
SP-LKF	Boeing 737-55D	2603/27368			Lsd fr Marta Lsg
SP-LKG	Boeing 737-53C	1894/24825	ex F-GHOL		Lsd fr BNP Lease
SP-LKH	Boeing 737-53C	2041/24826	ex F-GHUL		Lsd fr BNP Lease
SP-LKI	Boeing 737-53C	2243/24827	ex F-GINL		Lsd fr BNP Lease
SP-LKK	Boeing 737-5L9	2998/28996	ex OY-APL		Lsd fr DAN
SP-LLA	Boeing 737-45D	2458/27131			Lsd fr Marta Lsg
SP-LLB	Boeing 737-45D	2492/27156			Lsd fr Marta Lsg; sublsd to AEW
SP-LLC	Boeing 737-45D	2502/27157			Lsd fr Marta Lsg
SP-LLD	Boeing 737-45D	2589/27256			Lsd fr Marta Lsg
SP-LLE	Boeing 737-45D	2804/27914			Lsd fr Marta Lsg
SP-LLF	Boeing 737-45D	2874/28752			Lsd fr WFBN
SP-LMC	Boeing 737-36N	2890/28668			Lsd fr GECAS
SP-LMD	Boeing 737-36N	2897/28669			Lsd fr GECAS

Two Boeing 737-85Ds are on order for delivery in 2005
Four Boeing 737-400s and six 737-500s sold to GECAS and leased back

SP-LOA	Boeing 767-25DER	261/24733	ex N6046P	Gniejeno	Lsd fr Avn Capital
SP-LOB	Boeing 767-25DER	266/24734		Krakow	Lsd fr Avn Capital
SP-LPA	Boeing 767-35DER	322/24865		Warszawa	Lsd fr Boullioun
SP-LPB	Boeing 767-35DER	577/27902		Gdansk	Lsd fr WFBN
SP-LPC	Boeing 767-35DER	659/28656		Poznan	

SP-LGA	Embraer EMB.145EP	145155	ex PT-SEJ	
SP-LGB	Embraer EMB.145EP	145165	ex PT-SEK	
SP-LGC	Embraer EMB.145EP	145227	ex PT-SHM	
SP-LGD	Embraer EMB.145EP	145244	ex PT-SII	
SP-LGE	Embraer EMB.145EP	145285	ex PT-SKC	
SP-LGF	Embraer EMB.145EP	145308	ex PT-SKZ	
SP-LGG	Embraer EMB.145EP	145319	ex PT-SMK	
SP-LGH	Embraer EMB.145EP	145329	ex PT-SMV	
SP-LGI	Embraer EMB.145MP	145336	ex PT-SNC	
SP-LGK	Embraer EMB.145MP	145339	ex PT-SNF	
SP-LGL	Embraer EMB.145MP	145406	ex PT-STD	
SP-LGM	Embraer EMB.145MP	145408	ex PT-STF	
SP-LGN	Embraer EMB.145MP	145441	ex PT-SUM	
SP-LGO	Embraer EMB.145EP	145560	ex PT-S	
SP-LGP	Embraer EMB.145EP			on order 03
SP-LGR	Embraer EMB.145EP			on order 03

SP-LDA	Embraer 170-100ST	170-00023	ex PT-	on order 04
SP-LDB	Embraer 170-100ST	170-00024	ex PT-	on order 04
SP-LDC	Embraer 170-100ST	170-00025	ex PT-	on order 04
SP-	Embraer 170-100ST		ex PT-	on order 04
SP-	Embraer 170-100ST		ex PT-	on order 04
SP-	Embraer 170-100ST		ex PT-	on order 04

Four more Embraer 170s are on order for delivery in 2005 with eight EMB.145s transferring to Eurolot. Four of the Embraer 170s are to be leased from GECAS
Owns Euro-LOT. Joined Star Alliance on 26 October 2003

POLONIA AIRLINES believed to have ceased operations

SILESIAN AIR

Wroclaw-Strachowice (WRO)

| SP-KTL | LET L-410UVP-E16A | 902414 | ex SP-KXB |

To change name to GetJet

WHITE EAGLE GENERAL AVIATION

White Eagle (WEA)   Warsaw-Okecie (WAW)

SP-FTN	LET L-410UVP-E10	902515	ex SP-FGI		
SP-FTV	LET L-410UVP-E	882038	ex SP-TAA		
SP-FTX	LET L-410UVP-E10	892301	ex SP-TAB		
SP-FTY	LET L-410UVP-E10	892317	ex SP-TAC		
SP-KTB	LET L-410UVP-E	902504	ex HA-LAZ	DHL c/s	
SP-FNS	Beech B300 Super King Air	FL-134	ex N3252V		
SP-KCA	Aerospatiale/Alenia ATR 42-300	085	ex F-WQNY	Freighter	Lsd fr ATR Asset Mgt

ST - SUDAN (The Republic of the Sudan)

AVIA TRANS AIR TRANSPORT

(VTT)   Khartoum (KRT)

ST-AVI	Antonov An-26	77305807	ex UR-26007

AZZA AIR TRANSPORT

Azza Transport (AZZ)   Khartoum (KRT)

ST-AKW	Boeing 707-330C	788/20123	ex (P4-AKW)	Lsd fr Ibis Aviation
ST-APS	Ilyushin Il-76TD	1023409316	ex RA-76837	
ST-APV	Antonov An-26	47302303		
ST-AQB	Ilyushin Il-76TD	0053460795	ex EP-ALA	
ST-AQG	Antonov An-12BP	401907	ex RA-11234	
ST-AQY	Ilyushin Il-76TD	0033448404	ex 9L-LCW	
ST-DAS	Antonov An-12	7345209	ex ER-AXC	
ST-JCC	Boeing 707-384C (Comtran 2)	495/18948	ex P4-JCC	Lsd fr Comtran

BEN AIR believed to have ceased operations

BENTIU AIR TRANSPORT

                                                                        Khartoum (KRT)

ST-SRA	Antonov An-26	17311801	ex

COPTRADE AIR TRANSPORT

Coptrade Air (CCW)   Khartoum (KRT)

ST-CAT	LET L-410UVP-E	902527	ex SP-FGM	Lsd fr BRQ
ST-CAU	LET L-410UVP-E	892340	ex RA-67612	Lsd fr BRQ

DATA INTERNATIONAL AVIATION

Data Air (DTN)   Khartoum (KRT)

ST-APJ	Antonov An-12

EAST/WEST EXPRESS

(AXD)   Khartoum (KRT)

ST-AWU	Antonov An-12BP	8345804	ex
ST-AWR	Ilyushin Il-76TD	0033447365	ex RDPL-34138
ST-EWC	Ilyushin Il-76MD	0023438129	ex EX-86919

ELDINDER AVIATION

Dinder (DND)   Khartoum (KRT)

ST-DND	LET L-410UVP-E10A	912528	ex SP-FGH

ELISRA AIRLINES ceased operations

EL MAGAL AVIATION

                                                                        Khartoum (KRT)

ST-HIS	Antonov An-26	07310310	ex UN-26026	
ST-MGC	Tupolev Tu-134			operator not confirmed
ST-MGL	Antonov An-26	9709	ex TC-ACS	
ST-SIG	Antonov An-12BP	1400101	ex UR-48975	

EL WAHA AVIATION ceased operations

FEDERAL AIRLINES believed to have ceased operations, both aircraft were stored

FORMER AIRLINES believed to have ceased operations

KATA TRANSPORTATION COMPANY

Khartoum (KRT)

ST-AZM	Antonov An-12			

MARSLAND AVIATION

Khartoum (KRT)

ST-MRS	Tupolev Tu-134B-3	63333	ex UN-85699	

MID AIRLINES

ST-ARB	Fokker 50	20201	ex PH-PRI	

SARIT AIRLINES

Saria (SRW) — *Khartoum (KRT)*

ST-SAL	Antonov An-26B	17311907	ex RA-26100	
UN-76499	Ilyushin Il-76TD	0023441186	ex RA-76499	Lsd fr BMK

SPIRIT OF AFRICA AIRLINES

Blue Nile (SDN) — *Sharjah (SHJ)*

ST-AQI	Boeing 707-307C	756/19999	ex 5Y-GFF	Lsd fr Sky Avn
ST-AQL	Boeing 747-246B	181/20504	ex 3D-PAJ	Lsd fr Sky Avn
ST-AQN	Boeing 747-246B	166/20333	ex 3D-PAH	Lsd fr Sky Avn
ST-AQW	Boeing 707-336C	854/20517	ex 3D-GFG	Lsd fr Sky Avn
Also wear Blue Nile titles				

SUDAN AIRWAYS

Sudanair (SD/SUD) (IATA 200) — *Khartoum (KRT)*

C5-SMM	Boeing 727-251	665/19973	ex HK-3871X	Lsd fr Mahfooz
EK-47318	Antonov An-24RV	67310505	ex RA-47318	Lsd fr V-Bard Avia
EK-49273	Antonov An-24T	7910405	ex RA-49273	Lsd fr V-Bard Avia
EK-49275	Antonov An-24T	9911102	ex RA-49275	Lsd fr V-Bard Avia
F-ODTK	Airbus Industrie A300B4-622	252	ex F-WZLR	Lsd fr Credit Lyonnais
JY-JAV	Airbus Industrie A310-222	357	ex 3B-STK	Lsd fr JAV
ST-AFA	Boeing 707-3J8C	885/20897	Blue Nile	
ST-AFB	Boeing 707-3J8C	887/20898	Cargo titles	
ST-AIX	Boeing 707-369C	764/20086	ex 9K-ACL	stored KRT
TS-IOE	Boeing 737-2H3	758/22624	Zarzis	Lsd fr TAR
TS-IOF	Boeing 737-2H3	776/22625	Sousse	Lsd fr TAR
Also leases aircraft from Fly Air as required				

SUDANAIR EXPRESS

Sudanese (SNV) — *Khartoum (KRT)*

EK-46507	Antonov An-24RV	37308403	ex RA-46507	Lsd fr V-Bard Avia
ST-ANH	Beech 65-C90 King Air	LJ-823	ex N580C	EMS
ST-AQQ	Antonov An-12BP	9346504	ex D2-FCT	
ST-SFS	Beech 200 Super King Air	BB-539	ex N555SK	EMS
Same company as Sudanese States Aviation, or a trading name?				

TAAT – TRANS ARABIAN AIR TRANSPORT

Trans Arabian (TRT) — *Khartoum (KRT)*

ST-AMF	Boeing 707-321C (Comtran 2)	637/19367	ex VR-HKL	

TRANS ATTICO

Tranattico Sudan (ML/ETC) — *Khartoum (KRT)*

ST-AQD	Antonov An-26B	11008	ex EX-26057	no titles
ST-AQF	Antonov An-12B	8345504	ex RA-12953	
ST-AQM	Antonov An-26	1404	ex RA-48099	

ST-AQP	Antonov An-12B	4342305	ex TN-AGC		
ST-AQR	Ilyushin Il-76TD	0043453575	ex 9L-LCX		
ST-CAC	Ilyushin Il-76TD	0023437076	ex T9-CAC	no titles	Joint ops with PHG
UN-76004	Ilyushin Il-76TD	0013434018	ex RA-76004		Lsd fr BMK

Trans Attico is the trading name of African Transport, Trading and Investment Co

UNITED ARABIAN COMPANY

United Arabian (UAB)　　　　　　　　　　　　　　　　　　　　　　　　　*Khartoum (KRT)*

ST-AQE	Antonov An-12BP	1400196	ex RA-12188

SU - EGYPT (Arab Republic of Egypt)

AIR CAIRO

(MSC)　　　　　　　　　　　　　　　　　　　　　　　　　　　　*Cairo-Intl (CAI)*

SU-EAF	Tupolev Tu-204-120	1450743764027	ex RA-64027	stored CAI	Lsd fr Sirocco
SU-EAG	Tupolev Tu-204-120S	1450743764028	ex RA-64028		Lsd fr Sirocco; jt ops with TAY
SU-EAH	Tupolev Tu-204-120	1450743164023			Lsd fr Sirocco
SU-EAI	Tupolev Tu-204-120	1450743164025		Cairo Avn titles	
SU-EAJ	Tupolev Tu-204-120	1450743164029	ex RA-64029		Jt ops with TAY
SU-EAK	Tupolev Tu-204-120S	1450743164033	ex RA-64033		on order

Air Cairo is the trading name of Cairo Air Transport Co, wholly owned by Sirocco Leasing

AIR MEMPHIS

Air Memphis (MHS)　　　　　　　　　　　　　　　　　　　　　　　*Cairo-Intl (CAI)*

SU-AVZ	Boeing 707-366C (BAC Stage 3)	868/20762			Lsd fr Tristar Lsg
SU-PBB	Boeing 707-336C (Comtran 2)	762/19916	ex SU-DAA	stored CAI	
SU-PBO	Douglas DC-9-31 (ABS 3)	940/48131	ex N928VJ		

Air Memphis Uganda is an affiliated company

AIR SINAI

Air Sinai (4D/ASD)　　　　　　　　　　　　　　　　　　　　　　　*Cairo-Intl (CAI)*

A subsidiary of Egyptair; operates aircraft from the parent

AMC AVIATION

AMC (AMV)　　　　　　　　　　　　　　　　　　　　　　　　　　*Cairo-Intl (CAI)*

SU-AYK	Boeing 737-266	455/21194			
SU-BMM	Airbus Industrie A300B4-203	175	ex SU-DAR	Zeiad	
SU-BOW	Airbus Industrie A310-322	437	ex PK-LEP		
SU-BOY	McDonnell-Douglas MD-83	2151/53191	ex N191AJ		Lsd fr WTCo
SU-BOZ	McDonnell-Douglas MD-83	2155/53192	ex N192AJ		Lsd fr WTCo

AMC Aviation is the trading name of Aviation Maintenance Company

EGYPTAIR

Egyptair (MS/MSR) (IATA 077)　　　　　　　　　　　　　　　　*Cairo-Intl (CAI)*

SU-BDG	Airbus Industrie A300B4-203F	200	ex F-WZMN	Toshki	
SU-GAC	Airbus Industrie A300B4-203F	255	ex F-WZMY	New Valley	
SU-GAR	Airbus Industrie A300B4-622R	557	ex F-WWAQ	Zoser	Lsd fr Airbus
SU-GAS	Airbus Industrie A300B4-622R	561	ex F-WWAN	Cheops	Lsd fr Airbus
SU-GAT	Airbus Industrie A300B4-622R	572	ex F-WWAE	Chephren	
SU-GAU	Airbus Industrie A300B4-622R	575	ex F-WWAF	Mycerinus	
SU-GAV	Airbus Industrie A300B4-622R	579	ex F-WWAJ	Menes	
SU-GAW	Airbus Industrie A300B4-622R	581	ex F-WWAL	Ahmose	
SU-GAY	Airbus Industrie A300B4-622R	607	ex F-WWAB	Seti 1	
SU-GBA	Airbus Industrie A320-231	0165	ex F-WWDV	Aswan	
SU-GBB	Airbus Industrie A320-231	0166	ex F-WWID	Luxor	
SU-GBC	Airbus Industrie A320-231	0178	ex F-WWIQ	Hurghada	
SU-GBD	Airbus Industrie A320-231	0194	ex F-WWIZ	Taba	
SU-GBE	Airbus Industrie A320-231	0198	ex F-WWDG	El Alamein	
SU-GBF	Airbus Industrie A320-231	0351	ex F-WWDM	Sharm El Sheikh	
SU-GBG	Airbus Industrie A320-231	0366	ex F-WWDD	Saint Catherine	
SU-GBT	Airbus Industrie A321-231	0680	ex D-AVZB	Red Sea	
SU-GBU	Airbus Industrie A321-231	0687	ex D-AVZR	Sinai	
SU-GBV	Airbus Industrie A321-231	0715	ex D-AVZX	Mediterranean	
SU-GBW	Airbus Industrie A321-231	0725	ex D-AVZA	The Nile; Air Cairo titles	
SU-GBZ	Airbus Industrie A320-232	2070	ex F-WWDJ		
SU-GCA	Airbus Industrie A320-232	2073	ex F-WWIO		
SU-GCB	Airbus Industrie A320-232	2079	ex F-WWDV		

SU-GCC	Airbus Industrie A320-232	2088	ex F-WWBH		
SU-GCD	Airbus Industrie A320-232	2094	ex F-WWBX		
SU-	Airbus Industrie A330-200	600	ex F-WW	on order Jul04	
SU-	Airbus Industrie A330-200	610	ex F-WW	on order 04	
SU-	Airbus Industrie A330-200		ex F-WW	on order 04	
SU-GBM	Airbus Industrie A340-212	156	ex F-WWJK	Osiris Express	
SU-GBN	Airbus Industrie A340-212	159	ex F-WWJV	Cleo Express	
SU-GBO	Airbus Industrie A340-212	178	ex F-WWJD	Hathor Express	

Four more Airbus Industrie A330-200s are on order for delivery in 2005

F-GPYL	Aerospatiale/Alenia ATR 42-500	542	ex F-WWLB		Lsd fr LIT
F-GPYO	Aerospatiale/Alenia ATR 42-500	544	ex F-WWLH		Lsd fr LIT
SU-APD	Boeing 707-366C (Comtran 2)	834/20341		Khafrah	
SU-GAL	Boeing 747-366M	704/24161	ex N6038E	Hatshepsut	
SU-GAM	Boeing 747-366M	707/24162	ex N6018N	Cleopatra	
SU-GBH	Boeing 737-566	2019/25084		Karnak; no titles	
SU-GBJ	Boeing 737-566	2169/25352		Philae	
SU-GBK	Boeing 737-566	2276/26052		Kalabsha	
SU-GBL	Boeing 737-566	2282/26051		Ramesseum	
SU-GBP	Boeing 777-266	71/28423		Nefertiti	
SU-GBR	Boeing 777-266	80/28424		Nefertari	
SU-GBS	Boeing 777-266	85/28425		Tyie	
SU-GBX	Boeing 777-266ER	362/32629			
SU-GBY	Boeing 777-266ER	368/32630		Titi	
YR-ATE	Aerospatiale/Alenia ATR 42-500	596	ex F-WWLY	Olt	Lsd fr ROT

Owns Air Sinai; the Boeing 747s and Boeing 777-200ERs will be withdrawn when the Airbus A330s are delivered

FLASH AIRLINES

Flash (FSH)   *Cairo-Intl (CAI)*

SU-ZCD	Boeing 737-3Q8	2424/26286	ex N171LF		Lsd fr ILFC

LOTUS AIR

Lotus Flower (/TAS)   *Cairo-Intl (CAI)*

SU-LBB	Airbus Industrie A320-212	0814	ex F-WWII		Lsd fr ILFC
SU-LBC	Airbus Industrie A320-214	0937	ex F-WWIS		Lsd fr debis
SU-LBD	Airbus Industrie A320-214	1372	ex F-WWIK	Lsd fr Flightlease; sublsd to GHA	
SU-LBE	Airbus Industrie A320-214	1413	ex EI-CWT		Lsd fr CIT Lsg
SU-LBF	Airbus Industrie A319-112	0629	ex HB-IPZ	Marmara-Nouvelles Itapes	
SU-	Airbus Industrie A320-214	2178	ex F-WWIP	on order 04	Lsd fr CIT Lsg
SU-	Airbus Industrie A320-214		ex F-WW	on order 04	Lsd fr CIT Lsg

LUXOR AIR

(LU)   *Luxor (LXR)*

SU-BME	McDonnell-Douglas MD-83	1582/49628	ex F-GRML		
SU-BMF	McDonnell-Douglas MD-83	1968/53199	ex EI-CNR		Lsd fr GECAS

MIDWEST AIRLINES EGYPT

(MY/MWA)   *Cairo-Intl (CAI)*

SU-MWA*	Airbus Industrie A310-304	652	ex F-WJKS	Almahrousa	

*Leased from Credit Lyonnais

ORCA AIR ceased operations

PETROLEUM AIR SERVICES

           Cairo-Intl (CAI)

SU-CAB	Bell 212	31223	
SU-CAJ	Bell 212	31247	
SU-CAL	Bell 212	31215	ex N3889A
SU-CAM	Bell 212	31249	
SU-CAN	Bell 212	31250	
SU-CAO	Bell 212	31260	
SU-CAQ	Bell 212	31262	
SU-CAR	Bell 212	31263	
SU-CAS	Bell 212	31264	
SU-CAU	Bell 212	35036	
SU-CAV	Bell 412HP	36037	ex XA-TNO
SU-CAW	Bell 412HP	36038	ex XA-SMW
SU-CAX	Bell 412HP	36081	ex N2156S
SU-CAY	Bell 412EP	36158	ex N6489P

SU-CAZ	Bell 412EP	36184	ex N55248		
SU-CBA	de Havilland DHC-7-102	93	ex C-GFYI		
SU-CBB	de Havilland DHC-7-102	96	ex C-GEWQ		
SU-CBC	de Havilland DHC-7-102	97	ex C-GFQL		
SU-CBD	de Havilland DHC-7-102	98	ex C-GEWQ		
SU-CBE	de Havilland DHC-7-102	99	ex C-GFBW		
SU-CAC	Bell 206L-3 LongRanger III	51004			
SU-CAE	Bell 206L-3 LongRanger III	51030			
SU-CAF	Bell 206L-3 LongRanger III	51031			
SU-CAG	Bell 206B JetRanger III	3574			
SU-CAH	Bell 206B JetRanger III	3581			
SU-CAI	Bell 206L-3 LongRanger III	51018			
SU-CBF	de Havilland DHC-8Q-315	584	ex C-FDHX		
SU-CBG	de Havilland DHC-8Q-315	585	ex C-FDHY		
SU-CBH	de Havilland DHC-8Q-315	594	ex C-FPJH		

PHAROAH AIRLINES ceased operations

RASLAN AIR current status is uncertain, sole aircraft sold in the USA

SCORPIO AIRLINES suspended operations in 2002 but did not restart as planned in 2003

SHOROUK AIR ceased operations in 4Q03

TRISTAR AIR

Triple Star (TSY)   *Cairo-Intl (CAI)*

SU-BMZ	Airbus Industrie A300B4-203F	129	ex N825SC

Also leases freighter aircraft from other operators as and when required

SU-Y PALESTINE

PALESTINIAN AIRLINES

Palestinian (PF/PNW) (IATA 400)   *El Arish*

SU-YAH	Fokker 50	20123	ex PH-FZJ	stored WOE	
SU-YAI	Fokker 50	20143	ex PH-FZI	stored WOE	
SU-YAK	Boeing 727-230	1425/21621	ex TC-AFR	stored AMM	Lsd fr Kingdom Ltd
SU-YAM	de Havilland DHC-8Q-315	546	ex C-FDHO	Hebron	

SX - GREECE (Hellenic Republic)

AEGEAN AIRLINES

Aegean (A3/AEE) (IATA 390)   *Athens-Eleftherios Venizelos Intl (ATH)*

SX-DVA	Avro RJ100	E3341	ex G-6-341		
SX-DVB	Avro RJ100	E3343	ex G-6-343		
SX-DVC	Avro RJ100	E3358	ex G-6-358		
SX-DVD	Avro RJ100	E3362	ex G-6-362		
SX-DVE	Avro RJ100	E3374	ex G-6-374		
SX-DVF	Avro RJ100	E3375	ex G-6-375		
SX-BBT	Boeing 737-33A	2012/25011	ex F-GRSA	Kastalia	Lsd fr AWAS
SX-BBU	Boeing 737-33A	2206/25743	ex EC-FMP	Joanna	Lsd fr AWAS
SX-BGH	Boeing 737-4Y0	1589/23866	ex N4360W	Iniochos	Lsd fr Boullioun
SX-BGJ	Boeing 737-4S3	2233/25595	ex N280CD		Lsd fr Boullioun
SX-BGK	Boeing 737-3Y0	1897/24679	ex 9V-TRA	Thessaloniki	Lsd fr SALE
SX-BGR	Boeing 737-408	2032/25063	ex TF-FID		Lsd fr Boullioun
SX-BGS	Boeing 737-4Q8	2221/26279	ex TC-AFM		Lsd fr PGT
SX-BGV	Boeing 737-4Q8	2665/26308	ex HL7235		Lsd fr ILFC
SX-BLM	Boeing 737-42C	2062/24813	ex D-ABDD		Lsd fr Unicapital
SX-BGN	Boeing 737-45D	2895/28753	ex SP-LLG		Lsd fr WFBN

AIR MILES

                                                            Athens-Eleftherios Venizelos Intl (ATH)

TF-ELV	Boeing 737-4S3	24796	ex G-TREN		Lsd fr /op by ICB

AVIATOR AIRWAYS

Aviator (AVW)   *Athens-Eleftherios Venizelos Intl (ATH)*

SX-APJ	Beech 200 Super King Air	BB-401	ex OY-JAO	Captain John	Lsd fr AHA
SX-BST	Beech 1900D	UE-236	ex SE-KXY		Lsd fr Air Express

BELLAVIA now operates light helicopter only

ELECTRA AIRLINES grounded by Greek authorities due to poor maintenance records

---

GEE BEE AIR

(GEB)   *Athens-Eleftherios Venizelos Intl (ATH)*

SX-BTK	Fokker 50	20199	ex PH-ZDI	o/o	Lsd fr A/c Finance & Trading

Current status is uncertain, one aircraft returned, one not delivered and one still on order

---

GREEK AIRLINES

                                              Athens-Eleftherios Venizelos Intl (ATH)

SX-BLV	Boeing 757-2G5	671/26278	ex G-JMCG	Lsd fr ILFC; sublsd to Air Scotland

---

HELLAS JET

(T4/HEJ) (IATA 681)   *Athens-Eleftherios Venizelos Intl (ATH)*

SX-BVA	Airbus Industrie A320-232	0425	ex N340LA	Pegasus	Lsd fr CIT Lsg
SX-BVB	Airbus Industrie A320-232	1992	ex F-WWBJ	Hermes	Lsd fr CIT Lsg
SX-BVC	Airbus Industrie A320-232	2016	ex F-WWBS	Orion	Lsd fr CIT Lsg

Wholly owned by Cyprus Airways and due to commence services in May 2003

HELLAS WINGS

Hellas Wings (LJR)   *Athens-Eleftherios Venizelos Intl (ATH)*

SX-BNJ	British Aerospace Jetstream 31	829	ex C-GMDJ	Patri	
SX-BNV	Piper PA-31-350 Navajo Chieftain	31-7952088	ex N112GD	Elpis	
SX-BSR	British Aerospace Jetstream 31	718	ex G-OAKI		Lsd fr Airfan Enterprises

---

HELLENIC STAR AVIATION

Hellenic Star (HJ/HST)   *Athens-Eleftherios Venizelos Intl (ATH)*

SX-BNA	de Havilland DHC-7-102	090	ex C-GELW	std	Lsd fr Bakoum Mediterranean

Current status is uncertain

MACEDONIAN AIRLINES became part of 'new' Olympic Airlines in December 2003

MEDITERRANEAN AIR FREIGHT

(MDF)   *Athens-Eleftherios Venizelos Intl (ATH)*

EC-HJO	Swearingen SA.227AC Metro III	AC-615B	ex N972GA		Lsd fr CKM
SX-BGT	Swearingen SA.226AT Merlin IVA	AT-038	ex EC-FUX	all-white	Lsd fr BCS

Operates for DHL

OLYMPIC AIRLINES

Olympic (OA/OAL) (IATA 050)   *Athens-Eleftherios Venizelos Intl (ATH)*

Previously listed as Olympic Airways, reformed 12 December 2003 prior to privatisation through integration of flight division of Olympic Airways with Macedonian Airlines and Olympic Aviation

SX-BIA	Aerospatiale/Alenia ATR 42-320	169	ex F-WWEW	Plato	
SX-BIB	Aerospatiale/Alenia ATR 42-320	182	ex F-WWER	Socrates	
SX-BIC	Aerospatiale/Alenia ATR 42-320	197	ex F-WWEE	Aristotle	
SX-BID	Aerospatiale/Alenia ATR 42-320	219	ex F-WWEG	Pythagoras	
SX-BIE	Aerospatiale/Alenia ATR 72-202	239	ex F-WWED	Thales	
SX-BIF	Aerospatiale/Alenia ATR 72-202	241	ex F-WWEA	Democritus	
SX-BIG	Aerospatiale/Alenia ATR 72-202	290	ex F-WWLQ	Homer	
SX-BIH	Aerospatiale/Alenia ATR 72-202	305	ex F-WWLC	Herodotus	
SX-BII	Aerospatiale/Alenia ATR 72-202	353	ex F-WWEK	Hippocrates	
SX-BIK	Aerospatiale/Alenia ATR 72-202	350	ex F-WWEG	Archimedes	
SX-BIL	Aerospatiale/Alenia ATR 72-202	437	ex F-WWLC	Melina-Eliada	
SX-BIM	Aerospatiale/Alenia ATR 42-202	337	ex F-WQNQ	Sptros Louis	
SX-BIN	Aerospatiale/Alenia ATR 42-202	291	ex F-WQNZ	Kostas Tsiklitiras	
SX-BIO*	de Havilland DHC-8-102	330	ex C-GZQZ	Katerina Thanou	
SX-BIP	de Havilland DHC-8-102	347	ex C-GZRA		
SX-BIQ*	de Havilland DHC-8-102	361	ex C-GZRD	Kahi Kahiasvili	
SX-BIR*	de Havilland DHC-8-102	364	ex C-GZRF	Kostas Kenteris	
SX-BIS	de Havilland DHC-8-106	355	ex OE-LLE		Lsd fr TYR

*Athens 04 Olympic Games titles

SX-BKA	Boeing 737-484	2109/25313		Vergina	
SX-BKB	Boeing 737-484	2124/25314		Olynthos	

SX-BKC	Boeing 737-484	2130/25361		Philippi; Olympic Games c/s	
SX-BKD	Boeing 737-484	2142/25362		Amphipoli; Olympic Games c/s	
SX-BKE	Boeing 737-484	2160/25417		Stagira	
SX-BKF	Boeing 737-484	2174/25430		Dion	
SX-BKG	Boeing 737-484	2471/27149		Pella	
SX-BKH	Boeing 737-4Q8	1828/24703	ex N407KW		Lsd fr ILFC
SX-BKI	Boeing 737-4Q8	1855/24704	ex N405KW		Lsd fr ILFC
SX-BKK	Boeing 737-4Q8	2195/25371	ex N404KW		Lsd fr ILFC
SX-BKL	Boeing 737-4Y0	2055/24915	ex 9M-MJT		Lsd fr Qatar Bank
SX-BKM	Boeing 737-4Q8	2115/24709	ex N406KW		Lsd fr Avn Capital
SX-BKN	Boeing 737-4Q8	2380/26281	ex N401KW		Lsd fr ILFC
SX-BLA	Boeing 737-33R	2887/28869	ex N964WP		Lsd fr Boullioun
SX-BMA	Boeing 737-46J	2465/27171	ex D-ABAE	City of Athens	Lsd fr Pembroke
SX-BMB	Boeing 737-46J	2585/27213	ex D-ABAG	City of Thessaloniki	Lsd fr Pembroke
SX-BMC	Boeing 737-42J	2457/27143	ex N734AB	City of Alexandroupoli	Lsd fr OASIS
SX-BEK	Airbus Industrie A300B4-605R	632	ex F-WWAG	Macedonia	
SX-BEL	Airbus Industrie A300B4-605R	696	ex F-WWAK	Athena	
SX-BEM	Airbus Industrie A300B4-605R	603	ex B-2310	Creta	Lsd fr GECAS
SX-BOA	Boeing 717-2K9	5015/55056		Andromeda; std ATH	Lsd Bavaria Lsg
SX-BOB	Boeing 717-2K9	5016/55053		Kassiopi; std ATH	Lsd Bavaria Lsg
SX-BOC	Boeing 717-23S	5048/55065		Iridanos; std ATH	Lsd fr Pembroke
SX-DFA	Airbus Industrie A340-313X	235	ex F-WWJN	Olympia	
SX-DFB	Airbus Industrie A340-313X	239	ex F-WWJC	Delphi	
SX-DFC	Airbus Industrie A340-313X	280	ex F-WWJJ	Marathon	
SX-DFD	Airbus Industrie A340-313X	292	ex F-WWJB		

OLYMPIC AIRWAYS renamed Olympic Airlines in December 2003 prior to privatisation and absorbed Macedonian Airlines and Olympic Aviation

OLYMPIC AVIATION became part of 'new' Olympic Airlines in December 2003

TRANSEUROPEAN AIRLINES

Eurolines (TEG) *Athens-Eleftherios Venizelos Intl (ATH)*

| SX-BNL | Embraer EMB.110P1 Bandeirante | 110224 | ex N614KC | ZS-PCY resd | Lsd fr Western Lsg |

VER-AVIA

Night Rider (GRV) *Athens-Eleftherios Venizelos Intl (ATH)*

SX-BBX	Swearingen SA.227AC Metro III	AC-657	ex N26902		Lsd fr Finova
SX-BMM	Swearingen SA.227AC Metro III	BC-774B	ex N774MW		
SX-BMO	Swearingen SA.227AC Metro III	AC-430	ex N778C		Lsd fr First A/c Lsg
SX-BNN	Swearingen SA.227AC Metro III	BC-771B	ex N771MW		

S2 - BANGLADESH (People's Republic of Bangladesh)

AIR BANGLADESH

(B9BGD) *Dhaka (DAC)*

Operates cargo charter flights with Antonov An-12s leased from other operators as required

AIR PARABAT

(PBT) *Dhaka (DAC)*

Current status is uncertain, had planned to restart operations but may not have recommenced services

BIMAN BANGLADESH AIRLINES

Bangladesh (BG/BBC) (IATA 997) *Dhaka (DAC)*

S2-ACO	Douglas DC-10-30	263/46993	ex 9V-SDB	City of Hazrat Shah Makhdoom (RA)	
S2-ACP	Douglas DC-10-30	275/46995	ex 9V-SDD	City of Dhaka	
S2-ACQ	Douglas DC-10-30	300/47817	ex 9V-SDF	City of Hazrat Shah Jalal (RA)	
S2-ACR	Douglas DC-10-30	445/48317		The New Era	
S2-ACS	Douglas DC-10-30ER	341/46543	ex C-GCPF		Lsd fr Pegasus
S2-ADN	Douglas DC-10-30ER	295/46542	ex N946PG		Lsd fr Pegasus
S2-ACH	Fokker F.28 Fellowship 4000	11172	ex PH-EXX		
S2-ACW	Fokker F.28 Fellowship 4000	11148	ex PK-YPJ		
S2-ADE	Airbus Industrie A310-325	698	ex F-WWCF	City of Hazrat Khan Jahan Ali (RA)	
S2-ADF	Airbus Industrie A310-325	700	ex F-WWCB	City of Chittagong	
S2-ADH	Airbus Industrie A310-325	650	ex N835AB		Lsd fr Airbus
S2-ADK	Airbus Industrie A310-325	594	ex N594RC		Lsd fr Crane Aircraft
S2-AEA	Boeing 737-377	1622/24304	ex S7-ABC		Lsd fr RGA
S2-AEB	Boeing 737-377	1620/24303	ex S7-ABD		Lsd fr RGA

| S2- | Fokker F.28 Fellowship 4000 | | ex | on order |
| S2- | Fokker F.28 Fellowship 4000 | | ex | on order |

BISMILLAH AIRLINES

Bismillah (5Z/BML)   *Dhaka/Sharjah (DAC/SHJ)*

| S2-ADR | Lockheed L-1011- Tristar 1 | 1129 | ex XU-300 | Freighter; stored BKK? |

Also operates cargo flights with freighters leased from other operators as and when required

GMG AIRLINES

(Z5) (IATA 009)   *Dhaka (DAC)*

S2-AAA	de Havilland DHC-8-102	245	ex N802MA	In memory of Bangabondu
S2-ACT	de Havilland DHC-8-311	307	ex OE-LRW	Hazrat Bayazid Bistami
S2-ADJ	de Havilland DHC-8-102	054	ex N816PH	. Lsd fr CIT Leasing

SOUTH ASIAN AIRLINES

(BDS)   *Dhaka (DAC)*

Current fleet details unknown

S5 - SLOVENIA (Republic of Slovenia)

ADRIA AIRWAYS

Adria (JP/ADR) (IATA 165)   *Ljubljana (LJU)*

S5-AAA	Airbus Industrie A320-231	0043	ex SX-BAS	
S5-AAB	Airbus Industrie A320-231	0113	ex SX-BAT	
S5-AAC	Airbus Industrie A320-231	0114	ex SX-BAU	
S5-AAD	Canadair CL-600-2B19	7166	ex C-FZWS	
S5-AAE	Canadair CL-600-2B19	7170	ex C-GAIK	
S5-AAF	Canadair CL-600-2B19	7272	ex C-FMND	
S5-AAG	Canadair CL-600-2B19	7384	ex C-FMMT	
S7-AAH	Canadair CL-600-2B19	7032	ex HA-LNX	Lsd fr Bombardier Capital

ALPE AIR

Alps (LPS)   *Ljubljana (LJU)*

Operates charter flights with aircraft leased from other operators as and when required

SOLINAIR

Solinair (SOP)   *Portoroz (POW)*

S5-BAE	LET L-410UVP-E	902503	ex RA-67650	op for DHL
S5-BAF	LET L-410UVP-E8C	912540	ex OM-WDA	
S5-CAI	Rockwell Commander 690A	11121	ex D-IGAF	

S7 - SEYCHELLES (Republic of Seychelles)

AIR SEYCHELLES

Seychelles (HM/SEY) (IATA 061)   *Mahe (SEZ)*

S7-AAA	Britten-Norman BN-2A-27 Islander	540	ex G-BDZP	Isle of Remire	stored
S7-AAF	de Havilland DHC-6 Twin Otter 300	623	ex S7-AAO	Isle of Praslin	
S7-AAJ	de Havilland DHC-6 Twin Otter 300	499	ex PH-STB	Isle of Desroches	
S7-AAR	de Havilland DHC-6 Twin Otter 300	539	ex PH-STF	Isle of Farquhar	
S7-AHM	Boeing 767-37DER	637/26328	ex (S7-AAZ)	Vailee de Mai	Lsd fr ILFC
S7-ASY	Boeing 767-3Q8ER	831/29386		Isle of Aldabra	Lsd fr ILFC
S7-PAL	Short SD.3-60	SH3758	ex G-KBAC		Lsd fr BAC Lsg
S7-SEZ	Boeing 737-7Q8	1005/30727	ex N1787B	Amirantes	Lsd fr ILFC

IDC AIRCRAFT

                                                                            Mahe (SEZ)

(Island Development Corporation)

S7-AAI	Reims Cessna F406 Caravan II	F406-0051	ex N7148P	
S7-AAU	Britten-Norman BN-2A-21 Islander	589	ex A2-01M	Op for Coast Guard
S7-SMB	Beech 1900D	UE-212	ex S7-IDC	

REGIONAIR now listed under 9V- Singapore

S9 - SAO TOME (Democratic Republic of Sao Tome & Principe)

AIR LUXOR STP
Luxorjet (C2/ALU)   Sao Tome (TMS)

Wholly owned subsidiary of Air Luxor and uses Airbus Industrie A320 aircraft leased from the parent when required

AIR SAO TOME E PRINCIPE
Equatorial (KY/EQL) (IATA 980)   Sao Tome (TMS)

S9-BAL	de Havilland DHC-6 Twin Otter 300	648	ex CS-TFD	Lsd fr TAP Lease

BRITISH GULF INTERNATIONAL AIRLINES now listed under Kyrgyzstan, although based at Sharjah

NATALCO AIR LINES

EK-12148	Antonov An-12		
TN-AGQ	Antonov An-12	402111 ex S9-BAN	id not confirmed
TN-AHD	Antonov An-12		

SAL EXPRESS
                                                                                      Sao Tome/Luanda (TMS/LAD)

S9-BAK	Beech 1900D	UE-358	ex N23610	Lsd fr Raytheon
S9-CAG	Beech 1900C-1	UC-157	ex N157YV	Lsd fr Raytheon

TRANSAFRIK INTERNATIONAL
                                                                                      Sao Tome/Luanda (TMS/LAD)

S9-BAE	Boeing 727-31F	147/18903	ex N210NE	
S9-BAG	Boeing 727-30C	411/19313	ex PP-ITP	
S9-BAV	Boeing 727-223 (Raisbeck 3)	1324/21383	ex N871AA	
S9-BOC	Boeing 727-23F	127/18447	ex ZS-NMY	all-white
S9-BOD	Boeing 727-25F	223/18968	ex PP-ITA	
S9-BOE	Boeing 727-22C	388/19192	ex N706DH	
S9-BOG	Boeing 727-90C	332/19170	ex N270AX	all-white
S9-CAA	Boeing 727-95F	494/19836	ex HR-AMR	
S9-CAB	Boeing 727-23F	266/19182	ex HR-AMI	
S9-TAO	Boeing 727-23F	350/19390	ex N931FT	

All except S9-TAO leased from T.W.L. Ltd

S9-BAS	Lockheed L-382G Hercules	4472	ex N905SJ	
S9-BAT	Lockheed L-382G Hercules	4134	ex N916SJ	
S9-BOF	Lockheed L-382G Hercules	4586	ex N921SJ	
S9-BOQ	Lockheed L-382E Hercules	4388	ex N912SJ	
S9-BOR	Lockheed L-382E Hercules	4362	ex N522SJ	
S9-CAI	Lockheed L-382E Hercules	4562	ex N904SJ	
S9-CAJ	Lockheed L-382E Hercules	4565	ex N902SJ	
S9-CAV	Lockheed L-382E Hercules	4301	ex N923SJ	
S9-CAW	Lockheed L-382E Hercules	4300	ex N908SJ	
S9-CAX	Lockheed L-382E Hercules	4248	ex N907SJ	
S9-CAY	Lockheed L-382E Hercules	4208	ex N918SJ	
S9-NAL	Lockheed L-382E Hercules	4385	ex 9Q-CHZ	
S9-	Lockheed L-382G Hercules	4299	ex N901SJ	

All leased from T.W.L. Ltd, some operate for aid agencies

TC - TURKEY (Republic of Turkey)

AIR ANATOLIA
Air Anatolia (NTL)   Antalya (AYT)

Operates charter flights with Airbus Industrie A300 and Boeing 757 aircraft leased from Fly Air when required

ATLAS JET INTERNATIONAL
Atlasjet (2U/OGE)   Istanbul (IST)

TC-OGA*	Boeing 757-225	115/22688	ex D-AMUU	Yanikali	Lsd fr Unicapital
TC-OGB	Boeing 757-225	117/22689	ex D-AMUK	Perihan	Lsd fr Unicapital
TC-OGC*	Boeing 757-2G5	161/23983	ex D-AMUX	Sait	Lsd fr Unicapital
TC-OGD	Boeing 757-2G5	173/24176	ex N500GX		Lsd fr WTCo

*Subleased to Thaijet as HS-OGA/OGB respectively

BON AIR now operate executive jets only

BOSPHORUS EUROPEAN AIRWAYS

Bosphorus (BHY)   *Istanbul (IST)*

TC-COA	Airbus Industrie A300B4-120	128	ex OY-CNL	stored IST	
TC-OIM	Airbus Industrie A300B4-120	094	ex OY-CNK	Kaan; stored IST	

CAT CARGO

Istanbul (IST)

TC-KET	Antonov An-12	

FLY AIR

Fly World (FLM)   *Istanbul (IST)*

TC-ANI	Airbus Industrie A300B4-203	046	ex EI-TLM	stored IST	Lsd fr GECAS
TC-FLA	Airbus Industrie A300B4-203	127	ex TC-GTB		Lsd fr GECAS
TC-FLE	Airbus Industrie A300B2K-3C	163	ex JA8472		
TC-FLF	Airbus Industrie A300B4-2C	194	ex JA8293	Sultan Reizen titles	
TC-FLG	Airbus Industrie A300B4-203	110	ex JA8292	Pasa Tours titles	
TC-OYC	Airbus Industrie A300B4-120	079	ex OY-CNA	Hakan	
TC-FLB	Boeing 757-236ER	187/24122	ex TC-ANM	HTC Reizen tls	Lsd fr IEM Airfinance
TC-FLC	Boeing 757-27B	169/24136	ex TC-ANN	Corendon tls	Lsd fr IEM Airfinance
TC-FLD	Boeing 757-256	616/26244	ex N508NA	stored QLA	Lsd fr Sunrock
TC-FLH	Boeing 737-3Q8	1666/24300	ex EI-PAR		Lsd fr Sunrock

Aircraft leased to Air Anatolia as required; also operates for Sudan Airways

FREEBIRD AIRLINES

Free Turk (FHY)   *Istanbul (IST)*

TC-FBB	McDonnell-Douglas MD-83	2090/53185	ex N879RA		Lsd fr AWAS
TC-FBD	McDonnell-Douglas MD-83	2092/53186	ex N880RA		Lsd fr AWAS
TC-FBE	Airbus Industrie A320-212	0132	ex SE-RCG		Lsd fr GATX
TC-FBG	McDonnell-Douglas MD-83	2088/53184	ex N878RA		Lsd fr AWAS
TC-FBT	McDonnell-Douglas MD-83	1906/49949	ex N882RA		Lsd fr AeroUSA

INTER EXPRESS

Inter-Euro (6K/INX) (IATA 821)

TC-IEA	Boeing 737-8CX	1098/32361			Lsd fr GATX JetPartners
TC-IEB	Boeing 737-8CX	1139/32363			Lsd fr GATX JetPartners
TC-IEC	Boeing 737-8CX			on order	Lsd fr GATX

KIBRIS TURK HAVA YOLLARI / KTHY CYPRUS TURKISH AIRLINES

Airkibris (YK/KYV) (IATA 056)   *Ercan (ECN)*

TC-JCO	Airbus Industrie A310-203	386	ex F-WWBC	Levkosa	
TC-JYK	Airbus Industrie A310-203	172	ex F-GEMF	Erenköy	
TC-MAO	Boeing 737-86N	840/28645	ex N1795B	Karpaz	Lsd fr GECAS
TC-MSO	Boeing 737-8S3	475/29246	ex N1787B	Magusa	Lsd fr Sunrock
TC-MZZ	Boeing 737-8S3	493/29247		Guzelyurt	Lsd fr Sunrock
EI-DDS	Airbus Industrie A321-211	1451	ex I-PEKM		Lsd fr GECAS
3D-ABV	McDonnell-Douglas MD-82	1070/49119	ex N820US	Back-up	Lsd fr Jetran

50% owned by THY- Turkish Airlines

MNG AIRLINES

Black Sea (MB/MNB) (IATA 716)   *Istanbul (IST)*

TC-MNA	Airbus Industrie A300B4-203F	019	ex N742SC		Lsd fr C-S Avn
TC-MNB	Airbus Industrie A300B4-203F	292	ex HL7279		Lsd fr KAL
TC-MNC	Airbus Industrie A300B4-203F	277	ex HL7278		Lsd fr KAL
TC-MND	Airbus Industrie A300C4-203F	212	ex ZS-SDG		
TC-MNE*	Airbus Industrie A300B4-203	222	ex ZS-SDH	Topkapi	
TC-MNJ	Airbus Industrie A300B4-203F	123	ex PH-JLH		Lsd fr C-S Avn

*Operates in full TUI colours with Jetair titles

TC-MNF	Boeing 737-4K5	1697/24126	ex D-AHLK		Lsd fr Defag
TC-MNH	Boeing 737-448	1850/24773	ex EI-BXC		Lsd fr ILFC
TC-MNI	Boeing 737-4K5	1715/24428	ex SP-KEN		Lsd fr Defag
TC-MNL	Boeing 737-4Q8	2598/25375	ex TC-ANH		Lsd fr ILFC
TC-MNM	Boeing 737-4Q8	2562/25374	ex TC-ANL		Lsd fr ILFC

Passenger flights are operated as MNG Pax and cargo flights as MNG Cargo

ONUR AIR

Onur Air (8Q/OHY) — Istanbul (IST)

TC-OAA	Airbus Industrie A300B4-605R	744	ex F-WQRD		Lsd fr ILFC
TC-OAB	Airbus Industrie A300B4-605R	749	ex F-WQRC	Safuan 1	Lsd fr ILFC
TC-OAG	Airbus Industrie A300B4-605R	747	ex F-OHLN		Lsd fr ILFC
TC-OAH	Airbus Industrie A300B4-605R	584	ex S7-RGO		
TC-ONK	Airbus Industrie A300B4-103	086	ex TC-TKA	Pinar	
TC-ONL	Airbus Industrie A300B4-103	087	ex TC-TKB	Selin	
TC-ONT	Airbus Industrie A300B4-203	138	ex ZS-SDE	Kaptan Bilal Basar	
TC-ONU	Airbus Industrie A300B4-203	192	ex ZS-SDF		
TC-ONY	Airbus Industrie A300B2K-3C	037	ex ZS-SDB		
TC-OAC	Airbus Industrie A320-212	0313	ex TC-ABG		Lsd fr Oasis Intl Lsg
TC-OAD	Airbus Industrie A320-212	0345	ex TC-ABH		Lsd fr Oasis Intl Lsg
TC-OAE	Airbus Industrie A321-231	0663	ex F-OHMP	on order	Lsd fr ILFC
TC-OAF	Airbus Industrie A321-231	0668	ex F-OHMQ	on order	Lsd fr ILFC
TC-OAI	Airbus Industrie A321-231	0787	ex D-ALAG		Lsd fr ILFC
TC-OAK	Airbus Industrie A321-231	0954	ex D-ALAI		Lsd fr ILFC
TC-ONJ	Airbus Industrie A321-131	0385	ex D-AVZG	Kaptan Koray Sahin	
TC-ONS	Airbus Industrie A321-131	0364	ex D-AVZD	Funda	
TC-ONM	McDonnell-Douglas MD-88	2167/53546		Yasemin	Lsd to IBE
TC-ONN	McDonnell-Douglas MD-88	2170/53547		Ece	
TC-ONO	McDonnell-Douglas MD-88	2180/53548		Yonca	
TC-ONP	McDonnell-Douglas MD-88	2185/53549		Esra	
TC-ONR	McDonnell-Douglas MD-88	2187/53550		Evren	

Began low-cost domestic services in mid December 2003

ORBIT EXPRESS AIRLINES

(ORX)

TC-ORH	Airbus Industrie A300C4-203F	083	ex TC-MNG	Aida	Lsd fr GECAS
TC-ORI	Airbus Industrie A300B4-203F	183	ex N512TA		Lsd fr Windshear Lsg
TC-	Airbus Industrie A300B4-203F	173	ex N511TA		Lsd fr WFBN
TC-	Boeing 747-2B5F	454/22481	ex HL7452	on order Mar04	
TC-	Boeing 747-2B5F	520/22486	ex HL7459	on order May04	

Orex Cargo titles

PEGASUS AIRLINES

Sunturk (1I/PGT) — Istanbul (IST)

TC-AFM	Boeing 737-4Q8	2221/26279			Lsd fr Triton; sublsd to AEE
TC-APD	Boeing 737-42R	2997/29107			
TC-APR	Boeing 737-4Y0	1859/24685	ex EC-GXR		Lsd fr BBAM
TC-AAP	Boeing 737-86N	1113/32736			Lsd fr GECAS
TC-APF	Boeing 737-86N	813/28642	ex N1787B		Lsd fr GECAS
TC-APG	Boeing 737-82R	224/29329			Lsd to Myanmar Intl
TC-APH	Boeing 737-8S3	792/29250	ex N1787B		Lsd fr Sunrock
TC-API	Boeing 737-86N	1056/32732			Lsd fr GECAS
TC-APJ	Boeing 737-86N	1104/32735			Lsd fr GECAS
TC-APM	Boeing 737-809	117/28403	ex B-18602		Lsd fr GECAS
TC-APN	Boeing 737-86N	573/28628	ex N5573L		Lsd fr GECAS; sublsd to DAH
TC-APU	Boeing 737-82R	849/29344			Lsd fr ILFC
TC-APY	Boeing 737-86N	233/28591	ex TC-IAH		Lsd fr GECAS
TC-APZ	Boeing 737-809	129/29103	ex B-18603		Lsd fr GECAS

SKY AIRLINES

Antalya Bird (SHY) — Antalya (AYT)

TC-SKA	Boeing 737-4Y0	1582/23865	ex PH-BPA	Sun	Lsd fr ICON Aircraft
TC-SKB	Boeing 737-430	2344/27004	ex EI-CPU	Star	Lsd fr Flightlease
TC-SKC	Boeing 737-85F	997/30478	ex N1787B	Moon	Lsd fr GATX
TC-SKD	Boeing 737-4Q8	2280/25372	ex TC-JDI	Black Eagle	Lsd fr ILFC

Sky Airlines is the trading name of Excelairways Cyprus

SUNEXPRESS AIR

Sunexpress (XQ/SXS) (IATA 564) — Antalya (AYT)

TC-SUA	Boeing 737-86N	455/28612		Lsd fr GECAS
TC-SUC	Boeing 737-86N	483/28616		Lsd fr GECAS
TC-SUD	Boeing 737-86N	542/28620		Lsd fr GECAS
TC-SUG	Boeing 737-8CX	1209/32365		Lsd fr GATX JetPartners
TC-SUH	Boeing 737-8CX	1235/32366		Lsd fr GATX JetPartners

| TC-SUI | Boeing 737-8CX | 1253/32367 | Lsd fr GATX JetPartners |
| TC-SUJ | Boeing 737-8CX | 1289/32368 | Lsd fr GATX JetPartners |

A subsidiary of THY (40%) and Condor (40%)

TOP AIR did not restart operations as planned

TURK HAVA KURUMU

Hur Kus (THK)   Ankara (ANK)

TC-CAU	Cessna 208 Caravan I	20800248	ex N1123X
TC-CAV	Cessna 208 Caravan I	20800256	ex N1249T
TC-FAH	Piper PA-42-720 Cheyenne IIIA	42-5501033	
TC-THK	Piper PA-42-720 Cheyenne IIIA	42-5501031	ex TC-FAG

TURKISH AIRLINES

Turkair (TK/THY) (IATA 235)   Istanbul (IST)

TC-JCV	Airbus Industrie A310-304	476	ex F-WWCT	Aras	
TC-JCY	Airbus Industrie A310-304	478	ex F-WWCX	Coruh	
TC-JCZ	Airbus Industrie A310-304	480	ex F-WWCZ	Ergene	
TC-JDA	Airbus Industrie A310-304	496	ex F-WWCV	Aksu	Lsd fr Itoh
TC-JDB	Airbus Industrie A310-304ER	497	ex F-WWCH	Goksu	Lsd fr Itoh

Four to be withdrawn from service pending possible sale to Mahan Air

TC-JDJ	Airbus Industrie A340-311	023	ex F-WWJN	Istanbul	Lsd fr Anatolia Lsg
TC-JDK	Airbus Industrie A340-311	025	ex F-WWJP	Isparta	Lsd fr Anatolia Lsg
TC-JDL	Airbus Industrie A340-311	057	ex F-WWJF	Ankara	Lsd fr Anatolia Lsg
TC-JDM	Airbus Industrie A340-311	115	ex F-WWJN	Izmir	Lsd fr Anatolia Lsg
TC-JDN	Airbus Industrie A340-313X	180	ex F-WWJU	Adana	
TC-JIH	Airbus Industrie A340-313X	270	ex F-WWJP	Hakkari	
TC-JII	Airbus Industrie A340-313X	331	ex F-WWJQ	Aydin	

TC-THA	Avro RJ100	E3232	ex G-6-232	Denizli	
TC-THB	Avro RJ100	E3234	ex G-6-234	Erzurum	
TC-THC	Avro RJ100	E3236	ex G-6-236	Samsum	
TC-THD	Avro RJ100	E3237	ex G-6-237	Van	
TC-THE	Avro RJ100	E3238	ex G-6-238	Gaziantep	
TC-THH	Avro RJ100	E3243	ex G-6-243	Kutahya	
TC-THI	Avro RJ70	E1229	ex G-BUFI	Erzincan	
TC-THJ	Avro RJ70	E1230	ex G-6-230	Usak	
TC-THM	Avro RJ100	E3264	ex G-6-264	Siirt	
TC-THN	Avro RJ70	E1252	ex G-6-252	Mus	
TC-THO	Avro RJ100	E3265	ex G-6-265	Tokat	

All leased from BAE Systems

TC-JDF	Boeing 737-4Y0	2071/24917		Ayvalik	Lsd fr GECAS
TC-JDG	Boeing 737-4Y0	2203/25181		Marmaris	Lsd fr GECAS
TC-JDH	Boeing 737-4Y0	2227/25184		Amasra	Lsd fr GECAS
TC-JDT	Boeing 737-4Y0	2258/25261	ex N600SK	Alanya	Lsd fr GECAS
TC-JDU*	Boeing 737-5Y0	2286/25288	ex (EI-CFT)	Trabzon	Lsd fr GECAS
TC-JDV*	Boeing 737-5Y0	2288/25289	ex (EI-CFU)	Bursa	Lsd fr GECAS
TC-JDY	Boeing 737-4Y0	2284/26065	ex (EI-CFS)	Antalya	Lsd fr GECAS
TC-JEN	Boeing 737-4Q8	2689/25376		Gelibolu	Lsd fr ILFC
TC-JEO	Boeing 737-4Q8	2717/25377		Anadolu	Lsd fr ILFC
TC-JER	Boeing 737-4Y0	2735/26073		Mugla	Lsd fr GECAS
TC-JET	Boeing 737-4Y0	2425/26077		Cannakkale	Lsd fr GECAS
TC-JEU	Boeing 737-4Y0	2431/26078		Samsun	Lsd fr GECAS
TC-JEV	Boeing 737-4Y0	2468/26085		Efes	Lsd fr GECAS
TC-JEY	Boeing 737-4Y0	2475/26086		Side	Lsd fr GECAS
TC-JEZ	Boeing 737-4Y0	2487/26088		Bergama	Lsd fr GECAS
TC-JKA	Boeing 737-4Y0	2604/26300	ex SX-BFA	Kars	Lsd fr ILFC

*To be withdrawn from service during 2004 along with six Boeing 737-400s

TC-JFC	Boeing 737-8F2	80/29765		Diyarbakir	
TC-JFD	Boeing 737-8F2	87/29766		Rize	
TC-JFE	Boeing 737-8F2	95/29767		Hatay	
TC-JFF	Boeing 737-8F2	99/29768		Afyon	
TC-JFG	Boeing 737-8F2	102/29769	ex N1787B	Mardin	
TC-JFH	Boeing 737-8F2	114/29770	ex N1787B	Igdir	
TC-JFI	Boeing 737-8F2	228/29771	ex N1795B	Sivas	
TC-JFJ	Boeing 737-8F2	242/29772		Agri	
TC-JFK	Boeing 737-8F2	259/29773		Zonguldak	
TC-JFL	Boeing 737-8F2	269/29774		Ordu	
TC-JFM	Boeing 737-8F2	279/29775		Nigde	
TC-JFN	Boeing 737-8F2	308/29776		Bitlis	
TC-JFO	Boeing 737-8F2	309/29777		Batman	
TC-JFP	Boeing 737-8F2	349/29778	ex N1787B	Amasya	
TC-JFR	Boeing 737-8F2	370/29779			
TC-JFT	Boeing 737-8F2	454/29780	ex N1787B	Kastamonu	

TC-JFU	Boeing 737-8F2	461/29781	ex N1795B	Elazig
TC-JFV	Boeing 737-8F2	490/29782		
TC-JFY	Boeing 737-8F2	497/29783		Manisa
TC-JFZ	Boeing 737-8F2	539/29784		Bolu
TC-JGA	Boeing 737-8F2	544/29785		Malatya
TC-JGB	Boeing 737-8F2	566/29786		
TC-JGC	Boeing 737-8F2	771/29787		
TC-JGD	Boeing 737-8F2	791/29788	ex N1787B	Nevsehir
TC-JGE	Boeing 737-8F2	1065/29789		Tekirdag
TC-JGF	Boeing 737-8F2	1088/29790		Ardahan
TC-JGG	Boeing 737-8F2	29791		on order

All to be retro-fitted with blended winglets

| TC-JCA | Boeing 727-2F2F | 1804/22992 | | all white; stored IST |

UENSPED PAKET SERVISI / UPS

Unsped (UNS) Istanbul (IST)

| TC-APS | Cessna 340A | 340A0247 | ex N3964G | | |
| TC-UPS | Swearingen SA.226TC Merlin IVA | AT-044 | ex TC-BPS | Beril | Op for UPS |

TF - ICELAND (Republic of Iceland)

AIR ATLANTA ICELAND

Atlanta (CC/ABD) Keflavik (KEF))

TF-ABA	Boeing 747-267B	531/22530	ex B-HID		Lsd fr CPA
TF-ABP	Boeing 747-267B	493/22429	ex B-HIC		Lsd fr CPA
TF-ARF	Boeing 747-236B	506/22305	ex G-BDXL		Lsd fr Avn Exposure Mgt
TF-ARG	Boeing 747-236B	495/22303	ex G-BDXK		Lsd fr Avn Exposure Mgt
TF-ARH	Boeing 747-230B (SF)	549/22669	ex N742SA		Lsd fr WFBN
TF-ARJ	Boeing 747-236M	674/23735	ex G-BDXN		
TF-ARL	Boeing 747-230B (SF)	574/22671	ex N743SA		Lsd fr WFBN
TF-ARM	Boeing 747-230B (SF)	490/22363	ex N744SA		Lsd fr GECAS
TF-ARN	Boeing 747-2F6B (SF)	498/22382	ex N745SA		Lsd fr GECAS
TF-ARO	Boeing 747-243B	618/23301	ex N73718		Lsd fr Boeing
TF-ARQ	Boeing 747-206M (EUD)	539/22380	ex PH-BUT		Lsd
TF-ARS	Boeing 747-357	586/22996	ex ZS-SKA		Lsd fr Flightlease
TF-ARU	Boeing 747-344	577/22970	ex ZS-SAT		Lsd fr SAA
TF-ATC*	Boeing 747-267B	466/22149	ex B-HIB		Lsd fr CPA
TF-ATD	Boeing 747-267B	446/21966	ex B-HIA		Lsd fr CPA
TF-ATE	Boeing 747-246B	197/20531	ex N557SW	std MZJ	Lsd fr Jumbo Jet Lsg
TF-ATF+	Boeing 747-246B	137/19825	ex N556SW	std MZJ	Lsd fr Jumbo Jet Lsg
TF-ATI	Boeing 747-341	702/24107	ex N824DS		Lsd fr ILFC, sublsd to IBE
TF-ATJ	Boeing 747-341	703/24108	ex N420DS		Lsd fr ILFC, sublsd to IBE
TF-ATN	Boeing 747-219B	527/22723	ex G-VBEE		Lsd fr Finova Capital; sublsd to VIR
TF-ATW	Boeing 747-219B	528/22724	ex G-VSSS		Lsd fr/op for VIR
TF-ATX	Boeing 747-236B(SF)	672/23711	ex G-BDXM		Lsd fr Snapdragon; sublsd to MAS
TF-ATZ	Boeing 747-236B(SF)	697/24088	ex G-BDXP		Lsd fr Snapdragon; sublsd to MAS
TF-	Boeing 747-230F	625/23348	ex D-ABZB		on order
TF-	Boeing 747-230B (SF)	660/23621	ex D-ABZF		std MZJ; on order
TF-	Boeing 747-230F	706/24138	ex D-ABZI		on order

*named Capt Johannes R Snorrason   +Named Jan Skuli Sigurdarson

TF-ATO	Boeing 767-204ER	210/24013	ex G-BNYS		Lsd fr Sumitomo
TF-ATP	Boeing 767-204ER	243/24239	ex G-BOPB		Lsd fr Sumitomo
TF-ATR	Boeing 767-204ER	256/24457	ex EC-GHM		Lsd fr GECAS; sublsd to EUK
TF-ATT	Boeing 767-383ER	263/24358	ex OY-KDH		Lsd fr BBAM; sublsd to UVG
TF-ATU	Boeing 767-3Y0ER	464/26204	ex N204GE		Lsd fr debis; sublsd to EUK
TF-ATY	Boeing 767-204ER	107/23072	ex N10698		Lsd fr Heller Air

TF-ARD	Boeing 757-225	74/22211	ex G-OOOV		Lsd fr GATX
TF-ARE	Boeing 757-225	75/22611	ex G-OOOW		Lsd fr GATX
TF-ARI	Boeing 757-2Y0ER	388/25240	ex G-OOOU		Lsd fr Buckingham Partners
TF-ARK	Boeing 757-225	114/22612	ex G-OOOM		Lsd fr Airfund Corp

Specialises in short and long term leases to other operators, mainly as back-up. Aircraft are often stored for short periods.
Air Atlanta Europe (EUK) is a wholly owned subsidiary

AIR ICELAND

Faxi (NY/FXI) (IATA 882) Akureyri/Reykjavik (AEY/REK)

TF-JMG	Fokker 50	20144	ex PH-DMD		Lsd fr Elmo Avn
TF-JMR	Fokker 50	20243	ex TF-FIR	Asdis	
TF-JMS	Fokker 50	20244	ex TF-FIS	Sigdis	
TF-JMT	Fokker 50	20250	ex TF-FIT	Freydis	
TF-JMU	Fokker 50	20264	ex T9-BBC		Lsd fr Elmo Avn

TF-JMC	de Havilland DHC-6 Twin Otter 300	413	ex C-GIZR	
TF-JMD	de Havilland DHC-6 Twin Otter 300	475	ex C-GDAA	
TF-JME	Swearingen SA.227DC Metro 23	DC-880B	ex N3002K	Lsd fr Millennium Lsg
TF-JMK	Swearingen SA.227AC Metro III	AC-467	ex N3046L	
TF-JML	Swearingen SA.227DC Metro 23	DC-881B	ex N3004D	Lsd fr Millennium Lsg

Subsidiary of Icelandair; also known as Flugfelag Islands

BLUEBIRD CARGO

Blue Cargo (BF/BBD) (IATA 290)   Keflavik (KEF)

TF-BBC	Boeing 737-3Q4	1493/24209	ex N209PK	Lsd fr PK Airfinance
TF-BBD	Boeing 737-3Y0F	1701/24463	ex OY-SEE	Op for UPS
TF-BBX	Boeing 737-3Y0(QC)	1242/23499	ex N499AY	Lsd fr Airplanes Holdings
TF-BBY	Boeing 737-3Y0(QC)	1243/23500	ex N500AY	Lsd fr GECAS

ICEBIRD AIRWAYS   now listed under Islandsflug, the parent organisation

---

ICELANDAIR

Iceair (FI/ICE) (IATA 108)   Keflavik/Reykjavik (KEF/REK)

TF-FIG	Boeing 757-23APF	237/24456	ex N571CA		Lsd fr AWAS
TF-FIH	Boeing 757-208	273/24739		Hafdis	Lsd fr BBAM
TF-FII	Boeing 757-208	281/24760		Fanndis	Lsd fr CIT Leasing
TF-FIJ	Boeing 757-208	368/25085	ex G-BTEJ	Svandis	
TF-FIK	Boeing 757-28A	704/26276		Soldis	Lsd fr ILFC
TF-FIN	Boeing 757-208	780/28989	ex N1790B	Bryndis	
TF-FIO	Boeing 757-208	859/29436		Valdis	
TF-FIP	Boeing 757-208	916/30423	ex N1006K	Leifur Erik	Lsd fr Hekla
TF-FIR	Boeing 757-256	593/26242	ex EC-FYJ		Lsd fr Itoh
TF-FIS*	Boeing 757-256	617/26245	ex N542NA		Lsd fr Sunrock
TF-FIT	Boeing 757-23APF	314/24868	ex N868AN		Lsd fr AWMS
TF-FIV	Boeing 757-208	956/30424			
TF-FIW	Boeing 757-27B	302/24838	ex D-ABNX	Loftleidir	Lsd fr Aviation Investors
TF-FIX	Boeing 757-308	1004/29434	ex N60659		

* Operates for Sierra National Airlines and Africa One

| TF-FIA | Boeing 767-3Y0ER | 405/24953 | ex N632TW | Lsd fr CIT Leasing; sublsd to MNF |
| TF-FIB | Boeing 767-383ER | 25365 | ex N365SR | Lsd fr Sunrock; sublsd to MNF |

Air Iceland is a wholly owned subsidiary

ICELANDIC EXPRESS

Keflavik/Reykjavik (KEF/REK)

| G-STRB | Boeing 737-3Y0 | 1625/24255 | ex G-OBWX | Lsd fr/op by AEU |

Commenced services on 27 February 2003

ISLANDSFLUG

Icebird (HH/ICB) (IATA 652)   Reykjavik (REK)

TF-ELC	Boeing 737-3M8	2024/25041	ex OO-LTL	Lsd fr Aerco, sublsd to/op for EXS
TF-ELD	Boeing 737-46B	1679/24124	ex EC-IFN	Lsd fr FUA
TF-ELM	Boeing 737-3M8(QC)	1630/24021	ex F-GIXP	Lsd fr AerCo; sublsd to EXS
TF-ELN	Boeing 737-3Q8QC	1375/23766	ex OO-ILK	Lsd fr Intl A/C Investors
TF-ELO	Boeing 737-33A(QC)	1599/24028	ex F-GIXK	Lsd fr Transcontinental Avn
TF-ELQ	Boeing 737-3Q8	1301/23535	ex TF-SUN	Lsd fr GECAS
TF-ELV	Boeing 737-4S3	1887/24796	ex G-TREN	Lsd fr Triton; op for Airmiles

TF-ELB	Airbus Industrie A300B4-622RF	659	ex N622DS	DHL titles	Lsd fr Treby Worldwide
TF-ELE	Airbus Industrie A310-304F	502	ex N502AN		Lsd fr WFBN
TF-ELF	Dornier 228-202K	8046	ex LN-NVC		Lsd fr Euro Investments
TF-ELG	Airbus Industrie A300C4-605R	758	ex D-ANDY	DHL titles Lsd fr debis; sublsd to AHK
TF-ELH	Dornier 228-201K	8070	ex G-RDGT		
TF-ELS	Airbus Industrie A310-304F	552	ex N283TR	DHL titles	Lsd fr Cloud Partners
TF-ELU	Airbus Industrie A300B4-622RF	657	ex N622RG		Lsd fr Azis Worldwide
TF-ELW	Airbus Industrie A300C4-605R	755	ex D-ABFH		Lsd fr debis

Some aircrft operate as Icebird Airways

JORVIK AVIATION

Icelandic (JVK)   Reykajvik (REK)

TF-JVB	Cessna 402B	402B0875	ex TF-SUD	Lsd fr Glitnir
TF-JVF	Piper PA-31Turbo Navajo B	31-779	ex TF-MYF	Lsd fr Glitnir
TF-JVG	Cessna 404 Titan	404-0033	ex TF-GTX	
TF-JVH	Cessna 402C	402C0355	ex TF-GTC	
TF-JVI	Partenavia P.68B	79	ex TF-GTM	

MD AIRLINES all aircraft returned to lessors and ceased operations

MYFLUG

Myflug (MYA)   *Myvatn (MVA)*

| TF-MYV | Piper PA-31-350 Navajo Chieftain | 31-7852139 | ex TF-OOJ |
| TF-MYY | Cessna U206F Stationair | U20602831 | ex N35960 |

TG - GUATEMALA (Republic of Guatemala)

AEREO RUTA MAYA

Guatemala City-la Aurora (GUA)

| TG-JFT | Cessna 208B Caravan I | 208B0622 |

AGUILAS MAYAS INTERNACIONAL now operate single engine aircraft only

AVCOM / AVIONES COMERCIALES DE GUATEMALA

Guatemala City-la Aurora (GUA)

TG-CAC	de Havilland DHC-6 Twin Otter 300	449	
TG-JAC	de Havilland DHC-6 Twin Otter 300	755	ex C-FCSG
TG-JAJ	de Havilland DHC-6 Twin Otter 300M	774	ex C-GFJQ
TG-JAZ	de Havilland DHC-6 Twin Otter 300	435	ex TF-ORN
TG-JEL	de Havilland DHC-6 Twin Otter 300	722	ex N3H
TG-JAB	Shrike Commander 500S	3303	
TG-JAY	de Havilland DHC-7-102	46	ex C-FYMK	Mundo Maya
TG-JWC	Shrike Commander 500S	3209	

AVIATECA GUATEMALA

Aviateca (GU/GUG) (IATA 240)   *Guatemala City-la Aurora (GUA)*

| N123GU | Boeing 737-2H6 (Nordam 3) | 308/20587 | ex TG-AYA | Lsd fr debis |

A member of Grupo TACA. Inter is a wholly owned subsidiary

DHL DE GUATEMELA

(L3/JOS)   *Guatemala City-la Aurora (GUA)*

| TG-DHL | Swearingen SA.227AC Metro III | AC-520 | ex HC-BQR |

Operate in full DHLcolurs

INTER – TRANSPORTES AEREOS INTER

Transpo-Inter (TSP)   *Guatemala City-la Aurora (GUA)*

TG-EAA	Cessna 208B Caravan I	208B0637	ex N1002Y
TG-JCB	Cessna 208 Caravan I	20800325	ex N5212M
TC-JCS	Cessna 208 Caravan I	20800327	ex N5268E

Wholly owned subisidiary and operates feeder services for AVIATECA using GU flight numbers.

RACSA (RUTAS AEREAS CENTRO AMERICANOS)

Guatemala City-la Aurora (GUA)

| TG-NTR | Nord 262 | 32 | ex N344PL | La Aurora |

TIKAL JET AIRLINES

Tikal (WU/TKC)   *Guatemala City-la Aurora (GUA)*

TG-AGW	LET L-410UVP	831137	ex HR-IAZ	
TG-ALE	Douglas DC-9-51 (ABS 3)	987/48135	ex OH-LYY	
TG-JII	Douglas DC-9-51 (ABS 3)	993/48136	ex OH-LYZ	
TG-TJD	LET L-410UVP	851421	ez CCCP-67157	Petenitza
TG-TJG	LET L-410UVP-E	902419	ex CCCP-67626	
TG-TJK	BAC One-Eleven 401AK	063	ex N217CA	Ciudad Flores
TG-	Douglas DC-9-32 (ABS 3)	625/47529	ex N823AT	

TRANSPORTES AEREOS GUATEMALTECOS

(GUM)   *Guatemala City-la Aurora (GUA)*

| TG-TAG | LET L-410UVP-E | 882028 | ex 2028 |

TG-TAJ   LET L-410UVP   800527   ex N26RZ
TG-TAY   LET L-410UVP   882029   ex Russian AF 2029
Trading name of TAG International Cargo.

TI - COSTA RICA (Republic of Costa Rica)

AEROFAST AIRLINES

San José-Juan Santamaria (SJO)

Reg	Type	c/n	ex	Notes
TI-AYM	Beech 99	U-2	ex N208BH	stored YPQ
TI-AYN	Beech 100	B-84	ex	stored YPQ
TI-AYQ	de Havilland DHC-6 Twin Otter 300	422	ex F-OGJV	stored YPQ

All stored and for sale after Aerofast Airlines were unable to pay for the repaint

AERO COSTA SOL

Costa Sol (CSG)   San José-Juan Santamaria (SJO)

Reg	Type	c/n	ex		Notes
N326BA	Swearingen SA.226TC Metro III	TC-269	ex N43RA		Lsd fr GAS Wilson
N4206M	Swearingen SA.226TC Metro III	TC-230	ex C-GBXE	Freighter	Lsd fr GAS Wilson
TI-ALD	Piper PA-31 Turbo Navajo C/R	31-7712080			
TI-ATF	Piper PA-31 Turbo Navajo C/R	31-7512053			
TI-ATR	Piper PA-31Turbo Navajo	31-677			
TI-AVU	LET L-410UVP-E9	952623	ex OK-ADS		

AVIONES TAXI AEREO

San José-Juan Santamaria (SJO)

Reg	Type	c/n	ex
TI-ASR	Piper PA-31 Turbo Navajo C/R		
TI-ATZ	de Havilland DHC-6 Twin Otter 200	169	ex N931MA

LACSA - COSTA RICA

Lacsa (LR/LRC) (IATA 133)   San José-Juan Santamaria (SJO)

Reg	Type	c/n	ex	Notes
N464TA	Airbus Industrie A320-233	1353	ex F-WWBB	Lsd fr TAI
N481TA	Airbus Industrie A320-233	1500	ex F-WWIE	Lsd fr TAI
N482TA	Airbus Industrie A320-233	1482	ex F-WWDU	Lsd fr TAI
N981LR	Airbus Industrie A320-233	0558	ex F-WWDF	Lsd fr TAI
N991LR	Airbus Industrie A320-233	0561	ex F-WWDM	Lsd fr TAI
N281LF	Boeing 737-2L9 (Nordam 3)	620/22071	ex VR-HKP	Lsd fr TAI

Member of Grupo TACA possibly renamed TACA Costa Rica which has code TAT

NATUREAIR

San José-Juan Santamaria (SJO)

Formerly listed as Travelair

Reg	Type	c/n	ex	Notes
TI-AYA	Britten-Norman BN-2A-8 Islander	626	ex N66177	
TI-AYB	Cessna U206E Stationair	U20601624	ex N9424G	
TI-AYU	Britten-Norman BN-2A-6 Islander	198	ex N104PC	
TI-AZC	de Havilland DHC-6 Twin Otter 300	697	ex N178GC	
TI-	de Havilland DHC-6 Twin Otter 300	433	ex N239SA	Lsd fr CVU

SANSA / SERVICIOS AEREOS NACIONALES

Sansa (RZ/LRS)   San José-Juan Santamaria (SJO)

Reg	Type	c/n	ex
TI-LRU	Cessna 208B Caravan I	208B0570	ex N1024Y
TI-LRV	Cessna 208B Caravan I	208B0614	ex N12397
TI-LRY	Cessna 208B Caravan I	208B0572	ex N1266Z

A subsidiary of LACSA, operates scheduled services for LACSA and TACA using LR codes

TACSA / TAXI AEREO CENTROAMERICANO

San José-Toblas Bolanos/Juan Santamaria (-/SJO)

Reg	Type	c/n	ex
TI-ADT	Piper PA-31 Turbo Navajo	31-403	ex F-OCOE
TI-ATT	Piper PA-31 Turbo Navajo C/R	31-7512030	ex N500PM
TI-ATU	Piper PA-31 Turbo Navajo C/R	31-7512011	ex N111MM
TI-AVF	Piper PA-31 Turbo Navajo	31-582	

TRANS COSTA RICA

Ticos (TCR)   San José-Toblas Bolanos/Juan Santamaria (-/SJO)

Reg	Type	c/n	ex	Notes
TI-AGM	Cessna U206F Stationair	U20601624	ex N9424G	
TI-TRB	Cessna 207 Skywagon	20700067	ex TI-AJR	Principe de Paz

TRAVELAIR now operates as Natureair

TJ - CAMEROON (Republic of Cameroon)

AIR INTER CAMEROUN – AIC

Inter-Cameroun (ICM)   Douala (DLA)

TJ-AIO	Boeing 737-229 (Nordam 3)	437/21139	ex G-BYZN		Sublsd to UYC
					Lsd fr Sterling Air Services

CAMEROON AIRLINES

Cam-Air (UY/UYC) (IATA 604)   Douala (DLA)

TJ-AIO	Boeing 737-229 (Nordam 3)	437/21139	ex G-BYZN		Lsd fr ICM
TJ-CAC	Boeing 767-33AER	822/28138		Le Dja	Lsd fr AWAS
TJ-CAD	Boeing 767-231ER	14/22564	ex N601TW	stored Douala	Lsd fr Rothwell Mgt
TJ-CAE	Boeing 747-312	23033	ex N122KH	Big Boss	Lsd fr Rothwell Mgt
TJ-CCG	Hawker Siddeley HS.748 Srs.2B/435	1805	ex G-11-11	Menchum	stored DLA
YU-AJK	Douglas DC-9-32	689/47568	ex Z3-ARD		Lsd fr JAT
YU-AJL	Douglas DC-9-32 (ABS 3)	695/47571	ex Z3-AAB		Lsd fr JAT

NATIONAL AIRWAYS CAMEROON

Yaounde (YAO)

ZS-NTT	Beech 200 Super King Air	BB-350	ex N125MS		Lsd fr NAC Sales & Lsg
ZS-OLY	Beech 1900D	UE-39	ex N39ZV	Afamba	Lsd fr NAC Sales & Lsg
Wholly owned by NAC Airways, South Africa					

SCHREINER AIRWAYS CAMEROON

Douala (DLA)

TJ-ALL	de Havilland DHC-6 Twin Otter 310	572	ex 5N-AKY	
TJ-CQE	de Havilland DHC-6 Twin Otter 310	662	ex 5N-EVS	
TJ-SAC	de Havilland DHC-6 Twin Otter 310	476	ex 5N-AKP	
TJ-SAD	de Havilland DHC-6 Twin Otter 300	600	ex N612BA	
TJ-SAE	de Havilland DHC-6 Twin Otter 300	675	ex 5N-BCL	
TJ-	Aerospatiale SA.365N3 Dauphin	6571	ex PH-SLW	
TJ-CQD	Aerospatiale SA.365N Dauphin 2	6062	ex 5N-ARM	
TJ-SAB	de Havilland DHC-8-311A	276	ex PH-SDT	Lsd fr GECAS
TJ-SAZ	Aerospatiale SA.365C2 Dauphin	5050	ex 5N-ALV	
Wholly owned subsidiary of Schreiner Airways				

TL - CENTRAL AFRICAN REPUBLIC

AFRICAN AIRLINES

TL-ADJ	Boeing 707-329C	828/20200	ex 9Q-CBW	stored Vatry

TN - CONGO BRAZZAVILE (People's Republic of Congo)

AERO-FRET BUSINESS

Brazzaville (BZV)

TN-AGY	Antonov An-12
TN-AHA	Antonov An-12

AEROSERVICE

Congoserv (BF/RSR)   Brazzaville/Pointe Noire (BZV/PNR)

EK-46656	Antonov An-24RV	47309302	
ER-AZP	Antonov An-24RV	17307002	
EX-42342	Yakovlev Yak-42D	4520421706302	ex UN-42342
TN-ACY	Cessna 402B	402B0810	ex TR-LTN
TN-ADN	Britten-Norman BN-2A-9 Islander	647	ex TL-AAQ
TN-ADY	Britten-Norman BN-2A-9 Islander	764	ex TR-LWL
TN-AEK	Cessna 404 Titan	404-0132	ex TR-LXI
TN-AEL	Cessna U206G Stationair 6	U20604793	
TN-AFA	CASA C.212-100 Aviocar	CB13-1-151	ex HB-LKX
TN-AFD	CASA C.212-300 Aviocar	DF72-2-398	ex D4-CBB
TN-AGY	Antonov An-12		
TN-AHA	Antonov An-12		

AIR ATLANTIC-CONGO current status is uncertain, sole aircraft returned to lessor

CARGO EXPRESS CONGO ceased operations

CONGO AIRLINES

Brazzaville (BZV)

3D-ALB	Boeing 727-256	912/20600	ex (9L-LCY)	
9L-	Boeing 727-247 (FedEx 3)	1341/21482	ex N830WA	Lsd fr Al-Barka Pty
9L-	Boeing 737-2B7 (Nordam 3)	966/22885	ex N273AU	Lsd fr Business Avn

EQUAFLIGHT SERVICE

Equaflight Congo (5E/EKA)   *Pointe Noir (PNR)*

F-HBCA	Beech 1900D	UE-188	ex SE-KXV	Lsd fr OJF

Associated with Occitania Jet Fleet

INTER CONGO

Brazzaville (BZV)

TN-AGU	Antonov An-26		
TN-AHB	Antonov An-26	99901908	ex RA-47183

LINA CONGO status uncertain; sole aircraft returned to lessor

REGIONAL AIR sole aircraft stored and believed to have ceased operations

TRANSAIR CONGO

Trans-Congo (Q8/TSG)   *Brazzaville/Pointe Noir (BZV/PNR)*

A6-ZYA	Boeing 737-2S2C	597/21926	ex N720A	Lsd fr FDN
RA-46495	Antonov An-24RV	27308208	ex CCCP-46495	Lsd fr Aquiline Lsg
RA-47811	Antonov An-24RV	17307003	ex TC-KHT	Lsd fr Aquiline Lsg
TN-AFL	Antonov An-24B	07306103	ex RA-46380	Lsd fr Aquiline Lsg
TN-AFZ	Boeing 727-23	542/19839	ex D2-FLZ	Lsd fr Kirra
TN-AGD	LET L-410MU	781116		
TN-AGK	Antonov An-12BP	402006	ex RA-11991	
ZS-XGW	Fokker F.28 Fellowship 4000	11130	ex SE-DGN	Lsd fr AQU

TR - GABON (Gabonese Republic)

AIR AFFAIRES GABON

Libreville (LBV)

TR-LEM	Cessna 208B Caravan I	0585	ex N1205M	
TR-LFO	Beech 1900D	UE-313	ex ZS-OCW	Lsd fr Rossair
TR-LFX	Cessna 208B Caravan I	208B0796	ex N99FX	
ZS-OCX	Beech 1900D	UE-321	ex N22978	Lsd fr Rossair

AIR EXCELLENCE

Libreville (LBV)

ZS-NWW	Hawker Siddeley.748 Srs.2B/378	1786	ex G-HDBC	Lsd fr EAS

AIR GABON

Golf November (GN/AGN) (IATA 185)   *Libreville (LBV)*

F-ODJG	Boeing 747-2Q2M	324/21468	ex (TR-LXK)	President Leon Mba
TR-LEV	Boeing 727-228	1605/22083	ex F-OHOA	stored LBV
TR-LFH	Boeing 767-266ER	97/23178	ex N767ER	Lsd fr Leopard Lsg
TR-LFU	Boeing 737-408	1721/24353	ex TF-FIB	Lsd fr CIT Leasing
TR-LST	Fokker F.28 Fellowship 2000	11080	ex PH-EXC	Libreville; stored LBV
TR-LXL	Boeing 737-2Q2C	515/21467		Le Makokou
TR-	Fokker F.28 Fellowship 4000	11126	ex SE-DGL	
3D-AAJ	Boeing 737-222	97/19075	ex 3C-AAJ	Lsd fr Avn Consultants

AIR GABON EXPRESS

Libreville (LBV)

TR-LFW	Hawker Siddeley HS.748 Srs 2A	1611	ex 9L-LBH	Lsd fr Liberavia

Same organisation as Gabon Express?

576

AIR MAX GABON

Libreville (LBV)

TR-LGH	Fokker F.27 Friendship 300M	10154	ex TN-AGX	Lsd fr Orcom Trading
S9-SSA	Antonov An-26		ex	

AIR SERVICE GABON

(G8/AQB)   *Libreville (LBV)*

TR-LFJ	de Havilland DHC-8-311	332	ex N106AV	retd or on overhaul in Canada?
TR-LGC	de Havilland DHC-8-102	241	ex PH-TTB	Lsd fr debis
TR-LGR	de Havilland DHC-8-102A	237	ex PH-TTA	Lsd fr SCH
TR-LZW	CASA C.212-200 Aviocar	CC29-180	ex N1710U	

AVIREX

Avirex-Gabon (G2/VXG)   *Libreville (LBV)*

TR-LBM	Cessna 404 Titan	404-0453	ex D-ICRG		
TR-LCN	Britten-Norman BN-2A-9 Islander	744	ex TR-LYU		
TR-LEB	Cessna 402B	402B1078	ex TN-AEZ		Lsd fr Beretford
TR-LEI	Piper PA-31 Turbo Navajo B	31-7300904	ex N4330B		Lsd fr Beretford
TR-LEQ	Reims Cessna F406 Caravan II	F406-0007	ex LX-LMS		Lsd fr Relwood
TR-LFG	Cessna 404 Titan	404-0844	ex TJ-AHY		
TR-LFP	Beech 1900C-1	UC-74	ex F-GOPK		
TR-LFS	Aerospatiale/Alenia ATR 42-300	031	ex F-WQNA	on order	
TR-LGA	Aerospatiale/Alenia ATR 42-300	041	ex F-WQNJ		Lsd fr ATR Asset Mgt
TR-LGP	Fokker F.28 Fellowship 4000	11126	ex SE-DGL		Lsd fr Jet Aviation
TR-LVR	Cessna 207 Skywagon	20700310	ex N1710U		

GABON EXPRESS

Gabex (GBE)   *Libreville (LBV)*

3D-DLN	Grumman G-159 Gulfstream I	25	ex 4X-ARH		
3D-DYS	NAMC YS-11A	2051	ex 3C-QRM		Lsd fr Fields Airmotive
3D-JCP	Fokker F.27 Friendship	10430	ex TT-WAK	Le Chari	Lsd fr Fields Airmotive
3D-TRE	Grumman G-159 Gulfstream I	042	ex ZS-OCA		Lsd fr Fields Airmotive

Same organisation as Air Gabon Express?

NATIONAL AIRWAYS GABON

Libreville (LBV)

9G-AIR	Fokker F.27 Friendship 100	10266	ex SE-KZF	Lsd fr/op by Sobel Air
9G-BEL	Fokker F.27 Friendship 100	10319	ex SE-KZH	Lsd fr/op by Sobel Air
9G-SOB	Fokker F.27 Friendship 100	10287	ex SE-KZG	Lsd fr/op by Sobel Air

Aircraft wear La Nationale titles

TS - TUNISIA

KARTHAGO AIRLINES

Karthago (5R/KAJ)   *Tunis-Carthage/Djerba-Zarzis (TUN/DJE)*

TS-IEC	Boeing 737-33A	2008/25010	ex OO-LTW	Lsd fr AWAS
TS-IED	Boeing 737-33A	2014/25032	ex OO-LTP	Lsd fr AWAS
TS-IEE	Boeing 737-33A	1955/24790	ex 5H-TCA	Lsd fr AWAS
TS-IEF	Boeing 737-3Q8	2674/26309	ex N73380	Lsd fr MSA V

Karthago Airlines is the trading name of Tunis Karthago Airlines

MEDITERRANEAN AIR SERVICE sole aircraft returned to lessor and believed to have ceased operations

NOUVELAIR

Nouvelair (BJ/LBT)   *Monastir (MIB)*

TS-INA	Airbus Industrie A320-214	1121	ex F-WWBT	Dora	Lsd to IRA
TS-INB	Airbus Industrie A320-214	1175	ex F-WWDO		Lsd fr GECAS
TS-INC	Airbus Industrie A320-214	1744	ex F-WWBS	Youssef	Lsd to IRA
TS-IND	Airbus Industrie A320-212	0348	ex OY-CNN		Lsd fr GECAS
TS-INE	Airbus Industrie A320-212	0222	ex OY-CNC		Lsd fr GECAS
TS-INF	Airbus Industrie A320-212	0299	ex G-JDFW		Lsd fr ALPS 94-1
TS-ING	Airbus Industrie A320-211	0140	ex D-AKFW		Lsd to AAW
TS-INH	Airbus Industrie A320-211	0157	ex D-AKFY		Lsd to AAW
EI-CEK	McDonnell-Douglas MD-83	1596/49631	ex EC-FMY		Lsd fr GECAS
EI-CNO	McDonnell-Douglas MD-83	1494/49672	ex EC-FTU		Lsd fr GECAS

F-GRMI   McDonnell-Douglas MD-83   2134/53488
Nouvelair is the trading name of Nouvel Air Tunisie (Nouvelair). Nouvelair International is a sister company

NOUVELAIR INTERNATIONAL

Nouvinter (NVJ)   Tunis-Carthage (TUN)

TS-IAX	Airbus Industrie A300B4-622R	601	ex JY-GAX	Lsd fr/op for LAA
TS-IAY	Airbus Industrie A300B4-620	354	ex A6-SHZ	Lsd to AAW
TS-IAZ	Airbus Industrie A300B4-622R	616	ex JY-GAZ	Lsd fr/op for LAA
TS-IGU	Airbus Industrie A310-203	295	ex JY-AGU	Lsd fr/op for LAA
TS-IGV	Airbus Industrie A310-203	306	ex JY-AGV	Lsd fr/op for LAA

TUNINTER

(UG/TUI)   Tunis-Carthage (TUN)

TS-LBA	Aerospatiale/Alenia ATR 42-300	245	ex G-BXBV	stored TUN
TS-LBB	Aerospatiale/Alenia ATR 72-202	258	ex F-WWLE	Habib Bourghiba
TS-LBC	Aerospatiale/Alenia ATR 72-202	281	ex F-WWLK	Tahar Haddad

40% owned by Tunis Air

TUNISAIR

Tunair (TU/TAR) (IATA 199)   Tunis-Carthage (TUN)

TS-IMB	Airbus Industrie A320-211	0119	ex F-WWIJ	Fahrat Hached	
TS-IMC	Airbus Industrie A320-211	0124	ex F-WWIS	7 Novembre	
TS-IMD	Airbus Industrie A320-211	0205	ex F-WWDO	Khereddine	
TS-IME	Airbus Industrie A320-211	0123	ex F-OGYC	Tabarka	
TS-IMF	Airbus Industrie A320-211	0370	ex F-WWIP	Djerba	
TS-IMG	Airbus Industrie A320-211	0390	ex F-WWDL	Abou el Kacem Chebbi	
TS-IMH	Airbus Industrie A320-211	0402	ex F-WWBN	Ali Belhaouane	
TS-IMI	Airbus Industrie A320-211	0511	ex F-WWDC	Jughurta	
TS-IMJ	Airbus Industrie A319-114	0869	ex D-AVYW	El Kantaoui	
TS-IMK	Airbus Industrie A319-114	0880	ex D-AVYD	Kerkenah	
TS-IML	Airbus Industrie A320-211	0958	ex F-WWBI	Gafsa El Ksar	
TS-IMM	Airbus Industrie A320-211	0975	ex F-WWIR	Le Bardo	
TS-IMN	Airbus Industrie A320-211	1187	ex F-WWDU	Ibn Khaldoun	
TS-IMO	Airbus Industrie A319-114	1479	ex D-AVYT	Hannibal	
TS-IMP	Airbus Industrie A320-211	1700	ex F-WWIS	La Galite	
TS-IOC	Boeing 737-2H3	607/21973		Salammbo	stored TUN
TS-IOD	Boeing 737-2H3C	615/21974		Bulla Regia	stored TUN
TS-IOE	Boeing 737-2H3	758/22624		Zarzis	Lsd to SUD
TS-IOF	Boeing 737-2H3	776/22625		Sousse	Lsd to SUD
TS-IOG	Boeing 737-5H3	2253/26639		Sfax	
TS-IOH	Boeing 737-5H3	2474/26640		Hammamet	
TS-IOI	Boeing 737-5H3	2583/27257		Mahdia	
TS-IOJ	Boeing 737-5H3	2701/27912		Monastir	
TS-IOK	Boeing 737-6H3	268/29496		Kairouan	
TS-IOL	Boeing 737-6H3	282/29497		Tozeur-Nefta	
TS-IOM	Boeing 737-6H3	310/29498		Carthage	
TS-ION	Boeing 737-6H3	510/29499		Utioue	
TS-IOP	Boeing 737-6H3	543/29500		El Jem	
TS-IOQ	Boeing 737-6H3	563/29501		Bizerte	
TS-IOR	Boeing 737-6H3	816/29502		Tahar Haddad	
TS-IPA	Airbus Industrie A300B4-605R	558	ex A6-EKD	Sidi Bou Said	
TS-IPB	Airbus Industrie A300B4-605R	563	ex A6-EKE	Tunis	
TS-IPC	Airbus Industrie A300B4-605R	505	ex F-OIHB	Amilcar	

Owns 40% of Tuninter

TUNISAVIA

Tunisavia (TAJ)   Tunis-Carthage (TUN)

TS-HSD	Aerospatiale SA.365N Dauphin 2	6117	
TS-HSE	Aerospatiale SA.365N Dauphin 2	6150	
TS-LIB	de Havilland DHC-6 Twin Otter 300	716	ex TS-DIB
TS-LSF	de Havilland DHC-6 Twin Otter 300	575	ex TS-DSF

TT - TCHAD (Republic of Chad)

AIR HORIZON AFRIQUE

Tchad-Horizon (TPK)   N'djamena (NDJ)

Operates cargo flights with Antonov An-12 freighters leased from other operators as required

578

AIR TCHAD current status uncertain, sole aircraft disposed of and believed to have ceased operations

TU - IVORY COAST (Republic of the Ivory Coast)

AFRIC'AIR CHARTERS now correctly listed under Benin

AFRIQUE REGIONAL AIRWAYS
Afrair (AFW)   *Abidjan (ABJ)*

Operates charter services with aircraft leased from Euralair Horizons as required

AIR CONTINENTAL
Abidjan (ABJ)

TU-TOD	Cessna U206F Stationair	U20601893	ex TT-BAR
TU-TOG	Swearingen SA.226AT Merlin IV	AT-051	ex C-FTJC
XT-OAG	Nord 262C-50P	36	ex XT-MAJ

AIR INTER IVOIRE
Inter Ivoire (NTV)   *Abidjan (ABJ)*

TU-TGF	Piper PA-31-350 Navajo Chieftain	31-7305072	ex N74930
TU-TJL	Piper PA-31T Cheyenne II	31T-7720033	ex N82152
TU-TJN	Beech 58 Baron	TH-776	ex HB-GGE

AIR IVOIRE
Air Ivoire (VU/VUN)   *Abidjan (ABJ)*

TU-TIW	Fokker F.28 Fellowship 4000	11233	ex N483US	Lsd fr ING Lease
TU-TIX	Fokker F.28 Fellowship 4000	11237	ex N486US	Lsd fr ING Lease
TU-TIY	Fokker F.28 Fellowship 4000	11238	ex N487US	Lsd fr ING Lease

Air Ivoire is the trading name of Nouvelle Air Ivoire

PANAFRICAN AIRWAYS
(PQ/PNF)

Current fleet details are not known at the time of publication

TY - BENIN (Republic of Benin)

AERO BENIN
(EM/AEB) (IATA 282)   *Cotonou (COO)*

Operates services with Boeing 727 aircraft leased from Interair as and when required

AFRICAIR CHARTERS
Benin Charters (7A/AFF)   *Cotonou (COO)*

Operates charter flights with Airbus Industrie A310 aircraft leased from Euralair Horizons as required

AFRIQUE AIRLINES
(X5/FBN)   *Cotonou (COO)*

F-GEMO	Airbus Industrie A310-304	504	F-WWCF	Lsd fr EGN

BENIN GOLF AIR
(A8/BGL)   *Cotonou (COO)*

Operates freight charters with Boeing 707 or Ilyushin Il-76 aircraft leased from other operators as and when required

TRANS AIR BENIN
Trans-Benin (Y7/TNB)   *Cotonou (COO)*

Operates services with aircraft leased from Airquarius Aviation or TransAir Congo as required

TZ - MALI (Republic of Mali)

<u>AFRICAN AIRLINES</u> believed to have ceased operations

AFRIQUE AIR AFFAIRES

Air Affaires (FAS)   *Bamako (BKO)*

Operates charters with Cessna 402Bs leased from Sahel Aviation Services as and when required

<u>AIR MALI INTERNATIONAL</u> ceased operations and liquidated at auction 07 April 2003

AVION EXPRESS

Avion Express (VXP)   *Bamako (BKO)*

3X-GDL	LET L-410UVP	

MALI AIRWAYS

(Z8)   *Bamako (BKO)*

Current fleet details are uncertain

NAS-AIR

Air Bane NCM)   *Bamako (BKO)*

Operates charter flights with Airbus Industrie A310 aircraft leased from Euralair Horizons as required

SAHEL AVIATION SERVICES

Savser (SAO)   *Bamako (BKO)*

TZ-AMS	Cessna 402C	402C0517	ex N68802	
TZ-ZBC	Beech 200 Super King Air	BB-86	ex N577BC	CatPass 250 conv

<u>STA-MALI</u> renamed STA-Trans African Airlines

STA - TRANS AFRICAN AIRLINES

STA Mali (T8/SBA)   *Bamako (BKO)*

3X-GDK	LET L-410UVP				
3X-GDL	LET L-410UVP				
5V-TTF	LET L-410UVP-E3	871921	ex 9L-LBU		
5V-TTG	LET L-410UVP	871926	ex S9-LBT		
5V-TTH	LET L-410UVP	871911	ex 9L-LBJ (2)		
TZ-ASM	Britten-Norman BN-2A-9 Islander	700	ex 6V-AES		Lsd fr Gestfin
3D-MES	Douglas DC-9-32 (ABS 3)	719/47598	ex C-FTMZ	Toumbouctou	Lsd fr C-S Avn
5V-TTB	Britten-Norman BN-2A-26 Islander	717			
5V-TTK	Douglas DC-9-32 (ABS 3)	302/47198	ex C-FTLW		

T3 - KIRIBATI (Republic of Kiribati)

AIR KIRIBATI

Tarawa-Bonriki Intl (TRW)

T3-ATI	Harbin Y-12 II	0077		
T3-ATJ	CASA C.212-200 Aviocar	356	ex N398FL	
T3-ATR	Aerospatiale/Alenia ATR 72-200	456	ex F-OHJA	Lsd fr ATR Asset Mgt

T8A - PALAU (Republic of Palau)

T8A103	Britten-Norman BN-2A-26 Islander	2043	ex RP-C693	Operator unknown

PALAU AIR MICRONESIA

Koror-Airai (ROR)

	Boeing 737-33A	1729/24094	ex F-ODGX	on order	Lsd fr Volito

Operated under Air New Zealand AOC

580

PALAU TRANS PACIFIC AIRLINES

Transpacific (6P/PTP)   *Koror-Airai (ROR)*

Operates scheduled passenger services with Boeing 737-809 aircraft leased from Mandarin Airlines as required

T9 - BOSNIA-HERZEGOVINA (Republic of Bosnia-Herzegovina)

AIR BOSNA suspended operations and filed for bankruptcy

AIR SRPSKA ceased operations in late October 2003 and sole aircraft returned to lessor

BIOAIR ceased operations

BOSNIA AIRLINES

(BSL)   *Sarajevo (SJJ)*

Current fleet details are unknown

DARDAN AIR did not restart operations

UK - UZBEKISTAN (Republic of Uzbekistan)

Note: It is reported that only some a/c registered in Uzbekistan carry the "-" in the registration.

AVIALEASING

Twinarrow (EC/TWN)   *Tashkent-Yuzhny/Miami-Opa Locka,FL (TAS/OPF)*

UK 11418	Antonov An-12BP	7344705	ex 3C-QRN	based OPF	Lsd fr TBS Aviation
UK 26001	Antonov An-26B	67314402	ex UK 26213	based OPF	Lsd fr TSS Aviation
UK 26002	Antonov An-26	07309104	ex UK 93914	based OPF	
UK 26003	Antonov An-26	07310406	ex S9-BOW	based OPF, The Skies the Limit	
UR-GLS	Antonov An-26B	10109	ex RA-26017	based OPF	Lsd fr GOR
4K-86810	Ilyushin Il-76MD	053404094	ex RA-86810		

Those based at Opa Locka, FL operate cargo flights for Bahamasair and DHL

INTER-CARGO SERVICE

Inter Cargo (ICF)   *Tashkent-Yuzhny (TAS)*

Operates cargo flights with Ilyushin Il-76TD freighters, leased from other operators as required

TAPO-AVIA

Tapoavia (3S/TPR)   *Tashkent-Vostochny*

UK 11804	Antonov An-12BP	2400806	ex CCCP-11804	
UK 11807	Antonov An-12BK	00346910	ex CCCP-11807	
UK 58644	Antonov An-12BP	2340303	ex CCCP-58644	
UK 76375	Ilyushin Il-76TD	1033414496		
UK 76427	Ilyushin Il-76TD	1013406207	ex 06207	Lsd to ASE
UK 76821	Ilyushin Il-76TD	0023441200	ex YI-ALR	Lsd to ASE
UK 76831	Ilyushin Il-76TD	1013409287	ex CCCP-76831	Lsd to AJC
UK 91006	Antonov An-140	202		

Tapo-Avia is a division of Chkalov Tashkent Aircraft Factory; aircraft registered to Republic of Uzbekistan

UZBEKISTAN AIRWAYS / UZBEKISTAN HAVO YULLARI

Uzbek (HY/UZB)   *Tashkent-Yuzhny (TAS)*

UK 46223	Antonov An-24B	67303102	ex CCCP-46223	
UK 46360	Antonov An-24B	07305901	ex RA-46360	stored TAS
UK 46373	Antonov An-24B	07306004	ex CCCP-46373	stored TAS
UK 46387	Antonov An-24B	07306110	ex CCCP-46387	
UK 46392	Antonov An-24B	07306205	ex CCCP-46392	
UK 46410	Antonov An-24RV	77304005	ex CCCP-46410	
UK 46573	Antonov An-24B	87304807	ex CCCP-46573	stored TAS
UK 46594	Antonov An-24B	97305104	ex CCCP-46594	
UK 46623	Antonov An-24RV	37308710	ex CCCP-46623	stored
UK 46658	Antonov An-24RV	47309304	ex CCCP-46658	
UK 47274	Antonov An-24B	07306404	ex CCCP-47274	
UK 86569	Ilyushin Il-62M	1356234		VIP; op for govt
UK 86573	Ilyushin Il-62M	4140536	ex CCCP-86573	
UK 86574	Ilyushin Il-62M	3344833	ex CCCP-86574	stored TAS
UK 86575	Ilyushin Il-62M	1647928	ex CCCP-86575	

Registration	Type	Serial	Ex	Notes
UK 86576	Ilyushin Il-62M	4546257	ex CCCP-86576	
UK 86577	Ilyushin Il-62M	2748552	ex CCCP-86577	
UK 86578	Ilyushin Il-62M	1951525	ex CCCP-86578	
UK 86579	Ilyushin Il-62M	2951636	ex CCCP-86579	
UK 76351	Ilyushin Il-76TD	1013408240	ex RA-76351	
UK 76353	Ilyushin Il-76TD	1023414454	ex 76353	
UK 76358	Ilyushin Il-76TD	1023410339		
UK 76359	Ilyushin Il-76TD	1033414483		
UK 76426	Ilyushin Il-76TD	1043419644	ex RA-76426	
UK 76428	Ilyushin Il-76TD	1043419648	ex CCCP-76427	
UK 76448	Ilyushin Il-76TD	1023413443	ex CCCP-76448	Lsd to ESL
UK 76449	Ilyushin Il-76TD	1023413443	ex CCCP-76449	
UK 76782	Ilyushin Il-76TD	0093498971	ex 9Q-CLF	stored TAS
UK 76793	Ilyushin Il-76TD	0093498951	ex CCCP-76793	
UK 76794	Ilyushin Il-76TD	0093498954	ex RA-76794	stored TAS
UK 76805	Ilyushin Il-76TD	1003403109	ex CCCP-76805	
UK 76811	Ilyushin Il-76TD	1013407223	ex CCCP-76811	stored TAS
UK 76813	Ilyushin Il-76TD	1013408246	ex CCCP-76813	stored TAS
UK-76824	Ilyushin Il-76TD	1023410327	ex CCCP-76824	stored TAS
UK 86012	Ilyushin Il-86	0010	ex CCCP-86012	
UK 86016	Ilyushin Il-86	51483202014	ex CCCP-86016	stored TAS
UK 86052	Ilyushin Il-86	51483202019	ex CCCP-86052	stored TAS
UK 86053	Ilyushin Il-86	51483203020	ex CCCP-86053	stored TAS
UK 86056	Ilyushin Il-86	51483203023	ex CCCP-86056	
UK 86057	Ilyushin Il-86	51483203024	ex CCCP-86057	stored TAS
UK 86064	Ilyushin Il-86	51483203031	ex CCCP-86064	
UK 86072	Ilyushin Il-86	51483204039	ex CCCP-86072	stored TAS
UK 86083	Ilyushin Il-86	51483206054	ex 86083	stored TAS
UK 86090	Ilyushin Il-86	51483207061	ex CCCP-86090	stored TAS
UK 85286	Tupolev Tu-154B	78A-286	ex CCCP-85286	stored MRV
UK 85344	Tupolev Tu-154B-2	79A-344	ex CCCP-85344	
UK 85356	Tupolev Tu-154B-2	79A-356	ex CCCP-85356	Freighter; stored TAS
UK 85370	Tupolev Tu-154B-2	79A-370	ex CCCP-85370	stored TAS
UK 85397	Tupolev Tu-154B-2	80A-397	ex CCCP-85397	stored TAS
UK 85398	Tupolev Tu-154B-2	80A-398	ex CCCP-85398	
UK 85401	Tupolev Tu-154B-2	80A-401	ex CCCP-85401	stored TAS
UK 85416	Tupolev Tu-154B-2	80A-416	ex CCCP-85416	stored TAS
UK 85438	Tupolev Tu-154B-2	80A-438	ex CCCP-85438	stored TAS
UK 85449	Tupolev Tu-154B-2	80A-449	ex CCCP-85449	
UK 85575	Tupolev Tu-154B-2	83A-575	ex CCCP-85575	
UK 85578	Tupolev Tu-154B-2	83A-578	ex CCCP-85578	
UK 85600	Tupolev Tu-154B-2	84A-600	ex CCCP-85600	Op for Govt
UK 85711	Tupolev Tu-154M	91A-887	ex CCCP-85711	
UK 85764	Tupolev Tu-154M	93A-947	ex RA-85764	
UK 85776	Tupolev Tu-154M	93A-958		
UK 87289	Yakovlev Yak-40	9320428	ex CCCP-87289	
UK 87367	Yakovlev Yak-40	9341731	ex CCCP-87367	dbr 09Apr03?
UK 87378	Yakovlev Yak-40	9421425	ex RA-87378	VIP
UK 87396	Yakovlev Yak-40	9410833	ex CCCP-87396	
UK 87799	Yakovlev Yak-40	9040316	ex CCCP-87799	
UK 87923	Yakovlev Yak-40	9741455	ex CCCP-87923	VIP
UK 87989	Yakovlev Yak-40	9541344	ex CCCP-87989	
UK 87996	Yakovlev Yak-40	9542044	ex CCCP-87996	
UK 88194	Yakovlev Yak-40	9621448	ex CCCP-88194	
UK 88217	Yakovlev Yak-40	9630350	ex CCCP-88217	VIP
UK 88242	Yakovlev Yak-40	9641551	ex CCCP-88242	
UK 11369	Antonov An-12BP	6343810	ex RA-11369	
UK 11372	Antonov An-12BP	5343204	ex CCCP-12130	stored TAS
UK 31001	Airbus Industrie A310-324	574	ex F-OGQY	Tashkent
UK 31002	Airbus Industrie A310-324	576	ex F-OGQZ	Fergana
UK 31003	Airbus Industrie A310-324	706	ex F-WWCM	Bukhara
UK 75700	Boeing 757-23P	731/28338		Op for Govt
UK 80001	Avro RJ85	E2312	ex G-6-312	VIP a/c
UK 80002	Avro RJ85	E2309	ex G-6-309	
UK 80003	Avro RJ85	E2319	ex G-6-319	
UK 91102	Ilyushin Il-114-100	1063800202	ex UK 91009	
UK-76701*	Boeing 767-33PER	635/28370	ex VP-BUA	Samarkand
VP-BUB*	Boeing 757-23P	875/30060	ex UK-75701	Urgench
VP-BUD*	Boeing 757-23P	886/30061	ex N6066Z	Shahrisbaz
VP-BUE	Boeing 767-3CBER	904/33469	ex N594HA	Lsd fr BCC Equipment
VP-BUZ*	Boeing 767-33PER	650/28392	ex (UK 76702)	Khiva
	Boeing 767-300ER			on order 4Q04

*Leased from Uzbekistan Finance Ltd

UN - KAZAKHSTAN (Republic of Kazakhstan)

ABSOLUTE KAZAKSTAN COMPANY believed to have ceased operations

AEROTRANS

Bachyt (ATG)   *Taraz (DMB)*

| UN-85422 | Tupolev Tu-154B-2 | 80A-422 | ex LZ-BTS |
| UN-85569 | Tupolev Tu-154B-2 | 82A-569 | ex CCCP-85569 |

AIR ASTANA

Astanaline (4L/SXA)   *Astana (TSE)*

P4-BAS	Boeing 737-8Q8	752/30627	ex N800SY	Primo	Lsd fr ILFC
P4-CAS	Boeing 737-7Q8	1011/30629	ex N710SY		Lsd fr ILFC
P4-DAS	Boeing 737-7Q8	1097/30642	ex N711SY		Lsd fr ILFC
P4-EAS	Boeing 757-2G5	830/29488	ex D-AMUG		Lsd fr Pegasus Avn
P4-FAS	Boeing 757-2G5	834/29489	ex D-AMUH		Lsd fr Pegasus Avn
P4-GAS	Boeing 757-2G5	708/28112	ex D-AMUI		Lsd fr Unicapital

Began operating key ex-Air Kazakstan routes from August 2002; joint venture between BAE Systems and government

AIR KAZAKSTAN

Air Kazakstan (9Y/KZK) (IATA 452)   *Almaty/Astana (ALA/TSE)*
Believed ceased operations from 12th February 2004

UN-46396	Antonov An-24B	07306210	ex CCCP-46396	
UN-46492	Antonov An-24RV	27308205?	ex CCCP-46492	
UN-46500	Antonov An-24RV	37308305	ex CCCP-46500	
UN-46626	Antonov An-24RV	37308805	ex CCCP-46626	
UN-46664	Antonov An-24RV	473099505?	ex RA-46664	
UN-47277	Antonov An-24B	07306407	ex CCCP-47277	
UN-47284	Antonov An-24B	07306504	ex CCCP-47284	
UN-47293	Antonov An-24RV	07306603	ex CCCP-47293	
UN-47299	Antonov An-24RV	.7306702?	ex CCCP-47299	
UN-47350	Antonov An-24RV	67310509	ex CCCP-47350	stored ALA
UN-47822	Antonov An-24RV	17307203	ex CCCP-47822	stored ALA
UN-47832	Antonov An-24B	17307304	ex CCCP-47832	stored ALA
UN-47833	Antonov An-24B	17307305?	ex CCCP-47833	
(UN-86068)	Ilyushin Il-86	51483204035	ex RA-86144	Lsd to ESL
UN-86069	Ilyushin Il-86	51483240036	ex CCCP-86069	stored ALA
UN-86071	Ilyushin Il-86	51483204038	ex CCCP-86071	stored ALA
UN-86077	Ilyushin Il-86	51483205047	ex CCCP-86077	
UN-86086	Ilyushin Il-86	51483206057	ex CCCP-86086	stored ALA
UN-86101	Ilyushin Il-86	51483207069	ex CCCP-86101	stored ALA
UN-85521	Tupolev Tu-154B-2	82A-521	ex CCCP-85521	
UN-85589	Tupolev Tu-154B-2	82A-589	ex CCCP-85589	stored VKO
UN-85775	Tupolev Tu-154M	93A-957	ex RA-85775	Lsd fr Makmir Leasing
UN-85780	Tupolev Tu-154M	93A-964	ex RA-85780	
UN-85781	Tupolev Tu-154M	93A-965	ex RA-85781	
UN-85782	Tupolev Tu-154M	93A-966	ex RA-85782	still wears VIP Air titles
				Lsd fr Makmir Leasing
UN-87202	Yakovlev Yak-40K	9812056	ex EP-EAK	
UN-87213	Yakovlev Yak-40K	9641050	ex OK-GEK	Uralsk
UN-87274	Yakovlev Yak-40	9311027	ex CCCP-87274	
UN-87491	Yakovlev Yak-40	9621647	ex 87491	
UN-87492	Yakovlev Yak-40	9541545	ex CCCP-87492	
UN-87498	Yakovlev Yak-40	9540146	ex 87498	
UN-87501	Yakovlev Yak-40	9512039	ex CCCP-87501	stored PWQ
UN-87543	Yakovlev Yak-40	9530842	ex CCCP-87543	
UN-87909	Yakovlev Yak-40	9731454	ex CCCP-87909	
UN-87934	Yakovlev Yak-40K	9740556	ex CCCP-87934	
UN-88154	Yakovlev Yak-40	9610846	ex CCCP-88154	
UN-88249	Yakovlev Yak-40	9640252	ex CCCP-88249	
UN-A3101	Airbus Industrie A310-322	399	ex D-ASRA	Lsd fr Boeing Capital
UN-A3102	Airbus Industrie A310-322	412	ex D-ASRB	Lsd fr Boeing Capital
UN-B3703	Boeing 737-2T4	1154/23444	ex N234GE	Lsd fr debis
UN-B3705	Boeing 737-2Q8	748/22453	ex UR-BVZ	Lsd fr GECAS
UN-B3706	Boeing 737-2M8	664/22090	ex HA-LEB	Almaty	Lsd fr GECAS
UN-B6701	Boeing 767-2DXER	861/32954		Op for Government
UN-26579	Antonov An-26B	46313406	ex CCCP-26579	
UN-42703	Yakovlev Yak-42D	4520424116690	ex UN-42407	
UN-42712	Yakovlev Yak-42D	4520423309017	ex UN-42447	
UN-42721	Yakovlev Yak-42D	4520424310017	ex UN-42448	

UN-42730	Yakovlev Yak-42D	4520423307017	ex UN-42558		
UN-65147	Tupolev Tu-134A-3	61012	ex CCCP-65147	stored ALA	
UN-65787	Tupolev Tu-134A	62798	ex CCCP-65787	stored ALA	
UN-76371	Ilyushin Il-76TD	1033414485	ex 76371		Joint ops with TIS
UN-76374	Ilyushin Il-76TD	1033416520			
UN-76810	Ilyushin Il-76TD	1013409282	ex CCCP-76810		

ALMATY AVIA CARGO

Almaty (6T/LMT)   **Almaty (ALA)**

UN-11650	Antonov An-12BP	6344305	ex LZ-BFG
UN-98102	Antonov An-12BP	5343005	ex LZ-BFD

ASIA CONTINENTAL believed to have ceased operations

ATYRAU AIR WAYS

Edil (IP/JOL) (IATA 312)   **Atyrau (GUW)**

UN-46582	Antonov An-24B	97305001	ex CCCP-46582		
UN-65069	Tupolev Tu-134A-3	49908	ex RA-65069	Kashagan	
UN-65070	Tupolev Tu-134A-3	49912	ex RA-65070	Tungysh	
UN-65610	Tupolev Tu-134A	40150	ex RA-65610	Bayterek	
UN-65619	Tupolev Tu-134A	31218	ex RA-65619	Venera; VIP	
UN-85742	Tupolev Tu-154B-2	78A-320	ex RA-85742	Terra Incognita	Lsd fr JAK
UN-85855	Tupolev Tu-154M	89A-823	ex B-2621		

AVIA JAYNAR

Almaty (ALA)

UR-47153	Antonov An-24B	88901605

AVIA PUSK

Apusk (GFR)   **Almaty (ALA)**

UN-11001	Antonov An-12	5343408	ex CCCP-11001

AVIATRACK ceased operations

AZAMAT ceased operations

BERKHUT AIR

Berkut (BEK)   **Uralsk (URA)**

UN-B1111	BAC One-Eleven 401AK	078	ex P4-CCL	Govt	Lsd fr Air Finance Europe
UN-11373	Antonov An-12BP	02348304			Lsd to Intrasarana
UN-75001	Ilyushin Il-18D	187009904	ex YR-IMM		Lsd to UGN
UN-85464	Tupolev Tu-154B-2	464	ex CCCP-85464	VIP	
UN-85478	Tupolev Tu-154B-2	478	ex CCCP-85478		
UN-87912	Yakovlev Yak-40K	9732054	ex RA-87912	VIP	
UN-88191	Yakovlev Yak-40	9621148	ex CCCP-88191		
UN-88260	Yakovlev Yak-40	9711552	ex CCCP-88260		
UN-88266	Yakovlev Yak-40K	9710453	ex CCCP-88266		

Berkhut Air is the trading name of AK Kanat Aviakompania

BERKHUT AVIAKOMPANIA

Venera (BPX)   **Uralsk (URA)**

UN-67462	LET L-410UVP	841227	ex CCCP-67642
UN-67463	LET L-410UVP	841228	ex CCCP-67643
UN-87306	Yakovlev Yak-40	9320229	ex CCCP-87306

BURUNDAI AVIA AIR

Rurun (BRY)   **Almaty (ALA)**

UN-26020	Antonov An-26B	10205	ex CCCP-26020	
UN-26075	Antonov An-26B	11508	ex CCCP-26075	
UN-26582	Antonov An-26B	47313504	ex CCCP-26582	all white
UN-26649	Antonov An-26	87307506	ex CCCP-26649	
UN-30003	Antonov An-30	1404	ex CCCP-30003	
UN-30029	Antonov An-30	0604	ex CCCP-30029	
UN-30031	Antonov An-30	0606	ex CCCP-30031	
UN-30038	Antonov An-30	0708	ex CCCP-30038	

UN-30046	Antonov An-30	0908	ex CCCP-30046
UN-30057	Antonov An-30	1106	ex CCCP-30057
UN-30060	Antonov An-30	1109	ex CCCP-30060
UN-30071	Antonov An-30	1302	ex CCCP-30071

All survey/combi configuration

EURO ASIA AIR INTERNATIONAL
Eakaz (5B/EAK)   Almaty (ALA)

UN-87337	Yakovlev Yak-40	9510639	ex CCCP-87337
UN-87403	Yakovlev Yak-40	9411533	ex CCCP-87403
UN-87935	Yakovlev Yak-40K	9741856	ex CCCP-87935
UN-87990	Yakovlev Yak-40	9541444	ex CCCP-87990
UN-88173	Yakovlev Yak-40	9621147	ex CCCP-88173
UN-65551	Tupolev Tu-134A-3	66212	ex CCCP-65551
UN-65776	Tupolev Tu-134A-3	62545	ex CCCP-65776

FLAMINGO AIRLINE believed to only operate light aircraft

GST AERO
Murat (BMK)   Almaty (ALA)

UN-76002	Ilyushin Il-76TD	0023442218	ex ST-AQA		
UN-76004	Ilyushin Il-76TD	0013434018	ex RA-76004		Lsd to ETC
UN-76005	Ilyushin Il-76TD	0073479392	ex 76749		Lsd to BRQ
UN-76007	Ilyushin Il-76				
UN-76496	Ilyushin Il-76TD	073410301	ex RA-76496		Op for United Nations
UN-76499	Ilyushin Il-76TD	0023441186	ex RA-76499		Lsd to SRW
UN-11002	Antonov An-12B	4341705	ex		Lsd fr TLR
UN-11006	Antonov An-12	01347909	ex 3C-QRI		Lsd to NFS
UN-28054	Antonov An-26B	10910	ex ER-AFD		
UN-87249	Yakovlev Yak-40	9540244	ex CCCP-87249		Lsd to UTG
UN-87537	Yakovlev Yak-40	9520242	ex CCCP-87537		Lsd to TLR
UN-88162	Yakovlev Yak-40	9611646	ex CCCP-88162	stored Fujirah	
UN-88268	Yakovlev Yak-40	9720653	ex CCCP-88268	all-white	Lsd to TLR

GVG AIRLINES ceased operations

IRBIS AIR ceased operations

ITRASARANA
Almaty (ALA)

UN-11373	Antonov An-12BP	02348304	Lsd fr BEK

JANA ARTA ceased operations

KAZ TRANSAIR both aircraft now operated by Euro-Asia Air; ceased operations

KAZAIR WEST
Kazwest (KAW)   Atyrau (GUW)

UN-65799	Tupolev Tu-134B-3	63187	ex YL-LBN	VIP; operates for ChevronTexaco
UN-65900	Tupolev Tu-134A-3	63684	ex CCCP-65900	
UN-67566	LET L-410UVP-E	861606	ex HA-LAK	
UN-67611	LET L-410UVP-E	892339	ex OM-UDX	
UN-87271	Yakovlev Yak-40	9310727	ex CCCP-87271	VIP
UN-87926	Yakovlev Yak-40K	9741755	ex CCCP-87926	

Owned by Clintondale Aviation and operates mainly VIP flights

KHOZU AVIA

UN-42323	Yakovlev Yak-42D	4520423402116	ex RA-42323	VIP
UN-42640	Yakovlev Yak-42D	4520423914323	ex UN-42373	Aurela titles
UN-42641	Yakovlev Yak-42D	4520423302017	ex RA-42557	VIP

KOKSHETAU AIRLINES
Kokta (KRT)   Kokchetav (KOV)

UN-86505	Ilyushin Il-62M	4934847	ex RA-86505	no titles
UN-87813	Yakovlev Yak-40	9230324	ex CCCP-87813	
UN-87913	Yakovlev Yak-40	9730255	ex CCCP-87913	

UN-87932	Yakovlev Yak-40	9740356	ex CCCP-87932
UN-88198	Yakovlev Yak-40	9632048	ex CCCP-88198
UN-88221	Yakovlev Yak-40	9630750	ex CCCP-88221
UN-88271	Yakovlev Yak-40K	9720953	ex CCCP-88271
UN-88277	Yakovlev Yak-40	9721953	ex CCCP-88277

QUADROTOUR AERO now listed under Kyrgystan although based in Kazakhstan

SAMAGU believed not to have commenced operations

SATQUAR AIR TRANSPORT

Almaty (ALA)

| UN-47176 | Antonov An-24B | 89901810 | ex CCCP-47176 |

SAYAKHAT
Sayakhat (W7/SAH)

Almaty (ALA)

UN-76384	Ilyushin Il-76TD	1003401015	
UN-76385	Ilyushin Il-76TD	1033416515	
UN-76434	Ilyushin Il-76	1023412395	ex CCCP-76434
UN-76442	Ilyushin Il-76TD	1023414450	ex CCCP-76442
UN-85835	Tupolev Tu-154M	85A-716	ex B-2601
UN-85837	Tupolev Tu-154M	86A-724	ex B-2604
UN-85852	Tupolev Tu-154M	86A-726	ex B-2611
UN-85853	Tupolev Tu-154M	86A-728	ex B-2606
UN-85854	Tupolev Tu-154M	86A-729	ex B-2607

SBS AVIATION ceased operations

SCAT AIRCOMPANY
Vlasta (DV/VSV)

Shymkent

UN-46265	Antonov An-24B	77303508	ex CCCP-46265
UN-46271	Antonov An-24B	77303804	ex CCCP-46271
UN-46310	Antonov An-24B	87305305	ex CCCP-46310
UN-46340	Antonov An-24B	97305608	ex CCCP-46340
UN-46368	Antonov An-24B	07305909	ex RA-46368
UN-46381	Antonov An-24B	07306104	ex CCCP-46381
UN-46421	Antonov An-24B	87341068	ex CCCP-46421
UN-46438	Antonov An-24B	87304309	ex CCCP-46438
UN-46699	Antonov An-24RV	47309910	ex UR-46699
UN-47270	Antonov An-24B	07306308	ex CCCP-47270
UN-47692	Antonov An-24RV	27307509	ex CCCP-47692
UN-47763	Antonov An-24B	79901307	ex CCCP-47763

SEMEYAVIA
Ertis (SMK)

Semipalatinsk (PLX)

UN-87204	Yakovlev Yak-40K	9810157	ex CCCP-87204
UN-87208	Yakovlev Yak-40K	9810557	ex CCCP-87208
UN-88259	Yakovlev Yak-40	9711452	ex CCCP-88259

TARAZ WINGS ceased operations

TSELINA now operates single engined aircraft only

TULPAR AIR SERVICE
Tulpar (TUX)

Almaty (ALA)

| UN-26006 | Antonov An-26 | 9810 | ex RA-26006 |
| UN-46253 | Antonov An-24B | 77303305 | ex RA-46253 |

VARTY PACIFIC AIRLINES
Varty (MDO)

Almaty (ALA)

| UN-11005 | Antonov An-12BP | 9346602 | ex RA-12960 |

VEGA AIR COMPANY ceased operations

VIP AVIA ceased operations

586

YUZHNAYA AIR COMPANY

Pluton (UGN)   *Almaty (ALA)*

UN-47736	Antonov An-24B	69901004	ex CCCP-47736 HO HA titles
UN-75005*	Ilyushin Il-18D	187010204	ex 3C-KKL
EX-017	Tupolev Tu-154B-1	78A-262	ex UN-85777

*Also operates services for other operators such as Ibis and Lignes Aeriennes Tchad

ZHETYSU AVIA

Zhetysu Avia (ZAV)   *Almaty (ALA)*

UN-87927	Yakovlev Yak-40K	9741855	ex CCCP-87927
UN-87931	Yakovlev Yak-40	9740256	ex CCCP-87931

ZHEZAIR / ZHEZKAZGAN AIR

Ulutau (KZH)   *Khezkazgan (DZN)*

UN-87920	Yakovlev Yak-40	9731055	ex CCCP-87920
UN-87929	Yakovlev Yak-40	9742055	ex CCCP-87931

UR - UKRAINE

AAR AIRLINES current status is uncertain, sole aircraft now operated by Ukriane Air Alliance

AERO CHARTER UKRAINE

Charter Ukraine (DW/UCR)   *Kiev-Borispol (KBP)*

UR-LUX	Yakovlev Yak-40	9541542	ex UR-87230	Lsd fr KAD
UR-87245	Yakovlev Yak-40	9531343	ex RA-87245	Lsd fr KAD
UR-87479	Yakovlev Yak-40	9441838	ex CCCP-87479	
UR-88290	Yakovlev Yak-40K	9840459	ex CCCP-88290 no titles	Lsd fr Lyra Enterprise
UR-BWZ	Antonov An-26B	27312208	ex UR-26119	
UR-DWA	Antonov An-26B	13905	ex EX-26598	
UR-74007	Antonov An-74-200	36547095903	ex HK-3809	Lsd fr WKH

AEROMIST KHARKIV

(HT)   *Kharkov (HRK)*

UR-14002	Antonov An-140	36525302006	
UR-14004	Antonov An-140		Lsd fr ODS
UR-14006	Antonov An-140		

AEROSTAR

Aerostar (UAR)   *Kiev-Zhulyany (IEV)*

UR-ECL	Yakovlev Yak-40K	9932059	ex RA-87219
UR-MIG	Yakovlev Yak-40	9641250	ex RA-88225
UR-87566	Yakovlev Yak-40	9211821	ex SP-FYU
UR-87961	Yakovlev Yak-40K	9820458	ex CCCP-87961
UR-87998	Yakovlev Yak-40	9540245	ex CCCP-87998 VIP

AEROSVIT AIRLINES

Aerosvit (VV/AEW) (IATA 870)   *Kiev-Borispol (KBP)*

SP-LLB	Boeing 737-45D	2492/27156		Lsd fr LOT
UR-BVY	Boeing 737-2Q8	852/22760	ex F-GEXJ	
UR-VVA	Boeing 737-3Q8	1808/24492	ex N492GD	Lsd fr Triton
UR-VVB	Boeing 737-529	2296/26537	ex OO-SYJ	Lsd fr CIT Leasing; op fr AUI
UR-VVD	Boeing 737-529	2165/25419	ex N419CT	Lsd fr CIT Aerospace
UR-VVE	Boeing 737-448	1778/24521	ex EI-BXB	Lsd fr ILFC
UR-VVF	Boeing 767-383ER	274/24476	ex N4476F	Lsd fr Kuta-Two Aircraft
UR-VVG	Boeing 767-383ER	358/24729	ex N102AB	Lsd fr Nordea Finans
UR-VVH	Boeing 737-45D		ex SP-LL	

Subsidiary of Air Ukraine;

AEROTRANS ceased operations

AEROVIS AIRLINES

(VIZ)

UR-CBG	Antonov An-12BP	6343705	ex	
UR-CBH	Antonov An-12BK	8345710		id not confirmed

AIR BOYOMA

UR-47311	Antonov An-24RV	57310402	ex CCCP-47311

AIR COMPANY HELIOS

(HEO)

Fleet details unknown

AIR KHARKOV

Air Kharkov (KHV)   Kharkov (HRK)

UR-65037	Tupolev Tu-134A-3	48850	ex CCCP-65037		
UR-65073	Tupolev Tu-134A	49980	ex CCCP-65073		
UR-65114	Tupolev Tu-134A-3	60395	ex CCCP-65114		
UR-65746	Tupolev Tu-134A-3	2351608	ex CCCP-65746		
UR-65752	Tupolev Tu-134A-3	61079	ex CCCP-65752		
UR-65761	Tupolev Tu-134A-3	62244	ex CCCP-65761		
UR-65764	Tupolev Tu-134A-3	62305	ex CCCP-65764		
UR-65773	Tupolev Tu-134A-3	62495	ex CCCP-65773		Lsd to OTL
UR-65877	Tupolev Tu-134A-3	31250	ex CCCP-65877		
UR-CAO	Antonov An-24B	97395997	ex ER-AFC	c/n unlikely	
UR-26514	Antonov An-26	6907	ex CCCP-26514		
UR-26555	Antonov An-26	3203	ex CCCP-26555		
UR-26651	Antonov An-26	7508	ex CCCP-26651		

Associated with Air Ukraine

AIR KIROVOGRAD renamed Kirovohradavia

AIR RWENZORI current status is uncertain; sole aircraft with Ukraine Air Alliance Airlines

AIR UKRAINE / AVIALINII UKRAINY

Air Ukraine (6U/UKR) (IATA 891)   Kiev-Borispol (KBP)

UR-65076	Tupolev Tu-134A-3	60001	ex CCCP-65076
UR-65077	Tupolev Tu-134A-3	60028	ex 65077
UR-65107	Tupolev Tu-134A	60328	ex CCCP-65107
UR-65135	Tupolev Tu-134A-3	60648	ex CCCP-65135
UR-65757	Tupolev Tu-134A-3	62215	ex CCCP-65757
UR-65765	Tupolev Tu-134A	62315	ex CCCP-65765
UR-85379	Tupolev Tu-154B-2	79A-379	ex CCCP-85379
UR-85460	Tupolev Tu-154B-2	81A-460	ex CCCP-85460
UR-85482	Tupolev Tu-154B-2	81A-482	ex CCCP-85482
UR-85490	Tupolev Tu-154B-2	81A-490	ex CCCP-85490
UR-85513	Tupolev Tu-154B-2	81A-513	ex CCCP-85513
UR-85526	Tupolev Tu-154B-2	82A-526	ex CCCP-85526
UR-85535	Tupolev Tu-154B-2	82A-535	ex CCCP-85535
UR-85701	Tupolev Tu-154M	91A-876	ex 85701
UR-85707	Tupolev Tu-154M	91A-882	ex CCCP-85707
UR-86133	Ilyushin Il-62M	1138234	ex CCCP-86133
UR-86135	Ilyushin Il-62M	1748445	ex CCCP-86135
UR-86580	Ilyushin Il-62M	2343554	ex CCCP-86580

Domestic services are operated under the name of Ukraine National Airlines

AIR URGA

Urga (3N/URG)   Kirovograd (KGO)

UR-ELC	Antonov An-24RV	57310410	ex UR-47313	
UR-ELL	Antonov An-24RV	67310503	ex UR-47316	
UR-ELM	Antonov An-24RV	67310506	ex UR-47319	
UR-ELN	Antonov An-24B	89901607	ex UR-47155	
UR-46558	Antonov An-24B	87304605	ex CCCP-46558	no props
UR-46577	Antonov An-24B	87304902	ex CCCP-46577	no props
UR-47300	Antonov An-24RV	57310203	ex CCCP-47300	

588

UR-ELA	Antonov An-26B	13505	ex UR-28583	Lsd to United Nations
UR-ELB	Antonov An-26B	58314005	ex UR-26201	
UR-ELD	Antonov An-26B	14010	ex UR-26203	
UR-ELE	Antonov An-26B	27312108	ex UR-26111	Lsd to United Nations
UR-ELF	Antonov An-26B	27312204	ex UR-26115	
UR-ELG	Antonov An-26B	37312902	ex UR-26140	Lsd to United Nations
UR-ELI	Antonov An-26B	57314009	ex UR-26202	
UR-ELR	Antonov An-26B	07309807	ex UR-26004	Lsd to United Nations
UR-26143	Antonov An-26B	12908	ex CCCP-26143	
UR-26580	Antonov An-26B	13408	ex TC-GZT	Lsd to United Nations

Air Urga is the commercial operation of Ukraine State Flight Academy

AIRTECH SERVICE believed not to have commenced operations

ANTONOV AIRLINES

Antonov Bureau (ADB)   *Kiev-Gostomel*
(International Cargo Transporter)

UR-82008	Antonov An-124-100	19530501006	ex CCCP-82008	
UR-82009	Antonov An-124-100	19530501007	ex CCCP-82009	
UR-82027	Antonov An-124-100	19530502288	ex CCCP-82027	
UR-82029	Antonov An-124-100	19530502630	ex CCCP-82029	
UR-82070	Antonov An-124-100	9773051359127	ex RA-82070	
UR-82072	Antonov An-124-100	9773053359136	ex RA-82072	
UR-82073	Antonov An-124-100	9773054359139	ex RA-82073	
UR-09307	Antonov An-22A	043481244	ex CCCP-09307	
UR-11315	Antonov An-12BP	4342307	ex CCCP-11315	
UR-11765	Antonov An-12BP	401705	ex LZ-SFM	
UR-13395	Antonov An-26	2605	ex CCCP-13395	
UR-21510	Antonov An-12BP	0901404	ex 88 red Soviet AF	
UR-48004	Antonov An-32	1306	ex CCCP-48004	Firefighter
UR-48093	Antonov An-32P	0703	ex CCCP-48093	
UR-74010	Antonov An-74T	36547030450	ex CCCP-74010	
UR-82060	Antonov An-225	01-01	ex CCCP-82060	

International cargo services operated in conjunction with Antonov Airlines (UK) using the An-225, eight An-124s, three An-12s and the An-22

ARP 410 AIRLINES

Air-Arp (URP)   *Kiev*

UR-PWA	Antonov An-24RV	57310308	ex RA-46820	
UR-46464	Antonov An-24RV	27307810		
UR-46477	Antonov An-24RV	27308101	ex CCCP-46477	
UR-46517	Antonov An-24RV	37308503	ex CCCP-46517	
UR-47256	Antonov An-24RV	27307708	ex TC-MOB	
UR-47265	Antonov An-24RV	27307807	ex CCCP-47265	
UR-47278	Antonov An-24B	07306408	ex CCCP-47278	
UR-47297	Antonov An-24RV	07306610	ex CCCP-47297	
UR-47308	Antonov An-24RV	57310308	ex CCCP-47308	
UR-47824	Antonov An-24RV	17307205	ex CCCP-47824	Getra titles
UR-BWY	Antonov An-26	97308205	ex UR-26670	Lsd to RPK
UR-26072	Antonov An-26B	17311409	ex RA-26072	
UR-26581	Antonov An-26B	57313503	ex RA-26581	Lsd to RPK
UR-26676	Antonov An-26B	13503	ex RA-26676	Lsd fr PER
UR-26689	Antonov An-26B	9005	ex CCCP-26689	
UR-30000	Antonov An-30A-100	1401	ex CCCP-30000	
UR-30044	Antonov An-30	0906	ex CCCP-30044	

Division of Kiev Aircraft Repair Plant 410

ARTEM AVIA

Artem Avia (ABA)   *Kiev-Zhulyany (IEV)*

UR-26094	Antonov An-26B	12706	ex CCCP-26094
UR-26214	Antonov An-26B	67314403	ex CCCP-26214

AS AVIAKOMPANIA merged into Kirovohradavia

ATI INTERNATIONAL ceased operations

AVIAEXPRESS AIRCOMPANY

Expressavia (VXX)   *Kiev-Zhulyany*

UR-67199	LET L-410UVP	790305	ex CCCP-67119
UR-67419	LET L-410UVP	831110	ex CCCP-67419

AVIAKOMPANIA TRANSAVIA ceased operations

AVIANT / KIEV AVIATION PLANT

Aviation Plant (UAK)   *Kiev-Gostomel*

UR-26175	Antonov An-24RV	77310810A	ex CCCP-26175	Lsd to EGA
UR-26194	Antonov An-26	0202	ex CCCP-26194	
UR-46777	Antonov An-24B	77301504	ex CCCP-46777	
UR-48023	Antonov An-32B	3409	ex HK-4006X	
UR-48086	Antonov An-32P	2901	ex CCCP-48086	Firefighter
UR-48087	Antonov An-32B	2904	ex CCCP-48087	
UR-69312	Antonov An-26	2906	ex CCCP-69312	
UR-79165	Antonov An-26	5409	ex CCCP-26219	

Aviant is the trading name of Kiev Aviation Plant

AVIRCITI ceased operations

AZOV-AVIA

Azov Avia (AZV)   *Melitopol*

UR-ZVA	Ilyushin Il-76MD	0063468036	ex UR-76684	no titles
UR-ZVB	Ilyushin Il-76MD	0053463902	ex UR-76658	op for UN/WFP
UR-ZVC	Ilyushin Il-76			

Also operates cargo charter flights with Ilyushin Il-76s leased from Ukrainian Cargo Airways when required

BUKOVYNA

Bukovyna (BKV)   *Chernovtsy (CWC)*

UR-65089	Tupolev Tu-134A	60180	ex CCCP-65089	Lsd to UKM
UR-65790	Tupolev Tu-134A-3	63100	ex CCCP-65790	

CABI

Cabi (CBI)   *Donetsk (DOK)*

UR-74057	Antonov An-74-200	36547098960	Lsd to AAG

CHAIKA AVIA COMPANY believed to have ceased operations

COLUMBUS AVIA

Columbus Avia (CBS)   *Dnepropetrovsk (DNK)*

UR-87308	Yakovlev Yak-40	9320429	ex CCCP-87308

CONSTANTA AIRLINES

Constanta (UZA)   *Zaporozhye (OZH)*

UR-ETG	Yakovlev Yak-40	9531143	ex RA-87243
UR-FRU	Yakovlev Yak-40	9440737	ex RA-87211
UR-87389	Yakovlev Yak-40	9410133	ex CCCP-87389
UR-87463	Yakovlev Yak-40	9430237	ex CCCP-87463
UR-87512	Yakovlev Yak-40	9521440	ex CCCP-87512
UR-87660	Yakovlev Yak-40	9240425	ex CCCP-87660
UR-87806	Yakovlev Yak-40	9231223	ex CCCP-87806

CRIMEA AIRLINES

Crimea Air (OR/CRF)   *Simferopol (SIP)*

UR-46622	Antonov An-24RV	37308709	ex RA-46622
UR-46675	Antonov An-24RV	47309607	ex CCCP-46675
UR-46688	Antonov An-24RV	47309805	ex CCCP-46688
UR-46833	Antonov An-24RV	17306710	ex CCCP-46833

Also leases Tupolev Tu-154s from Air Ukraine as and when required

DESNA ceased operations

DNIEPROAVIA / DNEPR-AIR

Dniepro (Z6/UDN)   *Dnepropetrovsk (DNK)*

UR-BWE	Yakovlev Yak-40	9530943	ex RA-87241	VIP	Joint ops with MLD
UR-BWF	Yakovlev Yak-40	9711352	ex RA-88258	VIP; op for Commercialii Bank	
UR-LEV	Yakovlev Yak-40	9720154	ex LY-AAA		
UR-ORO	Yakovlev Yak-40K	9740656	ex RA-98106		

UR-PIT	Yakovlev Yak-40	9610647	ex RA-88168	
UR-XYZ	Yakovlev Yak-40	9610946	ex RA-88155	
UR-87918	Yakovlev Yak-40	9730855	ex 87918	dbr 28Apr03?
UR-87965	Yakovlev Yak-40	9820858	ex RA-87965	VIP
UR-88237	Yakovlev Yak-40	9640751	ex CCCP-88237	
UR-88309	Yakovlev Yak-40	9840859	ex 5R-MUA	VIP; op for Interpipe Group
UR-88310	Yakovlev Yak-40	9940760	ex 5R-MUB	VIP; op for Interpipe Group
UR-42376	Yakovlev Yak-42D	4520424914477	ex EP-CPK	Lsd to SAI
UR-42405	Yakovlev Yak-42D	4520423116624	ex CCCP-42405	
UR-42409	Yakovlev Yak-42D	4520421216709	ex ER-42409	
UR-42426	Yakovlev Yak-42D	4520423304016	ex TC-IYI	
UR-42449	Yakovlev Yak-42D	4520421401018	ex EP-CPC	Lsd to SAI

DONBASS AIRLINES ceased operations

DONBASS EASTERN UKRAINIAN AIRLINES renamed DonbassAero 01 October 2003 following reorganisation

DONBASSAERO

Aviation Donbass (7D/UDC)   Donetsk (DOK)
Previously listed as Donbass Eastern Ukrainian Airlines and reorganised 01 October 2003

UR-46254	Antonov An-24B	77303402	ex RA-46254	
UR-46302	Antonov An-24B	97305202	ex CCCP-46302	
UR-46585	Antonov An-24B	97305004	ex CCCP-46585	
UR-46586	Antonov An-24B	97305006	ex CCCP-46586	
UR-46647	Antonov An-24RV	37309107	ex CCCP-46647	
UR-47296	Antonov An-24RV	07306609	ex CCCP-47296	
UR-47846	Antonov An-24B	17307408	ex CCCP-47846	
UR-42308	Yakovlev Yak-42	11040303	ex CCCP-42308	
UR-42318	Yakovlev Yak-42	4520423402051	ex RA-42318	
UR-42319	Yakovlev Yak-42	4520423402062	ex CCCP-42319	
UR-42327	Yakovlev Yak-42	4520424402161	ex T9-ABF	
UR-42366	Yakovlev Yak-42	4520421814047	ex T9-ABH	
UR-42372	Yakovlev Yak-42D	4520423914266	ex CCCP-42372	no titles
UR-42377	Yakovlev Yak-42D	4520421014479	ex CCCP-42377	
UR-42381	Yakovlev Yak-42D	4520422014576	ex EP-SAF	
UR-42383	Yakovlev Yak-42D	4520422016201	ex T9-ABD	
UR-42530	Yakovlev Yak-42	11120204	ex CCCP-42530	

EUROPEAN UKRAINE AIRLINES believed to have ceased operations

GALAIRCERVIS ceased operations

GORLITSA AIRLINES

Golitsa (GOR)   Kiev-Zhulynay (IEV)

UR-BXU	Antonov An-26B	11703	ex RA-26081	
UR-BXV	Antonov An-26B	12110	ex UR-26113	
UR-GLS	Antonov An-26B	07310109	ex RA-26017	Lsd to TWN
UR-YMR	Antonov An-12BK	9346302	ex UR-11349	Lsd to VPB
UR-46666	Antonov An-24RV	47309507	ex YL-LCG	

CAR AIRLINES / INDEPENDENT CARRIER ceased operations

ISD AVIA

Isdavia (ISD)   Donetsk (DOK)

UR-BYY	Tupolev Tu-134B-3	62820	ex RA-65720
UR-ISD	Yakovlev Yak-40	9530541	ex RA-88291

KHARKOV AVIATION PRODUCTION ASSOCIATION

West-Kharkov (WKH)   Kharkov (HRK)

UR-67472	LET L-410UVP	841237	ex CCCP-67472	
UR-74007	Antonov An-74-200	36547095903	ex HK-3809	Lsd to UCR
UR-74038	Antonov An-74TK-200	36547097933	ex RA-74038	VIP
UR-98104	Antonov An-24RV	67302310	ex CCCP-98104	

KHORIV AVIA

Khoriv-Avia (KRV)   Kiev-Zhulyany (IEV)

UR-BYH	Antonov An-74	39547098946	ex LZ-MNM
UR-CAC	Antonov An-74	47136013	ex UN-74011

KHORS AIR

Aircompany Khors (X9/KHO)   **Kiev-Borispol (KBP)**

UR-BYL	Douglas DC-9-51	787/47657	ex N2248F	Lsd fr Scanair Greece, sublsd to RSO
UR-CBV	Douglas DC-9-51 (ABS 3)	890/47772	ex OH-LYV	
UR-CBY	Douglas DC-9-51 (ABS 3)	891/47773	ex OH-LYW	Lsd to UKM
UR-CBZ	Douglas DC-9-51 (ABS 3)	980/48134	ex OH-LYX	
UR-CCK	Douglas DC-9-51 (ABS 3)	827/47736	ex OH-LYR	Lsd to RSO
UR-CCR	Douglas DC-9-51 (ABS 3)	808/47696	ex OH-LYP	
UR-CCS	Douglas DC-9-51 (ABS 3)	829/47737	ex OH-LYS	Lsd to UKM

Last two not confirmed, may be reversed

UR-TSI	Antonov An-12BP	6344701	ex UR-UAA	Op for WFP, UN
UR-11326	Antonov An-12BP	2400802	ex CCCP-11326	
UR-11332	Antonov An-12BP	4342202	ex T9-CAD	

KIROVOHRADAVIA

Air Kirovograd (KAD)   **Kirovograd (KGO)**
Previously listed as Air Kirovograd

UR-LUX	Yakovlev Yak-40	9541542	ex UR-87230	Lsd to UCR
UR-87245	Yakovlev Yak-40	9531343	ex RA-87245	Lsd to UCR
UR-87276	Yakovlev Yak-40	9311227	ex CCCP-87276	
UR-87405	Yakovlev Yak-40	9421733	ex RA-87405	
UR-87435	Yakovlev Yak-40	9431135	ex CCCP-87435	stored KGO
UR-87562	Yakovlev Yak-40	9211321	ex CCCP-87562	
UR-87814	Yakovlev Yak-40	9230524	ex RA-87814	based Africa

KROONK AIR LINES

Kroonk (KRO)   **Kiev-Zhulyany (IEV)**

UR-26129	Antonov An-26B	12703	ex CCCP-26129	
UR-26244	Antonov An-26	97307705	ex CCCP-26244	Lsd as HA-TCN

LUGANSK AVIATION ENTERPRISE

Enterprise Lugansk (LHS)   **Lugansk (VSG)**

UR-46475	Antonov An-24RV	27308003	ex CCCP-46475	no titles
UR-46514	Antonov An-24RV	37308410	ex RA-46514	
UR-47312	Antonov An-24RV	57310403	ex RA-47312	
UR-85316	Tupolev Tu-154B-2	78A-316	ex CCCP-85316	
UR-85362	Tupolev Tu-154B-2	79A-362	ex 4K-85362	

LVIV AIRLINES

Ukraine West (5V/UKW)   **Lviv (LWO)**

UR-46249	Antonov An-24B	77303207	ex UR-46569 (1)	
UR-46278	Antonov An-24B	77303701	ex CCCP-46278	
UR-46301	Antonov An-24B	97305201	ex CCCP-46301	
UR-46305	Antonov An-24B	97305205	ex CCCP-46305	
UR-46326	Antonov An-24B	97305503	ex CCCP-46326	
UR-46383	Antonov An-24B	07306106	ex CCCP-46383	
UR-46813	Antonov An-24B	673024027?	ex CCCP-46813	

UR-42317	Yakovlev Yak-42	4520422202039	ex 42317	
UR-42358	Yakovlev Yak-42	4520422811413	ex CCCP-42358	Lsd to SAI
UR-42369	Yakovlev Yak-42	4520422914190	ex CCCP-42369	Lsd to SAI
UR-42403	Yakovlev Yak-42D	4520422116588	ex CCCP-42403	no titles	Lsd to SAI
UR-42527	Yakovlev Yak-42	11040903	ex CCCP-42527	
UR-42540	Yakovlev Yak-42	11140604	ex T9-ABC (2)	
UR-42544	Yakovlev Yak-42	11151004	ex T9-ABC (1)	

UR-BXD	Ilyushin Il-18D	172011401	ex Soviet AF	
UR-11314	Antonov An-12BK	8345604	RA-13357	
UR-11346	Antonov An-12BK	8345702	ex 54 Red, Ukraine AF	no titles
UR-76705	Ilyushin Il-76MD	0063472158	ex RA-76705	Lsd to UKR
UR-76717	Ilyushin Il-76MD	0073474216	ex 4K-76717	dam 27Jul02
UR-76778	Ilyushin Il-76MD	0083483502	ex CCCP-76778	

MOTOR SICH AVIAKOMPANIA

Motor Sich (M9/MSI)   **Zaporozhye (OZH)**

UR-BXC	Antonov An-24RV		
UR-MSI	Antonov An-24RV	27307608	ex UR-47699
UR-11316	Antonov An-12BK	9346810	ex RA-11316

UR-11819	Antonov An-12B	6344009		
UR-14005	Antonov An-140			
UR-47258	Antonov An-24RV	27307609	ex CCCP-47269	
UR-74026	Antonov An-74-200	36547096919	ex HK-3810X	
UR-87215	Yakovlev Yak-40	9510540	ex OK-FEJ	VIP
UR-88219	Yakovlev Yak-40K	9630550	ex CCCP-88219	

ODESSA AIRLINES

Odessa Air (5K/ODS)   Odessa (ODS)

UR-14001	Antonov An-140	36525301003	ex UR-PWO		Lsd fr Ukrtranslizing
UR-14004	Antonov An-140				Lsd to Aeromist Kharkiv
UR-	Antonov An-140			on order	
UR-87327	Yakovlev Yak-40	9330630	ex CCCP-87327		
UR-87421	Yakovlev Yak-40	9421734	ex CCCP-87421		
UR-87469	Yakovlev Yak-40	9441437	ex CCCP-87469		
UR-88299	Yakovlev Yak-40	9321028	ex OK-BYI		Op for Ironimpex

PODILIA AVIA

Podilia (PDA)   Khmelnitsky (HMJ)

UR-26077	Antonov An-26B	17311603	ex RA-26077
UR-46397	Antonov An-24B	07306301	ex RA-46397

POLAVA UNIVERSAL AVIA

UR-UTN	LET L-410UVP-E19A	912614	ex UR-67716

ROVNO UNIVERSAL AIR

Rivne Universal   Rovno (RWN)

UR-67069	LET L-410UVP	810705	ex CCCP-67069
UR-67082	LET L-410UVP	810719	ex CCCP-67082
UR-67083	LET L-410UVP	810720	ex CCCP-67083
UR-67084	LET L-410UVP	810721	ex CCCP-67084
UR-67085	LET L-410UVP	810722	ex CCCP-67085
UR-67102	LET L-410UVP	841328	ex HA-LAP
UR-67372	LET L-410UVP	830940	ex CCCP-67372
UR-67439	LET L-410UVP	841204	ex YL-KAH
UR-67477	LET L-410UVP	841302	ex CCCP-67477
UR-67492	LET L-410UVP	841317	ex ES-LLD
UR-67504	LET L-410UVP	851408	ex HA-LAN
UR-67524	LET L-410UVP	851431	ex CCCP-67524
UR-67663	LET L-410UVP-E	902525	ex CCCP-67663

SANAIR ceased operations

SEVASTOPOL AVIA

Sevastopol

UR-BXA	Antonov An-24B	99902107	ex 01 blue
UR-TMD	Ilyushin Il-18E	186009102	ex ER-ICJ

SHOVKOVIY SHIYAH Current status is uncertain as sole aircraft disposed of

SIRIUS AIR

Sirius (IRS)   Ivano-Frankovsk (IFO)

UR-RPC	Yakovlev Yak-40	9721353	ex YL-TRB	
UR-87987	Yakovlev Yak-40	9541144	ex CCCP-87987	VIP

SOUTH AIRLINES

Southline (YG/OTL)   Odessa (ODS)

UR-BZY	Tupolev Tu-134A-3	48565	ex ER-TCH	Lsd fr Transcargo Ltd
UR-65773	Tupolev Tu-134A-3	62495	ex CCCP-65773	Lsd fr KHV

TAVRIA AVIAKOMPANIA

Tavrey (T6/TVR) (IATA 204)   Odessa (ODS)

UR-42337	Yakovlev Yak-42D	4520423606235	ex YL-	Lsd fr FKZS Leasing

TAVRIA-MAK

Tavria Mak (BE/TVM)   *Simferopol (SIP)*

UR-BXB	Antonov An-26	6207	ex 45 blue

TRANS KIEV
ceased operations

UES AVIA

Aviasystem (UES)   *Dnepropetrovsk (DNK)*

UR-ORG	Yakovlev Yak-40K	9741056	ex UR-87591	Executive
UR-87590	Yakovlev Yak-40K	9741156	ex OK-HER	Executive
UR-78734	Ilyushin Il-76TD	1013409303	ex HA-TCA	stored JNB

UES Avia is a division of United Energy System of Ukraine

UHURU AIRLINES

UR-26215	Antonov An-26B	67304707	ex LZ-NHB
UR-48084	Antonov An-32	2601	ex CCCP-48084

UKRAINE AIR ENTERPRISE

Enterprise Ukraine (UKN) (IATA 416)   *Kiev-Borispol (KBP)*

UR-65556	Tupolev Tu-134A-3	66372	ex CCCP-65556
UR-65718	Tupolev Tu-134A-3	63668	ex 65718
UR-65782	Tupolev Tu-134A-3	62672	ex CCCP-65782
UR-86527	Ilyushin Il-62M	4037758	ex CCCP-86527
UR-86528	Ilyushin Il-62M	4038111	ex CCCP-86528
UR-87964	Yakovlev Yak-40	9820758	ex CCCP-87964

Operates flights for Ukrainian Government as well as some commercial flights

UKRAINE AIR ALLIANCE

Ukraine Airalliance (UKL)   *Kiev-Borispol (KBP)*

UR-CAP	Ilyushin Il-76TD	0063466989	ex UR-76394	Jt ops with KGA
UR-CAT	Ilyushin Il-76TD	0053464922	ex UR-76663	
UR-CBR	Ilyushin Il-76TD			
UR-26042	Antonov An-26B	10710	ex CCCP-26042	
UR-26519	Antonov An-26B	7010	ex CCCP-26519	
UR-26650	Antonov An-26B	7507	ex UN-26650	
UR-28737	PZL-Mielec/Antonov An-28	1AJ007-25	ex RA-28737	
UR-48083	Antonov An-32B	3001	ex CCCP-48083	Lsd to Airmark

UKRAINE FLIGHT STATE ACADEMY

Flight Academy (UFA)   *Kirovograd (KGO)*

UR-46205	Antonov An-24B	67302803	ex RA-46205	no titles
UR-46311	Antonov An-24B	97305307	ex LZ-MND	
UR-47179	Antonov An-24B	99901904	ex CCCP-47179	
UR-47702	Antonov An-24B	59900203	ex CCCP-47702	
UR-47711	Antonov An-24B	69900501	ex CCCP-47711	
UR-47743	Antonov An-24B	79901106	ex CCCP-47743	
UR-47791	Antonov An-24B	67303004	ex LZ-MNF	
UR-67129	LET L-410UVP	790325	ex CCCP-67129	
UR-67169	LET L-410UVP	790205	ex CCCP-67169	
UR-67197	LET L-410UVP	790303	ex CCCP-67197	
UR-67357	LET L-410UVP	820917	ex CCCP-67357	
UR-67389	LET L-410UVP	831017	ex CCCP-67389	
UR-67392	LET L-410UVP	831020	ex CCCP-67392	
UR-67395	LET L-410UVP	831023	ex CCCP-67395	
UR-67411	LET L-410UVP	831039	ex CCCP-67411	
UR-67417	LET L-410UVP	831108	ex CCCP-67417	
UR-67449	LET L-410UVP	841214	ex CCCP-67449	
UR-67526	LET L-410UVP	851433	ex CCCP-67526	
UR-67527	LET L-410UVP	851434	ex CCCP-67527	
UR-67543	LET L-410UVP	851510	ex CCCP-67543	
UR-67555	LET L-410UVP	851519	ex LZ-MNC	
UR-67658	LET L-410UVP E	902512	ex CCCP-67658	
UR-67659	LET L-410UVP E	902513	ex CCCP-67659	

Commercial operations are also conducted as Air Urga

UKRAINE INTERNATIONAL AIRLINES

Ukraine International (PS/AUI) (IATA 566)   *Kiev-Borispol (KBP)*

UR-GAC	Boeing 737-247 (Nordam 3)	1071/23188	ex B-2509		Lsd fr GECAS
UR-GAH	Boeing 737-32Q	3105/29130	ex N1779B	Mayrni	
UR-GAJ	Boeing 737-5Y0	2262/25192	ex PT-SSA		Lsd fr GECAS
UR-GAK	Boeing 737-5Y0	2374/26075	ex PT-SLN		Lsd fr GECAS
UR-GAL	Boeing 737-341	1637/24275	ex PP-VOD		Lsd fr GECAS; sublsd to BPA
UR-GAM	Boeing 737-4Y0	2256/25190	ex HA-LEU		Lsd fr GECAS
UR-GAN	Boeing 737-36N	2996/28569	ex F-GRFC		Lsd fr Lift France
UR-GAP	Boeing 737-529	2165/25419	ex N419CT		Lsd fr CIT Leasing
UR-GA	Boeing 737-4Y0	2256/25190	ex HA-LEU	on order	Lsd fr GECAS
UR-UFB	Airbus Industrie A320-211	0027	ex N270SE	Mary-Lyn1	Lsd fr WFBN

Associated with Air Ukraine

UKRAINE NATIONAL AIRLINES

(UR/UNL)   *Kiev-Zhulyany (IEV)*

UR-46293	Antonov An-24B	77303805	ex CCCP-46293
UR-46330	Antonov An-24B	97305507	ex CCCP-46330
UR-46372	Antonov An-24B	07306003	ex CCCP-46372
UR-46434	Antonov An-24B	87304304	ex CCCP-46434
UR-46440	Antonov An-24B	87304401	ex CCCP-46440
UR-46469	Antonov An-24RV	27307907	ex CCCP-46469
UR-46527	Antonov An-24RV	47310006	ex CCCP-46527
UR-46596	Antonov An-24B	97305106	ex CCCP-46596
UR-47257	Antonov An-24RV	27307709	ex CCCP-47257
UR-47266	Antonov An-24RV	07306304	ex CCCP-47266
UR-47281	Antonov An-24B	07306501	ex CCCP-47281
UR-47287	Antonov An-24B	07306507	ex CCCP-47287
UR-47801	Antonov An-24RV	17306810	ex CCCP-47801
UR-47836	Antonov An-24B	17307308	ex CCCP-47836
UR-47837	Antonov An-24B	17307309	ex CCCP-47837
UR-30005	Antonov An-30	1406	ex CCCP-30005
UR-30022	Antonov An-30	0404	ex CCCP-30022
UR-30025	Antonov An-30	0503	ex CCCP-30025
UR-30026	Antonov An-30	0505	ex CCCP-30026
UR-30030	Antonov An-30	0605	ex CCCP-30030
UR-30036	Antonov An-30	0703	ex CCCP-30036
UR-46633	Antonov An-30	0202	ex CCCP-46633

Operates domestic services for Air Ukraine

UKRAINIAN CARGO AIRWAYS

Cargotrans (6Z/UKS) (IATA 516)   *Zaporozhye (OZH)*

UR-UCA	Ilyushin Il-76MD	0073479394	ex UR-76715	
UR-UCC	Ilyushin Il-76MD	0083489647	ex UR-78775	
UR-UCD	Ilyushin Il-76MD	0083488643	ex UR-78774	
UR-UCE	Ilyushin Il-76MD	0083484522	ex UR-76398	
UR-UCF	Ilyushin Il-76MD	0083488638	ex UR-76412	
UR-UCG	Ilyushin Il-76MD	0083482478	ex UR-76414	
UR-UCH	Ilyushin Il-76MD	0083484536	ex UR-78756	Op for UN
UR-UCL	Ilyushin Il-76MD	0043456692	ex UR-76620	all-white
UR-UCO	Ilyushin Il-76MD	0053458749	ex UR-76630	Op for UN
UR-UCQ	Ilyushin Il-76MD	0063465963	ex UR-76671	Op for UN
UR-UCR	Ilyushin Il-76MD	0073475270	ex UR-76728	
UR-UCS	Ilyushin Il-76TD	0063470113	ex RA-76444	
UR-UCU	Ilyushin Il-76MD	0073476275	ex UR-76729	
UR-UCV	Ilyushin Il-76TD	0043451517	ex UR-76397	Op for UN
UR-UCW	Ilyushin Il-76MD	0054358733	ex UR-76317	
UR-UCX	Ilyushin Il-76MD	0063470112	ex UR-76695	
UR-UCY	Ilyushin Il-76MD	0083485566	ex UR-76399	
UR-UDB	Ilyushin Il-76MD	0043455686	ex UR-76320	
UR-UDC	Ilyushin Il-76MD	0063467011	ex CCCP-76678	

Often operate for aid agencies

UR-UCK	Antonov An-12BP	0346905	ex UR-11304
UR-UCP	Antonov An-26B	4407	ex UR-26602
UR-UCZ	Tupolev Tu-154B-2	82A-561	ex RA-85561

Associated with the Ukraine Air Force and operates civil cargo charters

UKRAINIAN PILOT SCHOOL

Pilot School (UPL)   *Kiev-Chaika*

UR-28721	WSK-PZL/Antonov An-28	1AJ007-08	ex RA-28721

Operates some commercial services as well as training school

UKRAIR AVIACOMPANY ceased operations

UM AIR

Mediterranee Ukraine (UF/UKM)   Kiev-Borispol (BPL)

UR-CBY	Douglas DC-9-51 (ABS 3)	891/47773	ex OH-LYW	Lsd fr KHO
UR-CCS	Douglas DC-9-51 (ABS 3)	829/47737	ex OH-LYS	Lsd fr KHO
UR-UFA	Airbus Industrie A320-			
UR-65076	Tupolev Tu-134A-3	60001	ex CCCP-65076	

UNIVERSAL AVIA ceased operations

VETERAN AIRLINES

Veteran (VPB)   Simferopol (SIP)

UR-PAS	Antonov An-12AP	2401105		Adrey
UR-PLV	Antonov An-12	4342308	ex 61 red	
UR-YMR	Antonov An-12BP	9346302	ex UR-11349	Lsd fr GOR

VOLARE AVIATION ENTERPRISE

Ukraine Volare (F7/VRE)   Rovno (RWN)

UR-BWM	Antonov An-12BP	00347004	ex Ukraine AF 20 blue
UR-LAI	Antonov An-12V	8345505	ex RA-12954
UR-LMI	Antonov An-12BK	6344605	ex Ukraine AF 73 blue
UR-LTG	Antonov An-12V	00347201	ex RA-12986
UR-SMA	Antonov An-12BK	7345208	ex UR-11348
UR-SVG	Antonov An-12BK	04342409	ex TN-AGE
UR-76628	Ilyushin Il-76TD	0053458741	ex CCCP-76628
UR-76636	Ilyushin Il-76TD	0053459781	ex CCCP-76636
UR-76687	Ilyushin Il-76TD	0063469051	ex CCCP-76687
UR-76704	Ilyushin Il-76MD	0063471150	ex CCCP-76704
UR-76727	Ilyushin Il-76TD	0073475268	ex CCCP-76727

YUZHMASHAVIA

Yuzhmash (2N/UMK)   Dnepropetrovsk (DNK)

UR-78785	Ilyushin Il-76MD	0083489691	ex RA-78785	
UR-78786	Ilyushin Il-76MD	0083490693	ex CCCP-78786	
UR-87298	Yakovlev Yak-40	9241325	ex CCCP-87298	VIP
UR-87508	Yakovlev Yak-40	9521040	ex CCCP-87508	
UR-87951	Yakovlev Yak-40K	9810957	ex CCCP-87951	
UR-88151	Yakovlev Yak-40	9610546	ex CCCP-88151	

YUZHNOYE ceased operations

VH - AUSTRALIA (Commonwealth of Australia)

ABORIGINAL AIR SERVICES

Alice Springs, NT (ASP)

Services are operated with aircraft from Janami Air, Ngaanyatjarra Air and Ngurratjuta Air as and when required

AEROLINK AIR SERVICES

Sydney-Bankstown, NSW (BWU)

VH-MWF	Embraer EMB.110P1 Bandeirante	110447	ex N216EB	
VH-WBI	Embraer EMB.110P1 Bandeirante	110292	ex PT-SCA	Lsd to FAJ as DQ-WBI

AEROPELICAN AIR SERVICES

Aeropelican (OT/PEL)   Newcastle-Belmont, NSW (BEO)

VH-KZN	de Havilland DHC-6 Twin Otter 320	652	ex N479WW
VH-KZO	de Havilland DHC-6 Twin Otter 320	753	ex C-GFBS
Owned by International Air Parts			

AERO TROPICS

(HC/ATI)   Cairns/Horn Island, QLD (CNS/HID)

VH-CSU	Britten-Norman BN-2A-26 Islander	81	ex YJ-RV6
VH-HPL	Britten-Norman BN-2A-26 Islander	3004	ex RP-C662

VH-WZD	Britten-Norman BN-2A-21 Islander	450	ex VH-USD	
VH-WZE	Britten-Norman BN-2A-20 Islander	354	ex VH-PNJ	
VH-WZF	Britten-Norman BN-2A-21 Islander	537	ex 5Y-RAJ	
VH-WZK	Britten-Norman BN-2A-20 Islander	421	ex VH-UBN	

VH-TFU	Swearingen SA.227DC Metro 23	DC-818B	ex N818GL	Lsd fr Transair
VH-WZG	Partenavia P.68B	63	ex VH-PNQ	
VH-WZN	Piper PA-31 Turbo Navajo	31-657	ex VH-NOS	
VH-WZO	Beech 95-E55 Baron	TE-979	ex VH-EGJ	
VH-WZP	Partenavia P.68C	228	ex VH-AJX	
VH-WZR	Beech 58 Baron	TH-383	ex VH-ATL	

Aero Tropics is the scheduled service division of Lip Air

AIR CAIRNS current status is uncertain as sole aircraft disposed of

AIR CHARTER AUSTRALIA

Adelaide-Parafield, SA (ADL)

VH-JVN	Reims Cessna F406 Caravan II	F406-0033	ex VH-RCB
VH-KEZ	Cessna 402C	402C0262	ex N40BH
VH-OCS	Cessna 441 Conquest II	441-0030	ex N441MM
VH-ROS	Cessna 402C	402C0038	ex N5764C

AIRCRUISING AUSTRALIA

Cruiser (AIX) 　　　　　　　　　　　　　　　　　　　　　　　　　　 *Sydney-Kingsford Smith, NSW (SYD)*

VH-NLS	Fokker F.27 Friendship 100	10105	ex ZK-NAH	
VH-WAN	Fokker F.27 Friendship 600	10315	ex ZK-RTA	Freighter

AIR FACILITIES current status is uncertain

AIR FRASER ISLAND

Maryborough, QLD

VH-BFS	Gippsland GA-8 Airvan	GA8-03-035
VH-BNX	Gippsland GA-8 Airvan	GA8-03-032

AIR FRONTIER

Darwin, NT (DRW)

VH-LIL	Piper PA-31-350 Navajo Chieftain	31-7852061	ex N27399

AIRLINES OF SOUTH AUSTRALIA

(RT/LRT) 　　　　　　　　　　　　　　　　　　　　　　　　　　 *Port Augusta, SA (PUG)*

VH-ANZ	Embraer EMB.120ER Brasilia	120135	ex VH-XFR
VH-FNP	Embraer EMB.110P1 Bandeirante	110157	ex (VH-PAG)
VH-LNB	Embraer EMB.110P1 Bandeirante	110441	ex N141EM

Owned by Air North

AIRLINES OF TASMANIA

Hobart, Tas (HBA)

VH-BSF	Piper PA-31P Pressurised Navajo	31P-58	ex N7305L
VH-BTD	Piper PA-31 Turbo Navajo C	31-7912041	ex VH-ATG
VH-BTI	Piper PA-31 Turbo Navajo C	31-8212003	ex ZK-VNA
VH-BTN	Aero Commander 680FLP	1695-35	ex D-IBME
VH-EXP	Rockwell Commander 680FL	1490-94	ex N361K
VH-IFF	Cessna 310Q	310Q0765	ex N2994Q
VH-LAD	Cessna 404	404-0224	
VH-LAM	Cessna 404 Titan II	404-0627	ex VH-ANN
VH-LCD	Cessna U206G Stationair 6	U20604523	ex N673AA
VH-MYS	Cessna U206G Stationair 6	U20605162	ex N4921U
VH-SGA	Piper PA-31P Navajo	31P-7300166	

First service 29 April 2003

AIR LINK

(DR) 　　　　　　　　　　　　　　　　　　　　　　　　　　 *Dubbo, NSW (DBO)*

VH-DVR	Piper PA-31-350 Navajo Chieftain	31-7952052	ex N27936
VH-DVW	Piper PA-31-350 Navajo Chieftain	31-7952011	ex VH-LHH
VH-MWP	Piper PA-31-350 Chieftain	31-8352005	ex N4109C
VH-MZF	Piper PA-31-350 Chieftain	31-8252039	ex N41064

VH-MZM	Piper PA-31-350 Chieftain	31-8252187	ex N4069Y

VH-BWQ	Cessna 310R	310R1401	ex N4915A
VH-HSL	Cessna 310R	310R0946	ex N8643G
VH-JMP	Cessna 310R	310R1270	ex N125SP
VH-MXY	Cessna 310R	310R1648	ex N2636N
VH-RUE	Beech 1900D	UE-53	ex ZK-JNG
VH-TDL	Piper PA-39 Twin Comanche C/R	30-152	ex VH-NHC

Operates flights for QantasLink in NSW

AIR MOUNT ISA

Mount Isa, QLD (ISA)

VH-ABP	Beech 58 Baron	TH-709	ex N67715
VH-HOA	Cessna 404 Titan	404-0408	ex VH-SBV
VH-LAP	Beech 58 Baron	TH-646	ex 5N-ATC
VH-RDZ	Cessna 402A	402A0125	ex VH-TMY
VH-SQT	Cessna 210M Centurion	21062874	ex N6005N
VH-TLH	Embraer EMB.110P1 Bandeirante	110407	ex (ZK-TZP)

AIR NGUKURR

Darwin, NT (DRW)

VH-HJR	Piper PA-31-350 Chieftain	31-8252016	ex VH-MZX
VH-IEK	Piper PA-31 Turbo Navajo	31-759	ex VH-TFK
VH-MZV	Piper PA-31-350 Chieftain	31-8152092	ex N4083C

AIR NOSTALGIA

Melbourne-Essendon, VIC (MES)

VH-TMQ	Douglas DC-3	16136/32884	ex A65-91

AIR SOUTH

VH-BQB	Embraer EMB.110P1 Bandeirante	110298	ex ZK-VJG

AIR WHITSUNDAY SEAPLANES

(RWS) — *Whitsunday/Airlie Beach, QLD (WSY)*

VH-AQV	de Havilland DHC-2 Beaver	1257	ex N67685
VH-AWD	de Havilland DHC-2 Beaver	1066	ex VH-AYS
VH-AWI	de Havilland DHC-2 Beaver	298	ex VH-HQE
VH-AWR	de Havilland DHC-2 Beaver	665	ex ZS-NVC
VH-AWY	de Havilland DHC-2 Beaver	1444	ex VH-SSG
VH-AWZ	de Havilland DHC-2 Beaver	1618	ex VH-BSL

All floatplanes; Air Whitsunday Seaplanes is the trading name of Coral Air Whitsunday

AIRNORTH REGIONAL

Topend (TL/ANO) — *Darwin, NT (DRW)*

VH-ANB	Embraer EMB.120ER Brasilia	120116	ex VH-XFX	
VH-ANJ	Embraer EMB.120ER Brasilia	120163	ex N455UE	Op for United Nations
VH-ANK	Embraer EMB.120RT Brasilia	120155	ex VH-YDD	
VH-ASN	Embraer EMB.120ER Brasilia	120056	ex N334JS	
VH-DIL	Embraer EMB.120ER Brasilia	120153	ex N285UE	
VH-ANA	Swearingen SA.227DC Metro 23	DC-871B	ex VH-HCB	
VH-ANW	Swearingen SA.227DC Metro 23	DC-873B	ex N3031Q	
VH-ANY	Swearingen SA.227DC Metro 23	DC-840B	ex N3022L	
VH-EVP	Cessna 441 Conquest	441-0088	ex N8936N	
VH-CAJ	Cessna 402C	402C0026	ex N5717C	Wfs
VH-NMQ	Cessna 402C	402C0451	ex VH-RMQ	Wfs
VH-RUY	Cessna 402C	402C0273	ex N1774G	Wfs
VH-TFM	Cessna 402C	402C0067	ex N2610Y	Wfs

AirNorth Regional is the trading name of Capiteq

AIRTEX AVIATION

Sydney-Bankstown, NSW (BWU)

VH-HJE	Piper PA-31-350 Navajo Chieftain	31-7852074	ex N5038X
VH-HJS	Piper PA-31-350 Navajo Chieftain	31-7652091	ex VH-TWB
VH-OZG	Piper PA-31-350 Navajo Chieftain	31-7952023	ex VH-LGI
VH-OZP	Piper PA-31-350 Navajo Chieftain	31-7725050	ex VH-MBP
VH-OZT	Piper PA-31-350 Navajo Chieftain	31-7405157	ex VH-MBT

VH-OZV	Piper PA-31-350 Navajo Chieftain	31-7405470	ex VH-TYV

VH-DEG	Cessna 421B Golden Eagle	421B0637	
VH-IAW	Swearingen SA.227AC Metro III	AC-600	ex N3117A
VH-IGN	Piper PA-61 Aerostar 601P	61-0682-7962142	ex N60700
VH-OZN	Piper PA-31 Turbo Navajo	31-285	ex VH-MBY
VH-PDN	Piper PA-31 Turbo Navajo	31-177	ex N9131Y
VH-PWY	Ted Smith Aerostar 601P	61P-0378-123	ex N9785Q
VH-UJF	Cessna 310R	310R1342	ex N6215C
VH-WGV	Swearingen SA.226TC Metro II	TC-287	ex ZK-SWD

Airtex Aviation is the trading name of Avtex Air Services

ALLIANCE AIRLINES

(QQ/QQA)   *Brisbane, QLD (BNE)*

VH-FKC	Fokker 100	11349	ex N887US		
VH-FKE	Fokker 100	11358	ex N889US		
VH-FWH	Fokker 100	11316	ex G-BXNF	City of Townsville	Op for ANG
VH-FWI	Fokker 100	11318	ex G-FIOR	City of Rockhampton	

Operates in joint Alliance/Norfolk Jet colours

ALLIGATOR AIRWAYS

Kununurra, WA (KNX)

VH-EDE	Cessna 210L Centurion	21060517	ex (N94140)
VH-FAP	Partenavia P.68B	45	
VH-IXE	Partenavia P.68B	178	
VH-PQJ	Cessna U206F Stationair	U20602245	ex N1537U
VH-RAS	Cessna 207 Skywagon	20700158	ex N1558U
VH-WNI	Cessna 210M Centurion	21062462	ex N761RR
VH-WOG	Gippsland GA-8 Airvan	GA8-02-012	
VH-WOT	Cessna 207 Skywagon	20700267	ex ZK-DEW
VH-WOU	Cessna 207 Skywagon	20700099	ex N91164
VH-WOV	Gippsland GA-8 Airvan	GA8-01-006	
VH-WOY	Cessna 207A Stationair 8	20700707	ex N9592M

ANINDILYAKWA AIR

Darwin, NT (DRW)

VH-BSE	Beech 58 Baron	TH-526	ex N8182R
VH-COQ	Cessna 310R	310R1643	ex N2635Y
VH-CYY	Piper PA-31 Turbo Navajo B	31-7401241	ex N913BT
VH-ENT	Cessna 404 Titan	404-0818	ex ZK-ECP
VH-KUZ	Cessna 441 Conquest	441-0138	ex N311KR
VH-PZO	Cessna 210L Centurion	21060298	ex N93185
VH-RDH	Cessna 210N Centurion	21064374	ex N6427Y

ANSETT AUSTRALIA CARGO ceased operations 9 January 2003

ASIAN EXPRESS AIRLINES

Freightexpress (HJ/AXF)   *Sydney-Kingsford Smith, NSW (SYD)*

VH-DHE	Boeing 727-2J4F (FedEx 3)	1598/22080	ex N729DH	DHL Express c/s	Lsd fr BCS

AUSTRALIAN AIR EXPRESS

(XM/XME) (IATA 524)   *Melbourne-Tullamarine, VIC*

(VH-VLE)	Boeing 727-277F (FedEx 3)	989/20549	ex VH-TXH		Lsd fr/op by NJS
VH-VLF	Boeing 727-277F (FedEx 3)	1481/21695	ex VH-AUP		Lsd fr/op by NJS
VH-VLG	Boeing 727-277F (Duganair 3)	1054/20551	ex VH-RMX	Julie	Lsd fr/op by NJS
VH-VLH	Boeing 727-277F (FedEx 3)	1759/22642	ex OO-DLB		Lsd fr/op by NJS
VH-VLI	Boeing 727-277F (FedEx 3)	1753/22641	ex EC-HIG		Lsd fr/op by NJS

Operated by NJS from 17 October 2003 using callsign 'Jetex8'

VH-EEN	Swearingen SA.227AT Expediter	AT-563	ex N563UP		Joint ops with QWA
VH-EEO	Swearingen SA.227AT Expediter	AT-564	ex N564UP		Joint ops with QWA
VH-EEP	Swearingen SA.227AT Expediter	AT-567	ex N565UP		Joint ops with QWA
VH-EER	Swearingen SA.226TC Metro II	TC-284	ex VH-WGW		Joint ops with QWA
VH-NJF	British Aerospace 146 Srs.300QT	E3198	ex G-BTLD		Lsd fr/op by NJS
VH-NJM	British Aerospace 146 Srs.300QT	E3194	ex G-BTHT		Lsd fr/op by NJS
VH-NJV	British Aerospace 146 Srs.100QT	E1002	ex G-BSTA		Lsd fr/op by NJS

Jointly owned by Australia Post and Qantas

AUSTRALIAN AIRLINES

(AO/AUZ)   *Cairns, QLD (CNS)*

VH-OGI	Boeing 767-338ER	387/25246		Lsd fr QFA
VH-OGJ	Boeing 767-338ER	396/25274		Lsd fr QFA
VH-OGK	Boeing 767-338ER	397/25316	ex N6018N	Lsd fr QFA
VH-OGL	Boeing 767-338ER	402/25363	ex N6018N	Lsd fr QFA
VH-OGV	Boeing 767-338ER	796/30186		Lsd fr QFA
VH-	Boeing 767-338ER		on order 04	

Wholly owned by Qantas as low-cost subsidiary operating to Asian destinations.

AUSTRALIAWIDE AIRLINES listed under trading name, Rex - Regional Express

BIG SKY EXPRESS

Granted AOC in January 2004 and flight in NSW operated with Transair Metros [Transair also have rights to fly the same routes!]

BRINDABELLA AIRLINES

(FQ)   *Canberra, ACT*

VH-TAO	Swearingen SA.227AC Metro III	AC-513	ex N513FA
VH-TAR	Piper PA-31-350 Navajo Chieftain	31-7405207	ex ZK-PKC
VH-TAS	Piper PA-31-350 Navajo Chieftain	31-7652012	ex N38335
VH-WAL	Piper PA-31 Turbo Navajo	31-7300943	ex N71TC

Frist service 28 April 2003; operates services for Qantas

CAPE YORK AIR SERVICES

Cairns, QLD (CNS)

VH-CYC	Cessna 208 Caravan I	20800108	ex N977A	Sir Bob Norman
VH-CYV	Piper PA-31 Turbo Navajo	31-18	ex VH-DZZ	
VH-DMF	Piper PA-31 Turbo Navajo	31-447	ex N6483L	
VH-IYI	Partenavia P.68B	136		
VH-RTP	Britten-Norman BN-2A-6 Islander	79	ex G-AXIN	

Operations for sale

CHARTAIR sold by previous owner and now just a air taxi/charter operator

CHC HELICOPTERS (AUSTRALIA)

Hems (HEM)   *Adelaide, SA (ADL)*

VH-LAF	Aerospatiale SA.332L1 Super Puma	2319	ex LN-OBT	Lsd to United Nations
VH-LAG	Aerospatiale SA.332L1 Super Puma	2352	ex LN-OBU	
VH-LHG	Aerospatiale SA.332L1 Super Puma	2317	ex LN-OBR	
VH-LHJ	Aerospatiale AS.332L Super Puma	2063	ex G-BSOI	
VH-LHK	Aerospatiale AS.332L Super Puma	2107	ex G-BKZH	Lsd fr SHZ
VH-PVA*	Aerospatiale SA.365C1 Dauphin 2	5025	ex F-WYMH	based MEN
VH-PVF*	Aerospatiale SA.365C1 Dauphin 2	5042		wfs MEN
VH-PVG*	Aerospatiale AS.365N3 Dauphin 2	6539	ex HB-XQS	based MEN
VH-PVH*	Aerospatiale AS.365N3 Dauphin 2	6604		based MEN
VH-PVK*	Aerospatiale SA.365C1 Dauphin 2	5033	ex F-WYMA	wfs MEN
VH-BZH	Bell 412	33044	ex N18098	
VH-EWA	Bell 412	36312	ex C-GUOP	
VH-NSC	Bell 412	33029	ex VH-CRQ	
VH-NSP	Bell 412	33091	ex N22976	
VH-NSV	Bell 412	33084	ex VH-AHH	
VH-UAH	Bell 412	33034	ex N2141B	
VH-VAA	Bell 412EP	36274	ex C-GLZM	Op for Victoria Ambulance Service
VH-VAB	Bell 412EP	36275		Op for Victoria Ambulance Service
VH-HRP	Sikorsky S-76A	760122	ex N176CH	based East Sale
VH-LAH	Sikorsky S-76A	760089	ex RJAF 725	based NTL
VH-LAI	Sikorsky S-76A	760103	ex RJAF 727	
VH-LAQ	Sikorsky S-76A	760112	ex G-BNSH	Lsd as RP-C176
VH-LHN	Sikorsky S-76A	760300	ex B-HZE	
VH-LHY	Sikorsky S-76A	760105	ex RJAF 729	based Pearce
VH-LHZ	Sikorsky S-76A	760113	ex RJAF 732	RAAF rescue
VH-BJX	Bell 206L-1 LongRanger III	45337	ex ZK-HQS	
VH-HHS	Bell 206L-1 LongRanger III	45404	ex N5735N	
VH-LAL	Bell 206B JetRanger III	2626	ex C-GJET	
VH-LHP	Bell 206L-3 LongRanger III	51002	ex G-CJCB	
VH-LHL	Bell 212	31160	ex C-GSQM	

VH-LHX	Bell 212	30680	ex C-GOKX	
VH-NSA	Bell 212	30550	ex G-BAFN	
VH-NSY	Bell 212	30849	ex ZS-RKN	
VH-PVM*	Aerospatiale AS.350B Ecureuil	2058	ex JA9705	based MEN
VH-UBH	Bell 206B JetRanger III	3350		

*Operated for Victoria Police Force
Owned by CHC-Helicopters (C-); also trades as Lloyds Offshore Helicopters

CIRRUS AIRLINES current status uncertain: all aircraft disposed of

COASTAL AIR SERVICES ceased operations

COMPLETE AIR SERVICES

Perth, WA (PER))

VH-BEB	Piper PA-31 Turbo Navajo	31-41	ex N9030Y
VH-KGX	Swearingen SA.226TC Metro II	TC-326	ex VH-UUK
VH-RMT	Piper PA-31 Turbo Navajo	31-7401216	ex N7600L

CORAL SEA AIRLINES ceased operations

CORPORATE AIRLINES

(FX)   *Canberra, ACT (CBR)*

VH-VEA	Cessna 404 Titan	404-0219	ex VH-ARQ
VH-VEC	Cessna 404 Titan	404-0217	ex VH-CSV
VH-VEH	Swearingen SA-227AC Metro III	AC-663B	ex N2697V
VH-VEM	Cessna 441 Conquest	441-0174	ex VH-IJG
VH-VEZ	Cessna 441 Conquest	441-0182	ex VH-AZB

DAKOTA DOWNUNDER

Albury, NSW (ABX)

VH-JGL	Douglas DC-3	15195/26640	ex A65-64	Louise

DAKOTA NATIONAL AIR

Sydney-Bankstown, NSW (BWU)

VH-BPN	Douglas DC-3	16197/32945	ex P2-ANV	07; stored BWU
VH-DNA	Douglas DC-3	15685/27130	ex P2-004	04
VH-MIN	Douglas DC-3	13459	ex VH-SNI	08; wings of VH-SBL
VH-PWN	Douglas DC-3	14556/26001	ex P2-005	05; stored BWU
VH-SBL	Douglas DC-3	12056	ex P2-ANR	03 Captain Jack Curtiss
VH-UPQ	Douglas DC-3	16552/33300	ex A65-105	06; stored BWU

DENIS BEAHAN AVIATION

Roma, QLD (RMA)

VH-AMD	Beech 65-B80 Queen Air	LD-504	ex TR-LUU	
VH-AMQ	Beech 65-B80 Queen Air	LD-443	ex N9235Q	Excalibur Queenaire 8800 conv
VH-BQL	Beech 65-B80 Queen Air	LD-288	ex DQ-FCQ	
VH-MWK	Beech 65-B80 Queen Air	LD-472	ex N25728	
VH-RUU	Beech 65-B80 Queen Air	LD-311	ex N7643N	Excalibur Queenaire 8200 conv
VH-BPZ	Cessna 402	402-0103	ex N4003Q	
VH-BUS	Cessna 402	402-0198	ex N991SA	

DERBY AIR SERVICES integrated into parent company Slingair

DIRECT AIR SERVICES

Warners Bay, NSW

VH-BYG	Piper PA-31-350 Navajo Chieftain	31-7852130	ex N350PA
VH-HJH	Piper PA-31-350 Navajo Chieftain	31-7752127	ex VH-WZW
VH-HJK	Piper PA-31-350 Chieftain	31-8052153	ex VH-JNX
VH-OZM	Piper PA-31-350 Navajo Chieftain	31-7852003	ex N710AN
VH-XLB	Piper PA-31-350 Navajo Chieftain	31-7852104	ex VH-LHG

EASTERN AUSTRALIA AIRLINES

(UN/EAQ)   *Sydney-Kingsford Smith, NSW (SYD)*

A wholly-owned subsidiary of Qantas and operates scheduled services in full colours as QantasLink

ELITE AIRWAYS

VH-FIA	Piper PA-31-350 Navajo Chieftain	31-7752032 ex ZK-FIA

EMU AIRWAYS

VH-CEM	Cessna 402B	402B1067	ex N98754	stored
VH-EMI	Beech 1900C	UC-109	ex N109YV	
VH-EMK	Beech 1900C-1	UC-159	ex N159GL	

G.A.M. AIR SERVICES

Aircraft also used as Reefwatch Air Tours

VH-KAK	Shrike Commander 500S	3269	ex N57163
VH-LET	Shrike Commander 500S	3264	ex N70343
VH-LTP	Shrike Commander 500S	3323	ex N12RS
VH-MDW	Shrike Commander 500S	3158	ex N801AC
VH-MEH	Shrike Commander 50)S	3258	ex N57213
VH-PAR	Shrike Commander 500S	3311	ex N84SA
VH-UJE	Shrike Commander 500S	3120	ex VH-BGE
VH-UJI	Shrike Commander 500S	3301	ex VH-TWS
VH-UJL	Shrike Commander 500S	3088	ex N9120N
VH-UJM	Shrike Commander 500S	3117	ex N5007H
VH-UJU	Shrike Commander 500S	3055	ex VH-PWO
VH-UJV	Shrike Commander 500S	3161	ex N712PC
VH-UJX	Shrike Commander 500S	1839-31	ex VH-EXL
VH-UJY	Shrike Commander 500S	3170	ex VH-TSS
VH-UJZ	Shrike Commander 500S	3279	ex VH-EXY
VH-YJC	Shrike Commander 500S	3176	ex VH-ACZ
VH-YJE	Shrike Commander 500S	3053	ex VH-EXE
VH-YJI	Shrike Commander 500S	3130	ex VH-BAJ
VH-YJL	Shrike Commander 500S	1875-48	ex VH-ACL
VH-YJO	Shrike Commander 500B	1506-180	ex VH-WRU
VH-YJR	Shrike Commander 500S	3231	ex VH-PCO
VH-YJS	Shrike Commander 500S	3315	ex VH-FGS
VH-YJU	Aero Commander 500U	1765-49	ex F-ODHD
VH-AAG	Rockwell Commander 690	11101	ex N57101
VH-FVJ	Rockwell Commander 685	12034	ex VH-UJR
VH-NBT	Rockwell Commander 681B	6047	ex VH-NYE
VH-NYC	Rockwell Commander 690	11026	ex N9226N
VH-UJA	Aero Commander 680FL	1521-100	ex PK-MAG
VH-UJG	Rockwell Commander 690	11062	ex VH-NEY
VH-YJZ	Beech 95-B55 Baron	TC-1933	ex VH-ARL

GOLDEN EAGLE AVIATION

VH-AEC	Britten-Norman BN-2B-26 Islander	2164	ex G-BKJO
VH-AEU	Britten-Norman BN-2B-26 Islander	2130	ex G-BJON
VH-AEX	Cessna U206G Stationair 6	U20606587	ex N9635Z
VH-EGE	Britten-Norman BN-2A-26 Islander	3015	ex VH-WRM
VH-FML	Piper PA-31 Turbo Navajo	31-8112015	ex N40540
VH-KTS	Piper PA-31 Turbo Navajo	31-7912014	ex N27833
VH-LCK	Piper PA-34-200 Seneca	34-7350236	ex N55663
VH-NMK	Piper PA-31-350 Chieftain	31-8152163	
VH-NPA	Piper PA-31-350 Chieftain	31-8452016	ex N41171
VH-PJY	Cessna U206G Stationair 6	U20605120	ex N4829U
VH-UPK	Cessna U206G Stationair 6	U20605477	ex (N6399U)

GOLDFIELDS AIR SERVICES

VH-ALY	Cessna 310R	310R1310	ex N6173X
VH-CSO	Cessna 310R	310R1854	
VH-HOR	Cessna 402C	402C0106	ex P2-KSR
VH-LAE	Cessna 402C	402C0097	ex N2614Z
VH-LCO	Cessna 310R	310R1216	ex N1386G
VH-MFF	Cessna 402B	402B0874	ex N5187J
VH-TYG	Cessna 210M Centurion	21061893	ex N1694C
VH-WXC	Cessna 210M Centurion	21062883	ex N6015N

GREAT WESTERN AVIATION

(MT)

Brisbane, QLD (BNE)

VH-DEH	Piper PA-31 Turbo Navajo C	31-7812123	ex N27792
VH-FMO	Piper PA-31 Turbo Navajo C	31-8012052	ex N35574
VH-FMU	Piper PA-31 Turbo Navajo C	31-8212015	ex N41033
VH-KTU	Piper PA-31 Turbo Navajo C	31-7912079	ex N35301
VH-SGV	Beech 200 Super King Air	BB-718	ex N6728N

First service 10 February 2003

GREAT WESTERN AVIATION

Perth, WA (PER)

VH-FWA	Beech 1900C	UB-61	ex N818BE
VH-FWJ	Piper PA-31 Turbo Navajo C	31-7712092	ex ZK-PNX
VH-IYP	Beech 1900C	UB-62	ex N819BE

HAMILTON ISLAND AVIATION

Hamilton Island, QLD (HTI)

VH-AAM	de Havilland DHC-2 Beaver	1492	Floatplane
VH-BKE	MBB BK117B-1	1042	
VH-BVA	de Havilland DHC-2 Beaver	245	Floatplane

HARDY AVIATION

Darwin, NT (DRW)

VH-ANM	Cessna 404 Titan	404-0010	ex VH-BPM
VH-ANS	Cessna 210M Centurion	21062784	ex N784ED
VH-ARJ	Cessna 402B	402B0629	ex N3784C
VH-HMA	Cessna 404 Titan	404-0122	ex N37158
VH-HMZ	Cessna 441	441-0017	ex N500UW
VH-HPA	Cessna U206G Stationair 6	U20605002	ex VH-WIW
VH-JZL	Cessna TU206G Stationair 6	U20604721	ex N732TS
VH-MKS	Swearingen SA.226TC Metro II	TC-262	ex N94GW
VH-MMA	Douglas DC-3	9583	ex VH-MWQ
VH-NOK	Cessna 210M Centurion	21062063	ex N9127M
VH-RAP	Cessna U206F Stationair	U20602989	ex VH-DXU
VH-SQL	Cessna 402C	402C0236	ex VH-OAS
VH-SGO	Beech 58 Baron	TH-1185	ex N3702D

HEAVYLIFT CARGO AIRLINES

(HVY)

Sydney, NSW

9L-LDQ	Short SC.5 Belfast	SH1819	ex G-HLFT

First service 26 September 2003; owned by Transpacific

HORIZON AIR

(BN/HZA)

Sydney-Bankstown, NSW (BWU)

VH-IMG	Hawker Siddeley HS.748 Srs.2/228 LFD	1604	ex A10-604	stored BWU
VH-IMI	Hawker Siddeley HS.748 Srs.2B/287 LFD	1736	ex G-BCOE	
VH-IMJ	Hawker Siddeley HS.748 Srs.2B/426	1799	ex 9N-ACX	
VH-IMK	Hawker Siddeley HS.748 Srs.2B/287 LFD	1737	ex G-BCOF	The Beast
VH-IPA	Hawker Siddeley HS.748 Srs.2B/361	1772	ex 5R-MJA	
VH-IPB	Hawker Siddeley HS.748 Srs.2B/361LFD	1773	ex 5R-MJB	stored BWU
VH-	Hawker Siddeley HS.748 Srs.2/228	1709	ex 3C-QQP	stored BWU
VH-HPB	Swearingen SA.227DC Metro 23	DC-808B	ex N808SK	

Entered administration 14 October 2003 and sold to Macair. Status of 748s uncertain as freight flights for Australian air Express have ceased

IAF AIR FREIGHTERS

Independent (IDP)

Melbourne-Essendon, VIC (MEB)

IAF Air Freighters is the trading name of Independent Air Freighters; still exists but owns no aircraft

IMPULSE AIRLINES

Sydney-Kingsford-Smith, NSW (SYD)

Wholly owned by Qantas and operates scheduled services in full colours as QantasLink (q.v.). To form nucleus of Jetstar, a new low-cost domestic airline being formed by Qantas, in May 2004 with fourteen Boeing 717s; these will be replaced by 23 Airbus Industrie A320s in due course

INLAND PACIFIC AIR

VH-BEM	Cessna 402C	402C0492	ex N6841L
VH-IPD	de Havilland DHC-6 Twin Otter 200	218	ex VH-MBC
VH-TRC	Cessna 421C Golden Eagle	421C0079	ex N98516
VH-TSI	Cessna 402B	402B0590	
VH-UCD	Cessna 402C	402C0049	ex N5825C

ISLAND AIR SERVICES

VH-BWC	Embraer EMB.110P1 Bandeirante	110261	ex LN-FAP

ISLAND AIR TAXIS

VH-ABX	Partenavia P.68B	99	ex (VH-ECO)
VH-ISD	Britten-Norman BN-2A-20 Islander	145	ex VH-UQN
VH-ISL	Britten-Norman BN-2B-26 Islander	2131	ex P2-MCA
VH-PNP	Partenavia P.68B	51	

ISLAND AIRLINES TASMANIA

VH-KGE	Piper PA-31-350 Navajo Chieftain	31-7752114	ex N27240
VH-XLA	Piper PA-31-350 Navajo Chieftain	31-7952206	ex ZK-FQW

Current status is uncertain, into administration and AOC suspended

JANAMI AIR

VH-HXH	Cessna 210N Centurion	21063847	ex N6260C
VH-MTJ	Cessna 210N Centurion	21064132	ex N5234Y

See also comments under Aboriginal Air

JETCRAFT

Jetcraft (JCC)

VH-UUG	Swearingen SA.227AC Metro III	AC-517	ex N3108X	
VH-UUO	Swearingen SA.227AC Metro III	AC-530	ex ZK-NST	
VH-UZA	Swearingen SA.227AT Merlin IVC	AT-502	ex VH-UUA	
VH-UZD	Swearingen SA.227AC Metro III	AC-490	ex N30693	
VH-UZG	Swearingen SA.227AC Metro III	AC-553	ex N220CT	Mayne Logistics titles
VH-UZI	Swearingen SA.227AT Expediter	AT-570	ex N570UP	
VH-UZP	Swearingen SA.227AC Metro III	AC-498	ex OY-BPL	David Fell
VH-UZQ	Swearingen SA.226TC Metro II	TC-259	ex C-FEPZ	
VH-UZW	Swearingen SA.227AC Metro III	AC-526	ex OY-GAW	Mount Hotham Falls Creek c/s

Metros operate services for Security Express in QLD, NSW and Victoria
Owns Transtate Airlines; purchased by Pearl Aviation but continues to operate separately

JETSTAR

VH-	Airbus Industrie A320-231	ex F-WW	on order Jun04	Lsd fr SALE
VH-	Airbus Industrie A320-231	ex F-WW	on order 04	Lsd fr SALE
VH-	Airbus Industrie A320-231	ex F-WW	on order 04	Lsd fr SALE
VH-	Airbus Industrie A320-231	ex F-WW	on order 04	
VH-	Airbus Industrie A320-231	ex F-WW	on order 04	
VH-	Airbus Industrie A320-231	ex F-WW	on order 04	
VH-	Airbus Industrie A320-231	ex F-WW	on order 04	
VH-	Airbus Industrie A320-231	ex F-WW	on order 04	
VH-	Airbus Industrie A320-231	ex F-WW	on order 04	
VH-	Airbus Industrie A320-231	ex F-WW	on order 04	
VH-	Airbus Industrie A320-231	ex F-WW	on order 04	
VH-	Airbus Industrie A320-231	ex F-WW	on order 04	

A total of 23 are on order for delivery by mid-2005 to replace the Boeing 717s including three leased from SALE

VH-IMD	Boeing 717-2K9	5014/55055	ex N9012S	Lsd fr Bavaria
VH-IMP	Boeing 717-2K9	5013/55054	ex N9012J	Lsd fr Bavaria
VH-LAX	Boeing 717-2K9	5020/55057	ex N6202S	Lsd fr Bavaria
VH-VQA	Boeing 717-2CM	5002/55001	ex N717XB	
VH-VQB	Boeing 717-2CM	5003/55002	ex N717XC	
VH-VQC	Boeing 717-2CM	5041/55151	ex N6202S	

VH-VQD	Boeing 717-23S	5031/55062	ex VH-AFR	Lsd fr Pembroke
VH-VQE	Boeing 717-23S	5034/55063	ex VH-SMH	Lsd fr Pembroke
VH-VQF	Boeing 717-231	5077/55092	ex N2425A	Lsd fr Pembroke
VH-VQG	Boeing 717-231	5083/55093	ex N426TW	Lsd fr Pembroke
VH-VQH	Boeing 717-231	5084/55094	ex N2427A	Lsd fr Pembroke
VH-VQI	Boeing 717-231	5087/55095	ex N428TW	Lsd fr Pembroke
VH-VQJ	Boeing 717-231	5093/55096	ex N429TW	Lsd fr Pembroke
VH-VQK	Boeing 717-231	5095/55097	ex N430TW	Lsd fr Pembroke

Boeing 717s will be removed from service as Airbus Industrie A320s are delivered
Wholly owned subsidiary of Qantas; to begin operations May 2004 as a low cost domestic operation based on Impulse
Airlines

KAKADU AIR SERVICES

Darwin, NT (DRW)

Also operates as Outback NT Air Services

VH-GKZ	Cessna 207 Skywagon	20700171	ex P2-SEB
VH-KAX	Cessna T207A Turbo Stationair 8	20700630	ex N154SP
VH-KQA	Cessna 402B	402B0567	
VH-LFU	Cessna 207 Skywagon	20700296	ex ZK-DXT
VH-NIV	Cessna 207 Skywagon 8	20700627	ex N41JF
VH-TFL	Cessna 210N Centurion	21063678	ex N671AA
VH-UBW	Cessna 207 Skywagon	20700137	ex N1537U

KARRATHA FLYING SERVICES

Karratha, WA (KTA)

VH-KFF	Piper PA-31-350 Navajo Chieftain	31-7952125	ex VH-UOT
VH-KFG	Beech C90 King Air	LJ-777	ex N9AN
VH-KFK	Beech 58 Baron	TH-969	ex VH-XMU
VH-KFM	Beech 58 Baron	TH-1339	ex VH-MOS
VH-KFQ	Piper PA-31 Turbo Navajo B	31-7401250	ex VH-SRZ
VH-KFW	Piper PA-31 Turbo Navajo	31-366	ex VH-WGU

KARUMBA AIR SERVICES   ceased operations

KING ISLAND AIRLINES

(KG)

Melbourne-Moorabbin, VIC (MBW)

VH-DMV	Piper PA-31-350 Navajo Chieftain	31-7405487	ex N61477
VH-KGN	Piper PA-31-350 Navajo Chieftain	31-7952061	ex N27952
VH-KIB	Piper PA-31-350 Navajo Chieftain	31-7305035	ex VH-TXD
VH-KIG	Piper PA-31-350 Navajo Chieftain	31-7852146	ex VH-HRL
VH-KGQ	Embraer EMB.110P1 Bandeirante	110221	ex VH-XFD	stored MBW

LAYNHAPUY AVIATION

Grove, NT (GOV)

VH-LGN	Cessna U206G Stationair	U20603773	ex N8190G
VH-LHA	Britten-Norman BN-2A-26 Islander	856	ex JA5265
VH-NTC	Cessna 208B Caravan I	208B0418	ex VH-DEX	Lsd fr debis
VH-PIY	Cessna U206G Stationair 6	U20604583	ex P2-PIY
VH-RXT	Cessna U206B Super Skylane	U206-0701	ex N3401L
VH-STK	Cessna U206G Stationair 6	U20603555	ex (N8845Q)

MACAIR AIRLINES

(CC/MCK)

Townsville, QLD (TSV)

VH-MYI	Swearingen SA.227DC Metro 23	DC-869B	ex 9M-APB
VH-HAN	Swearingen SA.227DC Metro 23	DC-822B	ex N822MM
VH-HPE	Swearingen SA.227DC Metro 23	DC-823B	ex N823MM
VH-UUA	Swearingen SA.227DC Metro 23	DC-824B	ex N824GL	Lsd fr Lambert Lsg
VH-UUB	Swearingen SA.227DC Metro 23	DC-894B	ex N3032F
VH-UUC	Swearingen SA.227AC Metro III	AC-679	ex N364AE	Lsd fr CRI Intl
VH-UUD	Swearingen SA.227AC Metro III	DC-817B	ex N817JE
VH-UUF	Swearingen SA.227AC Metro III	AC-616	ex VH-UZS	Copper Connection
VH-UUN	Swearingen SA.227AC Metro III	AC-686	ex N686AV
VH-UUQ	Swearingen SA.227AC Metro III	AC-714	ex N433MA
VH-UZY	Swearingen SA.226TC Metro II	TC-343	ex N342PL
VH-UQC	Embraer EMB.110P2 Bandeirante	110194	ex VH-XFM	stored CNS
VH-UQY	de Havilland DHC-6 Twin Otter 310	551	ex VH-ZRP
VH-XDA	SAAB SF.340B	340B-333	ex F-GMVX	Lsd fr SAAB
VH-XDZ	SAAB SF.340B	340B-328	ex F-GMVV	Lsd fr SAAB

Merged with Transtate Airlines; part of the Transjet Group

MAROOMBA AIR SERVICE

(KN)   *Perth, WA (PER)*

VH-SMN	Cessna 310R	310R0531	ex VH-AJB
VH-SMO	Cessna 441 Conquest	441-0132	ex VH-ANJ
VH-SMQ	British Aerospace Jetstream 31	665	ex VH-ESW
VH-SMT	Beech 200 Super King Air	BB-162	ex RP-C22
VH-SMZ	Beech B200 Super King Air	BB-1490	ex N122LC

MARTHAKAL YOLNGU AIRLINES

Elcho Island, NT (ELC)

VH-FUY	Cessna U206G Stationair 6	U20604939	ex N735MF
VH-SOP	Cessna U206G Stationair 6	U20606216	ex N6284Z
VH-UBE	Cessna 207A Super Skywagon	20700475	ex N6307H
VH-UBP	Cessna U206G Stationair	U20603716	ex P2-MAX

MISSIONARY AVIATION FELLOWSHIP now has no connection with any airline operation

NATIONAL JET SYSTEMS

National Jet (NC/NJS)   *Adelaide, SA (ADL)*

VH-TBS	Boeing 727-77C (FedEx 3)	768/20278	ex C2-RN7	wfs BNE
(VH-VLE)	Boeing 727-277F (FedEx 3)	989/20549	ex VH-TXH	
VH-VLF	Boeing 727-277F (FedEx 3)	1481/21695	ex VH-AUP	
VH-VLG	Boeing 727-277F (Duganair 3)	1054/20551	ex VH-RMX	Sandra
VH-VLH	Boeing 727-277F (FedEx 3)	1759/22642	ex OO-DLB	Joanne
VH-VLI	Boeing 727-277F (FedEx 3)	1753/22641	ex EC-HIG	Tania

Operated from 17 October 2003 on behalf of Australian air Express (XME) using call-sign 'Jetex8'

VH-NJA*	British Aerospace 146 Srs.100	E1004	ex G-DEBJ	
VH-NJC	British Aerospace 146 Srs.100	E1013	ex G-6-013	City of Cairns
VH-NJD*	British Aerospace 146 Srs.100	E1160	ex VH-JSF	Op for QantasLink
VH-NJF*	British Aerospace 146 Srs.300QT	E3198	ex G-BTLD	Op for XME
VH-NJG*	British Aerospace 146 Srs.200	E2170	ex G-BSOH	Op for QantasLink
VH-NJH*	British Aerospace 146 Srs.200	E2178	ex G-BTCP	Op for QantasLink
VH-NJJ*	British Aerospace 146 Srs.200	E2184	ex G-BTKC	Op for QantasLink
VH-NJL*	British Aerospace 146 Srs.300	E3213	ex G-BVPE	Op for QantasLink
VH-NJM*	British Aerospace 146 Srs.300QT	E3194	ex G-BTHT	Op for XME
VH-NJN*	British Aerospace 146 Srs.300	E3217	ex G-BUHW	Op for QantasLink
VH-NJQ*	British Aerospace 146 Srs.200	E2072	ex G-BNJI	based BNE
VH-NJR*	British Aerospace 146 Srs.100	E1152	ex G-BRLN	
VH-NJT*	Avro RJ70A	E1228	ex G-OLXX	based PER
VH-NJU*	British Aerospace 146 Srs.200	E2073	ex G-BVFV	Op for Dept of Immigration
VH-NJV*	British Aerospace 146 Srs.100QT	E1002	ex G-BSTA	Op for XME
VH-NJW	British Aerospace 146 Srs.200	E2034	ex (VH-FRB)	Lsd fr ANZ Bank, op for QantasLink
VH-NJX	British Aerospace 146 Srs.100	E1003	ex EI-CPY	Op for QantasLink
VH-NJY*	British Aerospace 146 Srs.100	E1005	ex G-SCHH	City of Mackay Op for QantasLink
VH-NJZ	British Aerospace 146 Srs.100	E1009	ex G-6-009	City of Rockhampton
				Op for QantasLink

*Leased from BAE Systems

VH-ZZT	Britten-Norman BN-2B-20 Islander	2279	ex G-BVNC	Op for Coastguard
VH-ZZU	Britten-Norman BN-2B-20 Islander	2280	ex G-BVND	Op for Coastguard
VH-ZZV	Britten-Norman BN-2B-20 Islander	2281	ex G-BVNE	Op for Coastguard
VH-ZZW	Britten-Norman BN-2B-20 Islander	2282	ex G-BVNF	Op for Coastguard
VH-ZZX	Britten-Norman BN-2B-20 Islander	2283	ex G-BVSG	Op for Coastguard
VH-ZZY	Britten-Norman BN-2B-20 Islander	2284	ex G-BVSH	Op for Coastguard

VH-JSH	de Havilland DHC-8-202	411	ex C-GHRI	
VH-JSI	de Havilland DHC-8-103	229	ex VH-LAR	Lsd to Fubilan as P2-NAX
VH-JSJ	de Havilland DHC-8-103	170	ex VH-NJD	
VH-JSQ	de Havilland DHC-8-311A	399	ex VH-NJT	Lsd fr Avline Lsg, op for Santos
VH-LCL	de Havilland DHC-8Q-202	492	ex C-GEOA	Op for RAN
VH-ZZA	de Havilland DHC-8-202	419	ex C-FWWU	Op for Coastguard
VH-ZZB	de Havilland DHC-8-202	424	ex C-FXBC	Op for Coastguard
VH-ZZC	de Havilland DHC-8-202	433	ex C-FXFK	Op for Coastguard
VH-ZZI	de Havilland DHC-8-202	550	ex C-GDLD	Op for Coastguard
VH-ZZJ	de Havilland DHC-8-202	551	ex C-FDHI	Op for Coastguard

VH-ZZE	Reims Cessna F406 Vigilant	F406-0076	ex F-WZDX	
VH-ZZF	Reims Cessna F406 Vigilant	F406-0078	ex (VH-BPH)	
VH-ZZG	Reims Cessna F406 Vigilant	F406-0079		
VH-ZZS	Shrike Commander 500S	3071	ex N45WS	

Owned by Cobham Group, parent of FR Aviation

NAUTILUS AVIATION

Townsville, QLD (TSV)

VH-OPH For sale	Cessna 208 Caravan I	20800157	ex PT-OZA	Orpheus Island	Floatplane

NETWORK AVIATION AUSTRALIA

Perth, WA (PER)

VH-AZW	Cessna 441 Conquest	441-0026	ex VH-FWA	
VH-NAX	Cessna 441 Conquest	441-0106	ex VH-YOL	
VH-NIF	Embraer EMB.120ER Brasilia	120054	ex VH-FNQ	
VH-SGT	Beech 200 Super King Air	BB-73		
VH-TLZ	Embraer EMB.120ER Brasilia	120152	ex N152CA	Lsd
VH-XDB	Beech 200 Super King Air	BB-533	ex LN-PAH	

NGAANYATJARRA AIR

Alice Springs, NT (ASP)

VH-HXH	Cessna 210N Centurion	21063847	ex N6260C	
VH-NGC	Pilatus PC-12/45	102	ex HB-FOE	
VH-NGD	Cessna P210N Centurion	21000459	ex VH-DXA	
VH-NGE	Cessna P210N Centurion	21000830	ex VH-JPL	
VH-NGS	Cessna 208B Caravan I	208B0416	ex N1114W	

See also comments under Aboriginal Air

NGURRATJUTA AIR

Alice Springs, NT (ASP)

VH-MTJ	Cessna 210N Centurion	21064132	ex N5234Y	
VH-NTQ	Cessna 208B Caravan I	208B0635	ex N1216Q	

See also comments under Aboriginal Air

NORFOLK JET EXPRESS

(NC)   *Brisbane, QLD/Norfolk Island, NSW (BNE/NLK)*

VH-RON Also leases Alliance Fokker 100s	Boeing 737-4L7	2483/26960	ex C2-RN10	Op by RON

NORTHERN AIR SERVICES ceased operations

NORTHWEST REGIONAL AIRLINES

(FY/NWR)   *Broome, WA (BME)*

VH-BBN	Cessna 210L Centurion	21060311	ex (N92303)	
VH-KDM	Cessna 210N Centurion	21063041	ex N6467N	
VH-PBV	Cessna 210M Centurion	21062350	ex N761LW	
VH-SKQ	Cessna 210L Centurion	21061243	ex N1629C	
VH-SMC	Cessna 210M Centurion	21062023	ex N1883C	
VH-TCI	Cessna 210L Centurion	21060548	ex N94225	
VH-WTX	Cessna 210L Centurion	21060222	ex (N93025)	
VH-DLF	Cessna 404 Titan	404-0683	ex N6763K	
VH-JOR	Cessna 404 Titan	404-0642	ex D-IEEE	
VH-UOP	Cessna 404 Titan	404-0636	ex N5280J	
VH-DAW	Cessna 310R	310R0148	ex N5028J	
VH-OTV	de Havilland DHC-3 Turbo Otter	250	ex N573A	

NUMBURINDI AIR

Katherine, NT (KTR)

VH-AEE	Cessna U206G Stationair 6	U20605226	ex N5345U	
VH-ASJ	Cessna U206G Stationair 6	U20605867	ex N6402X	

O'CONNOR AIRLINES

O'Connor (UQ/OCM)   *Mount Gambier, SA (MGB)*

VH-OAA	Cessna 441 Conquest	441-0102	ex N4246Z	
VH-OAB*	British Aerospace Jetstream 32EP	853	ex N853JX	Spirit of Tantanoola
VH-OAE*	British Aerospace Jetstream 32EP	851	ex N851JX	Spirit of Mount Gambier
VH-OAL	Cessna 210N Centurion	21063031	ex N6457N	
VH-OAM*	British Aerospace Jetstream 32EP	859	ex N859AE	

VH-PNX	Partenavia P.68B	66			
VH-YFD	Cessna 441 Conquest	441-0157	ex N51LR		

*Leased from BAE Systems

PACIFIC AIR EXPRESS (INTERNATIONAL)

Solpac (PAQ)   *Brisbane, QLD (BNE)*

ER-AXE	Antonov An-12BK	7345201		Lsd fr/op by MCC

PACIFIC AIR FREIGHTERS

Brisbane, QLD (BNE)

VH-PAF	Douglas DC-4	27352	ex N9013V	for sale	Lsd fr Airfreighters Intl

PACIFIC AVIATION

Pacav (PCV)   *Sydney-Bankstown, NSW (BWU)*

VH-SMH	Cessna 208B Caravan I	208B0916	ex N1254D

PACIFIC RIM AIRWAYS   did not start operations

PALACE AIR

Coolangatta

Plans to start operations with a Boeing 747SP in March 2004 on charters

PAR AVION   now listed as Airlines of Tasmania

PEARL AVIATION

Perth, WA (PER)

VH-FII	Beech 200 Super King Air	BB-653	ex VH-MXK	Op for Flight Inspection Alliance
VH-LKF	Beech 200 Super King Air	BB-660	ex N200TK	EMS
VH-NTE	Beech 200 Super King Air	BB-529	ex VH-SWP	Op for NT Aerial Medical Services
VH-NTG	Beech 200C Super King Air	BL-9	ex VH-KZL	Op for NT Aerial Medical Services
VH-NTH	Beech 200C Super King Air	BL-12	ex VH-SWO	Op for NT Aerial Medical Services
VH-OYA	Beech 200 Super King Air	BB-365	ex P2-SML	Lsd to RAAF
VH-OYD	Beech 200 Super King Air	BB-1041	ex N200BK	EMS
VH-OYE	Beech 200 Super King Air	BB-355	ex VH-SMB	EMS
VH-OYH	Beech 200 Super King Air	BB-148	ex VH-WNH	Op for Granites Gold Mines
VH-OYK	Beech 200C Super King Air	BL-41	ex VH-HEO	
VH-TLX	Beech 200 Super King Air	BB-550	ex P2-MBM	EMS
VH-TNQ	Beech 200C Super King Air	BL-30	ex N3723Y	Op for NT Aerial Medical Services
VH-FIX	Beech 300 Super King Air	FL-90	ex D-CKRA	Calibrator	Op for AirServices
VH-OYB	Swearingen SA.227DC Metro 23	DC-848B	ex N452LA	
VH-OYG	Swearingen SA.227DC Metro 23	DC-875B	ex VH-SWM	
VH-OYI	Swearingen SA.227DC Metro 23	DC-839B	ex VH-DMI	
VH-OYN	Swearingen SA.227DC Metro 23	DC-870B	ex VH-DMO	
VH-PPE	Grumman G-73AT Turbo Mallard	J-22	ex VH-LAW	
VH-PPI	Grumman G-73 Mallard	J-23	ex VH-OAW	
VH-PPT	Grumman G-73AT Turbo Mallard	J-26	ex VH-JAW	

Owns Jetcraft

PEARL COAST AIRWAYS

Perth, WA (PER)

VH-MOX	Cessna 208 Caravan I	20800227	ex VH-NGD	Floatplane
VH-MQX	Cessna U206G Stationair 6	U20604924	ex N735HQ	

PEL-AIR AVIATION

Questair (QWA)   *Sydney-Mascot, NSW*

VH-AJG	IAI 1124 Westwind	281	ex N1124F	Freighter
VH-AJJ	IAI 1124 Westwind	248	ex N25RE	
VH-AJK	IAI 1124 Westwind	256	ex 4X-CNB	Freighter
VH-AJP	IAI 1124 Westwind	238	ex 4X-CMJ	Freighter
VH-AJV	IAI 1124 Westwind	282	ex N186G	
VH-AJV	IAI 1124 Westwind	282	ex N186G	
VH-KNS	IAI 1124 Westwind	323	ex N816H	Freighter
VH-KNU	IAI 1124 Westwind	317	ex VH-UUZ	Freighter
VH-NGA	IAI 1124A Westwind II	387	ex N97AL	

608

VH-EEJ	Swearingen SA.227AC Metro III	AC-617	ex VH-SSV	Combi	
VH-EEN	Swearingen SA.227AT Expediter	AT-563	ex N563UP	Freighter	Jt ops with XME
VH-EEO	Swearingen SA.227AT Expediter	AT-564	ex N564UP	Freighter	Jt ops with XME
VH-EEP	Swearingen SA.227TT Expediter	AT-567	ex N565UP	Freighter	Jt ops with XME
VH-EEQ	Swearingen SA.227AC Metro III	AC-612	ex VH-SST	Combi	
VH-EER	Swearingen SA.227AC Metro III	AC-632	ex VH-SSW	Combi	
VH-EES	Swearingen SA.227AC Metro III	AC-614	ex VH-SSZ	Combi	
VH-EET	Swearingen SA.227AC Metro III	AC-494	ex VH-SSM	Combi	Op for TNT
VH-EEU	Swearingen SA.227AC Metro III	AC-619B	ex VH-OYC	Combi	
VH-AFR	Beech 1900C-1	UC-112	ex N112YV		Op as Pel-Air Express
VH-EEY	Beech 1900C-1	UC-130	ex N130UE		Op as Pel-Air Express
VH-SLD	Learjet 35A	35A-145	ex N145GJ	Freighter	
VH-SLE	Learjet 35A	35A-428	ex N17LH		
VH-SLF	Learjet 36A	36A-049	ex N136ST		
VH-SLJ	Learjet 36	36-014	ex N200Y	Freighter	

All Learjets used on Fleet Support and based at NAS Nowra (NOA)

QANTAS AIRWAYS

Qantas (QF/QFA) (IATA 081)   *Sydney-Kingsford Smith, NSW (SYD)*

VH-EBA	Airbus Industrie A330-201	508	ex F-WWKM	Cradle Mountain	
VH-EBB	Airbus Industrie A330-201	522	ex F-WWYQ	Albany	
VH-EBC	Airbus Industrie A330-201	506	ex F-WWYU	Surfers Paradise	
VH-EBD	Airbus Industrie A330-201	513	ex F-WWYV	Traralgon	
VH-QPA	Airbus Industrie A330-303	553	ex F-WWKS	Kununurra	
VH-QPB	Airbus Industrie A330-303	558	ex F-WWYQ	Freycinet Peninsula	
VH-QPC	Airbus Industrie A330-303	564	ex F-WWYQ	Broken Hilll	
VH-QPD	Airbus Industrie A330-303	574	ex F-WWYU	on order 04	
VH-QPE	Airbus Industrie A330-303	593	ex F-WW	on order	
VH-QPE	Airbus Industrie A330-303		ex F-WW	on order	

Operate with Cityjet titles

Twelve Airbus Industrie A380-800s, (registered VH-OQA to -OQL), for delivery between 2006 and 2011

VH-CZR^	Boeing 737-33A	1831/24460	ex G-OBMH		Sublsd to QNZ as ZK-CZR
VH-CZS^	Boeing 737-33A	1654/24030	ex XA-SGJ		Sublsd to QNZ as ZK-CZS
VH-CZU^	Boeing 737-33A	2600/27267			Sublsd to QNZ as ZK-CZU
VH-JNE^	Boeing 737-33A	2069/25119	ex PT-TER		Sublsd to QNZ as ZK-JNE
VH-TAG	Boeing 737-376	1251/23478		Advance	Lsd to QNZ as ZK-JNG
VH-TAH	Boeing 737-376	1259/23479		Adventure	
VH-TAK	Boeing 737-376	1277/23485		Daring	
VH-TAU	Boeing 737-376	1286/23486		Enterprise	Lsd to QNZ as ZK-JNF
VH-TAV	Boeing 737-376	1306/23487		Intrepid	
VH-TAW	Boeing 737-376	1352/23488		Progress	Lsd to QNZ as ZK-JNH
VH-TAX	Boeing 737-376	1356/23489		Success	
VH-TAY	Boeing 737-376	1390/23490		Valiant	Lsd to QNZ as ZK-JNA
VH-TAZ	Boeing 737-376	1391/23491		Victory	
VH-TJA	Boeing 737-376	1649/24295		Resolute	
VH-TJB	Boeing 737-376	1653/24296		Guadalcanal	
VH-TJC	Boeing 737-376	1740/24297		Endeavour	
VH-TJD	Boeing 737-376	1761/24298		Gallant	
VH-TJE	Boeing 737-476	1820/24430		Kookaburra	
VH-TJF	Boeing 737-476	1863/24431		Brolga	
VH-TJG	Boeing 737-476	1879/24432	ex 9M-MLE	Eagle	
VH-TJH	Boeing 737-476	1881/24433		Falcon	
VH-TJI	Boeing 737-476	1912/24434	ex 9M-MLD	Swan	
VH-TJJ	Boeing 737-476	1959/24435		Heron	
VH-TJK	Boeing 737-476	1998/24436		Ibis	
VH-TJL	Boeing 737-476	2162/24437		Swift	
VH-TJM	Boeing 737-476	2171/24438		Kestrel	
VH-TJN	Boeing 737-476	2265/24439		Egret	
VH-TJO	Boeing 737-476	2324/24440		Lorikeet	
VH-TJP	Boeing 737-476	2363/24441		Petrel	
VH-TJQ	Boeing 737-476	2371/24442		Bellbird	
VH-TJR	Boeing 737-476	2398/24443		Cockatiel	
VH-TJS	Boeing 737-476	2454/24444		Jabiru	
VH-TJT	Boeing 737-476	2539/24445		Kingfisher	
VH-TJU	Boeing 737-476	2569/24446		Currawong	
VH-TJV	Boeing 737-4Q8	2264/25163	ex H4-SOL	Swan	Lsd fr ILFC
VH-TJW	Boeing 737-4L7	2517/26961	ex C2-RN11	Strahan	
VH-TJX	Boeing 737-476	2773/28150		Stawell	
VH-TJY	Boeing 737-476	2785/28151			
VH-TJZ	Boeing 737-476	2829/28152			

^Leased from Australian Wetleasing Operations and will not return to Qantas. All -300s to be retired by the end of 2004

VH-VXA	Boeing 737-838	1042/29551	ex (N979AN)	Broome	
VH-VXB	Boeing 737-838	1045/30101	ex (N980AN)	Yanani Dreaming	
VH-VXC	Boeing 737-838	1049/30897	ex (N981AN)	Gippsland	
VH-VXD	Boeing 737-838	1063/29552	ex (N982AN)	Tenterfield	
VH-VXE	Boeing 737-838	1071/30899	ex (N983AN)	Coffs Harbour	

VH-VXF	Boeing 737-838	1096/29553	ex (N984AN)	Sunshine Coast	
VH-VXG	Boeing 737-838	1102/30901	ex (N985AM)	Port Douglas	
VH-VXH	Boeing 737-838	1137/33478	ex (N986AM)	Warrnambool	
VH-VXI	Boeing 737-838	1141/33479	ex (N987AM)	Oonadatta	
VH-VXJ	Boeing 737-838	1157/33480	ex (N988AM)	Coober Pedy	
VH-VXK	Boeing 737-838	1160/33481	ex (N989AM)	Katherine	
VH-VXL	Boeing 737-838	1172/33482		Charlville	
VH-VXM	Boeing 737-838	1177/33483	ex N6055X	Mount Hotham	
VH-VXN	Boeing 737-838	1180/33484		Freemantle	
VH-VXO	Boeing 737-838	1183/33485		Kakadu	
VH-VXP	Boeing 737-838	1324/33722		Logan	
VH-VXQ	Boeing 737-838	1335/33723		Redlands	
VH-VXR	Boeing 737-838	1340/33724		Shepparton	
VH-VXS	Boeing 737-838	1352/33725			
VH-VXT	Boeing 737-838	1412/33760	ex N1787B		
VH-VXU	Boeing 737-838	1420/33761			

Seven more Boeing 737-838s are on order for future delivery
First eleven 737-838s from deferred order of American Airlines, originally ordered as 737-823s

VH-EBT	Boeing 747-338	602/23222	ex N1784B	City of Wagga Wagga	
VH-EBU	Boeing 747-338	606/23223	ex N5573P	Nalanji Dreaming	
VH-EBV	Boeing 747-338	610/23224	ex N6005C	City of Geraldton; stored Avalon	
VH-EBW	Boeing 747-338	638/23408	ex N6055X	City of Tamworth; stored Avalon	
VH-EBX	Boeing 747-338	662/23688	ex N6005C	City of Wodonga	
VH-EBY	Boeing 747-338	678/23823	ex N6005C	City of Mildura	
VH-OEB	Boeing 747-48E	983/25778	ex HL7416		
VH-OEC	Boeing 747-4H6	808/24836	ex 9M-MHN		
VH-OED	Boeing 747-4H6	858/25126	ex 9M-MHO		
VH-OEE	Boeing 747-438ER	1308/32909	ex N747ER	Nullarbor	
VH-OEF	Boeing 747-438ER	1313/32910	ex N60659	City of Sydney	
VH-OEG	Boeing 747-438ER	1320/32911		Parkes	
VH-OEH	Boeing 747-438ER	1321/32912	ex N5020K		
VH-OEI	Boeing 747-438ER	1330/32913		Hervey Bay	
VH-OEJ	Boeing 747-438ER	1331/32914	ex N60668	Wanula Dreaming	
VH-OJA	Boeing 747-438	731/24354	ex N6046P	City of Canberra	
VH-OJB	Boeing 747-438	746/24373		Mount Isa	
VH-OJC	Boeing 747-438	751/24406		City of Melbourne	
VH-OJD	Boeing 747-438	764/24481		City of Brisbane	
VH-OJE	Boeing 747-438	765/24482		City of Adelaide	
VH-OJF	Boeing 747-438	781/24483		City of Perth	
VH-OJG	Boeing 747-438	801/24779	ex N6009F	City of Hobart	
VH-OJH	Boeing 747-438	807/24806		City of Darwin	
VH-OJI	Boeing 747-438	826/24887	ex N6009F	Longreach	
VH-OJJ	Boeing 747-438	835/24974		Winton	
VH-OJK	Boeing 747-438	857/25067		Newcastle	
VH-OJL	Boeing 747-438	865/25151		City of Ballarat	
VH-OJM	Boeing 747-438	875/25245		Gosford	
VH-OJN	Boeing 747-438	883/25315	ex N6009F	City of Dubbo	
VH-OJO	Boeing 747-438	894/25544	ex N6005C	City of Toowoomba	
VH-OJP	Boeing 747-438	916/25545		City of Albury	
VH-OJQ	Boeing 747-438	924/25546	ex N6005C	Manduran	
VH-OJR	Boeing 747-438	936/25547	ex N6018N	City of Bathurst	
VH-OJS	Boeing 747-438	1230/25564			
VH-OJT	Boeing 747-438	1233/25565			
VH-OJU	Boeing 747-438	1239/25566			

VH-EAL*	Boeing 767-238ER	125/23306	ex N6009F	City of Geelong; stored MHV	
VH-EAM*	Boeing 767-238ER	129/23309	ex N6018N	Lake MacQuarie	
VH-EAN*	Boeing 767-238ER	133/23402	ex N6018N	Alice Springs	
VH-EAO*	Boeing 767-238ER	137/23403	ex N6046P	City of Cairns	
VH-EAQ*	Boeing 767-238ER	183/23896	ex N6009F	City of Launceston	
VH-OGA	Boeing 767-338ER	231/24146	ex N6055X	City of Whyalla	
VH-OGB	Boeing 767-338ER	242/24316	ex N6005C	City of Kalgoorlie/Boulder	
VH-OGC	Boeing 767-338ER	246/24317	ex N6005C	City of Bendigo	
VH-OGD	Boeing 767-338ER	247/24407	ex N6009F	City of Maitland	
VH-OGE	Boeing 767-338ER	278/24531		City of Orange	
VH-OGF	Boeing 767-338ER	319/24853		City of Lismore	
VH-OGG	Boeing 767-338ER	343/24929		City of Rockhampton	
VH-OGH	Boeing 767-338ER	344/24930		City of Parramatta	
VH-OGI	Boeing 767-338ER	387/25246		City of Port Augusta	Lsd to AUZ
VH-OGJ	Boeing 767-338ER	396/25274		Port MacQuarie	Lsd to AUZ
VH-OGK	Boeing 767-338ER	397/25316	ex N6018N	City of Mackay	Lsd to AUZ
VH-OGL	Boeing 767-338ER	402/25363	ex N6018N	City of Wangaratta	Lsd to AUZ
VH-OGM	Boeing 767-338ER	451/25575		City of Bundaberg	Lsd to AUZ
VH-OGN	Boeing 767-338ER	549/25576		Partnership	
VH-OGO	Boeing 767-338ER	550/25577		Unity	
VH-OGP	Boeing 767-338ER	615/28153			
VH-OGQ	Boeing 767-338ER	623/28154			
VH-OGR	Boeing 767-338ER	662/28724			
VH-OGS	Boeing 767-338ER	665/28725			
VH-OGT	Boeing 767-338ER	710/29117			
VH-OGU	Boeing 767-338ER	713/29118			

VH-OGV	Boeing 767-338ER	796/30186		Lsd to AUZ
VH-ZXA	Boeing 767-336ER	288/24337 ex G-BNWE		Lsd fr BAW
VH-ZXB	Boeing 767-336ER	293/24338 ex G-BNWF		Lsd fr BAW
VH-ZXC	Boeing 767-336ER	298/24339 ex G-BNWG		Lsd fr BAW
VH-ZXD	Boeing 767-336ER	363/24342 ex G-BNWJ		Lsd fr BAW
VH-ZXE	Boeing 767-336ER	364/24343 ex G-BNWK		Lsd fr BAW
VH-ZXF	Boeing 767-336ER	365/25203 ex G-BNWL		Lsd fr BAW
VH-ZXG	Boeing 767-336ER	419/25443 ex G-BNWP		Lsd fr BAW

*Sold via Blue Star Aviation and due to leave fleet

VH-AES	Douglas DC-3	6021 ex VH-SBA	Hawdon - historic flight	

22.5% owned by British Airways; in turn owns Impulse Airlines, Southern Australia Airlines, Sunstate Airlines which operate as QantasLink plus 46% of Air Pacific. Owns 4.99% and plans to purchase 22.5% of Air New Zealand Australian Airlines is low-cost division while Jetconnect operates domestic services in New Zealand in full Qantas colours. Member of oneworld alliance.
Jetstar is a new low fare domestic unit that will initially operate using Impulse Airlines as operating entity.

QANTASLINK

(QF/QFA)   *various*

VH-IMD	Boeing 717-2K9	5014/55055 ex N9012S	Impulse	Lsd fr Bavaria
VH-IMP	Boeing 717-2K9	5013/55054 ex N9012J	Impulse	Lsd fr Bavaria
VH-LAX	Boeing 717-2K9	5020/55057 ex N6202S	Impulse	Lsd fr Bavaria
VH-VQA	Boeing 717-2CM	5002/55001 ex N717XB	Impulse	
VH-VQB	Boeing 717-2CM	5003/55002 ex N717XC	Impulse	
VH-VQC	Boeing 717-2CM	5041/55151 ex N6202S	Impulse	
VH-VQD	Boeing 717-23S	5031/55062 ex VH-AFR	Impulse	Lsd fr Pembroke
VH-VQE	Boeing 717-23S	5034/55063 ex VH-SMH	Impulse	Lsd fr Pembroke
VH-VQF	Boeing 717-231	5077/55092 ex N2425A	Impulse	Lsd fr Pembroke
VH-VQG	Boeing 717-231	5083/55093 ex N426TW	Impulse	Lsd fr Pembroke
VH-VQH	Boeing 717-231	5084/55094 ex N2427A	Impulse	Lsd fr Pembroke
VH-VQI	Boeing 717-231	5087/55095 ex N428TW	Impulse	Lsd fr Pembroke
VH-VQJ	Boeing 717-231	5093/55096 ex N429TW	Impulse	Lsd fr Pembroke
VH-VQK	Boeing 717-231	5095/55097 ex N430TW	Impulse	Lsd fr Pembroke

To transfer initially to Jetstar, the new low-cost domestic carrier of Qantas

VH-NJD	British Aerospace 146 Srs.100	E1160 ex VH-JSF	Airlink	Lsd fr NJS
VH-NJG	British Aerospace 146 Srs.200	E2170 ex G-BSOH	Airlink	Lsd fr NJS
VH-NJH	British Aerospace 146 Srs.200	E2178 ex G-BTCP	Airlink	Lsd fr NJS
VH-NJJ	British Aerospace 146 Srs.200	E2184 ex G-BTKC	Airlink	Lsd fr NJS
VH-NJL	British Aerospace 146 Srs.300	E3213 ex G-BVPE	Airlink	Lsd fr NJS
VH-NJN	British Aerospace 146 Srs.300	E3217 ex G-BUHW	Airlink	Lsd fr NJS
VH-NJW	British Aerospace 146 Srs.200	E2034 ex G-DEBD	Airlink	Lsd fr ANZ Bank
VH-NJX	British Aerospace 146 Srs.100	E1003 ex EI-CPY	Airlink	Lsd fr NJS
VH-NJY	British Aerospace 146 Srs.100	E1005 ex G-SCHH	Airlink; City of Macka	Lsd fr NJS
VH-NJZ	British Aerospace 146 Srs.100	E1009 ex G-6-009	Airlink; City of Rockhampton	
				Lsd fr NJS
VH-YAF*	British Aerospace 146 Srs.200	E2040 ex G-DEBG	Mildura-Rural City	Lsd fr BAES

*Operated by Eastern Australia Airlines but to be returned to lessor

VH-SBB	de Havilland DHC-8Q-311	539 ex C-FDHO	Sunstate	
VH-SBG	de Havilland DHC-8Q-315	575 ex C-GSAH	Sunstate; City of Gladstone	
VH-SBJ	de Havilland DHC-8Q-315	578 ex C-FDHI	Sunstate	
VH-SBT	de Havilland DHC-8Q-315	580 ex C-FDHP	Sunstate	
VH-SBV	de Havilland DHC-8Q-315	595 ex C-GIHK	Sunstate	
VH-SBW	de Havilland DHC-8Q-315	599 ex C-	Sunstate	
VH-SCE	de Havilland DHC-81-315	602 ex C-	Sunstate	
VH-SDA	de Havilland DHC-8Q-202	482 ex C-GFQL	Sunstate; Torres Strait	
VH-SDE	de Havilland DHC-8Q-202	453 ex N453DS	Sunstate	
VH-TND	de Havilland DHC-8-102	036 ex N806MX	Sunstate	
VH-TNG	de Havilland DHC-8-102	041 ex N807MX	Sunstate	
VH-TNU	de Havilland DHC-8-103	203 ex OE-LLM	Sunstate	
VH-TNW	de Havilland DHC-8-103A	243 ex D-BFRA	Sunstate	
VH-TNX	de Havilland DHC-8-102	033 ex N805MX	Sunstate	
VH-TQC	de Havilland DHC-8Q-315	596 ex C-GDOE	Eastern Australia	
VH-TQD	de Havilland DHC-8Q-315	598 ex C-	Eastern Australia	
VH-TQE	de Havilland DHC-8Q-315	600 ex C-GZPO	Eastern Australia	
VH-TQF	de Havilland DHC-8-102	067 ex N801AW	Eastern Australia	
VH-TQG	de Havilland DHC-8-201	430 ex C-GDNG	Eastern Australia	
VH-TQH	de Havilland DHC-8Q-315	597 ex C-GZDM	Eastern Australia	
VH-TQN	de Havilland DHC-8-102	062 ex D-BEST	Eastern Australia	
VH-TQO	de Havilland DHC-8-102	004 ex C-GGPJ	Eastern Australia	
VH-TQP	de Havilland DHC-8-102	135 ex C-GFQL	Eastern Australia	
VH-TQQ	de Havilland DHC-8-102	204 ex C-GFUM	Eastern Australia	
VH-TQR	de Havilland DHC-8-102	208 ex C-GESR	Eastern Australia	
VH-TQS	de Havilland DHC-8-202	418 ex C-GFRP	Eastern Australia	
VH-TQT	de Havilland DHC-8-102A	349 ex C-GBSW	Eastern Australia	
VH-TQU	de Havilland DHC-8-102A	346 ex N848MA	Eastern Australia	
VH-TQV	de Havilland DHC-8-102A	362 ex C-GCWZ	Eastern Australia	
VH-TQW	de Havilland DHC-8-103A	306 ex C-GGEW	Eastern Australia	
VH-TQX	de Havilland DHC-8-202	439 ex N439SD	Eastern Australia	

VH-TQY	de Havilland DHC-8-315	552	ex C-FDHP	Eastern Australia	
VH-TQZ	de Havilland DHC-8-315	555	ex C-GDNK	Eastern Australia	
VH-WZI*	de Havilland DHC-8-102	014	ex N814CL	Spirit of Sunraysia	Lsd fr Volvo A/S
VH-WZJ*	de Havilland DHC-8-102	027	ex N27CL	City of Devonport	Lsd fr Volvo A/S
VH-WZS*	de Havilland DHC-8-102	005	ex N4229R	City of Burnie	Lsd fr Volvo A/S
VH-	de Havilland DHC-8Q-315	603		Eastern Australia on order Jul04	
VH-	de Havilland DHC-8Q-315	604		Eastern Australia on order Aug04	

*Operated by Eastern Australia Airlines.
Some DHC-8-102s will be retired as the new srs 300 aircraft are delivered
QantasLink is the feeder services of Eastern Australia, Impulse and Sunstate, all of whom are wholly owned by Qantas

QUEENSLAND REGIONAL AIRLINES

| VH-JSZ | de Havilland DHC-8-102 | 8 | ex P2-NAY | | Lsd fr Aeromil |

REDPATH REGIONAL AIR SERVICES

Port Macquarie, NSW

| VH-OZH | Cessna 208B Caravan I | 208B0464 | ex N13313 | |

REGIONAIR

Melbourne-Moorabin, VIC (MBW)

| VH-TBJ | Piper PA-31-350 Navajo Chieftain | 31-7552128 | ex VH-SAJ |
| VH-VTR | Piper PA-31-350 Navajo Chieftain | 31-7952165 | ex VH-MYF |

REGIONAL PACIFIC AIR

Horn Island, QLD (HID)

| VH-FNU | de Havilland DHC-6 Twin Otter 300 | 286 | ex P2-RDI | Lsd fr FNU Pty |
| VH-RPZ | de Havilland DHC-6 Twin Otter 300 | 381 | ex 6Y-JMV | |

REX – REGIONAL EXPRESS

(ZL/RXA)   *Orange, NSW/Wagga Wagga, NSW (OAG/WGA)*

VH-EKD	SAAB SF.340A	155	ex SE-F55		
VH-EKH	SAAB SF.340B	369	ex SE-C69		
VH-EKX	SAAB SF.340B	257	ex (F-GNVQ)		
VH-KDB	SAAB SF.340A	008	ex PH-KJK		
VH-KDI	SAAB SF.340A	131	ex SE-F31		
VH-KDQ	SAAB SF.340B	325	ex SE-KVO		
VH-KDV	SAAB SF.340B	322	ex SE-KVN		
VH-KEQ	SAAB SF.340A	011	ex 9M-NSB		
VH-KRX	SAAB SF.340B	290	ex N361BE	on order	Lsd fr SAAB
VH-LIH	SAAB SF.340B	316	ex SE-C16		Lsd fr Scania Finance
VH-NRX	SAAB SF.340B	291	ex N362BE	on order	Lsd fr SAAB
VH-OLL	SAAB SF.340B	175	ex N143NC		Lsd fr Newcourt Capital
VH-OLM	SAAB SF.340B	205	ex SE-G05		Lsd fr Macquarie Bank
VH-OLN	SAAB SF.340B	207	ex SE-G07		Lsd fr Macquarie Bank
VH-ORX	SAAB SF.340B	293	ex N363BE	on order	Lsd fr SAAB
VH-PRX	SAAB SF.340B	303	ex N366BE	on order	Lsd fr SAAB
VH-RXX	SAAB SF.340B	209	ex N355BE		Lsd fr SAAB
VH-RXE	SAAB SF.340B	275	ex N275CJ		Lsd fr SAAB
VH-RXN	SAAB SF.340B	279	ex N358BE		Lsd fr SAAB
VH-RXS	SAAB SF.340B	285	ex N359BE		Lsd fr SAAB
VH-SBA	SAAB SF.340B	311	ex SE-KXA		Lsd fr Macquarie Bank
VH-TCH	SAAB SF.340B	362	ex SE-C62		Lsd fr SAAB

Some aircraft are for trade-in to SAAB and replacement by the aircraft on order (originally planned to be the older aircraft but this is not happening in practice)

VH-KAN	Swearingen SA.227DC Metro 23	DC-836B	ex N3021U
VH-KDJ	Swearingen SA.227DC Metro 23	DC-797B	ex N30042
VH-KDO	Swearingen SA.227DC Metro 23	DC-837B	ex N3021N
VH-KDT	Swearingen SA.227DC Metro 23	DC-800B	ex N3005U
VH-KED	Swearingen SA.227DC Metro 23	DC-845B	ex N3023Q
VH-KEU	Swearingen SA.227DC Metro 23	DC-846B	ex N30236
VH-KEX	Swearingen SA.227DC Metro 23	DC-872B	ex N3030X

Rex/Regional Express is the trading name of Australiawide Airlines

ROSSAIR

(RFS)   *Adelaide, SA (ADL)*

VH-XMD	Cessna 441 Conquest	441-0025	ex N441HD
VH-XMG	Cessna 441 Conquest	441-0130	ex VH-KDN
VH-XMJ	Cessna 414 Conquest	441-0113	ex N27TA

RUDGE AIR

VH-DHI	de Havilland DH.104 Dove 5	04410	ex XJ324	Belle's Dove

Current status is uncertain

SCHUTT AIR SERVICES operates as Regionair

SEAIR PACIFIC GOLD COAST

VH-LMD	Cessna 208 Caravan I	20800217	ex 9M-FBA	Floatplane
VH-LMZ	Cessna 208 Caravan I	20800173	ex LN-SEA	Floatplane
VH-MSF	GAF N22C Nomad	N22C-69		Lsd fr Whitaker

SHARP AVIATION

VH-CCL	Piper PA-31-350 Navajo Chieftain	31-7752015	ex N62999
VH-JCH	Piper PA-31-350 Chieftain	31-8152106	ex N4084T
VH-LCE	Piper PA-31-350 Navajo Chieftain	31-7305088	ex N305SP

SHINE AIR SERVICES

VH-ADE	Piper PA-31-325 Navajo C/R	31-7712006	ex N62996
VH-ITF	Piper PA-31 Turbo Navajo C	31-7812014	ex N27435
VH-VHT	Cessna 404 Titan	404-0226	ex ZS-OJN

SHORTSTOP AIR CHARTER

VH-OVM	Douglas DC-3	16354/33102	ex VH-JXD	Arthur Schutt MBE

SKIPPERS AVIATION

VH-FMQ	Cessna 441 Conquest	441-0109	ex N26226
VH-LBA	Cessna 441 Conquest	441-0042	ex N46MR
VH-LBX	Cessna 441 Conquest	441-0091	ex VH-AZY
VH-LBY	Cessna 441 Conquest	441-0023	ex VH-TFW
VH-LBZ	Cessna 441 Conquest	441-0038	ex VH-HWD
VH-HWR	Swearingen SA.227DC Metro 23	DC-851B	ex N3025T
VH-WAI	Swearingen SA.227DC Metro 23	DC-874B	ex N3032L
VH-WAJ	Swearingen SA.227DC Metro 23	DC-876B	ex N3033U
VH-WAX	Swearingen SA.227DC Metro 23	DC-877B	ex N30337
VH-WBA	Swearingen SA.227DC Metro 23	DC-883B	ex N30042
VH-WBQ	Swearingen SA.227DC Metro 23	DC-884B	ex N30046
VH-XFT	de Havilland DHC-8-102	052	ex ZK-NEW
VH-XFU	de Havilland DHC-8-102	151	ex ZK-NEV
VH-XUC	Embraer EMB.120ER Brasilia	120208	ex VH-XFV
VH-XUA	Embraer EMB.120ER Brasilia	120045	ex N272UE
VH-XUB	Embraer EMB.120RT Brasilia	120181	ex VH-XFW
VH-XUD	Embraer EMB.120ER Brasilia	120140	ex VH-XFZ

SKYLINK AUSTRALIA

VH-XMM	Piper PA-31-350 Chieftain	31-8052020	ex N3546L

SKYTRADERS

VH-	CASA C.212 Srs 400		on order
VH-	CASA C.212 Srs.400		on order

Plans to operate between Tasmania and Antarctic research bases; also expects to use a Falcon executive jet

SKYTRANS

(NP)

VH-JOB	Cessna 310R	310R1236	ex G-BOAT
VH-JOF	Cessna 310R	310R0548	ex VH-HCB

VH-SKH	Cessna 310R	310R1221	ex VH-LAF	
VH-SKN	Cessna 310R	310R1681	ex ZK-ETM	
VH-SKX	Cessna 310R	310R0935	ex VH-UFS	
VH-SKJ	Cessna 404 Titan	404-0086	ex VH-BPO	
VH-SKV	Cessna 404 Titan	404-0412	ex VH-TLE	
VH-SKW	Cessna 404 Titan	404-0042	ex VH-PNY	
VH-SKZ	Cessna 404 Titan	404-0080	ex VH-JOH	
VH-SZA	Cessna 404 Titan	404-0205	ex VH-JOA	
VH-SZO	Cessna 404 Titan	404-0834	ex VH-WZL	Lsd fr Titan Enterprise
VH-TWZ	Cessna 404 Titan	404-0404	ex VH-EOS	
VH-JAQ	Piper PA-34-220T Seneca III	34-8133184	ex VH-SKJ	
VH-JOH	Cessna 402C	402C0486	ex VH-JOC	
VH-JOV	Cessna 402C	402C0087	ex VH-JOC	
VH-SKG	Britten-Norman BN-2A-27 Islander	609	ex ZK-CRA	
VH-SKU	Beech 200 Super King Air	BB-165	ex VH-XRF	
VH-SQS	Britten-Norman BN-2A-21 Islander	494	ex G-BEGC	

SKYWEST AIRLINES

(XR)   *Perth, WA (PER)*

VH-FNA	Fokker 50	20106	ex PH-EXG
VH-FNB	Fokker 50	20107	ex PH-EXF
VH-FND	Fokker 50	20129	ex PH-EXB
VH-FNH	Fokker 50	20113	ex PH-EXY
VH-FNI	Fokker 50	20114	ex PH-EXZ
VH-FNY	Fokker 100	11484	ex N108ML

SLINGAIR

Kununurra, WA (KNX)

VH-AOI	Cessna 210N Centurion	21064609	ex N8721Y
VH-BKD	Cessna 210N Centurion	21063127	ex N6635N
VH-FOK	Cessna 210N Centurion	21063109	ex N6559N
VH-HOC	Cessna 210N Centurion	21064689	ex N1360U
VH-NLV	Cessna 210N Centurion	21063093	ex VH-APU
VH-NLZ	Cessna 210N Centurion	21063769	ex VH-RZZ
VH-OCM	Cessna 210N Centurion	21064466	ex N9300Y
VH-STB	Cessna 210M Centurion	21062771	ex N6467B
VH-TWD	Cessna 210N Centurion	21064356	ex N6372Y
VH-URX	Cessna 210N Centurion	21064449	ex N6595Y
VH-AZD	Gippsland GA-8 Airvan	GA8-01-005	
VH-DER	Piper PA-31 Turbo Navajo C	31-7912110	ex N3539D
VH-IEU	Cessna 207 Skywagon	20700231	ex N69336
VH-IEW	Cessna U206G Stationair	U20603695	ex (N7591N)
VH-JVO	Cessna 310R	310R0539	ex N145FB
VH-KSA	Cessna 208B Caravan I	208B0516	ex N6302B
VH-MPZ	Cessna 310R	310R0551	ex N310WB
VH-NLG	Cessna U206G Stationair	U20603930	ex ZS-JGH
VH-RGE	Cessna U206F Stationair	U20601981	ex N51221
VH-RKD	Piper PA-31-350 Chieftain	31-8152048	ex N4076Z
VH-TWY	Cessna 310R	310R0090	ex N69336

Derby Air Services is a wholly owned subsidiary

SOUTH PACIFIC AIR status uncertain; believed to be operating as HeavyLift Airlines

SUNSHINE EXPRESS AIRLINES

(CQ/EXL)   *Maroochydore-Sunshine Coast, QLD*

VH-SEF	Swearingen SA.227AC Metro III	AC-641	ex ZK-SDA	Spirit of Biloela
VH-SEG	Short SD.3-60	SH3760	ex RP-C3318	
VH-SEZ	Swearingen SA.227AC Metro III	AC-637	ex ZK-RCA	
VH-SUR	Short SD.3-60	SH3728	ex G-BNYF	

Operates on behalf of QantasLink

SUNSTATE AIRLINES

(QF/SSQ) (IATA)   *Brisbane, QLD (BNE)*

Wholly owned by Qantas and operates scheduled services in full colours as QantasLink (q.v.)

TASAIR

Hobart, TAS (HBT)

| VH-EXC | Shrike Commander 500S | 3251 | ex N57162 |
| VH-EXF | Shrike Commander 500S | 1797-12 | ex N5024E |

VH-JVD	Piper PA-31-350 Navajo Chieftain	31-7952041	ex N27523
VH-LST	Shrike Commander 500S	3111	ex N9157N
VH-LTW	Piper PA-31-350 Chieftain	31-8152025	ex N40725
VH-MZI	Piper PA-31-350 Chieftain	31-8152131	ex N4087S
VH-TZY	Piper PA-31-350 Navajo Chieftain	31-7405166	ex N662WR

TASFAST AIR FREIGHT

Upper Beaconsfield, VIC

| VH-MYX | Piper PA-31-350 Navajo Chieftain | 31-7552098 | ex P2-SAS |

TRANSAIR

(JT)   *Brisbane, QLD (BNE)*

VH-NEL	Swearingen SA.227AC Metro III	AC-611B	ex N611AV	Lsd fr ABN Amroc Australia
VH-TFG	Swearingen SA.227AC Metro III	AC-504	ex N31072	
VH-TFQ	Swearingen SA.226TC Metro II	TC-395	ex N20849	
VH-TFU	Swearingen SA.227DC Metro 23	DC-818B	ex N818GL	Lsd to ATI
VH-UUZ	Swearingen SA.227AC Metro III	AC-610B	ex VH-CUZ	

Also lease aircraft to Big Sky Express

TRANSAUSTRALIAN AIR EXPRESS ceased operations and aircraft transferred to National Jet Systems

TRANSPAC EXPRESS did not restart operations as planned

TROPICAIR

Carnarvon, WA (CVQ)

| VH-AFY | Piper PA-31 Turbo Navajo C | 31-8012084 | ex ZK-CJO |
| VH-PNS | Partenavia P.68B | 71 | |

TWINPIONAIR AIRLINES

Coolangatta, QLD (OOL)

| VH-AIS | Scottish Aviation Twin Pioneer 3 | 540 | ex G-APPH | Lsd to Hamilton |
| VH-EVB | Scottish Aviation Twin Pioneer 3 | 586 | ex 9M-ART | |

VALLEY AIR CHARTER SERVICES never commenced scheduled operations

VIRGIN BLUE AIRLINES

Virgin Blue (DJ/VOZ)   *Brisbane, QLD (BNE)*

VH-VBA	Boeing 737-7Q8	817/28238	ex N1791B	Brizzie Lizzie	Lsd fr ILFC
VH-VBB	Boeing 737-7Q8	832/28240	ex N1787B	Barossa Belle	Lsd fr ILFC
VH-VBC	Boeing 737-7Q8	858/30638		Betty Blue	Lsd fr ILFC
VH-VBD	Boeing 737-7Q8	975/30707		Sassy Sydney	Lsd fr ILFC
VH-VBF	Boeing 737-7Q8	1032/30630		Mellie Melbourne	Lsd fr ILFC
VH-VBH	Boeing 737-7Q8	1080/30641		Spirit of Sally	Lsd fr ILFC
VH-VBI	Boeing 737-7Q8	1107/30644		Smurfette	Lsd fr ILFC
VH-VBJ	Boeing 737-7Q8	1159/30647		Perth Princess	Lsd fr ILFC
VH-VBK	Boeing 737-7Q8	1171/30648		Lady Victoria	Lsd fr ILFC
VH-VBL	Boeing 737-7Q8	1220/30633		Victoria Vixen	Lsd fr ILFC
VH-VBM	Boeing 737-76N	1090/32734	ex N734SH	Tassie Tigress	
					Lsd fr AFS Investments
VH-VBN	Boeing 737-76N	1134/33005	ex N330SF	Southern Belle	Lsd fr GECAS
VH-VBO	Boeing 737-76N	1226/33418		Tropical Temptress	Lsd fr GECAS
VH-VBP	Boeing 737-7BX	922/30743	ex N368ML	Deja Blue	Lsd fr Boullioun
VH-VBQ	Boeing 737-7BX	989/30744	ex N369ML	La Blue Femme	Lsd fr Boullioun
VH-VBR	Boeing 737-7BX	1027/30745	ex N370ML	Mackay Maiden	Lsd fr Boullioun
VH-VBS	Boeing 737-7BX	1085/30746	ex N371ML	Blue Baroness	Lsd fr Boullioun
VH-VBT	Boeing 737-7BX	776/30740	ex N365ML	Launie Lass	Lsd fr Boullioun
VH-VBU	Boeing 737-76Q	1322/30288		Darwin Diva	Lsd fr Boullioun
VH-VBV	Boeing 737-7BK	1384/33015		Moulin Blue	Lsd fr CIT Aerospace
VH-VBW	Boeing 737-705	230/29091	ex LN-TUE	Blue Tongue Lizzie	Lsd fr BBAM
VH-VBX	Boeing 737-705	260/29092	ex LN-TUG	Sultry Sapphire	Lsd fr BBAM
VH-	Boeing 737-7			on order 04	
VH-	Boeing 737-7			on order 04	
VH-	Boeing 737-7			on order 04	
VH-VOA	Boeing 737-8BK	991/30620		Blue Belle	Lsd fr CIT Aerospace
VH-VOB	Boeing 737-8BK	1108/30622		Matilda Blue	Lsd fr CIT Aerospace
VH-VOC	Boeing 737-8BK	1136/30623		Skye Blue	Lsd fr CIT Aerospace
VH-VOD	Boeing 737-8BK	1193/30624	ex N60656	Blue Moon	Lsd fr CIT Aerospace
VH-VOE	Boeing 737-86Q	824/30272	ex N90CD	Peaka Blue	Lsd fr Boullioun
VH-VOF	Boeing 737-86Q	845/30274	ex N91CD	Baby Blue	Lsd fr Boullioun
VH-VOG	Boeing 737-86N	839/28644	ex OO-CYS	Misty Blue	Lsd fr GECAS

VH-VOH	Boeing 737-86N	1094/29884		Jazzy Blue	Lsd fr GECAS
VH-VOI	Boeing 737-81Q	1138/30786	ex (N734MA)	Blue Bambino	Lsd fr CIT Lsg
VH-VOJ	Boeing 737-81Q	1234/30787	ex (N738MA)	Lulu Blue	Lsd fr CIT Lsg
VH-VOK	Boeing 737-8FE	1359/33758		Smoochy Maroochy	
VH-VOL	Boeing 737-8FE	1364/33759		Goldie Coast	
VH-VOM	Boeing 737-8FE	1373/33794		Little Blue Peep	
VH-VON	Boeing 737-8FE	1375/33795		Scarlett Blue	
VH-VOO	Boeing 737-8FE	1377/33796		Bonnie Blue	Lsd to PBI
VH-VOP	Boeing 737-8FE	1389/33797		Whitney Sundays	Lsd to PBI
VH-VOQ	Boeing 737-8FE	1391/33798		Peta Pan	Lsd to PBI
VH-VOR	Boeing 737-8FE	33722		on order 04	
VH-VOS	Boeing 737-8FE	33800		on order 04	
VH-VOT	Boeing 737-8FE	33801		on order 04	
VH-VOU	Boeing 737-8Q8	30665		Blue Billie; on order	Lsd fr ILFC
VH-VOV	Boeing 737-82R	1325/30658		Alluring Alice	Lsd fr ILFC
VH-VOW	Boeing 737-8Q8	1436/32798			Lsd fr ILFC
VH-VOX	Boeing 737-8BK	1446/33017		Brindabella Blue	Lsd fr CIT Lsg
					Lsd to PBI as ZK-PBC
VH-VOY	Boeing 737-8FE	33996		on order 04	
VH-VUA	Boeing 737-8FE	33997		on order 04	
VH-VUB	Boeing 737-8FE	34013		on order 04	
VH-VUC	Boeing 737-8FE	34014		on order 04	

Being retro-fitted with blended winglets. Pacific Blue is wholly owned and operates international services from New Zealand

WETTENHALL AIR SERVICES

Deniliguin, NSW (DNQ)

VH-MAB	Piper PA-39-160 Twin Comanche C/R	39-96	ex VH-MED
VH-MAV	Shrike Commander 500S	3280	ex N81512

WHITAKER AIR CHARTERS

Maryborough/Hervey Bay, QLD (MBH/HVB)

VH-MBF	Britten-Norman BN-2A-8 Islander	646	ex P2-MBF	
VH-MBK	Britten-Norman BN-2A-8 Islander	158	ex P2-MBD	Great Keppel Island Resort c/s
VH-TZL	de Havilland DHC-6 Twin Otter 100	43	ex SE-FTO	Great Keppel Island Resort c/s
VH-TZR	de Havilland DHC-6 Twin Otter 200	145	ex DQ-FDD	

Some operate with Lady Elliot Island titles

WILDERNESS AIR

Strahan, TAS (SRN)

VH-JBM	Cessna A185F Skywagon	18502204	ex VH-AER
VH-SCH	Cessna A185F Skywagon	18503071	ex N21941
VH-KLP	Cessna 208 Caravan	20800260	ex N12324
VH-TLO	Cessna A185F Skywagon	18503658	ex N8332Q

WINRYE AVIATION

Sydney-Bankstown, NSW (BWU)

VH-SSD	Swearingen SA.226T Merlin III	T-210	ex N173SP
VH-SSM	Swearingen SA.226T Merlin III	T-204	ex VH-EGC

VN - VIETNAM (The Socialist Republic of Vietnam)

PACIFIC AIRLINES

Pacific Airlines (BL/PIC)   *Ho Chi Minh City (SGN)*

S7-RGJ	Airbus Industrie A321-131	0604	ex N225LF	Lsd fr/op by RGA
S7-RGK	Airbus Industrie A321-131	0614	ex N511LF	Lsd fr/op by RGA
S7-RGL	Airbus Industrie A320-232	0542	ex PK-AWE	Lsd fr/op by RGA

VASCO

Vasco Air (VFC)   *Ho Chi Minh City (SGN)*

N218AS	Embraer EMB.120RT Brasilia	120015	ex PT-SIK	Freighter	Lsd fr CPT
VN-B376	Antonov An-30	1009		Survey	
VN-B378	Antonov An-30	1205		Survey	
VN-B594	Beech 200 Super King Air	BB-1329	ex VH-SWC		

Vasco is the trading name of Vietnam Air Service Co

VIETNAM AIRLINES

Vietnam Airlines (VN/HVN)   Hanoi (HAN)

VN-B202	Aerospatiale/Alenia ATR 72-201	215	ex F-OKVN	
VN-B204	Aerospatiale/Alenia ATR 72-201	341	ex F-OKVM	
VN-B206	Aerospatiale/Alenia ATR 72-212	419	ex F-WWLW	
VN-B208	Aerospatiale/Alenia ATR 72-212	416	ex F-WWLE	
VN-B210	Aerospatiale/Alenia ATR 72-212A	678	ex F-WWET	
VN-B212	Aerospatiale/Alenia ATR 72-212A	685	ex F-WWEH	
VN-B214	Aerospatiale/Alenia ATR 72-212A	688	ex F-WWEK	
VN-B246	Aerospatialei/Alenia ATR 72-202	523	ex G-UKTL	Lsd fr ATR Asset Mgt
S7-ASA*	Airbus Industrie A320-214	0590	ex F-WWBE	Lsd fr Aerostar
S7-ASB*	Airbus Industrie A320-214	0594	ex F-WWBG	Lsd fr Aerostar
S7-ASC*	Airbus Industrie A320-214	0601	ex F-WWBJ	Lsd fr Aerostar
S7-ASD*	Airbus Industrie A320-214	0605	ex F-WWBM	Lsd fr Aerostar
S7-ASE*	Airbus Industrie A320-214	0607	ex F-WWBN	Lsd fr Aerostar
S7-ASF*	Airbus Industrie A320-214	0611	ex F-WWBP	Lsd fr Aerostar
S7-ASG*	Airbus Industrie A320-214	0617	ex F-WWBS	Lsd fr Aerostar
S7-ASH*	Airbus Industrie A320-214	0619	ex F-WWBT	Lsd fr Aerostar
S7-ASI*	Airbus Industrie A320-214	0648	ex F-WWDP	Lsd fr Aerostar
S7-ASJ*	Airbus Industrie A320-214	0650	ex F-WWDS	Lsd fr Aerostar
VN-A123	Airbus Industrie A320-211	0024	ex N240SE	Op for LAO
VN-A341	Airbus Industrie A321-131	0550	ex N550BR	Lsd fr ILFC
VN-A342	Airbus Industrie A321-131	0591	ex N591KB	Lsd fr ILFC
VN-A346	Airbus Industrie A321-131	0597	ex N291LF	Lsd fr ILFC
VN-	Airbus Industrie A320-233	0789	ex N454TA	Lsd fr Pegasus
VN-	Airbus Industrie A321-231	2255	ex D-AV	on order 04
VN-	Airbus Industrie A321-231	2261	ex D-AV	on order 04
VN-	Airbus Industrie A321-231	2267	ex D-AV	on order 04

Two more Airbus Industrie A321-231s are on order for delivery in 2005.   *Operated by Regionair

VN-A761	Boeing 767-33AER	780/27477	ex N477AN	Lsd fr AWMS
VN-A762	Boeing 767-324ER	568/27392	ex S7-RGV	Lsd fr GECAS
VN-A763	Boeing 767-352ER	575/26261	ex N261LF	Lsd fr ILFC
VN-A764	Boeing 767-324ER	571/27393	ex S7-RGW	Lsd fr GECAS
VN-A765	Boeing 767-324ER	593/27568	ex S7-RGU	Lsd fr GECAS
VN-A766	Boeing 767-33AER	591/27909	ex N279AN	Lsd fr AWAS
VN-A769	Boeing 767-352ER	583/26262	ex EI-CLS	Lsd fr ILFC
VN-A502	Fokker 70	11580	ex PH-EZL	VIP
VN-A504	Fokker 70	11585	ex PH-EZM	VIP
VN-A141	Boeing 777-2Q8ER	436/28688		Lsd fr ILFC
VN-A142	Boeing 777-2Q8ER	443/32701		Lsd fr ILFC
VN-A143	Boeing 777-26KER	450/33502		
VN-A144	Boeing 777-26KER	453/33503		
VN-	Boeing 777-26KER			on order 04

One more Boeing 777-26KER is on order for delivery in 2005

VP-A - ANGUILLA (UK Dependency)

AIR ANGUILLA   ceased operations

TRANS ANGUILLA AIRLINES

                              Anguilla-Wallbake/St Thomas-Cyril E King, VI (AXA/STT)

VP-AAA	Britten-Norman BN-2A-21 Islander	382	ex N361RA	
VP-AAF	Britten-Norman BN-2B-21 Islander	2024	ex N21DA	

TYDEN AIR

                              Anguilla-Wallbake/St Thomas-Cyril E King, VI (AXA/STT)

N62TA	Britten-Norman BN-2A-21 Islander	515	ex N56JA	
VP-AAB	Britten-Norman BN-2A-26 Islander	3008	ex V3-HEZ	Lsd fr GA Roe

VP-C - CAYMAN ISLANDS (UK Colony)

CANCUN EXPRESS

                              Georgetown, Grand Cayman (GCM)

VP-CEX	British Aerospace Jetstream 32EP	903	ex N242RH	Lsd fr Finova

CAYMAN AIRWAYS

Cayman (KX/CAY)   *Georgetown, Grand Cayman (GCM)*

VP-CAL	Boeing 737-205 (Nordam 3)	616/22022	ex VR-CAL	Lsd fr CI Government
VP-CKX	Boeing 737-236 (AvAero 3)	1056/23162	ex VR-CKX	Lsd fr Boullioun
VP-CKY	Boeing 737-3Q8	2355/26282	ex N262KS	Lsd fr Castle 2003-1A
VP-CYB	Boeing 737-2S2C (Nordam 3)	608/21929	ex N716A	Lsd fr WFBN

ISLAND AIR

(G5)   *Georgetown, Grand Cayman (GCM)*

VP-CII	Britten-Norman BN-2A Islander	883	ex VR-CII
VP-CIN	Piper PA-31-350 Chieftain	31-8152184	ex VR-CIN
VP-CTO	de Havilland DHC-6 Twin Otter 300	773	ex VR-CTO

VP-F - FALKLAND ISLANDS (UK Dependency)

BRITISH ANTARCTIC SURVEY

Penguin (BAN)   *Rothera Base, Antarctica*

VP-FAZ	de Havilland DHC-6 Twin Otter 310	748	ex C-GEOA
VP-FBB	de Havilland DHC-6 Twin Otter 310	783	ex C-GDKL
VP-FBC	de Havilland DHC-6 Twin Otter 310	787	ex C-GDIU
VP-FBL	de Havilland DHC-6 Twin Otter 300	839	ex C-GDCZ
VP-FBQ	de Havilland DHC-7-110	111	ex G-BOAX

One de Havilland DHC-6 damaged on landing in Antarctic

FIGAS – FALKLAND ISLANDS GOVERNMENT AIR SERVICES

                                                       Port Stanley (PSY)

VP-FBD	Britten-Norman BN-2B-26 Islander	2160	ex G-BKJK	
VP-FBI	Britten-Norman BN-2B-26 Islander	2188	ex G-BLNI	
VP-FBM	Britten-Norman BN-2B-26 Islander	2200	ex G-BLNZ	
VP-FBN	Britten-Norman BN-2B-26 Islander	2216	ex G-BRFY	Fishery Patrol
VP-FBO	Britten-Norman BN-2B-26 Islander	2218	ex G-BRGA	Fishery Patrol
VP-FBR	Britten-Norman BN-2B-26 Islander	2252	ex G-BTLX	

VP-L - BRITISH VIRGIN ISLANDS (UK Colony)

FLY BVI

                                                          Beef Island (EIS)

| N18AU | Cessna 404 Titan | 404-0823 | ex ST-AWD |
| N6884A | Piper PA-23-250 Aztec F | 27-7954105 | |

VQ-T - TURKS & CAICOS ISLANDS (UK Colony)

INTERISLAND AIRWAYS

Islandways (JY/IWY)   *Providenciales (PLS)*

VQ-TDA	Britten-Norman BN-2A-27 Islander	504	ex HI-704CT		
VQ-TIG	Cessna 401A	401A0018	ex N2020C		
VQ-TRG	Cessna 401A	401A0061	ex N60EM	Island Voayager	
VQ-TVG	de Havilland DHC-6 Twin Otter 300	410	ex N974SW	Island Spirit	Lsd fr Molo Lsg

SKYKING AIRLINES

Skyking (RU/SKI)   *Providenciales (PLS)*

VQ-TBL	Beech 1900C-1	UC-104	ex N104GL
VQ-TGK	Beech 1900C-1	UC-128	ex N15553
VQ-TPT	Beech 1900C-1	UC-125	ex N125GL

TURKS & CAICOS NATIONAL AIRLINES ceased operations

VT - INDIA (Republic of India)

AIR DECCAN

(DN)   *Bangalore (BLR)*

| VT-ADA | Aerospatiale/Alenia ATR 42-320 | 388 | ex F-WQNC | Lsd fr ATR Asset Mgt |
| VT-ADB | Aerospatiale/Alenia ATR 42-320 | 128 | ex F-WQNT | Lsd fr ATR Asset Mgt |

618

VT-ADC	Aerospatiale/Alenia ATR 42-320	333	ex F-WQNJ	Lsd fr ATR Asset Mgt
VT-ADD	Aerospatiale/Alenia ATR 42-320	208	ex F-WQNN	Lsd fr ATR Asset Mgt

Air Deccan is the trading name of Deccan Aviation

AIR INDIA

Airindia (AI/AIC) (IATA 098) *Mumbai-Chatrapati Shivaji Intl (BOM)*

VT-EJG	Airbus Industrie A310-304	406	ex F-WWCG	Yamuna	
VT-EJH	Airbus Industrie A310-304	407	ex F-WWCH	Teesta	
VT-EJI	Airbus Industrie A310-304	413	ex F-WWCJ	Saraswati	
VT-EJJ	Airbus Industrie A310-304	428	ex F-WWCR	Beas	
VT-EJK	Airbus Industrie A310-304	429	ex F-WWCS	Gomati	
VT-EJL	Airbus Industrie A310-304	392	ex F-WWCB	Maturandi	
VT-EQS	Airbus Industrie A310-304	538	ex F-WWCP	Krishna	
VT-EQT	Airbus Industrie A310-304	544	ex F-WWCL	Narmada	Lsd fr Indus Bank
VT-EVE	Airbus Industrie A310-324	501	ex 9V-STS	Periyar	Lsd fr Osprey A/c Lsg
VT-EVF	Airbus Industrie A310-324	548	ex 9V-STU	Mahanadi	Lsd fr Osprey A/c Lsg
VT-EVG	Airbus Industrie A310-304	447	ex F-OHLH	Kosi	Lsd fr GECAS
VT-EVH	Airbus Industrie A310-304	481	ex F-OHLI	Tungabhadra	Lsd fr GECAS
VT-EVI	Airbus Industrie A310-304	519	ex 5Y-BFT	Brahmaputra	Lsd fr ILFC
VT-EVU	Airbus Industrie A310-324	634	ex 9V-STY	Godavari	Lsd fr SIA
VT-EVW	Airbus Industrie A310-324	598	ex F-WIHQ	Cauveri	Lsd fr Airbus
VT-EVX	Airbus Industrie A310-324	695	ex F-WIHR	Luni	Lsd fr Airbus
VT-EVY	Airbus Industrie A310-324	589	ex 9V-STW	Ganga	Lsd fr SIA
VT-AIA	Airbus Industrie A310-324	665	ex 9V-STA		Lsd fr SIA
VT-AIB	Airbus Industrie A310-324		ex 9V-		Lsd fr SIA
VT-AIC	Boeing 747-4B5	1170/26409	ex HL7407		Lsd fr KAL
VT-AID	Boeing 747-4B5	830/24261	ex HL7481	Kaziranca	Lsd fr KAL
VT-EFU	Boeing 747-237B	390/21829		Krishna Deva Raya	
VT-EGA	Boeing 747-237B	414/21993		Samudragupta	
VT-EGB	Boeing 747-237B	431/21994		Mahendra Varman	
VT-EGC	Boeing 747-237B	434/21995		Harsha Vardhana	
VT-EPW	Boeing 747-337M	711/24159	ex N6018N	Shivaji	
VT-EPX	Boeing 747-337M	719/24160	ex N6046P	Narasimha Varman	
VT-ESM	Boeing 747-437	987/27078		Konark	
VT-ESN	Boeing 747-437	1003/27164		Tanjiere	
VT-ESO	Boeing 747-437	1009/27165		Khajurao	
VT-ESP	Boeing 747-437	1034/27214		Ajanta	
VT-EVA	Boeing 747-437	1089/28094		Agra	Lsd fr Veena Lsg
VT-EVB	Boeing 747-437	1093/28095		Velha Goa	Lsd fr Veena Lsg
VT-EVJ	Boeing 747-4B5	739/24199	ex HL7409	Fatehpur Sikri	Lsd fr KAL

Owns 8% of Air Mauritius

AIR SAHARA

Sahara (S2) (IATA 705) *Delhi-Indira Gandhi Intl (DEL)*

VT-SAW*	Boeing 737-31S	2923/29055	ex D-ADBK	Lsd fr Deutsche Structured Finance
VT-SAX*	Boeing 737-31S	2925/29056	ex D-ADBL	Lsd fr Deutsche Structured Finance
VT-SID	Boeing 737-4Q8	1971/24705	ex N621LF	Lsd fr ILFC
VT-SIF	Boeing 737-2K9	709/22416	ex VT-PDB	stored DEL
VT-SIG	Boeing 737-73A	216/28497	ex N700AZ	Lsd fr AWAS
VT-SIJ	Boeing 737-81Q	424/29049	ex N8253J	Lsd fr Trim Lsg
VT-SIK	Boeing 737-81Q	444/29050	ex N8253V	Lsd fr Lift Lsg
VT-SIQ	Boeing 737-4Q8	1627/24234	ex N234AN	Lsd fr ILFC
VT-SIR	Boeing 737-76Q	1010/30279	ex N73749	Lsd fr Boullioun
VT-SIS	Boeing 737-76Q	1025/30280	ex N73750	Lsd fr Boullioun
VT-SIU	Boeing 737-7K9	205/28090	ex SX-BLT	Lsd fr Bavaria Intl Lsg
VT-SIV	Boeing 737-7K9	223/28091	ex SX-BLU	Lsd fr Bavaria Intl Lsg
VT-SIY	Boeing 737-4S3	1722/24166	ex N768BC	Lsd fr Hanway Corp

*Exact tie-up not confirmed

VT-SAL	Canadair CL-600-2B19	7224	ex N572ML	Lsd fr Canadian Regional A/c
VT-SAO	Canadair CL-600-2B19	7227	ex N573ML	Lsd fr Canadian Regional A/c
VT-SAP	Canadair CL-600-2B19	7242	ex N574ML	Lsd fr State Street
VT-SAQ	Canadair CL-600-2B19	7345	ex G-JECA	
VT-SAR	Canadair CL-600-2B19	7393	ex G-JECB	
VT-SAS	Canadair CL-600-2B19	7434	ex G-JECC	Lsd fr Travel Yan Ltd
VT-SAU	Canadair CL-600-2B19	7469	ex G-JECD	

ALLIANCE AIR

Allied (CD/LLR) (IATA 296) *Delhi-Indira Gandhi Intl (DEL)*

VT-ABA	Aerospatiale/Alenia ATR 42-320	390	ex F-WQNK	Lsd fr ATRiam Capital
VT-ABB	Aerospatiale/Alenia ATR 42-320	392	ex F-WQNL	Lsd fr ATRiam Capital
VT-ABC	Aerospatiale/Alenia ATR 42-320	315	ex F-WQNB	
VT-ABD	Aerospatiale/Alenia ATR 42-320	356	ex F-FWNF	Lsd fr Merinos Leasing

VT-EGE	Boeing 737-2A8	679/22281	ex N8291V		
VT-EGF	Boeing 737-2A8	681/22282	ex N8292V		
VT-EGG	Boeing 737-2A8	689/22283	ex N8290V		
VT-EGH	Boeing 737-2A8	739/22284			
VT-EGI	Boeing 737-2A8	798/22285			
VT-EGJ	Boeing 737-2A8	799/22286			
VT-EGM	Boeing 737-2A8C	747/22473			
VT-EHF	Boeing 737-2A8	902/22861			
VT-EHG	Boeing 737-2A8	903/22862			
VT-EHH	Boeing 737-2A8	907/22863			

Six leased Aerospatiale/Alenia ATR 42s are on order
A subsidiary of Indian Airlines

BLUE DART AVIATION

Chennai (MAA)

VT-BDE	Boeing 737-2A8F	434/21163	ex VT-EDR	Vision II	Lsd fr Icici Ltd
VT-BDF	Boeing 737-2A8F	435/21164	ex VT-EDS		Lsd fr Icici Ltd
VT-BDG	Boeing 737-2K9F	702/22415	ex VT-SIE		Lsd fr Infrastructure Lsg
VT-BDH	Boeing 737-25C	1585/24236	ex B-2524	Freighter	

Operates services for Federal Express

GESCO AIR LOGISTICS SERVICE

Mumbai Juhu

VT-HGB	Bell 212	31124	ex A7-HAN	Lsd fr Gulf H/c
VT-HGC	Bell 212	31149	ex A7-HAT	Lsd fr Gulf H/c

Joint venture between Gulf Helicopters and GESCO - The Great Eastern Shipping Co

INDIAN AIRLINES

Indair (IC/IAC) (IATA 058)   *Delhi-Indira Gandhi Intl (DEL)*

VT-EHC	Airbus Industrie A300B4-203	181	ex F-WZMY		
VT-EHD	Airbus Industrie A300B4-203	182	ex F-WZMZ		
VT-EVD	Airbus Industrie A300B4-203	240	ex EI-CEB	50 years titles	Lsd fr GECAS

All to be withdrawn from service

VT-EPB	Airbus Industrie A320-231	0045	ex F-WWDY		
VT-EPC	Airbus Industrie A320-231	0046	ex F-WWDG		
VT-EPD	Airbus Industrie A320-231	0047	ex F-WWDP		
VT-EPE	Airbus Industrie A320-231	0048	ex F-WWDU		
VT-EPF	Airbus Industrie A320-231	0049	ex F-WWIA		
VT-EPG	Airbus Industrie A320-231	0050	ex F-WWDR		
VT-EPH	Airbus Industrie A320-231	0051	ex F-WWIB		
VT-EPI	Airbus Industrie A320-231	0056	ex F-WWIC		
VT-EPJ	Airbus Industrie A320-231	0057	ex F-WWIF	50 years titles	
VT-EPK	Airbus Industrie A320-231	0058	ex F-WWID		
VT-EPL	Airbus Industrie A320-231	0074	ex F-WWIQ		
VT-EPM	Airbus Industrie A320-231	0075	ex F-WWIR	50 years titles	
VT-EPO	Airbus Industrie A320-231	0080	ex F-WWIX		
VT-EPP	Airbus Industrie A320-231	0089	ex F-WWDT		
VT-EPQ	Airbus Industrie A320-231	0090	ex F-WWDX		
VT-EPR	Airbus Industrie A320-231	0095	ex F-WWDS		
VT-EPS	Airbus Industrie A320-231	0096	ex F-WWDU		
VT-EPT	Airbus Industrie A320-231	0097	ex F-WWDV		
VT-ESA	Airbus Industrie A320-231	0396	ex F-WWBK		
VT-ESB	Airbus Industrie A320-231	0398	ex F-WWDQ		
VT-ESC	Airbus Industrie A320-231	0416	ex F-WWBP		
VT-ESD	Airbus Industrie A320-231	0423	ex F-WWIT		
VT-ESE	Airbus Industrie A320-231	0431	ex F-WWBQ		
VT-ESF	Airbus Industrie A320-231	0432	ex F-WWBS		
VT-ESG	Airbus Industrie A320-231	0451	ex F-WWIN		
VT-ESH	Airbus Industrie A320-231	0469	ex F-WWBD		
VT-ESI	Airbus Industrie A320-231	0486	ex F-WWBH	50 years titles	
VT-ESJ	Airbus Industrie A320-231	0490	ex F-WWDT	50 years titles	
VT-ESK	Airbus Industrie A320-231	0492	ex F-WWBU	50 years titlles	
VT-ESL	Airbus Industrie A320-231	0499	ex F-WWDO		
VT-EVO	Airbus Industrie A320-231	0247	ex N247RX		Lsd fr ORIX
VT-EVP	Airbus Industrie A320-231	0257	ex N257RX		Lsd fr ORIX
VT-EVQ	Airbus Industrie A320-231	0327	ex G-OOAC	50 years titles	Lsd fr ORIX
VT-EVR	Airbus Industrie A320-231	0336	ex G-OOAD	50 years titles	Lsd fr ORIX
VT-EVS	Airbus Industrie A320-231	0308	ex EC-GUR		Lsd fr ORIX
VT-EVT	Airbus Industrie A320-231	0314	ex EC-GLT		Lsd fr ORIX
VT-EYA	Airbus Industrie A320-231	0376	ex G-MEDB		Lsd fr debis
VT-EYB	Airbus Industrie A320-231	0386	ex G-MEDD		Lsd fr debis
VT-EYC	Airbus Industrie A320-231	0362	ex G-YJBM	on order	Lsd fr ALPS 941
VT-EYD	Airbus Industrie A320-231	0168	ex N168BN		Lsd fr Loki Lsg
VT-EYE	Airbus Industrie A320-231	0179	ex N971GT		Lsd fr Sigmund Lsg

| VT-EIO | Dornier 228-201 | 8037 | ex D-IDBG |
| VT-EJO | Dornier 228-201 | 8054 | ex D-CALI |

Alliance Air is a wholly owned subsidiary
Nineteen Airbus Industrie A319s [to replace the 737-200s with Alliance Air], four Airbus Industrie A320s and twenty Airbus Industrie A321s are on order for delivery from 2005 to 2008

JAGSON AIRLINES

Delhi-Indira Gandhi Intl (DEL)

VT-ESQ	Dornier 228-201	8006	ex A5-RGB	
VT-ESS	Dornier 228-201	8017	ex A5-RGC	
VT-EUM	Dornier 228-201	8096	ex D-CAAL	Lsd fr Dornier

JET AIRWAYS

Jet Airways (9W/JAI) (IATA 589)   *Mumbai-Chatrapati Shivaji Intl (BOM)*

VT-JCA	Aerospatiale/Alenia ATR 72-212A	572	ex F-WQKD	Lsd fr Pentavana
VT-JCB	Aerospatiale/Alenia ATR 72-212A	575	ex F-WQKE	Lsd fr Pentavana
VT-JCC	Aerospatiale/Alenia ATR 72-212A	593	ex F-WQKP	Lsd fr Pentavana
VT-JCD	Aerospatiale/Alenia ATR 72-212A	636	ex F-WQMC	Lsd fr Pentavana
VT-JCE	Aerospatiale/Alenia ATR 72-212A	640	ex F-WQMD	Lsd fr Pentavana
VT-JCF	Aerospatiale/Alenia ATR 72-212A	674	ex F-WQMK	Lsd fr SFR
VT-JCG	Aerospatiale/Alenia ATR 72-212A	679	ex F-WQML	Lsd fr SFR
VT-JCH	Aerospatiale/Alenia ATR 72-212A	681	ex F-WQMM	Lsd fr SFR
VT-JAM	Boeing 737-48E	2905/25773	ex N773SR	Lsd fr Pinewatch
VT-JAN	Boeing 737-48E	2925/25775	ex N775SR	Lsd fr Pinewatch
VT-JAR	Boeing 737-45R	2943/29032		
VT-JAS	Boeing 737-45R	2963/29033		
VT-JAT	Boeing 737-45R	3015/29034		
VT-JGA	Boeing 737-85R	1228/30410		Lsd fr North American A/c Hire
VT-JGB	Boeing 737-71Q	1282/30411	ex N1787B	Lsd fr Tombo
VT-JGC	Boeing 737-95R	1314/30412		
VT-JGD	Boeing 737-95R	1350/33740		Lsd fr Washington Lease
VT-JNA	Boeing 737-86N	89/28578	ex N578GE	Lsd fr GECAS
VT-JNB	Boeing 737-86N	91/28575	ex N575GE	Lsd fr GECAS
VT-JNC	Boeing 737-85R	164/29036		
VT-JND	Boeing 737-85R	177/29037	ex N1787B	Lsd fr Washington A/c Hire
VT-JNE	Boeing 737-71Q	138/29043	ex N29879	Lsd fr Tombo
VT-JNF	Boeing 737-71Q	152/29044	ex N29887	Lsd fr Tombo
VT-JNG	Boeing 737-71Q	169/29045	ex N29975	Lsd fr Tombo
VT-JNH	Boeing 737-71Q	181/29046	ex N29976	Lsd fr Tombo
VT-JNJ	Boeing 737-85R	297/29038		Lsd fr Washington A/c Hire
VT-JNL	Boeing 737-85R	326/29039		Lsd fr Washington A/c Hire
VT-JNM	Boeing 737-85R	465/29040		Lsd fr Washington A/c Hire
VT-JNN	Boeing 737-85R	489/29041		Lsd fr North American A/c Hire
VT-JNP	Boeing 737-76N	664/28630	ex N630GE	Lsd fr GECAS
VT-JNQ	Boeing 737-76N	734/28635	ex N635GE	Lsd fr GECAS
VT-JNR	Boeing 737-85R	749/30403	ex N1781B	Lsd fr North American A/c Hire
VT-JNS	Boeing 737-73A	775/28498	ex N498AW	Lsd fr AWMS 1
VT-JNT	Boeing 737-76N	417/28609	ex N609LP	Lsd fr Zibal Lsg
VT-JNU	Boeing 737-75R	835/30404	ex N1787B	Lsd fr North American A/c Hire
VT-JNV	Boeing 737-75R	927/30405		Lsd fr North American A/c Hire
VT-JNW	Boeing 737-75R	1016/30406	ex N1787B	Lsd fr North American A/c Hire
VT-JNX	Boeing 737-85R	1073/30407		Lsd fr North American A/c Hire
VT-JNY	Boeing 737-85R	1146/30408	ex (VT-JGA)	Lsd fr North American A/c Hire
VT-JNZ	Boeing 737-85R	1185/30409	ex (VT-JGB)	Lsd fr North American A/c Hire

Ten Embraer 175s are on order for delivery but order may be cancelled if Indian Government do not relax regulations

PAWAN HANS HELICOPTERS

Pawan Hans (PHE)   *Delhi-Safdarjung*

VT-EKZ	Aerospatiale SA365 Dauphin 2	6209	
VT-ELB	Aerospatiale SA365 Dauphin 2	6211	ex F-WYMI
VT-ELE	Aerospatiale SA365 Dauphin 2	6214	
VT-ELF	Aerospatiale SA365 Dauphin 2	6215	
VT-ELG	Aerospatiale SA365 Dauphin 2	6217	
VT-ELI	Aerospatiale SA365 Dauphin 2	6236	
VT-ELJ	Aerospatiale SA365 Dauphin 2	6239	
VT-ELK	Aerospatiale SA365 Dauphin 2	6245	
VT-ELL	Aerospatiale SA365 Dauphin 2	6246	
VT-ELM	Aerospatiale SA365 Dauphin 2	6248	
VT-ELN	Aerospatiale SA365 Dauphin 2	6254	
VT-ELP	Aerospatiale SA365 Dauphin 2	6260	
VT-ELQ	Aerospatiale SA365 Dauphin 2	6261	
VT-ELR	Aerospatiale SA365 Dauphin 2	6268	
VT-ELS	Aerospatiale SA365 Dauphin 2	6273	

VT-ELT	Aerospatiale SA365 Dauphin 2	6278			
VT-ENW	Aerospatiale SA365 Dauphin 2	6094			
VT-ENZ	Aerospatiale SA365 Dauphin 2	6163			
VT-PHJ	Aerospatiale AS.365N3 Dauphin	6628			
VT-PHK	Aerospatiale AS.365N3 Dauphin	6631			
VT-ASM	Mil Mi-172	356C03			
VT-PHA	Bell 206L-4 LongRanger IV	52019	ex N6197Y		
VT-PHD	Bell 206L-4 LongRanger IV	52142	ex N64080	Op for Indian Customs	
VT-PHE	Bell 206L-4 LongRanger IV	52159	ex N9217Z	Op for Indian Customs	
VT-PHF	Mil Mi-172	356C06			
VT-PHG	Mil Mi-172	365C07			
VT-PHH	Bell 407	53210	ex N52263		
VT-PHI	Bell 407	53212	ex N52265		

TRANS BHARAT AVIATION

Delhi-Palam

VT-ERP	Beech 99	U-99	ex N217BH	Arjun	
VT-ESU	Beech 99	U-7	ex N205BH	Krishan Raj	

VISAA AIRWAYS

(9A)   *Mumbai-Chatrapati Shivaji Intl (BOM)*

VT-VAA	de Havilland DHC-8Q-202	536	ex D-BTHF	on order	Lsd fr AUB
VT-VAB	de Havilland DHC-8Q-202	463	ex D-BHAL	on order, stored AGB	Lsd fr AUB

Neither delivered and presumed not to have started operations

V2 - ANTIGUA (State of Antigua and Barbuda)

AEROWINGS Sole aircraft permanently retired at Opa Locka, FL

CARIB AVIATION

Red Tail (DEL)   *Antigua-VC Bird Intl (ANU)*

V2-LCL	Britten-Norman BN-2A-26 Islander	2006	ex G-BESR		
V2-LDI	Britten-Norman BN-2A-26 Islander	919	ex N662J		
V2-LDL	Britten-Norman BN-2A-27 Islander	532	ex V4-AAA		
V2-LDO	Beech A65 Queen Air	LC-291	ex N8312N	Excalibur Queenaire 8800 conv	
V2-LEW	Cessna 402B	402B1220	ex N797A		
V2-LFK	de Havilland DHC-6 Twin Otter 300	615	ex N220SA	Vistaliner	Lsd fr Twin Otter
V2-LFL	de Havilland DHC-6 Twin Otter 300	510	ex HK-1980		
V2-LFP	Britten-Norman BN-2B-20 Islander	2211	ex 8P-TAI		

CARIBBEAN STAR AIRWAYS

Carib Star (8B/GFI)   *Antigua-VC Bird Intl (ANU)*

V2-LFF	de Havilland DHC-8-314	410	ex N285BC	Lsd fr Bombardier Capital
V2-LFG	de Havilland DHC-8-106	268	ex N286BC	Lsd fr Bombardier Capital
V2-LFH	de Havilland DHC-8-106	253	ex N287DC	Lsd fr Bombardier Capital
V2-LFI	de Havilland DHC-8-106	317	ex N288BC	Lsd fr Bombardier Capital
V2-LFJ	de Havilland DHC-8-102	007	ex C-GFQI	Lsd fr Air Manitoba
V2-LFM	de Havilland DHC-8-311A	267	ex C-GFPZ	Lsd fr Bombardier Capital
V2-LFO	de Havilland DHC-8-102	106	ex N822PH	Lsd fr JetFleet III
V2-LFU	de Havilland DHC-8-311	250	ex N802SA	Lsd fr Bombardier Capital
V2-	de Havilland DHC-8-311A	266	ex C-GZTB	Lsd fr Bombardier Capital
V2-	de Havilland DHC-8-311A	232	ex C-GZTX	Lsd fr Bombardier Capital

Associated with Caribbean Sun Airlines, last two are V2-LGA/LGB but tie-up unknown

CBJ CARGO

Antigua-VC Bird Intl (ANU)

V2-	Lockheed L-1011-200F Tristar	1198	ex N102CK		

CBJ Cargo is the trading name of Caribjet; current status is uncertain

LIAT - THE CARIBBEAN AIRLINE

LIAT (LI/LIA)   *Antigua-VC Bird Intl (ANU)*

V2-LCY	de Havilland DHC-8-110	035	ex C-GESR		
V2-LDP	de Havilland DHC-8-102	140	ex EI-BZC		Lsd fr GECAS
V2-LDQ	de Havilland DHC-8-102	113	ex EI-BWX		Lsd fr GECAS
V2-LDU	de Havilland DHC-8-102A	270	ex EI-CBV	std Calgary	Lsd fr GECAS

V2-LEF	de Havilland DHC-8-103	144	ex HS-SKH	Lsd fr GECAS
V2-LES	de Havilland DHC-8-311B	412	ex C-GETI	Lsd fr Bombardier
V2-LET	de Havilland DHC-8-311B	416	ex C-GFOD	Lsd fr Bombardier
V2-LEU	de Havilland DHC-8-311	408	ex C-FWBB	
V2-LFT	de Havilland DHC-8-102	261	ex N819MA	
V2-LFV	de Havilland DHC-8-311A	283	ex PH-SDR	Lsd fr GECAS
V2-LFW	de Havilland DHC-8-311A	305	ex N305DC	
V2-LFX	de Havilland DHC-8-311A	315	ex N783BC	

LIAT controls Four Island Air and Inter Island Air Services
29% owned by BWIA

NORMAN AVIATION

Antigua

| V2-LDN | Piper PA-31 Turbo Navajo C/R | 31-7612017 | ex N99910 |

TRANSCARAIBE AIR INTERNATIONAL current status is uncertain

V3 - BELIZE (State of Antigua and Barbuda)

MAYA ISLAND AIR

Myland (MW/MYD)   *Belize City-Municipal/San Pedro (TZA/SPR)*

V3-HER	Cessna 207A Stationair 8	20700606	ex VP-HER	
V3-HFS	Cessna 208B Caravan I	208B0579	ex N52627	status uncertain
V3-HGD	Cessna 208B Caravan I	208B0910	ex N12522	
V3-HGE	Britten-Norman BN-2A-26 Islander	911	ex N103NE	
V3-HGF	Cessna 208B Caravan I	208B0927		
V3-HGI	Gippsland GA-8 Airvan	GA8-01-008	ex VH-AUV	
V3-HGJ	Cessna 208B Caravan I	208B0946	ex N52639	
V3-HGK	Britten-Norman BN-2A-27 Islander	853	ex N271RS	
V3-HGO	Cessna 208B Caravan I	208B0995	ex N1241G	
V3-HGP	Cessna 208B Caravan I	208B0998	ex N5213S	
V3-HGQ	Cessna 208B Caravan I			
V3-HMT	Cessna 207A Stationair 8	20700655		

TROPIC AIR COMMUTER

Tropiser (PM/TOS)   *San Pedro (SPR)*

V3-HFP	Cessna 208B Caravan I	208B0478	ex N1289Y
V3-HFQ	Cessna 208B Caravan I	208B0575	ex N52623
V3-HFV	Cessna 208B Caravan I	208B0647	ex N5268M
V3-HFW	Cessna 208B Caravan I	208B0791	ex N5262X
V3-HGB	Cessna 208B Caravan I	208B0871	ex N51612
V3-HIK	Cessna 208B Caravan I	208B0707	ex N23681
V3-HSS	Cessna 208B Caravan I	208B0407	ex N1116V
V3-HDT	Cessna 207A Stationair 8	20700716	ex (N9696M)	status?

V4 - ST KITTS & NEVIS (Federation of St Christopher and Nevis)

AIR ST KITTS & NEVIS

Sea Breeze (BEZ)   *Basseterre-Golden Rock (SKB)*

N90HL	Cessna 208B Caravan I	208B0693		Lsd fr Africair
N900HL	Cessna 208B Caravan I	208B0912	ex N5188W	Lsd fr Africair
N910HL	Cessna 208B Caravan I	208B0706	ex N1244Y	Lsd fr Africair

NEVIS EXPRESS

(VF)   *Nevis-Newcastle (NEV)*

| N102NE | Britten-Norman BN-2A-26 Islander | 311 | ex C-GAPZ | Lsd fr BN Aircraft |

Nevis Express is the trading name of Daystar Airlines

TROPICAL INTERNATIONAL AIRWAYS

Tropexpress (PQ/TKX)   *Basseterre-Golden Rock (SKB)*

Operates charter flights with aircraft leased from Omni Air International or American Trans Air as required

V5 - NAMIBIA (Republic of Namibia)

AIR NAMIBIA – NATIONAL AIRLINE OF THE REPUBLIC

Namibia (SW/NMB) (IATA 186)
Windhoek-Eros/Hosea Kutako Intl (ERS/WDH)

V5-ANA	Boeing 737-25A	1422/23790	ex N724ML	Ondekaremba	Lsd fr SFR
V5-ANB	Boeing 737-2L9	550/21686	ex ZS-OKF		Lsd fr SFR
V5-CAR	Cessna 208B Caravan I	208B0513	ex ZS-OTU		Lsd fr/op by Comav
V5-COX	Beech 1900D				
V5-NMA	Boeing 747-48EM	1131/28551	ex N6055X	Welwitschia; stored FRA	
V5-	Cessna 208B Caravan I	208B0544	ex ZS-OWC		Lsd fr/op by Comav
ZS-NYI	Reims Cessna F406 Caravan II	F406-0030	ex 5Y-MMJ		Lsd fr/op by Comav
ZS-OTT	Reims Cessna F406 Caravan II	F406-0040	ex 5Y-HHJ		Lsd fr/op by Comav
ZS-OUD	Beech 1900C	UB-73	ex V5-LTC	Kalahari	Lsd fr/op by Comav

BAY AIR AVIATION

Nomad Air (NMD)
Walvis Bay (WVB)

V5-FUR	Cessna 310Q	310Q0456	ex ZS-FUR

Bay Air is the trading name of Nomad Air

COMAV

Windhoek-Eros (ERS)

V5-CAR	Cessna 208B Caravan I	208B0513	ex ZS-OTU		Lsd to/op for NMB
V5-JIH	Cessna 402B	402B1057			
V5-SOS	Cessna 402C	402C0437	ex V5-AAS	EMS	
V5-	Cessna 208B Caravan I	208B0544	ex ZS-OWC		Lsd to/op for NMB
V5-	Beech 1900D	UE-10	ex ZS-OYB		Lsd to/op for NMB
ZS-NYI	Reims Cessna F406 Caravan II	F406-0030	ex 5Y-MMJ		Lsd to/op for NMB
ZS-OTT	Reims Cessna F406 Caravan II	F406-0040	ex 5Y-HHJ		Lsd to/op for NMB
ZS-OUB	Beech 1900C	UB-20	ex V5-MNN	Khomas	
ZS-OUD	Beech 1900C	UB-73	ex V5-LTC	Kalahari	Lsd to/op for NMB
ZS-OYA	Beech 1900D	UE-7	ex VH-IMA		Lsd to/op for NMB

NAMIBIA COMMERCIAL AIRWAYS

Med Rescue (MRE)
Windhoek-Eros (ERS)

V5-NCG	Douglas DC-6B	1040/45564	ex GBM112	Bateleur; stored ERS

WEST AIR AVIATION

Westair Wings (WAA)
Windhoek-Eros (ERS)

V5-DHL	Reims Cessna F406 Caravan II	F406-0062	ex N744C	DHL titles
V5-LWH	Cessna 310R	310R0571	ex ZS-LWH	
V5-MDY	Cessna 402B	402B1353		
V5-WAA	Cessna 404 Titan (RAM)	404-0210	ex N88668	Ghost Rider
V5-WAB	Cessna 310Q	310Q0727		
V5-WAC	Cessna 404 Titan	404-0616	ex ZS-KRJ	
V5-WAD	Cessna 310R	310R1340	ex ZS-KEE	
V5-WAE	Cessna 402C	402C0430	ex ZS-NPA	
V5-WAG	Cessna 310R	310R1668	ex V5-KRK	
V5-WAK	Reims Cessna F406 Caravan II	F406-0048	ex G-FLYN	DHL titles

V6 - MICRONESIA (Federated States of Micronesia)

CAROLINE PACIFIC AIR

Pohnpei (PNI)

V6-01FM	Britten-Norman BN-2A-27 Islander	2014	ex V6-SFM
V6-02FM	Beech 65-80 Queen Air	LC-84	ex N349N
V6-03FM	Britten-Norman BN-2A-21 Islander	660	ex VH-AUN

V7 - MARSHALL ISLANDS (Republic of the Marshall Islands)

AIRLINE OF THE MARSHALL ISLANDS

Marshall Islands (CW/MRS) (IATA 778)
Majuro Intl (MAJ)

V7-0210	de Havilland DHC-8-102	218	ex ZK-NEU	Lsd fr Finova
V7-9206	Dornier 228-212	8194	ex D-CAHD	
V7-9207	Dornier 228-212	8201	ex D-CAHE	

V8 - BRUNEI DARUSSALAM

ROYAL BRUNEI AIRLINES

Brunei (BI/RBA) (IATA 672)   Bandar Seri Begawan (BWN)

V8-RBF	Boeing 767-33AER	414/25530		
V8-RBG	Boeing 767-33AER	442/25532	ex N6055X	
V8-RBH	Boeing 767-33AER	477/25534	ex N6055X	
V8-RBJ	Boeing 767-33AER	454/25533	ex N67AW	
V8-RBK	Boeing 767-33AER	504/25536	ex N96AC	
V8-RBL	Boeing 767-33AER	521/27189	ex N1794B	
V8-RBM	Boeing 767-328ER	586/27428	ex S7-RGT	
V8-RBN	Boeing 767-328ER	579/27427	ex S7-AAB	
V8-RBA	Boeing 757-2M6	94/23452	ex N6066U	
V8-RBB	Boeing 757-2M6	100/23453		Lsd to HRH
V8-RBP	Airbus Industrie A319-132	2023	ex D-AVWW	Lsd fr CIT Lsg
V8-RBR	Airbus Industrie A319-132	2032	ex D-AVYK	Lsd fr CIT Lsg
V8-RBS	Airbus Industrie A320-232	2135	ex F-WWIV	Lsd fr CIT Lsg
V8-RBT	Airbus Industrie A320-232	2139	ex F-WWDO	Lsd fr CIT Lsg

XA - MEXICO (United Mexican States)

AERO CUAHONTE

Cuahonte (CUO)   Uruapan (UPN)

XA-KOC	Cessna 402C	402C0301	ex N3271M
XA-TGG	Swearingen SA.226TC Metro II	TC-385	ex N46GW
XA-TLS	Swearingen SA.227AC Metro III	AC-752	ex N27444

AERO JUAREZ

Juarez (JUA)   Guadalajara (GDL)

XA-SBM	Piper PA-31-350 Navajo Chieftain	31-7852138	ex N27749	Joint ops with Aero Freight

AEROCALIFORNIA

Aerocalifornia (JR/SER) (IATA 078)   La Paz (LAP)

XA-ACZ	Douglas DC-9-32 (ABS 3)	619/47514	ex N947ML	Lsd fr Interglobal
XA-ADA	Douglas DC-9-32 (ABS 3)	926/48112	ex N18513	Lsd fr PLM Financial
XA-ADK	Douglas DC-9-31 (ABS 3)	214/47131	ex N941ML	Lsd fr Interglobal
XA-AGS	Douglas DC-9-15	90/45786	ex N968E	Lsd fr GECAS
XA-BCS	Douglas DC-9-14	88/47043	ex N1302T	Lsd fr GECAS
XA-CSL	Douglas DC-9-14	29/45743	ex N8902E	Lsd fr GECAS
XA-GDL	Douglas DC-9-15	139/47085	ex EI-BZY	Lsd fr GECAS
XA-LAC	Douglas DC-9-15	405/47126	ex EI-BZW	Lsd fr GECAS
XA-LMM	Douglas DC-9-14	45/45736	ex N655TX	Lsd fr GECAS
XA-RKT	Douglas DC-9-15	224/47122	ex EI-BZZ	Lsd fr GECAS
XA-RNQ	Douglas DC-9-15	125/47059	ex EI-BZX	Lsd fr GECAS
XA-RRY	Douglas DC-9-15	64/45785	ex EI-CBB	Lsd fr GECAS
XA-RXG	Douglas DC-9-14	7/45714	ex N651TX	Lsd fr Polaris
XA-SWG	Douglas DC-9-32	395/47230	ex N277AW	Lsd fr Interglobal
XA-SWH	Douglas DC-9-32	450/47236	ex N274AW	Lsd fr Interglobal
XA-SYD	Douglas DC-9-32	397/47283	ex N2786S	Lsd fr Interglobal
XA-SYQ	Douglas DC-9-14	15/45702	ex HB-IEF	Lsd fr Interglobal
XA-TAF	Douglas DC-9-32	154/47039	ex N4157A	Lsd fr PLM Intl
XA-TBQ	Douglas DC-9-32 (ABS 3)	642/47553	ex N136AA	Lsd fr Jetfleet
XA-THB	Douglas DC-9-32 (ABS 3)	761/47648	ex N942VV	Lsd fr PLM Intl
XA-THC	Douglas DC-9-32 (ABS 3)	772/47666	ex N941VV	Lsd fr PLM Intl
XA-TNT	Douglas DC-9-32 (ABS 3)	930/48113	ex N12514	Lsd fr Interglobal

AEROCARIBE

Aerocaribe (QA/CBE) (IATA 723)   Cancun/Merida (CUN/MID)

N910AE	British Aerospace Jetstream 32EP	910	ex G-31-910		Lsd fr BAES
N915AE	British Aerospace Jetstream 32EP	915	ex G-31-915	Sir Francis Drake	Lsd fr BAES
N940AE	British Aerospace Jetstream 32EP	940	ex G-31-940	returned?	Lsd fr BAES
N943AE	British Aerospace Jetstream 32EP	943	ex G-31-943	Commander	Lsd fr BAES
XA-ABQ	Douglas DC-9-31 (ABS 3)	943/48119	ex N937VJ	VTP Cancun	Lsd fr USA Lsg
XA-ABR	Douglas DC-9-31 (ABS 3)	949/48120	ex N938VJ	Regionmontana	Lsd fr USA Lsg
XA-ABS	Douglas DC-9-31 (ABS 3)	942/48118	ex N929VJ	Veracruzana	Lsd fr USA Lsg
XA-ABT	Douglas DC-9-31 (ABS 3)	1030/48141	ex N921VJ		Lsd fr USA Lsg
XA-AEB	Douglas DC-9-31 (ABS 3)	1048/48147	ex N976VJ		Lsd fr USA Lsg
XA-AEC	Douglas DC-9-31 (ABS 3)	1050/48155	ex N977VJ		Lsd fr USA Lsg

XA-TVB	Douglas DC-9-31 (ABS 3)	1042/48145	ex N925VJ		Lsd fr Alameda Corp
XA-TVC	Douglas DC-9-31 (ABS 3)	1044/48146	ex N926VJ		Lsd fr Alameda Corp
XA-TXG	Douglas DC-9-31 (ABS 3)	919/48114	ex N934VJ		Lsd fr Alameda Corp

XA-NJI	Fairchild Hiller FH-227D	576	ex XC-UTB	Tatich

A subsidiary of CINTRA; operates some services as Mexicana Inter using MX flight numbers

---

AEROCEDROS

Ensenada (ESE)

XA-RYV	Convair 440	474	ex XB-CSE
XA-STJ	Cessna 402B	402B0801	ex N3792C
XA-TFY	Convair 440	472	ex N411GA
XA-TFZ	Convair 440	439	ex N44829

Operates Convair 440's for Soc Coop Prod Pesque Pescado

AEROFERINCO ceased operations

AEROLINEAS EJECUTIVAS current status is uncertain; believed to have ceased operations

---

AEROLINEAS INTERNACIONALES

Lineaint (N2/LNT)   *Cuernavaca (CVJ)*

XA-AAD	Boeing 727-223 (Raisbeck 3)	1185/20991	ex N850AA		
XA-AFB	Boeing 727-232 (Raisbeck 3)	1164/21149	ex N461S		Lsd fr Transcontinental Asset Mgt
XA-AFC	Boeing 727-225F (Raisbeck 3)	831/20383	ex N8840E	Brisa	Lsd fr Joda
XA-SKC	Boeing 727-23	265/19181	ex N1906	Cuernavaca	
XA-SNW	Boeing 727-23	140/18450	ex N1994		
XA-SPU	Boeing 727-223	699/20181	ex N6828	Tepoztian	
XA-TPV	Boeing 727-223	657/19493	ex N6818	Xochicalco	
XA-TQT	Boeing 727-223	730/20188	ex N6835	Cuautlia	

AEROLITORAL

Costera (5D/SLI)   *MonterreyEscobedo Intl/Vera Cruz (MTY/VER)*

XA-	Embraer EMB.145LR	145	ex PT-S	on order 04	
XA-	Embraer EMB.145LR	145	ex PT-S	on order 04	
XA-	Embraer EMB.145LR	145	ex PT-S	on order 04	
XA-	Embraer EMB.145LR	145	ex PT-S	on order 04	
XA-	Embraer EMB.145LR	145	ex PT-S	on order 04	
XA-AAO	SAAB SF.340B	164	ex HB-AKC		Lsd fr SWR
XA-ACB	SAAB SF.340B	179	ex N145NC		Lsd fr Newcourt
XA-ACK	SAAB SF.340B	183	ex N144NC		Lsd fr Newcourt
XA-ACR	SAAB SF.340B	186	ex N142NC		Lsd fr Newcourt
XA-ADH	SAAB SF.340B	178	ex N141NC		Lsd fr Newcourt
XA-ADY	SAAB SF.340B	363	ex SE-KCZ		Lsd fr SAAB
XA-AEM	SAAB SF.340B	161	ex HB-AKB		Lsd fr SWR
XA-AFR	SAAB SF.340B	176	ex HB-AKE		Lsd fr SWR
XA-ASM	SAAB SF.340B	197	ex N350BE		Lsd fr SAAB
XA-CGO	SAAB SF.340B	270	ex XA-TIU		Lsd fr Boeing Capital
XA-TJI	SAAB SF.340B	188	ex PH-KSF	Jalisco	Lsd fr Boeing Capital
XA-TJR	SAAB SF.340B	226	ex PH-KSK		Lsd fr Boeing Capital
XA-TKA	SAAB SF.340B	288	ex PH-KSM		Lsd fr Boeing Capital
XA-TKL	SAAB SF.340B	217	ex PH-KSI		Lsd fr Boeing Capital
XA-TKT	SAAB SF.340B	189	ex PH-KSG	Tamaulipas	Lsd fr Boeing Capital
XA-TQO	SAAB SF.340B	251	ex HK-4088X	Guanajuato	Lsd fr SAAB
XA-TQX	SAAB SF.340B	321	ex HK-4115X	Sinaloa	Lsd fr SAAB
XA-TTW	SAAB SF.340B	255	ex SE-G55		Lsd fr SAAB
XA-TUB	SAAB SF.340B	248	ex SE-KXD		Lsd fr SAAB
XA-TUC	SAAB SF.340B	196	ex N349BE		Lsd fr SAAB
XA-TUM	SAAB SF.340B	246	ex N354BE		Lsd fr SAAB
XA-TUN	SAAB SF.340B	187	ex N347BE		Lsd fr SAAB
XA-TUQ	SAAB SF.340B	190	ex N348BE		Lsd fr SAAB

Subsidiary of Aeromexico; operates scheduled services using AM flight numbers

---

AEROMAR AIRLINES

Trans-Aeromar (VW/TAO)   *Mexico City-Toluca (TLC)*

XA-RNP	Aerospatiale/Alenia ATR 42-320	213	ex F-WWEA	15th anniversary
XA-RXC	Aerospatiale/Alenia ATR 42-320	257	ex F-WWEO	
XA-SJJ	Aerospatiale/Alenia ATR 42-320	039	ex N71296	
XA-SYH	Aerospatiale/Alenia ATR 42-320	062	ex XA-PEP	Presidente Aleman
XA-TAH	Aerospatiale/Alenia ATR 42-500	471	ex F-WWLS	
XA-TAI	Aerospatiale/Alenia ATR 42-500	474	ex F-WWLF	
XA-TIC	Aerospatiale/Alenia ATR 42-320	058	ex F-OGNF	
XA-TKJ	Aerospatiale/Alenia ATR 42-500	561	ex F-WWLW	

XA-TLN	Aerospatiale/Alenia ATR 42-500	564	ex F-WWEC	15th anniversary
XA-TPR	Aerospatiale/Alenia ATR 42-500	586	ex F-WWEA	
XA-TPS	Aerospatiale/Alenia ATR 42-500	594	ex F-WWEX	
XA-TRI	Aerospatiale/Alenia ATR 42-500	607	ex F-WWEA	
XA-TRJ	Aerospatiale/Alenia ATR 42-500	608	ex F-WWEB	

AEROMEXICO

AeroMexico (AM/AMX) (IATA 139)　　　　　　　　　　　　　　　　　　**Mexico City-Benito Juarez Intl (MEX)**

XA-AAM	Boeing 737-752	1381/33783			Lsd fr RBS Avn
XA-BAM	Boeing 737-752	1393/33784			Lsd fr ILFC
XA-CAM	Boeing 737-752	1398/33785			Lsd fr ILFC
XA-DAM	Boeing 737-752	1403/33786			Lsd fr ILFC
XA-EAM	Boeing 737-752	1415/29363			Lsd fr ILFC
XA-FAM	Boeing 737-752	1421/33787			Lsd fr ILFC
XA-GAM	Boeing 737-752	1439/33788			Lsd fr ILFC
	Boeing 737-752			on order 04	Lsd fr ILFC
	Boeing 737-752			on order 04	Lsd fr ILFC

A further six Boeing 737-752s are on order for delivery in 2005; five leased from RBS Aviation and one from ILFC

N301AM	Boeing 757-2Q8	957/30045			Lsd fr ILFC
N490AM	Boeing 757-23A	510/25490	ex N53AW		LSd fr AWAS
N703AM	Boeing 757-29J	588/27203			Lsd fr WLL 27203 Inc
N801AM	Boeing 757-2Q8	541/25624	ex XA-SIK		Lsd fr Castle 2003-2A LLC
N802AM	Boeing 757-2Q8	558/26270	ex XA-SJD		Lsd fr MDFC Equipment Lsg
N803AM	Boeing 757-2Q8	590/26268	ex XA-SMJ		Lsd fr Castle 2003-2A LLC
N804AM	Boeing 757-2Q8	592/26271	ex XA-SMK		Lsd fr Castle 2003-1A LLC
N805AM	Boeing 757-2Q8	594/26272	ex XA-SML		Lsd fr ILFC
N806AM	Boeing 757-2Q8	597/26273	ex XA-SMM		Lsd fr ILFC

XA-APB	Boeing 767-3Q8ER	727/27618	ex (XA-TMG)		Lsd fr ILFC
XA-JBC	Boeing 767-284ER	307/24762	ex XA-RVY		Lsd fr AWAS
XA-RVZ	Boeing 767-284ER	297/24716	ex CC-CDH		Lsd fr AWAS
XA-TNS	Boeing 767-283ER	305/24728	ex N301AR		Lsd fr PLM Intl
XA-TOJ	Boeing 767-283ER	301/24727	ex PT-TAI		Lsd fr Boeing Capital

N1003P	Douglas DC-9-32	1014/48150	ex (XA-AMG)	stored MEX	Lsd fr Alameda Corp
XA-AMC	Douglas DC-9-32	961/48127		stored GYR	Lsd fr GECAS
XA-AMD	Douglas DC-9-32	964/48128			Lsd fr GECAS
XA-AME	Douglas DC-9-32	968/48129			Lsd fr GECAS
XA-DEI	Douglas DC-9-32	771/47650			
XA-DEK	Douglas DC-9-32	718/47602			
XA-DEL	Douglas DC-9-32	721/47607			Lsd fr GECAS
XA-DEM	Douglas DC-9-32	723/47609			
XA-JEB	Douglas DC-9-32	458/47394	ex YV-19C		
XA-JEC	Douglas DC-9-32	235/47106	ex YV-73C		
XA-SDF	Douglas DC-9-32	99/47006	ex VR-BMG		
XA-TFO	Douglas DC-9-32	1017/48151	ex N1003U		

EI-BTX	McDonnell-Douglas MD-82	1445/49660	ex (N59842)		Lsd fr Airplanes Holdings
EI-BTY	McDonnell-Douglas MD-82	1466/49667	ex (N12844)		Lsd fr Airplanes Holdings
N158PL	McDonnell-Douglas MD-88	1623/49761			Lsd fr Polaris
N160PL	McDonnell-Douglas MD-88	1626/49763			Lsd fr Polaris
N161PL	McDonnell-Douglas MD-88	1632/49764			Lsd fr Polaris
N162PL	McDonnell-Douglas MD-88	1645/49765			Lsd fr Polaris
N168PL	McDonnell-Douglas MD-88	1854/53174			Lsd fr Polaris
N169PL	McDonnell-Douglas MD-88	1868/53175			Lsd fr Polaris
N204AM	McDonnell-Douglas MD-87	1430/49404	ex OH-LMB		Lsd fr WFBN
N205AM	McDonnell-Douglas MD-87	1525/49405	ex OH-LMC		Lsd fr WFBN
N214AM	McDonnell-Douglas MD-87	1457/49585	ex LN-RMX		Lsd fr WFBN
N216AM	McDonnell-Douglas MD-87	1472/49586	ex LN-RMY		Lsd fr WFBN
N491SH	McDonnell-Douglas MD-82	1087/49150	ex OH-LMN		Lsd fr Ocean Aircraft Holdings
N501AM	McDonnell-Douglas MD-82	1172/49188	ex XA-AMO		Lsd fr Boeing Capital
N505MD	McDonnell-Douglas MD-82	1086/49149	ex XA-SFM		Lsd fr Finova
N583MD	McDonnell-Douglas MD-83	1438/49659	ex YV-39C		Lsd fr Boeing Capital
N753RA	McDonnell-Douglas MD-87	1541/49587	ex HB-IUC		Lsd fr BK Aircraft Holdings
N754RA	McDonnell-Douglas MD-87	1617/49641			Lsd fr WFBN
N755RA	McDonnell-Douglas MD-87	1621/49727			Lsd fr Pegasus
N803ML	McDonnell-Douglas MD-87	1610/49726			Lsd fr Triton
N831LF	McDonnell-Douglas MD-83	1704/53050	ex EC-EUZ		Lsd fr ILFC
N838AM	McDonnell-Douglas MD-83	1331/49397	ex N830VV		Lsd fr Boeing Capital
N861LF	McDonnell-Douglas MD-83	1578/49826	ex EC-EZR		Lsd fr Triton
N881LF	McDonnell-Douglas MD-83	1718/53051	ex EC-EVU		Lsd fr Triton
N944AM	McDonnell-Douglas MD-83	1304/49440	ex D-ALLT		Lsd fr Pacific
N945AS	McDonnell-Douglas MD-83	1423/49643	ex G-BNSA		Lsd fr WFBN
N946AS	McDonnell-Douglas MD-83	1461/49658	ex G-BNSB		Lsd fr WFBN
N957AS	McDonnell-Douglas MD-82	1080/49126	ex N780JA		Lsd fr CIT Leasing
N1003Y	McDonnell-Douglas MD-82	1031/48068	ex XA-SFK		Lsd fr WTCo
N1075T	McDonnell-Douglas MD-87	1549/49724	ex SU-DAP		Lsd fr CIT Leasing
XA-AMQ	McDonnell-Douglas MD-82	1180/49190		stored GYR	Lsd fr GECAS

XA-AMS	McDonnell-Douglas MD-88	1715/49926	ex (N164PL)		Lsd fr Polaris
XA-AMT	McDonnell-Douglas MD-88	1716/49927	ex (N165PL)		Lsd fr Polaris
XA-AMU	McDonnell-Douglas MD-88	1732/49928	ex N166PL		Lsd fr Polaris
XA-AMV	McDonnell-Douglas MD-88	1741/49929	ex (N167PL)		Lsd fr Polaris
XA-MRM	McDonnell-Douglas MD-82	1938/53066	ex B-28005		Lsd fr WLL 53066 Inc
XA-SFO	McDonnell-Douglas MD-87	1508/49673	ex (EI-CBU)		Lsd fr GECAS
(XA-SHJ)	McDonnell-Douglas MD-87	1670/49779	ex N751RA		Lsd fr CIT Leasing
XA-SWW	McDonnell-Douglas MD-83	1592/49848	ex SU-DAM		Lsd fr Pegasus
XA-SXJ	McDonnell-Douglas MD-83	1573/49845	ex SU-DAL		Lsd fr Pegasus
XA-TLH	McDonnell-Douglas MD-82	1956/53119	ex B-28013		Lsd fr World Lease
XA-TPM	McDonnell-Douglas MD-87	1463/49671	ex PZ-TCG	District of Para	Lsd fr ILFC
XA-TRD	McDonnell-Douglas MD-82	1016/48079	ex N956AS		Lsd fr GATX
XA-TWA	McDonnell-Douglas MD-87	1674/49780	ex N132NJ		Lsd fr Pacific Aircorp
XA-TWT	McDonnell-Douglas MD-87	1614/49706	ex EC-GKG		Lsd fr Air Trade Capital
XA-TXC	McDonnell-Douglas MD-87	1333/49389	ex EC-GKF		Lsd fr Air Trade Capital
XA-TXH	McDonnell-Douglas MD-87	1681/49413	ex N136NJ		Lsd fr Pacific Aircorp
XA-	McDonnell-Douglas MD-82	1088/49151	ex N619DB	on order	Lsd fr Airfund Intl
XA-	McDonnell-Douglas MD-83	1630/49741	ex N959PG		Lsd fr Pacific Aircorp
XA-	McDonnell-Douglas MD-83	1680/49904	ex N960PG		Lsd fr Pacific Aircorp

Subsidiary of CINTRA
Founder member of SkyTeam Alliance with Air France, Korean Air and Delta

AEROMEXPRESS CARGO

Aeromexpress (QO/MPX) (IATA 976)   Mexico City-Benito Juarez Intl (MEX)

N909PG	Boeing 727-2K5F (FedEx 3)	1553/21852	ex (XA-SXL)	Icaro	Lsd fr ART 21852

Subsidiary of CINTRA

AERO-MITLA

Oaxaca (OAX)

XA-KIK	Douglas DC-3	4369	ex TG-ASA

AEROSAFIN current status is uncertain, possibly did not commence operations

AEROPACIFICO

XA-AFE	LET L-410UVP	902508	ex

AEROSERVICIOS MONTERREY

Servimonte (SVM)   Monterrey-General Mariano Ecobedo Intl (MTY)

XA-HAC	Piper PA-31 Turbo Navajo C/R	31-7912088	ex N3532K

AEROTRANSCARGO current status is uncertain, possibly did not commence operations

AEROUNION

AeroUnion(6R/TNO)   Mexico City-Benito Juarez Intl (MEX)

XA-TUE	Airbus Industrie A300B4-203F	078	ex C-FICB	Fata	Lsd fr CIC
XA-TVU	Airbus Industrie A300B4-203F	074	ex G-HLAC	Nina	Lsd fr S-C Avn
XA-TWQ	Airbus Industrie A300B4-203F	045	ex G-HLAB		Lsd fr RBS Avn

AeroUnion is the trading name of Aerotransporte de Carga Union

AEROVIAS CASTILLO

Aerocastillo (CLL)   Guadalajara (GDL)

XA-COJ	Cessna U206G Stationair 6	U20605484	ex XB-ZIC
XA-IUL	Cessna 402C	402C0091	
XA-JIO	Cessna U206G Stationair 6	U20605330	
XA-JON	Cessna 402C	402C0230	ex N2718R
XA-KEB	Cessna T207A Stationair 8	20700615	
XA-PEA	Cessna TU206G Stationair 6	U20606379	
XA-POM	Cessna 421C Golden Eagle	421C0695	ex N546RP
XA-RWO	Cessna T210L Turbo Centurion	21061474	
XA-SCE	Lear Jet 24D	24D-271	ex N4305U

AEROVIAS MONTES AZULES

Montes Azules (MZL)   Tuxtla Gutierrez (TGZ)

XA-SOF	Cessna A185F Skywagon	18504177	ex XB-EFP
XA-SOG	Piper PA-31 Turbo Navajo C/R	31-7612056	ex XB-EGX
XA-TMQ	Cessna TU206G Turbo Stationair 6	U20604578	ex N9569E

628

ALCON SERVICIOS AEREOS

Alcon (AOA)
Saltillo (SLW)

| XA-TND | NAMC YS-11A-600 | 2073 | ex N111PH | Freighter |
| XA-TQP | NAMC YS-11A-600 | 2070 | ex S9-CAP | Freighter |

ALLEGRO AIR

Allegro (LL/GRO)
Monterrey-General Mariano Ecobedo Intl (MTY)

XA-	Boeing 727-2A1 (Super 27)	1320/21343	ex N102RK	Lsd fr ART 21343
XA-	Boeing 727-2K5 (FedEx 3)	1551/21851	ex N369FA	Lsd fr Pacific AirCorp
XA-AAQ	Boeing 727-231 (Super 27)	1454/21628	ex N54341	Lsd fr Pegasus
XA-GRO	Boeing 727-231 (Super 27)	1466/21634	ex N64347	Lsd fr PALS VI
XA-TRR	Boeing 727-231 (Super 27)	1456/21629	ex N54342	Lsd fr Pegasus
XA-TSW	McDonnell-Douglas MD-83	1630/49741	ex N959PG	Lsd fr Pacific AirCorp
XA-TTC	McDonnell-Douglas MD-83	1680/49904	ex N960PG	Lsd fr Pacific AirCorp
XA-TUP	McDonnell-Douglas MD-82	1594/49877	ex OH-LMT	stored TUS	Lsd fr Pegasus
XA-TWL	McDonnell-Douglas MD-83	1380/49568	ex N963PG	Lsd fr Pacific AirCorp
XA-TWM	McDonnell-Douglas MD-83	1581/49846	ex	Lsd fr GECAS
XA-TYB	McDonnell-Douglas MD-82	1140/49229	ex N137NJ	
XA-XPW	McDonnell-Douglas MD-82	1071/49120	ex N83872	Lsd fr WFBN

AVIACSA

Aviacsa (6A/CHP)
Tuxtla Gutierrez (TGZ)

XA-SDR	Boeing 727-276	1056/20555	ex VH-TBJ	
XA-SIE	Boeing 727-276 (Duganair 3)	1661/22069	ex VH-TBR	
XA-SIJ	Boeing 727-276	1564/22017	ex VH-TBQ	
XA-SJE	Boeing 727-276	1357/21479	ex VH-TBN	
XA-SJU	Boeing 727-276	906/20552	ex VH-TBG	
XA-SLG	Boeing 727-276 (Duganair 3)	1232/21171	ex VH-TBM	
XA-SLM	Boeing 727-276 (Duganair 3)	1483/21696	ex VH-TBP	
XA-SMB	Boeing 727-276	1434/21646	ex VH-TBO	
XA-SXC	Boeing 727-225	902/20619	ex N8857E	stored MEX
XA-SXE	Boeing 727-225	898/20615	ex N8852E	
XA-AAV	Boeing 737-3K9	1796/24214	ex EC-HNO	Lsd fr TED
XA-ABC	Boeing 737-205 (Nordam 3)	1245/23467	ex N713A	
XA-NAF	Boeing 737-219 (Nordam 3)	1186/23470	ex ZK-NAT	
XA-NAK	Boeing 737-219 (Nordam 3)	1199/23474	ex ZK-NAX	
XA-NAV	Boeing 737-219 (Nordam 3)	1194/23472	ex ZK-NAV	Lsd fr debis
XA-SIW	Boeing 737-2T4	716/22370	ex N139AW	Lsd fr GECAS
XA-SIX	Boeing 737-2T4	717/22371	ex N140AW	Lsd fr GECAS
XA-TTM	Boeing 737-201 (Nordam 3)	865/22753	ex N246US	
XA-TTP	Boeing 737-201 (Nordam 3)	963/22868	ex N262AU	
XA-TUK	Boeing 737-201 (Nordam 3)	961/22867	ex N261AU	
XA-TVD	Boeing 737-201 (Nordam 3)	889/22758	ex N252AU	
XA-TVL	Boeing 737-201 (Nordam 3)	964/22869	ex N263AU	
XA-TVN	Boeing 737-201 (Nordam 3)	845/22752	ex N244US	
XA-TWJ	Boeing 737-219 (Nordam 3)	1189/23471	ex ZK-NAU	
XA-TWO	Boeing 737-219 (Nordam 3)	1203/23475	ex ZK-NAY	
XA-TWW	Boeing 737-219 (Nordam 3)	1197/23473	ex ZK-NAW	
XA-TXD	Boeing 737-201 (Nordam 3)	651/22018	ex N232US	
XA-TXF	Boeing 737-201 (Nordam 3)	984/22961	ex N264AU	
XA-	Boeing 737-201 (Nordam 3)	987/22962	ex N265AU	
XA-	Boeing 737-201 (Nordam 3)	873/22755	ex N248US	Lsd fr Jetran Intl
XA-	Boeing 737-201 (Nordam 3)	879/22756	ex N249US	
XA-TIM	Douglas DC-9-15	82/45778	ex N1064T	
XA-TJS	Douglas DC-9-15 (ABS 3)	140/45784	ex N1070T	

AVIONES DE SONORA

Sonorav (ADS)
Hermosillo (HMO)

| XA-KEA | Cessna 310R | 310R1880 | |
| XA-KOA | Cessna 340A | 340A0978 | ex YV-1886P |

AVIOQUINTANA

Avioquintana (AQT)
Chetumal (CTM)

| XA-SXB | Swearingen SA.226TC Metro IIA | TC-412 | ex N253AM |

Avioqunitana is the trading name of Aviones de Renta de Quintana Roo

AZTECA AIRLINES

(ZE/TED) (IATA 994)   *Mexico City-Benito Juarez Intl (MEX)*

XA-AAU	Boeing 737-3K9	1623/24211	ex EC-HLM	Lsd fr Bavaria
XA-AAV	Boeing 737-3K9	1796/24214	ex EC-HNO	Lsd fr Bavaria; sublsd to CHP
XA-AEP	Boeing 737-7EA	859/32406	ex N1787B	
XA-AEQ	Boeing 737-7EA	904/32407		
XA-TWF	Boeing 737-76N	124/28577	ex N966PG	Lsd fr PALS VII Inc
XA-TWG	Boeing 737-3K2	1198/23412	ex N551FA	Lsd fr PALS I Inc

Azteca Airlines is the trading name of Aero Servicios Azteca/Lineas Aereas Azteca

ESTAFETA CARGA AEREA

(E7/ESF) (IATA 355)   *San Luis Potosi (SLP)*

XA-ABX	Boeing 737-210C (Nordam 3)	344/20917	ex N4906W	Lsd fr Facts Air
XA-ACP	Boeing 737-2T4C (Nordam 3)	989/23065	ex N230GE	Lsd fr GECAS
XA-ADV	Boeing 737-2T4C (Nordam 3)	992/23066	ex N306GE	
XA-TRW	Boeing 737-275C (Nordam 3)	139/19743	ex C-GWJK	Lsd fr GECAS
XA-TWP	Boeing 737-229C (Nordam 3)	576/21738	ex G-BYYF	Lsd fr LaserLine Lease Finance

GACELA AIR CARGO current status is uncertain, believed to have ceased operations

GLOBAL AIR

Mexico City-Benito Juarez Intl (MEX)

XA-TWR	Boeing 737-2H4 (AVA 3)	/21812	ex N60SW	Lsd fr WFBN

HELI MIDWEST DE MEXICO operates light helicopters only

HELISERVICIO CAMPECHE

Helicampeche (HEC)   *Campeche/Mexico City*

XA-AAC	Bell 212	31147	ex N24HS	Lsd fr OLOG
XA-IUR	Bell 212	30938		Lsd fr OLOG
XA-TOB	Bell 212	30817	ex N16785	Lsd fr OLOG
XA-TQG	Bell 212	30687	ex 9Y-TFA	Lsd fr OLOG
XA-TRP	Bell 212	30869	ex N71AL	Lsd fr OLOG
XA-TVM	Bell 212	30934	ex HC-CAY	Lsd fr OLOG
XA-TWU	Bell 212	30932	ex HK-4221X	Lsd fr OLOG
XA-	Bell 212	30934	ex N68AL	Lsd fr OLOG
XA-AAB	Bell 412EP	36253	ex N4217U	Lsd fr OLOG
XA-AAN	Bell 412EP	36254	ex N24171	Lsd fr OLOG
XA-AAR	Bell 412EP	36255	ex N2416X	Lsd fr OLOG
XA-SBZ	Bell 412SP	33213	ex N399AL	Lsd fr OLOG
XA-SMW	Bell 412HP	36038	ex SU-CAW	Lsd fr OLOG
XA-SYL	Bell 412EP	36101	ex N87746	
XA-TAM	Bell 412SP	33169	ex N396AL	Lsd fr OLOG
XA-TLO	Bell 412SP	36012	ex N397AL	Lsd fr OLOG
XA-TRC	Bell 412EP	36157	ex N1174X	Lsd fr OLOG
XA-TSH	Bell 412EP	36256	ex XA-ABO	Lsd fr OLOG
XA-TTF	Bell 412EP	36273	ex N508AL	Lsd fr OLOG
XA-TTL	Bell 412HP	36065	ex D-HHZZ	Lsd fr OLOG
XA-TUW	Bell 412	33065	ex C-GAUY	Lsd fr OLOG
XA-TXP	Bell 412EP	36311	ex N24129	
XA-TXQ	Bell 412EP	36268	ex N61318	
XA-TXR	Bell 412EP	36289	ex N2029N	
XA-TXV	Bell 412EP	36317	ex N7020C	
XA-TXZ	Bell 412EP	36314	ex N7030B	
XA-TYA	Bell 412EP	36315	ex N7007Q	
XA-TYQ	Bell 412EP	33210	ex 9Y-BCL	
XA-	Bell 412	36309	ex N24113	
XA-	Bell 412	36310	ex N2413V	
XA-JMB	Bell 407	53274		Lsd fr OLOG
XA-JOL	Bell 206B JetRanger III	786	ex N31AL	Lsd fr OLOG
XA-LOC	Bell 206B JetRanger III	3284		Lsd fr OLOG
XA-TKU	Bell 206L-1 LongRanger II	45697	ex N2092U	Lsd fr OLOG

Subsidiary of Offshore Logistics (OLOG)

MAGNICHARTERS

Grupomonterrey (GMT)   *Monterrey-General Mariano Ecobedo Intl (MTY)*

XA-MAA	Boeing 737-377	1274/23655	ex N812AR	
XA-MAB	Boeing 737-2C3	406/21016	ex XA-NBM	Lsd fr AAR Engine
XA-MAC	Boeing 737-2C3	397/21014	ex N302AR	

XA-MAD	Boeing 737-277 (Nordam 3)			
XA-MAE	Boeing 737-277 (Nordam 3)	789/22648	ex N181AW	
XA-MAF	Boeing 737-2K9 (Nordam 3)	815/22505	ex N303AR	Lsd fr AT Aircraft
XA-MAG	Boeing 737-205	440/21184	ex N1999L	Lsd fr AAR Engine

MAS AIR CARGO

Mas Carga (MY/MAA)   Mexico City-Benito Juarez Intl (MEX)

N314LA	Boeing 767-316ERF	848/32573		Lsd fr LCO

Mas Air Cargo is the trading name of Aerotransportes Mas de Carga. 25% owned by LANChile and operates as LANCargo Group with LANCargo Chile, ABSA Brasil and Florida West International

MEXICANA

Mexicana (MX/MXA) (IATA 132)   Mexico City-Benito Juarez Intl (MEX)

N62TY	Airbus Industrie A319-112	1625	ex D-AVYZ	Mexicali	Lsd fr CIT Leasing
N429MX	Airbus Industrie A319-112	1429	ex N50074	Mexico	Lsd fr Boullioun
N588MX	Airbus Industrie A319-112	0588	ex D-ANNE	Vancouver	Lsd fr WTCo
N612MX	Airbus Industrie A319-112	1612	ex EI-CXA	Merida	Lsd fr O'Farrell Lsg Corp
N618MX	Airbus Industrie A319-112	1618	ex D-AVWH	Caracas	Lsd fr WFBN
N634MX	Airbus Industrie A319-112	1634	ex D-AVYH	Panama	Lsd fr WFBN
N706MX	Airbus Industrie A319-112	1706	ex D-AVYQ	Sacramento	Lsd fr Boullioun
N750MX	Airbus Industrie A319-112	1750	ex D-AVYB	Vamos por Todo	Lsd fr Boullioun
N866MX	Airbus Industrie A319-112	1866	ex D-AVYB	Cancun	Lsd fr ILFC
N872MX	Airbus Industrie A319-112	1872	ex D-AVYF	Villahermosa	Lsd fr ILFC
N882MX	Airbus Industrie A319-112	1882	ex D-AVYO	Los Cabos	Lsd fr ILFC
N925MX	Airbus Industrie A319-112	1925	ex D-AVYS		Lsd fr ILFC
XA-CMA	Airbus Industrie A319-112	2066	ex D-AVYF		Lsd fr ILFC
XA-MXA	Airbus Industrie A319-112	2078	ex D-AVYO		Lsd fr ILFC
XA-NCA	Airbus Industrie A319-112	2126	ex D-AVWM		Lsd fr ILFC
F-OHME	Airbus Industrie A320-231	0252	ex XA-RZU	Nueva York	
F-OHMF	Airbus Industrie A320-231	0259	ex XA-RYQ	Ciudad del Carmen	
F-OHMG	Airbus Industrie A320-231	0260	ex XA-RYS	Monterrey	
F-OHMH	Airbus Industrie A320-231	0261	ex XA-RYT	Chetumal	Star Alliance c/s
F-OHMI	Airbus Industrie A320-231	0275	ex XA-RJW	Playa del Carmen	
F-OHMJ	Airbus Industrie A320-231	0276	ex XA-RJX	Cozumel	
F-OHMK	Airbus Industrie A320-231	0296	ex XA-RJY	San Jose California	
F-OHML	Airbus Industrie A320-231	0320	ex XA-RJZ	Puerto Vallarta	
F-OHMM	Airbus Industrie A320-231	0321	ex XA-RKA	Querétaro	
F-OHMN	Airbus Industrie A320-231	0353	ex XA-RKB	San Luis Potosi	
N225RX	Airbus Industrie A320-231	0225	ex EC-HCR		Lsd fr ORIX
N280RX	Airbus Industrie A320-231	0280	ex G-BVZU	Orlando	Lsd fr ORIX
N291MX	Airbus Industrie A320-231	0291	ex G-OOAA	Morelia	Lsd fr ORIX
N292MX	Airbus Industrie A320-231	0292	ex G-OOAB	Oaxaca	Lsd fr ORIX
N304ML	Airbus Industrie A320-231	0373	ex F-WQBD	Veracruz	Lsd fr AFT Trust
N332MX	Airbus Industrie A320-231	0332	ex B-22301	Denver	Lsd fr ACG Acq
N347TM	Airbus Industrie A320-231	0347	ex B-22307	San Salvador	Lsd fr East Trust
N361DA	Airbus Industrie A320-231	0361	ex PH-FHA	Montreal	Lsd fr WFBN
N368MX	Airbus Industrie A320-231	0368	ex F-OHMA	Oakland	Lsd fr ACG Acqs
N369MX	Airbus Industrie A320-231	0369	ex B-22302	Toronto	Lsd fr WFBN
N405MX	Airbus Industrie A320-231	0405	ex EI-TLI	1960s colours	Lsd fr ILFC
N415MX	Airbus Industrie A320-231	0415	ex EI-TLT	Tijuana	Lsd fr WFBN
N428MX	Airbus Industrie A320-231	0428	ex	Toluca	
N447MX	Airbus Industrie A320-231	0447	ex C-FRAR	Minatitlan	Lsd fr ILFC
N467RX	Airbus Industrie A320-231	0467	ex G-BVJW	San Francisco	Lsd fr ORIX
XA-TXT	Airbus Industrie A320-231	0430	ex 5B-DBK		Lsd fr ILFC
XA-HOH	Boeing 727-264 (FedEx 3)	1379/21577		Tijuana; stored MEX	
XA-HOV	Boeing 727-264 (FedEx 3)	1429/21637		Mexicali	
XA-IEU	Boeing 727-264 (FedEx 3)	1497/21836		Huatulco	
XA-MEB	Boeing 727-264 (FedEx 3)	1545/21837	ex XA-IEV	Zacatecas; stored MEX	
XA-MEC	Boeing 727-264 (FedEx 3)	1547/21838	ex XA-IEW	Miami; stored MEX	
XA-MEE	Boeing 727-264 (FedEx 3)	1619/22157		Los Cabos; stored MEX	
XA-MEF	Boeing 727-264 (FedEx 3)	1642/22158		Campeche; stored MEX	
XA-MEH	Boeing 727-264 (FedEx 3)	1676/22409		Nuevo Laredo	
XA-MEI	Boeing 727-264 (FedEx 3)	1678/22410		Leon; stored MEX	

Last 727 service performed by XA-MEE on 30 May 2003

N101LF	Boeing 757-2Q8	688/26332	ex LV-WMH	Las Vegas	Lsd fr ILFC
N380RM^	Boeing 757-2Q8	836/29380	ex N1795B	Buenos Aires	Lsd fr ILFC
N755MX	Boeing 757-2Q8	424/24964	ex N754AT	No que no..?	Lsd fr ILFC
N758MX	Boeing 757-2Q8	438/24965	ex N755AT	Vamos por mas	Lsd fr MSA V
N762MX	Boeing 757-2Q8	819/29442		SS Juan Pablo	Lsd fr ILFC
N763MX*	Boeing 757-2Q8	821/29443		Ciudad de Mexico	Lsd fr ILFC
N764MX	Boeing 757-2Q8	639/27351	ex N809AM	Ciudad de Mexico	Lsd fr ILFC
N765MX	Boeing 757-2Q8	954/30044		Buenos Aires	Lsd fr ILFC
XA-TRA	Boeing 757-230	267/24737	ex D-ABNA	Los Angeles	Lsd fr Pegasus

*Star Alliance c/s   ^1960's colours

PH-JXW	Fokker 100	11390	ex XA-SGS	Mazatlan	Lsd fr debis
PH-KXJ	Fokker 100	11400	ex XA-SGT	Ixtapa Zihuatanejo	Lsd MAF II
XA-SGE*	Fokker 100	11382	ex PH-JXS	Cuernavaca	
XA-SGF*	Fokker 100	11384	ex PH-JXU	Puebla	
XA-SHI*	Fokker 100	11309	ex PH-LMZ	Chihuahua	
XA-SHJ*	Fokker 100	11319	ex PH-LNB	Torreon	
XA-TCG*	Fokker 100	11374	ex PH-JXX	Tuxpan	
XA-TCH*	Fokker 100	11375	ex PH-JXR	Guatamela	
XA-TKP*	Fokker 100	11266	ex PK-JGD	San Antonio	
XA-TKR*	Fokker 100	11339	ex PK-JGH	San Luis Potosi	

*Leased from Airplanes 100 Finance

| XA-MXB | Boeing 767-383ER | 273/24475 | ex LN-RCG | | Lsd fr AFG Inv Trust |
| N365SR | Boeing 767-383ER | 395/25365 | ex LN-RCL | | Lsd fr WFBN |

Subsidiary of CINTRA
Member of Star Alliance but will resign on 31 March 2004

MEXICANA INTER

Ops a network of services in conjunction with Aerocaribe and Aero Cozumel

PEGASO – TRANSPORTES AEREOS PEGASO

Transpegaso (TPG)   *Mexico City-Benito Juarez Intl (MEX)*

XA-MBB	MBB Bo105CBS-4	S-676	ex N4573H
XA-NAT	MBB Bo105LS-A3	2044	ex XA-TTT
XA-TFP	MBB Bo105LS-A3	2043	ex XA-SSS
XA-THI	MBB Bo105LS-A3	2046	ex C-GERG
XA-THJ	MBB Bo105LS-A3	2049	ex D-HSLA
XA-THK	MBB BK117B-2	7131	ex D-HBCZ
XA-THM	MBB BK117B-2	7252	ex D-HAEC
XA-TRF	MBB BK117B-2	7070	ex CC-CSW

SAEMSA / SERVICIOS AEREOS ESPECIALIZADOS MEXICANOS

Servimex (SXM)   *Campeche, Tampico & Toluca (CPE/TAM/TLC)*

XA-SRL	Aerospatiale SA330J Puma	1625	ex XC-CME
XA-SRN	Aerospatiale SA330J Puma	1644	ex XC-FOI
XA-SRO	Aerospatiale SA330J Puma	1615	ex XC-IMP
XA-SRP	Aerospatiale SA330J Puma	1616	ex XC-OPS
XA-SRQ	Aerospatiale SA330J Puma	1613	ex XC-SDE
XA-TFT	Aerospatiale AS365N2 Dauphin	6495	
XA-TFU	Aerospatiale AS365N2 Dauphin	6512	
XA-TFV	Aerospatiale AS365N2 Dauphin	6513	
XA-TGS	Aerospatiale AS365N2 Dauphin	6515	
XA-TGY	Aerospatiale AS365N2 Dauphin	6516	
XA-TGZ	Aerospatiale AS365N2 Dauphin	6517	
HK-4232	Bell 212	30983	ex XA-SRZ
XA-SSB	Bell 212	30845	ex XC-DAH
XA-SSC	Bell 212	30992	ex XC-DIA
XA-SSD	Bell 212	30988	ex XC-DIF
XA-SSF	Bell 212	30987	ex XC-SER
XA-SSG	Bell 212	30939	ex XC-SET
XA-SSK	Bell 212	30924	ex XC-HFI
XA-SSL	Bell 212	35031	ex XC-HHN
XA-SRF	Cessna U206G Stationair 6	U20605823	ex XC-DOJ
XA-SRG	Cessna U206G Stationair 6	U20604684	
XA-SRI	Cessna U206G Stationair 6	U20604133	ex XC-MTT
XA-SRJ	Cessna U206C Super Skywagon	U206-1135	
XA-SST	Cessna U206G Stationair 6	U20605820	ex XC-DOI
XA-SRK	Cessna T210M Turbo Centurion	21062532	
XA-SRW	Sikorsky S-76A	760142	ex XC-FEK
XA-SRX	Sikorsky S-76A	760094	ex XC-FES
XA-SSO	Bell 206B JetRanger	1250	ex XC-GIJ
XA-SSP	Bell 206B JetRanger III	3962	ex XC-HIB
XA-SSQ	Aerospatiale SA316B Alouette III	1744	ex XC-DOL

SETRA / SERVICIOS DE TRANSPORTES AEREOS

Setra (SVI)   *Mexico City-Benito Juarez Intl (MEX)*

| XC-BCO | de Havilland DHC-8Q-202 | 558 | ex XA-BCO | Combi |
| XC-BDM | de Havilland DHC-8Q-202 | 559 | ex XA-AEA | Combi |

Subsidiary of Banco de Mexico

SUDPACIFICO ceased operations

TACSA / TRANSPORTES AEREOS DE COAHUILA ceased operations

TANSA / TRANSPORTES AEREOS DE NAYARIT

Tepic (TPQ)

XA-FAL	Cessna 402B	402B0205	ex XA-CAV
XA-IUI	Douglas DC-3	11719	ex N4007C	damaged
XA-RZF	Douglas DC-3	12192	ex C-FDTV

WESTAIR DE MEXICO ceased operations

XT - BURKINA FASO (People's Democratic Republic of Burkina Faso)

AIR BURKINA

Burkina (2J/VBW)   *Ouagadougou (OUA)*

XT-FDC	Fokker F.28 Fellowship 4000	11173	ex N497US
XT-FZP	Fokker F.28 Fellowship 4000	11185	ex PH-ZCF	Bonkougou
XT-TIB	Fokker F.28 Fellowship 2000	11108	ex F-GDUU

BURKINA AIRLINES

(BFR)   *Ouagadougou (OUA)*

Current fleet details are unknown

FASO AIRWAYS

Faso (F3/FSW)   *Ouagadougou (OUA)*

XT-FBD	LET L-410UVP	851414	ex UR-67510
XT-FCB	Ilyushin Il-76TD	1023408265	ex T9-CAB

XU - CAMBODIA (Kingdom of Cambodia)

CAMBODIA AIRLINES

(Y6/KHM)   *Phnom Penh-Pochentong (PNH)*

Operates services with aircraft leased from Far Eastern Air Transport as and when required

FIRST CAMBODIA AIRLINES

(F6)   *Phnom Penh-Pochentong (PNH)*

Current fleet details unknown

IMTREC AVIATION CAMBODIA

Imtrec (IMT)   *Phnom Penh-Pochentong (PNH)*

XU-315	Antonov An-12BP	2400702		idenity not confirmed
XU-365	Antonov An-12BP	01348005	ex UK 11109

KAMPUCHEA AIRWAYS

Kampuchea (KT/KMP)   *Phnom Penh-Pochentong (PNH)*

XU-100	Lockheed L-1011-1 Tristar 1	1156	ex N309GB

MEKONG AIR INTERNATIONAL ceased operations May 2003

PHNOM PENH AIRWAYS

Phnom Penh-Pochentong (PNH)

XU-054	Antonov An-24RV	27307809	ex RA-46463

PRESIDENT AIRLINES

(TO/PSD)   *Phnom Penh-Pochentong (PNH)*

XU-325	Antonov An-26B	12808	ex RA-26136
XU-335	Antonov An-24B	9990208	ex RA-79152
XU-375	Antonov An-24B			Lsd to SEQ
XU-385	Antonov An-24B	

XU-881	Fokker F.27 Friendship 100	10168	ex RP-C5888	stored PNH	
XU-888	Fokker F.28 Fellowship 1000	11012	ex XU-001	stored PNH	
YU-ANP	Boeing 737-2K3 (Nordam 3)	1401/23912		Zadar	Lsd fr AGX

Also leases Boeing 737-8Q8 aircraft from Mandarin Airlines when required

ROYAL PHNOM PENH AIRWAYS

Phnom-Penh-Air (RL/PPW)　　　　　　　　　　　　　　　　　　*Phnom Penh-Pochentong (PNH)*

XU-070	Xian Y-7-100C	09706	ex B-3448
XU-071	Xian Y-7-100C	08708	ex B-3449
XU-072	Xian Y-7-100C	08705	ex B-3494

SIEM REAP AIR INTERNATIONAL

Siemreap Air (FT/SRH) (IATA 084)　　　　　　　　　　　　　　　　　　*Siem Reap (REP)*

A wholly owned subsidiary of Bangkok Air and leases aircraft from parent as required - some wear joint titles

XY - MYANMAR (Union of Myanmar)

AIR MANDALAY

(6T)　　　　　　　　　　　　　　　　　　*Mandalay/Yangon (MDL/RGN)*

F-OHFS	Aerospatiale/Alenia ATR 72-212	393	ex F-WWLI		Lsd fr ATR Asset Mgt
F-OHFZ	Aerospatiale/Alenia ATR 72-212	469	ex		Lsd fr ATRiam Capital
F-OHOT	Aerospatiale/Alenia ATR 42-300	020	ex F-WQNU	stored TLS	Lsd fr ATRiam Capital
F-OHRN	Aerospatiale/Alenia ATR 42-300	268	ex F-WQNF		Lsd fr Merinos Lsg

MYANMA AIRWAYS

Unionair (UB/UBA)　　　　　　　　　　　　　　　　　　*Yangon (RGN)*

XY-ADT	Fokker F.27 Friendship 600	10523	ex PH-EXE	
XY-ADZ	Fokker F.27 Friendship 600	19574	ex PH-EXF	
XY-AEQ	Fokker F.27 Friendship 400	10294	ex 5Y-BIP	
XY-AER	Fokker F.27 Friendship 100	10124	ex 5001	
XY-AEU	Fokker F.27 Friendship 600	10343	ex CU-T1287	
XY-AEV	Fokker F.27 Friendship 600	10347	ex CU-T1288	
XY-AEW	Fokker F.27 Friendship 600	10352	ex CU-T1290	
XY-ADU	Fokker F.28 Fellowship 1000	11019	ex PH-ZAO	
XY-ADW	Fokker F.28 Fellowship 4000	11114	ex PH-EXU	
XY-AFA	Aerospatiale SA.330J Puma	1422		stored RGN
XY-AFB	Aerospatiale SA.330J Puma	1437		stored RGN
XY-AFC	Aerospatiale SA.330J Puma	1450		
XY-AGA	Fokker F.28 Fellowship 4000	11232	ex PH-EZG	
XY-AGB	Fokker F.28 Fellowship 4000	11184	ex YU-AOH	

MYANMAR AIRWAYS INTERNATIONAL

(8M) (IATA 599)　　　　　　　　　　　　　　　　　　*Yangon (RGN)*

TC-APG	Boeing 737-82R	224/29329		Lsd fr PGT
S7-ASK	McDonnell-Douglas MD-82	2145/53481	ex PK-LME	Lsd fr/op by RGA

Joint venture between Myanma Airways and Regionair

YANGON AIRLINES

(HK)　　　　　　　　　　　　　　　　　　*Yangon (RGN)*

F-OIYA	Aerospatiale/Alenia ATR 72-212	479	ex F-WWEL	Lsd fr EVA Lsg
F-OIYB	Aerospatiale/Alenia ATR 72-212	481	ex F-WWEQ	Lsd fr EVA Lsg

YA - AFGHANISTAN (Islamic State of Afghanistan)

ARIANA AFGHAN AIRLINES

Ariana (FG/AFG) (IATA 255)　　　　　　　　　　　　　　　　　　*Kabul (KBL)*

YA-FAK	Boeing 727-223 (Raisbeck 3)	1276/21370	ex N865AA
YA-FAL	Boeing 727-223 (Raisbeck 3)	1267/21090	ex N863AA
YA-FAM	Boeing 727-223 (Raisbeck 3)	1255/21088	ex N861AA
YA-FAS	Boeing 727-223 (Raisbeck 3)	1345/21388	ex N876AA
YA-FAY	Boeing 727-228	1719/22289	ex F-GCDH
YA-BAB	Airbus Industrie A300B4-203	180	ex VT-EHO
YA-BAC	Airbus Industrie A300B4-203	190	ex VT-EHQ
YA-BAD	Airbus Industrie A300B4-203	177	ex VT-EHN

KAM AIR

(RQ/KMF)
Kabul (KBL)

3D-	Boeing 727-251 (FedEx 3)	746/20289	ex N267US	Lsd fr Financial Advisory Grp

KHYBER AFGHAN AIRLINES

Khyber (KHY)
Jalalabad/Sharjah (-/SHJ)

Operates cargo flights with Antonov An-12 and Ilyushin Il-76 aircraft leased from other operators as and when required

YI - IRAQ (Republic of Iraq)

IRAQI AIRWAYS

Iraqi (IA/IAW) (IATA 073)
Baghdad-Al Muthana/Saddam Intl (BGW/SDA)

YI-AGK	Boeing 727-270	1186/21197		Ninevah	stored AMM
YI-AGL	Boeing 727-270	1191/21198		Basrah	stored AMM
YI-AGM	Boeing 727-270	1203/21199		Al Habbania	stored MIR
YI-AGQ	Boeing 727-270	1647/22261	ex N8284V	Ataameem	stored AMM
YI-AGS	Boeing 727-270	1809/22263	ex N1780B		stored AMM
YI-AOD	Boeing 727-256	1006/20814	ex 9L-LCK	id unconfirmed	wfu BGW 04
YI-AOE	Boeing 727-2H3	1210/21235	ex 3D-BOB		wfu BGW 04
YI-AOW	Boeing 727-224	1151/20666	ex 3D-SGH		wfu BGW 04
YI-AOY	Boeing 727-2H3	1252/21318	ex 3D-JAB		wfu BGW 04
YI-AOZ	Boeing 727-256	910/20598	ex 9L-LCS		wfu BGW 04

Last five believed to have been recently active but noted wfu and stripped at BGW 2.04

YI-AGE	Boeing 707-370C (Comtran 2)	889/20889			stored AMM
YI-AGF	Boeing 707-370C (Comtran 2)	891/20890			stored AMM
YI-AGG	Boeing 707-370C	892/20891		Baghdad	stored AMM
YI-AGN	Boeing 747-270C	287/21180		Tigris	stored TOE
YI-AGO	Boeing 747-270C	289/21181		Euphrates	stored THR
YI-AGP	Boeing 747-270C	565/22366		Shat-al-Arab	stored TOE
YI-ALM	Boeing 747SP-70	567/22858		Al Qadissiya	stored TOE
YI-ALV	Ilyushin Il-76				
YI-AOF	Boeing 737-281	266/20451	ex EX-451		
YI-AOX	Boeing 747SP-09	445/22298	ex 3D-GFD		

Most aircraft in the country were destroyed or damaged beyond repair during second Gulf War. Stored aircraft are extant outside Iraq, others reported active recently

UNITED IRAQI AIRLINES
Arbil

	Boeing 727-223 (Raisbeck 3)		ex

Commenced operations in early December 2003

YJ - VANUATU (Republic of Vanuatu)

AIR TROPICANA
Port Vila (VLI)

YJ-RV3	Beech 95 Travel Air	TD-24	ex N8273D

AIR VANUATU

Air Van (NF/AVN) (IATA 218)
Port Vila (VLI)

YJ-AV18	Boeing 737-3Q8	3016/28054		Spirit of Vanuatu	Lsd fr ILFC
YJ-AV42	Aerospatiale/Alenia ATR 42-300	223	ex N223AT	Spirit of Vanuatu	

Expected to merge with Vanair in 2004

UNITY AIRLINES
Port Vila (VLI)

YJ-009	Britten-Norman BN-2A-8 Islander	65	ex V7-0009

VANAIR

(X4)
Port Vila (VLI)

YJ-RV1	de Havilland DHC-6 Twin Otter 300	491	ex HP-730APP	Freedom
YJ-RV2	Britten-Norman BN-2A Islander	172	ex (P2-ISW)	
YJ-RV5	de Havilland DHC-6 Twin Otter 300	520	ex 5U-ABU	

YJ-RV8	de Havilland DHC-6 Twin Otter 310	703	ex F-ODGL	Unity	ZS-OUL reserved
YJ-RV10	de Havilland DHC-6 Twin Otter 300	679	ex OY-SLI	Melanesian Princess	
YJ-RV12	Embraer EMB.110P1 Bandeirante	110347	ex VH-SJP		
YJ-RV16	Britten-Norman BN-2A-27 Islander	104	ex ZK-FLU		

Expected to merge with Air Vanuatu in 2004

YK - SYRIA (Syrian Arab Republic)

SYRIANAIR

Syrianair (RB/SYR) (IATA 070)   Damascus (DAM)

YK-AKA	Airbus Industrie A320-232	0886	ex F-WWDH	Ugarit	
YK-AKB	Airbus Industrie A320-232	0918	ex F-WWIJ	Ebla	
YK-AKC	Airbus Industrie A320-232	1032	ex F-WWDV	Afamia	
YK-AKD	Airbus Industrie A320-232	1076	ex F-WWIK	Mari	
YK-AKE	Airbus Industrie A320-232	1085	ex F-WWIX	Bosra	
YK-AKF	Airbus Industrie A320-232	1117	ex F-WWBN	Amrit	
YK-ANC	Antonov An-26	3007			Govt operated
YK-AND	Antonov An-26	3008			Govt operated
YK-ANE	Antonov An-26	3103			Govt operated
YK-ANF	Antonov An-26	3104			Govt operated
YK-ANG	Antonov An-26B	10907			Govt operated
YK-ANH	Antonov An-26B	11406			Govt operated
YK-AGA	Boeing 727-294	1188/21203		6 Octobre	
YK-AGB	Boeing 727-294	1194/21204		Damascus	
YK-AGC	Boeing 727-294	1198/21205		Palmyra	
YK-AGD	Boeing 727-269	1670/22360	ex 9K-AFB		
YK-AGE	Boeing 727-269	1716/22361	ex 9K-AFC		
YK-AGF	Boeing 727-269	1788/22763	ex 9K-AFD		
YK-AQA	Yakovlev Yak-40	9341932			Govt operated
YK-AQB	Yakovlev Yak-40	9530443			Govt operated
YK-AQD	Yakovlev Yak-40	9830158			Govt operated
YK-AQE	Yakovlev Yak-40	9830258			Govt operated
YK-AQF	Yakovlev Yak-40	9931859			Govt operated
YK-AQG	Yakovlev Yak-40K	9941959			Govt operated
YK-AHA	Boeing 747SP-94	284/21174		16 Novembre	
YK-AHB	Boeing 747SP-94	290/21175		Arab Solidarity	
YK-ANA	Antonov An-24B	87304203			
YK-ATA	Ilyushin Il-76M	093421613			Govt operated
YK-ATB	Ilyushin Il-76T	093421619			Govt operated
YK-ATC	Ilyushin Il-76M	0013431911			Govt operated
YK-ATD	Ilyushin Il-76M	0013431915			Govt operated
YK-AYE	Tupolev Tu-134B-3	66187			

Those aircraft shown as Government operated are flown by the Syrian Air Force in Syrianair colours

YL - LATVIA (Republic of Latvia)

AIR BALTIC

AirBaltic (BT/BTI) (IATA 657)   Riga-Spilve (RIX)

YL-BAR	Fokker 50	20149	ex PH-LVL	Cesis	Lsd fr Finova
YL-BAS	Fokker 50	20162	ex OY-KAE	Zemgale	Lsd fr SAS
YL-BAT	Fokker 50	20163	ex OY-KAF	Riga	Lsd fr SAS
YL-BAU	Fokker 50	20126	ex PH-AAO		Lsd fr Finova
YL-BAW	Fokker 50	20148	ex OY-MMS		Lsd fr Finova
YL-	Fokker 50	20153	ex ES-AFM		Lsd fr ILFC
YL-BAK	Avro RJ70	E1223	ex EI-CUO	Kurzeme	Lsd fr BAES
YL-BAL	Avro RJ70	E1224	ex N833BE	Latgale; all-white	Lsd fr BAES
YL-BAN	Avro RJ70	E1225	ex N834BE	Vidzeme; all-white	Lsd fr BAES
YL-BBA	Boeing 737-505	2138/24646	ex N646LS		Lsd fr AFSI
YL-BBB	Boeing 737-505	2018/24273	ex LN-BRJ		Lsd fr BRA

Also operates as Baltic International; 36.5% owned by SAS
Plans to replace its Avro RJ70s with three more Boeing 737-500s

AIR LIVONIA current status is uncertain, believed to have ceased operations

AVIAVILSA current status is uncertain, believed to have ceased operations

CONCORS

Concors (COS)   Riga-Spilve (RIX)

| YL-KAE | LET L-410UVP-E | 790209 | ex RA-67173 | | Lsd fr Banke Paritate |

INVERSIJA

Inver (INV) — Riga-Spilve (RIX)

YL-LAJ	Ilyushin Il-76T		possibly second use of marks
YL-LAK	Ilyushin Il-76T	0003424707 ex RA-76522	
YL-LAL	Ilyushin Il-76T	0013433984 ex RA-76755	

LAT CHARTER

LatCharter (6Y/LTC) — Riga-Spilve (RIX)

YL-BBC	Airbus Industrie A320-211	0142 ex D-AKFX	Lsd fr Wiederaufbrau
YL-LBT	Yakovlev Yak-42D	4520424404018 ex B-2758	
YL-LBU	Yakovlev Yak-42D	4520423403018 ex B-2757	

LATPASS AIRLINES

Latpass (QJ/LTP) — Riga-Spilve (RIX)

YL-LAB	Tupolev Tu-154B-2	81A-515 ex CCCP-85515

RAF-AVIA

Mitavia (MTL) — Riga-Spilve (RIX)

YL-RAA	Antonov An-26B	97311206 ex RA-26064	DHL c/s	
YL-RAB	Antonov An-26	07310508 ex RA-26032	DHL c/s	Lsd to AAG
YL-RAC	Antonov An-26	07309903 ex CCCP-79169	DHL c/s	Lsd to AAG
YL-RAD	Antonov An-26B	47313909 ex RA-26589	DHL c/s	Lsd to Silver Air
YL-RAE	Antonov An-26B	57314004 ex UN-26200		
YL-RAZ	Antonov An-26B			
YL-RAF	Antonov An-74TK	36547095905 ex UR-CAE		Lsd fr CBI

RIGA AEROCLUB

Sport Club (RAK) — Riga-Spilve (RIX)

YL-KAB	WSK/PZL-Antonov An-28	1AJ009-15 ex RA-28949	Lsd fr RTS Co
YL-KAD	WSK/PZL-Antonov An-28	1AJ004-02 ex UR-28753	
YL-KAF	WSK/PZL-Antonov An-28	1AJ009-09 ex RA-28943	
YL-LCK	Antonov An-24B	79901110 ex CCCP-47727	

Riga Aeroclub is the trading name of Latvian Professional Air Sport Center

YN - NICARAGUA (Republic of Nicaragua)

AEROSEGOVIA

Segovia (SGV) — Managua (MGA)

YN-CBV	Antonov An-32	1809 ex HK-4132X
YN-CGC	Antonov An-26	77305109 ex RA-26622
YN-CGD	Antonov An-24B	77302903 ex 2903

Also operates cargo charters with Ilyushin Il-76s leased from other operators as required

AIR CHARTER CARGO believed to have ceased operations

ATLANTIC AIRWAYS

Atlantic Nicaragua (AYN) — Managua (MGA)

YN-CFL	LET L-410UVP-E3	871917 ex OK-SDH	
YN-CFM	LET L-410UVP-E	871017 ex OK-SGH	
YN-CFR	LET L-410UVP	861705 ex TG-CFE	no titles

LA COSTENA

Lacostena — Managua (MGA)

HP-1317APP	Short SD.3-60	SH3602 ex N360MQ	Lsd fr APP
HP-1318APP	Short SD.3-60	SH3612 ex N362MQ	Lsd fr APP
HP-1407APP	Cessna 208B Caravan I	208B0611 ex TI-LRS	Lsd fr APP
YN-CEQ	Cessna 208B Caravan I	208B0444 ex N1265C	
YN-CFD	Cessna 208B Caravan I	208B0758	
YN-CFK	Cessna 208B Caravan I	208B0691	

Member of Grupo TACA

YR - ROMANIA (Republic of Romania)

CARPATAIR

Carpatair (V3/KRP)   Bucharest-Baneasa (BBU)

YR-VGM	SAAB SF.340B	208	ex HB-AKI		Lsd fr SWR
YR-VGN	SAAB SF.340B	200	ex HB-AKH		Lsd fr SWR
YR-VGO	SAAB SF.340B	215	ex HB-AKL		Lsd fr SWR
YR-VGP	SAAB SF.340B	228	ex HB-AKO		Lsd fr SWR
YR-VGR	SAAB SF.340B	225	ex HB-AKN		Lsd fr SWR
YR-	SAAB SF.340B	168	ex HB-AKP		Lsd fr SWR
HB-IYD	SAAB 2000	059	ex SE-059		Lsd fr SWR
HB-IZO	SAAB 2000	029	ex SE-029		Lsd fr SWR
YR-SBA	SAAB 2000	038	ex HB-IZV		
HB-	SAAB 2000			on order	
HB-	SAAB 2000			on order	
HB-	SAAB 2000			on order	
YR-VGA	Yakovlev Yak-40	9810757	ex ER-JGE		

ION TIRIAC AIR

Tiriac Air (TIH)   Bucharest-Otopeni (OTP)

OE-ITA	Boeing 737-3L9	1760/27924	ex N730PA		Lsd fr FSG Privatair
YR-ITA	Antonov An-26	6407	ex LZ-MNH	DHL c/s	

ROMAVIA

Aeromavia (WQ/RMV)   Bucharest-Baneasa/Otopeni (BBU/OTP)

YR-ABB	Boeing 707-3K1C (Comtran 2)	883/20804		Romania titles	
YR-BRE	Rombac/BAC One-Eleven 561RC	405	ex (EI-BUQ)	Romania titles	
YR-BRH	Rombac/BAC One-Eleven 561RC	408			
YR-BRI	Rombac/BAC One-Eleven 561RC	409			
YR-IMZ	Ilyushin Il-18GrM	187009802		Freighter	Lsd to EXV as 4R-EXD

TAROM

Tarom (RO/ROT) (IATA 281)   Bucharest-Otopeni (OTP)

YR-ATA	Aerospatiale/Alenia ATR 42-500	566	ex F-WWLF	Dunarea	
YR-ATB	Aerospatiale/Alenia ATR 42-500	569	ex F-WWLH	Bistrita	
YR-ATC	Aerospatiale/Alenia ATR 42-500	589	ex F-WWLR	Mures	
YR-ATD	Aerospatiale/Alenia ATR 42-500	591	ex F-WWLS	Cris	
YR-ATE	Aerospatiale/Alenia ATR 42-500	596	ex F-WWLY	Olt	Lsd to MSR
YR-ATF	Aerospatiale/Alenia ATR 42-500	599	ex F-WWEB	Arges	
YR-ATG	Aerospatiale/Alenia ATR 42-500	605	ex F-WWLG	Dambovita	
YR-BGA	Boeing 737-38J	2524/27179	ex N5573K	Alba Iulia	
YR-BGB	Boeing 737-38J	2529/27180		Bucuresti	
YR-BGC	Boeing 737-38J	2662/27181		Constanta	
YR-BGD	Boeing 737-38J	2663/27182		Deva; special c/s	
YR-BGE	Boeing 737-38J	2671/27395		Timisoara	
YR-BGF	Boeing 737-78J	795/28440		Brâila	
YR-BGG	Boeing 737-78J	827/28442			
YR-BGH	Boeing 737-78J	1394/28438			
YR-BGI	Boeing 737-78J	1419/28439			
YR-ABA	Boeing 707-3K1C (Comtran 2)	878/20803		no titles	
YR-LCA	Airbus Industrie A310-325	636	ex F-WWCG	Transilvania	
YR-LCB	Airbus Industrie A310-325	644	ex F-WWCO	Moldova	

Four Airbus Industrie A318s are on order for delivery in 2005/06

YS - EL SALVADOR (Republic of El Salvador)

TACA INTERNATIONAL AIRLINES

Taca (TA/TAI) (IATA 202)   San Salvador-Comalapa Intl (SAL)

N471TA	Airbus Industrie A319-132	1066	ex D-AVWE		Lsd fr WFBN; sublsd to TPU
N472TA	Airbus Industrie A319-132	1113	ex D-AVWU		Lsd fr WFBN; sublsd to TPU
N473TA	Airbus Industrie A319-132	1140	ex D-AVYP		Lsd fr WFBN; sublsd to TPU
N474TA	Airbus Industrie A319-132	1159	ex D-AVWD		Lsd fr WFBN; sublsd to PTU
N475TA	Airbus Industrie A319-132	1575	ex D-AVWP		Lsd fr IEM Airfinance
N476TA	Airbus Industrie A319-132	1934	ex D-AVWE		Lsd fr debis
N477TA	Airbus Industrie A319-132	1952	ex D-AVWK		Lsd fr WFBN
N	Airbus Industrie A319-132		ex D-AV	on order	

N	Airbus Industrie A319-132		ex D-AV	on order
EI-TAA	Airbus Industrie A320-233	0912	ex N458TA	Lsd fr Rockshaw; sublsd to CUB
EI-TAB	Airbus Industrie A320-233	1624	ex N485TA	Mensajero de Esperanza
				Lsd fr CIT Ireland Lsg; sublsd CUB
EI-TAC	Airbus Industrie A320-233	1676	ex (N486TA)	Lsd fr CIT Ireland Lsg
N340LA	Airbus Industrie A320-232	0425	ex HC-BUH	Lsd fr CIT Leasing; sublsd to LRC
N451TA	Airbus Industrie A320-233	0733	ex F-WWBR	Lsd fr WFBN
N452TA	Airbus Industrie A320-233	0741	ex F-WWBK	Lsd fr WFBN
N453TA	Airbus Industrie A320-233	0747	ex F-WWIH	Lsd fr WFBN
N455TA	Airbus Industrie A320-233	0874	ex F-WWBV	Lsd fr Pegasus
N457TA	Airbus Industrie A320-233	0902	ex F-WWDN	Lsd fr Pegasus
N461TA	Airbus Industrie A320-233	1300	ex F-WWBP	Lsd fr WFBN
N462TA	Airbus Industrie A320-233	1334	ex F-WWDM	Lsd fr WFBN
N463TA	Airbus Industrie A320-233	1339	ex F-WWDN	Lsd fr WFBN; sublsd to TPU
N464TA	Airbus Industrie A320-233	1353	ex F-WWBB	Lsd fr WFBN; sublsd to LRC
N465TA	Airbus Industrie A320-233	1374	ex F-WWIM	Lsd fr WFBN; sublsd to CUB
N470TA	Airbus Industrie A320-233	1400	ex F-WWIZ	Lsd fr WFBN
N481TA	Airbus Industrie A320-233	1500	ex F-WWIE	Lsd fr IEM Airfinance; sublsd to LRC
N482TA	Airbus Industrie A320-233	1482	ex F-WWDU	Lsd fr IEM Airfinance; sublsd to LRC
N483TA	Airbus Industrie A320-214	1509	ex F-WWBD	Lsd fr IEM Airfinance
N484TA	Airbus Industrie A320-233	1523	ex F-WWIL	Lsd fr WFBN
N486TA	Airbus Industrie A320-233	1730	ex F-WWBJ	Lsd fr WFBN
N487TA	Airbus Industrie A320-233	2084	ex F-WWIG	Lsd fr WFBN
N488TA	Airbus Industrie A320-233	2118	ex F-WWIK	Lsd fr WFBN
N489TA	Airbus Industrie A320-233	2102	ex F-WWBQ	Lsd fr WFBN
N981LR	Airbus Industrie A320-233	0558	ex F-WWDF	Lsd fr debis; sublsd to TAI
N991LR	Airbus Industrie A320-233	0561	ex F-WWDM	Lsd fr debis; sublsd to TAI

Fourteen more Airbus Industrie A320-233s are on order for delivery up to 2007

Owns 30% of AVIATECA and 10% of LACSA while TACA Peru is wholly owned; feeder services are operated by AeroPerlas, Inter, Islena, La Costena and SANSA, known collectively as Grupo TACA.

YU - SERBIA & MONTENEGRO (Federation of Serbia & Montenegro)

AIR YUGOSLAVIA

Yugair (YRG)   *Belgrade (BEG)*

Operates charter services using aircraft leased from parent, JAT Airways, as required

AVIOGENEX

Genex (AGX)   *Belgrade (BEG)*

YU-AKD	Boeing 727-2L8	1142/21040	ex OY-SBJ	Zagreb	stored BEG
YU-AKH	Boeing 727-2L8	1146/21080	ex OY-SBP	Beograd	
YU-AKM	Boeing 727-243	1814/22702	ex HK-3618X	Pula	
YU-ANP	Boeing 737-2K3 (Nordam 3)	1401/23912		Zadar	Lsd to PSD

INTERAIR LINK

                                                                                    Belgrade (BEG)

YU-ALN	Aerospatiale/Alenia ATR 72-201	180	ex F-WWEP
YU-ALO	Aerospatiale/Alenia ATR 72-201	186	ex F-WWEW
YU-ALP	Aerospatiale/Alenia ATR 72-201	189	ex F-WWED
YU-ALR	Aerospatiale/Alenia ATR 72-202	357	ex G-BVTK

Low cost regional carrier wholly owned by JAT Airways

JAT AIRWAYS

JAT (JU/JAT) (IATA 115)   *Belgrade (BEG)*
Previously listed as JAT-Jugoslovenski Aerotransport / Yugoslav Airlines

YU-AKB	Boeing 727-2H9	1045/20931		stored BEG
YU-AKE	Boeing 727-2H9	1094/21037		stored BEG
YU-AKF	Boeing 727-2H9	1118/21038		stored BEG
YU-AKG	Boeing 727-2H9	1119/21039		stored BEG
YU-AKI	Boeing 727-2H9	1681/22393		Lsd to West African
YU-AKJ	Boeing 727-2H9	1691/22394	ex N8281V	stored BEG
YU-AKK	Boeing 727-2H9	1786/22665	ex TS-JEA	Lsd to West African
YU-AKL	Boeing 727-2H9	1790/22666	ex TS-JEB	
YU-AND	Boeing 737-3H9	1134/23329		City of Krusevac
YU-ANF	Boeing 737-3H9	1136/23330		
YU-ANH	Boeing 737-3H9	1171/23415	ex TC-CYO	
YU-ANI	Boeing 737-3H9	1175/23416		Lsd to MAK as Z3-AAA
YU-ANJ	Boeing 737-3H9	1305/23714	ex TC-MIO	
YU-ANK	Boeing 737-3H9	1310/23715		

639

YU-ANL	Boeing 737-3H9	1321/23716	ex TS-IEC		Lsd to MAK as Z3-ARF
YU-ANV	Boeing 737-3H9	1524/24140			
YU-ANW	Boeing 737-3H9	1526/24141	ex TS-IED	all-white	
YU-AON	Boeing 737-3Q4	1490/24208	ex N181LF		Lsd fr ILFC
YU-AOO	Boeing 737-4Q8	1665/24070	ex N240LF		Lsd fr WFBN
YU-AOS	Boeing 737-4B7	1795/24551	ex N429US	o/o 3.04	Lsd fr CIT
YU-AJH	Douglas DC-9-32	685/47562	ex N1345U		Lsd to OSL
YU-AJI	Douglas DC-9-32	687/47563	ex N1346U		Lsd to BLV
YU-AJJ	Douglas DC-9-32 (ABS 3)	688/47567	ex Z3-ARE	all-white	
YU-AJK	Douglas DC-9-32	689/47568	ex Z3-ARD		Lsd to UYC
YU-AJL	Douglas DC-9-32 (ABS 3)	695/47571	ex Z3-AAB	all-white	Lsd to UYC
YU-AJM	Douglas DC-9-32	701/47582			Lsd to BLV
YU-ALN	Aerospatiale/Alenia ATR 72-201	180	ex F-WWEP		Op by Interair Link
YU-ALO	Aerospatiale/Alenia ATR 72-201	186	ex F-WWEW		Op by Interair Link
YU-ALP	Aerospatiale/Alenia ATR 72-201	189	ex F-WWED		Op by Interair Link
YU-ALR	Aerospatiale/Alenia ATR 72-202	357	ex G-BVTK		Op by Interair Link
YU-AMB	Douglas DC-10-30	278/46988		City of Belgrade	

Leases aircraft to Savannah Airlines and Sosoliso Airlines as required as well as Air Yugoslavia. InterAir Link is low cost regional carrier

MONTENEGRO AIRLINES

Motairo (YM/MGX) (IATA 409)   *Podgorica/Tivat (TGD/TIV)*

YU-AOJ	Fokker F.28 Fellowship 2000	11187	ex F-WQPL		Lsd to Air One Nine
YU-AOK	Fokker 100	11272	ex G-UKFP	Sveti Petar Cetinjski	Lsd to VDR
YU-AOL	Fokker 100	11268	ex G-UKFL		Lsd fr Transasian
YU-AOM	Fokker 100	11321	ex G-BYDP		
YU-AOP	Fokker 100	11332	ex PT-MQW		

PELIKAN BLUE LINE

Pelikan Line (PBL)   *Podgorica/Tivat (TGD/TIV)*

YU-BXX	LET L-410UVP-E	902422	ex RA-67629
YU-BYY	LET L-410UVP-E	892316	ex RA-67619

YV - VENEZUELA (Bolivarian Republic of Venezuela)

AEROBOL – AEROVIAS BOLIVAR

Ciudad Bolivar (CBL)

YV-315C	Cessna U206G Stationair 6	U20604323	ex YV-1465P
YV-387C	Cessna U206G Stationair 6	U20605398	
YV-389C	Cessna U206G Stationair 6		
YV-408C	Cessna U206G Stationair 6		
YV-540C	Cessna U206G Stationair 6		
YV-615C	Cessna U206G Stationair 6		
YV-849C	Cessna U206G Stationair 6		
YV-946C	Cessna U206G Stationair 6		
YV-948C	Cessna U206G Stationair 6		
YV-270C	Britten-Norman BN-2A-20 Islander	573	ex YV-142CP
YV-288C	Cessna 207A Stationair 8	20700708	ex YV-2143P
YV-380C	Cessna 207A Stationair		

AERO EJECUTIVOS

Venejecutiv (VEJ)   *Caracas-Simon Bolivar Intl (CCS)*

YV-223C	Convair 440	144	ex YV-58C	
YV-426C	Douglas DC-3	4093	ex N10DC	
YV-440C	Douglas DC-3	2201	ex N31PB	Caballo Viejo
YV-500C	Douglas DC-3	6135	ex C-FDBJ	

AEROLINEAS SOSA believed to have ceased operations after sole aircraft sold

AEROPOSTAL / ALAS DE VENEZUELA

Aeropostal (VH/LAV) (IATA 152)   *Caracas-Simon Bolivar Intl (CCS)*

YV-10C	Douglas DC-9-51	820/47713	ex N6388Z	Lsd fr Amtec Corp
YV-11C	Douglas DC-9-21 (ABS 3)	462/47306	ex N339CA	Lsd fr Amtec Corp
YV-12C	Douglas DC-9-21 (ABS 3)	475/47360	ex N338CA	Lsd fr Amtec Corp
YV-13C	Douglas DC-9-21 (ABS 3)	382/47301	ex N316CA	Lsd fr Amtec Corp
YV-14C	Douglas DC-9-51 (ABS 3)	830/47738	ex OH-LYT	Lsd fr FIN
YV-15C	Douglas DC-9-51 (ABS 3)	883/47771	ex OH-LYU	Lsd fr FIN

YV-20C	Douglas DC-9-51	842/47705		El Guayanes	
YV-21C	Douglas DC-9-51	845/47719		El Zuliano	
YV-22C	Douglas DC-9-51	841/47703		El Margariteno	
YV-24C	Douglas DC-9-32	848/47727		El Falconiano	
YV-25C	Douglas DC-9-32	847/47721		El Andino	
YV-32C	Douglas DC-9-51	892/47770		El Caraqueno	
YV-33C	Douglas DC-9-51	893/47782	ex N1002N	El Venezolano	
YV-35C	Douglas DC-9-51	815/47712	ex N649HA	El Larense	
YV-37C	Douglas DC-9-34CF	872/47752	ex 9Y-TFI	El Llanero	
YV-42C	Douglas DC-9-51	783/47656	ex N148CA		Lsd fr Amtec Corp
YV-43C	Douglas DC-9-51	805/47694	ex HP-1388ALV		
YV-44C	Douglas DC-9-51	806/47695	ex HP-1389ALV		
YV-46C	Douglas DC-9-32	610/47535	ex N70542		
YV-47C	Douglas DC-9-32	560/47490	ex N14564		
YV-48C	Douglas DC-9-32	394/45847	ex N17531		
YV-49C	Douglas DC-9-32	637/47539	ex N14524		
YV-17C	Boeing 727-277	907/20548	ex HK-3977X	on order	Lsd fr Pegasus
YV-18C	Boeing 727-231 (Super 27)	1574/21984	ex N54352		Lsd fr Pegasus
YV-40C	Boeing 727-231 (Super 27)	1462/21632	ex N54345		Lsd fr Pegasus
YV-41C	Boeing 727-231 (Super 27)	1565/21968	ex N54349		Lsd fr Pegasus
N64346	Boeing 727-231 (FedEx 3)	1464/21633			Lsd fr FAO
N79749	Boeing 727-224 (FedEx 3)	1767/22451			Lsd fr FAO
N79750	Boeing 727-224 (FedEx 3)	1772/22452		Patricia; std TUC	Lsd fr FAO
YV-01C	McDonnell-Douglas MD-83	1539/49822	ex N822AN		Lsd fr MSA I

AEROSERVICIOS GUYANA believed to have ceased operations

AEROSERVICIOS RANGER

Caracas-La Carlota/Lagunillas/Tumeremo (-/LGY/TMO)

YV-429C	Bell 206B JetRanger III	1959	ex N9910K
YV-431C	Bell 206B JetRanger III	2598	
YV-433C	Bell 206B JetRanger II	2106	ex YV-330CP
YV-455C	Bell 206B JetRanger	1481	ex N218AL
YV-457C	Bell 206B JetRanger III	2470	ex N50056
YV-571C	Bell 206B JetRanger	273	ex N59Q
YV-572C	Bell 206B JetRanger	644	ex N7906J
YV-920C	Britten-Norman BN-2A-26 Islander	56	ex YR-BNY
YV-921C	Britten-Norman BN-2A-26 Islander	149	ex G-AXWR

AEROTECHNICA

Acarigua (AGV)

YV-101C	Bell 206B JetRanger	459	ex YV-C-GAA
YV-102C	Bell 206B JetRanger	506	ex YV-C-GAB
YV-103C	Bell 206B JetRanger III	3211	
YV-104C	Bell 206B JetRanger	467	ex YV-C-GAH
YV-105C	Bell 206B JetRanger	889	ex YV-C-GAL
YV-106C	Bell 206B JetRanger	414	ex YV-C-GAM
YV-108C	Bell 206B JetRanger III	2384	
YV-109C	Bell 206B JetRanger III	2402	
YV-110C	Bell 206B JetRanger	1119	ex N83005
YV-112C	Bell 206B JetRanger III	3213	
YV-115C	Bell 206B JetRanger II	2099	
YV-116C	Bell 206B JetRanger II	2190	ex N103K
YV-117C	Bell 206B JetRanger III	2692	
YV-118C	Bell 206B JetRanger III	3409	
YV-122C	Bell 206B JetRanger II	1984	
YV-124C	Bell 206B JetRanger III	2215	
YV-251C	Bell 206B JetRanger	1106	ex YV-T-AIN
YV-254C	Bell 206B JetRanger II	2059	ex N9934K
YV-320C	Bell 206B JetRanger III	2248	
YV-321C	Bell 206B JetRanger III	2496	
YV-322C	Bell 206B JetRanger III	3359	
YV-323C	Bell 206B JetRanger	874	
YV-325C	Bell 206B JetRanger II	2095	ex GN7635
YV-326C	Bell 206B JetRanger	1858	
YV-327C	Bell 206B JetRanger	1355	ex YV-235CP
YV-328C	Bell 206B JetRanger III	3308	
YV-329C	Bell 206B JetRanger III	3336	
YV-333C	Bell 206B JetRanger	1699	ex YV-141CP
YV-111C	Bell 206L-1 LongRanger II	45343	
YV-121C	Bell 206L-1 LongRanger II	45501	
YV-118CP	Beech 65-E90 King Air	LW-234	

YV-1032C	Sikorsky S-61N Helipro	61711	ex C-GHJU	Lsd fr CHC Helicopters
YV-1033C	Sikorsky S-61N	61222	ex C-GROV	Lsd fr CHC Helicopters

AEREO TRANSPORTE LA MONTANA

Ciudad-Bolivar (CBL)

YV-336C	Cessna U206G Stationair 6	U20604672	ex YV-360C
YV-337C	Cessna U206G Stationair 6	U20605562	ex YV-364C
YV-338C	Cessna U206G Stationair 6		
YV-339C	Cessna U206G Stationair 6		
YV-340C	Cessna U206G Stationair 6		
YV-491C	Cessna U206G Stationair 6		
YV-521C	Cessna U206G Stationair 6		
YV-746C	Cessna U206G Stationair 6		
YV-522C	Britten-Norman BN-2A-8 Islander	310	ex HP-1079KN
YV-523C	Cessna 207A Stationair		

ASERCA AIRLINES

Aserca (R7/OCA) (IATA 717)   *Caracas-Simon Bolivar Intl (CCS)*

YV-705C*	Douglas DC-9-31	283/45867	ex N8952E	Virgen del Valle
YV-706C	Douglas DC-9-31	365/45875	ex YV-815C	Virgen de la Chinita
YV-707C	Douglas DC-9-31	390/47272	ex YV-816C	Virgen de la Coromoto
YV-708C	Douglas DC-9-31	130/45864	ex N8927E	Virgen de Socorro
YV-709C	Douglas DC-9-31	151/47005	ex N937ML	Madre Maria de San Jose
YV-710C	Douglas DC-9-31	389/47271	ex N975ML	Virgen de Loreto
YV-714C	Douglas DC-9-31	87/47007	ex N938ML	El Pilar
YV-718C*	Douglas DC-9-31	282/47187	ex N8951E	El Viajero
YV-719C	Douglas DC-9-31	322/47157	ex N8959E	El Ejecutivas
YV-720C*	Douglas DC-9-31	103/45837	ex N8922E	El Industrial

*Leased from ATASCO

AVENSA / AEROVIAS VENEZOLANOS ceased operations

AVIOR EXPRESS / AVIONES DE ORIENTE

Avior (3B/ROI) (IATA 863)   *Barcelona (BLA)*

YV-401C	Beech 1900D	UE-270	ex N11024
YV-402C	Beech 1900D	UE-268	ex N11002
YV-403C	Beech 1900D	UE-279	ex N11252
YV-404C	Beech 1900D	UE-298	ex N21693
YV-406C	Beech 1900D	UE-304	ex N22675
YV-438C	Beech 1900D	UE-342	ex N23369
YV-466C	Beech 1900D	UE-343	ex N23373
YV-503C	Beech 1900D	UE-344	ex N23376
YV-660C	Beech 1900D	UE-331	ex N2820B
YV-663C	Beech 1900D	UE-355	ex N23538
YV-664C	Beech 1900D	UE-356	ex N23593
YV-659C	Cessna 208B Caravan I	208B0729	
YV-100C	Embraer EMB.120RT Brasilia	1200675	ex N276UE
YV-662C	Embraer EMB.120ER Brasilia	120356	ex PT-SHK
YV-667C	Embraer EMB.120ER Brasilia	120355	ex PT-SSO
YV-925C	Cessna 208B Caravan I	208B0793	ex N52627

CIACA AIRLINES

Ciudad Bolivar (CBL)

YV-953C	LET L-410UVP	831114	ex 3C-KKU
YV-978C	LET L-410UVP	810702	ex CCCP-67066 stored
YV-981C	LET L-410UVP	841303	ex CCCP-67478
YV-1025C	LET L-410UVP	831010	ex RA-67382
YV-1027C	LET L-410UVP		

COMERAVIA

Cuidad Bolivar (CBL)

YV-179C	Cessna P206B Super Skylane	P206-0355	ex YV-C-CMD
YV-180C	Cessna U206G Stationair 6	U20604092	ex YV-1279P
YV-188C	Cessna U206G Stationair 6		
YV-317C	Cessna U206G Stationair 6		
YV-673C	Cessna U206G Stationair 6		
YV-578C	WSK-PZL Mielec/Antonov An-28		El Abuelo
YV-1071C	LET L-410UVP		

EL SOL DE AMERICA

Solamerica (ESC)   *Caracas-Simon Bolivar Intl (CCS)*

YV-811C	Douglas DC-3			also reported as YV-911C
YV-872C	Britten-Norman BN-2A MkIII-2 Trislander	1034	ex N414WA	
YV-1029C	LET L-410UVP	831027	ex PZ-TGR	
YV-1120C	LET L-410UVP	841329	ex YV-982CP	

HELITEC

Maturin (MUN)

YV-696CP	Swearingen SA.227TT Merlin IIIC	TT-465	ex OY-CRU
YV-808CP	Swearingen SA.227TT Merlin 300	TT-435	ex N92RC

IAACA / LINEA AEREA IAACA

Air Barinas (KG/BNX)   *Barinas (BNS)*

YV-951C	Aerospatiale/Alenia ATR 42-320	400	ex F-WWLA
YV-1004C	Aerospatiale/Alenia ATR 72-212	482	ex F-WWES
YV-1005C	Aerospatiale/Alenia ATR 72-212	485	ex F-WWLE
YV-1073C	Aerospatiale/Alenia ATR 72-212	486	ex F-WWLG

JET AIR INTERNATIONAL CHARTERS ceased operations

LABSA / LINEA AEREA BOLIVARIANA

Labsa (LBS)   *Caracas-Simon Bolivar Intl (CCS)*

YV-1083C	British Aerospace Jetstream 31	752	ex OB-1735	Lsd fr ACQ

LASER / LINEAS AEREAS DE SERVICIO EJECUTIVO REGIONAL

Laser (8Z/LER) (IATA 722)   *Caracas-Simon Bolivar Intl (CCS)*

YV-881C	Douglas DC-9-32	217/45789	ex N17543		Lsd fr Pacific AirCorp
YV-977C	Douglas DC-9-14	32/45745	ex YV-852C	Aldebaran	Lsd fr Intl Air Support
YV-1121C	Douglas DC-9-32	437/47281	ex N922LG		Lsd fr Pacific AirCorp
YV-1122C	Douglas DC-9-32	325/47219	ex N18544		Lsd fr Pacific AirCorp

LINEA TURISTICA AEREOTUY

Aereotuy (LD/TUY)   *Caracas-Simon Bolivar Intl (CCS)*

YV-638C	de Havilland DHC-7-102	5	ex N702AC		Lsd fr Volvo A/S
YV-639C	de Havilland DHC-7-102	30	ex N4309N		Lsd fr Volvo A/S
YV-640C	de Havilland DHC-7-102	17	ex N47RM	stored CCS	Lsd fr Volvo A/S
YV-861C	Cessna 208B Caravan	208B0690	ex N506C		Lsd fr Cessna Finance Corp
YV-862C	Cessna 208B Caravan	208B0695	ex N504C		Lsd fr Cessna Finance Corp
YV-863C	Cessna 208B Caravan	208B0955	ex N5262Z		Lsd fr Cessna Finance Corp

YV-638C and YV-639C also reported with identities reversed

MIDAS AIR ceased operations

RUTACA – RUTAS AEREAS

Rutaca (RUC)   *Ciudad Bolivar (CBL)*

YV-206C	Cessna U206D Super Skywagon	U206-1338	
YV-210C	Cessna U206G Stationair 6	U20605354	
YV-214C	Cessna U206F Stationair	U20602386	
YV-219C	Cessna U206G Stationair	U20603977	ex YV-1296P
YV-229C	Cessna U206G Stationair	U20603541	
YV-379C	Cessna U206G Stationair 6	U20604150	
YV-785C	Cessna U206G Stationair	U20603889	ex YV-1314P
YV-786C	Cessna U206G Stationair 6	U20605125	
YV-789C	Cessna U206G Stationair 6	U20604803	
YV-793C	Cessna U206F Stationair	U20603192	
YV-245C	Embraer EMB.110P1 Bandeirante	110325	ex N103TN
YV-246C	Embraer EMB.110P1 Bandeirante	110363	ex N104TN
YV-247C	Embraer EMB.110P1 Bandeirante	110293	ex N901A
YV-248C	Embraer EMB.110P1 Bandeirante	110376	ex N61DA
YV-249C	Embraer EMB.110P1 Bandeirante	110382	ex N63DA
YV-787C	Embraer EMB.110P1 Bandeirante	110403	ex N202EB	Curacao
YV-215C	Boeing 737-2M6	462/21231	ex CC-CYN	Lsd fr Pacific Coast Group
YV-216C	Boeing 737-2S3 (Nordam 3)	563/21774	ex N367DL

YV-217C	Cessna 207A Stationair 7	20700440		
YV-218C	Douglas DC-3	43079	ex YV-108C	stored CBL
YV-222C	Douglas DC-3	7386	ex PP-CED	stored CBL
YV-226C	Douglas DC-3	19121	ex YV-12C	stored CBL
YV-227C	Douglas DC-3	19000	ex YV-115C	stored CBL; Freighter
YV-790C	Cessna 208B Caravan I	208B0527	ex N5283S	
YV-791C	Cessna 208B Caravan I	208B0555	ex N5095N	
YV-792C	Cessna 208B Caravan I	208B0608	ex N5180K	
YV-794C	Cessna 208B Caravan I	208B0795	ex N5264U	

SANTA BARBARA AIRLINES

Santa Barbara (S3/BBR)   **Maracaibo (MAR)**

YV-1014C	Aerospatiale/Alenia ATR 42-320	368	ex F-WSFB	Mi Chinita
YV-1015C	Aerospatiale/Alenia ATR 42-320	360	ex F-GMGI	Virgen del Carmen
YV-1017C	Aerospatiale/Alenia ATR 42-320	300	ex PP-PSG	
YV-1018C	Aerospatiale/Alenia ATR 42-320	340	ex F-WQNH	
YV-1019C	Aerospatiale/Alenia ATR 42-320	363	ex F-WQNV	

All leased from ATR Asset Management

YV-1037C	Cessna 208B Caravan I	208B0888		Lsd fr Cessna Finance Corp
YV-1038C	Cessna 208B Caravan I	208B0889		Lsd fr Cessna Finance Corp
YV-1039C	Cessna 208B Caravan I	208B0901		Lsd fr Cessna Finance Corp
YV-1040C	Douglas DC-10-30	178/47867	ex N41068	Lsd fr Pegasus
YV-1052C	Douglas DC-10-30	133/46944	ex N940PG	Lsd fr Pegasus
YV-1056C	Boeing 727-2D3 (Super 27)	1701/22269	ex N969PG	Lsd fr ART 22269 LLC

SASCA / SERVICIOS AEREOS SUCRE

Isla Margarita

YV-980C	LET L-410UVP	830939	ex CCCP-67371
YV-1070C	Beech 1900C-1	UC-	
YV-1126C	Cessna 208B Caravan I	208B0781	ex N5268A

SERVIVENSA / SERVICIOS AVENSA   ceased operations

SUNDANCE AIR

Caracas-Metropolitano

YV-1029C	LET L-410UVP	831027	ex

TRANSAVEN / TRANSPORTE AEREO VENEZUELA

Caracas-Simon Bolivar Intl (CCS)

YV-479C	Cessna 401A	401A0078	ex YV-479P
YV-943C	Britten-Norman BN-2A Mk III Trislander	1040	ex N420WA
YV-1114C	LET L-410UVP	831032	ex YV-983CP
YV-1115C	Britten-Norman BN-2A-8 Islander	296	ex HP-1209PS
YV-1116C	Britten-Norman BN-2A-7 Islander	242	ex HP-1220PS
YV-1117C	Britten-Norman BN-2A MkIII Trislander	1007	ex HP-899PS

TRANSCARGA

Tiaca (TIW)   **Caracas-Simon Bolivar Intl (CCS)**

YV-940C	Swearingen SA.226TC Metro II	TC-247	ex N5448M	Lsd fr Leland Lsg

VENESCAR INTERNACIONAL

Vecar (V4/VEC)   **Caracas-Simon Bolivar Intl (CCS)**

YV-846C	Boeing 727-35F (FedEx 3)	325/19167	ex OO-DHQ	DHL c/s	Lsd fr BCS
YV-848C	Boeing 727-31F (FedEx 3)	712/20114	ex OO-DHM	DHL c/s	Lsd fr BCS
YV-	AMD Falcon 20C	200	ex N12AR	DHL c/s; regn not confirmed	
YV-876C	Aerospatiale/Alenia ATR 42-300F	052	ex TG-DHP		Op for DHL
YV-913C	Aerospatiale/Alenia ATR 42-300F	061	ex F-WQOE		Op for DHL

Venescar International is the trading name of Venezolana Servicios Expresos de Carga Internacional

Z - ZIMBABWE (Republic of Zimbabwe)

AIR ZAMBEZI   did not restart operations

AIR ZIMBABWE

Air Zimbabwe (UM/AZW) (IATA 168)

Harare International (HRE)

Z-WPA	Boeing 737-2N0	1313/23677		Mbuya Nehanda	Lsd to LAM
Z-WPB	Boeing 737-2N0	1405/23678		Great Zimbabwe	
Z-WPC	Boeing 737-2N0	1415/23679		Matojeni	
Z-WPD	British Aerospace 146 Srs.200	E2065	ex G-5-065	Jongu'e	Lsd fr Govt
Z-WPE	Boeing 767-2N0ER	287/24713		Victoria Falls	
Z-WPF	Boeing 767-2N0ER	333/24867		Chimanimani	

AIRLINK ZIMBABWE

Flywell (FEM)

Harare-International (HRE)

ZS-NRG	British Aerospace Jststream 41	41051	ex G-4-051	Lsd fr LNK
ZS-OUV	Embraer EMB.135LR	145493	ex PT-SXM	Lsd fr LNK
49% owned by SA Airlink.				

DHL AVIATION (ZIMBABWE)

Harare-International (HRE)

Z-KPS	Cessna 208B Caravan I	208B0303	ex N31SE	Lsd fr Whelson Air Touring

EXEC-AIR

Axair (AXE)

Harare-Charles Prince

Z-WFP	Cessna 402A	402A0013	
Z-WLW	Cessna 210M Centurion	21061178	ex N732UE
Z-WOR	Piper PA-31 Turbo Navajo	31-35	ex ZS-JWF
Z-WOU	Piper PA-31 Turbo Navajo	31-118	ex ZS-SWA
Z-WRB	Cessna 402B	402B0032	ex N9475P

FALCON AIR

Harare-Charles Prince

Z-DDD	Reims Cessna F406 Caravan II	F406-0069	ex F-GIQD
Z-DDE	Reims Cessna F406 Caravan II	F406-0068	ex F-GIQC
Z-DDF	Reims Cessna F406 Caravan II	F406-0071	ex F-GIQE
Z-DDG	Reims Cessna F406 Caravan II	F406-0067	ex F-GEUG
Z-WKN	Cessna T207 Skywagon	20700243	ex VP-WKN
Operates for District Development Fund			

MAJESTIC AIR did not commence operations

SOUTHERN CROSS AVIATION

Victoria Falls (VFA)

Z-THL	Cessna U206F Stationair	U20603233	ex N8372Q
Z-WFA	Cessna T207 Staionair 8	20700098	ex VP-WFA

UNITED AIR CHARTERS

Unitair (UAC)

Harare Charles Prince

Z-BWK	Cessna U206G Stationair	U20603546	
Z-WKL	Cessna U206F Stationair	U20601707	ex ZS-ILV
Z-WMG	Cessna U206 Super Skywagon	U206-0323	ex VP-WMG
Z-WTA	Cessna U206F Stationair	U20602547	ex OO-SPX
Z-YHS	Cessna U206C Super Skywagon	U206-1029	ex VP-YHS
Z-UAC	Beech 58 Baron	TH-211	ex 9J-ADK
Z-UAS	Britten-Norman BN-2A Islander	162	ex CR-ALR
Z-UTD	Britten-Norman BN-2A Mk.III-2 Trislander		
		1055	ex A2-AGY
Z-WEX	Britten-Norman BN-2A Islander	619	ex VP-WEX
Z-WHG	Beech 95-D55 Baron	TE-761	ex VP-WHG
Z-WHH	Beech 65-80 Queen Air	LD-101	ex VP-WHH
Z-WHX	Britten-Norman BN-2A-7 Islander	192	ex VP-WHX
Z-WTF	Cessna 414A Chancellor	414A0062	ex G-METR
Z-WTG	Beech 58 Baron	TH-262	ex ZS-BSP

645

ZA - ALBANIA (Republic of Albania)

ADA AIR

Ada Air (ZY/ADE) (IATA 121)　　　　　　　　　　　　　　　　　　　　Tirana (TIA)

LZ-DOM	Yakovlev Yak-40	9620447			Lsd fr HMS
ZA-ADA	Embraer EMB.110P2 Bandeirante	110303	ex F-GCMQ		

ALBANIAN AIRLINES

Albanian (LV/LBC) (IATA 639)　　　　　　　　　　　　　　　　　　　Tirana (TIA)

LZ-DOB	Yakovlev Yak-40	9340432			Lsd fr HMS
YU-AJL	Douglas DC-9-32 (ABS 3)	695/47571	ex Z3-AAB	all-white	Lsd fr/op by JAT
ZA-MAK	British Aerospace 146 Srs.100	E1085	ex G-CCLN		
ZA-MAL	British Aerospace 146 Srs.200	E2054	ex G-BZWP		Lsd fr BAES; op by HMS
ZA-MEV	British Aerospace 146 Srs.300	E3197	ex VH-EWS		Op by HMS

ZK - NEW ZEALAND (Dominion of New Zealand)

AIR CHATHAMS

Chatham (CV/CVA)　　　　　　　　　　　　　　　　　　　Chatham Island (CHT)

ZK-CIA	Beech 65-B80 Queen Air	LD-430	ex N640K		
ZK-CIB	Convair 580	327A	ex C-FCIB		Lsd fr KFA
ZK-CIC	Swearingen SA.227AC Metro III	AC-623B	ex N623AV		Lsd to OGN
ZK-JSV	Swearingen SA.227DC Metro 23	DC-868B	ex C-FAFI		
ZK-KAI	Cessna U206G Stationair	U20603711			
ZK-KSA	Convair 580	507	ex C-GTTE		Lsd to Pionair

Air Chathams is the trading name of Air Transport (Chatham Islands) Ltd

AIR COROMANDEL　ceased operations

AIR FREIGHT NZ

　　　　　　　　　　　　　　　　　　　　　　　　Auckland-Intl (AKL)

ZK-FTA	Convair 580	168	ex C-GKFP	Freighter	Op for Parceline
ZK-KFH	Convair 580	42	ex C-FKFL	Freighter	
ZK-KFJ	Convair 580	114	ex C-GKFJ	Freighter	
ZK-KFL	Convair 580	372	ex C-FKFL	Freighter	Op for Parceline

AIR NAPIER

(NPR)　　　　　　　　　　　　　　　　　　　　　　　　Napier (NPE)

ZK-ELK	Piper PA-32-260 Cherokee Six	32-7600009	ex N8768C	
ZK-MSL	Piper PA-34-200T Seneca II	34-7770224	ex N5600V	
ZK-NPR	Piper PA-31 Turbo Navajo B	31-777	ex ZK-DOM	
ZK-WUG	Piper PA-34-200T Seneca II	34-7970329	ex N2891R	

AIR NATIONAL

　　　　　　　　　　　　　　　　　　　　　　　Auckland-Intl (AKL)

ZK-ECM	Embraer EMB.110P1 Bandeirante	110383	ex SE-KEL		
ZK-ECN	British Aerospace Jetstream 32EP	967	ex N967JS	City of Rotorua	Lsd fr BAES
ZK-ECP	British Aerospace Jetstream 32EP	878	ex VH-BAE		Lsd fr BAES
ZK-ECR	de Havilland DHC-8Q-202	475	ex ET-AKY		
ZK-NEZ	de Havilland DHC-8-102	60	ex C-GEOA		

AIR NELSON

Link (RLK)　　　　　　　　　　　　　　　　　　　　　　　Nelson (NSN)

Wholly owned by Air New Zealand; operates as part of Air New Zealand Link (q.v.).

AIR NEW ZEALAND

NewZealand (NZ/ANZ) (IATA 086)　　　　　　Auckland-Intl/Wellington-Intl (AKL/WLG)

ZK-OJA	Airbus Industrie A320-232	2085	ex F-WWIN	Lord of the Rings c/s	Lsd fr ILFC
ZK-OJB	Airbus Industrie A320-232	2090	ex F-WWBM		Lsd fr RBS Avn
ZK-OJC	Airbus Industrie A320-232	2112	ex F-WWDQ		Lsd fr RBS Avn
ZK-OJD	Airbus Industrie A320-232	2130	ex F-WWDK		Lsd fr RBS Avn
ZK-OJE	Airbus Industrie A320-232	2148	ex F-WWIH		Lsd fr RBS Avn
ZK-OJF	Airbus Industrie A320-232	2153	ex F-WWIS		Lsd fr RBS Avn
ZK-OJG	Airbus Industrie A320-232	2173	ex F-WWDJ	on order 04	Lsd fr ILFC
ZK-OJH	Airbus Industrie A320-232		ex F-WW	on order 04	Lsd fr RBS Avn

ZK-OJI	Airbus Industrie A320-232		ex F-WW	on order 04	Lsd fr RBS Avn
ZK-OJJ	Airbus Industrie A320-232		ex F-WW	on order 04	Lsd fr ILFC
ZK-OJK	Airbus Industrie A320-232		ex F-WW	on order 04	
ZK-OJL	Airbus Industrie A320-232		ex F-WW	on order 04	

Four more Airbus Industrie A320-232s are on order for delivery in 2005 (ZK-OJM-P)

ZK-FRE	Boeing 737-3U3	2992/28742	ex N360PR		Lsd fr GECAS
ZK-NGA	Boeing 737-33R	2975/28873	ex N1787B		Lsd fr GECAS
ZK-NGB	Boeing 737-36Q	3013/29140			Lsd fr Boullioun
ZK-NGC	Boeing 737-36Q	3057/29189			Lsd fr Boullioun
ZK-NGD	Boeing 737-3U3	2966/28732	ex N930WA		
ZK-NGE	Boeing 737-3U3	2969/28733	ex N931WA		Lsd fr debis
ZK-NGF	Boeing 737-3U3	2974/28734	ex N309FL		Lsd fr debis
ZK-NGG	Boeing 737-319	3123/25606	ex N1795B		
ZK-NGH	Boeing 737-319	3126/25607			
ZK-NGI	Boeing 737-319	3128/25608			
ZK-NGJ	Boeing 737-319	3130/25609		Last 737-300 built	
ZK-NGK	Boeing 737-3K2	2731/26318	ex PH-TSX		Lsd fr ILFC
ZK-NGM	Boeing 737-3K2	2722/28085	ex PH-TSY		Lsd fr ILFC
ZK-NGN	Boeing 737-33S	3012/29072	ex (N308L)		Lsd fr Pembroke
ZK-NGO	Boeing 737-37Q	2961/28548	ex G-OAMS		Lsd fr GECAS

ZK-NBS	Boeing 747-419	756/24386	ex (ZK-NZE)	Mataatua	
ZK-NBT	Boeing 747-419	815/24855	ex N6018N		
ZK-NBU	Boeing 747-419	933/25605			
ZK-NBV	Boeing 747-419	1180/26910		Lord of the Rings c/s	
ZK-NBW	Boeing 747-419	1228/29375			Lsd fr ILFC
ZK-SUH	Boeing 747-419	855/24896	ex N891LF		Lsd fr ILFC
ZK-SUI	Boeing 747-441	971/24957	ex N821LF		Lsd fr ILFC
ZK-SUJ	Boeing 747-4F6	1161/27602	ex N756PR	Lord of the Rings c/s	Lsd fr ILFC

ZK-NBA	Boeing 767-219ER	124/23326	ex VH-RMC	Aotearoa	
ZK-NBB	Boeing 767-219ER	134/23327	ex N6055X	Arahina	
ZK-NBC	Boeing 767-219ER	149/23328	ex N6009F	Atarau	
ZK-NCF	Boeing 767-319ER	413/24876			Lsd fr ILFC
ZK-NCG	Boeing 767-319ER	509/26912			
ZK-NCH	Boeing 767-319ER	555/26264			Lsd fr ILFC
ZK-NCI	Boeing 767-319ER	558/26913	ex N6009F		
ZK-NCJ	Boeing 767-319ER	574/26915	ex N6018N		
ZK-NCK	Boeing 767-319ER	663/26971			
ZK-NCL	Boeing 767-319ER	677/28745			
ZK-NCN	Boeing 767-319ER	785/29388			Lsd fr ILFC
ZK-NCO	Boeing 767-319ER	808/30586			Lsd fr ILFC

Owns 77% of Mount Cook Airlines and 50% of Eagle Airways while Air Nelson is wholly owned. These three operate as Air New Zealand Link in full colours. Air New Zealand Express is wholly owned subsidiary operating domestic services, first service 27 October 2002. 4.99% owned by Qantas who plan to purchase 22.5% but plans blocked by administrators. Member of Star Alliance

---

AIR NEW ZEALAND LINK

New Zealand (NZ/NZA)   **Christchurch-Intl/Nelson/Hamilton (CHC/NSN/HLZ)**

ZK-MCA	Aerospatiale/Alenia ATR 72-212A	597	ex F-WQKC	Mount Cook	
ZK-MCB	Aerospatiale/Alenia ATR 72-212A	598	ex F-WQKG	Mount Cook	
ZK-MCF	Aerospatiale/Alenia ATR 72-212A	600	ex F-WQKH	Mount Cook	
ZK-MCJ	Aerospatiale/Alenia ATR 72-212A	624	ex F-WQKI	Mount Cook	
ZK-MCO	Aerospatiale/Alenia ATR 72-212A	628	ex F-WQKJ	Mount Cook	
ZK-MCP	Aerospatiale/Alenia ATR 72-212A	630	ex F-WQKK	Mount Cook	
ZK-MCU	Aerospatiale/Alenia ATR 72-212A	632	ex F-WQKL	Mount Cook	
ZK-MCW	Aerospatiale/Alenia ATR 72-212A	646	ex F-WQMG	Mount Cook	
ZK-MCX	Aerospatiale/Alenia ATR 72-212A	687	ex F-WQMN	Mount Cook	
ZK-MCY	Aerospatiale/Alenia ATR 72-212A	703	ex F-WQMR	Mount Cook	

ZK-EAA	Beech 1900D	UE-424	ex N2335Y	Eagle	Lsd fr Raytheon
ZK-EAB	Beech 1900D	UE-425	ex N2335Z	Eagle	Lsd fr Raytheon
ZK-EAC	Beech 1900D	UE-426	ex N51226	Eagle	Lsd fr Raytheon
ZK-EAD	Beech 1900D	UE-427	ex N50127	Eagle	Lsd fr Raytheon
ZK-EAE	Beech 1900D	UE-428	ex N3188L	Eagle	Lsd fr Raytheon
ZK-EAF	Beech 1900D	UE-429	ex N50069	Eagle	Lsd fr Raytheon
ZK-EAG	Beech 1900D	UE-430	ex N50430	Eagle	Lsd fr Raytheon
ZK-EAH	Beech 1900D	UE-431	ex N51321	Eagle	Lsd fr Raytheon
ZK-EAI	Beech 1900D	UE-432	ex N5032L	Eagle	Lsd fr Raytheon
ZK-EAJ	Beech 1900D	UE-433	ex N4469Q	Eagle	Lsd fr Raytheon
ZK-EAK	Beech 1900D	UE-434	ex N4474P	Eagle	Lsd fr Raytheon
ZK-EAL	Beech 1900D	UE-435	ex N50815	Eagle	Lsd fr Raytheon
ZK-EAM	Beech 1900D	UE-436	ex N5016C	Eagle	Lsd fr Raytheon
ZK-EAN	Beech 1900D	UE-437	ex N50307	Eagle	Lsd fr Raytheon
ZK-EAO	Beech 1900D	UE-438	ex N4470D	Eagle	Lsd fr Raytheon
ZK-EAP	Beech 1900D	UE-439	ex N50899	Eagle	Lsd fr Raytheon

ZK-FXA	SAAB SF.340A	120	ex HB-AHP	Air Nelson	
ZK-FXB	SAAB SF.340A	122	ex HB-AHQ	Air Nelson	

ZK-FXD	SAAB SF.340A	088	ex HB-AHN	Air Nelson	
ZK-NLC	SAAB SF.340A	132	ex SE-LMT	Air Nelson	Lsd fr SAAB
ZK-NLE	SAAB SF.340A	067	ex SE-ISX	Air Nelson	
ZK-NLG	SAAB SF.340A	151	ex VH-LPI	Air Nelson	Lsd fr SAAB
ZK-NLH	SAAB SF.340A	137	ex SE-ISN	Air Nelson	
ZK-NLI	SAAB SF.340A	159	ex SE-KRN	Air Nelson	Lsd fr SKX
ZK-NLM	SAAB SF.340A	038	ex VH-ZLZ	Air Nelson	
ZK-NLN	SAAB SF.340A	136	ex N136AN	Air Nelson	Lsd fr MCC Financial
ZK-NLO	SAAB SF.340A	153	ex N153AN	Air Nelson	Lsd fr MCC Financial
ZK-NLP	SAAB SF.340A	042	ex SE-ISU	Air Nelson	
ZK-NLQ	SAAB SF.340A	124	ex D-CDID	Air Nelson	
ZK-NLR	SAAB SF.340A	097	ex SE-ISZ	Air Nelson	
ZK-NLS	SAAB SF.340A	134	ex HB-AHT	Air Nelson	Lsd fr SAAB
ZK-NLT	SAAB SF.340A	116	ex D-CDIC	Air Nelson	
ZK-NSK	SAAB SF.340A	084	ex HB-AHM	Air Nelson	

Services are operated by Air Nelson (wholly owned), Eagle Airways (50% owned) and Mount Cook Airlines (77% owned). The Beech 1900Ds replace the Bandeirantes and Metros

AIR POST

Post (PST)   Auckland-Intl/Christchurch/Nelson/Wellington-Intl (AKL/CHC/NSN/WLG)

ZK-NSS	Swearingen SA.227AC Metro III	AC-692B	ex N2707D		
ZK-POA	Swearingen SA.227AC Metro III	AC-551B	ex D-CABF		
ZK-POB	Swearingen SA.227AC Metro III	AC-606B	ex D-CABG		
ZK-POE	Swearingen SA.227CC Metro 23	CC-843B	ex N30228		
ZK-POF	Swearingen SA.227CC Metro 23	CC-844B	ex N30229		
ZK-NAO	Fokker F.27 Friendship 500	10364	ex 9V-BFK		
ZK-NQC	Boeing 737-219C (Nordam 3)	928/22994		all-white	
ZK-POH	Fokker F.27 Friendship 500	10680	ex VT-NEH		

A joint venture between New Zealand Post and Airwork (NZ) 1984 Ltd; all freighters

AIR RAROTONGA

(GZ)   Rarotonga (RAR)

ZK-EFS	SAAB SF.340	049	ex G-GNTA	Lsd fr SAAB
ZK-FTS	Embraer EMB.110P1 Bandeirante	110239	ex N107CA	
ZK-TAI	Embraer EMB.110P1 Bandeirante	110387	ex N134EM	
ZK-TAK	Embraer EMB.110P1 Bandeirante	110448	ex VH-KHA	

AIR SAFARIS & SERVICES

Airsafari (SRI)   Lake Tekapo

ZK-FJH	Cessna P206E Super Skywagon	206-0634		
ZK-NMC	GAF N24A Nomad	N24A-034	ex VH-DHP	
ZK-NMD	GAF N24A Nomad	N24A-060	ex VH-DHU	
ZK-NME	GAF N24A Nomad	N24A-122	ex 5W-FAT	
ZK-SAF	Gippsland GA-8 Airvan	GA8-02-017	ex VH-AAP	
ZK-SEU	Cessna 207A Stationair 8	20700713	ex ZK-EWC	
ZK-SEY	Cessna T207A Turbo Stationair 8	20700661	ex N76012	
ZK-SRI	Cessna 208B Caravan I	208B0636	ex N208PR	

AIR WANGANUI COMMUTER

Wanganui (WAG)

| ZK-WLV | Beech 58 Baron | TH-698 | ex VH-WLV | |
| ZK-WTH | Piper PA-31P-350 Mojave | 31P-8414003 | ex N9187Y | |

AIRWORK NEW ZEALAND

(PST)   Auckland-Ardmore/Christchurch/Wellington (AMZ/CHC/WLG)

ZK-EBT	Piper PA-31-350 Navajo Chieftain	31-7552044	ex N59929		
ZK-FOP	Piper PA-31-350 Navajo Chieftain	31-7405227	ex N888SG	EMS	Op for Childflight Trust
ZK-FPL	Piper PA-31T3-T1040	31T-8475001	ex N2464W		
ZK-HLF	MBB BK.117B-1	1070	ex JA6641		
ZK-LFT	Swearingen SA.227AC Metro III	AC-582	ex ZK-PAA	EMS	Op for Childflight Trust
ZK-PAX	Fokker F.27 Friendship 500	10596	ex HB-ILJ		
ZK-SLA	Boeing 737-377	1260/23653	ex VH-CZA		Lsd fr Airlift Trading

Owns 50% of Air Post which operates on Airwork (NZ) ICAO's designator

ASPIRING AIR

(OI)   Wanaka (WKA)

| ZK-EVO | Britten-Norman BN-2A-26 Islander | 785 | ex 5W-FAQ | |
| ZK-EVT | Britten-Norman BN-2A-26 Islander | 152 | ex YJ-RV19 | Lake Wanaka |

EAGLE AIRWAYS

(EX)   *Hamilton (HLZ)*

50% owned by Air New Zealand; operates as part of Air New Zealand Link (q.v.)

FLIGHT CORPORATION

Flightcorp (FCP)   *Nelson (NSN)*

ZK-OSE	Cessna 207 Skywagon	20700226	ex VH-SBT

FLIGHT 2000

Ardmore (AMZ)

ZK-DAK	Douglas DC-3	15035/26480	ex VH-SBT	RAF D-Day colours

FREEDOM AIR

Free Air (SJ/FOM)   *Auckland-Intl (AKL)*

ZK-FDM	Boeing 737-3M8	2004/25016	ex HB-IIC	
ZK-SJB	Boeing 737-33R	2881/28868	ex PP-SFK	Lsd fr ORIX
ZK-SJC	Boeing 737-3U3	2988/28738	ex N308FL	Lsd fr GECAS
ZK-SJE	Boeing 737-3K2	2721/27635	ex PH-TSZ	

Owned by Mount Cook Airline

GREAT BARRIER AIRLINES

(GB)   *Auckland-Intl (AKL)*

ZK-CNS	Piper PA-32-260 Cherokee Six	32-686		Stitchbird
ZK-ENZ	Piper PA-32-260 Cherokee Six	32-1117	ex ZK-DBP	Tomtit
ZK-FVD	Britten-Norman BN-2A-26 Islander	316	ex G-BJWN	NZ Pigeon
ZK-LGC	Britten-Norman BN-2A Mk III-1 Trislander	381	ex VH-NKW	
ZK-LGR	Britten-Norman BN-2A Mk III-1 Trislander	372	ex VH-BSP	
ZK-NAD	GAF Nomad N24A	N24A-30	ex VH-DHF	Koka
ZK-NSN	Piper PA-31 Turbo Navajo	31-687	ex VH-CFP	Bellbird
ZK-PLA	Partenavia P.68B	86	ex A6-ALO	Tui
ZK-RDT	Embraer EMB.820C Navajo	820517	ex PT-RDT	
ZK-REA	Britten-Norman BN-2A-26 Islander	43	ex ZK-FWH	Brown Teal

HELICOPTERS NEW ZEALAND

Nelson (NSN)

ZK-HBV	Aerospatiale AS.350D Ecureuil	1265	ex N3208R
ZK-HDE	Aerospatiale AS.350BA Ecureuil	1491	ex N5449B
ZK-HDK	Aerospatiale AS.350BA Ecureuil	1466	ex F-ODVZ
ZK-HDQ	Aerospatiale AS.350BA Ecureuil	1932	ex VH-BHX
ZK-HDR	Aerospatiale AS.350B2 Ecureuil	2382	ex HB-XJC
ZK-HDV	Aerospatiale AS.350B3 Ecureuil	3195	ex HB-ZBR
ZK-HFE	Aerospatiale AS.350BA Ecureuil	2518	
ZK-HFH	Aerospatiale AS.350BA Ecureuil	2132	ex VH-WCU
ZK-HFK	Aerospatiale AS.350B Ecureuil	1397	ex VH-WCD
ZK-HJE	Aerospatiale AS.350BA Ecureuil	1307	
ZK-HJQ	Aerospatiale AS.350D Ecureuil	1295	ex C-FBXE
ZK-HJY	Aerospatiale AS.350BA Ecureuil	2005	ex JA9463
ZK-HKR	Aerospatiale AS.350D Ecureuil	1234	ex N3606X
ZK-HND	Aerospatiale AS.350B Ecureuil	1661	ex VH-HRD
ZK-HNE	Aerospatiale AS.350B2 Ecureuil	2811	ex HB-XLJ
ZK-HNG	Aerospatiale AS.350B3 Ecureuil	3190	ex HB-ZBH
ZK-HNK	Aerospatiale AS.350B2 Ecureuil	2349	ex VH-WCS
ZK-HNL	Aerospatiale AS.350B Ecureuil	1550	
ZK-HNN	Aerospatiale AS.350B Ecureuil	1572	ex VH-WCG
ZK-HNQ	Aerospatiale AS.350BA Ecureuil	1972	ex JA9450
ZK-HNU	Aerospatiale AS.350BA Ecureuil	1120	ex N3595G
ZK-HNX	Aerospatiale AS.350BA Ecureuil	1828	ex RP-C2777
ZK-HNZ	Aerospatiale AS.350B2 Ecureuil	2463	ex HB-XVT
ZK-HZK	Aerospatiale AS.350B Ecureuil	1827	
ZK-HDA	Bell 412	33066	ex N626LH
ZK-HNI	Bell 412SP	33204	ex 9M-AYW
ZK-HNO	Bell 212	31139	ex VH-BQH
ZK-HZE	Bell 206B JetRanger	769	ex C-FTPG

HELI–HARVEST

ER-MHA	Mil Mi-8MTV-1	95626	ex RA-25481
ER-MHH	Mil Mi-8MTV-1	96121	ex RA-25746
ER-MHZ	Mil Mi-8MTV-1	96078	ex RA-22503

HELIPRO

Helipro (HPR)   *Palmerston North (PMR)*

ZK-HRS	Bell 206B JetRanger	877	ex JA9087
ZK-HYD	Aerospatiale AS.350D Ecureuil	1258	ex N36079
ZK-HYG	Bell UH-1H	4568	ex N205HA
ZK-HYN	Aerospatiale AS.355F1 Ecureuil 2	5286	ex JA9588
ZK-HYO	Aerospatiale AS.350D Ecureuil	1186	ex N155EH
ZK-HYW	Aerospatiale AS.350D Ecureuil	1420	ex N5782G
ZK-HYZ	Kawasaki/MBB BK117A-3	1010	ex ZK-HRQ

JETCONNECT

Qantas Jetconnect (QNZ)   *Auckland-Intl (AKL)*

ZK-CZR	Boeing 737-33A	1831/24460	ex VH-CZR	Lsd fr QFA
ZK-CZS	Boeing 737-33A	1654/24030	ex VH-CZS	Lsd fr QFA
ZK-CZU	Boeing 737-33A	2600/27267	ex VH-CZU	Lsd fr QFA
ZK-JNA	Boeing 737-376	1390/23490	ex VH-TAY	Lsd fr QFA
ZK-JNE	Boeing 737-33A	2069/25119	ex VH-JNE	Lsd fr QFA
ZK-JNF	Boeing 737-376	1286/23486	ex VH-TAU	Lsd fr QFA
ZK-JNG	Boeing 737-376	1251/23478	ex VH-TAG	Lsd fr QFA
ZK-JNH	Boeing 737-376	1352/23488	ex VH-TAW	Lsd fr QFA

Wholly owned by Qantas and operates in full colours

LAKELAND HELICOPTERS

ZK-HCH	Bell 206B JetRanger III	2258	ex N16859
ZK-HIX	Bell 206B JetRanger	869	ex N-YDA
ZK-HSP	Bell UH-1H	5352	ex N226MS
ZK-HWO	Bell 206B JetRanger	838	ex N38AL
ZK-HZX	Bell UH-1H	11892	ex N3061A

MILFORD SOUND FLIGHTSEEING

ZK-DBV	Britten-Norman BN-2A Islander	164	ex VH-EQX	
ZK-MCD	Britten-Norman BN-2A-26 Islander	719	ex G-BCAG	
ZK-MCE	Britten-Norman BN-2A-26 Islander	724	ex G-BCHB	
ZK-MFN	Britten-Norman BN-2B-27 Islander	2168	ex N2407B	
ZK-MSF	Britten-Norman BN-2A-26 Islander	2037	ex OY-PPP	
ZK-ZQN	Britten-Norman BN-2B-26 Islander	2197	ex G-BLNW	on order
ZK-LAW	Cessna 207A Stationair 8	20700723	ex N9750M	

MILFORD SOUND SCENIC FLIGHTS

ZK-DEW	Cessna 207 Skywagon	20700161	ex VH-UBQ
ZK-DRY	Cessna 207 Skywagon	20700196	ex 5W-FAL
ZK-SEW	Cessna T207A Stationair 6	20700584	ex N73394
ZK-SEX	Cessna T207A Stationair 6	20700609	ex N73622
ZK-WET	Cessna 207A Skywagon	20700375	ex VH-SLD
ZK-OBL	Britten-Norman BN-2A-20 Islander	2035	ex VH-OBL

MOUNTAIN AIR

ZK-DOV	Cessna 206 Super Skywagon	206-0248	ex N5248U
ZK-PIW	Piper PA-23-250 Aztec E	27-7305089	ex VH-RCI
ZK-PIX	Piper PA-23-250 Aztec E	27-4738	ex N14174
ZK-PIY	Britten-Norman BN-2A-20 Islander	344	ex JA5218
ZK-PIZ	Britten-Norman BN-2B-26 Islander	2012	ex N2132M

MOUNT COOK AIRLINE

Mountcook (NM/NZM) (IATA 445)   Christchurch-Intl (CHC)

77% owned by Air New Zealand; operates scheduled services as Air New Zealand Link in full colours using NZ flight numbers

ORIGIN PACIFIC AIRWAYS

Origin (QO/OGN)   Nelson (NSN)

ZK-JSE	British Aerospace Jetstream 41	41046	ex C-FTVI	
ZK-JSK	British Aerospace Jetstream 41	41049	ex C-FTVK	
ZK-JSM	British Aerospace Jetstream 41	41052	ex C-FTVN	
ZK-JSN	British Aerospace Jetstream 41	41053	ex C-FTVP	on order 02
ZK-NSO	British Aerospace Jetstream 41	41056	ex C-FTVQ	
ZK-JSA	British Aerospace Jetstream 31	839	ex G-GLAM	Lsd fr Inglis Aircraft
ZK-JSH	British Aerospace Jetstream 31	838	ex G-IBLW	Lsd fr Inglis Aircraft
ZK-JSI	British Aerospace Jetstream 31	761	ex G-LOGV	
ZK-JSQ	British Aerospace Jetstream 32EP	968	ex ZK-REW	Lsd fr BAES
ZK-JSR	British Aerospace Jetstream 32EP	969	ex ZK-RES	Lsd fr BAES
ZK-JSU	British Aerospace Jetstream 32EP	946	ex ZK-TPC	Lsd fr BAES
ZK-JSY	Aerospatiale/Alenia ATR 72-212	379	ex D-ACCC	Lsd fr Flair Avn
ZK-JSZ	Aerospatiale/Alenia ATR 72-212	385	ex D-ADDD	Lsd fr Flair Avn

PACIFIC BLUE

(PBI)

ZK-PBA	Boeing 737-8FE	1377/33796	ex VH-VOO	Lsd fr VOZ
ZK-PBB	Boeing 737-8FE	1389/33797	ex VH-VOP	Lsd fr VOZ
ZK-PBC	Boeing 737-8BK	1446/33017	ex VH-VOX	Lsd fr VOZ
ZK-	Boeing 737-8FE	1391/33798	ex VH-VOQ	Lsd fr VOZ

Wholly owned subsidiary of Virgin Blue

PIONAIR ADVENTURES

Queenstown (ZQN)

ZK-AMS	Douglas DC-3	9286	ex VH-PWN (1)	Dulcie
ZK-AMY	Douglas DC-3	13506	ex VH-CAN	
ZK-AWP	Douglas DC-3	16387/33135	ex 5W-FAI	
ZK-KSA	Convair 580	507	ex C-GTTE	Lsd fr Air Chathams
ZK-PAL	Convair 580	501	ex N631AR	

SALT AIR

Auckland-Intl (AKL)

ZK-FOO	Cessna 207 Skywagon	20700075	ex P2-SED	
ZK-HBC	Bell 206B JetRanger	2112		
ZK-JCB	Cessna U206C Super Skywagon	U206-0922	ex VH-LCJ	

SOUNDSAIR

Wellington (WLG)

ZK-ENT	Cessna U206G Stationair	U20603667	ex N7551N
ZK-KLC	Gippsland GA-8 Airvan	GA8-03-040	ex VH-BQR
ZK-PDM	Cessna 208 Caravan I	20800240	ex N1289N
ZK-REA	Britten-Norman BN-2A-26 Islander	43	ex ZK-FWH

SOUTH EAST AIR

Invercargill (IVC)

ZK-DIV	Piper PA-32-260 Cherokee Six	32-7400015	ex N57306
ZK-FWZ	Britten-Norman BN-2A-26 Islander	52	ex T3-ATH
ZK-FXE	Britten-Norman BN-2A-26 Islander	110	ex F-OCFR
ZK-JEM	Cessna A185E Skywagon	18501780	
ZK-RTS	Piper PA-32-300 Cherokee Six	32-7340070	

TOURISM FLIGHTSEEING now listed as Milford Sound Flightseeing and The Helicopter Line

THE HELICOPTER LINE

ZK-HKF	Aerospatiale AS.355F1 Ecureuil 2	5200	ex VH-HJK
ZK-HKY	Aerospatiale AS.355F1 Ecureuil 2	5123	ex N909CH
ZK-HMI	Aerospatiale AS.355F1 Ecureuil 2	5029	ex N5775Y
ZK-HML	Aerospatiale AS.355F1 Ecureuil 2	5032	ex N5776A
ZK-HPE	Aerospatiale AS.355F1 Ecureuil 2	5229	ex N58021
ZK-HPI	Aerospatiale AS.355F1 Ecureuil 2	5211	ex N5802N
ZK-HPZ	Aerospatiale AS.355F1 Ecureuil 2	5107	ex N87906
ZK-HAH	Aerospatiale AS.350BA Ecureuil	1615	ex VH-EBB
ZK-HMM	Aerospatiale AS.350BA Ecureuil	2436	ex ZK-IWJ

VINCENT AVIATION

ZK-CII	Reims Cessna F406 Caravan II	F406-0012	ex 5Y-WAW	
ZK-VAA	Reims Cessna F406 Caravan II	f4060012	ex ZK-CII	
ZK-VAB	Beech 1900D	UE-302	ex ZK-JND	
ZK-VAE	Beech 1900C	UC-56	ex VH-OST	Op for UN; based DRW
ZK-VAF	Reims Cessna F406 Caravan II	F406-0057	ex F-ODYZ	

ZP - PARAGUAY (Republic of Paraguay)

AEROLINEAS PARAGUAYAS / ARPA

Arpa (A8/PAY)

ZP-CAD	Cessna 208B Caravan I	208B0621	ex N5260Y
ZP-CAR	Cessna 208 Caravan I	20800033	ex PT-OGZ

Wholly owned by TAM Group, Brazil

TAM PARAGUAY

Paraguaya (PZ/LAP) (IATA 692)

Operates services with Fokker 100 aircraft leased from parent company, TAM Brasil, as required
TAM Paraguay is the trading name of Transportes Aereos del Mercosur

ZS - SOUTH AFRICA (Republic of South Africa)

AERONEXUS

ZS-ANX	Boeing 737-217	20197	ex N780TJ	on order
ZS-TIC	McDonnell-Douglas MD-82	1203/49233	ex N932AS	1 Time
ZS-TOC	McDonnell-Douglas MD-82	1204/49234	ex N933AS	1 Time

AIRQUARIUS AVIATION

Quarius (AQU)

ZS-BAL	Fokker F.28 Fellowship 4000	11190	ex SE-DGO		Lsd fr Shanike Invest; sublsd LVB
ZS-DRF	Fokker F.28 Friendship 4000	11239	ex 5Y-LLL		Lsd fr Foster Aero Intl
ZS-GAV	Fokker F.28 Fellowship 4000	11191	ex SE-DGP		Lsd fr Shanike Investments
ZS-JAL	Fokker F.28 Fellowship 3000	11151	ex V5-KEA	stored HLA	
ZS-JAP	Fokker F.28 Fellowship 3000	11143	ex V5-KEX	stored HLA	
ZS-JAS	Fokker F.28 Fellowship 4000	11225	ex 5H-JAZ	Bella Donna	Lsd to UN
ZS-JAV	Fokker F.28 Fellowship 4000	11183	ex VH-AHT		
ZS-JEN	Fokker F.28 Fellowship 4000	11204	ex SE-DGR		
ZS-JES	Fokker F.28 Fellowship 4000	11236	ex SE-DGS	Op for UN, based ISB	
ZS-OPS	Fokker F.28 Fellowship 4000	11241	ex SE-DGU		Lsd fr Shanike Invest
ZS-XGV	Fokker F.28 Fellowship 4000	11128	ex SE-DGM		
ZS-XGW	Fokker F.28 Fellowship 4000	11130	ex SE-DGN		Lsd to TSG
ZS-XGX	Fokker F.28 Fellowship 4000	11115	ex SE-DGF		

Two operate for South African Airlink

VH-IMJ	Hawker Siddeley.748 Srs.2B/426	1799	ex 9N-ACX		Lsd fr HZA
ZS-IRS	Boeing 727-223A (Raisbeck 3)		ex N		Lsd to LVB
ZS-NPX	Boeing 727-23F	218/19131	ex N512FE		Lsd fr Mic-Dav Air
ZS-OJE	Douglas DC-3	16096/32844	ex 5Y-AAE		
ZS-XGE	Hawker Siddeley 748 Srs.2A/351	1770	ex G-BGPR		
ZS-XGY	Hawker Siddeley 748 Srs.2A/344	1764	ex TN-AFI	stored JNB	
ZS-XGZ	Hawker Siddeley 748 Srs.2A/286LFD	1740	ex 5H-WDL		

Specialise in short term leases to other African operators

AIRWORLD

Speed Service (SPZ)   Pretoria-Wonderboom (PRY)

ZS-OBN	Boeing 727-232F (FedEx 3)	920/20637	ex N68782	Lsd fr SFR

Operate for Speed Service Couriers

CAMPION AVIATION believed to have ceased operations

CENTRAL AIR CARGO ceased operations

CHARLAN AIR CHARTERS

(S8/CAH)   Johannesburg-Grand Central (GCJ)

ZS-CAB	Embraer EMB.120ER Brasilia	120098	ex (3D-BIN)	
ZS-CAC	Swearingen SA.227BC Metro III	BC-780B	ex XA-SCI	
ZS-CAE	Embraer EMB.120ER Brasilia	120078	ex C-GOAB	
ZS-OMV	Swearingen SA.227BC Metro III	BC-773B	ex XA-RVS	Lsd fr Brazprops 17 (Pty)

CHC AIR

Court Air (CUT)   Cape Town-International (CPT)

ZS-KEI	Convair 580	141	ex N5822
ZS-LYL	Convair 580	39	ex N511GA

Associated with CHC Helicopters

CHC HELICOPTERS (AFRICA)

Cape Town-International (CPT)

ZS-HSZ	Sikorsky S-61N	61473	ex 8Q-BUZ	
ZS-HVJ	Sikorsky S-61N	61493	ex N9119Z	
ZS-RDV	Sikorsky S-61N	61716	ex G-BIHH	
ZS-RLK	Sikorsky S-61N	61772	ex G-BEWM	
ZS-RLL	Sikorsky S-61N	61778	ex G-BFFK	
ZS-HNU	Sikorsky S-76A	760073	ex N721EW	Op in Brazil as PT-YVM
ZS-RBE	Sikorsky S-76A	760268	ex V5-HAB	Lsd to Sonair as D2-EXH
ZS-REI	Sikorsky S-76A	760016	ex (ZS-RNS)	
ZS-RGZ	Sikorsky S-76A	760051	ex VH-EMM	Op in Brazil as PT-YQM
ZS-RJK	Sikorsky S-76A	760067	ex VH-EMN	Op in Brazil as PT-YGM
ZS-RJS	Sikorsky S-76A	760160	ex 5N-DGS	Lsd to Sonair as D2-EXF
ZS-RKE	Sikorsky S-76A	760042	ex LX-HUD	Lsd to Sonair as D2-EXG
ZS-RKO	Sikorsky S-76A	760135	ex VH-LAX	
ZS-RKP	Sikorsky S-76A	760198	ex VH-LAY	
ZS-RNG	Sikorsky S-76A	760036	ex G-CHCE	Lsd to Sonair as D2-EXJ
ZS-RNT	Sikorsky S-76A	760131	ex C-GIMU	
ZS-RPI	Sikorsky S-76A+	760049	ex G-BHGK	
ZS-HJN	Bell 206L-1 LongRanger II	45571		
ZS-RDI	Bell 206L-3 LongRanger III	51392	ex N521EV	
ZS-RGV	Bell 212	30952	ex C-FRUU	
ZS-RKL	MBB Bo105DB	S-35	ex G-BAFD	
ZS-RNP	Bell 212	30893	ex C-FPKW	based Malabo
ZS-RNR	Bell 212	30829	ex C-FRWL	based Malabo

A member of CHC Helicopter Corp

CIVAIR

(CIW)   Cape Town

ZS-	Douglas DC-9-32	750/47643	ex 9L-LDH	stored JNB

Also operates light twins and helicopters

COMAIR

Commercial (MN/CAW) (IATA 161)   Johannesburg-Jan Smuts (JNB)

ZS-NNG	Boeing 737-236	635/21793	ex PH-TSE		Lsd fr Boullioun
ZS-NNH	Boeing 737-236	653/21797	ex PH-TSD		
ZS-OKB	Boeing 737-376	1225/23477	ex VH-TAF		
ZS-OKC	Boeing 737-376	1270/23484	ex VH-TAJ		
ZS-OKD	Boeing 737-236	677/21803	ex G-BGDO		Lsd fr GECAS
ZS-OKE	Boeing 737-236	710/21807	ex G-BGDT		Lsd fr Laroc Avn
ZS-OKF	Boeing 737-2L9	550/21686	ex V5-ANB	Desert Rose	Lsd fr SFR
ZS-OKG	Boeing 737-376	1264/23483	ex VH-TAI		
ZS-OLA	Boeing 737-236	1058/23163	ex G-BKYE		
ZS-OLB	Boeing 737-236	1074/23167	ex G-BKYI		
ZS-OLC	Boeing 737-230	714/22119	ex N219AS		Lsd fr SFR

ZS-OTF	Boeing 737-436	2147/25305	ex G-DOCC		Lsd fr SFR: op by Kulula
ZS-OTG	Boeing 737-436	2197/25840	ex G-DOCJ		Lsd fr SFR:op by Kulula
ZS-OTH	Boeing 737-436	2222/25841	ex G-DOCK		Lsd fr SFR; op by Kulula
ZS-SBN	Boeing 737-244	214/20229	ex (ZS-FKH)		
ZS-SBO	Boeing 737-244	250/20329			
ZS-SBR	Boeing 737-244	260/20331		Back-up aircraft	
ZS-SIN	Boeing 737-236	670/21802	ex CC-CHS		Lsd fr SFR
ZS-SIP	Boeing 737-230	701/22116	ex N392AS		Lsd fr SFR
ZS-SIR	Boeing 737-236	697/21805	ex G-BGDR		Lsd fr SFR
ZS-SIS	Boeing 737-236	669/21801	ex G-BGDL		Lsd fr SFR
ZS-NVR	Boeing 727-230	922/20673	ex 5N-NEC	stored JNB	Op for UN

British Airways franchise carrier, operates in BA Union Flag c/s
Kulula.com is a low-cost wholly owned subsidiary operating Boeing 737s although switching to MD-83s leased from Safair

DHL AVIATION
Worldstar (DHV) — Lanseria (HLA)

ZS-ADL	Cessna 208B Caravan I	208B0381	ex 5Y-TAS	DHL c/s	Lsd fr/op by Solenta Avn
ZS-NIZ	Cessna 208B Caravan I	208B0353	ex 5Y-NIZ	DHL c/s	Lsd fr/op by Solenta Avn
ZS-NYR	Cessna 208B Caravan I	208B0382	ex N10YR	DHL c/s	Lsd fr/op by Solenta Avn
ZS-OBY	Cessna 208B Caravan I	208B0345	ex 9Q-COI	DHL c/s	Lsd fr/op by Solenta Avn
ZS-OER	Cessna 208B Caravan I	208B0296	ex 5Y-BNB	DHL c/s	Lsd fr/op by Solenta Avn
ZS-OFK	Cessna 208B Caravan I	208B0668	ex 7Q-YKR	DHL c/s	Lsd fr/op by Solenta Avn
ZS-OJF	Cessna 208B Caravan I	208B0481	ex N72ED	DHL c/s	Lsd fr/op by Solenta Avn
ZS-ORI	Cessna 208B Caravan I	208B0525	ex N208BC	DHL c/s	Lsd fr/op by Solenta Avn
ZS-ORK	Cessna 208B Caravan I	208B0336	ex D4-CBJ	DHL c/s	Lsd fr/op by Solenta Avn
ZS-OTV	Cessna 208B Caravan I	208B0545	ex PT-MHE	DHL c/s	Lsd fr/op by Solenta Avn
ZS-SLO	Cessna 208B Caravan I	208B0485	ex F-OGXI	DHL c/s	Lsd fr/op by Solenta Avn
ZS-SLR*	Cessna 208B Caravan I	208B0497	ex N497AC	DHL c/s	Lsd fr/op by Solenta Avn
ZS-SLT	Cessna 208B Caravan I	208B0459	ex F-OGXK	DHL c/s	Lsd fr/op by Solenta Avn
5Y-BNH	Cessna 208B Caravan I	208B0385	ex ZS-NYS	DHL c/s	Lsd fr/op by Solenta Avn
5Y-NHB	Cessna 208B Caravan I	208B0328	ex ZS-NHB	DHL c/s	Lsd fr/op by Solenta Avn
9J-DHL	Cessna 208B Caravan I	208B0261	ex ZS-NOM	DHL c/s	Lsd fr/op by Solenta Avn
ZS-ATR	Aerospatiale/Alenia ATR 42-300	060	ex PH-XLC		Lsd fr/op by Solenta Avn
ZS-OVP	Aerospatiale/Alenia ATR 42-300	088	ex F-WQNG		Lsd fr/op by Solenta Avn
ZS-OVR	Aerospatiale/Alenia ATR 42-300	116	ex F-WQNB		Lsd fr/op by Solenta Avn
ZS-OVS	Aerospatiale/Alenia ATR 42-300	075	ex F-WQNU	DHL c/s	Lsd fr/op by Solenta Avn

EAST COAST AIRWAYS
Eastway (ECT) — Durban-Virginia (VIR)

ZS-LFM	Beech 200 Super King Air	BB-954	ex N1839S	
ZS-NGC	Beech 200 Super King Air	BB-215	ex 7Q-YTC	Lsd fr KanBerri Air

EXECUTIVE AEROSPACE
Aerospace (EAS) — Johannesburg-Jan Smuts (JNB)

ZS-AGB	Hawker Siddeley.748 Srs.2B/501	1807	ex 9N-AEH	Lsd to LEO as 4R-LPV
ZS-LSO*	Hawker Siddeley.748 Srs.2B/FAA	1783	ex G-BMJU	Op by Pelican Air
ZS-NNW	Hawker Siddeley.748 Srs.2B/378	1785	ex G-BOHZ	stored DUR
ZS-NWW*	Hawker Siddeley.748 Srs.2B/378	1786	ex G-HDBC	Sublsd to Air Excellence
ZS-ODJ*	Hawker Siddeley.748 Srs.2A/263	1680	ex F-GHKA	
ZS-PLO*	Hawker Siddeley.748 Srs.2B/378	1797	ex G-EMRD	
ZS-TPW	Hawker Siddeley.748 Srs.2B/378	1784	ex (ZS-KLC)	

*Leased from Aerospace Express

EXECUTIVE HELICOPTERS
Lanseria (HLA)

ZS-NAT	Britten-Norman BN-2T Turbine Islander	2158	ex 7Q-YAV

FEDERAL AIR
Fedair (FDR) — Durban-Intl (DUR)

ZS-JML	Cessna 208B Caravan I	208B0582		
ZS-NDV	Cessna 208B Caravan I	208B0374	ex N1117Y	
ZS-NFY	Cessna 208B Caravan I	208B0294	ex N5275B	Lsd fr Grand Caravan Charter
ZS-NGO	Cessna 208B Caravan I	208B0322	ex N1027S	Lsd to STA, Mozambique
ZS-NLM	Cessna 208B Caravan I	208B0375	ex TZ-NLM	Lsd fr Caravan Air
ZS-NPD	Cessna 208B Caravan I	208B-369	ex A2-NPD	
ZS-NVH	Cessna 208B Caravan I	208B0473	ex N1287N	Lsd fr Caravan Transport
ZS-NXZ	Cessna 208B Caravan I	208B0357	ex N1115N	
ZS-ODS	Cessna 208B Caravan I	208B0538	ex C-FKAC	
ZS-PAT	Cessna 208B Caravan I	208B0437		Lsd fr Flying Fish Airlines

ZS-THR	Cessna 208B Caravan I	208B0571		
ZS-AMB	Pilatus PC-12/45	203	ex	Lsd fr Union Charter Trust
ZS-DAT	Pilatus PC-12/45	242	ex HB-FRM	Lsd fr Union Charter Trust
ZS-FDR	Beech 200 Super King Air	BB-1234	ex N971LE	Lsd fr New Federal Avn Partnership

HYDRO AIR

Hydro Cargo (HYC)   Johannesburg-Jan Smuts (JNB)

| ZS-OOS | Boeing 747-258C | 272/21190 | ex 4X-AXD | dbr LOS 28Nov03? | Ops for DHL |

Hydro Air is the trading name of FJC Aviation

INTER-AIR AIRLINES

Inline (D6/ILN) (IATA 625)   Johannesburg-Jan Smuts (JNB)

ZS-IJH	Boeing 727-116C	594/19813	ex N77AZ	Lsd fr Avn Consultants
ZS-IJI	Boeing 707-323C (Comtran 2)	614/19517	ex N29AZ	Lsd fr Avn Consultants
ZS-IJJ	Boeing 737-2H7C	309/20591	ex N24AZ	
3D-ZZM	Boeing 737-2H7C	304/20590	ex 3C-ZZM	Lsd to MRT

Inter-Air is the trading name of InterAviation Services

INTERLINK AIRLINES

Interlink (ID/ITK)   Johannesburg-Jan Smuts (JNB)

| (ZS-MRJ) | Douglas DC-9-32 | 621/47466 | ex 3D-MRJ | |

JAM AIR

Lanseria (HLA)

| ZS-JAM | Swearingen SA.227AC Metro III | AC-696B | ex N748JA | |

JAM Air is the trading name of Jesus Alive Ministeries

KING AIR PARTNERSHIP

Melville

| ZS-NRC | Douglas DC-9-32 | 190/47090 | ex | |
| ZS-NRD | Douglas DC-9-32 | 121/47037 | ex | |

KULULA.COM

Johannesburg-Jan Smuts (JNB)

ZS-OTF	Boeing 737-436	2147/25305	ex G-DOCC	Lsd fr SFR
ZS-OTG	Boeing 737-436	2197/25840	ex G-DOCJ	Lsd fr SFR
ZS-OTH	Boeing 737-436	2222/25841	ex G-DOCK	Lsd fr SFR

Wholly owned low cost, no frills subsidiary of Comair

LUFT CARGO ceased operations

MILLIONAIR CHARTER

Lanseria (HLA)

ZS-IJF	Boeing 727-23	114/18444	ex N1988	Faith; no titles	stored JNB
ZS-NNN	Douglas DC-9-32	630/47516	ex N1294L		Lsd to Sunair
ZS-NRA	Douglas DC-9-32	609/47430	ex G-BMAK		Lsd to Sunair
ZS-NRB	Douglas DC-9-32	611/47468	ex G-BMAM		Lsd to Sunair
ZS-OLN	Douglas DC-9-32	312/47218	ex N12538	Charity; all-white	

NAC – NATIONAL AIRWAYS CORPORATION

Natchair (NTN)   Lanseria (HLA)

ZS-OLY	Beech 1900D	UE-37	ex N37YV	
ZS-ORV	Beech 1900D	UE-42	ex N42YV	Lsd to Air Express Algeria
ZS-OWN	Beech 1900D	UE-4	ex (ZS-OWB)	Lsd fr FTR Partnerships
ZS-OYA	Beech 1900D	UE-7	ex VH-IMA	Lsd fr Compion; sublsd to Comav
ZS-OYC	Beech 1900D	UE-117	ex VH-NTL	
ZS-OYD	Beech 1900D	UE-191	ex VH-IAR	Lsd fr Awesome Avn
ZS-OYE*	Beech 1900D	UE-200	ex VH-IAV	
ZS-OYF*	Beech 1900D	UE-214	ex VH-IMS	Lsd fr SkyInvest Administration
ZS-OYG	Beech 1900D	UE-230	ex VH-IMH	
ZS-OYH*	Beech 1900D	UE-250	ex VH-IAY	Lsd fr SkyInvest Administration
ZS-OYJ	Beech 1900D	UE-273	ex 5Y-NAC	Op for United Nations
ZS-OYK	Beech 1900D	UE-318	ex VH-NBN	
ZS-OYL	Beech 1900D	UE-324	ex VH-IMR	

ZS-PBY	Beech 1900C-1	UC-96	ex N130GA	on order
ZS-PBZ	Beech 1900C-1	UC-126	ex N139GA	
ZS-PCC	Beech 1900C-1	UC-143	ex N152GA	on order
ZS-PCE	Beech 1900C-1	UC-150	ex N150GA	on order

*Operates as Air Express Algerie

ZS-ARL	Beech 200 Super King Air	BB-1537	ex N3237M	
ZS-KNG	Cessna 402C	402C0287	ex N3175M	
ZS-NBJ	Beech 200 Super King Air	BB-1070	ex SE-KND	Op as NAC Charter
ZS-OCI	Beech 200 Super King Air	BB-121	ex TR-LDX	
ZS-ODI	Beech 200 Super King Air	BB-1542	ex N202JT	Op as NAC Charter
ZS-ORP	Cessna 404 Titan	404-0212	ex 5Y-HCN	
ZS-OVX	Beech 200 Super King Air	BB-1253	ex A2-AEO	
ZS-OZZ	Beech 1900C	UC-73	ex N1570B	LSd fr Straovest

Subsidiary of Safair;

NATIONAL AIRLINES

(KUS)   ***Cape Town-Intl (CPT)***

Current fleet details unknown, possible misquote for National Airways

NATIONAL AIRWAYS

(YJ)   ***Cape Town-Intl (CPT)***

| ZS-MKI | Beech 65-C90A King Air | LJ-1099 | ex Z-MKI | Lsd fr SPH Group |
| ZS-OUI | Beech 200 Super King Air | BB-688 | ex 5R-MGH | CatPass 250 conv Lsd fr Skyeinvest |

NATIONWIDE AIR CHARTER

Nationwide Air (CE/NTW)   ***Lanseria (HLA)***

ZS-NNM	BAC One-Eleven 409AY	108	ex G-BGTU	stored HLA
ZS-NUI	BAC One-Eleven 537GF	258	ex 5B-DAH	
ZS-NUJ	BAC One-Eleven 537GF	261	ex 5B-DAJ	
ZS-OAG	BAC One-Eleven 401AK	066	ex G-BBME	stored HLA
ZS-OAH	BAC One-Eleven 408EF	115	ex G-BBMG	
ZS-OEZ	Boeing 737-230	704/22118	ex 9A-CTC	Lsd fr Finova
ZS-OIV	Boeing 737-230	840/22634	ex 9A-CTE	Lsd fr Aerotrans Inc
ZS-OMG	Boeing 737-230	793/22140	ex 9A-CTD	Lsd fr Finova
ZS-OOC	Boeing 737-258	910/22856	ex 4X-ABN	
ZS-OOD	Boeing 737-258	919/22857	ex 4X-ABO	
ZS-OVE	Boeing 737-228	944/23006	ex EI-CTX	Lsd fr Rancemont Lease
ZS-OVF	Boeing 737-228	952/23008	ex EI-CRN	Lsd fr Rancemont Lease
ZS-OVG	Boeing 737-236	661/21800	ex N705S	
ZS-OWM	Boeing 737-2R8C	573/21711	ex 5H-MRK	Lsd fr VSA Aviation; sublsd to Filair
ZS-NYY	Boeing 727-95	315/19251	ex CC-CHC	
ZS-ODO	Boeing 727-231	1063/20843	ex N54338	
ZS-OZP	Boeing 727-281	881/20572	ex JU-1036	stored HLA
ZS-OZR	Boeing 727-281	888/20573	ex JU-1037	
ZS-PBI	Boeing 767-370ER	450/26200	ex C-GGOH	Lsd fr GECAS

NATURELINK WEST AFRICA

Naturelink Southafri (NRK)   ***Pretoria-Wonderboom (PRY)***

ZS-KMN	Beech 58 Baron	TH-153		
ZS-LXB	Cessna 402B	402B0513		
ZS-MRU	Douglas DC-3	4363	ex N234Z	Lsd fr Gallovents Ten
ZS-MSK	Beech Super King Air 200	BB-597	ex 5Y-BJC	
ZS-NDN	Piper PA-31-350 Navajo Chieftain	31-7952196		Panther conv
ZS-NUV	Cessna 208B Caravan I	208B0596		Lsd fr Allied Farms
ZS-OJJ	Douglas DC-3-TP65	32961	ex N8194	Lsd fr Dodson Intl
ZS-OJK	Douglas DC-3-TP65	14165/25610	ex SAAF 6844	Lsd fr Dodson Intl
ZS-OOZ	Embraer EMB.110P1 Bandeirante	110219	ex TG-TWO	
ZS-OPE	Cessna 208B Caravan I	208B0687	ex N955PA	Lsd to STA Mozambique
ZS-OUM	Embraer EMB.110P1 Bandeirante	110195	ex TR-LYK	Lsd fr Bandit Partnership
ZS-OWO	Embraer EMB.110P1 Bandeirante	110311	ex 8P-TIA	
ZS-OWR	CASA C.212	263	ex N263MA	Lsd to Kivu Air
ZS-OWS	Cessna U206F Stationair	U20602307	ex 9Q-COK	
ZS-OXV	Cessna 208B Caravan I	208B0563	ex N330AK	
ZS-OZJ	Embraer EMB.110P1 Bandeirante	110439	ex OH-EBD	Lsd fr Bandit Partnership

NELAIR CHARTERS

Nelspruit (NLP)

ZS-EDG	Cessna U206 Super Skywagon	U206-0382	ex N2182F	
ZS-EVB	Piper PA-30 Twin Comanche 160B	30-1218	ex N8134Y	
ZS-IKZ	Piper PA-32-300 Cherokee Six E	32-7240070	ex ZS-XAS	
ZS-JGW	Cessna 401B	401B0106	ex N7966Q	
ZS-JTX	Piper PA-31-350 Navajo Chieftain	31-7652059	ex N59800	
ZS-JZX	Piper PA-34-200T Seneca II	34-7770269	ex N5911V	
ZS-LVR	Douglas DC-3	20475	ex N5000E	Memphis Belle
ZS-MHE	Piper PA-31-350 Navajo Chieftain	31-7305096		
ZS-MMY	Piper PA-34-200T Seneca II	34-7670051	ex N4469X	
ZS-MSO	Piper PA-32-300 Cherokee Six	32-7540083	ex N33050	
ZS-NSM	Cessna U206D Super Skywagon	U206-1444		
ZS-PCN	Cessna U206F Stationair	U20602450	ex N1080V	

NORSE AIR

ZS-	Swearingen SA.227BC Metro III	BC-786B	ex
ZS-	Swearingen SA.227BC Metro III	BC-798B	ex
ZS-	Swearingen SA.227DC Metro 23	DC-820B	ex
ZS-PBU	Swearingen SA.227DC Metro 23	DC-826B	ex XA-SNF

ORION AIR CHARTER ceased operations

PELICAN AIR SERVICES

Johannesburg (JNB)

ZS-LSO*	Hawker Siddeley.748 Srs.2B/FAA	1783	ex G-BMJU	Lsd fr EAS

PHOEBUS APOLLO AVIATION

Phoebus (PHB)   *Johannesburg-Rand*

ZS-DIW	Douglas DC-3	11991	ex SAAF 6871	Pegasus
ZS-PAI	Douglas C-54E	27319	ex N4989K	Atlas
ZS-PAJ	Douglas C-54D	22192	ex C9-ATS	
ZS-	Douglas DC-3	1984	ex C9-ATG	on rebuild
9J-PAA	ATEL ATL-98 Carvair	13/27314	ex N5459M	

Phoebus Apollo Zambia is a wholly owned subsidiary using code KZM

PROFESSIONAL AVIATION

Lanseria (HLA)

ZS-LJI	Douglas DC-3-TP65	34225	ex SAAF 6871	Ruzizi; stored BEW

PROGRESS AIR

Lanseria (HLA)

ZS-SDM	Swearingen SA.227AC Metro III	AC-756	ex C-FAFW

ROSSAIR

Ross Charter (RSS)   *Lanseria (HLA)*

ZS-NPT	Beech 1900C-1	UC-113	ex 5Y-HAC	all-white
ZS-ODG	Beech 1900C-1	UC-158	ex N158YV	
ZS-OHE	Beech 1900C-1	UC-48	ex 9J-AFJ	
ZS-OKA	Beech 1900C-1	UC-144	ex 5Y-BND	Op for UN
ZS-OLP	Beech 1900C	UB-18	ex Z-DHS	
ZS-OLV	Beech 1900C-1	UC-137	ex 9G-FAN	
ZS-ONJ	Beech 1900C-1	UC-63	ex TR-LEU	
5Y-ROS	Beech 1900C-1	UC-65	ex ZK-OGZ	Lsd to Rossair Kenya
PH-RAE	Beech 1900D	UE-21	ex ZS-OLX	Lsd to ROS
PH-RAG	Beech 1900D	UE-29	ex OY-GMP	Lsd to ROS
PH-RAH	Beech 1900D	UE-31	ex (OY-GEP)	Lsd to ROS
PH-RAR	Beech 1900D	UE-372	ex ZS-ONS	Lsd to ROS
PH-RAT	Beech 1900D	UE-350	ex ZS-OOV	Lsd to ROS
ZS-OCW	Beech 1900D	UE-313	ex N11354	Lsd to Air Affaires
ZS-OCX	Beech 1900D	UE-321	ex N22978	Lsd fr Air Affaires
ZS-OLW	Beech 1900D	UE-33	ex N33YV	
ZS-OMC	Beech 1900D	UE-18	ex N18YV	Op for UN
ZS-ONH	Beech 1900D	UE-310	ex TR-LFE	
ZS-OOW	Beech 1900D	UE-57	ex N57ZV	
ZS-OWN	Beech 1900D	UE-4	ex N4ZV	

5Y-OKL	Beech 1900D	UE-48	ex ZS-OKL		Lsd to Rossair Kenya
ZS-LGN	de Havilland DHC-6 Twin Otter 300	424	ex ZS-OVJ		
ZS-MZB	de Havilland DHC-6 Twin Otter 300	691	ex N230BV	based Angola	
ZS-NJK	de Havilland DHC-6 Twin Otter 300	598	ex N403CA	based Kenya	
ZS-OEF	de Havilland DHC-6 Twin Otter 310	838	ex N451RS		
ZS-OVD	de Havilland DHC-6 Twin Otter 300	288	ex HB-LSP		
ZS-OVN	de Havilland DHC-6 Twin Otter 300	719	ex N719DK		
ZS-OVT	de Havilland DHC-6 Twin Otter 300	721	ex S7-AAT		Lsd to Tassili
5Y-BOS	de Havilland DHC-6 Twin Otter 300	513	ex ZS-OHS	Op for Red Cross, based Kenya	
ZS-KMA	Beech 65-C90 King Air	LJ-930	ex N3717J		
ZS-MES	Beech 200 Super King Air	BB-1038	ex N223MH		
ZS-MIN	Beech 200 Super King Air	BB-941	ex N36801		
ZS-MWF	Cessna 414A Chancellor II	414A0106			
ZS-NAX	Beech 200C Super King Air	BL-8	ex 5Y-NAX		
ZS-NUF	Beech 200C Super King Air	BL-4	ex V5-AAL		Lsd to Red Cross
PH-RAK	Aerospatiale/Alenia ATR 42-300	032	ex ZS-OUY		Lsd to ROS
PH-RAQ	Aerospatiale/Alenia ATR 42-300	139	ex ZS-OSN		Lsd to ROS
ZS-OJJ	Douglas DC-3-TP65	32961/16213	ex N8194	dam 24Aug01	
ZS-OVU	Cessna 404 Titan	404-0637	ex 5H-AMK		
ZS-OXE	Reims Cessna F406 Caravan II	F406-0058			

Owns Air Lesotho

ROVOS AIR

(VOS) *Pretoria-Wonderboom (PRY)*

ZS-ARV	Convair 440	228	ex CP-2237
ZS-BRV	Convair 440	215	ex CP-2236
ZS-CRV	Douglas DC-3	13331	ex ZS-PTG

RYON BLAKE AIR

Johannesburg-Rand

ZS-OJH	Swearingen SA.227AC Metro III	AC-727	ex N100GS	Lsd to STA Mozambique
ZS-OLS	Swearingen SA.227AC Metro III	AC-748B	ex OY-NPC	

SAFAIR

Cargo (FA/SFR) (IATA 640) *Johannesburg-Jan Smuts (JNB)*

ZS-JAG	Lockheed L-382G Hercules	5027	ex B-3004		
ZS-JIV	Lockheed L-382G Hercules	4673	ex D2-THE		Lsd to/op for ABR
ZS-JIX	Lockheed L-382G Hercules	4684	ex D2-THZ	EARL logo	
ZS-JIY	Lockheed L-382G Hercules	4691	ex D2-THS		
ZS-JIZ	Lockheed L-382G Hercules	4695	ex F-GNMM		Op for UN/WFP
ZS-JVL	Lockheed L-382G Hercules	4676	ex EI-JVL		
ZS-RSC	Lockheed L-382G Hercules	4475	ex S9-NAD		
ZS-RSI	Lockheed L-328G Hercules	4600	ex F-GIMV		
ZS-NZV	Boeing 727-230	1023/20792			
ZS-OPC	Boeing 727-225F (FedEx 3)	825/20382	ex EI-HCA		
ZS-PDL	Boeing 727-281F (FedEx 3)	865/20466	ex EI-LCH		Lsd fr TTC Hunt

Also owns a large fleet of Boeing 727s, Boeing 737s and McDonnell-Douglas MD-80s that are leased out to other operators including Air Namibia, Comair, Macedonian Airlines and South African Airlines while 3 ATR 72-212As are leased to Jet Airways and five Airbus Industrie A300B4-203Fs to European Air Transport/DHL International

SOLENTA AVIATION

Lanseria (HLA)

ZS-ADL	Cessna 208B Caravan I	208B0381	ex 5Y-TAS	Op for DHV
ZS-NIZ	Cessna 208B Caravan I	208B0353	ex 5Y-NIZ	Op for DHV
ZS-NYR	Cessna 208B Caravan I	208B0382	ex N10YR	Op for DHV
ZS-OBY	Cessna 208B Caravan I	208B0345	ex 9Q-COI	Op for DHV
ZS-OFK	Cessna 208B Caravan I	208B0668	ex 7Q-YKR	Op for DHV
ZS-OJF	Cessna 208B Caravan I	208B0481	ex N72ED	Op for DHV
ZS-ORI	Cessna 208B Caravan I	208B0525	ex N208BC	Op for DHV
ZS-ORK	Cessna 208B Caravan I	208B0336	ex D4-CBJ	Op for DHV
ZS-OTV	Cessna 208B Caravan I	208B0545	ex PT-MHE	Op for DHV
ZS-SLO	Cessna 208B Caravan I	208B0485	ex F-OGXI	Op for DHV
ZS-SLR	Cessna 208B Caravan I	208B0497	ex N497AC	Op for DHV
ZS-SLT	Cessna 208B Caravan I	208B0459	ex F-OGXK	Op for DHV
ZS-TLC	Cessna 208B Caravan I	208B0472	ex 5Y-TLC	Op for DHV
5Y-BNB	Cessna 208B Caravan I	208B0296	ex ZS-OER	Op for DHV
5Y-BNH	Cessna 208B Caravan I	208B0385	ex ZS-NYS	Op for DHV
5Y-NHB	Cessna 208B Caravan I	208B0328	ex ZS-NHB	Op for DHV

658

9J-DHL	Cessna 208B Caravan I	208B0261	ex ZS-NOM		Op for DHV
ZS-ATR	Aerospatiale/Alenia ATR 42-300F	060	ex PH-XLC		Op for DHV
ZS-OUJ	de Havilland DHC-6 Twin Otter 300	582	ex 5H-MUG		
ZS-OVP	Aerospatiale/Alenia ATR 42-300F	088	ex F-WQNG		Op for DHV
ZS-OVR	Aerospatiale/Alenia ATR 42-300F	116	ex F-WQNB		Op for DHV
ZS-OVS	Aerospatiale/Alenia ATR 42-300F	075	ex F-WQNU		Op for DHY

SOUTH AFRICAN AIRLINK

Link (4Z/LNK) (IATA 749) — Johannesburg-Jan Smuts (JNB)

ZS-NRE^	British Aerospace Jetstream 41	41048	ex G-4-048		
ZS-NRF^	British Aerospace Jetstream 41	41050	ex G-4-050		
ZS-NRG^	British Aerospace Jetstream 41	41051	ex G-4-051	Pietermaritzburg	
ZS-NRH^	British Aerospace Jetstream 41	41054	ex G-4-054	Pietersburg	
ZS-NRI^	British Aerospace Jetstream 41	41061	ex G-4-061		
ZS-NRJ^	British Aerospace Jetstream 41	41062	ex G-4-062		
ZS-NRK^	British Aerospace Jetstream 41	41065	ex G-4-065		Lsd to SZL
ZS-NRL^	British Aerospace Jetstream 41	41068	ex G-4-068		
ZS-NRM^	British Aerospace Jetstream 41	41069	ex G-4-069	Nelspruit	
ZS-NUO*	British Aerospace Jetstream 41	41044	ex VH-IMS		Op for Mocambique Express
ZS-NYK	British Aerospace Jetstream 41	41095	ex G-4-095		Lsd fr Kwazulu-Natal Govt
ZS-OEX	British Aerospace Jetstream 41	41103	ex G-4-103		
ZS-OMF^	British Aerospace Jetstream 41	41034	ex G-MSKJ		Lsd fr BAES
ZS-OMS	British Aerospace Jetstream 41	41035	ex VH-JSX		
ZS-OMY	British Aerospace Jetstream 41	41036	ex VH-CCJ		
ZS-OMZ	British Aerospace Jetstream 41	41037	ex VH-CCW		

^Leased from Midlands Aviation   *Leased from Foster Webb Partnership

ZS-OTM	Embraer EMB.135LR	145485	ex PT-SXE		
ZS-OTN	Embraer EMB.135LR	145491	ex PT-SXK		
ZS-OUV	Embraer EMB.135LR	145493	ex PT-SXM		Op as Airlink Zimbabwe
ZS-OUW	Embraer EMB.135LR			on order	
ZS-SJW	Embraer EMB.135LR	145423	ex PT-STU		
ZS-SJX	Embraer EMB.135LR	145428	ex PT-STZ		
ZS-	Embraer EMB.135LR			on order 03	
ZS-	Embraer EMB.135LR			on order 03	
ZS-	Embraer EMB.135LR			on order 04	
ZS-	Embraer EMB.135LR			on order 04	

A further twenty Embraer EMB.135LRs are on order for delivery up to 2008 through Coronation Aircraft Leasing
Owns 49% of Kalahari Express Airways and Airlink Zimbabwe

SOUTH AFRICAN AIRWAYS

Springbok (SA/SAA) (IATA 083) — Johannesburg-Jan Smuts (JNB)

ZS-SLA	Airbus Industrie A340-211	008	ex D-AIBA		Lsd fr Airbus
ZS-SLB	Airbus Industrie A340-211	011	ex D-AIBC		Lsd fr Airbus
ZS-SLC	Airbus Industrie A340-211	018	ex D-AIBD		Lsd fr Airbus
ZS-SLD	Airbus Industrie A340-211	019	ex D-AIBE		Lsd fr Airbus
ZS-SLE	Airbus Industrie A340-211	021	ex D-AIBH		Lsd fr Airbus
ZS-SNA	Airbus Industrie A340-642	410	ex F-WWCE		
ZS-SNB	Airbus Industrie A340-642	417	ex F-WWCG		
ZS-SNC	Airbus Industrie A340-642	426	ex F-WWCH		
ZS-SND	Airbus Industrie A340-642	531	ex F-WWCX		
ZS-SNE	Airbus Industrie A340-642	534	ex F-WWCY		Lsd fr ILFC
ZS-SNF	Airbus Industrie A340-642	547	ex F-WWCI		
ZS-SNG	Airbus Industrie A340-642	557	ex F-WWCG		Lsd fr ILFC
ZS-SNI	Airbus Industrie A340-642	630	ex F-WWCG	on order	Lsd fr ILFC
ZS-SXA	Airbus Industrie A340-313X	544	ex F-WWJS	on order 03	
ZS-SXB	Airbus Industrie A340-313X	582	ex F-WWJT	on order 03	
ZS-SXC	Airbus Industrie A340-313X	590	ex F-WW	on order 04	

Three more A340-300s are on order for delivery in 2005.

ZS-SIA	Boeing 737-244	787/22580	ex PP-SNW	Tugela	Lsd fr SFR
ZS-SIB	Boeing 737-244	796/22581	ex D6-CAJ	Limpopo	Lsd fr SFR
ZS-SIC	Boeing 737-244	805/22582		Vaal	Lsd fr SFR
ZS-SID	Boeing 737-244F	809/22583		Oranje	Lsd fr SFR
ZS-SIE	Boeing 737-244	821/22584		Letaba	Lsd fr SFR
ZS-SIF	Boeing 737-244F	828/22585		Komati	Lsd fr SFR
ZS-SIG	Boeing 737-244	829/22586		Marico	Lsd fr SFR
ZS-SIH	Boeing 737-244	835/22587		Kei	Lsd fr SFR
ZS-SII	Boeing 737-244	836/22588		Berg	Lsd fr SFR
ZS-SIJ	Boeing 737-244	843/22589	ex CC-CHK	Caledon	Lsd fr SFR
ZS-SIL	Boeing 737-244	859/22591		Wilge	Lsd fr SFR
ZS-SIM	Boeing 737-244	881/22828		Umgeni	Lsd fr SFR
ZS-SIO	Boeing 737-236	628/21792	ex CC-CHR		Lsd fr SFR
ZS-SIT	Boeing 737-236	599/21790	ex G-BGDA	stored JNB	Lsd fr SFR
ZS-SIU	Boeing 737-236	644/22026	ex G-BGJE		Lsd fr SFR
ZS-SIV	Boeing 737-236	662/22029	ex CC-CZN		Lsd fr GECAS; sublsd to ATC

ZS-SIW	Boeing 737-236	722/22031	ex CC-CZP		Lsd fr GECAS; sublsd to ATC
ZS-SJA	Boeing 737-8S3	561/29248			Lsd fr GATX
ZS-SJB	Boeing 737-8S3	653/29249			Lsd fr GATX
ZS-SJC	Boeing 737-85F	565/28828			Lsd fr GATX
ZS-SJD	Boeing 737-85F	582/28829			Lsd fr GATX
ZS-SJE	Boeing 737-85F	669/28830			Lsd fr GATX
ZS-SJF	Boeing 737-85F	688/30006	ex N1787B		Lsd fr GATX
ZS-SJG	Boeing 737-8S3	711/32353			Lsd fr GATX
ZS-SJH	Boeing 737-8S3	725/32354	ex N1787B		Lsd fr GATX
ZS-SJI	Boeing 737-85F	746/30007	ex N1787B		Lsd fr GATX
ZS-SJJ	Boeing 737-85F	761/30567	ex N1787B		Lsd fr GATX
ZS-SJK	Boeing 737-8BG	807/32355	ex PH-HZT		Lsd fr GATX
ZS-SJL	Boeing 737-8BG	819/32356	ex PH-HZZ		Lsd fr GATX
ZS-SJM	Boeing 737-85F	789/30476	ex N1014X		Lsd fr GATX
ZS-SJN	Boeing 737-85F	850/30569			Lsd fr GATX
ZS-SJO	Boeing 737-8BG	918/32357	ex PH-HZS		Lsd fr GATX
ZS-SJP	Boeing 737-8BG	955/32358	ex PH-HZU		Lsd fr GATX
ZS-SJR	Boeing 737-844	1176/32631			Lsd fr Safair Lease; sublsd to XLA
ZS-SJS	Boeing 737-844	1205/32632			Lsd fr Safair Lease
ZS-SJT	Boeing 737-844	1225/32633			Lsd fr Safair Lease
ZS-SJU	Boeing 737-844	1383/32634			Lsd fr Safair Lease
ZS-SJV	Boeing 737-844	1407/32635	ex N1787B		Lsd fr Safair Lease

All fitted with as new, or being retrofitted, with blended winglets
All Boeing 737s are to be replaced by eleven Airbus Industrie A319s from 2005 (to replace the 737 Classics) and fifteen Airbus Industrie A320s (to replace the 737-800s) from 2010

ZS-SAC	Boeing 747-312	598/23031	ex N120KF	Shosholoza	
ZS-SAJ	Boeing 747-312	583/23027	ex N116KB	Ndizani	
ZS-SAK	Boeing 747-444	1162/28468	ex N60697	Ebhayi	
ZS-SAL	Boeing 747-244B	154/20237	ex N1795B	Tafelberg	
ZS-SAM	Boeing 747-244B	158/20238	ex PP-VNW	Drakensberg	
ZS-SAN	Boeing 747-244B	160/20239		Lebombo	
ZS-SAT	Boeing 747-344	577/22970	ex N8279V	Johannesburg	Lsd to ABD
ZS-SAU	Boeing 747-344	578/22971	ex N8296V	Cape Town	
ZS-SAV	Boeing 747-444	827/24976	ex N6009F	Durban	
ZS-SAW	Boeing 747-444	861/25152	ex N60668	Bloemfontein	
ZS-SAX	Boeing 747-444	943/26637		Kempton Park	
ZS-SAY	Boeing 747-444	995/26638		Vulindlela	
ZS-SAZ	Boeing 747-444	1187/29119		Monti	
ZS-SBK	Boeing 747-4F6	1158/28959	ex N1785B	The Great North	
ZS-SBS	Boeing 747-4F6	1167/28960	ex N60668		
ZS-SPC	Boeing 747SP-44	288/21134	ex 3B-NAG	Maluti	
ZS-SPE	Boeing 747SP-44	298/21254	ex V5-SPE	Hantam	
PT-MVA	Airbus Industrie A330-222	232	ex F-WWKV		Lsd fr TAM to Apr04
PT-MVB	Airbus Industrie A330-222	238	ex F-WWKY		Lsd fr TAM to Apr04
ZS-SRB	Boeing 767-266ER	98/23179	ex N573SW	Syaya	Lsd fr UT Finance
ZS-SRC	Boeing 767-266ER	99/23180	ex N575SW	Ngomeza	Lsd fr UT Finance

Owns 49% of Air Tanzania. To take a 30% stake in Nigeria Eagle Airline

SOUTH AFRICAN EXPRESS AIRLINES

Expressways (YB/EXY)   **Johannesburg-Jan Smuts (JNB)**

ZS-NMI	Canadair CL-600-2B19	7153	ex C-FZAN	
ZS-NMJ	Canadair CL-600-2B19	7161	ex C-GAUG	
ZS-NMK	Canadair CL-600-2B19	7198	ex C-GBMF	
ZS-NML	Canadair CL-600-2B19	7201	ex C-GBLX	
ZS-NMM	Canadair CL-600-2B19	7234		
ZS-NMN	Canadair CL-600-2B19	7237		
ZS-NLW	de Havilland DHC-8-315	338	ex ZS-NLY	301
ZS-NLX	de Havilland DHC-8-315	348	ex C-GDKL	302
ZS-NLY	de Havilland DHC-8-315	352	ex ZS-NLW	303
ZS-NLZ	de Havilland DHC-8-315	354	ex C-GFRP	304
ZS-NMA	de Havilland DHC-8-315	358	ex C-GDFT	305
ZS-NMB	de Havilland DHC-8-315	368	ex C-GGIU	306
ZS-NMP	de Havilland DHC-8-315B	420	ex ZS-NNJ	307

Scheduled flights are operated as SA Connector using SA flight numbers

SUNAIR

Sunstream (AG/SJE)   **Lanseria (HLA)**

ZS-NRA	Douglas DC-9-32	609/47430	ex G-BMAK	Lsd to Million Air
ZS-NRB	Douglas DC-9-32	611/47468	ex G-BMAM	Lsd to Million Air

Subsidiary of AirQuarius and Million Air

VSA AVIATION

Lanseria (HLA)

ZS-NGW	Dornier 228-101	7036	ex A2-ABA	Lsd to STA Mozambique
ZS-NRN	Dornier 228-200	8021	ex OY-CHK	
ZS-OOU	Cessna 404 Titan	404-0415	ex 9Q-CMX	Lsd to STA Mozambique
ZS-OVM	Dornier 228-201	8056	ex F-GOAH	Lsd to ATC
ZS-OWM	Boeing 737-2R8C	573/21711	ex 5H-MRK	Lsd to Nationwide

Z3 - MACEDONIA (Republic of Macedonia)

AIR VARDAR

(VDR) *Skopje (SKP)*

Z3-AA	Fokker 100	11272	ex YU-AOK	Lsd fr MGX

Also reported as Vardar Air; stored at Skopje since delivery

MACEDONIAN AIR TRANSPORT - MAT

Makavio (IN/MAK) (IATA 367) *Skopje (SKP)*

Z3-AAA	Boeing 737-3H9	1175/23416	ex YU-ANI	Lsd fr JAT
Z3-ARF	Boeing 737-3H9	1321/23716	ex YU-ANL	Lsd fr JAT

3A - MONACO (Principality of Monaco)

HELI AIR MONACO

Heli Air (YO/MCM) *Monte Carlo (MCM)*

3A-MAC	Aerospatiale AS.350B Ecureuil	1673	ex HB-XBC
3A-MCM	Aerospatiale SA.365N Dauphin	6076	ex N9UW
3A-MIK	Aerospatiale AS.350BA Ecureuil	1091	ex I-ELIL
3A-MJP	Aerospatiale SA.365C3 Dauphin 2	5015	ex N90049
3A-MPJ	Eurocopter EC.130B4	3662	
3A-MTP	Aerospatiale AS.350B2 Ecureuil	1996	ex I-LOLO
3A-MTT	Aerospatiale AS.350B2 Ecureuil	1967	ex I-LUPJ
3A-MXL	Aerospatiale AS.355N Ecureuil 2	5713	

MONACAIR

Monacair (MCR) *Monte Carlo (MCM)*

3A-MLV	Aerospatiale AS.350B1 Ecureuil	2271	ex EC-ERR
3A-MTV	Aerospatiale AS.365N Dauphin	6096	ex F-OHNZ

3B - MAURITIUS (Republic of Mauritius)

AIR MAURITIUS

AirMauritius (MK/MAU) (IATA 239) *Plaisance (MRU)*

3B-NAU	Airbus Industrie A340-312	076	ex F-WWJG	Pink Pigeon	
3B-NAV	Airbus Industrie A340-312	094	ex F-WWJF	Kestrel	Lsd fr ILFC
3B-NAY	Airbus Industrie A340-313X	152	ex F-WWJX	Cardinal	Lsd fr ILFC
3B-NBD	Airbus Industrie A340-313X	194	ex F-WWJP	Parakeet	
3B-NBE	Airbus Industrie A340-313X	268	ex F-WWJG	Paille en Queue	
3B-NAK	Boeing 767-23BER	206/23973	ex N6046P	City of Curepipe	
3B-NAL	Boeing 767-23BER	214/23974	ex N6018N	City of Port Louis	
3B-NBA	Aerospatiale/Alenia ATR 42-500	534	ex F-WWLF	Saint Brendan	
3B-NBB	Aerospatiale/Alenia ATR 42-500	554	ex F-WWLL	Coin de Mire	
3B-NBF	Airbus Industrie A319-112	1592	ex D-AVYX	Mon Choisy	
3B-NBG	Aerospatiale/Alenia ATR 72-212A	690	ex F-WWEM	Port Mathurin	
3B-NBH	Airbus Industrie A319-112	1936	ex D-AVWF	Blue Bay	
3B-NZD	Bell 206B JetRanger III	4464			
3B-NZE	Bell 206B JetRanger III	4465			
3B-NZF	Bell 206B JetRanger III	4496			

12.8% owned by British Airways and Air France, 8.5% owned by Air India

3C - EQUATORIAL GUINEA (Republic of Equatorial Guinea)

AEROLINEAS DE GUINEA
(AG)

RA-47741	Antonov An-24B	79901104	ex CCCP-47741		Lsd fr TYM

AIR BAS
Aviabas (RBS)
Previously listed as Air Cess

Sharjah (SHJ)

UN-11007	Antonov An-12V	9346509	ex 3C-OOZ	
UN-75002	Ilyushjn Il-18E	185008603	ex 3C-KKR	
UN-75003	Ilyushin Il-18V	184996903	ex 3C-KKJ	
UN-75004	Ilysuhin Il-18D	186009202	ex 3C-KKK	Irbus

AIR CARGO PLUS now listed as Cargo Plus Aviation

AIR CONSUL
Aeroconsul (RCS)

Malabo (SSG)

EC-CIY	Piper PA-31-350 Navajo Chieftain	31-7405181	ex N66875
3C-JJG	Piper PA-31-350 Navajo Chieftain	31-7552059	ex TR-LUQ

AIR GUINEE EQUATORIAL

Malabo (SSG)

ES-LLC	LET L-410UVP-E20C	912609	ex OK-WDH	Lsd fr AIT

AVIREX GUINEE EQUATORIALE
Avirex (AXG)

Malabo (SSG)

Operates charters with Cessna twin aircraft leased from parent Avirex (TR-) as and when required

CARGO PLUS AVIATION
Cargo Plus (8L/CGP)
Previously listed as Air Cargo Plus

Sharjah (SHJ)

Operates cargo flights using Russian freighters leased from other operators as required

CET AVIATION ENTERPRISE believed to have ceased operations

COAGE AIR LINES
Coage (COG)

Malabo (SSG)

EY-46602	Antonov An-24RV	37308509	ex CCCP-46602	Lsd fr TZK

Coage Air Lines is the trading name of Compania Aerea de Guinea Ecuatorial

DUCOR WORLD AIRWAYS
Ducor World (DWA)

Ostend (OST)

3C-QRL	Lockheed L-1011-1 Tristar	1093	ex G-BBAF	stored MST
A8-AAA	Lockheed L-1011- Tristar	1101	ex 3C-QRQ	Lsd to IAX

Registered in Guinea but based at Ostend

ECUATO GUINEANA DE AVIACION
EcuatoGuinea (ECV)

Malabo (SSG)

UR-26175	Antonov An-24RV	77310810A	ex 26175		Lsd fr UAK
3C-QQH	Embraer EMB.145LR	145076	ex LX-LGT	Immaculada; stored DNR	

Also leases Airbus A321s from Spanair as required plus other aircraft as and when required. Part owned by Spanair

EQUATORIAL CARGO
Equa-Cargo (EQC)

Malabo (SSG)

3C-HAV	Ilyushin Il-76MD	0073479386	ex UR-76748

GATS GUINEA

GATS Air (GTS)
Malabo/Abu Dhabi (SSG/AUH)

3C-KKE	Ilyushin Il-76TD	1023411368	ex YN-CEX
3C-KKF	Ilyushin Il-76TD	1023411384	ex YN-CEV
3C-KKG	Ilyushin Il-76TD	1023410360	ex YN-CEW

Two possibly reregistered EX-436 and EX-832 but not confirmed, may be 'new' aircraft

GUINEA CARGO

(GNC)
Malabo (SSG)

Current fleet details unknown

GUINEE AIRWAYS

(GIJ)
Malabo (SSG)

Current fleet details unknown

GEASA

Geasa (GEA)
Malabo (SSG)

RA-87956	Yakovlev Yak-40K	9821757	ex CCCP-87956	Lsd fr Aquiline Lsg

GEASA is the trading name of Guinee Ecuatorial Airlines

GETRA

Getra (GET)
Malabo (SSG)

ER-AWD	Antonov An-24			
UN-46469	Antonov An-24RV	27307907	ex CCCP-46460	Lsd fr UNL

JETLINE INC

Equajet (JLE)
Ras al Khaimah (RKT)

ER-AFN	Antonov An-26	27312602	ex RA-26093		
P4-CBH	BAC One Eleven 401AK	088	ex HZ-MAJ		
P4-DCE	Douglas DC-8-62H (BAC 3)	469/46071	ex VP-BLG		Lsd fr Sunningdale Investments
P4-JLI	Boeing 727-2K5	1640/21853	ex HZ-HR1	based Mitiga	
TL-ABW	Ilyushin Il-62M	3052657	ex 3C-OQZ	Jalal	
VP-CJL	BAC One Elevan 401AK	086	ex N325V		
3C-QRF	BAC One Elevan 401AK	061	ex P4-CBI		Op for Cen-Sad
5A-DKR	Ilyushin Il-62M	4053514	ex		Op for Cen-Sad
5A-DKS	Ilyushin Il-76TD	1033418584	ex RA-76843		Op for Cen-Sad cargo
5A-DKT	Ilyushin Il-62M	4648414	ex 3C-QQR	Rayane	Op for Cen-Sad

Operates VIP flights for CEN-SAD (Community of Sahel-Saharan States) [also reported as Sin-Sad]

KNG – TRANSAVIA CARGO

Viacargo (VCG)
Sharjah (SHJ)

3C-AAG	Antonov An-12BP	7344801	ex RA-98119		Lsd fr CGT
3C-AAL	Antonov An-12BP	00347003	ex RA-98103	no titles	Lsd fr CGT

KODA AIR CARGO

9L-LDU	Boeing 707-373C	500/19179	ex 3C-GIG	Lsd to RLL

LOTUS INTERNATIONAL AIR

Lotmore (LUS)
Sharjah (SHJ)

3C-ZZD	Antonov An-12V	00347305	ex EL-ALA

ROYAL AIRLINES CARGO

Sharjah (SHJ)

3C-QRN	Antonov An-12

SAN AIR current status is uncertain, believed to have ceased operations

748 AIR SERVICES

Nairobi-Wilson

| 3C-JJX | Hawker Siddeley Andover C.1 | Set 6 | ex EL-VDD |
| 3C-KKB | Hawker Siddeley Andover C.1 | Set 9 | ex NZ7622 |

TRANS AFRICAN AIRLINES believed to have ceased operations, both aircraft now operated by Jetline

UTAGE

Utage (UTG)
Malabo (SSG)

ER-AZB	Antonov An-24			
RA-46624	Antonov An-24RV	37308801		
UN-65695	Tupolev Tu-134B-3	63285	ex YL-LBE	Lsd fr Aqualine
UN-87249	Yakovlev Yak-40	9540244	ex CCCP-87249	Lsd fr BMK

Utage is the trading name of Union de Transporte Aereo de Guinea Ecuatorial

3D - SWAZILAND (Kingdom of Swaziland)

OPERATOR UNKNOWN:

| 3D- | Boeing 727-251 | 746/20289 | ex N267US | see also Kam Air (YA-) |
| 3D- | Boeing 727-2F2 | 1222/21260 | ex N103AZ | |

AFRICAN INTERNATIONAL AIRWAYS

Fly Cargo (AIN)
Manzini-Matsapha (MTS)

ZS-OSI	Douglas DC-8-62F (BAC 3)	516/46098	ex 3D-AIA	
ZS-OZV	Douglas DC-8-62F (BAC 3)	379/45986	ex 3D-CDL	
3D-ADV	Douglas DC-8F-54 (BAC 2)	410/46012	ex 5N-AWZ	ZS-OZI resd
3D-AFR	Douglas DC-8F-54 (QNC 2)	247/45802	ex N46UA	ZS-OZH resd
3D-ETR	Douglas DC-8-54F (BAC 2)	189/45663	ex N565FA	

AIRLINKS SWAZILAND

Swazilink (SZL) (IATA 141)
Manzini-Matsapha (MTS)

| ZS-NRK | British Aerospace Jetstream 41 | 41065 | ex G-4-065 | Lsd fr/op by LNK |

Joint venture between South African Airlink and the Swaziland Government; leases other aircraft from the former

CITY AIR SERVICES

Beira

3D-ENG	LET L-410UVP			
3D-NEB	LET L-410UVP			
3D-NVA	LET L-410UVP	882035		
3D-NVC	LET L-410UVP	831033	ex RA-67405	

Operates for SENA, a sugar company

INTERFLIGHT

Intercon (JMV)
Manzini-Matsapha (MTS)

| 3D-JNM | Boeing 727-89 (FedEx 3) | 255/19139 | ex N511DB | Lsd to TTG |
| 3D-KIM | LET L-410UVP | 851416 | ex 3C-ZZC | Lsd to Jetair |

NORTHEAST AIRLINES

(NEY)
Manzini-Matsapha (MTS)

3D-NEC	Lockheed L-1011-50 Tristar	1096	ex N310SS	Lsd fr Sound Corp
3D-NEG	Lockheed L-1011-50 Tristar	1066	ex N31019	Lsd fr Tristar Capital
3D-NEL	Lockheed L-1011-50 Tristar	1066	ex N31019	Lsd fr Tristar Capital
3D-NE	Lockheed L-1011-50 Tristar	1100	ex N312GB	
3D-	Douglas DC-8-63	391/45931	ex N4935C	
3D-NED	Boeing 747-283B	147/20009	ex SE-RBP	on order
3D-NEE	Boeing 747-212B	283/21162	ex SE-RBN	on order
3D-NEF	Boeing 747-212B	309/21316	ex SE-RBH	on order

ROM ATLANTIC INTERNATIONAL status uncertain as sole aircraft disposed of

SKY AVIATION leasing company only - some aircraft listed under Spirit of Africa Airlines

SWAZI EXPRESS AIRWAYS

Swazi Express (Q4/SWX)   *Manzini-Matsapha (MTS)*

3D-SEA   Swearingen SA.227AC Metro III   AC-573 ex ZS-OWK   Lsd fr Steffen Air

WESTAIR CARGO AIRLINES

3D-PHS   Boeing 737-268C   295/20575 ex HZ-AGB

3X - GUINEA (Republic of Guinea)

AIR GUINÉE ceased operations and replaced by Air Guinee Express

AIR GUINÉE EXPRESS

(2U/GIP)   *Conakry (CKY)*

3X-GCB	Boeing 737-2R6C	779/22627		
3X-GCM	Boeing 737-205	1266/23469	ex N469NA	Lsd fr NI Aircraft Lsg
3X-	Boeing 737-266		ex HZ-	on order
3X-GDN	Douglas DC-8F			

GUINÉE AIR SERVICES

Gass (GIS)   *Conakry (CKY)*

Operates charter services with Antonov An-24/26s leased from other operators as required

SOCIETÉ DES TRANSPORTS AÉRIENS DE GUINÉE

Sotag (GIT)   *Conakry (CKY)*

Operates charter flights with Tu-154 aircraft leased from Russian operators as required

SUD AIR TRANSPORT

Sud Transport (GID)   *Conakry (CKY)*

Operates charter flights with Antonov An-24/26 aircraft leased from Russian operators as required

UNION DES TRANSPORTS AFRICAINS DE GUINÉE

Transport Africain (GIH)   *Conakry (CKY)*

9L-LBG   Antonov An-24   ex

4K - AZERBAIJAN (Republic of Azerbaijan)

AZAL AZERBAIJAN AIRLINES

Azal (J2/AHY) (IATA 771)   *Baku-Bina (BAK)*

4K-65496	Tupolev Tu-134B-3	63468		Op for Govt	Lsd fr Azerbaijan AF
4K-65704	Tupolev Tu-134B-3	63410	ex YL-LBJ	
4K-65705	Tupolev Tu-134B-3	63415	ex CCCP-65705	stored BAK
4K-65708	Tupolev Tu-134B-3	63447	ex AL-65708	stored BAK
4K-65710	Tupolev Tu-134B-3	63490	ex AL-65710	stored BAK
4K-65711	Tupolev Tu-134B-3	63498	ex AL-65711	stored BAK
4K-65712	Tupolev Tu-134B-3	63515	ex YL-LBL	
4K-65713	Tupolev Tu-134B-3	63520	ex CCCP-65713	
4K-65714	Tupolev Tu-134B-3	63527	ex CCCP-65714	
4K-87257	Yakovlev Yak-40	9311426	ex CCCP-87257	
4K-87415	Yakovlev Yak-40	9420734	ex CCCP-87415	
4K-87478	Yakovlev Yak-40	9440638	ex CCCP-87478	
4K-87812	Yakovlev Yak-40	9230424	ex CCCP-87812	
4K-88174	Yakovlev Yak-40	9621247	ex CCCP-88174	
4K-AZ1	Boeing 727-235 (FedEx 3)	531/19460	ex 4K-4201	
4K-AZ8	Boeing 727-230	870/20525	ex OM-AHK	
4K-AZ10	Tupolev Tu-154M	98A-1013		Op for Govt
4K-AZ38	Boeing 757-256	620/26246	ex N262CT	Lsd fr CIT Lsg
4K-85548	Tupolev Tu-154B-2	82A-548	ex 85548	
4K-85729	Tupolev Tu-154M	92A-911	ex CCCP-85729	VIP
4K-85734	Tupolev Tu-154M	92A-916	ex RA-85734	
4K-85738	Tupolev Tu-154M	92A-921	ex LZ-LCC	

| VP-BBR | Boeing 757-22L | 894/29305 | ex N6046P | Lsd fr Azerbaijan Finance |
| VP-BBS | Boeing 757-22L | 947/30834 | | Lsd fr Azerbaijan Finance |

AZAL CARGO

Azalaviacargo (AHC)   *Baku-Bina (BAK)*

4K-AZ14	Ilyushin Il-76TD	1023412389	ex UR-76447	
4K-AZ15	Ilyushin Il-76TD	1033417569	ex RA-76379	
4K-AZ16	Ilyushin Il-76TD	1023412411	ex UK 76410	
4K-AZ19	Ilyushin Il-76MD	0053460820	ex UR-76408	
4K-AZ22	Ilyushin Il-76TD	0053464926	ex UR-76664	
4K-AZ27	Ilyushin Il-76MD	0053460287	ex EP-IBS	Lsd fr AZQ
4K-AZ28	Ilyushin Il-76TD	0063471147	ex ER-IBB	
4K-78129	Ilyushin Il-76MD	0083489683	ex UR-78129	Lsd fr TII
4K-86810	Ilyushin Il-76M	053404094	ex RA-86810	
4K-AZ18	Antonov An-12B	9346308	ex RA-12108	all white
4K-AZ20	Antonov An-26B			ATIR titles
4K-AZ30	Antonov An-12BP	5343410		all-white
4K-AZ32	Antonov An-12	5343006	ex	
4K-AZ35	Antonov An-12BK	00347102		Lsd fr Applex AAC Lsg
4K-AZ36	Antonov An-12BK	8345807		
4K-AZ39	Antonov An-26	97307805		
4K-26584	Antonov An-26B	13509	ex 26584	

Division of Azerbaijan Airlines; leases further Ilyushin Il-76s as required

ETRAMAIR WING

Baku-Bina (BAK)

| 4K-48136 | Antonov An-32 | 3103 | ex 48136 |

IMAIR

Improtex (IK/ITX)   *Baku-Bina (BAK)*

| 4K-AZ17 | Tupolev Tu-154M | 85A-718 | ex B-2603 |
| 4K-85732 | Tupolev Tu-154M | 92A-914 | ex CCCP-85732 |

SILK WAY AIRLINES

Silk Line (ZP/AZQ)   *Baku Bina (BAK)*

4K-AZ23	Antonov An-12BK	8345605	ex RA-11715	all-white	
4K-AZ27	Ilyushin Il-76TD	0053460827	ex ER-IBS		Op for AHC
4K-AZ31	Ilyushin Il-76TD	1013405184	ex RA-76426		
4K-AZ33	Antonov An-12BK	8346201	ex RA-11267		

TURANAIR

Turan (3T/URN)   *Baku-Bina (BAK)*

4K-325	Tupolev Tu-154B-2	78A-325	ex HA-LCM	
4K-473	Tupolev Tu-154B-2	81A-473	ex HA-LCO	
4K-474	Tupolev Tu-154B-2	81A-474	ex 4K-85474	
4K-727*	Tupolev Tu-154M	86A-727	ex SP-LCA	Sub-lsd to BUC as LZ-LGS
4K-733*	Tupolev Tu-154M	86A-733	ex SP-LCB	Sub-lsd to BUC as LZ-LGV
4K-85524	Tupolev Tu-154B-2	82A-524	ex YL-LAG	

*Leased from VARZ

4L - GEORGIA (Republic of Georgia)

ABAVIA status uncertain, sole aircraft now operated by Air Bisec

ADJARIA AIRLINES

(MNM)   *Tbilisi (TBS)*

| 4L-AAM | Yakovlev Yak-42D | 4520423116579 | ex B-2754 | |
| 4L-AAR | Yakovlev Yak-42D | 4520423116650 | ex B-2751 | no titles |

AIR BISEC

Tbilisi (TBS)

| 4L-65061 | Tupolev Tu-134A-3 | 49874 | ex CCCP-65061 |

AIRZENA GEORGIAN AIRLINES

Tamazi (A9/TGZ) (IATA 606)   *Tbilisi (TBS)*

D-AHLF	Boeing 737-5K5	1968/24927	Tbilisi	Lsd fr HLF
D-AHLI	Boeing 737-5K5	2022/25037	Kakheti	Lsd fr HLF
4L-TGA	Boeing 737-529	2111/25218 ex N218CT	Kakhi Asatiani	Lsd fr CIT Lsg
4L-85496	Tupolev Tu-154B-2	81A-496 ex RA-85496		Lsd to TLR

AVIAEXPRESSCRUISE

(GGO)   *Tbilisi (TBS)*

Current status is uncertain, believed to have ceased operation before code allocated

CAUCASUS AIRLINES

Silk Road (NS/SRJ)   *Tbilisi (TBS)*

4L-XLA	Embraer EMB.120RT Brasilia	120081 ex PH-XLA	
4L-XLF	Embraer EMB.120ER Brasilia	120082 ex PH-XLF	

GEORGIAN AIRLINES

(GEO)   *Tbilisi (TBS)*

4L-AVC	Yakovlev Yak-40	9342031	
4L-AVD	Yakovlev Yak-40	9430537 ex 4L-87466	
4L-AVK	Yakovlev Yak-40	9311526 ex 4L-87258	

LASARE AIR

Aero Lasare (LRE)   *Tbilisi (TBS)*

4L-CAA	Antonov An-12BP	402102 ex 4L-11241		Lsd to Sant Air
4L-11304	Antonov An-12BP	0901304 ex EK-11304	stored TBS	

TBILAVIAMSHENI

Tbilavia (L6/VNZ)   *Tbilisi (TBS)*

4L-AAJ	Tupolev Tu-134A	63860 ex 4L-65993	Georgia titles	
4L-AAK	Yakovlev Yak-40	9531043 ex 4L-87242		
4L-26087	Antonov An-26B	12601 ex GR-26087		
4L-86558	Ilyushin Il-62M	1052128 ex RA-86558	Op for Govt	

4R - SRI LANKA (Democratic Socialist Republic of Sri Lanka)

AERO LANKA

AeroLanka   *Colombo-Bandaranayike Intl (CMB)*

N6819	Boeing 727-223F (FedEx3)	661/19494	Lsd fr Prewitt Lsg

EXPO AVIATION

Expoavia (8D/EXV)   *Colombo-Bandaranayike Intl (CMB)*

EX-24808	Antonov An-24RV	77310808 ex YR-BMN	Lsd fr AAP
4R-EXC	Ilyushin Il-18		
4R-EXD	Ilyushin Il-18GrM	187009802 ex YR-IMZ	Lsd fr RMV
4R-EXE	Ilyushin Il-18GrM	187010403 ex EX-75466	Lsd fr PHG
4R-EXF	Fokker F.27 Friendship 500RF	10631 ex A4O-FC	
4R-EXG	Fokker F.27 Friendship 500RF	10630 ex A4O-FB	
4R-EXH	Fokker F.27 Friendship 500RF	10642 ex A4O-FG	

LION AIR

Sri-Lion (LEO)   *Colombo-Bandaranayike Intl (CMB)*

(4R-LPV)	Hawker Siddeley.748 Srs.2B/501	1807 ex ZS-AGB	Lsd fr EAS

SERENDIB EXPRESS

Serendib (QL/RNL)   *Sharjah (SHJ)*

4R-SEL	Antonov An-24RV	77310807 ex EX24807	Lsd fr AAP
4R-SEM	Boeing 727-223F (FedEx 3)	661/19494 ex N6819	
4R-SEN	Swearingen SA.227AC Metro III	AC-485 ex N890MA	
4R-	Swearingen SA.227AC Metro III	AC-652 ex N26877	

SRILANKAN

Srilankan (UL/ALK) (IATA 603)
Colombo-Bandaranaike Intl (CMB)

4R-ABB	Airbus Industrie A320-231	0406	ex F-WWDB	Lsd fr Boullioun
4R-ABC	Airbus Industrie A320-230	0304	ex N304RX	Lsd fr WTCo
4R-ABD	Airbus Industrie A320-231	0315	ex N643AW	Lsd fr WTCo
4R-ADA	Airbus Industrie A340-311	032	ex F-WWJT	Lsd fr Serendib Ltd
4R-ADB	Airbus Industrie A340-311	033	ex F-WWJU	Lsd fr Serendib Ltd
4R-ADC	Airbus Industrie A340-311	034	ex F-WWJY	
4R-ADE	Airbus Industrie A340-313X	367	ex F-GTUA	
4R-ADF	Airbus Industrie A340-313X	374	ex F-GTUB	
4R-ALA	Airbus Industrie A330-243	303	ex F-WWYH	Lsd fr Taprobane
4R-ALB	Airbus Industrie A330-243	306	ex F-WWYL	Lsd fr Taprobane
4R-ALC	Airbus Industrie A330-243	311	ex F-WWYN	Lsd fr Taprobane
4R-ALD	Airbus Industrie A330-243	313	ex F-WWYP	Lsd fr Taprobane

Partially owned and controlled by Emirates. Cargo operations use code ULC as SriLanka Cargo
SriLankan Air Taxi is a wholly owned subsidiary

SRILANKAN AIR TAXI

Colombo-Bandaranaike Intl (CMB)

4R-	Cessna 208 Caravan		amphibian
4R-	Cessna 208 Caravan		amphibian

Wholly owned subsidiary of SriLankan

4X - ISRAEL (State of Israel)

ARKIA ISRAELI AIRLINES

Arkia (IZ/AIZ) (IATA 238)
Tel Aviv-Ben Gurion/Sde Dov (TLV/SDV)

4X-AHA	de Havilland DHC-7-102	60	ex 5N-BDS	stored SDV
4X-AHC	de Havilland DHC-7-102	82	ex 5N-BDT	stored SDV
4X-AHD	de Havilland DHC-7-102	55	ex 5N-EMR	stored SDV
4X-AHF	de Havilland DHC-7-102	77	ex N76598	
4X-AHG	de Havilland DHC-7-102	33	ex N235SL	Metulla
4X-AHH	de Havilland DHC-7-102	45	ex N7156J	
4X-AHI	de Havilland DHC-7-102	8	ex	stored SDV
4X-AHJ	de Havilland DHC-7-102	50	ex G-BRYE	
4X-AHM	de Havilland DHC-7-102	73	ex 5N-SKA	stored SDV
4X-AVU	Aerospatiale/Alenia ATR 72-212A	587	ex F-WWES	
4X-AVW	Aerospatiale/Alenia ATR 72-212A	583	ex F-WWER	
4X-AVX	Aerospatiale/Alenia ATR 72-212A	656	ex F-WWEJ	
4X-AVZ	Aerospatiale/Alenia ATR 72-212A	577	ex F-WWEN	
4X-AYT	Britten-Norman BN-2A Islander	96	ex IAF 4X-FN-/00	
4X-BAU	Boeing 757-3E7	906/30178	ex N1003M	
4X-BAW	Boeing 757-3E7	912/30179		
4X-BAZ	Boeing 757-236	183/24121	ex EC-HUT	Lsd fr BBAM

AYEET AVIATION

Ayeet (AYT)
Beer-Sheba (BEV)

4X-AHP	de Havilland DHC-6 Twin Otter 100	75	ex C-FCSF	Lsd fr Lev-David Hotels
4X-AYS	Britten-Norman BN-2A-8 Islander	376	ex (G-BJWL)	
4X-CAH	Britten-Norman BN-2A-26 Islander	150	ex G-PASW	

CARGO AIR LINES

CAL (5C/ICL) (IATA 700)
Tel Aviv-Ben Gurion (TLV)

4X-ICL	Boeing 747-271C	416/21964	ex N538MC	Lsd fr GTI
4X-ICM	Boeing 747-271C	438/21965	ex N539MC	Lsd fr GTI
4X-ICN	Boeing 747-2B5B(SF)	513/222485	ex N285SW	Lsd fr UT Finance

EL AL ISRAEL AIRLINES

ElAl (LY/ELY) (IATA 114)
Tel Aviv-Ben Gurion (TLV)

4X-EKA	Boeing 737-858	204/29957		801	Tiberias
4X-EKB	Boeing 737-858	249/29958		802	Eilat
4X-EKC	Boeing 737-858	314/29959		803	Beit Shean
4X-EKD	Boeing 737-758	327/29960		701	Beth-Shean
4X-EKE	Boeing 737-758	442/29961		702	Nazareth
4X-EKI	Boeing 737-86N	192/28587	ex N802NA	804	Lsd fr GECAS
4X-EKJ	Boeing 737-86N			on order	

Reg	Type	Serial	ex	Fleet	Notes
4X-AXF	Boeing 747-258C	327/21594		405	Freighter
4X-AXH	Boeing 747-258B (SCD)	418/22254		407	
4X-AXK	Boeing 747-245F	478/22151	ex 9V-SQU	410	
4X-AXL	Boeing 747-245F	476/22150	ex 9V-SQT	411	all-white
4X-AXQ	Boeing 747-238B	233/20841	ex VH-EBG	408	
4X-ELA	Boeing 747-458	1027/26055		201	
4X-ELB	Boeing 747-458	1032/26056	ex N60697	202	Haifa
4X-ELC	Boeing 747-458	1062/27915	ex N6009F	203	
4X-ELD	Boeing 747-458	1215/29328		204	Jerusalem

All Boeing 747-200s are for sale
Two Boeing 747-458Fs are reserved as 4X-ELK/ELL, for future delivery

Reg	Type	Serial	ex	Fleet	Notes
4X-EBI	Boeing 757-258	745/27622		508	Lsd fr ILFC; sublsd to ISR
4X-EBM	Boeing 757-258	156/23918		502	Op for ISR
4X-EBO	Boeing 757-236ER	174/24120	ex G-BPEF		Lsd fr BBAM; op for ERO
4X-EBS	Boeing 757-258ER	325/24884		504	
4X-EBT	Boeing 757-258ER	356/25036		505	Lsd to/op for ERO
4X-EBU	Boeing 757-258	529/26053		506	
4X-EBV	Boeing 757-258	547/26054		507	
4X-EAA	Boeing 767-258	62/22972	ex N6066Z	601	
4X-EAB	Boeing 767-258	68/22973	ex N6018N	602	
4X-EAC	Boeing 767-258ER	86/22974	ex N6018N	603	
4X-EAD	Boeing 767-258ER	89/22975	ex N6046P	604	
4X-EAE	Boeing 767-27EER	316/24832	ex F-GHGD	605	
4X-EAF	Boeing 767-27EER	326/24854	ex F-GHGE	606	
4X-ECA	Boeing 777-258ER	319/30831		101	
4X-ECB	Boeing 777-258ER	325/30832		102	
4X-ECC	Boeing 777-258ER	335/30833		103	
4X-ECD	Boeing 777-258ER	405/33169		104	

EL-ROM AIRLINES

(ELR)   Tel Aviv-Sde Dov (SDV)

4X-CCD	Piper PA-31-350 Navajo Chieftain	31-7652166	ex N62919
4X-CCF	Piper PA-31-350 Navajo Chieftain	31-7652169	ex N62921

ISRAIR

Israir (6H/ISR)   Tel Aviv-Ben Gurion (TLV)

4X-ATL	Aerospatiale/Alenia ATR 42-320	089	ex F-WQCY		
4X-ATM	Aerospatiale/Alenia ATR 42-320	069	ex F-WQFS		
4X-ATN	Aerospatiale/Alenia ATR 42-320	053	ex F-WQGN		
4X-ATO	Aerospatiale/Alenia ATR 42-320	064	ex F-GPEC		
4X-EBI	Boeing 757-258	745/27622		all-white	Op by ELY
4X-EBM	Boeing 757-258	156/23918			Op by ELY

MOONAIR AVIATION

Tel Aviv-Sde Dov (SDV)

4X-CCJ	Piper PA-31-350 Navajo Chieftain	31-7405140	ex G-FOEL

NESHER AVIATION & TOURISM

Tel Aviv-Sde Dov (SDV)

4X-AYH	Britten-Norman BN-2A-21 Islander	446	ex N93JA
4X-CAY	Britten-Norman BN-2A-26 Islander	640	ex G-AYOC
4X-CBZ	Cessna 402B	402B0531	ex EC-CJE
4X-DZP	Cessna T310R	310R0731	ex N816P

SUN D'OR INTERNATIONAL AIRLINES

Echo Romeo (7L/ERO)   Tel Aviv-Ben Gurion (TLV)

4X-EBO	Boeing 757-236ER	174/24120	ex G-BPEF		Lsd fr ELY
4X-EBT	Boeing 757-258ER	356/25036		505	Lsd fr ELY
4X-EKI	Boeing 737-86N	192/28587	ex N802NA	804	Lsd fr ELY

Operates charter service with aircraft leased from parent, El Al Israel Airlines, or Arkia as required

5A - LIBYA (Socialist People's Libyan Arab Jamahiriya)

AFRIQIYAH AIRWAYS

D-AHLU	Boeing 737-4K5	2677/27831		Lsd fr BPA
TS-IAY	Airbus Industrie A300B4-620	354	ex A6-SHZ	Lsd fr NVJ, op for Govt of Libya
TS-ING	Airbus Industrie A320-211	0140	ex D-AKFW	Lsd fr LBT
TS-INH	Airbus Industrie A320-211	0157	ex D-AKFY	Lsd fr LBT

Afriqiyah Airways is the trading name of African Airlines Corporation

AIR LIBYA TIBESTI

Air Libya (7Q/TLR)   *Benghazi (BEN)*
Previously listed as Tibesti Air Libya

EX-87228	Yakovlev Yak-40D	9841659	ex RA-87228	Sara	Lsd fr AAP
EX-87250	Yakovlev Yak-40	9310726	ex CCCP-87250		Lsd fr KGA
EX-87412	Yakovlev Yak-40	9420434	ex RA-87412		Lsd fr AAP
EX-87426	Yakovlev Yak-40	9420235	ex CCCP-8726		Lsd fr AAP
EX-88207	Yakovlev Yak-40	9631149	ex RA-88207		Lsd fr AAP
EX-88270	Yakovlev Yak-40	9720853	ex RA-88270		Lsd fr AAP
UN-87357	Yakovlev Yak-40	9520242	ex CCCP-87357		Lsd fr VDA
UN-88268	Yakovlev Yak-40	9720653	ex CCCP-88268	all-white	Lsd fr BMK
9L-LDK	Yakovlev Yak-40				
EK-13399	Antonov An-26	2606	ex RA-13399		Lsd fr URT
EK-46630	Antonov An-24RV	37308809	ex UR-46630		Lsd fr URT
UN-11002	Antonov An-12	4341705	ex		Lsd fr BMK
UN-65699	Tupolev Tu-134B-3	63333	ex YL-LBG		Lsd fr Aqualine
4L-85496	Tupolev Tu-154B-2	81A-496	ex RA-85496		Lsd fr TGZ
5A-DBM	Cessna 421C Golden Eagle	421C0142	ex N3913C		
5A-DEP	Cessna A185F Skywagon	18502650			
5A-DKZ	Cessna 402C	402C0089	ex N2614D		
5A-	Antonov An-140			on order Jun04	
5A-	Antonov An-140			on order 4Q04	

Three more Antonov An-140s are on order for delivery in 2005

AIR ONE NINE

YU-AOJ	Fokker F.28 Fellowship 2000	11187	ex F-WQPL	Lsd fr MGX

BURAQ AIR TRANSPORT

EX-417	LET L-410UVP	851417	ex CCCP-67513	Lsd fr AAP
ST-CAT	LET L-410UVP	902527	ex SP-FGM	Lsd fr CCW
ST-CAU	LET L-410UVP	892340	ex RA-67612	Lsd fr CCW
ST-DND	LET L-410UVP-E10A	912528	ex SP-FGH	Lsd fr DND
UN-76005	Ilyushin Il-76TD	0073479392	ex 76649	Lsd fr BMK
5A-DMN	Boeing 727-228	1710/22287	ex TC-JEC	
5A-DMO	Boeing 727-2F2	1088/20983	ex TC-JBJ	
5A-DMP	Boeing 727-2F2	1086/20981	ex TC-JBG	

LIBYAN ARAB AIR CARGO

5A-DOA	Antonov An-26		ex Libyan AF	
5A-DOB	Antonov An-26	27312307	ex Libyan AF	
5A-DOC	Antonov An-26		ex Libyan AF	
5A-DOF	Antonov An-26	13007	ex 8908 Libyan AF	
5A-DOU	Antonov An-26	27313109	ex Libyan AF	
5A-DOV	Antonov An-26	27313201	ex Libyan AF	
5A-DNB	Ilyushin Il-76TD	0023437086		
5A-DNC	Ilyushin Il-76TD	0023437084		stored TIP
5A-DND	Ilyushin Il-76TD	0033445299		
5A-DNE	Ilyushin Il-76T	0013432952		
5A-DNG	Ilyushin Il-76TD	0013432961		
5A-DNH	Ilyushin Il-76TD	0033446356		stored TIP
5A-DNI	Ilyushin Il-76T	0013430878		airworthy
5A-DNJ	Ilyushin Il-76T	0013430869		
5A-DNK	Ilyushin Il-76T	0013430882		
5A-DNO	Ilyushin Il-76TD	0043451509		
5A-DNP	Ilyushin Il-76TD	0043451516		

5A-DNQ	Ilyushin Il-76TD	0043454641			
5A-DNS	Ilyushin Il-76TD	0023439145			
5A-DNT	Ilyushin Il-76TD	0023439141			
5A-DNU	Ilyushin Il-76TD	0043454651			
5A-DNV	Ilyushin Il-76TD	0043454645			
5A-DRR	Ilyushin Il-76M	083415469			
5A-DZZ	Ilyushin Il-76M	093416501			
5A-DJR	Lockheed L-382E Hercules	4302	ex RP-C99		
5A-DKL	Antonov An-124	19530502761	ex UR-82066	Susa	
5A-DKN	Antonov An-124				
5A-DOM	Lockheed L-382G Hercules	4992	ex N4268M		

LIBYAN ARAB AIRLINES

Libair(LN/LAA) (IATA 148)   *Tripoli-Ben Gashir Intl (TIP)*

3D-AAK	Boeing 727-223	1263/21089	ex 3X-GDM		
5A-DIB	Boeing 727-2L5	1109/21051			
5A-DIC	Boeing 727-2L5	1110/21052		stored TIP	
5A-DID	Boeing 727-2L5	1213/21229		stored TIP	
5A-DIE	Boeing 727-2L5	1215/21230		stored TIP	
5A-DIF	Boeing 727-2L5	1257/21332			
5A-DIH	Boeing 727-2L5	1371/21539	ex N1253E		
5A-DII	Boeing 727-2L5	1386/21540	ex N1261E		
5A-DCT	de Havilland DHC-6 Twin Otter 300	627			
5A-DCV	de Havilland DHC-6 Twin Otter 300	637			
5A-DCX	de Havilland DHC-6 Twin Otter 300	641			
5A-DCZ	de Havilland DHC-6 Twin Otter 300	645			
5A-DDB	de Havilland DHC-6 Twin Otter 300	653			
5A-DDC	de Havilland DHC-6 Twin Otter 300	670			
5A-DDE	de Havilland DHC-6 Twin Otter 300	677			
5A-DHN	de Havilland DHC-6 Twin Otter 300	712		Op for Agoco-Arabian Gulf Oil	
5A-DHY	de Havilland DHC-6 Twin Otter 300	661	ex C-GELZ		
5A-DJG	de Havilland DHC-6 Twin Otter 300	744	ex C-GFHQ		
5A-DJH	de Havilland DHC-6 Twin Otter 300	747			
5A-DJI	de Havilland DHC-6 Twin Otter 300	757			
5A-DJJ	de Havilland DHC-6 Twin Otter 300	769			
TS-IAX	Airbus Industrie A300B4-622R	601	ex JY-GAX		Lsd fr/op by NVJ
TS-IAZ	Airbus Industrie A300B4-622R	616	ex JY-GAZ		Lsd fr/op by NVJ
TS-IGU	Airbus Industrie A310-203	295	ex JY-AGU		Lsd fr/op by NVJ
TS-IGV	Airbus Industrie A310-203	306	ex JY-AGV		Lsd fr/op by NVJ
5A-DDG	BAC One-Eleven 414EG	158	ex C5-LKI		
5A-DGC	Cessna 402C	402C0045	ex N5800C		
5A-DHG	Cessna 402C	402C0464	ex N8737Q		
5A-DHH	Cessna 402C	402C0444	ex N6790F		
5A-DHZ	Swearingen SA.226AT Merlin III	T-345	ex OO-HSC		
5A-DJB	Swearingen SA.226AT Merlin III	T-388	ex OO-XSC		
5A-AGU	Airbus Industrie A310-203	295	ex JY-AGU		Lsd fr RJA
5A-DLV	Fokker F.28 Fellowship 4000	11200	ex PH-EXV		
5A-DLW	Fokker F.28 Fellowship 4000	11194	ex PH-EXZ		
5A-DTG	Fokker F.28 Fellowship 4000	11139	ex PK-MSU		
5A-DTH	Fokker F.28 Fellowship 4000	11140	ex PK-MSV		

TIBESTI AIR LIBYA   now listed as Air Libya Tibesti

TOBRUK AIR

Tobruk Air (TOB)   *Tripoli-Ben Gashir Intl (TIP)*

Operates cargo flights with Ilyushin Il-76 aircraft as and when required

5B - CYPRUS (Republic of Cyprus)

AEROTRANS   ceased operations

CYPRUS AIRWAYS

Cyprus (CY/CYP) (IATA 048)   *Larnaca (LCA)*

5B-DAT	Airbus Industrie A320-231	0028	ex YU-AOB	Praxandros	
5B-DAU	Airbus Industrie A320-231	0035	ex F-WWDX	Evelthon	
5B-DAV	Airbus Industrie A320-231	0037	ex F-WWDN	Kinyras	
5B-DAW	Airbus Industrie A320-231	0038	ex F-WWDZ	Agapinor	
5B-DBA	Airbus Industrie A320-231	0180	ex F-WWIT	Evagoras	
5B-DBB	Airbus Industrie A320-231	0256	ex F-WWBH	Akamas	
5B-DBC	Airbus Industrie A320-231	0295	ex F-WWIE	Tefkros	

5B-DBD	Airbus Industrie A320-231	0316	ex F-WWBC	Onisillos	
5B-DBO	Airbus Industrie A319-112	1729	ex D-AVWR	Nikoklis	
5B-DBP	Airbus Industrie A319-112	1768	ex D-AVWB	Chalkanor	
5B-DBS	Airbus Industrie A330-243	505	ex F-WWKO	Ammochostos	Lsd fr ILFC
5B-DBT	Airbus Industrie A330-243	526	ex F-WWKY	Keryneia	Lsd fr ILFC

Eurocypria is 51% owned subsidiary

EUROCYPRIA AIRWAYS

Eurocypria (UI/ECA)   *Larnaca (LCA)*

5B-DBU	Boeing 737-8Q8	1272/32796	ex N6055X	Zephyros	Lsd fr ILFC
5B-DBV	Boeing 737-8Q8	1295/30654		Levantes	Lsd fr ILFC
5B-DBW	Boeing 737-8Q8	1307/30671			Lsd fr ILFC
5B-DBX	Boeing 737-8Q8	1309/33699		Gregos	Lsd fr ILFC

51% owned by Cyprus Airways

HELIOS AIRWAYS

Helios (ZU/HCY) (IATA 032)   *Larnaca (LCA)*

| 5B-DBH | Boeing 737-86N | 790/30806 | | Zela | Lsd fr GECAS |
| 5B-DBI | Boeing 737-86N | 829/30807 | | Veni | Lsd fr GECAS |

5H - TANZANIA (United Republic of Tanzania)

AIR EXCEL

(XLL)   *Arusha (ARK)*

5H-AEL	Cessna 404 Titan	404-0835	ex 5H-THF	
5H-AXL	Cessna 208B Caravan I	208B0401	ex D-FHEW	Lsd fr Aviation Finance Group
5H-EMK	Cessna TU206G Stationair 6	U20604638	ex 5H-SDA	
5H-SMK	Cessna 208B Caravan I	208B0654	ex VT-TAP	Lsd fr Nordic Avn Contractor
5H-WOW	Reims Cessna F406 Caravan II	F406-0060	ex PH-GUG	Lsd fr Gen Air Services

AIR EXPRESS ZANZIBAR

Khaki Express (ZG/AEJ)   *Zanzibar*

| ZS-OBS | LET L-410UVP | 932731 | ex S9-TBA | Lsd fr IYU Partnership |

AIR TANZANIA

Tanzania (TC/ATC) (IATA 197)   *Dar-es-Salaam (DAR)*

ZS-OVM	Dornier 228-201	8056	ex (ZS-STA)		Lsd fr VSA Aviation
5H-ATC	Boeing 737-2R8C	546/21710		Kilimanjaro	
5H-MUZ	Boeing 737-236	662/22029	ex ZS-SIV		Lsd fr SAA
5H-MVA	Boeing 737-236	722/22031	ex ZS-SIW		Lsd fr SAA

49% owned by South African Airways;

COASTAL AVIATION

    Dar-es-Salaam (DAR)

5H-BAT	Cessna 208B Caravan I	208B1030	ex N12554	
5H-	Cessna 208B Caravan I	208B0929	ex N1129K	
5H-CCT	Cessna TU206G Stationair 6	U20604597	ex ZS-MXV	
5H-CTL	Cessna TU206F Staionair	U20601988		
5H-ELO	Beech Baron 58	TH-1492	ex 5Y-DTD	
5H-EXC	Pilatus PC-12/45	220	ex ZS-EXC	Lsd fr Swiss Avn
5H-GUN	Cessna U206G Stationair 6	U20605223	ex 5H-TGT	
5H-HOT	Cessna 208B Caravan I	208B0677	ex N1256N	
5H-JAY	Cessna 340	340-0225	ex 5Y-ATC	
5H-JET	Piper PA-34-200T Seneca II	34-7870345		
5H-MAD	Cessna 208B Caravan I	208B0872	ex N1294K	Lsd fr Cessna Finance
5H-POA	Cessna 208B Caravan I	208B0965	ex N1129Y	
5H-SRP	Pilatus PC-12/45	317	ex HB-	Lsd fr Swiss Avn
5H-TOY	Cessna 404 Titan	404-0668	ex 5Y-MCK	

NAHALO AIR SAFARIS ceased operations

NORTHERN AIR

    Arusha (ARK)

5H-NAA	Cessna 208 Caravan I	20800109	ex N9628F
5H-NAC	Cessna 208B Caravan I	208B0757	ex N1307D
5H-SJF	Cessna 208B Caravan I	208B0950	ex N1130T

PRECISIONAIR

Precisionair (PW/PRF) (IATA 031)   *Zanzibar (ZNZ)*

5H-PAA	Aerospatiale/Alenia ATR 42-320	308	ex F-WQHB	City of Arusha
5H-PAC	LET L-410UVP-E20	922711	ex OK-XDI	Lsd fr LET Aircraft
5H-PAD	LET L-410UVP-E20	871811	ex OK-SDO	Lsd fr LET Aircraft
5H-PAE	LET L-410UVP-E20	982631	ex OK-DDE	Lsd fr Pamco spol
5H-PAF	Cessna 208B Caravan I	208B0754	ex N1772E	
5H-PAG	Aerospatiale/Alenia ATR 42-320	384	ex F-WQJO	
5H-PAJ	LET L-410UVP	871920	ex ZS-OOF	

REGIONAL AIR SERVICES

Arusha (ARK)

5H-MUA	Cessna 208B Caravan I	208B0481	ex ZS-OJF	
5H-MUC	de Havilland DHC-6 Twin Otter 300	580	ex 5Y-BIJ	
5H-MUR	Cessna 208 Caravan I	20800004	ex 5Y-MAK	Lsd fr Aircraft Lsg Svs
5H-MUW	de Havilland DHC-6 Twin Otter 300	149	ex ZS-ORJ	Lsd fr Executive Turbine

Subsidiary of AirKenya

SKYAIR

Dar-es-Salaam (DAR)

5H-SKT	Piper PA-31-350 Chieftain	31-8152058	ex A2-AHP	
5H-SKV	Piper PA-31-350 Navajo Chieftain	31-7752181	ex 5H-TAP	
5H-SKX	Cessna 402B	402B0829	ex 5Y-EAL	

TANZANAIR – TANZANIAN AIR SERVICES

Dar-es-Salaam (DAR)

5H-LDS	Cessna 310I	310I0029	ex 5Y-AJN	
5H-TZA	Cessna 310R	310R1333	ex N6200C	
5H-TZE	Reims Cessna F406 Caravan II	F406-0046	ex OY-PED	

ZANAIR

Zanzibar (ZNZ)

5H-LET	LET L-410UVP	831125	ex 9L-LBK	
5H-ZAL	Cessna 402B	402B0640	ex TU-TJA	
5H-ZAP	LET L-410UVP	871824	ex 9L-LBV	
5H-ZAY	Cessna 404 Titan	404-0207	ex N798A	
5H-ZAZ	Cessna 402C	402C0029	ex 5Y-NNM	

ZANTAS AIR SERVICE

Zanzibar (ZNZ)

5H-TAK	Cessna 208B Caravan I	208B0891	ex	Lsd fr Cessna Finance

5N - NIGERIA (Federal Republic of Nigeria)

ADC AIRLINES

Adco (ADK)   *Lagos (LOS)*

5N-BED	Boeing 737-204 (Nordam 3)	858/22638	ex ZK-NAA	Lsd fr debis
5N-BEE	Boeing 737-204 (Nordam 3)	700/22365	ex ZK-NAI	Lsd fr debis
5N-BFJ	Boeing 737-2B7 (Nordam 3)	986/22890	ex N278AU	
5N-BFK	Boeing 737-2B7 (Nordam 3)	/22891	ex N279AU	

AERO CONTRACTORS

Aeroline (AJ/NIG)   *Lagos (LOS)*

5N-AQK	Aerospatiale SA.365N Dauphin 2	6108		Op for NNPC	
5N-AQL	Aerospatiale SA.365N Dauphin 2	6109		Op for NNPC	
5N-BAF	Aerospatiale SA.365N2 Dauphin 2	6430	ex F-WYMC	Op for NNPC	
5N-BBR	Aerospatiale SA.365N2 Dauphin 2	6446	ex OY-HMY		
5N-BDA	Aerospatiale SA.365N Dauphin 2	6077	ex PH-SST		
5N-BFP	Aerospatiale SA.365N1 Dauphin	6319	ex LN-OPQ		
5N-ESO	Aerospatiale SA.365N Dauphin 2	6072	ex PH-SSP		
5N-STO	Aerospatiale SA.365N Dauphin 2	6106	ex PH-SSV		
5N-	Aerospatiale SA.365N3 Dauphin	6593	ex PH-SHH		
5N-BEH	de Havilland DHC-8-311	300	ex PH-SDP	stored MST	Lsd fr GECAS

Reg	Type	MSN	ex	Notes
5N-BFB	de Havilland DHC-8-311	298	ex PH-SDM	Lsd fr GECAS
5N-DAP	de Havilland DHC-8-311A	244	ex C-GCDO	
5N-EVD	de Havilland DHC-8-311	216	ex PH-SDI	Lsd fr SCI
5N-MGV	de Havilland DHC-8-102	024	ex C-GMOK	
5N-AOA	Aerospatiale AS.355F Ecureuil 2	5277	ex F-WZFB	Op for NNPC
5N-AOB	Aerospatiale AS.355F Ecureuil 2	5278		Op for NNPC
5N-ASP	de Havilland DHC-6 Twin Otter 310	704	ex PH-SSF	Op for Delta Steel Co
5N-AVG	de Havilland DHC-6 Twin Otter 310	634		Op for NNPC
5N-BBK	Sikorsky S-76B	760310	ex PH-KHA	
5N-BCX	Sikorsky S-76C+	760466	ex SE-JFA	
5N-SDW	Sikorsky S-76B	760350	ex PH-KHC	

An affiliate of Schreiner Airways

AFRIJET AIRLINES

Afrijet (FRJ) — Lagos (LOS)

Reg	Type	MSN	ex	Notes
5N-BCB	Fairchild FH-227B	558	ex XA-SQT	
5N-BCC	Fairchild FH-227B	575	ex HK-1411	
5N-FRJ	Fairchild F-27J	126	ex 3C-ZZE	Freighter

AIR NIGERIA

(NGP) — Lagos (LOS)

Current details unknown

ALBARKA AIR SERVICES

Al-Air (F4/NBK) (IATA -) — Abuja (ABV)

Reg	Type	MSN	ex	Notes
5N-BBP	BAC One-Eleven 518FG	202	ex G-OBWB	stored MLA
5N-BBQ	BAC One-Eleven 520FN	230	ex G-OBWC	stored MLA
5N-BBU	BAC One-Eleven 561RC	252	ex YR-BCI	stored LOS
5N-IMM	Boeing 727-256	915/20603	ex EC-GCK	
5N-AMM	Boeing 727-256	916/20604	ex EC-GCL	

AL-DAWOOD AIR

Bambi (AJK) — Lagos (LOS)

Reg	Type	MSN	ex	Notes
9Q-CAD	Douglas DC-8-63F	386/46000	ex N964R	Lsd fr WFBN

ALLIED AIR

Bambi (AJK) — Lagos (LOS)

Reg	Type	MSN	ex	Notes
5N-OTI	Boeing 727-247 (FedEx 3)	1738/22534	ex N297WA	

Also conducts cargo services with leased Boeing 707C and Douglas DC-10-30Fs as and when required

AMAKO AIR

Amako Air (OBK) — Lagos (LOS)

Reg	Type	MSN	ex	Notes
5N-KHA	Boeing 707-347C (Comtran 2)	745/19967	ex SU-PBC	
5N-KMA	Boeing 707-3K1C (Comtran 2)	884/20805	ex YR-ABC	stored LOS

BELLVIEW AIRLINES

Bellview Airlines (B3/BLV) (IATA 208) — Lagos (LOS)

Reg	Type	MSN	ex	Name	Notes
F-GHXK	Boeing 737-2A1	514/21599	ex N171AW		Lsd fr Alter Bail Avn
F-GHXL	Boeing 737-2S3	570/21775	ex G-BMOR		Lsd fr Alter Bail Avn
5N-BFJ	Boeing 737-				
5N-BFM	Boeing 737-2L9	22733	ex N270FL		
5N-BFN	Boeing 737-2L9	22734	ex N271FL		
5N-BFX	Boeing 737-291	909/22743	ex CC-CVH	Hope	Lsd fr Hawk Avn Mgt
YU-AJI	Douglas DC-9-32	687/47563	ex N1346U		Lsd fr JAT
YU-AJK	Douglas DC-9-32	689/47568	ex Z3-ARD		Lsd fr JAT
YU-AJM	Douglas DC-9-32	701/47582			Lsd fr JAT

CHANCHANGI AIRLINES

Chanchangi (3U/NCH) — Kaduna (KAD)

Reg	Type	MSN	ex	Notes
5N-BCF	Boeing 727-2M7	1452/21655	ex CC-CSW	
5N-BDE	Boeing 727-2M7	1675/21346	ex XA-MXI	
5N-BDF	Boeing 727-2M7	1302/21457	ex N79751	Lsd fr Aero Capital Corp

5N-BDG	Boeing 727-225 (FedEx 3)	1798/22558	ex N282SC	
5N-BEU	Boeing 727-225 (FedEx 3)	1800/22559	ex N283SC	
5N-BCG	BAC One-Eleven 510ED	141	ex G-AVMM	stored LOS
5N-BCH	BAC One-Eleven 510ED	140	ex G-AVML	stored LOS

CHROME AIR SERVICES

Chrome Air (CHO)   Lagos (LOS)

5N-SEO	BAC One-Eleven 487GK	267	ex YR-BCR	Freighter
5N-UJC	BAC One-Eleven 525FT	255	ex YR-BCL	

DANA / DORNIER AVIATION NIGERIA

Dana Air (DAV)   Kaduna (KAD)

5N-ARP	Dornier 228-201	8013	ex D-IDMI	non-airworthy
5N-AUN	Dornier 228-201	8076	ex D-CEPT	
5N-DOA	Dornier 228-202	8025	ex N228RP	non-airworthy
5N-DOB	Dornier 228-202	8026	ex N232RP	airworthy
5N-DOC	Dornier 228-202	8041	ex N234RP	airworthy
5N-DOD	Dornier 228-202	8048	ex N235RP	non-airworthy
5N-DOE	Dornier 228-202	8049	ex N236RP	non-airworthy
5N-DOF	Dornier 228-202	8125	ex N245RP	non-airworthy
5N-DOG	Dornier 228-202	8040	ex N233RP	non-airworthy
5N-DOI	Dornier 228-202	8137	ex N237RP	non-airworthy
5N-DOJ	Dornier 228-202	8138	ex N238RP	non-airworthy
5N-DOK	Dornier 228-202	8140	ex N240RP	non-airworthy
5N-DOL	Dornier 228-202	8145	ex N241RP	non-airworthy
5N-DOM	Dornier 228-202	8147	ex N242RP	non-airworthy

All registered to Aeronautical Industrial Engineering & Production Management

5N-SAG	Dornier 328-110	3016	ex D-CASU	on order

DAS AIR current status is uncertain

DASAB AIR

Dasab Air (DSQ)   Lagos (LOS)

5N-BEG	Boeing 727-256	914/20602	ex EC-GCJ	

EARTH AIRLINES SERVICES current status is uncertain

EAS AIR LINES

Echoline (EXW)   Lagos (LOS)

F-GYAL	Boeing 737-222	95/19074	ex N468AT	Lsd fr BIE
5N-BEY	Boeing 737-2K9	804/22504	ex PP-VNF	
5N-ESD	RomBAC One-Eleven 561RC	402	ex YR-BRB	stored LOS
5N-ESE	BAC One-Eleven 525FT	254	ex YR-BCK	stored LOS

EAS Air Lines is the trading name of Executive Airline Services

EASY LINK

                                                           Lagos (LOS)

5N-BCM	LET L-410UVP-E	902435	ex HI-692CT	
5N-BEA	LET L-410UVP	902435	ex OK-VDT	
5N-BEB	LET L-410UVP	882103	ex OK-TDS	
5N-BEK	LET L-410UVP	872002	ex OK-SDR	

FREEDOM AIR SERVICES

Inter Freedom (FFF)   Lagos (LOS)

5N-BCY	Boeing 727-235	538/19461	ex N461RD	Hajiya Asmal	Lsd fr IAL Lsg

FRESH AIR CARGO

Fresh Air (FRR)   Lagos (LOS)

5N-BCN	Antonov An-12B	9346409	ex RA-12965	
5N-BFQ	Boeing 737-2B7 (AVA 3)	990/22892	ex N128NJ	

Also leases other aircraft from Phoenix Aviation when required

IRS AIRLINES

(LVB)
Lagos (LOS)

EK-74101	Boeing 747-238B	310/21352	ex YA-EAG		
ZS-BAL	Fokker F.28 Fellowship 4000	11190	ex SE-DGO		Lsd fr AQU
ZS-IRS	Boeing 727-223A (Raisbeck 3)		ex		Lsd fr AQU
3D-BOX	Boeing 747-238B	260/21054	ex YA-EAH		Lsd fr Pegasus
5N-AKR*	Boeing 727-223A (Raisbeck 3)	1121/20984	ex N860AA		
5N-RIR*	Boeing 727-223A (Raisbeck 3)	1250/21087	ex N843AA	Khalifa Isiyaku Rabiu	
5N-	Boeing 727-223A (Raisbeck 3)	1459/21519	ex N880AA		stored HLA

*Leased from Aerospace Sales & Leasing

KABO AIR

Kabo (QNK)
Kano (KAN)

5N-HHH	BAC One-Eleven 401AK	064	ex HZ-NB2	VIP; stored SEN	
5N-EEE	Boeing 747-243B	134/19732	ex G-VGIN		
5N-JJJ	Boeing 747-136	111/19766	ex G-AWNF		
5N-NNN	Boeing 747-287B	274/21189	ex G-VIRG		
5N-OOO	Boeing 747-136	246/20952	ex G-AWNP		
5N-PDP	Boeing 747-238B	238/20842	ex G-VJFK		Lsd fr Aeronautics Leasing
5N-PPP	Boeing 747-238B	241/20921	ex G-VLAX		Lsd fr Aeronautics Leasing
5N-RRR	Boeing 747-136	109/19765	ex G-AWNE	Emir of Kano	

KELIX AIR believed not to have commenced operations

MILLENIUM AIR

5N-BFL	LET L-410UVP	902406	ex OK-JOB	reported dbr	

Current status uncertain as sole aircraft reported dbr in Nigeria when another aircraft taxied into it

NIGERIA AIRWAYS liquidated by new Nigerian Government in 2Q03, also reported as early 2004; to be replaced by Nigeria Eagle

NIGERIAN EAGLE AIRLINE
Lagos (LOS)

Being set-up to replace Nigeria Airways as the new National carrier, 30% to be owned by South African Airways

NIGERIAN GLOBAL

(NGI)
Lagos (LOS)

Operated scheduled services with Airbus Industrie A310-300 aircraft leased from Euralair as required although the latter entered receivership in late 2003 and the aircraft stored

OKADA AIR ceased operations

ORIENTAL AIRLINES ceased operations

OVERLAND AIRWAYS

5N-	Beech 1900D	UE-225	ex N225GL
5N-	Beech 1900D	UE-116	ex N116YV

One is believed to be 5N-BCP

PAN AFRICAN AIRLINES
Lagos (LOS)

5N-APL	Bell 206B JetRanger II	1527		non-airworthy
5N-BAJ	Bell 206B JetRanger III	2424	ex N5002D	
5N-BAP	Bell 206B JetRanger III	3235	ex G-OCHL	

PREMIUM AIR SHUTTLE

Blue Shuttle (EMI)
Lagos (LOS)

5N-BOS	Yakovlev Yak-40	9341431	ex LZ-DOA
5N-DAN	Yakovlev Yak-40	9340632	ex LZ-DOD
5N-MAR	Yakovlev Yak-40		

SAVANNAH AIRLINES ceased operations

SKYLINE ceased operations and aircraft returned to Arkia in June 2003

SKYPOWER EXPRESS AIRWAYS

Nigeria Express (EAN)   *Lagos (LOS)*

5N-AXK	Embraer EMB.110P1 Bandeirante	110449	ex (N212PB)	Op for Sobel
5N-AXR	Embraer EMB.110P1 Bandeirante	110459	ex PT-SHM	

Operates services for Nigerian Postal Services

SOSOLISO AIRLINES

Sosoliso (OSL)   *Enugu (ENU)*

YU-AJH	Douglas DC-9-32	685/47562	ex N1345U	Rose of Enugu	Lsd fr JAT
5N-BFA	Douglas DC-9-31	1033/48142	ex N922VJ		
5N-BFS	Douglas DC-9-31	1027/48140	ex N920VJ		
5N-BGL	McDonnell-Douglas MD-81	1067/48099	ex N819US		

SPACE WORLD AIRLINES

Lagos (LOS)

5N-BGA	Boeing 737-291	740/22456	ex N996UA
5N-BGB	Boeing 737-291	757/22457	ex N997UA

SUPERIOR INTERNATIONAL AIRLINES believed not to have commenced operations

TRANSAHARAN AIRLINES

5N-BEC	Boeing 727-256	1080/20975	ex EC-CIE

WEST AFRICAN AIRLINES

(WZ)   *Lagos (LOS)*

YU-AKI	Boeing 727-2H9	1681/22393		Lsd fr JAT
YU-AKK	Boeing 727-2H9	1786/22665	ex TS-JEA	Lsd fr JAT

5R - MADAGASCAR (Democratic Republic of Madagascar)

AIR MADAGASCAR

Air Madagascar (MD/MDG) (IATA 258)   *Antananarivo (TNR)*

5R-MFA	Boeing 737-2B2	204/20231		Boina	
5R-MFB	Boeing 737-2B2	314/20680		Sambirano	
5R-MFF	Boeing 767-3S1ER	384/25221	ex C-GGBK		Lsd fr GECAS
5R-MFH	Boeing 737-3Q8	2651/26305			Lsd fr Triton
5R-MFI	Boeing 737-3Q8	2623/26301	ex N319FL		Lsd fr Castle 2003-1B
5R-MGC	de Havilland DHC-6 Twin Otter 300	328			
5R-MGD	de Havilland DHC-6 Twin Otter 300	329			
5R-MGE	de Havilland DHC-6 Twin Otter 300	330			
5R-MJA	Hawker Siddeley HS.748 Srs.2B /360LFD	1772		Kandreho	
5R-MJC	Aerospatiale/Alenia ATR 42-300	132	ex 5R-MVK		
5R-MJD	Aerospatiale/Alenia ATR 42-310	155	ex 5R-MVX		
5R-MVT	Aerospatiale/Alenia ATR 42-300	044	ex F-WQAD		Lsd fr ATR Asset Mgt

Owns 34% of TAM (Travaux Aeriens de Madagascar)

MADAGASCAR FLYING SERVICES current status is uncertain

MALAGASY AIRLINES

(MLG)   *Antananarivo (TNR)*

5R-MDB	Cessna 402B	402B0572		
5R-MHJ	Piper PA-23-250 Aztec A	27-409	ex 5R-MVJ	
5R-MKS	Cessna 402B	402B0014	ex 5R-MVC	
5R-MLZ	Cessna TU206G Stationair 6	U20604526	ex F-BVQK	Lsd fr Aerotour Development
5R-MVL	Cessna 208 Caravan I	20800001	ex HB-CLD	Lsd fr ADF, Paris

TAM – TRANSPORTS & TRAVAUX AÉRIENS DE MADAGASCAR ceased operations

TIKO AIR

Antananarivo (TNR)

5R-MKM	CASA CN.235-10	14-C012	ex ZS-OGF	Lsd fr NAC Leasing
5R-MRM	Boeing 737-3Z9	1515/24081	ex OE-ILG	Op for Govt

5T - MAURITANIA (Islamic Republic of Mauritania)

AIR MAURITANIE

Mike Romeo (MR/MRT)   *Nouakchott (NKC)*

3D-ZZM	Boeing 737-2H7C	304/20590	ex 3C-ZZM	Lsd fr ILN
5T-CLG	Fokker F.28 Fellowship 4000	11093	ex PH-ZBL	
5T-CLH	Fokker F.28 Fellowship 4000	11138	ex PH-CHB	Lsd fr Caskett Trading
5T-CLK	Boeing 737-7Q8	22/28210	ex N341LF	Lsd fr ILFC
5T-CLM	Boeing 737-7Q8	30037	on order	Lsd fr ILFC
5T-CLP	Boeing 727-294 (Dugan 3)	1561/22004	ex ZS-OBM	

COMPAGNIE MAURITANIENNE DE TRANSPORTS - CTM

(CPM)   *Nouakchott (NKC)*

RA-26107	Antonov An-26B	27312008	ex LY-LVR	Lsd fr Pskovavia

Also leased other cargo aircraft as and when required

LIGNES MAURITANIENNES AIR EXPRESS current status is uncertain, believed not to have commenced operations

5U - NIGER (Republic of Niger)

AIR INTER NIGER

Inter Niger (AWH)   *Niamey (NIM)*

Operates flights with Embraer EMB.110P1 Bandeirante aircraft leased from Air Burkina as required

AIR NIGER INTERNATIONAL believed not to have commenced operations

NIGER AIR SERVICE ceased operations

NIGERAVIA

                                                                                   Niamey (NIM)

5U-ABY	Beech 200 Super King Air	BB-431	ex F-GILH
5U-ABZ	Britten-Norman BN-2A-9 Islander	702	ex OY-DZV

5V - TOGO (Togolese Republic)

AFRICA WEST

West Togo (FK/WTA)   *Lome (LFW)*

Operates cargo services with aircraft (Antonov An-12/Antonov An-32) leased from Dvin Avia (EK-) and Veteran Airlines (ER) as and when required

AIR TOGO

Air Togo (YT/TGA) (IATA 030)   *Lome (LFW)*

Operated scheduled services with Airbus Industrie A310-300 aircraft leased from Euralair as required although the latter entered receivership in late 2003 and the aircraft stored

ELITE AIR

Elair (EAI)   *Lome (LFW)*

5V-TTA	Piper PA-31-350 Navajo Chieftain	31-7405448	ex 9J-JLP	
5V-TTB	Britten-Norman BN-2A-26 Islander	717		based Mali
5V-TTC	Cessna 310Q	310Q0711	ex F-BUFK	

FINALAIR

Finalair (FIT)

Operates charter flights with aircraft leased from other operators as required

TRANS AFRICAN believed to have ceased operations; sole aircraft disposed of

TRANSTEL

Transtel (TTG)   *Lome (LFW)*

3D-JNM	Boeing 727-89	255/19139	ex N511DB	Lsd fr JMV

5W - SAMOA (Independent State of Western Samoa)

POLYNESIAN AIRLINES OF SAMOA

Polynesian (PH/PAO) (IATA 162)   *Apia (APW)*

5W-FAV	Britten-Norman BN-2A-8 Islander	42	ex ZK-FMS	Samoa Star	
5W-FAY	de Havilland DHC-6 Twin Otter 310	690	ex VH-UQW	Gillian	
5W-PAH	de Havilland DHC-6 Twin Otter 310	516	ex VH-FNX		
5W-SAO	Boeing 737-8Q8	935/30639		Island of Savaii	Lsd fr ILFC

5X - UGANDA (Republic of Uganda)

AFRICA ONE

(Y2/AFI) (IATA 693)   *Entebbe/Lagos (EBB/LOS)*

5X-ONE	Douglas DC-10-30	185/46952	ex 5Y-MBA	Trans Sahara titles; stored Kemble	

Africa One Zambia and Africa One [9Q] are wholly owned subsidiaries. Africa One is the trading name of African Joint Air Services. Current status is uncertain although it is possible services are operated by Icelandair in associaition with Sierra National Airlines

AIR MEMPHIS UGANDA

5X-AMU   Boeing 707-3
Sister company of Air Memphis (SU)

AIR UGANDA INTERNATIONAL did not start operations

DAS AIR CARGO

Dairair (WD/DSR)   *Entebbe (EBB)*

N400JR	Douglas DC-10-30F	254/46976	ex N602DC		Lsd fr GECAS
N401JR	Douglas DC-10-30F	266/46590	ex N68065		Lsd fr Boeing Capital
N402JR	Douglas DC-10-30F	327/47831	ex LX-TLD		Lsd fr Finova
5X-BON	Douglas DC-10-30F	214/46921	ex N608GC		Lsd fr Finova
5X-JOE	Douglas DC-10-30CF	115/47906	ex N116WA		
5X-ROY	Douglas DC-10-30F	305/47818	ex N537MD		Lsd fr Boeing Capital

DAS Air Cargo is the trading name of Dairo Air Service. Two McDonnell-Douglas MD-11s are on order by 1Q05

EAGLE AIR

African Eagle (H7/EGU)   *Entebbe (EBB)*

5X-DIV	LET L-410UVP-E8B	912539	ex 9J-EAZ	
5X-GNF	LET L-410UVP-E8	892320	ex OK-UDA	

EAST AFRICAN AIRWAYS

(QU/UGX)   *Entebbe (EBB)*

5X-EAA	Boeing 737-291	871/22741	ex N998UA	

FIKA SALAAMA AIRLINES ceased operations

GREAT LAKE AIRWAYS

Lakes Cargo (GLU)   *Entebbe (EBB)*

5X-GLA	Boeing 707-379C (Comtran 2)	718/19821	ex 5X-JEF	all-white	Lsd fr Jet Com

RELIANCE AIR

Entebbe (EBB)

N9732F	Cessna 208 Caravan I	20800156		Lsd fr Airserv Intl

UGANDA AIR CARGO ceased operations

UNITED AIRLINES

Entebbe (EBB)

5X-UAG	LET L-410UVP-E3	871904	ex OK-SDL	

5Y - KENYA

AD AVIATION

Nairobi-Wilson (WIL)

5Y-JMR	Beech 200C Super King Air	BL-17	ex F-GJMR

AFRICAN AIRLINES INTERNATIONAL

African Airlines (AIK)   *Nairobi-Jomo Kenyatta Intl (NBO)*

5Y-AXI	Boeing 707-330B (Comtran 2)	454/18927	ex Z-WKV	Isiolo	Lsd fr Avn Consultants

Associated with African Express Airways

AFRICAN EXPRESS AIRWAYS

Express Jet (XU/AXK)   *Nairobi-Jomo Kenyatta Intl (NBO)*

5Y-AXB	Boeing 727-231	603/19565	ex 5V-TPB	
5Y-AXD	Douglas DC-9-32	180/47088	ex 9L-LDF	Lsd fr RLL
5Y-AXF	Douglas DC-9-32	237/47093	ex 9L-LDG	Lsd fr RLL

Associated with African Airlines International

AIM -AIR

Nairobi-Wilson (WIL)

N206KA	Cessna TU206A Skywagon	U206-0514	
N342EA	Cessna U206G Stationair 6	U20606197	
N343EA	Cessna U206G Stationair	U20603699	
N345EA	Cessna U206G Stationair 6	U20604764	
N347EA	Cessna U206G Stationair 6	U20604797	
N756MS	Cessna U206G Stationair 6	U20604205	
5Y-BMD	Cessna U206G Stationair 6	U20605494	ex N348EA
N761FB	Cessna 210M Centurion	21062212	
5Y-BLG	Cessna 210M Centurion	21061898	ex N346EA
5Y-SPK	Cessna 208B Caravan I	208B0243	ex N349EA	Lsd fr Samaritans Purse

Aim Air is the trading name of Africa Inland Missionary International Services

AIR EXPRESS

Nairobi-Wilson (WIL)

5Y-BRN	Fokker F.27 Friendship 100	10155	ex ZS-OEI

AIRCRAFT LEASING SERVICES

Nairobi-Wilson (WIL)

5Y-APZ	Cessna 402B	402B0232	ex N2956Q	
5Y-BAF	Cessna 310R	310R0633	ex N98890	
5Y-BLA	Beech 200C Super King Air	BL-10	ex C-FAMB	
5Y-BRB	Aerospatiale/Alenia ATR 42-300	240	ex ZS-OWU	
5Y-DHL	Beech 1900C-1	UC-100	ex N15305	Op for UN
5Y-GSV	Cessna 208 Caravan I	20800024	ex N9358F	Op for UNICEF
5Y-HAA	Cessna 208 Caravan I	20800021	ex N9349F	
5Y-LKG	Beech 1900C	UB-63	ex C-FUCB	Op for Kenya Airlink
5Y-MAK	Cessna 208 Caravan I	20800004	ex HB-CLI	Lsd to Regional Air Svs as 5H-MUR
5Y-SGL	Beech 1900C-1	UC-114	ex V5-SGL	Of for UN Humanitarian Service

AIRKENYA

(QP) (IATA 853)   *Nairobi-Wilson (WIL)*

5Y-BEK	de Havilland DHC-6 Twin Otter 200	181	ex 5X-UWV	stored WIL	
5Y-BGH	de Havilland DHC-6 Twin Otter 300	574	ex N4226J		
5Y-BIO	de Havilland DHC-6 Twin Otter 300	579	ex 5H-MRB	UN/WFP titles	
5Y-BKP*	Short SD.3-60	SH3750	ex G-BWMW	std HLA	Lsd fr Lynrise Air Lease
5Y-BKW	Short SD.3-60	SH3717	ex G-BWMZ		
5Y-BMJ	de Havilland DHC-7-102	83	ex N721AS		
5Y-BMP	de Havilland DHC-7-102	80	ex N780MG		
5Y-BNN	Cessna 208B Caravan I	208B0683	ex N1126T		
5Y-BPD	de Havilland DHC-7-102	32	ex 7O-ACZ		

Owns Regional Air

ASA – AFRICAN SAFARI AIRWAYS
Zebra (QSC)   *Mombasa (MBA)*

5Y-VIP	Airbus Industrie A310-308	620	ex D-AHLC	Lsd fr Defag

AVIATION ASSISTANCE INTERNATIONAL
Nairobi-Wilson (WIL)

Reg	Type	Serial	ex	Notes	
OY-GEB	Beech B200C Super King Air	BL-40	ex VH-NSR		
OY-GEW	Beech 1300	BB-1342	ex VT-SAE	B200 Super King Air conv	
5Y-BMA*	Beech 200C Super King Air	BB-155	ex OY-GEH		
5Y-BMC*	Beech 200 Super King Air	BB-211	ex OY-BTR		
5Y-ECO*	Beech 1300	BB-1343	ex OY-GER	B 200Super King Air conv	
5Y-EKO*	Beech 200C Super King Air	BL-2	ex OY-BVE		
5Y-EOB*	Beech 1300	BB-1305	ex OY-GES	B 200Super King Air conv	
5Y-BVI*	Beech 1900C-1	UC-55	ex OY-BVI		
5Y-EOC	Cessna 208B Caravan I	208B0737	ex N1266A		
5Y-EOD	Cessna 208B Caravan I	208B0738	ex N1266A	Op for ECHO	
5Y-EOE	Beech 1900C-1	UC-90	ex N90YV	UN/WFP titles	Lsd fr Raytheon
5Y-NBB	Beech 65-C90 King Air	LJ-528	ex N883AV		

Associated with Aviation Assistance (OY-); *leased from Aviation Assistance

BLUEBIRD AVIATION
Cobra (BBZ)   *Nairobi -Wilson (WIL)*

Reg	Type	Serial	ex	Notes
5Y-HHB	LET L-410AB	730209	ex OK-DDV	
5Y-HHC	LET L-410A	720204	ex OK-DDU	
5Y-HHF	LET L-410AB	710002	ex OK-ADR	
5Y-HHL	LET L-410UVP-E9	872018	ex OK-SDA	
5Y-VVA	LET L-410UVP-E9	962633	ex OK-BDL	
5Y-VVB	LET L-410UVP-E9	942704	ex OK-BDG	
5Y-VVC	LET L-410UVP-E20	922728	ex ZS-NIJ	
5Y-VVE	LET L-410UVP-E20	922726	ex 5Y-YYY	
5Y-VVF	Fokker 50	20136	ex N136NM	
5Y-VVG	Fokker 50	20137	ex N137NM	on order
5Y-VVH	Fokker 50	20203	ex N203NM	
5Y-HHE	Beech 200 Super King Air	BB-547	ex ZS-NIP	Lsd ff Amazon Air Contracts
5Y-HHK	Beech 200 Super King Air	BB-696	ex 5Y-TWB	

BLUE SKY AVIATION
Nairobi-Wilson (WIL)

5Y-BOD	LET L-410UVP-E20	982727	ex OK-DDF
5Y-BPX	LET L-410UVP-E9	962632	ex 5H-PAH
5Y-BSA	LET L-410UVP-E9	892323	ex OK-UDC

DAS AIR CARGO
Dasair (DAZ)   *Nairobi-Jomo Kenyatta Intl (NBO)*

Operates cargo charters with aircraft leased from parent company, DAS Air Cargo (DSR), as required

EAGLE AVIATION
Magnum (Y4/EQA)   *Mombasa (MBA)*

5Y-LNT	Aerospatiale/Alenia ATR 42-320	205	ex N521JS

EAST AFRICAN AIR CHARTERS
(S9/HAS) (IATA 895)   *Nairobi-Wilson (WIL)*

Reg	Type	Serial	ex
5Y-AHL	Cessna 401	401-0193	ex PH-MPS
5Y-ALY	Cessna U206F Stationair	U20602266	ex N15588U
5Y-AOO	Cessna U206F Stationair	U20601710	
5Y-ART	Cessna 210L Centurion	21059817	
5Y-BIX	Reims Cessna F406 Caravan II	F406-0055	ex N65912
5Y-BLN	Cessna 208B Caravan I	208B0558	ex N50398
5Y-BMH	Cessna 310R	310R0501	
5Y-BOX	Cessna 208B Caravan I	208B0500	ex 9M-PMV

EAST AFRICAN EXPRESS

5Y-EEE	Fokker F.28 Fellowship 4000	11229	ex 5Y-MNT	
5Y-NNN	Fokker F.28 Fellowship 4000	11231	ex 5Y-NNT	
5Y-XXX	Grumman G.159 Gulfstream	1	ex 5Y-EMK	stored HLA

Associated with East African Safari Air, possibly a subsidiary

EAST AFRICAN SAFARI AIR

Car Hire (S9/HSA)

5Y-CCC	Boeing 767-3Y0ER	380/24948	ex C-GHML	Mary Rosamond	Lsd fr GECAS
5Y-TTT	LET L-410UVP-E20	922726	ex ZS-NIK		
5Y-QQQ	Boeing 767-31AER	595/27619	ex PH-MCV	Elizabeth	Lsd fr ILFC

Associated with East African Express

FLAMINGO AIRLINES

Batian (F7/KFL)

5Y-FLA	SAAB SF.340B	163	ex SE-KCG	Lsd fr SAAB
5Y-FLB	SAAB SF.340B	171	ex SE-KCH	Lsd fr SAAB

Subsidiary of Kenya Airways

KASKAZI AVIATION

SE-KKX	Dornier 228-100	7004	ex LN-HPE

KENYA AIRWAYS

Kenya (KQ/KQA) (IATA 706)

5Y-KQA	Boeing 737-3U8	2863/28746		Lsd fr Simba Finance
5Y-KQB	Boeing 737-3U8	2884/28747		Lsd fr Simba Finance
5Y-KQC	Boeing 737-3U8	3034/29088		Lsd fr Simba Finance
5Y-KQD	Boeing 737-3Q8	3095/29750	ex N5573L	
5Y-KQJ	Boeing 737-248	565/21714	ex N1714T	Lsd fr European Capital
5Y-KQK	Boeing 737-248	579/21715	ex N1715Z	Lsd fr European Capital
5Y-KQN	Boeing 737-229C	401/20915	ex G-BZKP	
5Y-KQV	Boeing 767-3Y0ER	487/26206	ex EC-GSU	Lsd fr GECAS
5Y-KQW	Boeing 767-3Y0ER	503/26207	ex EC-GTI	Lsd fr GECAS
5Y-KQX	Boeing 767-36NER	844/30854		Lsd fr GECAS
5Y-KQY	Boeing 767-36NER	841/30841		Lsd fr GECAS
5Y-KQZ	Boeing 767-36NER	837/30853		Lsd fr GECAS
5Y-KQE	Boeing 737-76N	877/30133		Lsd fr GECAS
5Y-KQF	Boeing 737-76N	1145/30136		Lsd fr GECAS
5Y-KQG	Boeing 737-7U8	1242/32371	ex N715BA	
5Y-KQH	Boeing 737-7U8	1327/32372		
5Y-	Boeing 777-2U8ER		on order 04	
5Y-	Boeing 777-2U8ER		on order 04	
5Y-	Boeing 777-2U8ER		on order 04	

26% owned by KLM while Flamingo Airlines is a wholly owned subsidiary
Some commuter services are operated by Aircraft Leasing Services using Beech 1900C with Kenya Airlink titles

KNIGHT AVIATION believed to have ceased operations

MOMBASA AIR SAFARI

(RRV)

5Y-NIK	LET L-410UVP	912619	ex OK-WDW	Lsd fr Skoda Trading
5Y-UVP	LET L-410UVP	912627	ex OK-WDY	Lsd fr Skoda Trading

QUEENSWAY AIR SERVICES

5Y-BNS	Cessna 208B Caravan I	208B0394	ex N894MA
5Y-BOL	Cessna 208B Caravan I	208B0155	ex ZS-ODL

REGIONAL AIR

Sunbird (QPSAL)

3D-CAY	Fokker F.28 Fellowship 3000	11136	ex 9Q-CAY

5Y-BPI	Boeing 737-2P6	496/21356	ex N213MT		Lsd fr GECAS
5Y-BPP	Boeing 737-2U4	652/22161	ex N161DF	all-white	Lsd fr Aergo Capital
5Y-BPZ	Boeing 737-2P6	564/21733	ex LV-YEB	Op fpr BAW	Lsd fr Aergo Capital
5Y-BRC	Boeing 737-2Q3	1565/24103	ex N241AG		Lsd fr Aergo Capital

Subsidiary of AirKenya

ROSSAIR KENYA

Nairobi-Wilson (WIL)

5Y-BOS	de Havilland DHC-6 Twin Otter 300	513	ex ZS-OHS		Lsd fr RSS
5Y-OKL	Beech 1900D	UE-48	ex ZS-OKL		Lsd fr RSS
5Y-RDS	Douglas DC-3TP65	15640/27085	ex N146JR		Lsd fr Sembar Avn
5Y-ROS	Beech 1900C-1	UC-65	ex ZS-OGZ	Op for Red Cross	Lsd fr RSS

SALAAM EXPRESS AIR SERVICES current status uncertain; operated aircraft for Air Rum but later reregistered

SKYTRAILS

Skytrails

Mombasa (MBA)

5Y-AFD	Cessna TU206B Skywagon	U206-0724	ex N3424L
5Y-EDH	Cessna 404 Titan	404-0241	ex N88728
5Y-SKA	de Havilland DHC-6 Twin Otter 300	518	ex D-IDWT
5Y-SKL	de Havilland DHC-6 Twin Otter 300	715	ex N8489H
5Y-SKS	de Havilland DHC-6 Twin Otter 300	682	ex G-BGZP
5Y-SKT	de Havilland DHC-6 Twin Otter 300	503	ex PH-STC

Skytrails is the trading name of African Safaris and Skytrails

SKYWAYS KENYA

Nairobi-Wilson (WIL)

5Y-BMB	Douglas DC-3	34375	ex N2025A	stored	Lsd fr Legion Express

Also leases Antonov An-26/32s as required

SUPERIOR AVIATION SERVICES

Skycargo (M7/SUK)

Nairobi-Wilson (WIL)

5Y-ATH	Piper PA-23-250 Aztec E	27-7305138	
5Y-BGN	Cessna 404 Titan II	404-0239	ex D-IEBB
5Y-PEA	Beech 58 Baron	TH-1067	ex N60664

TRACK MARK

Nairobi-Wilson (WIL)

5Y-TAV	Cessna 208B Caravan I	208B0668

TRANSWORLD SAFARIS

Nairobi-Wilson (WIL)

5Y-ROH	Piper PA-31-350 Chieftain	31-8152038	ex N217JP	
5Y-TWA	Beech 200 Super King Air	BB-803	ex G-WPLC	
5Y-TWC	Beech 200C Super King Air	BL-37	ex G-IFTB	Lsd fr Aerolite Investments
5Y-TWG	Cessna 208B Caravan I	208B0674	ex N1286N	Lsd fr Aerolite Investments
5Y-TWH	Cessna 208B Caravan I	208B0784	ex N1253M	Lsd fr Aerolite Investments
5Y-TWJ	Cessna 208B Caravan I	208B0896	ex N1128S	Lsd fr Aerolite Investments

UNITED AIR LINES

Nairobi-Wilson (WIL)

5Y-LAV	Cessna 310R	310R0882	ex N3644G

WESTERN AIRWAYS

Nairobi-Wilson (WIL)

5Y-BIY	Cessna 404 Titan	404-0061		
5Y-LEA	Cessna 404 Titan	404-0614	ex 5Y-EAG	Lsd fr Commuter Air Svs

ZB AIR

Bosky (ZBA)

Nairobi-Wilson (WIL)

5Y-OPM	Cessna 208B Caravan I	208B0330	ex N1034S
5Y-ZBI	Cessna 208B Caravan I	208B0324	ex N1029P

| 5Y-ZBR | Cessna 208B Caravan I | 208B0446 | ex N12922 | |
| 5Y-ZBW | Cessna 208B Caravan I | 208B0409 | ex N1115W | |

5Y-AIS	Beech 95-D55 Baron	TE-680		
5Y-AUN	Cessna U206F Stationair	U20602531	ex N1244V	
5Y-AYZ	Cessna 310R	310R0121	ex N4940J	
5Y-AZS	Cessna 310R	310R0524	ex N87350	
5Y-SAB	Cessna 404 Titan	404-0675	ex N6761X	
5Y-ZBK	Beech B200 Super King Air	BB-1714	ex N3214D	
5Y-ZBM	Cessna U206H Stationair 6	U20608114	ex N259ME	
5Y-ZBO	Cessna U206H Stationair	U20608131	ex N373ME	

ZB Air is the trading name of Z Boskovic Air Charters

6O - SOMALIA (Democratic Republic of Somalia)

DAMAL AIRLINES
Malabo/Sharjah (SSG/SHJ)

| UN-75002 | Ilyushjn Il-18E | 185008603 | ex 3C-KKR | Lsd fr/op by RBS |

JUBA AIRWAYS
Juba (JUB)   *Dubai/Sharjah (DXB/SHJ)*

| EX-005 | Ilyushin Il-18D | 188011105 | ex EX-105 | Jt ops with PHG |
| EX-201 | Ilyushin Il-18D | 188011201 | ex EX-74268 | Jt ops with PHG |

STAR AFRICAN AIR
(STU)   *Sharjah (SHJ)*

Operates flights with Antonov An-24 and Ilyushin Il-18 aircraft leased from Aerovista and Renan as and when required

6V - SENEGAL (Republic of Senegal)

AERO SERVICE ASF
Dakar (DKR)

| 6V-AHF | Cessna 208B Caravan I | 208B0634 | ex N12386 | |
| 6V-AHI | Cessna 402C | 402C0120 | ex F-OHCM | |

AFRIQUE CARGO SERVICES
Dakar (DKR)

| UN-11006 | Antonov An-12 | 01347909 | ex 3C-QRI | Lsd fr BMK |

AIR SENEGAL INTERNATIONAL
Air Senegal (V7/SNG) (IATA 407)   *Dakar (DKR)*

6V-AHK	Boeing 737-2B6 (Nordam 3)	456/21216	ex CN-RMK	Lsd fr RAM
6V-AHL	de Havilland DHC-8-202	556	ex C-GDSG	
6V-AHN	Boeing 737-7BX	716/30738	ex N363ML	Lsd fr Aircraft 30738 LLC
6V-AHO	Boeing 737-7BX	758/30739	ex N364ML	Lsd fr GECAS

Operates as Royal Air Maroc Express franchise with Groupe Royal Air Maroc stickers

ASECNA
(XKX)   *Dakar (DKR)*

| 6V-AFW | Aerospatiale/Alenia ATR 42-300 | 117 | ex F-WWEN | Calibrator/Pax |

Operates as intergovernmental organisation conducting calibration flights in West Africa as well as some services; ASECNA is the Agence pour la Securité de la Navigation Aérienne en Afrique et à Madagascar

ATLANTIS AIRLINES
Atlantis-lines(9V/ELS)   *Dakar (DKR)*

Operates cargo flights with McDonnell-Douglas MD-11 and Douglas DC-10 aircraft leased from Gemini Air Cargo

SENEGALAIR
Senair (SGL)   *Dakar (DKR)*

| 6V-AGS | Beech 200 Super King Air | BB-28 | ex F-GKPL | |

SUNU AIR

Dakar (DKR)

| 6V-AHS | Fokker F.27 Friendship 200 | 10675 | ex OY-EBC | Lsd fr Elgin A/c |

6Y - JAMAICA

AIR JAMAICA

Jamaica (JM/AJM) (IATA 201)   *Kingston-Norman Manley Intl (KIN)*

6Y-JAF+	Airbus Industrie A320-214	0624	ex N624AJ	624	The Caribbean	Lsd fr WTCo
6Y-JAG+	Airbus Industrie A320-214	0626	ex N626AJ	626	Barbados	Lsd fr WTCo
6Y-JAI+	Airbus Industrie A320-214	0628	ex N628AJ	628	Montego Bay	Lsd fr debis
6Y-JAJ+	Airbus Industrie A320-214	0630	ex N630AJ	630	Ocho Rios	Lsd fr debis
6Y-JMA	Airbus Industrie A320-212	0528	ex TC-ONE	622		Lsd fr ILFC
6Y-JMB	Airbus Industrie A320-212	0422	ex G-OZBA	620		Lsd fr GECAS
6Y-JMD	Airbus Industrie A321-211	0666	ex G-BXAW	566	Westmoreland	Lsd fr ILFC
6Y-JME	Airbus Industrie A321-211	0775	ex G-BXNP	575		Lsd fr ILFC
6Y-JMF	Airbus Industrie A320-214	1213	ex F-WWBE	632	Freedom	Lsd fr GECAS
6Y-JMG	Airbus Industrie A320-214	1390	ex F-WWIU	634	America	Lsd fr Mystic River
6Y-JMH	Airbus Industrie A321-211	1503	ex D-AVZU	515	May Pen	Lsd fr GECAS
6Y-JMI	Airbus Industrie A320-214	1747	ex F-WWDI	636		Lsd fr CIT Leasing
6Y-JMJ	Airbus Industrie A320-214	1751	ex F-WWDE	638		Lsd fr CIT Leasing
6Y-JMK	Airbus Industrie A320-214	2048	ex F-WWIH			Lsd fr ILFC
6Y-JMR	Airbus Industrie A321-211	1905	ex D-AVZP			Lsd fr ILFC
6Y-JMS	Airbus Industrie A321-211	1966	ex D-AVZH	517		Lsd fr ILFC
6Y-JMW	Airbus Industrie A321-211	1988	ex D-AVXH			Lsd fr ILFC

+Not current on October 2003 register, status?

6Y-JMC	Airbus Industrie A340-312	048	ex 3B-NAT	348	New York	Lsd fr ILFC
6Y-JMM	Airbus Industrie A340-313X	216	ex C-GBQM	350	Jamaica	Lsd fr ILFC
6Y-JMP	Airbus Industrie A340-313X	257	ex C-GDVV	351	Atlantic Limousine II	Lsd fr ILFC

All names prefixed 'Spirit of'
Owns 55% of Air Jamaica Express which operates feeder services using JM flights number

AIR JAMAICA EXPRESS

Jamaica Express (JQ/JMX) (IATA 100)   *Kingston-Tinson Peninsula/Montego Bay (KTP/MBJ)*

6Y-JEB	de Havilland DHC-8-102	059	ex C-GAAM	954	Spirit of Jamaica
					Lsd fr CIT Leasing
6Y-JEC	de Havilland DHC-8-102	043	ex N814PH	955	Lsd fr CIT Leasing
6Y-JED	de Havilland DHC-8-102	050	ex N815PH	956	Lsd fr CIT Leasing
6Y-JMT	de Havilland DHC-8-102	104	ex N821PH	951	Lsd fr Aerocentury
6Y-JMZ	de Havilland DHC-8-102	110	ex N823PH	953	Lsd fr Aerocentury

55% owned by Air Jamaica

AIRSPEED JAMAICA

Kingston-Tinson Peninsula (KTP)

| 6Y-JSX | Britten-Norman BN-2A-27 Islander | 78 | ex 6Y-JLB |

JAMAICA AIRLINK

Kingston-Tinson Peninsula (KTP)

6Y-JRD	Cessna U206G Stationair 6	U20604522	ex N9019M	
6Y-JRF	Cessna T207A Super Skywagon	20700365		Lsd fr M&M Leasing
6Y-JRG	Cessna 208B Caravan I	208B0311	ex YN-CDR	Lsd fr Caravan 311 Ltd

Jamaica AirLink is the trading name of Rutair

RUTAIR now listed as Jamaica AirLink

TIMAIR

Montego Bay (MBJ)

6Y-JLU	Britten-Norman BN-2B-26 Islander	2170	ex 6Y-JLG
6Y-JNA	Cessna U206G Stationair	U20603837	ex N4515C
6Y-JNJ	Cessna U206G Stationair 6	U20606359	ex N2447N
6Y-JNL	Cessna U206G Stationair 6	U20605620	ex N712RS

7O - YEMEN (Republic of Yemen)

YEMENIA

Yemeni (IY/IYE) (IATA 635)   San'a (SAH)

F-OGYO	Airbus Industrie A310-324ET	568	ex F-WGYO	Lsd fr Murgab Ltd
F-OHPR	Airbus Industrie A310-325	702	ex F-WWCG	Lsd fr Airbus
F-OHPS	Airbus Industrie A310-325	704	ex F-WWCL	Lsd fr Airbus
7O-ACL	de Havilland DHC-7-103	23		
7O-ACM	de Havilland DHC-7-103	31		stored ADE
7O-ACQ	Boeing 737-2R4C	1034/23129		
7O-ACR	Boeing 737-2R4C	1040/23130		Freighter
7O-ACU	Boeing 737-2N8	478/21296	ex 4W-ABZ	
7O-ACV	Boeing 727-2N8	1518/21844	ex 4W-ACF	
7O-ACX	Boeing 727-2N8	1549/21846	ex 4W-ACH	
7O-ACY	Boeing 727-2N8	1557/21847	ex 4W-ACI	
7O-ADA	Boeing 727-2N8	1512/21842	ex 4W-ACJ	Op for Govt
7O-ADD	Lockheed L-382C Hercules	4827	ex 1160	Jt ops with Air Force
7O-ADE	Lockheed L-382C Hercules	4825	ex 1150	Jt ops with Air Force
7O-ADF	Ilyushin Il-76TD	1033418578	ex RA-76380	
7O-ADG	Ilyushin Il-76TD	1023412402	ex RA-76405	Jt ops with Air Force
7O-ADH	de Havilland DHC-6 Twin Otter 310	764	ex G-BBAC	Lsd fr BAC Lsg
7O-ADI	de Havilland DHC-6 Twin Otter 300	664	ex HB-LRT	Lsd fr FAT
7O-ADJ	Airbus Industrie A310-324	535	ex F-WQKB	Lsd fr ILFC
7O-ADK	de Havilland DHC-6 Twin Otter 310	813	ex A4O-DB	
7O-ADL	Boeing 737-8Q8	1129/30645		Lsd fr ILFC
7O-ADM	Boeing 737-8Q8	1195/28252		Lsd fr ILFC
7O-ADN	Boeing 737-8Q8	1186/30661		Lsd fr ILFC
7O-	Airbus Industrie A330-243	625	ex F-WW	on order	Lsd fr ILFC

49% owned by Saudi Arabian Airlines

7P - LESOTHO (Kingdom of Lesotho)

AFRICAN INTERNATIONAL AIRLINES current ststus is uncertain, believed to have ceased operations

7Q - MALAWI (Republic of Malawi)

AIR MALAWI

Malawi (QM/AML) (IATA 167)   Blantyre (BLZ)

7Q-YKP	Boeing 737-33A	2045/25056		Kwacha
7Q-YKQ	Aerospatiale/Alenia ATR 42-320	236	ex F-WWES	Shire
7Q-YKU	Cessna 208B Caravan I	208B0679	ex N1239A	

7T - ALGERIA (Democratic & Popular Republic of Algeria)

AIR ALGERIE

Air Algerie (AH/DAH) (IATA 124)   Algiers (ALG)

7T-VUI	Aerospatiale/Alenia ATR 72-202	644	ex F-OHGM	
7T-VUJ	Aerospatiale/Alenia ATR 72-202	648	ex F-OHGN	
7T-VUK	Aerospatiale/Alenia ATR 72-202	652	ex F-OHGO	
7T-VUM	Aerospatiale/Alenia ATR 72-202	677	ex F-OHGQ	
7T-VUN	Aerospatiale/Alenia ATR 72-500	684	ex F-OHGR	
7T-	Aerospatiale/Alenia ATR 72-202	699	ex F-WWEV	on order 04
7T-VEA	Boeing 727-2D6	850/20472		Tassili
7T-VEB	Boeing 727-2D6	855/20473		Hoggar
7T-VEI	Boeing 727-2D6	1111/21053		Djebel Amour
7T-VEM	Boeing 727-2D6	1204/21210		Mont du Ksall
7T-VEP	Boeing 727-2D6	1233/21284		Mont du Tessala
7T-VET	Boeing 727-2D6	1662/22372		Gorges du Rhumel
7T-VEU	Boeing 727-2D6 (Raisbeck 3)	1664/22373		Djurdjura
7T-VEV	Boeing 727-2D6 (Raisbeck 3)	1711/22374	ex N8292V	
7T-VEW	Boeing 727-2D6 (Raisbeck 3)	1723/22375	ex N8295V	
7T-VEX	Boeing 727-2D6 (Raisbeck 3)	1801/22765		Djemila
7T-VEF	Boeing 737-2D6	332/20759		Saoura
7T-VEG	Boeing 737-2D6	361/20884		Monts des Oulad Nails
7T-VEJ	Boeing 737-2D6	407/21063		Chrea
7T-VEK	Boeing 737-2D6	409/21064		Edough
7T-VEL	Boeing 737-2D6	416/21065		Akfadou
7T-VEN	Boeing 737-2D6	454/21211		La Soummam
7T-VEO	Boeing 737-2D6	459/21212		Titteri
7T-VEQ	Boeing 737-2D6	473/21285		Le Zaccar

7T-VER	Boeing 737-2D6	482/21286		Le Souf	
7T-VES	Boeing 737-2D6C (Nordam 3)	486/21287		Le Tadmait	
7T-VEY	Boeing 737-2D6 (Nordam 3)	853/22766		Rhoufi	
7T-VJA	Boeing 737-2T4 (Nordam 3)	897/22800	ex N4556L	Monts des Babors	
7T-VJB	Boeing 737-2T4 (Nordam 3)	900/22801	ex N4558L	Monts des Biban	
TC-APN	Boeing 737-86N	573/28628	ex N5573L		Lsd fr PGT
7T-VJJ	Boeing 737-8D6	610/30202		Jugurtha	
7T-VJK	Boeing 737-8D6	640/30203	ex N1781B	Mansourah	
7T-VJL	Boeing 737-8D6	652/30204		Allizi	
7T-VJM	Boeing 737-8D6	691/30205			
7T-VJN	Boeing 737-8D6	751/30206			
7T-VJO	Boeing 737-8D6	868/30207	ex N1787B		
7T-VJP	Boeing 737-8D6	896/30208	ex N1787B		
7T-VJQ	Boeing 737-6D6	1115/30209			
7T-VJR	Boeing 737-6D6	1131/30545			
7T-VJS	Boeing 737-6D6	1150/30210	ex N60559		
7T-VJT	Boeing 737-6D6	1152/30546			
7T-VJU	Boeing 737-6D6	1164/30211			

Three more Boeing 737-8D6s are on order

7T-VIH	Cessna 208B Caravan I	208B0384	ex N1120A
7T-VII	Cessna 208B Caravan I	208B0393	ex N1123G
7T-VIJ	Cessna 208B Caravan I	208B0552	ex N1123M
7T-VIK	Cessna 208B Caravan I	208B0573	ex N1009M
7T-VIL	Cessna 208B Caravan I	208B0601	ex N1247H
7T-VIM	Cessna 208B Caravan I	208B0602	ex N1247K
7T-VRJ	Fokker F.27 Friendship 400M	10547	ex 7T-WAS
7T-VRK	Fokker F.27 Friendship 400M	10553	ex 7T-WAT
7T-VRL	Fokker F.27 Friendship 400M	10495	ex 7T-WAK
7T-VRQ	Fokker F.27 Friendship 400M	10526	ex 7T-WAO
7T-VRR	Fokker F.27 Friendship 400M	10555	ex 7T-WAU
7T-VRU	Fokker F.27 Friendship 400M	10494	ex 7T-WAI
7T-VRV	Fokker F.27 Friendship 400M	10543	ex 7T-WAQ
7T-VCV	Beech A100 King Air	B-93	ex N9369Q
7T-VHG	Lockheed L-100-30T Hercules	4880	ex N4148M
7T-VHL	Lockheed L-100-30T Hercules	4886	ex N4160M
7T-VIN	Beech 1900D	UE-365	ex N31685
7T-VIQ	Beech 1900D	UE-381	ex N31683
7T-VJC	Airbus Industrie A310-203	291	ex F-WZED
7T-VJD	Airbus Industrie A310-203	293	ex F-WZEE
7T-VJG	Boeing 767-3D6ER	310/24766	
7T-VJH	Boeing 767-3D6ER	323/24767	
7T-VJI	Boeing 767-3D6ER	332/24768	ex N6009F
7T-VRF	Beech A100 King Air	B-147	ex N1828W

Five Airbus Industrie A330-200s on order for delivery from 1Q2005

AIR EXPRESS ALGERIA

Algiers (ALG)

ZS-ORV	Beech 1900D	UE-42	ex N42YV	Lsd fr NTN
ZS-OXR	LET L-410UVP	922730	ex	Lsd fr Orsmond Avn
ZS-OYE	Beech 1900D	UE-200	ex VH-IAV	Lsd fr NTN
ZS-OYF	Beech 1900D	UE-214	ex VH-IMS	Lsd fr NTN
ZS-OYH	Beech 1900D	UE-250	ex VH-IAY	Lsd fr NTN

ANTINEA AIRLINES was a member of Groupe Khalifa; current status uncertain following collapse of the parent

KHALIFA AIRWAYS ceased intl operations late March 2003, then domestic on 04/05/2003 and declared bankrupt

SAHARA AIRLINES ceased operations

RYM AIRLINES

Oran

7T-V	Boeing 737-291 (Nordam 3)	632/22089	ex N992UA	on order, stored SAT
7T-V	Boeing 737-291 (Nordam 3)	713/22383	ex N993UA	on order, stored SAT
7T-V	Boeing 737-291 (Nordam 3)	718/22384	ex N994UA	on order

Initial sale fell through

TASSILI AIRLINES

Tassili Air (SF/DTH) (IATA 515)   *Hassi Messaoud (HME)*

| 7T-VCG | Pilatus PC-6/B2-H4 Turbo Porter | 917 | ex HB-FLJ |
| 7T-VCH | Pilatus PC-6/B2-H4 Turbo Porter | 929 | ex HB-FLX |

7T-VCI	Pilatus PC-6/B2-H4 Turbo Porter	933	ex HB-FLY
7T-VCJ	Pilatus PC-6/B2-H4 Turbo Porter	934	ex HB-FLZ
7T-VCK	Pilatus PC-6/B2-H4 Turbo Porter	930	ex HB-FMA

F-GPYC	Aerospatiale/Alenia ATR 42-500	484	ex F-WWEB	Lsd fr Brice Bail
F-GPYD	Aerospatiale/Alenia ATR 42-500	490	ex F-WWLJ	Lsd fr Brice Bail
F-GVZA	Aerospatiale/Alenia ATR 42-300	503	ex F-WQLI	Lsd fr/op by RLA
7T-VIN	Beech 1900D	UE-365	ex N31685	
7T-VIP	Beech 1900D	UE-369	ex N30538	
7T-VIQ	Beech 1900D	UE-381	ex N31683	

8P - BARBADOS

TRANS ISLAND AIR 2000

Trans Island (TRD)   *Bridgetown-Grantley Adams (BGI)*

8P-BGC	de Havilland DHC-6 Twin Otter 300	604	ex N604ML	Lsd fr Acquisition Air
8P-BJK	Aero Commander 500B	1400-144	ex N13SK	
8P-JML	de Havilland DHC-6 Twin Otter 300	406	ex N171GC	
8P-MLK	de Havilland DHC-6 Twin Otter 300	477	ex HK-3777	

8Q - MALDIVES (Republic of Maldives)

ISLAND AVIATION SERVICES

(Q2/DQA) (IATA 986)   *Male (MLE)*

8Q-AMB	Dornier 228-212	8178	ex D-COLT	
8Q-AMC	Dornier 228-212	8179	ex D-CISS	
8Q-AMD	de Havilland DHC-8-202	429	ex C-GDKL	Lsd fr Fulhangi Lsg
8Q-IAS	Dornier 228-212	8239	ex F-OHQJ	

MALDIVIAN AIR TAXI

Male (MLE)

8Q-CSL	de Havilland DHC-6 Twin Otter 100	64	ex C-FCSL
8Q-MAA	de Havilland DHC-6 Twin Otter 300	693	ex C-GKCS
8Q-MAB	de Havilland DHC-6 Twin Otter 300	287	ex C-GKBV
8Q-MAC	de Havilland DHC-6 Twin Otter 100	60	ex C-GTKB
8Q-MAE	de Havilland DHC-6 Twin Otter 300	464	ex C-FPOQ
8Q-MAG	de Havilland DHC-6 Twin Otter 200	224	ex C-GENT
8Q-MAH	de Havilland DHC-6 Twin Otter 300	374	ex C-FMYV
8Q-MAI	de Havilland DHC-6 Twin Otter 300	279	ex C-GKBM
8Q-MAK	de Havilland DHC-6 Twin Otter 300	276	ex C-FBBA
8Q-MAL	de Havilland DHC-6 Twin Otter 300	321	ex C-GBBU
8Q-MAM	de Havilland DHC-6 Twin Otter 300	339	ex C-GOKB
8Q-MAO	de Havilland DHC-6 Twin Otter 300	259	ex C-FKBI
8Q-MAP	de Havilland DHC-6 Twin Otter 310	571	ex C-GKBX
8Q-MAQ	de Havilland DHC-6 Twin Otter 300	611	ex C-FBKB
8Q-NTA	de Havilland DHC-6 Twin Otter 200	146	ex C-GNTA
8Q-OEQ	de Havilland DHC-6 Twin Otter 100	44	ex C-FOEQ
8Q-QBU	de Havilland DHC-6 Twin Otter 100	99	ex C-FQBU
8Q-QHC	de Havilland DHC-6 Twin Otter 100	21	ex C-FQHC

All leased from Kenn Borek and operate as Floatplanes

TRANS MALDIVIAN AIRWAYS

Hum (HUM)   *Male (MLE)*

8Q-TMA	de Havilland DHC-6 Twin Otter 100	82	ex 8Q-HIA	
8Q-TMB	de Havilland DHC-6 Twin Otter 310	587	ex C-GASV	
8Q-TMC	de Havilland DHC-6 Twin Otter 300	434	ex 8Q-SUM	
8Q-TMD	de Havilland DHC-6 Twin Otter 300	530	ex 8Q-HIG	
8Q-TME	de Havilland DHC-6 Twin Otter 300	798	ex 8Q-HIH	
8Q-TMF	de Havilland DHC-6 Twin Otter 300	657	ex 8Q-HII	Lsd fr Zimex
8Q-TMG	de Havilland DHC-6 Twin Otter 310	597	ex 8Q-HIJ	
8Q-TMH	de Havilland DHC-6 Twin Otter 310	668	ex HK-4194X	
8Q-TMI	de Havilland DHC-6 Twin Otter 300	751	ex N710PV	Lsd fr Aerocentury Corp
8Q-TMJ	de Havilland DHC-6 Twin Otter 300	781	ex N781JM	Lsd fr Aerocentury Corp
8Q-TMK	de Havilland DHC-6 Twin Otter 300	754	ex N107JM	Lsd fr Aerocentury Corp
8Q-TML	de Havilland DHC-6 Twin Otter 300	640	ex N709PV	Lsd fr Jetfleet III

All Floatplanes
Trans Maldivian Airways is the trading name of Hummingbird Helicopters

8R - GUYANA (Co-operative Republic of Guyana)

AIR SERVICES

Georgetown-Ogle

8R-GAA	Piper PA-34-200T Seneca II	34-7870451	ex 8R-GGJ	
8R-GET	Britten-Norman BN-2A-27 Islander	484	ex G-BDLG	
8R-GFI	Britten-Norman BN-2A-9 Islander	677	ex G-AZGU	on rebuild
8R-GFM	Cessna U206F Stationair	U20601731	ex N9531G	
8R-GGE	Cessna U206G Stationair	U20603358	ex N8501Q	Floatplane
8R-GHB	Cessna U206G Stationair 6	U20604889	ex 8R-GPF	
8R-GHE	Britten-Norman BN-2A-6 Islander	269	ex 8R-GHB	
8R-GYA	Cessna U206G Stationair	U20603654	ex 8R-GGF	R/STOL conv

LAPARKAN AIRWAYS

(LE) (IATA 959)   *Georgetown-Cheddi Jagan Intl (GEO)*

Operates cargo services with Douglas DC-8F aircraft leased from Fine Air and Florida West as and when required

RORAIMA AIRWAYS

Roraima (ROR)   *Georgetown-Ogle*

8R-GRA	Britten-Norman BN-2A-26 Islander	3006	ex N42540
8R-GRC	Britten-Norman BN-2B-27 Islander	2114	ex SX-DKA

TRANS GUYANA AIRWAYS

Trans Guyana (TGY)   *Georgetown-Ogle*

8R-GGT	Britten-Norman BN-2A-26 Islander	635	ex VQ-TAG	
8R-GHD	Britten-Norman BN-2A-27 Islander	622	ex C-GKES	on rebuild
8R-GHM	Britten-Norman BN-2A-27 Islander	216	ex PT-IAS	
8R-GRS	Cessna U206G Stationair 6	U20606202	ex N206GX	
8R-GTG	Cessna 208B Caravan I	208B0397	ex N397TA	

UNIVERSAL AIRLINES

Guyana Jet (UW/UVG) (IATA 761)   *Georgetown-Cheddi Jagan Intl (GEO)*

TF-ATT	Boeing 767-383ER	263/24358	ex OY-KDH	Lsd fr ABD

9A - CROATIA (Republic of Croatia)

AIR ADRIATIC

Adriatic (AHR)   *Rijeka (RJK)*

9A-CBC	McDonnell-Douglas MD-82	1095/49143	ex N824US	My Dream	Lsd fr Elmo Avn
9A-CBD	McDonnell-Douglas MD-82	1055/48095	ex N815US		Lsd fr Elmo Avn

CROATIA AIRLINES

Croatia (OU/CTN) (IATA 831)   *Zagreb (ZAG)*

9A-CTF	Airbus Industrie A320-212	0258	ex F-OKAI	Rijeka	Lsd fr debis
9A-CTG	Airbus Industrie A319-112	0767	ex D-AVYA	Zadar	
9A-CTH	Airbus Industrie A319-112	0833	ex D-AVYJ	Zagreb	
9A-CTI	Airbus Industrie A319-112	1029	ex D-AVYC	Vukovar	
9A-CTJ	Airbus Industrie A320-214	1009	ex F-WWDN	Dubrovnik	
9A-CTK	Airbus Industrie A320-214	1237	ex F-WWIK	Split	
9A-CTL	Airbus Industrie A319-112	1252	ex D-AVYS	Pula	
9A-CTS	Aerospatiale/Alenia ATR 42-300QC	312	ex F-WWEK	Istra	
9A-CTT	Aerospatiale/Alenia ATR 42-300QC	317	ex F-WWEO	Dalmacija	
9A-CTU	Aerospatiale/Alenia ATR 42-320	394	ex F-WWLJ	Slavonija	

LAUS AIR

Laus Aur (LSU)   *Zagreb (ZAG)*

9A-BAL	LET L-410UVP	871924	ex HA-LAS	Farnair titles

NORTH ADRIA AVIATION

North-Adria (NAI)   *Vrsar*

9A-BAN	LET L-410UVP	851407	ex UN-67503
9A-BNA	LET L-410UVP	851518	ex CCCP-67554

TRADE AIR

Tradair (TDR) — Zagreb (ZAG)

9A-BTA	LET L-410UVP-E19A	912538	ex OK-WDO
9A-BTB	LET L-410UVP-E3	902506	ex LZ-KLA
9A-BTC	LET L-410UVP-E3	902507	ex LZ-KLB

9G - GHANA (Republic of Ghana)

AEROGEM AIRLINES

Aerogem (GCK) — Accra (ACC)

Operates cargo flights with Antonov An-32 aircraft leased from other operators as required

GHANA AIRWAYS

Ghana (GH/GHA) (IATA 237) — Accra (ACC)

5X-TRE	Douglas DC-9-51	864/47746	ex N414EA		Lsd fr Boeing Capital
5X-TWO	Douglas DC-9-51	861/47732	ex N411EA		Lsd fr Boeing Capital
9G-ADT	Douglas DC-9-51	796/47665	ex YV-90C	stored ACC	
9G-ADU	Douglas DC-9-51	803/47692	ex YV-80C		
9G-ANA	Douglas DC-10-30	369/48286		stored FCO	
9G-ANB	Douglas DC-10-30	234/46959	ex 9M-MAW	stored ACC	Lsd fr PKG Lease
9G-ANC	Douglas DC-10-30	159/46933	ex 9M-MAZ	stored FCO	Lsd fr Aeronautics
9G-AND	Douglas DC-10-30	106/46712	ex N140AA		Lsd fr BCI Aircraft Holdings
9G-ANE	Douglas DC-10-30	165/46713	ex N141AA		Lsd fr BCI Aircraft Holdings

JOHNSON'S AIR

Johnsonsair (JON) — Accra (ACC)

9G-FIA	Boeing 707-331C (Comtran 2)	815/20069	ex P4-YYY	stored SHJ	Lsd fr ALG Group
9G-IRL	Boeing 707-320C				
9G-JET	Boeing 707-323C (Comtran 2)	655/19372	ex HS-TFS	all-white	
9G-LAD*	Boeing 707-323C (Comtran 2)	439/18940	ex 5N-MXX	no titles	Lsd fr ALG Group
9G-OLD*	Boeing 707-324C (Comtran 2)	537/19350	ex (9G-DUC)	all-white	Lsd fr ALG Group
*Jointly operated with First International A/W					
9G-LCA	Canadair CL-44-0 Guppy	16	ex 4K-GUP	stored BOH	
9G-PEL	Douglas DC-8F-62 (BAC 3)	481/46085	ex 4K-AZ29		

MK AIRLINES

(7G/MKA) — Manston (MSE)

9G-MKA	Douglas DC-8F-55 (QNC 2)	254/45804	ex N855BC	stored MSE	
9G-MKC	Douglas DC-8F-55 (QNC 2)	207/45692	ex 5V-TAF	stored MSE	
9G-MKE	Douglas DC-8-55F (QNC 2)	223/45753	ex 5N-OCM		
9G-MKF	Douglas DC-8F-55 (QNC 2)	246/45820	ex C-FIWW		Lsd to NGE
9G-MKG	Douglas DC-8-62F (BAC 3)	437/46027	ex TF-MKG		
9G-MKH	Douglas DC-8-62AF (BAC 3)	551/46153	ex TF-MKH		
9G-MKK	Douglas DC-8-62F (BAC 3)	417/46022	ex N187SK		
9G-MKN	Douglas DC-8-63CF (BAC 3)	540/46151	ex N815CK		
9G-MKO	Douglas DC-8-63AF (BAC 3)	549/46147	ex N811CK		
9G-	Douglas DC-8F-55 (QNC 2)	251/45764	ex N812TC		
9G-MKJ	Boeing 747-244SF	486/22170	ex ZS-SAR		Lsd fr Finova
9G-MKL	Boeing 747-2R7F	354/21650	ex N639FE		Lsd fr US Bancorp
9G-MKM	Boeing 747-2B5B (SF)	484/22482	ex N207BA		Lsd fr Boeing A/c
9G-MKP	Boeing 747-245F	396/21841	ex N638FE		Lsd fr US Bancorp
9G-MKQ	Boeing 747-2S4F	472/22169	ex N713BA		Lsd fr Boeing A/c Holding
9G-	Boeing 747-2B2M	353/21614	ex 5R-MFT		

RACE CARGO AIRLINES

FastCargo (RCN) — Accra (ACC)

Joint operations with First International Airlines

SOBEL AIR

Accra (ACC)

9G-AIR	Fokker F.27 Friendship 100	10266	ex SE-KZF
9G-BEL	Fokker F.27 Friendship 100	10319	ex SE-KZH
9G-SOB	Fokker F.27 Friendship 100	10287	ex SE-KZG

All leased to/operated for Air National Gabon with La Nationale titles

9H - MALTA (Republic of Malta)

AIR MALTA

Air Malta (KM/AMC) (IATA 643)   Luqa (MLA)

9H-ABE	Boeing 737-2Y5 (Nordam 3)	1414/23847		Mellieha	Lsd fr Celsius Amtec
9H-ABF	Boeing 737-2Y5 (Nordam 3)	1418/23848		Zurieq	Lsd fr Celsius Amtec
9H-ABR	Boeing 737-3Y5	2446/25613		Juan de Homedes	Lsd fr ILFC
9H-ABS	Boeing 737-3Y5	2467/25614		Antoine de Paule	Lsd fr ILFC
9H-ABT	Boeing 737-3Y5	2478/25615		Ferdinand von Hompesch	Lsf ILFC
9H-ADH	Boeing 737-33A	3007/27459	ex N1787B		Lsd fr AWAS
9H-ADI	Boeing 737-33A	3021/27460			Lsd fr AWAS
9H-ADM	Boeing 737-382	1695/24365	ex CS-TIB		Lsd fr ILFC
9H-ADN	Boeing 737-382	2226/25161	ex CS-TIK		Lsd fr ILFC
9H-ADY	Airbus Industrie A320-214	1769	ex F-WWDK		Lsd fr GATX
9H-ADZ	Airbus Industrie A320-211	0331	ex VH-HYY		Lsd fr GATX
9H-AED	Airbus Industrie A320-212	0288	ex SE-RCC		
9H-AEF	Airbus Industrie A320-214	2142	ex F-WWBZ		Lsd fr ILFC
9H-AEG	Airbus Industrie A319-112	2113	ex D-AVWQ		Lsd fr ILFC
9H-AEH	Airbus Industrie A319-112	2122	ex D-AVWA		Lsd fr ILFC
9H-AEI	Airbus Industrie A320-214	2189	ex F-WWDL	on order	Lsd fr ILFC
9H-AEJ	Airbus Industrie A319-112	2186	ex D-AVWX	on order 04	Lsd fr ILFC

Owns Malta Air Charter. A further four Airbus Industrie A319-112s are on order for delivery up to 2007 plus three more A320-214s up to 2008, all leased from ILFC. To introduce Fare4U as low cost operation using three Boeing 737-300s by the end of March 2004

EUROPE 2000 AIRLINES

                                                                                     Luqa (MLA)

N715MQ	Swearingen SA.227DC Metro 23	DC-805B
N3084W	Swearingen SA.227DC Mtero 23	DC-902B

MALTA AIR CHARTER

Malta Charter (R5/MAC)   Luqa (MLA)

LZ-CAR	Mil Mi-8P	8606	ex RA-24639
LZ-CAX	Mil Mi-8	7666	ex RA-22847

MEDAVIA

Medavia (MDM)   Luqa (MLA)

PH-ACY	Beech 1900D	UE-44	ex D-CBSG	Lsd fr ROS
9H-AAP	CASA C.212-100 Aviocar	TC15-1-009	ex EC-CRV	
9H-AAR	CASA C.212-200 Aviocar	CC15-1-161		
9H-AAS	CASA C.212-200 Aviocar	CC15-2-162		

9J - ZAMBIA (Republic of Zambia)

AFRICA ONE ZAMBIA

(AZL)

Wholly owned subsidiary of Africa One Airlines

NATIONWIDE AIRLINES (ZAMBIA)

Zamnaat (4J/NWZ)   Lusaka (LUN)

Operates services with Boeing 737-200s leased from Nationwide Airlines (ZS) as and when required

PHOEBUS APOLLO ZAMBIA

(KZM)   Lusaka (LUN)

9J-PAA	ATEL ATL-98 Carvair	13/27314	ex N5459M

Wholly owned subsidiary of Phoebus Appollo Aviation

ZAMBIAN AIRWAYS

Zambiani (Q3/MBN) (IATA 391)   Lusaka (LUN)

9J-MAS	Beech 1900D	UE-323	ex N23047	Mukango
9J-MBO	Beech 1900D	UE-319	ex N23004	Kaingo

Operates franchise services on behalf of British Airways in full colours with Boeing 737-200 leased from Comair
Owned by Comair and Roan Air

ZAMBIA SKYWAYS

Zambia Skies (X7/ZAK) — Lusaka (LUN)

9J-DCF	Beech 65-C90 King Air	LJ-575	ex N12RF
9J-YVZ	Beech 65-B90 King Air	LJ-338	ex ZS-LWZ

9K - KUWAIT (State of Kuwait)

KUWAIT AIRWAYS

Kuwaiti (KU/KAC) (IATA 229) — Kuwait (KWI)

9K-AHI	Airbus Industrie A300C4-620	344	ex PK-MAY	Op for Govt	
9K-AMA	Airbus Industrie A300B4-605R	673	ex F-WWAQ	Failaka	
9K-AMB	Airbus Industrie A300B4-605R	694	ex F-WWAV	Burghan	
9K-AMC	Airbus Industrie A300B4-605R	699	ex F-WWAM	Wafra	
9K-AMD	Airbus Industrie A300B4-605R	719	ex F-WWAB	Wara	
9K-AME	Airbus Industrie A300B4-605R	721	ex F-WWAG	Al-Rawdhatain	
9K-ALA	Airbus Industrie A310-308	647	ex F-WWCQ	Al-Jahra	
9K-ALB	Airbus Industrie A310-308	649	ex F-WWCV	Gharnada	
9K-ALC	Airbus Industrie A310-308	663	ex JY-AGT	Kadhma	
9K-ALD	Airbus Industrie A310-308	648	ex F-WWCR	Al-Salmiya; op for Govt	
9K-ADB	Boeing 747-269M	335/21542		stored, for sale	
9K-ADD	Boeing 747-269M	553/22740		Al-Salmiya, stored - for sale	
9K-ADE	Boeing 747-469M	1046/27338		Al-Jabariya; op for Govt	
9K-AKA	Airbus Industrie A320-212	0181	ex F-WWIU	Bubbyan	
9K-AKB	Airbus Industrie A320-212	0182	ex F-WWIV	Kubber	
9K-AKC	Airbus Industrie A320-212	0195	ex F-WWDP	Qurtoba	
9K-AKD	Airbus Industrie A320-212	2046	ex F-WWBG	Al-Mobarakiya	Op for Govt
9K-ANA	Airbus Industrie A340-313	089	ex F-WWJX	Warba	
9K-ANB	Airbus Industrie A340-313	090	ex F-WWJZ	Al-Sabahiya	
9K-ANC	Airbus Industrie A340-313	101	ex F-WWJE	Al-Mobarakia	
9K-AND	Airbus Industrie A340-313	104	ex F-WWJJ	Al-Riggah	
9K-AOA	Boeing 777-269ER	125/28743		Al-Grain	
9K-AOB	Boeing 777-269ER	145/28744		Qarph	

9L - SIERRA LEONE (Republic of Sierra Leone)

AEROLIFT — Freetown (FNA)

D2-FED	Antonov An-32A	1408	ex RA-69356	
9L-LCY	Ilyushin Il-76TD	1003499994	ex RA-76796	
9L-LDO	Antonov An-32A	2206	ex RA-48117	stored WIL
9L-LDP	Yakovlev Yak-42D	452042??07018	ex RA-42450	for sale
9L-LDT	Yakovlev Yak-42D	10018	ex RA-42	

AFRIK AIR LINKS

Africa Links (AFK) — Freetown (FNA)

9L-LBW	Boeing 727-227 (Raisbeck 3)	1132/21044	ex N13759

AIR LEONE

Aeroleone (RLL) — Freetown (FNA)

9L-LCA	LET L-410UVP	841319	ex 3C-DDC	Lsd to Bat Systems
9L-LCB	LET L-410UVP-E	892807	ex 3C-DDD	Lsd to Bat Systems
9L-LCE	LET L-410UVP	800524	ex 9L-LBW	Lsd to Sunshine Coast Skydivers
9L-LCP	LET L-410UVP	790216	ex LZ-MNP	based Kenya
9L-LCQ	Antonov An-28	1AJ006-07	ex SP-DDC	
9L-LDF	Douglas DC-9-32	180/47088	ex EC-BIM	Lsd to AXK
9L-LDG	Douglas DC-9-32	237/47093	ex EC-BIR	Lsd to AXK
9L-LDI	Yakovlev Yak-40	9542043	ex PLW-043	
9L-LDJ	BAC One-Eleven Srs 531FS	242	ex G-OBWE	stored MLA
9L-LDL	BAC One-Eleven Srs 518FG	232	ex G-OBWA	stored MLA
9L-LDU	Boeing 707-373C	500/19179	ex 3C-GIG	Lsd fr Koda

AIR UNIVERSAL

Uni-Leone (UVS) — Freetown/Amman (FNA/AMM)

9L-LDC	Lockheed 1011-100 Tristar	1231	ex TF-ABT
9L-LDE	Lockheed 1011-250 Tristar	1244	ex N740DA

HA AIRLINES

Freetown/Beirut (FNA/BEY)

9L-LCU	Boeing 727-256	1010/20818	ex EC-CFH

QUIKMAY AIRLINES

Freetown/Amman (FNA/AMM)

Current situation unknown, both aircraft to Iraqi Airways and cannibalised

SIERRA NATIONAL AIRLINES

Selair (LJ/SLA) (IATA 690)

Freetown (FNA)

TF-FIS	Boeing 757-256	617/26245	ex N542NA	Lsd fr ICE

STAR AIR

Freetown/Amman (FNA/AMM)

9L-LDN	Lockheed L-1011 Tristar 100	1221	ex XU-122
9L-LDR	Lockheed L-1011 Tristar 500	1179	ex 9Y-TGJ
9L-LDS	Lockheed L-1011 Tristar 500	1233	ex N3140D
9L-LDV	Lockheed L-1011 Tristar-1	1200	ex 5Y-RUM
9L-LDZ	Lockheed L-1011 Tristar 200F	1212	ex V2-LFQ
9L-LED	Lockheed L-1011 Tristar 500	1222	ex 9Y-THA

TRANS ATLANTIC AIRLINES

(KC)

Freetown (FNA)

Current fleet details are unknown

WEST COAST AIRLINES

West Leone (WCA)

Freetown (FNA)

9L-LBJ	LET L-410UVP	841202	ex RA-67438
9L-LBK	LET L-410UVP	831125	ex RA-67434
9L-LBL	LET L-410UVP	841201	ex
9L-LBM	LET L-410UVP	841338	ex RA-67109
9L-LBN	LET L-410UVP	851337	ex RA-67108

9L-LBQ	Antonov An-24			Jt ops with GIH

9M - MALAYSIA (Federation of Malaysia)

AIR ASIA

Asian express (AK/AXM)

Kuala Lumpur-Sultan Abdul Aziz Shah (KUL)

9M-AAA	Boeing 737-3Y0	2013/24907	ex UR-GAE	Lsd fr GECAS
9M-AAC	Boeing 737-3Q8	2854/28200	ex N282LF	Lsd fr ILFC
9M-AAD	Boeing 737-3Y0	2001/24905	ex N905AF	Lsd fr Airplanes Finance
9M-AAE	Boeing 737-3L9	1800/24570	ex B-2653	Lsd fr SALE
9M-AAF	Boeing 737-33A	1739/24096	ex N496AN	Lsd fr AWMS II
9M-AAG	Boeing 737-3L9	2347/27061	ex SX-BGI	Lsd fr Tombo
9M-AAH	Boeing 737-375	1434/23808	ex LY-AGP	Lsd fr Inter Leasing
9M-AAI	Boeing 737-301	1248/23510	ex N341US	
9M-AAJ	Boeing 737-301	1268/23511	ex N342US	
9M-AAL	Boeing 737-301	1214/23235	ex N337US	Lsd fr AFS Investments
9M-AAN*	Boeing 737-301	1208/23234	ex N338US	Lsd fr AFS Investments
9M-AAO	Boeing 737-301	1219/23236	ex N339US	Lsd fr AFS Investments
9M-	Boeing 737-3M8	2039/25071	ex N250AT	

*Leased to Thai AirAsia, a wholly owned subisiary

BERJAYA AIR CHARTER

Berjaya (J8/BVT)

Kuala Lumpur-Sultan Abdul Aziz Shah (KUL)

9M-TAH	de Havilland DHC-7-110	109	ex G-BRYD
9M-TAK	de Havilland DHC-7-110	110	ex G-BOAW
9M-TAL	de Havilland DHC-7-110	112	ex G-BOAY
9M-TAO	de Havilland DHC-7-110	62	ex G-BRYA

BOSKYM UDARA ceased operations

HORNBILL SKYWAYS

Koching (KCH)

9M-AVL	Bell 206B JetRanger II	1047	ex 9V-BFR
9M-AVM	Bell 206B JetRanger II	2169	
9M-AVY	Bell 206B JetRanger III	2259	
9M-AWE	Bell 206B JetRanger III	2363	
9M-AYP	Bell 206B JetRanger III	3612	ex N2292Z
9M-AYQ	Bell 206B JetRanger III	3584	ex N2297L
9M-SGH	Bell 206B JetRanger III	4103	ex N7107Z
9M-SGJ	Bell 206B JetRanger III	4059	ex N8129Y
9M-BCT	Bell 206L-4 LongRanger IV	52150	
9M-BCU	Bell 206L-4 LongRanger IV	52151	

ISLAND AIR current status uncertain, believed to have ceased operations

KENARI AIR current status uncertain, believed to have ceased operations

LAYANG LAYANG AEROSPACE

(LAY)   Miri (MYY)

N149AC	Garlick-Bell 205A-1 (UH-1H)	5229	ex 66-00746	Lsd fr Erickson
RA-41901	Antonov An-38	1416384701001		Lsd fr VTK
9M-LLA	Short SC.7 Skyvan 3	SH1977	ex ZS-LFG	
9M-LLB	GAF N22C Nomad	N22C-95	ex VH-SNL	
(9M-LLC)	Antonov An-38-100	010003	ex RA-41903	Lsd fr VTK

MALAYSIA AIRLINES

Malaysian (MH/MAS) (IATA 232)   Kuala Lumpur-Sultan Abdul Aziz Shah (KUL)

9M-MKA	Airbus Industrie A330-322	067	ex F-WWKK		
9M-MKC	Airbus Industrie A330-322	069	ex F-WWKM		
9M-MKD	Airbus Industrie A330-322	073	ex F-WWKN		
9M-MKE	Airbus Industrie A330-322	077	ex F-WWKO		
9M-MKF	Airbus Industrie A330-322	100	ex F-WWKZ		
9M-MKG	Airbus Industrie A330-322	107	ex F-WWKV		
9M-MKH	Airbus Industrie A330-322	110	ex F-WWKE		
9M-MKI	Airbus Industrie A330-322	116	ex F-WWKT		
9M-MKJ	Airbus Industrie A330-322	119	ex F-WWKJ		
9M-MKT	Airbus Industrie A330-223	262	ex HB-IQF		Lsd fr Sierra Lsg
9M-MKU	Airbus Industrie A330-223	255	ex HB-IQE		Lsd fr Sierra Lsg
9M-MKV	Airbus Industrie A330-223	296	ex EI-CZS		Lsd fr Calliope Ltd
9M-MKW	Airbus Industrie A330-223	300	ex EI-CZT		Lsd fr Calliope Ltd
9M-MKX	Airbus Industrie A330-223	290	ex EI-CZR		Lsd fr Calliope Ltd
9M-	Airbus Industrie A330-322	095	ex C-FBUS	on order	Lsd fr ILFC
9M-	Airbus Industrie A330-322	143	ex C-FRAE	on order	Lsd fr ILFC
9M-MMA	Boeing 737-4H6	2272/26443			
9M-MMB	Boeing 737-4H6	2308/26444			
9M-MMC	Boeing 737-4H6	2332/26453			
9M-MMD	Boeing 737-4H6	2340/26464			
9M-MME	Boeing 737-4H6	2362/26465			
9M-MMF	Boeing 737-4H6	2372/26466			
9M-MMG	Boeing 737-4H6	2378/26467			
9M-MMH	Boeing 737-4H6	2391/27084			Lsd to UBA
9M-MMI	Boeing 737-4H6	2395/27096			
9M-MMJ	Boeing 737-4H6	2399/27097			
9M-MMK	Boeing 737-4H6	2403/27083			
9M-MML	Boeing 737-4H6	2407/27085			
9M-MMM	Boeing 737-4H6	2410/27166			
9M-MMN	Boeing 737-4H6	2419/27167			
9M-MMQ	Boeing 737-4H6	2441/27087			
9M-MMR	Boeing 737-4H6	2445/26468			
9M-MMS	Boeing 737-4H6	2450/27169			
9M-MMT	Boeing 737-4H6	2462/27170			
9M-MMU	Boeing 737-4H6	2479/26447	ex VT-JAV		
9M-MMV	Boeing 737-4H6	2491/26449			
9M-MMW	Boeing 737-4H6	2496/26451			
9M-MMX	Boeing 737-4H6	2501/26452			
9M-MMY	Boeing 737-4H6	2507/26455			
9M-MMZ	Boeing 737-4H6	2521/26457			
9M-MQA	Boeing 737-4H6	2525/26458			
9M-MQB	Boeing 737-4H6	2530/26459			
9M-MQC	Boeing 737-4H6	2533/26460			Lsd fr GECAS
9M-MQD	Boeing 737-4H6	2536/26461			
9M-MQE	Boeing 737-4H6	2542/26462			
9M-MQF	Boeing 737-4H6	2560/26463			

9M-MQG	Boeing 737-4H6	2568/27190		
9M-MQH	Boeing 737-4H6	2624/27352		Lsd fr GECAS
9M-MQI	Boeing 737-4H6	2632/27353	ex 9H-ADJ	
9M-MQJ	Boeing 737-4H6	2657/27383		Lsd fr Tombo
9M-MQK	Boeing 737-4H6	2673/27384		
9M-MQL	Boeing 737-4H6	2676/27191		Lsd fr GECAS
9M-MQM	Boeing 737-4H6	2685/27306		Lsd fr Tombo
9M-MQN	Boeing 737-4H6	2852/27673	ex 9H-ADK	
9M-MQO	Boeing 737-4H6	2877/27674	ex 9H-ADL	
TF-ATX	Boeing 747-236B (SF)	672/23711	ex G-BDXM	Lsd fr ABD
TF-ATZ	Boeing 747-236B (SF)	697/24088	ex G-BDXP	Lsd fr ABD
9M-MHI*	Boeing 747-236 (SCD)	502/22304	ex (G-BDXL)	Kuching
9M-MHJ*	Boeing 747-236 (SCD)	526/22442	ex (G-BDXN)	Jahor Bahru
9M-MPA	Boeing 747-4H6	932/27042		Ipoh
9M-MPB	Boeing 747-4H6	965/25699		Shah Alam
9M-MPC	Boeing 747-4H6	974/25700		Kuantan
9M-MPD	Boeing 747-4H6	997/25701		Seremban
9M-MPE	Boeing 747-4H6	999/25702		Kangar
9M-MPF	Boeing 747-4H6	1017/27043		Kota Bharu
9M-MPG	Boeing 747-4H6	1025/25703		Kuala Terengganu
9M-MPH	Boeing 747-4H6	1041/27044	ex N6066B	Langkawi
9M-MPI	Boeing 747-4H6	1091/27672		Tioman
9M-MPJ	Boeing 747-4H6	1130/28426		Labuan
9M-MPK	Boeing 747-4H6	1147/28427		Lsd fr GECAS
9M-MPL*	Boeing 747-4H6	1150/28428		
9M-MPM*	Boeing 747-4H6	1152/28435		
9M-MPN*	Boeing 747-4H6	1247/28432		
9M-MPO*	Boeing 747-4H6	1290/28433		Alor Setar
9M-MPP*	Boeing 747-4H6	1296/29900		Putrajaya
9M-MPQ*	Boeing 747-4H6	1301/29901		

*Leased from Aircraft Business Malaysia. Two more Boeing 747-4H6s are on order for delivery in 2008/2009

9M-MRA	Boeing 777-2H6ER	64/28408	ex N5017V	
9M-MRB	Boeing 777-2H6ER	74/28409	ex N50217	Lsd fr GECC
9M-MRC	Boeing 777-2H6ER	78/28410		Lsd fr GECC
9M-MRD	Boeing 777-2H6ER	84/28411		
9M-MRE	Boeing 777-2H6ER	115/28412		
9M-MRF	Boeing 777-2H6ER	128/28413		Lsd fr GECC
9M-MRG	Boeing 777-2H6ER	140/28414		
9M-MRH	Boeing 777-2H6ER	151/28415		
9M-MRI	Boeing 777-2H6ER	155/28416		Lsd fr GECAS
9M-MRJ	Boeing 777-2H6ER	222/28417		
9M-MRK	Boeing 777-2H6ER	231/28418		
9M-MRL	Boeing 777-2H6ER	329/29065		Lsd fr SALE
9M-MRM	Boeing 777-2H6ER	336/29066		Lsd fr SALE
9M-MRN	Boeing 777-2H6ER	394/28419		Lsd fr Aircraft Business Malaysia
9M-MRO	Boeing 777-2H6ER	404/28420		Lsd fr Aircraft Business Malaysia
9M-MRP	Boeing 777-2H6ER	28421		on order
9M-MRQ	Boeing 777-2H6ER	28422		on order
9M-	Boeing 777-3H6			on order Jun03
9M-	Boeing 777-3H6			on order Aug03
9M-	Boeing 777-3H6			on order Oct03
9M-	Boeing 777-3H6			on order Dec03
9M-MDK	de Havilland DHC-6 Twin Otter 310	792	ex C-GESR	
9M-MDL	de Havilland DHC-6 Twin Otter 310	802	ex C-GECV	
9M-MDM	de Havilland DHC-6 Twin Otter 310	804	ex C-GDKL	
9M-MDN	de Havilland DHC-6 Twin Otter 300	844	ex C-FDQL	
9M-MDO	de Havilland DHC-6 Twin Otter 300	629	ex ZK-KHA	
9M-MGA	Fokker 50	20150	ex PH-EXM	
9M-MGB	Fokker 50	20156	ex PH-EXP	
9M-MGC	Fokker 50	20161	ex PH-EXK	
9M-MGD	Fokker 50	20164	ex PH-EXL	
9M-MGE	Fokker 50	20166	ex PH-EXN	
9M-MGF	Fokker 50	20167	ex PH-EXO	
9M-MGG	Fokker 50	20170	ex PH-EXS	
9M-MGI	Fokker 50	20175	ex PH-EXB	
9M-MGJ	Fokker 50	20204	ex PH-EXM	
9M-MGK	Fokker 50	20248	ex PH-EXR	

Cargo operations are undertaken by MASKargo, a wholly owned subsidiary of Malaysia Airlines
Six Airbus Industrie A380-800s are on order for delivery from 2007

MHS AVIATION

Kerteh/Miri (KTE/MYY)

9M-AVO	Sikorsky S-61N	61766	ex G-BEKI
9M-AVP	Sikorsky S-61N	61768	ex G-BEKJ
9M-AVQ	Sikorsky S-61N	61736	ex G-BCLB

9M-AVT	Sikorsky S-61N	61735	ex 9M-ELF(2)	
9M-AWN	Sikorsky S-61N	61714	ex G-BBHN	
9M-PCM	Sikorsky S-61N	61720	ex G-BBVB	
9M-SSR	Sikorsky S-61N	61719	ex LN-OSK	
9M-SSS	Sikorsky S-61N	61474	ex LN-OQL	
9M-STA	Sikorsky S-76C	760383		
9M-STB	Sikorsky S-76C	760384		
9M-STC	Sikorsky S-76C	760392		
9M-STD	Sikorsky S-76C	760397		
9M-STE	Sikorsky S-76C	760398		
9M-STF	Sikorsky S-76C	760400		
9M-PHB	Aerospatiale AS.355F2 Ecureuil 2	5418		
9M-SSE	Aerospatiale SA.330J Puma	1557	ex G-BFTV	stored Kerteh
9M-SSN	de Havilland DHC-6 Twin Otter 300	659	ex VH-AHI	
9M-SSV	Aerospatiale AS.355F2 Ecureuil 2	5476		
9M-STL	Beech 1900D	UE-373	ex N31110	
9M-STS	Aerospatiale AS.332L1 Super Puma	2387		
9M-STT	Aerospatiale AS.332L1 Super Puma	2405		
9M-STV	Aerospatiale AS.332L1 Super Puma	2408		

PAN-MALAYSIAN AIR TRANSPORT

Pan Malaysian (PMA)   *Kuala Lumpur-Sultan Abdul Aziz Shah (KUL)*

9M-PIH	Short SC.7 Skyvan 3	SH1962	ex G-BFUM

SABAH AIR / PENERBANGAN SABAH

Sabah Air (SAX)   *Kota Kinabalu-Intl (BKI)*

9M-AWB	Bell 206B JetRanger III	2330	
9M-AWC	Bell 206B JetRanger III	2336	
9M-AWD	Bell 206B JetRanger III	2351	
9M-AXH	Bell 206B JetRanger III	2480	
9M-AYN	Bell 206B JetRanger III	3022	ex N5738M
9M-SAC	Bell 206B JetRanger III	2510	
9M-ATC	Bell 212	30718	
9M-AUA	GAF N22B Nomad	N22B-7	
9M-AZK	Bell 206L-3 LongRanger III	51484	ex N4196G
9M-BDM	Bell 206L-4 LongRanger IV	52261	ex N61504
9M-KNS	Beech 200 Super King Air	BB-294	ex N18494
9M-TPS	Britten-Norman BN-2T-4S Islander	4009	ex G-BWPO

TRANSMILE AIR SERVICES

Transmile (TH/TSE)   *Kuala Lumpur-Sultan Abdul Aziz Shah (KUL)*

9M-TGA	Boeing 727-2F2F (Duganair 3)	1808/22993	ex TC-JCB		Lsd to AMU
9M-TGB	Boeing 727-2F2F (Duganair 3)	1810/22998	ex TC-JCD		Lsd to AMU
9M-TGE	Boeing 727-247F (FedEx 3)	1471/21697	ex N210UP		
9M-TGF	Boeing 727-247F (FedEx 3)	1474/21698	ex N209UP		
9M-TGG	Boeing 727-247F (FedEx 3)	1485/21699	ex N207UP		
9M-TGG	Boeing 727-247F (FedEx 3)	1493/21701	ex N208UP		
9M-TGH	Boeing 727-223F (FedEx 3)	661/19494	ex N6819		Lsd fr Prewitt Lsg
9M-TGJ	Boeing 727-247F (FedEx 3)	1489/21700	ex N211UP		
9M-TGK	Boeing 727-247F (FedEx 3)	1305/21392	ex N212UP		
9M-PML	Boeing 737-275C	427/21116	ex C-GDPW	Freighter	Op for Poslaju Kurier
9M-PMM	Boeing 737-205C	278/20458	ex RP-C2906	Freighter	
9M-PMP	Boeing 737-248C	215/20220	ex EI-ASE	Freighter	Lsd to TSD
9M-PMQ	Boeing 737-230C	230/20254	ex F-GFVJ	Freighter	Lsd to TSD
9M-PMW	Boeing 737-209	1581/24197	ex B-1878		Lsd to Seulawah
9M-PMZ	Boeing 737-209	1420/23796	ex PK-BYA		Lsd to Kartika Air
9M-PMA	Cessna 208B Caravan I	208B0800			
9M-PMB	Cessna 208B Caravan I	208B0801			

Operates freight services for Malaysian Post Office

VISION AIR

     Miri (MYY)

9M-VAA	Dornier 228-202K	8165	ex N419VA	Lsd fr Vegas Jet
9M-VAM	Dornier 228-212	8216	ex N420VA	Lsd fr Vegas Jet

Joint venture between Vision Air (N) and Government of Sarawak

WIRA KRIS

     Miri (MYY)

9M-WKB	Short SC.7 Skyvan 3	SH1965	ex ZS-KMX

9N - NEPAL (Kingdom of Nepal)

AIR ANAYA

9N-ADD	Mil Mi-17-1 (Mi-8ATM)	59489607385	ex RA-22160	
9N-ADL	Mil Mi-17-1 (Mi-8ATM)	59489605283	ex RA-27093	
9N-ADN	Mil Mi-17-1V (Mi-8MTV-1)	95985	ex RA-27135	stored KTM

ASIAN AIRLINES ceased operations

BUDDHA AIR

Buddha Air (BHA)   **Kathmandu (KTM)**

9N-AEE	Beech 1900D	UE-286	ex N11194
9N-AEK	Beech 1900D	UE-295	ex N21540
9N-AEW	Beech 1900D	UE-328	ex N23179
9N-AGH	Beech 1900D	UE-409	ex N4192N

COSMIC AIR

(F5)   **Kathmandu/Pokhara (KTM/PKR)**

9N-AEP	Dornier 228-201	8078	ex D-CBMI	
9N-AGM	SAAB SF.340A	064	ex N464EA	Lsd fr Elmo Finance
9N-AGY	Dornier 228-100	7022	ex SE-KTM	

GORKHA AIRLINES

9N-ADS	Mil Mi-17-1V (Mi-8MTV-1)	95603	ex RA-25459	stored KTM
9N-ADS	Mil Mi-17-1V (Mi-8MTV-1)	95604	ex RA-25460	
9N-AEO	Dornier 228-200	8010	ex SE-KTO	stored KTM

MOUNTAIN AIR current status is uncertain as both aircraft returned to USA

NECON AIR

Necon Air (3Z/NEC)   **Kathmandu (KTM)**

9N-AFU	Aerospatiale/Alenia ATR 42-320	144	ex F-WQIH	Lsd fr ATR Asset Mgt
9N-AGI	Beech 1900C-1	UC-97	ex N97YV	
9N-AGL	Beech 1900C-1	UC-108	ex N15656	stored KTM
9N-AGP	Aerospatiale/Alenia ATR 42-320	149	ex F-WQNP	Lsd fr ATR Asset Mgt

ROYAL NEPAL AIRLINES

Royal Nepal (RA/RNA)   **Kathmandu (KTM)**

9N-ABB	de Havilland DHC-6 Twin Otter 300	302		
9N-ABM	de Havilland DHC-6 Twin Otter 300	455	ex N302EH	
9N-ABO	de Havilland DHC-6 Twin Otter 300	638		
9N-ABQ	de Havilland DHC-6 Twin Otter 300	655		stored KTM
9N-ABT	de Havilland DHC-6 Twin Otter 300	812	ex C-GHHI	
9N-ABU	de Havilland DHC-6 Twin Otter 300	814	ex C-GHHY	
9N-ABX	de Havilland DHC-6 Twin Otter 300	830	ex C-GIQS	
9N-ACA	Boeing 757-2F8	142/23850		Karnali
9N-ACB	Boeing 757-2F8C	182/23863	ex N5573K	Garnadi

SHANGRI-LA AIR

9N-AFA	de Havilland DHC-6 Twin Otter 310	665	ex VT-ERV	
9N-AFX	de Havilland DHC-6 Twin Otter 310	805	ex N805AA	stored KTM

SITA AIRLINES

9N-AHA	Dornier 228-202K	8123	ex F-ODZG
9N-AHB	Dornier 228-202K	8169	ex F-OGPI

SKYLINE AIRWAYS

9N-AEQ	de Havilland DHC-6 Twin Otter 310	708	ex C-GBQD

YETI AIRLINES

9N-AET	de Havilland DHC-6 Twin Otter 300	619	ex C-GBQA
9N-AFD	de Havilland DHC-6 Twin Otter 300	651	ex (9N-AEA)
9N-AFE	de Havilland DHC-6 Twin Otter 300	720	ex (9N-AEB)

9Q - CONGO KINSHASA (Democratic Republic of Congo)

AFRICA ONE
(CFR)

Wholly owned subsidiary of Africa One Airlines

AFRICAN BUSINESS AIR TRANSPORT

ER-AFI	Antonov An-32B	3205	ex ER-ADI	Lsd fr RAN

AFRICAINE D'AVIATION

9Q-CAA	Ilyushin Il-18		
9Q-CAB	Antonov An-26		
9Q-CHB	Ilyushin Il-18D	180002003	
9Q-CIB	Antonov An-26	1701	ex YL-RAB
9Q-CJB	Antonov An-26		

AIR KASAI

3Q-CRM	NAMC YS-11A	2051	ex N911AX	Lsd fr Fields Airmotive
9Q-CFQ	Piper PA-23-250 Aztec C	27-2880	ex TN-ABH	
9Q-CJA	Britten-Norman BN-2A-21 Islander	898	ex I-301	
9Q-CKO	Nord 2501TC Noratlas	169	ex F-WFYJ	
9Q-CTR	Douglas DC-3	9452	ex ZS-EDX	
9Q-CUW	Vickers 798D Viscount	391	ex XA-RJL	A la Grace de Dieu
9Q-CYC	Douglas DC-3	18977	ex N9984Q	
9Q-CYE	Douglas DC-3	19771	ex 79004	

AIR KATANGA

9Q-CAP	Nord 262A-32	35	ex F-BPNT	
9Q-CJJ	Douglas DC-3	10110	ex ZS-NZA	
9Q-COE	Hawker Siddeley Andover C Mk.1	Set 20	ex 3C-KKS	
9Q-CSJ	BAC One-Eleven Srs.201AC	013	ex EI-BWM	Fatima
9Q-CYA	Britten-Norman BN-2A Islander	617	ex G-AYBB	
9Q-CYB	Hawker Siddeley Andover C Mk.1	Set 29	ex 9Q-CVC	

AIR TROPIQUES

9Q-CEJ	Beech 1900C	UB-74	ex ZS-ODR

AL-DAWOOD AIR now correctly listed under Nigeria

ATO - AIR TRANSPORT OFFICE

9Q-CTO	Lockheed L-188A Electra	1073	ex 9Q-CRM
9Q-CVK	Hawker Siddeley Andover C.Mk.1	Set17	ex P4-BLL

Cargo Express Congo (TN) is a wholly owned subsidiary

BUSINESS AVIATION OF CONGO

(4P)
Kinshasa-Ndolo (NLO)

ZS-CAI	Douglas DC-3	13541	ex 6638	
ZS-DOC	Dornier 228-202	8104	ex MAAW-R1	
9Q-CAF	Antonov An-32			
9Q-CLN	Fokker F.27 Friendship 300M	10152	ex ZS-OEH	
9Q-CMX	Cessna 404 Titan	404-0415	ex N8801K	
9Q-CTM	LET L-410UVP	882031	ex 2031	(also reported as 9Q-CMT)
9Q-CYM	LET L-410UVP-E3	902402	ex RA-67620	

GLOBAL AIRWAYS fleet details unknown, Possibly did not commence operations

HEWA BORA AIRWAYS

Allcongo (EO/ALX)
Kinshasa-Ndjili (FIH)

9Q-CHC	Lockheed L-1011-500 Tristar	1209	ex N767DA	
9Q-CHE	Boeing 727-232 (FedEx 3)	1785/22677	ex N546DA	
9Q-CHF	Boeing 727-232 (FedEx 3)	1749/22494	ex N545DA	
9Q-CKK	Boeing 707-366C	867/20761	ex 9Q-CKB	
9Q-CKZ	Boeing 737-293	47/19309	ex N777EC	Ville de Lubumbashi dam FIH Apr00
9Q-CRG	Boeing 727-30	28/18361	ex N18477	Ville de Goma
9Q-CRS	Boeing 727-214	573/19687	ex 5H-ARS	
9Q-CWA	Boeing 727-227	998/20775	ex N554PE	Ville de Bakavu

KINSHASA AIRWAYS

Kinshasa Airways (KNS)
Kinshasa-Ndjili (FIH)

9Q-CAN	Douglas DC-8F-54 (QNC 2)	274/45858	ex 3C-QRG	
9Q-CBP	Boeing 727-2H3	1271/21320	ex 3D-PAI	Lsd fr Sky Aviation
9Q-CKS	Boeing 707-399C (Comtran 2)	601/19415	ex 3D-NGK	no titles
9Q-CMG	Douglas DC-8F-55 (QNC 2)	208/45683	ex 3D-FNK	stored SHJ
9Q-CWY	Boeing 747SP-09	304/21300	ex 3D-PAJ	Lsd fr Sky Aviation

(also reported as ex 3D-PAF)

KIVU AIR

Goma (GOM)

9Q-	Short SC.7 Skyvan	SH1831	ex ZS-ORN	Lsd fr NRK
ZS-OWR	CASA C.212	263	ex N263MA	Lsd fr NRK

LIGNES AÉRIENNES CONGOLAISES

(6V/LCG)
Kinshasa-Ndjili (FIH)

9Q-CLV	Douglas DC-8-54F (QNC 2)	122/45610	ex N803CK	stored GOM
9Q-CNK	Boeing 737-298C	348/20795		stored FIH

MALIFT AIR

Malila (MLC)
Kinshasa-Ndjil/Khartoum (FIH/KRT)

9Q-CMD	Antonov An-32B	2210	ex 9Q-CMD	Kevin; stored SHJ
9Q-CMK	Antonov An-24RV			Kenzo
9Q-CMM	Britten-Norman BN-2A-21 Islander	812	ex 9U-BRV	
9Q-CPG	WSK-PZL/Antonov An-28	1AJ004-12		Audrey

MALU AVIATION

Kinshasa-Ndolo (NDO)

9Q-CDV	Partenavia P.68B	207		
9Q-CSP	WSK-PZL/Antonov An-28	1AJ008-09	ex RA-28923	
3D-MKX	Hawker Siddeley Andover C.1	Set 19	ex 3C-CPX	

SABINAIR

9Q-CUG	LET L-410UVP

TMK AIR COMMUTER

Goma (GOM)

9Q-CBO	de Havillamd DHC-6 Twin Otter	738	ex N123SL	

TRANS INTERNATIONAL AIR believed to have ceased operations, sole aircraft written off April 2003

VIRUNGA AIR CHARTER

Goma (GOM)

9Q-CAM	Douglas DC-3	34409	ex 45-1139	Simba Mzee
9Q-CDD	Dornier 28D-1 Skyservant	4025	ex D-IFAQ	
9Q-CTL	Partenavia P.68B	145	ex 5Y-BCG	
9Q-CTN	Partenavia P.68C-TC	238-04-TC	ex OO-TZT	
9Q-CTX	Dornier 128-6 Turbo Skyservant	6007	ex D-IDOQ	

WALTAIR

Kinshasa-Ndjili (FIH)

9Q-CAN	Aerospatiale SE.210 Caravelle 11R	240	ex 3D-CNA
9Q-CPI	Aerospatiale SE.210 Caravelle 10B3	169	ex 9Q-CPY
9Q-CPW	Hawker Siddeley Andover C.Mk.1	Set14	ex XS607
9Q-CVH	Douglas DC-8F-55 (QNC 2)	255/45821	ex3D-CWH

WETRAFA AIRLIFT

Kinshasa-Ndjili (FIH)

9Q-CWT	Boeing 727-25	204/18291	ex N904TS	stored FIH

WIMBI DIRA AIRWAYS

(9C/WDA)

Kinshasa-Ndjili (FIH)

9Q-CLK	Boeing 707-323C	686/29587	ex 3D-ROK
9Q-CWC	Antonov An-12		
9Q-CWD	Boeing 727-231F	576/19562	ex N12305
9Q	Boeing 727-232 (FedEx 3)	/22494	ex N545DA
9Q-	Boeing 727-232 (FedEx 3)	/22677	ex N546DA

9U - BURUNDI (Republic of Burundi)

AIR BURUNDI

Air Burundi (8Y/PBU) (IATA)

Bujumbura (BJM)

9U-BHB	de Havilland DHC-6 Twin Otter 300	560		
9U-BHG	Beech 1900C-1	UC-147	ex 9U-BHD	
9U-BHO	Antonov An-12	8345503		stored JNB
9U-BHQ	Antonov An-26	17311102		

VOLGA ATLANTIC Current status uncertain, believed to have ceased operations

9V - SINGAPORE (Republic of Singapore)

AIRMARK SINGAPORE

Singapore-Changi (SIN)

UR-48083	Antonov An-32B	3001	ex CCCP-48083	Lsd fr UKL

REGIONAIR

Orchid (7S/RGA)

Singapore-Changi (SIN)

S7-ABA	Boeing 737-377	1641/24305	ex VH-CZP		Lsd fr Ansett Australia
S7-ABB	Boeing 737-377	1618/24302	ex VH-CZM	stored QPG	Lsd fr Ansett Australia
S7-ABC	Boeing 737-377	1622/24304	ex VH-CZO	stored QPG	Lsd to BBC
S7-ABD	Boeing 737-377	1620/24303	ex VH-CZN		Lsd to BBC
S7-ASK	McDonnell-Douglas MD-82	2145/53481	ex PK-LME		Lsd fr STAR; sublsd to 8M
S7-RGJ	Airbus Industrie A321-131	0604	ex N225LF		Lsd fr ILFC; sublsd to PIC
S7-RGK	Airbus Industrie A321-131	0614	ex N511LF		Lsd fr ILFC; sublsd to PIC
S7-RGL	Airbus Industrie A320-232	0542	ex PK-AWE		Lsd fr ILFC; sublsd to PIC

Also operates 767s registered S7- for Air Vietnam (q.v.)
Owns 49% of Myanmar Airways

SILKAIR

Silkair (MI/SLK)

Singapore-Changi (SIN)

9V-SBA	Airbus Industrie A319-132	1074	ex D-AVWH
9V-SBB	Airbus Industrie A319-132	1098	ex D-AVWQ
9V-SBC	Airbus Industrie A319-132	1228	ex D-AVYL

9V-SBD	Airbus Industrie A319-132	1698	ex D-AVYE	
9V-SBE	Airbus Industrie A319-132		ex D-AV	on order 04
9V-SLA	Airbus Industrie A320-232	0872	ex F-WWBC	Lsd fr Volito Avn
9V-SLB	Airbus Industrie A320-232	0899	ex F-WWDL	
9V-SLC	Airbus Industrie A320-232	0969	ex F-WWBO	
9V-SLD	Airbus Industrie A320-232	1422	ex F-WWBK	
9V-SLE	Airbus Industrie A320-232	1561	ex F-WWBC	
9V-SLF	Airbus Industrie A320-232	2058	ex F-WWBK	
9V-SLG	Airbus Industrie A320-232		ex F-WW	on order 04
9V-SLH	Airbus Industrie A320-232		ex F-WW	on order 04

Two more Airbus Industrie A320-232s and one more A319-132 is on order for delivery in 2005
Wholly owned subsidiary of Singapore Airlines

SINGAPORE AIRLINES

Singapore (SQ/SIA) (IATA 618)   Singapore-Changi (SIN)

9V-STA	Airbus Industrie A310-324	665	ex F-WWCL	Lsd to AIC
9V-STB	Airbus Industrie A310-324	669	ex F-WWCC	stored SIN
9V-STC	Airbus Industrie A310-324	680	ex F-WWCT	stored SIN
9V-STD	Airbus Industrie A310-324	684	ex F-WWCJ	stored SIN
9V-STE	Airbus Industrie A310-324	693	ex F-WWCI	stored SIN
9V-STF	Airbus Industrie A310-324	697	ex F-WWAN	stored SIN
9V-STQ	Airbus Industrie A310-324	493	ex F-WWCN	stored SIN
9V-STU	Airbus Industrie A310-324	548	ex F-WWCV	stored SIN
9V-STW	Airbus Industrie A310-324	589	ex F-WWCO	Lsd to AIC
9V-STY	Airbus Industrie A310-324	634	ex F-WWCF	Lsd to AIC
9V-STZ	Airbus Industrie A310-324	654	ex F-WWCJ	stored SIN

All withdrawn by the end of June 2003

9V-SGA	Airbus Industrie A340-541	492	ex F-WWTP	
9V-SGB	Airbus Industrie A340-541	499	ex F-WWTR	
9V-SGC	Airbus Industrie A340-541	478	ex F-WWTG	
9V-SGD	Airbus Industrie A340-541	560	ex F-WWTM	on order
9V-SGE	Airbus Industrie A340-541	563	ex F-WWTU	on order

N127LC	Boeing 747-412	859/25127	ex 9V-SMK	Lsd fr WFBN
9V-SMA	Boeing 747-412	717/24061	ex N5573B	stored SIN
9V-SMB	Boeing 747-412	722/24062	ex VH-ANA	Lsd to FJI
9V-SMC	Boeing 747-412	736/24063	ex 3B-SMC	
9V-SMD	Boeing 747-412	755/24064	ex VH-ANB	Lsd to FJI
9V-SME	Boeing 747-412	761/24065		stored SIN
9V-SMH	Boeing 747-412	831/24227	ex N6009F	stored VCV
9V-SMI	Boeing 747-412	838/24975		
9V-SMJ	Boeing 747-412	852/25068	ex N6005C	
9V-SMM	Boeing 747-412	921/26547	ex N6038E	
9V-SMN	Boeing 747-412	923/26548		stored SIN
9V-SMO	Boeing 747-412	940/27066		
9V-SMP	Boeing 747-412	953/27067		
9V-SMQ	Boeing 747-412	955/27132		
9V-SMR	Boeing 747-412	962/27133		
9V-SMS	Boeing 747-412	981/27134		
9V-SMT	Boeing 747-412	990/27137	ex N60697	
9V-SMU	Boeing 747-412	1000/27068		
9V-SMV	Boeing 747-412	1010/27069		
9V-SMW	Boeing 747-412	1015/27178	ex N6018N	
9V-SMY	Boeing 747-412	1023/27217		
9V-SMZ	Boeing 747-412	1030/26549	ex N6018N	
9V-SPA	Boeing 747-412	1040/26550		
9V-SPB	Boeing 747-412	1045/26551		
9V-SPC	Boeing 747-412	1049/27070		
9V-SPD	Boeing 747-412	1056/26552	ex N6009F	
9V-SPE	Boeing 747-412	1070/26554		
9V-SPF	Boeing 747-412	1072/27071		
9V-SPG	Boeing 747-412	1074/26562		
9V-SPH	Boeing 747-412	1075/26555		
9V-SPI	Boeing 747-412	1082/28022		
9V-SPJ	Boeing 747-412	1084/26556		
9V-SPL	Boeing 747-412	1101/26557		
9V-SPM	Boeing 747-412	1241/29950		
9V-SPN	Boeing 747-412	1266/28031		
9V-SPO	Boeing 747-412	1270/28028		
9V-SPP	Boeing 747-412	1276/28029		
9V-SPQ	Boeing 747-412	1289/28025		

9V-SQA	Boeing 777-212ER	67/28507		
9V-SQB	Boeing 777-212ER	83/28508		Jubilee
9V-SQC	Boeing 777-212ER	86/28509		
9V-SQD	Boeing 777-212ER	90/28510		
9V-SQE	Boeing 777-212ER	122/28511		
9V-SQF	Boeing 777-212ER	126/28512		
9V-SQG	Boeing 777-212ER	226/28518		

9V-SQH	Boeing 777-212ER	237/28519		
9V-SQI	Boeing 777-212ER	390/28530	ex N5023Q	
9V-SQJ	Boeing 777-212ER	406/30875		
9V-SQK	Boeing 777-212ER	428/33368		
9V-SQL	Boeing 777-212ER	451/33370		
9V-SQM	Boeing 777-212ER	33372		on order
9V-SQN	Boeing 777-212ER	33373		on order
9V-SRA	Boeing 777-212ER	144/28513		
9V-SRB	Boeing 777-212ER	149/28998		
9V-SRC	Boeing 777-212ER	150/28999		
9V-SRD	Boeing 777-212ER	153/28514		
9V-SRE	Boeing 777-212ER	239/28523		
9V-SRF	Boeing 777-212ER	330/28521		
9V-SRG	Boeing 777-212ER	337/28522		
9V-SRH	Boeing 777-212ER	343/30866		
9V-SRI	Boeing 777-212ER	348/30867		
9V-SRJ	Boeing 777-212ER	372/28527		
9V-SRK	Boeing 777-212ER	389/28529	ex N5022E	
9V-SRL	Boeing 777-212ER	409/32334		
9V-SRM	Boeing 777-212ER	438/32320		
9V-SRN	Boeing 777-212ER	441/32318		
9V-SRO	Boeing 777-212ER	447/32321		stored PAE
9V-SRP	Boeing 777-212ER	448/33369		stored PAE
9V-SRQ	Boeing 777-212ER	449/33371		stored PAE
9V-SVA	Boeing 777-212ER	350/28524		
9V-SVB	Boeing 777-212ER	353/28525		
9V-SVC	Boeing 777-212ER	355/28526		
9V-SVD	Boeing 777-212ER	366/30869		
9V-SVE	Boeing 777-212ER	374/30870		
9V-SVF	Boeing 777-212ER	378/30871		
9V-SVG	Boeing 777-212ER	398/30872		
9V-SVH	Boeing 777-212ER	407/28532	ex N5022E	
9V-SVI	Boeing 777-212ER	412/32316		
9V-SVJ	Boeing 777-212ER	415/32335		
9V-SVK	Boeing 777-212ER	419/28520		
9V-SVL	Boeing 777-212ER	422/32336		
9V-SVM	Boeing 777-212ER	430/30874		
9V-SVN	Boeing 777-212ER	431/30873		
9V-SVO	Boeing 777-212ER	28533		on order
9V-	Boeing 777-212ER			on order

Four more are on order for delivery through 2007

9V-SYA	Boeing 777-312			
9V-SYB	Boeing 777-312	184/28516		
9V-SYC	Boeing 777-312	188/28517		
9V-SYD	Boeing 777-312	192/28534		
9V-SYE	Boeing 777-312	244/28531		
9V-SYF	Boeing 777-312	360/30868		
9V-SYG	Boeing 777-312	364/28528		
9V-SYH	Boeing 777-312	420/32317	ex N5020K	
9V-SYI	Boeing 777-312	32327		on order
9V-	Boeing 777-312			on order

Three more are on order for delivery through 2007
Those in the -SQx series have three class cabins while those in -SRx and SYx series are two class configuration

VH-SQD	Lear Jet 45	45-033	ex N50162	Trainer
VH-SQM	Lear Jet 45	45-035	ex N5013U	Trainer
VH-SQR	Lear Jet 45	45-195		Trainer
VH-SQV	Lear Jet 45	45-207		Trainer

Owns SilkAir and Singapore Airlines Cargo, 49% of Virgin Atlantic and Tiger Airways, 5.9% of Air New Zealand and 10% of China Airlines. Ten Airbus Industrie A380-841s are on order for delivery in 2006 (5) and 2007 (5)

SINGAPORE AIRLINES CARGO

Singapore Cargo (SQ/SQC) (IATA -)   Singapore-Changi (SIN)

9V-SFA	Boeing 747-412F	1036/26563	ex N60659	
9V-SFB	Boeing 747-412F	1042/26561		
9V-SFC	Boeing 747-412F	1052/26560		Lsd to CCA as B-2409
9V-SFD	Boeing 747-412F	1069/26553		
9V-SFE	Boeing 747-412F	1094/28263		
9V-SFF	Boeing 747-412F	1105/28026		
9V-SFG	Boeing 747-412F	1173/26558		
9V-SFH	Boeing 747-412F	1224/28032		
9V-SFI	Boeing 747-412F	1256/28027		
9V-SFJ	Boeing 747-412F	1285/26559		
9V-SFK	Boeing 747-412F	1298/28030		
9V-SFL	Boeing 747-412F	1322/32897	ex N5022E	
9V-SFM	Boeing 747-412F	1333/32898		
9V-SFN	Boeing 747-412F	1342/32899		
9V-SFO	Boeing 747-412F			on order 04

Two more Boeing 747-412F's are on order for delivery in 2005
Wholly owned subsidiary of Singapore Airlines

TIGER AIRWAYS

Singapore-Changi (SIN)

Low cost carrier due to commence services in 3Q04; 49% owned by Singapore Airlines

VALUAIR

(VLU)   *Singapore-Changi (SIN)*

9V-VLA	Airbus Industrie A320-232	2156	ex F-WWDC		Lsd fr SALE
9V-VLB	Airbus Industrie A320-232	2164	ex F-WWIF	on order 04	Lsd fr SALE

9XR - RWANDA (Rwanda Republic)

ALLIANCE EXPRESS RWANDA
ceased operations

RWANDA AIRLINES
ceased operations

RWANDAIR EXPRESS

Rwandair (RWD) (IATA 459)   *Kigali (KGL)*

OY-APH	Boeing 737-5L9	2856/28721	Lsd fr DAN

SILVERBACK CARGO FREIGHTERS

Silverback (VRB)   *Kigali (KGL)*

9XR-SC	Douglas DC-8-62F	463/46068	ex N990CF	
9XR-SD	Douglas DC-8-62F	376/45956	ex N994CF	Lsd fr Debden Investment

9Y - TRINIDAD & TOBAGO (Republic of Trinidad & Tobago)

BRISTOW CARIBBEAN

Galeota Point

9Y-BCL	Bell 412SP	33210	ex N412SA	Lsd fr OLOG
9Y-EVS	Bell 412SP	33212	ex XA-SBJ	Lsd fr OLOG
9Y-OLG	Bell 412	33011	ex XA-TXA	Lsd fr OLOG
9Y-TEY	Bell 212	30640	ex VR-BFE	
9Y-TIF	Bell 212	30615	ex G-BTYA	
9Y-TIG	Bell 212	30544	ex G-BHDL	
9Y-TJM	Bell 412SP	33159	ex PT-HUO	Lsd fr Aeroleo
9Y-TJW	Sikorsky S-76B	760296	ex C-GZIL	

Associated with Bristow Helicopters, subsidiary of Air Logistics

BWEE EXPRESS ceased operations

BWIA WEST INDIES AIRWAYS

West Indian (BW/BWA) (IATA 106)   *Port of Spain (POS)*

9Y-ANU	Boeing 737-8Q8	697/28235	(ex 9Y-SLU)		Lsd fr ILFC
9Y-BGI	Boeing 737-8Q8	547/28232			Lsd fr ILFC
9Y-GEO	Boeing 737-8Q8	433/28225	ex N1787B		Lsd fr ILFC
9Y-GND	Boeing 737-86N	1251/33419			Lsd fr GECAS
9Y-KIN	Boeing 737-8Q8	680/28234	(ex 9Y-ANU)		Lsd fr ILFC
9Y-POS	Boeing 737-8Q8	506/28230			Lsd fr ILFC
9Y-TAB	Boeing 737-8Q8	598/28233			Lsd fr ILFC
9Y-JIL	Airbus Industrie A340-313	016	ex G-VSKY		Lsd fr ILFC
9Y-TJN	Airbus Industrie A340-313	093	ex C-FTNP		Lsd fr ILFC
9Y-WIL	de Havilland DHC-8Q-311	489	ex C-GFCW	stored POS	Lsd fr WI Aircraft
9Y-WIN	de Havilland DHC-8Q-311	499	ex C-GDSG	stored POS	Lsd fr WI Aircraft
9Y-WIP	de Havilland DHC-8Q-311	538	ex C-FDHI		Lsd fr WI Aircraft; sublsd to TBX

Owns 29% of LIAT

TOBAGO EXPRESS

Tabex (TBX)

9Y-WIP	de Havilland DHC-8Q-311	538	ex C-FDHI	Lsd fr TBX
9Y-WIT	de Havilland DHC-8Q-314B	487	ex OE-LSA	
9Y-WIZ	de Havilland DHC-8Q-311	557	ex C-GEMU	

JET AND TURBOPROP AIRLINERS IN NON-AIRLINE SERVICE

* Indicates a/c believed to be flown by stated operator. Aircraft are listed in alphabetical order of manufacturer

Aerospatiale/Alenia ATR-42

F-GFJH*	(300)	049		Direction Generale de l'Aviation Civile (calibrator)
F-WEGB	(200)	002		ATR second prototype, stored TLS
F-WWEZ*	(500)	443		ATR - Srs 500 prototype (ff 16Sep94)
mm62165*	(420MP)	500	ex F-WWEW	Guardia di Finanza/Italian Customs
mm62166*	(420MP)	502	ex CM-X-62166	Guardia di Finanza/Italian Customs
mm62170*	(420MP)	466	ex CS-X-62170	Guardia Costiera/Italian Coast Guard
mm62208	(420MP)	615	ex F-WQMJ	Guardia Costiera/Italian Coast Guard
mm	(420MP)	620	ex F-W	Guardia di Finanza/Italian Customs
N212AZ*	(300)	016	ex F-WHHS	Kramer Investment Co /Summit Aviation
N315CR*	(320)	252	ex F-WWEE	Jefferson Financial Co
N470JF*	(320)	247	ex N106LM	Jefferson Financial Co
TR-KJD*	(F-300)	131	ex F-WWEB	Government of Gabon

Aerospatiale/Alenia ATR-72

F-WWEY	(212A)	098		ATR (Prototype, ff 27Oct88) stored TLS

Airbus Industrie A300

TS-IAY*	(C4-620)	354	ex A6-SHZ	Government of Libya [Op by NVJ]
9K-AHI*	(C4-620)	344	ex PK-MAY	State of Kuwait [op by KU/KAC]

Airbus Industrie A310

418*	(304)	418	ex F-WQIC	Armée de l'Air (call sign F-RADC)
421*	(304)	421	ex F-ODVD	Armée de l'Air (call sign F-RADA)
422*	(304)	422	ex F-ODVE	Armée de l'Air (call sign F-RADB)
1021*	(304)	498	ex D-AOAA	Bundersrepublik Deutschland/Luftwaffe [GAF]
1022*	(304)	499	ex D-AOAB	Bundersrepublik Deutschland/Luftwaffe 'Theodor Heuss' [GAF]
1023*	(304)	503	ex D-AOAC	Bundersrepublik Deutschland/Luftwaffe 'Kurt Schumacher' [GAF]
1024*	(304MRTT)	434	ex D-AIDA	Bundersrepublik Deutschland/Luftwaffe [GAF]
1025*	(304MRTT)	484	ex D-AIDB	Bundersrepublik Deutschland/Luftwaffe 'Helmut Köhl' [GAF]
1026*	(304MRTT)	522	ex D-AIDE	Bundersrepublik Deutschland/Luftwaffe 'Hans Grade' [GAF]
1027*	(304MRTT)	523	ex D-AIDI	Bundersrepublik Deutschland/Luftwaffe 'August Euler' [GAF]
15001*	(304F)	446	ex F-WQCQ	Canadian Armed Forces/437Sqdn [CFC]
15002*	(304F)	482	ex C-GLWD	Canadian Armed Forces/437Sqdn [CFC]
15003*	(304F)	425	ex C-FWDX	Canadian Armed Forces/437Sqdn [CFC]
15004*	(304F)	444	ex C-FNWD	Canadian Armed Forces/437Sqdn [CFC]
15005*	(304MRTT)	441	ex F-ZJCP	Canadian Armed Forces/437Sqdn [CFC]
44-444*	(324)	591	ex (HS-TYQ)	Royal Thai Air Force/Royal Flight
CA-01*	(222)	372	ex 9V-STN	Belgian Defence [BAF]
CA-02*	(222)	367	ex 9V-STM	Belgian Defence [BAF]
P4-ABU*	(304)	431	ex P4-DPD	Praeda A.V.V
T.22-1	(304)	550	ex F-WEMP	Fuerza Aereas Espanolas/Spanish Air Force
T.22-2	(304)	551	ex F-WEMQ	Fuerza Aereas Espanolas/Spanish Air Force (coded 45-51)
9K-ALD*	(308)	648	ex F-WWCR	Kuwait Government [op by KU/KAC]

Airbus Industrie A318

F-WWIA	(111)	1599	Airbus Industrie (prototype, ff 15Jan02 with PW engines, re-engined with CFM-56s and ff 29Aug02)
F-WWIB	(111)	1660	Airbus Industrie (2nd prototype, ff 03Jun02) For Frontier 04

Airbus Industrie A319

0001*	(133X)	1468	ex D-AVYQ	Government of Venezuela/Fuerza Aérea Venezolana [CJ]
1485*	(115X)	1485	ex F-GXFA	Armée de l'Air (callsign F-RBFA) [CJ]
1556*	(115X)	1556	ex F-GXFB	Armée de l'Air (callsign F-RBFB) [CJ]
A6-ESH*	(113X)	0910	ex D-AWFR	Sharjah Ruler's Flight [SHJ] [CJ]
A7-ABZ*	(133X)	1335	ex D-AVYX	Government of Qatar [op by QTR] [CJ]
A7-	(133X)	1656	ex F-GMRO	Government of Qatar [op by QTR]; on order [CJ]
D-ADNA*	(133X)	1053	ex D-AVYN	DaimlerChrysler Aerospace [DCS] [CJ]
F-GSVU*	(133X)	1256	ex (VP-BCS)	Aero Services Executive/Vivendi International [W4/BES] [CJ]
F-GYAS	(133X)	1999	ex D-AVYQ	Aero Services Executive/CIT Leasing [Op for Ukraine Govt] [CJ]

G-OMAK*	(132)	0913	ex F-WWIF	Al Kharafi Avn/Twinjet Leasing [TWJ]
HS-TYR	(133X)	1908	ex D-AIJO	Royal Thai Air Force [CJ]
mm62173*	(115X)	1002	ex D-AJWF	Aeronautica Militare Italiana (Republica Italiana) [CJ]
mm62174*	(115X)	1157	ex D-AACI	Aeronautica Militare Italiana (Republica Italiana) [CJ]
mm62209	(115X)	1795	ex D-AWOR	Aeronautica Militare Italiana (Republica Italiana) [CJ]
N320NP	(112)	1494	ex F-WQRZ	Blue Moon Aviation (56 seat VIP) [Op by Frontier]
VP-CIE	(133X)	1589	ex D-AVYF	Bugshan Group [CJ]
VP-CVX*	(133X)	1212	ex (D-AIKA)	Volkswagen Group/VW Air Services [WGT] [CJ]
	(133X)	1880	ex D-AVYM	Customer unknown [CJ]
	(133X)	1727	ex D-AVWQ	Customer unknown [CJ]
	(115X)	2192	ex D-AV	Customer unknown [CJ]

One of the unidentified customers may be Brazil for use as a presidential aircraft

Airbus Industrie A320

A7-AAG*	(232)	0927	ex F-WWBA	Government of Qatar [Op by QTR]
F-WWBA*	(131)	0001	ex F-WWFT	Airbus Industrie (prototype, ff 22Feb87)
9K-AKD	(212)	2046	ex F-WWBG	Kuwait Government 'Al-Mobarakiya' [op by KAC]

Airbus Industrie A330

A7-HJJ*	(203)	487	ex F-WWYM	Government of Qatar [Op by QTR]

Airbus Industrie A340

A7-HHK*	(211)	026	ex F-WWJQ	Government of Qatar [Op by QTR]
A7-	(541)	495	ex F-WWTQ	Government of Qatar (on order)
F-WWAI*	(311)	001		Airbus Industrie (Development aircraft, ff 25Oct91)
F-WWCA*	(642)	360	ex F-WWTA	Airbus Industrie Srs 600 prototype
F-WWTE	(541)	394		Airbus Industrie Srs 500 prototype (ff 11Feb02)
(HZ-124)*	(211)	004	ex D-ACME	Royal Embassy of Saudi Arabia [conv to flying hospital]
HZ-WBT4*	(213)	151	ex V8-JBB	Kingdom Holdings "Khaled & Reem"
JY-ABH*	(211)	009	ex V8-AM1	Jordanian Royal Flight [op by RJ/RJA]
SU-GGG*	(212)	061	ex F-WWJI	Government of Arab Republic of Egypt
V8-AC3*	(213X)	204	ex D-ASFB	Sultan's Flight [V8-HB3 also reported]
V8-BKH*	(212)	046	ex V8-PJB	Sultan's Flight

Antonov An-12

ER-AXB	(BP)		ex	
RA-13341	(BP)	9346904		United Nations
S9-CDB	(BP)	401901	ex D2-FCV	
UR-11352*	(BP)	401810?	ex CCCP-11352	Government of Ukraine
3C-AAG	(BP)	7344801	ex RA-98119 (2)	
3C-AAL	(BP)	00347003		
4K-12425		2401103	ex CCCP-12425	Azerbaijan Ministry of Defence
4L-TAS				
9U-BHN		3341506	ex RA-11318	

Antonov An-24

D2-FBQ				
D2-FEH				
JU-7050				Government of Mongolia
JU-7070				Government of Mongolia
ST-GRD	(RV)	77310709	ex RA-47364	(identity not confirmed)
S9-CAU				
UR-46464	(RV)	27307810	ex ER-46464	
XU-052				
XU-054				
9Q-CMK				

Antonov An-26

D2-EPN*		7804		Government of Angola
D2-FBN				
D2-MOP*		13607		Government of Republic of Angola
D2-MPG*		13704		Government of Republic of Angola
ER-AFQ		27312503		
EX-26780		97307809	ex ER-AFR	
RA-26661*		8009	ex CCCP-26661	Firefighter
RDPL 34039*		2302		Government of Laos
RDPL 34114*				Government of Laos
ST-GRG				
TN-AFL				
UN-26167		17311505		Kazakstan Government

YV-1101CP		17309810	UN-26005	
5R-MVP	(B)	07310208	ex RA-26021	Armee de l'Air Malgache
9Q-CTJ				
9U-BHM				

Antonov An-28/WSK-PZL M.28

SP-DFC*	(M)	AJE001-10		PZL-Mielec, based Venezuela
RA-28717		1AJ007-02		Oil Trans Avia
UR-28737		1AJ007-25		Air Space Agency
UR-28764		IAJ004-13	ex CCCP-28764	

Antonov An-30

RA-27205	0709	ex CCCP-27205	Russian Air Force 'Open Skies'

Antonov An-32

D2-FDG				
D2-FDP				
D2-FDQ				
D2-FOG				Giro Global Aeronautics
D2-MAX		2102	ex RA-48098	
D2-MBF				
D2-MBG				
ER-AWT				
OB-1612/AT-530		3403		Peruvian Navy
OB-1613/AT-531		3408		Peruvian Navy
OB-1624/PNP-227		3307	ex YL-LDD	Peruvian Police
OB-1625/PNP-228		3308	ex YL-LDE	Peruvian Police
ST-GRJ		3110	ex ER-AEX	
S9-BOI		2109	ex 4K-66756	Chik Oil, Angola (also reported as S9-BOH)
YN-CGA		3007	ex HP-1217AVL	
3C-5GE*		1609		Government of Equatorial Guines
3D-DRO		2207	ex RA-48118	AMA Property Ltd
9A-BAB/707*	(B)	3310		Government of Croatia/Croatian Air Force
9A-BAC/727*	(B)	2810	ex 021	Government of Croatia/Croatian Air Force
9Q-CLD				
9XR-NS		2105	ex HK-4113X	

Antonov An-38

3810001*	3801001		Antonov
41910	28.02.002		NAPO Aviatrans

Antonov An-72

D2-FEP			
ER-72932*	36572070696		Moldovan Ministry of Defence
ER-72933*			Moldovan Ministry of Defence
ER-72935*			Moldovan Ministry of Defence
UR-72003*	00-03	ex CCCP-72003	Southern Engine Factory
UR-72984			Ukraine Ministry of Defence
4L-AAL			GPS Angola

Antonov An-74

RA-74051*		0102P		Russian Min for Civil Air & Protection
RA-74300	(TK-300)		ex UR-74300	Kharkov APO/Antonov
				(Progress D-436T1 engines)
RDPL 34018*	(TK-100)			Government of Laos
UR-74033				ARTOS
UR-74038	(TK-200)			Antonov

Avro RJ

A9C-BDF	(RJ85)	E2390	ex G-6-390	Bahrain Royal Flight [BAH]

Beech 99

D-IEXE		U-46	ex LN-SAX	Air Service Wildgruber
JA8801*	(B99)	U-163	ex N9387S	Senpaku Gijyutsu Kenkyu-jo
N9FH		U-94	ex	Ozark Aircraft Sales
N33TN		U-28	ex N99TA	Grand Slam LLC
N84SD*		U-10	ex N99NN	Skydive Factory
N204FW	(99A)	U-134	ex N140Z	US Dept of Justice
N199SD*		U-26	ex C-FRQC	Aerolease of America [status?]
N205TC		U-4	ex N133PM	Flanagan Enterprises (Nevada)
N213AV	(C99)	U-213	ex N6656N	Anthem Aircraft Leasing
N7899R		U-88		Aircraft Guaranty Trust
N42417	(C99)	U-165		Pineapple Air U165 Inc
PT-FSC*		U-65	ex PP-FSC	Ministry of the Interior

Beech 1900

1901*	(C-1)	UC-23	ex N3188K	Republic of China Air Force
1902*	(C-1)	UC-25	ex N3189F	Republic of China Air Force
1903*	(C-1)	UC-27	ex N31904	Republic of China Air Force
1904*	(C-1)	UC-29	ex N3192E	Republic of China Air Force
1906*	(C-1)	UC-6	ex N72423	Republic of China Air Force
1907*	(C-1)	UC-7	ex N72424	Republic of China Air Force
1908*	(C-1)	UC-8	ex N3179U	Republic of China Air Force
1909*	(C-1)	UC-34	ex N3206K	Republic of China Air Force
1910*	(C-1)	UC-35	ex N3214Z	Republic of China Air Force
1911*	(C-1)	UC-30	ex N3199H	Republic of China Air Force
1912*	(C-1)	UC-32	ex N3206C	Republic of China Air Force
96-0112	(D)	UE-256	ex N10931	US Army
FAB-043		UA-3	ex N1900J	Ministerio de Defensa Nacional
AP-BGH	(C-1)	UC-165	ex N55456	Leni Overseas Development/Aircraft Sales & Services
C-GSLB	(D)	UE-264	ex N10759	Pentastar Transportation
D-CSAG	(D)	UE-353		Vidair Technology Inside
F-HCHA	(D)		N37YV	Regourd Aviation
HZ-PC2*	(C-1)	UC-4	ex N3078C	Saudi Arabian CAA
N19NG*	(C-1)	UC-2	ex N19NA	Northrop Grumman Aviation
N20RA*	(C)	UB-42	ex (N272HK)	Dept of the Air Force/EG & G Group
N23BD*	(C)	UB-64	ex N93BD	Bill Davis Racing
N27RA*	(C)	UB-37	ex N7214K	Dept of the Air Force/EG & G Group
N45AR	(D)	UE-12	ex N138MA	Autec Aviation Services [op for USN]
N46AR	(D)	UE-27		Autec Aviation Services [op for USN]
N60GH	(C)	UB-68	ex N521M	Haas CNC Racing
N61HA*	(D)	UE-175	ex N995WS	Wachovia Bank NA
N125BA	(C)	UB-6	ex N125GP	San Juan Jet Charter/Raytheon
N166K	(D)	UE-63	ex N82890	Raytheon Aircraft Company (corporate shuttle)
N181GA	(C)	UB-24		APA Enterprises
N196NW*	(D)	UE-362	ex N23627	WFBN/Intel Corp
N305PC*	(D)	UE-299		BCC Equipment Lsg/Peabody Western Coal
N368DC*	(D)	UE-368	ex N30535	Dow Chemical Co
N378SA	(C)	UB-31	ex N196GA	Joda Inc/Hartford Holding Corp
N413CM	(C-1)	UC-13	ex N33014	Chip Ganassi Racing/Profile Avn Services
N470MM*	(D)	UE-394	ex N41255	Schwans Shared Services
N502CG*	(C)	UB-39	ex N2TS	SABCO Racing
N503RH*	(C-1)	UC-78	ex N1568D	Hendrick Motorsports Inc
N504RH*	(C)	UB-72	ex OY-JRS	Hendrick Motorsports Inc
N505RH*	(C)	UB-56	ex OY-JRP	Hendrick Motorsports Inc
N506RH	(C-1)	UC-139	ex N500PR	Hendrick Motorsports Inc
N534M*	(D)	UE-333	ex N23235	Menard Inc
N535M*	(D)	UE-332		Menard Inc
N536M*	(D)	UE-334		Menard Inc
N640MW*	(C-1)	UC-1	ex N3114B	Marvin Lumber Co
N800CA	(D)	UE-383	ex N31686	Ruand Inc
N896FM*	(C)	UB-48	ex N810BE	Intel Corp
N869SC*	(C)	UB-40	ex N809BE	Intel Corp
N1883M	(D)	UE-354	ex N30414	Meijer Distribution Inc
N1900K*	(D)	UE-412	ex N44828	Raytheon Aircraft Company
N3188L	(D)	UE-428		Raytheon
N4469Q	(D)	UE-433		Raytheon Aircraft Company
N11284	(D)	UE-280	ex VT-AGD	US Army
N22889	(D)	UE-314		Air King Aviation
SU-BLA	(C-1)	UC-33	ex N7242U	Arab Republic of Egypt Air Force (also 4802)
VH-AFR	(D)	UC-112	ex N112YV	Pacific Aviation (Australasia)
VH-RUE	(D)	UE-53	ex ZK-JNG	Hawker Pacific
VT-KDA	(D)	UE-284	ex VT-AMA	Reliance Industries
YV-687C	(C)	UB-57	ex N816BE	
YV-837C	(D)	UE-157	ex N157AX	
YV-955C	(D)	UE-294	ex N21334	
YV-1070C	(C-1)	UC-119	ex N119YV	
5N-MPA*	(D)	UE-149	ex N3217L	Mobil Producing Nigeria
5N-MPN*	(D)	UE-77	ex N82936	Mobil Producing Nigeria
9G-AGF*	(D)	UE-136	ex N3212K	Ashanti Goldfields

Beriev BE-12P

RA-00041		Avialesoochrana
RA-00046		Avialesoochrana
RA-00049		Avialesoochrana

Boeing 707

242*	(344C)	800/20110	ex 4X-BYQ	Israeli Air Force (VIP/transport a/c) [also 4X-JYQ]
260*	(3J6B)	880/20716	ex 4X-BYN	Israeli Air Force (VIP/tanker a/c) [also 4X-JYN]
264*	(3J6C)	875/20721	ex 4X-BYH	Israeli Air Force (VIP/transport a/c) [also 4X-JYH]
272*	(3L6C)	900/21096	ex P4-MDJ	Israeli Air Force (VIP/transport a/c)
275*	(3P1C)	923/21334	ex A7-AAA	Israeli Air Force (VIP/tanker a/c)
290*	(3W6C)	941/21956	ex 4X-980	Israeli Air Force (VIP/tanker a/c)

319	(323C)	714/19575	ex OB-1371	Fuerza Aérea del Peru/Peruvian Air Force [FPR]
902*	(351C)	611/19443	ex CC-CCK	Fuerza Aérea de Chile
905*	385C)	447/19000	ex 4X-JYI	Fuerza Aérea de Chile
1001*	(368C)	928/21396	ex EP-NHY	Government of Islamic Republic of Iran [op by IRIAF]
1002*	(300C)			Government of Islamic Republic of Iran [op by IRIAF]
1415*	(328C)	596/19522	ex (ZS-LSK)	South African Air Force [also AF-615]
1417*	(328C)	665/19723	ex (ZS-LSJ)	South African Air Force [also AF-617]
1419*	(328C)	763/19917	ex (ZS-LSJ)	South African Air Force [also AF-619]
1421*	(344C)	831/20283	ex EL-TBA	South African Air Force [also AF-621]
1423*	(344C)	691/19706	ex 3D-ASC	South African Air Force [also AF-623]
(1902)*	(YE8B)	1001/24503	ex N707UM	Royal Saudi Air Force
2401*	(345C)	679/19840	ex PP-VJY	Forca Aerea Brasileira
2402*	(345C)	712/19842	ex PP-VJX	Forca Aerea Brasileira status?
6944*	(384C)	715/19760	ex SX-DBD	Fuerza Aerea Venezolena
68-19635*	(351C)	706/19635	ex AP-BAA	Pakistan Air Force 'Pakistan 1'
68-19866*	(340C)	738/19866	ex AP-AWY	Pakistan Air Force
A-7002*	(3M1C)	899/21092	ex PK-GAU	TNI-AU - Indonesian Air Force
A20-261*	(368C)	919/21261	ex N7486B	Royal Australian Air Force
A20-623*	(338C)	671/19623	ex C-GRYN	Royal Australian Air Force 'City of Sydney'
A20-624*	(338C)	689/19624	ex VH-EAD	Royal Australian Air Force 'Richmond Town'
A20-629*	(338C)	737/19629	ex C-GGAB	Royal Australian Air Force
ARC-101*	(373C)	835/20301	ex OB-1592	Armada Nacional - Republica de Colombiana
CNA-NS*	(138B)	229/18334	ex N58937	Government of Morocco
D2-MAN*	(321B)	780/20025	ex N707KS	Government of Angola
D2-MAY	(321B)	658/19374	ex CC-PBZ	Angola Air Force (undergoing upgrade with IAI, Tel Aviv)
D2-TPR*	(3J6B)	870/20715	ex B-2404	Government of Angola
FAP-01*	(321B)	472/18957	ex ZP-CCF	Fuerza Aerea Paraguaya
HZ-123	(138B)	29/17696	ex 17696	Government of Kingdom of Saudi Arabia [stored]
K-2899*	(337C)	736/19988	ex VT-DXT	Indian Air Force/Aviation Research Centre
LX-N20199*	(329C)	816/20199	ex OO-SJN	NATO/AEWF
mm62148*	(382B)	676/19740	ex CS-TBC	Aeronautica Militaire Italiana (Italian AF)
mm62149*	(382B)	840/20298	ex CS-TBG	Aeronautica Militaire Italiana (Italian AF)
mm62150*	(3F5C)	857/20514	ex CS-TBT	Aeronautica Militaire Italiana (Italian AF)
mm62151*	(3F5C)	859/20515	ex CS-TBU	Aeronautica Militaire Italiana (Italian AF)
N88ZL*	(330B)	457/18928	ex N5381X	DB Air Ltd (stored)
N404PA*	(321B)	408/18835		United States Material Command (test a/c)
N677R	(351C)	708/19774	ex PP-BRH	Omega Air
N707AR*	(321B)	790/20029	ex EL-AKS	Omega Air (tanker/transport conversion)
N707CA	(351B)	345/18586	ex P4-FDH	Omega Air (status?)
N707GE	(321)	122/17608	ex N37681	General Electric Co (stored Mojave)
N707MQ	(368C)	925/21368	ex HZ-HM3	Alameda Corp
N707RE*	(330C)	806/20124	ex N707HE	Omega Air (707RE test aircraft; ff as such 9 Aug2001)
N707JT*	(138B)	388/18740	ex N707XX	Jett Clipper Johnny LLC (J Travolta) [BAC Stage 3]
N931NA*	(KC-135A)	18615	ex 63-7998	NASA,Johnson Space Center
SU-AXJ*	(366C)	888/20919		Government of Arab Republic of Egypt
T.17-1	(331B)	773/20060	ex N275B	Ejercito del Aire Espanol
T.17-3	(368C)	922/21367	ex N7667B	Ejercito del Aire Espanol
TM.17-4	(351C)	505/19164	ex SX-DBO	Ejercito del Aire Espanol
VT-DVB*	(337B)	549/19248	ex K-2900	Indian Air Force/Aviation Research Centre
3C-JZW	(351C)	369/18747	ex N21AZ	
5A-DAK	(3L5C)	911/21228		Government of Libya [op by LN/LAA]
5V-TAG*	(312B)	765/19739	ex N600CS	Government of Togo
5V-TGE*	(3L6B)	896/21049	ex P4-TBN	Government of Togo [BAC Stage 3 conv]
9Q-CGC*	(327C)	646/19531	ex ET-AIV	Government of Democratic Republic of Congo (status?)
9Q-CLK*	(138B)	64/17702	ex N707SK	Government of Democratic Republic of Congo

Boeing 717

N717XA*	(200)	5001/55000	ex (N9530)	Boeing Corp [prototype, ff 02Sep98]

Boeing 720

C-FETB*	(023B)	177/18024	ex OD-AFQ	Pratt & Whitney Canada (engine testbed) [PWC]
N720H*	(051B)	237/18384	ex N720GT	Honeywell International Inc (engine testbed)
N720JR*	(047B)	307/18451	ex N2143J	JAR A/C Services
N720PW*	(023B)	173/18021	ex C-FWXI	Pratt & Whitney Engine Services (engine testbed)
P4-NJR*	(047B)	314/18453	ex HZ-KA4	JR Executive Aruba [stage 2]

Boeing 727

3501*	(14)	169/18912	ex TP-10501	Forcea Aerea Mexicana [also XA-FAD]
3505*	(264)	1757/22661	ex XA-MXA	Forcea Aerea Mexicana [FedEx 3]
3506*	(264)	1776/22662	ex XA-MXB	Forcea Aerea Mexicana [FedEx 3]
3507*	(264)	1720/22412	ex XA-MEK	Forcea Aerea Mexicana [FedEx 3]
10503*	(14)	133/18908	ex XA-SER	Forcea Aerea Mexicana [also XA-FAY]
10504*	(14)	150/18909	ex XA-SEU	Forcea Aerea Mexicana [also XA-FAZ]
A9C-BA*	(2M7)	1595/21824	ex N740RW	Bahrain Royal Flight [Super 27 conv] [BAH]

Registration	Line	MSN	Ex	Operator
EP-GDS*	(81)	405/19557	ex 1002	Government of Islamic Republic of Iran (stored Teheran)
EP-PLN*	(30)	35/18363	ex EP-SHP	Government of Islamic Republic of Iran (stored Teheran)
HR-	(227)	1216/21246	ex N14GA	Rohr Inc (stored MIA)
HZ-AB3*	(2U5)	1657/22362	ex V8-BG1	Al-Anwa Establishment [Super 27 conv] (stored QLA)
HZ-DG1*	(51)	347/19124	ex N604NA	Dallah-Albaraka [FedEx 3]
HZ-HR3*	(2Y4)	1815/22968	ex HZ-RH3	Rafic B Hariri/Saudi Oger Ltd [Super 27 conv]
HZ-OCV*	(21)	262/19006	ex HZ-TFA	Salem Bin Zaid Ahmed Al Hassan [FedEx 3]
JY-HS1*	(76)	766/20228	ex VR-CHS	HMS Aviation
JY-HS2*	(2L4)	1100/21010	ex VR-CCA	HMS Aviation (stored FTW)
J2-KBA*	(191)	418/19394	ex N727X	Presidence de la Republique de Djibouti
N30MP*	(21)	239/18998	ex N111JL	MP Global Charter [Super 27 conve]
N31TR*	(212)	1510/21948	ex VR-COJ	Triangle A/C Services [Super 27 conv]
N40*	(25C)	628/19854	ex N8171G	FAA [Dugan 3]
N67JR*	(30)	249/18936	ex N18HH	Cityair LLC [Super 27 conv]
N113*	(30)	234/18935	ex N18G	US Dept of Justice (FedEx 3) [JUD]
N143AZ	(294)	1559/22043	ex C5-GAL	Grecoarir [Raisbeck 3]
N143KT	(269)	1652/22359	ex N169KT	Wilmington Trust Co (stored, status?)
N252RL	(281)	1318/21456	ex HL7536	DV Air Freight Services (stored)
(N274CL)*	(232)	936/20641	ex N7270B	Clay Lacy Aviation [FedEx 3]
N289MT	(223)	1765/22467	ex N710AA	Raytheon Company [FedEx 3]
N311AG*	(17)	858/20512	ex N767RV	Gordon P & Anne Getty [Super 27 conv]
N359PA*	(230)	1015/20789	ex D-ABSI	GM Aviation Services (stored Perpignan)
N400RG*	(22)	481/19149	ex N7085U	WTCo/MBI Aviation 'Al Bashaer' [Super 27 conv]
N502MG*	(191)	309/19391	ex N502RA	Roush Racing/RD Aviation [FedEx 3]
N503MG*	(191)	317/19392	ex N503RA	Roush Racing/RD Aviation [FedEx 3]
N504MG*	(191)	431/19395	ex N810SC	Roush Racing/RD Aviation [FedEx 3]
N530KF*	(61)	290/19176	ex N2777	US Dept of Justice (FedEx 3) [JUD]
N570C	(243)	1635/22165	ex 5Y-AXD	The O Corporation
N624VA*	(17)	797/20327	ex N529AC	Enterprise Aviation [Super 27 conv]
N698SS	(223)	1275/21369	ex N864AA	Southwest Sports Aviation/Texas Rangers [Raisbeck 3]
N720DC*	(77)	296/19253	ex N448DR	Americana Aviation Inc
N721MF*	(2X8)	1784/22687	ex N4532N	Wistair Corp/727 Aeroplane Corp
N724CL*	(51)	264/19121	ex N299LA	Clay Lacy Aviation [Raisbeck3]
N724YS*	(281)	1378/21474	ex N240RC	Horta LLC [Op for San Jose Sabre Cats]
N727AN	(251)	1700/22543	ex N203US	Antonov Aircraft Sealer Corp
N727CF*	(22)	136/18323	ex VP-BMC	PDC 1999 LLC, stored OKC
N727EC*	(30)	52/18365	ex N700TE	Atlantic Aircraft Inc
N727GG*	(95)	327/19252	ex HZ-WBT2	Trans Gulf Corporation
N727HC*	(35)	501/19835	ex N900CH	Jerrold Perenchio/Clay Lacy Aviation [FedEx 3]
N727LA*	(21)	412/19260	ex N727SG	Funair Corp, stored TLV [FedEx 3]
N727M*	(221)	1797/22541	ex N369PA	Nomads [Super 27]
N727NK*	(212)	1502/21945	ex N317NE	Funair Corp/Miami Heat [Dugan 3]
N727NY	(232)	967/20646	ex N523PE	727 Exec-Jet LLC
N727PX*	(21)	422/19261	ex N260GS	Paxson Communications [Raisbeck 3]
N727RE*	(282)	1715/22430	ex N6167D	Imperial Palace Air/PetcoAir [Dugan 3/winglets]
N727VJ*	(44)	348/19318	ex N44MD	United Breweries Holdings (based India)
N727WF	(23)	596/20045	ex N2913	Penisula Aviation LLC/WFBN
N753AS	(22C)	434/19203	ex N753AL	Jet Midwest Inc
N766JS*	(27)	456/19535	ex N60FM	Aircraft Guaranty Title LLC Trustee (stored San Antonio, TX)
N777KY*	(2B6)	1107/21068	ex N119GA	Team Aviation/New Orleans Hornets
N908JE*	(31)	735/20115	ex N505LS	JEGE Inc [Super 27]
N2034*	(251)	1169/21155	ex N109KM	US Dept of Justice (FedEx 3) [JUD]
N7455U	(222)	1562/21909		Elegaire Ltd [FedEx 3]
N37270	(63UDF)	555/19846	ex OB-R-902	Boeing (USD test-bed; stored Marana)
NZ7271*	(22C)	640/19892	ex N7435U	Royal Air New Zealand Air Force
P4-JLD*	(193)	377/19620	ex VR-CWC	Tatarstan Flights AVV [Raisbeck 3]
P4-MMG*	(30)	117/18368	ex VP-CMM	Amel Aruba/MME Aviation [Raisbeck 3]
P4-ONE*	(22)	473/19148	ex N341TC	Joss AVV [FedEx 3] (stored?)
P4-SKI*	(212)	1340/21460	ex (P4-MER)	Precision International [Super 27]
P4-YJR*	(30)	98/18366	ex N727JR	JAR Executive Aruba [FedEx 3] (based Beirut)
TJ-AAM*	(2R1)	1414/21636		Government of Cameroon
VP-BAA*	(51)	334/19215	ex N727AK	Marbyia Investments
VP-BAB*	(76)	298/19254	ex N682G	Occidental Petroleum [Super 27 conv]
VP-BDJ*	(23)	605/20046	ex VR-BDJ	DJ Aerospace/Donald Trump
VP-BIF*	(1H2)	869/20533	ex VP-BKC	New Century Freight Partners [Super 27]
VP-BNA*	(21RE)	426/19262	ex VR-BNA	Arapho Ltd/Mid-East Jet [FedEx 3]
VP-CJN*	(76)	822/20371	ex 5X-AMM	Starling Aviation [FedEx 3]
VP-CKA*	(82)	856/20489	ex VR-CKA	SAMCO Aviation [FedEx 3]
VP-CMN*	(46)	495/19282	ex VP-CMN	IDG (Cayman) Ltd (stored San Antonio, TX)
VP-CZY *	(2P1)	1406/21595	ex N727MJ	Dunview Ltd [Super 27] [op by PJS]
XC-FPA	(264)	1728/22413	ex XA-MEL	Policia Federal Preventiva/Mexican Federal Police [FedEx 3]
XC-MPF	(264)	1780/22664	ex XA-MXD	Policia Federal Preventiva/Mexican Federal Police [FedEx 3]
XC-NPF	(264)	1778/22663	ex XA-MXC	Policia Federal Preventiva/Mexican Federal Police [FedEx 3]

XC-OPF	(264)	1754/22676	ex XA-MEZ	Policia Federal Preventiva/Mexican Federal Police [FedEx 3]
XT-BBE*	(14)	238/18990	ex N21UC	Government of Burkina Faso
3D-BOE	(30)	185/18933	ex N7271P	Government of DRC (Dugan 3/winglets, stored VCV)
5B-DBE*	(30)	145/18371	ex 9M-SAS	Aimes Company [FedEx 3]
5N-FGN*	(2N5)	1805/22825	ex 5N-AGY	Federal Government of Nigeria [Super 27]
6V-AEF*	(2M1)	1134/21091	ex N40104	Government of Senegal 'Pointe de Sangomar' [Super 27]
9Q-CDC*	(30)	222/18934	ex 9Q-RDZ	Government of Democratic Republic of Congo
9Q-CPJ*	(22F)	365/19088	ex N743EV	MIBA "Dibindi"

Boeing 737

0207*	(2N1)	442/21167	ex 0001	Republica Bolivariana de Venezuela
165829	(7AF)	496/29979	ex N1003N	United States Navy [C-40A] 'City of Dallas'
165830	(7AF)	568/29980	ex N1003M	United States Navy [C-40A] 'Spirit of New York City'
165831	(7AF)	651/30200		United States Navy [C-40A] 'City of Fort Worth'
165832	(7AF)	742/30781	ex N1787B	United States Navy [C-40A] 'City of St Augustine'
165833	(7AFC)	1069/32597		United States Navy [C-40A
165834	(7AFC)	1174/32598		United States Navy [C-40A]
	(7AFC)			United States Navy [C-40A]
	(7AFC)			United States Navy [C-40A]
01-0005	(7DM)	1089/33080	ex N374BJ	United States Air Force/89AW [C-40B] [BBJ]
01-0015	(7DM)	979/32916	ex N378BJ	United States Air Force/15ABW[C-40B] [winglets] [BBJ]
01-0040*	(7DM)	684/29971	ex N371BJ	United States Air Force [C-40B] [BBJ]
02-0201*	(7CP)	545/30755	ex N752BC	United States Air Force/201ALS [winglets] [BBJ]
02-0202*	(7CP)	481/30753	ex N754BC	United States Air Force/201ALS [winglets] [BBJ]
02-0203	(7FD)	1223/33500	ex N708BC	United States Air Force [BBJ]
2115*	(2N3)	441/21165		Forca Aerea Brasileira
2116*	(2N3)	445/21166		Forca Aerea Brasileira
3701*	(8AR)	428/30139	ex N1787B	Republic of China Air Force
22-222*	(2Z6)	980/23059	ex N45733	Royal Thai Air Force/Royal Flight (stored BKK)
55-555*	(4Z6)	2698/27906	ex (HS-RTA)	Royal Thai Air Force/Royal Flight
85101*	(3Z8)	1073/23152		Republic of Korea
921*	(58N)	2929/28866	ex N1786B	Fuerza Aérea de Chile
922*	(330F)	1272/23524	ex D-ABXC	Fuerza Aérea de Chile
A36-001	(7DT)	738/30829	ex N372BJ	Royal Australian Air Force [BBJ]
A36-002	(7DF)	613/30790	ex N10040	Royal Australian Air Force [BBJ]
A -	(7ES)	1245/33474	ex N378BC	Royal Australian Air Force (Wedgetail AEW) (on order 06)
A -	(7ES)	1232/33542	ex N358BJ	Royal Australian Air Force (Wedgetail AEW) (on order 06)
A -	(700IGW)		o/o 07	Royal Australian Air Force (AEW)
A -	(700IGW)		o/o 08	Royal Australian Air Force (AEW)
AI-7301*	(2X9)	868/22777	ex N1779B	TNI-AU - Indonesian Air Force
AI-7302*	(2X9)	947/22778	ex N8288V	TNI-AU - Indonesian Air Force
AI-7303*	(2X9)	985/22779		TNI-AU - Indonesian Air Force
AP-BEH*	(33A)	2341/25504		Government of Pakistan 'Pakistan 2'
A6-AIN*	(7Z5)	280/29268	ex N1786B	Abu Dhabi Amiri Flight [MO/AUH] [BBJ]
A6-AUH	(8EX)	1196/33473	ex N379BC	Abu Dhabi Amiri Flight [MO/AUH] [BBJ2]
A6-DAS*	(7Z5)	530/29858		Abu Dhabi Amiri Flight [MO/AUH] [BBJ]
A6-HRS*	(7EO)	150/29251		Dubai Air Wing [DUB] [BBJ]
A6-LIW*	(7Z5)	445/29857	ex (A6-AUH)	Abu Dhabi Amiri Flight [MO/AUH] [BBJ]
A6-MRM*	(8EC)	787/32450	ex N1787B	Dubai Air Wing [DUB] [BBJ2]
A6-RJZ*	(7Z5)	432/29269	ex A6-SIR	Royal Jet [BBJ]
B-4008*	(3T0)	1507/23839	ex N19357	CAAC Special Services [Op by CUA]
B-4009*	(3T0)	1516/23840	ex N27358	CAAC Special Services [Op by CUA]
B-4020*	(34N)	2746/28081		North China Administration [Op by CUA]
B-4021*	(34N)	2747/28082		North China Administration [Op by CUA]
EP-AGA*	(286)	483/21317		Government of Islamic Republic of Iran
EP-IGA*	(270C)	368/20892	ex YI-AGH	Government of Islamic Republic of Iran (stored Teheran)
EP-IGD*	(270C)	371/20893	ex YI-AGI	Government of Islamic Republic of Iran (stored Teheran)
EW-001PA	(8EV)	1075/33079	ex N375BC	Government of Belarus [BBJ2]
FAC	(74V)	323/29272	ex N7378P	Government of Colombia [BBJ]
FAP-356*	(528)	2739/27426	ex PRP-001	Fuerza Aerea del Peru
G-OBBJ*	(8DR)	882/32777	ex N379BJ	Multiflight Jet Charter [BBJ2]
HL7270	(7EG)	926/32807	ex N375BJ	Samsung Techwin Aerospace [BBJ]
(HZ-DG5)*	(7BQ)	423/30547	ex N79711	Dallah AVCO Flight Operations (Lsd fr WFBN) [BBJ]
HZ-101*	(8DP)	836/32451	ex N374BJ	Royal Saudi Air Force [BBJ2]
HZ-102*	(7DP)	940/32805	ex N372BC	Royal Saudi Air Force [BBJ]
HZ-MF1	(7FG)	1204/33405	ex N373JM	Saudi Ministry of Finance & Economy [BBJ]
HZ-MF2	(7AJ)	1217/33499	ex N355BJ	Saudi Ministry of Finance & Economy [BBJ]
HZ-MIS*	(2K5)	816/22600	ex D-AHLH	Sheikh M Edress [Nordam 3]
HZ-TAA*	(7P3)	217/29188	ex N1779B	HRH Talal bin Abdul Aziz [BBJ]
HZ-	(8EF)	996/32971	ex N371BC	WFBN/Executive Jets Ltd [BBJ2]

K2412*	(2A8)	977/23036	ex VT-EHW	Indian Air Force	
K2413*	(2A8)	982/23037	ex VT-EHX	Indian Air Force	
K3186*	(2A8)	275/20484	ex VT-EAK	Indian Air Force	
K3187*	(2A8)	273/20483	ex VT-EAJ	Indian Air Force	
K	(2A8)	899/22860	ex VT-EHE	Indian Air Force	
M53-01	(7H6)	397/29274	ex 9M-BBJ	Royal Malaysian Air Force	[BBJ]
N4AS*	(74U)	197/29233		Air Shamrock	[BBJ]
N37NY*	(4Y0)	1651/23976	ex N773RA	New York Knicks & Rangers (op by PACE A/l)	
N50TC*	(72T)	131/29024		Tracinda Corp	[BBJ]
N90R	(7EL)	889/32775		Swiflite Aircraft Corp	[BBJ]
N108MS	(7BC)	1111/33102	ex N105QS	Yona Aviation II	[BBJ]
N127QS*	(7BC)	356/30327		Netjets (Lsd fr WFBN)	[BBJ]
N129QS*	(7BC)	384/30329	ex N1787B	Netjets (Lsd fr WFBN)	[BBJ]
N134AR	(7AH)	456/29749	ex C6-TTB	BB Five Inc	[BBJ]
N135TA*	(222)	171/19940	ex N135AW	Sky King Inc (Nordam Stage 3)	
N147AW	(297)	860/22630	ex N729AL	Sky King Inc	
N156QS*	(7BC)	569/30756	ex N1003W	Netjets (Lsd fr WFBN)	[BBJ]
N159PL*	(242)	438/21186	ex C-GNDL	Compass Capital Corp (op by PACE Airlines)	
N164RJ*	(7BC)	377/30328	ex N128QS	Netjets (Lsd fr WFBN) 'Capt James Cook' [winglets]	[BBJ]
N165W*	(247)	57/19605	ex N4508W	Northrop Grumman Corp	
N171QS*	(7BC)	491/30572	ex N1005S	Netjets (Lsd fr WFBN)	[BBJ]
N180AD*	(7BF)	301/30496	ex N180SM	Funair Corporation	[BBJ]
N181QS*	(7BC)	586/30782	ex N1006F	Netjets	[BBJ]
N182QS	(7BC)	861/32575		Boeing Company (stored BFI)	[BBJ]
N191QS*	(7BC)	623/30791		TRW Ventures LLC	[BBJ]
N201YT	(266)	451/21192	ex LV-ZRD	DS Hall t/a Wings of Eagles	
N222TM	(2K9)	1176/23404	ex	Boeing Capital Corporation	
N223US*	(201)	534/21665	ex N761N	L-3 Communications Corp/USN [Nordam 3]	
N227AU*	(201)	592/21816	ex C-FRYH	L-3 Communications Corp/USN [Nordam 3]	
N253DV*	(39A)	1409/23800	ex N117DF	Aviation /NBA Orlando Magics	
N313P	(7ET)	1037/33010	ex (N104QS)	Premier Executive Transport Services	[BBJ]
N315TS*	(7CU)	554/30772	ex N1784B	Tutor-Saliba Corp	[BBJ]
N349BA*	(73Q)	602/30789		BCC Equipment Lsg/The Boeing Company	[BBJ]
N358BJ	(7ES)	1232/23542		Boeing Business Jets	
N364BJ	(8DP)	836/32451		Boeing Aircraft Holding	[BBJ2]
N366G*	(75V)	126/28561	ex N1787B	GE Air Transport Services/GECC	[BBJ]
N367G*	(75V)	312/28579		GE Air Transport Services/GECC	[BBJ]
N368CE*	(33A)	2749/27456	ex 9M-CHG	Club Excellence (Op by Premier)	
N370BC*	(205)	1262/23468	ex HZ-TBA	Basic Capital Management	
N374BC	(7DM)	1089/33080		Boeing Aircraft Holding	[BBJ]
N375SP	(8EQ)	33361		Boeing Business Jets	[BBJ2]
N465AT*	(2L9)	517/21528	ex N359AS	Sky King Inc	
N487GS*	(247)	44/19600	ex N307VA	Charlotte Hornets (op by PACE Airlines) stored Lake City, FL	
N500LS*	(73T)	143/29054	ex N6067E	Hays Productions Inc (The Limited)	[BBJ]
N515GM	(7BC)	586/30782		KevinAir LLC	
N583CC*	(291)	415/21069		Pride Air/Gund Sports Marketing	
N703BC	(7BC)	1211/33434	ex N109QS	BCC Equipment Leasing Corp	[BBJ]
N707BZ*	(7BC)	988/32970	ex N103QS	SJ 2003-1 Trust	[BBJ]
N733PA*	(205)	1236/23466	ex N733AR	Phillips 66 Petroleum [Nordam 3]	
N734MA*	(81Q)	30786		Boeing Co	[BBJ2]
N736BP*	(205)	1226/23465	ex LN-SUU	BP Exploration/WFBN [Nordam 3]	
N737A*	(7AX)	648/30181		ARAMCO Associated Company	
N737BG*	(247)	93/19612	ex N903LC	Boeing JSF Avionics Flying Laboratory [AVA 3]	
N737BZ*	(73Q)	101/29102		BCC Equipment Lsg Co/Boeing Co	[BBJ]
N737CC*	(74Q)	206/29135	ex N60436	WFBN/Mid East Jet	[BBJ]
N737DX*	(408)	1851/24804	ex TF-FIC	Sports Jet (Phoenix Suns/Arizona Cardinals)	
N737ER*	(7CJ)	516/30754	ex N61MJ	BBJ One Inc	[BBJ]
N737GG*	(74Q)	225/29136	ex N1787B	WFBN/Boeing Business Jets	[BBJ]
(N737M)	(8EQ)	1124/33361	ex N737SP	EIE Eagle / WFBN	[BBJ2]
N737Q	(2L9)	480/21279	ex C6-BEQ	BCC Equipment Lsg Co/Sky King [AVA 3]	
N737WH*	(75T)	167/29142	ex N700WH	Southern A/C Svs/Wayne Huizenga [Fleet National Bank]	[BBJ]
N738A*	(7AX)	690/30182	ex N1785B	ARAMCO Associated Company	
N739A*	(7AX)	702/30183		ARAMCO Associated Company	
N743A*	(7AXC)	925/30184		ARAMCO Capital Company	
N743NV	(6Z9)	526/30137	ex OE-LNL	US Navy [Lsd fr WFBN]	
N745A*	(7AXC)	978/30185		ARAMCO Capital Company	
N742PB*	(73U)	234/29200		Chartwell Partners LLC	[BBJ]
N747BX	(86Q)			Boeing Co	[BBJ2]
N787WH*	(2V6)	803/22431	ex N737WH	Southern A/C Svs	
N888YF	(7BC)	1060/33036	ex N110QS	AVN Air LLC/Evergreen International SA	[BBJ]
N889NC*	(7AV)	244/30070	ex N18NC	WFBN/Newsflight II Inc	[BBJ]
N902WG*	(2H6)	822/22620	ex N22620	Gary 737 LLC	
N977UA	(291)	518/21508	ex N7391F	Sky King Inc	
N982UA	(291)	536/21640	ex N7396F	Sky King Inc	
N1011N*	(79U)	111/29441	ex N1101N	Boeing Capital Corp	[BBJ]
N4529W*	(247)	335/20785		Dept of the Air Force/EG & G Group [Nordam 3]	
N5175U*	(T43A)	334/20689	ex 72-0282	Dept of the Air Force/EG & G Group [Nordam 3]	
N5176Y*	(T43A)	339/20692	ex 72-0285	Dept of the Air Force/EG & G Group [Nordam 3]	
N5177C*	(T43A)	340/20693	ex 72-0286	Dept of the Air Force/EG & G Group [Nordam 3]	

N5294E*	(T43A)	337/20691	ex 72-0284	Dept of the Air Force/EG & G Group [Nordam 3]
N5294M*	(T43A)	343/20694	ex 72-0287	Dept of the Air Force/EG & G Group [Nordam 3]
N7600K*	(7BC)	953/32628	ex N102QS	SAS Institute [BBJ]
N60669	(42C)	1871/24231	ex PH-BPD	WFBN/Boeing Corp (Connexion by Boeing)
P4-GJC*	(7CG)	401/30751	ex N888GW	Silver Arrows [BBJ]
P4-PHS*	(53A)	1977/24970	ex P4-FZT	SEB Investments Corporation/Pacific Sky
P4-TBN*	(7BH)	336/29791	ex N348BA	TBN Aircraft Corp/Tango Aircraft Holdings [BBJ]
RP-C4007*	(332)	2488/25996	ex RP-C2000	Government of the Philippines
TP-02*	(33A)	1737/24095	ex N731XL	Fuerza Aerea Mexicana [also XC-UJB]
TP-03*	(112)	217/19772	ex XB-IBV	Fuerza Aerea Mexicana [also XC-UJL]
3520	(2B7)	1049/23133	ex N286AU	Fuerza Aerea Mexicana
TS-IOO*	(7H3)	348/29149	ex N5573L	Government of Tunisia [op by TAR] [BBJ]
VP-BBJ*	(72U)	146/29273	ex N1011N	Picton Ltd [BBJ]
VP-BBT	(705)	83/29089	ex LN-TUB	Ford Motor Co [FOB]
VP-BBU	(705)	109/29090	ex LN-TUC	Ford Motor Co [FOB]
VP-BEL*	(74T)	189/29139	ex N21KR	Magenta Aviation [BBJ]
VP-BHN*	(8AN)	779/32438	ex VP-BNH	Saudi Oger [BBJ2]
VP-BJB*	(7BC)	415/30330	ex N130QS	Sigair Ltd [winglets] [BBJ]
VP-BRM*	(75U)	158/28956	ex N1786B	Dobro Ltd/Theberton USA Inc [BBJ]
VP-BWR*	(79T)	265/29317	ex N1787B	Usal Ltd/Bel Air Ltd [BBJ]
VP-BYA*	(7AN)	642/29972		Saudi Oger/Boeing Business Jets [BBJ]
VP-BZL*	(8DV)	969/33915	ex D-ABZL	Lowa Inc (Lsd fr WFBN) [BBJ2]
VP-BBW*	(7BJ)	179/30076	ex N737BF	GAMA Avn/Dunview Co Ltd [BBJ]
VP-B	(7BC)	747/30884	ex N184QS	Boeing Business Jets [BBJ]
VP-CBB	(8AW)	912/32806	ex N73721	WFBN/AS Bugshan & Brothers
				(Bosco Aviation) [BBJ2]
VP-CEC*	(7AW)	251/30031	ex N73715	Boeing Business Jets [BBJ]
VP-CHK*	(2S9)	618/21957	ex N39BL	Executive Jet Aviation/Harry Akande [AVA 3]
VP-CSA*	(2W8)	820/22628	ex A6-ESH	SAMCO Aviation
XA-AEX*	(7EJ)	853/32774	ex N1784B	Grupo Omnilife 'Nilambara' [BBJ]
ZS-SRA*	(7ED)	826/32627	ex N373BJ	Republic of South Africa/SAAF [BBJ]
3C-EGE	(7FB)	1189/33367	ex N377JC	Boeing Aircraft Holding Co (stored BFI) [BBJ]
4X-AOT*	(297)	562/21740	ex N70724	ELTA Electronics (research aircraft)
5R-MRM	(3Z9)	1515/24081	ex OE-ILG	Government of Madagascar
5U-BAG*	(2N9C)	513/21499	ex (5U-MAF)	Government of Niger

Four 737 AEW&C aircraft are on order for Turkey with delivery between 2006-8

Boeing 747

20-1101*	(47C)	816/24730	ex JA8091	Government of Japan/
				Japan Air Self-Defence Force
20-1102*	(47C)	839/24731	ex JA8092	Government of Japan/
				Japan Air Self-Defence Force
73-1676	(E-4B)	202/20682		USAF
73-1677	(E-4B)	204/20683		USAF
74-0787	(E-4B)	232/20684		USAF
75-0125	(E-4B)	257/20949		USAF
82-8000*	(VC25A)	679/23824	ex N6005C	USAF/89AW
92-9000*	(VC25A)	685/23825	ex N60659	USAF/89AW
00-0001	(4G4F)	1238/30201		USAF (as YAL-1A)
A4O-SO*	(SP-27)	405/21785	ex N351AS	Oman Royal Flight [RS/ORF]
A4O-SP*	(SP-27)	447/21992	ex N150UA	Oman Royal Flight [RS/ORF]
A4O-OMN	(430)	1292/32445	ex D-ARFO	Oman Royal Flight [RS/ORF]
A6-GDP*	(2B4SF)	263/21098	ex N712CK	Dubai Air Wing [DUB]
A6-HRM	(422)	1171/26903	ex N108UA	Dubai Air Wing [DUB]
A6-MMM	(422)	1185/26906	ex N109UA	Dubai Air Wing [DUB]
A6-SMM*	(SP-31)	441/21963	ex N602AA	Dubai Air Wing [DUB]
A6-SMR*	(SP-31)	415/21961	ex N58201	Dubai Air Wing [DUB]
A6-YAS*	(4F6)	1174/28961	ex N1794B	Abu Dhabi Amiri Flight [MO/AUH]
A6-ZSN*	(SP-Z5)	676/23610	ex N60659	Abu Dhabi Amiri Flight [MO/AUH]
A9C-HMH*	(SP-21)	373/21649	ex A9C-HHH	Bahrain Royal Flight 'Gulf of Bahrain' [BAH]
A9C-HMK	(4P8)	1324/33684		Bahrain Royal Flight [BAH]
HZ-AIJ*	(SP-68)	560/22750	ex N6046P	Saudi Arabian Royal flight [SVA]
HZ-HM1A*	(3G1)	592/23070	ex N1784B	Saudi Arabian Royal flight [SVA]
HZ-HM1B*	(SP-68)	329/21652	ex HZ-HM1	Saudi Arabian Royal flight (Flying hospital) [SVA]
HZ-WBT6	(4J6)	926/25880	ex N747BZ	Kingdom Holding II LLC/WFBN
N145UA*	(SP-21)	306/21441	ex N536PA	NASA, Ames Research Center (SOIA project)
N708BA	(SP-B5)	507/22484	ex HL7457	Wings World Wide-The Air Medical Foundation
N709BA	(SP-B5)	501/22483	ex HL7456	Wings World Wide-The Air Medical Foundation
N747BC	(4J6)	904/25879	ex B-2464	Boeing Aircraft Holding Corp (stored MZJ)
N747GE*	(121)	25/19651	ex N744PA	General Electric Co (engine test-bed)
N747KV	(SP-44)	21133	ex N747KS	Panair Inc
N747UT	(SP-J6)	21934	ex N139SW	UT Finance Corp
N905NA*	(123)	86/20107	ex N9668	NASA, Johnson Space Center
				(Shuttle Transporter)
N911NA*	(SR-46)	221/20781	ex N747BL	NASA, Johnson Space Center
				(Shuttle Transporter)
N4522V	(SP-09)	564/22805		Global Peace Initiative
VP-BAT*	(SP-21)	367/21648	ex VR-BAT	Worldwide A/C Holding (Bermuda) (stored BOH)
V8-ALI*	(430)	910/26426	ex N6009F	Sultan's Flight
7O-YMN	(SP-27)	413/21786	ex A7-AHM	People's Republic of Yemen [Op by IYE]

Boeing 757

98-0001*	(VC-32A)	783/29025	ex N3519L	USAF/89AW
98-0002*	(VC-32A)	787/29026	ex N3519M	USAF/89AW
99-0003*	(VC-32A)	824/29027		USAF/89AW
99-0004*	(VC-32A)	829/29028		USAF/89AW
09001				USAF
HZ-HMED*	(23A)	599/25495	ex N275AW	Saudi Arabian Royal Flight, (Flying Hospital) [SVA]
N84WA*	(23A)	523/25493	ex N757AV	Kodiak Associates
N226G*	(23A)	511/25491	ex N38383	L-3 Capital LLC
N557NA*	(225)	2/22191	ex N501EA	NASA/Langley Research Center
N610G*	(22L)	870/29304	ex N1018N	L-3 Capital LLC
N756AF*	(23A)	332/24923	ex N680FM	Vulcan Aircraft Inc
N757A*	(200)	1/22212		Boeing Logistics Spares
N757AF*	(2J4)	371/25155	ex N115FS	Vulcan Aircraft Inc
N757BJ*	(236)	14/22176	ex N261PW	US Bancorp Leasing & Financial
N757MA*	(24Q)	739/28463		WFBN/Mid East Jet
N770BB*	(2J4)	387/25220	ex VP-CAU	The Yucaipa Companies
NZ7571	(2K2)	519/26633	ex PH-TKA	Royal New Zealand Air Force
NZ7572	(2K2)	26634	ex PH-TKB	Royal New Zealand Air Force
T-01*	(23A)	470/25487		Fuerza Aerea Argentina "Virgen de Lujan"
TP-01*	(225)	151/22690		Fuerza Aerea Mexicana [also XC-UJM]
UN-B5701	(2M6ER)	102/23454	ex P4-NSN	Kazakhstan Government [op by BEC]

Boeing 767

64-3501*	(27CER)	557/27385	ex N767JA	JASDF (AWACS)
64-3502*	(27CER)	588/27391	ex N767JB	JASDF (AWACS)
74-3503*	(27CER)	618/28016	ex N767JC	JASDF (AWACS)
74-3504*	(27CER)	642/28017	ex N767JD	JASDF (AWACS)
A6-SUL*	(341ER)	768/30341	ex N60659	Abu Dhabi Amiri Flight [MO/AUH]
HZ-	(231)	30/22567	ex (N515DL)	Jetlease Air Cargo/Sheikh M Edress
HZ-WBT3*	(3P6ER)	525/27255	ex N255KD	Kingdom Holding
N767A*	(2AXER)	903/33685		Aramco Aircraft
N767BA*	(200)	1/22233		The Boeing Company
N767KS*	(29NER)	629/28270	ex N6038E	WFBN/Mid East Jet
N767TT	(2EYER)	912/33686		Boeing Integrated Defence & Space (for Italian Air Force)
UN-B7601	(2DXER)	861/32954		Kazakhstan Government [op by BEC]
VP-BKS*	(3P6ER)	522/27254	ex A4O-GW	Kalair Inc
V8-MHB*	(27GER)	517/25537	ex V8-MJB	Sultan's Flight
	(33AER)	909/33425	ex N595HA	Silver Wings [SVV]

Three more 767 Tanker Transports are on order for Italian Air Force for delivery 2005-2008

Boeing 777

N777AS*	(24QER)	174/29271		WFBN/Mid East Jet [stored BOH]
VP-BRH*	(2ANER)	252/29953		Saudi Oger/Eastern Skys Ltd

British Aircraft Corp One-Eleven

551*	(485GD)	247	ex 1001	Sultan of Oman Air Force
552*	(485GD)	249	ex 1002	Sultan of Oman Air Force
553*	(485GD)	251	ex 1003	Sultan of Oman Air Force
G-MAAH*	(488GH)	259	ex VP-CDA	Gazelle Ltd [stored BOH]
HZ-ABM2*	(401AK)	060	ex HZ-MAA	AMC - Aviation Management Consortium
N17MK*	(410AQ)	054	ex N17VK	Go Jet Inc
N62WH*	(401AK)	078	ex HZ-TA1	S & J Enterprises
N101PC*	(401AK)	073	ex N401SK	Sky King Inc
N111JX*	(414EG)	163	ex N123H	Select Aviation Inc
N111RZ*	(401AK)	056	ex N491ST	Rotec Industries
N161NG*	(401AK)	067	ex N765CF	Northrop-Grumman Corp
N162W*	(401AK)	087	ex N173FE	Northrop Grumman Corp (research a/c)
N164W*	(401AK)	090	ex G-AXCK	Northrop Grumman Corp (research a/c)
N200EE*	(212AR)	083	ex N490ST	Select Aviation Inc
N200JX*	(203AE)	015	ex N583CQ	Select Aviation Inc
N789CF*	(422EQ)	119	ex N114MX	Kori Air Inc
N999BW*	(419EP)	120	ex N87BL	Jet Place Inc
PK-PJF*	(401AK)	065	ex N117MR	Citra Avn
P4-JLB*	(492GM)	260	ex VP-CHM	Arabsco/Mercury Aviation
VP-CCG*	(401AK)	081	ex VR-CCG	ARAVCO [QTV 3]
VP-CLM*	(401AK)	072	ex N119DA	Aravco [Stage 2]
VP-CMI*	(212AR)	183	ex VR-CMI	Kinyaa Ltd 'Sabah'
VP-CJL	(401AK)	086	ex N325V	Jetline International
XA-ADC*	(211AH)	084	ex S9-TAE	Aerotax Monse (stored San Antonio, TX)
XA-CMG	(401AK)	079	ex N880P	Grupo Adelac
XX105*	(201AC)	008	ex G-ASJD	Air Fleet Dept, MoD
ZE432*	(479FU)	250	ex DQ-FBV	Empire Test Pilots School
ZE433*	(479FU)	245	ex DQ-FBQ	GEC-Ferranti/Air Fleet Dept, MoD
ZH763*	(539GL)	263	ex G-BGKE	QinetiQ
5N-BDC*	(412EB)	111	ex EL-LIB	Eagle Aviation/Al Amrani Group (dam LBV 28Aug01)

British Aerospace 146

G-BLRA*	(100)	E1017	ex N117TR	BAE Systems Corporate Air Travel [BAE]
G-LUXE	(301)	E3001	ex G-5-300	FAAM (Atmospheric Research Aircraft) [Op by DCT]
G-OFOA	(100)	E1006	ex G-BKMN	Formula One Management
G-OFOM*	(100)	E1144	ex N3206T	Formula One Management
G-TBAE	(200)	E2018	ex G-JEAR	Corporate Air Travel / BAE Systems
N114M*	(100)	E1068	ex N861MC	Montex Drilling "Lucky Liz"
PK-OSP	(100)	E1124	ex G-CBXY	Surya Paloh, Golkar Party (op by AFE)
ZE700*	(100)	E1021	ex G-6-021	Royal Air Force 32 Sqdn
ZE701*	(100)	E1029	ex G-6-029	Royal Air Force 32 Sqdn

British Aerospace (Hawker Siddeley/)748/Andover/(Hindustan Aeronautics) HAL 748

11-111*	(2A/208)	1570	ex HS-TAF	Royal Thai Air Force/Royal Flight
99-999*	(2A/208)	1715	ex HS-TAF	Royal Thai Air Force/Royal Flight
AF602*	(2A/265)	1688		Zambia Air Force (status?)
F-GODD	(2A/245)	1658	ex G-BFLL	Societé Commerciale de Metaux et Mineruax Rene Aumas
RP-2001*	(2/209)	1641	ex RP-211	Philippine Air Transportation Office (calibrator)
VT-DXH*	(2/224)	513		Border Security Force (stored DEL)
VT-EAT*	(2/224)	540		Border Security Force
VT-EAV*	(2/224)	542		Border Security Force
VT-EFN*	(2/224)	548		National Remote Sensing Agency
VT-EFR*	(2/224)	547	ex VT-EBA	National Airports Authority [YXA]
VT-EHL*	(2/224)	549		Border Security Force
VT-EIR*	(2M LFD)	587		Border Security Force; (stored DEL)
XT-MAL*	(2A/320 LFD)	1754		Government of Burkina Faso
XT-MAN*	(2B/369 LFD)	1775	ex G-11-13	Government of Burkina Faso
3C-JJX	(C.Mk1)	Set 6	ex EL-VDD	JAM Air
3C-KKB*	(C.Mk1)	Set 9	ex NZ7622	748 Air Services
3C-KKC*	(C.Mk1)	Set 18	ex NZ7625	748 Air Services
5Y-IAK	(CC2)	1564	ex G-BVZS	ex-Arch Avn
9N-CAN	(2A)	1667	ex	Clewer Avn (stored HLA)
9Q-CMJ	(C.Mk1)	Set 4	ex 3D-ATS	
9Q-COE	(C.Mk1)	Set 28	ex VR-BOI	Air Aid

British Aerospace ATP

G-BTPH		2015	ex EC-HFM	BAE Systems, LFD prototype (under conversion)
G-BUWM		2009	ex CS-TGB	BAE Systems (Operations) Ltd (stored Woodford)
G-CORP*		2037	ex G-BTNK	Trident Avn Leasing (stored SEN)

British Aerospace Jetstream 31/32

C-GEMQ	(3102)	747	ex N103XV	Advanced Air Ambulance
C-GNRG	(3102)	791	ex N791JZ	Advanced Air Ambulance
C-GZOS				
CP-	(3101)	807	ex N429UE	LET America
G-BRGN*	(3102)	637	ex G-BLHC	Cranfield University
G-BWWW*	(3102)	614	ex G-31-614	BAE Systems (Operations) Ltd
HH-DPL	(3102)	769	ex N845JS	Quiver Overseas/WFBN (stored FXE)
HI-	(3101)	660	ex N411MX	Britannia Aviation Services
HL5214*	(3200)	945	ex G-BTYU	Dong Ah Construction Co
HR-	(3102)	725	ex N833JS	
HR-	(3102)	726	ex N834JS	
HS-DCA*	(3200)	960	ex HS-ASD	Director of Civil Aviation
N10UP	(3101)	635	ex N635JX	Hvizdak Holdings
N93BA	(3217)	923	ex JA8876	Triple Diamond Jet Centre
N127UM	(3101)	762	ex N443PE	Ultra Motorsports
N148JH*	(32EP)	819	ex N3107	MidAmerica Jet
N170PC	(3101)	717	ex G-31-717	N &J Aviation LLC (VIP)
N242BM	(32EP)	902	ex N3155	Jetstream Air/Corporate Flight
N418UE	(3101)	780	ex N331QS	Sum Air Services/Paradise Air [RN]
N492UE	(3201)	790	ex	Corporate Flight
N493UE	(3201)	805	ex	Corporate Flight
N494UE	(3201)	810	ex	Corporate Flight
N643JX*	(3101)	643	ex N421MX	Jetstream Air/Corporate Flight
N646VN*	(3100)	646	ex N646SA	Air East (executive)
N651VN*	(3101)	651	ex ZK-JSX	Air East (executive)
N657BA*	(3101)	657	ex N412MX	Jetstream Air/Corporate Flight
N664JX*	(3101)	664	ex N408AE	Premiere Aero
N685RD	(3101)	685	ex N455PE	Pinney Leasing
N694AM	(3101)	694	ex N168PC	Atkins Aviation
N723VN	(3102)	723	ex N342PF	Hartford Holding Corp; stored LAS
N733VN*	(3112)	733	ex N8000J	Canadian Aero Technic/WFBN
N743PE*	(3101)	755	ex N755SP	HBJ Leasing
N752VN	(3101)	752	ex N120HR	Air East (executive)
N849JS	(3102)	812	ex	J&R Aviation LLC/Picerne Military Procurement

714

N855JS*	(3101)	739	ex N105XV	730 Flight Management/Corporate Flight
N858CY*	(32EP)	858	ex N423AM	Corporate Aircraft Partners [stored IGM]
N862JX	(3201)	862	ex N862AE	Corporate Flight
N865CY*	(32EP)	865	ex N424AM	Corporate Flight Mgt [stored IGM]
N870CY*	(32EP)	870	ex N425AM	Corporate Aircraft Partners [stored IGM]
N874CP*	(32EP)	874	ex N426AM	Corporate Aircraft Partners [stored IGM]
N876CP*	(32EP)	876	ex N427AM	Corporate Aircraft Partners [stored Mena, AR]
N877CP*	(32EP)	877	ex N428AM	Corporate Aircraft Partners [stored Mena, AR]
N879CP*	(32EP)	879	ex N429AM	Corporate Aircraft Partners [stored IGM]
N886CP*	(32EP)	886	ex N3136	Corporate Aircraft Partners [stored IGM]
N888CY*	(32EP)	888	ex N3137	Corporate Aircraft Partners [stored IGM]
N896CP *	(32EP)	896	ex N3140	Corporate Aircraft Partners [stored IGM]
N903EH	(3101)	605	ex N903FH	Club Air Inc/First Capital Group
N904EH	(3101)	613	ex N904FH	Club Air Inc/First Capital Group
N22746*	(3112)	745	ex C-GJPQ	Sky Mapping
N78019	(31)	604	ex LN-FAL	Personal Airliner Ltd
OM-NKD*	(3100)	612	ex HB-AEA	Tatravagonka Poprad
TG-TAK	(3101)	811	ex N427UE	Axis Development
VH-OZD	(3100)	668	ex N668SA	ex-Sakhalin Energy Aviation; stored Sydney
VP-B*	(3100)	691	ex N217FN	Dekkers Aviation Group
YR-TRG	(32EP)	835	ex G-BUIO	RomPetrol Logistics [RDP]
9Q-CFI*	(3200)	852	ex G-31-852	Gecamines

British Aerospace Jetstream 41

1060*	(4100)	41060	ex G-BWGW	Royal Thai Army
1094*	(4100)	41094	ex G-BWTZ	Royal Thai Army
B-HRS*	(4100)	41102	ex G-BXWM	Government Flying Service
B-HRT*	(4100)	41104	ex G-BXWN	Government Flying Service
N410TJ*	(4100)	41038	ex N514GP	Stuart Jet
N941H*	(4100)	41030	ex N680AS	Honeywell Aviation Services/BCC Equipment Lsg

Canadair CL-600-2B-19 (RJ-100/200/Challenger 800)

B-4	(200LR)	7455	ex C-GHUT	Poly Technologies/China Ocean
B-4071	(200LR)	7639	ex C-GKAK	Poly Technologies/China Ocean
C-FNRJ	(100LR)	7002		Bombardier Inc (2nd prototype)
G-ELNX	(200)	7508	ex VH-KXJ	Eurolynx Corporation/Anadarko Petroleum
HB-IDJ*	(100)	7136	ex VP-CRJ	TAG Aviation Service [FP/FPG]
N135BC*	(100SE)	7075	ex N877SE	Executive Aircraft Sales/DJ Burrell
N260BD	(100)	7039	ex LV-YVA	Bombardier Services Corporation
N261BD	(100)	7137	ex LV-ZTB	Bombardier Services Corporation
N351BA	(200)	7351	ex ZS-OGH	Bombardier Aerospace Corp
N405CC*	(100SE)	7099	ex N305CC	Bombardier Capital Inc
N501LS	(200)	7584	ex C-GJVI	Boston Enterprises LLC
N529DB*	(100SE)	7152	ex N655CC	Hardwicke Properties
N601LS*	(100ER)	7008	ex N501LS	Directional Visions
N711WM*	(200)	7140	ex N140WC	Coast Hotels & Casinos Inc
N787BC	(200)	7139	ex LV-ZTC	Bombardier Services Corporation
N846PR	(800)	7846	ex C-GZLM	Penske Jet (Challenger 800)
P4-CRJ*	(100)	7176	ex LX-GJC	HCX Aviation
VP-BCC	(200)	7717	ex C-GZSQ	

Canadair CL-600-2C10 (RJ-700)/ CL-600-2D24 (RJ-900)

C-FRJX	(900)	15991		Bombardier Inc (prototype CRJ-900, conv from CRJ-700)
N1RL	(700)	10004	ex N400MS	Indycar Aviation/Banc One Leasing

CASA C.212

90-0177	(200)	332	ex N8005R	USAF
90-0178	(200)	347	ex N8005L	USAF
EC-HAP*	(400)	465		Secretaria Generale de Pesca Maritima
EC-HTU	(400MP)	470		TRAGSA (Op for MAPA)
EC-INX	(400MP)	472		Secretaria Generale de Pesca Maritima
F-GIQO	(200)	A12-04-387	ex F-ZVMR	Aerostock
I-MAFE*	(200)	CC79-1-273	ex EC-DVD	Cia Generale Ripreseaeree [CGR]
N99TF*	(100)	CB8-1-89		Raeford Aviation (skydiving)
N433CA*	(200)	CC50-7-272	ex TI-AVV	Carolina Sky Sports/Fayard Enterprises
N434CA*	(200)	CC50-8-286		Carolina Sky Sports/Fayard Enterprises
N515RL*	(200)	DF-2-405	ex N405AC	ConocoPhillips Alaska Inc
(N960BW)	(200)	CC40-8-248	ex N202FN	Aviation Worldwide Services LLC
(N961BW)	(200)	CC40-3-231	ex N203FN	Aviation Worldwide Services LLC
N962BW*	(200)	CC44-1-290	ex N439CA	Presidential Airlines
N963BW	(200)	379	ex N204FN	Blackwater Aviation
N7214E*	(200)	CD51-6318	ex FAC 1155	Carolina Sky Sports
PK-ABM*	(200)	33N/AB4-5-182	ex PK-XAG	Mantrust Asahi
SAF-212	(400)	466		Surinam Air Force
SAF-214	(400)	467		Surinam Air Force
SE-IVE*	(200)	CE61-1-343		Swedish Coastguard
SE-IVF*	(200)	CE61-2-346		Swedish Coastguard

SE-KVG*	(200)	AS28-1-229	ex EC-502	Swedish Coastguard
SE-LBD	(100)	CB20-2-154	ex N125JM	Flygtransporter i Nykoping
SE-LDG	(100)	CC35-1-192	ex N192MA	Flygtransporter i Nykoping
T9-ABA	(200)	A48-1-302	ex F-GHOX	Air Salzburg
VH-TEM*	(200)	CC37-1-138	ex P2-CNP	Fugro Airborne Surveys

CASA-Nurtanio CN.235

A4O-CU	(M-100)	C062		Royal Oman Police [ROP]
A4O-CV	(M-100)	C063		Royal Oman Police [ROP]
EC-100	(100MP)	P1	ex ECT-130	CASA, prototype ff 11Nov83
EC-HTU*	(400)			Secretaria Generale de Pesca Maritima
N168D	(300)	C135		Devon Holding & Leasing
N196D	(300)	C139		Devon Holding & Leasing
N235TF		C036	ex EC-HAU	EADS CASA
N385RS	(200QC)	C042	ex N9858H	Turbo Flight Avn Co
PK-XNC	(200MPA)	01N		Nurtanio, prototype ff 30Dec83
XC-PFH	(200QC)	C041	ex EC-GEJ	Policia Federal Preventiva/ Mexican Federal Police
XC-PFW	(10M)	C011	ex N100FN	Policia Federal Preventiva/ Mexican Federal Police

CASA CN.295

EC-295		P-001		CASA (prototype, ff Nov97)
EC-296		S-1		CASA (1st production a/c, ff 22Dec98)

Convair

C-FNRC*	(580)	473	ex CF-NRC	NRC Flight Research Laboratory
C-GRSC*	(580)	72	ex N8EG	Innotech Aviation (remote sensing a/c)
N24DR*	(440)	393	ex CF-GLM	San Francisco Iron Goods & Trade
N30KE*	(580)	364	ex N30KA	Sierra Industries (stored OPF)
N39*	(580)	480	ex N74	FAA
N49*	(580)	479	ex N103	FAA
N57RD*	(580)	509	ex N12FV	RDC Marine [Lsd fr ERH]
N115BF*	(440)	461	ex N29KE	San Francisco Iron Goods & Trade
N131CW*	(C-131D)	205	ex N6288Y	Classic Wings
N145GT	(C-131B)	256		Richard Air
N442JM*	(440)	438	ex XA-TDL	Wings of Hope
N580AS*	(580)	2	ex N113AP	Honeywell Aviation Services (testbed)
(N580ES)*	(580)	500	ex N580HH	Raytheon Company
N8277Q	(640)	282	ex P4-SSG	Kestrel Inc
N41626	(340)	274	ex 53-7822	Miami Air Lease
N51211*	(580)	489	ex N5121	Veridian Systems Division
N51255*	(580)	383	ex N45LC	Veridian Systems Division
N70636	(C-131A)	53-11	ex XA-TDF	Wings of Hope
XA-SQG	(C-131B)	266	ex N7814B	California Aeroservicios (stored San Diego)
ZS-ARV	(340)	228	ex (ZS-OTE)	Rovos Rail Tours
ZS-BRV	(340)	215	ex (ZS-OTD)	Rovos Rail Tours

de Havilland DHC-6 Twin Otter

298*	(300)	298	ex F-BTOR	French AF (c/s F-SCOY)
300*	(300)	300	ex F-BTOT	French AF (c/s F-SCOZ)
AP-BRR*	(300)	782	ex (FAE 782)	Pakistan Oil & Gas Development Corp
A6-MAR	(300)	841	ex N9045S	Mohammed Abdul Rahim al Ali
B-3512*	(300)	831	ex VR-BJP	ATB Island Creek of China Coal
C-FCSU*	(300)	352		Transport Canada [TGO]
C-FCSW*	(300)	355		Transport Canada (for sale) [TGO]
C-FCSX*	(300)	357		Transport Canada (for sale) [TGO]
C-FPOK*	(200)	116	ex (N31TW)	NRC Flight Research Laboratory
C-GGPM	(300)	613	ex CC-PII	Barrick Gold Corporation
C-GIGK	(300)	492	ex N300BC	Ashe Aircraft Enterprises
C-GJDI*	(300)	837	ex N565GA	Irving Oil (Raisbeck conv)
C-GZVH	(300)	671	ex HZ-FO2	Paul's Aircraft Services
C-GZXV	(200)	208	ex RP-C663	Ashe Aircraft Enterprises
CC-PQQ	(300)	793	ex C-FWZB	Compania Minerva Nevada
CP-1019*	(300)	368		YPF Bolivianos (ZS-OUH reserved)
D-IDHB	(200)	132	ex RP-C1776	Air America titles
D-IDHC	(100)	71	ex C-FCIJ	Air Service Wildgruber
D-IVER	(300)	411	ex SE-IYP	Businesswings
D-IXXY	(300)	233	ex 5N-BBT	Nordic Aviation Leasing
EC-ISV	(200)	205	ex OY-PAE	
FAP-02	(200)	137	ex FAP-01	Fuerza Aerea Paraguaya
F-BTAU*	(200)	153	ex (N33TW)	Centre de Parachutisme Sportif
F-GHRK*	(200)	144	ex N202E	Samevi 98 SL/Parachutisme Tallard
F-GJDS	(300)	375	ex TR-LDH	Savoie Air Lines (used for skydiving)
F-OIQF	(300)	815	ex N45KH	Polynesie Francaise
HC-	(300)	667	ex N546WA	ex HMHC
HZ-ATO*	(300)	836	ex C-GDCZ	Saudi Arabian Airlines, Special Flight Services [SVA]
LV- *	(200)	136	ex AE-100	YPF Argentina

LV-APT*	(200)	138	ex AE-258	Lobos
N3PY	(300)	767	ex N2670X	Westwind Air
N10EA	(200)	199	ex C-FRXU	Eagle Air Transport/Skydive Chicago
N16NG	(300)	596	ex N16NA	Northrop Grumman Aviation
N24HV	(100)	109	ex N911BX	Vertical Air/Skydive Leland
N28SP	(300)	601		Taylor, Taylor & associates
N30EA	(200)	191		Eagle Air Transport/Skydive Chicago
N34KH	(300)	542	ex PJ-WIE	JAS Aircraft Sales & Leasing
N46RF	(300)	824	ex C-GIUZ	NOAA/US Dept of Commerce
N48RF*	(300)	740	ex N600LJ	National Oceanic & Atmospheric Administration [NAA]
N49SJ*	(300)	423	ex N490AS	US Dept of the Interior
N53AR	(300)	350	ex YV-1034C	Twin Otter International Ltd
N57RF*	(310)	688	ex N485RF	National Oceanic & Atmospheric Administration [NAA]
N61UT*	(300)	549	ex N160CA	Union Texas Pakistan
N63AR	(300)	432	ex N254SA	Twin Otter International Ltd
N73WD*	(100)	73	ex C-FPPD	Alberta Aircraft Leasing
N83NX*	(UV-18A)	496	ex 76-22566	US Dept of Navy
N98VA	(100)	65	ex N666PV	Twin Otter International Ltd
N100AP*	(100)	22	ex HP-772	Carolina Sky Sports
N121PM*	(100)	14		One Papa Mike Corp/ Southern California Skydiving Club
N122PM*	(100)	15	ex N348MA	Raeford Parachute Center (skydiving)
N123FX*	(310)	200	ex G-BUOM	Freefall Express
N125SA	(100)	104	ex N125SR	Perris Valley Aviation
N128WJ*	(200)	128	ex N63128	Skydive Arizona
N129PM*	(100)	114	ex N67CA	Freefall Express
N148DE*	(300)	493	ex N72348	US Dept of Energy [Op by NRG]
N157KM	(100)	57	ex RNoAF 57	Kevin McCole
N162DE*	(300)	429	ex N35062	US Dept of Energy [Op by NRG]
N166DH*	(100)	66	ex CF-ARC	Freefall Express
N167WC	(300)	343	ex N3434	Washington Corp
N169BA	(100)	103	ex C-FQBV	Desert Sand Aircraft Leasing
N169TH	(100)	93	ex N951SM	Summerfield Aviation
N184KM	(200)	184	ex RNoAF 184	Kevin McCole
N186AL	(200)	186	ex C-GKNR	Alberta A/C Leasing
N200DZ*	(200)	112	ex N491AL	Monterey Bay Aero Sportsplex
N202EH*	(100)	48	ex N4914	The Skydive Factory
N203E*	(200)	53		Adventure Aviation LLC
N203SF*	(200)	151	ex C-FJCL	The Skydive Factory
N204BD	(200)	204	ex C-FISO	Skydive Arizona
N204EH*	(100)	61	ex N8082N	The Skydive Factory
N204SA	(300)	402	ex HP-1308APP	Aire Express
N220EA*	(200)	190	ex N930MA	Eagle Air Transport/Skydive Chicago
N223AL	(200)	223	ex C-FYPP	Win Win Aviation Inc
(N225CS)	(100)	29	ex N229YK	F&M Aviation
N227CS*	(100)	27	ex ZK-FQK	Carolina Sky Sports
N228CS*	(300)	608	ex HK-3523	Carolina Sky Sports
N228YK*	(300)	228	ex C-FPAE	Skydiving Productions over Texas
N233SA	(300)	440	ex N547N	Airborne Research
N244MV	(300)	244	ex P2-IAA	Joda LLC
N255SA	(300)	723		Airborne Research
N270CM	(300)	270	ex VH-UQR	Orion Aviation LLC
N300DZ	(300)	644	ex C-GIMG	Westwind Air
N300WH	(320)	647	ex VH-XFC	Southern Aircraft Services (Floatplane)
N301CL	(200)	221	ex DQ-FIL	Win Win Aviation
N332MA	(100)	32	ex C-GGNI	Pace Aviation
N353PM	(300)	351	ex C-FCST	N353PM LLC
N512AR	(100)	59	ex	Twin Otter International
N607NA*	(100)	4	ex N508NA	NASA, John H Glenn Research Center
N622JM	(300)	548	ex N548X	Musha Transportation Ltd
N660MA*	(300)	231		ARAMCO
N663MA*	(300)	593		ARAMCO
N669JW*	(200)	88	ex P2-RDB	Carolina Sky Sports
N690MF	(200)	121	ex C-FQXW	Desert Sand Aircraft Lsg
N705PV	(300)	234	ex N279WW	Flanagan Enterprises
N708PV	(300)	489	ex C-GDMP	PM Leasing
N711AF*	(300)	711	ex C-GIFG	Vulcan Inc
N711AS*	(200)	202		Skydive Productions over Texas
N716NC*	(100)	110	ex N952SM	Freefall Express
N719AS*	(200)	139	ex N711SD	Skydive Productions over Texas
N753AF	(200)	206	ex F-GCVR	Twin Otter International
N776BF	(300)	672	ex N776BE	Continental Aviation Services
N823X	(300)	823	ex B-3507	Transport Services LLC
N826X	(300)	826	ex B-3509	Transport Services
N842AR*	(300)	842	ex C-FDHA	ConocoPhillips Alaska
N894S*	(300)	779	ex N89HP	Hewlett Packard Co
N899AS	(300)	347	ex LN-FKB	Air Service International
N901BS*	(200)	160	ex N921MA	Raeford Aviation (skydiving)
N923MA*	(200)	168	ex N923HM	Speedstar Express LLC
N924MA*	(200)	216	ex N653HM	ex-Paracentrum Provincie Leopoldsburg

N926MA*	(200)	133	ex N953SM	Speed Star Express [Skydive Elsinore]
N932MA*	(200)	211	ex V3-HTD	CASC Inc/East Troy, IL Sky Sports
N974SW	(300)	410	ex CC-CHL	Molo Leasing Inc
N1022S*	(100)	79	ex C-GHYH	Carolina Sky Sports
N3434*	(200)	193	ex HK-3643X	Aerohio Aviation/Carolina Sky Sports
N6151Q	(300)	633	ex N6151C	Aviation Specialities
N38535	(300)	414		Ironwood Investments
N40269	(200)	152	ex F-GHXY	Freefall Express
N64116	(200)	157	ex 5X-UVL	Twin Otter International Ltd
N64150*	(200)	150		Perris Valley Aircraft
OB-1704	(300)	701	ex C-GBGC	Minera Barrick Misquichitica
OH-SLK*	(300)	260	ex SE-GEG	Finnish Parachuting Club
PJ-	(300)	359	ex N149SA	Twin Otter International
PNC-201*	(300)	727	ex HK-2777G	Policia Nacional Fondo Rotatoria
PNC-202*	(300)	829	ex C-GDIU	Policia Nacional Fondo Rotatoria
SE-GEE*	(300)	364	ex F-GFAH	Skydive Airlines
ST-AOQ*	(300)	778	ex HB-LRE	AMC Arab Mining Company
T-741*	(300)	466	ex HB-LID	Swiss Federal Office for Topography
TY-BBS*	(300)	807	ex C-GESR	Force Aerienne du Benin
VH-HPT*	(320)	707	ex VH-USW	Hawker Pacific (op by Australian Army)
VH-OHP*	(300)	527	ex VH-FNY	Hawker Pacific (op by Australian Army)
VH-OTA*	(100)	90	ex N950SM	Sydney Skydiving Centre
VT-ELX*	(300)	825	ex C-GIIG	Scintrex/Dept of Mines
XC-ALA				Procurador General de la Republica (Drug Enforcement)
XC-DIO*	(300)	687	ex (N549N)	Procurador General de la Republica (Drug Enforcement)
YI-AKY	(300)	736		Iraqi Northern Petroleum
YV-184CP*	(300)	557		Fundavair
ZS-OVD	(300)	288	ex HB-LSP	New Millen 130 Investments
ZS-OVJ	(300)	424	ex 5Y-BHR	Executive Turbine P/L
ZS-	(310)	838	ex N451RA	ex-Ricart Aviation Sales
ZS-PDY	(200)	119	ex N63119	Iron Mountain Plant Sales
3X-GAY*	(300)	553	ex N888LA	Cie des Bauxites de Guinee
5A-DAS*	(300)	567		Waha Oil Company
5A-DAT*	(300)	569		Waha Oil Company
5A-DAU*	(300)	570		Oasis Oil Company
5A-DBF	(300)	705		Veba Oil Company
5A-DBH*	(300)	808	ex C-GDFT	Umm Al Jawaby Petroleum Company
5A-DBJ	(300)	444		Occidental Oil of Libya
5A-DCA*	(300)	599		Libyan Ministry of Agriculture
5A-DCJ*	(300)	595		Occidental Oil of Libya
5A-DHN*	(300)	712		Agoco-Arabian Gulf Oil Company [op by LJA]
5A-DSC*	(300)	636	ex HB-LRN	Sirte Oil Company [op by IMX]
5N-MPU	(300)			Mobil
5Y-JHZ	(310)	336	ex HB-LOI	Aircraft Lsg Services Ltd/Ashraf
6V-AFF*	(300)	788	ex C-GBOD	Government of Senegal (surveillance a/c)
9Q-CJD*	(300)	797	ex C-GDIU	Siforzal Company

de Havilland DHC-7

HK-3111W*	(102)	87	ex HK-3111G	Intercor/Carbocol [op by HEL]
HK-3340W*	(102)	108	ex C-GFBW	Intercor/Carbocol [op by HEL]
N34HG	(102)	34	ex ZS-IRS	US Dept of the Army
N56HG	(102)	56	ex VH-UUX	Northrop Grumman California Microwave Systems
N59AG	(102)	59	ex C-GYMC	US Dept of Defense
N67DA*	(102R)	102	ex (RP-__)	DGV
N158CL*	(102)	58	ex N42RA	US Dept of Defense
N176RA	(102)	76	ex C-GFOD	US Dept of the Army
N177RA	(102)	85	ex C-GFOD	US Dept of the Army
N341DS	(102)	57	ex C-GTAZ	Telford Air Spares (stored BGR)
N701GA	(102)	19	ex N4860J	Regional Airlines Support Group
N705GG*	(102)	48		US Government Dept of Army
N765MG	(102)	65	ex N2655P	US Government Dept of Army
N53993*	(103)	104	ex C-GFUM	US Government Dept of Army
N89068	(102)	88	ex HK-3112G	Wilmington Trust Co (op by Dept of Defense)

de Havilland DHC-8

C-FDHX	(315)			Bombardier
C-FJJA*	(Q-401)	4001		Bombardier Inc (Srs 400 prototype, ff 31Jan98)
C-GCFJ*	(101)	020		Canadian Department of Transport
C-GFPZ	(311A)	267		Bombardier (stored Maastricht)
C-GGMP*	(Q200)	002		Bombardier Inc
C-GHQP	(Q-402)	4004	ex C-GIHK	Hydro-Quebec [APZ] (Op by AIE)
C-GHGQ*	(Q-402)	4003	ex C-FPJH	Hydro-Quebec [APZ] (Op by AIE)
C-GHQZ	(314)	370	ex OE-LLY	Hydro-Quebec [APZ] (Op by AIE)
C-GJNL	(311)	422	ex G-BXPZ	Hydro-Quebec [APZ] (Op by AIE)
C-GJVB	(102)	046	ex CAF 142802	Field Aviation
HK-3997W*	(202)	391	ex C-GFBW	BP Oil Exploration Colombia [BPX]
KAF304*	(103)	189	ex C-GLOT	Kenya Air Force
KAF305*	(103)	219	ex C-GFCF	Kenya Air Force

KAF306*	(103)	223	ex C-GFBW	Kenya Air Force
LN-ILS	(103)	396		Avinor A/S (for sale)
MTX-05	(202)	572	ex C-GFBW	Armada de Mexico
N108TY	(301)	108	ex B-3533	CIT Leasing Corp; stored Winston-Salem
N116TY	(301)	116	ex B-3531	CIT Leasing Corp; stored Winston-Salem
N194TY	(301)	194	ex B-3532	CIT Leasing Corp
N308RD*	(102A)	265	ex N228H	RDC Marine Inc
N381BC	(102)	121	ex 6V-AHD	Wells Fargo Bank Northwest
N387BC	(106)	351	ex C-GILX	Bombardier Services Corp
N505LL	(311)	415	ex N600SR	Path Corporation
N713M*	(102)	030	ex N444T	US Department of Justice/JPATS [JUD]
N724A*	(202)	440	ex C-GFBW	ARAMCO Associated Co
N725A*	(202)	441	ex C-GFCF	ARAMCO Associated Co
N759A*	(202)	435	ex C-GDIU	ARAMCO Associated Co
N819MA	(102A)	251	ex C-GJNZ	WFBN
VH-JSX	(102)	008	ex	Aeromil (Aircraft) Pty
VH-LCL*	(Q-202)	492	ex C-GEOA	LADS/Surveillance Australia
5H-KMC	(103)	010	ex N802WP	Kahama Mining Corp
5N-MGV	(101)	024	ex C-GMOK	Mobil Oil Nigeria
5N-*	(101)	028	ex C-GCFK	Mobil Producing Nigeria

Dornier 228

A4O-CQ*	(100)	7028	ex D-IBLN	Royal Oman Police Air Wing [ROP]
D-CALM*	(101)	7051		DLR Flugbetriebe [GPL]
D-CAWI*	(101)	7014	ex D-IAWI	DLR Flugbetriebe/Alfred Wegener Institute "Polar 2"
D-CFFU*	(212)	8180		DLR Flugbetriebe [GPL]
D-CICE*	(101)	7073		DLR Flugbetriebe/Alfred Wegener Institute "Polar 4"
D-CODE*	(101)	7083	ex(D-CEVA)	DLR Flugbetriebe [GPL]
D-IROL	(100)	7003	ex SE-KHL	Business Wings
D4-CBK	(212)	8222	ex 7Q-YKS	Guarda Costeira de Cabo Verde (stored OBF)
EP-TCC*	(212)	8195	ex D-CNCC	National Cartographic Center
EP-THA*	(212)	8207	ex D-CIME	National Cartographic Center
EP-TKH*	(212)	8204	ex D-CIMO	National Cartographic Center
EP-TZA*	(212)	8208	ex D-CIMU	National Cartographic Center
JA8858*	(201)	8128	ex D-CBDU	National Aerospace Laboratory
PH-MNZ	(212)	8206	ex D-CDIV	Netherlands Coast Guard, op by MPH
VT-EIX*	(100)	7032	ex D-IBLP	Oil & Natural Gas Commission (wfs)
VT-ENK*	(201)	8086	ex D-CANA	National Airports Authority
VT-EPU*	(200)	8090/2016		National Airports Authority
ZS-CCC	(201)	8092	ex MAAW-T01	Execujet Aircraft Sales
ZS-DOC	(202)	8104	ex MAAW-R1	Interactive Trading 102
ZS-	(202K)	8148	ex MAAW-T303	
5N-ACT*	(201)	8130	ex D-CAOS	MFCT
5N-AUM*	(100)	7023	ex D-IBLE	NNPC
5N-AUV*	(101)	7011	ex D-ICIP	Air Border Patrol Unit
5N-AUW*	(101)	7018	ex D-IBLB	Air Border Patrol Unit
5N-AUX*	(101)	7095	ex D-CAGE	Air Border Patrol Unit
5N-AUY*	(101)	7116	ex D-CIMA	Air Border Patrol Unit
5N-AUZ*	(101)	7167	ex D-CAFA	Air Border Patrol Unit
5N-MPS*	(202)	8146	ex D-CALO	NEPA-National Electric Power Authority
5U-MBI*	(201)	8074	ex D-CELO	Government of Niger/Escadrille Nationale du Niger

Dornier 328 (new build aircraft due in 4Q04 from AvCraft)

C-FSCO	(100)	3109	ex D-CDXV.	Shell Canada
D-BDMO	(300)	3200	ex D-BDXN	Fairchild-Dornier
D-BEJR	(300)	3102		Dornier, 3rd Srs.300 prototype
D-BJET	(JET)	3002	ex D-CATI	Dornier Srs.300 prototype ff 20Jan98, stored Oberpfaffenhofen
D-BWAL	(300)	3099		Dornier 2nd Srs.300 prototype
D-CDOL*	(100)	3003		Dornier (stored Oberpfaffenhofen)
D-CDXA	(130)	3100		Dornier (stored Oberpfaffenhofen)
D-CITI*	(100)	3004	ex HB-AEJ	Dornier (stored Oberpfaffenhofen)
D-CMTM*	(110)	3094		Bonair (Lsd fr Millennium Leasing)
D-CMUC*	(110)	3096	ex D-CDXM	Bonair (Lsd fr Millennium Leasing)
N28CG*	(110)	3024	ex N95CG	Corning Inc
N38CG*	(110)	3034	ex D-CDXA	Corning Inc
N328AC	(300)	3132		Dornier (stored TUL)
N328DC*	(110)	3019	ex D-CDHD	Pacific Gas & Electric
N328FA*	(110)	3095	ex D-CATI	WFBN/Fairchild Aerospace (stored TUL)
N328FD	(300)	3196		WFBN
N328GT*	(Envoy 3)	3183	ex N328FD	Ultimate Air Charters
N328JT*	(300)	3105	ex D-BALL	Fairchild-Dornier (stored TUL)
N328PM*	(Envoy 3)	3184		Altria Corporate Services
N328PT	(Envoy 3)	3199		WFBN
N404SS*	(110)	3090	ex D-CDYY	BellSouth Communications and Telecoms Inc
N653JC*	(110)	3027	ex N653PC	Johnson Control
N873JC*	(Envoy 3)	3118	ex D-BDXB	St Thomas Energy Exports

OE-LKA*	(110)	3110	ex D-CDXI	JetAlliance [JAF]
XA-	(Envoy 3)	3216	ex D-BDXD	Grupo Protexa
5N-SPE*	(Envoy 3)	3120	ex D-BABA	Shell Petroleum [Op by BHN]
5N-SPM*	(Envoy 3)	3141	ex D-BDXR	Shell Petroleum [Op by BHN]
5N-SPN*	(Envoy 3)	3151	ex D-BDXT	Shell Petroleum [Op by BHN]

Dornier 728

D-ADLH	(100)	7002		Dornier GmbH
D-AEVA	(100)	7001		Dornier GmbH (ro 21Mar02)

Programme put on hold after manufacturer entered liquidation and assets sold; neither aircraft flown

Douglas DC-8

46013*	(72CF)	427/46013	ex OH-LFT	Armée de l'Air (callsign F-RAFG)
46043*	(72CF)	443/46043	ex OH-LFV	Armée de l'Air (callsign F-ZVMT)
46130*	(72CF)	542/46130	ex OH-LFY	Armée de l'Air (callsign F-RAFF)
HB-IGH*	(72)	455/46067	ex VP-BJR	Al Nassr Ltd
N698SN	(F-54)	283/45886	ex N698QS	Stage 3 Nacelle Inc (stored MHV)
N728A*	(72)	471/46081	ex N8971U	ARAMCO
N817NA*	(72)	458/46082	ex N717NA	NASA, Dryden Flight Research Center
TR-LTZ*	(73CF)	446/46053	ex N8638	Government of Gabon
VP-BHM*	(62)	491/46111	ex VR-BHM	Brisair Ltd

Douglas DC-9

71-0874	(C-9A)	647/47467		USAF/374TAW (stored Davis-Monthan AFB, AZ)
71-0876	(C-9A)	653/47475		USAF/435TAW
71-0878	(C-9A)	659/47536		USAF/435TAW
71-0882	(C-9A)	670/47541		USAF/435TAW (stored Davis-Monthan AFB, AZ)
73-1681	(VC-9C)	765/47668		USAF/89AW
73-1682	(VC-9C)	769/47670		USAF/89AW
73-1683	(VC-9C)	774/47671		USAF/89AW
F-GVTH	(21)	474/47308	ex F-WTVH	Thales Systèmes Aéroportes
				(electronics test-bed)
mm62012*	(32)	709/47595		Aeronautica Militare Italiane (Italian AF)
N13FE*	(14)	61/45706	ex N5NE	Tuckahoe LLC/Flight Service Group [stored MZJ]
N112PS*	(15RC)	129/47013	ex N557AS	Sky Way Enterprises [ABS 3]
N120NE*	(15)	34/45731	ex HB-IFA	AC Aiello [ABS 3]
N133NK	(32)	923/48111	ex N13512	US Dept of Justice/JPATS (ABS) [Op by NKS]
N338CA	(21)	475/47360	ex OY-KID	Celsius Amtec
N305PA*	(15)	62/45740	ex N911KM	Pharmair Corp
N697BJ	(32)	918/47799	ex N926LG	McAir Inc/Blue Jackets
N724HB	(32CF)	843/47690	ex KAF321	Comtran Intl (stored San Antonio)
N813TL*	(15)	41/45732	ex N29	US Dept of Justice/JPATS (ABS 3) [JUD]
N814RW*	(15F)	102/47011	ex N179DE	US Dept of Justice/JPATS (ABS 3) [JUD]
N682RW*	(51)	862/47733	ex	Detroit Red Wings & Tigers
N880DP*	(32)	754/47635	ex N880RB	Round Ball One /Detroit Pistons [ABS 3]
N900SA*	(15)	71/45775	ex N40SH	HW Aviation LLC
N941NE*	(41)	752/47633	ex SE-DBM	Private Jet [ABS 3]
N950VJ*	(31)	681/47564		US Dept of Justice/JPATS [JUD]
N8860*	(15)	51/45797	ex N8953U	RM Scaife

Douglas DC-10

N910SF	(10)	65/46524	ex 99-0910	United States of America, st Davis-Monthan AFB
T-235*	(KC-10F)	235/46956	ex PH-MBP	Klu/Royal Netherlands Air Force
				'Jan Scheffer' [NAF]
T-236*	(KC-10F)	264/46985	ex PH-MBT	Klu/Royal Netherlands Air Force
				'Prins Bernhard' [NAF]
N10MB*	(30CF)	157/47907	ex OO-SLB	Omega Air Inc (stored San Antonio, TX)
N220AU*	(10)	2/46501	ex G-GCAL	Project Orbis Intl (flying hospital)
N285CR	(30)	352/48285	ex C-GCPG	WFBN
N296CR	(30)	370/48296	ex C-GCPI	WFBN
N482CR	(30)	364/48288	ex C-GCPH	WFBN

Embraer EMB.110 Bandeirante

D2-EUN	(P1A)	110467	ex PT-SHV	Government of Angola
D2-EUT	(P1A)	110485	ex PT-SHT	Government of Angola
N102TN	(P1)	110312	ex PT-SCS	Beason Simons
PP-EAM*	(P1A)	110498	ex PT-SBS	Governo do Estado do Amazonas
PP-EIX*	(P1A)	110468	ex PT-SHW	Governo de Amapa
PP-EMG	(E)	110032	ex PT-GJV	Policia Civil de Minas Gerais
PP-EON*	(C)	110038	ex PT-KOK	Governo de Roraima
PP-EOO*	(C)	110025	ex PT-FVH	Governo de Roraima
PP-ERN*	(P1)	110344	ex PT-FAV	Governo de Rio Grande do Norte
PP-FFV*	(B1)	110284	ex PT-SBO	INPE Instituto Pesquisas Espacias
PP-SBI	(C)	110030		stored Sao Jose dos Campos
PT-EDO*	(C)	110016	ex PP-SBD	Carlos Alberto Edo Palma
PT-FRF*	(EJ)	110115	ex PT-GKK	Departamento Nac Est de Rodagem
PT-LRA*	(P1)	110415	ex N39174	Disri Dist Com Prod Alim Beb

PT-LRE*	(P1)	110428	ex PP-EUO	Sao Raimundo Mineracao Ltda
PT-ODJ*	(C)	110034	ex FAB 2144	Mineracao Taboca
PT-SCE*	(P1)	110296		Cia Hidroeletr San Francisco
PT-SCY*	(P2)	110319		CODARGO
PT-SGM*	(P1)	110420	ex 8R-GFO	World Air Taxi
PT-SHN*	(P1A)	110460		Paulo Guimareas e Cia
PT-SHO*	(P1A)	110461		Furnas Centrais Electricas
PT-SHP*	(P1A)	110462		Cia Hidroeletr San Francisco
PT-SHR*	(P1A)	110464		Furnas Centrais Electricas
PT-SHU*	(P1A)	110466		Cia Energetica de Minas Gerais
PT-SRM*	(P1A)	110463	ex PT-SHQ	Sao Raimundo Mineracao Itaituba
PT-WAW	(C)	110122	ex FAB2189	Fulvio Kain
PT-WTL*	(C)	110104	ex FAB2180	Viviam Marafugi Fukkissima
S9-DAI	(P1)	110381	ex OO-SKW	Island Oil Exploration
TR-KMA*	(P1K)	110268	ex PT-SBG	Government of Gabon
TR-KNB*	(P1K)	110297	ex PT-SCF	Government of Gabon
TR-KNC*	(P1K)	110360		Government of Gabon
VH-JAX	(P2)	110190	ex VH-MWV	Australian East Coast Airsports
VH-UQA	(P2)	110245	ex VH-XFL	Australian East Coast Airsports
YV-100C				
ZS-PHB	(P1)	110198	ex G-ONEW	TM Bengis t/a Microzate Trading 789CC
ZS-TMB	(P1)	110288	ex OO-SKU	TM Bengis t/a Microzate Trading 789CC

Embraer EMB.120 Brasilia

550/CX-BTZ*	(ER)	120089	ex N12705	Uruguayan Air Force
2000		120003	ex PT-ZBB	Brazilain Air Force
C-FPAW*	(ER)	120018	ex N516P	Pratt & Whitney Canada [PWC]
C-GOAB	(ER)	120078	ex N16702	Go Air
C-GOAD	(ER)	120086	ex N19704	PPI Motorsports/Go Air
N130G	(RT)	120130	ex PT-SNW	Jones Aviation Trading Co
N138DE*	(ER)	120095	ex N27707	Champion Air/Dale Earnhardt
N221CR	(ER)	120171	ex N16724	RCR Air Inc
N233RD	(ER)	120260	ex N205SW	Bill Davis Racing
N284UE	(ER)	120145	ex PT-SPL	Players Air/Hinckley Inc
N331CR	(ER)	120121	ex PH-XLG	RCR Air Inc
(N400GG)	(ER)	120035	ex N331JS	North American Jet Charter
N500DE*	(ER)	120118	ex N26714	Champion Air/Dale Earnhardt
N919EM*	(ER)	120160	ex N132PP	Evernham Motorsports
OY-PAO	(ER)	120016	ex SE-LKB	NAC Nordic Aviation Contractors
PP-PSC	(ER)	120213	ex F-GTSK	Embraer (corporate shuttle)
PT-SRE	(ER)	120324	ex PT-SXQ	Embraer, stored
PT-SRG	(ER)	120331		Embraer, stored
PT-XSP	(ER)	120323		Embraer, stored
PT-ZBA*		120001		Embraer prototype, ff 27Jul83, stored
T-500	(ER)	120357	ex PT-SOJ	Angolan Air Force -ntu?
T-501	(ER)	120358	ex PT-SOK	Angolan Air Force -ntu?

Embraer EMB.135/EMB.140/EMB.145/Legacy

209*	(135LR)	145209	ex PP-SFX	Hellenic Air Force	
374*	(145AEW)	145374	ex PP-SQZ	Hellenic Air Force	
484*	(135BJ)	145484	ex PT-SAD	Hellenic Air Force	[Legacy}
	(135SA)	145	ex PT-XJU	Hellenic Air Force	[Legacy]
6702*	(145SA)	145263	ex PP-XSC	Brazilian Air Force (as R-99A)	
6703*	(145SA)	145365	ex PP-XSD	Brazilian Air Force	(145AEW)
6704*	(145SA)	145392	ex PT-XSE	Brazilian Air Force	(145AEW)
6751*	(145RS)	145154	ex PP-XRT	Brazilian Air Force	
6752*	(145RS)	145257	ex PP-XRU	Brazilian Air Force	
	(145ER)	145020	ex PT-SPA	Brazilian Air Force	
	(145ER)	145023	ex PT-SPB	Brazilian Air Force	
	(145ER)	145027	ex PT-SPC	Brazilian Air Force	
	(145ER)	145028	ex PT-SPD	Brazilian Air Force	
	(145ER)	145034	ex PT-SPG	Brazilian Air Force	
	(145SA)	145190	ex PT-XJN	Mexican Air Force (on order)	
	(145MPA)			Mexican Air Force (on order)	
	(145MPA)			Mexican Air Force (on order)	
	(135BJ)		ex PT-	Indian Government (on order)	[Legacy]
	(135BJ)		ex PT-	Indian Government (on order)	[Legacy]
	(135BJ)		ex PT-	Indian Government (on order)	[Legacy]
	(135BJ)		ex PT-	Indian Government (on order)	[Legacy]
	(135BJ)		ex PT-	Indian Government (on order)	[Legacy]
CE-01*	(135LR)	145449	ex PT-SUU	Belgian Air Force [BAF]	
CE-02*	(135LR)	145486	ex PT-SVZ	Belgian Air Force [BAF]	
CE-03*	(145LR)	145526	ex PT-STR	Belgian Air Force [BAF]	
CE-04*	(145LR)	145548	ex PT-SZL	Belgian Air Force [BAF]	
EC-IIR	(135BJ)	145540	ex (PT-SAI)	FADESA	[Legacy]
HB-JEA	(135BJ)	145555	ex PR-SC	G5 Executive/Pisco Overseas	[Legacy]
HB-JED	(135BJ)	145644	ex PT-SAR	DiaMair/GE Lisca AG [Legacy]	
N135SG	(135BJ)	145706	ex PT-SAX	Gulf Aviation Services Group	[Legacy]
N135SL	(135BJ)	145711	ex PT-SAY	United Aviation	[Legacy]

N201CP	(135LR)	145726	ex PT-SHC	Pfizer Inc/Charlie Papa Operations (corporate shuttle)
N202CP	(135LR)	145728	ex PT-SHE	Pfizer Inc/Charlie Papa Operations (corporate shuttle)
N302GC*	(135LR)	145600	ex PT-SCJ	Indigo Air t/a Air Serv/WFBN [stored BNA]
N303GC*	(135LR)	145608	ex PT-SCR	Indigo Air t/a Air Serv/WFBN [stored BNA]
N325JF	(135ER)	145499	ex PT-S	Executive Jet Management [EJM] (Op for Intel Corp)
N386CH*	(135ER)	145467	ex PT-SVM	WFBN/Executive Jet Management [EJM] (Op for Intel Corp)
N486TM*	(135ER)	145364	ex PT-SOM	Executive Jet Management [EJM] (Op for Intel Corp)
N642AG	(135BJ)	145642	ex PT-SAQ	Yo Pegasus LLC/Hermes Investment Group [Legacy]
N686SG	(135BJ)	145686	ex PT-S	Interstate Equipment Leasing [Legacy]
N691AN	(135BJ)	145699	ex PT-S	Wind Spirit LLC [Legacy]
N730BH	(135BJ)	145730	ex PT-SHG	Briad Restaurant Group/Redeye II [Legacy]
N829RN*	(135ER)	145361	ex PT-SOP	Executive Jet Management [EJM] (Op for Intel Corp)
N912CW	(135BJ)	145412	ex PT-SAB	Flight Options [OPT] [Legacy]
N928CW	(135BJ)	145528	ex VP-CVD	Flight Options/WFBN [OPT] [Legacy]
N948AL*	(135ER)	145450	ex PT-SUV	Executive Jet Management [EJM] (Op for Intel Corp)
N962CW	(135BJ)	145462	ex PP-XGM	Flight OptionsWFBN [OPT] [Legacy]
N962FM*	(135ER)	145466	ex PT-SVL	Executive Jet Management [EJM] (Op for Intel Corp)
N995CW	(135BJ)	145495	ex PR-LEG	Flight OptionsWFBN [OPT] [Legacy]
N1023C*	(135LR)	145550	ex PT-SZN	Conoco/PNC Bank
PP-XHL	(145H)	145374		Embraer
PP-XJM		145723		Embraer
PP-XJR		145757		Embraer
PP-XJV		145694		Embraer (belly-mounted radar)
PR-RIO	(135BJ)	145717	ex PT-SAZ	Unibanco [Legacy]
(PT-SAA)	(145BJ)	145363	ex PP-XJO	Embraer (First Legacy, f/f 31Mar01) [Legacy]
PT-SAF	(135BJ)	145505		Embraer [Legacy]
PT-SAG	(135BJ)	145516		Embraer [Legacy]
PT-SAS	(135BJ)	145678		Embraer [Legacy]
PT-SDN	(135BJ)	145625		Embraer [Legacy]
PT-XIT	(135BJ)	145729		Embraer [Legacy]
PT-ZJA	(135KE)	145801		Embraer (EMB.140 prototype, conv from EMB.135, ff 27Jun00)
PT-ZJB	(145XR)	145001		Embraer (second prototype 145, ff 17Nov95)
PT-ZJC	(135ER)	145002		Embraer (EMB.135 secondprototype, conv from EMB.145)
PT-ZJD	(145)	145003		Embraer (third prototype and demonstrator)
P4-VVP	(135BJ)	145549	ex PT-SAJ	Kung Fung Trading/Evolga of Moscow [Legacy]
VP-CFA	(135BJ)	145637	ex PT-SAP	Samco Aviation/Sheikh Fahad Al Athel [Legacy]

Embraer 170/175/190

PP-XJA	(100)	17000005		Embraer
PP-XJB	(100)	17000003		Embraer, ff 25May02
PP-XJC	(100)	17000002		Embraer, ff 09Apr02
PP-XJD	(200)	17000014		Embraer (prototype 175, ff 16Jun03)
PP-XJE	(100SL)	17000001		Embraer, 1st prototype (ff 19Feb02)
PP-XJF	(100)	17000004		Embraer
PP-XJG	(200)	17000017		Embraer (second 175)
PP-XJI	(100)	17000007		Embraer
PP-XJS	(100)	17000006		Embraer

Fairchild F-27

N19HE*	(F)	110	ex C-GQCM	19th Hole Corporation (stored Stuart, FL)
N235KT*		16	ex N101FG	Fritz GH Abbing (Fokker Friendship Assn)
N366SB*	(F)	97	ex N20W	Sunbelt Communications Inc (stored)
N432NA*	(F)	35	ex N768RL	Southeastern Oklahoma State University

Fairchild-Hiller FH-227

5002	(E)	501	ex N2657	Myanmar Air Force
5004	(B/LCD)	552	ex N708U	Myanmar Air Force
5006	(B/LCD)	554	ex N709U	Myanmar Air Force
N7820M*	(B/LCD)	558	ex XA-SQT	Flight Source
XB-DOU*	(D)	578	ex N2783R	Secretaria de Asientos Humanos

Fokker F.27 Friendship

AR-NZE	(200)	10262	ex	Pakistan Navy
44/AR-NZZ	(200)	10444	ex ZK-DCA	Pakistan Navy
45/AR-NZV	(200)	10445	ex ZK-DCB	Pakistan Navy

5001	(600)	10392	ex OY-SRR	Myanma Air Force [also XY-AER]
F-BYAO*	(102A)	10127	ex F-WYAO	Institut Geographique National
F-GKPY	(100)	10224	ex LX-LGA	Burlington Engineering
J-752	(200)	10281	ex AP-ATW	Pakistan Air Force (VIP)
PH-FBP	(100)	10150	ex C-3	Royal Dutch Airforce Historical Flight
PH-KFG*	(200)	10249	ex I-ATIM	Fokker Friendship Association
TF-SYN*	(200)	10545	ex PH-EXC	Icelandic Coastguard/Landhelgisgaezlan [ICG]
VH-CAT*	(100)	10132	ex PH-FAZ	Omega Aviation
VH-EWP*	(500RF)	10534	ex PH-EXW	Executive Airlines Engineering/RAN (surveyor)
3C-QSJ	(100)	10149	ex C-2	Trygon Ltd (stored Southend)
7T-VRN*	(600)	10527	ex 7T-WAN	Government of Algeria
7T-VRW*	(400M)	10556	ex 7T-WAV	Government of Algeria

Fokker F.28 Fellowship

0740*	(3000)	11147	ex PH-EXW	Armada Argentine
0741*	(3000RC)	11145	ex PH-EXV	Armada Argentine
0742*	(3000RC)	11150	ex PH-EXX	Armada Argentine
A-2801*	(1000)	11042	ex PK-PJT	TNI-AU - Indonesian Air Force
A-2802*	(3000R)	11113	ex PK-GFR	TNI-AU - Indonesian Air Force
A-2803*	(3000R)	11117	ex PK-GFQ	TNI-AU - Indonesian Air Force
EP-PAZ*	(1000)	11104	ex F-GIAK	Iranian Government [op by IRC]
FAC001*	(1000)	11992	ex PH-EXF	Fuerza Aerea Colombiana
G530*	(3000)	11125	ex PH-ZBP	Ghana Air Force
M28-01*	(1000)	11088	ex FM2101	Royal Malaysian Air Force [RMF]
N159AD	(4000)	11227	ex N478US	Aerodynamics
N500WN*	(1000)	11016	ex N43AE	Desert Eagle
RP-1250*	(3000)	11153	ex RP-C1250	Philippines Government
T-02* (2)	(4000)	11203	ex PH-RRC	Fuerza Aerea Argentina
T-03	(1000)	11028	ex T-04	Fuerza Aerea Argentina
VH-AHT	(4000)	11183	ex VH-FKI	IAP Group Australia
5A-DSO*	(2000)	11110	ex HB-AAS	Sirte Oil Company
5H-CCM*	(3000)	11137	ex PH-ZBS	Government of Tanzania 'Uhuru na Umoja'
5V-TAI*	(1000)	11079	ex 5V-MAB	Government of Togo

Fokker 50/60

5001		20229	ex PH-JXE	Republic of China Air Force
5002		20238	ex PH-JXH	Republic of China Air Force
5003		20242	ex PH-JXI	Republic of China Air Force
U-01	604	20321	ex PH-UTL	KLu/Royal Netherlands Air Force 'Marinus van Meel' [NAF]
U-02	604	20324	ex PH-UTN	KLu/Royal Netherlands Air Force 'Willem Versteegh' [NAF]
U-03	604	20327	ex PH-UTP	KLu/Royal Netherlands Air Force 'Jan Borghouts' [NAF]
U-04	604	20329	ex PH-UTR	KLu/Royal Netherlands Air Force 'Jules Zeegers' [NAF]
U-05	502	20253	ex PH-KXO	KLu/Royal Netherlands Air Force 'Fonse Aler' [NAF]
U-06	502	20287	ex PH-MXI	KLu/Royal Netherlands Air Force 'Robbie Wijting'[NAF]
5H-TGF		20231	ex PH-JXG	Government of Tanzania

Fokker 70

KAF308*		11557	ex PH-MXM	Kenyan Government
N322K*		11521	ex PH-MKS	Ford Motor Co/WFBN [FRD]
N324K*		11545	ex PH-EZH	Ford Motor Co/WFBN [FRD]
PH-KBX*		11547		Dutch Royal Flight [op by MPH]

Fokker 100

F-GIOH		11424	ex PH-LXV	Sairgroup
G-FMAH		11286	ex N856US	Gazelle Ltd
G-MABH		11291	ex N858US	Gazelle Ltd (Aravco)
PK-TWI		11293	ex G-MAMH	PT Arutmin [op by Transwisata Airlines]
TU-VAA*		11245	ex PH-CDI	Government of Cote d'Ivoire

Ilyushin Il-62

86612		41804	ex UR-86612	Ukraine Government [replaced by A319CJ?]

Ilyushin Il-76

RA-76529	(LL)	073410308	ex CCCP-76529	D-236T propfan eng testbed
RA-78764	(MD)	0083486586	ex CCCP-78764	Ministry of Defence
RA-86628	(M)	063405144	ex CCCP-86628	Russian Air Force
ST-AQR	(TD)	0043453575	ex 9L-LCX	
(4K-86810)	(M)	053404094	ex RA-86810	Azerbaijan Ministry of Defence
4X-AGI		0093486579	ex RA-78740	Israel Aircraft Industries (stored Tel Aviv)

Ilyushin Il-96

RA-96000	(M)	0101	ex CCCP-96000	Ilyushin Design Bureau (prototype, ff 28Sep88)
RA-96001	(300)	30000103	ex CCCP-96001	Ilyushin Design Bureau

Ilyushin Il-114

RA-54000		0101	ex CCCP-54000	Ilyushin prototype, ff 29Mar90
RA-91002		1033830030		Ilyushin OKB
RA-91005	(T)	0301		Ilyushin, Freighter prototype
UK 91009	(100)	1063860202		TAPO (Srs 100 prototype)

IR.AN 140

HESA.01				HESA (Hevapeimasazi-Iran Aircraft Manufacturing Industries Co) (licence buit Antonov An-140)

ITPN N-250

PK-XNG	(-50)	PA1/A9996		ITPN (prototype) [IPN]

LET L-410

D-COXB*	(UVP)	820924	ex DDR-SXB	AeroClub Braunschweig
D-COXC	(UVP)	820925	ex S9-TBT	Antares Airtransport
D6-CAL	(UVP)	800526	ex HA-LAB	H Juergen Uebrig
D6-GDH	(UVP)	851336	ex 3X-GDH	
HI-	(UVP)	861702	ex N808LT	International Flight Center
HK-	(UVP)	841224	ex N408LT	International Flight Center
HK-4142	(UVP-E)	861703	ex N5957J	AVIHECO
JU-2030	(UVP-E1)	861801	ex OK-RDE	VK Programme
J2-MBA	(UVP)	841205	ex 3D-NVR	Djibouti Air Force [also reported as J2-MDA]
J2-MBB	(UVP)			
LZ-KLC	(UVP)	902514	ex	
N28RZ	(UVP)	902430	ex RA-67637	Aztec Capital Corp
N30RZ	(UVP)	892314	ex LY-AZR	Aztec Capital Corp
N514CK				
N40252	(UVP)	841308	ex RA-67483	Caribbean Eagle Inc
2710*	(UVP-E20C)	912710	ex OK-BYF	SLU - Statni Letecky Utvar (op by Czech AF) [CEF]
OK-CDB	(UVP-E20)	972730	ex OK-YDB	LET
OK-DZA	(MA)	730207	ex OK-158	Slovacky Aeroklub
OK-PDB	(FG)	851522	ex Czech AF1522	P Navratil (stored Precov)
OK-PDO	(UVP)	851411	ex UR-67507	P Navratil
OK-SDY	(UVP)	851418	ex CCCP-67514	VZLU Letnany
OK-UDB	(UVP-E14)	892312	ex Czech AF2312	LET Factories
OK-WDC	(UVP-E8D)	912531		
OK-WYI	(UVP-E)	912616	ex CCCP-67685	UCL, Flight Inspection division [CBA]
OK-XDJ	(UVP-E20)	922701		LET
OM-SYI	(UVP-E6)	882019	ex OK-SYI	Letecky Urad Slovenskel Republiky [CIA]
RA-67673	(UVP)	872011	ex RussAF 2011	LET
SP-TPA	(UVP-E15)	892318		PPL Porty Lotnicze (calibrator)
SP-TPB	(UVP-E15)	892329		PPL Porty Lotnicze (calibrator)
S9-BOX	(UVP)	882102	ex 2102/65 red	
TG-AGW	(UVP)	831137	ex HR-IAZ	
UN-67666	(UVP)	912612	ex (CCCP-67666)	Akzol Uralsk
XT-FBD	(UVP)	851414	ex CCCP-67510	
YV-831CP	(UVP)	831115	ex	
YV-861C	(UVP)	820840	ex UR-67340	
YV-867CP	(UVP)	872010	ex 2010	
YV-875CP	(UVP)	892343		
YV-953C	(UVP)	831114	ex	
YV-991C	(UVP)	820835	ex 3C-JJG	
YV-1060C	(UVP)	902505		
Z-OMS	(UVP)			
ZS-OMI	(UVP-E20)	872017	ex 9J-ZSL	Aircraft Systems South Africa
ZS-OOF	(UVP)	871920	ex	Aircraft Systems South Africa
ZS-OOH	(UVP-E20)	871922	ex 5X-UAZ	Aircraft Systems South Africa
3C-DDC	(UVP)	841319	ex N550AG	Ibis Air
3C-DDD	(UVP-E)	892307	ex N551AG	Ibis Air
3C-FFK	(UVP)	770101	ex OK-IYA	Ocean Wonders
3C-QRH	(UVP)	871934	ex RussAF 1934	David Jones
3D-ALC	(UVP)	831036	ex 9L-LCI	
3D-BHK	(UVP)	810724	ex 9U-BHK	Dorgale Investment
3D-GAM	(UVP)	851423	ex 9U-BHF	Privately owned
3D-HVR	(UVP)	841205	ex 3D-NVH	Hernic Pty
3D-KIM	(UVP)	851416	ex 3C-ZZC	no titles
3D-MCG	(UVP)	841206	ex 3D-NVG	Meridian
5R-MGZ	(UVP)	820837		Eric Nadal/Veronique Boeuf
5Y-BCM	(UVP)	902502	ex HI-692CT	
9L-LCE	(UVP)			East Air (based Caloundra, Qld for skydiving)
9L-LCW	(UVP-E)	902519	ex RA-67661	
9Q-CGU	(UVP)	810701	ex 3C-KKU	

```
9XR-JT          (UVP)          810707   ex XT-FAS
```
Several other LET L-410's are flying in non-airline service but are difficult to identify and seem to change identities regularly

LET L-420

ZS-OSE	922729A	
ZS-OUE	012735A ex OK-GDM	Aircraft Systems SA

LET 610

OK-130*	X-01 ex OK-TZB	LET (prototype, ff 20Dec88, stored)
OK-CZD	970301 ex (9U-)	LET
OK-UZB*	900003/X03 ex OK-024	VZLU Letnany
OK-WDC		LET
OK-XZA	970102 ex (9U-)	LET

Lockheed Electra

N145CS*	(P-3AEW)	185B-5409 ex N91LC	US Customs Service
N146CS*	(P-3AEW)	185-5286 ex N96LW	US Customs Service
TP-201*	(A)	1051 ex TP-0201	Fuerza Aerea Mexicana [also XC-UTA]

Lockheed Hercules

HZ-114*	(130H)	4843 ex HZ-HM5	Saudi Arabian Airlines, Royal Flight [SVA]
HZ-115*	(130H)	4845 ex HZ-HM6	Saudi Arabian Airlines, Royal Flight [SVA]
HZ-116*	(VC-130H)	4915 ex N4185M	Saudi Arabian Airlines, Royal Flight [SVA]
HZ-117*	(-30)	4954	Saudi Arabian Airlines, Royal Flight [SVA]
HZ-MS 02*	(VC-130H)	4918 ex HZ-MS21	Saudi Aeromedical Evacuation (flying hospital)
HZ-MS 06*	(-30)	4952 ex HZ-MS6	Saudi Aeromedical Evacuation (flying hospital)
HZ-MS 07*	(VC-130H)	4922 ex HZ-MS7	Saudi Aeromedical Evacuation (flying hospital)
HZ-MS 08*	(-30)	4986 ex HZ-MS8	Saudi Aeromedical Evacuation (flying hospital)
HZ-MS 19*	(VC-130H)	4837 ex HZ-MS19	Saudi Aeromedical Evacuation (flying hospital)
N130AR*	(C-130H)	4984 ex Bu162312	National Center for Atmospheric Research
(N130HL)*	(C-130A)	3052 ex N226LS	GIA Capital LLC
N427NA*	(C-130Q)	4901 ex Bu161495	NASA, Goddard Space Center
N8213G	(-30)	5055	HSL Co
N8218J	(-30)	5056	Ruftberg LLC
SU-BAM*		4803 ex 78-0760	Arab Republic of Egypt Air Force
TP-300*		3087 ex 56-0479	Fuerza Aerea Mexicana [also XC-UTP]
9J-BTM*		3095 ex 9J-AFV	Chani Enterprises

Lockheed L-1011 Tristar

ZD948*	(KC.1)	1157 ex G-BFCA	Royal Air Force [RR/RRR]
ZD949*	(K.1)	1159 ex G-BFCB	Royal Air Force [RR/RRR]
ZD950*	(KC.1)	1164 ex G-BFCC	Royal Air Force [RR/RRR]
ZD951*	(K.1)	1165 ex G-BFCD	Royal Air Force [RR/RRR]
ZD952*	(KC.1)	1168 ex G-BFCE	Royal Air Force [RR/RRR]
ZD953*	(KC.1)	1174 ex G-BFCF	Royal Air Force [RR/RRR]
ZE704*	(C.2)	1186 ex N508PA	Royal Air Force [RR/RRR]
ZE705*	(C.2)	1188 ex N509PA	Royal Air Force [RR/RRR]
ZE706*	(C.2A)	1177 ex N503PA	Royal Air Force [RR/RRR]
HZ-AB1*	(500)	1247 ex JY-HKJ	Prince Abdul Aziz Al Ibrahim/Al Anwae Avn
HZ-HM5*	(500)	1250 ex N5129K	Saudi Arabian Airlines, Royal flight [SVA]
HZ-HM6*	(500)	1249 ex VR-CZZ	Saudi Arabian Airlines, Royal flight [SVA]
N140SC*	(100)	1067 ex C-FTNJ	Orbital Sciences Corp (space booster conversion)
N727DA	(-1)	1167	US Marshals Service
P4-MED*	(100)	1064 ex N787M	The Flying Hospital [op by Eagle Jet Aviation]; stored TUS
VP-CGF	(500)	1195 ex VR-CGF	Jetstream Holdings (VIP a/c)

McDonnell-Douglas MD-11

HZ-HM7*		532/48532 ex N9093P	Saudi Arabian Airlines, Royal flight [SVA]; stored SAT
HZ-AFA1*		544/48533 ex HZ-HM8	Saudi Arabian Airlines, Royal flight [SVA]

McDonnell-Douglas MD-80

N143G*	(87)	1453/49670 ex N3H	JEM Investments/422 Holdings Inc
N287KB*	(87)	1595/49768 ex D-ALLJ	KEB Aircraft
N312TT	(81)	944/48003 ex N480LP	WFBN
N721MM*	(87)	1587/49767 ex N721EW	MGM Mirage Aviation
N806US	(81)	1002/48038 ex N930PS	CSI Avn Services/US Dept of Justice/JPATS [JUD]
N807US	(81)	1003/48039 ex N931PS	CSI Avn Services/US Dept of Justice/JPATS [JUD]
N16894	(82)	1279/49393 ex EI-BTC	CSI Avn Services/US Dept of Justice/JPATS [JUD]
N16895	(82)	1285/49394 ex EI-BTD	CSI Avn Services/US Dept of Justice/JPATS [JUD]
OE-IFA	(83)	1843/49809 ex 3B-AGC	JetAlliance

McDonnell-Douglas MD-90-30

N901DC*		2018/53367		McDonnell-Douglas/Boeing prototype, ff 22Feb93; stored IGM
P4-MDG		2242/53579		Hwa-Hsia Leasing/Kingsair Aviation Corp
P4-MDH		2246/53580		Hwa-Hsia Leasing/Leader Aviation Corp

NAMC YS-11

JA8701*	(A)	2093		Japan Maritime Safety Agency
JA8702*	(A)	2175		Japan Maritime Safety Agency
JA8709*	(A)	2084	ex PP-SMN	JCAB Flight Inspection [calibrator]
JA8720*		2047		JCAB Flight Inspection [calibrator]
JA8780*	(A)	2164		Japan Maritime Safety Agency
JA8782*	(A)	2167		Japan Maritime Safety Agency
JA8791*	(A)	2177		Japan Maritime Safety Agency
N171RV*	(A)	2071	ex JA8713	San Francisco Iron Goods & Trade
N173RV*	(A)	2173	ex JA8789	San Francisco Iron Goods & Trade

Nord 262

TR-KJC*	(C)	97		Government of Gabon
XT-MAK*	(C)	98		Government of Burkina Faso (Lsd to Air Continental)
5Y-DCA*	(C)	96	ex F-WNDA	Kenya Directorate of Civil Aviation (calibrator)

SAAB SF.340

Fv100001*	(B)	170	ex SE-F70	Royal Swedish Air Force (VIP) [SEC]
Fv100002*	(B)	342	ex SE-C42	Royal Swedish Air Force (AEW version) [SEC]
Fv100003*	(B)	379	ex SE-C79	Hellenic Air Force (AEW version) [Lsd fr RSwAF]
Fv100004*	(B)	395	ex SE-C95	Hellenic Air Force (AEW version) [Lsd fr RSwAF]
Fv100005*	(B)	409	ex SE-B09	Royal Swedish Air Force 'Argus' [SEC]
Fv100006*	(B)	431	ex SE-B31	Royal Swedish Air Force (AEW version) [SEC]
Fv100007*	(B)	455	ex SE-B55	Royal Swedish Air Force (AEW version) [SEC]
JA8951*	(B)	385	ex SE-C85	Japan Maritime Safety Agency
JA8952*	(B)	405	ex SE-B05	Japan Maritime Safety Agency
N44KS*	(A)	050	ex N340SA	Goodyear Tire & Rubber
N72VN	(A)	072	ex N4340P	Vee Neal Aviation/Lambert Leasing
N102VN	(A)	103	ex N102XJ	Vee Neal Aviation (Lsd fr SAAB)
N184K*	(A)	029	ex N98AL	Indiana University Foundation
N340SL	(A)	069	ex N69LP	Lambert Leasing
N340SS*	(A)	022	ex N804CE	Meregrass Inc (19-seat VIP)
N346AM	(A)	032	ex SE-E32	Worthington Aviation
N727DL	(A)	036	ex ZS-ABM	Napleton Aviation Group

SAAB 2000

JA003G*	051	ex SE-051	JCAB Flight Inspection
JA004G*	054	ex SE-054	JCAB Flight Inspection
N500PR*	030	ex N5125	Omicron Transportation/Penske Racing (N5125 reserved)
N5123*	020	ex N5123L	General Motors (for disposal) [GMC]
N5124*	027	ex SE-027	General Motors (for disposal) [GMC]

Short SC.7 Skyvan

G-BVXW*	SH1889	ex LX-DEF	Babcock Support Services Ltd
G-PIGY*	SH1943	ex LX-JUL	Babcock Support Services Ltd (dam Jan03)
HZ-ZAL*	SH1956	ex G-BERZ	Saudi Min of Petroleum
HZ-ZAP*	SH1957	ex G-BFHZ	Saudi Min of Petroleum
HZ-ZAS*	SH1969	ex G-BHCH	Saudi Min of Petroleum
HZ-ZAT*	SH1970	ex G-BHHT	Saudi Min of Petroleum
LX-GHI*	SH1890	ex PA-53	CAE Aviation
N4NE*	SH1885	ex YV802CP	Perris Valley Aviation
N26LH	SH1925	ex PK-TRT	LE Hill
N28LH	SH1851	ex PK-TRQ	LE Hill
N46HB	SH1847	ex	Advanced Air Inc
N50DA	SH1852	ex G-AWVM	All West Freight Inc
N80GB*	SH1888	ex LX-ABC	GB Airlink
N101FX*	SH1845	ex C-FGSC	Vertical Air [Skydive Deland]
N642M*	SH1917	ex VH-IBS	Collier County Mosquito Control District
N643M*	SH1939	ex VH-IBT	Collier County Mosquito Control District
N644M*	SH1912	ex VH-IBR	Collier County Mosquito Control District
(N931MA)*	SH1842	ex N101UV	Skydive Arizona
N1846*	SH1846	ex N4916	Aire Express (skydive)
OH-SBA*	SH1908	ex SE-GEY	Deltacraft [4L/DEC]
OE-FDE*	SH1886	ex C9-ASN	Pink Aviation Services
PT-PQD*	SH1951	ex C-FSDZ	Skylift Skydive & Air Cargo
SE-LDK*	SH1870	ex SX-BBO	Goteborg Fallskarmsklubb
VH-IBO*	SH1916	ex SAF-704	Sydney Skydiving Centre
VH-WGQ*	SH1915	ex SAF-702	Violetta Laiketsion (canx to Kenya)

VH-WGT*		SH1960 ex ZS-MJS	Fugro Airborne Survey (stored Umm Al Qawain)
XB-ICT		SH1950 ex N24107	unknown (stored Tamiami)
XC-UTN*		SH1950 ex XC-UTI	Government of Mexico
YV-*		SH1955 ex YV-0-SAR-1	Cia Aerea de Viajes Expresso
ZS-OIO		SH1954 ex (9U-)	Avia Air Charter
3D-ALH			
8R-GGK*		SH1980 ex 8P-ASG	Guyana Defense Force
8R-GRR*		SH1976 ex G-BJDA	Guyana Defense Force
			(believed w/o 14Oct94 but still current)

Short SD.3-30

N8154G		SH3010 ex 85-25342	K&K Aircraft Inc
YV-0-GUR-1*		SH3123 ex G-14-3123	CVG Edelca

Short SD.3-60

FAV-1952*		SH3727 ex YV-O-GUR-1-2	Venezuelan Air Force

(Fairchild-)Swearingen SA.226AT Merlin IV

F-GERP*		AT-012 ex N111MV	Travel Air Service International
F-GMTO*	(A)	AT-031 ex N22KW	Meteorologique Nationale
JA8828*		AT-016 ex N76MX	Showa Aviation
N44GL	(A)	AT-032 ex N44PB	Southbank
N54GP*	(A)	AT-034 ex N717CC	Double EE Ranch
N55CE*		AT-004	US Army Corp of Engineers
N69ST*	(A)	AT-030 ex N5440F	OM Enterprises Inc
N120SC	(A)	AT-067 ex N120AS	Southern Cross Aviation
N202WS*	(A)	AT-037 ex N216GA	Dash 10 Charters
N427SP		AT-018 ex N600TA	5th Third Bank of Columbus
N582JF	(A)	AT-027 ex N824MD	Joseph G Fabick t/a PGF Farms
N727DP*	(A)	AT-039 ex N439BW	Mark A Kyle
N750AA		AT-011 ex PT-WGH	Damax Inc
N836MA		AT-068 ex F-GFPR	Javelin Conversions Inc
N4679K*		AT-006 ex XC-UTF	Hurley Aircraft
OB-1146	(A)	AT-064E ex N21PC	Shougang Hirro Peru

(Fairchild-)Swearingen SA.226TC Metro II

LQ-MLV*		TC-257 ex LV-MLV	Ministero de Accion Social (EMS)
N71Z*		TC-245	Suncoast Media
N226BA		TC-321 ex N105UR	Halair
N226FA		TC-311 ex N116BS	Air Metro III Inc (stored San Antonio, TX)
N323LB*		TC-323	South Florida Expeditions
N324TA		TC-298 ex N324BA	Tellico Air Services
N911HF*		TC-215 ex N62SA	Eagle Helicopters
N2510R		TC-292	Jorge Araya Coromias
PH-NLZ*		TC-277 ex N5651M	NLR-National Lucht & Ruimtevaartlaboratorium
VH-IAU		TC-289 ex VH-KDR	S&T Income Tax Aid Specialists
V5-		TC-392 ex N392CA	Johann Wilhelm Je Beer
XA-HUO			Enrique Cuahonte Delgado/Martha AD
9Q-		TC-208E ex N5336M	Sitco Mine

(Fairchild-)Swearingen SA.227AC Metro III

C6-		AC-599 ex N3116B	
LV-WEE*		AC-516 ex N45ML	Provincia de Catamarca
N6UP		TT-441 ex N125RG	Sunlight Corp
N75X		TT-421 ex N90BJ	Dyer Investment
N90GT		TT-534 ex N139F	E C Menzies Electrical
N98EB		AC-497 ex N110AV	SHO Enterprises
N115GS		AC-715 ex CP-2301	Worldwide Aircraft Services
N227LC		AC-707 ex N84GM	Metro-Jet LLC
N239LC		AC-735 ex N523WA	PCG Acquisition I
N345PA		AC-472 ex XB-RFQ	Mociva Inc
N345TJ		AC-744B ex N32TJ	Tyler Jet
N767FA		AC-767B ex ZK-NSJ	Air Metro III
N2699Y		AC-666	River City Aviation
PH-DYM		AC-523 ex D-CABE	Dynamic Airlines [QG/DYE]
YV-		TT-507 ex N507TT	

(Fairchild-)Swearingen SA.227AT Merlin IVC

N9UA		AT-495B ex C-FNAL	Robert E Morris (N9U resd)
N45MW		AT-452 ex N3010Q	Wilder Avn Sales & Leasing
N66GA*		AT-427 ex D-CAIR	Thomas D Ganley (N629TG res)
N120JM*		AT-577 ex N31136	Breeze Investment
N313D*		AT-464 ex N30364	Mana-Igreja Crista Inc
N318DH		AT-469 ex C-GCAU	Pacific Assembly Inc
N471CD		AT-549B ex N3111K	National Guard Bureau
N762VM		AT-695B ex N2709Z	F Mahor LLC

N919CK		AT-585	ex N227JW	JM Smith
N999MX*		AT-501	ex N3051H	Fair Weather Avn
N8897Y		AT-492	ex C-FJTA	Career Aviation Academy

(Fairchild-)Swearingen SA.227DC Metro 23

N5LN		DC-878B		M7 Aviation LP
N510FS		CC-842B		Textron Financial Corp

Tupolev Tu-134

63957*	(A-3)	63957	ex 01 Yellow	Ukraine Air Force
D2-ECC*	(A)	49830		Government of Republic of Angola
EW-63955*	(M)	63955	ex CCCP-63955	Belarus Government
LZ-TUG*	(A-3)	49858	ex OK-BYT	Government of Bulgaria/Aviodetachment 28 [BGF]
RA-65079	(A-3)	60054	ex LY-ASK	Avcom [J6/AOC]
RA-65557*	(A-3)	66380	ex CCCP-65557	Aero Rent/Itera Company [NRO]
RA-65624*	(A-3)	8350601	ex CCCP-65624	Tupolev Design Bureau
RA-65701	(B-3)	63365	ex YL-LBI	Avcom [J6/AOC]
RA-65725	(A-3M)	66472	ex CCCP-65725	Meridian Air [MMM]
RA-65917*	(A3-CX)	63991	ex CCCP-65917	Meridian Air [MMM]
RA-65919*	(A-3)	66168	ex CCCP-65919	Aero Rent [NRO]
RA-65945	(UBL)	64010	ex CCCP-65945	Avcom [J6/AOC]
UN-65551*	(A-3)	66212	ex CCCP-65551	Standard Oil/Kaz TransAir
UR-65556*	(A-3)	66372	ex CCCP-65556	Government of Ukraine
UN-65799*	(B-3)	63187	ex YL-LBN	Government of Kazakhstan
4K-65496*	(A-3)	63468	ex 4K-65985	Azerbaijan Ministry of Defence
4L-65993*	(A)	63860	ex RA-65993	Georgia Ministry of Defence

Tupolev Tu-154

LZ-BTZ*	(M)	88A-781		Government of Bulgaria/Aviodetachment 28 [BGF]
0601*	(B-2)	84A-601	ex OK-BYD	SLU - Statni Letecky Utvar (op by Czech AF) [CEF]
101*	(M)	90A-837	ex 837	Polskie Wojska Lotnicze (Polish AF)
102*	(M)	90A-862	ex 862	Polskie Wojska Lotnicze (Polish AF)
1003*	(M)	98A-1003		SLU - Statni Letecky Utvar (op by Czech AF) [CEF]
1016*	(M)	98A-1016	ex OK-BYZ	SLU - Statni Letecky Utvar (op by Czech AF) [CEF]
UK 85050*	(B)	73A-050	ex CCCP-85050	Uzbekistan Ministry of Defence
UN-85464*	(B-2)	80A-464	ex CCCP-85464	Kazakhstan Ministry of Defence
3D-RTP	(M)	91A-895	ex YL-LAI	

Tupolev Tu-204

RA-64006	(120)	1450743164006	ex CCCP-64006	Scirocco Aerospace (for sale)
RA-64007		1450743164007		Tupolev Design Bureau
RA-64009	(C)	1450743164009		Tupolev Design Bureau

Tupolev Tu-214

RA-64501		145744452001	Tupolev Design Bureau

Tupolev Tu-234

RA-64001	(300)	1450743164001	ex CCCP-64001	Tupolev Design Bureau (conv from Tu-204)
RA-64026	(300)	1450743164026		Tupolev Design Bureau (1st production aircraft)

Tupolev Tu-334

RA-94001	(100)	01-001	Tupolev Design Bureau (prototype, ff 08Feb99)

VFW 614

D-ADAM*		G17	ex D-BABP	DLR Flugbetriebe [GPL]

Yakovlev Yak-40

0260*	(K)	9940260	ex OK-BYK	SLU - Statni Letecky Utvar (op by Czech AF) [CEF]
1257*	(K)	9821257	ex OK-BYJ	SLU - Statni Letecky Utvar (op by Czech AF) [CEF]
D2-EAG*		9230122	ex I-JAKO	Government of Republic of Angola
HA-YLR		9541044		Hungarian CAA, Flight Inspection A/C
LY-ARZ		9641851	ex SP-FYT	Lietuvos Svedijos UAB Svedijos Preke
OK-020		9431436	ex OK-EXB	VZLU (stored)
OM-DYA		9341230	ex OK-DHA	Letecky Urad Slovenskej Republiky [CIA]
RA-21500	(K)	9741356	ex CCCP-21500	Baltic Finance Industrial Group [Op by RNB]
RA-87572		9220422	ex	Youshnii Express
RA-87655		9211820	ex	Interprobusiness; VSA titles
RA-87807		9231723	ex	Unitemp-M
RA-87908		9721354	ex CCCP-87908	Garry Kasparov
RA-87953	(K)	9811157	ex CCCP-87953	Aist-M Airclub [ISM]
RA-87977		9321128	ex OK-BYH	Avcom [J6/AOC]

RA-87983		9540644	ex CCCP-87983	Aist-M Airclub [ISM]
RA-88308		9230224	ex SP-GEA	
RDPL 34002*		9840559		Government of Laos
S9-BAP		9441938	ex RA-87474	Agua Limpa
UR-87908		9721354		Kolsto Ural/Ural Ring
UR-88310				Groupe Aero Pipe
UR-BWF*		0711352	ex RA-88258	Ukraine Bank
UR-BWH		9640951	ex RA-88238	Concern Regions of Ukraine
UR-FRU				SUMY MV Frunze Sciene & Production Association
UR-LEV		9720154	ex LY-AAA	
UR-XYZ		9610496	ex RA-88155	
UR-88309				Interpipe Group
YU-AKT/71503*		9222020		Federal Air Traffic Control Agency (calibrator)
YU-AKV/71505*		9630849		Federal Air Traffic Control Agency (calibrator)
3C-CGE*		9821557	ex 3C-MNB	Government of Equatorial Guines
4K-87218		9440937	ex HA-LJC	ECT Trade Co
4L-MGC				
5R-MUA*		9840859		Armee de l'Air Malgache
5R-MUB*		9940760		Armee de l'Air Malgache
9L-LEE	(K)			

Yakovlev Yak-42

B-2757	(D)	4520423403018		Saratov Factory (stored)
B-2758	(D)	4520424404018		Saratov Factory (stored)
B-4012	(D)	4520424914375		Chinese Navy
B-4013	(D)	4520424914..?		Chinese Navy
RA-42423	(D)	4520424216606		Yakovlev Design Bureau (City Star 100 demonstrator)
RA-42533				Krivoy Rog Tech School

IATA TWO LETTER DESIGNATORS

1I	Executive Jet Aviation (N) [c]
1I	Novair Airlines (SE)
1I	Pegasus Airlines (TC)
2B	AeroCondor (CS)
2C	SNCF (F) [train]
2D	AeroVIP (LV)
2E	Smokey Bay Air (N)
2F	Frontier Flying Service (N)
2G	Northwest Seaplanes (N)
2J	Air Burkina (XT)
2K	Aerogal (HC)
2L	Lineas Aereas Entre Rios (LV)
2M	Moldavian Airlines (ER)
2N	Yuzhmashavia (UR)
2P	Air Philippines (RP)
2R	VIA Rail Canada (C) [train]
2S	Island Express (N)
2U	Sunaire Express (N)
2U	Atlas International (TC)
2U	Air Guinee Express (3X)
2V	Amtrak (N) [train]
2W	Welcome Air (OE)
2Y	Air Andaman (HS)
2Z	Air Plus Comet (EC)
2Z	Chang An Airlines (B)
3A	Alliance Airlines (N)
3B	AVIOR Express (YV)
3B	Burkina Airlines (XT)
3C	Corporate Airlines (N)
3D	Air People International (HS)
3D	Denim Air (PH)
3F	Pacific Airways (N) [c]
3G	Atlant-Soyuz Airlines (RA)
3H	Air Inuit (C)
3H	Hapag-Lloyd Express (D)
3J	Zip Air (C)
3K	Everts Air Cargo (N)
3K	Everts Air Alaska (N)
3L	Intersky (OE)
3M	Gulfstream International (N)
3N	Air Urga (UR)
3P	Thai Pacific Airlines (HS)
3P	Inter Tropical Aviation (PZ)
3R	Avia Air (P4)
3S	Air Antilles Express (F-O)
3S	TAPO Avia (UK)
3S	Air Guyane (F-O)
3T	Contactair (D)
3T	Turanair (4K)
3U	Air Cargo Carriers (N)
3U	Sichuan Airlines (B)
3U	Chanchangi Airlines (5N)
3V	TNT Airways (OO)
3W	Wanair (F-O)
3W	Woodgate Executive Air Charter (G)
3X	Japan Air Commuter (JA)
3Z	Necon Air (9N)
4A	FS Air Service (N)
4B	Olson Air Service (N)
4C	AIRES (HK)
4C	Tashkent Aircraft Production (UR) [prod]
4D	Air Sinai (SU)
4E	Tanana Air Service (N)
4F	Air City (D)
4G	Shenzen Airlines (B)
4G	Gazpromavia (RA)
4H	Fly Linhas Aereas (PP)
4J	Nationwide Airlines (9J)
4K	Kenn Borek Air (C)
4L	Deltacraft (OY)
4L	Air Astana (UN)
4M	LAN Dominicana (HI)
4N	Air North (C)
4O	Ocean Airlines (D6)
4P	Business Aviation (9Q)
4Q	Anderson Aviation (N)
4R	Hamburg International (D)
4S	Sol Air (HR)
4T	Belair (HB)
4U	TAVAJ (PT)
4U	Germanwings (D)
4V	Varig Log (PP)
4W	Warbelow's Air Ventures (N)
4Y	Flight Alaska (N)
4Z	South African Airlink (ZS)
5A	Alpine Air (N)
5B	Euro-Asia Air (UN)
5C	Cargo Airlines (4X)
5C	Air Tahoma (N)
5D	Aerolittoral (XA)
5D	DutchBird (PH)
5E	Equaflight Services (TN)
5F	Arctic Circle Air Service (N)
5H	Star Air (PK)
5J	Cebu Pacific Air (RP)
5K	Odessa Air (UR)
5L	AeroSur (CP)
5M	Sibaviatrans (RA)
5N	Arkhangelskie Linii (RA)
5N	North Cariboo Air (C)
5P	SkyEurope Airlines (HA)
5P	PENTA (PT)
5Q	Keen Airways (G)
5R	Custom Air Transport (N)
5R	Karthago Airlines (TS)
5S	Sapair (HI)
5T	Canadian North (C)
5U	LADE (LV)
5V	Lvov Airlines (UR)
5W	Astraeus Airlines (G)
5X	United Parcel Service (N)
5Y	Atlas Air (N)
5Y	Isle of Scilly Airbus (G)
5Z	Air Freight Express (G)
5Z	Bismillah Airlines (S2)
6A	Aviacsa (XA)
6B	Britannia Airways Sweden (SE)
6C	Cape Smythe Air Service (N)
6D	Pelita Air (PK)
6E	City Air (D)
6G	Air Wales (G)
6H	Israir (4X)
6J	Sky Net Asia Airlines (JA)
6J	Skyservice Airlines (C)
6K	Asian Spirit (RP)
6K	Inter Express (TC)
6L	Aklak Air (C)
6N	Aerosucre (HK)
6N	Air Emilia (I) [c]
6P	Clubair Sixgo (I)
6P	Palau Trans Pacific Airlines (T-8A)
6Q	Slovak Airlines (OM)
6R	AeroUnion (XA)
6R	Georgian Airlines (4L)
6S	Kato Airlines (LN)
6T	Almaty Avia Cargo (UN)
6T	Air Mandalay (XY)
6U	Air Ukraine (UR)
6V	Air Vegas (N)
6V	Lignes Aeriennes Congolaises (9Q)
6W	Saravia (RA)
6X	Belgian Air Force (OO) [m]
6Y	LAT Charter (YL)
6Z	Panavia (HP)
6Z	Ukrainian Cargo Airlines (UR)
7A	Afric'Air Charters (TY)
7B	Kras Air (RA)
7C	Columbia Pacific Airlines (N) [c]
7C	Coyne Airways (G)
7D	Donbass Aero (UR)
7E	Aeroline (D)
7F	First Air (C)
7G	Bellair (N)
7G	MK Air Cargo (9G)
7H	ERA Helicopters (N)
7H	Jet Alaska (N)
7J	Skagway Air Service (N)
7J	Tajikistan Airlines (EY)

7K	Kogalymavia (RA)	AG	Air Contractors (EI)
7L	Aero Caribbean (CU)	AH	Air Algerie (7T)
7L	Sun d'Or International Airlines (4X)	AI	Air India (VT)
7M	Tyumen Airlines (RA)	AJ	Aero Contractors (5N)
7N	Inland Aviation Services (N)	AK	Air Asia (9M)
7P	Batavia Air (PK)	AL	Midwest Connect (N)
7Q	Air Libya Tibesti (5A)	AL	Trans Avia Export Cargo Airlines (EW)
7S	Region Air (9V)	AM	Aeromexico (XA)
7S	Arctic Transportation Services (N)	AO	Australian Airlines (VH)
7T	Air Glaciers (HB)	AP	Air One (I)
7T	Trans Am (HC)	AQ	Aloha Airlines (N)
7U	Aviaenergo (RA)	AR	Aerolineas Argentinas (LV)
7W	Aviation Assistance (OY)	AS	Alaska Airlines (N)
7Y	Air Industria (I)	AT	Royal Air Maroc (CN)
7Z	Laker Airways (C6)	AU	Austral LIneas Aereas (LV)
8B	Caribbean Star Airlines (V2-L)	AV	AVIANCA (HK)
8C	ATI-Air Transport International (N)	AW	Dirgantara-Air Service (PK)
8D	Expo Aviation (4R)	AW	Schreiner Airways (PH)
8D	Servant Air (N) [c]	AX	American Connection (N)
8E	Bering Air (N)	AY	Finnair (OH)
8F	Fischer Air (OK)	AZ	Alitalia (I)
8G	Angel Airlines (HS)	B2	Belavia Belarussian Airlines (EW)
8G	Gulf and Caribbean Air (N)	B3	Bellview Airlines (5N)
8J	Komiinteravia (RA)	B4	Bankair (N)
8L	Cargo Plus Aviation (3C)	B4	Bachflug (OE) [c]
8L	Newair Air Service (OY)	B5	Flightline (G)
8M	Myanmar Airways International (XY)	B5	Amadeus Flugdienst (D)
8N	Nordkalottflyg (SE)	B6	jetBlue Airways (N)
8O	West Coast Air (C)	B7	UNI Air (B)
8P	Pacific Coastal Airlines (C)	B8	Botir Avia (EX)
8P	Payam International Air (EP)	B8	Eritrean Airlines (E3)
8Q	Baker Aviation (N)	B9	Air Bangladesh (S2)
8Q	Onur Air (TC)	B9	Iran Air Tours (EP)
8R	Edelweiss Air (HB)	BA	British Airways (G)
8R	TRIP (PP)	BA	British Asia Airways (G)
8T	Air Tindi (C)	BB	Seaborne Airlines (N)
8U	Afriqiyah Airways (5A)	BC	Skymark Airlines (JA)
8V	Wright Air Service (N)	BD	bmi-british midland international (G)
8W	BAX Global (N)	BE	British European (G)
8Y	Air Burundi (9U)	BE	Tavria Mak (UR)
8Z	LASER (YV)	BF	Aero Service (TN)
9A	Visaa Airlines (VT)	BF	Bluebird cargo (TF)
9B	AccessRail (C) [train]	BG	Biman Bangladesh Airlines (S2)
9C	Haiti Caribbean Airlines (HI)	BH	Hawk Air (C)
9C	Wimbi Dira Airways (9Q)	BI	Royal Brunei Airlines (V8)
9D	Aero Continente Dominicana (HI)	BJ	Nouvelair (TS)
9E	Pinnacle Airlines (N)	BL	Pacific Airlines (VN)
9F	Eurostar (G) [train]	BN	Forward Air International (N) [broker]
9H	Ecoair International (7T)	BN	Horizon Airlines (VH)
9H	Dutch Eagle Express (PJ)	BO	Bali Air (PK)
9J	Pacific Island Airways (N)	BO	Bouraq Indonesia Airlines (PK)
9K	Cape Air (N)	BO	Aboitiz Air (RP)
9L	Colgan Air (N)	BP	Air Botswana (A2)
9M	Central Mountain Air (C)	BR	EVA Airways (B)
9N	Trans States Airlines (N)	BS	British International (G)
9N	SATENA (HK)	BT	AirBaltic (YL)
9P	Pelangi Air (9M)	BU	Braathens Airways (LN)
9Q	PB Air (HS)	BV	Blue Panorama (I)
9R	Phuket Airlines (HS)	BW	BWIA West Indies Airways (9Y)
9S	Southern Air (N)	BX	Coast Air (LN)
9T	Transwest Air (C)	BY	Britannia Airways (G)
9U	Air Moldova (ER)	BZ	Keystone Air Service (C)
9V	VIP Avia (UN)	C2	Air Luxor STP (S9)
9V	Atlantis Airways (6V)	C4	Zimex Aviation (HB)
9W	Jet Airways (VT)	C5	Commutair (N)
9X	Transporti Aerei Italiani (I)	C6	Canjet Airlines (C)
9Y	Air Kazakstan (UN)	C7	Rico Linhas Aereos (PP)
A2	Cielos del Peru (OB)	C8	Chicago Express Airlines (N)
A3	Aegean Airlines (SX)	C9	Cirrus Air (D)
A4	Southern Winds (LV)	CA	Air China (B)
A5	Airlinair (F)	CB	Kalitta Charters (N)
A6	Air Alps Aviation (OE	CB	ScotAirways (G)
A7	Air Comet Plus (EC)	CC	Air Atlanta Iceland (TF)
A8	Benin Gulf Air (TZ)	CC	Macair Airlines (VH)
A8	ARPA (ZP)	CD	Alliance Air (VT)
A9	Air Zena Georgian Airlines (4L)	CE	Nationwide Airlines (ZS)
AA	American Airlines (N)	CF	City Airline (SE)
AB	Air Berlin (D)	CG	Airlines of Papua-New Guinea (P2)
AC	Air Canada (C)	CH	Bemidji Airlines (N)
AD	Air Paradise International (PK)	CI	China Airlines (B)
AE	Mandarin Airlines (B)	CK	China Cargo Airlines (B)
AF	Air France (F)	CL	Lufthansa Cityline (D)

CM	COPA Airlines (HP)		EU	Ecuatoriana (HC)
CN	Islands Nationair (P2)		EV	Atlantic Southeast Airlines (N)
CO	Continental Airlines (N)		EW	Eurowings (D)
CO	Continental Express (N)		EX	Eagle Airways (ZK)
CQ	Sunshine Express Airlines (VH)		EX	Air Santo Domingo (HI)
CR	OAG Worldwide (G) [data]		EY	Etihad Airways (A6)
CS	Continental Micronesia (N)		EY	Eagle Air (5V)
CT	Air Sofia (LZ)		EZ	Evergreen International Airlines (N)
CU	Cubana (CU)		EZ	Sun-Air of Scandinavia (OY)
CV	Air Chathams (ZK)		F2	Falcon Air Express (N)
CV	Cargolux Airlines International (LX)		F3	Faso AirAsia (XT)
CW	Air Marshall Islands (V7)		F4	Albarka Air Service (5N)
CX	Cathay Pacific Airways (B)		F5	Cosmic Air (9N)
CY	Cyprus Airways (5B)		F6	CNAC-Zheijang Airlines (B)
D2	Severstal (RA)		F6	First Air (C)
D3	Daallo Airlines (J2)		F6	First Cambodian Airlines (XU)
D4	Alidaunia (I)		F7	Flamingo Airways (5Y)
D5	DHL Aero Express (HP)		F7	Volare Aviation Enterprise (UR)
D6	Inter-Air Airlines (ZS)		F8	Freedom Airlines (N)
D8	Djibouti Airlines (J2)		F9	Frontier Airlines (N)
D9	Aeroflot-Don Airlines (RA)		FA	Safair (ZS)
DB	Brit'air (F)		FA	FreshAer Airlines (EI)
DC	Golden Air (SE)		FB	Bulgaria Air (LZ)
DE	Condor Flug (D)		FC	Falcon Express Cargo Airlines (A6)
DF	Aerolineas Baleares (EC)		FC	FinnComm Airlines (OH)
DG	SEAir Asian Airlines (RP)		FD	Thai AirAsia (HS)
DH	Atlantic Coast Airlines (N)		FG	Ariana Afghan Airlines (YA)
DI	Deutsche BA (D)		FH	Futura International (EC)
DJ	Virgin Blue (VH)		FI	Icelandair (TF)
DK	MyTravel Airways (OY)		FJ	Air Pacific (DQ)
DL	Delta Air Lines (N)		FK	Keewatin Air (C)
DM	Maersk Air (OY)		FK	Africa West (5V)
DN	VASO Airlines (RA)		FL	Airtran Airways (N)
DN	Air Deccan (VT)		FM	Shanghai Airlines (B)
DO	Air Vallee (I)		FN	Regional Air Lines (CN)
DP	First Choice Airways (G)		FO	Airlines of Tasmania (VH)
DQ	Coastal Air Transport (N)		FP	TAG Aviation (HB) [c]
DR	Air Link (VH)		FP	Freedom Air (N)
DS	easyJet Switzerland (HB)		FQ	Thomas Cook Airlines (OO)
DT	TAAG Angola Airlines (D2)		FQ-	Brindabella Airlines (VH)
DU	Hemus Air (LZ)		FR	Ryanair (EI)
DV	Lufttaxi Flug (D)		FS	MAF (VH)
DV	SCAT (UN)		FS	Staf Carga (LV)
DW	Aero Charter Ukraine (UR)		FT	Siam Reap Air (XU)
DX	Danish Air Transport (OY)		FU	Air Littoral (F)
DY	Norwegian Air Shuttles (LN)		FV	Pulkovo Airlines (RA)
DZ	Transcaraibes Air International (F-O)		FW	Fair Inc (JA)
E3	Domodedeovo Airlines (RA)		FX	Corporate Airlines Canberra (VH)
E4	Aero Asia International (AP)		FX	FedEx (N)
E5	Samara Airlines (RA)		FY	Northwest Regional (N)
E6	Aviaexpresscruise (RA)		FZ	Alisea (I)
E6	Grizoldubova Air (RA)		FZ	Air Facilities (VH)
E7	European Aviation (G)		G2	Avirex (TR)
E7	Estafeta Carga Aerea (XA)		G2	Dobrolet Airlines (RA)
E8	Alpi Eagles (I)		G3	GOL Transporte Aereos (PP))
E9	AJT Air International (RA)		G4	Allegiant Airlines (N)
E9	Boston-Maine Airways (N)		G5	Enkor (RA)
EA	European Air Express (D)		G6	Guinea Bissau Airlines (J5)
EC	Heli-Inter (F) [c]		G7	Gandalf Airlines (I)
EC	Avialeasing (UK)		G8	Air Service Gabon (TR)
ED	Air Blue (AP) [c]		G9	Continental Wings (C5)
EE	Aero Airlines (ES)		G9	Air Arabia (A6)
EF	Far Eastern Air Transport (B)		GA	Garuda Indonesia (PK)
EG	Japan Asia Airways (JA)		GB	ABX Air (N)
EH	SAETA (HK)		GB	Great Barrier Airlines (ZK)
EH	Air Nippon Network (JA)		GC	Gambia International Airways (C5)
EI	Aer Lingus - Irish International Airlines (EI)		GD	Air Alpha Greenland (OY)
EJ	New England Airlines (N)		GE	Transasian Airlines (B)
EK	Emirates (A6)		GF	Gulf Air (A4O)
EL	Air Nippon (JA)		GF	Gulf Helicopters (A7)
EM	Western Airlines (VH)		GH	Ghana Airways (9G)
EM	Empire Airlines (N)		GI	Itek Air (EX)
EM	Aero Benin (TY)		GJ	Eurofly (I)
EN	Air Dolomiti (I)		GL	Air Greenland (OY)
EO	Hewa Bora Airways (9Q)		GL	Miami Air International (N)
EO	Express One International (N)		GM	Air Slovakia (OM)
EP	Iran Aseman Airlines (EP)		GN	Air Gabon (TR)
EQ	TAME (HC)		GO	Go Fly (G)
ER	AStar Air Cargo (N)		GP	Gestair (EC) [c]
ES	DHL International (A9C)		GQ	Big Sky Airlines (N)
ES	TACA Peru (OB)		GR	Aurigny Air Services (G)
ET	Ethiopian Airlines (ET)		GR	Gemini Air Cargo (N)

GS	Grant Aviation (N)	JL	Japan Air Lines (JA)
GT	GB Airways (G)	JM	Air Jamaica (6Y)
GU	Aviateca - Aerolineas de Guatemala (TG)	JN	Excel Airways (G)
GV	Trans Gulf Express (A6) [c]	JO	JALways (JA)
GW	Kuban Airlines (RA)	JP	Adria Airways (S5)
GX	JetMagic (EI)	JQ	Air Jamaica Express (6Y)
GX	Pacificair (RP)	JR	Aero California (XA)
GZ	Air Rarotonga (ZK)	JS	Air Koryo (P)
H2	Sky Airline (CC)	JT	Lion Airlines (PK)
H3	Harbour Air (C)	JT	Transair (VH)
H5	Mavial (RA)	JU	JAT Airways (YU)
H6	Hageland Aviation Services (N)	JV	Bearskin Lake Air Service (C)
H7	Eagle Aviation (5X)	JW	Arrow Air (N)
H9	Air d'Ayiti (HH)	JX	Nice Helicopters (F) [c]
HA	Hawaiian Airlines (N)	JY	Interisland Airways (VQ-T)
HB	Homer Air (N)	JZ	Skyways Express (SE)
HC	Aero Tropics/Lip Air (VH)	K1	Venescar (YV)
HD	Air Do (JA)	K2	Eurolot (SP)
HE	LGW (D)	K2	Kyrghyzstan Airlines (EY)
HF	Hapag-Lloyd (D)	K5	Wings of Alaska (N)
HG	NIKI (OE)	K7	Yakutia Avia (RA)
HH	Islandsflug (TF)	K7	Arizona Express Airlines (N)
HI	Papillon Airways (N)	K8	Dutch Caribbean (PJ)
HJ	Asian Express Airlines (VH)	K9	Krylo Air (RA)
HJ	Swedeways Airlines (SE)	K9	Skyward Aviation (C)
HJ	Hellenic Star Airways (SX)	KA	Dragonair (B-H)
HK	Four Star Air Cargo (N)	KB	Druk Air (A5)
HK	Yangon Airlines (XY)	KC	TransAtlantic Airlines (N) [c]
HM	Air Seychelles (S7)	KD	Kaliningrad Avia (RA)
HO	Antinea Airlines (7T)	KE	Korean Air (HL)
HP	America West Airlines (N)	KF	Blue I (OH)
HQ	HMY Airlines (C)	KG	King Island Airlines (VH)
HR	Hahn Airlines (D)	KG	IAACA (YV)
HS	Direktfly (SE)	KJ	British Mediterranean Airways (G)
HT	Aeromist Kharkiv (UR)	KL	KLM - Royal Dutch Airlines (PH)
HU	Shanxi Aviation (B)	KM	Air Malta (9H)
HV	Transavia Airlines (PH)	KN	Maroomba Air Services (VH)
HW	North-Wright Airways (C)	KO	Alaska Central Express (N)
HX	Trans North Aviation (N)	KQ	Kenya Airways (5Y)
HY	Uzbekistan Airways (UK)	KR	Kitty Hawk Air Cargo (N)
HZ	SAT-Sakhalinske Aviatrossy (RA)	KS	Peninsula Airways (N)
I9	Indigo Airlines (N) [c]	KT	Kampuchea Airlines (XU)
IA	Iraqi Airways (YI)	KU	Kuwait Airways (9K)
IB	Iberia Lineas Aereas de España (EC)	KV	KMV - Kavkaskie Mineralnye Vody (RA)
IC	Indian Airlines (VT)	KW	KAS Air Company (EX)
ID	Air Normandie (F)	KW	Kelowna Flightcraft Air Charter (C)
ID	Interlink Airlines (ZS)	KX	Cayman Airways (VR-C)
IE	Solomons (H4)	KY	Air Sao Tome e Principe (S9)
IF	Italy First (I)	KZ	Nippon Cargo Airlines (JA)
IF	Islas Airways (EC)	L1	Kalitta Air (N)
IG	Meridiana (I)	L2	Lynden Air Cargo (N)
IH	Falcon Aviation (SE)	L3	DHL de Guatemala (TG)
II	IBC Airways (N)	L4	Lauda Air SpA (I)
IK	Imair (4K)	L4	Livingston (I)
IM	Menajet (A7)	L5	CHC-Helikopter Service (LN)
IN	Macedonian Air Transport (Z3)	L6	TbilAviensheni (4L)
IO	Indonesian Airlines (PK)	L7	Laoagi International Airways (RP)
IP	Atyrau Airlines (UN)	L8	Air Luxor GB (J5)
IQ	Augsburg Airways (D)	LA	LAN - Chile (CC)
IR	Iranair (EP)	LB	LAB - Lloyd Aereo Boliviano (CP)
IS	Island Airlines (N)	LD	Aereotuy (YV)
IU	HeviLift (P2)	LD	Air Hong Kong (B)
IV	Windjet (I)	LE	Helgoland Airlines (D)
IX	Select Air (OE) [c]	LE	Laparkam Airways (8R)
IY	Yemenia (7O)	LF	Nordic AirLink (LN)
IZ	Arkia Israeli Airlines (4X)	LG	Luxair (LX)
J2	Azerbaijan Airlines (4K)	LH	Lufthansa Cargo (D)
J3	Northwestern Air (C)	LH	Lufthansa (D)
J4	Buffalo Airways (N)	LI	LIAT - The Caribbean Airline (V2)
J5	Alaska Seaplane Servcies (N) [c]	LJ	Sierra National Airlines (9L)
J6	Larry's Flying Services (N)	LK	Air Luxor (CS)
J6	AVCOM (RA) [c]	LK	Goldfields Air Services (VH)
J7	Centrre Avia (RA)	LL	Allegro Air (XA)
J8	Berjaya Air Chater (9M)	LN	Libyan Arab Airlines (5A)
JB	Helijet International Airways (C)	LO	LOT - Polski Linie Lotnicze (SP)
JC	JAL Express (JA)	LP	LAN Peru (OB)
JD	Japan Air System (JA)	LQ	Air Astana (UN)
JF	LAB Flying Service (N)	LQ	Air Guinea Cargo (3C)
JH	Harlequin Air (JA)	LR	LACSA (TI)
JH	Nordeste Linhas Aereas Regionais (PT)	LS	Channel Express/Jet 2 (G)
JJ	TAM Linhas Aereas (PT)	LT	LTU International Airways (D)
JK	Spanair (EC)	LU	Luxor Airlines (SU)

LV	Albanian Airlines (ZA)	OE	Asia Overnight Express (RP)
LW	Pacific Wings (N)	OF	Air Finland (OH)
LX	Swiss International Airlines (HB)	OH	Comair (N)
LY	El Al Israel Airlines (4X)	OI	Aspiring Air (ZK)
M2	Mahfooz Aviation (C5)	OK	CSA Czech Airlines (OK)
M3	ABSA Cargo (PP)	OL	OLT - Ostfriesische Lufttransport (D)
M4	Macedonian Airlines (Z3)	OM	MIAT (JU)
M5	Kenmore Air (N)	ON	Air Nauru (C2)
M6	Amerijet International (N)	OO	Skywest Airlines (N)
M7	Superior Aviation Services (5Y)	OP	Chalks Ocean Airways (N)
M7	Tropical Airways d'Haiti (HH)	OQ	Queen Air (HI)
M9	Motor Sich (UR)	OQ	Sunrise Airlines (N)
MA	Malev (HA)	OR	Crimea Airlines (UR)
MB	Execaire (C) [c]	OS	Austrian Airlines (OE)
MB	MNG Airlines (TC)	OT	Aeropelican Air Services (VH)
MC	USAF Air Mobility Command (N) [m]	OU	Croatia Airlines (9A)
MD	Air Madagascar (5R)	OV	Estonian Air (ES)
ME	MEA - Middle East Airlines (OD)	OX	Orient Thai Airlines (HS)
MF	Xiamen Airlines (B)	OY	Omni Air Express (N) [c]
MG	Champion Air (N)	OZ	Asiana Airlines (HL)
MG	Djibouti Airlines (J2)	P2	UTAir (RA)
MH	Malaysia Airlines (9M)	P2	Panair (I)
MI	Silkair (9V)	P3	Phoenix Aviation (EX)
MK	Air Mauritius (3B)	P3	Premier Trans Air (N) [c]
ML	Trans Attico (N)	P4	Aerolineas Sosa (HR)
ML	Asia Pacific Airlines (N)	P5	Aerorepublica Colombia (HK)
MM	EuroAtlantic Airways (CS)	P6	Trans-Air (N)
MM	SAM (HK)	P7	East Line Express (RA)
MN	Comair (ZS)	P8	Pantanal (PT)
MO	Amiri Flight (A7) [c]	PB	Provincial Airlines (C)
MO	Calm Air International (C)	PC	Air Fiji (DQ)
MP	Martinair Holland (PH)	PC	Continental Airways (RA)
MQ	American Eagle Airlines (N)	PD	Pluto Airlines (A6) [c]
MR	Air Mauritanie (5T)	PE	Air Europe Italy (I)
MS	Egyptair (SU)	PF	Palestine Airlines (SU)
MT	Great Western Aviation (VH) [c]	PG	Bangkok Airways (HS)
MT	Thomas Cook Airlines (G)	PH	Polynesian Airlines (5W)
MU	China Eastern Airlines (B)	PI	Sun Airlines (DQ)
MV	Armenian International Airlines (EK)	PJ	Air St Pierre (F-O)
MW	Maya Island Air (V3)	PK	Pakistan International Airlines (AP)
MX	Mexicana (XA)	PL	AirStars (RA)
MY	Masair Cargo (XA)	PM	Tropic Air Commuter (V3)
MY	Midwest Airlines (SU)	PN	Pan Am (N)
MZ	Merpati Nusantara Airlines (PK)	PO	Polar Air Cargo (N)
N2	Aerolineas Internacionales (XA)	PP	Jet Aviation Business Jets (HB) [c]
N3	Omskavia (RA)	PQ	PanAfrican Airways (TU)
N4	Minerva Airlines (I)	PQ	Tropical International Airways (V4)
N5	Kyrgyz International Airlines (EX)	PQ	PTL Luftfahrtunternehmen (D)
N6	Aero Continente (OB)	PR	Philippine Airlines (RP)
N7	LagunAir (EC)	PS	Ukraine International Airlines (UR)
N9	North Coast Aviation (P2)	PT	Capital Cargo International (N)
NA	North American Airlines (N)	PT	West Air Sweden (SE)
NB	Sterling European Airlines (OY)	PU	PLUNA (CX)
NC	National Jet Systems (VH)	PV	St Barth Commuter (F-O)
NC	Norfolk Jet Express (VH)	PW	Precisionair (5H)
NC	Northern Air Cargo (N)	PX	Air Niugini (P2)
ND	Airlink (P2)	PY	Surinam Airways (PZ)
NE	Sky Europe Airlines (OM)	PZ	TAM Paraguay (ZP)
NF	Air Vanuatu (YJ)	Q1	Expo Aviation (4R)
NG	Lauda Air (OE)	Q2	Island Aviation Services (8Q)
NH	All Nippon Airways (JA)	Q3	Zambian Airways (9J)
NI	Portugalia (CS)	Q4	Swazi Express Airways (3D)
NK	Spirit Airlines (N)	Q5	Forty Mile Air (40 Mile Air) (N)
NL	Shaheen Air International (AP)	Q6	Aero Condor (OB)
NM	Mount Cook Airline (ZK)	Q7	Sobelair (OO)
NO	Neos (I)	Q8	Trans Air Congo (TN)
NP	Skytrans (VH)	QA	Aerocaribe (XA)
NQ	Air Japan (JA)	QA	Afrinat International (C5)
NR	Pamir Air (YA)	QD	Aerovip (CX)
NS	Silk Route Airways (4L)	QE	Crossair Europe (F)
NT	Binter Canarias (EC)	QF	QantasLink (VH)
NU	Japan Transocean Air (JA)	QF	Qantas Airways (VH)
NV	Northern Executive Aviation (G) [c]	QI	Cimber Air (OY)
NV	Nakanihon Airlines (JA)	QJ	Latpass Airlines (YL)
NW	Northwest Airlines (N)	QK	Jazz Air (C)
NW	Northwest Airlink (N)	QL	Serendip Express (4R)
NX	Air Macau (B-M)	QN	Air Armenia (EK)
NY	Air Iceland (TF)	QM	Air Malawi (7Q)
NZ	Air New Zealand (ZK)	QN	Air Armenia (ER)
OA	Olympic Airways (SX)	QO	Aeromexpress Cargo (XA)
OB	Astrakan Airlines (RA)	QO	Origin Pacific Airways (ZK)
OC	Omni (CS)	QP	Airkenya (5Y)

QP	Regional Air (5Y)	T7	Twin Jet (F)
QQ	Alliance Airlines (VH)	T8	STA-Trans African Airlines (TZ)
QR	Qatar Airways (A7)	T9	Transmeridian Airways (N)
QS	Travel Service Airline (OK)	TA	TACA International Airlines (YS)
QT	TAMPA Airlines (HK)	TC	Air Tanzania (5H)
QT	Regional Pacific Airways (P2)	TE	Lithuanian Airlines (LY)
QV	Lao Aviation (RDPL)	TF	Malmo Aviation (SE)
QX	Horizon Airlines (N)	TG	Thai Airways International (HS)
QY	European Air Transport (OO)	TH	British Airways CitiExpress (G)
R2	Orenburg Avia (RA)	TH	Transmile Air Services (9M)
R3	Armenian Airlines (EK)	TI	Tol Air Services (N)
R4	Russia State Transport Co (RA)	TJ	TANS (OB)
R5	Malta Air Charter (9H)	TK	THY - Turkish Airlines (TC)
R7	ASERCA (YV)	TL	Airnorth Regional (VH)
R8	Royal Aruban Airlines (P4)	TL	TMA Cargo (OD)
R8	Kyrgystan Airlines (EX)	TM	LAM - Linhas aereas de Mocambique (C9)
R9	Village Aviation (N)	TN	Air Tahiti Nui (F-O)
R9	Camai Air	TO	President Airlines (XU)
RA	Royal Nepal Airlines (9N)	TP	Air Portugal (CS)
RB	Syrianair (YK)	TQ	Tandem Aero (ER)
RC	Atlantic Airways (OY)	TS	Air Transat (C)
RD	Ryan International (N)	TT	Air Lithuania (LY)
RE	Aer Arann (EI)	TU	Tunis Air (TS)
RF	Florida West International Airlines (N)	TV	Virgin Express (OO)
RG	VARIG (PP)	TX	Air Caraibes (F-O)
RH	RPX Airlines (PK)	TY	Air Caledonie (F-O)
RI	Mandala Airlines (PK)	TY	Iberworld (EC)
RJ	Royal Jordanian (JY)	TZ	ATA Airlines (N)
RL	Royal Phnom Penh Airways (XU)	UI	San Juan Aviation (N) [c]
RN	Euralair International (F)	U2	easyJet Airlines (G)
RO	TAROM (YR)	U5	International Business Air (SE)
RP	Chautauqua Airlines (N)	U5	USA 3000 (N)
RQ	Kam-Air (YA)	U6	Ural Airlines (RA)
RR	Royal Air Force (G) [m]	U7	USA Jet Airlines (N)
RS	Oman Royal Flight (A4O) [c]	U7	Northern Dene Airwaysr (C)
RS	Aerofreight Airlines (RA)	U8	Armavia (ER)
RS	Intercontinental de Aviacion (HK)	U9	Tatarstan Air (RA)
RT	Airlines of South Australia (VH)	UA	United Airlines (N)
RU	Skyking Airlines (VQ-T)	UB	Myanma Airways (XY)
RV	Redair (C5)	UD	Hex'Air (F)
RY	European Executive Express (SE)	UF	UM Airlines (UR)
RZ	SANSA (TI)	UG	Tuninter (TS)
S2	Air Sahara (VT)	UI	EuroCypria (5B)
S3	Santa Barbara Airlines (YV)	UI	Alaska Seaplane Service (N) [c]
S4	SATA International (CS)	UJ	Montair Aviation (C)
S5	Shuttle America (N)	UK	Buzz (G)
S7	Sibir Airlines (RA)	UL	SriLankan (4R)
S8	AirEst (ES)	UM	Air Zimbabwe (Z)
S8	Shovkoviy Shiyah (UR)	UN	Transaero (RA)
S8	Charlan Air Charter (ZS)	UP	Bahamasair (C6)
S9	East African Safari Air (5Y)	UQ	O'Connor Airlines (VH)
SA	South African Airways (ZS)	UR	Ukraine National Airlines (UR)
SB	Air Caledonie International (F-O)	US	Allegheny Airlines (N)
SC	Shandong Airlines (B)	US	US Airways (N)
SD	Sudan Airways (ST)	US	US Airways Express (N)
SE	Star Airlines (F)	UU	Air Austral (F-O)
SE	Samoa Air (N)	UV	Helisureste (EC)
SF	Tassili Airlines (7T)	UW	Universal Airlines (8R)
SG	JetsGo (C)	UX	Air Europa (EC)
SI	Sierra Pacific Airlines (N)	UX	Air Europa Express (EC)
SI	Skynet Airlines (EI)	UY	Cameroon Airlines (TJ)
SJ	Aviandina (OB)	UZ	Tesis (RA)
SJ	Freedom Air International (ZK)	UZ	Buraq Air Transport (5A)
SK	Scandinavian Airlines System (LN/OY/SE)	V1	Africa West (5V)
SL	Rio-Sul Servicios Aereos Regionais SA (PT)	V2	Karat Air Company (RA)
SM	Sunworld International Airlines (N)	V3	Carpatair (YR)
SM	Swedline Express (SE)	V4	Valair (F) [c]
SN	SN Brussels Airlines (OO)	V5	Royal Aruban Airlines (P4)
SO	Superior Aviation (N)	V6	Air Atlantique (F)
SP	SATA - Air Acores (CS)	V7	Air Senegal International (6V)
SQ	Singapore Airlines (9V)	V8	Air Mikisew (C)
SS	Corsair (F)	V8	Duo Airways (G)
ST	Germania Flug (D)	V8	Atran (RA)
SU	Aeroflot Russian Airlines (RA)	V8	Tapsa Aviation (LV)
SV	Saudi Arabian Airlines (HZ)	V8	Iliamna Air Taxi (N)
SW	Air Namibia (V5)	V9	Bashkirian Airlines (RA)
SY	Sun Country Airlines (N)	VA	Volare Airlines (I)
T2	Thai Air Cargo (HS)	VB	Maersk Air (G)
T3	Eastern Airways (G)	VF	Nevis Express (V4)
T4	Hellas Jet (SX)	VG	VLM Airlines (OO)
T5	Turkmenistan Airlines (EZ)	VH	ALAS de Venezuela (YV)
T6	Tavria Aviakompania (UR)	VI	Vieques Air Link (N)

1135

VI	Volga-Dnepr Airlines (RA)		Y8	Yangtze River Express (b)
VJ	Jatayu Air (PK)		YB	South African Express Airlines (ZS)
VL	Inter Express Air Charter (C)		YG	South Airlines (RA)
VL	VIA - Bulgarian Airways (LZ)		YH	West Caribbean Airways (HK)
VM	Viaggio Air (LZ)		YI	Air Sunshine (N)
VN	Vietnam Airlines (VN)		YJ	National Airways (ZS)
VO	Tyrolean Airways (OE)		YK	KTHY Cyprus Turkish Airlines (TC)
VP	VASP (PP)		YL	Executive Airlines (East Hampton) (N)
VQ	Vintage Props & Jets (N) [c]		YL	Yamal Airlines (RA)
VR	TACV (D4)		YM	Montenegro Airlines (YU)
VS	Virgin Atlantic Airways (G)		YN	Air Creebec (C)
VT	Air Tahiti (F-O)		YO	Heli Air Monaco (3A)
VU	Air Ivoire (TU)		YP	Aero Lloyd (D)
VV	Aerosvit Airlines (UR)		YQ	Helikopterservice Euro Air (SE)
VW	Aeromar Airlines (XA)		YR	Scenic Airlines (N)
VZ	MyTravel Airways (G)		YS	Regional Airlines (F)
VZ	MyTravel Lite (G)		YV	Mesa Airlines (N)
W2	Canada Western Airlines (C)		YW	Air Nostrum (EC)
W2	Southwest Air (P2)		YX	Midwest Airlines (N)
W4	Aero Services Executive (F) [c]		YZ	TACA Ecuador (HC)
W4	M&N Aviation (N)		Z2	Zhongyuan Airlines (B)
W5	Mahan Air (EP)		Z2	Styrian Spirit (OE)
W7	Sayakhat (UN)		Z3	Pro Mech Air (N)
W8	CargoJet Airways (C)		Z5	GMG Airlines (S2)
W9	British North West Airlines (G)		Z6	Dnieproavia (UR)
WA	KLM Cityhopper (PH)		Z7	ADC Airlines (5N)
WB	RwandAir Express (9XR)		Z8	Mali Airways (TZ)
WC	Islena Airlines (HR)		ZA	Astair (RA)
WD	DAS Air Cargo (5X)		ZB	Monarch Airlines (G)
WE	Centurion Air Cargo (N)		ZD	Flying Dandy Airlines (LZ)
WF	Wideroe's Flyveselskap (LN)		ZE	Azteca Airlines (XA)
WG	Wasaya Airways (C)		ZF	Atlantic Airlines (HR)
WI	Tradewinds Airlines (N)		ZG	Air Express Zanzibar (5H)
WJ	Air Labrador (C)		ZH	Shenzen Airlines (B)
WK	American Falcon (LV)		ZI	Aigle Azur
WL	Aeroperlas (HP)		ZK	Great Lakes Airlines (N)
WM	Winair (PJ)		ZL	Rex-Regional Express (VH)
WN	Southwest Airlines (N)		ZN	Air Mediterranee (F)
WO	World Airways (N)		ZN	Air Bourbon (F-O)
WP	Island Air (N)		ZP	Air St Thomas (N)
WQ	Romavia (YR)		ZP	Silk Way Airlines (4K)
WR	Royal Tongan Airlines (A3)		ZQ	Caribbean Sun Airlines (N)
WS	Westjet (C)		ZR	Aviacom Zitotrans (RA)
WT	Nigeria Airways (5N)		ZR	Muk Air (OY)
WU	Tikal Jets (TG)		ZS	AzzurraAir (I)
WV	Swefly (SE)		ZT	Voronezh Avia (RA)
WW	bmi Regional (G)		ZU	Helios Airways (5B)
WW	bmibaby (G)		ZV	Air Midwest (N)
WX	CityJet (EI)		ZY	Ada Air (ZA)
WY	Omanair (A4O)			
WZ	West African Airlines (5N)			
X3	HapagLloyd Express (D)			
X4	Vanair (YJ)			
X5	Afrique Airlines (TY)			
X7	Zambia Skyways (9J)			
X8	ICARO Express (HC)			
X9	Khors Air (UR)			
X9	Omni Air International(N)			
XB	IATA (C) [non operator[			
XC	KD Air (C)			
XE	Edelweiss Air (HB)			
XF	Vladivostok Air (RA)			
XG	Cygnes Air (EC)			
XG	Air Mali International (TZ)			
XJ	Mesaba Airlines (N)			
XK	CCM Airlines (F)			
XL	Country Connection Airlines (VH)			
XL	LAN Ecuador (HC)			
XM	Alitalia Express (I)			
XM	Australian air Express (VH)			
XN	Axon Airlines (SX)			
XO	Volar Airlines (EC)			
XQ	Sun Express Air (TC)			
XR	Skywest Airlines (VH)			
XT	KLM exel (PH)			
XU	African Express Airlines (5Y)			
XW	China Xinhua Airlines (B)			
XZ	Air Georgian/Calm Air/Central Mountain Air (C)			
Y2	Africa One (5H)			
Y4	Eagle Aviation (5Y)			
Y6	Cambodia Airlines (XU)			
Y7	Trans Air Benin (TN)			

ICAO THREE LETTER DESIGNATORS

The three-letter codes listed below are those allocated by States (countries) that are members of ICAO [International Civil Aviation Organisation] and checked against several lists available on the inernet.. The call-signs listed in the main section are also taken from this list.

AAB	Abelag Aviation (OO) [c]		AGD	Agderfly (LN) [c]
AAC	Army Air Corp (G) [m]		AGK	TAG Aviation Ukraine (UR) [c]
AAD	Aero Aviation Centre (C) [c]		AGL	Air Angouleme (F) [c]
AAE	Express Air (N) [c]		AGN	Air Gabon (TR)
AAF	Aigle Azur Transports Aeriens (F)		AGO	Angola Air Charter (D2)
AAG	Atlantic Air Lines (G)		AGP	AerFi Group (EI) [lessor]
AAH	Aloha Airlines (N)		AGU	Angara Air (RA)
AAI	Air Aurora (N) [c]		AGV	Air Glaciers (HB)
AAK	Alaska Island Air (N) [c]		AGX	Aviogenex (YU)
AAL	American Airlines (N)		AGZ	Agrolet (OM) [agricultural]
AAM	Aviation Management Corp (N) [c]		AHA	Air Alpha Greenland (OY)
AAQ	Copterline (OH)		AHC	AZAL Cargo (4K)
AAR	Asiana Airlines (HL)		AHE	Airport Heli Basel (HB) [c]
AAV	Astro Air International (RP) [c]		AHF	Aspen Helicopters (N) [c]
AAW	African Airlines (5A)		AHG	Aerochago (HI)
AAY	Allegiant Air (N)		AHH	Airplanes Holdings (EI) [ferry]
ABA	Artem Avia (UR)		AHK	Air Hong Kong (B)
ABD	Air Atlanta Iceland (TF)		AHT	HTA Helicopters (CS)
ABG	Abakan-Avia (RA)		AHU	ABC Air Hungary (HA)
ABH	Aerolineas Baleares (EC)		AHW	Aeromist-Kharkiv (UR)
ABJ	Abaete Linhas Aereas (PT)		AHY	Azerbaijan Airlines (4K)
ABK	Alberta Citylink (C)		AIA	Avies Air (ES)
ABO	APSA (HK)		AIB	Airbus Industrie (F/D)
ABP	ABA Air (OK)		AIC	Air India (VT)
ABR	Air Contractors Ireland (EI)		AIE	Air Inuit (C)
ABV	Antrak Air Ghana (9G)		AIH	Alpine Air Express Chile (CC)
ABX	ABX Air (N)		AIK	African Airlines Intl (5Y)
ABZ	ATA-Brasil (PP)		AIM	Avones y Helicopteros Baleares (EC)
ACA	Air Canada (C)		AIN	African International Airways (3D)
ACD	Academy Airlines (N)		AIP	Alpine Aviation (N)
ACG	Air Partner (G) [c]		AIT	AirEst (ES)
ACH	ACS - Air Charter Service (EL)		AIX	Aircruising Australia (VH)
ACI	AirCalin (F-O)		AIZ	Arkia Israeli Airlines (4X)
ACP	Astral Aviation (5Y) [c]		AJE	Aero Jet Express (XA) [c]
ACQ	Aero Continente (OB)		AJI	Ameristar Jet Charters (N)
ACT	Flightline (N)		AJK	Allied Air (5N)
ADB	Antonov Airlines (UR)		AJM	Air Jamaica (6Y)
ADD	Advanced Air Company (JA)		AJS	Central Charter de Colombia (HK) [c]
ADE	Ada Air (ZA)		AJT	Amerijet International (N)
ADH	Air One (I)		AJU	AirJetSul (CS) [c]
ADI	Audeli Air Express (EC)		AJW	Alpha Jet International (N) [c]
ADJ	Abidjan Air Cargo (TU)		AJX	Air Japan (JA)
ADK	ADC Airlines (5N)		AKF	Gulf Falcon Air Services (5Y)
ADN	Aero-Dienst (D) [c]		AKK	Aklak Air (C)
ADO	Air Do (JA)		AKN	Alkan Air (C)
ADR	Adria Airways (S5)		AKP	Antex-Polus (RA)
ADS	Aviones de Sonora (XA)		AKR	Arctic Air (LN)
ADU	Airdeal (OH) [c]		AKT	Karat Air Company (RA)
ADW	Air Andanam (HS)		AKX	Air Nippon Network (JA)
ADX	Anderson Aviation (N)		AKY	Yak Service (RA)
AEA	Air Europa (EC)		ALG	Air Logistics (N)
AEB	Aero Benin (TY)		ALH	Atlantic Airlines (G)
AED	Aeronord (I) [c]		ALK	SriLankan (4R)
AEE	Aegean Airlines (SX)		ALL	Aliserio (I) [c]
AEF	Aero Lloyd (D)		ALO	Allegheny Airlines (N)
AEJ	Air Express Zanzibar (5H)		ALP	Alpliner (HB) [c]
AEL	Air Europe Italy (I)		ALR	Alaire (EC)
AEN	Air Enterprise (F) [c]		ALU	Air Luxor STP (S9)
AEP	Aerotec (EC) [c]		ALX	Hewa Bora Airways (9Q)
AEQ	AviaExpressCruise (4L)		ALZ	Alta Flights (C)
AER	Alaska Central Express (N)		AMB	Deutsche Rettungsflugwacht-
AEU	Astreaus (G)			German Air Rescue (D)
AEW	AeroSvit Airlines (UR)		AMC	Air Malta (9H)
AFB	American Falcon (LV)		AME	Spanish Air Force (EC) [m]
AFD	Panorama Flight Service (N) [c]		AMF	Ameriflight (N)
AFE	Airfast Indonesia (PK)		AMG	Air Minas (PP)
AFF	Afric'Air Charters (TY)		AMH	Alan Mann Helicopters (G) [c]
AFG	Ariana Afghan Airlines (YA)		AMK	Amerer Air (OE)
AFK	Africa Air Lines (9L)		AML	Air Malawi (7Q)
AFL	Aeroflot Russian Airlines (RA)		AMP	Aerotransporte (OB)
AFO	Aero Empresa Mexicana (XA) [c]		AMS	Air Muskoka (C)
AFP	Forca Aerea Portuguesa (CS) [m]		AMT	ATA Airlines (N)
AFR	Air France (F)		AMU	Air Macau (B-M)
AFW	Afrique Regional Airways (TU)		AMV	AMC Aviation (SU)
AFX	Airfreight Express (G)		AMW	Air Midwest (N)

AMX	Aeromexico (XA)	AVE	AVENSA (YV)
ANA	All Nippon Airways (JA)	AVG	Air Falcon (J2) [c]
ANB	ANT Air Taxi (G) [c]	AVH	Aviser (EC)
ANF	Alpine Aviation (G) [c]	AVJ	Avia Traffic Co (EX)
ANG	Air Niugini (P2)	AVM	Avemex (XA) [c]
ANK	Air Nippon (JA)	AVN	Air Vanuatu (YJ)
ANL	Air Nacoia (D2)	AVO	Avisto (HB) [c]
ANM	Antares Airtransport (D)	AVR	Active Aero Charter (N) [c]
ANO	Airnorth Regional (VH)	AVS	Artac Aviation (EC)
ANP	Anton Air International (7P)	AVT	Asia Avia Megatama (PK)
ANQ	Aerolineas de Antioqua (HK)	AVU	Aviasud Aerotaxi (F) [c]
ANS	Air Nostrum (EC)	AVW	Aviator (SX)
ANT	Air North (C)	AWC	Titan Airways (G)
ANU	Avion Air (C)	AWD	Providence Aviation Services (AP) [c]
ANX	Air Norterra (C)	AWE	America West Airlines (N)
ANZ	Air New Zealand (ZK)	AWH	Air Inter Niger (5U)
AOA	Alcon Servicios Aereos (XA)	AWI	Air Wisconsin (N)
AOC	Avcom (RA) [c]	AWL	Ansett Worldwide (VH) [lsg]
AOD	Aero Vodochody (OK) [c]	AWP	Air Niger International (5U)
AOO	AS Aviakompania (UR)	AWR	Arctic Wings & Rotors (C)
AOP	Aeropiloto (CS) [c]	AWS	Royal Wings (JY)
AOT	Asia Overnight Express (RP)	AWT	Air West (C)
AOV	Aero Vision (F) [c]	AWU	Aeroline (D)
AOW	Air Omega (D)	AWW	Air Wales (G)
APB	Air Atlantique (F)	AXD	Air West Express (ST)
APC	Airpac Air Lines (N)	AXE	Exec-Air (Z)
APG	Air People International (HS)	AXF	Asian Express Airlines (VH)
APN	Air Polonia (SP)	AXG	Avirex (3X)
APO	Aeropro (C)	AXK	African Express Airways (5Y)
APP	Aeroperlas (HP)	AXL	KLM exel (PH)
APR	Air Provence (F)	AXM	Air Asia (9M)
APT	LAP Colombia (HK)	AXQ	Action Airlines ((N) [c]
APW	Fine Air Services (N)	AXU	Abu Dhabi Aviation (A6)
APZ	HydroQuebec (C)	AXX	Macedonian Airlines (Z3)
AQB	Air Service Gabon (TR)	AXY	Axis Airways (F)
AQO	Alcoa Aircraft Operations (N) [c]	AYB	Belgian Army (OO)
AQT	Avioqunitana (XA)	AYM	Airman (EC) [c]
AQU	Airquarius Aviation (ZS)	AYN	Atlantic Airways (YN)
ARB	Avia Air Charter Services (P4)	AYP	Nike (OE)
ARE	AIRES (HK)	AYT	Ayeet Aviation (4X)
ARG	Aerolineas Argentinas (LV)	AYZ	Atlant-Soyuz Airlines (RA)
ARI	Everts Air Fuel (N)	AZA	Alitalia (I)
ARL	Airlec Air Espace (F)	AZE	Arcus Air (D)
ARN	Jazz Air (C)	AZF	Air Zermatt (HB)
ARN	Astra Airlines (HB) [c]	AZI	AzzurraAir (I)
ARN	Avia Service (EK)	AZK	Azal Helikopter Air Company (4K) [c]
ARV	Aravco (G) [c]-	AZL	Africa One Zambia (9J)
ASA	Alaska Airlines (N)	AZQ	Silk Way (4K)
ASB	Air Spray (C)	AZS	Aviacon Zitotrans (RA)
ASD	Air Sinai (SU)	AZT	Azimut (EC) [c]
ASE	AeroStars (RA)	AZV	Azov-Avia (UR)
ASH	Mesa Airlines (N)	AZW	Air Zimbabwe (Z)
ASJ	Air Satellite (C)	AZZ	Azza Air Transport (ST)
ASM	Awesome Flight Services (ZS) [c]	BAC	BAC Leasing (G)
ASN	Air & Sea Transport (RA)	BAE	British Aerospace Corp Flight Ops (G) [c]
ASO	Aero Slovakia (OM) [c]	BAF	Belgian Air Force (OO) [m]
AST	Air Astana (UN)	BAG	dba (D)
ASW	Air Southwest (C)	BAH	Bahrain Amiri Flight (A9C) [c]
ASZ	Astrakhan Airlines (RA)	BAJ	Baker Aviation (N)
ATC	Air Tanzania (5H)	BAL	Britannia Airways (G)
ATG	Aerotrans (UN)	BAN	British Antarctic Survey (VP-F)
ATI	Aero Tropics (VH)	BAP	Trans International Express (N)
ATJ	Air Traffic (D) [c]	BAR	Bradley Air (Charter) Service (C) [c]
ATK	Aerotaca (HK)	BAT	Swissjet (HB) [c]
ATN	Air Transport Intl (N)	BAW	British Airways (G)
ATT	Aer Turas Teoranta (EI)	BAY	Bayon Airlines (XU)
ATU	Atlant Hungary Airlines (HA)	BBA	Bannert Air (OE) [c]
ATV	Avanti-Air (OE) [c]	BBC	Biman Bangladesh A/L (S2)
ATX	Air Taxis (G) [c]	BBD	Bluebird Cargo (TF)
AUA	Austrian Airlines (OE)	BBG	Alisea Airlines (I)
AUB	Augsburg Airways (D)	BBL	IBM Euroflight (F/HB) [c]
AUF	Augusta Air (D)	BBR	Santa Barbara Airlines (YV)
AUH	Abu Dhabi Amiri Flight (A6) [c]	BBZ	Bluebird Aviation (5Y)
AUI	Ukraine Intl Airlines (UR)	BCA	Brasmex (PP)
AUL	Arkhangelskie Linii (RA)	BCF	Bachflug (OE) [c]
AUR	Aurigny Air Services (G)	BCS	European Air Transport (OO)
AUT	Cielos del Sur (LV)	BCY	CityJet (EI)
AUV	Atruvera Aviation Transportation (RA)	BDI	Benair (OY)
AUY	Aerolineas Uruguayas (CX)	BDN	A&AEE Boscombe Down (G) [m]
AUZ	Australian Airlines (VH)	BDS	South Asian Airlines (S2)
AVA	AVIANCA (HK)	BDY	Birdy Airlines (OO)
AVB	Aviation Beauport (G) [c]	BEA	Benair (HB) [c]

BEC	Berkut Avia (UN)
BED	Belgorod Air Enterprise (RA)
BEE	flybe. (G)
BEI	Benair (I) [c]
BEK	Berkhut Air (UN)
BEN	AirNow (N)
BER	Air Berlin (D)
BES	Aero Services Executive (F) [c]
BET	BETA Cargo Airlines (PP)
BEZ	Air St Kitts & Nevis (V4)
BFC	Basler Airlines (N)
BFF	Air Nunavut (C)
BFL	Buffalo Airways (C)
BFR	Burkina Airlines (XT)
BGA	Air Transport Intl (F)
BGD	Air Bangladesh (S2)
BGF	Aviodetachment 28 (LZ) [g]
BGH	BH Air (LZ)
BGI	British Gulf International (EX)
BGL	Benin Gulf Air (TY)
BGM	Bugulma Air Enterprise (RA)
BGS	Bundesgrenzschutz (D) [federal]
BGT	Bergen Air Transport (LN)
BHA	Buddha Air (9N)
BHL	Bristow Helicopters (G)
BHN	Bristow Helicopters (Nigeria) (5N)
BHP	Belair (HB)
BHR	Bighorn Airways (N)
BHS	Bahamasair (C6)
BHV	Spetsavia (RA)
BHY	Bosphorus European Airways (TC)
BIB	Michelin Air Services (F) [c]
BID	Binair (D)
BIE	Air Mediterranee (F)
BIG	Big Island Air (N)
BIH	British International Helicopters (G)
BIL	Billund Air Center (OY) [c]
BKA	Bankair (N)
BKF	BF Lento (OH) [c]
BKN	Khakasia Air (RA)
BKP	Bangkok Airways (HS)
BKS	Aviaexpresscruise (RA)
BKV	Bukovyna (UR)
BLA	All Charter (G) [c]
BLF	Blue I (OH)
BLN	Bali Air (PK)
BLR	Atlantic Coast Airlines (N)
BLS	Bearskin Lake Air Service (C)
BLV	Bellview Airlines (5N)
BLX	Britannia Airways Sweden (SE)
BLY	Starair (EI) [c]
BMA	bmi -british midland international (G)
BMH	Bristow Masayu Helicopters (PK)
BMI	bmibaby (G)
BMJ	Bemidji Airlines (N)
BMK	GST Aero (UN)
BML	Bismillah Airlines (S2)
BMM	Burman Aviation (G) [c]
BMN	Bowman Aviation (N)
BMW	BMW Flugdienst (D) [c]
BMX	Banco de Mexico (XA) [c]
BMY	Bimini Island Air (N)
BNC	Sundance Air (N)
BND	Bond Helicopters (G)
BNG	BN Group (G) [manufacturer]
BNS	Banc One Management Corp (N) [c]
BNX	IAACA (YV)
BOA	Boniair (Z3) [c]
BOB	Bonair (D) [c]
BOD	Bond Air Services (G)
BOE	Boeing Commercial Airplane Group (N)
BOI	Aboitiz Air Transport (RP)
BOL	TAB Airlines (CP)
BOT	Air Botswana (A2)
BOU	Bouraq Indonesia A/L (PK)
BPA	Blue Panorama Airlines (I)
BPS	Budapest Air Services (HA)
BPX	Berkut Aviakompomia (UN)
BRA	Braathens Airways (LN)
BRD	Brock Air Services (C) [c]
BRE	Breeze (UR)
BRG	Bering Air (N)

BRI	Air-Bor (F) [c]
BRK	Bryansk Avia Enterprise (RA)
BRP	Aerobratsk (RA)
BRQ	Buraq Air Transport (5A)
BRT	British Airways CitiExpress (G)
BRU	Belavia Belarussian Airlines (EW)
BRW	Bright Aviation Services (LZ)
BRY	Burundi Avia Air (UN)
BRZ	Samara Airlines (RA)
BSK	Miami Air International (N)
BSL	Bosnia Airlines (T9)
BSP	Global Airways (9Q)
BSR	Guine Bissau Airlines (J5)
BSY	Big Sky Airlines (N)
BTA	ExpressJet Airlines (N)
BTC	Bashkirian Airlines (RA)
BTI	AirBaltic (YL)
BTR	Botik Air (EX)
BTU	Rolls-Royce (G) [c]
BTV	Batavia Air (PK)
BUB	Air Bourbon (F-O)
BUC	Bulgarian Air Charter (LZ)
BUE	Orebro Aviation (SE)
BUN	Burat Airlines (RA)
BUZ	Buzz Stansted (G)
BVN	Baron Aviation Services (N)
BVR	ACM Air Charter (D) [c]
BVT	Berjaya Air Charter (9M)
BWA	BWIA West Indies Airways (9Y)
BWE	CorpJet (N) [c]
BWG	Blue Wings (D)
BXA	Bexair (A9C) [c]
BXH	Bar XH Air (C)
BXL	Bonair exel (PJ)
BXR	Redding Aero Enterprises (N)
BYA	Berry Aviation (N)
BYL	Bylina (RA)
BYR	Berytos Airlines (OD) [c]
BYU	Bayu Indonesia (PK)
BZF	Jet Aviation Business Jets (N) [c]
BZH	Brit'air (F)
CAA	Atlantic Southeast Airlines (N)
CAG	CNAC (B)
CAH	Charlan Air Charter (ZS)
CAL	China Airlines (B)
CAM	Village Aviation (N)
CAP	Capital Airlines (N) [c]
CAT	Copenhagen Air Taxi (OY)
CAV	Calm Air International (C)
CAX	Central Air Express (9Q)
CAW	Comair (ZS)
CAY	Cayman Airways (VR-C)
CBA	UCL (OK) [calibration]
CBC	Caribair (HI)
CBE	Aerocaribe (XA)
CBI	Cabi (OY)
CBK	Cheboksary Air Enterprise (RA)
CBR	Cabair Helicopters (G) [c]
CBS	Columbus Avia (UR)
CBT	Catalina Flying Boats (N)
CCA	Air China (B)
CCF	CCF Manager Airline (D) [c]
CCI	Capital Cargo Interl (N)
CCK	Flight Trac (N) -[survey]
CCL	Continental Cargo A/L (9G)
CCM	CCM Airlines (F)
CCP	Champion Air (N)
CCQ	Capital City Air Carrier (N)
CCW	Coptrade Air Transport (ST)
CCY	Cherry Air (N)
CDA	Aerocardal (CC)
CDF	Vulcan Air (I) - trainer
CDG	Shandong Airlines (B)
CDP	Aero Condor (OB)
CDS	Central Districts A/L (RA)
CDX	Cloudex (OH) [c]
CEA	Corporate Airlines (N) [c]
CEB	Cebu Pacific Air (RP)
CEE	Servicios Aereos Centrales (XA)
CEF	Czech Air Force (OK) [m]
CEG	CEGA Aviation (G) [c]
CEM	Central Mongolian Airways (JU)

CEP	Chipola Aviation (N) [c]		CPB	Corporate Express (C)
CER	Creston Aviation (N) [c]		CPD	Capital Airlines (5Y) [c]
CES	China Eastern Airlines (B)		CPH	Champagne Airlines (F)
CFA	China Flying Dragon Aviation Co (B)		CPI	CAI (I) - [EMS/c]
CFC	Canadian Forces (C) [m]		CPM	CTM- Compagnie Mauritanneene de
CFG	Condor Flugdienst (D)			Transportes (5T)
CFM	ACEF Cargo (CS)		CPN	Caspian Airlines (EP)
CFR	Africa One (9Q)		CPS	Compass International Airways (G)
CFZ	Zhongfei Airlines (B)		CPT	Corporate Air (Billings) (N)
CGI	Rusair (RA)		CPV	Air Corporrate (I) [c]
CGL	Seagle Air (OM)		CRC	Conair Aviation (C)
CGN	Chang An Airlines (B)		CRF	Crimea Airlines (UR)
CGP	Cargo Plus Aviation (3C)		CRJ	Air Cruzal (D2)
CGR	Compagnie Gen. Ripresearee (I) [c]		CRK	CR Airways (B-H)
CGT	CNG Transavia (RA)		CRL	Corsair (F)
CHA	Central Flying Service (N) [c]		CRM	Commander Mexicana (XA) [c]
CHC	CITIC Offshore Helicopters (B)		CRN	Aero Caribbean (CU)
CHF	Chitaavia (RA)		CRQ	Air Creebec (C)
CHH	Hainan Airlines (B)		CSA	CSA Czech Airlines (OK)
CHI	Cougar Helicopter (C)		CSC	Sichuan Airlines (B)
CHJ	Air Chayka International (UR) [c]		CSG	Aero Costa Rica (TI)
CHK	Chalks Ocean Airways (N)		CSH	Shanghai Airlines (B)
CHN	Channel Islands Aviation (N)		CSJ	Castle Aviation (N)
CHO	Chrome Air Services (5N)		CSK	Flightcraft (N) [c]
CHP	Aviacsa (XA)		CSO	Casino Airlines (N)
CHQ	Chautauqua Airlines (N)		CSQ	IBC Airways (N)
CHW	Charter Air (OE)		CSR	CIS-Air International (OK) [c]
CIA	Letecky Urad Slovenskie (OM) [calibration]		CST	Coast Air (LN)
CIB	Condor Berlin (D)		CSY	Shuangyang Avn (B)
CIE	Czech Government Flying Service (OK)		CSZ	Shenzen Airlines (B)
CIG	Sirius Aero (RA)		CTA	AeroCharter (N)
CII	City Fly (I)		CTK	East Midlands Helicopters (G) [c]
CIL	Cecil Air (G) [c]		CTL	Central Air Southwest (N)
CIM	Cimber Air (OY)		CTN	Croatia Airlines (9A)
CIO	Il Ciocco Intl Travel Services (I) [c]		CTO	Cape Air Transport (VH) [c]
CIP	City Air (D)		CTS	Center-South Airlines (RA)
CIR	Arctic Circle Air Service (N)		CTT	Custom Air Charter (N)
CIU	Cielos del Peru (OB)		CTZ	CATA (LV)
CIW	Civair (ZS) [c]		CUA	China United Airlines (B)
CJA	Canjet (C)		CUB	Cubana (CU)
CJC	Colgan Air (N)		CUK	Polo Aviation (G) [c]
CJE	CIP Transports (F) [c]		CUO	Aero Cuahonte (XA)
CJT	CargoJet Canada (C)		CUT	CHC Air (ZS)
CKK	China Cargo Airlines (B)		CVA	Air Chathams (ZK)
CKL	Kokomo Aviation (N) [c]		CVC	Centre Avia (RA)
CKM	Air BKS (EC)		CVF	Dassault Falcon Jet (F) [c]
CKS	Kalitta Air (N)		CVG	Carill Aviation (G) [c]
CLB	Flight Precision (G) [calibration]		CVO	Center Vol (EC) [c]
CLC	Classic Air (HB)		CVU	Grand Canyon Airlines (N)
CLE	Colemill Enterprises (N) [c]		CWA	Canada Western Airlines (C)
CLF	Centreline Air Charter (G) [c]		CWC	Centurion Air Cargo (N)
CLG	Chalair (F)		CWE	Celtic West (G) [c]
CLH	Lufthansa Cityline (D)		CWG	Continental Wings (D6)
CLL	Aerovias Castillo (XA)		CWK	Comores Airlines (D6)
CLS	Challenge Air (D) [c]		CWX	Crow Executive Air (N) [c]
CLU	Air Luxor STP (S9)		CXA	Xiamen Airlines (B)
CLX	Cargolux Airlines Intl (LX)		CXH	China Xinhua Airlines (B)
CME	Prince Edward Air (C)		CXI	Shanxi Airlines (B)
CMI	Continental Micronesia (N)		CXP	Casino Express (N)
CMK	Black Sea Airlines (RA)		CXS	Boston-Maine Airways (N)
CMN	Cimarron Aire (N)		CXT	Coastal Air Transport (N)
CMP	COPA Airlines (HP)		CYO	Air Transport (N)
CMS	Aviation Commercial Aviation (C)		CYP	Cyprus Airways (5B)
CMX	El Caminante Taxi Aereo (XA) [c]		CYR	Ryanair UK (G)
CMY	Cape Smythe Air Service (N)		CYZ	China Postal Airlines (B)
CNB	Cityline Hungary (HA)		DAB	Dassault Aviation (F) [manufacturer]
CND	Aero Continente Dominicana (HI)		DAE	DHL Aero Expresso (HP)
CNI	Aerotaxi (CU)		DAG	Daghestan Airlines (RA)
CNK	Sunwest Airlines (C)		DAH	Air Algerie (7T)
CNS	Centennial Air (C)		DAL	Delta Air Lines (N)
CNT	CNET (F) corporate		DAN	Maersk Air (OY)
CNX	All Canada Express (C)		DAO	Daallo Airlines (J2)
COA	Continental Airlines (N)		DAP	DAP Airways (CC)
COC	Conseta Luftfahrt (D)-[c]		DAR	Danish Army (OY) [m]
COD	Concordavia (UR) [c]		DAV	DANA (5N)
COE	Comtel Air Luftverkehrs (D) [c]		DAW	Duo Airways (G)
COF	Confortair (C)		DAZ	DAS Air Cargo (5Y)
COG	Coage Airlines (3X)		DBJ	Duchess of Jersey (G) [c]
COM	Comair (N)		DBR	DutchBird (PH)
COS	Latvian Air Service (YL)		DCA	Dreamcatcher Airways (G) [c]
COY	Coyne Airways (G)		DCE	Dutch Caribbean Express (PJ)
CPA	Cathay Pacific Airways (B-H)		DCN	Federal Armed Forces (D) [m]

DCS	DaimlerChrysler Aviation (D) [c]
DCT	Directflight (G)
DCV	Discover Air (N)
DCX	DaimlerChrysler Aviation (N) [c]
DDD	Flying Dandy Airlines (LZ)
DEA	Delta AirTaxi (I) [c]
DEC	Deltacraft (OH)
DEI	Ecoair International (7T)
DEL	Carib Aviation (V2)
DER	Deerjet (B) [c]
DFT	Skydrift (G)
DGX	Dasnair (HB) [c]
DHK	DHL Air (G)
DHL	AStar Air Cargo (N)
DHV	DHL Aviation (ZS)
DHX	DHL International (A9C)
DIR	Dirgantara Air Service (PK)
DJA	Antinea Airlines (7T)
DJB	Djibouti Airlines (J2)
DKT	Business Aviation Centre (N)
DLA	Air Dolomiti (I)
DLH	Lufthansa (D)
DLO	Nauta (I) [c]
DMO	Domodedovo Civil Airlines (RA)
DMS	Air Dimension (I) [c]
DND	Eldinder Aviation (ST)
DNM	Denim Air (PH)
DNV	Aeroflot-Don Airlines (RA)
DOB	Dobrolet Airlines (RA)
DOC	Norsk Luftsmbulsnce A/S (LN)
DRA	Dravidian Air Services (G) [c]
DRK	Druk Air (A5)
DRR	Airdirect (OE) [c]
DRT	Darta (F) [c]
DRU	Alrosa-Mirny Air Enterprise (RA)
DRY	Deraya Air Taxi (PK)
DSO	Dassault Falcon Service (F) [c]
DSQ	Dasab Airlines (5N)
DSR	DAS Air Cargo (5X)
DST	AEX Air (N)
DTA	TAAG Angola Airlines (D2)
DTH	Tassili Airlines (7T)
DTN	Data International Aviation (ST)
DUB	Dubai Air Wing (A6) [c]
DUK	Ducair (LX) [c]
DWA	Ducor World Airways (3C)
DYE	Dynamic Airlines (PH) [c]
DYN	Aero Dynamics (N)
EAB	Swiss Eagle (HB) [c]
EAD	Aerocondor (CS)
EAF	European Air Charter (G)
EAI	Elite Air (5V)
EAK	Euro Asia Air (UN)
EAL	European Air Express (SE)
EAM	Embassy Airlines (5N)
EAN	Skypower Express A/W (5N)
EAQ	Eastern Australia A/L (VH)
EAS	Executive Aerospace (ZS)
EAT	Air Transport Europe (OM)
EAW	European Airways (G)
EAX	Eastern Air Executive (G) [c]
EAY	Aer Airlines (ES)
EBA	Bond Aviation (I) [c]
EBF	MSR Flug (D) [c]
EBS	Eli-Fly (I)
EBU	Delta AirElite (N) [c]
ECA	EuroCypria (5B)
ECC	Crossair Europe (F)
ECM	Aerolineas Comerciales (XA) [c]
ECN	Euro Continental Air (EC)
ECQ	EcoAir (5N)
ECT	East Coast Airways (ZS)
ECU	Ecuavia (HC)
ECV	Ecuato Guineana de Aviacion (3C)
EDC	Edinburgh Air Charter (G) [c]
EDJ	Edwards Jet Center (N)
EDO	Elidolomiti (I)
EDW	Edelweiss Air (HB)
EEA	Ecuatoriana (HC)
EEC	Carry Air (F) [c]
EEI	Elisystem (I) [c]
EEJ	Euro Executive Jet (G) [c]
EEU	Eurofly Service (I) [c]
EEV	Ex.Av Executive Aviation (I) [c]
EEX	Avanti Air (D)
EEZ	Eurofly (I)
EFF	Westair Aviation (EI) [c]
EFG	Elifriula (I)
EGF	American Eagle (N)
EGL	Capital Aviation (G) [c]
EGM	Aero Esztergom (HA) [c]
EGN	Eagle Aviation (F)
EGU	Eagle Aviation (5X)
EGY	Egyptian Air Force (SU) [m]
EHD	Alpha Jet international (N) [c]
EIA	Evergreen Intl Airlines (N)
EIN	Aer Lingus - Irish Intl A/L (EI)
EIS	EIS Aircraft (D) [target towing]
EJM	Executive Jet Management (N) [c]
EJO	Execujet MiddleEast (A6) [c]
EJT	Eclipse Aviation (N) [manufacturer]
EKA	Equaflight Service (TN)
ELB	Elilombardia (I) [c]
ELE	WPD Helicopter Unit (G) [survey]
ELG	Alpi Eagles (I)
ELJ	Delta AirElite Business Jets (N) [c]
ELL	Estonian Air (ES)
ELN	Elilario (I)
ELO	EuroLOT (SP)
ELR	El-Rom Airlines (4X)
ELS	Atlantis Airways (6V)
ELT	Elliott Aviation (N) [c]
ELV	TANS (OB)
ELW	Elitorino (I) [c]
ELY	El Al Israel Airlines (4X)
EMD	Ballards Flying Service (N) [c/EMS]
EMI	Premium Air Shuttle (5N)
EMU	EAA Helicopters (B-M)
EMX	Euromanx (G)
ENI	Enimex (ES)
ENK	Enknor (RA)
ENV	Fly Victoria (G) [c]
ENW	AirNor - Aeronaves del Noroeste (EC) [c]
EOL	Airailes (F) [c]
EOS	Eliossola (I) [c]
EPA	Express Airways (D)
EPE	Aeroempresarial (XA) [c]
EPS	Epps Aviation Charter (N)
EQC	Equatorial Cargo (3C)
EQL	Air Sao Tome e Principe (S9)
ERG	Aviaenergo (RA)
ERH	ERA Aviation (N)
ERJ	Eurojet Italy (I) [c]
ERL	Euralair Executive (F) [c]
ERM	AeroMaan (XA) [c]
ERN	Aerolinair (F)
ERO	Sun d'Or Intl Airlines (4X)
ERT	Eritrean Airlines (E3)
ERV	Yerevan Avia (EK)
ESC	El Sol de America (YV)
ESF	Estafeta Carga Aerea (XA)
ESI	Eliservizi Italiani (I) [c]
ESK	Sky Europe Airlines (OM)
ESL	East Line Express (RA)
ESN	EuroSun (TC)
ESX	EuroSkylink (G) [c]
ETC	Trans Attico (ST)
ETH	Ethiopian Airlines (ET)
ETI	Elitaliana (I) [c]
ETS	Flygtransporter I Nykoping (SE) [c]
ETV	European Executive (G) [c]
EUF	Eurojet Airlines (F)
EUH	Euralair Horizons (F)
EUK	Air Atlanta Europe (G)
EUY	EUJet (EI)
EVA	EVA Airways (B)
EVE	Air Evex (D) [c]
EVN	Euraviation (I) [c]
EWG	Eurowings (D)
EXA	Execaire (C) [c]
EXC	European Executive Airlines (SE)
EXH	G5 Executive (HB) [c]
EXJ	Executive Jet Charter (G) [c]
EXL	Sunshine Express Airlines (VH)

EXN	Exin (SP)
EXR	Flight Express (N)
EXS	Channel Express (G)
EXT	Nightexpress (D)
EXV	Expo Aviation (4R)
EXW	EAS Air Lines (5N)
EXY	South African Express A/L (ZS)
EYE	FS Air Services (N)
EZD	Grizoldubova Air (RA)
EZE	Eastern Airways (G)
EZS	easyJet Switzerland (HB)
EZY	easyJet Airlines (G)
FAB	First Air (C)
FAE	FreshAer (EI)
FAF	Force Aerienne Francaise (F) [m]
FAG	Fuerza Aerea Argentina (LV) [m]
FAH	Farnair Hungary (HA)
FAI	Falcon Air (N) [c]
FAJ	Air Fiji (DQ)
FAM	FAASA Aviacion (EC)
FAO	Falcon Air Express (N)
FAS	Afrique Air Affaires (TZ)
FAT	Farnair Switzerland (HB)
FAU	Falcon Airlines (5N)
FAW	Falwell Aviation (N) [c]
FAZ	Flint Air Service (N) [c]
FBM	Airlink Zimbabwe (Z)
FBN	Afrique Airlines (TN)
FCA	First Choice Airlines (G)
FCC	First Cambodia Airlines (XY)
FCI	Air Carriers (N)
FCN	Falcon Aviation (SE)
FCP	Flight Corp (ZK)
FCR	Flying Carpet (OD)
FCV	Nav Air Charter (C)
FDN	Dolphin Air (A6)
FDO	Douanes Francais - French Customs (F)
FDR	Fedair (ZS)
FDX	FedEx (N)
FDY	Gulfstream Air Charter (N) [c]
FEA	Far Eastern Air Transport (B)
FEX	CEC Flightexec [c]
FFD	SFD Stuttgarter Flugdienst (D) [c]
FFF	Freedom Air Services (5N)
FFG	Flugdienst Fehlhaber (D)
FFR	Fischer Air (OK)
FFT	Frontier Airlines (N)
FFW	Flying Finn Airways (OH)
FGN	Gendarmerie Nationale (F) [police]
FGS	Elitellina (I) [c]
FHL	Fast Helicopters (G) [c]
FHY	Freebird Airlines (TC)
FIF	Air Finland (OH)
FII	German Flight Inspection (D)
FIN	Finnair (OH)
FIT	Finalair (5V)
FIV	CitationShares Sales (N) [c]
FJC	Falcon Jet Centre (G) [c]
FJE	FlyJet (G)
FJI	Air Pacific (DQ)
FJT	Fly Jet (I) [c]
FLB	Fly Linhas Aereas (PP)
FLG	Pinnacle Airlines (N)
FLI	Atlantic Airways (OY)
FLL	Federal Airlines (ST)
FLM	Fly Air (TC)
FLT	Flightline (G)
FLU	Flugschule Basel (HB) [c]
FLV	Flight Air Company (RA)
FNE	Farnair Europe (PH)
FNF	Finnish Air Force (OY) [m]
FNG	Frontier Guard (OH) [govt]
FNK	Feniks Airlines (UN)
FNM	Avio Nord (I) [agricultural]
FOB	Fordair (G) [c]
FOC	STAC (HB) [govt]
FOM	Freedom Air Intl (ZK)
FOR	Formula One Management (G) [c]
FPC	Lillbacka Jetair (OH) [c]
FPG	TAG Aviation (HB) [c]
FPO	Europe Airpost (F)
FPR	Fuerza Aerea del Peru (OB)
FRA	FR Aviation (G) [c/m]
FRC	Icare Franche Comte (F) [c]
FRD	Ford Motor Co (N) [c]
FRE	Freedom Air (N)
FRG	Freight Runners Express (N)
FRI	Fair Inc (JA)
FRJ	Afrijet (5N)
FRL	Freedom Airlines (N)
FRR	Fresh Air (5N)
FRT	Aerofreight Airlines (RA)
FRW	Farwest Airlines (N)
FSC	Four Star Air Cargo (N)
FSD	EFS Flug Service (D) [c]
FSH	Flash Airlines (SU)
FSW	Faso Airlines (XT)
FTA	Frontier Flying Service (N)
FTL	Flightline (EC)
FTM	Flyteam Aviation (G) [c]
FTR	Finist'air (F)
FTY	Fly Tyrol (OE)
FUA	Futura Internacional (EC)
FUE	Aviastar (RA)
FUJ	Fujairah Aviation Centre (A6) [c]
FUP	Foxair (D) [c]
FUR	Air Poitiers (F) [c]
FWA	West Air France (F)
FWI	Air Caraibes (F-O)
FWL	Florida West Intl Airlines (N)
FXI	Air Iceland (TF)
FXJ	Flexjet Operations (OY) [c]
FXR	Foxair (I) [c]
FYN	Comfort Air (D) [f]
GAE	Grand Aire Express (N)
GAF	German Air Force/Luftwaffe (D) [m]
GAG	Global Air Operations (D6)
GAI	Gromov Air (RA)
GAM	German Army (D) [m]
GAO	Golden Air (SE)
GAP	Air Philippines (RP)
GAZ	Global Aviation (9V) [c]
GBE	Gabon Express (TR)
GBJ	WM Aero Charter (D) [c]
GBL	GB Airways (G)
GBR	Rader Aviation (N) [c]
GCC	GECAS (EI) [lessor]
GCK	Aerogem Cargo (9G)
GCO	Gemini Air Cargo (N)
GDA	Gold Air International (G) [c]
GDB	Belgian Gendarmerie (OO) [police]
GDH	Guneydogu Aviation (TC) [c]
GDM	EAS Aeroservizi (I) [c]
GEA	GEASA (3C)
GEB	Gee Bee Air (SX)
GEC	Lufthansa Cargo (D)
GED	Europe Air Lines (F) [c]
GEO	Georgian Airlines (4R)
GES	Gestair Executive Jet (EC) [c]
GET	GETRA (3C)
GEV	Gestavi (EC)
GEX	TransGulf Express (A6) [c]
GFA	Gulf Air (A4O)
GFD	GFD (D) [target towing]
GFI	Caribbean Star Airlines (V2)
GFR	Avia Pusk (UN)
GFT	Gulfstream International (N)
GGG	Air Cargo Georgia (4R)
GGN	Air Alliance (C)
GGO	Avial (4R)
GHA	Ghana Airways (9G)
GHP	US Jets (N) [c]
GHS	Gatari Air Service (PK)
GIA	Garuda Indonesia (PK)
GID	Sud Air Transport (3X)
GIH	Union des Transportes Africain de Guinee (3X)
GIJ	Guinee Airways (3C)
GIP	Air Guinee Express (3X)
GIQ	Guinee Paramount Airlines)3X)
GIS	Guinee Air Services Inter (3X)
GIT	Societe des Transportes Aeriens de Guinee (3X)
GIV	Grivco Air (YR) [c]
GJB	Trans Air Link (N)
GJT	GIR Jet (EC)

GLA	Great Lakes Airlines (N)	HIN	Heli-Inter (F) [c]
GLB	Air Castle Corp (N) [c]	HIT	Heli-Italia (I)
GLG	Aerogal (HC)	HJA	Air Adeah (HH)
GLL	Air Gemini (D2)	HKA	Superior Aviation (N)
GLN	Gulf Air Falcon (3D)	HKL	Hak Air (5N)
GLO	Gol Transportes Aereos (PR)	HKN	Jim Hankins Air Service (N)
GLR	Central Mountain Air (C)	HKR	Hawk Air (LV)
GLT	Galata Aviacharter (ER)	HKS	CHC-Helikopter Service (LN)
GLU	Great Lakes Airways (5X)	HLC	Helicap (F) [c]
GMA	GAMA Aviation (G) [c]	HLF	Hapag-Lloyd (D)
GMC	General Motors (N) [c]	HLG	Helog (HB) [c]
GMG	GMG Airlines (S2)	HLN	Air Holland (PH)
GMI	Germania Flug (D)	HLQ	Harlequin Air (JA)
GMT	Magnicharters (XA)	HLR	Heli-Air (LZ)
GNC	Guinea Cargo (3C)	HLU	Heli-Union (F)
GNF	Gandalf Airlines (I)	HLX	Hapag-Lloyd Express (D)
GNS	Eastern Executive Air Charter (G) [c]	HMA	Air Tahoma (N)
GNT	bmi-british midland Regional (G)	HMD	Hammonds Air Service (N)
GNV	General Avia (EK)	HMF	Norrlandsflyg (SE) [EMS]
GNY	German Navy (D) [m]	HMR	North American Charter (C)
GOA	Alberta Government Air Transportation Svcs (C)	HMS	Hemus Air (LZ)
GOI	Gofir Aerotaxi (HB) [c]	HMY	HMY Airways (C)
GOJ	Eurojet Aviation (G) [c]	HNA	Greek Navy (SX) [m]
GOM	Gomelavia (EW)	HOA	Hola Airlines (EC)
GOR	Golitsa Ailines (UR)	HPJ	Hop-A-Jet (N) [c]
GOS	Goldfields Air Services (VH)	HPL	Heliportugal (CS) [c]
GPH	Sterling Helicopters (G) [c}	HPR	Helipro (ZK)
GPL	DLR-Flugbetriebe (D) [research]	HPT	Heli-Pet (UR) [c]
GRD	National Grid Helicopters (G) [survey]	HRA	Heli-Iberica (EC) [c]
GRF	Aerogryf (SP)	HRH	Royal Tongan Airlines (A3)
GRL	Air Greenland (OY)	HRM	Servicios Aereos Helios (EC) [c]
GRN	Rio Grande Air(N)	HRS	Hellas Jet (SX)
GRO	Allegro Air (XA)	HRZ	Croatian Air Force (9A) [m]
GRP	Great Plains Airlines (N)	HSE	Helisureste (EC)
GRR	Agroar (CS) [c]	HSI	Heliswiss (HB)
GRV	Ver-Avia (SX)	HSS	Transportes Aereos del Sur (EC) [c]
GRX	AirCompany Grodno (EW) [c]	HST	Hellenic Star Aviation (SX)
GSL	Geographic Air Survey (C) [survey]	HSU	Helisul (CS)
GSS	Global Supply Systems (G)	HSV	Svenska Direktfly (SE)
GTI	Atlas Air (N)	HSW	Heliswiss Iberia (EC) [c]
GTS	GATS Guinee (3X)	HTA	Heli-Trans (LN)
GTV	Aerogaviota (CU)	HTG	Grossman Air Service (OE) [c]
GTY	National Aviation Co (SU)	HTR	HAL Holsteiner Lubeck (D) [target towing]
GUF	Gulf African Airlines (3C)	HUK	Hungarian Ukrainian Heavylift (HA)
GUG	Aviateca (TG)	HUM	Trans Maldivian Airlines (8Q)
GUY	Air Guyane (F-O)	HUV	Hunair (HA)
GWI	Germanwings (D)	HVN	Vietnam Airlines (VN)
GWY	USA 3000 (N)	HVY	Heavylift Airlines (VH)
GZA	Excellent Air (D) [c]	HWY	Highland Airways (G)
GZP	Gazprom Avia (RA)	HYC	Hydro Air (ZS)
HAA	Helicopteros Agroforestal (CC)	HYR	Airlink Airways (EI) [c]
HAF	Hellenic Air Force (SX) [m]	HZA	Horizon Airlines (VH)
HAG	Hageland Aviation Services (N)	IAA	Indonesian Airlines (PK)
HAL	Hawaiian Airlines (N)	IAC	Indian Airlines (VT)
HAS	East African Safari Air (5Y)	IAD	AirDay (I)
HAT	Air Taxi (F) [c]	IAF	Israeli Air Force (4X)
HAX	Benair Norway (LN)	IAJ	Islandair (G)
HBI	CHC Denmark (OY)	IAM	ARA Flugrettungs (OE)
HCN	Naske Air (D) [c]	IAR	Iliamna Air Taxi (N)
HCP	Helicopter spol (OK) [EMS]	IAT	IATA (C)
HCY	Helios Airways (5B)	IAV	Island Flyer (G) [broker]
HDA	Dragonair (B-H)	IAW	Iraqi Airways (YI)
HDI	Hoteles Dinamicos (XA) [c]	IBB	Binter Canarias (EC)
HEA	Heliavia (CS) [c]	IBE	Iberia Lineas Aereas de España (EC)
HEC	Heliservicios Campeche (XA)	IBT	Ibertrans Aerea (EC)
HEJ	Hellas Jet (SX)	IBU	Indigo LLC (N) [c]
HEL	Helicol (HK)	IBZ	Intl Business Air (SE)
HEM	CHC Helicopters Australia (VH)	ICA	Icaro (I)
HER	Hex'Air (F)	ICB	Islandsflug (TF)
HET	TAF Helicopters (EC)	ICC	Institut Cartographic de Catalunia (EC) [survey]
HFR	Helifrance (F) [c]	ICE	Icelandair (TF)
HGA	Hoganair (N)	ICF	Inter-Cargo Services (UK)
HGD	Hangard Airlines (JU)	ICG	Landhelgisgaezlan (TF) [coastguard]
HHA	Atlantic Airlines de Honduras (HR)	ICL	Cargo Air Lines (4X)
HHE	Heli-Holland (PH) [c]	ICM	Air Inter Cameron (TJ)
HHH	Helicsa Helicopters (EC)	ICT	Inter (HK)
HHI	Hamburg International (D)	IDA	Indonesia Air Transport (PK)
HHK	Heli Hong Kong (B-H)	IDP	IAFAir Freighters (VH)
HHN	Hahn Airlines (D)	IDR	Indicator Aviation (HA) [c]
HHO	Houston Helicopters (N)	IDU	Air Industria (I)
HIB	Helibravo Aviacao (CS)	IEA	Intermedicacion Aerea (EC) [c]
HIG	Heli-Inter Guyane (F-O) [c]	IEP	Elipiu (I) [c]

IFA	FAI Airservice (D) [c]	JDP	JDP Lux (LX) [c]
IFC	Indian Air Force (VT) [m]	JEF	Jetflite (OH) [c]
IFT	Interflight (G) [c]	JEJ	Jets Ejecutivos (XA) [c]
IIL	India International Airways (VT) [c]	JEK	Jet Link (4X) [c]
IJA	International Jet Aviation (N) [c]	JEL	Tal Air Charters (C)
IKA	Itek Air (EX)	JEM	Emerald Airways (G)
IKK	Iki International Airlines (JA)	JET	Windjet (I)
IKR	Ikaros Fly (OY) [c]	JEX	JAL Express (JA)
IKT	Sakha Avia (RA)	JFK	Keenair Charter (G)
ILN	Inter-Air Airlines (ZS)	JFL	Jetfly Airlines (OE)
ILV	Ilavia (RA)	JGO	Jetsgo (C)
IMT	Imtrec Aviation Cambodia (XU)	JIA	PSA Airlines (N)
IMX	Zimex Aviation (HB)	JKK	Spanair (EC)
INC	Jet Air International Charters (YV)	JLE	Jetline International (3C)
INJ	Interjet Hellenic Aviation (SX) [c]	JLN	Eurojet (9H) [c]
INR	Inter Air (SE) [c]	JMC	Thomas Cook Airlines (G)
INV	Inversija (YL)	JMG	Jetmagic (EI)
INX	Inter Express (TC)	JMV	Interflight (3D)
IOI	Atol Milano (I) [c]	JMX	Air Jamaica Express (6Y)
IOS	Isles of Scilly Skybus (G)	JOL	Atyrau Airways (UN)
IPN	IPTN (PK) [manufacturer]	JON	Johnson's Air (9G)
IRA	Iranair (EP)	JOS	DHL Guatemala (TG)
IRB	Iran Air Tours (EP)	JRN	Jet Rent (XA) [c]
IRC	Iran Aseman Airlines (EP)	JSP	Palmer Aviation (G) [c]
IRD	Arvand Air (EP)	JTA	Japan TransOcean Air (JA)
IRG	NAFT Air Line (EP)	JTR	Executive Aviation Services (G) [c]
IRI	Navid Air (EP) [c]	JTT	Jet 2000 (RA) [c]
IRJ	Bon-Air (EP)	JTV	Air Independence (D) [c]
IRK	Kish Air (EP)	JTY	Jatayu Airlines (PK)
IRL	Irish Air Corp (EI) [m]	JUA	Aero Juarez (XA)
IRM	Mahan Air (EP)	JUC	Juba Airways (6O)
IRO	CSA Air (N)	JUD	US Department of Justice (N) - prisoner
IRP	Payam International Air (EP)		transport
IRQ	Qeshm Air (EP)	JUS	USA Jet Airlines (N)
IRR	Tara Airlines (EP) [c]	JVK	Jorvik Aviation (TF)
IRS	Sirius Air (UR)	JWY	Jetways (N) [c]
IRX	Aria Air (EP)	JZA	Air Canada Jazz (C)
IRZ	Saha Airline (EP)	KAB	Avia Baltila Aviation (LY) [c]
ISA	Island Airlines (N)	KAC	Kuwait Airways (9K)
ISD	ISD Avia (UR)	KAD	Kirovohradavia (UR)
ISK	Intersky (OE)	KAE	Kartika Airlines (PK)
ISR	Israir (4X)	KAI	Kaiserair (N) [c]
ISS	Meridiana (I)	KAJ	Karthargo Airlines (TS)
IST	Istanbul Airways (TC)	KAL	Korean Air (HL)
ISV	Islena Airlines (HR)	KAO	KAPO (RA)
ISW	Islas Airways (EC)	KAP	Cape Air (N)
ITD	Inter Trans Avia Cargo (EX)	KAT	Kato Air (LN)
ITH	International Trans-Air (5N)	KAW	Kazair West (UN)
ITK	Interlink Airways (ZS)	KAZ	Tatarstan Air (RA)
ITL	MIKMA (ER)	KBA	Kenn Borek Air (C)
ITN	Industrias Avia (EC) [c]	KDC	KD Air (C)
ITT	Inter Trans Air (LZ)	KDZ	Avior Technologies (N) [c]
ITX	Imair (4K)	KEE	Keystone Air Service (C)
IUS	Icarus Elicotteri (I) [c]	KFA	Kelowna Flightcraft Air Charter (C)
IVJ	Flight International Aviation (N)	KFL	Flamingo Airways (5Y)
IVT	Interaviatrans (UR) [c]	KFS	Kalitta Charters (N)
IWD	Iberworld (EC)	KGA	Kyrghyzstan Airlines (EX)
IWY	Interisland Airways (VQ-T)	KGL	Kolavia (RA)
IXT	Lineas Aereas Ixtlan (XA) [c]	KHA	Kitty Hawk Air Cargo (N)
IYE	Yemenia (7O)	KHM	Cambodia Airlines (XU)
IZA	Izhavia-Izhevsk Air Enterprise (RA)	KHO	Khors Air (UR)
JAA	Japan Asia Airways (JA)	KHV	Air Kharkov (UR)
JAC	Japan Air Commuter (JA)	KHX	Knighthawk Express (N)
JAF	JetAlliance (OE) [c]	KHY	Khyber Afghan Airlines (YA)
JAI	Jet Airways (VT)	KIL	Kuban Airlines (RA)
JAL	Japan Air Lines (JA)	KIP	Kinnarps (SE) [c]
JAM	Sunline Airlines (5Y)	KIS	Contactair (D)
JAR	Airlink (OE) [c]	KJC	Kras Air (RA)
JAS	Japan Air System (JA)	KLA	Air Lithuania (LY)
JAT	JAT Airways (YU)	KLB	Air Mali International (TZ)
JAV	Jordan Air (JY)	KLC	KLM Cityhopper (PH)
JAZ	JALways (JA)	KLD	Air Klaipeda (LY) [c]
JBA	Helijet International Airways (C)	KLG	Karlog Air (OY) [c]
JBR	Job Air ((OK) [c]	KLM	KLM - Royal Dutch A/L (PH)
JBU	jetBlue Airways (N)	KLO	Flight-Ops International (C) [c]
JCB	JCB Aviation Dept (G) [c]	KLX	Kelix Air (5N)
JCC	Jetcraft Aviation (VH)	KMA	Komiaviatrans (RA) [c]
JCK	Jackson Air Services (C)	KMF	Kam-Air (YA)
JCR	Rotterdam Jet Centre (PH) [c]	KMP	Kampuchea Airlines (XU)
JCS	Jetclub (HB) [c]	KMV	Komiinteravia (RA)
JCX	Jet Connections (D) [c]	KNI	Kaliningrad Avia (RA)
JDA	JD Aviation (G) [c]	KNM	KNAAPO (RA)

KNS	Kinshasa Airways (9Q)
KNX	KnightHawk Air Express (C)
KOA	Euro-Flite (OY) [c]
KOP	Copters (CC)
KOR	Air Koryo (P)
KPH	KVZ (RA)
KQA	Kenya Airways (5Y)
KRC	New Zealand Defence Force (ZK) [m]
KRE	Aerosucre (HK)
KRG	Krimaviamontazh (UR) [c]
KRI	Krylo Air (RA)
KRM	Crimea Universal Avia (UR) [c]
KRO	Kroonk Air Agency (UR)
KRP	Carpatair (YR)
KRT	Kok Shetau Airlines (UN)
KRV	Khoriv Avia (UR)
KSI	Air Kissari (D2) [c]
KSM	Kosmos Aviakompania (RA)
KSP	SAEP (HK)
KST	PTL Luftfahrtunternehman (D)
KTA	Kirov Avia Enterprise (RA)
KTB	Transaviabaltika (LY) [c]
KTK	Karekavia (RA)
KTR	Helikoptertransport (SE) [c]
KUS	National Airlines (ZS)
KYL	Kyrgyz International Airlines (EX)
KYM	Krym International Airlines (UR)
KYV	KTHY Cyprus Turkish A/L (TC)
KZE	Euro-Asia Air International (EX)
KZH	Zhezair (UN)
KZK	Air Kazakstan (UN)
KZM	Phoebus Apollo Zambia (9J)
LAA	Libyan Arab Airlines (5A)
LAB	LAB Flying Service (N)
LAC	Lockheed (N) [manufacturer]
LAJ	British Mediterranean A/W (G)
LAL	Air Labrador (C)
LAM	LAM - Linhas aereas de Mocambique (C9)
LAN	LAN - Chile (CC)
LAO	Lao Aviation (RDPL)
LAP	TAM Paraguay (ZP)
LAU	Lineas Aereas Suramericanas Colombia (HK)
LAV	Aeropostal (YV)
LAY	Layang-Layang Aerospace (9M)
LBC	Albanian Airlines (ZA)
LBH	Laker Airways (C6)
LBQ	Quest Diagnostics (N) [c]
LBR	Elbe Air (D) [c]
LBS	LABSA (YV)
LBT	Nouvellair (TS)
LCB	LC Busre (OB)
LCG	Lignes Aeriennes Congolaises (9Q)
LCH	Lynch Flying Service (N)
LCI	Lotsiya (UR)
LCO	LANChile Cargo (CC)
LCR	Libyan Arab Air Cargo (5A)
LCT	Stellair (EC) [c]
LCY	London City Airport Jet Centre (G) [c]
LDA	Lauda Air (OE)
LDE	LADE - Lineas Aereas del Estado (LV)
LDI	Lauda Air SpA (I)
LDO	Elisusa (I) [c]
LEA	Unijet (F) [c]
LEC	Linex (TL)
LEO	Lion Air (4R)
LER	LASER (YV)
LET	Aerolineas Ejecutivos (XA) [c]
LEU	Lions Air (HB) [c]
LFI	NAC Helicopters (ZK) [c]
LFT	Aerolift Company (9L) [c]
LGL	Luxair (LX)
LGO	Lego Company (OY) [c]
LGW	LGW (D)
LHN	Express One Inl (N)
LHS	Lugansk Aviation Enterprise (UR)
LIA	LIAT - The Caribbean Airline (V2)
LID	Alidauncia (I)
LIL	Lithuanian Airlines (LY)
LIM	Air Limo (OO) [c]
LIO	Air Charter Iceland (TF) [c]
LIQ	Lid Air (SE)
LIT	Air Littoral (F)
LIV	Air Livonia (ES)
LJA	Air Jamahiriya (5A)
LJR	Hellas Wings (SX)
LKN	Lankair (4R)
LLB	Lloyd Aereo Boliviano (CP)
LLM	Yamal Airlines (RA)
LLR	Alliance Air (VT)
LMB	Aviakomi (4L)
LMG	South African Air Force (ZS) [m]
LMS	Lomas Helicopters (G) [c]
LMT	Almaty Avia Cargo (UN)
LNC	LAN Dominicana (HI)
LNE	LAN Ecuador (HC)
LNI	Lion Airlines (PK)
LNK	South African Airlink (ZS)
LNT	Aerolineas Internacionales (XA)
LOD	Malmo Air Taxi (SE) [c]
LOF	Trans States Airlines (N)
LOG	Loganair (G)
LOT	LOT - Polski Linie Lotnicze (SP)
LPC	Alpine Aviation (ZS)
LPE	LAN Peru (OB)
LPN	Laoag Intl Airways (RP)
LPR	LAPA (LV)
LPS	Alpe Air (S5)
LPV	Air Alps Aviation (OE)
LRA	Little Red Air Service (C)
LRB	LR Airlines (OK)
LRC	LACSA (TI)
LRE	Lasare Air (4L)
LRK	L-Air (F) [c]
LRN	LRC Linhas Aereas (PP)
LRO	Alrosa Aviation (RA)
LRR	Lorraine Aviation (F) [c]
LRS	SANSA (TI)
LRT	Airlines of South Australia (VH)
LSB	Lensibavia (RA) [training]
LSE	Lansa (CC)
LSK	Aurela (LY)
LSR	Alsair - Alsace Air Service (F)
LSU	Laus Air (9A)
LSY	Lindsay Aviation (N)
LTC	LAT Charter (YL)
LTE	Volar Airlines (EC)
LTF	Lufttaxi Flug (D)
LTP	Latpass Airlines (YL)
LTR	Lufttransport (LN)
LTU	LTU Intl Airways (D)
LUR	Atlantis European Airways (EK)
LUS	Lotus Airways Cargo (3C)
LVB	IRS Airlines (5N)
LVG	Livingston (I)
LVL	Livian Air (EC) [c]
LVN	Aliven (I) [c]
LVR	Aviavilsa (LY)
LXA	Luxaviation (LX)
LXF	Lynx Air International (N)
LXG	Air Luxor GB (J5)
LXJ	Bombardier Business Jet Solution (N) [c]
LXO	Luxor Air (SU)
LXP	LANExpress (CC)
LXR	Air Luxor (CS)
LYC	Lynden Air Cargo (N)
LYM	Key Lime Air (N)
LYN	Altyn Air (EK)
LYT	Apatas Airlines (LY)
LZD	Bulgaria Air (LZ)
LZT	Lanzarote Aerocargo (EC)
MAA	Mas Air Cargo (XA)
MAC	Malta Air Charter (9H)
MAF	Missionary Aviation Fellowship (PK)
MAH	Malev (HA)
MAK	Macedonian Air Transport (Z3)
MAL	Morningstar Air Express (C)
MAP	National Oceanic & Atmospheric Administration (N) [govt]
MAS	Malaysia Airlines (9M)
MAT	Maine Aviation (N) [c]
MAU	Air Mauritius (3B)
MAV	Marina Aeroservice (EC) [c]
MAW	Mustique Airways (J8)
MAX	Max Aviation (C)

MBA	Automobilvertriebs (OE) [c]
MBI	Mountain Bird (N) [c]
MBL	First City Air (G) [c]
MBN	Zambian Airways (9J)
MBO	Exxon Mobil Aviation (C) [c]
MBR	Brazilian Navy (PP) [m]
MBV	Aeriantur-M Airlines(ER)
MCC	Aerocom (ER)
MCD	Air Med (G) [EMS]
MCE	Marshalls of Cambridge (G) [c]
MCG	SOS Helikoptern Gotland (SE) [EMS]
MCH	McAlpine Helicopters (G) [c]
MCI	Morocco Aiways (CN)
MCK	Macair (VH)
MCL	Medical Aviation Services (G) [EMS]
MCM	Heli Air Monaco (3A)
MCN	Mac Dan Aviation (N)
MCO	Aerolineas Marcos (XA) [c]
MCR	Monacair (3A)
MDA	Mandarin Airlines (B)
MDC	Mid-Atlantic Freight (N)
MDF	Mediterranean Air Freight (SX)
MDG	Air Madagascar (5R)
MDL	Mandala Airlines (PK)
MDM	Med-Avia (9H)
MDO	Varty Pacific Airlines (UN)
MDR	Compania Mexicana de Aeroplanas (XA) [c]
MDS	McNeely Charter Services (N)
MDT	Sundt Air (LN) [c]
MDV	Moldavian Airlines (ER)
MEA	MEA - Middle East A/L (OD)
MEE	Elimediterranea (I) [c]
MEH	Malev Express (HA)
MEI	Merlin Express (N)
MEJ	Medjet International (N) [EMS]
MEP	Midwest Airlines (N)
MER	Methow Aviation (N)
MES	Mesaba Airlines (N)
MGE	Asia Pacific International (N)
MGL	MIAT (JU)
MGM	MG Aviation (F) [c]
MGX	Montenegro Airlines (YU)
MHA	Mountain High Aviation (N) [c]
MHN	Manhattan Air (G) [c]
MHS	Air Memphis (SU)
MHU	Air Memphis Uganda (5X)
MIV	MI-Avia (RA) [police]
MJL	Jet Line International (ER)
MJM	ETI 2000 (I) [c]
MJN	Royal Air Force of Oman (A4O) [m]
MJR	Million Air Owensboro (N) [c]
MKA	MK Air Cargo (9G)
MKK	Malasa Aviatsia Dona (RA) [c]
MKU	Island Air (N)
MKV	Myachkovo Air Services (RA)
MLA	Forty Mile Air (40 Mile Air) (N)
MLC	Malift Air (9Q)
MLD	Air Moldova (ER)
MLE	Moldaeroservice (ER) [c]
MLG	Malagasy Airlines (5R)
MLT	Moldtransavia (ER)
MMA	Mondair (CN)
MMC	Aermarche (I) [c]
MMD	Air Alsie (OY) [c]
MMM	Meridian Air (RA) [c]
MMZ	EuroAtlantic Airways (CS)
MNA	Merpati Nusantara A/L (PK)
MNB	MNG Airlines (TC)
MNE	Aeroamanecer (XA) [c]
MNF	AV8Air (G)
MNG	Aero Mongolia (JU)
MNI	Aeromilenio (XA)
MNL	Farnair Europe-Miniliner (I)
MNM	Adjaria Airlines (4L)
MON	Monarch Airlines (G)
MOU	Anglo American Airmotive (G) [c]
MOV	VIM Airlines (RA)
MOZ	Amadeus Air (OE)
MPD	Air Plus Comet (EC)
MPH	Martinair Holland (PH)
MPX	Aeromexpress Cargo (XA)
MRA	Martinaire (N)

MRE	Namibia Commercial Airways (V5)
MRG	Manag'Air (F) [c]
MRP	ABAS spol (OK) [c]
MRS	Air Marshall Islands (V7)
MRT	Air Mauritanie (5T)
MSA	Mistral Air (I)
MSC	Air Cairo (SU)
MSH	US Marshalls Service (N) [govt]
MSI	Motor Sich Aviakompania (UR)
MSK	Maersk Air (G)
MSM	Aeromas (CX)
MSP	Vigilancia Aerea (TI) [c]
MSQ	Mesquita Taxi Aerea (PT)
MSR	Egyptair (SU)
MSV	Aero Kamov (RA)
MTC	Minerva (I)
MTE	Aeromet Linea Aerea (CC)
MTF	Interjet (I) [c]
MTG	Servicios Aereos MTT (XA) [c]
MTJ	Metrojet (B-H) [c]
MTK	Air Metack (D2)
MTL	RAF-Avia (YL)
MTM	MTM Aviation (D) [c]-[c]
MTN	Mountain Air Cargo (N)
MTX	Multi Taxi (XA) [c]
MTZ	Mali Airways (TZ)
MUA	Murray Air (N)
MUI	Trans-Air (N)
MUK	Muk Air (OY)
MUN	Aeromundo Executivo (XA) [c]
MVD	KMV - Kavakaskie Mineralnye Vody (RA)
MVK	Helicopter Training & Hire (G) [c]
MVL	Mavial (RA)
MWA	Midwest Airline Egypt (SU)
MWT	Midwest Aviation (N)
MXA	Mexicana (XA)
MXP	May Air X-Press (N)
MYA	Myflug (TF)
MYD	Maya Island Airways (V3)
MYL	MyTravel Lite (G)
MYO	Mayoral (EC) [c]
MYT	MyTravel Airways (G)
MZL	Aerovias Montes Acules (XA)
MZS	Mahfooz Aviation (C5)
NAA	NOAA Aircraft Operations (N) [research]
NAD	Seulawah Nad Air (PK)
NAC	Northern Air Cargo (N)
NAF	Royal Netherlands Air Force (PH) [m]
NAG	Northern Air Charter (D)
NAI	North Adria Aviation (9A)
NAL	Northway Aviation (C)
NAO	North American Airlines (N)
NAV	Nav Canada (C) [calibrator]
NAW	Newair Air Service (OY)
NAX	Norwegian Air Shuttle (LN)
NAY	Naysa Aerotaxis (EC)
NBK	Albarka Air Services (5N)
NCA	Nippon Cargo Airlines (JA)
NCB	North Cariboo Flying Service(C)
NCG	Netherlands Coast Guard (PH) [survey]
NCH	Chanchangi Airlines (5N)
NCM	NAS Air (TZ)
NCN	Niger Air Continental (5U)
NCT	Nacional Transportes Aereos (PP)
NCY	NAT Executive (F) [c]
NDC	Nordic Airlink (SE)
NDN	Aerolineas Andinas (YV)
NDS	Nordstress (VH) [leasing co]
NDU	University of North Dakota (N) [research]
NEA	New England Airlines (N)
NEC	Necon Air (9N)
NEF	Nordflyg (SE)
NES	Nordeste Linhas Aereas Regionais (PT)
NEX	Northern Executive Avn (G) [c]
NEY	Northeast Airlines (3D)
NFA	North Flying (OY)
NFF	Aircraft Support & Services (OD)
NGA	Nigeria Airways (5N)
NGE	Angel Airlines (HS)
NGI	Nigerian Global (5N)
NGK	Oriental Air Bridge (JA)
NGP	Air Nigeria (5N)

NGR	Nigerian Air Force (5N) [m]	OHY	Onur Air (TC)
NHA	Air Nove (LZ)	OJF	Occitania Jet Freight (F)
NHK	Federal Aviation Administration (N)	OKJ	Okada Air (5N)
NIA	Nordavia Flug (D) [c]	OLC	Solar Cargo (YV)
NIG	Aerocontractors (5N)	OLT	OLT - Ostfriesische Lufttransport (D)
NIN	Nurman Air (PK)	OMG	Aeromega Helicopters (G) [c]
NIR	SAAB Norsk Flytjeneste (LN) [target tug]	OMN	Sultan of Oman's Air Force (A4O) [m]
NJA	Sky Air Cargo [EL]	OMS	Omsk Avia (RA)
NJE	Netjets Transportes Aereos (CS)	OND	Condomett (I) [c]
NJS	National Jet Systems (VH)	ONE	Oceanair Linhas Aereas (PP)
NKF	Nordkalottflyg (SE)	ONG	Sonnig AG (HB) [c]
NKS	Spirit Airlines (N)	OOM	Zoom Airlines (C)
NKT	North Country Aviation (N) [c]	OPC	Krystel Air Charter (G) [c]
NKV	Nikolaev Air (UR) [c]	OPE	Aerope 3S Aviation (F) [c]
NKZ	Aerokuzbass (RA)	OPT	Flight Options (N) [c]
NLE	Boston-Maine Airways (N)	ORA	Executive Airlines (East Hampton) (N)
NLK	Elbrus Avia (RA)	ORB	Orenburg Avia (RA)
NLS	Nationale Luchtvaart School (PH) [trainer]	ORC	Air Cordial (G)
NLT	Newfoundland Labrador Air Transport (C)	ORF	Oman Royal Flight (A4O) [c]
NMB	Air Namibia (V5)	ORJ	OrangeCargo (JA)
NMD	Bay Air (V5)	ORM	Orel Air Enterprisevia (RA)
NMI	Pacific Wings (N)	ORO	Clipper National Air (EC) [c]
NOE	Air Tropical (F-O)	ORS	Action Air (I) [c]
NOF	Fonnalfly A/S (LN) [c]	ORX	Orbit Express Airlines (TC)
NOL	National Overseas Airline (SU) [c]	ORZ	Zorex (EC)
NOR	Norsk Helikopter (LN)	OSL	Sololiso Airlines (5N)
NOS	Neos (I)	OST	Alania Leasing Airline (RA)
NOW	Royal Norwegian Air Force (LN) [m]	OSV	Vladikavkaz Air Enterprise (RA)
NOY	Noy Aviation (4X) [c]	OTL	South Airlines (UR)
NPO	Napo Aviatrans (RA)	OVA	Aero Nova (EC)
NPP	NPP Mir Aviakompania (RA)	OVC	Aerovic (HC)
NPR	Air Napier (ZK)	OWL	Miami Valley Air (N)
NRG	Ross Aviation (N)	OWR	Crown Air (OK) [c]
NRK	Naturelink Charter (ZS)	OXE	Oxaero (G) [c]
NRL	Nolinor Aviation (C)	OXO	Millon Air (N) [c]
NRN	Royal Dutch Navy (PH) [m]	OZB	Zona Blava (EC) [c]
NRO	Aero Rent (RA) [c]	OZR	Ozark Airlines (N)
NRS	Atlantic Richfield Corp (N) [c]	PAA	Pan Am (N)
NRT	Norest Air (EC) [c]	PAC	Polar Air Cargo (N)
NRV	International Express Air Charter (C)	PAG	Perimeter Airlines (C)
NSE	SATENA (HK)	PAJ	Aliparma (I) [c]
NSW	Country Connection A/L (VH)	PAL	Philippine Airlines (RP)
NTA	NT Air (C)	PAM	Phoenix Air (D) [c]
NTB	Servicios Aereos del Norte (XA) [c]	PAO	Polynesian Airlines (5W)
NTC	Heartland Aviation (N)	PAQ	Pacific Air International (VH)
NTH	Hokkaido Air System (JA)	PAS	Pelita Air Service (PK)
NTL	Air Anatolia (TC)	PAU	Locavions Aero Services (F) [c]
NTM	North American Airlines (C)	PAX	Pan Air (N) [c]
NTN	National Airways Corp (ZS)	PBA	PB Air (HS)
NTV	Air Inter Ivoire (TU)	PBL	Pelikan Blue Line (YU)
NTW	Nationwide Air Charter (ZS)	PBT	Air Parabat (S2)
NVG	Novgorod Avia Enterprise (RA)	PBU	Air Burundi (9U)
NVI	Avial Air (RA)	PCE	Pace Airlines (N)
NVJ	Nouvelair International (TS)	PCM	West Air (N)
NVR	Novair (SE)	PCO	Pacific Coastal Airlines (C)
NVY	Royal Navy (G) [m]	PCV	Pacific Aviation (VH)
NWA	Northwest Airlines (N)	PDA	Podililia Avia (RA)
NWD	New World Jet Corp (N) [c]	PDD	Phillips Petroleum (N) [c}
NWL	North-Wright Airways (C)	PDF	Pelican Air Services (ZS)
NWR	Northwest Regional Airlines (VH)	PDG	PDG Helicopters (G) [c]
NWZ	Nationwide Airlines (9J)	PDT	Piedmont Airlines (N)
NYB	Belgian Navy (OO) [m]	PEA	Pan Europeenne Air Service (F)
NZM	Mount Cook Airline (ZK)	PEG	Pelangi Air (9M)
NZP	Alliance Air (RA)	PEL	Aeropelican Air Services (VH)
OAE	Omni Air International(N)	PEN	Peninsula Airways (N)
OAF	Aerzzterflugambulanz (OE) [EMS]	PEP	PENTA (PT)
OAL	Olympic Airlines (SX)	PER	Pioneer Cargo Airlines (AP)
OAO	Arkhangelsk 2nd Avn Enterprise (RA)	PFA	Pacific Flight Services (9V) [c]
OAS	Omanair (A4O)	PFN	Pan African Air Services (9L)
OAV	Omni Aviacao e Technologia (CS)	PFT	Air Cargo Express International (N)
OAW	Odette Airways (HB)	PGA	Portugalia (CS)
OBA	Aerobanana (XA) [c]	PGP	Perm Airlines (RA)
OBK	Amako Air (5N)	PGT	Pegasus Airlines (TC)
OBM	Aviaobshchemash (RA)	PGX	Paragon Air Express (N)
OCA	ASERCA (YV)	PHA	Phoeinix Air (N)
OCE	Heliocean (F-O) [c]	PHB	Phoebus Apollo Aviation (ZS)
OCM	O'Connor Airlines (VH)	PHD	Duncan Aviation (N) [c]
OCN	Octavia Airlines (F)	PHE	Pawan Hans Helicopters (VT)
ODS	Odessa Air (UR)	PHG	Phoenix Aviation (EX)
OEA	Orient Thai Airlines (HS)	PHM	Petroleum Helicopters (N)
OGE	Atlas International (TC)	PIA	Pakistan Intl Airlines (AP)
OGN	Origin Pacific Airways (ZK)	PIC	Pacific Airlines (VN)

PIL	Canada Jet Charters (C) [c]
PIT	Panair (I) [c]
PJS	Jet Aviation Business Jets (HB) [c]
PKR	Pakker Avio (ES) [c]
PKW	Sierra West Airlines (N)
PLC	Police Aviation Services (G)
PLF	Polish Air Force (SP) [m]
PLK	Pulkova Airlines (RA)
PLM	Air Pullmantur (EC)
PLR	Northwestern Air (C)
PLS	Palio Air Service (I) [c]
PLZ	Planet Airways (N)
PMA	Pan-Malaysian Air Transport (9M)
PMC	Primac Courier (N)
PML	Eliair (I) [c]
PMM	Primair (RA)
PMS	Planemaster Air Charters (N)
PNA	Universal Airlines (N)
PNF	Pan African Airways (TU)
PNH	Pankh Joint Stock Co (RA) [c]
PNL	Aero Personal (XA) [c]
PNR	Pan Air Lineas Aereas (EC)
PNS	Penas Air Cargo (PK) [surveyor]
PNV	Panavia Panama (HP)
PNW	Palestine Airlines (SU)
POA	Portuguese Army (CS) [m]
PON	Portuguese Navy (CS) [m]
POV	Poltava Universal Aivia (UR) [c]
PPK	Ramp 66 (N)
PPS	Butte Aviation (N) [c]
PPW	Royal Phnom Penh Airways (XU)
PRF	Precisionair (5H)
PRG	ASPAR - Aeroservcios Parrague (CC)
PRI	Island air Honolulu (N)
PRL	Pearl Aviation (AP) [c]
PRO	Propair (C)
PRP	PRT Aviation (EC) [c]
PRZ	Air Paradise International (PK)
PSA	Pacific Island Aviation (N)
PSC	Pascan Aviation (C) [c]
PSD	President Airlines (XU)
PSV	Sapair (HI)
PSW	Pskovn Avia (RA)
PTI	PrivatAir (HB)
PTK	Petropavlovsk Kamchatsky Air Enterprise (RA)
PTN	Pantanal (PT)
PTO	North West Geomatics (C) [survey]
PTP	Palau Trans Pacific Airline (T8A)
PTR	Province of Nova Scotia (C)
PTZ	Avialesookhrana (RA) [fire-fighting]
PUA	PLUNA (CX)
PVV	Continental Airways (RA)
PWC	Pratt & Whitney Canada (C) [testbed]
PWF	Private Wings (D)
PXX	Aroostook Aviation (N) [c]
PYN	Haverfordwest Air Charter (G) [c]
PYR	Pyramid Airlines (SU) [c]
PZL	PZL (SP) [manufacturer]
QAC	Qatar Air Cargo (A7)
QAF	Qatar Amiri Flight (A7) [c]
QAH	Quick Airways (PH)
QAJ	Quick Air Jet Charter (D) [c]
QCL	Air Class Lineas Aereas (CX)
QDR	Quadrotour Avia (UN)
QFA	Qantas Airways (VH)
QGA	Windrose Air JetCharter (D) [c]
QKC	Aero Taxi (N) [c]
QNK	Kabo Air (5N)
QNZ	JetConnect (ZK)
QQA	Alliance Airlines (VH)
QSC	African Safari Airways (5Y)
QTR	Qatar Airways (A7)
QUE	Gouvernement du Quebec (C)
QVR	Quadratour Avia (EX)
QWA	Quest-Air (VH)
QXE	Horizon Airlines (N)
RAB	Rila Airlines (LZ)
RAD	Alada Empresa de Transportes Aereos (D2)
RAE	Regional (F)
RAG	Regio-Air (D) [c]
RAK	Riga Aeroclub ((YL)
RAM	Royal Air Maroc (CN)
RAN	Renan Air (ER)
RAX	Royal Air Freight (N)
RBA	Royal Brunei Airlines (V8)
RBB	Rabbit Air (HB) [c]
RBD	American Connection (N)
RBN	Red Baron Aviation (N)
RBS	Air Bas (3C)
RBW	Shandong Airlines Rainbow Jet (B) [c]
RCA	Richland Aviation (N) [c]
RCN	Race Cargo Airlines (9G)
RCS	Air Consul (3C)
RCX	Air Service Center (I) [c]
RDA	Redair Gambia (C5)
RDD	Adygheya Avia (RA)
RDP	Rompetrol Logistics (YR) [c]
RDS	Rhoades International (N)
REA	Aer Arann (EI)
RED	Red Cross (HB) [humanitarian]
REN	Aerorent (XA) [c]
REU	Air Austral (F-O)
REV	Rostvertol (RA) [c]
REX	Ram Air Freight (N)
REY	Aero-Rey (XA) [c]
RFF	Russian Air Force (RA) [m]
RFL	Interfly (I) [c]
RFS	Rossair Charter (VH)
RGA	Region Air (9V)
RGL	Regional Air Lines (CN)
RGN	Cygnus Air (EC)
RHC	Redhill Charters (G) [c]
RHL	Air Archipels (F-O)
RIN	Airline Transport (ER)
RIT	Asian Spirit (RP)
RJA	Royal Jordanian (JY)
RLA	Airlinair (F)
RLE	Rico Linhas Aereas (PT)
RLK	Air Nelson (ZK)
RMA	Rocky Mountain Helicopters (N)
RMC	RMC Aviation Dept (G) [c]
RME	Armenian Airlines (EK)
RMF	Royal Malaysian Air Force (9M) [m]
RMI	Point Airlines (5N)
RML	Armenian International Airways (EK)
RMO	Saturn Aviakompania (RA)
RMV	Romavia (YR)
RMX	Air Max (LZ)
RNA	Royal Nepal Airlines (9N)
RNB	Rosneft-Baltika (RA)
RNL	Serendip Express (4R)
RNO	Air Normandie (F)
RNV	Armavia (EK)
ROF	Romanian Air Force (YR) [m]
ROI	Avior Express (YV)
ROJ	Royal Jet (A6) [c]
RON	Air Nauru (C2)
ROO	Aeriltalia (I) [c]
ROP	Royal Oman Police (A4O) [c]
ROR	Roraima Air (8R)
ROS	Rossair Europe (YR)
ROT	TAROM (YR)
RPA	Provence Aero Service (F) [c]
RPB	Aerorepublica Colombia (HK)
RPC	Aerolineas del Pacifico (HC)
RPH	RPX Airlines (PK)
RPK	Royal Airlines (AP)
RPS	Global Air Response (N)
RPX	BAC Express (G)
RRL	Rolls-Royce (G) [c/manufacturer]
RRM	Acvila Air (YR) [c]
RRR	Royal Air Force (G) [m]
RRV	Mombasa Air Safari (5Y)
RRZ	Rollrights Aviation (G) [c]
RSE	SNAS Aviation (HZ)
RSI	Air Sunshine (N)
RSL	Rio-Sul Servicios Aereos Regionals SA (PT)
RSM	Air Somalia (6O)
RSO	Aero Asia International (AP)
RSR	Aero Service (TN)
RSS	Rossair Executive Air Charter (ZS)
RSU	Aerosur (CP)
RTE	Aeronorte (CS) [c]
RTM	Trans Am (HC)

RTN	Raytheon (N) [manufacturer]		SGS	Saskatchewan Govt Executive Air Service (C)
RTS	Relief Transport Services (G) [humanitarian]		SGV	Aerosegovia (YN)
RTT	Titan Aero (RA)		SGY	Skagway Air Service (N)
RUC	RUTACA (YV)		SHE	Shell Aircraft (G) [c]
RUM	RUM Airlines (JY)		SHJ	Sharjah Ruler's Flight (A6) [c
RUS	Cirrus Airlines (D)		SHM	Sheltham Aviation (ZS) [c]
RVC	Richards Aviation (N) [c]		SHP	SAF Helicopters (F) [c/EMS]
RVE	Airventure (OO)		SHT	British Airways Shuttle (G)
RVL	Air Vallee (I)		SHU	SAT-Sakhalinske Aviatrossy (RA)
RVP	AirVIP (CS) [c]		SHX	Sagawa Helicopter Express (JA) [c]
RVR	Ravenair (G) [c]		SHY	Sky Airlines (TC)
RVT	AirCompany Veteran (EK)		SHZ	CHC Scotia Helicopters (G)
RWD	Rwanda Express (9XR)		SIA	Singapore Airlines (9V)
RWL	RWL-German Flight Academy (D)[trainer]		SIB	Sibaviatrans (RA)
RWS	Air Whitsunday Seaplanes (VH)		SIG	Signature Aircraft Charter (G) [c]
RXA	Rex-Regional Airlines (VH)		SIH	Skynet Airlines (EI)
RYA	Arctic Transportation Services (N)		SIJ	Seco International (JA)
RYL	Royal Aruban Airlines (P4)		SIN	Servizi Aerei Industrali (I)
RYM	Atlantic Express (G)		SIO	Sirio (I) [c]
RYN	Ryan Intl Airlines (N)		SJE	Sunair 2000 (ZS)
RYR	Ryanair (EI)		SJT	Swiss Jet (HB) [c]
RYZ	Ryazan Avia Trans (RA)		SKC	Skymaster Airlines (PP)
RZN	Aero Zano (XA) [c]		SKH	British Sky Broadcasting (G)
RZO	SATA International (CS)		SKI	Skyking Airlines (VQ-T)
RZV	Rzhevka Air Enterprise		SKK	Skylink Aviation (C)
SAA	South African Airways (ZS)		SKL	Skycharter (C) [c]
SAB	SN Brussels Airlines (OO)		SKS	Sky Service (OO)
SAF	Republic of Singapore Air Force (9V) [m]		SKT	Sky Services Aviation (EC) [c]
SAG	SOS Flygambulans (SE) [EMS]		SKU	Sky Airline (CC)
SAH	Sayakhat (UN)		SKW	Skywest Airlines (N)
SAI	Shaheen Air Intl (AP)		SKY	Skymark Airlines (JA)
SAL	Regional Air (5Y)		SKZ	Skyway Enterprises (N)
SAM	SAM (HK)		SLA	Sierra National Airlines (9L)
SAO	Sahel Aviation Services (TU)		SLB	Slok Air (5N)
SAS	Scandinavian Airlines System (LN/OY/SE)		SLD	Silver Air (OK)
SAT	SATA - Air Acores (CS)		SLF	Skyline Flights (D) [c]
SAX	Sabah Air (9M)		SLG	Saskatchewan Government Air Ambulance (C)
SAY	ScotAirways (G)			[EMS]
SAZ	Swiss Air Ambulance (HB) [EMS]		SLH	Silverhawk Aviation Charter (N) [c]
SBA	STA-Mali (TZ)		SLI	Aerolitoral (XA)
SBD	SIBIA Aviakompania (RA) [c]		SLK	Silkair (9V)
SBF	SB Air (N)		SLL	Slovak Airlines (OM)
SBI	Sibir Airlines (RA)		SLM	Surinam Airways (PZ)
SBJ	Trans Sahara Air (5N)		SLN	Sloane Helicopters (G) [c]
SBU	St Barth Commuter (F-O)		SLR	Sobelair (OO)
SBX	North Star Air Cargo (N)		SMC	Sabang Merauke Air Charter (PK)
SCE	Scenic Airlines (N)		SMH	Smithair (N)
SCH	Schreiner Airways (PH)		SMK	Semeavia (UN)
SCJ	Business Air Sweden (SE) [c]		SMX	Alitalia Express (I)
SCO	Helikopterservice Euro Air (SE)		SNA	Senator Aviation Charter (D) [c]
SCR	Si-Chang Flying Service (HS) [c]		SNB	Sterling European A/L (OY)
SCT	SAAB (SE) [manufacturer]		SNC	Air Cargo Carriers (N)
SCW	Malmo Aviation (SE)		SNF	Shans Air (RA)
SCX	Sun Country Airlines (N)		SNG	Air Senegal International (6V)
SCY	Air Scandic (G)		SNJ	Skynet Asia Airways (JA)
SDB	Sukhoi Design Bureau Air Transport Co (RA)		SNK	Southeast Airlines (N)
SDC	Royal Swedish Air Force (SE) [m]		SNM	Servizi Aerei (I) [c]
SDE	Soder Air (OH)		SNV	Sudanair Express (ST)
SDK	SADELCA (HK)		SOC	SSA Joint Stock Company (RA) [c]
SDL	Skydrift Aircharter (G) [c]		SOF	Solis Aviation (LZ)
SDM	Russia State Transport Co (RA)		SOK	Sokol Atck (UR) [c]
SDO	Air Santo Domincana (HI)		SOL	Solomons (H4)
SDR	City Airlines (SE)		SOO	Southern Air (N)
SDV	SELVA (HK)		SOP	Solinair (S5)
SDY	Island Express (N)		SOV	Saratov Air (RA)
SEE	Shaheen Air Cargo (AP)		SOW	Sowind Air (C)
SEQ	Sky Eyes (HS) [c]		SOY	A Soriano Aviation (RP)
SER	Aero California (XA)		SPA	Sierra Pacific Airlines (N)
SEU	Star Airlines (F)		SPB	Springbok Classic Air (ZS)
SEY	Air Seychelles (S7)		SPD	Airspeed Aviation (C)
SFB	Air Sofia (LZ)		SPG	Springdale Air Service (N)
SFC	Shuswap Air (C) [c]		SPH	Sapphire Executive Air (ZS) [c]
SFF	Safewing Aviation (N) [c]		SPJ	Air Service (Z3)
SFG	Caribbean Sun Airlines (N)		SPK	North-South Airways (N)
SFN	Safarin Airlines (EP)		SPM	Air St Pierre (F-O)
SFP	Safe Air International (AP) [n]		SPN	Skorpion Air (LZ)
SFR	Safair (ZS)		SPS	Servicios Politecnicos Aereos (EC) [survey]
SFU	Solent Flight (G) [c]		SPU	Southeast Airmotive (N) [c]
SGB	Sky King Inc (N) [c]		SPW	Speedwings (HB) [c]
SGK	Skyward Aviation (C)		SPZ	Airworld (ZS)
SGL	Senegalair (6V)		SQC	Singapore Airlines Cargo (9V)
SGO	Space Cargo (3C)		SQF	Slovak Air Force (OM) [m]

SRC	SEARCA (HK)	TAI	TACA Intl Airlines (YS)
SRH	Siem Reap Airways International (XU)	TAJ	Tunisavia (TS)
SRI	Air Safaris & Services (ZK)	TAM	TAM Brasil (PP)
SRJ	Caucasus Airways (4L)	TAO	Aeromar Airlines (XA)
SRK	Sky Work (HB) [c]	TAP	Air Portugal (CS)
SRL	Swedeline Express (SE)	TAQ	Taunus Air (D) [c]
SRN	Sirair (RA)	TAR	Tunis Air (TS)
SRO	Saereo (HC)	TAS	Lotus Airlines (SU)
SRQ	SEAir Asian Airlines (RP)	TAT	TACA (TI)
SRR	Star Air (OY)	TAU	Transportes Aereos Tauro (XA) [c]
SRS	Selkirk Remote Sensing (C) [survey]	TAX	Travel Air Flug (D) [c]
SRU	Star Up (OB)	TAY	TNT Airways (OO)
SRW	Sarit Airlines (ST)	TBC	Turbine Air (G)
SSA	SISAV (I) [c}	TBG	Tropical Air d'Haiti (HH)
SSC	Southern Seaplanes (N)	TBX	Tobago Express (9Y)
SSD	Star Service International (F) [c]	TCF	Shuttle America (N)
SSG	Slovak Government Flying Service (OM)	TCG	Thai Air Cargo (HS)
SSN	Airquarius Air Charter (ZS)	TCJ	TCB-Transportes Charter do Brasil (PT)
SSP	Starspeed (G) [c}	TCL	Coastal Air Transport (N)
SSQ	Sunstate Airlines (VH)	TCR	Trans Costa Rica (TI)
SSS	SAESA (EC)	TCT	Transcontinental Sur (CX)
SSV	Skyservice Airlines (C)	TCU	Inter Tropical Aviation (PZ)
SSZ	Specsavers Aviation (G) [c]	TCV	TACV (D4)
STB	Staero (RA)	TCW	Thomas Cook Airlines (OO)
STI	Sontair (C)	TCX	Thomas Cook Airlines (G)
STJ	Stella Aviation Charter (PH) [c}	TCY	Twin Cities Air Service (N) [c]
STQ	Star Air (PK)	TDB	Welch Aviation (N) [c]
STT	Air St Thomas (N)	TDC	Tadair (EC)
STW	Aircompany Starway (EX)	TDG	Air Cargo Express (N)
STY	Styrian Spirit (OE)	TDM	Tandem Aero (ER)
SUA	Silesian Airlines (SP)	TDR	Trade Air (9A)
SUB	Suburban Air Freight (N)	TDX	Tradewinds Airlines (N)
SUD	Sudan Airways (ST)	TED	Azteca Airlines (XA)
SUF	Sun Airlines (DQ)	TEG	Transeuropean Airlines (SX)
SUG	Sunu Air (6V)	TEL	Telford Aviation (N)
SUI	Swiss Air Force (HB) [m]	TEM	Tech-Mont Helicopters (OM) [c]
SUK	Superior Aviation Services (5Y)	TET	Tepavia Trans (ER)
SUM	MCHS Rossii (RA)	TEX	CATEX (F) [c]
SUS	Sun-Air of Scandinavia (OY)	TFA	Trans Florida Airlines (N)
SUV	Sundance Air (YV)	TFH	Thai Flying Helicopter Service (HS) [h]
SUW	Astair (RA)	TFR	Trans-African Airways (3X)
SUZ	Premiair Charters (G) [c]	TFT	Thai Flying Service (HS)
SVA	Saudi Arabian Airlines (HZ)	TGA	Air Togo (5V)
SVB	Swefly (SE)	TGC	TG Aviation (G) [c]
SVD	SVG Air (J8)	TGE	TASA-Trabajos Aereos (EC) [c]
SVF	Swedish Armed Forces (SE) [m]	TGN	Trigana Air Service (PK)
SVI	SETRA (XA)	TGO	Transport Canada (C)
SVK	Air Slovakia (OM)	TGT	SAAB Nyge Aero (SE) [c]
SVM	Aeroservicios Monterrey (XA)	TGV	SNCF (F) [railways]
SVN	Savanair (D2)	TGY	Trans Guyana Airways (8R)
SVP	Saratov Aviation Plant (RA)	TGZ	Air Zena Georgian A/L (4L)
SVR	Ural Airlines (RA)	THA	Thai Airways Intl (HS)
SVT	Sakhalin Airlines (RA)	THK	Turk Hava Kurumu (TC)
SVW	Silver Arrows (LX) [c]	THT	Air Tahiti Nui (F-O)
SVX	Security Aviation (N) [c]	THU	Thunder Airlines (C)
SVY	Cooper Aerial Surveys (G) [survey]	THY	THY-Turkish Airlines (TC)
SWA	Southwest Airlines (N)	THZ	THS Helicopters (F) [c]
SWB	Swissboogie (HB) [c]	TIC	Travel Intl Air Charter (9J) [c]
SWD	Southern Winds (LV)	TIH	Ion Tiriac Air (YR)
SWE	Swedeways (SE)	TIL	Tajikstan International Airlines (EY)
SWH	Adler Aviation (C)	TIM	Team Air Lines (PP)
SWI	Sunworld Intl Airlines (N)	TIN	Taino Airlines (HI)
SWN	West Air Sweden (SE)	TIS	Tesis (RA)
SWP	Star Work Sky (I) [c]	TIW	Transcarga (YV)
SWR	Swiss International Airlines (HB)	TJN	Tian-Shan (UN) [c]
SWT	Swiftair (EC)	TJT	Twin Jet (F)
SWX	Swazi Express Airways (3D)	TKC	Tikal Jet Airlines (TG)
SWZ	Servair (HB) [c]	TKO	Tretyakovo Airlines (RA)
SXA	Southern Cross Avn (N) [ferry]	TKX	Tropical International Airways (V4)
SXM	SAEMSA (XA)	TLB	Atlantique Air Assistance (F)
SXS	Sun Express Air (TC)	TLE	Aero Util (XA)
SYB	Symbol Compania de Aviacion (EC) [c]	TLP	Tulip Air (PH)
SYJ	Slate Falls Airways (C)	TLR	Air Libya Tibesti (5A)
SYL	Yakutia Airlines (RA)	TLT	Turtle Airways (DQ)
SYR	Syrianair (YK)	TLY	TopFly (EC)
SYX	Midwest Connect (N)	TMA	TMA Cargo (OD)
SYY	South African Historic Flight (ZS)	TMG	Tri MG Airlines (PK)
SZL	Airlinks Swaziland (3D)	TMH	Transmanche Aviation (F) [c]
TAE	TAME (HC)	TMM	TMC Airlines (N)
TAF	Aerea Transportes Aereos del Pacifico (XA) [c]	TMN	UTAir (RA)
TAG	TAG Aviation (N) [c]	TMP	Arizona Express Airways (N)
TAH	Air Moorea (F-O)	TMS	Temsco Helicopter A/L (N)

TMX	Tramon Air (ZS)	UCH	US Airports Air Charter (N) [c]
TNA	Transasia Airways (B)	UCR	Aero Charter Ukraine (UR)
TNB	Trans-Air Benin (TY)	UDC	Donbass Aero (UR)
TNO	Aerotransporte de Carga Union (XA)	UDN	Dnieproavia (UR)
TNR	Tanana Air Service (N)	UEJ	JetCorp (N) [c]
TNT	Trans North Helicopters (C)	UES	UES Avia (UR)
TNX	Trener Air (ha) [c]	UFA	Ukraine State Flying School (UR)
TOB	Tobruk Air (5A)	UGL	Inter Island Express (N)
TOL	Tol Air Services (N)	UGN	Yuzhnaya Air Company (UN)
TOO	Alieurope (I)	UGP	Shar Ink (RA)
TOS	Tropic Air Commuter (V3)	UGX	East African Airways (5X)
TPA	TAMPA Airlines (HK)	UHS	Ulyanovsk Higher Civil Aviation School (RA)
TPC	Air Caledonie (F-O)	UIA	UNI Air (B)
TPG	Pegaso (XA)	UJT	Universal Jet Aviation (N) [c]
TPK	Air Horizon Afrique (TT)	UKA	Buzz (G)
TPM	Transpais Aereo (XA) [c]	UKL	Ukraine Air Alliance (UR)
TPR	TAPO Avia (UK)	UKM	UM Airlines (UR)
TPS	TAPSA Aviation (LV)	UKN	Ukraine Air Enterprise (UR)
TPU	TACA Peru (OB)	UKO	Yuros Bulgarian Air Co (LZ) [c]
TPV	Thai Pacific Airlines (HS)	UKR	Air Ukraine (UR)
TRA	Transavia Airlines (PH)	UKS	Ukrainian Cargo Airways (UR)
TRD	Trans Island Air (8P)	UKU	Sverdlovsk 2nd Air Enterprise (RA)
TRI	Ontario Ministry of National Resources Air Services(C)	UKW	Lvov Airlines (UR)
		ULC	AirLanka Cargo (4R)
TRJ	AJT Air International (RA)	UMB	Airumbria (I) [c]
TRN	Servicios Aereos Corporativos (XA) [c]	UMK	Yuzhmashavia (UR)
TRS	Airtran Airways (N)	UNC	Uni-Fly (OY) [c]
TRT	TAAT -Trans Arabian Air Transport (ST)	UNE	Aerolineas Universal (HK)
TRZ	Transmeridian Airways (N)	UNF	Union Flights (N)
TSC	Air Transat (C)	UNL	Ukraine National Airlines (UR)
TSD	TAF Linhas Aereas (PT)	UNO	United Nations (-) [humanitarian]
TSE	Transmile Air Services (9M)	UNR	Rovno Universal Air (UR)
TSG	Trans Air Congo (TN)	UNS	Uesnsped Paket Servisi (TC)
TSI	Transport Air (F) [c]	UPL	Ukrainian Pilot School (UR)
TSK	Tomsk Airways (RA)	UPS	United Parcel Service (N)
TSO	Transaero Airlines (RA)	URG	Air Urga (UR)
TSP	Inter Transportes Aereos (TG)	URJ	Star Air Aviation (AP)
TSS	Tri-State Aero (N) [c]	URN	Turanair (4K)
TSU	Contract Air Cargo (N)	URP	ARP 410 Airlines (UR)
TSY	Tristar Air (SU)	URT	Avia Urartu (EK)
TTA	TTA (C9)	URV	Uraiavia (RA) [c]
TTG	Transtel (5V)	USA	US Airways (N)
TTL	Total Lineas Aereas (PP)	USB	Tusheti (4L) [c]
TUA	Turkmenistan Airlines (EZ)	USC	Airnet Systems (N)
TUD	Flight Alaska (N) [c]	USS	US Airways Shuttle (N)
TUI	Tuninter (TS)	UST	Austro Aereo (HC)
TUQ	Air Turquoise (F) [c]	USX	US Airways Express (N)
TUS	ABSA Cargo (PP)	UTG	UTAGE (3C)
TUV	Turavia Air Transport (SP) [c]	UTK	Irkut-Avia (RA)
TUX	Tulpar Air Services (UN)	UTL	Aviatia Utilitara Bucuresti (YR) [c]
TUY	Aereotuy (YV)	UVG	Universal Airlines (8R)
TVH	Tavasa (EC) [c]	UVS	Air Universal (9L)
TVI	Tiramavia (ER)	UYA	Flight Alaska (N)
TVJ	TAVAJ (PT)	UYC	Cameroon Airlines (TJ)
TVL	Travel Service Hungary (HA)	UZA	Constanta Airlines (UR)
TVM	Tavria-Mak (UR)	UZB	Uzbekistan Airways (UK)
TVR	Tavria Aviakompania (UR)	UZL	Uzavialeasing (UK)
TVS	Travel Service Airlines (OK)	VAL	Voyageur Airways (C)
TWE	Transair Sweden (SE)	VAP	Phuket Aviation (HS)
TWG	Trans Wing (LN)	VAS	Atran (RA)
TWJ	Twinjet Aircraft (G) [c]	VAV	Angkor Air Co (XU)
TWM	Transairways (C9)	VAZ	Airlines 400 (RA)
TWN	Avialeasing (UK)	VBG	Vyborg (RA)
TXC	Trans Avia Export Cargo Airlines (EW)	VBI	Pacific Blue (ZK)
TXE	Transaero Express (RA)	VBS	Avbase Aviation (N) [c]
TXI	ATSA (XA) [c]	VBW	Air Burkina (XT)
TYJ	Tyrolean Jet Services (OE)	VCG	KNG Transavia Cargo (3C)
TYM	Tyumen Airlines (RA)	VCN	Execujet Charter (HB) [c]
TYR	Tyrolean Airways (OE)	VDA	Volga-Dnepr Airlines (RA)
TYW	Tyrol Air Ambulance (OE) [EMS]	VDR	Air Vardar (Z3)
TZA	Aero Tomza (XA) [c]	VEA	Vega Airlines (LZ)
TZK	Tajikistan Airlines (EY)	VEC	Venescar Internacional (YV)
TZU	Servicios Aereos Tamazula (XA) [c]	VEE	Victor Echo (EC) [c]
UAB	United Arabian Company (ST)	VEJ	Aeroejecutivos (YV)
UAC	United Air Charters (Z)	VES	Vieques Air Link (N)
UAE	Emirates (A6)	VEX	Virgin Express (OO)
UAF	United Arab Emirates Air Force (A6) [m]	VFC	VASCO (VN)
UAK	Aviant (UR)	VGA	Air Vegas (N)
UAL	United Airlines (N)	VGE	Air Service Vosges (F)
UAR	Aerostar (UN)	VGV	Vologda State Aviation Enterprise (RA)
UBA	Myanma Airways (XY)	VHM	VHM Charterflug (D) [c]
UCA	Commutair (N)	VIB	VibroAir (D) [c]

VID	Avia Prad (RA)
VIH	Vichi Airlines (ER)
VIK	Viking Airlines (SE)
VIM	VIA - Bulgarian Airways (LZ)
VIN	Vinair Aeroservicios (CS) [c]
VIR	Virgin Atlantic Airways (G)
VIS	Aerovis Airlines (OY)
VJG	Avioriprese Jet Executive (I) [c]
VKG	MyTravel Airways(OY)
VLA	Valan International Cargo Charter (ZS)
VLE	Volare (I)
VLK	Vladivostok Air (RA)
VLM	VLM Airlines (OO)
VLN	Valan International Cargo (ER)
VLO	VARIG Logistica (PP)
VLT	Vertical T Air Transport (RA) [c]
VLU	ValuAir (9V)
VLV	Avialift Vladivostock (RA) [c]
VMM	Grupo Vuelos Mediterraneo (EC) [c]
VMP	Execujet Scandinavia (OY) [c]
VNR	Wanair (F-O)
VNZ	Tbilaviamsheni (4L)
VOA	Viaggio Air (LZ)
VOL	Blue Chip Jet (SE) [c]
VOS	Rovos Air (ZS)
VOZ	Virgin Blue (VH)
VPB	Veteran Airlines (UR)
VRB	Silverback Cargo Freighters (9XR)
VRE	Volare Aviation Enterprise (UR)
VRG	VARIG - Viacao Aerea Rio Grandense (PP)
VRL	Air Vallee (I)
VRN	Voronezh Avia (RA)
VRT	Averitt Air Charter (N) [c]
VSO	VASO Airlines (RA)
VSP	VASP - Viacao Aerea Sao Paulo (PP)
VSR	Aviostart (LZ)
VSU	Aerolineas Saso (HR)
VSV	SCAT (UN)
VTA	Air Tahiti (F-O)
VTE	Corporate Flight Management (N)
VTK	Vostock Airlines (RA)
VTS	Everts Air Alaska/Everts Cargo (N)
VTT	Avia Trans Air Transport (ST)
VUE	Ad Aviation (G) [c]
VUL	Elios (I) [c]
VUN	Air Ivoire (TU)
VUR	Vuelos Internos Privados (HC)
VVA	Aviast (RA)
VVI	Vivant Air (LZ)
VXG	Avirex (TR)
VXP	Avion Express (TZ)
VXX	AviaExpress Aircompany (UR)
VZL	VZ Let (RA) [c]
VZR	Aviazur (F-O)
WAA	West Air Aviation (V5)
WAB	Aero Industries (N)
WAE	Western Air Express (N)
WAK	Wings of Alaska (N)
WAS	Walsten Air Service (C)
WAV	Warbelow's Air Ventures (N)
WAY	Airways (F) [c]
WBA	Westbird Aviation (OH) [c]
WCA	West Coast Airlines (9L)
WCO	Columbia Helicopters (N)
WCR	West Caribbean Costa Rica (TS)
WCW	West Caribbean Airways (HK)
WDA	Wimbi Dira Airways (9Q)
WDK	Oxford Helicopters (G) [c]
WDL	WDL Aviation (D)
WEA	White Eagle General Avn (SP)
WES	Westex (C)
WEW	West Wind Aviation (C)
WFA	Westflug Aachen (D) [c]
WGP	Williams Grand Prix Racing (G) [c]
WGT	VW Air Services (D) [c]
WHE	Westland Helicopters (G) [manufacturers]
WHS	Wiking Helikopter Service (D) [c]
WIA	Winair (PJ)
WIF	Wideroe's Flyveselskap (LN)
WIG	Wiggins Airways (N)
WIL	West Isle Air (N)
WJA	Westjet Airlines (C)

WKH	Kharkov Aviation Production Association (UR)
WLA	Airwaves Airlink (G)
WLC	Welcome Air (OE)
WLG	Volga Aviaexpress (RA)
WLR	Air Walser (I) [c]
WML	Chantilly Air (N) [c]
WNC	Wenic Air Services (9V)
WNT	CargoJet Airways (C)
WOA	World Airways (N)
WOD	Woodgate Executive Air Services (G)
WON	Wings Air (PK)
WRA	White River Air Service (C)
WSF	West African Airways (TY)
WSG	Wasaya Airways (C)
WTA	Africa West (5V)
WTC	Weasua Airtransport (A8)
WTV	Air Colorado (N)
XAR	Travel Express Aviation Services (PK)
XAX	Rockhopper (G)
XER	Xerox (N) [c]
XIA	Irving Oil (C) [c]
XKX	ASECNA (6V)
XLA	Excel Airways (G)
XLL	Air Excel (5H)
XMS	British Airways Santa (G)
XNA	Express.net Airlines (N)
XNR	Taxi Aereo del Norte (XA)
YRG	Air Yugoslavia (YU)
YSS	Yes (CS)
YXA	National Airports Authority (VT) [calibration]
YZR	Yangtze River Express (B)
ZAK	Zambian Skyways (9J)
ZAN	Zantop Intl Airlines (N)
ZAV	Zhetysu Avia (UK)
ZBA	ZB Air (5Y)
ZIP	Zip Air (C)

Key: [c] is corporate operator and [m] is military

AIRPORT 3-LETTER CODE INDEX

Code	Location	Code	Location	Code	Location
BYG	Buffalo-Municipal, WY	COS	Colorado Springs Memorial, CO	DNA	Okinawa-Kadena
BZE	Belize City-Philip SW Goldson Intl	COU	Columbia Regional, MO	DND	Dundee-Riverside Park
		CPE	Campeche-Intl	DNK	Dnepropetrovsk
BZK	Bryansk	CPH	Copenhagen-Kastrup	DNQ	Deniliquin
BZV	Brazzaville Maya-Maya	CPQ	Campinhas	DNR	Dinard-Pleurtuit
CAE	Columbia Metropolitan, SC	CPR	Casper-Natrona County Intl, WY	DOH	Doha Intl
CAG	Cagliari-Elmas	CPT	Cape Town-DF Malan Intl	DOK	Donetsk
CAI	Cairo Intl	CRD	Comodoro Rivadavia/Gen Mosconi	DPA	Chicago-du Page, IL
CAK	Akron-Canton Regional, OH			DPS	Denpasar-Ngurah Rai
CAN	Guangzhou-Baiyun	CRE	Myrtle Beach-Grand Strand, SC	DRS	Dresden
CAP	Cap Haitien Intl	CRK	Clark Air Base	DRT	Del Rio Intl, TX
CAS	Casablanca-Anfa	CRU	Carriacou Island	DRW	Darwin
CAY	Cayenne-Rochambeau	CRZ	Chardzhev	DSM	Des Moines Intl, IA
CBB	Cochabamba-Jorge Wilsterman	CSE	Crested Butte, CO	DTM	Dortmund-Wickede
		CSL	San Luis Obispo-O'Sullivan, CA	DTN	Shreveport-Downtown, LA
CBG	Cambridge	CSN	Carson City, NV	DTW	Detroit Metropolitan, MI
CBL	Cuidad Bolivar	CSY	Cheboksary	DUB	Dublin
CBR	Canberra	CTC	Catamarca	DUD	Dunedin
CCL	Chinchilla	CTG	Cartagena-Rafael Nunez	DUJ	DuBois-Jefferson County, PA
CCP	Concepcion-Carriel Sur	CTM	Chetumal	DUQ	Duncan
CCS	Caracas-Simon Bolivar Intl	CTN	Cooktown	DUR	Durban-Louis Botha Intl
CCU	Calcutta-Chadra Bose Intl	CTS	Sapporo-New Chitose	DUS	Dusseldorf
CDB	Cold Bay, AK	CTU	Chengdu-Shuangliu	DUT	Dutch Harbor, AK
CDG	Paris-Charles de Gaulle	CUB	Columbus-Owens Field, SC	DVT	Phoenix-Deer Valley, AZ
CDU	Camden	CUD	Caloundra	DXB	Dubai Intl
CDW	Caldwell-Essex Co, NJ	CUE	Cuenca	DYR	Anadyr-Ugolny
CEB	Cebu-Lahug	CUG	Cudal	DYU	Dushanbe
CEE	Cherepovets	CUH	Cushing-Municipal, OK	DZN	Zhezkazgan
CEJ	Chernigov	CUM	Cumana-Antonio Jose de Sucre	EAT	Wenatchee-Pangborn, WA
CEK	Chelyabinsk-Balandino	CUN	Cancun Intl	EAU	Eau-Claire County, WI
CEQ	Cannes-Mandelieu	CUR	Curacao-Williemstadt	EBB	Entebbe Intl
CER	CherbourgMaupertun	CUU	Chihuahua/Gen Villalobos Intl	EBJ	Esbjerg
CEW	Crestview-Bob Sikes, FL	CUZ	Cuzco-Velaazco Astete	ECN	Ercan-Leskofa
CFE	Clermont-Ferrand	CVF	Courchevel	EDF	Anchorage-Elmendorf AFB, AK
CFN	Donegal-Carrickfin	CVG	Cincinnati-Covington Intl, OH	EDI	Edinburgh
CFR	Caen-Carpiquet	CVJ	Cuernavaca	EDM	La Roche-sur-Yon
CFS	Coffs Harbour	CVN	Clovis-Municipal, NM	EFD	Houston-Ellington Field, TX
CFU	Kerkira	CVQ	Carnarvon	EGO	Belgorod
CGH	Sao Paulo-Congonhas	CVR	Culver City, CA	EGS	Eglisstadir
CGK	Jakarta-Soekarno Hatta Intl	CVT	Coventry-Baginton	EGV	Eagle River, WI
CGN	Cologne-Bonn	CWA	Wausau, WI	EIN	Eindhoven
CGO	Zhengzhou	CWB	Curitiba-Alfonso Pena	EIS	Beef Island
CGP	Chittagong Intl	CWC	Chernovtsy	EKO	Elko Municipal, NV
CGQ	Changchun	CWL	Cardiff-Wales	EKT	Eskilstuna-Eskeby
CGR	Campo Grande Intl	CXH	Vancouver-Coal Harbour	EKX	Elizabethtown, KY
CHA	Chattanooga, TN	CYM	Chathanm SPB, AK	ELC	Elcho Island
CHC	Christchurch Intl	CYS	Cheyenne, WY	ELM	Elmira-Corning Regional, NY
CHD	Chandler-Williams AFB, AZ	CZM	Cozumel Intl	ELP	El Paso Intl, TX
CHR	Chateauroux-Deols	CZS	Cruzeiro do Sul-Campo Intl	ELS	East London-Ben Schoeman
CHS	Charleston Intl, SC	CZX	Changzhou	EMA	East Midlands
CHT	Chathams Island-Karewa	DAB	Daytona Beach-Regional, FL	EME	Emden
CIA	Rome-Ciampino	DAC	Dhaka-Zia Intl	EMK	Emmonak, AK
CIC	Chico, CA	DAL	Dallas-Love Field, TX	ENA	Kenai Municipal, AK
CIH	Changzhi	DAM	Damascus Intl	ENS	Twente-Enschede
CIX	Chiclayo-Cornel Ruiz	DAR	Dar-es-Salaam Intl	ENU	Enugu
CJN	El Cajun, CA	DAY	Dayton-James M Cox Intl, OH	EOH	Medellin-Enrique Olaya Herrara
CKC	Cherkassy	DBO	Dubbo	EOR	El Dorado
CKG	Chongqing	DBV	Dubrovnik	EPH	Ephrata, WA
CKY	Conakry-Gbessia	DCA	Washington-Reagan National, DC	EPL	Epinal-Mirecourt
CLD	Carlsbad, CA	DCF	Dominica-Cane Field	ERF	Erfurt
CLE	Cleveland-Hopkins Intl, OH	DEL	Delhi-Indira Gandhi Intl	ERI	Erie Intl, CO
CLO	Cali-Alfonso Bonilla Aragon	DEN	Denver Intl, CO	ERS	Windhoek-Eros
CLT	Charlotte-Douglas Intl, NC	DET	Detroit City, MI	ESE	Ensenada
CLU	Columbus-Municipal, IN	DFW	Dallas-Forth Worth Intl, TX	ESF	Alexandria-Regional, LA
CMB	Colombo-Bandaranaike Intl	DGO	Durango-Guadelupe Victoria	ESL	Elista
CMD	Cootamundra	DHA	Dhahran Intl	ESS	Essen-Mülheim
CMF	Chambery/Aix les Bains	DHF	Abu Dhabi-Al Dhaffra	ETH	Eliat-Hozman
CMH	Columbus-Port Intl, OH	DHN	Dothan, AL	EUG	Eugene-Mahlon Sweet, OR
CMN	Casablanca-Mohammed V	DHR	Den Holder/de Kooy	EVE	Harstad-Norvik
CMR	Colmar-Houssen	DIJ	Dijon-Longvic	EVG	Sveg
CMU	Kundiawa-Chimbu	DIL	Dili-Comoro	EVN	Yerevan-Zvartnots
CMV	Coromandel	DJE	Djerba-Zarziz	EWR	Newark Liberty Intl, NJ
CNF	Belo Horizonte-Neves Intl	DJJ	Jayapura	EXT	Exeter
CNI	Shanghai	DJN	Delta Junction	EYP	El Yopal
CNL	Sindal	DKR	Dakar-Yoff	EYW	Key West Intl, FL
CNS	Cairns	DLA	Douala	EZE	Buenos Aires-Ezeiza
CNW	Waco-James Connolly, TX	DLG	Dillingham, AK	FAE	Vagar-Faroe Islands
COA	Columbia, CA	DLH	Duluth Intl, MN	FAI	Fairbanks Intl, AK
COE	Coeur d'Alene, ID	DMA	Davis-Monthan AFB, AZ	FAM	Farmington Regional, MO
CON	Concord-Municipal, NH	DMB	Taraz-Zhambyl	FAO	Faro
COO	Cotonou-Cadjehoun	DME	Moscow-Domodedovo	FAT	Fresno Air Terminal, CA
COR	Cordoba-Pajas Blancas			FBK	Fairbanks-Fort Wainwright, AK

FBM	Lubumbashi-Luano
FCO	Rome-Fiumicino
FDE	Forde
FDF	Fort de France-le Lamentin
FDH	Friedrichshafen
FEW	Cheyenne/Warren AFB, WY
FGI	Apia-Faqali'l
FIH	Kinshasa-N'Djili
FJR	Fujairah Intl
FKB	Karlsruhe-Baden Baden
FKI	Kisangani
FLF	Flensburg
FLL	Fort Lauderdale-Hollywood Intl, FL
FLR	Florence-Peretola
FLS	Finders Island
FMN	Farmington-Four Counties Regional, NM
FMO	Munster/Osnabruck
FNA	Freetown-Lungi Intl
FNC	Funchal-Madeira
FNI	Nimes-Garons
FNJ	Pyongyang-Sunan
FNT	Flint-Bishop Intl, MI
FOC	Fuzhou
FOG	Foggia-Gino Lisa
FOR	Fortaleza-Pinto Martins
FPO	Freeport Intl
FPR	Fort Pierce-St Lucie Co, FL
FRA	Frankfurt Intl
FRD	Friday Harbor, WA
FRG	Farmingdale-Republic Field, NY
FRJ	Frejus-Saint Raphael
FRL	Forli-Luigi Ridolfi
FRU	Bishkek-Manas
FSD	Sioux Falls-Foss Field, SD
FSP	St Pierre et Miquelon
FTW	Fort Worth-Meacham, TX
FTY	Atlanta-Fulton Co, GA
FUK	Fukuoka
FWA	Fort Wayne Intl, IN
FXE	Fort Lauderdale Executive, FL
FZO	Bristol-Filton
GAJ	Yamaguchi
GBE	Gaborone-Sir Sertse Khama Intl
GBI	Grand Bahama Island
GBL	Goulburn Island, NT
GCI	Guernsey
GCJ	Johannesburg-Grand Central
GCM	Georgetown-Owen Roberts Intl
GCN	Grand Canyon National Park, AZ
GDL	Guadalajara-Costilla Intl
GDN	Gdansk
GDT	Grand Turk
GDX	Magadan-Sokol
GEA	Noumea-Magenta
GEN	Oslo-Gardermoen
GEO	Georgetown-Cheddi Jagan
GET	Geraldtown, VIC
GEX	Geelong
GEY	Greybull-South Big Horn, WY
GHN	Guanghan
GIB	Gibraltar
GIG	Rio de Janeiro-Galeao
GIS	Gisborne
GJT	Grand Junction-Walker Field, CO
GKA	Goroka
GKH	Gorkha
GLA	Glasgow
GLO	Gloucester
GLZ	Gilze-Rijen
GME	Gomel-Pokalubishi
GNB	Grenoble-St Geoirs
GOA	Genoa-Cristoforo Colombo
GOH	Godthaab-Nuuk
GOI	Goa-Dabolim
GOJ	Nizhny Novogorod-Streigino
GOM	Goma
GON	Groton-New London, CT
GOT	Gothenburg-Landvetter
GOV	Grove-Nhulunbuy
GPT	Gulfport-Biloxi Regional, MS

GRO	Gerona-Costa Brava
GRQ	Groningen-Eelde
GRR	Grand Rapids-Kent County, MI
GRU	Sao Paulo-Guarulhos
GRV	Grozny
GRZ	Graz-Thalerhof
GSE	Gothenburg-Save
GSO	Greensboro-Piedmont Triad Intl, SC
GTR	Columbus-Golden Triangle Regional, GA
GUA	Guatemala City-La Aurora
GUB	Guerrero Negro
GUM	Guam-Ab Won Pat Intl
GUW	Akyrau
GVA	Geneva-Cointrin
GVT	Greenville-Majors Field, TX
GWO	Greenwood-le Floor, MS
GWT	Westerland-Sylt
GWY	Galway-Carnmore
GXQ	Coyhaique-Teniente Vidal
GYE	Guayaquil-Simon Bolivar
GYN	Goioma
GYR	Goodyear-Litchfield, AZ
GZA	Gaza Intl
GZM	Gozo
HAH	Moroni-Prince Said Ibrahim
HAJ	Hannover
HAK	Haikou-Dayingshan
HAM	Hamburg-Fuhlsbüttel
HAN	Hanoi-Gialam
HAO	Hamilton, OH
HAU	Haugesund
HAV	Havana-Jose Marti Intl
HBA	Hobart
HDD	Hyderabad
HEL	Helsinki-Vantaa
HEM	Helsinki-Malmi
HER	Heraklion
HEX	Santo Domingo-la Herrara
HGH	Hangzhou-Jianqio
HGL	Helgoland-Dune
HGR	Hagerstown, MD
HGU	Mount Hagen-Kagamuga
HHN	Hahn
HHR	Hawthorne, CA
HID	Horn Island
HIG	Highbury
HII	Lake Havasu
HIK	Honolulu-Oahu Island, HI
HIR	Honiara-Henderson
HKG	Hong Kong Intl
HKT	Phuket Intl
HLA	Lanseria
HLF	Hultsfred
HLP	Jakarta-Halim Perdanakusuma
HLT	Hamilton, VIC
HLZ	Hamilton
HME	Hassi Messaoud
HMJ	Khmelnitsky
HMO	Hermosillo-Gen Garcia Intl
HMT	Hemet-Ryan Field, CA
HND	Tokyo-Haneda Intl
HNL	Honolulu Intl, HI
HNS	Haines Municipal, AK
HOH	Hohenems-Dornbirn
HOM	Homer, AK
HOT	East Hampton, NY
HOU	Houston-Hobby, TX
HRB	Harbin-Yanjiagang
HRE	Harare Intl
HRK	Kharkov
HSH	Las Vegas-Henderson, NV
HSM	Horsham, VIC
HST	Homestead, FL
HTA	Chita-Kadala
HTI	Hamilton Island
HTO	East Hampton, NY
HUF	Terre Haute-Hulman Regional, IN
HUM	Houma, LA

HUV	Hudiksvall
HUY	Humberside
HVB	Hervey Bay, QLD
HVN	New Haven-Tweed, CT
HWO	Hollywood-North Perry, FL
HYA	Hyannis-Barnstable Municipal, MA
HZB	Mervilel-Calonnel
IAB	Wichita-McConnell AFB, KS
IAD	Washington-Dulles Intl, DC
IAG	Niagara Falls-Intl, NY
IAH	Houston Intercontinental, TX
IBA	Ibadan
IBE	Ibague-Perales
IBZ	Ibiza
ICN	Seoul-Incheon
ICT	Wichita-Mid Continent, KS
IEV	Kiev-Zhulyany
IFJ	Isafjordur
IFN	Isfahan
IFO	Ivano-Frankovsk
IFP	Laughlin-Bullhead Intl, AZ
IGM	Kingman, AZ
IJK	Izhevsk
IKI	Iki
IKT	Irkutsk
ILG	Wilmington-Newcastle, DE
ILI	Iliamna, AK
ILN	Wilmington-Airborne, OH
ILR	Ilorin
IMT	Iron Mountain-Ford, MI
IND	Indianapolis Intl, IN
INN	Innsbruck-Kranebitten
INT	Winston-Salem-Smith Reynolds, NC
INU	Nauru Island Intl
INV	Inverness-Dalcross
IOM	Ronaldsway
IQQ	Iquique-Diego Aracena
IQT	Iquitos-Coronel Vignetta
IRK	Kirksville-Regional, MO
ISA	Mount Isa
ISB	Islamabad-Chaklala
ISM	Kissimmee Municipal, FL
ISO	Kinston-Stalling Field, NC
IST	Istanbul-Ataturk
ITB	Itaituba
ITM	Osaka-Itami Intl
ITO	Hilo Intl, HI
IVC	Invercargill
IWA	Ivanovo
JAN	Jackson Intl, MS
JAV	Ilulissat-Jakobshavn
JAX	Jacksonville Intl, FL
JDP	Paris-Heliport
JED	Jeddah-King Abdul Aziz Intl
JER	Jersey
JFK	New York-JFK, NY
JGC	Grand Canyon Heliport, AZ
JHB	Johor Bahru-Sultan Ismail Intl
JHE	Helsingborg Heliport
JHW	Jamestown-Chautauqua Co, NY
JIB	Djibouti-Ambouli
JKG	Jonkoping-Axamo
JNB	Johannesburg-Jan Smuts Intl
JNU	Juneau Intl, AK
JVL	Janesville-Rock County, WI
KAD	Kaduna
KAN	Kano-Mallam Aminu Intl
KBL	Kabul-Khwaja Rawash
KBP	Kiev-Borispol
KCH	Koching
KDH	Kandahar
KDK	Kodiak Municipal, AK
KEF	Keflavik Intl
KEH	Kenmore Air Harbor, WA
KEJ	Kemorovo
KEP	Nepalgunj
KER	Kerman
KGC	Kingscote
KGD	Kaliningrad-Khrabovo
KGF	Karaganda

KGI	Kalgoorlie	LEH	le Havre-Octeville	MEM	Memphis Intl, TN
KGL	Kigali-Gregoire Kayibanda	LEJ	Leipzig-Halle	MES	Medan-Polonia
KGO	Kirovograd	LEQ	Lands End-St Just	MEX	Mexico City-Juarez Intl
KGP	Kogalym	LFT	Lafayette-Regional, AL	MFE	McAllen-Miller, TX
KHH	Kaoshiung Intl	LFW	Lome-Tokoin	MFM	Macau Intl
KHI	Karachi Quaid-e-Azam Intl	LGA	New York-La Guardia, NY	MFN	Milford Sound
KHV	Khabarovsk-Novy	LGB	Long Beach-Daugherty Field, CA	MGA	Managua-Sandino
KIH	Kish Island	LGG	Liege-Biersit	MGB	Mount Gambier
KIN	Kingston-Norman Manley Intl	LGW	London Gatwick	MGL	Mönchengladbach
KIV	Kishinev-Chisinau	LGY	Lagunillas	MGQ	Mogadishu Intl
KIW	Kitwe-Southdowns	LHE	Lahore Intl	MHB	Auckland-Mechanics Bay
KIX	Osaka-Kansai Intl	LHR	London-Heathrow	MHD	Mashad-Shahid Hashemi
KJA	Krasnoyarsk-Yemelyanovo	LIG	Limoges-Bellegarde		Nejad Intl
KJK	Kortrijk-Wevelgem	LIL	Lille-Lesquin	MHG	Mannheim-Neu Ostheim
KLF	Kaluga	LIM	Lima-Jorge Chavez Intl	MHH	Marsh Harnour
KLU	Klagenfurt	LIN	Milan-Linate	MHP	Minsk 2 Intl
KMG	Kunming-Wujiaba	LIS	Lisbon	MHQ	Mariehamn
KMI	Miyazaki	LIT	Little Rock-Adams Field, AR	MHR	Sacramento-Mather, CA
KMJ	Kumamoto	LJU	Ljubljana-Brnik	MHV	Mojave-Kern Co, CA
KMW	Kostroma	LKE	Seattle-Lake Union, WA	MIA	Miami Intl, FL
KNX	Kununurra	LKO	Lucknow-Amausi	MIB	Monastir
KOA	Kailua Kona, HI	LKP	Lake Placid, NY	MID	Merida
KOV	Kokhshetan	LLA	Lulea-Kallax	MIE	Newcastle, IN
KOW	Ganzhou	LLW	Lilongwe-Tilange Intl	MIR	Monastir-Habib Bourguiba Intl
KRB	Karumba	LME	Le Mans-Arnage	MIU	Maiduguri
KRH	Redhill	LNA	West Palm Beach, FL	MJM	Mbuji Mayi
KRK	Krakow Intl	LNX	Smolensk	MJZ	Mirny
KRO	Kurgan	LNZ	Linz-Hoersching	MKC	Kansas City Downtown, KS
KRP	Karup	LOS	Lagos-Murtala Mohammed	MKE	Milwaukee-Mitchell Field, WI
KRR	Krasnodar-Pashkovsky	LPA	Las Palmas-Gran Canaria	MKY	MacKay
KRS	Kristiansand-Kjevik	LPB	La Paz-El Alto	MLA	Luqa
KRT	Khartoum-Civil	LPI	Linkoping-Malmen	MLB	Melbourne-Cape Kennedy, FL
KSC	Kosice-Barca	LPK	Lipetsk	MLC	McAlester-Regional, OK
KSD	Karlstad	LPL	Liverpool Intl	MLE	Male Intl
KSF	Kassel-Calden	LPY	Le Puy-Loudes	MLH	Basle-Mulhouse EuroAirport
KSK	Karlskoga	LRD	Laredo Intl, TX	MLU	Monroe-Regional, LA
KSM	St Mary's Bethel, AK	LRE	Longreach, QL	MLW	Monrovia-Spriggs Payne
KSN	Kustanay	LRH	La Rochelle-Laleu	MMK	Murmansk
KSZ	Kotlas	LSI	Sumburgh	MML	Marshall-Ryan Field, MN
KTA	Karratha	LST	Launceston	MMX	Malmo-Sturup
KTE	Kerteh	LTN	London-Luton	MNL	Manila-Nino Aquino Intl
KTM	Kathmandu-Tribhuvan Intl	LUG	Lugano	MNZ	Manassas, VA
KTN	Ketchikan Intl, AK	LUK	Cincinatti Municipal, OH	MOB	Mobile-Regional, AL
KTP	Kingston-Tinson Peninsula	LUN	Lusaka Intl	MOR	Morristown, TN
KTR	Katherine-Tindal	LUX	Luxembourg	MPB	Miami-Watson Island, FL
KTW	Katowice-Pyrzowice	LWB	Lewisburg-Greenbrier Valley, WV	MPL	Montpellier-Mediterranean
KUF	Samara-Kurumoch	LWO	Lvov-Snilow	MPM	Maputo
KUL	Kuala Lumpur Intl	LWR	Leeuwarden	MPR	McPherson, KS
KUN	Kaunus-Karlelava Intl	LXR	Luxor	MQF	Magnitogorsk
KVB	Skovde	LYN	Lyon-Bron	MQL	Mildura
KVX	Kirov	LYP	Faisalabad	MQS	Mustique Intl
KWE	Guiyang	LYS	Lyon-Satolas	MQT	Marquette-Sawyer, MI
KWI	Kuwait Intl	LYT	Lady Elliott Island	MQY	Smyrna, TN
KXK	Komsomolsk	LYX	Lydd Intl	MRI	Anchorage-Merrill Field, AK
KYZ	Kyzyi	MAA	Chennai	MRO	Masterton
KZN	Kazan-Bonsoglebskow	MAD	Madrid-Barajas	MRS	Marseille-Marignane
KZO	Kzyl-Orda	MAG	Madang	MRU	Plaisance Intl
LAD	Luanda-4 de Fevereiro	MAH	Menorca-Mahon	MRV	Mineralnye Vody
LAE	Lae-Nadzab	MAJ	Majuro-Amata Kabua Intl	MSC	Mesa-Falcon Field, AZ
LAF	Lafayette-Purdue University, IN	MAN	Manchester Intl	MSE	Manston-Kent Intl
LAO	Laoag Intl	MAO	Manaus-Eduardo Gomes	MSO	Missoula Johnson-Bell Field, MT
LAP	La Paz Gen Leon Intl	MAR	Maracaibo-La Chinita Intl	MSP	Minneapolis-St Paul Intl, MN
LAS	Las Vegas-McCarran Intl, NV	MAW	Malden, MO	MSQ	Minsk-Velikiydvor (Minsk I Intl)
LAW	Lawton, OK	MBA	Mombasa-Moi Intl	MST	Maastricht-Aachen
LAX	Los Angeles Intl, CA	MBD	Mmbatho Intl	MSU	Maseru-Moshoeshoe
LBA	Leeds-Bradford	MBH	Maryborough	MSY	New Orleans Intl, LA
LBB	Lubbock, TX	MBJ	Montego Bay-Sangster Intl	MTM	Metlakatla, AK
LBD	Khudzhand	MBW	Melbourne-Moorabin	MTN	Baltimore-Glenn L Martin, MD
LBE	Latrobe-Westmoreland Co, PA	MBX	Maribor	MTS	Manzini-Matsapha
LBG	Paris-le Bourget	MCI	Kansas City Intl, MO	MTY	Monterey-Gen Escobedo Intl
LBH	Sydney-Palm Beach	MCM	Monte Carlo Heliport	MUB	Maun
LBV	Libreville-Leon M'Ba	MCO	Orlando Intl, FL	MUC	Munich-Franz Joseph Straus
LCA	Larnaca Intl	MCT	Muscat-Seeb Intl	MUN	Maturin
LCE	La Ceibe-Goloson Intl	MCW	Mason City Municipal, IA	MVA	Myvatri-Rykiahlid
LCH	Lake Charles-Regional, LA	MCX	Makhachkala-Uytash	MVD	Montevideo-Carrasco Intl
LCK	Columbus-Rickenbacker, OH	MDE	Medellin-Olaya Herrera	MVQ	Mogilev
LCY	London-City	MDL	Mandalay	MVY	Martha's Vineyard, MA
LDB	Londrina	MDT	Harrisburg Intl, PA	MWO	Middletown-Hook Field
LDE	Tarbes-Ossun Lourdes	MDU	Mendi		Memorial, OH
LDH	Lord Howe Island	MDW	Chicago-Midway, IL	MXE	Maxton, NC
LDK	Lidkoping-Hovby	MEB	Melbourne-Essendon	MXN	Morlaix-Ploujean
LED	St Petersburg-Pulkovo	MEL	Melbourne-Tullamarine	MXP	Milan-Malpensa

Code	Location	Code	Location	Code	Location
MXX	Mora	OSH	Oshkosh-Wittman Field, WI	PPT	Papeete-Faaa
MYR	Myrtle Beach, SC	OSL	Oslo Intl	PRA	Parana
MYY	Miri	OSR	Ostrava-Mosnov	PRC	Prescott, AZ
MZJ	Marana-Pinal Airpark, AZ	OST	Ostend	PRG	Prague-Ruzyne
NAL	Nalchik	OTP	Bucharest-Otopeni Intl	PRN	Pristina
NAN	Nadi Intl	OTS	Anacortes, WA	PRV	Prerov
NAP	Naples-Capodichino	OTZ	Kotzebue-Wien Memorial, AK	PRY	Pretoria-Wonderboom
NAS	Nassau Intl	OUA	Ouagadougou	PSA	Pisa-Galileo
NAY	Beijing-Nan Yuan	OUL	Oulu	PSM	Portsmouth-Pease Intl, NH
NBO	Nairobi-Jomo Kenyatta Intl	OVB	Novosibirsk-Tolmachevo	PSR	Pescara
NCE	Nice-Cote d'Azur	OWD	Norwood Memorial, MA	PSY	Port Stanley
NCL	Newcastle	OXB	Bissau Vierira Intl	PTA	Port Alsworth, AK
NDJ	N'djamena	OXC	Oxford-Waterbury, CT	PTG	Pietersburg
NEV	Nevis-Newcastle	OZH	Zaporozhye-Mokraya	PTI	Port Douglas
NFG	Nefteyugansk	PAC	Paitilla, Panama City	PTK	Pontiac-Oakland, MI
NGO	Nagoya-Komaki	PAD	Paderborn-Lippstadt	PTP	Pointe a Pitre-Le Raizet
NGS	Nagasaki	PAE	Everett-Paine Field, WA	PTY	Panama City-Tocumen Intl
NHT	RAF Northolt	PAP	Port-au-Prince Intl	PUF	Pau-Pyrenees
NIC	Nicosia	PAQ	Palmer Municipal, AK	PUG	Port Agusta
NIM	Niamey-Diori Hamani	PBG	Plattsburgh, NY	PUQ	Punta Arenas
NKC	Nouakchott	PBH	Paro	PUU	Puerto Asi
NKG	Nanjing	PBI	Palm Beach Intl, FL	PUY	Pula
NLK	Norfolk Island, NSW	PBM	Paramaribo-Pengel Intl	PVH	Porto Velho
NLO	Kinshasa-N'dolo	PCL	Pucalipa-Rolden	PVU	Provo-Municipal. UT
NLP	Nelspruit	PCM	Playa del Carmen	PWK	Chicago-Pal Waukee, IL
NNK	Naknek, AK	PDK	Atlanta-Peachtree, GA	PWM	Portland Intl Jetport, ME
NNR	Connemara	PDC	La Verne-Bracketts Field, CA	PWQ	Pavlodar
NOA	Nowra	PDL	Ponta Delgada	PYL	Perry Island SPB, AK
NOE	Norden-Norddeich	PDV	Plovdiv	PZE	Penzance
NOU	Noumea-La Tontouta	PDX	Portland Intl, OR	QLA	Lasham
NOZ	Novokuznetsk	PEE	Perm-Bolshoe-Savino	RAB	Rabaul
NPE	Napier	PEK	Beijing-Capital	RAI	Praia-Mendes
NQN	Neuquen	PEN	Penang-Intl	RAK	Marrakesh
NQY	Newquay-St Mawgan	PER	Perth Intl	RAO	Ribeirao Preto
NRK	Norrkoping	PEZ	Penza	RAR	Rarotonga
NRT	Tokyo-Narita Intl	PFO	Paphos Intl	RAS	Rasht
NSI	Yaounde	PGA	Page, AZ	RBA	Rabat-Sale
NSK	Norilsk	PGF	Perpignan-Rivesaltes	RBR	Rio Branco-Medici
NSN	Nelson	PHC	Port Harcourt	RBY	Ruby, AK
NSO	Scone, NSW	PHE	Port Hedland	RCM	Richmond, Qld
NTB	Notodden	PHF	Newport News, VA	RDD	Redding-Municipal, CA
NTE	Nantes-Atlantique	PHL	Philadelphia Intl, PA	RDG	Reading-Gen Spaatz Field, PA
NTL	Newcastle-Williamstown	PHX	Phoenix-Sky Harbor Intl, AZ	RDM	Redmond-Roberts Field, OR
NTY	Sun City-Pilansberg	PIE	St Petersburg-Clearwater Intl, FL	RDU	Raleigh-Durham Intl, NC
NUE	Nurenburg	PIK	Prestwick	REC	Recife-Guararapes
NVA	Neiva-La Marquita	PIR	Pierre-Regional, SD	REK	Reykjavik
NVR	Novgorod	PIT	Pittsburgh Intl, PA	REN	Orenburg
NWI	Norwich	PKC	Petropavlovsk	REP	Siem Reap
NYM	Nadym	PKR	Pokhara	RFD	Rockford, IL
NYO	Nykoping-Skavsta	PKV	Pskov	RGN	Yangon Intl
OAG	Orange, NSW	PLB	Plattsburg-Clinton Co, NY	RHE	Reims Champagne
OAJ	Jacksonville, NC	PLH	Plymouth	RHI	Rhinelander-Oneida Co, WI
OAK	Oakland Intl, CA	PLL	Manaus-Ponta Pelada	RIC	Richmond-Byrd Intl, VA
OAX	Oaxaca-Xoxocotlan	PLS	Providenciales Intl	RIX	Riga-Skulte Intl
OBF	Oberpfaffenhofen	PLU	Belo Horizonte-Pampulha	RJK	Rijeka
OBN	Oban	PLX	Semipalatisnk	RKD	Rockland-Knox County, ME
OCF	Ocala-Taylor Field, FL	PMB	Pembina, ND	RKE	Roskilde
ODB	Cordoba-Palma del Rio	PMD	Palmdale, CA	RKT	Ras al Khaimah Intl
ODE	Odense-Beldringe	PMF	Parma	RMA	Roma
ODS	Odessa-Tsentralny	PMI	Palma de Mallorca	RMI	Rimini
ODW	Oak Harbor, WA	PMO	Palermo-Punta Raisi	RML	Colombo-Ratmalana
OEL	Orel	PMR	Palmerston-North	RNC	McMinnville-Warren Co, OR
OGG	Kahului, HI	PNA	Pamplona	RNO	Reno-Cannon Intl, NV
OGZ	Vladivkavkaz-Beslan	PNE	Philadelphia-Northern, PA	RNS	Rennes-St Jacques
OKA	Okinawa-Naha	PNH	Phnom Penh-Pochentong	RNT	Seattle-Renton, WA
OKC	Oklahoma City-Will Roger, OK	PNI	Pohnpei-Caroline Islands	ROB	Monrovia Roberts Intl
OKD	Sappor-Okadama	PNK	Pontianak-Supadio	ROK	Rockhampton, IL
OLB	Olbia-Costa Smeralda	PNR	Pointe Noire	ROM	Rome Urbe
OMA	Omaha-Eppley Field, NE	PNS	Pensacola-Regional, FL	ROR	Koror-Airai
OME	Nome, AK	PNX	Sherman-Denison, TX	ROT	Rotorua
OMS	Omsk-Severny	POA	Porto Alegre-Canoas	ROV	Rostov-on-Don
ONT	Ontario Intl, CA	POC	La Verne-Brackett Field, CA	ROW	Roswell
OOL	Coolangatta	POG	Port Gentil	RPM	Ngukurr
OPF	Opa Locka, FL	POM	Port Moresby	RSE	Sydney-Au Rose, QLD
OPO	Porto	POP	Puerto Plata Intl	RTM	Rotterdam
ORB	Orebro-Bofors	POS	Port of Spain-Piarco	RTW	Saratov-Tsentrainy
ORD	Chicago-O'Hare Intl, IL	POW	Portoroz	RUH	Riyadh-King Khalid Intl
ORG	Paramaribo-Zorg en Hoop	POX	Pontoise-Cormeilles	RUN	St Denis-Gilot
ORK	Cork	PPB	Presidente Prudente	RVH	St Petersburg-Rzhevka
ORL	Orlando-Executive, FL	PPG	Pago Pago Intl	RWN	Rovno
ORY	Paris-Orly	PPK	Petropavlovsk	RYB	Rybinsk-Staroselye
OSC	Oscoda-Wurtsmith	PPQ	Paraparaumu	RZN	Ryazan

Code	Name	Code	Name	Code	Name
SAH	Sana'a Intl	SPN	Saipan Island Intl	TNA	Jinan
SAL	San Salvador Intl	SPR	San Pedro	TNF	Toussus-le-Noble
SAN	San Diego-Lindbergh Intl, CA	SPW	Spencer Municipal, IA	TNN	Tainan
SAT	San Antonio Intl, TX	SPZ	Springdale, AR	TNR	Antananarivo
SBA	Santa Barbara Municipal, CA	SRN	Strahan	TOA	Torrance, CA
SBH	St Barthelemy	SRQ	Sarasota-Bradenton Intl, FL	TOE	Tozeur-Nefta
SBP	San Luis Obispo, CA	SRZ	Santa Cruz-El Trompillo	TOF	Tomsk
SBY	Salisbury-Wicomico, MD	SSA	Salvador-Dois de Julho	TOL	Toledo-Express, OH
SCC	Prudhoe Bay, AK	SSG	Malabo	TPA	Tampa Intl, FL
SCH	Schenectady County, NY	SSH	Sharm el Sheikh	TPE	Taipei-Chiang Kai Shek Intl
SCI	San Cristobal-Paramilio	STA	Stauning	TPQ	Tepic
SCK	Stockton Metropolitan, CA	STI	Santiago Intl	TPS	Trapani
SCL	Santiago-Benitez Intl	STL	St Louis-Lambert Intl, MO	TRD	Trondheim-Vaernes
SCN	Saarbrucken-Ensheim	STM	Santarem-Gomez Intl	TRG	Tauranga
SCU	Santiago de Cuba	STN	London-Stansted	TRN	Turin-Caselle
SCW	Syktyvkor	STR	Stuttgart	TRS	Trieste
SDA	Damascus-Saddam Intl	STS	Santa Rosa-Sonoma, CA	TRW	Tarawa
SDF	Louisville-Standiford Field, KY	STT	St Thomas-King	TSA	Taipei-Sung Shan
SDJ	Sendai	STU	Santa Cruz	TSE	Astana
SDQ	Santo Domingo Intl	STW	Stavropol-Shpakovskoye	TSM	Taos-Municipal, NM
SDU	Rio de Janeiro-Santos Dumont	STX	St Croix -Hamilton Airport	TSN	Tianjin
SDV	Tel Aviv-Sde Dov	SUA	Stuart-Witham Field, FL	TSV	Townsville
SEA	Seattle-Tacoma Intl, WA	SUB	Surabaya-Juanda	TTD	Portland-Troutdale, OR
SEL	Seoul-Kimpo Intl	SUI	Sukhumi	TTN	Mercer-County, Trenton, NJ
SEN	Southend	SUS	St Louis-Spirit of St Louis, MO	TUL	Tulsa Intl, OK
SEZ	Mahe-Seychelles Intl	SUV	Suva-Nausori	TUN	Tunis-Carthage
SFA	Sioux Falls, SD	SVD	Kingstown, St Vincent	TUO	Taupo
SFB	Sanford Regional, FL	SVG	Stavanger-Sola	TUS	Tucson Intl, AZ
SFC	St Francois	SVH	Statesville Municipal, NC	TWB	Toowoomba
SFJ	Kangerlussuaq-Sondre Stromfjord	SVO	Moscow-Sheremetyevo	TXK	Texarkana Municipal, AR
		SVX	Ekaterinburg-Koitsovo	TXL	Berlin-Tegel
SFO	San Francisco Intl	SWH	Swan Hill	TYA	Tula
SFS	Subic Bay Intl	SXF	Berlin-Schönefeld	TYF	Torsby-Frylanda
SFT	Skelleftea	SXM	St Maarten-Philipsburg	TYN	Taiyuan-Wusu
SGD	Sondeberg	SYD	Sydney-Kingsford Smith Intl	TZA	Belize-Municipal
SGH	Springfield-Beckley, OH	SYR	Syracuse-Hancock Intl, NY	UBS	Columbus-Lowndes Co, MS
SGL	Manila-Sangley Point	SYY	Stornoway	UCT	Ukhta
SGN	Ho Chi Minh City-Tansonnhat	SZB	Subang-Sultan Abdul Aziz Shah Intl	UFA	Ufa
SGU	St George Municipal UT			UIK	Ust-Ilimsk
SGW	Saginaw Bay, AK	SZG	Salzburg	UIO	Quito-Mariscal Sucre
SGY	Skagway Municipal, AK	SZO	Shanzhou	UKX	Ust-Kut
SGZ	Songkhla	SZX	Shenzen-Huangtian	ULC	Santiago-los Cerillos
SHA	Shanghai-Hongqiao	SZZ	Szczecin-Goleniow	ULN	Ulan Bator
SHE	Shenyang	TAM	Tampico	ULY	Ulyanovsk
SHJ	Sharjah Intl	TAR	Taranto	UME	Umea
SHR	Sheridan County, WY	TAS	Tashkent-Yuzhny	UNK	Unalakleet Municipal, AK
SIA	Xi'an-Xiguan	TAT	Tatry-Poprad	UNU	Juneau-Dodge Co, AK
SID	Sal	TBG	Tabubil	UPG	Ujang Pendang
SIG	San Juan-Isla Grande, PR	TBS	Tbilisi-Novo Alexeyevka	UPN	Uruapan
SIN	Singapore-Changi	TBU	Tongatapu-Fua'Amotu Intl	URA	Uratsk
SIP	Simferopol	TBW	Tambov	URC	Urumqi-Diwopou
SIR	Sion	TEB	Teterboro, NJ	URS	Kursk
SIT	Sitka, AK	TED	Thisted	UTP	Utapao
SIX	Singleton	TER	Lajes-Terceira Island	UTT	Umtata
SJC	San Jose Intl, CA	TFN	Tenerife-Norte los Rodeos	UUA	Bugulma
SJJ	Sarajevo-Butmir	TFS	Tenerife-Sur Reine Sofia	UUD	Ulan Ude-Mukhino
SJK	Sao Jose-dos Campos	TGD	Podgorica	UUS	Yuzhno-Sakhalinsk
SJO	San Jose-Juan Santamaria Intl	TGR	Touggourt	VAI	Vanimo
SJU	San Juan-Marin Intl, PR	TGU	Tegucigalpa-Toncontin Intl	VAR	Varna Intl
SJY	Deinajoki-Ilmajoki	TGZ	Tuxtla-Gutierrez	VBS	Brescia
SKB	Basseterre-Golden Rock	THE	Terresina	VCE	Venice-Marco Polo
SKD	Samarkand	THF	Berlin-Tempelhof	VCP	Sao Paulo-Viracopos
SKE	Skien-Geiteryggen	THN	Trollhattan-Vanersborg	VCT	Victoria-Regional, TX
SKF	San Antonio-Kelly AFB, TX	THR	Teheran-Mehrabad Intl	VCV	Victorville, CA
SKP	Skopje	TIA	Tirana-Rinas	VDM	Viedma-Castello
SKX	Saransk	TIJ	Tijuana-Rodriguez Intl	VDZ	Valdez-Municipal, AK
SKY	Sandusky, OH	TIP	Tripoli Intl	VER	Vera Cruz-Jara Intl
SLA	San Luis Potois	TIS	Thursday Island	VFA	Victoria Falls
SLC	Salt Lake City Intl, UT	TIV	Tivat	VGD	Vologda
SLM	Salamanca Matacan	TJM	Tyumen-Roschino	VGT	Las Vegas-North, NV
SLU	Castries	TKA	Talkeetna, AK	VIE	Vienna-Schwechat
SLW	Saltillo	TKJ	Tok, AK	VIH	Vichy-Rolla National, MO
SMF	Sacramento-Metropolitan, CA	TKU	Turku	VIR	Durban-Virginia
SMN	Salmon, ID	TLC	Toluca-Alfonso Lopez	VIS	Visalia-Municipal, CA
SMO	Santa Monica, CA	TLL	Tallinn-Ylemiste	VKO	Moscow-Vnukovo
SMX	Santa Maria-Public, CA	TLR	Tulare-Mefford Field, CA	VLC	Valencia
SNA	John Wayne-Orange Co, CA	TLS	Toulouse-Blagnac	VLE	Valle-J Robidoux , AZ
SNN	Shannon	TLV	Tel Aviv-Ben Gurion Intl	VLI	Port Vila-Bauerfield
SOF	Sofia-Vrazhdebna Intl	TML	Tamale	VLK	Volgodonsk
SOU	Southampton Intl	TMO	Tumeremo	VLN	Valencia Intl, CA
SPB	St Thomas Seaplane, VI	TMS	Sao Tome Intl	VNC	Venice, FL
SPI	Springfield Capital, IL	TMW	Tamworth-Westdale	VNE	Vannes

Code	Location	Code	Location	Code	Location
VNO	Vilnius Intl	YIP	Detroit-Willow Run, MI	YXH	Medicine Hat
VNY	Van Nuys, CA	YJF	Fort Liard	YXJ	Fort St John
VOG	Volgograd-Gumrak	YJN	St Jean	YXK	Rimouski
VOZ	Voronezh-Chertovtskye	YKC	Toronto-Buttonville	YXL	Sioux Lookout
VPC	Cartersville, GA	YKE	Knee Lake	YXS	Prince George
VQS	Vieques, PR	YKF	Kitchener-Waterloo	YXT	Terrace
VRN	Verona-Villafranca	YKL	Schefferville	YXU	London
VSG	Lugansk	YKS	Yakutsk	YXX	Abbotsford
VTE	Vientiane-Wattay	YLB	Lac la Biche	YXY	Whitehorse
VTG	Vung Tau	YLP	Mingan	YXZ	Wawa-Hawk Junction
VVC	Villavicencio-La Vanguardia	YLQ	La Tuque	YYB	North Bay
VVI	Santa Cruz-Viru Viru Intl	YLT	Alert	YYC	Calgary
VVO	Vladivostock-Knevichi	YLW	Kelowna	YYD	Smithers
WAG	Wanganui	YMM	Fort McMurray	YYE	Fort Nelson
WAT	Waterford	YMO	Moosonee	YYF	Penticton
WAW	Warsaw-Okecie	YMP	Port McNeil	YYG	Charlottetown
WDH	Windhoek-Hosea Kutako Intl	YMX	Montreal-Mirabel Intl	YYJ	Victoria
WDR	Winder-Barrow Co, GA	YMY	Ear Falls	YYQ	Churchill, Man
WFB	Ketchikan Waterfront SPB, AK	YNA	Natashquan	YYR	Goose Bay
WGA	Wagga Wagga	YNC	Wemindji	YYT	St Johns
WHP	Los Angeles-Whiteman Field, CA	YND	Ottawa-Gatineau, Que	YYW	Armstrong
WIL	Nairobi-Wilson	YNF	Corner Brook	YYZ	Toronto-Lester B Pearson Intl
WIR	Wairoa	YNR	Arnes	YZF	Yellowknife
WKA	Wanaka	YOJ	High Level	YZH	Slave Lake
WLG	Wellington Intl	YOO	Oshawa	YZT	Port Hardy
WOE	Woensdrecht	YOW	Ottawa-McDonald Cartier Intl	YZU	Whitecourt
WOW	Willow, AK	YPA	Prince Albert	YZV	Sept-Iles
WRO	Wroclaw-Strachowice	YPB	Port Alberni-Sproat Lake	YZY	Mackenzie
WST	Westerly State, RI	YPD	Parry Sound	ZAG	Zagreb-Pieso
WSY	Airlie Beach-Whitsunday	YPE	Peace River	ZAM	Zamboanga Intl
WUH	Wuhan	YPL	Pickle Lake	ZFD	Fond du Lac, Sask
WVB	WalvisBay	YPQ	Peterborough	ZFM	Fort McPherson
WVL	Waterville-Lafleur, ME	YPR	Prince Rupert-Digby Island	ZJN	Swan River
WVN	Wilhelmshaven-Mariensiel	YQA	Muskoka	ZNZ	Zanzibar-Kisuani
WWA	Wasilla, AK	YQB	Quebec	ZPB	Sachigo Lake
WYA	Whyalla	YQD	The Pas	ZQN	Queenstown-Frankton
WYN	Wyndham	YQF	Red Deer	ZRH	Zurich-Kloten
XBE	Bearskin Lake	YQH	Watson Lake	ZSI	Sandy Lake
XCM	Chatham	YQK	Kenora	ZTR	Zhitomyr
XFW	Hamburg-Finkenwerder	YQN	Nakina	ZUC	Ignace
XLW	Lemwerder	YQR	Regina	ZUH	Zhuhai
XMN	Xiamen-Gaoqi	YQS	St Thomas		
XSP	Singapore-Seletar	YQT	Thunder Bay		
YAG	Fort Frances Municipal	YQU	Grande Prairie		
YAM	Sault Ste Marie	YQV	Yorkton		
YAO	Yaounde	YRB	Resolute Bay, Nun		
YAW	Halifax	YRJ	Roberval		
YBC	Baie Comeau	YRL	Red Lake		
YBL	Campbell River	YRO	Ottawa-Rockcliffe		
YBX	Lourdes-de-Blanc Sablon	YRP	Carp		
YCA	Courtenay	YRT	Rankin Inlet		
YCB	Cambridge Bay	YSB	Sudbury		
YCD	Nanaimo-Cassidy	YSE	Squamishr		
YCL	Charlo	YSF	Stony Rapids		
YCN	Cochrane-Lillabelle Lake	YSM	Fort Smith		
YCR	Cross Lake-Sinclair Memorial	YSN	Salmon Arm		
YCW	Chilliwack	YSQ	Atlin		
YDF	Deer Lake	YTA	Pembroke		
YDQ	Dawson Creek	YTF	Alma		
YDT	Vancouver-Boundary Bay	YTH	Thompson		
YEG	Edmonton-Intl	YTP	Tofino SPB		
YEL	Elliott Lake-Municipal	YTZ	Toronto-City Centre		
YEV	Inuvik-Mike Zubko	YUL	Montreal-Pierre Elliot Trudeau		
YFB	Iqaluit	YUY	Rouyn-Noranda		
YFC	Fredericton	YVA	Moroni-Iconi		
YFO	Flin Flon	YVC	La Ronge		
YFS	Fort Simpson	YVG	Vermillion Bay		
YGG	Ganges Harbour	YVJ	Victoria		
YGL	La Grande	YVO	Val d'Or/La Grande		
YGM	Gimli	YVP	Kuujjuaq		
YGR	Madelaine Island	YVQ	Norman Wells		
YGV	Havre St Pierre	YVR	Vancouver Intl		
YGX	Gillam	YVT	Buffalo Narrows		
YHF	Hearst	YWF	Halifax-Waterfront Heliport		
YHM	Hamilton	YWG	Winnipeg Intl		
YHN	Homepayne	YWH	Victoria-Inner Harbour		
YHR	Chevery	YWJ	Deline		
YHS	Sechelt-Gibson	YWK	Wabush		
YHU	Montreal-St Hubert, Que	YWR	White River		
YHY	Hay River	YWS	Whistler		
YHZ	Halifax Intl	YXD	Edmonton Municipal		
YIB	Atikokan Municipal	YXE	Saskatoon-Diefenbacker		

NATIONALITY INDEX

This index lists the world's current registration prefixes and is a guide to their location in the main part of the book

OPERATOR INDEX

NOTES

NOTES

AIR-BRITAIN SALES

Companion volumes to this publication are also available by post-free mail order from

Air-Britain Sales Department (Dept AF04)
41 Penshurst Road, Leigh,
Tonbridge, Kent TN11 8HL

For a full list of current titles and details of how to order, visit our e-commerce site at
www.air-britain.co.uk
Visa / Mastercard / Delta / Switch accepted - please give full details of card number and expiry date.

ANNUAL PUBLICATIONS - 2004 - NOW AVAILABLE

UK and IRELAND QUICK REFERENCE 2004 £5.95 (Members) £6.95 (Non-members)
New, basic easy-to-carry registration and type listing, UK-based foreign aircraft, current military serials, aircraft museums and base index. A5 size, 144 pages.

BUSINESS JETS QUICK REFERENCE 2004 £4.50 (Members) £4.95 (Non-members)
The latest addition to the Quick Reference range, listing all purpose-built business jets, in both civil and military use, in registration or serial order by country. Easy-to-carry A5 size, 76 pages.

AIRLINE FLEETS QUICK REFERENCE 2004 £5.95 (Members) £6.95 (Non-members)
New pocket guide now expanded to airliners of over 19 seats of major operators likely to be seen worldwide; regn, type, c/n, fleet nos. Listed by country and airline. A5 size, 192 pages.

CIVIL AIRCRAFT REGISTERS of UK & IRELAND 2004 £17.50 (Members) £22.00 (Non-members)
The most comprehensive coverage of all current and extant G- and EI- registered aircraft, full identities and CofA details, military/civil marks decode, full type/regn index, overseas-registered aircraft based here, glider and preservation registers, now with complete listing of museums and other significant aircraft collections. Over 550 pages lie-flat hardback.

BUSINESS JETS INTERNATIONAL 2004 *(Prices to be announced, available May/June)*
Complete production listings of all business jet types in c/n order, giving full identities, fates and a comprehensive cross-reference index. Available in hardback or softback at approx 400 pages.

EUROPEAN REGISTERS HANDBOOK 2004 *(Prices to be announced, available May/June)*
Current civil registers of 42 European countries, all powered aircraft, balloons, gliders, microlights. Full previous identities and many extra permit and reservation details. Now in new A4 softback format approx 600 pages.

OTHER PUBLICATIONS CURRENTLY AVAILABLE:

JET AIRLINERS OF THE WORLD 1949-2001 £16.00 (Members) £20.00 (Non-members)
Detailed production lists of over 70 jet airliner types with expanded coverage of Russian-built types and purely military jet transports. Full cross-reference index containing over 56,000 registrations and serials.

BUSINESS TURBOPROPS INTERNATIONAL 2000 £15.00 (Members) £19.00 (Non-members)
Complete production lists of over 75 types including all B-N Islanders, with 42,000+ cross-reference index. 360 pages, hardback.

WORLD MILITARY TRANSPORT FLEETS 2002 £15.00 (Members) £19.00 (Non-members)
The complete country-by-country guide of all the fixed-wing military and government operated transport and patrol aircraft. C/ns, units and bases are given where known. Over 10,000 entries including future plans. 280 pages.

Air-Britain also publishes a comprehensive range of military titles, please check for latest details of RAF Serial Registers, detailed RAF aircraft type "Files", Squadron Histories and Royal Navy Aircraft Histories.

IMPORTANT NOTE – Members receive substantial discounts on prices of all the above Air-Britain publications.
For details of membership see the following page or visit our website at http://www.air-britain.co.uk

AIR-BRITAIN MEMBERSHIP

Join on-line at www.air-britain.co.uk

If you are not currently a member of Air-Britain, the publishers of this book, you may be interested in what we have on offer to provide for your interest in aviation.

About Air-Britain
Formed over 50 years ago, we are the world's most progressive aviation society, and exist to bring together aviation enthusiasts with every type of interest. Our members include aircraft historians, aviation writers, spotters and pilots – and those who just have a fascination with aircraft and aviation. Air-Britain is a non-profit organisation, which is independently audited, and any financial surpluses are used to provide services to the ever-growing membership. In the last 7 years, our membership has increased annually, and our current membership now stands at over 4,200.

Membership of Air-Britain
Membership is open to all. A basic membership fee is charged and every member receives a copy of the quarterly house magazine, Air-Britain Aviation World, and is entitled to use all the Air-Britain specialist services and to buy **Air-Britain publications at discounted prices**. A membership subscription includes the choice to add any or all of our other 3 magazines, News and/or Archive and/or Aeromilitaria. Air-Britain publishes 10-20 books per annum (around 70 titles in stock at any one time). Membership runs January - December each year, but new members have a choice of options periods to get their initial subscription started.

Air-Britain Aviation World is the quarterly 48-page house magazine containing not only news of Air-Britain activities, but also a wealth of features, often illustrated in colour, on many different aviation subjects, contemporary and historical, contributed by our 4,200 members.

Air-Britain News is the world aviation news monthly, containing data on Aircraft Registrations worldwide, and news of Airlines and Airliners, Business Jets, Local Airfield News, Civil and Military Air Show Reports and International Military Aviation. An average 160 pages of lavishly–illustrated information for the dedicated enthusiast.

Air-Britain Archive is the quarterly 48 page specialist journal of civil aviation history. Packed with the results of historical research by Air-Britain specialists into aircraft types, overseas registers and previously   unpublished photographs and facts about the rich heritage of civil aviation. Around 100 photographs per issue, some in colour.

Air-Britain Aeromilitaria is the quarterly 48-page unique source for meticulously researched details of military aviation history edited by the acclaimed authors of Air-Britain's military monographs, featuring British, Commonwealth, European and U.S. Military aviation articles. Illustrated in colour and black and white.

Other Benefits
Additional to the above, members have exclusive access to the Air-Britain e-mail Information Exchange Service (ab-ix) where they can exchange information and solve each other's queries, and to an on-line UK airfield residents database. Other benefits include numerous Branches, use of the Specialists' Information Service; Air-Britain trips and access to black and white and colour photograph libraries. During the summer we also host our own popular FLY-IN. Each autumn, we host an Aircraft Recognition Contest.

Membership Subscription Rates – from £15 per annum.
Membership subscription rates start from as little as £15 per annum, and this amount provides a copy of 'Air-Britain Aviation World' quarterly as well as all the other benefits covered above. Subscriptions to include any or all of our other three magazines vary between £24 and £59 per annum (slightly higher to overseas).

Join on-line at www.air-britain.co.uk   or, write to 'Air-Britain' at 1 Rose Cottages, 179 Penn Road, Hazlemere, High Wycombe, Bucks HP15 7NE, UK, or telephone/fax on 01394 450767 (+44 1394 450767) and ask for a membership pack containing the full details of subscription rates, samples of our magazines and a book list.